The Sporting News
NBA GUIDE
1 9 9 2 - 9 3 E D I T I O N

Editors/NBA Guide

CRAIG CARTER
ALEX SACHARE

Contributing Editors/NBA Guide

CLARE MARTIN
DAVE SLOAN

The Sporting News

PUBLISHING CO.

Thomas G. Osenton, President and Chief Operating Officer; **Kathy Kinkeade**, Vice President/Production; **William N. Topaz**, Director/Information Development; **Gary Levy**, Editor; **Mike Nahrstedt**, Managing Editor; **Joe Hoppel**, Senior Editor; **Tom Dienhart**, Associate Editor; **Mark Shimabukuro**, Assistant Editor; **Bill Bayer and Kevin Hormuth**, Editorial Assistants; **Bill Perry**, Director of Graphic Presentation; **Mike Bruner**, Art Director/Yearbooks and Books; **Gary Brinker**, Director of Information Systems.

A Times Mirror
Company

TABLE OF CONTENTS

ON THE COVER: Scottie Pippen (dunking over Portland's Clyde Drexler), Michael Jordan (left) and the Chicago Bulls defeated the Trail Blazers in the 1992 NBA Finals to capture their second straight NBA championship.

Photo by Andrew D. Bernstein/NBA Photos

NBA statistics compiled by Elias Sports Bureau, New York.

ISBN: 0-89204-436-5   10 9 8 7 6 5 4 3 2 1

REVIEW OF 1991-92 SEASON

Including

Review of the Regular Season

Final Standings

Final Statistics

Top Performances

Active Career Leaders

Review of the NBA Finals

NBA Finals Box Scores, Statistics

Playoff Results, Statistics

NBA Draft Review, Round-by-Round List

Team-by-Team No. 1 Draft Choices

Abracadabra! NBA sees Magic again

By JAN HUBBARD

The announcement was met with shock and disbelief. Magic Johnson, the Los Angeles Lakers' superstar and a man who seemed to take absolute delight in any basketball endeavor, stunned the sports world on November 7, 1991, when he announced that he had contracted the human immunodeficiency virus (HIV) that causes AIDS.

In calm and reassuring tones, Johnson said that although he would be forced to retire prematurely at age 32 after 12 spectacular years as the Lakers' point guard, he would not disappear from the public eye.

Johnson's many fans and admirers were jolted by the suddenness of his retirement and saddened by the ramifications of the disease. But as the season unfolded, they again were reminded of Johnson's remarkable ability to create something special out of something that seemed hopeless.

Only this time, Johnson was not sparking a rally or leading a comeback or making a last-second shot to win a championship game. This time, Johnson was fighting the notion that individuals who are HIV positive should be neither seen nor heard.

He succeeded beyond anyone's wildest expectations—except, perhaps, his own. Johnson was a fixture at Lakers games. He worked out by himself before games, then sat on the bench and cheered his former teammates.

Johnson passionately embraced his new role as an AIDS educator as he toured the country and spoke to numerous groups and reporters. He said his goal was to increase awareness, and he seemed to be succeeding.

He did not completely go away in a basketball sense, either. Since he did not officially retire but instead was placed on the Lakers' injured list, Johnson was allowed to receive votes to play in the All-Star Game. The fans paid him the ultimate compliment by voting him to the team, and Johnson paid them back by creating a fairy tale in front of a worldwide audience.

On February 9, 1992, despite three

Magic Johnson's 1992 All-Star Game performance was astonishing.

months away from organized competition, Johnson scored 25 points and collected nine assists, five rebounds and two steals as he led the West to a 153-113 victory over the East. Johnson was named Most Valuable Player of the 42nd annual All-Star Game.

Johnson obviously had worked hard to prepare for the game, and he continued his routine of working out six hours per day. Over the summer, he achieved another goal when he joined the U.S. Olympic team. Magic was immediately named co-captain, along with Larry Bird.

Johnson said the combination of physical exercise, proper diet and rest had helped him fight off any negative effects of the HIV.

Regardless of whether he plays again or achieves his goal of owning a team, there was no argument that Johnson had performed in an extraordinary manner. He clearly created many positive headlines out of a difficult situation.

"I think good things are coming out of what happened to me," Johnson said. "And I always step back and say, 'That's incredible.' I've said all along that I have no fear about what's going to happen to me, and I still don't. There's no sense in being scared. God has already blessed me. I'm still healthy and strong. I have the virus, but I'm dealing with it. I want people to know that I don't have bad days. I don't sit around and say, 'Why me?' I'm just trying to say I have it, let's deal with it, and make sure other people don't get it."

CENTRAL DIVISION

Chicago Bulls (67-15)—Michael Jordan won his third MVP award, meaning that he and Magic have combined to win the last six. Jordan continued to excel as a leader and the best all-around player in the NBA, prodding the Bulls to a tie for the fourth-best record in league history. Jordan won his sixth consecutive scoring title, but his 30.1-point average was the lowest of those six seasons. Scottie Pippen continued his stellar play with a 21-point scoring average and, for the first time, had more rebounds and assists than Jordan. And Horace Grant again was the premier role player in the league. He averaged 10 rebounds per game.

Cleveland Cavaliers (57-25)—Mark Price returned from a major knee injury and the Cavaliers equaled the best regular-season record in their history. More important, the Cavs, who had lost in the first playoff round the previous six times they had advanced to postseason play, did not fold in the playoffs. They went to the Eastern Conference finals before losing to the Bulls in six games. The Cavs had one of the best front lines in the league in four-time All-Star Brad Daugherty (21.5 points, 10.4 rebounds), Larry Nance and John (Hot Rod) Williams.

Detroit Pistons (48-34)—For the first time in six years, the Pistons did not advance as far as the Eastern finals. In fact, they lost in the first playoff round to New York—and that led to massive changes. Coach Chuck Daly left after the season and was hired by New Jersey. General Manager Jack McCloskey departed for the Minnesota Timberwolves. The Pistons had severe problems scoring points because their two leading scorers were jump shooters Joe Dumars (19.9 points) and Isiah Thom-

Forward Horace Grant played his role with the Chicago Bulls to perfection.

as (18.5). Each made fewer than 45 percent of his field-goal attempts. The Pistons again led the league in defense, allowing only 96.9 points per game. But they averaged only 98.9 on offense, the second-fewest in the league. Detroit, 1989 and 1990 NBA champions, is facing a rebuilding project.

Indiana Pacers (40-42)—The Pacers continued to be "next year's team" as their high expectations went unanswered. Indiana lost nine of its first 13 games and struggled the rest of the season. Reggie Miller again led the Pacers in scoring, but his average fell almost two points to 20.7. Chuck Person averaged 18.5 points, but he was up and down. The Pacers' best player was Detlef Schrempf, who won his second consecutive Sixth Man Award. Schrempf posted career-high averages in points (17.3), rebounds (9.6) and assists (3.9). His 82.8 percent figure from the free-throw line also was a personal high.

Atlanta Hawks (38-44)—The Hawks' grand plan of a staggered rebuilding program went up in flames when Dominique Wilkins suffered a major knee injury and missed the last 40 games of the season.

Still, the Hawks fought for a playoff berth until the last two weeks of the season as Coach Bob Weiss did a masterful job of motivating and juggling. Forward Kevin Willis was one of the most improved players in the league, averaging 15.5 rebounds. And Stacey Augmon had a solid rookie season, notching 13.3 points per game while shooting 49 percent from the field. The Hawks had planned to blend youth with experience and not dip into the lottery, but that plan was delayed by Wilkins' injury.

Charlotte Hornets (31-51) —The Hornets made a major advancement, thanks to the presence of Rookie of the Year Larry Johnson, who averaged 19.2 points and 11 rebounds. Along with second-year guard Kendall Gill (20.5 points), the Hornets have two future All-Stars. Charlotte also added Georgetown center Alonzo Mourning in the draft, so the Hornets could be poised for a playoff run. In amassing their best record, the Hornets managed two consecutive winning months, February (9-4) and March (8-6).

Milwaukee Bucks (31-51) —The Bucks failed to make the playoffs for the first time in 13 years, and that led to notable changes. Del Harris resigned as coach early in the season and was replaced by Frank Hamblen. At the end of the season, however, former Bucks assistant Mike Dunleavy was lured from the Lakers and given an eight-year contract. The Bucks then traded Dale Ellis, Jay Humphries and Larry Krystkowiak and added veterans Blue Edwards, Eric Murdock and Alaa Abdelnaby and rookies Todd Day and Lee Mayberry.

ATLANTIC DIVISION

Boston Celtics (51-31) —The Celtics trailed the Knicks by five games with two weeks left in the regular season, but the Knicks folded and the Celtics surged. The result: For the 14th time in 20 years, the Celtics won a division title. That achievement, however, was marred by the continuing back problems of Larry Bird, who missed 37 games and the first playoff round. Reggie Lewis emerged as an All-Star with a 20.8 scoring average, but with Bird and Kevin McHale (sidelined 26 games because of assorted injuries) ailing, the Celtics lost to Cleveland in the second playoff round.

New York Knicks (51-31) —Although the Knicks crumbled late, they drew on the considerable playoff experience of first-year Coach Pat Riley and took the champion Bulls to seven games before losing in the second round. Riley preached hard-nosed play and defense, and the Knicks re- sponded by lowering their points-allowed average nearly six points to 97.7 per game, which was second in the league. Patrick Ewing again was a dominant force with averages of 24 points and 11.2 rebounds. And after two years of struggling, Mark Jackson reasserted himself with averages of 11.3 points and 8.6 assists.

New Jersey Nets (40-42) —The Nets flopped to a 2-11 start and then were ravaged by rumors that Bill Fitch would be fired in December. The Nets overcame all the distractions, however, and made the playoffs for the first time in six years. They lost in the first round, but they gained experience and confidence. And after the season, they also gained a new coach as Fitch resigned and Chuck Daly was hired. Derrick Coleman missed 17 games with various injuries, but he averaged 19.8 points and 9.5 rebounds. And guard Drazen Petrovic came into his own by leading the Nets in scoring with a 20.6 mark.

Miami Heat (38-44) —The fourth-year Heat thrilled its fans by becoming the first of the four newest expansion teams to make the playoffs. It was a brief experience as the Heat was eliminated in three games by the Bulls, but it still was a significant achievement. The youthful Heat players—Rony Seikaly, Glen Rice and Steve Smith—will only get better, and the Heat got a gift in the draft as guard Harold Miner fell to Miami at No. 12.

Philadelphia 76ers (35-47) —It was another year of distractions and disappointment as the 76ers struggled and Charles Barkley criticized. At the end of the season, Philadelphia decided it was time to move in a new direction. Coach Jim Lynam was promoted to general manager and Doug Moe was hired as coach. But the biggest change came when the 76ers traded Barkley to Phoenix for guard Jeff Hornacek, center Andrew Lang and forward Tim Perry. They then drafted Barkley clone Clarence Weatherspoon.

Washington Bullets (25-57) —The Bullets were hurt by Bernard King's knee injury and John Williams' weight problems—both players missed the entire season. Pervis Ellison emerged as one of the better centers in the league, collecting 20 points and 11.2 rebounds per contest, but he also missed 16 games with injuries. Forward Harvey Grant missed 18 games. The Bullets acquired guard Rex Chapman from Charlotte, but he was unable to play until the last game of the season because of a leg problem. The Bullets ended the year simply wishing for good health.

Orlando Magic (21-61) —The Magic was 10 games worse than the previous season, but there was a bright spot: The team acquired the rights to center Shaquille O'Neal by winning the draft lottery. The Magic also had injury problems, with Dennis Scott missing 64 games because of a nerve problem in his leg and Nick Anderson sidelined for 22 games with an eye injury. Plus, Scott Skiles had a subpar year after winning the league's Most Improved Player Award the previous season. If O'Neal lives up to expectations and the Magic can stay healthy, there will be a lot of excitement in Orlando.

MIDWEST DIVISION

Utah Jazz (55-27) —For the fourth consecutive year, the Jazz won more than 50 games. But unlike previous years when its postseason ended early, the Jazz advanced to the Western Conference finals before losing to Portland. Karl Malone again was the Jazz's foundation, averaging 28 points and 11.2 rebounds. And John Stockton led the league in assists for the fifth consecutive year, averaging 13.7. Jeff Malone was more comfortable with his role in his second year with the Jazz and popped in 20.2 points per outing. But the Jazz needed more depth, and after the season, Utah traded Blue Edwards, Eric Murdock and a No. 1 draft pick to Milwaukee in a deal that netted veteran guard Jay Humphries, who should combine with Stockton and Jeff Malone to give the Jazz one of the best three-guard rotations in the league.

San Antonio Spurs (47-35) —The Spurs had averaged 55.5 victories in the previous two seasons, but they were in a state of flux throughout 1991-92. Larry Brown was fired in January and replaced by Bob Bass. David Robinson had surgery on his thumb in March and was lost for the remainder of the season. After the season, troubled Rod Strickland was released. Jerry Tarkanian was hired as coach, but he quickly lost Terry Cummings because of a major off-season knee injury. The Spurs hope to find the stability needed for a successful team.

Houston Rockets (42-40) —Less than half a season after he won Coach of the Year honors, Don Chaney was fired. Hakeem Olajuwon was suspended during the season when, during a contract dispute, he said he could not play and the Rockets accused him of faking an injury. The bright spot on the court was the play of power forward Otis Thorpe, who earned All-Star status for the first time. Under Coach Rudy Tomjanovich, the Rockets rallied to post a winning record but barely missed their eighth straight playoff berth.

Denver Nuggets (24-58) —The Nuggets' rebuilding program took a small step forward in the standings as they improved by four victories over the previous year. But in the middle, the Nuggets took a huge step with rookie Dikembe Mutombo, who racked up 16.6 points and 12.3 rebounds per game. Along with the Nuggets' other youthful players, he gives the franchise hope for the future.

Dallas Mavericks (22-60) —Four years ago, the Mavericks were in the Western Conference finals. Last season, they were the third-worst team in the league. There have been problems galore, most notably the drug-related banishment of Roy Tarpley. The Mavericks ended the season with six players 30 or older, but then embarked on a building program. They traded Rolando Blackman to New York for a No. 1 draft choice and hoped to replace Blackman with former Ohio State guard Jim Jackson.

Minnesota Timberwolves (15-67) —The Wolves won the fewest games in their three-year history, but they hope the playing-time investment in young players Pooh Richardson, Doug West and Gerald Glass will eventually pay off. The Timberwolves selected Duke's Christian Laettner in the draft, hoping his versatility and toughness will solve their power forward problems.

PACIFIC DIVISION

Portland Trail Blazers (57-25) —The Blazers advanced to the NBA Finals for the second time in three years, but, for the second time, they were defeated. That left them in a most delicate situation. Should they make a major change, or should they avoid tampering with a winning combination? The Blazers still depend on Clyde Drexler, who finished second in MVP voting and averaged 25 points. But they did tamper with the bench, adding free agent Rod Strickland and rookie shooter Tracy Murray, whose draft rights were acquired from Milwaukee for reserve Alaa Abdelnaby. The Blazers did lose guard Danny Ainge, a free agent who signed with Phoenix.

Golden State Warriors (55-27) —Don Nelson won the Coach of the Year award—and deservedly so. Nelson may have done his finest job in 1991-92. The day before the season opener, he traded star guard Mitch Richmond to Sacramento for rookie Billy Owens. Despite that major change, Nelson directed the Warriors to their best season since 1975-76. All-Stars Chris Mullin and Tim Hardaway led a prolific offensive attack, averaging 25.6 and

George Karl (left) and Larry Brown helped to revitalize the SuperSonics and Clippers, respectively, after taking over coaching duties in midseason.

23.4 points, respectively. And Sarunas Marciulionis developed into one of the league's best sixth men as he averaged a career-high 18.9 points.

Phoenix Suns (53-29) —The Suns won more than 50 games for the fourth consecutive year, but they again came up short in the playoffs, losing to Portland. Despite their success, the Suns knew they had to do something dramatic if they were going to challenge for a championship. So, in the off-season, they sent All-Star Jeff Hornacek, Andrew Lang and Tim Perry to Philadelphia for Charles Barkley. They also signed free agent Danny Ainge. Add those two to a core group that features Kevin Johnson (19.7 points, 10.7 assists) and sixth man deluxe Dan Majerle (17.3 points), and the Suns could make a run at the Western Conference title.

Seattle SuperSonics (47-35) —The SuperSonics made a major switch at midseason, firing coach K.C. Jones and hiring George Karl, the former Golden State coach who had been directing a team in Spain. Karl is one of the most creative coaches in the business, and his offbeat approach went over well in Seattle. Karl moved Nate McMillan from guard to small forward, but assigned him most of the ball-handling duties. Karl used forward Shawn Kemp off the bench to prevent foul trouble. He employed a variety of lineups, and by the end of the season the Sonics were one of the hottest teams in the league. They upset the Warriors in the first round of the playoffs before losing to the Jazz.

Los Angeles Clippers (45-37) —The Clippers had not made the playoffs in 16 years, but in February they hired Larry Brown, who finally gave the franchise the on-court leadership it had lacked. Brown had been fired by the Spurs, but he was exactly what the young, talented Clippers needed. Danny Manning returned to the form that made him the No. 1 pick of the 1988 draft, averaging 19.3 points, and Ron Harper provided assistance with an 18.2 figure.

Los Angeles Lakers (43-39) —Despite losing Magic Johnson, the Lakers battled throughout the year and managed to win a playoff spot on the last day of the regular season. By then, they also had lost James Worthy and Sam Perkins because of injuries. They were too thin to challenge in the playoffs, losing in the first round to the Trail Blazers. But, considering the ongoing obstacles they encountered, the Lakers had a surprisingly good season.

Sacramento Kings (29-53) —The Kings also changed coaches at midseason, with Rex Hughes taking over for Dick Motta, who was fired. The Kings acquired Mitch Richmond in a trade the day before the season started, and he provided them with 22.5 points per game. Spud Webb ran the team and had the best season of his career, averaging 16 points and 7.1 assists. The Kings also got good scoring from forwards Lionel Simmons (17.1 points) and Wayman Tisdale (16.6). But the Kings lacked the bulk and experience needed to compete in the tough Western Conference. After the season, they hired Warriors assistant Garry St. Jean as their new coach.

1991-92 NBA STATISTICS

1991-92 NBA CHAMPION CHICAGO BULLS

Front row (from left to right): Bobby Hansen, Stacey King, Will Perdue, Cliff Levingston, Scott Williams, Craig Hodges. Middle row: B.J. Armstrong, Michael Jordan, Horace Grant, Bill Cartwright, Scottie Pippen, John Paxson. Back row: assistant coach Tex Winter, assistant coach Jim Cleamons, head coach Phil Jackson, assistant coach John Bach.

FINAL STANDINGS

ATLANTIC DIVISION

Team	Atl.	Bos.	Char.	Chi.	Cle.	Dal.	Den.	Det.	G.S.	Hou.	Ind.	L.A.C.	L.A.L.	Mia.	Mil.	Min.	N.J.	N.Y.	Orl.	Phi.	Pho.	Por.	Sac.	S.A.	Sea.	Uta.	Was.	W.	L.	Pct.	G.B.
Boston	1	..	3	1	3	1	1	4	1	1	2	2	3	2	0	2	3	5	3	1	1	2	1	2	1		3	51	31	.622	..
New York	2	2	4	0	0	2	2	2	1	1	3	2	0	4	3	2	3	..	4	3	1	1	1	0	2	2	4	51	31	.622	..
New Jersey	1	3	3	0	2	2	1	2	0	1	2	1	0	2	4	2	..	2	3	3	1	1	1	0	0		2	40	42	.488	11
Miami	2	2	3	0	1	1	2	2	1	0	1	0	0	..	4	2	2	1	3	1	0	0	2	1	1	1	5	38	44	.463	13
Philadelphia	2	1	1	1	0	2	0	1	1	2	1	0	4	1	2	2	1	2	..	1	0	0	0	2	0	0	5	35	47	.427	16
Washington	2	1	2	0	0	2	1	1	0	0	2	1	0	1	2	3	0	3	0		0	0	0	2	0	0	..	25	57	.305	26
Orlando	2	0	1	1	1	1	0	0	0	2	0	0	1	1	2	1	1		..	3	0	0	0	1	1	0	2	21	61	.256	30

CENTRAL DIVISION

Team	Atl.	Bos.	Char.	Chi.	Cle.	Dal.	Den.	Det.	G.S.	Hou.	Ind.	L.A.C.	L.A.L.	Mia.	Mil.	Min.	N.J.	N.Y.	Orl.	Phi.	Pho.	Por.	Sac.	S.A.	Sea.	Uta.	Was.	W.	L.	Pct.	G.B.
Chicago	5	3	4	..	3	2	2	4	1	1	3	2	1	4	3	2	4	4	3	3	1	2	2	1	2	1	4	67	15	.817	..
Cleveland	5	1	3	2	..	1	1	3	1	1	5	1	2	3	3	2	2	4	3	4	1	0	2	1	1	1	4	57	25	.695	10
Detroit	4	0	4	1	1	2	2	..	1	2	2	0	2	3	1	2	2	1	3	0	2	2	1	1	1	1	3	48	34	.585	19
Indiana	4	2	2	1	0	1	2	2	0	1	..	0	2	3	4	2	2	1	2	2	2	0	1	0	1	1	2	40	42	.488	27
Atlanta	..	3	2	0	0	2	2	1	1	2	1		1	0	2	3	2	3	2	2	2	2	0	1	0	1	2	38	44	.463	29
Charlotte	2	1	..	0	2	1	1	1	1	0	3	0	1	1	2	1	1	0	3	3	1	0	3	1	0	1	2	31	51	.378	36
Milwaukee	1	2	3	2	1	1	2	0	1	1	0	1	0	..	2	0	1	3	3	0	0	0	1	1	1	1	3	31	51	.378	36

MIDWEST DIVISION

Team	Atl.	Bos.	Char.	Chi.	Cle.	Dal.	Den.	Det.	G.S.	Hou.	Ind.	L.A.C.	L.A.L.	Mia.	Mil.	Min.	N.J.	N.Y.	Orl.	Phi.	Pho.	Por.	Sac.	S.A.	Sea.	Uta.	Was.	W.	L.	Pct.	G.B.
Utah	1	1	2	1	1	4	5	1	3	4	1	3	3	1	1	3	2	0	2	2	2	2	3	4	1	..	2	55	27	.671	..
San Antonio	2	1	0	1	1	5	4	1	2	2	0	2	3	1	1	6	1	2	1	1	1	2	3	..	3	1	0	47	35	.573	8
Houston	0	1	2	1	1	2	3	0	2	..	1	2	2	2	1	3	1	1	2	1	3	3	3	1	1	1	1	42	40	.512	13
Denver	0	1	1	0	1	2	..	0	0	2	0	0	1	0	1	2	1	0	2	2	1	1	2	1	0	1	1	24	58	.293	31
Dallas	0	1	1	0	1	..	3	0	0	4	1	1	0	1	1	3	0	0	1	0	0	1	0	0	1	0		22	60	.268	33
Minnesota	0	2	1	0	0	2	3	1	0	2	0	0	1	0	0	..	0	0	0	0	0	0	1	0	0	2	0	15	67	.183	40

PACIFIC DIVISION

Team	Atl.	Bos.	Char.	Chi.	Cle.	Dal.	Den.	Det.	G.S.	Hou.	Ind.	L.A.C.	L.A.L.	Mia.	Mil.	Min.	N.J.	N.Y.	Orl.	Phi.	Pho.	Por.	Sac.	S.A.	Sea.	Uta.	Was.	W.	L.	Pct.	G.B.
Portland	2	1	2	0	2	4	3	0	3	1	2	3	4	2	2	4	1	1	2	1	2	..	5	2	4	2	2	57	25	.695	..
Golden State	1	1	1	1	1	4	4	1	..	2	2	3	3	1	2	4	2	1	2	1	3	2	5	2	3	1	2	55	27	.671	2
Phoenix	0	1	1	1	1	2	3	2	2	3	1	2	3	2	2	4	1	1	2	2	..	3	4	3	3	2	2	53	29	.646	4
Seattle	1	0	1	0	1	4	3	1	2	3	2	3	4	1	1	4	2	0	1	0	2	1	4	1	..	3	2	47	35	.573	10
L.A. Clippers	1	0	2	0	1	3	4	2	2	2	2	..	2	2	2	4	1	0	2	1	3	2	2	2	1	0		45	37	.549	12
L.A. Lakers	2	0	1	1	0	4	3	0	2	2	0	3	..	2	1	3	2	2	2	2	2	1	4	1	1	1	1	43	39	.524	14
Sacramento	1	0	1	0	0	3	2	0	0	1	1	3	1	0	2	3	1	1	2	1	0	..	1	1	1	2		29	53	.354	28

HOME-ROAD RECORDS OF ALL TEAMS

Team	Home	Road	Total	Team	Home	Road	Total
Atlanta	23- 18	15- 26	38- 44	Milwaukee	25- 16	6- 35	31- 51
Boston	34- 7	17- 24	51- 31	Minnesota	9- 32	6- 35	15- 67
Charlotte	22- 19	9- 32	31- 51	New Jersey	25- 16	15- 26	40- 42
Chicago	36- 5	31- 10	67- 15	New York	30- 11	21- 20	51- 31
Cleveland	35- 6	22- 19	57- 25	Orlando	13- 28	8- 33	21- 61
Dallas	15- 26	7- 34	22- 60	Philadelphia	23- 18	12- 29	35- 47
Denver	18- 23	6- 35	24- 58	Phoenix	36- 5	17- 24	53- 29
Detroit	25- 16	23- 18	48- 34	Portland	33- 8	24- 17	57- 25
Golden State	31- 10	24- 17	55- 27	Sacramento	21- 20	8- 33	29- 53
Houston	28- 13	14- 27	42- 40	San Antonio	31- 10	16- 25	47- 35
Indiana	26- 15	14- 27	40- 42	Seattle	28- 13	19- 22	47- 35
L.A. Clippers	29- 12	16- 25	45- 37	Utah	37- 4	18- 23	55- 27
L.A. Lakers	24- 17	19- 22	43- 39	Washington	14- 27	11- 30	25- 57
Miami	28- 13	10- 31	38- 44	Totals	699- 408	408- 699	1107- 1107

OFFENSIVE TEAM STATISTICS

Team	G.	FG Att.	FG Made	FG Pct.	FT Att.	FT Made	FT Pct.	Off.	Def.	Tot.	Ast.	PF	Disq.	Stl.	Turn Over	Blk. Sh.	Pts.	Avg.
Golden State..	82	7427	3767	.507	2606	1944	.746	1137	2376	3513	2064	2049	24	854	1353	375	9732	118.7
Indiana	82	7079	3498	.494	2364	1868	.790	1083	2564	3647	2398	2137	25	705	1402	393	9197	112.2
Phoenix	82	7219	3553	.492	2397	1861	.776	1088	2558	3646	2202	1852	14	673	1242	582	9194	112.1
Portland	82	7352	3476	.473	2463	1858	.754	1294	2549	3843	2065	1983	25	753	1328	410	9135	111.4
Chicago	82	7168	3643	.508	2132	1587	.744	1173	2439	3612	2279	1693	4	672	1088	480	9011	109.9
Charlotte	82	7568	3613	.477	2168	1637	.755	1164	2367	3531	2284	1819	14	822	1273	309	8980	109.5
Cleveland	82	7025	3427	.488	2259	1819	.805	1041	2450	3491	2260	1556	8	616	1073	621	8926	108.9
Utah	82	6866	3379	.492	2490	1961	.788	1097	2543	3640	2188	1746	11	715	1264	448	8877	108.3
Boston	82	7196	3543	.492	1917	1549	.808	1095	2583	3678	2072	1686	14	636	1165	484	8745	106.6
Seattle	82	7128	3380	.474	2263	1772	.783	1282	2257	3539	1877	1952	22	775	1323	448	8737	106.5
Atlanta	82	7476	3492	.467	2074	1517	.731	1288	2498	3786	2123	1771	8	793	1255	320	8711	106.2
New Jersey	82	7580	3473	.458	2009	1471	.732	1512	2392	3904	1937	1834	19	736	1392	615	8641	105.4
Milwaukee	82	7216	3321	.460	2104	1596	.759	1297	2172	3469	2018	1904	25	863	1350	317	8609	105.0
Miami	82	7061	3256	.461	2329	1839	.790	1187	2366	3553	1749	1819	14	670	1377	373	8608	105.0
Sacramento	82	7189	3348	.466	2162	1615	.747	1054	2354	3408	1957	1763	10	727	1360	618	8549	104.3
San Antonio	82	7090	3377	.476	2246	1652	.736	1229	2552	3781	2010	1799	14	729	1308	608	8524	104.0
L.A. Clippers	82	7076	3347	.473	2223	1601	.720	1132	2393	3525	2053	1873	15	824	1269	498	8440	102.9
Washington	82	7301	3364	.461	1956	1521	.778	1069	2345	3414	2011	1852	12	713	1254	422	8395	102.4
Houston	82	6894	3273	.475	2020	1491	.738	1074	2432	3506	2058	1769	23	656	1378	571	8366	102.0
Philadelphia	82	6761	3187	.471	2267	1757	.775	1058	2309	3367	1755	1582	8	692	1238	482	8358	101.9
Orlando	82	7102	3220	.453	2268	1693	.746	1171	2329	3500	1792	1977	24	643	1389	367	8330	101.6
New York	82	6947	3312	.477	2049	1503	.734	1185	2489	3674	2130	1905	15	634	1242	382	8328	101.6
Minnesota	82	7342	3366	.458	1857	1379	.743	1167	2168	3335	2025	1866	13	619	1157	526	8237	100.5
L.A. Lakers	82	6977	3183	.456	2278	1744	.766	1156	2196	3352	1803	1543	6	756	1089	400	8229	100.4
Denver	82	7380	3262	.442	2067	1526	.738	1350	2352	3702	1553	1984	18	773	1447	461	8176	99.7
Detroit	82	6867	3191	.465	2108	1566	.743	1210	2421	3631	1899	1646	3	546	1212	357	8113	98.9
Dallas	82	7104	3120	.439	1999	1499	.750	1194	2439	3633	1630	1867	15	536	1202	349	8007	97.6

DEFENSIVE TEAM STATISTICS

Team	FG Att.	FG Made	FG Pct.	FT Att.	FT Made	FT Pct.	Off.	Def.	Tot	Ast.	PF	Disq.	Stl.	Turn Over	Blk. Sh.	Pts.	Avg.	Pt. Dif.
Detroit	6973	3157	.453	1866	1421	.762	1115	2255	3370	1894	1916	21	642	1117	373	7946	96.9	+2.0
New York	6727	3082	.458	2172	1666	.767	1014	2241	3255	1778	1803	19	669	1249	396	8009	97.7	+3.9
Chicago	6970	3206	.460	1985	1525	.768	1081	2171	3252	1841	1800	15	631	1288	352	8155	99.5	+10.4
San Antonio	7098	3211	.452	2061	1587	.770	1103	2362	3465	1882	1810	14	753	1252	463	8252	100.6	+3.3
L.A. Lakers	7095	3408	.480	1744	1329	.762	1234	2384	3618	2173	1831	22	594	1256	389	8319	101.5	-1.1
L.A. Clippers	6997	3211	.459	2249	1706	.759	1151	2445	3596	1784	1870	21	705	1396	432	8352	101.9	+1.1
Utah	7178	3292	.459	2056	1535	.747	1146	2255	3401	1925	1958	24	646	1205	458	8353	101.9	+6.4
Boston	7293	3323	.456	2084	1601	.768	1178	2333	3511	1923	1634	11	680	1414	414	8448	103.0	+3.6
Philadelphia	7145	3449	.483	1772	1375	.776	1171	2365	3536	2226	1766	11	686	1184	454	8462	103.2	-1.3
Cleveland	7435	3496	.470	1683	1294	.769	1236	2376	3612	2156	1874	9	649	1150	417	8479	103.4	+5.5
Houston	7317	3391	.463	1985	1529	.770	1232	2406	3638	2131	1673	13	743	1174	384	8507	103.7	-1.7
Portland	7150	3249	.454	2367	1797	.759	1097	2336	3433	1980	1957	23	688	1369	433	8539	104.1	+7.3
Seattle	6864	3263	.475	2460	1848	.751	1122	2228	3350	1832	1850	14	697	1320	479	8583	104.7	+1.9
Dallas	7051	3314	.470	2368	1823	.770	1157	2631	3788	1936	1735	19	723	1054	456	8634	105.3	-7.6
Phoenix	7477	3429	.459	2207	1669	.756	1218	2345	3563	1909	1931	11	659	1258	493	8707	106.2	+5.9
Milwaukee	6911	3445	.498	2195	1638	.746	1170	2319	3489	2118	1780	9	730	1420	473	8749	106.7	-1.7
Washington	7174	3431	.478	2240	1687	.753	1197	2636	3833	1902	1689	10	710	1325	450	8761	106.8	-4.5
New Jersey	7175	3422	.477	2318	1775	.766	1215	2355	3570	1789	1722	10	806	1343	484	8780	107.1	-1.7
Minnesota	7116	3453	.485	2337	1738	.744	1311	2534	3845	2088	1675	7	660	1215	574	8815	107.5	-7.0
Denver	6967	3346	.480	2513	1943	.773	1109	2530	3639	1811	1787	11	780	1393	593	8821	107.6	-7.9
Atlanta	7342	3523	.480	2006	1537	.766	1160	2545	3705	2168	1732	13	711	1253	393	8834	107.7	-1.5
Orlando	7045	3426	.486	2437	1830	.751	1107	2445	3552	2095	1895	16	791	1271	534	8897	108.5	-6.9
Miami	7157	3529	.493	2242	1685	.752	1134	2415	3549	2070	1968	21	731	1316	447	8953	109.2	-4.2
Indiana	7312	3425	.468	2627	1976	.752	1241	2325	3566	2165	1984	21	816	1247	386	9042	110.3	+1.9
Sacramento	7420	3557	.479	2297	1728	.752	1311	2639	3950	2128	1816	14	816	1357	530	9046	110.3	-6.1
Charlotte	7495	3717	.496	2241	1661	.741	1253	2581	3834	2366	1750	8	621	1392	524	9300	113.4	-3.9
Golden State	7507	3616	.482	2563	1923	.750	1324	2436	3760	2122	2021	15	794	1512	435	9412	114.8	+3.9

Disq.—Individual player disqualified (fouled out of game).

INDIVIDUAL LEADERS

POINTS
Minimum 70 games or 1,400 points

	G.	FG	FT	Pts.	Avg.
Jordan, Chicago	80	943	491	2404	30.1
K. Malone, Utah	81	798	673	2272	28.0
Mullin, Golden State	81	830	350	2074	25.6
Drexler, Portland	76	694	401	1903	25.0
Ewing, New York	82	796	377	1970	24.0
Hardaway, Golden State	81	734	298	1893	23.4
Robinson, San Antonio	68	592	393	1578	23.2
Barkley, Philadelphia	75	622	454	1730	23.1
Richmond, Sacramento	80	685	330	1803	22.5
Rice, Miami	79	672	266	1765	22.3

STEALS
Minimum 70 games or 125 steals

	G.	No.	Avg.
Stockton, Utah	82	244	2.98
M. Williams, Indiana	79	233	2.95
Robertson, Milwaukee	82	210	2.56
Blaylock, New Jersey	72	170	2.36
Robinson, San Antonio	68	158	2.32
Jordan, Chicago	80	182	2.28
Mullin, Golden State	81	173	2.14
Bogues, Charlotte	82	170	2.07
Threatt, L.A. Lakers	82	168	2.05
Macon, Denver	76	154	2.03

FIELD GOALS
Minimum 300 FG made

	FGA	FGM	Pct.
Williams, Portland	563	340	.604
Thorpe, Houston	943	558	.592
Grant, Chicago	790	457	.578
Daugherty, Cleveland	1010	576	.570
Cage, Seattle	542	307	.566
Barkley, Philadelphia	1126	622	.552
Robinson, San Antonio	1074	592	.551
Manning, L.A. Clippers	1199	650	.542
Ellison, Washington	1014	547	.539
Nance, Cleveland	1032	556	.539
Rodman, Detroit	635	342	.539

REBOUNDS
Minimum 70 games or 800 rebounds

	G.	Off.	Def.	Tot.	Avg.
Rodman, Detroit	82	523	1007	1530	18.7
Willis, Atlanta	81	418	840	1258	15.5
Mutombo, Denver	71	316	554	870	12.3
Robinson, San Antonio	68	261	568	829	12.2
Olajuwon, Houston	70	246	599	845	12.1
Seikaly, Miami	79	307	627	934	11.8
Anderson, Denver	82	337	604	941	11.5
Ewing, New York	82	228	693	921	11.2
K. Malone, Utah	81	225	684	909	11.2
Barkley, Philadelphia	75	271	559	830	11.1

FREE THROWS
Minimum 125 made

	FTA	FTM	Pct.
Price, Cleveland	285	270	.947
Bird, Boston	162	150	.926
Pierce, Seattle	455	417	.916
Blackman, Dallas	266	239	.898
J. Malone, Utah	285	256	.898
Skiles, Orlando	277	248	.895
Hornacek, Phoenix	315	279	.886
Gamble, Boston	157	139	.885
Dawkins, Philadelphia	186	164	.882
Anderson, Philadelphia	163	143	.877

BLOCKED SHOTS
Minimum 70 games or 100 blocked shots

	G.	No.	Avg.
Robinson, San Antonio	68	305	4.49
Olajuwon, Houston	70	304	4.34
Nance, Cleveland	81	243	3.00
Ewing, New York	82	245	2.99
Mutombo, Denver	71	210	2.96
Bol, Philadelphia	71	205	2.89
Causwell, Sacramento	80	215	2.69
Ellison, Washington	66	177	2.68
Eaton, Utah	81	205	2.53
Lang, Phoenix	81	201	2.48

ASSISTS
Minimum 70 games or 400 assists

	G.	No.	Avg.
Stockton, Utah	82	1126	13.7
Johnson, Phoenix	78	836	10.7
Hardaway, Golden State	81	807	10.0
Bogues, Charlotte	82	743	9.1
Strickland, San Antonio	57	491	8.6
Jackson, New York	81	694	8.6
Richardson, Minnesota	82	685	8.4
M. Williams, Indiana	79	647	8.2
Adams, Washington	78	594	7.6
Price, Cleveland	72	535	7.4

3-PT. FIELD GOALS
Minimum 50 made

	FGA	FGM	Pct.
Barros, Seattle	186	83	.446
Petrovic, New Jersey	277	123	.444
Hornacek, Phoenix	189	83	.439
Iuzzolino, Dallas	136	59	.434
Ellis, Milwaukee	329	138	.419
Ehlo, Cleveland	167	69	.413
Stockton, Utah	204	83	.407
Bird, Boston	128	52	.406
Curry, Charlotte	183	74	.404
Hawkins, Philadelphia	229	91	.397

TEAM-BY-TEAM INDIVIDUAL STATISTICS

ATLANTA HAWKS

Player	G.	Min.	FGA	FGM	Pct.	FTA	FTM	Pct.	Off. Reb.	Def. Reb.	Tot. Reb.	Ast.	PF	Disq.	Stl.	Blk. Sh.	Pts.	Avg.	Hi.
Wilkins	42	1601	914	424	.464	352	294	.835	103	103	158	77	0	52	24	1179	28.1	52
Willis	81	2962	1224	591	.483	363	292	.804	418	840	1258	173	223	0	72	54	1480	18.3	32
Augmon	82	2505	899	440	.489	320	213	.666	191	229	420	201	161	0	124	27	1094	13.3	32
Robinson	81	2220	928	423	.456	275	175	.636	64	155	219	446	178	0	105	24	1055	13.0	31
Ferrell	66	1598	632	331	.524	218	166	.761	105	105	210	92	134	0	49	17	839	12.7	27
Graham	78	1718	682	305	.447	170	126	.741	72	159	231	175	193	3	96	21	791	10.1	24
Rasmussen	81	1968	726	347	.478	40	30	.750	94	299	393	107	233	1	35	48	729	9.0	18
Volkov	77	1516	569	251	.441	198	125	.631	103	162	265	250	178	2	66	30	662	8.6	25
Mays	2	32	14	6	.429	2	2	1.000	1	1	2	1	4	0	0	0	17	8.5	15
Cheeks	56	1086	249	115	.462	43	26	.605	29	66	95	185	73	0	83	6	259	4.6	11
Sanders	12	117	45	20	.444	9	7	.778	9	17	26	9	15	0	5	3	47	3.9	9
Wiley (Tot)	53	870	193	83	.430	35	24	.686	24	57	81	180	89	0	47	3	204	3.8	12
Wiley (Atl)	41	767	160	71	.444	30	21	.700	22	51	73	166	73	0	43	3	177	4.3	12
Monroe	38	313	144	53	.368	23	19	.826	12	21	33	27	19	0	12	2	131	3.4	13
Koncak	77	1489	284	111	.391	29	19	.655	62	199	261	132	207	2	50	67	241	3.1	11
Leonard	5	13	6	4	.667	2	2	1.000	3	2	5	1	3	0	1	0	10	2.0	4

3-Pt. FG: Atlanta 210-671 (.313)—Wilkins 37-128 (.289); Willis 6-37 (.162); Augmon 1-6 (.167); Robinson 34-104 (.327); Ferrell 11-33 (.333); Graham 55-141 (.390); Rasmussen 5-23 (.217); Volkov 35-110 (.318); Mays 3-6 (.500); Cheeks 3-6 (.500); Wiley 14-38 (.368); Monroe 6-27 (.222); Koncak 0-12 (.000). Opponents 251-732 (.343).

BOSTON CELTICS

Player	G.	Min.	FGA	FGM	Pct.	FTA	FTM	Pct.	Off. Reb.	Def. Reb.	Tot. Reb.	Ast.	PF	Disq.	Stl.	Blk. Sh.	Pts.	Avg.	Hi.
Lewis	82	3070	1397	703	.503	343	292	.851	117	277	394	185	258	4	125	105	1703	20.8	38
Bird	45	1662	758	353	.466	162	150	.926	46	388	434	306	82	0	42	33	908	20.2	49
Parish	79	2285	874	468	.535	232	179	.772	219	486	705	70	172	2	68	97	1115	14.1	31

Player	G.	Min.	FGA	FGM	Pct.	FTA	FTM	Pct.	Off. Reb.	Def. Reb.	Tot. Reb.	Ast.	PF	Disq.	Stl.	Blk. Sh.	Pts.	Avg.	Hi.
McHale	56	1398	634	323	.509	163	134	.822	119	211	330	82	112	1	11	59	780	13.9	26
Gamble	82	2496	908	480	.529	157	139	.885	80	206	286	219	200	2	75	37	1108	13.5	34
Brown	31	883	350	149	.426	78	60	.769	15	64	79	164	74	0	33	7	363	11.7	23
Shaw	17	436	164	70	.427	40	35	.875	11	58	69	89	29	0	12	10	175	10.3	24
Fox	81	1535	525	241	.459	184	139	.755	73	147	220	126	230	3	78	30	644	8.0	31
Pinckney	81	1917	378	203	.537	255	207	.812	252	312	564	62	158	1	70	56	613	7.6	17
Douglas(Tot)	42	752	253	117	.462	107	73	.682	13	50	63	172	78	0	25	9	308	7.3	20
Douglas(Bos)	37	654	222	101	.455	100	68	.680	12	45	57	153	68	0	21	9	271	7.3	20
Bagley	73	1742	506	223	.441	95	68	.716	38	123	161	480	123	1	57	4	524	7.2	18
Kleine	70	991	293	144	.491	48	34	.708	94	202	296	32	99	0	23	14	326	4.7	15
Pritchard	11	136	34	16	.471	18	14	.778	1	10	11	30	17	0	3	4	46	4.2	10
Green	26	367	103	46	.447	18	13	.722	3	21	24	68	28	0	17	1	106	4.1	10
Robinson	1	6	5	1	.200	0	0	---	2	0	2	1	3	0	0	0	2	2.0	2
Vrankovic	19	110	32	15	.469	12	7	.583	8	20	28	5	22	0	0	17	37	1.9	5
Battle	8	46	4	3	.750	8	8	1.000	3	6	9	0	4	0	1	0	14	1.8	10
Massenburg	7	46	9	4	.444	4	2	.500	2	5	7	0	7	0	0	1	10	1.4	5

3-Pt. FG: Boston 110-359 (.306)—Lewis 5-21 (.238); Bird 52-128 (.406); McHale 0-13 (.000); Gamble 9-31 (.290); Brown 5-22 (.227); Shaw 0-7 (.000); Fox 23-70 (.329); Pinckney 0-1 (.000); Douglas 1-9 (.111); Bagley 10-42 (.238); Kleine 4-8 (.500); Pritchard 0-3 (.000); Green 1-4 (.250). Opponents 201-652 (.308).

CHARLOTTE HORNETS

Player	G.	Min.	FGA	FGM	Pct.	FTA	FTM	Pct.	Off. Reb.	Def. Reb.	Tot. Reb.	Ast.	PF	Disq.	Stl.	Blk. Sh.	Pts.	Avg.	Hi.
Gill	79	2906	1427	666	.467	381	284	.745	165	237	402	329	237	1	154	46	1622	20.5	32
Johnson	82	3047	1258	616	.490	409	339	.829	323	576	899	292	225	3	81	51	1576	19.2	34
Curry	77	2020	1038	504	.486	152	127	.836	57	202	259	177	156	1	93	20	1209	15.7	29
Newman	55	1651	618	295	.477	308	236	.766	71	108	179	146	181	4	70	14	839	15.3	41
Gattison	82	2223	799	423	.529	285	196	.688	177	403	580	131	273	4	59	69	1042	12.7	24
Chapman	21	545	240	108	.450	53	36	.679	9	45	54	86	47	0	14	8	260	12.4	27
Reid	51	1257	435	213	.490	190	134	.705	96	221	317	81	159	0	49	23	560	11.0	23
Bogues	82	2790	671	317	.472	120	94	.783	58	177	235	743	156	0	170	6	730	8.9	22
Frederick	66	852	370	161	.435	92	63	.685	75	69	144	71	91	0	40	26	389	5.9	21
Gminski	35	499	199	90	.452	28	21	.750	37	81	118	31	37	0	11	16	202	5.8	22
Lynch	55	819	223	93	.417	46	35	.761	30	55	85	83	107	0	37	9	224	4.1	12
Grandison	3	25	4	2	.500	10	6	.600	3	8	11	1	4	0	1	1	10	3.3	7
Leckner	59	716	154	79	.513	51	38	.745	49	157	206	31	114	1	9	18	196	3.3	11
Perry(Tot)	50	437	129	49	.380	41	27	.659	14	25	39	78	36	0	34	3	126	2.5	12
Perry(Cha)	40	371	114	43	.377	39	26	.667	12	20	32	64	26	0	25	2	113	2.8	12
Ansley(Tot)	10	45	18	8	.444	6	5	.833	2	4	6	2	7	0	0	0	21	2.1	9
Ansley(Cha)	2	13	7	3	.429	0	0	---	0	2	2	1	0	0	0	0	6	3.0	6
Massenburg	3	13	3	0	.000	2	1	.500	1	3	4	0	2	0	1	0	1	0.3	1
Grant	13	57	8	0	.000	2	1	.500	1	3	4	18	3	0	8	0	1	0.1	1
Hunter	1	1	0	0	---	0	0	---	0	0	0	0	0	0	0	0	0	0.0	0

3-Pt. FG: Charlotte 117-369 (.317)—Gill 6-25 (.240); Johnson 5-22 (.227); Curry 74-183 (.404); Newman 13-46 (.283); Gattison 0-2 (.000); Chapman 8-27 (.296); Reid 0-3 (.000); Bogues 2-27 (.074); Frederick 4-17 (.235); Gminski 1-3 (.333); Lynch 3-8 (.375); Leckner 0-1 (.000); Perry 1-5 (.200). Opponents 205-632 (.324).

CHICAGO BULLS

Player	G.	Min.	FGA	FGM	Pct.	FTA	FTM	Pct.	Off. Reb.	Def. Reb.	Tot. Reb.	Ast.	PF	Disq.	Stl.	Blk. Sh.	Pts.	Avg.	Hi.
Jordan	80	3102	1818	943	.519	590	491	.832	91	420	511	489	201	1	182	75	2404	30.1	51
Pippen	82	3164	1359	687	.506	434	330	.760	185	445	630	572	242	2	155	93	1720	21.0	41
Grant	81	2859	790	457	.578	317	235	.741	344	463	807	217	196	0	100	131	1149	14.2	28
Armstrong	82	1875	697	335	.481	129	104	.806	19	126	145	266	88	0	46	5	809	9.9	22
Cartwright	64	1471	445	208	.467	159	96	.604	93	231	324	87	131	0	22	14	512	8.0	17
Paxson	79	1946	487	257	.528	37	29	.784	21	75	96	241	142	0	49	9	555	7.0	16
King	79	1268	425	215	.506	158	119	.753	87	118	205	77	129	0	21	25	551	7.0	23
Perdue	77	1007	278	152	.547	91	45	.495	108	204	312	80	133	1	16	43	350	4.5	16
Hodges	56	555	242	93	.384	17	16	.941	7	17	24	54	33	0	14	1	238	4.3	21
Levingston	79	1020	251	125	.498	96	60	.625	109	118	227	66	134	0	27	45	311	3.9	13
Williams	63	690	172	83	.483	74	48	.649	90	157	247	50	122	0	13	36	214	3.4	12
Hansen(Tot)	68	809	178	79	.444	22	8	.364	17	60	77	69	134	0	27	3	173	2.5	13
Hansen(Chi)	66	769	169	75	.444	22	8	.364	15	58	73	68	128	0	26	3	165	2.5	13
Randall	15	67	22	10	.455	8	6	.750	4	5	9	7	8	0	0	0	26	1.7	8
Hopson	2	10	2	1	.500	0	0	---	0	0	0	0	2	0	1	0	2	1.0	2
Sparrow	4	18	8	1	.125	0	0	---	0	1	1	4	2	0	0	0	3	0.8	3
Nevitt	4	9	3	1	.333	0	0	---	0	1	1	1	2	0	0	0	2	0.5	2

3-Pt. FG: Chicago 138-454 (.304)—Jordan 27-100 (.270); Pippen 16-80 (.200); Grant 0-2 (.000); Armstrong 35-87 (.402); Paxson 12-44 (.273); King 2-5 (.400); Perdue 1-2 (.500); Hodges 36-96 (.375); Levingston 1-6 (.167); Williams 0-3 (.000); Hansen 7-25 (.280); Randall 0-2 (.000); Sparrow 1-2 (.500). Opponents 218-657 (.332).

CLEVELAND CAVALIERS

Player	G.	Min.	FGA	FGM	Pct.	FTA	FTM	Pct.	Off. Reb.	Def. Reb.	Tot. Reb.	Ast.	PF	Disq.	Stl.	Blk. Sh.	Pts.	Avg.	Hi.
Daugherty	73	2643	1010	576	.570	533	414	.777	191	569	760	262	190	1	65	78	1566	21.5	32
Price	72	2138	897	438	.488	285	270	.947	38	135	173	535	113	0	94	12	1247	17.3	30
Nance	81	2880	1032	556	.539	320	263	.822	213	457	670	232	200	2	80	243	1375	17.0	35
Ehlo	63	2016	684	310	.453	123	87	.707	94	213	307	238	150	0	78	22	776	12.3	29
Williams	80	2432	678	341	.503	359	270	.752	228	379	607	196	191	2	60	182	952	11.9	30
Battle	76	1637	659	316	.480	171	145	.848	19	93	112	159	116	0	36	5	779	10.3	21
Brandon	82	1605	601	252	.419	124	100	.806	49	113	162	316	107	0	81	22	605	7.4	19
Sanders(Tot)	31	633	161	92	.571	47	36	.766	27	69	96	53	83	1	24	10	221	7.1	23
Sanders(Cle)	21	552	139	81	.583	41	31	.756	27	61	88	42	75	1	22	9	194	9.2	23
Kerr	48	847	237	121	.511	54	45	.833	14	64	78	110	29	0	27	10	319	6.6	24
James	65	866	403	164	.407	76	61	.803	35	77	112	25	94	1	16	11	418	6.4	19
Ferry	68	937	328	134	.409	73	61	.836	53	160	213	75	135	0	22	15	346	5.1	15
Bennett	52	831	209	79	.378	50	35	.700	62	99	161	38	121	1	19	9	193	3.7	14

Player	G.	Min.	FGA	FGM	Pct.	FTA	FTM	Pct.	Off. Reb.	Def. Reb.	Tot. Reb.	Ast.	PF	Disq.	Stl.	Blk. Sh.	Pts.	Avg.	Hi.
Oliver	27	252	98	39	.398	22	17	.773	9	18	27	20	22	0	9	2	96	3.6	11
Morton	4	54	12	3	.250	9	8	.889	3	4	7	5	3	0	1	0	14	3.5	7
Phills	10	65	28	12	.429	11	7	.636	4	4	8	4	3	0	3	1	31	3.1	11
Brown	6	50	10	5	.500	8	5	.625	2	4	6	3	7	0	3	0	15	2.5	5

3-Pt. FG: Cleveland 253-708 (.357)—Daugherty 0-2 (.000); Price 101-261 (.387); Nance 0-6 (.000); Ehlo 69-167 (.413); Williams 0-4 (.000); Battle 2-17 (.118); Brandon 1-23 (.043); Sanders 1-3 (.333); Kerr 32-74 (.432); James 29-90 (.322); Ferry 17-48 (.354); Bennett 0-1 (.000); Oliver 1-9 (.111); Morton 0-1 (.000); Phills 0-2 (.000). Opponents 193-581 (.332).

DALLAS MAVERICKS

Player	G.	Min.	FGA	FGM	Pct.	FTA	FTM	Pct.	Off. Reb.	Def. Reb.	Tot. Reb.	Ast.	PF	Disq.	Stl.	Blk. Sh.	Pts.	Avg.	Hi.
Blackman	75	2527	1161	535	.461	266	239	.898	78	161	239	204	134	0	50	22	1374	18.3	31
Harper	65	2252	1011	448	.443	261	198	.759	49	121	170	373	150	0	101	17	1152	17.7	38
Williams	75	2040	851	367	.431	171	124	.725	106	348	454	94	189	2	35	98	859	11.5	26
Lever	31	884	349	135	.387	80	60	.750	56	105	161	107	73	0	46	12	347	11.2	32
T. Davis	68	2149	531	256	.482	285	181	.635	228	444	672	57	202	1	26	29	693	10.2	20
Iuzzolino	52	1280	355	160	.451	128	107	.836	27	71	98	194	79	0	33	1	486	9.3	23
McCray	75	2106	622	271	.436	153	110	.719	149	319	468	219	180	2	48	30	677	9.0	24
Smith	76	1707	702	291	.415	121	89	.736	129	262	391	129	259	5	62	34	671	8.8	26
Moore	42	782	325	130	.400	78	65	.833	31	51	82	48	97	0	32	4	355	8.5	19
Hodge	51	1058	328	163	.497	150	100	.667	118	157	275	39	128	2	25	23	426	8.4	24
White	65	1021	382	145	.380	162	124	.765	96	140	236	31	157	1	31	22	418	6.4	20
Donaldson	44	994	227	107	.471	84	59	.702	97	173	270	31	86	0	8	44	273	6.2	15
Howard	27	318	104	54	.519	31	22	.710	17	34	51	14	55	2	11	8	131	4.9	14
Garrick (Tot)	40	549	143	59	.413	26	18	.692	12	44	56	98	54	0	36	4	137	3.4	13
Garrick (Dal)	6	63	17	4	.235	2	2	1.000	2	4	6	17	7	0	8	0	10	1.7	4
Quinnett (Tot)	39	326	124	43	.347	26	16	.615	16	35	51	12	32	0	16	8	115	2.9	14
Quinnett (Dal)	15	136	51	15	.294	12	8	.667	7	20	27	5	11	0	9	2	41	2.7	8
B. Davis	33	429	86	38	.442	15	11	.733	4	29	33	66	57	0	11	3	92	2.8	8
Vianna	1	9	2	1	.500	0	0	---	0	0	0	2	3	0	0	2	2	2.0	2

3-Pt. FG: Dallas 268-797 (.336)—Blackman 65-169 (.385); Harper 58-186 (.312); Williams 1-6 (.167); Lever 17-52 (.327); T. Davis 0-5 (.000); Iuzzolino 59-136 (.434); McCray 25-85 (.294); Smith 1-1 (.000); Moore 30-84 (.357); White 4-27 (.148); Howard 1-2 (.500); Garrick 0-1 (.000); Quinnett 3-15 (.200); B. Davis 5-18 (.278). Opponents 183-599 (.306).

DENVER NUGGETS

Player	G.	Min.	FGA	FGM	Pct.	FTA	FTM	Pct.	Off. Reb.	Def. Reb.	Tot. Reb.	Ast.	PF	Disq.	Stl.	Blk. Sh.	Pts.	Avg.	Hi.
Williams	81	2623	1277	601	.471	269	216	.803	145	90	235	270	4	148	68	1474	18.2	32
Mutombo	71	2716	869	428	.493	500	321	.642	316	554	870	156	273	1	43	210	1177	16.6	39
Anderson	82	2793	854	389	.456	268	167	.623	337	640	941	78	263	3	88	65	945	11.5	30
Garland	78	2209	750	333	.444	199	171	.859	67	123	190	411	206	1	98	22	846	10.8	26
Macon	76	2304	889	333	.375	185	135	.730	80	140	220	168	242	4	154	14	805	10.6	23
Jackson	81	1538	845	356	.421	108	94	.870	22	92	114	192	130	0	44	4	837	10.3	29
Davis	46	741	403	185	.459	94	82	.872	20	50	70	68	69	0	29	1	457	9.9	20
Liberty	75	1527	621	275	.443	180	131	.728	144	164	308	58	165	3	66	29	698	9.3	25
Lichti	68	1176	376	173	.460	118	99	.839	36	82	118	74	131	0	43	12	446	6.6	17
Wolf	67	1160	277	100	.361	66	53	.803	97	143	240	61	124	1	32	14	254	3.8	15
Lane	9	141	40	10	.250	19	8	.421	22	22	44	13	18	0	2	1	28	3.1	10
Brooks	37	270	97	43	.443	21	17	.810	13	26	39	11	19	0	8	2	105	2.8	13
Scheffler (Tot)	11	61	9	6	.667	12	9	.750	10	4	14	0	10	0	3	1	21	1.9	7
Scheffler (Den)	7	46	7	4	.571	6	4	.667	8	3	11	0	8	0	3	0	12	1.7	6
Cook	22	115	25	15	.600	6	4	.667	13	21	34	2	10	0	5	4	34	1.5	7
Hastings	40	421	50	17	.340	28	24	.857	30	68	98	26	56	0	10	15	58	1.5	10

3-Pt. FG: Denver 126-418 (.301)—Williams 56-156 (.359); Anderson 0-4 (.000); Garland 9-28 (.321); Macon 4-30 (.133); Jackson 31-94 (.330); Davis 5-16 (.313); Liberty 17-50 (.340); Lichti 1-9 (.111); Wolf 1-11 (.091); Brooks 2-11 (.182); Hastings 0-9 (.000). Opponents 186-532 (.350).

DETROIT PISTONS

Player	G.	Min.	FGA	FGM	Pct.	FTA	FTM	Pct.	Off. Reb.	Def. Reb.	Tot. Reb.	Ast.	PF	Disq.	Stl.	Blk. Sh.	Pts.	Avg.	Hi.
Dumars	82	3192	1311	587	.448	475	412	.867	82	106	188	375	145	0	71	12	1635	19.9	45
I. Thomas	78	2918	1264	564	.446	378	292	.772	68	179	247	560	194	2	118	15	1445	18.5	44
Woolridge	82	2113	907	452	.498	353	241	.683	109	151	260	88	154	0	41	33	1146	14.0	34
Aguirre	75	1582	787	339	.431	230	158	.687	67	169	236	126	171	0	51	11	851	11.3	27
Rodman	82	3301	635	342	.539	140	84	.600	523	1007	1530	191	248	0	68	70	800	9.8	20
Laimbeer	81	2234	727	342	.470	75	67	.893	104	347	451	160	225	0	51	54	783	9.7	26
Salley	72	1774	486	249	.512	260	186	.715	106	190	296	116	222	1	49	110	684	9.5	23
Walker	74	1541	381	161	.423	105	65	.619	85	153	238	205	134	0	63	18	387	5.2	19
Bedford	32	363	121	50	.413	22	14	.636	24	39	63	12	56	0	6	18	114	3.6	11
Sellers	43	226	88	41	.466	26	20	.769	15	27	42	14	20	0	1	10	102	2.4	13
Henderson (Tot)	16	96	32	12	.375	11	9	.818	1	7	8	10	12	0	3	0	36	2.3	8
Henderson (Det)	8	62	21	8	.381	5	5	1.000	0	6	6	5	8	0	3	0	24	3.0	8
Blanks	43	189	55	25	.455	11	8	.727	9	13	22	19	26	0	14	1	64	1.5	12
C. Thomas	37	156	51	18	.353	15	10	.667	6	16	22	22	20	0	4	1	48	1.3	11
McCann	26	129	33	13	.394	13	4	.308	12	18	30	6	23	0	6	4	30	1.2	10

3-Pt. FG: Detroit 165-526 (.314)—Dumars 49-120 (.408); I. Thomas 25-86 (.291); Woolridge 1-9 (.111); Aguirre 15-71 (.211); Rodman 32-101 (.317); Laimbeer 32-85 (.376); Salley 0-3 (.000); Walker 0-10 (.000); Bedford 0-1 (.000); Sellers 0-1 (.000); Henderson 3-5 (.600); Blanks 6-16 (.375); C. Thomas 2-17 (.118); McCann 0-1 (.000). Opponents 211-625 (.338).

GOLDEN STATE WARRIORS

Player	G.	Min.	FGA	FGM	Pct.	FTA	FTM	Pct.	Off. Reb.	Def. Reb.	Tot. Reb.	Ast.	PF	Disq.	Stl.	Blk. Sh.	Pts.	Avg.	Hi.
Mullin	81	3346	1584	830	.524	420	350	.833	127	323	450	286	171	1	173	62	2074	25.6	40
Hardaway	81	3332	1592	734	.461	389	298	.766	81	229	310	807	208	1	164	13	1893	23.4	43
Marciulionis	72	2117	912	491	.538	477	376	.788	68	140	208	243	237	4	116	10	1361	18.9	35

Player	G.	Min.	FGA	FGM	Pct.	FTA	FTM	Pct.	Off. Reb.	Def. Reb.	Tot. Reb.	Ast.	PF	Disq.	Stl.	Blk. Sh.	Pts.	Avg.	Hi.
Owens	80	2510	891	468	.525	312	204	.654	243	396	639	188	276	4	90	65	1141	14.3	30
Higgins	25	535	211	87	.412	59	48	.814	30	55	85	22	75	2	15	13	255	10.2	23
Hill	82	1886	487	254	.522	235	163	.694	182	411	593	47	315	7	73	43	671	8.2	20
Elie	79	1677	424	221	.521	182	155	.852	69	158	227	174	159	3	68	15	620	7.8	27
Alexander	80	1350	459	243	.529	149	103	.691	106	230	336	32	176	0	45	62	589	7.4	28
Askew	80	1496	379	193	.509	160	111	.694	89	144	233	188	128	1	47	23	498	6.2	16
Gatling	54	612	206	117	.568	109	72	.661	75	107	182	16	101	0	31	36	306	5.7	18
Jackson	5	54	23	11	.478	6	4	.667	5	5	10	3	7	1	2	0	26	5.2	11
Lister	26	293	79	44	.557	33	14	.424	21	71	92	14	61	0	5	16	102	3.9	15
Tolbert	35	310	86	33	.384	40	22	.550	14	41	55	21	73	0	10	6	90	2.6	9
Buechler (Tot)	28	290	71	29	.408	21	12	.571	18	34	52	23	31	0	19	7	70	2.5	8
Buechler (GS)	15	121	33	10	.303	12	9	.750	10	18	28	10	11	0	9	3	29	1.9	7
Battle (Tot)	16	92	17	11	.647	12	10	.833	4	12	16	4	10	0	2	2	32	2.0	10
Battle (GS)	8	46	13	8	.615	4	2	.500	1	6	7	4	6	0	1	2	18	2.3	6
Massenburg (Tot)	18	90	25	10	.400	15	9	.600	7	18	25	0	21	0	1	1	29	1.6	6
Massenburg (GS)	7	22	8	5	.625	9	6	.667	4	8	12	0	10	0	0	0	16	2.3	6
Petersen	27	169	40	18	.450	10	7	.700	12	33	45	9	35	0	5	6	43	1.6	6
Thompson	1	1	0	0	---	0	0	---	0	0	0	0	0	0	0	0	0	0.0	0
Smrek	2	3	0	0	---	0	0	---	0	1	1	0	0	0	0	0	0	0.0	0

3-Pt. FG: Golden State 254-763 (.333)—Mullin 64-175 (.366); Hardaway 127-376 (.338); Marciulionis 3-10 (.300); Owens 1-9 (.111); Higgins 33-95 (.347); Hill 0-1 (.000); Elie 23-70 (.329); Alexander 0-1 (.000); Askew 1-10 (.100); Gatling 0-4 (.000); Tolbert 2-8 (.250); Buechler 0-1 (.000); Battle 0-1 (.000); Petersen 0-2 (.000). Opponents 257-776 (.331).

HOUSTON ROCKETS

Player	G.	Min.	FGA	FGM	Pct.	FTA	FTM	Pct.	Off. Reb.	Def. Reb.	Tot. Reb.	Ast.	PF	Disq.	Stl.	Blk. Sh.	Pts.	Avg.	Hi.
Olajuwon	70	2636	1177	591	.502	428	328	.766	246	599	845	157	263	7	127	304	1510	21.6	40
Thorpe	82	3056	943	558	.592	463	304	.657	285	577	862	250	307	7	52	37	1420	17.3	33
Maxwell	80	2700	1216	502	.413	267	206	.772	37	206	243	326	200	3	104	28	1372	17.2	35
K. Smith	81	2735	910	432	.475	253	219	.866	34	143	177	562	112	0	104	7	1137	14.0	35
Floyd	82	1662	704	286	.406	170	135	.794	34	116	150	239	128	0	57	21	744	9.1	31
B. Johnson	80	2202	633	290	.458	143	104	.727	95	217	312	158	234	2	72	49	685	8.6	20
Bullard	80	1278	447	205	.459	50	38	.760	73	150	223	75	129	1	26	21	512	6.4	20
A. Johnson (Tot)	69	1235	330	158	.479	101	66	.653	13	67	80	266	89	1	61	9	386	5.6	22
A. Johnson (Hou)	49	772	222	103	.464	69	42	.609	8	37	45	166	46	0	40	6	251	5.1	22
Herrera	43	566	161	83	.516	44	25	.568	33	66	99	27	60	0	16	25	191	4.4	14
Jamerson	48	378	191	79	.414	27	25	.926	22	21	43	33	39	0	17	0	191	4.0	16
Turner	42	345	98	43	.439	59	31	.525	38	40	78	12	40	0	6	4	117	2.8	15
L. Smith	45	800	92	50	.543	11	4	.364	107	149	256	33	121	3	21	7	104	2.3	15
Rollins	59	697	86	46	.535	30	26	.867	61	110	171	15	85	0	14	62	118	2.0	13
Henderson	8	34	11	4	.364	6	4	.667	1	1	2	5	4	0	0	0	12	1.5	6
Winchester	4	17	3	1	.333	0	0	---	0	0	0	0	1	0	0	0	2	0.5	2
Godfread	1	2	0	0	---	0	0	---	0	0	0	0	0	0	0	0	0	0.0	0

3-Pt. FG: Houston 329-959 (.343)—Olajuwon 0-1 (.000); Thorpe 0-7 (.000); Maxwell 162-473 (.342); K. Smith 54-137 (.394); Floyd 37-123 (.301); B. Johnson 1-9 (.111); Bullard 64-166 (.386); A. Johnson 3-10 (.300); Herrera 0-1 (.000); Jamerson 8-28 (.286); L. Smith 0-1 (.000); Henderson 0-3 (.000). Opponents 196-574 (.341).

INDIANA PACERS

Player	G.	Min.	FGA	FGM	Pct.	FTA	FTM	Pct.	Off. Reb.	Def. Reb.	Tot. Reb.	Ast.	PF	Disq.	Stl.	Blk. Sh.	Pts.	Avg.	Hi.
Miller	82	3120	1121	562	.501	515	442	.858	82	236	318	314	210	1	105	26	1695	20.7	37
Person	81	2923	1284	616	.480	197	133	.675	114	312	426	382	247	5	68	18	1497	18.5	41
Schrempf	80	2605	925	496	.536	441	365	.828	202	568	770	312	286	4	62	37	1380	17.3	35
M. Williams	79	2750	824	404	.490	427	372	.871	73	209	282	647	262	7	233	22	1188	15.0	28
Smits	74	1772	855	436	.510	193	152	.788	124	293	417	116	231	4	29	100	1024	13.8	31
Fleming	82	1737	610	294	.482	179	132	.737	69	140	209	266	134	0	56	7	726	8.9	28
McCloud	51	892	313	128	.409	64	50	.781	45	87	132	116	95	1	26	11	338	6.6	20
Davis	64	1301	279	154	.552	152	87	.572	158	252	410	30	191	2	27	74	395	6.2	19
Thompson	80	1299	359	168	.468	71	58	.817	98	283	381	102	207	0	52	34	394	4.9	16
K. Williams	60	565	218	113	.518	43	26	.605	64	65	129	40	99	0	20	41	252	4.2	23
Green	35	256	158	62	.392	28	15	.536	22	20	42	22	31	0	13	6	141	4.0	15
Sanders	10	81	22	11	.500	6	5	.833	0	8	8	11	8	0	2	1	27	2.7	8
Lane	3	30	5	3	.600	6	0	.000	9	9	18	4	9	0	0	0	6	2.0	4
Dreiling	60	509	87	43	.494	40	30	.750	22	74	96	25	123	1	10	16	117	2.0	15
Wittman	24	115	19	8	.421	2	1	.500	1	8	9	11	4	0	2	0	17	0.7	4

3-Pt. FG: Indiana 333-940 (.354)—Miller 129-341 (.378); Person 132-354 (.373); Schrempf 23-71 (.324); M. Williams 8-33 (.242); Smits 0-2 (.000); Fleming 6-27 (.222); McCloud 32-94 (.340); Davis 0-1 (.000); Thompson 0-2 (.000); K. Williams 0-4 (.000); Green 2-10 (.200); Dreiling 1-1 (1.000). Opponents 216-640 (.338).

LOS ANGELES CLIPPERS

Player	G.	Min.	FGA	FGM	Pct.	FTA	FTM	Pct.	Off. Reb.	Def. Reb.	Tot. Reb.	Ast.	PF	Disq.	Stl.	Blk. Sh.	Pts.	Avg.	Hi.
Manning	82	2904	1199	650	.542	385	279	.725	229	335	564	285	293	5	135	122	1579	19.3	34
Harper	82	3144	1292	569	.440	398	293	.736	120	327	447	417	199	0	152	72	1495	18.2	30
Smith	49	1310	539	251	.466	270	212	.785	95	206	301	56	159	2	41	98	714	14.6	30
Norman	77	2009	821	402	.490	226	121	.535	158	290	448	125	145	0	53	66	929	12.1	27
Do. Rivers	59	1657	533	226	.424	196	163	.832	23	124	147	233	166	2	111	19	641	10.9	23
Edwards	72	1437	538	250	.465	271	198	.731	55	147	202	53	236	1	24	33	698	9.7	26
Polynice	76	1834	470	244	.519	201	125	.622	195	341	536	46	165	0	45	20	613	8.1	23
Grant	78	2049	595	275	.462	54	44	.815	34	150	184	538	181	4	138	14	609	7.8	20
Vaught	79	1687	551	271	.492	69	55	.797	160	352	512	71	165	1	37	31	601	7.6	23
Brown	22	254	89	39	.438	29	18	.621	9	19	28	16	31	0	12	1	103	4.7	13
Young (Tot)	62	1023	255	100	.392	67	57	.851	16	59	75	172	53	0	46	4	280	4.5	13
Young (LAC)	44	889	215	84	.391	53	47	.887	16	50	66	152	47	0	40	4	235	5.3	13
Mayes (Tot)	24	255	99	30	.303	36	24	.667	3	13	16	35	41	0	16	2	99	4.1	12
Mayes (LAC)	3	40	5	2	.400	6	4	.667	0	1	1	3	9	0	2	1	9	3.0	5
Kimble	34	277	111	44	.396	31	20	.645	13	19	32	17	37	0	10	6	112	3.3	15

Player	G.	Min.	FGA	FGM	Pct.	FTA	FTM	Pct.	Off. Reb.	Def. Reb.	Tot. Reb.	Ast.	PF	Disq.	Stl.	Blk. Sh.	Pts.	Avg.	Hi.
Da. Rivers	15	122	30	10	.333	11	10	.909	10	9	19	21	14	0	7	1	30	2.0	9
Copeland	10	48	23	7	.304	2	2	1.000	1	6	7	5	5	0	2	0	16	1.6	8
Ellis	29	103	50	17	.340	19	9	.474	12	12	24	1	11	0	6	9	43	1.5	6
Perry	10	66	15	6	.400	2	1	.500	2	5	7	14	10	0	9	1	13	1.3	7

3-Pt. FG: L.A. Clippers 145-502 (.289)—Manning 0-5 (.000); Harper 64-211 (.303); Smith 0-6 (.000); Norman 4-28 (.143); Do. Rivers 26-92 (.283); Edwards 0-1 (.000); Polynice 0-1 (.000); Grant 15-51 (.294); Vaught 4-5 (.800); Brown 7-22 (.318); Young 20-60 (.333); Mayes 1-2 (.500); Kimble 4-13 (.308); Da. Rivers 0-1 (.000); Copeland 0-2 (.000); Perry 0-2 (.000). Opponents 224-648 (.346).

LOS ANGELES LAKERS

Player	G.	Min.	FGA	FGM	Pct.	FTA	FTM	Pct.	Off. Reb.	Def. Reb.	Tot. Reb.	Ast.	PF	Disq.	Stl.	Blk. Sh.	Pts.	Avg.	Hi.
Worthy	54	2108	1007	450	.447	204	166	.814	98	207	305	252	89	0	76	23	1075	19.9	37
Perkins	63	2332	803	361	.450	372	304	.817	192	364	556	141	192	1	64	62	1041	16.5	29
Threatt	82	3070	1041	509	.489	243	202	.831	43	210	253	593	231	1	168	16	1240	15.1	42
Scott	82	2679	1005	460	.458	291	244	.838	74	236	310	226	140	0	105	28	1218	14.9	31
Green	82	2902	803	382	.476	457	340	.744	306	456	762	117	141	0	91	36	1116	13.6	28
Divac	36	979	317	157	.495	112	86	.768	87	160	247	60	114	3	55	35	405	11.3	32
Teagle	82	1602	805	364	.452	197	151	.766	91	92	183	113	148	0	66	9	880	10.7	28
Campbell	81	1876	491	220	.448	223	138	.619	155	268	423	59	203	1	53	159	578	7.1	25
Smith	63	820	283	113	.399	75	49	.653	31	45	76	109	91	0	39	8	275	4.4	18
Brown (Tot)	42	431	128	60	.469	49	30	.612	31	51	82	26	48	0	12	7	150	3.6	16
Brown (LAL)	36	381	118	55	.466	41	25	.610	29	47	76	23	41	0	9	7	135	3.8	16
Robinson	9	78	27	11	.407	8	7	.875	7	12	19	9	4	0	5	0	29	3.2	10
Sparrow (Tot)	46	489	151	58	.384	13	8	.615	3	25	28	83	57	0	12	5	127	2.8	12
Sparrow (LAL)	42	471	143	57	.399	13	8	.615	3	24	27	79	55	0	12	5	124	3.0	12
Calip	7	58	18	4	.222	3	2	.667	1	4	5	12	8	0	1	0	11	1.6	3
Haley	49	394	84	31	.369	29	14	.483	31	64	95	7	75	0	7	8	76	1.6	11
Owens	20	80	32	9	.281	10	8	.800	8	7	15	3	11	0	5	4	26	1.3	8

3-Pt. FG: L.A. Lakers 119-445 (.267)—Worthy 9-43 (.209); Perkins 15-69 (.217); Threatt 20-62 (.323); Scott 54-157 (.344); Green 12-56 (.214); Divac 5-19 (.263); Teagle 1-4 (.250); Campbell 0-2 (.000); Smith 0-11 (.000); Brown 0-3 (.000); Robinson 0-1 (.000); Sparrow 2-13 (.154); Calip 1-5 (.200). Opponents 174-596 (.292).

MIAMI HEAT

Player	G.	Min.	FGA	FGM	Pct.	FTA	FTM	Pct.	Off. Reb.	Def. Reb.	Tot. Reb.	Ast.	PF	Disq.	Stl.	Blk. Sh.	Pts.	Avg.	Hi.
Rice	79	3007	1432	672	.469	318	266	.836	84	310	394	184	170	0	90	35	1765	22.3	46
Seikaly	79	2800	947	463	.489	505	370	.733	307	627	934	109	278	2	40	121	1296	16.4	28
Long	82	3063	890	440	.494	404	326	.807	259	432	691	225	248	2	139	40	1212	14.8	29
Smith	61	1806	654	297	.454	127	95	.748	81	107	188	278	162	1	59	19	729	12.0	24
Burton	68	1585	622	280	.450	245	196	.800	76	168	244	123	186	2	46	37	762	11.2	28
Edwards	81	1840	716	325	.454	191	162	.848	56	155	211	170	138	1	99	20	819	10.1	26
Coles	81	1976	649	295	.455	262	216	.824	69	120	189	366	151	3	73	13	816	10.1	22
Shaw (Tot)	63	1423	513	209	.407	91	72	.791	50	154	204	250	115	0	57	22	495	7.9	24
Shaw (Mia)	46	987	349	139	.398	51	37	.725	39	96	135	161	86	0	45	12	320	7.0	20
Douglas	5	98	31	16	.516	7	5	.714	1	5	6	19	10	0	4	0	37	7.4	11
Kessler	77	1197	383	158	.413	115	94	.817	114	200	314	34	185	3	17	32	410	5.3	15
Morton (Tot)	25	270	93	36	.387	38	32	.842	6	20	26	32	23	0	13	1	106	4.2	16
Morton (Mia)	21	216	81	33	.407	29	24	.828	3	16	19	27	20	0	12	1	92	4.4	16
Askins	59	843	205	84	.410	37	26	.703	65	77	142	38	109	0	40	15	219	3.7	18
Bennett (Tot)	54	833	211	80	.379	50	35	.700	63	99	162	38	122	1	19	9	195	3.6	14
Bennett (Mia)	2	2	2	1	.500	0	0	---	1	0	1	0	1	0	0	0	2	1.0	2
Ogg	43	367	84	46	.548	30	16	.533	30	44	74	7	73	0	5	28	108	2.5	10
Babic	9	35	13	6	.462	8	6	.750	2	9	11	6	0	0	1	0	18	2.0	6
Sundvold	3	8	3	1	.333	0	0	---	0	0	0	2	2	0	0	0	3	1.0	3

3-Pt. FG: Miami 257-751 (.342)—Rice 155-396 (.391); Seikaly 0-3 (.000); Long 6-22 (.273); Smith 40-125 (.320); Burton 6-15 (.400); Edwards 7-32 (.219); Coles 10-52 (.192); Shaw 5-16 (.313); Douglas 0-1 (.000); Morton 2-15 (.133); Askins 25-73 (.342); Sundvold 1-1 (1.000). Opponents 210-606 (.347).

MILWAUKEE BUCKS

Player	G.	Min.	FGA	FGM	Pct.	FTA	FTM	Pct.	Off. Reb.	Def. Reb.	Tot. Reb.	Ast.	PF	Disq.	Stl.	Blk. Sh.	Pts.	Avg.	Hi.
Ellis	81	2191	1034	485	.469	212	164	.774	92	161	253	104	151	0	57	18	1272	15.7	31
Malone	82	2511	929	440	.474	504	396	.786	320	424	744	93	136	0	74	64	1279	15.6	30
Humphries	71	2261	803	377	.469	249	195	.783	44	140	184	466	210	2	119	13	991	14.0	28
Robertson	82	2463	922	396	.430	198	151	.763	175	175	350	360	263	5	210	32	1010	12.3	30
Brickowski	65	1556	584	306	.524	163	125	.767	97	247	344	122	223	11	60	23	740	11.4	26
Roberts	80	1746	645	311	.482	171	128	.749	103	154	257	122	177	0	52	40	769	9.6	25
Krystkowiak	79	1848	660	293	.444	169	128	.757	131	298	429	114	218	2	54	12	714	9.0	21
Grayer	82	1659	689	309	.448	153	102	.667	129	128	257	150	142	0	64	13	739	9.0	27
Lohaus	70	1081	360	162	.450	41	27	.659	65	184	249	74	144	5	40	71	408	5.8	24
Schayes	43	726	199	83	.417	96	74	.771	58	110	168	34	98	0	19	19	240	5.6	25
Conner	81	1420	239	103	.431	115	81	.704	63	121	184	294	86	0	97	10	287	3.5	15
Henson	50	386	144	52	.361	29	23	.793	17	24	41	82	50	0	15	1	150	3.0	17
Lane (Tot)	14	177	46	14	.304	27	9	.333	32	34	66	17	28	0	2	1	37	2.6	10
Lane (Mil)	2	6	1	1	1.000	2	1	.500	1	3	4	0	1	0	0	0	3	1.5	3
Popson	5	26	7	3	.429	2	1	.500	2	3	5	3	5	0	2	1	7	1.4	3

3-Pt. FG: Milwaukee 371-1005 (.369)—Ellis 138-329 (.419); Malone 3-8 (.375); Humphries 42-144 (.292); Robertson 67-210 (.319); Brickowski 3-6 (.500); Roberts 19-37 (.514); Krystkowiak 0-5 (.000); Grayer 19-66 (.288); Lohaus 57-144 (.396); Conner 0-7 (.000); Henson 23-48 (.479); Popson 0-1 (.000). Opponents 221-603 (.367).

MINNESOTA TIMBERWOLVES

Player	G.	Min.	FGA	FGM	Pct.	FTA	FTM	Pct.	Off. Reb.	Def. Reb.	Tot. Reb.	Ast.	PF	Disq.	Stl.	Blk. Sh.	Pts.	Avg.	Hi.
Campbell	78	2441	1137	527	.464	299	240	.803	141	145	286	229	206	1	84	31	1307	16.8	36
Richardson	82	2922	1261	587	.466	178	123	.691	91	210	301	685	152	0	119	25	1350	16.5	27
Corbin	11	344	142	57	.401	53	44	.830	24	45	69	33	31	0	12	6	158	14.4	23
West	80	2540	894	463	.518	231	186	.805	107	150	257	281	239	1	66	26	1116	14.0	28
Glass	75	1822	871	383	.440	125	77	.616	107	153	260	175	171	0	66	30	859	11.5	31
Bailey (Tot)	84	2104	836	368	.440	270	215	.796	122	363	485	78	160	1	35	117	951	11.3	22

Player	G.	Min.	FGA	FGM	Pct.	FTA	FTM	Pct.	Off. Reb.	Def. Reb.	Tot. Reb.	Ast.	PF	Disq.	Stl.	Blk. Sh.	Pts.	Avg.	Hi.
Bailey (Min)	71	1777	735	329	.448	215	171	.795	99	308	407	59	129	1	30	102	829	11.7	22
Mitchell	82	2151	725	307	.423	266	209	.786	158	315	473	94	230	3	53	39	825	10.1	24
Spencer	61	1481	331	141	.426	178	123	.691	167	268	435	53	241	7	27	79	405	6.6	20
Breuer	67	1176	344	161	.468	77	41	.532	98	183	281	89	117	0	27	99	363	5.4	18
Brooks	82	1082	374	167	.447	63	51	.810	27	72	99	205	82	0	66	7	417	5.1	21
Frank	10	140	33	18	.545	15	10	.667	8	18	26	8	24	0	5	4	46	4.6	13
Longley	66	991	249	114	.458	80	53	.663	67	190	257	53	157	0	35	64	281	4.3	20
Randall (Tot)	54	441	149	68	.456	43	32	.744	39	32	71	33	39	0	12	3	171	3.2	14
Randall (Min)	39	374	127	58	.457	35	26	.743	35	27	62	26	31	0	12	3	145	3.7	14
Brown	4	23	6	4	.667	0	0	---	0	3	3	6	2	0	1	0	9	2.3	4
Murphy	47	429	80	39	.488	34	19	.559	36	74	110	11	40	0	9	8	98	2.1	13
Garrick	15	112	33	11	.333	8	6	.750	2	7	9	18	14	0	7	3	29	1.9	7

3-Pt. FG: Minnesota 126-394 (.320)—Campbell 13-37 (.351); Richardson 53-155 (.342); Corbin 0-1 (.000); West 4-23 (.174); Glass 16-54 (.296); Bailey 0-1 (.000); Mitchell 2-11 (.182); Breuer 0-1 (.000); Brooks 32-90 (.356); Randall 3-14 (.214); Brown 1-3 (.333); Murphy 1-2 (.500); Garrick 1-2 (.500). Opponents 171-483 (.354).

NEW JERSEY NETS

Player	G.	Min.	FGA	FGM	Pct.	FTA	FTM	Pct.	Off. Reb.	Def. Reb.	Tot. Reb.	Ast.	PF	Disq.	Stl.	Blk. Sh.	Pts.	Avg.	Hi.
Petrovic	82	3027	1315	668	.508	287	232	.808	97	161	258	252	248	3	105	11	1691	20.6	39
Coleman	65	2207	958	483	.504	393	300	.763	203	415	618	205	168	2	54	98	1289	19.8	38
Bowie	71	2179	947	421	.445	280	212	.757	203	375	578	186	212	2	41	120	1062	15.0	34
Blaylock	72	2548	993	429	.432	177	126	.712	101	168	269	492	182	1	170	40	996	13.8	27
Morris	77	2394	726	346	.477	231	165	.714	199	295	494	197	211	2	129	81	879	11.4	22
Mills	82	1714	670	310	.463	152	114	.750	187	266	453	84	200	3	48	41	742	9.0	25
Anderson	64	1086	480	187	.390	98	73	.745	38	89	127	203	68	0	67	9	450	7.0	18
George	70	1037	386	165	.427	106	87	.821	36	69	105	162	98	0	41	3	418	6.0	22
Addison	76	1175	432	187	.433	76	56	.737	65	100	165	68	109	1	28	28	444	5.8	19
Dudley	82	1902	472	190	.403	171	80	.468	343	396	739	58	275	5	38	179	460	5.6	16
Buechler	2	29	8	4	.500	0	0	---	2	0	2	2	2	0	2	1	8	4.0	6
Lee	46	307	116	50	.431	19	10	.526	17	18	35	22	39	0	11	1	120	2.6	9
Feitl	34	175	77	33	.429	19	16	.842	21	40	61	6	22	0	2	3	82	2.4	8

3-Pt. FG: New Jersey 224-670 (.334)—Petrovic 123-277 (.444); Coleman 23-76 (.303); Bowie 8-25 (.320); Blaylock 12-54 (.222); Morris 22-110 (.200); Mills 8-23 (.348); Anderson 3-13 (.231); George 1-6 (.167); Addison 14-49 (.286); Lee 10-37 (.270). Opponents 161-508 (.317).

NEW YORK KNICKERBOCKERS

Player	G.	Min.	FGA	FGM	Pct.	FTA	FTM	Pct.	Off. Reb.	Def. Reb.	Tot. Reb.	Ast.	PF	Disq.	Stl.	Blk. Sh.	Pts.	Avg.	Hi.
Ewing	82	3150	1525	796	.522	511	377	.738	228	693	921	156	277	2	88	245	1970	24.0	45
Starks	82	2118	902	405	.449	302	235	.778	45	146	191	276	231	4	103	18	1139	13.9	30
McDaniel	82	2344	1021	488	.478	192	137	.714	176	284	460	149	241	3	57	24	1125	13.7	37
Wilkins	82	2344	964	431	.447	159	116	.730	74	132	206	219	195	4	76	17	1016	12.4	28
Jackson	81	2461	747	367	.491	222	171	.770	95	210	305	694	153	0	112	13	916	11.3	30
Mason	82	2198	399	203	.509	260	167	.642	216	357	573	106	229	0	46	20	573	7.0	17
Vandeweghe	67	956	383	188	.491	81	65	.802	31	57	88	57	87	0	15	8	467	7.0	25
Oakley	82	2309	402	210	.522	117	86	.735	256	444	700	133	258	2	67	15	506	6.2	17
Anthony	82	1510	435	161	.370	158	117	.741	33	103	136	314	170	0	59	9	447	5.5	20
Donaldson (Tot)	58	1075	245	112	.457	86	61	.709	99	190	289	33	103	0	8	49	285	4.9	15
Donaldson (NY)	14	81	18	5	.278	2	2	1.000	2	17	19	2	17	0	0	5	12	0.9	2
Quinnett	24	190	73	28	.384	14	8	.571	9	15	24	7	21	0	7	6	74	3.1	14
McKinney	2	9	9	2	.222	0	0	---	0	1	1	0	1	0	0	0	4	2.0	2
McCormick	22	108	33	14	.424	21	14	.667	14	20	34	9	18	0	2	0	42	1.9	7
Winchester (Tot)	19	81	30	13	.433	10	8	.800	6	9	15	8	5	0	2	2	35	1.8	4
Winchester (NY)	15	64	27	12	.444	10	8	.800	6	9	15	8	4	0	2	2	33	2.2	4
Eddie	4	13	9	2	.222	0	0	---	0	1	1	0	3	0	0	0	4	1.0	2

3-Pt. FG: New York 201-618 (.325)—Ewing 1-6 (.167); Starks 94-270 (.348); McDaniel 12-39 (.308); Wilkins 38-108 (.352); Jackson 11-43 (.256); Vandeweghe 26-66 (.394); Oakley 0-3 (.000); Anthony 8-55 (.145); Quinnett 10-26 (.385); Winchester 1-2 (.500). Opponents 179-606 (.295).

ORLANDO MAGIC

Player	G.	Min.	FGA	FGM	Pct.	FTA	FTM	Pct.	Off. Reb.	Def. Reb.	Tot. Reb.	Ast.	PF	Disq.	Stl.	Blk. Sh.	Pts.	Avg.	Hi.
Scott	18	608	331	133	.402	71	64	.901	14	52	66	35	49	1	20	9	359	19.9	29
Anderson	60	2203	1042	482	.463	302	202	.667	98	286	384	163	132	0	97	33	1196	19.9	37
Catledge	78	2430	922	457	.496	346	240	.694	257	292	549	109	196	2	58	16	1154	14.8	30
Bowie	52	1721	633	312	.493	136	117	.860	70	175	245	163	101	1	55	38	758	14.6	31
Skiles	75	2377	868	359	.414	277	248	.895	36	166	202	544	188	0	74	5	1057	14.1	41
Reynolds	46	1159	518	197	.380	189	158	.836	47	102	149	151	69	0	63	17	555	12.1	30
Vincent	39	885	349	150	.430	130	110	.846	19	82	101	148	55	1	35	4	411	10.5	35
Roberts	55	1118	446	236	.529	196	101	.515	113	223	336	39	221	7	22	83	573	10.4	24
Williams	48	905	324	171	.528	142	95	.669	115	157	272	33	139	2	41	53	437	9.1	24
Higgins (Tot)	38	616	277	127	.458	36	31	.861	29	73	102	41	58	0	16	6	291	7.7	29
Higgins (Orl)	32	580	262	123	.469	29	24	.828	27	67	94	37	52	0	14	6	276	8.6	29
Turner	75	1591	499	225	.451	114	79	.693	62	184	246	92	229	6	24	16	530	7.1	21
Smith	55	877	316	116	.365	91	70	.769	40	76	116	57	85	1	36	13	310	5.6	22
Corchiani	51	741	193	77	.399	104	91	.875	18	60	78	141	90	0	45	2	255	5.0	11
Kite	72	1479	215	94	.437	68	40	.588	156	246	402	44	212	2	30	57	228	3.2	11
Acres	68	926	151	78	.517	67	51	.761	97	155	252	22	140	1	25	15	208	3.1	13
Wiley	9	90	28	9	.321	5	3	.600	2	5	7	13	13	0	4	0	21	2.3	7
Thompson	1	15	3	1	.333	0	0	---	0	1	1	1	2	0	2	0	2	2.0	2

3-Pt. FG: Orlando 197-608 (.324)—Scott 29-89 (.326); Anderson 30-85 (.353); Catledge 0-4 (.000); Bowie 17-44 (.386); Skiles 91-250 (.364); Reynolds 3-24 (.125); Vincent 1-13 (.077); Roberts 0-1 (.000); Higgins 6-24 (.250); Turner 1-8 (.125); Smith 8-21 (.381); Corchiani 10-37 (.270); Kite 0-1 (.000); Acres 1-3 (.333); Wiley 0-4 (.000). Opponents 215-609 (.353).

PHILADELPHIA 76ers

Player	G.	Min.	FGA	FGM	Pct.	FTA	FTM	Pct.	Off. Reb.	Def. Reb.	Tot. Reb.	Ast.	PF	Disq.	Stl.	Blk. Sh.	Pts.	Avg.	Hi.
Barkley	75	2881	1126	622	.552	653	454	.695	271	559	830	308	196	2	136	44	1730	23.1	38
Hawkins	81	3013	1127	521	.462	461	403	.874	53	218	271	248	174	0	157	43	1536	19.0	43

Player	G.	Min.	FGA	FGM	Pct.	FTA	FTM	Pct.	Off. Reb.	Def. Reb.	Tot. Reb.	Ast.	PF	Disq.	Stl.	Blk. Sh.	Pts.	Avg.	Hi.
Gilliam	81	2771	1001	512	.511	425	343	.807	234	426	660	118	176	1	51	85	1367	16.9	31
Anderson	82	2432	1008	469	.465	163	143	.877	96	182	278	135	128	0	86	11	1123	13.7	34
Dawkins	82	2815	902	394	.437	186	164	.882	42	185	227	567	158	0	89	5	988	12.0	26
Shackleford	72	1399	422	205	.486	95	63	.663	145	270	415	46	205	3	38	51	473	6.6	17
Wiggins	49	569	229	88	.384	51	35	.686	43	51	94	22	67	0	20	1	211	4.3	19
Mayes	21	215	94	28	.298	30	20	.667	3	12	15	32	32	0	14	1	90	4.3	12
Williams	50	646	206	75	.364	88	56	.636	62	83	145	12	110	1	20	20	206	4.1	12
Ruland	13	209	38	20	.526	16	11	.688	16	31	47	5	45	0	7	4	51	3.9	9
Grant (Tot)	68	891	225	99	.440	24	20	.833	14	55	69	217	76	0	45	2	225	3.3	15
Grant (Phi)	55	834	217	99	.456	22	19	.864	13	52	65	199	73	0	37	2	224	4.1	15
Payne	49	353	145	65	.448	13	9	.692	13	41	54	17	34	0	16	8	144	2.9	24
Oliver	34	279	100	33	.330	22	15	.682	10	20	30	20	33	0	10	2	81	2.4	12
Ansley	8	32	11	5	.455	6	5	.833	2	2	4	2	6	0	0	0	15	1.9	9
Bol	71	1267	128	49	.383	26	12	.462	54	168	222	22	139	1	11	205	110	1.5	8
Hoppen	11	40	7	2	.286	10	5	.500	1	9	10	2	6	0	0	0	9	0.8	5

3-Pt. FG: Philadelphia 227-680 (.334)—Barkley 32-137 (.234); Hawkins 91-229 (.397); Gilliam 0-2 (.000); Anderson 42-127 (.331); Dawkins 36-101 (.356); Shackleford 0-1 (.000); Wiggins 0-1 (.000); Mayes 14-39 (.359); Grant 7-18 (.389); Payne 5-12 (.417); Oliver 0-4 (.000); Bol 0-9 (.000). Opponents 189-615 (.307).

PHOENIX SUNS

Player	G.	Min.	FGA	FGM	Pct.	FTA	FTM	Pct.	Off. Reb.	Def. Reb.	Tot. Reb.	Ast.	PF	Disq.	Stl.	Blk. Sh.	Pts.	Avg.	Hi.
Hornacek	81	3078	1240	635	.512	315	279	.886	106	301	407	411	218	1	158	31	1632	20.1	35
Johnson	78	2899	1125	539	.479	555	448	.807	61	231	292	836	180	0	116	23	1536	19.7	44
Majerle	82	2853	1153	551	.478	303	229	.756	148	335	483	274	158	0	131	43	1418	17.3	37
Chambers	69	1948	989	426	.431	311	258	.830	86	315	401	142	196	1	57	37	1128	16.3	36
Perry	80	2483	789	413	.523	215	153	.712	204	347	551	134	237	2	44	116	982	12.3	27
Lang	81	1965	475	248	.522	164	126	.768	170	376	546	43	306	8	48	201	622	7.7	21
Ceballos	64	725	365	176	.482	148	109	.736	60	92	152	50	52	0	16	11	462	7.2	27
West	82	1436	310	196	.632	171	109	.637	134	238	372	22	239	2	14	81	501	6.1	16
Burtt	31	356	160	74	.463	54	38	.704	10	24	34	59	58	0	16	4	187	6.0	23
Knight	42	631	217	103	.475	48	33	.688	16	30	46	112	58	0	24	3	243	5.8	19
Mustaf	52	545	193	92	.477	71	49	.690	45	100	145	45	59	0	21	16	233	4.5	19
Rambis	28	381	82	38	.463	18	14	.778	23	83	106	37	46	0	12	14	90	3.2	11
Nealy	52	505	121	62	.512	24	16	.667	25	86	111	37	45	0	16	2	160	3.1	17

3-Pt. FG: Phoenix 227-596 (.381)—Hornacek 83-189 (.439); Johnson 10-46 (.217); Majerle 87-228 (.382); Chambers 18-49 (.367); Perry 3-8 (.375); Lang 0-1 (.000); Ceballos 1-6 (.167); Knight 4-13 (.308); Nealy 20-50 (.400). Opponents 180-586 (.307).

PORTLAND TRAIL BLAZERS

Player	G.	Min.	FGA	FGM	Pct.	FTA	FTM	Pct.	Off. Reb.	Def. Reb.	Tot. Reb.	Ast.	PF	Disq.	Stl.	Blk. Sh.	Pts.	Avg.	Hi.
Drexler	76	2751	1476	694	.470	505	401	.794	166	334	500	512	229	2	138	70	1903	25.0	48
Porter	82	2784	1129	521	.461	368	315	.856	51	204	255	477	155	1	127	12	1485	18.1	31
Kersey	77	2553	852	398	.467	262	174	.664	241	392	633	243	254	1	114	71	971	12.6	28
Robinson	82	2124	854	398	.466	330	219	.664	140	276	416	137	274	11	85	107	1016	12.4	22
Williams	80	2519	563	340	.604	293	221	.754	260	444	704	108	244	4	62	41	901	11.3	23
Duckworth	82	2222	786	362	.461	226	156	.690	151	346	497	99	264	5	38	37	880	10.7	23
Ainge	81	1595	676	299	.442	131	108	.824	40	108	148	202	148	0	73	13	784	9.7	27
Abdelnaby	71	934	361	178	.493	101	76	.752	81	179	260	30	132	1	25	16	432	6.1	20
Pack	72	894	272	115	.423	127	102	.803	32	65	97	140	101	0	40	4	332	4.6	16
Bryant	56	800	198	95	.480	60	40	.667	87	114	201	41	105	0	26	8	230	4.1	18
Whatley	23	209	51	21	.412	31	27	.871	6	15	21	34	12	0	14	3	69	3.0	12
Strothers	4	17	12	4	.333	4	2	.500	1	0	1	1	2	0	1	1	10	2.5	7
Young	18	134	40	16	.400	14	10	.714	0	9	9	20	6	0	6	0	45	2.5	12
Cooper	35	344	82	35	.427	11	7	.636	38	63	101	21	57	0	4	27	77	2.2	10

3-Pt. FG: Portland 325-944 (.344)—Drexler 114-338 (.337); Porter 128-324 (.395); Kersey 1-8 (.125); Robinson 1-11 (.091); Williams 0-1 (.000); Duckworth 0-3 (.000); Ainge 78-230 (.339); Pack 0-10 (.000); Bryant 0-3 (.000); Whatley 0-4 (.000); Strothers 0-2 (.000); Young 3-10 (.300). Opponents 244-805 (.303).

SACRAMENTO KINGS

Player	G.	Min.	FGA	FGM	Pct.	FTA	FTM	Pct.	Off. Reb.	Def. Reb.	Tot. Reb.	Ast.	PF	Disq.	Stl.	Blk. Sh.	Pts.	Avg.	Hi.
Richmond	80	3095	1465	685	.468	406	330	.813	62	257	319	411	231	1	92	34	1803	22.5	37
Simmons	78	2895	1162	527	.454	365	281	.770	149	485	634	337	205	0	135	132	1336	17.1	33
Tisdale	72	2521	1043	522	.500	198	151	.763	135	334	469	106	248	3	55	79	1195	16.6	29
Webb	77	2724	1006	448	.445	305	262	.859	30	193	223	547	193	1	125	24	1231	16.0	28
Thomas	1	31	12	5	.417	2	1	.500	0	0	0	1	3	0	1	0	12	12.0	12
Hopson (Tot)	71	1314	593	276	.465	253	179	.708	105	101	206	102	115	0	67	39	743	10.5	26
Hopson (Sac)	69	1304	591	275	.465	253	179	.708	105	101	206	102	113	0	66	39	741	10.7	26
Bonner	79	2287	658	294	.447	241	151	.627	192	293	485	125	194	0	94	26	740	9.4	21
Causwell	80	2291	455	250	.549	222	136	.613	196	384	580	59	281	4	47	215	636	8.0	19
Hansen	2	40	9	4	.444	0	0	---	2	2	4	1	6	0	1	0	8	4.0	6
Les	62	712	192	74	.385	47	38	.809	11	52	63	143	58	0	31	3	231	3.7	17
Chilcutt	69	817	250	113	.452	28	23	.821	78	109	187	38	70	0	32	17	251	3.6	19
Brown	56	535	169	77	.456	58	38	.655	26	43	69	59	60	0	35	12	192	3.4	12
Schintzius	33	400	117	50	.427	12	10	.833	43	75	118	20	67	1	6	28	110	3.3	12
Scheffler	4	15	2	2	1.000	6	5	.833	2	1	3	0	2	0	0	1	9	2.3	7
Thompson (Tot)	19	91	37	14	.378	8	3	.375	11	8	19	8	9	0	6	3	31	1.6	5
Thompson (Sac)	18	76	34	13	.382	8	3	.375	11	7	18	7	7	0	6	3	29	1.6	5
Jepsen	31	87	24	9	.375	11	7	.636	12	18	30	1	17	0	1	5	25	0.8	4

3-Pt. FG: Sacramento 238-675 (.353)—Richmond 103-268 (.384); Simmons 1-5 (.200); Tisdale 0-2 (.000); Webb 73-199 (.367); Thomas 1-2 (.500); Hopson 12-47 (.255); Bonner 1-4 (.250); Causwell 0-1 (.000); Hansen 0-2 (.000); Les 45-131 (.344); Chilcutt 2-2 (1.000); Brown 0-6 (.000); Schintzius 0-4 (.000); Thompson 0-1 (.000); Jepsen 0-1 (.000). Opponents 204-616 (.331).

SAN ANTONIO SPURS

Player	G.	Min.	FGA	FGM	Pct.	FTA	FTM	Pct.	Off. Reb.	Def. Reb.	Tot. Reb.	Ast.	PF	Disq.	Stl.	Blk. Sh.	Pts.	Avg.	Hi.
Robinson	68	2564	1074	592	.551	561	393	.701	261	568	829	181	219	2	158	305	1578	23.2	39
Cummings	70	2149	1053	514	.488	249	177	.711	247	384	631	102	210	4	58	34	1210	17.3	35

Player	G.	Min.	FGA	FGM	Pct.	FTA	FTM	Pct.	Off. Reb.	Def. Reb.	Tot. Reb.	Ast.	PF	Disq.	Stl.	Blk. Sh.	Pts.	Avg.	Hi.
Elliott	82	3120	1040	514	.494	331	285	.861	143	296	439	214	149	0	84	29	1338	16.3	33
Strickland	57	2053	659	300	.455	265	182	.687	92	173	265	491	122	0	118	17	787	13.8	28
Anderson	57	1889	685	312	.455	138	107	.775	62	238	300	302	151	2	54	51	744	13.1	36
Carr	81	1867	732	359	.490	212	162	.764	128	218	346	63	264	5	32	96	881	10.9	30
V. Johnson	60	1350	499	202	.405	85	55	.647	67	115	182	145	93	0	41	14	478	8.0	17
A. Johnson	20	463	108	55	.509	32	24	.750	5	30	35	100	43	1	21	3	135	6.8	15
Tucker (Tot)	24	415	129	60	.465	20	16	.800	8	29	37	27	39	0	21	3	155	6.5	15
Tucker (SA)	24	415	129	60	.465	20	16	.800	8	29	37	27	39	0	21	3	155	6.5	15
Garrick	19	374	93	44	.473	16	10	.625	8	33	41	63	33	0	21	1	98	5.2	13
Green	80	1127	344	147	.427	89	73	.820	92	250	342	36	148	0	29	11	367	4.6	15
Royal	60	718	178	80	.449	133	92	.692	65	59	124	34	73	0	25	7	252	4.2	18
Sutton	67	601	240	93	.388	45	34	.756	6	41	47	91	111	0	26	9	246	3.7	14
Buechler	11	140	30	15	.500	9	3	.333	6	16	22	11	18	0	8	3	33	3.0	8
Pressey	56	759	161	60	.373	41	28	.683	22	73	95	142	86	0	29	19	151	2.7	11
Higgins	6	36	15	4	.267	7	7	1.000	2	6	8	4	6	0	2	0	15	2.5	7
Massenburg	1	9	5	1	.200	0	0	---	0	0	0	2	0	0	0	0	2	2.0	2
Wiley	3	13	5	3	.600	0	0	---	0	1	1	1	3	0	0	0	6	2.0	4
Copa	33	132	40	22	.550	13	4	.308	14	22	36	3	29	0	2	6	48	1.5	5
Bardo	1	1	0	0	---	0	0	---	0	0	0	0	0	0	0	0	0	0.0	0

3-Pt. FG: San Antonio 118-404 (.292)—Robinson 1-8 (.125); Cummings 5-13 (.385); Elliott 25-82 (.305); Strickland 5-15 (.333); Anderson 13-56 (.232); Carr 1-5 (.200); V. Johnson 19-60 (.317); A. Johnson 1-5 (.200); Tucker 19-48 (.396); Garrick 0-1 (.000); Sutton 26-89 (.292); Pressey 3-21 (.143); Higgins 0-1 (.000). Opponents 243-700 (.347).

SEATTLE SUPERSONICS

Player	G.	Min.	FGA	FGM	Pct.	FTA	FTM	Pct.	Off. Reb.	Def. Reb.	Tot. Reb.	Ast.	PF	Disq.	Stl.	Blk. Sh.	Pts.	Avg.	Hi.
Pierce	78	2658	1306	620	.475	455	417	.916	93	140	233	241	213	2	86	20	1690	21.7	34
Johnson	81	2366	1164	534	.459	338	291	.861	118	174	292	161	199	0	55	11	1386	17.1	39
Kemp	64	1808	718	362	.504	361	270	.748	264	401	665	86	261	13	70	124	994	15.5	27
McKey	52	1757	604	285	.472	222	188	.847	95	173	268	120	142	2	61	47	777	14.9	29
Benjamin	63	1941	740	354	.478	249	171	.687	130	383	513	76	185	1	39	118	879	14.0	27
Payton	81	2549	734	331	.451	148	99	.669	123	172	295	506	248	0	147	21	764	9.4	22
Cage	82	2461	542	307	.566	171	106	.620	266	462	728	92	237	0	99	55	720	8.8	23
Barros	75	1331	493	238	.483	79	60	.759	17	64	81	125	84	0	51	4	619	8.3	19
McMillan	72	1652	405	177	.437	84	54	.643	92	160	252	359	218	4	129	29	435	6.0	20
Brown (Tot)	57	655	249	102	.410	66	48	.727	32	52	84	48	82	0	30	5	271	4.8	13
Brown (Sea)	35	401	160	63	.394	37	30	.811	23	33	56	32	51	0	18	4	168	4.8	12
Dailey	11	98	37	9	.243	16	13	.813	2	10	12	4	6	0	5	1	31	2.8	13
Conlon	45	381	101	48	.475	32	24	.750	33	36	69	12	40	0	9	7	120	2.7	14
King	40	213	71	27	.380	45	34	.756	20	29	49	12	42	0	4	5	88	2.2	10
Kofoed	44	239	53	25	.472	26	15	.577	6	20	26	51	26	0	2	2	66	1.5	15

3-Pt. FG: Seattle 205-647 (.317)—Pierce 33-123 (.268); Johnson 27-107 (.252); Kemp 0-3 (.000); McKey 19-50 (.380); Benjamin 0-2 (.000); Payton 3-23 (.130); Cage 0-5 (.000); Barros 83-186 (.446); McMillan 27-98 (.276); Brown 12-41 (.293); Dailey 0-1 (.000); King 0-1 (.000); Kofoed 1-7 (.143). Opponents 209-621 (.337).

UTAH JAZZ

Player	G.	Min.	FGA	FGM	Pct.	FTA	FTM	Pct.	Off. Reb.	Def. Reb.	Tot. Reb.	Ast.	PF	Disq.	Stl.	Blk. Sh.	Pts.	Avg.	Hi.
K. Malone	81	3054	1516	798	.526	865	673	.778	225	684	909	241	226	2	108	51	2272	28.0	44
J. Malone	81	2922	1353	691	.511	285	256	.869	49	184	233	180	126	1	56	5	1639	20.2	35
Stockton	82	3002	939	453	.482	366	308	.842	68	202	270	1126	234	3	244	22	1297	15.8	27
Edwards	81	2283	830	433	.522	146	113	.774	86	212	298	137	236	1	81	46	1018	12.6	30
Corbin (Tot)	80	2207	630	303	.481	201	174	.866	163	309	472	140	193	1	82	20	780	9.8	23
Corbin (Utah)	69	1863	488	246	.504	148	130	.878	139	264	403	107	162	1	70	14	622	9.0	21
Bailey	13	327	101	39	.386	55	44	.800	23	55	78	19	31	0	5	15	122	9.4	21
Brown	82	1783	488	221	.453	285	190	.667	187	289	476	81	196	1	42	34	632	7.7	24
Benoit	77	1161	375	175	.467	100	81	.810	105	191	296	34	124	0	19	44	434	5.6	15
Murdock	50	478	183	76	.415	61	46	.754	21	33	54	92	52	0	30	7	203	4.1	12
Eaton	81	2023	240	107	.446	87	52	.598	150	341	491	40	239	2	36	205	266	3.3	14
Rudd	65	538	188	75	.399	42	32	.762	15	39	54	109	64	0	15	1	193	3.0	12
Crowder	51	328	112	43	.384	18	15	.833	16	25	41	17	35	0	7	2	114	2.2	10
Thornton	2	6	7	1	.143	2	2	1.000	2	0	2	0	1	0	0	0	4	2.0	4
Austin	31	112	46	21	.457	30	19	.633	11	24	35	5	20	0	2	2	61	2.0	7

3-Pt. FG: Utah 158-458 (.345)—K. Malone 3-17 (.176); J. Malone 1-12 (.083); Stockton 83-204 (.407); Edwards 39-103 (.379); Corbin 0-3 (.000); Bailey 0-1 (.000); Brown 0-1 (.000); Benoit 3-14 (.214); Murdock 5-26 (.192); Rudd 11-47 (.234); Crowder 13-30 (.433). Opponents 234-695 (.337).

WASHINGTON BULLETS

Player	G.	Min.	FGA	FGM	Pct.	FTA	FTM	Pct.	Off. Reb.	Def. Reb.	Tot. Reb.	Ast.	PF	Disq.	Stl.	Blk. Sh.	Pts.	Avg.	Hi.
Ellison	66	2511	1014	547	.539	312	227	.728	217	523	740	190	222	2	62	177	1322	20.0	31
Adams	78	2795	1233	485	.393	360	313	.869	58	252	310	594	162	1	145	9	1408	18.1	40
Grant	64	2388	1022	489	.478	220	176	.800	157	275	432	170	178	1	74	67	1155	18.0	33
Eackles	65	1463	759	355	.468	187	139	.743	39	139	178	125	145	1	47	7	856	13.2	40
Chapman (Tot)	22	567	252	113	.448	53	36	.679	10	48	58	89	51	0	15	8	270	12.3	27
Chapman (Was)	1	22	12	5	.417	0	0	---	1	3	4	3	4	0	1	0	10	10.0	10
Hammonds	37	984	400	195	.488	82	50	.610	49	136	185	36	118	1	22	13	440	11.9	31
English	81	1665	846	366	.433	176	148	.841	74	94	168	143	160	1	32	9	886	10.9	27
Stewart	76	2229	590	303	.514	233	188	.807	186	263	449	120	225	3	51	44	794	10.4	23
Wingate	81	2127	572	266	.465	146	105	.719	80	189	269	247	162	1	123	21	638	7.9	18
A. King	6	59	30	11	.367	8	7	.875	1	10	11	5	7	0	3	0	31	5.2	11
Smith	48	708	246	100	.407	56	45	.804	30	51	81	99	98	0	44	1	247	5.1	17
Foster	49	548	193	89	.461	49	35	.714	43	102	145	35	83	0	6	12	213	4.3	17
Turner	70	871	261	111	.425	77	61	.792	17	73	90	177	59	0	57	2	284	4.1	15
Strong	1	12	4	0	.000	4	3	.750	1	4	5	1	1	0	0	0	3	3.0	3
Sampson	10	108	29	9	.310	6	4	.667	11	19	30	4	14	1	3	8	22	2.2	7
Jones	75	1365	90	33	.367	40	20	.500	105	212	317	62	214	0	43	92	86	1.1	6

3-Pt. FG: Washington 146-537 (.272)—Ellison 1-3 (.333); Adams 125-386 (.324); Grant 1-8 (.125); Eackles 7-35 (.200); Chapman 0-2 (.000); Hammonds 0-1 (.000); English 6-34 (.176); Stewart 0-3 (.000); Wingate 1-18 (.056); A. King 2-7 (.286); Smith 2-21 (.095); Foster 0-1 (.000); Turner 1-16 (.063); Sampson 0-2 (.000). Opponents 212-601 (.353).

TOP 1991-92 PERFORMANCES

*Denotes each overtime period.

MOST POINTS IN A GAME

	FG.	FT.	Pts.
Dominique Wilkins, Atlanta vs. New York, December 7, 1991	**17	16	52
Michael Jordan, Chicago at Washington, March 19, 1992	19	12	51
Michael Jordan, Chicago vs. Denver, March 24, 1992	18	12	50
Larry Bird, Boston vs. Portland, March 15, 1992	**19	9	49
Clyde Drexler, Portland vs. San Antonio, November 24, 1991	17	11	48
Michael Jordan, Chicago at Milwaukee, November 2, 1991	19	7	46
Michael Jordan, Chicago vs. Cleveland, February 17, 1992	21	4	46
Glen Rice, Miami vs. Orlando, April 11, 1992	19	4	46
Patrick Ewing, New York vs. Detroit, November 30, 1991	17	11	45
Joe Dumars, Detroit at Golden State, March 12, 1992	17	9	45
Michael Jordan, Chicago at Boston, November 6, 1991	16	9	44
Isiah Thomas, Detroit vs. Utah, November 15, 1991	15	12	44
Kevin Johnson, Phoenix vs. Utah, November 30, 1991	*16	10	44
Michael Jordan, Chicago at Milwaukee, January 3, 1992	19	6	44
Karl Malone, Utah at Golden State, March 3, 1992	16	12	44
Michael Jordan, Chicago vs. Cleveland, March 28, 1992	21	2	44
Hersey Hawkins, Philadelphia at Orlando, November 13, 1991	13	13	43
Patrick Ewing, New York at Atlanta, December 7, 1991	**18	7	43
Dominique Wilkins, Atlanta at Chicago, December 21, 1991	16	10	43
Karl Malone, Utah vs. Phoenix, January 31, 1992	*13	17	43
Tim Hardaway, Golden State vs. Boston, February 19, 1992	14	13	43
Sedale Threatt, L.A. Lakers at New York, March 10, 1992	16	9	42
Karl Malone, Utah vs. Golden State, April 13, 1992	11	20	42
Karl Malone, Utah at Phoenix, November 30, 1991	*15	11	41
Dominique Wilkins, Atlanta vs. Milwaukee, December 10, 1991	17	7	41
Scott Skiles, Orlando at Indiana, January 17, 1992	14	9	41
Johnny Newman, Charlotte vs. Indiana, January 25, 1992	14	12	41
Chuck Person, Indiana vs. Sacramento, February 19, 1992	14	8	41
Scottie Pippen, Chicago at Milwaukee, February 28, 1992	17	7	41
Clyde Drexler, Portland at Boston, March 15, 1992	**12	13	41
Michael Adams, Washington vs. Boston, November 2, 1991	*15	5	40
Michael Jordan, Chicago vs. Golden State, November 5, 1991	17	5	40
Tim Hardaway, Golden State at Philadelphia, November 8, 1991	17	4	40
Michael Jordan, Chicago at Portland, November 29, 1991	**16	8	40
Chris Mullin, Golden State vs. Portland, December 20, 1991	15	10	40
Michael Jordan, Chicago at Miami, January 8, 1992	17	6	40
Hakeem Olajuwon, Houston at Seattle, February 11, 1992	16	8	40
Kevin Johnson, Phoenix at Portland, February 18, 1992	17	6	40
Ledell Eackles, Washington at Atlanta, February 19, 1992	*16	6	40
Karl Malone, Utah at Sacramento, March 12, 1992	14	12	40
Michael Jordan, Chicago at New Jersey, March 17, 1992	16	8	40

MOST FIELD GOALS MADE IN A GAME

	FGA	FGM
Michael Jordan, Chicago vs. Cleveland, February 17, 1992	32	21
Michael Jordan, Chicago vs. Cleveland, March 28, 1992	32	21
Michael Jordan, Chicago at Milwaukee, November 2, 1991	29	19
Michael Jordan, Chicago at Milwaukee, January 3, 1992	29	19
Larry Bird, Boston vs. Portland, March 15, 1992	**35	19
Michael Jordan, Chicago at Washington, March 19, 1992	30	19
Glen Rice, Miami vs. Orlando, April 11, 1992	32	19
Patrick Ewing, New York at Atlanta, December 7, 1991	**33	18
Michael Jordan, Chicago vs. Denver, March 24, 1992	31	18
Michael Jordan, Chicago vs. Golden State, November 5, 1991	22	17
Tim Hardaway, Golden State at Philadelphia, November 8, 1991	30	17
Clyde Drexler, Portland vs. L.A. Clippers, November 19, 1991	30	17
Patrick Ewing, New York vs. Philadelphia, November 23, 1991	28	17
Clyde Drexler, Portland vs. San Antonio, November 24, 1991	28	17
Reggie Lewis, Boston vs. Washington in Hartford, November 25, 1991	24	17
Patrick Ewing, New York vs. Detroit, November 30, 1991	26	17
Dominique Wilkins, Atlanta vs. New York, December 7, 1991	**30	17
Dominique Wilkins, Atlanta vs. Milwaukee, December 10, 1991	27	17
Scottie Pippen, Chicago vs. Atlanta, December 21, 1991	26	17
Michael Jordan, Chicago at Miami, January 8, 1992	27	17
Eddie A. Johnson, Seattle at Orlando, January 28, 1992	31	17
Kevin Johnson, Phoenix at Portland, February 18, 1992	24	17
Scottie Pippen, Chicago at Milwaukee, February 28, 1992	24	17
Joe Dumars, Detroit at Golden State, March 12, 1992	33	17
Drazen Petrovic, New Jersey vs Boston in Hartford, March 13, 1992	26	17
Reggie Lewis, Boston at Cleveland, April 7, 1992	27	17
Hakeem Olajuwon, Houston vs. Phoenix, April 19, 1992	34	17
Michael Jordan, Chicago at Boston, November 6, 1991	26	16
Michael Jordan, Chicago at Portland, November 29, 1991	**39	16
Kevin Johnson, Phoenix vs. Utah, November 30, 1991	*29	16
Clyde Drexler, Portland at Philadelphia, December 6, 1991	*27	16

	FGA	FGM
Xavier McDaniel, New York vs. Boston, December 14, 1991	20	16
Michael Jordan, Chicago vs. Atlanta, December 21, 1991	24	16
Dominique Wilkins, Atlanta at Chicago, December 21, 1991	26	16
Willie Anderson, San Antonio at Golden State, January 10, 1992	18	16
Clyde Drexler, Portland at Golden State, January 28, 1992	*30	16
Tim Hardaway, Golden State vs. Portland, January 28, 1992	*33	16
Nick Anderson, Orlando at Washington, February 2, 1992	25	16
Hakeem Olajuwon, Houston at Seattle, February 11, 1992	22	16
Orlando Woolridge, Detroit at Philadelphia, February 16, 1992	21	16
Ledell Eackles, Washington at Atlanta, February 19, 1992	*27	16
Larry Johnson, Charlotte vs. Denver, February 19, 1992	25	16
David Robinson, San Antonio vs. Minnesota, February 19, 1992	30	16
Karl Malone, Utah at Golden State, March 3, 1992	21	16
Larry Nance, Cleveland at Atlanta, March 7, 1992	22	16
Sedale Threatt, L.A. Lakers at New York, March 10, 1992	22	16
Michael Jordan, Chicago at New Jersey, March 17, 1992	32	16
Michael Jordan, Chicago at Indiana, April 10, 1992	30	16
Danny Manning, L.A. Clippers at L.A. Lakers, April 19, 1992	*23	16

MOST FREE THROWS MADE IN A GAME

	FTA	FTM
Karl Malone, Utah vs. Golden State, April 13, 1992	24	20
Karl Malone, Utah vs. Orlando, December 10, 1991	19	17
Sam Vincent, Orlando at Seattle, January 8, 1992	18	17
Karl Malone, Utah vs. Phoenix, January 31, 1992	*21	17
Charles Barkley, Philadelphia vs. Boston, February 1, 1992	20	17
Patrick Ewing, New York at Indiana, February 12, 1992	22	17
Dominique Wilkins, Atlanta vs. New York, December 7, 1991	**18	16
Ricky Pierce, Seattle vs. Miami, January 2, 1992	*17	16
Tom Chambers, Phoenix vs. Portland, January 19, 1992	*17	16
Eddie A. Johnson, Seattle at Utah, February 27, 1992	*18	16
Michael Williams, Indiana at Miami, March 18, 1992	*17	16
Moses Malone, Milwaukee at Seattle, March 27, 1992	19	16
Charles Barkley, Philadelphia vs. New Jersey, November 6, 1991	20	15
Charles Barkley, Philadelphia vs. Golden State, November 8, 1991	15	15
Derrick McKey, Seattle vs. Chicago, November 22, 1991	*15	15
Brad Daugherty, Cleveland at Philadelphia, November 26, 1991	16	15
Hersey Hawkins, Philadelphia vs. Portland, December 6, 1991	*15	15
John Stockton, Utah vs. L.A. Clippers, December 26, 1991	16	15
A.C. Green, L.A. Lakers vs. Orlando, January 12, 1992	15	15
Dikembe Mutombo, Denver at Minnesota, February 3, 1992	21	15
Karl Malone, Utah at L.A. Clippers, February 25, 1992	17	15

MOST REBOUNDS IN A GAME

	OFF	DEF	TOT
Dennis Rodman, Detroit vs. Indiana, March 4, 1992	*18	16	34
Kevin Willis, Atlanta vs. Washington, February 19, 1992	*16	17	33
Dennis Rodman, Detroit at Charlotte, January 28, 1992	*12	20	32
Kevin Willis, Atlanta at Dallas, December 3, 1991	11	20	31
Dennis Rodman, Detroit at Sacramento, March 14, 1992	9	22	31
Dennis Rodman, Detroit at Minnesota, January 23, 1992	9	18	27
Dennis Rodman, Detroit vs. Orlando, February 18, 1992	9	18	27
Dennis Rodman, Detroit at Cleveland, February 6, 1992	8	18	26
Dennis Rodman, Detroit at Philadelphia, February 16, 1992	10	16	26
Dennis Rodman, Detroit at Portland, December 13, 1991	5	20	25
Dennis Rodman, Detroit vs. Miami, January 31, 1992	6	19	25
Dennis Rodman, Detroit at New Jersey, February 19, 1992	10	15	25
Dennis Rodman, Detroit vs. Philadelphia, March 18, 1992	9	16	25
Dennis Rodman, Detroit vs. Boston, March 20, 1992	*9	16	25
Kevin Willis, Atlanta at Washington, November 23, 1991	7	17	24
David Robinson, San Antonio at Sacramento, December 3, 1991	12	12	24
Rony Seikaly, Miami vs. Cleveland, December 11, 1991	11	13	24
Dennis Rodman, Detroit at San Antonio, January 6, 1992	6	18	24
Dennis Rodman, Detroit at New Jersey, January 11, 1992	9	15	24
David Robinson, San Antonio vs. Golden State, February 27, 1992	10	14	24
Terry Cummings, San Antonio vs. Orlando, April 3, 1992	*8	16	24
Kevin Willis, Atlanta at Philadelphia, November 22, 1991	6	17	23
Michael Cage, Seattle vs. Minnesota, December 6, 1991	7	16	23
Dennis Rodman, Detroit at Phoenix, December 10, 1991	9	14	23
Hakeem Olajuwon, Houston at Golden State, December 12, 1991	6	17	23
Dennis Rodman, Detroit vs. Sacramento, January 8, 1992	7	16	23
Hakeem Olajuwon, Houston vs. Minnesota, January 28, 1992	4	19	23
Kevin Willis, Atlanta vs. Seattle, February 3, 1992	4	19	23
Detlef Schrempf, Indiana at Orlando, February 11, 1992	8	15	23
Dennis Rodman, Detroit at Orlando, February 21, 1992	4	19	23
Dennis Rodman, Detroit vs. New Jersey, February 29, 1992	9	14	23
Larry Johnson, Charlotte vs. Minnesota, March 10, 1992	11	12	23
Charles Barkley, Philadelphia vs. New Jersey, November 6, 1991	5	17	22
Michael Cage, Seattle vs. Indiana, November 9, 1991	10	12	22
Terry Catledge, Orlando vs. Philadelphia, November 13, 1991	12	10	22

	OFF	DEF	TOT
Kevin Willis, Atlanta vs. Boston, November 30, 1991	6	16	22
Cadillac Anderson, Denver vs. L.A. Clippers, December 6, 1991	*10	12	22
Dennis Rodman, Detroit vs. L.A. Lakers, December 20, 1991	4	18	22
Dikembe Mutombo, Denver vs. Golden State, December 26, 1991	9	13	22
Pervis Ellison, Washington vs. Indiana, January 14, 1992	**6	16	22
Dennis Rodman, Detroit vs. Cleveland, January 29, 1992	8	14	22
Dennis Rodman, Detroit vs. Milwaukee, February 27, 1992	7	15	22
Kevin Willis, Atlanta vs. Boston, February 28, 1992	10	12	22
Kevin Willis, Atlanta vs. Orlando, March 18, 1992	8	14	22
Otis Thorpe, Houston at L.A. Lakers, November 15, 1991	11	10	21
Dennis Rodman, Detroit vs. Cleveland, December 5, 1991	9	12	21
Dennis Rodman, Detroit at Washington, December 6, 1991	9	12	21
Dennis Rodman, Detroit vs. Charlotte, December 18, 1991	8	13	21
Kevin Willis, Atlanta at New Jersey, December 23, 1991	6	15	21
Kevin Willis, Atlanta vs. Minnesota, December 28, 1991	*8	13	21
Terry Davis, Dallas at Detroit, January 13, 1992	8	13	21
Dennis Rodman, Detroit vs. Dallas, January 13, 1992	5	16	21
Patrick Ewing, New York at Golden State, January 24, 1992	6	15	21
Rony Seikaly, Miami vs. Seattle, January 29, 1992	2	19	21
Shawn Kemp, Seattle at Charlotte, January 31, 1992	9	12	21
Karl Malone, Utah vs. Chicago, February 3, 1992	***6	15	21
Dikembe Mutombo, Denver at Minnesota, February 3, 1992	13	8	21
Dennis Rodman, Detroit vs. Milwaukee, February 5, 1992	10	11	21
Kevin Willis, Atlanta vs. Orlando, February 6, 1992	4	17	21
Kevin Willis, Atlanta vs. Charlotte, February 11, 1992	3	18	21
Dennis Rodman, Detroit vs. Washington, March 2, 1992	7	14	21
Dennis Rodman, Detroit at Golden State, March 12, 1992	4	17	21
Dennis Rodman, Detroit vs. Golden State, March 25, 1992	7	14	21
Dennis Rodman, Detroit vs. L.A. Clippers, March 31, 1992	9	12	21
Patrick Ewing, New York vs. Washington, April 14, 1992	4	17	21
Kevin Willis, Atlanta vs. New York, April 15, 1992	7	14	21

MOST ASSISTS IN A GAME

	AST
John Stockton, Utah vs. Golden State, November 29, 1991	23
John Stockton, Utah vs. Minnesota, April 17, 1992	23
John Stockton, Utah at San Antonio, April 19, 1992	21
Kevin Johnson, Phoenix vs. Portland, March 31, 1992	20
John Stockton, Utah at Indiana, November 2, 1991	19
John Stockton, Utah at Boston, December 20, 1991	19
John Stockton, Utah at Cleveland, December 23, 1991	19
John Stockton, Utah vs. Atlanta, January 16, 1992	19
John Stockton, Utah vs. San Antonio, January 22, 1992	19
Kevin Johnson, Phoenix vs. Chicago, February 5, 1992	19
Mark Jackson, New York vs. Houston, February 6, 1992	19
John Stockton, Utah vs. Cleveland, February 11, 1992	19
Michael Adams, Washington at Sacramento, February 12, 1992	19
John Stockton, Utah vs. Seattle, February 27, 1992	*19
Rod Strickland, San Antonio at Minnesota, March 3, 1992	19
Micheal Williams, Indiana vs. New York, November 13, 1991	18
John Stockton, Utah at Philadelphia, December 18, 1991	18
John Stockton, Utah at Minnesota, January 11, 1992	18
Kevin Johnson, Phoenix at Utah, January 31, 1992	*18
John Stockton, Utah vs. L.A. Lakers, February 13, 1992	18
John Stockton, Utah at Phoenix, March 1, 1992	18
Kevin Johnson, Phoenix at Cleveland, March 10, 1992	18
Muggsy Bogues, Charlotte vs. Dallas, December 11, 1991	17
Mark Jackson, New York vs. Boston, December 14, 1991	17
Michael Adams, Washington at Dallas, December 20, 1991	17
Mark Jackson, New York vs. Utah, December 21, 1991	17
John Stockton, Utah vs. L.A. Clippers, December 26, 1991	17
Rod Strickland, San Antonio at Chicago, January 17, 1992	17
Kevin Johnson, Phoenix vs. Portland, January 19, 1992	*17
Kevin Johnson, Phoenix vs. Cleveland, February 26, 1992	17
Kevin Johnson, Phoenix vs. Houston, March 3, 1992	*17
Pooh Richardson, Minnesota at Washington, March 13, 1992	17
Mark Jackson, New York vs. Orlando, March 24, 1992	17
Tim Hardaway, Golden State vs. Philadelphia, March 30, 1992	17
Kenny Smith, Houston vs. L.A. Lakers, March 31, 1992	17

MOST STEALS IN A GAME

	STL
Michael Adams, Washington at Indiana, November 1, 1991	9
Doc Rivers, L.A. Clippers vs. Phoenix, November 6, 1991	9
Nick Anderson, Orlando at Washington, November 12, 1991	8
Micheal Williams, Indiana vs. Chicago, December 30, 1991	8
Reggie Williams, Denver vs. San Antonio, November 5, 1991	7
Doc Rivers, L.A. Clippers vs. Denver, November 8, 1991	7
Fat Lever, Dallas at Milwaukee, November 9, 1991	7

STL

Micheal Williams, Indiana at L.A. Lakers, January 3, 1992 7
John Stockton, Utah vs. Cleveland, February 11, 1992 7
Kendall Gill, Charlotte at Milwaukee, February 13, 1992 7
Reggie Williams, Denver vs. Dallas, February 14, 1992 7
Ed Pinckney, Boston vs. Indiana, February 26, 1992 7
Mark Macon, Denver vs. Sacramento, March 17, 1992 7
Kendall Gill, Charlotte at New Jersey, March 23, 1992 7
John Stockton, Utah vs. Philadelphia, March 25, 1992 7
Micheal Williams, Indiana vs. Golden State, March 27, 1992 7
Lester Conner, Milwaukee vs. Detroit, April 14, 1992 .... *7

MOST BLOCKED SHOTS IN A GAME

BLK

David Robinson, San Antonio vs. Portland, February 4, 1992 11
Dikembe Mutombo, Denver at Orlando, March 10, 1992 10
David Robinson, San Antonio at Portland, November 24, 1991 9
David Robinson, San Antonio at Minnesota, December 11, 1991 9
Hakeem Olajuwon, Houston vs. Denver, January 14, 1992 9
Hakeem Olajuwon, Houston vs. Golden State, January 16, 1992 9
Hakeem Olajuwon, Houston vs. Indiana, February 3, 1992 9
Hakeem Olajuwon, Houston at L.A. Clippers, February 12, 1992 9
Mark Eaton, Utah vs. Sacramento, November 11, 1991 8
Larry Nance, Cleveland vs. Philadelphia, November 27, 1991 8
David Robinson, San Antonio at L.A. Clippers, December 4, 1991 8
David Robinson, San Antonio at Indiana, December 10, 1991 8
David Robinson, San Antonio at Dallas, December 17, 1991 8
Andrew Lang, Phoenix at Denver, December 18, 1991 8
Hakeem Olajuwon, Houston at Charlotte, December 20, 1991 8
Hakeem Olajuwon, Houston at Orlando, December 22, 1991 8
David Robinson, San Antonio at New York, December 26, 1991 8
Hakeem Olajuwon, Houston at Miami, January 10, 1992 .... *8
David Robinson, San Antonio vs. Chicago, January 28, 1992 8
Hakeem Olajuwon, Houston vs. Chicago, January 30, 1992 8
Duane Causwell, Sacramento at Denver, March 17, 1992 8
Mark Eaton, Utah vs. Portland, March 21, 1992 8
Hakeem Olajuwon, Houston vs. Orlando, April 4, 1992 8
Larry Nance, Cleveland at New Jersey, April 10, 1992 8

1991-92 Edge NBA Players of the Week

Nov. 11—Chris Mullin, Golden State
Nov. 18—Brad Daugherty, Cleveland
Nov. 25—Kevin Willis, Atlanta
Dec.   2—David Robinson, San Antonio
Dec.   9—Jeff Malone, Utah
Dec. 16—Dennis Rodman, Detroit
Dec. 23—Pervis Ellison, Washington
Dec. 30—Scottie Pippen, Chicago
Jan.   6—Patrick Ewing, New York
Jan. 13—Michael Jordan, Chicago
Jan. 20—Tim Hardaway, Golden State
Jan. 27—Nick Anderson, Orlando

Feb.   3—Larry Nance, Cleveland
Feb. 17—John Stockton, Utah
Feb. 24—Tim Hardaway, Golden State
Mar.   2—Danny Manning, L.A. Clippers
Mar.   9—Karl Malone, Utah
Mar. 16—Joe Dumars, Detroit
Mar. 23—Larry Johnson, Charlotte
Mar. 30—Mark Jackson, New York
Apr.   6—Mookie Blaylock, New Jersey
Apr. 13—Reggie Lewis, Boston
Apr. 20—Karl Malone, Utah

1991-92 Edge NBA Players of the Month

November—Clyde Drexler, Portland
December—Jeff Hornacek, Phoenix
January—Dennis Rodman, Detroit

February—Detlef Schrempf, Indiana
March—Michael Jordan, Chicago
April—Glen Rice, Miami

1991-92 Coaches of the Month

November—Mike Dunleavy, L.A. Lakers
December—Cotton Fitzsimmons, Phoenix
January—Phil Jackson, Chicago

February—George Karl, Seattle
March—Larry Brown, L.A. Clippers
April—Chris Ford, Boston

1991-92 Rookies of the Month

November—Dikembe Mutombo, Denver
December—Larry Johnson, Charlotte
January—Dikembe Mutombo, Denver

February—Larry Johnson, Charlotte
March—Larry Johnson, Charlotte
April—Stacey Augmon, Atlanta

ACTIVE CAREER LEADERS
(Players who were on active rosters or on injured list during 1991-1992 season)

MOST GAMES PLAYED		MOST FIELD GOALS ATTEMPTED		MOST FREE THROWS ATTEMPTED	
Robert Parish	1,260	Moses Malone	18,916	Moses Malone	10,910
Moses Malone	1,246	Larry Bird	17,334	Magic Johnson	5,649
Maurice Cheeks	1,066	Dominique Wilkins	16,163	Tom Chambers	5,564
Walter Davis	1,033	Walter Davis	15,871	Dominique Wilkins	5,557
Wayne Rollins	1,018	Robert Parish	15,656	Michael Jordan	5,456
James Edwards	1,015	Bernard King	14,932	Bernard King	5,387
Wayne Cooper	984	Mark Aguirre	14,095	Charles Barkley	5,347
Vinnie Johnson	984	Isiah Thomas	13,883	Karl Malone	5,318
Bill Laimbeer	978	Tom Chambers	13,825	Robert Parish	5,048
Brad Davis	961	Terry Cummings	13,775	Buck Williams	4,827

MOST MINUTES PLAYED		MOST FIELD GOALS MADE		MOST FREE THROWS MADE	
Moses Malone	44,200	Moses Malone	9,307	Moses Malone	8,395
Robert Parish	38,727	Larry Bird	8,591	Magic Johnson	4,788
Larry Bird	34,443	Robert Parish	8,493	Michael Jordan	4,620
Maurice Cheeks	34,335	Walter Davis	8,118	Dominique Wilkins	4,494
Magic Johnson	32,287	Bernard King	7,739	Tom Chambers	4,490
Bill Laimbeer	31,775	Dominique Wilkins	7,581	Larry Bird	3,960
Buck Williams	31,002	Michael Jordan	7,087	Bernard King	3,933
Isiah Thomas	30,844	Mark Aguirre	6,851	Charles Barkley	3,920
Rolando Blackman	29,684	Terry Cummings	6,740	Karl Malone	3,826
Tom Chambers	29,028	Kevin McHale	6,532	Robert Parish	3,648

HIGHEST FIELD GOAL PERCENTAGE
(2,000 FGM minimum)

	FGA	FGM	Pct.
Charles Barkley	8,722	5,025	.576
James Donaldson	5,354	3,053	.570
Jeff Ruland	3,723	2,100	.564
Kevin McHale	11,685	6,532	.559
Buck Williams	9,146	5,092	.557
Otis Thorpe	7,343	4,064	.553
Larry Nance	10,379	5,684	.548
David Robinson	3,740	2,036	.544
Robert Parish	15,656	8,493	.542
James Worthy	11,224	6,028	.537

HIGHEST FREE THROW PERCENTAGE
(1,200 FTM minimum)

	FTA	FTM	Pct.
Mark Price	1,343	1,208	.899
Larry Bird	4,471	3,960	.886
Jeff Malone	2,768	2,426	.876
Ricky Pierce	2,790	2,438	.874
Chris Mullin	2,928	2,558	.874
Kiki Vandeweghe	3,931	3,426	.872
Reggie Miller	2,268	1,973	.870
Hersey Hawkins	1,737	1,510	.869
Michael Adams	1,931	1,646	.852
Walter Davis	3,676	3,128	.851

MOST REBOUNDS		MOST ASSISTS		MOST FOULS	
Moses Malone	15,894	Magic Johnson	9,921	Robert Parish	3,800
Robert Parish	12,691	Isiah Thomas	7,991	James Edwards	3,725
Bill Laimbeer	9,925	John Stockton	7,365	Bill Laimbeer	3,391
Buck Williams	9,831	Maurice Cheeks	7,285	Wayne Rollins	3,216
Larry Bird	8,974	Larry Bird	5,695	Wayne Cooper	3,144
Larry Smith	7,857	Rickey Green	5,221	Tom Chambers	3,109
Hakeem Olajuwon	7,441	Eric Floyd	4,816	Buck Williams	3,020
James Donaldson	7,356	Brad Davis	4,709	Moses Malone	3,003
Charles Barkley	7,079	Lafayette Lever	4,483	Larry Smith	2,833
Kevin McHale	6,764	Terry Porter	4,366	Bernard King	2,832

MOST STEALS		MOST BLOCKED SHOTS		MOST DISQUALIFICATIONS	
Maurice Cheeks	2,277	Mark Eaton	2,985	James Edwards	95
Alvin Robertson	1,791	Wayne Rollins	2,456	Wayne Rollins	91
Magic Johnson	1,698	Hakeem Olajuwon	2,102	Robert Parish	80
Isiah Thomas	1,670	Robert Parish	2,049	Alton Lister	72
John Stockton	1,633	Manute Bol	1,942	Tom Chambers	70
Michael Jordan	1,594	Larry Nance	1,774	Hakeem Olajuwon	62
Larry Bird	1,556	Moses Malone	1,705	Larry Smith	62
Clyde Drexler	1,528	Kevin McHale	1,631	Bill Laimbeer	59
Lafayette Lever	1,507	Patrick Ewing	1,606	Danny Schayes	59
Rickey Green	1,348	Wayne Cooper	1,535	Wayne Cooper	55
				LaSalle Thompson	55

HIGHEST SCORING AVERAGE
(400 Games or 10,000 Points minimum)

	G.	FGM	FTM	Pts.	Avg.
Michael Jordan	589	7,087	4,620	19,000	32.3
Dominique Wilkins	762	7,581	4,494	19,975	26.2
Karl Malone	570	5,458	3,826	14,770	25.9
Larry Bird	897	8,591	3,960	21,791	24.3
Patrick Ewing	520	4,862	2,567	12,293	23.6
Charles Barkley	610	5,025	3,920	14,184	23.3
Bernard King	842	7,739	3,933	19,432	23.1
Hakeem Olajuwon	594	5,365	2,843	13,575	22.9
Chris Mullin	520	4,353	2,558	11,536	22.2
Moses Malone	1,246	9,307	8,395	27,016	21.7

HIGHEST 3-PT. FIELD GOAL PERCENTAGE
(100 3-PT. FGM minimum)

	FGA	FGM	Pct.
Steve Kerr	297	141	.475
Drazen Petrovic	416	180	.433
Dana Barros	505	210	.416
Mark Price	1,117	459	.411
Hersey Hawkins	865	354	.409
Trent Tucker	1,279	523	.409
Dale Ellis	1,891	763	.403
Craig Hodges	1,408	563	.400
Jon Sundvold	576	226	.392
Jeff Hornacek	615	240	.390

MOST 3-PT. FIELD GOALS MADE		MOST 3-PT. FIELD GOALS ATTEMPTED		MOST POINTS	
Michael Adams	783	Michael Adams	2,332	Moses Malone	27,016
Dale Ellis	763	Dale Ellis	1,891	Larry Bird	21,791
Danny Ainge	694	Danny Ainge	1,821	Robert Parish	20,634
Larry Bird	649	Larry Bird	1,727	Dominique Wilkins	19,975
Craig Hodges	563	Derek Harper	1,492	Walter Davis	19,521
Reggie Miller	550	Reggie Miller	1,441	Bernard King	19,432
Trent Tucker	523	Eric Floyd	1,419	Michael Jordan	19,000
Derek Harper	507	Craig Hodges	1,408	Tom Chambers	17,736
Byron Scott	478	Chuck Person	1,330	Mark Aguirre	17,542
Terry Porter	476	Trent Tucker	1,279	Magic Johnson	17,239

Jordan just too much as Bulls win 2nd title

By PAUL ATTNER

The first one was for the city itself.

"We wanted it for the people of Chicago," Michael Jordan said after the Chicago Bulls won their first National Basketball Association championship in 1991.

The second one, in 1992, was different.

"This one is for the players and coaches," Jordan declared.

Who's to argue? After all, the world's greatest individual basketball player proved last spring to be its most impressive team player as well. His magical handiwork enabled the Bulls to defeat the Portland Trail Blazers in six games to become only the fourth team (after the Lakers, Celtics and Pistons) to win two championships in a row. But it's doubtful any of those teams relied as heavily on the talents of a single player as the Bulls did.

Although it appeared Chicago may have been ripe for an upset after grueling series with the New York Knicks (seven games) and Cleveland Cavaliers (six) prior to the Finals, it never happened. In truth, both the physical Knicks and the pesky Cavs gave the Bulls a rougher time than the Trail Blazers, who probably should have been ousted in four or five games. Two inexplicable fourth-quarter collapses by Chicago (in Games 2 and 4) made this series seem a lot closer than it really was.

The Trail Blazers never did stop Jordan, even though they had the league's second-best player, Clyde Drexler, guarding him. Jordan averaged 35.8 points in the series, the second-highest total ever in a six-game NBA Finals.

"Going into the series, I thought Michael had 2,000 moves," Drexler said. "I was wrong. He has 3,000."

Jordan's performances were particularly memorable in Games 1, 5 and 6. In the opener, he scored a record 35 points in the first half and 39 in the game in a 122-89 Bulls romp at Chicago Stadium. He tied a Finals record with six three-point baskets as Chicago rolled to a commanding 66-51 halftime lead. In Game 5 at Portland, with the series tied 2-2, Jordan exploded for 46 points in a 119-106 victory that put the Bulls back in control of the series. And in

The Trail Blazers couldn't control Chicago's Michael Jordan no matter how hard they tried.

the decisive Game 6—after scoring just two points in the first quarter—Jordan scored 12 of his game-high 33 points in the fourth period, including Chicago's last six points of the game.

It surprised no one when Jordan was unanimously named the series' Most Valuable Player, becoming the first player to win the award in back-to-back seasons.

The tone of the '92 Finals was established in the first game when Jordan, who made just 27 three-point field goals during the regular season (and only five more in Chicago's first 16 playoff games), connected for six in the first half alone. Jordan's performance surprised even him.

"Sometimes I fascinate myself," he said. "I can't explain it. I just felt good and I kept shooting. I got into a zone. But I don't expect it to happen again."

The Bulls, whose 33-point margin of victory in Game 1 was just two shy of the NBA

Portland's 115-104 overtime victory in Game 2 was a stunner, but the Blazers failed to capitalize on the momentum gained in the come-from-behind win.

Finals record, were well on their way to another victory in Game 2 as well before a late collapse cost them the win. Chicago led, 92-82, with 4 minutes, 36 seconds left before Portland went on a 15-5 tear to force overtime and eventually won the game, 115-104.

The Trail Blazers, who often had been criticized for their inability to execute in pressure situations, proved to be much more proficient in that area than the Bulls. And the Blazers made their comeback with Drexler, their leading scorer with 26 points, on the bench after fouling out. Center Kevin Duckworth's jumper with eight seconds left sent the game into overtime, where reserve guard Danny Ainge scored a Finals record-tying nine points to help Portland pull out the victory.

The series moved to Portland's Memorial Coliseum for Games 3, 4 and 5, which may not have been as great an advantage for the Blazers as it seemed on paper. Although they were undefeated (8-0) at home in the 1992 playoffs, the Blazers had lost three straight games at home to Detroit in the 1990 Finals. And the league's Western Conference representative had lost its last eight games at home in the NBA Finals since 1989.

The streak soon reached nine. Despite the importance of the game and the need to maintain momentum, the Blazers inexplicably came out flat in Game 3. Jordan led the Bulls with 26 points and Scottie Pippen contributed 18 points, eight rebounds and seven assists in a 94-84 Chicago victory.

Portland shot just 35.9 percent from the field and finished with its second-lowest playoff point total ever.

"I can't explain it," forward Jerome Kersey said of the Trail Blazers' lackluster effort. "We knew we had to win it but we didn't play like it. We need to increase our intensity or we're in trouble."

The Blazers got their act together for Game 4, but it still almost wasn't enough. The Bulls led throughout before Portland scored 19 of the game's final 27 points to come away with a series-tying 93-88 victory. Drexler and Kersey scored 21 points apiece and reserve forward Cliff Robinson added 17.

Jordan, who again led Chicago with 32 points, did not score in the final 10:26. And the Bulls, who felt they should have been celebrating a four-game sweep, instead found themselves in a 2-2 deadlock.

NBA Finals MVP Michael Jordan was the easy winner in the head-to-head duel between him and Portland star Clyde Drexler.

"This series by all rights and purposes should be over," Bulls Coach Phil Jackson said. "We are in control of this series. . . ."

Jackson's players were equally upset.

"I think it's important they feel that way," Jackson said. "I agree with them. I am angry, too."

What was the Blazers' response to the Bulls' attitude?

"Arrogance," guard Terry Porter said bluntly. "All I know is the series is tied. You've still got to win this thing on the court, not by talking."

Chicago backed up its talk with a very solid performance in Game 5, taking back the home-court edge with a 119-106 win. The Bulls put together runs of 10-0, 7-0 and 12-4 in the first half en route to a 56-44 halftime lead.

Jordan shot 14-for-23 from the field in racking up his 46 points while Pippen again was a major contributor with 24 points, 11 rebounds and nine assists.

Pippen's performance, in fact, may have been as important as Jordan's. When he played well in what for him was a roller-coaster 1992 postseason, the Bulls rarely were challenged; when he played poorly, they struggled.

"You've got to hand it to them," Portland forward Buck Williams said. "They said they had to win and they did. But this isn't over yet."

It was over in Chicago two days later. The Bulls, who trailed by 17 points late in the third quarter and 79-64 entering the final period, put together the biggest fourth-quarter rally in NBA Finals history to win the game and the championship, 97-93.

The way the Bulls won Game 6 was perhaps as stunning as the victory itself. With a tired Jordan on the bench, Jackson opened the fourth quarter with four reserves—Scott Williams, B.J. Armstrong, Bobby Hansen and Stacey King—on the floor along with Pippen. The Bulls outscored the Blazers, 14-2, in the opening minutes of the period to cut Portland's lead to 81-78. Jordan, who reentered the game with 8:36 left, then combined with Pippen to score the Bulls' last 19 points.

"We needed a different matchup," Jackson said. "That's what we got from those young guys. They had fresh legs. Either it's daring or stupid, depending on which way it comes out."

"Our guys just ran out of gas," said Portland Coach Rick Adelman, whose team was held to only 14 points in the final quarter. "When the game was on the line, the Bulls turned the intensity up and took control."

The Trail Blazers, who entered the NBA Finals brimming with confidence after impressive playoff triumphs over the Lakers, Phoenix and Utah, simply committed too many turnovers and played too inconsistently to dethrone the Bulls. Although Portland thought it had the one player, Drexler, who could neutralize Jordan in a one-on-one matchup, Jordan's dominance over the six games only served to illustrate that the gap between him and all other players in the league is huge.

"To see him up close like this for a long series, you realize how great he is," Williams said. "He is the best there ever was. No question about it. When they need him, he produces. You can't stop him. The pressure on him is unbelievable but he still comes through. You've got to appreciate that."

You sure do.

1992 NBA FINALS

Game No. 1

AT CHICAGO, JUNE 3, 1992

Portland	Pos.	Min.	FGA	FGM	FTA	FTM	—REBOUNDS— Off.	Def.	Tot.	Ast.	PF	Stls.	Pts.
Kersey, Jerome	F	27	8	3	1	1	1	6	7	3	3	0	7
Williams, Buck	F	18	1	1	2	1	1	1	2	0	4	1	3
Duckworth, Kevin	C	25	5	3	1	1	1	4	5	2	3	0	7
Drexler, Clyde	G	31	14	5	7	6	4	1	5	7	4	2	16
Porter, Terry	G	32	9	5	4	3	1	5	6	2	2	0	13
Robinson, Cliff		24	14	7	2	2	0	2	2	0	5	0	16
Bryant, Mark		21	8	5	0	0	3	2	5	0	1	0	10
Ainge, Danny		22	8	3	2	1	0	0	0	1	1	1	8
Whatley, Ennis		13	5	2	0	0	0	1	1	0	1	2	4
Pack, Robert		13	5	1	2	2	0	1	1	1	1	1	4
Cooper, Wayne		8	0	0	0	0	0	2	2	0	1	0	0
Abdelnaby, Alaa		6	1	0	2	1	0	2	2	0	0	0	1
Totals		240	78	35	23	18	11	27	38	16	26	7	89

FG Pct.: .449. FT Pct.:.783. Team Rebounds: 5. Turnovers: Kersey 5, Drexler 4, Williams 4, Bryant 2, Duckworth 2, Abdelnaby 1, Ainge 1, Pack 1, Porter 1. Total—21.

Chicago	Pos.	Min.	FGA	FGM	FTA	FTM	—REBOUNDS— Off.	Def.	Tot.	Ast.	PF	Stls.	Pts.
Pippen, Scottie	F	33	14	8	9	8	3	6	9	10	2	2	24
Grant, Horace	F	31	8	5	2	1	3	4	7	2	0	1	11
Cartwright, Bill	C	16	4	1	4	3	3	2	5	0	3	0	5
Paxson, John	G	19	4	2	0	0	0	0	0	5	4	1	4
Jordan, Michael	G	34	27	16	1	1	2	1	3	11	0	2	39
Williams, Scott		28	6	6	0	0	4	5	9	1	4	0	12
Armstrong, B.J.		29	11	5	0	0	0	3	3	6	3	0	11
Hansen, Bobby		14	4	2	2	1	0	1	1	2	1	0	5
Levingston, Cliff		15	7	4	0	0	0	3	3	1	1	0	8
King, Stacey		15	3	0	2	1	1	1	2	0	2	1	1
Perdue, Will		6	3	1	2	0	2	0	2	0	1	0	2
Totals		240	91	50	22	15	16	28	44	38	21	7	122

FG Pct.: .549. FT Pct.:.682. Team Rebounds: 9. Turnovers: Armstrong 3, Cartwright 2, Williams 2, Jordan 1, King 1, Levingston 1, Pippen 1, Team 1. Total—11.

Score by Periods:	1st	2nd	3rd	4th	Totals
Portland	30	21	17	21 —	89
Chicago	33	33	38	18 —	122

Blocked Shots: Grant 3, Cooper 2, S. Williams 2, Ainge 1, Duckworth 1, King 1, Pippen 1.
3-Pt. Field Goals: Ainge 1-2, Drexler 0-2, Porter 0-2, Armstrong 1-1, Jordan 6-10, Hansen 0-1, Levingston 0-1, Paxson 0-1, Pippen 0-1.
Officials: Dick Bavetta, Hue Hollins, Jake O'Donnell.
Attendance: 18,676.
Time of Game: 2:15.

Game No. 2

AT CHICAGO, JUNE 5, 1992

Portland	Pos.	Min.	FGA	FGM	FTA	FTM	—REBOUNDS— Off.	Def.	Tot.	Ast.	PF	Stls.	Pts.
Kersey, Jerome	F	41	11	6	0	0	4	4	8	4	6	2	12
Williams, Buck	F	48	9	7	5	5	3	11	14	2	2	1	19
Duckworth, Kevin	C	43	15	6	2	2	0	8	8	4	3	1	14
Drexler, Clyde	G	38	20	8	10	10	2	5	7	8	6	2	26
Porter, Terry	G	49	17	8	9	7	0	1	1	3	1	1	24
Robinson, Cliff		18	2	0	8	3	0	2	2	2	4	0	3
Ainge, Danny		23	10	7	4	3	1	1	2	4	0	0	17
Whatley, Ennis		5	0	0	0	0	0	0	0	0	0	0	0
Totals		265	84	42	38	30	10	32	42	27	26	7	115

FG Pct.: .500. FT Pct.:.789. Team Rebounds: 12. Turnovers: Porter 3, Williams 3, Duckworth 2, Kersey 1, Team 1. Total—9.

Chicago	Pos.	Min.	FGA	FGM	FTA	FTM	Off.	Def.	Tot.	Ast.	PF	Stls.	Pts.
Pippen, Scottie	F	48	19	6	6	4	3	5	8	10	4	3	16
Grant, Horace	F	46	6	4	3	2	2	10	12	7	4	1	10
Cartwright, Bill	C	34	4	4	4	2	1	3	4	1	3	0	10
Paxson, John	G	42	14	6	0	0	0	1	1	4	2	0	16
Jordan, Michael	G	50	32	16	9	7	1	4	5	10	5	1	39
Williams, Scott		20	3	1	2	1	1	8	9	0	2	0	3
Levingston, Cliff		9	6	3	2	1	1	0	1	1	2	0	7
Armstrong, B.J.		7	1	0	0	0	0	0	0	1	2	0	0
Perdue, Will		3	0	0	0	0	1	0	1	0	2	0	0
Hansen, Bobby		6	1	1	0	0	0	0	0	0	3	0	3
Totals		265	86	41	26	17	10	31	41	34	29	5	104

FG Pct.: .477. FT Pct.:.654. Team Rebounds: 9. Turnovers: Pippen 6, Jordan 5, Cartwright 1, Hansen 1, Paxson 1, Williams 1. Total—15.

Score by Periods:	1st	2nd	3rd	4th	OT	Totals
Portland	31	23	16	27	18	— 115
Chicago	23	22	32	20	7	— 104

Blocked Shots: Grant 5, Cartwright 1, Duckworth 1, Porter 1, B. Williams 1, S. Williams 1.
3-Pt. Field Goals: Porter 1-5, Ainge 0-3, Drexler 0-4, Hansen 1-1, Paxson 4-7, Pippen 0-3, Jordan 0-4.
Officials: Hugh Evans, Jess Kersey, Paul Mihalak.
Attendance: 18,676.
Time of Game: 2:56.

Game No. 3

AT PORTLAND, JUNE 7, 1992

Chicago	Pos.	Min.	FGA	FGM	FTA	FTM	Off.	Def.	Tot.	Ast.	PF	Stls.	Pts.
Pippen, Scottie	F	43	15	6	8	6	1	7	8	7	4	1	18
Grant, Horace	F	37	12	7	5	4	1	7	8	6	4	1	18
Cartwright, Bill	C	25	7	3	2	0	2	5	7	3	6	0	6
Paxson, John	G	32	5	3	2	2	0	0	0	2	1	2	8
Jordan, Michael	G	41	22	11	4	4	2	5	7	4	4	3	26
Williams, Scott		19	5	1	0	0	1	5	6	2	4	1	2
Armstrong, B.J.		17	5	2	2	0	0	0	0	1	1	1	4
Hansen, Bobby		10	3	1	0	0	0	0	0	0	0	0	3
Levingston, Cliff		7	0	0	2	1	0	2	2	0	1	0	1
King, Stacey		9	4	3	4	2	2	2	4	0	1	0	8
Totals		240	78	37	29	19	9	33	42	25	26	9	94

FG Pct.: .474. FT Pct.:.655. Team Rebounds: 13. Turnovers: Jordan 5, Pippen 5, Armstrong 2, Cartwright 1, Grant 1, King 1, Paxson 1. Total—16.

Portland	Pos.	Min.	FGA	FGM	FTA	FTM	Off.	Def.	Tot.	Ast.	PF	Stls.	Pts.
Kersey, Jerome	F	36	13	4	6	3	6	6	12	1	4	3	11
Williams, Buck	F	41	5	1	4	4	1	8	9	2	5	1	6
Duckworth, Kevin	C	25	11	5	2	1	2	2	4	0	6	1	11
Drexler, Clyde	G	42	17	9	12	12	1	8	9	3	4	0	32
Porter, Terry	G	44	7	3	2	1	1	4	5	4	2	0	7
Robinson, Cliff		25	11	2	2	1	1	2	3	1	3	1	5
Ainge, Danny		23	12	4	4	3	1	0	1	1	2	0	12
Whatley, Ennis		4	2	0	0	0	0	0	0	0	0	0	0
Totals		240	78	28	32	25	13	30	43	12	26	6	84

FG Pct.: .359. FT Pct.:.781. Team Rebounds: 10. Turnovers: Drexler 5, Duckworth 4, Kersey 4, Porter 3, Ainge 2, Robinson 2. Total—20.

Score by Periods:	1st	2nd	3rd	4th	Totals
Chicago	34	20	16	24	— 94
Portland	26	19	15	24	— 84

Blocked Shots: Pippen 2, S. Williams 2, Grant 1, Kersey 1, Robinson 1.
3-Pt. Field Goals: Hansen 1-1, Jordan 0-1, Paxson 0-1, Pippen 0-1, Drexler 2-4, Ainge 1-5, Porter 0-1, Robinson 0-1.
Officials: Mike Mathis, Ed T. Rush, Bill Oakes.
Attendance: 12,888.
Time of Game: 2:33.

Game No. 4

AT PORTLAND, JUNE 10, 1992

Chicago	Pos.	Min.	FGA	FGM	FTA	FTM	Off.	Def.	Tot.	Ast.	PF	Stls.	Pts.
Pippen, Scottie	F	33	13	8	4	1	3	6	9	6	4	1	17
Grant, Horace	F	44	10	4	0	0	1	9	10	1	4	1	8
Cartwright, Bill	C	38	8	4	2	1	0	4	4	2	3	2	9
Paxson, John	G	30	7	3	2	1	0	0	0	0	4	1	9
Jordan, Michael	G	44	26	11	8	8	0	5	5	6	4	0	32
Armstrong, B.J.		18	7	3	1	0	1	0	1	2	2	1	6
Williams, Scott		14	1	1	3	3	0	1	1	0	4	0	5
Levingston, Cliff		15	4	0	0	0	2	1	3	1	1	0	0
Hodges, Craig		5	1	1	0	0	0	0	0	0	1	1	2
Totals		240	77	35	20	14	7	26	33	18	27	7	88

FG Pct.: .455. FT Pct.:.700. Team Rebounds: 11. Turnovers: Jordan 5, Pippen 3, Cartwright 2, Hodges 2, Armstrong 1, Grant 1, Paxson 1, Williams 1, Team 2. Total—16.

Portland	Pos.	Min.	FGA	FGM	FTA	FTM	Off.	Def.	Tot.	Ast.	PF	Stls.	Pts.
Kersey, Jerome	F	43	12	8	6	5	1	3	4	5	3	2	21
Williams, Buck	F	32	7	3	0	0	3	1	4	0	3	1	6
Duckworth, Kevin	C	26	11	3	1	1	3	8	11	2	3	0	7
Drexler, Clyde	G	43	22	9	6	3	3	5	8	9	2	2	21
Porter, Terry	G	45	10	5	4	3	1	5	6	4	0	1	14
Robinson, Cliff		27	11	6	10	5	2	4	6	4	4	2	17
Ainge, Danny		21	8	3	0	0	2	4	6	3	4	2	7
Whatley, Ennis		3	0	0	0	0	0	0	0	1	0	1	0
Totals		240	81	37	27	17	15	30	45	28	19	11	93

FG Pct.: .457. FT Pct.:.630. Team Rebounds: 13. Turnovers: Williams 3, Ainge 2, Drexler 2, Kersey 2, Porter 2, Duckworth 1, Robinson 1. Total—13.

Score by Periods:	1st	2nd	3rd	4th	Totals
Chicago	26	22	21	19 — 88	
Portland	18	27	21	27 — 93	

Blocked Shots: Drexler 3, Duckworth 1, Robinson 1, B. Williams 1, S. Williams 1.
3-Pt. Field Goals: Paxson 2-4, Jordan 2-6, Armstrong 0-1, Grant 0-1, Ainge 1-2, Porter 1-3, Drexler 0-4.
Officials: Darrell Garretson, Joe Crawford, Dick Bavetta.
Attendance: 12,888.
Time of Game: 2:31.

Game No. 5

AT PORTLAND, JUNE 12, 1992

Chicago	Pos.	Min.	FGA	FGM	FTA	FTM	Off.	Def.	Tot.	Ast.	PF	Stls.	Pts.
Pippen, Scottie	F	45	15	8	9	8	3	8	11	9	4	2	24
Grant, Horace	F	33	4	2	5	2	0	5	5	3	6	1	6
Cartwright, Bill	C	19	4	2	0	0	1	2	3	3	4	1	4
Paxson, John	G	33	11	6	0	0	0	1	1	3	2	2	12
Jordan, Michael	G	42	23	14	19	16	0	5	5	4	5	0	46
Williams, Scott		23	4	2	4	3	3	1	4	3	5	0	7
Armstrong, B.J.		17	4	2	4	4	0	0	0	0	1	0	8
Levingston, Cliff		13	3	2	2	2	2	1	3	1	1	0	6
King, Stacey		8	4	1	2	2	0	1	1	0	4	0	4
Hansen, Bobby		5	1	1	0	0	1	0	1	0	1	0	2
Hodges, Craig		1	0	0	0	0	0	0	0	0	0	0	0
Perdue, Will		1	0	0	0	0	0	0	0	0	0	0	0
Totals		240	73	40	45	37	10	24	34	26	33	6	119

FG Pct.: .548. FT Pct.:.822. Team Rebounds: 8. Turnovers: Jordan 4, Grant 3, Pippen 3, Cartwright 2, Armstrong 1, Paxson 1. Total—14.

Portland	Pos.	Min.	FGA	FGM	FTA	FTM	Off.	Def.	Tot.	Ast.	PF	Stls.	Pts.
Kersey, Jerome	F	36	17	7	0	0	8	4	12	3	5	2	14
Williams, Buck	F	31	6	3	0	0	3	4	7	0	3	0	6

Portland	Pos.	Min.	FGA	FGM	FTA	FTM	Off.	Def.	Tot.	Ast.	PF	Stls.	Pts.
							—REBOUNDS—						
Duckworth, Kevin	C	28	6	3	11	7	2	5	7	0	5	0	13
Drexler, Clyde	G	41	21	9	14	12	5	5	10	3	6	0	30
Porter, Terry	G	46	12	5	8	7	1	1	2	8	3	3	17
Ainge, Danny		28	13	5	4	3	0	3	3	3	5	0	14
Robinson, Cliff		26	4	3	5	5	1	3	4	4	6	0	11
Whatley, Ennis		1	0	0	0	0	0	0	0	0	0	0	0
Pack, Robert		3	1	0	2	1	0	0	0	0	1	0	1
Totals		240	80	35	44	35	20	25	45	21	34	5	106

FG Pct.: .438. FT Pct.:.795. Team Rebounds: 8. Turnovers: Kersey 6, Drexler 4, Duckworth 3, Porter 3, Ainge 1, Williams 1. Total—18.

Score by Periods:	1st	2nd	3rd	4th	Totals
Chicago	39	27	28	25	— 119
Portland	26	28	24	28	— 106

Blocked Shots: Grant 4, Drexler 1, Jordan 1, Levingston 1, Porter 1, B. Williams 1.
3-Pt. Field Goals: Jordan 2-4, Paxson 0-1, Pippen 0-1, Ainge 1-4, Drexler 0-3.
Officials: Jake O'Donnell, Jess Kersey, Hue Hollins.
Attendance: 12,888.
Time of Game: 2:43.

Game No. 6

AT CHICAGO, JUNE 14, 1992

Portland	Pos.	Min.	FGA	FGM	FTA	FTM	Off.	Def.	Tot.	Ast.	PF	Stls.	Pts.
							—REBOUNDS—						
Kersey, Jerome	F	45	20	11	2	2	6	3	9	4	4	2	24
Williams, Buck	F	41	4	1	5	5	1	7	8	2	4	1	7
Duckworth, Kevin	C	17	3	2	0	0	2	4	6	1	5	1	4
Drexler, Clyde	G	43	24	8	7	7	3	5	8	2	5	2	24
Porter, Terry	G	47	15	7	7	7	1	5	6	7	3	1	22
Robinson, Cliff		26	10	5	0	0	0	1	1	2	1	2	10
Ainge, Danny		21	2	1	0	0	0	0	0	3	2	2	2
Totals		240	78	35	21	21	13	25	38	21	24	11	93

FG Pct.: .449. FT Pct.:1.000. Team Rebounds: 9. Turnovers: Kersey 6, Porter 4, Williams 4, Drexler 3, Duckworth 2, Ainge 1, Robinson 1, Team 1. Total—21.

Chicago	Pos.	Min.	FGA	FGM	FTA	FTM	Off.	Def.	Tot.	Ast.	PF	Stls.	Pts.
							—REBOUNDS—						
Pippen, Scottie	F	43	17	9	6	6	4	1	5	4	3	0	26
Grant, Horace	F	36	1	1	2	0	0	5	5	5	2	0	2
Cartwright, Bill	C	19	5	2	0	0	0	1	1	0	2	0	4
Paxson, John	G	29	9	6	0	0	0	3	3	2	2	2	13
Jordan, Michael	G	43	24	13	5	5	1	3	4	4	3	4	33
Williams, Scott		24	5	2	0	0	3	5	8	0	2	0	4
Armstrong, B.J.		19	7	3	0	0	0	1	1	4	3	0	6
Hansen, Bobby		5	1	1	0	0	0	0	0	1	1	1	3
Levingston, Cliff		6	0	0	4	1	1	0	1	0	1	1	1
King, Stacey		16	4	1	4	3	0	3	3	0	0	0	5
Totals		240	73	38	21	15	9	22	31	20	19	8	97

FG Pct.: .521. FT Pct.:.714. Team Rebounds: 6. Turnovers: Pippen 5, Cartwright 4, Jordan 4, Armstrong 2, Paxson 2, King 1, Team 1. Total—18.

Score by Periods:	1st	2nd	3rd	4th	Totals
Portland	25	25	29	14	— 93
Chicago	19	25	20	33	— 97

Blocked Shots: Drexler 2, Robinson 2, S. Williams 2, Duckworth 1, Grant 1, Jordan 1, Pippen 1.
3-Pt. Field Goals: Porter 1-2, Drexler 1-3, Ainge 0-1, Kersey 0-1, Hansen 1-1, Jordan 2-3, Pippen 2-3, Paxson 1-4, Armstrong 0-2.
Officials: Hugh Evans, Mike Mathis, Ed. T. Rush.
Attendance: 18,676.
Time of Game: 2:29.

1992 NBA FINALS

CHICAGO BULLS VS. PORTLAND TRAIL BLAZERS

Player	G.	Min.	FGA	FGM	Pct.	FTA	FTM	Pct.	Off. Reb.	Def. Reb.	Tot. Reb.	Ast.	PF	Disq.	Stl.	Blk. Sh.	Pts.	Avg.	Hi.
Jordan	6	254	154	81	.526	46	41	.891	6	23	29	39	21	0	10	2	215	35.8	46
Pippen	6	244	93	45	.484	42	33	.786	17	33	50	46	21	0	9	4	125	20.8	26
Paxson	6	185	50	26	.520	4	3	.750	0	5	5	16	15	0	8	0	62	10.3	16
Grant	6	227	41	23	.561	17	9	.529	7	40	47	24	20	1	5	14	55	9.2	18
Cartwright	6	151	32	16	.500	12	6	.500	7	17	24	9	21	1	3	1	38	6.3	10
Armstrong	3	107	35	15	.429	7	4	.571	1	4	5	14	12	0	2	0	35	5.8	11
Williams	6	128	24	13	.542	9	7	.778	12	25	37	6	21	0	1	8	33	5.5	12
King	4	48	15	5	.333	12	8	.667	3	7	10	0	7	0	1	1	18	4.5	8
Levingston	6	65	20	9	.450	10	5	.500	6	7	13	4	7	0	1	1	23	3.8	8
Hansen	5	40	10	6	.600	2	1	.500	1	1	2	3	6	0	1	0	16	3.2	5
Hodges	2	6	1	1	1.000	0	0	---	0	0	0	0	1	0	1	0	2	1.0	2
Perdue	3	10	3	1	.333	2	0	.000	1	2	3	0	3	0	0	0	2	0.7	2

3-Pt. FG: Chicago 25-65 (.385)—Jordan 12-28 (.429); Pippen 2-9 (.222); Paxson 7-18 (.389); Grant 0-1 (.000); Armstrong 1-4 (.250); Levingston 0-1 (.000); Hansen 3-4 (.750).

PORTLAND TRAIL BLAZERS VS. CHICAGO BULLS

Player	G.	Min.	FGA	FGM	Pct.	FTA	FTM	Pct.	Off. Reb.	Def. Reb.	Tot. Reb.	Ast.	PF	Disq.	Stl.	Blk. Sh.	Pts.	Avg.	Hi.
Drexler	6	238	118	48	.407	56	50	.893	18	29	47	32	27	2	8	6	149	24.8	32
Porter	6	263	70	33	.471	34	28	.824	5	21	26	28	11	0	6	2	97	16.2	24
Kersey	6	228	81	39	.481	15	11	.733	26	26	52	20	25	1	11	1	89	14.8	24
Robinson	6	146	52	23	.442	27	16	.593	4	14	18	13	23	1	5	4	62	10.3	17
Ainge	6	138	53	23	.434	14	10	.714	4	8	12	15	18	0	5	1	60	10.0	17
Bryant	1	21	8	5	.625	0	0	---	3	2	5	0	1	0	0	0	10	10.0	10
Duckworth	6	164	51	22	.431	17	12	.706	10	31	41	9	25	1	3	4	56	9.3	14
Williams	6	211	32	16	.500	16	15	.938	12	32	44	6	21	0	5	3	47	7.8	19
Pack	2	16	6	1	.167	4	3	.750	0	1	1	1	2	0	1	0	5	2.5	4
Abdelnaby	1	6	1	0	.000	2	1	.500	0	2	2	0	0	0	0	1	1	1.0	1
Whatley	5	26	7	2	.286	0	0	---	0	1	1	1	1	0	3	0	4	0.8	4
Cooper	1	8	0	0	---	0	0	---	0	2	2	1	0	0	0	0	0	0.0	0

3-Pt. FG: Portland 10-52 (.192)—Drexler 3-20 (.150); Porter 3-13 (.231); Kersey 0-1 (.000); Robinson 0-1 (.000); Ainge 4-17 (.235).

OFFENSIVE TEAM STATISTICS

		FIELD GOALS			FREE THROWS			REBOUNDS			MISCELLANEOUS				Turn Over	Blk. Sh.	SCORING	
Team	G.	Att.	Made	Pct.	Att.	Made	Pct.	Off.	Def.	Tot.	Ast.	PF	Disq.	Stl.			Pts.	Avg.
Phoenix	8	710	345	.486	278	229	.824	103	225	328	219	205	6	60	115	40	948	118.5
Golden State	4	352	170	.483	154	111	.721	55	90	145	93	109	1	41	49	19	468	117.0
Portland	21	1760	848	.482	712	535	.751	292	603	895	541	553	10	184	325	97	2309	110.0
Indiana	3	242	111	.459	103	81	.786	28	77	105	70	83	1	26	40	12	323	107.7
Boston	10	886	442	.499	236	181	.767	142	280	422	249	220	4	73	117	53	1071	107.1
Seattle	9	731	355	.486	267	211	.790	130	234	364	184	238	3	59	145	56	950	105.6
Cleveland	17	1357	655	.483	483	400	.828	203	496	699	448	347	3	125	241	104	1761	103.6
San Antonio	3	253	123	.486	81	54	.667	42	72	114	53	72	2	23	47	26	310	103.3
Utah	16	1234	592	.480	536	433	.808	201	428	629	367	354	0	119	227	76	1646	102.9
New Jersey	4	381	168	.441	83	59	.711	64	99	163	103	113	1	43	53	31	407	101.8
Chicago	22	1750	852	.487	612	450	.735	285	592	877	531	520	5	172	298	121	2208	100.4
Miami	3	239	108	.452	89	65	.730	33	66	99	60	68	1	21	44	9	298	99.3
L.A. Clippers	5	406	195	.480	133	94	.707	67	136	203	111	129	3	30	65	28	491	98.2
L.A. Lakers	4	311	134	.431	130	101	.777	44	91	135	80	102	2	36	62	15	378	94.5
New York	12	940	409	.435	320	238	.744	186	334	520	273	300	3	76	165	50	1083	90.3
Detroit	5	377	158	.419	126	96	.762	54	130	184	108	117	1	29	76	23	424	84.8

3-Pt. FG: Phoenix 29-78 (.372); Golden State 17-47 (.362); Portland 78-221 (.353); Indiana 20-45 (.444); Boston 6-31 (.194); Seattle 29-99 (.293); Cleveland 51-148 (.345); San Antonio 10-24 (.417); Utah 29-98 (.296); New Jersey 12-41 (.293); Chicago 54-145 (.372); Miami 17-38 (.447); L.A. Clippers 7-27 (.259); L.A. Lakers 9-20 (.450); New York 27-106 (.255); Detroit 10-36 (.278).

DEFENSIVE TEAM STATISTICS

	FIELD GOALS			FREE THROWS			REBOUNDS			MISCELLANEOUS				Turn Over	Blk. Sh.	SCORING		Pt. Dif.
Team	Att.	Made	Pct.	Att.	Made	Pct.	Off.	Def.	Tot	Ast.	PF	Disq.	Stl.			Pts.	Avg.	
New York	893	358	.401	336	242	.720	137	295	432	262	276	3	78	161	60	1071	89.3	+1.0
Detroit	418	173	.414	138	103	.746	92	150	242	107	122	1	36	69	25	463	92.6	-7.8
Chicago	1708	767	.449	615	473	.769	281	584	865	502	539	10	155	328	88	2072	94.2	+6.2
Cleveland	1496	710	.475	361	272	.753	246	456	702	407	395	4	143	214	109	1718	101.1	+2.5
L.A. Clippers	380	183	.482	173	134	.775	63	144	207	115	112	0	37	71	31	511	102.2	-4.0
Utah	1288	620	.481	453	344	.759	205	400	605	371	405	3	108	213	85	1640	102.5	+0.4
Portland	1720	812	.472	695	547	.787	249	548	797	522	543	10	156	322	96	2239	106.6	+3.3
Boston	799	400	.501	283	232	.820	94	276	370	270	207	2	75	129	56	1070	107.0	+0.1
Seattle	732	357	.488	305	238	.780	110	223	333	205	206	1	82	116	40	977	108.6	-3.0
L.A. Lakers	328	165	.503	131	88	.672	64	126	190	118	98	3	40	66	17	437	109.3	-14.8
New Jersey	332	155	.467	144	122	.847	65	132	197	97	85	0	29	68	29	440	110.0	-8.3
San Antonio	253	130	.514	88	72	.818	42	83	125	78	64	0	23	38	14	337	112.3	-9.0
Indiana	273	132	.484	103	79	.767	53	98	151	75	75	2	23	37	13	345	115.0	-7.3
Golden State	343	171	.499	141	112	.794	66	122	188	88	117	3	27	75	25	466	116.5	+0.5
Phoenix	712	353	.496	204	147	.721	114	228	342	187	217	4	74	124	57	937	117.1	+1.4
Miami	254	136	.535	94	76	.809	48	88	136	86	69	0	31	38	15	352	117.3	-18.0

3-Pt. FG against: New York 27-82 (.329); Detroit 14-46 (.304); Chicago 65-206 (.316); Cleveland 26-94 (.277); L.A. Clippers 11-27 (.407); Utah 56-161 (.348); Portland 68-187 (.364); Boston 38-101 (.376); Seattle 25-75 (.333); L.A. Lakers 19-41 (.463); New Jersey 8-36 (.222); San Antonio 5-19 (.263); Indiana 2-6 (.333); Golden State 12-41 (.293); Phoenix 27-76 (.355); Miami 4-9 (.444).

1992 PLAYOFF RESULTS, STATISTICS

EASTERN CONFERENCE FIRST ROUND
Chicago 3, Miami 0
Apr. 24—Fri.—Miami 94 at Chicago 113
Apr. 26—Sun.—Miami 90 at Chicago 120
Apr. 29—Wed.—Chicago 119 at Miami 114

Boston 3, Indiana 0
Apr. 23—Thur.—Indiana 113 at Boston 124
Apr. 25—Sat.—Indiana 112 at Boston ....°119
Apr. 27—Mon.—Boston 102 at Indiana 98

Cleveland 3, New Jersey 1
Apr. 23—Thur.—New Jersey 113 at Cleveland 120
Apr. 25—Sat.—New Jersey 96 at Cleveland 118
Apr. 28—Tue.—Cleveland 104 at New Jersey 109
Apr. 30—Thur.—Cleveland 98 at New Jersey 89

New York 3, Detroit 2
Apr. 24—Fri.—Detroit 75 at New York 109
Apr. 26—Sun.—Detroit 89 at New York 88
Apr. 28—Tue.—New York 90 at Detroit ....°87
May 1—Fri.—New York 82 at Detroit 86
May 3—Sun.—Detroit 87 at New York 94

EASTERN CONFERENCE SEMIFINALS
Cleveland 4, Boston 3
May 2—Sat.—Boston 76 at Cleveland 101
May 4—Mon.—Boston 104 at Cleveland 98
May 8—Fri.—Cleveland 107 at Boston 110
May 10—Sun.—Cleveland 114 at Boston ....°112
May 13—Wed.—Boston 98 at Cleveland 114
May 15—Fri.—Cleveland 91 at Boston 122
May 17—Sun.—Boston 104 at Cleveland 122

Chicago 4, New York 3
May 5—Tue.—New York 94 at Chicago 89
May 7—Thur.—New York 78 at Chicago 86
May 9—Sat.—Chicago 94 at New York 86
May 10—Sun.—Chicago 86 at New York 93
May 12—Tue.—New York 88 at Chicago 96
May 14—Thur.—Chicago 86 at New York 100
May 17—Sun.—New York 81 at Chicago 110

EASTERN CONFERENCE FINALS
Chicago 4, Cleveland 2
May 19—Tue.—Cleveland 89 at Chicago 103
May 21—Thur.—Cleveland 107 at Chicago 81
May 23—Sat.—Chicago 105 at Cleveland 96
May 25—Mon.—Chicago 85 at Cleveland 99
May 27—Wed.—Cleveland 89 at Chicago 112
May 29—Fri.—Chicago 99 at Cleveland 94

WESTERN CONFERENCE FIRST ROUND
Portland 3, L.A. Lakers 1
Apr. 23—Thur.—L.A. Lakers 102 at Portland 115
Apr. 25—Sat.—L.A. Lakers 79 at Portland 101

Apr. 29—Wed.—Portland 119 at L.A. Lakers......................°121
May 3—Sun.—Portland 102 at L.A. Lakers†......................76
†Game played in Las Vegas.

Utah 3, L.A. Clippers 2
Apr. 24—Fri.—L.A. Clippers 97 at Utah 115
Apr. 26—Sun.—L.A. Clippers 92 at Utah 103
Apr. 28—Tue.—Utah 88 at L.A. Clippers...........................98
May 3—Sun.—Utah 107 at L.A. Clippers†.........................115
May 4—Mon.—L.A. Clippers 89 at Utah 98
†Game played in Anaheim.

Seattle 3, Golden State 1
Apr. 23—Thur.—Seattle 117 at Golden State 109
Apr. 25—Sat.—Seattle 101 at Golden State 115
Apr. 28—Tue.—Golden State 128 at Seattle 129
Apr. 30—Thur.—Golden State 116 at Seattle 119

Phoenix 3, San Antonio 0
Apr. 24—Fri.—San Antonio 111 at Phoenix........................117
Apr. 26—Sun.—San Antonio 107 at Phoenix 119
Apr. 29—Wed.—Phoenix 101 at San Antonio 92

WESTERN CONFERENCE SEMIFINALS
Portland 4, Phoenix 1
May 5—Tue.—Phoenix 111 at Portland 113
May 7—Thur.—Phoenix 119 at Portland 126
May 9—Sat.—Portland 117 at Phoenix 124
May 11—Mon.—Portland 153 at Phoenix ....°°151
May 14—Thur.—Phoenix 106 at Portland 118

Utah 4, Seattle 1
May 6—Wed.—Seattle 100 at Utah 108
May 8—Fri.—Seattle 97 at Utah 103
May 10—Sun.—Utah 98 at Seattle 104
May 12—Tue.—Utah 89 at Seattle 83
May 14—Thur.—Seattle 100 at Utah 111

WESTERN CONFERENCE FINALS
Portland 4, Utah 2
May 16—Sat.—Utah 88 at Portland 113
May 19—Tue.—Utah 102 at Portland 119
May 22—Fri.—Portland 89 at Utah 97
May 24—Sun.—Portland 112 at Utah 121
May 26—Tue.—Utah 121 at Portland ....°127
May 28—Thur.—Portland 105 at Utah 97

NBA FINALS
Chicago 4, Portland 2
June 3—Wed.—Portland 89 at Chicago 122
June 5—Fri.—Portland 115 at Chicago ....°104
June 7—Sun.—Chicago 94 at Portland 84
June 10—Wed.—Chicago 88 at Portland 93
June 12—Fri.—Chicago 119 at Portland 106
June 14—Sun.—Portland 93 at Chicago 97

°Indicates overtime period.

BOSTON CELTICS

Player	G.	Min.	FGA	FGM	Pct.	FTA	FTM	Pct.	Off. Reb.	Def. Reb.	Tot. Reb.	Ast.	PF	Disq.	Stl.	Blk. Sh.	Pts.	Avg.	Hi.
Lewis	10	408	218	115	.528	63	48	.762	11	32	43	39	38	2	24	8	280	28.0	42
McHale	10	306	126	65	.516	44	35	.795	21	46	67	13	34	0	5	5	165	16.5	23
Gamble	10	335	131	62	.473	15	12	.800	13	29	42	23	26	0	12	6	136	13.6	22
Parish	10	335	101	50	.495	28	20	.714	38	59	97	14	22	0	7	15	120	12.0	27
Bird	4	107	42	21	.500	4	3	.750	2	16	18	21	7	0	1	2	45	11.3	16
Bagley	10	308	95	42	.442	37	26	.703	8	19	27	85	17	0	9	1	111	11.1	35
Pinckney	10	314	58	35	.603	31	26	.839	36	48	84	7	30	0	12	9	96	9.6	17
Brown	6	120	44	22	.500	6	4	.667	3	9	12	31	16	2	1	4	48	8.0	18
Fox	8	67	23	11	.478	4	4	1.000	3	3	6	4	11	0	2	2	29	3.6	8
Douglas	6	65	25	9	.360	2	1	.500	1	3	4	10	8	0	0	0	19	3.2	5
Kleine	9	82	22	9	.409	2	2	1.000	6	16	22	1	11	0	1	2	20	2.2	12
Vrankovic	1	3	1	1	1.000	0	0	---	0	0	0	0	0	0	0	0	2	2.0	2

3-Pt. FG: Boston 6-31 (.194)—Lewis 2-6 (.333); McHale 0-1 (.000); Gamble 0-2 (.000); Bird 0-5 (.000); Bagley 1-4 (.250); Pinckney 0-1 (.000); Brown 0-3 (.000); Fox 3-6 (.500); Douglas 0-2 (.000); Kleine 0-1 (.000); Armstrong 5-17 (.294). Opponents 38-101 (.376).

CHICAGO BULLS

Player	G.	Min.	FGA	FGM	Pct.	FTA	FTM	Pct.	Off. Reb.	Def. Reb.	Tot. Reb.	Ast.	PF	Disq.	Stl.	Blk. Sh.	Pts.	Avg.	Hi.
Jordan	22	920	581	290	.499	189	162	.857	37	100	137	127	62	0	44	16	759	34.5	56
Pippen	22	899	325	152	.468	155	118	.761	59	134	193	147	72	1	41	25	428	19.5	31
Grant	22	856	183	99	.541	76	51	.671	76	118	194	66	68	1	24	39	249	11.3	20
Paxson	22	598	139	73	.525	19	16	.842	0	22	22	61	53	1	14	1	174	7.9	16

Player	G.	Min.	FGA	FGM	Pct.	FTA	FTM	Pct.	Off. Reb.	Def. Reb.	Tot. Reb.	Ast.	PF	Disq.	Stl.	Blk. Sh.	Pts.	Avg.	Hi.
Armstrong	22	434	139	63	.453	38	30	.789	2	22	24	47	33	0	14	0	161	7.3	18
Cartwright	22	612	116	55	.474	31	13	.419	29	69	98	38	70	1	11	4	123	5.6	12
Williams	22	321	70	34	.486	28	20	.714	33	62	95	7	65	0	6	18	88	4.0	12
King	14	111	40	18	.450	23	15	.652	7	13	20	5	12	0	5	2	53	3.8	13
Levingston	22	191	57	25	.439	28	14	.500	17	24	41	9	31	0	4	6	64	2.9	12
Perdue	18	157	37	18	.486	20	9	.450	18	22	40	9	34	1	3	10	45	2.5	16
Hodges	17	137	41	16	.390	2	1	.500	3	1	4	5	10	0	5	0	42	2.5	7
Hansen	9	69	22	9	.409	3	1	.333	4	5	9	10	10	0	1	0	22	2.4	5

3-Pt. FG: Chicago 54-145 (.372)—Jordan 17-44 (.386); Pippen 6-24 (.250); Grant 0-2 (.000); Paxson 12-27 (.444); Armstrong 5-17 (.294); Williams 0-1 (.000); King 2-2 (1.000); Levingston 0-1 (.000); Perdue 0-1 (.000); Hodges 9-20 (.450); Hansen 3-6 (.500). Opponents 65-206 (.316).

CLEVELAND CAVALIERS

Player	G.	Min.	FGA	FGM	Pct.	FTA	FTM	Pct.	Off. Reb.	Def. Reb.	Tot. Reb.	Ast.	PF	Disq.	Stl.	Blk. Sh.	Pts.	Avg.	Hi.
Daugherty	17	687	235	124	.528	145	118	.814	37	137	174	58	47	0	11	17	366	21.5	40
Price	17	603	238	118	.496	73	66	.904	10	32	42	128	34	0	24	4	327	19.2	35
Nance	17	681	251	124	.494	70	58	.829	45	112	157	43	56	1	14	46	306	18.0	32
Williams	17	567	154	84	.545	109	87	.798	50	80	130	42	58	2	24	17	255	15.0	20
Ehlo	17	552	152	63	.414	21	16	.762	22	55	77	77	40	0	21	5	163	9.6	21
Sanders	17	418	115	56	.487	21	17	.810	20	35	55	37	62	0	15	12	130	7.6	17
Battle	15	202	82	34	.415	23	21	.913	4	8	12	15	11	0	5	1	89	5.9	14
Brandon	12	157	55	22	.400	4	3	.750	4	18	22	30	17	0	3	1	47	3.9	6
Kerr	12	149	41	18	.439	5	5	1.000	1	5	6	10	12	0	5	0	44	3.7	9
Phills	5	12	9	4	.444	4	3	.750	2	4	6	5	1	0	1	0	11	2.2	4
Ferry	9	55	15	7	.467	4	4	1.000	7	9	16	1	7	0	1	1	19	2.1	8
James	8	22	10	1	.100	4	2	.500	1	1	2	2	2	0	1	0	4	0.5	4

3-Pt. FG: Cleveland 51-148 (.345)—Daugherty 0-1 (.000); Price 25-69 (.362); Nance 0-1 (.000); Ehlo 21-51 (.412); Sanders 1-3 (.333); Battle 0-2 (.000); Brandon 0-3 (.000); Kerr 3-11 (.273); Phills 0-1 (.000); Ferry 1-3 (.333); James 0-3 (.000). Opponents 26-94 (.277).

DETROIT PISTONS

Player	G.	Min.	FGA	FGM	Pct.	FTA	FTM	Pct.	Off. Reb.	Def. Reb.	Tot. Reb.	Ast.	PF	Disq.	Stl.	Blk. Sh.	Pts.	Avg.	Hi.
Dumars	5	221	68	32	.471	19	15	.789	5	3	8	16	11	0	5	1	84	16.8	23
I. Thomas	5	200	65	22	.338	28	22	.786	3	23	26	37	18	0	5	0	70	14.0	31
Salley	5	149	44	20	.455	28	23	.821	10	20	30	14	18	0	3	14	63	12.6	20
Woolridge	5	128	52	23	.442	16	9	.563	5	5	10	3	14	0	1	1	55	11.0	16
Aguirre	5	113	48	16	.333	16	12	.750	4	5	9	12	9	0	2	1	45	9.0	13
Laimbeer	5	145	46	17	.370	5	5	1.000	5	28	33	8	18	1	4	1	41	8.2	15
Rodman	5	156	27	16	.593	8	4	.500	16	35	51	9	17	0	4	2	36	7.2	12
McCann	1	13	6	3	.500	0	0	---	1	1	2	0	2	0	1	6	6.0	6
Bedford	1	9	6	3	.500	0	0	---	0	2	2	1	0	1	0	6	6.0	6
Sellers	2	13	4	2	.500	2	2	1.000	0	0	0	2	0	0	2	6	3.0	6
Walker	5	68	9	3	.333	4	4	1.000	5	7	12	4	7	0	1	0	10	2.0	6
Blanks	1	10	2	1	.500	0	0	---	0	1	1	3	2	0	3	0	2	2.0	2

3-Pt. FG: Detroit 12-39 (.308)—Dumars 5-10 (.500); I. Thomas 4-11 (.364); Salley 0-1 (.000); Aguirre 1-5 (.200); Laimbeer 2-10 (.200); Rodman 0-2 (.000). Opponents 14-46 (.304).

GOLDEN STATE WARRIORS

Player	G.	Min.	FGA	FGM	Pct.	FTA	FTM	Pct.	Off. Reb.	Def. Reb.	Tot. Reb.	Ast.	PF	Disq.	Stl.	Blk. Sh.	Pts.	Avg.	Hi.
Hardaway	4	176	80	32	.400	37	24	.649	6	9	15	29	14	0	13	0	98	24.5	27
Marciulionis	4	133	47	25	.532	41	34	.829	3	6	9	20	15	0	3	1	85	21.3	27
Owens	4	157	57	30	.526	27	17	.630	13	20	33	13	14	0	8	2	77	19.3	25
Mullin	4	168	63	27	.429	14	13	.929	3	9	12	12	8	0	5	2	71	17.8	24
Elie	4	80	36	23	.639	3	2	.667	11	11	22	10	11	1	5	0	50	12.5	22
Gatling	4	81	29	18	.621	22	14	.636	9	16	25	0	14	0	2	10	50	12.5	16
Lister	4	47	15	6	.400	5	4	.800	3	8	11	1	9	0	0	4	16	4.0	7
Higgins	2	17	5	2	.400	2	2	1.000	0	0	0	1	1	0	1	0	6	3.0	4
Alexander	4	24	5	3	.600	1	1	1.000	1	5	6	1	8	0	2	0	7	1.8	4
Hill	4	47	7	3	.429	2	0	.000	3	5	8	1	12	0	2	0	6	1.5	4
Askew	4	30	8	1	.125	0	0	---	3	1	4	5	3	0	0	0	2	0.5	2

3-Pt. FG: Golden State 17-47 (.362)—Hardaway 10-29 (.345); Marciulionis 1-2 (.500); Mullin 4-12 (.333); Elie 2-2 (1.000); Higgins 0-2 (.000). Opponents 12-41 (.293).

INDIANA PACERS

Player	G.	Min.	FGA	FGM	Pct.	FTA	FTM	Pct.	Off. Reb.	Def. Reb.	Tot. Reb.	Ast.	PF	Disq.	Stl.	Blk. Sh.	Pts.	Avg.	Hi.
Miller	3	130	43	25	.581	30	24	.800	4	3	7	14	12	1	4	0	81	27.0	32
Schrempf	3	120	47	18	.383	28	25	.893	12	27	39	7	10	0	2	1	63	21.0	23
Person	3	118	47	19	.404	12	8	.667	1	8	9	7	11	0	2	0	51	17.0	32
M. Williams	3	106	43	18	.419	15	11	.733	1	7	8	24	12	0	9	0	50	16.7	18
McCloud	2	53	12	6	.500	11	8	.727	0	2	2	6	5	0	2	1	23	11.5	17
Fleming	3	51	18	10	.556	3	1	.333	0	2	2	6	5	0	3	0	21	7.0	13
Thompson	3	63	11	7	.636	2	2	1.000	2	11	13	4	11	0	1	4	16	5.3	8
Smits	3	28	11	4	.364	2	2	1.000	3	3	6	0	7	0	2	1	10	3.3	6
Davis	3	69	10	4	.400	0	0	---	5	14	19	2	8	0	0	5	8	2.7	4
K. Williams	1	1	0	0	---	0	0	---	0	0	0	0	0	0	1	0	0	0.0	0
Green	1	3	0	0	---	0	0	---	0	0	0	0	0	0	0	0	0	0.0	0
Dreiling	3	3	0	0	---	0	0	---	0	2	2	0	0	0	0	0	0	0.0	0

3-Pt. FG: Indiana 20-45 (.444)—Miller 7-11 (.636); Schrempf 2-4 (.500); Person 5-15 (.333); M. Williams 3-9 (.333); McCloud 3-6 (.500). Opponents 2-6 (.333).

LOS ANGELES CLIPPERS

Player	G.	Min.	FGA	FGM	Pct.	FTA	FTM	Pct.	Off. Reb.	Def. Reb.	Tot. Reb.	Ast.	PF	Disq.	Stl.	Blk. Sh.	Pts.	Avg.	Hi.
Manning	5	194	81	46	.568	31	20	.645	15	13	28	14	21	1	5	4	113	22.6	33
Harper	5	206	87	39	.448	14	11	.786	10	22	32	23	13	0	5	4	90	18.0	26
Do. Rivers	5	187	56	25	.446	27	22	.815	4	15	19	21	16	0	6	0	76	15.2	23
Norman	5	184	53	27	.509	17	9	.529	19	30	49	15	18	0	4	3	63	12.6	14
Smith	5	148	56	22	.393	15	14	.933	10	18	28	9	24	2	4	12	58	11.6	16
Edwards	5	87	24	10	.417	19	12	.632	5	8	13	3	11	0	1	1	32	6.4	9
Grant	5	77	21	10	.476	2	2	1.000	0	4	4	18	10	0	3	2	22	4.4	8
Vaught	5	36	11	7	.636	2	2	1.000	2	10	12	4	3	0	1	1	17	3.4	8
Polynice	5	63	12	7	.583	6	2	.333	2	16	18	2	11	0	1	1	16	3.2	6
Young	3	11	4	2	.500	0	0	---	0	0	0	1	0	0	0	0	4	1.3	4
Kimble	3	5	1	0	.000	0	0	---	0	0	0	1	2	0	0	0	0	0.0	0
Ellis	1	2	0	0	---	0	0	---	0	0	0	0	0	0	0	0	0	0.0	0

3-Pt. FG: L.A. Clippers 7-27 (.259)—Manning 1-3 (.333); Harper 1-9 (.111); Do. Rivers 4-8 (.500); Norman 0-2 (.000); Grant 0-2 (.000); Vaught 1-1 (1.000); Young 0-2 (.000) Opponents 11-27 (.407).

LOS ANGELES LAKERS

Player	G.	Min.	FGA	FGM	Pct.	FTA	FTM	Pct.	Off. Reb.	Def. Reb.	Tot. Reb.	Ast.	PF	Disq.	Stl.	Blk. Sh.	Pts.	Avg.	Hi.
Scott	4	148	44	22	.500	27	24	.889	3	7	10	14	10	0	6	1	75	18.8	22
Teagle	4	126	55	27	.491	20	16	.800	3	10	13	8	18	1	5	2	70	17.5	26
Threatt	4	162	46	24	.522	12	9	.750	0	8	8	17	11	0	2	0	59	14.8	24
Green	4	153	39	16	.410	23	19	.826	15	21	36	7	10	0	7	0	51	12.8	19
Campbell	4	117	37	14	.378	18	12	.667	9	16	25	6	14	0	3	6	40	10.0	13
Divac	4	143	43	15	.349	10	9	.900	6	16	22	15	17	1	5	3	39	9.8	18
Brown	3	44	19	8	.421	6	3	.500	3	8	11	2	3	0	2	1	19	6.3	8
Robinson	3	24	10	3	.300	8	5	.625	2	4	6	1	6	0	3	1	11	3.7	7
Smith	4	40	10	3	.300	2	1	.500	1	1	2	5	5	0	4	0	7	1.8	5
Sparrow	3	16	4	1	.250	4	3	.750	1	0	1	4	5	0	1	0	5	1.7	4
Haley	2	12	4	1	.250	0	0	---	1	0	1	1	3	0	0	0	2	1.0	2

3-Pt. FG: L.A. Lakers 9-20 (.450)—Scott 7-12 (.583); Threatt 2-3 (.667); Divac 0-2 (.000); Brown 0-1 (.000); Smith 0-2 (.000). Opponents 19-41 (.463).

MIAMI HEAT

Player	G.	Min.	FGA	FGM	Pct.	FTA	FTM	Pct.	Off. Reb.	Def. Reb.	Tot. Reb.	Ast.	PF	Disq.	Stl.	Blk. Sh.	Pts.	Avg.	Hi.
Seikaly	3	117	35	19	.543	32	24	.750	11	19	30	4	15	1	1	5	62	20.7	26
Rice	3	119	64	24	.375	7	6	.857	3	7	10	5	7	0	2	0	57	19.0	25
Smith	3	100	34	18	.529	6	5	.833	3	3	6	15	2	0	4	1	48	16.0	19
Long	3	120	36	15	.417	10	7	.700	7	8	15	8	11	0	5	0	37	12.3	17
Shaw	3	85	30	14	.467	8	5	.625	2	11	13	12	13	0	2	0	36	12.0	19
Coles	3	45	10	7	.700	10	8	.800	2	5	7	6	5	0	3	0	23	7.7	9
Edwards	3	55	13	5	.385	8	5	.625	1	6	7	7	3	0	2	0	15	5.0	8
Askins	3	48	11	5	.455	2	0	.000	4	5	9	3	7	0	1	0	13	4.3	8
Morton	1	2	0	0	---	2	2	1.000	0	0	0	0	0	0	0	0	2	2.0	2
Ogg	3	15	3	1	.333	2	1	.500	0	1	1	0	3	0	1	3	3	1.0	3
Kessler	2	12	2	0	.000	2	2	1.000	0	1	1	0	1	0	0	0	2	1.0	2
Sundvold	1	2	1	0	.000	0	0	---	0	0	0	0	1	0	0	0	0	0.0	0

3-Pt. FG: Miami 17-38 (.447)—Rice 3-12 (.250); Smith 7-11 (.636); Long 0-4 (.000); Shaw 3-5 (.600); Coles 1-1 (1.000); Askins 3-5 (.600). Opponents 4-9 (.444).

NEW JERSEY NETS

Player	G.	Min.	FGA	FGM	Pct.	FTA	FTM	Pct.	Off. Reb.	Def. Reb.	Tot. Reb.	Ast.	PF	Disq.	Stl.	Blk. Sh.	Pts.	Avg.	Hi.
Petrovic	4	163	76	41	.539	13	11	.846	4	6	10	13	13	0	4	1	97	24.3	40
Coleman	4	162	74	36	.486	21	16	.762	13	32	45	21	12	0	7	4	89	22.3	24
Morris	4	135	58	32	.552	9	7	.778	11	9	20	5	11	0	7	7	75	18.8	28
Blaylock	4	148	55	17	.309	4	3	.750	5	11	16	31	16	0	15	2	38	9.5	12
Bowie	4	112	33	14	.424	12	8	.667	8	11	19	9	19	0	3	5	37	9.3	16
Mills	4	77	27	10	.370	11	7	.636	9	15	24	8	18	0	1	2	27	6.8	9
Addison	1	9	7	2	.286	0	0	---	0	0	0	1	0	0	0	0	5	5.0	5
George	4	44	23	7	.304	3	1	.333	0	0	0	8	8	0	3	1	15	3.8	5
Dudley	4	77	14	5	.357	8	4	.500	13	12	25	3	14	1	2	10	14	3.5	5
Anderson	3	24	9	3	.333	2	2	1.000	1	2	3	3	1	0	1	0	8	2.7	6
Feitl	1	3	2	1	.500	0	0	---	0	1	1	0	0	0	0	0	2	2.0	2
Lee	2	6	3	0	.000	0	0	---	0	0	0	0	1	0	0	1	0	0.0	0

3-Pt. FG: New Jersey 12-41 (.293)—Petrovic 4-12 (.333); Coleman 1-6 (.167); Morris 4-10 (.400); Blaylock 1-6 (.167); Bowie 1-2 (.500); Mills 0-1 (.000); Addison 1-2 (.500); Lee 0-2 (.000). Opponents 8-36 (.222).

NEW YORK KNICKERBOCKERS

Player	G.	Min.	FGA	FGM	Pct.	FTA	FTM	Pct.	Off. Reb.	Def. Reb.	Tot. Reb.	Ast.	PF	Disq.	Stl.	Blk. Sh.	Pts.	Avg.	Hi.
Ewing	12	482	239	109	.456	73	54	.740	33	100	133	27	49	1	7	31	272	22.7	34
McDaniel	12	458	197	94	.477	49	36	.735	43	43	86	23	34	1	9	2	226	18.8	24
Starks	12	295	123	46	.374	52	42	.808	7	23	30	38	45	1	17	0	145	12.1	27
Wilkins	12	344	109	45	.413	23	16	.696	12	18	30	34	35	0	5	1	107	8.9	19
Jackson	12	368	92	37	.402	27	22	.815	12	15	27	86	26	0	10	0	100	8.3	18
Oakley	12	354	58	22	.379	27	20	.741	44	64	108	8	36	0	8	5	64	5.3	13
Anthony	12	213	46	19	.413	33	20	.606	4	13	17	41	28	0	16	1	63	5.3	14
Mason	12	288	43	19	.442	28	22	.786	28	48	76	10	34	0	2	8	60	5.0	13
Vandeweghe	8	75	24	13	.542	7	6	.857	3	3	6	4	10	0	2	1	36	4.5	12
Winchester	3	11	5	3	.600	1	0	.000	0	0	0	2	0	0	0	0	6	2.0	4
Donaldson	2	11	2	2	1.000	0	0	---	0	4	4	0	2	0	0	1	4	2.0	4
McCormick	1	6	2	0	.000	0	0	---	0	3	3	0	1	0	0	1	0	0.0	0

3-Pt. FG: New York 27-106 (.255)—Ewing 0-1 (.000); McDaniel 2-8 (.250); Starks 11-46 (.239); Wilkins 1-13 (.077); Jackson 4-21 (.190); Anthony 5-12 (.417); Vandeweghe 4-5 (.800). Opponents 27-82 (.329).

PHOENIX SUNS

Player	G.	Min.	FGA	FGM	Pct.	FTA	FTM	Pct.	Off. Reb.	Def. Reb.	Tot. Reb.	Ast.	PF	Disq.	Stl.	Blk. Sh.	Pts.	Avg.	Hi.
Johnson	8	335	128	62	.484	72	62	.861	8	25	33	93	24	1	12	2	189	23.6	35
Hornacek	8	343	128	62	.484	34	31	.912	12	39	51	42	23	0	14	2	163	20.4	31
Majerle	7	266	111	48	.432	26	25	.962	13	31	44	20	11	0	10	0	130	18.6	25
Chambers	7	194	85	39	.459	32	27	.844	8	23	31	19	25	1	2	5	109	15.6	29
Ceballos	8	188	80	44	.550	30	20	.667	20	31	51	12	14	0	6	6	108	13.5	20
Perry	8	185	63	38	.603	32	23	.719	12	27	39	11	24	1	3	6	99	12.4	31
Burtt	8	104	38	16	.421	21	18	.857	3	9	12	14	18	0	5	0	50	6.3	14
Lang	8	192	40	15	.375	19	15	.789	15	17	32	2	33	2	3	15	45	5.6	14
West	8	96	19	14	.737	8	4	.500	8	9	17	2	21	1	2	4	32	4.0	13
Nealy	8	67	18	7	.389	4	4	1.000	4	14	18	4	12	0	3	0	23	2.9	10

3-Pt. FG: Phoenix 29-78 (.372)—Johnson 3-6 (.500); Hornacek 8-17 (.471); Majerle 9-33 (.273); Chambers 4-7 (.571); Burtt 0-2 (.000); Nealy 5-13 (.385). Opponents 27-76 (.355).

PORTLAND TRAIL BLAZERS

Player	G.	Min.	FGA	FGM	Pct.	FTA	FTM	Pct.	Off. Reb.	Def. Reb.	Tot. Reb.	Ast.	PF	Disq.	Stl.	Blk. Sh.	Pts.	Avg.	Hi.
Drexler	21	847	425	198	.466	171	138	.807	60	95	155	147	77	2	31	20	553	26.3	42
Porter	21	870	285	147	.516	143	119	.832	25	72	97	141	49	0	22	3	450	21.4	41
Kersey	21	756	257	131	.510	114	79	.693	59	103	162	75	85	2	41	19	341	16.2	29
Duckworth	21	647	216	107	.495	53	35	.660	40	77	117	41	76	1	11	12	249	11.9	24
Robinson	21	522	197	91	.462	77	44	.571	25	63	88	43	84	3	22	21	227	10.8	24
Ainge	21	449	169	81	.479	47	39	.830	8	32	40	49	58	1	15	1	222	10.6	25
Williams	21	758	130	66	.508	91	69	.758	61	118	179	22	73	1	27	17	201	9.6	21
Bryant	12	116	29	10	.345	4	3	.750	11	18	29	1	22	0	3	0	23	1.9	10
Abdelnaby	8	25	10	5	.500	4	2	.500	0	4	4	2	4	0	0	0	12	1.5	5
Cooper	3	27	4	2	.500	0	0	---	1	7	8	0	4	0	3	4	1.3	2
Whatley	14	96	20	6	.300	4	4	1.000	0	10	10	13	11	0	7	0	16	1.1	4
Pack	15	52	18	4	.222	4	3	.750	2	4	6	7	10	0	5	1	11	0.8	6

3-Pt. FG: Portland 78-221 (.353)—Drexler 19-81 (.235); Porter 37-78 (.474); Kersey 0-3 (.000); Robinson 1-6 (.167); Ainge 21-52 (.404); Whatley 0-1 (.000). Opponents 68-187 (.364).

SAN ANTONIO SPURS

Player	G.	Min.	FGA	FGM	Pct.	FTA	FTM	Pct.	Off. Reb.	Def. Reb.	Tot. Reb.	Ast.	PF	Disq.	Stl.	Blk. Sh.	Pts.	Avg.	Hi.
Cummings	3	122	66	34	.515	20	10	.500	15	19	34	7	9	0	4	4	78	26.0	31
Elliott	3	137	40	19	.475	18	16	.889	4	9	13	8	6	0	3	4	59	19.7	22
Carr	3	109	44	24	.545	16	10	.625	8	15	23	3	14	1	2	11	59	19.7	20
Strickland	2	80	22	13	.591	8	5	.625	0	7	7	19	8	0	3	2	31	15.5	20
V. Johnson	3	69	24	11	.458	2	1	.500	3	5	8	7	7	0	5	1	25	8.3	12
Royal	3	57	9	5	.556	9	5	.556	5	7	12	0	7	0	2	2	15	5.0	6
Tucker	3	38	14	6	.429	1	1	1.000	1	2	3	2	3	0	0	0	14	4.7	5
Pressey	3	46	18	6	.333	0	0	---	1	2	3	3	9	1	3	1	13	4.3	11
Sutton	2	15	6	2	.333	3	3	1.000	0	0	0	2	3	0	1	1	7	3.5	5
Green	3	47	10	3	.300	4	3	.750	5	6	11	2	6	0	0	0	9	3.0	4

3-Pt. FG: San Antonio 10-24 (.417)—Cummings 0-1 (.000); Elliott 5-8 (.625); Carr 1-2 (.500); V. Johnson 2-4 (.500); Tucker 1-5 (.200); Pressey 1-2 (.500); Sutton 0-2 (.000). Opponents 5-19 (.263).

SEATTLE SUPERSONICS

Player	G.	Min.	FGA	FGM	Pct.	FTA	FTM	Pct.	Off. Reb.	Def. Reb.	Tot. Reb.	Ast.	PF	Disq.	Stl.	Blk. Sh.	Pts.	Avg.	Hi.
Pierce	9	316	131	63	.481	54	47	.870	9	13	22	28	24	0	5	1	176	19.6	31
Johnson	9	247	137	65	.474	34	32	.941	8	19	27	8	19	0	3	3	166	18.4	26
Kemp	9	338	101	48	.475	80	61	.763	47	63	110	4	41	0	5	14	157	17.4	28
McKey	9	315	99	52	.525	45	38	.844	17	27	44	24	37	1	7	12	147	16.3	27
McMillan	9	246	83	35	.422	14	10	.714	14	19	33	63	35	1	16	3	86	9.6	17
Payton	8	221	58	27	.466	12	7	.583	6	15	21	38	26	1	8	2	61	7.6	15
Barros	7	96	40	21	.525	0	0	---	1	6	7	8	11	0	4	0	52	7.4	10
Benjamin	9	161	41	23	.561	18	9	.500	18	36	46	5	20	0	5	13	55	6.1	14
Cage	9	197	34	19	.559	1	1	1.000	18	33	51	4	22	0	6	8	39	4.3	10
Conlon	1	1	1	0	.000	2	2	1.000	0	1	1	0	0	0	0	0	2	2.0	2
Brown	5	22	6	2	.333	7	4	.571	0	2	2	2	3	0	0	0	9	1.8	5

3-Pt. FG: Seattle 29-99 (.293)—Pierce 3-11 (.273); Johnson 4-22 (.182); McKey 5-16 (.313); McMillan 6-26 (.231); Payton 0-2 (.000); Barros 10-17 (.588); Benjamin 0-1 (.000); Brown 1-4 (.250). Opponents 25-75 (.333).

UTAH JAZZ

Player	G.	Min.	FGA	FGM	Pct.	FTA	FTM	Pct.	Off. Reb.	Def. Reb.	Tot. Reb.	Ast.	PF	Disq.	Stl.	Blk. Sh.	Pts.	Avg.	Hi.
K. Malone	16	688	284	148	.521	210	169	.805	43	138	181	42	57	0	22	19	465	29.1	44
J. Malone	16	610	275	134	.487	72	62	.861	12	27	39	31	33	0	8	2	331	20.7	33
Stockton	16	623	182	77	.423	78	65	.833	10	37	47	217	38	0	34	5	237	14.8	24
Corbin	16	447	137	69	.504	54	42	.778	39	49	88	17	45	0	12	3	180	11.3	28
Edwards	16	354	111	52	.468	32	23	.719	22	29	51	17	45	0	23	3	129	8.1	16
Benoit	13	257	84	36	.429	11	11	1.000	18	32	50	6	30	0	6	5	89	6.8	16
Brown	16	274	75	30	.400	41	32	.780	22	43	65	11	43	0	2	2	92	5.8	12
Eaton	16	473	46	26	.565	27	21	.778	30	60	90	4	47	0	7	36	73	4.6	14
Murdock	3	11	5	3	.600	2	2	1.000	0	3	3	1	1	0	1	1	8	2.7	6
Rudd	10	84	21	10	.476	4	3	.750	0	4	4	19	11	0	3	0	25	2.5	8
Crowder	4	12	9	5	.556	1	0	.000	1	1	2	1	1	0	1	0	10	2.5	4
Thornton	2	32	5	2	.400	4	3	.750	5	4	9	1	3	0			7	3.5	5

3-Pt. FG: Utah 29-98 (.296)—K. Malone 0-2 (.000); J. Malone 1-3 (.333); Stockton 18-58 (.310); Corbin 0-2 (.000); Edwards 2-10 (.200); Benoit 6-13 (.462); Murdock 0-1 (.000); Rudd 2-7 (.286); Crowder 0-2 (.000). Opponents 56-161 (.348).

1992 PLAYOFF HIGHS

SCORING

Player	Points	Opponents	Date
Jordan, Chicago	56	at Miami	April 29
Jordan, Chicago	46	Miami	April 24
Jordan, Chicago	46	at Portland	June 12

REBOUNDS

Player	Rebounds	Opponents	Date
Kemp, Seattle	20	Golden State	April 30
Kemp, Seattle	19	at Golden State	April 25
Ewing, New York	19	Detroit	May 3
K. Malone, Utah	19	Portland	May 28

ASSISTS

Player	Assists	Opponents	Date
Stockton, Utah	21	L.A. Clippers	April 24
Johnson, Phoenix	19	San Antonio	April 26
Stockton, Utah	19	L.A. Clippers	April 26

INDIVIDUAL HIGHS

Most Minutes Played, Game..52, Williams, Portland vs. Utah, May 26*
48, Elliott, San Antonio at Phoenix, April 26
Hardaway, Golden State at Seattle, April 30
Most Points, Game..56, Jordan, Chicago at Miami, April 29
Most Field Goals Made, Game..21, Jordan, Chicago vs. Miami, April 24
Most Field Goal Attempts, Game..34, Jordan, Chicago vs. Miami, April 24
Most 3-Pt. Field Goals Made, Game..6, Porter, Portland vs. Utah, May 16
Jordan, Chicago vs. Portland, June 3
Most 3-Pt. Field Goal Attempts, Game..13, Hardaway, Golden State at Seattle, April 30
Most Free Throws Made, Game..22, K. Malone, Utah at L.A. Clippers, May 3
Most Free Throw Attempts, Game..24, K. Malone, Utah at L.A. Clippers, May 3
Most Rebounds, Game..20, Kemp, Seattle vs. Golden State, April 30
Most Offensive Rebounds, Game..9, Williams, Cleveland at New Jersey, April 28
Parish, Boston vs. Cleveland, May 8
Most Defensive Rebounds, Game..14, Ewing, New York at Chicago, May 7
Parish, Boston vs. Cleveland, May 10*
Most Assists, Game..21, Stockton, Utah vs. L.A. Clippers, April 24
Most Blocked Shots, Game..7, Carr, San Antonio vs. Phoenix, April 29
Most Steals, Game..8, Hardaway, Golden State at Seattle, April 30

TEAM HIGHS & LOWS

Most Points, Game..153, Portland at Phoenix, May 11**
129, Seattle vs. Golden State, April 28
Fewest Points, Game..75, Detroit at New York, April 24
Most Points, Half..75, Portland vs. L.A. Lakers, April 23
Fewest Points, Half..30, New York at Chicago, May 17
Most Points, Quarter..42, Portland at Phoenix, May 11
Fewest Points, Quarter..12, Detroit at New York, May 3
L.A. Clippers at Utah, May 4
Highest Field Goal Percentage, Game...615, Seattle vs. Golden State, April 28
Lowest Field Goal Percentage, Game...359, Portland vs. Chicago, June 7
Most Field Goals Made, Game..54, Portland at Phoenix, May 11**
52, Boston vs. Cleveland, May 15
Fewest Field Goals Made, Game..27, New York at Detroit, May 1
Most 3-Pt. Field Goals Made, Game..8, Indiana at Boston, April 23
Portland vs. Utah, May 19
Most Free Throws Made, Game..48, Utah vs. Portland, May 24
Fewest Free Throws Made, Game..4, Boston at Cleveland, May 2
Most Rebounds, Game..60, Seattle vs. Golden State, April 30
Fewest Rebounds, Game..22, Golden State at Seattle, April 28
Most Assists, Game..42, Cleveland vs. Boston, May 17
Most Steals, Game..15, New York vs. Detroit, April 24
Chicago vs. Miami, April 26
Portland vs. Phoenix, May 5
Most Personal Fouls, Game..38, Phoenix vs. Portland, May 11**
35, Seattle at Golden State, April 25
Portland at Phoenix, May 9
Fewest Personal Fouls, Game..9, Cleveland vs. Boston, May 2
Most Blocked Shots, Game..16, Seattle at Utah, May 14
Most Turnovers, Game..24, Seattle vs. Golden State, April 28
Fewest Turnovers, Game..6, New York vs. Detroit, April 26
Chicago at New York, May 10
Phoenix vs. Portland, May 11**

*Denotes overtime period.

ACTIVE CAREER PLAYOFF LEADERS
(Players who were on active rosters or on injured list during 1991-1992 season)

MOST GAMES PLAYED

Magic Johnson	186
Robert Parish	174
Kevin McHale	165
Larry Bird	164
Danny Ainge	149
Kurt Rambis	139
James Worthy	138
Byron Scott	137
Maurice Cheeks	128
Vinnie Johnson	116

MOST FIELD GOALS ATTEMPTED

Larry Bird	3,090
Magic Johnson	2,513
Michael Jordan	2,290
James Worthy	2,243
Robert Parish	2,164
Kevin McHale	2,090
Isiah Thomas	1,869
Byron Scott	1,672
Moses Malone	1,566
Clyde Drexler	1,543

MOST FREE THROWS ATTEMPTED

Magic Johnson	1,241
Larry Bird	1,012
Michael Jordan	960
Kevin McHale	958
Robert Parish	758
Moses Malone	756
Isiah Thomas	689
James Worthy	647
Karl Malone	552
Clyde Drexler	543

MOST MINUTES PLAYED

Magic Johnson	7,403
Larry Bird	6,886
Robert Parish	5,942
Kevin McHale	5,603
James Worthy	5,149
Maurice Cheeks	4,766
Byron Scott	4,517
Isiah Thomas	4,216
Danny Ainge	4,080
Michael Jordan	3,862

MOST FIELD GOALS MADE

Larry Bird	1,458
Magic Johnson	1,276
James Worthy	1,235
Kevin McHale	1,172
Michael Jordan	1,160
Robert Parish	1,094
Byron Scott	828
Isiah Thomas	825
Maurice Cheeks	761
Moses Malone	750

MOST FREE THROWS MADE

Magic Johnson	1,040
Larry Bird	901
Michael Jordan	806
Kevin McHale	754
Moses Malone	576
Robert Parish	548
Isiah Thomas	530
James Worthy	471
Clyde Drexler	429
Karl Malone	424

HIGHEST FIELD GOAL PERCENTAGE
(150 FGM minimum)

	FGA	FGM	Pct.
Kurt Rambis	495	284	.574
Charles Barkley	726	413	.569
Kevin McHale	2,090	1,172	.561
Bernard King	474	265	.559
James Worthy	2,243	1,235	.551
Horace Grant	718	389	.542
Hakeem Olajuwon	948	512	.540
Randy Wittman	417	225	.540
Danny Schayes	308	166	.539
Larry Nance	705	379	.538

HIGHEST FREE THROW PERCENTAGE
(100 FTM minimum)

	FTA	FTM	Pct.
Hersey Hawkins	128	120	.938
Mark Price	143	134	.937
Jeff Hornacek	160	146	.913
Kiki Vandeweghe	259	235	.907
Larry Bird	1,012	901	.890
Rolando Blackman	250	218	.872
Ricky Pierce	279	242	.867
Jeff Malone	210	181	.862
Chris Mullin	147	126	.857
Joe Dumars	449	381	.849

MOST REBOUNDS

Robert Parrish	1,714
Larry Bird	1,683
Magic Johnson	1,431
Moses Malone	1,295
Kevin McHale	1,224
Bill Laimbeer	1,097
Buck Williams	777
Dennis Rodman	766
Kurt Rambis	764
James Worthy	730

MOST ASSISTS

Magic Johnson	2,320
Larry Bird	1,062
Isiah Thomas	987
Maurice Cheeks	908
John Stockton	717
Michael Jordan	624
Clyde Drexler	604
Danny Ainge	569
Terry Porter	506
Joe Dumars	478

MOST PERSONAL FOULS

Robert Parish	599
Kevin McHale	565
Magic Johnson	521
Larry Bird	466
Danny Ainge	431
Bill Laimbeer	408
Kurt Rambis	373
Byron Scott	367
Isiah Thomas	363
John Salley	358

MOST STEALS

Magic Johnson	358
Larry Bird	296
Maurice Cheeks	289
Isiah Thomas	234
Michael Jordan	219
Byron Scott	198
Clyde Drexler	177
James Worthy	172
Danny Ainge	149
Scottie Pippen	145

MOST BLOCKED SHOTS

Robert Parrish	297
Kevin McHale	274
Mark Eaton	201
Hakeem Olajuwon	178
Moses Malone	151
John Salley	146
Larry Bird	145
Alton Lister	141
Larry Nance	130
Wayne Rollins	127

MOST DISQUALIFICATIONS

Robert Parish	16
Bill Laimbeer	13
Alton Lister	10
Wayne Rollins	10
Kevin McHale	8
Isiah Thomas	8
Buck Williams	8
Jerome Kersey	7
7 players tied at	6

HIGHEST SCORING AVERAGE
(25 Games or 625 Points minimum)

	G.	FGM	FTM	Pts.	Avg.
Michael Jordan	92	1,160	806	3,184	34.6
Karl Malone	53	520	424	1,464	27.6
Bernard King	25	265	148	679	27.2
Hakeem Olajuwon	50	512	302	1,326	26.5
Dominique Wilkins	48	456	327	1,255	26.1
Larry Bird	164	1,458	901	3,897	23.8
Patrick Ewing	38	339	191	870	22.9
Terry Cummings	61	558	252	1,369	22.4
Charles Barkley	51	413	303	1,144	22.4
Moses Malone	94	750	576	2,077	22.1

HIGHEST 3-PT. FIELD GOAL PERCENTAGE
(15 3-PT. FGM minimum)

	FGA	FGM	Pct.
Bob Hansen	76	38	.500
Reggie Miller	37	18	.486
Chris Mullin	37	17	.459
Eric Floyd	67	28	.418
Hersey Hawkins	67	28	.418
Lafayette Lever	44	18	.409
Terry Porter	252	102	.405
Trent Tucker	94	38	.404
Byron Scott	260	104	.400
Chuck Person	64	25	.391

MOST 3-PT. FIELD GOALS MADE

Danny Ainge	110
Byron Scott	104
Terry Porter	102
Craig Hodges	90
Isiah Thomas	81
Larry Bird	80
Michael Jordan	58
Clyde Drexler	51
Magic Johnson	48
Mark Aguirre	45
Scottie Pippen	45

MOST 3-PT. FIELD GOALS ATTEMPTED

Danny Ainge	286
Byron Scott	260
Terry Porter	252
Larry Bird	249
Craig Hodges	248
Isiah Thomas	234
Clyde Drexler	203
Magic Johnson	203
Michael Jordan	172
Mark Aguirre	142

MOST POINTS

Larry Bird	3,897
Magic Johnson	3,640
Michael Jordan	3,184
Kevin McHale	3,106
James Worthy	2,953
Robert Parish	2,736
Isiah Thomas	2,261
Byron Scott	2,104
Moses Malone	2,077
Maurice Cheeks	1,888

Orlando is big winner in Shaq sweepstakes

By CHRIS BRIENZA

Most lottery winners dream of mansions. But Pat Williams, the president and general manager of the Orlando Magic, had his eyes set squarely on a shack.

Or "Shaq," as two-time consensus All-America center Shaquille O'Neal of Louisiana State is often called.

This Shaq, at 7-foot-1 and about 300 pounds, is almost as big as a real shack—and more expensive.

Eleven teams took part in the NBA Draft Lottery on May 17 to determine the order of selection for the June 24 draft. Regardless of which team won the right to pick first in May, there was no doubt about who that player would be in June.

"As a result of winning the lottery," Williams said wryly, "our interviewing process was not very complicated."

The consensus No. 1 pick was O'Neal, who declared for the draft after his junior season at LSU. Often compared to elite centers like Patrick Ewing, David Robinson and Hakeem Olajuwon, O'Neal is one of those rare talents around whom entire franchises are built. He averaged 24.1 points, 14 rebounds and 5.2 blocked shots for the Tigers last season and figures to be the Magic's man in the middle for many years to come.

"I feel very fortunate to be drafted by the Magic," O'Neal said. "I think they might have been lacking a little at center. I'm not promising we'll win a championship in the first year; things take time. But I'll learn the ropes, get my feet wet, and after that I'm going to be a good player. I think I'll be pretty hard to stop."

He certainly was on the collegiate level. O'Neal, the first early-entry candidate to be selected No. 1 overall in the NBA since the Houston Rockets drafted Olajuwon in 1984, led the nation in blocked shots last season and was second in rebounding.

In 1990-91, O'Neal did exactly the opposite, leading the nation in rebounding and finishing second in blocks. That season, he became the first player in Southeastern Conference history to lead the league in scoring, rebounding, blocked shots and field-goal percentage in the same season.

He also is the first player since Auburn's Charles Barkley (1982-84) to lead the SEC in rebounding for three straight years. In his three seasons at LSU, O'Neal averaged 13.5 rebounds per game.

"We all have to remember he's only 20 years old," Orlando Coach Matt Guokas said. "He still has a long way to go. He's been preaching patience, and I've been doing that for three years.

"But while we're waiting for him to develop into the kind of player that we expect him to be, he still has the ability to do a lot of things to help us."

The Magic, 21-61 last year, was not the only team to improve itself via the draft or through trades.

The Charlotte Hornets, who made big strides in 1991-92 thanks to the emergence of Kendall Gill and Rookie of the Year Larry Johnson, filled a big void at center by selecting Georgetown's 6-10 Alonzo Mourning with the second overall pick. Mourning averaged 21.3 points, 10.7 rebounds and five blocks per game as a senior while earning Big East Conference Player of the Year and Defensive Player of the Year honors.

"I think he'll have an immediate impact on our rebounding, our shot-blocking and our interior defense," said Dave Twardzik, Charlotte's director of player personnel. "Offensively, he has a way to go. Because of the double-teams and the triple-teams in college, he really has not progressed as much offensively as he should have. But here, he won't have (double- and triple-teams)."

Minnesota, selecting third, took 6-10 Duke center Christian Laettner, last season's consensus college Player of the Year. Laettner, the all-time leading scorer in NCAA Tournament history, led the Blue Devils to their second straight NCAA championship in 1991-92.

"Obviously, I'm very thrilled," said Laettner, who won a gold medal with the U.S. Olympic team. "It should be an easy adjustment for me. I'm not expecting anything difficult. Contrary to popular belief, I'm a fairly easy person to get along with, especially with my teammates. At times I may be too competitive, but I think they appreciate that and they want that."

The versatile Laettner could see action at both power forward and center with the Timberwolves.

Dallas, choosing fourth, took two-time Big Ten Player of the Year Jimmy Jackson of Ohio State, another early-entry candidate. Jackson averaged 22.4 points, 6.8 rebounds and four assists in leading the Buckeyes to a 26-6 record and into the round of eight in the 1992 NCAA Tournament.

The versatile 6-6 guard will be counted on to fill the void created by the loss of Rolando Blackman, the Mavericks' all-time leading scorer who was traded to the New York Knicks on draft day.

"I expect (Jackson) to get a lot of playing time," said Rick Sund, Dallas' vice president of basketball operations. "And that's one of the reasons we traded Ro Blackman, because we wanted to get a lot of minutes (for Jackson)."

The Denver Nuggets, with the Nos. 5 and 13 overall picks, used those choices on 6-8 forward LaPhonso Ellis of Notre Dame and 6-5 swingman Bryant Stith of Virginia.

Ellis, the third all-time leading rebounder in Notre Dame history, averaged 17.7 points and 11.7 rebounds in his senior year. Stith was a three-time All-Atlantic Coast Conference selection and Virginia's all-time leading scorer. Ironically, Stith's Cavaliers beat Ellis' Fighting Irish, 81-76 in overtime, in the NIT title game last spring.

Like Denver, the Milwaukee Bucks also had two first-round picks, Nos. 8 and 23 overall. The Bucks acquired the 23rd choice from Utah in a draft-day deal that sent guard Jay Humphries and forward Larry Krystkowiak to the Jazz for guard Eric Murdock, forward Blue Edwards and a first-round pick. The Bucks used that choice to select Arkansas guard Lee Mayberry. Earlier in the first round, Milwaukee had used the No. 8 selection on Arkansas swingman Todd Day, marking the first time since 1981 (when New Jersey selected Maryland's Buck Williams and Albert King) that two players from the same school were drafted in the first round by the same NBA team in the same year.

Right before Milwaukee nabbed Mayberry, Phoenix drafted Arkansas center Oliver Miller, marking only the fifth time in history that three players from one school were taken in the first round of the same draft. A fourth Razorback, forward Isaiah Morris, was picked by Miami early in the second round.

Shaquille O'Neal (right) and Christian Laettner, the draft's Nos. 1 and 3 overall selections, battle it out in a February 1991 Duke-LSU game.

The suddenly youth-oriented Bucks, who were the NBA's oldest team in 1991-92 (their average age at the end of the season was 29.8 years), got even younger on July 1 when they shipped 31-year-old shooting guard Dale Ellis to San Antonio in a three-way deal with Portland that sent 24-year-old forward Alaa Abdelnaby to Milwaukee.

The NBA's biggest off-season trade involved one of its headliners.

One week before the draft, the Philadelphia 76ers sent six-time All-Star Charles Barkley to the Phoenix Suns for guard Jeff Hornacek, center Andrew Lang and forward Tim Perry.

"This team was in a position to end up with one of the top basketball players in the world," Suns President Jerry Colangelo said. "This adds some of the things we've needed for a long time. When you're talking physical presence on the court, leadership on the court, it is there."

The 76ers, meanwhile, were pleased with what they received in return.

"We are extremely happy to acquire these three players," Philadelphia General Manager Jim Lynam said. "We feel they will mesh tremendously in the Doug Moe (motion-offense) system." Moe replaced Lynam as the 76ers' coach after the end of last season.

Philadelphia may have acquired a replacement for Barkley in Southern Missis-sippi forward Clarence Weatherspoon, a three-time Metro Conference Player of the Year. Sometimes referred to as "Baby Barkley," the 6-6 Weatherspoon will be given every opportunity to live up to that nickname in the years to come.

OFFICIAL NBA DRAFT—JUNE 24, 1992

FIRST ROUND

	TEAM	NAME	COLLEGE	HT.
1.	Orlando	Shaquille O'Neal	Louisiana State	7:00
2.	Charlotte	Alonzo Mourning	Georgetown	6:10
3.	Minnesota	Christian Laettner	Duke	6:10
4.	Dallas	Jimmy Jackson	Ohio State	6:04
5.	Denver	LaPhonso Ellis	Notre Dame	6:08
6.	Washington	Tom Gugliotta	North Carolina State	6:09
7.	Sacramento	Walt Williams	Maryland	6:07
8.	Milwaukee	Todd Day	Arkansas	6:07
9.	Philadelphia	Clarence Weatherspoon	Southern Mississippi	6:05
10.	Atlanta	Adam Keefe	Stanford	6:09
11.	Houston	Robert Horry	Alabama	6:08
12.	Miami	Harold Miner	Southern California	6:04
13.	Denver (from New Jersey)	Bryant Stith	Virginia	6:05
14.	Indiana	Malik Sealy	St. John's	6:06
15.	L.A. Lakers	Anthony Peeler	Missouri	6:03
16.	L.A. Clippers	Randy Woods	La Salle	6:00
17.	Seattle	Doug Christie	Pepperdine	6:06
18.	San Antonio	Tracy Murray*	UCLA	6:06
19.	Detroit	Don MacLean†	UCLA	6:09
20.	New York	Hubert Davis	North Carolina	6:03
21.	Boston	Jon Barry	Georgia Tech	6:04
22.	Phoenix	Oliver Miller	Arkansas	6:07
23.	Milwaukee (from Utah)	Lee Mayberry	Arkansas	6:01
24.	Golden State	Latrell Sprewell	Alabama	6:05
25.	L.A. Clippers (from Cleveland)	Elmore Spencer	UNLV	6:11
26.	Portland	David Johnson	Syracuse	6:05
27.	Chicago	Byron Houston	Oklahoma State	6:04

*Draft rights traded by San Antonio to Portland in a three-way deal that included Dale Ellis going from Milwaukee to San Antonio and Alaa Abdelnaby going from Portland to Milwaukee.

†Draft rights traded by Detroit with William Bedford to Los Angeles Clippers for Olden Polynice and 1996 and 1997 second round draft choices.

SECOND ROUND

	TEAM	NAME	COLLEGE	HT.
28.	Minnesota	Marlon Maxey	Texas-El Paso	6:08
29.	New Jersey (from Orlando via Chicago)	P.J. Brown	Louisiana Tech	6:10
30.	Dallas	Sean Rooks	Arizona	6:09
31.	Portland (from Denver)	Reggie Smith	Texas Christian	6:08
32.	Washington	Brent Price	Oklahoma	6:00
33.	Chicago (from Sacramento)	Corey Williams	Oklahoma State	6:00
34.	Minnesota (from Milwaukee)	Chris Smith	Connecticut	6:02
35.	Charlotte	Tony Bennett	Wisconsin-Green Bay	5:11
36.	L.A. Lakers (from Phi. via Minn. and Mil.)	Duane Cooper	Southern California	6:01
37.	Miami	Isaiah Morris	Arkansas	6:08
38.	Atlanta	Elmer Bennett	Notre Dame	6:00
39.	Chicago (from Indiana)	Litterial Green‡	Georgia	6:01
40.	New Jersey	Steve Rogers	Alabama State	6:03
41.	Houston	Ronald (Popeye) Jones	Murray State	6:07
42.	Miami (from L.A. Lakers)	Matt Geiger	Georgia Tech	6:11
43.	Golden State (from L.A. Clippers)	Predrag Danilovic	Partizan (Yugoslavia)	6:04
44.	San Antonio	Henry Williams	UNC Charlotte	6:02
45.	Seattle	Chris King	Wake Forest	6:06
46.	Denver (from Detroit)	Robert Werdann	St. John's	6:11
47.	Boston	Darren Morningstar	Pittsburgh	6:10
48.	Phoenix (from New York)	Brian Davis	Duke	6:06
49.	Phoenix	Ron Ellis	Louisiana Tech	6:06
50.	Golden State	Matt Fish	UNC Wilmington	6:09
51.	Minnesota (from Utah)	Tim Burroughs	Jacksonville	6:07
52.	Chicago (from Portland)	Matt Steigenga	Michigan State	6:07
53.	Houston (from Cleveland)	Curtis Blair	Richmond	6:01
54.	Sacramento (from Chicago via Portland)	Brett Roberts	Morehead State	6:06

‡Draft rights traded by Chicago to Orlando for a 1993 second round draft choice.

TEAM-BY-TEAM NO. 1 DRAFT CHOICES

*—Designates first player chosen in draft.

ATLANTA HAWKS

1950—Bob Cousy, Holy Cross
1951—Mel Hutchins, Brigham Young
1952—Not available
1953—Bob Houbregs, Washington
1954—Bob Pettit, Louisiana State
1955—Not available
1956—None
1957—Win Wilfong, Memphis State
1958—Dave Gambee, Oregon State
1959—Bob Ferry, St. Louis
1960—Fred LaCour, San Francisco
1961—Cleo Hill, Winston-Salem
1962—Zelmo Beaty, Prairie View
1963—Jerry Ward, Boston College
1964—Jeff Mullins, Duke
1965—Jim Washington, Villanova
1966—Lou Hudson, Minnesota
1967—Tim Workman, Seattle
1968—Skip Harlicka, South Carolina
1969—Butch Beard, Louisville
1970—Pete Maravich, Louisiana State
    John Vallely, UCLA
1971—Tom Payne, Kentucky†
    George Trapp, Long Beach State
1972—None
1973—Dwight Jones, Houston
    John Brown, Missouri
1974—Tom Henderson, Hawaii
    Mike Sojourner, Utah
1975—David Thompson, North Carolina State*
    Marvin Webster, Morgan State
1976—Armond Hill, Princeton
1977—Wayne Rollins, Clemson
1978—Butch Lee, Marquette
    Jack Givens, Kentucky
1979—None
1980—Don Collins, Washington State
1981—Al Wood, North Carolina
1982—Keith Edmonson, Purdue
1983—None
1984—Kevin Willis, Michigan State
1985—Jon Koncak, Southern Methodist
1986—Billy Thompson, Louisville
1987—Dallas Comegys, DePaul
1988—None
1989—Roy Marble, Iowa
1990—Rumeal Robinson, Michigan
1991—Stacey Augmon, Nevada-Las Vegas
    Anthony Avent, Seton Hall
1992—Adam Keefe, Stanford

†Payne was selected by Atlanta in the 1971 supplementary draft of hardship cases. Atlanta had to forfeit its 1972 first-round choice.

BOSTON CELTICS

1947—Eddie Ehlers, Purdue
1948—George Hauptfuehrer, Harvard
1949—Tony Lavelli, Yale
1950—Charlie Share, Bowling Green
1951—Ernie Barrett, Kansas State
1952—Bill Stauffer, Missouri
1953—Frank Ramsey, Kentucky
1954—Togo Palazzi, Holy Cross
1955—Jim Loscutoff, Oregon
1956—Bill Russell, San Francisco
    Tom Heinsohn, Holy Cross
1957—Sam Jones, North Carolina College
1958—Ben Swain, Texas Southern
1959—John Richter, North Carolina State
1960—Tom Sanders, New York University
1961—Gary Phillips, Houston
1962—John Havlicek, Ohio State
1963—Bill Green, Colorado State
1964—Mel Counts, Oregon State
1965—Ollie Johnson, San Francisco
1966—Jim Barnett, Oregon
1967—Mal Graham, New York University
1968—Don Chaney, Houston
1969—Jo Jo White, Kansas
1970—Dave Cowens, Florida State
1971—Clarence Glover, Western Kentucky
1972—Paul Westphal, Southern California
1973—Steve Downing, Indiana
1974—Glenn McDonald, Long Beach State
1975—Tom Boswell, South Carolina
1976—Norm Cook, Kansas
1977—Cedric Maxwell, North Carolina-Charlotte
1978—Larry Bird, Indiana State
    Freeman Williams, Portland State
1979—None
1980—Kevin McHale, Minnesota
1981—Charles Bradley, Wyoming
1982—Darren Tillis, Cleveland State
1983—Greg Kite, Brigham Young
1984—Michael Young, Houston
1985—Sam Vincent, Michigan State
1986—Len Bias, Maryland
1987—Reggie Lewis, Northeastern
1988—Brian Shaw, Cal.-Santa Barbara
1989—Michael Smith, Brigham Young
1990—Dee Brown, Jacksonville
1991—Rick Fox, North Carolina
1992—Jon Barry, Georgia Tech

CHARLOTTE HORNETS

1988—Rex Chapman, Kentucky
1989—J.R. Reid, North Carolina
1990—Kendall Gill, Illinois
1991—Larry Johnson, Nevada-Las Vegas*
1992—Alonzo Mourning, Georgetown

CHICAGO BULLS

1966—Dave Schellhase, Purdue
1967—Clem Haskins, Western Kentucky
1968—Tom Boerwinkle, Tennessee
1969—Larry Cannon, La Salle
1970—Jimmy Collins, New Mexico State
1971—Kennedy McIntosh, Eastern Michigan
1972—Ralph Simpson, Michigan State
1973—Kevin Kunnert, Iowa
1974—Maurice Lucas, Marquette
    Cliff Pondexter, Long Beach State
1975—None
1976—Scott May, Indiana
1977—Tate Armstrong, Duke
1978—Reggie Theus, Nevada-Las Vegas
1979—David Greenwood, UCLA
1980—Kelvin Ransey, Ohio State
1981—Orlando Woolridge, Notre Dame
1982—Quintin Dailey, San Francisco
1983—Sidney Green, Nevada-Las Vegas
1984—Michael Jordan, North Carolina
1985—Keith Lee, Memphis State
1986—Brad Sellers, Ohio State
1987—Olden Polynice, Virginia
1988—Will Perdue, Vanderbilt
    Horace Grant, Clemson
1989—Stacey King, Oklahoma
    B.J. Armstrong, Iowa
    Jeff Sanders, Georgia Southern
1990—None
1991—Mark Randall, Kansas
1992—Byron Houston, Oklahoma State

CLEVELAND CAVALIERS

1970—John Johnson, Iowa
1971—Austin Carr, Notre Dame*
1972—Dwight Davis, Houston
1973—Jim Brewer, Minnesota
1974—Campy Russell, Michigan
1975—John Lambert, Southern California

The Charlotte Hornets were ecstatic to get Georgetown center Alonzo Mourning with the No. 2 pick.

1976—Chuckie Williams, Kansas State
1977—None
1978—Mike Mitchell, Auburn
1979—None
1980—Chad Kinch, North Carolina-Charlotte
1981—None
1982—John Bagley, Boston College
1983—Roy Hinson, Rutgers
        Stewart Granger, Villanova
1984—Tim McCormick, Michigan
1985—Charles Oakley, Virginia Union
1986—Brad Daugherty, North Carolina*
        Ron Harper, Miami (O.)
1987—Kevin Johnson, California
1988—Randolph Keys, Southern Miss.
1989—John Morton, Seton Hall
1990—None
1991—Terrell Brandon, Oregon
1992—None

DALLAS MAVERICKS

1980—Kiki Vandeweghe, UCLA
1981—Mark Aguirre, DePaul*
        Rolando Blackman, Kansas State
1982—Bill Garnett, Wyoming
1983—Dale Ellis, Tennessee
        Derek Harper, Illinois
1984—Sam Perkins, North Carolina
        Terence Stansbury, Temple
1985—Detlef Schrempf, Washington
        Bill Wennington, St. John's
        Uwe Blab, Indiana

1986—Roy Tarpley, Michigan
1987—Jim Farmer, Alabama
1988—None
1989—Randy White, Louisiana Tech
1990—None
1991—Doug Smith, Missouri
1992—Jim Jackson, Ohio State

DENVER NUGGETS

1967—Walt Frazier, Southern Illinois
1968—Tom Boerwinkle, Tennessee
1969—Bob Presley, California
1970—Spencer Haywood, Detroit
1971—Cliff Meely, Colorado
1972—John Belcher, Arkansas State
1973—Mike Bantom, St. Joseph's
1974—James Williams, Austin Peay
1975—Marvin Webster, Morgan State
1976—None
1977—Tom LaGarde, North Carolina
        Anthony Roberts, Oral Roberts
1978—Rod Griffin, Wake Forest
        Mike Evans, Kansas State
1979—None
1980—James Ray, Jacksonville
        Carl Nicks, Indiana State
1981—None
1982—Rob Williams, Houston
1983—Howard Carter, Louisiana State
1984—None
1985—Blair Rasmussen, Oregon
1986—Maurice Martin, St. Joseph's
        Mark Alarie, Duke
1987—None
1988—Jerome Lane, Pittsburgh
1989—Todd Lichti, Stanford
1990—Chris Jackson, Louisiana State
1991—Dikembe Mutombo, Georgetown
        Mark Macon, Temple
1992—LaPhonso Ellis, Notre Dame
        Bryant Stith, Virginia

DETROIT PISTONS

1949—Bob Harris, Oklahoma A & M
1950—George Yardley, Stanford
1951—Zeke Sinicola, Niagara
1952—Not available
1953—Jack Molinas, Columbia
1954—Dick Rosenthal, Notre Dame
1955—Not available
1956—Ron Sobieszczk, DePaul
1957—Charles Tyra, Louisville
1958—None
1959—Bailey Howell, Mississippi State
1960—Jackie Moreland, Louisiana Tech
1961—Ray Scott, Portland
1962—Dave DeBusschere, Detroit
1963—Eddie Miles, Seattle
1964—Joe Caldwell, Arizona State
1965—Bill Buntin, Michigan
1966—Dave Bing, Syracuse
1967—Jimmy Walker, Providence*
        Sonny Dove, St. John's
1968—Otto Moore, Pan American
1969—Terry Driscoll, Boston College
1970—Bob Lanier, St. Bonaventure*
1971—Curtis Rowe, UCLA
1972—Bob Nash, Hawaii
1973—None
1974—Al Eberhard, Missouri
1975—None
1976—Leon Douglas, Alabama
1977—None
1978—None
1979—Greg Kelser, Michigan State
        Roy Hamilton, UCLA
        Phil Hubbard, Michigan
1980—Larry Drew, Missouri

1981—Isiah Thomas, Indiana
     Kelly Tripucka, Notre Dame
1982—Cliff Levingston, Wichita State
     Ricky Pierce, Rice
1983—Antoine Carr, Wichita State
1984—Tony Campbell, Ohio State
1985—Joe Dumars, McNeese State
1986—John Salley, Georgia Tech
1987—None
1988—None
1989—Kenny Battle, Illinois
1990—Lance Blanks, Texas
1991—None
1992—Don MacLean, UCLA

GOLDEN STATE WARRIORS

1947—Francis Crossin, Pennsylvania
1948—Phil Farbman, CCNY
1949—Vern Gardner, Utah
1950—Paul Arizin, Villanova
1951—Don Sunderlage, Illinois
1952—Bill Mlkvy, Temple
1953—Ernie Beck, Pennsylvania
1954—Gene Shue, Maryland
1955—Tom Gola, La Salle
1956—Hal Lear, Temple
1957—Len Rosenbluth, North Carolina
1958—Guy Rodgers, Temple
1959—Wilt Chamberlain, Kansas
1960—Al Bunge, Maryland
1961—Tom Meschery, St. Mary's (Cal.)
1962—Wayne Hightower, Kansas
1963—Nate Thurmond, Bowling Green
1964—Barry Kramer, New York University
1965—Rick Barry, Miami (Fla.)
     Fred Hetzel, Davidson
1966—Clyde Lee, Vanderbilt
1967—Dave Lattin, Texas Western
1968—Ron Williams, West Virginia
1969—Bob Portman, Creighton
1970—None
1971—Cyril Baptiste, Creighton†
     Darnell Hillman, San Jose State
1972—None
1973—Kevin Joyce, South Carolina
1974—Jamaal Wilkes, UCLA
1975—Joe Bryant, La Salle
1976—Robert Parish, Centenary
     Sonny Parker, Texas A & M
1977—Rickey Green, Michigan
     Wesley Cox, Louisville
1978—Purvis Short, Jackson State
     Raymond Townsend, UCLA
1979—None
1980—Joe Barry Carroll, Purdue*
     Rickey Brown, Mississippi State
1981—None
1982—Lester Conner, Oregon State
1983—Russell Cross, Purdue
1984—None
1985—Chris Mullin, St. John's
1986—Chris Washburn, North Carolina State
1987—Tellis Frank, Western Kentucky
1988—Mitch Richmond, Kansas State
1989—Tim Hardaway, Texas-El Paso
1990—Tyrone Hill, Xavier
1991—Chris Gatling, Old Dominion
     Victor Alexander, Iowa State
     Shaun Vandiver, Colorado
1992—Latrell Sprewell, Alabama

†Baptiste was selected by Golden State in the 1971 supplementary draft of hardship cases. Golden State had to forfeit its 1972 first-round choice.

HOUSTON ROCKETS

1967—Pat Riley, Kentucky
1968—Elvin Hayes, Houston*
1969—Bobby Smith, Tulsa

1970—Rudy Tomjanovich, Michigan
1971—Cliff Meely, Colorado
1972—None
1973—Ed Ratleff, Long Beach State
1974—Bobby Jones, North Carolina
1975—Joe Meriweather, Southern Illinois
1976—John Lucas, Maryland*
1977—None
1978—None
1979—Lee Johnson, East Texas State
1980—None
1981—None
1982—Terry Teagle, Baylor
1983—Ralph Sampson, Virginia*
     Rodney McCray, Louisville
1984—Hakeem Olajuwon, Houston*
1985—Steve Harris, Tulsa
1986—Buck Johnson, Alabama
1987—None
1988—Derrick Chievous, Missouri
1989—None
1990—Alec Kessler, Georgia
1991—John Turner, Phillips
1992—Robert Horry, Alabama

INDIANA PACERS

1967—Jimmy Walker, Providence
1968—Don May, Dayton
1969—None
1970—Rick Mount, Purdue
1971—None
1972—George McGinnis, Indiana
1973—Steve Downing, Indiana
1974—Billy Knight, Pittsburgh
1975—Dan Roundfield, Central Michigan
1976—None
1977—None
1978—Rick Robey, Kentucky
1979—Dudley Bradley, North Carolina
1980—None
1981—Herb Williams, Ohio State
1982—Clark Kellogg, Ohio State
1983—Steve Stipanovich, Missouri
     Mitchell Wiggins, Florida State
1984—Vern Fleming, Georgia
1985—Wayman Tisdale, Oklahoma
1986—Chuck Person, Auburn
1987—Reggie Miller, UCLA
1988—Rik Smits, Marist (N.Y.)
1989—George McCloud, Florida State
1990—None
1991—Dale Davis, Clemson
1992—Malik Sealy, St. John's

LOS ANGELES CLIPPERS

1970—John Hummer, Princeton
1971—Elmore Smith, Kentucky State
1972—Bob McAdoo, North Carolina
1973—Ernie DiGregorio, Providence
1974—Tom McMillen, Maryland
1975—None
1976—Adrian Dantley, Notre Dame
1977—None
1978—None
1979—None
1980—Michael Brooks, La Salle
1981—Tom Chambers, Utah
1982—Terry Cummings, DePaul
1983—Byron Scott, Arizona State
1984—Lancaster Gordon, Louisville
     Michael Cage, San Diego State
1985—Benoit Benjamin, Creighton
1986—None
1987—Reggie Williams, Georgetown
     Joe Wolf, North Carolina
     Ken Norman, Illinois
1988—Danny Manning, Kansas*
     Hersey Hawkins, Bradley
1989—Danny Ferry, Duke

1990—Bo Kimble, Loyola Marymount
    Loy Vaught, Michigan
1991—LeRon Ellis, Syracuse
1992—Randy Woods, La Salle
    Elmore Spencer, UNLV

LOS ANGELES LAKERS

1948—Arnie Ferrin, Utah
1949—Vern Mikkelsen, Hamline
1950—Kevin O'Shea, Notre Dame
1951—Whitey Skoog, Minnesota
1952—Not available
1953—Jim Fritsche, Hamline
1954—Ed Kalafat, Minnesota
1955—Not available
1956—Jim Paxson, Dayton
1957—Jim Krebs, Southern Methodist
1958—Elgin Baylor, Seattle*
1959—Tom Hawkins, Notre Dame
1960—Jerry West, West Virginia
1961—Wayne Yates, Memphis State
1962—Leroy Ellis, St. John's
1963—Roger Strickland, Jacksonville
1964—Walt Hazzard, UCLA
1965—Gail Goodrich, UCLA
1966—Jerry Chambers, Utah
1967—None
1968—Bill Hewitt, Southern California
1969—Willie McCarter, Drake
    Rick Roberson, Cincinnati
1970—Jim McMillian, Columbia
1971—Jim Cleamons, Ohio State
1972—Travis Grant, Kentucky State
1973—Kermit Washington, American University
1974—Brian Winters, South Carolina
1975—David Meyers, UCLA
    Junior Bridgeman, Louisville
1976—None
1977—Kenny Carr, North Carolina State
    Brad Davis, Maryland
    Norm Nixon, Duquesne
1978—None
1979—Magic Johnson, Michigan State*
    Brad Holland, UCLA
1980—None
1981—Mike McGee, Michigan
1982—James Worthy, North Carolina*
1983—None
1984—Earl Jones, District of Columbia
1985—A.C. Green, Oregon State
1986—Ken Barlow, Notre Dame
1987—None
1988—David Rivers, Notre Dame
1989—Vlade Divac, Partizan Belgrade
1990—Elden Campbell, Clemson
1991—None
1992—Anthony Peeler, Missouri

MIAMI HEAT

1988—Rony Seikaly, Syracuse
    Kevin Edwards, DePaul
1989—Glen Rice, Michigan
1990—Willie Burton, Minnesota
    Dave Jamerson, Ohio
1991—Steve Smith, Michigan State
1992—Harold Miner, Southern California

MILWAUKEE BUCKS

1968—Charlie Paulk, Northeastern Oklahoma
1969—Kareem Abdul-Jabbar, UCLA*
1970—Gary Freeman, Oregon State
1971—Collis Jones, Notre Dame
1972—Russell Lee, Marshall
    Julius Erving, Massachusetts
1973—Swen Nater, UCLA
1974—Gary Brokaw, Notre Dame
1975—None
1976—Quinn Buckner, Indiana

1977—Kent Benson, Indiana*
    Marques Johnson, UCLA
    Ernie Grunfeld, Tennessee
1978—George Johnson, St. John's
1979—Sidney Moncrief, Arkansas
1980—None
1981—Alton Lister, Arizona State
1982—Paul Pressey, Tulsa
1983—Randy Breuer, Minnesota
1984—Kenny Fields, UCLA
1985—Jerry Reynolds, Louisiana State
1986—Scott Skiles, Michigan State
1987—None
1988—Jeff Grayer, Iowa State
1989—None
1990—Terry Mills, Michigan
1991—Kevin Brooks, Southwestern Louisiana
1992—Todd Day, Arkansas
    Lee Mayberry, Arkansas

MINNESOTA TIMBERWOLVES

1989—Pooh Richardson, UCLA
1990—Felton Spencer, Louisville
    Gerald Glass, Mississippi
1991—Luc Longley, New Mexico
1992—Christian Laettner, Duke

NEW JERSEY NETS

1967—Sonny Dove, St. John's
1968—Joe Allen, Bradley
1969—Kareem Abdul-Jabbar, UCLA
1970—Bob Lanier, St. Bonaventure
1971—Charles Davis, Wake Forest
1972—Jim Chones, Marquette
1973—Doug Collins, Illinois State
1974—Brian Winters, South Carolina
1975—John Lucas, Maryland
1976—None
1977—Bernard King, Tennessee
1978—Winford Boynes, San Francisco
1979—Calvin Natt, Northeast Louisiana
    Cliff Robinson, Southern California
1980—Mike O'Koren, North Carolina
    Mike Gminski, Duke
1981—Buck Williams, Maryland
    Albert King, Maryland
    Ray Tolbert, Indiana
1982—Eric Floyd, Georgetown
    Eddie Phillips, Alabama
1983—None
1984—Jeff Turner, Vanderbilt
1985—None
1986—Dwayne Washington, Syracuse
1987—Dennis Hopson, Ohio State
1988—Chris Morris, Auburn
1989—Mookie Blaylock, Oklahoma
1990—Derrick Coleman, Syracuse*
    Tate George, Connecticut
1991—Kenny Anderson, Georgia Tech
1992—None

NEW YORK KNICKERBOCKERS

1947—Wat Misaka, Utah
1948—Harry Gallatin, NE Missouri State
1949—Dick McGuire, St. John's
1950—Not available
1951—Not available
1952—Ralph Polson, Whitworth
1953—Walter Dukes, Seton Hall
1954—Jack Turner, Western Kentucky
1955—Ken Sears, Santa Clara
1956—Ronnie Shavlik, North Carolina State
1957—Brendan McCann, St. Bonaventure
1958—Pete Brannan, North Carolina
1959—Johnny Green, Michigan State
1960—Darrall Imhoff, California
1961—Tom Stith, St. Bonaventure
1962—Paul Hogue, Cincinnati

1963—Art Heyman, Duke
1964—Jim Barnes, Texas Western
1965—Bill Bradley, Princeton
    Dave Stallworth, Wichita State
1966—Cazzie Russell, Michigan*
1967—Walt Frazier, Southern Illinois
1968—Bill Hosket, Ohio State
1969—John Warren, St. John's
1970—Mike Price, Illinois
1971—Dean Meminger, Marquette
1972—Tom Riker, South Carolina
1973—Mel Davis, St. John's
1974—None
1975—Eugene Short, Jackson State
1976—None
1977—Ray Williams, Minnesota
1978—Micheal Ray Richardson, Montana
1979—Bill Cartwright, San Francisco
    Larry Demic, Arizona
    Sly Williams, Rhode Island
1980—Mike Woodson, Indiana
1981—None
1982—Trent Tucker, Minnesota
1983—Darrell Walker, Arkansas
1984—None
1985—Patrick Ewing, Georgetown*
1986—Kenny Walker, Kentucky
1987—Mark Jackson, St. John's
1988—Rod Strickland, DePaul
1989—None
1990—Jerrod Mustaf, Maryland
1991—Greg Anthony, Nevada-Las Vegas
1992—Hubert Davis, North Carolina

ORLANDO MAGIC

1989—Nick Anderson, Illinois
1990—Dennis Scott, Georgia Tech
1991—Brian Williams, Arizona
    Stanley Roberts, Louisiana State
1992—Shaquille O'Neal, Louisiana State*

PHILADELPHIA 76ers

1964—Luke Jackson, Pan American
1965—Billy Cunningham, North Carolina
1966—Matt Guokas, St. Joseph's
1967—Craig Raymond, Brigham Young
1968—Shaler Halimon, Utah State
1969—Bud Ogden, Santa Clara
1970—Al Henry, Wisconsin
1971—Dana Lewis, Tulsa
1972—Fred Boyd, Oregon State
1973—Doug Collins, Illinois State*
    Raymond Lewis, Los Angeles State
1974—Marvin Barnes, Providence
1975—Darryl Dawkins, No College
1976—Terry Furlow, Michigan State
1977—Glenn Mosley, Seton Hall
1978—None
1979—Jim Spanarkel, Duke
1980—Andrew Toney, Southwestern Louisiana
    Monti Davis, Tennessee State
1981—Franklin Edwards, Cleveland State
1982—Mark McNamara, California
1983—Leo Rautins, Syracuse
1984—Charles Barkley, Auburn
    Leon Wood, Fullerton State
    Tom Sewell, Lamar
1985—Terry Catledge, South Alabama
1986—None
1987—Chris Welp, Washington
1988—Charles Smith, Pittsburgh
1989—Kenny Payne, Louisville
1990—None
1991—None
1992—Clarence Weatherspoon, Mississippi

PHOENIX SUNS

1968—Gary Gregor, South Carolina

1969—Neal Walk, Florida
1970—Greg Howard, New Mexico
1971—John Roche, South Carolina
1972—Corky Calhoun, Pennsylvania
1973—Mike Bantom, St. Joseph's
1974—John Shumate, Notre Dame
1975—Alvan Adams, Oklahoma
    Ricky Sobers, Nevada-Las Vegas
1976—Ron Lee, Oregon
1977—Walter Davis, North Carolina
1978—Marty Byrnes, Syracuse
1979—Kyle Macy, Kentucky
1980—None
1981—Larry Nance, Clemson
1982—David Thirdkill, Bradley
1983—None
1984—Jay Humphries, Colorado
1985—Ed Pinckney, Villanova
1986—William Bedford, Memphis State
1987—Armon Gilliam, Nevada-Las Vegas
1988—Tim Perry, Temple
    Dan Majerle, Central Michigan
1989—Anthony Cook, Arizona
1990—Jayson Williams, St. John's
1991—None
1992—Oliver Miller, Arkansas

PORTLAND TRAIL BLAZERS

1970—Geoff Petrie, Princeton
1971—Sidney Wicks, UCLA
1972—LaRue Martin, Loyola*
1973—Barry Parkhill, Virginia
1974—Bill Walton, UCLA*
1975—Lionel Hollins, Arizona State
1976—Wally Walker, Virginia
1977—Rich Laurel, Hofstra
1978—Mychal Thompson, Minnesota*
    Ron Brewer, Arkansas
1979—Jim Paxson, Dayton
1980—Ronnie Lester, Iowa
1981—Jeff Lamp, Virginia
    Darnell Valentine, Kansas
1982—Lafayette Lever, Arizona State
1983—Clyde Drexler, Houston
1984—Sam Bowie, Kentucky
    Bernard Thompson, Fresno State
1985—Terry Porter, Wisconsin-Stevens Point
1986—Walter Berry, St. John's
    Arvidas Sabonis, Soviet Union
1987—Ronnie Murphy, Jacksonville
1988—Mark Bryant, Seton Hall
1989—Byron Irvin, Missouri
1990—Alaa Abdelnaby, Duke
1991—None
1992—Dave Johnson, Syracuse

SACRAMENTO KINGS

1949—Frank Saul, Seton Hall
1950—Joe McNamee, San Francisco
1951—Sam Ranzino, North Carolina State
1952—Not available
1953—Richie Regan, Seton Hall
1954—Tom Marshall, Western Kentucky
1955—Not available
1956—Si Green, Duquesne
1957—Rod Hundley, West Virginia*
1958—Archie Dees, Indiana
1959—Bob Boozer, Kansas State*
1960—Oscar Robertson, Cincinnati*
1961—Larry Siegfried, Ohio State
1962—Jerry Lucas, Ohio State
1963—Tom Thacker, Cincinnati
1964—George Wilson, Cincinnati
1965—Nate Bowman, Wichita State
1966—Walt Wesley, Kansas
1967—Mel Daniels, New Mexico
1968—Don Smith (Abdul Aziz), Iowa State
1969—Herm Gilliam, Purdue
1970—Sam Lacey, New Mexico State

1971—Ken Durrett, La Salle
1972—Nate Williams, Utah State
1973—Ron Behagen, Minnesota
1974—Scott Wedman, Colorado
1975—Bill Robinzine, DePaul
　　　　Bob Bigelow, Pennsylvania
1976—Richard Washington, UCLA
1977—Otis Birdsong, Houston
1978—Phil Ford, North Carolina
1979—Reggie King, Alabama
1980—Hawkeye Whitney, North Carolina State
1981—Steve Johnson, Oregon State
　　　　Kevin Loder, Alabama State
1982—LaSalle Thompson, Texas
　　　　Brook Steppe, Georgia Tech
1983—Ennis Whatley, Alabama
1984—Otis Thorpe, Providence
1985—Joe Kleine, Arkansas
1986—Harold Pressley, Villanova
1987—Kenny Smith, North Carolina
1988—Ricky Berry, San Jose State
1989—Pervis Ellison, Louisville*
1990—Lionel Simmons, La Salle
　　　　Travis Mays, Texas
　　　　Duane Causwell, Temple
　　　　Anthony Bonner, St. Louis
1991—Billy Owens, Syracuse
　　　　Pete Chilcutt, North Carolina
1992—Walt Williams, Maryland

SAN ANTONIO SPURS

1967—Matt Aitch, Michigan State
1968—Shaler Halimon, Utah State
1969—Willie Brown, Middle Tennessee
1970—Nate Archibald, Texas-El Paso
1971—Stan Love, Oregon
1972—LaRue Martin, Loyola
1973—Kevin Kunnert, Iowa
1974—Leonard Robinson, Tennessee
1975—Mark Olberding, Minnesota
1976—None
1977—None
1978—Frankie Sanders, Southern
1979—Wiley Peck, Mississippi State
1980—Reggie Johnson, Tennessee
1981—None
1982—None
1983—John Paxson, Notre Dame
1984—Alvin Robertson, Arkansas
1985—Alfredrick Hughes, Loyola (Ill.)
1986—Johnny Dawkins, Duke
1987—David Robinson, Navy*
　　　　Greg Anderson, Houston
1988—Willie Anderson, Georgia
1989—Sean Elliott, Arizona
1990—Dwayne Schintzius, Florida
1991—None
1992—Tracy Murray, UCLA

SEATTLE SUPERSONICS

1967—Al Tucker, Oklahoma Baptist
1968—Bob Kauffman, Guilford
1969—Lucius Allen, UCLA
1970—Jim Ard, Cincinnati
1971—Fred Brown, Iowa
1972—Bud Stallworth, Kansas
1973—Mike Green, Louisiana Tech
1974—Tom Burleson, North Carolina State
1975—Frank Oleynick, Seattle University
1976—Bob Wilkerson, Indiana
1977—Jack Sikma, Illinois Wesleyan
1978—None
1979—James Bailey, Rutgers
　　　　Vinnie Johnson, Baylor
1980—Bill Hanzlik, Notre Dame
1981—Danny Vranes, Utah
1982—None
1983—Jon Sundvold, Missouri
1984—None

1985—Xavier McDaniel, Wichita State
1986—None
1987—Scottie Pippen, Central Arkansas
　　　　Derrick McKey, Alabama
1988—Gary Grant, Michigan
1989—Dana Barros, Boston College
　　　　Shawn Kemp, Trinity Valley JC
1990—Gary Payton, Oregon State
1991—Rich King, Nebraska
1992—Doug Christie, Pepperdine

UTAH JAZZ

1974—None
1975—Rich Kelley, Stanford
1976—None
1977—None
1978—James Hardy, San Francisco
1979—Larry Knight, Loyola
1980—Darrell Griffith, Louisville
　　　　John Duren, Georgetown
1981—Danny Schayes, Syracuse
1982—Dominique Wilkins, Georgia
1983—Thurl Bailey, North Carolina State
1984—John Stockton, Gonzaga
1985—Karl Malone, Louisiana Tech
1986—Dell Curry, Virginia Tech
1987—Jose Ortiz, Oregon State
1988—Eric Leckner, Wyoming
1989—Blue Edwards, East Carolina
1990—None
1991—Eric Murdock, Providence
1992—None

WASHINGTON BULLETS

1961—Walt Bellamy, Indiana
1962—Billy McGill, Utah
1963—Rod Thorn, West Virginia
1964—Gary Bradds, Ohio State
1965—Jerry Sloan, Evansville
1966—Jack Marin, Duke
1967—Earl Monroe, Winston-Salem
1968—Wes Unseld, Louisville
1969—Mike Davis, Virginia Union
1970—George Johnson, Stephen F. Austin
1971—Phil Chenier, California†
　　　　Stan Love, Oregon
1972—None
1973—Nick Weatherspoon, Illinois
1974—Len Elmore, Maryland
1975—Kevin Grevey, Kentucky
1976—Mitch Kupchak, North Carolina
　　　　Larry Wright, Grambling
1977—Greg Ballard, Oregon
　　　　Bo Ellis, Marquette
1978—Roger Phegley, Bradley
　　　　Dave Corzine, DePaul
1979—None
1980—Wes Matthews, Wisconsin
1981—Frank Johnson, Wake Forest
1982—None
1983—Jeff Malone, Mississippi State
　　　　Randy Wittman, Indiana
1984—Melvin Turpin, Kentucky
1985—Kenny Green, Wake Forest
1986—John Williams, Louisiana State
　　　　Anthony Jones, Nevada-Las Vegas
1987—Tyrone Bogues, Wake Forest
1988—Harvey Grant, Oklahoma
1989—Tom Hammonds, Georgia Tech
1990—None
1991—LaBradford Smith, Louisville
1992—Tom Gugliotta, N.C. State

†Chenier was selected by Baltimore in the 1971 supplementary draft of hardship cases. Baltimore had to forfeit its 1972 first-round choice.

NOTE: The first-round selections of Denver, Indiana, New Jersey and San Antonio between 1967-75 were made while those clubs were members of the American Basketball Association.

1992-93 INFORMATION

Including

NBA Office Directories

Directories of NBA Teams

Team Schedules/1991-92 Results

Rosters of NBA Teams

Day-by-Day Schedule/TV Schedule

Divisional Alignment/Playoff Format

CBA Information

National Basketball Association

OFFICE: Olympic Tower, 645 Fifth Avenue, New York, N.Y. 10022
TELEPHONE: (212) 826-7000

Commissioner: David J. Stern
Deputy Commissioner & Chief Operating Officer:
Russell T. Granik
Senior Vice President & General Counsel:
Gary B. Bettman
Director of Business Affairs: Valerie B. Ackerman
Special Assistant to the Commissioner: Adam Silver
Assistant to the Deputy Commissioner: Nancy Hayward
Assistant to the Senior Vice President & General Counsel:
Debbie Walsh
Administrative Assistant to the Commissioner:
Marilyn Coughlin
Administrative Assistant to the Commissioner:
Linda Tosi

David J. Stern

Administration
Director of Administration: Noreen Reilly
Director of Personnel: Loretta Hackett
Office Services Coordinator: Paul Marxen
Personnel Coordinator: Ada Williams
Office Administration Coordinator: Ellen Vorel
Personnel Assistant: Anne Faughnan

Broadcasting
Vice President, Broadcasting: John Kosner
Executive Producer, NBA Radio: Tom Carelli
Manager, Broadcast Production: Brian Sherriffe
Broadcasting Coordinator: Jim Griffel
NBA Radio Assistant: Tim Lindsey
Broadcasting Assistant: Jordan Schlachter

Corporate Affairs
Vice President, Corporate Affairs: Carolyn Blitz Sonn
Corporate Affairs Manager: Steve Martin
Corporate Affairs Coordinator: Lynn Breidenbach
Corporate Affairs Assistant: Kelly Kennedy

Editorial
Vice President, Editorial: Alex Sachare
Editorial Manager: Mark Hurlman
Editorial Manager: Clare Martin
Editorial Assistant: Chris Ekstrand
Staff Writer: Jamie Rosenberg
Fan Services Assistant: Nicole Anderson

Finance
Vice President, Finance: Robert Criqui
Controller: Michael Galloway
Director of Computer Services: Timothy Kolp
Assistant Controller: Rutheen Neville
Manager, User Services: Mignon Kolp
PC Support Coordinator: Richard D'Addario
Assistant Systems Manager: Constantine Terzopoulos
Assistant, User Services: Johanna Carter
Administrative Assistant: Edythe Verdonck
Benefits Coordinator: Meryl Steinberg

Legal
Deputy General Counsel: Joel M. Litvin
Assistant General Counsel: William S. Koenig

Operations
Vice President, Operations: Rod Thorn
Director of Scheduling and Game Operations: Matt Winick
Manager, Basketball Operations: Gary Brokaw
Chief of Officiating Staff: Darell Garretson
Operations Coordinator: Theresa Sanzari
Operations Assistant: Sandi Bittler

Player Programs
Vice President, Player Programs: Tom (Satch) Sanders
Player Programs Manager: Randolph Smith
Program Development Coordinator: Melvyn Davis

Public Relations
Vice President, Public Relations: Brian McIntyre
Director of Media Relations: Terry Lyons
Director of International Public Relations: Josh Rosenfeld
Director of Business Public Relations: Mary Neagoy
Assistant Director of Media Relations: Chartese Dean
Public Relations Manager/Business: Seth Sylvan
Public Relations Manager/Entertainment: Karen Spina
Public Relations Coordinator: Chris Brienza
Public Relations Assistant: Peter Steber
Public Relations Assistant: Hope Newton
International Public Relations Consultant: Barbara Colangelo

Security
Vice President and Director of Security: Horace Balmer
Assistant Director of Security: Larry Richardson
Security Coordinator: Jim Wilson

Special Events
Vice President, Special Events: Steve Mills
Director of Special Events: Regina McDonald
Director of Special Events: Ski Austin
Director of Special Events: Michael Golub
Event Manager: Mary Kate Shea
International Event Manager: Kim Bohuny
Event Planner: Perle Zablow
Event Coordinator: Bradley Dillon
Event Coordinator: Paul Lambert
Event Coordinator: Kenneth Payne
Special Events Assistant: Siobhan Greene

NBA Properties, Inc.

OFFICE: Olympic Tower, 645 Fifth Avenue, New York, N.Y. 10022
TELEPHONE: (212) 826-7000

International Offices

NBA Australia, Ltd. :
7 Barnacle Mews, Templestowe 3106, Victoria, Australia
TELEPHONE: 613 846 4325   FAX: 613 846 6235

NBA Asia, Ltd. :
Banyan Villas 2C, 9 Stanley Village Road, Hong Kong
TELEPHONE: 852 813 5694   FAX: 852 813 7471

NBA Europe, SA:
Freixa 26-28, 08021 Barcelona, Spain
TELEPHONE: 343 447 3709   FAX: 343 232 2388

President: Rick Welts
Special Assistant to the President: Bill Daugherty

Business Development
Vice President: William Jemas, Jr.
Senior Product Manager: Donna Goldsmith
Senior Publishing Manager: Frank Fochetta
Product Manager: Christopher Malone
Product Manager: Kim McBride
Product Manager: Carlton Smith
Business Development Manager: Avonda Perna
Manager, Direct Response Programs: Diane Naughton
Manager, Manufacturing: Gerard McCarrick
Manager, Manufacturing: Lee Newell
Business Development Assistant: Maria Credle
Assistant Product Manager: Anne Goldman
Assistant Product Manager: Joanne Masso
Product Assistant: Joy Dellapina
Manufacturing Assistant: Carolyn Zucker
Direct Marketing Assistant: Stacey Smith

Finance
Vice President and Controller: Richard C. Coiro
Assistant Controller: Gary Etkin
Accounting Manager: Margaret Norton
Staff Accountant: Lionel McCloud
Staff Accountant: Hillary Mohel
Accounting Assistant: Laurie Coleman

Legal
Vice President and General Counsel: John T. Rose II
Assistant General Counsel: Gary D. Way
Trademark Counsel: Terese R. Cohen
Staff Attorney: Sheryl L. Goodman
Trademark Assistant: Beverly Hand

Licensing Group

Group Vice President and General Manager: Bill Marshall
Special Assistant: Mark Sage
Vice President, International: Rob Millman
Director and Group Manager, Premium Sales: John Killen
Director and Group Manager, Retail Sales: Mark Appleman
Director of Licensing, Non-Apparel: Carol Blazejowski
Director of Licensing, Children's: Sue Koten
Director of Licensing, Adult Apparel: Sal LaRocca
Director of Licensing, Non-Apparel: Michelle Savadge-Brown
Director of Quality Control: Chris Tripucka
International Sales Manager: Mike Newman
Regional Sales Manager, Midwest Division: Carl Bassewitz
Regional Sales Manager, Atlantic Division: Paul Clarke
Regional Sales Manager, Central Division: Nat Handler
Premium Account Manager: Ron Pence
National Account Manager: Deirdre Wharton
Licensing Manager: Elizabeth Irwin
Premium Account Manager: Mike Caligiure
Premium Account Manager: Jill Gilson
International Licensing Coordinator: Laura Dail
International Sales Coordinator: Juan Gutierrez
International Sales Assistant: Michael Wozniak
Licensing Assistant, International: Rhonda Bugg
Licensing Assistant, Non-Apparel: Lori Dolce
Licensing Assistant, Non-Apparel: Nancy Fitzpatrick
Licensing Assistant, Children's: David Moroknek
Licensing Assistant, Adult Apparel: Peter Sparaco
Licensing Assistant, Traffic: Deborah Morton-Edwards
Quality Control Assistant: Lynn Rist
Retail Sales Assistant: Lisa Steinberg
Sales Services Assistant: Bill Terrell

Marketing

Vice President: Judy Shoemaker
Creative Director: Tom O'Grady
Computer Graphics Director: Kim Mason
Production Manager: Denise Apelian
Traffic Manager: Amy Straut
Marketing Manager: Tim Taylor
Marketing Projects Coordinator: Anne Rabasca
Computer Graphics Coordinator: Lisa Ruckel
Assistant Art Director: Barry Gottlieb
Production Assistant: Jennifer Levine

Media and Sponsor Programs

Vice President, Media & Sponsor Programs: David Schreff
Director & Group Manager, Media Programs: Michael Dresner
Director & Group Manager, Sponsor Programs: Ted Howard
Director & Group Manager, Sponsor Programs: Michael Stevens
Director of Sponsor Programs: David Grant
Director of Sponsor Programs: Peter Gumas
Director of Sponsor Programs: James Howe
Director of Sponsor Programs: Royce Wolfe
Director, International Media Marketing: Jayne Ferguson
Director of Media Programs: Barry Schwartz
Manager, Media Programs: Donna Daniels
Account Executive: Robin Nero

Team Services
Vice President: Paula Hanson
Team Services Manager: Randy Hersh
Community Relations Manager: Jeff Price
Team Services Assistant: Pam Sulzer
Team Services Assistant: Julie Bosley
Team Services Assistant: Nikki Edgecombe
Team Services Assistant: Adam Holzer
Team Services Assistant: Howard Shelton

International Group
Vice President and General Manager: Paul Zilk
Vice President, International Business Affairs: Harvey E. Benjamin
Vice President, International Television: Ed Desser
Vice President, International Licensing: Rob Millman
Director, International Media Marketing: Jayne Ferguson
Director, International Group: Paul Kayaian
Director of International Public Relations: Josh Rosenfeld
Director of Production and Technical Operations, International Television: Peter Skrodelis
Assistant Controller: Gary Etkin
Licensing Manager: Mike Bantom
International Event Manager: Kim Bohuny
Scheduling and Client Services Manager, International Television: Suze Foley
Programming Sales Manager, International Television: Anne Murray
International Sales Manager: Mike Newman
International Licensing Coordinator: Laura Dail
International Sales Coordinator: Juan Gutierrez
Business Operations Coordinator: Shannon Whitefischer
Licensing Assistant, International: Rhonda Bugg
International Sales Assistant: Michael Wozniak
International Public Relations Consultant: Barbara Colangelo

———————————

Vice President and Managing Director, NBA Australia, Ltd.: Ian Campbell
Vice President and Managing Director, NBA Asia, Ltd.: Rob Levine
Director of Licensing, NBA Europe, SA: Francisco Roca

NBA Television Ventures

OFFICE: 450 Harmon Meadow Boulevard, Secaucus, N.J. 07094
TELEPHONE: (201) 865-1500

President: Ed Desser
Research Coordinator: Douglas Kirk

NBA Entertainment, Inc.

OFFICE: 450 Harmon Meadow Boulevard, Secaucus, N.J. 07094
TELEPHONE: (201) 865-1500

Vice President and Executive Producer: Don Sperling
Vice President, Programming: Jon Miller
Vice President, Operations: Stephen Hellmuth

Production
Director of Production: Gil Kerr
Director of Player/Talent Relations: Leah Wilcox
Supervising Producer: Gregg Winik
Creative Director: David Gavant
Senior Producer: Ken Rosen
Senior Producer: Charles Bloom
Senior Producer: Timothy Kane
Senior Producer: James Podhoretz
Editorial Manager: Laurence Weitzman
Producers: Kenneth Adelson, Michael Antinoro, Scott Bantle, Todd Caso (Archivist),
David Check, Rich Docherty, David Goldfield, Steve Koontz, Richard Kopilnick,
James Most, Barry Small, Andy Thompson, Scott Weinstock
Writer for "Inside Stuff": William Rubens
Associate Producers: Jon Clateman, Paul Goldberg, Steve Herbst, Darryl Lepik, Denise Lynam,
Danny Meiseles, Chris Oden, John Oliver, Robert Santarlasci, Michael Tolajian
Player/Talent Relations Coordinator: Lisa Holmes-Cross
Broadcast Associate: Danielle Maged

Operations
Director of Videotape Operations: Alan Goldstein
Director of Engineering: James Parkinson
Production Manager: Geraldine Lavin
Assignment Manager: Paul Hirschheimer
Technical Manager: Roger Miller
Editors: William Clancy, Dion Cocoros, Marc Feldman, Maureen Hassett, Patrick Kelleher,
Sean Kelly, Steve Michaud, Keith Norris, Scott Robblee, James Schwartz

Programming
Home Video Marketing Manager: Judy Harper
Marketing Coordinator: Colleen Martin
Account Coordinator: Matthew Hendison

International Broadcasting
Vice President, International Television: Ed Desser
Director, International Media Marketing: Jayne Ferguson
Director of Production and Technical Operations, International Television: Peter Skrodelis
Scheduling and Client Services Manager, International Television: Suze Foley
Programming Sales Manager, International Television: Anne Murray
Business Operations Coordinator: Shannon Whitefischer

Administration/Accounting/Legal/Licensing/Photos
Director of Business Affairs: Charles L. Rosenzweig
Director of Administration: Michael Scott
Project Manager: Stephanie Schwartz
Office Manager: Martha Randolph
Accounting Manager: John Inguagiato
Unit Coordinator: Cherie Alleyne
Licensing Coordinator: Sheila O'Brien
Licensing Assistant: Christina Magliocco
Photo Assistant: Renee Duff
Photo Assistant: Paul White
Official NBA Photographer: Andy Bernstein
Official NBA Photographer: Nathaniel Butler

ATLANTA HAWKS

Office: One CNN Center, Suite 405, South Tower, Atlanta, GA 30303

Telephone: (404) 827-3800

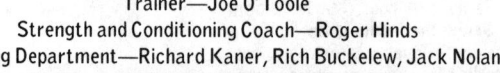

Board of Directors—R.E. (Ted) Turner,
J. Michael Gearon (Chairman),
Stan Kasten, M.B. (Bud) Seretean, Bruce B. Wilson
President—Stan Kasten
Executive Vice President—Lee Douglas
Vice President/General Manager—Pete Babcock
Vice President/Business Manager—Bob Wolfe
Head Coach—Bob Weiss
Assistant Coaches—Johnny Davis, Bob Weinhauer
Trainer—Joe O'Toole
Strength and Conditioning Coach—Roger Hinds
Scouting Department—Richard Kaner, Rich Buckelew, Jack Nolan
Director of Media Relations—Arthur Triche
Director of Corporate Sales and Promotions—Frank Timmerman
Director of Sales—Cheryl Dukes
Director of Community Affairs—Mel Pender
Manager of Corporate Sales and Promotions—Tracy White
Manager of Client Relations—Kim Coleman
Manager of Game Operations and Marketing Services—Donna Feazell
Accounting Assistant—Whitney Grant
Ticket Coordinator—Margie Smith-Sikes
Office Manager/Executive Assistant—Tracey Hammaren
Staff—Mike Adams, Hannah-Catherine Allport, Louis Artiaga, Bryan Bartley, Scott Bowers,
Sharon Bradley, John Carey, Barrie Cohn, Jeff Crawford, Michael Epps, Don Hensley, Dale Hendricks,
Katherine Ingram, Belinda Johnson, David Lawrence, Darrin May, Teyon McCoy, Charley Smith,
Dan Taylor, Chuck Washington, Amanda Wimbush, Warnette Zanders
Team Physicians—Dr. David Apple, Dr. Milton Frank III
Team Dentist—Dr. Louis Freedman
Home Court—The Omni (16,510, built in 1972)
Team Colors—Red, White and Gold
Radio—WGST (640 AM) Steve Holman
Television—TBS Superstation, SportSouth
Game Time—7:30 p.m.

Ted Turner

Pete Babcock

Bob Weiss

ATLANTA HAWKS

1991-92 Record (Won 38, Lost 44)   **1992-93 SCHEDULE**

					W-L
Nov.	2—Detroit	87	89—		0-1
	5—Utah	98	94		1-1
	6—At Charlotte	104	114—		1-2
	8—At Boston	100	95		2-2
	9—Miami	97	93		3-2
	12—Charlotte	118	100		4-2
	14—At Sacramento	96	98—		4-3
	15—At Phoenix	119	115		5-3
	17—At L.A. Lakers	89	111—		5-4
	20—Sacramento	116	104		6-4
	22—At Philadelphia	99	92		7-4
	23—At Washington	115	126—		7-5
	26—Detroit	93	103—		7-6
	27—At Detroit	91	100—		7-7
	29—San Antonio	85	88—		7-8
	30—Boston	129	102		8-8
Dec.	3—At Dallas	103	99		9-8
	5—At Houston	109	97		10-8
	7—New York	*128	137—		10-9
	10—Milwaukee	118	104		11-9
	12—At Cleveland	107	134—		11-10
	14—At Miami	101	121—		11-11
	17—Indiana	117	113		12-11
	20—Cleveland	99	122—		12-12
	21—At Chicago	103	117—		12-13
	23—At New Jersey	93	105—		12-14
	26—Chicago	111	122—		12-15
	28—Minnesota	*125	122		13-15
Jan.	2—Phoenix	123	105		14-15
	4—L.A. Clippers	97	95		15-15
	6—Houston	109	97		16-15
	7—At New York	109	94		17-15
	9—Dallas	124	108		18-15
	11—At Indiana	115	138—		18-16
	14—Milwaukee	93	88		19-16
	16—At Utah	111	116—		19-17
	17—At L.A. Clippers	*107	111—		19-18
	19—At Denver	119	93		20-18
	21—At Seattle	128	119		21-18
	22—At Golden State	124	136—		21-19
	24—At Portland	117	125—		21-20
	28—Philadelphia	110	109		22-20
	29—At Milwaukee	110	100		23-20
	31—At Indiana	*106	115—		23-21
Feb.	1—Detroit	80	89—		23-22
	3—Seattle	110	112—		23-23
	6—Orlando	123	112		24-23
	11—Charlotte	108	113—		24-24
	13—At Miami	119	121—		24-25
	14—At Orlando	112	107		25-25
	17—At Washington	117	110		26-25
	19—Washington	*102	103—		26-26
	21—Chicago	88	103—		26-27
	22—New Jersey	119	107		27-27
	24—Denver	117	95		28-27
	28—Boston	102	90		29-27
Mar.	1—At Milwaukee	*106	109—		29-28
	4—At Philadelphia	102	107—		29-29
	6—Indiana	*113	115—		29-30
	7—Cleveland	94	110—		29-31
	10—At San Antonio	92	103—		29-32
	11—L.A. Lakers	98	109—		29-33
	13—Portland	95	106—		29-34
	14—Miami	115	102		30-34
	16—At Detroit	89	77		31-34
	18—Orlando	96	99—		31-35
	20—At Charlotte	112	110		32-35
	22—At Cleveland	80	123—		32-36
	23—Golden State	*126	125		33-36
	26—Washington	107	95		34-36
	27—At Minnesota	105	103		35-36
	29—At Boston	93	117—		35-37
Apr.	1—At Indiana	117	137—		35-38
	3—At New York	94	115—		35-39
	4—Philadelphia	121	126—		35-40
	7—At New Jersey	104	97		36-40
	9—At Orlando	94	96—		36-41
	11—New Jersey	118	98		37-41
	13—At Chicago	93	100—		37-42
	15—New York	95	94		38-42
	17—Chicago	95	121—		38-43
	19—At Cleveland	108	112—		38-44

*Denotes overtime game.

Nov.	Fri.	6—New York
	Sat.	7—At Chicago
	Wed.	11—At Houston
	Thu.	12—At San Antonio
	Sat.	14—At Dallas
	Tue.	17—Milwaukee
	Thu.	19—New Jersey
	Sat.	21—Boston
	Mon.	23—At Boston°
	Wed.	25—At Philadelphia
	Fri.	27—At Cleveland
	Sat.	28—Miami
Dec.	Tue.	1—Indiana
	Wed.	2—At New Jersey
	Fri.	4—At Indiana
	Sat.	5—San Antonio
	Tue.	8—Chicago
	Fri.	11—Denver
	Sat.	12—Philadelphia
	Tue.	15—Detroit
	Wed.	16—At Detroit
	Fri.	18—At Miami
	Sat.	19—Orlando
	Tue.	22—Charlotte
	Sat.	26—At Minnesota
	Mon.	28—At Washington
	Tue.	29—Cleveland
Jan.	Sat.	2—Milwaukee
	Tue.	5—Washington
	Thu.	7—At Milwaukee
	Fri.	8—At Detroit
	Tue.	12—Golden State
	Thu.	14—Detroit
	Sat.	16—At Cleveland
	Tue.	19—At Charlotte
	Wed.	20—At Boston
	Fri.	22—New Jersey
	Sat.	23—Phoenix
	Mon.	25—Sacramento
	Tue.	26—At Orlando
	Thu.	28—At New York
	Sat.	30—Philadelphia
Feb.	Tue.	2—Seattle
	Wed.	3—At Miami
	Sat.	6—Cleveland
	Tue.	9—At Golden State
	Thu.	11—At Sacramento
	Sat.	13—At Utah
	Sun.	14—At L.A. Lakers
	Tue.	16—At Portland
	Thu.	18—At Phoenix
	Tue.	23—Washington
	Wed.	24—At Philadelphia
	Fri.	26—Boston
	Sat.	27—At Chicago
Mar.	Tue.	2—At New York
	Thu.	4—At Indiana
	Sat.	6—Utah
	Mon.	8—L.A. Clippers
	Tue.	9—At Milwaukee
	Fri.	12—Orlando
	Sun.	14—L.A. Lakers
	Tue.	16—At Charlotte
	Wed.	17—At New Jersey
	Fri.	19—Minnesota
	Tue.	23—Dallas
	Thu.	25—Houston
	Sat.	27—Miami
	Mon.	29—Portland
	Wed.	31—At Denver
Apr.	Fri.	2—At L.A. Clippers
	Sat.	3—At Seattle
	Tue.	6—New York
	Fri.	9—Chicago
	Sat.	10—At Charlotte
	Tue.	13—Cleveland
	Wed.	14—At Detroit
	Sat.	17—Charlotte
	Tue.	20—Indiana
	Wed.	21—At Washington
	Fri.	23—Milwaukee
	Sat.	24—At Orlando

°Game played in Hartford.

BOSTON CELTICS

Office: 151 Merrimac Street, Boston, MA 02114

Telephone: (617) 523-6050

Chairman of the Board—Don F. Gaston
Vice President and Secretary—Paul R. Dupee
Vice Chairman and Treasurer—Alan N. Cohen
President—Arnold (Red) Auerbach
Senior Exec. Vice President—Dave Gavitt
Asst. to the Senior Exec. Vice President—Larry Bird
Exec. V.P. and General Manager—Jan Volk
V.P./Finance—Joseph G. DiLorenzo
V.P./Marketing and Communications—Tod Rosensweig
V.P./Sales—Stephen Riley
Executive Assistant to Mr. Auerbach—Mary A. Faherty
Head Coach—Chris Ford
Asst. Coaches—Don Casey, Jon Jennings (Scouting Coordinator)
Head Scout—Rick Weitzman
Scouts—Dennis Johnson, John Kuester
Special Assignment Scout—Forddy Anderson
Physical Therapist/Trainer—Ed Lacerte
Travel Coord./Equipment Manager—Wayne Lebeaux
Director of Sales—Duane Johnson
Director of Public Relations—R. Jeffrey Twiss
Director of Publications and Information—David Zuccaro
Director of Community Relations—M.L. Carr
Community Relations Coordinator—Wayne Levy
Marketing Coordinator—Mark Lev
Unitholder Relations—Barbara J. Reed
Accountant—Joseph Durkin
Assistant Director of Sales—Don Vendetti
Hartford Sales—Dan Jones
Assistant Director of Public Relations—Eric Hutcherson
Special Programs Coordinator—Susan Trodden Gramolini
Secretaries—Mildred P. Duggan, Carolyn Hughes,
Carol Shackelford, Dianela Correia, Patricia Vetrano, Tiffanie Halpin
Team Physician—Arnold Scheller, M.D.
Home Court—Boston Garden (14,890, built in 1928)
Team Colors—Green and White
Radio—WEEI (590 AM), Glenn Ordway and Jerry Sichting
Television—WFXT (Channel 25), Tom Heinsohn and Bob Cousy;
SportsChannel, Mike Gorman and Tom Heinsohn
Game Times—7:30 or 8 p.m. Mon.-Sat., Sun. as listed.

Red Auerbach   **Dave Gavitt**   **Chris Ford**

BOSTON CELTICS

1991-92 Record (Won 51, Lost 31)

Date	Opponent			W-L
Nov.	1—Charlotte	111	108	1-0
	2—At Washington	118	126—	1-1
	5—At Miami	93	89	2-1
	6—Chicago	113	132—	2-2
	8—Atlanta	95	100—	2-3
	10—At Portland	90	116—	2-4
	12—At Sacramento	126	103	3-4
	13—At Phoenix	117	111	4-4
	15—Philadelphia	122	97	5-4
	16—At Charlotte	109	118—	5-5
	20—Indiana	116	101	6-5
	23—At New Jersey	125	107	7-5
	25—Washington	121	108	8-5
	27—Orlando	101	92	9-5
	29—L.A. Lakers	114	91	10-5
	30—At Atlanta	102	129—	10-6
Dec.	4—Miami	124	97	11-6
	6—New York	103	92	12-6
	9—Denver	132	94	13-6
	13—Seattle	117	97	14-6
	14—At New York	101	111—	14-7
	17—At Orlando	105	98	15-7
	18—Milwaukee	131	117	16-7
	20—Utah	112	101	17-7
	21—At Miami	101	112—	17-8
	25—At Chicago	99	121—	17-9
	27—At Seattle	110	87	18-9
	28—At Denver	90	97—	18-10
	30—At L.A. Clippers	97	86	19-10
Jan.	3—Cleveland	100	111—	19-11
	4—At Minnesota	96	100—	19-12
	6—Sacramento	110	108	20-12
	8—New York	99	95	21-12
	10—Minnesota	94	104—	21-13
	11—At New York	96	100—	21-14
	15—New Jersey	120	130—	21-15
	17—Philadelphia	98	95	22-15
	19—San Antonio	98	89	23-15
	20—At Cleveland	107	102	24-15
	22—Orlando	107	95	25-15
	24—Phoenix	93	100—	25-16
	26—Detroit	106	91	26-16
	28—At Washington	98	87	27-16
	31—At Milwaukee	100	102—	27-17
Feb.	1—At Philadelphia	110	126—	27-18
	5—Houston	98	85	28-18
	11—At San Antonio	84	100—	28-19
	12—At Dallas	100	108—	28-20
	14—At Houston	99	105—	28-21
	16—At L.A. Lakers	114	107	29-21
	17—At Utah	83	88—	29-22
	19—At Golden State	112	117—	29-23
	21—Charlotte	113	110	30-23
	23—At Indiana	95	102—	30-24
	25—At New Jersey	95	109—	30-25
	26—Indiana	130	109	31-25
	28—At Atlanta	90	102—	31-26
Mar.	1—Dallas	101	91	32-26
	4—Orlando	125	100	33-26
	6—L.A. Clippers	117	100	34-26
	8—At Orlando	111	93	35-26
	10—At Miami	101	108—	35-27
	11—At Chicago	85	119—	35-28
	13—New Jersey	108	110—	35-29
	15—Portland	**152	148	36-29
	17—At Milwaukee	106	127—	36-30
	18—Cleveland	96	94	37-30
	20—At Detroit	*104	99	38-30
	22—Golden State	114	97	39-30
	25—At New Jersey	118	110	40-30
	27—Detroit	106	87	41-30
	29—Atlanta	117	93	42-30
Apr.	1—Washington	120	106	43-30
	3—At Indiana	97	101—	43-31
	5—Chicago	97	86	44-31
	7—At Cleveland	100	97	45-31
	8—New York	93	89	46-31
	10—Milwaukee	109	100	47-31
	12—At Charlotte	128	102	48-31
	14—At Philadelphia	99	94	49-31
	15—At Detroit	92	89	50-31
	19—Miami	109	93	51-31

*Denotes overtime game.

1992-93 SCHEDULE

Nov.	Fri.	6—Minnesota
	Sat.	7—At Milwaukee
	Tue.	10—At Miami
	Wed.	11—At Charlotte
	Fri.	13—Philadelphia
	Sat.	14—At New York
	Tue.	17—At Washington
	Wed.	18—Utah
	Sat.	21—At Atlanta
	Mon.	23—Atlanta°
	Wed.	25—Washington
	Fri.	27—Charlotte
	Sat.	28—At Philadelphia
Dec.	Tue.	1—At Cleveland
	Wed.	2—Chicago
	Fri.	4—Miami
	Sat.	5—At Chicago
	Tue.	8—At Orlando
	Wed.	9—Denver
	Fri.	11—Seattle
	Tue.	15—At Minnesota
	Wed.	16—At Indiana
	Fri.	18—New York
	Tue.	22—At New Jersey
	Wed.	23—Houston
	Sat.	26—At Utah
	Sun.	27—At Sacramento
	Tue.	29—At Seattle
	Wed.	30—At L.A. Clippers
Jan.	Sun.	3—L.A. Clippers
	Tue.	5—At Charlotte
	Wed.	6—Indiana
	Fri.	8—New Jersey
	Sun.	10—At New York
	Tue.	12—At Cleveland
	Wed.	13—Washington
	Fri.	15—Orlando
	Sat.	16—At Milwaukee
	Mon.	18—At Chicago
	Wed.	20—Atlanta
	Wed.	27—At Detroit
	Fri.	29—At Orlando
	Sun.	31—L.A. Lakers
Feb.	Fri.	5—Philadelphia
	Sun.	7—Golden State
	Tue.	9—Milwaukee°
	Fri.	12—At Dallas
	Sat.	13—At San Antonio
	Tue.	16—At Phoenix
	Thu.	18—At Houston
	Tue.	23—At Indiana
	Wed.	24—New Jersey
	Fri.	26—At Atlanta
	Sun.	28—Portland
Mar.	Mon.	1—At Detroit
	Wed.	3—San Antonio
	Fri.	5—Detroit
	Sun.	7—Cleveland
	Wed.	10—At Philadelphia
	Fri.	12—Milwaukee
	Sun.	14—Charlotte
	Tue.	16—At Golden State
	Thu.	18—At Denver
	Fri.	19—At L.A. Lakers
	Sun.	21—At Portland
	Wed.	24—Miami
	Fri.	26—Dallas
	Sun.	28—Washington°
	Mon.	29—Sacramento
	Wed.	31—Philadelphia
Apr.	Fri.	2—Phoenix
	Sun.	4—Chicago
	Thu.	8—At New York
	Fri.	9—Detroit
	Sun.	11—New York
	Tue.	13—Indiana
	Thu.	15—At New Jersey
	Sat.	17—At Miami
	Sun.	18—At Orlando
	Wed.	21—Orlando
	Fri.	23—Cleveland
	Sun.	25—At Washington

°Game played in Hartford.

CHARLOTTE HORNETS

Office: One Hive Drive, Charlotte, NC 28217

Telephone: (704) 357-0252

Owner—George Shinn
President—Spencer Stolpen
Player Personnel Director—Dave Twardzik
Vice President of Business—Sam Russo
Vice President of Marketing—Tom Ward
V.P. of Corporate Development—Roger Schweickert
Vice President of Finance—Wayne J. DeBlander
Head Coach—Allan Bristow
Asst. Coaches—Bill Hanzlik, T.R. Dunn
Trainer—Terry Kofler
Director of Media Relations—Harold Kaufman
Director of Broadcast Operations—Steve Martin
Dir. of Community Relations/Special Events—Marilynn Bowler
Director of Publications—Bo Hussey
Controller—Shoon Ledyard
Director of Customer Service—Emily Nantz
Director of Ticket Operations—Clayton Smith
Media Relations Assistant—Jason Brannon
Sales Representatives—Tony Bates, Carmen Girouard, Pamela Pruitt
Game Operations/Youth Programs—Steve Iannarino, Jim Wilson
Youth Program Coordinator—David Thompson
Sponsor Services Representatives—Susie Bunch, Tracy Wheeler,
Jill Cornwell, Jan King
Promotions Manager—Renea Bared
Community Relations Assistant—Suzanne Conley
Crown Club Dir./Publications Asst.—Stephanie Williams
Strength and Conditioning Coach—Chip Sigmon
Administrative Assistant/Scout—Bill Branch
Administrative Assistant—Irene Lavelle
Equipment Manager—David Jovanovic
Mascot Coordinator/Community Relations—John Guagliano
Telecommunications Administrator—Cathy Montgomery
Basketball Secretary—Leslie Jones
Home Court—Charlotte Coliseum (23,698, built in 1988)
Team Colors—Teal, Purple and White
Radio—WBT (1110 AM) Matt Pinto and Gerry Vaillancourt
Television—WJZY-TV (Channel 46 - Cable 8);
SportSouth (cable), Steve Martin and Gil McGregor
Game Times—Mon.-Sat. 7:35 p.m., Sun. 2:05

George Shinn   **Spencer Stolpen**   **Allan Bristow**

CHARLOTTE HORNETS

1991-92 Record (Won 31, Lost 51)

Date	Opponent	Score		W-L
Nov.	1—At Boston	108	111—	0-1
	2—New Jersey	108	116—	0-2
	5—At Detroit	93	117—	0-3
	6—Atlanta	114	104	1-3
	8—Milwaukee	°122	125—	1-4
	9—At New York	113	118—	1-5
	12—At Atlanta	100	118—	1-6
	13—Chicago	95	117—	1-7
	15—At Miami	105	120—	1-8
	16—Boston	118	109	2-8
	19—At Milwaukee	104	127—	2-9
	20—Cleveland	109	108	3-9
	22—Indiana	112	110	4-9
	26—At Denver	97	103—	4-10
	27—At Utah	107	113—	4-11
	29—At Phoenix	111	131—	4-12
	30—At L.A. Clippers	112	130—	4-13
Dec.	2—New York	97	99—	4-14
	4—L.A. Lakers	124	106	5-14
	6—At Chicago	96	114—	5-15
	7—At Orlando	109	95	6-15
	11—Dallas	103	106—	6-16
	13—Miami	108	112—	6-17
	14—At New Jersey	109	102	7-17
	17—Utah	102	122—	7-18
	18—At Detroit	97	117—	7-19
	20—Houston	95	99—	7-20
	21—At Cleveland	111	120—	7-21
	23—At Philadelphia	114	106	8-21
	27—New Jersey	120	136—	8-22
	28—At Washington	124	129—	8-23
Jan.	2—L.A. Clippers	°102	109—	8-24
	4—Phoenix	113	108	9-24
	9—Sacramento	109	96	10-24
	11—Portland	93	115—	10-25
	14—At Seattle	°117	116	11-25
	15—At L.A. Lakers	93	95—	11-26
	17—At Portland	104	120—	11-27
	18—At Sacramento	113	119—	11-28
	20—At Golden State	119	135—	11-29
	22—Chicago	112	115—	11-30
	25—Indiana	107	105	12-30
	28—Detroit	°95	100—	12-31
	31—Seattle	105	122—	12-32
Feb.	2—At Miami	100	118—	12-33
	4—Washington	115	99	13-33
	6—Golden State	132	113	14-33
	11—At Atlanta	113	108	15-33
	13—At Milwaukee	118	127—	15-34
	16—Miami	126	109	16-34
	17—At Indiana	117	128—	16-35
	19—Denver	106	104	17-35
	21—At Boston	110	113—	17-36
	22—Orlando	130	110	18-36
	25—Milwaukee	94	82	19-36
	27—Philadelphia	136	84	20-36
	29—Indiana	121	119	21-36
Mar.	4—At Milwaukee	119	110	22-36
	7—At New York	78	107—	22-37
	10—Minnesota	105	96	23-37
	11—At Dallas	120	105	24-37
	13—At Houston	100	118—	24-38
	16—At San Antonio	117	112	25-38
	19—At Philadelphia	°123	116	26-38
	20—Atlanta	110	112—	26-39
	22—Detroit	113	101	27-39
	23—At New Jersey	120	123—	27-40
	25—San Antonio	113	108	28-40
	27—Cleveland	115	121—	28-41
	28—At Washington	97	113—	28-42
	30—Orlando	123	112	29-42
Apr.	1—At Chicago	94	100—	29-43
	2—New York	96	117—	29-44
	4—Washington	118	109	30-44
	7—At Orlando	110	135—	30-45
	9—At Cleveland	134	141—	30-46
	10—At Detroit	106	125—	30-47
	12—Boston	102	128—	30-48
	14—At Indiana	96	123—	30-49
	15—Cleveland	115	107	31-49
	17—Philadelphia	112	122—	31-50
	19—At Minnesota	107	130—	31-51

°Denotes overtime game.

1992-93 SCHEDULE

Nov.	Fri.	6—Washington
	Sun.	8—At Cleveland
	Tue.	10—At Orlando
	Wed.	11—Boston
	Fri.	13—At Indiana
	Sat.	14—Miami
	Tue.	17—Dallas
	Fri.	20—Golden State
	Sat.	21—At Miami
	Tue.	24—Philadelphia
	Wed.	25—At Detroit
	Fri.	27—At Boston
	Sat.	28—Indiana
Dec.	Tue.	1—At Phoenix
	Wed.	2—At Golden State
	Fri.	4—At Sacramento
	Sat.	5—At L.A. Clippers
	Wed.	9—Phoenix
	Thu.	10—At New York
	Sat.	12—Denver
	Tue.	15—At Chicago
	Wed.	16—Utah
	Sat.	19—At Washington
	Tue.	22—At Atlanta
	Wed.	23—Detroit
	Mon.	28—At New Jersey
	Tue.	29—Chicago
Jan.	Sat.	2—New Jersey
	Tue.	5—Boston
	Fri.	8—L.A. Clippers
	Mon.	11—At Dallas
	Thu.	14—At Houston
	Sat.	16—At San Antonio
	Tue.	19—Atlanta
	Wed.	20—At New York
	Fri.	22—At Chicago
	Sun.	24—Indiana
	Wed.	27—Sacramento
	Fri.	29—L.A. Lakers
	Sat.	30—At Washington
Feb.	Mon.	1—Seattle
	Wed.	3—At Philadelphia
	Fri.	5—Milwaukee
	Tue.	9—Cleveland
	Thu.	11—Orlando
	Fri.	12—At Miami
	Sun.	14—Detroit
	Mon.	15—At Milwaukee
	Wed.	17—New York
	Tue.	23—New Jersey
	Thu.	25—San Antonio
	Fri.	26—At Indiana
	Sun.	28—At Denver
Mar.	Mon.	1—At Utah
	Thu.	4—At Seattle
	Fri.	5—At Portland
	Sun.	7—At L.A. Lakers
	Tue.	9—Washington
	Thu.	11—At Cleveland
	Fri.	12—At Chicago
	Sun.	14—At Boston
	Tue.	16—Atlanta
	Thu.	18—Minnesota
	Fri.	19—At Indiana
	Sun.	21—At Minnesota
	Tue.	23—Houston
	Wed.	24—At New Jersey
	Fri.	26—At Detroit
	Sun.	28—Portland
	Tue.	30—Miami
Apr.	Thu.	1—At Orlando
	Fri.	2—Cleveland
	Wed.	7—Orlando
	Fri.	9—At Philadelphia
	Sat.	10—Atlanta
	Mon.	12—Philadelphia
	Wed.	14—New York
	Fri.	16—Detroit
	Sat.	17—At Atlanta
	Wed.	21—Milwaukee
	Fri.	23—Chicago
	Sat.	24—At Milwaukee

CHICAGO BULLS

Office: One Magnificent Mile, 980 North Michigan Avenue, Suite 1600, Chicago, IL 60611

Telephone: (312) 943-5800

Chairman—Jerry Reinsdorf
Alt. NBA Governors—Robert A. Judelson, Sanford Takiff
V.P./Basketball Operations—Jerry Krause
V.P./Financial & Legal—Irwin Mandel
V.P./Marketing & Broadcasting—Steve Schanwald
Head Coach—Phil Jackson
Asst. Coaches—John Bach, Jim Cleamons, Tex Winter
Trainer—Robert (Chip) Schaefer
Strength & Conditioning Consultant—Al Vermeil
Scouts/Special Assistants—Clarence Gaines Jr., Jim Stack
Supervisor of European Scouting—Ivica Dukan
European Rep./Asst. Coach/Scout—Herb Brown
Controller—Stu Bookman
Director of Promotions & Corporate Sales—David Brenner
Director of Ticket Sales—Keith Brown
Director of Community Services—Sara Kalstone
Director of Ticket & Stadium Operations—Joe O'Neil
Manager, Promotions—Greg Bradshaw
Media Services Assistants—John Diamond, Joyce Szymanski
Assistant to the Chairman—Anita Fasano
Community Services Assistant—Dave Kurland
Ticket Assistant—Kevin Riley
Asst. to the V.P./Basketball Operations—Karen Stack
Financial & Legal Assistant—Judy Canter
Accountants—Jan Angell, Michele Cunningham
Office Manager/Receptionist—Anna Halverson
Team Physician—Dr. John Hefferon
Home Court—Chicago Stadium (17,339, built in 1929)
Team Colors—Red, White and Black
Radio—WMAQ (670 AM), Neil Funk, Tom Boerwinkle;
WIND (560 AM—Spanish), Hector Molina
Television—WGN-TV (Channel 9), Wayne Larrivee, John Kerr;
SportsChannel (cable), Tom Dore, John Kerr
Game Time—7:30 p.m.

Jerry Reinsdorf

Jerry Krause

Phil Jackson

CHICAGO BULLS

1991-92 Record (Won 67, Lost 15)

Date	Opponent			W-L
Nov.	1—Philadelphia	110	90	1-0
	2—At Milwaukee	107	109—	1-1
	5—Golden State	110	118—	1-2
	6—At Boston	132	113	2-2
	8—Dallas	108	92	3-2
	9—Orlando	107	76	4-2
	12—Detroit	110	93	5-2
	13—At Charlotte	117	95	6-2
	15—Milwaukee	114	101	7-2
	20—At Golden State	112	108	8-2
	22—At Seattle	°112	109	9-2
	23—At Denver	107	100	10-2
	26—At L.A. Clippers	116	79	11-2
	29—At Portland	°°116	114	12-2
	30—At Sacramento	118	102	13-2
Dec.	4—Cleveland	108	102	14-2
	6—Charlotte	114	96	15-2
	7—At Philadelphia	100	103—	15-3
	10—Seattle	108	103	16-3
	13—New York	99	89	17-3
	14—At Washington	113	100	18-3
	17—L.A. Lakers	89	102—	18-4
	20—At New Jersey	115	98	19-4
	21—Atlanta	117	103	20-4
	25—Boston	121	99	21-4
	26—At Atlanta	122	111	22-4
	28—Sacramento	127	118	23-4
	30—At Indiana	109	104	24-4
Jan.	3—At Milwaukee	108	113—	24-5
	4—New Jersey	140	96	25-5
	7—Washington	102	89	26-5
	8—At Miami	108	106	27-5
	10—Utah	105	90	28-5
	11—Miami	108	99	29-5
	14—Philadelphia	103	80	30-5
	16—At Cleveland	100	85	31-5
	17—San Antonio	102	96	32-5
	19—At Detroit	87	85	33-5
	21—Phoenix	108	102	34-5
	22—At Charlotte	115	112	35-5
	24—Detroit	117	93	36-5
	25—Houston	114	100	37-5
	28—At San Antonio	104	109—	37-6
	30—At Houston	102	105—	37-7
	31—At Dallas	107	92	38-7
Feb.	2—At L.A. Lakers	103	97	39-7
	3—At Utah	°°°123	126—	39-8
	5—At Phoenix	114	126—	39-9
	11—New Jersey	133	113	40-9
	13—At New York	106	85	41-9
	15—New York	99	98	42-9
	17—Cleveland	112	113—	42-10
	19—At Orlando	112	99	43-10
	21—At Atlanta	103	88	44-10
	22—Minnesota	105	90	45-10
	25—At Detroit	106	108—	45-11
	26—Washington	122	103	46-11
	28—At Milwaukee	109	105	47-11
Mar.	1—Portland	111	91	48-11
	3—Indiana	101	103—	48-12
	5—At Minnesota	113	100	49-12
	6—Miami	123	81	50-12
	8—At Philadelphia	103	99	51-12
	11—Boston	119	85	52-12
	14—At Orlando	112	96	53-12
	16—At Miami	116	100	54-12
	17—At New Jersey	90	79	55-12
	19—At Washington	106	100	56-12
	21—Orlando	108	111—	56-13
	24—Denver	116	103	57-13
	28—Cleveland	126	102	58-13
	31—At New York	96	90	59-13
Apr.	1—Charlotte	100	94	60-13
	3—L.A. Clippers	114	103	61-13
	5—At Boston	86	97—	61-14
	7—Milwaukee	116	101	62-14
	10—At Indiana	108	96	63-14
	11—Indiana	108	106	64-14
	13—Atlanta	100	93	65-14
	14—At Cleveland	100	115—	65-15
	17—At Atlanta	121	95	66-15
	19—Detroit	103	85	67-15

°Denotes overtime game.

1992-93 SCHEDULE

Nov.	Fri.	6—At Cleveland
	Sat.	7—Atlanta
	Mon.	9—Indiana
	Wed.	11—Detroit
	Fri.	13—At Milwaukee
	Sat.	14—Denver
	Tue.	17—At Minnesota
	Thu.	19—At Seattle
	Fri.	20—At L.A. Lakers
	Sun.	22—At Phoenix
	Tue.	24—At Golden State
	Sat.	28—At New York
Dec.	Wed.	2—At Boston
	Fri.	4—Portland
	Sat.	5—Boston
	Tue.	8—At Atlanta
	Wed.	9—Cleveland
	Fri.	11—Houston
	Sat.	12—New Jersey
	Tue.	15—Charlotte
	Thu.	17—At Washington
	Sat.	19—Philadelphia
	Mon.	21—Miami
	Wed.	23—Washington
	Fri.	25—New York
	Sat.	26—At Indiana
	Tue.	29—At Charlotte
	Wed.	30—At Miami
Jan.	Sat.	2—Indiana
	Tue.	5—L.A. Lakers
	Wed.	6—At Cleveland
	Fri.	8—Milwaukee
	Sat.	9—At Philadelphia
	Tue.	12—At Orlando
	Fri.	15—Golden State
	Sat.	16—Orlando
	Mon.	18—Boston
	Thu.	21—At New Jersey
	Fri.	22—Charlotte
	Sun.	24—At San Antonio
	Tue.	26—At Dallas
	Thu.	28—At Houston
	Sat.	30—At Denver
Feb.	Mon.	1—At Utah
	Wed.	3—At Sacramento
	Thu.	4—At L.A. Clippers
	Sun.	7—At Portland
	Wed.	10—At Indiana
	Fri.	12—New York
	Sat.	13—Cleveland
	Mon.	15—Sacramento
	Wed.	17—Utah
	Tue.	23—Milwaukee
	Thu.	25—At Orlando
	Sat.	27—Atlanta
Mar.	Tue.	2—At New Jersey
	Wed.	3—Dallas
	Fri.	5—San Antonio
	Tue.	9—Seattle
	Thu.	11—At Miami
	Fri.	12—Charlotte
	Sun.	14—At Detroit
	Mon.	15—L.A. Clippers
	Fri.	19—Washington
	Sat.	20—At Washington
	Tue.	23—Minnesota
	Wed.	24—At Philadelphia
	Fri.	26—Orlando
	Tue.	30—Phoenix
Apr.	Fri.	2—New Jersey
	Sun.	4—At Boston
	Tue.	6—At Milwaukee
	Fri.	9—At Atlanta
	Sat.	10—At Indiana
	Mon.	12—At Detroit
	Wed.	14—Miami
	Fri.	16—Milwaukee
	Sun.	18—At Cleveland
	Tue.	20—Philadelphia
	Thu.	22—Detroit
	Fri.	23—At Charlotte
	Sun.	25—At New York

CLEVELAND CAVALIERS

Office: The Coliseum, 2923 Streetsboro Rd., Richfield, OH 44286
Telephone: (216) 659-9100

Chairman of the Board—Gordon Gund
Senior Vice Chairman—George Gund III
Secretary and Legal Counsel—Richard T. Watson
Chief Executive Officer—John W. Graham
President—Tom Chestnut
Executive Vice President/General Manager—Wayne Embry
Vice Chairman—J. Richard Kelso
Head Coach—Lenny Wilkens
Director of Player Personnel—Gary Fitzsimmons
Assistant Coaches—Dick Helm, Brian Winters
Trainer/Director of Travel—Gary Briggs
Senior Vice President of Sales and Marketing—Jim Kahler
Vice President Corporate Sales—Bill Enders
Vice President, Broadcasting—Joe Tait
Director of Community & School Relations—Rich Rollins
Director of Public Relations—Bob Price
Asst. Dir. of Public Relations—Bob Zink
Admin. Asst. to General Manager—Judy Berger
Staff Assistant—Debbie Nelson
Director of Finance—Gene Weber
Director of Marketing—Gayle Bibby-Creme
Director of Ticket Sales—Andy Malitz
Director of Suite Sales—Dave Auker
Director of Community Business Development—Austin Carr
Manager Creative Services—Mark Heffernan
Director of Broadcast Services—David Dombrowski
Account Executives—Dave Westphal, Tim Guthrie, Richard Bloom,
Doug Sanborn, Randy Newell, Robert Winfield, Brian Hopkins
Team Physicians—Dr. Robert Dimeff, Dr. John Bergfeld
Strength and Conditioning Consultant—Stan Kellers
Equipment Managers—Andy Bell, Dan Minor
Home Court—The Coliseum (20,273, built in 1974)
Team Colors—Royal Blue, Burnt Orange, White
Radio—WWWE (1100 AM), Joe Tait
Television—WOIO (Channel 19), TBA;
SportsChannel Ohio (cable), TBA
Game Time—7:30 p.m.

Gordon Gund

Wayne Embry

Lenny Wilkens

CLEVELAND CAVALIERS

1991-92 Record (Won 57, Lost 25)   **1992-93 SCHEDULE**

Month	Game			W-L
Nov.	1—At Portland	106	117—	0-1
	2—At L.A. Clippers	105	106—	0-2
	5—At Dallas	112	101	1-2
	7—At Houston	86	105—	1-3
	8—At San Antonio	°101	107—	1-4
	12—Milwaukee	119	113	2-4
	14—Seattle	°115	109	3-4
	16—Indiana	127	117	4-4
	20—At Charlotte	108	109—	4-5
	21—New Jersey	116	112	5-5
	23—Detroit	96	89	6-5
	26—At Philadelphia	95	91	7-5
	27—Philadelphia	107	97	8-5
	29—Orlando	115	104	9-5
Dec.	4—At Chicago	102	108—	9-6
	5—At Detroit	110	101	10-6
	7—Washington	99	97	11-6
	11—At Miami	103	105—	11-7
	12—Atlanta	134	107	12-7
	14—Dallas	97	99—	12-8
	17—Miami	148	80	13-8
	18—At New Jersey	93	102—	13-9
	20—At Atlanta	122	99	14-9
	21—Charlotte	120	111	15-9
	23—Utah	113	112	16-9
	26—At Milwaukee	111	94	17-9
	27—San Antonio	103	97	18-9
	30—Houston	121	89	19-9
Jan.	2—At New York	110	103	20-9
	3—At Boston	111	100	21-9
	7—At Minnesota	113	98	22-9
	9—At Washington	99	92	23-9
	11—Philadelphia	108	102	24-9
	14—Portland	114	121—	24-10
	16—Chicago	85	100—	24-11
	18—New York	108	106	25-11
	20—Boston	102	107—	25-12
	22—Indiana	°119	115	26-12
	24—At Indiana	104	102	27-12
	25—At Orlando	96	99—	27-13
	29—At Detroit	95	90	28-13
	30—Orlando	115	98	29-13
Feb.	2—Minnesota	106	95	30-13
	5—At Philadelphia	°110	108	31-13
	6—Detroit	95	112—	31-14
	11—At Utah	109	111—	31-15
	12—At Denver	102	108—	31-16
	15—New Jersey	128	92	32-16
	17—At Chicago	113	112	33-16
	18—At Milwaukee	116	128—	33-17
	20—At New York	92	89	34-17
	21—Sacramento	119	102	35-17
	23—Milwaukee	103	89	36-17
	26—At Phoenix	100	103—	36-18
	28—At L.A. Lakers	101	90	37-18
Mar.	1—At Seattle	107	113—	37-19
	4—At Sacramento	109	108	38-19
	5—At Golden State	108	116—	38-20
	7—At Atlanta	110	94	39-20
	10—Phoenix	102	100	40-20
	13—L.A. Lakers	°109	107	41-20
	15—Denver	100	91	42-20
	16—At Washington	111	102	43-20
	18—At Boston	94	96—	43-21
	20—Golden State	122	107	44-21
	22—Atlanta	123	80	45-21
	24—Indiana	128	113	46-21
	25—At Orlando	106	96	47-21
	27—At Charlotte	121	115	48-21
	28—At Chicago	102	126—	48-22
	31—Miami	123	114	49-22
Apr.	2—L.A. Clippers	115	98	50-22
	3—At Miami	103	100	51-22
	5—New York	97	93	52-22
	7—Boston	97	100—	52-23
	9—Charlotte	141	134	53-23
	10—At New Jersey	86	110—	53-24
	12—Washington	114	91	54-24
	14—Chicago	115	100	55-24
	15—At Charlotte	107	115—	55-25
	17—At Indiana	107	102	56-25
	19—Atlanta	112	108	57-25

°Denotes overtime game.

1992-93 SCHEDULE

Month	Day	Date	Opponent
Nov.	Fri.	6	Chicago
	Sun.	8	Charlotte
	Tue.	10	Washington
	Thu.	12	At Golden State
	Fri.	13	At Portland
	Sun.	15	At Sacramento
	Tue.	17	At San Antonio
	Thu.	19	At Houston
	Sat.	21	At Dallas
	Tue.	24	Milwaukee
	Wed.	25	At Milwaukee
	Fri.	27	Atlanta
	Sat.	28	At Orlando
Dec.	Tue.	1	Boston
	Thu.	3	New York
	Sat.	5	Portland
	Tue.	8	L.A. Clippers
	Wed.	9	At Chicago
	Fri.	11	At Detroit
	Sat.	12	Seattle
	Tue.	15	Houston
	Wed.	16	At Philadelphia
	Fri.	18	Sacramento
	Sat.	19	Utah
	Wed.	23	Indiana
	Sat.	26	New Jersey
	Mon.	28	Detroit
	Tue.	29	At Atlanta
Jan.	Sat.	2	L.A. Lakers
	Tue.	5	At New York
	Wed.	6	Chicago
	Sat.	9	Minnesota
	Tue.	12	Boston
	Wed.	13	At New Jersey
	Fri.	15	At Indiana
	Sat.	16	Atlanta
	Mon.	18	At Washington
	Wed.	20	Phoenix
	Fri.	22	At L.A. Clippers
	Sat.	23	At Denver
	Tue.	26	At Utah
	Thu.	28	Orlando
	Sat.	30	At Miami
Feb.	Tue.	2	Golden State
	Wed.	3	At Milwaukee
	Fri.	5	Detroit
	Sat.	6	At Atlanta
	Tue.	9	At Charlotte
	Wed.	10	At Orlando
	Fri.	12	Milwaukee
	Sat.	13	At Chicago
	Mon.	15	Indiana
	Wed.	17	Dallas
	Tue.	23	Miami
	Fri.	26	At L.A. Lakers
	Sun.	28	At Phoenix
Mar.	Tue.	2	At Seattle
	Thu.	4	At Minnesota
	Sun.	7	At Boston
	Mon.	8	Denver
	Thu.	11	Charlotte
	Sat.	13	At Washington°
	Tue.	16	Philadelphia
	Thu.	18	New York
	Sat.	20	At Miami
	Tue.	23	San Antonio
	Fri.	26	At Philadelphia
	Sun.	28	At Detroit
Apr.	Thu.	1	At New York
	Fri.	2	At Charlotte
	Sun.	4	New Jersey
	Tue.	6	Miami
	Fri.	9	Washington
	Sat.	10	At New Jersey
	Tue.	13	At Atlanta
	Thu.	15	At Milwaukee
	Fri.	16	Orlando
	Sun.	18	Chicago
	Tue.	20	Detroit
	Wed.	21	At Indiana
	Fri.	23	At Boston
	Sun.	25	Philadelphia

°Game played in Baltimore.

DALLAS MAVERICKS

Office: Reunion Arena, 777 Sports Street, Dallas TX 75207

Telephone: (214) 748-1808

Owner/President—Donald Carter
Chief Operating Officer/General Manager—Norm Sonju
V.P./Basketball Operations—Rick Sund
V.P./Counsel—Doug Adkins
Head Coach—Richie Adubato
Assistant Coaches—Gar Heard, Bob Zuffelato
Strength & Conditioning Coach—Bob King
Special Assignment Coach—Clifford Ray
Trainer—Doug Atkinson
Director of Scouting—Keith Grant
Director of Finance—Jim Livingston
Director of Broadcasting & Communications—Allen Stone
Director of Media Services—Kevin Sullivan
Director of Operations/Marketing—Steve Letson
Director of Reunion Production Company—Kevin Spivey
Controller—Tom Kelly
Manager of Group Sales/Game Operations—Marty Faulkner
Ticket/Box Office Manager—Mary Jean Gaines
Account Executives—Louise Farrage (Sr. Acct. Exec.), Bill Woods
Sales Representatives—Berry Carter, Mitchell Glieber, Lynne Sonju
Media Services Assistant—Tony Fay
Account Coordinator—Jodi Benefiel
Community Services Coordinator—Marla Thomas
Marketing/Public Relations Representative—Brad Davis
Accountants—Karen Bright, Lisa Tyner
Staff—Doug Baker (Equipment Mgr.), Linda Bloom, Kelli Boyer, Paul Brown, Nina Clayton,
Donna Coach, Johnnie Godkin, Jim Guy, Bryan Hague, Leland Johnson, Cheryl Karalla,
Tresa Rhoades, Bobby Rhoden, Pat Russell
Team Physicians—J. Pat Evans, M.D., T.O. Souryal, M.D., J.R. Zamorano, M.D.
Chaplain/Counselor—Dr. Tony Evans
Home Court—Reunion Arena (17,502, built in 1980)
Team Colors—Blue & Green
Radio—WBAP (820 AM), Ted Davis, Allen Stone
Television—KTVT (Channel 11), Allen Stone, Bill Walton;
Home Sports Entertainment, Allen Stone, Bob Ortegel
Game Time—7:30 p.m.

Donald Carter

Norm Sonju

Richie Adubato

DALLAS MAVERICKS

1991-92 Record (Won 22, Lost 60)   **1992-93 SCHEDULE**

					W-L				
Nov.	1—At San Antonio	99	140—		0-1	Nov.	Sat.	7—Utah	
	2—L.A. Lakers	*113	114—		0-2		Tue.	10—At Minnesota	
	5—Cleveland	101	112—		0-3		Wed.	11—Milwaukee	
	6—At Minnesota	97	94		1-3		Sat.	14—Atlanta	
	8—At Chicago	92	108—		1-4		Tue.	17—At Charlotte	
	9—At Milwaukee	95	111—		1-5		Thu.	19—At San Antonio	
	12—Houston	92	98—		1-6		Sat.	21—Cleveland	
	14—L.A. Clippers	95	88		2-6		Wed.	25—L.A. Clippers	
	16—Phoenix	91	88		3-6		Fri.	27—Seattle	
	19—At Denver	96	93		4-6		Sun.	29—At L.A. Lakers	
	20—New York	89	92—		4-7	Dec.	Tue.	1—At Utah	
	23—Utah	*121	109		5-7		Thu.	3—At Seattle	
	27—Indiana	113	106		6-7		Sat.	5—Houston	
	29—New Jersey	91	97—		6-8		Tue.	8—Miami	
	30—Minnesota	79	78		7-8		Thu.	10—Minnesota	
Dec.	3—Atlanta	99	103—		7-9		Sat.	12—San Antonio	
	5—At Golden State	107	117—		7-10		Wed.	16—L.A. Lakers	
	7—At Seattle	101	104—		7-11		Fri.	18—At San Antonio	
	8—At L.A. Lakers	88	103—		7-12		Sat.	19—At Houston	
	10—Miami	*114	110		8-12		Tue.	22—At L.A. Clippers	
	11—At Charlotte	106	103		9-12		Wed.	23—At Golden State	
	13—At Indiana	108	124—		9-13		Sat.	26—Golden State	
	14—At Cleveland	99	97		10-13		Tue.	29—At Sacramento	
	17—San Antonio	87	98—		10-14		Wed.	30—At Portland	
	20—Washington	99	107—		10-15	Jan.	Sat.	2—At Minnesota	
	21—Sacramento	109	85		11-15		Tue.	5—Portland	
	23—At Houston	105	85		12-15		Thu.	7—Phoenix	
	26—At Portland	88	113—		12-16		Sat.	9—Utah	
	28—At Phoenix	103	121—		12-17		Mon.	11—Charlotte	
Jan.	3—Detroit	96	106—		12-18		Wed.	13—At Detroit	
	4—At Utah	78	113—		12-19		Fri.	15—New York	
	7—L.A. Lakers	80	104—		12-20		Sat.	16—At Denver	
	9—At Atlanta	108	124—		12-21		Tue.	19—Detroit	
	10—Seattle	82	94—		12-22		Thu.	21—Denver	
	13—At Detroit	81	84—		12-23		Sat.	23—At Orlando	
	14—At New Jersey	88	97—		12-24		Sun.	24—At Miami	
	16—Denver	90	101—		12-25		Tue.	26—Chicago	
	18—Golden State	141	143—		12-26		Fri.	29—Sacramento	
	22—Milwaukee	118	116		13-26		Sat.	30—At Phoenix	
	24—At Orlando	103	121—		13-27	Feb.	Mon.	1—New Jersey	
	25—At Miami	101	103—		13-28		Wed.	3—Houston	
	29—San Antonio	93	108—		13-29		Fri.	5—Indiana	
	31—Chicago	92	107—		13-30		Sat.	6—At Denver	
Feb.	1—Utah	90	104—		13-31		Mon.	8—At L.A. Lakers	
	3—At Sacramento	95	99—		13-32		Wed.	10—Washington	
	4—At L.A. Clippers	80	97—		13-33		Fri.	12—Boston	
	6—Portland	98	103—		13-34		Sat.	13—Philadelphia	
	12—Boston	108	100		14-34		Tue.	16—At New York	
	14—At Denver	85	105—		14-35		Wed.	17—At Cleveland	
	15—Houston	103	99		15-35		Wed.	24—Denver	
	18—Philadelphia	90	94—		15-36		Fri.	26—At Minnesota	
	19—At Utah	96	118—		15-37		Sun.	28—At Indiana	
	21—Minnesota	109	94		16-37	Mar.	Tue.	2—At Milwaukee	
	24—Golden State	131	138—		16-38		Wed.	3—At Chicago	
	26—At Minnesota	105	106—		16-39		Fri.	5—Houston	
	28—Phoenix	115	107		17-39		Sat.	6—Phoenix	
Mar.	1—At Boston	91	101—		17-40		Tue.	9—At San Antonio	
	3—At New York	83	102—		17-41		Wed.	10—Portland	
	5—At Washington	109	119—		17-42		Fri.	12—At Phoenix	
	6—At Philadelphia	86	88—		17-43		Sat.	13—At Sacramento	
	8—San Antonio	81	93—		17-44		Mon.	15—Utah	
	10—At Houston	93	116—		17-45		Wed.	17—Orlando	
	11—Charlotte	105	120—		17-46		Fri.	19—At Philadelphia	
	13—At L.A. Clippers	97	105—		17-47		Sun.	21—At New Jersey	
	15—At Seattle	100	109—		17-48		Tue.	23—At Atlanta	
	17—At Phoenix	81	92—		17-49		Wed.	24—At Washington	
	18—L.A. Clippers	86	117—		17-50		Fri.	26—At Boston	
	20—Sacramento	96	125—		17-51		Sun.	28—San Antonio	
	22—Seattle	105	113—		17-52		Wed.	31—Seattle	
	24—At Portland	83	109—		17-53	Apr.	Fri.	2—Golden State	
	26—At L.A. Lakers	92	115—		17-54		Sun.	4—At L.A. Clippers	
	29—Denver	105	98		18-54		Tue.	6—At Seattle	
Apr.	1—Orlando	102	89		19-54		Thu.	8—At Portland	
	3—Minnesota	95	104—		19-55		Sat.	10—At Golden State	
	5—At Sacramento	89	103—		19-56		Mon.	12—At Utah	
	8—At Golden State	91	110—		19-57		Wed.	14—L.A. Lakers	
	9—At Utah	90	113—		19-58		Fri.	16—Denver	
	11—At Houston	99	92		20-58		Sat.	17—Sacramento	
	14—At San Antonio	108	120—		20-59		Tue.	20—L.A. Clippers	
	15—At Portland	94	100—		20-60		Wed.	21—At Denver	
	17—Houston	109	106		21-60		Fri.	23—Minnesota	
	19—At Denver	104	92		22-60		Sat.	24—At Houston	

*Denotes overtime game.

DENVER NUGGETS

Office: McNichols Sports Arena, 1635 Clay Street, Denver, CO 80204-1799
Telephone: (303) 893-6700

Owner—COMSAT Denver Inc.
General Manager—Bernie Bickerstaff
President—Timothy J. Leiweke
V.P./General Counsel—Glen Grunwald
V.P./Sales & Marketing—Shawn Hunter
V.P./Corporate Sales—Mike Sheehan
Assistant General Manager—Todd Eley
Head Coach—Dan Issel
Assistant Coaches—Gene Littles, Mike Evans
Basketball Operations Asst.—Lisa Sloan
Trainer—Jim Gillen
Controller—Mark Waggoner
Director of Broadcasting—Lou Personett

Director of Ticket Operations—Penny Harris
Assistant Director of Ticket Operations—Laura Joines
Director of Corporate Services & Advertising—Michael Blake
Director of Corporate Sales—Scott Zebedis
Senior Corporate Account Executives—Susan Cohig, Deanna Poyfair, Chris Whitney
Director of Ticket Sales—Joe Levy
Director of Community Relations—George White
Director of Player and Community Programs—John Outlaw
Director of Graphic Services—Dan Price
Director of Media Services—Jay L. Clark
Assistant Director of Media Services—Brian J. Bain
Broadcast Coordinator—Mark Hulsey
Director of Game Operations/Special Events—John Iacino
Junior Corporate Account Executives—Rick Cord, John Greene, Tracy Hartman
Executive Assistant—Charlotte Grahame
Account Executives—Paul Andrews, Eric Becker, Greg Conrad, Dave Larm, John Liotta,
Troy Ralston, Dave Smrek, Robert Winston
Team Physicians—Dr. Michael Dunn, Dr. Allen Schreiber, Dr. Steve Traina
Home Court—McNichols Sports Arena (17,022, built in 1975)
Team Colors—White, Blue, Yellow, Green, Red, Purple and Orange
Radio—KOA (850 AM) Jeff Kingery
Television—KWGN (Channel 2), Al Albert, TBA;
PSN (cable)
Game Times—2 p.m. and 7 p.m.

Bernie Bickerstaff   **Timothy J. Leiweke**   **Dan Issel**

DENVER NUGGETS

1991-92 Record (Won 24, Lost 58)

Date	Opponent			W-L
Nov.	1—Golden State	105	108—	0-1
	2—Houston	°109	101	1-1
	5—San Antonio	97	96	2-1
	7—Minnesota	88	77	3-1
	8—At L.A. Clippers	82	106—	3-2
	12—At Portland	82	120—	3-3
	16—Portland	122	111	4-3
	19—Dallas	93	96—	4-4
	20—At Phoenix	97	113—	4-5
	22—At Utah	96	121—	4-6
	23—Chicago	100	107—	4-7
	26—Charlotte	103	97	5-7
	27—At Minnesota	92	101—	5-8
	29—Seattle	101	90	6-8
	30—New Jersey	107	97	7-8
Dec.	3—At Houston	110	100	8-8
	6—L.A. Clippers	°100	102—	8-9
	9—At Boston	94	132—	8-10
	11—At Philadelphia	98	88	9-10
	12—At New Jersey	81	121—	9-11
	14—At Indiana	108	129—	9-12
	16—At Detroit	89	103—	9-13
	18—Phoenix	123	109	10-13
	19—At Seattle	106	119—	10-14
	21—Washington	102	117—	10-15
	26—Golden State	100	110—	10-16
	28—Boston	97	90	11-16
	30—Philadelphia	109	93	12-16
Jan.	2—At Golden State	111	125—	12-17
	4—Orlando	93	91	13-17
	7—Seattle	99	106—	13-18
	8—At Phoenix	114	135—	13-19
	10—At L.A. Lakers	88	102—	13-20
	11—San Antonio	85	96—	13-21
	13—Sacramento	111	109	14-21
	14—At Houston	94	111—	14-22
	16—At Dallas	101	90	15-22
	19—Atlanta	93	119—	15-23
	21—At Sacramento	85	94—	15-24
	23—Utah	115	111	16-24
	25—Milwaukee	°107	100	17-24
	30—L.A. Lakers	96	106—	17-25
	31—At Golden State	103	124—	17-26
Feb.	2—Indiana	122	128—	17-27
	3—At Minnesota	99	114—	17-28
	6—At Milwaukee	97	106—	17-29
	11—At Portland	112	121—	17-30
	12—Cleveland	108	102	18-30
	14—Dallas	105	85	19-30
	15—At Utah	93	106—	19-31
	19—At Charlotte	104	106—	19-32
	21—At Washington	106	99	20-32
	22—At New York	87	98—	20-33
	24—At Atlanta	95	117—	20-34
	26—Miami	98	105—	20-35
	28—Houston	81	84—	20-36
	29—At San Antonio	112	115—	20-37
Mar.	3—At Seattle	92	111—	20-38
	4—Portland	100	129—	20-39
	6—Detroit	91	106—	20-40
	8—Utah	88	112—	20-41
	10—At Orlando	89	82	21-41
	13—At Miami	109	113—	21-42
	15—At Cleveland	91	100—	21-43
	17—Sacramento	118	100	22-43
	19—At Utah	100	115—	22-44
	21—L.A. Clippers	87	114—	22-45
	23—At Minnesota	100	95	23-45
	24—At Chicago	103	116—	23-46
	26—New York	104	106—	23-47
	28—Phoenix	101	121—	23-48
	29—At Dallas	98	105—	23-49
	31—Minnesota	°114	121—	23-50
Apr.	2—At Houston	114	137—	23-51
	5—San Antonio	87	90—	23-52
	7—Utah	101	124—	23-53
	9—At Sacramento	107	124—	23-54
	11—At L.A. Clippers	88	122—	23-55
	13—At L.A. Lakers	93	100—	23-56
	15—L.A. Lakers	110	107	24-56
	17—At San Antonio	94	108—	24-57
	19—Dallas	92	104—	24-58

°Denotes overtime game.

1992-93 SCHEDULE

Nov.	Sat.	7—San Antonio
	Sun.	8—At Portland
	Tue.	10—Utah
	Sat.	14—At Chicago
	Sun.	15—At Milwaukee
	Tue.	17—At Indiana
	Thu.	19—Detroit
	Sat.	21—Minnesota
	Sun.	22—At L.A. Lakers
	Wed.	25—Sacramento
	Fri.	27—At L.A. Clippers
	Sat.	28—L.A. Clippers
Dec.	Tue.	1—Houston
	Fri.	4—Golden State
	Sat.	5—At Utah
	Wed.	9—At Boston
	Fri.	11—At Atlanta
	Sat.	12—At Charlotte
	Mon.	14—At New York
	Wed.	16—Portland
	Sat.	19—L.A. Clippers
	Tue.	22—At San Antonio
	Wed.	23—Phoenix
	Sat.	26—At Houston
	Sun.	27—At Phoenix
	Wed.	30—San Antonio
Jan.	Sat.	2—At Seattle
	Tue.	5—At Sacramento
	Fri.	8—Houston
	Sat.	9—Seattle
	Tue.	12—At Portland
	Wed.	13—New York
	Fri.	15—At Minnesota
	Sat.	16—Dallas
	Tue.	19—At San Antonio
	Thu.	21—At Dallas
	Sat.	23—Cleveland
	Mon.	25—Minnesota
	Wed.	27—At Golden State
	Thu.	28—New Jersey
	Sat.	30—Chicago
Feb.	Wed.	3—At Utah
	Fri.	5—Sacramento
	Sat.	6—Dallas
	Tue.	9—At Seattle
	Wed.	10—At L.A. Lakers
	Fri.	12—Philadelphia
	Sat.	13—Washington
	Mon.	15—At Miami
	Wed.	17—At Orlando
	Tue.	23—Seattle
	Wed.	24—At Dallas
	Sat.	27—At Houston
	Sun.	28—Charlotte
Mar.	Tue.	2—L.A. Lakers
	Thu.	4—Portland
	Sat.	6—At New Jersey
	Mon.	8—At Cleveland
	Wed.	10—At Washington
	Thu.	11—At Detroit
	Sat.	13—At Philadelphia
	Mon.	15—Miami
	Tue.	16—At Minnesota
	Thu.	18—Boston
	Sat.	20—Orlando
	Mon.	22—Utah
	Thu.	25—Golden State
	Sat.	27—Indiana
	Mon.	29—At Utah
	Wed.	31—Atlanta
Apr.	Fri.	2—Milwaukee
	Sun.	4—Minnesota
	Tue.	6—At Sacramento
	Fri.	9—At Phoenix
	Sat.	10—At L.A. Clippers
	Mon.	12—At Golden State
	Wed.	14—Houston
	Fri.	16—At Dallas
	Sun.	18—L.A. Clippers
	Wed.	21—Dallas
	Thu.	22—At San Antonio
	Sun.	25—Phoenix

DETROIT PISTONS

Office: The Palace of Auburn Hills, Two Championship Drive,
Auburn Hills, MI 48326

Telephone: (313) 377-0100

Managing Partner—William M. Davidson
Legal Counsel—Oscar H. Feldman
Advisory Board—Warren J. Coville, Milt Dresner,
Bud Gerson, Dorothy Gerson, David Mondry,
Ann Newman, Herbert Tyner, William M. Wetsman
President—Thomas S. Wilson
Director of Player Personnel—Billy McKinney
Asst. to Director of Player Personnel—Will Robinson
Head Coach—Ron Rothstein
Assistant Coaches—Don Chaney, Brendan Malone, Alan Srebnick
Player Personnel Assistant/Scout—Doug Gardner
Director of Scouting—Walt Perrin
Trainer—Tony Harris
Strength and Conditioning Coach—Arnie Kander
Director of Public Relations—Matt Dobek
Exec. V.P. of Marketing—Dan Hauser
Exec. V.P. of Corporate Sales—John Ciszewski
V.P. of Finance—Ron Campbell
V.P. of Marketing and Broadcasting—Harry E. Hutt
V.P. of Advertising Sales—Lou Korpas
V.P. of Sales—Andy Appleby
Public Relations Assistants—Sue Emerick, Dave Wieme
Statistician—Morris Moorawnick
Dir. of Multimedia Communications—Pete Skorich
Basketball Executive Assistant—Nancy Bontumasi
Team Physician—Dr. Ben Paolucci
Team Photographer—Allen Einstein
Locker Room/Equipment Manager—Jerry Dziedzic
Home Court—The Palace of Auburn Hills (21,454, built in 1988)
Team Colors—Red, White and Blue
Radio—Pistons Network WWJ (950 AM) George Blaha,
Mark Champion, Greg Kelser
Television—WKBD (Channel 50) George Blaha
Game Times—Mon., Thur., Sat. 7:30 p.m., Fri. 8 p.m., Sun. 7 p.m.

William Davidson

Tom Wilson

Ron Rothstein

DETROIT PISTONS

1991-92 Record (Won 48, Lost 34)

				W-L
Nov.	1—Milwaukee	99	109—	0-1
	2—At Atlanta	89	87	1-1
	5—Charlotte	117	93	2-1
	9—At New Jersey	110	100	3-1
	10—Washington	85	79	4-1
	12—At Chicago	93	110—	4-2
	13—At Miami	102	107—	4-3
	15—Utah	123	115	5-3
	16—Philadelphia	86	89—	5-4
	18—At Indiana	101	118—	5-5
	20—Seattle	86	91—	5-6
	22—New York	90	99—	5-7
	23—At Cleveland	89	96—	5-8
	26—At Atlanta	103	93	6-8
	27—Atlanta	100	91	7-8
	30—At New York	96	103—	7-9
Dec.	1—Houston	94	87	8-9
	3—Indiana	99	108—	8-10
	5—Cleveland	101	110—	8-11
	6—At Washington	105	94	9-11
	10—At Phoenix	93	102—	9-12
	11—At L.A. Clippers	96	101—	9-13
	13—At Portland	113	103	10-13
	14—At Utah	100	102—	10-14
	16—Denver	103	89	11-14
	18—Charlotte	117	97	12-14
	20—L.A. Lakers	112	93	13-14
	26—At Orlando	112	100	14-14
	27—Orlando	106	94	15-14
	30—Phoenix	103	110—	15-15
Jan.	2—At Houston	106	83	16-15
	3—At Dallas	106	96	17-15
	6—At San Antonio	90	100—	17-16
	8—Sacramento	114	95	18-16
	10—Portland	86	81	19-16
	11—New Jersey	90	88	20-16
	13—Dallas	84	81	21-16
	15—At Indiana	118	104	22-16
	19—Chicago	85	87—	22-17
	23—At Minnesota	111	100	23-17
	24—At Chicago	93	117—	23-18
	26—At Boston	91	106—	23-19
	28—At Charlotte	°100	95	24-19
	29—Cleveland	90	95—	24-20
	31—Miami	109	98	25-20
Feb.	1—At Atlanta	89	80	26-20
	5—Milwaukee	102	94	27-20
	6—At Cleveland	112	95	28-20
	11—At Milwaukee	87	104—	28-21
	13—Minnesota	93	96—	28-22
	16—At Philadelphia	90	83	29-22
	18—Orlando	117	95	30-22
	19—At New Jersey	102	106—	30-23
	21—At Orlando	114	100	31-23
	22—At Miami	98	107—	31-24
	25—Chicago	108	106	32-24
	27—Milwaukee	104	97	33-24
	29—New Jersey	90	99—	33-25
Mar.	2—Washington	99	89	34-25
	4—Indiana	°110	107	35-25
	6—At Denver	106	91	36-25
	8—At L.A. Lakers	98	93	37-25
	10—At Seattle	98	92	38-25
	12—At Golden State	119	112	39-25
	14—At Sacramento	89	83	40-25
	16—Atlanta	77	89—	40-26
	18—Philadelphia	91	85	41-26
	20—Boston	°99	104—	41-27
	22—At Charlotte	101	113—	41-28
	25—Golden State	99	103—	41-29
	27—At Boston	87	106—	41-30
	29—San Antonio	107	103	42-30
	31—L.A. Clippers	81	97—	42-31
Apr.	3—At Washington	85	119—	42-32
	5—Miami	104	80	43-32
	7—At New York	103	94	44-32
	8—At Philadelphia	89	71	45-32
	10—Charlotte	125	106	46-32
	12—New York	72	61	47-32
	14—At Milwaukee	°98	94	48-32
	15—Boston	89	92—	48-33
	19—At Chicago	85	103—	48-34

°Denotes overtime game.

1992-93 SCHEDULE

Nov.	Fri.	6—Milwaukee
	Sat.	7—At Indiana
	Wed.	11—At Chicago
	Thu.	12—Miami
	Sat.	14—Indiana
	Tue.	17—At L.A. Clippers
	Thu.	19—At Denver
	Sat.	21—At Seattle
	Sun.	22—At Portland
	Wed.	25—Charlotte
	Sat.	28—At Minnesota
	Sun.	29—New York
Dec.	Fri.	4—At Philadelphia
	Sat.	5—Philadelphia
	Wed.	9—Orlando
	Fri.	11—Cleveland
	Sat.	12—At New York
	Tue.	15—At Atlanta
	Wed.	16—Atlanta
	Fri.	18—Indiana
	Sat.	19—At Milwaukee
	Tue.	22—Houston
	Wed.	23—At Charlotte
	Sat.	26—At Washington°
	Mon.	28—At Cleveland
	Wed.	30—Washington
Jan.	Sat.	2—At Orlando
	Tue.	5—At Miami
	Wed.	6—L.A. Clippers
	Fri.	8—Atlanta
	Sat.	9—Golden State
	Mon.	11—San Antonio
	Wed.	13—Dallas
	Thu.	14—At Atlanta
	Sat.	16—At Philadelphia
	Tue.	19—At Dallas
	Thu.	21—At Houston
	Fri.	22—At San Antonio
	Mon.	25—Phoenix
	Wed.	27—Boston
	Fri.	29—Minnesota
	Sat.	30—At Indiana
Feb.	Fri.	5—At Cleveland
	Sun.	7—Seattle
	Tue.	9—Miami
	Wed.	10—At New Jersey
	Fri.	12—New Jersey
	Sun.	14—At Charlotte
	Tue.	16—Orlando
	Wed.	17—At Miami
	Tue.	23—Philadelphia
	Fri.	26—New York
	Sat.	27—Milwaukee
Mar.	Mon.	1—Boston
	Wed.	3—Utah
	Fri.	5—At Boston
	Sun.	7—At Milwaukee
	Tue.	9—L.A. Lakers
	Thu.	11—Denver
	Sun.	14—Chicago
	Tue.	16—At Sacramento
	Wed.	17—At Utah
	Fri.	19—At Phoenix
	Sun.	21—At L.A. Lakers
	Mon.	22—At Golden State
	Fri.	26—Charlotte
	Sun.	28—Cleveland
	Tue.	30—At Orlando
	Wed.	31—Portland
Apr.	Fri.	2—Sacramento
	Tue.	6—Washington
	Thu.	8—At New Jersey
	Fri.	9—At Boston
	Sun.	11—At Washington
	Mon.	12—Chicago
	Wed.	14—Atlanta
	Fri.	16—At Charlotte
	Sat.	17—At New York
	Tue.	20—At Cleveland
	Thu.	22—At Chicago
	Fri.	23—Indiana
	Sun.	25—New Jersey

°Game played in Baltimore.

GOLDEN STATE WARRIORS

Office: Oakland Coliseum Arena, 7000 Coliseum Way, Oakland, CA 94621-1918

Telephone: (510) 638-6300

Chairman—James F. Fitzgerald
President—Daniel F. Finnane
Head Coach & General Manager—Don Nelson
V.P. & Asst. General Manager—Alvin Attles
Sr. V.P. of Marketing & Broadcasting—Richard Rogers
V.P. of Marketing—John Rizzardini
V.P. of Broadcasting—David McGahey
Controller—Dan Bernert
Director of Player Personnel—Sam Schuler
Assistant Coaches—Gregg Popovich, Donn Nelson
Director of Scouting—Ed Gregory
Executive Assistant—Jean Schuler
Athletic Trainer—Tom Abdenour
Conditioning Coach—Mark Grabow
Equipment Manager—Shane Salazar
Director of Media Relations—Julie Marvel
Asst. Director of Media Relations—Mike Nelson
Director of Events & Game Operations—Jim Rogers
Directors of Community Relations—Nate Thurmond, Fran Endicott
TV Producer/Director—Dan Becker
Ticket Manager—John Copeland
Merchandise Manager—Jim Sweeney
Director of Publications—Steve Schaefer
Director of Media Sales—Todd Santino
Staff—Don Addis, Tim Baggs, Tim Barrett, Joe Casey, Andy Dallin, Bryan Deierling,
Barbara Edmiston, Rayschael Eison, Paula Epps, Rikki Field, Xenia Fountaine, Sandria Frost,
Asya Gerlovin, Mary Haro, Andee Henrotin, Gary Hershon, Patty McCartney, David Perry,
Vera Pollard, Jerrie Powell, Scott Pruneau, Vivian Schumann, Eunice Smith-Harpe,
Susan Stafford, Lauren Walls, Furdae Williams
Team Physician—Dr. Robert Albo
Home Court—Oakland Coliseum Arena (15,025, built in 1966)
Team Colors—Gold and Blue
Radio—KNBR (680 AM) Greg Papa
Television—KPIX (Channel 5), KICU (Channel 36) & SportsChannel,
Steve Albert, Jim Barnett
Game Times—Mon.-Sat. 7:30 p.m., Sun. 1:30 p.m.

James Fitzgerald   **Daniel Finnane**   **Don Nelson**

GOLDEN STATE WARRIORS

1991-92 Record (Won 55, Lost 27)   **1992-93 SCHEDULE**

				W-L				
Nov.	1—At Denver	108	105	1-0	Nov.	Fri.	6—At Utah	
	2—Sacramento	153	91	2-0		Sat.	7—At Minnesota	
	5—At Chicago	118	110	3-0		Tue.	10—L.A. Lakers	
	6—At Milwaukee	120	114	4-0		Thu.	12—Cleveland	
	8—At Philadelphia	116	126—	4-1		Sat.	14—Portland	
	9—At Washington	127	119	5-1		Sun.	15—At L.A. Lakers	
	12—Phoenix	119	116	6-1		Tue.	17—At Miami	
	14—L.A. Lakers	112	115—	6-2		Thu.	19—At Orlando	
	16—At L.A. Clippers	123	105	7-2		Fri.	20—At Charlotte	
	20—Chicago	108	112—	7-3		Sun.	22—At New Jersey	
	22—At Portland	116	112	8-3		Tue.	24—Chicago	
	23—Milwaukee	120	115	9-3		Fri.	27—At Phoenix	
	26—At Seattle	°130	136—	9-4		Sat.	28—Phoenix	
	29—At Utah	108	135—	9-5	Dec.	Wed.	2—Charlotte	
Dec.	3—Utah	108	103	10-5		Fri.	4—At Denver	
	5—Dallas	117	107	11-5		Sat.	5—Orlando	
	7—Sacramento	124	120	12-5		Tue.	8—Indiana	
	10—L.A. Clippers	117	127—	12-6		Thu.	10—Milwaukee	
	12—Houston	96	99—	12-7		Sat.	12—At Sacramento	
	14—Orlando	128	107	13-7		Tue.	15—L.A. Clippers	
	17—Minnesota	119	105	14-7		Wed.	16—At L.A. Clippers	
	18—At L.A. Clippers	104	100	15-7		Sat.	19—Minnesota	
	20—Portland	123	118	16-7		Sun.	20—At Portland	
	21—At Seattle	112	120—	16-8		Tue.	22—At Phoenix	
	26—At Denver	110	100	17-8		Wed.	23—Dallas	
	27—At Minnesota	°106	102	18-8		Sat.	26—At Dallas	
	30—At L.A. Lakers	114	99	19-8		Mon.	28—At San Antonio	
Jan.	2—Denver	125	111	20-8		Tue.	29—At Houston	
	4—Indiana	140	121	21-8	Jan.	Sat.	2—Houston	
	10—San Antonio	120	128—	21-9		Tue.	5—At Seattle	
	11—At Phoenix	118	130—	21-10		Thu.	7—Miami	
	14—At San Antonio	124	123	22-10		Sat.	9—At Detroit	
	16—At Houston	98	91	23-10		Tue.	12—At Atlanta	
	18—At Dallas	143	141	24-10		Wed.	13—At Philadelphia	
	20—Charlotte	135	119	25-10		Fri.	15—At Chicago	
	22—Atlanta	136	124	26-10		Sat.	16—At Indiana	
	24—New York	109	114—	26-11		Mon.	18—Sacramento	
	28—Portland	°116	124—	26-12		Wed.	20—Utah	
	29—At L.A. Lakers	99	112—	26-13		Fri.	22—Seattle	
	31—Denver	124	103	27-13		Tue.	26—At Portland	
Feb.	2—At New York	120	113	28-13		Wed.	27—Denver	
	3—At Orlando	122	114	29-13		Fri.	29—L.A. Clippers	
	5—At Miami	124	126—	29-14	Feb.	Mon.	1—At Milwaukee	
	6—At Charlotte	113	132—	29-15		Tue.	2—At Cleveland	
	11—Washington	139	127	30-15		Thu.	4—At New York	
	13—San Antonio	109	94	31-15		Fri.	5—At Washington	
	15—Seattle	140	122	32-15		Sun.	7—At Boston	
	17—L.A. Lakers	116	100	33-15		Tue.	9—Atlanta	
	19—Boston	117	112	34-15		Thu.	11—Phoenix	
	21—Phoenix	123	115	35-15		Sat.	13—At Sacramento	
	22—At L.A. Lakers	126	124	36-15		Sun.	14—Washington	
	24—At Dallas	138	131	37-15		Tue.	16—San Antonio	
	26—At Houston	116	118—	37-16		Thu.	18—Seattle	
	27—At San Antonio	103	124—	37-17		Wed.	24—Utah	
	29—Miami	136	110	38-17		Fri.	26—L.A. Clippers	
Mar.	2—At Sacramento	118	98	39-17		Sat.	27—At Seattle	
	3—Utah	101	123—	39-18	Mar.	Mon.	1—Philadelphia	
	5—Cleveland	116	108	40-18		Wed.	3—L.A. Lakers	
	7—Houston	110	100	41-18		Sun.	7—Portland	
	8—At L.A. Clippers	96	97—	41-19		Wed.	10—At Phoenix	
	10—New Jersey	129	122	42-19		Thu.	11—New Jersey	
	12—Detroit	112	119—	42-20		Tue.	16—Boston	
	17—At Seattle	119	107	43-20		Thu.	18—Houston	
	18—Minnesota	123	120	44-20		Fri.	19—At Sacramento	
	20—At Cleveland	107	122—	44-21		Mon.	22—Detroit	
	22—At Boston	97	114—	44-22		Thu.	25—At Denver	
	23—At Atlanta	°125	126—	44-23		Fri.	26—At Minnesota	
	25—At Detroit	103	99	45-23		Sun.	28—New York	
	27—At Indiana	125	117	46-23		Tue.	30—Minnesota	
	28—At New Jersey	°153	148	47-23	Apr.	Fri.	2—At Dallas	
	30—Philadelphia	124	106	48-23		Sat.	3—At Houston	
	31—At Sacramento	**°148	136	49-23		Tue.	6—At San Antonio	
Apr.	2—At Phoenix	105	109—	49-24		Thu.	8—L.A. Lakers	
	3—Sacramento	°124	116	50-24		Sat.	10—Dallas	
	5—Portland	122	130—	50-25		Mon.	12—Denver	
	7—At Portland	101	110—	50-26		Wed.	14—San Antonio	
	8—Dallas	110	91	51-26		Fri.	16—At L.A. Clippers	
	11—Phoenix	134	125	52-26		Sun.	18—At L.A. Lakers	
	13—At Utah	99	138—	52-27		Tue.	20—At Portland	
	14—At Minnesota	122	100	53-27		Wed.	21—Sacramento	
	17—L.A. Clippers	116	104	54-27		Fri.	23—At Utah	
	19—Seattle	108	106	55-27		Sun.	25—Seattle	

°Denotes overtime game.

HOUSTON ROCKETS

Office: The Summit, Ten Greenway Plaza, Houston, TX 77046
Telephone: (713) 627-0600

Chairman of the Board—Charlie Thomas
Vice-Chairman of the Board—Gary Bradley
President—Ed Schmidt
General Manager/Alt. Governor—Steve Patterson
Director of Communications—Jim Foley
Head Coach—Rudy Tomjanovich
Assistant Coaches—Carroll Dawson, Bill Berry,
John Killilea (Personnel), Calvin Murphy (Community Relations),
Joe Ash (Scout), Jim Boylen (Video Coordinator)
Strength Coach—Robert Barr
Film Coach—Ed Bernholz
Trainer—Ray Melchiorre
Equipment Manager—David Nordstrom

Media Information Director—Jay Goldberg
Assistant Media Information Director—David Spangler
Marketing Director—Brad Ewing
Director of Corporate Sales—Neal Talmadge
Director of Ticket Operations—Jeff Gaines
Executive Assistant—Kathleen Price
Community Services Administrator—Bob Rockwell
Box Office Manager—Larry Chu
Group Sales—Ed Penn
Sales Marketing Coordinator—Tracy Mitchell
Advertising Sales—John Kopack, Mark Shainbrown
Sponsor Services Coordinator—Shari Rainey
Front Office—Sharon Scott (Receptionist), Sally Clack (Administrative Assistant)
Physician—Dr. Charles Baker, M.D.
Dentist—Dr. Tom O'Brien, D.D.S.
Limited Partners Advisory Board—Chairman: Larry Gerdes; Will Hardee,
Bill Gamble, Don Quast, Tillman Fertitta
Home Court—The Summit (16,279, built in 1975)
Team Colors—Red and Gold
Radio—KTRH (740 AM) Gene Peterson, Jim Foley;
KXYZ (Spanish, 1320 AM) Rolando Becerra, Alex Lopez-Negrete
Television—KTXH-TV (Channel 20);
Home Sports Entertainment, Bill Worrell, Calvin Murphy
Game Time—7:30 p.m.

Charlie Thomas   **Steve Patterson**   **Rudy Tomjanovich**

HOUSTON ROCKETS

1991-92 Record (Won 42, Lost 40)

					W-L
Nov.	1—L.A. Lakers	°126	121		1-0
	2—At Denver	°101	109—		1-1
	5—Portland	106	99		2-1
	7—Cleveland	105	86		3-1
	9—Phoenix	96	95		4-1
	12—At Dallas	98	92		5-1
	15—At L.A. Lakers	74	86—		5-2
	16—At Sacramento	102	93		6-2
	19—New York	90	79		7-2
	21—Minnesota	106	102		8-2
	23—At Minnesota	89	102—		8-3
	26—New Jersey	118	109		9-3
	29—At Indiana	121	141—		9-4
Dec.	1—At Detroit	87	94—		9-5
	3—Denver	100	110—		9-6
	5—Atlanta	97	109—		9-7
	7—Utah	91	96—		9-8
	10—At Portland	108	106		10-8
	12—At Golden State	99	96		11-8
	14—San Antonio	100	107—		11-9
	17—Washington	100	97		12-9
	19—Sacramento	109	102		13-9
	20—At Charlotte	99	95		14-9
	22—At Orlando	99	94		15-9
	23—Dallas	85	105—		15-10
	26—At New Jersey	93	99—		15-11
	27—At Washington	107	100		16-11
	29—At Milwaukee	100	110—		16-12
	30—At Cleveland	89	121—		16-13
Jan.	2—Detroit	83	106—		16-14
	4—At San Antonio	°°112	110		17-14
	6—At Atlanta	97	109—		17-15
	8—At Philadelphia	104	114—		17-16
	10—At Miami	°111	107		18-16
	11—Seattle	119	115		19-16
	14—Denver	111	94		20-16
	16—Golden State	91	98—		20-17
	18—At Utah	80	108—		20-18
	21—Milwaukee	117	107		21-18
	23—L.A. Clippers	109	96		22-18
	25—At Chicago	100	114—		22-19
	28—Minnesota	111	102		23-19
	30—Chicago	105	102		24-19
Feb.	1—At Phoenix	92	106—		24-20
	3—Indiana	122	111		25-20
	5—At Boston	85	98—		25-21
	6—At New York	85	102—		25-22
	11—At Seattle	99	105—		25-23
	12—At L.A. Clippers	95	97—		25-24
	14—Boston	105	99		26-24
	15—At Dallas	99	103—		26-25
	17—Minnesota	°122	124—		26-26
	20—Philadelphia	110	101		27-26
	21—At Utah	97	124—		27-27
	23—San Antonio	90	83		28-27
	26—Golden State	118	116		29-27
	28—At Denver	84	81		30-27
Mar.	1—At L.A. Lakers	105	97		31-27
	3—At Phoenix	°107	112—		31-28
	5—Miami	114	93		32-28
	7—At Golden State	100	110—		32-29
	8—At Sacramento	109	108		33-29
	10—Dallas	116	93		34-29
	12—At San Antonio	98	104—		34-30
	13—Charlotte	118	100		35-30
	15—Utah	106	97		36-30
	17—L.A. Clippers	100	92		37-30
	19—Seattle	91	112—		37-31
	21—Sacramento	97	100—		37-32
	24—At Seattle	106	128—		37-33
	26—At L.A. Clippers	95	109—		37-34
	28—At Portland	95	115—		37-35
	31—L.A. Lakers	101	107—		37-36
Apr.	2—Denver	137	114		38-36
	4—Orlando	110	101		39-36
	7—At San Antonio	95	92		40-36
	9—At Minnesota	117	102		41-36
	11—Dallas	92	99—		41-37
	14—Portland	108	96		42-37
	15—At Utah	98	130—		42-38
	17—At Dallas	106	109—		42-39
	19—Phoenix	97	100—		42-40

°Denotes overtime game.

1992-93 SCHEDULE

Nov.	Fri.	6—Seattle°
	Sat.	7—At Seattle°
	Wed.	11—Atlanta
	Sat.	14—At San Antonio
	Tue.	17—Sacramento
	Thu.	19—Cleveland
	Sat.	21—San Antonio
	Tue.	24—L.A. Clippers
	Wed.	25—At Orlando
	Fri.	27—At Miami
	Sat.	28—Utah
Dec.	Tue.	1—At Denver
	Thu.	3—L.A. Lakers
	Sat.	5—At Dallas
	Tue.	8—Minnesota
	Fri.	11—At Chicago
	Sat.	12—At Minnesota
	Tue.	15—At Cleveland
	Thu.	17—San Antonio
	Sat.	19—Dallas
	Tue.	22—At Detroit
	Wed.	23—At Boston
	Sat.	26—Denver
	Tue.	29—Golden State
	Wed.	30—At Phoenix
Jan.	Sat.	2—At Golden State
	Sun.	3—At Portland
	Tue.	5—Phoenix
	Thu.	7—Portland
	Fri.	8—At Denver
	Sun.	10—Utah
	Tue.	12—At L.A. Clippers
	Thu.	14—Charlotte
	Sat.	16—New York
	Mon.	18—At L.A. Lakers
	Tue.	19—At Sacramento
	Thu.	21—Detroit
	Sat.	23—At Indiana
	Sun.	24—At New Jersey
	Tue.	26—At Milwaukee
	Thu.	28—Chicago
	Sat.	30—New Jersey
Feb.	Tue.	2—Indiana
	Wed.	3—At Dallas
	Fri.	5—Minnesota
	Mon.	8—Washington
	Wed.	10—At Philadelphia
	Thu.	11—At New York
	Sat.	13—At Minnesota
	Tue.	16—Philadelphia
	Thu.	18—Boston
	Tue.	23—At Utah
	Thu.	25—Phoenix
	Sat.	27—Denver
Mar.	Tue.	2—At L.A. Clippers
	Wed.	3—At Sacramento
	Fri.	5—At Dallas
	Sat.	6—Sacramento
	Tue.	9—Miami
	Thu.	11—Portland
	Sat.	13—Utah
	Tue.	16—Orlando
	Thu.	18—At Golden State
	Fri.	19—At Portland
	Sun.	21—Seattle
	Tue.	23—At Charlotte
	Thu.	25—At Atlanta
	Fri.	26—At Washington
	Sun.	28—At Minnesota
Apr.	Thu.	1—Milwaukee
	Sat.	3—Golden State
	Tue.	6—L.A. Clippers
	Thu.	8—At Utah
	Sat.	10—San Antonio
	Tue.	13—L.A. Lakers
	Wed.	14—At Denver
	Fri.	16—At L.A. Lakers
	Sat.	17—At Seattle
	Mon.	19—At Phoenix
	Thu.	22—Minnesota
	Sat.	24—Dallas
	Sun.	25—At San Antonio

°Game played in Japan.

INDIANA PACERS

Office: 300 E. Market St., Indianapolis, IN 46204

Telephone: (317) 263-2100

Pacers Basketball Corp. Owners—Melvin Simon, Herb Simon
President—Donnie Walsh
V.P./Business Operations—Greg Jamison
V.P./Administration & Media Relations—Dale Ratermann
V.P./Basketball—George Irvine
Head Coach—Bob Hill
Assistant Coaches—Bob Ociepka, Billy Knight, Ed Badger
Scout—Mel Daniels
Athletic Trainer/Team Administrator—David Craig
Chief Financial Officer—Bob Metelko
Controller—Doug McKee
Sponsor Sales/Promotions Director—Malcolm Bordelon
Ticket Sales/Game Op. Dir.—Mark Andrew Zwartynski
Community Relations Director—Kathy Jordan
Broadcast Production Director—Larry Mago
Advertising Director—Wendy Sommers
Tickets/Game Operations—Vicki Corhn, Mark Davenport,
Steve LaCroix, Alice Laskowski, Thorpe Miller
Group Sales Manager—Mike Henn
Ticket Manager—Tina Brennan
Ticket Promotions/Game Operations Manager—Kim Kelsh
Sponsor Sales/Promotions—Keith Hendricks, Rick Heliste, Mike White
Media Relations Assistant—Tim Edwards
Broadcast Production Coordinator—Dean McDowell
Sponsor Sales/Promotions Coordinator—Jana Youree Miller
Community Relations Assistant—Chris Clawson
Basketball Video Coordinator/Scout—Courtney Witte
Administrative Assistant—Vicki Cappola
Benefits Administrator—Colleen Moore
Home Court—Market Square Arena (16,530, built in 1974)
Team Colors—Blue and Yellow
Radio—WNDE (1260 AM) Mark Boyle
Television—WXIN (Channel 59), Prime Sports Network—Midwest (Cable),
Clark Kellogg, Bob Leonard, Jerry Baker
Game Time—7:30 p.m.

Melvin Simon

Herb Simon

Bob Hill

INDIANA PACERS

1991-92 Record (Won 40, Lost 42)

				W-L
Nov.	1—Washington	103	109—	0-1
	2—Utah	127	112—	1-1
	5—At Phoenix	111	105	2-1
	6—At Sacramento	102	112—	2-2
	8—At Portland	96	121—	2-3
	9—At Seattle	111	118—	2-4
	11—At L.A. Clippers	97	106—	2-5
	13—New York	110	107	3-5
	15—Seattle	108	124—	3-6
	16—At Cleveland	117	127—	3-7
	18—Detroit	118	101	4-7
	20—At Boston	101	116—	4-8
	22—At Charlotte	110	112—	4-9
	23—Miami	119	83	5-9
	27—At Dallas	106	113—	5-10
	29—Houston	141	121	6-10
	30—At Milwaukee	119	137—	6-11
Dec.	3—At Detroit	108	99	7-11
	4—Phoenix	108	114—	7-12
	6—Milwaukee	126	106	8-12
	7—Portland	112	115—	8-13
	10—San Antonio	109	102	9-13
	13—Dallas	124	108	10-13
	14—Denver	129	108	11-13
	17—At Atlanta	113	117—	11-14
	18—At Miami	°112	118—	11-15
	21—New Jersey	°118	109	12-15
	26—Philadelphia	110	113—	12-16
	28—At New York	°106	115—	12-17
	30—Chicago	104	109—	12-18
Jan.	3—At L.A. Lakers	114	87	13-18
	4—At Golden State	121	140—	13-19
	6—At Utah	108	124—	13-20
	8—L.A. Clippers	102	104—	13-21
	11—Atlanta	138	115	14-21
	14—At Washington	°°118	127—	14-22
	15—Detroit	104	118—	14-23
	17—Orlando	120	127—	14-24
	18—Miami	127	103	15-24
	20—At New York	97	105—	15-25
	22—At Cleveland	°115	119—	15-26
	24—Cleveland	102	104—	15-27
	25—At Charlotte	105	107—	15-28
	29—At Philadelphia	115	90	16-28
	31—Atlanta	°115	106	17-28
Feb.	2—At Denver	128	122	18-28
	3—At Houston	111	122—	18-29
	6—At San Antonio	117	106	19-29
	11—At Orlando	100	98	20-29
	12—New York	104	111—	20-30
	14—Milwaukee	107	100	21-30
	15—At Minnesota	117	101	22-30
	17—Charlotte	128	117	23-30
	19—Sacramento	129	115	24-30
	21—At New Jersey	101	105—	24-31
	23—Boston	102	95	25-31
	26—At Boston	109	130—	25-32
	28—Orlando	114	109	26-32
	29—At Charlotte	119	121—	26-33
Mar.	3—At Chicago	103	101	27-33
	4—At Detroit	°107	110—	27-34
	6—At Atlanta	°115	113	28-34
	7—Minnesota	108	97	29-34
	10—Washington	101	91	30-34
	11—At Philadelphia	93	111—	30-35
	13—At Orlando	97	98—	30-36
	16—L.A. Lakers	98	85	31-36
	18—At Miami	°116	111	32-36
	20—Milwaukee	°102	97	33-36
	22—Philadelphia	108	100	34-36
	24—At Cleveland	113	128—	34-37
	25—At Washington	131	109	35-37
	27—Golden State	117	125—	35-38
Apr.	1—Atlanta	137	117	36-38
	3—Boston	101	97	37-38
	5—New Jersey	120	128—	37-39
	8—At Milwaukee	122	107	38-39
	10—Chicago	96	108—	38-40
	11—At Chicago	106	108—	38-41
	14—Charlotte	123	96	39-41
	16—At New Jersey	119	113	40-41
	17—Cleveland	102	107—	40-42

°Denotes overtime game.

1992-93 SCHEDULE

Nov.	Sat.	7—Detroit
	Mon.	9—At Chicago
	Wed.	11—Philadelphia
	Fri.	13—Charlotte
	Sat.	14—At Detroit
	Tue.	17—Denver
	Fri.	20—Utah
	Sat.	21—At Milwaukee
	Tue.	24—Miami
	Wed.	25—At Miami
	Fri.	27—Orlando
	Sat.	28—At Charlotte
Dec.	Tue.	1—At Atlanta
	Wed.	2—Portland
	Fri.	4—Atlanta
	Sat.	5—At Washington
	Tue.	8—At Golden State
	Thu.	10—At Sacramento
	Fri.	11—At Portland
	Sun.	13—At L.A. Clippers
	Wed.	16—Boston
	Fri.	18—At Detroit
	Sat.	19—New Jersey
	Mon.	21—At Philadelphia
	Wed.	23—At Cleveland
	Sat.	26—Chicago
	Tue.	29—At New York
	Wed.	30—New York
Jan.	Sat.	2—At Chicago
	Tue.	5—L.A. Clippers
	Wed.	6—At Boston
	Sat.	9—At Orlando
	Tue.	12—Philadelphia
	Fri.	15—Cleveland
	Sat.	16—Golden State
	Mon.	18—At New Jersey
	Tue.	19—Washington
	Thu.	21—Milwaukee
	Sat.	23—Houston
	Sun.	24—At Charlotte
	Wed.	27—At Philadelphia
	Thu.	28—L.A. Lakers
	Sat.	30—Detroit
Feb.	Tue.	2—At Houston
	Thu.	4—At San Antonio
	Fri.	5—At Dallas
	Wed.	10—Chicago
	Fri.	12—Minnesota
	Sat.	13—At Milwaukee
	Mon.	15—At Cleveland
	Wed.	17—Sacramento
	Tue.	23—Boston
	Wed.	24—At Washington
	Fri.	26—Charlotte
	Sun.	28—Dallas
Mar.	Tue.	2—San Antonio
	Thu.	4—Atlanta
	Sun.	7—At Miami
	Mon.	8—Seattle
	Wed.	10—At Orlando
	Sat.	13—At New York
	Wed.	17—Milwaukee
	Fri.	19—Charlotte
	Sun.	21—At Phoenix
	Tue.	23—At Utah
	Thu.	25—At Seattle
	Sat.	27—At Denver
	Sun.	28—At L.A. Lakers
	Wed.	31—Washington
Apr.	Fri.	2—Orlando
	Sun.	4—Phoenix
	Tue.	6—At New Jersey
	Wed.	7—At Minnesota
	Sat.	10—Chicago
	Tue.	13—At Boston
	Wed.	14—New Jersey
	Fri.	16—New York
	Sun.	18—At Milwaukee
	Tue.	20—At Atlanta
	Wed.	21—Cleveland
	Fri.	23—At Detroit
	Sat.	24—Miami

LOS ANGELES CLIPPERS

Office: L.A. Memorial Sports Arena, 3939 S. Figueroa Street, Los Angeles, CA 90037

Telephone: (213) 748-8000

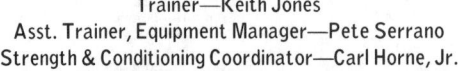

Chairman of the Board & Owner—Donald T. Sterling
Exec. V.P./General Manager—Elgin Baylor
Exec. V.P./Business Operations—Andrew Roeser
Executive Vice President—Harley Frankel
Head Coach—Larry Brown
Assistant Coaches—R.C. Buford, John Hammond,
Quin Snyder, Mack Calvin
Asst. Coach/Director of Scouting—Barry Hecker
Asst. Director of Scouting—Jeff Weltman
Trainer—Keith Jones
Asst. Trainer, Equipment Manager—Pete Serrano
Strength & Conditioning Coordinator—Carl Horne, Jr.
Team Physician—Dr. Tony Daly
Vice President/Marketing & Broadcasting—Mitch Huberman
Vice President/Marketing—Carl Lahr
Vice President/Public Relations—Mike Williams
Director of Corporate Sponsorships—Kevin Smith
Director of Sponsor Services—Diane Thibert
Media Relations Manager—Lori Hamamoto
Public Relations Assistant—Cary Collins
Controller—Susan Lewis
Accounting Assistant—Amy Fowler
Director of Promotions—Lou Rosenberg
Group Sales Manager—Staci Davis
Director of Ticket Operations—TBA
Asst. Director of Ticket Operations—Don Petraska
Assistant to the General Manager—Belinda Cline
Executive Assistants—Shirley McIntyre, Joe-Ann Arellano
Team Photographer—Andrew D. Bernstein and Associates
Home Court—L.A. Memorial Sports Arena (15,925, built in 1959)
Team Colors—Red, White and Blue
Radio—KMPC (710 AM) Ralph Lawler, Rich Marotta
Television—KCOP-TV (Channel 13) Ralph Lawler, Mike Fratello;
SportsChannel (cable), Joel Meyers
Game Times—Mon.-Sat. 7:30 p.m., Sun. 6 p.m.

Donald T. Sterling   **Elgin Baylor**   **Larry Brown**

LOS ANGELES CLIPPERS

1991-92 Record (Won 45, Lost 37)   **1992-93 SCHEDULE**

	1991-92 Results			W-L			1992-93 Schedule
Nov.	1—At Sacramento	90	94—	0-1	Nov.	Fri.	6—L.A. Lakers
	2—Cleveland	106	105	1-1		Sat.	7—At Phoenix
	5—At L.A. Lakers	°114	109	2-1		Tue.	10—At Sacramento
	6—Phoenix	111	87	3-1		Wed.	11—Sacramento
	8—Denver	106	82	4-1		Fri.	13—At L.A. Lakers
	9—At Utah	84	101—	4-2		Sat.	14—At Utah
	11—Indiana	106	97	5-2		Tue.	17—Detroit
	13—At San Antonio	93	107—	5-3		Thu.	19—New York
	14—At Dallas	88	95—	5-4		Sat.	21—Phoenix
	16—Golden State	105	123—	5-5		Tue.	24—At Houston
	19—At Portland	112	132—	5-6		Wed.	25—At Dallas
	21—Portland	91	106—	5-7		Fri.	27—Denver
	22—At Phoenix	97	105—	5-8		Sat.	28—At Denver
	24—Seattle	89	86	6-8	Dec.	Thu.	3—Orlando
	26—Chicago	79	116—	6-9		Sat.	5—Charlotte
	29—Washington	94	101—	6-10		Tue.	8—At Cleveland
	30—Charlotte	130	112	7-10		Thu.	10—At New Jersey
Dec.	4—San Antonio	92	81	8-10		Fri.	11—At Philadelphia
	6—At Denver	°102	100	9-10		Sun.	13—Indiana
	7—Minnesota	101	87	10-10		Tue.	15—At Golden State
	10—At Golden State	127	117	11-10		Wed.	16—Golden State
	11—Detroit	101	96	12-10		Fri.	18—Minnesota
	13—Utah	°102	101	13-10		Sat.	19—At Seattle
	15—Orlando	119	104	14-10		Tue.	22—Dallas
	17—At Seattle	99	116—	14-11		Fri.	25—San Antonio
	18—Golden State	100	104—	14-12		Sun.	27—Philadelphia
	21—At Minnesota	100	87	15-12		Wed.	30—Boston
	25—L.A. Lakers	75	85—	15-13	Jan.	Sat.	2—At New York
	26—At Utah	115	123—	15-14		Sun.	3—At Boston
	28—Philadelphia	102	95	16-14		Tue.	5—At Indiana
	30—Boston	86	97—	16-15		Wed.	6—At Detroit
Jan.	2—At Charlotte	°109	102	17-15		Fri.	8—At Charlotte
	4—At Atlanta	95	97—	17-16		Sun.	10—At Milwaukee
	6—At New Jersey	90	105—	17-17		Tue.	12—Houston
	8—At Indiana	104	102	18-17		Thu.	14—L.A. Lakers
	10—At Philadelphia	90	102—	18-18		Fri.	15—At Seattle
	11—At Washington	96	107—	18-19		Mon.	18—At Minnesota
	13—Seattle	98	94	19-19		Fri.	22—Cleveland
	16—At Seattle	98	101—	19-20		Sun.	24—Seattle
	17—Atlanta	°111	107	20-20		Wed.	27—Utah
	21—At San Antonio	100	114—	20-21		Fri.	29—At Golden State
	23—At Houston	96	109—	20-22		Sat.	30—At Utah
	25—New York	93	100—	20-23	Feb.	Tue.	2—Phoenix
	31—At Sacramento	109	112—	20-24		Thu.	4—Chicago
Feb.	1—New Jersey	99	88	21-24		Sat.	6—Sacramento
	4—Dallas	97	80	22-24		Tue.	9—At San Antonio
	5—At L.A. Lakers	95	100—	22-25		Wed.	10—At Phoenix
	12—Houston	97	95	23-25		Fri.	12—Portland
	14—Phoenix	104	97	24-25		Sun.	14—At Portland
	16—At Portland	107	106	25-25		Mon.	15—San Antonio
	17—San Antonio	124	110	26-25		Thu.	18—Washington
	19—L.A. Lakers	125	94	27-25		Tue.	23—Sacramento
	21—Portland	116	123—	27-26		Fri.	26—At Golden State
	22—At Phoenix	112	130—	27-27		Sun.	28—At L.A. Lakers
	25—Utah	101	106—	27-28	Mar.	Tue.	2—Houston
	28—Miami	108	92	28-28		Thu.	4—At Washington
Mar.	1—At Orlando	101	96	29-28		Fri.	5—At Miami
	3—At Miami	117	116	30-28		Sun.	7—At Orlando
	5—At New York	91	101—	30-29		Mon.	8—At Atlanta
	6—At Boston	100	117—	30-30		Wed.	10—New Jersey
	8—Golden State	97	96	31-30		Fri.	12—Minnesota
	10—At Sacramento	120	109	32-30		Sun.	14—At Minnesota
	11—Seattle	96	104—	32-31		Mon.	15—At Chicago
	13—Dallas	105	97	33-31		Thu.	18—Miami
	15—Sacramento	131	105	34-31		Sat.	20—Utah
	17—At Houston	92	100—	34-32		Tue.	23—At Sacramento
	18—At Dallas	117	86	35-32		Wed.	24—Milwaukee
	20—At Phoenix	114	101	36-32		Fri.	26—At Portland
	21—At Denver	114	87	37-32		Sat.	27—At Seattle
	26—Houston	109	95	38-32		Tue.	30—L.A. Lakers
	28—Milwaukee	103	95	39-32	Apr.	Fri.	2—Atlanta
	31—At Detroit	97	81	40-32		Sun.	4—Dallas
Apr.	2—At Cleveland	98	115—	40-33		Tue.	6—At Houston
	3—At Chicago	103	114—	40-34		Thu.	8—At San Antonio
	5—At Milwaukee	97	96	41-34		Sat.	10—Denver
	7—At Minnesota	115	108	42-34		Mon.	12—Phoenix
	9—Portland	106	100	43-34		Tue.	13—At Portland
	11—Denver	122	88	44-34		Fri.	16—Golden State
	14—Sacramento	97	103—	44-35		Sun.	18—At Denver
	16—Minnesota	96	93	45-35		Tue.	20—At Dallas
	17—At Golden State	104	116—	45-36		Thu.	22—Seattle
	19—At L.A. Lakers	°108	109—	45-37		Sun.	25—Portland

°Denotes overtime game.

LOS ANGELES LAKERS

Office: Great Western Forum, 3900 West Manchester Blvd., P.O. Box 10,
Inglewood, CA 90306

Telephone: (310) 419-3100

Owner—Dr. Jerry Buss
California Sports President—Lou Baumeister
CEO, California Sports Marketing—Frank Mariani
General Manager—Jerry West
Assistant General Manager—Mitchell Kupchak
Assistant to the General Manager—Michael Cooper
Special Consultant—Bill Sharman
Head Coach—Randy Pfund
Assistant Coaches—Bill Bertka, Chet Kammerer, Larry Drew
Scouts—Gene Tormohlen, Ronnie Lester
Trainer—Gary Vitti
Executive Vice President—Ken Doi
Assistant to the Owner—John Jackson
General Counsel—Jim Perzik
Vice President, Advertising—Jim Harkins
Vice President, Finance—Joe McCormack
Vice President, Booking and General Manager—Claire Rothman
Controller—Ross Cote
Director of Sales—Steve Chase
Director of Combination Sales—John Roth
Director of Broadcasting—Keith Harris
Director of Public Relations—John Black
Assistant General Manager (Forum)—Rob Collins
Box Office Director—Vern Ausmus
Administrative Assistant—Mary Lou Liebich
Equipment Manager—Rudy Garciduenas
Director of Personnel/Payroll—Joan McLaughlin
Director of Operations—Lee Zeidman
Assistant Public Relations Directors—Raymond Ridder, Rhonda Windham
Team Physicians—Dr. Robert Kerlan, Dr. Stephen Lombardo, Dr. Michael Mellman
Home Court—The Great Western Forum (17,505, built in 1967)
Team Colors—Royal Purple and Gold
Radio—KLAC (570 AM) Chick Hearn, Stu Lantz
Television—KCAL (Channel 9); Prime Ticket (cable), Chick Hearn, Stu Lantz
Game Time—7:30 p.m.

Jerry Buss

Jerry West

Randy Pfund

LOS ANGELES LAKERS

1991-92 Record (Won 43, Lost 39)

Date	Opponent	Score		W-L
Nov.	1—At Houston	*121	126—	0-1
	2—At Dallas	*114	113	1-1
	5—L.A. Clippers	*109	114—	1-2
	8—At Phoenix	85	113—	1-3
	10—Minnesota	96	86	2-3
	14—At Golden State	115	112	3-3
	15—Houston	86	74	4-3
	17—Atlanta	111	89	5-3
	19—Phoenix	103	95	6-3
	22—San Antonio	98	96	7-3
	24—Milwaukee	102	97	8-3
	26—At Orlando	98	87	9-3
	27—At Miami	89	87	10-3
	29—At Boston	91	114—	10-4
	30—At Philadelphia	93	91	11-4
Dec.	3—At Milwaukee	94	126—	11-5
	4—At Charlotte	106	124—	11-6
	6—At New Jersey	98	89	12-6
	8—Dallas	103	88	13-6
	10—At Sacramento	92	90	14-6
	11—Utah	95	101—	14-7
	15—Sacramento	110	94	15-7
	17—At Chicago	102	89	16-7
	19—At Minnesota	85	93—	16-8
	20—At Detroit	93	112—	16-9
	22—Phoenix	88	100—	16-10
	25—At L.A. Clippers	85	75	17-10
	28—Portland	88	98—	17-11
	30—Golden State	99	114—	17-12
Jan.	3—Indiana	87	114—	17-13
	5—Miami	123	111	18-13
	7—At Dallas	104	80	19-13
	8—At San Antonio	87	103—	19-14
	10—Denver	102	88	20-14
	12—Orlando	112	99	21-14
	15—Charlotte	95	93	22-14
	18—At Seattle	108	112—	22-15
	20—Seattle	116	110	23-15
	21—At Portland	92	131—	23-16
	23—At Sacramento	108	105	24-16
	24—Sacramento	95	92	25-16
	29—Golden State	112	99	26-16
	30—At Denver	106	96	27-16
Feb.	2—Chicago	97	103—	27-17
	3—At Phoenix	104	113—	27-18
	5—L.A. Clippers	100	95	28-18
	11—At Minnesota	116	108	29-18
	13—At Utah	91	97—	29-19
	14—Washington	92	108—	29-20
	16—Boston	107	114—	29-21
	17—At Golden State	100	116—	29-22
	19—At L.A. Clippers	94	125—	29-23
	20—At Seattle	103	105—	29-24
	22—Golden State	124	126—	29-25
	26—New York	81	68	30-25
	28—Cleveland	90	101—	30-26
Mar.	1—Houston	97	105—	30-27
	3—At Portland	101	105—	30-28
	4—New Jersey	101	92	31-28
	8—Detroit	93	98—	31-29
	10—At New York	106	104	32-29
	11—At Atlanta	109	98	33-29
	13—At Cleveland	*107	109—	33-30
	14—At Washington	92	89	34-30
	16—At Indiana	85	98—	34-31
	18—Portland	93	98—	34-32
	20—Minnesota	131	121	35-32
	26—Dallas	115	92	36-32
	27—At Utah	103	92	37-32
	29—Philadelphia	117	88	38-32
	31—At Houston	107	101	39-32
Apr.	1—At San Antonio	86	104—	39-33
	3—Seattle	91	96—	39-34
	5—Phoenix	109	104	40-34
	7—At Seattle	88	117—	40-35
	9—San Antonio	94	102—	40-36
	11—Utah	90	93—	40-37
	13—Denver	100	93	41-37
	15—At Denver	107	110—	41-38
	16—At Sacramento	94	102—	41-39
	18—At Portland	109	101	42-39
	19—L.A. Clippers	*109	108	43-39

*Denotes overtime game.

1992-93 SCHEDULE

Nov.	Fri.	6—At L.A. Clippers
	Sun.	8—Sacramento
	Tue.	10—At Golden State
	Thu.	12—At Seattle
	Fri.	13—L.A. Clippers
	Sun.	15—Golden State
	Fri.	20—Chicago
	Sun.	22—Denver
	Wed.	25—New Jersey
	Fri.	27—At Portland
	Sun.	29—Dallas
Dec.	Tue.	1—At Sacramento
	Thu.	3—At Houston
	Fri.	4—At Phoenix
	Sun.	6—Minnesota
	Wed.	9—Portland
	Fri.	11—Washington
	Sun.	13—Milwaukee
	Tue.	15—At San Antonio
	Wed.	16—At Dallas
	Fri.	18—Phoenix
	Sat.	19—At Denver
	Wed.	23—Seattle
	Sat.	26—San Antonio
	Mon.	28—At Miami
	Wed.	30—At Orlando
Jan.	Sat.	2—At Cleveland
	Sun.	3—At Milwaukee
	Tue.	5—At Chicago
	Wed.	6—At Minnesota
	Fri.	8—Sacramento
	Sun.	10—Miami
	Thu.	14—At L.A. Clippers
	Fri.	15—Portland
	Mon.	18—Houston
	Wed.	20—Seattle
	Fri.	22—At Utah
	Sun.	24—At Washington
	Tue.	26—At New Jersey
	Thu.	28—At Indiana
	Fri.	29—At Charlotte
	Sun.	31—At Boston
Feb.	Tue.	2—Orlando
	Thu.	4—Utah
	Fri.	5—At Phoenix
	Mon.	8—Dallas
	Wed.	10—Denver
	Sun.	14—Atlanta
	Thu.	18—At Portland
	Wed.	24—At Sacramento
	Fri.	26—Cleveland
	Sun.	28—L.A. Clippers
Mar.	Tue.	2—At Denver
	Wed.	3—At Golden State
	Fri.	5—Philadelphia
	Sun.	7—Charlotte
	Tue.	9—At Detroit
	Wed.	10—At New York
	Fri.	12—At Philadelphia
	Sun.	14—At Atlanta
	Mon.	15—At San Antonio
	Wed.	17—San Antonio
	Fri.	19—Boston
	Sun.	21—Detroit
	Wed.	24—Phoenix
	Fri.	26—New York
	Sun.	28—Indiana
	Tue.	30—At L.A. Clippers
	Wed.	31—Minnesota
Apr.	Sun.	4—Utah
	Tue.	6—At Phoenix
	Thu.	8—At Golden State
	Fri.	9—Portland
	Sun.	11—Seattle
	Tue.	13—At Houston
	Wed.	14—At Dallas
	Fri.	16—Houston
	Sun.	18—Golden State
	Tue.	20—At Minnesota
	Wed.	21—At Utah
	Fri.	23—At Seattle
	Sat.	24—Sacramento

MIAMI HEAT

Office: The Miami Arena, Miami, FL 33136-4102

Telephone: (305) 577-4328

Partners—Ted Arison, Zev Bufman
Billy Cunningham, Lewis Schaffel
Managing General Partner—Lewis Schaffel
Limited Partners—Julio Iglesias, Raanan Katz,
Amancio Suarez, Robert Sturges
Executive Vice President—Pauline Winick
Vice President, Finance—Sammy Schulman
Vice President, Special Projects—Kip Hunter-Epstein
Vice President, Sponsor Relations—Joy Behrman
Vice President, Corporate Sales—Roger Green
Vice President, Community Relations—Wali Jones
Head Coach—Kevin Loughery
Assistant Coaches—Bob Staak, Alvin Gentry
Trainer/Travel Coordinator—Ron Culp
Player Personnel Director Emeritus—Stu Inman
Scouting Coordinator—Tony Fiorentino
Strength & Conditioning Coach—Bill Foran
Special Assignment Scout—Al Bianchi
Director of Public Relations—Mark Pray
Director of Corporate Education—Sybil Wilson-George
Director of Marketing & Community Services—Jorge Cunill
Director of Corporate Sales—Kimberly Terranova
Director of Customer Relations—Jeff Craney
Director of Sales—Mike Weiss
Box Office Manager—Anthony Franco
Executive Administrative Assistant—Nuria Pardo
Communications Coordinator—Carmen Green
Public Relations Assistant—Andy Elisburg
Team Physicians—Dr. Harlan Selesnick, Dr. Allen Herskowitz
Counsel—Alan Fein, Joel Arnold
Home Court—Miami Arena (15,008, built in 1988)
Team Colors—Orange, Red, Yellow, Black, White
Radio—WQAM (560 AM), Dave Halberstam;
WRFM (830 AM), Jose Paneda
Television—SportsChannel Florida/WBFS (Channel 33) Eric Reid, TBA
Game Times—Mon.-Fri. 7:30 p.m., Sat. 3:30 p.m. or 7:30 p.m., Sun. 4 p.m. or 6 p.m.

Lewis Schaffel

Kevin Loughery

MIAMI HEAT

1991-92 Record (Won 38, Lost 44)

				W-L
Nov.	2—New York	107	93	1-0
	5—Boston	89	93—	1-1
	7—At New Jersey	111	89	2-1
	9—At Atlanta	93	97—	2-2
	13—Detroit	107	102	3-2
	15—Charlotte	120	105	4-2
	16—At Milwaukee	°120	116	5-2
	19—Utah	111	91	6-2
	20—At Philadelphia	107	114—	6-3
	22—Sacramento	118	112	7-3
	23—At Indiana	83	119—	7-4
	26—At New York	81	98—	7-5
	27—L.A. Lakers	87	89—	7-6
	29—Philadelphia	95	92	8-6
	30—At Orlando	99	105—	8-7
Dec.	3—Portland	94	124—	8-8
	4—At Boston	97	124—	8-9
	7—Phoenix	108	109—	8-10
	10—At Dallas	°110	114—	8-11
	11—Cleveland	105	103	9-11
	13—At Charlotte	112	108	10-11
	14—Atlanta	121	101	11-11
	17—At Cleveland	80	148—	11-12
	18—Indiana	°118	112	12-12
	20—At Philadelphia	99	127—	12-13
	21—Boston	112	101	13-13
	23—Orlando	113	102	14-13
	26—At Phoenix	104	132—	14-14
	28—At Utah	103	128—	14-15
	29—At Portland	96	129—	14-16
Jan.	2—At Seattle	°109	113—	14-17
	4—At Sacramento	110	98	15-17
	5—At L.A. Lakers	111	123—	15-18
	8—Chicago	106	108—	15-19
	10—Houston	°107	111—	15-20
	11—At Chicago	99	108—	15-21
	15—Milwaukee	134	115	16-21
	16—At Washington	102	94	17-21
	18—At Indiana	103	127—	17-22
	20—Minnesota	121	106	18-22
	22—Washington	125	112	19-22
	24—At New Jersey	117	123—	19-23
	25—Dallas	103	101	20-23
	29—Seattle	119	114	21-23
	31—At Detroit	98	109—	21-24
Feb.	2—Charlotte	118	100	22-24
	4—At New York	91	122—	22-25
	5—Golden State	126	124	23-25
	11—Philadelphia	102	114—	23-26
	13—Atlanta	121	119	24-26
	16—At Charlotte	109	126—	24-27
	17—New York	102	104—	24-28
	20—At Milwaukee	111	109	25-28
	22—Detroit	107	98	26-28
	25—At San Antonio	101	123—	26-29
	26—At Denver	105	98	27-29
	28—At L.A. Clippers	92	108—	27-30
	29—At Golden State	110	136—	27-31
Mar.	3—L.A. Clippers	116	117—	27-32
	5—At Houston	93	114—	27-33
	6—At Chicago	81	123—	27-34
	8—Washington	112	98	28-34
	10—Boston	108	101	29-34
	13—Denver	113	109	30-34
	14—At Atlanta	102	115—	30-35
	16—Chicago	100	116—	30-36
	18—Indiana	°111	116—	30-37
	21—At New York	88	105—	30-38
	22—New Jersey	107	100	31-38
	25—At Minnesota	105	97	32-38
	27—San Antonio	118	101	33-38
	28—At Orlando	109	100	34-38
	31—At Cleveland	114	123—	34-39
Apr.	1—At Philadelphia	91	108—	34-40
	3—Cleveland	100	103—	34-41
	5—At Detroit	80	104—	34-42
	7—Washington	100	89	35-42
	10—At Washington	108	93	36-42
	11—Orlando	105	101	37-42
	14—New Jersey	100	105—	37-43
	16—Milwaukee	95	87	38-43
	19—At Boston	93	109—	38-44

°Denotes overtime game.

1992-93 SCHEDULE

Nov.	Fri.	6—At Orlando
	Sat.	7—New Jersey
	Tue.	10—Boston
	Thu.	12—At Detroit
	Sat.	14—At Charlotte
	Tue.	17—Golden State
	Fri.	20—At Philadelphia
	Sat.	21—Charlotte
	Tue.	24—At Indiana
	Wed.	25—Indiana
	Fri.	27—Houston
	Sat.	28—At Atlanta
Dec.	Wed.	2—At Milwaukee
	Fri.	4—At Boston
	Sat.	5—New Jersey
	Tue.	8—At Dallas
	Thu.	10—At San Antonio
	Sat.	12—Phoenix
	Tue.	15—Sacramento
	Fri.	18—Atlanta
	Sat.	19—At New York
	Mon.	21—At Chicago
	Wed.	23—Utah
	Sat.	26—Orlando
	Mon.	28—L.A. Lakers
	Wed.	30—Chicago
Jan.	Sat.	2—At Washington
	Tue.	5—Detroit
	Thu.	7—At Golden State
	Sat.	9—At Sacramento
	Sun.	10—At L.A. Lakers
	Tue.	12—At Utah
	Thu.	14—At Portland
	Fri.	15—At Phoenix
	Wed.	20—Philadelphia
	Fri.	22—At Orlando
	Sun.	24—Dallas
	Tue.	26—At Washington
	Thu.	28—Milwaukee
	Sat.	30—Cleveland
Feb.	Wed.	3—Atlanta
	Fri.	5—New York
	Sun.	7—At New York
	Tue.	9—At Detroit
	Wed.	10—At Minnesota
	Fri.	12—Charlotte
	Sun.	14—At New Jersey
	Mon.	15—Denver
	Wed.	17—Detroit
	Tue.	23—At Cleveland
	Wed.	24—Portland
	Fri.	26—San Antonio
	Sun.	28—Minnesota
Mar.	Wed.	3—Washington
	Fri.	5—L.A. Clippers
	Sun.	7—Indiana
	Tue.	9—At Houston
	Thu.	11—Chicago
	Sat.	13—Seattle
	Mon.	15—At Denver
	Tue.	16—At Seattle
	Thu.	18—At L.A. Clippers
	Sat.	20—Cleveland
	Tue.	23—At Orlando
	Wed.	24—At Boston
	Fri.	26—New Jersey
	Sat.	27—At Atlanta
	Tue.	30—At Charlotte
Apr.	Thu.	1—At New Jersey
	Fri.	2—New York
	Sun.	4—Orlando
	Tue.	6—At Cleveland
	Thu.	8—At Milwaukee
	Sat.	10—Philadelphia
	Mon.	12—Milwaukee
	Wed.	14—At Chicago
	Thu.	15—At Washington
	Sat.	17—Boston
	Tue.	20—New York
	Wed.	21—At Philadelphia
	Fri.	23—Washington
	Sat.	24—At Indiana

MILWAUKEE BUCKS

Office: Bradley Center, 1001 N. Fourth St., Milwaukee, WI 53203-1312

Telephone: (414) 227-0500

President—Herb Kohl
Vice President of Basketball Operations—TBA
Vice President of Business Operations—John Steinmiller
Head Coach—Mike Dunleavy
Director of Player Personnel—Lee Rose
Assistant Coaches—Frank Hamblen, Jim Eyen, Butch Carter
Scout—Larry Riley
Scout/Video Coordinator—Larry Harris
Trainer—Mark Pfeil
Director of Finance—Jim Woloszyk
Director of Publicity—Bill King II
Ticket Manager—Bea Westfahl
Director of Sales—Jim Grayson
Director of Team Services—Tom Hoffer
Executive Secretary—Rita Huber
Sales Representatives—Tony Shields, David Snyder, Steve Tarachow, Dave Trattner
Staff—Marie Miller, Marie Montalbano-Stachurski, Susan Satterthwaite, Sandy Short,
Carole Szczech, Sue Thompson, Kim Van Deraa, Wade Waugus, Rich Wermager
Assistant Trainer—Phil Horton
Equipment Manager—Harold Lewis
Publicity Assistant—Scott Johnson
Medical Advisors—David Haskell, M.D.; Conrad Heinzelmann, M.D.; John Krebs, D.D.S.
Chiropractic Consultant—Craig Jordan, D.C.
Physical Therapy Consultant—John Crowe, R.P.T.
Assistant Video Coordinator—Bob Peterson
Home Court—Bradley Center (18,633, built in 1988)
Team Colors—Forest Green, Kelly Green, Lime & White
Television—WCGV-Fox (Channel 24), Jim Paschke, Jon McGlocklin
Radio—WTMJ (620 AM), Jim Irwin, Jon McGlocklin
Game Times—Mon.-Thur. 7:30 p.m., Fri.-Sat. 8 p.m., Sun. 1:30 or 7:30 p.m.

Herb Kohl

John Steinmiller

Mike Dunleavy

MILWAUKEE BUCKS

1991-92 Record (Won 31, Lost 51)

Date	Opponent	Bucks	Opp	W-L
Nov.	1—At Detroit	109	99	1-0
	2—Chicago	109	107	2-0
	5—At New York	85	113—	2-1
	6—Golden State	114	120—	2-2
	8—At Charlotte	*125	122	3-2
	9—Dallas	111	95	4-2
	11—At Philadelphia	99	102—	4-3
	12—At Cleveland	113	119—	4-4
	15—At Chicago	101	114—	4-5
	16—Miami	*116	120—	4-6
	19—Charlotte	127	104	5-6
	21—Washington	112	87	6-6
	23—At Golden State	115	120—	6-7
	24—At L.A. Lakers	97	102—	6-8
	26—At Portland	*98	107—	6-9
	30—Indiana	137	119	7-9
Dec.	3—L.A. Lakers	126	94	8-9
	5—New Jersey	101	109—	8-10
	6—At Indiana	106	126—	8-11
	8—San Antonio	102	83	9-11
	10—At Atlanta	104	118—	9-12
	12—At Washington	109	97	10-12
	14—Minnesota	103	92	11-12
	18—At Boston	117	131—	11-13
	19—At Orlando	95	87	12-13
	21—Philadelphia	110	97	13-13
	26—Cleveland	94	111—	13-14
	29—Houston	110	100	14-14
Jan.	2—At Minnesota	92	91	15-14
	3—Chicago	113	108	16-14
	8—Utah	99	98	17-14
	10—At New Jersey	97	104—	17-15
	11—Sacramento	*105	106—	17-16
	14—At Atlanta	88	93—	17-17
	15—At Miami	115	134—	17-18
	17—New York	90	85	18-18
	19—Orlando	108	98	19-18
	21—At Houston	107	117—	19-19
	22—At Dallas	116	118—	19-20
	24—At San Antonio	86	115—	19-21
	25—At Denver	*100	107—	19-22
	29—Atlanta	100	110—	19-23
	31—Boston	102	100	20-23
Feb.	2—Seattle	122	106	21-23
	5—At Detroit	94	102—	21-24
	6—Denver	106	97	22-24
	11—Detroit	104	87	23-24
	13—Charlotte	127	118	24-24
	14—At Indiana	100	107—	24-25
	16—At Orlando	104	118—	24-26
	18—Cleveland	128	116	25-26
	20—Miami	109	111—	25-27
	23—At Cleveland	89	103—	25-28
	25—At Charlotte	82	94—	25-29
	27—At Detroit	97	104—	25-30
	28—Chicago	105	109—	25-31
Mar.	1—Atlanta	*109	106	26-31
	4—Charlotte	110	119—	26-32
	6—Orlando	124	102	27-32
	7—At Washington	90	94—	27-33
	10—Portland	112	126—	27-34
	12—Phoenix	100	106—	27-35
	14—Philadelphia	110	105	28-35
	17—Boston	127	106	29-35
	19—At New York	92	96—	29-36
	20—At Indiana	*97	102—	29-37
	22—Washington	109	88	30-37
	24—At Sacramento	102	113—	30-38
	25—At Phoenix	104	132—	30-39
	27—At Seattle	95	96—	30-40
	28—At L.A. Clippers	95	103—	30-41
	30—At Utah	100	120—	30-42
Apr.	1—New Jersey	117	121—	30-43
	3—At New Jersey	103	122—	30-44
	5—L.A. Clippers	96	97—	30-45
	7—At Chicago	101	116—	30-46
	8—Indiana	107	122—	30-47
	10—At Boston	100	109—	30-48
	12—At Philadelphia	94	90	31-48
	14—Detroit	*94	98—	31-49
	16—At Miami	87	95—	31-50
	18—New York	103	114—	31-51

*Denotes overtime game.

1992-93 SCHEDULE

Nov.	Fri.	6—At Detroit
	Sat.	7—Boston
	Tue.	10—At San Antonio
	Wed.	11—At Dallas
	Fri.	13—Chicago
	Sun.	15—Denver
	Tue.	17—At Atlanta
	Sat.	21—Indiana
	Tue.	24—At Cleveland
	Wed.	25—Cleveland
	Fri.	27—At Philadelphia
	Sat.	28—Washington
Dec.	Wed.	2—Miami
	Thu.	3—At Washington
	Sat.	5—At New York
	Sun.	6—Phoenix
	Tue.	8—At Portland
	Thu.	10—At Golden State
	Sat.	12—At Utah
	Sun.	13—At L.A. Lakers
	Tue.	15—At Seattle
	Thu.	17—New Jersey
	Sat.	19—Detroit
	Tue.	22—Sacramento
	Sat.	26—New York
	Mon.	28—At Orlando
Jan.	Sat.	2—At Atlanta
	Sun.	3—L.A. Lakers
	Tue.	5—Minnesota
	Thu.	7—Atlanta
	Fri.	8—At Chicago
	Sun.	10—L.A. Clippers
	Tue.	12—At Washington
	Thu.	14—San Antonio
	Sat.	16—Boston
	Tue.	19—Portland
	Thu.	21—At Indiana
	Sat.	23—Philadelphia
	Tue.	26—Houston
	Thu.	28—At Miami
	Sat.	30—At Minnesota
Feb.	Mon.	1—Golden State
	Wed.	3—Cleveland
	Fri.	5—At Charlotte
	Sun.	7—New Jersey
	Tue.	9—At Boston*
	Fri.	12—At Cleveland
	Sat.	13—Indiana
	Mon.	15—Charlotte
	Tue.	16—At New Jersey
	Thu.	18—Utah
	Tue.	23—At Chicago
	Wed.	24—New York
	Fri.	26—At Philadelphia
	Sat.	27—At Detroit
Mar.	Tue.	2—Dallas
	Fri.	5—Orlando
	Sun.	7—Detroit
	Tue.	9—Atlanta
	Thu.	11—Seattle
	Fri.	12—At Boston
	Tue.	16—At New York
	Wed.	17—At Indiana
	Fri.	19—At New Jersey
	Sat.	20—Philadelphia
	Wed.	24—At L.A. Clippers
	Fri.	26—At Phoenix
	Sat.	27—At Sacramento
	Mon.	29—Washington
Apr.	Thu.	1—At Houston
	Fri.	2—At Denver
	Tue.	6—Chicago
	Thu.	8—Miami
	Sat.	10—Orlando
	Mon.	12—At Miami
	Tue.	13—At Orlando
	Thu.	15—Cleveland
	Fri.	16—At Chicago
	Sun.	18—Indiana
	Wed.	21—At Charlotte
	Fri.	23—At Atlanta
	Sat.	24—Charlotte

*Game played in Hartford.

MINNESOTA TIMBERWOLVES

Office: Target Center, 600 First Ave. North, Minneapolis, MN 55403

Telephone: (612) 673-1600

Owners—Harvey Ratner, Marv Wolfenson
President—Bob Stein
General Manager—Jack McCloskey
Vice President of Sales—Len Komoroski
Vice President of Marketing—Chris Wright
Vice President of Administration—Joe Pettirossi
Assistant to the General Manager/Asst. Coach—Jim Brewer
Head Coach—Jimmy Rodgers
Assistant Coach—Sidney Lowe
Asst. Coach/Advance Scout/Video Coordinator—Chuck Davisson
Scout—Stan Novak
Trainer—Jay Jensen
Strength/Conditioning Coordinator—Sol Brandys
Controller—Dave Carlson
Director of Media Services—Bill Robertson
Director of Ticket Operations—Brenda Tinnen
Director of Corporate Sales—Ron Minegar
Ticket Sales Manager—Jeff Munneke
Manager of Corporate Services—Sandy Hill
Manager of Basketball Community Relations—Tom Moore
Broadcasting Manager—Charley Frank
Audio/Visual Manager—Duffer Schultz
Community Relations Manager—Bill McMoore
Executive Director of Timberwolves Foundation—Kristy Pierce
Medical Director—Sheldon Burns, M.D.
Orthopedic Surgeon—David Fischer, M.D.
Legal Counsel—Bill Busch, Esq.
Home Court—Target Center (19,006, built in 1990)
Team Colors—Royal Blue, Kelly Green and Silver
Television—KARE (Channel 11), KITN (Channel 29), Kevin Harlan,
Tom Hanneman and Quinn Buckner; Prime Sports Network-Upper Midwest (cable),
Jerry Schemmel and Greg Kessler
Radio—KFAN Sports Radio (1130 AM) Kevin Harlan, Tom Hanneman and
Chad Hartman
Game Times—7 p.m., Sundays 2:30 p.m.

Bob Stein   **Jack McCloskey**   **Jimmy Rodgers**

MINNESOTA TIMBERWOLVES

1991-92 Record (Won 15, Lost 67)   **1992-93 SCHEDULE**

	1991-92 Results			W-L			1992-93 Schedule
Nov.	1—Utah	97	112—	0-1	Nov.	Fri.	6—At Boston
	6—Dallas	94	97—	0-2		Sat.	7—Golden State
	7—At Denver	77	88—	0-3		Tue.	10—Dallas
	9—At Sacramento	84	80	1-3		Thu.	12—At New Jersey
	10—At L.A. Lakers	86	96—	1-4		Sat.	14—Phoenix
	13—Washington	°114	119—	1-5		Tue.	17—Chicago
	15—Portland	102	107—	1-6		Fri.	20—Washington
	17—Seattle	91	101—	1-7		Sat.	21—At Denver
	20—At San Antonio	106	113—	1-8		Wed.	25—New York
	21—At Houston	102	106—	1-9		Fri.	27—At Washington°
	23—Houston	102	89	2-9		Sat.	28—Detroit
	27—Denver	101	92	3-9	Dec.	Thu.	3—At Utah
	30—At Dallas	78	79—	3-10		Sat.	5—At Seattle
Dec.	3—Phoenix	95	101—	3-11		Sun.	6—At L.A. Lakers
	6—At Seattle	94	96—	3-12		Tue.	8—At Houston
	7—At L.A. Clippers	87	101—	3-13		Thu.	10—At Dallas
	11—San Antonio	85	98—	3-14		Sat.	12—Houston
	13—Philadelphia	95	104—	3-15		Tue.	15—Boston
	14—At Milwaukee	92	103—	3-16		Fri.	18—At L.A. Clippers
	16—At Portland	104	119—	3-17		Sat.	19—At Golden State
	17—At Golden State	105	119—	3-18		Wed.	23—Sacramento
	19—L.A. Lakers	93	85	4-18		Sat.	26—Atlanta
	21—L.A. Clippers	87	100—	4-19		Mon.	28—At Utah
	23—New York	91	97—	4-20		Wed.	30—New Jersey
	27—Golden State	°102	106—	4-21	Jan.	Sat.	2—Dallas
	28—At Atlanta	°122	125—	4-22		Tue.	5—At Milwaukee
	30—Sacramento	109	117—	4-23		Wed.	6—L.A. Lakers
Jan.	2—Milwaukee	91	92—	4-24		Fri.	8—Seattle
	4—Boston	100	96	5-24		Sat.	9—At Cleveland
	7—Cleveland	98	113—	5-25		Wed.	13—San Antonio
	8—At New Jersey	97	103—	5-26		Fri.	15—Denver
	10—At Boston	104	94	6-26		Mon.	18—L.A. Clippers
	11—Utah	101	96	7-26		Wed.	20—Portland
	13—At Phoenix	111	131—	7-27		Sat.	23—At Sacramento
	14—At Utah	110	116—	7-28		Mon.	25—At Denver
	16—San Antonio	111	125—	7-29		Wed.	27—Phoenix
	18—New Jersey	100	112—	7-30		Fri.	29—At Detroit
	20—At Miami	106	121—	7-31		Sat.	30—Milwaukee
	21—At Orlando	92	105—	7-32	Feb.	Tue.	2—At Portland
	23—Detroit	100	111—	7-33		Wed.	3—At Phoenix
	24—At Philadelphia	86	119—	7-34		Fri.	5—At Houston
	28—At Houston	102	111—	7-35		Sat.	6—At San Antonio
	31—At San Antonio	101	103—	7-36		Wed.	10—Miami
Feb.	2—At Cleveland	95	106—	7-37		Fri.	12—At Indiana
	3—Denver	114	99	8-37		Sat.	13—Houston
	5—Orlando	102	109—	8-38		Mon.	15—Utah
	11—L.A. Lakers	108	116—	8-39		Thu.	18—Sacramento
	13—At Detroit	96	93	9-39		Tue.	23—At New York
	15—Indiana	101	117—	9-40		Wed.	24—Seattle
	17—At Houston	°124	122	10-40		Fri.	26—Dallas
	19—At San Antonio	103	113—	10-41		Sun.	28—At Miami
	21—At Dallas	94	109—	10-42	Mar.	Tue.	2—At Orlando
	22—At Chicago	90	105—	10-43		Thu.	4—Cleveland
	24—Seattle	91	106—	10-44		Sat.	6—San Antonio
	26—Dallas	106	105	11-44		Mon.	8—Philadelphia
	29—At New York	87	103—	11-45		Tue.	9—At Utah
Mar.	3—San Antonio	102	103—	11-46		Thu.	11—At Sacramento
	5—Chicago	100	113—	11-47		Fri.	12—At L.A. Clippers
	7—At Indiana	97	108—	11-48		Sun.	14—L.A. Clippers
	10—At Charlotte	96	105—	11-49		Tue.	16—Denver
	11—Portland	113	124—	11-50		Thu.	18—At Charlotte
	13—At Washington	115	118—	11-51		Fri.	19—At Atlanta
	15—Phoenix	113	118—	11-52		Sun.	21—Charlotte
	17—At Portland	91	111—	11-53		Tue.	23—At Chicago
	18—At Golden State	120	123—	11-54		Wed.	24—San Antonio
	20—At L.A. Lakers	121	131—	11-55		Fri.	26—Golden State
	21—At Phoenix	105	121—	11-56		Sun.	28—Houston
	23—Denver	95	100—	11-57		Tue.	30—At Golden State
	25—Miami	97	105—	11-58		Wed.	31—At L.A. Lakers
	27—Atlanta	103	105—	11-59	Apr.	Fri.	2—At San Antonio
	29—Sacramento	86	112—	11-60		Sun.	4—At Denver
	31—At Denver	°121	114	12-60		Wed.	7—Indiana
Apr.	3—At Dallas	104	95	13-60		Fri.	9—Orlando
	5—Utah	93	91	14-60		Sun.	11—At Portland
	7—L.A. Clippers	108	115—	14-61		Tue.	13—At Seattle
	9—Houston	102	117—	14-62		Wed.	14—At Phoenix
	11—At Sacramento	94	114—	14-63		Fri.	16—Portland
	12—At Seattle	116	126—	14-64		Sun.	18—At Philadelphia
	14—Golden State	100	122—	14-65		Tue.	20—L.A. Lakers
	16—At L.A. Clippers	93	96—	14-66		Thu.	22—At Houston
	17—At Utah	106	120—	14-67		Fri.	23—At Dallas
	19—Charlotte	130	107	15-67		Sun.	25—Utah

°Denotes overtime game.

°Game played in Baltimore.

NEW JERSEY NETS

Office: Meadowlands Arena, East Rutherford, NJ 07073

Telephone: (201) 935-8888

Board of Directors—Alan L. Aufzien, David B. Gerstein,
Jerry L. Cohen, Henry Taub, Joseph Taub,
Bernie Mann, Donald J. Unger
Chairman of the Board & C.E.O.—Alan L. Aufzien
Vice Chairman of the Board & Treasurer—David B. Gerstein
President & C.O.O.—Jerry L. Cohen
Senior Vice President—Arnold J. Prives
Senior Vice President/Basketball Operations—Willis Reed
Senior V.P./Operations & Asst. to President—James Lampariello
Senior V.P./Finance & Controller—Ray Schaetzle
Head Coach—Chuck Daly
Assistant Coaches—Brendan Suhr, Paul Silas, Rick Carlisle
Trainer—Ted Arzonico
V.P./Television & Corporate Sales—Robert Moran
V.P./Broadcasting & Corporate Sales—Lou Terminello
Vice President/Ticket Sales—Jim Leahy
Vice President/Ticket Operations—Joseph P. Macdonell
Senior Sales Manager/Season Tickets—Rick Lottermann
Director of Public Relations—John Mertz
Staff—Thomas Bates, Rosemarie Currey, Janet Daly, Octavia Fisher, Dan Harris, Jennie Kerner,
Donna Mastropolo, Maura Miller, Dottie Moretto, Dolores O'Dowd, Judi Osur, Bill Paige,
Debbie Richards, Len Rivers, Amy Scheer, Callie Smith, John Tudhope
Team Physicians—Dr. Jeffrey Minkoff, Dr. Orrin Sherman, Dr. John J. Sonzogni, Jr.
Team Dentist—Dr. H. Hugh Gardy
Home Court—Meadowlands Arena (20,029, built in 1981)
Team Colors—Red, White and Blue
Television—SportsChannel (cable); WWOR (Channel 9), Spencer Ross &
Bill Raftery
Radio—WNEW (1130 AM), Howard David, Jim Spanarkel, Mike O'Koren
Game Time—7:30 p.m.

Willis Reed

Chuck Daly

NEW JERSEY NETS

1991-92 Record (Won 40, Lost 42)

Date	Opponent			W-L
Nov.	2—At Charlotte	116	108	1-0
	6—At Philadelphia	105	107—	1-1
	7—Miami	89	111—	1-2
	9—Detroit	100	110—	1-3
	12—At New York	96	98—	1-4
	13—Utah	92	98—	1-5
	15—Washington	°111	116—	1-6
	16—At Orlando	100	102—	1-7
	19—Sacramento	122	118	2-7
	21—At Cleveland	112	116—	2-8
	23—Boston	107	125—	2-9
	26—At Houston	109	118—	2-10
	27—At San Antonio	100	106—	2-11
	29—At Dallas	97	91	3-11
	30—At Denver	97	107—	3-12
Dec.	3—Philadelphia	88	86	4-12
	5—At Milwaukee	109	101	5-12
	6—L.A. Lakers	89	98—	5-13
	10—New York	88	114—	5-14
	12—Denver	121	81	6-14
	14—Charlotte	102	109—	6-15
	17—At New York	94	102—	6-16
	18—Cleveland	102	93	7-16
	20—Chicago	98	115—	7-17
	21—At Indiana	°109	118—	7-18
	23—Atlanta	105	93	8-18
	26—Houston	99	93	9-18
	27—At Charlotte	136	120	10-18
	30—Orlando	122	112	11-18
Jan.	3—Washington	108	112—	11-19
	4—At Chicago	96	140—	11-20
	6—L.A. Clippers	105	90	12-20
	8—Minnesota	103	97	13-20
	10—Milwaukee	104	97	14-20
	11—At Detroit	88	90—	14-21
	14—Dallas	97	88	15-21
	15—At Boston	130	120	16-21
	18—At Minnesota	112	100	17-21
	22—Phoenix	106	104	18-21
	24—Miami	123	117	19-21
	25—At Philadelphia	94	115—	19-22
	28—At Sacramento	118	124—	19-23
	29—At Phoenix	95	128—	19-24
	31—At Portland	108	113—	19-25
Feb.	1—At L.A. Clippers	88	99—	19-26
	5—Seattle	85	95—	19-27
	6—At Washington	108	124—	19-28
	11—At Chicago	113	133—	19-29
	12—At Philadelphia	102	87	20-29
	14—Philadelphia	107	99	21-29
	15—At Cleveland	92	128—	21-30
	19—Detroit	106	102	22-30
	21—Indiana	105	101	23-30
	22—At Atlanta	107	119—	23-31
	25—Boston	109	95	24-31
	27—Portland	98	96	25-31
	29—At Detroit	99	90	26-31
Mar.	1—New York	90	75	27-31
	4—At L.A. Lakers	92	101—	27-32
	6—At Utah	96	117—	27-33
	7—At Seattle	98	109—	27-34
	10—At Golden State	122	129—	27-35
	13—At Boston	110	108	28-35
	14—At New York	°96	94	29-35
	17—Chicago	79	90—	29-36
	20—Washington	99	96	30-36
	22—At Miami	100	107—	30-37
	23—Charlotte	123	120	31-37
	25—Boston	110	118—	31-38
	28—Golden State	°148	153—	31-39
	30—San Antonio	117	109	32-39
Apr.	1—At Milwaukee	121	117	33-39
	3—Milwaukee	122	103	34-39
	5—At Indiana	128	120	35-39
	7—Atlanta	97	104—	35-40
	8—At Washington	109	103	36-40
	10—Cleveland	110	86	37-40
	11—At Atlanta	98	118—	37-41
	13—At Orlando	110	104	38-41
	14—At Miami	105	100	39-41
	16—Indiana	113	119—	39-42
	18—Orlando	127	111	40-42

°Denotes overtime game.

1992-93 SCHEDULE

Nov.	Fri.	6—At Philadelphia
	Sat.	7—At Miami
	Tue.	10—At New York
	Thu.	12—Minnesota
	Sat.	14—Orlando
	Sun.	15—Washington
	Tue.	17—Utah
	Thu.	19—At Atlanta
	Sat.	21—Philadelphia
	Sun.	22—Golden State
	Tue.	24—At Seattle
	Wed.	25—At L.A. Lakers
	Fri.	27—At Utah
	Sat.	28—At Sacramento
Dec.	Wed.	2—Atlanta
	Fri.	4—San Antonio
	Sat.	5—At Miami
	Tue.	8—Phoenix
	Thu.	10—L.A. Clippers
	Sat.	12—At Chicago
	Tue.	15—New York
	Thu.	17—At Milwaukee
	Sat.	19—At Indiana
	Sun.	20—Sacramento
	Tue.	22—Boston
	Sat.	26—At Cleveland
	Mon.	28—Charlotte
	Wed.	30—At Minnesota
Jan.	Sat.	2—At Charlotte
	Tue.	5—At Orlando
	Wed.	6—At Philadelphia
	Fri.	8—At Boston
	Sat.	9—Washington
	Wed.	13—Cleveland
	Fri.	15—Philadelphia
	Sat.	16—At Washington°
	Mon.	18—Indiana
	Thu.	21—Chicago
	Fri.	22—At Atlanta
	Sun.	24—Houston
	Tue.	26—L.A. Lakers
	Thu.	28—At Denver
	Sat.	30—At Houston
Feb.	Mon.	1—At Dallas
	Tue.	2—At San Antonio
	Thu.	4—Seattle
	Sun.	7—At Milwaukee
	Wed.	10—Detroit
	Fri.	12—At Detroit
	Sun.	14—Miami
	Tue.	16—Milwaukee
	Tue.	23—At Charlotte
	Wed.	24—At Boston
	Fri.	26—Portland
	Sun.	28—New York
Mar.	Tue.	2—Chicago
	Thu.	4—Orlando
	Sat.	6—Denver
	Wed.	10—At L.A. Clippers
	Thu.	11—At Golden State
	Sat.	13—At Phoenix
	Mon.	15—At Portland
	Wed.	17—Atlanta
	Fri.	19—Milwaukee
	Sun.	21—Dallas
	Mon.	22—At Washington
	Wed.	24—Charlotte
	Fri.	26—At Miami
	Sat.	27—At Orlando
	Tue.	30—Philadelphia
Apr.	Thu.	1—Miami
	Fri.	2—At Chicago
	Sun.	4—At Cleveland
	Tue.	6—Indiana
	Thu.	8—Detroit
	Sat.	10—Cleveland
	Wed.	14—At Indiana
	Thu.	15—Boston
	Sat.	17—At Washington
	Wed.	21—At New York
	Fri.	23—Orlando
	Sun.	25—At Detroit

°Game played in Baltimore.

NEW YORK KNICKERBOCKERS

Office: Madison Square Garden, Two Pennsylvania Plaza, New York, NY 10121-0091
Telephone: (212) 465-6499

Governor/President and Chief Operating Officer,
Paramount Communications, Inc.—Stanley R. Jaffe
President and Chief Executive Officer,
Madison Square Garden—Robert M. Gutkowski
President—David W. Checketts
Vice President, Player Personnel—Ernie Grunfeld
Vice President and General Counsel—Kenneth W. Munoz
Vice President, Public Relations—John Cirillo
Vice President, Business Affairs—Francis P. Murphy
Alternate Governors—David W. Checketts,
Robert M. Gutkowski, Kenneth W. Munoz
Head Coach—Pat Riley
Assistant Coaches—Dick Harter, Jeff Van Gundy
Video Coordinator—Bob Salmi
Trainer/Traveling Secretary—Mike Saunders
Director of Administration—Ed Tapscott
Director of Scouting Services—Dick McGuire
Director of Marketing—Pam Harris
Director of Community Relations—Cal Ramsey
Manager, Publications and Information—Dennis D'Agostino
Manager, Media Relations—Tim Donovan
Manager, Promotions—Billie Streets
Manager, Dance Team—Petra Belton
Basketball Consultant—William "Red" Holzman
Assistant Trainer—Tim Walsh
Strength and Conditioning Coach—Greg Brittenham
Marketing Assistant—Mark Pannes
Business Affairs Coordinator—Jim Pfeifer
Administrative Assistant—Jehudith Cohen
Senior Secretary—Pat Hazelton
Administrative Assistant—Mari LaRocca
Executive Administrative Assistant—Maggie McLoughlin-McEvoy
Administrative Assistant—Dawn Owens
Administrative Assistant—Debbie Sturniolo
Team Physician—Dr. Norman Scott
Team Dentist—Dr. George Bergofin
Scout—Andrew "Fuzzy" Levane
Receptionist—Gerri Bell
Home Court—Madison Square Garden (19,763, built in 1968)
Team Colors—Orange, White and Blue
Television—MSG Network (cable), Marv Albert, John Andariese
Radio—WFAN (660 AM), Mike Breen, Walt Frazier
Game Time—7:30 p.m.

Stanley R. Jaffe

David W. Checketts

Pat Riley

NEW YORK KNICKERBOCKERS

1991-92 Record (Won 51, Lost 31)   **1992-93 SCHEDULE**

				W-L
Nov.	1—At Orlando	96	106—	0-1
	2—At Miami	93	107—	0-2
	5—Milwaukee	113	85	1-2
	7—Orlando	128	100	2-2
	9—Charlotte	118	113	3-2
	12—New Jersey	98	96	4-2
	13—At Indiana	107	110—	4-3
	16—At San Antonio	89	106—	4-4
	19—At Houston	79	90—	4-5
	20—At Dallas	92	89	5-5
	22—At Detroit	99	90	6-5
	23—Philadelphia	100	92	7-5
	26—Miami	98	81	8-5
	30—Detroit	103	96	9-5
Dec.	2—At Charlotte	99	97	10-5
	6—At Boston	92	103—	10-6
	7—At Atlanta	**137	128	11-6
	10—At New Jersey	114	88	12-6
	11—Seattle	96	87	13-6
	13—At Chicago	89	99—	13-7
	14—Boston	111	101	14-7
	17—New Jersey	102	94	15-7
	21—Utah	106	97	16-7
	23—At Minnesota	97	91	17-7
	26—San Antonio	89	118—	17-8
	28—Indiana	*115	106	18-8
Jan.	2—Cleveland	103	110—	18-9
	4—At Washington	113	99	19-9
	5—Phoenix	*108	104	20-9
	7—Atlanta	94	109—	20-10
	8—At Boston	95	99—	20-11
	11—Boston	100	96	21-11
	14—At Orlando	115	111	22-11
	15—Portland	91	96—	22-12
	17—At Milwaukee	85	90—	22-13
	18—At Cleveland	106	108—	22-14
	20—Indiana	105	97	23-14
	22—At Philadelphia	109	119—	23-15
	24—At Golden State	114	109	24-15
	25—At L.A. Clippers	100	93	25-15
	27—At Utah	97	80	26-15
	29—Washington	101	89	27-15
	31—At Washington	*125	114	28-15
Feb.	2—Golden State	113	120—	28-16
	4—Miami	122	91	29-16
	6—Houston	102	85	30-16
	12—At Indiana	111	104	31-16
	13—At Chicago	85	106—	31-17
	15—At Chicago	98	99—	31-18
	17—At Miami	104	102	32-18
	18—Sacramento	110	97	33-18
	20—Cleveland	89	92—	33-19
	22—Denver	98	87	34-19
	24—At Phoenix	95	104—	34-20
	26—At L.A. Lakers	68	81—	34-21
	27—At Sacramento	*109	110—	34-22
	29—Minnesota	103	87	35-22
Mar.	1—At New Jersey	75	90—	35-23
	3—Dallas	102	83	36-23
	5—L.A. Clippers	101	91	37-23
	7—Charlotte	107	78	38-23
	9—At Philadelphia	111	99	39-23
	10—L.A. Lakers	104	106—	39-24
	14—New Jersey	*94	96—	39-25
	17—At Orlando	99	86	40-25
	19—Milwaukee	96	92	41-25
	21—Miami	105	88	42-25
	24—Orlando	126	117	43-25
	26—At Denver	106	104	44-25
	28—At Seattle	92	87	45-25
	29—At Portland	107	96	46-25
	31—Chicago	90	96—	46-26
Apr.	2—At Charlotte	117	96	47-26
	3—Atlanta	115	94	48-26
	5—At Cleveland	93	97—	48-27
	7—At Detroit	94	103—	48-28
	8—At Boston	89	93—	48-29
	10—Philadelphia	115	99	49-29
	12—At Detroit	61	72—	49-30
	14—Washington	93	90	50-30
	15—At Atlanta	94	95—	50-31
	18—At Milwaukee	114	103	51-31

*Denotes overtime game.

1992-93 SCHEDULE

Nov.	Fri.	6—At Atlanta
	Sat.	7—Philadelphia
	Tue.	10—New Jersey
	Fri.	13—At Washington
	Sat.	14—Boston
	Mon.	16—At Portland
	Tue.	17—At Seattle
	Thu.	19—At L.A. Clippers
	Sat.	21—Orlando
	Tue.	24—Washington
	Wed.	25—At Minnesota
	Sat.	28—Chicago
	Sun.	29—At Detroit
Dec.	Tue.	1—Portland
	Thu.	3—At Cleveland
	Sat.	5—Milwaukee
	Tue.	8—Seattle
	Thu.	10—Charlotte
	Sat.	12—Detroit
	Mon.	14—Denver
	Tue.	15—At New Jersey
	Fri.	18—At Boston
	Sat.	19—Miami
	Fri.	25—At Chicago
	Sat.	26—At Milwaukee
	Tue.	29—Indiana
	Wed.	30—At Indiana
Jan.	Sat.	2—L.A. Clippers
	Tue.	5—Cleveland
	Fri.	8—At Orlando
	Sun.	10—Boston
	Tue.	12—At Sacramento
	Wed.	13—At Denver
	Fri.	15—At Dallas
	Sat.	16—At Houston
	Mon.	18—Phoenix
	Wed.	20—Charlotte
	Fri.	22—At Philadelphia
	Tue.	26—Philadelphia
	Thu.	28—Atlanta
Feb.	Tue.	2—Washington
	Thu.	4—Golden State
	Fri.	5—At Miami
	Sun.	7—Miami
	Mon.	8—At Philadelphia
	Thu.	11—Houston
	Fri.	12—At Chicago
	Sun.	14—At Orlando
	Tue.	16—Dallas
	Wed.	17—At Charlotte
	Tue.	23—Minnesota
	Wed.	24—At Milwaukee
	Fri.	26—At Detroit
	Sun.	28—At New Jersey
Mar.	Tue.	2—Atlanta
	Thu.	4—Utah
	Mon.	8—Orlando
	Wed.	10—L.A. Lakers
	Fri.	12—At Washington
	Sat.	13—Indiana
	Tue.	16—Milwaukee
	Thu.	18—At Cleveland
	Sun.	21—San Antonio
	Tue.	23—At Phoenix
	Thu.	25—At Utah
	Fri.	26—At L.A. Lakers
	Sun.	28—At Golden State
	Tue.	30—Sacramento
Apr.	Thu.	1—Cleveland
	Fri.	2—At Miami
	Sun.	4—At San Antonio
	Tue.	6—At Atlanta
	Thu.	8—Boston
	Sun.	11—At Boston
	Tue.	13—Washington
	Wed.	14—At Charlotte
	Fri.	16—At Indiana
	Sat.	17—Detroit
	Tue.	20—At Miami
	Wed.	21—New Jersey
	Fri.	23—At Philadelphia
	Sun.	25—Chicago

ORLANDO MAGIC

Office: One Magic Place, Orlando Arena, Orlando, FL 32801-1114

Telephone: (407) 649-3200

Chairman—Rich DeVos
President/Chief Executive Officer—Dick DeVos
General Manager/Chief Operating Officer—Pat Williams
Exec. Vice President/Asst. General Manager—Jack Swope
Vice President of Basketball Operations—Bob Vander Weide
Director of Player Personnel—John Gabriel
Head Coach—Matt Guokas
Assistant Coach—Brian Hill
Trainer—Lenny Currier
Director of Sponsorship/Broadcast Sales—Edgar Allen
Director of Box Office Operations—Ashleigh Bizzelle
Director of Marketing—Cari Coats
Director of Broadcasting—John Cook
Director of Finance/Business Manager—Danny Durso
Director of Novelty Sales—Kathy Farkas
Director of Publicity/Media Relations—Alex Martins
Advertising Manager—Carol Beeler
Controller—Scott Herring
Office Manager—Betty Johnson
Assistant Director of Box Office Operations—Mike Marini
Promotions Manager—Jodie Pennington
Assistant Controllers—Amy Racicot, Sylvia Pagan
Assistant Director of Publicity/Media Relations—Travis Stanley, Traci Blue
Executive Assistant to the General Manager—Marlin Ferrell
Broadcast Coordinator—Dennis Neumann
Strength & Flexibility Coach—David Oliver
Equipment Manager—Rodney Powell
Video Scout—Tom Sterner
Sponsorship Sales—Brian Crews, Chris D'Orso, Ralph Gray, John Payne
Promotions/Publicity Coordinator—Mike Burch
Marketing Coordinator—Darla Hancock
Box Office Representatives—Cathy Deiter, Bill Mauger, Joe Whitehurst
Administrative Assistants—Jo Carol Flohr, Barbara Jones, Toni Sandberg, Page Willner, Mary Woods
Talent Network—Curly Neal, Mike Stevens
Home Court—Orlando Arena (15,151, built in 1989)
Team Colors—Electric Blue, Quick Silver and Magic Black
Television—WKCF-TV (Channel 18); Sunshine Network (cable), Chip Caray, Jack Givens
Radio—WDBO (580 AM) David Steele
Game Times—7:30 p.m., 2 p.m.

Richard M. DeVos

Pat Williams

Matt Guokas

ORLANDO MAGIC

1991-92 Record (Won 21, Lost 61)

Month	Date—Opponent			W-L
Nov.	1—New York	106	96	1-0
	2—At Philadelphia	122	115	2-0
	6—Washington	105	88	3-0
	7—At New York	100	128—	3-1
	9—At Chicago	76	107—	3-2
	12—At Washington	95	82	4-2
	13—Philadelphia	100	121—	4-3
	16—New Jersey	102	100	5-3
	20—Utah	102	107—	5-4
	23—Sacramento	93	95—	5-5
	26—L.A. Lakers	87	98—	5-6
	27—At Boston	92	101—	5-7
	29—At Cleveland	104	115—	5-8
	30—Miami	105	99	6-8
Dec.	4—Portland	115	124—	6-9
	6—Phoenix	105	122—	6-10
	7—Charlotte	95	109—	6-11
	10—At Utah	103	122—	6-12
	12—At Sacramento	100	106—	6-13
	14—At Golden State	107	128—	6-14
	15—At L.A. Clippers	104	119—	6-15
	17—Boston	98	105—	6-16
	19—Milwaukee	87	95—	6-17
	22—Houston	94	99—	6-18
	23—At Miami	102	113—	6-19
	26—Detroit	100	112—	6-20
	27—At Detroit	94	106—	6-21
	29—San Antonio	87	96—	6-22
	30—At New Jersey	112	122—	6-23
Jan.	4—At Denver	91	93—	6-24
	7—At Portland	89	104—	6-25
	8—At Seattle	104	103	7-25
	10—At Phoenix	107	118—	7-26
	12—At L.A. Lakers	99	112—	7-27
	14—New York	111	115—	7-28
	17—At Indiana	127	120	8-28
	19—At Milwaukee	98	108—	8-29
	21—Minnesota	105	92	9-29
	22—At Boston	95	107—	9-30
	24—Dallas	121	103	10-30
	25—Cleveland	99	96	11-30
	28—Seattle	97	102—	11-31
	30—At Cleveland	98	115—	11-32
	31—At Philadelphia	88	112—	11-33
Feb.	2—At Washington	104	114—	11-34
	3—Golden State	114	122—	11-35
	5—At Minnesota	109	102	12-35
	6—At Atlanta	112	123—	12-36
	11—Indiana	98	100—	12-37
	14—Atlanta	107	112—	12-38
	16—Milwaukee	118	104	13-38
	18—At Detroit	95	117—	13-39
	19—Chicago	99	112—	13-40
	21—Detroit	100	114—	13-41
	22—At Charlotte	110	130—	13-42
	26—Philadelphia	95	89	14-42
	28—At Indiana	109	114—	14-43
Mar.	1—L.A. Clippers	96	101—	14-44
	3—Washington	93	106—	14-45
	4—At Boston	100	125—	14-46
	6—At Milwaukee	102	124—	14-47
	8—Boston	93	111—	14-48
	10—Denver	82	89—	14-49
	13—Indiana	98	97	15-49
	14—Chicago	96	112—	15-50
	17—New York	86	99—	15-51
	18—At Atlanta	99	96	16-51
	21—At Chicago	111	108	17-51
	24—At New York	117	126—	17-52
	25—Cleveland	96	106—	17-53
	28—Miami	100	109—	17-54
	30—At Charlotte	112	123—	17-55
Apr.	1—At Dallas	89	102—	17-56
	3—At San Antonio	°113	106	18-56
	4—At Houston	101	110—	18-57
	7—Charlotte	135	110	19-57
	9—Atlanta	96	94	20-57
	11—At Miami	101	105—	20-58
	13—New Jersey	104	110—	20-59
	15—Philadelphia	102	99	21-59
	16—At Washington	106	119—	21-60
	18—At New Jersey	111	127—	21-61

°Denotes overtime game.

1992-93 SCHEDULE

Nov.	Fri.	6—Miami
	Sat.	7—At Washington
	Tue.	10—Charlotte
	Thu.	12—Washington
	Sat.	14—At New Jersey
	Wed.	18—At Philadelphia
	Thu.	19—Golden State
	Sat.	21—At New York
	Wed.	25—Houston
	Fri.	27—At Indiana
	Sat.	28—Cleveland
Dec.	Tue.	1—At Seattle
	Thu.	3—At L.A. Clippers
	Sat.	5—At Golden State
	Tue.	8—Boston
	Wed.	9—At Detroit
	Fri.	11—Phoenix
	Tue.	15—Philadelphia
	Thu.	17—Sacramento
	Sat.	19—At Atlanta
	Tue.	22—Utah
	Sat.	26—At Miami
	Mon.	28—Milwaukee
	Wed.	30—L.A. Lakers
Jan.	Sat.	2—Detroit
	Tue.	5—New Jersey
	Fri.	8—New York
	Sat.	9—Indiana
	Tue.	12—Chicago
	Fri.	15—At Boston
	Sat.	16—At Chicago
	Mon.	18—At Philadelphia
	Fri.	22—Miami
	Sat.	23—Dallas
	Tue.	26—Atlanta
	Thu.	28—At Cleveland
	Fri.	29—Boston
Feb.	Mon.	1—At Sacramento
	Tue.	2—At L.A. Lakers
	Fri.	5—At Portland
	Sun.	7—At Phoenix
	Mon.	8—At Utah
	Wed.	10—Cleveland
	Thu.	11—At Charlotte
	Sun.	14—New York
	Tue.	16—At Detroit
	Wed.	17—Denver
	Tue.	23—Portland
	Thu.	25—Chicago
	Fri.	26—At Washington
	Sun.	28—San Antonio
Mar.	Tue.	2—Minnesota
	Thu.	4—At New Jersey
	Fri.	5—At Milwaukee
	Sun.	7—L.A. Clippers
	Mon.	8—At New York
	Wed.	10—Indiana
	Fri.	12—At Atlanta
	Sun.	14—Seattle
	Tue.	16—At Houston
	Wed.	17—At Dallas
	Fri.	19—At San Antonio
	Sat.	20—At Denver
	Tue.	23—Miami
	Fri.	26—At Chicago
	Sat.	27—New Jersey
	Tue.	30—Detroit
Apr.	Thu.	1—Charlotte
	Fri.	2—At Indiana
	Sun.	4—At Miami
	Tue.	6—Philadelphia
	Wed.	7—At Charlotte
	Fri.	9—At Minnesota
	Sat.	10—At Milwaukee
	Tue.	13—Milwaukee
	Thu.	15—At Philadelphia
	Fri.	16—At Cleveland
	Sun.	18—Boston
	Tue.	20—Washington
	Wed.	21—At Boston
	Fri.	23—At New Jersey
	Sat.	24—Atlanta

PHILADELPHIA 76ers

Office: Veterans Stadium, P.O. Box 25040, Philadelphia, PA 19147-0240

Telephone: (215) 339-7600

President—Harold Katz
Vice President—David Katz
General Manager—Jim Lynam
Head Coach—Doug Moe
Assistant Coaches—Fred Carter, David Moe, Tony DiLeo (Scout)
Player Personnel Director—Gene Shue
Trainer—Mike Abdenour
Equipment Manager—Allen Lumpkin, Sr.
Team Physician—Dr. Jack McPhilemy
Business Manager—Gerry Ryan
Controller—Andy Speiser
Director of Marketing—Alan Sharavsky
Director of Broadcast Sales—Fred Liedman
Director of Promotions—Toni Amendolia-Carelli
Director of Ticket Sales—Karen Gallagher
Director of Public Relations/Publicity—Zack Hill
Director of Group Sales—Ron Dick
Director of Statistical Information—Harvey Pollack
Sales Manager—Joel Doliner
Assistant Public Relations Director—Marty Mack
Assistant Marketing Director—Amy Cummins
Assistant Promotions Director—Dawn Mycock
Assistant Controller—Pat DeMarco
Box Office Manager—Pat Thornton
Office Manager—Marlene Barnes
Admin. Assistants—Barbara Bunker, Jeanette Edwards, Mary Purcell, Jodi Silverman
Account Executives—Anet Baghdasarian, Julius Banzet, Tim Curran, Nina McElroy,
Rocco Piccone Jr., Dean DiPietro, Steve Jacobs, J. Scott Loft, Mary McCrossen,
Sherri Miller, Steve Smith, Dan Waskow
Home Court—The Spectrum (18,168, built in 1967)
Team Colors—Red, White and Blue
Television—PRISM (cable), Jon Gurevitch, Jack Ramsay;
SportsChannel Philadelphia (cable) Marc Zumoff, Steve Mix;
WPHL (Channel 17), Greg Gumbel, Steve Mix
Radio—WIP (610 AM) Jim Kozimor
Game Time—7:30 p.m.

Harold Katz

Jim Lynam

Doug Moe

PHILADELPHIA 76ers

1991-92 Record (Won 35, Lost 47)

Date	Opponent	Score	Opp	W-L
Nov.	1—At Chicago	90	110—	0-1
	2—Orlando	115	122—	0-2
	5—At Washington	107	106	1-2
	6—New Jersey	107	105	2-2
	8—Golden State	126	116	3-2
	11—Milwaukee	102	99	4-2
	13—At Orlando	121	100	5-2
	15—At Boston	97	122—	5-3
	16—At Detroit	89	86	6-3
	20—Miami	114	107	7-3
	22—Atlanta	92	99—	7-4
	23—At New York	92	100—	7-5
	26—Cleveland	91	95—	7-6
	27—At Cleveland	97	107—	7-7
	29—At Miami	92	95—	7-8
	30—L.A. Lakers	91	93—	7-9
Dec.	3—At New Jersey	86	88—	7-10
	6—Portland	°105	102	8-10
	7—Chicago	103	100	9-10
	11—Denver	88	98—	9-11
	13—At Minnesota	104	95	10-11
	14—Seattle	104	95	11-11
	18—Utah	105	107—	11-12
	20—Miami	127	99	12-12
	21—At Milwaukee	97	110—	12-13
	23—Charlotte	106	114—	12-14
	26—At Indiana	113	110	13-14
	28—At L.A. Clippers	95	102—	13-15
	30—At Denver	93	109—	13-16
Jan.	2—At Sacramento	110	114—	13-17
	4—At Seattle	112	93	14-17
	5—At Portland	102	115—	14-18
	8—Houston	114	104	15-18
	10—L.A. Clippers	102	90	16-18
	11—At Cleveland	102	108—	16-19
	14—At Chicago	80	103—	16-20
	17—At Boston	95	98—	16-21
	18—At Washington	105	101	17-21
	20—Washington	99	91	18-21
	22—New York	119	109	19-21
	24—Minnesota	119	86	20-21
	25—New Jersey	115	94	21-21
	28—At Atlanta	109	110—	21-22
	29—Indiana	90	115—	21-23
	31—Orlando	112	88	22-23
Feb.	1—Boston	126	110	23-23
	5—Cleveland	°108	110—	23-24
	11—At Miami	114	102	24-24
	12—New Jersey	87	102—	24-25
	14—At New Jersey	99	107—	24-26
	16—Detroit	83	90—	24-27
	18—At Dallas	94	90	25-27
	20—At Houston	101	110—	25-28
	21—At San Antonio	90	100—	25-29
	24—Sacramento	108	96	26-29
	26—At Orlando	89	95—	26-30
	27—At Charlotte	84	136—	26-31
	29—At Washington	101	92	27-31
Mar.	4—Atlanta	107	102	28-31
	6—Dallas	88	86	29-31
	8—Chicago	99	103—	29-32
	9—New York	99	111—	29-33
	11—Indiana	111	93	30-33
	13—Phoenix	104	108—	30-34
	14—At Milwaukee	105	110—	30-35
	18—At Detroit	85	91—	30-36
	19—Charlotte	°116	123—	30-37
	22—At Indiana	100	108—	30-38
	23—San Antonio	105	92	31-38
	25—At Utah	94	100—	31-39
	27—At Phoenix	113	117—	31-40
	29—At L.A. Lakers	88	117—	31-41
	30—At Golden State	106	124—	31-42
Apr.	1—Miami	108	91	32-42
	4—At Atlanta	126	121	33-42
	8—Detroit	71	89—	33-43
	10—At New York	99	115—	33-44
	12—Milwaukee	90	94—	33-45
	14—Boston	94	99—	33-46
	15—At Orlando	99	102—	33-47
	17—At Charlotte	122	112	34-47
	18—Washington	111	104	35-47

°Denotes overtime game.

1992-93 SCHEDULE

Nov.	Fri.	6—New Jersey
	Sat.	7—At New York
	Wed.	11—At Indiana
	Fri.	13—At Boston
	Wed.	18—Orlando
	Fri.	20—Miami
	Sat.	21—At New Jersey
	Tue.	24—At Charlotte
	Wed.	25—Atlanta
	Fri.	27—Milwaukee
	Sat.	28—Boston
Dec.	Wed.	2—San Antonio
	Fri.	4—Detroit
	Sat.	5—At Detroit
	Wed.	9—Seattle
	Fri.	11—L.A. Clippers
	Sat.	12—At Atlanta
	Tue.	15—At Orlando
	Wed.	16—Cleveland
	Fri.	18—Utah
	Sat.	19—At Chicago
	Mon.	21—Indiana
	Sat.	26—At Portland
	Sun.	27—At L.A. Clippers
	Wed.	30—At Utah
Jan.	Sat.	2—At Sacramento
	Wed.	6—New Jersey
	Fri.	8—At Washington
	Sat.	9—Chicago
	Tue.	12—At Indiana
	Wed.	13—Golden State
	Fri.	15—At New Jersey
	Sat.	16—Detroit
	Mon.	18—Orlando
	Wed.	20—At Miami
	Fri.	22—New York
	Sat.	23—At Milwaukee
	Tue.	26—At New York
	Wed.	27—Indiana
	Fri.	29—Washington
	Sat.	30—At Atlanta
Feb.	Wed.	3—Charlotte
	Fri.	5—At Boston
	Mon.	8—New York
	Wed.	10—Houston
	Fri.	12—At Denver
	Sat.	13—At Dallas
	Tue.	16—At Houston
	Thu.	18—At San Antonio
	Tue.	23—At Detroit
	Wed.	24—Atlanta
	Fri.	26—Milwaukee
Mar.	Mon.	1—At Golden State
	Wed.	3—At Phoenix
	Fri.	5—At L.A. Lakers
	Sat.	6—At Seattle
	Mon.	8—At Minnesota
	Wed.	10—Boston
	Fri.	12—L.A. Lakers
	Sat.	13—Denver
	Tue.	16—At Cleveland
	Wed.	17—Washington
	Fri.	19—Dallas
	Sat.	20—At Milwaukee
	Wed.	24—Chicago
	Fri.	26—Cleveland
	Sun.	28—Phoenix
	Tue.	30—At New Jersey
	Wed.	31—At Boston
Apr.	Fri.	2—Portland
	Sun.	4—Sacramento
	Tue.	6—At Orlando
	Wed.	7—At Washington
	Fri.	9—Charlotte
	Sat.	10—At Miami
	Mon.	12—At Charlotte
	Thu.	15—Orlando
	Sun.	18—Minnesota
	Tue.	20—At Chicago
	Wed.	21—Miami
	Fri.	23—New York
	Sun.	25—At Cleveland

PHOENIX SUNS

Office: P.O. Box 1369, Phoenix, AZ 85001
Telephone: (602) 379-7900

President & Chief Executive Officer—Jerry Colangelo
Senior Executive Vice President—Lowell (Cotton) Fitzsimmons
Vice President/Director of Player Personnel—Dick Van Arsdale
Vice President, Marketing—Harvey T. Shank
Vice President, Public Relations—Thomas P. Ambrose
Vice President/Chief Operating Officer—Richard H. Dozer
Head Coach—Paul Westphal
Assistant Coaches—Lionel Hollins, Scotty Robertson
Chief Scout—Dick Percudani
NBA Scout—Todd Quinter
Video Coordinator/Scout—Garrick Barr
Assistant Director of Player Personnel—Bryan Colangelo
Trainer—Joe Proski
Team Physician—Dr. Richard Emerson
Team Physician Emeritus—Dr. Paul Steingard
Strength & Conditioning Coach—Robin Pound
Assistant to the President—Ruth Dryjanski
Controller—Kelvin R. Hansen
Director of Ticket Operations—Dianne Yaeger
Assistant Director of Ticket Operations—Mary McGlynn
Ticket Manager—Gordon Volden
Sales Manager—Blake Edwards
Director of Corporate Sales—Stephen Weber
Media Relations Director—Julie Fie
Media Relations Assistant—Seth Sulka
Director of Game Operations—Kenny Glenn
Merchandising Manager—Jason Cohn
Marketing Assistant—Marliss Stahle
Publications Director—Jim Brewer
Speakers Bureau Coordinator—Neal Walk
Community Relations Manager—TBA
Community Relations Representative—Connie Hawkins
Home Court—America West Arena (Approx. 19,000, dedicated in 1992)
Team Colors—Purple, Orange and Copper
Television—KUTP (Channel 45), Al McCoy, Cotton Fitzsimmons
Dimension Cable (ASPN), George Allen
Radio—KTAR (620 AM), Al McCoy, Cotton Fitzsimmons
Game Times—Mon.-Sat. 7:30 p.m., Sun. TBA

Jerry Colangelo   **Paul Westphal**

PHOENIX SUNS

1991-92 Record (Won 53, Lost 29)   **1992-93 SCHEDULE**

Date	Opponent			W-L
Nov.	1—At Seattle	99	95	1-0
	2—At Portland	100	76	2-0
	5—Indiana	105	111—	2-1
	6—At L.A. Clippers	87	111—	2-2
	8—L.A. Lakers	113	85	3-2
	9—At Houston	95	96—	3-3
	12—At Golden State	116	119—	3-4
	13—Boston	111	117—	3-5
	15—Atlanta	115	119—	3-6
	16—At Dallas	88	91—	3-7
	19—At L.A. Lakers	95	103—	3-8
	20—Denver	113	97	4-8
	22—L.A. Clippers	105	97	5-8
	26—At Sacramento	89	104—	5-9
	27—Sacramento	141	100	6-9
	29—Charlotte	131	111	7-9
	30—Utah	°134	125	8-9
Dec.	3—At Minnesota	101	95	9-9
	4—At Indiana	114	108	10-9
	6—At Orlando	122	105	11-9
	7—At Miami	109	108	12-9
	10—Detroit	102	93	13-9
	13—At San Antonio	112	107	14-9
	18—At Denver	109	123—	14-10
	20—San Antonio	116	91	15-10
	22—At L.A. Lakers	100	88	16-10
	26—Miami	132	104	17-10
	28—Dallas	121	103	18-10
	30—At Detroit	110	103	19-10
Jan.	2—At Atlanta	105	123—	19-11
	4—At Charlotte	108	113—	19-12
	5—At New York	°104	108—	19-13
	8—Denver	135	114	20-13
	10—Orlando	118	107	21-13
	11—Golden State	130	118	22-13
	13—Minnesota	131	111	23-13
	15—At Sacramento	128	111	24-13
	17—Sacramento	134	94	25-13
	19—Portland	°132	128	26-13
	21—At Chicago	102	108—	26-14
	22—At New Jersey	104	106—	26-15
	24—At Boston	100	93	27-15
	25—At Washington	121	115	28-15
	29—New Jersey	128	95	29-15
	31—At Utah	°116	117—	29-16
Feb.	1—Houston	106	92	30-16
	3—L.A. Lakers	113	104	31-16
	5—Chicago	126	114	32-16
	12—Portland	97	107—	32-17
	14—At L.A. Clippers	97	104—	32-18
	15—Washington	124	98	33-18
	17—At Seattle	96	98—	33-19
	18—At Portland	116	129—	33-20
	21—At Golden State	115	123—	33-21
	22—L.A. Clippers	130	112	34-21
	24—New York	104	95	35-21
	26—Cleveland	103	100	36-21
	28—At Dallas	107	115—	36-22
Mar.	1—Utah	114	109	37-22
	3—Houston	°112	107	38-22
	5—Seattle	118	105	39-22
	7—At San Antonio	109	122—	39-23
	10—At Cleveland	100	102—	39-24
	12—At Milwaukee	106	100	40-24
	13—At Philadelphia	108	104	41-24
	15—At Minnesota	118	113	42-24
	17—Dallas	92	81	43-24
	20—L.A. Clippers	101	114—	43-25
	21—Minnesota	121	105	44-25
	25—Milwaukee	132	104	45-25
	27—Philadelphia	117	113	46-25
	28—At Denver	121	101	47-25
	31—Portland	128	111	48-25
Apr.	2—Golden State	109	105	49-25
	3—At Utah	94	113—	49-26
	5—At L.A. Lakers	104	109—	49-27
	7—Sacramento	103	101	50-27
	9—At Seattle	104	119—	50-28
	11—At Golden State	125	134—	50-29
	14—Seattle	122	100	51-29
	16—San Antonio	121	101	52-29
	19—At Houston	100	97	53-29

°Denotes overtime game.

1992-93 SCHEDULE

Nov.	Sat.	7—L.A. Clippers
	Tue.	10—At Portland
	Thu.	12—At Utah
	Sat.	14—At Minnesota
	Mon.	16—Seattle
	Wed.	18—Sacramento
	Sat.	21—At L.A. Clippers
	Sun.	22—Chicago
	Wed.	25—Portland
	Fri.	27—Golden State
	Sat.	28—At Golden State
Dec.	Tue.	1—Charlotte
	Fri.	4—L.A. Lakers
	Sun.	6—At Milwaukee
	Tue.	8—At New Jersey
	Wed.	9—At Charlotte
	Fri.	11—At Orlando
	Sat.	12—At Miami
	Tue.	15—Washington
	Fri.	18—At L.A. Lakers
	Tue.	22—Golden State
	Wed.	23—At Denver
	Sat.	26—Seattle
	Sun.	27—Denver
	Wed.	30—Houston
Jan.	Sun.	3—At San Antonio
	Tue.	5—At Houston
	Thu.	7—At Dallas
	Tue.	12—At Seattle
	Thu.	14—At Sacramento
	Fri.	15—Miami
	Mon.	18—At New York
	Wed.	20—At Cleveland
	Fri.	22—At Washington
	Sat.	23—At Atlanta
	Mon.	25—At Detroit
	Wed.	27—At Minnesota
	Fri.	29—San Antonio
	Sat.	30—Dallas
Feb.	Tue.	2—At L.A. Clippers
	Wed.	3—Minnesota
	Fri.	5—L.A. Lakers
	Sun.	7—Orlando
	Wed.	10—L.A. Clippers
	Thu.	11—At Golden State
	Sat.	13—At Seattle
	Tue.	16—Boston
	Thu.	18—Atlanta
	Tue.	23—At San Antonio
	Thu.	25—At Houston
	Fri.	26—Utah
	Sun.	28—Cleveland
Mar.	Tue.	2—At Portland
	Wed.	3—Philadelphia
	Fri.	5—Sacramento
	Sat.	6—At Dallas
	Tue.	9—At Sacramento
	Wed.	10—Golden State
	Fri.	12—Dallas
	Sat.	13—New Jersey
	Wed.	17—Portland
	Fri.	19—Detroit
	Sun.	21—Indiana
	Tue.	23—New York
	Wed.	24—At L.A. Lakers
	Fri.	26—Milwaukee
	Sun.	28—At Philadelphia
	Tue.	30—At Chicago
Apr.	Fri.	2—At Boston
	Sun.	4—At Indiana
	Tue.	6—L.A. Lakers
	Thu.	8—At Sacramento
	Fri.	9—Denver
	Sun.	11—Utah
	Mon.	12—At L.A. Clippers
	Wed.	14—Minnesota
	Fri.	16—Seattle
	Sat.	17—At Utah
	Mon.	19—Houston
	Thu.	22—At Portland
	Sat.	24—San Antonio
	Sun.	25—At Denver

PORTLAND TRAIL BLAZERS

Office: Port of Portland Bldg., 700 N.E. Multnomah St., Suite 600, Portland, OR 97232
Telephone: (503) 234-9291

Governor—Paul Allen
Vice Chairman—Bert Kolde
President—Harry Glickman
Chairman Emeritus—Larry Weinberg
Senior Vice President, Operations—Geoff Petrie
Senior Vice President, Marketing—Marshall Glickman
Vice President, General Counsel—Mike Fennell
Vice President, Player Personnel—Brad Greenberg
Vice President, Finance—Charlene Hodges
Vice President, Administration—Berlyn Hodges
Vice President, Sponsor Sales—Mick Dowers
Vice President, Special Events—Wally Scales

Head Coach—Rick Adelman
Assistant Coaches—Jack Schalow, John Wetzel, Kip Motta
Senior Scouting Consultant—Morris "Bucky" Buckwalter
Trainer—Mike Shimensky
Video Coordinator—Dan Burke
Equipment Manager—Roger Sabrowski
Director, Sports Communications—John Lashway
Assistant Director, Sports Communications—John Christensen
Director, Corporate Communications—Christee Sweeney
Director, Sponsor Services—Dennis Paye
Director, Marketing Services—Pat Lafferty
Director, Game Operations—Jose Ayala
Controller—Linda Glasser
Ticket Manager—Lori Ryan-Spencer
Executive Producer/Director—George Wasch
Coordinating Producer—J.R. Hellman
Computer Systems Engineer—Ken Spencer
Executive Assistant—Linda Temple
Administrative Assistants—Sandy Chisholm, Ann Carroll
Team Physician—Dr. Robert Cook
Home Court—Memorial Cbliseum (12,888, built in 1960)
Team Colors—Scarlet, Black and White
Television—KGW (Channel 8), Steve Jones, TBA
Radio—KEX (1190 AM), Bill Schonely, Mike Rice
Game Times—Mon.-Fri. 7:30 p.m., Sat., Sun. and Holidays 5 p.m. or 7 p.m.

Paul Allen   **Rick Adelman**

PORTLAND TRAIL BLAZERS

1991-92 Record (Won 57, Lost 25)

				W-L
Nov.	1—Cleveland	117	106	1-0
	2—Phoenix	76	100—	1-1
	5—At Houston	99	106—	1-2
	6—At San Antonio	93	119—	1-3
	8—Indiana	121	96	2-3
	10—Boston	116	90	3-3
	12—Denver	120	82	4-3
	15—At Minnesota	107	102	5-3
	16—At Denver	111	122—	5-4
	19—L.A. Clippers	132	112	6-4
	21—At L.A. Clippers	106	91	7-4
	22—Golden State	112	116—	7-5
	24—San Antonio	116	111	8-5
	26—Milwaukee	*107	98	9-5
	29—Chicago	**114	116—	9-6
Dec.	1—Washington	91	87	10-6
	3—At Miami	124	94	11-6
	4—At Orlando	124	115	12-6
	6—At Philadelphia	*102	105—	12-7
	7—At Indiana	115	112	13-7
	10—Houston	106	108—	13-8
	13—Detroit	103	113—	13-9
	14—Sacramento	115	110	14-9
	16—Minnesota	119	104	15-9
	20—At Golden State	118	123—	15-10
	22—Seattle	96	87	16-10
	26—Dallas	113	88	17-10
	28—At L.A. Lakers	98	88	18-10
	29—Miami	129	96	19-10
Jan.	2—At Utah	103	107—	19-11
	5—Philadelphia	115	102	20-11
	7—Orlando	104	89	21-11
	10—At Detroit	81	86—	21-12
	11—At Charlotte	115	93	22-12
	14—At Cleveland	121	114	23-12
	15—At New York	96	91	24-12
	17—Charlotte	120	104	25-12
	19—At Phoenix	*128	132—	25-13
	21—L.A. Lakers	131	92	26-13
	23—At Seattle	113	109	27-13
	24—Atlanta	125	117	28-13
	28—At Golden State	*124	116	29-13
	31—New Jersey	113	108	30-13
Feb.	2—Sacramento	147	107	31-13
	4—At San Antonio	88	95—	31-14
	6—At Dallas	103	98	32-14
	11—Denver	121	112	33-14
	12—At Phoenix	107	97	34-14
	14—At Sacramento	107	106	35-14
	16—L.A. Clippers	106	107—	35-15
	18—Phoenix	129	116	36-15
	21—At L.A. Clippers	123	116	37-15
	22—At Seattle	104	113—	37-16
	24—Utah	110	107	38-16
	27—At New York	96	98—	38-17
	28—At Washington	117	96	39-17
Mar.	1—At Chicago	91	111—	39-18
	3—L.A. Lakers	105	101	40-18
	4—At Denver	129	100	41-18
	6—Sacramento	114	106	42-18
	8—Seattle	109	97	43-18
	10—At Milwaukee	126	112	44-18
	11—At Minnesota	124	113	45-18
	13—At Atlanta	106	95	46-18
	15—At Boston	**148	152—	46-19
	17—Minnesota	111	91	47-19
	18—At L.A. Lakers	98	93	48-19
	21—At Utah	77	95—	48-20
	24—Dallas	109	83	49-20
	26—At Sacramento	128	106	50-20
	28—Houston	115	95	51-20
	29—New York	96	107—	51-21
	31—At Phoenix	111	128—	51-22
Apr.	2—Utah	118	86	52-22
	5—At Golden State	130	122	53-22
	7—Golden State	110	101	54-22
	9—At L.A. Clippers	100	106—	54-23
	10—Seattle	113	106	55-23
	12—San Antonio	123	97	56-23
	14—At Houston	96	108—	56-24
	15—At Dallas	100	94	57-24
	18—L.A. Lakers	101	109—	57-25

*Denotes overtime game.

1992-93 SCHEDULE

Nov.	Sun.	8—Denver
	Tue.	10—Phoenix
	Fri.	13—Cleveland
	Sat.	14—At Golden State
	Mon.	16—New York
	Fri.	20—At Sacramento
	Sun.	22—Detroit
	Tue.	24—San Antonio
	Wed.	25—At Phoenix
	Fri.	27—L.A. Lakers
	Sun.	29—Sacramento
Dec.	Tue.	1—At New York
	Wed.	2—At Indiana
	Fri.	4—At Chicago
	Sat.	5—At Cleveland
	Tue.	8—Milwaukee
	Wed.	9—At L.A. Lakers
	Fri.	11—Indiana
	Sun.	13—Washington
	Wed.	16—At Denver
	Fri.	18—At Seattle
	Sun.	20—Golden State
	Tue.	22—Seattle
	Sat.	26—Philadelphia
	Wed.	30—Dallas
Jan.	Sat.	2—Utah
	Sun.	3—Houston
	Tue.	5—At Dallas
	Thu.	7—At Houston
	Sat.	9—At San Antonio
	Tue.	12—Denver
	Thu.	14—Miami
	Fri.	15—At L.A. Lakers
	Sun.	17—Seattle
	Tue.	19—At Milwaukee
	Wed.	20—At Minnesota
	Fri.	22—Sacramento
	Sun.	24—At Utah
	Tue.	26—Golden State
	Sat.	30—At Seattle
Feb.	Tue.	2—Minnesota
	Fri.	5—Orlando
	Sun.	7—Chicago
	Fri.	12—At L.A. Clippers
	Sun.	14—L.A. Clippers
	Tue.	16—Atlanta
	Thu.	18—L.A. Lakers
	Tue.	23—At Orlando
	Wed.	24—At Miami
	Fri.	26—At New Jersey
	Sun.	28—At Boston
Mar.	Tue.	2—Phoenix
	Thu.	4—At Denver
	Fri.	5—Charlotte
	Sun.	7—At Golden State
	Wed.	10—At Dallas
	Thu.	11—At Houston
	Sat.	13—At San Antonio
	Mon.	15—New Jersey
	Wed.	17—At Phoenix
	Fri.	19—Houston
	Sun.	21—Boston
	Tue.	23—At Seattle
	Thu.	25—At Sacramento
	Fri.	26—L.A. Clippers
	Sun.	28—At Charlotte
	Mon.	29—At Atlanta
	Wed.	31—At Detroit
Apr.	Fri.	2—At Philadelphia
	Sat.	3—At Washington
	Tue.	6—Utah
	Thu.	8—Dallas
	Fri.	9—At L.A. Lakers
	Sun.	11—Minnesota
	Tue.	13—L.A. Clippers
	Thu.	15—At Utah
	Fri.	16—At Minnesota
	Sun.	18—San Antonio
	Tue.	20—Golden State
	Thu.	22—Phoenix
	Fri.	23—At Sacramento
	Sun.	25—At L.A. Clippers

SACRAMENTO KINGS

Office: One Sports Parkway, Sacramento, CA 95834
Telephone: (916) 928-0000

Owners of General Partner—Jim Thomas, Eli Broad, Rob Maguire,
Ned Fox, Rick Gilchrist
Managing General Partner—Jim Thomas
President—Rick Benner
General Manager—Jerry Reynolds
Head Coach—Garry St. Jean
Vice President Arena Operations—Mike Duncan
Vice President Concessions Operations—Tom Petersen
Vice President Marketing—Joe Marsalla
Vice President Finance—Steve Schmidt
Vice President Business Development—Michael McCullough
Assistant Coaches—Mike Schuler, Dave Wohl, Eddie Jordan
Trainer—Bill Jones
Chief Scout—Scotty Stirling
Director of Public Relations—TBA
Director of Ticket Sales and Customer Relations—Philip Hess
Director of Broadcasting—Michael Hansen
Director of Promotions and Game Operations—Sally Simonds
Business Manager—Marie Hurt
Assistant Director of Public Relations—Troy Hanson
Player Relations/Equipment Manager—Larry Heslin
Basketball Assistant—Liz Schneider
Marketing Assistant—Debora Parker
Marketing Staff—Art Collins, Steve Ebbage, Mike Klemin
Arena Operations—Betty Ansel, Bob Canfield, Bernie Church, Mike Cleveland,
John DeGrace, Patty Greenwalt, Tim Higgins, Michelle Holzmer, Susan Laudi,
Leslie Roath, Steve Schneider, Paula Thompson
Concessions Personnel—Roger Castillo, Ted Hansen, Rosemary Kittle, Lee Lehman,
Tim Mitchell, Tracy Newton, Lisa Paterno, Bruce Richards, John Sanders, Roger Toy
Receptionists—Shannon Rogers, Mona Klotz
Team Physicians—Dr. Richard Marder, Dr. James J. Castles
Strength Coach—Al Biancani
Home Court—ARCO Arena (17,280, built in 1988)
Team Colors—Red, White and Blue
Television—KRBK (Channel 31), Grant Napear, Ted Green
Radio—KFBK (1530 AM), Gary Gerould, Tim Roye
Game Times—Mon.-Sat. 7:30 p.m., Sun. 6 p.m.

Jim Thomas

Jerry Reynolds

Garry St. Jean

SACRAMENTO KINGS

1991-92 Record (Won 29, Lost 53)

				W-L
Nov.	1—L.A. Clippers	94	90	1-0
	2—At Golden State	91	153—	1-1
	5—At Seattle	87	98—	1-2
	6—Indiana	112	102	2-2
	9—Minnesota	80	84—	2-3
	11—At Utah	90	106—	2-4
	12—Boston	103	126—	2-5
	14—Atlanta	98	96	3-5
	16—Houston	93	102—	3-6
	19—At New Jersey	118	122—	3-7
	20—At Atlanta	104	116—	3-8
	22—At Miami	112	118—	3-9
	23—At Orlando	95	93	4-9
	26—Phoenix	104	89	5-9
	27—At Phoenix	100	141—	5-10
	30—Chicago	102	118—	5-11
Dec.	3—San Antonio	99	94	6-11
	7—At Golden State	120	124—	6-12
	10—L.A. Lakers	90	92—	6-13
	12—Orlando	106	100	7-13
	14—At Portland	110	115—	7-14
	15—At L.A. Lakers	94	110—	7-15
	19—At Houston	102	109—	7-16
	21—At Dallas	85	109—	7-17
	23—At San Antonio	90	101—	7-18
	26—Seattle	106	115—	7-19
	28—At Chicago	118	127—	7-20
	30—At Minnesota	117	109	8-20
Jan.	2—Philadelphia	114	110	9-20
	4—Miami	98	110—	9-21
	6—At Boston	108	110—	9-22
	8—At Detroit	95	114—	9-23
	9—At Charlotte	96	109—	9-24
	11—At Milwaukee	*106	105	10-24
	13—At Denver	109	111—	10-25
	15—Phoenix	111	128—	10-26
	17—At Phoenix	94	134—	10-27
	18—Charlotte	119	113	11-27
	21—Denver	94	85	12-27
	23—L.A. Lakers	105	108—	12-28
	24—At L.A. Lakers	92	95—	12-29
	28—New Jersey	124	118	13-29
	29—At Utah	105	124—	13-30
	31—L.A. Clippers	112	109	14-30
Feb.	2—At Portland	107	147—	14-31
	3—Dallas	99	95	15-31
	5—Utah	100	98	16-31
	12—Washington	98	97	17-31
	14—Portland	106	107—	17-32
	16—San Antonio	106	112—	17-33
	18—At New York	97	110—	17-34
	19—At Indiana	115	129—	17-35
	21—At Cleveland	102	119—	17-36
	23—At Washington	124	117	18-36
	24—At Philadelphia	96	108—	18-37
	27—New York	*110	109	19-37
	29—Seattle	115	110	20-37
Mar.	2—Golden State	98	118—	20-38
	4—Cleveland	108	109—	20-39
	6—At Portland	106	114—	20-40
	8—Houston	108	109—	20-41
	10—L.A. Clippers	109	120—	20-42
	12—Utah	103	114—	20-43
	14—Detroit	83	89—	20-44
	15—At L.A. Clippers	105	131—	20-45
	17—At Denver	100	118—	20-46
	18—At San Antonio	89	118—	20-47
	20—At Dallas	125	96	21-47
	21—At Houston	100	97	22-47
	24—Milwaukee	113	102	23-47
	26—Portland	106	128—	23-48
	29—At Minnesota	112	86	24-48
	31—Golden State	**136	148—	24-49
Apr.	2—Seattle	103	111—	24-50
	3—At Golden State	*116	124—	24-51
	5—Dallas	103	89	25-51
	7—At Phoenix	101	103—	25-52
	9—Denver	124	107	26-52
	11—Minnesota	114	94	27-52
	14—At L.A. Clippers	103	97	28-52
	16—L.A. Lakers	102	94	29-52
	17—At Seattle	106	130—	29-53

*Denotes overtime game.

1992-93 SCHEDULE

Nov.	Fri.	6—San Antonio
	Sun.	8—At L.A. Lakers
	Tue.	10—L.A. Clippers
	Wed.	11—At L.A. Clippers
	Sat.	14—At Seattle
	Sun.	15—Cleveland
	Tue.	17—At Houston
	Wed.	18—At Phoenix
	Fri.	20—Portland
	Mon.	23—Seattle
	Wed.	25—At Denver
	Sat.	28—New Jersey
	Sun.	29—At Portland
Dec.	Tue.	1—L.A. Lakers
	Fri.	4—Charlotte
	Tue.	8—Washington
	Thu.	10—Indiana
	Sat.	12—Golden State
	Tue.	15—At Miami
	Thu.	17—At Orlando
	Fri.	18—At Cleveland
	Sun.	20—At New Jersey
	Tue.	22—At Milwaukee
	Wed.	23—At Minnesota
	Sun.	27—Boston
	Tue.	29—Dallas
Jan.	Sat.	2—Philadelphia
	Tue.	5—Denver
	Fri.	8—At L.A. Lakers
	Sat.	9—Miami
	Tue.	12—New York
	Thu.	14—Phoenix
	Sat.	16—At Utah
	Mon.	18—At Golden State
	Tue.	19—Houston
	Fri.	22—At Portland
	Sat.	23—Minnesota
	Mon.	25—At Atlanta
	Wed.	27—At Charlotte
	Fri.	29—At Dallas
	Sat.	30—At San Antonio
Feb.	Mon.	1—Orlando
	Wed.	3—Chicago
	Fri.	5—At Denver
	Sat.	6—At L.A. Clippers
	Tue.	9—Utah
	Thu.	11—Atlanta
	Sat.	13—Golden State
	Mon.	15—At Chicago
	Wed.	17—At Indiana
	Thu.	18—At Minnesota
	Tue.	23—At L.A. Clippers
	Wed.	24—L.A. Lakers
	Fri.	26—Seattle
	Sat.	27—At Utah
Mar.	Wed.	3—Houston
	Fri.	5—At Phoenix
	Sat.	6—At Houston
	Tue.	9—Phoenix
	Thu.	11—Minnesota
	Sat.	13—Dallas
	Tue.	16—Detroit
	Thu.	18—At Seattle
	Fri.	19—Golden State
	Tue.	23—L.A. Clippers
	Thu.	25—Portland
	Sat.	27—Milwaukee
	Mon.	29—At Boston
	Tue.	30—At New York
Apr.	Thu.	1—At Washington
	Fri.	2—At Detroit
	Sun.	4—At Philadelphia
	Tue.	6—Denver
	Thu.	8—Phoenix
	Fri.	9—At Seattle
	Tue.	13—San Antonio
	Fri.	16—At San Antonio
	Sat.	17—At Dallas
	Tue.	20—Utah
	Wed.	21—At Golden State
	Fri.	23—Portland
	Sat.	24—At L.A. Lakers

SAN ANTONIO SPURS

Office: 600 E. Market St., Suite 102, San Antonio, TX 78205
Telephone: (512) 554-7787

Chairman—Red McCombs
President—Gary Woods
Executive Vice President—Russ Bookbinder
Vice President of Basketball Operations—Bob Bass
Head Coach—Jerry Tarkanian
Assistant Coaches—Ron Adams, Rex Hughes,
Tom Thibodeau, Ed Manning
Trainer/Director of Travel—John Andersen
Basketball Assistant—Yvonne Quinn
Vice President of Broadcasting—Lawrence Payne
Broadcast Sales Executives—Jesse Mendiola, Jay Wisse
Broadcast Producer/Assistant—Mike Kickirillo, Darr Weeks
Director of Media Services—Dave Senko
Media Services Department—Tom James, Becky Salini
Community Relations Asst./Rep.—Niki Simpson, George Gervin
Director of Marketing—Bruce Guthrie
Promotions Manager/Coordinator—Cheryl Jividen, Lori McDowell
Director of Sales—Joe Clark
Account Executives—J. Altman, B. Beasley, R. Davis, C. Domhoff, B. Houston, C. Valdez
Retail Merchandising Manager—Kenton Nelson
Controller—Julie Daleiden
Executive Assistant—Diane Flack
Ticket Manager—Jeanne Adams
Staff—Todd Caflisch, Ian Campos, John Coleman, Kelli Collier, Moe Guerrero,
Grace Guzman, Ed Hunt, Kim Kellel, Melinda Keller, Cathi Ladd, Carla Martinez,
Susan Maxwell, Anthony Mitchell, Eleanor Ortiz, Pat Quinn, Clinton Rathmell,
Mary Ann Sanchez, Tina Sandlin, Evelyn Vargas, Dawn Vordenbaum
Team Physician—Dr. Jack Henry
Home Court—HemisFair Arena (16,057, built in 1968)
Team Colors—Metallic Silver, Black, Teal/Fuschia/Orange
Radio—WOAI (1200 AM, English), Jay Howard;
KSAH (720 AM, Spanish), Armando Quintero
Television—KSAT 12, HSE (Cable 23), Dave Barnett, Greg Simmons
Game Time—7:30 p.m.

Red McCombs   **Gary Woods**   **Jerry Tarkanian**

SAN ANTONIO SPURS

1991-92 Record (Won 47, Lost 35)

				W-L
Nov.	1—Dallas	140	99	1-0
	3—At Seattle	106	98	2-0
	5—At Denver	96	97—	2-1
	6—Portland	119	93	3-1
	8—Cleveland	°107	101	4-1
	13—L.A. Clippers	107	93	5-1
	16—New York	106	89	6-1
	20—Minnesota	113	106	7-1
	22—At L.A. Lakers	96	98—	7-2
	24—At Portland	111	116—	7-3
	27—New Jersey	106	100	8-3
	29—At Atlanta	88	85	9-3
	30—Seattle	119	101	10-3
Dec.	3—At Sacramento	94	99—	10-4
	4—At L.A. Clippers	81	92—	10-5
	6—Utah	92	93—	10-6
	8—At Milwaukee	83	102—	10-7
	10—At Indiana	102	109—	10-8
	11—At Minnesota	98	85	11-8
	13—Phoenix	107	112—	11-9
	14—At Houston	107	100	12-9
	17—At Dallas	98	87	13-9
	18—Washington	93	96—	13-10
	20—At Phoenix	91	116—	13-11
	23—Sacramento	101	90	14-11
	26—At New York	118	89	15-11
	27—At Cleveland	97	103—	15-12
	29—At Orlando	96	87	16-12
	30—At Washington	84	94—	16-13
Jan.	4—Houston	°°110	112—	16-14
	6—Detroit	100	90	17-14
	8—L.A. Lakers	103	87	18-14
	10—At Golden State	128	120	19-14
	11—At Denver	96	85	20-14
	14—Golden State	123	124—	20-15
	16—At Minnesota	125	111	21-15
	17—At Chicago	96	102—	21-16
	19—At Boston	89	98—	21-17
	21—L.A. Clippers	114	100	22-17
	22—At Utah	98	100—	22-18
	24—Milwaukee	115	86	23-18
	28—Chicago	109	104	24-18
	29—At Dallas	108	93	25-18
	31—Minnesota	103	101	26-18
Feb.	4—Portland	95	88	27-18
	6—Indiana	106	117—	27-19
	11—Boston	100	84	28-19
	13—At Golden State	94	109—	28-20
	14—At Seattle	91	108—	28-21
	16—At Sacramento	112	106	29-21
	17—At L.A. Clippers	110	124—	29-22
	19—At Minnesota	113	103	30-22
	21—Philadelphia	100	90	31-22
	23—At Houston	83	90—	31-23
	25—Miami	123	101	32-23
	27—Golden State	124	103	33-23
	29—Denver	115	112	34-23
Mar.	3—At Minnesota	103	102	35-23
	4—At Utah	93	102—	35-24
	7—Phoenix	122	109	36-24
	8—At Dallas	93	81	37-24
	10—Atlanta	103	92	38-24
	12—Houston	104	98	39-24
	14—Utah	113	106	40-24
	16—Charlotte	112	117—	40-25
	18—Sacramento	118	89	41-25
	21—Seattle	101	96	42-25
	23—At Philadelphia	92	105—	42-26
	25—At Charlotte	108	113—	42-27
	27—At Miami	101	118—	42-28
	29—At Detroit	103	107—	42-29
	30—At New Jersey	109	117—	42-30
Apr.	1—L.A. Lakers	104	86	43-30
	3—Orlando	°106	113—	43-31
	5—At Denver	90	87	44-31
	7—Houston	92	95—	44-32
	9—At L.A. Lakers	102	94	45-32
	12—At Portland	97	123—	45-33
	14—Dallas	120	108	46-33
	16—At Phoenix	101	121—	46-34
	17—Denver	108	94	47-34
	19—Utah	90	101—	47-35

°Denotes overtime game.

1992-93 SCHEDULE

Nov.	Fri.	6—At Sacramento
	Sat.	7—At Denver
	Tue.	10—Milwaukee
	Thu.	12—Atlanta
	Sat.	14—Houston
	Tue.	17—Cleveland
	Thu.	19—Dallas
	Sat.	21—At Houston
	Tue.	24—At Portland
	Wed.	25—At Utah
	Sat.	28—Seattle
Dec.	Tue.	1—At Washington
	Wed.	2—At Philadelphia
	Fri.	4—At New Jersey
	Sat.	5—At Atlanta
	Tue.	8—Utah
	Thu.	10—Miami
	Sat.	12—At Dallas
	Tue.	15—L.A. Lakers
	Thu.	17—At Houston
	Fri.	18—Dallas
	Tue.	22—Denver
	Fri.	25—At L.A. Clippers
	Sat.	26—At L.A. Lakers
	Mon.	28—Golden State
	Wed.	30—At Denver
Jan.	Sun.	3—Phoenix
	Tue.	5—At Utah
	Thu.	7—Utah
	Sat.	9—Portland
	Mon.	11—At Detroit
	Wed.	13—At Minnesota
	Thu.	14—At Milwaukee
	Sat.	16—Charlotte
	Tue.	19—Denver
	Fri.	22—Detroit
	Sun.	24—Chicago
	Wed.	27—At Seattle
	Fri.	29—At Phoenix
	Sat.	30—Sacramento
Feb.	Tue.	2—New Jersey
	Thu.	4—Indiana
	Sat.	6—Minnesota
	Tue.	9—L.A. Clippers
	Thu.	11—Washington
	Sat.	13—Boston
	Mon.	15—At L.A. Clippers
	Tue.	16—At Golden State
	Thu.	18—Philadelphia
	Tue.	23—Phoenix
	Thu.	25—At Charlotte
	Fri.	26—At Miami
	Sun.	28—At Orlando
Mar.	Tue.	2—At Indiana
	Wed.	3—At Boston
	Fri.	5—At Chicago
	Sat.	6—At Minnesota
	Tue.	9—Dallas
	Sat.	13—Portland
	Mon.	15—L.A. Lakers
	Wed.	17—At L.A. Lakers
	Fri.	19—Orlando
	Sun.	21—At New York
	Tue.	23—At Cleveland
	Wed.	24—At Minnesota
	Fri.	26—Utah
	Sun.	28—At Dallas
	Tue.	30—Seattle
	Wed.	31—At Utah
Apr.	Fri.	2—Minnesota
	Sun.	4—New York
	Tue.	6—Golden State
	Thu.	8—L.A. Clippers
	Sat.	10—At Houston
	Tue.	13—At Sacramento
	Wed.	14—At Golden State
	Fri.	16—Sacramento
	Sun.	18—At Portland
	Mon.	19—At Seattle
	Thu.	22—Denver
	Sat.	24—At Phoenix
	Sun.	25—Houston

SEATTLE SUPERSONICS
Office: 190 Queen Anne Ave. N., Box C 900911, Seattle, WA 98109-9711
Telephone: (206) 281-5800

Chairman of the Board—Barry Ackerley
President—Bob Whitsitt
Executive Vice President—John Dresel
Vice President/Marketing & Promotions—Kim Cleworth
Asst. Vice President/Marketing & Promotions—Janet Magelby
Vice President/Sponsorship Sales & Broadcasting—Gary Spinnell
Head Coach—George Karl
Assistant Coaches—Bob Kloppenburg, Tim Grgurich
Scout—Mark Warkentien
Trainer—Frank Furtado
Strength & Conditioning Coach—Bob Medina
Director of Public/Media Relations—TBA
Assistant Director of Public/Media Relations—Bill Boehlke
Public/Media Relations Assistant—Mary Rucker
Editor-in-Chief, Sonics Fastbreak Magazine—Tim Quam
Controller—Krista Mann
Sponsorship Sales Manager—Scott Patrick
Marketing Coordinator—Anne Marie Mastor
Sponsor Account Executive—Douglas Ramsey
Director of Game Operations—Jeff Olsen
Director of Community Relations—Jim Marsh
Assistant Director of Game Operations/Community Relations—Rob Martin
Director of Broadcasting—Rick Turner
Director of Sales—Bob Boustead
Assistant Director of Sales—Sharon Wortman
Ticket Manager—Kathy Loomis
Executive Assistant—Sarah Furtado
Administrative Assistant/Office Manager—Julie Wilder
Receptionist—Melissa Robinson
Team Physician (Orthopedist)—Dr. Richard Zorn
Internist Consultant—Dr. Howard Maron
Team Dentist—Dr. Jack Nichols
Team Ophthalmologist—Dr. Walter Rotkis
Home Court—The Coliseum (14,252, built in 1962)
Team Colors—Green and Yellow
Television—Prime Sports Northwest (Channel 6), TBA, Kevin Calabro
Radio—KJR (950 AM), Kevin Calabro
Game Time—7 p.m.

SEATTLE SUPERSONICS

Barry Ackerley

Bob Whitsitt

George Karl

SEATTLE SUPERSONICS

1991-92 Record (Won 47, Lost 35)

Date	Opponent			W-L
Nov.	1—Phoenix	95	99—	0-1
	3—San Antonio	98	106—	0-2
	5—Sacramento	98	87	1-2
	7—At Utah	103	95	2-2
	9—Indiana	118	111	3-2
	14—At Cleveland	°109	115—	3-3
	15—At Indiana	124	108	4-3
	17—At Minnesota	101	91	5-3
	19—At Washington	113	106	6-3
	20—At Detroit	91	86	7-3
	22—Chicago	°109	112—	7-4
	24—At L.A. Clippers	86	89—	7-5
	26—Golden State	°136	130	8-5
	29—At Denver	90	101—	8-6
	30—At San Antonio	101	119—	8-7
Dec.	3—Washington	91	90	9-7
	6—Minnesota	96	94	10-7
	7—Dallas	104	101	11-7
	10—At Chicago	103	108—	11-8
	11—At New York	87	96—	11-9
	13—At Boston	97	117—	11-10
	14—At Philadelphia	95	104—	11-11
	17—L.A. Clippers	116	99	12-11
	19—Denver	119	106	13-11
	21—Golden State	120	112	14-11
	22—At Portland	87	96—	14-12
	26—At Sacramento	115	106	15-12
	27—Boston	87	110—	15-13
Jan.	2—Miami	°113	109	16-13
	4—Philadelphia	93	112—	16-14
	7—At Denver	106	99	17-14
	8—Orlando	103	104—	17-15
	10—At Dallas	94	82	18-15
	11—At Houston	115	119—	18-16
	13—At L.A. Clippers	94	98—	18-17
	14—Charlotte	°116	117—	18-18
	16—At Minnesota	101	98	19-18
	18—L.A. Lakers	112	108	20-18
	20—At L.A. Lakers	110	116—	20-19
	21—Atlanta	119	128—	20-20
	23—Portland	109	113—	20-21
	25—Utah	103	104—	20-22
	28—At Orlando	102	97	21-22
	29—At Miami	114	119—	21-23
	31—At Charlotte	122	105	22-23
Feb.	2—At Milwaukee	106	122—	22-24
	3—At Atlanta	112	110	23-24
	5—At New Jersey	95	85	24-24
	11—Houston	105	99	25-24
	14—San Antonio	108	91	26-24
	15—At Golden State	122	140—	26-25
	17—Phoenix	98	96	27-25
	20—L.A. Lakers	105	103	28-25
	22—Portland	113	104	29-25
	24—At Minnesota	106	91	30-25
	27—At Utah	°130	124	31-25
	29—At Sacramento	110	115—	31-26
Mar.	1—Cleveland	113	107	32-26
	3—Denver	111	92	33-26
	5—At Phoenix	105	118—	33-27
	7—New Jersey	109	98	34-27
	8—At Portland	97	109—	34-28
	10—Detroit	92	98—	34-29
	11—At L.A. Clippers	104	96	35-29
	15—Dallas	109	100	36-29
	17—Golden State	107	119—	36-30
	19—At Houston	112	91	37-30
	21—At San Antonio	96	101—	37-31
	22—At Dallas	113	105	38-31
	24—Houston	128	106	39-31
	27—Milwaukee	96	95	40-31
	28—New York	87	92—	40-32
	31—Utah	122	103	41-32
Apr.	2—At Sacramento	111	103	42-32
	3—At L.A. Lakers	96	91	43-32
	7—L.A. Lakers	117	88	44-32
	9—Phoenix	119	104	45-32
	10—At Portland	106	113—	45-33
	12—Minnesota	126	116	46-33
	14—At Phoenix	100	122—	46-34
	17—Sacramento	130	106	47-34
	19—At Golden State	106	108—	47-35

°Denotes overtime game.

1992-93 SCHEDULE

Nov.	Fri.	6—At Houston°
	Sat.	7—Houston°
	Thu.	12—L.A. Lakers
	Sat.	14—Sacramento
	Mon.	16—At Phoenix
	Tue.	17—New York
	Thu.	19—Chicago
	Sat.	21—Detroit
	Mon.	23—At Sacramento
	Tue.	24—New Jersey
	Fri.	27—At Dallas
	Sat.	28—At San Antonio
Dec.	Tue.	1—Orlando
	Thu.	3—Dallas
	Sat.	5—Minnesota
	Tue.	8—At New York
	Wed.	9—At Philadelphia
	Fri.	11—At Boston
	Sat.	12—At Cleveland
	Tue.	15—Milwaukee
	Fri.	18—Portland
	Sat.	19—L.A. Clippers
	Tue.	22—At Portland
	Wed.	23—At L.A. Lakers
	Sat.	26—At Phoenix
	Tue.	29—Boston
Jan.	Sat.	2—Denver
	Tue.	5—Golden State
	Fri.	8—At Minnesota
	Sat.	9—At Denver
	Tue.	12—Phoenix
	Thu.	14—At Utah
	Fri.	15—L.A. Clippers
	Sun.	17—At Portland
	Mon.	18—Utah
	Wed.	20—At L.A. Lakers
	Fri.	22—At Golden State
	Sun.	24—At L.A. Clippers
	Wed.	27—San Antonio
	Sat.	30—Portland
Feb.	Mon.	1—At Charlotte
	Tue.	2—At Atlanta
	Thu.	4—At New Jersey
	Sat.	6—At Washington
	Sun.	7—At Detroit
	Tue.	9—Denver
	Thu.	11—Utah
	Sat.	13—Phoenix
	Tue.	16—Washington
	Thu.	18—At Golden State
	Tue.	23—At Denver
	Wed.	24—At Minnesota
	Fri.	26—At Sacramento
	Sat.	27—Golden State
Mar.	Tue.	2—Cleveland
	Thu.	4—Charlotte
	Sat.	6—Philadelphia
	Mon.	8—At Indiana
	Tue.	9—At Chicago
	Thu.	11—At Milwaukee
	Sat.	13—At Miami
	Sun.	14—At Orlando
	Tue.	16—Miami
	Thu.	18—Sacramento
	Fri.	19—At Utah
	Sun.	21—At Houston
	Tue.	23—Portland
	Thu.	25—Indiana
	Sat.	27—L.A. Clippers
	Tue.	30—At San Antonio
	Wed.	31—At Dallas
Apr.	Sat.	3—Atlanta
	Tue.	6—Dallas
	Fri.	9—Sacramento
	Sun.	11—At L.A. Lakers
	Tue.	13—Minnesota
	Fri.	16—At Phoenix
	Sat.	17—Houston
	Mon.	19—San Antonio
	Thu.	22—At L.A. Clippers
	Fri.	23—L.A. Lakers
	Sun.	25—At Golden State

°Game played in Japan.

UTAH JAZZ

Office: Delta Center, 301 West So. Temple, Salt Lake City, UT 84101

Telephone: (801) 325-2500

Owner—Larry H. Miller
General Manager—R. Tim Howells
President—Frank Layden
Director of Basketball Operations—Scott Layden
Executive Assistant—Judy Adams
Head Coach—Jerry Sloan
Assistant Coaches—Phil Johnson, Gordon Chiesa, David Fredman
Trainer—Don Sparks
Assistant Trainer/Equipment Manager—Terry Clark
Vice President Public Relations/Special Events—David Allred
Vice President Sales—Larry Baum
Vice President Marketing—Jay Francis
Vice President Finance/Retail Operations—Bob Hyde
Vice President Broadcasting/National Sales Manager—Randy Rigby
Director of Broadcasting—Brian Douglas
Director of Promotions—Grant Harrison
Director of Local Sales—Mike Snarr
Director of Media Services—Kim Turner
Director of Customer Service Center—Nola Wayman
Director of Youth Basketball Programs—David Wilson
Broadcast Coordinator—J'Neil Romero
Controller—John Larson
Team Counsel/Basketball Operations—Philip Marantz
Team Counsel/Business Operations—Dennis Haslam
Team Orthopedic Surgeons—Dr. Lyle Mason, Dr. Gordon Affleck, Dr. Robert W. Jordan
Team Internist—Dr. Russell B. Shields
Home Court—Delta Center (19,911, built in 1991)
Team Colors—Purple, Green and Gold
Television—KSTU (Channel 13-Fox), Rod Hundley, Ron Boone
Prime Sports Network—Rod Hundley, Ron Boone
Radio—KISN (570 AM), Rod Hundley, Ron Boone
Game Time—7 p.m.

Larry H. Miller

R. Tim Howells

Jerry Sloan

UTAH JAZZ

	1991-92 Record (Won 55, Lost 27)			
				W-L
Nov.	1—At Minnesota	112	97	1-0
	2—At Indiana	112	127—	1-1
	5—At Atlanta	94	98—	1-2
	7—Seattle	95	103—	1-3
	9—L.A. Clippers	101	84	2-3
	11—Sacramento	106	90	3-3
	13—At New Jersey	98	92	4-3
	15—At Detroit	115	123—	4-4
	16—At Washington	107	98	5-4
	19—At Miami	91	111—	5-5
	20—At Orlando	107	102	6-5
	22—Denver	121	96	7-5
	23—At Dallas	°109	121—	7-6
	27—Charlotte	113	107	8-6
	29—Golden State	135	108	9-6
	30—At Phoenix	°125	134—	9-7
Dec.	3—At Golden State	103	108—	9-8
	4—Washington	101	74	10-8
	6—At San Antonio	93	92	11-8
	7—At Houston	96	91	12-8
	10—Orlando	122	103	13-8
	11—At L.A. Lakers	101	95	14-8
	13—At L.A. Clippers	°101	102—	14-9
	14—Detroit	102	100	15-9
	17—At Charlotte	122	102	16-9
	18—At Philadelphia	107	105	17-9
	20—At Boston	101	112—	17-10
	21—At New York	97	106—	17-11
	23—At Cleveland	112	113—	17-12
	26—L.A. Clippers	123	115	18-12
	28—Miami	128	103	19-12
Jan.	2—Portland	107	103	20-12
	4—Dallas	113	78	21-12
	6—Indiana	124	108	22-12
	8—At Milwaukee	98	99—	22-13
	10—At Chicago	90	105—	22-14
	11—At Minnesota	96	101—	22-15
	14—Minnesota	116	110	23-15
	16—Atlanta	116	111	24-15
	18—Houston	108	80	25-15
	22—San Antonio	100	98	26-15
	23—At Denver	111	115—	26-16
	25—At Seattle	104	103	27-16
	27—New York	80	97—	27-17
	29—Sacramento	124	105	28-17
	31—Phoenix	°117	116	29-17
Feb.	1—At Dallas	104	90	30-17
	3—Chicago	°°°126	123	31-17
	5—At Sacramento	98	100—	31-18
	11—Cleveland	111	109	32-18
	13—L.A. Lakers	97	91	33-18
	15—Denver	106	93	34-18
	17—Boston	88	83	35-18
	19—Dallas	118	96	36-18
	21—Houston	124	97	37-18
	24—At Portland	107	110—	37-19
	25—At L.A. Clippers	106	101	38-19
	27—Seattle	°124	130—	38-20
Mar.	1—At Phoenix	109	114—	38-21
	3—At Golden State	123	101	39-21
	4—San Antonio	102	93	40-21
	6—New Jersey	117	96	41-21
	8—At Denver	112	88	42-21
	12—At Sacramento	114	103	43-21
	14—At San Antonio	106	113—	43-22
	15—At Houston	97	106—	43-23
	19—At Denver	115	100	44-23
	21—Portland	95	77	45-23
	25—Philadelphia	100	94	46-23
	27—L.A. Lakers	92	103—	46-24
	30—Milwaukee	120	100	47-24
	31—At Seattle	103	122—	47-25
Apr.	2—At Portland	86	118—	47-26
	3—Phoenix	113	94	48-26
	5—At Minnesota	91	93—	48-27
	7—At Denver	124	101	49-27
	9—Dallas	113	90	50-27
	11—At L.A. Lakers	93	90	51-27
	13—At Golden State	138	99	52-27
	15—Houston	130	98	53-27
	17—Minnesota	120	106	54-27
	19—At San Antonio	101	90	55-27

°Denotes overtime game.

		1992-93 SCHEDULE
Nov.	Fri.	6—Golden State
	Sat.	7—At Dallas
	Tue.	10—At Denver
	Thu.	12—Phoenix
	Sat.	14—L.A. Clippers
	Tue.	17—At New Jersey
	Wed.	18—At Boston
	Fri.	20—At Indiana
	Sat.	21—At Washington
	Wed.	25—San Antonio
	Fri.	27—New Jersey
	Sat.	28—At Houston
Dec.	Tue.	1—Dallas
	Thu.	3—Minnesota
	Sat.	5—Denver
	Tue.	8—At San Antonio
	Thu.	10—Washington
	Sat.	12—Milwaukee
	Wed.	16—At Charlotte
	Fri.	18—At Philadelphia
	Sat.	19—At Cleveland
	Tue.	22—At Orlando
	Wed.	23—At Miami
	Sat.	26—Boston
	Mon.	28—Minnesota
	Wed.	30—Philadelphia
Jan.	Sat.	2—At Portland
	Tue.	5—San Antonio
	Thu.	7—At San Antonio
	Sat.	9—At Dallas
	Sun.	10—At Houston
	Tue.	12—Miami
	Thu.	14—Seattle
	Sat.	16—Sacramento
	Mon.	18—At Seattle
	Wed.	20—At Golden State
	Fri.	22—L.A. Lakers
	Sun.	24—Portland
	Tue.	26—Cleveland
	Wed.	27—At L.A. Clippers
	Sat.	30—L.A. Clippers
Feb.	Mon.	1—Chicago
	Wed.	3—Denver
	Thu.	4—At L.A. Lakers
	Mon.	8—Orlando
	Tue.	9—At Sacramento
	Thu.	11—At Seattle
	Sat.	13—Atlanta
	Mon.	15—At Minnesota
	Wed.	17—At Chicago
	Thu.	18—At Milwaukee
	Tue.	23—Houston
	Wed.	24—At Golden State
	Fri.	26—At Phoenix
	Sat.	27—Sacramento
Mar.	Mon.	1—Charlotte
	Wed.	3—At Detroit
	Thu.	4—At New York
	Sat.	6—At Atlanta
	Tue.	9—Minnesota
	Sat.	13—At Houston
	Mon.	15—At Dallas
	Wed.	17—Detroit
	Fri.	19—Seattle
	Sat.	20—At L.A. Clippers
	Mon.	22—At Denver
	Tue.	23—Indiana
	Thu.	25—New York
	Fri.	26—At San Antonio
	Mon.	29—Denver
	Wed.	31—San Antonio
Apr.	Sun.	4—At L.A. Lakers
	Tue.	6—At Portland
	Thu.	8—Houston
	Sun.	11—At Phoenix
	Mon.	12—Dallas
	Thu.	15—Portland
	Sat.	17—Phoenix
	Tue.	20—At Sacramento
	Wed.	21—L.A. Lakers
	Fri.	23—Golden State
	Sun.	25—At Minnesota

WASHINGTON BULLETS

Office: Capital Centre, Landover, MD 20785

Telephone: (301) 773-2255

Chairman of the Board—Abe Pollin
Vice Chairman—Jerry Sachs
President—Susan O'Malley
Vice President/General Manager—John Nash
Vice President/Head Coach—Wes Unseld
Secretary and Legal Counsel—David Osnos
Assistant Coaches—Bill Blair, Jeff Bzdelik
Assistant General Manager—Chuck Douglas
Scout—Bill Gardiner
Trainer—John Lally
Strength and Conditioning Coach—Dennis Householder
Equipment Managers—Charlie Butler, Jerry Walters
Assistant to the General Manager—Rosemary Donohue
Assistant to the President—Ellen Ward
Assistant to the Head Coach—Joan Green
Vice President—Judy Holland
Vice President—Rick Moreland
Vice President of Sales—Dave Lanzi
Controller—Kathy Muth
Senior Director of Client Services—Rhonda Ballute
Director of Advertising/Promotions—Minerva Conrad
Director of Community Relations—Bonnie Downing
Director of Public Relations—Matt Williams
Area Sales Managers—Terry Dawkins, Ralph Rosello, Mark Schiponi, Ron Schneider
Assistant Director of Public Relations—Maureen Lewis
Assistant Director of Game Operations—Glenn Morrill
Assistant to the Controller—Joyce Freeman
Public Relations Assistant—Jim Delaney
Customer Service Representatives—Sharon Bouchard, Joe Moyer
Team Physicians—Dr. Steve Haas, Dr. Carl MacCartee
Home Court—Capital Centre (18,756, built in 1973)
Team Colors—Red, White and Blue
Radio—WTOP (1500 AM), Charlie Slowes
Television—WDCA (Channel 20), Mel Proctor, Phil Chenier, Al Koken;
Home Team Sports (cable), Mel Proctor, Phil Chenier, Al Koken
Game Times—Mon.-Sat. 7:30 p.m.; Sun. 1 p.m.

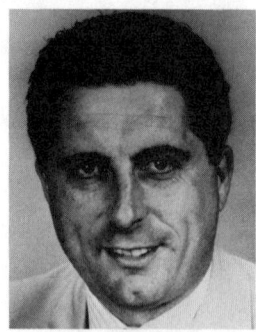

Susan O'Malley   **John Nash**   **Wes Unseld**

WASHINGTON BULLETS

1991-92 Record (Won 25, Lost 57)

Month	Game			W-L
Nov.	1—At Indiana	109	103	1-0
	2—Boston	126	118	2-0
	5—Philadelphia	106	107—	2-1
	6—At Orlando	88	105—	2-2
	9—Golden State	119	127—	2-3
	10—At Detroit	79	85—	2-4
	12—Orlando	82	95—	2-5
	13—At Minnesota	°119	114	3-5
	15—At New Jersey	°116	111	4-5
	16—Utah	98	107—	4-6
	19—Seattle	106	113—	4-7
	21—At Milwaukee	87	112—	4-8
	23—Atlanta	126	115	5-8
	25—At Boston	108	121—	5-9
	29—At L.A. Clippers	101	94	6-9
Dec.	1—At Portland	87	91—	6-10
	3—At Seattle	90	91—	6-11
	4—At Utah	74	101—	6-12
	6—Detroit	94	105—	6-13
	7—At Cleveland	97	99—	6-14
	12—Milwaukee	97	109—	6-15
	14—Chicago	100	113—	6-16
	17—At Houston	97	100—	6-17
	18—At San Antonio	96	93	7-17
	20—At Dallas	107	99	8-17
	21—At Denver	117	102	9-17
	27—Houston	100	107—	9-18
	28—Charlotte	129	124	10-18
	30—San Antonio	94	84	11-18
Jan.	3—At New Jersey	112	108	12-18
	4—New York	99	113—	12-19
	7—At Chicago	89	102—	12-20
	9—Cleveland	92	99—	12-21
	11—L.A. Clippers	107	96	13-21
	14—Indiana	°°127	118	14-21
	16—Miami	94	102—	14-22
	18—Philadelphia	101	105—	14-23
	20—At Philadelphia	91	99—	14-24
	22—At Miami	112	125—	14-25
	25—Phoenix	115	121—	14-26
	28—Boston	87	98—	14-27
	29—At New Jersey	89	101—	14-28
	31—New York	°114	125—	14-29
Feb.	2—Orlando	114	104	15-29
	4—At Charlotte	99	115—	15-30
	6—New Jersey	124	108	16-30
	11—At Golden State	127	139—	16-31
	12—At Sacramento	97	98—	16-32
	14—At L.A. Lakers	108	92	17-32
	15—At Phoenix	98	124—	17-33
	17—Atlanta	110	117—	17-34
	19—At Atlanta	°103	102	18-34
	21—Denver	99	106—	18-35
	23—Sacramento	117	124—	18-36
	26—At Chicago	103	122—	18-37
	28—Portland	96	117—	18-38
	29—Philadelphia	92	101—	18-39
Mar.	2—At Detroit	89	99—	18-40
	3—At Orlando	106	93	19-40
	5—Dallas	119	109	20-40
	7—Milwaukee	94	90	21-40
	8—At Miami	98	112—	21-41
	10—At Indiana	91	101—	21-42
	13—Minnesota	118	115	22-42
	14—L.A. Lakers	89	92—	22-43
	16—Cleveland	102	111—	22-44
	19—Chicago	100	106—	22-45
	20—At New Jersey	96	99—	22-46
	22—At Milwaukee	88	109—	22-47
	25—Indiana	109	131—	22-48
	26—At Atlanta	95	107—	22-49
	28—Charlotte	113	97	23-49
Apr.	1—At Boston	106	120—	23-50
	3—Detroit	119	85	24-50
	4—At Charlotte	109	118—	24-51
	7—At Miami	89	100—	24-52
	8—New Jersey	103	109—	24-53
	10—Miami	93	108—	24-54
	12—At Cleveland	91	114—	24-55
	14—At New York	90	93—	24-56
	16—Orlando	119	106	25-56
	18—At Philadelphia	104	111—	25-57

°Denotes overtime game.

1992-93 SCHEDULE

Nov.	Fri.	6—At Charlotte
	Sat.	7—Orlando
	Tue.	10—At Cleveland
	Thu.	12—At Orlando
	Fri.	13—New York
	Sun.	15—At New Jersey
	Tue.	17—Boston
	Fri.	20—At Minnesota
	Sat.	21—Utah
	Tue.	24—At New York
	Wed.	25—At Boston
	Fri.	27—Minnesota†
	Sat.	28—At Milwaukee
Dec.	Tue.	1—San Antonio
	Thu.	3—Milwaukee
	Sat.	5—Indiana
	Tue.	8—At Sacramento
	Thu.	10—At Utah
	Fri.	11—At L.A. Lakers
	Sun.	13—At Portland
	Tue.	15—At Phoenix
	Thu.	17—Chicago
	Sat.	19—Charlotte
	Wed.	23—At Chicago
	Sat.	26—Detroit†
	Mon.	28—Atlanta
	Wed.	30—At Detroit
Jan.	Sat.	2—Miami
	Tue.	5—At Atlanta
	Fri.	8—Philadelphia
	Sat.	9—At New Jersey
	Tue.	12—Milwaukee
	Wed.	13—At Boston
	Sat.	16—New Jersey†
	Mon.	18—Cleveland
	Tue.	19—At Indiana
	Fri.	22—Phoenix
	Sun.	24—L.A. Lakers
	Tue.	26—Miami
	Fri.	29—At Philadelphia
	Sat.	30—Charlotte
Feb.	Tue.	2—At New York
	Fri.	5—Golden State
	Sat.	6—Seattle
	Mon.	8—At Houston
	Wed.	10—At Dallas
	Thu.	11—At San Antonio
	Sat.	13—At Denver
	Sun.	14—At Golden State
	Tue.	16—At Seattle
	Thu.	18—At L.A. Clippers
	Tue.	23—At Atlanta
	Wed.	24—Indiana
	Fri.	26—Orlando
Mar.	Wed.	3—At Miami
	Thu.	4—L.A. Clippers
	Tue.	9—At Charlotte
	Wed.	10—Denver
	Fri.	12—New York
	Sat.	13—Cleveland†
	Wed.	17—At Philadelphia
	Fri.	19—At Chicago
	Sat.	20—Chicago
	Mon.	22—New Jersey
	Wed.	24—Dallas
	Fri.	26—Houston
	Sun.	28—At Boston°
	Mon.	29—At Milwaukee
	Wed.	31—At Indiana
Apr.	Thu.	1—Sacramento
	Sat.	3—Portland
	Tue.	6—At Detroit
	Wed.	7—At Cleveland
	Fri.	9—At Cleveland
	Sun.	11—Detroit
	Tue.	13—At New York
	Thu.	15—Miami
	Sat.	17—New Jersey
	Tue.	20—At Orlando
	Wed.	21—Atlanta
	Fri.	23—At Miami
	Sun.	25—Boston

°Game played in Hartford.
†Game played in Baltimore.

ROSTERS OF NBA CLUBS

ATLANTA HAWKS
Coach—Bob Weiss
Assistant coaches—Johnny Davis, Bob Weinhauer

No.	Name	Pos.	Hgt.	Wgt.	Birthdate	College
2	Stacey Augmon	G/F	6-8	205	8-1-68	UNLV
10	Elmer Bennett	G	6-0	171	2-13-70	Notre Dame
33	Duane Ferrell	F	6-7	215	2-28-65	Georgia Tech
25	Paul Graham	F	6-6	200	11-28-67	Ohio University
31	Adam Keefe	F	6-9	241	2-22-70	Stanford
32	Jon Koncak	C	7-0	250	5-17-63	Southern Methodist
1	Travis Mays	G	6-2	190	6-19-68	Texas
12	Rodney Monroe	G	6-3	185	4-16-68	North Carolina State
41	Blair Rasmussen	C	7-0	260	11-13-62	Oregon
22	Rumeal Robinson	G	6-2	200	11-13-66	Michigan
34	Jeff Sanders	F	6-8	240	1-14-66	Georgia Southern
11	Morlon Wiley	G	6-4	192	9-24-66	Long Beach State
21	Dominique Wilkins	F	6-8	215	1-12-60	Georgia
42	Kevin Willis	F/C	7-0	240	9-6-62	Michigan State

BOSTON CELTICS
Coach—Chris Ford
Assistant coaches—Don Casey, Jon Jennings

No.	Name	Pos.	Hgt.	Wgt.	Birthdate	College
5	John Bagley	G	6-0	205	4-23-60	Boston College
4	Jon Barry	G	6-5	195	7-25-69	Georgia Tech
7	Dee Brown	G	6-1	161	11-29-68	Jacksonville
20	Sherman Douglas	G	6-1	180	9-15-66	Syracuse
44	Rick Fox	G/F	6-7	231	7-24-69	North Carolina
34	Kevin Gamble	G/F	6-5	210	11-13-65	Iowa
53	Joe Kleine	C	7-0	271	1-4-62	Arkansas
35	Reggie Lewis	G/F	6-7	195	11-21-65	Northeastern
32	Kevin McHale	F/C	6-10	225	12-19-57	Minnesota
50	Darren Morningstar	C	6-10	235	4-22-69	Pittsburgh
00	Robert Parish	C	7-0	230	8-30-53	Centenary (La.)
54	Ed Pinckney	F	6-9	215	3-27-63	Villanova
11	Stojko Vrankovic	C	7-2	260	1-22-64	

CHARLOTTE HORNETS
Coach—Allan Bristow
Assistant coaches—T.R. Dunn, Bill Hanzlik

No.	Name	Pos.	Hgt.	Wgt.	Birthdate	College
25	Tony Bennett	G	6-0	175	6-1-69	Wis.-Green Bay
1	Tyrone Bogues	G	5-3	140	1-9-65	Wake Forest
30	Dell Curry	G	6-5	200	6-25-64	Virginia Tech
44	Kenny Gattison	F	6-8	252	5-23-64	Old Dominion
13	Kendall Gill	G	6-5	200	5-25-68	Illinois
42	Mike Gminski	C	6-11	260	8-3-59	Duke
20	Tom Hammonds	F	6-9	225	3-27-67	Georgia Tech
2	Larry Johnson	F	6-7	250	3-14-69	UNLV
9	Kevin Lynch	G/F	6-5	197	12-24-68	Minnesota
33	Alonzo Mourning	C	6-10	240	2-8-70	Georgetown
22	John Newman	F	6-7	190	11-28-63	Richmond
34	J.R. Reid	F/C	6-9	256	3-31-68	North Carolina

CHICAGO BULLS
Coach—Phil Jackson
Assistant coaches—John Bach, Jim Cleamons, Tex Winter

No.	Name	Pos.	Hgt.	Wgt.	Birthdate	College
10	B.J. Armstrong	G	6-2	175	9-9-67	Iowa
24	Bill Cartwright	C	7-1	245	7-30-57	San Francisco
54	Horace Grant	F	6-10	220	7-4-65	Clemson
20	Bobby Hansen	G	6-6	195	1-18-61	Iowa
	Byron Houston	F	6-7	250	11-22-69	Oklahoma State
23	Michael Jordan	G	6-6	198	2-17-63	North Carolina
21	Stacey King	F/C	6-11	230	1-29-67	Oklahoma
53	Cliff Levingston	F	6-8	220	1-4-61	Wichita State
5	John Paxson	G	6-2	185	9-29-60	Notre Dame
32	Will Perdue	C	7-0	240	8-29-65	Vanderbilt
33	Scottie Pippen	G/F	6-7	210	9-25-65	Central Arkansas
	Matt Steigenga	F	6-7	225	3-27-70	Michigan State
	Corey Williams	G	6-2	190	4-24-70	Oklahoma State
42	Scott Williams	C	6-10	230	3-21-68	North Carolina

CLEVELAND CAVALIERS
Coach—Lenny Wilkens
Assistant coaches—Dick Helm, Brian Winters

No.	Name	Pos.	Hgt.	Wgt.	Birthdate	College
10	John Battle	G	6-2	190	11-9-62	Rutgers
11	Terrell Brandon	G	6-0	180	5-20-70	Oregon
43	Brad Daugherty	C	7-0	263	10-19-65	North Carolina
3	Craig Ehlo	G/F	6-7	205	8-11-61	Washington State
35	Danny Ferry	F	6-10	245	10-17-66	Duke
4	Steve Kerr	G	6-3	180	9-27-65	Arizona
22	Larry Nance	F/C	6-10	235	2-12-59	Clemson
14	Bobby Phills	G	6-5	217	12-20-69	Southern (La.)
25	Mark Price	G	6-0	178	2-15-64	Georgia Tech
33	Mike Sanders	F	6-6	215	5-7-60	UCLA
18	John Williams	F/C	6-11	245	8-9-62	Tulane

DALLAS MAVERICKS
Coach—Richie Adubato
Assistant coaches—Gar Heard, Bob Zuffelato

No.	Name	Pos.	Hgt.	Wgt.	Birthdate	College
43	Terry Davis	F/C	6-10	246	6-17-67	Virginia Union
12	Derek Harper	G	6-4	206	10-13-61	Illinois
35	Donald Hodge	C	7-0	233	2-25-69	Temple
41	Brian Howard	F	6-7	215	10-19-67	North Carolina State
13	Mike Iuzzolino	G	5-11	175	1-22-68	St. Francis (Ind.)
24	Jim Jackson	G	6-6	220	10-14-70	Ohio State
21	Fat Lever	G	6-3	182	8-18-60	Arizona State
1	Rodney McCray	F	6-8	248	8-29-61	Louisville
20	Tracy Moore	G	6-4	200	12-28-65	Tulsa
45	Sean Rooks	C	6-10	250	9-9-69	Arizona
34	Doug Smith	F	6-10	220	9-17-69	Missouri
33	Randy White	F	6-8	244	11-4-67	Louisiana Tech
32	Herb Williams	C/F	6-11	260	2-16-58	Ohio State

DENVER NUGGETS
Coach — Dan Issel
Assistant coaches — Mike Evans, Gene Littles

No.	Name	Pos.	Hgt.	Wgt.	Birthdate	College
43	Kevin Brooks	F	6-8	200	10-12-69	SW Louisiana
00	Anthony Cook	F/C	6-10	250	3-19-67	Arizona
6	Walter Davis	G	6-6	200	9-9-54	North Carolina
20	LaPhonso Ellis	F	6-8	240	5-5-70	Notre Dame
12	Winston Garland	G	6-2	175	12-19-64	SW Missouri State
10	Scott Hastings	F/C	6-11	245	6-3-60	Arkansas
3	Chris Jackson	G	6-1	170	3-9-69	Louisiana State
30	Marcus Liberty	F	6-8	205	10-27-68	Illinois
21	Todd Lichti	G	6-4	205	1-8-67	Stanford
1	Mark Macon	G	6-5	185	4-14-69	Temple
55	Dikembe Mutombo	C	7-2	245	6-25-66	Georgetown
23	Bryant Stith	G	6-5	208	12-10-70	Virginia
28	Robert Werdann	C	6-11	250	9-12-70	St. John's
34	Reggie Williams	F/G	6-7	195	3-5-64	Georgetown

DETROIT PISTONS
Coach — Ron Rothstein
Assistant coaches — Don Chaney, Brendan Malone, Alan Srebnick

No.	Name	Pos.	Hgt.	Wgt.	Birthdate	College
23	Mark Aguirre	F	6-6	232	12-10-59	DePaul
32	Lance Blanks	G	6-4	195	9-9-66	Texas
4	Joe Dumars	G	6-3	195	5-24-63	McNeese State
40	Bill Laimbeer	C	6-11	260	5-19-57	Notre Dame
34	Olden Polynice	C	7-0	250	11-21-64	Virginia
10	Dennis Rodman	F	6-8	210	5-13-61	SE Oklahoma State
22	John Salley	F/C	6-11	244	5-16-64	Georgia Tech
2	Brad Sellers	F	7-0	227	12-17-62	Ohio State
14	Charles Thomas	G	6-3	175	10-3-69	Eastern Michigan
11	Isiah Thomas	G	6-1	182	4-30-61	Indiana
5	Darrell Walker	G	6-4	180	3-9-61	Arkansas
0	Orlando Woolridge	F	6-9	215	12-16-59	Notre Dame

GOLDEN STATE WARRIORS
Coach — Don Nelson
Assistant coaches — Donn Nelson, Gregg Popovich

No.	Name	Pos.	Hgt.	Wgt.	Birthdate	College
52	Victor Alexander	F/C	6-9	265	8-31-69	Iowa State
4	Vincent Askew	G	6-6	226	2-28-66	Memphis State
35	Jud Buechler	F	6-6	220	6-19-68	Arizona
4	Dell Demps	G	6-3	205	2-12-70	Pacific
25	Chris Gatling	F	6-10	220	9-3-67	Old Dominion
	Jeff Grayer	F/G	6-5	210	12-17-65	Iowa State
10	Tim Hardaway	G	6-0	195	9-1-66	Texas-El Paso
32	Tyrone Hill	F	6-9	243	3-17-68	Xavier
14	Keith Jennings	G	5-7	160	11-2-68	East Tenn. State
53	Alton Lister	C/F	7-0	245	10-1-58	Arizona State
13	Sarunas Marciulionis	G	6-5	215	6-13-64	Lithuania
17	Chris Mullin	F	6-7	215	7-30-63	St. John's
30	Billy Owens	F/G	6-9	220	5-1-69	Syracuse
43	Jim Petersen	F/C	6-10	240	2-22-62	Minnesota
15	Latrell Sprewell	G	6-5	190	9-8-70	Alabama
3	Tom Tolbert	F	6-7	240	10-16-65	Arizona

HOUSTON ROCKETS
Coach — Rudy Tomjanovich
Assistant coaches — Bill Berry, Jim Boylen, Carroll Dawson,
John Killilea, Calvin Murphy

No.	Name	Pos.	Hgt.	Wgt.	Birthdate	College
12	Curtis Blair	G	6-3	187	9-24-70	Richmond
50	Matt Bullard	F	6-10	225	6-5-67	Iowa
21	Sleepy Floyd	G	6-3	183	3-6-60	Georgetown
7	Carl Herrera	F	6-9	215	12-14-66	Houston
25	Robert Horry	F	6-9	220	8-25-70	Alabama
32	Dave Jamerson	G	6-5	192	8-13-67	Ohio University
6	Avery Johnson	G	5-11	175	3-25-65	Southern (La.)
54	Popeye Jones	F	6-8	270	6-17-70	Murray State
11	Vernon Maxwell	G	6-4	190	9-12-65	Florida
34	Hakeem Olajuwon	C	7-0	255	1-21-63	Houston
15	Tree Rollins	C	7-1	255	6-16-55	Clemson
30	Kenny Smith	G	6-3	170	3-8-65	North Carolina
13	Larry Smith	F/C	6-8	251	1-18-58	Alcorn State
33	Otis Thorpe	F	6-10	246	8-5-62	Providence
40	John Turner	F	6-8	245	11-30-67	Phillips (Okla.)
10	David Wood	F	6-9	230	11-30-64	Nevada

INDIANA PACERS
Coach — Bob Hill
Assistant coaches — Ed Badger, Billy Knight, Bob Oceipka

No.	Name	Pos.	Hgt.	Wgt.	Birthdate	College
32	Dale Davis	F	6-11	230	3-25-69	Clemson
54	Greg Dreiling	C	7-1	250	11-7-63	Kansas
10	Vern Fleming	G	6-5	185	2-4-62	Georgia
23	Sean Green	G	6-5	210	2-2-70	Iona
20	George McCloud	G/F	6-8	215	5-27-67	Florida State
31	Reggie Miller	G	6-7	185	8-24-65	UCLA
45	Chuck Person	F	6-8	225	6-27-64	Auburn
11	Detlef Schrempf	F	6-10	230	1-21-63	Washington
21	Malik Sealy	F	6-8	192	2-1-70	St. John's
24	Rik Smits	C	7-4	265	8-23-66	Marist (N.Y.)
41	LaSalle Thompson	F/C	6-10	260	6-23-61	Texas
44	Kenny Williams	F	6-9	205	6-9-69	Eliz. City St. (N.C.)
4	Micheal Williams	G	6-2	175	7-23-66	Baylor
14	Randy Wittman	G	6-6	210	10-28-59	Indiana

LOS ANGELES CLIPPERS
Coach — Larry Brown
Assistant coaches — Mack Calvin, John Hammond, Barry Hecker

No.	Name	Pos.	Hgt.	Wgt.	Birthdate	College
00	William Bedford	C	7-1	252	12-3-63	Memphis State
22	LeRon Ellis	C/F	6-10	240	4-28-69	Syracuse
23	Gary Grant	G	6-3	195	4-21-65	Michigan
4	Ron Harper	G	6-6	198	1-20-64	Miami of Ohio
30	Bo Kimble	G	6-4	190	4-9-66	Loyola Marymount
42	Don MacLean	F	6-10	240	1-16-70	UCLA
5	Danny Manning	F	6-10	234	5-17-66	Kansas
3	Ken Norman	F	6-8	223	9-5-64	Illinois
25	Doc Rivers	G	6-4	185	10-13-61	Marquette
54	Charles Smith	C/F	6-10	244	7-16-65	Pittsburgh
42	Elmore Spencer	C	7-0	270	12-6-69	UNLV
35	Loy Vaught	F	6-9	240	2-27-67	Michigan
14	Randy Woods	G	6-0	185	9-23-70	La Salle
21	Danny Young	G	6-4	175	7-26-62	Wake Forest

LOS ANGELES LAKERS
Coach — Randy Pfund
Assistant coaches — Bill Bertka, Larry Drew, Chet Kammerer

No.	Name	Pos.	Hgt.	Wgt.	Birthdate	College
	Alex Blackwell	F	6-7	235	6-27-70	Monmouth (N.J.)
6	Chucky Brown	F	6-8	214	2-29-68	North Carolina State
41	Elden Campbell	F/C	6-11	230	7-23-68	Clemson
5	Duane Cooper	G	6-1	185	6-25-69	Southern California
12	Vlade Divac	C	7-1	250	2-3-68	
	James Edwards	C	7-1	252	11-22-55	Washington
45	A.C. Green	F	6-9	225	10-4-63	Oregon State
54	Jack Haley	F/C	6-10	250	1-27-64	UCLA
	Sean Higgins	G/F	6-9	215	12-30-68	Michigan
32	Magic Johnson	G	6-9	225	8-14-59	Michigan State
25	Keith Owens	C/F	6-7	225	5-31-69	UCLA
	Anthony Peeler	G	6-4	215	11-25-69	Missouri
14	Sam Perkins	F/C	6-9	257	6-14-61	North Carolina
43	Cliff Robinson	F	6-9	240	3-13-60	Southern California
4	Byron Scott	G	6-4	200	3-28-61	Arizona State
34	Tony Smith	G	6-4	205	6-14-68	Marquette
2	Rory Sparrow	G	6-2	175	6-12-58	Villanova
3	Sedale Threatt	G	6-2	185	9-10-61	West Virginia Tech
42	James Worthy	F	6-9	225	2-27-61	North Carolina

MIAMI HEAT
Coach — Kevin Loughery
Assistant coaches — Alvin Gentry, Bob Staak

No.	Name	Pos.	Hgt.	Wgt.	Birthdate	College
2	Keith Askins	G/F	6-8	205	12-15-67	Alabama
34	Willie Burton	G/F	6-8	219	5-26-68	Minnesota
12	Bimbo Coles	G	6-2	182	4-22-68	Virginia Tech
21	Kevin Edwards	G	6-3	197	10-30-65	DePaul
52	Matt Geiger	C	7-1	251	9-10-69	Georgia Tech
33	Alec Kessler	F/C	6-11	241	1-13-67	Georgia
43	Grant Long	F	6-9	230	3-12-66	Eastern Michigan
32	Harold Miner	G	6-5	210	5-5-71	Southern California
23	John Morton	G	6-3	195	5-18-67	Seton Hall
53	Alan Ogg	C	7-2	245	7-5-67	Ala.-Birmingham
41	Glen Rice	F/G	6-8	220	5-28-67	Michigan
4	Rony Seikaly	C	6-11	252	5-10-65	Syracuse
22	Brian Shaw	G	6-6	190	3-22-66	UC Santa Barbara
3	Steve Smith	G	6-8	202	3-31-69	Michigan State
20	Jon Sundvold	G	6-2	175	7-2-61	Missouri

MILWAUKEE BUCKS
Coach — Mike Dunleavy
Assistant coaches — Butch Carter, Jim Eyen, Frank Hamblen

No.	Name	Pos.	Hgt.	Wgt.	Birthdate	College
5	Alaa Abdelnaby	F	6-10	240	6-24-68	Duke
00	Anthony Avent	F	6-10	235	10-18-69	Seton Hall
40	Frank Brickowski	F/C	6-10	248	8-15-59	Penn State
	Todd Day	G/F	6-8	200	1-7-70	Arkansas
30	Blue Edwards	G/F	6-5	200	10-31-65	East Carolina
8	Moses Malone	C	6-10	255	3-23-55	Petersburg (Va.) HS
11	Lee Mayberry	G	6-2	175	6-12-70	Arkansas
20	Eric Murdock	G	6-1	190	6-14-68	Providence
34	Fred Roberts	F	6-10	218	8-14-60	Brigham Young
21	Alvin Robertson	G	6-4	208	7-22-62	Arkansas
10	Dan Schayes	C	6-11	260	5-10-59	Syracuse
	Sam Vincent	G	6-2	185	5-18-63	Michigan State

MINNESOTA TIMBERWOLVES
Coach—Jimmy Rodgers
Assistant coaches—Jim Brewer, Chuck Davisson, Sidney Lowe

No.	Name	Pos.	Hgt.	Wgt.	Birthdate	College
41	Thurl Bailey	F	6-11	232	4-7-61	North Carolina State
1	Scott Brooks	G	5-11	165	7-31-65	UC Irvine
19	Tony Campbell	G/F	6-7	215	5-7-62	Ohio State
4	Gerald Glass	G/F	6-6	221	11-12-67	Mississippi
	Christian Laettner	F	6-11	235	8-17-69	Duke
13	Luc Longley	C	7-2	265	1-19-69	New Mexico
	Marlon Maxey	F	6-8	250	2-19-69	Texas-El Paso
17	Bob McCann	F	6-7	248	4-22-64	Morehead State
42	Sam Mitchell	F	6-7	210	9-2-63	Mercer (Ga.)
52	Mark Randall	F	6-9	235	9-30-67	Kansas
24	Pooh Richardson	G	6-1	180	5-14-66	UCLA
	Chris Smith	G	6-3	191	5-17-70	Connecticut
50	Felton Spencer	C	7-0	265	1-5-68	Louisville
	Gundars Vetra	G/F	6-6	196	5-22-67	
5	Doug West	G	6-6	200	5-27-67	Villanova

NEW JERSEY NETS
Coach—Chuck Daly
Assistant coaches—Rick Carlisle, Paul Silas, Brendan Suhr

No.	Name	Pos.	Hgt.	Wgt.	Birthdate	College
21	Rafael Addison	F/G	6-7	226	7-22-64	Syracuse
7	Kenny Anderson	G	6-1	168	10-9-70	Georgia Tech
10	Mookie Blaylock	G	6-1	185	3-20-67	Oklahoma
31	Sam Bowie	C	7-1	240	3-17-61	Kentucky
52	P.J. Brown	C	6-11	225	10-14-68	Louisiana Tech
44	Derrick Coleman	F	6-10	230	6-21-67	Syracuse
22	Chris Dudley	C	6-11	240	2-22-65	Yale
12	Tate George	G	6-5	190	5-29-68	Connecticut
6	Roy Hinson	F	6-9	215	5-2-61	Rutgers
20	Doug Lee	G	6-6	200	10-24-64	Purdue
5	Terry Mills	F	6-10	230	12-21-67	Michigan
34	Chris Morris	F	6-8	210	1-20-66	Auburn
54	Dan O'Sullivan	C	6-10	250	3-3-68	Fordham
3	Drazen Petrovic	G	6-5	208	10-22-64	Zagreb (Yugo.)
14	Steve Rogers	G	6-5	190	7-30-68	Alabama State

NEW YORK KNICKERBOCKERS
Coach—Pat Riley
Assistant coaches—Dick Harter, Jeff Van Gundy

No.	Name	Pos.	Hgt.	Wgt.	Birthdate	College
2	Greg Anthony	G	6-2	185	11-15-67	UNLV
20	Rolando Blackman	G	6-6	206	2-26-59	Kansas State
44	Hubert Davis	G	6-5	183	5-17-70	North Carolina
33	Patrick Ewing	C	7-0	240	8-5-62	Georgetown
13	Mark Jackson	G	6-3	192	4-1-65	St. John's
14	Anthony Mason	F	6-7	250	12-14-66	Tennessee State
40	Tim McCormick	C	7-0	240	3-10-62	Michigan
32	Xavier McDaniel	F	6-8	205	6-4-63	Wichita State
34	Charles Oakley	F	6-9	245	12-18-63	Virginia Union
3	John Starks	G	6-5	185	8-10-65	Oklahoma State
21	Gerald Wilkins	G	6-6	210	9-11-63	Tennessee-Chattanooga

ORLANDO MAGIC
Coach—Matt Guokas
Assistant coach—Brian Hill

No.	Name	Pos.	Hgt.	Wgt.	Birthdate	College
25	Nick Anderson	G/F	6-6	205	1-20-68	Illinois
33	Terry Catledge	F	6-8	230	8-22-63	South Alabama
	Lester Conner	G	6-4	180	9-17-59	Oregon State
13	Chris Corchiani	G	6-1	186	3-28-68	North Carolina State
	Litterial Green	G	6-1	185	3-7-70	Georgia
	Greg Kite	C	6-11	270	8-5-61	Brigham Young
	Shaquille O'Neal	C	7-1	301	3-6-72	Louisiana State
35	Jerry Reynolds	G/F	6-8	206	12-23-62	Louisiana State
53	Stanley Roberts	C	7-0	285	2-7-70	Louisiana State
3	Dennis Scott	G/F	6-8	229	9-5-68	Georgia Tech
4	Scott Skiles	G	6-1	180	3-5-64	Michigan State
31	Jeff Turner	F	6-9	240	4-9-62	Vanderbilt
8	Brian Williams	F/C	6-11	242	4-6-69	Arizona

PHILADELPHIA 76ers
Coach—Doug Moe
Assistant coaches—Fred Carter, Tony DiLeo, David Moe

No.	Name	Pos.	Hgt.	Wgt.	Birthdate	College
20	Ron Anderson	F	6-7	215	10-15-58	Fresno State
11	Manute Bol	C	7-7	225	10-16-62	Bridgeport (Conn.)
12	Johnny Dawkins	G	6-2	170	9-28-63	Duke
35	Armon Gilliam	F	6-9	245	5-28-64	UNLV
3	Greg Grant	G	5-7	140	8-29-66	Trenton State (N.J.)
33	Hersey Hawkins	G	6-3	190	9-29-65	Bradley
	Jeff Hornacek	G	6-4	190	5-3-63	Iowa State
28	Andrew Lang	C	6-11	250	6-28-66	Arkansas
31	Brian Oliver	G	6-4	210	6-1-68	Georgia Tech
21	Kenny Payne	F	6-8	220	11-25-66	Louisville
	Tim Perry	F	6-9	220	6-4-65	Temple
43	Jeff Ruland	C	6-11	275	12-16-58	Iona
14	Charles Shackleford	C	6-11	245	4-22-66	North Carolina State
	Clarence Weatherspoon	F	6-6	240	9-8-70	Southern Miss.
55	Jayson Williams	F	6-10	240	2-22-68	St. John's

PHOENIX SUNS
Coach—Paul Westphal
Assistant coaches—Lionel Hollins, Scotty Robertson

No.	Name	Pos.	Hgt.	Wgt.	Birthdate	College
22	Danny Ainge	G	6-5	185	3-17-59	Brigham Young
34	Charles Barkley	F	6-6	252	2-20-63	Auburn
15	Steve Burtt	G	6-2	195	11-5-62	Iona
23	Cedric Ceballos	F	6-6	210	8-2-69	Cal State Fullerton
24	Tom Chambers	F	6-10	230	6-21-59	Utah
	Brian Davis	F	6-7	200	6-21-70	Duke
12	Richard Dumas	F	6-7	204	5-19-69	Oklahoma State
	Ron Ellis	F	6-7	215	9-18-68	Louisiana Tech
7	Kevin Johnson	G	6-1	190	3-4-66	California
32	Negele Knight	G	6-1	182	3-6-67	Dayton
9	Dan Majerle	G/F	6-6	220	9-9-65	Central Michigan
	Oliver Miller	F/C	6-9	290	4-6-70	Arkansas
0	Jerrod Mustaf	F	6-10	245	10-28-69	Maryland
45	Ed Nealy	F	6-7	240	2-19-60	Kansas State
31	Kurt Rambis	F	6-8	213	2-25-58	Santa Clara
41	Mark West	C	6-10	246	11-5-60	Old Dominion

PORTLAND TRAIL BLAZERS
Coach — Rick Adelman
Assistant coaches — Kip Motta, Jack Schalow, John Wetzel

No.	Name	Pos.	Hgt.	Wgt.	Birthdate	College
2	Mark Bryant	F	6-9	245	4-25-65	Seton Hall
22	Clyde Drexler	G	6-7	222	6-22-62	Houston
00	Kevin Duckworth	C	7-0	280	4-1-64	Eastern Illinois
	Mario Elie	G	6-5	210	11-26-63	American International
	Dave Johnson	G/F	6-7	210	11-16-70	Syracuse
25	Jerome Kersey	F	6-7	225	6-26-62	Longwood (Va.)
	Tracy Murray	F	6-8	225	7-25-71	UCLA
14	Robert Pack	G	6-2	180	2-3-69	Southern California
30	Terry Porter	G	6-3	195	4-8-63	Wisconsin-Stevens Point
3	Cliff Robinson	F	6-10	225	12-16-66	Connecticut
	Reggie Smith	C	6-10	240	8-21-70	Texas Christian
	Rod Strickland	G	6-3	175	7-11-66	DePaul
7	Lamont Strothers	G	6-4	195	5-10-68	Christopher Newport (Va.)
8	Ennis Whatley	G	6-3	180	8-11-62	Alabama
52	Buck Williams	F	6-8	225	3-8-60	Maryland

SACRAMENTO KINGS
Coach — Garry St. Jean
Assistant coaches — Eddie Jordan, Mike Schuler, Dave Wohl

No.	Name	Pos.	Hgt.	Wgt.	Birthdate	College
24	Anthony Bonner	F	6-8	225	6-8-68	St. Louis
3	Randy Brown	G	6-3	190	5-22-68	New Mexico State
31	Duane Causwell	C	7-0	240	5-31-68	Temple
32	Pete Chilcutt	F/C	6-10	232	9-14-68	North Carolina
51	Les Jepsen	C	7-0	237	6-24-67	Iowa
33	Jim Les	G	5-11	165	8-18-63	Bradley
2	Mitch Richmond	G	6-5	215	6-30-65	Kansas State
	Brett Roberts	F	6-8	230	3-24-70	Morehead State
22	Lionel Simmons	F	6-7	210	11-14-68	La Salle
23	Wayman Tisdale	F	6-9	260	6-9-64	Oklahoma
4	Spud Webb	G	5-7	135	7-13-63	North Carolina State
42	Walt Williams	F	6-8	220	4-16-70	Maryland

SAN ANTONIO SPURS
Coach — Jerry Tarkanian
Assistant coaches — Ron Adams, Rex Hughes, Ed Manning, Tom Thibodeau

No.	Name	Pos.	Hgt.	Wgt.	Birthdate	College
40	Willie Anderson	G/F	6-8	202	1-8-67	Georgia
35	Antoine Carr	F	6-9	265	7-23-61	Wichita State
34	Terry Cummings	F	6-9	235	3-15-61	DePaul
24	Lloyd Daniels	G	6-7	210	9-4-67	Andrew Jackson (N.Y.) HS
15	Vinny Del Negro	G	6-4	195	8-9-66	N.C. State
32	Sean Elliott	F	6-8	210	2-2-68	Arizona
3	Dale Ellis	G/F	6-7	215	8-6-60	Tennessee
21	Sidney Green	F	6-9	240	1-4-61	UNLV
50	David Robinson	C	7-1	235	8-6-65	Navy
2	Larry Smith	F/C	6-8	245	1-18-58	Alcorn State
23	Greg Sutton	G	6-2	170	12-3-67	Oral Roberts
4	Henry Williams	G	6-1	170	6-6-70	UNC Charlotte

SEATTLE SUPERSONICS
Coach—George Karl
Assistant coaches—Tim Grgurich, Bob Kloppenburg

No.	Name	Pos.	Hgt.	Wgt.	Birthdate	College
3	Dana Barros	G	5-11	165	4-13-67	Boston College
00	Benoit Benjamin	C	7-0	265	11-22-64	Creighton
21	Tony Brown	F	6-6	195	7-29-60	Arkansas
44	Michael Cage	C/F	6-9	230	1-28-62	San Diego State
35	Doug Christie	G	6-6	200	5-9-70	Pepperdine
24	Marty Conlon	F	6-10	224	1-19-68	Providence
8	Eddie Johnson	F	6-7	215	5-1-59	Illinois
40	Shawn Kemp	F	6-10	245	11-26-69	Trinity Valley C.C. (Tex.)
14	Chris King	F	6-8	215	7-24-69	Wake Forest
25	Rich King	C	7-2	265	4-4-69	Nebraska
23	Bart Kofoed	G	6-4	210	3-24-64	Kearney State (Neb.)
31	Derrick McKey	F	6-10	225	10-10-66	Alabama
10	Nate McMillan	G/F	6-5	197	8-3-64	North Carolina State
20	Gary Payton	G	6-4	190	7-23-68	Oregon State
22	Ricky Pierce	G	6-4	215	8-19-59	Rice

UTAH JAZZ
Coach—Jerry Sloan
Assistant coaches—Gordon Chiesa, David Fredman, Phil Johnson

No.	Name	Pos.	Hgt.	Wgt.	Birthdate	College
50	Isaac Austin	C	6-10	260	8-18-69	Arizona State
21	David Benoit	F	6-8	225	5-9-68	Alabama
40	Mike Brown	F	6-10	260	7-19-63	George Washington
23	Tyrone Corbin	F	6-6	222	12-31-62	DePaul
15	Corey Crowder	G/F	6-5	214	4-13-69	Kentucky Wesleyan
53	Mark Eaton	C	7-4	290	1-24-57	UCLA
	Jay Humphries	G	6-3	185	10-17-62	Colorado
	Larry Krystkowiak	F/C	6-9	240	9-23-64	Montana
24	Jeff Malone	G	6-4	205	6-28-61	Mississippi State
32	Karl Malone	F	6-9	256	7-24-63	Louisiana Tech
11	Delaney Rudd	G	6-2	195	11-8-62	Wake Forest
12	John Stockton	G	6-1	175	3-26-62	Gonzaga
33	Bob Thornton	F/C	6-10	225	7-10-62	UC Irvine

WASHINGTON BULLETS
Coach—Wes Unseld
Assistant coaches—Bill Blair, Jeff Bzdelik

No.	Name	Pos.	Hgt.	Wgt.	Birthdate	College
10	Michael Adams	G	5-10	175	1-19-63	Boston College
31	Mark Alarie	F	6-8	225	12-11-63	Duke
3	Rex Chapman	G	6-4	205	10-5-67	Kentucky
21	Ledell Eackles	G	6-5	225	11-24-66	New Orleans
43	Pervis Ellison	F/C	6-10	225	4-3-67	Louisville
14	A.J. English	G	6-3	180	7-11-67	Virginia Union
42	Greg Foster	F/C	6-11	240	10-3-68	Texas-El Paso
44	Harvey Grant	F	6-9	235	7-4-65	Oklahoma
24	Tom Gugliotta	F	6-10	240	12-19-69	North Carolina State
23	Charles Jones	F/C	6-9	235	4-3-57	Albany State (Ga.)
30	Bernard King	F	6-7	205	12-4-56	Tennessee
20	Brent Price	G	6-1	165	12-9-68	Oklahoma
22	LaBradford Smith	G	6-3	200	4-3-69	Louisville
33	Larry Stewart	F	6-8	220	9-21-68	Coppin State
1	Andre Turner	G	5-11	160	12-13-64	Memphis State
34	John Williams	F	6-9	260	10-26-66	Louisiana State
55	David Wingate	G	6-5	185	12-15-63	Georgetown

1992-93 NBA SCHEDULE

(All Times Shown Are Local, Except Games In Japan, Which Are Eastern Standard)

FRIDAY, NOVEMBER 6
Minnesota at Boston, 7:30
New Jersey at Philadelphia, 7:30
Miami at Orlando, 7:30
Washington at Charlotte, 8:00
New York at Atlanta, 7:30
Chicago at Cleveland, 8:00
Milwaukee at Detroit, 8:00
Seattle at Houston*, 10:30
Golden State at Utah, 7:00
L.A. Lakers at L.A. Clippers, 7:30
San Antonio at Sacramento, 7:30
*Game played in Japan.

SATURDAY, NOVEMBER 7
Philadelphia at New York, 7:30
Orlando at Washington, 7:30
New Jersey at Miami, 7:30
Detroit at Indiana, 7:30
Atlanta at Chicago, 7:30
Boston at Milwaukee, 8:00
Golden State at Minnesota, 7:00
Utah at Dallas, 7:30
San Antonio at Denver, 7:00
L.A. Clippers at Phoenix, 7:30
Houston at Seattle*, 10:00
*Game played in Japan.

SUNDAY, NOVEMBER 8
Charlotte at Cleveland, 7:30
Sacramento at L.A. Lakers, 7:30
Denver at Portland, 7:00

MONDAY, NOVEMBER 9
Indiana at Chicago, 7:30

TUESDAY, NOVEMBER 10
New Jersey at New York, 7:30
Charlotte at Orlando, 8:00
Boston at Miami, 7:30
Washington at Cleveland, 7:30
Dallas at Minnesota, 7:00
Milwaukee at San Antonio, 7:30
Utah at Denver, 7:00
L.A. Lakers at Golden State, 7:30
L.A. Clippers at Sacramento, 7:30
Phoenix at Portland, 7:30

WEDNESDAY, NOVEMBER 11
Boston at Charlotte, 7:30
Philadelphia at Indiana, 7:30
Detroit at Chicago, 7:30
Milwaukee at Dallas, 7:30
Atlanta at Houston, 7:30
Sacramento at L.A. Clippers, 7:30

THURSDAY, NOVEMBER 12
Minnesota at New Jersey, 7:30
Washington at Orlando, 7:30
Miami at Detroit, 7:30
Atlanta at San Antonio, 7:30
Phoenix at Utah, 7:00
Cleveland at Golden State, 7:30
L.A. Lakers at Seattle, 7:00

FRIDAY, NOVEMBER 13
Philadelphia at Boston, 7:30
New York at Washington, 8:00
Charlotte at Indiana, 7:30
Chicago at Milwaukee, 8:00
L.A. Clippers at L.A. Lakers, 7:30
Cleveland at Portland, 7:30

SATURDAY, NOVEMBER 14
Boston at New York, 7:30
Orlando at New Jersey, 7:30
Miami at Charlotte, 7:30

Indiana at Detroit, 7:30
Denver at Chicago, 7:30
Phoenix at Minnesota, 7:00
Atlanta at Dallas, 7:30
Houston at San Antonio, 7:30
L.A. Clippers at Utah, 7:00
Portland at Golden State, 7:30
Sacramento at Seattle, 7:00

SUNDAY, NOVEMBER 15
Washington at New Jersey, 7:00
Denver at Milwaukee, 7:30
Golden State at L.A. Lakers, 7:30
Cleveland at Sacramento, 6:00

MONDAY, NOVEMBER 16
Seattle at Phoenix, 7:30
New York at Portland, 7:30

TUESDAY, NOVEMBER 17
Utah at New Jersey, 7:30
Boston at Washington, 7:30
Golden State at Miami, 7:30
Dallas at Charlotte, 7:30
Milwaukee at Atlanta, 8:00
Denver at Indiana, 7:30
Chicago at Minnesota, 7:00
Sacramento at Houston, 7:30
Cleveland at San Antonio, 7:30
Detroit at L.A. Clippers, 7:30
New York at Seattle, 7:00

WEDNESDAY, NOVEMBER 18
Utah at Boston, 7:30
Orlando at Philadelphia, 7:30
Sacramento at Phoenix, 7:30

THURSDAY, NOVEMBER 19
Golden State at Orlando, 7:30
New Jersey at Atlanta, 7:30
Cleveland at Houston, 7:30
Dallas at San Antonio, 7:30
Detroit at Denver, 7:00
New York at L.A. Clippers, 7:30
Chicago at Seattle, 7:00

FRIDAY, NOVEMBER 20
Miami at Philadelphia, 7:30
Golden State at Charlotte, 7:30
Utah at Indiana, 7:30
Washington at Minnesota, 7:00
Chicago at L.A. Lakers, 7:30
Portland at Sacramento, 5:00

SATURDAY, NOVEMBER 21
Orlando at New York, 8:30
Philadelphia at New Jersey, 7:30
Utah at Washington, 7:30
Charlotte at Miami, 7:30
Boston at Atlanta, 7:30
Indiana at Milwaukee, 8:00
Cleveland at Dallas, 7:30
San Antonio at Houston, 7:30
Minnesota at Denver, 7:00
Phoenix at L.A. Clippers, 7:30
Detroit at Seattle, 7:00

SUNDAY, NOVEMBER 22
Golden State at New Jersey, 7:00
Chicago at Phoenix, 7:00
Denver at L.A. Lakers, 7:30
Detroit at Portland, 7:00

MONDAY, NOVEMBER 23
Atlanta at Boston*, 7:30
Seattle at Sacramento, 7:30
*Game played in Hartford.

TUESDAY, NOVEMBER 24
Washington at New York, 7:30
Philadelphia at Charlotte, 7:30
Milwaukee at Cleveland, 7:30
Miami at Indiana, 7:30
L.A. Clippers at Houston, 7:30
Chicago at Golden State, 7:30
San Antonio at Portland, 5:00
New Jersey at Seattle, 7:00

WEDNESDAY, NOVEMBER 25
Washington at Boston, 7:30
Atlanta at Philadelphia, 7:30
Houston at Orlando, 7:30
Indiana at Miami, 7:30
Charlotte at Detroit, 7:30
Cleveland at Milwaukee, 7:30
New York at Minnesota, 7:00
L.A. Clippers at Dallas, 7:30
Sacramento at Denver, 7:00
San Antonio at Utah, 7:00
Portland at Phoenix, 7:30
New Jersey at L.A. Lakers, 7:30

FRIDAY, NOVEMBER 27
Charlotte at Boston, 7:30
Milwaukee at Philadelphia, 7:30
Minnesota at Washington*, 7:30
Houston at Miami, 7:30
Atlanta at Cleveland, 7:30
Orlando at Indiana, 7:30
Seattle at Dallas, 7:30
New Jersey at Utah, 7:00
Golden State at Phoenix, 7:30
Denver at L.A. Clippers, 7:30
L.A. Lakers at Portland, 7:30
*Game played in Baltimore.

SATURDAY, NOVEMBER 28
Chicago at New York, 1:00
Boston at Philadelphia, 7:30
Cleveland at Orlando, 7:30
Indiana at Charlotte, 7:30
Miami at Atlanta, 7:30
Washington at Milwaukee, 8:00
Detroit at Minnesota, 7:00
Utah at Houston, 7:30
Seattle at San Antonio, 7:30
L.A. Clippers at Denver, 7:00
Phoenix at Golden State, 7:30
New Jersey at Sacramento, 7:30

SUNDAY, NOVEMBER 29
New York at Detroit, 7:00
Dallas at L.A. Lakers, 7:30
Sacramento at Portland, 7:00

TUESDAY, DECEMBER 1
Portland at New York, 7:30
San Antonio at Washington, 7:30
Indiana at Atlanta, 7:30
Boston at Cleveland, 7:30
Houston at Denver, 7:00
Dallas at Utah, 7:00
Charlotte at Phoenix, 7:30
L.A. Lakers at Sacramento, 7:30
Orlando at Seattle, 7:00

WEDNESDAY, DECEMBER 2
Chicago at Boston, 8:00
Atlanta at New Jersey, 7:30
San Antonio at Philadelphia, 7:30
Portland at Indiana, 7:30
Miami at Milwaukee, 7:30
Charlotte at Golden State, 7:30

THURSDAY, DECEMBER 3
Milwaukee at Washington, 7:30
New York at Cleveland, 7:30
L.A. Lakers at Houston, 7:30
Minnesota at Utah, 7:00
Orlando at L.A. Clippers, 7:30
Dallas at Seattle, 7:00

FRIDAY, DECEMBER 4
Miami at Boston, 7:30
San Antonio at New Jersey, 7:30
Detroit at Philadelphia, 7:30
Atlanta at Indiana, 7:30
Portland at Chicago, 7:00
Golden State at Denver, 7:00
L.A. Lakers at Phoenix, 7:30
Charlotte at Sacramento, 7:30

SATURDAY, DECEMBER 5
Milwaukee at New York, 1:00
Indiana at Washington, 7:30
New Jersey at Miami, 7:30
San Antonio at Atlanta, 7:30
Portland at Cleveland, 7:30
Philadelphia at Detroit, 7:30
Boston at Chicago, 7:30
Houston at Dallas, 7:30
Denver at Utah, 7:00
Charlotte at L.A. Clippers, 7:30
Orlando at Golden State, 7:30
Minnesota at Seattle, 7:00

SUNDAY, DECEMBER 6
Phoenix at Milwaukee, 7:30
Minnesota at L.A. Lakers, 7:30

TUESDAY, DECEMBER 8
Seattle at New York, 7:30
Phoenix at New Jersey, 7:30
Boston at Orlando, 8:00
Chicago at Atlanta, 7:30
L.A. Clippers at Cleveland, 7:30
Miami at Dallas, 7:30
Minnesota at Houston, 7:30
Utah at San Antonio, 7:30
Indiana at Golden State, 7:30
Washington at Sacramento, 7:30
Milwaukee at Portland, 7:30

WEDNESDAY, DECEMBER 9
Denver at Boston, 7:30
Seattle at Philadelphia, 7:30
Phoenix at Charlotte, 7:30
Orlando at Detroit, 7:30
Cleveland at Chicago, 7:30
Portland at L.A. Lakers, 7:30

THURSDAY, DECEMBER 10
Charlotte at New York, 7:30
L.A. Clippers at New Jersey, 7:30
Minnesota at Dallas, 7:30
Miami at San Antonio, 7:30
Washington at Utah, 7:00
Milwaukee at Golden State, 7:30
Indiana at Sacramento, 7:30

FRIDAY, DECEMBER 11
Seattle at Boston, 7:30
L.A. Clippers at Philadelphia, 7:30
Phoenix at Orlando, 7:30
Denver at Atlanta, 7:30
Cleveland at Detroit, 8:00
Houston at Chicago, 7:30
Washington at L.A. Lakers, 7:30
Indiana at Portland, 7:30

SATURDAY, DECEMBER 12
Detroit at New York, 7:30
Phoenix at Miami, 7:30
Denver at Charlotte, 7:30
Philadelphia at Atlanta, 7:30
Seattle at Cleveland, 7:30
New Jersey at Chicago, 7:30

Houston at Minnesota, 7:00
San Antonio at Dallas, 7:30
Milwaukee at Utah, 7:00
Golden State at Sacramento, 7:30

SUNDAY, DECEMBER 13
Indiana at L.A. Clippers, 6:00
Milwaukee at L.A. Lakers, 7:30
Washington at Portland, 5:00

MONDAY, DECEMBER 14
Denver at New York, 7:30

TUESDAY, DECEMBER 15
New York at New Jersey, 7:30
Philadelphia at Orlando, 7:30
Sacramento at Miami, 7:30
Detroit at Atlanta, 7:30
Houston at Cleveland, 7:30
Charlotte at Chicago, 7:30
Boston at Minnesota, 7:00
L.A. Lakers at San Antonio, 7:30
Washington at Phoenix, 7:30
L.A. Clippers at Golden State, 7:30
Milwaukee at Seattle, 7:00

WEDNESDAY, DECEMBER 16
Cleveland at Philadelphia, 7:30
Utah at Charlotte, 7:30
Atlanta at Detroit, 7:30
Boston at Indiana, 7:30
L.A. Lakers at Dallas, 7:30
Portland at Denver, 7:00
Golden State at L.A. Clippers, 7:30

THURSDAY, DECEMBER 17
Chicago at Washington, 7:30
Sacramento at Orlando, 7:30
New Jersey at Milwaukee, 7:30
San Antonio at Houston, 7:30

FRIDAY, DECEMBER 18
New York at Boston, 7:30
Utah at Philadelphia, 7:30
Atlanta at Miami, 7:30
Sacramento at Cleveland, 7:30
Indiana at Detroit, 8:00
Dallas at San Antonio, 7:00
Minnesota at L.A. Clippers, 7:30
Phoenix at L.A. Lakers, 7:30
Portland at Seattle, 7:00

SATURDAY, DECEMBER 19
Miami at New York, 7:30
Charlotte at Washington, 7:30
Orlando at Atlanta, 7:30
Utah at Cleveland, 7:30
New Jersey at Indiana, 7:30
Philadelphia at Chicago, 7:30
Detroit at Milwaukee, 8:00
Dallas at Houston, 7:30
L.A. Lakers at Denver, 7:00
Minnesota at Golden State, 7:30
L.A. Clippers at Seattle, 7:00

SUNDAY, DECEMBER 20
Sacramento at New Jersey, 7:00
Golden State at Portland, 7:00

MONDAY, DECEMBER 21
Indiana at Philadelphia, 7:30
Miami at Chicago, 7:30

TUESDAY, DECEMBER 22
Boston at New Jersey, 7:30
Utah at Orlando, 7:30
Charlotte at Atlanta, 7:30
Houston at Detroit, 7:30
Sacramento at Milwaukee, 7:30
Denver at San Antonio, 7:30
Golden State at Phoenix, 6:00
Dallas at L.A. Clippers, 7:30
Seattle at Portland, 7:30

WEDNESDAY, DECEMBER 23
Houston at Boston, 7:30
Utah at Miami, 7:30
Detroit at Charlotte, 7:30
Indiana at Cleveland, 7:30
Washington at Chicago, 7:30
Sacramento at Minnesota, 7:00
Phoenix at Denver, 7:00
Seattle at L.A. Lakers, 7:30
Dallas at Golden State, 7:30

FRIDAY, DECEMBER 25
New York at Chicago, 8:00
San Antonio at L.A. Clippers, 12:30

SATURDAY, DECEMBER 26
Detroit at Washington*, 7:30
Orlando at Miami, 7:30
New Jersey at Cleveland, 1:30
Chicago at Indiana, 7:30
New York at Milwaukee, 8:00
Atlanta at Minnesota, 7:00
Golden State at Dallas, 7:30
Denver at Houston, 7:30
Boston at Utah, 1:30
Seattle at Phoenix, 7:30
San Antonio at L.A. Lakers, 7:30
Philadelphia at Portland, 7:00
*Game played in Baltimore.

SUNDAY, DECEMBER 27
Denver at Phoenix, 7:00
Philadelphia at L.A. Clippers, 6:00
Boston at Sacramento, 6:00

MONDAY, DECEMBER 28
Charlotte at New Jersey, 7:30
Atlanta at Washington, 7:30
Milwaukee at Orlando, 7:30
L.A. Lakers at Miami, 7:30
Detroit at Cleveland, 7:30
Golden State at San Antonio, 7:30
Minnesota at Utah, 7:00

TUESDAY, DECEMBER 29
Indiana at New York, 7:30
Chicago at Charlotte, 7:30
Cleveland at Atlanta, 7:30
Golden State at Houston, 7:30
Dallas at Sacramento, 7:30
Boston at Seattle, 7:00

WEDNESDAY, DECEMBER 30
L.A. Lakers at Orlando, 7:30
Chicago at Miami, 7:30
Washington at Detroit, 7:30
New York at Indiana, 7:30
New Jersey at Minnesota, 7:00
San Antonio at Denver, 7:00
Philadelphia at Utah, 7:00
Houston at Phoenix, 7:30
Boston at L.A. Clippers, 7:30
Dallas at Portland, 7:30

SATURDAY, JANUARY 2
L.A. Clippers at New York, 1:00
Miami at Washington, 7:30
Detroit at Orlando, 7:30
New Jersey at Charlotte, 7:30
Milwaukee at Atlanta, 8:00
L.A. Lakers at Cleveland, 7:30
Indiana at Chicago, 7:30
Dallas at Minnesota, 7:00
Houston at Golden State, 7:30
Philadelphia at Sacramento, 7:30
Utah at Portland, 7:00
Denver at Seattle, 7:00

SUNDAY, JANUARY 3
L.A. Clippers at Boston, 7:00
L.A. Lakers at Milwaukee, 7:30
Phoenix at San Antonio, 7:00
Houston at Portland, 7:00

TUESDAY, JANUARY 5

Cleveland at New York, 7:30
New Jersey at Orlando, 7:30
Detroit at Miami, 7:30
Boston at Charlotte, 7:30
Washington at Atlanta, 7:30
L.A. Clippers at Indiana, 7:30
L.A. Lakers at Chicago, 7:00
Minnesota at Milwaukee, 7:30
Portland at Dallas, 7:30
Phoenix at Houston, 7:30
San Antonio at Utah, 7:00
Denver at Sacramento, 7:30
Golden State at Seattle, 7:00

WEDNESDAY, JANUARY 6

Indiana at Boston, 7:30
New Jersey at Philadelphia, 7:30
Chicago at Cleveland, 7:30
L.A. Clippers at Detroit, 7:30
L.A. Lakers at Minnesota, 7:00

THURSDAY, JANUARY 7

Atlanta at Milwaukee, 7:30
Phoenix at Dallas, 7:30
Portland at Houston, 7:30
Utah at San Antonio, 7:30
Miami at Golden State, 7:30

FRIDAY, JANUARY 8

New Jersey at Boston, 7:30
Philadelphia at Washington, 7:30
New York at Orlando, 8:00
L.A. Clippers at Charlotte, 7:30
Atlanta at Detroit, 8:00
Milwaukee at Chicago, 7:30
Seattle at Minnesota, 7:00
Houston at Denver, 7:00
Sacramento at L.A. Lakers, 7:30

SATURDAY, JANUARY 9

Washington at New Jersey, 7:30
Chicago at Philadelphia, 7:30
Indiana at Orlando, 7:30
Minnesota at Cleveland, 7:30
Golden State at Detroit, 7:30
Utah at Dallas, 7:30
Portland at San Antonio, 7:30
Seattle at Denver, 7:00
Miami at Sacramento, 7:30

SUNDAY, JANUARY 10

Boston at New York, 8:00
L.A. Clippers at Milwaukee, 7:30
Utah at Houston, 7:30
Miami at L.A. Lakers, 7:30

MONDAY, JANUARY 11

San Antonio at Detroit, 7:30
Charlotte at Dallas, 7:30

TUESDAY, JANUARY 12

Milwaukee at Washington, 7:30
Chicago at Orlando, 7:30
Golden State at Atlanta, 7:30
Boston at Cleveland, 7:30
Philadelphia at Indiana, 7:30
Miami at Utah, 7:00
Houston at L.A. Clippers, 7:30
New York at Sacramento, 7:30
Denver at Portland, 7:30
Phoenix at Seattle, 7:00

WEDNESDAY, JANUARY 13

Washington at Boston, 7:30
Cleveland at New Jersey, 7:30
Golden State at Philadelphia, 7:30
Dallas at Detroit, 7:30
San Antonio at Minnesota, 7:00
New York at Denver, 7:00

THURSDAY, JANUARY 14

Detroit at Atlanta, 7:30

San Antonio at Milwaukee, 7:30
Charlotte at Houston, 7:30
Seattle at Utah, 7:00
L.A. Lakers at L.A. Clippers, 7:30
Phoenix at Sacramento, 7:30
Miami at Portland, 7:30

FRIDAY, JANUARY 15

Orlando at Boston, 7:30
Philadelphia at New Jersey, 7:30
Cleveland at Indiana, 8:00
Golden State at Chicago, 7:30
Denver at Minnesota, 7:00
New York at Dallas, 7:30
Miami at Phoenix, 7:30
Portland at L.A. Lakers, 7:30
L.A. Clippers at Seattle, 7:00

SATURDAY, JANUARY 16

Detroit at Philadelphia, 7:30
New Jersey at Washington*, 7:30
Atlanta at Cleveland, 7:30
Golden State at Indiana, 7:30
Orlando at Chicago, 7:30
Boston at Milwaukee, 8:00
New York at Houston, 7:30
Charlotte at San Antonio, 7:30
Dallas at Denver, 7:00
Sacramento at Utah, 7:00
*Game played in Baltimore.

SUNDAY, JANUARY 17

Seattle at Portland, 5:00

MONDAY, JANUARY 18

Phoenix at New York, 1:00
Indiana at New Jersey, 7:30
Orlando at Philadelphia, 2:00
Cleveland at Washington, 1:00
Boston at Chicago, 2:30
L.A. Clippers at Minnesota, 7:00
Houston at L.A. Lakers, 1:30
Sacramento at Golden State, 2:00
Utah at Seattle, 7:00

TUESDAY, JANUARY 19

Atlanta at Charlotte, 7:30
Washington at Indiana, 7:30
Portland at Milwaukee, 7:30
Detroit at Dallas, 7:30
Denver at San Antonio, 7:30
Houston at Sacramento, 7:30

WEDNESDAY, JANUARY 20

Atlanta at Boston, 7:30
Charlotte at New York, 7:30
Philadelphia at Miami, 7:30
Phoenix at Cleveland, 7:30
Portland at Minnesota, 7:00
Seattle at L.A. Lakers, 7:30
Utah at Golden State, 7:30

THURSDAY, JANUARY 21

Chicago at New Jersey, 7:30
Milwaukee at Indiana, 7:30
Denver at Dallas, 7:30
Detroit at Houston, 7:30

FRIDAY, JANUARY 22

New York at Philadelphia, 7:30
Phoenix at Washington, 7:30
Miami at Orlando, 7:30
New Jersey at Atlanta, 7:30
Charlotte at Chicago, 7:30
Detroit at San Antonio, 7:30
L.A. Lakers at Utah, 6:00
Cleveland at L.A. Clippers, 7:30
Seattle at Golden State, 7:30
Sacramento at Portland, 7:30

SATURDAY, JANUARY 23

Dallas at Orlando, 7:30
Phoenix at Atlanta, 7:30

Houston at Indiana, 7:30
Philadelphia at Milwaukee, 8:00
Cleveland at Denver, 7:00
Minnesota at Sacramento, 7:30

SUNDAY, JANUARY 24

Houston at New Jersey, 7:00
L.A. Lakers at Washington, 1:00
Dallas at Miami, 6:00
Indiana at Charlotte, 7:30
Chicago at San Antonio, 12:00
Portland at Utah, 1:30
Seattle at L.A. Clippers, 6:00

MONDAY, JANUARY 25

Sacramento at Atlanta, 7:30
Phoenix at Detroit, 8:00
Minnesota at Denver, 7:00

TUESDAY, JANUARY 26

Philadelphia at New York, 7:30
L.A. Lakers at New Jersey, 7:30
Miami at Washington, 7:30
Atlanta at Orlando, 7:30
Houston at Milwaukee, 7:30
Chicago at Dallas, 7:30
Cleveland at Utah, 7:00
Golden State at Portland, 7:30

WEDNESDAY, JANUARY 27

Indiana at Philadelphia, 7:30
Sacramento at Charlotte, 7:30
Boston at Detroit, 7:30
Phoenix at Minnesota, 7:00
Utah at L.A. Clippers, 7:30
Denver at Golden State, 7:30
San Antonio at Seattle, 7:00

THURSDAY, JANUARY 28

Atlanta at New York, 7:30
Milwaukee at Miami, 7:30
Orlando at Cleveland, 7:30
L.A. Lakers at Indiana, 7:30
Chicago at Houston, 7:30
New Jersey at Denver, 7:00

FRIDAY, JANUARY 29

Washington at Philadelphia, 7:30
Boston at Orlando, 7:30
L.A. Lakers at Charlotte, 7:30
Minnesota at Detroit, 8:00
Sacramento at Dallas, 7:30
San Antonio at Phoenix, 6:00
L.A. Clippers at Golden State, 7:30

SATURDAY, JANUARY 30

Charlotte at Washington, 7:30
Cleveland at Miami, 7:30
Philadelphia at Atlanta, 7:30
Detroit at Indiana, 7:30
Milwaukee at Minnesota, 7:00
New Jersey at Houston, 7:30
Sacramento at San Antonio, 7:30
Chicago at Denver, 7:00
L.A. Clippers at Utah, 7:00
Dallas at Phoenix, 7:30
Portland at Seattle, 7:00

SUNDAY, JANUARY 31

L.A. Lakers at Boston, 12:30

MONDAY, FEBRUARY 1

Seattle at Charlotte, 7:30
Golden State at Milwaukee, 7:30
New Jersey at Dallas, 7:30
Chicago at Utah, 6:00
Orlando at Sacramento, 7:30

TUESDAY, FEBRUARY 2

Washington at New York, 7:30
Seattle at Atlanta, 7:30
Golden State at Cleveland, 7:30
Indiana at Houston, 7:30

New Jersey at San Antonio, 7:30
Phoenix at L.A. Clippers, 7:30
Orlando at L.A. Lakers, 7:30
Minnesota at Portland, 7:30

WEDNESDAY, FEBRUARY 3
Charlotte at Philadelphia, 7:30
Atlanta at Miami, 7:30
Cleveland at Milwaukee, 7:30
Houston at Dallas, 7:30
Denver at Utah, 7:00
Minnesota at Phoenix, 7:30
Chicago at Sacramento, 7:30

THURSDAY, FEBRUARY 4
Golden State at New York, 7:30
Seattle at New Jersey, 7:30
Indiana at San Antonio, 7:30
Chicago at L.A. Clippers, 7:30
Utah at L.A. Lakers, 7:30

FRIDAY, FEBRUARY 5
Philadelphia at Boston, 7:30
Golden State at Washington, 7:30
New York at Miami, 8:00
Milwaukee at Charlotte, 7:30
Detroit at Cleveland, 7:30
Indiana at Dallas, 7:30
Minnesota at Houston, 7:30
Sacramento at Denver, 7:00
L.A. Lakers at Phoenix, 7:30
Orlando at Portland, 7:30

SATURDAY, FEBRUARY 6
Seattle at Washington, 7:30
Cleveland at Atlanta, 7:30
Minnesota at San Antonio, 7:30
Dallas at Denver, 7:00
Sacramento at L.A. Clippers, 7:30

SUNDAY, FEBRUARY 7
Golden State at Boston, 1:00
Miami at New York, 6:00
Seattle at Detroit, 7:00
New Jersey at Milwaukee, 1:30
Orlando at Phoenix, 7:00
Chicago at Portland, 12:30

MONDAY, FEBRUARY 8
New York at Philadelphia, 7:30
Washington at Houston, 7:30
Orlando at Utah, 7:00
Dallas at L.A. Lakers, 7:30

TUESDAY, FEBRUARY 9
Milwaukee at Boston*, 7:30
Cleveland at Charlotte, 7:30
Miami at Detroit, 7:30
L.A. Clippers at San Antonio, 7:30
Atlanta at Golden State, 7:30
Utah at Sacramento, 7:30
Denver at Seattle, 7:00
*Game played in Hartford.

WEDNESDAY, FEBRUARY 10
Detroit at New Jersey, 8:00
Houston at Philadelphia, 7:30
Cleveland at Orlando, 7:30
Chicago at Indiana, 7:30
Miami at Minnesota, 7:00
Washington at Dallas, 7:30
L.A. Clippers at Phoenix, 7:30
Denver at L.A. Lakers, 7:30

THURSDAY, FEBRUARY 11
Houston at New York, 7:30
Orlando at Charlotte, 7:30
Washington at San Antonio, 7:30
Phoenix at Golden State, 7:30
Atlanta at Sacramento, 7:30
Utah at Seattle, 7:00

FRIDAY, FEBRUARY 12
Charlotte at Miami, 7:30

Milwaukee at Cleveland, 7:30
New Jersey at Detroit, 8:00
Minnesota at Indiana, 7:30
New York at Chicago, 7:00
Boston at Dallas, 7:30
Philadelphia at Denver, 8:30
Portland at L.A. Clippers, 7:30

SATURDAY, FEBRUARY 13
Cleveland at Chicago, 7:30
Indiana at Milwaukee, 8:00
Houston at Minnesota, 7:00
Philadelphia at Dallas, 7:30
Boston at San Antonio, 7:30
Washington at Denver, 7:00
Atlanta at Utah, 7:00
Golden State at Sacramento, 7:30
Phoenix at Seattle, 7:00

SUNDAY, FEBRUARY 14
Miami at New Jersey, 5:00
New York at Orlando, 1:30
Detroit at Charlotte, 1:30
Atlanta at L.A. Lakers, 7:30
Washington at Golden State, 7:30
L.A. Clippers at Portland, 5:00

MONDAY, FEBRUARY 15
Denver at Miami, 7:30
Indiana at Cleveland, 6:00
Sacramento at Chicago, 2:30
Charlotte at Milwaukee, 7:30
Utah at Minnesota, 7:00
San Antonio at L.A. Clippers, 7:30

TUESDAY, FEBRUARY 16
Dallas at New York, 7:30
Milwaukee at New Jersey, 7:30
Orlando at Detroit, 7:30
Philadelphia at Houston, 7:30
Boston at Phoenix, 6:00
San Antonio at Golden State, 7:30
Atlanta at Portland, 7:30
Washington at Seattle, 7:00

WEDNESDAY, FEBRUARY 17
Denver at Orlando, 7:30
Detroit at Miami, 7:30
New York at Charlotte, 7:30
Dallas at Cleveland, 7:30
Sacramento at Indiana, 7:30
Utah at Chicago, 7:30

THURSDAY, FEBRUARY 18
Utah at Milwaukee, 7:30
Sacramento at Minnesota, 7:00
Boston at Houston, 7:30
Philadelphia at San Antonio, 7:30
Atlanta at Phoenix, 7:30
Washington at L.A. Clippers, 7:30
Seattle at Golden State, 7:30
L.A. Lakers at Portland, 7:30

SUNDAY, FEBRUARY 21
All-Star Game at Utah, 4:00

TUESDAY, FEBRUARY 23
Minnesota at New York, 7:30
Portland at Orlando, 7:30
New Jersey at Charlotte, 7:30
Washington at Atlanta, 7:30
Miami at Cleveland, 7:30
Philadelphia at Detroit, 7:30
Boston at Indiana, 7:30
Milwaukee at Chicago, 7:30
Phoenix at San Antonio, 7:30
Seattle at Denver, 7:30
Houston at Utah, 7:00
Sacramento at L.A. Clippers, 7:30

WEDNESDAY, FEBRUARY 24
New Jersey at Boston, 7:30
Atlanta at Philadelphia, 7:30

Indiana at Washington, 7:30
Portland at Miami, 8:00
New York at Milwaukee, 7:30
Seattle at Minnesota, 7:00
Denver at Dallas, 7:30
Utah at Golden State, 7:30
L.A. Lakers at Sacramento, 7:30

THURSDAY, FEBRUARY 25
Chicago at Orlando, 7:30
San Antonio at Charlotte, 7:30
Phoenix at Houston, 7:30

FRIDAY, FEBRUARY 26
Portland at New Jersey, 7:30
Milwaukee at Philadelphia, 7:30
Orlando at Washington, 7:30
San Antonio at Miami, 7:30
Boston at Atlanta, 7:30
New York at Detroit, 8:00
Charlotte at Indiana, 7:30
Dallas at Minnesota, 7:00
Utah at Phoenix, 7:30
Cleveland at L.A. Lakers, 7:30
L.A. Clippers at Golden State, 7:30
Seattle at Sacramento, 7:30

SATURDAY, FEBRUARY 27
Milwaukee at Detroit, 7:30
Atlanta at Chicago, 7:30
Denver at Houston, 7:30
Sacramento at Utah, 7:00
Golden State at Seattle, 7:00

SUNDAY, FEBRUARY 28
Portland at Boston, 7:00
New York at New Jersey, 1:00
San Antonio at Orlando, 1:00
Minnesota at Miami, 4:00
Dallas at Indiana, 2:30
Charlotte at Denver, 7:00
Cleveland at Phoenix, 1:30
L.A. Clippers at L.A. Lakers, 12:30

MONDAY, MARCH 1
Boston at Detroit, 8:00
Charlotte at Utah, 7:00
Philadelphia at Golden State, 7:30

TUESDAY, MARCH 2
Atlanta at New York, 7:30
Chicago at New Jersey, 8:00
Minnesota at Orlando, 7:30
San Antonio at Indiana, 7:30
Dallas at Milwaukee, 7:30
L.A. Lakers at Denver, 7:00
Houston at L.A. Clippers, 7:30
Phoenix at Portland, 7:30
Cleveland at Seattle, 7:00

WEDNESDAY, MARCH 3
San Antonio at Boston, 7:30
Washington at Miami, 7:30
Utah at Detroit, 7:30
Dallas at Chicago, 7:30
Philadelphia at Phoenix, 7:30
L.A. Lakers at Golden State, 7:30
Houston at Sacramento, 7:30

THURSDAY, MARCH 4
Utah at New York, 7:30
Orlando at New Jersey, 7:30
L.A. Clippers at Washington, 7:30
Atlanta at Indiana, 7:30
Cleveland at Minnesota, 7:00
Portland at Denver, 7:00
Charlotte at Seattle, 7:00

FRIDAY, MARCH 5
Detroit at Boston, 7:30
L.A. Clippers at Miami, 7:30
San Antonio at Chicago, 7:00
Orlando at Milwaukee, 8:00

Houston at Dallas, 7:30
Sacramento at Phoenix, 7:30
Philadelphia at L.A. Lakers, 7:30
Charlotte at Portland, 7:30

SATURDAY, MARCH 6
Denver at New Jersey, 7:30
Utah at Atlanta, 7:30
San Antonio at Minnesota, 7:00
Phoenix at Dallas, 7:30
Sacramento at Houston, 7:30
Philadelphia at Seattle, 7:00

SUNDAY, MARCH 7
Cleveland at Boston, 1:00
L.A. Clippers at Orlando, 2:00
Indiana at Miami, 4:00
Detroit at Milwaukee, 1:30
Charlotte at L.A. Lakers, 7:30
Portland at Golden State, 12:30

MONDAY, MARCH 8
Orlando at New York, 8:00
L.A. Clippers at Atlanta, 7:30
Denver at Cleveland, 7:30
Seattle at Indiana, 7:30
Philadelphia at Minnesota, 7:00

TUESDAY, MARCH 9
Washington at Charlotte, 7:30
L.A. Lakers at Detroit, 7:30
Seattle at Chicago, 7:30
Atlanta at Milwaukee, 7:30
Miami at Houston, 7:30
Dallas at San Antonio, 7:30
Minnesota at Utah, 7:00
Phoenix at Sacramento, 7:30

WEDNESDAY, MARCH 10
L.A. Lakers at New York, 7:30
Boston at Philadelphia, 7:30
Denver at Washington, 7:30
Indiana at Orlando, 7:30
Portland at Dallas, 7:30
Golden State at Phoenix, 7:30
New Jersey at L.A. Clippers, 7:30

THURSDAY, MARCH 11
Chicago at Miami, 7:30
Charlotte at Cleveland, 7:30
Denver at Detroit, 7:30
Seattle at Milwaukee, 7:30
Portland at Houston, 7:30
New Jersey at Golden State, 7:30
Minnesota at Sacramento, 7:30

FRIDAY, MARCH 12
Milwaukee at Boston, 7:30
L.A. Lakers at Philadelphia, 7:30
New York at Washington, 7:30
Orlando at Atlanta, 7:30
Charlotte at Chicago, 7:30
Dallas at Phoenix, 7:30
Minnesota at L.A. Clippers, 7:30

SATURDAY, MARCH 13
Indiana at New York, 8:30
Denver at Philadelphia, 7:30
Cleveland at Washington*, 7:30
Seattle at Miami, 7:30
Utah at Houston, 7:30
Portland at San Antonio, 7:30
New Jersey at Phoenix, 7:30
Dallas at Sacramento, 7:30
*Game played in Baltimore.

SUNDAY, MARCH 14
Charlotte at Boston, 8:00
Seattle at Orlando, 7:30
L.A. Lakers at Atlanta, 7:00
Chicago at Detroit, 12:00
L.A. Clippers at Minnesota, 2:30

MONDAY, MARCH 15
L.A. Clippers at Chicago, 7:30
Utah at Dallas, 7:30
L.A. Lakers at San Antonio, 7:00
Miami at Denver, 7:00
New Jersey at Portland, 7:30

TUESDAY, MARCH 16
Milwaukee at New York, 7:30
Atlanta at Charlotte, 7:30
Philadelphia at Cleveland, 7:30
Denver at Minnesota, 7:00
Orlando at Houston, 7:30
Boston at Golden State, 5:00
Detroit at Sacramento, 7:30
Miami at Seattle, 7:00

WEDNESDAY, MARCH 17
Atlanta at New Jersey, 7:30
Washington at Philadelphia, 7:30
Milwaukee at Indiana, 7:30
Orlando at Dallas, 7:30
Detroit at Utah, 7:00
Portland at Phoenix, 7:30
San Antonio at L.A. Lakers, 7:30

THURSDAY, MARCH 18
Minnesota at Charlotte, 7:30
New York at Cleveland, 7:30
Boston at Denver, 7:00
Miami at L.A. Clippers, 7:30
Houston at Golden State, 7:30
Sacramento at Seattle, 7:00

FRIDAY, MARCH 19
Milwaukee at New Jersey, 7:30
Dallas at Philadelphia, 7:30
Minnesota at Atlanta, 7:30
Charlotte at Indiana, 7:30
Washington at Chicago, 7:30
Orlando at San Antonio, 7:30
Seattle at Utah, 7:00
Detroit at Phoenix, 7:30
Boston at L.A. Lakers, 7:30
Golden State at Sacramento, 7:30
Houston at Portland, 7:30

SATURDAY, MARCH 20
Chicago at Washington, 7:30
Cleveland at Miami, 7:30
Philadelphia at Milwaukee, 8:00
Orlando at Denver, 7:00
Utah at L.A. Clippers, 7:30

SUNDAY, MARCH 21
San Antonio at New York, 12:00
Dallas at New Jersey, 7:00
Charlotte at Minnesota, 2:30
Seattle at Houston, 7:30
Indiana at Phoenix, 7:00
Detroit at L.A. Lakers, 5:00
Boston at Portland, 5:00

MONDAY, MARCH 22
New Jersey at Washington, 7:30
Utah at Denver, 7:00
Detroit at Golden State, 7:30

TUESDAY, MARCH 23
Miami at Orlando, 7:30
Houston at Charlotte, 7:30
Dallas at Atlanta, 7:30
San Antonio at Cleveland, 8:00
Minnesota at Chicago, 7:30
Indiana at Utah, 7:00
New York at Phoenix, 7:30
L.A. Clippers at Sacramento, 7:30
Portland at Seattle, 7:00

WEDNESDAY, MARCH 24
Miami at Boston, 7:30
Charlotte at New Jersey, 7:30
Chicago at Philadelphia, 7:30

Dallas at Washington, 7:30
San Antonio at Minnesota, 7:00
Milwaukee at L.A. Clippers, 7:30
Phoenix at L.A. Lakers, 7:30

THURSDAY, MARCH 25
Houston at Atlanta, 7:30
Golden State at Denver, 7:00
New York at Utah, 7:00
Portland at Sacramento, 7:30
Indiana at Seattle, 7:00

FRIDAY, MARCH 26
Dallas at Boston, 7:30
Cleveland at Philadelphia, 7:30
Houston at Washington, 7:30
New Jersey at Miami, 7:30
Charlotte at Detroit, 8:00
Orlando at Chicago, 7:30
Golden State at Minnesota, 7:00
Utah at San Antonio, 7:30
Milwaukee at Phoenix, 7:30
New York at L.A. Lakers, 7:30
L.A. Clippers at Portland, 7:30

SATURDAY, MARCH 27
New Jersey at Orlando, 7:30
Miami at Atlanta, 7:30
Indiana at Denver, 7:00
Milwaukee at Sacramento, 7:30
L.A. Clippers at Seattle, 7:00

SUNDAY, MARCH 28
Washington at Boston*, 2:30
Phoenix at Philadelphia, 12:00
Portland at Charlotte, 12:00
Cleveland at Detroit, 12:00
Houston at Minnesota, 2:30
San Antonio at Dallas, 7:00
Indiana at L.A. Lakers, 7:30
New York at Golden State, 5:00
*Game played in Hartford.

MONDAY, MARCH 29
Sacramento at Boston, 7:30
Portland at Atlanta, 7:30
Washington at Milwaukee, 7:30
Denver at Utah, 7:00

TUESDAY, MARCH 30
Sacramento at New York, 7:30
Philadelphia at New Jersey, 7:30
Detroit at Orlando, 7:30
Miami at Charlotte, 7:30
Phoenix at Chicago, 7:00
Seattle at San Antonio, 7:30
L.A. Lakers at L.A. Clippers, 7:30
Minnesota at Golden State, 7:30

WEDNESDAY, MARCH 31
Philadelphia at Boston, 7:30
Portland at Detroit, 7:30
Washington at Indiana, 7:30
Seattle at Dallas, 7:30
Atlanta at Denver, 7:00
San Antonio at Utah, 7:00
Minnesota at L.A. Lakers, 7:30

THURSDAY, APRIL 1
Cleveland at New York, 7:30
Miami at New Jersey, 7:30
Sacramento at Washington, 7:30
Charlotte at Orlando, 7:30
Milwaukee at Houston, 7:30

FRIDAY, APRIL 2
Phoenix at Boston, 8:00
Portland at Philadelphia, 7:30
New York at Miami, 7:30
Cleveland at Charlotte, 7:30
Sacramento at Detroit, 8:00
Orlando at Indiana, 7:30
New Jersey at Chicago, 7:30

Golden State at Dallas, 7:30
Minnesota at San Antonio, 7:30
Milwaukee at Denver, 7:00
Atlanta at L.A. Clippers, 7:30

SATURDAY, APRIL 3

Portland at Washington, 7:30
Golden State at Houston, 7:30
Atlanta at Seattle, 7:00

SUNDAY, APRIL 4

Chicago at Boston, 1:30
Sacramento at Philadelphia, 12:30
Orlando at Miami, 4:00
New Jersey at Cleveland, 1:30
Phoenix at Indiana, 2:30
New York at San Antonio, 7:00
Minnesota at Denver, 2:00
Dallas at L.A. Clippers, 6:00
Utah at L.A. Lakers, 7:30

TUESDAY, APRIL 6

Indiana at New Jersey, 7:30
Philadelphia at Orlando, 7:30
New York at Atlanta, 7:30
Miami at Cleveland, 7:30
Washington at Detroit, 7:30
Chicago at Milwaukee, 7:30
L.A. Clippers at Houston, 7:30
Golden State at San Antonio, 7:30
L.A. Lakers at Phoenix, 7:30
Denver at Sacramento, 7:30
Utah at Portland, 7:30
Dallas at Seattle, 7:00

WEDNESDAY, APRIL 7

Philadelphia at Washington, 7:30
Orlando at Charlotte, 7:30
Indiana at Minnesota, 7:00

THURSDAY, APRIL 8

Boston at New York, 8:00
Detroit at New Jersey, 7:30
Miami at Milwaukee, 7:30
L.A. Clippers at San Antonio, 7:30
Houston at Utah, 7:00
L.A. Lakers at Golden State, 7:30
Phoenix at Sacramento, 7:30
Dallas at Portland, 7:30

FRIDAY, APRIL 9

Detroit at Boston, 7:30
Charlotte at Philadelphia, 7:30
Chicago at Atlanta, 7:30
Washington at Cleveland, 7:30
Orlando at Minnesota, 7:00
Denver at Phoenix, 7:30
Portland at L.A. Lakers, 7:30
Sacramento at Seattle, 7:00

SATURDAY, APRIL 10

Cleveland at New Jersey, 7:30
Philadelphia at Miami, 7:30
Atlanta at Charlotte, 7:30
Chicago at Indiana, 7:30
Orlando at Milwaukee, 8:00
San Antonio at Houston, 7:30
Denver at L.A. Clippers, 7:30
Dallas at Golden State, 7:30

SUNDAY, APRIL 11

New York at Boston, 1:00
Detroit at Washington, 1:00
Utah at Phoenix, 12:30
Seattle at L.A. Lakers, 12:30
Minnesota at Portland, 5:00

MONDAY, APRIL 12

Milwaukee at Miami, 7:30
Philadelphia at Charlotte, 7:30
Chicago at Detroit, 7:30
Dallas at Utah, 7:00
Phoenix at L.A. Clippers, 7:30
Denver at Golden State, 7:30

TUESDAY, APRIL 13

Indiana at Boston, 7:30
Washington at New York, 7:30
Milwaukee at Orlando, 7:30
Cleveland at Atlanta, 7:30
L.A. Lakers at Houston, 7:30
San Antonio at Sacramento, 7:30
L.A. Clippers at Portland, 7:30
Minnesota at Seattle, 7:00

WEDNESDAY, APRIL 14

New York at Charlotte, 7:30
Atlanta at Detroit, 7:30
New Jersey at Indiana, 7:30
Miami at Chicago, 7:30
L.A. Lakers at Dallas, 7:30
Houston at Denver, 7:00
Minnesota at Phoenix, 7:30
San Antonio at Golden State, 7:30

THURSDAY, APRIL 15

Boston at New Jersey, 7:30
Orlando at Philadelphia, 7:30
Miami at Washington, 7:30
Cleveland at Milwaukee, 7:30
Portland at Utah, 6:00

FRIDAY, APRIL 16

Detroit at Charlotte, 7:30
Orlando at Cleveland, 7:30
New York at Indiana, 7:30
Milwaukee at Chicago, 7:30
Portland at Minnesota, 7:00
Denver at Dallas, 7:30
Sacramento at San Antonio, 7:30
Seattle at Phoenix, 7:30
Golden State at L.A. Clippers, 7:30
Houston at L.A. Lakers, 7:30

SATURDAY, APRIL 17

Detroit at New York, 8:30
New Jersey at Washington, 7:30
Boston at Miami, 3:30
Charlotte at Atlanta, 7:30
Sacramento at Dallas, 7:30
Phoenix at Utah, 7:00
Houston at Seattle, 7:00

SUNDAY, APRIL 18

Minnesota at Philadelphia, 1:00
Boston at Orlando, 12:30
Chicago at Cleveland, 5:30
Indiana at Milwaukee, 1:30

L.A. Clippers at Denver, 7:00
Golden State at L.A. Lakers, 12:00
San Antonio at Portland, 5:00

MONDAY, APRIL 19

Houston at Phoenix, 7:30
San Antonio at Seattle, 7:00

TUESDAY, APRIL 20

Washington at Orlando, 7:30
New York at Miami, 7:30
Indiana at Atlanta, 7:30
Detroit at Cleveland, 7:30
Philadelphia at Chicago, 7:30
L.A. Lakers at Minnesota, 7:00
L.A. Clippers at Dallas, 7:30
Utah at Sacramento, 7:30
Golden State at Portland, 7:30

WEDNESDAY, APRIL 21

Orlando at Boston, 7:30
New Jersey at New York, 7:30
Miami at Philadelphia, 7:30
Atlanta at Washington, 7:30
Milwaukee at Charlotte, 7:30
Cleveland at Indiana, 7:30
Dallas at Denver, 7:30
L.A. Lakers at Utah, 7:00
Sacramento at Golden State, 7:30

THURSDAY, APRIL 22

Detroit at Chicago, 7:30
Minnesota at Houston, 7:30
Denver at San Antonio, 7:30
Seattle at L.A. Clippers, 7:30
Phoenix at Portland, 5:00

FRIDAY, APRIL 23

Cleveland at Boston, 7:30
Orlando at New Jersey, 7:30
New York at Philadelphia, 7:30
Washington at Miami, 7:30
Chicago at Charlotte, 7:30
Milwaukee at Atlanta, 7:30
Indiana at Detroit, 8:00
Minnesota at Dallas, 7:30
Golden State at Utah, 7:00
Portland at Sacramento, 7:30
L.A. Lakers at Seattle, 7:00

SATURDAY, APRIL 24

Atlanta at Orlando, 7:30
Miami at Indiana, 7:30
Charlotte at Milwaukee, 8:00
Dallas at Houston, 7:30
San Antonio at Phoenix, 12:30
Sacramento at L.A. Lakers, 7:30

SUNDAY, APRIL 25

Chicago at New York, 1:00
Boston at Washington, 1:00
Philadelphia at Cleveland, 3:30
New Jersey at Detroit, 3:30
Utah at Minnesota, 2:30
Houston at San Antonio, 7:30
Phoenix at Denver, 7:00
Portland at L.A. Clippers, 12:30
Seattle at Golden State, 12:30

1992-93 NBA Games on Television

(All times Eastern)

NBC Schedule

Dec. 25—San Antonio at L.A. Clippers.........................3:30
New York at Chicago.....................................9:00
Jan. 24—Chicago at San Antonio................................1:00
Portland at Utah 3:30
Jan. 31—L.A. Lakers at Boston 12:30
Feb. 7—Golden State at Boston 1:00
Chicago at Portland 3:30
Feb. 14—Detroit at Charlotte or
New York at Orlando..................................1:30
Feb. 21—43rd NBA ALL-STAR GAME 6:00
(Salt Lake City)
Feb. 28—New York at New Jersey or
San Antonio at Orlando................................1:00
L.A. Clippers at L.A. Lakers or
Cleveland at Phoenix 3:30
Mar. 7—Cleveland at Boston..................................1:00
Portland at Golden State............................3:30
Mar. 14—Chicago at Detroit 12:00

Mar. 21—San Antonio at New York 12:00
Mar. 28—Phoenix at Philadelphia or
Portland at Charlotte or
Cleveland at Detroit 12:00
Apr. 4—Chicago at Boston 1:30
Apr. 11—New York at Boston 1:00
Seattle at L.A. Lakers or
Utah at Phoenix 3:30
Apr. 17—Boston at Miami 3:30
Apr. 18—Golden State at L.A. Lakers 3:00
Chicago at Cleveland 5:30
Apr. 24—San Antonio at Phoenix............................3:30
Apr. 25—Chicago at New York....................................1:00
New Jersey at Detroit or
Portland at L.A. Clippers or
Philadelphia at Cleveland or
Seattle at Golden State............................3:30

TNT Schedule

Nov. 3—Naismith Hall of Fame Game 8:00
(From Springfield, Mass.)
Portland vs. Charlotte
Nov. 6—Chicago at Cleveland 8:00
Seattle vs. Houston at Japan 10:30
Nov. 10—Charlotte at Orlando 8:00
Nov. 13—New York at Washington............................8:00
L.A. Clippers at L.A. Lakers................10:30
Nov. 17—Milwaukee at Atlanta................................8:00
Nov. 20—Portland at Sacramento............................8:00
Chicago at L.A. Lakers................. 10:30
Nov. 24—San Antonio at Portland............................8:00
Dec. 2—Chicago at Boston 8:00
Dec. 4—Portland at Chicago...................................8:00
Dec. 8—Boston at Orlando....................................8:00
Dec. 11—Cleveland at Detroit 8:00
Dec. 15—Boston at Minnesota................................8:00
Dec. 18—Dallas at San Antonio...............................8:00
Dec. 22—Golden State at Phoenix.........................8:00
Jan. 3—Phoenix at San Antonio............................8:00
Jan. 5—L.A. Lakers at Chicago..............................8:00
Jan. 8—New York at Orlando................................8:00
Jan. 10—Boston at New York 8:00
Jan. 15—Cleveland at Indiana.................................8:00
Jan. 17—Seattle at Portland 8:00
Jan. 22—L.A. Lakers at Utah..................................8:00
Jan. 25—Phoenix at Detroit 8:00
Jan. 29—San Antonio at Phoenix............................8:00

Feb. 1—Chicago at Utah 8:00
Feb. 5—New York at Miami...................................8:00
Feb. 10—Detroit at New Jersey...............................8:00
Feb. 12—New York at Chicago................................8:00
Philadelphia at Denver.............................10:30
Feb. 14—L.A. Clippers at Portland 8:00
Feb. 16—Boston at Phoenix 8:00
Feb. 19—NBA All-Star Friday Night..........................TBA
Feb. 20—NBA All-Star Saturday...............................7:00
Feb. 24—Portland at Miami 8:00
Feb. 26—New York at Detroit 8:00
Mar. 1—Boston at Detroit 8:00
Mar. 2—Chicago at New Jersey..............................8:00
Mar. 5—San Antonio at Chicago............................8:00
Mar. 8—Orlando at New York 8:00
Mar. 14—Charlotte at Boston 8:00
Mar. 15—L.A. Lakers at San Antonio 8:00
Mar. 16—Boston at Golden State............................8:00
Mar. 21—Detroit at L.A. Lakers 8:00
Mar. 23—San Antonio at Cleveland.........................8:00
Mar. 28—New York at Golden State.........................8:00
Mar. 30—Phoenix at Chicago............................... 8:00
Apr. 2—Phoenix at Boston 8:00
Apr. 4—New York at San Antonio 8:00
Apr. 8—Boston at New York..................................8:00
Apr. 15—Portland at Utah..8:00
Apr. 22—Phoenix at Portland...................................8:00

1992-93 NBA Games on Radio

(All times Eastern)

Jan. 24—Chicago at San Antonio..................... 12:30
Jan. 31—L.A. Lakers at Boston 12:00
Feb. 7—Chicago at Portland....................................3:00
Feb. 14—Detroit at Charlotte or
New York at Orlando..................................1:00
Feb. 21—43rd NBA ALL-STAR GAME....................5:30
(Salt Lake City)
Feb. 28—New York at New Jersey or
San Antonio at Orlando......................... 12:30
Mar. 7—Portland at Golden State............................3:00

Mar. 14—Chicago at Detroit 11:30
Mar. 21—San Antonio at New York 11:30
Mar. 28—Phoenix at Philadelphia or
Cleveland at Detroit or
Portland at Charlotte..............................11:30
Apr. 4—Chicago at Boston 1:00
Apr. 11—Seattle at L.A. Lakers or
Utah at Phoenix 3:00
Apr. 18—Chicago at Cleveland 5:00
Apr. 25—Chicago at New York.................................12:30

Divisional Alignment 1992-93 Season

EASTERN CONFERENCE	WESTERN CONFERENCE
Atlantic Division	**Midwest Division**

Boston Celtics	Dallas Mavericks
Miami Heat	Denver Nuggets
New Jersey Nets	Houston Rockets
New York Knicks	Minnesota Timberwolves
Orlando Magic	San Antonio Spurs
Philadelphia 76ers	Utah Jazz
Washington Bullets	

Central Division	**Pacific Division**
Atlanta Hawks	Golden State Warriors
Charlotte Hornets	Los Angeles Clippers
Chicago Bulls	Los Angeles Lakers
Cleveland Cavaliers	Phoenix Suns
Detroit Pistons	Portland Trail Blazers
Indiana Pacers	Sacramento Kings
Milwaukee Bucks	Seattle SuperSonics

1992-93 Playoff Format

Under the National Basketball Association's playoff format, 16 teams qualify for postseason. Four of the playoff berths will go to division champions and the remaining spots to the six teams in each conference with the best regular-season winning percentage. The first-round series are best-of-five and include every team. All succeeding rounds are best-of-seven.

The playoff pairings will look like this:

Western Conference   **Eastern Conference**

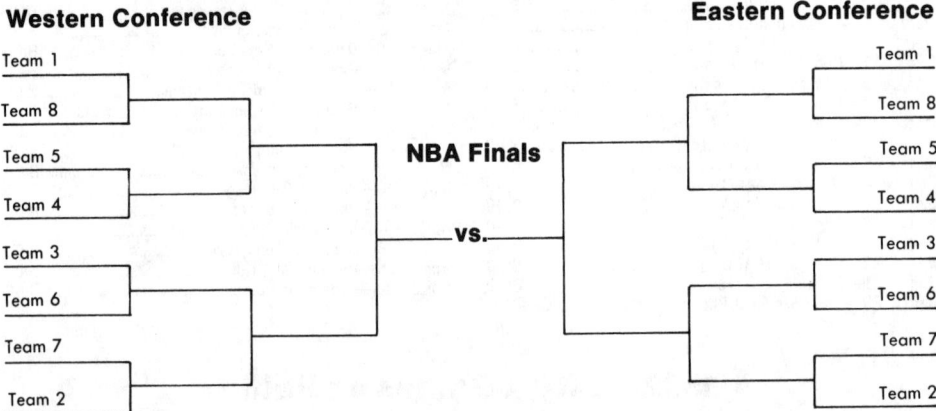

Note: Team 1 in each conference is the division winner with the better record, Team 2 is the other division winner and Teams 3 through 8 are ranked according to their regular-season winning percentage.

Continental Basketball Association

425 South Cherry Street, Suite 230, Denver, CO 80222, 303/331-0404
Fax: 303/377-9452; Scorephone: 617/951-0724

Commissioner: .... Terdema L. Ussery II
Deputy Commissioner: ....Arnold D. Fielkow
Vice President, Operations: .... Jim Tooley
Operations Assistant: .... Bret Mactavish
Vice President, Public Relations: .... Greg Anderson
Assistant Director of Public Relations: ....Brett Meister
Vice President, Marketing: .... Alex J. Vergara
Marketing Assistant: ....Lara Price
Marketing Administrative Assistant: .... Andrea Vignaroli
Director of Scouting Services: .... Marty Blake
Business Manager: .... Alma Bennet
Executive Assistant: ....Cinderella Epstein
Receptionist .... Kathleen Atnip

CBA EXPECTS CONTINUED GROWTH AND NBA IMPACT IN 1992-93

Impact and growth. Two staples for the fast-rising Continental Basketball Association in recent years, are expected to again be key elements as the league enters its 47th season of play in 1992-93, and its 13th year as the Official Developmental League of the NBA.

Impact: There were a record 72 CBA veterans on NBA rosters last season, as every NBA club signed at least one former CBA player. "The NBA, players, agents, and college coaches are starting to understand that the CBA is another valuable option for players to improve their skills and move up," said Marty Blake, NBA/CBA director of scouting services.

Those figures are particularly impressive when considering that in 1978-79 (the first year of the CBA-NBA developmental agreement), there were only two NBA players with CBA experience. The CBA veterans in the NBA are no longer just practice players; nine former CBA players were full-time NBA starters last year, and 11 ranked among the top-20 NBA statistical leaders, including Washington All-Star guard Michael Adams, and Indiana guard Micheal Williams, a second team NBA All-Defensive selection.

The CBA's impact in the NBA is not reserved for players. Three current NBA head coaches are CBA veterans—Chicago's Phil Jackson, who led the Bulls to a second consecutive NBA World Championship in 1992, Seattle's George Karl, and Indiana's Bob Hill; and 33 of the 55 NBA referees last year had CBA experience.

Growth: League attendance soared to a record 1.7 million last season—a 7.4 percent increase from the previous all-time mark set in 1990-91. As league attendance increased for the 10th straight season, the CBA also sent 27 player call-ups to the NBA last year. Perhaps the most notable was Quad City Thunder guard Anthony Bowie, who became a part-time starter for the Orlando Magic.

In April, the La Crosse Catbirds won what CBA Commissioner Terdema L. Ussery II phrased as "perhaps the greatest Championship Series in league history." Led by star guard David Rivers, the CBA Playoff Most Valuable Player, La Crosse topped the Rapid City Thrillers, four-games-to-three. It was the second time in three years that La Crosse edged Rapid City for the crown.

The 1992-93 campaign will feature a lineup of 16 CBA clubs, including new franchises in Fargo (ND)-Moorhead (MN) and Rochester (MN). This year's 56-game CBA schedule will begin November 20 and conclude March 28. An annual attraction for NBA scouts, the CBA All-Star Classic will be staged January 12 in Oklahoma City's 14,000-seat Myriad Convention Center.

Following are the final standings, award winners and statistical leaders for the 1991-92 CBA season and the 1992-93 divisional lineup:

1991-92 FINAL STANDINGS

AMERICAN CONFERENCE

EASTERN DIVISION

	W	L	QW*	PTS.
Grand Rapids Hoops	28	28	110.5	194.5
Birmingham Bandits	25	31	114.5	189.5
Albany Patroons	24	32	109.0	181.0
Columbus Horizon	18	38	88.0	142.0

MIDWEST DIVISION

	W	L	QW*	PTS.
Quad City Thunder	42	14	136.5	262.5
La Crosse Catbirds	40	16	140.0	260.0
Rockford Lightning	21	35	98.0	161.0
Fort Wayne Fury	21	35	87.0	150.0

NATIONAL CONFERENCE

NORTHERN DIVISION

	W	L	QW*	PTS.
Rapid City Thrillers	37	19	130.0	241.0
Omaha Racers	37	19	127.0	238.0
Tri-City Chinook	29	27	112.0	199.0
Sioux Falls Skyforce	24	32	104.0	176.0
Yakima Sun Kings	13	43	82.5	121.5

SOUTHERN DIVISION

	W	L	QW*	PTS.
Oklahoma City Cavalry	33	23	114.5	213.5
Wichita Falls Texans	28	28	126.5	210.5
Tulsa Zone	24	32	108.0	180.0
Bakersfield Jammers	16	8	52.0	100.0

*QW—Quarters won. Teams get 3 points for a win, 1 point for each quarter won and ½ point for any quarter tied.

PLAYOFF RESULTS

American Conference First Round Shootout
Birmingham defeated Albany, 1-0

American Conference Second Round
La Crosse defeated Grand Rapids, 3-1
Quad City defeated Birmingham, 3-1

American Conference Finals
La Crosse defeated Quad City, 3-2

National Conference First Round Shootout
Wichita defeated Tri-City, 1-0

National Conference Second Round
Omaha defeated Oklahoma City, 3-2
Rapid City defeated Wichita Falls, 3-1

National Conference Finals
Rapid City defeated Omaha, 3-2

CBA Championship
La Crosse defeated Rapid City, 4-3

AWARD WINNERS

Most Valuable Player: Barry Mitchell, Quad City
Rookie of the Year: Marcus Kennedy, Grand Rapids
Newcomer of the Year: Stanley Brundy, Rapid City
Defensive Player of the Year: Barry Mitchell, Quad City

Co-Coaches of the Year: Dan Panaggio, Quad City
Flip Saunders, La Crosse
Executive of the Year: Brooks Ellison, Yakima
Playoff MVP: David Rivers, La Crosse

ALL-LEAGUE

FIRST TEAM		SECOND TEAM
Ronnie Grandison, Omaha	Forward	Stanley Brundy, Rapid City
Barry Mitchell, Quad City	Forward	Stephen Thompson, Oklahoma City
Marcus Kennedy, Grand Rapids	Center	Steve Scheffler, Quad City
Mark Davis, La Crosse	Guard	Steve Bardo, Whichita Falls
David Rivers, La Crosse	Guard	Jeff Martin, Grand Rapids

ALL-DEFENSIVE

Forward—Barry Mitchell, Quad City
Forward—Kurt Portmann, Wichita Falls
Center—Jawann Oldham, Tulsa
Guard—A.J. Wynder, Quad City
Guard—Steve Bardo, Wichita Falls
Darryl McDonald, Sioux Falls

ALL-ROOKIE

Forward—Walter Bond, Wichita Falls
Forward—Kermit Holmes, Columbus
Center—Marcus Kennedy, Grand Rapids
Guard—Bobby Phills, Sioux Falls
Guard—Gary Waites, Grand Rapids

CBA STATISTICAL LEADERS

POINTS

		G	Pts.	Avg.
1.	Stephen Thompson, Oklahoma City	39	1004	25.7
2.	Mark Davis, La Crosse	56	1382	24.7
3.	Jeff Martin, Grand Rapids	56	1377	24.6
4.	Steve Burtt, Oklahoma City	43	1019	23.7
5.	Derrick Gervin, La Crosse	42	991	23.6
6.	Kenny Travis, Albany	47	1099	23.4
7.	Bobby Phills, Sioux Falls	34	785	23.1
8.	Marcus Kennedy, Grand Rapids	29	656	22.6
9.	Byron Irvin, Columbus	55	1226	22.3
10.	Skeeter Henry, Birmingham	56	1158	20.7

ASSISTS

		G	Ast.	Avg.
1.	David Rivers, La Crosse	32	414	12.9
2.	Shawn McDaniel, Tulsa	52	444	8.5
3.	Craig Neal, Rapid City	38	316	8.3
4.	Cedric Hunter, Omaha	50	406	8.1
5.	Corey Gaines, Sioux Falls	53	424	8.0
6.	Anthony Houston, Yakima	58	456	7.9
7.	Michael Anderson, Tri-City	43	332	7.7
8.	Mark Wade, Omaha	34	247	7.3
9.	A.J. Wynder, Quad City	56	402	7.2
10.	Byron Dinkins, Columbus	43	286	6.7

FIELD GOALS

		FGM	FGA	Pct.
1.	Jarvis Basnight, Rapid City	338	528	.640
2.	Willie Simms, Tri-City	249	397	.627
3.	Steve Scheffler, Quad City	233	381	.612
4.	Darryl McDonald, Sioux Falls	193	321	.601
5.	Stanley Brundy, Rapid City	237	397	.597
6.	Steve Wright, Albany	180	302	.596
7.	Marcus Kennedy, Grand Rapids	262	444	.590
8.	Cedric Hunter, Omaha	248	442	.561
9.	Vince Hamilton, La Crosse	109	199	.548
10.	Sam Johnson, Tulsa	187	344	.544

BLOCKED SHOTS

		G	BS	Avg.
1.	Jawann Oldham, Tulsa	49	160	3.3
2.	Cedric Lewis, Albany	52	154	3.0
3.	Nate Johnston, Rapid City	56	144	2.6
4.	Kurt Portmann, Wichita Falls	54	135	2.5
5.	Cedric Jenkins, Wichita Falls	29	65	2.2
6.	Jim Usevitch, Tri-City	56	123	2.2
7.	Jackie Jones, Yakima	41	87	2.1
8.	Jarvis Basnight, Rapid City	52	95	1.8
9.	Dave Popson, Birmingham	39	59	1.5
10.	William Hunter, Yakima	49	74	1.5

REBOUNDS

		G	Reb.	Avg.
1.	Stanley Brundy, Rapid City	45	501	11.1
2.	Greg Wiltjer, Omaha	56	605	10.8
3.	Jawann Oldham, Tulsa	49	526	10.7
4.	Wayne Tinkle, Tri-City	55	585	10.6
5.	Marcus Kennedy, Grand Rapids	29	305	10.5
6.	Ronnie Grandison, Omaha	43	432	10.0
7.	Lee Campbell, Yakima	41	397	9.7
8.	Cedric Jenkins, Wichita Falls	29	272	9.4
9.	Brian Rahilly, La Crosse	55	511	9.3
10.	Jeff Sanders, Fort Wayne	44	405	9.2

STEALS

		G	St.	Avg.
1.	Kenny Battle, La Crosse	32	95	3.0
2.	Barry Mitchell, Quad City	55	160	2.9
3.	Kieth Wilson, Tulsa	55	145	2.6
4.	David Rivers, La Crosse	32	82	2.6
5.	Darryl McDonald, Sioux Falls	56	132	2.4
	Kelsey Weems, Oklahoma City	56	132	2.4
7.	A.J. Wynder, Quad City	56	130	2.3
8.	Eric Johnson, Birmingham	54	125	2.3
9.	Melvin Newbern, Tulsa	45	104	2.3
10.	Mark Davis, La Crosse	56	128	2.3

1992-93 DIVISIONAL ALIGNMENT

AMERICAN CONFERENCE

EASTERN DIVISION

Albany (NY) Patroons
Columbus (OH) Horizon
Fort Wayne (IN) Fury
Grand Rapids (MI) Hoops

MIDEAST DIVISION

La Crosse (WI) Catbirds
Quad City (IL) Thunder
Rochester (MN) Renegade
Rockford (IL) Lightning

NATIONAL CONFERENCE

MIDWEST DIVISION

Fargo (ND)-Moorhead (MN) Fever
Omaha (NE) Racers
Rapid City (SD) Thrillers
Sioux Falls (SD) Skyforce

WESTERN DIVISION

Oklahoma City (OK) Cavalry
Tri-City (WA) Chinook
Wichita Falls (TX) Texans
Yakima (WA) Sun Kings

TOP NBA, ABA PERFORMERS

Including

Year-by-Year NBA Award Winners

Year-by-Year NBA All-Rookie Teams

Year-by-Year NBA All-Defensive Teams

Year-by-Year All-NBA Teams

Players Who Have Made All-NBA Teams

NBA All-Star Game Box Score, 1992

NBA All-Star Game Records

Basketball Hall of Fame

ABA All-Stars, Award Winners

POST-SEASON AWARDS
EDGE NBA MOST VALUABLE PLAYER
(Maurice Podoloff Trophy)
Selected by vote of NBA players until 1979-80; by Writers and Broadcasters since 1980-81

1955-56—Bob Pettit, St. Louis	1974-75—Bob McAdoo, Buffalo
1956-57—Bob Cousy, Boston	1975-76—Kareem Abdul-Jabbar, L.A.
1957-58—Bill Russell, Boston	1976-77—Kareem Abdul-Jabbar, L.A.
1958-59—Bob Pettit, St. Louis	1977-78—Bill Walton, Portland
1959-60—Wilt Chamberlain, Philadelphia	1978-79—Moses Malone, Houston
1960-61—Bill Russell, Boston	1979-80—Kareem Abdul-Jabbar, L.A.
1961-62—Bill Russell, Boston	1980-81—Julius Erving, Philadelphia
1962-63—Bill Russell, Boston	1981-82—Moses Malone, Houston
1963-64—Oscar Robertson, Cincinnati	1982-83—Moses Malone, Philadelphia
1964-65—Bill Russell, Boston	1983-84—Larry Bird, Boston
1965-66—Wilt Chamberlain, Philadelphia	1984-85—Larry Bird, Boston
1966-67—Wilt Chamberlain, Philadelphia	1985-86—Larry Bird, Boston
1967-68—Wilt Chamberlain, Philadelphia	1986-87—Magic Johnson, L.A. Lakers
1968-69—Wes Unseld, Baltimore	1987-88—Michael Jordan, Chicago
1969-70—Willis Reed, New York	1988-89—Magic Johnson, L.A. Lakers
1970-71—Kareem Abdul-Jabbar, Milwaukee	1989-90—Magic Johnson, L.A. Lakers
1971-72—Kareem Abdul-Jabber, Milwaukee	1990-91—Michael Jordan, Chicago
1972-73—Dave Cowens, Boston	1991-92—Michael Jordan, Chicago
1973-74—Kareem Abdul-Jabbar, Milwaukee	

IBM NBA COACH OF THE YEAR
(Red Auerbach Trophy)
Selected by Writers and Broadcasters

1962-63—Harry Gallatin, St. Louis	1977-78—Hubie Brown, Atlanta
1963-64—Alex Hannum, San Francisco	1978-79—Cotton Fitzsimmons, Kansas City
1964-65—Red Auerbach, Boston	1979-80—Bill Fitch, Boston
1965-66—Dolph Schayes, Philadelphia	1980-81—Jack McKinney, Indiana
1966-67—Johnny Kerr, Chicago	1981-82—Gene Shue, Washington
1967-68—Richie Guerin, St. Louis	1982-83—Don Nelson, Milwaukee
1968-69—Gene Shue, Baltimore	1983-84—Frank Layden, Utah
1969-70—Red Holzman, New York	1984-85—Don Nelson, Milwaukee
1970-71—Dick Motta, Chicago	1985-86—Mike Fratello, Atlanta
1971-72—Bill Sharman, Los Angeles	1986-87—Mike Schuler, Portland
1972-73—Tom Heinsohn, Boston	1987-88—Doug Moe, Denver
1973-74—Ray Scott, Detroit	1988-89—Cotton Fitzsimmons, Phoenix
1974-75—Phil Johnson, Kansas City-Omaha	1989-90—Pat Riley, L.A. Lakers
1975-76—Bill Fitch, Cleveland	1990-91—Don Chaney, Houston
1976-77—Tom Nissalke, Houston	1991-92—Don Nelson, Golden State

COCA-COLA CLASSIC NBA ROOKIE OF THE YEAR
(Eddie Gottlieb Trophy)
Selected by Writers and Broadcasters

1952-53—Don Meineke, Fort Wayne	1972-73—Bob McAdoo, Buffalo
1953-54—Ray Felix, Baltimore	1973-74—Ernie DiGregorio, Buffalo
1954-55—Bob Pettit, Milwaukee	1974-75—Keith Wilkes, Golden State
1955-56—Maurice Stokes, Rochester	1975-76—Alvan Adams, Phoenix
1956-57—Tom Heinsohn, Boston	1976-77—Adrian Dantley, Buffalo
1957-58—Woody Sauldsberry, Philadelphia	1977-78—Walter Davis, Phoenix
1958-59—Elgin Baylor, Minneapolis	1978-79—Phil Ford, Kansas City
1959-60—Wilt Chamberlain, Philadelphia	1979-80—Larry Bird, Boston
1960-61—Oscar Robertson, Cincinnati	1980-81—Darrell Griffith, Utah
1961-62—Walt Bellamy, Chicago	1981-82—Buck Williams, New Jersey
1962-63—Terry Dischinger, Chicago	1982-83—Terry Cummings, San Diego
1963-64—Jerry Lucas, Cincinnati	1983-84—Ralph Sampson, Houston
1964-65—Willis Reed, New York	1984-85—Michael Jordan, Chicago
1965-66—Rick Barry, San Francisco	1985-86—Patrick Ewing, New York
1966-67—Dave Bing, Detroit	1986-87—Chuck Person, Indiana
1967-68—Earl Monroe, Baltimore	1987-88—Mark Jackson, New York
1968-69—Wes Unseld, Baltimore	1988-89—Mitch Richmond, Golden State
1969-70—Kareem Abdul-Jabbar, Milwaukee	1989-90—David Robinson, San Antonio
1970-71—(tie) Dave Cowens, Boston	1990-91—Derrick Coleman, New Jersey
Geoff Petrie, Portland	1991-92—Larry Johnson, Charlotte
1971-72—Sidney Wicks, Portland	

NBA MOST IMPROVED PLAYER
Selected by Writers and Broadcasters

1985-86—Alvin Robertson, San Antonio	1989-90—Rony Seikaly, Miami
1986-87—Dale Ellis, Seattle	1990-91—Scott Skiles, Orlando
1987-88—Kevin Duckworth, Portland	1991-92—Pervis Ellison, Washington
1988-89—Kevin Johnson, Phoenix	

NBA EXECUTIVE OF THE YEAR

Selected by NBA Executives for The Sporting News

1972-73—Joe Axelson, Kansas City-Omaha
1973-74—Eddie Donovan, Buffalo
1974-75—Dick Vertlieb, Golden State
1975-76—Jerry Colangelo, Phoenix
1976-77—Ray Patterson, Houston
1977-78—Angelo Drossos, San Antonio
1978-79—Bob Ferry, Washington
1979-80—Red Auerbach, Boston
1980-81—Jerry Colangelo, Phoenix
1981-82—Bob Ferry, Washington

1982-83—Zollie Volchok, Seattle
1983-84—Frank Layden, Utah
1984-85—Vince Boryla, Denver
1985-86—Stan Kasten, Atlanta
1986-87—Stan Kasten, Atlanta
1987-88—Jerry Krause, Chicago
1988-89—Jerry Colangelo, Phoenix
1989-90—Bob Bass, San Antonio
1990-91—Bucky Buckwalter, Portland
1991-92—Wayne Embry, Cleveland

J. WALTER KENNEDY CITIZENSHIP AWARD

Selected by the Pro Basketball Writers Association of America

1974-75—Wes Unseld, Washington
1975-76—Slick Watts, Seattle
1976-77—Dave Bing, Washington
1977-78—Bob Lanier, Detroit
1978-79—Calvin Murphy, Houston
1979-80—Austin Carr, Cleveland
1980-81—Mike Glenn, New York
1981-82—Kent Benson, Detroit
1982-83—Julius Erving, Philadelphia
1983-84—Frank Layden, Utah

1984-85—Dan Issel, Denver
1985-86—(tie) Michael Cooper, L.A. Lakers
         Rory Sparrow, New York
1986-87—Isiah Thomas, Detroit
1987-88—Alex English, Denver
1988-89—Thurl Bailey, Utah
1989-90—Glenn Rivers, Atlanta
1990-91—Kevin Johnson, Phoenix
1991-92—Magic Johnson, L.A. Lakers

NBA DEFENSIVE PLAYER OF THE YEAR

Selected by Writers and Broadcasters

1982-83—Sidney Moncrief, Milwaukee
1983-84—Sidney Moncrief, Milwaukee
1984-85—Mark Eaton, Utah
1985-86—Alvin Robertson, San Antonio
1986-87—Michael Cooper, L.A. Lakers

1987-88—Michael Jordan, Chicago
1988-89—Mark Eaton, Utah
1989-90—Dennis Rodman, Detroit
1990-91—Dennis Rodman, Detroit
1991-92—David Robinson, San Antonio

MILLER GENUINE DRAFT NBA SIXTH MAN AWARD

Selected by Writers and Broadcasters

1982-83—Bobby Jones, Philadelphia
1983-84—Kevin McHale, Boston
1984-85—Kevin McHale, Boston
1985-86—Bill Walton, Boston
1986-87—Ricky Pierce, Milwaukee

1987-88—Roy Tarpley, Dallas
1988-89—Eddie Johnson, Phoenix
1989-90—Ricky Pierce, Milwaukee
1990-91—Detlef Schrempf, Indiana
1991-92—Detlef Schrempf, Indiana

SCHICK AWARD

Determined by Computer Formula

1983-84—Magic Johnson, Los Angeles
1984-85—Michael Jordan, Chicago
1985-86—Charles Barkley, Philadelphia
1986-87—Charles Barkley, Philadelphia
1987-88—Charles Barkley, Philadelphia

1988-89—Michael Jordan, Chicago
1989-90—David Robinson, San Antonio
1990-91—David Robinson, San Antonio
1991-92—Dennis Rodman, Detroit

ALL-ROOKIE TEAMS

Selected by NBA Coaches

1962-63
Terry Dischinger, Chicago
Chet Walker, Syracuse
Zelmo Beaty, St. Louis
John Havlicek, Boston
Dave DeBusschere, Detroit

1963-64
Jerry Lucas, Cincinnati
Gus Johnson, Baltimore
Nate Thurmond, San Francisco
Art Heyman, New York
Rod Thorn, Baltimore

1964-65
Willis Reed, New York
Jim Barnes, New York
Howard Komives, New York
Lucious Jackson, Philadelphia
Wally Jones, Baltimore
Joe Caldwell, Detroit

1965-66
Rick Barry, San Francisco
Billy Cunningham, Philadelphia
Tom Van Arsdale, Detroit
Dick Van Arsdale, New York
Fred Hetzel, San Francisco

1966-67
Lou Hudson, St. Louis
Jack Marin, Baltimore
Erwin Mueller, Chicago
Cazzie Russell, New York
Dave Bing, Detroit

1967-68
Earl Monroe, Baltimore
Bob Rule, Seattle
Walt Frazier, New York
Al Tucker, Seattle
Phil Jackson, New York

1968-69
Wes Unseld, Baltimore
Elvin Hayes, San Diego
Bill Hewitt, Los Angeles
Art Harris, Seattle
Gary Gregor, Phoenix

1969-70
K. Abdul-Jabbar, Milwaukee
Bob Dandridge, Milwaukee
Jo Jo White, Boston
Mike Davis, Baltimore
Dick Garrett, Los Angeles

1970-71
Geoff Petrie, Portland
Dave Cowens, Boston
Pete Maravich, Atlanta
Calvin Murphy, San Diego
Bob Lanier, Detroit

1971-72
Elmore Smith, Buffalo
Sidney Wicks, Portland
Austin Carr, Cleveland
Phil Chenier, Baltimore
Clifford Ray, Chicago

1972-73
Bob McAdoo, Buffalo
Lloyd Neal, Portland
Fred Boyd, Philadelphia
Dwight Davis, Cleveland
Jim Price, Los Angeles

1973-74
Ernie DiGregorio, Buffalo
Ron Behagen, Kansas City-Omaha
Mike Bantom, Phoenix
John Brown, Atlanta
Nick Weatherspoon, Capital

1974-75
Keith Wilkes, Golden State
John Drew, Atlanta
Scott Wedman, Kan. City-Omaha
Tom Burleson, Seattle
Brian Winters, Los Angeles

1975-76
Alvan Adams, Phoenix
Gus Williams, Golden State
Joe Meriweather, Houston
John Shumate, Phoenix-Buffalo
Lionel Hollins, Portland

1976-77
Adrian Dantley, Buffalo
Scott May, Chicago
Mitch Kupchak, Washington
John Lucas, Houston
Ron Lee, Phoenix

1977-78
Walter Davis, Phoenix
Marques Johnson, Milwaukee
Bernard King, New Jersey
Jack Sikma, Seattle
Norm Nixon, Los Angeles

1978-79
Phil Ford, Kansas City
Mychal Thompson, Portland
Ron Brewer, Portland
Reggie Theus, Chicago
Terry Tyler, Detroit

1979-80
Larry Bird, Boston
Magic Johnson, Los Angeles
Bill Cartwright, New York
Calvin Natt, Portland
David Greenwood, Chicago

1980-81
Joe Barry Carroll, Golden State
Darrell Griffith, Utah
Larry Smith, Golden State
Kevin McHale, Boston
Kelvin Ransey, Portland

1981-82
Kelly Tripucka, Detroit
Jay Vincent, Dallas
Isiah Thomas, Detroit
Buck Williams, New Jersey
Jeff Ruland, Washington

1982-83
Terry Cummings, San Diego
Clark Kellogg, Indiana
Dominique Wilkins, Atlanta
James Worthy, Los Angeles
Quintin Dailey, Chicago

1983-84
Ralph Sampson, Houston
Steve Stipanovich, Indiana
Byron Scott, Los Angeles
Jeff Malone, Washington
Thurl Bailey, Utah, tie
Darrell Walker, New York, tie

1984-85
Michael Jordan, Chicago
Hakeem Olajuwon, Houston
Sam Bowie, Portland
Charles Barkley, Philadelphia
Sam Perkins, Dallas

1985-86
Xavier McDaniel, Seattle
Patrick Ewing, New York
Karl Malone, Utah
Joe Dumars, Detroit
Charles Oakley, Chicago

1986-87
Brad Daugherty, Cleveland
Ron Harper, Cleveland
Chuck Person, Indiana
Roy Tarpley, Dallas
John Williams, Cleveland

1987-88
Mark Jackson, New York
Armon Gilliam, Phoenix
Kenny Smith, Sacramento
Greg Anderson, San Antonio
Derrick McKey, Seattle

1988-89
FIRST TEAM
Mitch Richmond, Golden State
Willie Anderson, San Antonio
Hersey Hawkins, Philadelphia
Rik Smits, Indiana
Charles Smith, L.A. Clippers

SECOND TEAM
Brian Shaw, Boston
Rex Chapman, Charlotte
Chris Morris, New Jersey
Rod Strickland, New York
Kevin Edwards, Miami

1989-90
FIRST TEAM
David Robinson, San Antonio
Tim Hardaway, Golden State
Vlade Divac, L.A. Lakers
Sherman Douglas, Miami
Pooh Richardson, Minnesota

SECOND TEAM
J.R. Reid, Charlotte
Sean Elliott, San Antonio
Stacey King, Chicago
Blue Edwards, Utah
Glen Rice, Miami

1990-91
FIRST TEAM
Kendall Gill, Charlotte
Dennis Scott, Orlando
Dee Brown, Boston
Lionel Simmons, Sacramento
Derrick Coleman, New Jersey

SECOND TEAM
Chris Jackson, Denver
Gary Payton, Seattle
Felton Spencer, Minnesota
Travis Mays, Sacramento
Willie Burton, Miami

1991-92
FIRST TEAM
Larry Johnson, Charlotte
Dikembe Mutombo, Denver
Billy Owens, Golden State
Steve Smith, Miami
Stacey Augmon, Atlanta

SECOND TEAM
Rick Fox, Boston
Terrell Brandon, Cleveland
Larry Stewart, Washington
Stanley Roberts, Orlando
Mark Macon, Denver

ALL-DEFENSIVE TEAMS

Selected by NBA Coaches

FIRST	1968-69	SECOND
Dave DeBusschere, New York		Rudy LaRusso, San Francisco
Nate Thurmond, San Francisco		Tom Sanders, Boston
Bill Russell, Boston		John Havlicek, Boston
Walt Frazier, New York		Jerry West, Los Angeles
Jerry Sloan, Chicago		Bill Bridges, Atlanta

FIRST	1969-70	SECOND
Dave DeBusschere, New York		John Havlicek, Boston
Gus Johnson, Baltimore		Bill Bridges, Atlanta
Willis Reed, New York		Kareem Abdul-Jabbar, Milwaukee
Walt Frazier, New York		Joe Caldwell, Atlanta
Jerry West, Los Angeles		Jerry Sloan, Chicago

FIRST	1970-71	SECOND
Dave DeBusschere, New York		John Havlicek, Boston
Gus Johnson, Baltimore		Paul Silas, Phoenix
Nate Thurmond, San Francisco		Kareem Abdul-Jabbar, Milwaukee
Walt Frazier, New York		Jerry Sloan, Chicago
Jerry West, Los Angeles		Norm Van Lier, Cincinnati

FIRST	1971-72	SECOND
Dave DeBusschere, New York		Paul Silas, Phoenix
John Havlicek, Boston		Bob Love, Chicago
Wilt Chamberlain, Los Angeles		Nate Thurmond, Golden State
Jerry West, Los Angeles		Norm Van Lier, Chicago
Walt Frazier, New York, tie		Don Chaney, Boston
Jerry Sloan, Chicago, tie		

FIRST	1972-73	SECOND
Dave DeBusschere, New York		Paul Silas, Boston
John Havlicek, Boston		Mike Riordan, Baltimore
Wilt Chamberlain, Los Angeles		Nate Thurmond, Golden State
Jerry West, Los Angeles		Norm Van Lier, Chicago
Walt Frazier, New York		Don Chaney, Boston

FIRST	1973-74	SECOND
Dave DeBusschere, New York		Elvin Hayes, Capital
John Havlicek, Boston		Bob Love, Chicago
Kareem Abdul-Jabbar, Milwaukee		Nate Thurmond, Golden State
Norm Van Lier, Chicago		Don Chaney, Boston
Walt Frazier, New York, tie		Dick Van Arsdale, Phoenix, tie
Jerry Sloan, Chicago, tie		Jim Price, Los Angeles, tie

FIRST	1974-75	SECOND
John Havlicek, Boston		Elvin Hayes, Washington
Paul Silas, Boston		Bob Love, Chicago
Kareem Abdul-Jabbar, Milwaukee		Dave Cowens, Boston
Jerry Sloan, Chicago		Norm Van Lier, Chicago
Walt Frazier, New York		Don Chaney, Boston

FIRST	1975-76	SECOND
Paul Silas, Boston		Jim Brewer, Cleveland
John Havlicek, Boston		Jamaal Wilkes, Golden State
Dave Cowens, Boston		Kareem Abdul-Jabbar, Los Angeles
Norm Van Lier, Chicago		Jim Cleamons, Cleveland
Don Watts, Seattle		Phil Smith, Golden State

FIRST	1976-77	SECOND
Bobby Jones, Denver		Jim Brewer, Cleveland
E.C. Coleman, New Orleans		Jamaal Wilkes, Golden State
Bill Walton, Portland		Kareem Abdul-Jabbar, Los Angeles
Don Buse, Indiana		Brian Taylor, Kansas City
Norm Van Lier, Chicago		Don Chaney, Los Angeles

FIRST	1977-78	SECOND
Bobby Jones, Denver		E.C. Coleman, Golden State
Maurice Lucas, Portland		Bob Gross, Portland
Bill Walton, Portland		Kareem Abdul-Jabbar, Los Angeles, tie
		Artis Gilmore, Chicago, tie
Lionel Hollins, Portland		Norm Van Lier, Chicago
Don Buse, Phoenix		Quinn Buckner, Milwaukee

FIRST	1978-79	SECOND
Bobby Jones, Philadelphia		Maurice Lucas, Portland
Bobby Dandridge, Washington		M.L. Carr, Detroit
Kareem Abdul-Jabbar, Los Angeles		Moses Malone, Houston
Dennis Johnson, Seattle		Lionel Hollins, Portland
Don Buse, Phoenix		Eddie Johnson, Atlanta

FIRST	1979-80	SECOND
Bobby Jones, Philadelphia		Scott Wedman, Kansas City
Dan Roundfield, Atlanta		Kermit Washington, Portland
Kareem Abdul-Jabbar, Los Angeles		Dave Cowens, Boston
Dennis Johnson, Seattle		Quinn Buckner, Milwaukee
Don Buse, Phoenix, tie		Eddie Johnson, Atlanta
Micheal Ray Richardson, New York, tie		

FIRST	1980-81	SECOND
Bobby Jones, Philadelphia		Dan Roundfield, Atlanta
Caldwell Jones, Philadelphia		Kermit Washington, Portland
Kareem Abdul-Jabbar, Los Angeles		George Johnson, San Antonio
Dennis Johnson, Phoenix		Quinn Buckner, Milwaukee
Micheal Ray Richardson, New York		Dudley Bradley, Indiana, tie
		Michael Cooper, Los Angeles, tie

FIRST	1981-82	SECOND
Bobby Jones, Philadelphia		Larry Bird, Boston
Dan Roundfield, Atlanta		Lonnie Shelton, Seattle
Caldwell Jones, Philadelphia		Jack Sikma, Seattle
Michael Cooper, Los Angeles		Quinn Buckner, Milwaukee
Dennis Johnson, Phoenix		Sidney Moncrief, Milwaukee

FIRST	1982-83	SECOND
Bobby Jones, Philadelphia		Larry Bird, Boston
Dan Roundfield, Atlanta		Kevin McHale, Boston
Moses Malone, Philadelphia		Wayne Rollins, Atlanta
Sidney Moncrief, Milwaukee		Michael Cooper, Los Angeles
Dennis Johnson, Phoenix (tie)		T.R. Dunn, Denver
Maurice Cheeks, Philadelphia (tie)		

FIRST	1983-84	SECOND
Bobby Jones, Philadelphia		Larry Bird, Boston
Michael Cooper, Los Angeles		Dan Roundfield, Atlanta
Wayne Rollins, Atlanta		Kareem Abdul-Jabbar, Los Angeles
Maurice Cheeks, Philadelphia		Dennis Johnson, Boston
Sidney Moncrief, Milwaukee		T.R. Dunn, Denver

FIRST	1984-85	SECOND
Sidney Moncrief, Milwaukee		Bobby Jones, Philadelphia
Paul Pressey, Milwaukee		Danny Vranes, Seattle
Mark Eaton, Utah		Hakeem Olajuwon, Houston
Michael Cooper, L.A. Lakers		Dennis Johnson, Boston
Maurice Cheeks, Philadelphia		T.R. Dunn, Denver

FIRST	1985-86	SECOND
Paul Pressey, Milwaukee		Michael Cooper, L.A. Lakers
Kevin McHale, Boston		Bill Hanzlik, Denver
Mark Eaton, Utah		Manute Bol, Washington
Sidney Moncrief, Milwaukee		Alvin Robertson, San Antonio
Maurice Cheeks, Philadelphia		Dennis Johnson, Boston

FIRST	1986-87	SECOND
Kevin McHale, Boston		Paul Pressey, Milwaukee
Michael Cooper, L.A. Lakers		Rodney McCray, Houston
Hakeem Olajuwon, Houston		Mark Eaton, Utah
Alvin Robertson, San Antonio		Maurice Cheeks, Philadelphia
Dennis Johnson, Boston		Derek Harper, Dallas

FIRST	1987-88	SECOND
Kevin McHale, Boston		Buck Williams, New Jersey
Rodney McCray, Houston		Karl Malone, Utah
Hakeem Olajuwon, Houston		Mark Eaton, Utah, tie
Michael Cooper, L.A. Lakers		Patrick Ewing, New York, tie
Michael Jordan, Chicago		Alvin Robertson, San Antonio
		Lafayette Lever, Denver

FIRST	1988-89	SECOND
Dennis Rodman, Detroit		Kevin McHale, Boston
Larry Nance, Cleveland		A.C. Green, L.A. Lakers
Mark Eaton, Utah		Patrick Ewing, New York
Michael Jordan, Chicago		John Stockton, Utah
Joe Dumars, Detroit		Alvin Robertson, San Antonio

FIRST	1989-90	SECOND
Dennis Rodman, Detroit		Kevin McHale, Boston
Buck Williams, Portland		Rick Mahorn, Philadelphia
Hakeem Olajuwon, Houston		David Robinson, San Antonio
Michael Jordan, Chicago		Derek Harper, Dallas
Joe Dumars, Detroit		Alvin Robertson, Milwaukee

FIRST	1990-91	SECOND
Michael Jordan, Chicago		Joe Dumars, Detroit
Alvin Robertson, Milwaukee		John Stockton, Utah
David Robinson, San Antonio		Hakeem Olajuwon, Houston
Dennis Rodman, Detroit		Scottie Pippen, Chicago
Buck Williams, Portland		Dan Majerle, Phoenix

FIRST	1991-92	SECOND
Dennis Rodman, Detroit		Larry Nance, Cleveland
Scottie Pippen, Chicago		Buck Williams, Portland
David Robinson, San Antonio		Patrick Ewing, New York
Michael Jordan, Chicago		John Stockton, Utah
Joe Dumars, Detroit		Micheal Williams, Indiana

NBA FINALS MOST VALUABLE PLAYER

Presented by Jeep/Eagle

1969—Jerry West, Los Angeles
1970—Willis Reed, New York
1971—Kareem Abdul-Jabbar, Milwaukee
1972—Wilt Chamberlain, Los Angeles
1973—Willis Reed, New York
1974—John Havlicek, Boston
1975—Rick Barry, Golden State
1976—JoJo White, Boston
1977—Bill Walton, Portland
1978—Wes Unseld, Washington
1979—Dennis Johnson, Seattle
1980—Magic Johnson, Los Angeles

1981—Cedric Maxwell, Boston
1982—Magic Johnson, Los Angeles
1983—Moses Malone, Philadelphia
1984—Larry Bird, Boston
1985—Kareem Abdul-Jabbar, L.A. Lakers
1986—Larry Bird, Boston
1987—Magic Johnson, L.A. Lakers
1988—James Worthy, L.A. Lakers
1989—Joe Dumars, Detroit
1990—Isiah Thomas, Detroit
1991—Michael Jordan, Chicago
1992—Michael Jordan, Chicago

ALL-NBA TEAMS

Selected by Writers and Broadcasters

FIRST	**1946-47**	SECOND
Joe Fulks (Philadelphia)		Ernie Calverley (Providence)
Bob Feerick (Washington)		Frank Baumholtz (Cleveland)
Stan Miasek (Detroit)		John Logan (St. Louis)
Bones McKinney (Washington)		Chuck Halbert (Chicago)
Max Zaslofsky (Chicago)		Fred Scolari (Washington)

FIRST	**1947-48**	SECOND
Joe Fulks (Philadelphia)		John Logan (St. Louis)
Max Zaslofsky (Chicago)		Carl Braun (New York)
Ed Sadowski (Boston)		Stan Miasek (Chicago)
Howie Dallmar (Philadelphia)		Fred Scolari (Washington)
Bob Feerick (Washington)		Buddy Jeannette (Baltimore)

FIRST	**1948-49**	SECOND
George Mikan (Minneapolis)		Arnie Risen (Rochester)
Joe Fulks (Philadelphia)		Bob Feerick (Washington)
Bob Davies (Rochester)		Bones McKinney (Washington)
Max Zaslofsky (Chicago)		Ken Sailors (Providence)
Jim Pollard (Minneapolis)		John Logan (St. Louis)

FIRST	**1949-50**	SECOND
George Mikan (Minneapolis)		Frank Brian (Anderson)
Jim Pollard (Minneapolis)		Fred Schaus (Fort Wayne)
Alex Groza (Indianapolis)		Dolph Schayes (Syracuse)
Bob Davies (Rochester)		Al Cervi (Syracuse)
Max Zaslofsky (Chicago)		Ralph Beard (Indianapolis)

FIRST	**1950-51**	SECOND
George Mikan (Minneapolis)		Dolph Schayes (Syracuse)
Alex Groza (Indianapolis)		Frank Brian (Tri-Cities)
Ed Macauley (Boston)		Vern Mikkelsen (Minneapolis)
Bob Davies (Rochester)		Joe Fulks (Philadelphia)
Ralph Beard (Indianapolis)		Dick McGuire (New York)

FIRST	**1951-52**	SECOND
George Mikan (Minneapolis)		Larry Foust (Fort Wayne)
Ed Macauley (Boston)		Vern Mikkelsen (Minneapolis)
Paul Arizin (Philadelphia)		Jim Pollard (Minneapolis)
Bob Cousy (Boston)		Bob Wanzer (Rochester)
Bob Davies (Rochester)		Andy Phillip (Philadelphia)
Dolph Schayes (Syracuse)		

FIRST	**1952-53**	SECOND
George Mikan (Minneapolis)		Bill Sharman (Boston)
Bob Cousy (Boston)		Vern Mikkelsen (Minneapolis)
Neil Johnston (Philadelphia)		Bob Wanzer (Rochester)
Ed Macauley (Boston)		Bob Davies (Rochester)
Dolph Schayes (Syracuse)		Andy Phillip (Philadelphia)

FIRST	**1953-54**	SECOND
Bob Cousy (Boston)		Ed Macauley (Boston)
Neil Johnston (Philadelphia)		Jim Pollard (Minneapolis)
George Mikan (Minneapolis)		Carl Braun (New York)
Dolph Schayes (Syracuse)		Bob Wanzer (Rochester)
Harry Gallatin (New York)		Paul Seymour (Syracuse)

FIRST	1954-55	SECOND
Neil Johnston (Philadelphia)		Vern Mikkelsen (Minneapolis)
Bob Cousy (Boston)		Harry Gallatin (New York)
Dolph Schayes (Syracuse)		Paul Seymour (Syracuse)
Bob Pettit (Milwaukee)		Slater Martin (Minneapolis)
Larry Foust (Fort Wayne)		Bill Sharman (Boston)

FIRST	1955-56	SECOND
Bob Pettit (St. Louis)		Dolph Schayes (Syracuse)
Paul Arizin (Philadelphia)		Maurice Stokes (Rochester)
Neil Johnston (Philadelphia)		Clyde Lovellette (Minneapolis)
Bob Cousy (Boston)		Slater Martin (Minneapolis)
Bill Sharman (Boston)		Jack George (Philadelphia)

FIRST	1956-57	SECOND
Paul Arizin (Philadelphia)		George Yardley (Fort Wayne)
Dolph Schayes (Syracuse)		Maurice Stokes (Rochester)
Bob Pettit (St. Louis)		Neil Johnston (Philadelphia)
Bob Cousy (Boston)		Dick Garmaker (Minneapolis)
Bill Sharman (Boston)		Slater Martin (St. Louis)

FIRST	1957-58	SECOND
Dolph Schayes (Syracuse)		Cliff Hagan (St. Louis)
George Yardley (Detroit)		Maurice Stokes (Cincinnati)
Bob Pettit (St. Louis)		Bill Russell (Boston)
Bob Cousy (Boston)		Tom Gola (Philadelphia)
Bill Sharman (Boston)		Slater Martin (St. Louis)

FIRST	1958-59	SECOND
Bob Pettit (St. Louis)		Paul Arizin (Philadelphia)
Elgin Baylor (Minneapolis)		Cliff Hagan (St. Louis)
Bill Russell (Boston)		Dolph Schayes (Syracuse)
Bob Cousy (Boston)		Slater Martin (St. Louis)
Bill Sharman (Boston)		Richie Guerin (New York)

FIRST	1959-60	SECOND
Bob Pettit (St. Louis)		Jack Twyman (Cincinnati)
Elgin Baylor (Minneapolis)		Dolph Schayes (Syracuse)
Wilt Chamberlain (Philadelphia)		Bill Russell (Boston)
Bob Cousy (Boston)		Richie Guerin (New York)
Gene Shue (Detroit)		Bill Sharman (Boston)

FIRST	1960-61	SECOND
Elgin Baylor (Los Angeles)		Dolph Schayes (Syracuse)
Bob Pettit (St. Louis)		Tom Heinsohn (Boston)
Wilt Chamberlain (Philadelphia)		Bill Russell (Boston)
Bob Cousy (Boston)		Larry Costello (Syracuse)
Oscar Robertson (Cincinnati)		Gene Shue (Detroit)

FIRST	1961-62	SECOND
Bob Pettit (St. Louis)		Tom Heinsohn (Boston)
Elgin Baylor (Los Angeles)		Jack Twyman (Cincinnati)
Wilt Chamberlain (Philadelphia)		Bill Russell (Boston)
Jerry West (Los Angeles)		Richie Guerin (New York)
Oscar Robertson (Cincinnati)		Bob Cousy (Boston)

FIRST	1962-63	SECOND
Elgin Baylor (Los Angeles)		Tom Heinsohn (Boston)
Bob Pettit (St. Louis)		Bailey Howell (Detroit)
Bill Russell (Boston)		Wilt Chamberlain (San Francisco)
Oscar Robertson (Cincinnati)		Bob Cousy (Boston)
Jerry West (Los Angeles)		Hal Greer (Syracuse)

FIRST	1963-64	SECOND
Bob Pettit (St. Louis)		Tom Heinsohn (Boston)
Elgin Baylor (Los Angeles)		Jerry Lucas (Cincinnati)
Wilt Chamberlain (San Francisco)		Bill Russell (Boston)
Oscar Robertson (Cincinnati)		John Havlicek (Boston)
Jerry West (Los Angeles)		Hal Greer (Philadelphia)

FIRST	1964-65	SECOND
Elgin Baylor (Los Angeles)		Bob Pettit (St. Louis)
Jerry Lucas (Cincinnati)		Gus Johnson (Baltimore)
Bill Russell (Boston)		Wilt Chamberlain (S.F.-Phila.)
Oscar Robertson (Cincinnati)		Sam Jones (Boston)
Jerry West (Los Angeles)		Hal Greer (Philadelphia)

FIRST	1965-66	SECOND
Rick Barry (San Francisco)		John Havlicek (Boston)
Jerry Lucas (Cincinnati)		Gus Johnson (Baltimore)
Wilt Chamberlain (Philadelphia)		Bill Russell (Boston)
Oscar Robertson (Cincinnati)		Sam Jones (Boston)
Jerry West (Los Angeles)		Hal Greer (Philadelphia)

FIRST	1966-67	SECOND
Rick Barry (San Francisco)		Willis Reed (New York)
Elgin Baylor (Los Angeles)		Jerry Lucas (Cincinnati)
Wilt Chamberlain (Philadelphia)		Bill Russell (Boston)
Jerry West (Los Angeles)		Hal Greer (Philadelphia)
Oscar Robertson (Cincinnati)		Sam Jones (Boston)

FIRST	1967-68	SECOND
Elgin Baylor (Los Angeles)		Willis Reed (New York)
Jerry Lucas (Cincinnati)		John Havlicek (Boston)
Wilt Chamberlain (Philadelphia)		Bill Russell (Boston)
Dave Bing (Detroit)		Hal Greer (Philadelphia)
Oscar Robertson (Cincinnati)		Jerry West (Los Angeles)

FIRST	1968-69	SECOND
Billy Cunningham (Philadelphia)		John Havlicek (Boston)
Elgin Baylor (Los Angeles)		Dave DeBusschere (Detroit-New York)
Wes Unseld (Baltimore)		Willis Reed (New York)
Earl Monroe (Baltimore)		Hal Greer (Philadelphia)
Oscar Robertson (Cincinnati)		Jerry West (Los Angeles)

FIRST	1969-70	SECOND
Billy Cunningham (Philadelphia)		John Havlicek (Boston)
Connie Hawkins (Phoenix)		Gus Johnson (Baltimore)
Willis Reed (New York)		Kareem Abdul-Jabbar (Milwaukee)
Jerry West (Los Angeles)		Lou Hudson (Atlanta)
Walt Frazier (New York)		Oscar Robertson (Cincinnati)

FIRST	1970-71	SECOND
John Havlicek (Boston)		Gus Johnson (Baltimore)
Billy Cunningham (Philadelphia)		Bob Love (Chicago)
Kareem Abdul-Jabbar (Milwaukee)		Willis Reed (New York)
Jerry West (Los Angeles)		Walt Frazier (New York)
Dave Bing (Detroit)		Oscar Robertson (Milwaukee)

FIRST	1971-72	SECOND
John Havlicek (Boston)		Bob Love (Chicago)
Spencer Haywood (Seattle)		Billy Cunningham (Philadelphia)
Kareem Abdul-Jabbar (Milwaukee)		Wilt Chamberlain (Los Angeles)
Jerry West (Los Angeles)		Nate Archibald (Cincinnati)
Walt Frazier (New York)		Archie Clark (Phila.-Balt.)

FIRST	1972-73	SECOND
John Havlicek (Boston)		Elvin Hayes (Baltimore)
Spencer Haywood (Seattle)		Rick Barry (Golden State)
Kareem Abdul-Jabbar (Milwaukee)		Dave Cowens (Boston)
Nate Archibald (Kansas City-Omaha)		Walt Frazier (New York)
Jerry West (Los Angeles)		Pete Maravich (Atlanta)

FIRST	1973-74	SECOND
John Havlicek (Boston)		Elvin Hayes (Capital)
Rick Barry (Golden State)		Spencer Haywood (Seattle)
Kareem Abdul-Jabbar (Milwaukee)		Bob McAdoo (Buffalo)
Walt Frazier (New York)		Dave Bing (Detroit)
Gail Goodrich (Los Angeles)		Norm Van Lier (Chicago)

FIRST	1974-75	SECOND
Rick Barry (Golden State)		John Havlicek (Boston)
Elvin Hayes (Washington)		Spencer Haywood (Seattle)
Bob McAdoo (Buffalo)		Dave Cowens (Boston)
Nate Archibald (Kansas City-Omaha)		Phil Chenier (Washington)
Walt Frazier (New York)		Jo Jo White (Boston)

FIRST	1975-76	SECOND
Rick Barry (Golden State)		Elvin Hayes (Washington)
George McGinnis (Philadelphia)		John Havlicek (Boston)
Kareem Abdul-Jabbar (Los Angeles)		Dave Cowens (Boston)
Nate Archibald (Kansas City)		Randy Smith (Buffalo)
Pete Maravich (New Orleans)		Phil Smith (Golden State)

FIRST	1976-77	SECOND
Elvin Hayes (Washington)		Julius Erving (Philadelphia)
David Thompson (Denver)		George McGinnis (Philadelphia)
Kareem Abdul-Jabbar (L. Angeles)		Bill Walton (Portland)
Pete Maravich (New Orleans)		George Gervin (San Antonio)
Paul Westphal (Phoenix)		Jo Jo White (Boston)

FIRST	1977-78	SECOND
Leonard Robinson (New Orleans)		Walter Davis (Phoenix)
Julius Erving (Philadelphia)		Maurice Lucas (Portland)
Bill Walton (Portland)		Kareem Abdul-Jabbar (Los Angeles)
George Gervin (San Antonio)		Paul Westphal (Phoenix)
David Thompson (Denver)		Pete Maravich (New Orleans)

FIRST	1978-79	SECOND
Marques Johnson (Milwaukee)		Walter Davis (Phoenix)
Elvin Hayes (Washington)		Bobby Dandridge (Washington)
Moses Malone (Houston)		Kareem Abdul-Jabbar (Los Angeles)
George Gervin (San Antonio)		Lloyd Free (San Diego)
Paul Westphal (Phoenix)		Phil Ford (Kansas City)

FIRST	1979-80	SECOND
Julius Erving (Philadelphia)		Dan Roundfield (Atlanta)
Larry Bird (Boston)		Marques Johnson (Milwaukee)
Kareem Abdul-Jabbar (Los Angeles)		Moses Malone (Houston)
George Gervin (San Antonio)		Dennis Johnson (Seattle)
Paul Westphal (Phoenix)		Gus Williams (Seattle)

FIRST	1980-81	SECOND
Julius Erving (Philadelphia)		Marques Johnson (Milwaukee)
Larry Bird (Boston)		Adrian Dantley (Utah)
Kareem Abdul-Jabbar (Los Angeles)		Moses Malone (Houston)
George Gervin (San Antonio)		Otis Birdsong (Kansas City)
Dennis Johnson (Phoenix)		Nate Archibald (Boston)

FIRST	1981-82	SECOND
Larry Bird (Boston)		Alex English (Denver)
Julius Erving (Philadelphia)		Bernard King (Golden State)
Moses Malone (Houston)		Robert Parish (Boston)
George Gervin (San Antonio)		Magic Johnson (Los Angeles)
Gus Williams (Seattle)		Sidney Moncrief (Milwaukee)

FIRST	1982-83	SECOND
Larry Bird (Boston)		Alex English (Denver)
Julius Erving (Philadelphia)		Buck Williams (New Jersey)
Moses Malone (Philadelphia)		Kareem Abdul-Jabbar (Los Angeles)
Magic Johnson (Los Angeles)		George Gervin (San Antonio)
Sidney Moncrief (Milwaukee)		Isiah Thomas (Detroit)

FIRST	1983-84	SECOND
Larry Bird (Boston)		Julius Erving (Philadelphia)
Bernard King (New York)		Adrian Dantley (Utah)
Kareem Abdul-Jabbar (Los Angeles)		Moses Malone (Philadelphia)
Magic Johnson (Los Angeles)		Sidney Moncrief (Milwaukee)
Isiah Thomas (Detroit)		Jim Paxson (Portland)

FIRST	1984-85	SECOND
Larry Bird (Boston)		Terry Cummings (Milwaukee)
Bernard King (New York)		Ralph Sampson (Houston)
Moses Malone (Philadelphia)		Kareem Abdul-Jabbar (L.A. Lakers)
Magic Johnson (L.A. Lakers)		Michael Jordan (Chicago)
Isiah Thomas (Detroit)		Sidney Moncrief (Milwaukee)

FIRST	1985-86	SECOND
Larry Bird (Boston)		Charles Barkley (Philadelphia)
Dominique Wilkins (Atlanta)		Alex English (Denver)
Kareem Abdul-Jabbar (L.A. Lakers)		Hakeem Olajuwon (Houston)
Magic Johnson (L.A. Lakers)		Sidney Moncrief (Milwaukee)
Isiah Thomas (Detroit)		Alvin Robertson (San Antonio)

FIRST	1986-87	SECOND
Larry Bird (Boston)		Dominique Wilkins (Atlanta)
Kevin McHale (Boston)		Charles Barkley (Philadelphia)
Hakeem Olajuwon (Houston)		Moses Malone (Washington)
Magic Johnson (L.A. Lakers)		Isiah Thomas (Detroit)
Michael Jordan (Chicago)		Lafayette Lever (Denver)

FIRST	**1987-88**	SECOND
Larry Bird (Boston)		Karl Malone (Utah)
Charles Barkley (Philadelphia)		Dominique Wilkins (Atlanta)
Hakeem Olajuwon (Houston)		Patrick Ewing (New York)
Michael Jordan (Chicago)		Clyde Drexler (Portland)
Magic Johnson (L.A. Lakers)		John Stockton (Utah)

1988-89

FIRST	SECOND	THIRD
Karl Malone (Utah)	Tom Chambers (Phoenix)	Dominique Wilkins (Atlanta)
Charles Barkley (Philadelphia)	Chris Mullin (Golden State)	Terry Cummings (Milwaukee)
Hakeem Olajuwon (Houston)	Patrick Ewing (New York)	Robert Parish (Boston)
Magic Johnson (L.A. Lakers)	John Stockton (Utah)	Dale Ellis (Seattle)
Michael Jordan (Chicago)	Kevin Johnson (Phoenix)	Mark Price (Cleveland)

1989-90

FIRST	SECOND	THIRD
Karl Malone (Utah)	Larry Bird (Boston)	James Worthy (L.A. Lakers)
Charles Barkley (Philadelphia)	Tom Chambers (Phoenix)	Chris Mullin (Golden State)
Patrick Ewing (New York)	Hakeem Olajuwon (Houston)	David Robinson (San Antonio)
Magic Johnson (L.A. Lakers)	John Stockton (Utah)	Clyde Drexler (Portland)
Michael Jordan (Chicago)	Kevin Johnson (Phoenix)	Joe Dumars (Detroit)

1990-91

FIRST	SECOND	THIRD
Karl Malone (Utah)	Dominique Wilkins (Atlanta)	James Worthy (L.A. Lakers)
Charles Barkley (Philadelphia)	Chris Mullin (Golden State)	Bernard King (Washington)
David Robinson (San Antonio)	Patrick Ewing (New York)	Hakeem Olajuwon (Houston)
Michael Jordan (Chicago)	Kevin Johnson (Phoenix)	John Stockton (Utah)
Magic Johnson (L.A. Lakers)	Clyde Drexler (Portland)	Joe Dumars (Detroit)

1991-92

FIRST	SECOND	THIRD
Karl Malone (Utah)	Scottie Pippen (Chicago)	Dennis Rodman (Detroit)
Chris Mullin (Golden State)	Charles Barkley (Philadelphia)	Kevin Willis (Atlanta)
David Robinson (San Antonio)	Patrick Ewing (New York)	Brad Daugherty (Cleveland)
Michael Jordan (Chicago)	Tim Hardaway (Golden State)	Mark Price (Cleveland)
Clyde Drexler (Portland)	John Stockton (Utah)	Kevin Johnson (Phoenix)

PLAYERS WHO HAVE MADE ALL-NBA TEAMS

(Official All-Star Teams at End of Season; Active 1991-92 Players in CAPS)

Player	1st Team	2nd	3rd
Kareem Abdul-Jabbar	10	5	0
Bob Cousy	10	2	0
Jerry West	10	2	0
Bob Pettit	10	1	0
Elgin Baylor	10	0	0
Oscar Robertson	9	2	0
LARRY BIRD	9	1	0
MAGIC JOHNSON	9	1	0
Wilt Chamberlain	7	3	0
Dolph Schayes	6	6	0
MICHAEL JORDAN	6	1	0
George Mikan	6	0	0
Julius Erving	5	2	0
George Gervin	5	2	0
Rick Barry	5	1	0
John Havlicek	4	7	0
MOSES MALONE	4	4	0
CHARLES BARKLEY	4	3	0
Bill Sharman	4	3	0
Walt Frazier	4	2	0
Bob Davies	4	1	0
Neil Johnston	4	1	0
KARL MALONE	4	1	0
Max Zaslofsky	4	0	0
Bill Russell	3	8	0
Elvin Hayes	3	3	0
HAKEEM OLAJUWON	3	2	1
Nate Archibald	3	2	0
Jerry Lucas	3	2	0
ISIAH THOMAS	3	2	0
Paul Arizin	3	1	0
Billy Cunningham	3	1	0
Joe Fulks	3	1	0
Ed Macauley	3	1	0
Paul Westphal	3	1	0
Spencer Haywood	2	2	0
Pete Maravich	2	2	0
Jim Pollard	2	2	0
Bernard King	2	1	1
Dave Bing	2	1	0
Bob Feerick	2	1	0
DAVID ROBINSON	2	0	1
Alex Groza	2	0	0
David Thompson	2	0	0
PATRICK EWING	1	4	0
Sidney Moncrief	1	4	0
Willis Reed	1	4	0
DOMINIQUE WILKINS	1	3	1
CLYDE DREXLER	1	2	1
CHRIS MULLIN	1	2	1
Marques Johnson	1	2	0
Ralph Beard	1	1	0
Larry Foust	1	1	0
Harry Gallatin	1	1	0
Dennis Johnson	1	1	0
Bob McAdoo	1	1	0
George McGinnis	1	1	0
Bones McKinney	1	1	0
Stan Miasek	1	1	0
Gene Shue	1	1	0
Bill Walton	1	1	0
Gus Williams	1	1	0
George Yardley	1	1	0
Howard Dallmar	1	0	0
Gail Goodrich	1	0	0
Connie Hawkins	1	0	0
KEVIN McHALE	1	0	0
Earl Monroe	1	0	0
Truck Robinson	1	0	0
Wes Unseld	1	0	0
Hal Greer	0	7	0
Slater Martin	0	5	0
JOHN STOCKTON	0	4	1
Tom Heinsohn	0	4	0
Gus Johnson	0	4	0
Vern Mikkelsen	0	4	0
KEVIN JOHNSON	0	3	1
Dave Cowens	0	3	0
Alex English	0	3	0
Richie Guerin	0	3	0
Sam Jones	0	3	0
John Logan	0	3	0
Maurice Stokes	0	3	0
Bob Wanzer	0	3	0
Carl Braun	0	2	0
Frank Brian	0	2	0
TOM CHAMBERS	0	2	0
Adrian Dantley	0	2	0
WALTER DAVIS	0	2	0
Cliff Hagan	0	2	0
Bob Love	0	2	0
Andy Phillip	0	2	0
Fred Scolari	0	2	0
Paul Seymour	0	2	0
Jack Twyman	0	2	0
Jo Jo White	0	2	0
TERRY CUMMINGS	0	1	1
ROBERT PARISH	0	1	1
Frank Baumholtz	0	1	0
Otis Birdsong	0	1	0
Ernie Calverley	0	1	0
Al Cervi	0	1	0
Phil Chenier	0	1	0
Archie Clark	0	1	0
Larry Costello	0	1	0
Bobby Dandridge	0	1	0
Dave DeBusschere	0	1	0
Phil Ford	0	1	0
World Free	0	1	0
Dick Garmaker	0	1	0
Jack George	0	1	0
Tom Gola	0	1	0
Chuck Halbert	0	1	0
Tim Hardaway	0	1	0
Bailey Howell	0	1	0
Lou Hudson	0	1	0
Buddy Jeannette	0	1	0
LAFAYETTE LEVER	0	1	0
Clyde Lovellette	0	1	0
Maurice Lucas	0	1	0
Dick McGuire	0	1	0
Jim Paxson	0	1	0
Scottie Pippen	0	1	0
Arnie Risen	0	1	0
ALVIN ROBERTSON	0	1	0
Dan Roundfield	0	1	0
Ken Sailors	0	1	0
RALPH SAMPSON	0	1	0
Fred Schaus	0	1	0
Phil Smith	0	1	0
Randy Smith	0	1	0
Norm Van Lier	0	1	0
BUCK WILLIAMS	0	1	0
JOE DUMARS	0	0	2
MARK PRICE	0	0	2
JAMES WORTHY	0	0	2
BRAD DAUGHERTY	0	0	1
DALE ELLIS	0	0	1
DENNIS RODMAN	0	0	1
KEVIN WILLIS	0	0	1

East-West All-Star Game
FEBRUARY 9, 1992 AT ORLANDO

Magic Johnson of the Los Angeles Lakers came out of retirement to lead the West to a convincing 153-113 win over the East in front of 14,272 emotional fans at Orlando Arena. With his game-high 25 points and nine assists, Johnson dazzled the crowd on the way to his second All-Star Most Valuable Player award, while Johnson's West teammate Clyde Drexler put up some MVP numbers of his own with 22 points and nine rebounds. The East was led by Michael Jordan's 18 points, 15 points from Isiah Thomas and 13 rebounds from Dennis Rodman. The West team's 153 points tied an All-Star record for most points scored in a non-overtime game, and it set an All-Star record for field goal percentage with a .653 mark (64-of-98).

West Coach—Don Nelson, Golden State
East Coach—Phil Jackson, Chicago
Most Valuable Player—Magic Johnson, L.A. Lakers

WEST ALL-STARS (153)

Player and Team	Pos.	Min.	FGA	FGM	FTA	FTM	Off.	Def.	Tot.	Ast.	PF	Stls.	Pts.
Malone, Utah	F	19	7	5	2	1	0	7	7	3	1	1	11
Mullin, Golden State	F	24	7	6	0	0	0	1	1	3	0	0	13
Robinson, San Antonio	C	18	9	7	8	5	1	4	5	2	3	3	19
Drexler, Portland	G	28	15	10	0	0	2	7	9	6	2	0	22
Johnson, L.A. Lakers	G	29	12	9	4	4	3	2	5	9	0	2	25
Hardaway, Golden State		20	10	5	2	2	0	0	0	7	2	1	14
Olajuwon, Houston		20	6	3	2	1	0	4	4	2	3	2	7
Hornacek, Phoenix		24	7	5	0	0	1	1	2	3	0	1	11
Thorpe, Houston		4	1	1	0	0	0	0	0	0	0	0	2
Worthy, L.A. Lakers		14	7	4	2	1	0	4	4	1	0	1	9
Stockton, Utah		18	8	5	0	0	0	1	1	5	2	3	12
Majerle, Phoenix		12	5	2	0	0	0	3	3	2	0	0	4
Mutombo, Denver		10	4	2	0	0	1	1	2	1	0	1	4
Totals		240	98	64	20	14	8	35	43	44	13	15	153

FG Pct.: .653. FT Pct.:.700. Team Rebounds: 13. Turnovers: Johnson 7, Olajuwon 3, Stockton 3, Hardaway 2, Mutombo 2, Drexler 1, Majerle 1, Malone 1, Mullin 1. Total—21.

EAST ALL-STARS (113)

Player and Team	Pos.	Min.	FGA	FGM	FTA	FTM	Off.	Def.	Tot.	Ast.	PF	Stls.	Pts.
Pippen, Chicago	F	21	13	6	3	2	4	0	4	1	0	2	14
Barkley, Philadelphia	F	28	14	6	0	0	2	7	9	1	3	0	12
Ewing, New York	C	17	7	4	5	2	2	2	4	0	3	2	10
Thomas, Detroit	G	28	14	7	0	0	0	1	1	5	0	3	15
Jordan, Chicago	G	31	17	9	0	0	1	0	1	5	2	2	18
Price, Cleveland		15	5	1	4	4	0	0	0	3	1	1	6
Daugherty, Cleveland		15	8	3	0	0	3	3	6	1	0	1	6
Dumars, Detroit		17	7	2	0	0	0	1	1	3	0	0	4
Rodman, Detroit		25	7	2	0	0	7	6	13	0	1	1	4
Lewis, Boston		15	7	3	2	1	0	4	4	2	3	0	7
Willis, Atlanta		14	10	4	0	0	4	0	4	0	1	0	8
Adams, Washington		14	8	4	0	0	1	0	1	1	1	4	9
Totals		240	117	51	14	9	28	20	48	22	15	16	113

FG Pct.: .436. FT Pct.:.643. Team Rebounds: 7. Turnovers: Barkley 3, Daugherty 3, Price 3, Thomas 3, Dumars 2, Ewing 2, Rodman 2, Adams 1, Jordan 1, Lewis 1, Pippen 1. Total—22.

Score by Periods:	1st	2nd	3rd	4th	Totals
West	44	35	36	38	— 153
East	31	24	28	30	— 113

Blocked Shots: Drexler 2, Malone 1, Olajuwon 1, Robinson 1, Ewing 1, Lewis 1, Pippen 1.
3-Pt. Field Goals: Johnson 3-3, Stockton 2-3, Drexler 2-4, Hardaway 2-5, Mullin 1-1, Hornacek 1-2, Majerle 0-2, Adams 1-3, Thomas 1-3, Barkley 0-2, Dumars 0-2, Price 0-3.
Officials: Darrell Garretson, Joe Crawford and Tommy Nunez.
Attendance: 14,272.
Time of Game: 2:01.

RESULTS OF ALL-STAR GAMES

Year—Result and Location	Winning Coach	Losing Coach	Most Valuable Player
1951—East 111, West 94 at Boston	Joe Lapchick	John Kundla	Ed Macauley, Boston
1952—East 108, West 91 at Boston	Al Cervi	John Kundla	Paul Arizin, Philadelphia
1953—West 79, East 75 at Fort Wayne	John Kundla	Joe Lapchick	George Mikan, Minnesota
1954—East 98, West 93 (OT) at New York	Joe Lapchick	John Kundla	Bob Cousy, Boston
1955—East 100, West 91 at New York	Al Cervi	Charley Eckman	Bill Sharman, Boston
1956—West 108, East 94 at Rochester	Charley Eckman	George Senesky	Bob Pettit, St. Louis
1957—East 109, West 97 at Boston	Red Auerbach	Bobby Wanzer	Bob Cousy, Boston
1958—East 130, West 118 at St. Louis	Red Auerbach	Alex Hannum	Bob Pettit, St. Louis
1959—West 124, East 108 at Detroit	Ed Macauley	Red Auerbach	E. Baylor, Mn. & B. Pettit, St.L.
1960—East 125, West 115 at Philadelphia	Red Auerbach	Ed Macauley	Wilt Chamberlain, Philadelphia
1961—West 153, East 131 at Syracuse	Paul Seymour	Red Auerbach	Oscar Robertson, Cincinnati
1962—West 150, East 130 at St. Louis	Fred Schaus	Red Auerbach	Bob Pettit, St. Louis
1963—East 115, West 108 at Los Angeles	Red Auerbach	Fred Schaus	Bill Russell, Boston
1964—East 111, West 107 at Boston	Red Auerbach	Fred Schaus	Oscar Robertson, Cincinnati
1965—East 124, West 123 at St. Louis	Red Auerbach	Alex Hannum	Jerry Lucas, Cincinnati
1966—East 137, West 94 at Cincinnati	Red Auerbach	Fred Schaus	Adrian Smith, Cincinnati
1967—West 135, East 120 at San Francisco	Fred Schaus	Red Auerbach	Rick Barry, San Francisco
1968—East 144, West 124 at New York	Alex Hannum	Bill Sharman	Hal Greer, Philadelphia
1969—East 123, West 112 at Baltimore	Gene Shue	Richie Guerin	Oscar Robertson, Cincinnati
1970—East 142, West 135 at Philadelphia	Red Holzman	Richie Guerin	Willis Reed, New York
1971—West 108, East 107 at San Diego	Larry Costello	Red Holzman	Lenny Wilkens, Seattle
1972—West 112, East 110 at Los Angeles	Bill Sharman	Tom Heinsohn	Jerry West, Los Angeles
1973—East 104, West 84 at Chicago	Tom Heinsohn	Bill Sharman	Dave Cowens, Boston
1974—West 134, East 123 at Seattle	Larry Costello	Tom Heinsohn	Bob Lanier, Detroit
1975—East 108, West 102 at Phoenix	K.C. Jones	Al Attles	Walt Frazier, New York
1976—East 123, West 109 at Philadelphia	Tom Heinsohn	Al Attles	Dave Bing, Washington
1977—West 125, East 124 at Milwaukee	Larry Brown	Gene Shue	Julius Erving, Philadelphia
1978—East 133, West 125 at Atlanta	Billy Cunningham	Jack Ramsay	Randy Smith, Buffalo
1979—West 134, East 129 at Detroit	Lenny Wilkens	Dick Motta	David Thompson, Denver
1980—East 144, West 136 (OT) at Landover	Billy Cunningham	Lenny Wilkens	George Gervin, San Antonio
1981—East 123, West 120 at Cleveland	Billy Cunningham	John MacLeod	Nate Archibald, Boston
1982—East 120, West 118 at E. Rutherford	Bill Fitch	Pat Riley	Larry Bird, Boston
1983—East 132, West 123 at Los Angeles	Billy Cunningham	Pat Riley	Julius Erving, Philadelphia
1984—East 154, West 145 (OT) at Denver	K.C. Jones	Frank Layden	Isiah Thomas, Detroit
1985—West 140, East 129 at Indianapolis	Pat Riley	K.C. Jones	Ralph Sampson, Houston
1986—East 139, West 132 at Dallas	K.C. Jones	Pat Riley	Isiah Thomas, Detroit
1987—West 154, East 149 (OT) at Seattle	Pat Riley	K.C. Jones	Tom Chambers, Seattle
1988—East 138, West 133 at Chicago	Mike Fratello	Pat Riley	Michael Jordan, Chicago
1989—West 143, East 134 at Houston	Pat Riley	Lenny Wilkens	Karl Malone, Utah
1990—East 130, West 113 at Miami	Chuck Daly	Pat Riley	Magic Johnson, L.A. Lakers
1991—East 116, West 114 at Charlotte	Chris Ford	Rick Adelman	Charles Barkley, Philadelphia
1992—West 153, East 113 at Orlando	Don Nelson	Phil Jackson	Magic Johnson (retired)

ALL-TIME EAST-WEST ALL-STAR RECORDS

(Active players in capital letters)

Player	G.	Min.	FGA	FGM	Pct.	FTA	FTM	Pct.	Reb.	Ast.	PF	Disq.	Pts.	Avg.
Kareem Abdul-Jabbar°	18	449	213	105	.493	50	41	.820	149	51	57	1	251	13.9
Oscar Robertson	12	380	172	88	.512	98	70	.714	69	81	41	0	246	20.5
Bob Pettit	11	350	193	81	.420	80	62	.775	178	23	25	0	224	20.4
Julius Erving	11	316	178	85	.478	63	50	.794	70	35	31	0	221	20.1
Elgin Baylor	11	321	164	70	.427	98	78	.796	99	38	31	0	218	19.8
Wilt Chamberlain	13	388	122	72	.590	94	47	.500	197	36	23	0	191	14.7
John Havlicek	13	303	154	74	.481	41	31	.756	46	31	20	0	179	13.8
ISIAH THOMAS°	10	286	126	72	.571	33	27	.818	25	93	15	0	177	17.7
MAGIC JOHNSON°	11	331	131	64	.489	42	38	.905	57	127	25	0	176	16.0
Jerry West°°	12	341	137	62	.453	50	36	.720	47	55	28	0	160	13.3
Bob Cousy	13	368	158	52	.329	51	43	.843	78	86	27	2	147	11.3
MICHAEL JORDAN°	7	208	126	64	.508	23	18	.783	27	24	17	0	147	21.0
Dolph Schayes°	11	248	109	48	.440	50	42	.840	105	17	32	1	138	11.5
Paul Arizin°	10	206	116	54	.466	35	29	.829	47	6	29	1	137	13.7
George Gervin	9	215	108	54	.500	36	28	.778	33	12	25	0	137	15.2
LARRY BIRD°	10	287	123	52	.423	32	27	.844	79	41	28	0	134	13.4
Rick Barry°	7	195	111	54	.486	24	20	.833	29	31	30	2	128	18.3
MOSES MALONE°	11	271	98	44	.449	67	40	.597	108	15	26	0	128	11.6
Elvin Hayes	12	264	129	52	.403	34	22	.647	92	17	37	0	126	10.5
Hal Greer	10	207	102	47	.461	37	26	.703	45	28	29	0	120	12.0
Bill Russell	12	343	111	51	.459	34	18	.529	139	39	37	1	120	10.0
Bill Sharman	8	194	104	40	.385	27	22	.815	31	16	16	0	102	12.8
Paul Westphal	5	128	68	43	.632	16	11	.688	7	24	14	0	97	19.4
Jerry Lucas	7	183	64	35	.547	21	19	.905	64	12	20	0	89	12.7
Jack Twyman	6	117	68	38	.559	20	13	.650	21	8	14	0	89	14.8
Walt Frazier	7	183	78	35	.449	21	18	.857	27	26	10	0	88	12.6
Bob McAdoo	5	126	64	37	.578	19	14	.737	30	6	18	0	88	17.6
Willis Reed	7	161	84	38	.452	16	12	.750	58	7	20	1	88	12.6
ROBERT PARISH	9	142	68	36	.529	21	14	.667	53	8	15	0	86	9.6
DOMINIQUE WILKINS	6	124	75	32	.427	28	21	.750	18	11	10	0	86	14.3
Lenny Wilkens	9	182	75	30	.400	32	25	.781	22	26	15	0	85	9.4
Ed Macauley	7	154	63	24	.381	41	35	.854	32	18	13	0	83	11.9
George Mikan	4	100	80	28	.350	27	22	.815	51	7	5	0	78	19.5
TOM CHAMBERS	4	84	56	29	.518	22	17	.773	16	5	11	0	77	19.3
Dave DeBusschere	8	167	81	37	.457	4	3	.750	51	11	12	0	77	9.6
KARL MALONE°	4	109	54	32	.593	19	13	.684	37	12	9	0	77	19.3
CLYDE DREXLER	6	121	61	31	.508	12	12	1.000	38	18	15	0	77	12.8
Dave Cowens°	6	154	66	33	.500	14	10	.714	81	12	21	0	76	12.7
David Thompson	4	115	49	33	.673	17	9	.529	16	10	13	0	75	18.8
Nate Archibald	6	162	60	27	.450	24	20	.833	18	40	10	0	74	12.3
CHARLES BARKLEY	6	136	62	29	.468	25	15	.600	47	6	13	0	74	12.3
Bob Lanier	8	121	55	32	.582	12	10	.833	45	12	15	0	74	9.3

Player	G.	Min.	FGA	FGM	Pct.	FTA	FTM	Pct.	Reb.	Ast.	PF	Disq.	Pts.	Avg.
JAMES WORTHY	7	142	77	34	.442	9	6	.667	26	9	10	0	74	10.6
Alex English	8	148	72	36	.500	2	1	.500	18	15	8	0	73	9.1
ROLANDO BLACKMAN	4	88	49	29	.592	16	13	.813	13	13	5	0	71	17.8
Neil Johnston	6	132	63	27	.429	23	16	.696	52	6	13	0	70	11.7
Gus Johnson	5	99	56	24	.429	25	19	.760	35	6	12	0	67	13.4
Vern Mikkelsen	6	110	70	27	.386	20	13	.650	52	8	20	0	67	11.2
HAKEEM OLAJUWON	7	160	61	23	.377	38	21	.553	59	12	19	1	67	9.6
Lou Hudson	6	99	61	26	.426	15	14	.933	13	6	11	0	66	11.0
Gene Shue	5	130	52	29	.558	12	8	.667	20	19	11	0	66	13.2
Jo Jo White	7	124	60	29	.483	11	6	.545	27	21	6	0	64	9.1
George Yardley	6	131	60	26	.433	17	12	.706	35	4	13	0	64	10.7
Adrian Dantley	6	130	54	23	.426	19	17	.895	23	7	13	0	63	10.5
Richie Guerin	6	122	56	23	.411	26	17	.654	19	18	17	0	63	10.5

*Also selected but did not play in one additional game.

EAST-WEST ALL-STAR GAME RECORDS

Most Games Played
18—Kareem Abdul-Jabbar
13—Wilt Chamberlain
13—Bob Cousy
13—John Havlicek
12—Elvin Hayes
12—Oscar Robertson
12—Bill Russell
12—Jerry West

Most Minutes Played
449—Kareem Abdul-Jabbar
388—Wilt Chamberlain
380—Oscar Robertson

Best Scoring Average
(60 Points Minimum)
21.0—Michael Jordan
20.5—Oscar Robertson
20.4—Bob Pettit

Most Field Goals Attempted
213—Kareem Abdul-Jabbar
193—Bob Pettit
178—Julius Erving

Most Field Goals Made
105—Kareem Abdul-Jabbar
88—Oscar Robertson
85—Julius Erving

Best Field Goal Percentage
(15 FGM Minimum)
.714—Randy Smith
.673—David Thompson
.643—Eddie Johnson

Most Free Throws Attempted
98—Elgin Baylor
98—Oscar Robertson
94—Wilt Chamberlain

Most Free Throws Made
78—Elgin Baylor
70—Oscar Robertson
62—Bob Pettit

Best Free Throw Percentage
(10 FTM Minimum)
1.000—Archie Clark
1.000—Clyde Drexler
.938—Larry Foust

Most 3-Point Field Goals Made
10—Magic Johnson
6—Isiah Thomas
3—by many

Most 3-Point Field Goal Attempts
21—Magic Johnson
14—Isaih Thomas
13—Larry Bird

Most Rebounds
197—Wilt Chamberlain
178—Bob Pettit
149—Kareem Abdul-Jabbar

Most Assists
127—Magic Johnson
93—Isiah Thomas
86—Bob Cousy

Most Steals
29—Isiah Thomas
23—Larry Bird
23—Michael Jordan

Most Blocked Shots
31—Kareem Abdul-Jabbar
13—Patrick Ewing
13—Hakeem Olajuwon

Most Personal Fouls
57—Kareem Abdul-Jabbar
41—Oscar Robertson
37—Elvin Hayes
37—Bill Russell

—PLAYER—SINGLE GAME—

Most Minutes Played
42—Oscar Robertson (1964)
42—Bill Russell (1964)
42—Jerry West (1964)
42—Nate Thurmond (1967)

Most Points Scored
42—Wilt Chamberlain (1962)

Most Field Goals Attempted
27—Rick Barry (1967)

Most Field Goals Scored
17—Wilt Chamberlain (1962)
Michael Jordan (1988)

Most Free Throws Attempted
16—Wilt Chamberlain (1962)

Most Free Throws Scored
12—Elgin Baylor (1962)
12—Oscar Robertson (1965)

Most Rebounds
27—Bob Pettit (1962)

Most Assists
22—Magic Johnson (1984)(OT)

Most Personals
6—Bob Wanzer (1954)
6—Paul Arizin (1956)
6—Bob Cousy (1956 and 1961)
6—Dolph Schayes (1959)
6—Walt Bellamy (1962)
6—Richie Guerin (1962)
6—Bill Russell (1965)
6—John Green (1965)
6—Rick Barry (1966 and 1978)
6—Kareem Abdul-Jabbar (1970)
6—Willis Reed (1970)
6—Hakeem Olajuwon (1987)

PLAYER—ONE HALF

Most Points—23 by Wilt Chamberlain, 1962
23 by Tom Chambers, 1987
Most FGA—16 by Dominique Wilkins, 1988
Most FGM—10 by Wilt Chamberlain, 1962
Most FTA—12 by Zelmo Beaty, 1966

Most FTM—10 by Zelmo Beaty, 1966
Most Rebounds—16 by Wilt Chamberlain, 1960
16 by Bob Pettit, 1962
Most Assists—13 by Magic Johnson, 1984
Most Personals—5 by Randy Smith, 1978

PLAYER—ONE QUARTER

Most Points—19 by Hal Greer, 1968
Most FGA—12 by Bill Sharman, 1960
Most FGM—8 by Dave DeBusschere, 1967
Most FTA—11 by Julius Erving, 1978
Most FTM—9 by Zelmo Beaty, 1966
        9 by Julius Erving, 1978
Most Rebounds—10 by Bob Pettit, 1962

Most Assists—9 by John Stockton, 1989
Most Personals—4 by Vern Mikkelsen, 1955
        4 by Cliff Hagan, 1959
        4 by Bob McAdoo, 1976
        4 by Randy Smith, 1978
        4 by David Robinson, 1991

—————————— FOR ONE TEAM ——————————

FULL GAME

Most Points—154 by East, 1984 (OT)
       154 by West, 1987 (OT)
Most FGA—135 by East, 1960
Most FGM—64 by West, 1992
Most FTA—57 by West, 1970
Most FTM—40 by East, 1959
Most Rebounds—83 by East, 1966
Most Assists—46 by West, 1984 (OT)
Most Personals—36 by East, 1965
Most Disqualifications—2 by East, 1956
       2 by East, 1965
       2 by East, 1970

ONE HALF

Most Points—87 by West, 1989
Most FGA—73 by East, 1960
Most FGM—36 by West, 1989
Most FTA—31 by East, 1959
Most FTM—26 by East, 1959
Most Rebounds—51 by East, 1966
Most Assists—28 by West, 1984

Most Peronsals—18 by West, 1954
       18 by East, 1962
       18 by East, 1970
       18 by West, 1986
       18 by East, 1987
Most Disqualifications—2 by East, 1956
       2 by East, 1970

ONE QUARTER

Most Points—50 by West, 1970
Most FGA—38 by East, 1960
Most FGM—19 by West, 1962
       19 by West, 1979
       19 by East, 1983
       19 by West, 1989
Most FTA—25 by West, 1970
Most FTM—19 by East, 1986
Most Rebounds—29 by West, 1962
       29 by East, 1962
Most Assists—15 by West, 1977
       15 by West, 1984
Most Personals—13 by East, 1970
Most Disqualifications—2 by East, 1956
       2 by East, 1970

———————— FOR TWO TEAMS ————————

FULL GAME

Most Pts.—303 (West 154, East 149), 1987 (OT)
Most FGA—256 (East 135, West 121), 1960
Most FGM—126 (East 63, West 63), 1984 (OT)
Most FTA—94 (West 47, East 47), 1961
Most FTM—71 (West 39, East 32), 1987 (OT)
Most Rebounds—151 (East 79, West 72), 1960
Most Assists—85 (West 46, East 39), 1984 (OT)
Most Personals—64 (East 36, West 28), 1965
Most Disqualifications—2 (East 2, West 0), 1956
       2 (East 1, West 1), 1962
       2 (East 2, West 0), 1970

ONE HALF

Most Points—157 (West 79, East 78), 1988
Most FGA—135 (East 73, West 62), 1960
Most FGM—65 (West 35, East 30), 1962
Most FTA—57 (West 29, East 28), 1962
Most FTM—36 (West 20, East 16), 1961
Most Rebounds—98 (East 50, West 48), 1962
       98 (East 51, West 47), 1966

Most Assists—45 (West 28, East 17), 1984
Most Personals—37 (West 22, East 15), 1980
Most Disqualifications—2 (East 2, West 0), 1956
       2 (East 1, West 1), 1962
       2 (East 2, West 0), 1970

ONE QUARTER

Most Points—86 (West 50, East 36), 1970
Most FGA—71 (East 37, West 34), 1962
Most FGM—36 (West 19, East 17), 1962
Most FTA—33 (East 20, West 13), 1962
Most FTM—27 (East 19, West 8), 1986
Most Rebounds—58 (West 30, East 28), 1966
Most Assists—25 (West 15, East 10), 1984
Most Personals—20 (East 11, West 9), 1985
       20 (East 12, West 8), 1987
Most Disqualifications—2 (East 2, West 0), 1956
       2 (East 1, West 1), 1962
       2 (East 2, West 0), 1970

NBA ALL-STAR SATURDAY RESULTS

American Airlines/ITT Sheraton Shootout
1986—Larry Bird, Boston
1987—Larry Bird, Boston
1988—Larry Bird, Boston
1989—Dale Ellis, Seattle
1990—Craig Hodges, Chicago
1991—Craig Hodges, Chicago
1992—Craig Hodges, Chicago

Gatorade Slam-Dunk Championship
1984—Larry Nance, Phoenix
1985—Dominique Wilkins, Atlanta
1986—Spud Webb, Atlanta
1987—Michael Jordan, Chicago
1988—Michael Jordan, Chicago
1989—Kenny Walker, New York
1990—Dominique Wilkins, Atlanta
1991—Dee Brown, Boston
1992—Cedric Ceballos, Phoenix

Schick Legends Classic
1984—West 64, East 63
1985—East 63, West 53
1986—West 53, East 44
1987—West 54, East 43
1988—East 47, West 45 (OT)
1989—West 54, East 53
1990—East 37, West 36
1991—East 41, West 34
1992—West 46, East 38

ALL-TIME ALL-STAR GAME LEADERS
(Active players in 1991-92 in capital letters)

GAMES

Kareem Abdul-Jabbar	18
Wilt Chamberlain	13
Bob Cousy	13
John Havlicek	13
Elvin Hayes	12
Oscar Robertson	12
Bill Russell	12
Jerry West	12
Six players tied at	11

MINUTES

Kareem Abdul-Jabbar	449
Wilt Chamberlain	388
Oscar Robertson	380
Bob Cousy	368
Bob Pettit	360
Bill Russell	343
Jerry West	341
MAGIC JOHNSON	341
Elgin Baylor	321
Julius Erving	316

FIELD GOAL ATTEMPTS

Kareem Abdul-Jabbar	213
Bob Pettit	193
Julius Erving	178
Oscar Robertson	172
Elgin Baylor	164
Bob Cousy	158
John Havlicek	154
Jerry West	137
MAGIC JOHNSON	131
Elvin Hayes	129

FIELD GOALS MADE

Kareem Abdul-Jabbar	105
Oscar Robertson	88
Julius Erving	85
Bob Pettit	81
John Havlicek	74
Wilt Chamberlain	72
ISIAH THOMAS	72
Elgin Baylor	70
MAGIC JOHNSON	64
MICHAEL JORDAN	64

FREE THROW ATTEMPTS

Elgin Baylor	98
Oscar Robertson	98
Wilt Chamberlain	94
Bob Pettit	80
MOSES MALONE	67
Julius Erving	63
Bob Cousy	51
Kareem Abdul-Jabbar	50
Dolph Schayes	50
Jerry West	50

FREE THROWS MADE

Elgin Baylor	78
Oscar Robertson	70
Bob Pettit	62
Julius Erving	50
Wilt Chamberlain	47
Bob Cousy	43
Dolph Schayes	42
Kareem Abdul-Jabbar	41
MOSES MALONE	40
MAGIC JOHNSON	38

FIELD GOAL PERCENTAGE
(15 FGM minimum)

Randy Smith	.714
David Thompson	.673
Eddie Johnson	.643
RALPH SAMPSON	.636
Paul Westphal	.632
Artis Gilmore	.621
KARL MALONE	.593
ROLANDO BLACKMAN	.592
Wilt Chamberlain	.590
DAVID ROBINSON	.588

FREE THROW PERCENTAGE
(10 FTM minimum)

Archie Clark	1.000
CLYDE DREXLER	1.000
Larry Foust	.938
Lou Hudson	.933
Don Ohl	.933
MAGIC JOHNSON	.905
Jerry Lucas	.905
Adrian Dantley	.895
Dennis Johnson	.864
Sidney Moncrief	.864

REBOUNDS

Wilt Chamberlain	197
Bob Pettit	178
Kareem Abdul-Jabbar	149
Bill Russell	139
MOSES MALONE	108
Dolph Schayes	105
Elgin Baylor	99
Elvin Hayes	92
Dave Cowens	81
LARRY BIRD	79

ASSISTS

MAGIC JOHNSON	127
ISIAH THOMAS	93
Bob Cousy	86
Oscar Robertson	81
Jerry West	55
Kareem Abdul-Jabbar	51
LARRY BIRD	41
Nate Archibald	40
Bill Russell	39
Elgin Baylor	38
Dick McGuire	38

STEALS

ISIAH THOMAS	29
LARRY BIRD	23
MICHAEL JORDAN	23
MAGIC JOHNSON	21
Julius Erving	18
Rick Barry	16
George Gervin	16
Sidney Moncrief	12
Nate Archibald	11
Seven players tied at	9

BLOCKED SHOTS

Kareem Abdul-Jabbar	31
PATRICK EWING	12
HAKEEM OLAJUWON	13
KEVIN MCHALE	12
Julius Erving	11
George Gervin	9
ROBERT PARISH	8
MAGIC JOHNSON	7
Jack Sikma	7
Elvin Hayes	6
MICHAEL JORDAN	6
MOSES MALONE	6

PERSONAL FOULS

Kareem Abdul-Jabbar	57
Oscar Robertson	41
Elvin Hayes	37
Bill Russell	37
Dolph Schayes	32
Elgin Baylor	31
Julius Erving	31
Rick Barry	30
Paul Arizin	29
Hal Greer	29

DISQUALIFICATIONS

Rick Barry	2
Bob Cousy	2
Kareem Abdul-Jabbar	1
Paul Arizin	1
Walt Bellamy	1
John Green	1
Richie Guerin	1
HAKEEM OLAJUWON	1
Willis Reed	1
Bill Russell	1
Dolph Schayes	1
Bobby Wanzer	1

3-POINT FIELD GOAL ATTEMPTS

MAGIC JOHNSON	21
ISIAH THOMAS	14
LARRY BIRD	13
CLYDE DREXLER	7
TIM HARDAWAY	7
MARK PRICE	7
CHARLES BARKLEY	7
MICHAEL JORDAN	6
JOHN STOCKTON	6
Three players tied at	5

3-POINT FIELD GOALS MADE

MAGIC JOHNSON	10
ISIAH THOMAS	6
DANNY AINGE	3
LARRY BIRD	3
CLYDE DREXLER	3
JOHN STOCKTON	3
MARK AGUIRRE	2
TOM CHAMBERS	2
JOE DUMARS	2
CHRIS MULLIN	2

POINTS

Kareem Abdul-Jabbar	251
Oscar Robertson	246
Bob Pettit	224
Julius Erving	221
Elgin Baylor	218
Wilt Chamberlain	191
John Havlicek	179
ISIAH THOMAS	177
MAGIC JOHNSON	176
Jerry West	160

SCORING AVERAGE
(60 points minimum)

MICHAEL JORDAN	21.0
Oscar Robertson	20.5
Bob Pettit	20.4
Julius Erving	20.1
Elgin Baylor	19.8
George Mikan	19.5
Paul Westphal	19.4
TOM CHAMBERS	19.3
KARL MALONE	19.3
David Thompson	18.8

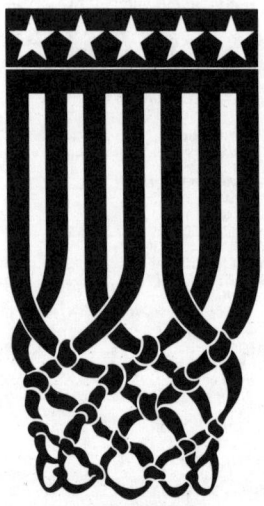

Basketball Hall of Fame

SPRINGFIELD, MASSACHUSETTS

CONTRIBUTORS

Name	Year Elected
Abbott, Senda	1984
Allen, Dr. Forrest C. (Phog)	1959
BEE, CLAIR F.	**1967**
BROWN, WALTER A.	**1965**
Bunn, John W.	1964
Douglas, Robert L. (Bob)	1971
Duer, Al	1981
Fagan, Clifford	1983
Fisher, Harry A.	1973
FLEISHER, LARRY	**1990**
GOTTLIEB, EDWARD	**1971**
Gulick, Dr. Luther H.	1959
HARRISON, LESTER	**1979**
Hepp, Ferenc	1980
Hickox, Edward J.	1959
Hinkle, Paul D. (Tony)	1965
IRISH, NED	**1964**
Jones, R. William	1964
KENNEDY, J. WALTER	**1980**
Liston, Emil S.	1974
McLendon, John B.	1978
MOKRAY, WILLIAM G. (BILL)	**1965**
Morgan, Ralph	1959
Morgenweck, Frank	1962
Naismith, Dr. James	1959
NEWELL, PETER F.	**1978**
O'Brien, John J.	1961
O'BRIEN, LARRY	**1990**
OLSEN, HAROLD G.	**1959**
PODOLOFF, MAURICE	**1973**
Porter, H. V.	1960

Name	Year Elected
Reid, William A.	1963
Ripley, Elmer	1972
St. John, Lynn W.	1962
Saperstein, Abe	1970
Schabinger, Arthur A.	1961
Stagg, Amos Alonzo	1959
Stankovich, Boris	1990
Steitz, Edward	1983
Taylor, Charles H. (Chuck)	1968
Tower, Oswald	1959
Trester, Arthur L.	1961
Wells, Clifford	1971
Wilke, Lou	1982

PLAYERS

Name	Year Elected
ARCHIBALD, NATHANIEL (NATE)	**1990**
ARIZIN, PAUL J.	**1977**
Barlow, Thomas B.	1980
BARRY, RICHARD F.D. (Rick)	**1986**
BAYLOR, ELGIN	**1976**
Beckman, John	1972
Belov, Sergei	1991
BING, DAVE	**1989**
Borgmann, Bennie	1961
BRADLEY, BILL	**1982**
Brennan, Joseph	1974
CERVI, AL	**1984**
CHAMBERLAIN, WILT	**1978**
COOPER, CHARLES (Tarzan)	**1976**
COUSY, ROBERT J.	**1970**
COWENS, DAVID (DAVE)	**1990**
CUNNINGHAM, WILLIAM J.	**1985**
DAVIES, ROBERT E. (BOB)	**1969**

The first player chosen in the 1970 NBA Draft, Bob Lanier (right) averaged 20.1 points and 10.1 rebounds in 14 seasons with Detroit and Milwaukee en route to induction in the Naismith Memorial Basketball Hall of Fame.

DeBernardi, Forrest S.	1961
DeBUSSCHERE, DAVE	**1982**
Dehnert, H. G. (Dutch)	1968
Endacott, Paul	1971
Foster, Harold (Bud)	1964
FRAZIER, WALTER (Clyde)	**1986**
Friedman, Max (Marty)	1971
FULKS, JOSEPH F. (JOE)	**1977**
Gale, Lauren (Laddie)	1976
GALLATIN, HARRY J.	**1990**
Gates, William	1988
GOLA, TOM	**1975**
GREER, HAL	**1981**
Gruenig, Robert (Ace)	1963
HAGAN, CLIFFORD O.	**1977**
Hanson, Victor	1960
Harris, Lusia	1991
HAVLICEK, JOHN	**1983**
HAWKINS, CONNIE	**1991**
HAYES, ELVIN	**1989**
HEINSOHN, THOMAS W.	**1985**
Holman, Nat	1964
HOUBREGS, ROBERT J.	**1986**
Hyatt, Charles (Chuck)	1959
Johnson, William C.	1976
JOHNSTON, D. NEIL	**1989**
JONES, K.C.	**1988**
JONES, SAM	**1983**
Krause, Edward (Moose)	1975
Kurland, Robert (Bob)	1961
LANIER, BOB	**1991**
LAPCHICK, JOE	**1966**
LOVELLETTE, CLYDE	**1987**
LUCAS, JERRY	**1979**
Luisetti, Angelo (Hank)	1959
McCracken, Branch	1960
McCracken, Jack	1962
McDermott, Bobby	1987
MACAULEY, C. EDWARD	**1960**
MARAVICH, PETER P.	**1986**
MARTIN, SLATER	**1981**
MIKAN, GEORGE L.	**1959**
MONROE, EARL	**1989**
Murphy, Charles (Stretch)	1960
Page, H.O. (Pat)	1962
PETTIT, ROBERT L.	**1970**
PHILLIP, ANDY	**1961**
POLLARD, JAMES C. (JIM)	**1977**
RAMSEY, FRANK	**1981**
REED, WILLIS	**1981**
ROBERTSON, OSCAR	**1979**
Roosma, Col. John S.	1961
RUSSELL, JOHN (HONEY)	**1964**
RUSSELL, WILLIAM (BILL)	**1974**
SCHAYES, ADOLPH	**1972**
Schmidt, Ernest J.	1973
Schommer, John J.	1959
Sedran, Barney	1962
SHARMAN, BILL	**1975**
Steinmetz, Christian	1961
Thompson, John A. (Cat)	1962
THURMOND, NATE	**1984**
TWYMAN, JACK	**1982**
UNSELD, WES	**1987**
Vandivier, Robert (Fuzzy)	1974
Wachter, Edward A.	1961
WANZER, ROBERT F.	**1986**
WEST, JERRY	**1979**
White, Nera	1991
WILKENS, LENNY	**1988**
Wooden, John R.	1960

COACHES

Name	Year Elected
Anderson, Harold	1984
AUERBACH, A. J. (RED)	**1968**
Barry, Sam	1978
Blood, Ernest A.	1960
Cann, Howard G.	1967
Carlson, Dr. H. Clifford	1959
Carnesecca, Lou	1991
Carnevale, Ben	1969
Case, Everett	1981
Dean, Everett S.	1966
Diddle, Edgar A.	1971
Drake, Bruce	1972
Gaines, Clarence	1981
Gardner, Jack	1983
Gill, Amory T. (Slats)	1967
Harshman, Marv	1984
Hickey, Edgar S.	1978
Hobson, Howard A.	1965
HOLZMAN, WILLIAM	**1985**
Iba, Henry P. (Hank)	1968
JULIAN, ALVIN F. (DOGGIE)	**1967**
Keaney, Frank W.	1960
Keogan, George E.	1961
Knight, Bob	1990
Lambert, Ward L.	1960
LITWACK, HARRY	**1975**
LOEFFLER, KENNETH D.	**1964**
Lonborg, A. C. (Dutch)	1972
McCutchan, Arad A.	1980
McGuire, Al	1991
McGUIRE, FRANK	**1976**
Meanwell, Dr. Walter E.	1959
Meyer, Raymond J.	1978
Miller, Ralph	1987
RAMSAY, JACK	**1991**
Rupp, Adolph F.	1968
Sachs, Leonard D.	1961
Shelton, Everett F.	1979
Smith, Dean	1982
Taylor, Fred R.	1985
Teague, Bertha	1984
Wade, Margaret	1984
Watts, Stanley H.	1985
Wooden, John R.	1972
Woolpert, Phil	1991

REFEREES

ENRIGHT, JAMES E.	**1978**
Hepbron, George T.	1960
Hoyt, George	1961
KENNEDY, MATTHEW P.	**1959**
Leith, Lloyd	1982
Mihalik, Zigmund J.	1985
NUCATOLA, JOHN P.	**1977**
Quigley, Ernest C.	1961
SHIRLEY, J. DALLAS	**1979**
Tobey, David	1961
Walsh, David H.	1961

TEAMS

First Team	1959
Original Celtics	1959
Buffalo Germans	1961
Renaissance	1963

Individuals associated with the NBA in bold face type.

Individuals elected—189.

Teams elected—4.

ABA CHAMPIONSHIP SERIES RESULTS

1968—Pittsburgh defeated New Orleans, four games to two
1969—Oakland defeated Indiana, four games to one
1970—Indiana defeated Los Angeles, four games to two
1971—Utah defeated Kentucky, four games to three
1972—Indiana defeated New York, four games to two
1973—Indiana defeated Kentucky, four games to three
1974—New York defeated Utah, four games to one
1975—Kentucky defeated Indiana, four games to one
1976—New York defeated Denver, four games to two

Players Who Made All-ABA Teams

	1st Team	2nd		1st Team	2nd
Marvin Barnes	0	1	Dan Issel	1	4
Rick Barry	4	0	Warren Jabali	1	0
John Beasley	0	2	Bobby Jones	0	1
Zelmo Beaty	0	2	James Jones	3	0
Ron Boone	1	1	Larry Jones	3	0
John Brisker	0	1	Billy Knight	1	0
Larry Brown	0	1	George McGinnis	2	1
Roger Brown	1	2	Bill Melchionni	1	0
Don Buse	0	1	Doug Moe	1	1
Joe Caldwell	0	1	Swen Nater	0	2
Mack Calvin	3	1	Bob Netolicky	0	1
Larry Cannon	0	1	Cincy Powell	0	1
Billy Cunningham	1	0	Red Robbins	0	2
Louie Dampier	0	4	Charlie Scott	1	1
Mel Daniels	4	1	James Silas	1	1
Julius Erving	4	1	Ralph Simpson	1	2
Don Freeman	1	3	Brian Taylor	0	1
George Gervin	0	2	David Thompson	0	1
Artis Gilmore	5	0	Bob Verga	1	0
Connie Hawkins	2	0	Charlie Williams	1	0
Spencer Haywood	1	0	Willie Wise	0	2

ABA Most Valuable Players

1976—Julius Erving, New York
1975—Julius Erving, New York
　　　George McGinnis, Indiana (tie)
1974—Julius Erving, New York
1973—Billy Cunningham, Carolina

1972—Artis Gilmore, Kentucky
1971—Mel Daniels, Indiana
1970—Spencer Haywood, Denver
1969—Mel Daniels, Indiana
1968—Connie Hawkins, Pittsburgh

ABA Rookies of the Year

1976—David Thompson, Denver
1975—Marvin Barnes, St. Louis
1974—Swen Nater, San Antonio
1973—Brian Taylor, New York
1972—Artis Gilmore, Kentucky

1971—Charlie Scott, Virginia
　　　Dan Issel, Kentucky (tie)
1970—Spencer Haywood, Denver
1969—Warren Armstrong, Oakland
1968—Mel Daniels, Minnesota

ABA Coaches of the Year

1976—Larry Brown, Denver
1975—Larry Brown, Denver
1974—Babe McCarthy, Kentucky
　　　Joe Mullaney, Utah (tie)
1973—Larry Brown, Carolina
1972—Tom Nissalke, Dallas

1971—Al Bianchi, Virginia
1970—Bill Sharman, Los Angeles
　　　Joe Belmont, Denver (tie)
1969—Alex Hannum, Oakland
1968—Vince Cazetta, Pittsburgh

ALL-TIME RECORDS OF ABA TEAMS

	Years	Regular Season			Playoffs		
		Won	Lost	Pct.	Won	Lost	Pct.
Anaheim Amigos	1	25	53	.321	0	0	.000
Carolina Cougars	5	215	205	.512	7	9	.438
Dallas Chaparrals	5	202	206	.408	9	16	.360
Denver Nuggets	2	125	43	.744	13	13	.500
Denver Rockets	7	288	288	.500	14	22	.389
Floridians	2	73	95	.435	2	8	.250
Houston Mavericks	2	52	104	.333	0	3	.000
Indiana Pacers	9	427	317	.574	69	50	.580
Kentucky Colonels	9	448	296	.602	55	46	.545
Los Angeles Stars	2	76	86	.469	10	7	.588

		Regular Season				Playoffs		
	Years	Won	Lost	Pct.		Won	Lost	Pct.
Memphis Sounds	5	139	291	.323		1	8	.111
Miami Floridians	2	66	96	.407		5	7	.417
Minnesota Muskies	1	50	28	.641		4	6	.400
Minnesota Pipers	1	36	42	.462		3	4	.429
New Jersey Americans	1	36	42	.462		0	0	.000
New Orleans Buccaneers	3	136	104	.567		14	14	.500
New York Nets	8	338	328	.508		37	32	.536
Oakland Oaks	2	82	74	.526		12	4	.750
Pittsburgh Condors	2	61	107	.363		0	0	.000
Pittsburgh Pipers	2	83	79	.512		11	4	.733
San Antonio Spurs	3	146	106	.579		8	12	.400
San Diego Conquistadors	4	101	173	.369		2	8	.250
San Diego Sails	1	3	8	.273		0	0	.000
Spirits of St. Louis	2	67	101	.399		5	5	.500
Texas Chaparrals	1	30	54	.357		0	4	.000
Utah Stars	6	265	171	.608		36	27	.571
Virginia Squires	6	200	303	.398		15	18	.455
Washington Capitols	1	44	40	.524		3	4	.429

Anaheim moved to Los Angeles after 1967-68 season and then to Utah after 1969-70 season. Houston moved to Carolina after 1968-69 season. Minnesota Muskies moved to Miami after 1967-68 season. New Jersey moved to New York after 1967-68 season. Oakland moved to Washington after 1968-69 season and then to Virginia after 1969-70 season. Pittsburgh moved to Minnesota and retained nickname after 1967-68 season and returned to Pittsburgh after 1968-69 season and changed nickname to Condors in 1970-71. New Orleans moved to Memphis after 1969-70 season. Dallas moved to San Antonio after 1972-73 season. San Diego was an expansion team in 1972-73 and changed nickname to Sails in 1975-76 before folding after 11 games. Carolina moved to St. Louis after 1973-74 season. Baltimore (not shown) folded before 1975-76 season even started and Utah folded after 16 games of 1975-76 season.

ABA YEARLY STATISTICAL LEADERS

Year	Scoring	Rebounding	Assists
1968	Connie Hawkins, 26.8	Mel Daniels, 15.6	Larry Brown, 6.5
1969	Rick Barry, 34.0	Mel Daniels, 16.5	Larry Brown, 7.1
1970	Spencer Haywood, 30.0	Spencer Haywood, 19.5	Larry Brown, 7.1
1971	Dan Issel, 29.9	Mel Daniels, 18.0	Bill Melchionni, 8.3
1972	Charlie Scott, 34.6	Artis Gilmore, 17.8	Bill Melchionni, 8.4
1973	Julius Erving, 31.9	Artis Gilmore, 17.5	Bill Melchionni, 7.5
1974	Julius Erving, 27.4	Artis Gilmore, 18.3	Al Smith, 8.2
1975	George McGinnis, 29.8	Swen Nater, 16.4	Mack Calvin, 7.7
1976	Julius Erving, 29.3	Artis Gilmore, 15.5	Don Buse, 8.2

ABA ALL-STAR GAMES AT A GLANCE

East 5, West 3

Date	Site	Att.	East Coach	Score	West Coach	MVP
Jan. 9, 1968	Indianapolis	10,872	Pollard	East, 126-120	McCarthy	L. Brown
Jan. 28, 1969	Louisville	5,407	Rhodes	West, 133-127	Hannum	J. Beasley
Jan. 24, 1970	Indianapolis	11,932	Leonard	West, 128- 98	McCarthy	S. Haywood
Jan. 23, 1971	Greensboro	14,407	Bianchi	East, 126-122	Sharman	M. Daniels
Jan. 29, 1972	Louisville	15,738	Mullaney	East, 142-115	Andersen	Dan Issel
Feb. 6, 1973	Salt Lake City	12,556	Brown	West, 123-111	Andersen	W. Jabali
Jan. 30, 1974	Norfolk	10,624	McCarthy	East, 128-112	Mullaney	A. Gilmore
Jan. 28, 1975	San Antonio	10,449	Loughery	East, 151-124	L. Brown	F. Lewis
Jan. 27, 1976	Denver	17,798	*Loughery	144-138	*L. Brown	D. Thompson

*The final ABA All-Star Game in 1976 was a contest between the Denver Nuggets, coached by Larry Brown, and a team of ABA All-Stars, coached by Kevin Loughery.

ALL-TIME, CAREER RECORDS

Including

NBA Championship Teams

Year-by-Year Statistical Leaders

All-Time NBA Leaders

Top NBA Career Scorers

Top Regular-Season Performances

Combined NBA/ABA All-Time Leaders

All-Time NBA Team Records

Top Ten Team Winning Percentages

All-Time Team Winning, Losing Streaks

Winningest NBA Coaches

Wilt Chamberlain's "100-Point" Box Score

"Highest Scoring Game" Box Score

"Lowest Scoring Game" Box Score

All-Time Regular-Season Records

All-Time Playoff Records

NBA Finals Records

NBA CHAMPIONS OVER THE YEARS

Season	Champion	Eastern Div./Conf. W.	L.		Western Div./Conf. W.	L.		Top Scorer Pts.	
1946-47—Philadelphia		35	25	Philadelphia	39	22	Chicago	1389	Joe Fulks (Phil.)
1947-48—Baltimore		27	21	Philadelphia	28	20	Baltimore	1007	Max Zaslofsky (Chi.)
1948-49—Minneapolis		38	22	Washington	44	16	Minneapolis	1698	George Mikan (Mpls.)
1949-50—Minneapolis		51	13	Syracuse	51	17	Minneapolis	1865	George Mikan (Mpls.)
1950-51—Rochester		36	30	New York	41	27	Rochester	1932	George Mikan (Mpls.)
1951-52—Minneapolis		37	29	New York	40	26	Minneapolis	1674	Paul Arizin (Phil.)
1952-53—Minneapolis		47	23	New York	48	22	Minneapolis	1564	Neil Johnston (Phil.)
1953-54—Minneapolis		42	30	Syracuse	46	26	Minneapolis	1759	Neil Johnston (Phil.)
1954-55—Syracuse		43	29	Syracuse	43	29	Fort Wayne	1631	Neil Johnston (Phil.)
1955-56—Philadelphia		45	27	Philadelphia	37	35	Fort Wayne	1849	Bob Pettit (St. Louis)
1956-57—Boston		44	28	Boston	34	38	St. Louis	1817	Paul Arizin (Phil.)
1957-58—St. Louis		49	23	Boston	41	31	St. Louis	2001	George Yardley (Det.)
1958-59—Boston		52	20	Boston	33	39	Minneapolis	2105	Bob Pettit (St. Louis)
1959-60—Boston		59	16	Boston	46	29	St. Louis	2707	Wilt Chamberlain (Phil.)
1960-61—Boston		57	22	Boston	51	28	St. Louis	3033	Wilt Chamberlain (Phil.)
1961-62—Boston		60	20	Boston	54	26	Los Angeles	4029	Wilt Chamberlain (Phil.)
1962-63—Boston		58	22	Boston	53	27	Los Angeles	3586	Wilt Chamberlain (S.F.)
1963-64—Boston		59	21	Boston	48	32	San Francisco	2948	Wilt Chamberlain (S.F.)
1964-65—Boston		62	18	Boston	49	31	Los Angeles	2534	W. Cha'lain (S.F.-Phil.)
1965-66—Boston		54	26	Boston	45	35	Los Angeles	2649	Wilt Chamberlain (Phil.)
1966-67—Philadelphia		68	13	Philadelphia	44	37	San Francisco	2775	Rick Barry (San Fran.)
1967-68—Boston		54	28	Boston	52	30	Los Angeles	2142	Dave Bing (Detroit)
1968-69—Boston		48	34	Boston	55	27	Los Angeles	2327	Elvin Hayes (San Diego)
1969-70—New York		60	22	New York	46	36	Los Angeles	†31.2	Jerry West (L.A.)
1970-71—Milwaukee		42	40	Baltimore	66	16	Milwaukee	†31.7	K. Abdul-Jabbar (Mil.)
1971-72—Los Angeles		48	34	New York	69	13	Los Angeles	†34.8	K. Abdul-Jabbar (Mil.)
1972-73—New York		57	25	New York	60	22	Los Angeles	†34.0	Nate Archibald (KC-O)
1973-74—Boston		56	26	Boston	59	23	Milwaukee	†30.6	Bob McAdoo (Buffalo)
1974-75—Golden State		60	22	Washington	48	34	Golden State	†34.5	Bob McAdoo (Buffalo)
1975-76—Boston		54	28	Boston	42	40	Phoenix	†31.1	Bob McAdoo (Buffalo)
1976-77—Portland		50	32	Philadelphia	49	33	Portland	†31.1	Pete Maravich (N.O.)
1977-78—Washington		44	38	Washington	47	35	Seattle	†27.2	George Gervin (S.A.)
1978-79—Seattle		54	28	Washington	52	30	Seattle	†29.6	George Gervin (S.A.)
1979-80—Los Angeles		59	23	Philadelphia	60	22	Los Angeles	†33.1	George Gervin (S.A.)
1980-81—Boston		62	20	Boston	40	42	Houston	†30.7	Adrian Dantley (Utah)
1981-82—Los Angeles		58	24	Philadelphia	57	25	Los Angeles	†32.3	George Gervin (S.A.)
1982-83—Philadelphia		65	17	Philadelphia	58	24	Los Angeles	†28.4	Alex English (Den.)
1983-84—Boston		62	20	Boston	54	28	Los Angeles	†30.6	Adrian Dantley (Utah)
1984-85—L.A. Lakers		63	19	Boston	62	20	L.A. Lakers	†32.9	Bernard King (New York)
1985-86—Boston		67	15	Boston	51	31	Houston	†30.3	Dominique Wilkins (Atl.)
1986-87—L.A. Lakers		59	23	Boston	65	17	L.A. Lakers	†37.1	Michael Jordan (Chicago)
1987-88—L.A. Lakers		54	28	Detroit	62	20	L.A. Lakers	†35.0	Michael Jordan (Chicago)
1988-89—Detroit		63	19	Detroit	57	25	L.A. Lakers	†32.5	Michael Jordan (Chicago)
1989-90—Detroit		59	23	Detroit	59	23	Portland	†33.6	Michael Jordan (Chicago)
1990-91—Chicago		61	21	Chicago	58	24	L.A. Lakers	†31.5	Michael Jordan (Chicago)
1991-92—Chicago		67	15	Chicago	57	25	Portland	†30.1	Michael Jordan (Chicago)

†Scoring champion based on average.

ALL-TIME STATISTICAL LEADERS

Season	FG Pct. Leaders		FT Pct. Leaders		Top Rebounders	
1946-47—.401	Bob Feerick (Wash.)	.811	Fred Scolari (Wash.)		....	
1947-48—.340	Bob Feerick (Wash.)	.788	Bob Feerick (Wash.)		....	
1948-49—.423	Arnie Risen (Roch.)	.859	Bob Feerick (Wash.)		....	
1949-50—.478	Alex Groza (Indpls.)	.843	Max Zaslofsky (Chi.)			
1950-51—.470	Alex Groza (Indpls.)	.855	Joe Fulks (Phil.)		1080	Dolph Schayes (Syr.)
1951-52—.448	Paul Arizin (Phil.)	.904	Bob Wanzer (Roch.)		880	Larry Foust (Ft.W.)
						Mel Hutchins (Milw.)
1952-53—.452	Neil Johnston (Phil.)	.850	Bill Sharman (Bos.)		1007	George Mikan (Mpls.)
1953-54—.486	Ed Macauley (Boston)	.844	Bill Sharman (Bos.)		1098	Harry Gallatin (N.Y.)
1954-55—.487	Larry Foust (Ft. W.)	.897	Bill Sharman (Bos.)		1085	Neil Johnston (Phil.)
1955-56—.457	Neil Johnston (Phil.)	.867	Bill Sharman (Bos.)		1164	Bob Pettit (St. Louis)
1956-57—.447	Neil Johnston (Phil.)	.905	Bill Sharman (Bos.)		1256	Maurice Stokes (Roch.)
1957-58—.452	Jack Twyman (Cinn.)	.904	Dolph Schayes (Syr.)		1564	Bill Russell (Boston)
1958-59—.490	Ken Sears (N.Y.)	.932	Bill Sharman (Bos.)		1612	Bill Russell (Boston)
1959-60—.477	Ken Sears (N.Y.)	.892	Dolph Schayes (Syr.)		1941	W. Chamberlain (Phil.)
1960-61—.509	Wilt Chamberlain (Phil.)	.921	Bill Sharman (Bos.)		2149	W. Chamberlain (Phil.)
1961-62—.519	Walt Bellamy (Chi.)	.896	Dolph Schayes (Syr.)		2052	W. Chamberlain (Phil.)
1962-63—.528	Wilt Chamberlain (S.F.)	.881	Larry Costello (Syr.)		1946	W. Chamberlain (S.F.)
1963-64—.527	Jerry Lucas (Cinn.)	.853	Oscar Robertson (Cin.)		1930	Bill Russell (Boston)
1964-65—.510	Wilt Cham'ain (S.F.-Phil.)	.877	Larry Costello (Phil.)		1878	Bill Russell (Boston)
1965-66—.540	Wilt Chamberlain (Phil.)	.881	Larry Siegfried (Bos.)		1943	W. Chamberlain (Phil.)
1966-67—.683	Wilt Chamberlain (Phil.)	.903	Adrian Smith (Cin.)		1957	W. Chamberlain (Phil.)
1967-68—.595	Wilt Chamberlain (Phil.)	.873	Oscar Robertson (Cin.)		1952	W. Chamberlain (Phil.)
1968-69—.583	Wilt Chamberlain (L.A.)	.864	Larry Siegfried (Bos.)		1712	W. Chamberlain (L.A.)
1969-70—.559	Johnny Green (Cinn.)	.898	Flynn Robinson (Mil.)		16.9*	Elvin Hayes (S.D.)
1970-71—.587	Johnny Green (Cinn.)	.859	Chet Walker (Chi.)		18.2*	W. Chamberlain (L.A.)
1971-72—.649	Wilt Chamberlain (L.A.)	.894	Jack Marin (Balt.)		19.2*	W. Chamberlain (L.A.)
1972-73—.727	Wilt Chamberlain (L.A.)	.902	Rick Barry (G.S.)		18.6*	W. Chamberlain (L.A.)
1973-74—.547	Bob McAdoo (Buff.)	.902	Ernie DiGregorio (Buff.)		18.1*	Elvin Hayes (Capital)
1974-75—.539	Don Nelson (Boston)	.904	Rick Barry (Golden State)		14.8*	Wes Unseld (Wash.)
1975-76—.561	Wes Unseld (Wash.)	.923	Rick Barry (Golden State)		16.9*	K. Abdul-Jabbar (L.A.)
1976-77—.579	K. Abdul-Jabbar (L.A.)	.945	Ernie DiGregorio (Buff.)		14.4*	Bill Walton (Port.)
1977-78—.578	Bobby Jones (Den.)	.924	Rick Barry (Golden State)		15.7*	Len Robinson (N.O.)
1978-79—.584	Cedric Maxwell (Bos.)	.947	Rick Barry (Hou.)		17.6*	Moses Malone (Hou.)
1979-80—.609	Cedric Maxwell (Bos.)	.935	Rick Barry (Hou.)		15.0*	Swen Nater (S.D.)
1980-81—.670	Artis Gilmore (Chi.)	.958	Calvin Murphy (Hou.)		14.8*	Moses Malone (Hou.)
1981-82—.652	Artis Gilmore (Chi.)	.899	Kyle Macy (Phoe.)		14.7*	Moses Malone (Hou.)
1982-83—.626	Artis Gilmore (S.A.)	.920	Calvin Murphy (Hou.)		15.3*	Moses Malone (Phil.)
1983-84—.631	Artis Gilmore (S.A.)	.888	Larry Bird (Boston)		13.4*	Moses Malone (Phil.)

Season	FG Pct. Leaders	FT Pct. Leaders	Top Rebounders
1984-85	.637 James Donaldson (L.A.C.)	.907 Kyle Macy (Phoenix)	13.1* Moses Malone (Phil.)
1985-86	.632 Steve Johnson (S.A.)	.896 Larry Bird (Boston)	13.1* Bill Laimbeer (Det.)
1986-87	.604 Kevin McHale (Boston)	.910 Larry Bird (Boston)	14.6* Charles Barkley (Phil.)
1987-88	.604 Kevin McHale (Boston)	.922 Jack Sikma (Milw.)	13.03* Michael Cage (L.A.C.)
1988-89	.595 Dennis Rodman (Detroit)	.911 Magic Johnson (L.A. Lakers)	13.5* H. Olajuwon (Hou.)
1989-90	.625 Mark West (Phoenix)	.930 Larry Bird (Boston)	14.0* H. Olajuwon (Hou.)
1990-91	.602 Buck Williams (Portland)	.918 Reggie Miller (Indiana)	13.0* David Robinson (S.A.)
1991-92	.604 Buck Williams (Portland)	.947 Mark Price (Cleveland)	18.7* Dennis Rodman (Detroit)

*Based on highest average per game.

Season	Most Assists	Most Minutes No.	Most Personals No.
1946-47	202 Ernie Calverly (Prov.)	....	208 Stan Miasek (Detroit)
1947-48	120 Howie Dallmar (Phil.)	....	231 Charles Gilmur (Chi.)
1948-49	321 Bob Davies (Roch.)	....	273 Ed Sadowski (Phi.)
1949-50	396 Dick McGuire (N. Y.)	....	297 George Mikan (Mpls.)
1950-51	414 Andy Phillip (Phil.)	....	308 George Mikan (Mpls.)
1951-52	539 Andy Phillip (Phil.)	2939 Paul Arizin (Phil.)	286 George Mikan (Mpls.)
1952-53	547 Bob Cousy (Boston)	3166 Neil Johnston (Phil.)	334 Don Meineke (Ft. W.)
1953-54	578 Bob Cousy (Boston)	3296 Neil Johnston (Phil.)	303 Earl Lloyd (Syracuse)
1954-55	557 Bob Cousy (Boston)	2953 Paul Arizin (Phil.)	319 Vern Mikkelsen (Mpls.)
1955-56	642 Bob Cousy (Boston)	2838 Slater Martin (Mpls.)	319 Vern Mikkelsen (Mpls.)
1956-57	478 Bob Cousy (Boston)	2851 Dolph Schayes (Syr.)	312 Vern Mikkelsen (Mpls.)
1957-58	463 Bob Cousy (Boston)	2918 Dolph Schayes (Syr.)	311 Walt Dukes (Detroit)
1958-59	557 Bob Cousy (Boston)	2979 Bill Russell (Boston)	332 Walt Dukes (Detroit)
1959-60	715 Bob Cousy (Boston)	3338 W. Chamberlain (Phil.) / Gene Shue (Detroit)	311 Tom Gola (Phil.)
1960-61	690 Oscar Robertson (Cinn.)	3773 W. Chamberlain (Phil.)	335 Paul Arizin (Phil.)
1961-62	899 Oscar Robertson (Cinn.)	3882 W. Chamberlain (Phil.)	330 Tom Meschery (Phil.)
1962-63	825 Guy Rodgers (S.F.)	3806 W. Chamberlain (S.F.)	312 Zelmo Beaty (St. Louis)
1963-64	868 Oscar Robertson (Cinn.)	3689 W. Chamberlain (S.F.)	325 Wayne Embry (Cinn.)
1964-65	861 Oscar Robertson (Cinn.)	3466 Bill Russell (Boston)	345 Bailey Howell (Balt.)
1965-66	847 Oscar Robertson (Cinn.)	3737 W. Chamberlain (Phil.)	344 Zelmo Beaty (St. Louis)
1966-67	908 Guy Rodgers (Chi.)	3682 W. Chamberlain (Phil.)	344 Joe Strawder (Detroit)
1967-68	702 Wilt Chamberlain (Phil.)	3836 W. Chamberlain (Phil.)	366 Bill Bridges (St. Louis)
1968-69	772 Oscar Robertson (Cinn.)	3695 Elvin Hayes (S.D.)	329 Billy Cunningham (Phil.)
1969-70	9.1* Lenny Wilkens (Sea.)	3665 Elvin Hayes (S.D.)	335 Jim Davis (Atlanta)
1970-71	10.1* Norm Van Lier (Cinn.)	3678 John Havlicek (Bos.)	350 Dave Cowens (Boston)
1971-72	9.7* Jerry West (L.A.)	3698 John Havlicek (Bos.)	314 Dave Cowens (Boston)
1972-73	11.4* Nate Archibald (KC-O)	3681 Nate Archibald (KC-O)	323 Neal Walk (Phoenix)
1973-74	8.2* Ernie DiGregorio (Buff.)	3602 Elvin Hayes (Capital)	319 Kevin Porter (Capital)
1974-75	8.0* Kevin Porter (Wash.)	3539 Bob McAdoo (Buff.)	330 Bob Dandridge (Mil.) / Phil Jackson (N.Y.)
1975-76	8.1* Don Watts (Seattle)	3379 K. Abdul-Jabbar (L.A.)	356 Charlie Scott (Boston)
1976-77	8.5* Don Buse (Indiana)	3364 Elvin Hayes (Wash.)	363 Lonnie Shelton (Knicks)
1977-78	10.2* Kevin Porter (Det.-N.J.)	3638 Len Robinson (N.O.)	350 Lonnie Shelton (N.Y.)
1978-79	13.4* Kevin Porter (Det.)	3390 Moses Malone (Hou.)	367 Bill Robinzine (K.C.)
1979-80	10.1* Micheal Richardson (N.Y.)	3226 Norm Nixon (L.A.)	328 Darryl Dawkins (Phil.)
1980-81	9.1* Kevin Porter (Wash.)	3417 Adrian Dantley (Utah)	342 Ben Poquette (Utah)
1981-82	9.6* Johnny Moore (S.A.)	3398 Moses Malone (Hou.)	372 Steve Johnson (K.C.)
1982-83	10.5* Magic Johnson (L.A.)	3093 Isiah Thomas (Det.)	379 Darryl Dawkins (N.J.)
1983-84	13.1* Magic Johnson (L.A.)	3082 Jeff Ruland (Wash.)	386 Darryl Dawkins (N.J.)
1984-85	13.98* Isiah Thomas (Det.)	3182 Buck Williams (N.J.)	344 Hakeem Olajuwon (Hou.)
1985-86	12.6* Magic Johnson (L.A.L.)	3270 Maurice Cheeks (Phil.)	333 Charles Barkley (Phil.)
1986-87	12.2* Magic Johnson (L.A.L.)	3281 Michael Jordan (Chi.)	340 Steve Johnson (Port.)
1987-88	13.8* John Stockton (Utah)	3311 Michael Jordan (Chi.)	332 Patrick Ewing (N.Y.)
1988-89	13.6* John Stockton (Utah)	3255 Michael Jordan (Chi.)	337 Grant Long (Miami)
1989-90	14.5* John Stockton (Utah)	3238 Rodney McCray (Sac.)	328 Rik Smits (Indiana)
1990-91	14.2* John Stockton (Utah)	3315 Chris Mullin (G.S.)	338 Sam Mitchell (Minn.)
1991-92	13.7* John Stockton (Utah)	3346 Chris Mullin (G.S.)	315 Tyrone Hill (G.S)

Most Disqualifications

Season	No.		Season	No.	
1946-47	—		1974-75	12	Kevin Porter (Washington)
1947-48	—		1975-76	19	Bill Robinzine (Kansas City)
1948-49	—		1976-77	21	Joe Meriweather (Atlanta)
1949-50	—		1977-78	20	George Johnson (New Jersey)
1950-51	19	Cal Christensen (Tri-City)	1978-79	19	John Drew (Atlanta)
1951-52	18	Don Boven (Milwaukee)			Wayne Rollins (Atlanta)
1952-53	26	Don Meineke (Ft. Wayne)	1979-80	12	Wayne Rollins (Atlanta)
1953-54	12	Earl Lloyd (Syracuse)			James Edwards (Indiana)
1954-55	17	Charley Share (Milwaukee)			George McGinnis (Indiana)
1955-56	17	Vern Mikkelsen (Minneapolis)	1980-81	18	Ben Poquette (Utah)
		Arnie Risen (Boston)	1981-82	25	Steve Johnson (K.C.)
1956-57	18	Vern Mikkelsen (Minneapolis)	1982-83	23	Darryl Dawkins (N.J.)
1957-58	20	Vern Mikkelsen (Minneapolis)	1983-84	22	Darryl Dawkins (N.J.)
1958-59	22	Walt Dukes (Detroit)	1984-85	16	Ken Bannister (N.Y.)
1959-60	20	Walt Dukes (Detroit)	1985-86	13	Joe Barry Carroll (G.S.)
1960-61	16	Walt Dukes (Detroit)			Steve Johnson (S.A.)
1961-62	20	Walt Dukes (Detroit)	1986-87	16	Steve Johnson (Port.)
1962-63	13	Frank Ramsey (Boston)	1987-88	11	Jack Sikma (Milw.)
1963-64	11	Zelmo Beaty (St. Louis)			Frank Brickowski (S.A.)
		Gus Johnson (Baltimore)	1988-89	14	Rik Smits (Indiana)
1964-65	15	Tom Sanders (Boston)	1989-90	11	Grant Long (Miami)
1965-66	19	Tom Sanders (Boston)			Rik Smits (Indiana)
1966-67	19	Joe Strawder (Detroit)			LaSalle Thompson (Indiana)
1967-68	18	John Tresvant (Det.-Cinn.)	1990-91	15	Blair Rasmussen (Denver)
		Joe Strawder (Detroit)	1991-92	13	Shawn Kemp (Seattle)
1968-69	14	Art Harris (Seattle)			
1969-70	18	Norm Van Lier (Cincinnati)			
1970-71	16	John Trapp (San Diego)			
1971-72	14	Curtis Perry (Hous.-Milw.)			
1972-73	16	Elmore Smith (Buffalo)			
1973-74	15	Mike Bantom (Phoenix)			

Seattle guard Dana Barros led the NBA in three-point field goal percentage last season.

Season	No.	Most Steals	No.	Most Blocked Shots
1973-74	2.68*	Larry Steele (Portland)	4.85*	Elmore Smith (Los Angeles)
1974-75	2.85*	Rick Barry (Golden State)	3.26*	K. Abdul-Jabbar (Milwaukee)
1975-76	3.18*	Don Watts (Seattle)	4.12*	K. Abdul-Jabbar (Los Angeles)
1976-77	3.47*	Don Buse (Indiana)	3.25*	Bill Walton (Portland)
1977-78	2.74*	Ron Lee (Phoenix)	3.38*	George Johnson (New Jersey)
1978-79	2.46*	M. L. Carr (Detroit)	3.95*	K. Abdul-Jabbar (Los Angeles)
1979-80	3.23*	Micheal Richardson (New York)	3.41*	K. Abdul-Jabbar (Los Angeles)
1980-81	3.43*	Magic Johnson (Los Angeles)	3.39*	George Johnson (San Antonio)
1981-82	2.67*	Magic Johnson (Los Angeles)	3.12*	George Johnson (San Antonio)
1982-83	2.84*	Micheal Richardson (Golden St.-New Jer.)	4.29*	Wayne Rollins (Atlanta)
1983-84	2.65*	Rickey Green (Utah)	4.28*	Mark Eaton (Utah)
1984-85	2.96*	Micheal Richardson (New Jersey)	5.56*	Mark Eaton (Utah)
1985-86	3.67*	Alvin Robertson (San Antonio)	4.96*	Manute Bol (Washington)
1986-87	3.21*	Alvin Robertson (San Antonio)	4.06*	Mark Eaton (Utah)
1987-88	3.16*	Michael Jordan (Chicago)	3.71*	Mark Eaton (Utah)
1988-89	3.21*	John Stockton (Utah)	4.31*	Manute Bol (Golden State)
1989-90	2.77*	Michael Jordan (Chicago)	4.59*	Hakeem Olajuwon (Houston)
1990-91	3.04*	Alvin Robertson (Milwaukee)	3.95*	Hakeem Olajuwon (Houston)
1991-92	2.98*	John Stockton (Utah)	4.49*	David Robinson (San Antonio)

Three-Point FG Pct. Leaders

Season	Pct.		Season	Pct.	
1979-80	.443	Fred Brown (Seattle)	1985-86	.451	Craig Hodges (Milwaukee)
1980-81	.383	Brian Taylor (San Diego)	1986-87	.481	Kiki Vandeweghe (Portland)
1981-82	.439	Campy Russell (New York)	1987-88	.491	Craig Hodges (Milw.-Phoe.)
1982-83	.345	Mike Dunleavy (San Antonio)	1988-89	.522	Jon Sundvold (Miami)
1983-84	.361	Darrell Griffith (Utah)	1989-90	.507	Steve Kerr (Cleveland)
1984-85	.433	Byron Scott (L.A. Lakers)	1990-91	.461	Jim Les (Sacramento)
		*Based on highest average per game.	1991-92	.446	Dana Barros (Seattle)

ALL-TIME NBA LEADERS
(Active 1991-92 players in capital letters)

MOST GAMES PLAYED

Kareem Abdul-Jabbar	1,560
Elvin Hayes	1,303
John Havlicek	1,270
ROBERT PARISH	1,260
Paul Silas	1,254
MOSES MALONE	1,246
Alex English	1,193
Hal Greer	1,122
Jack Sikma	1,107
Dennis Johnson	1,100

MOST FIELD GOALS MADE

Kareem Abdul-Jabbar	15,837
Wilt Chamberlain	12,681
Elvin Hayes	10,976
Alex English	10,659
John Havlicek	10,513
Oscar Robertson	9,508
MOSES MALONE	9,307
Jerry West	9,016
Elgin Baylor	8,693
LARRY BIRD	8,591

MOST FIELD GOALS ATTEMPTED

Kareem Abdul-Jabbar	28,307
Elvin Hayes	24,272
John Havlicek	23,930
Wilt Chamberlain	23,497
Alex English	21,036
Elgin Baylor	20,171
Oscar Robertson	19,620
Jerry West	19,032
MOSES MALONE	18,916
Hal Greer	18,811

MOST MINUTES PLAYED

Kareem Abdul-Jabbar	57,446
Elvin Hayes	50,000
Wilt Chamberlain	47,859
John Havlicek	46,471
MOSES MALONE	44,200
Oscar Robertson	43,866
Bill Russell	40,726
Hal Greer	39,788
Walt Bellamy	38,940
ROBERT PARISH	38,727

MOST FREE THROWS MADE

MOSES MALONE	8,395
Oscar Robertson	7,694
Jerry West	7,160
Dolph Schayes	6,979
Adrian Dantley	6,832
Kareem Abdul-Jabbar	6,712
Bob Pettit	6,182
Wilt Chamberlain	6,057
Elgin Baylor	5,763
Len Wilkens	5,394

MOST FREE THROWS ATTEMPTED

Wilt Chamberlain	11,862
MOSES MALONE	10,910
Kareem Abdul-Jabbar	9,304
Oscar Robertson	9,185
Jerry West	8,801
Adrian Dantley	8,351
Dolph Schayes	8,273
Bob Pettit	8,119
Walt Bellamy	8,088
Elvin Hayes	7,999

MOST REBOUNDS

Wilt Chamberlain	23,924
Bill Russell	21,620
Kareem Abdul-Jabbar	17,440
Elvin Hayes	16,279
MOSES MALONE	15,894
Nate Thurmond	14,464
Walt Bellamy	14,241
Wes Unseld	13,769
Jerry Lucas	12,942
Bob Pettit	12,849

MOST STEALS

MAURICE CHEEKS	2,277
ALVIN ROBERTSON	1,791
MAGIC JOHNSON	1,698
ISIAH THOMAS	1,670
Gus Williams	1,638
JOHN STOCKTON	1,633
MICHAEL JORDAN	1,594
LARRY BIRD	1,556
CLYDE DREXLER	1,528
Julius Erving	1,508

MOST ASSISTS

MAGIC JOHNSON	9,921
Oscar Robertson	9,887
ISIAH THOMAS	7,991
JOHN STOCKTON	7,365
MAURICE CHEEKS	7,285
Len Wilkens	7,211
Bob Cousy	6,955
Guy Rodgers	6,917
Nate Archibald	6,476
John Lucas	6,454

MOST BLOCKED SHOTS

Kareem Abdul-Jabbar	3,189
MARK EATON	2,985
WAYNE ROLLINS	2,456
HAKEEM OLAJUWON	2,102
George T. Johnson	2,082
ROBERT PARISH	2,049
MANUTE BOL	1,942
LARRY NANCE	1,774
Elvin Hayes	1,771
Artis Gilmore	1,747

MOST PERSONAL FOULS

Kareem Abdul-Jabbar	4,657
Elvin Hayes	4,193
Jack Sikma	3,879
Hal Greer	3,855
ROBERT PARISH	3,800
JAMES EDWARDS	3,725
Dolph Schayes	3,664
Walt Bellamy	3,536
Caldwell Jones	3,527
Bailey Howell	3,499

MOST DISQUALIFICATIONS

Vern Mikkelsen	127
Walter Dukes	121
Charlie Share	105
Paul Arizin	101
Darryl Dawkins	100
JAMES EDWARDS	95
Tom Gola	94
Tom Sanders	94
Steve Johnson	93
WAYNE ROLLINS	91

HIGHEST FIELD GOAL PERCENTAGE
(2,000 FGM minimum)

	FGA	FGM	Pct.
Artis Gilmore	9,570	5,732	.599
CHARLES BARKLEY	8,722	5,025	.576
Steve Johnson	4,965	2,841	.572
Darryl Dawkins	6,079	3,477	.572
JAMES DONALDSON	5,354	3,053	.570
JEFF RULAND	3,723	2,100	.564
Kareem Abdul-Jabbar	28,307	15,837	.559
KEVIN McHALE	11,685	6,532	.559
BUCK WILLIAMS	9,146	5,092	.557
OTIS THORPE	7,343	4,064	.553

HIGHEST FREE THROW PERCENTAGE
(1,200 FTM minimum)

	FTA	FTM	Pct.
Rick Barry	4,243	3,818	.900
MARK PRICE	1,343	1,208	.899
Calvin Murphy	3,864	3,445	.892
LARRY BIRD	4,471	3,960	.886
Bill Sharman	3,559	3,143	.883
JEFF MALONE	2,768	2,426	.876
RICKY PIERCE	2,790	2,438	.874
CHRIS MULLIN	2,928	2,558	.874
KIKI VANDEWEGHE	3,931	3,426	.872
REGGIE MILLER	2,268	1,973	.870

HIGHEST 3-POINT FIELD GOAL PERCENTAGE
(100 3-PT. FGM minimum)

	FGA	FGM	Pct.
STEVE KERR	297	141	.475
DRAZEN PETROVIC	416	180	.433
DANA BARROS	505	210	.416
MARK PRICE	1,117	459	.411
HERSEY HAWKINS	865	354	.409
TRENT TUCKER	1,279	523	.409
DALE ELLIS	1,891	763	.403
CRAIG HODGES	1,408	563	.400
JON SUNDVOLD	576	226	.392
JEFF HORNACEK	615	240	.390

MOST 3-PT. FIELD GOALS ATTEMPTED

MICHAEL ADAMS	2,332
DALE ELLIS	1,891
DANNY AINGE	1,821
LARRY BIRD	1,727
Darrell Griffith	1,596
DEREK HARPER	1,492
REGGIE MILLER	1,441
ERIC FLOYD	1,419
CRAIG HODGES	1,408
CHUCK PERSON	1,330

MOST 3-PT. FIELD GOALS MADE

MICHAEL ADAMS	783
DALE ELLIS	763
DANNY AINGE	694
LARRY BIRD	649
CRAIG HODGES	563
REGGIE MILLER	550
Darrell Griffith	530
TRENT TUCKER	523
DEREK HARPER	507
BYRON SCOTT	478

HIGHEST SCORING AVERAGE
(400 Games or 10,000 Points minimum)

	G.	FGM	FTM	Pts.	Avg.
MICHAEL JORDAN	589	7,087	4,620	19,000	32.3
Wilt Chamberlain	1045	12,681	6,057	31,419	30.1
Elgin Baylor	846	8,693	5,763	23,149	27.4
Jerry West	932	9,016	7,160	25,192	27.0
Bob Pettit	792	7,349	6,182	20,880	26.4
DOMINIQUE WILKINS	762	7,581	4,494	19,975	26.2
George Gervin	791	8,045	4,541	20,708	26.2
KARL MALONE	570	5,458	3,826	14,770	25.9
Oscar Robertson	1040	9,508	7,694	26,710	25.7
Kareem Abdul-Jabbar	1560	15,837	6,712	38,387	24.6

TOP NBA CAREER SCORERS

(10,000 or more points)

(Active players in capital letters)

Figures from National Basketball League are included below; NBL did not record field goal attempts, however, so all field goal percentages listed here are based only on field goals and attempts in NBA competition. Minutes played not compiled prior to 1952; rebounds not compiled prior to 1951.

Player	Yrs.	G.	Min.	FGM	FGA	Pct.	FTM	FTA	Pct.	Reb.	Ast.	PF	Pts.	Avg.	Career
Kareem Abdul-Jabbar	20	1560	57446	15837	28307	.559	6712	9304	.721	17440	5660	4657	38387	24.6	70-89
Wilt Chamberlain	14	1045	47859	12681	23497	.540	6057	11862	.511	23924	4643	2075	31419	30.1	60-73
Elvin Hayes	16	1303	50000	10976	24272	.452	5356	7999	.670	16279	2398	4193	27313	21.0	69-84
MOSES MALONE	16	1246	44200	9307	18916	.492	8395	10910	.769	15894	1749	3003	27016	21.7	77-92
Oscar Robertson	14	1040	43886	9508	19620	.485	7694	9185	.838	7804	9887	2931	26710	25.7	61-74
John Havlicek	16	1270	46471	10513	23930	.439	5369	6589	.815	8007	6114	3281	26395	20.8	63-78
Alex English	15	1193	38063	10659	21036	.507	4277	5141	.832	6538	4351	3027	25613	21.5	77-91
Jerry West	14	932	36571	9016	19032	.474	7160	8801	.814	5376	6238	2435	25192	27.0	61-74
Adrian Dantley	15	955	34151	8169	15121	.540	6832	8351	.818	5455	2830	2550	23177	24.3	77-91
Elgin Baylor	14	846	33863	8693	20171	.431	5763	7391	.780	11463	3650	2596	23149	27.4	59-72
LARRY BIRD	13	897	34443	8591	17334	.496	3960	4471	.886	8974	5695	2279	21791	24.3	80-92
Hal Greer	15	1122	39788	8504	18811	.452	4578	5717	.801	5665	4540	3855	21586	19.2	59-73
Walt Bellamy	14	1043	38940	7914	15340	.516	5113	8088	.632	14241	2544	3536	20941	20.1	62-75
Bob Pettit	11	792	30690	7349	16872	.436	6182	8119	.761	12849	2369	2529	20880	26.4	55-65
George Gervin	10	791	26536	8045	15747	.511	4541	5383	.844	3607	2214	2331	20708	26.2	77-86
ROBERT PARISH	16	1260	38727	8493	15656	.542	3648	5048	.723	12691	1942	3800	20634	16.4	77-92
DOMINIQUE WILKINS	10	762	28211	7581	16163	.469	4494	5557	.809	5332	1980	1570	19975	26.2	83-92
WALTER DAVIS	15	1033	28859	8118	15871	.511	3128	3676	.851	3053	3878	2454	19521	18.9	78-92
BERNARD KING	13	842	28987	7739	14932	.518	3933	5387	.730	4984	2845	2832	19432	23.1	78-91
Dolph Schayes	16	1059	29800	6135	15427	.380	6979	8273	.844	11256	3072	3664	19249	18.2	49-64
Bob Lanier	14	959	32103	7761	15092	.514	3724	4858	.767	9698	3007	3048	19248	20.1	71-84
Gail Goodrich	14	1031	33527	7431	16300	.456	4319	5354	.807	3279	4805	2775	19181	18.6	66-79
Reggie Theus	13	1026	34603	7057	14973	.471	4663	5644	.826	3349	6453	3008	19015	18.5	79-91
MICHAEL JORDAN	8	589	22775	7087	13644	.519	4620	5456	.847	3697	3507	1756	19000	32.3	85-92
Chet Walker	13	1032	33433	6876	14628	.470	5079	6384	.796	7314	2126	2727	18831	18.2	63-75
Bob McAdoo	14	852	28327	7420	14751	.503	3944	5229	.754	8048	1951	2726	18787	22.1	73-86
Rick Barry	10	794	28825	7252	16163	.449	3818	4243	.900	5168	4017	2264	18395	23.2	66-80
Julius Erving	11	836	28677	7237	14276	.507	3844	4950	.777	5601	3224	2286	18364	22.0	77-87
Dave Bing	12	901	32769	6962	15769	.441	4403	5683	.775	3420	5397	2615	18327	20.3	67-78
World B. Free	13	886	26893	6512	14294	.456	4718	6264	.753	2430	3319	2270	17955	20.3	76-88
Calvin Murphy	13	1002	30607	7247	15030	.482	3445	3864	.892	2103	4402	3250	17949	17.9	71-83
Lou Hudson	13	890	29794	7392	15129	.489	3156	3960	.797	3926	2432	2439	17940	20.2	67-79
Lenny Wilkens	15	1077	38064	6189	14327	.432	5394	6973	.774	5030	7211	3285	17772	16.5	61-75
Bailey Howell	12	950	30627	6515	13585	.480	4740	6224	.762	9383	1853	3498	17770	18.7	60-71
TOM CHAMBERS	11	860	29028	6525	13825	.472	4490	5564	.807	5803	2026	3109	17736	20.6	82-92
MARK AGUIRRE	11	833	25815	6851	14095	.486	3515	4743	.741	4310	2662	2400	17542	21.1	82-92
Earl Monroe	13	926	29636	6906	14898	.464	3642	4513	.807	2796	3594	2416	17454	18.8	68-80
Jack Sikma	14	1107	36943	6396	13792	.464	4292	5053	.849	10816	3488	3879	17287	15.6	78-91
EARVIN JOHNSON	12	874	32287	6074	11657	.521	4788	5649	.848	6376	9921	2002	17239	19.7	80-91
Bob Cousy	14	924	30165	6168	16448	.375	4624	5756	.803	4786	6955	2242	16960	18.4	51-70
ROLANDO BLACKMAN	11	865	29684	6487	13061	.497	3501	4166	.840	3083	2748	1405	16643	19.2	82-92
ISIAH THOMAS	11	842	30844	6350	13883	.457	3577	4681	.764	3087	7991	2623	16575	19.7	82-92
KEVIN McHALE	12	900	28462	6532	11685	.559	3470	4359	.796	6764	1597	2632	16573	18.4	81-92
Nate Archibald	13	876	31159	5899	12628	.467	4664	5760	.810	2046	6476	2002	16481	18.8	71-84
TERRY CUMMINGS	10	768	26217	6740	13775	.489	2845	3978	.715	6663	1823	2695	16364	21.3	83-92
Paul Arizin	10	713	24897	5628	13356	.421	5010	6189	.810	6129	1665	2764	16266	22.8	51-62
Randy Smith	12	976	31444	6676	14218	.470	2893	3705	.781	3597	4487	2556	16262	16.7	72-83
Pete Maravich	10	658	24316	6187	14025	.441	3564	4344	.820	2747	3563	1865	15948	24.2	71-80
Jack Twyman	11	823	26147	6237	13873	.450	3366	4325	.778	5424	1861	2782	15840	19.2	56-66
KIKI VANDEWEGHE	12	769	24027	6047	11496	.526	3426	3931	.872	2737	1643	1515	15726	20.4	81-92
EDDIE A. JOHNSON	11	852	25852	6352	13277	.478	2615	3125	.837	3890	2080	2369	15645	18.4	82-92
Walt Frazier	13	825	30965	6130	12516	.490	3321	4226	.786	4830	5040	2180	15581	18.9	68-80
Artis Gilmore	12	909	29685	5732	9570	.599	4114	5768	.713	9161	1777	2986	15579	17.1	77-88
Dennis Johnson	14	1100	35954	5832	13100	.445	3791	4754	.797	4249	5499	3087	15535	14.1	77-90
Bob Dandridge	13	839	29502	6445	13317	.484	2638	3382	.780	5715	2846	2940	15530	18.5	70-82
Sam Jones	12	871	24285	6271	13745	.456	2869	3572	.803	4305	2209	1735	15411	17.7	58-69
Dick Barnett	14	971	28937	6034	13227	.456	3290	4324	.761	2812	2729	2514	15358	15.8	60-74
John Drew	11	739	21828	5481	11658	.470	4319	5774	.748	5088	1224	2641	15291	20.7	75-85
Dick Van Arsdale	12	921	31771	5413	11661	.464	4253	5385	.790	3807	3060	2575	15079	16.4	66-77
Mike Mitchell	10	759	24537	6371	12912	.493	2255	2894	.779	4246	1010	2012	15016	19.8	79-88
CLYDE DREXLER	9	709	24063	5761	11792	.489	3060	3908	.783	4351	4114	2221	14857	21.0	84-92
KARL MALONE	7	570	21134	5458	10398	.525	3826	5318	.719	6199	1549	1953	14770	25.9	86-92
Richie Guerin	13	848	27449	5174	12451	.416	4328	5549	.780	4278	4211	2769	14676	17.3	57-70
Dan Issel	9	718	22342	5424	10711	.506	3792	4756	.797	5707	1804	2022	14659	20.4	77-85
Jamaal Wilkes	12	828	27275	6226	12471	.499	2185	2878	.759	5117	2050	2296	14644	17.7	75-86
Purvis Short	12	842	24549	5934	12507	.474	2614	3174	.824	3625	2123	2479	14607	17.3	79-90
Spencer Haywood	12	760	25600	5790	12447	.465	3011	3766	.800	7038	1351	2167	14592	19.2	71-83
Bill Russell	13	963	40726	5687	12930	.440	3148	5614	.561	21620	4100	2592	14522	15.1	57-69
Nate Thurmond	14	964	35875	5521	13105	.421	3395	5089	.667	14464	2575	2624	14437	15.0	64-77
Jo Jo White	12	837	29941	6169	13884	.444	2060	2471	.834	3345	4095	2056	14399	17.2	70-81
JAMES WORTHY	10	764	26045	6028	11224	.537	2176	2838	.767	4280	2359	1808	14287	18.7	83-92
Tom Van Arsdale	12	929	28682	5505	12763	.431	3222	4226	.762	3942	2085	2922	14232	15.3	66-77
CHARLES BARKLEY	8	610	22761	5025	8722	.576	3920	5347	.733	7079	2276	2045	14184	23.3	85-92
JAMES EDWARDS	15	1015	26730	5529	11093	.498	3092	4426	.699	5756	1417	3725	14151	13.9	78-92
Gus Williams	11	825	25645	5793	12570	.461	2399	3173	.756	2222	4597	1637	14093	17.1	76-87
Dave DeBusschere	12	875	31202	5722	13249	.432	2609	3730	.699	9618	2497	2801	14053	16.1	63-74
Jerry Lucas	11	829	32131	5709	11441	.499	2635	3365	.783	12942	2730	2389	14053	17.0	64-74
LARRY NANCE	11	810	27035	5684	10379	.548	2673	3560	.751	6457	2121	2384	14049	17.3	82-92
Fred Brown	13	963	24422	6006	12568	.478	1896	2211	.858	2637	3160	1937	14018	14.6	72-84
JEFF MALONE	9	698	23372	5759	11911	.484	2426	2768	.876	1897	1846	1395	14004	20.1	84-92
Alvan Adams	13	988	27203	5709	11464	.498	2490	3160	.788	6937	4012	3214	13910	14.1	76-88
Bob Love	11	789	25120	5447	12688	.429	3001	3728	.805	4653	1123	2130	13895	17.6	67-77
Marques Johnson	11	691	23694	5733	11065	.518	2412	3265	.739	4817	2502	1766	13892	20.1	78-90

Player	Yrs.	G.	Min.	FGM	FGA	Pct.	FTM	FTA	Pct.	Reb.	Ast.	PF	Pts.	Avg.	Career
Billy Cunningham	9	654	22406	5116	11467	.446	3394	4717	.720	6638	2625	2431	13626	20.8	66-76
HAKEEM OLAJUWON	8	594	21812	5365	10464	.513	2843	4100	.693	7441	1302	2360	13575	22.9	85-92
Dave Cowens	11	766	29565	5744	12499	.460	2027	2590	.783	10444	2910	2920	13516	17.6	71-83
Cliff Hagan	10	745	21733	5239	11630	.450	2969	3722	.798	5116	2242	2388	13447	18.0	57-66
BUCK WILLIAMS	11	877	31002	5092	9146	.557	3202	4827	.663	9831	1297	3020	13388	15.3	82-92
Rudy Tomjanovich	11	768	25714	5630	11240	.501	2089	2666	.784	6198	1573	1937	13383	17.4	71-81
Jeff Mullins	12	802	24574	5383	11631	.463	2251	2764	.814	3427	3023	2165	13017	16.2	65-76
BILL LAIMBEER	12	978	31775	5235	10534	.497	2336	2799	.835	9925	2043	3391	12995	13.3	81-92
Bob Boozer	11	874	25449	4961	10738	.462	3042	3998	.761	7119	1237	2519	12964	14.8	61-71
Mychal Thompson	12	935	27764	5191	10306	.504	2427	3707	.655	6951	2141	2692	12810	13.7	79-91
Paul Westphal	12	823	20947	5079	10084	.504	2596	3166	.820	1580	3591	1705	12809	15.6	73-84
Sidney Wicks	10	760	25762	5046	11002	.459	2711	3955	.685	6620	2437	2524	12803	16.8	72-81
Mickey Johnson	12	904	25005	4733	10544	.449	3253	4066	.800	6465	2677	3101	12748	14.1	75-86
Bill Sharman	11	711	21793	4761	11168	.426	3143	3559	.883	2779	2101	1925	12665	17.8	51-61
Otis Birdsong	12	696	21627	5347	10562	.506	1801	2748	.655	2072	2260	1783	12544	18.0	78-89
Jack Marin	11	849	24590	5068	10890	.465	2405	2852	.843	4405	1813	2416	12541	14.8	67-77
Mike Newlin	11	837	24574	4720	10133	.466	3005	3456	.870	2494	3364	2542	12507	14.9	72-82
John Kerr	12	905	27784	4909	11751	.418	2662	3682	.723	10092	2004	2287	12480	13.8	55-66
Joe Barry Carroll	10	705	22838	5021	10583	.474	2413	3232	.747	5404	1264	2212	12455	17.7	82-91
Darrell Griffith	10	765	21403	5237	11305	.463	1387	1961	.707	2519	1627	1689	12391	16.2	81-91
Cazzie Russell	12	817	22213	5172	11154	.464	2033	2459	.827	3068	1838	1693	12377	15.1	67-78
Maurice Lucas	12	855	24787	4870	10297	.473	2595	3399	.763	7520	1987	2865	12339	14.4	77-88
PATRICK EWING	7	520	18838	4862	9175	.530	2567	3463	.741	5141	1101	1971	12293	23.6	86-92
Johnny Green	14	1057	24624	4973	10091	.493	2335	4226	.553	9083	1449	2856	12281	11.6	60-73
Tom Heinsohn	9	654	19254	4773	11787	.405	2648	3353	.790	5749	1318	2454	12194	18.6	57-65
Willis Reed	10	650	23073	4859	10202	.476	2465	3298	.747	8414	1186	2411	12183	18.7	65-74
Kelly Tripucka	10	707	20959	4434	9380	.473	3106	3660	.849	2703	2090	1634	12142	17.2	82-91
MAURICE CHEEKS	14	1066	34335	4855	9281	.523	2307	2911	.793	3046	7285	2223	12069	11.3	79-92
Norm Nixon	10	768	27250	5219	10805	.483	1527	1978	.772	1991	6386	1983	12065	15.7	78-89
BILL CARTWRIGHT	12	829	25028	4390	8265	.531	3275	4233	.774	5634	1240	2526	12055	14.5	80-92
John Long	13	861	22310	5062	10812	.468	1789	2076	.862	2452	1717	1840	12002	13.9	79-91
Len Robinson	11	772	25141	4816	9971	.483	2355	3556	.662	7267	1348	2253	11988	15.5	75-85
ORLANDO WOOLRIDGE	11	719	20531	4497	8665	.519	2987	4022	.743	3213	1355	1858	11988	16.7	82-92
Clyde Lovellette	11	704	19075	4784	10795	.443	2379	3141	.757	6663	1097	2289	11947	17.0	54-64
Sidney Moncrief	11	767	23150	4117	8198	.502	3587	4319	.831	3575	2793	1635	11931	15.6	80-91
Scott Wedman	13	906	25927	5153	10713	.481	1526	1923	.794	4355	1771	2549	11916	13.2	75-87
VINNIE JOHNSON	13	984	24308	4882	10515	.464	1978	2673	.740	3109	3212	2063	11825	12.0	80-92
Archie Clark	10	725	23581	4693	9784	.480	2433	3163	.769	2427	3498	1806	11819	16.3	67-76
Paul Silas	16	1254	34989	4293	9949	.432	3196	4748	.673	12357	2572	3105	11782	9.4	65-80
George Mikan	9	520	8350	4097	8783	.404	3570	4588	.778	4167	1245	2162	11764	22.6	47-56
Dick Snyder	13	964	25676	4890	10019	.488	1975	2398	.824	2732	2767	2453	11755	12.2	67-79
Jimmy Walker	9	698	23590	4624	10039	.461	2407	2903	.829	1860	2429	1735	11655	16.7	68-76
Kevin Loughery	11	755	22208	4477	10829	.413	2621	3262	.803	2254	2803	2543	11575	15.3	63-73
Don Ohl	10	727	22413	4685	10806	.434	2179	2975	.732	2163	2243	2014	11549	15.9	61-70
CHRIS MULLIN	7	520	18385	4353	8409	.518	2558	2928	.874	2340	2005	1150	11536	22.2	86-92
ERIC FLOYD	10	804	23948	4183	9289	.450	2683	3270	.820	2284	4816	1769	11518	14.3	83-92
Junior Bridgeman	12	849	21257	4801	10099	.475	1875	2216	.846	2995	2066	1969	11517	13.6	76-87
Rudy LaRusso	10	736	24487	4102	9521	.431	3303	4308	.767	6936	1556	2553	11507	15.6	60-69
Harold Hairston	11	776	24330	4240	8872	.478	3025	4080	.741	8019	1268	2334	11505	14.8	65-75
BYRON SCOTT	9	709	22416	4667	9423	.495	1650	1985	.831	2282	2109	1552	11462	16.2	84-92
DALE ELLIS	9	637	18160	4425	9078	.487	1765	2267	.779	2449	1057	1399	11378	17.9	84-92
Dan Roundfield	11	746	23443	4289	8852	.485	2733	3702	.738	7243	1620	2561	11318	15.2	77-87
Willie Naulls	10	716	20620	4526	11145	.406	2253	2774	.812	6508	1114	2216	11305	15.8	57-66
David Thompson	8	509	16305	4213	8365	.504	2815	3616	.778	1921	1631	1287	11264	22.1	77-84
Ed Macauley	10	641	18071	3742	8589	.436	3750	4929	.761	4325	2079	1667	11234	17.5	50-59
John Johnson	12	869	25681	4575	10254	.446	2050	2633	.779	4778	3285	2505	11200	12.9	71-82
Jim Paxson	11	784	21357	4545	9134	.498	2011	2493	.807	1593	2300	1442	11199	14.3	80-90
Larry Foust	12	817	21890	3814	9414	.405	3570	4816	.741	8041	1368	2909	11198	13.7	51-62
HERB WILLIAMS	11	823	25429	4678	9944	.470	1779	2541	.700	5893	1746	2449	11142	13.5	82-92
Bill Bridges	13	926	30878	4181	9463	.442	2650	3824	.693	11054	2553	3375	11012	11.9	63-75
Mike Woodson	11	786	20021	4368	9364	.466	2125	2615	.813	1838	1822	1847	10981	14.0	81-91
Ricky Sobers	11	821	22992	4250	9262	.459	2272	2695	.843	2132	3525	2622	10902	13.3	76-86
Don Nelson	14	1053	21685	4017	8373	.480	2864	3744	.765	5192	1526	2451	10898	10.3	63-76
Bobby Smith	11	865	22407	4776	10642	.449	1307	1637	.798	3630	1734	2059	10882	12.6	70-80
Cliff Robinson	12	620	19206	4482	9569	.468	1823	2525	.722	5218	1240	1866	10794	17.4	80-89
MIKE GMINSKI	12	875	23498	4130	8861	.466	2508	2974	.843	6321	1185	1523	10774	12.3	81-92
OTIS THORPE	8	649	21798	4064	7343	.553	2540	3610	.704	5861	1572	2159	10671	16.4	85-92
Carl Braun	13	788	18409	3912	10211	.383	2801	3484	.804	2122	2892	2164	10625	13.5	48-62
Wes Unseld	13	984	35832	4369	8586	.509	1883	2976	.633	13769	3822	2762	10624	10.8	69-81
XAVIER McDANIEL	7	556	18235	4435	8991	.493	1692	2370	.714	3775	1304	1802	10609	19.1	86-92
Jerry Sloan	11	755	25750	4116	9646	.427	2339	3239	.722	5615	1925	2700	10571	14.0	66-76
Billy Knight	9	671	18412	4064	8026	.506	2399	2892	.830	3037	1435	1204	10561	15.7	77-85
THURL BAILEY	9	736	21757	4240	8980	.472	2061	2538	.812	4194	1157	1584	10545	14.3	84-92
Brian Winters	9	650	19938	4490	9457	.475	1443	1713	.842	1688	2674	1830	10537	16.2	75-83
Austin Carr	10	682	19660	4359	9714	.449	1753	2181	.804	1990	1878	1394	10473	15.4	72-81
Cedric Maxwell	11	835	23769	3433	6293	.546	3598	4592	.784	5261	1862	2273	10465	12.5	78-88
Robert Reid	13	919	25109	4443	9706	.458	1459	1992	.732	4168	2500	2893	10448	11.4	78-91
RICKY PIERCE	10	639	16656	3929	7793	.504	2438	2790	.874	1655	1260	1604	10440	16.3	83-92
Guy Rodgers	12	891	28661	4125	10907	.378	2165	3006	.720	3791	6907	2630	10415	11.7	59-70
DEREK HARPER	9	707	22774	4077	8499	.480	1732	2310	.750	1917	4358	1677	10393	14.7	84-92
Wayne Embry	11	831	21763	3993	9067	.440	2394	3741	.640	7544	1194	2838	10380	12.5	59-69
Sam Lacey	13	1002	31873	4276	9693	.441	1748	2369	.738	9687	3754	3473	10300	10.3	71-83
Calvin Natt	11	599	18818	4003	7580	.528	2269	2954	.768	4070	1306	1386	10291	17.2	80-90
Ray Scott	9	684	21339	3906	9641	.405	2472	3293	.720	7154	1618	2035	10184	14.9	62-70
Leroy Ellis	14	1048	27520	4143	9378	.442	1890	2595	.728	8709	1405	2661	10176	9.7	63-76
Eddie Johnson	10	675	19975	4015	8436	.476	2029	2564	.791	1522	3436	1706	10163	15.1	78-87
Ray Williams	10	655	18462	3962	8794	.451	2143	2673	.802	2370	3779	2165	10158	15.5	78-87
Gene Shue	10	699	23338	3715	9378	.396	2638	3273	.806	2855	2608	1405	10068	14.4	55-64
Vern Mikkelsen	10	699	18443	3547	8812	.403	2969	3874	.766	5940	1515	2812	10063	14.4	50-59
Charlie Scott	9	560	19278	4113	9266	.444	1809	2344	.772	2034	2696	2059	10037	17.9	72-80
Neil Johnston	8	516	18298	3303	7435	.444	3417	4447	.768	5856	1269	1681	10023	19.4	52-59

ALL-TIME TOP PERFORMANCES

(IN REGULAR-SEASON PLAY)

*Denotes each overtime period played.

MOST POINTS SCORED IN ONE GAME

	FG.	FT.	Pts.
Wilt Chamberlain, Philadelphia vs. New York at Hershey, Pa., March 2, 1962	36	28	100
Wilt Chamberlain, Philadelphia vs. Los Angeles at Philadelphia, December 8, 1961	***31	16	78
Wilt Chamberlain, Philadelphia vs. Chicago at Philadelphia, January 13, 1962	29	15	73
Wilt Chamberlain, San Francisco at New York, November 16, 1962	29	15	73
David Thompson, Denver at Detroit, April 9, 1978	28	17	73
Wilt Chamberlain, San Francisco at Los Angeles, November 3, 1962	29	14	72
Elgin Baylor, Los Angeles at New York, November 15, 1960	28	15	71
Wilt Chamberlain, San Francisco at Syracuse, March 10, 1963	27	16	70
Michael Jordan, Chicago at Cleveland, March 28, 1990	*23	21	69
Wilt Chamberlain, Philadelphia at Chicago, December 16, 1967	30	8	68
Pete Maravich, New Orleans vs. Knicks, February 25, 1977	26	16	68
Wilt Chamberlain, Philadelphia vs. New York at Philadelphia, March 9, 1961	27	13	67
Wilt Chamberlain, Philadelphia at St. Louis, February 17, 1962	26	15	67
Wilt Chamberlain, Philadelphia vs. New York at Philadelphia, February 25, 1962	25	17	67
Wilt Chamberlain, San Francisco vs. Los Angeles at San Francisco, January 11, 1963	28	11	67
Wilt Chamberlain, Los Angeles vs. Phoenix, February 9, 1969	29	8	66
Wilt Chamberlain, Philadelphia at Cincinnati, February 13, 1962	24	17	65
Wilt Chamberlain, Philadelphia at St. Louis, February 27, 1962	25	15	65
Wilt Chamberlain, Philadelphia vs. Los Angeles at Philadelphia, February 7, 1966	28	9	65
Elgin Baylor, Minneapolis vs. Boston at Minneapolis, November 8, 1959	25	14	64
Rick Barry, Golden State vs. Portland at Oakland, March 26, 1974	30	4	64
Joe Fulks, Philadelphia vs. Indianapolis at Philadelphia, February 10, 1949	27	9	63
Elgin Baylor, Los Angeles at Philadelphia, December 8, 1961	***23	17	63
Jerry West, Los Angeles vs. New York at Los Angeles, January 17, 1962	22	19	63
Wilt Chamberlain, San Francisco vs. Los Angeles at San Francisco, December 14, 1962	24	15	63
Wilt Chamberlain, San Francisco at Philadelphia, November 26, 1964	27	9	63
George Gervin, San Antonio at New Orleans, April 9, 1978	23	17	63
Wilt Chamberlain, Philadelphia at Boston, January 14, 1962	27	8	62
Wilt Chamberlain, Philadelphia at St. Louis at Detroit, January 17, 1962	*24	14	62
Wilt Chamberlain, Philadelphia vs. Syracuse at Utica, N. Y., January 21, 1962	*25	12	62
Wilt Chamberlain, San Francisco at New York, January 29, 1963	27	8	62
Wilt Chamberlain, San Francisco at Cincinnati, November 15, 1964	26	10	62
Wilt Chamberlain, Philadelphia vs. San Francisco at Philadelphia, March 3, 1966	26	10	62
George Mikan, Minneapolis vs. Rochester at Minneapolis, January 20, 1952	**22	17	61
Wilt Chamberlain, Philadelphia vs. Chicago at Philadelphia, December 9, 1961	28	5	61
Wilt Chamberlain, Philadelphia vs. St. Louis at Philadelphia, February 22, 1962	21	19	61
Wilt Chamberlain, Philadelphia at Chicago, February 28, 1962	24	13	61
Wilt Chamberlain, San Francisco vs. Cincinnati at San Francisco, November 21, 1962	27	7	61
Wilt Chamberlain, San Francisco vs. Syracuse at San Francisco, December 11, 1962	27	7	61
Wilt Chamberlain, San Francisco vs. St. Louis at San Francisco, December 18, 1962	26	9	61
Michael Jordan, Chicago at Detroit, March 4, 1987	*22	17	61
Michael Jordan, Chicago vs. Atlanta, April 16, 1987	22	17	61
Karl Malone, Utah vs. Milwaukee, January 27, 1990	21	19	61
Wilt Chamberlain, Philadelphia at Los Angeles, December 1, 1961	22	16	60
Wilt Chamberlain, Philadelphia vs. Los Angeles at Hershey, Pa., December 29, 1961	24	12	60
Wilt Chamberlain, Los Angeles vs. Cincinnati at Cleveland, January 26, 1969	22	16	60
Bernard King, New York vs. New Jersey, December 25, 1984	19	22	60
Larry Bird, Boston vs. Atlanta at New Orleans, March 12, 1985	22	15	60
Tom Chambers, Phoenix vs. Seattle, March 24, 1990	22	16	60
Jack Twyman, Cincinnati vs. Minneapolis at Cincinnati, January 15, 1960	21	17	59
Wilt Chamberlain, Philadelphia at New York, December 25, 1961	***23	13	59
Wilt Chamberlain, Philadelphia vs. New York at Syracuse, February 8, 1962	23	13	59
Wilt Chamberlain, San Francisco vs. New York at San Francisco, October 30, 1962	24	11	59
Wilt Chamberlain, San Francisco at Cincinnati, November 18, 1962	24	11	59
Wilt Chamberlain, San Francisco vs. St. Louis at San Francisco, December 2, 1962	25	9	59
Wilt Chamberlain, San Francisco vs. Los Angeles at San Francisco, December 6, 1963	22	15	59
Wilt Chamberlain, San Francisco at Philadelphia, January 28, 1964	24	11	59
Wilt Chamberlain, San Francisco at Detroit, February 11, 1964	*25	9	59
Purvis Short, Golden State vs. New Jersey, November 17, 1984	20	15	59
Michael Jordan, Chicago at Detroit, April 3, 1988	21	17	59
Wilt Chamberlain, Philadelphia vs. Detroit at Bethlehem, Pa., January 25, 1960	24	10	58
Wilt Chamberlain, Philadelphia at New York, February 21, 1960	26	6	58
Wilt Chamberlain, Philadelphia at Cincinnati, February 25, 1961	25	8	58
Wilt Chamberlain, Philadelphia vs. Detroit at Philadelphia, November 4, 1961	24	10	58
Wilt Chamberlain, Philadelphia at Detroit, November 8, 1961	23	12	58
Wilt Chamberlain, Philadelphia at New York, March 4, 1962	24	10	58
Wilt Chamberlain, San Francisco vs. Detroit at Bakersfield, Calif., January 24, 1963	25	8	58
Wilt Chamberlain, San Francisco at New York, December 15, 1964	*25	8	58
Wilt Chamberlain, Philadelphia vs. Cincinnati at Philadelphia, February 13, 1967	26	6	58
Fred Brown, Seattle at Golden State, March 23, 1974	24	10	58
Michael Jordan, Chicago vs. New Jersey, February 26, 1987	16	26	58

	FG.	FT.	Pts.
Richie Guerin, New York vs. Syracuse at New York, December 11, 1959	18	21	57
Elgin Baylor, Los Angeles at Detroit, February 16, 1961	23	11	57
Bob Pettit, St. Louis at Detroit, February 18, 1961	25	7	57
Wilt Chamberlain, Philadelphia vs. Los Angeles at Philadelphia, October 20, 1961	24	9	57
Wilt Chamberlain, Philadelphia at Cincinnati, December 19, 1961	24	9	57
Wilt Chamberlain, San Francisco vs. Chicago at San Francisco, November 10, 1962	24	9	57
Rick Barry, San Francisco at New York, December 14, 1965	18	21	57
Rick Barry, San Francisco at Cincinnati, October 29, 1966	21	15	57
Lou Hudson, Atlanta vs. Chicago at Auburn, Ala., November 10, 1969	25	7	57
Calvin Murphy, Houston vs. New Jersey at Houston, March 18, 1978	24	9	57
Adrian Dantley, Utah vs. Chicago, December 4, 1982	20	17	57
Purvis Short, Golden State vs. San Antonio, January 7, 1984	24	7	57
Dominique Wilkins, Atlanta vs. New Jersey, April 10, 1986	21	15	57
Dominique Wilkins, Atlanta vs. Chicago, December 10, 1986	19	19	57
Wilt Chamberlain, Philadelphia vs. New York at Philadelphia, January 2, 1961	23	10	56
Wilt Chamberlain, Philadelphia vs. Syracuse at Philadelphia, January 5, 1961	20	16	56
Wilt Chamberlain, Philadelphia vs. Los Angeles at Philadelphia, January 21, 1961	25	6	56
Elgin Baylor, Los Angeles vs. Syracuse at Los Angeles, January 24, 1961	19	18	56
Wilt Chamberlain, Philadelphia at Syracuse, March 1, 1961	22	12	56
Wilt Chamberlain, Philadelphia vs. Los Angeles at Philadelphia, November 17, 1961	24	8	56
Wilt Chamberlain, San Francisco vs. Detroit at San Francisco, October 23, 1962	23	10	56
Wilt Chamberlain, San Francisco at Cincinnati, February 7, 1963	23	10	56
Wilt Chamberlain, San Francisco at Los Angeles, February 16, 1963	**26	4	56
Wilt Chamberlain, San Francisco vs. Baltimore at San Francisco, December 1, 1964	**22	12	56
Oscar Robertson, Cincinnati vs. Los Angeles at Cincinnati, December 18, 1964	17	22	56
Earl Monroe, Baltimore vs. Los Angeles, February 13, 1968	*20	16	56
Chet Walker, Chicago vs. Cincinnati at Chicago, February 6, 1972	22	12	56
Kelly Tripucka, Detroit vs. Chicago, January 29, 1983	18	20	56
Kevin McHale, Boston vs. Detroit, March 3, 1985	22	12	56
Michael Jordan, Chicago vs. Philadelphia, March 24, 1987	22	12	56
Tom Chambers, Phoenix at Golden State, February 18, 1990	19	16	56

MOST FIELD GOALS SCORED IN ONE GAME

	FGA	FGM
Wilt Chamberlain, Philadelphia vs. New York at Hershey, Pa., March 2, 1962	63	36
Wilt Chamberlain, Philadelphia vs. Los Angeles at Philadelphia, December 8, 1961	***62	31
Wilt Chamberlain, Philadelphia at Chicago, December 16, 1967	40	30
Rick Barry, Golden State vs. Portland at Oakland, March 26, 1974	45	30
Wilt Chamberlain, Philadelphia vs. Chicago at Philadelphia, January 13, 1962	48	29
Wilt Chamberlain, San Francisco at Los Angeles, November 3, 1962	48	29
Wilt Chamberlain, San Francisco at New York, November 16, 1962	43	29
Wilt Chamberlain, Los Angeles vs. Phoenix, February 9, 1969	35	29
Elgin Baylor, Los Angeles at New York, November 15, 1960	48	28
Wilt Chamberlain, Philadelphia vs. Chicago at Philadelphia, December 9, 1961	48	28
Wilt Chamberlain, San Francisco vs. Los Angeles at San Francisco, January 11, 1963	47	28
Wilt Chamberlain, Philadelphia vs. Los Angeles at Philadelphia, February 7, 1966	43	28
David Thompson, Denver at Detroit, April 9, 1978	38	28
Joe Fulks, Philadelphia vs. Indianapolis at Philadelphia, February 10, 1949	56	27
Wilt Chamberlain, Philadelphia vs. New York at Philadelphia, March 9, 1961	37	27
Wilt Chamberlain, Philadelphia at Boston, January 14, 1962	45	27
Wilt Chamberlain, San Francisco vs. Cincinnati at San Francisco, November 21, 1962	52	27
Wilt Chamberlain, San Francisco vs. Syracuse at San Francisco, December 11, 1962	57	27
Wilt Chamberlain, San Francisco at New York, January 29, 1963	44	27
Wilt Chamberlain, San Francisco at Syracuse, March 10, 1963	38	27
Wilt Chamberlain, San Francisco at Philadelphia, November 26, 1964	58	27
Wilt Chamberlain, Philadelphia at New York, February 21, 1960	47	26
Wilt Chamberlain, Philadelphia at St. Louis, February 17, 1962	44	26
Wilt Chamberlain, San Francisco vs. St. Louis at San Francisco, December 18, 1962	53	26
Wilt Chamberlain, San Francisco at Los Angeles, February 16, 1963	**47	26
Wilt Chamberlain, San Francisco at Cincinnati, November 15, 1964	44	26
Wilt Chamberlain, Philadelphia vs. San Francisco at Philadelphia, March 3, 1966	39	26
Wilt Chamberlain, Philadelphia vs. Cincinnati at Philadelphia, February 13, 1967	34	26
Pete Maravich, New Orleans vs. Knicks at New Orleans, February 25, 1977	43	26
Elgin Baylor, Minneapolis vs. Boston at Minneapolis, November 8, 1959	47	25
Wilt Chamberlain, Philadelphia vs. Boston at New York, February 23, 1960	44	25
Wilt Chamberlain, Philadelphia vs. Los Angeles at Philadelphia, January 21, 1961	46	25
Bob Pettit, St. Louis at Detroit, February 18, 1961	42	25
Wilt Chamberlain, Philadelphia at Cincinnati, February 25, 1961	38	25
Wilt Chamberlain, Philadelphia vs. Syracuse at Utica, N.Y., January 21, 1962	*42	25
Wilt Chamberlain, Philadelphia vs. New York at Philadelphia, February 25, 1962	38	25
Wilt Chamberlain, Philadelphia at St. Louis, February 27, 1962	43	25
Wilt Chamberlain, San Francisco vs. St. Louis at San Francisco, December 2, 1962	36	25
Wilt Chamberlain, San Francisco vs. Detroit at Bakersfield, Calif., January 24, 1963	36	25
Wilt Chamberlain, San Francisco at Detroit, February 11, 1964	*50	25
Wilt Chamberlain, San Francisco at New York, December 15, 1964	**45	25
Lou Hudson, Atlanta vs. Chicago at Auburn, Ala., November 10, 1969	34	25

MOST FREE THROWS MADE IN ONE GAME

	FTA	FTM
Wilt Chamberlain, Philadelphia vs. New York at Hershey, Pa., March 2, 1962	32	28
Adrian Dantley, Utah vs. Houston, at Las Vegas, January 4, 1984	29	28

	FTA	FTM
Adrian Dantley, Utah vs. Denver, November 25, 1983	31	27
Adrian Dantley, Utah vs. Dallas at Utah, October 31, 1980	29	26
Michael Jordan, Chicago vs. New Jersey, February 26, 1987	27	26
Frank Selvy, Milwaukee vs. Minneapolis at Ft. Wayne, December 2, 1954	26	24
Dolph Schayes, Syracuse vs. Minneapolis at Syracuse, January 17, 1952	***27	23
Nate Archibald, Cincinnati vs. Detroit at Cincinnati, February 5, 1972	*24	23
Nate Archibald, K.C.-Omaha vs. Portland at Kansas City, January 21, 1975	25	23
Pete Maravich, New Orleans vs. New York, October 26, 1975	**26	23
Kevin Johnson, Phoenix vs. Utah, April 9, 1990	*24	23
Larry Foust, Minneapolis vs. St. Louis at Minneapolis, November 30, 1957	26	22
Richie Guerin, New York at Boston, February 11, 1961	23	22
Oscar Robertson, Cincinnati vs. Los Angeles at Cincinnati, December 18, 1964	23	22
Oscar Robertson, Cincinnati at Baltimore, December 27, 1964	26	22
Oscar Robertson, Cincinnati vs. Baltimore at Cincinnati, November 20, 1966	23	22
John Williamson, New Jersey vs. San Diego at New Jersey, December 9, 1978	24	22
Lloyd Free, San Diego at Atlanta, January 13, 1979	29	22
Bernard King, New York vs. New Jersey, December 25, 1984	26	22
Rolando Blackman, Dallas at New Jersey, February 17, 1986	23	22
Eric Floyd, Houston vs. Golden State, February 3, 1991	**27	22
Dolph Schayes, Syracuse vs. New York at Syracuse, February 15, 1953	25	21
Richie Guerin, New York vs. Syracuse at New York, December 11, 1959	26	21
Rick Barry, San Francisco at New York, December 14, 1965	22	21
Rick Barry, San Francisco vs. Baltimore at San Francisco, November 6, 1966	25	21
Flynn Robinson, Milwaukee vs. Atlanta at Baltimore, February 17, 1969	22	21
Lenny Wilkens, Seattle at Philadelphia, November 8, 1969	25	21
Connie Hawkins, Phoenix vs. Seattle, January 17, 1970	25	21
Spencer Haywood, Seattle vs. K.C.-Omaha at Seattle, January 3, 1973	27	21
John Drew, Atlanta at Phoenix, April 5, 1977	28	21
Rich Kelley, New Orleans vs. New Jersey at New Orleans, March 21, 1978	25	21
Moses Malone, Houston vs. Washington, February 27, 1980	23	21
Jack Sikma, Seattle vs. Kansas City at Seattle, November 14, 1980	23	21
Moses Malone, Philadelphia vs. New York, February 13, 1985	23	21
Moses Malone, Washington vs. Golden State, December 29, 1986	22	21
Charles Barkley, Philadelphia at Atlanta, February 9, 1988	26	21
Michael Jordan, Chicago at Cleveland, March 28, 1990	*23	21
George Mikan, Minneapolis at Anderson, November 19, 1949	23	20
George Mikan, Minneapolis at Chicago, December 3, 1949	23	20
Dolph Schayes, Syracuse at Cincinnati, October 26, 1957	22	20
George Yardley, Detroit at St. Louis, December 26, 1957	24	20
Walter Dukes, Detroit at Los Angeles, November 19, 1960	24	20
Elgin Baylor, Los Angeles at St. Louis, December 21, 1962	21	20
Jerry West, Los Angeles vs. San Francisco at Los Angeles, October 30, 1965	21	20
Oscar Robertson, Cincinnati at Los Angeles, December 3, 1965	24	20
Jerry West, Los Angeles at New York, January 8, 1966	24	20
Jerry West, Los Angeles vs. San Francisco at Los Angeles, January 21, 1966	23	20
Zelmo Beaty, St. Louis at Seattle, December 3, 1967	23	20
Kareem Abdul-Jabbar, Milwaukee at Boston, March 8, 1970	25	20
Lenny Wilkens, Seattle vs. Baltimore at U. of Washington, January 14, 1971	21	20
Artis Gilmore, Chicago vs. Kansas City at Chicago, March 18, 1977	25	20
David Thompson, Denver at New Orleans, April 10, 1977	22	20
Nate Archibald, Boston vs. Chicago, January 16, 1980	22	20
Rolando Blackman, Dallas vs. San Antonio, January 5, 1983	21	20
Kelly Tripucka, Detroit vs. Chicago, January 29, 1983	22	20
Moses Malone, Philadelphia vs. Golden State, February 20, 1985	22	20
Michael Jordan, Chicago at New York, November 1, 1986	22	20
Moses Malone, Washington vs. Houston, November 21, 1986	23	20
Dominique Wilkins, Atlanta at Seattle, February 10, 1987	22	20
Moses Malone, Washington at Atlanta, November 6, 1987	23	20
Moses Malone, Washington at San Antonio, March 14, 1988	22	20
Charles Barkley, Philadelphia vs. New York, March 16, 1988	24	20
Karl Malone, Utah at Minnesota, December 17, 1989	24	20
Karl Malone, Utah vs. Golden State, April 13, 1992	24	20

MOST REBOUNDS IN ONE GAME

	Reb.
Wilt Chamberlain, Philadelphia vs. Boston at Philadelphia, November 24, 1960	55
Bill Russell, Boston vs. Syracuse at Boston, February 5, 1960	51
Bill Russell, Boston vs. Philadelphia at Boston, November 16, 1957	49
Bill Russell, Boston vs. Detroit at Providence, March 11, 1965	49
Wilt Chamberlain, Philadelphia vs. Syracuse at Philadelphia, February 6, 1960	45
Wilt Chamberlain, Philadelphia vs. Los Angeles at Philadelphia, January 21, 1961	45
Wilt Chamberlain, Philadelphia vs. New York at Philadelphia, November 10, 1959	43
Wilt Chamberlain, Philadelphia vs. Los Angeles at Philadelphia, December 8, 1961	***43
Bill Russell, Boston vs. Los Angeles at Boston, January 20, 1963	43
Wilt Chamberlain, Philadelphia vs. Boston at Philadelphia, March 6, 1965	43
Wilt Chamberlain, Philadelphia vs. Boston at Philadelphia, January 15, 1960	42
Wilt Chamberlain, Philadelphia vs. Detroit at Bethlehem, Pa., January 25, 1960	42
Nate Thurmond, San Francisco vs. Detroit at San Francisco, November 9, 1965	42
Wilt Chamberlain, Philadelphia vs. Boston at Philadelphia, January 14, 1966	42
Wilt Chamberlain, Los Angeles vs. Boston, March 7, 1969	*42

Reb.
Bill Russell, Boston vs. Syracuse at Boston, February 12, 1958 41
Wilt Chamberlain, San Francisco vs. Detroit at San Francisco, October 26, 1962 .... *41
Bill Russell, Boston vs. San Francisco at Boston, March 14, 1965 41
Bill Russell, Boston vs. Cincinnati at Boston, December 12, 1958 .... *40
Wilt Chamberlain, Philadelphia vs. Syracuse at Philadelphia, November 4, 1959 40
Bill Russell, Boston vs. Philadelphia at Boston, February 12, 1961 40
Jerry Lucas, Cincinnati at Philadelphia, February 29, 1964 40
Wilt Chamberlain, San Francisco vs. Detroit at San Francisco, November 22, 1964 40
Wilt Chamberlain, Philadelphia vs. Boston at Philadelphia, December 28, 1965 40
Neil Johnston, Philadelphia vs. Syracuse at Philadelphia, December 4, 1954 39
Bill Russell, Boston vs. Detroit at Boston, January 25, 1959 39
Bill Russell, Boston vs. New York at Boston, December 19, 1959 39
Wilt Chamberlain, Philadelphia vs. Cincinnati at St. Louis, December 28, 1959 39
Wilt Chamberlain, Philadelphia vs. Syracuse at Boston, January 13, 1960 .... *39
Wilt Chamberlain, Philadelphia vs. Boston at Philadelphia, January 29, 1960 39
Wilt Chamberlain, Philadelphia vs. Detroit at Philadelphia, November 4, 1960 39
Bill Russell, Boston vs. New York at Providence, R.I., December 21, 1961 39
Maurice Stokes, Rochester vs. Syracuse at Rochester, January 14, 1956 38
Bill Russell, Boston vs. Philadelphia at Providence, February 23, 1958 38
Bill Russell, Boston vs. New York at Boston, December 4, 1959 38
Wilt Chamberlain, Philadelphia vs. Los Angeles at New York, November 29, 1960 38
Wilt Chamberlain, Philadelphia at Cincinnati, December 18, 1960 38
Wilt Chamberlain, Philadelphia vs. Chicago at Philadelphia, November 25, 1961 38
Bill Russell, Boston at San Francisco, February 21, 1963 38
Wilt Chamberlain, San Francisco vs. Boston at San Francisco, February 21, 1963 38
Wilt Chamberlain, San Francisco vs. Boston at San Francisco, April 24, 1964 38
Bill Russell, Boston at New York, January 30, 1965 38
Bill Russell, Boston vs. Los Angeles at Boston, March 3, 1965 38
Wilt Chamberlain, Philadelphia vs. San Francisco at Philadelphia, March 2, 1967 38
Wilt Chamberlain, Philadelphia at Seattle, December 20, 1967 38
Wilt Chamberlain, Los Angeles vs. Baltimore at Los Angeles, March 9, 1969 38

MOST ASSISTS IN ONE GAME

Ast.
Scott Skiles, Orlando vs. Denver at Orlando, December 30, 1990 30
Kevin Porter, New Jersey vs. Houston at New Jersey, February 24, 1978 29
Bob Cousy, Boston vs. Minneapolis at Boston, February 27, 1959 28
Guy Rodgers, San Francisco vs. St. Louis at San Francisco, March 14, 1963 28
John Stockton, Utah vs. San Antonio, January 15, 1991 28
Geoff Huston, Cleveland vs. Golden State at Cleveland, January 27, 1982 27
John Stockton, Utah at New York, December 19, 1989 27
John Stockton, Utah at Portland, April 14, 1988 26
Ernie DiGregorio, Buffalo at Portland, January 1, 1974 25
Kevin Porter, Detroit vs. Boston at Detroit, March 9, 1979 25
Kevin Porter, Detroit at Phoenix, April 1, 1979 25
Isiah Thomas, Detroit vs. Dallas, February 13, 1985 25
Nate McMillan, Seattle vs. L.A. Clippers, February 23, 1987 25
Guy Rodgers, Chicago vs. New York at Chicago, December 21, 1966 24
Kevin Porter, Washington vs. Detroit, March 23, 1980 24
John Lucas, San Antonio vs. Denver, April 15, 1984 24
Isiah Thomas, Detroit at Washington, February 7, 1985 .... **24
John Stockton, Utah at Houston, January 3, 1989 24
Magic Johnson, L.A. Lakers vs. Denver, November 17, 1989 24
Magic Johnson, L.A. Lakers at Phoenix, January 9, 1990 .... *24
Jerry West, Los Angeles vs. Philadelphia at Los Angeles, February 1, 1967 23
Kevin Porter, Detroit vs. Houston at Detroit, December 27, 1978 23
Kevin Porter, Detroit at Los Angeles, March 30, 1979 23
Nate Archibald, Boston vs. Denver at Boston, February 5, 1982 23
Magic Johnson, Los Angeles vs. Seattle, February 21, 1984 23
Magic Johnson, L.A. Lakers at Dallas, April 20, 1988 23
Lafayette Lever, Denver at Golden State, April 21, 1989 23
John Stockton, Utah vs. L.A. Lakers, April 12, 1990 23
John Stockton, Utah at L.A. Clippers, December 8, 1990 23
John Stockton, Utah vs. Golden State, November 29, 1991 23
John Stockton, Utah vs. Minnesota, April 17, 1992 23
Oscar Robertson, Cincinnati vs. Syracuse at Cincinnati, October 29, 1961 22
Oscar Robertson, Cincinnati vs. New York at Cincinnati, March 5, 1966 .... *22
Art Williams, San Diego at Phoenix, December 28, 1968 22
Art Williams, San Diego vs. San Francisco, February 14, 1970 22
Kevin Porter, Washington vs. Atlanta at Washington, March 5, 1975 22
Kevin Porter, Detroit vs. San Antonio at Detroit, December 23, 1978 22
Phil Ford, Kansas City vs. Milwaukee at Kansas City, February 21, 1979 22
Kevin Porter, Detroit at Chicago, February 27, 1979 22
John Lucas, Golden State at Denver, February 27, 1981 22
Allan Leavell, Houston vs. New Jersey, January 25, 1983 22
Magic Johnson, Los Angeles vs. Cleveland, November 17, 1983 22
Ennis Whatley, Chicago vs. New York, January 14, 1984 22
Ennis Whatley, Chicago vs. Atlanta, March 3, 1984 22
John Stockton, Utah vs. L.A. Lakers, January 8, 1987 22

Ast.

John Stockton, Utah vs. Cleveland, December 11, 1989	*22
Magic Johnson, L.A. Lakers vs. Portland, November 6, 1990	*22
Richie Guerin, New York vs. St. Louis at New York, December 12, 1958	21
Bob Cousy, Boston vs. St. Louis at Boston, December 21, 1960	21
Oscar Robertson, Cincinnati vs. New York at Cincinnati, February 14, 1964	21
Guy Rodgers, Chicago vs. San Francisco at Chicago, October 18, 1966	21
Wilt Chamberlain, Philadelphia vs. Detroit, February 2, 1968	21
Guy Rodgers, Milwaukee vs. Detroit, October 31, 1968	21
Clem Haskins, Chicago vs. Boston, December 6, 1969	*21
Larry Siegfried, San Diego at Portland, November 16, 1970	21
Nate Archibald, K.C.-Omaha vs. Detroit at Omaha, December 15, 1972	*21
Kevin Porter, Washington vs. Los Angeles at Washington, March 2, 1975	21
Kevin Porter, Detroit at Houston, February 6, 1979	21
Phil Ford, Kansas City vs. Phoenix at Kansas City, February 23, 1979	21
Maurice Cheeks, Philadelphia vs. New Jersey, October 30, 1982	21
Magic Johnson, Los Angeles at Atlanta, January 15, 1983	21
Isiah Thomas, Detroit at Kansas City, December 22, 1984	21
Ennis Whatley, Chicago vs. Golden State, February 23, 1985	21
Norm Nixon, L.A. Clippers vs. Detroit, March 18, 1985	21
Isiah Thomas, Detroit vs. Washington, April 12, 1985	21
Doc Rivers, Atlanta vs. Philadelphia, March 4, 1986	21
Nate McMillan, Seattle vs. Sacramento, March 31, 1987	21
John Stockton, Utah at L.A. Clippers, February 19, 1988	21
John Stockton, Utah vs. L.A. Clippers, February 20, 1988	21
John Stockton, Utah vs. Phoenix, March 22, 1988	21
John Stockton, Utah at L.A. Clippers, April 20, 1988	21
John Stockton, Utah vs. Phoenix, November 19, 1988	21
Magic Johnson, L.A. Lakers at L.A. Clippers, December 6, 1988	21
John Stockton, Utah vs. Denver, February 14, 1989	21
Kevin Johnson, Phoenix at L.A. Lakers, February 26, 1989	21
Magic Johnson, L.A. Lakers vs. Seattle, April 23, 1989	21
Gary Grant, L.A. Clippers vs. Milwaukee, November 29, 1989	21
Magic Johnson, L.A. Lakers at Boston, December 15, 1989	21
Gary Grant, L.A. Clippers vs. Seattle, January 18, 1990	21
John Stockton, Utah vs. Portland, March 1, 1990	21
John Stockton, Utah vs. Phoenix, March 13, 1990	21
John Stockton, Utah vs. Golden State, December 11, 1990	21
Magic Johnson, L.A. Lakers vs. Indiana, December 16, 1990	21
John Stockton, Utah at San Antonio, April 19, 1992	21

MOST STEALS IN ONE GAME

Stl.

Larry Kenon, San Antonio at Kansas City, December 26, 1976	11
Jerry West, Los Angeles vs. Seattle at Los Angeles, December 7, 1973	10
Larry Steele, Portland vs. Los Angeles at Portland, November 16, 1974	10
Fred Brown, Seattle at Philadelphia, December 3, 1976	10
Gus Williams, Seattle at New Jersey, February 22, 1978	10
Eddie Jordan, New Jersey at Philadelphia, March 23, 1979	10
Johnny Moore, San Antonio vs. Indiana, March 6, 1985	10
Lafayette Lever, Denver vs. Indiana, March 9, 1985	10
Clyde Drexler, Portland at Milwaukee, January 10, 1986	10
Alvin Robertson, San Antonio vs. Phoenix, February 18, 1986	10
Alvin Robertson, San Antonio at L.A. Clippers, November 22, 1986	10
Ron Harper, Cleveland vs. Philadelphia, March 10, 1987	10
Michael Jordan, Chicago vs. New Jersey, January 29, 1988	10
Alvin Robertson, San Antonio vs. Houston, January 11, 1989	*10
Alvin Robertson, Milwaukee vs. Utah, November 19, 1990	10
Calvin Murphy, Houston vs. Boston at Houston, December 14, 1973	9
Larry Steele, Portland vs. Los Angeles at Portland, March 5, 1974	9
Rick Barry, Golden State vs. Buffalo at Oakland, October 29, 1974	9
Don Watts, Seattle vs. Philadelphia at Seattle, February 23, 1975	9
Larry Steele, Portland vs. Phoenix at Portland, March 7, 1975	9
Larry Steele, Portland vs. Detroit at Portland, March 14, 1976	9
Quinn Buckner, Milwaukee vs. Indiana at Milwaukee, January 2, 1977	9
Don Watts, Seattle vs. Phoenix at Seattle, March 27, 1977	9
Earl Tatum, Detroit at Los Angeles, November 28, 1978	9
Gus Williams, Seattle at Washington, January 23, 1979	9
Ron Lee, Detroit vs. Houston, March 16, 1980	9
Dudley Bradley, Indiana at Utah, November 10, 1980	9
Dudley Bradley, Indiana vs. Cleveland at Indiana, November 29, 1980	9
Micheal Ray Richardson, New York at Chicago, December 23, 1980	9
Johnny High, Phoenix at Washington, January 28, 1981	9
Magic Johnson, Los Angeles vs. Phoenix at Los Angeles, November 6, 1981	9
Jack Sikma, Seattle vs. Kansas City at Kansas City, January 27, 1982	9
Rickey Green, Utah vs. Denver, November 10, 1982	9
Rickey Green, Utah at Philadelphia, November 27, 1982	9
Micheal Ray Richardson, Golden State vs. San Antonio, February 5, 1983	9
Darwin Cook, New Jersey vs. Portland, December 3, 1983	*9
Gus Williams, Washington vs. Atlanta, October 30, 1984	9
Johnny Moore, San Antonio vs. Golden State, January 8, 1985	9

Stl.
Larry Bird, Boston at Utah, February 18, 1985...9
Micheal Ray Richardson, New Jersey vs. Indiana, October 30, 1985.................................***9
Maurice Cheeks, Philadelphia vs. L.A. Clippers, January 5, 1987.......................................9
T.R. Dunn, Denver at New Jersey, January 6, 1988..9
Michael Jordan, Chicago at Boston, November 9, 1988..9
Hersey Hawkins, Philadelphia vs. Boston, January 25, 1991..9
John Stockton, Utah vs. Houston, February 12, 1991...9
Michael Adams, Washington at Indiana, November 1, 1991..9
Doc Rivers, L.A. Clippers vs. Phoenix, November 6, 1991..9

MOST BLOCKED SHOTS IN ONE GAME

Blk.
Elmore Smith, Los Angeles vs. Portland at Los Angeles, October 28, 1973.........................17
Manute Bol, Washington vs. Atlanta, January 25, 1986 15
Manute Bol, Washington vs. Indiana, February 26, 1987...15
Elmore Smith, Los Angeles vs. Detroit at Los Angeles, October 26, 1973..........................14
Elmore Smith, Los Angeles vs. Houston at Los Angeles, November 4, 1973 14
Mark Eaton, Utah vs. Portland, January 18, 1985 14
Mark Eaton, Utah vs. San Antonio, February 18, 1989 14
George Johnson, San Antonio vs. Golden State at San Antonio, February 24, 1981 13
Mark Eaton, Utah vs. Portland, February 18, 1983 13
Darryl Dawkins, New Jersey vs. Philadelphia, November 5, 1983 13
Ralph Sampson, Houston at Chicago, December 9, 1983..*13
Manute Bol, Golden State vs. New Jersey, February 2, 1990 13
Nate Thurmond, Chicago vs. Atlanta at Chicago, October 18, 1974 12
George Johnson, New Jersey at New Orleans, March 21, 1978..12
Wayne Rollins, Atlanta vs. Portland at Atlanta, February 21, 1979....................................12
Mark Eaton, Utah at Denver, February 5, 1983 12
Mark Eaton, Utah vs. Dallas, March 17, 1984..12
Mark Eaton, Utah at Dallas, February 26, 1985...12
Manute Bol, Washington vs. Milwaukee, December 12, 1985...*12
Mark Eaton, Utah vs. Portland, November 1, 1986 12
Manute Bol, Washington vs. Cleveland, February 5, 1987 12
Akeem Olajuwon, Houston vs. Seattle, March 10, 1987...**12
Manute Bol, Washington vs. Boston, March 26, 1987 12
Manute Bol, Golden State at San Antonio, February 22, 1989...12
Akeem Olajuwon, Houston vs. Utah, November 11, 1989...12
David Robinson, San Antonio vs. Minnesota, February 23, 1990...12

COMBINED NBA/ABA ALL-TIME LEADERS
(Active 1991-92 players in capital letters)

MOST GAMES PLAYED

Kareem Abdul-Jabbar	1,560
MOSES MALONE	1,372
Artis Gilmore	1,329
Elvin Hayes	1,303
Caldwell Jones	1,299
John Havlicek	1,270
ROBERT PARISH	1,260
Paul Silas	1,254
Julius Erving	1,243
Dan Issel	1,218

MOST FIELD GOALS MADE

Kareem Abdul-Jabbar	15,837
Wilt Chamberlain	12,681
Julius Erving	11,818
Elvin Hayes	10,976
Alex English	10,659
John Havlicek	10,513
Dan Issel	10,431
George Gervin	10,368
MOSES MALONE	10,149
Rick Barry	9,695

MOST FIELD GOALS ATTEMPTED

Kareem Abdul-Jabbar	28,307
Elvin Hayes	24,272
John Havlicek	23,930
Wilt Chamberlain	23,497
Julius Erving	23,370
Rick Barry	21,283
Alex English	21,036
Dan Issel	20,894
George Gervin	20,583
Moses Malone	20,441

MOST MINUTES PLAYED

Kareem Abdul-Jabbar	57,446
Elvin Hayes	50,000
MOSES MALONE	48,573
Wilt Chamberlain	47,859
Artis Gilmore	47,134
John Havlicek	46,471
Julius Erving	45,227
Oscar Robertson	43,866
Dan Issel	41,786
Bill Russell	40,726

MOST FREE THROWS MADE

MOSES MALONE	8,882
Oscar Robertson	7,694
Jerry West	7,160
Dolph Schayes	6,979
Adrian Dantley	6,832
Kareem Abdul-Jabbar	6,712
Dan Issel	6,591
Julius Erving	6,256
Bob Pettit	6,182
Artis Gilmore	6,132

MOST FREE THROWS ATTEMPTED

Wilt Chamberlain	11,862
MOSES MALONE	11,684
Kareem Abdul-Jabbar	9,304
Oscar Robertson	9,185
Jerry West	8,801
Artis Gilmore	8,790
Adrian Dantley	8,351
Dan Issel	8,315
Dolph Schayes	8,273
Bob Pettit	8,119

MOST REBOUNDS

Wilt Chamberlain	23,924
Bill Russell	21,620
MOSES MALONE	17,516
Kareem Abdul-Jabbar	17,440
Artis Gilmore	16,330
Elvin Hayes	16,279
Nate Thurmond	14,464
Walt Bellamy	14,241
Wes Unseld	13,769
Jerry Lucas	12,942

MOST STEALS

MAURICE CHEEKS	2,277
Julius Erving	2,272
Don Buse	1,818
ALVIN ROBERTSON	1,791
MAGIC JOHNSON	1,698
ISIAH THOMAS	1,670
Gus Williams	1,638
JOHN STOCKTON	1633
MICHAEL JORDAN	1,594
LARRY BIRD	1,556

MOST ASSISTS

MAGIC JOHNSON	9,921
Oscar Robertson	9,887
ISIAH THOMAS	7,991
JOHN STOCKTON	7,365
MAURICE CHEEKS	7,285
Len Wilkens	7,211
Bob Cousy	6,955
Guy Rodgers	6,917
Nate Archibald	6,476
John Lucas	6,454

MOST BLOCKED SHOTS

Kareem Abdul-Jabbar	3,189
Artis Gilmore	3,178
MARK EATON	2,985
WAYNE ROLLINS	2,456
Caldwell Jones	2,297
HAKEEM OLAJUWON	2,102
George T. Johnson	2,082
ROBERT PARISH	2,049
MANUTE BOL	1,942
Julius Erving	1,941

MOST PERSONAL FOULS

Kareem Abdul-Jabbar	4,657
Artis Gilmore	4,529
Caldwell Jones	4,436
Elvin Hayes	4,193
Jack Sikma	3,879
Hal Greer	3,855
ROBERT PARISH	3,800
JAMES EDWARDS	3,725
Dolph Schayes	3,664
Walt Bellamy	3,536

MOST DISQUALIFICATIONS

Vern Mikkelsen	127
Walter Dukes	121
Charlie Share	105
Paul Arizin	101
Darryl Dawkins	100
JAMES EDWARDS	95
Tom Gola	94
Tom Sanders	94
Steve Johnson	92
WAYNE ROLLINS	91

HIGHEST FIELD GOAL PERCENTAGE
(2,000 FGM minimum)

	FGA	FGM	Pct.
Artis Gilmore	16,158	9,403	.582
CHARLES BARKLEY	8,722	5,025	.576
STEVE JOHNSON	4,965	2,841	.572
Darryl Dawkins	6,079	3,477	.572
JAMES DONALDSON	5,354	3,053	.570
JEFF RULAND	3,723	2,100	.564
Bobby Jones	7,953	4,451	.560
Kareem Abdul-Jabbar	28,307	15,837	.559
KEVIN McHALE	11,685	6,532	.559
BUCK WILLIAMS	9,146	5,092	.557

HIGHEST FREE THROW PERCENTAGE
(1,200 FTM minimum)

	FTA	FTM	Pct.
MARK PRICE	1,343	1,208	.899
Rick Barry	6,397	5,713	.893
Calvin Murphy	3,864	3,445	.892
LARRY BIRD	4,471	3,960	.886
Bill Sharman	3,559	3,143	.883
JEFF MALONE	2,768	2,426	.876
RICKY PIERCE	2,790	2,438	.874
CHRIS MULLIN	2,928	2,558	.874
Billy Keller	1,378	1,202	.872
KIKI VANDEWEGHE	3,931	3,426	.872

HIGHEST SCORING AVERAGE
(400 Games or 10,000 Points minimum)

	G.	FGM	FTM	Pts.	Avg.
MICHAEL JORDAN	589	7,087	4,620	19,000	32.3
Wilt Chamberlain	1,045	12,681	6,057	31,419	30.1
Elgin Baylor	846	8,693	5,763	23,149	27.4
Jerry West	932	9,016	7,160	25,192	27.0
Bob Pettit	792	7,349	6,182	20,880	26.4
DOMINIQUE WILKINS	762	7,581	4,494	19,975	26.2
KARL MALONE	570	5,458	3,826	14,770	25.9
Oscar Robertson	1,040	9,508	7,694	26,710	25.7
George Gervin	1,060	10,368	5,737	26,595	25.1
Rick Barry	1,020	9,695	5,713	25,279	24.8

HIGHEST 3-POINT FIELD GOAL PERCENTAGE
(100 3FGM Minimum)

	FGA	FGM	Pct.
STEVE KERR	297	141	.475
DRAZEN PETROVIC	416	180	.433
DANA BARROS	505	210	.416
MARK PRICE	1,117	459	.411
HERSEY HAWKINS	865	354	.409
TRENT TUCKER	1,279	523	.409
DALE ELLIS	1,891	763	.403
CRAIG HODGES	1,408	563	.400
JON SUNDVOLD	576	226	.392
JEFF HORNACEK	615	240	.390

MOST 3-PT. FIELD GOALS ATTEMPTED

MICHAEL ADAMS	2,332
Louie Dampier	2,217
DALE ELLIS	1,891
DANNY AINGE	1,821
LARRY BIRD	1,727
Darrell Griffith	1,596
Billy Keller	1,495
DEREK HARPER	1,492
REGGIE MILLER	1,441
ERIC FLOYD	1,419

MOST 3-PT. FIELD GOALS MADE

Louie Dampier	794
MICHAEL ADAMS	783
DALE ELLIS	763
DANNY AINGE	694
LARRY BIRD	649
CRAIG HODGES	563
REGGIE MILLER	550
Darrell Griffith	530
TRENT TUCKER	523
DEREK HARPER	507

COMBINED NBA/ABA ALL-TIME SCORERS
(Active 1991-92 players in capital letters)

	Yrs.	G.	Pts.	Avg.
Kareem Abdul-Jabbar	20	1,560	38,387	24.6
Wilt Chamberlain	14	1,045	31,419	30.1
Julius Erving	16	1,243	30,026	24.2
MOSES MALONE	18	1,372	29,187	21.3
Dan Issel	15	1,218	27,482	22.6
Elvin Hayes	16	1,303	27,313	21.0
Oscar Robertson	14	1,040	26,710	25.7
George Gervin	14	1,060	26,595	25.1
John Havlicek	16	1,270	26,395	20.8
Alex English	15	1,193	25,613	21.5
Rick Barry	14	1,020	25,279	24.8
Jerry West	14	932	25,192	27.0
Artis Gilmore	17	1,329	24,941	18.8
Adrian Dantley	15	955	23,177	24.3
Elgin Baylor	14	846	23,149	27.4
LARRY BIRD	13	897	21,791	24.3
Hal Greer	15	1,122	21,586	19.2
Walt Bellamy	14	1,043	20,941	20.1
Bob Pettit	11	792	20,880	26.4
ROBERT PARISH	16	1,260	20,634	16.4
DOMINIQUE WILKINS	10	762	19,975	26.2
WALTER DAVIS	15	1,033	19,521	18.9
BERNARD KING	13	842	19,432	23.1
Dolph Schayes	16	1,059	19,249	18.2
Bob Lanier	14	959	19,248	20.1
Gail Goodrich	14	1,031	19,181	18.6
Reggie Theus	13	1,026	19,015	18.5
MICHAEL JORDAN	8	589	19,000	32.3
Chet Walker	13	1,032	18,831	18.2
Bob McAdoo	14	852	18,787	22.1
Dave Bing	12	901	18,327	20.3
World B. Free	13	886	17,955	20.3
Calvin Murphy	13	1,002	17,949	17.9
Lou Hudson	13	890	17,940	20.2
Len Wilkens	15	1,077	17,772	16.5
Bailey Howell	12	950	17,770	18.7
TOM CHAMBERS	11	860	17,736	20.6
MARK AGUIRRE	11	833	17,542	21.1
Earl Monroe	13	926	17,454	18.8
Ron Boone	13	1,041	17,437	16.8
Jack Sikma	14	1,107	17,287	15.6
MAGIC JOHNSON	12	874	17,239	19.7
Spencer Haywood	13	844	17,111	20.3
George McGinnis	11	842	17,009	20.2
Bob Cousy	14	924	16,960	18.4
ROLANDO BLACKMAN	11	865	16,643	19.2
ISIAH THOMAS	11	842	16,575	19.7
KEVIN MCHALE	12	900	16,573	18.4
Nate Archibald	13	876	16,481	18.8
TERRY CUMMINGS	10	768	16,364	21.3
Billy Cunningham	11	770	16,310	21.2
Paul Arizin	10	713	16,266	22.8
Randy Smith	12	976	16,262	16.7
Pete Maravich	10	658	15,948	24.2
Jack Twyman	11	823	15,840	19.2
KIKI VANDEWEGHE	12	769	15,726	20.4
EDDIE A. JOHNSON	11	852	15,645	18.4
Walt Frazier	13	825	15,581	18.9
Dennis Johnson	14	1,100	15,535	14.1
Bob Dandridge	13	839	15,530	18.5
Sam Jones	12	871	15,411	17.7
Dick Barnett	14	971	15,358	15.8
John Drew	11	739	15,291	20.7
Louie Dampier	12	960	15,279	15.9

NBA All-Time Overall Records

Team	W.	L.	Pct.
Boston Celtics	2274	1285	.639
Los Angeles Lakers	2119	1330	.614
Chicago Stags*	145	92	.612
Milwaukee Bucks	1164	804	.591
Washington Capitols*	157	114	.579
Anderson Packers*	37	27	.578
Philadelphia 76ers	1942	1442	.574
San Antonio Spurs	689	623	.525
Portland Trail Blazers	943	861	.523
Phoenix Suns	1028	940	.522
St. Louis Bombers*	122	115	.515
Chicago Bulls	1085	1046	.509
Denver Nuggets	662	650	.505
Atlanta Hawks	1696	1690	.501
Cleveland Rebels*	30	30	.500
New York Knickerbockers	1760	1795	.495
Seattle SuperSonics	1014	1036	.495
Indianapolis Olympians*	132	137	.491
Golden State Warriors	1732	1822	.487
Washington Bullets	1228	1303	.485
Detroit Pistons	1649	1799	.478
Utah Jazz	702	774	.476
Houston Rockets	960	1090	.468
Sacramento Kings	1600	1849	.464
Dallas Mavericks	455	529	.462
Cleveland Cavaliers	762	1042	.422
Indiana Pacers	545	767	.415
New Jersey Nets	512	800	.390
Los Angeles Clippers	664	1140	.368
Toronto Huskies*	22	38	.367
Sheboygan Redskins*	22	40	.355
Baltimore Bullets*	158	292	.351
Detroit Falcons*	20	40	.333
Waterloo Hawks*	19	43	.306
Indianapolis Jets*	18	42	.300
Charlotte Hornets	96	232	.293
Miami Heat	95	233	.290
Orlando Magic	70	176	.285
Providence Steamrollers*	46	122	.274
Minnesota Timberwolves	66	180	.268
Pittsburgh Ironmen*	15	45	.250
Denver Nuggets*	11	51	.177
Totals	28466	28466	.500

*Defunct

NBA All-Time Road Records

Team	W.	L.	Pct.
Chicago Stags*	63	58	.521
Boston Celtics	847	830	.505
Los Angeles Lakers	781	815	.489
Milwaukee Bucks	441	530	.454
Washington Capitols*	58	72	.446
Cleveland Rebels*	13	17	.433
Philadelphia 76ers	665	892	.427
St. Louis Bombers*	45	71	.388
Chicago Bulls	392	631	.383
Anderson Packers*	11	18	.379
New York Knickerbockers	624	1024	.379
San Antonio Spurs	237	419	.361
Atlanta Hawks	547	986	.357
Phoenix Suns	344	621	.356
Washington Bullets	419	760	.355
Portland Trail Blazers	313	578	.351
Detroit Pistons	530	1007	.345
Seattle SuperSonics	345	656	.345
Golden State Warriors	565	1089	.342
Dallas Mavericks	167	325	.339
Houston Rockets	317	675	.320
Denver Nuggets	204	452	.311
Sacramento Kings	483	1106	.304
Utah Jazz	218	520	.295
Cleveland Cavaliers	251	640	.282
Detroit Falcons*	8	22	.267
New Jersey Nets	174	482	.265
Indiana Pacers	171	485	.261
Inaianapolis Olympians*	31	89	.258
Los Angeles Clippers	210	678	.236
Toronto Huskies*	7	23	.233
Providence Steamrollers*	17	65	.207
Baltimore Bullets*	36	141	.203
Charlotte Hornets	32	132	.195
Sheboygan Redskins*	5	22	.185
Orlando Magic	21	102	.171
Miami Heat	26	138	.159
Minnesota Timberwolves	19	104	.154
Indianapolis Jets*	4	22	.154
Pittsburgh Ironmen*	4	26	.133
Waterloo Hawks*	1	22	.043
Denver Nuggets*	1	26	.037
Totals	9647	17371	.357

*Defunct

NBA All-Time Home Records

Team	W.	L.	Pct.
Boston Celtics	1225	367	.769
Los Angeles Lakers	1199	394	.753
Milwaukee Bucks	699	259	.730
Philadelphia 76ers	1116	417	.728
Washington Capitols*	97	37	.724
Anderson Packers*	23	9	.719
Indianapolis Olympians*	86	37	.699
Portland Trail Blazers	628	271	.699
Denver Nuggets	458	198	.698
Phoenix Suns	675	301	.692
San Antonio Spurs	452	204	.689
Chicago Stags*	70	33	.680
Utah Jazz	484	254	.656
Atlanta Hawks	1022	541	.654
Seattle Supersonics	651	349	.651
St. Louis Bombers*	73	41	.640
Chicago Bulls	662	382	.634
Washington Bullets	752	449	.626
Golden State Warriors	1002	603	.624
Houston Rockets	618	383	.617
Sacramento Kings	968	601	.617
Detroit Pistons	975	610	.615
New York Knickerbockers	1006	638	.612
Dallas Mavericks	288	204	.585
Indiana Pacers	374	282	.570
Cleveland Rebels*	17	13	.567
Cleveland Cavaliers	505	397	.560
Sheboygan Redskins*	17	14	.548
Waterloo Hawks*	17	15	.531
Baltimore Bullets*	111	100	.526
New Jersey Nets	338	318	.515
Los Angeles Clippers	444	444	.500
Toronto Huskies*	15	15	.500
Indianapolis Jets*	14	15	.483
Miami Heat	69	95	.421
Detroit Falcons*	12	18	.400
Orlando Magic	49	74	.399
Charlotte Hornets	64	100	.390
Minnesota Timberwolves	47	76	.382
Denver Nuggets*	9	15	.375
Pittsburgh Ironmen*	11	19	.367
Providence Steamrollers*	29	55	.345
Totals	17371	9647	.643

*Defunct

NBA All-Time Neutral Court Records

Team	W.	L.	Pct.
Anderson Packers*	3	0	1.000
Chicago Stags*	12	1	.923
Boston Celtics	202	88	.697
Milwaukee Bucks	24	15	.615
Indianapolis Olympians*	15	11	.577
St. Louis Bombers*	4	3	.571
Golden State Warriors	165	130	.559
Philadelphia 76ers	161	133	.548
Cleveland Cavaliers	6	5	.545
Los Angeles Lakers	139	121	.535
Sacramento Kings	149	142	.512
New York Knickerbockers	130	133	.494
Chicago Bulls	31	33	.484
Detroit Pistons	144	182	.442
Houston Rockets	25	32	.439
Atlanta Hawks	127	163	.438
Washington Bullets	57	94	.377
Seattle SuperSonics	18	31	.367
Los Angeles Clippers	10	18	.357
Phoenix Suns	9	18	.333
Washington Capitols*	2	5	.286
Baltimore Bullets*	11	51	.177
Portland Trail Blazers	2	12	.143
Waterloo Hawks*	1	6	.143
Denver Nuggets*	1	10	.091
Providence Steamrollers*	0	2	.000
Sheboygan Redskins*	0	4	.000
Indianapolis Jets*	0	5	.000
Totals	1448	1448	.500

*Defunct

ALL-TIME RECORDS OF NBA TEAMS

ANDERSON PACKERS

Season	Coach	Reg. W.	L.	Sea'n W.	L.	Playoffs W.	L.
1949-50	Howard Schultz, 21-14	..	..	..	..	..	..
	Ike Duffey, 1-2	..	..	..	..	..	..
	Doxie Moore, 15-11	37	27	..	..	4	4

ATLANTA HAWKS

Season	Coach	Reg. W.	L.	Sea'n W.	L.	Playoffs W.	L.
1949-50	Roger Potter, 1-6	..	..	..	..	..	..
	Red Auerbach, 28-29	29	35	..	..	1	2
1950-51	Dave McMillan, 9-14	..	..	..	..	..	..
	John Logan, 2-1	..	..	..	..	..	..
	Marko Todorovich, 14-28	25	43	..	..	..	..
1951-52*	Doxie Moore	17	49	..	..	..	..
1952-53	Andrew Levane	27	44	..	..	..	..
1953-54	Andrew Levane, 11-35	..	..	..	..	..	..
	Red Holzman, 10-16	21	51	..	..	..	..
1954-55	Red Holzman	26	46	..	..	..	..
1955-56†	Red Holzman	33	39	..	..	4	4
1956-57	Red Holzman, 14-19	..	..	..	..	..	..
	Slater Martin, 5-3	..	..	..	..	..	..
	Alex Hannum, 15-16	34	38	..	..	6	4
1957-58	Alex Hannum	41	31	..	..	8	3
1958-59	Andy Phillip, 6-4	..	..	..	..	..	..
	Ed Macauley, 43-19	49	23	..	..	2	4
1959-60	Ed Macauley	46	29	..	..	7	7
1960-61	Paul Seymour	51	28	..	..	5	7
1961-62	Paul Seymour, 5-9	..	..	..	..	..	..
	Andrew Levane, 20-40	..	..	..	..	..	..
	Bob Pettit, 4-2	29	51	..	..	..	..
1962-63	Harry Gallatin	48	32	..	..	6	5
1963-64	Harry Gallatin	46	34	..	..	6	6
1964-65	Harry Gallatin, 17-16	..	..	..	..	..	..
	Richie Guerin, 28-19	45	35	..	..	1	3
1965-66	Richie Guerin	36	44	..	..	6	4
1966-67	Richie Guerin	39	42	..	..	5	4
1967-68	Richie Guerin	56	26	..	..	2	4
1968-69‡	Richie Guerin	48	34	..	..	5	6
1969-70	Richie Guerin	48	34	..	..	4	5
1970-71	Richie Guerin	36	46	..	..	1	4
1971-72	Richie Guerin	36	46	..	..	2	4
1972-73	Cotton Fitzsimmons	46	36	..	..	2	4
1973-74	Cotton Fitzsimmons	35	47	..	..	..	.
1974-75	Cotton Fitzsimmons	31	51	..	..	..	..
1975-76	C. Fitzsimmons, 28-46	..	..	..	..	..	..
	Gene Tormohlen, 1-7	29	53	..	..	..	..
1976-77	Hubie Brown	31	51	..	..	..	..
1977-78	Hubie Brown	41	41	..	..	0	2
1978-79	Hubie Brown	46	36	..	..	5	4
1979-80	Hubie Brown	50	32	..	..	1	4
1980-81	Hubie Brown, 31-48	..	..	..	..	..	..
	Mike Fratello, 0-3	31	51	..	..	..	..
1981-82	Kevin Loughery	42	40	..	..	0	2
1982-83	Kevin Loughery	43	39	..	..	1	2
1983-84	Mike Fratello	40	42	..	..	2	3
1984-85	Mike Fratello	34	48	..	..	..	..
1985-86	Mike Fratello	50	32	..	..	4	5
1986-87	Mike Fratello	57	25	..	..	4	5
1987-88	Mike Fratello	50	32	..	..	6	6
1988-89	Mike Fratello	52	30	..	..	2	3
1989-90	Mike Fratello	41	41	..	..	..	..
1990-91	Bob Weiss	43	39	..	..	2	3
1991-92	Bob Weiss	38	44	..	..	..	..
Totals		1696	1690			100	119

*Team moved from Tri-Cities to Milwaukee.
†Team moved from Milwaukee to St. Louis.
‡Team moved from St. Louis to Atlanta.

BALTIMORE BULLETS

Season	Coach	Reg. W.	L.	Sea'n W.	L.	Playoffs W.	L.
1947-48	Buddy Jeannette	28	20	8	3		
1948-49	Buddy Jeannette	29	31	1	2		
1949-50	Buddy Jeannette	25	43	..	..		
1950-51	Buddy Jeannette, 14-23	..	..	..	..		
	Walter Budko, 10-19	24	42	..	..		

Season	Coach	Reg. W.	L.	Sea'n W.	L.	Playoffs W.	L.
1951-52	Fred Scolari, 12-27	..	..	..	..		
	Chick Reiser, 8-19	20	46	..	..		
1952-53	Chick Reiser, 0-3	..	..	..	..		
	Clair Bee, 16-51	16	54	..	..	0	2
1953-54	Clair Bee	16	56	..	..	..	..
1954-55	Clair Bee, 2-9	..	..	..	..	..	..
	Al Barthelme, 1-2	3	11	..	..	..	..
Totals		161	303			9	7

*Team disbanded November 27.

BOSTON CELTICS

Season	Coach	Reg. W.	L.	Sea'n W.	L.	Playoffs W.	L.
1946-47	John Russell	22	38				
1947-48	John Russell	20	28			1	2
1948-49	Alvin Julian	25	35			..	..
1949-50	Alvin Julian	22	46			..	..
1950-51	Red Auerbach	39	30			0	2
1951-52	Red Auerbach	39	27			1	2
1952-53	Red Auerbach	46	25			3	3
1953-54	Red Auerbach	42	30			2	4
1954-55	Red Auerbach	36	36			3	4
1955-56	Red Auerbach	39	33			1	2
1956-57	Red Auerbach	44	28			7	3
1957-58	Red Auerbach	49	23			6	5
1958-59	Red Auerbach	52	20			8	3
1959-60	Red Auerbach	59	16			8	5
1960-61	Red Auerbach	57	22			8	2
1961-62	Red Auerbach	60	20			8	6
1962-63	Red Auerbach	58	22			8	5
1963-64	Red Auerbach	59	21			8	2
1964-65	Red Auerbach	62	18			8	4
1965-66	Red Auerbach	54	26			11	6
1966-67	Bill Russell	60	21			4	5
1967-68	Bill Russell	54	28			12	7
1968-69	Bill Russell	48	34			12	6
1969-70	Tom Heinsohn	34	48			..	..
1970-71	Tom Heinsohn	44	38			..	..
1971-72	Tom Heinsohn	56	26			5	6
1972-73	Tom Heinsohn	68	14			7	6
1973-74	Tom Heinsohn	56	26			12	6
1974-75	Tom Heinsohn	60	22			6	5
1975-76	Tom Heinsohn	54	28			12	6
1976-77	Tom Heinsohn	44	38			5	4
1977-78	Tom Heinsohn, 11-23	..	..			..	..
	Tom Sanders, 21-27	32	50			..	..
1978-79	Tom Sanders, 2-12	..	..			..	..
	Dave Cowens, 27-41	29	53			..	..
1979-80	Bill Fitch	61	21			5	4
1980-81	Bill Fitch	62	20			12	5
1981-82	Bill Fitch	63	19			7	5
1982-83	Bill Fitch	56	26			2	5
1983-84	K.C. Jones	62	20			15	8
1984-85	K.C. Jones	63	19			13	8
1985-86	K.C. Jones	67	15			15	3
1986-87	K.C. Jones	59	23			13	10
1987-88	K.C. Jones	57	25			9	8
1988-89	Jimmy Rodgers	42	40			0	3
1989-90	Jimmy Rodgers	53	30			2	3
1990-91	Chris Ford	56	26			5	6
1991-92	Chris Ford	51	31			6	4
Totals		2274	1285			270	183

CHARLOTTE HORNETS

Season	Coach	Reg. W.	L.	Sea'n W.	L.	Playoffs W.	L.
1988-89	Dick Harter	20	62			..	..
1989-90	Dick Harter, 8-32	..	..				
	Gene Littles, 11-31	19	63			..	..
1990-91	Gene Littles	26	56			..	..
1991-92	Allan Bristow	31	51			..	..
Totals		96	232			..	..

CHICAGO BULLS

Season	Coach	Reg. Sea'n W.	L.	Playoffs W.	L.
1966-67	John Kerr	33	48	0	3
1967-68	John Kerr	29	53	1	4
1968-69	Dick Motta	33	49	..	..
1969-70	Dick Motta	39	43	1	4
1970-71	Dick Motta	51	31	3	4
1971-72	Dick Motta	57	25	0	4
1972-73	Dick Motta	51	31	3	4
1973-74	Dick Motta	54	28	4	7
1974-75	Dick Motta	47	35	7	6
1975-76	Dick Motta	24	58	..	..
1976-77	Ed Badger	44	38	1	2
1977-78	Ed Badger	40	42	..	..
1978-79	Larry Costello, 20-36				
	Scotty Robertson, 11-15	31	51	..	..
1979-80	Jerry Sloan	30	52	..	..
1980-81	Jerry Sloan	45	37	2	4
1981-82	Jerry Sloan, 19-32				
	Phil Johnson, 0-1				
	Rod Thorn, 15-15	34	48	..	..
1982-83	Paul Westhead	28	54	..	..
1983-84	Kevin Loughery	27	55	..	..
1984-85	Kevin Loughery	38	44	1	3
1985-86	Stan Albeck	30	52	0	3
1986-87	Doug Collins	40	42	0	3
1987-88	Doug Collins	50	32	4	6
1988-89	Doug Collins	47	35	9	8
1989-90	Phil Jackson	55	27	10	6
1990-91	Phil Jackson	61	21	15	2
1991-92	Phil Jackson	67	15	15	7
Totals		1085	1046	76	80

CHICAGO STAGS

Season	Coach	Reg. Sea'n W.	L.	Playoffs W.	L.
1946-47	Harold Olsen	39	22	5	6
1947-48	Harold Olsen	28	20	2	3
1948-49	Harold Olsen, 28-21	38	22	0	2
	*Philip Brownstein, 10-1	..	..	..	..
1949-50	Philip Brownstein	40	28	0	2
Totals		145	92	7	13

*Substituted during Olsen's illness.

CLEVELAND CAVALIERS

Season	Coach	Reg. Sea'n W.	L.	Playoffs W.	L.
1970-71	Bill Fitch	15	67	..	..
1971-72	Bill Fitch	23	59	..	..
1972-73	Bill Fitch	32	50	..	..
1973-74	Bill Fitch	29	53	..	..
1974-75	Bill Fitch	40	42	..	..
1975-76	Bill Fitch	49	33	6	7
1976-77	Bill Fitch	43	39	1	2
1977-78	Bill Fitch	43	39	0	2
1978-79	Bill Fitch	30	52	..	..
1979-80	Stan Albeck	37	45	..	..
1980-81	Bill Musselman, 25-46				
	Don Delaney, 3-8	28	54	..	..
1981-82	Don Delaney, 4-11				
	Bob Kloppenburg, 0-3				
	Chuck Daly, 9-32				
	Bill Musselman, 2-21	15	67	..	..
1982-83	Tom Nissalke	23	59	..	..
1983-84	Tom Nissalke	28	54	..	..
1984-85	George Karl	36	46	1	3
1985-86	George Karl, 25-42				
	Gene Littles, 4-11	29	53	..	..
1986-87	Lenny Wilkens	31	51	..	..
1987-88	Lenny Wilkens	42	40	2	3
1988-89	Lenny Wilkens	57	25	2	3
1989-90	Lenny Wilkens	42	40	2	3
1990-91	Lenny Wilkens	33	49	..	..
1991-92	Lenny Wilkens	57	25	9	8
Totals		762	1042	23	31

CLEVELAND REBELS

Season	Coach	Reg. Sea'n W.	L.	Playoffs W.	L.
1946-47	Dutch Dehnert, 17-20				
	Roy Clifford, 13-10	30	30	1	2

DALLAS MAVERICKS

Season	Coach	Reg. Sea'n W.	L.	Playoffs W.	L.
1980-81	Dick Motta	15	67	..	..
1981-82	Dick Motta	28	54	..	..
1982-83	Dick Motta	38	44	..	..
1983-84	Dick Motta	43	39	4	6
1984-85	Dick Motta	44	38	1	3
1985-86	Dick Motta	44	38	5	5
1986-87	Dick Motta	55	27	1	3
1987-88	John MacLeod	53	29	10	7
1988-89	John MacLeod	38	44	..	..
1989-90	John MacLeod, 5-6				
	Richie Adubato, 42-29	47	35	0	3
1990-91	Richie Adubato	28	54	..	..
1991-92	Richie Adubato	22	60	..	..
Totals		455	529	21	27

DENVER NUGGETS

Season	Coach	Reg. Sea'n W.	L.	Playoffs W.	L.
1949-50	James Darden	11	51	..	..

DENVER NUGGETS

Season	Coach	Reg. Sea'n W.	L.	Playoffs W.	L.
1967-68	Bob Bass	45	33	2	3
1968-69	Bob Bass	44	34	3	4
1969-70	John McLendon, 9-19				
	Joe Belmont, 42-14	51	33	5	7
1970-71	Joe Belmont, 3-10				
	Stan Albeck, 27-44	30	54	..	..
1971-72	Alex Hannum	34	50	3	4
1972-73	Alex Hannum	47	37	1	4
1973-74	Alex Hannum	37	47	..	..
1974-75	Larry Brown	65	19	7	6
1975-76	Larry Brown	60	24	6	7
1976-77	Larry Brown	50	32	2	4
1977-78	Larry Brown	48	34	6	7
1978-79	Larry Brown, 28-25				
	Donnie Walsh, 19-10	47	35	1	2
1979-80	Donnie Walsh	30	52	..	..
1980-81	Donnie Walsh, 11-20				
	Doug Moe, 26-25	37	45	..	..
1981-82	Doug Moe	46	36	1	2
1982-83	Doug Moe	45	37	3	5
1983-84	Doug Moe	38	44	2	3
1984-85	Doug Moe	52	30	8	7
1985-86	Doug Moe	47	35	5	5
1986-87	Doug Moe	37	45	0	3
1987-88	Doug Moe	54	28	5	6
1988-89	Doug Moe	44	38	0	3
1989-90	Doug Moe	43	39	0	3
1990-91	Paul Westhead	20	62	..	..
1991-92	Paul Westhead	24	58	..	..
ABA Totals		413	331	27	35
NBA Totals		662	650	33	50

DETROIT FALCONS

Season	Coach	Reg. Sea'n W.	L.	Playoffs W.	L.
1946-47	Glenn Curtis, 12-22				
	Philip Sachs, 8-18	20	40	..	..

DETROIT PISTONS

Season	Coach	Reg. Sea'n W.	L.	Playoffs W.	L.
1948-49	Carl Bennett, 0-6				
	Paul Armstrong, 22-32	22	38	..	..
1949-50	Murray Mendenhall	40	28	2	2
1950-51	Murray Mendanhall	32	36	1	2
1951-52	Paul Birch	29	37	0	2
1952-53	Paul Birch	36	33	4	4
1953-54	Paul Birch	40	32	0	4
1954-55	Charles Eckman	43	29	6	5
1955-56	Charles Eckman	37	35	4	6
1956-57	Charles Eckman	34	38	0	2
1957-58	*Charles Eckman, 9-16				
	Red Rocha, 24-23	33	39	3	4

Season	Coach	Reg. Sea'n W	L	Playoffs W	L
1958-59	Red Rocha	28	44	1	2
1959-60	Red Rocha, 13-21	..	..	..	..
	Dick McGuire, 17-24	30	45	0	2
1960-61	Dick McGuire	34	45	2	3
1961-62	Dick McGuire	37	43	5	5
1962-63	Dick McGuire	34	46	1	3
1963-64	Charles Wolf	23	57	..	..
1964-65	Charles Wolf, 2-9	..	..	..	..
	D. DeBusschere, 29-40	31	49	..	..
1965-66	Dave DeBusschere	22	58	..	..
1966-67	D. DeBusschere, 28-45	30	51	..	..
	Donnis Butcher, 2-6				
1967-68	Donnis Butcher	40	42	2	4
1968-69	D. Butcher, 10-12	..	..	..	..
	Paul Seymour, 22-38	32	50	..	..
1969-70	Bill van Breda Kolff	31	51	..	..
1970-71	Bill van Breda Kolff	45	37	..	..
1971-72	B. van Breda Kolff, 6-4	..	..	..	..
	Terry Dischinger, 0-2	..	..	..	..
	Earl Lloyd, 20-50	26	56	..	..
1972-73	Earl Lloyd, 2-5	..	..	..	..
	Ray Scott, 38-37	40	42	..	..
1973-74	Ray Scott	52	30	3	4
1974-75	Ray Scott	40	42	1	2
1975-76	Ray Scott, 17-25	..	..	..	..
	Herb Brown, 19-21	36	46	4	5
1976-77	Herb Brown	44	38	1	2
1977-78	Herb Brown, 9-15	..	..	..	..
	Bob Kauffman, 29-29	38	44	..	..
1978-79	Dick Vitale	30	52	..	..
1979-80	Dick Vitale, 4-8	..	..	..	..
	Richie Adubato, 12-58	16	66	..	..
1980-81	Scotty Robertson	21	61	..	..
1981-82	Scotty Robertson	39	43	..	..
1982-83	Scotty Robertson	37	45	..	..
1983-84	Chuck Daly	49	33	2	3
1984-85	Chuck Daly	46	36	5	4
1985-86	Chuck Daly	46	36	1	3
1986-87	Chuck Daly	52	30	10	5
1987-88	Chuck Daly	54	28	14	9
1988-89	Chuck Daly	63	19	15	2
1989-90	Chuck Daly	59	23	15	5
1990-91	Chuck Daly	50	32	7	8
1991-92	Chuck Daly	48	34	2	3
Totals		1649	1799	111	105

*Team moved from Fort Wayne to Detroit.

GOLDEN STATE WARRIORS

Season	Coach	Reg. Sea'n W	L	Playoffs W	L
1946-47	Edward Gottlieb	35	25	8	2
1947-48	Edward Gottlieb	27	21	6	7
1948-49	Edward Gottlieb	28	32	0	2
1949-50	Edward Gottlieb	26	42	0	2
1950-51	Edward Gottlieb	40	26	0	2
1951-52	Edward Gottlieb	33	33	1	2
1952-53	Edward Gottlieb	12	57	..	..
1953-54	Edward Gottlieb	29	43	..	..
1954-55	Edward Gottlieb	33	39	..	..
1955-56	George Senesky	45	27	7	3
1956-57	George Senesky	37	35	0	2
1957-58	George Senesky	37	35	3	5
1958-59	Al Cervi	32	40	..	..
1959-60	Neil Johnston	49	26	4	5
1960-61	Neil Johnston	46	33	0	3
1961-62	Frank McGuire	49	31	6	6
1962-63	*Bob Feerick	31	49	..	..
1963-64	Alex Hannum	48	32	5	7
1964-65	Alex Hannum	17	63	..	..
1965-66	Alex Hannum	35	45	..	..
1966-67	Bill Sharman	44	37	9	6
1967-68	Bill Sharman	43	39	4	6
1968-69	George Lee	41	41	2	4
1969-70	George Lee, 22-30	..	..	..	..
	Al Attles, 8-22	30	52	..	..
1970-71	Al Attles	41	41	1	4
1971-72	†Al Attles	51	31	1	4
1972-73	Al Attles	47	35	5	6
1973-74	Al Attles	44	38	..	..
1974-75	Al Attles	48	34	12	5
1975-76	Al Attles	59	23	7	6
1976-77	Al Attles	46	36	5	5
1977-78	Al Attles	43	39	..	..
1978-79	Al Attles	38	44	..	..
1979-80	Al Attles, 18-43	..	..	..	..
	John Bach, 6-15	24	58	..	..
1980-81	Al Attles	39	43	..	..
1981-82	Al Attles	45	37	..	..
1982-83	Al Attles	30	52	..	..
1983-84	John Bach	37	45	..	..
1984-85	John Bach	22	60	..	..
1985-86	John Bach	30	52	..	..
1986-87	George Karl	42	40	4	6
1987-88	George Karl, 16-48	..	..	..	..
	Ed Gregory, 4-14	20	62	..	..
1988-89	Don Nelson	43	39	4	4
1989-90	Don Nelson	37	45	..	..
1990-91	Don Nelson	44	38	4	5
1991-92	Don Nelson	55	27	1	3
Totals		1732	1822	99	112

*Team moved from Philadelphia to San Francisco.
†Team moved from San Francisco to Golden State (Oakland).

HOUSTON ROCKETS

Season	Coach	Reg. Sea'n W	L	Playoffs W	L
1967-68	Jack McMahon	15	67	..	..
1968-69	Jack McMahon	37	45	2	4
1969-70	Jack McMahon, 9-17	..	..	..	..
	Alex Hannum, 18-38	27	55	..	..
1970-71	Alex Hannum	40	42	..	..
1971-72	*Tex Winter	34	48	..	..
1972-73	Tex Winter, 17-30	..	..	..	..
	John Egan, 16-19	33	•49	..	..
1973-74	John Egan	32	50	..	..
1974-75	John Egan	41	41	3	5
1975-76	John Egan	40	42	..	..
1976-77	Tom Nissalke	49	33	6	6
1977-78	Tom Nissalke	28	54	..	..
1978-79	Tom Nissalke	47	35	0	2
1979-80	Del Harris	41	41	2	5
1980-81	Del Harris	40	42	12	9
1981-82	Del Harris	46	36	1	2
1982-83	Del Harris	14	68	..	..
1983-84	Bill Fitch	29	53	..	..
1984-85	Bill Fitch	48	34	2	3
1985-86	Bill Fitch	51	31	13	7
1986-87	Bill Fitch	42	40	5	5
1987-88	Bill Fitch	46	36	1	3
1988-89	Don Chaney	45	37	1	3
1989-90	Don Chaney	41	41	1	3
1990-91	Don Chaney	52	30	0	3
1991-92	Don Chaney, 26-26	..	..	..	..
	Rudy Tomjanovich, 16-14	42	40	..	..
Totals		960	1090	49	60

*Team moved from San Diego to Houston.

INDIANA PACERS

Season	Coach	Reg. Sea'n W	L	Playoffs W	L
1967-68	Larry Staverman	38	40	0	3
1968-69	Larry Staverman, 2-7	..	..	..	..
	Bob Leonard, 42-27	44	34	9	8
1969-70	Bob Leonard	59	25	12	3
1970-71	Bob Leonard	58	26	7	4
1971-72	Bob Leonard	47	37	12	8
1972-73	Bob Leonard	51	33	12	6
1973-74	Bob Leonard	46	38	7	7
1974-75	Bob Leonard	45	39	9	9
1975-76	Bob Leonard	39	45	1	2
1976-77	Bob Leonard	36	46	..	..
1977-78	Bob Leonard	31	51	..	..
1978-79	Bob Leonard	38	44	..	..
1979-80	Bob Leonard	37	45	..	..
1980-81	Jack McKinney	44	38	0	2
1981-82	Jack McKinney	35	47	..	..

Season	Coach	Reg. Sea'n W.	L.	Playoffs W.	L.
1982-83	Jack McKinney	20	62	..	..
1983-84	Jack McKinney	26	56	..	..
1984-85	George Irvine	22	60	..	..
1985-86	George Irvine	26	56	..	..
1986-87	Jack Ramsay	41	41	1	3
1987-88	Jack Ramsay	38	44	..	..
1988-89	Jack Ramsay, 0-7	..	..	..	..
	Mel Daniels, 0-2	..	..	..	..
	George Irvine, 6-14	..	..	..	..
	Dick Versace, 22-31	28	54	..	..
1989-90	Dick Versace	42	40	0	3
1990-91	Dick Versace, 9-16	..	..	..	..
	Bob Hill, 32-25	41	41	2	3
1991-92	Bob Hill	40	42	0	3
ABA Totals		427	317	69	50
NBA Totals		545	767	3	14

INDIANAPOLIS JETS

Season	Coach	Reg. Sea'n W.	L.	Playoffs W.	L.
1948-49	Bruce Hale, 4-13	..	..	..	..
	Burl Friddle, 14-29	18	42	..	..

INDIANAPOLIS OLYMPIANS

Season	Coach	Reg. Sea'n W.	L.	Playoffs W.	L.
1949-50	Clifford Barker	39	25	3	3
1950-51	Clifford Barker	24	32	..	..
	Wallace Jones	7	5	1	2
1951-52	Herman Schaefer	34	32	0	2
1952-53	Herman Schaefer	28	43	0	2
Totals		132	137	4	9

LOS ANGELES CLIPPERS

Season	Coach	Reg. Sea'n W.	L.	Playoffs W.	L.
1970-71	Dolph Schayes	22	60	..	..
1971-72	Dolph Schayes, 0-1	..	..	..	..
	John McCarthy, 22-59	22	60	..	..
1972-73	Jack Ramsay	21	61	..	..
1973-74	Jack Ramsay	42	40	2	4
1974-75	Jack Ramsay	49	33	3	4
1975-76	Jack Ramsay	46	36	4	5
1976-77	Tates Locke, 16-30	..	..	..	..
	Bob MacKinnon, 3-4	..	..	..	..
	Joe Mullaney, 11-18	30	52	..	..
1977-78	Cotton Fitzsimmons	27	55	..	..
1978-79*	Gene Shue	43	39	..	..
1979-80	Gene Shue	35	47	..	..
1980-81	Paul Silas	36	46	..	..
1981-82	Paul Silas	17	65	..	..
1982-83	Paul Silas	25	57	..	..
1983-84	Jim Lynam	30	52	..	..
1984-85†	Jim Lynam, 22-39	..	..	..	..
	Don Chaney, 9-12	31	51	..	..
1985-86	Don Chaney	32	50	..	..
1986-87	Don Chaney	12	70	..	..
1987-88	Gene Shue	17	65	..	..
1988-89	Gene Shue, 10-28	..	..	..	..
	Don Casey, 11-33	21	61	..	..
1989-90	Don Casey	30	52	..	..
1990-91	Mike Schuler	31	51	..	..
1991-92	Mike Schuler, 21-24	..	..	..	..
	Mack Calvin, 1-1	..	..	..	..
	Larry Brown, 23-12	45	37	2	3
Totals		664	1140	11	16

*Team moved from Buffalo to San Diego.
†Team moved from San Diego to Los Angeles.

LOS ANGELES LAKERS

Season	Coach	Reg. Sea'n W.	L.	Playoffs W.	L.
1948-49	John Kundla	44	16	8	2
1949-50	John Kundla	51	17	10	2
1950-51	John Kundla	44	24	3	4
1951-52	John Kundla	40	26	9	4
1952-53	John Kundla	48	22	9	3
1953-54	John Kundla	46	26	9	4
1954-55	John Kundla	40	32	3	4
1955-56	John Kundla	33	39	1	2
1956-57	John Kundla	34	38	2	3
1957-58	George Mikan, 9-30	..	..	..	..
	John Kundla, 10-23	19	53	..	..
1958-59	John Kundla	33	39	6	7
1959-60	John Castellani, 11-25	..	..	..	..
	Jim Pollard, 14-25	25	50	5	4
1960-61*	Fred Schaus	36	43	6	6
1961-62	Fred Schaus	54	26	7	6
1962-63	Fred Schaus	53	27	6	7
1963-64	Fred Schaus	42	38	2	3
1964-65	Fred Schaus	49	31	5	6
1965-66	Fred Schaus	45	35	7	7
1966-67	Fred Schaus	36	45	0	3
1967-68	Bill van Breda Kolff	52	30	10	5
1968-69	Bill van Breda Kolff	55	27	11	7
1969-70	Joe Mullaney	46	36	11	7
1970-71	Joe Mullaney	48	34	5	7
1971-72	Bill Sharman	69	13	12	3
1972-73	Bill Sharman	60	22	9	8
1973-74	Bill Sharman	47	35	1	4
1974-75	Bill Sharman	30	52	..	..
1975-76	Bill Sharman	40	42	..	..
1976-77	Jerry West	53	29	4	7
1977-78	Jerry West	45	37	1	2
1978-79	Jerry West	47	35	3	5
1979-80	Jack McKinney, 10-4	..	..	..	..
	Paul Westhead, 50-18	60	22	12	4
1980-81	Paul Westhead	54	28	1	2
1981-82	Paul Westhead, 7-4	..	..	..	..
	Pat Riley, 50-21	57	25	12	2
1982-83	Pat Riley	58	24	8	7
1983-84	Pat Riley	54	28	14	7
1984-85	Pat Riley	62	20	15	4
1985-86	Pat Riley	62	20	8	6
1986-87	Pat Riley	65	17	15	3
1987-88	Pat Riley	62	20	15	9
1988-89	Pat Riley	57	25	11	4
1989-90	Pat Riley	63	19	4	5
1990-91	Mike Dunleavy	58	24	12	7
1991-92	Mike Dunleavy	43	39	1	3
Totals		2119	1330	293	195

*Team moved from Minneapolis to Los Angeles.

MIAMI HEAT

Season	Coach	Reg. Sea'n W.	L.	Playoffs W.	L.
1988-89	Ron Rothstein	15	67	..	..
1989-90	Ron Rothstein	18	64	..	..
1990-91	Ron Rothstein	24	58	..	..
1991-92	Kevin Loughery	38	44	0	3
Totals		95	233	0	3

MILWAUKEE BUCKS

Season	Coach	Reg. Sea'n W.	L.	Playoffs W.	L.
1968-69	Larry Costello	27	55	..	..
1969-70	Larry Costello	56	26	5	5
1970-71	Larry Costello	66	16	12	2
1971-72	Larry Costello	63	19	6	5
1972-73	Larry Costello	60	22	2	4
1973-74	Larry Costello	59	23	11	5
1974-75	Larry Costello	38	44	..	..
1975-76	Larry Costello	38	44	1	2
1976-77	Larry Costello, 3-15	..	..	..	..
	Don Nelson, 27-37	30	52	..	..
1977-78	Don Nelson	44	38	5	4
1978-79	Don Nelson	38	44	..	..
1979-80	Don Nelson	49	33	3	4
1980-81	Don Nelson	60	22	3	4
1981-82	Don Nelson	55	27	2	4
1982-83	Don Nelson	51	31	5	4
1983-84	Don Nelson	50	32	8	8
1984-85	Don Nelson	59	23	3	5
1985-86	Don Nelson	57	25	7	7

Season	Coach	Reg. W.	Sea'n L.	Playoffs W.	L.
1986-87	Don Nelson	50	32	6	6
1987-88	Del Harris	42	40	2	3
1988-89	Del Harris	49	33	3	6
1989-90	Del Harris	44	38	1	3
1990-91	Del Harris	48	34	0	3
1991-92	Del Harris, 8-9	..	..		
	Frank Hamblen, 23-42	31	51	..	..
Totals		1164	804	85	84

MINNESOTA TIMBERWOLVES

Season	Coach	Reg. W.	Sea'n L.	Playoffs W.	L.
1989-90	Bill Musselman	22	60	..	..
1990-91	Bill Musselman	29	53	..	..
1991-92	Jimmy Rodgers	15	67	..	..
Totals		66	180	..	..

NEW JERSEY NETS

Season	Coach	Reg. W.	Sea'n L.	Playoffs W.	L.
1967-68	Max Zaslofsky	36	42	..	..
1968-69	Max Zaslofsky	17	61	..	..
1969-70	York Larese	39	45	3	4
1970-71	Lou Carnesecca	40	44	2	4
1971-72	Lou Carnesecca	44	40	10	9
1972-73	Lou Carnesecca	30	54	1	4
1973-74	Kevin Loughery	55	29	12	2
1974-75	Kevin Loughery	58	26	1	4
1975-76	Kevin Loughery	55	29	8	5
1976-77	Kevin Loughery	22	60	..	..
1977-78	*Kevin Loughery	24	58	..	..
1978-79	Kevin Loughery	37	45	0	2
1979-80	Kevin Loughery	34	48	..	..
1980-81	Kevin Loughery, 12-23	..	..	..	..
	Bob MacKinnon, 12-35	24	58	..	..
1981-82	Larry Brown	44	38	0	2
1982-83	Larry Brown, 47-29	..	..	..	..
	Bill Blair, 2-4	49	33	0	2
1983-84	Stan Albeck	45	37	5	6
1984-85	Stan Albeck	42	40	0	3
1985-86	Dave Wohl	39	43	0	3
1986-87	Dave Wohl	24	58	..	..
1987-88	Dave Wohl, 2-13	..	..	..	..
	Bob MacKinnon, 10-29	..	..	..	..
	Willis Reed, 7-21	19	63	..	..
1988-89	Willis Reed	26	56	..	..
1989-90	Bill Fitch	17	65	..	..
1990-91	Bill Fitch	26	56	..	..
1991-92	Bill Fitch	40	42	1	3
ABA Totals		374	370	37	32
NBA Totals		512	800	6	21

*Team moved from New York to New Jersey.

NEW YORK KNICKERBOCKERS

Season	Coach	Reg. W.	Sea'n L.	Playoffs W.	L.
1946-47	Neil Cohalan	33	27	2	3
1947-48	Joe Lapchick	26	22	1	2
1948-49	Joe Lapchick	32	28	3	3
1949-50	Joe Lapchick	40	28	3	2
1950-51	Joe Lapchick	36	30	8	6
1951-52	Joe Lapchick	37	29	8	6
1952-53	Joe Lapchick	47	23	6	5
1953-54	Joe Lapchick	44	28	0	4
1954-55	Joe Lapchick	38	34	1	2
1955-56	Joe Lapchick, 26-25	..	..	..	..
	Vince Boryla, 9-12	35	37	..	..
1956-57	Vince Boryla	36	36	..	..
1957-58	Vince Boryla	35	37	..	..
1958-59	Andrew Levane	40	32	0	2
1959-60	Andrew Levane, 8-19	..	..	..	..
	Carl Braun, 19-29	27	48	..	..
1960-61	Carl Braun	21	58	..	..
1961-62	Eddie Donovan	29	51	..	..
1962-63	Eddie Donovan	21	59	..	..
1963-64	Eddie Donovan	22	58	..	..

Season	Coach	Reg. W.	Sea'n L.	Playoffs W.	L.
1964-65	Eddie Donovan, 12-26	..	..	..	..
	Harry Gallatin, 19-23	31	49	..	..
1965-66	Harry Gallatin, 6-15	..	..	..	..
	Dick McGuire, 24-35	30	50	..	..
1966-67	Dick McGuire	36	45	1	3
1967-68	Dick McGuire, 15-22	..	..	..	..
	Red Holzman, 28-17	43	39	2	4
1968-69	Red Holzman	54	28	6	4
1969-70	Red Holzman	60	22	12	7
1970-71	Red Holzman	52	30	7	5
1971-72	Red Holzman	48	34	9	7
1972-73	Red Holzman	57	25	12	5
1973-74	Red Holzman	49	33	5	7
1974-75	Red Holzman	40	42	1	2
1975-76	Red Holzman	38	44	..	..
1976-77	Red Holzman	40	42	..	..
1977-78	Willis Reed	43	39	2	4
1978-79	Willis Reed, 6-8	..	..	..	..
	Red Holzman, 25-43	31	51	..	..
1979-80	Red Holzman	39	43	..	..
1980-81	Red Holzman	50	32	0	2
1981-82	Red Holzman	33	49	..	..
1982-83	Hubie Brown	44	38	2	4
1983-84	Hubie Brown	47	35	6	6
1984-85	Hubie Brown	24	58	..	..
1985-86	Hubie Brown	23	59	..	..
1986-87	Hubie Brown, 4-12	..	..	..	..
	Bob Hill, 20-46	24	58	..	..
1987-88	Rick Pitino	38	44	1	3
1988-89	Rick Pitino	52	30	5	4
1989-90	Stu Jackson	45	37	4	6
1990-91	Stu Jackson, 7-8	..	..	..	..
	John MacLeod, 32-35	39	43	0	3
1991-92	Pat Riley	51	31	6	6
Totals		1760	1795	113	117

ORLANDO MAGIC

Season	Coach	Reg. W.	Sea'n L.	Playoffs W.	L.
1989-90	Matt Guokas	18	64	..	..
1990-91	Matt Guokas	31	51	..	..
1991-92	Matt Guokas	21	61	..	..
Totals		70	176	..	..

PHILADELPHIA 76ERS

Season	Coach	Reg. W.	Sea'n L.	Playoffs W.	L.
1949-50	Al Cervi	51	13	6	5
1950-51	Al Cervi	32	34	4	3
1951-52	Al Cervi	40	26	3	4
1952-53	Al Cervi	47	24	0	2
1953-54	Al Cervi	42	30	9	4
1954-55	Al Cervi	43	29	7	4
1955-56	Al Cervi	35	37	4	4
1956-57	Al Cervi, 4-8	..	..	..	..
	Paul Seymour, 34-26	38	34	2	3
1957-58	Paul Seymour	41	31	1	2
1958-59	Paul Seymour	35	37	5	4
1959-60	Paul Seymour	45	30	1	2
1960-61	Alex Hannum	38	41	4	4
1961-62	Alex Hannum	41	39	2	3
1962-63	Alex Hannum	48	32	2	3
1963-64	*Dolph Schayes	34	46	2	3
1964-65	Dolph Schayes	40	40	6	5
1965-66	Dolph Schayes	55	25	1	4
1966-67	Alex Hannum	68	13	11	4
1967-68	Alex Hannum	62	20	7	6
1968-69	Jack Ramsay	55	27	1	4
1969-70	Jack Ramsay	42	40	1	4
1970-71	Jack Ramsay	47	35	3	4
1971-72	Jack Ramsay	30	52	..	..
1972-73	Roy Rubin, 4-47	..	..	..	..
	Kevin Loughery, 5-26	9	73	..	..
1973-74	Gene Shue	25	57	..	..
1974-75	Gene Shue	34	48	..	..
1975-76	Gene Shue	46	36	1	2
1976-77	Gene Shue	50	32	10	9

Season	Coach	Reg. Sea'n W.	L.	Playoffs W.	L.
1977-78	Gene Shue, 2-4	..	..	..	..
	Billy Cunningham, 53-23	55	27	6	4
1978-79	Billy Cunningham	47	35	5	4
1979-80	Billy Cunningham	59	23	12	6
1980-81	Billy Cunningham	62	20	9	7
1981-82	Billy Cunningham	58	24	12	9
1982-83	Billy Cunningham	65	17	12	1
1983-84	Billy Cunningham	52	30	2	3
1984-85	Billy Cunningham	58	24	8	5
1985-86	Matt Guokas	54	28	6	6
1986-87	Matt Guokas	45	37	2	3
1987-88	Matt Guokas, 20-23	..	..	..	..
	Jim Lynam, 16-23	36	46	..	..
1988-89	Jim Lynam	46	36	0	3
1989-90	Jim Lynam	53	29	4	6
1990-91	Jim Lynam	44	38	4	4
1991-92	Jim Lynam	35	47	..	..
Totals		1942	1442	175	153

*Team moved from Syracuse to Philadelphia.

PHOENIX SUNS

Season	Coach	Reg. Sea'n W.	L.	Playoffs W.	L.
1968-69	Johnny Kerr	16	66	..	..
1969-70	Johnny Kerr, 15-23	..	..	..	..
	Jerry Colangelo, 24-20	39	43	3	4
1970-71	Cotton Fitzsimmons	48	34	..	..
1971-72	Cotton Fitzsimmons	49	33	..	..
1972-73	B. van Breda Kolff, 3-4	..	..	..	..
	Jerry Colangelo, 35-40	38	44	..	..
1973-74	John MacLeod	30	52	..	..
1974-75	John MacLeod	32	50	..	..
1975-76	John MacLeod	42	40	10	9
1976-77	John MacLeod	34	48	..	..
1977-78	John MacLeod	49	33	0	2
1978-79	John MacLeod	50	32	9	6
1979-80	John MacLeod	55	27	3	5
1980-81	John MacLeod	57	25	3	4
1981-82	John MacLeod	46	36	2	5
1982-83	John MacLeod	53	29	1	2
1983-84	John MacLeod	41	41	9	8
1984-85	John MacLeod	36	46	0	3
1985-86	John MacLeod	32	50	..	..
1986-87	John MacLeod, 22-34	..	..	..	..
	Dick Van Arsdale, 14-12	36	46	..	..
1987-88	John Wetzel	28	54	..	..
1988-89	Cotton Fitzsimmons	55	27	7	5
1989-90	Cotton Fitzsimmons	54	28	9	7
1990-91	Cotton Fitzsimmons	55	27	1	3
1991-92	Cotton Fitzsimmons	53	29	4	4
Totals		1028	940	61	67

PITTSBURGH IRONMEN

Season	Coach	Reg. Sea'n W.	L.	Playoffs W.	L.
1946-47	Paul Birch	15	45	..	..

PORTLAND TRAIL BLAZERS

Season	Coach	Reg. Sea'n W.	L.	Playoffs W.	L.
1970-71	Rolland Todd	29	53	..	..
1971-72	Rolland Todd, 12-44	..	..	..	..
	Stu Inman, 6-20	18	64	..	..
1972-73	Jack McCloskey	21	61	..	..
1973-74	Jack McCloskey	27	55	..	..
1974-75	Lenny Wilkens	38	44	..	..
1975-76	Lenny Wilkens	37	45	..	..
1976-77	Jack Ramsay	49	33	14	5
1977-78	Jack Ramsay	58	24	2	4
1978-79	Jack Ramsay	45	37	1	2
1979-80	Jack Ramsay	38	44	1	2
1980-81	Jack Ramsay	45	37	1	2
1981-82	Jack Ramsay	42	40	..	..
1982-83	Jack Ramsay	46	36	3	4
1983-84	Jack Ramsay	48	34	2	3
1984-85	Jack Ramsay	42	40	4	5
1985-86	Jack Ramsay	40	42	1	3
1986-87	Mike Schuler	49	33	1	3
1987-88	Mike Schuler	53	29	1	3
1988-89	Mike Schuler, 25-22	..	..	..	..
	Rick Adelman, 14-21	39	43	0	3
1989-90	Rick Adelman	59	23	12	9
1990-91	Rick Adelman	63	19	9	7
1991-92	Rick Adelman	57	25	13	8
Totals		943	861	65	63

PROVIDENCE STEAMROLLERS

Season	Coach	Reg. Sea'n W.	L.	Playoffs W.	L.
1946-47	Robert Morris	28	32	..	..
1947-48	Albert Soar, 2-17	..	..	..	..
	Nat Hickey, 4-25	6	42	..	..
1948-49	Ken Loeffler	12	48	..	..
Totals		46	122	..	..

SACRAMENTO KINGS

Season	Coach	Reg. Sea'n W.	L.	Playoffs W.	L.
1948-49	Les Harrison	45	15	2	2
1949-50	Les Harrison	51	17	0	2
1950-51	Les Harrison	41	27	9	5
1951-52	Les Harrison	41	25	3	3
1952-53	Les Harrison	44	26	1	2
1953-54	Les Harrison	44	28	3	3
1954-55	Les Harrison	29	43	1	2
1955-56	Bob Wanzer	31	41	..	..
1956-57	Bob Wanzer	31	41	..	..
1957-58*	Bob Wanzer	33	39	0	2
1958-59	Bob Wanzer, 3-15	..	..	..	..
	Tom Marshall, 16-38	19	53	..	..
1959-60	Tom Marshall	19	56	..	..
1960-61	Charles Wolf	33	46	..	..
1961-62	Charles Wolf	43	37	1	3
1962-63	Charles Wolf	42	38	6	6
1963-64	Jack McMahon	55	25	4	6
1964-65	Jack McMahon	48	32	1	3
1965-66	Jack McMahon	45	35	2	3
1966-67	Jack McMahon	39	42	1	3
1967-68	Ed Jucker	39	43	..	..
1968-69	Ed Jucker	41	41	..	..
1969-70	Bob Cousy	36	46	..	..
1970-71	Bob Cousy	33	49	..	..
1971-72	Bob Cousy	30	52	..	..
1972-73†	Bob Cousy	36	46	..	..
1973-74	Bob Cousy, 6-16	..	..	..	..
	Draff Young, 0-3	..	..	..	..
	Phil Johnson, 27-30	33	49	..	..
1974-75	Phil Johnson	44	38	2	4
1975-76‡	Phil Johnson	31	51	..	..
1976-77	Phil Johnson	40	42	..	..
1977-78	Phil Johnson, 13-24	..	..	..	..
	Larry Staverman, 18-27	31	51	..	..
1978-79	Cotton Fitzsimmons	48	34	1	4
1979-80	Cotton Fitzsimmons	47	35	1	2
1980-81	Cotton Fitzsimmons	40	42	7	8
1981-82	Cotton Fitzsimmons	30	52	..	..
1982-83	Cotton Fitzsimmons	45	37	..	..
1983-84	Cotton Fitzsimmons	38	44	0	3
1984-85	Jack McKinney, 1-8	..	..	..	..
	Phil Johnson, 30-43	31	51	..	..
1985-86§	Phil Johnson	37	45	0	3
1986-87	Phil Johnson, 14-32	..	..	..	..
	Jerry Reynolds, 15-21	29	53	..	..
1987-88	Bill Russell, 17-41	..	..	..	..
	Jerry Reynolds, 7-17	24	58	..	..
1988-89	Jerry Reynolds	27	55	..	..
1989-90	Jerry Reynolds, 7-21	..	..	..	..
	Dick Motta, 16-38	23	59	..	..
1990-91	Dick Motta	25	57	..	..
1991-92	Dick Motta, 7-18	..	..	..	..
	Rex Hughes, 22-35	29	53	..	..
Totals		1600	1849	45	69

*Team moved from Rochester to Cincinnati.
†Team moved from Cincinnati to Kansas City-Omaha.
‡Team moved from Kansas City-Omaha to Kansas City.
§Team moved from Kansas City to Sacramento.

ST. LOUIS BOMBERS

Season	Coach	Reg. W.	Sea'n L.	Playoffs W.	L.
1946-47	Ken Loeffler	38	23	1	2
1947-48	Ken Loeffler	29	19	3	4
1948-49	Grady Lewis	29	31	0	2
1949-50	Grady Lewis	26	42	..	..
Totals		122	115	4	8

SAN ANTONIO SPURS

Season	Coach	Reg. W.	Sea'n L.	Playoffs W.	L.
1967-68	Cliff Hagan	46	32	4	4
1968-69	Cliff Hagan	41	37	3	4
1969-70	Cliff Hagan, 22-21	..	..	..	..
	Max Williams, 23-18	45	39	2	4
1970-71	Max Williams, 5-14	..	..	..	..
	Bill Blakely, 25-40	30	54	0	4
1971-72	Tom Nissalke	42	42	0	4
1972-73	Babe McCarthy, 24-48	..	..	..	..
	Dave Brown, 4-8	28	56	..	..
1973-74	Tom Nissalke	45	39	3	4
1974-75	Tom Nissalke, 17-10	..	..	..	..
	Bob Bass, 34-23	51	33	2	4
1975-76	Bob Bass	50	34	3	4
1976-77	Doug Moe	44	38	0	2
1977-78	Doug Moe	52	30	2	4
1978-79	Doug Moe	48	34	7	7
1979-80	Doug Moe, 33-33	..	..	..	..
	Bob Bass, 8-8	41	41	1	2
1980-81	Stan Albeck	52	30	3	4
1981-82	Stan Albeck	48	34	4	5
1982-83	Stan Albeck	53	29	6	5
1983-84	Morris McHone, 11-20	..	..	..	..
	Bob Bass, 26-25	37	45	..	..
1984-85	Cotton Fitzsimmons	41	41	2	3
1985-86	Cotton Fitzsimmons	35	47	0	3
1986-87	Bob Weiss	28	54	..	..
1987-88	Bob Weiss	31	51	0	3
1988-89	Larry Brown	21	61	..	..
1989-90	Larry Brown	56	26	6	4
1990-91	Larry Brown	55	27	1	3
1991-92	Larry Brown, 21-17	..	..	..	..
	Bob Bass, 26-18	47	35	0	3
ABA Totals		378	366	17	32
NBA Totals		689	623	32	48

SEATTLE SUPERSONICS

Season	Coach	Reg. W.	Sea'n L.	Playoffs W.	L.
1967-68	Al Bianchi	23	59	..	..
1968-69	Al Bianchi	30	52	..	..
1969-70	Lenny Wilkens	36	46	..	..
1970-71	Lenny Wilkens	38	44	..	..
1971-72	Lenny Wilkens	47	35	..	..
1972-73	Tom Nissalke, 13-32	..	..	..	..
	Bucky Buckwalter, 13-24	26	56	..	..
1973-74	Bill Russell	36	46	..	..
1974-75	Bill Russell	43	39	4	5
1975-76	Bill Russell	43	39	2	4
1976-77	Bill Russell	40	42	..	..
1977-78	Bob Hopkins, 5-17	..	..	..	..
	Lenny Wilkens, 42-18	47	35	13	9
1978-79	Lenny Wilkens	52	30	12	5
1979-80	Lenny Wilkens	56	26	7	8
1980-81	Lenny Wilkens	34	48	..	..
1981-82	Lenny Wilkens	52	30	3	5
1982-83	Lenny Wilkens	48	34	0	2
1983-84	Lenny Wilkens	42	40	2	3
1984-85	Lenny Wilkens	31	51	..	..
1985-86	Bernie Bickerstaff	31	51	..	..
1986-87	Bernie Bickerstaff	39	43	7	7
1987-88	Bernie Bickerstaff	44	38	2	3
1988-89	Bernie Bickerstaff, 46-30	47	35	3	5
	☆Tom Newell, 0-1	..	..	..	..
	☆Bob Kloppenburg, 1-4	..	..	..	..
1989-90	Bernie Bickerstaff	41	41	..	..
1990-91	K.C. Jones	41	41	2	3
1991-92	K.C. Jones, 18-18	..	..	..	..
	Bob Kloppenburg, 2-2	..	..	..	..
	George Karl, 27-15	47	35	4	5
Totals		1014	1036	61	64

☆Substituted during Bickerstaff's illness

SHEBOYGAN REDSKINS

Season	Coach	Reg. W.	Sea'n L.	Playoffs W.	L.
1949-50	Ken Suesens	22	40	1	2

TORONTO HUSKIES

Season	Coach	Reg. W.	Sea'n L.	Playoffs W.	L.
1946-47	Ed Sadowski, 3-9	..	..	..	..
	Lew Hayman, 0-1	..	..	..	..
	Dick Fitzgerald, 2-1	..	..	..	..
	Robert Rolfe, 17-27	22	38	..	..

UTAH JAZZ

Season	Coach	Reg. W.	Sea'n L.	Playoffs W.	L.
1974-75	Scotty Robertson, 1-14	..	..	..	..
	Elgin Baylor, 0-1	..	..	..	..
	Bill van Breda Kolff, 22-44	23	59	..	..
1975-76	Bill van Breda Kolff	38	44	..	..
1976-77	Bill van Breda Kolff, 14-12	..	..	..	..
	Elgin Baylor, 21-35	35	47	..	..
1977-78	Elgin Baylor	39	43	..	..
1978-79	Elgin Baylor	26	56	..	..
1979-80	☆Tom Nissalke	24	58	..	..
1980-81	Tom Nissalke	28	54	..	..
1981-82	Tom Nissalke, 8-12	..	..	..	..
	Frank Layden, 17-45	25	57	..	..
1982-83	Frank Layden	30	52	..	..
1983-84	Frank Layden	45	37	5	6
1984-85	Frank Layden	41	41	4	6
1985-86	Frank Layden	42	40	1	3
1986-87	Frank Layden	44	38	2	3
1987-88	Frank Layden	47	35	6	5
1988-89	Frank Layden, 11-6	..	..	..	..
	Jerry Sloan, 40-25	51	31	0	3
1989-90	Jerry Sloan	55	27	2	3
1990-91	Jerry Sloan	54	28	4	5
1991-92	Jerry Sloan	55	27	9	7
Totals		702	774	33	41

☆Team moved from New Orleans to Utah.

WASHINGTON BULLETS

Season	Coach	Reg. W.	Sea'n L.	Playoffs W.	L.
1961-62	☆Jim Pollard	18	62	..	..
1962-63	†Jack McMahon, 12-26	..	..	..	..
	Bob Leonard, 13-29	25	55	..	..
1963-64	‡Bob Leonard	31	49	..	..
1964-65	Buddy Jeannette	37	43	5	5
1965-66	Paul Seymour	38	42	0	3
1966-67	Mike Farmer, 1-8	..	..	..	..
	Buddy Jeannette, 3-13	..	..	..	..
	Gene Shue, 16-40	20	61	..	..
1967-68	Gene Shue	36	46	..	..
1968-69	Gene Shue	57	25	0	4
1969-70	Gene Shue	50	32	3	4
1970-71	Gene Shue	42	40	8	10
1971-72	Gene Shue	38	44	2	4
1972-73	Gene Shue	52	30	1	4
1973-74	§K.C. Jones	47	35	3	4
1974-75	★K.C. Jones	60	22	8	9
1975-76	K.C. Jones	48	34	3	4
1976-77	Dick Motta	48	34	4	5
1977-78	Dick Motta	44	38	14	7
1978-79	Dick Motta	54	28	9	10
1979-80	Dick Motta	39	43	0	2
1980-81	Gene Shue	39	43	..	..
1981-82	Gene Shue	43	39	3	4
1982-83	Gene Shue	42	40	..	..
1983-84	Gene Shue	35	47	1	3

Season	Coach	Reg. W.	L.	Sea'n W.	L.
1984-85	Gene Shue	40	42	1	3
1985-86	Gene Shue, 32-37	..	..	..	..
	Kevin Loughery, 7-6	39	43	2	3
1986-87	Kevin Loughery	42	40	0	3
1987-88	Kevin Loughery, 8-19	..	..	..	..
	Wes Unseld, 30-25	38	44	2	3
1988-89	Wes Unseld	40	42	..	..
1989-90	Wes Unseld	31	51	..	..
1990-91	Wes Unseld	30	52	..	..
1991-92	Wes Unseld	25	57	..	..
Totals		1228	1303	69	94

*Known as Chicago Packers.
†Name changed to Chicago Zephyrs.
‡Moved from Chicago to Baltimore and known as Baltimore Bullets.
§Moved from Baltimore to Washington and known as Capital Bullets.
*Name changed to Washington Bullets.

WASHINGTON CAPITOLS

Season	Coach	Reg. W.	L.	Sea'n W.	L.
1946-47	Red Auerbach	49	11	2	4
1947-48	Red Auerbach	28	20	..	..
1948-49	Red Auerbach	38	22	6	5
1949-50	Robert Feerick	32	36	0	2
1950-51	*Horace McKinney	10	25	..	..
Totals		157	114	8	11

*Team disbanded January 9.

WATERLOO HAWKS

Season	Coach	Reg. W.	L.	Sea'n W.	L.
1949-50	Charles Shipp	8	27	..	..
	Jack Smiley	11	16	..	..
Totals		19	43	..	..

ALL-TIME WINNINGEST NBA COACHES

Coach	W-L	Pct.
Red Auerbach	938-479	.662
Jack Ramsay	864-783	.525
DICK MOTTA	856-863	.498
BILL FITCH	845-877	.491
LENNY WILKENS	815-721	.531
COTTON FITZSIMMONS	805-745	.519
Gene Shue	784-861	.477
DON NELSON	719-493	.593
John MacLeod	707-657	.518
Red Holzman	696-604	.535
Doug Moe	609-492	.553
PAT RILEY	584-225	.722
Alvin Attles	557-518	.518
K.C. JONES	522-252	.674
CHUCK DALY	476-303	.611
Alex Hannum	471-412	.533
Billy Cunningham	454-196	.698
Larry Costello	430-300	.589
Tom Heinsohn	427-263	.619
John Kundla	423-302	.583
LARRY BROWN	393-301	.566
KEVIN LOUGHERY	379-547	.409
Hubie Brown	341-410	.454
Bill Russell	341-290	.540
Bill Sharman	333-240	.581
DEL HARRIS	332-341	.493
Richie Guerin	327-291	.529
Al Cervi	326-241	.575
Joe Lapchick	326-247	.569
Mike Fratello	324-253	.562
Fred Schaus	315-245	.563
Stan Albeck	307-267	.535
JERRY SLOAN	298-228	.567
Lester Harrison	295-181	.620
Frank Layden	277-294	.485
Paul Seymour	271-241	.529
Bill Van Breda Kolff	266-255	.511
Eddie Gottlieb	263-318	.453
Jack McMahon	260-289	.474
Tom Nissalke	248-391	.388
JIM LYNAM	246-264	.482
Phil Johnson	236-306	.435
DON CHANEY	217-266	.449
Bernie Bickerstaff	202-208	.493
Dick McGuire	197-260	.431
RICK ADELMAN	193-88	.687
MATT GUOKAS	189-264	.417
Bob Leonard	186-264	.413
PHIL JACKSON	183-63	.744
PAUL WESTHEAD	183-224	.450
MIKE SCHULER	179-159	.530
WES UNSELD	156-227	.407
Dolph Schayes	151-172	.467
Ray Scott	147-134	.523
GEORGE KARL	146-191	.433
Jerry West	145-101	.589
Charles Wolf	143-187	.433
Bob Cousy	141-209	.403
BOB WEISS	140-188	.427
Doug Collins	137-109	.557
Harry Gallatin	136-120	.531
Buddy Jeannette	136-173	.440
Jack McKinney	136-215	.387
John Egan	129-152	.459
Charles Eckman	123-118	.510
Paul Birch	120-147	.449

1991-92 head coaches in capital letters.

ALL-TIME COACHES RANKED BY GAMES

Coach	G.
BILL FITCH	1722
DICK MOTTA	1719
Jack Ramsay	1647
Gene Shue	1645
COTTON FITZSIMMONS	1550
LENNY WILKENS	1536
Red Auerbach	1417
John MacLeod	1364
Red Holzman	1300
DON NELSON	1212
Doug Moe	1101
Alvin Attles	1075
KEVIN LOUGHERY	926
Alex Hannum	883
PAT RILEY	809

1991-92 head coaches in capital letters.

ALL-TIME COACHES RANKED BY WINNING PCT.
(400 games minimum)

Coach	Pct.	W.	L.
PAT RILEY	.722	584	225
Billy Cunningham	.698	454	196
K.C. JONES	.674	522	252
Red Auerbach	.662	938	479
Lester Harrison	.620	295	181
Tom Heinsohn	.619	427	263
CHUCK DALY	.611	476	303
DON NELSON	.593	719	493
Larry Costello	.589	430	300
John Kundla	.583	423	302
Bill Sharman	.581	333	240
Al Cervi	.575	326	241
Joe Lapchick	.569	326	247
JERRY SLOAN	.567	298	228
LARRY BROWN	.566	393	301

1991-92 head coaches in capital letters.

LONGEST SINGLE-SEASON WINNING & LOSING STREAKS BY TEAM

Team	Winning Streak			Losing Streak		
Atlanta	(12)	12- 8-68 to	1- 3-69	(16)	3-11-76 to	4- 9-76
Boston	(18)	2-24-82 to	3-26-82	(10)	1- 7-49 to	1-25-49
Charlotte	(5)	2-22-92 to	3- 4-92	(12)	1-19-90 to	2-14-90
Chicago	(14)	11- 6-91 to	12- 6-91	(13)	10-29-76 to	12- 3-76
Cleveland	(11)	12-15-88 to	1- 7-89	(19)	3-19-82 to	4-18-82
		12-20-91 to	1-11-92			
Dallas	(11)	2-14-88 to	3- 4-88	(15)	1-18-81 to	2-20-81
					3- 1-92 to	3-26-92
Denver	(12)	3-10-82 to	4- 2-82	(11)	3-24-92 to	4-13-92
Detroit	(13)	1-23-90 to	2-21-90	(14)	3- 7-80 to	3-30-80
Golden State	(11)	12-29-71 to	1-22-72	(17)	*12-20-64 to	1-26-65
				(16)	12-29-84 to	1-31-85
Houston	(13)	3- 3-91 to	3-28-91	(17)	†1-18-68 to	2-16-68
				(13)	2-27-78 to	3-22-78
Indiana	(7)	1- 2-81 to	1-14-81	(12)	2-16-83 to	3-11-83
		2- 4-88 to	2-21-88		3-14-85 to	4- 3-85
					1-26-89 to	2-23-89
L.A. Clippers	(11)	‡11- 3-74 to	11-23-74	(19)	†3-11-82 to	4-13-82
	(8)	11-30-91 to	12-15-91		12-30-88 to	2- 6-89
L.A. Lakers	(33)	11- 5-71 to	1- 7-72	(11)	§1- 1-59 to	1-20-59
				(7)	2-13-92 to	2-22-92
Miami	(4)	11-13-91 to	11-19-91	(17)	11- 5-88 to	12-12-88
		3-22-92 to	3-28-92			
Milwaukee	(20)	2- 6-71 to	3- 8-71	(11)	10-25-74 to	11-16-74
					3-24-92 to	4-10-92
Minnesota	(4)	2-14-90 to	2-20-90	(16)	2-29-92 to	3-29-92
New Jersey	(11)	12-23-82 to	1-12-83	(16)	1- 5-78 to	2- 3-78
New York	(18)	10-24-69 to	11-28-69	(12)	3-23-85 to	4-13-85
Orlando	(4)	2- 2-91 to	2-12-91	(17)	12- 4-91 to	1- 7-92
		2-22-91 to	2-27-91			
		3-21-91 to	3-27-91			
Philadelphia	(14)	12-21-82 to	1-21-83	(20)	1- 9-73 to	2-11-73
Phoenix	(10)	1- 9-90 to	1-25-90	(12)	11-14-68 to	12- 3-68
					2-19-77 to	3-13-77
Portland	(16)	3-20-91 to	4-19-91	(13)	2-12-72 to	3- 4-72
Sacramento	(15)	★2-17-50 to	3-19-50	(14)	•1-16-60 to	2-10-60
	(6)	2-18-86 to	2-28-86		•12-12-71 to	1- 9-72
				(10)	12- 9-89 to	12-27-89
					3- 2-92 to	3-18-92
San Antonio	(8)	1-17-78 to	2- 2-78	(13)	2- 4-89 to	3- 2-89
		12-13-78 to	12-26-78			
		10-14-80 to	10-28-80			
		12- 8-90 to	12-21-90			
Seattle	(12)	10-29-82 to	11-19-82	(10)	12-12-68 to	12-29-68
					1-16-76 to	2- 8-76
Utah	(10)	◆1-14-78, to	2- 1-78	(18)	2-24-82 to	3-29-82
	(9)	1- 6-90 to	1-27-90			
Washington	(9)	■12- 4-68 to	12-25-68	(13)	■12-17-66 to	1- 8-67
		11-14-78 to	12- 1-78	(9)	1- 7-83 to	1-22-83
					1- 7-84 to	1-20-84
					2-19-91 to	3- 9-91

*Club located in San Francisco. ‡Club located in Buffalo. ★Club located in Rochester. ◆Club located in New Orleans.
†Club located in San Diego. §Club located in Minneapolis. •Club located in Cincinnati. ■Club located in Baltimore.

TOP TEN WINNING PERCENTAGES IN NBA HISTORY

Home

1.	.976	1986—Boston	(40- 1)
2.	.971	1950—Rochester	(33- 1)
3.	.969	1950—Syracuse	(31- 1)
4.	.968	1950—Minneapolis	(30- 1)
5.	.967	1947—Washington	(29- 1)
6.	.951	1987—Boston	(39- 2)
7.	.944	1971—Milwaukee	(34- 2)
8.	.941	1953—Syracuse	(32- 2)
9.	.933	1967—Philadelphia	(28- 2)
10.	.926	1960—Boston	(25- 2)

Road

1.	.816	1972—Los Angeles	(31- 7)
2.	.800	1973—Boston	(32- 8)
3.	.780	1975—Boston	(32- 9)
4.	.765	1967—Philadelphia	(26- 8)
5.	.756	1992—Chicago	(31-10)
6.	.732	1983—Philadelphia	(30-11)
7.	.730	1970—New York	(27-10)
8.	.719	1960—Boston	(23- 9)
9.	.718	1973—Los Angeles	(28-11)
10.	.711	1965—Boston	(27-11)

Overall

1.	.841	1972—Los Angeles	(69-13)	6.	.817	1947—Washington	(49-11)
2.	.840	1967—Philadelphia	(68-13)	7.	.805	1971—Milwaukee	(66-16)
3.	.829	1973—Boston	(68-14)	8.	.797	1950—Syracuse	(51-13)
4.	.817	1986—Boston	(67-15)	9.	.793	1987—L. A. Lakers	(65-17)
5.	.817	1992—Chicago	(67-15)	10.	.793	1983—Philadelphia	(65-17)

NBA ALL-TIME ATTENDANCE

REGULAR SEASON

61,983—January 29, 1988
   Boston at Detroit (Silverdome)
52,745—February 14, 1987
   Philadelphia at Detroit (Silverdome)
49,551—April 17, 1990
   Denver at Minnesota (Metrodome)
47,692—March 30, 1988
   Atlanta at Detroit (Silverdome)
45,458—April 13, 1990
   Orlando at Minnesota (Metrodome)

44,970—February 21, 1987
   Atlanta at Detroit (Silverdome)
44,180—February 15, 1986
   Philadelphia at Detroit (Silverdome)
43,816—February 16, 1985
   Philadelphia at Detroit (Silverdome)
43,606—March 17, 1990
   L. A. Lakers at Minnesota (Metrodome)
41,311—March 14, 1987
   Philadelphia at Detroit (Silverdome)

PLAYOFFS

41,732—June 16, 1988
   L. A. Lakers at Detroit (Silverdome)
   1988 NBA Finals, Game 5
40,172—April 15, 1980
   Milwaukee at Seattle (Kingdome)
   1980 Western Conference
   Semifinals, Game 5
39,457—May 30, 1978
   Washington at Seattle (Kingdome)
   1978 NBA Finals, Game 4

39,188—June 12, 1988
   L. A. Lakers at Detroit (Silverdome)
   1988 NBA Finals, Game 3
37,552—May 17, 1979
   Phoenix at Seattle (Kingdome)
   1979 Western Conference Finals, Game 7

ALL-STAR GAMES

44,735—February 12, 1989
   Houston, Tex. (Astrodome)
43,146—February 10, 1985
   Indianapolis, Ind. (Hoosier Dome)
34,275—February 8, 1987
   Seattle, Wash. (Kingdome)

31,745—February 4, 1979
   Pontiac, Mich. (Silverdome)
23,530—February 10, 1991
   Charlotte, N. C. (Charlotte Coliseum)

1991-92 REGULAR-SEASON ATTENDANCE

(Ranked according to overall total)

Team	HOME Total	HOME Avg.	ROAD Total	ROAD Avg.	OVERALL Total	OVERALL Avg.
1. Charlotte	971,618	23,698	610,100	14,880	1,581,718	19,289
2. Detroit	879,614	21,454	669,797	16,337	1,549,411	18,895
3. Chicago	759,969	18,536	749,780	18,287	1,509,749	18,412
4. Utah	806,663	19,675	622,661	15,187	1,429,324	17,431
5. New York	731,371	17,838	680,729	16,603	1,412,100	17,221
6. L.A. Lakers	699,240	17,055	692,386	16,887	1,391,626	16,971
7. Minnesota	769,035	18,757	607,804	14,824	1,376,839	16,791
8. Boston	610,976	14,902	743,731	18,140	1,354,707	16,521
9. San Antonio	658,337	16,057	657,352	16,033	1,315,689	16,045
10. Cleveland	677,408	16,522	635,346	15,496	1,312,754	16,009
11. Sacramento	697,574	17,014	604,602	14,746	1,302,176	15,880
12. Golden State	616,025	15,025	650,970	15,877	1,266,995	15,451
13. Dallas	649,741	15,847	606,212	14,786	1,255,953	15,317
14. Milwaukee	635,515	15,500	620,089	15,124	1,255,604	15,312
15. Philadelphia	574,128	14,003	674,844	16,460	1,248,972	15,231
16. Houston	592,790	14,458	644,456	15,718	1,237,246	15,088
17. Orlando	621,191	15,151	612,906	14,949	1,234,097	15,050
18. Phoenix	594,336	14,496	632,459	15,426	1,226,795	14,961
19. Miami	613,583	14,965	606,727	14,798	1,220,310	14,882
20. Portland	528,408	12,888	679,246	16,567	1,207,654	14,727
21. Seattle	586,929	14,315	601,990	14,683	1,188,919	14,499
22. Denver	534,323	13,032	636,655	15,528	1,170,978	14,280
23. Indiana	517,352	12,618	633,502	15,451	1,150,854	14,035
24. Atlanta	511,903	12,485	638,892	15,583	1,150,795	14,034
25. New Jersey	517,356	12,618	619,140	15,101	1,136,496	13,860
26. Washington	511,655	12,479	613,565	14,965	1,125,220	13,722
27. L.A. Clippers	500,200	12,200	621,299	15,154	1,121,499	13,677
Totals	17,367,240	15,689	17,367,240	15,689	34,734,480	15,689

WILT CHAMBERLAIN'S 100-POINT GAME

March 2, 1962 at Hershey, Pa.

Philadelphia Warriors (169)

Player	Pos.	FGA	FGM	FTA	FTM	Pts.
Paul Arizin	F	18	7	2	2	16
Tom Meschery	F	12	7	2	2	16
Wilt Chamberlain	C	63	36	32	28	100
Guy Rodgers	G	4	1	12	9	11
Al Attles	G	8	8	1	1	17
York Larese		5	4	1	1	9
Ed Conlin		4	0	0	0	0
Joe Ruklick		1	0	2	0	0
Ted Luckenbill		0	0	0	0	0
Totals		115	63	52	43	169

FG Pct.: .548. FT Pct.: .827. Team Rebounds: 3.

New York Knickerbockers (147)

Player	Pos.	FGA	FGM	FTA	FTM	Pts.
Willie Naulls	F	22	9	15	13	31
Johnny Green	F	7	3	0	0	6
Darrall Imhoff	C	7	3	1	1	7
Richie Guerin	G	29	13	17	13	39
Al Butler	G	13	4	0	0	8
Cleveland Buckner		26	16	1	1	33
Dave Budd		8	6	1	1	13
Donnie Butcher		6	3	6	4	10
Totals		118	57	41	33	147

FG Pct.: .483. FT Pct.: .805. Team Rebounds: 4.

Score by Periods:	1st	2nd	3rd	4th	Totals
Philadelphia	42	37	46	44	169
New York	26	42	38	41	147

Officials: Willie Smith and Pete D'Ambrosio.
Attendance: 4,124.

CHAMBERLAIN'S SCORING BY PERIODS

	Min.	FGA	FGM	FTA	FTM	Reb	Ast	Pts
1st	12	14	7	9	9	10	0	23
2nd	12	12	7	5	4	4	1	18
3rd	12	16	10	8	8	6	1	28
4th	12	21	12	10	7	5	0	31
Totals	48	63	36	32	28	25	2	100

LOWEST-SCORING GAME IN NBA HISTORY

November 22, 1950 at Minneapolis

Fort Wayne Pistons (19)

Player	Pos.	FGA	FGM	FTA	FTM	Pts.
Fred Schaus	F	1	0	3	3	3
Jack Kerris	F	1	0	4	2	2
Larry Foust	C	2	1	1	1	3
John Hargis	G	1	1	0	0	2
John Oldham	G	5	1	4	3	5
Paul Armstrong		2	1	2	2	4
Bob Harris		0	0	1	0	0
Ralph Johnson		1	0	0	0	0
Totals		13	4	15	11	19

FG Pct.: .308. FT Pct.: .733. Rebounds—Oldham 4, Kerris 2, Foust 1, Harris 1. Assists—Hargis 1, Johnson 1, Schaus 1. Personal Fouls—Kerris 5, Foust 3, Oldham 2, Armstrong 1, Harris 1, Johnson 1.

Minneapolis Lakers (18)

Player	Pos.	FGA	FGM	FTA	FTM	Pts.
Jim Pollard	F	1	0	1	1	1
Vern Mikkelsen	F	2	0	0	0	0
George Mikan	C	11	4	11	7	15
Slater Martin	G	2	0	3	0	0
Bob Harrison	G	2	0	2	2	2
Bud Grant		0	0	0	0	0
Joe Hutton		0	0	0	0	0
Arnie Ferrin		0	0	0	0	0
Totals		18	4	17	10	18

FG Pct.: .222. FT Pct.: .588. Rebounds—Mikan 4, Mikkelsen 3, Martin 1, Pollard 1. Assists—Martin 2, Grant 1, Pollard 1. Personal Fouls—Harrison 3, Martin 2, Mikkelsen 2, Pollard 2, Grant 1, Mikan 1.

Score by Periods:	1st	2nd	3rd	4th	Totals
Fort Wayne	8	3	5	3	19
Minneapolis	7	6	4	1	18

Referees: Jocko Collins and Stan Stutz. Attendance: 7,021.

HIGHEST-SCORING GAME IN NBA HISTORY

December 13, 1983 at Denver

Detroit Pistons (186)

Player	Pos.	FGA	FGM	FTA	FTM	Pts.
Kelly Tripucka	F	25	14	9	7	35
Cliff Levingston	F	2	1	0	0	2
Bill Laimbeer	C	10	6	9	5	17
Isiah Thomas	G	34	18	19	10	47
John Long	G	25	18	6	5	41
Terry Tyler		15	8	3	2	18
Vinnie Johnson		12	4	5	4	12
Earl Cureton		6	3	5	3	9
Ray Tolbert		4	1	4	1	3
Walker Russell		2	1	0	0	2
Kent Benson		1	0	0	0	0
David Thirdkill		0	0	0	0	0
Totals		136	74	60	37	186

FG Pct.: .544. FT Pct.: .617. Team Rebounds: 16. Minutes Played—Thomas 52, Laimbeer 47, Long 46, Tripucka 39, Cureton 34, Tyler 28, Johnson 21, Tolbert 15, Benson 13, Levingston 13, Russell 6, Thirdkill 1. Total Rebounds—Laimbeer 12, Tyler 8, Cureton 7, Long 6, Tolbert 6, Johnson 5, Thomas 5, Tripucka 4, Levingston 2, Benson 1. Assists—Thomas 17, Johnson 8, Long 8, Laimbeer 6, Cureton 2, Tolbert 2, Tripucka 2, Russell 1, Tyler 1.

Denver Nuggets (184)

Player	Pos.	FGA	FGM	FTA	FTM	Pts.
Alex English	F	30	18	13	11	47
Kiki Vandeweghe	F	29	21	11	9	51
Dan Issel	C	19	11	8	6	28
Rob Williams	G	8	3	4	3	9
T.R. Dunn	G	3	3	2	1	7
Mike Evans		13	7	2	2	16
Richard Anderson		6	5	3	2	13
Danny Schayes		1	0	12	11	11
Bill Hanzlik		4	0	2	2	2
Howard Carter		1	0	0	0	0
Ken Dennard		1	0	0	0	0
Totals		115	68	57	47	184

FG Pct.: .591. FT Pct.: .825. Team Rebounds: 13. Minutes Played—English 50, Vandeweghe 50, Evans 40, Hanzlik 38, Dunn 36, Issel 35, Schayes 24, Williams 21, Anderson 14, Carter 4, Dennard 3. Total Rebounds—English 12, Vandeweghe 9, Issel 8, Hanzlik 7, Schayes 7, Anderson 5, Dunn 4, Williams 3, Evans 2. Assists—Vandeweghe 8, English 7, Evans 7, Hanzlik 7, Issel 5, Williams 5, Dunn 2, Schayes 2, Anderson 1, Carter 1, Dennard 1.

Score by Periods:	1st	2nd	3rd	4th	OT	OT	OT	Totals
Detroit	38	36	34	37	14	12	15	186
Denver	34	40	39	32	14	12	13	184

3-Pt. Field Goals: Thomas 1-2, Anderson 1-1, Issel 0-1. Officials: Joe Borgia and Jesse Hall. Attendance: 9,655. Time of Game: 3:11.

All-Time Regular-Season NBA Records

Compiled by Elias Sports Bureau

Throughout this all-time NBA record section, records for "fewest" and "lowest" exclude games and seasons before 1954-55, when the 24-second clock was introduced.

INDIVIDUAL
SEASONS

Most Seasons

20—Kareem Abdul-Jabbar, Milwaukee, 1969-70—1974-75; L.A. Lakers, 1975-76—1988-89
16—Dolph Schayes, Syracuse (NBL), 1948-49; Syracuse, 1949-50—1962-63; Philadelphia 1963-64
   John Havlicek, Boston, 1962-63—1977-78
   Paul Silas, St. Louis, 1964-65—1967-68; Atlanta, 1968-69; Phoenix, 1969-70—1971-72; Boston, 1972-73—1975-76; Denver, 1976-77; Seattle, 1977-78—1979-80
   Elvin Hayes, San Diego, 1968-69—1970-71; Houston, 1971-72; Baltimore, 1972-73; Capital, 1973-74; Washington, 1974-75—1980-81; Houston, 1981-82—1983-84.
   Moses Malone, Buffalo, 1976-77; Houston, 1976-77—1981-82; Philadelphia, 1982-83—1985-86; Washington, 1986-87—1987-88; Atlanta, 1988-89—1990-91; Milwaukee, 1991-92
   Robert Parish, Golden State, 1976-77—1979-80; Boston, 1980-81—1991-92
15—Hal Greer, Syracuse, 1958-59—1962-63; Philadelphia, 1963-64—1972-73
   Lenny Wilkens, St. Louis, 1960-61—1967-68; Seattle, 1968-69—1971-72; Cleveland, 1972-73—1973-74; Portland, 1974-75
   Adrian Dantley, Buffalo, 1976-77; Indiana, 1977-78; Los Angeles, 1977-78—1978-79; Utah, 1979-80—1985-86; Detroit, 1986-87—1988-89; Dallas, 1988-89—1989-90; Milwaukee, 1990-91
   Alex English, Milwaukee, 1976-77—1977-78; Indiana, 1978-79—1979-80; Denver, 1979-80—1989-90; Dallas, 1990-91
   Brad Davis, Los Angeles, 1977-78—1978-79; Indiana, 1978-79—1979-80; Utah, 1979-80; Dallas, 1980-81—1991-92
   Walter Davis, Phoenix, 1977-78—1987-88; Denver, 1988-89—1990-91; Portland, 1990-91; Denver, 1991-92
   James Edwards, Los Angeles, 1977-78; Indiana, 1977-78—1980-81; Cleveland, 1981-82—1982-83; Phoenix, 1982-83—1987-88; Detroit, 1987-88—1990-91; L.A. Clippers, 1991-92
   Wayne Rollins, Atlanta, 1977-78—1987-88; Cleveland, 1988-89—1989-90; Detroit, 1990-91; Houston, 1991-92

GAMES

Most Games, Career

1,560—Kareem Abdul-Jabbar, Milwaukee, 1969-70—1974-75; L.A. Lakers, 1975-76—1988-89
1,303—Elvin Hayes, San Diego, 1968-69—1970-71; Houston, 1971-72; Baltimore, 1972-73; Capital, 1973-74; Washington, 1974-75—1980-81; Houston, 1981-82—1983-84
1,270—John Havlicek, Boston, 1962-63—1977-78
1,260—Robert Parish, Golden State, 1976-77—1979-80; Boston, 1980-81—1991-92
1,254—Paul Silas, St. Louis, 1964-65—1967-68; Atlanta, 1968-69; Phoenix, 1969-70—1971-72; Boston, 1972-73—1975-76; Denver, 1976-77; Seattle, 1977-78—1979-80

Most Consecutive Games, Career

906—Randy Smith, Buffalo, San Diego, Cleveland, New York, San Diego, February 18, 1972—March 13, 1983
844—John Kerr, Syracuse, Philadelphia, Baltimore, October 31, 1954—November 4, 1965
706—Dolph Schayes, Syracuse, February 17, 1952—December 26, 1961

Most Games, Season

88—Walt Bellamy, New York, Detroit, 1968-69
87—Tom Henderson, Atlanta, Washington, 1976-77
86—McCoy McLemore, Cleveland, Milwaukee, 1970-71

MINUTES
Minutes have been compiled since 1951-52

Most Seasons Leading League, Minutes

8—Wilt Chamberlain, Philadelphia, 1959-60—1961-62; San Francisco, 1962-63—1963-64; Philadelphia, 1965-66—1967-68
4—Elvin Hayes, San Diego, 1968-69—1969-70; Capital, 1973-74; Washington, 1976-77

Most Consecutive Seasons Leading League, Minutes

5—Wilt Chamberlain, Philadelphia, 1959-60—1961-62; San Francisco, 1962-63-1963-64
3—Wilt Chamberlain, Philadelphia, 1965-66—1967-68
   Michael Jordan, Chicago, 1986-87—1988-89

Most Minutes, Career

57,446—Kareem Abdul-Jabbar, Milwaukee, 1969-70—1974-75; L.A. Lakers, 1975-76—1988-89
50,000—Elvin Hayes, San Diego, 1968-69—1970-71; Houston, 1971-72; Baltimore, 1972-73; Capital, 1973-74; Washington, 1974-75—1980-81; Houston, 1981-82—1983-84

47,859—Wilt Chamberlain, Philadelphia, 1959-60—1961-62; San Francisco, 1962-63—1964-65; Philadelphia, 1964-65—1967-68; Los Angeles, 1968-69—1972-73
46,471—John Havlicek, Boston, 1962-63—1977-78
44,200—Moses Malone, Buffalo, 1976-77; Houston, 1976-77—1981-82; Philadelphia, 1982-83—1985-86; Washington, 1986-87—1987-88; Atlanta, 1988-89—1990-91; Milwaukee, 1991-92

Highest Average, Minutes per Game, Career (minimum: 400 games)

45.8—Wilt Chamberlain, Philadelphia, 1959-60—1961-62; San Francisco, 1962-63—1964-65; Philadelphia, 1964-65—1967-68; Los Angeles, 1968-69—1972-73 (47,859/1,045)
42.3—Bill Russell, Boston, 1956-57—1968-69 (40,726/963)
42.2—Oscar Robertson, Cincinnati, 1960-61—1969-70; Milwaukee, 1970-71—1973-74 (43,866/1,040)

Most Minutes, Season

3,882—Wilt Chamberlain, Philadelphia, 1961-62
3,836—Wilt Chamberlain, Philadelphia, 1967-68
3,806—Wilt Chamberlain, San Francisco, 1962-63
3,773—Wilt Chamberlain, Philadelphia, 1960-61
3,737—Wilt Chamberlain, Philadelphia, 1965-66
3,698—John Havlicek, Boston, 1971-72

Highest Average, Minutes per Game, Season

48.5—Wilt Chamberlain, Philadelphia, 1961-62 (3,882/80)
47.8—Wilt Chamberlain, Philadelphia, 1960-61 (3,773/79)
47.6—Wilt Chamberlain, San Francisco, 1962-63 (3,806/80)
47.3—Wilt Chamberlain, Philadelphia, 1965-66 (3,737/79)
46.8—Wilt Chamberlain, Philadelphia, 1967-68 (3,836/82)
46.4—Wilt Chamberlain, Philadelphia, 1959-60 (3,338/72)
46.1—Wilt Chamberlain, San Francisco, 1963-64 (3,689/80)
46.0—Nate Archibald, KC-Omaha, 1972-73 (3,681/80)

Most Minutes, Rookie, Season

3,695—Elvin Hayes, San Diego, 1968-69
3,534—Kareem Abdul-Jabbar, Milwaukee, 1969-70
3,344—Walt Bellamy, Chicago, 1961-62

Most Minutes, Game

69—Dale Ellis, Seattle at Milwaukee, November 9, 1989 (5 ot)
68—Xavier McDaniel, Seattle at Milwaukee, November 9, 1989 (5 ot)
64—Norm Nixon, Los Angeles at Cleveland, January 29, 1980 (4 ot)
    Eric Floyd, Golden State vs. New Jersey, February 1, 1987 (4 ot)

COMPLETE GAMES

Most Complete Games, Season

79—Wilt Chamberlain, Philadelphia, 1961-62

Most Consecutive Complete Games, Season

47—Wilt Chamberlain, Philadelphia, January 5—March 14, 1962

SCORING

Most Seasons Leading League

7—Wilt Chamberlain, Philadelphia, 1959-60—1961-62; San Francisco, 1962-63—1963-64; San Francisco, Philadelphia, 1964-65; Philadelphia, 1965-66
6—Michael Jordan, Chicago, 1986-87—1991-92
4—George Gervin, San Antonio, 1977-78—1979-80, 1981-82

Most Consecutive Seasons Leading League

7—Wilt Chamberlain, Philadelphia, 1959-60—1961-62; San Francisco, 1962-63—1963-64; San Francisco, Philadelphia, 1964-65; Philadelphia, 1965-66
6—Michael Jordan, Chicago, 1986-87—1991-92
3—George Mikan, Minneapolis, 1948-49—1950-51
    Neil Johnston, Philadelphia, 1952-53—1954-55
    Bob McAdoo, Buffalo, 1973-74—1975-76
    George Gervin, San Antonio, 1977-78—1979-80

Most Points, Lifetime

38,387—Kareem Abdul-Jabbar, Milwaukee, 1969-70—1974-75; L.A. Lakers, 1975-76—1988-89
31,419—Wilt Chamberlain, Philadelphia, 1959-60—1961-62; San Francisco, 1962-63—1964-65; Philadelphia, 1964-65—1967-68; Los Angeles, 1968-69—1972-73
27,313—Elvin Hayes, San Diego, 1968-69—1970-71; Houston, 1971-72; Baltimore, 1972-73; Capital, 1973-74; Washington, 1974-75—1980-81; Houston, 1981-82—1983-84
27,016—Moses Malone, Buffalo, 1976-77; Houston, 1976-77—1981-82; Philadelphia, 1982-83—1985-86; Washington, 1986-87—1987-88; Atlanta, 1988-89—1990-91; Milwaukee, 1991-92
26,710—Oscar Robertson, Cincinnati, 1960-61—1969-70; Milwaukee, 1970-71—1973-74

Highest Average, Points per Game, Career (minimum: 400 games)

32.3—Michael Jordan, Chicago, 1984-85—1991-92 (19,000/589)
30.1—Wilt Chamberlain, Philadelphia, 1959-60—1961-62; San Francisco, 1962-63—1964-65; Philadelphia, 1964-65—1967-68; Los Angeles, 1968-69—1972-73 (31,419/1,045)
27.4—Elgin Baylor, Minneapolis, 1958-59—1959-60; Los Angeles, 1960-61—1971-72; (23,149/846)

27.0—Jerry West, Los Angeles, 1960-61—1973-74 (25,192/932)
26.4—Bob Pettit, Milwaukee, 1954-55; St. Louis, 1955-56—1964-65 (20,880/792)

Most Points, Season

4,029—Wilt Chamberlain, Philadelphia, 1961-62
3,586—Wilt Chamberlain, San Francisco, 1962-63
3,041—Michael Jordan, Chicago, 1986-87
3,033—Wilt Chamberlain, Philadelphia, 1960-61
2,948—Wilt Chamberlain, San Francisco, 1963-64

Highest Average, Points per Game, Season (minimum: 70 games)

50.4—Wilt Chamberlain, Philadelphia, 1961-62 (4,029/80)
44.8—Wilt Chamberlain, San Francisco, 1962-63 (3,586/80)
38.4—Wilt Chamberlain, Philadelphia, 1960-61 (3,033/79)
37.6—Wilt Chamberlain, Philadelphia, 1959-60 (2,707/72)
37.1—Michael Jordan, Chicago, 1986-87 (3,041/82)
36.9—Wilt Chamberlain, San Francisco, 1963-64 (2,948/80)

Most Points, Rookie, Season

2,707—Wilt Chamberlain, Philadelphia, 1959-60
2,495—Walt Bellamy, Chicago, 1961-62
2,361—Kareem Abdul-Jabbar, Milwaukee, 1969-70

Highest Average, Points per Game, Rookie, Season

37.6—Wilt Chamberlain, Philadelphia, 1959-60 (2,707/72)
31.6—Walt Bellamy, Chicago, 1961-62 (2,495/79)
30.5—Oscar Robertson, Cincinnati, 1960-61 (2,165/71)

Most Seasons, 2,000-or-More Points

9—Kareem Abdul-Jabbar, Milwaukee, 1969-70—1973-74; Los Angeles, 1975-76—1976-77, 1979-80—1980-81
8—Alex English, Denver, 1981-82—1988-89
7—Wilt Chamberlain, Philadelphia, 1959-60—1961-62, San Francisco, 1962-63—1963-64; San Francisco, Philadelphia, 1964-65; Philadelphia, 1965-66
   Oscar Robertson, Cincinnati, 1960-61—1966-67
   Dominique Wilkins, Atlanta, 1984-85—1990-91
   Michael Jordan, Chicago, 1984-85, 1986-87—1991-92

Most Consecutive Seasons, 2,000-or-More Points

8—Alex English, Denver, 1981-82—1988-89
7—Wilt Chamberlain, Philadelphia, 1959-60—1961-62; San Francisco, 1962-63—1963-64; San Francisco, Philadelphia, 1964-65; Philadelphia, 1965-66
   Oscar Robertson, Cincinnati, 1960-61—1966-67
   Dominique Wilkins, Atlanta, 1984-85—1990-91
6—George Gervin, San Antonio, 1977-78—1982-83
   Michael Jordan, Chicago, 1986-87—1991-92

Most Seasons, 1,000-or-More Points

19—Kareem Abdul-Jabbar, Milwaukee, 1969-70—1974-75; L.A. Lakers, 1975-76—1987-88
16—John Havlicek, Boston, 1962-63—1977-78
15—Elvin Hayes, San Diego, 1968-69—1970-71; Houston, 1971-72; Baltimore, 1972-73; Capital, 1973-74; Washington, 1974-75—1980-81; Houston, 1981-82—1982-83
   Moses Malone, Buffalo, Houston, 1976-77; Houston, 1977-78—1981-82; Philadelphia, 1982-83—1985-86;
   Washington, 1986-87—1987-88; Atlanta, 1988-89—1989-90; Milwaukee, 1991-92
   Robert Parish, Golden State, 1977-78—1979-80; Boston, 1980-81—1991-92

Most Consecutive Seasons, 1,000-or-More Points

19—Kareem Abdul-Jabbar, Milwaukee, 1969-70—1974-75; L.A. Lakers, 1975-76—1987-88
16—John Havlicek, Boston, 1962-63—1977-78
15—Elvin Hayes, San Diego, 1968-69—1970-71; Houston, 1971-72; Baltimore, 1972-73; Capital, 1973-74; Washington, 1974-75—1980-81; Houston, 1981-82—1982-83
   Robert Parish, Golden State, 1977-78—1979-80; Boston, 1980-81—1991-92

Most Points, Game

100—Wilt Chamberlain, Philadelphia vs. New York, at Hershey, Pa., March 2, 1962
78—Wilt Chamberlain, Philadelphia vs. Los Angeles, December 8, 1961 (3 ot)
73—Wilt Chamberlain, Philadelphia vs. Chicago, January 13, 1962
   Wilt Chamberlain, San Francisco at New York, November 16, 1962
   David Thompson, Denver at Detroit, April 9, 1978
72—Wilt Chamberlain, San Francisco at Los Angeles, November 3, 1962
71—Elgin Baylor, Los Angeles at New York, November 15, 1960

Most Points, Rookie, Game

58—Wilt Chamberlain, Philadelphia vs. Detroit, at Bethlehem, Pa., January 25, 1960
   Wilt Chamberlain, Philadelphia at New York, February 21, 1960
57—Rick Barry, San Francisco at New York, December 14, 1965
56—Earl Monroe, Baltimore vs. Los Angeles, February 13, 1968 (ot)

Most Games, 50-or-More Points, Career

118—Wilt Chamberlain, Philadelphia, 1959-60—1961-62; San Francisco, 1962-63—1964-65; Philadelphia, 1964-
   65—1967-68; Los Angeles, 1968-69—1972-73
22—Michael Jordan, Chicago, 1984-85—1991-92
17—Elgin Baylor, Minneapolis, 1958-59—1959-60; Los Angeles, 1960-61—1971-72
14—Rick Barry, San Francisco, 1965-66—1966-67; Golden State, 1972-73—1977-78; Houston, 1978-
   79—1979-80

Most Games, 50-or-More Points, Season

45—Wilt Chamberlain, Philadelphia, 1961-62
30—Wilt Chamberlain, San Francisco, 1962-63
 9—Wilt Chamberlain, San Francisco, 1963-64
   Wilt Chamberlain, San Francisco, Philadelphia, 1964-65

Most Consecutive Games, 50-or-More Points

7—Wilt Chamberlain, Philadelphia, December 16—December 29, 1961
6—Wilt Chamberlain, Philadelphia, January 11—January 19, 1962
5—Wilt Chamberlain, Philadelphia, December 8—December 13, 1961
  Wilt Chamberlain, Philadelphia, February 25—March 4, 1962

Most Games, 40-or-More Points, Career

271—Wilt Chamberlain, Philadelphia, 1959-60—1961-62, San Francisco, 1962-63—1964-65; Philadelphia, 1964-
    65—1967-68; Los Angeles, 1968-69—1972-73
121—Michael Jordan, Chicago, 1984-85—1991-92
 87—Elgin Baylor, Minneapolis, 1958-59—1959-60; Los Angeles, 1960-61—1971-72

Most Games, 40-or-More Points, Season

63—Wilt Chamberlain, Philadelphia, 1961-62
52—Wilt Chamberlain, San Francisco, 1962-63
37—Michael Jordan, Chicago, 1986-87

Most Consecutive Games, 40-or-More Points

14—Wilt Chamberlain, Philadelphia, December 8—December 30, 1961
   Wilt Chamberlain, Philadelphia, January 11—February 1, 1962
10—Wilt Chamberlain, San Francisco, November 9—November 25, 1962
 9—Michael Jordan, Chicago, November 28—December 12, 1986

Most Consecutive Games, 30-or-More Points

65—Wilt Chamberlain, Philadelphia, November 4, 1961—February 22, 1962
31—Wilt Chamberlain, Philadelphia, San Francisco, February 25—December 8, 1962
25—Wilt Chamberlain, Philadelphia, November 11—December 27, 1960

Most Consecutive Games, 20-or-More Points

126—Wilt Chamberlain, Philadelphia, San Francisco, October 19, 1961—January 19, 1963
 92—Wilt Chamberlain, San Francisco, February 26, 1963—March 18, 1964
 72—Michael Jordan, Chicago, December 29, 1987—December 6, 1988

Most Consecutive Games, 10-or-More Points

787—Kareem Abdul-Jabbar, L.A. Lakers, December 4, 1977—December 2, 1987
526—Moses Malone, Houston, Philadelphia, November 4, 1978—March 4, 1985
499—Michael Jordan, Chicago, March 25, 1986—April 19, 1992 (current)

Most Points, One Half

59—Wilt Chamberlain, Philadelphia vs. New York, at Hershey, Pa., March 2, 1962 (2nd Half)
53—David Thompson, Denver at Detroit, April 9, 1978 (1st Half)
   George Gervin, San Antonio at New Orleans, April 9, 1978 (1st Half)
45—Wilt Chamberlain, San Francisco at New York, November 16, 1962
   Rick Barry, Golden State vs. Portland, March 26, 1974 (2nd Half)

Most Points, One Quarter

33—George Gervin, San Antonio at New Orleans, April 9, 1978 (2nd Qtr.)
32—David Thompson, Denver at Detroit, April 9, 1978 (1st Qtr.)
31—Wilt Chamberlain, Philadelphia vs. New York, at Hershey, Pa., March 2, 1962 (4th Qtr.)

Most Points, Overtime Period

14—Butch Carter, Indiana vs. Boston, March 20, 1984
13—Earl Monroe, Baltimore vs. Detroit, February 6, 1970
   Joe Caldwell, Atlanta vs. Cincinnati, at Memphis, February 18, 1970

FIELD GOAL PERCENTAGE

Most Seasons, Leading League

9—Wilt Chamberlain, Philadelphia, 1960-61; San Francisco, 1962-63; San Francisco, Philadelphia, 1964-65; Philadelphia, 1965-66—1967-68; Los Angeles, 1968-69, 1971-72—1972-73
4—Artis Gilmore, Chicago, 1980-81—1981-82; San Antonio, 1982-83—1983-84
3—Neil Johnston, Philadelphia, 1952-53, 1955-56—1956-57

Most Consecutive Seasons Leading League

5—Wilt Chamberlain, San Francisco, Philadelphia, 1964-65; Philadelphia, 1965-66—1967-68; Los Angeles, 1968-69
4—Artis Gilmore, Chicago, 1980-81—1981-82; San Antonio, 1982-83—1983-84

Highest Field Goal Percentage, Career (minimum: 2,000 field goals)

.599 —Artis Gilmore, Chicago, 1976-77—1981-82; San Antonio, 1982-83—1986-87; Chicago, 1987-88; Boston,
      1987-88.
.576 —Charles Barkley, Philadelphia, 1984-85—1991-92
.5722—Steve Johnson, Kansas City, 1981-82—1983-84; Chicago, 1983-84—1984-85; San Antonio, 1985-86; Port-
      land, 1986-87—1988-89; Minnesota, 1989-90; Seattle, 1989-90; Golden State, 1990-91
.5720—Darryl Dawkins, Philadelphia, 1975-76—1981-82; New Jersey, 1982-83—1986-87; Utah, 1987-88; Detroit,
      1987-88—1988-89
.570 —James Donaldson, Seattle, 1980-81—1982—83; San Diego, 1983-84; L.A. Clippers, 1984-85—1985-86;
      Dallas, 1985-86—1991-92; New York, 1991-92

Highest Field Goal Percentage, Season (Qualifiers)

.727—Wilt Chamberlain, Los Angeles, 1972-73 (426/586)
.683—Wilt Chamberlain, Philadelphia, 1966-67 (785/1,150)
.670—Artis Gilmore, Chicago, 1980-81 (547/816)
.652—Artis Gilmore, Chicago, 1981-82 (546/837)
.649—Wilt Chamberlain, Los Angeles, 1971-72 (496/764)

Highest Field Goal Percentage, Rookie, Season (Qualifiers)

.613—Steve Johnson, Kansas City, 1981-82 (395/644)
.600—Otis Thorpe, Kansas City, 1984-85 (411/685)
.582—Buck Williams, New Jersey, 1981-82 (513/881)

Highest Field Goal Percentage, Game (minimum: 15 field goals)

1.000—Wilt Chamberlain, Philadelphia vs. Los Angeles, January 20, 1967 (15/15)
　　　　Wilt Chamberlain, Philadelphia vs. Baltimore, at Pittsburgh, February 24, 1967 (18/18)
　　　　Wilt Chamberlain, Philadelphia at Baltimore, March 19, 1967 (16/16)
　.947—Wilt Chamberlain, San Francisco vs. New York, at Boston, November 27, 1963 (18/19)
　.941—Wilt Chamberlain, Philadelphia at Baltimore, November 25, 1966 (16/17)
　　　　Scottie Pippen, Chicago vs. Charlotte, February 23, 1991 (16/17)

Most Field Goals, No Misses, Game

18—Wilt Chamberlain, Philadelphia vs. Baltimore, at Pittsburgh, February 24, 1967
16—Wilt Chamberlain, Philadelphia at Baltimore, March 19, 1967
15—Wilt Chamberlain, Philadelphia vs. Los Angeles, January 20, 1967
14—Bailey Howell, Baltimore vs. San Francisco, January 3, 1965
　　　Wilt Chamberlain, Los Angeles vs. Detroit, March 11, 1969
　　　Billy McKinney, Kansas City vs. Boston at St. Louis, December 27, 1978

Most Field Goal Attempts, None Made, Game

17—Tim Hardaway, Golden State at San Antonio, December 27, 1991 (ot)
15—Howie Dallmar, Philadelphia vs. New York, November 27, 1947
　　　Howie Dallmar, Philadelphia vs. Washington, November 25, 1948
　　　Dick Ricketts, Rochester vs. St. Louis, March 7, 1956
　　　Corky Devlin, Ft. Wayne vs. Minneapolis, at Rochester, December 25, 1956
　　　Charlie Tyra, New York at Philadelphia, November 7, 1957
　　　Frank Ramsey, Boston vs. Cincinnati, at Philadelphia, December 8, 1960
　　　Ray Williams, New Jersey vs. Indiana, December 28, 1981
　　　Rodney McCray, Sacramento at Utah, November 9, 1988
14—Ed Leede, Boston at Washington, December 13, 1950
　　　Jack George, Philadelphia at Syracuse, November 1, 1953
　　　Sihugo Green, St. Louis vs. Boston, at Philadelphia, December 14, 1961
　　　Bailey Howell, Detroit vs. St. Louis, January 4, 1963
　　　Bill Russell, Boston vs. Philadelphia, at Syracuse, January 23, 1965
　　　Adrian Smith, Cincinnati at New York, December 18, 1965
　　　Connie Dierking, Cincinnati at San Francisco, November 1, 1969

FIELD GOALS

Most Seasons Leading League

7—Wilt Chamberlain, Philadelphia, 1959-60—1961-62; San Francisco, 1962-63—1963-64; San Francisco, Philadel-
　　phia, 1964-65; Philadelphia, 1965-66
6—Michael Jordan, Chicago, 1986-87—1991-92
5—Kareem Abdul-Jabbar, Milwaukee, 1969-70—1971-72, 1973-74; Los Angeles, 1976-77
4—George Gervin, San Antonio, 1977-78—1979-80, 1981-82

Most Consecutive Seasons Leading League

7—Wilt Chamberlain, Philadelphia, 1959-60—1961-62; San Francisco, 1962-63—1963-64; San Francisco, Philadel-
　　phia, 1964-65; Philadelphia, 1965-66
6—Michael Jordan, Chicago, 1986-87—1991-92
3—George Mikan, Minneapolis, 1948-49—1950-51
　　Kareem Abdul-Jabbar, Milwaukee, 1969-70—1971-72
　　George Gervin, San Antonio, 1977-78—1979-80

Most Field Goals, Career

15,837—Kareem Abdul-Jabbar, Milwaukee, 1969-70—1974-75; L.A. Lakers, 1975-76—1988-89
12,681—Wilt Chamberlain, Philadelphia, 1959-60—1961-62; San Francisco, 1962-63—1964-65; Philadelphia, 1964-
　　　　65—1967-68; Los Angeles, 1968-69—1972-73
10,976—Elvin Hayes, San Diego, 1968-69—1970-71; Houston, 1971-72; Baltimore, 1972-73; Capital, 1973-74;
　　　　Washington, 1974-75—1980-81; Houston, 1981-82—1983-84

Most Field Goals, Season

1,597—Wilt Chamberlain, Philadelphia, 1961-62
1,463—Wilt Chamberlain, San Francisco, 1962-63
1,251—Wilt Chamberlain, Philadelphia, 1960-61

Most Consecutive Field Goals, No Misses, Season

35—Wilt Chamberlain, Philadelphia, February 17—February 28, 1967

Most Field Goals, Game

36—Wilt Chamberlain, Philadelphia vs. New York, at Hershey, Pa., March 2, 1962
31—Wilt Chamberlain, Philadelphia vs. Los Angeles, December 8, 1961 (3 OT)

30—Wilt Chamberlain, Philadelphia at Chicago, December 16, 1967
   Rick Barry, Golden State vs. Portland, March 26, 1974

Most Field Goals, One Half

22—Wilt Chamberlain, Philadelphia vs. New York, at Hershey, Pa., March 2, 1962 (2nd Half)
21—Rick Barry, Golden State vs. Portland, March 26, 1974 (2nd Half)
20—David Thompson, Denver at Detroit, April 9, 1978 (1st Half)

Most Field Goals, One Quarter

13—David Thompson, Denver at Detroit, April 9, 1978 (1st Qtr.)
12—Cliff Hagan, St. Louis at New York, February 4, 1958 (4th Qtr.)
   Wilt Chamberlain, Philadelphia vs. New York, at Hershey, Pa., March 2, 1962 (4th Qtr.)
   George Gervin, San Antonio at New Orleans, April 9, 1978 (2nd Qtr.)
   Jeff Malone, Washington at Phoenix, February 27, 1988 (3rd Qtr.)

FIELD GOAL ATTEMPTS

Most Seasons Leading League

7—Wilt Chamberlain, Philadelphia, 1959-60—1961-62; San Francisco, 1962-63—1963-64; San Francisco, Philadelphia, 1964-65; Philadelphia, 1965-66
5—Michael Jordan, Chicago, 1986-87—1987-88, 1989-90—1991-92
3—Joe Fulks, Philadelphia, 1946-47—1948-49
   George Mikan, Minneapolis, 1949-50—1951-52
   Elvin Hayes, San Diego, 1968-69—1970-71
   George Gervin, San Antonio, 1978-79—1979-80, 1981-82

Most Consecutive Seasons Leading League

7—Wilt Chamberlain, Philadelphia, 1959-60—1961-62; San Francisco, 1962-63—1963-64; San Francisco, Philadel-
   phia, 1964-65; Philadelphia, 1965-66
3—Joe Fulks, Philadelphia, 1946-47—1948-49
   George Mikan, Minneapolis, 1949-50—1951-52
   Elvin Hayes, San Diego, 1968-69—1970-71
   Michael Jordan, Chicago, 1989-90—1991-92

Most Field Goal Attempts, Career

28,307—Kareem Abdul-Jabbar, Milwaukee, 1969-70—1974-75; L.A. Lakers, 1975-76—1988-89
24,272—Elvin Hayes, San Diego, 1968-69—1970-71; Houston, 1971-72; Baltimore, 1972-73; Capital, 1973-74;
       Washington, 1974-75—1980-81; Houston, 1981-82—1983-84
23,930—John Havlicek, Boston, 1962-63—1977-78

Most Field Goal Attempts, Season

3,159—Wilt Chamberlain, Philadelphia, 1961-62
2,770—Wilt Chamberlain, San Francisco, 1962-63
2,457—Wilt Chamberlain, Philadelphia, 1960-61

Most Field Goal Attempts, Game

63—Wilt Chamberlain, Philadelphia vs. New York, at Hershey, Pa., March 2, 1962
62—Wilt Chamberlain, Philadelphia vs. Los Angeles, December 8, 1961 (3 OT)
60—Wilt Chamberlain, San Francisco at Cincinnati, October 28, 1962 (OT)

Most Field Goal Attempts, One Half

37—Wilt Chamberlain, Philadelphia vs. New York, at Hershey, Pa., March 2, 1962 (2nd Half)
34—George Gervin, San Antonio at New Orleans, April 9, 1978 (1st Half)
32—Wilt Chamberlain, Philadelphia vs. Chicago, at Boston, January 24, 1962

Most Field Goal Attempts, One Quarter

21—Wilt Chamberlain, Philadelphia vs. New York, at Hershey, Pa., March 2, 1962 (4th Qtr.)
20—Wilt Chamberlain, Philadelphia vs. Chicago, at Boston, January 24, 1962
   George Gervin, San Antonio at New Orleans, April 9, 1978 (2nd Qtr.)
19—Bob Pettit, St. Louis at Philadelphia, December 6, 1961

THREE-POINT FIELD GOAL PERCENTAGE

Most Seasons Leading League

2—Craig Hodges, Milwaukee, 1985-86; Milwaukee-Phoenix, 1987-88
1—Fred Brown, Seattle, 1979-80
   Brian Taylor, San Diego, 1980-81
   Campy Russell, New York, 1981-82
   Mike Dunleavy, San Antonio, 1982-83
   Darrell Griffith, Utah, 1983-84
   Byron Scott, L.A. Lakers, 1984-85
   Kiki Vandeweghe, Portland, 1986-87
   Jon Sundvold, Miami, 1988-89
   Steve Kerr, Cleveland, 1989-90
   Jim Les, Sacramento, 1990-91
   Dana Barros, Seattle, 1991-92

Highest Three-Point Field Goal Percentage, Career (minimum: 100 three-point FGs)

.475—Steve Kerr, Phoenix, 1988-89; Cleveland, 1989-90—1991-92 (141/297)
.433—Drazen Petrovic, Portland, 1989-90—1990-91; New Jersey, 1990-91—1991-92 (180/416)
.416—Dana Barros, Seattle, 1989-90—1991-92 (210/505)

Highest Three-Point Field Goal Percentage, Season (Qualifiers)

.522—Jon Sundvold, Miami, 1988-89 (48/92)
.507—Steve Kerr, Cleveland, 1989-90 (73/144)
.491—Craig Hodges, Milwaukee-Phoenix, 1987-88 (86/175)

Most Three-Point Field Goals, No Misses, Game

6—Chuck Person, Indiana at Phoenix, February 11, 1987
Danny Ainge, Boston at Utah, January 4, 1988
Charles Barkley, Philadelphia at Miami, February 22, 1989
Mark Price, Cleveland at Golden State, March 9, 1989
5—by many

Most Three-Point Field Goals Attempts, None Made, Game

8—Michael Adams, Denver vs. Washington, February 15, 1989
Michael Adams, Denver vs. Indiana, March 17, 1991
Vernon Maxwell, Houston at Orlando, March 30, 1991
Reggie Miller, Indiana at New York, December 28, 1991
7—by many

THREE-POINT FIELD GOALS

Most Seasons Leading League

2—Darrell Griffith, Utah, 1983-84—1984-85
Larry Bird, Boston, 1985-86—1986-87
Michael Adams, Denver, 1988-89—1989-90
Vernon Maxwell, Houston, 1990-91—1991-92
1—Brian Taylor, San Diego, 1979-80
Mike Bratz, Cleveland, 1980-81
Don Buse, Indiana, 1981-82
Mike Dunleavy, San Antonio, 1982-83
Danny Ainge, Boston, 1987-88

Most Three-Point Field Goals, Career

783—Michael Adams, Sacramento, 1985-86; Washington, 1986-87; Denver, 1987-88—1990-91; Washington, 1991-92
763—Dale Ellis, Dallas, 1983-84—1985-86; Seattle, 1986-87—1990-91; Milwaukee, 1990-91—1991-92
694—Danny Ainge, Boston, 1981-82—1988-89; Sacramento, 1988-89—1989-90; Portland, 1990-91—1991-92

Most Three-Point Field Goals, Season

172—Vernon Maxwell, Houston, 1990-91
167—Michael Adams, Denver, 1990-91
166—Michael Adams, Denver, 1988-89

Most Consecutive Three-Point Field Goals, No Misses, Season

11—Scott Wedman, Boston, December 21, 1984—March 31, 1985
10—Trent Tucker, New York, December 28, 1984—January 15, 1985
Brad Davis, Dallas, January 23—February 3, 1988
Kenny Smith, Houston, January 22—February 6, 1991
9—Craig Hodges, Chicago, February 3—February 8, 1990

Most Three-Point Field Goals, Game

9—Dale Ellis, Seattle vs. L.A. Clippers, April 20, 1990
Michael Adams, Denver at L.A. Clippers, April 12, 1991
8—Rick Barry, Houston vs. Utah, February 9, 1980
John Roche, Denver vs. Seattle, January 9, 1982
Michael Adams, Denver vs. Milwaukee, January 21, 1989
Vernon Maxwell, Houston at Denver, April 5, 1991
John Starks, New York vs. Chicago, March 31, 1992

Most Consecutive Games, Three-Point Field Goals Made, Season

43—Michael Adams, Denver, January 28—April 23, 1988
36—Michael Adams, Denver, November 4, 1988—January 23, 1989
34—Mark Price, Cleveland, December 5, 1989—February 17, 1990

Most Three-Point Field Goals, Rookie, Season

125—Dennis Scott, Orlando, 1990-91
95—Dana Barros, Seattle, 1989-90
72—Travis Mays, Sacramento, 1990-91

Most Three-Point Field Goals Made, One Half

7—John Roche, Denver vs. Seattle, January 9, 1982
Michael Adams, Denver vs. Milwaukee, January 21, 1989
6—Norm Nixon, L.A. Clippers at San Antonio, March 7, 1986
Jack Sikma, Milwaukee at San Antonio, December 22, 1990
Michael Adams, Denver vs. Milwaukee, March 23, 1991
John Starks, New York vs. Chicago, March 31, 1992

Most Three-Point Field Goals Made, One Quarter

7—John Roche, Denver vs. Seattle, January 9, 1982
5—Norm Nixon, L.A. Clippers at San Antonio, March 7, 1986
Michael Adams, Denver vs. Milwaukee, January 21, 1989
Mark Price, Cleveland at Golden State, March 9, 1989

Craig Hodges, Chicago vs. Indiana, March 13, 1989
Jack Sikma, Milwaukee vs. San Antonio, November 14, 1989
Steve Kerr, Cleveland at Orlando, January 6, 1990

THREE-POINT FIELD GOAL ATTEMPTS

Most Seasons Leading League

4—Michael Adams, Denver, 1987-88—1990-91
2—Darrell Griffith, Utah, 1983-84—1984-85
1—Brian Taylor, San Diego, 1979-80
  Mike Bratz, Cleveland, 1980-81
  Joey Hassett, Golden State, 1981-82
  Mike Dunleavy, San Antonio, 1982-83
  Larry Bird, Boston, 1985-86
  Dale Ellis, Seattle, 1986-87
  Vernon Maxwell, Houston, 1991-92

Most Three-Point Field Goal Attempts, Career

2,332—Michael Adams, Sacramento, 1985-86; Washington, 1986-87; Denver, 1987-88—1990-91; Washington, 1991-92
1,891—Dale Ellis, Dallas, 1983-84—1985-86; Seattle, 1986-87—1990-91; Milwaukee, 1990-91—1991-92
1,821—Danny Ainge, Boston, 1981-82—1988-89; Sacramento, 1988-89—1989-90; Portland, 1990-91—1991-92

Most Three-Point Field Goal Attempts, Season

564—Michael Adams, Denver, 1990-91
510—Vernon Maxwell, Houston, 1990-91
473—Vernon Maxwell, Houston, 1991-92

Most Three-Point Field Goal Attempts, Game

20—Michael Adams, Denver at L.A. Clippers, April 12, 1991
16—Michael Adams, Denver vs. Milwaukee, March 23, 1991 (OT)
15—Michael Adams, Denver vs. Utah, March 14, 1988
  Michael Adams, Denver vs. Houston, April 5, 1991
  John Starks, New York vs. Chicago, March 31, 1992

Most Three-Point Field Goal Attempts, One Half

13—Michael Adams, Denver at L.A. Clippers, April 12, 1991
11—John Roche, Denver vs. Seattle, January 9, 1982
  Michael Adams, Denver vs. San Antonio, April 19, 1991

FREE THROW PERCENTAGE

Most Seasons Leading League

7—Bill Sharman, Boston, 1952-53—1956-57, 1958-59, 1960-61
6—Rick Barry, Golden State, 1972-73, 1974-75—1975-76, 1977-78; Houston, 1978-79—1979-80
4—Larry Bird, Boston, 1983-84, 1985-86—1986-87, 1989-90

Most Consecutive Seasons, Leading League

5—Bill Sharman, Boston, 1952-53—1956-57
3—Rick Barry, Golden State, 1977-78; Houston, 1978-79—1979-80
2—Bob Feerick, Washington, 1947-48—1948-49
  Rick Barry, Golden State, 1974-75—1975-76
  Larry Bird, Boston, 1985-86—1986-87

Highest Free Throw Percentage, Career (minimum: 1,200 free throws made)

.900—Rick Barry, San Francisco, 1965-66—1966-67; Golden State, 1972-73—1977-78; Houston, 1978-79—1979-80 (3,818)/4,243)
.899—Mark Price, Cleveland, 1986-87—1991-92 (1,208/1,343)
.892—Calvin Murphy, San Diego, 1970-71; Houston, 1971-72—1982-83 (3,445/3,864)
.886—Larry Bird, Boston, 1979-80—1991-92 (3,960/4,471)

Highest Free Throw Percentage, Season (Qualifiers)

.958 —Calvin Murphy, Houston, 1980-81 (206/215)
.9473—Mark Price, Cleveland, 1991-92 (270/285)
.9467—Rick Barry, Houston, 1978-79 (160/169)
.945 —Ernie DiGregorio, Buffalo, 1976-77 (138/146)
.9352—Ricky Sobers, Chicago, 1980-81 (231/247)

Highest Free Throw Percentage, Rookie, Season (Qualifiers)

.902—Ernie DiGregorio, Buffalo, 1973-74 (174/193)
.896—Chris Mullin, Golden State, 1985-86 (189/211)
.879—Winston Garland, Golden State, 1987-88 (138/157)

Most Free Throws Made, No Misses, Game

19—Bob Pettit, St. Louis at Boston, November 22, 1961
  Bill Cartwright, New York vs. Kansas City, November 17, 1981
  Adrian Dantley, Detroit vs. Chicago, December 15, 1987 (OT)
18—Dolph Schayes, Syracuse vs. Minneapolis, January 10, 1957
  Dolph Schayes, Syracuse vs. Boston, March 9, 1957
  Dolph Schayes, Syracuse vs. Los Angeles, October 29, 1960
  Oscar Robertson, Cincinnati at St. Louis, January 30, 1962

Jerry West, Los Angeles vs. Detroit, November 10, 1965
Jerry West, Los Angeles vs. New York, November 9, 1969
Pete Maravich, Atlanta vs. Buffalo, November 28, 1973
Rick Barry, Golden State vs. Portland, December 26, 1974
Rick Barry, Golden State vs. Washington, February 6, 1975
Bob McAdoo, Buffalo at Portland, November 29, 1975
Dominique Wilkins, Atlanta at San Antonio, January 13, 1988
Danny Schayes, Denver vs. Houston, April 15, 1988
Mark Price, Cleveland vs. Charlotte, April 9, 1989
Magic Johnson, L.A. Lakers vs. Utah, April 11, 1991

Most Free Throw Attempts, None Made, Game

10—Wilt Chamberlain, Philadelphia vs. Detroit, November 4, 1960
 9—Wilt Chamberlain, Philadelphia at St. Louis, February 19, 1967
 8—Elvin Hayes, Houston vs. Portland, March 26, 1972
 7—Connie Simmons, Rochester vs. Philadelphia at New Haven, January 2, 1956
   Frank Selvy, Los Angeles vs. New York, January 19, 1962
   Jerome Lane, Denver vs. Houston, December 13, 1988

FREE THROWS MADE

Most Seasons Leading League

5—Adrian Dantley, Indiana, Los Angeles, 1977-78; Utah, 1980-81—1981-82, 1983-84, 1985-86
4—Oscar Robertson, Cincinnati, 1963-64—1964-65, 1967-68—1968-69
   Karl Malone, Utah, 1988-89—1991-92
3—George Mikan, Minneapolis, 1948-49—1950-51
   Neil Johnston, Philadelphia, 1952-53—1954-55
   Bob Pettit, St. Louis, 1955-56, 1958-59, 1962-63
   Nate Archibald, Cincinnati, 1971-72; Kansas City-Omaha, 1972-73, 1974-75

Most Consecutive Seasons Leading League

4—Karl Malone, Utah, 1988-89—1991-92
3—George Mikan, Minneapolis, 1948-49—1950-51
   Neil Johnston, Philadelphia, 1952-53—1954-55

Most Free Throws Made, Career

8,395—Moses Malone, Buffalo, 1976-77; Houston, 1976-77—1981-82; Philadelphia, 1982-83—1985-86;
      Washington, 1986-87—1987-88; Atlanta, 1988-89—1990-91; Milwaukee, 1991-92
7,694—Oscar Robertson, Cincinnati, 1960-61—1969-70; Milwaukee, 1970-71—1973-74
7,160—Jerry West, Los Angeles, 1960-61—1973-74

Most Free Throws Made, Season

840—Jerry West, Los Angeles, 1965-66
835—Wilt Chamberlain, Philadelphia, 1961-62
833—Michael Jordan, Chicago, 1986-87

Most Consecutive Free Throws Made, Season

78—Calvin Murphy, Houston, December 27, 1980—February 28, 1981
75—Ricky Pierce, Seattle, November 15, 1991—December 11, 1991
71—Larry Bird, Boston, December 19, 1989—February 13, 1990

Most Free Throws Made, Game

28—Wilt Chamberlain, Philadelphia vs. New York, at Hershey, Pa., March 2, 1962
   Adrian Dantley, Utah vs. Houston, at Las Vegas, January 4, 1984
27—Adrian Dantley, Utah vs. Denver, November 25, 1983
26—Adrian Dantley, Utah vs. Dallas, October 31, 1980
   Michael Jordan, Chicago vs. New Jersey, February 26, 1987

Most Free Throws Made, One Half

19—Oscar Robertson, Cincinnati at Baltimore, December 27, 1964
18—Michael Jordan, Chicago vs. New York, January 21, 1990 (2nd Half)
17—Rick Barry, San Francisco at New York, December 6, 1966 (2nd Half)
   Adrian Dantley, Detroit vs. Sacramento, December 10, 1986 (2nd Half)

Most Free Throws Made, One Quarter

14—Rick Barry, San Francisco at New York, December 6, 1966 (3rd Qtr.)
   Pete Maravich, Atlanta vs. Buffalo, November 28, 1973 (3rd Qtr.)
   Adrian Dantley, Detroit vs. Sacramento, December 10, 1986 (4th Qtr.)
   Michael Jordan, Chicago at Utah, November 15, 1989 (4th Qtr.)
13—Ken Sears, New York at Boston, November 3, 1956
   Oscar Robertson, Cincinnati at Baltimore, December 27, 1964
   John Drew, Atlanta vs. New Orleans, January 20, 1979 (3rd Qtr.)

FREE THROW ATTEMPTS

Most Seasons Leading League

9—Wilt Chamberlain, Philadelphia, 1959-60—1961-62; San Francisco, 1962-63—1963-64; San
   Francisco, Philadelphia, 1964-65; Philadelphia, 1966-67—1967-68; Los Angeles, 1968-69
5—Moses Malone, Houston, 1979-80—1981-82; Philadelphia, 1982-83, 1984-85

Most Consecutive Seasons Leading League

6—Wilt Chamberlain, Philadelphia, 1959-60—1961-62; San Francisco, 1962-63—1963-64; San Francisco, Philadelphia, 1964-65
4—Moses Malone, Houston, 1979-80—1981-82; Philadelphia, 1982-83
   Karl Malone, Utah, 1988-89—1991-92
3—Wilt Chamberlain, Philadelphia, 1966-67—1967-68; Los Angeles, 1968-69

Most Free Throw Attempts, Career

11,862—Wilt Chamberlain, Philadelphia, 1959-60—1961-62; San Francisco, 1962-63—1964-65; Philadelphia, 1964-65—1967-68; Los Angeles, 1968-69—1972-73
10,910—Moses Malone, Buffalo, 1976-77; Houston, 1976-77—1981-82; Philadelphia, 1982-83—1985-86; Washington, 1986-87—1987-88; Atlanta, 1988-89—1990-91; Milwaukee, 1991-92
9,304—Kareem Abdul-Jabbar, Milwaukee, 1969-70—1974-75; L.A. Lakers, 1975-76—1988-89

Most Free Throw Attempts, Season

1,363—Wilt Chamberlain, Philadelphia, 1961-62
1,113—Wilt Chamberlain, San Francisco, 1962-63
1,054—Wilt Chamberlain, Philadelphia, 1960-61

Most Free Throw Attempts, Game

34—Wilt Chamberlain, Philadelphia vs. St. Louis, February 22, 1962
32—Wilt Chamberlain, Philadelphia vs. New York, at Hershey, Pa., March 2, 1962
31—Adrian Dantley, Utah vs. Denver, November 25, 1983

Most Free Throw Attempts, One Half

22—Oscar Robertson, Cincinnati at Baltimore, December 27, 1964
   Tony Campbell, Minnesota vs. L.A. Clippers, March 8, 1990
21—Adrian Dantley, Utah vs. New Jersey, February 25, 1981
20—Nate Thurmond, San Francisco at Philadelphia, January 5, 1971

Most Free Throw Attempts, One Quarter

16—Oscar Robertson, Cincinnati at Baltimore, December 27, 1964
   Stan McKenzie, Phoenix at Philadelphia, February 15, 1970
   Pete Maravich, Atlanta at Chicago, January 2, 1973 (2nd Qtr.)
15—George Yardley, Detroit vs. Minneapolis, December 25, 1957 (3rd Qtr.)
   Wilt Chamberlain, Philadelphia vs. Syracuse, November 9, 1961
   Wilt Chamberlain, Philadelphia at Cincinnati, February 13, 1962
   Rick Barry, San Francisco at New York, December 6, 1966
   Wilt Chamberlain, Philadelphia vs. Seattle at New York, December 12, 1967
   John Drew, Atlanta vs. New Orleans, January 20, 1979 (3rd Qtr.)
   Adrian Dantley, Detroit vs. Sacramento, December 10, 1986 (4th Qtr.)
   Shawn Kemp, Seattle at Phoenix, April 14, 1992 (4th Qtr.)

REBOUNDS
Rebounds have been compiled since 1950-51

Most Seasons Leading League

11—Wilt Chamberlain, Philadelphia, 1959-60—1961-62; San Francisco, 1962-63; Philadelphia, 1965-66—1967-68; Los Angeles, 1968-69, 1970-71—1972-73
6—Moses Malone, Houston, 1978-79, 1980-81—1981-82; Philadelphia, 1982-83—1984-85
4—Bill Russell, Boston, 1957-58—1958-59, 1963-64—1964-65

Most Consecutive Seasons Leading League

5—Moses Malone, Houston, 1980-81—1981-82; Philadelphia, 1982-83—1984-85
4—Wilt Chamberlain, Philadelphia, 1959-60—1961-62; San Francisco, 1962-63
   Wilt Chamberlain, Philadelphia, 1965-66—1967-68; Los Angeles, 1968-69

Most Rebounds, Career

23,924—Wilt Chamberlain, Philadelphia, 1959-60—1961-62; San Francisco, 1962-63—1964-65; Philadelphia, 1964-65—1967-68; Los Angeles, 1968-69—1972-73
21,620—Bill Russell, Boston, 1956-57—1968-69
17,440—Kareem Abdul-Jabbar, Milwaukee, 1969-70—1974-75; L.A. Lakers, 1975-76—1988-89
16,279—Elvin Hayes, San Diego, 1968-69—1970-71; Houston, 1971-72; Baltimore, 1972-73; Capital, 1973-74; Washington, 1974-75—1980-81; Houston, 1981-82—1983-84
15,894—Moses Malone, Buffalo, 1976-77; Houston, 1976-77—1981-82; Philadelphia, 1982-83—1985-86; Washington, 1986-87—1987-88; Atlanta, 1988-89—1990-91; Milwaukee, 1991-92

Highest Average, Rebounds per Game, Career (minimum: 400 games)

22.9—Wilt Chamberlain, Philadelphia, 1959-60—1961-62; San Francisco, 1962-63—1964-65; Philadelphia, 1964-65—1967-68; Los Angeles, 1968-69—1972-73 (23,924/1,045)
22.5—Bill Russell, Boston, 1956-57—1968-69 (21,620/963)
16.2—Bob Pettit, Milwaukee, 1954-55; St. Louis, 1955-56—1964-65 (12,849/792)
15.6—Jerry Lucas, Cincinnati, 1963-64—1969-70; San Francisco, 1969-70—1970-71; New York, 1971-72—1973-74 (12,942/829)
15.0—Nate Thurmond, San Francisco, 1963-64—1970-71; Golden State, 1971-72—1973-74; Chicago, 1974-75—1975-76; Cleveland, 1975-76—1976-77 (14,464/964)

Most Rebounds, Season

2,149—Wilt Chamberlain, Philadelphia, 1960-61
2,052—Wilt Chamberlain, Philadelphia, 1961-62

1,957—Wilt Chamberlain, Philadelphia, 1966-67
1,952—Wilt Chamberlain, Philadelphia, 1967-68
1,946—Wilt Chamberlain, San Francisco, 1962-63
1,943—Wilt Chamberlain, Philadelphia, 1965-66
1,941—Wilt Chamberlain, Philadelphia, 1959-60
1,930—Bill Russell, Boston, 1963-64

Most Rebounds, Rookie, Season

1,941—Wilt Chamberlain, Philadelphia, 1959-60
1,500—Walt Bellamy, Chicago, 1961-62
1,491—Wes Unseld, Baltimore, 1968-69

Most Seasons, 1,000-or-More Rebounds

13—Wilt Chamberlain, Philadelphia, 1959-60—1961-62; San Francisco, 1962-63—1963-64; San Francisco, Philadelphia, 1964-65; Philadelphia, 1965-66—1967-68; Los Angeles, 1968-69, 1970-71—1972-73
12—Bill Russell, Boston, 1957-58—1968-69
9—Bob Pettit, St. Louis, 1955-56—1963-64
Walt Bellamy, Chicago, 1961-62—1962-63; Baltimore, 1963-64—1964-65; Baltimore, New York, 1965-66;
New York, 1966-67; New York, Detroit, 1968-69; Atlanta, 1970-71—1971-72
Elvin Hayes, San Diego, 1968-69—1970-71; Houston, 1971-72; Baltimore, 1972-73; Capital, 1973-74; Washington, 1974-75, 1976-77—1977-78

Most Consecutive Seasons, 1,000-or-More Rebounds

12—Bill Russell, Boston, 1957-58—1968-69
10—Wilt Chamberlain, Philadelphia, 1959-60—1961-62; San Francisco, 1962-63—1963-64; San Francisco, Philadelphia, 1964-65; Philadelphia, 1965-66—1967-68; Los Angeles, 1968-69
9—Bob Pettit, St. Louis, 1955-56—1963-64

Highest Average, Rebounds per Game, Season

27.2—Wilt Chamberlain, Philadelphia, 1960-61 (2,149/79)
27.0—Wilt Chamberlain, Philadelphia, 1959-60 (1,941/72)
25.7—Wilt Chamberlain, Philadelphia, 1961-62 (2,052/80)
24.7—Bill Russell, Boston, 1963-64 (1,930/78)
24.6—Wilt Chamberlain, Philadelphia, 1965-66 (1,943/79)

Most Rebounds, Game

55—Wilt Chamberlain, Philadelphia vs. Boston, November 24, 1960
51—Bill Russell, Boston vs. Syracuse, February 5, 1960
49—Bill Russell, Boston vs. Philadelphia, November 16, 1957
Bill Russell, Boston vs. Detroit at Providence, March 11, 1965
45—Wilt Chamberlain, Philadelphia vs. Syracuse, February 6, 1960
Wilt Chamberlain, Philadelphia vs. Los Angeles, January 21, 1961

Most Rebounds, Rookie, Game

45—Wilt Chamberlain, Philadelphia vs. Syracuse, February 6, 1960
43—Wilt Chamberlain, Philadelphia vs. New York, November 10, 1959
42—Wilt Chamberlain, Philadelphia vs. Boston, January 15, 1960
Wilt Chamberlain, Philadelphia vs. Detroit, at Bethlehem, Pa., January 25, 1960

Most Rebounds, One Half

32—Bill Russell, Boston vs. Philadelphia, November 16, 1957
31—Wilt Chamberlain, Philadelphia vs. Boston, November 24, 1960
28—Wilt Chamberlain, Philadelphia vs. Syracuse, February 6, 1960

Most Rebounds, One Quarter

18—Nate Thurmond, San Francisco at Baltimore, February 28, 1965
17—Bill Russell, Boston vs. Philadelphia, November 16, 1957
Bill Russell, Boston vs. Cincinnati, December 12, 1958
Bill Russell, Boston vs. Syracuse, February 5, 1960
Wilt Chamberlain, Philadelphia vs. Syracuse, February 6, 1960

OFFENSIVE REBOUNDS
Offensive Rebounds have been compiled since 1973-74

Most Offensive Rebounds, Career

6,583—Moses Malone, Buffalo, 1976-77; Houston, 1976-77—1981-82; Philadelphia, 1982-83—1985-86; Washington, 1986-87—1987-88; Atlanta, 1988-89—1990-91; Milwaukee, 1991-92
3,987—Robert Parish, Golden State, 1976-77—1979-80; Boston, 1980-81—1991-92
3,325—Buck Williams, New Jersey, 1981-82—1988-89; Portland, 1989-90—1991-92

Highest Average, Offensive Rebounds Per Game, Career (minimum: 400 games)

5.3—Moses Malone, Buffalo, 1976-77; Houston, 1976-77—1981-82; Philadelphia, 1982-83—1985-86; Washington, 1986-87—1987-88; Atlanta, 1988-89—1990-91; Milwaukee, 1991-92 (6,583/1,246)
4.4—Charles Barkley, Philadelphia, 1984-85—1991-92 (2,688/610)
4.2—Hakeem Olajuwon, Houston, 1984-85—1991-92 (2,492/594)

Most Offensive Rebounds, Season

587—Moses Malone, Houston, 1978-79
573—Moses Malone, Houston, 1979-80
558—Moses Malone, Houston, 1981-82

Most Offensive Rebounds, Game

21—Moses Malone, Houston vs. Seattle, February 11, 1982
19—Moses Malone, Houston at New Orleans, February 9, 1979
18—Charles Oakley, Chicago vs. Milwaukee, March 15, 1986 (ot)
  Dennis Rodman, Detroit vs. Indiana, March 4, 1992 (ot)

DEFENSIVE REBOUNDS
Defensive Rebounds have been compiled since 1973-74

Most Defensive Rebounds, Career

9,394—Kareem Abdul-Jabbar, Milwaukee, 1973-74—1974-75; L.A. Lakers, 1975-76—1988-89
9,311—Moses Malone, Buffalo, 1976-77; Houston, 1976-77—1981-82; Philadelphia, 1982-83—1985-86; Washington, 1986-87—1987-88; Atlanta, 1988-89—1990-91; Milwaukee, 1991-92
8,704—Robert Parish, Golden State, 1976-77-1979-80; Boston, 1980-81—1991-92

Highest Average, Defensive Rebounds Per Game, Career (minimum: 400 games)

9.8—Dave Cowens, Boston, 1973-74—1979-80; Milwaukee, 1982-83 (5,122/524)
8.4—Wes Unseld, Capital, 1973-74; Washington, 1974-75—1980-81 (4,974/591)
8.3—Hakeem Olajuwon, Houston, 1984-85—1991-92 (4,949/594)

Most Defensive Rebounds, Season

1,111—Kareem Abdul-Jabbar, Los Angeles, 1975-76
1,109—Elvin Hayes, Capital, 1973-74
1,007—Dennis Rodman, Detroit, 1991-92

Most Defensive Rebounds, Game

29—Kareem Abdul-Jabbar, Los Angeles vs. Detroit, December 14, 1975
28—Elvin Hayes, Capital at Atlanta, November 17, 1973
25—Elvin Hayes, Capital vs. Seattle, February 27, 1974
  Artis Gilmore, Chicago vs. San Antonio, December 22, 1978
  Robert Parish, Golden State vs. New York, March 30, 1979
  Swen Nater, San Diego vs. Denver, December 14, 1979
  Herb Williams, Indiana vs. Denver, January 23, 1989

ASSISTS

Most Seasons Leading League

8—Bob Cousy, Boston, 1952-53—1959-60
6—Oscar Robertson, Cincinnati, 1960-61—1961-62, 1963-64—1965-66, 1968-69
5—John Stockton, Utah, 1987-88—1991-92

Most Consecutive Seasons Leading League

8—Bob Cousy, Boston, 1952-53—1959-60
5—John Stockton, Utah, 1987-88—1991-92
3—Oscar Robertson, Cincinnati, 1963-64—1965-66

Most Assists, Career

9,921—Magic Johnson, L.A. Lakers, 1979-80—1990-91
9,887—Oscar Robertson, Cincinnati, 1960-61—1969-70; Milwaukee, 1970-71—1973-74
7,991—Isiah Thomas, Detroit, 1981-82—1991-92
7,365—John Stockton, Utah, 1984-85—1991-92
7,285—Maurice Cheeks, Philadelphia, 1978-79—1988-89; San Antonio, 1989-90; New York, 1989-90—1990-91; Atlanta, 1991-92

Highest Average, Assists per Game, Career (minimum: 400 games)

11.4 —Magic Johnson, L.A. Lakers, 1979-80—1990-91 (9,921/874)
11.3 —John Stockton, Utah, 1984-85—1991-92 (7,365/652)
9.51—Oscar Robertson, Cincinnati, 1960-61—1969-70; Milwaukee, 1970-71—1973-74 (9,887/1,040)
9.49—Isiah Thomas, Detroit, 1981-82—1991-92 (7,991/842)

Most Assists, Season

1,164—John Stockton, Utah, 1990-91
1,134—John Stockton, Utah, 1989-90
1,128—John Stockton, Utah, 1987-88

Most Assists, Rookie, Season

868—Mark Jackson, New York, 1987-88
690—Oscar Robertson, Cincinnati, 1960-61
689—Tim Hardaway, Golden State, 1989-90

Highest Average, Assists per Game, Season (minimum: 70 games)

14.5—John Stockton, Utah, 1989-90 (1,134/78)
14.2—John Stockton, Utah, 1990-91 (1,164/82)
13.9—Isiah Thomas, Detroit, 1984-85 (1,123/81)
13.8—John Stockton, Utah, 1987-88 (1,128/82)

Most Assists, Game

30—Scott Skiles, Orlando vs. Denver, December 30, 1990
29—Kevin Porter, New Jersey vs. Houston, February 24, 1978
28—Bob Cousy, Boston vs. Minneapolis, February 27, 1959
  Guy Rodgers, San Francisco vs. St. Louis, March 14, 1963
  John Stockton, Utah vs. San Antonio, January 15, 1991

Most Assists, Rookie, Game

> 25—Ernie DiGregorio, Buffalo at Portland, January 1, 1974
>   Nate McMillan, Seattle vs. L.A. Clippers, February 23, 1987
> 22—Phil Ford, Kansas City vs. Milwaukee, February 21, 1979
>   Ennis Whatley, Chicago vs. New York, January 14, 1984
>   Ennis Whatley, Chicago vs. Atlanta, March 3, 1984
> 21—Phil Ford, Kansas City vs. Phoenix, February 23, 1979
>   Nate McMillan, Seattle vs. Sacramento, March 31, 1987

Most Assists, One Half

> 19—Bob Cousy, Boston vs. Minneapolis, February 27, 1959
> 18—Magic Johnson, Los Angeles vs. Seattle, February 21, 1984 (1st Half)
> 17—Nate McMillan, Seattle vs. L.A. Clippers, February 23, 1987 (2nd Half)

Most Assists, One Quarter

> 14—John Lucas, San Antonio vs. Denver, April 15, 1984 (2nd Qtr.)
> 12—Bob Cousy, Boston vs. Minneapolis, February 27, 1959
>   John Lucas, Houston vs. Milwaukee, October 27, 1977 (3rd Qtr.)
>   John Lucas, Golden State vs. Chicago, November 17, 1978 (1st Qtr.)
>   Magic Johnson, Los Angeles vs. Seattle, February 21, 1984 (1st Qtr.)
> 11—John McCarthy, St. Louis vs. Detroit, March 8, 1960 (1st Qtr.)
>   Isiah Thomas, Detroit vs. Golden State, January 24, 1985 (1st Qtr.)
>   Nate McMillan, Seattle vs. L.A. Clippers, February 23, 1987 (3rd Qtr.)
>   John Stockton, Utah vs. Chicago, November 30, 1988 (2nd Qtr.)
>   Michael Holton, Charlotte vs. Philadelphia, December 1, 1988 (1st Qtr.)
>   Isiah Thomas, Detroit vs. Cleveland, November 24, 1989 (1st Qtr.)
>   Avery Johnson, Seattle vs. Miami, January 5, 1990 (3rd Qtr.)
>   John Stockton, Utah vs. Portland, March 1, 1990 (3rd Qtr.)
>   Magic Johnson, L.A. Lakers at Charlotte, January 24, 1991 (1st Qtr.)

PERSONAL FOULS

Most Seasons Leading League

> 3—George Mikan, Minneapolis, 1949-50—1951-52
>   Vern Mikkelsen, Minneapolis, 1954-55—1956-57
>   Darryl Dawkins, Philadelphia, 1979-80; New Jersey, 1982-83—1983-84
> 2—Walter Dukes, Detroit, 1957-58—1958-59
>   Zelmo Beaty, St. Louis, 1962-63, 1965-66
>   Dave Cowens, Boston, 1970-71—1971-72
>   Lonnie Shelton, New York Knicks, 1976-77—1977-78
>   Steve Johnson, Kansas City, 1981-82; Portland, 1986-87

Most Consecutive Seasons Leading League

> 3—George Mikan, Minneapolis, 1949-50—1951-52
>   Vern Mikkelsen, Minneapolis, 1954-55—1956-57
> 2—Walter Dukes, Detroit, 1957-58—1958-59
>   Dave Cowens, Boston, 1970-71—1971-72
>   Lonnie Shelton, New York Knicks, 1976-77—1977-78
>   Darryl Dawkins, New Jersey, 1982-83—1983-84

Most Personal Fouls, Career

> 4,657—Kareem Abdul-Jabbar, Milwaukee, 1969-70—1974-75; L.A. Lakers, 1975-76—1988-89
> 4,193—Elvin Hayes, San Diego, 1968-69—1970-71; Houston, 1971-72; Baltimore, 1972-73; Capital, 1973-74; Washington, 1974-75—1980-81; Houston, 1981-82—1983-84
> 3,879—Jack Sikma, Seattle, 1977-78—1985-86; Milwaukee, 1986-87—1990-91

Most Personal Fouls, Season

> 386—Darryl Dawkins, New Jersey, 1983-84
> 379—Darryl Dawkins, New Jersey, 1982-83
> 372—Steve Johnson, Kansas City, 1981-82

Most Personal Fouls, Game

> 8—Don Otten, Tri-Cities at Sheboygan, November 24, 1949
> 7—Alex Hannum, Syracuse at Boston, December 26, 1950
> 6—By many players

Most Personal Fouls, One Half

> 6—By many players

Most Personal Fouls, One Quarter

> 6—By many players

DISQUALIFICATIONS
Disqualifications have been compiled since 1950-51

Most Seasons Leading League

> 4—Walter Dukes, Detroit, 1958-59—1961-62
> 3—Vern Mikkelsen, Minneapolis, 1955-56—1957-58
>   Steve Johnson, Kansas City, 1981-82, San Antonio, 1985-86, Portland, 1986-87

Most Consecutive Seasons Leading League

    4—Walter Dukes, Detroit, 1958-59—1961-62
    3—Vern Mikkelsen, Minneapolis, 1955-56—1957-58

Most Disqualifications, Career

  127—Vern Mikkelsen, Minneapolis, 1950-51—1958-59
  121—Walter Dukes, New York, 1955-56; Minneapolis, 1956-57; Detroit, 1957-58—1962-63
  105—Charlie Share, Ft. Wayne, 1951-52—1953-54; Milwaukee, 1953-54—1954-55; St. Louis, 1955-56—1958-59; St. Louis, Minneapolis, 1959-60

Highest Percentage, Games Disqualified, Career (minimum: 400 games)

  21.88—Walter Dukes, New York, 1955-56; Minneapolis, 1956-57; Detroit, 1957-58—1962-63 (121/553)
  20.13—Vern Mikkelsen, Minneapolis, 1950-51—1958-59 (127/631)
  18.14—Alex Hannum, Syracuse, 1950-51; Baltimore, 1951-52; Rochester, 1951-52—1953-54; Milwaukee, 1954-55; St. Louis, 1955-56; Fort Wayne, 1956-57; St. Louis, 1956-57 (82/452)

Lowest Percentage, Games Disqualified, Career (minimum: 400 games)

  0.00—Wilt Chamberlain, Philadelphia, 1959-60—1961-62; San Francisco, 1962-63—1964-65; Philadelphia, 1964-65—1967-68; Los Angeles, 1968-69—1972-73 (0/1,045)
       Rolando Blackman, Dallas, 1981-82—1991-92 (0/865)
       Don Buse, Indiana, 1976-77; Phoenix, 1977-78—1979-80; Indiana, 1980-81—1981-82; Portland, 1982-83; Kansas City, 1983-84—1984-85 (0/648)
       Jerry Sichting, Indiana, 1980-81—1984-85; Boston, 1985-86—1987-88; Portland, 1987-88—1988-89; Charlotte, 1989-90; Milwaukee, 1989-90 (0/598)
       Randy Wittman, Atlanta, 1983-84—1987-88; Sacramento, 1988-89; Indiana, 1988-89—1991-92 (0/543)
       Danny Young, Seattle, 1984-85—1987-88; Portland, 1988-89—1991-92; L.A. Clippers, 1991-92 (0/502)
       John Battle, Atlanta, 1985-86—1990-91; Cleveland, 1991-92 (0/492)
       Steve Colter, Portland, 1984-85—1985-86; Chicago, 1986-87; Philadelphia, 1986-87—1987-88; Washington, 1987-88—1989-90; Sacramento, 1990-91 (0/469)
       Charlie Criss, Atlanta, 1977-78—1981-82; San Diego, 1981-82; Milwaukee, 1982-83—1983-84; Atlanta, 1983-84—1984-85 (0/418)
  0.11—Mike Gminski, New Jersey, 1980-81—1987-88; Philadelphia, 1987-88—1990-91; Charlotte, 1990-91—1991-92 (1/875)
  0.14—Larry Drew, Detroit, 1980-81; Kansas City, 1981-82—1984-85; Sacramento, 1985-86; L.A. Clippers, 1986-87—1987-88; L.A. Lakers, 1989-90—1990-91 (1/714)

Most Consecutive Games Without Disqualification, Career

  1,129—Moses Malone, Houston, Philadelphia, Washington, Atlanta, Milwaukee, January 7, 1978—April 18, 1992 (current)
  1,045—Wilt Chamberlain, Philadelphia, San Francisco, Philadelphia, Los Angeles, October 24, 1959—March 28, 1973
    865—Rolando Blackman, Dallas, October 30, 1981—April 19, 1992 (current)

Most Disqualifications, Season

  26—Don Meineke, Ft. Wayne, 1952-53
  25—Steve Johnson, Kansas City, 1981-82
  23—Darryl Dawkins, New Jersey, 1982-83

Fewest Minutes, Disqualified, Game

  5—Dick Farley, Syracuse at St. Louis, March 12, 1956
  6—Bill Bridges, St. Louis at New York, October 29, 1963
      Johnny Green, Baltimore vs. San Francisco, October 28, 1966
      Jim Barnes, Los Angeles at Philadelphia, December 2, 1966
      Leonard Gray, Washington at Philadelphia, April 9, 1977
      Chris Engler, Golden State vs. Utah, March 5, 1983
      Sam Mitchell, Minnesota vs. L.A. Lakers, March 17, 1990

STEALS
Steals have been compiled since 1973-74

Most Seasons Leading League

  3—Micheal Ray Richardson, New York, 1979-80; Golden State, New Jersey, 1982-83; New Jersey, 1984-85
    Alvin Robertson, San Antonio, 1985-86—1986-87; Milwaukee, 1990-91
  2—Magic Johnson, Los Angeles, 1980-81—1981-82
    Michael Jordan, Chicago, 1987-88, 1989-90
    John Stockton, Utah, 1988-89, 1991-92

Most Consecutive Seasons Leading League

  2—Magic Johnson, Los Angeles, 1980-81—1981-82
    Alvin Robertson, San Antonio, 1985-86—1986-87

Most Steals, Career

  2,277—Maurice Cheeks, Philadelphia, 1978-79—1988-89; San Antonio, 1989-90; New York, 1989-90—1990-91; Atlanta, 1991-92
  1,791—Alvin Robertson, San Antonio, 1984-85—1988-89; Milwaukee, 1989-90—1991-92
  1,698—Magic Johnson, L.A. Lakers, 1979-80—1990-91

Highest Average, Steals per Game, Career (minimum: 400 games)

  2.83—Alvin Robertson, San Antonio, 1984-85—1988-89; Milwaukee, 1989-90—1991-92 (1,791/633)
  2.71—Michael Jordan, Chicago, 1984-85—1991-92 (1,594/589)
  2.63—Micheal Ray Richardson, New York, 1978-79—1981-82; Golden State, New Jersey, 1982-83; New Jersey, 1983-84—1985-86 (1,463/556)

Most Steals, Season

301—Alvin Robertson, San Antonio, 1985-86
281—Don Buse, Indiana, 1976-77
265—Micheal Ray Richardson, New York, 1979-80

Highest Average, Steals per Game, Season (Qualifiers)

3.67—Alvin Robertson, San Antonio, 1985-86 (301/82)
3.47—Don Buse, Indiana, 1976-77 (281/81)
3.43—Magic Johnson, Los Angeles, 1980-81 (127/37)

Most Steals, Rookie, Season

211—Dudley Bradley, Indiana, 1979-80
209—Ron Harper, Cleveland, 1986-87
205—Mark Jackson, New York, 1987-88

Highest Average, Steals per Game, Rookie, Season (Qualifiers)

2.57—Dudley Bradley, Indiana, 1979-80 (211/82)
2.55—Ron Harper, Cleveland, 1986-87 (209/82)
2.50—Mark Jackson, New York, 1987-88 (205/82)

Most Steals, Game

11—Larry Kenon, San Antonio at Kansas City, December 26, 1976
10—Jerry West, Los Angeles vs. Seattle, December 7, 1973
     Larry Steele, Portland vs. Los Angeles, November 16, 1974
     Fred Brown, Seattle at Philadelphia, December 3, 1976
     Gus Williams, Seattle at New Jersey, February 22, 1978
     Eddie Jordan, New Jersey at Philadelphia, March 23, 1979
     Johnny Moore, San Antonio vs. Indiana, March 6, 1985
     Lafayette Lever, Denver vs. Indiana, March 9, 1985
     Clyde Drexler, Portland at Milwaukee, January 10, 1986
     Alvin Robertson, San Antonio vs. Phoenix, February 18, 1986
     Alvin Robertson, San Antonio at L.A. Clippers, November 22, 1986
     Ron Harper, Cleveland vs. Philadelphia, March 10, 1987
     Michael Jordan, Chicago vs. New Jersey, January 29, 1988
     Alvin Robertson, San Antonio vs. Houston, January 11, 1989 (ot)
     Alvin Robertson, Milwaukee vs. Utah, November 19, 1990

Most Steals, One Half

8—Quinn Buckner, Milwaukee vs. N.Y. Nets, November 27, 1976
     Fred Brown, Seattle at Philadelphia, December 3, 1976
     Gus Williams, Seattle at Washington, January 23, 1979
     Eddie Jordan, New Jersey at Chicago, October 23, 1979
     Dudley Bradley, Indiana at Utah, November 10, 1980
     Rob Williams, Denver at New Jersey, February 17, 1983
     Lafayette Lever, Denver vs. Indiana, March 9, 1985
     Michael Jordan, Chicago at Boston, November 9, 1988

Most Steals, One Quarter

8—Lafayette Lever, Denver vs. Indiana, March 9, 1985
7—Quinn Buckner, Milwaukee vs. N.Y. Nets, November 27, 1976

BLOCKED SHOTS
Blocked shots have been compiled since 1973-74

Most Seasons Leading League

4—Kareem Abdul-Jabbar, Milwaukee, 1974-75; Los Angeles, 1975-76, 1978-79—1979-80
     Mark Eaton, Utah, 1983-84—1984-85; 1986-87—1987-88
3—George T. Johnson, New Jersey, 1977-78; San Antonio, 1980-81—1981-82

Most Consecutive Seasons Leading League

2—Kareem Abdul-Jabbar, Milwaukee, 1974-75; Los Angeles, 1975-76
     Kareem Abdul-Jabbar, Los Angeles, 1978-79—1979-80
     George T. Johnson, San Antonio, 1980-81—1981-82
     Mark Eaton, Utah, 1983-84—1984-85
     Mark Eaton, Utah, 1986-87—1987-88
     Hakeem Olajuwon, Houston, 1989-90—1990-91

Most Blocked Shots, Career

3,189—Kareem Abdul-Jabbar, Milwaukee, 1973-74—1974-75; L.A. Lakers, 1975-76—1988-89
2,985—Mark Eaton, Utah, 1982-83—1991-92
2,456—Wayne Rollins, Atlanta, 1977-78—1987-88; Cleveland, 1988-89—1989-90; Detroit, 1990-91; Houston, 1991-92

Highest Average, Blocked Shots per Game, Career (minimum: 400 games)

3.68—Mark Eaton, Utah, 1982-83—1991-92 (2,985/811)
3.55—Manute Bol, Washington, 1985-86—1987-88; Golden State, 1988-89—1989-90; Philadelphia, 1990-91—1991-92 (1,942/547)
3.54—Hakeem Olajuwon, Houston, 1984-85—1991-92 (2,102/594)

Most Blocked Shots, Season

456—Mark Eaton, Utah, 1984-85

397—Manute Bol, Washington, 1985-86
393—Elmore Smith, Los Angeles, 1973-74

Highest Average, Blocked Shots per Game, Season (Qualifiers)

5.56—Mark Eaton, Utah, 1984-85 (456/82)
4.97—Manute Bol, Washington, 1985-86 (397/80)
4.85—Elmore Smith, Los Angeles, 1973-74 (393/81)

Most Blocked Shots, Rookie, Season

397—Manute Bol, Washington, 1985-86
319—David Robinson, San Antonio, 1989-90
275—Mark Eaton, Utah, 1982-83

Highest Average, Blocked Shots per Game, Rookie, Season (Qualifiers)

4.97—Manute Bol, Washington, 1985-86 (397/80)
3.89—David Robinson, San Antonio, 1989-90 (319/82)
3.40—Mark Eaton, Utah, 1982-83 (275/81)

Most Blocked Shots, Game

17—Elmore Smith, Los Angeles vs. Portland, October 28, 1973
15—Manute Bol, Washington vs. Atlanta, January 25, 1986
     Manute Bol, Washington vs. Indiana, February 26, 1987
14—Elmore Smith, Los Angeles vs. Detroit, October 26, 1973
     Elmore Smith, Los Angeles vs. Houston, November 4, 1973
     Mark Eaton, Utah vs. Portland, January 18, 1985
     Mark Eaton, Utah vs. San Antonio, February 18, 1989

TURNOVERS
Turnovers have been compiled since 1977-78

Most Turnovers, Career

3,724—Moses Malone, Houston, 1977-78—1981-82; Philadelphia, 1982-83—1985-86; Washington, 1986-
          87—1987-88; Atlanta, 1988-89—1990-91; Milwaukee, 1991-92
3,493—Reggie Theus, Chicago, 1978-79—1983-84; Kansas City, 1983-84—1984-85; Sacramento, 1985-86—1987-
          88; Atlanta, 1988-89; Orlando, 1989-90; New Jersey, 1990-91
3,403—Magic Johnson, L.A. Lakers, 1979-80—1990-91

Most Turnovers, Season

366—Artis Gilmore, Chicago, 1977-78
360—Kevin Porter, Detroit, New Jersey, 1977-78
359—Micheal Ray Richardson, New York, 1979-80

Most Turnovers, Game

14—John Drew, Atlanta at New Jersey, March 1, 1978
13—Chris Mullin, Golden State at Utah, March 31, 1988
12—Kevin Porter, New Jersey at Philadelphia, November 9, 1977
     Artis Gilmore, Chicago vs. Atlanta, January 31, 1978 (ot)
     Kevin Porter, Detroit at Philadelphia, February 7, 1979
     Maurice Lucas, Portland vs. Phoenix, November 25, 1979
     Moses Malone, Houston at Phoenix, February 6, 1981
     Eric Floyd, Golden State vs. Denver, October 25, 1985
     Scottie Pippen, Chicago at New Jersey, February 25, 1990 (ot)

TEAM
GAMES WON & LOST

Highest Winning Percentage, Season

.841 —Los Angeles, 1971-72 (69-13)
.840 —Philadelphia, 1966-67 (68-13)
.829 —Boston, 1972-73 (68-14)
.8170—Boston, 1985-86 (67-15)
.8170—Chicago, 1991-92 (67-15)
.8167—Washington, 1946-47 (49-11)

Lowest Winning Percentage, Season

.110—Philadelphia, 1972-73 (9-73)
.125—Providence, 1947-48 (6-42)
.146—L.A. Clippers, 1986-87 (12-70)

Most Consecutive Games Won

33—Los Angeles, November 5, 1971—January 7, 1972
20—Washington, March 13—December 4, 1948 (5 games in 1947-48, 15 games in 1948-49)
     Milwaukee, February 6—March 8, 1971
18—Rochester, February 17—November 11, 1950 (15 games in 1949-50, 3 games in 1950-51)
     Philadelphia, March 3—November 4, 1966 (11 games in 1965-66, 7 games in 1966-67)
     New York, October 24—November 28, 1969
     Boston, February 24—March 26, 1982

Most Consecutive Games Won, One Season

 33—Los Angeles, November 5, 1971—January 7, 1972
 20—Milwaukee, February 6—March 8, 1971
 18—New York, October 24—November 28, 1969
   Boston, February 24—March 26, 1982

Most Consecutive Games Won, Start of Season

 15—Washington, November 3—December 4, 1948
 14—Boston, October 22—November 27, 1957
 12—Seattle, October 29—November 19, 1982

Most Consecutive Games Won, End of Season

 15—Rochester, February 17—March 19, 1950
 14—Milwaukee, February 28—March 27, 1973
 11—Philadelphia, March 3—March 20, 1966

Most Consecutive Games Lost

 24—Cleveland, March 19—November 5, 1982 (19 games in 1981-82; 5 games in 1982-83)
 21—Detroit, March 7—October 22, 1980 (14 games in 1979-80; 7 games in 1980-81)
 20—Philadelphia, January 9—February 11, 1973
 19—Philadelphia, March 21—November 10, 1972 (4 games in 1971-72; 15 games in 1972-73)
   San Diego, March 11—April 13, 1982
   L.A. Clippers, December 30, 1988—February 6, 1989

Most Consecutive Games Lost, One Season

 20—Philadelphia, January 9—February 11, 1973
 19—Cleveland, March 19—April 18, 1982
   San Diego, March 11—April 13, 1982
   L.A. Clippers, December 30, 1988—February 6, 1989
 18—Utah, February 24—March 29, 1982

Most Consecutive Games Lost, Start of Season

 17—Miami, November 5—December 12, 1988
 15—Denver, October 29—November 25, 1949
   Cleveland, October 14—November 10, 1970
   Philadelphia, October 10—November 10, 1972

Most Consecutive Games Lost, End of Season

 19—Cleveland, March 19—April 18, 1982
 15—San Diego, February 23—March 20, 1968
 14—Detroit, March 7—March 30, 1980
   L.A. Clippers, March 27—April 19, 1987

Highest Winning Percentage, Home Games, Season

 .976—Boston, 1985-86 (40-1)
 .971—Rochester, 1949-50 (33-1)
 .969—Syracuse, 1949-50 (31-1)
 .968—Minneapolis, 1949-50 (30-1)
 .967—Washington, 1946-47 (29-1)

Lowest Winning Percentage, Home Games, Season

 .125—Providence, 1947-48 (3-21)
 .161—Philadelphia, 1972-73 (5-26)
 .195—San Diego, 1967-68 (8-33)

Most Consecutive Home Games Won

 38—Boston, December 10, 1985—November 28, 1986 (31 games in 1985-86; 7 games in 1986-87)
 36—Philadelphia, January 14, 1966—January 20, 1967 (14 games in 1965-66; 22 games in 1966-67)
 34—Portland, March 5, 1977—February 3, 1978 (8 games in 1976-77; 26 games in 1977-78)

Most Consecutive Home Games Lost

 16—Orlando, March 1—November 6, 1990 (14 games in 1989-90; 2 games in 1990-91)
 15—Cleveland, March 20—November 26, 1982 (9 games in 1981-82; 6 games in 1982-83)
 14—Charlotte, February 28—November 3, 1989 (13 games in 1988-89; 1 game in 1989-90)

Highest Winning Percentage, Road Games, Season

 .816—Los Angeles, 1971-72 (31-7)
 .800—Boston, 1972-73 (32-8)
 .780—Boston, 1974-75 (32-9)
 .765—Philadelphia, 1966-67 (26-8)
 .756—Chicago, 1991-92 (31-10)

Lowest Winning Percentage, Road Games, Season

 .000—Baltimore, 1953-54 (0-20)
 .024—Sacramento, 1990-91 (1-40)
 .034—Philadelphia, 1952-53 (1-28)

Most Consecutive Road Games Won

 16—Los Angeles, November 6, 1971—January 7, 1972
 12—New York, October 15—December 10, 1969
   Los Angeles, October 15—December 20, 1972
   Portland, April 10—December 8, 1990 (four games in 1989-90; eight games in 1990-91)

Most Consecutive Road Games Lost

43—Sacramento, November 21, 1990—November 22, 1991 (37 games in 1990-91; 6 games in 1991-92)
34—New Jersey, December 23, 1989—November 21, 1990 (28 games in 1989-90; 6 games in 1990-91)
32—Baltimore, January 2, 1953—March 14, 1954 (12 games in 1952-53; 20 games in 1953-54)

OVERTIME GAMES

Most Overtime Games, Season

14—Philadelphia, 1990-91
13—New York, 1950-51
12—Baltimore, 1952-53
　　Milwaukee, 1952-53
　　Rochester, 1952-53

Most Consecutive Overtime Games, Season

3—Ft. Wayne, November 14-17-18, 1951
　Rochester, November 18-20-22, 1951
　San Francisco, October 26-27-28, 1962
　Houston, November 17-20-24, 1976
　Milwaukee, February 24-26-28, 1978
　Kansas City, March 2-4-7, 1979
　Phoenix, April 4-6-7, 1987
　L.A. Lakers, November 1-2-5, 1991

Most Overtime Games Won, Season

8—Milwaukee, 1977-78
　Philadelphia, 1990-91
7—New York, 1949-50
　New York, 1955-56
　Boston, 1958-59
　Los Angeles, 1961-62
　Chicago, 1969-70
　New York, 1990-91

Most Overtime Games Won, No Losses, Season

7—Los Angeles, 1961-62
5—New York, 1946-47
　Boston, 1966-67
　San Antonio, 1980-81
　Philadelphia, 1982-83
　Portland, 1986-87

Most Consecutive Overtime Games Won

11—San Antonio, November 13, 1979—February 8, 1983 (2 games in 1979-80, 5 games in 1980-81, 1
　　game in 1981-82, 3 games in 1982-83)
10—Milwaukee, February 26, 1972—November 30, 1974 (3 games in 1971-72, 3 games in 1972-73, 3
　　games in 1973-74, 1 game in 1974-75)
9—Boston, March 24, 1974—October 23, 1976 (1 game in 1973-74, 3 games in 1974-75, 3 games in
　　1975-76, 2 games in 1976-77)
　Houston, November 3, 1976—January 19, 1979 (4 games in 1976-77, 2 games in 1977-78, 3 games
　　in 1978-79)
　New York, November 11, 1988—February 17, 1990 (4 games in 1988-89; 5 games in 1989-90)

Most Overtime Games Lost, Season

10—Baltimore, 1952-53
8—Milwaukee, 1952-53
　Golden State, 1979-80

Most Overtime Games Lost, No Wins, Season

8—Golden State, 1979-80
6—Ft. Wayne, 1951-52
　Seattle, 1990-91

Most Consecutive Overtime Games Lost

10—Golden State, October 13, 1979—March 15, 1981 (8 games in 1979-80, 2 games in 1980-81)
9—Boston, November 14, 1946—vs. St.L. in 9th game of **48-49)
　Baltimore, January 14, 1953—February 22, 1954 (6 games in 1952-53, 3 games in 1953-54)
　Syracuse, January 13, 1960—January 21, 1962 (2 games in 1959-60, 4 games in 1960-61, 3 games
　　in 1961-62)
　New Jersey, March 18, 1986—April 19, 1988 (1 game in 1985-86; 4 games in 1986-87; 4 games in
　　1987-88)

Most Overtime Periods, Game

6—Indianapolis (75) at Rochester (73), January 6, 1951
5—Anderson (123) at Syracuse (125), November 24, 1949
　Seattle (154) at Milwaukee (155), November 9, 1989
4—New York (92) at Rochester (102), January 23, 1951
　Indianapolis (96) at Rochester (99), November 8, 1952
　Cleveland (129) at Portland (131), October 18, 1974
　Los Angeles (153) at Cleveland (154), January 29, 1980
　Atlanta (127) at Seattle (122), February 19, 1982
　Chicago (156) at Portland (155), March 16, 1984
　New Jersey (147) at Golden State (150), February 1, 1987

OFFENSE
SCORING

Highest Average, Points per Game, Season

126.5—Denver, 1981-82 (10,371/82)
125.4—Philadelphia, 1961-62 (10,035/80)
125.2—Philadelphia, 1966-67 (10,143/81)

Lowest Average, Points per Game, Season

87.4—Milwaukee, 1954-55 (6,291/72)
90.8—Rochester, 1954-55 (6,535/72)
91.1—Syracuse, 1954-55 (6,557/72)

Most Consecutive Games, 100+ Points

136—Denver, January 21, 1981—December 8, 1982
129—San Antonio, December 12, 1978—March 14, 1980
 81—Cincinnati, December 6, 1961—December 2, 1962

Most Consecutive Games, 100+ Points, Season

82—Denver, October 30, 1981—April 17, 1982 (entire season)
77—New York, October 23, 1966—March 19, 1967
73—Syracuse, November 4, 1961—March 14, 1962
    Philadelphia, November 8, 1966—March 19, 1967

Most Consecutive Games, Fewer Than 100 Points, Season

25—Milwaukee, December 18, 1954—January 30, 1955
15—Ft. Wayne, January 28—February 20, 1956
14—New York, November 27—December 19, 1954
    Ft. Wayne, December 11, 1955—January 5, 1956

Most Points, Game

186—Detroit at Denver, December 13, 1983 (3 ot)
184—Denver vs. Detroit, December 13, 1983 (3 ot)
173—Boston vs. Minneapolis, February 27, 1959
    Phoenix vs. Denver, November 10, 1990
171—San Antonio vs. Milwaukee, March 6, 1982 (3 ot)
169—Philadelphia vs. New York, at Hershey, Pa., March 2, 1962

Fewest Points, Game

57—Milwaukee vs. Boston, at Providence, February 27, 1955
59—Sacramento at Charlotte, January 10, 1991
61—New York at Detroit, April 12, 1992
62—Boston vs. Milwaukee, at Providence, February 27, 1955
63—Buffalo vs. Milwaukee, October 21, 1972

Most Points, Both Teams, Game

370—Detroit (186) at Denver (184), December 13, 1983 (3 ot)
337—San Antonio (171) vs. Milwaukee (166), March 6, 1982 (3 ot)
320—Golden State (162) at Denver (158), November 2, 1990
318—Denver (163) vs. San Antonio (155), January 11, 1984
316—Philadelphia (169) vs. New York (147), at Hershey, Pa., March 2, 1962
    Cincinnati (165) vs. San Diego (151), March 12, 1970
    Phoenix (173) vs. Denver (143), November 10, 1990

Fewest Points, Both Teams, Game

119—Milwaukee (57) vs. Boston (62), at Providence, February 27, 1955
133—New York (61) at Detroit (72), April 12, 1992
135—Syracuse (66) vs. Ft. Wayne (69), at Buffalo, January 25, 1955

Largest Margin of Victory, Game

68—Cleveland vs. Miami, December 17, 1991 (148-80)
63—Los Angeles vs. Golden State, March 19, 1972 (162-99)
62—Syracuse vs. New York, December 25, 1960 (162-100)
    Golden State vs. Sacramento, November 2, 1991 (153-91)
59—Golden State vs. Indiana, March 19, 1977 (150-91)
    Milwaukee vs. Detroit, December 26, 1978 (143-84)
58—Milwaukee vs. Sacramento, December 15, 1985 (140-82)

BY HALF

Most Points, First Half

107—Phoenix vs. Denver, November 10, 1990
 90—Denver at San Antonio, November 7, 1990
 89—Cincinnati vs. San Diego, March 12, 1970
    L.A. Lakers vs. Phoenix, January 2, 1987

Fewest Points, First Half

20—New Orleans at Seattle, January 4, 1975
22—Milwaukee vs. Syracuse, February 12, 1955

25—Rochester vs. Boston, at New York, February 26, 1957
Philadelphia vs. Milwaukee, March 3, 1972
Golden State vs. Chicago, January 1, 1974
Detroit at Indiana, November 8, 1989
Washington vs. Detroit, February 1, 1991

Most Points, Both Teams, First Half

174—Phoenix (107) vs. Denver (67), November 10, 1990
173—Denver (90) at San Antonio (83), November 7, 1990
170—Golden State (87) at Denver (83), November 2, 1990

Fewest Points, Both Teams, First Half

58—Syracuse (27) vs. Ft. Wayne (31), at Buffalo, January 25, 1955
61—Milwaukee (26) vs. Minneapolis (35), at Buffalo, November 6, 1954
Rochester (30) vs. New York (31), December 15, 1956

Most Points, Second Half

97—Atlanta at San Diego, February 11, 1970
95—Philadelphia at Seattle, December 20, 1967
94—Houston at Denver, January 10, 1991

Fewest Points, Second Half

25—Boston vs. Milwaukee, at Providence, February 27, 1955
St. Louis vs. Boston, December 26, 1964
Golden State vs. Boston, February 14, 1978
Washington vs. New York, December 22, 1985
New Jersey at Seattle, November 21, 1989
26—Milwaukee vs. Boston, at Providence, February 27, 1955
St. Louis vs. Rochester, November 23, 1955
New York at Chicago, February 23, 1973
Miami vs. Boston, November 15, 1988
Houston at L.A. Lakers, November 15, 1991

Most Points, Both Teams, Second Half

172—San Antonio (91) at Denver (81), January 11, 1984
170—Philadelphia (90) vs. Cincinnati (80), March 19, 1971
169—Philadelphia (90) vs. New York (79), at Hershey, Pa., March 2, 1962

Fewest Points, Both Teams, Second Half

51—Boston (25) vs. Milwaukee (26), at Providence, February 27, 1955
58—St. Louis (26) vs. Rochester (32), November 23, 1955
60—Detroit (30) vs. New York (30), April 12, 1992

BY QUARTER

Most Points, First Quarter

50—Syracuse at San Francisco, December 16, 1962
Boston vs. Denver, February 5, 1982
Utah vs. Denver, April 10, 1982
Milwaukee vs. Orlando, November 16, 1989
Phoenix vs. Denver, November 10, 1990
49—Atlanta vs. New Jersey, January 5, 1985
Portland vs. San Antonio, November 25, 1990
48—Boston at San Diego, February 12, 1982
Denver at Golden State, November 17, 1983
Philadelphia vs. San Antonio, March 24, 1989
Denver at San Antonio, November 7, 1990
Washington vs. Denver, December 29, 1990
Golden State vs. Sacramento, November 2, 1991

Fewest Points, First Quarter

4—Sacramento at L.A. Lakers, February 4, 1987
5—Syracuse at Milwaukee, November 13, 1954
New York vs. Ft. Wayne, at Boston, November 21, 1956
Cleveland at Chicago, December 15, 1990
6—Los Angeles vs. Chicago, November 20, 1977

Most Points, Both Teams, First Quarter

91—Utah (50) vs. Denver (41), April 10, 1982
87—Denver (47) vs. San Antonio (40), January 11, 1984
Phoenix (50) vs. Denver (37), November 10, 1990
86—Denver (47) vs. San Antonio (39), November 20, 1987
Houston (44) vs. Denver (42), November 6, 1990

Fewest Points, Both Teams, First Quarter

18—Ft. Wayne (9) at Syracuse (9), November 29, 1956
25—Minneapolis (11) at Rochester (14), December 11, 1954
Boston (7) at Milwaukee (18), November 12, 1974

Most Points, Second Quarter

57—Phoenix vs. Denver, November 10, 1990
52—Baltimore vs. Detroit, December 18, 1965

50—San Diego vs. Utah, April 14, 1984
   San Antonio at Houston, November 17, 1984

Fewest Points, Second Quarter

5—Utah at Los Angeles, December 1, 1981
6—Boston at New Jersey, January 9, 1990
7—Golden State at Portland, January 1, 1983
   Portland at Philadelphia, December 6, 1991

Most Points, Both Teams, Second Quarter

91—Seattle (46) at Golden State (45), March 23, 1974
90—New York (47) at Philadelphia (43), November 18, 1988
89—Denver (45) at Dallas (44), January 14, 1983
   San Antonio (47) vs. Denver (42), November 7, 1990

Fewest Points, Both Teams, Second Quarter

23—Rochester (10) at Milwaukee (13), January 4, 1955
24—Portland (7) at Philadelphia (17), December 6, 1991

Most Points, Third Quarter

57—Golden State vs. Sacramento, March 4, 1989
54—Atlanta at San Diego, February 11, 1970

Fewest Points, Third Quarter

4—Buffalo vs. Milwaukee, October 21, 1972
6—New York at Milwaukee, December 29, 1974

Most Points, Both Teams, Third Quarter

89—Atlanta (49) vs. Philadelphia (40), March 4, 1973
88—Los Angeles (44) vs. San Diego (44), March 23, 1979

Fewest Points, Both Teams, Third Quarter

23—Houston (11) at Philadelphia (12), February 2, 1975
   Detroit (10) vs. New York (13), April 12, 1992
24—Rochester (10) vs. Philadelphia (14), at New Haven, Conn., February 17, 1955
   Charlotte (7) vs. Utah (17), February 8, 1990

Most Points, Fourth Quarter

58—Buffalo at Boston, October 20, 1972
54—Boston vs. San Diego, February 25, 1970

Fewest Points, Fourth Quarter

7—Houston at L.A. Lakers, November 15, 1991
8—Phoenix at Detroit, February 18, 1976
   Seattle at Denver, October 31, 1985

Most Points, Both Teams, Fourth Quarter

99—San Antonio (53) at Denver (46), January 11, 1984
96—Boston (52) vs. Minneapolis (44), February 27, 1959
   Detroit (53) vs. Cincinnati (43), January 7, 1972

Fewest Points, Both Teams, Fourth Quarter

23—Boston (10) vs. Philadelphia (13), November 21, 1956
25—Milwaukee (12) vs. Boston (13), at Providence, February 27, 1955
   Minneapolis (10) at Ft. Wayne (15), February 12, 1956
   Dallas (9) at Minnesota (16), December 13, 1989

OVERTIME

Most Points, Overtime Period

24—Sacramento vs. Utah, March 17, 1990
23—L.A. Clippers vs. Phoenix, November 12, 1988
   Dallas at L.A. Lakers, December 12, 1990
   Indiana vs. Golden State, March 31, 1991

Fewest Points, Overtime Period

0—Houston vs. Portland, January 22, 1983
   L.A. Lakers vs. Detroit, December 1, 1989
   Seattle at Philadelphia, February 16, 1990
1—Washington at Atlanta, March 16, 1983
2—Minneapolis vs. New York, November 7, 1954
   Rochester vs. Ft. Wayne, December 1, 1954
   Cincinnati vs. Minneapolis, November 21, 1959
   K.C.-Omaha vs. Chicago, December 1, 1972
   New Jersey at Milwaukee, December 4, 1977
   Seattle at San Antonio, January 30, 1988
   Seattle at Chicago, February 23, 1988
   New Jersey vs. Atlanta, April 19, 1988
   Seattle at Cleveland, December 23, 1988
   Charlotte at Phoenix, January 15, 1990
   Washington vs. Philadelphia, March 24, 1990

Most Points, Both Teams, Overtime Period

39—Indiana (23) vs. Golden State (16), March 31, 1991
37—Los Angeles (21) at Baltimore (16), October 21, 1969

Fewest Points, Both Teams, Overtime Period

4—Seattle (0) at Philadelphia (4), February 16, 1990
6—Philadelphia (3) vs. Washington (3), November 15, 1975 (2nd ot)
  Washington (2) vs. Philadelphia (4), March 24, 1990

Largest Margin of Victory, Overtime Game

17—Portland at Houston, January 22, 1983 (113-96 game, 17-0 overtime)
16—Milwaukee vs. New Jersey, December 4, 1977 (134-118 game, 18-2 overtime)
15—Boston at San Francisco, January 2, 1963 (135-120 game, 21-6 overtime)
  Dallas at L.A. Lakers, December 12, 1990 (112-97 game, 23-8 overtime)

PLAYERS SCORING

Most Players, 2,000-or-More Points, Season

2—Los Angeles, 1964-65 (West 2,292, Baylor 2,009)
  Atlanta, 1972-73 (Maravich 2,063, Hudson 2,029)
  Denver, 1982-83 (English 2,326, Vandeweghe 2,186)
  Denver, 1983-84 (Vandeweghe 2,295, English 2,167)
  Boston, 1986-87 (Bird 2,076, McHale, 2,008)

Most Players, 1,000-or-More Points, Season

6—Syracuse, 1960-61 (Schayes 1,868, Greer 1,551, Barnett 1,320, Gambee 1,085, Costello 1,084, Kerr 1,056)
  Denver, 1987-88 (English 2,000, Lever 1,546, Adams 1,137, Schayes 1,129, Vincent 1,124, Rasmussen 1,002)
  Boston, 1990-91 (Lewis 1,478, Gamble 1,281, McHale 1,251, Parish 1,207, Bird 1,164, Shaw 1,091)

Most Players, 40-or-More Points, Game

2—Baltimore vs. Los Angeles, November 14, 1964 (Johnson 41, Bellamy 40)
  Los Angeles at San Francisco, February 11, 1970 (Baylor 43, West 43)
  New Orleans vs. Denver, April 10, 1977 (Maravich 45, Williams 41)
  Phoenix at Boston, January 5, 1978 (Westphal 43, Davis 40)
  San Antonio vs. Milwaukee, March 6, 1982 (3 ot) (Gervin 50, Mitchell 45)
  Detroit at Denver, December 13, 1983 (3 ot) (Thomas 47, Long 41)
  Denver vs. Detroit, December 13, 1983 (3 ot) (Vandeweghe 51, English 47)
  Utah vs. Detroit, March 19, 1984 (Dantley 43, Drew 42)

Most Players, 40-or-More Points, Both Teams, Game

4—Denver vs. Detroit, December 13, 1983 (3 ot) (Detroit: Thomas 47, Long 41; Denver: Vandeweghe 51, English 47)
3—New Orleans (2) vs. Denver (1), April 10, 1977 (New Orleans: Maravich 45, Williams 41; Denver: Thompson 40)
  San Antonio (2) vs. Milwaukee (1), March 6, 1982 (3 ot) (San Antonio: Gervin 50, Mitchell 45; Milwaukee: Winters 42)

FIELD GOAL PERCENTAGE

Highest Field Goal Percentage, Season

.545—L.A. Lakers, 1984-85 (3,952/7,254)
.532—Los Angeles, 1983-84 (3,854/7,250)
.529—Los Angeles, 1979-80 (3,898/7,368)

Lowest Field Goal Percentage, Season

.362 —Milwaukee, 1954-55 (2,187/6,041)
.3688—Syracuse, 1956-57 (2,550/6,915)
.3695—Rochester, 1956-57 (2,515/6,807)

Highest Field Goal Percentage, Game

.707—San Antonio at Dallas, April 16, 1983 (53/75)
.705—Chicago at Golden State, December 2, 1981 (43/61)
.699—Chicago vs. Detroit, January 22, 1980 (58/83)
.697—Portland vs. L.A. Clippers, February 1, 1986 (62/89)
.696—Phoenix at Golden State, March 12, 1980 (48/69)

Lowest Field Goal Percentage, Game

.229—Milwaukee vs. Minneapolis, at Buffalo, November 6, 1954 (22/96)
.235—New York vs. Milwaukee, at Providence, December 31, 1954 (24/102)
.238—Cleveland at San Francisco, November 10, 1970 (25/105)

Highest Field Goal Percentage, Both Teams, Game

.632—Boston (.650) vs. New Jersey (.615) at Hartford, December 11, 1984 (108/171)
.630—Portland (.697) vs. L.A. Clippers (.560), February 1, 1986 (109/173)
.628—New York (.642) vs. Denver (.612), December 8, 1981 (113/180)
.625—Chicago (.699) vs. Detroit (.559), January 22, 1980 (110/176)
  Phoenix (.696) at Golden State (.566), March 12, 1980 (95/152)

Lowest Field Goal Percentage, Both Teams, Game

.246—Milwaukee (.229) vs. Minneapolis (.263), at Buffalo, November 6, 1954 (48/195)
.260—Rochester (.250) at St. Louis (.270), November 23, 1955 (61/235)
.273—St. Louis (.239) vs. Syracuse (.315), November 12, 1955 (56/205)

FIELD GOALS

Most Field Goals per Game, Season

    49.9—Boston, 1959-60 (3,744/75)
    49.0—Philadelphia, 1961-62 (3,917/80)
    48.5—Denver, 1981-82 (3,980/82)

Fewest Field Goals per Game, Season

    30.4—Milwaukee, 1954-55 (2,187/72)
    32.4—Ft. Wayne, 1954-55 (2,333/72)
    32.8—Syracuse, 1954-55 (2,360/72)

Most Field Goals, Game

    74—Detroit at Denver, December 13, 1983 (3 ot)
    72—Boston vs. Minneapolis, February 27, 1959
    69—Syracuse vs. San Francisco, March 10, 1963
        Los Angeles vs. Golden State, March 19, 1972
        Detroit vs. Boston, March 9, 1979
        Milwaukee vs. New Orleans, March 14, 1979
        Los Angeles vs. Denver, April 9, 1982

Fewest Field Goals, Game

    19—Indiana at New York, December 10, 1985
    20—Rochester vs. Milwaukee, February 19, 1955
    21—Syracuse vs. Milwaukee, January 2, 1955

Most Field Goals, Both Teams, Game

    142—Detroit (74) at Denver (68), December 13, 1983 (3 ot)
    136—Milwaukee (68) at San Antonio (68), March 6, 1982 (3 ot)
    134—Cincinnati (67) vs. San Diego (67), March 12, 1970

Fewest Field Goals, Both Teams, Game

    46—Boston (23) vs. Milwaukee (23), at Providence, February 27, 1955
    48—Milwaukee (22) vs. Minneapolis (26), at Buffalo, November 6, 1954
        Syracuse (21) vs. Milwaukee (27), January 2, 1955
        Philadelphia (23) at New York (25), December 27, 1955
        Minneapolis (23) vs. St. Louis (25), at Ft. Wayne, December 29, 1955

Most Field Goals, One Half

    43—Phoenix vs. Denver, November 10, 1990 (1st Half)

Most Field Goals, Both Teams, One Half

    71—Denver (37) at San Antonio (34), November 7, 1990 (1st Half)

Most Field Goals, One Quarter

    24—Phoenix vs. Denver, November 10, 1990 (2nd Qtr.)

Most Field Goals, Both Teams, One Quarter

    40—Boston (23) vs. Minneapolis (17), February 27, 1959 (4th Qtr.)

FIELD GOAL ATTEMPTS

Most Field Goal Attempts per Game, Season

    119.6—Boston, 1959-60 (8,971/75)
    117.7—Boston, 1960-61 (9,295/79)
    115.7—Philadelphia, 1959-60 (8,678/75)

Fewest Field Goal Attempts per Game, Season

    79.72—Utah, 1990-91 (6,537/82)
    80.40—Utah, 1989-90 (6,593/82)
    80.43—Utah, 1988-89 (6,595/82)

Most Field Goal Attempts, Game

    153—Philadelphia vs. Los Angeles, December 8, 1961 (3 ot)
    150—Boston vs. Philadelphia, March 2, 1960
    149—Boston vs. Detroit, January 27, 1961

Fewest Field Goal Attempts, Game

    55—Ft. Wayne at Milwaukee, February 20, 1955
        Philadelphia vs. Atlanta, April 1, 1988
    58—Chicago vs. Atlanta, February 14, 1989
        Utah at Minnesota, December 17, 1989

Most Field Goal Attempts, Both Teams, Game

    291—Philadelphia (153) vs. Los Angeles (138), December 8, 1961 (3 ot)
    274—Boston (149) vs. Detroit (125), January 27, 1961
        Philadelphia (141) at Boston (133), March 5, 1961

Fewest Field Goal Attempts, Both Teams, Game

    132—Chicago (65) vs. New York (67), December 27, 1983
    133—Minneapolis (66) vs. Milwaukee (67), at Huron, January 27, 1955
        Philadelphia (59) vs. Milwaukee (74), at Albany, N.Y., March 14, 1955

134—New Jersey (67) at New York (67), November 9, 1982
Philadelphia (55) vs. Atlanta (79), April 1, 1988

Most Field Goal Attempts, One Half
83—Philadelphia vs. Syracuse, November 4, 1959
Boston at Philadelphia, December 27, 1960

Most Field Goal Attempts, Both Teams, One Half
153—Boston (80) vs. Minneapolis (73), February 27, 1959 (2nd Half)

Most Field Goal Attempts, One Quarter
47—Boston vs. Minneapolis, February 27, 1959 (4th Qtr.)

Most Field Goal Attempts, Both Teams, One Quarter
86—Boston (47) vs. Minneapolis (39), February 27, 1959 (4th Qtr.)

THREE-POINT FIELD GOAL PERCENTAGE

Highest Three-Point Field Goal Percentage, Season
.407 —Cleveland, 1989-90 (346/851)
.3844—Boston, 1987-88 (271/705)
.3838—Boston, 1979-80 (162/422)

Lowest Three-Point Field Goal Percentage, Season
.104—Los Angeles, 1982-83 (10/96)
.122—Atlanta, 1980-81 (10/82)
.138—Los Angeles, 1981-82 (13/94)

Most Three-Point Field Goals, No Misses, Game
6—Cleveland at Utah, January 24, 1985
L.A. Lakers at Portland, January 1, 1987
Houston vs. Denver, February 17, 1989
San Antonio vs. Milwaukee, December 22, 1990
5—New York vs. Sacramento, January 10, 1987
Utah at Denver, February 4, 1989
Atlanta at L.A. Clippers, March 30, 1990
4—by many

Most Three-Point Field Goals, No Misses, Both Teams, Game
5—San Antonio (4) at Philadelphia (1), December 19, 1984
4—Washington (4) at Kansas City (0), January 8, 1981
Washington (3) vs. Atlanta (1), December 3, 1987

THREE-POINT FIELD GOALS

Most Three-Point Field Goals per Game, Season
4.71—New York, 1988-89 (386/82)
4.52—Milwaukee, 1991-92 (371/82)
4.22—Cleveland, 1989-90 (346/82)
4.16—Portland, 1990-91 (341/82)

Fewest Three-Point Field Goals per Game, Season
0.12—Atlanta, 1980-81 (10/82)
Los Angeles, 1982-83 (10/82)
0.16—Atlanta, 1979-80 (13/82)
Detroit, 1980-81 (13/82)
Los Angeles, 1981-82 (13/82)

Most Three-Point Field Goals, Game
16—Sacramento vs. Golden State, February 9, 1989
13—Sacramento at Golden State, March 4, 1989
12—Seattle vs. L.A. Clippers, April 20, 1990
Milwaukee vs. Portland, December 30, 1990
Houston at Denver, April 5, 1991
Portland at L.A. Clippers, February 21, 1992

Most Three-Point Field Goals, Both Teams, Game
21—Milwaukee (12) vs. Portland (9), December 30, 1990
20—Sacramento (16) vs. Golden State (4), February 9, 1989
19—Sacramento (13) at Golden State (6), March 4, 1989
Denver (10) vs. Milwaukee (9), March 23, 1991 (ot)
Houston (12) at Denver (7), April 5, 1991
Atlanta (10) at Portland (9), January 24, 1992

Most Three-Point Field Goals, One Half
9—Sacramento vs. Golden State, February 9, 1989
New York vs. Chicago, March 4, 1989
Sacramento at Golden State, March 4, 1989
Milwaukee vs. Portland, December 30, 1990

Most Three-Point Field Goals, One Quarter
8—Denver vs. Seattle, January 9, 1982

THREE-POINT FIELD GOAL ATTEMPTS

Most Three-Point Field Goal Attempts per Game, Season

13.98—New York, 1988-89 (1,147/82)
12.91—Denver, 1990-91 (1,059/82)
12.25—Milwaukee, 1991-92 (1,005/82)

Fewest Three-Point Field Goal Attempts per Game, Season

0.91—Atlanta, 1979-80 (75/82)
1.00—Atlanta, 1980-81 (82/82)
1.02—Detroit, 1980-81 (84/82)
     Philadelphia, 1980-81 (84/82)

Most Three-Point Field Goal Attempts, Game

31—Sacramento vs. Golden State, February 9, 1989
29—New York vs. Golden State, March 31, 1989
28—New York at Golden State, January 18, 1989
     Sacramento at Golden State, March 4, 1989

Most Three-Point Field Goal Attempts, Both Teams, Game

46—Indiana (26) at Golden State (20), March 2, 1989 (ot)
45—Sacramento (31) vs. Golden State (14), February 9, 1989
44—Sacramento (28) at Golden State (16), March 4, 1989

Most Three-Point Field Goal Attempts, One Half

17—New York at Golden State, January 18, 1989
     Sacramento vs. Golden State, February 9, 1989
     Sacramento at Golden State, March 4, 1989

FREE THROW PERCENTAGE

Highest Free Throw Percentage, Season

.832 —Boston, 1989-90 (1,791/2,153)
.824 —Boston, 1990-91 (1,646/1,997)
.8207—Milwaukee, 1988-89 (1,955/2,382)
.8205—K.C.-Omaha, 1974-75 (1,797/2,190)

Lowest Free Throw Percentage, Season

.635—Philadelphia, 1967-68 (2,121/3,338)
.638—San Francisco, 1963-64 (1,800/2,821)
.640—San Francisco, 1964-65 (1,819/2,844)

Most Free Throws Made, No Misses, Game

39—Utah at Portland, December 7, 1982
35—Boston vs. Miami, April 12, 1990
33—Boston vs. New Jersey, March 18, 1990
     Golden State vs. Houston, April 11, 1991
30—Buffalo vs. Los Angeles, November 18, 1975
     Utah vs. Boston, December 28, 1985
     Portland at Indiana, November 30, 1986
29—Syracuse at Boston, November 2, 1957
     Utah at Boston, December 14, 1984

Lowest Free Throw Percentage, Game

.200—New Orleans at Houston, November 19, 1977 (1/5)
.214—Houston vs. Portland, February 22, 1983 (3/14)
.231—Miami at L.A. Lakers, April 5, 1991 (3/13)
.308—Minnesota vs. Houston, November 25, 1990 (4/13)
.310—Seattle at Phoenix, October 16, 1979 (9/29)

Highest Free Throw Percentage, Both Teams, Game

.971—Boston (1.000) vs. Seattle (.947), March 20, 1987 (33/34)
.970—Phoenix (1.000) at Indiana (.929), January 7, 1983 (32/33)
.968—Milwaukee (1.000) at Detroit (.941), January 2, 1974 (30/31)

Lowest Free Throw Percentage, Both Teams, Game

.410—Los Angeles (.386) at Chicago (.471), December 7, 1968 (25/61)
.450—Milwaukee (.375) at Cleveland (.500), November 3, 1977 (9/20)
.465—Kansas City (.440) at Dallas (.500), March 26, 1982 (20/43)

FREE THROWS MADE

Most Free Throws Made per Game, Season

31.9—New York, 1957-58 (2,300/72)
31.2—Minneapolis, 1957-58 (2,246/72)
30.9—Syracuse, 1952-53 (2,197/71)

Fewest Free Throws Made per Game, Season

15.5—Milwaukee, 1972-73 (1,271/82)
15.8—Baltimore, 1972-73 (1,294/82)
15.9—Cleveland, 1974-75 (1,301/82)

Most Free Throws Made, Game

> 61—Phoenix vs. Utah, April 9, 1990 (ot)
> 60—Washington vs. New York, November 13, 1987
> 59—Syracuse vs. Anderson, November 24, 1949 (5 ot)

Fewest Free Throws Made, Game

> 1—New Orleans at Houston, November 19, 1977
> 2—Chicago vs. Seattle, March 13, 1973
>   N.Y. Knicks vs. Chicago, January 25, 1977
>   Houston at Denver, January 27, 1978
>   Los Angeles vs. San Diego, March 28, 1980
>   Seattle vs. Dallas, January 7, 1985

Most Free Throws Made, Both Teams, Game

> 116—Syracuse (59) vs. Anderson (57), November 24, 1949 (5 ot)
> 103—Boston (56) at Minneapolis (47), November 28, 1954
> 96—Philadelphia (48) vs. Minneapolis (48), November 2, 1957

Fewest Free Throws Made, Both Teams, Game

> 7—Milwaukee (3) vs. Baltimore (4), January 1, 1973
> 9—Milwaukee (3) at Cleveland (6), November 3, 1977
>   Los Angeles (2) vs. San Diego (7), March 28, 1980

Most Free Throws Made, One Half

> 36—Chicago vs. Phoenix, January 8, 1970
>   Golden State vs. Utah, March 29, 1990
>   Seattle at Denver, April 7, 1991

Most Free Throws Made, Both Teams, One Half

> 58—Utah (34) at Minnesota (24), December 17, 1989

Most Free Throws Made, One Quarter

> 26—Atlanta at Milwaukee, March 3, 1991

Most Free Throws Made, Both Teams, One Quarter

> 39—Cincinnati (24) at Baltimore (15), December 27, 1964
>   Chicago (22) vs. Denver (17), December 29, 1978

FREE THROW ATTEMPTS

Most Free Throw Attempts per Game, Season

> 42.4—New York, 1957-58 (3,056/72)
> 42.3—St. Louis, 1957-58 (3,047/72)
> 42.1—Philadelphia, 1966-67 (3,411/81)

Fewest Free Throw Attempts per Game, Season

> 20.6 —Milwaukee, 1972-73 (1,687/82)
> 21.20—New York, 1973-74 (1,738/82)
> 21.21—New York, 1972-73 (1,739/82)

Most Free Throw Attempts, Game

> 86—Syracuse vs. Anderson, November 24, 1949 (5 ot)
> 80—Phoenix vs. Utah, April 9, 1990 (ot)
> 74—Anderson at Syracuse, November 24, 1949 (5 ot)
>   San Francisco vs. New York, November 6, 1964 (2 ot)
> 71—Chicago vs. Phoenix, January 8, 1970

Fewest Free Throw Attempts, Game

> 3—Los Angeles vs. San Diego, March 28, 1980
> 4—New York at Atlanta, March 6, 1974
>   Milwaukee at K.C.-Omaha, February 25, 1975
>   Golden State vs. Chicago, March 6, 1977
>   Houston at Denver, January 27, 1978
>   Seattle vs. Dallas, January 7, 1985

Most Free Throw Attempts, Both Teams, Game

> 160—Syracuse (86) vs. Anderson (74), November 24, 1949 (5 ot)
> 136—Baltimore (70) vs. Syracuse (66), November 15, 1952 (ot)
> 127—Ft. Wayne (67) vs. Minneapolis (60), December 31, 1954

Fewest Free Throw Attempts, Both Teams, Game

> 12—Los Angeles (3) vs. San Diego (9), March 28, 1980
> 14—Milwaukee (6) vs. Baltimore (8), January 1, 1973
> 15—New Orleans (5) at Houston (10), November 19, 1977

Most Free Throw Attempts, One Half

> 48—Chicago vs. Phoenix, January 8, 1970

Most Free Throw Attempts, Both Teams, One Half

> 76—New York (40) at St. Louis (36), December 14, 1957

Most Free Throw Attempts, One Quarter

    30—Boston at Chicago, January 9, 1963
         Seattle vs. Dallas, March 15, 1992

Most Free Throw Attempts, Both Teams, One Quarter

    50—New York (26) at St. Louis (24), December 14, 1957
         Cincinnati (29) at Baltimore (21), December 27, 1964

REBOUNDS
Rebounds have been compiled since 1950-51
Team Rebounds Not Included

Most Rebounds per Game, Season

    71.5—Boston, 1959-60 (5,365/75)
    70.7—Boston, 1960-61 (5,582/79)

Fewest Rebounds per Game, Season

    38.7—Charlotte, 1989-90 (3,173/82)
    39.2—New York, 1984-85 (3,218/82)
    39.4—Charlotte, 1990-91 (3,227/82)

Most Rebounds, Game

    109—Boston vs. Detroit, December 24, 1960
    105—Boston vs. Minneapolis, February 26, 1960
    104—Philadelphia vs. Syracuse, November 4, 1959
         Philadelphia vs. Cincinnati, November 8, 1959

Fewest Rebounds, Game

    20—New York vs. Ft. Wayne, at Miami, February 14, 1955
         Buffalo at Houston, February 17, 1974
    21—New York vs. Golden State, February 18, 1975

Most Rebounds, Both Teams, Game

    188—Philadelphia (98) vs. Los Angeles (90), December 8, 1961 (3 ot)
    177—Philadelphia (104) vs. Syracuse (73), November 4, 1959
         Boston (89) at Philadelphia (88), December 27, 1960

Fewest Rebounds, Both Teams, Game

    48—New York (20) vs. Ft. Wayne (28), at Miami, February 14, 1955
    53—Denver (26) vs. Indiana (27), February 2, 1992
    55—Phoenix (25) at Philadelphia (30), January 7, 1985

Most Rebounds, One Half

    65—Boston vs. Cincinnati, January 12, 1962

Most Rebounds, One Quarter

    40—Philadelphia vs. Syracuse, November 9, 1961

OFFENSIVE REBOUNDS
Offensive Rebounds have been compiled since 1973-74

Most Offensive Rebounds per Game, Season

    18.5—Denver, 1990-91 (1,520/82)
    18.4—New Jersey, 1991-92 (1,512/82)
    17.8—Seattle, 1977-78 (1,456/82)

Fewest Offensive Rebounds per Game, Season

    10.6—Utah, 1990-91 (867/82)
    11.2—Golden State, 1989-90 (915/82)
    11.3—Boston, 1987-88 (930/82)

Most Offensive Rebounds, Game

    39—Boston at Capital, October 20, 1973
    37—Kansas City at Denver, January 4, 1983
         San Antonio at Golden State, February 28, 1990 (ot)
         New Jersey vs. Golden State, April 6, 1990
    36—Detroit at Los Angeles, December 14, 1975

Fewest Offensive Rebounds, Game

    1—Cleveland vs. Houston, March 23, 1975
       New York vs. Boston, March 4, 1978
    2—Houston at Cleveland, November 9, 1973
       Detroit vs. Portland, January 23, 1974
       Atlanta at K.C.-Omaha, March 18, 1975
       Phoenix vs. New Orleans, December 21, 1975
       Phoenix at Golden State, March 12, 1980
       San Antonio at Chicago, November 4, 1986
       L.A. Lakers vs. Chicago, February 2, 1988
       Houston at Portland, December 19, 1989

Most Offensive Rebounds, Both Teams, Game

57—Los Angeles (29) vs. Cleveland (28), January 22, 1974 (ot)
    Detroit (29) vs. Indiana (28), January 30, 1977
56—Los Angeles (30) vs. Utah (26), November 13, 1983
55—New Orleans (31) vs. Buffalo (24), November 6, 1974
    San Antonio (37) at Golden State (18), February 28, 1990 (ot)

Fewest Offensive Rebounds, Both Teams, Game

 8—Detroit (4) at Boston (4), November 11, 1988
10—Detroit (5) at K.C.-Omaha (5), November 19, 1974
    Utah (3) vs. Portland (7), December 28, 1989
11—Golden State (4) vs. Milwaukee (7), March 19, 1974
    Chicago (5) vs. New York (6), February 11, 1975
    Portland (5) vs. Boston (6), February 15, 1975
    Buffalo (5) vs. N.Y. Knicks (6), April 8, 1977
    Atlanta (4) at Dallas (7), March 27, 1982
    Atlanta (4) at Cleveland (7), December 7, 1982
    Phoenix (5) vs. Dallas (6), December 28, 1984
    Dallas (4) at Utah (7), December 7, 1989
    Houston (4) at Utah (7), February 12, 1991

DEFENSIVE REBOUNDS
Defensive Rebounds have been compiled since 1973-74

Most Defensive Rebounds per Game, Season

37.5—Boston, 1973-74 (3,074/82)
37.0—Golden State, 1973-74 (3,035/82)
36.2—Boston, 1975-76 (2,972/82)

Fewest Defensive Rebounds per Game, Season

25.0—Minnesota, 1989-90 (2,053/82)
25.6—New York, 1984-85 (2,102/82)
25.7—San Diego, 1982-83 (2,108/82)

Most Defensive Rebounds, Game

61—Boston vs. Capital, March 17, 1974
58—Los Angeles vs. Seattle, October 19, 1973
56—Portland vs. Cleveland, October 18, 1974 (4 ot)

Fewest Defensive Rebounds, Game

10—Utah at L.A. Lakers, April 1, 1990
12—Indiana at New Jersey, February 27, 1987
    Philadelphia at Boston, January 20, 1989

Most Defensive Rebounds, Both Teams, Game

106—Portland (56) vs. Cleveland (50), October 18, 1974 (4 ot)
103—Philadelphia (54) vs. Washington (49), November 15, 1975 (3 ot)
101—Indiana (53) vs. Denver (48), January 23, 1989

Fewest Defensive Rebounds, Both Teams, Game

31—Utah (10) at L.A. Lakers (21), April 1, 1990
33—Philadelphia (16) at Milwaukee (17), December 14, 1984
34—Philadelphia (16) vs. Phoenix (18), January 7, 1985
    New York (14) at Philadelphia (20), January 20, 1986
    New Jersey (15) at Miami (19), January 26, 1991

ASSISTS

Most Assists per Game, Season

31.4—L.A. Lakers, 1984-85 (2,575/82)
31.2—Milwaukee, 1978-79 (2,562/82)
30.7—Los Angeles, 1982-83 (2,519/82)

Fewest Assists per Game, Season

16.6—Minneapolis, 1956-57 (1,195/72)
17.3—N.Y. Nets, 1976-77 (1,422/82)
17.6—Detroit, 1957-58 (1,264/72)

Most Assists, Game

53—Milwaukee vs. Detroit, December 26, 1978
52—Chicago vs. Atlanta, March 20, 1971
    Seattle vs. Denver, March 18, 1983
    Denver at Golden State, April 21, 1989
51—Sheboygan vs. Denver, March 10, 1950
    Phoenix vs. San Antonio, February 2, 1979
    Los Angeles vs. Denver, February 23, 1982

Fewest Assists, Game

3—Boston vs. Minneapolis, at Louisville, November 28, 1956
    Baltimore vs. Boston, October 16, 1963

Cincinnati vs. Chicago, at Evansville, December 5, 1967
New York at Boston, March 28, 1976

Most Assists, Both Teams, Game

93—Detroit (47) at Denver (46), December 13, 1983 (3 ot)
89—Detroit (48) at Cleveland (41), March 28, 1973 (ot)
88—Phoenix (47) vs. San Diego (41), at Tucson, March 15, 1969
　　San Antonio (50) vs. Denver (38), April 15, 1984

Fewest Assists, Both Teams, Game

10—Boston (3) vs. Minneapolis (7), at Louisville, November 28, 1956
11—Baltimore (3) vs. Boston (8), October 16, 1963
12—Ft. Wayne (6) vs. New York (6), at Miami, February 17, 1955
　　Chicago (6) vs. St. Louis (6), October 27, 1961

Most Assists, One Half

33—Phoenix vs. Denver, November 10, 1990

Most Assists, Both Teams, One Half

51—Denver (27) at San Antonio (24), November 7, 1990

Most Assists, One Quarter

19—Milwaukee vs. Detroit, December 26, 1978
　　San Antonio vs. Denver, April 15, 1984 (2nd Qtr.)

Most Assists, Both Teams, One Quarter

28—Minnesota (15) vs. Charlotte (13), April 19, 1992

PERSONAL FOULS

Most Personal Fouls per Game, Season

32.1—Tri-Cities, 1949-50 (2,057/64)
31.6—Rochester, 1952-53 (2,210/70)
30.8—Tri-Cities, 1950-51 (2,092/68)

Since 1954-55 Season

30.1—Atlanta, 1977-78 (2,470/82)

Fewest Personal Fouls per Game, Season

18.6—L.A. Lakers, 1990-91 (1,524/82)
18.8—L.A. Lakers, 1991-92 (1,543/82)
19.0—Cleveland, 1991-92 (1,556/82)

Most Personal Fouls, Game

66—Anderson at Syracuse, November 24, 1949 (5 ot)
60—Syracuse at Baltimore, November 15, 1952
56—Syracuse vs. Anderson, November 24, 1949 (5 ot)
55—Milwaukee at Baltimore, November 12, 1952

Since 1954-55 Season

52—Utah at Phoenix, April 9, 1990 (ot)

Since 1954-55 Season (Regulation Game)

46—New York at Phoenix, December 3, 1987

Fewest Personal Fouls, Game

7—San Antonio at Houston, April 13, 1984 (ot)
8—Detroit at Phoenix, March 27, 1975
　　Indiana at New Jersey, November 3, 1984
　　Dallas at Seattle, January 7, 1985
　　Utah vs. Washington, December 4, 1991
9—by many

Most Personal Fouls, Both Teams, Game

122—Anderson (66) at Syracuse (56), November 24, 1949 (5 ot)
114—Syracuse (60) at Baltimore (54), November 15, 1952 (ot)
　97—Syracuse (50) vs. New York (47), February 15, 1953

Since 1954-55 Season

87—Portland (44) vs. Chicago (43), March 16, 1984 (4 ot)

Since 1954-55 Season (Regulation Game)

84—Indiana (44) vs. Kansas City (40), October 22, 1977

Fewest Personal Fouls, Both Teams, Game

22—New Jersey (10) at Philadelphia (12), December 22, 1984
23—Detroit (8) at Phoenix (15), March 27, 1975
　　Cleveland (10) at Washington (13), March 16, 1992
24—Philadelphia (9) at Rochester (15), January 5, 1957
　　New York (12) at Philadelphia (12), February 25, 1960
　　Washington (9) at L.A. Clippers (15), December 15, 1984
　　Dallas (8) at Seattle (16), January 7, 1985
　　Philadelphia (12) at Chicago (12), March 7, 1989

Most Personal Fouls, One Half

30—Rochester at Syracuse, January 15, 1953

Most Personal Fouls, Both Teams, One Half

51—Syracuse (28) at Boston (23), December 26, 1950

Most Personal Fouls, One Quarter

19—Dallas at Denver, January 15, 1982

Most Personal Fouls, Both Teams, One Quarter

32—Dallas (19) at Denver (13), January 15, 1982

DISQUALIFICATIONS
Disqualifications have been compiled since 1950-51

Most Disqualifications per Game, Season

1.53—Rochester, 1952-53 (107/70)
1.41—Fort Wayne, 1952-53 (97/69)
1.31—Baltimore, 1952-53 (93/71)
        Milwaukee, 1952-53 (93/71)

Since 1954-55 Season

0.98—Atlanta, 1977-78 (80/82)

Fewest Disqualifications per Game, Season

0.02—L.A. Lakers, 1988-89 (2/82)
0.03—Detroit, 1991-92 (3/82)
0.05—Chicago, 1991-92 (4/82)

Most Disqualifications, Game

8—Syracuse at Baltimore, November 15, 1952 (ot)
6—Syracuse at Boston, December 26, 1950
5—Pittsburgh at Philadelphia, November 7, 1946
    Boston vs. Syracuse, December 26, 1950
    Baltimore vs. Syracuse, November 15, 1952 (ot)
    Rochester at Philadelphia, December 11, 1952
    Minneapolis vs. St. Louis, February 17, 1957 (ot)
    Indiana at New Jersey, February 8, 1978 (ot)
    Kansas City at Denver, November 11, 1978
    Chicago at Portland, March 16, 1984 (4 ot)
    Atlanta at Utah, February 19, 1986 (ot)

Most Disqualifications, Both Teams, Game

13—Syracuse (8) at Baltimore (5), November 15, 1952 (ot)
11—Syracuse (6) at Boston (5), December 26, 1950
9—Minneapolis (5) vs. St. Louis (4), February 17, 1957 (ot)

Since 1954-55 Season (Regulation Game)

8—Kansas City (5) at Denver (3), November 11, 1978

STEALS
Steals have been compiled since 1973-74

Most Steals per Game, Season

12.9—Phoenix, 1977-78 (1,059/82)
11.9—Golden State, 1974-75 (972/82)
11.7—San Antonio, 1988-89 (961/82)

Fewest Steals per Game, Season

5.94—Detroit, 1990-91 (487/82)
6.20—Boston, 1976-77 (506/82)
6.24—Detroit, 1989-90 (512/82)

Most Steals, Game

25—Golden State vs. Los Angeles, March 25, 1975
    Golden State vs. San Antonio, February 15, 1989
24—Golden State vs. Los Angeles, January 21, 1975
    Phoenix vs. San Antonio, November 20, 1977
    Philadelphia vs. Detroit, November 11, 1978
    Portland vs. Golden State, March 17, 1984
    Charlotte at Houston, November 30, 1989
    Milwaukee vs. Orlando, March 6, 1992

Fewest Steals, Game

0—Golden State at New York, November 24, 1973
    Seattle at Cleveland, November 27, 1973
    Cleveland vs. Philadelphia, March 15, 1975
    Chicago at Boston, March 24, 1976
    Denver at Atlanta, October 21, 1978
    Utah at Dallas, December 23, 1980
    Dallas at Phoenix, April 12, 1984

Boston at Detroit, October 26, 1984
Sacramento at Houston, January 23, 1986
Sacramento vs. Portland, April 23, 1988
Boston at Minnesota, February 2, 1990
Utah vs. Sacramento, April 16, 1991
Houston at Dallas, November 12, 1991

Most Steals, Both Teams, Game

40—Golden State (24) vs. Los Angeles (16), January 21, 1975
Philadelphia (24) vs. Detroit (16), November 11, 1978
Golden State (25) vs. San Antonio (15), February 15, 1989
39—Golden State (25) vs. Los Angeles (14), March 25, 1975
Atlanta (22) vs. Detroit (17), January 3, 1978
Phoenix (20) at New York (19), February 25, 1978

Fewest Steals, Both Teams, Game

2—Detroit (1) at New York (1), October 9, 1973
3—New York (1) vs. Chicago (2), October 20, 1973
Golden State (0) at New York (3), November 24, 1973
Cleveland (1) at Boston (2), January 30, 1974
Phoenix (1) at Utah (2), March 5, 1981

Most Steals, One Half

17—Golden State vs. San Antonio, February 15, 1989

Most Steals, One Quarter

11—Los Angeles vs. Chicago, March 12, 1982
New Jersey vs. L.A. Clippers, March 1, 1988
Miami at L.A. Clippers, February 28, 1992
Milwaukee vs. Orlando, March 6, 1992

BLOCKED SHOTS
Blocked Shots have been compiled since 1973-74

Most Blocked Shots per Game, Season

8.7—Washington, 1985-86 (716/82)
8.5—Utah, 1984-85 (697/82)
8.4—Washington, 1986-87 (685/82)

Fewest Blocked Shots per Game, Season

2.6—Dallas, 1980-81 (214/82)
2.7—Philadelphia, 1973-74 (220/82)
2.8—Atlanta, 1974-75 (227/82)

Most Blocked Shots, Game

22—New Jersey vs. Denver, December 12, 1991
21—Detroit vs. Atlanta, October 18, 1980 (2 ot)
Los Angeles vs. Denver, April 9, 1982
Cleveland vs. New York, January 7, 1989
20—San Antonio vs. Golden State, February 24, 1981
Detroit vs. Chicago, November 3, 1982
Philadelphia vs. Seattle, March 9, 1984
Houston at Denver, November 16, 1984
Washington vs. Indiana, February 26, 1987

Fewest Blocked Shots, Game

0—By many teams

Most Blocked Shots, Both Teams, Game

34—Detroit (19) vs. Washington (15), November 19, 1981
32—New Jersey (19) at New Orleans (13), March 21, 1978
New Orleans (19) vs. Indiana (13), March 27, 1979
Philadelphia (20) vs. Seattle (12), March 9, 1984
31—Houston (20) at Denver (11), November 16, 1984
Washington (20) vs. Indiana (11), February 26, 1987

Fewest Blocked Shots, Both Teams, Game

0—Seattle at Portland, November 22, 1973
Atlanta at Phoenix, December 3, 1974
Kansas City at New York, October 30, 1975
Detroit at New York, November 29, 1975
Houston at Los Angeles, January 22, 1978
Buffalo at Atlanta, January 29, 1978
Phoenix at Portland, November 25, 1979
Washington at Dallas, February 10, 1982

TURNOVERS
Turnovers have been compiled since 1970-71

Most Turnovers per Game, Season

    24.5—Denver, 1976-77 (2,011/82)
    24.4—Buffalo, 1972-73 (2,001/82)
    23.4—Philadelphia, 1976-77 (1,915/82)

Fewest Turnovers per Game, Season

    13.0—Minnesota, 1990-91 (1,062/82)
    13.1—Cleveland, 1991-92 (1,073/82)
    13.3—Chicago, 1991-92 (1,088/82)

Most Turnovers, Game

    43—Los Angeles vs. Seattle, February 15, 1974
    41—New Jersey vs. Detroit, November 16, 1980
    40—Boston vs. Portland, at Philadelphia, January 5, 1971
         Los Angeles vs. Atlanta, December 1, 1972 (ot)
         K.C.-Omaha at Detroit, February 18, 1973
         Buffalo at Detroit, March 16, 1973
         Portland at Phoenix, March 7, 1976
         San Antonio vs. Phoenix, November 3, 1977
         New York vs. Milwaukee, December 3, 1977
         San Antonio at Golden State, February 15, 1989

Fewest Turnovers, Game

    3—Portland vs. Phoenix, February 22, 1991
    4—New York vs. Milwaukee, January 3, 1972
         Washington at Utah, March 3, 1981
         Dallas vs. Utah, February 1, 1985
         Houston vs. Sacramento, January 23, 1986
         Dallas vs. Sacramento, November 26, 1986
         Washington vs. Boston, January 25, 1990
         Philadelphia at New York, January 21, 1991 (ot)
    5—By many

Most Turnovers, Both Teams, Game

    73—Philadelphia (38) vs. San Antonio (35), October 22, 1976
         Denver (38) vs. Phoenix (35), October 24, 1980
    71—New Jersey (41) vs. Detroit (30), November 16, 1980

Fewest Turnovers, Both Teams, Game

    13—Detroit (6) vs. Philadelphia (7), April 21, 1989
    14—Dallas (6) at Phoenix (8), January 6, 1989
         Washington (6) at Dallas (8), February 25, 1989
         Seattle (5) vs. Sacramento (9), April 9, 1990
         Minnesota (5) vs. L.A. Lakers (9), December 6, 1990
         Charlotte (6) vs. Detroit (8), February 22, 1991
         Dallas (5) vs. Houston (9), November 12, 1991

DEFENSE
POINTS

Fewest Points Allowed per Game, Season

    89.7—Syracuse, 1954-55 (6,457/72)
    90.0—Ft. Wayne, 1954-55 (6,480/72)
    90.4—Milwaukee, 1954-55 (6,510/72)

Most Points Allowed per Game, Season

    130.8—Denver, 1990-91 (10,723/82)
    126.0—Denver, 1981-82 (10,328/82)
    125.1—Seattle, 1967-68 (10,261/82)

Most Consecutive Games, Fewer Than 100 Points Allowed, Season

    28—Ft. Wayne, October 30—December 30, 1954
    20—Ft. Wayne, January 30—March 1, 1955
    16—Philadelphia, November 13—December 15, 1954

Most Consecutive Games, 100+ Points Allowed, Season

    82—Denver, October 30, 1981—April 17, 1982 (entire season)
         Denver, November 2, 1990—April 21, 1991 (entire season)
    80—Seattle, October 13, 1967—March 16, 1968

Michael Jordan scorched Miami for a record 135 points in Chicago's three-game playoff sweep of the Heat last season.

FIELD GOAL PERCENTAGE
Opponents' Field Goal Percentage has been compiled since 1970-71

Lowest Opponents' Field Goal Percentage, Season

   .420—Milwaukee, 1971-72 (3,370/8,025)
   .422—Milwaukee, 1972-73 (3,385/8,028)
   .424—Milwaukee, 1970-71 (3,489/8,224)

Highest Opponents' Field Goal Percentage, Season

   .536—Golden State, 1984-85 (3,839/7,165)
   .529—San Diego, 1982-83 (3,652/6,910)
   .526—San Diego, 1981-82 (3,739/7,105)

TURNOVERS
Opponents' Turnovers have been compiled since 1970-71

Most Opponents' Turnovers per Game, Season

   24.1—Atlanta, 1977-78 (1,980/82)
   24.0—Phoenix, 1977-78 (1,969/82)
   23.7—Denver, 1976-77 (1,944/82)

Fewest Opponents' Turnovers per Game, Season

   12.2—Boston, 1989-90 (1,003/82)
   12.9—Dallas, 1991-92 (1,054/82)
   13.6—Boston, 1991-92 (1,114/82)

NBA Playoff Records

Individuals (Series)

MOST POINTS

2-Game Series
68—Bob McAdoo, New York vs. Cleveland 1978
65—Elgin Baylor, Minneapolis vs. Detroit 1960
    Gus Williams, Seattle vs. Portland, 1983

3-Game Series
135—Michael Jordan, Chicago vs. Miami 1992
131—Michael Jordan, Chicago vs. Boston 1986

4-Game Series
150—Akeem Olajuwon, Houston vs. Dallas 1988
147—Michael Jordan, Chicago vs. Milw. 1990

5-Game Series
226—Michael Jordan, Chicago vs. Cleveland 1988
215—Michael Jordan, Chicago vs. Phila. 1990

6-Game Series
278—Jerry West, Los Angeles vs. Baltimore 1965
245—Rick Barry, San Fran. vs. Phila. 1967

7-Game Series
284—Elgin Baylor, Los Angeles vs. Boston 1962
270—Wilt Chamberlain, San Fran. vs. St. L. 1964

MOST MINUTES PLAYED

2-Game Series
95—John Kerr, Syracuse vs. New York, 1959
92—John Williamson, N. Jersey vs. Phila. 1979
    Elvin Hayes, Wash. vs. Phila. 1980

3-Game Series
144—Wilt Chamberlain, Phila. vs. Syr. 1961
142—Wilt Chamberlain, Phila. vs. Syr. 1960
    Bill Bridges, St. Louis vs. Baltimore 1966
    Bob McAdoo, Buffalo vs. Philadelphia, 1976
    Moses Malone, Houston vs. L.A. 1981

4-Game Series
195—Wilt Chamberlain, Phila. vs. Cinn. 1965
    Jerry Lucas, Cinn. vs. Phila. 1965
    Oscar Robertson, Cinn. vs. Phila. 1965
    Wilt Chamberlain, Los Ang. vs. Atl. 1970

192—Wilt Chamberlain, Phila. vs. Cin. 1967
    Wilt Chamberlain, Los Ang. vs. Chi. 1972

5-Game Series
243—Oscar Robertson, Cin. vs. Syr. 1963
242—Kareem Abdul-Jabbar, L.A. vs. Sea. 1979

6-Game Series
296—Wilt Chamberlain, Phila. vs. N.Y. 1968
292—Bill Russell, Boston vs. Los Angeles 1968

7-Game Series
345—Kareem Abdul-Jabbar, Milw. vs. Bos. 1974
341—Wilt Chamberlain, Phila. vs. Boston 1965

HIGHEST FIELD GOAL PERCENTAGE
(minimum: 4 FG per game)

2-Game Series
.773—Darryl Dawkins, New Jersey vs. N.Y. 1983
.750—Mike Bantom, Indiana vs. Phila. 1981

3-Game Series
.778—Rick Mahorn, Philadelphia vs. Milw. 1991
.750—Alton Lister, Milwaukee vs. N.J. 1986

4-Game Series
.739—Derrek Dickey, Golden St. vs. Wash. 1975
.731—James Donaldson, Dallas vs. Houston 1988

5-Game Series
.721—James Worthy, L.A. Lakers vs. Denver 1985
.714—Bobby Jones, Philadelphia vs. Boston 1985
    Robert Parish, Boston vs. Indiana 1991

6-Game Series
.781—James Donaldson, Dal. vs. L.A. Lakers 1986
.675—Clifford Ray, Golden State vs. Detroit 1976

7-Game Series
.744—James Donaldson, Dal. vs. L.A. Lakers 1988
.686—Robert Parish, Boston vs. Atlanta 1988

MOST FIELD GOALS

2-Game Series
28—Bob McAdoo, New York vs. Cleveland 1978
27—Jo Jo White, Boston vs. San Antonio 1977

3-Game Series
53—Michael Jordan, Chicago vs. Miami 1992
51—Wilt Chamberlain, Phila. vs. Syracuse 1960

4-Game Series
65—Kareem Abdul-Jabbar, Milw. vs. Chi. 1974
56—Akeem Olajuwon, Houston vs. Dallas 1988

5-Game Series
86—Michael Jordan, Chicago vs. Phila. 1990
85—Michael Jordan, Chicago vs. Cleveland 1988

6-Game Series
96—Jerry West, Los Angeles vs. Baltimore 1965
94—Rick Barry, San Fran. vs. Phila. 1967

7-Game Series
113—Wilt Chamberlain, San Fran. vs. St. L. 1964
104—Bob McAdoo, Buffalo vs. Washington 1975

MOST FIELD GOAL ATTEMPTS

2-Game Series
62—John Williamson, N. Jersey vs. Phila. 1979
53—Neil Johnston, Philadelphia vs. Syracuse 1957
    George Yardley, Ft. Wayne vs. Minn., 1957
    Elgin Baylor, Minneapolis vs. Detroit, 1960

3-Game Series
104—Wilt Chamberlain, Phila. vs. Syr. 1960
96—Wilt Chamberlain, Phila. vs. Syr. 1961

4-Game Series

114—Earl Monroe, Baltimore vs. New York 1969
    Dominique Wilkins, Atlanta vs. Det. 1986
108—Elgin Baylor, Los Ang. vs. San Fran. 1968
    Dominique Wilkins, Atlanta vs. Ind. 1987

5-Game Series

159—Wilt Chamberlain, Phila. vs. Syr. 1962
157—Michael Jordan, Chicago vs. Phila. 1990

6-Game Series

235—Rick Barry, San Fran. vs. Phila. 1967
212—Jerry West, Los Angeles vs. Baltimore 1965

7-Game Series

235—Elgin Baylor, Los Angeles vs. Boston 1962
216—Elgin Baylor, Los Angeles vs. St. Louis 1961
    Bob McAdoo, Buffalo vs. Washington 1975

MOST THREE-POINT FIELD GOALS MADE, NONE MISSED

2-Game Series

4—Kevin Grevey, Washington vs. N.J. 1982
1—Dudley Bradley, Indiana vs. Philadelphia 1981
    Sly Williams, New York vs. New Jersey 1983

3-Game Series

2—Mike McGee, L.A. Lakers vs. Phoenix 1985
    Drazen Petrovic, Portland vs. Dallas 1990
1—by many

4-Game Series

4—Dana Barros, Seattle vs. Golden State 1992
2—Lafayette Lever, Denver vs. Portland 1986

    B.J. Armstrong, Chicago vs. Detroit 1991
    Mario Elie, Golden State vs. Seattle, 1992

5-Game Series

4—Ricky Pierce, Milwaukee vs. Atlanta 1989
3—Kiki Vandeweghe, New York vs. Detroit 1992

6-Game Series

3—Norm Nixon, Los Angeles vs. San Antonio 1983
    Lafayette Lever, Denver vs. Dallas 1988
1—by many

7-Game Series

2—David Wingate, San Antonio vs. Portland 1990
1—by many

MOST THREE-POINT FIELD GOALS MADE

2-Game Series

5—Kevin Grevey, Washington vs. Phila. 1980
4—Kevin Grevey, Washington vs. N.J. 1982

3-Game Series

10—Michael Adams, Denver vs. Phoenix 1989
9—Byron Scott, L.A. Lakers vs. Portland 1989
    Vernon Maxwell, Hous. vs. L.A. Lakers 1991

4-Game Series

10—Tim Hardaway, Golden State vs. Seattle 1992
9—Larry Bird, Boston vs. Milwaukee 1986
    Bob Hansen, Utah vs. Portland 1988
    Michael Cooper, L.A. Lakers vs. Detroit 1989

    Tim Hardaway, Golden State vs. San Ant. 1991
    Terry Porter, Portland vs. L.A. Lakers 1992

5-Game Series

17—Chuck Person, Indiana vs. Boston 1991
12—Eddie Johnson, Phoenix vs. Utah 1990

6-Game Series

18—Terry Porter, Portland vs. Utah 1992
16—Craig Hodges, Chicago vs. Detroit 1989

7-Game Series

16—Terry Porter, Portland vs. San Antonio 1990
14—Danny Ainge, Boston vs. Milwaukee 1987

MOST THREE-POINT FIELD GOAL ATTEMPTS

2-Game Series

10—Kevin Grevey, Washington vs. Phila. 1980
6—John Williamson, Washington vs. Phila. 1980

3-Game Series

27—Vernon Maxwell, Hous. vs. L.A. Lakers 1991
22—Michael Adams, Denver vs. Phoenix 1989

4-Game Series

29—Tim Hardaway, Golden State vs. Seattle 1992
27—Michael Cooper, L.A. Lakers vs. Detroit 1989

5-Game Series

31—Chuck Person, Indiana vs. Boston 1991
28—Michael Adams, Denver vs. Seattle 1988

6-Game Series

37—Craig Hodges, Chicago vs. Detroit 1989
34—Magic Johnson, L.A. Lakers vs. Portland 1991
    Terry Porter, Portland vs. Utah 1992

7-Game Series

35—Terry Porter, Portland vs. San Antonio 1990
28—Craig Hodges, Chicago vs. Detroit 1990

MOST FREE THROWS MADE, NONE MISSED

2-Game Series

8—Jo Jo White, Boston vs. Seattle 1977
    Rick Barry, Houston vs. Atlanta 1979
    Caldwell Jones, Phila. vs. N. Jersey 1979
    Mike Newlin, Houston vs. Atlanta 1979
    Bobby Jones, Phila. vs. Wash. 1980

3-Game Series

18—Kiki Vandeweghe, Denver vs. Phoenix 1982
15—Walter Davis, Denver vs. Phoenix 1989

4-Game Series

32—Kiki Vandeweghe, Portland vs. Denver 1986
27—Kevin Johnson, Phoenix vs. L.A. Lakers 1989

5-Game Series

30—Mark Price, Cleveland vs. Philadelphia 1990
25—Jeff Malone, Utah vs. Portland 1991

6-Game Series

17—Bob Lanier, Milwaukee vs. New Jersey 1984
14—Bobby Leonard, Minneapolis vs. St.L. 1959
    Dave Twardzik, Portland vs. Seattle 1978

7-Game Series

35—Jack Sikma, Milwaukee vs. Boston 1987
23—Calvin Murphy, Houston vs. San Antonio 1981

MOST FREE THROWS MADE

2-Game Series

21—George Yardley, Detroit vs. Cincinnati 1958
19—Larry Foust, Fort Wayne vs. Minn. 1957
    Reggie Theus, Chicago vs. New York 1981

3-Game Series

43—Kevin Johnson, Phoenix vs. Denver 1989
42—Dolph Schayes, Syracuse vs. Boston 1957

4-Game Series

49—Jerry West, Los Angeles vs. Atlanta 1970
48—Michael Jordan, Chicago vs. Milwaukee 1985
    Sidney Moncrief, Milwaukee vs. Chicago 1985

5-Game Series

62—Oscar Robertson, Cinn. vs. Phila. 1964
61—Oscar Robertson, Cincinnati vs. Boston 1966
    Karl Malone, Utah vs. L.A. Clippers 1992

6-Game Series

86—Jerry West, Los Angeles vs. Baltimore 1965
68—Michael Jordan, Chicago vs. New York 1989

7-Game Series

83—Dolph Schayes, Syracuse vs. Boston 1959
82—Elgin Baylor, Los Angeles vs. Boston 1962

MOST FREE THROW ATTEMPTS

57—Jerry West, Los Angeles vs. Atlanta 1970

2-Game Series

24—George Yardley, Detroit vs. Cincinnati 1958
    Bernard King, New Jersey vs. Phila. 1979
    Calvin Natt, Portland vs. Seattle 1983
23—Larry Foust, Ft. Wayne vs. Minneapolis 1957

3-Game Series

47—Dolph Schayes, Syracuse vs. Boston 1957
46—Kevin Johnson, Phoenix vs. Denver 1989

4-Game Series

58—Michael Jordan, Chicago vs. Milwaukee 1985

5-Game Series

79—Karl Malone, Utah vs. L.A. Clippers 1992
72—Oscar Robertson, Cincinnati vs. Phila. 1964

6-Game Series

95—Jerry West, Los Angeles vs. Baltimore 1965
86—George Mikan, Minneapolis vs. Syracuse 1950

7-Game Series

100—Charles Barkley, Phila. vs. Milw. 1986
 99—Elgin Baylor, Los Angeles vs. Boston 1962

MOST REBOUNDS

2-Game Series

41—Moses Malone, Houston vs. Atlanta 1979
39—John Kerr, Syracuse vs. Philadelphia 1957

3-Game Series

84—Bill Russell, Boston vs. Syracuse 1957
69—Wilt Chamberlain, Philadelphia vs. Syr. 1961

4-Game Series

118—Bill Russell, Boston vs. Minneapolis 1959
106—Wilt Chamberlain, Phila. vs. Cin. 1967

5-Game Series

160—Wilt Chamberlain, Phila. vs. Bos. 1967
155—Bill Russell, Boston vs. Syracuse 1961

6-Game Series

171—Wilt Chamberlain, Phila. vs. San Fran. 1967
165—Wilt Chamberlain, Phila. vs. Bos. 1960

7-Game Series

220—Wilt Chamberlain, Phila. vs. Bos. 1965
189—Bill Russell, Boston vs. Los Angeles 1962

MOST OFFENSIVE REBOUNDS

2-Game Series

25—Moses Malone, Houston vs. Atlanta 1979
13—Dan Roundfield, Atlanta vs. Houston 1979
    Lonnie Shelton, Seattle vs. Portland 1983

3-Game Series

28—Moses Malone, Houston vs. Seattle 1982
22—Karl Malone, Utah vs. Golden State 1989

4-Game Series

27—Moses Malone, Phila. vs. Los Angeles 1983
25—Shawn Kemp, Seattle vs. Golden State 1992

5-Game Series

36—Larry Smith, Golden St. vs. L.A. Lakers 1987
35—Charles Barkley, Phila. vs. Chicago 1990

6-Game Series

46—Moses Malone, Houston vs. Boston 1981
45—Moses Malone, Houston vs. Philadelphia 1977

7-Game Series

45—Wes Unseld, Washington vs. San Antonio 1979
44—Roy Tarpley, Dallas vs. L.A. Lakers 1988

MOST DEFENSIVE REBOUNDS

2-Game Series

23—Wes Unseld, Washington vs. Atlanta 1978
21—Wes Unseld, Washington vs. Phila. 1980

3-Game Series

43—Bob McAdoo, Buffalo vs. Philadelphia 1976
41—Elvin Hayes, Washington vs. Cleveland 1977
    Tom Chambers, Phoenix vs. Denver 1989

4-Game Series

62—Kareem Abdul-Jabbar, Milw. vs. Chi. 1974
53—Wes Unseld, Washington vs. G.S. 1975

5-Game Series

62—Jack Sikma, Seattle vs. Washington 1979
    Karl Malone, Utah vs. Portland 1991
61—Kareem Abdul-Jabbar, Milw. vs. L.A. 1974

6-Game Series

91—Bill Walton, Portland vs. Philadelphia 1977
79—Sam Lacey, K.C.-Omaha vs. Chicago 1975

7-Game Series

95—Kareem Abdul-Jabbar, L.A. vs. G.S. 1977
86—Dave Cowens, Boston vs. Philadelphia 1977

MOST ASSISTS

2-Game Series

20—Frank Johnson, Washington vs. N.J. 1982
19—Paul Westphal, Phoenix vs. Milwaukee 1978

3-Game Series

48—Magic Johnson, L.A. Lakers vs. S.A. 1986
47—Kevin Johnson, Phoenix vs. San Antonio 1992

4-Game Series

57—Magic Johnson, L.A. Lakers vs. Phoenix 1989
54—Magic Johnson, L.A. Lakers vs. Houston 1990

5-Game Series

85—Magic Johnson, L.A. Lakers vs. Portland 1985
81—Magic Johnson, L.A. Lakers vs. Houston 1986

6-Game Series

90—Johnny Moore, San Ant. vs. Los Ang. 1983
87—Magic Johnson, Los Angeles vs. Phoenix 1984

7-Game Series

115—John Stockton, Utah vs. L.A. Lakers 1988
96—Magic Johnson, L.A. Lakers vs. Dallas 1988

MOST PERSONAL FOULS

2-Game Series

12—Bob Lochmueller, Syracuse vs. Boston 1953
Walter Dukes, Detroit vs. Cincinnati 1958
Ray Felix, New York vs. Syracuse 1959
Dave Cowens, Boston vs. San Antonio 1977
Dan Roundfield, Atlanta vs. Houston 1979
Albert King, New Jersey vs. N.Y. 1983
Buck Williams, New Jersey vs. N.Y. 1983

3-Game Series

18—Charlie Share, St. Louis vs. Minneapolis 1956
Vern Mikkelsen, Minneapolis vs. St. L. 1957
17—Walter Dukes, Minneapolis vs. St. Louis 1957
Paul Arizin, Philadelphia vs. Syracuse 1961
Larry Costello, Syracuse vs. Phila. 1961
Kevin Duckworth, Port. vs. L.A. Lakers 1989
Sam Perkins, Dallas vs. Portland 1990
Jay Humphries, Milwaukee vs. Phil. 1991

4-Game Series

22—Al Attles, San Francisco vs. Los Angeles 1968
Doc Rivers, Atlanta vs. Detroit 1986

21—Akeem Olajuwon, Houston vs. Portland 1987
Mark Eaton, Utah vs. Portland 1988
Roy Tarpley, Dallas vs. Houston 1988

5-Game Series

27—George Mikan, Minneapolis vs. N.Y. 1953
Red Rocha, Syracuse vs. Philadelphia 1956
Larry Costello, Syracuse vs. Cincinnati 1963
26—Tom Gola, Philadelphia vs. Syracuse 1962
Bailey Howell, Boston vs. Philadelphia 1969

6-Game Series

35—Charlie Scott, Boston vs. Phoenix 1976
33—Tom Heinsohn, Boston vs. St. Louis 1958
Tom Meschery, San Fran. vs. Phila. 1967

7-Game Series

37—Arnie Risen, Boston vs. St. Louis 1957
Tom Sanders, Boston vs. Philadelphia 1965
36—Vern Mikkelsen, Minneapolis vs. N.Y. 1952
Jack McMahon, St. Louis vs. Boston 1957

MOST DISQUALIFICATIONS

2-Game Series

2—Bob Lochmueller, Syracuse vs. Boston 1953
Walter Dukes, Detroit vs. Cincinnati 1958
Ray Felix, New York vs. Syracuse 1959
Dave Cowens, Boston vs. San Antonio 1977
Dan Roundfield, Atlanta vs. Houston 1979
Albert King, New Jersey vs. N.Y. 1983
Buck Williams, New Jersey vs. N.Y. 1983

3-Game Series

3—Charlie Share, St. Louis vs. Minneapolis 1956
Vern Mikkelsen, Minneapolis vs. St. Louis 1957

4-Game Series

2—Walter Dukes, Detroit vs. Cincinnati 1962
Zelmo Beaty, St. Louis vs. Detroit 1963
Al Attles, San Francisco vs. Los Angeles 1968
Lou Hudson, Atlanta vs. Los Angeles 1970
Dennis Johnson, Phoenix vs. Los Angeles 1982

Lonnie Shelton, Cleveland vs. Boston 1985
Ben Poquette, Cleveland vs. Boston 1985
Sam Bowie, Portland vs. Dallas 1985
Doc Rivers, Atlanta vs. Detroit 1986
Alton Lister, Seattle vs. L.A. Lakers 1987
Mark Eaton, Utah vs. Portland 1988
Greg Anderson, Milwaukee vs. Chicago 1990
Tyrone Hill, Golden State vs. San Antonio 1991

5-Game Series

5—Art Hillhouse, Philadelphia vs. Chicago 1947
4—Chuck Gilmur, Chicago vs. Philadelphia 1947

6-game Series

5—Charlie Scott, Boston vs. Phoenix 1976

7-Game Series

5—Arnie Risen, Boston vs. St. Louis 1957
4—Frank Ramsey, Boston vs. Syracuse 1959
Hal Greer, Philadelphia vs. Balt. 1971

MOST STEALS

2-Game Series

10—Maurice Cheeks, Philadelphia vs. N.J. 1979
9—Maurice Cheeks, Philadelphia vs. Ind. 1981

3-Game Series

13—Clyde Drexler, Portland vs. Dallas 1990
Hersey Hawkins, Philadelphia vs. Mil. 1991
12—Alvin Robertson, S.A. vs. L.A. Lakers 1988

4-Game Series

17—Lionel Hollins, Portland vs. L.A. 1977
15—Mookie Blaylock, New Jersey vs. Cleveland 1992

5-Game Series

21—Micheal Ray Richardson, N.J. vs. Phil. 1984
Isiah Thomas, Detroit vs. Washington 1988
20—Michael Jordan, Chicago vs. Phila. 1990

6-Game Series

19—Rick Barry, Golden State vs. Seattle 1975
18—Slick Watts, Seattle vs. Golden State 1975
Gus Williams, Seattle vs. Portland 1978

7-Game Series

28—John Stockton, Utah vs. L.A. Lakers 1988
27—Maurice Cheeks, Phila. vs. San Ant. 1979

MOST BLOCKED SHOTS

2-Game Series

10—Darryl Dawkins, Phila. vs. Atlanta 1982
9—Artis Gilmore, Chicago vs. New York 1981

3-Game Series

18—Manute Bol, Golden State vs. Utah 1989
15—Kareem Abdul-Jabbar, L.A. vs. Denver 1979

4-Game Series

23—Akeem Olajuwon, Hou. vs. L.A. Lakers 1990
20—Akeem Olajuwon, Houston vs. Portland 1987

5-Game Series

29—Mark Eaton, Utah vs. Houston 1985

Manute Bol, Wash. vs. Phila. 1986
25—Kareem Abdul-Jabbar, L.A. vs. S.A., 1983

6-Game Series

27—Marvin Webster, Seattle vs. Denver 1978
23—Kareem Abdul-Jabbar, L.A. vs. Phila. 1980
Akeem Olajuwon, Houston vs. Seattle 1987

7-Game Series

29—David Robinson, S.A. vs. Portland 1990
28—Elvin Hayes, Washington vs. Cleveland 1976

MOST TURNOVERS

2-Game Series
14—John Williamson, N.J. vs. Phila. 1979
12—Wes Unseld, Washington vs. Atlanta 1978
Frank Johnson, Washington vs. N.J. 1982

3-Game Series
17—Walter Davis, Phoenix vs. Portland 1979
15—Billy Ray Bates, Portland vs. Seattle 1980
Charles Barkley, Philadelphia vs. Milw. 1991

4-Game Series
24—Magic Johnson, Los Angeles vs. Phila. 1983
23—Jeff Ruland, Washington vs. Phila. 1985

5-Game Series
29—Larry Bird, Boston vs. Milwaukee 1984
28—Charles Barkley, Phila. vs. Wash. 1986

6-Game Series
30—Magic Johnson, Los Angeles vs. Phila. 1980
Sidney Moncrief, Milwaukee vs. N.J. 1984
29—George McGinnis, Phila. vs. Wash. 1978

7-Game Series
37—Charles Barkley, Phila. vs. Milw. 1986
34—John Johnson, Seattle vs. Phoenix 1979

Teams (Series)

MOST POINTS

2-Game Series
260—Syracuse vs. New York 1959
241—Minneapolis vs. Ft. Wayne 1957
New York vs. Cleveland 1978

3-Game Series
408—L.A. Lakers vs. Phoenix 1985
407—L.A. Lakers vs. Denver 1987

4-Game Series
498—Philadelphia vs. New York 1978
492—Portland vs. Dallas 1985

5-Game Series
664—San Antonio vs. Denver 1983
662—L.A. Lakers vs. Denver 1985

6-Game Series
747—Philadelphia vs. San Francisco 1967
735—Los Angeles vs. Detroit 1962

7-Game Series
869—Boston vs. Syracuse 1959
867—Boston vs. Cincinnati 1963

FEWEST POINTS

2-Game Series
171—Atlanta vs. Philadelphia 1982
175—New Jersey vs. Washington 1982

3-Game Series
258—New York vs. Chicago 1991
261—Houston vs. Seattle 1982

4-Game Series
356—Milwaukee vs. Detroit 1989
371—Minneapolis vs. Ft. Wayne 1955

5-Game Series
424—Detroit vs. New York 1992
431—Kansas City vs. Houston 1981

6-Game Series
520—Houston vs. Boston 1981
543—Chicago vs. Detroit 1989

7-Game Series
620—New York vs. Chicago 1992
623—Kansas City vs. Phoenix 1981

HIGHEST FIELD GOAL PERCENTAGE

2-Game Series
.555—New York vs. Cleveland 1978
.541—Philadelphia vs. Atlanta 1982

3-Game Series
.600—L.A. Lakers vs. Phoenix 1985
.596—L.A. Lakers vs. San Antonio 1986

4-Game Series
.561—Milwaukee vs. Chicago 1974
.554—Boston vs. Chicago 1981

5-Game Series
.565—L.A. Lakers vs. Denver 1985
.560—Los Angeles vs. Dallas 1984

6-Game Series
.536—Los Angeles vs. Phoenix 1984
.534—L.A. Lakers vs. Dallas 1986

7-Game Series
.534—L.A. Lakers vs. Dallas 1988
.526—Detroit vs. Boston 1987

LOWEST FIELD GOAL PERCENTAGE

2-Game Series
.321—Cincinnati vs. Detroit 1958
.355—Philadelphia vs. Syracuse 1957

3-Game Series
.308—Syracuse vs. Boston 1957
.324—Syracuse vs. Philadelphia 1958

4-Game Series
.323—Minneapolis vs. Ft. Wayne 1955
.384—Baltimore vs. Milwaukee 1971

5-Game Series
.348—Syracuse vs. Boston 1961
.352—Cincinnati vs. Boston 1964

6-Game Series
.355—Boston vs. St. Louis 1958
.363—San Francisco vs. Los Angeles 1969

7-Game Series
.339—Syracuse vs. Ft. Wayne 1955
.369—Boston vs. St. Louis 1957

MOST FIELD GOALS

2-Game Series
101—New York vs. Cleveland 1978
93—Minneapolis vs. Ft. Wayne 1957

3-Game Series
165—L.A. Lakers vs. Phoenix 1985
156—San Antonio vs. Denver 1990

4-Game Series
206—Portland vs. Dallas 1985
198—Milwaukee vs. Chicago 1974

5-Game Series
274—San Antonio vs. Denver 1983
      L.A. Lakers vs. Denver 1985
252—Los Angeles vs. Dallas 1984

6-Game Series
293—Boston vs. Atlanta 1972
292—Houston vs. Denver 1986

7-Game Series
333—Boston vs. Cincinnati 1963
332—New York vs. Los Angeles 1970
      Milwaukee vs. Denver 1978

FEWEST FIELD GOALS

2-Game Series
63—Atlanta vs. Philadelphia 1982
69—Cincinnati vs. Detroit 1958

3-Game Series
88—Syracuse vs. Boston 1957
93—St. Louis vs. Minneapolis 1956

4-Game Series
118—Minneapolis vs. Ft. Wayne 1955
134—Milwaukee vs. Detroit 1989
      L.A. Lakers vs. Portland 1992

5-Game Series
155—St. Louis vs. Ft. Wayne 1956
158—Detroit vs. New York 1992

6-Game Series
194—Chicago vs. Detroit 1989
201—New Jersey vs. Milwaukee 1984

7-Game Series
207—Syracuse vs. Ft. Wayne 1955
217—Ft. Wayne vs. Syracuse 1955

MOST FIELD GOAL ATTEMPTS

2-Game Series
248—New York vs. Syracuse 1959
215—Cincinnati vs. Detroit 1958
      Detroit vs. Minneapolis 1960

3-Game Series
349—Philadelphia vs. Syracuse 1960
344—Minneapolis vs. St. Louis 1957

4-Game Series
464—Minneapolis vs. Boston 1959
463—Boston vs. Minneapolis 1959

5-Game Series
568—Boston vs. Los Angeles 1965
565—Boston vs. Philadelphia 1967

6-Game Series
743—San Francisco vs. Philadelphia 1967
712—Boston vs. Philadelphia 1960

7-Game Series
835—Boston vs. Syracuse 1959
799—Boston vs. St. Louis 1957

FEWEST FIELD GOAL ATTEMPTS

2-Game Series
150—Atlanta vs. Philadelphia 1982
157—Milwaukee vs. Phoenix 1978
      Philadelphia vs. Atlanta 1982

3-Game Series
219—New York vs. Chicago 1991
228—Indiana vs. Detroit 1990

4-Game Series
288—Indiana vs. Atlanta 1987
293—Milwaukee vs. Chicago 1990
      Chicago vs. Detroit 1991

5-Game Series
366—Philadelphia vs. Chicago 1991
368—Kansas City vs. Houston 1981

6-Game Series
437—Chicago vs. Detroit 1989
448—Milwaukee vs. New Jersey 1984

7-Game Series
516—Chicago vs. New York 1992
522—New York vs. Chicago 1992

MOST THREE-POINT FIELD GOALS MADE

2-Game Series
7—Washington vs. Philadelphia 1980
4—Washington vs. New Jersey 1982

3-Game Series
20—Indiana vs. Boston 1992
18—L.A. Lakers vs. Portland 1989

4-Game Series
20—Golden State vs. San Antonio 1991
19—Portland vs. L.A. Lakers 1992

5-Game Series
26—Indiana vs. Boston 1991
25—Detroit vs. Portland 1990

6-Game Series
32—Portland vs. Utah 1992
30—New York vs. Chicago 1989

7-Game Series
26—Portland vs. San Antonio 1990
24—Chicago vs. Detroit 1990

MOST THREE-POINT FIELD GOAL ATTEMPTS

2-Game Series
19—Washington vs. Philadelphia 1980
10—New York vs. Chicago 1981

3-Game Series
45—Indiana vs. Boston 1992
39—Denver vs. Phoenix 1989
      Houston vs. L.A. Lakers 1991

4-Game Series
52—Golden State vs. San Antonio 1991
47—New York vs. Boston 1988
      Golden State vs. Seattle 1992

5-Game Series
67—Golden State vs. Phoenix 1989
65—Golden State vs. L.A. Lakers 1991

6-Game Series
81—New York vs. Chicago 1989
79—Chicago vs. Detroit 1989

7-Game Series
81—Chicago vs. Detroit 1990
68—Portland vs. San Antonio 1990

HIGHEST FREE THROW PERCENTAGE

2-Game Series
.865—Syracuse vs. New York 1959
.839—Chicago vs. New York 1981

3-Game Series
.872—Denver vs. San Antonio 1990
.852—Chicago vs. Boston 1987

4-Game Series
.882—Houston vs. Boston 1980
.869—Cincinnati vs. Philadelphia 1965

5-Game Series
.894—Dallas vs. Seattle 1984
.881—Utah vs. Portland 1991

6-Game Series
.849—Boston vs. Detroit 1985
.824—Los Angeles vs. Baltimore 1965

7-Game Series
.840—Syracuse vs. Boston 1959
.839—Cleveland vs. Boston 1992

LOWEST FREE THROW PERCENTAGE

2-Game Series
.610—New Jersey vs. Washington 1982
.629—San Antonio vs. Boston 1977

3-Game Series
.611—Baltimore vs. St. Louis 1966
.618—Kansas City vs. Phoenix 1980

4-Game Series
.657—Seattle vs. L.A. Lakers 1989
.667—Houston vs. L.A. Lakers 1990

5-Game Series
.567—Houston vs. Utah 1985
.613—Los Angeles vs. Milwaukee 1971

6-Game Series
.603—Philadelphia vs. Boston 1960
.613—Philadelphia vs. San Francisco 1967

7-Game Series
.582—San Francisco vs. St. Louis 1964
.606—Philadelphia vs. Boston 1968

MOST FREE THROWS MADE

2-Game Series
90—Syracuse vs. New York 1959
62—Detroit vs. Cincinnati 1958

3-Game Series
131—Minneapolis vs. St. Louis 1956
121—St. Louis vs. Minneapolis 1956

4-Game Series
147—Los Angeles vs. San Francisco 1968
144—L.A. Lakers vs. Seattle 1987

5-Game Series
183—Philadelphia vs. Syracuse 1956
176—Boston vs. Syracuse 1961

6-Game Series
232—Boston vs. St. Louis 1958
215—St. Louis vs. Boston 1958

7-Game Series
244—St. Louis vs. Boston 1957
239—Los Angeles vs. Boston 1962

FEWEST FREE THROWS MADE

2-Game Series
25—New Jersey vs. Washington 1982
31—Phoenix vs. Milwaukee 1978
      Washington vs. Philadelphia 1980

3-Game Series
37—Kansas City vs. Portland 1981
38—Seattle vs. Detroit 1975
      Portland vs. Chicago 1977
      Houston vs. L.A. Lakers 1991

4-Game Series
46—Milwaukee vs. Chicago 1974
52—Baltimore vs. Milwaukee 1971

5-Game Series
63—Seattle vs. Dallas 1984
70—Baltimore vs. New York 1973

6-Game Series
84—Cleveland vs. Boston 1976
86—Boston vs. Buffalo 1974

7-Game Series
100—Milwaukee vs. Boston 1974
102—New York vs. Capital 1974
      Golden State vs. Chicago 1975
      Boston vs. Cleveland 1992

MOST FREE THROW ATTEMPTS

2-Game Series
104—Syracuse vs. New York 1959
82—Detroit vs. Cincinnati 1958

3-Game Series
174—St. Louis vs. Minneapolis 1956
173—Minneapolis vs. St. Louis 1956

4-Game Series
186—Syracuse vs. Boston 1955
180—Minneapolis vs. Ft. Wayne 1955

5-Game Series
238—Philadelphia vs. Syracuse 1956
232—Boston vs. Syracuse 1961

6-Game Series
298—Boston vs. St. Louis 1958
292—St. Louis vs. Boston 1958

7-Game Series
341—St. Louis vs. Boston 1957
303—Cincinnati vs. Boston 1963

FEWEST FREE THROW ATTEMPTS

2-Game Series
38—Phoenix vs. Milwaukee 1978
40—Atlanta vs. Washington 1978

3-Game Series
49—Houston vs. L.A. Lakers 1991
51—Seattle vs. Detroit 1975
      Kansas City vs. Portland 1981

4-Game Series
57—Milwaukee vs. Chicago 1974
72—Washington vs. Boston 1984

5-Game Series
88—Seattle vs. Dallas 1984
92—Milwaukee vs. Los Angeles 1974
    Chicago vs. L.A. Lakers 1991

6-Game Series
105—Boston vs. Buffalo 1974
116—Houston vs. Washington 1977

7-Game Series
128—New York vs. Capital 1974
133—Boston vs. Cleveland 1992

HIGHEST REBOUND PERCENTAGE

2-Game Series
.585—Boston vs. San Antonio 1977
.559—Washington vs. Atlanta 1978

3-Game Series
.652—L.A. Lakers vs. San Antonio 1986
.590—Boston vs. Indiana 1992

4-Game Series
.585—Portland vs. L.A. Lakers 1992
.572—Detroit vs. Milwaukee 1989

5-Game Series
.591—Boston vs. New York 1974
.577—Seattle vs. Los Angeles 1979

6-Game Series
.580—Los Angeles vs. Philadelphia 1980
.570—Boston vs. Phoenix 1976

7-Game Series
.5561—San Francisco vs. St. Louis 1964
.5556—Seattle vs. Phoenix 1979

MOST REBOUNDS

2-Game Series
137—New York vs. Syracuse 1959
127—Cincinnati vs. Detroit 1958
    Detroit vs. Cincinnati 1958

3-Game Series
225—Philadelphia vs. Syracuse 1960
212—San Francisco vs. Los Angeles 1967

4-Game Series
295—Boston vs. Minneapolis 1959
268—Minneapolis vs. Boston 1959

5-Game Series
396—Boston vs. Syracuse 1961
371—Boston vs. Philadelphia 1958

6-Game Series
457—Boston vs. Philadelphia 1960
435—San Francisco vs Philadelphia 1967

7-Game Series
525—Boston vs. Syracuse 1959
517—Boston vs. Philadelphia 1962

FEWEST REBOUNDS

2-Game Series
71—Atlanta vs. Philadelphia 1982
76—San Antonio vs. Boston 1977

3-Game Series
79—San Antonio vs. L.A. Lakers 1986
99—Miami vs. Chicago 1992

4-Game Series
134—Milwaukee vs. Chicago 1990
135—L.A. Lakers vs. Portland 1992

5-Game Series
176—Kansas City vs. Houston 1981
    Seattle vs. Utah 1992
178—L.A. Lakers vs. Chicago 1991
    Philadelphia vs. Chicago 1991

6-Game Series
214—L.A. Lakers vs. Portland 1991
222—Philadelphia vs. Milwaukee 1982

7-Game Series
248—Chicago vs. New York 1992
250—Houston vs. San Antonio 1981

MOST OFFENSIVE REBOUNDS

2-Game Series
51—Houston vs. Atlanta 1979
43—Philadelphia vs. New Jersey 1979

3-Game Series
72—Golden State vs. Detroit 1977
65—Sacramento vs. Houston 1986

4-Game Series
77—Seattle vs. L.A. Lakers 1989
76—San Antonio vs. Los Angeles 1982
    Seattle vs. L.A. Lakers 1987
    Portland vs. Utah 1988

5-Game Series
111—Phoenix vs. Golden State 1989
110—Houston vs. Utah 1985

6-Game Series
124—Golden State vs. Detroit 1976
117—Washington vs. Philadelphia 1978

7-Game Series
142—Washington vs. San Antonio 1979
141—Boston vs. Philadelphia 1982

FEWEST OFFENSIVE REBOUNDS

2-Game Series
19—Milwaukee vs. Phoenix 1978
22—Portland vs. Seattle 1983

3-Game Series
20—Milwaukee vs. Detroit 1976
21—Portland vs. Chicago 1977
    San Antonio vs. L.A. Lakers 1986

4-Game Series
33—Utah vs. Portland 1988
34—Golden State vs. San Antonio 1991

5-Game Series
40—Los Angeles vs. Seattle 1979
46—Cleveland vs. Philadelphia 1990

6-Game Series
54—Kansas City-Omaha vs. Chicago 1975
56—Buffalo vs. Boston 1976

7-Game Series
66—Cleveland vs. Boston 1992
70—Boston vs. Detroit 1987

MOST DEFENSIVE REBOUNDS

2-Game Series
79—Boston vs. San Antonio 1977
77—Milwaukee vs. Phoenix 1978

3-Game Series
119—L.A. Lakers vs. Denver 1987
118—Phoenix vs. Denver 1989
      San Antonio vs. Denver 1990

4-Game Series
161—New York vs. Philadelphia 1978
158—Milwaukee vs. Chicago 1974

5-Game Series
208—San Antonio vs. Denver 1983
197—Boston vs. New York 1974

6-Game Series
240—Boston vs. Phoenix 1976
234—Golden State vs. Phoenix 1976

7-Game Series
245—Washington vs. Cleveland 1976
      Washington vs. San Antonio 1979
239—Detroit vs. Chicago 1974
      Washington vs. Buffalo 1975
      Chicago vs. Golden State 1975
      Philadelphia vs. Boston 1977

FEWEST DEFENSIVE REBOUNDS

2-Game Series
45—Atlanta vs. Philadelphia 1982
49—Cleveland vs. New York 1978

3-Game Series
58—San Antonio vs. L.A. Lakers 1986
66—Miami vs. Chicago 1992

4-Game Series
84—Detroit vs. Chicago 1991
89—Seattle vs. L.A. Lakers 1987

5-Game Series
108—Golden State vs. L.A. Lakers 1987
112—Seattle vs. Utah 1992

6-Game Series
134—Milwaukee vs. Philadelphia 1982
144—Houston vs. Boston 1981

7-Game Series
162—Dallas vs. L.A. Lakers 1988
165—Chicago vs. New York 1992

MOST ASSISTS

2-Game Series
62—New York vs. Cleveland 1978
      Philadelphia vs. New Jersey 1979
59—Boston vs. San Antonio 1977

3-Game Series
107—L.A. Lakers vs. Denver 1987
104—L.A. Lakers vs. Phoenix 1985

4-Game Series
129—Los Angeles vs. San Antonio 1982
123—Portland vs. Dallas 1985

5-Game Series
181—San Antonio vs. Denver 1983
179—L.A. Lakers vs. Denver 1985

6-Game Series
197—Los Angeles vs. Phoenix 1984
196—Los Angeles vs. San Antonio 1983

7-Game Series
233—Milwaukee vs. Denver 1978
218—Los Angeles vs. Phoenix 1970

FEWEST ASSISTS

2-Game Series
24—Cincinnati vs. Detroit 1958
30—Detroit vs. Cincinnati 1958

3-Game Series
36—Syracuse vs. Philadelphia 1958
39—Syracuse vs. Boston 1957

4-Game Series
58—Minneapolis vs. Ft. Wayne 1955
62—Baltimore vs. New York 1969

5-Game Series
77—Chicago vs. Los Angeles 1968
79—Cincinnati vs. Boston 1966

6-Game Series
93—Minneapolis vs. St. Louis 1959
96—Detroit vs. Boston 1968

7-Game Series
105—Washington vs. Cleveland 1976
119—Baltimore vs. New York 1971
      New York vs. Baltimore 1971

MOST PERSONAL FOULS

2-Game Series
70—New York vs. Syracuse 1959
61—Atlanta vs. Philadelphia 1982

3-Game Series
99—Minneapolis vs. St. Louis 1957
98—New Jersey vs. Milwaukee 1986

4-Game Series
126—Detroit vs. Chicago 1991
124—New York vs. Philadelphia 1978
      Portland vs. Denver 1986

5-Game Series
165—Syracuse vs. Boston 1961
157—Los Angeles vs. Detroit 1961

6-Game Series
197—Boston vs. Philadelphia 1962
      Milwaukee vs. New Jersey 1984

7-Game Series
221—Boston vs. St. Louis 1957
216—Boston vs. Cincinnati 1963

FEWEST PERSONAL FOULS

2-Game Series
- 40—Milwaukee vs. Phoenix 1978
- 41—Philadelphia vs. Washington 1980

3-Game Series
- 55—Chicago vs. New York 1991
  - L.A. Lakers vs. Houston 1991
- 58—Detroit vs. Seattle 1975
  - Kansas City vs. Phoenix 1980

4-Game Series
- 69—Chicago vs. Milwaukee 1974
- 72—Philadelphia vs. Cincinnati 1967

5-Game Series
- 89—Philadelphia vs. Boston 1958
- 90—Los Angeles vs. Milwaukee 1971

6-Game Series
- 108—Los Angeles vs. Milwaukee 1972
- 116—L.A. Lakers vs. Portland 1991

7-Game Series
- 124—Cleveland vs. Boston 1992
- 135—L.A. Lakers vs. Dallas 1988

MOST DISQUALIFICATIONS

2-Game Series
- 4—New York vs. Syracuse 1959
  - New Jersey vs. New York 1983
- 3—San Antonio vs. Boston 1977
  - Atlanta vs. Philadelphia 1982

3-Game Series
- 8—Minneapolis vs. St. Louis 1957
- 7—St. Louis vs. Minneapolis 1956

4-Game Series
- 5—Minneapolis vs. Ft. Wayne 1955
  - Cleveland vs. Philadelphia 1985
  - Atlanta vs. Detroit 1986
- 4—St. Louis vs. Detroit 1963
  - New York vs. Boston 1967

Milwaukee vs. Philadelphia 1985
Portland vs. Dallas 1985
Seattle vs. Dallas 1987

5-Game Series
- 9—Chicago vs. Philadelphia 1947
- 8—Philadelphia vs. Chicago 1947

6-Game Series
- 11—Boston vs. St. Louis 1958
- 10—Detroit vs. Los Angeles 1962

7-Game Series
- 10—Boston vs. St. Louis 1957
- 9—Minneapolis vs. New York 1952
  - St. Louis vs. Boston 1957
  - Boston vs. Los Angeles 1962

MOST STEALS

2-Game Series
- 23—Philadelphia vs. Washington 1980
- 22—Indiana vs. Philadelphia 1981
  - Philadelphia vs. Indiana 1981

3-Game Series
- 37—Chicago vs. New York 1991
- 36—Philadelphia vs. Milwaukee 1991

4-Game Series
- 57—Portland vs. Los Angeles 1977
- 55—Golden State vs. Washington 1975

5-Game Series
- 66—Kansas City vs. Phoenix 1979
- 59—Golden State vs. L.A. Lakers 1987

6-Game Series
- 81—Golden State vs. Seattle 1975
- 71—Philadelphia vs. Portland 1977

7-Game Series
- 94—Golden State vs. Phoenix 1976
- 78—Los Angeles vs. Golden State 1977

FEWEST STEALS

2-Game Series
- 10—New York vs. Cleveland 1978
  - Atlanta vs. Washington 1982
- 11—Portland vs. Seattle 1983
  - Seattle vs. Portland 1983

3-Game Series
- 11—Indiana vs. Detroit 1990
- 12—Denver vs. Phoenix 1983

4-Game Series
- 10—Detroit vs. Milwaukee 1989
- 16—Detroit vs. L.A. Lakers 1989

5-Game Series
- 17—Dallas vs. Seattle 1984
- 19—Boston vs. New York 1974

6-Game Series
- 24—Detroit vs. Boston 1991
- 26—Boston vs. Detroit 1991

7-Game Series
- 21—Milwaukee vs. Boston 1974
- 25—Detroit vs. Chicago 1974

MOST BLOCKED SHOTS

2-Game Series
- 22—Philadelphia vs. Atlanta 1982
- 20—Houston vs. Atlanta 1979

3-Game Series
- 34—L.A. Lakers vs. Denver 1987
  - Golden State vs. Utah 1989
- 32—Los Angeles vs. Kansas City 1984

4-Game Series
- 35—Seattle vs. Houston 1989
- 32—Golden State vs. Washington 1975
  - Los Angeles vs. San Antonio 1982

Philadelphia vs. Los Angeles 1983
Seattle vs. Dallas 1987

5-Game Series
- 53—Boston vs. Washington 1982
- 46—Philadelphia vs. Atlanta 1980
  - Los Angeles vs. Dallas 1984

6-Game Series
- 60—Philadelphia vs. Los Angeles 1980
- 51—Philadelphia vs. Los Angeles 1982

7-Game Series
- 62—Philadelphia vs. Milwaukee 1981
- 60—Boston vs. Philadelphia 1982

FEWEST BLOCKED SHOTS

2-Game Series
4—New York vs. Chicago 1981
5—Boston vs. San Antonio 1977
    Indiana vs. Philadelphia 1981

3-Game Series
4—Seattle vs. Los Angeles 1978
5—Seattle vs. Houston 1982
    Denver vs. Phoenix 1989
    Milwaukee vs. Philadelphia 1991

4-Game Series
6—Indiana vs. Atlanta 1987
8—Boston vs. Milwaukee 1983
    Milwaukee vs. Detroit 1989

5-Game Series
10—Houston vs. Boston 1975
11—New York vs. Boston 1974
    Milwaukee vs. Atlanta 1989

6-Game Series
10—Boston vs. Phoenix 1976
11—Boston vs. Washington 1975

7-Game Series
5—Boston vs. Milwaukee 1974
21—Boston vs. Philadelphia 1977
    L.A. Lakers vs. Detroit 1988

MOST TURNOVERS

2-Game Series
47—Boston vs. San Antonio 1977
46—Philadelphia vs. New Jersey 1979

3-Game Series
82—Chicago vs. Portland 1977
67—New York vs. Chicago 1991

4-Game Series
94—Golden State vs. Washington 1975
92—Milwaukee vs. Baltimore 1971

5-Game Series
128—Phoenix vs. Kansas City 1979
113—San Antonio vs. Denver 1985

6-Game Series
149—Portland vs. Philadelphia 1977
144—Boston vs. Phoenix 1976

7-Game Series
147—Phoenix vs. Golden State 1976
146—Seattle vs. Phoenix 1979

FEWEST TURNOVERS

2-Game Series
23—Seattle vs. Portland 1983
24—Portland vs. Seattle 1983

3-Game Series
28—Houston vs. Seattle 1982
31—Boston vs. Chicago 1987

4-Game Series
36—Milwaukee vs. Detroit 1989
44—Utah vs. Dallas 1986

5-Game Series
52—Chicago vs. Philadelphia 1991
55—Chicago vs. Los Angeles 1972

6-Game Series
46—Detroit vs. Boston 1991
60—Boston vs. Detroit 1991

7-Game Series
76—Atlanta vs. Boston 1988
80—Milwaukee vs. Boston 1987
    Boston vs. Cleveland 1992

Individual Records
MINUTES

Most Minutes, Game
67—Red Rocha, Syracuse at Boston, March 21, 1953 (4 ot)
    Paul Seymour, Syracuse at Boston, March 21, 1953 (4 ot)
66—Bob Cousy, Boston vs. Syracuse, March 21, 1953 (4 ot)

Highest Average, Minutes Per Game, One Playoff Series
49.33—Wilt Chamberlain, Philadelphia vs. New York, 1968 (296/6)
49.29—Kareem Abdul-Jabbar, Milwaukee vs. Boston, 1974 (345/7)
48.75—Wilt Chamberlain, Philadelphia vs. Cincinnati, 1965 (195/4)
    Jerry Lucas, Cincinnati vs. Philadelphia, 1965 (195/4)
    Oscar Robertson, Cincinnati vs. Philadelphia, 1965 (195/4)
    Wilt Chamberlain, Los Angeles vs. Atlanta, 1970 (195/4)

SCORING

Highest Scoring Average, One Playoff Series
46.3—Jerry West, Los Angeles vs. Baltimore, 1965 (278/6)
45.2—Michael Jordan, Chicago vs. Cleveland, 1988 (226/5)
45.0—Michael Jordan, Chicago vs. Miami, 1992 (135/3)

Most Points, Game
63—Michael Jordan, Chicago at Boston, April 20, 1986 (2 ot)
61—Elgin Baylor, Los Angeles at Boston, April 14, 1962
56—Wilt Chamberlain, Philadelphia vs. Syracuse, March 22, 1962
    Michael Jordan, Chicago at Miami, April 29, 1992

Most Points, Rookie, Game
53—Wilt Chamberlain, Philadelphia vs. Syracuse, March 14, 1960
50—Wilt Chamberlain, Philadelphia at Boston, March 22, 1960
46—Kareem Abdul-Jabbar, Milwaukee vs. Philadelphia at Madison, Wis., April 3, 1970

Most Consecutive Games, 20+ Points

　　57—Kareem Abdul-Jabbar, Milwaukee, Los Angeles, April 13, 1973—April 5, 1981
　　56—Michael Jordan, Chicago, June 2, 1989—June 14, 1992 (current)
　　49—Elgin Baylor, Minneapolis, Los Angeles, March 17, 1960—March 30, 1964

Most Consecutive Games, 30+ Points

　　11—Elgin Baylor, Los Angeles, March 27, 1962—April 18, 1962
　　　9—Kareem Abdul-Jabbar, Milwaukee, March 25, 1970—April 19, 1970
　　　　　Bob McAdoo, Buffalo, April 12, 1974—April 15, 1976
　　　8—Michael Jordan, Chicago, April 23, 1987—May 8, 1988

Most Consecutive Games, 40+ Points

　　6—Jerry West, Los Angeles, April 3—April 13, 1965
　　4—Bernard King, New York, April 19—April 27, 1984
　　3—Kareem Abdul-Jabbar, Los Angeles, April 26—May 1, 1977
　　　　Michael Jordan, Chicago, May 3—May 7, 1989
　　　　Michael Jordan, Chicago, May 9—May 13, 1990

Most Points, One Half

　　39—Eric Floyd, Golden State vs. L.A. Lakers, May 10, 1987
　　37—Michael Jordan, Chicago at Miami, April 29, 1992

Most Points, One Quarter

　　29—Eric Floyd, Golden State vs. L.A. Lakers, May 10, 1987
　　27—Mark Aguirre, Dallas at Houston, May 5, 1988

Most Points, Overtime Period

　　13—Clyde Drexler, Portland at L.A. Lakers, April 29, 1992

FIELD GOALS

Highest Field Goal Percentage, Game (minimum: 8 field goals)

　1.000—Wilt Chamberlain, Los Angeles at Atlanta, April 17, 1969 (9/9)
　　　　　Tom Kozelko, Capital at New York, April 12, 1974 (8/8)
　　　　　Larry McNeill, K.C.-Omaha vs. Chicago, April 13, 1975 (12/12)
　　　　　Scott Wedman, Boston vs. L.A. Lakers, May 27, 1985 (11/11)
　　　　　Brad Davis, Dallas at Utah, April 25, 1986 (8/8)
　　　　　Bob Hansen, Utah vs. Dallas, April 25, 1986 (9/9)
　　　　　Robert Parish, Boston at Atlanta, May 16, 1988 (8/8)
　　　　　John Paxson, Chicago vs. L.A. Lakers, June 5, 1991 (8/8)
　　.923—Wes Unseld, Washington vs. San Antonio, May 6, 1979 (12/13)
　　.917—Bill Bradley, New York at Los Angeles, April 26, 1972 (11/12)
　　　　　James Worthy, Los Angeles at Boston, May 31, 1984 (ot) (11/12)
　　　　　Clint Richardson, Philadelphia at Milwaukee, April 28, 1985 (11/12)

Most Field Goals, None Missed, Game

　　12—Larry McNeill, K.C.-Omaha vs. Chicago, April 13, 1975
　　11—Scott Wedman, Boston vs. L.A. Lakers, May 27, 1985
　　　9—Wilt Chamberlain, Los Angeles at Atlanta, April 17, 1969
　　　　　Bob Hansen, Utah vs. Dallas, April 25, 1986

Most Field Goals, Game

　　24—Wilt Chamberlain, Philadelphia vs. Syracuse, March 14, 1960
　　　　　John Havlicek, Boston vs. Atlanta, April 1, 1973
　　　　　Michael Jordan, Chicago vs. Cleveland, May 1, 1988
　　22—Wilt Chamberlain, Philadelphia at Boston, March 22, 1960
　　　　　Wilt Chamberlain, Philadelphia vs. Syracuse, March 22, 1962
　　　　　Elgin Baylor, Los Angeles at Boston, April 14, 1962
　　　　　Wilt Chamberlain, San Francisco vs. St. Louis, April 10, 1964
　　　　　Rick Barry, San Francisco vs. Philadelphia, April 18, 1967
　　　　　Billy Cunningham, Philadelphia vs. Milwaukee, April 1, 1970
　　　　　Michael Jordan, Chicago at Boston, April 20, 1986 (2 ot)

Most Field Goals, One Half

　　15—Eric Floyd, Golden State vs. L.A. Lakers, May 10, 1987
　　14—John Havlicek, Boston vs. Atlanta, April 1, 1973
　　　　　Gus Williams, Seattle at Dallas, April 17, 1984
　　　　　Michael Jordan, Chicago vs. Cleveland, May 1, 1988
　　　　　Isiah Thomas, Detroit at L.A. Lakers, June 19, 1988
　　　　　Michael Jordan, Chicago at Philadelphia, May 11, 1990
　　　　　Michael Jordan, Chicago vs. Portland, June 3, 1992

Most Field Goals, One Quarter

　　12—Eric Floyd, Golden State vs. L.A. Lakers, May 10, 1987
　　11—Gus Williams, Seattle at Dallas, April 17, 1984
　　　　　Isiah Thomas, Detroit at L.A. Lakers, June 19, 1988

Most Field Goal Attempts, Game

　　48—Wilt Chamberlain, Philadelphia vs. Syracuse, March 22, 1962
　　　　　Rick Barry, San Francisco vs. Philadelphia, April 18, 1967
　　46—Elgin Baylor, Los Angeles at Boston, April 14, 1962
　　45—Elgin Baylor, Los Angeles at St. Louis, March 27, 1961
　　　　　Michael Jordan, Chicago vs. Cleveland, May 1, 1988

Most Field Goal Attempts, None Made, Game

    14—Chick Reiser, Baltimore at Philadelphia, April 10, 1948
         Dennis Johnson, Seattle vs. Washington, June 7, 1978
    12—Tom Gola, Philadelphia at Boston, March 23, 1958
         Guy Rodgers, San Francisco at Boston, April 18, 1964
         Paul Pressey, Milwaukee at Boston, May 5, 1987

Most Field Goal Attempts, One Half

    25—Wilt Chamberlain, Philadelphia vs. Syracuse, March 22, 1962
         Elgin Baylor, Los Angeles at Boston, April 14, 1962
         Michael Jordan, Chicago vs. Cleveland, May 1, 1988

Most Field Goal Attempts, One Quarter

    17—Rick Barry, San Francisco at Philadelphia, April 14, 1967

THREE-POINT FIELD GOALS

Most Three-Point Field Goals, None Missed, Game

    5—Brad Davis, Dallas at Utah, April 25, 1986
        Byron Scott, L.A. Lakers vs. Golden State, May 5, 1991
    4—Kevin Grevey, Washington vs. New Jersey, April 23, 1982
        Scott Wedman, Boston vs. L.A. Lakers, May 27, 1985
        John Lucas, Milwaukee vs. Boston, May 8, 1987
        Scottie Pippen, Chicago at Cleveland, April 28, 1989
        Dale Ellis, Seattle at Houston, May 5, 1989
        Scottie Pippen, Chicago vs. New York, May 19, 1989
        Michael Cooper, L.A. Lakers at Phoenix, May 26, 1989
        Craig Hodges, Chicago vs. Detroit, June 1, 1990
        Chris Mullin, Golden State at L.A. Lakers, May 8, 1991
        Byron Scott, L.A. Lakers at Portland, May 21, 1991
        Steve Smith, Miami vs. Chicago, April 29, 1992

Most Three-Point Field Goals, Game

    7—Chuck Person, Indiana at Boston, April 28, 1991
    6—Michael Cooper, L.A. Lakers vs. Boston, June 4, 1987
        Michael Adams, Denver at Phoenix, April 30, 1989
        Eddie Johnson, Phoenix at Golden State, May 13, 1989
        Eddie Johnson, Phoenix vs. Utah, May 4, 1990
        Bill Laimbeer, Detroit vs. Portland, June 7, 1990 (ot)
        Vernon Maxwell, Houston at L.A. Lakers, April 27, 1991
        Terry Porter, Portland vs. Utah, May 16, 1992
        Michael Jordan, Chicago vs. Portland, June 3, 1992

Most Three-Point Field Goal Attempts, Game

    13—Vernon Maxwell, Houston at L.A. Lakers, April 27, 1991
         Tim Hardaway, Golden State at Seattle, April 30, 1992
    12—Michael Adams, Denver at Phoenix, April 30, 1989
         Craig Hodges, Chicago at Detroit, June 3, 1990

FREE THROWS

Most Free Throws Made, None Missed, Game

    17—Gail Goodrich, Los Angeles at Chicago, March 28, 1971
         Bob Love, Chicago at Golden State, April 27, 1975
    16—Dolph Schayes, Syracuse vs. Boston, March 25, 1959
         Chet Walker, Chicago vs. Golden State, April 30, 1975
         Tom Chambers, Phoenix at Utah, May 6, 1990
         Kevin Johnson, Phoenix at Portland, May 7, 1992

Most Free Throws Made, Game

    30—Bob Cousy, Boston vs. Syracuse, March 21, 1953 (4 ot)
    23—Michael Jordan, Chciago vs. New York, May 14, 1989
    22—Michael Jordan, Chicago vs. Cleveland, May 5, 1989 (ot)
         Karl Malone, Utah at L.A. Clippers, May 3, 1992

Most Free Throws Made, One Half

    19—Magic Johnson, L.A. Lakers vs. Golden State, May 8, 1991
         Karl Malone, Utah at Portland, May 9, 1991

Most Free Throws Made, One Quarter

    13—Michael Jordan, Chicago vs. Detroit, May 21, 1991
    11—Larry Spriggs, L.A. Lakers vs. Dallas, April 28, 1984
         John Stockton, Utah at Portland, April 30, 1988
         Terry Porter, Portland vs. Dallas, April 26, 1990
         Michael Jordan, Chicago vs. Detroit, May 28, 1990
         Magic Johnson, L.A. Lakers vs. Golden State, May 8, 1991

Most Free Throw Attempts, Game

    32—Bob Cousy, Boston vs. Syracuse, March 21, 1953 (4 ot)
    28—Michael Jordan, Chicago vs. New York, May 14, 1989

Most Free Throw Attempts, One Half

    21—Magic Johnson, L.A. Lakers vs. Golden State, May 8, 1991
    20—Karl Malone, Utah at Portland, May 9, 1991

Most Free Throw Attempts, One Quarter

    14—Michael Jordan, Chicago vs. Detroit, May 21, 1991
    13—Julius Erving, Philadelphia vs. Milwaukee, April 5, 1981
           Charles Barkley, Philadelphia vs. Chicago, May 11, 1990

REBOUNDS

Highest Average, Rebounds per Game, One Playoff Series

    32.0—Wilt Chamberlain, Philadelphia vs. Boston, 1967 (160/5)
    31.4—Wilt Chamberlain, Philadelphia vs. Boston, 1965 (220/7)
    31.0—Bill Russell, Boston vs. Syracuse, 1961 (155/5)

Most Rebounds, Game

    41—Wilt Chamberlain, Philadelphia vs. Boston, April 5, 1967
    40—Bill Russell, Boston vs. Philadelphia, March 23, 1958
         Bill Russell, Boston vs. St. Louis, March 29, 1960
         Bill Russell, Boston vs. Los Angeles, April 18, 1962 (ot)

Most Rebounds, Rookie, Game

    35—Wilt Chamberlain, Philadelphia at Boston, March 22, 1960

Most Rebounds, One Half

    26—Wilt Chamberlain, Philadelphia vs. San Francisco, April 16, 1967

Most Rebounds, One Quarter

    19—Bill Russell, Boston vs. Los Angeles, April 18, 1962

Most Offensive Rebounds, Game

    15—Moses Malone, Houston vs. Washington, April 21, 1977 (ot)
    13—Moses Malone, Houston at Atlanta, April 13, 1979
    12—Moses Malone, Houston vs. Atlanta, April 11, 1979
         Moses Malone, Houston vs. Seattle, April 23, 1982
         Larry Smith, Golden State at L.A. Lakers, May 12, 1987

Most Defensive Rebounds, Game

    20—Dave Cowens, Boston at Houston, April 22, 1975
         Dave Cowens, Boston at Philadelphia, May 1, 1977
         Bill Walton, Portland at Philadelphia, June 3, 1977
         Bill Walton, Portland vs. Philadelphia, June 5, 1977
    19—Sam Lacey, K.C.-Omaha vs. Chicago, April 13, 1975
         Dave Cowens, Boston at Buffalo, April 28, 1976
         Elvin Hayes, Washington at Cleveland, April 15, 1977
         Larry Bird, Boston at Philadelphia, April 23, 1980
         Akeem Olajuwon, Houston at Dallas, April 30, 1988

ASSISTS

Highest Average, Assists per Game, One Playoff Series

    17.0—Magic Johnson, L.A. Lakers vs. Portland, 1985 (85/5)
    16.4—John Stockton, Utah vs. L.A. Lakers, 1988 (115/7)
    16.2—Magic Johnson, L.A. Lakers vs. Houston, 1986 (81/5)

Most Assists, Game

    24—Magic Johnson, Los Angeles vs. Phoenix, May 15, 1984
         John Stockton, Utah at L.A. Lakers, May 17, 1988
    23—Magic Johnson, L.A. Lakers at Portland, May 3, 1985
    22—Doc Rivers, Atlanta vs. Boston, May 16, 1988

Most Assists, Rookie, Game

    18—Spud Webb, Atlanta vs. Detroit, April 19, 1986

Most Assists, One Half

    15—Magic Johnson, L.A. Lakers at Portland, May 3, 1985
         Doc Rivers, Atlanta vs. Boston, May 16, 1988

Most Assists, One Quarter

    10—Magic Johnson, L.A. Lakers vs. Denver, May 22, 1985
         Magic Johnson, L.A. Lakers vs. Houston, April 27, 1991
         Magic Johnson, L.A. Lakers at Portland, May 18, 1991

PERSONAL FOULS

Most Personal Fouls, Game

    8—Jack Toomay, Baltimore at New York, March 26, 1949 (ot)
    7—Al Cervi, Syracuse at Boston, March 21, 1953 (4 ot)
    6—By many players

Most Personal Fouls, One Half

6—By many players

Most Personal Fouls, One Quarter

6—Paul Mokeski, Milwaukee vs. Philadelphia, May 7, 1986
5—Arnie Risen, Boston vs. Syracuse, March 21, 1957
  Jim Krebs, Los Angeles at Boston, April 21, 1963
  Brian Winters, Milwaukee vs. Philadelphia, April 10, 1981
  Mark West, Dallas at Los Angeles, April 28, 1984
  Akeem Olajuwon, Houston vs. Denver, April 26, 1986
  Greg Kite, Boston at Houston, June 1, 1986
  Robert Parish, Boston at Chicago, April 28, 1987
  Roy Tarpley, Dallas at Denver, May 17, 1988
  Derrick Chievous, Houston at Seattle, April 28, 1989
  Walter Davis, Denver at Phoenix, April 30, 1989
  Tony Brown, Milwaukee at Detroit, May 12, 1989
  Michael Jordan, Chicago at Detroit, May 21, 1989
  Danny Ainge, Portland at Utah, May 11, 1991
  Karl Malone, Utah vs. Portland, May 11, 1991
  Joe Dumars, Detroit at Chicago, May 21, 1991

Most Minutes Played, No Personal Fouls, Game

54—Randy Wittman, Atlanta at Detroit, April 25, 1986 (2 ot)
50—Jo Jo White, Boston at Milwaukee, April 30, 1974 (ot)
49—Gus Williams, Seattle at Dallas, April 26, 1984 (ot)
  James Worthy, L.A. Lakers vs. Golden State, May 14, 1991 (ot)

DISQUALIFICATIONS

Fewest Minutes Played, Disqualified Player, Game

7—Bob Lochmueller, Syracuse vs. Boston, March 19, 1953
  Will Perdue, Chicago at New York, May 14, 1992
8—Dick Schnittker, Minneapolis vs. Ft. Wayne at Indianapolis, March 22, 1955
  Al Bianchi, Syracuse vs. Boston, March 25, 1959
  Jim Krebs, Los Angeles vs. Detroit, March 19, 1961
  Elston Turner, Denver vs. Portland, April 20, 1986
  Antoine Carr, Atlanta vs. Boston, May 15, 1988

STEALS

Most Steals, Game

8—Rick Barry, Golden State vs. Seattle, April 14, 1975
  Lionel Hollins, Portland at Los Angeles, May 8, 1977
  Maurice Cheeks, Philadelphia vs. New Jersey, April 11, 1979
  Craig Hodges, Milwaukee at Philadelphia, May 9, 1986
  Tim Hardaway, Golden State at L.A. Lakers, May 8, 1991
  Tim Hardaway, Golden State at Seattle, April 30, 1992
7—Rick Barry, Golden State at Chicago, May 11, 1975
  Rick Barry, Golden State vs. Detroit, April 28, 1976
  Bobby Jones, Denver at Portland, April 24, 1977
  Magic Johnson, Los Angeles vs. Portland, April 24, 1983
  Darrell Walker, New York at Detroit, April 17, 1984
  T.R. Dunn, Denver vs. Portland, April 20, 1986
  Dennis Johnson, Boston vs. Atlanta, April 29, 1986
  Derek Harper, Dallas at L.A. Lakers, April 30, 1986
  Patrick Ewing, New York vs. Boston, May 4, 1990
  Byron Scott, L.A. Lakers at Golden State, May 10, 1991

BLOCKED SHOTS

Most Blocked Shots, Game

10—Mark Eaton, Utah vs. Houston, April 26, 1985
  Akeem Olajuwon, Houston at L.A. Lakers, April 29, 1990
 9—Kareem Abdul-Jabbar, Los Angeles vs. Golden State, April 22, 1977
  Manute Bol, Washington at Philadelphia, April 18, 1986
 8—George Johnson, Golden State at Seattle, April 24, 1975
  Elvin Hayes, Washington vs. Cleveland, April 26, 1976 (ot)
  Kareem Abdul-Jabbar, Los Angeles at Portland, May 10, 1977
  Bill Walton, Portland vs. Philadelphia, June 5, 1977
  Caldwell Jones, Philadelphia vs. Washington, May 3, 1978
  Darryl Dawkins, Philadelphia vs. Atlanta, April 21, 1982
  Kareem Abdul-Jabbar, Los Angeles at Portland, May 1, 1983
  Mark Eaton, Utah at Houston, April 19, 1985
  Manute Bol, Washington at Philadelphia, April 20, 1986
  Manute Bol, Washington vs. Philadelphia, April 22, 1986
  Akeem Olajuwon, Houston vs. Boston, June 5, 1986
  Akeem Olajuwon, Houston vs. Portland, April 28, 1987
  Alton Lister, Seattle vs. Houston, April 28, 1989
  David Robinson, San Antonio vs. Portland, May 10, 1990
  David Robinson, San Antonio vs. Golden State, April 25, 1991

TURNOVERS

Most Turnovers, Game

    11—John Williamson, New Jersey at Philadelphia, April 11, 1979
    10—Quinn Buckner, Milwaukee vs. Phoenix, April 14, 1978
         Magic Johnson, Los Angeles vs. Philadelphia, May 14, 1980
         Larry Bird, Boston vs. Chicago, April 7, 1981
         Moses Malone, Philadelphia at New Jersey, April 24, 1984
         Kevin Johnson, Phoenix at L.A. Lakers, May 23, 1989

Most Minutes Played, No Turnovers, Game

    51—Marques Johnson, Milwaukee at Seattle, April 8, 1980 (ot)
         Jeff Hornacek, Phoenix vs. Portland, May 11, 1992 (2 ot)
    49—Buck Williams, Portland vs. San Antonio, May 19, 1990 (ot)

Team Records
WON-LOST

Most Consecutive Games Won, All Playoff Series

    13—L.A. Lakers, 1988-89
    12—Detroit, 1989-90

Most Consecutive Games Won, One Playoff Series

    11—L.A. Lakers, 1989
     9—Los Angeles, 1982

Most Consecutive Games Won At Home, All Playoff Series

    15—Chicago, 1990-91
    14—Minneapolis, 1949-51
         Boston, 1986-87
         Detroit, 1989-90

Most Consecutive Games Won At Home, One Playoff Series

    10—Portland, 1977
         Boston, 1986
         L.A. Lakers, 1987
         Detroit, 1990
     9—Boston, 1976
         Seattle, 1978
         Boston, 1984
         Boston, 1985
         Portland, 1990

Most Consecutive Games Won On Road, All Playoff Series

     8—Chicago, 1991-92
     5—Minneapolis, 1950
         Boston, 1968-69
         Los Angeles, 1982
         L.A. Lakers, 1989
         Detroit, 1989-90

Most Consecutive Games Won On Road, One Playoff Series

     6—Chicago, 1991
     5—Minneapolis, 1950
         Los Angeles, 1982
         L.A. Lakers, 1989

Most Consecutive Games Lost, All Playoff Series

    11—Baltimore, 1965-66, 1969-70
    10—New Jersey, 1984-86, 1992

Most Consecutive Games Lost At Home, All Playoff Series

     9—Philadelphia, 1968-71
     6—Cincinnati, 1965-67
         Baltimore, 1965-66, 1968-69
         New Jersey, 1979, 1982-84

Most Consecutive Games Lost At Home, One Playoff Series

     3—New York, 1953
         Philadelphia, 1969
         San Francisco, 1969
         New Jersey, 1984
         Philadelphia, 1984
         Milwaukee, 1989
         Portland, 1990
         L.A. Lakers, 1991

Most Consecutive Games Lost On Road, All Playoff Series

    18—Chicago, 1967-68, 1970-73
    14—Los Angeles, 1973-74, 1977-79
         Cleveland, 1976-78, 1985, 1988-89

Most Consecutive Games Lost On Road, One Playoff Series

    7—Boston, 1987
    6—Los Angeles, 1971

Most Games, One Playoff Series

    24—L.A. Lakers, 1988
    23—Boston, 1984
         Boston, 1987
         Detroit, 1988
    22—Seattle, 1978
         Chicago, 1992

Most Home Games, One Playoff Series

    14—L.A. Lakers, 1988
    13—Boston, 1984
         Boston, 1987

Most Road Games, One Playoff Series

    12—Houston, 1981
    11—Washington, 1978
         Detroit, 1988

Most Wins, One Playoff Series

    15—Boston, 1984
         L.A. Lakers, 1985
         Boston, 1986
         L.A. Lakers, 1987
         L.A. Lakers, 1988
         Detroit, 1989
         Detroit, 1990
         Chicago, 1991
         Chicago, 1992
    14—Portland, 1977
         Washington, 1978
         Los Angeles, 1984
         Detroit, 1988

Most Wins At Home, One Playoff Series

    12—Boston, 1984
         L.A. Lakers, 1988
    11—Boston, 1987

Most Wins On Road, One Playoff Series

    8—Houston, 1981
    7—Boston, 1968
         Detroit, 1989
         Chicago, 1991

Most Games Lost, One Playoff Series

    10—Baltimore, 1971
         Washington, 1979
         Boston, 1987
     9—Washington, 1975
         Phoenix, 1976
         Philadelphia, 1977
         Seattle, 1978
         Houston, 1981
         Philadelphia, 1982
         Detroit, 1988
         L.A. Lakers, 1988
         Portland, 1990

Most Games Lost At Home, One Playoff Series

    5—Washington, 1979
         Houston, 1981
    4—Boston, 1966
         Boston, 1968
         Baltimore, 1971
         Seattle, 1980
         Kansas City, 1981

Most Losses On Road, One Playoff Series

    8—Boston, 1987
    7—Phoenix, 1976
         Seattle, 1978
         Boston, 1984
         L.A. Lakers, 1988

Most Games Won At Home Without A Loss, One Playoff Series

    10—Portland, 1977
         Boston, 1986
         L.A. Lakers, 1987
     9—Boston, 1976

Most Games Lost On Road Without A Win, One Playoff Series

    6—Los Angeles, 1971
    5—Cincinnati, 1964
       Los Angeles, 1977
       Philadelphia, 1990

Highest Won-Lost Pct., One Playoff Series

    .923—Philadelphia, 1983 (12-1)
    .883—Detroit, 1989 (15-2)
        Chicago, 1991 (15-2)

SCORING

Most Points, Game

    157—Boston vs. New York, April 28, 1990
    156—Milwaukee at Philadelphia, March 30, 1970
    153—L.A. Lakers vs. Denver, May 22, 1985
        Portland at Phoenix, May 11, 1992 (2 ot)

Fewest Points, Game

    70—Golden State vs. Los Angeles, April 21, 1973
       Seattle at Houston, April 23, 1982
    71—Syracuse vs. Ft. Wayne at Indianapolis, April 7, 1955
       Houston vs. Boston, May 9, 1981

Most Points, Both Teams, Game

    304—Portland (153) at Phoenix (151), May 11, 1992 (2 ot)
    285—San Antonio (152) vs. Denver (133), April 26, 1983
       Boston (157) vs. New York (128), April 28, 1990
    280—Dallas (151) vs. Seattle (129), April 23, 1987

Fewest Points, Both Teams, Game

    145—Syracuse (71) vs. Ft. Wayne (74) at Indianapolis, April 7, 1955
    157—Phoenix (81) at Kansas City (76), April 17, 1981
       Boston (79) at Detroit (78), May 30, 1988
    158—Ft. Wayne (74) at St. Louis (84), March 24, 1956
       Golden State (86) at Chicago (72), May 11, 1975

Largest Margin Of Victory, Game

    58—Minneapolis vs. St. Louis, March 19, 1956 (133-75)
    56—Los Angeles at Golden State, April 21, 1973 (126-70)
    50—Milwaukee vs. San Francisco, April 4, 1971 (136-86)

BY HALF

Most Points, First Half

    82—San Antonio vs. Denver, April 26, 1983
       L.A. Lakers vs. Denver, April 23, 1987
    80—L.A. Lakers vs. Denver, May 11, 1985

Fewest Points, First Half

    28—Los Angeles at Milwaukee, April 7, 1974
    30—St. Louis at Minneapolis, March 19, 1956
       Golden State at Los Angeles, April 22, 1977
       Houston vs. Boston, May 9, 1981
       Houston at Seattle, April 25, 1982

Most Points, Both Teams, First Half

    150—San Antonio (82) vs. Denver (68), April 26, 1983
    147—L.A. Lakers (79) at Denver (68), May 17, 1985

Fewest Points, Both Teams, First Half

    69—Syracuse (31) vs. Ft. Wayne (38) at Indianapolis, April 7, 1955
    71—Milwaukee (37) at Los Angeles (34), April 9, 1972
       Phoenix (33) vs. Boston (38), June 6, 1976
       Houston (30) vs. Boston (41), May 9, 1981

Largest Lead At Halftime

    40—Detroit vs. Washington, April 26, 1987 (led 76-36; won 128-85)
    36—Milwaukee at Philadelphia, March 30, 1970 (led 77-41; won 156-120)

Largest Deficit At Halftime Overcome To Win Game

    21—Baltimore at Philadelphia, April 13, 1948 (trailed 20-41; won 66-63)
    18—Los Angeles at Seattle, April 27, 1980 (trailed 39-57; won 98-93)
       Philadelphia vs. New York, April 27, 1983 (trailed 41-59; won 98-91)
       Milwaukee at New Jersey, April 22, 1986 (trailed 55-73, won 118-113)
       Phoenix at Denver, May 2, 1989 (trailed 54-72, won 130-121)
       Portland vs. Phoenix, May 23, 1990 (trailed 41-59; won 108-107)

Most Points, Second Half

    87—Milwaukee vs. Denver, April 23, 1978

83—Houston vs. San Antonio, April 6, 1980
Detroit vs. Boston, May 24, 1987
Boston vs. New York, April 28, 1990

Fewest Points, Second Half

27—Philadelphia vs. Boston, May 21, 1982
30—Capital at New York, April 12, 1974
Golden State vs. Detroit, April 12, 1977
Washington vs. Seattle, May 24, 1979
Boston vs. Detroit, May 2, 1989
New York at Chicago, May 17, 1992

Most Points, Both Teams, Second Half

158—Milwaukee (79) at Philadelphia (79), March 30, 1970
152—Boston (83) vs. New York (69), April 28, 1990

Fewest Points, Both Teams, Second Half

65—Boston (32) at Philadelphia (33), May 1, 1977
67—Capital (33) vs. New York (34), April 5, 1974

BY QUARTER, OVERTIME PERIOD

Most Points, First Quarter

45—L.A. Lakers vs. Phoenix, April 18, 1985
Dallas vs. L.A. Lakers, May 4, 1986
43—Philadelphia vs. San Francisco, April 14, 1967
Philadelphia at San Francisco, April 24, 1967
Denver vs. Utah, May 7, 1985

Fewest Points, First Quarter

8—Utah at L.A. Lakers, May 8, 1988
9—Atlanta at Boston, May 13, 1988

Most Points, Both Teams, First Quarter

84—Philadelphia (43) at San Francisco (41), April 24, 1967
79—Boston (41) vs. New York (38), April 28, 1990

Fewest Points, Both Teams, First Quarter

26—Detroit (10) vs. Boston (16), May 30, 1988
30—Chicago (13) vs. Detroit (17), April 5, 1974

Largest Lead End Of First Quarter

26—Milwaukee at Philadelphia, March 30, 1970 (led 40-14; won 156-120)
22—Phoenix vs. Portland, May 25, 1990 (led 40-18; won 123-89)

Largest Deficit End Of First Quarter Overcome To Win

20—L.A. Lakers at Seattle, May 14, 1989 (trailed 12-32, won 97-95)
18—San Francisco at St. Louis, April 12, 1967 (trailed 21-39; won 112-107)

Most Points, Second Quarter

46—Boston vs. St. Louis, March 27, 1960
Boston vs. Detroit, March 24, 1968
45—New York vs. Boston, March 19, 1955
St. Louis vs. Ft. Wayne, March 14, 1957

Fewest Points, Second Quarter

10—Houston at Seattle, April 25, 1982
Boston at Detroit, April 28, 1989
11—Golden State at Los Angeles, April 22, 1977

Most Points, Both Teams, Second Quarter

76—Cincinnati (41) at Boston (35), March 31, 1963
Boston (39) vs. Milwaukee (37), May 6, 1987
75—Boston (46) vs. Detroit (29), March 24, 1968
Golden State (39) vs. Phoenix (36), May 13, 1989

Fewest Points, Both Teams, Second Quarter

25—Golden State (11) at Los Angeles (14), April 22, 1977
29—Syracuse (13) vs. Ft. Wayne (16) at Indianapolis, April 7, 1955
Houston (10) at Seattle (19), April 25, 1982

Most Points, Third Quarter

49—L.A. Lakers vs. Golden State, May 5, 1987
47—Milwaukee at Philadelphia, March 30, 1970
Los Angeles vs. Boston, June 3, 1984

Fewest Points, Third Quarter

6—Atlanta at Boston, May 6, 1986
8—Los Angeles vs. Milwaukee, April 9, 1972

Most Points, Both Teams, Third Quarter

82—San Francisco (44) vs. St. Louis (38), April 1, 1967
80—Los Angeles (47) vs. Boston (33), June 3, 1984

Fewest Points, Both Teams, Third Quarter

 26—Capital (10) at New York (16), April 12, 1974
 30—Capital (11) vs. New York (19), April 5, 1974

Largest Lead End Of Third Quarter

 52—Milwaukee at Philadelphia, March 30, 1970 (led 124-72; won 156-120)
 48—Milwaukee vs. San Francisco, April 4, 1971 (led 105-57; won 136-86)

Largest Deficit End Of Third Quarter Overcome To Win

 16—New York vs. Boston, April 22, 1973 (trailed 56-72; won 117-110 in 2ot)
 15—Chicago vs. Portland, June 14, 1992 (trailed 64-79; won 97-93)

Most Points, Fourth Quarter

 51—Los Angeles vs. Detroit, March 31, 1962
 49—Golden State at San Antonio, April 25, 1991

Fewest Points, Fourth Quarter

  9—Boston vs. Milwaukee, April 29, 1983
 10—Detroit vs. Boston, May 30, 1988

Most Points, Both Teams, Fourth Quarter

 86—Golden State (49) at San Antonio (37), April 25, 1991
 83—Milwaukee (47) vs. Denver (36), April 23, 1978

Fewest Points, Both Teams, Fourth Quarter

 26—Philadelphia (12) vs. Boston (14), May 1, 1977
 29—Detroit (10) vs. Boston (19), May 30, 1988

Most Points, Overtime Period

 22—Los Angeles vs. New York, May 1, 1970
 20—Portland vs. Utah, May 26, 1992

Fewest Points, Overtime Period

  4—Minneapolis vs. St. Louis, March 25, 1957
  Boston vs. Milwaukee, May 10, 1974
  Milwaukee at Boston, May 10, 1974
  Portland at Denver, May 1, 1977
  Seattle vs. Milwaukee, April 9, 1980
  Utah at Denver, May 2, 1985
  Boston vs. Detroit, June 1, 1988
  L.A. Lakers vs. Chicago, June 7, 1991

Most Points, Both Teams, Overtime Period

 38—Los Angeles (22) vs. New York (16), May 1, 1970
 36—L.A. Lakers (19) vs. Portland (17), April 29, 1992

Fewest Points, Both Teams, Overtime Period

  8—Boston (4) vs. Milwaukee (4), May 10, 1974
 10—Seattle (4) vs. Milwaukee (6), April 9, 1980

PLAYERS SCORING

Most Players, 30+ Points, Game

 3—Denver at Utah, April 19, 1984
  San Antonio vs. Golden State, April 25, 1991
 2—by many

Most Players, 30+ Points, Both Teams, Game

 3—Accomplished 48 times. Most recent:
  Cleveland (2) vs. New Jersey (1), April 23, 1992
  Phoenix (2) vs. San Antonio (1), April 26, 1992
  Portland (2) at Phoenix (1), May 11, 1992 (2 ot)

Most Players, 20+ Points, Game

 5—Boston vs. Los Angeles, April 19, 1965
  Philadelphia vs. Boston, April 11, 1967
  Phoenix at Los Angeles, May 23, 1984
  Boston vs. Milwaukee, May 15, 1986
  L.A. Lakers vs. Boston, June 4, 1987
  Boston vs. L.A. Lakers, June 11, 1987

Most Players, 20+ Points, Both Teams, Game

 8—Cincinnati (4) at Detroit (4), March 16, 1962
  Boston (4) at Los Angeles (4), April 26, 1966
  Phoenix (5) at Los Angeles (3), May 23, 1984
  Boston (5) vs. Milwaukee (3), May 15, 1986
  L.A. Lakers (5) vs. Boston (3), June 4, 1987
  Portland (4) at Phoenix (4), May 11, 1992 (2 ot)

Most Players, 10+ Points, Game

 10—Minneapolis vs. St. Louis, March 19, 1956
  9—Cincinnati at Boston, March 31, 1963
  Dallas vs. Seattle, April 23, 1987

Most Players, 10+ Points, Both Teams, Game

15—Philadelphia (8) vs. Milwaukee (7), March 30, 1970
    L.A. Lakers (8) vs. Phoenix (7), April 18, 1985
    Dallas (9) vs. Seattle (6), April 23, 1987
    Dallas (8) vs. Houston (7), April 28, 1988
14—Ft. Wayne (7) at Minneapolis (7), March 17, 1957
    St. Louis (7) at Boston (7), March 27, 1960
    Detroit (7) at Cincinnati (7), March 17, 1962
    Boston (7) at Detroit (7), March 25, 1968
    Philadelphia (7) at Washington (7), May 5, 1978
    Phoenix (7) at L.A. Lakers (7), April 20, 1985
    Denver (7) at L.A. Lakers (7), April 25, 1987
    Boston (8) vs. New York (6), April 28, 1990

Fewest Players, 10+ Points, Game

1—Golden State vs. Los Angeles, April 21, 1973
2—In many games

Fewest Players, 10+ Points, Both Teams, Game

5—Rochester (2) at Minneapolis (3), March 16, 1955
    Ft. Wayne (2) vs. Philadelphia (3), April 1, 1956
    Los Angeles (2) at Boston (3), April 29, 1969
    Chicago (2) at Detroit (3), May 20, 1990

FIELD GOAL PERCENTAGE

Highest Field Goal Percentage, Game

.670—Boston vs. New York, April 28, 1990 (63-94)
.663—L.A. Lakers vs. San Antonio, April 17, 1986 (57-86)

Lowest Field Goal Percentage, Game

.233—Golden State vs. Los Angeles, April 21, 1973 (27-116)
.242—St. Louis at Minneapolis, March 19, 1956 (22-91)

Highest Field Goal Percentage, Both Teams, Game

.591—L.A. Lakers (.640) vs. Denver (.543), May 11, 1985
.588—Boston (.608) vs. Atlanta (.571), May 22, 1988
    Boston (.670) vs. New York (.510), April 28, 1990

Lowest Field Goal Percentage, Both Teams, Game

.277—Syracuse (.275) vs. Ft. Wayne (.280) at Indianapolis, April 7, 1955
.288—Minneapolis (.283) vs. Rochester (.293), March 16, 1955

FIELD GOALS

Most Field Goals, Game

67—Milwaukee at Philadelphia, March 30, 1970
    San Antonio vs. Denver, May 4, 1983
    L.A. Lakers vs. Denver, May 22, 1985
64—Milwaukee vs. Denver, April 23, 1978

Fewest Field Goals, Game

22—St. Louis at Minneapolis, March 19, 1956
23—Ft. Wayne vs. Syracuse at Indianapolis, April 7, 1955
    New Jersey at Milwaukee, May 8, 1984

Most Field Goals, Both Teams, Game

119—Milwaukee (67) at Philadelphia (52), March 30, 1970
114—San Antonio (62) vs. Denver (52), April 26, 1983
    Boston (63) vs. New York (51), April 28, 1990

Fewest Field Goals, Both Teams, Game

48—Ft. Wayne (23) vs. Syracuse (25) at Indianapolis, April 7, 1955
52—Boston (26) at Detroit (26), May 30, 1988

FIELD GOAL ATTEMPTS

Most Field Goal Attempts, Game

140—Boston vs. Syracuse, March 18, 1959
    San Francisco at Philadelphia, April 14, 1967 (ot)
135—Boston vs. Syracuse, April 1, 1959
    Boston vs. Philadelphia, March 22, 1960

Fewest Field Goal Attempts, Game

59—Chicago at Detroit, May 31, 1989
61—Milwaukee at New Jersey, May 3, 1984

Most Field Goal Attempts, Both Teams, Game

257—Boston (135) vs. Philadelphia (122), March 22, 1960
256—San Francisco (140) at Philadelphia (116), April 14, 1967 (ot)

Fewest Field Goal Attempts, Both Teams, Game

    136—Atlanta (65) at Indiana (71), April 29, 1987
    137—Indiana (66) vs. Atlanta (71), May 1, 1987
          Chicago (68) vs. New York (69), May 12, 1992

THREE-POINT FIELD GOALS

Most Three-Point Field Goals, Game

    9—Denver at Phoenix, April 30, 1989
      Phoenix at Golden State, May 13, 1989
      Portland vs. San Antonio, May 15, 1990 (2 ot)
      Indiana at Boston, April 28, 1991
    8—Boston at Milwaukee, May 18, 1986
      L.A. Lakers vs. Portland, April 27, 1989
      Chicago vs. New York, May 19, 1989
      Detroit vs. Portland, June 7, 1990 (ot)
      Detroit at Atlanta, April 30, 1991
      Indiana at Boston, April 23, 1992
      Portland vs. Utah, May 19, 1992

Most Three-Point Field Goals, Both Teams, Game

    15—Chicago (8) vs. New York (7), May 19, 1989
    14—Houston (7) at L.A. Lakers (7), April 27, 1991

Most Three-Point Field Goals, None Missed, Game

    5—Dallas at Utah, April 25, 1986
      Dallas vs. L.A. Lakers, May 4, 1986
    4—Washington vs. New Jersey, April 23, 1982
      L.A. Lakers vs. Denver, May 11, 1985

THREE-POINT FIELD GOAL ATTEMPTS

Most Three-Point Field Goal Attempts, Game

    20—Denver at Phoenix, April 30, 1989
      Chicago vs. Detroit, May 29, 1989
    19—Chicago at Detroit, June 3, 1990
      Golden State at San Antonio, April 25, 1991
      Houston at L.A. Lakers, April 27, 1991

Most Three-Point Field Goal Attempts, Both Teams, Game

    34—Houston (19) at L.A. Lakers (15), April 27, 1991
    33—Chicago (18) at New York (15), May 11, 1989

FREE THROW PERCENTAGE

Highest Free Throw Percentage, Game

    1.000—Detroit at Milwaukee, April 18, 1976 (15-15)
          Dallas vs. Seattle, April 19, 1984 (24-24)
          Detroit vs. Chicago, May 18, 1988 (23-23)
          Phoenix vs. Golden State, May 9, 1989 (28-28)
          Chicago vs. Cleveland, May 19, 1992 (19-19)
          Portland at Chicago, June 14, 1992 (21-21)
    .971—Denver vs. San Antonio, May 1, 1990 (34-35)

Lowest Free Throw Percentage, Game

    .261—Philadelphia at Boston, March 19, 1960 (6-23)
    .429—New Jersey vs. Philadelphia, April 22, 1984 (9-21)
          Denver at L.A. Lakers, April 23, 1987 (9-21)

Highest Free Throw Percentage, Both Teams, Game

    .957—Chicago (.964) at Boston (.947), April 23, 1987
    .946—Phoenix (1.000) vs. Golden State (.893), May 9, 1989

Lowest Free Throw Percentage, Both Teams, Game

    .500—Philadelphia (.261) at Boston (.762), March 19, 1960
    .523—New York (.455) at Detroit (.591), May 8, 1990

FREE THROWS MADE

Most Free Throws Made, Game

    57—Boston vs. Syracuse, March 21, 1953 (4 ot)
    54—St. Louis vs. Minneapolis, March 17, 1956

Fewest Free Throws Made, Game

    3—Houston vs. Washington, April 19, 1977
      Los Angeles at Philadelphia, May 26, 1983
    4—Kansas City at Portland, April 1, 1981
      Boston at Cleveland, May 2, 1992

Most Free Throws Made, Both Teams, Game

108—Boston (57) vs. Syracuse (51), March 21, 1953 (4 ot)
98—New York (51) vs. Baltimore (47), March 26, 1949 (ot)
91—St. Louis (54) vs. Minneapolis (37), March 17, 1956

Fewest Free Throws Made, Both Teams, Game

12—Boston (6) at Buffalo (6), April 6, 1974
17—Chicago (9) at Los Angeles (8), April 1, 1973
Boston (9) vs. Buffalo (8), April 21, 1976

FREE THROW ATTEMPTS

Most Free Throw Attempts, Game

70—St. Louis vs. Minneapolis, March 17, 1956
68—Minneapolis vs. St. Louis, March 21, 1956

Fewest Free Throw Attempts, Game

5—Los Angeles at Philadelphia, May 26, 1983
Boston at Cleveland, May 2, 1992
6—Houston vs. Washington, April 19, 1977

Most Free Throw Attempts, Both Teams, Game

128—Boston (64) vs. Syracuse (64), March 21, 1953 (4 ot)
122—St. Louis (70) vs. Minneapolis (52), March 17, 1956
Minneapolis (68) vs. St. Louis (54), March 21, 1956

Fewest Free Throw Attempts, Both Teams, Game

18—Boston (7) at Buffalo (11), April 6, 1974
24—Atlanta (10) vs. Washington (14), April 20, 1979

TOTAL REBOUNDS

Highest Rebound Percentage, Game

.723—L.A. Lakers vs. San Antonio, April 17, 1986 (47-65)
.685—New York vs. Detroit, April 24, 1992 (50-73)

Most Rebounds, Game

97—Boston vs. Philadelphia, March 19, 1960
95—Boston vs. Syracuse, March 18, 1959

Fewest Rebounds, Game

18—San Antonio at L.A. Lakers, April 17, 1986
22—Golden State at Seattle, April 28, 1992

Most Rebounds, Both Teams, Game

169—Boston (89) vs. Philadelphia (80), March 22, 1960
San Francisco (93) at Philadelphia (76), April 16, 1967
163—Boston (95) vs. Syracuse (68), March 18, 1959

Fewest Rebounds, Both Teams, Game

51—Milwaukee (25) vs. Philadelphia (26), May 1, 1982
57—Golden State (22) at Seattle (35), April 28, 1992

OFFENSIVE REBOUNDS

Highest Offensive Rebounding Percentage, Game

.583—Houston vs. Philadelphia, May 11, 1977 (28-48)
.571—Milwaukee vs. Philadelphia, April 17, 1981 (24-42)

Most Offensive Rebounds, Game

30—Seattle vs. Portland, April 23, 1978
29—Washington at Atlanta, April 26, 1979
Kansas City at Phoenix, April 27, 1979

Fewest Offensive Rebounds, Game

2—New York at Boston, April 19, 1974
Golden State at Chicago, April 30, 1975
3—Boston at Buffalo, April 6, 1974
K.C.-Omaha at Chicago, April 20, 1975
Milwaukee at Detroit, April 15, 1976
Boston vs. L.A. Lakers, May 30, 1985
Atlanta at Indiana, April 29, 1987
Phoenix at Utah, May 6, 1990
Chicago vs. New York, April 28, 1991
Boston at Detroit, May 13, 1991

Most Offensive Rebounds, Both Teams, Game

51—Houston (27) vs. Atlanta (24), April 11, 1979
Utah (27) at Houston (24), April 28, 1985
50—Washington (28) at San Antonio (22), May 11, 1979

Fewest Offensive Rebounds, Both Teams, Game

   13—Indiana (6) vs. Atlanta (7), May 1, 1987
      Cleveland (6) vs. Boston (7), May 4, 1992
      Phoenix (6) at Portland (7), May 14, 1992
   14—Atlanta (3) at Indiana (11), April 29, 1987

DEFENSIVE REBOUNDS

Highest Defensive Rebounding Percentage, Game

   .952—Chicago vs. Golden State, April 30, 1975 (40-42)
   .947—Boston vs. New York, April 19, 1974 (36-38)

Most Defensive Rebounds, Game

   56—San Antonio vs. Denver, May 4, 1983
   49—Philadelphia vs. New York, April 16, 1978
      Denver vs. Portland, May 1, 1977 (ot)

Fewest Defensive Rebounds, Game

   12—Golden State at Seattle, April 28, 1992
   13—San Antonio at L.A. Lakers, April 17, 1986

Most Defensive Rebounds, Both Teams, Game

   92—Denver (49) vs. Portland (43), May 1, 1977 (ot)
   86—San Antonio (56) vs. Denver (30), May 4, 1983

Fewest Defensive Rebounds, Both Teams, Game

   34—Milwaukee (15) vs. Philadelphia (19), May 1, 1982
   35—Golden State (12) at Seattle (23), April 28, 1992

ASSISTS

Most Assists, Game

   51—San Antonio vs. Denver, May 4, 1983
   46—Milwaukee at Philadelphia, March 30, 1970
      Milwaukee vs. Denver, April 23, 1978
      Boston vs. New York, April 28, 1990

Fewest Assists, Game

   5—Boston at St. Louis, April 3, 1960
     Detroit at Chicago, April 5, 1974
   6—Chicago vs. Los Angeles, March 29, 1968

Most Assists, Both Teams, Game

   79—L.A. Lakers (44) vs. Boston (35), June 4, 1987
   78—Denver (40) at San Antonio (38), April 26, 1983

Fewest Assists, Both Teams, Game

   16—Chicago (6) vs. Los Angeles (10), March 29, 1968
   17—Cincinnati (7) at Detroit (10), March 15, 1958

PERSONAL FOULS

Most Personal Fouls, Game

   55—Syracuse at Boston, March 21, 1953 (4 ot)
   53—Baltimore at New York, March 26, 1949 (ot)
   51—Boston vs. Syracuse, March 21, 1953 (4 ot)
   47—New York vs. Baltimore, March 26, 1949 (ot)
   45—Syracuse at New York, April 8, 1952

Fewest Personal Fouls, Game

   9—Cleveland vs. Boston, May 2, 1992
   12—Philadelphia at Boston, March 23, 1958
      Los Angeles at Golden State, April 21, 1973

Most Personal Fouls, Both Teams, Game

   106—Syracuse (55) at Boston (51), March 21, 1953 (4 ot)
   100—Baltimore (53) at New York (47), March 26, 1949 (ot)
    82—Syracuse (45) at New York (37), April 8, 1952

Fewest Personal Fouls, Both Teams, Game

   27—Philadelphia (12) at Boston (15), March 23, 1958
   29—Golden State (14) at Milwaukee (15), March 30, 1972
      Cleveland (9) vs. Boston (20), May 2, 1992

DISQUALIFICATIONS

Most Disqualifications, Game

   7—Syracuse at Boston, March 21, 1953 (4 ot)
   6—Baltimore at New York, March 26, 1949 (ot)
   5—New York vs. Baltimore, March 26, 1949 (ot)
     Boston vs. Syracuse, March 21, 1953 (4 ot)
   4—by many

Most Disqualifications, Both Teams, Game

    12—Syracuse (7) at Boston (5), March 21, 1953 (4 ot)
    11—Baltimore (6) at New York (5), March 26, 1949 (ot)
     7—Los Angeles (4) at Detroit (3), April 3, 1962
        Boston (4) vs. Los Angeles (3), April 18, 1962 (ot)

STEALS

Most Steals, Game

    22—Golden State vs. Seattle, April 14, 1975
    20—Golden State vs. Phoenix, May 2, 1976

Fewest Steals, Game

    0—Buffalo at Boston, March 30, 1974
      Phoenix at Seattle, April 15, 1976
    1—Detroit at Chicago, March 30, 1974
      New York at Boston, April 14, 1974
      Milwaukee at Boston, May 10, 1974 (2 ot)
      Boston vs. Phoenix, May 23, 1976
      Seattle at Portland, April 26, 1978
      Dallas at Seattle, April 24, 1984
      Chicago at Boston, April 26, 1987
      Detroit vs. Milwaukee, May 10, 1989
      Chicago at Detroit, May 31, 1989
      Cleveland at Philadelphia, April 29, 1990
      Phoenix at Portland, May 27, 1990
      Detroit at Atlanta, April 30, 1991
      Chicago vs. New York, May 5, 1992

Most Steals, Both Teams, Game

    35—Golden State (22) vs. Seattle (13), April 14, 1975
    32—Seattle (18) at Golden State (14), April 16, 1975
        Los Angeles (19) vs. Golden State (13), May 4, 1977
        Milwaukee (19) at Philadelphia (13), May 9, 1986

Fewest Steals, Both Teams, Game

    2—Phoenix (0) at Seattle (2), April 15, 1976
    3—New York (1) at Boston (2), April 14, 1974

BLOCKED SHOTS

Most Blocked Shots, Game

    20—Philadelphia vs. Milwaukee, April 5, 1981
    16—Seattle at Utah, May 14, 1992

Fewest Blocked Shots, Game

    0—New York at Boston, April 19, 1974
      Boston vs. Milwaukee, May 5, 1974
      Boston vs. Milwaukee, May 10, 1974 (2 ot)
      Boston at Washington, May 11, 1975
      Boston at Buffalo, May 2, 1976
      Boston vs. Phoenix, June 4, 1976 (3 ot)
      Philadelphia vs. Portland, May 22, 1977
      Denver at Milwaukee, April 23, 1978
      Philadelphia at Washington, May 7, 1978
      Washington at Seattle, May 21, 1978
      Boston at Houston, May 14, 1981
      New York vs. Philadelphia, May 1, 1983
      Portland vs. Phoenix, April 26, 1984
      Portland vs. Dallas, April 25, 1985
      L.A. Lakers vs. Boston, June 5, 1985
      Dallas vs. L.A. Lakers, May 8, 1986
      Detroit at Washington, April 29, 1987
      Chicago vs. Detroit, May 15, 1988
      L.A. Lakers vs. Detroit, June 7, 1988
      New York vs. Boston, May 2, 1990
      Chicago vs. New York, April 25, 1991
      Milwaukee vs. Philadelphia, April 27, 1991 (ot)
      Philadelphia at Chicago, May 6, 1991
      Portland at L.A. Lakers, May 24, 1991
      Miami at Chicago, April 24, 1992

Most Blocked Shots, Both Teams, Game

    29—Philadelphia (20) vs. Milwaukee (9), April 5, 1981
    25—Washington (13) vs. Philadelphia (12), April 22, 1986
    24—Denver (14) at Milwaukee (10), April 30, 1978

Fewest Blocked Shots, Both Teams, Game

    1—Dallas (1) at Portland (0), April 25, 1985
    2—New York (0) at Boston (2), April 19, 1974

Larry Bird ended his NBA career as the third leading scorer in playoff history.

Philadelphia (1) at Milwaukee (1), April 12, 1981
Boston (0) at Houston (2), May 14, 1981
Boston (1) at Milwaukee (1), May 18, 1986
Chicago (0) vs. New York (2), April 25, 1991

TURNOVERS

Most Turnovers, Game

36—Chicago at Portland, April 17, 1977
34—Portland at Philadelphia, May 22, 1977
31—Golden State at Washington, May 25, 1975
    Denver vs. Milwaukee, April 21, 1978
    Seattle at Phoenix, May 6, 1979

Fewest Turnovers, Game

4—Detroit at Boston, May 9, 1991
5—Chicago vs. Los Angeles, March 30, 1971
    Boston vs. Chicago, April 26, 1987
    Detroit vs. Milwaukee, May 12, 1989
    Boston at Detroit, May 13, 1991
    Chicago at L.A. Lakers, June 9, 1991

Most Turnovers, Both Teams, Game

60—Golden State (31) at Washington (29), May 25, 1975
55—Chicago (36) at Portland (19), April 17, 1977
    Denver (31) vs. Milwaukee (24), April 21, 1978
    Phoenix (29) vs. Kansas City (26), April 22, 1979

Fewest Turnovers, Both Teams, Game

13—Detroit (4) at Boston (9), May 9, 1991
14—Boston (5) at Detroit (9), May 13, 1991

TOP SCORERS IN PLAYOFF HISTORY

(Active players in 1991-92 in capital letters)

Figures from National Basketball League are included below; NBL did not record field goal attempts, however, so all field goal percentages listed here are based only on field goals and attempts in NBA competition. Minutes played not compiled prior to 1952; rebounds not compiled prior to 1951.

Player	Yrs.	G.	Min.	FGA	FGM	Pct.	FTA	FTM	Pct.	Reb.	Ast.	PF	Pts.	Avg.
Kareem Abdul-Jabbar	18	237	8851	4422	2356	.533	1419	1050	.740	2481	767	797	5762	24.3
Jerry West	13	153	6321	3460	1622	.469	1507	1213	.805	855	970	451	4457	29.1
LARRY BIRD	12	164	6886	3090	1458	.472	1012	901	.890	1683	1062	466	3897	23.8
John Havlicek	13	172	6860	3329	1451	.436	1046	874	.836	1186	825	517	3776	22.0
EARVIN JOHNSON	12	186	7403	2513	1276	.508	1241	1040	.838	1431	2320	521	3640	19.6
Elgin Baylor	12	134	5510	3161	1388	.439	1101	847	.769	1725	541	445	3623	27.0
Wilt Chamberlain	13	160	7559	2728	1425	.522	1627	757	.465	3913	673	412	3607	22.5
MICHAEL JORDAN	8	92	3862	2290	1160	.507	960	806	.840	613	624	311	3184	34.6
Dennis Johnson	13	180	7004	1167	2661	.439	756	943	.802	781	1006	575	3116	17.3
KEVIN MCHALE	12	165	5603	2090	1172	.561	958	754	.787	1224	271	565	3106	18.8
Julius Erving	11	141	5288	2441	1187	.486	908	707	.779	994	594	403	3088	21.9
JAMES WORTHY	8	138	5149	2243	1235	.551	647	471	.728	730	450	341	2953	21.4
Sam Jones	12	154	4654	2571	1149	.447	753	611	.811	718	358	391	2909	18.9
ROBERT PARISH	13	174	5942	2164	1094	.506	758	548	.723	1714	228	599	2736	15.7
Bill Russell	13	165	7497	2335	1003	.430	1106	667	.603	4104	770	546	2673	16.2
ISIAH THOMAS	9	111	4216	1869	825	.441	689	530	.769	524	987	363	2261	20.4
Bob Pettit	9	88	3545	1834	766	.418	915	708	.744	1304	241	277	2240	25.5
Elvin Hayes	10	96	4160	1901	883	.464	656	428	.652	1244	185	378	2194	22.9
George Mikan	9	91	1500	1394	723	.404	906	695	.767	665	155	390	2141	23.5
BYRON SCOTT	9	137	4517	1672	828	.495	421	344	.817	455	334	367	2104	15.4
MOSES MALONE	12	94	3796	1566	750	.479	756	576	.762	1295	136	244	2077	22.1
Tom Heinsohn	9	104	3203	2035	818	.402	568	422	.743	954	215	417	2058	19.8
Bob Cousy	13	109	4140	2016	689	.342	799	640	.801	546	937	314	2018	18.5
Dolph Schayes	15	103	2687	1491	609	.390	918	755	.822	1051	257	397	1973	19.2
Bob Dandridge	8	98	3882	1716	823	.480	422	321	.761	754	365	377	1967	20.1
Walt Frazier	8	93	3953	1500	767	.511	523	393	.751	666	599	285	1927	20.7
Gus Williams	10	99	3205	1644	781	.475	483	356	.737	308	469	243	1927	19.5
Chet Walker	13	105	3688	1531	687	.449	689	542	.787	737	212	286	1916	18.2
Oscar Robertson	10	86	3673	1466	675	.460	655	560	.855	578	769	267	1910	22.2
MAURICE CHEEKS	12	128	4766	1486	761	.512	465	362	.778	447	908	321	1888	14.8
Hal Greer	13	92	3642	1657	705	.425	574	466	.812	505	393	357	1876	20.4
CLYDE DREXLER	9	87	3353	1543	697	.452	543	429	.790	610	604	313	1874	21.5
Cliff Hagan	9	90	2965	1544	701	.454	540	432	.800	744	305	320	1834	20.4
Rick Barry	7	74	2723	1688	719	.426	448	392	.875	418	340	232	1833	24.8
Jamaal Wilkes	10	113	3799	1689	785	.465	344	250	.727	718	246	326	1820	16.1
MARK AGUIRRE	9	102	2958	1435	696	.485	417	310	.743	537	262	281	1747	17.1
Jo Jo White	6	80	3428	1629	732	.449	309	256	.828	348	452	241	1720	21.5
Bob McAdoo	9	94	2714	1423	698	.491	442	320	.724	711	127	318	1718	18.3
Dave Cowens	7	89	3768	1627	733	.451	293	218	.744	1285	333	398	1684	18.9
Alex English	10	68	2427	668	1328	.503	325	377	.862	371	293	188	1661	24.4
George Gervin	9	59	2202	1225	622	.508	424	348	.821	341	186	207	1592	27.0
JOE DUMARS	7	99	3607	1263	589	.466	449	381	.849	228	478	204	1591	16.1
Michael Cooper	11	168	4744	582	1244	.468	293	355	.825	574	703	474	1581	9.4
Don Nelson	11	150	3209	1175	585	.498	498	407	.817	719	210	399	1577	10.5
DANNY AINGE	9	149	4080	1304	607	.465	286	237	.829	350	569	431	1561	10.5
Adrian Dantley	7	73	2515	1012	531	.525	623	496	.796	395	169	188	1558	21.3
Dick Barnett	11	102	3027	1317	603	.458	445	333	.748	273	247	282	1539	15.1
Dave DeBusschere	8	96	3682	1253	634	.416	384	268	.698	1155	253	327	1536	16.0
Sidney Moncrief	11	93	3226	1033	491	.475	602	488	.811	469	317	285	1487	16.0
Earl Monroe	8	82	2715	1292	567	.439	426	337	.791	266	264	216	1471	17.9
KARL MALONE	7	53	2248	1079	520	.482	552	424	.768	609	113	203	1464	27.6
Jack Sikma	11	102	3558	1249	557	.446	407	338	.830	945	244	432	1463	14.3
Bobby Jones	10	125	3431	1034	553	.535	429	347	.809	614	284	400	1453	11.6
WALTER DAVIS	10	78	2184	1192	591	.496	317	263	.830	240	312	186	1450	18.6
Gail Goodrich	8	80	2622	1227	542	.442	447	366	.819	250	333	219	1450	18.1
Bill Sharman	10	78	2573	1262	538	.426	406	370	.911	285	201	220	1446	18.5
SCOTTIE PIPPEN	5	81	3128	1098	528	.481	413	306	.741	633	420	288	1407	17.4
Bailey Howell	11	86	2712	1165	542	.465	433	317	.732	697	130	376	1401	16.3
TERRY PORTER	7	73	2771	944	467	.495	436	365	.837	256	506	177	1401	19.2
VINNIE JOHNSON	10	116	2671	1275	578	.453	284	214	.754	364	306	234	1387	12.0
Willis Reed	7	78	2641	1203	570	.474	285	218	.765	801	149	295	1385	17.4
Darryl Dawkins	10	109	2734	992	542	.546	414	291	.703	665	119	438	1375	12.6
TERRY CUMMINGS	8	61	2202	1085	558	.514	353	252	.714	540	143	229	1369	22.4
TOM CHAMBERS	7	63	2300	1096	497	.453	413	345	.835	446	157	233	1363	21.6
BILL LAIMBEER	9	113	3735	1174	549	.468	259	212	.819	1097	195	408	1354	12.0
Rudy LaRusso	9	93	3188	1152	467	.405	546	410	.751	779	194	366	1344	14.5
Paul Westphal	9	107	2449	1149	553	.481	285	225	.789	153	353	241	1337	12.5
Frank Ramsey	9	98	2396	1105	469	.424	476	393	.826	494	151	362	1331	13.6
HAKEEM OLAJUWON	7	50	1956	948	512	.540	444	302	.680	623	104	214	1326	26.5
Lou Hudson	9	61	2199	1164	519	.446	326	262	.804	318	164	196	1300	21.3
JEROME KERSEY	8	81	2595	1034	492	.476	415	302	.728	544	198	306	1286	-15.9
Wes Unseld	12	119	4889	1040	513	.493	385	234	.608	1777	453	317	1260	10.6
DOMINIQUE WILKINS	7	48	1906	1063	456	.429	396	327	.826	316	126	108	1255	26.1
Andrew Toney	6	72	2146	1015	485	.478	346	272	.786	168	323	265	1254	17.4
Bob Lanier	9	67	2426	955	508	.532	297	228	.768	645	235	233	1244	18.6
Bill Bradley	8	95	3161	1165	510	.438	251	202	.805	333	263	313	1222	12.9
Fred Brown	8	83	1900	1082	499	.461	227	186	.819	196	193	144	1197	14.4
Jim McMillian	7	72	2722	1101	497	.451	253	200	.791	377	137	169	1194	16.6
Paul Arizin	8	49	1815	1001	411	.411	439	364	.829	404	128	117	1186	24.2
Bill Bridges	12	113	3521	1135	475	.419	349	235	.673	1305	219	408	1185	10.5
Marques Johnson	6	54	2112	964	471	.489	311	218	.701	427	198	156	1163	21.5
Maurice Lucas	9	82	2426	975	472	.484	289	215	.744	690	225	310	1159	14.1
CHARLES BARKLEY	6	51	1995	726	413	.569	453	303	.669	670	212	190	1144	22.4
Tom Sanders	11	130	3039	1066	465	.436	296	212	.716	763	127	508	1142	8.8
Vern Mikkelsen	9	85	2102	999	396	.396	446	349	.783	585	152	377	1141	13.5
Mychal Thompson	11	104	2708	897	449	.501	361	234	.648	627	126	309	1132	10.9

Player	Yrs.	G.	Min.	FGA	FGM	Pct.	FTA	FTM	Pct.	Reb.	Ast.	PF	Pts.	Avg.
Archie Clark	10	71	2387	977	444	.454	307	237	.772	229	297	197	1125	15.8
Paul Silas	14	163	4619	998	396	.397	480	332	.692	1527	335	469	1124	6.9
Cedric Maxwell	8	102	2731	688	375	.545	471	366	.777	553	194	260	1116	10.9
Jim Pollard	8	82	1724	1029	397	.339	413	306	.741	407	259	234	1100	13.4
KIKI VANDEWEGHE	11	67	1881	816	417	.511	259	235	.907	188	133	132	1089	16.3
Phil Chenier	7	60	2088	974	438	.450	251	212	.845	230	131	152	1088	18.1
Jeff Mullins	10	83	2255	1030	462	.449	213	160	.751	304	259	217	1084	13.1
Alvan Adams	9	78	2288	930	440	.473	256	196	.766	588	320	251	1076	13.8
Bob Love	6	47	2061	1023	441	.431	250	194	.776	352	87	144	1076	22.9
Zelmo Beaty	7	63	2345	857	399	.466	380	273	.718	696	98	267	1071	17.0
ROLANDO BLACKMAN	6	48	1889	409	822	.498	218	250	.872	180	198	91	1039	21.6
Lenny Wilkens	7	64	2403	899	359	.399	407	313	.769	373	372	258	1031	16.1
Dan Issel	7	53	1599	810	402	.496	269	223	.829	393	145	157	1029	19.4
Norm Nixon	6	58	2287	921	440	.478	186	142	.763	195	465	201	1027	17.7
Robert Reid	9	79	2740	983	430	.437	217	157	.724	391	335	277	1025	13.0
BUCK WILLIAMS	8	79	2992	706	367	.520	426	285	.669	777	101	292	1019	12.9
JAMES EDWARDS	8	101	2166	839	392	.467	336	229	.682	348	84	313	1013	10.0
RICKY PIERCE	8	65	1784	770	368	.478	279	242	.867	166	123	197	996	15.3
Arnie Risen	12	73	1023	684	330	.385	747	325	.686	561	86	300	985	13.5
Nate Thurmond	9	81	2875	912	379	.416	335	208	.621	1101	227	266	966	11.9
Clyde Lovellette	10	69	1642	892	371	.416	323	221	.684	557	89	232	963	14.0
HORACE GRANT	5	82	3062	718	389	.542	254	177	.697	728	195	267	955	11.6
Calvin Murphy	6	51	1660	817	388	.475	177	165	.932	78	213	197	945	18.5
BILL CARTWRIGHT	8	96	2863	724	357	.493	315	225	.714	539	122	335	939	9.8
John Kerr	12	76	2275	759	370	.386	281	193	.687	827	152	173	933	12.3
George Yardley	7	46	1693	767	324	.442	349	285	.817	457	112	143	933	20.3
LARRY NANCE	7	59	2099	705	379	.538	226	167	.739	461	139	187	925	15.7
Slater Martin	11	92	2876	867	304	.351	442	316	.715	270	354	342	924	10.0
JOHN STOCKTON	8	63	2223	643	310	.482	311	256	.823	205	717	200	918	14.6
Lionel Hollins	8	77	2293	897	369	.411	236	173	.733	207	344	221	911	11.8
Bob Davies	10	67	571	508	311	.612	371	282	.760	78	162	193	904	13.5
SAM PERKINS	6	57	2091	686	332	.484	292	224	.767	459	112	198	903	15.8
Larry Foust	10	73	1920	763	301	.394	384	300	.781	707	94	255	902	12.4
A.C. GREEN	7	98	2644	645	317	.491	354	263	.743	689	74	227	901	9.2
Max Zaslofsky	8	63	732	850	306	.360	372	287	.772	121	101	174	899	14.3
Jerry Lucas	8	72	2370	786	367	.467	206	162	.786	717	214	197	896	12.4
THURL BAILEY	8	58	2002	778	347	.446	237	198	.835	367	96	177	892	15.4
JEFF MALONE	7	46	1659	747	353	.473	210	181	.862	125	107	112	889	19.3
Scott Wedman	8	85	1961	812	368	.453	171	119	.696	322	150	189	882	10.4
PAUL PRESSEY	9	75	2269	682	321	.471	313	228	.728	316	420	261	881	11.7
Keith Erickson	7	87	2393	806	364	.452	189	144	.762	386	216	286	872	10.0

TOP PERFORMANCES IN PLAYOFFS

*Denotes each overtime period played.

MOST POINTS SCORED IN ONE GAME

	FG.	FT.	Pts.
Michael Jordan, Chicago at Boston, April 20, 1986	**22	19	63
Elgin Baylor, Los Angeles at Boston, April 14, 1962	22	17	61
Wilt Chamberlain, Philadelphia vs. Syracuse at Philadelphia, March 22, 1962	22	12	56
Michael Jordan, Chicago at Miami, April 29, 1992	20	16	56
Rick Barry, San Francisco vs. Philadelphia at San Francisco, April 18, 1967	22	11	55
Michael Jordan, Chicago vs. Cleveland, May 1, 1988	24	7	55
John Havlicek, Boston vs. Atlanta at Boston, April 1, 1973	24	6	54
Wilt Chamberlain, Philadelphia vs. Syracuse at Philadelphia, March 14, 1960	24	5	53
Jerry West, Los Angeles vs. Boston, April 23, 1969	21	11	53
Jerry West, Los Angeles vs. Baltimore at Los Angeles, April 5, 1965	16	20	52
Sam Jones, Boston at New York, March 28, 1967	19	13	51
Eric Floyd, Golden State vs. L.A. Lakers, May 10, 1987	18	13	51
Bob Cousy, Boston vs. Syracuse at Boston, March 21, 1953	****10	30	50
Bob Pettit, St. Louis vs. Boston at St. Louis, April 12, 1958	19	12	50
Wilt Chamberlain, Philadelphia at Boston, March 22, 1960	22	6	50
Wilt Chamberlain, San Francisco vs. St. Louis at San Francisco, April 10, 1964	22	6	50
Billy Cunningham, Philadelphia vs. Milwaukee at Philadelphia, April 1, 1970	22	8	50
Bob McAdoo, Buffalo vs. Washington at Buffalo, April 18, 1975	20	10	50
Dominique Wilkins, Atlanta vs. Detroit, April 19, 1986	19	12	50
Michael Jordan, Chicago vs. Cleveland, April 28, 1988	19	12	50
Michael Jordan, Chicago vs. Cleveland, May 5, 1989	*14	22	50
Elgin Baylor, Los Angeles vs. Detroit at Los Angeles, March 15, 1961	17	15	49
Jerry West, Los Angeles vs. Baltimore at Los Angeles, April 3, 1965	15	19	49
Michael Jordan, Chicago at Boston, April 17, 1986	18	13	49
Akeem Olajuwon, Houston at Seattle, May 14, 1987	**19	11	49
Michael Jordan, Chicago at Philadelphia, May 11, 1990	19	7	49
Jerry West, Los Angeles at Baltimore, April 9, 1965	20	8	48
Michael Jordan, Chicago at Milwaukee, May 1, 1990	20	7	48
George Mikan, Minneapolis at Rochester, March 29, 1952	15	17	47
Elgin Baylor, Los Angeles at Detroit, March 18, 1961	17	13	47
Elgin Baylor, Los Angeles at St. Louis, March 27, 1961	17	13	47
Sam Jones, Boston vs. Cincinnati at Boston, April 10, 1963	18	11	47
Rick Barry, San Francisco vs. St. Louis at San Francisco, Apirl 1, 1967	17	13	47
Dominique Wilkins, Atlanta at Boston, May 22, 1988	19	8	47
Michael Jordan, Chicago vs. New York, May 14, 1989	12	23	47
Michael Jordan, Chicago vs. Detroit, May 26, 1990	17	11	47

	FG.	FT.	Pts.
Wilt Chamberlain, Philadelphia vs. Syracuse at Philadelphia, March 14, 1961	19	8	46
Wilt Chamberlain, San Francisco at St. Louis, April 5, 1964	19	8	46
Wilt Chamberlain, Philadelphia vs. Boston at Philadelphia, April 12, 1966	19	8	46
Zelmo Beaty, St. Louis vs. San Francisco, March 23, 1968	14	18	46
Kareem Abdul-Jabbar, Milwaukee vs. Philadelphia at Madison, Wisc., April 3, 1970	18	10	46
Elvin Hayes, Washington vs. Buffalo at Washington, April 20, 1975	19	8	46
George Gervin, San Antonio vs. Washington at San Antonio, April 18, 1978	17	12	46
Bernard King, New York at Detroit, April 19, 1984	18	10	46
Bernard King, New York vs. Detroit, April 22, 1984	19	8	46
Adrian Dantley, Utah vs. Phoenix, May 8, 1984	16	14	46
Michael Jordan, Chicago vs. Detroit, May 27, 1989	16	14	46
Michael Jordan, Chicago at Philadelphia, May 10, 1991	20	6	46
Michael Jordan, Chicago vs. Miami, April 24, 1992	21	4	46
Michael Jordan, Chicago at Portland, June 12, 1992	14	16	46

MOST FIELD GOALS SCORED IN ONE GAME

	FGA	FGM
Wilt Chamberlain, Philadelphia vs. Syracuse at Philadelphia, March 14, 1960	42	24
John Havlicek, Boston vs. Atlanta at Boston, April 1, 1973	36	24
Michael Jordan, Chicago vs. Cleveland, May 1, 1988	45	24
Wilt Chamberlain, Philadelphia at Boston, March 22, 1960	42	22
Wilt Chamberlain, Philadelphia vs. Syracuse at Philadelphia, March 22, 1962	48	22
Elgin Baylor, Los Angeles at Boston, April 14, 1962	46	22
Wilt Chamberlain, San Francisco vs. St. Louis at San Francisco, April 10, 1964	32	22
Rick Barry, San Francisco vs. Philadelphia at San Francisco, April 18, 1967	48	22
Billy Cunningham, Philadelphia vs. Milwaukee at Philadelphia, April 1, 1970	39	22
Michael Jordan, Chicago at Boston, April 20, 1986	**41	22
Jerry West, Los Angeles vs. Boston, April 23, 1969	41	21
Bob McAdoo, Buffalo vs. Boston at Buffalo, April 6, 1974	40	21
Michael Jordan, Chicago vs. Miami, April 24, 1992	34	21
Jerry West, Los Angeles at Baltimore, April 9, 1965	43	20
Wilt Chamberlain, Los Angeles vs. New York at Los Angeles, May 6, 1970	27	20
Kareem Abdul-Jabbar, Milwaukee at Chicago, April 18, 1974	29	20
Bob McAdoo, Buffalo vs. Washington at Buffalo, April 18, 1975	32	20
Xavier McDaniel, Seattle vs. L.A. Lakers, May 23, 1987	29	20
Michael Jordan, Chicago at Milwaukee, May 1, 1990	35	20
Michael Jordan, Chicago at Philadelphia, May 10, 1991	34	20
Michael Jordan, Chicago at Miami, April 29, 1992	30	20
Bob Pettit, St. Louis vs. Boston at St. Louis, April 12, 1958	34	19
Wilt Chamberlain, Philadelphia vs. Syracuse at Philadelphia, March 14, 1961	36	19
Wilt Chamberlain, San Francisco at St. Louis, April 5, 1964	36	19
Wilt Chamberlain, San Francisco vs. St. Louis at San Francisco, April 16, 1964	29	19
Wilt Chamberlain, Philadelphia vs. Boston at Philadelphia, April 12, 1966	34	19
Jerry West, Los Angeles vs. Boston at Los Angeles, April 22, 1966	31	19
Wilt Chamberlain, Philadelphia vs. Cincinnati at Philadelphia, March 21, 1967	30	19
Sam Jones, Boston at New York, March 28, 1967	30	19
Gail Goodrich, Los Angeles vs. Golden State at Los Angeles, April 25, 1973	26	19
Elvin Hayes, Capital at New York, March 29, 1974	29	19
Elvin Hayes, Washington vs. Buffalo at Washington, April 20, 1975	26	19
Fred Brown, Seattle vs. Phoenix at Seattle, April 15, 1976	35	19
George Gervin, San Antonio vs. Washington at San Antonio, May 11, 1979	31	19
George Gervin, San Antonio vs. Houston, April 4, 1980	29	19
Kareem Abdul-Jabbar, Los Angeles vs. Philadelphia, May 7, 1980	31	19
Calvin Murphy, Houston at San Antonio, April 17, 1981	28	19
Bernard King, New York vs. Detroit, April 22, 1984	27	19
Rolando Blackman, Dallas vs. Portland, April 18, 1985	**33	19
Dominique Wilkins, Atlanta vs. Detroit, April 19, 1986	28	19
Akeem Olajuwon, Houston at Seattle, May 14, 1987	**33	19
Michael Jordan, Chicago vs. Cleveland, April 28, 1988	35	19
Dominique Wilkins, Atlanta at Boston, May 22, 1988	33	19
Michael Jordan, Chicago at Philadelphia, May 11, 1990	34	19

MOST FREE THROWS SCORED IN ONE GAME

	FTA	FTM
Bob Cousy, Boston vs. Syracuse at Boston, March 21, 1953	****32	30
Michael Jordan, Chicago vs. New York, May 14, 1989	28	23
Michael Jordan, Chicago vs. Cleveland, May 5, 1989	**27	22
Karl Malone, Utah vs. L.A. Clippers at Anaheim, May 3, 1992	24	22
Oscar Robertson, Cincinnati at Boston, April 10, 1963	22	21
Bob Cousy, Boston vs. Syracuse at Boston, March 17, 1954	**25	20
Jerry West, Los Angeles at Detroit, April 3, 1962	23	20
Jerry West, Los Angeles vs. Baltimore at Los Angeles, April 5, 1965	21	20
Magic Johnson, L.A. Lakers vs. Golden State, May 8, 1991	22	20
Karl Malone, Utah at Portland, May 9, 1991	22	20
Bob Pettit, St. Louis at Boston, April 9, 1958	24	19
Jerry West, Los Angeles vs. Baltimore at Los Angeles, April 3, 1965	21	19
Michael Jordan, Chicago at Boston, April 20, 1986	**21	19

MOST REBOUNDS IN ONE GAME

	RB.
Wilt Chamberlain, Philadelphia vs. Boston at Philadelphia, April 5, 1967	41
Bill Russell, Boston vs. Philadelphia at Boston, March 23, 1958	40
Bill Russell, Boston vs. St. Louis at Boston, March 29, 1960	40
Bill Russell, Boston vs. Los Angeles at Boston, April 18, 1962	*40
Bill Russell, Boston vs. Philadelphia at Boston, March 19, 1960	39
Bill Russell, Boston vs. Syracuse at Boston, March 23, 1961	39
Wilt Chamberlain, Philadelphia vs. Boston at Philadelphia, April 6, 1965	39
Bill Russell, Boston vs. St. Louis at Boston, April 11, 1961	38
Bill Russell, Boston vs. Los Angeles at Boston, April 16, 1963	38
Wilt Chamberlain, San Francisco vs. Boston at San Francisco, April 24, 1964	38
Wilt Chamberlain, Philadelphia vs. San Francisco at Philadelphia, April 16, 1967	38

MOST ASSISTS IN ONE GAME

	AST.
Earvin (Magic) Johnson, Los Angeles vs. Phoenix, May 15, 1984	24
John Stockton, Utah at L.A. Lakers, May 17, 1988	24
Earvin (Magic) Johnson, L.A. Lakers at Portland, May 3, 1985	23
Glenn (Doc) Rivers, Atlanta vs. Boston, May 16, 1988	22
Earvin (Magic) Johnson, Los Angeles vs. Boston, June 3, 1984	21
Earvin (Magic) Johnson, L.A. Lakers vs. Houston, April 27, 1991	21
Earvin (Magic) Johnson, L.A. Lakers at Portland, May 18, 1991	21
John Stockton, Utah vs. L.A. Clippers, April 24, 1992	21
Johnny Moore, San Antonio vs. Denver, April 27, 1983	20
Earvin (Magic) Johnson, L.A. Lakers at Houston, May 16, 1986	20
Earvin (Magic) Johnson, L.A. Lakers vs. Boston, June 4, 1987	20
John Stockton, Utah at L.A. Lakers, May 21, 1988	20
Earvin (Magic) Johnson, L.A. Lakers at Dallas, May 31, 1988	20
Earvin (Magic) Johnson, L.A. Lakers at Phoenix, May 28, 1989	20
Tim Hardaway, Golden State at L.A. Lakers, May 14, 1991	*20
Earvin (Magic) Johnson, L.A. Lakers vs. Chicago, June 12, 1991	20
Bob Cousy, Boston vs. St. Louis at Boston, April 9, 1957	19
Bob Cousy, Boston at Minneapolis, April 7, 1959	19
Wilt Chamberlain, Philadelphia vs. Cincinnati at Philadelphia, March 24, 1967	19
Walt Frazier, New York vs. Los Angeles at New York, May 8, 1970	19
Jerry West, Los Angeles vs. Chicago at Los Angeles, April 1, 1973	19
Norm Nixon, Los Angeles vs. Seattle at Los Angeles, April 22, 1979	19
Earvin (Magic) Johnson, Los Angeles vs. San Antonio, May 18, 1983	19
Earvin (Magic) Johnson, L.A. Lakers vs. Phoenix, April 18, 1985	19
Earvin (Magic) Johnson, L.A. Lakers vs. Portland, May 7, 1985	19
Earvin (Magic) Johnson, L.A. Lakers vs. Denver, May 22, 1985	19
Earvin (Magic) Johnson, L.A. Lakers vs. Houston, May 13, 1986	19
Earvin (Magic) Johnson, L.A. Lakers vs. Boston, June 14, 1987	19
Earvin (Magic) Johnson, L.A. Lakers vs. Dallas, May 25, 1988	19
Earvin (Magic) Johnson, L.A. Lakers vs. Detroit, June 19, 1988	19
John Stockton, Utah at Phoenix, May 2, 1990	19
Earvin (Magic) Johnson, L.A. Lakers vs. Portland, May 24, 1991	19
Kevin Johnson, Phoenix vs. San Antonio, April 26, 1992	19
John Stockton, Utah vs. L.A. Clippers, April 26, 1992	19

NBA Playoff Home Records

Team	W.	L.	Pct.
Cleveland Rebels*	1	0	1.000
Sheboygan Redskins*	1	0	1.000
Baltimore Bullets*	7	1	.875
Anderson Packers*	3	1	.750
Los Angeles Lakers	193	65	.748
Boston Celtics	180	63	.741
Portland Trail Blazers	48	18	.727
Philadelphia 76ers	111	49	.694
Chicago Bulls	52	23	.693
New York Knickerbockers	77	36	.681
Detroit Pistons	71	34	.676
Seattle SuperSonics	43	21	.672
Cleveland Cavaliers	18	9	.667
Los Angeles Clippers	8	4	.667
Utah Jazz	25	13	.658
Atlanta Hawks	69	36	.657
Dallas Mavericks	15	8	.652
Phoenix Suns	41	22	.651
Golden State Warriors	65	38	.631
Milwaukee Bucks	53	33	.616
Washington Bullets	48	32	.600
Washington Capitols*	6	4	.600
Indianapolis Olympians*	4	3	.571
Houston Rockets	30	23	.566
Denver Nuggets	23	18	.561
San Antonio Spurs	21	17	.553
Sacramento Kings	28	25	.528
St. Louis Bombers*	3	4	.429
Chicago Stags*	3	5	.375
Indiana Pacers	2	5	.286
New Jersey Nets	2	10	.167
Miami Heat	0	1	.000
Totals	1251	621	.668

*Defunct

NBA Playoff Road Records

Team	W.	L.	Pct.
Los Angeles Lakers	100	130	.435
Boston Celtics	90	120	.429
Milwaukee Bucks	32	51	.386
Philadelphia 76ers	64	104	.381
Detroit Pistons	40	71	.360
Houston Rockets	19	37	.339
Chicago Stags*	4	8	.333
Golden State Warriors	34	74	.318
New York Knickerbockers	36	81	.308
Phoenix Suns	20	45	.308
Chicago Bulls	24	57	.296
Seattle SuperSonics	18	43	.295
Sacramento Kings	17	44	.279
Portland Trail Blazers	17	45	.274
Atlanta Hawks	31	83	.272
New Jersey Nets	4	11	.267
San Antonio Spurs	11	31	.262
Washington Bullets	21	62	.253
Anderson Packers*	1	3	.250
Baltimore Bullets*	2	6	.250
Dallas Mavericks	6	19	.240
Denver Nuggets	10	32	.238
Utah Jazz	8	28	.222
Washington Capitols*	2	7	.222
Los Angeles Clippers	3	12	.200
St. Louis Bombers*	1	4	.200
Cleveland Cavaliers	5	22	.185
Indiana Pacers	1	9	.100
Cleveland Rebels*	0	2	.000
Indianapolis Olympians*	0	6	.000
Miami Heat	0	2	.000
Sheboygan Redskins*	0	2	.000
Totals	621	1251	.332

*Defunct

NBA Playoff Series Won-Lost Records

Team	W.	L.	Pct.
Boston Celtics	63	23	.733
Los Angeles Lakers	72	30	.706
Anderson Packers*	2	1	.667
Baltimore Bullets*	3	2	.600
Seattle SuperSonics	14	12	.538
Philadelphia 76ers	36	34	.514
New York Knickerbockers	26	25	.510
Chicago Bulls	16	16	.500
Portland Trail Blazers	14	14	.500
Golden State Warriors	22	23	.489
Phoenix Suns	13	14	.481
Detroit Pistons	23	25	.479
Milwaukee Bucks	16	18	.471
Houston Rockets	10	14	.417
Washington Bullets	13	19	.406
Dallas Mavericks	4	6	.400
Utah Jazz	6	9	.400
Washington Capitols*	2	3	.400
Atlanta Hawks	16	28	.364
Chicago Stags*	2	4	.333
Denver Nuggets	6	12	.333
Sacramento Kings	9	19	.321
Cleveland Cavaliers	3	8	.273
San Antonio Spurs	4	13	.235
Indianapolis Olympians*	1	4	.200
Los Angeles Clippers	1	4	.200
New Jersey Nets	1	7	.125
Cleveland Rebels*	0	1	.000
Indiana Pacers	0	5	.000
Miami Heat	0	1	.000
St. Louis Bombers*	0	3	.000
Sheboygan Redskins*	0	1	.000
Totals	398	398	.500

*Defunct

NBA All-Time Playoff Records

Team	W.	L.	Pct.
Los Angeles Lakers	293	195	.600
Boston Celtics	270	183	.596
Baltimore Bullets*	9	7	.563
Philadelphia 76ers	175	153	.534
Detroit Pistons	111	105	.514
Portland Trail Blazers	65	63	.508
Milwaukee Bucks	85	84	.503
Anderson Packers*	4	4	.500
New York Knickerbockers	113	117	.491
Seattle SuperSonics	61	64	.488
Chicago Bulls	76	80	.487
Phoenix Suns	61	67	.477
Golden State Warriors	99	112	.469
Atlanta Hawks	100	119	.457
Houston Rockets	49	60	.450
Utah Jazz	33	41	.446
Dallas Mavericks	21	27	.438
Cleveland Cavaliers	23	31	.426
Washington Bullets	69	94	.423
Washington Capitols*	8	11	.421
Los Angeles Clippers	11	16	.407
San Antonio Spurs	32	48	.400
Denver Nuggets	33	50	.398
Sacramento Kings	45	69	.395
Chicago Stags*	7	13	.350
Cleveland Rebels*	1	2	.333
St. Louis Bombers*	4	8	.333
Sheboygan Redskins*	1	2	.333
Indianapolis Olympians*	4	9	.308
New Jersey Nets	6	21	.222
Indiana Pacers	3	14	.176
Miami Heat	0	3	.000
Totals	1872	1872	.500

*Defunct

In just three years, Phil Jackson has compiled the NBA's top winning percentage among playoff coaches.

Highest Winning Percentages by Coaches in NBA Playoffs
(25 games minimum)

Coach	W.	L.	Pct.
PHIL JACKSON	40	15	.727
PAT RILEY	108	53	.671
Butch van Breda Kolff	21	12	.636
John Kundla	60	35	.632
Billy Cunningham	66	39	.629
CHUCK DALY	71	42	.628
Larry Costello	37	23	.617
Red Auerbach	99	69	.589
Tom Heinsohn	47	33	.588
K.C. JONES	81	57	.587
Alex Hannum	45	34	.570
Bill Sharman	35	27	.565
Al Cervi	33	26	.559
RICK ADELMAN	34	27	.557
Bill Russell	34	27	.557

Most Playoff Games by NBA Coaches

Coach	G.
Red Auerbach	168
PAT RILEY	161
K.C. JONES	138
DICK MOTTA	126
CHUCK DALY	113
DON NELSON	109
BILL FITCH	106
Billy Cunningham	105
Red Holzman	105
Jack Ramsay	102
John MacLeod	101
LENNY WILKENS	101
John Kundla	95
Doug Moe	83
COTTON FITZSIMMONS	80
Tom Heinsohn	80

Most Victories by Coaches in NBA Playoffs

Coach	W.	L.	Pct.
PAT RILEY	108	53	.671
Red Auerbach	99	69	.589
K.C. JONES	81	57	.587
CHUCK DALY	71	42	.628
Billy Cunningham	66	39	.629
John Kundla	60	35	.632
Red Holzman	58	47	.552
DICK MOTTA	56	70	.444
BILL FITCH	55	51	.519
LENNY WILKENS	52	49	.515
DON NELSON	51	58	.468
Tom Heinsohn	47	33	.588
John MacLeod	47	54	.465
Alex Hannum	45	34	.570
Jack Ramsay	44	58	.431
PHIL JACKSON	40	15	.727
Larry Costello	37	23	.617
Bill Sharman	35	27	.565
RICK ADELMAN	34	27	.557
COTTON FITZSIMMONS	34	46	.425
Bill Russell	34	27	.557
Al Cervi	33	26	.559
Doug Moe	33	50	.398
Fred Schaus	33	38	.465
Alvin Attles	31	30	.508
Joe Lapchick	30	30	.500
Gene Shue	30	47	.390
Richie Guerin	26	34	.433
DEL HARRIS	21	31	.404
Butch van Breda Kolff	21	12	.636

ALL-TIME NBA PLAYOFF LEADERS

(Active players in 1991-92 in capital letters)

MOST YEARS PLAYED

Kareem Abdul-Jabbar	18
Dolph Schayes	15
Paul Silas	14
Wilt Chamberlain	13
Bob Cousy	13
Hal Greer	13
John Havlicek	13
Dennis Johnson	13
ROBERT PARISH	13
Bill Russell	13
Chet Walker	13
Jerry West	13

MOST GAMES PLAYED

Kareem Abdul-Jabbar	237
MAGIC JOHNSON	186
Dennis Johnson	180
ROBERT PARISH	174
John Havlicek	172
Michael Cooper	168
KEVIN McHALE	165
Bill Russell	165
LARRY BIRD	164
Paul Silas	163

MOST MINUTES PLAYED

Kareem Abdul-Jabbar	8,851
Wilt Chamberlain	7,559
Bill Russell	7,497
MAGIC JOHNSON	7,403
Dennis Johnson	7,004
LARRY BIRD	6,886
John Havlicek	6,860
Jerry West	6,321
ROBERT PARISH	5,942
KEVIN McHALE	5,603

MOST FIELD GOALS ATTEMPTED

Kareem Abdul-Jabbar	4,422
Jerry West	3,460
John Havlicek	3,329
Elgin Baylor	3,161
LARRY BIRD	3,090
Wilt Chamberlain	2,728
Dennis Johnson	2,661
Sam Jones	2,571
MAGIC JOHNSON	2,513
Julius Erving	2,441

MOST FIELD GOALS MADE

Kareem Abdul-Jabbar	2,356
Jerry West	1,622
LARRY BIRD	1,458
John Havlicek	1,451
Wilt Chamberlain	1,425
Elgin Baylor	1,388
MAGIC JOHNSON	1,276
JAMES WORTHY	1,235
Julius Erving	1,187
KEVIN McHALE	1,172

MOST FREE THROWS ATTEMPTED

Wilt Chamberlain	1,627
Jerry West	1,507
Kareem Abdul-Jabbar	1,419
MAGIC JOHNSON	1,241
Bill Russell	1,106
Elgin Baylor	1,101
John Havlicek	1,046
LARRY BIRD	1,012
MICHAEL JORDAN	960
KEVIN McHALE	958

HIGHEST SCORING AVERAGE
(25 games or 625 points minimum)

	G.	FGM	FTM	Pts.	Avg.
MICHAEL JORDAN	92	1,160	806	3,184	34.6
Jerry West	153	1,622	1,213	4,457	29.1
KARL MALONE	53	520	424	1,464	27.6
BERNARD KING	25	265	148	679	27.2
Elgin Baylor	134	1,388	847	3,623	27.0
George Gervin	59	622	348	1,592	27.0
HAKEEM OLAJUWON	50	512	302	1,326	26.5
DOMINIQUE WILKINS	48	456	327	1,255	26.1
Bob Pettit	88	766	708	2,240	25.5
Rick Barry	74	719	392	1,833	24.8

MOST FREE THROWS MADE

Jerry West	1,213
Kareem Abdul-Jabbar	1,050
MAGIC JOHNSON	1,040
LARRY BIRD	901
John Havlicek	874
Elgin Baylor	847
MICHAEL JORDAN	806
Wilt Chamberlain	757
Dennis Johnson	756
Dolph Schayes	755

HIGHEST FIELD GOAL PERCENTAGE
(150 FGM minimum)

	FGA	FGM	Pct.
KURT RAMBIS	495	284	.574
CHARLES BARKLEY	726	413	.569
Artis Gilmore	316	179	.566
KEVIN McHALE	2,090	1,172	.561
BERNARD KING	474	265	.559
JAMES WORTHY	2,243	1,235	.551
Darryl Dawkins	992	542	.546
Cedric Maxwell	688	375	.545
HORACE GRANT	718	389	.542
HAKEEM OLAJUWON	948	512	.540

HIGHEST FREE THROW PERCENTAGE
(100 FTM minimum)

	FTA	FTM	Pct.
HERSEY HAWKINS	128	120	.938
MARK PRICE	143	134	.937
Calvin Murphy	177	165	.932
JEFF HORNACEK	160	146	.913
Bill Sharman	406	370	.911
KIKI VANDEWEGHE	259	235	.907
LARRY BIRD	1,012	901	.890
Vince Boryla	135	120	.889
Rick Barry	448	392	.875
Bobby Wanzer	270	236	.874

MOST REBOUNDS

Bill Russell	4,104
Wilt Chamberlain	3,913
Kareem Abdul-Jabbar	2,481
Wes Unseld	1,777
Elgin Baylor	1,725
ROBERT PARISH	1,714
LARRY BIRD	1,683
Paul Silas	1,527
MAGIC JOHNSON	1,431
Bill Bridges	1,305

MOST STEALS

MAGIC JOHNSON	358
LARRY BIRD	296
MAURICE CHEEKS	289
Dennis Johnson	247
Julius Erving	235
ISIAH THOMAS	234
MICHAEL JORDAN	219
Michael Cooper	203
BYRON SCOTT	198
Kareem Abdul-Jabbar	189

MOST ASSISTS

MAGIC JOHNSON	2,320
LARRY BIRD	1,062
Dennis Johnson	1,006
ISIAH THOMAS	987
Jerry West	970
Bob Cousy	937
MAURICE CHEEKS	908
John Havlicek	825
Bill Russell	770
Oscar Robertson	769

MOST BLOCKED SHOTS

Kareem Abdul-Jabbar	476
ROBERT PARISH	297
KEVIN McHALE	274
Julius Erving	239
Caldwell Jones	223
Elvin Hayes	222
MARK EATON	201
HAKEEM OLAJUWON	178
Darryl Dawkins	165
Bobby Jones	156

MOST PERSONAL FOULS

Kareem Abdul-Jabbar	797
ROBERT PARISH	599
Dennis Johnson	575
KEVIN McHALE	565
Bill Russell	546
MAGIC JOHNSON	521
John Havlicek	517
Tom Sanders	508
Michael Cooper	474
Paul Silas	469

MOST DISQUALIFICATIONS

Tom Sanders	26
Vern Mikkelsen	24
Bailey Howell	21
Jack Sikma	17
Darryl Dawkins	16
ROBERT PARISH	16
Charlie Share	16
Dave Cowens	15
4 players tied at	14

MOST 3-PT. FIELD GOALS ATTEMPTED

Michael Cooper	316
DANNY AINGE	286
BYRON SCOTT	260
TERRY PORTER	252
LARRY BIRD	249
CRAIG HODGES	248
ISIAH THOMAS	234
CLYDE DREXLER	203
MAGIC JOHNSON	203
MICHAEL JORDAN	172

MOST 3-PT. FIELD GOALS MADE

Michael Cooper	124
DANNY AINGE	110
BYRON SCOTT	104
TERRY PORTER	102
CRAIG HODGES	90
ISIAH THOMAS	81
LARRY BIRD	80
MICHAEL JORDAN	58
CLYDE DREXLER	51
MAGIC JOHNSON	48

HIGHEST 3-PT. FIELD GOAL PERCENTAGE
(15 3-PT. FGM minimum)

	FGA	FGM	Pct.
BOB HANSEN	76	38	.500
REGGIE MILLER	37	18	.486
CHRIS MULLIN	37	17	.459
ERIC FLOYD	67	28	.418
HERSEY HAWKINS	67	28	.418
LAFAYETTE LEVER	44	18	.409
TERRY PORTER	252	102	.405
TRENT TUCKER	94	38	.404
BYRON SCOTT	260	104	.400
Brian Winters	48	19	.396

NBA FINALS YEAR-BY-YEAR

Year	Dates		Winner (Coach)	Loser (Coach)	Games
1947—Apr.	16-Apr.	22	Philadelphia (Gottlieb)	Chicago (Olsen)	4-1
1948—Apr.	10-Apr.	21	Baltimore (Jeannette)	Philadelphia (Gottlieb)	4-2
1949—Apr.	4-Apr.	13	Minneapolis (Kundla)	Washington (Auerbach)	4-2
1950—Apr.	8-Apr.	23	Minneapolis (Kundla)	*Syracuse (Cervi)	4-2
1951—Apr.	7-Apr.	21	Rochester (Harrison)	New York (Lapchick)	4-3
1952—Apr.	12-Apr.	25	Minneapolis (Kundla)	New York (Lapchick)	4-3
1953—Apr.	4-Apr.	10	*Minneapolis (Kundla)	New York (Lapchick)	4-1
1954—Mar.	31-Apr.	12	*Minneapolis (Kundla)	Syracuse (Cervi)	4-3
1955—Mar.	31-Apr.	10	*Syracuse (Cervi)	*Ft. Wayne (Eckman)	4-3
1956—Mar.	31-Apr.	7	*Philadelphia (Senesky)	Ft. Wayne (Eckman)	4-1
1957—Mar.	30-Apr.	13	*Boston (Auerbach)	St. Louis (Hannum)	4-3
1958—Mar.	29-Apr.	12	St. Louis (Hannum)	*Boston (Auerbach)	4-2
1959—Apr.	4-Apr.	9	*Boston (Auerbach)	Minneapolis (Kundla)	4-0
1960—Mar.	27-Apr.	9	*Boston (Auerbach)	St. Louis (Macauley)	4-3
1961—Apr.	2-Apr.	11	*Boston (Auerbach)	St. Louis (Seymour)	4-1
1962—Apr.	7-Apr.	18	*Boston (Auerbach)	Los Angeles (Schaus)	4-3
1963—Apr.	14-Apr.	24	*Boston (Auerbach)	Los Angeles (Schaus)	4-2
1964—Apr.	18-Apr.	26	*Boston (Auerbach)	San Francisco (Hannum)	4-1
1965—Apr.	18-Apr.	25	*Boston (Auerbach)	Los Angeles (Schaus)	4-1
1966—Apr.	17-Apr.	28	Boston (Auerbach)	Los Angeles (Schaus)	4-3
1967—Apr.	14-Apr.	24	*Philadelphia (Hannum)	San Francisco (Sharman)	4-2
1968—Apr.	21-May	2	Boston (Russell)	Los Angeles (van Breda Kolff)	4-2
1969—Apr.	23-May	5	Boston (Russell)	Los Angeles (van Breda Kolff)	4-3
1970—Apr.	24-May	8	*New York (Holzman)	Los Angeles (Mullaney)	4-3
1971—Apr.	21-Apr.	30	*Milwaukee (Costello)	Baltimore (Shue)	4-0
1972—Apr.	26-May	7	*Los Angeles (Sharman)	New York (Holzman)	4-1
1973—May	1-May	10	New York (Holzman)	Los Angeles (Sharman)	4-1
1974—May	28-May	12	Boston (Heinsohn)	*Milwaukee (Costello)	4-3
1975—May	18-May	25	Golden State (Attles)	*Washington (Jones)	4-0
1976—May	23-June	6	Boston (Heinsohn)	Phoenix (MacLeod)	4-2
1977—May	22-June	5	Portland (Ramsay)	Philadelphia (Shue)	4-2
1978—May	21-June	7	Washington (Motta)	Seattle (Wilkens)	4-3
1979—May	20-June	1	Seattle (Wilkens)	*Washington (Motta)	4-1
1980—May	4-May	16	Los Angeles (Westhead)	Philadelphia (Cunningham)	4-2
1981—May	5-May	14	*Boston (Fitch)	Houston (Harris)	4-2
1982—May	27-June	8	Los Angeles (Riley)	Philadelphia (Cunningham)	4-2
1983—May	22-May	31	*Philadelphia (Cunningham)	Los Angeles (Riley)	4-0
1984—May	27-June	12	*Boston (Jones)	Los Angeles (Riley)	4-3
1985—May	27-June	9	L.A. Lakers (Riley)	*Boston (Jones)	4-2
1986—May	26-June	8	*Boston (Jones)	Houston (Fitch)	4-2
1987—June	2-June	14	*L.A. Lakers (Riley)	Boston (Jones)	4-2
1988—June	7-June	21	*L.A. Lakers (Riley)	Detroit (Daly)	4-3
1989—June	6-June	13	*Detroit (Daly)	L.A. Lakers (Riley)	4-0
1990—June	5-June	14	Detroit (Daly)	Portland (Adelman)	4-1
1991—June	2-June	12	Chicago (Jackson)	L.A. Lakers (Dunleavy)	4-1
1991—June	3-June	14	*Chicago (Jackson)	Portland (Adelman)	4-2

*Had best record (or tied for best record) during regular season.

NBA Finals—Series Records

Team	W.	L.	Pct.
Chicago Bulls	2	0	1.000
Baltimore Bullets*	1	0	1.000
Sacramento Kings	1	0	1.000
Boston Celtics	16	3	.842
Golden State Warriors	3	3	.500
Milwaukee Bucks	1	1	.500
Seattle SuperSonics	1	1	.500
Los Angeles Lakers	11	13	.458
Detroit Pistons	2	3	.400
Philadelphia 76ers	3	5	.375
New York Knickerbockers	2	4	.333
Portland Trail Blazers	1	2	.333
Atlanta Hawks	1	3	.250
Washington Bullets	1	3	.250
Chicago Stags*	0	1	.000
Phoenix Suns	0	1	.000
Washington Capitols*	0	1	.000
Houston Rockets	0	2	.000
Totals	46	46	.500

*Defunct

NBA Finals—Overall Records

Team	W.	L.	Pct.
Chicago Bulls	8	3	.727
Baltimore Bullets*	4	2	.667
Milwaukee Bucks	7	4	.636
Boston Celtics	70	46	.603
Seattle SuperSonics	7	5	.583
Sacramento Kings	4	3	.571
Golden State Warriors	17	14	.548
Detroit Pistons	15	13	.536
Philadelphia 76ers	23	25	.479
Los Angeles Lakers	66	75	.468
New York Knickerbockers	16	20	.444
Atlanta Hawks	11	14	.440
Portland Trail Blazers	7	10	.412
Houston Rockets	4	8	.333
Phoenix Suns	2	4	.333
Washington Capitols*	2	4	.333
Washington Bullets	5	15	.250
Chicago Stags*	1	4	.200
Totals	269	269	.500

*Defunct

NBA Finals—Home Records

Team	W.	L.	Pct.
Baltimore Bullets*	3	0	1.000
Detroit Pistons	9	3	.750
Golden State Warriors	12	4	.750
Sacramento Kings	3	1	.750
Boston Celtics	44	17	.721
Philadelphia 76ers	16	8	.667
Phoenix Suns	2	1	.333
Seattle SuperSonics	4	2	.667
Washington Capitols*	2	1	.667
Atlanta Hawks	7	4	.636
Chicago Bulls	3	2	.600
Los Angeles Lakers	40	31	.563
New York Knickerbockers	9	8	.529
Chicago Stags*	1	1	.500
Houston Rockets	3	3	.500
Milwaukee Bucks	3	3	.500
Portland Trail Blazers	4	5	.444
Washington Bullets	3	7	.300
Totals	168	101	.625

*Defunct

NBA Finals—Road Records

Team	W.	L.	Pct.
Chicago Bulls	5	1	.833
Milwaukee Bucks	4	1	.800
Seattle SuperSonics	3	3	.500
Boston Celtics	26	29	.473
Detroit Pistons	6	10	.375
Portland Trail Blazers	3	5	.375
Los Angeles Lakers	26	44	.371
New York Knickerbockers	7	12	.368
Baltimore Bullets	1	2	.333
Golden State Warriors	5	10	.333
Sacramento Kings	1	2	.333
Philadelphia 76ers	7	17	.292
Atlanta Hawks	4	10	.286
Washington Bullets	2	8	.200
Houston Rockets	1	5	.167
Chicago Stags*	0	3	.000
Phoenix Suns	0	3	.000
Washington Capitols*	0	3	.000
Totals	101	168	.375

*Defunct

NBA FINALS RECORDS
Individual (Series)

MOST POINTS

4 Games
118—Rick Barry, Golden State 1975
109—Joe Dumars, Detroit 1989

5 Games
169—Jerry West, Los Angeles 1965
156—Michael Jordan, Chicago 1991

6 Games
245—Rick Barry, San Francisco 1967
215—Michael Jordan, Chicago 1992

7 Games
284—Elgin Baylor, Los Angeles 1962
265—Jerry West, Los Angeles 1969

MOST MINUTES PLAYED

4 Games
186—Bob Cousy, Boston 1959
    Bill Russell, Boston 1959
179—Magic Johnson, Los Angeles 1983

5 Games
240—Wilt Chamberlain, Los Angeles 1973
236—Wilt Chamberlain, Los Angeles 1972

6 Games
292—Bill Russell, Boston 1968
291—John Havlicek, Boston 1968

7 Games
345—K. Abdul-Jabbar, Milwaukee 1974
338—Bill Russell, Boston 1962

HIGHEST FIELD GOAL PERCENTAGE
(minimum: 4 FG per game)

4 Games
.739—Derrek Dickey, Golden State 1975
.605—Kareem Abdul-Jabbar, Milwaukee 1971

5 Games
.702—Bill Russell, Boston 1965
.653—John Paxson, Chicago 1991

6 Games
.667—Bob Gross, Portland 1977
.622—Bill Walton, Boston 1986

7 Games
.638—James Worthy, Los Angeles 1984
.625—Wilt Chamberlain, Los Angeles 1970

MOST FIELD GOALS

4 Games
46—Kareem Abdul-Jabbar, Milwaukee 1971
44—Rick Barry, Golden State 1975

5 Games
63—Michael Jordan, Chicago 1991
62—Wilt Chamberlain, San Francisco 1964

6 Games
94—Rick Barry, San Francisco 1967
81—Michael Jordan, Chicago 1992

7 Games
101—Elgin Baylor, Los Angeles 1962
97—K. Abdul-Jabbar, Milwaukee 1974

MOST FIELD GOAL ATTEMPTS

4 Games
102—Elgin Baylor, Minneapolis 1959
99—Rick Barry, Golden State 1975

5 Games
139—Jerry West, Los Angeles 1965
129—Paul Arizin, Philadelphia 1956

6 Games
235—Rick Barry, San Francisco 1967
163—Elgin Baylor, Los Angeles 1963

7 Games
235—Elgin Baylor, Los Angeles 1962
196—Jerry West, Los Angeles 1969

MOST THREE-POINT FIELD GOALS MADE

4 Games

9—Michael Cooper, L.A. Lakers 1989
2—Bob McAdoo, Los Angeles 1983
Bill Laimbeer, Detroit 1989
Isiah Thomas, Detroit 1989
James Worthy, L.A. Lakers 1989

5 Games

11—Isiah Thomas, Detroit 1990
8—Bill Laimbeer, Detroit 1990

6 Games

14—Michael Cooper, L.A. Lakers 1987
12—Michael Jordan, Chicago 1992

7 Games

5—Michael Cooper, Los Angeles 1984
Byron Scott, L.A. Lakers 1988
Isiah Thomas, Detroit 1988
4—Larry Bird, Boston 1984

MOST THREE-POINT FIELD GOAL ATTEMPTS

4 Games

27—Michael Cooper, L.A. Lakers 1989
6—Isiah Thomas, Detroit 1989

5 Games

25—Terry Porter, Portland 1990
22—Bill Laimbeer, Detroit 1990

6 Games

28—Michael Jordan, Chicago 1992
23—Michael Cooper, L.A. Lakers 1987

7 Games

20—Michael Cooper, L.A. Lakers 1988
17—Isiah Thomas, Detroit 1988

HIGHEST FREE THROW PERCENTAGE
(minimum: 2 FTM per game)

4 Games

.944—Phil Chenier, Washington 1975
.941—Bill Sharman, Boston 1959

5 Games

1.000—Bill Laimbeer, Detroit 1990
Vlade Divac, L.A. Lakers 1991
.957—Jim McMillian, Los Angeles 1972

6 Games

.968—Bill Sharman, Boston 1958
.960—Magic Johnson, L.A. Lakers 1987

7 Games

.959—Bill Sharman, Boston 1957
.947—Don Meineke, Fort Wayne 1955

MOST FREE THROWS MADE

4 Games

34—Phil Chenier, Washington 1975
33—Joe Dumars, Detroit 1989

5 Games

51—Jerry West, Los Angeles 1965
48—Bob Pettit, St. Louis 1961

6 Games

67—George Mikan, Minneapolis 1950
61—Joe Fulks, Philadelphia 1948

7 Games

82—Elgin Baylor, Los Angeles 1962
75—Jerry West, Los Angeles 1970

MOST FREE THROW ATTEMPTS

4 Games

47—Moses Malone, Philadelphia 1983
38—Joe Dumars, Detroit 1989

5 Games

60—Bob Pettit, St. Louis 1961
59—Jerry West, Los Angeles 1965

6 Games

86—George Mikan, Minneapolis 1950
79—Bob Pettit, St. Louis 1958

7 Games

99—Elgin Baylor, Los Angeles 1962
97—Bob Pettit, St. Louis 1957

MOST REBOUNDS

4 Games

118—Bill Russell, Boston 1959
76—Wes Unseld, Baltimore 1971

5 Games

144—Bill Russell, Boston 1961
138—Wilt Chamberlain, San Francisco 1964

6 Games

171—Wilt Chamberlain, Philadelphia 1967
160—Nate Thurmond, San Francisco 1967

7 Games

189—Bill Russell, Boston 1962
175—Wilt Chamberlain, Los Angeles 1969

MOST OFFENSIVE REBOUNDS

4 Games

27—Moses Malone, Philadelphia 1983
16—George Johnson, Golden State 1975

5 Games

21—Elvin Hayes, Washington 1979
20—Wes Unseld, Washington 1979

6 Games

46—Moses Malone, Houston 1981
34—Cedric Maxwell, Boston 1981

7 Games

33—Elvin Hayes, Washington 1978
Marvin Webster, Seattle 1978
30—Robert Parish, Boston 1984

MOST DEFENSIVE REBOUNDS

4 Games

53—Wes Unseld, Washington 1975
45—Moses Malone, Philadelphia 1983

5 Games

62—Jack Sikma, Seattle 1979
55—Bill Laimbeer, Detroit 1990

6 Games

91—Bill Walton, Portland 1977
76—Larry Bird, Boston 1981

7 Games

72—Larry Bird, Boston 1984
64—Marvin Webster, Seattle 1978

MOST ASSISTS

4 Games

51—Bob Cousy, Boston 1959
50—Magic Johnson, Los Angeles 1983

5 Games

62—Magic Johnson, L.A. Lakers 1991
57—Michael Jordan, Chicago 1991

6 Games

84—Magic Johnson, L.A. Lakers 1985
78—Magic Johnson, L.A. Lakers 1987

7 Games

95—Magic Johnson, Los Angeles 1984
91—Magic Johnson, L.A. Lakers 1988

MOST PERSONAL FOULS

4 Games

20—Michael Cooper, Los Angeles 1983
19—Kevin Porter, Washington 1975
Tony Campbell, L.A. Lakers 1989

5 Games

27—George Mikan, Minneapolis 1953
25—Art Hillhouse, Philadelphia 1947
Lonnie Shelton, Seattle 1979
Bill Laimbeer, Detroit 1990

6 Games

35—Charlie Scott, Boston 1976
33—Tom Heinsohn, Boston 1958
Tom Meschery, San Francisco 1967

7 Games

37—Arnie Risen, Boston 1957
36—Vern Mikkelsen, Minneapolis 1952
Jack McMahon, St. Louis 1957

MOST DISQUALIFICATIONS

4 Games

1—John Tresvant, Baltimore 1971
Elvin Hayes, Washington 1975
George Johnson, Golden State 1975
Kevin Porter, Washington 1975
Marc Iavaroni, Philadelphia 1983
Michael Cooper, Los Angeles 1983
Tony Campbell, L.A. Lakers 1989
A.C. Green, L.A. Lakers 1989
Rick Mahorn, Detroit 1989

5 Games

5—Art Hillhouse, Philadelphia 1947
4—Chuck Gilmur, Chicago 1947

6 Games

5—Charlie Scott, Boston 1976

7 Games

5—Arnie Risen, Boston 1957
3—Mel Hutchins, Fort Wayne 1955
Jack McMahon, St. Louis 1957

MOST STEALS

4 Games

14—Rick Barry, Golden State 1975
11—Maurice Cheeks, Philadelphia 1983

5 Games

14—Michael Jordan, Chicago 1991
12—Scottie Pippen, Chicago 1991

6 Games

16—Julius Erving, Philadelphia 1977
Magic Johnson, Los Angeles 1980

Larry Bird, Boston 1986
15—Maurice Cheeks, Philadelphia 1980
Magic Johnson, Los Angeles 1982
Byron Scott, L.A. Lakers 1985
Danny Ainge, Boston 1986

7 Games

20—Isiah Thomas, Detroit 1988
15—Larry Bird, Boston 1984

MOST BLOCKED SHOTS

4 Games

11—Elvin Hayes, Washington 1975
George Johnson, Golden State 1975
Julius Erving, Philadelphia 1983
John Salley, Detroit 1989
9—Kareem Abdul-Jabbar, Los Angeles 1983
Bobby Jones, Philadelphia 1983

5 Games

16—Jack Sikma, Seattle 1979

12—John Salley, Detroit 1990
Vlade Divac, L.A. Lakers 1991

6 Games

23—Kareem Abdul-Jabbar, Los Angeles 1980
22—Bill Walton, Portland 1977

7 Games

18—Marvin Webster, Seattle 1978
17—Dennis Johnson, Seattle 1978

MOST TURNOVERS

4 Games

24—Magic Johnson, Los Angeles 1983
18—Andrew Toney, Philadelphia 1983
14—Kareem Abdul-Jabbar, Los Angeles 1983

5 Games

25—Isiah Thomas, Detroit 1990
22—Terry Porter, Portland 1990
Magic Johnson, L.A. Lakers 1991

6 Games

30—Magic Johnson, Los Angeles 1980
26—Magic Johnson, Los Angeles 1982

7 Games

31—Magic Johnson, Los Angeles 1984
26—Gus Williams, Seattle 1978
Isiah Thomas, Detroit 1988

Teams (Series)

MOST POINTS

4 Games

487—Boston vs. Minneapolis 1959
446—Minneapolis vs. Boston 1959

5 Games

617—Boston vs. Los Angeles 1965
605—Boston vs. St. Louis 1961

6 Games

747—Philadelphia vs. San Francisco 1967
707—San Francisco vs. Philadelphia 1967

7 Games

827—Boston vs. Los Angeles 1966
824—Boston vs. Los Angeles 1962

FEWEST POINTS

4 Games

376—Baltimore vs. Milwaukee 1971
382—Washington vs. Golden State 1975

5 Games

458—L.A. Lakers vs. Chicago 1991
467—Fort Wayne vs. Philadelphia 1956

6 Games

520—Houston vs. Boston 1981
579—Boston vs. Houston 1981

7 Games

636—Syracuse vs. Fort Wayne 1955
640—Fort Wayne vs. Syracuse 1955

HIGHEST FIELD GOAL PERCENTAGE

4 Games

.527—Detroit vs. L.A. Lakers 1989
.504—Milwaukee vs. Baltimore 1971

5 Games

.527—Chicago vs. L.A. Lakers 1991
.470—New York vs. Los Angeles 1972

6 Games

.515—L.A. Lakers vs. Boston 1987
.512—L.A. Lakers vs. Boston 1985

7 Games

.515—Los Angeles vs. Boston 1984
.494—Los Angeles vs. New York 1970

LOWEST FIELD GOAL PERCENTAGE

4 Games

.384—Baltimore vs. Milwaukee 1971
.388—Minneapolis vs. Boston 1959

5 Games

.365—Fort Wayne vs. Philadelphia 1956
.372—St. Louis vs. Boston 1961

6 Games

.355—Boston vs. St. Louis 1958
.379—Houston vs. Boston 1981

7 Games

.339—Syracuse vs. Fort Wayne 1955
.369—Boston vs. St. Louis 1957

MOST FIELD GOALS

4 Games

188—Boston vs. Minneapolis 1959
180—Minneapolis vs. Boston 1959

5 Games

243—Boston vs. Los Angeles 1965
238—Boston vs. St. Louis 1961

6 Games

287—Philadelphia vs. San Francisco 1967
   San Francisco vs. Philadelphia 1967
280—L.A. Lakers vs. Boston 1987

7 Games

332—New York vs. Los Angeles 1970
327—Los Angeles vs. Boston 1984

FEWEST FIELD GOALS

4 Games

144—L.A. Lakers vs. Detroit 1989
147—Washington vs. Golden State 1975

5 Games

163—Ft. Wayne vs. Philadelphia 1956
167—L.A. Lakers vs. Chicago 1991

6 Games

203—Houston vs. Boston 1981
211—St. Louis vs. Boston 1958

7 Games

207—Syracuse vs. Fort Wayne 1955
217—Fort Wayne vs. Syracuse 1955

MOST FIELD GOAL ATTEMPTS

4 Games

464—Minneapolis vs. Boston 1959
463—Boston vs. Minneapolis 1959

5 Games

568—Boston vs. Los Angeles 1965
555—Boston vs. St. Louis 1961

6 Games

743—San Francisco vs. Philadelphia 1967
640—Boston vs. Los Angeles 1963

7 Games

799—Boston vs. St. Louis 1957
769—Boston vs. St. Louis 1960

FEWEST FIELD GOAL ATTEMPTS

4 Games

310—L.A. Lakers vs. Detroit 1989
317—Detroit vs. L.A. Lakers 1989

5 Games

374—L.A. Lakers vs. Chicago 1991
404—Chicago vs. L.A. Lakers 1991

6 Games

478—Chicago vs. Portland 1992
479—Portland vs. Chicago 1992

7 Games

531—L.A. Lakers vs. Detroit 1988
558—Fort Wayne vs. Syracuse 1955

MOST THREE-POINT FIELD GOALS MADE

4 Games

13—L.A. Lakers vs. Detroit 1989
5—Detroit vs. L.A. Lakers 1989

5 Games

25—Detroit vs. Portland 1990
13—L.A. Lakers vs. Chicago 1991

6 Games

25—Chicago vs. Portland 1992
16—L.A. Lakers vs. Boston 1987

7 Games

10—L.A. Lakers vs. Detroit 1988
9—Boston vs. Los Angeles 1984
   Detroit vs. L.A. Lakers 1988

MOST THREE-POINT FIELD GOAL ATTEMPTS

4 Games
43—L.A. Lakers vs. Detroit 1989
20—Detroit vs. L.A. Lakers 1989

5 Games
56—Detroit vs. Portland 1990
47—Portland vs. Detroit 1990

6 Games
65—Chicago vs. Portland 1992
52—Portland vs. Chicago 1992

7 Games
40—L.A. Lakers vs. Detroit 1988
31—Detroit vs. L.A. Lakers 1988

HIGHEST FREE THROW PERCENTAGE

4 Games
.785—Los Angeles vs. Philadelphia 1983
.776—Detroit vs. L.A. Lakers 1989

5 Games
.826—Chicago vs. L.A. Lakers 1991
.810—L.A. Lakers vs. Chicago 1991

6 Games
.821—Boston vs. Phoenix 1976
.813—Los Angeles vs. Philadelphia 1980

7 Games
.827—Boston vs. Los Angeles 1966
.805—Los Angeles vs. Boston 1962

LOWEST FREE THROW PERCENTAGE

4 Games
.675—Baltimore vs. Milwaukee 1971
.698—Boston vs. Minneapolis 1959

5 Games
.616—San Francisco vs. Boston 1964
.647—Los Angeles vs. New York 1973

6 Games
.613—Philadelphia vs. San Francisco 1967
.672—Los Angeles vs. Philadelphia 1982

7 Games
.641—Los Angeles vs. Boston 1969
.688—Los Angeles vs. New York 1970

MOST FREE THROWS MADE

4 Games
111—Boston vs. Minneapolis 1959
108—L.A. Lakers vs. Detroit 1989

5 Games
146—Los Angeles vs. Boston 1965
145—New York vs. Minneapolis 1953

6 Games
232—Boston vs. St. Louis 1958
215—St. Louis vs. Boston 1958

7 Games
244—St. Louis vs. Boston 1957
239—Los Angeles vs. Boston 1962

FEWEST FREE THROWS MADE

4 Games
52—Baltimore vs. Milwaukee 1971
72—Golden State vs. Washington 1975

5 Games
73—New York vs. Los Angeles 1973
76—Chicago vs. L.A. Lakers 1991

6 Games
94—Boston vs. Houston 1981
105—Houston vs. Boston 1986

7 Games
100—Milwaukee vs. Boston 1974
117—Boston vs. Milwaukee 1974

MOST FREE THROW ATTEMPTS

4 Games
159—Boston vs. Minneapolis 1959
144—L.A. Lakers vs. Detroit 1989

5 Games
211—San Francisco vs. Boston 1964
199—New York vs. Minneapolis 1953
Los Angeles vs. Boston 1965

6 Games
298—Boston vs. St. Louis 1958
292—St. Louis vs. Boston 1958

7 Games
341—St. Louis vs. Boston 1957
299—Boston vs. St. Louis 1957

FEWEST FREE THROW ATTEMPTS

4 Games
77—Baltimore vs. Milwaukee 1971
93—Los Angeles vs. Philadelphia 1983

5 Games
92—Chicago vs. L.A. Lakers 1991
96—New York vs. Los Angeles 1973

6 Games
129—Boston vs. Houston 1981
144—Los Angeles vs. Philadelphia 1980
Philadelphia vs. Los Angeles 1980

7 Games
137—Milwaukee vs. Boston 1974
151—Boston vs. Milwaukee 1974

HIGHEST REBOUND PERCENTAGE

4 Games
.557—Golden State vs. Washington 1975
.533—Milwaukee vs. Baltimore 1971

5 Games
.548—Boston vs. St. Louis 1961
.542—Los Angeles vs. New York 1972

6 Games
.580—Los Angeles vs. Philadelphia 1980
.570—Boston vs. Phoenix 1976

7 Games
.541—Rochester vs. New York 1951
.538—Boston vs. Los Angeles 1966

MOST REBOUNDS

4 Games
295—Boston vs. Minneapolis 1959
268—Minneapolis vs. Boston 1959

5 Games
369—Boston vs. St. Louis 1961
316—Boston vs. Los Angeles 1965

6 Games
435—San Francisco vs. Philadelphia 1967
425—Philadelphia vs. San Francisco 1967

7 Games
487—Boston vs. St. Louis 1957
448—Boston vs. St. Louis 1960

FEWEST REBOUNDS

4 Games
145—L.A. Lakers vs. Detroit 1989
160—Detroit vs. L.A. Lakers 1989

5 Games
178—L.A. Lakers vs. Chicago 1991
196—Chicago vs. L.A. Lakers 1991

6 Games
223—Philadelphia vs. Los Angeles 1980
225—Chicago vs. Portland 1992

7 Games
263—L.A. Lakers vs. Detroit 1988
297—Boston vs. Milwaukee 1974

HIGHEST OFFENSIVE REBOUND PERCENTAGE

4 Games
.396—Philadelphia vs. Los Angeles 1983
.375—Golden State vs. Washington 1975

5 Games
.336—Washington vs. Seattle 1979
.332—Detroit vs. Portland 1990

6 Games
.410—Boston vs. Houston 1981
.407—Philadelphia vs. Los Angeles 1982

7 Games
.384—Boston vs. Los Angeles 1984
.366—Seattle vs. Washington 1978

MOST OFFENSIVE REBOUNDS

4 Games
72—Golden State vs. Washington 1975
   Philadelphia vs. Los Angeles 1983

5 Games
82—Washington vs. Seattle 1979
72—Detroit vs. Portland 1990

6 Games
112—Houston vs. Boston 1981
111—Houston vs. Boston 1986

7 Games
131—Boston vs. Los Angeles 1984
127—Seattle vs. Washington 1978

FEWEST OFFENSIVE REBOUNDS

4 Games
45—Detroit vs. L.A. Lakers 1989
47—L.A. Lakers vs. Detroit 1989

5 Games
55—Chicago vs. L.A. Lakers 1991
57—Portland vs. Detroit 1990

6 Games
57—Philadelphia vs. Los Angeles 1980
61—Chicago vs. Portland 1992

7 Games
72—L.A. Lakers vs. Detroit 1988
86—Milwaukee vs. Boston 1974

HIGHEST DEFENSIVE REBOUND PERCENTAGE

4 Games
.737—Washington vs. Golden State 1975
.710—Detroit vs. L.A. Lakers 1989

5 Games
.718—Detroit vs. Portland 1990
.705—Chicago vs. L.A. Lakers 1991

6 Games
.782—Los Angeles vs. Philadelphia 1980
.769—Boston vs. Phoenix 1976

7 Games
.745—Detroit vs. L.A. Lakers 1988
.735—Portland vs. Chicago 1992

MOST DEFENSIVE REBOUNDS

4 Games
143—Golden State vs. Washington 1975
120—Washington vs. Golden State 1975
   Philadelphia vs. Los Angeles 1983

5 Games
162—Seattle vs. Washington 1979
151—Washington vs. Seattle 1979

6 Games
240—Boston vs. Phoenix 1976
228—Portland vs. Philadelphia 1977

7 Games
223—Seattle vs. Washington 1978
220—Milwaukee vs. Boston 1974
   Washington vs. Seattle 1978

FEWEST DEFENSIVE REBOUNDS

4 Games
98—L.A. Lakers vs. Detroit 1989
110—Los Angeles vs. Philadelphia 1983

5 Games
119—L.A. Lakers vs. Chicago 1991
141—Chicago vs. L.A. Lakers 1991

6 Games
144—Houston vs. Boston 1981
160—Philadelphia vs. Los Angeles 1982

7 Games
191—L.A. Lakers vs. Detroit 1988
206—Boston vs. Los Angeles 1984

MOST ASSISTS

4 Games
114—Boston vs. Minneapolis 1959
104—Philadelphia vs. Los Angeles 1983

5 Games
139—Chicago vs. L.A. Lakers 1991
130—Boston vs. St. Louis 1961

6 Games
192—L.A. Lakers vs. Boston 1985
188—Los Angeles vs. Philadelphia 1982

7 Games
198—Los Angeles vs. Boston 1984
192—New York vs. Los Angeles 1970

FEWEST ASSISTS

4 Games
78—Baltimore vs. Milwaukee 1971
82—Golden State vs. Washington 1975

5 Games
88—San Francisco vs. Boston 1964
   Los Angeles vs. New York 1973
94—Detroit vs. Portland 1990

6 Games
105—Los Angeles vs. Boston 1963
108—Houston vs. Boston 1981

7 Games
121—Seattle vs. Washington 1978
135—Los Angeles vs. Boston 1962
   Boston vs. Los Angeles 1969

MOST PERSONAL FOULS

4 Games
120—Los Angeles vs. Philadelphia 1983
116—Golden State vs. Washington 1975

5 Games
149—Portland vs. Detroit 1990
146—Boston vs. San Francisco 1964

6 Games
194—Boston vs. St. Louis 1958
   St. Louis vs. Boston 1958
182—San Francisco vs. Philadelphia 1967
   Portland vs. Philadelphia 1977

7 Games
221—Boston vs. St. Louis 1957
210—Boston vs. Los Angeles 1962

FEWEST PERSONAL FOULS

4 Games
84—Milwaukee vs. Baltimore 1971
89—Philadelphia vs. Los Angeles 1983

5 Games
96—L.A. Lakers vs. Chicago 1991
106—Los Angeles vs. New York 1972

6 Games
121—Houston vs. Boston 1981
124—Boston vs. Houston 1986

7 Games
150—Los Angeles vs. New York 1970
153—Boston vs. Milwaukee 1974

MOST DISQUALIFICATIONS

4 Games
2—Washington vs. Golden State 1975
   L.A. Lakers vs. Detroit 1989
1—Baltimore vs. Milwaukee 1971
   Golden State vs Washington 1975
   Los Angeles vs. Philadelphia 1983
   Philadelphia vs. Los Angeles 1983
   Detroit vs. L.A. Lakers 1989

5 Games
9—Chicago vs. Philadelphia 1947
8—Philadelphia vs. Chicago 1947

6 Games
11—Boston vs. St. Louis 1958
9—Minneapolis vs. Syracuse 1950

7 Games
10—Boston vs. St. Louis 1957
9—Minneapolis vs. New York 1952
   St. Louis vs. Boston 1957
   Boston vs. Los Angeles 1962

FEWEST DISQUALIFICATIONS

4 Games
0—Boston vs. Minneapolis 1959
   Minneapolis vs. Boston 1959
   Milwaukee vs. Baltimore 1971

5 Games
0—Los Angeles vs. New York 1972
1—New York vs. Los Angeles 1972
   Chicago vs. L.A. Lakers 1991

6 Games
0—Los Angeles vs. Philadelphia 1980
   Boston vs. Houston 1986
   Houston vs. Boston 1986
1—By seven teams

7 Games
0—St. Louis vs. Boston 1960
   L.A. Lakers vs. Detroit 1988
1—Los Angeles vs. Boston 1969
   Los Angeles vs. New York 1970

MOST STEALS

4 Games
55—Golden State vs. Washington 1975
45—Washington vs. Golden State 1975

5 Games
49—Chicago vs. L.A. Lakers 1991
38—Seattle vs. Washington 1979

6 Games
71—Philadelphia vs. Portland 1977
64—Portland vs. Philadelphia 1977
   Los Angeles vs. Philadelphia 1982

7 Games
65—Boston vs. Los Angeles 1984
59—Los Angeles vs. Boston 1984

FEWEST STEALS

4 Games
16—Detroit vs. L.A. Lakers 1989
22—L.A. Lakers vs. Detroit 1989

5 Games
28—Detroit vs. Portland 1990
29—Washington vs. Seattle 1979

6 Games

    30—Boston vs. L.A. Lakers 1987
    40—Boston vs. Houston 1981

7 Games

    21—Milwaukee vs. Boston 1974
    40—Seattle vs. Washington 1978

MOST BLOCKED SHOTS

4 Games

    32—Golden State vs. Washington 1975
        Philadelphia vs. Los Angeles 1983
    29—Los Angeles vs. Philadelphia 1983

5 Games

    39—Seattle vs. Washington 1979
    25—Detroit vs. Portland 1990
        Chicago vs. L.A. Lakers 1991

6 Games

    60—Philadelphia vs. Los Angeles 1980
    51—Philadelphia vs. Los Angeles 1982

7 Games

    49—Seattle vs. Washington 1978
    41—Los Angeles vs. Boston 1984

FEWEST BLOCKED SHOTS

4 Games

    16—L.A. Lakers vs. Detroit 1989
    20—Washington vs. Golden State 1975

5 Games

    17—Portland vs. Detroit 1990
    22—L.A. Lakers vs. Chicago 1991

6 Games

    10—Boston vs. Phoenix 1976
    21—Phoenix vs. Boston 1976

7 Games

     5—Boston vs. Milwaukee 1974
    21—L.A. Lakers vs. Detroit 1988

MOST TURNOVERS

4 Games

    94—Golden State vs. Washington 1975
    92—Milwaukee vs. Baltimore 1971

5 Games

    104—Los Angeles vs. New York 1973
     88—New York vs. Los Angeles 1972

6 Games

    149—Portland vs. Philadelphia 1977
    144—Boston vs. Phoenix 1976

7 Games

    142—Milwaukee vs. Boston 1974
    126—Seattle vs. Washington 1978

FEWEST TURNOVERS

4 Games

    46—Detroit vs. L.A. Lakers 1989
    47—L.A. Lakers vs. Detroit 1989

5 Games

    66—Chicago vs. L.A. Lakers 1991
    74—New York vs. Los Angeles 1973

6 Games

    68—L.A. Lakers vs. Boston 1987
    76—L.A. Lakers vs. Boston 1985

7 Games

    87—Detroit vs. L.A. Lakers 1988
    94—L.A. Lakers vs. Detroit 1988

Individual Records

MINUTES

Most Minutes, Game

    61—Garfield Heard, Phoenix at Boston, June 4, 1976 (3 ot)
    60—Jo Jo White, Boston vs. Phoenix, June 4, 1976 (3 ot)
    58—Bob Cousy, Boston vs. St. Louis, April 13, 1957 (2 ot)
        Kareem Abdul-Jabbar, Milwaukee at Boston, May 10, 1974 (2 ot)
        John Havlicek, Boston vs. Milwaukee, May 10, 1974 (2 ot)
        Oscar Robertson, Milwaukee at Boston, May 10, 1974 (2 ot)
        John Havlicek, Boston vs. Phoenix, June 4, 1976 (3 ot)

Most Minutes per Game, One Championship Series

    49.3—Kareem Abdul-Jabbar, Milwaukee vs. Boston, 1974 (345/7)
    48.7—Bill Russell, Boston vs. Los Angeles, 1968 (292/6)
    48.5—John Havlicek, Boston vs. Los Angeles, 1968 (291/6)

SCORING

Most Points, Game

    61—Elgin Baylor, Los Angeles at Boston, April 14, 1962
    55—Rick Barry, San Francisco vs. Philadelphia, April 18, 1967
    53—Jerry West, Los Angeles vs. Boston, April 23, 1969

Most Points, Rookie, Game

    42—Magic Johnson, Los Angeles at Philadelphia, May 16, 1980
    37—Joe Fulks, Philadelphia vs. Chicago, April 16, 1947
        Tom Heinsohn, Boston vs. St. Louis, April 13, 1957 (2 ot)
    34—Joe Fulks, Philadelphia vs. Chicago, April 22, 1947
        Elgin Baylor, Minneapolis at Boston, April 4, 1959

Highest Scoring Average, One Championship Series

    40.8—Rick Barry, San Francisco vs. Philadelphia, 1967 (245/6)
    40.6—Elgin Baylor, Los Angeles vs. Boston, 1962 (284/7)
    37.9—Jerry West, Los Angeles vs. Boston, 1969 (265/7)

Highest Scoring Average, Rookie, One Championship Series

26.2—Joe Fulks, Philadelphia vs. Chicago, 1947 (131/5)
24.0—Tom Heinsohn, Boston vs. St. Louis, 1957 (168/7)
23.0—Alvan Adams, Phoenix vs. Boston, 1976 (138/6)

Most Consecutive Games, 20+ Points

25—Jerry West, Los Angeles, April 20, 1966—May 8, 1970
19—Julius Erving, Philadelphia, May 22, 1977—May 22, 1983
18—Kareem Abdul-Jabbar, Milwaukee-Los Angeles, April 21, 1971—May 30, 1982

Most Consecutive Games, 30+ Points

13—Elgin Baylor, Minneapolis-Los Angeles, April 9, 1959—April 21, 1963
6—Rick Barry, San Francisco, April 14, 1967—April 24, 1967
5—Bob Pettit, St. Louis, April 7, 1957—March 29, 1958
   Jerry West, Los Angeles, April 20, 1966—April 28, 1966
   John Havlicek, Boston, April 30, 1968—April 27, 1969
   Jerry West, Los Angeles, May 5, 1969—May 1, 1970

Most Consecutive Games, 40+ Points

2—Jerry West, Los Angeles, April 19-21, 1965
   Rick Barry, San Francisco, April 18-20, 1967
   Jerry West, Los Angeles, April 23-25, 1969

Scoring 30+ Points in All Games in Championship Series

Elgin Baylor, Los Angeles vs. Boston, 1962 (7-game series)
Rick Barry, San Francisco vs. Philadelphia, 1967 (6-game series)

Scoring 20+ Points in All Games of 7-Game Championship Series

Bob Pettit, St. Louis vs. Boston, 1960
Elgin Baylor, Los Angeles vs. Boston, 1962
Jerry West, Los Angeles vs. Boston, 1962
Jerry West, Los Angeles vs. Boston, 1969
Jerry West, Los Angeles vs. New York, 1970
Kareem Abdul-Jabbar, Milwaukee vs. Boston, 1974
Larry Bird, Boston vs. Los Angeles, 1984

Most Points, One Half

35—Michael Jordan, Chicago vs. Portland, June 3, 1992

Most Points, One Quarter

25—Isiah Thomas, Detroit at L.A. Lakers, June 19, 1988

Most Points, Overtime Period

9—John Havlicek, Boston vs. Milwaukee, May 10, 1974
   Bill Laimbeer, Detroit vs. Portland, June 7, 1990
   Danny Ainge, Portland at Chicago, June 5, 1992

FIELD GOALS

Highest Field Goal Percentage, Game (minimum: 8 field goals)

1.000—Scott Wedman, Boston vs. L.A. Lakers, May 27, 1985 (11/11)
       John Paxson, Chicago vs. L.A. Lakers, June 5, 1991 (8/8)
 .917—Bill Bradley, New York at Los Angeles, April 26, 1972 (11/12)
       James Worthy, Los Angeles at Boston, May 31, 1984 (11/12) (ot)

Most Field Goals, Game

22—Elgin Baylor, Los Angeles at Boston, April 14, 1962
   Rick Barry, San Francisco vs. Philadelphia, April 18, 1967
20—Wilt Chamberlain, Los Angeles vs. New York, May 6, 1970

Most Field Goals, One Half

14—Isiah Thomas, Detroit at L.A. Lakers, June 19, 1988
   Michael Jordan, Chicago vs. Portland, June 3, 1992

Most Field Goals, One Quarter

11—Isiah Thomas, Detroit at L.A. Lakers, June 19, 1988

Most Field Goal Attempts, Game

48—Rick Barry, San Francisco vs. Philadelphia, April 18, 1967
46—Elgin Baylor, Los Angeles at Boston, April 14, 1962
43—Rick Barry, San Francisco at Philadelphia, April 14, 1967 (ot)

Most Field Goal Attempts, One Half

25—Elgin Baylor, Los Angeles at Boston, April 14, 1962

Most Field Goal Attempts, One Quarter

17—Rick Barry, San Francisco at Philadelphia, April 14, 1967

THREE-POINT FIELD GOALS

Most Three-Point Field Goals, None Missed, Game

4—Scott Wedman, Boston vs. L.A. Lakers, May 27, 1985
3—Danny Ainge, Boston at L.A. Lakers, June 2, 1987
   Isiah Thomas, Detroit at Portland, June 14, 1990

Most Three-Point Field Goals, Game

    6—Michael Cooper, L.A. Lakers vs. Boston, June 4, 1987
       Bill Laimbeer, Detroit vs. Portland, June 7, 1990 (ot)
       Michael Jordan, Chicago vs. Portland, June 3, 1992
    5—Danny Ainge, Boston vs. L.A. Lakers, June 11, 1987

Most Three-Point Field Goal Attempts, Game

    10—Michael Jordan, Chicago vs. Portland, June 3, 1992
     9—Bill Laimbeer, Detroit vs. Portland, June 7, 1990 (ot)
       Terry Porter, Portland vs. Detroit, June 14, 1990

FREE THROWS

Most Free Throws Made, None Missed, Game

    15—Terry Porter, Portland at Detroit, June 7, 1990 (ot)
    14—Magic Johnson, Los Angeles at Philadelphia, May 16, 1980

Most Free Throws Made, Game

    19—Bob Pettit, St. Louis at Boston, April 9, 1958
    17—Cliff Hagan, St. Louis at Boston, March 30, 1958
       Elgin Baylor, Los Angeles at Boston, April 14, 1962
       Jerry West, Los Angeles vs. Boston, April 21, 1965
       Jerry West, Los Angeles vs. Boston, April 25, 1969

Most Free Throws Made, One Half

    12—Rick Barry, San Francisco vs. Philadelphia, April 24, 1967
       Dennis Johnson, Boston vs. Los Angeles, June 12, 1984

Most Free Throws Made, One Quarter

    9—Frank Ramsey, Boston vs. Minneapolis, April 4, 1959

Most Free Throw Attempts, Game

    24—Bob Pettit, St. Louis at Boston, April 9, 1958
    22—Bob Pettit, St. Louis vs. Boston, April 11, 1957
    21—Elgin Baylor, Los Angeles at Boston, April 18, 1962 (ot)

Most Free Throw Attempts, One Half

    15—Bill Russell, Boston vs. St. Louis, April 11, 1961

Most Free Throw Attempts, One Quarter

    11—Bob Pettit, St. Louis at Boston, April 9, 1958
       Wilt Chamberlain, Philadelphia vs. San Francisco, April 16, 1967

REBOUNDS

Most Rebounds, Game

    40—Bill Russell, Boston vs. St. Louis, March 29, 1960
       Bill Russell, Boston vs. Los Angeles, April 18, 1962 (ot)
    38—Bill Russell, Boston vs. St. Louis, April 11, 1961
       Bill Russell, Boston vs. Los Angeles, April 16, 1963
       Wilt Chamberlain, San Francisco vs. Boston, April 24, 1964
       Wilt Chamberlain, Philadelphia vs. San Francisco, April 16, 1967

Most Rebounds, Rookie, Game

    32—Bill Russell, Boston vs. St. Louis, April 13, 1957 (2 ot)
    25—Bill Russell, Boston vs. St. Louis, March 31, 1957
    23—Bill Russell, Boston vs. St. Louis, April 9, 1957
       Bill Russell, Boston at St. Louis, April 11, 1957
       Tom Heinsohn, Boston vs. St. Louis, April 13, 1957 (2 ot)

Highest Average, Rebounds per Game, One Championship Series

    29.5—Bill Russell, Boston vs. Minneapolis, 1959 (118/4)
    28.8—Bill Russell, Boston vs. St. Louis, 1961 (144/5)
    28.5—Wilt Chamberlain, Philadelphia vs. San Francisco, 1967 (171/6)

Highest Average, Rebounds per Game, Rookie, One Championship Series

    22.9—Bill Russell, Boston vs. St. Louis, 1957 (160/7)
    13.0—Nate Thurmond, San Francisco vs. Boston, 1964 (65/5)
    12.6—Tom Heinsohn, Boston vs. St. Louis, 1957 (88/7)

Most Consecutive Games, 20+ Rebounds

    15—Bill Russell, Boston, April 9, 1960—April 16, 1963
    12—Wilt Chamberlain, San Francisco—Philadelphia—Los Angeles, April 18, 1964—April 23, 1969

Most Consecutive Games, 30+ Rebounds

    3—Bill Russell, Boston, April 5, 1959—April 9, 1959
    2—Bill Russell, Boston, April 9, 1960—April 2, 1961
       Wilt Chamberlain, Philadelphia, April 14, 1967—April 16, 1967
       Wilt Chamberlain, Los Angeles, April 29, 1969—May 1, 1969

20+ Rebounds in All Championship Series Games

    Bill Russell, Boston vs. Minneapolis, 1959 (4-game series)
    Bill Russell, Boston vs. St. Louis, 1961 (5-game series)

Bill Russell, Boston vs. Los Angeles, 1962 (7-game series)
Wilt Chamberlain, San Francisco vs. Boston, 1964 (5-game series)
Wilt Chamberlain, Philadelphia vs. San Francisco, 1967 (6-game series)
Nate Thurmond, San Francisco vs. Philadelphia, 1967 (6-game series)

Most Rebounds, One Half

26—Wilt Chamberlain, Philadelphia vs. San Francisco, April 16, 1967

Most Rebounds, One Quarter

19—Bill Russell, Boston vs. Los Angeles, April 18, 1962

Most Offensive Rebounds, Game

11—Elvin Hayes, Washington at Seattle, May 27, 1979
10—Marvin Webster, Seattle vs. Washington, June 7, 1978
     Robert Reid, Houston vs. Boston, May 10, 1981
     Moses Malone, Houston vs. Boston, May 14, 1981

Most Defensive Rebounds, Game

20—Bill Walton, Portland at Philadelphia, June 3, 1977
     Bill Walton, Portland vs. Philadelphia, June 5, 1977
18—Dave Cowens, Boston vs. Phoenix, May 23, 1976

ASSISTS

Most Assists, Game

21—Magic Johnson, Los Angeles vs. Boston, June 3, 1984
20—Magic Johnson, L.A. Lakers vs. Boston, June 4, 1987
     Magic Johnson, L.A. Lakers vs. Chicago, June 12, 1991

Highest Average, Assists per Game, One Championship Series

14.0—Magic Johnson, L.A. Lakers vs. Boston, 1985 (84/6)
13.6—Magic Johnson, Los Angeles vs. Boston, 1984 (95/7)

Most Assists, Rookie, Game

11—Magic Johnson, Los Angeles vs. Philadelphia, May 7, 1980
10—Tom Gola, Philadelphia vs. Ft. Wayne, March 31, 1956
     Walt Hazzard, Los Angeles at Boston, April 25, 1965
     Magic Johnson, Los Angeles vs. Philadelphia, May 4, 1980
     Magic Johnson, Los Angeles vs. Philadelphia, May 14, 1980

Highest Average, Assists per Game, Rookie, One Championship Series

8.7—Magic Johnson, Los Angeles vs. Philadelphia, 1980 (52/6)
6.0—Tom Gola, Philadelphia vs. Ft. Wayne, 1956 (30/5)
5.2—Walt Hazzard, Los Angeles vs. Boston, 1965 (26/5)

Most Consecutive Games, 10+ Assists

13—Magic Johnson, L.A. Lakers, June 3, 1984—June 4, 1987
 6—Magic Johnson, Los Angeles, June 8, 1982—May 27, 1984

Most Assists, One Half

14—Magic Johnson, L.A. Lakers vs. Detroit, June 19, 1988
13—Robert Reid, Houston vs. Boston, June 5, 1986
     Magic Johnson, L.A. Lakers vs. Boston, June 4, 1987

Most Assists, One Quarter

8—Bob Cousy, Boston vs. St. Louis, April 9, 1957
     Magic Johnson, Los Angeles vs. Boston, June 3, 1984
     Robert Reid, Houston vs. Boston, June 5, 1986
     Michael Cooper, L.A. Lakers vs. Boston, June 4, 1987
     Magic Johnson, L.A. Lakers vs. Boston, June 4, 1987
     Magic Johnson, L.A. Lakers at Detroit, June 16, 1988
     Magic Johnson, L.A. Lakers vs. Detroit, June 19, 1988

PERSONAL FOULS

Most Minutes Played, No Personal Fouls, Game

50—Jo Jo White, Boston at Milwaukee, April 30, 1974 (ot)
48—Bill Russell, Boston at St. Louis, April 3, 1960
     Bill Russell, Boston at Los Angeles, April 17, 1963
     Wilt Chamberlain, Los Angeles vs. Boston, May 1, 1969
     Magic Johnson, L.A. Lakers vs. Chicago, June 12, 1991

DISQUALIFICATIONS

Most Consecutive Games Disqualified

5—Art Hillhouse, Philadelphia, 1947
     Charlie Scott, Boston, 1976
4—Arnie Risen, Boston, 1957

Fewest Minutes Played, Disqualified Player, Game

9—Bob Harrison, Minneapolis vs. New York, April 13, 1952
10—Bob Harrison, Minneapolis vs. New York, April 4, 1953

STEALS

Most Steals, Game

    6—John Havlicek, Boston vs. Milwaukee, May 3, 1974
        Steve Mix, Philadelphia vs. Portland, May 22, 1977
        Maurice Cheeks, Philadelphia at Los Angeles, May 7, 1980
        Isiah Thomas, Detroit at L.A. Lakers, June 19, 1988

BLOCKED SHOTS

Most Blocked Shots, Game

    8—Bill Walton, Portland vs. Philadelphia, June 5, 1977
        Akeem Olajuwon, Houston vs. Boston, June 5, 1986
    7—Dennis Johnson, Seattle at Washington, May 28, 1978

TURNOVERS

Most Turnovers, Game

   10—Magic Johnson, Los Angeles vs. Philadelphia, May 14, 1980
    9—Magic Johnson, Los Angeles vs. Philadelphia, May 31, 1983

Most Minutes Played, No Turnovers, Game

  48—Rodney McCray, Houston vs. Boston, June 5, 1986
  47—Wes Unseld, Washington at Seattle, May 27, 1979
       Michael Cooper, Los Angeles vs. Boston, June 6, 1984 (ot)
  46—Dennis Johnson, Boston at L.A. Lakers, June 14, 1987
       Michael Cooper, L.A. Lakers vs. Detroit, June 13, 1989
       Horace Grant, Chicago vs. Portland, June 5, 1992 (ot)

Team Records
WON-LOST

Most Consecutive Games Won, All Championship Series

    5—Minneapolis, 1953-54
       Boston, 1959-60
       Los Angeles, 1972-73
       Detroit, 1989-90
       Chicago, 1991-92

Most Consecutive Games Won, One Championship Series

    4—Minneapolis vs. New York, 1953 (5-game series)
       Boston vs. Minneapolis, 1959 (4-game series)
       Milwaukee vs. Baltimore, 1971 (4-game series)
       Los Angeles vs. New York, 1972 (5-game series)
       New York vs. Los Angeles, 1973 (5-game series)
       Golden State vs. Washington, 1975 (4-game series)
       Portland vs. Philadelphia, 1977 (6-game series)
       Seattle vs. Washington, 1979 (5-game series)
       Philadelphia vs. Los Angeles, 1983 (4-game series)
       Detroit vs. L.A. Lakers, 1989 (4-game series)
       Chicago vs. L.A. Lakers, 1991 (5-game series)

Most Consecutive Games Won at Home, All Championship Series

    7—Minneapolis, 1949-52
    6—Boston, 1960-62
       Boston, 1964-65
       Syracuse/Philadelphia, 1955-67

Most Consecutive Games Won at Home, One Championship Series

    4—Syracuse vs. Ft. Wayne, 1955 (7-game series)

Most Consecutive Games Won on Road, All Championship Series

    5—Detroit, 1989-90
    4—Minneapolis, 1953-54
       Chicago, 1991-92

Most Consecutive Games Won on Road, One Championship Series

    3—Minneapolis vs. New York, 1953 (5-game series)
       Detroit vs. Portland, 1990 (5-game series)
       Chicago vs. L.A. Lakers, 1991 (5-game series)

Most Consecutive Games Lost, All Championship Series

    9—Baltimore/Washington, 1971-78
    5—Minneapolis/Los Angeles, 1959-62
       New York, 1972-73
       Philadelphia, 1977-80

Most Consecutive Games Lost at Home, All Championship Series

    5—L.A. Lakers, 1989-91 (current)
       Portland, 1990-92
    4—Baltimore/Washington, 1971-75

Most Consecutive Games Lost on Road, All Championship Series

    7—Ft. Wayne, 1955-56
    5—Philadelphia, 1947-56
       St. Louis, 1960-61
       Syracuse/Philadelphia, 1954-67
       Los Angeles, 1968-70
       Baltimore/Washington, 1971-78

SCORING

Most Points, Game

    148—Boston vs. L.A. Lakers (114), May 27, 1985
    142—Boston vs. Los Angeles (110), April 18, 1965
    141—Philadelphia vs. San Francisco (135), April 14, 1967 (ot)
         L.A. Lakers vs. Boston (122), June 4, 1987

Fewest Points, Game

    71—Syracuse vs. Ft. Wayne (74) at Indianapolis, April 7, 1955
       Houston vs. Boston (94), May 9, 1981
    74—Ft. Wayne vs. Syracuse (71) at Indianapolis, April 7, 1955
    80—Phoenix vs. Boston (87) June 6, 1976

Most Points, Both Teams, Game

    276—Philadelphia (141) vs. San Francisco (135), April 14, 1967 (ot)
    263—L.A. Lakers (141) vs. Boston (122), June 4, 1987

Fewest Points, Both Teams, Game

    145—Syracuse (71) vs. Ft. Wayne (74) at Indianapolis, April 7, 1955
    165—Houston (71) vs. Boston (94), May 9, 1981

Largest Margin of Victory, Game

    35—Washington vs. Seattle, June 4, 1978 (117-82)
    34—Boston vs. St. Louis, April 2, 1961 (129-95)
       Boston vs. L.A. Lakers, May 27, 1985 (148-114)
    33—Boston vs. Los Angeles, April 25, 1965 (129-96)
       Philadelphia vs. Los Angeles, June 6, 1982 (135-102)
       Los Angeles vs. Boston, June 3, 1984 (137-104)
       Chicago vs. Portland, June 3, 1992 (122-89)

BY HALF

Most Points, First Half

    79—Boston vs. L.A. Lakers, May 27, 1985
    76—Boston vs. St. Louis, March 27, 1960

Fewest Points, First Half

    30—Houston vs. Boston, May 9, 1981
    31—Syracuse vs. Ft. Wayne at Indianapolis, April 7, 1955

Most Points, Both Teams, First Half

    140—San Francisco (72) vs. Philadelphia (68), April 24, 1967
    138—Philadelphia (73) vs. San Francisco (65), April 14, 1967

Fewest Points, Both Teams, First Half

    69—Syracuse (31) vs. Ft. Wayne (38) at Indianapolis, April 7, 1955
    71—Phoenix (33) vs. Boston (38), June 6, 1976
       Houston (30) vs. Boston (41), May 9, 1981

Largest Lead at Halftime

    30—Boston vs. L.A. Lakers, May 27, 1985 (led 79-49; won 148-114)
    27—New York vs. Los Angeles, May 8, 1970 (led 69-42; won 113-99)

Largest Deficit at Halftime, Overcome to Win Game

    21—Baltimore at Philadelphia, April 13, 1948 (trailed 20-41; won 66-63)
    14—New York at Los Angeles, April 29, 1970 (trailed 42-56; won 111-108 in ot)
       Golden State at Washington, May 18, 1975 (trailed 40-54; won 101-95)
       Philadelphia at Los Angeles, May 31, 1983 (trailed 51-65; won 115-108)

Most Points, Second Half

    81—Philadelphia vs. Los Angeles, June 6, 1982
    80—Los Angeles vs. Boston, June 3, 1984

Fewest Points, Second Half

    30—Washington vs. Seattle, May 24, 1979
    31—St. Louis vs. Boston, April 2, 1960

Most Points, Both Teams, Second Half

139—Boston (78) vs. Los Angeles (61), April 18, 1965
138—Los Angeles (71) at Boston (67), April 21, 1963
      Los Angeles (80) vs. Boston (58), June 3, 1984

Fewest Points, Both Teams, Second Half

73—Washington (30) vs. Seattle (43), May 24, 1979
76—Ft. Wayne (38) at Syracuse (38), March 31, 1955
      Ft. Wayne (36) vs. Syracuse (40) at Indianapolis, April 7, 1955

BY QUARTER, OVERTIME PERIOD

Most Points, First Quarter

43—Philadelphia vs. San Francisco, April 14, 1967
      Philadelphia at San Francisco, April 24, 1967
41—San Francisco vs. Philadelphia, April 24, 1967

Fewest Points, First Quarter

13—Ft. Wayne at Syracuse, April 2, 1955
      Milwaukee at Boston, May 3, 1974
15—Los Angeles at Boston, April 29, 1969
      Milwaukee vs. Boston, May 7, 1974
      Philadelphia vs. Portland, June 3, 1977

Most Points, Both Teams, First Quarter

84—Philadelphia (43) at San Francisco (41), April 24, 1967
73—Philadelphia (43) vs. San Francisco (30), April 14, 1967

Fewest Points, Both Teams, First Quarter

31—Los Angeles (15) at Boston (16), April 29, 1969
33—Ft. Wayne (13) at Syracuse (20), April 2, 1955

Largest Lead at End of First Quarter

20—Los Angeles vs. New York, May 6, 1970 (led 36-16; won 135-113)
19—San Francisco vs. Boston, April 22, 1964 (led 40-21; won 115-91)
      Boston vs. Milwaukee, May 3, 1974 (led 32-13; won 95-83)

Largest Deficit at End of First Quarter, Overcome to Win

14—Los Angeles at Boston, April 17, 1966 (trailed 20-34; won 133-129 in ot)
12—Detroit at L.A. Lakers, June 13, 1989 (trailed 23-35; won 105-97)

Most Points, Second Quarter

46—Boston vs. St. Louis, March 27, 1960
43—Los Angeles at Boston, April 8, 1962

Fewest Points, Second Quarter

12—Boston vs. Milwaukee, May 5, 1974
13—Syracuse vs. Ft. Wayne at Indianapolis, April 7, 1955
      Phoenix vs. Boston, June 6, 1976
      Houston vs. Boston, May 9, 1981

Most Points, Both Teams, Second Quarter

73—St. Louis (38) vs. Boston (35), April 8, 1961
      Boston (38) vs. Los Angeles (35), April 14, 1962
72—St. Louis (42) at Boston (30), March 29, 1958
      Boston (46) vs. St. Louis (26), March 27, 1960

Fewest Points, Both Teams, Second Quarter

29—Syracuse (13) vs. Ft. Wayne (16) at Indianapolis, April 7, 1955
31—Phoenix (13) vs. Boston (18), June 6, 1976

Most Points, Third Quarter

47—Los Angeles vs. Boston, June 3, 1984
41—Portland vs. Philadelphia, May 31, 1977
      Los Angeles at Philadelphia, May 27, 1982

Fewest Points, Third Quarter

11—New York at Los Angeles, April 30, 1972
12—Boston at St. Louis, April 7, 1960
      Boston at L.A. Lakers, June 14, 1987

Most Points, Both Teams, Third Quarter

80—Los Angeles (47) vs. Boston (33), June 3, 1984
75—Boston (40) vs. Los Angeles (35), April 21, 1963

Fewest Points, Both Teams, Third Quarter

31—Portland (15) vs. Chicago (16), June 7, 1992
33—Washington (14) vs. Seattle (19), May 24, 1979

Largest Lead at End of Third Quarter

    36—Chicago vs. Portland, June 3, 1992 (led 104-68; won 122-89)
    31—Portland vs. Philadelphia, May 31, 1977 (led 98-67; won 130-98)

Largest Deficit at End of Third Quarter, Overcome to Win

    15—Chicago vs. Portland, June 14, 1992 (trailed 64-79; won 97-93)
    12—San Francisco at Philadelphia, April 23, 1967 (trailed 84-96; won 117-109)

Most Points, Fourth Quarter

    44—Philadelphia vs. Los Angeles, June 6, 1982
    42—Boston vs. Los Angeles, April 25, 1965
         Portland vs. Philadelphia, May 29, 1977

Fewest Points, Fourth Quarter

    13—Philadelphia vs. San Francisco, April 23, 1967
         Milwaukee vs. Boston, April 30, 1974
         L.A. Lakers at Detroit, June 8, 1989
    14—Boston at St. Louis, April 11, 1957
         St. Louis vs. Boston, April 2, 1960
         Houston at Boston, May 5, 1981
         Portland at Chicago, June 14, 1992

Most Points, Both Teams, Fourth Quarter

    76—Philadelphia (38) at Los Angeles (38), June 1, 1982
    75—Boston (40) vs. L.A. Lakers (35), May 27, 1985

Fewest Points, Both Teams, Fourth Quarter

    33—Boston (14) at St. Louis (19), April 11, 1957
    35—Ft. Wayne (17) at Syracuse (18), April 10, 1955
         Houston (16) vs. Boston (19), May 10, 1981

Most Points, Overtime Period

    22—Los Angeles vs. New York, May 1, 1970
    18—Portland at Chicago, June 5, 1992

Fewest Points, Overtime Period

    4—Boston vs. Milwaukee, May 10, 1974
        Milwaukee at Boston, May 10, 1974
        L.A. Lakers vs. Chicago, June 7, 1991
    6—Los Angeles vs. New York, April 29, 1970
        Boston at Milwaukee, April 30, 1974
        Boston vs. Phoenix, June 4, 1976
        Phoenix at Boston, June 4, 1976

Most Points, Both Teams, Overtime Period

    38—Los Angeles (22) vs. New York (16), May 1, 1970
    30—Boston (16) vs. Phoenix (14), June 4, 1976

Fewest Points, Both Teams, Overtime Period

    8—Boston (4) vs. Milwaukee (4), May 10, 1974
    12—Boston (6) vs. Phoenix (6), June 4, 1976

100-POINT GAMES

Most Consecutive Games, 100+ Points, All Championship Series

    20—Minneapolis/Los Angeles, 1959-65
         L.A. Lakers, 1983-87
    19—Boston, 1981-86
    18—Philadelphia, 1977-83 (current)

Most Consecutive Games Scoring Fewer Than 100 Points, All Championship Series

    6—Houston, 1981
    5—Boston, 1974
        Seattle, 1978-79
        Boston, 1976-81
        L.A. Lakers, 1989-91

PLAYERS SCORING

Most Players, 30+ Points, Game

    2—Accomplished 25 times. Most recent:
        Chicago at L.A. Lakers, June 12, 1991

Most Players, 30+ Points, Both Teams, Game

    3—Los Angeles (2) vs. Boston (1), April 16, 1962
        Los Angeles (2) at Boston (1), April 18, 1962 (ot)
        Los Angeles (2) vs. Boston (1), April 17, 1963
        Los Angeles (2) at Boston (1), April 21, 1963
        Los Angeles (2) at Boston (1), April 24, 1966

Philadelphia (2) vs. San Francisco (1), April 14, 1967 (ot)
Philadelphia (2) at San Francisco (1), April 20, 1967
Los Angeles (2) vs. Boston (1), April 25, 1969
Portland (2) vs. Detroit (1), June 12, 1990

Most Players, 20+ Points, Game

5—Boston vs. Los Angeles, April 19, 1965
    L.A. Lakers vs. Boston, June 4, 1987
    Boston vs. L.A. Lakers, June 11, 1987
4—By many teams.

Most Players, 20+ Points, Both Teams, Game

8—Boston (4) at Los Angeles (4), April 26, 1966
    L.A. Lakers (5) vs. Boston (3), June 4, 1987
7—Boston (5) vs. Los Angeles (2), April 19, 1965
    Philadelphia (4) vs. San Francisco (3), April 14, 1967 (ot)
    Boston (4) vs. Los Angeles (3), April 30, 1968 (ot)
    Philadelphia (4) at Los Angeles (3), May 31, 1983
    Los Angeles (4) vs. Boston (3), June 10, 1984
    Boston (4) at L.A. Lakers (3), June 7, 1985

Most Players, 10+ Points, Game

8—Boston vs. Los Angeles, May 31, 1984 (ot)
7—Accomplished 16 times. Most recent:
    Detroit at Portland, June 10, 1990

Most Players, 10+ Points, Both Teams, Game

14—Boston (7) vs. St. Louis (7), March 27, 1960
13—Los Angeles (7) at Boston (6), April 19, 1966
    Boston (8) vs. Los Angeles (5), May 31, 1984 (ot)

Fewest Players, 10+ Points, Game

2—Ft. Wayne vs. Philadelphia, April 1, 1956
    St. Louis at Boston, March 29, 1958
    St. Louis vs. Boston, April 12, 1958
    Los Angeles at Boston, April 29, 1969
    Chicago vs. L.A. Lakers, June 2, 1991
    Chicago at Portland, June 10, 1992

Fewest Players, 10+ Points, Both Teams, Game

5—Ft. Wayne (2) vs. Philadelphia (3), April 1, 1956
    Los Angeles (2) at Boston (3), April 29, 1969
6—Boston (3) vs. Los Angeles (3), April 18, 1962 (ot)
    Boston (3) at Los Angeles (3), April 25, 1969
    Baltimore (3) at Milwaukee (3), April 21, 1971
    Golden State (3) vs. Washington (3), May 20, 1975
    Chicago (2) vs. L.A. Lakers (4), June 2, 1991
    Chicago (2) at Portland (4), June 10, 1992

FIELD GOAL PERCENTAGE

Highest Field Goal Percentage, Game

.617—Chicago vs. L.A. Lakers, June 5, 1991 (50/81)
.615—L.A. Lakers vs. Boston, June 4, 1987 (56-91)
.608—Boston vs. L.A. Lakers, May 27, 1985 (62-102)

Lowest Field Goal Percentage, Game

.275—Syracuse vs. Ft. Wayne at Indianapolis, April 7, 1955 (25-91)
.280—Ft. Wayne vs. Syracuse at Indianapolis, April 7, 1955 (23-82)
.293—Boston at St. Louis, April 6, 1957 (29-99)
.295—San Francisco at Philadelphia, April 16, 1967 (38-129)
.302—Boston vs. St. Louis, April 9, 1958 (32-106)

Highest Field Goal Percentage, Both Teams, Game

.582—L.A. Lakers (.615) vs. Boston (.548), June 4, 1987 (107-184)
.553—L.A. Lakers (.556) vs. Boston (.549), June 2, 1987 (100-181)

Lowest Field Goal Percentage, Both Teams, Game

.277—Syracuse (.275) vs. Ft. Wayne (.280) at Indianapolis, April 7, 1955 (48-173)
.312—Boston (.304) at St. Louis (.320), April 11, 1957 (68-218)

Highest Field Goal Percentage, One Half

.706—Philadelphia vs. Los Angeles, June 6, 1982 (36/51)
.667—Philadelphia at Los Angeles, May 7, 1980 (26/39)
    Philadelphia at Los Angeles, June 8, 1982 (30/45)
    Los Angeles vs. Boston, June 6, 1984 (28/42)
.659—Chicago vs. L.A. Lakers, June 5, 1991 (27/41)

Highest Field Goal Percentage, One Quarter

.850—Chicago vs. L.A. Lakers, June 5, 1991 (17/20)

.824—Detroit vs. L.A. Lakers, June 6, 1989 (14/17)
.813—Los Angeles vs. Boston, June 6, 1984 (13/16)
      Boston at Houston, June 3, 1986 (13/16)

FIELD GOALS

Most Field Goals, Game

    62—Boston vs. L.A. Lakers, May 27, 1985
    61—Boston vs. St. Louis, March 27, 1960

Fewest Field Goals, Game

    23—Ft. Wayne vs. Syracuse at Indianapolis, April 7, 1955
    25—Syracuse vs. Ft. Wayne at Indianapolis, April 7, 1955

Most Field Goals, Both Teams, Game

    112—Philadelphia (57) vs. San Francisco (55), April 14, 1967 (ot)
    111—Boston (62) vs. L.A. Lakers (49), May 27, 1985

Fewest Field Goals, Both Teams, Game

    48—Ft. Wayne (23) vs. Syracuse (25) at Indianapolis, April 7, 1955
    57—Syracuse (26) vs. Ft. Wayne (31) at Indianapolis, April 3, 1955

FIELD GOAL ATTEMPTS

Most Field Goal Attempts, Game

    140—San Francisco at Philadelphia, April 14, 1967 (ot)
    133—Boston vs. St. Louis, March 27, 1960

Fewest Field Goal Attempts, Game

    66—Los Angeles at New York, May 4, 1970
        L.A. Lakers at Chicago, June 2, 1991
    70—Detroit at L.A. Lakers, June 13, 1989

Most Field Goal Attempts, Both Teams, Game

    256—San Francisco (140) at Philadelphia (116), April 14, 1967 (ot)
    250—Boston (130) vs. Minneapolis (120), April 4, 1959

Fewest Field Goal Attempts, Both Teams, Game

    146—L.A. Lakers (66) at Chicago (80), June 2, 1991
    149—Detroit (70) at L.A. Lakers (79), June 13, 1989

THREE-POINT FIELD GOALS MADE

Most Three-Point Field Goals Made, Game

    8—Detroit vs. Portland, June 7, 1990 (ot)
    7—Boston vs. L.A. Lakers, May 27, 1985
       Detroit at Portland, June 12, 1990
       Chicago vs. Portland, June 3, 1992

Most Three-Point Field Goals Made, Both Teams, Game

    10—Boston (6) vs. L.A. Lakers (4), June 11, 1987
    9—Boston (7) vs. L.A. Lakers (2), May 27, 1985
       Detroit (8) vs. Portland (1), June 7, 1990 (ot)
       Portland (5) vs. Detroit (4), June 14, 1990

THREE-POINT FIELD GOAL ATTEMPTS

Most Three-Point Field Goal Attempts, Game

    16—Detroit at Portland, June 12, 1990
    15—L.A. Lakers at Detroit, June 8, 1989
       Chicago vs. Portland, June 3, 1992
       Chicago vs. Portland, June 5, 1992 (ot)

Most Three-Point Field Goal Attempts, Both Teams, Game

    27—Chicago (15) vs. Portland (12), June 5, 1992 (ot)
    23—L.A. Lakers (15) at Detroit (8), June 8, 1989
       Portland (13) vs. Detroit (10), June 10, 1990

FREE THROW PERCENTAGE

Highest Free Throw Percentage, Game

    1.000—Portland at Chicago, June 14, 1992 (21-21)
    .958—Boston vs. Houston, May 29, 1986 (23-24)

Lowest Free Throw Percentage, Game

    .444—Philadelphia vs. San Francisco, April 16, 1967 (16-36)
       Golden State at Washington, May 25, 1975 (8-18)
    .476—Baltimore at Milwaukee, April 21, 1971 (10-21)

Highest Free Throw Percentage, Both Teams, Game

.933—L.A. Lakers (.955) at Chicago (.875), June 5, 1991 (28/30)
.903—Boston (.926) vs. Los Angeles (.889), April 14, 1962 (65-72)

Lowest Free Throw Percentage, Both Teams, Game

.538—Philadelphia (.444) vs. San Francisco (.655), April 16, 1967 (35-65)
.541—San Francisco (.478) at Boston (.615), April 18, 1964 (46-85)

FREE THROWS MADE

Most Free Throws Made, Game

45—St. Louis at Boston, April 13, 1957 (2 ot)
44—St. Louis at Boston, April 9, 1958

Fewest Free Throws Made, Game

3—Los Angeles at Philadelphia, May 26, 1983
7—Chicago vs. L.A. Lakers, June 5, 1991

Most Free Throws Made, Both Teams, Game

80—St. Louis (44) at Boston (36), April 9, 1958
77—Syracuse (39) vs. Ft. Wayne (38), April 9, 1955
    Boston (43) at St. Louis (34), April 12, 1958

Fewest Free Throws Made, Both Teams, Game

23—Milwaukee (9) vs. Boston (14), April 28, 1974
25—Baltimore (11) vs. Milwaukee (14), April 25, 1971
    Golden State (8) at Washington (17), May 25, 1975

FREE THROW ATTEMPTS

Most Free Throw Attempts, Game

64—Philadelphia at San Francisco, April 24, 1967
62—St. Louis at Boston, April 13, 1957 (2 ot)

Fewest Free Throw Attempts, Game

5—Los Angeles at Philadelphia, May 26, 1983
8—Chicago vs. L.A. Lakers, June 5, 1991

Most Free Throw Attempts, Both Teams, Game

116—St. Louis (62) at Boston (54), April 13, 1957 (2 ot)
107—Boston (60) at St. Louis (47), April 2, 1958
    St. Louis (57) at Boston (50), April 9, 1958

Fewest Free Throw Attempts, Both Teams, Game

30—Chicago (8) vs. L.A. Lakers (22), June 5, 1991
31—Milwaukee (13) vs. Boston (18), April 28, 1974

TOTAL REBOUNDS

Highest Rebound Percentage, Game

.667—Boston vs. St. Louis, April 9, 1960 (78-117)
.632—Los Angeles vs. New York, May 7, 1972 (67-106)

Most Rebounds, Game

93—Philadelphia vs. San Francisco, April 16, 1967
86—Boston vs. Minneapolis, April 4, 1959

Fewest Rebounds, Game

29—L.A. Lakers vs. Chicago, June 7, 1991 (ot)
31—L.A. Lakers at Detroit, June 16, 1988
    Chicago at Portland, June 14, 1992

Most Rebounds, Both Teams, Game

169—Philadelphia (93) vs. San Francisco (76), April 16, 1967
159—San Francisco (80) at Philadelphia (79), April 14, 1967 (ot)

Fewest Rebounds, Both Teams, Game

69—Detroit (34) at L.A. Lakers (35), June 7, 1988
    Chicago (31) at Portland (38), June 14, 1992
70—L.A. Lakers (34) at Chicago (36), June 5, 1991

OFFENSIVE REBOUNDS

Highest Offensive Rebound Percentage, Game

.556—Detroit vs. L.A. Lakers, June 16, 1988 (20-36)
.529—Seattle vs. Washington, June 7, 1978 (27-51)

Most Offensive Rebounds, Game

28—Houston vs. Boston, May 10, 1981
27—Seattle vs. Washington, June 7, 1978
    Boston at Los Angeles, June 6, 1984

Fewest Offensive Rebounds, Game

3—Boston vs. L.A. Lakers, May 30, 1985
5—Philadelphia at Los Angeles, May 7, 1980

Philadelphia vs. Los Angeles, May 11, 1980
Boston at L.A. Lakers, June 2, 1987
L.A. Lakers at Detroit, June 12, 1988

Most Offensive Rebounds, Both Teams, Game

45—Houston (28) vs. Boston (17), May 10, 1981
44—Seattle (27) vs. Washington (17), June 7, 1978
    Boston (25) vs. Houston (19), May 5, 1981

Fewest Offensive Rebounds, Both Teams, Game

15—L.A. Lakers (6) at Chicago (9), June 2, 1991
17—L.A. Lakers (14) at Boston (3), May 30, 1985
    L.A. Lakers (8) at Detroit (9), June 6, 1989

DEFENSIVE REBOUNDS

Highest Defensive Rebound Percentage, Game

.921—L.A. Lakers at Boston, May 30, 1985 (35-38)
.881—Los Angeles vs. Philadelphia, May 7, 1980 (37-42)

Most Defensive Rebounds, Game

48—Portland at Philadelphia, June 3, 1977
46—Philadelphia vs. Portland, May 26, 1977

Fewest Defensive Rebounds, Game

16—L.A. Lakers at Detroit, June 16, 1988
20—Philadelphia vs. Portland, May 22, 1977
    L.A. Lakers at Chicago, June 5, 1991
    L.A. Lakers vs. Chicago, June 7, 1991 (ot)

Most Defensive Rebounds, Both Teams, Game

84—Portland (48) at Philadelphia (36), June 3, 1977
82—Philadelphia (46) vs. Portland (36), May 26, 1977

Fewest Defensive Rebounds, Both Teams, Game

43—L.A. Lakers (21) at Detroit (22), June 8, 1989
45—L.A. Lakers (20) at Chicago (25), June 5, 1991

ASSISTS

Most Assists, Game

44—Los Angeles vs. New York, May 6, 1970
    L.A. Lakers vs. Boston, June 4, 1987
43—Boston vs. L.A. Lakers, May 27, 1985

Fewest Assists, Game

5—Boston at St. Louis, April 3, 1960
9—Los Angeles at Boston, April 28, 1966

Most Assists, Both Teams, Game

79—L.A. Lakers (44) vs. Boston (35), June 4, 1987
76—L.A. Lakers (40) vs. Boston (36), June 7, 1985

Fewest Assists, Both Teams, Game

21—Los Angeles (10) at Boston (11), April 29, 1969
24—Los Angeles (10) at Boston (14), May 3, 1969

PERSONAL FOULS

Most Personal Fouls, Game

42—Minneapolis vs. Syracuse, April 23, 1950
40—Portland vs. Philadelphia, May 31, 1977

Fewest Personal Fouls, Game

13—L.A. Lakers at Detroit, June 12, 1988
15—L.A. Lakers at Chicago, June 5, 1991

Most Personal Fouls, Both Teams, Game

77—Minneapolis (42) vs. Syracuse (35), April 23, 1950
76—Minneapolis (39) at New York (37), April 18, 1952 (ot)

Fewest Personal Fouls, Both Teams, Game

35—Boston (17) at Milwaukee (18), April 28, 1974
    Boston (17) at Houston (18), June 3, 1986
    L.A. Lakers (15) at Chicago (20), June 5, 1991
36—Baltimore (17) vs. Milwaukee (19), April 25, 1971
    Boston (17) vs. Houston (19), May 26, 1986
    L.A. Lakers (13) at Detroit (23), June 12, 1988

DISQUALIFICATIONS

Most Disqualificiations, Game

4—Minneapolis vs. Syracuse, April 23, 1950
    Minneapolis vs. New York, April 4, 1953
    New York vs. Minneapolis, April 10, 1953

St. Louis at Boston, April 13, 1957 (2 ot)
Boston vs. Los Angeles, April 18, 1962 (ot)

Most Disqualifications, Both Teams, Game

7—Boston (4) vs. Los Angeles (3), April 18, 1962 (ot)
6—St. Louis (4) at Boston (2), April 13, 1957 (2 ot)

STEALS

Most Steals, Game

17—Golden State vs. Washington, May 23, 1975
16—Philadelphia vs. Portland, May 22, 1977

Fewest Steals, Game

1—Milwaukee at Boston, May 10, 1974 (2 ot)
    Boston vs. Phoenix, May 23, 1976
2—Milwaukee at Boston, May 3, 1974
    Milwaukee at Boston, May 5, 1974
    Milwaukee vs. Boston, May 12, 1974
    Detroit vs. L.A. Lakers, June 6, 1989
    Detroit vs. Portland, June 7, 1990 (ot)

Most Steals, Both Teams, Game

31—Golden State (17) vs. Washington (14), May 23, 1975
28—Golden State (15) at Washington (13), May 25, 1975

Fewest Steals, Both Teams, Game

6—Detroit (3) vs. L.A. Lakers (3), June 8, 1989
    L.A. Lakers (3) vs. Detroit (3), June 13, 1989
8—Milwaukee (2) at Boston (6), May 5, 1974
    Milwaukee (1) at Boston (7), May 10, 1974 (2 ot)
    Seattle (4) vs. Washington (4), June 2, 1978
    Seattle (4) vs. Washington (4), May 29, 1979 (ot)
    Chicago (4) at L.A. Lakers (4), June 9, 1991

BLOCKED SHOTS

Most Blocked Shots, Game

13—Seattle at Washington, May 28, 1978
    Philadelphia at Los Angeles, May 4, 1980
    Philadelphia vs. Los Angeles, June 6, 1982
    Philadelphia at Los Angeles, May 22, 1983
    Houston vs. Boston, June 5, 1986
12—Golden State vs. Washington, May 20, 1975

Fewest Blocked Shots, Game

0—Boston vs. Milwaukee, May 5, 1974
    Boston vs. Milwaukee, May 10, 1974 (2 ot)
    Boston vs. Phoenix, June 4, 1976 (3 ot)
    Philadelphia vs. Portland, May 22, 1977
    Washington at Seattle, May 21, 1978
    Boston at Houston, May 14, 1981
    L.A. Lakers vs. Boston, June 5, 1985
    L.A. Lakers vs. Detroit, June 7, 1988

Most Blocked Shots, Both Teams, Game

22—Philadelphia (13) at Los Angeles (9), May 4, 1980
    Philadelphia (13) vs. Los Angeles (9), June 6, 1982
21—Philadelphia (13) vs. Los Angeles (8), May 22, 1983

Fewest Blocked Shots, Both Teams, Game

2—Boston (0) at Houston (2), May 14, 1981
3—Boston (0) vs. Milwaukee (3), May 5, 1974
    Boston (0) vs. Milwaukee (3), May 10, 1974 (2 ot)
    Boston (1) vs. Phoenix (2), May 23, 1976
    L.A. Lakers (1) vs. Detroit (2), June 21, 1988
    Chicago (1) vs. L.A. Lakers (2), June 5, 1991

TURNOVERS

Most Turnovers, Game

34—Portland at Philadelphia, May 22, 1977
31—Golden State at Washington, May 25, 1975

Fewest Turnovers, Game

5—Chicago at L.A. Lakers, June 9, 1991
7—L.A. Lakers vs. Detroit, June 13, 1989

Most Turnovers, Both Teams, Game

60—Golden State (31) at Washington (29), May 25, 1975
54—Phoenix (29) at Boston (25), June 4, 1976 (3 ot)
    Portland (34) at Philadelphia (20), May 22, 1977

Fewest Turnovers, Both Teams, Game

15—Chicago (5) at L.A. Lakers (10), June 9, 1991
16—L.A. Lakers (7) vs. Detroit (9), June 13, 1989

YEAR-BY-YEAR REGULAR-SEASON, PLAYOFF REVIEWS

Including

Statistical team and individual wrapups of NBA regular-season play and playoffs ranging from the 1990-91 season back to the NBA's first year, 1946-47.

1990-91 NBA STATISTICS

1990-91 NBA CHAMPION CHICAGO BULLS

Front row (from left to right): Craig Hodges, John Paxson, Horace Grant, Bill Cartwright, Scottie Pippen, Michael Jordan, B.J. Armstrong. Middle row: trainer Chip Schaefer, Cliff Levingston, Scott Williams, Will Perdue, Stacey King, Dennis Hopson, Vice President of Basketball Operations Jerry Krause. Back row: assistant coach Jim Cleamons, assistant coach Tex Winter, head coach Phil Jackson, assistant coach John Bach, scout Jim Stack, scout Clarence Gaines Jr.

FINAL STANDINGS

ATLANTIC DIVISION

Team	Atl.	Bos.	Char.	Chi.	Cle.	Dal.	Den.	Det.	G.S.	Hou.	Ind.	L.A.C.	L.A.L.	Mia.	Mil.	Min.	N.J.	N.Y.	Orl.	Phi.	Pho.	Por.	Sac.	S.A.	Sea.	Uta.	Was.	W.	L.	Pct.	G.B.
Boston	1	..	3	2	3	2	2	2	1	2	2	2	1	4	2	2	4	5	1	2	1	1	2	1	2	1	5	56	26	.683	..
Philadelphia	4	3	2	3	2	1	2	2	0	0	3	2	1	4	2	0	3	1	2	..	1	1	0	1	0	1	3	44	38	.537	12
New York	1	0	4	0	1	0	1	3	0	0	2	2	1	4	0	1	5	..	0	5	0	0	2	1	1	2	3	39	43	.476	17
Washington	2	1	2	1	3	0	1	1	2	1	2	2	0	2	1	1	3	2	1	2	0	0	0	0	0	0	..	30	52	.366	26
New Jersey	1	1	2	1	2	0	1	1	1	0	1	1	0	3	2	1	..	0	1	2	1	0	1	0	1	0	2	26	56	.317	30
Miami	0	1	2	0	1	2	2	1	0	0	2	2	0	..	0	0	3	1	1	1	0	0	1	0	0	1	3	24	58	.293	32

CENTRAL DIVISION

Team	Atl.	Bos.	Char.	Chi.	Cle.	Dal.	Den.	Det.	G.S.	Hou.	Ind.	L.A.C.	L.A.L.	Mia.	Mil.	Min.	N.J.	N.Y.	Orl.	Phi.	Pho.	Por.	Sac.	S.A.	Sea.	Uta.	Was.	W.	L.	Pct.	G.B.
Chicago	4	2	5	..	5	2	2	2	3	1	0	4	2	1	4	4	2	3	4	2	1	1	0	2	0	2	3	61	21	.744	..
Detroit	5	2	4	2	3	2	2	..	2	3	2	0	3	2	2	3	1	2	2	0	1	2	0	1	2	0	3	50	32	.610	11
Milwaukee	3	2	3	1	3	1	1	3	1	0	3	0	3	..	1	2	4	..	1	2	4	2	2	1	1	1	3	48	34	.585	13
Atlanta	..	3	1	1	3	2	1	0	1	1	4	2	1	4	2	..	1	3	3	1	0	0	1	2	2	1	2	43	39	.524	18
Indiana	1	2	5	1	4	0	2	2	1	1	..	1	0	2	2	1	3	2	1	1	0	2	1	1	2	2	2	41	41	.500	20
Cleveland	2	1	4	0	..	2	1	2	0	0	1	1	1	3	2	1	2	3	2	2	0	0	1	0	1	0	1	33	49	.402	28
Charlotte	4	1	..	0	1	1	0	1	1	0	0	1	0	2	2	1	2	0	2	2	0	0	2	1	0	0	2	26	56	.317	35

MIDWEST DIVISION

Team	Atl.	Bos.	Char.	Chi.	Cle.	Dal.	Den.	Det.	G.S.	Hou.	Ind.	L.A.C.	L.A.L.	Mia.	Mil.	Min.	N.J.	N.Y.	Orl.	Phi.	Pho.	Por.	Sac.	S.A.	Sea.	Uta.	Was.	W.	L.	Pct.	G.B.
San Antonio	0	1	1	2	2	4	4	2	2	3	1	2	1	2	1	4	2	1	3	2	3	2	3	..	3	2	2	55	27	.671	..
Utah	1	1	2	0	2	5	3	2	3	2	0	3	2	1	1	4	2	0	4	2	2	1	3	3	3	..	2	54	28	.659	1
Houston	1	0	2	2	2	3	5	0	2	..	2	1	2	2	5	2	2	3	2	3	0	3	2	2	2	1	2	52	30	.634	3
Orlando	1	1	0	0	0	4	3	0	2	1	3	0	1	0	2	1	2	..	0	2	0	2	1	1	1	1	1	31	51	.378	24
Minnesota	1	0	1	0	1	4	2	0	1	0	1	1	1	2	1	..	1	1	2	2	0	0	3	0	2	1	1	29	53	.354	26
Dallas	0	0	1	0	0	..	3	0	2	1	2	1	2	0	1	1	2	2	1	1	0	1	2	1	2	0	2	28	54	.341	27
Denver	1	0	2	0	1	1	..	0	1	0	0	0	0	1	3	1	1	2	0	0	3	1	0	1	1	1	1	20	62	.244	35

PACIFIC DIVISION

Team	Atl.	Bos.	Char.	Chi.	Cle.	Dal.	Den.	Det.	G.S.	Hou.	Ind.	L.A.C.	L.A.L.	Mia.	Mil.	Min.	N.J.	N.Y.	Orl.	Phi.	Pho.	Por.	Sac.	S.A.	Sea.	Uta.	Was.	W.	L.	Pct.	G.B.
Portland	1	1	2	2	2	3	4	1	3	4	2	3	3	2	1	4	2	2	4	1	2	..	3	2	4	3	2	63	19	.768	..
L.A. Lakers	1	1	2	1	1	2	4	3	3	2	4	..	2	0	3	2	1	4	1	3	2	4	3	3	2	2	2	58	24	.707	5
Phoenix	2	1	2	1	2	4	4	2	3	1	1	3	..	1	2	2	1	4	2	2	1	3	3	1	3	2	2	55	27	.671	8
Golden State	1	1	1	1	2	2	3	1	..	2	1	3	2	2	1	3	1	2	2	2	1	2	2	3	1	0	4	44	38	.537	19
Seattle	1	0	2	0	1	2	4	1	1	2	1	3	2	2	1	1	3	1	3	0	4	1	2	1	..	2	2	41	41	.500	22
L.A. Clippers	0	0	1	0	1	3	4	0	2	2	1	..	0	0	1	3	1	0	1	0	2	1	3	2	2	1	0	31	51	.378	32
Sacramento	0	0	0	0	1	2	1	0	3	1	0	2	0	1	1	1	0	2	1	1	2	1	..	1	1	1	2	25	57	.305	38

HOME-ROAD RECORDS OF ALL TEAMS

Team	Home	Road	Total	Team	Home	Road	Total
Atlanta	29- 12	14- 27	43- 39	Milwaukee	33- 8	15- 26	48- 34
Boston	35- 6	21- 20	56- 26	Minnesota	21- 20	8- 33	29- 53
Charlotte	17- 24	9- 32	26- 56	New Jersey	20- 21	6- 35	26- 56
Chicago	35- 6	26- 15	61- 21	New York	21- 20	18- 23	39- 43
Cleveland	23- 18	10- 31	33- 49	Orlando	24- 17	7- 34	31- 51
Dallas	20- 21	8- 33	28- 54	Philadelphia	29- 12	15- 26	44- 38
Denver	17- 24	3- 38	20- 62	Phoenix	32- 9	23- 18	55- 27
Detroit	32- 9	18- 23	50- 32	Portland	36- 5	27- 14	63- 19
Golden State	30- 11	14- 27	44- 38	Sacramento	24- 17	1- 40	25- 57
Houston	31- 10	21- 20	52- 30	San Antonio	33- 8	22- 19	55- 27
Indiana	29- 12	12- 29	41- 41	Seattle	28- 13	13- 28	41- 41
L.A. Clippers	23- 18	8- 33	31- 51	Utah	36- 5	18- 23	54- 28
L.A. Lakers	33- 8	25- 16	58- 24	Washington	21- 20	9- 32	30- 52
Miami	18- 23	6- 35	24- 58	Totals	730- 377	377- 730	1107- 1107

OFFENSIVE TEAM STATISTICS

Team	G.	FIELD GOALS Att.	Made	Pct.	FREE THROWS Att.	Made	Pct.	REBOUNDS Off.	Def.	Tot.	Ast.	MISCELLANEOUS PF	Disq.	Stl.	Turn Over	Blk. Sh.	SCORING Pts.	Avg.
Denver	82	8868	3901	.440	2263	1726	.763	1520	2530	4050	2005	2235	46	856	1332	406	9828	119.9
Golden State	82	7346	3566	.485	2761	2162	.783	1113	2306	3419	1954	2207	37	803	1359	378	9564	116.6
Portland	82	7369	3577	.485	2538	1912	.753	1202	2561	3763	2254	1975	19	724	1309	410	9407	114.7
Phoenix	82	7199	3573	.496	2680	2064	.770	1132	2598	3730	2209	1850	12	687	1302	535	9348	114.0
Indiana	82	6994	3450	.493	2479	2010	.811	1018	2376	3394	2181	2088	16	658	1355	357	9159	111.7
Boston	82	7214	3695	.512	1997	1646	.824	1088	2697	3785	2160	1695	12	672	1320	565	9145	111.5
Chicago	82	7125	3632	.510	1411	1605	.760	1148	2342	3490	2212	1751	7	822	1184	438	9024	110.0
Atlanta	82	7223	3349	.464	2544	2034	.800	1235	2420	3655	1864	1768	14	729	1231	374	9003	109.8
San Antonio	82	6988	3409	.488	2459	1883	.766	1131	2657	3788	2140	1896	22	670	1445	571	8782	107.1
Houston	82	7287	3403	.467	2200	1631	.741	1275	2508	3783	1906	1874	32	796	1402	409	8753	106.7
Seattle	82	7117	3500	.492	2143	1608	.750	1222	2173	3395	2042	1973	23	861	1404	380	8744	106.6
Milwaukee	82	6948	3337	.480	2241	1796	.801	1079	2162	3241	2075	2033	25	894	1321	330	8727	106.4
L.A. Lakers	82	6911	3343	.484	2261	1805	.798	1078	2440	3518	2091	1524	7	642	1203	384	8717	106.3
Orlando	82	7256	3298	.455	2447	1818	.743	1233	2429	3662	1809	1976	20	602	1391	306	8684	105.9
Philadelphia	82	6925	3289	.475	2366	1868	.790	984	2496	3480	1824	1629	11	678	1230	479	8641	105.4
Utah	82	6537	3214	.492	2472	1951	.789	867	2474	3341	2217	1796	14	652	1305	451	8527	104.0
L.A. Clippers	82	7315	3391	.464	2273	1596	.702	1246	2500	3746	2119	2043	23	725	1438	507	8491	103.5
New York	82	6822	3308	.485	2147	1654	.770	1053	2436	3489	2172	1764	8	638	1379	418	8455	103.1
New Jersey	82	7459	3311	.444	2245	1658	.739	1400	2348	3748	1782	1954	18	748	1423	600	8441	102.9
Charlotte	82	7033	3286	.467	2214	1725	.779	1027	2200	3227	2019	1946	23	759	1290	304	8428	102.8
Miami	82	7139	3280	.459	2307	1649	.715	1232	2302	3534	1904	2080	29	756	1551	387	8343	101.7
Cleveland	82	6857	3259	.475	2176	1665	.765	1011	2329	3340	2240	1672	12	643	1281	450	8313	101.4
Washington	82	7268	3390	.466	2028	1478	.729	1173	2390	3563	2081	1927	17	588	1359	468	8205	100.1
Detroit	82	6875	3194	.465	2211	1686	.763	1206	2452	3658	1825	1869	27	487	1181	367	8205	100.1
Dallas	82	6890	3245	.471	1986	1512	.761	984	2360	3344	1821	1840	14	581	1186	397	8195	99.9
Minnesota	82	7276	3265	.449	2082	1531	.735	1275	2113	3388	1885	1864	35	712	1062	440	8169	99.6
Sacramento	82	6818	3086	.453	2105	1540	.732	1027	2218	3245	1991	2075	28	631	1272	513	7928	96.7

DEFENSIVE TEAM STATISTICS

Team	FIELD GOALS Att.	Made	Pct.	FREE THROWS Att.	Made	Pct.	REBOUNDS Off.	Def.	Tot	Ast.	MISCELLANEOUS PF	Disq.	Stl.	Turn Over	Blk. Sh.	SCORING Pts.	Avg.	Pt. Dif.
Detroit	6743	3053	.453	2173	1674	.770	1002	2274	3276	1736	1987	24	581	1127	289	7937	96.8	+3.3
L.A. Lakers	7262	3354	.462	1700	1278	.752	1131	2187	3318	1998	1823	19	668	1175	334	8164	99.6	+6.7
Utah	7011	3217	.459	2090	1615	.773	1101	2278	3379	1858	1995	17	686	1254	409	8254	100.7	+3.3
Chicago	6884	3267	.475	2017	1554	.770	1062	2162	3224	2016	1826	17	633	1402	348	8278	101.0	+9.1
San Antonio	7289	3265	.448	2187	1664	.761	1122	2270	3392	1928	2008	31	801	1260	437	8412	102.6	+4.5
Houston	7316	3337	.456	2086	1609	.771	1242	2431	3673	1965	1786	20	711	1415	357	8466	103.2	+3.5
New York	7162	3410	.476	1903	1471	.773	1119	2336	3455	1999	1813	19	724	1239	368	8474	103.3	-0.2
Minnesota	6778	3320	.490	2219	1680	.757	1094	2379	3473	2142	1692	16	512	1238	511	8491	103.5	-3.9
Sacramento	6687	3142	.470	2686	2045	.761	1164	2543	3707	1912	1847	17	699	1312	448	8484	103.5	-6.8
Milwaukee	6775	3290	.486	2312	1755	.759	1108	2315	3423	2023	1912	17	704	1531	461	8524	104.0	+2.5
Cleveland	7117	3459	.486	1916	1464	.764	1097	2398	3495	2150	1895	20	710	1226	394	8545	104.2	-2.5
Dallas	6945	3346	.482	2296	1700	.740	1116	2489	3605	2025	1778	10	650	1147	400	8570	104.5	-4.6
Seattle	6738	3285	.488	2459	1866	.759	1107	2149	3256	1851	1820	20	729	1485	446	8643	105.4	+1.2
Philadelphia	7432	3536	.476	1794	1388	.774	1156	2519	3675	2220	1862	23	691	1177	391	8656	105.6	-0.2
Boston	7559	3419	.452	2084	1639	.786	1192	2204	3396	2052	1660	7	738	1127	381	8668	105.7	+5.8
Portland	7275	3320	.456	2341	1819	.777	1079	2354	3433	2048	2075	40	630	1397	352	8695	106.0	+8.7
Washington	7280	3396	.466	2288	1763	.771	1232	2473	3705	1861	1778	19	727	1254	492	8721	106.4	-5.0
L.A. Clippers	7151	3337	.467	2529	1901	.752	1115	2494	3609	1982	1887	23	773	1316	491	8774	107.0	-3.5
New Jersey	7206	3374	.468	2493	1927	.773	1287	2527	3814	1737	1896	18	831	1452	540	8811	107.5	-4.5
Phoenix	7499	3462	.462	2244	1705	.760	1195	2298	3493	1972	2059	24	682	1282	463	8811	107.5	+6.5
Miami	6974	3335	.478	2603	1997	.767	1176	2364	3540	2006	1960	13	853	1466	502	8840	107.8	-6.0
Charlotte	6915	3408	.493	2441	1884	.772	1151	2514	3665	2144	1841	19	675	1406	480	8858	108.0	-5.2
Atlanta	7219	3568	.494	2069	1587	.767	1080	2499	3579	2320	2034	29	688	1291	361	8940	109.0	+0.8
Orlando	7232	3454	.478	2451	1879	.767	1095	2500	3595	2118	1983	18	706	1215	654	9010	109.9	-4.0
Indiana	7299	3577	.490	2490	1851	.743	1202	2313	3515	2063	2037	21	729	1260	353	9191	112.1	-0.4
Golden State	7349	3544	.482	2797	2121	.758	1292	2480	3772	2164	2206	36	726	1534	437	9430	115.0	+1.6
Denver	7962	4076	.512	3068	2377	.775	1242	3067	4309	2492	1844	14	757	1527	525	10723	130.8	-10.9

Disq.—Individual player disqualified (fouled out of game).

INDIVIDUAL LEADERS

POINTS
Minimum 70 games or 1,400 points

	G.	FG	FT	Pts.	Avg.
Jordan, Chicago	82	990	571	2580	31.5
K. Malone, Utah	82	847	684	2382	29.0
King, Washington	64	713	383	1817	28.4
Barkley, Philadelphia	67	665	475	1849	27.6
Ewing, New York	81	845	464	2154	26.6
Adams, Denver	66	560	465	1752	26.5
Wilkins, Atlanta	81	770	476	2101	25.9
Mullin, Golden State	82	777	513	2107	25.7
Robinson, San Antonio	82	754	592	2101	25.6
Richmond, Golden State	77	703	394	1840	23.9

FIELD GOALS
Minimum 300 FG made

	FGA	FGM	Pct.
Williams, Portland	595	358	.602
Parish, Boston	811	485	.598
Gamble, Boston	933	548	.587
Barkley, Philadelphia	1167	665	.570
Divac, L.A. Lakers	637	360	.565
Polynice, Seattle-L.A. Clippers	564	316	.560
Thorpe, Houston	988	549	.556
McHale, Boston	912	504	.553
Robinson, San Antonio	1366	754	.552
Paxson, Chicago	578	317	.548

FREE THROWS
Minimum 125 made

	FTA	FTM	Pct.
Miller, Indiana	600	551	.918
J. Malone, Utah	252	231	.917
Pierce, Milwaukee-Seattle	471	430	.913
Tripucka, Charlotte	167	152	.910
Johnson, L.A. Lakers	573	519	.906
Skiles, Orlando	377	340	.902
Vandeweghe, New York	288	259	.899
Hornacek, Phoenix	224	201	.897
Johnson, Phoenix-Seattle	257	229	.891
Bird, Boston	183	163	.891

ASSISTS
Minimum 70 games or 400 assists

	G.	No.	Avg.
Stockton, Utah	82	1164	14.2
Johnson, L.A. Lakers	79	989	12.5
Adams, Denver	66	693	10.5
K. Johnson, Phoenix	77	781	10.1
Hardaway, Golden State	82	793	9.7
Thomas, Detroit	48	446	9.3
Richardson, Minnesota	82	734	9.0
Grant, L.A. Clippers	68	587	8.6
Douglas, Miami	73	624	8.5
Skiles, Orlando	79	660	8.4

STEALS
Minimum 70 games or 125 steals

	G.	No.	Avg.
Robertson, Milwaukee	81	246	3.04
Stockton, Utah	82	234	2.85
Jordan, Chicago	82	223	2.72
Hardaway, Golden State	82	214	2.61
Pippen, Chicago	82	193	2.35
Blaylock, New Jersey	72	169	2.35
Adams, Denver	66	147	2.23
Hawkins, Philadelphia	80	178	2.23
K. Johnson, Phoenix	77	163	2.12
Mullin, Golden State	82	173	2.11

REBOUNDS
Minimum 70 games or 800 rebounds

	G.	Off.	Def.	Tot.	Avg.
Robinson, San Antonio	82	335	728	1063	13.0
Rodman, Detroit	82	361	665	1026	12.5
Oakley, New York	76	305	615	920	12.1
K. Malone, Utah	82	236	731	967	11.8
Ewing, New York	81	194	711	905	11.2
Daugherty, Cleveland	76	177	653	830	10.9
Parish, Boston	81	271	585	856	10.6
Benjamin, L.A.C.-Seattle	70	157	566	723	10.3
Thorpe, Houston	82	287	559	846	10.3
Coleman, New Jersey	74	269	490	759	10.3

BLOCKED SHOTS
Minimum 70 games or 100 blocked shots

	G.	No.	Avg.
Olajuwon, Houston	56	221	3.95
Robinson, San Antonio	82	320	3.90
Ewing, New York	81	258	3.19
Bol, Philadelphia	82	247	3.01
Dudley, New Jersey	61	153	2.51
Nance, Cleveland	80	200	2.50
Eaton, Utah	80	188	2.35
McHale, Boston	68	146	2.15
Benjamin, L.A. Clippers-Seattle	70	145	2.07
Ellison, Washington	76	157	2.07

3-PT. FIELD GOALS
Minimum 50 made

	FGA	FGM	Pct.
Les, Sacramento	154	71	.461
Tucker, New York	153	64	.418
Hornacek, Phoenix	146	61	.418
Porter, Portland	313	130	.415
Skiles, Orlando	228	93	.408
Ainge, Portland	251	102	.406
Hawkins, Philadelphia	270	108	.400
Bird, Boston	198	77	.389
Rice, Miami	184	71	.386
Hardaway, Golden State	252	97	.385

TEAM-BY-TEAM INDIVIDUAL STATISTICS

ATLANTA HAWKS

Player	G.	Min.	FGA	FGM	Pct.	FTA	FTM	Pct.	Off. Reb.	Def. Reb.	Tot. Reb.	Ast.	PF	Disq.	Stl.	Blk. Sh.	Pts.	Avg.	Hi.
Wilkins	81	3078	1640	770	.470	574	476	.829	261	471	732	265	156	0	123	65	2101	25.9	45
Rivers	79	2586	1020	444	.435	262	221	.844	47	206	253	340	216	2	148	47	1197	15.2	36
Battle	79	1863	862	397	.461	316	270	.854	34	125	159	217	145	0	45	6	1078	13.6	28
Webb	75	2197	803	359	.447	266	231	.868	41	133	174	417	180	0	118	6	1003	13.4	32
Willis	80	2373	881	444	.504	238	159	.668	259	445	704	99	235	2	60	40	1051	13.1	29
Malone	82	1912	598	280	.468	372	309	.831	271	396	667	68	134	0	30	74	869	10.6	25
Ferrell	78	1165	356	174	.489	156	125	.801	97	82	179	55	151	3	33	27	475	6.1	20
Robinson	47	674	242	108	.446	80	47	.588	20	51	71	132	65	0	32	8	265	5.6	19
Moncrief	72	1096	240	117	.488	105	82	.781	31	97	128	104	112	0	50	9	337	4.7	16
McCormick	56	689	187	93	.497	90	66	.733	56	109	165	32	91	1	11	14	252	4.5	12
Koncak	77	1931	321	140	.436	54	32	.593	101	274	375	124	265	6	74	76	313	4.1	20
Wilson	25	162	70	21	.300	26	13	.500	16	24	40	11	13	0	5	1	55	2.2	8
Wright	4	20	3	2	.667	1	1	1.000	1	5	6	3	0	0	0	0	5	1.3	3
Leonard	4	9	3	0	0	....	4	2	.500	0	2	2	0	2	0	0	1	2	0.5	2

3-Pt. FG: Atlanta 271-836 (.324)—Wilkins 85-249 (.341); Rivers 88-262 (.336); Battle 14-49 (.286); Webb 54-168 (.321); Willis 4-10 (.400); Malone 0-7 (.000); Ferrell 2-3 (.667); Robinson 2-11 (.182); Moncrief 21-64 (.328); McCormick 0-3 (.000); Koncak 1-8 (.125); Wilson 0-2 (.000). Opponents 217-621 (.349).

BOSTON CELTICS

Player	G.	Min.	FGA	FGM	Pct.	FTA	FTM	Pct.	Off. Reb.	Def. Reb.	Tot. Reb.	Ast.	PF	Disq.	Stl.	Blk. Sh.	Pts.	Avg.	Hi.
Bird	60	2277	1017	462	.454	183	163	.891	53	456	509	431	118	0	108	58	1164	19.4	45
Lewis	79	2878	1219	598	.491	340	281	.826	119	291	410	201	234	1	98	85	1478	18.7	42
McHale	68	2067	912	504	.553	275	228	.829	145	335	480	126	194	2	25	146	1251	18.4	32
Gamble	82	2706	933	548	.587	227	185	.815	85	182	267	256	237	6	100	34	1281	15.6	33
Parish	81	2441	811	485	.598	309	237	.767	271	585	856	66	197	1	66	103	1207	14.9	29
Shaw	79	2772	942	442	.469	249	204	.819	104	266	370	602	206	1	105	34	1091	13.8	26
Brown	82	1945	612	284	.464	157	137	.873	41	141	182	344	161	0	83	14	712	8.7	22

Player	G.	Min.	FGA	FGM	Pct.	FTA	FTM	Pct.	Off. Reb.	Def. Reb.	Tot. Reb.	Ast.	PF	Disq.	Stl.	Blk. Sh.	Pts.	Avg.	Hi.
Pinckney	70	1165	243	131	.539	116	104	.897	155	186	341	45	147	0	61	43	366	5.2	19
M. Smith	47	389	200	95	.475	27	22	.815	21	35	56	43	27	0	6	2	218	4.6	23
Kleine	72	850	218	102	.468	69	54	.783	71	173	244	21	108	0	15	14	258	3.6	18
D. Smith	2	16	4	1	.250	4	3	.750	0	0	0	5	3	0	1	1	5	2.5	4
Wynder	6	39	12	3	.250	8	6	.750	1	2	3	8	1	0	1	0	12	2.0	4
Vrankovic	31	166	52	24	.462	18	10	.556	15	36	51	4	43	1	1	29	58	1.9	7
Popson	19	64	32	13	.406	10	9	.900	7	7	14	2	12	0	1	2	35	1.8	10
C. Smith	5	30	7	3	.429	5	3	.600	0	2	2	6	7	0	1	0	9	1.8	4

3-Pt. FG: Boston 109-346 (.315)—Bird 77-198 (.389); Lewis 1-13 (.077); McHale 15-37 (.405); Gamble 0-7 (.000); Parish 0-1 (.000); Shaw 3-27 (.111); Brown 7-34 (.206); Pinckney 0-1 (.000); M. Smith 6-24 (.250); Kleine 0-2 (.000); D. Smith 0-1 (.000); Wynder 0-1 (.000). Opponents 191-611 (.313).

CHARLOTTE HORNETS

Player	G.	Min.	FGA	FGM	Pct.	FTA	FTM	Pct.	Off. Reb.	Def. Reb.	Tot. Reb.	Ast.	PF	Disq.	Stl.	Blk. Sh.	Pts.	Avg.	Hi.
Gilliam	25	949	380	195	.513	128	104	.813	86	148	234	27	65	1	34	21	494	19.8	39
Newman	81	2477	1017	478	.470	476	385	.809	94	160	254	188	278	7	100	17	1371	16.9	40
Chapman	70	2100	922	410	.445	282	234	.830	45	146	191	250	167	1	73	16	1102	15.7	36
Reid	80	2467	773	360	.466	259	182	.703	154	348	502	89	286	6	87	47	902	11.3	26
Gill	82	1944	836	376	.450	182	152	.835	105	158	263	303	186	0	104	39	906	11.0	28
Curry	76	1515	715	337	.471	114	96	.842	47	152	199	166	125	0	75	25	802	10.6	26
Gminski (Tot)	80	2196	808	357	.442	158	128	.810	186	396	582	93	99	0	40	56	844	10.6	25
Gminski (Char)	50	1405	524	248	.473	95	75	.789	115	266	381	60	58	0	24	22	572	11.4	25
Gattison	72	1552	457	243	.532	248	164	.661	136	243	379	44	211	3	48	67	650	9.0	19
Tripucka	77	1289	412	187	.454	167	152	.910	46	130	176	159	130	0	33	13	541	7.0	23
Bogues	81	2299	524	241	.460	108	86	.796	58	158	216	669	160	2	137	3	568	7.0	16
Leckner (Tot)	72	1122	294	131	.446	111	62	.559	82	213	295	39	192	4	14	22	324	4.5	13
Leckner (Char)	40	744	198	92	.465	84	46	.548	55	153	208	21	123	3	10	11	230	5.8	13
Sanders	3	43	14	6	.429	2	1	.500	3	6	9	1	6	0	1	1	13	4.3	8
Keys	44	473	145	59	.407	33	19	.576	40	60	100	18	93	0	22	15	140	3.2	13
Haffner	7	50	21	8	.381	2	1	.500	2	2	4	9	4	0	3	1	17	2.4	6
Hoppen	19	112	32	18	.563	10	8	.800	14	16	30	3	18	0	2	1	44	2.3	5
Cureton	9	159	24	8	.333	3	1	.333	6	30	36	3	16	0	0	3	17	1.9	7
Scheffler	39	227	39	20	.513	21	19	.905	21	24	45	9	20	0	2	2	59	1.5	6

3-Pt. FG: Charlotte 131-417 (.314)—Newman 30-84 (.357); Chapman 48-148 (.324); Reid 0-2 (.000); Gill 2-14 (.143); Curry 32-86 (.372); Gminski 1-6 (.167); Gattison 0-2 (.000); Tripucka 15-45 (.333); Bogues 0-12 (.000); Keys 3-14 (.214); Haffner 0-2 (.000); Hoppen 0-1 (.000); Cureton 0-1 (.000). Opponents 158-500 (.316).

CHICAGO BULLS

Player	G.	Min.	FGA	FGM	Pct.	FTA	FTM	Pct.	Off. Reb.	Def. Reb.	Tot. Reb.	Ast.	PF	Disq.	Stl.	Blk. Sh.	Pts.	Avg.	Hi.
Jordan	82	3034	1837	990	.539	671	571	.851	118	374	492	453	229	1	223	83	2580	31.5	46
Pippen	82	3014	1153	600	.520	340	240	.706	163	432	595	511	270	3	193	93	1461	17.8	43
Grant	78	2641	733	401	.547	277	197	.711	266	393	659	178	203	2	95	69	1000	12.8	25
Cartwright	79	2273	649	318	.490	178	124	.697	167	319	486	126	167	0	32	15	760	9.6	20
Armstrong	82	1731	632	304	.481	111	97	.874	25	124	149	301	118	0	70	4	720	8.8	19
Paxson	82	1971	578	317	.548	41	34	.829	15	76	91	297	136	0	62	3	710	8.7	28
King	76	1198	334	156	.467	152	107	.704	72	136	208	65	134	0	24	42	419	5.5	16
Hodges	73	843	344	146	.424	27	26	.963	10	32	42	97	74	0	34	2	362	5.0	20
Hopson	61	728	244	104	.426	83	55	.663	49	60	109	65	79	0	25	14	264	4.3	14
Perdue	74	972	235	116	.494	112	75	.670	122	214	336	47	147	1	23	57	307	4.1	15
Levingston	78	1013	282	127	.450	91	59	.648	99	126	225	56	143	0	29	43	314	4.0	14
Williams	51	337	104	53	.510	28	20	.714	42	56	98	16	51	0	12	13	127	2.5	10

3-Pt. FG: Chicago 155-424 (.366)—Jordan 29-93 (.312); Pippen 21-68 (.309); Grant 1-6 (.167); Armstrong 15-30 (.500); Paxson 42-96 (.438); King 0-2 (.000); Hodges 44-115 (.383); Hopson 1-5 (.200); Perdue 0-3 (.000); Levingston 1-4 (.250); Williams 1-2 (.500). Opponents 190-626 (.304).

CLEVELAND CAVALIERS

Player	G.	Min.	FGA	FGM	Pct.	FTA	FTM	Pct.	Off. Reb.	Def. Reb.	Tot. Reb.	Ast.	PF	Disq.	Stl.	Blk. Sh.	Pts.	Avg.	Hi.
Daugherty	76	2946	1155	605	.524	579	435	.751	177	653	830	253	191	2	74	46	1645	21.6	38
Nance	80	2927	1211	635	.524	330	265	.803	201	485	686	237	219	3	66	200	1537	19.2	34
Price	16	571	195	97	.497	62	59	.952	8	37	45	166	23	0	42	2	271	16.9	26
Williams	43	1293	430	199	.463	164	107	.652	111	179	290	100	126	2	36	69	505	11.7	23
Ehlo	82	2766	773	344	.445	140	95	.679	142	246	388	376	209	0	121	34	832	10.1	24
Valentine	65	1841	496	230	.464	172	143	.831	37	135	172	351	170	2	98	12	609	9.4	28
Ferry	81	1661	643	275	.428	152	124	.816	99	187	286	142	230	1	43	25	697	8.6	21
Brown	74	1485	502	263	.524	144	101	.701	78	135	213	80	130	0	26	24	627	8.5	26
James	37	505	254	112	.441	72	52	.722	26	53	79	32	59	1	15	5	300	8.1	25
Paddio	70	1181	506	212	.419	93	74	.796	38	80	118	90	71	0	20	6	504	7.2	24
Morton	66	1207	274	120	.438	139	113	.813	41	62	103	243	112	1	61	18	357	5.4	21
Kerr	57	905	223	99	.444	53	45	.849	5	32	37	131	52	0	29	4	271	4.8	13
Woodson (Tot)	15	171	77	26	.338	13	11	.846	3	10	13	15	18	0	5	5	64	4.3	16
Woodson (Clev)	4	46	23	5	.217	1	1	1.000	1	1	2	5	7	0	1	0	11	2.8	9
Bennett	27	334	107	40	.374	47	35	.745	30	34	64	28	50	0	8	2	115	4.3	23
Chievous	18	110	46	17	.370	16	9	.563	11	7	18	2	16	0	3	1	43	2.4	9
Babic	12	52	19	6	.316	12	7	.583	6	3	9	4	7	0	1	1	19	1.6	5

3-Pt. FG: Cleveland 160-479 (.334)—Daugherty 0-3 (.000); Nance 2-8 (.250); Price 18-53 (.340); Williams 0-1 (.000); Ehlo 49-149 (.329); Valentine 6-25 (.240); Ferry 23-77 (.299); Brown 0-4 (.000); James 24-60 (.400); Paddio 6-24 (.250); Morton 4-12 (.333); Kerr 28-62 (.452); Woodson 0-1 (.000). Opponents 163-505 (.323).

DALLAS MAVERICKS

Player	G.	Min.	FGA	FGM	Pct.	FTA	FTM	Pct.	Off. Reb.	Def. Reb.	Tot. Reb.	Ast.	PF	Disq.	Stl.	Blk. Sh.	Pts.	Avg.	Hi.
Tarpley	5	171	79	43	.544	18	16	.889	16	39	55	12	20	0	6	9	102	20.4	29
Blackman	80	2965	1316	634	.482	326	282	.865	63	193	256	301	153	0	69	11	1590	19.9	37
Harper	77	2879	1226	572	.467	391	286	.731	59	174	233	548	222	1	147	14	1519	19.7	34
Williams	60	1832	655	332	.507	130	83	.638	86	271	357	95	197	3	30	88	747	12.5	31
McCray	74	2561	679	336	.495	198	159	.803	153	407	560	259	203	3	70	51	844	11.4	23
Donaldson	82	2800	615	327	.532	229	165	.721	201	526	727	69	181	0	34	93	819	10.0	25

Player	G.	Min.	FGA	FGM	Pct.	FTA	FTM	Pct.	Off. Reb.	Def. Reb.	Tot. Reb.	Ast.	PF	Disq.	Stl.	Blk. Sh.	Pts.	Avg.	Hi.
English	79	1748	734	322	.439	140	119	.850	108	146	254	105	141	0	40	25	763	9.7	27
White	79	1901	665	265	.398	225	159	.707	173	331	504	63	308	6	81	44	695	8.8	24
Lever	4	86	23	9	.391	14	11	.786	3	12	15	12	5	0	6	3	29	7.3	13
Upshaw	48	514	231	104	.450	64	55	.859	20	35	55	86	77	0	28	5	270	5.6	19
Davis	80	1426	373	159	.426	118	91	.771	13	105	118	230	212	1	45	17	431	5.4	15
Alford	34	236	117	59	.504	31	26	.839	10	14	24	22	11	0	8	1	151	4.4	15
Wright (Tot)	15	164	47	19	.404	24	16	.667	12	33	45	3	28	0	4	5	54	3.6	13
Wright (Dall)	3	8	3	2	.667	2	2	1.000	1	1	2	0	2	0	1	0	6	2.0	4
Grandholm	26	168	58	30	.517	21	10	.476	20	30	50	8	33	0	2	8	79	3.0	10
Shasky	57	510	116	51	.440	79	48	.608	58	76	134	11	75	0	14	20	150	2.6	13

3-Pt. FG: Dallas 193-600 (.322)—Tarpley 0-1 (.000); Blackman 40-114 (.351); Harper 89-246 (.362); Williams 0-4 (.000); McCray 13-39 (.333); English 0-1 (.000); White 6-37 (.162); Lever 0-3 (.000); Upshaw 7-29 (.241); Davis 22-85 (.259); Alford 7-23 (.304); Wright 0-1 (.000); Grandholm 9-17 (.529). Opponents 178-583 (.305).

DENVER NUGGETS

Player	G.	Min.	FGA	FGM	Pct.	FTA	FTM	Pct.	Off. Reb.	Def. Reb.	Tot. Reb.	Ast.	PF	Disq.	Stl.	Blk. Sh.	Pts.	Avg.	Hi.
Adams	66	2346	1421	560	.394	529	465	.879	58	198	256	693	162	1	147	6	1752	26.5	54
Woolridge	53	1823	983	490	.498	439	350	.797	141	220	361	119	145	2	69	23	1330	25.1	40
Davis	39	1044	667	316	.474	94	86	.915	52	71	123	84	108	2	62	3	728	18.7	41
Jackson	67	1505	1009	417	.413	98	84	.857	34	87	121	206	149	2	55	4	942	14.1	35
Lichti	29	860	378	166	.439	69	59	.855	49	63	112	72	65	1	46	8	405	14.0	29
Williams (Tot)	73	1896	855	384	.449	197	166	.843	133	173	306	133	253	9	113	41	991	13.6	28
Williams (Den)	51	1542	728	323	.444	156	131	.840	116	131	247	87	189	7	93	30	820	16.1	28
Rasmussen	70	2325	885	405	.458	93	63	.677	170	508	678	70	307	15	52	132	875	12.5	25
Farmer (Tot)	27	456	223	101	.453	65	48	.738	29	39	68	38	58	0	13	2	255	9.4	20
Farmer (Den)	25	443	216	99	.458	63	46	.730	27	36	63	38	58	0	13	2	249	10.0	20
Gaines	10	226	70	28	.400	26	22	.846	4	10	14	91	25	0	10	2	83	8.3	18
Mills	17	279	120	56	.467	22	16	.727	31	57	88	16	44	0	16	9	128	7.5	15
Lane	62	1383	461	202	.438	141	58	.411	280	298	578	123	192	1	51	40	463	7.5	22
Wolf	74	1593	519	234	.451	83	69	.831	136	264	400	107	244	8	60	31	539	7.3	18
Liberty	76	1171	513	216	.421	92	58	.630	117	104	221	64	153	2	48	19	507	6.7	19
Battle (Tot)	56	945	282	133	.472	93	70	.753	83	93	176	62	108	0	60	18	339	6.1	23
Battle (Den)	40	682	196	95	.485	64	50	.781	62	61	123	47	83	0	41	12	243	6.1	18
Legler	10	148	72	25	.347	6	5	.833	8	10	18	12	20	0	2	0	58	5.8	14
Cook	58	1121	283	118	.417	129	71	.550	134	192	326	26	100	1	35	72	307	5.3	14
Neal	10	125	35	14	.400	22	13	.591	2	16	18	37	26	1	4	0	44	4.4	14
Anderson (Tot)	68	924	270	116	.430	115	60	.522	97	221	318	16	140	3	35	45	292	4.3	16
Anderson (Den)	41	659	193	85	.440	87	44	.506	67	170	237	12	107	3	25	36	214	5.2	16
Johnson	21	217	68	29	.426	32	21	.656	9	12	21	77	22	0	14	2	79	3.8	15
Mason	3	21	4	2	.500	8	6	.750	3	2	5	0	6	0	1	0	10	3.3	7
Dunn	17	217	47	21	.447	10	9	.900	20	22	42	24	30	0	12	1	53	3.1	12

3-Pt. FG: Denver 300-1059 (.283)—Adams 167-564 (.296); Woolridge 0-4 (.000); Davis 10-33 (.303); Jackson 24-100 (.240); Lichti 14-47 (.298); Williams 43-131 (.328); Rasmussen 2-5 (.400); Farmer 5-22 (.227); Gaines 5-21 (.238); Mills 0-2 (.000); Lane 1-4 (.250); Wolf 2-15 (.133); Liberty 17-57 (.298); Battle 3-22 (.136); Legler 3-12 (.250); Cook 0-3 (.000); Neal 3-9 (.333); Johnson 0-4 (.000); Dunn 1-4 (.250). Opponents 194-502 (.386).

DETROIT PISTONS

Player	G.	Min.	FGA	FGM	Pct.	FTA	FTM	Pct.	Off. Reb.	Def. Reb.	Tot. Reb.	Ast.	PF	Disq.	Stl.	Blk. Sh.	Pts.	Avg.	Hi.
Dumars	80	3046	1292	622	.481	417	371	.890	62	125	187	443	135	0	89	7	1629	20.4	42
Thomas	48	1657	665	289	.435	229	179	.782	35	125	160	446	118	4	75	10	776	16.2	32
Aguirre	78	2006	909	420	.462	317	240	.757	134	240	374	139	209	2	47	20	1104	14.2	30
Edwards	72	1903	792	383	.484	295	225	.729	91	186	277	65	249	4	12	30	982	13.6	32
Johnson	82	2390	936	406	.434	209	135	.646	110	170	280	271	166	0	75	15	958	11.7	32
Laimbeer	82	2668	778	372	.478	147	123	.837	173	564	737	157	242	3	38	56	904	11.0	25
Rodman	82	2747	560	276	.493	176	111	.631	361	665	1026	85	281	7	65	55	669	8.2	34
Salley	74	1649	377	179	.475	256	186	.727	137	190	327	70	240	7	52	112	544	7.4	24
Henderson	23	392	117	50	.427	21	16	.762	8	29	37	62	43	0	12	2	123	5.3	24
Bedford	60	562	242	106	.438	78	55	.705	55	76	131	32	76	0	2	36	272	4.5	20
Long	25	256	85	35	.412	25	24	.960	9	23	32	18	17	0	9	2	96	3.8	14
Hastings	27	113	28	16	.571	13	13	1.000	14	14	28	7	23	0	0	0	48	1.8	7
Blanks	38	214	61	26	.426	14	10	.714	4	16	20	26	35	0	9	2	64	1.7	7
Rollins	37	202	33	14	.424	14	8	.571	13	29	42	4	35	0	2	20	36	1.0	6

3-Pt. FG: Detroit 131-440 (.298)—Dumars 14-45 (.311); Thomas 19-65 (.292); Aguirre 24-78 (.308); Edwards 1-2 (.500); Johnson 11-34 (.324); Laimbeer 37-125 (.296); Rodman 6-30 (.200); Salley 0-1 (.000); Henderson 7-21 (.333); Bedford 5-13 (.385); Long 2-6 (.333); Hastings 3-4 (.750); Blanks 2-16 (.125). Opponents 157-504 (.311).

GOLDEN STATE WARRIORS

Player	G.	Min.	FGA	FGM	Pct.	FTA	FTM	Pct.	Off. Reb.	Def. Reb.	Tot. Reb.	Ast.	PF	Disq.	Stl.	Blk. Sh.	Pts.	Avg.	Hi.
Mullin	82	3315	1449	777	.536	580	513	.884	141	302	443	329	176	2	173	63	2107	25.7	40
Richmond	77	3027	1424	703	.494	465	394	.847	147	305	452	238	207	0	126	34	1840	23.9	40
Hardaway	82	3215	1551	739	.476	381	306	.803	87	245	332	793	228	7	214	12	1881	22.9	40
Marciulionis	50	987	365	183	.501	246	178	.724	51	67	118	85	136	4	62	4	545	10.9	23
Higgins	82	2024	559	259	.463	226	185	.819	109	245	354	113	198	2	52	37	776	9.5	24
Tolbert	62	1371	433	183	.423	172	127	.738	87	188	275	76	195	4	35	38	500	8.1	19
Elie (Tot)	33	644	159	79	.497	89	75	.843	46	64	110	45	85	1	19	10	237	7.2	15
Elie (GS)	30	624	152	77	.507	87	74	.851	46	63	109	44	83	1	19	10	231	7.7	15
Lister	77	1552	393	188	.478	202	115	.569	121	362	483	93	282	4	20	90	491	6.4	19
Hill	74	1192	299	147	.492	152	96	.632	157	226	383	19	264	8	33	30	390	5.3	16
Askew	7	85	25	12	.480	11	9	.818	7	4	11	13	21	1	2	0	33	4.7	10
Petersen	62	834	236	114	.483	76	50	.658	49	131	200	27	153	2	13	41	279	4.5	25
Pritchard	62	773	229	88	.384	77	62	.805	16	49	65	81	104	1	30	8	243	3.9	15
Johnson	24	228	63	34	.540	37	22	.595	18	39	57	17	50	1	4	4	90	3.8	11
Smrek	5	25	11	6	.545	4	2	.500	3	4	7	1	9	0	2	0	14	2.8	4
Robinson	24	170	59	24	.407	15	8	.533	15	8	23	11	23	0	9	1	56	2.3	7
Mokeski	36	257	59	21	.356	15	12	.800	20	47	67	9	58	0	8	3	57	1.6	8
Jepsen	21	105	36	11	.306	9	6	.667	17	20	37	1	16	0	1	3	28	1.3	5
Kofoed	5	21	3	0	.000	6	3	.500	2	1	3	4	4	0	0	0	3	0.6	2

3-Pt. FG: Golden State 270-801 (.337)—Mullin 40-133 (.301); Richmond 40-115 (.348); Hardaway 97-252 (.385); Marciulionis 1-6 (.167); Higgins 73-220 (.332); Tolbert 7-21 (.333); Elie 3-8 (.375); Lister 0-1 (.000); Petersen 1-4 (.250); Pritchard 5-31 (.161); Mokeski 3-9 (.333); Jepsen 0-1 (.000). Opponents 221-686 (.322).

HOUSTON ROCKETS

Player	G.	Min.	FGA	FGM	Pct.	FTA	FTM	Pct.	Off. Reb.	Def. Reb.	Tot. Reb.	Ast.	PF	Disq.	Stl.	Blk. Sh.	Pts.	Avg.	Hi.
Olajuwon	56	2062	959	487	.508	277	213	.769	219	551	770	131	221	5	121	221	1187	21.2	39
K. Smith	78	2699	1003	522	.520	340	287	.844	36	127	163	554	131	0	106	11	1380	17.7	38
Thorpe	82	3039	988	549	.556	480	334	.696	287	559	846	197	278	10	73	20	1435	17.5	35
Maxwell	82	2870	1247	504	.404	296	217	.733	41	197	238	303	179	2	127	15	1397	17.0	51
Johnson	73	2279	873	416	.477	216	157	.727	108	222	330	142	240	5	81	47	991	13.6	32
Floyd	82	1850	939	386	.411	246	185	.752	52	107	159	317	122	0	95	17	1005	12.3	40
Wood	82	1421	349	148	.424	133	108	.812	107	139	246	94	236	4	58	16	432	5.3	27
Woodson	11	125	54	21	.389	12	10	.833	2	9	11	10	11	0	5	4	53	4.8	16
Winchester	64	607	245	98	.400	45	35	.778	34	33	67	25	70	0	16	13	239	3.7	18
L. Smith	81	1923	263	128	.487	50	12	.240	302	407	709	88	265	6	83	22	268	3.3	12
Jamerson	37	202	113	43	.381	27	22	.815	9	21	30	27	24	0	6	1	113	3.1	12
Feitl	52	372	140	52	.371	44	33	.750	29	71	100	8	52	0	3	12	137	2.6	12
Bullard	18	63	31	14	.452	17	11	.647	6	8	14	2	10	0	3	0	39	2.2	6
Caldwell	42	343	83	35	.422	17	7	.412	43	57	100	8	35	0	19	10	77	1.8	9

3-Pt. FG: Houston 316-989 (320)—Olajuwon 0-4 (.000); K. Smith 49-135 (.363); Thorpe 3-7 (.429); Maxwell 172-510 (.337); Johnson 2-15 (.133); Floyd 48-176 (.273); Wood 28-90 (.311); Woodson 1-6 (.167); Winchester 8-20 (.400); Jamerson 5-19 (.263); Feitl 0-3 (.000); Bullard 0-3 (.000); Caldwell 0-1 (.000). Opponents 183-621 (.295).

INDIANA PACERS

Player	G.	Min.	FGA	FGM	Pct.	FTA	FTM	Pct.	Off. Reb.	Def. Reb.	Tot. Reb.	Ast.	PF	Disq.	Stl.	Blk. Sh.	Pts.	Avg.	Hi.
Miller	82	2972	1164	596	.512	600	551	.918	81	200	281	331	165	1	109	13	1855	22.6	40
Person	80	2566	1231	620	.504	229	165	.721	121	296	417	238	221	1	56	17	1474	18.4	35
Schrempf	82	2632	831	432	.520	539	441	.818	178	482	660	301	262	3	58	22	1320	16.1	29
Fleming	69	1929	671	356	.531	221	161	.729	83	131	214	369	116	0	76	13	877	12.7	31
M. Williams	73	1706	523	261	.499	330	290	.879	49	127	176	348	202	1	150	17	813	11.1	29
Smits	76	1690	705	342	.485	189	144	.762	116	241	357	84	246	3	24	111	828	10.9	31
Thompson	82	1946	565	276	.488	104	72	.692	154	409	563	147	265	4	63	63	625	7.6	19
Sanders	80	1357	494	206	.417	57	47	.825	73	112	185	106	198	1	37	26	463	5.8	18
McCloud	74	1070	351	131	.373	49	38	.776	35	83	118	150	141	1	40	11	343	4.6	18
Dreiling	73	1031	194	98	.505	105	63	.600	66	189	255	51	178	1	24	29	259	3.5	12
Dinkins (Tot)	12	149	34	14	.412	9	8	.889	0	12	12	19	15	0	2	0	36	3.0	6
Dinkins (Ind)	2	5	1	1	1.000	0	0	.000	0	1	1	0	3	0	0	0	2	1.0	2
K. Williams	75	527	179	93	.520	50	34	.680	56	75	131	31	81	0	11	31	220	2.9	15
Wittman	41	355	79	35	.443	6	4	.667	6	27	33	25	9	0	10	4	74	1.8	12
Oldham	4	19	6	3	.500	0	0	.000	0	3	3	1	0	0	0	6	6	1.5	6

3-Pt. FG: Indiana 249-749 (.332)—Miller 112-322 (.348); Person 69-203 (.340); Schrempf 15-40 (.375); Fleming 4-18 (.222); M. Williams 1-7 (.143); Thompson 1-5 (.200); Sanders 4-20 (.200); McCloud 43-124 (.347); Dreiling 0-2 (.000); K. Williams 0-3 (.000); Wittman 0-5 (.000). Opponents 186-609 (.305).

LOS ANGELES CLIPPERS

Player	G.	Min.	FGA	FGM	Pct.	FTA	FTM	Pct.	Off. Reb.	Def. Reb.	Tot. Reb.	Ast.	PF	Disq.	Stl.	Blk. Sh.	Pts.	Avg.	Hi.
Smith	74	2703	1168	548	.469	484	384	.793	216	392	608	134	267	4	81	145	1480	20.0	52
Harper	39	1383	729	285	.391	217	145	.668	58	130	188	209	111	0	66	35	763	19.6	36
Norman	70	2309	1037	520	.501	275	173	.629	177	320	497	159	192	0	63	63	1219	17.4	34
Manning	73	2197	905	470	.519	306	219	.716	169	257	426	196	281	5	117	62	1159	15.9	31
Benjamin	39	1337	465	229	.492	169	123	.728	95	374	469	74	110	1	26	91	581	14.9	27
Polynice (Tot)	79	2092	564	316	.560	252	146	.579	220	333	553	42	192	1	43	32	778	9.8	30
Polynice (LAC)	31	1132	261	151	.579	138	79	.572	106	177	283	26	98	1	17	13	381	12.3	30
Grant	68	2105	587	265	.451	74	51	.689	69	140	209	587	192	4	103	12	590	8.7	24
Garland	69	1702	519	221	.426	157	118	.752	46	152	198	317	189	3	97	10	564	8.2	21
Martin	74	1334	507	214	.422	100	68	.680	53	78	131	65	104	0	37	31	523	7.1	25
Kimble	62	1004	418	159	.380	119	92	.773	42	77	119	76	158	2	30	8	429	6.9	27
Vaught	73	1178	359	175	.487	74	49	.662	124	225	349	40	135	2	20	23	399	5.5	17
Garrick	67	949	236	100	.424	79	60	.759	40	87	127	223	101	0	62	2	260	3.9	19
Bannister	47	339	81	43	.531	65	25	.385	34	62	96	9	73	0	5	7	111	2.4	16
Smrek (Tot)	15	95	27	9	.333	12	6	.500	7	19	26	4	27	1	3	3	24	1.6	4
Smrek (LAC)	10	70	16	3	.188	8	4	.500	4	15	19	3	18	1	1	3	10	1.0	4
Butler	9	37	19	5	.263	6	4	.667	8	8	16	1	9	0	0	1	14	1.6	5
Ball	7	26	8	3	.375	2	2	1.000	5	6	11	0	5	0	1	1	11	1.2	2

3-Pt. FG: L.A. Clippers 113-434 (.260)—Smith 0-7 (.000); Harper 48-148 (.324); Norman 6-32 (.188); Manning 0-3 (.000); Polynice 0-1 (.000); Grant 9-39 (.231); Garland 4-26 (.154); Martin 27-88 (.307); Kimble 19-65 (.292); Vaught 0-2 (.000); Garrick 0-22 (.000); Bannister 0-1 (.000). Opponents 199-593 (.336).

LOS ANGELES LAKERS

Player	G.	Min.	FGA	FGM	Pct.	FTA	FTM	Pct.	Off. Reb.	Def. Reb.	Tot. Reb.	Ast.	PF	Disq.	Stl.	Blk. Sh.	Pts.	Avg.	Hi.
Worthy	78	3008	1455	716	.492	266	212	.797	107	249	356	275	117	0	104	35	1670	21.4	36
Johnson	79	2933	976	466	.477	573	519	.906	105	446	551	989	150	0	102	17	1531	19.4	34
Scott	82	2630	1051	501	.477	148	118	.797	54	192	246	177	146	0	95	21	1191	14.5	32
Perkins	73	2504	744	368	.495	279	229	.821	167	371	538	108	247	2	64	78	983	13.5	31
Divac	82	2310	637	360	.565	279	196	.703	205	461	666	92	247	3	106	127	921	11.2	25
Teagle	82	1498	757	335	.443	177	145	.819	82	99	181	82	165	1	31	8	815	9.9	35
Green	82	2164	542	258	.476	302	223	.738	201	315	516	71	117	0	59	23	750	9.1	21
Thompson	72	1077	228	113	.496	88	62	.705	74	154	228	21	112	0	23	23	288	4.0	19
Smith	64	695	220	97	.441	57	40	.702	24	47	71	135	80	0	28	12	234	3.7	12
Drew	48	496	125	54	.432	22	17	.773	5	29	34	118	40	0	15	1	139	2.9	11
Campbell	52	380	123	56	.455	49	32	.653	40	56	96	10	71	1	11	38	144	2.8	12
Thomas	26	108	50	17	.340	21	12	.571	14	17	31	10	24	0	4	1	46	1.8	9
Brown	7	27	3	2	.667	0	0	.000	0	4	4	3	8	0	0	0	5	0.7	3

3-Pt. FG: L.A. Lakers 226-744 (.304)—Worthy 26-90 (.289); Johnson 80-250 (.320); Scott 71-219 (.324); Perkins 18-64 (.281); Divac 5-14 (.357); Teagle 0-9 (.000); Green 11-55 (.200); Thompson 0-2 (.000); Smith 0-7 (.000); Drew 14-33 (.424); Brown 1-1 (1.000). Opponents 178-573 (.311).

MIAMI HEAT

Player	G.	Min.	FGA	FGM	Pct.	FTA	FTM	Pct.	Off. Reb.	Def. Reb.	Tot. Reb.	Ast.	PF	Disq.	Stl.	Blk. Sh.	Pts.	Avg.	Hi.
Douglas	73	2562	1055	532	.504	414	284	.686	78	131	209	624	178	2	121	5	1352	18.5	42
Rice	77	2646	1193	550	.461	209	171	.818	85	296	381	189	216	0	101	26	1342	17.4	37
Seikaly	64	2171	822	395	.481	417	258	.619	207	502	709	95	213	2	51	86	1050	16.4	35
Edwards	79	2000	927	380	.410	213	171	.803	80	125	205	240	151	2	129	46	955	12.1	34
Burton	76	1928	773	341	.441	293	229	.782	111	151	262	107	275	6	72	24	915	12.0	27
Long	80	2514	561	276	.492	230	181	.787	225	343	568	176	295	10	119	43	734	9.2	22
Thompson	73	1481	411	205	.499	124	89	.718	120	192	312	111	161	3	32	48	499	6.8	20
Kessler	78	1259	468	199	.425	131	88	.672	115	221	336	31	189	1	17	26	486	6.2	21
Davis	55	996	236	115	.487	124	69	.556	107	159	266	39	129	2	18	28	300	5.5	13
Coles	82	1355	393	162	.412	95	71	.747	56	97	153	232	149	0	65	12	401	4.9	15
Wagner	13	116	57	24	.421	11	9	.818	0	7	7	15	14	0	2	3	63	4.8	15
Sundvold	24	225	107	43	.402	11	11	1.000	3	6	9	24	11	0	7	0	112	4.7	13
Askins	39	266	81	34	.420	25	12	.480	30	38	68	19	46	0	16	13	86	2.2	10
Ogg	31	261	55	24	.436	10	6	.600	15	34	49	2	53	1	6	27	54	1.7	11

3-Pt. FG: Miami 140-464 (.302)—Douglas 4-31 (.129); Rice 71-184 (.386); Seikaly 2-6 (.333); Edwards 24-84 (.286); Burton 4-30 (.133); Long 1-6 (.167); Thompson 0-4 (.000); Kessler 0-4 (.000); Davis 1-2 (.500); Coles 6-34 (.176); Wagner 6-17 (.353); Sundvold 15-35 (.429); Askins 6-25 (.240); Ogg 0-2 (.000). Opponents 173-514 (.337).

MILWAUKEE BUCKS

Player	G.	Min.	FGA	FGM	Pct.	FTA	FTM	Pct.	Off. Reb.	Def. Reb.	Tot. Reb.	Ast.	PF	Disq.	Stl.	Blk. Sh.	Pts.	Avg.	Hi.
Pierce	46	1327	720	359	.499	311	282	.907	37	80	117	96	90	0	38	11	1037	22.5	37
Ellis (Tot.)	51	1424	718	340	.474	166	120	.723	66	107	173	95	112	1	49	8	857	16.8	32
Ellis (Mil)	21	624	327	159	.486	82	58	.707	38	43	81	31	53	1	16	5	406	19.3	32
Humphries	80	2726	960	482	.502	239	191	.799	57	163	220	538	237	2	129	7	1215	15.2	36
Robertson	81	2598	904	438	.485	263	199	.757	191	268	459	444	273	5	246	16	1098	13.6	31
Brickowski	75	1912	706	372	.527	248	198	.798	129	297	426	131	255	4	86	43	942	12.6	32
Roberts	82	2114	670	357	.533	209	170	.813	107	174	281	135	190	2	63	29	888	10.8	34
Schayes	82	2228	597	298	.499	328	274	.835	174	361	535	98	264	4	55	61	870	10.6	31
Sikma	77	1940	691	295	.427	197	166	.843	108	333	441	143	218	4	65	64	802	10.4	29
Grayer	82	1422	485	210	.433	147	101	.687	111	135	246	123	98	0	48	9	521	6.4	23
Dantley	10	126	50	19	.380	26	18	.692	8	5	13	9	8	0	5	0	57	5.7	16
Lohaus	81	1219	415	179	.431	54	37	.685	59	158	217	75	170	3	50	74	428	5.3	23
Conner (Tot.)	74	1008	207	96	.464	94	68	.723	21	91	112	165	75	0	85	2	260	3.5	13
Conner (Mil)	39	519	96	38	.396	52	39	.750	10	45	55	107	37	0	48	1	115	2.9	13
Henson	68	690	189	79	.418	42	38	.905	14	37	51	131	83	0	32	0	214	3.1	16
Anderson	26	247	73	27	.370	28	16	.571	26	49	75	3	29	0	8	9	70	2.7	12
Stephens	3	6	3	2	.667	2	2	1.000	0	0	0	2	0	0	0	0	6	2.0	6
Kornet	32	157	62	23	.371	13	7	.538	10	14	24	9	28	0	5	1	58	1.8	11

3-Pt. FG: Milwaukee 257-753 (.341)—Pierce 37-93 (.398); Ellis 30-68 (.441); Humphries 60-161 (.373); Robertson 23-63 (.365); Brickowski 0-2 (.000); Roberts 4-25 (.160); Schayes 0-5 (.000); Sikma 46-135 (.341); Grayer 0-3 (.000); Dantley 1-3 (.333); Lohaus 33-119 (.277); Conner 0-3 (.000); Henson 18-54 (.333); Anderson 0-1 (.000); Kornet 5-18 (.278). Opponents 189-574 (.329).

MINNESOTA TIMBERWOLVES

Player	G.	Min.	FGA	FGM	Pct.	FTA	FTM	Pct.	Off. Reb.	Def. Reb.	Tot. Reb.	Ast.	PF	Disq.	Stl.	Blk. Sh.	Pts.	Avg.	Hi.
Campbell	77	2893	1502	652	.434	446	358	.803	161	185	346	214	204	0	121	48	1678	21.8	34
Corbin	82	3196	1311	587	.448	371	296	.798	185	404	589	347	257	3	162	53	1472	18.0	32
Richardson	82	3154	1350	635	.470	165	89	.539	82	204	286	734	114	0	131	13	1401	17.1	35
Mitchell	82	3121	1010	445	.441	396	307	.775	188	332	520	133	338	13	66	57	1197	14.6	37
Spencer	81	2099	381	195	.512	252	182	.722	272	369	641	25	337	14	48	121	572	7.1	23
Glass	51	606	340	149	.438	76	52	.684	54	48	102	42	76	2	28	9	352	6.9	32
Breuer	73	1505	435	197	.453	79	35	.443	114	231	345	73	132	1	35	80	429	5.9	20
Brooks	80	980	370	159	.430	72	61	.847	28	44	72	204	122	1	53	5	424	5.3	18
Murphy	52	1063	227	90	.396	105	70	.667	92	163	255	60	101	1	25	20	251	4.8	13
West	75	824	246	118	.480	84	58	.690	56	80	136	48	115	0	35	23	294	3.9	17
Thornton	12	110	13	4	.308	10	8	.800	1	14	15	1	18	0	3	1	16	1.3	6
Coffey	52	320	75	28	.373	22	12	.545	42	37	79	3	45	0	6	4	68	1.3	8
Godfread	10	20	12	5	.417	4	3	.750	0	2	2	0	5	0	1	4	13	1.3	4
Thomas	3	14	4	1	.250	0	0	....	0	0	0	1	0	0	0	0	2	0.7	2

3-Pt. FG: Minnesota 108-381 (.283)—Campbell 16-61 (.262); Corbin 2-10 (.200); Richardson 42-128 (.328); Mitchell 0-9 (.000); Spencer 0-1 (.000); Glass 2-17 (.118); Brooks 45-135 (.333); Murphy 1-17 (.059); West 0-1 (.000); Coffey 0-1 (.000); Godfread 0-1 (.000). Opponents 171-505 (.339).

NEW JERSEY NETS

Player	G.	Min.	FGA	FGM	Pct.	FTA	FTM	Pct.	Off. Reb.	Def. Reb.	Tot. Reb.	Ast.	PF	Disq.	Stl.	Blk. Sh.	Pts.	Avg.	Hi.
Theus	81	2955	1247	583	.468	343	292	.851	69	160	229	378	231	0	85	35	1510	18.6	36
Coleman	74	2602	1100	514	.467	442	323	.731	269	490	759	163	217	3	71	99	1364	18.4	42
Blaylock	72	2585	1039	432	.416	176	139	.790	67	182	249	441	180	0	169	40	1017	14.1	27
Morris	79	2553	962	409	.425	244	179	.734	210	311	521	220	248	5	138	96	1042	13.2	32
Bowie	62	1916	723	314	.434	231	169	.732	176	304	480	147	175	4	43	90	801	12.9	38
Petrovic (Tot.)	61	1015	493	243	.493	137	114	.832	51	59	110	86	132	0	43	1	623	10.2	27
Petrovic (NJ)	43	882	422	211	.500	115	99	.861	41	51	92	66	111	0	37	1	543	12.6	27
Anderson	1	18	4	4	1.000	0	0	.000	4	2	6	1	4	0	2	0	8	8.0	8
Gervin	56	743	394	164	.416	114	90	.789	40	70	110	30	88	0	19	19	425	7.6	34
Dudley	61	1560	417	170	.408	176	94	.534	229	282	511	37	217	6	39	153	434	7.1	20
Mills (Tot.)	55	819	288	134	.465	66	47	.712	82	147	229	33	100	0	35	29	315	5.7	20
Mills (NJ)	38	540	168	78	.464	44	31	.705	51	90	141	17	56	0	19	20	187	4.9	20
Haley	78	1178	343	161	.469	181	112	.619	140	216	356	31	199	0	20	21	434	5.6	18
Hinson	9	91	39	20	.513	3	1	.333	6	13	19	4	14	0	0	3	41	4.6	12
Conner	35	489	111	58	.523	42	29	.690	11	46	57	58	38	0	37	1	145	4.1	13
George	56	594	193	80	.415	40	32	.800	19	28	47	104	58	0	25	5	192	3.4	18
Buechler	74	859	226	94	.416	66	43	.652	61	80	141	51	79	0	33	15	232	3.1	12
Lee	48	265	71	19	.268	28	25	.893	7	23	30	34	39	0	11	2	66	1.4	8

3-Pt. FG: New Jersey 161-586 (.275)—Theus 52-144 (.361); Coleman 13-38 (.342); Blaylock 14-91 (.154); Morris 45-179 (.251); Bowie 4-22 (.182); Petrovic 22-59 (.373); Gervin 7-28 (.250); Mills 0-2 (.000); Conner 0-2 (.000); George 0-2 (.000); Buechler 1-4 (.250); Lee 3-15 (.200). Opponents 136-442 (.308).

NEW YORK KNICKERBOCKERS

Player	G.	Min.	FGA	FGM	Pct.	FTA	FTM	Pct.	Off. Reb.	Def. Reb.	Tot. Reb.	Ast.	PF	Disq.	Stl.	Blk. Sh.	Pts.	Avg.	Hi.
Ewing	81	3104	1645	845	.514	623	464	.745	194	711	905	244	287	3	80	258	2154	26.6	50
Vandeweghe	75	2420	927	458	.494	288	259	.899	78	102	180	110	122	0	42	10	1226	16.3	29
G. Wilkins	68	2164	804	380	.473	206	169	.820	78	129	207	275	181	0	82	23	938	13.8	27
Oakley	76	2739	595	307	.516	305	239	.784	305	615	920	204	288	4	62	17	853	11.2	24
Jackson	72	1595	508	250	.492	160	117	.731	62	135	197	452	81	0	60	9	630	8.8	26
Cheeks	76	2147	483	241	.499	129	105	.814	22	151	173	435	138	0	128	10	592	7.8	27
Starks	61	1173	410	180	.439	105	79	.752	30	101	131	204	137	1	59	17	466	7.6	25
Tucker	65	1194	434	191	.440	27	17	.630	33	72	105	111	120	0	44	9	463	7.1	19
Quinnett	68	1011	303	139	.459	36	26	.722	65	80	145	53	100	0	22	13	319	4.7	20
Mustaf	62	825	228	106	.465	87	56	.644	51	118	169	36	109	0	15	14	268	4.3	13
Walker	54	771	191	83	.435	82	64	.780	63	94	157	13	92	0	18	30	230	4.3	13
E. Wilkins	68	668	255	114	.447	90	51	.567	69	111	180	15	91	0	17	7	279	4.1	20
Gray	8	37	12	4	.333	3	3	1.000	2	8	10	0	6	0	0	1	11	1.4	4
Grant	22	107	27	10	.370	6	5	.833	1	9	10	20	9	0	9	0	26	1.2	8

3-Pt. FG: New York 185-558 (.332)—Ewing 0-6 (.000); Vandeweghe 51-141 (.362); G. Wilkins 9-43 (.209); Oakley 0-2 (.000); Jackson 13-51 (.255); Cheeks 5-20 (.250); Starks 27-93 (.290); Tucker 64-153 (.418); Quinnett 15-43 (.349); Mustaf 0-1 (.000); Walker 0-1 (.000); E. Wilkins 0-1 (.000); Grant 1-3 (.333). Opponents 183-545 (.336).

ORLANDO MAGIC

Player	G.	Min.	FGA	FGM	Pct.	FTA	FTM	Pct.	Off. Reb.	Def. Reb.	Tot. Reb.	Ast.	PF	Disq.	Stl.	Blk. Sh.	Pts.	Avg.	Hi.
Skiles	79	2714	1039	462	.445	377	340	.902	57	213	270	660	192	2	89	4	1357	17.2	34
Scott	82	2336	1183	503	.425	204	153	.750	62	173	235	134	203	1	62	25	1284	15.7	40
Catledge	51	1459	632	292	.462	258	161	.624	168	187	355	58	113	2	34	9	745	14.6	30
Anderson	70	1971	857	400	.467	259	173	.668	92	294	386	106	145	0	74	44	990	14.1	31
Smith	75	1885	902	407	.451	301	221	.734	176	213	389	169	190	1	85	35	1044	13.9	33
Reynolds	80	1843	793	344	.434	419	336	.802	88	211	299	203	123	0	95	56	1034	12.9	27
Turner	71	1683	532	259	.487	112	85	.759	108	255	363	97	234	5	29	10	609	8.6	28
Vincent	49	975	353	152	.431	120	99	.825	11	90	107	197	74	0	30	5	406	8.3	26
Ansley	67	877	263	144	.548	127	91	.717	122	131	253	25	125	0	27	7	379	5.7	16
Wright	8	136	41	15	.366	21	13	.619	10	27	37	3	23	0	3	5	43	5.4	13
Kite	82	2225	338	166	.491	123	63	.512	189	399	588	59	298	4	25	81	395	4.8	16
Acres	68	1313	214	109	.509	101	66	.653	140	219	359	25	218	4	25	25	285	4.2	12
Wiley	34	350	108	45	.417	25	17	.680	4	13	17	73	37	1	24	0	113	3.3	17
McNamara	2	13	1	0	.000	0	0	.000	0	4	4	0	1	0	0	0	0	0.0	0

3-Pt. FG: Orlando 270-754 (.358)—Skiles 93-228 (.408); Scott 125-334 (.374); Catledge 0-5 (.000); Anderson 17-58 (.293); Smith 9-46 (.196); Reynolds 10-34 (.294); Turner 6-15 (.400); Vincent 3-19 (.158); Acres 1-3 (.333); Wiley 6-12 (.500). Opponents 223-674 (.331).

PHILADELPHIA 76ers

Player	G.	Min.	FGA	FGM	Pct.	FTA	FTM	Pct.	Off. Reb.	Def. Reb.	Tot. Reb.	Ast.	PF	Disq.	Stl.	Blk. Sh.	Pts.	Avg.	Hi.
Barkley	67	2498	1167	665	.570	658	475	.722	258	422	680	284	173	2	110	33	1849	27.6	45
Hawkins	80	3110	1251	590	.472	550	479	.871	48	262	310	299	182	0	178	39	1767	22.1	39
Gilliam (Tot)	75	2644	1001	487	.487	329	268	.815	220	378	598	105	185	2	69	53	1242	16.6	39
Gilliam (Phil)	50	1695	621	292	.470	201	164	.816	134	230	364	78	120	1	35	32	748	15.0	29
Dawkins	4	124	41	26	.634	11	10	.909	0	16	16	28	4	0	3	0	63	15.8	25
Anderson	82	2340	1055	512	.485	198	165	.833	103	264	367	115	163	1	65	13	1198	14.6	28
Green	79	2248	722	334	.463	141	117	.830	33	104	137	413	130	0	57	6	793	10.0	27
Gminski	30	791	284	109	.384	63	53	.841	71	130	201	33	41	0	16	34	272	9.1	19
Mahorn	80	2439	559	261	.467	240	189	.788	151	470	621	118	276	6	79	56	711	8.9	19
Turner	70	1407	383	168	.439	87	64	.736	36	116	152	311	124	0	63	0	412	5.9	18
Oliver	73	800	272	111	.408	71	52	.732	18	62	80	88	76	0	34	4	279	3.8	19
Payne	47	444	189	68	.360	29	26	.897	17	49	66	16	43	0	10	6	166	3.5	15
Williams	52	508	161	72	.447	56	37	.661	41	70	111	16	92	1	9	6	182	3.5	17
Farmer	2	13	7	2	.286	2	2	1.000	2	3	5	0	0	0	0	0	6	3.0	6
Hoppen (Tot)	30	155	44	24	.545	22	16	.727	18	21	39	3	29	0	3	1	64	2.1	6
Hoppen (Phil)	11	43	12	6	.500	12	8	.667	4	5	9	0	11	0	1	0	20	1.8	6
Elie	3	20	7	2	.286	2	1	.500	0	1	1	1	2	0	0	0	6	2.0	6
Bol	82	1522	164	65	.396	41	24	.585	66	284	350	20	184	0	16	247	155	1.9	8
Harris	6	41	16	4	.250	4	2	.500	0	1	1	0	5	0	1	0	10	1.7	5
Reid	3	37	14	2	.143	0	0	.000	2	7	9	4	3	0	1	3	4	1.3	4

3-Pt. FG: Philadelphia 195-618 (.316)—Barkley 44-155 (.284); Hawkins 108-270 (.400); Gilliam 0-2 (.000); Dawkins 1-4 (.250); Anderson 9-43 (.209); Green 8-36 (.222); Gminski 1-8 (.125); Mahorn 0-9 (.000); Turner 12-33 (.364); Oliver 5-18 (.278); Payne 4-18 (.222); Williams 1-2 (.500); Farmer 0-1 (.000); Hoppen 0-1 (.000); Elie 1-2 (.500); Bol 1-14 (.071); Harris 0-2 (.000). Opponents 196-660 (.297).

PHOENIX SUNS

Player	G.	Min.	FGA	FGM	Pct.	FTA	FTM	Pct.	Off. Reb.	Def. Reb.	Tot. Reb.	Ast.	PF	Disq.	Stl.	Blk. Sh.	Pts.	Avg.	Hi.
K. Johnson	77	2772	1145	591	.516	616	519	.843	54	217	271	781	174	0	163	11	1710	22.2	38
Chambers	76	2475	1271	556	.437	459	379	.826	104	386	490	194	235	3	65	52	1511	19.9	39
McDaniel (Tot)	81	2634	1186	590	.497	267	193	.723	173	384	557	187	264	2	76	46	1373	17.0	41
McDaniel (Phoe)	66	2105	896	451	.503	198	144	.727	137	339	476	149	214	2	50	42	1046	15.8	34
Hornacek	80	2733	1051	544	.518	224	201	.897	74	247	321	409	185	1	111	16	1350	16.9	31
Majerle	77	2281	821	397	.484	298	227	.762	168	250	418	216	162	0	106	40	1051	13.6	26
E. Johnson	15	312	186	88	.473	29	21	.724	16	30	46	17	37	0	9	2	203	13.5	35
Ceballos	63	730	419	204	.487	166	110	.663	77	73	150	35	70	0	22	5	519	8.2	34
West	82	1957	382	247	.647	206	135	.655	171	393	564	37	266	2	32	161	629	7.7	21
Battle	16	263	86	38	.442	29	20	.690	21	32	53	15	25	0	19	6	96	6.0	23
Knight	64	792	308	131	.425	118	71	.602	20	51	71	191	83	0	20	7	339	5.3	27
Lang	63	1152	189	109	.577	130	93	.715	113	190	303	27	168	2	17	127	311	4.9	16
Perry	46	587	144	75	.521	70	43	.614	53	73	126	27	60	1	23	43	193	4.2	19
Lockhart	1	2	1	1	1.000	0	0		0	0	0	0	0	0	0	0	4	4.0	4
Rambis	62	900	167	83	.497	85	60	.706	77	189	266	64	107	1	25	11	226	3.6	10
Carroll	11	96	36	13	.361	12	11	.917	3	21	24	11	18	0	1	8	37	3.4	8
Nealy	55	573	97	45	.464	38	28	.737	44	107	151	36	46	0	24	4	123	2.2	9

3-Pt. FG: Phoenix 138-432 (.319)—K. Johnson 9-44 (.205); Chambers 20-73 (.274); McDaniel 0-5 (.000); Hornacek 61-146 (.418); Majerle 30-86 (.349); E. Johnson 6-21 (.286); Ceballos 1-6 (.167); Battle 0-2 (.000); Knight 6-25 (.240); Lang 0-1 (.000); Perry 0-5 (.000); Rambis 0-2 (.000); Nealy 5-16 (.313). Opponents 182-584 (.312).

PORTLAND TRAIL BLAZERS

Player	G.	Min.	FGA	FGM	Pct.	FTA	FTM	Pct.	Off. Reb.	Def. Reb.	Tot. Reb.	Ast.	PF	Disq.	Stl.	Blk. Sh.	Pts.	Avg.	Hi.
Drexler	82	2852	1338	645	.482	524	416	.794	212	334	546	493	226	2	144	60	1767	21.5	39
Porter	81	2665	944	486	.515	339	279	.823	52	230	282	649	151	2	158	12	1381	17.0	38
Duckworth	81	2511	1084	521	.481	240	177	.772	177	354	531	89	251	5	33	34	1282	15.8	27
Kersey	73	2359	887	424	.478	327	232	.709	169	312	481	227	251	4	101	76	1084	14.8	35
Davis (Tot)	71	1483	862	403	.468	117	107	.915	71	110	181	125	150	2	80	3	924	13.0	41
Davis (Port)	32	439	195	87	.446	23	21	.913	19	39	58	41	42	0	18	0	196	6.1	16
Robinson	82	1940	806	373	.463	314	205	.653	123	226	349	151	263	2	78	76	957	11.7	22
Williams	80	2582	595	358	.602	308	217	.705	227	524	751	97	247	2	47	47	933	11.7	26
Ainge	80	1710	714	337	.472	138	114	.826	45	160	205	285	195	2	63	13	890	11.1	20
Bryant	53	781	203	99	.488	101	74	.733	65	125	190	27	120	0	15	12	272	5.1	20
Petrovic	18	133	71	32	.451	22	15	.682	10	8	18	20	21	0	6	0	80	4.4	11
Young	75	897	271	103	.380	45	41	.911	22	53	75	141	49	0	50	7	283	3.8	21
Abdelnaby	43	290	116	58	.474	44	25	.568	27	62	89	12	39	0	4	12	135	3.1	15
Cooper	67	746	145	57	.393	42	33	.786	54	134	188	22	120	0	7	61	147	2.2	13

3-Pt. FG: Portland 341-904 (.377)—Drexler 61-191 (.319); Porter 130-313 (.415); Duckworth 0-2 (.000); Kersey 4-13 (.308); Davis 1-3 (.333); Robinson 6-19 (.316); Ainge 102-251 (.406); Bryant 0-1 (.000); Petrovic 1-6 (.167); Young 36-104 (.346); Cooper 0-1 (.000). Opponents 236-730 (.323).

SACRAMENTO KINGS

Player	G.	Min.	FGA	FGM	Pct.	FTA	FTM	Pct.	Off. Reb.	Def. Reb.	Tot. Reb.	Ast.	PF	Disq.	Stl.	Blk. Sh.	Pts.	Avg.	Hi.
Carr	77	2527	1228	628	.511	389	295	.758	163	257	420	191	315	14	45	101	1551	20.1	41
Tisdale	33	1116	542	262	.483	170	136	.800	75	178	253	66	99	0	23	28	660	20.0	36
Simmons	79	2978	1301	549	.422	435	320	.736	193	504	697	315	249	0	113	85	1421	18.0	42
Mays	64	2145	724	294	.406	331	255	.770	54	124	178	253	169	1	81	11	915	14.3	36
Sparrow	80	2375	756	371	.491	83	58	.699	45	141	186	362	189	1	83	16	831	10.4	32
Bonner	34	750	230	103	.448	76	44	.579	59	102	161	49	62	0	39	5	250	7.4	18
Les	55	1399	268	119	.444	103	86	.835	18	93	111	299	141	0	57	4	395	7.2	20
Causwell	76	1719	413	210	.508	165	105	.636	141	250	391	69	225	4	49	148	525	6.9	22
Wood	12	222	63	25	.397	21	19	.905	5	14	19	49	10	0	5	0	81	6.8	25
Hansen	36	811	256	96	.375	36	18	.500	33	63	96	90	72	1	20	5	229	6.4	18
Wennington	77	1455	415	181	.436	94	74	.787	101	239	340	69	230	4	46	59	437	5.7	15
Frederick	35	475	168	67	.399	60	43	.717	36	48	84	44	50	0	22	13	177	5.1	22
Calloway	64	678	192	75	.391	79	55	.696	25	53	78	61	98	1	22	7	205	3.2	16
Colter	19	251	56	23	.411	10	7	.700	5	21	26	37	27	0	11	1	58	3.1	17
Sampson	25	348	93	34	.366	19	5	.263	41	70	111	17	54	0	11	17	74	3.0	8
Leckner	32	378	96	39	.406	27	16	.593	27	60	87	18	69	1	4	11	94	2.9	10
Higgins	7	61	10	6	.600	7	4	.571	4	1	5	2	16	1	0	2	16	2.3	6
Dawson	4	17	7	4	.571	0	0	.000	2	4	6	9	2	0	0	0	9	2.3	4

3-Pt. FG: Sacramento 216-578 (.374)—Carr 0-3 (.000); Tisdale 0-1 (.000); Simmons 3-11 (.273); Mays 72-197 (.365); Sparrow 31-78 (.397); Les 71-154 (.461); Wood 12-38 (.316); Hansen 19-69 (.275); Wennington 1-5 (.200); Calloway 0-2 (.000); Colter 5-14 (.357); Sampson 1-5 (.200); Dawson 1-1 (1.000). Opponents 155-491 (.316).

SAN ANTONIO SPURS

Player	G.	Min.	FGA	FGM	Pct.	FTA	FTM	Pct.	Off. Reb.	Def. Reb.	Tot. Reb.	Ast.	PF	Disq.	Stl.	Blk. Sh.	Pts.	Avg.	Hi.
Robinson	82	3095	1366	754	.552	777	592	.762	335	728	1063	208	264	5	127	320	2101	25.6	43
Cummings	67	2195	1039	503	.484	240	164	.683	194	327	521	157	225	5	61	30	1177	17.6	31
Elliott	82	3044	976	478	.490	402	325	.808	142	314	456	238	190	2	69	33	1301	15.9	34
Anderson	75	2592	991	453	.457	213	170	.798	68	283	351	358	226	4	79	46	1083	14.4	28
Strickland	58	2076	651	314	.482	211	161	.763	57	162	219	463	125	0	117	11	800	13.8	27
Williams	22	354	127	61	.480	41	35	.854	17	42	59	46	64	2	20	11	171	7.8	22
Pressey	70	1683	426	201	.472	133	110	.827	50	126	176	271	174	1	63	32	528	7.5	18
Green	66	1099	384	177	.461	105	89	.848	98	215	313	52	172	0	32	13	443	6.7	19
Wingate	25	563	138	53	.384	41	29	.707	24	51	75	46	66	0	19	5	136	5.4	15
Lett	7	99	29	14	.483	9	6	.667	1	6	7	7	9	0	2	1	34	4.9	11
Johnson (Tot)	68	959	277	130	.469	87	59	.678	22	55	77	230	62	0	47	4	320	4.7	21
Johnson (SA)	47	742	209	101	.483	55	38	.691	13	43	56	153	40	0	33	2	241	5.1	21
Higgins	50	464	212	97	.458	33	28	.848	18	45	63	35	53	0	8	1	225	4.5	22
Greenwood	63	1018	169	85	.503	94	69	.734	61	160	221	52	172	3	29	25	239	3.8	15
Schintzius	42	398	155	68	.439	40	22	.550	28	93	121	17	64	0	2	29	158	3.8	16
Myers	8	103	23	10	.435	11	9	.818	2	16	18	14	14	0	3	3	29	3.6	8
Dinkins	10	144	33	13	.394	9	8	.889	0	11	11	19	12	0	2	0	34	3.4	6
Massenburg	35	161	60	27	.450	45	28	.622	23	35	58	4	26	0	4	9	82	2.3	19

3-Pt. FG: San Antonio 81-297 (.273)—Robinson 1-7 (.143); Cummings 7-33 (.212); Elliott 20-64 (.313); Anderson 7-35 (.200); Strickland 11-33 (.333); Williams 14-26 (.538); Pressey 16-57 (.281); Green 0-3 (.000); Wingate 1-9 (.111); Lett 0-1 (.000); Johnson 1-5 (.200); Higgins 3-19 (.158); Greenwood 0-2 (.000); Schintzius 0-2 (.000); Myers 0-1 (.000). Opponents 218-704 (.310).

SEATTLE SUPERSONICS

Player	G.	Min.	FGA	FGM	Pct.	FTA	FTM	Pct.	Off. Reb.	Def. Reb.	Tot. Reb.	Ast.	PF	Disq.	Stl.	Blk. Sh.	Pts.	Avg.	Hi.
McDaniel	15	529	290	139	.479	69	49	.710	36	45	81	38	50	0	26	4	327	21.8	41
Pierce (Tot)	78	2167	1156	561	.485	471	430	.913	67	124	191	168	170	1	60	13	1598	20.5	37
Pierce (Sea)	32	840	436	202	.463	160	148	.925	30	44	74	72	80	1	22	2	561	17.5	27
Johnson (Tot)	81	2085	1122	543	.484	257	229	.891	107	164	271	111	181	0	58	9	1354	16.7	35
Johnson (Sea)	66	1773	936	455	.486	228	208	.912	91	134	225	94	144	0	49	7	1151	17.4	34
McKey	73	2503	847	438	.517	278	235	.845	172	251	423	169	220	2	91	56	1115	15.3	33
Ellis	30	800	391	181	.463	84	62	.738	28	64	92	64	59	0	33	3	451	15.0	26
Kemp	81	2442	909	462	.508	436	288	.661	267	412	679	144	319	11	77	123	1214	15.0	31
Benjamin (Tot)	70	2236	778	386	.496	295	210	.712	157	566	723	119	184	1	54	145	982	14.0	28
Benjamin (Sea)	31	899	313	157	.502	126	87	.690	62	192	254	45	74	0	28	54	401	12.9	28
Threatt	80	2066	835	433	.519	173	137	.792	25	74	99	273	191	0	113	8	1013	12.7	31
Polynice	48	960	303	165	.545	114	67	.588	104	156	270	16	94	0	26	19	397	8.3	27
Payton	82	2244	575	259	.450	97	69	.711	108	135	243	528	249	3	165	15	588	7.2	19
Cage	82	2141	445	226	.508	112	70	.625	177	381	558	89	194	0	85	58	522	6.4	17
Barros	66	750	311	154	.495	85	78	.918	17	54	71	111	40	0	23	1	418	6.3	24
Dailey	30	299	155	73	.471	62	38	.613	11	21	32	16	25	0	7	1	184	6.1	29
McMillan	78	1434	305	132	.433	93	57	.613	71	180	251	371	211	6	104	20	338	4.3	12

Player	G.	Min.	FGA	FGM	Pct.	FTA	FTM	Pct.	Off. Reb.	Def. Reb.	Tot. Reb.	Ast.	PF	Disq.	Stl.	Blk. Sh.	Pts.	Avg.	Hi.
Corzine	28	147	38	17	.447	22	13	.591	10	23	33	4	18	0	5	5	47	1.7	10
Meents	13	53	28	7	.250	4	2	.500	3	7	10	8	5	0	7	4	17	1.3	4

3-Pt. FG: Seattle 136-427 (.319)—McDaniel 0-3 (.000); Pierce 9-23 (.391); Johnson 33-99 (.333); McKey 4-19 (.211); Ellis 27-89 (.303); Kemp 2-12 (.167); Threatt 10-35 (.286); Payton 1-13 (.077); Cage 0-3 (.000); Barros 32-81 (.395); Dailey 0-1 (.000); McMillan 17-48 (.354); Meents 1-1 (1.000). Opponents 207-633 (.327).

UTAH JAZZ

Player	G.	Min.	FGA	FGM	Pct.	FTA	FTM	Pct.	Off. Reb.	Def. Reb.	Tot. Reb.	Ast.	PF	Disq.	Stl.	Blk. Sh.	Pts.	Avg.	Hi.
K. Malone	82	3302	1608	847	.527	888	684	.770	236	731	967	270	268	2	89	79	2382	29.0	41
J. Malone	69	2466	1034	525	.508	252	231	.917	36	170	206	143	128	0	50	6	1282	18.6	43
Stockton	82	3103	978	496	.507	434	363	.836	46	191	237	1164	233	1	234	16	1413	17.2	28
Bailey	82	2486	872	399	.458	271	219	.808	101	306	407	124	160	0	53	91	1017	12.4	25
Edwards	62	1611	464	244	.526	117	82	.701	51	150	201	108	203	4	57	29	576	9.3	25
Griffith	75	1005	445	174	.391	45	34	.756	17	73	90	37	100	1	42	7	430	5.7	24
Eaton	80	2580	292	169	.579	112	71	.634	182	485	667	51	298	6	39	188	409	5.1	13
M. Brown	82	1391	284	129	.454	178	132	.742	109	228	337	49	166	0	29	24	390	4.8	16
Rudd	82	874	285	124	.435	71	59	.831	14	52	66	216	92	0	36	2	324	4.0	11
Cummings	4	26	6	4	.667	10	7	.700	3	2	5	0	8	0	0	0	15	3.8	10
Toolson	47	470	124	50	.403	33	25	.758	32	35	67	31	58	0	14	2	137	2.9	13
T. Brown (Tot)	30	294	80	30	.375	23	20	.870	24	19	43	16	47	0	4	0	83	2.8	10
T. Brown (Utah)	23	267	77	28	.364	23	20	.870	24	15	39	13	39	0	4	0	78	3.4	10
Palmer	28	85	45	15	.333	15	10	.667	6	15	21	6	20	0	3	4	40	1.4	6
Munk	11	29	7	3	.429	12	7	.583	4	9	14	1	5	0	1	2	13	1.2	4
O'Sullivan	21	85	16	7	.438	11	7	.636	5	12	17	4	18	0	1	1	21	1.0	5

3-Pt. FG: Utah 148-458 (.323)—K. Malone 4-14 (.286); J. Malone 1-6 (.167); Stockton 58-168 (.345); Bailey 0-3 (.000); Edwards 6-24 (.250); Griffith 48-138 (.348); Rudd 17-61 (.279); Toolson 12-32 (.375); T. Brown 2-11 (.182); Palmer 0-1 (.000). Opponents 205-667 (.307).

WASHINGTON BULLETS

Player	G.	Min.	FGA	FGM	Pct.	FTA	FTM	Pct.	Off. Reb.	Def. Reb.	Tot. Reb.	Ast.	PF	Disq.	Stl.	Blk. Sh.	Pts.	Avg.	Hi.
King	64	2401	1511	713	.472	485	383	.790	114	205	319	292	187	1	56	16	1817	28.4	52
Grant	77	2842	1224	609	.498	249	185	.743	179	378	557	204	232	2	91	61	1405	18.2	34
Eackles	67	1616	762	345	.453	222	164	.739	47	81	128	136	121	0	47	10	868	13.0	33
Williams	33	941	393	164	.417	97	73	.753	42	135	177	133	63	0	39	6	411	12.5	27
Ellison	76	1942	636	326	.513	214	139	.650	224	361	585	102	268	6	49	157	791	10.4	30
English	70	1443	572	251	.439	157	111	.707	66	81	147	177	127	1	25	15	616	8.8	31
Workman	73	2034	515	234	.454	133	101	.759	51	191	242	353	162	1	87	7	581	8.0	21
Walker	71	2305	535	230	.430	154	93	.604	140	358	498	459	199	2	78	33	553	7.8	22
Alarie	42	587	225	99	.440	48	41	.854	41	76	117	45	88	1	15	8	244	5.8	15
Hammonds	70	1023	336	155	.461	79	57	.722	58	148	206	43	108	0	15	7	367	5.2	21
Irvin	33	316	129	60	.465	61	50	.820	24	21	45	24	32	0	15	2	171	5.2	16
Foster	54	606	211	97	.460	61	42	.689	52	99	151	37	112	1	12	22	236	4.4	12
Robinson (Tot)	36	425	150	62	.413	27	15	.556	29	22	51	35	49	0	16	1	139	3.9	13
Robinson (Wash)	12	255	91	38	.418	12	7	.583	14	14	28	24	26	0	7	0	83	6.9	13
Jones	62	1499	124	67	.540	50	29	.580	119	240	359	48	199	2	51	124	163	2.6	10
Smith	5	45	4	2	.500	6	3	.500	2	2	4	4	3	0	1	0	7	1.4	2

3-Pt. FG: Washington 55-284 (.194)—King 8-37 (.216); Grant 2-15 (.133); Eackles 14-59 (.237); Williams 10-41 (.244); Ellison 0-6 (.000); English 3-31 (.097); Workman 12-50 (.240); Walker 0-9 (.000); Alarie 5-21 (.238); Hammonds 0-4 (.000); Irvin 1-5 (.200); Foster 0-5 (.000); Robinson 0-1 (.000). Opponents 166-555 (.299).

PLAYOFF RESULTS

EASTERN CONFERENCE FIRST ROUND
Chicago 3, New York 0
Apr. 25—Thur.—New York 85 at Chicago 126
Apr. 28—Sun.—New York 79 at Chicago 89
Apr. 30—Tue.—Chicago 103 at New York 94

Boston 3, Indiana 2
Apr. 26—Fri.—Indiana 120 at Boston 127
Apr. 28—Sun.—Indiana 130 at Boston 118
May 1—Wed.—Boston 112 at Indiana 105
May 3—Fri.—Boston 113 at Indiana 116
May 5—Sun.—Indiana 121 at Boston...............................124

Detroit 3, Atlanta 2
Apr. 26—Fri.—Atlanta 103 at Detroit 98
Apr. 28—Sun.—Atlanta 88 at Detroit 101
Apr. 30—Tue.—Detroit 103 at Atlanta 91
May 2—Thur.—Detroit 111 at Atlanta 123
May 5—Sun.—Atlanta 81 at Detroit.................................113

Philadelphia 3, Milwaukee 0
Apr. 25—Thur.—Philadelphia 99 at Milwaukee 90
Apr. 27—Sat.—Philadelphia 116 at Milwaukee........................*112
Apr. 30—Tue.—Milwaukee 100 at Philadelphia 121

EASTERN CONFERENCE SEMIFINALS
Chicago 4, Philadelphia 1
May 4—Sat.—Philadelphia 92 at Chicago 105
May 6—Mon.—Philadelphia 100 at Chicago 112
May 10—Fri.—Chicago 97 at Philadelphia...............................99
May 12—Sun.—Chicago 101 at Philadelphia...............................85
May 14—Tue.—Philadelphia 95 at Chicago 100

Detroit 4, Boston 2
May 7—Tue.—Detroit 86 at Boston..75
May 9—Thur.—Detroit 103 at Boston 109
May 11—Sat.—Boston 115 at Detroit 83
May 13—Mon.—Boston 97 at Detroit 104
May 15—Wed.—Detroit 116 at Boston 111
May 17—Fri.—Boston 113 at Detroit *117

EASTERN CONFERENCE FINALS
Chicago 4, Detroit 0
May 19—Sun.—Detroit 83 at Chicago 94
May 21—Tue.—Detroit 97 at Chicago 105
May 25—Sat.—Chicago 113 at Detroit 107
May 27—Mon.—Chicago 115 at Detroit 94

WESTERN CONFERENCE FIRST ROUND
Portland 3, Seattle 2
Apr. 26—Fri.—Seattle 102 at Portland 110
Apr. 28—Sun.—Seattle 106 at Portland 115

Apr. 30—Tue.—Portland 99 at Seattle...................................102
May 2—Thur.—Portland 89 at Seattle 101
May 4—Sat.—Seattle 107 at Portland...............................119

Golden State 3, San Antonio 1
Apr. 25—Thur.—Golden State 121 at San Antonio......................130
Apr. 27—Sat.—Golden State 111 at San Antonio...........................98
May 1—Wed.—San Antonio 106 at Golden State 109
May 3—Fri.—San Antonio 97 at Golden State 110

L.A. Lakers 3, Houston 0
Apr. 25—Thur.—Houston 92 at L.A. Lakers 94
Apr. 27—Sat.—Houston 98 at L.A. Lakers 109
Apr. 30—Tue.—L.A. Lakers 94 at Houston...............................90

Utah 3, Phoenix 1
Apr. 25—Thur.—Utah 129 at Phoenix 90
Apr. 27—Sat.—Utah 92 at Phoenix 102
Apr. 30—Tue.—Phoenix 98 at Utah.....................................107
May 2—Thur.—Phoenix 93 at Utah 101

WESTERN CONFERENCE SEMIFINALS
L.A. Lakers 4, Golden State 1
May 5—Sun.—Golden State 116 at L.A. Lakers 126
May 8—Wed.—Golden State 125 at L.A. Lakers 124
May 10—Fri.—L.A. Lakers 115 at Golden State 112
May 12—Sun.—L.A. Lakers 123 at Golden State......................107
May 14—Tue.—Golden State 119 at L.A. Lakers *124

Portland 4, Utah 1
May 7—Tue.—Utah 97 at Portland.......................................117
May 9—Thur.—Utah 116 at Portland 118
May 11—Sat.—Portland 101 at Utah 107
May 12—Sun.—Portland 104 at Utah 101
May 14—Tue.—Utah 96 at Portland 103

WESTERN CONFERENCE FINALS
L.A. Lakers 4, Portland 2
May 18—Sat.—L.A. Lakers 111 at Portland 106
May 21—Tue.—L.A. Lakers 98 at Portland 109
May 24—Fri.—Portland 92 at L.A. Lakers..............................106
May 26—Sun.—Portland 95 at L.A. Lakers 116
May 28—Tue.—L.A. Lakers 84 at Portland.................................95
May 30—Thur.—Portland 90 at L.A. Lakers 91

NBA FINALS
Chicago 4, L.A. Lakers 1
June 2—Sun.—L.A. Lakers 93 at Chicago............................91
June 5—Wed.—L.A. Lakers 86 at Chicago...........................107
June 7—Fri.—Chicago 104 at L.A. Lakers...........................*96
June 9—Sun.—Chicago 97 at L.A. Lakers............................82
June 12—Wed.—Chicago 108 at L.A. Lakers 101

1989-90 NBA STATISTICS

1989-90 NBA CHAMPION DETROIT PISTONS

Front row (left to right): trainer Mike Abdenour, assistant to General Manager Will Robinson, assistant coach Brendan Suhr, Coach Chuck Daly, Managing Partner William Davidson, General Manager Jack McCloskey, CEO Thomas Wilson, legal counsel Oscar Feldman, assistant coach Brendan Malone, chief scout Stan Novak, announcer George Blaha. Back row: Isiah Thomas, Joe Dumars, Mark Aguirre, David Greenwood, Bill Laimbeer, William Bedford, James Edwards, John Salley, Scott Hastings, Dennis Rodman, Ralph Lewis, Vinnie Johnson, Gerald Henderson.

FINAL STANDINGS

ATLANTIC DIVISION

Team	Atl.	Bos.	Char.	Chi.	Cle.	Dal.	Den.	Det.	G.S.	Hou.	Ind.	L.A.C.	L.A.L.	Mia.	Mil.	Min.	N.J.	N.Y.	Orl.	Phi.	Pho.	Por.	Sac.	S.A.	Sea.	Uta.	Was.	W.	L.	Pct.	G.B.
Philadelphia	2	2	2	2	2	1	1	3	1	1	4	2	1	5	3	1	4	3	2	..	1	1	1	1	1	1	5	53	29	.646	..
Boston	3	..	2	2	3	1	1	2	1	2	1	1	0	5	2	1	5	4	4	3	1	0	2	1	2	1	2	52	30	.634	1
New York	3	1	1	1	2	1	1	0	2	1	3	2	0	5	2	1	4	..	2	2	1	0	2	1	1	1	5	45	37	.549	8
Washington	2	3	2	1	1	1	1	0	1	1	1	1	1	3	1	1	3	0	4	1	0	1	1	0	0	0	..	31	51	.378	22
Miami	0	0	1	0	0	0	0	0	1	0	1	0	2	..	2	1	1	1	3	0	0	0	1	0	0	1	2	18	64	.220	35
New Jersey	2	1	1	1	0	0	0	0	0	1	0	0	0	4	0	1	..	1	1	1	0	0	1	0	0	0	2	17	65	.207	36

CENTRAL DIVISION

Team	Atl.	Bos.	Char.	Chi.	Cle.	Dal.	Den.	Det.	G.S.	Hou.	Ind.	L.A.C.	L.A.L.	Mia.	Mil.	Min.	N.J.	N.Y.	Orl.	Phi.	Pho.	Por.	Sac.	S.A.	Sea.	Uta.	Was.	W.	L.	Pct.	G.B.
Detroit	2	2	2	4	4	1	2	..	1	1	4	1	1	3	3	2	4	4	5	1	2	1	2	1	1	1	4	59	23	.720	..
Chicago	5	2	2	..	5	2	1	1	2	1	2	1	1	4	4	2	3	3	3	2	2	1	1	1	1	0	3	55	27	.671	4
Milwaukee	2	2	2	1	2	1	1	2	1	1	2	1	1	2	..	2	4	2	5	1	1	1	1	1	2	0	3	44	38	.537	15
Cleveland	3	1	1	0	..	0	0	1	1	0	3	1	1	4	3	1	4	2	4	2	1	1	2	1	1	1	3	42	40	.512	17
Indiana	3	3	1	3	2	0	2	1	1	1	..	0	0	3	3	1	4	1	4	0	1	1	1	1	1	1	3	42	40	.512	17
Atlanta	..	1	2	0	2	0	1	3	2	2	2	1	0	4	3	1	2	1	5	2	0	1	1	1	1	1	2	41	41	.500	18
Orlando	0	0	1	2	1	0	0	0	0	0	1	0	1	0	1	3	2	1	..	2	0	0	1	1	0	1	0	18	64	.220	41

MIDWEST DIVISION

Team	Atl.	Bos.	Char.	Chi.	Cle.	Dal.	Den.	Det.	G.S.	Hou.	Ind.	L.A.C.	L.A.L.	Mia.	Mil.	Min.	N.J.	N.Y.	Orl.	Phi.	Pho.	Por.	Sac.	S.A.	Sea.	Uta.	Was.	W.	L.	Pct.	G.B.
San Antonio	1	1	5	1	1	2	3	1	3	2	1	4	2	2	1	4	2	1	1	4	1	4	1	..	3	3	2	56	26	.683	..
Utah	1	1	5	2	1	3	4	1	2	2	1	4	2	1	2	5	2	1	1	1	2	3	2	3	2	..	2	55	27	.671	1
Dallas	2	1	3	0	2	..	2	1	3	4	2	3	0	2	1	4	2	1	2	1	1	0	3	3	2	1	1	47	35	.573	9
Denver	1	1	2	1	2	3	..	0	2	4	0	2	0	1	2	5	2	1	2	1	2	4	1	2	0	1	1	43	39	.524	13
Houston	0	0	4	1	2	1	1	2	..	1	2	2	1	2	1	1	2	1	2	1	4	2	2	3	1	1	1	41	41	.500	15
Minnesota	1	1	2	0	1	1	0	0	1	2	1	1	0	1	0	..	1	1	1	1	0	1	2	1	0	1	0	22	60	.268	34
Charlotte	0	0	..	0	1	1	3	0	2	1	1	2	0	1	0	2	1	1	1	0	1	0	1	1	0	0	0	19	63	.232	37

PACIFIC DIVISION

Team	Atl.	Bos.	Char.	Chi.	Cle.	Dal.	Den.	Det.	G.S.	Hou.	Ind.	L.A.C.	L.A.L.	Mia.	Mil.	Min.	N.J.	N.Y.	Orl.	Phi.	Pho.	Por.	Sac.	S.A.	Sea.	Uta.	Was.	W.	L.	Pct.	G.B.
L.A. Lakers	2	2	4	1	1	4	4	1	4	2	2	4	..	2	1	4	2	2	1	1	3	2	5	2	4	2	1	63	19	.768	..
Portland	1	2	4	1	1	4	2	1	2	3	1	5	3	2	1	1	2	2	2	1	3	..	4	3	3	2	1	59	23	.720	4
Phoenix	2	1	3	0	1	3	3	0	5	2	1	4	1	2	1	4	2	1	2	1	..	2	5	0	3	3	2	54	28	.659	9
Seattle	1	0	4	1	1	2	1	3	2	1	2	0	2	0	3	2	1	2	1	2	2	2	1	2	..	1	2	41	41	.500	22
Golden State	0	1	2	1	1	2	1	..	2	1	3	1	2	3	2	0	1	3	2	0	2	3	1	2	2	1	1	37	45	.451	26
L.A. Clippers	1	1	2	1	1	1	2	1	1	2	2	..	1	0	1	3	2	0	2	0	0	0	2	0	3	0	1	30	52	.366	33
Sacramento	1	0	3	1	0	1	0	0	2	0	1	3	0	1	1	2	1	0	1	1	0	0	..	0	2	1	1	23	59	.280	40

HOME-ROAD RECORDS OF ALL TEAMS

Team	Home	Road	Total	Team	Home	Road	Total
Atlanta	25- 16	16- 25	41- 41	Milwaukee	27- 14	17- 24	44- 38
Boston	30- 11	22- 19	52- 30	Minnesota	17- 24	5- 36	22- 60
Charlotte	13- 28	6- 35	19- 63	New Jersey	13- 28	4- 37	17- 65
Chicago	36- 5	19- 22	55- 27	New York	29- 12	16- 25	45- 37
Cleveland	27- 14	15- 26	42- 40	Orlando	12- 29	6- 35	18- 64
Dallas	30- 11	17- 24	47- 35	Philadelphia	34- 7	19- 22	53- 29
Denver	28- 13	15- 26	43- 39	Phoenix	32- 9	22- 19	54- 28
Detroit	35- 6	24- 17	59- 23	Portland	35- 6	24- 17	59- 23
Golden State	27- 14	10- 31	37- 45	Sacramento	16- 25	7- 34	23- 59
Houston	31- 10	10- 31	41- 41	San Antonio	34- 7	22- 19	56- 26
Indiana	28- 13	14- 27	42- 40	Seattle	30- 11	11- 30	41- 41
L.A. Clippers	20- 21	10- 31	30- 52	Utah	36- 5	19- 22	55- 27
L.A. Lakers	37- 4	26- 15	63- 19	Washington	20- 21	11- 30	31- 51
Miami	11- 30	7- 34	18- 64	Totals	713-394	394-713	1107-1107

OFFENSIVE TEAM STATISTICS

		FIELD GOALS			FREE THROWS			REBOUNDS			MISCELLANEOUS					SCORING	
Team	G.	Att.	Made	Pct.	Att.	Made	Pct.	Off.	Def.	Tot.	Ast.	PF	Disq.	Stl.	Turn Over	Blk. Sh.	Pts.	Avg.
Golden State	82	7208	3489	.484	2858	2313	.809	915	2385	3300	1978	2010	22	756	1415	488	9534	116.3
Phoenix	82	7139	3544	.496	2716	2159	.795	1053	2651	3704	2109	1825	20	668	1275	501	9423	114.9
Denver	82	8015	3716	.464	2201	1737	.789	1169	2532	3701	2275	2047	31	814	1136	329	9397	114.6
Portland	82	7547	3572	.473	2734	2031	.743	1355	2552	3907	2085	2048	21	749	1356	364	9365	114.2
Orlando	82	7525	3457	.459	2725	2060	.756	1304	2465	3769	1993	1975	15	617	1407	294	9090	110.9
L.A. Lakers	82	7010	3434	.490	2417	1902	.787	1097	2460	3557	2232	1737	9	655	1226	445	9079	110.7
Philadelphia	82	7028	3437	.489	2509	1976	.788	1111	2406	3517	1932	1697	10	687	1209	365	9039	110.2
Boston	82	7148	3563	.498	2153	1791	.832	1066	2707	3773	2423	1717	13	539	1256	455	9023	110.0
Chicago	82	7090	3531	.498	2140	1665	.778	1075	2279	3354	2172	1906	15	814	1247	388	8977	109.5
Indiana	82	6807	3381	.497	2335	1906	.816	940	2388	3328	2023	1972	32	552	1342	350	8962	109.3
Atlanta	82	7019	3417	.487	2544	1943	.764	1273	2187	3460	1820	1871	19	717	1270	353	8901	108.5
New York	82	7089	3434	.484	2349	1775	.756	1187	2426	3613	2140	1828	15	714	1412	492	8879	108.3
Washington	82	7581	3598	.475	2093	1599	.764	1198	2450	3648	2214	1929	18	561	1201	424	8832	107.7
Seattle	82	7243	3466	.479	2167	1606	.741	1323	2255	3578	1874	2064	21	701	1366	335	8769	106.9
Utah	82	6593	3330	.505	2484	1874	.754	953	2501	3454	2212	2031	14	677	1410	491	8760	106.8
Houston	82	7250	3483	.480	2267	1633	.720	1217	2638	3855	2194	1934	23	809	1513	551	8752	106.7
San Antonio	82	6997	3388	.484	2535	1888	.745	1163	2474	3637	2037	1854	18	799	1399	554	8718	106.3
Milwaukee	82	7146	3380	.473	2273	1722	.758	1108	2246	3354	2046	2086	24	826	1315	326	8691	106.0
Detroit	82	6980	3333	.478	2252	1713	.761	1185	2458	3643	1996	1961	20	512	1233	418	8556	104.3
L.A. Clippers	82	6853	3319	.484	2458	1815	.738	1056	2362	3418	1978	1859	20	782	1547	507	8509	103.8
Cleveland	82	6977	3214	.461	2201	1637	.744	1128	2380	3508	2106	1666	16	645	1243	512	8411	102.6
Dallas	82	6831	3246	.475	2261	1735	.767	1042	2419	3461	1776	1733	13	664	1228	398	8384	102.2
Sacramento	82	7056	3305	.468	1964	1515	.771	952	2363	3315	2052	1863	17	546	1239	392	8341	101.7
Miami	82	7345	3383	.461	2028	1393	.687	1242	2313	3555	1957	2123	31	736	1557	388	8247	100.6
Charlotte	82	7183	3270	.455	1967	1487	.756	962	2211	3173	2080	1889	15	778	1226	262	8232	100.4
New Jersey	82	7415	3157	.426	2350	1754	.746	1363	2324	3687	1475	1952	16	774	1360	481	8208	100.1
Minnesota	82	6876	3067	.446	2137	1596	.747	1196	2053	3249	1844	1901	25	789	1197	344	7803	95.2

DEFENSIVE TEAM STATISTICS

	FIELD GOALS			FREE THROWS			REBOUNDS			MISCELLANEOUS					SCORING		
Team	Att.	Made	Pct.	Att.	Made	Pct.	Off.	Def.	Tot.	Ast.	PF	Disq.	Stl.	Turn Over	Blk. Sh.	Pts.	Avg.	Pt. Dif.
Detroit	6809	3043	.447	2342	1785	.762	1040	2281	3321	1764	2072	29	606	1248	304	8057	98.3	+ 6.1
Minnesota	6391	3081	.482	2420	1859	.768	1050	2322	3372	1880	1748	11	578	1366	489	8150	99.4	− 4.2
Utah	6949	3164	.455	2452	1865	.761	1100	2210	3310	1885	1910	19	736	1241	452	8367	102.0	+ 4.8
Dallas	7013	3288	.469	2161	1627	.753	1142	2398	3540	1961	1832	17	649	1236	388	8378	102.2	+ 0.1
San Antonio	7090	3269	.461	2169	1663	.767	1125	2241	3366	1967	1919	20	760	1420	416	8432	102.8	+ 3.5
Cleveland	7135	3418	.479	1898	1444	.761	1134	2451	3585	2137	1893	19	680	1294	379	8436	102.9	− 0.3
L.A. Lakers	7247	3382	.467	2111	1584	.750	1131	2243	3374	2009	1909	22	669	1200	426	8523	103.9	+ 6.8
Philadelphia	7117	3417	.480	2054	1584	.771	1113	2356	3469	2155	1945	16	636	1234	380	8630	105.2	+ 5.0
Houston	7322	3399	.464	2256	1671	.741	1175	2460	3635	2010	1819	10	790	1428	392	8632	105.3	+ 1.5
Seattle	6704	3257	.486	2533	1992	.786	1007	2204	3211	1862	1796	23	634	1303	406	8684	105.9	+ 1.0
Boston	7383	3438	.466	2133	1648	.773	1046	2318	3364	2078	1845	18	736	1003	356	8696	106.0	+ 4.0
Chicago	6819	3361	.493	2392	1784	.746	1068	2296	3364	2110	1742	17	665	1411	383	8710	106.2	+ 3.3
Milwaukee	6871	3292	.479	2570	1990	.774	1158	2405	3563	2023	1879	27	685	1506	444	8755	106.8	− 0.8
Sacramento	7158	3384	.473	2324	1828	.787	1146	2531	3677	2022	1740	14	704	1168	391	8756	106.8	− 5.1
New York	7430	3497	.471	2100	1598	.761	1249	2285	3534	2126	1869	30	719	1287	418	8763	106.9	+ 1.4
L.A. Clippers	7207	3432	.476	2251	1737	.772	1149	2367	3516	2092	1950	22	828	1364	429	8787	107.2	− 3.4
Atlanta	6935	3438	.496	2279	1760	.772	1151	2236	3387	2144	1961	17	672	1294	389	8817	107.5	+ 1.0
Phoenix	7588	3528	.465	2163	1585	.733	1202	2335	3537	2125	2151	33	677	1254	395	8841	107.8	+ 7.1
Portland	7227	3351	.464	2500	1917	.767	1055	2357	3412	2026	2086	19	667	1489	432	8847	107.9	+ 6.3
New Jersey	7020	3403	.485	2491	1906	.765	1144	2590	3734	1871	1886	11	768	1419	478	8853	108.0	− 7.9
Charlotte	6922	3438	.497	2380	1865	.784	1063	2723	3786	2066	1754	11	638	1376	384	8873	108.2	− 7.8
Indiana	7225	3486	.482	2395	1804	.753	1173	2297	3470	1945	2021	16	716	1189	321	8949	109.1	+ 0.2
Washington	7403	3511	.474	2376	1845	.777	1198	2503	3701	1952	1780	16	644	1200	430	9009	109.9	− 2.2
Miami	7010	3418	.488	2716	2050	.755	1125	2467	3592	2076	1781	13	860	1473	477	9044	110.3	− 9.7
Denver	7334	3589	.489	2517	1939	.770	1021	2846	3867	2073	1911	19	613	1514	462	9281	113.2	+ 1.4
Golden State	7885	3766	.478	2633	1998	.759	1495	2594	4089	2331	2219	24	817	1422	430	9791	119.4	− 3.1
Orlando	7757	3864	.498	2502	1897	.758	1173	2569	3742	2333	2060	20	734	1216	556	9821	119.8	− 8.9

Disq.—Individual player disqualified (fouled out of game).

INDIVIDUAL LEADERS

POINTS
Minimum 70 games or 1,400 points

	G.	FG	FT	Pts.	Avg.
Jordan, Chicago	82	1034	593	2753	33.6
Malone, Utah	82	914	696	2540	31.0
Ewing, New York	82	922	502	2347	28.6
Chambers, Phoenix	81	810	557	2201	27.2
Wilkins, Atlanta	80	810	459	2138	26.7
Barkley, Philadelphia	79	706	557	1989	25.2
Mullin, Golden State	78	682	505	1956	25.1
Miller, Indiana	82	661	544	2016	24.6
Olajuwon, Houston	82	806	382	1995	24.3
Robinson, San Antonio	82	690	613	1993	24.3
Bird, Boston	75	718	319	1820	24.3
Malone, Washington	75	781	257	1820	24.3

FIELD GOALS
Minimum 300 FG Made

	FGA	FGM	Pct.
West, Phoenix	530	331	.625
Barkley, Philadelphia	1177	706	.600
Parish, Boston	871	505	.580
Malone, Utah	1627	914	.562
Woolridge, L.A. Lakers	550	306	.556
Ewing, New York	1673	922	.551
McHale, Boston	1181	648	.549
Thorpe, Houston	998	547	.548
Worthy, L.A. Lakers	1298	711	.548
Williams, Portland	754	413	.548

FREE THROWS
Minimum 125 Made

	FTA	FTM	Pct.
Bird, Boston	343	319	.930
E. Johnson, Phoenix	205	188	.917
Davis, Denver	227	207	.912
Dumars, Detroit	330	297	.900
McHale, Boston	440	393	.893
Porter, Portland	472	421	.892
Johnson, L.A. Lakers	637	567	.890
Mullin, Golden State	568	505	.889
Hawkins, Philadelphia	436	387	.888
Price, Cleveland	338	300	.888

ASSISTS
Minimum 70 games or 400 assists

	G.	No.	Avg.
Stockton, Utah	78	1134	14.5
Johnson, L.A. Lakers	79	907	11.5
K. Johnson, Phoenix	74	846	11.4
Bogues, Charlotte	81	867	10.7
Grant, L.A. Clippers	44	442	10.0
Thomas, Detroit	81	765	9.4
Price, Cleveland	73	666	9.1
Porter, Portland	80	726	9.1
Hardaway, Golden State	79	689	8.7
Walker, Washington	81	652	8.0

STEALS
Minimum 70 games or 125 steals

	G.	No.	Avg.
Jordan, Chicago	82	227	2.77
Stockton, Utah	78	207	2.65
Pippen, Chicago	82	211	2.57
Robertson, Milwaukee	81	207	2.56
Harper, Dallas	82	187	2.28
Corbin, Minnesota	82	175	2.13
Lever, Denver	79	168	2.13
Olajuwon, Houston	82	174	2.12
Conner, New Jersey	82	172	2.10
Hardaway, Golden State	79	165	2.09

REBOUNDS
Minimum 70 games or 800 rebounds

	G.	Off.	Def.	Tot.	Avg.
Olajuwon, Houston	82	299	850	1149	14.0
Robinson, San Antonio	82	303	680	983	12.0
Barkley, Philadelphia	79	361	548	909	11.5
Malone, Utah	82	232	679	911	11.1
Ewing, New York	82	235	658	893	10.9
Seikaly, Miami	74	253	513	766	10.4
Parish, Boston	79	259	537	796	10.1
Malone, Atlanta	81	364	448	812	10.0
Cage, Seattle	82	306	515	821	10.0
Williams, Portland	82	250	550	800	9.8

BLOCKED SHOTS
Minimum 70 games or 100 blocked shots

	G.	No.	Avg.
Olajuwon, Houston	82	376	4.59
Ewing, New York	82	327	3.99
Robinson, San Antonio	82	319	3.89
Bol, Golden State	75	238	3.17
Benjamin, L.A. Clippers	71	187	2.63
Eaton, Utah	82	201	2.45
Jones, Washington	81	197	2.43
West, Phoenix	82	184	2.24
Smits, Indiana	82	169	2.06
J. Williams, Cleveland	82	167	2.04

3-PT. FIELD GOALS
Minimum 25 made

	FGA	FGM	Pct.
Kerr, Cleveland	144	73	.507
Hodges, Chicago	181	87	.481
Petrovic, Portland	74	34	.459
Sundvold, Miami	100	44	.440
Scott, L.A. Lakers	220	93	.423
Hawkins, Philadelphia	200	84	.420
Ehlo, Cleveland	248	104	.419
Stockton, Utah	113	47	.416
Miller, Indiana	362	150	.414
Lever, Denver	87	36	.414

TEAM-BY-TEAM INDIVIDUAL STATISTICS

ATLANTA HAWKS

Player	G.	Min.	FGA	FGM	Pct.	FTA	FTM	Pct.	Off. Reb.	Def. Reb.	Tot. Reb.	Ast.	PF	Disq.	Stl.	Blk. Sh.	Pts.	Avg.	Hi.
Wilkins	80	2888	1672	810	.484	569	459	.807	217	304	521	200	141	0	126	47	2138	26.7	44
Malone	81	2735	1077	517	.480	631	493	.781	364	448	812	130	158	0	47	84	1528	18.9	31
Rivers	48	1526	480	218	.454	170	138	.812	47	153	200	264	151	2	116	22	598	12.5	24
Willis	81	2273	805	418	.519	246	168	.683	253	392	645	57	259	4	63	47	1006	12.4	30
Smith (Tot)	79	2421	811	378	.466	196	161	.821	18	139	157	445	143	0	79	8	943	11.9	24
Smith (Atl)	33	674	204	98	.480	65	55	.846	7	30	37	142	45	0	22	1	255	7.7	22
Battle	60	1477	544	275	.506	135	102	.756	27	72	99	154	115	0	28	3	654	10.9	27
Webb	82	2184	616	294	.477	186	162	.871	38	163	201	477	185	0	105	12	751	9.2	26
Long	48	1030	384	174	.453	55	46	.836	26	57	83	85	66	0	45	5	404	8.4	20
Carr	44	803	248	128	.516	102	79	.775	50	99	149	53	128	4	15	34	335	7.6	21
Levingston	75	1706	424	216	.509	122	83	.680	113	206	319	80	216	2	55	41	516	6.9	21
Volkov	72	937	284	137	.482	120	70	.583	52	67	119	83	166	3	36	22	357	5.0	17
Matthews	1	13	3	1	.333	2	2	1.000	0	0	0	5	0	0	0	0	4	4.0	4
Koncak	54	977	127	78	.614	79	42	.532	58	168	226	23	182	4	38	34	198	3.7	12
Toney	32	286	72	30	.417	25	21	.840	3	11	14	52	35	0	10	0	88	2.8	11
Marble	24	162	58	16	.276	29	19	.655	15	9	24	11	16	0	7	1	51	2.1	7
Workman	6	16	3	2	.667	2	2	1.000	0	3	3	2	3	0	3	0	6	1.0	4
Ferrell	14	29	14	5	.357	6	2	.333	3	4	7	2	3	0	1	0	12	0.9	4
Williams (Tot)	21	102	18	6	.333	6	3	.500	5	18	23	2	30	0	3	1	15	0.7	4
Williams (Atl)	5	14	4	0	.000	0	0	....	0	1	1	0	2	0	0	0	0	0.0	0

3-Pt. FG: Atlanta 124-411 (.302)—Wilkins 59-183 (.322); Malone 1-9 (.111); Rivers 24-66 (.364); Willis 2-7 (.286); Smith 4-24 (.167); Battle 2-13 (.154); Webb 1-19 (.053); Long 10-29 (.345); Carr 0-4 (.000); Levingston 1-5 (.200); Volkov 13-34 (.382); Matthews 0-1 (.000); Koncak 0-1 (.000); Toney 7-13 (.538); Marble 0-2 (.000); Ferrell 0-1 (.000). Opponents 181-533 (.340).

BOSTON CELTICS

Player	G.	Min.	FGA	FGM	Pct.	FTA	FTM	Pct.	Off. Reb.	Def. Reb.	Tot. Reb.	Ast.	PF	Disq.	Stl.	Blk. Sh.	Pts.	Avg.	Hi.
Bird	75	2944	1517	718	.473	343	319	.930	90	622	712	562	173	2	106	61	1820	24.3	50
McHale	82	2722	1181	648	.549	440	393	.893	201	476	677	172	250	3	30	157	1712	20.9	34
Lewis	79	2522	1089	540	.496	317	256	.808	109	238	347	225	216	2	88	63	1340	17.0	34
Parish	79	2396	871	505	.580	312	233	.747	259	537	796	103	189	2	38	69	1243	15.7	18
Johnson	75	2036	475	206	.434	140	118	.843	48	153	201	485	179	2	81	14	531	7.1	24
Paxson	72	1283	422	191	.453	90	73	.811	24	53	77	137	115	0	33	5	460	6.4	18
Kleine	81	1365	367	176	.480	100	83	.830	117	238	355	46	170	0	15	27	435	5.4	18
Gamble	71	990	301	137	.455	107	85	.794	42	70	112	119	77	1	28	8	362	5.1	18
M. Smith	65	620	286	136	.476	64	53	.828	40	60	100	79	51	0	9	1	327	5.0	24
Pinckney	77	1082	249	135	.542	119	92	.773	93	132	225	68	126	1	34	42	362	4.7	19
Bagley	54	1095	218	100	.459	39	29	.744	26	63	89	296	77	0	40	4	230	4.3	14
C. Smith	60	519	133	59	.444	76	53	.697	14	55	69	103	75	0	35	3	171	2.9	12
Upshaw	14	131	39	12	.308	6	4	.667	3	10	13	28	19	0	2	1	30	2.1	7

3-Pt. FG: Boston 106-404 (.262)—Bird 65-195 (.333); McHale 23-69 (.333); Lewis 4-15 (.267); Johnson 1-24 (.042); Paxson 5-20 (.250); Kleine 0-4 (.000); Gamble 3-18 (.167); M. Smith 2-28 (.071); Pinckney 0-1 (.000); Bagley 1-18 (.056); C. Smith 0-7 (.000); Upshaw 2-5 (.400). Opponents 172-539 (.319).

CHARLOTTE HORNETS

Player	G.	Min.	FGA	FGM	Pct.	FTA	FTM	Pct.	Off. Reb.	Def. Reb.	Tot. Reb.	Ast.	PF	Disq.	Stl.	Blk. Sh.	Pts.	Avg.	Hi.
Chapman	54	1762	924	377	.408	192	144	.750	52	127	179	132	113	0	46	6	945	17.5	38
Gilliam (Tot)	76	2426	940	484	.515	419	303	.723	211	388	599	99	212	4	69	51	1271	16.7	30
Gilliam (Char)	60	2159	819	432	.527	363	264	.727	185	344	529	91	184	4	63	46	1128	18.8	30
Curry	67	1860	990	461	.466	104	96	.923	31	137	168	159	148	0	98	26	1070	16.0	30
Tripucka	79	2404	1029	442	.430	351	310	.883	82	240	322	224	220	1	75	16	1232	15.6	31
J.R. Reid	82	2757	814	358	.440	289	192	.664	199	492	691	101	292	7	92	54	908	11.1	25
Bogues	81	2743	664	326	.491	134	106	.791	48	159	207	867	168	1	166	3	763	9.4	22
Rambis	16	448	116	58	.500	55	30	.545	48	72	120	28	45	0	32	10	146	9.1	21
Keys (Tot)	80	1615	678	293	.432	140	101	.721	100	153	253	88	224	1	68	8	701	8.8	22
Keys (Char)	32	723	319	142	.445	58	40	.690	48	68	116	49	107	1	30	6	336	10.5	20
Gattison	63	941	269	148	.550	110	75	.682	75	122	197	39	150	1	35	31	372	5.9	18
R. Reid (Tot)	72	1202	447	175	.391	86	54	.628	34	117	151	90	153	0	38	16	414	5.8	20
R. Reid (Char)	60	1117	414	162	.391	78	50	.641	33	110	143	82	136	0	36	14	383	6.4	20
Williams (Tot)	28	329	119	60	.504	46	36	.783	12	20	32	81	39	0	22	1	156	5.6	17
Williams (Char)	22	303	109	58	.532	44	35	.795	11	20	31	77	39	0	22	1	151	6.9	17
Rowsom	44	559	179	78	.436	83	68	.819	44	87	131	22	58	0	18	11	225	5.1	20
Anderson	54	604	211	88	.417	23	18	.783	33	94	127	55	64	0	20	9	231	4.3	19
Hoppen	10	135	41	16	.390	10	8	.800	19	17	36	6	26	0	2	1	40	4.0	8
Sichting	34	469	119	50	.420	18	15	.833	3	16	19	92	39	0	16	2	118	3.5	12
Gray	39	466	82	38	.463	39	25	.641	38	93	131	17	64	0	12	24	101	2.6	9
Dozier	9	92	27	9	.333	8	4	.500	7	8	15	3	10	0	6	2	22	2.4	6
Turner (Tot)	11	115	38	11	.289	4	4	1.000	4	4	8	23	6	0	8	0	26	2.4	8
Turner (Char)	8	84	25	9	.360	4	4	1.000	1	2	3	20	5	0	7	0	22	2.8	8
Holton	16	109	26	14	.538	2	1	.500	1	1	2	16	19	0	1	0	29	1.8	10
Lewis (Tot)	7	26	7	4	.571	2	2	1.000	4	2	6	0	3	0	1	0	10	1.4	4
Lewis (Char)	3	20	6	4	.667	2	2	1.000	4	2	6	0	2	0	1	0	10	3.3	4

3-Pt. FG: Charlotte 205-611 (.336)—Chapman 47-142 (.331); Gilliam 0-2 (.000); Curry 52-147 (.354); Tripucka 38-104 (.365); J.R. Reid 0-5 (.000); Bogues 5-26 (.192); Rambis 0-1 (.000); Keys 12-33 (.364); Gattison 1-1 (1.000); R. Reid 9-29 (.310); Williams 0-3 (.000); Rowsom 1-2 (.500); Anderson 37-100 (.370); Sichting 3-12 (.250); Gray 0-2 (.000); Dozier 0-1 (.000); Turner 0-1 (.000). Opponents 132-421 (.314).

CHICAGO BULLS

Player	G.	Min.	FGA	FGM	Pct.	FTA	FTM	Pct.	Off. Reb.	Def. Reb.	Tot. Reb.	Ast.	PF	Disq.	Stl.	Blk. Sh.	Pts.	Avg.	Hi.
Jordan	82	3197	1964	1034	.526	699	593	.848	143	422	565	519	241	0	227	54	2753	33.6	69
Pippen	82	3148	1150	562	.489	295	199	.675	150	397	547	444	298	6	211	101	1351	16.5	28
Grant	80	2753	853	446	.523	256	179	.699	236	393	629	227	230	1	92	84	1071	13.4	23
Cartwright	71	2160	598	292	.488	280	227	.811	137	328	465	145	243	6	38	34	811	11.4	24
Paxson	82	2365	708	365	.516	68	56	.824	27	92	119	335	176	1	83	6	819	10.0	27
King	82	1777	530	267	.504	267	194	.727	169	215	384	87	215	0	38	58	728	8.9	24
Hodges	63	1055	331	145	.438	33	30	.909	11	42	53	110	87	1	30	2	407	6.5	18
Armstrong	81	1291	392	190	.485	78	69	.885	19	83	102	199	105	0	46	6	452	5.6	20
Perdue	77	884	268	111	.414	104	72	.692	88	126	214	46	150	0	19	26	294	3.8	14
Davis	53	429	158	58	.367	8	7	.875	25	56	81	18	52	0	10	8	130	2.5	8
Haley	11	58	20	9	.450	7	7	1.000	7	11	18	4	7	0	0	1	25	2.3	7
Nealy	46	503	70	38	.529	41	30	.732	46	92	138	28	67	0	16	4	104	2.3	10
Lett	4	28	8	2	.250	0	0	....	0	0	0	1	8	0	0	0	4	1.0	2
Sanders	31	182	40	13	.325	4	2	.500	17	22	39	9	27	0	4	4	28	0.9	6

3-Pt. FG: Chicago 250-669 (.374)—Jordan 92-245 (.376); Pippen 28-112 (.250); Paxson 33-92 (.359); King 0-1 (.000); Hodges 87-181 (.481); Armstrong 3-6 (.500); Perdue 0-5 (.000); Davis 7-25 (.280); Nealy 0-2 (.000). Opponents 204-581 (.351).

CLEVELAND CAVALIERS

Player	G.	Min.	FGA	FGM	Pct.	FTA	FTM	Pct.	Off. Reb.	Def. Reb.	Tot. Reb.	Ast.	PF	Disq.	Stl.	Blk. Sh.	Pts.	Avg.	Hi.
Harper	7	262	138	61	.442	41	31	.756	19	29	48	49	25	1	14	9	154	22.0	36
Price	73	2706	1066	489	.459	338	300	.888	66	185	251	666	89	0	114	5	1430	19.6	37
J. Williams	82	2776	1070	528	.493	440	325	.739	220	443	663	168	214	2	86	167	1381	16.8	33
Daugherty	41	1438	509	244	.479	287	202	.704	77	296	373	130	108	1	29	22	690	16.8	30
Nance	62	2065	807	412	.511	239	186	.778	162	354	516	161	185	3	54	122	1011	16.3	31
Ehlo	81	2894	940	436	.464	185	126	.681	147	292	439	371	226	2	126	23	1102	13.6	31
Keys	48	892	359	151	.421	82	61	.744	52	85	137	39	117	0	38	2	365	7.6	22
Brown	75	1339	447	210	.470	164	125	.762	83	148	231	50	148	0	33	26	545	7.3	30
R. Williams	32	542	239	91	.381	41	30	.732	17	43	60	38	79	2	22	10	218	6.8	17
Kerr	78	1664	432	192	.444	73	63	.863	12	86	98	248	59	0	45	7	520	6.7	19
Bennett	55	990	286	137	.479	96	64	.667	84	104	188	54	133	1	23	10	338	6.1	20
Chievous (Tot)	55	591	220	105	.477	111	80	.721	35	55	90	31	70	0	26	5	293	5.3	17
Chievous (Clev)	14	99	42	15	.357	24	19	.792	7	8	15	4	11	0	3	1	49	3.5	12
Dudley	37	684	203	79	.389	77	26	.338	88	115	203	20	83	1	19	41	184	5.0	15

Player	G.	Min.	FGA	FGM	Pct.	FTA	FTM	Pct.	Off. Reb.	Def. Reb.	Tot. Reb.	Ast.	PF	Disq.	Stl.	Blk. Sh.	Pts.	Avg.	Hi.
Mokeski	38	449	150	63	.420	36	25	.694	27	72	99	17	76	0	8	10	151	4.0	14
Morton	37	402	161	48	.298	62	43	.694	7	25	32	67	30	0	18	4	146	3.9	14
Rollins	48	674	125	57	.456	16	11	.688	58	95	153	24	83	3	13	53	125	2.6	10
Voce	1	4	3	1	.333	0	0	....	2	0	2	0	0	0	0	0	2	2.0	2

3-Pt. FG: Cleveland 346-851 (.407)—Harper 1-5 (.200); Price 152-374 (.406); Daugherty 0-2 (.000); Nance 1-1 (1.000); Ehlo 104-248 (.419); Keys 2-10 (.200); Brown 0-7 (.000); R. Williams 6-27 (.222); Kerr 73-144 (.507); Chievous 0-1 (.000); Mokeski 0-1 (.000); Morton 7-30 (.233); Rollins 0-1 (.000). Opponents 156-500 (.312).

DALLAS MAVERICKS

Player	G.	Min.	FGA	FGM	Pct.	FTA	FTM	Pct.	Off. Reb.	Def. Reb.	Tot. Reb.	Ast.	PF	Disq.	Stl.	Blk. Sh.	Pts.	Avg.	Hi.
Blackman	80	2934	1256	626	.498	340	287	.844	88	192	280	289	128	0	77	21	1552	19.4	35
Harper	82	3007	1161	567	.488	315	250	.794	54	190	244	609	224	1	187	26	1473	18.0	42
Tarpley	45	1648	696	314	.451	172	130	.756	189	400	589	67	160	0	79	70	758	16.8	27
Perkins	76	2668	883	435	.493	424	330	.778	209	363	572	175	225	4	88	64	1206	15.9	45
Dantley	45	1300	484	231	.477	254	200	.787	78	94	172	80	99	0	20	7	662	14.7	30
Donaldson	73	2265	479	258	.539	213	149	.700	155	475	630	57	129	0	22	47	665	9.1	21
H. Williams	81	2199	665	295	.444	159	108	.679	76	315	391	119	243	4	51	106	700	8.6	21
Davis	73	1292	365	179	.490	100	77	.770	12	81	93	242	151	2	47	9	470	6.4	25
Wennington	60	814	234	105	.449	75	60	.800	64	134	198	41	144	2	20	21	270	4.5	14
White	55	707	252	93	.369	89	50	.562	78	95	173	21	124	0	24	6	237	4.3	18
Alford	41	302	138	63	.457	37	35	.946	2	23	25	39	22	0	15	3	168	4.1	16
Jones	66	650	194	72	.371	69	47	.681	33	49	82	29	77	0	32	16	195	3.0	13
McCann	10	62	21	7	.333	14	12	.857	4	8	12	6	7	0	2	2	26	2.6	8
Upshaw	3	4	3	1	.333	0	0	....	0	0	0	0	0	0	0	0	2	0.7	2
Wade	1	3	0	0	....	0	0	....	0	0	0	2	0	0	0	0	0	0.0	0

3-Pt. FG: Dallas 157-486 (.323)—Blackman 13-43 (.302); Harper 89-240 (.371); Tarpley 0-6 (.000); Perkins 6-28 (.214); Dantley 0-2 (.000); H. Williams 2-9 (.222); Davis 35-104 (.337); Wennington 0-4 (.000); White 1-14 (.071); Alford 7-22 (.318); Jones 4-13 (.308); Upshaw 0-1 (.000). Opponents 175-587 (.298).

DENVER NUGGETS

Player	G.	Min.	FGA	FGM	Pct.	FTA	FTM	Pct.	Off. Reb.	Def. Reb.	Tot. Reb.	Ast.	PF	Disq.	Stl.	Blk. Sh.	Pts.	Avg.	Hi.
Lever	79	2832	1283	568	.443	337	271	.804	230	504	734	517	172	1	168	13	1443	18.3	31
English	80	2211	1293	635	.491	183	161	.880	119	167	286	225	130	0	51	23	1433	17.9	38
Davis	69	1635	1033	497	.481	227	207	.912	46	133	179	155	160	1	59	9	1207	17.5	36
Adams	79	2690	989	398	.402	314	267	.850	49	176	225	495	133	0	121	3	1221	15.5	32
Rasmussen	81	1995	895	445	.497	134	111	.828	174	420	594	82	300	10	40	104	1001	12.4	26
Schayes	53	1194	330	163	.494	264	225	.852	117	225	342	61	200	7	41	45	551	10.4	28
Carroll (Tot)	76	1721	759	312	.411	177	137	.774	133	310	443	97	192	4	47	115	761	10.0	25
Carroll (Den)	30	719	354	153	.432	70	52	.743	51	142	193	54	70	0	28	59	358	11.9	25
Lichti	79	1326	514	250	.486	174	130	.747	49	102	151	116	145	1	55	13	630	8.0	20
Hanzlik	81	1605	396	179	.452	183	136	.743	67	140	207	186	249	7	78	29	500	6.2	19
Kempton	71	1061	312	153	.490	114	77	.675	51	167	218	118	144	2	30	9	383	5.4	17
Lane	67	956	309	145	.469	120	44	.367	144	217	361	105	189	1	53	17	334	5.0	18
Hughes	60	892	202	83	.411	34	23	.676	15	55	70	116	87	0	48	1	209	3.5	17
Higgins	5	32	8	3	.375	8	7	.875	1	2	3	2	1	0	1	0	13	2.6	6
Dunn	65	657	97	44	.454	39	26	.667	56	82	138	43	67	1	41	4	114	1.8	12

3-Pt. FG: Denver 228-677 (.337)—Lever 36-87 (.414); English 2-5 (.400); Davis 6-46 (.130); Adams 158-432 (.366); Rasmussen 0-1 (.000); Schayes 0-4 (.000); Lichti 0-14 (.000); Hanzlik 6-31 (.194); Kempton 0-1 (.000); Lane 0-5 (.000); Hughes 20-49 (.408); Dunn 0-2 (.000). Opponents 164-517 (.317).

DETROIT PISTONS

Player	G.	Min.	FGA	FGM	Pct.	FTA	FTM	Pct.	Off. Reb.	Def. Reb.	Tot. Reb.	Ast.	PF	Disq.	Stl.	Blk. Sh.	Pts.	Avg.	Hi.
Thomas	81	2993	1322	579	.438	377	292	.775	74	234	308	765	206	0	139	19	1492	18.4	37
Dumars	75	2578	1058	508	.480	330	297	.900	60	152	212	368	129	1	63	2	1335	17.8	34
Edwards	82	2283	928	462	.498	354	265	.749	112	233	345	63	295	4	23	37	1189	14.5	32
Aguirre	78	2005	898	438	.488	254	192	.756	117	188	305	145	201	2	34	19	1099	14.1	31
Laimbeer	81	2675	785	380	.484	192	164	.854	166	614	780	171	278	4	57	84	981	12.1	31
Johnson	82	1972	775	334	.431	196	131	.668	108	148	256	255	143	0	71	13	804	9.8	25
Rodman	82	2377	496	288	.581	217	142	.654	336	456	792	72	276	2	52	60	719	8.8	18
Salley	82	1914	408	209	.512	244	174	.713	154	285	439	67	282	7	51	153	593	7.2	21
Bedford	42	246	125	54	.432	22	9	.409	15	43	58	4	39	0	3	17	118	2.8	13
Henderson (Tot)	57	464	109	53	.486	15	12	.800	11	32	43	74	50	0	16	2	135	2.4	13
Henderson (Det)	46	335	83	42	.506	13	10	.769	8	23	31	61	36	0	8	2	108	2.3	13
Greenwood	37	205	52	22	.423	29	16	.552	24	54	78	12	40	0	4	9	60	1.6	6
Kimbrough	10	50	16	7	.438	2	2	1.000	4	3	7	5	4	0	4	0	16	1.6	4
Hastings	40	166	33	10	.303	22	19	.864	7	25	32	8	31	0	3	3	42	1.1	9
Lewis	4	6	1	0	.000	0	0	....	0	0	0	1	0	0	0	0	0	0.0	0

3-Pt. FG: Detroit 177-541 (.327)—Thomas 42-136 (.309); Dumars 22-55 (.400); Edwards 0-3 (.000); Aguirre 31-93 (.333); Laimbeer 57-158 (.361); Johnson 5-34 (.147); Rodman 1-9 (.111); Salley 1-4 (.250); Bedford 1-6 (.167); Henderson 14-31 (.452); Hastings 3-12 (.250). Opponents 186-558 (.333).

GOLDEN STATE WARRIORS

Player	G.	Min.	FGA	FGM	Pct.	FTA	FTM	Pct.	Off. Reb.	Def. Reb.	Tot. Reb.	Ast.	PF	Disq.	Stl.	Blk. Sh.	Pts.	Avg.	Hi.
Mullin	78	2830	1272	682	.536	568	505	.889	130	333	463	319	142	1	123	45	1956	25.1	39
Richmond	78	2799	1287	640	.497	469	406	.866	98	262	360	223	210	3	98	24	1720	22.1	32
Teagle	82	2376	1122	538	.480	294	244	.830	114	253	367	155	231	3	91	15	1323	16.1	44
Hardaway	79	2663	985	464	.471	276	211	.764	57	253	310	689	232	6	165	12	1162	14.7	28
Marciulionis	75	1695	557	289	.519	403	317	.787	84	137	221	121	230	5	94	7	905	12.1	33
Higgins	82	1993	632	304	.481	285	234	.821	120	302	422	129	184	0	47	53	909	11.1	28
Tolbert	70	1347	442	218	.493	241	175	.726	122	241	363	58	191	0	23	25	616	8.8	27
Garland	51	891	288	108	.375	63	53	.841	31	80	111	157	77	1	48	5	270	5.3	13
Johnson	10	99	32	12	.375	17	14	.824	8	9	17	9	12	0	0	1	40	4.0	10
Lister	3	40	8	4	.500	7	4	.571	5	3	8	2	8	0	1	0	12	4.0	7

Player	G.	Min.	FGA	FGM	Pct.	FTA	FTM	Pct.	Off. Reb.	Def. Reb.	Tot. Reb.	Ast.	PF	Disq.	Stl.	Blk. Sh.	Pts.	Avg.	Hi.
Petersen	43	592	141	60	.426	73	52	.712	49	111	160	23	103	0	17	20	172	4.0	14
Upshaw (Tot)	40	387	146	64	.438	37	28	.757	9	32	41	54	53	0	27	1	160	4.0	19
Upshaw (GS)	23	252	104	51	.490	31	24	.774	6	22	28	26	34	0	25	0	128	5.6	19
Welp (Tot)	27	198	61	23	.377	25	19	.760	18	30	48	9	58	0	6	8	65	2.4	10
Welp (GS)	14	142	38	16	.421	23	18	.783	11	25	36	4	37	0	5	8	50	3.6	10
Blab	40	481	87	33	.379	31	17	.548	28	71	99	24	93	0	1	22	83	2.1	8
Bol	75	1310	169	56	.331	49	25	.510	33	243	276	36	194	3	13	238	146	1.9	10
Smrek	13	107	24	10	.417	6	1	.167	11	23	34	1	18	0	4	11	21	1.6	6
Taylor	10	37	6	0	.000	16	11	.688	4	8	12	1	4	0	0	0	11	1.1	3
Shasky	14	51	14	4	.286	6	2	.333	4	9	13	1	10	0	1	2	10	0.7	3

3-Pt. FG: Golden State 243-750 (.324)—Mullin 87-234 (.372); Richmond 34-95 (.358); Teagle 3-14 (.214); Hardaway 23-84 (.274); Marciulionis 10-39 (.256); Higgins 67-193 (.347); Tolbert 5-18 (.278); Garland 1-10 (.100); Johnson 2-3 (.667); Lister 0-1 (.000); Petersen 0-1 (.000); Upshaw 2-9 (.222); Bol 9-48 (.188); Taylor 0-1 (.000). Opponents 261-733 (.356).

HOUSTON ROCKETS

Player	G.	Min.	FGA	FGM	Pct.	FTA	FTM	Pct.	Off. Reb.	Def. Reb.	Tot. Reb.	Ast.	PF	Disq.	Stl.	Blk. Sh.	Pts.	Avg.	Hi.
Olajuwon	82	3124	1609	806	.501	536	382	.713	299	850	1149	234	314	6	174	376	1995	24.3	52
Thorpe	82	2947	998	547	.548	446	307	.688	258	476	734	261	270	5	66	24	1401	17.1	33
Wiggins	66	1852	853	416	.488	237	192	.810	133	153	286	104	165	0	85	1	1024	15.5	34
Johnson	82	2832	1019	504	.495	270	205	.759	113	268	381	252	321	8	104	62	1215	14.8	30
Floyd	82	2630	803	362	.451	232	187	.806	46	152	198	600	159	0	94	11	1000	12.2	35
Maxwell (Tot)	79	1987	627	275	.439	211	136	.645	50	178	228	296	148	0	84	10	714	9.0	32
Maxwell (Hou)	30	869	321	142	.442	116	77	.664	15	72	87	150	69	0	42	5	374	12.5	32
Woodson	61	972	405	160	.395	86	62	.721	25	63	88	66	100	1	42	11	394	6.5	17
Chievous	41	492	178	90	.506	87	61	.701	28	47	75	27	59	0	23	4	244	6.0	17
Lucas	49	938	291	109	.375	55	42	.764	19	71	90	238	59	0	45	2	286	5.8	16
Bowie	66	918	293	119	.406	54	40	.741	36	82	118	96	80	0	42	5	284	4.3	18
Dinkins	33	362	109	44	.404	30	26	.867	13	27	40	75	30	0	19	2	115	3.5	12
Lloyd (Tot)	21	123	53	30	.566	16	9	.563	8	10	18	11	12	0	3	0	69	3.3	15
Lloyd (Hou)	19	113	51	29	.569	16	9	.563	8	10	18	11	9	0	3	0	67	3.5	15
Smith	74	1300	213	101	.474	55	20	.364	180	272	452	69	203	3	56	28	222	3.0	11
Caldwell	51	331	76	42	.553	28	13	.464	36	73	109	7	69	0	11	18	97	1.9	11
McCormick	18	116	29	10	.345	19	10	.526	8	19	27	3	24	0	3	1	30	1.7	6
Nevitt	3	9	2	2	1.000	0	0		0	3	3	1	3	0	1	4	1.3	2

3-Pt. FG: Houston 153-491 (.312)—Olajuwon 1-6 (.167); Thorpe 0-10 (.000); Wiggins 0-3 (.000); Johnson 2-17 (.118); Floyd 89-234 (.380); Maxwell 13-53 (.245); Woodson 12-41 (.293); Chievous 3-8 (.375); Lucas 26-87 (.299); Bowie 6-21 (.286); Dinkins 1-9 (.111); Smith 0-2 (.000). Opponents 163-556 (.293).

INDIANA PACERS

Player	G.	Min.	FGA	FGM	Pct.	FTA	FTM	Pct.	Off. Reb.	Def. Reb.	Tot. Reb.	Ast.	PF	Disq.	Stl.	Blk. Sh.	Pts.	Avg.	Hi.
Miller	82	3192	1287	661	.514	627	544	.868	95	200	295	311	175	1	110	18	2016	24.6	44
Person	77	2714	1242	605	.487	270	211	.781	126	319	445	230	217	1	53	20	1515	19.7	42
Schrempf	78	2573	822	424	.516	490	402	.820	149	471	620	247	271	6	59	16	1267	16.2	29
Smits	82	2404	967	515	.533	297	241	.811	135	377	512	142	328	11	45	169	1271	15.5	34
Fleming	82	2876	919	467	.508	294	230	.782	118	204	322	610	213	1	92	10	1176	14.3	30
Thompson	82	2126	471	223	.473	134	107	.799	175	455	630	106	313	11	65	71	554	6.8	16
Sanders	82	1531	479	225	.470	75	55	.733	78	152	230	89	220	1	43	23	510	6.2	19
Natt	14	164	31	20	.645	22	17	.773	10	25	35	9	14	0	1	0	57	4.1	16
Green	69	927	231	100	.433	51	43	.843	9	45	54	182	60	0	51	1	244	3.5	15
McCloud	44	413	144	45	.313	19	15	.789	12	30	42	45	56	0	19	3	118	2.7	13
Wittman	61	544	122	62	.508	6	5	.833	4	26	30	39	21	0	7	4	130	2.1	14
Nix	20	109	39	14	.359	16	11	.688	8	18	26	5	15	0	3	1	39	2.0	8
Dreiling	49	307	53	20	.377	34	25	.735	21	66	87	8	69	0	4	14	65	1.3	5

3-Pt. FG: Indiana 294-770 (.382)—Miller 150-362 (.414); Person 94-253 (.372); Schrempf 17-48 (.354); Smits 0-1 (.000); Fleming 12-34 (.353); Thompson 1-5 (.200); Sanders 5-14 (.357); Green 1-11 (.091); McCloud 13-40 (.325); Wittman 1-2 (.500). Opponents 173-541 (.320).

LOS ANGELES CLIPPERS

Player	G.	Min.	FGA	FGM	Pct.	FTA	FTM	Pct.	Off. Reb.	Def. Reb.	Tot. Reb.	Ast.	PF	Disq.	Stl.	Blk. Sh.	Pts.	Avg.	Hi.
Harper (Tot)	35	1367	637	301	.473	231	182	.788	74	132	206	182	105	1	81	41	798	22.8	39
Harper (LAC)	28	1105	499	240	.481	190	151	.795	55	103	158	133	80	0	67	32	644	23.0	39
Smith	78	2732	1145	595	.520	572	454	.794	177	347	524	114	294	6	86	119	1645	21.1	40
Manning	71	2269	826	440	.533	370	274	.741	142	280	422	187	261	4	91	39	1154	16.3	39
Norman	70	2334	949	484	.510	242	153	.632	143	327	470	160	196	0	78	59	1128	16.1	35
Benjamin	71	2313	688	362	.526	321	235	.732	156	501	657	159	217	3	59	187	959	13.5	29
Grant	44	1529	517	241	.466	113	88	.779	59	136	195	442	120	1	108	5	575	13.1	27
Williams	5	133	57	21	.368	21	18	.857	8	7	15	10	7	0	9	1	60	12.0	24
Garland (Tot)	79	1762	573	230	.401	122	102	.836	51	163	214	303	152	1	78	10	574	7.3	23
Garland (LAC)	28	871	285	122	.428	59	49	.831	20	83	103	146	75	0	30	5	304	10.9	23
Garrick	73	1721	421	208	.494	114	88	.772	34	128	162	289	151	4	90	7	508	7.0	23
Martin	69	1351	414	170	.411	129	91	.705	78	81	159	44	97	0	41	16	433	6.3	20
Young	45	459	194	92	.474	38	27	.711	36	50	86	24	47	0	25	3	219	4.9	27
Wolf	77	1325	392	155	.395	71	55	.775	63	169	232	62	129	0	30	24	370	4.8	19
Rivers	52	724	197	80	.406	78	59	.756	30	55	85	155	53	0	31	0	219	4.2	15
Bannister	52	589	161	77	.478	110	52	.473	39	73	112	18	92	1	17	7	206	4.0	15
Les (Tot)	7	92	14	5	.357	17	13	.765	3	4	7	21	9	0	3	0	23	3.3	11
Les (LAC)	6	86	14	5	.357	13	11	.846	3	4	7	20	6	0	3	0	21	3.5	11
McKinney	7	104	32	8	.250	4	2	.500	4	8	12	7	15	1	6	1	18	2.6	7
Harris	15	93	40	14	.350	4	3	.750	5	5	10	1	9	0	7	1	31	2.1	8
Edwards	4	26	7	3	.429	3	1	.333	1	1	2	4	4	0	1	0	7	1.8	5
Bryn	3	10	2	0	.000	6	4	.667	0	2	2	0	5	0	2	1	4	1.3	4
Turner	3	31	13	2	.154	0	0		0	2	2	5	2	0	1	0	4	1.3	2

3-Pt. FG: L.A. Clippers 56-230 (.243)—Harper 13-46 (.283); Smith 1-12 (.083); Manning 0-5 (.000); Norman 7-16 (.438); Benjamin 0-1 (.000); Grant 5-21 (.238); Williams 0-5 (.000); Garland 11-26 (.423); Garrick 4-21 (.190); Martin 2-15 (.133); Young 8-26 (.308); Wolf 5-25 (.200); Rivers 0-5 (.000); Bannister 0-1 (.000); Les 0-1 (.000); McKinney 0-1 (.000); Edwards 0-2 (.000); Turner 0-1 (.000). Opponents 186-576 (.323).

LOS ANGELES LAKERS

Player	G.	Min.	FGA	FGM	Pct.	FTA	FTM	Pct.	Off. Reb.	Def. Reb.	Tot. Reb.	Ast.	PF	Disq.	Stl.	Blk. Sh.	Pts.	Avg.	Hi.
Johnson	79	2937	1138	546	.480	637	567	.890	128	394	522	907	167	1	132	34	1765	22.3	38
Worthy	80	2960	1298	711	.548	317	248	.782	160	318	478	288	190	0	99	49	1685	21.1	35
Scott	77	2593	1005	472	.470	209	160	.766	51	191	242	274	180	2	77	31	1197	15.5	33
Green	82	2709	806	385	.478	370	278	.751	262	450	712	90	207	0	66	50	1061	12.9	27
Woolridge	62	1421	550	306	.556	240	176	.733	49	136	185	96	160	2	39	46	788	12.7	24
Thompson	70	1883	562	281	.500	204	144	.706	173	304	477	43	207	0	33	73	706	10.1	24
Divac	82	1611	549	274	.499	216	153	.708	167	345	512	75	240	2	79	114	701	8.5	25
Cooper	80	1851	493	191	.387	94	83	.883	59	168	227	215	206	1	67	36	515	6.4	16
Drew	80	1333	383	170	.444	60	46	.767	12	86	98	217	92	0	47	4	418	5.2	15
Vincent (Tot.)	41	459	183	86	.470	49	41	.837	20	42	62	18	52	0	18	5	214	5.2	19
Vincent (LAL)	24	200	78	41	.526	12	8	.667	7	19	26	10	29	0	8	3	90	3.8	16
McNamara	33	190	86	38	.442	40	26	.650	22	41	63	3	31	1	2	1	102	3.1	15
McCants	13	65	26	8	.308	8	6	.750	1	5	6	2	11	0	3	1	22	1.7	4
Oldham (Tot.)	6	45	6	3	.500	7	3	.429	4	12	16	1	9	0	2	3	9	1.5	3
Oldham (LAL)	3	9	3	2	.667	2	1	.500	0	1	1	1	3	0	0	0	5	1.7	3
Bucknall	18	75	33	9	.273	6	5	.833	5	2	7	10	10	0	2	1	23	1.3	4
Higgins	6	18	0	0	....	2	1	.500	1	0	1	1	4	0	1	2	1	0.2	1

3-Pt. FG: L.A. Lakers 309-841 (.367)—Johnson 106-276 (.384); Worthy 15-49 (.306); Scott 93-220 (.423); Green 13-46 (.283); Woolridge 0-5 (.000); Divac 0-5 (.000); Cooper 50-157 (.318); Drew 32-81 (.395); Vincent 0-1 (.000); Bucknall 0-1 (.000). Opponents 175-519 (.337).

MIAMI HEAT

Player	G.	Min.	FGA	FGM	Pct.	FTA	FTM	Pct.	Off. Reb.	Def. Reb.	Tot. Reb.	Ast.	PF	Disq.	Stl.	Blk. Sh.	Pts.	Avg.	Hi.
Seikaly	74	2409	968	486	.502	431	256	.594	253	513	766	78	258	8	124		1228	16.6	40
Douglas	81	2470	938	463	.494	326	224	.687	70	136	206	619	187	0	145	10	1155	14.3	37
Rice	77	2311	1071	470	.439	124	91	.734	100	252	352	138	198	1	61	27	1048	13.6	28
Edwards	78	2211	959	395	.412	183	139	.760	77	205	282	252	149	1	125	33	938	12.0	33
Thompson	79	2142	727	375	.516	185	115	.622	238	313	551	166	237	1	54	89	867	11.0	29
Frank	77	1762	607	278	.458	234	179	.765	151	234	385	85	282	6	51	27	735	9.5	24
Long	81	1856	532	257	.483	241	172	.714	156	246	402	96	300	11	91	38	686	8.5	22
Sundvold	63	867	363	148	.408	52	44	.846	15	56	71	102	69	0	25	0	384	6.1	18
Sparrow	82	1756	510	210	.412	77	59	.766	37	101	138	298	140	0	49	4	487	5.9	21
Davis	63	884	262	122	.466	87	54	.621	93	136	229	25	171	2	25	28	298	4.7	18
Cummings	37	391	159	77	.484	37	21	.568	28	65	93	13	60	1	12	4	175	4.7	14
Haffner	43	559	217	88	.406	25	17	.680	7	44	51	80	53	0	13	2	196	4.6	14
Rowinski	14	112	32	14	.438	26	22	.846	17	12	29	5	19	0	1	2	50	3.6	11

3-Pt. FG: Miami 88-300 (.293)—Seikaly 0-1 (.000); Douglas 5-31 (.161); Rice 17-69 (.246); Edwards 9-30 (.300); Thompson 2-4 (.500); Long 0-3 (.000); Sundvold 44-100 (.440); Sparrow 8-40 (.200); Davis 0-1 (.000); Haffner 3-21 (.143). Opponents 158-462 (.342).

MILWAUKEE BUCKS

Player	G.	Min.	FGA	FGM	Pct.	FTA	FTM	Pct.	Off. Reb.	Def. Reb.	Tot. Reb.	Ast.	PF	Disq.	Stl.	Blk. Sh.	Pts.	Avg.	Hi.
Pierce	59	1709	987	503	.510	366	307	.839	64	103	167	133	158	2	50	7	1359	23.0	45
Humphries	81	2818	1005	496	.494	285	224	.786	80	189	269	472	253	2	156	11	1237	15.3	29
Robertson	81	2599	946	476	.503	266	197	.741	230	329	559	445	280	2	207	17	1153	14.2	37
Sikma	71	2520	827	344	.416	260	230	.885	109	383	492	229	244	5	76	48	986	13.9	30
Pressey	57	1400	506	239	.472	190	144	.758	59	113	172	244	149	1	71	23	628	11.0	21
Roberts	82	2235	666	330	.495	249	195	.783	107	204	311	147	210	5	56	25	857	10.5	27
Lohaus (Tot.)	80	1943	663	305	.460	103	75	.728	98	300	398	168	211	3	58	88	732	9.2	25
Lohaus (Mil.)	52	1353	461	211	.458	77	54	.701	77	211	288	106	145	2	44	66	522	10.0	25
Anderson	60	1291	432	219	.507	170	91	.535	112	261	373	24	176	3	32	54	529	8.8	28
Grayer	71	1427	487	224	.460	152	99	.651	94	123	217	107	125	0	48	10	548	7.7	18
Krystkowiak	16	381	118	43	.364	33	26	.788	16	60	76	25	41	0	10	2	112	7.0	18
Breuer	30	554	186	86	.462	51	32	.627	43	84	127	13	63	0	9	33	204	6.8	18
Coleman	22	305	97	46	.474	41	34	.829	31	56	87	12	54	0	7	7	126	5.7	17
Brown	61	635	206	88	.427	56	38	.679	39	33	72	41	79	0	32	4	219	3.6	13
Sichting (Tot.)	35	496	125	50	.400	22	18	.818	3	16	19	94	40	0	16	2	121	3.5	12
Sichting (Mil.)	1	27	6	0	.000	4	3	.750	0	0	0	2	1	0	0	0	3	3.0	3
Dunleavy	5	43	14	4	.286	8	7	.875	0	2	2	10	7	0	1	0	17	3.4	9
Henderson	11	129	26	11	.423	2	2	1.000	3	9	12	13	14	0	8	0	27	2.5	7
Kornet	57	438	114	42	.368	39	24	.615	25	46	71	21	54	0	14	3	113	2.0	16
Horford	23	236	62	18	.290	24	15	.625	19	40	59	2	33	0	5	16	51	1.5	6

3-Pt. FG: Milwaukee 209-670 (.312)—Pierce 46-133 (.346); Humphries 21-70 (.300); Robertson 4-26 (.154); Sikma 68-199 (.342); Pressey 6-43 (.140); Roberts 2-11 (.182); Lohaus 46-121 (.380); Grayer 1-8 (.125); Krystkowiak 0-2 (.000); Coleman 0-1 (.000); Brown 5-20 (.250); Dunleavy 2-9 (.222); Henderson 3-7 (.429); Kornet 5-20 (.250). Opponents 181-564 (.321).

MINNESOTA TIMBERWOLVES

Player	G.	Min.	FGA	FGM	Pct.	FTA	FTM	Pct.	Off. Reb.	Def. Reb.	Tot. Reb.	Ast.	PF	Disq.	Stl.	Blk. Sh.	Pts.	Avg.	Hi.
Campbell	82	3164	1581	723	.457	569	448	.787	209	242	451	213	260	7	111	31	1903	23.2	44
Corbin	82	3011	1083	521	.481	209	161	.770	219	385	604	216	288	5	175	41	1203	14.7	36
Mitchell	80	2414	834	372	.446	349	268	.768	180	282	462	89	301	7	66	54	1012	12.7	31
Richardson	82	2581	925	426	.461	107	63	.589	55	162	217	554	143	0	133	25	938	11.4	27
Breuer (Tot.)	81	1879	696	298	.429	193	126	.653	154	263	417	97	196	2	42	108	722	8.9	40
Breuer (Min.)	51	1325	510	212	.416	142	94	.662	111	179	290	84	133	2	33	75	518	10.2	40
Murphy	82	2493	552	260	.471	203	144	.709	207	357	564	106	229	2	76	60	680	8.3	24
Lohaus	28	590	202	94	.465	26	21	.808	21	89	110	62	66	1	14	22	210	7.5	19
Roth	71	1061	420	159	.379	201	150	.746	34	78	112	115	144	1	51	6	486	6.8	24
Branch	11	91	61	25	.410	22	14	.636	8	12	20	4	14	0	6	0	65	5.9	14
Royal	66	746	255	117	.459	197	153	.777	69	68	137	43	107	0	32	8	387	5.9	23
Sellers (Tot.)	59	700	254	103	.406	73	58	.795	39	50	89	33	74	1	17	22	264	4.5	18
Sellers (Min.)	14	113	56	19	.339	12	9	.750	8	11	19	11	11	0	6	3	47	3.4	10
West	52	378	135	53	.393	32	26	.813	24	46	70	18	61	0	10	6	135	2.6	23
Lowe	80	1744	229	73	.319	54	39	.722	41	122	163	337	114	0	73	4	187	2.3	22
Leonard	22	127	31	13	.419	14	6	.429	10	17	27	1	26	0	3	9	32	1.5	6
Johnson	4	17	2	0	.000	0	0	....	0	3	3	1	4	0	0	0	0	0.0	0

3-Pt. FG: Minnesota 73-294 (.248)—Campbell 9-54 (.167); Corbin 0-11 (.000); Mitchell 0-9 (.000); Richardson 23-83 (.277); Breuer

0-1 (.000); Murphy 16-43 (.372); Lohaus 1-16 (.063); Roth 18-52 (.346); Branch 1-1 (1.000); Royal 0-1 (.000); Sellers 0-2 (.000); West 3-11 (.273); Lowe 2-9 (.222); Leonard 0-1 (.000). Opponents 129-391 (.330).

NEW JERSEY NETS

Player	G.	Min.	FGA	FGM	Pct.	FTA	FTM	Pct.	Off. Reb.	Def. Reb.	Tot. Reb.	Ast.	PF	Disq.	Stl.	Blk. Sh.	Pts.	Avg.	Hi.
Hopson	79	2551	1093	474	.434	342	271	.792	113	166	279	151	183	1	100	51	1251	15.8	29
Hinson	25	793	286	145	.507	99	86	.869	61	111	172	22	87	0	14	27	376	15.0	31
Morris	80	2449	1065	449	.422	316	228	.722	194	228	422	143	219	1	130	79	1187	14.8	33
Bowie	68	2207	834	347	.416	379	294	.776	206	484	690	91	211	5	38	121	998	14.7	29
Short	82	2213	950	432	.455	237	198	.835	101	147	248	145	202	2	66	20	1072	13.1	29
Gervin	21	339	197	93	.472	89	65	.730	29	36	65	8	47	0	20	7	251	12.0	25
Blaylock	50	1267	571	212	.371	81	63	.778	42	98	140	210	110	0	82	14	505	10.1	24
Carroll	46	1002	405	159	.393	107	85	.794	82	168	250	43	122	4	19	56	403	8.8	22
Shackleford	70	1557	535	247	.462	115	79	.687	180	299	479	56	183	1	40	35	573	8.2	23
Conner	82	2355	573	237	.414	214	172	.804	90	175	265	385	182	0	172	8	648	7.9	18
Dudley (Tot.)	64	1356	355	146	.411	182	58	.319	174	249	423	39	164	2	41	72	350	5.5	15
Dudley (NJ)	27	672	152	67	.441	105	32	.305	86	134	220	19	81	1	22	31	166	6.1	14
Haley (Tot.)	67	1084	347	138	.398	125	85	.680	115	185	300	26	170	1	18	12	361	5.4	19
Haley (NJ)	56	1026	327	129	.394	118	78	.661	108	174	282	22	163	1	18	11	336	6.0	19
Myers (Tot.)	52	751	225	89	.396	100	66	.660	33	63	96	135	109	0	35	11	244	4.7	16
Myers (NJ)	28	543	180	74	.411	69	50	.725	23	45	68	100	70	0	20	9	198	7.1	16
Taylor	17	114	52	21	.404	9	6	.667	5	6	11	5	9	0	5	3	51	3.0	8
Jackson	28	160	69	25	.362	21	17	.810	16	8	24	13	16	0	13	1	67	2.4	13
Brundy	16	128	30	15	.500	18	7	.389	15	11	26	3	24	0	6	5	37	2.3	12
Wood	28	200	49	16	.327	16	14	.875	1	11	12	47	16	0	6	0	50	1.8	11
Mason	21	108	40	14	.350	15	9	.600	11	23	34	7	20	0	2	2	37	1.8	8
Carlisle	5	21	7	1	.143	0	0	....	0	2	2	0	5	0	1	1	2	0.4	2

3-Pt. FG: New Jersey 140-506 (.277)—Hopson 32-101 (.317); Morris 61-193 (.316); Bowie 10-31 (.323); Short 10-35 (.286); Gervin 0-3 (.000); Blaylock 18-80 (.225); Carroll 0-2 (.000); Shackleford 0-1 (.000); Conner 2-13 (.154); Haley 0-1 (.000); Myers 0-6 (.000); Taylor 3-13 (.231); Jackson 0-3 (.000); Wood 4-21 (.190); Carlisle 0-3 (.000). Opponents 141-420 (.336).

NEW YORK KNICKERBOCKERS

Player	G.	Min.	FGA	FGM	Pct.	FTA	FTM	Pct.	Off. Reb.	Def. Reb.	Tot. Reb.	Ast.	PF	Disq.	Stl.	Blk. Sh.	Pts.	Avg.	Hi.
Ewing	82	3165	1673	922	.551	648	502	.775	235	658	893	182	325	7	78	327	2347	28.6	51
Oakley	61	2196	641	336	.524	285	217	.761	258	469	727	146	220	3	64	16	889	14.6	25
G. Wilkins	82	2609	1032	472	.457	259	208	.803	133	238	371	330	188	0	95	21	1191	14.5	30
Newman	80	2277	786	374	.476	299	239	.799	60	131	191	180	254	3	95	22	1032	12.9	30
Vandeweghe	22	563	231	102	.442	48	44	.917	15	38	53	41	28	0	15	3	258	11.7	24
Jackson	82	2428	749	327	.437	165	120	.727	106	212	318	604	121	0	109	4	809	9.9	33
Cheeks (Tot.)	81	2519	609	307	.504	202	171	.847	50	190	240	453	78	0	124	10	789	9.7	22
Cheeks (NY)	31	753	159	92	.579	65	57	.877	11	62	73	151	32	0	42	5	244	7.9	20
Strickland	51	1019	386	170	.440	130	83	.638	43	83	126	219	71	0	70	8	429	8.4	19
Tucker	81	1725	606	253	.417	86	66	.767	57	117	174	173	159	0	74	8	667	8.2	21
Walker	68	1595	384	204	.531	173	125	.723	131	212	343	49	178	1	33	52	535	7.9	24
E. Wilkins	79	972	310	141	.455	147	89	.605	114	151	265	16	152	1	18	18	371	4.7	14
Gray (Tot.)	58	560	99	42	.424	47	32	.681	40	105	145	19	90	0	15	26	116	2.0	9
Gray (NY)	19	94	17	4	.235	8	7	.875	2	12	14	2	26	0	3	2	15	0.8	2
Myers	24	208	45	15	.333	31	16	.516	10	18	28	35	39	0	15	2	46	1.9	9
Quinnett	31	193	58	19	.328	3	2	.667	9	19	28	11	27	0	3	4	40	1.3	6
Butler	13	33	12	3	.250	2	0	.000	3	6	9	1	8	0	0	0	6	0.5	4

3-Pt. FG: New York 236-710 (.332)—Ewing 1-4 (.250); Oakley 0-3 (.000); G. Wilkins 39-125 (.312); Newman 45-142 (.317); Vandeweghe 10-19 (.526); Jackson 35-131 (.267); Cheeks 3-7 (.429); Strickland 6-21 (.286); Tucker 95-245 (.388); Walker 2-5 (.400); E. Wilkins 0-2 (.000); Gray 0-3 (.000); Myers 0-1 (.000); Quinnett 0-2 (.000). Opponents 171-543 (.315).

ORLANDO MAGIC

Player	G.	Min.	FGA	FGM	Pct.	FTA	FTM	Pct.	Off. Reb.	Def. Reb.	Tot. Reb.	Ast.	PF	Disq.	Stl.	Blk. Sh.	Pts.	Avg.	Hi.
Catledge	74	2462	1152	546	.474	486	341	.702	271	292	563	72	201	0	36	17	1435	19.4	49
Theus	76	2350	1178	517	.439	443	378	.853	75	146	221	407	194	1	60	12	1438	18.9	36
Smith	65	1644	708	348	.492	222	169	.761	117	183	300	147	174	0	76	57	875	13.5	33
Reynolds	67	1817	741	309	.417	322	239	.742	91	232	323	180	162	1	93	64	858	12.8	34
Anderson	81	1785	753	372	.494	264	186	.705	107	209	316	124	140	0	69	34	931	11.5	29
Vincent	63	1657	564	258	.457	214	188	.879	37	157	194	354	108	1	65	20	705	11.2	29
Green	73	1860	667	312	.468	209	136	.651	166	422	588	99	231	4	50	26	761	10.4	36
Ansley	72	1221	465	231	.497	227	164	.722	187	175	362	40	152	0	24	17	626	8.7	26
Skiles	70	1460	464	190	.409	119	104	.874	23	136	159	334	126	0	36	4	536	7.7	23
Wiley	40	638	208	92	.442	38	28	.737	13	39	52	114	65	0	45	3	229	5.7	24
Turner	60	1105	308	132	.429	54	42	.778	52	175	227	53	161	4	23	12	308	5.1	18
Acres	80	1691	285	138	.484	120	83	.692	154	277	431	67	248	4	36	25	362	4.5	18
Corzine	6	79	29	11	.379	2	0	.000	7	11	18	2	7	0	2	0	22	3.7	12
Oldham	3	36	3	1	.333	5	2	.400	4	11	15	0	6	0	2	3	4	1.3	3

3-Pt. FG: Orlando 116-393 (.295)—Catledge 2-8 (.250); Theus 26-105 (.248); Smith 10-40 (.250); Reynolds 1-14 (.071); Anderson 1-17 (.059); Vincent 1-14 (.071); Green 1-3 (.333); Skiles 52-132 (.394); Wiley 17-46 (.370); Turner 2-10 (.200); Acres 3-4 (.750). Opponents 196-555 (.353).

PHILADELPHIA 76ers

Player	G.	Min.	FGA	FGM	Pct.	FTA	FTM	Pct.	Off. Reb.	Def. Reb.	Tot. Reb.	Ast.	PF	Disq.	Stl.	Blk. Sh.	Pts.	Avg.	Hi.
Barkley	79	3085	1177	706	.600	744	600	.749	361	548	909	307	250	2	148	50	1989	25.2	39
Hawkins	82	2856	1136	522	.460	436	387	.888	85	219	304	261	217	2	130	28	1515	18.5	31
Dawkins	81	2865	950	465	.489	244	210	.861	48	199	247	601	159	1	121	9	1162	14.3	30
Gminski	81	2659	1002	458	.457	235	193	.821	196	491	687	128	136	0	43	102	1112	13.7	26
Anderson	78	2089	841	379	.451	197	165	.838	81	214	295	143	143	0	72	13	926	11.9	30
Mahorn	75	2271	630	313	.497	256	183	.715	167	401	568	98	251	2	44	103	811	10.8	27
Smith	75	1405	514	261	.508	186	130	.699	62	110	172	109	198	2	35	20	668	8.9	20
Vincent	17	259	105	45	.429	37	33	.892	13	23	36	8	23	0	10	2	124	7.3	19
Brooks	72	975	276	119	.431	57	50	.877	15	49	64	207	105	0	47	0	319	4.4	20
Payne	35	216	108	47	.435	18	16	.889	11	15	26	10	37	0	7	6	114	3.3	10

Player	G.	Min.	FGA	FGM	Pct.	FTA	FTM	Pct.	Off. Reb.	Def. Reb.	Tot. Reb.	Ast.	PF	Disq.	Stl.	Blk. Sh.	Pts.	Avg.	Hi.
Copeland	23	110	68	31	.456	14	11	.786	4	6	10	9	12	0	1	1	74	3.2	8
Nimphius	38	314	91	38	.418	30	14	.467	22	39	61	6	45	0	4	18	90	2.4	9
Thornton	56	592	112	48	.429	51	26	.510	45	88	133	17	105	1	20	12	123	2.2	11
Gaines	9	81	12	4	.333	4	1	.250	1	4	5	26	11	0	4	0	10	1.1	4
Lloyd	2	10	2	1	.500	0	0	....	0	0	0	0	3	0	0	0	2	1.0	2
Shouse	3	18	4	0	.000	0	0	....	0	0	0	2	2	0	1	1	0	0.0	0

3-Pt. FG: Philadelphia 189-543 (.348)—Barkley 20-92 (.217); Hawkins 84-200 (.420); Dawkins 22-66 (.333); Gminski 3-17 (.176); Anderson 3-21 (.143); Mahorn 2-9 (.222); Smith 16-36 (.444); Vincent 1-1 (1.000); Brooks 31-79 (.392); Payne 4-10 (.400); Copeland 1-5 (.200); Nimphius 0-1 (.000); Thornton 1-3 (.333); Gaines 1-2 (.500); Shouse 0-1 (.000). Opponents 212-573 (.370).

PHOENIX SUNS

Player	G.	Min.	FGA	FGM	Pct.	FTA	FTM	Pct.	Off. Reb.	Def. Reb.	Tot. Reb.	Ast.	PF	Disq.	Stl.	Blk. Sh.	Pts.	Avg.	Hi.
Chambers	81	3046	1617	810	.501	647	557	.861	121	450	571	190	260	1	88	47	2201	27.2	60
K. Johnson	74	2782	1159	578	.499	598	501	.838	42	228	270	846	143	0	95	14	1665	22.5	44
Hornacek	67	2278	901	483	.536	202	173	.856	86	227	313	337	144	2	117	14	1179	17.6	30
E. Johnson	64	1811	907	411	.453	205	188	.917	69	177	246	107	174	4	32	10	1080	16.9	37
Majerle	73	2244	698	296	.424	260	198	.762	144	286	430	188	177	5	100	32	809	11.1	32
West	82	2399	530	331	.625	288	199	.691	212	516	728	45	277	5	36	184	861	10.5	20
Gilliam	16	267	121	52	.430	56	39	.696	26	44	70	8	28	0	6	5	143	8.9	22
McGee	14	280	87	42	.483	21	10	.476	11	25	36	16	28	0	8	1	102	7.3	25
Rambis (Tot.)	74	1904	373	196	.509	127	82	.646	156	369	525	135	208	0	100	37	462	6.2	21
Rambis (Phoe.)	58	1456	257	132	.514	72	52	.722	108	297	405	107	163	0	68	27	316	5.4	16
Perry	60	612	195	100	.513	90	53	.589	79	73	152	17	76	0	21	22	254	4.2	22
Battle	59	729	170	93	.547	82	55	.671	44	80	124	38	94	2	35	11	242	4.1	16
Lang	74	1011	174	97	.557	98	64	.653	83	188	271	21	171	1	22	133	258	3.5	16
Grant	67	678	216	83	.384	59	39	.661	16	43	59	168	58	0	36	1	208	3.1	14
Legler	11	83	29	11	.379	6	6	1.000	4	4	8	6	12	0	2	0	28	2.5	8
Morrison	36	153	68	23	.338	30	24	.800	7	13	20	11	20	0	2	0	72	2.0	11
Williams	6	26	10	2	.200	2	1	.500	1	0	1	4	0	0	0	0	5	0.8	2

3-Pt. FG: Phoenix 176-543 (.324)—Chambers 24-86 (.279); K. Johnson 8-41 (.195); Hornacek 40-98 (.408); E. Johnson 70-184 (.380); Majerle 19-80 (.238); McGee 8-23 (.348); Rambis 0-2 (.000); Perry 1-1 (1.000); Battle 1-4 (.250); Grant 3-16 (.188); Legler 0-1 (.000); Morrison 2-7 (.286). Opponents 200-563 (.355).

PORTLAND TRAIL BLAZERS

Player	G.	Min.	FGA	FGM	Pct.	FTA	FTM	Pct.	Off. Reb.	Def. Reb.	Tot. Reb.	Ast.	PF	Disq.	Stl.	Blk. Sh.	Pts.	Avg.	Hi.
Drexler	73	2683	1357	670	.494	430	333	.774	208	299	507	432	222	1	145	51	1703	23.3	41
Porter	80	2781	969	448	.462	472	421	.892	59	213	272	726	150	0	151	4	1406	17.6	31
Duckworth	82	2462	1146	548	.478	312	231	.740	184	325	509	91	271	2	36	34	1327	16.2	28
Kersey	82	2843	1085	519	.478	390	269	.690	251	439	690	188	304	7	121	63	1310	16.0	31
Williams	82	2801	754	413	.548	408	288	.706	250	550	800	116	285	4	69	39	1114	13.6	24
Robinson	82	1565	751	298	.397	251	138	.550	110	198	308	72	226	4	53	53	746	9.1	22
Petrovic	77	967	427	207	.485	160	135	.844	50	61	111	116	134	0	23	2	583	7.6	24
Irvin	50	488	203	96	.473	91	61	.670	30	44	74	47	40	0	28	1	258	5.2	23
Young	82	1393	328	138	.421	112	91	.813	29	93	122	231	84	0	82	4	383	4.7	16
Cooper	79	1176	304	138	.454	39	25	.641	128	221	339	44	211	2	18	95	301	3.8	12
Bryant	58	562	153	70	.458	50	28	.560	54	92	146	13	93	0	18	9	168	2.9	12
Reid	12	85	33	13	.394	8	4	.500	1	7	8	8	17	0	2	2	31	2.6	6
Johnston (Tot.)	21	87	48	18	.375	13	9	.692	13	10	23	1	11	1	3	8	46	2.2	8
Johnston (Port.)	15	74	37	14	.378	11	7	.636	11	10	21	1	11	1	3	7	35	2.3	8

3-Pt. FG: Portland 190-565 (.336)—Drexler 30-106 (.283); Porter 89-238 (.374); Kersey 3-20 (.150); Williams 0-1 (.000); Robinson 12-44 (.273); Petrovic 34-74 (.459); Irvin 5-14 (.357); Young 16-59 (.271); Cooper 0-3 (.000); Reid 1-3 (.333); Johnston 0-3 (.000). Opponents 228-688 (.331).

SACRAMENTO KINGS

Player	G.	Min.	FGA	FGM	Pct.	FTA	FTM	Pct.	Off. Reb.	Def. Reb.	Tot. Reb.	Ast.	PF	Disq.	Stl.	Blk. Sh.	Pts.	Avg.	Hi.
Tisdale	79	2937	1383	726	.525	391	306	.783	185	410	595	108	251	3	54	54	1758	22.3	40
Ainge	75	2727	1154	506	.438	267	222	.831	69	257	326	453	238	2	113	18	1342	17.9	39
McCray	82	3238	1043	537	.515	348	273	.784	192	477	669	377	176	0	60	70	1358	16.6	30
Smith	46	1747	607	280	.461	131	106	.809	11	109	120	303	98	0	57	7	688	15.0	24
Carr (Tot.)	77	1727	721	356	.494	298	237	.795	115	207	322	119	247	6	30	68	949	12.3	32
Carr (Sac.)	33	924	473	228	.482	196	158	.806	65	108	173	66	119	2	15	34	614	18.6	32
Del Negro	76	1858	643	297	.462	155	135	.871	39	159	198	250	182	2	64	10	739	9.7	28
Pressley	72	1603	566	240	.424	141	110	.780	94	215	309	149	148	0	58	36	636	8.8	23
Ellison	34	866	351	111	.442	78	49	.628	64	132	196	65	132	4	16	57	271	8.0	25
Turner	36	315	122	58	.475	65	40	.615	22	28	50	22	40	0	17	7	156	4.3	16
Sampson	26	417	129	48	.372	23	12	.522	11	73	84	28	66	1	14	22	109	4.2	16
Toney (Tot.)	64	968	250	87	.348	83	67	.807	14	46	60	174	106	1	33	0	264	4.1	16
Toney (Sac.)	32	682	178	57	.320	58	46	.793	11	35	46	122	71	1	23	0	176	5.5	16
Allen	63	746	239	106	.444	43	23	.535	49	89	138	23	102	0	16	19	235	3.7	14
Kite	71	1515	234	101	.432	54	27	.500	131	246	377	76	201	2	31	51	229	3.2	10
Williams	16	88	14	6	.429	6	3	.500	5	17	22	2	28	0	3	7	15	0.9	4
Jackson	17	58	11	3	.273	6	3	.500	2	5	7	8	3	0	5	0	10	0.6	6
Stokes	13	34	9	1	.111	2	2	1.000	2	3	5	4	8	0	0	0	4	0.2	2

3-Pt. FG: Sacramento 216-649 (.333)—Tisdale 0-6 (.000); Ainge 108-289 (.374); McCray 11-42 (.262); Smith 22-59 (.373); Carr 0-3 (.000); Del Negro 10-32 (.313); Pressley 46-148 (.311); Ellison 0-2 (.000); Turner 0-3 (.000); Sampson 1-4 (.250); Toney 16-50 (.320); Allen 0-7 (.000); Kite 1-1 (1.000); Williams 0-1 (.000); Jackson 1-2 (.500). Opponents 160-507 (.316).

SAN ANTONIO SPURS

Player	G.	Min.	FGA	FGM	Pct.	FTA	FTM	Pct.	Off. Reb.	Def. Reb.	Tot. Reb.	Ast.	PF	Disq.	Stl.	Blk. Sh.	Pts.	Avg.	Hi.
Robinson	82	3002	1300	690	.531	837	613	.732	303	680	983	164	259	3	138	319	1993	24.3	41
Cummings	81	2821	1532	728	.475	440	343	.780	226	451	677	219	286	1	110	52	1818	22.4	52
Anderson	82	2788	1082	532	.492	290	217	.748	115	257	372	364	252	0	111	58	1288	15.7	28
Cheeks	50	1766	450	215	.478	137	114	.832	39	128	167	302	46	0	82	5	545	10.9	22

Player	G.	Min.	FGA	FGM	Pct.	FTA	FTM	Pct.	Off. Reb.	Def. Reb.	Tot. Reb.	Ast.	PF	Disq.	Stl.	Blk. Sh.	Pts.	Avg.	Hi.
Strickland (Tot).....	82	2140	756	343	.454	278	174	.626	90	169	259	468	160	3	127	14	868	10.6	21
Strickland (SA)......	31	1121	370	173	.468	148	91	.615	47	86	133	249	89	3	57	6	439	14.2	21
Elliott	81	2032	647	311	.481	216	187	.866	127	170	297	154	172	0	45	14	810	10.0	24
Maxwell	49	1118	306	133	.435	95	59	.621	35	106	141	146	79	0	42	5	340	6.9	16
Williams (Tot)	47	743	338	131	.388	68	52	.765	28	55	83	53	102	2	32	14	320	6.8	24
Williams (SA)........	10	68	42	19	.452	6	4	.667	3	5	8	5	16	0	1	3	42	4.2	13
Wingate................	78	1856	491	220	.448	112	87	.777	62	133	195	208	154	2	89	18	527	6.8	19
Brickowski............	78	1438	387	211	.545	141	95	.674	89	238	327	105	226	4	66	37	517	6.6	16
Paspalj	28	181	79	27	.342	22	18	.818	15	15	30	10	37	0	3	7	72	2.6	13
Jones	72	885	144	67	.465	54	38	.704	76	154	230	20	146	2	20	27	173	2.4	11
Moore..................	53	516	126	47	.373	27	16	.593	16	36	52	82	55	0	32	3	118	2.2	11
Blab (Tot).............	47	531	98	39	.398	37	20	.541	29	79	108	25	102	0	1	22	98	2.1	8
Blab (SA)..............	7	50	11	6	.545	6	3	.500	1	8	9	1	9	0	0	0	15	2.1	5
Lebo	4	32	7	2	.286	2	2	1.000	2	2	4	3	7	0	2	0	6	1.5	4
Welp....................	13	56	23	7	.304	2	1	.500	7	5	12	5	21	0	1	0	15	1.2	4

3-Pt. FG: San Antonio 54-226 (.239)—Robinson 0-2 (.000); Cummings 19-59 (.322); Anderson 7-26 (.269); Cheeks 1-9 (.111); Strickland 2-9 (.222); Elliott 1-9 (.111); Maxwell 15-52 (.288); Williams 0-5 (.000); Wingate 0-13 (.000); Brickowski 0-2 (.000); Paspalj 0-1 (.000); Jones 1-5 (.200); Moore 8-34 (.235). Opponents 231-624 (.370).

SEATTLE SUPERSONICS

Player	G.	Min.	FGA	FGM	Pct.	FTA	FTM	Pct.	Off. Reb.	Def. Reb.	Tot. Reb.	Ast.	PF	Disq.	Stl.	Blk. Sh.	Pts.	Avg.	Hi.
Ellis....................	55	2033	1011	502	.497	236	193	.818	90	148	238	110	124	3	59	7	1293	23.5	53
McDaniel..............	69	2432	1233	611	.496	333	244	.733	165	282	447	171	231	2	73	36	1471	21.3	37
McKey.................	80	2748	949	468	.493	403	315	.782	170	319	489	187	247	2	87	81	1254	15.7	33
Threatt................	65	1481	599	303	.506	157	130	.828	43	72	115	216	164	0	65	8	744	11.4	36
Cage...................	82	2595	645	325	.504	212	148	.698	306	515	821	70	232	1	79	45	798	9.7	24
Barros.................	81	1630	738	299	.405	110	89	.809	35	97	132	205	97	0	53	1	782	9.7	28
Dailey.................	30	491	240	97	.404	66	52	.788	18	33	51	34	63	0	12	0	247	8.2	22
Kemp..................	81	1120	424	203	.479	159	117	.736	146	200	346	26	204	5	47	70	525	6.5	20
Farmer................	38	400	203	89	.438	80	57	.713	17	26	43	25	44	0	17	1	243	6.4	26
McMillan..............	82	2338	438	207	.473	153	98	.641	127	276	403	598	289	7	140	37	523	6.4	19
Sellers................	45	587	198	84	.424	61	49	.803	31	39	70	32	63	1	11	19	217	4.8	18
S. Johnson (Tot)....	25	259	92	48	.522	35	21	.600	19	34	53	17	56	0	3	5	117	4.7	13
S. Johnson (Sea)...	21	242	90	48	.533	35	21	.600	19	31	50	16	52	0	3	5	117	5.6	13
Polynice...............	79	1085	289	156	.540	99	47	.475	128	172	300	15	187	0	25	21	360	4.6	18
A. Johnson...........	53	575	142	55	.387	40	29	.725	21	22	43	162	55	0	26	1	140	2.6	12
Meents................	26	148	44	19	.432	23	17	.739	7	23	30	7	12	0	4	3	55	2.1	10

3-Pt. FG: Seattle 231-650 (.355)—Ellis 96-256 (.375); McDaniel 5-17 (.294); McKey 3-23 (.130); Threatt 8-32 (.250); Barros 95-238 (.399); Dailey 1-5 (.200); Kemp 2-12 (.167); Farmer 8-27 (.296); McMillan 11-31 (.355); Sellers 0-3 (.000); Polynice 1-2 (.500); A. Johnson 1-4 (.250). Opponents 178-520 (.342).

UTAH JAZZ

Player	G.	Min.	FGA	FGM	Pct.	FTA	FTM	Pct.	Off. Reb.	Def. Reb.	Tot. Reb.	Ast.	PF	Disq.	Stl.	Blk. Sh.	Pts.	Avg.	Hi.
Malone	82	3122	1627	914	.562	913	696	.762	232	679	911	226	259	1	121	50	2540	31.0	61
Stockton..............	78	2915	918	472	.514	432	354	.819	57	149	206	1134	233	3	207	18	1345	17.2	34
Bailey.................	82	2583	977	470	.481	285	222	.779	116	294	410	137	175	2	32	100	1162	14.2	27
Griffith................	82	1444	649	301	.464	78	51	.654	43	123	166	63	149	0	68	19	733	8.9	20
Edwards..............	82	1889	564	286	.507	203	146	.719	69	182	251	145	280	2	76	36	727	8.9	22
Hansen................	81	2174	568	265	.467	64	33	.516	66	163	229	149	194	2	52	11	617	7.6	23
M. Brown.............	82	1397	344	177	.515	199	157	.789	111	262	373	47	187	0	32	28	512	6.2	22
Eaton..................	82	2281	300	158	.527	118	79	.669	171	430	601	39	238	3	33	201	395	4.8	14
Leckner...............	77	764	222	125	.563	109	81	.743	48	144	192	19	157	0	15	23	331	4.3	16
Rudd...................	77	850	259	111	.429	53	35	.660	12	43	55	177	81	0	22	1	273	3.5	15
Ortiz...................	13	64	42	19	.452	5	3	.600	8	7	15	7	15	0	2	1	42	3.2	9
Les.....................	1	6	0	0	....	4	2	.500	0	0	0	1	3	0	0	0	2	2.0	2
Johnston..............	6	13	11	4	.364	2	2	1.000	2	0	2	0	0	0	1	0	11	1.8	5
Johnson...............	48	272	84	20	.238	17	13	.765	8	20	28	64	49	1	17	2	54	1.1	6
R. Brown..............	16	56	28	8	.286	2	0	.000	10	5	15	4	11	0	0	0	16	1.0	6

3-Pt. FG: Utah 226-630 (.359)—Malone 16-43 (.372); Stockton 47-113 (.416); Bailey 0-8 (.000); Griffith 80-215 (.372); Edwards 9-30 (.300); Hansen 54-154 (.351); M. Brown 1-2 (.500); Rudd 16-56 (.286); Ortiz 1-2 (.500); Johnston 1-1 (1.000); Johnson 1-6 (.167). Opponents 174-563 (.309).

WASHINGTON BULLETS

Player	G.	Min.	FGA	FGM	Pct.	FTA	FTM	Pct.	Off. Reb.	Def. Reb.	Tot. Reb.	Ast.	PF	Disq.	Stl.	Blk. Sh.	Pts.	Avg.	Hi.
Malone	75	2567	1592	781	.491	293	257	.877	54	152	206	243	116	1	48	6	1820	24.3	43
King....................	82	2687	1459	711	.487	513	412	.803	129	275	404	376	230	1	51	7	1837	22.4	42
Williams...............	18	632	274	130	.474	84	65	.774	27	109	136	84	33	0	21	9	327	18.2	29
Eackles................	78	1696	940	413	.439	280	210	.750	74	101	175	182	157	0	50	4	1055	13.5	40
Alarie..................	82	1893	785	371	.473	133	108	.812	151	223	374	142	219	2	60	39	860	10.5	20
Walker.................	81	2883	696	316	.454	201	138	.687	173	541	714	652	220	1	139	30	772	9.5	21
Grant	81	1846	601	284	.473	137	96	.701	138	204	342	131	194	1	52	43	664	8.2	24
Hammonds	61	805	295	129	.437	98	63	.643	61	107	168	50	98	0	14	11	321	5.3	17
Colter..................	73	977	297	142	.478	95	77	.811	55	121	176	148	98	0	47	10	361	4.9	25
Turpin.................	59	818	209	110	.526	71	56	.789	88	133	221	27	135	0	15	47	276	4.7	17
Horton.................	45	374	162	80	.494	69	42	.609	59	49	108	19	63	1	9	5	202	4.5	18
Jones..................	81	2240	185	94	.508	105	68	.648	145	359	504	139	296	10	50	197	256	3.2	14
Roth....................	42	412	86	37	.430	14	7	.500	44	76	120	20	70	1	8	13	81	1.9	8

3-Pt. FG: Washington 37-197 (.188)—Malone 1-6 (.167); King 3-23 (.130); Williams 2-18 (.111); Eackles 19-59 (.322); Alarie 10-49 (.204); Walker 2-21 (.095); Grant 0-8 (.000); Hammonds 0-1 (.000); Colter 0-5 (.000); Turpin 0-2 (.000); Horton 0-4 (.000); Roth 0-1 (.000). Opponents 142-474 (.300).

PLAYOFF RESULTS

EASTERN CONFERENCE FIRST ROUND
New York 3, Boston 2
Apr. 26—Thur.—New York 105 at Boston.....................................116
Apr. 28—Sat.—New York 128 at Boston......................................157
May 2—Wed.—Boston 99 at New York.......................................102
May 4—Fri.—Boston 108 at New York.......................................135
May 6—Sun.—New York 121 at Boston......................................114

Detroit 3, Indiana 0
Apr. 26—Thur.—Indiana 92 at Detroit 104
Apr. 28—Sat.—Indiana 87 at Detroit 100
May 1—Tue.—Detroit 108 at Indiana...96

Philadelphia 3, Cleveland 2
Apr. 26—Thur.—Cleveland 106 at Philadelphia.........................111
Apr. 29—Sun.—Cleveland 101 at Philadelphia..........................107
May 1—Tue.—Philadelphia 95 at Cleveland............................122
May 3—Thur.—Philadelphia 96 at Cleveland...........................108
May 5—Sat.—Cleveland 97 at Philadelphia.............................113

Chicago 3, Milwaukee 1
Apr. 27—Fri.—Milwaukee 97 at Chicago 111
Apr. 29—Sun.—Milwaukee 102 at Chicago................................109
May 1—Tue.—Chicago 112 at Milwaukee.................................119
May 3—Thur.—Chicago 110 at Milwaukee 86

EASTERN CONFERENCE SEMIFINALS
Chicago 4, Philadelphia 1
May 7—Mon.—Philadelphia 85 at Chicago 96
May 9—Wed.—Philadelphia 96 at Chicago...............................101
May 11—Fri.—Chicago 112 at Philadelphia 118
May 13—Sun.—Chicago 111 at Philadelphia 101
May 16—Wed.—Philadelphia 99 at Chicago..............................117

Detroit 4, New York 1
May 8—Tue.—New York 112 at Detroit 112
May 10—Thur.—New York 97 at Detroit 104
May 12—Sat.—Detroit 103 at New York 111
May 13—Sun.—Detroit 102 at New York 90
May 15—Tue.—New York 84 at Detroit 95

EASTERN CONFERENCE FINALS
Detroit 4, Chicago 3
May 20—Sun.—Chicago 77 at Detroit 86
May 22—Tue.—Chicago 93 at Detroit 102
May 26—Sat.—Detroit 102 at Chicago..107
May 28—Mon.—Detroit 101 at Chicago.......................................108
May 30—Wed.—Chicago 83 at Detroit 97
June 1—Fri.—Detroit 91 at Chicago..109
June 3—Sun.—Chicago 74 at Detroit 93

WESTERN CONFERENCE FIRST ROUND
L.A. Lakers 3, Houston 1
Apr. 27—Fri.—Houston 89 at L.A. Lakers...................................101

Apr. 29—Sun.—Houston 100 at L.A. Lakers...............................104
May 1—Tue.—L.A. Lakers 108 at Houston................................114
May 3—Thur.—L.A. Lakers 109 at Houston................................88

Phoenix 3, Utah 2
Apr. 27—Fri.—Phoenix 96 at Utah..113
Apr. 29—Sun.—Phoenix 105 at Utah..87
May 2—Wed.—Utah 105 at Phoenix..120
May 4—Fri.—Utah 105 at Phoenix...94
May 6—Sun.—Phoenix 104 at Utah...102

San Antonio 3, Denver 0
Apr. 26—Thur.—Denver 103 at San Antonio 119
Apr. 28—Sat.—Denver 120 at San Antonio 129
May 1—Tue.—San Antonio 131 at Denver.................................120

Portland 3, Dallas 0
Apr. 26—Thur.—Dallas 102 at Portland 109
Apr. 28—Sat.—Dallas 107 at Portland 114
May 1—Tue.—Portland 106 at Dallas..92

WESTERN CONFERENCE SEMIFINALS
Portland 4, San Antonio 3
May 5—Sat.—San Antonio 94 at Portland.................................107
May 8—Tue.—San Antonio 112 at Portland...............................122
May 10—Thur.—Portland 98 at San Antonio...............................121
May 12—Sat.—Portland 105 at San Antonio 115
May 15—Sun.—San Antonio 132 at Portland.............................**138
May 17—Thur.—Portland 97 at San Antonio 112
May 19—Sat.—San Antonio 105 at Portland *108

Phoenix 4, L.A. Lakers 1
May 8—Tue.—Phoenix 104 at L.A. Lakers.................................102
May 10—Thur.—Phoenix 100 at L.A. Lakers...............................124
May 12—Sat.—L.A. Lakers 103 at Phoenix.................................117
May 13—Sun.—L.A. Lakers 101 at Phoenix................................114
May 15—Tue.—Phoenix 106 at L.A. Lakers.................................103

WESTERN CONFERENCE FINALS
Portland 4, Phoenix 2
May 21—Mon.—Phoenix 98 at Portland 100
May 23—Wed.—Phoenix 107 at Portland 108
May 25—Fri.—Portland 89 at Phoenix..123
May 27—Sun.—Portland 107 at Phoenix....................................119
May 29—Tue.—Phoenix 114 at Portland.....................................120
May 31—Thur.—Portland 112 at Phoenix 109

NBA FINALS
Detroit 4, Portland 1
June 5—Tue.—Portland 99 at Detroit...105
June 7—Thur.—Portland 106 at Detroit *105
June 10—Sun.—Detroit 121 at Portland 106
June 12—Tue.—Detroit 112 at Portland 109
June 14—Thur.—Detroit 92 at Portland 90

1988-89 NBA STATISTICS

1988-89 NBA CHAMPION DETROIT PISTONS

Front row (left to right): Bill Laimbeer, John Long, Coach Chuck Daly, CEO Tom Wilson, Owner William Davidson, G.M. Jack McCloskey, legal counsel Oscar Feldman, John Salley, James Edwards, Rick Mahorn. Back row: trainer Mike Abdenour, scouting director Stan Novak, assistant G.M. Will Robinson, assistant coach Brendan Suhr, Michael Williams, Vinnie Johnson, Fennis Dembo, Dennis Rodman, Mark Aguirre, Joe Dumars, Isiah Thomas, assistant coach Brendan Malone, announcer George Blaha.

FINAL STANDINGS

ATLANTIC DIVISION

Team	Atl.	Bos.	Char.	Chi.	Cle.	Dal.	Den.	Det.	G.S.	Hou.	Ind.	L.A.C.	L.A.L.	Mia.	Mil.	N.J.	N.Y.	Phil.	Pho.	Por.	Sac.	S.A.	Sea.	Uta.	Was.	W.	L.	Pct.	G.B.
New York	2	3	4	2	2	2	1	4	0	2	5	2	1	1	3	4	..	2	1	2	1	1	1	1	5	52	30	.634	..
Philadelphia	2	3	3	3	2	1	1	0	1	2	4	2	0	2	1	5	4	..	0	1	2	1	1	1	4	46	36	.561	6
Boston	1	..	6	1	1	1	1	1	1	1	2	2	1	2	2	5	3	3	0	1	2	2	0	1	2	42	40	.512	10
Washington	1	4	5	1	2	1	1	0	1	2	3	2	1	2	1	5	1	2	0	1	2	1	1	0	..	40	42	.488	12
New Jersey	1	1	4	2	0	1	1	0	0	0	3	1	1	1	1	..	2	1	1	0	1	1	2	0	1	26	56	.317	26
Charlotte	1	0	..	1	0	0	0	0	0	0	2	2	0	1	0	2	2	3	0	0	1	2	1	1	1	20	62	.244	32

CENTRAL DIVISION

Team	Atl.	Bos.	Char.	Chi.	Cle.	Dal.	Den.	Det.	G.S.	Hou.	Ind.	L.A.C.	L.A.L.	Mia.	Mil.	N.J.	N.Y.	Phil.	Pho.	Por.	Sac.	S.A.	Sea.	Uta.	Was.	W.	L.	Pct.	G.B.
Detroit	5	3	4	6	3	2	1	..	1	1	4	2	2	2	2	4	0	5	2	1	2	2	2	2	5	63	19	.768	..
Cleveland	2	4	4	6	..	2	2	3	1	1	5	1	0	2	3	4	2	3	2	2	2	2	1	1	2	57	25	.695	6
Atlanta	..	3	4	4	4	1	0	1	1	1	5	2	1	1	6	4	2	2	1	1	2	1	1	1	3	52	30	.634	11
Milwaukee	0	2	4	0	3	2	2	4	2	1	4	2	1	2	..	4	1	3	1	2	2	1	1	1	4	49	33	.598	14
Chicago	2	3	4	..	0	2	1	0	1	1	4	1	2	2	6	2	3	1	1	2	2	2	2	0	3	47	35	.573	16
Indiana	1	3	2	2	1	1	1	2	1	0	..	1	0	1	2	1	0	0	1	2	1	2	1	1	1	28	54	.341	35

MIDWEST DIVISION

Team	Atl.	Bos.	Char.	Chi.	Cle.	Dal.	Den.	Det.	G.S.	Hou.	Ind.	L.A.C.	L.A.L.	Mia.	Mil.	N.J.	N.Y.	Phil.	Pho.	Por.	Sac.	S.A.	Sea.	Uta.	Was.	W.	L.	Pct.	G.B.
Utah	1	1	1	2	1	2	3	0	2	4	1	3	3	5	1	2	1	1	2	4	3	5	1	..	2	51	31	.622	..
Houston	1	1	2	1	1	5	2	1	3	..	2	2	1	4	1	2	0	0	1	3	2	6	2	2	0	45	37	.549	6
Denver	2	1	2	1	0	3	..	1	3	4	1	2	1	5	0	1	1	1	2	3	3	2	3	3	1	44	38	.537	7
Dallas	1	1	2	0	0	..	3	0	1	1	3	0	6	0	1	0	1	1	2	2	5	2	4	1	3	38	44	.463	13
San Antonio	1	0	0	0	0	1	3	0	1	0	0	1	1	4	1	1	1	1	0	2	..	0	1	1	0	21	61	.256	30
Miami	1	0	1	0	0	0	1	0	0	2	1	3	0	..	0	1	1	0	0	0	1	2	0	1	0	15	67	.183	36

PACIFIC DIVISION

Team	Atl.	Bos.	Char.	Chi.	Cle.	Dal.	Den.	Det.	G.S.	Hou.	Ind.	L.A.C.	L.A.L.	Mia.	Mil.	N.J.	N.Y.	Phil.	Pho.	Por.	Sac.	S.A.	Sea.	Uta.	Was.	W.	L.	Pct.	G.B.
L.A. Lakers	1	1	2	0	2	4	3	0	3	3	2	5	..	4	1	1	1	2	3	5	5	3	4	1	1	57	25	.695	..
Phoenix	1	2	2	1	0	3	3	0	4	3	1	5	3	4	1	1	1	2	..	2	5	3	4	2	2	55	27	.671	2
Seattle	1	2	1	0	1	2	2	0	4	2	1	4	2	4	1	0	1	1	4	5	4	..	3	1	1	47	35	.573	10
Golden State	1	1	2	1	1	3	1	1	..	1	1	5	2	4	0	2	2	1	2	2	3	2	2	1	1	43	39	.524	14
Portland	1	1	2	0	0	2	2	1	4	1	0	5	0	4	0	2	0	1	3	..	3	4	2	1	0	39	43	.476	18
Sacramento	0	0	1	0	0	2	1	0	3	2	1	3	1	3	0	1	1	0	1	3	..	2	1	1	0	27	55	.329	30
L.A. Clippers	0	0	0	1	1	1	2	0	1	2	1	..	1	1	0	1	0	0	1	2	3	1	1	0	0	21	61	.256	36

HOME-ROAD RECORDS OF ALL TEAMS

	Home	Road	Total		Home	Road	Total
Atlanta	33- 8	19- 22	52- 30	Miami	12- 29	3- 38	15- 67
Boston	32- 9	10- 31	42- 40	Milwaukee	31- 10	18- 23	49- 33
Charlotte	12- 29	8- 33	20- 62	New Jersey	17- 24	9- 32	26- 56
Chicago	30- 11	17- 24	47- 35	New York	35- 6	17- 24	52- 30
Cleveland	37- 4	20- 21	57- 25	Philadelphia	30- 11	16- 25	46- 36
Dallas	24- 17	14- 27	38- 44	Phoenix	35- 6	20- 21	55- 27
Denver	35- 6	9- 32	44- 38	Portland	28- 13	11- 30	39- 43
Detroit	37- 4	26- 15	63- 19	Sacramento	21- 20	6- 35	27- 55
Golden State	29- 12	14- 27	43- 39	San Antonio	18- 23	3- 38	21- 61
Houston	31- 10	14- 27	45- 37	Seattle	31- 10	16- 25	47- 35
Indiana	20- 21	8- 33	28- 54	Utah	34- 7	17- 24	51- 31
L.A. Clippers	17- 24	4- 37	21- 61	Washington	30- 11	10- 31	40- 42
L.A. Lakers	35- 6	22- 19	57- 25	Totals	694-331	331-694	1025-1025

OFFENSIVE TEAM STATISTICS

		FIELD GOALS			FREE THROWS			REBOUNDS			MISCELLANEOUS				Turn	Blk.	SCORING	
Team	G.	Att.	Made	Pct.	Att.	Made	Pct.	Off.	Def.	Tot.	Ast.	PF	Disq.	Stl.	Over	Sh.	Pts.	Avg.
Phoenix	82	7545	3754	.498	2594	2051	.791	1095	2619	3714	2280	1933	13	693	1279	416	9727	118.6
Denver	82	8140	3813	.468	2314	1821	.787	1206	2513	3719	2282	2088	26	811	1225	436	9675	118.0
New York	82	7611	3701	.486	2366	1779	.752	1322	2265	3587	2083	2053	16	900	1572	446	9567	116.7
Golden State	82	7977	3730	.468	2384	1904	.799	1323	2561	3884	2009	1946	21	831	1488	643	9558	116.6
L.A. Lakers	82	7143	3584	.502	2508	2011	.802	1094	2612	3706	2282	1672	2	724	1344	421	9406	114.7
Portland	82	7795	3695	.474	2416	1789	.740	1384	2381	3765	2212	2026	22	828	1435	388	9395	114.6
Seattle	82	7478	3564	.477	2379	1775	.746	1397	2238	3635	2083	2027	12	864	1403	494	9196	112.1
Philadelphia	82	7201	3500	.486	2504	1970	.787	1143	2356	3499	2110	1721	8	689	1214	354	9174	111.9
Atlanta	82	7230	3412	.472	2709	2168	.800	1372	2316	3688	1990	1880	14	817	1310	474	9102	111.0
Boston	82	7143	3520	.493	2349	1840	.783	1179	2442	3621	2189	1876	16	639	1336	418	8958	109.2
Milwaukee	82	7167	3399	.474	2382	1955	.821	1133	2272	3405	2071	1953	16	821	1305	323	8932	108.9
Cleveland	82	6904	3466	.502	2438	1821	.747	1033	2475	3508	2260	1592	5	791	1323	586	8923	108.8
Houston	82	7196	3412	.474	2527	1909	.755	1211	2554	3765	2016	2026	26	789	1569	501	8897	108.5
Washington	82	7591	3519	.464	2318	1789	.772	1254	2354	3608	2048	2054	17	694	1291	325	8879	108.3
Indiana	82	6945	3385	.487	2275	1795	.789	1065	2497	3562	2012	2105	48	563	1547	418	8767	106.9
Detroit	82	6879	3395	.494	2379	1830	.769	1154	2546	3700	2027	1939	15	522	1336	406	8740	106.6
Chicago	82	6968	3448	.495	2106	1656	.786	1018	2453	3471	2213	1855	17	722	1327	376	8726	106.4
L.A. Clippers	82	7428	3526	.475	2220	1606	.723	1156	2384	3540	2208	1937	17	815	1666	530	8712	106.2
San Antonio	82	7409	3469	.468	2367	1651	.698	1295	2181	3476	2037	2153	36	961	1712	423	8652	105.5
Sacramento	82	7351	3362	.457	2104	1620	.770	1141	2454	3595	1970	1877	28	624	1370	409	8651	105.5
Utah	82	6595	3182	.482	2742	2110	.770	1050	2607	3657	2108	1894	13	720	1532	583	8588	104.7
Charlotte	82	7430	3426	.461	2060	1580	.767	1138	2200	3338	2323	2068	20	515	1318	264	8566	104.5
New Jersey	82	7226	3333	.461	2260	1653	.731	1204	2419	3623	1793	1966	12	773	1449	431	8506	103.7
Dallas	82	6917	3244	.469	2263	1785	.789	1048	2397	3445	1867	1739	14	579	1233	476	8484	103.5
Miami	82	7116	3221	.453	2103	1477	.702	1309	2211	3520	1958	2124	38	744	1728	408	8016	97.8

DEFENSIVE TEAM STATISTICS

		FIELD GOALS			FREE THROWS			REBOUNDS			MISCELLANEOUS				Turn	Blk.	SCORING		Pt.
Team	Att.	Made	Pct.	Att.	Made	Pct.	Off.	Def.	Tot.	Ast.	PF	Disq.	Stl.	Over	Sh.	Pts.	Avg.	Dif.	
Utah	7170	3113	.434	2342	1765	.754	1220	2233	3453	1812	2086	26	779	1329	505	8176	99.7	+ 5.0	
Detroit	7022	3140	.447	2325	1826	.785	1131	2188	3319	1855	2088	28	646	1225	341	8264	100.8	+ 5.8	
Cleveland	7346	3385	.461	1748	1358	.777	1214	2283	3497	2043	1970	19	685	1429	363	8300	101.2	+ 7.6	
Dallas	7304	3422	.469	2090	1573	.753	1231	2500	3731	2133	1869	11	660	1175	386	8583	104.7	- 1.2	
Chicago	7098	3361	.474	2190	1693	.773	1078	2300	3378	2099	1781	13	686	1255	348	8608	105.0	+ 1.4	
Milwaukee	6901	3301	.478	2369	1838	.776	1094	2335	3429	2109	1935	14	707	1522	425	8636	105.3	+ 3.6	
Atlanta	7124	3363	.472	2329	1826	.784	1261	2325	3586	2037	2109	23	687	1487	348	8699	106.1	+ 4.9	
L.A. Lakers	7540	3541	.470	2051	1542	.752	1178	2222	3400	2157	1941	24	752	1263	432	8818	107.5	+ 7.2	
Houston	7290	3413	.468	2372	1806	.761	1145	2428	3573	2015	2013	28	800	1455	439	8819	107.5	+ 1.0	
Boston	7183	3475	.484	2294	1780	.776	1048	2222	3270	2124	1950	19	762	1191	387	8863	108.1	+ 1.1	
Miami	6928	3384	.488	2613	2021	.773	1188	2366	3554	2062	1830	15	926	1543	553	8937	109.0	-11.2	
Seattle	7067	3437	.486	2489	1915	.769	1188	2252	3440	1958	1881	15	670	1553	413	8958	109.2	+ 2.9	
New Jersey	7162	3560	.497	2286	1749	.765	1030	2476	3506	2134	1834	14	744	1376	485	9027	110.1	- 6.4	
Philadelphia	7296	3658	.501	2023	1565	.774	1149	2412	3561	2281	1984	26	640	1269	445	9051	110.4	+ 1.5	
Washington	7235	3486	.482	2510	1929	.769	1132	2538	3670	2082	1921	19	655	1381	523	9056	110.4	- 2.1	
Phoenix	7736	3589	.464	2308	1737	.753	1252	2458	3710	2166	2057	16	625	1368	427	9096	110.9	+ 7.7	
Sacramento	7420	3589	.484	2301	1747	.759	1171	2604	3775	2107	1821	22	759	1284	442	9106	111.0	- 5.5	
Indiana	7400	3453	.467	2606	2036	.781	1288	2312	3600	2034	2029	15	836	1206	389	9109	111.1	- 4.2	
San Antonio	7148	3486	.488	2714	2105	.776	1256	2462	3718	2062	1938	21	915	1728	545	9249	112.8	- 7.3	
New York	7358	3636	.494	2390	1834	.767	1213	2326	3539	2292	1898	19	778	1688	433	9258	112.9	+ 3.8	
Charlotte	7113	3555	.500	2629	2040	.776	1191	2621	3812	2061	1791	10	710	1425	441	9265	113.0	- 8.5	
Portland	7322	3572	.488	2504	1933	.772	1151	2391	3542	2073	1960	17	738	1569	358	9275	113.1	+ 1.5	
L.A. Clippers	7738	3747	.484	2400	1834	.764	1342	2550	3892	2384	1882	17	933	1440	551	9525	116.2	- 9.9	
Denver	7484	3701	.495	2683	1977	.737	1136	2864	4000	2136	2001	21	665	1597	485	9536	116.3	+ 1.7	
Golden State	8000	3693	.462	2501	1916	.766	1437	2639	4076	2215	1935	20	861	1554	485	9583	116.9	- 0.3	

Disq.—Individual player disqualified (fouled out of game).

INDIVIDUAL LEADERS

POINTS

Minimum 70 games or 1,400 points

	G.	FG	FT	Pts.	Avg.		G.	FG	FT	Pts.	Avg.
Jordan, Chicago	81	966	674	2633	32.5	Wilkins, Atlanta	80	814	442	2099	26.2
Malone, Utah	80	809	703	2326	29.1	Barkley, Philadelphia	79	700	602	2037	25.8
Ellis, Seattle	82	857	377	2253	27.5	Chambers, Phoenix	81	774	509	2085	25.7
Drexler, Portland	78	829	438	2123	27.2	Olajuwon, Houston	82	790	454	2034	24.8
Mullin, Golden State	82	830	493	2176	26.5	Cummings, Milwaukee	80	730	362	1829	22.9
English, Denver	82	924	325	2175	26.5	Ewing, New York	80	727	361	1815	22.7

POINTS—Continued

	G.	FG	FT	Pts.	Avg.
Tripucka, Charlotte	71	568	440	1606	22.6
McHale, Boston	78	661	436	1758	22.5
Johnson, L.A. Lakers	77	579	513	1730	22.5
Richmond, Golden State	79	649	410	1741	22.0
Malone, Washington	76	677	296	1651	21.7
Person, Indiana	80	711	243	1728	21.6
E. Johnson, Phoenix	70	608	217	1504	21.5
King, Washington	81	654	361	1674	20.7

FIELD GOALS
Minimum 300 FG Made

	FGA	FGM	Pct.
Rodman, Detroit	531	316	.595
Barkley, Philadelphia	1208	700	.579
Parish, Boston	1045	596	.570
Ewing, New York	1282	727	.567
Worthy, L.A. Lakers	1282	702	.548
McHale, Boston	1211	661	.546
Thorpe, Houston	961	521	.542
Benjamin, L.A. Clippers	907	491	.541
Nance, Cleveland	920	496	.539
Stockton, Utah	923	497	.538

FREE THROWS
Minimum 125 Made

	FTA	FTM	Pct.
Johnson, L.A. Lakers	563	513	.911
Sikma, Milwaukee	294	266	.905
Skiles, Indiana	144	130	903
Price, Cleveland	292	263	.901
Mullin, Golden State	553	493	.892
K. Johnson, Phoenix	576	508	.882
Kleine, Sacramento-Boston	152	134	.882
Davis, Denver	199	175	.879
Gminski, Philadelphia	341	297	.871
Malone, Washington	340	296	.871

ASSISTS
Minimum 70 games or 400 assists

	G.	No.	Avg.
Stockton, Utah	82	1118	13.6
Johnson, L.A. Lakers	77	988	12.8
K. Johnson, Phoenix	81	991	12.2
Porter, Portland	81	770	9.5
McMillan, Seattle	75	696	9.3
Floyd, Houston	82	709	8.6
Jackson, New York	72	619	8.6
Price, Cleveland	75	631	8.4
Thomas, Detroit	80	663	8.3
Jordan, Chicago	81	650	8.0

STEALS
Minimum 70 games or 125 steals

	G.	No.	Avg.
Stockton, Utah	82	263	3.21
Robertson, San Antonio	65	197	3.03
Jordan, Chicago	81	234	2.89
Lever, Denver	71	195	2.75
Drexler, Portland	78	213	2.73
Olajuwon, Houston	82	213	2.60
Rivers, Atlanta	76	181	2.38
Harper, Cleveland	82	185	2.26
Garland, Golden State	79	175	2.22
Conner, New Jersey	82	181	2.21

REBOUNDS
Minimum 70 games or 800 rebounds

	G.	Off.	Def.	Tot.	Avg.
Olajuwon, Houston	82	338	767	1105	13.5
Barkley, Philadelphia	79	403	583	986	12.5
Parish, Boston	80	342	654	996	12.5
Malone, Atlanta	81	386	570	956	11.8
Malone, Utah	80	259	594	853	10.7
Oakley, New York	82	343	518	861	10.5
Eaton, Utah	82	227	616	843	10.3
Thorpe, Houston	82	272	515	787	9.6
Laimbeer, Detroit	81	138	638	776	9.6
Cage, Seattle	80	276	489	765	9.6

BLOCKED SHOTS
Minimum 70 games or 100 blocked shots

	G.	No.	Avg.
Bol, Golden State	80	345	4.31
Eaton, Utah	82	315	3.84
Ewing, New York	80	281	3.51
Olajuwon, Houston	82	282	3.44
Nance, Cleveland	73	206	2.82
Benjamin, L.A. Clippers	79	221	2.80
Cooper, Denver	79	211	2.67
West, Phoenix	82	187	2.28
Lister, Seattle	82	180	2.20
Smits, Indiana	82	151	1.84

3-PT. FIELD GOALS
Minimum 25 made

	FGA	FGM	Pct.
Sundvold, Miami	92	48	.522
Ellis, Seattle	339	162	.478
Price, Cleveland	211	93	.441
Hawkins, Philadelphia	166	71	.428
Hodges, Phoenix-Chicago	180	75	.417
E. Johnson, Phoenix	172	71	.413
Berry, Sacramento	160	65	.406
Pressley, Sacramento	295	119	.403
Miller, Indiana	244	98	.402
Scott, L.A. Lakers	193	77	.399

TEAM-BY-TEAM INDIVIDUAL STATISTICS

ATLANTA HAWKS

Player	G.	Min.	FGA	FGM	Pct.	FTA	FTM	Pct.	Off. Reb.	Def. Reb.	Tot. Reb.	Ast.	PF	Disq.	Stl.	Blk. Sh.	Pts.	Avg.	Hi.
Wilkins	80	2997	1756	814	.464	524	442	.844	256	297	553	211	138	0	117	52	2099	26.2	41
Malone	81	2878	1096	538	.491	711	561	.789	386	570	956	112	154	0	79	100	1637	20.2	37
Theus	82	2517	1067	497	.466	335	285	.851	86	156	242	387	236	0	108	16	1296	15.8	32
Rivers	76	2462	816	371	.455	287	247	.861	89	197	286	525	263	6	181	40	1032	13.6	32
Battle	82	1672	628	287	.457	238	194	.815	30	110	140	197	125	0	42	9	779	9.5	21
Levingston	80	2184	568	300	.528	191	133	.696	194	304	498	75	270	4	97	70	734	9.2	23
Carr	78	1488	471	226	.480	152	130	.855	106	168	274	91	221	0	31	62	582	7.5	22
Koncak	74	1531	269	141	.524	114	63	.553	147	306	453	56	238	4	54	98	345	4.7	16
Webb	81	1219	290	133	.459	60	52	.867	21	102	123	284	104	0	70	6	319	3.9	21
Ferrell	41	231	83	35	.422	44	30	.682	19	22	41	10	33	0	7	6	100	2.4	16
Tolbert	50	341	94	40	.426	37	23	.622	31	57	88	16	55	0	13	13	103	2.1	9
Bradley	38	267	86	28	.326	16	8	.500	7	25	32	24	41	0	16	2	72	1.9	8
Mannion (Tot.)	10	32	8	4	.500	0	0	---	0	5	5	2	5	0	3	0	8	0.8	4
Mannion (Atl.)	5	18	6	2	.333	0	0	---	0	2	2	2	2	0	2	0	4	0.8	2

3-Pt. FG: Atlanta 110-397 (.277)—Wilkins 29-105 (.276); Malone 0-12 (.000); Theus 17-58 (.293); Rivers 43-124 (.347); Battle 11-34 (.324); Levingston 1-5 (.200); Carr 0-1 (.000); Koncak 0-3 (.000); Webb 1-22 (.045); Bradley 8-31 (.258); Mannion 0-2 (.000). Opponents 147-511 (.288).

BOSTON CELTICS

Player	G.	Min.	FGA	FGM	Pct.	FTA	FTM	Pct.	Off. Reb.	Def. Reb.	Tot. Reb.	Ast.	PF	Disq.	Stl.	Blk. Sh.	Pts.	Avg.	Hi.
McHale	78	2876	1211	661	.546	533	436	.818	223	414	637	172	223	2	26	97	1758	22.5	36
Bird	6	189	104	49	.471	19	18	.947	1	36	37	29	18	0	6	5	116	19.3	29
Parish	80	2840	1045	596	.570	409	294	.719	342	654	996	175	209	2	79	116	1486	18.6	34

Player	G.	Min.	FGA	FGM	Pct.	FTA	FTM	Pct.	Off. Reb.	Def. Reb.	Tot. Reb.	Ast.	PF	Disq.	Stl.	Blk. Sh.	Pts.	Avg.	Hi.
Lewis	81	2657	1242	604	.486	361	284	.787	116	261	377	218	258	5	124	72	1495	18.5	39
Ainge	45	1349	589	271	.460	128	114	.891	37	117	154	215	108	0	52	1	714	15.9	45
Pinckney (Tot)	80	2012	622	319	.513	350	280	.800	166	283	449	118	202	2	83	66	918	11.5	26
Pinckney (Bos)	29	678	176	95	.540	129	103	.798	60	88	148	44	77	1	29	23	293	10.1	22
Johnson	72	2309	638	277	.434	195	160	.821	31	159	190	472	211	3	94	21	721	10.0	24
Paxson	57	1138	445	202	.454	103	84	.816	18	56	74	107	96	0	38	8	492	8.6	21
Shaw	82	2301	686	297	.433	132	109	.826	119	257	376	472	211	1	78	27	703	8.6	31
Upshaw (Tot)	32	617	212	99	.467	26	18	.692	10	39	49	117	80	1	26	3	219	6.8	13
Upshaw (Bos)	23	473	149	73	.490	20	14	.700	6	30	36	97	62	1	19	3	162	7.0	13
Kleine (Tot)	75	1411	432	175	.405	152	134	.882	124	254	378	67	192	2	33	23	484	6.5	19
Kleine (Bos)	28	498	129	59	.457	64	53	.828	49	88	137	32	66	0	15	5	171	6.1	16
Lohaus	48	738	270	117	.433	46	35	.761	47	95	142	49	101	1	21	26	269	5.6	18
Gamble	44	375	136	75	.551	55	35	.636	11	31	42	34	40	0	14	3	187	4.3	31
Birdsong	13	108	36	18	.500	2	0	.000	4	9	13	9	10	0	3	1	37	2.8	11
Grandison	72	528	142	59	.415	80	59	.738	47	45	92	42	71	0	18	3	177	2.5	15
Acres	62	632	114	55	.482	48	26	.542	59	87	146	19	94	0	19	6	137	2.2	9
Rivas	28	91	31	12	.387	25	16	.640	9	15	24	3	21	0	4	1	40	1.4	8

3-Pt. FG: Boston 78-309 (.252)—McHale 0-4 (.000); Lewis 3-22 (.136); Ainge 58-155 (.374); Johnson 7-50 (.140); Paxson 4-24 (.167); Shaw 0-13 (.000); Upshaw 2-10 (.200); Kleine 0-1 (.000); Lohaus 0-4 (.000); Gamble 2-11 (.182); Birdsong 1-3 (.333); Grandison 0-10 (.000); Acres 1-1 (1.000); Rivas 0-1 (.000). Opponents 133-459 (.290).

CHARLOTTE HORNETS

Player	G.	Min.	FGA	FGM	Pct.	FTA	FTM	Pct.	Off. Reb.	Def. Reb.	Tot. Reb.	Ast.	PF	Disq.	Stl.	Blk. Sh.	Pts.	Avg.	Hi.
Tripucka	71	2302	1215	568	.467	508	440	.866	79	188	267	224	196	0	88	16	1606	22.6	40
Chapman	75	2219	1271	526	.414	195	155	.795	74	113	187	176	167	1	70	25	1267	16.9	37
Reid	82	2152	1214	519	.428	196	152	.776	82	220	302	153	235	2	53	20	1207	14.7	28
Curry	48	813	521	256	.491	46	40	.870	26	78	104	50	68	0	42	4	571	11.9	31
Rambis	75	2233	627	325	.518	248	182	.734	269	434	703	159	208	4	100	57	832	11.1	23
Holton	67	1696	504	215	.427	143	120	.839	30	75	105	424	165	0	66	12	553	8.3	22
Rowsom	34	517	162	80	.494	81	65	.802	56	81	137	24	69	1	10	12	226	6.6	17
Hoppen	77	1419	353	199	.564	139	101	.727	123	261	384	57	239	4	25	21	500	6.5	16
Cureton	82	2047	465	233	.501	123	66	.537	188	300	488	130	230	3	50	61	532	6.5	17
Kempton	79	1341	335	171	.510	207	142	.686	91	213	304	102	215	3	41	14	484	6.1	21
Bogues	79	1755	418	178	.426	88	66	.750	53	112	165	620	141	1	111	7	423	5.4	14
Green	33	370	132	57	.432	14	13	.929	4	19	23	82	16	0	18	0	128	3.9	14
Lewis	42	336	121	58	.479	39	19	.487	35	26	61	15	28	0	11	3	136	3.2	17
Tolbert	14	117	37	17	.459	12	6	.500	7	14	21	7	20	0	2	4	40	2.9	8
Kite (Tot)	70	942	151	65	.430	41	20	.488	81	162	243	36	161	1	27	54	150	2.1	9
Kite (Char)	12	213	30	16	.533	10	6	.600	15	38	53	7	43	1	4	8	38	3.2	6
Lowe	14	250	25	8	.320	11	7	.636	6	28	34	93	28	0	14	0	23	1.6	5

3-Pt. FG: Charlotte 134-430 (.312)—Tripucka 30-84 (.357); Chapman 60-191 (.314); Reid 17-52 (.327); Curry 19-55 (.345); Rambis 0-3 (.000); Holton 3-14 (.214); Rowsom 1-1 (1.000); Hoppen 1-2 (.500); Cureton 0-1 (.000); Kempton 0-1 (.000); Bogues 1-13 (.077); Green 1-5 (.200); Lewis 1-3 (.333); Tolbert 0-3 (.000); Lowe 0-2 (.000). Opponents 115-399 (.288).

CHICAGO BULLS

Player	G.	Min.	FGA	FGM	Pct.	FTA	FTM	Pct.	Off. Reb.	Def. Reb.	Tot. Reb.	Ast.	PF	Disq.	Stl.	Blk. Sh.	Pts.	Avg.	Hi.
Jordan	81	3255	1795	966	.538	793	674	.850	149	503	652	650	247	2	234	65	2633	32.5	53
Pippen	73	2413	867	413	.476	301	201	.668	138	307	445	256	261	8	139	61	1048	14.4	31
Cartwright	78	2333	768	365	.475	308	236	.766	152	369	521	90	234	2	21	41	966	12.4	23
Grant	79	2809	781	405	.519	199	140	.704	240	441	681	168	251	1	86	62	950	12.0	25
Vincent	70	1703	566	274	.484	129	106	.822	34	156	190	335	124	0	53	10	656	9.4	23
Hodges (Tot)	59	1204	430	203	.472	57	48	.842	23	66	89	146	90	0	43	4	529	9.0	23
Hodges (Chi)	49	1112	394	187	.475	53	45	.849	21	63	84	138	82	0	41	4	490	10.0	23
Paxson	78	1738	513	246	.480	36	31	.861	13	81	94	308	162	1	53	6	567	7.3	24
Sellers	80	1732	476	231	.485	101	86	.851	85	142	227	99	176	2	35	69	551	6.9	32
Corzine	81	1483	440	203	.461	96	71	.740	92	223	315	103	134	0	29	45	479	5.9	23
Davis	49	545	190	81	.426	26	19	.731	47	67	114	31	58	1	11	5	185	3.8	15
Perdue	30	190	72	29	.403	14	8	.571	18	27	45	11	38	0	4	6	66	2.2	9
Haley	51	289	78	37	.474	46	36	.783	21	50	71	10	56	0	11	0	110	2.2	12
Pressley (Tot)	13	124	31	9	.290	9	5	.556	3	12	15	26	11	0	4	0	23	1.8	4
Pressley (Chi)	3	17	6	1	.167	0	0	---	0	1	1	4	2	0	0	0	2	0.7	2
Jones	8	65	15	5	.333	2	2	1.000	4	4	8	4	7	0	2	1	12	1.5	8
Nealy	13	94	7	5	.714	2	1	.500	4	19	23	6	23	0	3	1	11	0.8	2
Wood	2	2	0	0	---	0	0	---	0	0	0	0	0	0	0	0	0	0.0	0

3-Pt. FG: Chicago 174-530 (.328)—Jordan 27-98 (.276); Pippen 21-77 (.273); Grant 0-5 (.000); Vincent 2-17 (.118); Hodges 71-168 (.423); Paxson 44-133 (.331); Sellers 3-6 (.500); Corzine 2-8 (.250); Davis 4-15 (.267); Pressley 0-2 (.000); Jones 0-1 (.000). Opponents 193-590 (.327).

CLEVELAND CAVALIERS

Player	G.	Min.	FGA	FGM	Pct.	FTA	FTM	Pct.	Off. Reb.	Def. Reb.	Tot. Reb.	Ast.	PF	Disq.	Stl.	Blk. Sh.	Pts.	Avg.	Hi.
Daugherty	78	2821	1012	544	.538	524	386	.737	167	551	718	285	175	1	63	40	1475	18.9	36
Price	75	2728	1006	529	.526	292	263	.901	48	178	226	631	98	0	115	7	1414	18.9	37
Harper	82	2851	1149	587	.511	430	323	.751	122	287	409	434	224	1	185	74	1526	18.6	32
Nance	73	2526	920	496	.539	334	267	.799	156	425	581	159	186	0	57	206	1259	17.2	33
Williams	82	2125	700	356	.509	314	235	.748	173	304	477	108	188	1	77	134	948	11.6	27
Sanders	82	2102	733	332	.453	135	97	.719	98	209	307	133	230	2	89	32	764	9.3	30
Ehlo	82	1867	524	249	.475	117	71	.607	100	195	295	266	161	0	110	19	608	7.4	25
Valentine	77	1086	319	136	.426	112	91	.813	22	81	103	174	88	0	57	7	366	4.8	15
Keys	42	331	172	74	.430	29	20	.690	23	33	56	19	51	0	12	6	169	4.0	19
Dudley	61	544	168	73	.435	107	39	.364	72	85	157	21	82	0	9	23	185	3.0	14
Hubbard	31	191	63	28	.444	25	17	.680	14	26	40	11	20	0	6	0	73	2.4	9
Rollins	60	583	138	62	.449	19	12	.632	38	101	139	19	89	0	11	38	136	2.3	8

3-Pt. FG: Cleveland 170-474 (.359)—Daugherty 1-3 (.333); Price 93-211 (.441); Harper 29-116 (.250); Nance 0-4 (.000); Williams 1-4 (.250); Sanders 3-10 (.300); Ehlo 39-100 (.390); Valentine 3-14 (.214); Keys 1-10 (.100); Dudley 0-1 (.000); Rollins 0-1 (.000). Opponents 172-508 (.339).

DALLAS MAVERICKS

Player	G.	Min.	FGA	FGM	Pct.	FTA	FTM	Pct.	Off. Reb.	Def. Reb.	Tot. Reb.	Ast.	PF	Disq.	Stl.	Blk. Sh.	Pts.	Avg.	Hi.
Aguirre	44	1529	829	373	.450	244	178	.730	90	145	235	189	128	0	29	29	953	21.7	41
Blackman	78	2946	1249	594	.476	370	316	.854	70	203	273	288	137	0	65	20	1534	19.7	37
Dantley (Tot)	73	2422	954	470	.493	568	460	.810	117	200	317	171	186	1	43	13	1400	19.2	35
Dantley (Dall)	31	1081	459	212	.462	263	204	.776	64	89	153	78	87	0	20	7	628	20.3	34
Harper	81	2968	1127	538	.477	284	229	.806	46	182	228	570	219	3	172	41	1404	17.3	38
Tarpley	19	591	242	131	.541	96	66	.688	77	141	218	17	70	2	28	30	328	17.3	35
Perkins	78	2860	959	445	.464	329	274	.833	235	453	688	127	224	1	76	92	1171	15.0	30
Williams (Tot)	76	2470	739	322	.436	194	133	.686	135	458	593	124	236	5	46	134	777	10.2	25
Williams (Dall)	30	903	197	78	.396	68	43	.632	48	149	197	36	80	2	15	54	199	6.6	15
Schrempf	37	845	263	112	.426	161	127	.789	56	110	166	86	118	3	24	9	353	9.5	24
Donaldson	53	1746	337	193	.573	124	95	.766	158	412	570	38	111	0	24	81	481	9.1	21
Davis	78	1395	379	183	.483	123	99	.805	14	94	108	242	151	0	48	18	497	6.4	17
Tyler	70	1057	360	169	.469	62	47	.758	74	135	209	40	90	0	24	39	386	5.5	20
Wennington	65	1074	275	119	.433	82	61	.744	82	204	286	46	211	3	16	35	300	4.6	21
Jones (Tot)	33	196	79	29	.367	16	14	.875	14	14	28	17	20	0	11	3	76	2.3	8
Jones (Dall)	25	131	64	24	.375	14	12	.857	10	10	20	13	13	0	9	2	64	2.6	8
Wiley	51	408	114	46	.404	16	13	.813	13	34	47	76	61	0	25	6	111	2.2	10
Blab	37	208	52	24	.462	25	20	.800	11	33	44	12	36	0	3	13	68	1.8	10
Alford	9	38	11	3	.273	2	1	.500	0	3	3	9	3	0	1	0	7	0.8	4

3-Pt. FG: Dallas 211-681 (.310)—Aguirre 29-99 (.293); Blackman 30-85 (.353); Dantley 0-1 (.000); Harper 99-278 (.356); Tarpley 0-1 (.000); Perkins 7-38 (.184); Williams 0-2 (.000); Schrempf 2-16 (.125); Davis 32-102 (.314); Tyler 1-9 (.111); Wennington 1-9 (.111); Jones 4-15 (.267); Wiley 6-24 (.250); Alford 0-2 (.000). Opponents 166-515 (.322).

DENVER NUGGETS

Player	G.	Min.	FGA	FGM	Pct.	FTA	FTM	Pct.	Off. Reb.	Def. Reb.	Tot. Reb.	Ast.	PF	Disq.	Stl.	Blk. Sh.	Pts.	Avg.	Hi.
English	82	2990	1881	924	.491	379	325	.858	148	178	326	383	174	0	66	12	2175	26.5	51
Lever	71	2745	1221	558	.457	344	270	.785	187	475	662	559	178	1	195	20	1409	19.8	38
Adams	77	2787	1082	468	.433	393	322	.819	71	212	283	490	149	0	166	11	1424	18.5	35
Davis	81	1857	1076	536	.498	199	175	.879	41	110	151	190	187	1	72	5	1267	15.6	33
Schayes	76	1918	607	317	.522	402	332	.826	142	358	500	105	320	8	42	81	969	12.8	37
Cook (Tot)	66	1143	478	218	.456	78	63	.808	34	73	107	127	121	0	71	10	507	7.7	21
Cook (Den)	30	386	163	71	.436	22	17	.773	13	35	48	43	44	0	28	6	161	5.4	21
Rasmussen	77	1308	577	257	.445	81	69	.852	105	182	287	49	194	2	29	41	583	7.6	24
Greenwood (Tot)	67	1403	395	167	.423	176	132	.750	140	262	402	96	201	5	47	52	466	7.0	23
Greenwood (Den)	29	491	148	62	.419	71	48	.676	48	116	164	41	78	3	17	28	172	5.9	17
Cooper	79	1864	444	220	.495	106	79	.745	212	407	619	78	302	7	36	211	520	6.6	20
Vincent	5	95	38	13	.342	9	5	.556	2	16	18	5	11	0	1	1	32	6.4	12
Hanzlik	41	701	151	66	.437	87	68	.782	18	75	93	86	82	1	25	5	201	4.9	22
Lane	54	550	256	109	.426	112	43	.384	87	113	200	60	105	1	20	4	261	4.8	18
Natt	14	168	50	22	.440	31	22	.710	12	34	46	7	13	0	6	1	66	4.7	12
Turner	78	1746	353	151	.428	56	33	.589	109	178	287	144	209	2	90	8	337	4.3	15
Hughes	26	224	64	28	.438	12	7	.583	6	13	19	35	30	0	17	2	70	2.7	9
Englestad	11	50	29	11	.379	10	6	.600	5	11	16	7	12	0	1	0	28	2.5	8

3-Pt. FG: Denver 228-676 (.337)—English 2-8 (.250); Lever 23-66 (.348); Adams 166-466 (.356); Davis 20-69 (.290); Schayes 3-9 (.333); Cook 2-10 (.200); Cooper 1-4 (.250); Vincent 1-2 (.500); Hanzlik 1-5 (.200); Lane 0-7 (.000); Natt 0-1 (.000); Turner 2-7 (.286); Hughes 7-22 (.318). Opponents 157-446 (.352).

DETROIT PISTONS

Player	G.	Min.	FGA	FGM	Pct.	FTA	FTM	Pct.	Off. Reb.	Def. Reb.	Tot. Reb.	Ast.	PF	Disq.	Stl.	Blk. Sh.	Pts.	Avg.	Hi.
Aguirre (Tot)	80	2597	1270	586	.461	393	288	.733	146	240	386	278	229	2	45	36	1511	18.9	41
Aguirre (Det)	36	1068	441	213	.483	149	110	.738	56	95	151	89	101	2	16	7	558	15.5	31
Dantley	42	1341	495	258	.521	305	256	.839	53	111	164	93	99	1	23	6	772	18.4	35
Thomas	80	2924	1227	569	.464	351	287	.818	49	224	273	663	209	0	133	20	1458	18.2	37
Dumars	69	2408	903	456	.505	306	260	.850	57	115	172	390	103	1	63	5	1186	17.2	42
Johnson	82	2073	996	462	.464	260	193	.734	109	146	255	242	155	0	74	17	1130	13.8	34
Laimbeer	81	2640	900	449	.499	212	178	.840	138	638	776	177	259	2	51	100	1106	13.7	32
Rodman	82	2208	531	316	.595	155	97	.626	327	445	772	99	292	4	55	76	735	9.0	32
Edwards	76	1254	422	211	.500	194	133	.686	68	163	231	49	226	1	11	31	555	7.3	18
Mahorn	72	1795	393	203	.517	155	116	.748	141	355	496	59	206	1	40	66	522	7.3	19
Salley	67	1458	333	166	.498	195	135	.692	134	201	335	75	197	3	40	72	467	7.0	19
Long (Tot)	68	919	359	147	.409	76	70	.921	18	59	77	80	84	1	29	3	372	5.5	25
Long (Det)	24	152	40	19	.475	13	11	.846	2	9	11	15	16	0	0	2	49	2.0	17
Williams	49	358	129	47	.364	47	31	.660	9	18	27	70	44	0	13	3	127	2.6	11
Dawkins	14	48	19	9	.474	18	9	.500	3	4	7	1	13	0	0	1	27	1.9	8
Harris	3	7	4	1	.250	2	2	1.000	0	2	2	0	1	0	1	0	4	1.3	4
Dembo	31	74	42	14	.333	10	8	.800	8	15	23	5	15	0	1	0	36	1.2	8
Mannion	5	14	2	2	1.000	0	0	---	0	3	3	0	3	0	1	0	4	0.8	4
Rowinski	6	8	2	0	.000	4	4	1.000	0	2	2	0	0	0	0	0	4	0.7	4

3-Pt. FG: Detroit 120-400 (.300)—Aguirre 22-75 (.293); Thomas 33-121 (.273); Dumars 14-29 (.483); Johnson 13-44 (.295); Laimbeer 30-86 (.349); Rodman 6-26 (.231); Edwards 0-2 (.000); Mahorn 0-2 (.000); Salley 0-2 (.000); Williams 2-9 (.222); Dembo 0-4 (.000). Opponents 158-554 (.285).

GOLDEN STATE WARRIORS

Player	G.	Min.	FGA	FGM	Pct.	FTA	FTM	Pct.	Off. Reb.	Def. Reb.	Tot. Reb.	Ast.	PF	Disq.	Stl.	Blk. Sh.	Pts.	Avg.	Hi.
Mullin	82	3093	1630	830	.509	553	493	.892	152	331	483	415	178	1	176	39	2176	26.5	47
Richmond	79	2717	1386	649	.468	506	410	.810	158	310	468	334	223	5	82	13	1741	22.0	47
Teagle	66	1569	859	409	.476	225	182	.809	110	153	263	96	173	2	79	17	1002	15.2	36
Garland	79	2661	1074	466	.434	251	203	.809	101	227	328	505	216	2	175	14	1145	14.5	31
Higgins	81	1887	633	301	.476	229	188	.821	111	265	376	160	172	2	39	42	856	10.6	30
O. Smith	80	1597	715	311	.435	218	174	.798	128	202	330	140	165	1	88	40	803	10.0	24
Sampson	61	1086	365	164	.449	95	62	.653	105	202	307	77	170	3	31	65	393	6.4	17
L. Smith	80	1897	397	219	.552	58	18	.310	272	380	652	118	248	2	61	54	456	5.7	18
Alford (Tot)	66	906	324	148	.457	61	50	.820	10	62	72	92	57	0	45	3	366	5.5	17
Alford (GS)	57	868	313	145	.463	59	49	.831	10	59	69	83	54	0	44	3	359	6.3	17

Player	G.	Min.	FGA	FGM	Pct.	FTA	FTM	Pct.	Off. Reb.	Def. Reb.	Tot. Reb.	Ast.	PF	Disq.	Stl.	Blk. Sh.	Pts.	Avg.	Hi.
Starks	36	316	125	51	.408	52	34	.654	15	26	41	27	36	0	23	3	146	4.1	14
Bol	80	1763	344	127	.369	66	40	.606	116	346	462	27	226	2	11	345	314	3.9	13
Jones (Tot)	9	105	30	12	.400	13	8	.615	8	10	18	9	8	0	5	2	32	3.6	7
Jones (GS)	2	13	5	3	.600	0	0	....	2	0	2	2	0	0	3	0	6	3.0	4
Frank	32	245	91	34	.374	51	39	.765	26	35	61	15	59	1	14	6	107	3.3	15
McDonald	11	103	19	13	.684	15	9	.600	4	8	12	5	11	0	4	0	35	3.2	12
Whitehead	5	42	6	3	.500	2	1	.500	0	5	5	2	8	0	1	0	7	1.4	5
Graham	7	22	10	3	.300	4	2	.500	8	3	11	0	6	0	0	0	8	1.1	2
Stroeder (Tot)	5	22	5	2	.400	0	0	....	5	9	14	3	3	0	0	2	4	0.8	4
Stroeder (GS)	4	20	5	2	.400	0	0	....	5	9	14	3	1	0	0	2	4	1.0	4

3-Pt. FG: Golden State 194-629 (.308)—Mullin 23-100 (.230); Richmond 33-90 (.367); Teagle 2-12 (.167); Garland 10-43 (.233); Higgins 66-168 (.393); O. Smith 7-37 (.189); Sampson 3-8 (.375); Alford 20-53 (.377); Starks 10-26 (.385); Bol 20-91 (.220); Frank 0-1 (.000). Opponents 281-821 (.342).

HOUSTON ROCKETS

Player	G.	Min.	FGA	FGM	Pct.	FTA	FTM	Pct.	Off. Reb.	Def. Reb.	Tot. Reb.	Ast.	PF	Disq.	Stl.	Blk. Sh.	Pts.	Avg.	Hi.
Olajuwon	82	3024	1556	790	.508	652	454	.696	338	767	1105	149	329	10	213	282	2034	24.8	43
Thorpe	82	3135	961	521	.542	450	328	.729	272	515	787	202	259	6	82	37	1370	16.7	37
Floyd	82	2788	893	396	.443	309	261	.845	48	258	306	709	196	1	124	11	1162	14.2	37
Woodson	81	2259	936	410	.438	237	195	.823	51	143	194	206	195	1	89	18	1046	12.9	29
B. Johnson	67	1850	515	270	.524	134	101	.754	114	172	286	126	213	4	64	35	642	9.6	24
Chievous	81	1539	634	277	.437	244	191	.783	114	142	256	77	161	1	48	11	750	9.3	27
Berry (Tot)	69	1355	501	254	.507	143	100	.699	86	181	267	77	183	1	29	48	609	8.8	26
Berry (Hou)	40	799	270	146	.541	80	57	.713	54	98	152	57	114	1	19	35	350	8.8	18
Short	65	1157	480	198	.413	89	77	.865	65	114	179	107	116	1	44	13	482	7.4	26
McCormick	81	1257	351	169	.481	129	87	.674	87	174	261	54	193	0	18	24	425	5.2	23
F. Johnson	67	879	246	109	.443	93	75	.806	22	57	79	181	91	0	42	0	294	4.4	17
Leavell	55	627	188	65	.346	60	44	.733	13	40	53	127	61	0	25	5	179	3.3	17
Thompson	23	222	59	20	.339	26	22	.846	9	19	28	13	33	0	13	1	62	2.7	10
Brown	14	91	45	14	.311	8	6	.750	7	8	15	5	14	0	3	0	36	2.6	14
Nevitt	43	228	62	27	.435	16	11	.688	17	47	64	3	51	1	5	29	65	1.5	8

3-Pt. FG: Houston 164-523 (.314)—Olajuwon 0-10 (.000); Thorpe 0-2 (.000); Floyd 109-292 (.373); Woodson 31-89 (.348); B. Johnson 1-9 (.111); Chievous 5-24 (.208); Berry 1-2 (.500); Short 9-33 (.273); McCormick 0-4 (.000); F. Johnson 1-6 (.167); Leavell 5-41 (.122); Thompson 0-2 (.000); Brown 2-9 (.222). Opponents 187-534 (.350).

INDIANA PACERS

Player	G.	Min.	FGA	FGM	Pct.	FTA	FTM	Pct.	Off. Reb.	Def. Reb.	Tot. Reb.	Ast.	PF	Disq.	Stl.	Blk. Sh.	Pts.	Avg.	Hi.
Person	80	3012	1453	711	.489	307	243	.792	144	372	516	289	280	12	83	18	1728	21.6	47
Tisdale	48	1326	564	285	.505	250	198	.792	99	211	310	75	181	5	35	32	768	16.0	39
Miller	74	2536	831	398	.479	340	287	.844	73	219	292	227	170	2	93	29	1181	16.0	36
Fleming	76	2552	814	419	.515	304	243	.799	85	225	310	494	212	4	77	12	1084	14.3	26
Thompson (Tot)	76	2329	850	416	.489	281	227	.808	224	494	718	81	285	12	79	94	1059	13.9	31
Thompson (Ind)	33	1053	314	169	.538	93	75	.806	104	222	326	37	132	6	33	39	413	12.5	24
Williams	46	1567	542	244	.450	126	90	.714	87	309	396	88	156	3	31	80	578	12.6	25
Schrempf (Tot)	69	1850	578	274	.474	350	273	.780	126	269	395	179	220	3	53	19	828	12.0	24
Schrempf (Ind)	32	1005	315	162	.514	189	146	.772	70	159	229	93	102	0	29	10	475	14.8	24
Smits	82	2041	746	386	.517	255	184	.722	185	315	500	70	310	14	37	151	956	11.7	27
Long	44	767	319	128	.401	63	59	.937	16	50	66	65	68	1	29	1	323	7.3	25
Skiles	80	1571	442	198	.448	144	130	.903	21	128	149	390	151	1	64	2	546	6.8	20
Wittman (Tot)	64	1120	286	130	.455	41	28	.683	26	54	80	111	43	0	23	2	291	4.5	17
Wittman (Ind)	33	704	169	80	.473	19	12	.632	20	34	54	79	31	0	13	2	173	5.2	17
Frederick	46	313	125	63	.504	34	24	.706	26	26	52	20	59	0	14	6	152	3.3	19
Morton	2	11	4	3	.750	0	0	....	0	0	0	1	2	0	0	0	6	3.0	6
Gray	72	783	153	72	.471	64	44	.688	84	161	245	29	128	0	11	21	188	2.6	14
Dreiling	53	396	77	43	.558	64	43	.672	39	53	92	18	100	0	5	11	129	2.4	12
Stephens	35	209	72	23	.319	22	17	.773	11	12	23	37	22	0	9	4	65	1.9	8
Toney	2	9	5	1	.200	1	0	.000	1	1	2	0	1	0	0	0	2	1.0	2

3-Pt. FG: Indiana 202-615 (.328)—Person 63-205 (.307); Tisdale 0-4 (.000); Miller 98-244 (.402); Fleming 3-23 (.130); Williams 0-3 (.000); Schrempf 5-19 (.263); Smits 0-1 (.000); Long 8-20 (.400); Skiles 20-75 (.267); Wittman 1-2 (.500); Frederick 2-5 (.400); Gray 0-1 (.000); Stephens 2-10 (.200); Toney 0-3 (.000). Opponents 167-547 (.305).

LOS ANGELES CLIPPERS

Player	G.	Min.	FGA	FGM	Pct.	FTA	FTM	Pct.	Off. Reb.	Def. Reb.	Tot. Reb.	Ast.	PF	Disq.	Stl.	Blk. Sh.	Pts.	Avg.	Hi.
Norman	80	3020	1271	638	.502	270	170	.630	245	422	667	277	223	2	106	66	1450	18.1	38
Manning	26	950	358	177	.494	103	79	.767	70	101	171	81	89	1	44	25	434	16.7	29
Benjamin	79	2585	907	491	.541	426	317	.744	164	532	696	157	221	4	57	221	1299	16.4	34
Smith	71	2161	878	435	.495	393	285	.725	173	292	465	103	273	6	68	89	1155	16.3	33
Dailey	69	1722	964	448	.465	286	217	.759	69	135	204	154	152	0	90	6	1114	16.1	36
Grant	71	1924	830	361	.435	162	119	.735	80	158	238	506	170	1	144	9	846	11.9	31
R. Williams	63	1303	594	260	.438	122	92	.754	70	109	179	103	181	1	81	29	642	10.2	29
Bannister	9	130	36	22	.611	53	30	.566	4	27	33	3	17	0	7	2	74	8.2	21
Nixon	53	1318	370	153	.414	65	48	.738	13	65	78	339	69	0	46	0	362	6.8	18
Garrick	71	1499	359	176	.490	127	102	.803	37	119	156	243	141	1	78	9	454	6.4	17
Wolf	66	1450	402	170	.423	64	44	.688	83	188	271	113	152	1	32	16	386	5.8	17
Whatley	8	90	33	12	.364	11	10	.909	2	14	16	22	15	0	7	1	34	4.3	11
K. Williams (Tot)	50	547	200	81	.405	59	46	.780	28	42	70	53	91	0	30	11	209	4.2	16
K. Williams (LAC)	9	114	32	14	.438	8	6	.750	9	11	20	17	17	0	5	3	34	3.8	9
White (Tot)	38	436	120	62	.517	42	34	.810	34	36	70	17	40	0	10	1	158	4.2	24
White (LAC)	37	434	119	62	.521	42	34	.810	34	36	70	17	39	0	10	1	158	4.3	24
Gondrezick	27	244	95	38	.400	40	26	.650	15	21	36	34	36	0	13	1	105	3.9	17
Popson	10	68	25	11	.440	2	1	.500	5	11	16	6	9	0	1	2	23	2.3	8
Kite	58	729	121	49	.405	31	14	.452	66	124	190	29	118	0	23	46	112	1.9	9
Lock	20	110	32	9	.281	15	12	.800	14	18	32	4	15	0	3	4	30	1.5	6
Rose	2	3	1	0	.000	0	0	....	1	1	2	0	0	0	0	0	0	0.0	0
Sumpter	1	1	1	0	.000	0	0	....	0	0	0	0	0	0	0	0	0	0.0	0

3-Pt. FG: L.A. Clippers 54-234 (.231)—Norman 4-21 (.190); Manning 1-5 (.200); Benjamin 0-2 (.000); Smith 0-3 (.000); Dailey 1-9 (.111); Grant 5-22 (.227); R. Williams 30-104 (.288); Bannister 0-1 (.000); Nixon 8-29 (.276); Garrick 0-13 (.000); Wolf 2-14 (.143); Gondrezick 3-11 (.273). Opponents 197-576 (.342).

LOS ANGELES LAKERS

Player	G.	Min.	FGA	FGM	Pct.	FTA	FTM	Pct.	Off. Reb.	Def. Reb.	Tot. Reb.	Ast.	PF	Disq.	Stl.	Blk. Sh.	Pts.	Avg.	Hi.
Johnson	77	2886	1137	579	.509	563	513	.911	111	496	607	988	172	0	138	22	1730	22.5	40
Worthy	81	2960	1282	702	.548	321	251	.782	169	320	489	288	175	0	108	56	1657	20.5	38
Scott	74	2605	1198	588	.491	226	195	.863	72	230	302	231	181	1	114	27	1448	19.6	35
Green	82	2510	758	401	.529	359	282	.786	258	481	739	103	172	0	94	55	1088	13.3	33
Abdul-Jabbar	74	1695	659	313	.475	165	122	.739	103	231	334	74	196	1	38	85	748	10.1	21
Woolridge	74	1491	494	231	.468	343	253	.738	81	189	270	58	130	0	30	65	715	9.7	29
Thompson	80	1994	521	291	.559	230	156	.678	157	310	467	48	224	0	58	59	738	9.2	27
Cooper	80	1943	494	213	.431	93	81	.871	33	158	191	314	186	0	72	32	587	7.3	18
Campbell	63	787	345	158	.458	83	70	.843	53	77	130	47	108	0	37	6	388	6.2	19
McNamara	39	318	64	32	.500	78	49	.628	38	62	100	10	51	0	4	3	113	2.9	10
Rivers	47	440	122	49	.402	42	35	.833	13	30	43	106	50	0	23	9	134	2.9	10
Lamp	37	176	69	27	.391	5	4	.800	6	28	34	15	27	0	8	2	60	1.6	7

3-Pt. FG: L.A. Lakers 227-667 (.340)—Johnson 59-188 (.314); Worthy 2-23 (.087); Scott 77-193 (.399); Green 4-17 (.235); Abdul-Jabbar 0-3 (.000); Woolridge 0-1 (.000); Thompson 0-1 (.000); Cooper 80-210 (.381); Campbell 2-21 (.095); Rivers 1-6 (.167); Lamp 2-4 (.500). Opponents 194-587 (.330).

MIAMI HEAT

Player	G.	Min.	FGA	FGM	Pct.	FTA	FTM	Pct.	Off. Reb.	Def. Reb.	Tot. Reb.	Ast.	PF	Disq.	Stl.	Blk. Sh.	Pts.	Avg.	Hi.
Edwards	79	2349	1105	470	.425	193	144	.746	85	177	262	349	154	0	139	27	1094	13.8	34
Sparrow	80	2613	982	444	.452	107	94	.879	55	161	216	429	168	0	103	17	1000	12.5	29
Long	82	2435	692	336	.486	406	304	.749	240	306	546	149	337	13	122	48	976	11.9	30
Seikaly	78	1962	744	333	.448	354	181	.511	204	345	549	55	258	8	46	96	848	10.9	30
Thompson	79	2273	716	349	.487	224	156	.696	241	331	572	176	260	8	56	105	854	10.8	30
Sundvold	68	1338	675	307	.455	57	47	.825	18	69	87	137	78	0	27	1	709	10.4	28
Cummings	53	1096	394	197	.500	97	72	.742	84	197	281	47	160	3	29	18	466	8.8	24
Gray	55	1220	398	167	.420	156	105	.673	117	169	286	117	144	1	36	25	440	8.0	25
Washington	54	1065	387	164	.424	104	82	.788	49	74	123	226	101	0	73	4	411	7.6	21
Wheeler	8	143	42	24	.571	10	8	.800	5	7	12	21	9	0	8	0	56	7.0	13
Taylor	21	368	151	60	.397	32	24	.750	11	23	34	43	37	0	22	5	144	6.9	21
Upshaw	9	144	63	26	.413	6	4	.667	4	9	13	20	18	0	7	0	57	6.3	13
Shasky	65	944	248	121	.488	167	115	.689	96	136	232	22	94	0	14	13	357	5.5	19
Mitchell	22	320	88	41	.466	60	36	.600	17	30	47	20	49	0	15	2	118	5.4	15
Hastings	75	1206	328	143	.436	107	91	.850	72	159	231	59	203	5	32	42	386	5.1	17
Neal (Tot)	53	500	123	45	.366	23	14	.609	7	22	29	118	70	0	24	4	114	2.2	9
Neal (Mia)	32	341	88	34	.386	21	13	.619	4	14	18	86	46	0	15	4	89	2.8	9
Popson (Tot)	17	106	40	16	.400	4	2	.500	12	15	27	8	17	0	1	3	34	2.0	8
Popson (Mia)	7	38	15	5	.333	2	1	.500	7	4	11	2	8	0	0	1	11	1.6	4

3-Pt. FG: Miami 97-298 (.326)—Edwards 10-37 (.270); Sparrow 18-74 (.243); Long 0-5 (.000); Seikaly 1-4 (.250); Thompson 0-4 (.000); Sundvold 48-92 (.522); Cummings 0-2 (.000); Gray 1-4 (.250); Washington 1-14 (.071); Taylor 0-2 (.000); Upshaw 1-5 (.200); Shasky 0-2 (.000); Hastings 9-28 (.321); Neal 8-25 (.320). Opponents 148-432 (.343).

MILWAUKEE BUCKS

Player	G.	Min.	FGA	FGM	Pct.	FTA	FTM	Pct.	Off. Reb.	Def. Reb.	Tot. Reb.	Ast.	PF	Disq.	Stl.	Blk. Sh.	Pts.	Avg.	Hi.
Cummings	80	2824	1563	730	.467	460	362	.787	281	369	650	198	265	5	106	72	1829	22.9	40
Pierce	75	2078	1018	527	.518	297	255	.859	82	115	197	156	193	1	77	19	1317	17.6	29
Sikma	80	2587	835	360	.431	294	266	.905	141	482	623	289	300	6	85	61	1068	13.4	30
Krystkowiak	80	2472	766	362	.473	351	289	.823	198	412	610	107	219	0	93	9	1017	12.7	31
Pressey	67	2170	648	307	.474	241	187	.776	73	189	262	439	221	2	119	44	813	12.1	25
Moncrief	62	1594	532	261	.491	237	205	.865	46	126	172	188	114	1	65	13	752	12.1	25
Humphries	73	2220	714	345	.483	158	129	.816	70	119	189	405	187	1	142	5	844	11.6	24
Grayer	11	200	73	32	.438	20	17	.850	14	21	35	22	15	0	10	1	81	7.4	18
Roberts	71	1251	319	155	.486	129	104	.806	68	141	209	66	126	0	36	23	417	5.9	19
Green (Tot)	63	871	264	129	.489	33	30	.909	11	58	69	187	35	0	40	2	291	4.6	14
Green (Mil)	30	501	132	72	.545	19	17	.895	7	39	46	105	19	0	22	2	163	5.4	14
Breuer	48	513	179	86	.480	51	28	.549	51	84	135	22	59	0	9	37	200	4.2	20
Davis (Tot)	33	258	102	49	.480	34	28	.824	16	21	37	14	39	0	13	5	127	3.8	17
Davis (Mil)	31	251	97	48	.495	32	26	.813	15	21	36	14	38	0	13	5	123	4.0	17
Brown (Tot)	43	365	118	50	.424	31	24	.774	22	22	44	26	42	0	15	4	128	3.0	15
Brown (Mil)	29	274	73	36	.493	23	18	.783	15	14	29	21	28	0	12	4	92	3.2	15
Mokeski	74	690	164	59	.360	51	40	.784	63	124	187	36	153	0	29	21	165	2.2	8
Horford	25	112	46	15	.326	19	12	.632	9	13	22	3	14	0	1	7	42	1.7	10
Dunleavy	2	5	2	1	.500	0	0	....	0	0	0	0	0	0	0	0	3	1.5	3
Turner	4	13	6	3	.500	0	0	....	3	3	3	0	2	0	2	0	6	1.5	4

3-Pt. FG: Milwaukee 179-567 (.316)—Cummings 7-15 (.467); Pierce 8-36 (.222); Sikma 82-216 (.380); Krystkowiak 4-12 (.333); Pressey 12-55 (.218); Moncrief 25-73 (.342); Humphries 25-94 (.266); Grayer 0-2 (.000); Roberts 3-14 (.214); Green 2-6 (.333); Davis 1-9 (.111); Brown 2-7 (.286); Mokeski 7-26 (.269); Dunleavy 1-2 (.500). Opponents 196-533 (.368).

NEW JERSEY NETS

Player	G.	Min.	FGA	FGM	Pct.	FTA	FTM	Pct.	Off. Reb.	Def. Reb.	Tot. Reb.	Ast.	PF	Disq.	Stl.	Blk. Sh.	Pts.	Avg.	Hi.
Hinson	82	2542	1027	495	.482	420	318	.757	152	370	522	71	298	3	34	121	1308	16.0	35
Morris	76	2096	905	414	.457	254	182	.717	188	209	397	119	250	4	102	60	1074	14.1	31
Carroll	64	1996	810	363	.448	220	176	.800	118	355	473	105	193	2	71	81	902	14.1	26
McGee	80	2027	917	434	.473	144	77	.535	73	116	189	116	184	1	80	12	1038	13.0	33
B. Williams	74	2446	702	373	.531	320	213	.666	249	447	696	78	223	0	61	36	959	13.0	27
Hopson	62	1551	714	299	.419	219	186	.849	91	111	202	103	150	0	70	30	788	12.7	32
Conner	82	2532	676	309	.457	269	212	.788	100	255	355	604	132	1	181	5	843	10.3	20
Berry	29	556	231	108	.468	63	43	.683	32	83	115	20	69	0	10	13	259	8.9	26
Bagley	68	1642	481	200	.416	123	89	.724	36	108	144	391	117	0	72	5	500	7.4	17
Lee	57	840	258	109	.422	71	53	.746	73	186	259	42	138	1	20	33	271	4.8	16
K. Williams	41	433	168	67	.399	51	40	.784	19	31	50	36	74	0	25	8	175	4.3	16

Player	G.	Min.	FGA	FGM	Pct.	FTA	FTM	Pct.	Off. Reb.	Def. Reb.	Tot. Reb.	Ast.	PF	Disq.	Stl.	Blk. Sh.	Pts.	Avg.	Hi.
Jones	37	307	102	50	.490	43	29	.674	20	27	47	20	38	0	17	6	129	3.5	14
Shackleford	60	484	168	83	.494	42	21	.500	50	103	153	21	71	0	15	18	187	3.1	13
Gaines	32	337	64	27	.422	16	12	.750	3	16	19	67	27	0	15	1	67	2.1	18
Cavenall	5	16	3	2	.667	5	2	.400	0	2	2	0	2	0	0	2	6	1.2	6

3-Pt. FG: New Jersey 187-568 (.329)—Hinson 0-2 (.000); Morris 64-175 (.366); McGee 93-255 (.365); B. Williams 0-3 (.000); Hopson 4-27 (.148); Conner 13-37 (.351); Bagley 11-54 (.204); Lee 0-2 (.000); K. Williams 1-6 (.167); Jones 0-1 (.000); Shackleford 0-1 (.000); Gaines 1-5 (.200). Opponents 158-512 (.309).

NEW YORK KNICKERBOCKERS

Player	G.	Min.	FGA	FGM	Pct.	FTA	FTM	Pct.	Off. Reb.	Def. Reb.	Tot. Reb.	Ast.	PF	Disq.	Stl.	Blk. Sh.	Pts.	Avg.	Hi.
Ewing	80	2896	1282	727	.567	484	361	.746	213	527	740	188	311	5	117	281	1815	22.7	45
Jackson	72	2477	1025	479	.467	258	180	.698	106	235	341	619	163	1	139	7	1219	16.9	34
Newman	81	2336	957	455	.475	351	286	.815	93	113	206	162	259	4	111	23	1293	16.0	35
G. Wilkins	81	2414	1025	462	.451	246	186	.756	95	149	244	274	166	1	115	22	1161	14.3	30
Oakley	82	2604	835	426	.510	255	197	.773	343	518	861	187	270	1	104	14	1061	12.9	27
Vandeweghe (Tot).	45	934	426	200	.469	89	80	.899	26	45	71	69	78	0	19	11	499	11.1	28
Vandeweghe (NY).	27	502	209	97	.464	56	51	.911	15	21	36	35	38	0	12	7	248	9.2	24
Strickland	81	1358	567	265	.467	231	172	.745	51	109	160	319	142	2	98	3	721	8.9	22
Tucker	81	1824	579	263	.454	55	43	.782	55	121	176	132	163	0	88	6	687	8.5	25
Green	82	1277	422	194	.460	170	129	.759	157	237	394	76	172	0	47	18	517	6.3	15
Walker	79	1163	356	174	.489	85	66	.776	101	129	230	36	190	1	41	45	419	5.3	19
E. Wilkins	71	584	245	114	.465	111	61	.550	72	76	148	7	110	1	10	16	289	4.1	12
Myers (Tot).	33	270	73	31	.425	48	33	.688	15	18	33	48	44	0	20	2	95	2.9	10
Myers (NY)	29	230	61	25	.410	44	31	.705	12	11	23	46	41	0	17	2	81	2.8	8
Butler	33	140	48	20	.417	20	16	.800	9	19	28	2	28	0	1	2	56	1.7	7

3-Pt. FG: New York 386-1147 (.337)—Ewing 0-6 (.000); Jackson 81-240 (.338); Newman 97-287 (.338); G. Wilkins 51-172 (.297); Oakley 12-48 (.250); Vandeweghe 3-10 (.300); Strickland 19-59 (.322); Tucker 118-296 (.399); Green 0-3 (.000); Walker 5-20 (.250); E. Wilkins 0-1 (.000); Myers 0-2 (.000); Butler 0-3 (.000). Opponents 152-534 (.285).

PHILADELPHIA 76ers

Player	G.	Min.	FGA	FGM	Pct.	FTA	FTM	Pct.	Off. Reb.	Def. Reb.	Tot. Reb.	Ast.	PF	Disq.	Stl.	Blk. Sh.	Pts.	Avg.	Hi.
Barkley	79	3088	1208	700	.579	799	602	.753	403	583	986	325	262	3	126	67	2037	25.8	43
Gminski	82	2739	1166	556	.477	341	297	.871	213	556	769	138	142	0	46	106	1409	17.2	29
Anderson	82	2618	1152	566	.491	229	196	.856	167	239	406	139	166	1	71	23	1330	16.2	36
Robinson	14	416	187	90	.481	44	32	.727	19	56	75	32	37	0	17	2	212	15.1	26
Hawkins	79	2577	971	442	.455	290	241	.831	51	174	225	239	184	0	120	37	1196	15.1	32
Cheeks	71	2298	696	336	.483	195	151	.774	39	144	183	554	114	0	105	17	824	11.6	24
Smith (Tot)	65	1295	496	216	.435	188	129	.686	61	106	167	128	164	4	43	23	568	8.7	27
Smith (Phil)	36	695	220	105	.477	93	65	.699	31	55	86	68	100	3	24	15	279	7.8	18
Henderson	65	986	348	144	.414	127	104	.819	17	51	68	140	121	1	42	3	425	6.5	20
Brooks	82	1372	371	156	.420	69	61	.884	19	75	94	306	116	0	69	3	428	5.2	18
Coleman	58	703	241	117	.485	77	61	.792	49	128	177	17	120	0	10	18	295	5.1	15
Jones (Tot)	49	669	204	90	.441	80	58	.725	30	81	111	40	58	0	18	15	238	4.9	20
Jones (Phil)	42	577	179	81	.453	67	50	.746	24	71	95	33	50	0	16	13	212	5.0	20
Wingate	33	372	115	54	.470	34	27	.794	12	25	37	73	43	0	9	2	137	4.2	19
Myers	4	40	12	6	.500	4	2	.500	3	7	10	2	3	0	3	0	14	3.5	10
Welp	72	843	222	99	.446	73	48	.658	59	134	193	29	176	0	23	41	246	3.4	12
Thornton	54	449	111	47	.423	60	32	.533	36	56	92	15	87	0	8	7	127	2.4	16
Rowinski (Tot)	9	15	4	1	.250	6	5	.833	1	4	5	0	0	0	0	0	7	0.8	4
Rowinski (Phil)	7	7	2	1	.500	2	1	.500	1	2	3	0	0	0	0	0	3	1.0	2

3-Pt. FG: Philadelphia 204-646 (.316)—Barkley 35-162 (.216); Gminski 0-6 (.000); Anderson 2-11 (.182); Robinson 0-1 (.000); Hawkins 71-166 (.428); Cheeks 1-13 (.077); Smith 4-16 (.250); Henderson 33-107 (.308); Brooks 55-153 (.359); Jones 0-1 (.000); Wingate 2-6 (.333); Welp 0-1 (.000); Thornton 1-3 (.333). Opponents 170-495 (.343).

PHOENIX SUNS

Player	G.	Min.	FGA	FGM	Pct.	FTA	FTM	Pct.	Off. Reb.	Def. Reb.	Tot. Reb.	Ast.	PF	Disq.	Stl.	Blk. Sh.	Pts.	Avg.	Hi.
Chambers	81	3002	1643	774	.471	598	509	.851	143	541	684	231	271	2	87	55	2085	25.7	42
E. Johnson	70	2043	1224	608	.497	250	217	.868	91	215	306	162	198	0	47	7	1504	21.5	45
K. Johnson	81	3179	1128	570	.505	576	508	.882	46	294	340	991	226	1	135	24	1620	20.4	41
Gilliam	74	2120	930	468	.503	323	240	.743	165	376	541	52	176	2	54	27	1176	15.9	41
Hornacek	78	2487	889	440	.495	178	147	.826	75	191	266	465	188	0	129	8	1054	13.5	32
Majerle	54	1354	432	181	.419	127	78	.614	62	147	209	130	139	1	63	14	467	8.6	25
Corbin	77	1655	454	245	.540	179	141	.788	176	222	398	118	222	2	82	13	631	8.2	30
West	82	2019	372	243	.653	202	108	.535	167	384	551	39	273	4	35	187	594	7.2	24
Perry	62	614	201	108	.537	65	40	.615	61	71	132	18	47	0	19	32	257	4.1	19
Hodges	10	92	36	16	.444	4	3	.750	2	3	5	8	8	0	2	0	39	3.9	9
Lang	62	526	117	60	.513	60	39	.650	54	93	147	9	112	1	17	48	159	2.6	21
Kerr	26	157	46	20	.435	9	6	.667	3	14	17	24	12	0	7	0	54	2.1	7
Davis	2	7	5	1	.200	2	2	1.000	1	0	1	0	1	0	0	0	4	2.0	2
Dunn	34	321	35	12	.343	12	9	.750	30	30	60	25	35	0	12	1	33	1.0	4
Nealy (Tot)	43	258	36	13	.361	9	4	.444	22	56	78	14	45	0	7	1	30	0.7	4
Nealy (Phoe)	30	164	29	8	.276	7	3	.429	18	37	55	8	22	0	4	0	19	0.6	4
Gattison	2	9	1	0	.000	2	1	.500	0	1	1	0	2	0	0	1	1	0.5	1
Crite	2	6	3	0	.000	0	0	---	1	0	1	0	1	0	0	0	0	0.0	0

3-Pt. FG: Phoenix 168-481 (.349)—Chambers 28-86 (.326); E. Johnson 71-172 (.413); K. Johnson 2-22 (.091); Hornacek 27-81 (.333); Majerle 27-82 (.329); Corbin 0-2 (.000); Perry 1-4 (.250); Hodges 4-12 (.333); Kerr 8-17 (.471); Davis 0-1 (.000); Nealy 0-2 (.000). Opponents 181-568 (.319).

PORTLAND TRAIL BLAZERS

Player	G.	Min.	FGA	FGM	Pct.	FTA	FTM	Pct.	Off. Reb.	Def. Reb.	Tot. Reb.	Ast.	PF	Disq.	Stl.	Blk. Sh.	Pts.	Avg.	Hi.
Drexler	78	3064	1672	829	.496	548	438	.799	289	326	615	450	269	2	213	54	2123	27.2	50
Duckworth	79	2662	1161	554	.477	428	324	.757	246	389	635	60	300	6	56	49	1432	18.1	32
Porter	81	3102	1146	540	.471	324	272	.840	85	282	367	770	187	1	146	8	1431	17.7	34

Player	G.	Min.	FGA	FGM	Pct.	FTA	FTM	Pct.	Off. Reb.	Def. Reb.	Tot. Reb.	Ast.	PF	Disq.	Stl.	Blk. Sh.	Pts.	Avg.	Hi.
Kersey	76	2716	1137	533	.469	372	258	.694	246	383	629	202	277	6	137	84	1330	17.5	33
Vandeweghe	18	432	217	103	.475	33	29	.879	11	24	35	34	40	0	7	4	251	13.9	28
Johnson	72	1477	565	296	.524	245	129	.527	135	223	358	105	254	3	20	44	721	10.0	27
Bowie	20	412	153	69	.451	49	28	.571	36	70	106	36	43	0	7	33	171	8.6	19
Branch	67	811	436	202	.463	120	87	.725	63	69	132	60	99	0	45	3	498	7.4	28
Young	48	952	250	115	.460	64	50	.781	17	57	74	123	50	0	55	3	297	6.2	19
Anderson	72	1082	348	145	.417	38	32	.842	62	169	231	98	100	1	44	12	371	5.2	20
Bryant	56	803	247	120	.486	69	40	.580	65	114	179	33	144	3	20	7	280	5.0	17
Sichting	25	390	104	46	.442	8	7	.875	9	20	29	59	17	0	15	0	102	4.1	11
Steppe	27	244	78	33	.423	37	32	.865	13	19	32	16	32	0	11	1	103	3.8	13
Wheeler (Tot)	28	354	87	45	.517	20	15	.750	17	14	31	54	26	0	27	0	105	3.8	13
Wheeler (Port)	20	211	45	21	.467	10	7	.700	12	7	19	33	17	0	19	0	49	2.5	8
Jones	72	1279	183	77	.421	61	48	.787	88	212	300	59	166	0	24	85	202	2.8	11
Neal	21	159	35	11	.314	2	1	.500	3	8	11	32	24	0	9	0	25	1.2	4
Ferreira	12	34	18	1	.056	8	7	.875	4	9	13	1	7	0	0	1	9	0.8	2

3-Pt. FG: Portland 216-645 (.335)—Drexler 27-104 (.260); Duckworth 0-2 (.000); Porter 79-219 (.361); Kersey 6-21 (.286); Vandeweghe 16-38 (.421); Bowie 5-7 (.714); Branch 7-31 (.226); Young 17-50 (.340); Anderson 49-141 (.348); Sichting 3-12 (.250); Steppe 5-9 (.556); Wheeler 0-1 (.000); Jones 0-1 (.000); Neal 2-9 (.222). Opponents 198-546 (.363).

SACRAMENTO KINGS

Player	G.	Min.	FGA	FGM	Pct.	FTA	FTM	Pct.	Off. Reb.	Def. Reb.	Tot. Reb.	Ast.	PF	Disq.	Stl.	Blk. Sh.	Pts.	Avg.	Hi.
Ainge (Tot)	73	2377	1051	480	.457	240	205	.854	71	184	255	402	186	1	93	8	1281	17.5	45
Ainge (Sac)	28	1028	462	209	.452	112	91	.813	34	67	101	187	78	1	41	7	567	20.3	45
Tisdale (Tot)	79	2434	1036	532	.514	410	317	.773	187	422	609	128	290	7	55	52	1381	17.5	39
Tisdale (Sac)	31	1108	472	247	.523	160	119	.744	88	211	299	53	109	2	20	20	613	19.8	34
K. Smith	81	3145	1183	547	.462	357	263	.737	49	177	226	621	173	0	102	7	1403	17.3	33
Thompson	43	1276	536	247	.461	188	152	.809	120	272	392	44	153	6	46	55	646	15.0	31
McCray	68	2435	729	340	.466	234	169	.722	143	371	514	293	121	0	57	36	854	12.6	29
Pressley	80	2257	873	383	.439	123	96	.780	216	269	485	174	215	1	93	76	981	12.3	26
Pinckney	51	1334	446	224	.502	221	177	.801	106	195	301	74	125	1	54	43	625	12.3	26
Berry	64	1406	567	255	.450	166	131	.789	57	140	197	80	197	4	37	22	706	11.0	34
Petersen	66	1633	606	278	.459	154	115	.747	121	292	413	81	236	8	47	68	671	10.2	25
D. Smith	29	600	276	111	.402	95	64	.674	30	51	81	60	64	1	19	8	289	10.0	27
Del Negro	80	1556	503	239	.475	100	85	.850	48	123	171	206	160	2	65	14	569	7.1	28
Kleine	47	913	303	116	.383	88	81	.920	75	166	241	35	126	2	18	18	313	6.7	19
Lohaus (Tot)	77	1214	486	210	.432	103	81	.786	84	172	256	66	161	3	30	56	502	6.5	29
Lohaus (Sac)	29	476	216	93	.431	57	46	.807	37	77	114	17	60	0	9	30	233	8.0	29
Wittman	31	416	117	50	.427	22	16	.727	6	20	26	32	12	0	10	0	118	3.8	15
Allen	7	43	19	8	.421	2	1	.500	3	4	7	0	7	0	1	1	17	2.4	6
Jackson	14	70	24	9	.375	2	1	.500	1	3	4	11	12	0	3	0	21	1.5	4
Gillery	24	84	19	6	.316	23	13	.565	7	16	23	2	29	0	2	4	25	1.0	5

3-Pt. FG: Sacramento 307-824 (.373)—Ainge 58-150 (.387); K. Smith 46-128 (.359); Thompson 0-1 (.000); McCray 5-22 (.227); Pressley 119-295 (.403); Pinckney 0-6 (.000); Berry 65-160 (.406); Petersen 0-8 (.000); D. Smith 3-15 (.200); Del Negro 6-20 (.300); Kleine 0-1 (.000); Lohaus 1-7 (.143); Wittman 2-4 (.500); Allen 0-1 (.333); Jackson 0-2 (.000). Opponents 181-573 (.316).

SAN ANTONIO SPURS

Player	G.	Min.	FGA	FGM	Pct.	FTA	FTM	Pct.	Off. Reb.	Def. Reb.	Tot. Reb.	Ast.	PF	Disq.	Stl.	Blk. Sh.	Pts.	Avg.	Hi.
W. Anderson	81	2738	1285	640	.498	289	224	.775	152	265	417	372	295	6	150	62	1508	18.6	36
Robertson	65	2287	962	465	.483	253	183	.723	157	227	384	393	259	6	197	36	1122	17.3	34
Dawkins	32	1083	400	177	.443	112	100	.893	32	69	101	224	64	0	55	0	454	14.2	30
G. Anderson	82	2401	914	460	.503	403	207	.514	255	421	676	61	221	2	102	103	1127	13.7	29
Brickowski	64	1822	654	337	.515	281	201	.715	148	258	406	131	252	10	102	35	875	13.7	27
Maxwell	79	2065	827	357	.432	243	181	.745	49	153	202	301	136	0	86	4	927	11.7	29
Cook	36	757	315	147	.467	56	46	.821	21	38	59	84	77	0	43	4	346	9.6	19
Bowie	18	438	144	72	.500	15	10	.667	25	31	56	29	43	1	18	4	155	8.6	24
Vincent (Tot)	29	646	257	104	.405	60	40	.667	38	72	110	27	63	0	6	4	249	8.6	21
Vincent (SA)	24	551	219	91	.416	51	35	.686	36	56	92	22	52	0	5	3	217	9.0	21
Greenwood	38	912	247	105	.425	105	84	.800	92	146	238	55	123	2	30	24	294	7.7	23
King	46	791	327	141	.431	48	37	.771	33	107	140	79	97	2	27	7	327	7.1	20
Comegys	67	1119	341	166	.487	161	106	.658	112	122	234	30	160	2	42	63	438	6.5	21
Natt (Tot)	24	353	116	47	.405	79	57	.722	28	50	78	18	32	0	8	3	151	6.3	16
Natt (SA)	10	185	66	25	.379	48	35	.729	16	16	32	11	19	0	2	2	85	8.5	16
M. Anderson	36	730	175	73	.417	82	57	.695	44	45	89	153	64	0	44	3	204	5.7	21
Mitchell (Tot)	24	353	97	43	.443	64	37	.578	18	32	50	21	51	0	16	2	123	5.1	15
Mitchell (SA)	2	33	9	2	.222	4	1	.250	1	2	3	1	2	0	1	0	5	2.5	3
Smrek	43	623	153	72	.471	76	49	.645	42	87	129	12	102	2	13	58	193	4.5	15
Gudmundsson	5	70	25	9	.360	4	3	.750	5	11	16	5	15	0	1	1	21	4.2	8
Jones	7	92	25	9	.360	13	8	.615	6	10	16	7	8	0	2	2	26	3.7	7
Whitehead (Tot)	57	622	182	72	.396	47	31	.660	49	85	134	19	115	1	23	4	175	3.1	12
Whitehead (SA)	52	580	176	69	.392	45	30	.667	49	80	129	17	107	1	21	4	158	3.2	12
Roth (Tot)	63	536	167	59	.353	87	60	.690	20	44	64	55	69	0	24	5	181	2.9	14
Roth (SA)	47	464	143	52	.364	76	52	.684	20	36	56	48	55	0	19	4	158	3.4	14
Smart	2	12	2	0	.000	2	2	1.000	0	1	1	2	0	0	0	0	2	1.0	2
Stroeder	1	2	2	0	---	0	0	---	0	0	0	2	0	0	0	0	0	0.0	0

3-Pt. FG: San Antonio 63-293 (.215)—W. Anderson 4-21 (.190); Robertson 9-45 (.200); Dawkins 0-4 (.000); G. Anderson 0-3 (.000); Brickowski 0-2 (.000); Maxwell 32-129 (.248); Cook 6-31 (.194); Bowie 1-5 (.200); Vincent 0-1 (.000); King 8-32 (.250); Comegys 0-2 (.000); M. Anderson 1-7 (.143); Roth 2-10 (.200); Smart 0-1 (.000). Opponents 172-532 (.323).

SEATTLE SUPERSONICS

Player	G.	Min.	FGA	FGM	Pct.	FTA	FTM	Pct.	Off. Reb.	Def. Reb.	Tot. Reb.	Ast.	PF	Disq.	Stl.	Blk. Sh.	Pts.	Avg.	Hi.
Ellis	82	3190	1710	857	.501	462	377	.816	156	186	342	164	197	0	108	22	2253	27.5	49
McDaniel	82	2385	1385	677	.489	426	312	.732	177	256	433	134	231	0	84	40	1677	20.5	39
McKey	82	2804	970	487	.502	375	301	.803	167	297	464	219	264	4	105	70	1305	15.9	34
Cage	80	2536	630	314	.498	265	197	.743	276	489	765	126	184	1	92	52	825	10.3	24
Threatt	63	1220	476	235	.494	77	63	.818	31	86	117	238	155	0	83	4	544	8.6	21
Lister	82	1806	543	271	.499	178	115	.646	207	338	545	54	310	3	28	180	657	8.0	20
Reynolds	56	737	357	149	.417	167	127	.760	49	51	100	62	58	0	53	26	428	7.6	25

Player	G.	Min.	FGA	FGM	Pct.	FTA	FTM	Pct.	Off. Reb.	Def. Reb.	Tot. Reb.	Ast.	PF	Disq.	Stl.	Blk. Sh.	Pts.	Avg.	Hi.
McMillan	75	2341	485	199	.410	189	119	.630	143	245	388	696	236	3	156	42	532	7.1	16
Schoene	69	774	349	135	.387	57	46	.807	58	107	165	36	136	1	37	24	358	5.2	20
Lucas	74	842	299	119	.398	77	54	.701	22	57	79	260	53	0	60	1	310	4.2	25
Ballard	2	15	8	1	.125	4	4	1.000	2	5	7	0	3	0	0	0	6	3.0	4
Polynice	80	835	180	91	.506	86	51	.593	98	108	206	21	164	0	37	30	233	2.9	12
Johnson	43	291	83	29	.349	16	9	.563	11	13	24	73	34	0	21	3	68	1.6	10
Champion	2	4	3	0	.000	0	0	---	0	0	0	0	2	0	0	0	0	0.0	0

3-Pt. FG: Seattle 293-774 (.379)—Ellis 162-339 (.478); McDaniel 11-36 (.306); McKey 30-89 (.337); Cage 0-4 (.000); Threatt 11-30 (.367); Reynolds 3-15 (.200); McMillan 15-70 (.214); Schoene 42-110 (.382); Lucas 18-68 (.265); Ballard 0-1 (.000); Polynice 0-2 (.000); Johnson 1-9 (.111); Champion 0-1 (.000). Opponents 169-543 (.311).

UTAH JAZZ

Player	G.	Min.	FGA	FGM	Pct.	FTA	FTM	Pct.	Off. Reb.	Def. Reb.	Tot. Reb.	Ast.	PF	Disq.	Stl.	Blk. Sh.	Pts.	Avg.	Hi.
Malone	80	3126	1559	809	.519	918	703	.766	259	594	853	219	286	3	144	70	2326	29.1	44
Bailey	82	2777	1272	615	.483	440	363	.825	115	332	447	138	185	0	48	91	1595	19.5	33
Stockton	82	3171	923	497	.538	452	390	.863	83	165	248	1118	241	3	263	14	1400	17.1	30
Griffith	82	2382	1045	466	.446	182	142	.780	77	253	330	130	175	0	86	22	1135	13.8	40
Hansen	46	964	300	140	.467	75	42	.560	29	99	128	50	105	0	37	6	341	7.4	20
Eaton	82	2914	407	188	.462	200	132	.660	227	616	843	83	290	6	40	315	508	6.2	15
Brown	66	1051	248	104	.419	130	92	.708	92	166	258	41	133	0	25	17	300	4.5	16
Leckner	75	779	220	120	.545	113	79	.699	48	151	199	16	174	1	8	22	319	4.3	21
Farmer	37	412	142	57	.401	41	29	.707	22	33	55	28	41	0	9	0	152	4.1	13
Ortiz	51	327	125	55	.440	52	31	.596	30	28	58	11	40	0	8	7	141	2.8	15
Iavaroni	77	796	163	72	.442	44	36	.818	41	91	132	32	99	0	11	13	180	2.3	10
Les	82	781	133	40	.301	73	57	.781	23	64	87	215	88	0	27	5	138	1.7	10
Kofoed	19	176	33	12	.364	11	6	.545	4	7	11	20	22	0	9	0	30	1.6	4
Roth	16	72	24	7	.292	11	8	.727	0	8	8	7	14	0	5	1	23	1.4	4
White	1	2	1	0	.000	0	0	---	0	0	0	0	1	0	0	0	0	0.0	0

3-Pt. FG: Utah 114-380 (.300)—Malone 5-16 (.313); Bailey 2-5 (.400); Stockton 16-66 (.242); Griffith 61-196 (.311); Hansen 19-54 (.352); Farmer 9-20 (.450); Ortiz 0-1 (.000); Iavaroni 0-1 (.000); Les 1-14 (.071); Kofoed 0-1 (.000); Roth 1-6 (.167). Opponents 185-606 (.305).

WASHINGTON BULLETS

Player	G.	Min.	FGA	FGM	Pct.	FTA	FTM	Pct.	Off. Reb.	Def. Reb.	Tot. Reb.	Ast.	PF	Disq.	Stl.	Blk. Sh.	Pts.	Avg.	Hi.
Malone	76	2418	1410	677	.480	340	296	.871	55	124	179	219	155	0	39	14	1651	21.7	38
King	81	2559	1371	654	.477	441	361	.819	133	251	384	294	219	1	64	13	1674	20.7	43
Williams	82	2413	940	438	.466	290	225	.776	158	415	573	356	213	1	142	70	1120	13.7	30
Eackles	80	1459	732	318	.434	346	272	.786	100	80	180	123	156	1	41	5	917	11.5	28
Catledge	79	2077	681	334	.490	254	153	.602	230	342	572	75	250	5	46	25	822	10.4	26
Walker	79	2565	681	286	.420	184	142	.772	135	372	507	496	215	2	155	23	714	9.0	23
Alarie	74	1141	431	206	.478	87	73	.839	103	152	255	63	160	1	25	22	498	6.7	22
Colter	80	1425	457	203	.444	167	125	.749	62	120	182	225	158	0	69	14	534	6.7	27
Grant	71	1193	390	181	.464	57	34	.596	75	88	163	79	147	2	35	29	396	5.6	14
Feitl	57	828	266	116	.436	65	54	.831	69	133	202	36	136	0	17	18	286	5.0	14
C. Jones	53	1154	125	60	.480	25	16	.640	77	180	257	42	187	4	39	76	136	2.6	9
C.A. Jones	43	516	82	38	.463	53	33	.623	54	86	140	18	49	0	18	16	110	2.6	10
Pressley	10	107	25	8	.320	9	5	.556	3	11	14	22	9	0	4	0	21	2.1	4

3-Pt. FG: Washington 52-243 (.214)—Malone 1-19 (.053); King 5-30 (.167); Williams 19-71 (.268); Eackles 9-40 (.225); Catledge 1-5 (.200); Walker 0-9 (.000); Alarie 13-38 (.342); Colter 3-25 (.120); Grant 0-1 (.000); Feitl 0-1 (.000); C. Jones 0-1 (.000); C.A. Jones 1-3 (.333). Opponents 155-510 (.304).

PLAYOFF RESULTS

EASTERN CONFERENCE FIRST ROUND
New York 3, Philadelphia 0

Apr. 27—Thur.—Philadelphia 96 at New York.............................102
Apr. 29—Sat.—Philadelphia 106 at New York.............................107
May   2—Tue.—New York 116 at Philadelphia.............................°115

Detroit 3, Boston 0

Apr. 28—Fri.—Boston 91 at Detroit..101
Apr. 30—Sun.—Boston 95 at Detroit...102
May   2—Tue.—Detroit 100 at Boston 85

Chicago 3, Cleveland 2

Apr. 28—Fri.—Chicago 95 at Cleveland 88
Apr. 30—Sun.—Chicago 88 at Cleveland.. 96
May   3—Wed.—Cleveland 94 at Chicago 101
May   5—Fri.—Cleveland 108 at Chicago ....°105
May   7—Sun.—Chicago 101 at Cleveland 100

Milwaukee 3, Atlanta 2

Apr. 27—Thur.—Milwaukee 92 at Atlanta.....................................100
Apr. 29—Sat.—Milwaukee 108 at Atlanta 98
May   2—Tue.—Atlanta 113 at Milwaukee ....°117
May   5—Fri.—Atlanta 113 at Milwaukee ....°106
May   7—Sun.—Milwaukee 96 at Atlanta 92

EASTERN CONFERENCE SEMIFINALS
Chicago 4, New York 2

May   9—Tue.—Chicago 120 at New York ....°109
May 11—Thur.—Chicago 97 at New York 114
May 13—Sat.—New York 88 at Chicago.......................................111
May 14—Sun.—New York 93 at Chicago......................................106
May 16—Tue.—Chicago 114 at New York 121
May 19—Fri.—New York 111 at Chicago......................................113

Detroit 4, Milwaukee 0

May 10—Wed.—Milwaukee 80 at Detroit 85
May 12—Fri.—Milwaukee 92 at Detroit.......................................112
May 14—Sun.—Detroit 110 at Milwaukee 90
May 15—Mon.—Detroit 96 at Milwaukee....................................... 94

EASTERN CONFERENCE FINALS
Detroit 4, Chicago 2

May 21—Sun.—Chicago 94 at Detroit 88
May 23—Tue.—Chicago 91 at Detroit..100
May 27—Sat.—Detroit 97 at Chicago 99
May 29—Mon.—Detroit 86 at Chicago 80
May 31—Wed.—Chicago 85 at Detroit 94
June 2—Fri.—Detroit 103 at Chicago 94

WESTERN CONFERENCE FIRST ROUND
L.A. Lakers 3, Portland 0

Apr. 27—Thur.—Portland 108 at L.A. Lakers 128
Apr. 30—Sun.—Portland 105 at L.A. Lakers.............................113
May   3—Wed.—L.A. Lakers 116 at Portland.............................108

Golden State 3, Utah 0

Apr. 27—Thur.—Golden State 123 at Utah 119
Apr. 29—Sat.—Golden State 99 at Utah 91
May   2—Tue.—Utah 106 at Golden State...................................120

Phoenix 3, Denver 0

Apr. 28—Fri.—Denver 103 at Phoenix.......................................104
Apr. 30—Sun.—Denver 114 at Phoenix 132
May   2—Tue.—Phoenix 130 at Denver 121

Seattle 3, Houston 1

Apr. 28—Fri.—Houston 107 at Seattle 111
Apr. 30—Sun.—Houston 97 at Seattle 109
May   3—Wed.—Seattle 107 at Houston......................................126
May   5—Fri.—Se)attle 98 at Houston 96

WESTERN CONFERENCE SEMIFINALS
Phoenix 4, Golden State 1

May   6—Sat.—Golden State 103 at Phoenix 130
May   9—Tue.—Golden State 127 at Phoenix.............................122
May 11—Thur.—Phoenix 113 at Golden State 104
May 13—Sat.—Phoenix 135 at Golden State 99
May 16—Tue.—Golden State 104 at Phoenix............................116

L.A. Lakers 4, Seattle 0

May   7—Sun.—Seattle 102 at L.A. Lakers 113
May 10—Wed.—Seattle 108 at L.A. Lakers...............................130
May 12—Fri.—L.A. Lakers 91 at Seattle.................................... 86
May 14—Sun.—L.A. Lakers 97 at Seattle 95

WESTERN CONFERENCE FINALS
L.A. Lakers 4, Phoenix 0

May 20—Sat.—Phoenix 119 at L.A. Lakers................................127
May 23—Tue.—Phoenix 95 at L.A. Lakers.................................101
May 26—Fri.—L.A. Lakers 110 at Phoenix................................107
May 28—Sun.—L.A. Lakers 122 at Phoenix...............................117

NBA FINALS
Detroit 4, L.A. Lakers 0

June 6—Tue.—L.A. Lakers 97 at Detroit 109
June 8—Thur.—L.A. Lakers 105 at Detroit................................108
June 11—Sun.—Detroit 114 at L.A. Lakers................................110
June 13—Tue.—Detroit 105 at L.A. Lakers 97

1987-88 NBA STATISTICS

1987-88 NBA CHAMPION LOS ANGELES LAKERS

Front row (left to right): Owner Jerry Buss, Kurt Rambis, James Worthy, Kareem Abdul-Jabbar, Michael Cooper, Byron Scott, Earvin (Magic) Johnson, assistant coach Bill Bertka. Back row: Coach Pat Riley, Wes Matthews, Billy Thompson, A.C. Green, Mike Smrek, Mychal Thompson, Jeff Lamp, Milt Wagner, assistant coach Randy Pfund, trainer Gary Vitti.

FINAL STANDINGS

ATLANTIC DIVISION

Team	Atl.	Bos.	Chi.	Cle.	Dal.	Den.	Det.	G.S.	Hou.	Ind.	L.A.C.	L.A.L.	Mil.	N.J.	N.Y.	Phil.	Pho.	Por.	Sac.	S.A.	Sea.	Uta.	Was.	W.	L.	Pct.	G.B.
Boston	4	..	3	2	2	0	3	2	1	5	2	0	3	5	5	4	2	2	2	2	1	2	5	57	25	.695	..
Washington	3	1	3	0	1	0	2	2	0	4	2	1	1	6	3	3	2	0	2	2	0	0	..	38	44	.463	19
New York	3	1	2	4	1	1	2	2	1	3	2	0	3	3	..	3	0	1	1	1	0	1	3	38	44	.463	19
Philadelphia	0	2	2	2	1	0	1	1	1	4	1	0	4	4	3	..	1	1	1	1	1	2	3	36	46	.439	21
New Jersey	0	1	1	1	1	0	1	0	1	0	2	0	2	..	3	2	1	0	1	1	0	1	0	19	63	.232	38

CENTRAL DIVISION

Team	Atl.	Bos.	Chi.	Cle.	Dal.	Den.	Det.	G.S.	Hou.	Ind.	L.A.C.	L.A.L.	Mil.	N.J.	N.Y.	Phil.	Pho.	Por.	Sac.	S.A.	Sea.	Uta.	Was.	W.	L.	Pct.	G.B.
Detroit	4	3	4	5	2	1	..	2	1	3	1	0	4	5	4	4	2	1	2	1	1	2	3	54	28	.659	..
Atlanta	..	2	2	5	2	1	2	2	1	4	2	0	3	5	3	6	1	0	1	2	2	1	3	50	32	.610	4
Chicago	3	3	..	3	0	1	2	2	2	3	2	1	5	5	3	4	2	1	1	1	1	2	3	50	32	.610	4
Cleveland	1	3	3	..	1	1	1	0	1	4	1	1	2	5	2	3	1	1	2	2	1	0	6	42	40	.512	12
Milwaukee	3	3	1	4	0	1	2	2	0	3	2	2	..	3	3	2	1	1	2	1	1	1	4	42	40	.512	12
Indiana	2	0	3	2	0	1	3	2	0	..	1	1	3	6	2	2	2	2	0	2	1	1	2	38	44	.463	16

MIDWEST DIVISION

Team	Atl.	Bos.	Chi.	Cle.	Dal.	Den.	Det.	G.S.	Hou.	Ind.	L.A.C.	L.A.L.	Mil.	N.J.	N.Y.	Phil.	Pho.	Por.	Sac.	S.A.	Sea.	Uta.	Was.	W.	L.	Pct.	G.B.
Denver	1	2	1	1	3	..	1	4	4	1	5	3	1	2	1	2	3	2	4	5	4	2	2	54	28	.659	..
Dallas	0	0	2	1	..	3	1	4	4	2	5	1	2	1	1	1	5	3	5	5	3	3	1	53	29	.646	1
Utah	1	0	0	2	3	4	0	4	3	1	4	1	1	1	0	3	4	5	3	4	..	..	2	47	35	.573	7
Houston	1	1	0	1	2	2	1	5	..	2	3	1	2	1	1	1	4	4	4	2	3	3	2	46	36	.561	8
San Antonio	0	0	1	0	1	1	1	2	4	0	5	0	1	1	1	1	3	0	3	..	3	0	3	31	51	.378	23
Sacramento	1	0	1	0	1	2	0	3	2	0	2	0	1	0	1	1	2	1	..	3	1	1	0	24	58	.293	30

PACIFIC DIVISION

Team	Atl.	Bos.	Chi.	Cle.	Dal.	Den.	Det.	G.S.	Hou.	Ind.	L.A.C.	L.A.L.	Mil.	N.J.	N.Y.	Phil.	Pho.	Por.	Sac.	S.A.	Sea.	Uta.	Was.	W.	L.	Pct.	G.B.
L.A. Lakers	2	2	1	1	4	2	2	6	4	1	5	..	0	2	2	2	5	3	4	5	4	4	1	62	20	.756	..
Portland	2	0	1	1	2	3	1	5	1	2	6	3	1	2	1	1	6	..	4	5	3	1	2	53	29	.646	9
Seattle	0	1	1	1	2	1	1	5	2	1	5	2	1	2	2	1	4	3	4	2	..	1	2	44	38	.537	18
Phoenix	1	0	0	1	0	2	0	4	1	0	4	1	1	1	2	1	..	0	3	2	2	2	0	28	54	.341	34
Golden State	0	0	0	2	1	1	0	..	0	0	3	0	0	2	0	1	2	1	2	3	1	1	0	20	62	.244	42
L.A. Clippers	0	0	0	1	0	0	1	3	2	1	..	1	0	0	1	2	0	3	0	1	1	0	0	17	65	.207	45

HOME-ROAD RECORDS OF ALL TEAMS

Team	Home	Road	Total	Team	Home	Road	Total
Atlanta	30-11	20-21	50-32	Milwaukee	30-11	12-29	42-40
Boston	36-5	21-20	57-25	New Jersey	16-25	3-38	19-63
Chicago	30-11	20-21	50-32	New York	29-12	9-32	38-44
Cleveland	31-10	11-30	42-40	Philadelphia	27-14	9-32	36-46
Dallas	33-8	20-21	53-29	Phoenix	22-19	6-35	28-54
Denver	35-6	19-22	54-28	Portland	33-8	20-21	53-29
Detroit	34-7	20-21	54-28	Sacramento	19-22	5-36	24-58
Golden State	16-25	4-37	20-62	San Antonio	23-18	8-33	31-51
Houston	31-10	15-26	46-36	Seattle	32-9	12-29	44-38
Indiana	25-16	13-28	38-44	Utah	33-8	14-27	47-35
L.A. Clippers	14-27	3-38	17-65	Washington	25-16	13-28	38-44
L.A. Lakers	36-5	26-15	62-20	Totals	640-303	303-640	943-943

OFFENSIVE TEAM STATISTICS

Team	G.	FIELD GOALS Att.	Made	Pct.	FREE THROWS Att.	Made	Pct.	REBOUNDS Off.	Def.	Tot.	Ast.	PF	Disq.	Stl.	Turn Over	Blk. Sh.	SCORING Pts.	Avg.
Denver	82	7961	3770	.474	2289	1841	.804	1163	2442	3605	2300	1982	18	832	1186	401	9573	116.7
Portland	82	7460	3661	.491	2701	2079	.770	1251	2491	3742	2307	2091	21	726	1351	347	9518	116.1
Boston	82	6905	3599	.521	2300	1846	.803	930	2440	3370	2448	1804	10	620	1304	415	9315	113.6
San Antonio	82	7559	3706	.490	2412	1769	.733	1184	2335	3519	2344	1991	27	739	1418	468	9314	113.6
L.A. Lakers	82	7078	3576	.505	2480	1956	.789	1073	2491	3564	2347	1715	9	672	1318	404	9250	112.8
Seattle	82	7443	3706	.476	2442	1826	.748	1313	2314	3627	2146	2380	21	775	1376	447	9135	111.4
Dallas	82	7191	3413	.475	2510	1980	.789	1341	2495	3836	1984	1734	14	645	1257	446	8960	109.3
Detroit	82	7018	3461	.493	2612	1977	.757	1181	2482	3663	2011	1957	20	588	1348	394	8957	109.2
Houston	82	7354	3465	.471	2483	1936	.780	1239	2530	3769	1936	1865	17	712	1367	502	8935	109.0
Phoenix	82	7302	3551	.486	2200	1681	.764	1113	2379	3492	2332	2045	19	675	1413	353	8901	108.5
Utah	82	7092	3484	.491	2404	1802	.750	1066	2553	3619	2407	1986	22	771	1481	627	8899	108.5
Sacramento	82	7337	3458	.471	2324	1795	.772	1232	2461	3693	2116	1895	14	582	1457	493	8855	108.0
Atlanta	82	7102	3443	.485	2441	1873	.767	1228	2379	3607	2062	2050	21	635	1225	537	8844	107.9
Golden State	82	7404	3463	.468	2204	1754	.796	1140	2252	3392	2005	2155	25	741	1395	283	8771	107.0
Milwaukee	82	7079	3366	.475	2364	1832	.775	1117	2335	3452	2194	1989	33	671	1275	380	8697	106.1
Philadelphia	82	6785	3214	.474	2731	2087	.764	1219	2307	3526	1897	1866	20	672	1433	465	8667	105.7
New York	82	7232	3363	.465	2306	1750	.759	1286	2194	3480	2012	2361	36	789	1518	445	8655	105.5
Washington	82	7164	3355	.468	2476	1914	.773	1229	2297	3526	1875	1922	16	698	1384	502	8653	105.5
Chicago	82	7015	3434	.490	2221	1685	.759	1170	2459	3629	2149	1849	14	712	1263	475	8609	105.0
Indiana	82	7154	3436	.480	1982	1546	.780	1078	2457	3535	1977	2038	20	619	1318	345	8581	104.6
Cleveland	82	6755	3313	.490	2438	1813	.744	1015	2289	3304	2070	1836	20	733	1439	526	8566	104.5
New Jersey	82	6857	3208	.468	2308	1682	.729	1075	2262	3337	1795	2042	27	727	1503	385	8235	100.4
L.A. Clippers	82	7194	3190	.443	2305	1644	.713	1191	2350	3541	1885	1908	18	721	1534	520	8103	98.8

DEFENSIVE TEAM STATISTICS

Team	FIELD GOALS Att.	Made	Pct.	FREE THROWS Att.	Made	Pct.	REBOUNDS Off.	Def.	Tot.	Ast.	PF	Disq.	Stl.	Turn Over	Blk. Sh.	Pts.	SCORING Avg.	Pt. Dif.
Chicago	6967	3276	.470	2205	1670	.757	1023	2268	3291	2079	1880	27	597	1244	415	8330	101.6	+ 3.4
Cleveland	7101	3383	.476	2044	1611	.788	1159	2255	3414	1989	2021	26	692	1439	449	8504	103.7	+ 0.8
Detroit	7134	3334	.467	2298	1751	.762	1144	2276	3420	1964	2164	32	649	1328	406	8533	104.1	+ 5.2
Atlanta	6885	3243	.471	2480	1927	.777	1156	2353	3509	1976	2008	18	640	1322	353	8549	104.3	+ 3.6
Utah	7283	3273	.449	2475	1905	.770	1277	2444	3721	1991	2013	16	771	1467	472	8597	104.8	+ 3.7
Dallas	7385	3468	.470	1957	1499	.766	1200	2323	3433	2240	1997	20	612	1228	436	8602	104.9	+ 4.4
Indiana	7060	3335	.472	2446	1858	.760	1160	2500	3660	1933	1859	8	700	1269	407	8646	105.4	- 0.8
Milwaukee	7063	3449	.473	2410	1832	.760	1172	2400	3572	2135	1952	22	621	1346	449	8653	105.5	+ 0.5
New York	6710	3202	.477	2806	2177	.776	1155	2284	3439	2005	1969	26	705	1631	447	8695	106.0	- 0.5
Washington	7235	3459	.478	2246	1670	.744	1228	2364	3592	2134	1966	20	690	1384	527	8711	106.3	- 0.8
L.A. Lakers	7467	3551	.476	2020	1538	.761	1175	2249	3424	2200	1940	20	732	1246	390	8771	107.0	+ 5.8
Philadelphia	7063	3501	.496	2163	1640	.758	1109	2225	3334	2217	2118	25	718	1280	441	8785	107.1	- 1.4
Houston	7420	3454	.465	2352	1805	.767	1261	2506	3767	1951	2012	17	737	1405	365	8821	107.6	+ 1.4
Boston	7260	3497	.482	2249	1724	.767	1122	2194	3316	2061	1989	25	734	1176	346	8828	107.7	+ 5.9
New Jersey	6918	3437	.497	2419	1895	.783	1034	2461	3495	1993	1942	19	809	1433	522	8900	108.5	- 8.1
L.A. Clippers	7360	3513	.477	2309	1799	.779	1241	2666	3907	2300	1912	13	842	1452	483	8949	109.1	-10.3
Seattle	6798	3298	.485	2992	2240	.748	1249	2306	3434	1964	1963	14	606	1533	423	8966	109.3	+ 2.1
Portland	7341	3492	.476	2632	2022	.768	1153	2400	3553	2154	2135	31	648	1443	376	9147	111.5	+ 4.5
Denver	7356	3608	.490	2508	1910	.762	1179	2748	3927	2171	1989	24	621	1606	510	9239	112.7	+ 4.1
Phoenix	7248	3609	.498	2506	1922	.767	1104	2416	3520	2225	1901	16	710	1296	441	9268	113.0	- 4.5
Sacramento	7465	3718	.498	2326	1771	.761	1153	2424	3577	2176	1951	20	784	1195	533	9327	113.7	- 5.8
Golden State	7244	3627	.501	2700	2047	.758	1209	2509	3718	2271	1811	10	747	1413	432	9453	115.3	- 8.3
San Antonio	7678	3851	.502	2390	1855	.776	1292	2513	3805	2470	1969	13	690	1427	537	9714	118.5	- 4.9

Disq.—Individual player disqualified (fouled out of game).

INDIVIDUAL LEADERS

POINTS
Minimum 70 games or 1,400 points

Player	G.	FG	FT	Pts.	Avg.	Player	G.	FG	FT	Pts.	Avg.
Jordan, Chicago	82	1069	723	2868	35.0	McHale, Boston	64	550	346	1446	22.6
Wilkins, Atlanta	78	909	541	2397	30.7	Scott, L.A. Lakers	81	710	272	1754	21.7
Bird, Boston	76	881	415	2275	29.9	Theus, Sacramento	73	619	320	1574	21.6
Barkley, Philadelphia	80	753	714	2264	28.3	McDaniel, Seattle	78	687	281	1669	21.4
Malone, Utah	82	858	552	2268	27.7	Cummings, Milwaukee	76	675	270	1621	21.3
Drexler, Portland	81	849	476	2185	27.0	Thorpe, Sacramento	82	622	460	1704	20.8
Ellis, Seattle	75	764	303	1938	25.8	J. Malone, Washington	80	648	335	1641	20.5
Aguirre, Dallas	77	746	388	1932	25.1	Chambers, Seattle	82	611	419	1674	20.4
English, Denver	80	843	314	2000	25.0	M. Malone, Washington	79	531	543	1607	20.3
Olajuwon, Houston	79	712	381	1805	22.8	Ewing, New York	82	656	341	1653	20.2

FIELD GOALS
Minimum 300 FG Made

	FGA	FGM	Pct.
McHale, Boston	911	550	.604
Parish, Boston	750	442	.589
Barkley, Philadelphia	1283	753	.587
Stockton, Utah	791	454	.574
Berry, San Antonio	960	540	.563
Rodman, Detroit	709	398	.561
Williams, New Jersey	832	466	.560
Levingston, Atlanta	564	314	.557
Ewing, New York	1183	656	.555
West, Clev.-Phoe.	573	316	.551

FREE THROWS
Minimum 125 FT Made

	FTA	FTM	Pct.
Sikma, Milwaukee	348	321	.922
Bird, Boston	453	415	.916
Long, Indiana	183	166	.907
Gminski, N.J.-Phil.	392	355	.906
Dawkins, San Antonio	221	198	.896
Davis, Phoenix	231	205	.887
Mullin, Golden State	270	239	.885
J. Malone, Washington	380	335	.882
Garland, Golden State	157	138	.879
Vandeweghe, Portland	181	159	.878

ASSISTS
Minimum 70 games or 400 assists

	G.	No.	Avg.
Stockton, Utah	82	1128	13.8
Johnson, L.A. Lakers	72	858	11.9
Jackson, New York	82	868	10.6
Porter, Portland	82	831	10.1
Rivers, Atlanta	80	747	9.3
McMillan, Seattle	82	702	8.6
Thomas, Detroit	81	678	8.4
Cheeks, Philadelphia	79	635	8.0
Lever, Denver	82	639	7.8
Johnson, Boston	77	598	7.8

STEALS
Minimum 70 games or 125 steals

	G.	No.	Avg.
Jordan, Chicago	82	259	3.16
Robertson, San Antonio	82	243	2.96
Stockton, Utah	82	242	2.95
Lever, Denver	82	223	2.72
Drexler, Portland	81	203	2.51
Jackson, New York	82	205	2.50
Cheeks, Philadelphia	79	167	2.11
McMillan, Seattle	82	169	2.06
Olajuwon, Houston	79	162	2.05
Adams, Denver	82	168	2.05
Harper, Dallas	82	168	2.05

REBOUNDS
Minimum 70 games or 800 rebounds

	G.	Off.	Def.	Tot.	Avg.
Cage, L.A. Clippers	72	371	567	938	13.03
Oakley, Chicago	82	326	740	1066	13.00
Olajuwon, Houston	79	302	657	959	12.1
Malone, Utah	82	277	709	986	12.0
Williams, New Jersey	70	298	536	834	11.9
Barkley, Philadelphia	80	385	566	951	11.9
Tarpley, Dallas	81	360	599	959	11.8
M. Malone, Washington	79	372	512	884	11.2
Thorpe, Sacramento	82	279	558	837	10.2
Laimbeer, Detroit	82	165	667	832	10.1

BLOCKED SHOTS
Minimum 70 games or 100 blocked shots

	G.	No.	Avg.
Eaton, Utah	82	304	3.71
Benjamin, L.A. Clippers	66	225	3.41
Ewing, New York	82	245	2.99
Olajuwon, Houston	79	214	2.71
Bol, Washington	77	208	2.70
Nance, Phoe.-Clev.	67	159	2.37
Oldham, Sacramento	54	110	2.04
Williams, Indiana	75	146	1.95
Williams, Cleveland	77	145	1.88
Hinson, Phil.-N.J.	77	140	1.82

3-PT. FIELD GOALS
Minimum 25 made

	FGA	FGM	Pct.
Hodges, Milw.-Phoe.	175	86	.491
Price, Cleveland	148	72	.486
Long, Indiana	77	34	.442
G. Henderson, N.Y.-Phil.	163	69	.423
Tripucka, Utah	74	31	.419
Ainge, Boston	357	148	.415
Bird, Boston	237	98	.414
Tucker, New York	167	69	.413
Ellis, Seattle	259	107	.413
Wood, S.A.-Atl.	127	52	.409

TEAM-BY-TEAM INDIVIDUAL STATISTICS

ATLANTA HAWKS

Player	G.	Min.	FGA	FGM	Pct.	FTA	FTM	Pct.	Off. Reb.	Def. Reb.	Tot. Reb.	Ast.	PF	Dsq.	Stl.	Blk. Sh.	Pts.	Avg.	Hi.
Wilkins	78	2948	1957	909	.464	655	541	.826	211	291	502	224	162	0	103	47	2397	30.7	51
Rivers	80	2502	890	403	.453	421	319	.758	83	283	366	747	272	3	140	41	1134	14.2	37
Willis	75	2091	687	356	.518	245	159	.649	235	312	547	28	240	2	68	41	871	11.6	27
Battle	67	1227	613	278	.454	188	141	.750	26	87	113	158	84	0	31	5	713	10.6	27
Wittman	82	2412	787	376	.478	89	71	.798	39	131	170	302	117	0	50	18	823	10.0	29
Levingston	82	2135	564	314	.557	246	190	.772	228	276	504	71	287	5	52	84	819	10.0	24
Carr	80	1483	517	281	.544	182	142	.780	94	195	289	103	272	7	38	83	705	8.8	24
Wood (Tot.)	52	909	312	136	.436	99	76	.768	17	40	57	174	50	0	26	1	400	7.7	27
Wood (Atl.)	14	79	30	16	.533	8	7	.875	1	5	6	19	6	0	4	0	48	3.4	10
Webb	82	1347	402	191	.475	131	107	.817	16	130	146	337	125	0	63	12	490	6.0	14
Koncak	49	1073	203	98	.483	136	83	.610	103	230	333	19	161	1	36	56	279	5.7	25
McGee	11	117	52	22	.423	6	2	.333	4	12	16	13	6	0	5	0	51	4.6	18
Rollins	76	1765	260	133	.512	80	70	.875	142	317	459	20	229	2	31	132	336	4.4	20
Washburn (Tot.)	37	260	81	36	.444	31	18	.581	28	47	75	6	29	0	5	8	90	2.4	10
Washburn (Atl.)	29	174	49	22	.449	23	13	.565	19	36	55	3	19	0	4	8	57	2.0	8
Whatley	5	24	9	4	.444	4	3	.750	0	4	4	2	3	0	2	0	11	2.2	3
Hastings	55	403	82	40	.488	27	25	.926	27	70	97	16	67	1	8	10	110	2.0	10

3-Pt. FG: Atlanta 85-282 (.301)—Wilkins 38-129 (.295); Rivers 9-33 (.273); Willis 0-2 (.000); Battle 16-41 (.390); Levingston 1-2 (.500); Carr 1-4 (.250); Wood 9-19 (.474); Webb 1-19 (.053); Koncak 0-2 (.000); McGee 5-19 (.263); Hastings 5-12 (.417). Opponents 136-406 (.335).

BOSTON CELTICS

Player	G.	Min.	FGA	FGM	Pct.	FTA	FTM	Pct.	Off. Reb.	Def. Reb.	Tot. Reb.	Ast.	PF	Dsq.	Stl.	Blk. Sh.	Pts.	Avg.	Hi.
Bird	76	2965	1672	881	.527	453	415	.916	108	595	703	467	157	0	125	57	2275	29.9	49
McHale	64	2390	911	550	.604	434	346	.797	159	377	536	171	179	1	27	92	1446	22.6	33

Player	G.	Min.	FGA	FGM	Pct.	FTA	FTM	Pct.	Off. Reb.	Def. Reb.	Tot. Reb.	Ast.	PF	Dsq.	Stl.	Blk. Sh.	Pts.	Avg.	Hi.
Ainge	81	3018	982	482	.491	180	158	.878	59	190	249	503	203	1	115	17	1270	15.7	33
Parish	74	2312	750	442	.589	241	177	.734	173	455	628	115	198	5	55	84	1061	14.3	26
Johnson	77	2670	803	352	.438	298	255	.856	62	178	240	598	204	0	93	29	971	12.6	24
Paxson (Tot.)	45	801	298	137	.460	79	68	.861	15	30	45	76	73	0	30	5	347	7.7	19
Paxson (Bos.)	28	538	191	94	.492	61	54	.885	7	20	27	49	44	0	23	4	244	8.7	19
Roberts	74	1032	330	161	.488	165	128	.776	60	102	162	81	118	0	16	15	450	6.1	20
Daye	47	655	217	112	.516	87	59	.678	30	46	76	71	68	0	29	4	283	6.0	27
Lewis	49	405	193	90	.466	57	40	.702	28	35	63	26	54	0	16	15	220	4.5	14
Lohaus	70	718	246	122	.496	62	50	.806	46	92	138	49	123	1	20	41	297	4.2	20
Sichting	24	370	82	44	.537	12	8	.667	5	16	21	60	30	0	14	0	98	4.1	17
Gilmore (Tot.)	71	893	181	99	.547	128	67	.523	69	142	211	21	148	0	15	30	265	3.7	15
Gilmore (Bos.)	47	521	101	58	.574	91	48	.527	54	94	148	12	94	0	10	18	164	3.5	15
Acres	79	1151	203	108	.532	111	71	.640	105	165	270	42	198	2	29	27	287	3.6	19
M'niefield (Tot.)	72	1070	221	108	.489	55	41	.745	30	66	96	228	133	0	59	3	261	3.6	16
M'niefield (Bos.)	61	868	173	83	.480	32	27	.844	22	53	75	190	107	0	44	3	196	3.2	16
Henry	10	81	28	11	.393	10	9	.900	2	8	10	12	11	0	1	1	34	3.4	10
Kite	13	86	23	9	.391	6	1	.167	10	14	24	2	16	0	3	8	19	1.5	4

3-Pt. FG: Boston 271-705 (.384)—Bird 98-237 (.414); Ainge 148-357 (.415); Parish 0-1 (.000); Johnson 12-46 (.261); Paxson 2-13 (.154); Roberts 0-6 (.000); Daye 0-1 (.000); Lewis 0-4 (.000); Lohaus 3-13 (.231); Sichting 2-8 (.250); Minniefield 3-11 (.273); Henry 3-8 (.375). Opponents 110-366 (.301).

CHICAGO BULLS

Player	G.	Min.	FGA	FGM	Pct.	FTA	FTM	Pct.	Off. Reb.	Def. Reb.	Tot. Reb.	Ast.	PF	Dsq.	Stl.	Blk. Sh.	Pts.	Avg.	Hi.
Jordan	82	3311	1998	1069	.535	860	723	.841	139	310	449	485	270	2	259	131	2868	35.0	59
Oakley	82	2816	776	375	.483	359	261	.727	326	740	1066	248	272	2	68	28	1014	12.4	26
Corzine	80	2328	715	344	.481	153	115	.752	170	357	527	154	149	1	36	95	804	10.1	21
Sellers	82	2212	714	326	.457	157	124	.790	107	143	250	141	174	0	34	66	777	9.5	24
Vincent (Tot.)	72	1501	461	210	.456	167	145	.868	35	117	152	381	145	0	55	16	573	8.0	23
Vincent (Chi.)	29	953	309	138	.447	107	99	.925	18	85	103	244	82	0	34	12	378	13.0	23
Pippen	79	1650	564	261	.463	172	99	.576	115	183	298	169	214	3	91	52	625	7.9	24
Paxson	81	1888	582	287	.493	45	33	.733	16	88	104	303	154	2	49	1	640	7.9	22
Grant	81	1827	507	254	.501	182	114	.626	155	292	447	89	221	3	51	53	622	7.7	20
Threatt	45	701	263	132	.502	41	32	.780	12	43	55	107	71	0	27	3	298	6.6	26
Sparrow (Tot.)	58	1044	293	117	.399	33	24	.727	15	57	72	167	79	1	41	3	260	4.5	19
Sparrow (Chi.)	55	992	274	112	.409	33	24	.727	14	56	70	162	72	1	37	3	250	4.5	19
Brown	46	591	174	78	.448	71	41	.577	66	93	159	28	85	0	11	4	197	4.3	15
Gilmore	24	372	80	41	.513	37	19	.514	15	48	63	9	54	0	5	12	101	4.2	13
Turner	17	98	30	8	.267	2	1	.500	8	2	10	9	5	0	8	0	17	1.0	4
Waiters	22	114	29	9	.310	2	0	.000	9	19	28	1	26	0	2	15	18	0.8	4
White	2	2	0	0	.000	0	0	.000	0	0	0	0	0	0	0	0	0	0.0	0

3-Pt. FG: Chicago 56-243 (.230)—Jordan 7-53 (.132); Oakley 3-12 (.250); Corzine 1-9 (.111); Sellers 1-7 (.143); Vincent 3-8 (.375); Pippen 4-23 (.174); Paxson 33-95 (.347); Grant 0-2 (.000); Threatt 2-20 (.100); Sparrow 2-12 (.167); Brown 0-1 (.000); Waiters 0-1 (.000). Opponents 108-368 (.293).

CLEVELAND CAVALIERS

Player	G.	Min.	FGA	FGM	Pct.	FTA	FTM	Pct.	Off. Reb.	Def. Reb.	Tot. Reb.	Ast.	PF	Dsq.	Stl.	Blk. Sh.	Pts.	Avg.	Hi.
Nance (Tot.)	67	2383	920	487	.529	390	304	.779	193	414	607	207	242	10	63	159	1280	19.1	45
Nance (Clev.)	27	906	304	160	.526	141	117	.830	74	139	213	84	90	3	18	63	437	16.2	29
Daugherty	79	2957	1081	551	.510	528	378	.716	151	514	665	333	235	2	48	54	1480	18.7	44
Price	80	2626	974	493	.506	252	221	.877	54	126	180	480	119	1	99	12	1279	16.0	32
Harper	57	1830	732	340	.464	278	196	.705	64	159	223	281	157	3	122	52	879	15.4	30
Williams	77	2106	663	316	.477	279	211	.756	159	347	506	103	203	2	61	145	843	10.9	24
Curry	79	1499	742	340	.458	101	79	.782	43	123	166	149	128	2	94	22	787	10.0	27
West	54	1183	316	182	.576	153	95	.621	83	198	281	50	158	2	25	79	459	8.5	17
Hubbard	78	1631	485	237	.489	243	182	.749	117	164	281	81	167	1	50	7	656	8.4	25
Ke. Johnson	52	1043	311	143	.460	112	92	.821	10	62	72	193	96	1	60	17	380	7.3	15
Corbin	54	1148	322	158	.491	98	77	.786	79	141	220	56	128	2	42	15	393	7.3	23
Ehlo	79	1709	485	226	.466	132	89	.674	86	188	274	206	182	0	82	30	563	7.1	20
Sanders (Tot.)	59	883	303	153	.505	76	59	.776	38	71	109	56	131	1	31	9	365	6.2	29
Sanders (Clev.)	24	417	132	71	.538	23	20	.870	10	37	47	26	58	1	13	5	162	6.8	20
Henderson (Tot.)	17	190	53	21	.396	26	15	.577	9	12	21	23	26	0	8	0	57	3.4	14
Henderson (Clev.)	5	20	5	2	.400	12	5	.417	3	1	4	2	2	0	0	0	9	1.8	7
Dudley	55	513	137	65	.474	71	40	.563	74	70	144	23	87	2	13	19	170	3.1	14
Rogers	24	168	61	26	.426	13	10	.769	8	19	27	3	23	0	4	3	62	2.6	11
Benson	2	12	2	2	1.000	2	1	.500	0	1	1	0	2	0	1	1	5	2.5	3
Ka. Johnson	4	12	3	1	.333	0	0	.000	0	0	0	1	0	0	1	0	2	0.5	2

3-Pt. FG: Cleveland 127-336 (.378)—Nance 0-1 (.000); Daugherty 0-2 (.000); Price 72-148 (.486); Harper 3-20 (.150); Williams 0-1 (.000); Curry 28-81 (.346); Hubbard 0-5 (.000); Ke. Johnson 2-9 (.222); Corbin 0-3 (.000); Ehlo 22-64 (.344); Rogers 0-2 (.000). Opponents 127-400 (.318).

DALLAS MAVERICKS

Player	G.	Min.	FGA	FGM	Pct.	FTA	FTM	Pct.	Off. Reb.	Def. Reb.	Tot. Reb.	Ast.	PF	Dsq.	Stl.	Blk. Sh.	Pts.	Avg.	Hi.
Aguirre	77	2610	1571	746	.475	504	388	.770	182	252	434	278	223	1	70	57	1932	25.1	38
Blackman	71	2580	1050	497	.473	379	331	.873	82	164	246	262	112	0	64	18	1325	18.7	32
Harper	82	3032	1167	536	.459	344	261	.759	71	175	246	634	164	0	168	35	1393	17.0	35
Perkins	75	2499	876	394	.450	332	273	.822	201	400	601	118	227	2	74	54	1066	14.2	26
Tarpley	81	2307	888	444	.500	277	205	.740	360	599	959	86	313	8	103	86	1093	13.5	29
Schrempf	82	1587	539	246	.456	266	201	.756	102	177	279	159	189	0	42	32	698	8.5	22
Davis	75	1480	415	208	.501	108	91	.843	18	84	102	303	149	0	51	18	537	7.2	25
Donaldson	81	2523	380	212	.558	189	147	.778	247	508	755	66	175	2	40	104	571	7.0	20
Blab	73	658	132	58	.439	65	46	.708	52	82	134	35	108	1	8	29	162	2.2	12
Alford	28	197	55	21	.382	17	16	.941	3	20	23	23	23	0	17	3	59	2.1	10
Wennington	30	125	49	25	.510	19	12	.632	14	25	39	4	33	0	5	9	63	2.1	10
Farmer	30	157	69	26	.377	10	9	.900	9	9	18	16	18	0	3	1	61	2.0	8

3-Pt. FG: Dallas 154-526 (.293)—Aguirre 52-172 (.302); Blackman 0-5 (.000); Harper 60-192 (.313); Perkins 5-30 (.167); Tarpley 0-5 (.000); Schrempf 5-32 (.156); Davis 30-74 (.405); Alford 1-8 (.125); Wennington 1-2 (.500); Farmer 0-6 (.000). Opponents 167-517 (.323).

DENVER NUGGETS

Player	G.	Min.	FGA	FGM	Pct.	FTA	FTM	Pct.	Off. Reb.	Def. Reb.	Tot. Reb.	Ast.	PF	Dsq.	Stl.	Blk. Sh.	Pts.	Avg.	Hi.
English	80	2818	1704	843	.495	379	314	.828	166	207	373	377	193	1	70	23	2000	25.0	37
Lever	82	3061	1360	643	.473	316	248	.785	203	462	665	639	214	0	223	21	1546	18.9	32
Vincent	73	1755	958	446	.466	287	231	.805	80	229	309	143	198	1	46	26	1124	15.4	42
Schayes	81	2166	668	361	.540	487	407	.836	200	462	662	106	323	9	62	92	1129	13.9	32
Adams	82	2778	927	416	.449	199	166	.834	40	183	223	503	138	0	168	16	1137	13.9	32
Rasmussen	79	1779	884	435	.492	170	132	.776	130	307	437	78	241	2	22	81	1002	12.7	35
Natt	27	533	208	102	.490	73	54	.740	35	61	96	47	43	0	13	3	258	9.6	26
Cooper	45	865	270	118	.437	67	50	.746	98	172	270	30	145	3	12	94	286	6.4	23
Smith	15	191	93	37	.398	28	21	.750	16	14	30	11	23	0	5	6	95	6.3	17
Evans	56	656	307	139	.453	37	30	.811	9	39	48	81	78	0	34	6	344	6.1	29
Hanzlik	77	1334	287	109	.380	163	129	.791	39	132	171	166	185	1	64	17	350	4.5	16
Moore	7	34	24	7	.292	6	6	1.000	5	7	12	5	4	0	2	1	20	2.9	10
Brooks	16	133	49	20	.408	4	3	.750	19	25	44	13	21	1	4	1	43	2.7	10
Dunn	82	1534	156	70	.449	52	40	.769	110	130	240	87	152	0	101	11	180	2.2	10
Martin	26	136	61	23	.377	21	10	.476	13	11	24	14	21	0	6	3	57	2.2	10
Wright	2	7	5	1	.200	0	0	.000	0	1	1	0	3	0	0	0	2	1.0	2

3-Pt. FG: Denver 192-562 (.342)—English 0-6 (.000); Lever 12-57 (.211); Vincent 1-4 (.250); Schayes 0-2 (.000); Adams 139-379 (.367); Natt 0-1 (.000); Cooper 0-1 (.000); Evans 36-91 (.396); Hanzlik 3-16 (.188); Dunn 0-1 (.000); Martin 1-4 (.250). Opponents 113-377 (.300).

DETROIT PISTONS

Player	G.	Min.	FGA	FGM	Pct.	FTA	FTM	Pct.	Off. Reb.	Def. Reb.	Tot. Reb.	Ast.	PF	Dsq.	Stl.	Blk. Sh.	Pts.	Avg.	Hi.
Dantley	69	2144	863	444	.514	572	492	.860	84	143	227	171	144	0	39	10	1380	20.0	45
Thomas	81	2927	1341	621	.463	394	305	.774	64	214	278	678	217	0	141	17	1577	19.5	42
Dumars	82	2732	960	453	.472	308	251	.815	63	137	200	387	155	1	87	15	1161	14.2	25
Laimbeer	82	2897	923	455	.493	214	187	.874	165	667	832	199	284	6	66	78	1110	13.5	30
Johnson	82	1935	959	425	.443	217	147	.677	90	141	231	267	164	0	58	18	1002	12.2	27
Edwards (Tot.)	69	1705	643	302	.470	321	210	.654	119	293	412	78	216	2	16	37	814	11.8	32
Edwards (Det.)	26	328	101	48	.475	61	45	.738	22	55	77	5	57	0	2	5	141	5.4	16
Rodman	82	2147	709	398	.561	284	152	.535	318	397	715	110	273	5	75	45	953	11.6	30
Mahorn	67	1963	481	276	.574	217	164	.756	159	406	565	60	262	4	43	42	717	10.7	34
Salley	82	2003	456	258	.566	261	185	.709	166	236	402	113	294	4	53	137	701	8.5	21
Bedford	38	298	101	44	.436	23	13	.565	27	38	65	4	47	0	8	17	101	2.7	14
Dawkins (Tot.)	6	33	9	2	.222	15	6	.400	2	3	5	2	14	0	0	2	10	1.7	4
Dawkins (Det.)	2	7	2	1	.500	3	2	.667	0	0	0	1	4	0	0	1	4	2.0	4
Lewis	50	310	87	27	.310	48	29	.604	17	34	51	14	36	0	13	4	83	1.7	10
Moore	9	25	13	4	.308	4	2	.500	2	0	2	1	8	0	2	0	10	1.1	4
Nevitt	17	63	21	7	.333	6	3	.500	4	14	18	0	12	0	1	5	17	1.0	4
Russell	1	1	1	0	.000	0	0	.000	0	0	0	1	0	0	0	0	0	0.0	0

3-Pt. FG: Detroit 58-202 (.287)—Dantley 0-2 (.000); Thomas 30-97 (.309); Dumars 4-19 (.211); Laimbeer 13-39 (.333); Johnson 5-24 (.208); Rodman 5-17 (.294); Mahorn 1-2 (.500); Lewis 0-1 (.000); Russell 0-1 (.000). Opponents 114-394 (.289).

GOLDEN STATE WARRIORS

Player	G.	Min.	FGA	FGM	Pct.	FTA	FTM	Pct.	Off. Reb.	Def. Reb.	Tot. Reb.	Ast.	PF	Dsq.	Stl.	Blk. Sh.	Pts.	Avg.	Hi.
Floyd	18	680	301	132	.439	139	116	.835	26	65	91	178	46	0	27	2	381	21.2	37
Mullin	60	2033	926	470	.508	270	239	.885	58	147	205	290	136	3	113	32	1213	20.2	38
Sampson (Tot.)	48	1663	682	299	.438	196	149	.760	140	322	462	122	164	3	41	88	749	15.6	34
Sampson (GS)	29	958	411	180	.438	111	86	.775	82	208	290	85	101	2	24	55	446	15.4	34
Carroll	14	408	209	79	.378	74	59	.797	21	72	93	19	46	1	13	25	217	15.5	25
Higgins	68	2188	725	381	.526	322	273	.848	94	199	293	188	188	2	70	31	1054	15.5	41
Teagle	47	958	546	248	.454	121	97	.802	41	40	81	61	95	0	32	4	594	12.6	28
Garland	67	2122	775	340	.439	157	138	.879	68	159	227	429	188	2	116	7	831	12.4	27
O. Smith (Tot.)	72	1549	662	325	.491	229	178	.777	126	121	247	155	160	0	91	42	841	11.7	29
O. Smith (GS)	57	1358	569	288	.506	201	157	.781	110	107	217	144	137	0	86	36	746	13.1	29
Harris (Tot.)	58	1084	487	223	.458	113	89	.788	53	73	126	87	89	0	50	8	535	9.2	24
Harris (GS)	44	885	401	189	.471	97	74	.763	41	64	105	70	74	0	42	6	452	10.3	24
Frank	78	1597	565	242	.428	207	150	.725	95	235	330	111	267	5	53	23	634	8.1	23
McDonald	81	2039	552	258	.467	111	87	.784	133	202	335	138	246	4	39	8	612	7.6	22
Feitl	70	1128	404	182	.450	134	94	.701	83	252	335	53	146	1	15	9	458	6.5	20
L. Smith	20	499	123	58	.472	27	11	.407	79	103	182	25	63	1	12	11	127	6.4	15
Minniefield	11	202	48	25	.521	23	14	.609	8	13	21	38	26	0	15	0	65	5.9	11
Hoppen (Tot.)	39	642	183	84	.459	62	54	.871	58	116	174	32	87	1	13	6	222	5.7	17
Hoppen (G.S.)	36	607	172	80	.465	59	51	.864	54	113	167	30	84	1	13	6	211	5.9	17
Whitehead	72	1221	360	174	.483	82	59	.720	109	212	321	39	209	3	32	21	407	5.7	19
White (Tot.)	49	581	249	111	.446	54	39	.722	12	19	31	59	57	0	20	2	261	5.3	24
White (GS)	35	462	203	94	.463	41	30	.732	11	17	28	49	43	0	19	2	218	6.2	24
Washburn	8	86	32	14	.438	8	5	.625	9	11	20	3	10	0	1	0	33	4.1	10
Henderson	12	170	48	19	.396	14	10	.714	6	11	17	21	24	0	8	0	48	4.0	14
Washington	6	56	14	7	.500	2	2	.500	9	10	19	0	13	0	4	4	16	2.7	4
Wade	11	123	20	3	.150	4	2	.500	3	12	15	34	13	0	7	1	8	0.7	4

3-Pt. FG: Golden State 91-312 (.292)—Floyd 1-20 (.050); Mullin 34-97 (.351); Sampson 0-5 (.000); Carroll 0-1 (.000); Higgins 19-39 (.487); Teagle 1-9 (.111); Garland 13-39 (.333); O. Smith 13-41 (.317); Harris 0-6 (.000); Frank 0-1 (.000); McDonald 9-35 (.257); Feitl 0-4 (.000); L. Smith 0-1 (.000); Minniefield 1-5 (.200); Hoppen 0-1 (.000); White 0-5 (.000); Henderson 0-1 (.000); Wade 0-2 (.000). Opponents 152-470 (.323).

HOUSTON ROCKETS

Player	G.	Min.	FGA	FGM	Pct.	FTA	FTM	Pct.	Off. Reb.	Def. Reb.	Tot. Reb.	Ast.	PF	Dsq.	Stl.	Blk. Sh.	Pts.	Avg.	Hi.
Olajuwon	79	2825	1385	712	.514	548	381	.695	302	657	959	163	324	7	162	214	1805	22.8	38
Sampson	19	705	271	119	.439	85	63	.741	58	114	172	37	63	1	17	33	303	15.9	31
Floyd (Tot.)	77	2514	969	420	.433	354	301	.850	77	219	296	544	190	1	95	12	1155	15.0	37
Floyd (Hou)	59	1834	668	288	.431	215	185	.860	51	154	205	366	144	1	68	10	774	13.1	27
Short	81	1949	986	474	.481	240	206	.858	71	151	222	162	197	0	58	14	1159	14.3	33
Carroll (Tot.)	77	2004	924	402	.435	225	172	.764	131	358	489	113	195	1	50	106	976	12.7	29

Player	G.	Min.	FGA	FGM	Pct.	FTA	FTM	Pct.	Off. Reb.	Def. Reb.	Tot. Reb.	Ast.	PF	Dsq.	Stl.	Blk. Sh.	Pts.	Avg.	Hi.
Carroll (Hou)	63	1596	715	323	.452	151	113	.748	110	286	396	94	149	0	37	81	759	12.0	29
McCray	81	2689	746	359	.481	367	288	.785	232	399	631	264	166	2	57	51	1006	12.4	24
Leavell	80	2150	666	291	.437	251	218	.869	22	126	148	405	162	1	124	9	819	10.2	26
Petersen	69	1793	488	249	.510	153	114	.745	145	291	436	106	203	3	36	40	613	8.9	22
Free	58	682	350	143	.409	100	80	.800	14	30	44	60	74	2	20	3	374	6.4	37
Reid	62	980	356	165	.463	63	50	.794	38	87	125	67	118	0	27	5	393	6.3	21
Harris	14	199	86	34	.395	16	15	.938	12	9	21	17	15	0	8	2	83	5.9	17
Johnson	70	879	298	155	.520	91	67	.736	77	91	168	49	127	0	30	26	378	5.4	19
Maxwell	71	848	171	80	.468	143	110	.769	74	105	179	60	75	0	22	12	270	3.8	23
Turner	12	99	34	12	.353	14	10	.714	4	4	8	23	13	0	7	1	35	2.9	8
Anderson	12	53	26	11	.423	5	4	.800	9	8	17	4	4	0	1	0	32	2.7	7
Conner	52	399	108	50	.463	41	32	.780	20	18	38	59	31	0	38	1	132	2.5	8

3-Pt. FG: Houston 69-291 (.237)—Olajuwon 0-4 (.000); Sampson 2-6 (.333); Floyd 13-52 (.250); Short 5-21 (.238); Carroll 0-1 (.000); McCray 0-4 (.000); Leavell 19-88 (.216); Petersen 1-6 (.167); Free 8-35 (.228); Reid 13-34 (.382); Harris 0-1 (.000); Johnson 1-8 (.125); Maxwell 0-2 (.000); Turner 1-7 (.143); Anderson 6-15 (.400); Conner 0-7 (.000). Opponents 108-393 (.275).

INDIANA PACERS

Player	G.	Min.	FGA	FGM	Pct.	FTA	FTM	Pct.	Off. Reb.	Def. Reb.	Tot. Reb.	Ast.	PF	Dsq.	Stl.	Blk. Sh.	Pts.	Avg.	Hi.
Person	79	2807	1252	575	.459	197	132	.670	171	365	536	309	266	4	73	9	1341	17.0	35
Tisdale	79	2378	998	511	.512	314	246	.783	168	323	491	103	274	5	54	34	1268	16.1	32
Fleming	80	2733	845	442	.523	283	227	.802	106	258	364	568	225	0	115	11	1111	13.9	30
Stipanovich	80	2692	828	411	.496	314	254	.809	157	505	662	183	302	8	90	69	1079	13.5	26
Long	81	2022	879	417	.474	183	166	.907	72	157	229	173	164	1	84	11	1034	12.8	32
Miller	82	1840	627	306	.488	186	149	.801	95	95	190	132	157	0	53	19	822	10.0	31
Williams	75	1966	732	311	.425	171	126	.737	116	353	469	98	244	1	37	146	748	10.0	24
Anderson	74	1097	436	217	.498	141	108	.766	89	127	216	78	98	0	41	6	542	7.3	25
Skiles	51	760	209	86	.411	54	45	.833	11	55	66	180	97	0	22	3	223	4.4	16
Gray	74	807	193	90	.466	73	44	.603	70	180	250	44	152	1	11	32	224	3.0	15
Wheeler	59	513	132	62	.470	34	25	.735	19	21	40	103	37	0	36	2	149	2.5	18
Dreiling	20	74	17	8	.471	26	18	.692	3	14	17	5	19	0	2	4	34	1.7	6
Rowsom	4	16	6	0	.000	6	6	1.000	1	4	5	1	3	0	1	0	6	1.5	4

3-Pt. FG: Indiana 163-485 (.336)—Person 59-177 (.333); Tisdale 0-2 (.000); Fleming 0-13 (.000); Stipanovich 3-15 (.200); Long 34-77 (.442); Miller 61-172 (.355); Williams 0-6 (.000); Anderson 0-2 (.000); Skiles 6-20 (.300); Gray 0-1 (.000). Opponents 118-368 (.321).

LOS ANGELES CLIPPERS

Player	G.	Min.	FGA	FGM	Pct.	FTA	FTM	Pct.	Off. Reb.	Def. Reb.	Tot. Reb.	Ast.	PF	Dsq.	Stl.	Blk. Sh.	Pts.	Avg.	Hi.
Woodson	80	2534	1263	562	.445	341	296	.868	64	126	190	273	210	1	109	26	1438	18.0	36
Cage	72	2660	766	360	.470	474	326	.688	371	567	938	110	194	1	91	58	1046	14.5	26
Dailey	67	1282	755	328	.434	313	243	.776	62	92	154	109	128	1	69	4	901	13.4	33
Benjamin	66	2171	693	340	.491	255	180	.706	112	418	530	172	203	2	50	225	860	13.0	30
White	17	352	124	66	.532	57	45	.789	31	31	62	9	32	0	7	3	178	10.5	20
Williams	35	857	427	152	.356	66	48	.727	55	63	118	58	108	1	29	21	365	10.4	34
Drew	74	2024	720	328	.456	108	83	.769	21	98	119	383	114	0	65	0	765	10.3	27
Burtt	19	312	138	62	.449	69	47	.681	6	21	27	38	56	0	10	5	171	9.0	17
Norman	66	1435	500	241	.482	170	87	.512	100	163	263	78	123	0	44	34	569	8.6	31
Wolf	42	1137	334	136	.407	54	45	.833	51	136	187	98	139	8	38	16	320	7.6	23
Fields	7	154	36	16	.444	26	20	.769	13	16	29	10	17	0	5	2	52	7.4	12
Valentine	79	1636	533	223	.418	136	101	.743	37	119	156	382	135	0	122	8	562	7.1	30
Gregory	23	313	134	61	.455	36	12	.333	37	58	95	16	37	0	9	13	134	5.8	21
Coleman	29	431	191	66	.346	36	20	.556	36	45	81	13	51	1	11	6	153	5.3	16
Murphy	1	19	1	1	1.000	4	3	.750	1	1	2	2	2	0	1	0	5	5.0	5
Phelps	2	23	7	3	.429	4	3	.750	0	2	2	3	1	0	5	0	9	4.5	7
Cureton	69	1128	310	133	.429	63	33	.524	97	174	271	63	135	1	32	36	299	4.3	21
Kite (Tot)	53	1063	205	92	.449	79	40	.506	85	179	264	47	153	1	19	58	224	4.2	16
Kite (LAC)	40	977	182	83	.456	73	39	.534	75	165	240	45	137	1	16	50	205	5.1	16
Gordon	8	65	31	11	.355	6	6	1.000	2	4	7	8	0	1	2	0	28	3.5	8
Nessley	35	295	49	18	.367	14	7	.500	20	53	73	16	78	1	7	11	43	1.2	6

3-Pt. FG: L.A. Clippers 79-317 (.249)—Woodson 18-78 (.231); Cage 0-1 (.000); Dailey 2-12 (.167); Benjamin 0-8 (.000); White 1-1 (1.000); Williams 13-58 (.224); Drew 26-90 (.289); Burtt 0-4 (.000); Norman 0-10 (.000); Wolf 3-15 (.200); Valentine 15-33 (.455); Gregory 0-1 (.000); Coleman 1-2 (.500); Cureton 0-3 (.000); Kite 0-1 (.000). Opponents 124-363 (.342).

LOS ANGELES LAKERS

Player	G.	Min.	FGA	FGM	Pct.	FTA	FTM	Pct.	Off. Reb.	Def. Reb.	Tot. Reb.	Ast.	PF	Dsq.	Stl.	Blk. Sh.	Pts.	Avg.	Hi.
Scott	81	3048	1348	710	.527	317	272	.858	76	257	333	335	204	2	155	27	1754	21.7	38
Worthy	75	2655	1161	617	.531	304	242	.796	129	245	374	289	175	1	72	55	1478	19.7	38
Johnson	72	2637	996	490	.492	489	417	.853	88	361	449	858	147	0	114	13	1408	19.6	39
Abdul-Jabbar	80	2308	903	480	.532	269	205	.762	118	360	478	135	216	1	48	92	1165	14.6	27
M. Thompson	80	2007	722	370	.512	292	185	.634	198	291	489	66	251	4	38	79	925	11.6	28
Green	82	2636	640	322	.503	379	293	.773	245	465	710	93	204	0	87	45	937	11.4	28
Campbell	13	242	101	57	.564	39	28	.718	8	19	27	15	41	0	11	2	143	11.0	28
Cooper	61	1793	482	189	.392	113	97	.858	50	178	228	289	136	1	66	26	532	8.7	21
Matthews	51	706	248	114	.460	65	54	.831	16	50	66	138	65	0	25	3	289	5.7	18
Rambis	70	845	186	102	.548	93	73	.785	103	165	268	54	103	0	39	13	277	4.0	17
Wagner	40	380	147	62	.422	29	26	.897	4	24	28	61	42	0	6	4	152	3.8	14
Tolbert (Tot)	25	259	69	35	.507	30	19	.633	23	32	55	10	39	0	8	5	89	3.6	9
Tolbert (LAL)	14	82	28	16	.571	13	10	.769	9	11	20	5	14	0	3	3	42	3.0	9
Smrek	48	421	103	44	.427	66	44	.667	27	58	85	8	105	3	7	42	132	2.8	12
B. Thompson	9	38	13	3	.231	10	8	.800	2	7	9	1	11	0	1	0	14	1.6	4
Lamp	3	7	0	0	.000	2	2	1.000	0	0	0	1	0	0	0	0	2	0.7	2

3-Pt. FG: L.A. Lakers 142-478 (.297)—Scott 62-179 (.346); Worthy 2-16 (.125); Johnson 11-56 (.196); Abdul-Jabbar 0-1 (.000); M. Thompson 0-3 (.000); Green 0-2 (.000); Campbell 1-3 (.333); Cooper 57-178 (.320); Matthews 7-30 (.233); Wagner 2-10 (.200). Opponents 131-439 (.298).

MILWAUKEE BUCKS

Player	G.	Min.	FGA	FGM	Pct.	FTA	FTM	Pct.	Off. Reb.	Def. Reb.	Tot. Reb.	Ast.	PF	Dsq.	Stl.	Blk. Sh.	Pts.	Avg.	Hi.
Cummings	76	2629	1392	675	.485	406	270	.665	184	369	553	181	274	6	78	46	1621	21.3	36
Sikma	82	2923	1058	514	.486	348	321	.922	195	514	709	279	316	11	93	80	1352	16.5	35
Pierce	37	965	486	248	.510	122	107	.877	30	53	83	73	94	0	21	7	606	16.4	29
Pressey	75	2484	702	345	.491	357	285	.798	130	245	375	523	233	6	112	34	983	13.1	25
Breuer	81	2258	788	390	.495	286	188	.657	191	360	551	103	198	3	46	107	968	12.0	33
Moncrief	56	1428	444	217	.489	196	164	.837	58	122	180	204	109	0	41	14	603	10.8	29
Humphries (Tot)	68	1809	538	284	.528	153	112	.732	49	125	174	395	177	1	81	5	683	10.0	26
Humphries (Mil)	18	252	54	20	.370	14	9	.643	5	18	23	41	23	0	20	1	49	2.7	9
Hodges	43	983	345	155	.449	39	32	.821	12	34	46	109	80	1	30	0	397	9.2	22
Lucas	81	1766	631	281	.445	162	130	.802	29	130	159	392	102	1	88	3	743	9.2	25
Reynolds	62	1161	419	188	.449	154	119	.773	70	90	160	104	97	0	74	32	498	8.0	24
Krystkowiak	50	1050	266	128	.481	127	103	.811	88	143	231	50	137	0	18	8	359	7.2	23
Mokeski	60	848	210	100	.476	72	51	.708	70	151	221	22	194	5	27	27	251	4.2	14
Hoppen	3	35	11	4	.364	3	3	1.000	4	3	7	2	3	0	0	0	11	3.7	5
Mannion	35	477	118	48	.407	37	25	.676	17	34	51	55	53	0	13	7	123	3.5	12
Davis	5	39	18	6	.333	0	0	.000	1	2	3	3	4	0	2	1	12	2.4	10
Moore (Tot)	10	50	27	9	.333	8	6	.750	6	8	14	6	6	0	2	1	24	2.4	10
Moore (Mil)	3	16	3	2	.667	2	0	.000	1	1	2	1	2	0	0	0	4	1.3	2
Henry	14	145	41	13	.317	7	4	.571	5	14	19	29	11	0	4	1	32	2.3	8
Stroeder	41	271	79	29	.367	30	20	.667	24	47	71	20	48	0	3	12	78	1.9	10
Winslow	7	45	13	3	.231	2	1	.500	3	4	7	2	9	0	1	0	7	1.0	5
Bradley	2	5	1	0	.000	0	0	.000	0	1	1	1	2	0	0	0	0	0.0	0

3-Pt. FG: Milwaukee 133-410 (.324)—Cummings 1-3 (.333); Sikma 3-14 (.214); Pierce 3-14 (.214); Pressey 8-39 (.205); Moncrief 5-31 (.161); Humphries 0-2 (.000); Hodges 55-118 (.466); Lucas 51-151 (.338); Reynolds 3-7 (.429); Krystkowiak 0-3 (.000); Mokeski 0-4 (.000); Mannion 2-12 (.167); Davis 0-2 (.000); Henry 2-6 (.333); Stroeder 0-2 (.000); Winslow 0-1 (.000); Bradley 0-1 (.000). Opponents 133-442 (.301).

NEW JERSEY NETS

Player	G.	Min.	FGA	FGM	Pct.	FTA	FTM	Pct.	Off. Reb.	Def. Reb.	Tot. Reb.	Ast.	PF	Dsq.	Stl.	Blk. Sh.	Pts.	Avg.	Hi.
Williams	70	2637	832	466	.560	346	245	.668	298	536	834	109	266	5	68	44	1279	18.3	30
Gminski	34	1194	474	215	.454	166	143	.861	82	238	320	55	78	0	28	33	573	16.9	27
Woolridge	19	622	247	110	.445	130	92	.708	31	60	91	71	73	2	13	20	312	16.4	29
Hinson (Tot)	77	2592	930	453	.487	351	272	.775	159	358	517	99	275	6	69	140	1178	15.3	27
Hinson (NJ)	48	1747	658	330	.502	227	183	.806	106	242	348	72	185	3	45	72	843	17.6	27
McCormick (Tot)	70	2114	648	348	.537	215	145	.674	146	321	467	118	234	3	32	23	841	12.0	27
McCormick (NJ)	47	1513	510	277	.543	162	108	.667	97	226	323	92	159	2	18	15	662	14.1	27
Bagley	82	2774	896	393	.439	180	148	.822	61	196	257	479	162	0	110	10	981	12.0	31
Coleman	27	657	240	116	.483	84	65	.774	58	115	173	39	110	4	28	16	297	11.0	23
Birdsong	67	1882	736	337	.458	92	47	.511	73	94	167	222	143	2	54	11	730	10.9	26
Hopson	61	1365	549	222	.404	177	131	.740	63	80	143	118	145	0	57	25	587	9.6	25
Dw. Washington	68	1379	547	245	.448	189	132	.698	54	64	118	206	163	2	91	4	633	9.3	27
Branch	20	308	134	56	.418	23	20	.870	20	28	48	16	41	1	16	11	133	6.7	20
Bradley (Tot)	65	1437	365	156	.427	97	74	.763	25	102	127	151	172	1	114	43	423	6.5	22
Bradley (NJ)	63	1432	364	156	.429	97	74	.763	25	101	126	150	170	1	114	43	423	6.7	22
Comegys	75	1122	363	156	.430	150	106	.707	54	164	218	65	175	3	36	70	418	5.6	21
Waller	9	91	40	16	.400	18	10	.556	9	4	13	3	13	0	4	1	42	4.7	10
O'Koren	4	52	16	9	.563	4	0	.000	1	3	4	2	2	0	3	2	18	4.5	8
McKenna	31	393	109	43	.394	25	24	.960	4	27	31	40	55	1	15	2	126	4.1	16
Du. Washington	15	156	42	18	.429	20	16	.800	5	17	22	34	23	0	12	0	54	3.6	18
Wilson	6	47	11	7	.636	11	6	.545	1	0	1	6	6	0	6	0	21	3.5	9
Engler	54	399	88	36	.409	35	31	.886	32	66	98	15	73	1	9	6	103	1.9	7
Moore (Tot)	5	61	10	4	.400	0	0	.000	2	4	6	12	1	0	3	0	8	1.6	8
Moore (NJ)	1	10	1	0	.000	0	0	.000	1	1	2	1	0	0	0	0	0	0.0	0

3-Pt. FG: New Jersey 137-455 (.301)—Williams 1-1 (1.000); Gminski 0-2 (.000); Woolridge 0-2 (.000); Hinson 0-1 (.000); McCormick 0-2 (.000); Bagley 47-161 (.292); Coleman 0-2 (.000); Birdsong 9-25 (.360); Hopson 12-45 (.267); Dw. Washington 11-49 (.224); Branch 1-5 (.200); Bradley 37-101 (.366); Comegys 0-1 (.000); Waller 0-2 (.000); O'Koren 0-1 (.000); McKenna 16-50 (.320); Du. Washington 2-4 (.500); Wilson 1-1 (1.000). Opponents 131-363 (.361).

NEW YORK KNICKERBOCKERS

Player	G.	Min.	FGA	FGM	Pct.	FTA	FTM	Pct.	Off. Reb.	Def. Reb.	Tot. Reb.	Ast.	PF	Dsq.	Stl.	Blk. Sh.	Pts.	Avg.	Hi.
Ewing	82	2546	1183	656	.555	476	341	.716	245	431	676	125	332	5	104	245	1653	20.2	42
Wilkins	81	2703	1324	591	.446	243	191	.786	106	164	270	326	183	1	90	22	1412	17.4	39
Jackson	82	3249	1013	438	.432	266	206	.774	120	276	396	868	244	2	205	6	1114	13.6	33
Cartwright	82	1676	528	287	.544	426	340	.798	127	257	384	85	234	4	43	43	914	11.1	23
Walker	82	2139	728	344	.473	178	138	.775	192	197	389	86	290	5	63	59	826	10.1	25
Newman	77	1589	620	270	.435	246	207	.841	87	72	159	62	204	5	72	11	773	10.0	29
Green	82	2049	585	258	.441	190	126	.663	221	421	642	93	318	9	65	32	642	7.8	20
Tucker	71	1248	455	193	.424	71	51	.718	32	87	119	117	158	3	53	6	506	7.1	18
Cummings	62	946	307	140	.456	80	59	.738	82	153	235	37	143	0	20	10	339	5.5	17
Tolbert	11	177	41	19	.463	17	9	.529	14	21	35	5	25	0	5	2	47	4.3	9
Scurry (Tot)	33	455	118	55	.466	39	27	.692	30	54	84	50	81	0	49	23	140	4.2	13
Scurry (NY)	4	8	2	1	.500	0	0	.000	1	2	3	1	3	0	2	1	2	0.5	2
White	12	117	46	17	.370	13	9	.692	1	2	3	10	14	0	1	0	43	3.6	10
McNealy	19	265	74	23	.311	31	21	.677	24	40	64	23	50	1	16	2	67	3.5	17
Sparrow	3	52	19	5	.263	0	0	.000	1	1	2	5	7	0	4	0	10	3.3	6
Carlisle	26	204	67	29	.433	11	10	.909	6	7	13	32	39	1	11	4	74	2.8	21
Toney	21	139	48	21	.438	11	10	.909	3	5	8	24	20	0	9	1	57	2.7	11
Thornton	7	85	19	6	.316	8	5	.625	5	8	13	4	23	0	2	0	17	2.4	6
Donovan	44	364	109	44	.404	21	17	.810	5	20	25	87	33	0	16	1	105	2.4	14
Henderson	6	69	14	5	.357	2	2	1.000	1	9	10	13	14	0	0	1	14	2.3	5
Orr	29	180	50	16	.320	16	8	.500	13	21	34	9	27	0	6	0	40	1.4	5

3-Pt. FG: New York 179-567 (.316)—Ewing 0-3 (.000); Wilkins 39-129 (.302); Jackson 32-126 (.254); Walker 0-1 (.000); Newman 26-93 (.280); Green 0-2 (.000); Tucker 69-167 (.413); Cummings 0-1 (.000); White 0-1 (.000); Sparrow 0-1 (.000); Carlisle 6-17 (.353); Toney 5-14 (.357); Donovan 0-7 (.000); Henderson 2-4 (.500); Orr 0-1 (.000). Opponents 114-375 (.304).

PHILADELPHIA 76ers

Player	G.	Min.	FGA	FGM	Pct.	FTA	FTM	Pct.	Off. Reb.	Def. Reb.	Tot. Reb.	Ast.	PF	Dsq.	Stl.	Blk. Sh.	Pts.	Avg.	Hi.
Barkley	80	3170	1283	753	.587	951	714	.751	385	566	951	254	278	6	100	103	2264	28.3	47
Robinson	62	2110	1041	483	.464	293	210	.717	116	289	405	131	192	4	79	39	1178	19.0	32
Gminski (Tot)	81	2961	1126	505	.448	392	355	.906	245	569	814	139	176	0	64	118	1365	16.9	30
Gminski (Phil)	47	1767	652	290	.445	226	212	.938	163	331	494	84	98	0	36	85	792	16.9	30
Cheeks	79	2871	865	428	.495	275	227	.825	59	194	253	635	116	0	167	22	1086	13.7	25
Hinson	29	845	272	123	.452	124	89	.718	53	116	169	27	90	3	24	68	335	11.6	22
Wingate	61	1419	545	218	.400	132	99	.750	44	57	101	119	125	0	47	22	545	8.9	28
Coleman (Tot)	70	1498	453	226	.499	185	141	.762	116	234	350	62	230	5	43	41	593	8.5	23
Coleman (Phil)	43	841	213	110	.516	101	76	.752	58	119	177	23	120	1	15	25	296	6.9	16
G. H'nd'rs'n(Tot)	75	1505	453	194	.428	170	138	.812	27	80	107	231	187	0	69	5	595	7.9	18
G. H'nd'rs'n (Phil)	69	1436	439	189	.431	168	136	.810	26	71	97	218	173	0	67	5	581	8.4	18
McCormick	23	601	138	71	.514	53	37	.698	49	95	144	26	75	1	14	8	179	7.8	18
Toney	29	522	171	72	.421	72	58	.806	8	39	47	108	35	0	11	6	211	7.3	16
King	72	1593	540	211	.391	103	78	.757	71	145	216	109	219	4	39	18	517	7.2	17
D. Henderson	22	351	116	47	.405	47	32	.681	11	24	35	34	41	0	12	5	126	5.7	15
Welp	10	132	31	18	.581	18	12	.667	11	13	24	5	25	0	5	5	48	4.8	18
Askew	14	234	74	22	.297	11	8	.727	6	16	22	33	12	0	10	6	52	3.7	9
McNamara	42	581	133	52	.391	66	48	.727	66	91	157	18	67	0	4	12	152	3.6	17
Thornton (Tot)	48	593	130	65	.500	55	34	.618	46	66	112	15	103	1	11	3	164	3.4	13
Thornton (Phil)	41	508	111	59	.532	47	29	.617	41	58	99	11	80	1	9	3	147	3.6	13
Colter	12	152	40	15	.375	9	7	.778	7	11	18	26	20	0	6	0	37	3.1	11
Vranes	57	772	121	53	.438	35	15	.429	45	72	117	36	100	0	27	33	121	2.1	10

3-Pt. FG: Philadelphia 152-471 (.323)—Barkley 44-157 (.280); Robinson 2-9 (.222); Cheeks 3-22 (.136); Hinson 0-1 (.000); Wingate 10-40 (.250); Coleman 0-1 (.000); G. Henderson 67-159 (.421); Toney 9-27 (.333); King 17-49 (.347); D. Henderson 0-1 (.000); Thornton 0-2 (.000); Vranes 0-3 (.000). Opponents 143-423 (.338).

PHOENIX SUNS

Player	G.	Min.	FGA	FGM	Pct.	FTA	FTM	Pct.	Off. Reb.	Def. Reb.	Tot. Reb.	Ast.	PF	Dsq.	Stl.	Blk. Sh.	Pts.	Avg.	Hi.
Nance	40	1477	616	327	.531	249	187	.751	119	275	394	123	152	7	45	96	843	21.1	45
Davis	68	1951	1031	488	.473	231	205	.887	32	127	159	278	131	0	86	3	1217	17.9	35
E. Johnson	73	2177	1110	533	.480	240	204	.850	121	197	318	180	190	0	33	9	1294	17.7	43
Edwards	43	1377	542	254	.469	260	165	.635	97	238	335	73	159	2	14	32	673	15.7	32
Gilliam	55	1807	720	342	.475	193	131	.679	134	300	434	72	143	1	58	29	815	14.8	25
Humphries	50	1557	484	264	.545	139	103	.741	44	107	151	354	154	1	61	4	634	12.7	26
West (Tot)	83	2098	573	316	.551	285	170	.596	165	358	523	74	265	4	47	147	802	9.7	23
West (Phoe)	29	915	257	134	.521	132	75	.568	82	160	242	24	107	2	22	68	343	11.8	23
Hodges (Tot)	66	1445	523	242	.463	71	59	.831	19	59	78	153	118	1	46	2	629	9.5	22
Hodges (Phoe)	23	462	178	87	.489	32	27	.844	7	25	32	44	38	0	16	2	232	10.1	19
Hornacek	82	2243	605	306	.506	185	152	.822	71	191	262	540	151	0	107	10	781	9.5	21
K. Johnson (Tot)	80	1917	596	275	.461	211	177	.839	36	155	191	437	155	1	103	24	732	9.2	31
K. Johnson (Phoe)	28	874	289	132	.463	99	85	.859	26	93	119	244	59	0	43	7	352	12.6	31
Adams	82	1646	506	251	.496	128	108	.844	118	247	365	183	245	3	82	41	611	7.5	18
Corbin (Tot)	84	1739	525	257	.490	138	110	.797	127	223	350	115	181	2	72	18	625	7.4	23
Corbin (Phoe)	30	591	203	99	.488	40	33	.825	48	82	130	59	53	0	30	3	232	7.7	18
Sanders	35	466	171	82	.480	53	39	.736	28	34	62	30	73	0	18	4	203	5.8	29
Thompson	37	566	159	74	.465	60	43	.717	40	36	76	51	75	1	21	1	191	5.2	23
Bailey	65	869	241	109	.452	89	70	.787	73	137	210	42	180	1	17	28	288	4.4	12
Martin	10	101	51	16	.314	13	8	.615	9	18	27	6	16	0	5	0	40	4.0	10
Crite	29	258	68	34	.500	25	19	.760	27	37	64	15	42	0	5	8	87	3.0	13
Moore (Tot)	14	59	29	9	.310	8	6	.750	2	6	8	1	21	0	5	0	24	1.7	6
Moore (Phoe)	5	34	16	5	.313	4	4	1.000	0	6	6	0	13	0	3	0	14	2.8	6
Cook	33	359	59	14	.237	28	23	.821	37	69	106	14	64	1	9	8	51	1.5	6

3-Pt. FG: Phoenix 118-357 (.331)—Nance 2-5 (.400); Davis 36-96 (.375); E. Johnson 24-94 (.255); Edwards 0-1 (.000); Humphries 3-16 (.188); West 0-1 (.000); Hodges 31-57 (.544); Hornacek 17-58 (.293); K. Johnson 3-15 (.200); Adams 1-2 (.500); Corbin 1-3 (.333); Sanders 0-1 (.000); Thompson 0-2 (.000); Bailey 0-4 (.000); Martin 0-1 (.000); Cook 0-1 (.000). Opponents 128-421 (.304).

PORTLAND TRAIL BLAZERS

Player	G.	Min.	FGA	FGM	Pct.	FTA	FTM	Pct.	Off. Reb.	Def. Reb.	Tot. Reb.	Ast.	PF	Dsq.	Stl.	Blk. Sh.	Pts.	Avg.	Hi.
Drexler	81	3060	1679	849	.506	587	476	.811	261	272	533	467	250	2	203	52	2185	27.0	42
Vandeweghe	37	1038	557	283	.508	181	159	.878	36	73	109	71	68	0	21	7	747	20.2	41
Kersey	79	2888	1225	611	.499	396	291	.735	211	446	657	243	302	8	127	65	1516	19.2	36
Duckworth	78	2223	907	450	.496	430	331	.770	224	352	576	66	280	5	31	32	1231	15.8	32
S. Johnson	43	1050	488	258	.529	249	146	.586	84	158	242	57	151	4	17	32	662	15.4	36
Porter	82	2991	890	462	.519	324	274	.846	65	313	378	831	204	1	150	16	1222	14.9	40
Lucas	73	1191	373	168	.450	148	109	.736	101	214	315	94	188	0	33	10	445	6.1	18
Paxson	17	263	107	43	.402	18	14	.778	8	10	18	27	29	0	7	1	103	6.1	14
Anderson (Tot)	74	1350	439	171	.390	77	58	.753	91	212	303	112	137	1	51	16	448	6.1	22
Anderson (Port)	62	1297	413	160	.387	72	54	.750	82	204	286	108	133	1	50	16	416	6.7	22
Holton	82	1279	353	163	.462	129	107	.829	50	99	149	211	154	0	41	10	436	5.3	18
Ca. Jones	79	1778	263	128	.487	106	78	.736	105	303	408	81	251	0	29	99	334	4.2	14
Sichting (Tot)	52	694	172	93	.541	23	17	.739	9	27	36	93	60	0	21	0	213	4.1	17
Sichting (Port)	28	324	90	49	.544	11	9	.818	4	11	15	33	30	0	7	0	115	4.1	14
Murphy	18	89	49	14	.286	11	7	.636	5	6	11	6	14	0	5	1	36	2.0	11
Ch. Jones	37	186	40	16	.400	33	19	.576	11	20	31	8	28	0	3	6	51	1.4	12
Wilson	15	54	23	7	.304	6	5	.833	2	9	11	3	7	0	0	0	19	1.3	5
Gamble	9	19	3	0	.000	0	0	.000	2	1	3	1	2	0	2	0	0	0.0	0

3-Pt. FG: Portland 117-380 (.308)—Drexler 11-52 (.212); Vandeweghe 22-58 (.379); Kersey 3-15 (.200); S. Johnson 0-1 (.000); Porter 24-69 (.348); Lucas 0-3 (.000); Paxson 3-8 (.375); Anderson 42-135 (.311); Holton 3-15 (.200); Ca. Jones 0-4 (.000); Sichting 8-14 (.571); Murphy 1-4 (.250); Ch. Jones 0-1 (.000); Gamble 0-1 (.000). Opponents 141-462 (.305).

SACRAMENTO KINGS

Player	G.	Min.	FGA	FGM	Pct.	FTA	FTM	Pct.	Off. Reb.	Def. Reb.	Tot. Reb.	Ast.	PF	Dsq.	Stl.	Blk. Sh.	Pts.	Avg.	Hi.
Theus	73	2653	1318	619	.470	385	320	.831	72	160	232	463	173	0	59	16	1574	21.6	36
Thorpe	82	3072	1226	622	.507	609	460	.755	279	558	837	266	264	3	62	56	1704	20.8	35

Player	G.	Min.	FGA	FGM	Pct.	FTA	FTM	Pct.	Off. Reb.	Def. Reb.	Tot. Reb.	Ast.	PF	Dsq.	Stl.	Blk. Sh.	Pts.	Avg.	Hi.
K. Smith	61	2170	694	331	.477	204	167	.819	40	98	138	434	140	1	92	8	841	13.8	30
D. Smith	35	899	364	174	.478	113	87	.770	35	68	103	89	108	2	21	17	443	12.7	30
McGee (Tot)	48	1003	530	223	.421	102	76	.745	55	73	128	71	81	0	52	6	575	12.0	30
McGee (Sac)	37	886	478	201	.421	96	74	.771	51	61	112	58	75	0	47	6	524	14.2	30
Kleine	82	1999	686	324	.472	188	153	.814	179	400	579	93	228	1	28	59	801	9.8	23
Pressley	80	2029	702	318	.453	130	103	.792	139	230	369	185	211	4	84	55	775	9.7	31
Edwards	16	414	115	54	.470	32	24	.750	4	15	19	92	10	0	10	1	132	8.3	19
Thompson	69	1257	456	215	.471	164	118	.720	138	289	427	68	217	1	54	73	550	8.0	20
Pinckney	79	1177	343	179	.522	178	133	.747	94	136	230	66	118	0	39	32	491	6.2	24
Tyler	74	1185	407	184	.452	64	41	.641	87	155	242	56	85	0	43	47	410	5.5	18
Oldham	54	946	250	119	.476	87	59	.678	82	222	304	33	143	2	12	110	297	5.5	19
Henry (Tot)	39	433	150	62	.413	47	39	.830	13	36	49	67	37	0	12	5	183	4.7	21
Henry (Sac)	15	207	81	38	.469	30	26	.867	6	14	20	26	15	0	7	3	117	7.8	21
Arlauckas	9	85	43	14	.326	8	6	.750	6	7	13	8	16	0	3	4	34	3.8	17
Jackson	58	760	171	64	.374	32	23	.719	17	42	59	179	81	0	20	5	157	2.7	11
Nessley (Tot)	44	336	52	20	.385	18	8	.444	23	59	82	16	89	1	8	12	48	1.1	6
Nessley (Sac)	9	41	3	2	.667	4	1	.250	3	6	9	0	11	0	1	1	5	0.6	2

3-Pt. FG: Sacramento 144-450 (.320)—Theus 16-59 (.271); Thorpe 0-6 (.000); K. Smith 12-39 (.308); D. Smith 8-23 (.348); McGee 48-141 (.340); Pressley 36-110 (.327); Edwards 0-2 (.000); Thompson 2-5 (.400); Pinckney 0-2 (.000); Tyler 1-7 (.143); Henry 15-31 (.484); Jackson 6-25 (.240). Opponents 120-370 (.324).

SAN ANTONIO SPURS

Player	G.	Min.	FGA	FGM	Pct.	FTA	FTM	Pct.	Off. Reb.	Def. Reb.	Tot. Reb.	Ast.	PF	Dsq.	Stl.	Blk. Sh.	Pts.	Avg.	Hi.
Robertson	82	2978	1408	655	.465	365	273	.748	165	333	498	557	300	4	243	69	1610	19.6	40
Berry	73	1922	960	540	.563	320	192	.600	176	219	395	110	207	2	55	63	1272	17.4	31
Brickowski	70	2227	805	425	.528	349	268	.768	167	316	483	266	275	11	74	36	1119	16.0	34
Dawkins	65	2179	835	405	.485	221	198	.896	66	138	204	480	95	0	88	2	1027	15.8	30
Mitchell	68	1501	784	378	.482	194	160	.825	54	144	198	68	101	0	31	13	919	13.5	36
Anderson	82	1984	756	379	.501	328	198	.604	161	352	513	79	228	1	54	122	957	11.7	31
Wood	38	830	282	120	.426	91	69	.758	16	35	51	155	44	0	22	1	352	9.3	27
Greenwood	45	1236	328	151	.460	111	83	.748	92	208	300	97	134	2	33	22	385	8.6	23
Sundvold	52	1024	379	176	.464	48	43	.896	14	34	48	183	54	0	27	2	421	8.1	25
Gudmundsson	69	1017	280	139	.496	145	117	.807	93	230	323	86	197	5	18	61	395	5.7	21
Wilson (Tot)	24	420	110	43	.391	40	29	.725	2	25	27	69	40	0	23	3	125	5.2	14
Wilson (SA)	18	373	99	36	.364	29	23	.793	1	25	26	63	34	0	17	3	104	5.8	14
Myers	22	328	95	43	.453	39	26	.667	11	26	37	48	30	0	17	6	112	5.1	13
Davis (Tot)	21	226	115	48	.417	10	7	.700	16	25	41	20	29	0	2	4	104	5.0	14
Davis (SA)	16	187	97	42	.433	10	7	.700	15	23	38	17	25	0	0	3	92	5.8	14
Nimphius	72	919	257	128	.498	83	60	.723	62	91	153	53	141	2	22	56	316	4.4	25
Rellford	4	42	8	5	.625	8	6	.750	2	5	7	1	3	0	0	3	16	4.0	8
Zevenbergen	8	58	27	15	.556	2	0	.000	4	9	13	3	12	0	3	1	30	3.8	8
Blackwell	10	112	41	15	.366	6	5	.833	2	4	6	18	16	0	3	0	37	3.7	10
Nealy	68	837	109	50	.459	63	41	.651	82	140	222	49	94	0	29	5	142	2.1	14
Moore	4	51	9	4	.444	0	0	.000	1	3	4	11	1	0	3	0	8	2.0	8

3-Pt. FG: San Antonio 133-412 (.323)—Robertson 27-95 (.284); Brickowski 1-5 (.200); Dawkins 19-61 (.311); Mitchell 3-12 (.250); Anderson 1-5 (.200); Wood 43-108 (.398); Greenwood 0-2 (.000); Sundvold 26-64 (.406); Gudmundsson 0-1 (.000); Wilson 9-25 (.360); Myers 0-4 (.000); Davis 1-15 (.067); Nimphius 0-1 (.000); Blackwell 2-11 (.182); Nealy 1-2 (.500); Moore 0-1 (.000). Opponents 157-450 (.349).

SEATTLE SUPERSONICS

Player	G.	Min.	FGA	FGM	Pct.	FTA	FTM	Pct.	Off. Reb.	Def. Reb.	Tot. Reb.	Ast.	PF	Dsq.	Stl.	Blk. Sh.	Pts.	Avg.	Hi.
Ellis	75	2790	1519	764	.503	395	303	.767	167	173	340	197	221	1	74	11	1938	25.8	47
McDaniel	78	2703	1407	687	.488	393	281	.715	206	312	518	263	230	2	96	52	1669	21.4	41
Chambers	82	2680	1364	611	.448	519	419	.807	135	355	490	212	297	4	87	53	1674	20.4	46
McKey	82	1706	519	255	.491	224	173	.772	115	213	328	107	237	3	70	63	694	8.5	20
McMillan	82	2453	496	235	.474	205	145	.707	117	221	338	702	238	1	169	47	624	7.6	21
Threatt (Tot)	71	1055	425	216	.508	71	57	.803	23	65	88	160	100	0	60	8	492	6.9	31
Threatt (Sea)	26	354	162	84	.519	30	25	.833	11	22	33	53	29	0	33	5	194	7.5	31
Williams	80	1084	450	199	.442	122	103	.844	61	66	127	96	207	1	62	7	502	6.3	21
Schoene	81	973	454	208	.458	63	51	.810	78	120	198	53	151	0	39	13	484	6.0	20
Lister	82	1812	343	173	.504	188	114	.606	200	427	627	58	319	8	27	140	461	5.6	19
Vincent	43	548	152	72	.474	60	46	.767	17	32	49	137	63	0	21	4	195	4.5	16
Polynice	82	1080	254	118	.465	158	101	.639	122	208	330	33	215	1	32	26	337	4.1	15
Young	77	949	218	89	.408	53	43	.811	18	57	75	218	69	0	52	2	243	3.2	13
Johnson	74	723	105	49	.467	32	22	.688	66	108	174	17	104	0	13	24	120	1.6	8

3-Pt. FG: Seattle 221-638 (.346)—Ellis 107-259 (.413); McDaniel 14-50 (.280); Chambers 33-109 (.303); McKey 11-30 (.367); McMillan 9-24 (.375); Threatt 1-7 (.143); Williams 1-7 (.143); Schoene 17-58 (.293); Lister 1-2 (.500); Vincent 5-13 (.385); Polynice 0-2 (.000); Young 22-77 (.286). Opponents 130-400 (.325).

UTAH JAZZ

Player	G.	Min.	FGA	FGM	Pct.	FTA	FTM	Pct.	Off. Reb.	Def. Reb.	Tot. Reb.	Ast.	PF	Dsq.	Stl.	Blk. Sh.	Pts.	Avg.	Hi.
Malone	82	3198	1650	858	.520	789	552	.700	277	709	986	199	296	2	117	50	2268	27.7	41
Bailey	82	2804	1286	633	.492	408	337	.826	134	397	531	158	186	1	49	125	1604	19.6	41
Stockton	82	2842	791	454	.574	324	272	.840	54	183	237	1128	247	5	242	16	1204	14.7	27
Griffith	52	1052	585	251	.429	92	59	.641	36	91	127	91	102	0	52	5	589	11.3	32
Hansen	81	1796	611	316	.517	152	113	.743	64	123	187	175	193	2	65	5	777	9.6	28
Tripucka	49	976	303	139	.459	68	59	.868	30	87	117	105	68	1	34	4	368	7.5	25
Eaton	82	2731	541	226	.418	191	119	.623	230	487	717	55	320	8	41	304	571	7.0	16
Turpin	79	1011	389	199	.512	98	71	.724	88	148	236	32	157	2	26	68	470	5.9	22
Green	81	1116	370	145	.424	83	75	.904	14	66	80	300	83	0	57	1	393	4.9	18
Scurry	29	447	116	54	.466	39	27	.692	29	52	81	49	78	0	47	22	138	4.8	13
Iavaroni	81	1238	308	143	.464	99	78	.788	94	174	268	67	162	1	23	25	364	4.5	17
Roth	26	201	74	30	.405	30	22	.733	7	21	28	16	37	0	12	0	84	3.2	12

Player	G.	Min.	FGA	FGM	Pct.	FTA	FTM	Pct.	Off. Reb.	Def. Reb.	Tot. Reb.	Ast.	PF	Dsq.	Stl.	Blk. Sh.	Pts.	Avg.	Hi.
Hughes	11	42	13	5	.385	6	6	1.000	3	1	4	8	5	0	0	0	17	1.5	6
Dawkins	4	26	7	1	.143	12	4	.333	2	3	5	1	10	0	1	1	6	1.5	3
Kofoed	36	225	48	18	.375	13	8	.615	4	11	15	23	42	0	6	1	46	1.3	8

3-Pt. FG: Utah 129-404 (.319)—Malone 0-5 (.000); Bailey 1-3 (.333); Stockton 24-67 (.358); Griffith 28-102 (.275); Hansen 32-97 (.330); Tripucka 31-74 (.419); Turpin 1-3 (.333); Green 4-19 (.211); Scurry 3-8 (.375); Iavaroni 0-2 (.000); Roth 2-11 (.182); Hughes 1-6 (.167); Kofoed 2-7 (.286). Opponents 146-464 (.315).

WASHINGTON BULLETS

Player	G.	Min.	FGA	FGM	Pct.	FTA	FTM	Pct.	Off. Reb.	Def. Reb.	Tot. Reb.	Ast.	PF	Dsq.	Stl.	Blk. Sh.	Pts.	Avg.	Hi.
J. Malone	80	2655	1360	648	.476	380	335	.882	44	162	206	237	198	1	51	13	1641	20.5	47
M. Malone	79	2692	1090	531	.487	689	543	.788	372	512	884	112	160	0	59	72	1607	20.3	36
King	69	2044	938	470	.501	324	247	.762	86	194	280	192	202	3	49	10	1188	17.2	34
Williams	82	2428	910	427	.469	256	188	.734	127	317	444	232	217	3	117	34	1047	12.8	28
Catledge	70	1610	585	296	.506	235	154	.655	180	217	397	63	172	0	33	9	746	10.7	27
Johnson	75	1258	498	216	.434	149	121	.812	39	82	121	188	120	0	70	4	554	7.4	23
Colter (Tot)	68	1513	441	203	.460	95	75	.789	58	115	173	261	132	0	62	14	484	7.1	29
Colter (Wash)	56	1361	401	188	.469	86	68	.791	51	104	155	235	112	0	56	14	447	8.0	29
Walker	52	940	291	114	.392	105	82	.781	43	84	127	100	105	2	62	10	310	6.0	20
Alarie	63	769	300	144	.480	49	35	.714	70	90	160	39	107	1	10	12	327	5.2	18
Bogues	79	1628	426	166	.390	74	58	.784	35	101	136	404	138	1	127	3	393	5.0	16
Jones	69	1313	177	72	.407	75	53	.707	106	219	325	59	226	5	53	113	197	2.9	11
Bol	77	1136	165	75	.455	49	26	.531	72	203	275	13	160	0	11	208	176	2.3	13
Murphy	9	46	23	8	.348	5	4	.800	4	12	16	1	5	0	0	0	20	2.2	5

3-Pt. FG: Washington 29-138 (.210)—J. Malone 10-24 (.417); M. Malone 2-7 (.286); King 1-6 (.167); Williams 5-38 (.132); Catledge 0-2 (.000); Johnson 1-9 (.111); Colter 3-10 (.300); Walker 0-6 (.000); Alarie 4-18 (.222); Bogues 3-16 (.188); Jones 0-1 (.000); Bol 0-1 (.000). Opponents 128-390 (.328).

New York's Mark Jackson was NBA Rookie of the Year in 1987-88 while dishing out a first-year record 868 assists.

PLAYOFF RESULTS

EASTERN CONFERENCE FIRST ROUND
Boston 3, New York 1
Apr. 29—Fri.—New York 92 at Boston 112
May   1—Sun.—New York 102 at Boston.......................128
May   4—Wed.—Boston 100 at New York 109
May   6—Fri.—Boston 102 at New York.........................94

Detroit 3, Washington 2
Apr. 28—Thur.—Washington 87 at Detroit 96
Apr. 30—Sat.—Washington 101 at Detroit....................102
May   2—Mon.—Detroit 106 at Washington.................*114
May   4—Wed.—Detroit 103 at Washington..................106
May   8—Sun.—Washington 78 at Detroit 99

Chicago 3, Cleveland 2
Apr. 28—Thur.—Cleveland 93 at Chicago 104
May   1—Sun.—Cleveland 101 at Chicago 106
May   3—Tue.—Chicago 102 at Cleveland 110
May   5—Thur.—Chicago 91 at Cleveland 97
May   8—Sun.—Cleveland 101 at Chicago 107

Atlanta 3, Milwaukee 2
Apr. 29—Fri.—Milwaukee 107 at Atlanta 110
May   1—Sun.—Milwaukee 97 at Atlanta 104
May   4—Wed.—Atlanta 115 at Milwaukee....................123
May   6—Fri.—Atlanta 99 at Milwaukee 105
May   8—Sun.—Milwaukee 111 at Atlanta 121

EASTERN CONFERENCE SEMIFINALS
Boston 4, Atlanta 3
May 11—Wed.—Atlanta 101 at Boston 110
May 13—Fri.—Atlanta 97 at Boston 108
May 15—Sun.—Boston 92 at Atlanta 110
May 16—Mon.—Boston 109 at Atlanta 118
May 18—Wed.—Atlanta 112 at Boston 104
May 20—Fri.—Boston 102 at Atlanta 100
May 22—Sun.—Atlanta 116 at Boston..........................118

Detroit 4, Chicago 1
May 10—Tue.—Chicago 82 at Detroit 93
May 12—Thur.—Chicago 105 at Detroit 95
May 14—Sat.—Detroit 101 at Chicago 79
May 15—Sun.—Detroit 96 at Chicago 77
May 18—Wed.—Chicago 95 at Detroit 102

EASTERN CONFERENCE FINALS
Detroit 4, Boston 2
May 25—Wed.—Detroit 104 at Boston 96
May 26—Thur.—Detroit 115 at Boston **119
May 28—Sat.—Boston 94 at Detroit.............................98
May 30—Mon.—Boston 79 at Detroit 78
June   1—Wed.—Detroit 102 at Boston *96
June   3—Fri.—Boston 90 at Detroit 95

WESTERN CONFERENCE FIRST ROUND
L.A. Lakers 3, San Antonio 0
Apr. 29—Fri.—San Antonio 110 at L.A. Lakers..............122
May   1—Sun.—San Antonio 112 at L.A. Lakers............130
May   3—Tue.—L.A. Lakers 109 at San Antonio............107

Denver 3, Seattle 2
Apr. 29—Fri.—Seattle 123 at Denver 126
May   1—Sun.—Seattle 111 at Denver...........................91
May   3—Tue.—Denver 125 at Seattle..........................114
May   5—Thur.—Denver 117 at Seattle 127
May   7—Sat.—Seattle 96 at Denver............................115

Dallas 3, Houston 1
Apr. 28—Thur.—Houston 110 at Dallas.........................120
Apr. 30—Sat.—Houston 119 at Dallas..........................108
May   3—Tue.—Dallas 93 at Houston.............................92
May   5—Thur.—Dallas 107 at Houston 97

Utah 3, Portland 1
Apr. 28—Thur.—Utah 96 at Portland 108
Apr. 30—Sat.—Utah 114 at Portland............................105
May   4—Wed.—Portland 108 at Utah 113
May   6—Fri.—Portland 96 at Utah 111

WESTERN CONFERENCE SEMIFINALS
L.A. Lakers 4, Utah 3
May   8—Sun.—Utah 91 at L.A. Lakers 110
May 10—Tue.—Utah 101 at L.A. Lakers 97
May 13—Fri.—L.A. Lakers 89 at Utah 96
May 15—Sun.—L.A. Lakers 113 at Utah 100
May 17—Tue.—Utah 109 at L.A. Lakers 111
May 19—Thur.—L.A. Lakers 80 at Utah 108
May 21—Sat.—Utah 98 at L.A. Lakers 109

Dallas 4, Denver 2
May 10—Tue.—Dallas 115 at Denver 126
May 12—Thur.—Dallas 112 at Denver 108
May 14—Sat.—Denver 107 at Dallas.............................105
May 15—Sun.—Denver 103 at Dallas............................124
May 17—Tue.—Dallas 110 at Denver 106
May 19—Thur.—Denver 95 at Dallas.............................108

WESTERN CONFERENCE FINALS
L.A. Lakers 4, Dallas 3
May 23—Mon.—Dallas 98 at L.A. Lakers 113
May 25—Wed.—Dallas 101 at L.A. Lakers 123
May 27—Fri.—L.A. Lakers 94 at Dallas 106
May 29—Sun.—L.A. Lakers 104 at Dallas.....................118
May 31—Tue.—Dallas 102 at L.A. Lakers 119
June   2—Thur.—L.A. Lakers 103 at Dallas 105
June   4—Sat.—Dallas 102 at L.A. Lakers 117

NBA FINALS
L.A. Lakers 4, Detroit 3
June   7—Tue.—Detroit 105 at L.A. Lakers 93
June   9—Thur.—Detroit 96 at L.A. Lakers 108
June 12—Sun.—L.A. Lakers 99 at Detroit........................86
June 14—Tue.—L.A. Lakers 86 at Detroit 111
June 16—Thur.—L.A. Lakers 94 at Detroit 104
June 19—Sun.—Detroit 102 at L.A. Lakers 103
June 21—Tue.—Detroit 105 at L.A. Lakers 108

*Overtime

1986-87 NBA STATISTICS

1986-87 NBA CHAMPION LOS ANGELES LAKERS

Front row (left to right): Owner Jerry Buss, Kurt Rambis, James Worthy, Kareem Abdul-Jabbar, Michael Cooper, Byron Scott, Earvin (Magic) Johnson, assistant coach Bill Bertka. Back row: Coach Pat Riley, Wes Matthews, Billy Thompson, A.C. Green, Mike Smrek, Mychal Thompson, Adrian Branch, assistant coach Randy Pfund, trainer Gary Vitti.

FINAL STANDINGS

ATLANTIC DIVISION

Team	Atl.	Bos.	Chi.	Cle.	Dal.	Den.	Det.	G.S.	Hou.	Ind.	L.A.C.	L.A.L.	Mil.	N.J.	N.Y.	Phil.	Pho.	Por.	Sac.	S.A.	Sea.	Uta.	Was.	W.	L.	Pct.	G.B.
Boston	3	..	6	3	2	2	3	2	2	5	2	0	3	4	4	3	2	2	2	2	2	1	4	59	23	.720	..
Philadelphia	3	3	3	4	0	2	0	1	2	4	2	0	3	3	3	..	1	2	2	1	2	1	3	45	37	.549	14
Washington	0	2	3	4	1	1	3	2	1	2	2	1	1	4	4	3	2	1	1	2	1	..		42	40	.512	17
New Jersey	0	2	2	2	0	0	1	0	1	1	1	0	2	..	5	3	1	0	0	0	0	1	2	24	58	.293	35
New York	1	2	2	1	0	0	0	0	1	2	2	0	2	1	..	3	1	0	2	1	0	1	2	24	58	.293	35

CENTRAL DIVISION

Team	Atl.	Bos.	Chi.	Cle.	Dal.	Den.	Det.	G.S.	Hou.	Ind.	L.A.C.	L.A.L.	Mil.	N.J.	N.Y.	Phil.	Pho.	Por.	Sac.	S.A.	Sea.	Uta.	Was.	W.	L.	Pct.	G.B.
Atlanta	..	3	4	4	2	2	3	1	1	3	2	1	3	5	5	3	1	1	2	2	2	2	5	57	25	.695	..
Detroit	3	2	3	5	1	2	..	1	1	3	2	1	3	5	6	5	1	0	1	1	2	1	3	52	30	.634	5
Milwaukee	3	3	2	5	0	1	3	2	2	4	2	1	..	4	4	2	2	0	2	1	2	1	4	50	32	.610	7
Indiana	3	1	2	3	2	1	3	2	0	..	2	0	2	5	3	2	1	0	1	2	1	1	4	41	41	.500	16
Chicago	2	0	..	5	1	1	3	0	0	3	2·	0	4	3	4	3	1	1	1	1	2	0	3	40	42	.488	17
Cleveland	2	2	1·	..	0	1	1	1	0	3	2	0	1	4	4	4	1	1	1	1	1	0	2	31	51	.378	26

MIDWEST DIVISION

Team	Atl.	Bos.	Chi.	Cle.	Dal.	Den.	Det.	G.S.	Hou.	Ind.	L.A.C.	L.A.L.	Mil.	N.J.	N.Y.	Phil.	Pho.	Por.	Sac.	S.A.	Sea.	Uta.	Was.	W.	L.	Pct.	G.B.
Dallas	0	0	1	2	..	4	1	5	3	0	5	3	2	2	2	2	3	2	5	4	5	3	1	55	27	.671	..
Utah	0	1	2	2	3	4	1	3	3	1	3	2	1	1	1	1	1	2	5	4	2	..	1	44	38	.537	11
Houston	1	0	2	2	3	3	1	..	2	4	1	0	1	0	3	2	5	5	1	3	1	4		42	40	.512	13
Denver	0	0	1	1	2	..	0	4	3	1	2	0	1	2	2	0	3	3	2	5	2	2	1	37	45	.451	18
Sacramento	0	0	1	1	1	4	1	1	1	1	4	0	0	2	0	0	3	2	..	3	2	1	1	29	53	.354	26
San Antonio	0	0	1	1	2	1	1	1	1	0	4	1	1	2	1	1	3	1	3	..	1	2	0	28	54	.341	27

PACIFIC DIVISION

Team	Atl.	Bos.	Chi.	Cle.	Dal.	Den.	Det.	G.S.	Hou.	Ind.	L.A.C.	L.A.L.	Mil.	N.J.	N.Y.	Phil.	Pho.	Por.	Sac.	S.A.	Sea.	Uta.	Was.	W.	L.	Pct.	G.B.
L.A. Lakers	1	2	2	2	2	5	1	4	4	2	6	..	1	2	2	2	5	5	5	4	4	3	1	65	17	.793	..
Portland	1	0	1	1	3	2	2	2	3	2	6	1	2	2	2	0	4	..	3	4	4	3	1	49	33	.598	16
Golden State	1	0	2	1	0	1	1	..	4	0	6	2	0	2	2	1	1	4	4	4	4	2	0	42	40	.512	23
Seattle	0	0	0	1	0	3	0	2	4	1	6	1	1	0	0	0	1	1	..	3	1	3	1	39	43	.476	26
Phoenix	1	0	1	1	2	2	1	5	2	1	5	1	0	1	1	1	..	2	2	2	1	4	0	36	46	.439	29
L.A. Clippers	0	0	0	0	0	3	0	0	1	0	..	0	0	0	1	0	0	1	0	1	1	2	2	0	12	70	.146	53

HOME-ROAD RECORDS OF ALL TEAMS

	Home	Road	Total		Home	Road	Total
Atlanta	35- 6	22- 19	57- 25	Milwaukee	32- 9	18- 23	50- 32
Boston	39- 2	20- 21	59- 23	New Jersey	19- 22	5- 36	24- 58
Chicago	29- 12	11- 30	40- 42	New York	18- 23	6- 35	24- 58
Cleveland	25- 16	6- 35	31- 51	Philadelphia	28- 13	17- 24	45- 37
Dallas	35- 6	20- 21	55- 27	Phoenix	26- 15	10- 31	36- 46
Denver	27- 14	10- 31	37- 45	Portland	34- 7	15- 26	49- 33
Detroit	32- 9	20- 21	52- 30	Sacramento	20- 21	9- 32	29- 53
Golden State	25- 16	17- 24	42- 40	San Antonio	21- 20	7- 34	28- 54
Houston	25- 16	17- 24	42- 40	Seattle	25- 16	14- 27	39- 43
Indiana	28- 13	13- 28	41- 41	Utah	31- 10	13- 28	44- 38
L.A. Clippers	9- 32	3- 38	12- 70	Washington	27- 14	15- 26	42- 40
L.A. Lakers	37- 4	28- 13	65- 17	Totals	627-316	316-627	943-943

OFFENSIVE TEAM STATISTICS

		FIELD GOALS			FREE THROWS			REBOUNDS				MISCELLANEOUS					SCORING	
Team	G.	Att.	Made	Pct.	Att.	Made	Pct.	Off.	Def.	Tot.	Ast.	PF	Disq.	Stl.	Turn Over	Blk. Sh.	Pts.	Avg.
Portland	82	7249	3650	.504	2928	2269	.775	1180	2413	3593	2359	2082	37	767	1546	387	9667	117.9
L.A. Lakers	82	7245	3740	.516	2550	2012	.789	1127	2515	3642	2428	1853	11	728	1358	482	9656	117.8
Denver	82	7951	3744	.471	2568	1975	.769	1294	2368	3662	2317	2184	22	754	1216	421	9569	116.7
Dallas	82	7373	3594	.487	2717	2148	.791	1219	2494	3713	2017	1873	15	688	1205	424	9567	116.7
Seattle	82	7451	3593	.482	2571	1948	.758	1373	2395	3768	2184	2224	33	705	1509	450	9325	113.7
Boston	82	7051	3645	.517	2153	1740	.808	933	2585	3518	2421	1710	15	561	1300	526	9237	112.6
Golden State	82	7412	3551	.479	2526	1970	.780	1193	2351	3544	2083	2138	18	715	1354	321	9188	112.0
Detroit	82	7237	3544	.490	2602	1991	.765	1245	2649	3894	2021	2078	21	643	1417	436	9118	111.2
Phoenix	82	7190	3575	.497	2499	1900	.760	1113	2366	3479	2354	2047	15	703	1498	397	9111	111.1
Sacramento	82	7413	3522	.475	2479	1974	.796	1282	2441	3723	2185	2007	31	513	1403	397	9095	110.9
Milwaukee	82	7282	3457	.475	2549	1953	.766	1119	2322	3441	2044	2180	35	845	1260	393	9052	110.4
Atlanta	82	7141	3435	.481	2661	2019	.759	1350	2478	3828	2077	2152	19	700	1279	511	9024	110.0
New Jersey	82	7083	3374	.476	2607	2000	.767	1169	2409	3578	1991	2353	56	643	1617	397	8893	108.5
San Antonio	82	7456	3532	.474	2292	1701	.742	1285	2347	3632	2220	1930	12	786	1406	325	8882	108.3
Utah	82	7514	3485	.464	2389	1735	.726	1194	2456	3650	2240	2040	13	835	1403	628	8844	107.9
Houston	82	7262	3465	.477	2355	1746	.741	1190	2481	3671	2227	1973	28	654	1384	555	8765	106.9
Philadelphia	82	6792	3335	.491	2617	1971	.753	1178	2327	3505	1943	1774	15	768	1519	540	8729	106.5
Indiana	82	7324	3454	.472	2170	1696	.782	1132	2464	3596	2170	2097	36	697	1361	314	8698	106.1
Washington	82	7397	3356	.454	2531	1935	.765	1305	2315	3620	1750	1775	5	755	1301	685	8690	106.0
Chicago	82	7155	3382	.473	2254	1754	.778	1248	2400	3648	2143	1922	16	677	1257	438	8596	104.8
L.A. Clippers	82	7332	3311	.452	2515	1866	.742	1231	2137	3368	1971	2004	30	751	1493	432	8566	104.5
Cleveland	82	7122	3349	.470	2554	1779	.697	1257	2420	3677	1912	1853	20	672	1619	559	8558	104.4
New York	82	7023	3329	.474	2362	1725	.730	1108	2162	3270	1941	2028	21	704	1420	396	8508	103.8

DEFENSIVE TEAM STATISTICS

		FIELD GOALS			FREE THROWS			REBOUNDS				MISCELLANEOUS					SCORING	
Team	Att.	Made	Pct.	Att.	Made	Pct.	Off.	Def.	Tot.	Ast.	PF	Disq.	Stl.	Turn Over	Blk. Sh.	Pts.	Avg.	Pt. Dif.
Atlanta	6998	3158	.451	2598	1987	.765	1196	2277	3473	1917	2034	21	619	1314	385	8431	102.8	+ 7.2
Chicago	6910	3337	.483	2255	1734	.769	1027	2317	3344	2028	1844	20	583	1269	492	8523	103.9	+ 0.9
Houston	7225	3348	.463	2422	1887	.779	1167	2364	3531	2126	1922	13	721	1366	368	8683	105.9	+ 1.0
Boston	7500	3470	.463	2148	1628	.758	1237	2287	3524	2060	1911	14	722	1156	338	8692	106.0	+ 6.6
Milwaukee	6906	3247	.470	2796	2117	.757	1191	2477	3668	2014	2024	27	659	1551	460	8731	106.5	+ 3.9
Philadelphia	7204	3537	.491	2049	1552	.757	1214	2202	3416	2202	1982	30	813	1372	446	8745	106.6	- 0.2
Indiana	6969	3344	.480	2584	1960	.759	1117	2584	3701	2019	1852	14	660	1416	472	8751	106.7	- 0.6
Washington	7453	3522	.473	2183	1654	.758	1334	2483	3817	2144	1938	14	699	1439	548	8802	107.3	- 1.4
Utah	7338	3347	.456	2564	1974	.770	1310	2637	3947	2011	1992	22	718	1579	457	8811	107.5	+ 0.4
Detroit	7307	3376	.462	2608	1951	.748	1143	2339	3482	2029	2067	28	670	1294	472	8836	107.8	+ 3.4
Cleveland	7441	3556	.478	2209	1664	.753	1254	2396	3650	2056	2076	23	810	1398	479	8871	108.2	- 3.8
L.A. Lakers	7531	3520	.467	2265	1731	.764	1280	2174	3454	2212	2004	16	721	1370	404	8893	108.5	+ 9.3
New York	7142	3500	.490	2534	1928	.761	1331	2448	3779	2152	1950	19	761	1417	400	9022	110.0	- 6.3
Dallas	7503	3586	.478	2293	1750	.763	1254	2386	3640	2304	2136	26	571	1332	421	9050	110.4	+ 6.3
Seattle	7329	3514	.479	2819	2166	.768	1236	2278	3514	2023	2027	23	731	1342	409	9287	113.3	+ 0.5
San Antonio	7310	3704	.507	2364	1786	.756	1100	2461	3561	2375	1844	16	699	1417	463	9300	113.4	- 5.1
New Jersey	7125	3418	.480	3018	2353	.780	1129	2352	3481	1958	2126	33	814	1357	566	9307	113.5	- 5.0
Phoenix	7336	3623	.494	2570	1942	.756	1235	2355	3590	2246	2034	20	799	1428	435	9311	113.5	- 2.4
Sacramento	7469	3656	.489	2500	1922	.769	1160	2355	3515	2154	2068	21	707	1210	487	9359	114.1	- 3.2
Golden State	7339	3615	.493	2665	1995	.749	1249	2481	3730	2174	2052	38	688	1412	450	9380	114.4	- 2.3
Portland	7523	3649	.485	2589	1996	.771	1208	2279	3487	2189	2228	42	735	1504	473	9410	114.8	+ 3.1
L.A. Clippers	7254	3522	.485	2515	1875	.746	1187	2643	3830	2416	2021	19	806	1533	534	9503	115.9	-11.4
Denver	7343	3636	.495	2901	2255	.777	1166	2720	3886	2189	2145	25	558	1564	452	9640	117.6	- 0.9

Disq.—Individual player disqualified (fouled out of game).

INDIVIDUAL LEADERS
POINTS
Minimum 70 games or 1,400 points

	G.	FG	FT	Pts.	Avg.		G.	FG	FT	Pts.	Avg.
Jordan, Chicago	82	1098	833	3041	37.1	Davis, Phoenix	79	779	288	1867	23.6
Wilkins, Atlanta	79	828	607	2294	29.0	Olajuwon, Houston	75	677	400	1755	23.4
English, Denver	82	965	411	2345	28.6	Chambers, Seattle	82	660	535	1909	23.3
Bird, Boston	74	786	414	2076	28.1	McDaniel, Seattle	82	806	275	1890	23.0
Vandeweghe, Portland	79	808	467	2122	26.9	Barkley, Philadelphia	68	557	429	1564	23.0
McHale, Boston	77	790	428	2008	26.1	Harper, Cleveland	82	734	386	1874	22.9
Aguirre, Dallas	80	787	429	2056	25.7	Nance, Phoenix	69	585	381	1552	22.5
Ellis, Seattle	82	785	385	2041	24.9	J. Malone, Washington	80	689	376	1758	22.0
M. Malone, Washington	73	595	570	1760	24.1	Drexler, Portland	82	707	357	1782	21.7
Johnson, L.A. Lakers	80	683	535	1909	23.9	Malone, Utah	82	728	323	1779	21.7

FIELD GOALS
Minimum 300 FG Made

	FGA	FGM	Pct.
McHale, Boston	1307	790	.604
Gilmore, San Antonio	580	346	.597
Barkley, Philadelphia	937	557	.594
Donaldson, Dallas	531	311	.586
Abdul-Jabbar, L.A. Lakers	993	560	.564
B. Williams, New Jersey	936	521	.557
Parish, Boston	1057	588	.556
Johnson, Portland	889	494	.556
McCray, Houston	783	432	.552
Nance, Phoenix	1062	585	.551

STEALS
Minimum 70 games or 125 steals

	G.	No.	Avg.
Robertson, San Antonio	81	260	3.21
Jordan, Chicago	82	236	2.88
Cheeks, Philadelphia	68	180	2.65
Harper, Cleveland	82	209	2.55
Drexler, Portland	82	204	2.49
Lever, Denver	82	201	2.45
Harper, Dallas	77	167	2.17
Stockton, Utah	82	177	2.16
Rivers, Atlanta	82	171	2.09
Porter, Portland	80	159	1.99

FREE THROWS
Minimum 125 FT Made

	FTA	FTM	Pct.
Bird, Boston	455	414	.910
Ainge, Boston	165	148	.897
Laimbeer, Detroit	274	245	.894
Scott, L.A. Lakers	251	224	.892
Hodges, Milwaukee	147	131	.891
Long, Indiana	246	219	.890
Vandeweghe, Portland	527	467	.886
J. Malone, Washington	425	376	.885
Blackman, Dallas	474	419	.884
Pierce, Milwaukee	440	387	.880

REBOUNDS
Minimum 70 games or 800 rebounds

	G.	Off.	Def.	Tot.	Avg.
Barkley, Philadelphia	68	390	604	994	14.6
Oakley, Chicago	82	299	775	1074	13.1
B. Williams, New Jersey	82	322	701	1023	12.5
Donaldson, Dallas	82	295	678	973	11.9
Laimbeer, Detroit	82	243	712	955	11.6
Cage, L.A. Clippers	80	354	568	922	11.5
L. Smith, Golden State	80	366	551	917	11.5
Olajuwon, Houston	75	315	543	858	11.4
M. Malone, Washington	73	340	484	824	11.3
Parish, Boston	80	254	597	851	10.6

ASSISTS
Minimum 70 games or 400 assists

	G.	No.	Avg.
Johnson, L.A. Lakers	80	977	12.2
Floyd, Golden State	82	848	10.3
Thomas, Detroit	81	813	10.0
Rivers, Atlanta	82	823	10.0
Porter, Portland	80	715	8.9
Theus, Sacramento	79	692	8.8
McMillan, Seattle	71	583	8.2
Stockton, Utah	82	670	8.2
Lever, Denver	82	654	8.0
Cheeks, Philadelphia	68	538	7.9

BLOCKED SHOTS
Minimum 70 games or 100 blocked shots

	G.	No.	Avg.
Eaton, Utah	79	321	4.06
Bol, Washington	82	302	3.68
Olajuwon, Houston	75	254	3.39
Benjamin, L.A. Clippers	72	187	2.60
Lister, Seattle	75	180	2.40
Ewing, New York	63	147	2.33
McHale, Boston	77	172	2.23
Nance, Phoenix	69	148	2.14
Hinson, Philadelphia	76	161	2.12
C. Jones, Washington	79	165	2.09

3-PT. FIELD GOALS
Minimum 25 made

	FGA	FGM	Pct.
Vandeweghe, Portland	81	39	.481
Schrempf, Dallas	69	33	.478
Ainge, Boston	192	85	.443
Scott, L.A. Lakers	149	65	.436
Tucker, New York	161	68	.422
McKenna, New Jersey	124	52	.419
Bird, Boston	225	90	.400
Cooper, L.A. Lakers	231	89	.385
Floyd, Golden State	190	73	.384
McGee, Atlanta	229	86	.376

TEAM-BY-TEAM INDIVIDUAL STATISTICS

ATLANTA HAWKS

Player	G.	Min.	FGA	FGM	Pct.	FTA	FTM	Pct.	Off. Reb.	Def. Reb.	Tot. Reb.	Ast.	PF	Disq.	Stl.	Blk. Sh.	Pts.	Avg.	Hi.
Wilkins	79	2969	1787	828	.463	742	607	.818	210	284	494	261	149	0	117	51	2294	29.0	57
Willis	81	2626	1003	538	.536	320	227	.709	321	528	849	62	313	4	65	61	1304	16.1	35
Rivers	82	2590	758	342	.451	441	365	.828	83	216	299	823	287	5	171	30	1053	12.8	27
Wittman	71	2049	792	398	.503	127	100	.787	30	94	124	211	107	0	39	16	900	12.7	30
McGee	76	1420	677	311	.459	137	80	.584	71	88	159	149	156	1	61	2	788	10.4	31
Levingston	82	1848	496	251	.506	212	155	.731	219	314	533	40	261	4	48	68	657	8.0	19
Webb	33	532	162	71	.438	105	80	.762	6	54	60	167	65	1	34	2	223	6.8	17
Battle	64	804	315	144	.457	126	93	.738	16	44	60	124	76	0	29	5	381	6.0	27
Koncak	82	1684	352	169	.480	191	125	.654	153	340	493	31	262	2	52	76	463	5.6	15
Rollins	75	1764	313	171	.546	87	63	.724	155	333	488	22	240	1	43	140	405	5.4	14
Carr	65	695	265	134	.506	103	73	.709	60	96	156	34	146	1	14	48	342	5.3	20
Williams	33	481	146	53	.363	40	27	.675	8	32	40	139	53	0	17	5	138	4.2	12
Hastings	40	256	68	23	.338	29	23	.793	16	54	70	13	35	0	10	7	71	1.8	7
Wilson (Tot.)	7	45	10	3	.300	2	2	1.000	1	3	4	7	10	0	1	0	8	1.1	4
Wilson (Atl.)	2	2	2	0	.000	0	0	...	0	0	0	1	1	0	0	0	0	0.0	0
Henderson	6	10	5	2	.400	1	1	1.000	0	0	0	3	1	0	0	0	5	0.8	3

3-Pt. FG: Atlanta 135-425 (.318)—Wilkins 31-106 (.292); Willis 1-4 (.250); Rivers 4-21 (.190); Wittman 4-12 (.333); McGee 86-229 (.376); Levingston 0-3 (.000); Webb 1-6 (.167); Battle 0-10 (.000); Koncak 0-1 (.000); Carr 1-3 (.333); Williams 5-18 (.278); Hastings 2-12 (.167). Opponents 128-426 (.300).

BOSTON CELTICS

Player	G.	Min.	FGA	FGM	Pct.	FTA	FTM	Pct.	Off. Reb.	Def. Reb.	Tot. Reb.	Ast.	PF	Disq.	Stl.	Blk. Sh.	Pts.	Avg.	Hi.
Bird	74	3005	1497	786	.525	455	414	.910	124	558	682	566	185	3	135	70	2076	28.1	47
McHale	77	3060	1307	790	.604	512	428	.836	247	516	763	198	240	1	38	172	2008	26.1	38
Parish	80	2995	1057	588	.556	309	227	.735	254	597	851	173	266	5	64	144	1403	17.5	34
Ainge	71	2499	844	410	.486	165	148	.897	49	193	242	400	189	3	101	14	1053	14.8	35
Johnson	79	2933	953	423	.444	251	209	.833	45	216	261	594	201	0	87	38	1062	13.4	27
Sichting	78	1566	398	202	.508	42	37	.881	22	69	91	187	124	0	40	1	448	5.7	20
Roberts	73	1079	270	139	.515	153	124	.810	54	136	190	62	129	1	22	20	402	5.5	23
Daye (Tot.)	62	731	202	101	.500	65	34	.523	37	88	125	76	100	0	25	7	236	3.8	14
Daye (Bos.)	61	724	202	101	.500	65	34	.523	37	87	124	75	98	0	25	7	236	3.9	14
Vincent	46	374	136	60	.441	55	51	.927	5	22	27	59	33	0	13	1	171	3.7	10
Wedman	6	78	27	9	.333	2	1	.500	3	6	9	6	6	0	2	2	20	3.3	9
Walton	10	112	26	10	.385	15	8	.533	11	20	31	9	23	0	1	10	28	2.8	9
Henry (Tot.)	54	323	136	46	.338	27	17	.630	7	27	34	35	34	0	9	1	122	2.3	12
Henry (Bos.)	36	231	103	38	.369	17	10	.588	7	20	27	27	27	0	6	1	98	2.7	12
Carlisle	42	297	92	30	.326	20	15	.750	8	22	30	35	28	0	8	0	80	1.9	10
Kite	74	745	110	47	.427	76	29	.382	61	108	169	27	148	2	17	46	123	1.7	10
Thirdkill	17	89	24	10	.417	16	5	.313	5	14	19	2	12	0	2	0	25	1.5	10
Turner	3	18	5	2	.400	0	0	....	1	1	2	1	1	0	0	0	4	1.3	2

3-Pt. FG: Boston 207-565 (.366)—Bird 90-225 (.400); McHale 0-4 (000); Parish 0-1 (.000); Ainge 85-192 (.443); Johnson 7-62 (.113); Sichting 7-26 (.269); Roberts 0-3 (.000); Wedman 1-2 (.500); Henry 12-31 (.387); Carlisle 5-16 (.313); Kite 0-1 (.000); Thirdkill 0-1 (.000); Turner 0-1 (.000). Opponents 124-405 (.306).

CHICAGO BULLS

Player	G.	Min.	FGA	FGM	Pct.	FTA	FTM	Pct.	Off. Reb.	Def. Reb.	Tot. Reb.	Ast.	PF	Disq.	Stl.	Blk. Sh.	Pts.	Avg.	Hi.
Jordan	82	3281	2279	1098	.482	972	833	.857	166	264	430	377	237	0	236	125	3041	37.1	61
Oakley	82	2980	1052	468	.445	357	245	.686	299	775	1074	296	315	4	85	36	1192	14.5	28
Paxson	82	2689	793	386	.487	131	106	.809	22	117	139	467	207	1	66	8	930	11.3	25
Banks	63	1822	462	249	.539	146	112	.767	115	193	308	170	173	3	52	17	610	9.7	24
Threatt (Tot.)	68	1446	534	239	.448	119	95	.798	26	82	108	259	164	0	74	13	580	8.5	27
Threatt (Chi.)	40	778	273	131	.480	66	53	.803	8	43	51	177	88	0	42	9	315	7.9	21
Sellers	80	1751	606	276	.455	173	126	.728	155	218	373	102	194	1	44	68	680	8.5	27
Corzine	82	2287	619	294	.475	129	95	.736	199	341	540	209	202	1	38	87	683	8.3	26
Cureton	43	1105	276	129	.467	73	39	.534	113	114	227	70	102	2	15	26	297	6.9	18
Colter	27	473	142	49	.345	39	33	.846	9	33	42	94	38	0	19	6	131	4.9	14
Brown	62	818	201	106	.527	72	46	.639	71	143	214	24	129	2	20	7	258	4.2	17
Turner	70	936	252	112	.444	31	23	.742	34	81	115	102	97	1	30	4	248	3.5	14
Poquette (Tot.)	58	604	122	62	.508	50	40	.800	30	71	101	35	77	1	9	34	164	2.8	13
Poquette (Chi.)	21	167	40	21	.525	11	9	.818	10	14	24	7	26	0	3	12	51	2.4	13
Myers	29	155	52	19	.365	43	28	.651	8	9	17	21	25	0	14	2	66	2.3	13
Waiters	44	534	93	40	.430	9	5	.556	38	49	87	22	83	1	10	31	85	1.9	6
Young	5	20	4	2	.500	2	1	.500	0	1	1	0	3	0	1	0	5	1.0	3
Cofield	5	27	11	2	.182	0	0	....	1	4	5	4	10	0	2	0	4	0.8	4
Daye	1	7	0	0	....	0	0	....	0	1	1	1	2	0	0	0	0	0.0	0

3-Pt. FG: Chicago 78-299 (.341)—Jordan 12-66 (.182); Oakley 11-30 (.367); Paxson 52-140 (.371); Banks 0-5 (.000); Threatt 0-16 (.000); Sellers 2-10 (.200); Corzine 0-5 (.000); Cureton 0-1 (.000); Colter 0-9 (.000); Turner 1-8 (.125); Poquette 0-1 (.000); Myers 0-6 (.000); Waiters 0-1 (.000); Cofield 0-1 (.000). Opponents 115-337 (.341).

CLEVELAND CAVALIERS

Player	G.	Min.	FGA	FGM	Pct.	FTA	FTM	Pct.	Off. Reb.	Def. Reb.	Tot. Reb.	Ast.	PF	Disq.	Stl.	Blk. Sh.	Pts.	Avg.	Hi.
Harper	82	3064	1614	734	.455	564	386	.684	169	223	392	394	247	3	209	84	1874	22.9	40
Daugherty	80	2695	905	487	.538	401	279	.696	152	495	647	304	248	3	49	63	1253	15.7	33
Williams	80	2714	897	435	.485	400	298	.745	222	407	629	154	197	0	58	167	1168	14.6	27
Hubbard	68	2083	605	321	.531	272	162	.596	178	210	388	136	224	6	66	7	804	11.8	23
Bagley	72	2182	732	312	.426	136	113	.831	55	197	252	379	114	0	91	7	768	10.7	24
Price	67	1217	424	173	.408	114	95	.833	33	84	117	202	75	1	43	4	464	6.9	27
West	78	1333	385	209	.543	173	89	.514	126	213	339	41	229	5	22	81	507	6.5	27
Corbin (Tot.)	63	1170	381	156	.409	124	91	.734	88	127	215	97	129	0	55	5	404	6.4	23
Corbin (Clev.)	32	438	117	43	.368	57	42	.737	36	60	96	17	48	0	17	2	129	4.0	14
Ehlo	44	890	239	99	.414	99	70	.707	55	106	161	92	80	0	40	30	273	6.2	26
Lee	67	870	374	170	.455	101	72	.713	93	158	251	69	147	0	25	40	412	6.1	20
Turpin	64	801	366	169	.462	77	55	.714	62	128	190	33	90	1	11	40	393	6.1	20
Newman	59	630	275	113	.411	76	66	.868	36	34	70	27	67	0	20	7	293	5.0	22
McCray	24	279	65	30	.462	41	20	.488	19	39	58	23	28	0	9	4	80	3.3	11
Poquette	37	437	82	41	.500	39	31	.795	20	57	77	28	51	1	6	22	113	3.1	10
Minniefield	11	122	42	13	.310	4	1	.250	1	9	10	13	8	0	6	1	27	2.5	4

3-Pt. FG: Cleveland 81-338 (.240)—Harper 20-94 (.213); Williams 0-1 (.000); Hubbard 0-4 (.000); Bagley 31-103 (.301); Price 23-70 (.329); West 0-2 (.000); Corbin 1-4 (.250); Ehlo 5-29 (.172); Lee 0-1 (.000); Newman 1-22 (.045); Poquette 0-3 (.000); Minniefield 0-5 (.000). Opponents 95-342 (.278).

DALLAS MAVERICKS

Player	G.	Min.	FGA	FGM	Pct.	FTA	FTM	Pct.	Off. Reb.	Def. Reb.	Tot. Reb.	Ast.	PF	Disq.	Stl.	Blk. Sh.	Pts.	Avg.	Hi.
Aguirre	80	2663	1590	787	.495	557	429	.770	181	246	427	254	243	4	84	30	2056	25.7	43
Blackman	80	2758	1264	626	.495	474	419	.884	96	182	278	266	142	0	64	21	1676	21.0	41
Harper	77	2556	993	497	.501	234	160	.684	51	148	199	609	195	0	167	25	1230	16.0	31
Perkins	80	2687	957	461	.482	296	245	.828	197	419	616	146	269	6	109	77	1186	14.8	29
Donaldson	82	3028	531	311	.586	329	267	.812	295	678	973	63	191	0	51	136	889	10.8	23
Schrempf	81	1711	561	265	.472	260	193	.742	87	216	303	161	224	2	50	16	756	9.3	19
Tarpley	75	1405	499	233	.467	139	94	.676	180	353	533	52	232	3	56	79	561	7.5	20
Davis	82	1582	436	199	.456	171	147	.860	27	87	114	373	159	0	63	10	577	7.0	24
Wood	54	657	310	121	.390	139	109	.784	39	55	94	34	83	0	19	11	358	6.6	25
Wennington	58	560	132	56	.424	60	45	.750	53	76	129	24	95	0	13	10	157	2.7	10
Nutt	25	91	40	16	.400	22	20	.909	1	7	8	16	6	0	7	0	57	2.3	11
Blab	30	160	51	20	.392	28	13	.464	11	25	36	13	33	0	4	9	53	1.8	7
Jackson	8	22	9	2	.222	8	7	.875	1	2	3	6	1	0	1	0	11	1.4	3

3-Pt. FG: Dallas 231-653 (.354)—Aguirre 53-150 (.353); Blackman 5-15 (.333); Harper 76-212 (.358); Perkins 19-54 (.352); Schrempf 33-69 (.478); Tarpley 1-3 (.333); Davis 32-106 (.302); Wood 7-25 (.280); Wennington 0-2 (.000); Nutt 5-17 (.294). Opponents 128-434 (.295).

1986-87 STATISTICS

DENVER NUGGETS

Player	G.	Min.	FGA	FGM	Pct.	FTA	FTM	Pct.	Off. Reb.	Def. Reb.	Tot. Reb.	Ast.	PF	Disq.	Stl.	Blk. Sh.	Pts.	Avg.	Hi.
English	82	3085	1920	965	.503	487	411	.844	146	198	344	422	216	0	73	21	2345	28.6	46
Lever	82	3054	1370	643	.469	312	244	.782	216	513	729	654	219	1	201	34	1552	18.9	36
Hanzlik	73	1990	746	307	.412	402	316	.786	79	177	256	280	245	3	87	28	952	13.0	33
Walker	81	2020	742	358	.482	365	272	.745	157	170	327	282	229	0	120	37	988	12.2	39
Evans	81	1567	729	334	.458	123	96	.780	36	92	128	185	149	1	79	12	817	10.1	27
Natt	1	20	10	4	.400	2	2	1.000	2	3	5	2	2	0	1	0	10	10.0	10
Rasmussen	74	1421	570	268	.470	231	169	.732	183	282	465	60	224	6	24	58	705	9.5	24
Schayes	76	1556	405	210	.519	294	229	.779	120	260	380	85	266	5	20	74	649	8.5	25
Cooper	69	1561	524	235	.448	109	79	.725	162	311	473	68	257	5	13	101	549	8.0	24
Alarie	64	1110	443	217	.490	101	67	.663	73	141	214	74	138	1	22	28	503	7.9	21
Martin	43	286	135	51	.378	66	42	.636	12	29	41	35	48	0	13	6	147	3.4	12
Dunn	81	1932	276	118	.428	55	36	.655	91	174	265	147	160	0	100	21	272	3.4	12
Smith	28	1168	79	33	.418	21	12	.571	17	17	34	22	30	0	1	1	78	2.8	12
Williams	5	10	2	1	.500	0	0	....	0	1	1	1	1	0	0	1	2	0.4	2

3-Pt. FG: Denver 106-391 (.271)—English 4-15 (.267); Lever 22-92 (.239); Hanzlik 22-80 (.275); Walker 0-4 (.000); Evans 53-169 (.314); Cooper 0-3 (.000); Alarie 2-9 (.222); Martin 3-15 (.200); Dunn 0-2 (.000); Smith 0-2 (.000).Opponents 113-361 (.313).

DETROIT PISTONS

Player	G.	Min.	FGA	FGM	Pct.	FTA	FTM	Pct.	Off. Reb.	Def. Reb.	Tot. Reb.	Ast.	PF	Disq.	Stl.	Blk. Sh.	Pts.	Avg.	Hi.
Dantley	81	2736	1126	601	.534	664	539	.812	104	228	332	162	193	1	63	7	1742	21.5	41
Thomas	81	3013	1353	626	.463	521	400	.768	82	237	319	813	251	5	153	20	1671	20.6	36
Johnson	78	2166	1154	533	.462	201	158	.786	123	134	257	300	159	0	92	16	1228	15.7	30
Laimbeer	82	2854	1010	506	.501	274	245	.894	243	712	955	151	283	4	72	69	1263	15.4	30
Dumars	79	2439	749	369	.493	246	184	.748	50	117	167	352	194	1	83	5	931	11.8	24
Green	80	1792	542	256	.472	177	119	.672	196	457	653	62	197	0	41	50	631	7.9	22
Rodman	77	1155	391	213	.545	126	74	.587	163	169	332	56	166	1	38	48	500	6.5	21
Mahorn	63	1278	322	144	.447	117	96	.821	93	282	375	38	221	4	32	50	384	6.1	17
Nimphius (Tot.)	66	1088	330	155	.470	120	81	.675	80	107	187	25	156	1	20	54	391	5.9	22
Nimphius (Det.)	28	277	78	36	.462	32	24	.750	22	32	54	7	38	0	4	13	96	3.4	12
Salley	82	1463	290	163	.562	171	105	.614	108	188	296	54	256	5	44	125	431	5.3	28
Campbell	40	332	145	57	.393	39	24	.615	21	37	58	19	40	0	12	1	138	3.5	17
McQueen	3	7	3	3	1.000	0	0	....	3	5	8	0	1	0	0	1	6	2.0	4
Nevitt	41	267	63	31	.492	24	14	.583	36	47	83	4	73	0	7	30	76	1.9	12
Taylor	12	44	10	6	.600	10	9	.900	1	3	4	3	4	0	2	1	21	1.8	6
Schweitz	3	7	1	0	.000	0	0	....	0	1	1	0	2	0	0	0	0	0.0	0

3-Pt. FG: Detroit 39-169 (.231)—Dantley 1-6 (.167); Thomas 19-98 (.194); Johnson 4-14 (.286); Laimbeer 6-21 (.286); Dumars 9-22 (.409); Green 0-2 (.000); Rodman 0-1 (.000); Nimphius 0-1 (.000); Salley 0-1 (.000); Campbell 0-3 (.000). Opponents 133-419 (.317).

GOLDEN STATE WARRIORS

Player	G.	Min.	FGA	FGM	Pct.	FTA	FTM	Pct.	Off. Reb.	Def. Reb.	Tot. Reb.	Ast.	PF	Disq.	Stl.	Blk. Sh.	Pts.	Avg.	Hi.
Carroll	81	2724	1461	690	.472	432	340	.787	173	416	589	214	255	2	92	123	1720	21.2	43
Floyd	82	3064	1030	503	.488	537	462	.860	56	212	268	848	199	1	146	18	1541	18.8	41
Short	34	950	501	240	.479	160	137	.856	55	82	137	86	103	1	45	7	621	18.3	34
Mullin	82	2377	928	477	.514	326	269	.825	39	142	181	261	217	1	98	36	1242	15.1	32
Teagle	82	1650	808	370	.458	234	182	.778	68	107	175	105	190	0	68	13	922	11.2	28
L. Smith	80	2374	544	297	.546	197	113	.574	366	551	917	95	295	7	71	56	707	8.8	23
Higgins	73	1497	412	214	.519	240	200	.833	72	165	237	96	145	0	40	21	631	8.6	26
Ballard	82	1579	564	248	.440	91	68	.747	99	241	340	108	167	0	50	15	579	7.1	20
McDonald	63	1284	360	164	.456	38	24	.632	63	120	183	84	200	5	27	8	353	5.6	20
Whitehead	73	937	327	147	.450	113	79	.699	110	152	262	24	175	1	16	12	373	5.1	15
Washburn	35	385	145	57	.393	51	18	.353	36	65	101	16	51	0	6	8	132	3.8	17
Moss	64	698	207	91	.440	69	49	.710	29	66	95	90	96	0	42	3	232	3.6	13
C. Smith	41	341	117	50	.427	36	27	.750	26	30	56	45	36	0	13	1	127	3.1	13
Henderson	5	45	8	3	.375	2	2	1.000	1	2	3	11	9	0	1	0	8	1.6	4

3-Pt. FG: Golden State 116-364 (.319)—Floyd 73-190 (.384); Short 4-17 (.235); Mullin 19-63 (.302); Teagle 0-10 (.000); L. Smith 0-1 (.000); Higgins 3-17 (.176); Ballard 15-40 (.375); McDonald 1-8 (.125); Whitehead 0-1 (.000); Washburn 0-1 (.000); Moss 1-14 (.071); C. Smith 0-2 (.000). Opponents 155-460 (.337).

HOUSTON ROCKETS

Player	G.	Min.	FGA	FGM	Pct.	FTA	FTM	Pct.	Off. Reb.	Def. Reb.	Tot. Reb.	Ast.	PF	Disq.	Stl.	Blk. Sh.	Pts.	Avg.	Hi.
Olajuwon	75	2760	1332	677	.508	570	400	.702	315	543	858	220	294	8	140	254	1755	23.4	44
Sampson	43	1326	566	277	.489	189	118	.624	88	284	372	120	169	6	40	58	672	15.6	33
McCray	81	3136	783	432	.552	393	306	.779	190	388	578	434	172	2	88	53	1170	14.4	28
Reid	75	2594	1006	420	.417	177	136	.768	47	242	289	323	232	2	75	21	1029	13.7	30
Lloyd	32	688	310	165	.532	86	65	.756	13	35	48	90	69	0	19	5	396	12.4	26
Petersen	82	2403	755	386	.511	209	152	.727	177	380	557	127	268	5	43	102	924	11.3	28
Wiggins	32	788	350	153	.437	65	49	.754	74	59	133	76	82	1	44	3	355	11.1	30
Maxwell (Tot.)	81	1968	477	253	.530	391	303	.775	175	260	435	197	178	1	39	14	809	10.0	25
Maxwell (Hou.)	46	836	188	100	.548	163	126	.773	72	112	184	75	76	0	13	5	332	7.2	17
Harris	74	1174	599	251	.419	130	111	.854	71	99	170	100	111	1	37	16	613	8.3	22
Leavell	53	1175	358	147	.411	119	100	.840	14	47	61	224	126	1	53	10	412	7.8	21
Minniefield (Tot.)	74	1600	482	218	.452	90	62	.689	29	111	140	348	174	2	72	7	509	6.9	20
Minniefield (Hou.)	63	1478	440	205	.466	86	61	.709	28	102	130	335	166	2	66	6	482	7.7	20
Johnson	60	520	201	94	.468	58	40	.690	38	50	88	40	81	0	17	15	228	3.8	12
Feitl	62	498	202	88	.436	71	53	.746	39	78	117	22	83	0	9	4	229	3.7	17
Anderson	51	312	139	59	.424	29	22	.759	24	55	79	33	37	0	7	3	144	2.8	10
Henry	18	92	33	8	.242	10	7	.700	0	7	7	8	7	0	3	0	24	1.3	5

3-Pt. FG: Houston 89-324 (.275)—Olajuwon 1-5 (.200); Sampson 0-3 (.000); McCray 0-9 (.000); Reid 53-162 (.327); Lloyd 1-7 (.143); Petersen 0-4 (.000); Wiggins 0-5 (.000); Maxwell 0-1 (.000); Harris 0-8 (.000); Leavell 18-57 (.316); Minniefield 11-34 (.324); Johnson 0-1 (.000); Feitl 0-1 (.000); Anderson 4-16 (.250); Henry 1-11 (.091). Opponents 100-355 (.282).

INDIANA PACERS

Player	G.	Min.	FGA	FGM	Pct.	FTA	FTM	Pct.	Off. Reb.	Def. Reb.	Tot. Reb.	Ast.	PF	Disq.	Stl.	Blk. Sh.	Pts.	Avg.	Hi.
Person	82	2956	1358	635	.468	297	222	.747	168	509	677	295	310	4	90	16	1541	18.8	42
Long	80	2265	1170	490	.419	246	219	.890	75	142	217	258	167	1	96	8	1218	15.2	44
Williams	74	2526	939	451	.480	269	199	.740	143	400	543	174	255	9	59	93	1101	14.9	32
Tisdale	81	2159	892	458	.513	364	258	.709	217	258	475	117	293	9	50	26	1174	14.5	35
Stipanovich	81	2761	760	382	.503	367	307	.837	184	486	670	180	304	9	106	97	1072	13.2	30
Fleming	82	2549	727	370	.509	302	238	.788	109	225	334	473	222	3	109	18	980	12.0	24
Richardson	78	1396	467	218	.467	74	59	.797	51	92	143	241	106	0	49	7	501	6.4	22
Anderson	63	721	294	139	.473	108	85	.787	73	78	151	54	65	0	31	3	363	5.8	27
Kellogg	4	60	22	8	.364	4	3	.750	7	4	11	6	12	0	5	0	20	5.0	6
Macy	76	1250	341	164	.481	41	34	.829	25	88	113	197	136	0	59	7	376	4.9	18
Brooks	10	148	37	13	.351	10	7	.700	9	19	28	11	19	0	9	0	33	3.3	10
Russell	48	511	165	64	.388	37	27	.730	18	37	55	129	62	0	20	5	157	3.3	16
Verhoeven	5	44	14	5	.357	0	0	....	2	5	7	2	11	1	2	1	10	2.0	4
Gray	55	456	101	41	.406	39	28	.718	39	90	129	26	93	0	10	28	110	2.0	13
Dreiling	24	128	37	16	.432	12	10	.833	12	31	43	7	42	0	2	2	42	1.8	8

3-Pt. FG: Indiana 94-316 (.297)—Person 49-138 (.355); Long 19-67 (.284); Williams 0-9 (.000); Tisdale 0-2 (.000); Stipanovich 1-4 (.250); Fleming 2-10 (.200); Richardson 6-17 (.353); Anderson 0-5 (.000); Kellogg 1-2 (.500); Macy 14-46 (.304); Russell 2-16 (.125). Opponents 103-345 (.299).

LOS ANGELES CLIPPERS

Player	G.	Min.	FGA	FGM	Pct.	FTA	FTM	Pct.	Off. Reb.	Def. Reb.	Tot. Reb.	Ast.	PF	Disq.	Stl.	Blk. Sh.	Pts.	Avg.	Hi.
Woodson	74	2126	1130	494	.437	290	240	.828	68	94	162	196	201	1	100	16	1262	17.1	37
M. Johnson	10	302	155	68	.439	42	30	.714	9	24	33	28	24	0	12	5	166	16.6	31
Cage	80	2922	878	457	.521	467	341	.730	354	568	922	131	221	1	99	67	1255	15.7	29
Maxwell	35	1132	289	150	.519	228	177	.776	103	148	251	122	102	1	26	9	477	13.6	25
Drew	60	1566	683	295	.432	166	139	.837	26	77	103	326	107	0	60	2	741	12.4	25
Benjamin	72	2230	713	320	.449	263	188	.715	134	452	586	135	251	7	60	187	828	11.5	28
Valentine	65	1759	671	275	.410	200	163	.815	38	112	150	447	148	3	116	10	726	11.2	24
Dailey	49	924	491	200	.407	155	119	.768	34	49	83	79	113	4	43	8	520	10.6	28
White	68	1545	552	265	.480	144	94	.653	90	104	194	79	159	1	47	19	624	9.2	30
Fields (Tot.)	48	883	352	159	.452	94	73	.777	63	85	148	61	123	2	32	11	394	8.2	22
Fields (LAC)	44	861	344	153	.445	89	72	.809	63	83	146	60	120	2	31	11	381	8.7	22
Nimphius	38	811	252	119	.472	88	57	.648	58	75	133	18	118	1	16	41	295	7.8	22
Gordon	70	1130	545	221	.406	95	70	.737	64	62	126	139	106	1	61	13	526	7.5	33
Cureton (Tot.)	78	1973	510	243	.476	152	82	.539	212	240	452	122	188	2	33	56	568	7.3	23
Cureton (LAC)	35	868	234	114	.487	79	43	.544	99	126	225	52	86	0	18	30	271	7.7	23
Huston	19	428	121	55	.455	34	18	.529	6	11	17	101	28	0	14	0	129	6.8	17
Kempton	66	936	206	97	.471	137	95	.693	70	124	194	53	162	6	38	12	289	4.4	18
S. Johnson	29	234	64	27	.422	38	20	.526	15	28	43	5	55	2	9	2	74	2.6	9
Polee	1	6	4	1	.250	0	0	....	0	0	0	3	0	1	0	2	2	2.0	2

3-Pt. FG: L.A. Clippers 78-348 (.224)—Woodson 34-123 (.276); M. Johnson 0-6 (.000); Cage 0-3 (.000); Drew 12-72 (.167); Benjamin 0-2 (.000); Valentine 13-56 (.232); Dailey 1-10 (.100); White 0-3 (.000); Fields 3-12 (.250); Nimphius 0-3 (.000); Gordon 14-48 (.292); Cureton 0-1 (.000); Huston 1-2 (.500); Kempton 0-1 (.000); S. Johnson 0-3 (.000); Polee 0-3 (.000). Opponents 110-320 (.344).

LOS ANGELES LAKERS

Player	G.	Min.	FGA	FGM	Pct.	FTA	FTM	Pct.	Off. Reb.	Def. Reb.	Tot. Reb.	Ast.	PF	Disq.	Stl.	Blk. Sh.	Pts.	Avg.	Hi.
Johnson	80	2904	1308	683	.522	631	535	.848	122	382	504	977	168	0	138	36	1909	23.9	46
Worthy	82	2819	1207	651	.539	389	292	.751	158	308	466	226	206	0	108	83	1594	19.4	31
Abdul-Jabbar	78	2441	993	560	.564	343	245	.714	152	371	523	203	245	2	49	97	1366	17.5	30
Scott	82	2729	1134	554	.489	251	224	.892	63	223	286	281	163	0	125	18	1397	17.0	33
M. Th'mpsn (To.)	82	1890	797	359	.450	297	219	.737	138	274	412	115	202	1	45	71	938	11.4	29
M. Th'mpsn (LA)	33	680	269	129	.480	101	75	.743	47	89	136	28	85	1	14	30	333	10.1	24
Green	79	2240	587	316	.538	282	220	.780	210	405	615	84	171	0	70	80	852	10.8	26
Cooper	82	2253	736	322	.438	148	126	.851	58	196	254	373	199	1	78	43	859	10.5	24
Rambis	78	1514	313	163	.521	157	120	.764	159	294	453	63	201	1	74	41	446	5.7	16
B. Thompson	59	762	261	142	.544	74	48	.649	69	102	171	60	148	1	15	30	332	5.6	13
Branch	32	219	96	48	.500	54	42	.778	23	30	53	16	39	0	16	3	138	4.3	12
Matthews	50	532	187	89	.476	36	29	.806	13	34	47	100	53	0	23	4	208	4.2	16
Brickowski	37	404	94	53	.564	59	40	.678	40	57	97	12	105	4	14	4	146	3.9	14
Smrek	35	233	60	30	.500	25	16	.640	13	24	37	5	70	1	4	13	76	2.2	8

3-Pt. FG: L.A. Lakers 164-447 (.367)—Johnson 8-39 (.205); Worthy 0-13 (.000); Abdul-Jabbar 1-3 (.333); Scott 65-149 (.436); M. Thompson 0-1 (.000); Green 0-5 (.000); Cooper 89-231 (.385); B. Thompson 0-1 (.000); Branch 0-2 (.000); Matthews 1-3 (.333). Opponents 122-431 (.283).

MILWAUKEE BUCKS

Player	G.	Min.	FGA	FGM	Pct.	FTA	FTM	Pct.	Off. Reb.	Def. Reb.	Tot. Reb.	Ast.	PF	Disq.	Stl.	Blk. Sh.	Pts.	Avg.	Hi.
Cummings	82	2770	1426	729	.511	376	249	.662	214	486	700	229	296	3	129	81	1707	20.8	39
Pierce	79	2505	1077	575	.534	440	387	.880	117	149	266	144	222	0	64	24	1540	19.5	32
Lucas	43	1358	624	285	.457	174	137	.787	29	96	125	290	82	0	71	6	753	17.5	29
Pressey	61	2057	616	294	.477	328	242	.738	98	198	296	441	213	4	110	47	846	13.9	27
Sikma	82	2536	842	390	.463	313	265	.847	208	614	822	203	328	14	88	90	1045	12.7	28
Moncrief	39	992	324	158	.488	162	136	.840	57	70	127	121	73	0	27	10	460	11.8	26
Hodges	78	2147	682	315	.462	147	131	.891	48	92	140	240	189	3	76	7	846	10.8	27
Breuer	76	1467	497	241	.485	202	118	.584	129	221	350	47	229	9	56	61	600	7.9	19
Reynolds	58	963	356	140	.393	184	118	.641	72	101	173	106	91	0	50	30	404	7.0	26
Bridgeman	34	418	171	79	.462	20	16	.800	14	38	52	35	50	0	10	2	175	5.1	12
Collins	6	57	28	10	.357	7	5	.714	11	4	15	2	11	0	2	1	25	4.2	11
Skiles	13	205	62	18	.290	12	10	.833	6	20	26	45	18	0	5	1	49	3.8	14
Glenn	4	34	13	5	.385	7	5	.714	0	2	2	1	3	0	1	0	15	3.8	9
Smith	42	461	150	57	.380	28	21	.750	13	19	32	43	74	0	25	3	138	3.3	15
Fields	4	22	8	6	.750	5	1	.200	0	2	2	1	3	0	1	0	13	3.3	6
McDowell	7	70	17	8	.471	7	6	.857	9	10	19	2	14	0	2	0	22	3.1	8
Bradley	68	900	213	76	.357	58	47	.810	11	71	102	66	118	2	105	8	212	3.1	12
Mokeski	62	626	129	52	.403	64	46	.719	45	93	138	22	126	0	18	13	150	2.4	11
J. Henderson	6	36	13	4	.308	4	4	1.000	2	5	7	0	12	0	1	1	12	2.0	4

Player	G.	Min.	FGA	FGM	Pct.	FTA	FTM	Pct.	Off. Reb.	Def. Reb.	Tot. Reb.	Ast.	PF	Disq.	Stl.	Blk. Sh.	Pts.	Avg.	Hi.
Webster	15	102	19	10	.526	8	6	.750	12	14	26	3	17	0	3	7	27	1.8	11
Engler	5	48	12	3	.250	1	1	1.000	3	13	16	3	10	0	1	1	7	1.4	5
C. H'ndrsn (To.)	8	16	8	4	.500	3	3	1.000	3	5	8	0	2	0	0	0	11	1.4	4
C. H'ndrsn (Mil.)	2	6	3	2	.667	2	2	1.000	1	4	5	0	1	0	0	0	6	3.0	4

3-Pt. FG: Milwaukee 185-572 (.323)—Cummings 0-3 (.000); Pierce 3-28 (.107); Lucas 46-126 (.365); Pressey 16-55 (.291); Sikma 0-2 (.000); Moncrief 8-31 (.258); Hodges 85-228 (.373); Reynolds 6-18 (.333); Bridgeman 1-6 (.167); Skiles 3-14 (.214); Smith 3-9 (.333); Bradley 13-50 (.260); Mokeski 0-1 (.000); Webster 1-1 (1.000). Opponents 120-415 (.289).

NEW JERSEY NETS

Player	G.	Min.	FGA	FGM	Pct.	FTA	FTM	Pct.	Off. Reb.	Def. Reb.	Tot. Reb.	Ast.	PF	Disq.	Stl.	Blk. Sh.	Pts.	Avg.	Hi.
Woolridge	75	2638	1067	556	.521	564	438	.777	118	249	367	261	243	4	54	86	1551	20.7	38
B. Williams	82	2976	936	521	.557	588	430	.731	322	701	1023	129	315	8	78	91	1472	18.0	35
Gminski	72	2272	947	433	.457	370	313	.846	192	438	630	99	159	0	52	69	1179	16.4	30
Brown	77	2339	810	358	.442	206	152	.738	84	135	219	259	273	12	89	14	873	11.3	29
R. Williams	32	800	290	131	.452	60	49	.817	26	49	75	185	111	4	38	9	318	9.9	25
King	61	1291	573	244	.426	100	81	.810	82	132	214	103	177	5	34	28	582	9.5	22
Dawkins	6	106	32	20	.625	24	17	.708	9	10	19	2	25	0	2	3	57	9.5	14
Washington	72	1600	538	257	.478	125	98	.784	37	92	129	301	184	5	92	7	616	8.6	29
Bailey	34	542	239	112	.469	80	58	.725	48	89	137	20	119	5	12	23	282	8.3	35
Wood	76	1733	501	187	.373	154	123	.799	23	97	120	370	126	0	48	3	557	7.3	22
McKenna	56	942	337	153	.454	57	43	.754	21	56	77	93	141	0	54	7	401	7.2	20
Coleman	68	1029	313	182	.581	121	88	.727	99	189	288	37	200	7	32	31	452	6.6	19
Birdsong	7	127	42	19	.452	9	6	.667	3	4	7	17	16	0	3	0	44	6.3	17
Turner	76	1003	325	151	.465	104	76	.731	80	117	197	60	200	6	33	13	378	5.0	17
Mannion	23	284	94	31	.330	31	18	.581	10	29	39	45	32	0	18	4	83	3.6	25
Engler (Tot.)	30	195	51	23	.451	16	12	.750	23	34	57	8	33	0	5	11	58	1.9	9
Engler (NJ)	18	130	31	16	.516	12	8	.667	14	19	33	4	23	0	3	9	40	2.2	9
Wilson	5	43	8	3	.375	2	2	1.000	1	3	4	6	9	0	1	0	8	1.6	4

3-Pt. FG: New Jersey 145-449 (.323)—Woolridge 1-8 (.125); B. Williams 0-1 (.000); Brown 5-20 (.250); R. Williams 7-28 (.250); King 13-32 (.406); Washington 4-24 (.167); Wood 60-200 (.300); McKenna 52-124 (.419); Coleman 0-1 (.000); Birdsong 0-1 (.000); Turner 0-1 (.000); Mannion 3-9 (.333). Opponents 118-366 (.322).

NEW YORK KNICKERBOCKERS

Player	G.	Min.	FGA	FGM	Pct.	FTA	FTM	Pct.	Off. Reb.	Def. Reb.	Tot. Reb.	Ast.	PF	Disq.	Stl.	Blk. Sh.	Pts.	Avg.	Hi.
King	6	214	105	52	.495	43	32	.744	13	19	32	19	14	0	2	0	136	22.7	31
Ewing	63	2206	1053	530	.503	415	296	.713	157	398	555	104	248	5	89	147	1356	21.5	43
G. Wilkins	80	2758	1302	633	.486	335	235	.701	120	174	294	354	165	0	88	18	1527	19.1	43
Cartwright	58	1989	631	335	.531	438	346	.790	132	313	445	96	188	2	40	26	1016	17.5	32
Tucker	70	1691	691	325	.470	101	77	.762	49	86	135	166	169	1	116	13	795	11.4	34
Henderson (Tot.)	74	2045	674	298	.442	230	190	.826	50	125	175	471	208	1	101	11	805	10.9	24
Henderson (N.Y.)	68	1890	624	273	.438	212	173	.816	44	122	166	439	191	1	95	11	738	10.9	24
Walker	68	1719	581	285	.491	185	140	.757	118	220	338	75	236	7	49	49	710	10.4	26
Cummings	49	1056	382	172	.450	110	79	.718	123	189	312	38	145	2	26	7	423	8.6	21
Sparrow	80	1951	590	263	.446	89	71	.798	29	86	115	432	160	0	67	6	608	7.6	24
Orr	65	1440	389	166	.427	172	125	.727	102	130	232	110	123	0	47	18	458	7.0	28
E. Wilkins	24	454	127	56	.441	58	27	.466	45	62	107	6	67	1	9	2	139	5.8	14
Oldham	44	776	174	71	.408	57	31	.544	51	128	179	19	95	1	22	71	173	3.9	13
McNealy	59	972	179	88	.492	80	52	.650	74	153	227	46	136	1	36	16	228	3.9	14
Wright	14	138	46	20	.435	28	12	.429	25	28	53	1	20	0	3	6	52	3.7	13
Granger	15	166	54	20	.370	11	9	.818	6	11	17	27	17	0	7	1	49	3.3	10
Martin	8	68	25	9	.360	8	7	.875	2	5	7	0	5	0	4	2	25	3.1	6
Thornton	33	282	67	29	.433	20	13	.650	18	38	56	8	48	0	4	3	71	2.2	11
Singleton	2	10	3	2	.667	0	0		0	0	0	1	1	0	0	0	4	2.0	2

3-Pt. FG: New York 125-375 (.333)—Ewing 0-7 (.000); G. Wilkins 26-74 (.351); Tucker 68-161 (.422); Henderson 19-74 (.257); Walker 0-4 (.000); Sparrow 11-42 (.262); Orr 1-5 (.200); E. Wilkins 0-1 (.000); Oldham 0-1 (.000); Wright 0-1 (.000); Granger 0-3 (.000); Thornton 0-1 (.000); Singleton 0-1 (.000). Opponents 94-358 (.263).

PHILADELPHIA 76ers

Player	G.	Min.	FGA	FGM	Pct.	FTA	FTM	Pct.	Off. Reb.	Def. Reb.	Tot. Reb.	Ast.	PF	Disq.	Stl.	Blk. Sh.	Pts.	Avg.	Hi.
Barkley	68	2740	937	557	.594	564	429	.761	390	604	994	331	252	5	119	104	1564	23.0	41
Erving	60	1918	850	400	.471	235	191	.813	115	149	264	191	137	0	76	94	1005	16.8	38
Cheeks	68	2624	788	415	.527	292	227	.777	47	168	215	538	109	0	180	15	1061	15.6	31
Robinson	55	1586	729	338	.464	184	139	.755	86	221	307	89	150	1	86	30	815	14.8	35
Hinson	76	2489	823	393	.478	360	273	.758	150	338	488	60	281	4	45	161	1059	13.9	28
McCormick	81	2817	718	391	.545	349	251	.719	180	431	611	114	270	4	36	64	1033	12.8	27
Toney	52	1058	437	197	.451	167	133	.796	16	69	85	188	78	0	18	8	549	10.6	32
Threatt	28	668	261	108	.414	53	42	.792	18	39	57	82	76	0	32	4	265	9.5	27
Ruland	5	116	28	19	.679	12	9	.750	12	16	28	10	13	0	4	4	47	9.4	19
Wingate	77	1612	602	259	.430	201	149	.741	70	86	156	155	169	1	93	19	680	8.8	28
Colter (Tot.)	70	1322	397	169	.426	107	82	.766	23	85	108	210	99	0	56	12	424	6.1	22
Colter (Phil.)	43	849	255	120	.471	68	49	.721	14	52	66	116	61	0	37	6	293	6.8	22
Free	20	285	123	39	.317	47	36	.766	5	14	19	30	26	0	5	4	116	5.8	12
Green	19	172	70	25	.357	19	14	.737	6	22	28	7	8	0	4	2	64	3.4	12
McNamara	11	113	30	14	.467	19	7	.368	17	19	36	2	17	0	1	0	35	3.2	10
Lampley	1	16	3	1	.333	2	1	.500	1	4	5	0	0	0	1	0	3	3.0	3
Vranes	58	817	138	59	.428	45	21	.467	51	95	146	30	127	0	35	25	140	2.4	10

3-Pt. FG: Philadelphia 88-340 (.259)—Barkley 21-104 (.202); Erving 14-53 (.264); Cheeks 4-17 (.235); Robinson 0-4 (.000); Hinson 0-1 (.000); McCormick 0-4 (.000); Toney 22-67 (.328); Threatt 7-16 (.438); Wingate 13-52 (.250); Colter 4-8 (.500); Free 2-9 (.222); Vranes 1-5 (.200). Opponents 119-416 (.286).

PHOENIX SUNS

Player	G.	Min.	FGA	FGM	Pct.	FTA	FTM	Pct.	Off. Reb.	Def. Reb.	Tot. Reb.	Ast.	PF	Disq.	Stl.	Blk. Sh.	Pts.	Avg.	Hi.
Davis	79	2646	1515	779	.514	334	288	.862	90	154	244	364	184	1	96	5	1867	23.6	45
Nance	69	2569	1062	585	.551	493	381	.773	188	411	599	233	223	4	86	148	1552	22.5	35

Player	G.	Min.	FGA	FGM	Pct.	FTA	FTM	Pct.	Off. Reb.	Def. Reb.	Tot. Reb.	Ast.	PF	Disq.	Stl.	Blk. Sh.	Pts.	Avg.	Hi.
Edwards	14	304	110	57	.518	70	54	.771	20	40	60	19	42	1	6	7	168	12.0	16
Humphries	82	2579	753	359	.477	260	200	.769	62	198	260	632	239	1	112	9	923	11.3	30
Adams	68	1690	618	311	.503	170	134	.788	91	247	338	223	207	3	62	37	756	11.1	25
Sanders	82	1655	722	357	.494	183	143	.781	101	170	271	126	210	1	61	23	859	10.5	23
Pinckney	80	2250	497	290	.584	348	257	.739	179	401	580	116	196	1	86	54	837	10.5	23
Bedford	50	979	358	142	.397	86	50	.581	79	167	246	57	125	1	18	37	334	6.7	17
Addison	62	711	331	146	.441	64	51	.797	41	65	106	45	75	1	27	7	359	5.8	22
Gondrezick	64	836	300	135	.450	107	75	.701	47	63	110	81	91	0	25	4	349	5.5	14
Hornacek	80	1561	350	159	.454	121	94	.777	41	143	184	361	130	0	70	5	424	5.3	14
Gattison	77	1104	311	148	.476	171	108	.632	87	183	270	36	178	1	24	33	404	5.2	29
Thompson	24	331	105	42	.400	33	27	.818	20	11	31	18	53	0	11	5	111	4.6	16
Vanos	57	640	158	65	.411	59	38	.644	67	113	180	43	94	0	19	23	168	2.9	14

3-Pt. FG: Phoenix 61-252 (.242)—Davis 21-81 (.259); Nance 1-5 (.200); Humphries 5-27 (.185); Adams 0-1 (.000); Sanders 2-17 (.118); Pinckney 0-2 (.000); Bedford 0-1 (.000); Addison 16-50 (.320); Gondrezick 4-17 (.235); Hornacek 12-43 (.279); Gattison 0-3 (.000); Thompson 0-3 (.000); Vanos 0-2 (.000). Opponents 123-395 (.311).

PORTLAND TRAIL BLAZERS

Player	G.	Min.	FGA	FGM	Pct.	FTA	FTM	Pct.	Off. Reb.	Def. Reb.	Tot. Reb.	Ast.	PF	Disq.	Stl.	Blk. Sh.	Pts.	Avg.	Hi.
Vandeweghe	79	3029	1545	808	.523	527	467	.886	86	165	251	220	137	0	52	17	2122	26.9	48
Drexler	82	3114	1408	707	.502	470	357	.760	227	291	518	566	281	7	204	71	1782	21.7	36
Johnson	79	2345	889	494	.556	490	342	.698	194	372	566	155	340	16	49	76	1330	16.8	40
Bowie	5	163	66	30	.455	30	20	.667	14	19	33	9	19	0	1	10	80	16.0	31
Porter	80	2714	770	376	.488	334	280	.838	70	267	337	715	192	0	159	9	1045	13.1	24
Kersey	82	2088	733	373	.509	364	262	.720	201	295	496	194	328	5	122	77	1009	12.3	28
Paxson	72	1798	733	337	.460	216	174	.806	41	98	139	237	134	0	76	12	874	12.1	22
Carr	49	1443	399	201	.504	169	126	.746	131	368	499	83	159	1	29	13	528	10.8	20
Duckworth (Tot.)	65	875	273	130	.476	134	92	.687	76	147	223	29	192	3	21	21	352	5.4	18
Duckworth (Port.)	51	753	228	112	.491	120	83	.692	63	129	192	23	165	3	16	18	307	6.0	18
Jones	78	1578	224	111	.496	124	97	.782	114	341	455	64	227	5	23	77	319	4.1	15
Holton	58	479	171	70	.409	55	44	.800	9	29	38	73	51	0	16	2	191	3.3	16
Berry	7	19	8	6	.750	1	1	1.000	4	3	7	1	8	0	2	0	13	1.9	7
Rowan	7	16	9	4	.444	4	3	.750	1	0	1	1	0	4	0	1	12	1.7	4
Engler	7	17	8	4	.500	3	3	1.000	6	2	8	1	0	0	1	1	11	1.6	6
Young (Tot.)	9	72	21	6	.286	2	1	.500	3	5	8	7	14	0	5	1	13	1.4	3
Young (Port.)	4	52	17	4	.235	0	0	....	3	4	7	7	11	0	4	1	8	2.0	2
Binion	11	51	10	4	.400	10	6	.600	8	10	18	1	5	0	2	2	14	1.3	5
Martin	24	146	31	9	.290	11	4	.364	8	20	28	9	24	0	7	1	22	0.9	6

3-Pt. FG: Portland 98-339 (.289)—Vandeweghe 39-81 (.481); Drexler 11-47 (.234); Porter 13-60 (.217); Kersey 1-23 (.043); Paxson 26-98 (.265); Carr 0-2 (.000); Duckworth 0-1 (.000); Jones 0-2 (.000); Holton 7-23 (.304); Rowan 1-1 (1.000); Martin 0-1 (.000). Opponents 116-421 (.276).

SACRAMENTO KINGS

Player	G.	Min.	FGA	FGM	Pct.	FTA	FTM	Pct.	Off. Reb.	Def. Reb.	Tot. Reb.	Ast.	PF	Disq.	Stl.	Blk. Sh.	Pts.	Avg.	Hi.
Theus	79	2872	1223	577	.472	495	429	.867	86	180	266	692	208	3	78	16	1600	20.3	33
Thorpe	82	2956	1050	567	.540	543	413	.761	259	560	819	201	292	11	46	60	1547	18.9	34
Johnson	81	2457	1309	606	.463	322	267	.829	146	207	353	251	218	4	42	19	1516	18.7	38
Smith	52	1658	757	338	.447	228	178	.781	60	122	182	204	184	3	46	23	863	16.6	31
Thompson	82	2166	752	362	.481	255	188	.737	237	450	687	122	290	6	69	126	912	11.1	27
Tyler	82	1930	664	329	.495	140	101	.721	116	212	328	73	151	1	55	78	760	9.3	23
Kleine	79	1658	543	256	.471	140	110	.786	173	310	483	71	213	2	35	30	622	7.9	22
Steppe	34	665	199	95	.477	88	73	.830	21	40	61	81	56	0	18	3	266	7.8	24
Pressley	67	913	317	134	.423	48	35	.729	68	108	176	120	96	1	40	21	310	4.6	19
Rogers	45	468	185	90	.486	15	9	.600	30	47	77	26	66	0	9	8	189	4.2	14
Wilson	53	789	185	82	.443	54	43	.796	28	53	81	207	67	0	42	4	210	4.0	12
Edwards	8	122	32	9	.281	14	10	.714	2	8	10	29	7	0	5	0	28	3.5	10
Olberding	76	1002	165	69	.418	131	116	.885	50	135	185	91	144	0	18	9	254	3.3	21
Douglas	8	98	24	7	.292	4	0	.000	5	9	14	17	9	0	9	0	14	1.8	6
Eaves	3	26	8	1	.125	2	2	1.000	0	1	1	0	6	0	1	0	4	1.3	4

3-Pt. FG: Sacramento 77-307 (.251)—Theus 17-78 (.218); Thorpe 0-3 (.000); Johnson 37-118 (.314); Smith 9-33 (.273); Thompson 0-5 (.000); Tyler 1-3 (.333); Kleine 0-1 (.000); Steppe 3-9 (.333); Pressley 7-28 (.250); Rogers 0-5 (.000); Wilson 3-18 (.167); Edwards 0-4 (.000); Olberding 0-1 (.000); Douglas 0-1 (.000). Opponents 125-395 (.316).

SAN ANTONIO SPURS

Player	G.	Min.	FGA	FGM	Pct.	FTA	FTM	Pct.	Off. Reb.	Def. Reb.	Tot. Reb.	Ast.	PF	Disq.	Stl.	Blk. Sh.	Pts.	Avg.	Hi.
Robertson	81	2697	1264	589	.466	324	244	.753	186	238	424	421	264	2	260	35	1435	17.7	34
Berry (Tot.)	63	1586	766	407	.531	288	187	.649	136	173	309	105	196	2	38	40	1001	15.9	29
Berry (SA)	56	1567	758	401	.529	287	186	.648	132	170	302	104	188	2	36	40	988	17.6	29
Mitchell	40	922	478	208	.435	112	92	.821	38	65	103	38	68	0	19	9	509	12.7	34
Thompson	49	1210	528	230	.436	196	144	.735	91	185	276	87	117	0	31	41	605	12.3	29
Greenwood	79	2587	655	336	.513	307	241	.785	256	527	783	237	248	3	71	50	916	11.6	31
Gilmore	82	2405	580	346	.597	356	242	.680	185	394	579	150	235	2	39	95	934	11.4	24
Sundvold	76	1765	751	365	.486	84	70	.833	20	78	98	315	109	1	35	0	850	11.2	25
Dawkins	81	1682	764	334	.437	191	153	.801	56	113	169	290	118	0	67	3	835	10.3	28
Corbin	31	732	264	113	.428	67	49	.731	52	67	119	80	81	0	38	3	275	8.9	23
Moore	55	1234	448	198	.442	70	56	.800	32	68	100	250	97	0	83	3	474	8.6	25
Krystkowiak	68	1004	373	170	.456	148	110	.743	77	162	239	85	141	1	22	12	451	6.6	24
Jones (Tot.)	65	858	322	133	.413	65	50	.769	40	64	104	73	79	0	42	19	323	5.0	24
Jones (SA)	49	744	289	119	.412	52	41	.788	39	56	95	66	68	0	32	18	286	5.8	24
Brickowski (Tot.)	44	487	124	63	.508	70	50	.714	48	68	116	17	118	4	20	6	176	4.0	14
Brickowski (SA)	7	83	30	10	.333	11	10	.909	8	11	19	5	13	0	6	2	30	4.3	11
Nealy	60	980	192	84	.438	69	51	.739	96	188	284	83	144	1	40	11	223	3.7	23
Duckworth	14	122	45	18	.400	14	9	.643	13	18	31	6	27	0	5	3	45	3.2	11
McKenzie	6	42	28	7	.250	2	2	1.000	2	5	7	1	9	0	1	0	17	2.8	8
Brittain	6			4			2	1	.500	2	2	4		9	0		1	9	1.5	5

3-Pt. FG: San Antonio 117-403 (.290)—Robertson 13-48 (.271); Berry 0-3 (.000); Mitchell 1-2 (.500); Thompson 1-1 (1.000); Greenwood 3-6 (.500); Sundvold 50-149 (.336); Dawkins 14-47 (.298); Moore 22-79 (.278); Krystkowiak 1-12 (.083); Jones 7-19 (.368); Brickowski 0-4 (.000); Nealy 4-31 (.129); McKenzie 1-2 (.500). Opponents 106-379 (.280).

1986-87 STATISTICS
SEATTLE SUPERSONICS

Player	G.	Min.	FGA	FGM	Pct.	FTA	FTM	Pct.	Off. Reb.	Def. Reb.	Tot. Reb.	Ast.	PF	Disq.	Stl.	Blk. Sh.	Pts.	Avg.	Hi.
Ellis	82	3073	1520	785	.516	489	385	.787	187	260	447	238	267	2	104	32	2041	24.9	41
Chambers	82	3018	1446	660	.456	630	535	.849	163	382	545	245	307	9	81	50	1909	23.3	42
McDaniel	82	3031	1583	806	.509	395	275	.696	338	367	705	207	300	4	115	52	1890	23.0	40
Lister	75	2288	687	346	.504	265	179	.675	223	482	705	110	289	11	32	180	871	11.6	25
Henderson	6	155	50	25	.500	18	17	.944	6	3	9	32	17	0	6	0	67	11.2	14
E. Johnson	24	508	186	85	.457	55	42	.764	11	35	46	115	36	0	12	1	217	9.0	22
Lucas	63	1120	388	175	.451	187	150	.802	88	219	307	65	171	1	34	21	500	7.9	22
McMillan	71	1972	301	143	.475	141	87	.617	101	230	331	583	238	4	125	45	373	5.3	15
Williams	65	703	296	132	.446	66	55	.833	47	36	83	66	154	1	45	8	319	4.9	15
Young	73	1482	288	132	.458	71	59	.831	23	90	113	353	72	0	74	3	352	4.8	17
Stansbury	44	375	156	67	.429	50	31	.620	8	16	24	57	78	0	13	0	176	4.0	16
C. Johnson	78	1051	178	88	.494	110	70	.636	106	171	277	21	137	0	21	42	246	3.2	12
Phelps	60	469	176	75	.426	44	31	.705	16	34	50	64	60	0	21	2	182	3.0	13
Schoene	63	579	190	71	.374	46	29	.630	52	65	117	27	94	1	20	11	173	2.7	15
Kitchen	6	31	6	3	.500	4	3	.750	4	5	9	1	4	0	2	3	9	1.5	5

3-Pt. FG: Seattle 191-571 (.335)—Ellis 86-240 (.358); Chambers 54-145 (.372); McDaniel 3-14 (.214); Lister 0-1 (.000); Henderson 0-3 (.000); E. Johnson 5-15 (.333); Lucas 0-5 (.000); McMillan 0-7 (.000); Williams 0-7 (.000); Young 29-79 (.367); Stansbury 11-29 (.379); C. Johnson 0-2 (.000); Phelps 1-10 (.100); Schoene 2-13 (.154); Kitchen 0-1 (.000). Opponents 93-324 (.287).

UTAH JAZZ

Player	G.	Min.	FGA	FGM	Pct.	FTA	FTM	Pct.	Off. Reb.	Def. Reb.	Tot. Reb.	Ast.	PF	Disq.	Stl.	Blk. Sh.	Pts.	Avg.	Hi.
Malone	82	2857	1422	728	.512	540	323	.598	278	577	855	158	323	6	104	60	1779	21.7	38
Griffith	76	1843	1038	463	.446	212	149	.703	81	146	227	129	167	0	97	29	1142	15.0	38
Bailey	81	2155	1036	463	.447	236	190	.805	145	287	432	102	150	0	38	88	1116	13.8	29
Tripucka	79	1865	621	291	.469	226	197	.872	54	188	242	243	147	0	85	11	798	10.1	27
Hansen	72	1453	601	272	.453	179	136	.760	84	119	203	102	146	0	44	6	696	9.7	26
Green	81	2090	644	301	.467	208	172	.827	38	125	163	541	108	0	110	2	781	9.6	24
Stockton	82	1858	463	231	.499	229	179	.782	32	119	151	670	224	1	177	14	648	7.9	21
Eaton	79	2505	585	234	.400	213	140	.657	211	486	697	105	273	5	43	321	608	7.7	17
Scurry	69	753	247	123	.498	134	94	.701	97	101	198	57	124	1	55	54	344	5.0	21
Curry	67	636	326	139	.426	38	30	.789	30	48	78	58	86	0	27	4	325	4.9	20
Benson	73	895	316	140	.443	58	47	.810	80	151	231	39	138	0	39	28	329	4.5	17
Iavaroni	78	845	215	100	.465	116	78	.672	64	109	173	36	154	0	16	11	278	3.6	13

3-Pt. FG: Utah 139-448 (.310)—Malone 0-7 (.000); Griffith 67-200 (.335); Bailey 0-2 (.000); Tripucka 19-52 (.365); Hansen 16-45 (.356); Green 7-19 (.368); Stockton 7-39 (.179); Scurry 4-13 (.308); Curry 17-60 (.283); Benson 2-7 (.286); Iavaroni 0-4 (.000). Opponents 143-451 (.317).

WASHINGTON BULLETS

Player	G.	Min.	FGA	FGM	Pct.	FTA	FTM	Pct.	Off. Reb.	Def. Reb.	Tot. Reb.	Ast.	PF	Disq.	Stl.	Blk. Sh.	Pts.	Avg.	Hi.
M. Malone	73	2488	1311	595	.454	692	570	.824	340	484	824	120	139	0	59	92	1760	24.1	50
J. Malone	80	2763	1509	689	.457	425	376	.885	50	168	218	298	154	0	75	13	1758	22.0	48
Vincent	51	1386	613	274	.447	169	130	.769	69	141	210	85	127	0	40	17	678	13.3	33
Catledge	78	2149	835	413	.495	335	199	.594	248	312	560	56	195	1	43	14	1025	13.1	32
Williams	78	1773	624	283	.454	223	144	.646	130	236	366	191	173	1	128	30	718	9.2	21
Johnson	18	399	128	59	.461	49	35	.714	10	20	30	58	31	0	21	0	153	8.5	18
Whatley	73	1816	515	246	.478	165	126	.764	58	136	194	392	172	0	92	10	618	8.5	20
Cook	82	1420	622	265	.426	103	82	.796	46	99	145	151	136	0	98	17	614	7.5	24
Adams	63	1303	393	160	.407	124	105	.847	38	85	123	244	88	0	86	6	453	7.2	17
Roundfield	36	669	220	90	.409	72	57	.792	64	106	170	39	77	0	11	16	238	6.6	22
C. Jones	79	1609	249	118	.474	76	48	.632	144	212	356	80	252	2	67	165	284	3.6	12
Murphy	21	141	72	31	.431	16	9	.563	17	22	39	5	21	0	3	2	71	3.4	8
Bol	82	1552	231	103	.446	67	45	.672	84	278	362	11	189	1	20	302	251	3.1	10
A. Jones	16	114	33	14	.424	13	9	.692	1	8	9	7	11	0	10	1	37	2.3	12
O'Koren	15	123	42	16	.381	2	0	.000	6	8	14	13	10	0	2	0	32	2.1	8

3-Pt. FG: Washington 43-218 (.197)—M. Malone 0-11 (.000); J. Malone 4-26 (.154); Vincent 0-3 (.000); Catledge 0-4 (.000); Williams 8-36 (.222); Johnson 0-1 (.000); Whatley 0-2 (.000); Cook 2-23 (.087); Adams 28-102 (.275); Roundfield 1-5 (.200); C. Jones 0-1 (.000); Bol 0-1 (.000); A. Jones 0-1 (.000); O'Koren 0-2 (.000). Opponents 104-358 (.291).

PLAYOFF RESULTS

EASTERN CONFERENCE FIRST ROUND
Boston 3, Chicago 0
Apr. 23—Thur.—Chicago 104 at Boston..................................108
Apr. 26—Sun.—Chicago 96 at Boston....................................105
Apr. 28—Tue.—Boston 105 at Chicago....................................94

Milwaukee 3, Philadelphia 2
Apr. 24—Fri.—Philadelphia 104 at Milwaukee............................107
Apr. 26—Sun.—Philadelphia 125 at Milwaukee.........................*122
Apr. 29—Wed.—Milwaukee 121 at Philadelphia..........................120
May 1—Fri.—Milwaukee 118 at Philadelphia..............................124
May 3—Sun.—Philadelphia 89 at Milwaukee.............................102

Detroit 3, Washington 0
Apr. 24—Fri.—Washington 92 at Detroit....................................106
Apr. 26—Sun.—Washington 85 at Detroit..................................128
Apr. 29—Wed.—Detroit 97 at Washington...................................96

Atlanta 3, Indiana 1
Apr. 24—Fri.—Indiana 94 at Atlanta...110
Apr. 26—Sun.—Indiana 93 at Atlanta...94
Apr. 29—Wed.—Atlanta 87 at Indiana..96
May 1—Fri.—Atlanta 101 at Indiana..97

EASTERN CONFERENCE SEMIFINALS
Detroit 4, Atlanta 1
May 3—Sun.—Detroit 112 at Atlanta.......................................111
May 5—Tue.—Detroit 102 at Atlanta.......................................115
May 8—Fri.—Atlanta 99 at Detroit..108
May 10—Sun.—Atlanta 88 at Detroit..89
May 13—Wed.—Detroit 104 at Atlanta.......................................96

Boston 4, Milwaukee 3
May 5—Tue.—Milwaukee 98 at Boston....................................111
May 6—Wed.—Milwaukee 124 at Boston...................................126
May 8—Fri.—Boston 121 at Milwaukee...................................*126
May 10—Sun.—Milwaukee 138 at Milwaukee...........................**137
May 13—Wed.—Milwaukee 129 at Boston...................................124
May 15—Fri.—Boston 111 at Milwaukee....................................121
May 17—Sun.—Milwaukee 113 at Boston....................................119

EASTERN CONFERENCE FINALS
Boston 4, Detroit 3
May 19—Tue.—Detroit 91 at Boston...104
May 21—Thur.—Detroit 101 at Boston.......................................110
May 23—Sat.—Boston 104 at Detroit..122
May 24—Sun.—Boston 119 at Detroit..145
May 26—Tue.—Detroit 107 at Boston..108
May 28—Thur.—Boston 105 at Detroit.......................................113
May 30—Sat.—Detroit 114 at Boston..117

WESTERN CONFERENCE FIRST ROUND
L.A. Lakers 3, Denver 0
Apr. 23—Thur.—Denver 95 at L.A. Lakers..................................128
Apr. 25—Sat.—Denver 127 at L.A. Lakers.................................139
Apr. 29—Wed.—L.A. Lakers 140 at Denver................................103

Golden State 3, Utah 2
Apr. 23—Thur.—Golden State 85 at Utah....................................99
Apr. 25—Sat.—Golden State 100 at Utah...................................103
Apr. 29—Wed.—Utah 95 at Golden State...................................110
May 1—Fri.—Utah 94 at Golden State.......................................98
May 3—Sun.—Golden State 118 at Utah...................................113

Houston 3, Portland 1
Apr. 24—Fri.—Houston 125 at Portland.....................................115
Apr. 26—Sun.—Houston 98 at Portland.....................................111
Apr. 28—Tue.—Portland 108 at Houston...................................117
Apr. 30—Thur.—Portland 101 at Houston..................................113

Seattle 3, Dallas 1
Apr. 23—Thur.—Seattle 129 at Dallas.......................................151
Apr. 25—Sat.—Seattle 112 at Dallas..110
Apr. 28—Tue.—Dallas 107 at Seattle..117
Apr. 30—Thur.—Dallas 98 at Seattle..124

WESTERN CONFERENCE SEMIFINALS
Seattle 4, Houston 2
May 2—Sat.—Seattle 111 at Houston.....................................*106
May 5—Tue.—Seattle 99 at Houston...97
May 7—Thur.—Houston 102 at Seattle......................................84
May 9—Sat.—Houston 102 at Seattle......................................117
May 12—Tue.—Seattle 107 at Houston......................................112
May 14—Thur.—Houston 125 at Seattle...................................**128

L.A. Lakers 4, Golden State 1
May 5—Tue.—Golden State 116 at L.A. Lakers.........................125
May 7—Thur.—Golden State 101 at L.A. Lakers........................116
May 9—Sat.—L.A. Lakers 133 at Golden State.........................108
May 10—Sun.—L.A. Lakers 121 at Golden State........................129
May 12—Tue.—Golden State 106 at L.A. Lakers........................118

WESTERN CONFERENCE FINALS
L.A. Lakers 4, Seattle 0
May 16—Sat.—Seattle 87 at L.A. Lakers.....................................92
May 19—Tue.—Seattle 104 at L.A. Lakers.................................112
May 23—Sat.—L.A. Lakers 122 at Seattle.................................121
May 25—Mon.—L.A. Lakers 133 at Seattle................................102

NBA FINALS
L.A. Lakers 4, Boston 2
June 2—Tue.—Boston 113 at L.A. Lakers.................................126
June 4—Thur.—Boston 122 at L.A. Lakers................................141
June 7—Sun.—L.A. Lakers 103 at Boston.................................109
June 9—Tue.—L.A. Lakers 107 at Boston.................................106
June 11—Thur.—L.A. Lakers 108 at Boston...............................123
June 14—Sun.—Boston 93 at L.A. Lakers..................................106

*Overtime.

1985-86 NBA STATISTICS

1985-86 NBA CHAMPION BOSTON CELTICS

Front row (left to right): Danny Ainge, Scott Wedman, Vice Chairman and Treasurer Alan Cohen, Executive Vice-President and General Manager Jan Volk, President Arnold (Red) Auerbach, Coach K.C. Jones, Chairman of the Board Don Gaston, Larry Bird, Dennis Johnson. Back row: Equipment Manager Wayne Lebeaux, Team Physician Dr. Thomas Silva, assistant coach Jimmy Rodgers, Sam Vincent, Rick Carlisle, Greg Kite, Robert Parish, Bill Walton, Kevin McHale, David Thirdkill, Jerry Sichting, assistant coach Chris Ford, Trainer Ray Melchiorre.

FINAL STANDINGS

ATLANTIC DIVISION

Team	Atl.	Bos.	Chi.	Cle.	Dal.	Den.	Det.	G.S.	Hou.	Ind.	L.A.C.	L.A.L.	Mil.	N.J.	N.Y.	Phi.	Pho.	Por.	Sac.	S.A.	Sea.	Uta.	Was.	W.	L.	Pct.	G.B.
Boston	6	..	5	5	1	1	4	2	2	5	2	2	5	4	5	4	1	1	1	2	2	2	5	67	15	.817	..
Philadelphia	1	2	5	6	2	1	4	1	1	6	2	0	1	4	6	..	2	2	2	1	1	1	3	54	28	.659	13
Washington	4	1	4	5	1	0	2	1	0	1	2	0	2	4	3	3	1	2	1	0	1	1	..	39	43	.476	28
New Jersey	2	2	3	3	0	1	2	1	1	3	0	1	2	..	5	2	2	2	2	1	0	2	2	39	43	.476	28
New York	1	1	2	1	1	1	1	1	0	4	0	1	0	1	..	0	2	0	1	1	1	0	3	23	59	.280	44

CENTRAL DIVISION

Team	Atl.	Bos.	Chi.	Cle.	Dal.	Den.	Det.	G.S.	Hou.	Ind.	L.A.C.	L.A.L.	Mil.	N.J.	N.Y.	Phi.	Pho.	Por.	Sac.	S.A.	Sea.	Uta.	Was.	W.	L.	Pct.	G.B.
Milwaukee	3	0	5	5	2	0	4	2	2	4	1	0	..	4	6	4	1	2	2	2	2	2	4	57	25	.695	..
Atlanta	..	0	5	4	1	1	4	1	1	5	2	1	3	4	5	4	2	2	2	1	1	0	1	50	32	.610	7
Detroit	2	1	4	5	2	1	..	1	1	5	2	1	2	4	4	2	0	1	0	1	2	1	4	46	36	.561	11
Chicago	1	1	..	3	0	2	2	1	3	1	0	1	2	4	1	1	1	0	1	1	1	1	1	30	52	.366	27
Cleveland	2	1	3	..	1	1	1	0	0	3	1	1	1	3	4	0	2	0	2	1	1	0	1	29	53	.354	28
Indiana	1	1	3	2	0	0	1	1	0	..	2	0	2	2	2	0	1	0	0	1	2	0	5	26	56	.317	31

MIDWEST DIVISION

Team	Atl.	Bos.	Chi.	Cle.	Dal.	Den.	Det.	G.S.	Hou.	Ind.	L.A.C.	L.A.L.	Mil.	N.J.	N.Y.	Phi.	Pho.	Por.	Sac.	S.A.	Sea.	Uta.	Was.	W.	L.	Pct.	G.B.
Houston	1	0	1	2	5	3	1	5	..	2	3	1	0	1	2	1	3	3	4	5	3	3	2	51	31	.622	..
Denver	1	1	0	1	3	..	1	3	3	2	4	3	2	1	1	1	4	3	3	3	2	3	2	47	35	.573	4
Dallas	1	1	2	1	..	3	0	4	1	2	2	1	0	2	1	0	5	2	3	4	3	5	1	44	38	.537	7
Utah	2	0	1	2	1	3	1	3	3	2	2	0	0	0	2	1	4	3	4	4	3	..	1	42	40	.512	9
Sacramento	0	1	2	0	3	3	2	3	2	2	0	0	0	1	0	3	2	..	5	5	2	2	1	37	45	.451	14
San Antonio	1	0	1	1	2	3	1	3	1	1	4	1	0	1	1	1	2	4	1	..	2	2	2	35	47	.427	16

PACIFIC DIVISION

Team	Atl.	Bos.	Chi.	Cle.	Dal.	Den.	Det.	G.S.	Hou.	Ind.	L.A.C.	L.A.L.	Mil.	N.J.	N.Y.	Phi.	Pho.	Por.	Sac.	S.A.	Sea.	Uta.	Was.	W.	L.	Pct.	G.B.
L.A. Lakers	1	0	2	1	4	2	1	4	4	2	4	..	2	1	1	2	5	6	5	4	4	5	2	62	20	.756	..
Portland	0	1	1	2	3	2	1	5	2	2	4	0	0	2	0	4	..	3	1	5	2	0		40	42	.488	22
L.A. Clippers	0	0	1	1	3	1	0	1	2	0	..	2	1	2	2	0	2	2	5	1	3	3	0	32	50	.390	30
Phoenix	0	1	1	0	0	1	2	4	2	1	4	1	1	0	0	0	..	2	2	3	5	1	1	32	50	.390	30
Seattle	1	0	1	1	2	3	0	4	2	0	3	2	0	2	1	1	1	1	0	3	..	2	1	31	51	.378	31
Golden State	1	0	0	2	1	2	1	..	0	1	5	2	0	1	1	1	2	1	2	2	2	2	1	30	52	.366	32

HOME-ROAD RECORDS OF ALL TEAMS

Team	Home	Road	Total	Team	Home	Road	Total
Atlanta	34- 7	16- 25	50- 32	Milwaukee	33- 8	24- 17	57- 25
Boston	40- 1	27- 14	67- 15	New Jersey	26- 15	13- 28	39- 43
Chicago	22- 19	8- 33	30- 52	New York	15- 26	8- 33	23- 59
Cleveland	16- 25	13- 28	29- 53	Philadelphia	31- 10	23- 18	54- 28
Dallas	26- 15	18- 23	44- 38	Phoenix	23- 18	9- 32	32- 50
Denver	34- 7	13- 28	47- 35	Portland	27- 14	13- 28	40- 42
Detroit	31- 10	15- 26	46- 36	Sacramento	25- 16	12- 29	37- 45
Golden State	24- 17	6- 35	30- 52	San Antonio	21- 20	14- 27	35- 47
Houston	36- 5	15- 26	51- 31	Seattle	24- 17	7- 34	31- 51
Indiana	19- 22	7- 34	26- 56	Utah	27- 14	15- 26	42- 40
L.A. Clippers	22- 19	10- 31	31- 51	Washington	26- 15	13- 28	39- 43
L.A. Lakers	35- 6	27- 14	62- 20	Totals	617-326	326-617	943-943

OFFENSIVE TEAM STATISTICS

Team	G.	FIELD GOALS Att.	Made	Pct.	FREE THROWS Att.	Made	Pct.	REBOUNDS Off.	Def.	Tot.	Ast.	MISCELLANEOUS PF	Disq.	Stl.	Turn Over	Blk. Sh.	SCORING Pts.	Avg.
L.A. Lakers	82	7343	3834	.522	2329	1812	.778	1101	2555	3656	2433	2031	8	693	1467	419	9618	117.3
Dallas	82	7254	3631	.501	2643	2050	.776	1059	2454	3513	2108	1733	17	605	1289	369	9453	115.3
Portland	82	7281	3610	.496	2799	2142	.765	1153	2316	3469	2180	2205	30	859	1529	356	9436	115.1
Denver	82	7868	3705	.471	2416	1929	.798	1223	2317	3540	2140	2164	23	826	1336	421	9410	114.8
Milwaukee	82	7310	3601	.493	2701	2063	.764	1189	2420	3609	2158	2210	34	805	1369	460	9390	114.5
Houston	82	7671	3759	.490	2434	1776	.730	1316	2434	3750	2318	1991	30	745	1374	551	9379	114.4
Detroit	82	7750	3754	.484	2300	1800	.783	1276	2461	3737	2319	2101	26	738	1343	340	9363	114.2
Boston	82	7312	3718	.508	2248	1785	.794	1054	2753	3807	2387	1756	15	641	1360	511	9359	114.1
Golden State	82	7567	3650	.482	2517	1912	.760	1271	2344	3615	2018	2032	37	751	1400	354	9299	113.4
San Antonio	82	7104	3596	.506	2523	1882	.746	1069	2413	3482	2260	2115	27	800	1624	390	9120	111.2
Philadelphia	82	7058	3435	.487	2810	2130	.758	1326	2378	3704	2017	1798	13	862	1595	490	9051	110.4
Phoenix	82	6993	3518	.503	2683	1949	.726	1034	2449	3483	2272	2260	29	773	1763	379	9023	110.0
Chicago	82	7227	3476	.481	2499	1922	.769	1280	2278	3558	2006	2166	34	609	1436	400	8962	109.3
New Jersey	82	7301	3548	.486	2396	1810	.755	1183	2483	3666	2128	2129	41	749	1575	345	8949	109.1
Sacramento	82	7220	3538	.490	2338	1818	.778	1135	2377	3512	2304	2134	19	602	1533	388	8924	108.8
L.A. Clippers	82	7165	3388	.473	2683	2067	.770	1159	2258	3417	1968	1931	23	694	1506	501	8907	108.6
Atlanta	82	7029	3447	.490	2704	1979	.732	1249	2405	3654	2025	2170	34	736	1483	434	8906	108.6
Utah	82	7083	3453	.488	2694	1930	.716	1068	2479	3547	2199	2038	14	717	1518	666	8871	108.2
Cleveland	82	7239	3478	.480	2325	1748	.752	1086	2455	3541	2064	2267	37	627	1411	436	8836	107.8
Seattle	82	7059	3335	.472	2331	1815	.779	1145	2256	3401	1977	2168	32	745	1435	295	8564	104.4
Indiana	82	7150	3441	.481	2183	1614	.739	1138	2613	3751	2159	2135	15	659	1515	381	8519	103.9
Washington	82	7148	3311	.463	2286	1704	.745	1066	2432	3498	1748	1796	15	626	1346	716	8442	103.0
New York	82	7034	3239	.460	2237	1534	.686	1081	2170	3251	1877	2213	47	714	1438	308	8094	98.7

DEFENSIVE TEAM STATISTICS

Team	FIELD GOALS Att.	Made	Pct.	FREE THROWS Att.	Made	Pct.	REBOUNDS Off.	Def.	Tot.	Ast.	MISCELLANEOUS PF	Disq.	Stl.	Turn Over	Blk. Sh.	SCORING Pts.	Avg.	Pt. Dif.
New York	6672	3192	.478	2744	2102	.766	1166	2587	3753	2007	2018	25	701	1629	444	8554	104.3	- 5.6
Seattle	6774	3301	.487	2491	1913	.768	1027	2308	3335	2038	2008	23	654	1467	406	8572	104.5	- 0.1
Boston	7476	3444	.461	2162	1617	.748	1089	2317	3406	1924	1966	22	725	1258	341	8587	104.7	+ 9.4
Washington	7360	3435	.467	2181	1649	.756	1249	2591	3840	2014	1907	17	712	1373	454	8590	104.8	- 1.8
Milwaukee	7043	3286	.467	2674	1980	.740	1169	2325	3494	1952	2139	26	633	1631	397	8649	105.5	+ 9.0
Atlanta	7074	3360	.475	2508	1905	.760	1202	2329	3531	1945	2129	30	697	1494	371	8712	106.2	+ 2.4
Indiana	7123	3372	.473	2571	1975	.768	1050	2479	3529	2057	1909	14	745	1315	445	8792	107.2	- 3.3
Philadelphia	7328	3615	.493	2041	1546	.757	1189	2228	3417	2255	2187	41	802	1520	469	8858	108.0	+ 2.4
Utah	7339	3470	.473	2483	1896	.764	1208	2510	3718	1977	2221	35	752	1531	464	8901	108.5	- 0.4
Cleveland	7239	3435	.475	2758	2115	.767	1131	2494	3625	2122	1945	23	711	1331	364	9071	110.6	- 2.9
L.A. Lakers	7450	3577	.480	2369	1778	.751	1104	2226	3330	2235	1992	26	792	1330	359	8983	109.5	+ 7.7
New Jersey	7124	3504	.492	2622	2008	.766	1036	2369	3405	2019	2002	19	783	1523	390	9112	111.1	- 2.0
Houston	7402	3638	.491	2406	1802	.749	1190	2389	3579	2196	1977	22	683	1464	386	9165	111.8	+ 2.6
Sacramento	7225	3566	.494	2609	1971	.755	1142	2339	3481	2118	2083	29	511	1409	478	9176	111.9	- 3.1
Detroit	7365	3620	.492	2589	1956	.756	1180	2538	3718	2083	1977	25	662	1490	500	9267	113.0	+ 1.2
Phoenix	7307	3569	.488	2692	2041	.758	1137	2265	3402	2149	2216	25	841	1515	466	9268	113.0	- 3.0
San Antonio	7365	3629	.493	2491	1916	.769	1157	2304	3461	2269	2108	32	800	1519	453	9272	113.1	- 1.9
Denver	7404	3638	.491	2693	1967	.730	1295	2732	4027	2106	2117	28	639	1741	484	9303	113.5	+ 1.3
Portland	7249	3637	.502	2638	1992	.755	1179	2362	3541	2254	2262	46	760	1645	426	9349	114.0	+ 1.1
Dallas	7689	3864	.503	2049	1545	.754	1219	2469	3688	2381	2196	33	617	1279	423	9363	114.2	+ 1.1
L.A. Clippers	7588	3849	.507	2280	1704	.747	1268	2458	3726	2469	2113	17	760	1396	457	9475	115.5	- 6.9
Golden State	7432	3863	.520	2401	1791	.746	1170	2519	3689	2325	2069	18	692	1487	442	9582	116.9	- 3.5

Disq.—Individual player disqualified (fouled out of game).

INDIVIDUAL LEADERS

POINTS

Minimum 70 games played or 1,400 points

Player	G.	FG	FT	Pts.	Avg.	Player	G.	FG	FT	Pts.	Avg.
Wilkins, Atlanta	78	888	577	2366	30.3	Abdul-Jabbar, L.A. Lakers	79	755	336	1846	23.4
Dantley, Utah	76	818	630	2267	29.8	Aguirre, Dallas	74	668	318	1670	22.6
English, Denver	81	951	511	2414	29.8	Malone, Washington	80	735	322	1795	22.4
Bird, Boston	82	796	441	2115	25.8	Davis, Phoenix	70	624	257	1523	21.8
Short, Golden State	64	633	351	1632	25.5	Blackman, Dallas	82	677	404	1762	21.5
Vandeweghe, Portland	79	719	523	1962	24.8	McHale, Boston	68	561	326	1448	21.3
Malone, Philadelphia	74	571	617	1759	23.8	Carroll, Golden State	79	650	377	1677	21.2
Olajuwon, Houston	68	625	347	1597	23.5	Thomas, Detroit	77	609	365	1609	20.9
Mitchell, San Antonio	82	802	317	1921	23.4	Woolridge, Chicago	70	540	364	1448	20.7
Free, Cleveland	75	652	379	1754	23.4	Johnson, L.A. Clippers	75	613	298	1525	20.3

FIELD GOALS
Minimum 300 FG made

	FGA	FGM	Pct.
Johnson, San Antonio	573	362	.632
Gilmore, San Antonio	684	423	.618
Nance, Phoenix	1001	582	.581
Worthy, L.A. Lakers	1086	629	.579
McHale, Boston	978	561	.574
Barkley, Philadelphia	1041	595	.572
Abdul-Jabbar, L.A. Lakers	1338	755	.564
Dantley, Utah	1453	818	.563
Lister, Milwaukee	577	318	.551
Parish, Boston	966	530	.549

FREE THROWS
Minimum 125 FT made

	FTA	FTM	Pct.
Bird, Boston	492	441	.8963
Mullin, Golden State	211	189	.8957
Gminski, New Jersey	393	351	.893
Paxson, Portland	244	217	.889
Gervin, Chicago	322	283	.879
Edwards, L.A. Clippers	151	132	.874
Johnson, L.A. Lakers	434	378	.871
Vandeweghe, Portland	602	523	.869
Davis, Dallas	228	198	.868
Malone, Washington	371	322	.868

ASSISTS
Minimum 70 games or 400 assists

	G.	No.	Avg.
Johnson, L.A. Lakers	72	907	12.6
Thomas, Detroit	77	830	10.8
Theus, Sacramento	82	788	9.6
Bagley, Cleveland	78	735	9.4
Cheeks, Philadelphia	82	753	9.2
Floyd, Golden State	82	746	9.1
Lucas, Houston	65	571	8.8
Nixon, L.A. Clippers	67	576	8.6
Rivers, Atlanta	53	443	8.4
Drexler, Portland	75	600	8.0

STEALS
Minimum 70 games or 125 steals

	G.	No.	Avg.
Robertson, San Antonio	82	301	3.67
Richardson, New Jersey	47	125	2.66
Drexler, Portland	75	197	2.63
Cheeks, Philadelphia	82	207	2.52
Lever, Denver	78	178	2.28
Thomas, Detroit	77	171	2.22
Barkley, Philadelphia	80	173	2.16
Pressey, Milwaukee	80	168	2.10
Bird, Boston	82	166	2.02
Cook, New Jersey	79	156	1.97

REBOUNDS
Minimum 70 games or 800 rebounds

	G.	Off.	Def.	Tot.	Avg.
Laimbeer, Detroit	82	305	770	1075	13.1
Barkley, Philadelphia	80	354	672	1026	12.8
B. Williams, New Jersey	82	329	657	986	12.0
Malone, Philadelphia	74	339	533	872	11.8
Sampson, Houston	79	258	621	879	11.1
Smith, Golden State	77	384	472	856	11.1
Bird, Boston	82	190	615	805	9.8
Thompson, Sacramento	80	252	518	770	9.6
Donaldson, LA Clippers-Dallas	83	171	624	795	9.6
Parish, Boston	81	246	524	770	9.5

BLOCKED SHOTS
Minimum 70 games or 100 blocked shots

	G.	No.	Avg.
Bol, Washington	80	397	4.96
Eaton, Utah	80	369	4.61
Olajuwon, Houston	68	231	3.40
Cooper, Denver	78	227	2.91
Benjamin, L.A. Clippers	79	206	2.61
Oldham, Chicago	52	134	2.58
Williams, Indiana	78	184	2.36
Rollins, Atlanta	74	167	2.26
Ewing, New York	50	103	2.06
McHale, Boston	68	134	1.97

3-PT. FIELD GOALS
Minimum 25 made

	FGA	FGM	Pct.
Hodges, Milwaukee	162	73	.4506
Tucker, New York	91	41	.4505
Grunfeld, New York	61	26	.426
Bird, Boston	194	82	.423
Free, Cleveland	169	71	.420
Macy, Chicago	141	58	.411
Cooper, L.A. Lakers	163	63	.387
Ellis, Dallas	173	63	.364
McKenna, Washington	75	27	.360
McGee, L.A. Lakers	114	41	.360
Wood, Philadelphia-Washington	114	41	.360

TEAM-BY-TEAM INDIVIDUAL STATISTICS

ATLANTA HAWKS

Player	G.	Min.	FGA	FGM	Pct.	FTA	FTM	Pct.	Off. Reb.	Def. Reb.	Tot. Reb.	Ast.	PF	Disq.	Stl.	Blk. Sh.	Pts.	Avg.	Hi.
Wilkins	78	3049	1897	888	.468	705	577	.818	261	357	618	206	170	0	138	49	2366	30.3	57
Wittman	81	2760	881	467	.530	135	104	.770	51	119	170	306	118	0	81	14	1043	12.9	24
Willis	82	2300	811	419	.517	263	172	.654	243	461	704	45	294	6	66	44	1010	12.3	39
Rivers	53	1571	464	220	.474	283	172	.608	49	113	162	443	185	2	120	13	612	11.5	29
Johnson	39	862	328	155	.473	110	79	.718	17	58	75	219	72	1	10	1	394	10.1	24
Levingston	81	1945	551	294	.534	242	164	.678	193	341	534	72	260	5	76	39	752	9.3	25
Williams	19	367	143	57	.399	48	41	.854	19	26	45	67	48	1	28	1	159	8.4	20
Koncak	82	1695	519	263	.507	257	156	.607	171	296	467	55	296	10	37	69	682	8.3	21
Webb	79	1229	412	199	.483	275	216	.785	27	96	123	337	164	1	82	5	616	7.8	23
Carr	17	258	93	49	.527	27	18	.667	16	36	52	14	51	1	7	15	116	6.8	14
Davis (Tot.)	66	1014	344	148	.430	138	118	.855	8	47	55	217	76	0	37	4	417	6.3	17
Davis (Atl.)	27	402	107	46	.430	59	51	.864	2	17	19	112	32	0	13	0	144	5.3	17
Rollins	74	1781	347	173	.499	90	69	.767	131	327	458	41	239	5	38	167	415	5.6	14
Battle	64	639	222	101	.455	103	75	.728	12	50	62	74	80	0	23	3	277	4.3	22
Charles	36	273	88	49	.557	36	24	.667	13	26	39	8	37	0	2	6	122	3.4	12
Hastings	62	650	159	65	.409	70	60	.857	44	80	124	26	118	2	14	8	193	3.1	12
Toney	3	24	7	2	.286	1	1	1.000	0	2	2	0	6	0	1	0	5	1.7	5

3-Pt. FG: Atlanta 33-166 (.199)—Wilkins 13-70 (.186); Wittman 5-16 (.313); Willis 0-6 (.000); Rivers 0-16 (.000); Johnson 5-20 (.250); Levingston 0-1 (.000); Williams 4-11 (.364); Koncak 0-1 (.000); Webb 2-11 (.182); Davis 1-2 (.500); Rollins 0-1 (.000); Battle 0-7 (.000); Hastings 3-4 (.750). Opponents 87-283 (.307).

BOSTON CELTICS

Player	G.	Min.	FGA	FGM	Pct.	FTA	FTM	Pct.	Off. Reb.	Def. Reb.	Tot. Reb.	Ast.	PF	Disq.	Stl.	Blk. Sh.	Pts.	Avg.	Hi.
Bird	82	3113	1606	796	.496	492	441	.896	190	615	805	557	182	0	166	51	2115	25.8	50
McHale	68	2397	978	561	.574	420	326	.776	171	380	551	181	192	2	29	134	1448	21.3	34
Parish	81	2567	966	530	.549	335	245	.731	246	524	770	145	215	3	65	116	1305	16.1	30
Johnson	78	2732	1060	482	.455	297	243	.818	69	199	268	456	206	3	110	35	1213	15.6	30
Ainge	80	2407	701	353	.504	136	123	.904	47	188	235	405	204	4	94	7	855	10.7	27
Wedman	79	1402	605	286	.473	68	45	.662	66	126	192	83	127	0	38	22	634	8.0	24
Walton	80	1546	411	231	.562	202	144	.713	136	408	544	165	210	1	38	106	606	7.6	22
Sichting	82	1596	412	235	.570	66	61	.924	27	77	104	188	118	0	50	0	537	6.5	17
Thirdkill	49	385	110	54	.491	88	55	.625	27	43	70	15	55	0	11	3	163	3.3	20
Vincent	57	432	162	59	.364	70	65	.929	11	37	48	69	59	0	17	4	184	3.2	12
Williams	6	54	21	5	.238	12	7	.583	7	8	15	2	15	0	1	1	17	2.8	7
Carlisle	77	760	189	92	.487	23	15	.652	22	55	77	104	92	1	19	4	199	2.6	10
Kite	64	464	91	44	.374	39	15	.385	35	93	128	17	81	1	3	28	83	1.3	8

3-Pt. FG: Boston 138-393 (.351)—Bird 82-194 (.423); Johnson 6-42 (.143); Ainge 26-73 (.356); Wedman 17-48 (.354); Sichting 6-16 (.375); Thirdkill 0-1 (.000); Vincent 1-4 (.250); Williams 0-4 (.000); Carlisle 0-10 (.000); Kite 0-1 (.000). Opponents 82-304 (.270).

CHICAGO BULLS

Player	G.	Min.	FGA	FGM	Pct.	FTA	FTM	Pct.	Off. Reb.	Def. Reb.	Tot. Reb.	Ast.	PF	Disq.	Stl.	Blk. Sh.	Pts.	Avg.	Hi.
Jordan	18	451	328	150	.457	125	105	.840	23	41	64	53	46	0	37	21	408	22.7	33
Woolridge	70	2248	1090	540	.495	462	364	.788	150	200	350	213	186	2	49	47	1448	20.7	44
Dailey	35	723	470	203	.432	198	163	.823	20	48	68	67	86	0	22	5	569	16.3	38
Gervin	82	2065	1100	519	.472	322	283	.879	78	137	215	144	210	4	49	23	1325	16.2	45
Green	80	2307	875	407	.465	335	262	.782	208	450	658	139	292	5	70	37	1076	13.5	31
Banks	82	2139	688	356	.517	255	183	.718	178	182	360	251	212	4	81	10	895	10.9	38
Oakley	77	1772	541	281	.519	269	178	.662	255	409	664	133	250	9	68	30	740	9.6	35
Corzine	67	1709	519	255	.491	171	127	.743	132	301	433	150	133	0	28	53	640	9.6	23
Macy	82	2426	592	286	.483	90	73	.811	41	137	178	446	201	1	81	11	703	8.6	22
Oldham	52	1276	323	167	.517	91	53	.582	112	194	306	37	206	6	28	134	387	7.4	17
Holton (Tot.)	28	512	175	77	.440	44	28	.636	11	22	33	55	47	1	25	0	183	6.5	21
Holton (Chi.)	24	447	155	73	.471	38	24	.632	10	20	30	48	40	1	23	0	171	7.1	21
Paxson	75	1570	328	153	.466	92	74	.804	18	76	94	274	172	2	55	2	395	5.3	23
Brown	10	42	18	18	.439	13	9	.692	5	11	16	16	16	0	5	1	45	4.5	15
Higgins (Tot.)	30	332	106	39	.368	27	19	.704	14	37	51	24	49	0	9	11	98	3.3	11
Higgins (Chi.)	5	81	23	9	.391	6	5	.833	3	4	7	5	11	0	4	3	23	4.6	7
Smrek	38	408	122	46	.377	29	16	.552	46	64	110	19	95	0	6	23	108	2.8	15
McKinney	9	83	23	10	.435	2	2	1.000	1	4	5	13	9	0	3	0	22	2.4	4
Brewer	4	18	9	3	.333	1	1	1.000	0	0	0	0	0	0	0	0	7	1.8	7

3-Pt. FG: Chicago 88-317 (.278)—Jordan 3-18 (.166); Woolridge 4-23 (.174); Dailey 0-8 (.000); Gervin 4-19 (.211); Green 0-8 (.000); Banks 0-19 (.000); Oakley 0-3 (.000); Corzine 3-12 (.250); Macy 58-141 (.411); Oldham 0-1 (.000); Holton 1-10 (.100); Paxson 15-50 (.300); Brown 0-2 (.000); Higgins 0-1 (.000); Smrek 0-2 (.000). Opponents 70-233 (.300).

CLEVELAND CAVALIERS

Player	G.	Min.	FGA	FGM	Pct.	FTA	FTM	Pct.	Off. Reb.	Def. Reb.	Tot. Reb.	Ast.	PF	Disq.	Stl.	Blk. Sh.	Pts.	Avg.	Hi.
Free	75	2535	1433	652	.455	486	379	.780	72	146	218	314	186	1	91	19	1754	23.4	43
Hinson	82	2834	1167	621	.532	506	364	.719	167	472	639	102	316	7	62	112	1606	19.6	39
Turpin	80	2292	838	456	.544	228	185	.811	182	374	556	55	260	6	65	106	1097	13.7	32
Bagley	78	2472	865	366	.423	215	170	.791	76	199	275	735	165	1	122	10	911	11.7	24
Hubbard	23	640	198	93	.470	112	76	.679	48	72	120	29	78	2	20	3	262	11.4	22
Johnson (Tot.)	71	1477	621	284	.457	155	112	.723	30	91	121	333	128	1	18	2	709	10.0	25
Johnson (Clev.)	32	615	293	129	.440	45	33	.733	13	33	46	114	56	0	8	1	315	9.8	25
Jones	53	1011	370	187	.505	178	132	.742	71	136	207	45	142	0	30	38	513	9.7	24
Lee	58	1197	380	177	.466	96	75	.781	116	235	351	67	204	9	29	37	431	7.4	25
Davis	39	612	237	102	.430	79	67	.848	6	30	36	105	44	0	24	4	273	7.0	17
Minniefield	76	1131	347	167	.481	93	73	.785	43	88	131	269	165	1	65	1	417	5.5	20
Anderson	17	207	74	37	.500	16	12	.750	5	21	26	8	20	0	1	0	86	5.1	14
Poquette	81	1496	348	166	.477	100	72	.720	121	252	373	78	187	2	33	32	406	5.0	15
Brewer (Tot.)	44	570	224	86	.384	38	34	.895	14	39	53	40	44	0	17	6	211	4.8	16
Brewer (Clev.)	40	552	215	83	.386	37	33	.892	14	39	53	40	43	0	17	6	204	5.1	16
Shelton	44	682	188	92	.489	16	14	.875	38	105	143	61	128	2	21	4	198	4.5	13
West	67	1172	209	113	.541	103	54	.524	97	225	322	20	235	6	27	62	280	4.2	14
McDonald	21	266	58	28	.483	8	5	.625	15	23	38	9	30	0	7	1	61	2.9	10
Whatley	8	66	19	9	.474	7	4	.571	2	5	7	13	8	0	5	0	22	2.8	14

3-Pt. FG: Cleveland 132-391 (.338)—Free 71-169 (.420); Hinson 0-4 (.000); Turpin 0-4 (.000); Bagley 9-37 (.243); Hubbard 0-1 (.000); Johnson 24-65 (.369); Jones 7-23 (.304); Lee 2-9 (.222); Davis 2-11 (.182); Minniefield 10-37 (.270); Anderson 0-1 (.000); Poquette 2-10 (.200); Brewer 5-17 (.294); Shelton 0-2 (.000); McDonald 0-1 (.000). Opponents 86-297 (.290).

DALLAS MAVERICKS

Player	G.	Min.	FGA	FGM	Pct.	FTA	FTM	Pct.	Off. Reb.	Def. Reb.	Tot. Reb.	Ast.	PF	Disq.	Stl.	Blk. Sh.	Pts.	Avg.	Hi.
Aguirre	74	2501	1327	668	.503	451	318	.705	177	268	445	339	229	6	62	14	1670	22.6	42
Blackman	82	2787	1318	677	.514	483	404	.836	88	203	291	271	138	0	79	25	1762	21.5	46
Perkins	80	2626	910	458	.503	377	307	.814	195	490	685	153	212	2	75	94	1234	15.4	32
Vincent	80	1994	919	442	.481	274	222	.810	107	261	368	180	193	2	66	21	1106	13.8	31
Harper	79	2150	730	390	.534	229	171	.747	75	151	226	416	166	1	153	23	963	12.2	26
Davis	82	1971	502	267	.532	228	198	.868	26	120	146	467	174	2	57	15	764	9.3	23
Donaldson (Tot.)	83	2682	459	256	.558	254	204	.803	171	624	795	96	189	0	28	139	716	8.6	20
Donaldson (Dall.)	69	2241	375	213	.568	184	147	.799	143	521	664	84	156	0	23	110	573	8.3	20
Ellis	72	1086	470	193	.411	82	59	.720	86	82	168	37	78	0	40	9	508	7.1	28
Nimphius	13	280	72	37	.514	29	17	.586	23	37	60	14	38	1	3	12	91	7.0	20
Schrempf	64	969	315	142	.451	152	110	.724	70	128	198	88	166	1	23	10	397	6.2	23
Wennington	56	562	153	72	.471	62	45	.726	32	100	132	21	83	0	11	22	189	3.4	15
Bryant	9	154	30	11	.367	11	6	.545	9	24	33	11	26	2	3	2	28	3.1	7
Blab	48	409	94	44	.468	67	36	.537	25	66	91	17	65	0	3	12	124	2.6	14
Keeling	20	75	39	17	.436	14	10	.714	3	3	6	10	9	0	7	0	44	2.2	7

3-Pt. FG: Dallas 141-446 (.316)—Aguirre 16-56 (.286); Blackman 4-29 (.138); Perkins 11-33 (.333); Vincent 0-3 (.000); Harper 12-51 (.235); Davis 32-89 (.360); Ellis 63-173 (.364); Nimphius 0-1 (.000); Schrempf 3-7 (.429); Wennington 0-4 (.000). Opponents 90-311 (.289).

DENVER NUGGETS

Player	G.	Min.	FGA	FGM	Pct.	FTA	FTM	Pct.	Off. Reb.	Def. Reb.	Tot. Reb.	Ast.	PF	Disq.	Stl.	Blk. Sh.	Pts.	Avg.	Hi.
English	81	3024	1888	951	.504	593	511	.862	192	213	405	320	235	1	73	29	2414	29.8	54
Natt	69	2007	930	469	.504	347	278	.801	125	311	436	164	143	0	58	13	1218	17.7	35
Lever	78	2616	1061	468	.441	182	132	.725	136	284	420	584	204	3	178	15	1080	13.8	31
Cooper	78	2112	906	422	.466	219	174	.795	190	420	610	81	315	6	42	227	1021	13.1	32
Hanzlik	79	1982	741	331	.447	405	318	.785	88	176	264	316	277	2	107	16	988	12.5	27
Evans	81	1389	715	304	.425	149	126	.846	30	71	101	177	159	1	61	1	773	9.5	28
Schayes	80	1654	440	221	.502	278	216	.777	154	285	439	79	298	7	42	63	658	8.2	25
Turner	73	1324	379	165	.435	53	39	.736	64	137	201	165	150	1	70	6	369	5.1	16
Dunn	82	2401	379	172	.454	88	68	.773	143	234	377	171	228	1	155	16	412	5.0	12
White	43	343	168	74	.440	23	19	.826	17	27	44	53	24	0	18	2	173	4.0	17
Rasmussen	48	330	150	61	.407	39	31	.795	37	60	97	16	63	0	3	10	153	3.2	15
Williams	53	573	111	67	.604	40	17	.425	47	99	146	14	68	1	19	23	151	2.8	16

3-Pt. FG: Denver 71-305 (.233)—English 1-5 (.200); Natt 2-6 (.333); Lever 12-38 (.316); Cooper 3-7 (.429); Hanzlik 8-41 (.195); Evans 39-176 (.222); Schayes 0-1 (.000); Turner 0-9 (.000); Dunn 0-1 (.000); White 6-21 (.286). Opponents 60-262 (.229).

DETROIT PISTONS

Player	G.	Min.	FGA	FGM	Pct.	FTA	FTM	Pct.	Off. Reb.	Def. Reb.	Tot. Reb.	Ast.	PF	Disq.	Stl.	Blk. Sh.	Pts.	Avg.	Hi.
Thomas	77	2790	1248	609	.488	462	365	.790	83	194	277	830	245	9	171	20	1609	20.9	39
Tripucka	81	2626	1236	615	.498	444	380	.856	116	232	348	265	167	0	93	10	1622	20.0	41
Laimbeer	82	2891	1107	545	.492	319	266	.834	305	770	1075	146	291	4	59	65	1360	16.6	29
Johnson	79	1978	996	465	.467	214	165	.771	119	107	226	269	180	2	80	23	1097	13.9	35
Long	62	1176	548	264	.482	104	89	.856	47	51	98	82	92	0	41	13	620	10.0	28
Dumars	82	1957	597	287	.481	238	190	.798	60	59	119	390	200	1	66	11	769	9.4	22
Cureton	80	2017	564	285	.505	211	117	.555	198	306	504	137	239	3	58	58	687	8.6	25
Campbell	82	1292	608	294	.484	73	58	.795	83	153	236	45	164	0	62	7	648	7.9	20
Benson	72	1344	415	201	.484	83	66	.795	118	258	376	80	196	3	58	51	469	6.5	21
Mahorn	80	1442	345	157	.455	119	81	.681	121	291	412	64	261	4	40	61	395	4.9	22
Nevitt (Tot.)	29	126	43	15	.349	26	19	.731	13	19	32	7	35	0	4	19	49	1.7	8
Nevitt (Det.)	25	101	32	12	.375	20	15	.750	10	15	25	5	29	0	2	17	39	1.6	8
Gibson	32	161	51	20	.392	11	8	.727	15	25	40	5	35	0	8	4	48	1.5	9
Crevier (Tot.)	3	4	3	0	.000	2	0	.000	1	0	1	0	2	0	0	0	0	0.0	0
Crevier (Det.)	2	3	2	0	.000	2	0	.000	1	0	1	0	2	0	0	0	0	0.0	0
Russell	1	2	1	0	.000	0	0	....	0	1	1	0	0	0	0	0	0	0.0	0

3-Pt. FG: Detroit 55-182 (.302)—Thomas 26-84 (.310); Tripucka 12-25 (.480); Laimbeer 4-14 (.286); Johnson 2-13 (.154); Long 3-16 (.188); Dumars 5-16 (.313); Cureton 0-2 (.000); Campbell 2-9 (.222); Benson 1-2 (.500); Mahorn 0-1 (.000). Opponents 71-258 (.275).

GOLDEN STATE WARRIORS

Player	G.	Min.	FGA	FGM	Pct.	FTA	FTM	Pct.	Off. Reb.	Def. Reb.	Tot. Reb.	Ast.	PF	Disq.	Stl.	Blk. Sh.	Pts.	Avg.	Hi.
Short	64	2427	1313	633	.482	406	351	.865	126	203	329	237	229	5	92	22	1632	25.5	44
Carroll	79	2801	1404	650	.463	501	377	.752	193	477	670	176	277	13	101	143	1677	21.2	34
Floyd	82	2764	1007	510	.506	441	351	.796	76	221	297	746	199	2	157	16	1410	17.2	32
Teagle	82	2158	958	475	.496	265	211	.796	96	139	235	115	241	2	71	34	1165	14.2	33
Mullin	55	1391	620	287	.463	211	189	.896	42	73	115	105	130	1	70	23	768	14.0	26
Smith	77	2441	586	314	.536	227	112	.493	384	472	856	95	286	7	62	50	740	9.6	21
Ballard	75	1792	570	272	.477	126	101	.802	132	285	417	83	174	0	65	8	662	8.8	25
Thibeaux	42	531	233	100	.429	48	29	.604	28	47	75	28	82	1	23	15	231	5.5	18
Huston	82	1208	273	140	.513	92	63	.685	10	55	65	342	67	0	38	4	345	4.2	13
Conner	36	413	136	51	.375	54	40	.741	25	37	62	43	23	0	24	1	144	4.0	11
Whitehead	81	1079	294	126	.429	97	60	.619	94	234	328	19	176	2	18	19	312	3.9	18
Verhoeven	61	749	167	90	.539	43	25	.581	65	95	160	29	141	3	29	17	206	3.4	16
Williams	5	25	5	2	.400	6	3	.500	0	6	6	0	7	1	1	2	7	1.4	2
Crevier	1	1	1	0	.000	0	0	....	0	0	0	0	0	0	0	0	0	0.0	0

3-Pt. FG: Golden State 87-278 (.313)—Short 15-49 (.306); Carroll 0-2 (.000); Floyd 39-119 (.328); Teagle 4-25 (.160); Mullin 5-27 (.185); Smith 0-1 (.000); Ballard 17-35 (.486); Thibeaux 2-5 (.400); Huston 2-6 (.333); Conner 2-7 (.286); Verhoeven 1-2 (.500). Opponents 65-229 (.284).

HOUSTON ROCKETS

Player	G.	Min.	FGA	FGM	Pct.	FTA	FTM	Pct.	Off. Reb.	Def. Reb.	Tot. Reb.	Ast.	PF	Disq.	Stl.	Blk. Sh.	Pts.	Avg.	Hi.
Olajuwon	68	2467	1188	625	.526	538	347	.645	333	448	781	137	271	9	134	231	1597	23.5	41
Sampson	79	2864	1280	624	.488	376	241	.641	258	621	879	283	308	12	99	129	1491	18.9	38
Lloyd	82	2444	1119	592	.529	236	199	.843	155	169	324	300	216	0	102	24	1386	16.9	38
Lucas	65	2120	818	365	.446	298	231	.775	33	110	143	571	124	0	77	5	1006	15.5	31
Reid	82	2157	881	409	.464	214	162	.757	67	234	301	222	231	3	91	16	986	12.0	25
McCray	82	2610	629	338	.537	222	171	.770	159	361	520	292	197	2	50	58	847	10.3	25
Leavell	74	1190	458	212	.463	158	135	.854	6	61	67	234	126	1	58	8	583	7.9	28
Wiggins	78	1198	489	222	.454	118	86	.729	87	72	159	101	155	1	59	5	531	6.8	22
Petersen	82	1664	411	196	.477	160	113	.706	149	247	396	85	231	2	38	54	505	6.2	19
Harris	57	482	233	103	.442	54	50	.926	25	32	57	50	55	0	21	4	257	4.5	16
McDowell	22	204	42	24	.571	25	17	.680	12	37	49	6	25	0	1	3	65	3.0	8
Ehlo	36	199	84	36	.429	29	23	.793	17	29	46	29	22	0	11	4	98	2.7	8
Waiters	43	156	39	13	.333	6	1	.167	15	13	28	8	30	0	4	10	27	0.6	6

3-Pt. FG: Houston 85-310 (.274)—Sampson 2-15 (.133); Lloyd 3-15 (.200); Lucas 45-146 (.308); Reid 6-33 (.182); McCray 0-3 (.000); Leavell 24-67 (.358); Wiggins 1-12 (.083); Petersen 0-3 (.000); Harris 1-5 (.200); McDowell 0-1 (.000); Ehlo 3-9 (.333); Waiters 0-1 (.000). Opponents 87-268 (.325).

INDIANA PACERS

Player	G.	Min.	FGA	FGM	Pct.	FTA	FTM	Pct.	Off. Reb.	Def. Reb.	Tot. Reb.	Ast.	PF	Disq.	Stl.	Blk. Sh.	Pts.	Avg.	Hi.
Williams	78	2770	1275	627	.492	403	294	.730	172	538	710	174	244	2	50	184	1549	19.9	40
Kellogg	19	568	294	139	.473	69	53	.768	51	117	168	57	59	2	28	8	335	17.6	30
Tisdale	81	2277	1002	516	.515	234	160	.684	191	393	584	79	290	3	32	44	1192	14.7	32
Fleming	80	2870	862	436	.506	353	263	.745	102	284	386	505	230	3	131	5	1136	14.2	27
Stipanovich	79	2397	885	416	.470	315	242	.768	173	450	623	206	261	1	75	69	1076	13.6	25

Player	G.	Min.	FGA	FGM	Pct.	FTA	FTM	Pct.	Off. Reb.	Def. Reb.	Tot. Reb.	Ast.	PF	Disq.	Stl.	Blk. Sh.	Pts.	Avg.	Hi.
Richardson	82	2224	736	335	.455	147	123	.837	69	182	251	372	153	1	58	8	794	9.7	21
Anderson (Tot)	77	1676	628	310	.494	127	85	.669	130	144	274	144	125	0	56	6	707	9.2	28
Anderson (Ind)	60	1469	554	273	.493	111	73	.658	125	123	248	136	105	0	55	6	621	10.4	28
Stansbury	74	1331	441	191	.433	132	107	.811	29	110	139	206	200	2	59	8	498	6.7	22
Warrick (Tot)	36	685	182	85	.467	68	54	.794	10	59	69	115	79	0	27	2	227	6.3	16
Warrick (Ind)	31	658	172	81	.471	67	53	.791	10	56	66	109	76	0	25	2	217	7.0	16
Martin	66	691	298	143	.480	54	46	.852	42	60	102	52	108	1	21	7	332	5.0	20
Garnett	80	1197	239	112	.469	162	116	.716	106	169	275	95	174	0	39	22	340	4.3	13
Buckner	32	419	104	49	.471	27	19	.704	9	42	51	86	80	0	40	3	117	3.7	13
McClain	45	461	180	69	.383	35	18	.514	14	16	30	67	61	0	38	4	157	3.5	15
Gray	67	423	108	54	.500	74	47	.635	45	73	118	15	94	0	8	11	155	2.3	11

3-Pt. FG: Indiana 23-143 (.161)—Williams 1-12 (.083); Kellogg 4-13 (.308); Tisdale 0-2 (.000); Fleming 1-6 (.167); Stipanovich 2-10 (.200); Richardson 1-9 (.111); Anderson 2-8 (.250); Stansbury 9-53 (.170); Warrick 2-10 (.200); Martin 0-8 (.000); Garnett 0-2 (.000); Buckner 0-1 (.000); McClain 1-9 (.111). Opponents 73-275 (.265).

LOS ANGELES CLIPPERS

Player	G.	Min.	FGA	FGM	Pct.	FTA	FTM	Pct.	Off. Reb.	Def. Reb.	Tot. Reb.	Ast.	PF	Disq.	Stl.	Blk. Sh.	Pts.	Avg.	Hi.
Smith	11	339	181	100	.552	84	58	.690	20	21	41	31	35	2	9	13	259	23.5	36
Johnson	75	2605	1201	613	.510	392	298	.760	156	260	416	283	214	2	107	50	1525	20.3	34
Nixon	67	2138	921	403	.438	162	131	.809	45	135	180	576	143	0	84	3	979	14.6	33
Maxwell	76	2458	661	314	.475	562	447	.795	241	383	624	215	252	2	61	29	1075	14.1	27
White	75	1761	684	355	.519	222	164	.739	82	99	181	74	161	2	74	8	875	11.7	32
Nimphius (Tot)	80	2226	694	351	.506	262	194	.740	152	301	453	62	267	8	33	105	896	11.2	26
Nimphius (LAC)	67	1946	622	314	.505	233	177	.760	129	264	393	48	229	7	30	93	805	12.0	26
Benjamin	79	2088	661	324	.490	307	229	.746	161	439	600	79	286	5	64	206	878	11.1	28
Donaldson	14	441	84	43	.512	70	57	.814	28	103	131	12	33	0	5	29	143	10.2	17
Edwards	73	1491	577	262	.454	151	132	.874	24	62	86	259	87	0	89	4	657	9.0	28
Bridgeman	58	1161	451	199	.441	119	106	.891	9	94	123	108	81	1	31	8	510	8.8	25
Valentine (Tot)	62	1217	388	161	.415	175	130	.743	32	93	125	246	123	0	72	2	456	7.4	21
Valentine (LAC)	34	483	182	69	.379	75	59	.787	12	41	53	107	45	0	23	1	200	5.9	21
Cage	78	1566	426	204	.479	174	113	.649	168	249	417	81	176	1	62	34	521	6.7	22
Wilkes	13	195	65	26	.400	27	22	.815	13	16	29	15	19	0	7	2	75	5.8	15
Gordon	60	704	345	130	.377	56	45	.804	24	44	68	60	91	1	33	10	312	5.2	22
Murphy	14	100	45	16	.356	14	9	.643	7	8	15	3	12	0	4	3	41	2.9	7
Bryant (Tot)	17	218	48	15	.313	19	11	.579	17	36	53	15	38	2	5	5	41	2.4	7
Bryant (LAC)	8	64	18	4	.222	8	5	.625	8	12	20	4	12	0	2	3	13	1.6	5
Thomas	6	69	15	6	.400	2	1	.500	3	5	8	12	12	0	5	1	13	2.2	5
Cross	21	128	24	6	.250	25	14	.560	9	21	30	1	38	0	2	3	26	1.2	7
Jones	3	18	2	0	.000	0	0		0	2	2	0	5	0	2	1	0	0.0	0

3-Pt. FG: L.A. Clippers—64-229 (.279)—Smith 1-2 (.500); Johnson 1-15 (.067); Nixon 42-121 (.347); Maxwell 0-3 (.000); White 1-9 (.111); Nimphius 0-2 (.000); Benjamin 1-3 (.333); Edwards 1-9 (.111); Bridgeman 6-18 (.333); Valentine 3-11 (.273); Cage 0-3 (.000); Wilkes 1-3 (.333); Gordon 7-28 (.250); Murphy 0-2 (.000). Opponents 73-261 (.280).

LOS ANGELES LAKERS

Player	G.	Min.	FGA	FGM	Pct.	FTA	FTM	Pct.	Off. Reb.	Def. Reb.	Tot. Reb.	Ast.	PF	Disq.	Stl.	Blk. Sh.	Pts.	Avg.	Hi.
Abdul-Jabbar	79	2629	1338	755	.564	439	336	.765	133	345	478	280	248	2	67	130	1846	23.4	46
Worthy	75	2454	1086	629	.579	314	242	.771	136	251	387	201	195	0	82	77	1500	20.0	37
Johnson	72	2578	918	483	.526	434	378	.871	85	341	426	907	133	0	113	16	1354	18.8	34
Scott	76	2190	989	507	.513	176	138	.784	55	134	189	164	167	0	85	15	1174	15.4	31
Lucas	77	1750	653	302	.462	230	180	.783	164	402	566	84	253	1	45	24	785	10.2	23
Cooper	82	2269	606	274	.452	170	147	.865	44	200	244	466	238	2	89	43	758	9.2	20
McGee	71	1213	544	252	.463	64	42	.656	51	89	140	83	131	0	53	7	587	8.3	34
Gudmundsson	8	128	37	20	.541	27	18	.667	17	21	38	3	25	1	3	4	58	7.3	15
Green	82	1542	388	209	.539	167	102	.611	160	221	381	54	229	2	49	49	521	6.4	21
Kupchak	55	783	257	124	.482	112	84	.750	69	122	191	17	102	0	12	7	332	6.0	15
Rambis	74	1573	269	160	.595	122	88	.721	156	361	517	69	198	0	66	33	408	5.5	17
Spriggs	43	471	192	88	.458	49	38	.776	28	53	81	49	78	0	18	9	214	5.0	18
Henderson	1	3	3	2	.667	0	0		0	1	1	0	1	0	0	0	4	4.0	4
Nevitt	4	25	11	3	.273	6	4	.667	3	4	7	2	6	0	2	2	10	2.5	4
Lester	7	222	52	26	.500	19	13	.684	0	14	14	54	27	0	9	3	67	2.5	8

3-Pt. FG: L.A. Lakers 138-409 (.337)—Abdul-Jabbar 0-2 (.000); Worthy 0-13 (.000); Johnson 10-43 (.233); Scott 22-61 (.361); Lucas 1-2 (.500); Cooper 63-163 (.387); McGee 41-114 (.360); Green 1-6 (.167); Kupchak 0-1 (.000); Spriggs 0-1 (.000); Lester 0-3 (.000). Opponents 51-247 (.206).

MILWAUKEE BUCKS

Player	G.	Min.	FGA	FGM	Pct.	FTA	FTM	Pct.	Off. Reb.	Def. Reb.	Tot. Reb.	Ast.	PF	Disq.	Stl.	Blk. Sh.	Pts.	Avg.	Hi.
Moncrief	73	2567	962	470	.489	580	498	.859	115	219	334	357	178	1	103	18	1471	20.2	35
Cummings	82	2669	1438	681	.474	404	265	.656	222	472	694	193	283	4	121	51	1627	19.8	35
Pressey	80	2704	843	411	.488	392	316	.806	127	272	399	623	247	4	168	71	1146	14.3	30
Pierce	81	2147	798	429	.538	310	266	.858	94	137	231	177	252	6	83	6	1127	13.9	32
Hodges	66	1739	568	284	.500	86	75	.872	39	78	117	229	157	3	74	2	716	10.8	29
Lister	81	1812	577	318	.551	266	160	.602	199	393	592	101	300	8	49	142	796	9.8	22
Breuer	82	1792	570	272	.477	198	141	.712	159	299	458	114	214	2	50	116	685	8.4	19
Davis	57	873	397	188	.474	75	61	.813	60	110	170	55	113	1	26	7	440	7.7	26
Fields	78	1120	398	204	.513	132	91	.689	59	144	203	79	170	3	51	15	499	6.4	23
Lamp	44	701	243	109	.449	64	55	.859	34	87	121	64	88	1	20	3	276	6.3	23
Glenn	38	573	190	94	.495	49	47	.959	4	53	57	39	42	0	9	3	235	6.2	14
Reynolds	55	508	162	72	.444	104	58	.558	37	43	80	86	57	0	43	19	203	3.7	17
Mokeski	45	521	139	59	.424	34	25	.735	36	103	139	30	92	1	6	6	143	3.2	12
Warrick	5	27	10	4	.400	1	1	1.000	0	3	3	6	3	0	2	0	10	2.0	4
Rowland	2	9	3	1	.333	2	1	.500	0	1	1	1	0	0	0	0	3	1.5	2
Jones	3	43	12	5	.417	4	3	.750	4	6	10	4	13	0	0	1	13	1.1	4

3-Pt. FG: Milwaukee 125-382 (.327)—Moncrief 33-103 (.320); Cummings 0-2 (.000); Pressey 8-44 (.182); Pierce 3-23 (.130); Hodges 73-162 (.451); Lister 0-2 (.000); Breuer 0-1 (.000); Davis 3-24 (.125); Fields 0-4 (.000); Lamp 3-13 (.231); Reynolds 1-2 (.500); Warrick 1-2 (.500). Opponents 97-329 (.295).

NEW JERSEY NETS

Player	G.	Min.	FGA	FGM	Pct.	FTA	FTM	Pct.	Off. Reb.	Def. Reb.	Tot. Reb.	Ast.	PF	Disq.	Stl.	Blk. Sh.	Pts.	Avg.	Hi.
Gminski	81	2525	949	491	.517	393	351	.893	206	462	668	133	163	0	56	71	1333	16.5	41
B. Williams	82	3070	956	500	.523	445	301	.676	329	657	986	131	294	9	73	96	1301	15.9	31
Birdsong	77	2395	1056	542	.513	210	122	.581	88	114	202	261	228	8	85	17	1214	15.8	31
Richardson	47	1604	661	296	.448	179	141	.788	77	173	250	340	163	2	125	11	737	15.7	38
Dawkins	51	1207	441	284	.644	297	210	.707	85	166	251	77	227	10	16	59	778	15.3	27
King	73	1998	961	438	.456	203	167	.823	116	250	366	181	205	4	58	24	1047	14.3	34
Cook	79	1965	627	267	.426	111	84	.757	51	126	177	390	172	0	156	22	629	8.0	23
Johnson	79	1574	507	214	.422	233	183	.785	98	234	332	217	248	1	67	25	616	7.8	25
R. Williams (Tot)	47	827	306	117	.382	126	115	.913	35	51	86	187	124	2	61	4	355	7.6	22
R. Williams (NJ)	5	63	32	10	.313	14	12	.857	3	1	4	9	12	0	5	0	32	6.4	13
Ransey	79	1504	505	231	.457	148	121	.818	34	82	116	252	128	0	51	4	586	7.4	21
O'Koren	67	1031	336	160	.476	39	23	.590	33	102	135	118	134	3	29	9	350	5.2	19
Turner	53	650	171	84	.491	78	58	.744	45	92	137	14	125	4	21	3	226	4.3	16
Cattage	29	185	83	28	.337	44	35	.795	15	19	34	4	23	0	6	0	92	3.2	12
Higgins (NJ)	2	29	16	3	.188	0	0	....	3	5	8	1	6	0	1	4	6	3.0	4
Joseph	1	5	0	0	....	2	2	1.000	0	0	0	0	1	0	0	0	2	2.0	2

3-Pt. FG: New Jersey 43-214 (.201)—Gminski 0-1 (.000); B. Williams 0-2 (.000); Birdsong 8-22 (.364); Richardson 4-27 (.148); Dawkins 0-1 (.000); King 4-23 (.174); Cook 11-53 (.208); Johnson 5-24 (.208); R. Williams 0-2 (.000); Ransey 3-24 (.125); O'Koren 7-27 (.259); Turner 0-1 (.000); Cattage 1-5 (.200); Higgins 0-2 (.000). Opponents 96-316 (.304).

NEW YORK KNICKERBOCKERS

Player	G.	Min.	FGA	FGM	Pct.	FTA	FTM	Pct.	Off. Reb.	Def. Reb.	Tot. Reb.	Ast.	PF	Disq.	Stl.	Blk. Sh.	Pts.	Avg.	Hi.
Ewing	50	1771	814	386	.474	306	226	.739	124	327	451	102	191	7	54	103	998	20.0	37
Cummings	31	1007	408	195	.478	139	97	.698	92	188	280	47	136	7	27	12	487	15.7	34
Wilkins	81	2025	934	437	.468	237	132	.557	92	116	208	161	155	0	68	9	1013	12.5	29
Orr	74	2237	741	330	.445	278	218	.784	123	189	312	179	177	4	61	26	878	11.9	28
Bailey	48	1245	443	202	.456	167	129	.772	102	232	334	50	207	12	33	40	533	11.1	31
Sparrow	74	2344	723	345	.477	127	101	.795	50	120	170	472	182	1	85	14	796	10.8	27
Tucker	77	1788	740	349	.472	100	79	.790	70	99	169	192	167	0	65	8	818	10.6	25
Walker	81	2023	753	324	.430	277	190	.686	100	120	220	337	216	1	146	36	838	10.3	28
Bannister	70	1405	479	235	.491	249	131	.526	89	233	322	42	208	5	42	24	601	8.6	35
Cartwright	2	36	7	3	.429	10	6	.600	2	8	10	5	6	0	1	1	12	6.0	11
McNealy	30	627	144	70	.486	47	31	.660	62	141	203	41	88	2	38	12	171	5.7	17
Grunfeld	76	1402	355	148	.417	108	90	.833	42	164	206	119	192	2	39	13	412	5.4	15
Thornton	71	1323	274	125	.456	162	86	.531	113	177	290	43	209	5	30	7	336	4.7	17
Green	7	72	27	13	.481	9	5	.556	12	15	27	2	8	0	4	0	31	4.4	11
Cofield	45	469	184	75	.408	20	12	.600	6	40	46	82	65	1	20	3	165	3.7	13
Carter	5	31	8	2	.250	1	1	1.000	2	1	3	6	1	0	0	0	5	1.0	3

3-Pt. FG: New York 82-239 (.343)—Ewing 0-5 (.000); Cummings 0-2 (.000); Wilkins 7-25 (.280); Orr 0-4 (.000); Bailey 0-4 (.000); Sparrow 5-20 (.250); Tucker 41-91 (.451); Walker 0-10 (.000); Bannister 0-1 (.000); Grunfeld 26-61 (.426); Cofield 3-15 (.200); Carter 0-1 (.000). Opponents 68-274 (.248).

PHILADELPHIA 76ers

Player	G.	Min.	FGA	FGM	Pct.	FTA	FTM	Pct.	Off. Reb.	Def. Reb.	Tot. Reb.	Ast.	PF	Disq.	Stl.	Blk. Sh.	Pts.	Avg.	Hi.
Malone	74	2706	1246	571	.458	784	617	.787	339	533	872	90	194	0	67	71	1759	23.8	42
Barkley	80	2952	1041	595	.572	578	396	.685	354	672	1026	312	333	8	173	125	1603	20.0	36
Erving	74	2474	1085	521	.480	368	289	.785	169	201	370	248	196	3	113	82	1340	18.1	31
Cheeks	82	3270	913	490	.537	335	282	.842	55	180	235	753	160	0	207	28	1266	15.4	31
McAdoo	29	609	251	116	.462	81	62	.765	25	78	103	35	64	0	10	18	294	10.1	28
Threatt	70	1754	684	310	.453	90	75	.833	21	100	121	193	157	1	93	5	696	9.9	24
Thompson	23	432	194	70	.361	43	37	.860	27	36	63	24	49	1	15	17	179	7.8	24
Catledge	64	1092	431	202	.469	139	90	.647	107	165	272	21	127	0	31	8	494	7.7	30
Jones	70	1519	338	189	.559	145	114	.786	49	120	169	126	159	0	48	49	492	7.0	21
Wood	29	455	136	57	.419	34	27	.794	9	18	27	75	24	0	14	0	154	5.3	15
Green (Tot)	41	453	192	83	.432	49	35	.714	27	46	73	9	53	0	5	9	201	4.9	20
Green (Phil)	21	232	91	39	.429	23	14	.609	10	25	35	6	27	0	1	2	92	4.4	13
Moss (Tot)	72	1012	292	116	.397	89	65	.730	34	81	115	108	132	1	56	15	304	4.2	14
Moss (Phil)	60	852	239	95	.397	74	54	.730	25	65	90	89	106	0	50	12	249	4.2	14
Toney	6	84	36	11	.306	8	3	.375	2	3	5	12	8	0	2	0	25	4.2	8
Stokes	31	350	119	56	.471	21	14	.667	27	30	57	17	56	0	14	11	126	4.1	16
Johnson	75	1069	223	105	.471	81	51	.630	106	149	255	15	129	0	23	62	261	3.5	12
Carter (Tot)	9	67	24	7	.292	7	6	.857	2	2	4	4	10	0	1	0	20	2.2	9
Carter (Phil)	4	36	16	5	.313	6	5	.833	0	1	1	1	8	0	0	0	15	3.8	9
Winters	4	17	13	3	.231	0	0	....	1	2	3	0	1	0	1	0	6	1.5	2
Young	2	2	2	0	.000	0	0	....	0	0	0	0	0	0	0	0	0	0.0	0

3-Pt. FG: Philadelphia 51-224 (.228)—Malone 0-1 (.000); Barkley 17-75 (.227); Erving 9-32 (.281); Cheeks 4-17 (.235); Threatt 1-24 (.042); Thompson 2-12 (.167); Catledge 0-4 (.000); Jones 0-1 (.000); Wood 13-29 (.448); Moss 5-25 (.200); Toney 0-2 (.000); Stokes 0-1 (.000); Winters 0-1 (.000). Opponents 82-282 (.291).

PHOENIX SUNS

Player	G.	Min.	FGA	FGM	Pct.	FTA	FTM	Pct.	Off. Reb.	Def. Reb.	Tot. Reb.	Ast.	PF	Disq.	Stl.	Blk. Sh.	Pts.	Avg.	Hi.
Davis	70	2239	1287	624	.485	305	257	.843	54	149	203	361	153	1	99	3	1523	21.8	43
Nance	73	2484	1001	582	.581	444	310	.698	169	449	618	240	247	6	70	130	1474	20.2	44
Edwards	52	1314	587	318	.542	302	212	.702	79	222	301	74	200	5	23	29	848	16.3	30
Humphries	82	2733	735	352	.479	257	197	.767	56	204	260	526	222	1	132	9	905	11.0	27
Sanders	82	1644	676	347	.513	257	208	.809	104	169	273	150	236	3	76	31	905	11.0	27
Adams	78	2005	679	341	.502	203	159	.783	148	329	477	324	272	7	103	46	841	10.8	28
Pinckney	80	1602	457	255	.558	254	171	.673	95	213	308	90	190	3	71	37	681	8.5	27
Thompson	61	1281	399	195	.489	157	127	.809	58	83	141	132	151	0	51	10	517	8.5	19
Toney (Tot)	13	230	66	28	.424	31	21	.677	3	22	25	26	24	0	6	0	80	6.2	22
Toney (Phoe)	10	206	59	26	.441	30	20	.667	3	20	23	26	18	0	5	0	75	7.5	22
Pittman	69	1132	218	127	.583	141	99	.702	99	147	246	58	140	2	37	23	353	5.1	22
Vanos	11	202	72	23	.319	23	8	.348	21	39	60	16	34	0	2	5	54	4.9	13
Glouchkov	49	772	209	84	.402	122	70	.574	31	132	163	32	124	0	26	25	239	4.9	13
Jones	43	742	164	75	.457	98	54	.510	65	128	193	52	87	0	32	25	200	4.7	19

Player	G.	Min.	FGA	FGM	Pct.	FTA	FTM	Pct.	Off. Reb.	Def. Reb.	Tot. Reb.	Ast.	PF	Disq.	Stl.	Blk. Sh.	Pts.	Avg.	Hi.
Durrant	4	51	21	8	.381	4	1	.250	2	6	8	5	10	0	3	0	17	4.3	9
Foster	48	704	218	85	.390	32	23	.719	9	49	58	121	77	0	22	1	202	4.2	13
Robey	46	629	191	72	.377	48	33	.688	40	108	148	58	92	1	19	5	177	3.8	12
Holton	4	65	20	4	.200	6	4	.667	1	2	3	7	7	0	2	0	12	3.0	7

3-Pt. FG: Phoenix 38-183 (.208)—Davis 18-76 (.237); Nance 0-8 (.000); Humphries 4-29 (.138); Sanders 3-15 (.200); Adams 0-2 (.000); Pinckney 0-2 (.000); Thompson 0-2 (.000); Toney 3-10 (.300); Glouchkov 1-1 (1.000); Jones 0-1 (.000); Foster 9-32 (.281); Robey 0-3 (.000); Holton 0-2 (.000). Opponents 89-279 (.319).

PORTLAND TRAIL BLAZERS

Player	G.	Min.	FGA	FGM	Pct.	FTA	FTM	Pct.	Off. Reb.	Def. Reb.	Tot. Reb.	Ast.	PF	Disq.	Stl.	Blk. Sh.	Pts.	Avg.	Hi.
Vandeweghe	79	2791	1332	719	.540	602	523	.869	92	124	216	187	161	0	54	17	1962	24.8	38
Drexler	75	2576	1142	542	.475	381	293	.769	171	250	421	600	270	8	197	46	1389	18.5	41
Thompson	82	2569	1011	503	.498	309	198	.641	181	427	608	176	267	5	76	35	1204	14.7	30
Paxson	75	1931	792	372	.470	244	217	.889	42	106	148	278	156	3	94	5	981	13.1	33
Bowie	38	1132	345	167	.484	161	114	.708	93	234	327	99	142	4	21	96	448	11.8	24
Carr	55	1557	466	232	.498	217	149	.687	146	346	492	70	203	5	38	30	613	11.1	27
Valentine	28	734	206	92	.447	100	71	.710	20	52	72	139	78	0	49	1	256	9.1	18
Colter	81	1868	597	272	.456	164	135	.823	41	136	177	257	188	0	113	10	706	8.7	26
Kersey	79	1217	470	258	.549	229	156	.681	137	156	293	83	208	2	85	32	672	8.5	22
Porter	79	1214	447	212	.474	155	125	.806	35	82	117	198	136	0	81	1	562	7.1	24
Jones	80	1437	254	126	.496	150	124	.827	105	250	355	74	244	2	38	61	376	4.7	21
Johnson	64	815	214	113	.528	85	37	.435	90	153	243	19	147	1	13	22	263	4.1	15
Martin (Tot)	8	21	7	3	.429	2	0	.000	1	3	4	0	7	0	1	6	6	0.8	2
Martin (Port)	5	14	5	2	.400	2	0	.000	0	0	0	0	5	0	0	4	0.8	2

3-Pt. FG: Portland 74-275 (.269)—Vandeweghe 1-8 (.125); Drexler 12-60 (.200); Paxson 20-62 (.323); Carr 0-4 (.000); Valentine 1-3 (.333); Colter 27-83 (.325); Kersey 0-6 (.000); Porter 13-42 (.310); Jones 0-7 (.000). Opponents 83-248 (.335).

SACRAMENTO KINGS

Player	G.	Min.	FGA	FGM	Pct.	FTA	FTM	Pct.	Off. Reb.	Def. Reb.	Tot. Reb.	Ast.	PF	Disq.	Stl.	Blk. Sh.	Pts.	Avg.	Hi.
Johnson	82	2514	1311	623	.475	343	280	.816	173	246	419	214	237	0	54	17	1530	18.7	38
Theus	82	2919	1137	546	.480	490	405	.827	73	231	304	788	232	3	112	20	1503	18.3	37
Woodson	81	2417	1073	510	.475	289	242	.837	94	132	226	197	215	1	92	37	1264	15.6	39
Thompson	80	2377	794	411	.518	276	202	.732	252	518	770	168	295	8	71	109	1024	12.8	25
Drew	75	1971	776	376	.485	161	128	.795	25	100	125	338	134	0	66	2	890	11.9	26
Thorpe	75	1675	492	289	.587	248	164	.661	137	283	420	84	233	3	35	34	742	9.9	28
Tyler	71	1651	649	295	.455	112	84	.750	109	204	313	94	159	0	64	108	674	9.5	26
Olberding	81	2157	403	225	.558	210	162	.771	113	310	423	266	276	3	43	23	612	7.6	17
Kleine	80	1180	344	160	.465	130	94	.723	113	260	373	46	224	1	24	34	414	5.2	14
Henry	28	149	67	31	.463	17	12	.706	8	11	19	4	11	0	5	0	78	2.8	18
Adams	18	139	44	16	.364	12	8	.667	2	4	6	22	9	0	9	1	40	2.2	10
Bratz	33	269	70	26	.371	18	14	.778	2	21	23	39	43	0	13	0	70	2.1	10
Kelley	37	324	49	28	.571	22	18	.818	29	52	81	43	62	0	10	3	74	2.0	8
Cooke	6	38	11	2	.182	10	5	.500	5	5	10	1	5	0	4	0	9	1.5	9

3-Pt. FG: Sacramento 30-134 (.224)—Johnson 4-20 (.200); Theus 6-35 (.171); Woodson 2-13 (.154); Thompson 0-1 (.000); Drew 10-31 (.323); Tyler 0-3 (.000); Olberding 0-2 (.000); Henry 4-10 (.400); Adams 0-3 (.000); Bratz 4-14 (.286); Kelley 0-2 (.000). Opponents 73-281 (.260).

SAN ANTONIO SPURS

Player	G.	Min.	FGA	FGM	Pct.	FTA	FTM	Pct.	Off. Reb.	Def. Reb.	Tot. Reb.	Ast.	PF	Disq.	Stl.	Blk. Sh.	Pts.	Avg.	Hi.
Mitchell	82	2970	1697	802	.473	392	317	.809	134	275	409	188	175	0	56	25	1921	23.4	44
Robertson	82	2878	1093	562	.514	327	260	.795	184	332	516	448	296	4	301	40	1392	17.0	41
Gilmore	71	2395	684	423	.618	482	338	.701	166	434	600	102	239	3	39	108	1184	16.7	33
Johnson	71	1828	573	362	.632	373	259	.694	143	319	462	95	291	13	44	66	983	13.8	31
Moore	28	856	303	150	.495	86	59	.686	25	61	86	252	78	0	70	6	363	13.0	30
Matthews	75	1853	603	320	.531	211	173	.820	30	101	131	476	168	1	87	32	817	10.9	29
Lamp (Tot)	74	1321	514	245	.477	133	111	.835	53	147	200	117	155	1	39	4	608	8.2	25
Lamp (SA)	30	620	271	136	.502	69	56	.812	19	60	79	53	67	0	19	1	332	11.1	25
Greenwood	68	1910	388	198	.510	184	142	.772	151	380	531	90	207	3	37	52	538	7.9	27
Williams (SA)	23	397	131	50	.382	64	62	.969	13	24	37	111	64	1	28	3	164	7.1	22
Sundvold	70	1150	476	220	.462	48	39	.813	22	58	80	261	110	0	34	0	500	7.1	18
Hughes	68	866	372	152	.409	84	49	.583	49	64	113	61	79	0	26	5	356	5.2	23
Wilkins (Tot)	75	1126	374	147	.393	93	58	.624	74	198	272	46	157	1	11	21	352	4.7	16
Wilkins (SA)	27	522	134	51	.381	46	28	.609	34	93	127	18	71	1	8	10	130	4.8	13
Iavaroni	42	669	163	74	.454	67	43	.642	42	90	132	53	109	0	22	14	191	4.5	17
Corbin	16	174	64	27	.422	14	10	.714	11	14	25	11	21	0	11	2	64	4.0	12
Higgins (SA)	11	128	40	18	.450	16	11	.688	5	19	24	12	21	0	2	3	47	4.3	11
Whatley (Tot)	14	107	35	15	.429	10	5	.500	4	10	14	23	10	0	5	1	35	2.5	14
Whatley (SA)	2	14	2	1	.500	0	0	......	0	0	0	3	1	0	0	0	2	1.0	2
Cook	34	356	67	28	.418	41	26	.634	31	50	81	21	64	0	13	11	82	2.4	9
Brittain	32	219	43	22	.512	19	10	.526	10	39	49	5	54	1	3	12	54	1.7	7

3-Pt. FG: San Antonio 46-196 (.235)—Mitchell 0-12 (.000); Robertson 8-29 (.276); Gilmore 0-1 (.000); Moore 4-22 (.182); Matthews 4-25 (.160); Lamp 4-17 (.235); Greenwood 0-1 (.000); Williams 2-6 (.333); Sundvold 21-60 (.350); Hughes 3-17 (.176); Iavaroni 0-2 (.000); Corbin 0-1 (.000); Higgins 0-2 (.000); Cook 0-1 (.000). Opponents 98-322 (.304).

SEATTLE SUPERSONICS

Player	G.	Min.	FGA	FGM	Pct.	FTA	FTM	Pct.	Off. Reb.	Def. Reb.	Tot. Reb.	Ast.	PF	Disq.	Stl.	Blk. Sh.	Pts.	Avg.	Hi.
Chambers	66	2019	928	432	.466	414	346	.836	126	305	431	132	248	6	55	37	1223	18.5	32
Sikma	80	2790	1100	508	.462	411	355	.864	146	602	748	301	293	4	92	73	1371	17.1	38
McDaniel	82	2706	1176	576	.490	364	250	.687	307	348	655	193	305	8	101	37	1404	17.1	36
Henderson	82	2568	900	434	.482	223	185	.830	89	98	187	487	230	2	138	11	1071	13.1	26
Wood	78	1749	817	355	.435	239	187	.782	80	164	244	114	171	2	57	19	902	11.6	27
McCormick	77	1705	444	253	.570	244	174	.713	140	263	403	83	219	4	19	28	681	8.8	21
Sobers	78	1279	541	240	.444	125	110	.880	29	70	99	180	139	1	44	2	603	7.7	23
Young	82	1901	449	227	.506	106	90	.849	29	91	120	303	113	0	110	9	568	6.9	20

Player	G.	Min.	FGA	FGM	Pct.	FTA	FTM	Pct.	Off. Reb.	Def. Reb.	Tot. Reb.	Ast.	PF	Disq.	Stl.	Blk. Sh.	Pts.	Avg.	Hi.
Phelps	70	880	286	117	.409	74	44	.595	29	60	89	71	86	0	45	1	279	4.0	18
Vranes	80	1569	284	131	.461	75	39	.520	115	166	281	68	218	3	63	31	301	3.8	13
Brickowski	40	311	58	30	.517	27	18	.667	16	38	54	21	74	2	11	7	78	2.0	11
Pope	11	74	20	9	.450	4	2	.500	6	5	11	4	11	0	2	1	21	1.9	16
Higgins	12	94	27	9	.333	5	3	.600	3	9	12	6	11	0	2	1	22	1.8	7
Stivrins	3	14	4	1	.250	4	1	.250	3	0	3	1	2	0	0	0	3	1.0	2
Johnson	41	264	23	12	.522	16	11	.688	26	34	60	13	46	0	6	37	35	0.9	5
Martin	3	7	2	1	.500	0	0	......	1	3	4	0	2	0	0	1	2	0.7	2

3-Pt. FG: Seattle 79-300 (.263)—Chambers 13-48 (.271); Sikma 0-13 (.000); McDaniel 2-10 (.200); Henderson 18-52 (.346); Wood 5-37 (.135); McCormick 1-2 (.500); Sobers 13-43 (.302); Young 24-74 (.324); Phelps 1-12 (.083); Vranes 0-4 (.000); Pope 1-1 (1.000); Higgins 1-4 (.250). Opponents 57-224 (.254).

UTAH JAZZ

Player	G.	Min.	FGA	FGM	Pct.	FTA	FTM	Pct.	Off. Reb.	Def. Reb.	Tot. Reb.	Ast.	PF	Disq.	Stl.	Blk. Sh.	Pts.	Avg.	Hi.
Dantley	76	2744	1453	818	.563	796	630	.791	178	217	395	264	206	2	64	4	2267	29.8	47
Malone	81	2475	1016	504	.496	405	195	.481	174	544	718	236	295	2	105	44	1203	14.9	29
Bailey	82	2358	1077	483	.448	277	230	.830	148	345	493	153	160	0	42	114	1196	14.6	26
Green	80	2012	758	357	.471	250	213	.852	32	103	135	411	130	0	106	6	932	11.7	27
Hansen	82	2032	628	299	.476	132	95	.720	82	162	244	193	205	1	74	9	710	8.7	25
Eaton	80	2551	589	277	.470	202	122	.604	172	503	675	101	282	5	33	369	676	8.5	20
Stockton	82	1935	466	228	.489	205	172	.839	33	146	179	610	227	2	157	10	630	7.7	19
Scurry	78	1168	301	142	.472	126	78	.619	97	145	242	85	171	2	78	66	363	4.7	15
Wilkins	48	604	240	96	.400	47	30	.638	40	105	145	28	86	0	3	11	222	4.6	16
Mannion	57	673	214	97	.453	82	53	.646	26	56	82	55	68	0	32	5	255	4.5	19
Iavaroni (Tot)	68	1014	244	110	.451	115	76	.661	63	146	209	82	163	0	32	17	296	4.4	17
Iavaroni (Utah)	26	345	81	36	.444	48	33	.688	21	56	77	29	54	0	10	3	105	4.0	10
Roberts	58	469	167	74	.443	87	67	.770	31	49	80	27	72	0	8	6	216	3.7	21
Cook (Tot)	36	373	73	31	.425	42	27	.643	33	53	86	21	65	0	13	11	89	2.5	9
Cook (Utah)	2	17	6	3	.500	1	1	1.000	2	3	5	0	1	0	0	0	7	3.5	7
Hayes	58	397	87	39	.448	36	11	.306	32	45	77	7	81	0	5	19	89	1.5	10

3-Pt. FG: Utah 35-169 (.207)—Dantley 1-11 (.091); Malone 0-2 (.000); Bailey 0-7 (.000); Green 5-29 (.172); Hansen 17-50 (.340); Stockton 2-15 (.133); Scurry 1-11 (.091); Mannion 8-42 (.190); Roberts 1-2 (.500). Opponents 65-251 (.259).

WASHINGTON BULLETS

Player	G.	Min.	FGA	FGM	Pct.	FTA	FTM	Pct.	Off. Reb.	Def. Reb.	Tot. Reb.	Ast.	PF	Disq.	Stl.	Blk. Sh.	Pts.	Avg.	Hi.
Malone	80	2992	1522	735	.483	371	322	.868	66	222	288	191	180	2	70	12	1795	22.4	43
Ruland	30	1114	383	212	.554	200	145	.725	107	213	320	159	100	1	23	25	569	19.0	30
Robinson	78	2563	1255	595	.474	353	269	.762	180	500	680	186	217	2	98	44	1460	18.7	38
G. Williams	77	2284	1013	434	.428	188	138	.734	52	114	166	453	113	0	96	15	1036	13.5	33
F. Johnson	14	402	154	69	.448	54	38	.704	7	21	28	76	30	0	11	1	176	12.6	27
Roundfield	79	2321	660	322	.488	362	273	.754	210	432	642	167	194	1	36	51	917	11.6	29
Daye	64	1075	399	198	.496	237	159	.671	71	112	183	109	121	0	46	11	556	8.7	22
Wood (Tot)	68	1198	466	184	.395	155	123	.794	25	65	90	182	70	0	34	0	532	7.8	30
Wood (Wash)	39	743	330	127	.385	121	96	.793	16	47	63	107	46	0	20	0	378	9.7	30
F. Williams	9	110	67	25	.373	17	12	.706	4	8	12	7	10	0	7	1	69	7.7	17
McMillen	56	863	285	131	.460	79	64	.810	44	69	113	35	85	0	9	10	326	5.8	21
McKenna	30	430	166	61	.367	30	25	.833	9	27	36	23	54	1	29	2	174	5.8	25
Green	20	221	101	44	.436	26	21	.808	17	21	38	3	26	0	4	7	109	5.5	20
Moss	12	160	53	21	.396	15	11	.733	9	16	25	19	26	1	6	3	55	4.6	14
Jones	81	1609	254	129	.508	86	54	.628	122	199	321	76	235	2	57	133	312	3.9	17
Bol	80	2090	278	128	.460	86	42	.488	123	354	477	23	255	5	28	397	298	3.7	18
Bradley	70	842	209	73	.349	56	32	.571	24	71	95	107	101	0	85	3	195	2.8	17
Whatley (Wash)	4	27	14	5	.357	3	1	.333	2	5	7	7	1	0	0	1	11	2.8	5
G. Johnson	2	7	3	1	.333	2	2	1.000	1	1	2	0	1	0	0	0	4	2.0	4
Gregory	2	2	2	1	.000	0	0	......	2	0	2	0	1	0	1	0	2	1.0	2

3-Pt. FG: Washington 116-408 (.284)—Malone 3-17 (.176); Ruland 0-4 (.000); Robinson 1-4 (.250); G. Williams 30-116 (.259); F. Johnson 0-3 (.000); Roundfield 0-6 (.000); Daye 1-3 (.333); Wood 28-85 (.329); F. Williams 7-14 (.500); McMillen 0-3 (.000); McKenna 27-75 (.360); Green 0-1 (.000); Moss 2-7 (.286); Jones 0-1 (.000). Bol 0-1 (.000); Bradley 17-68 (.250). Opponents 71-259 (.274).

PLAYOFF RESULTS

EASTERN CONFERENCE FIRST ROUND
Boston 3, Chicago 0
Apr. 17—Thur.—Chicago 104 at Boston 123
Apr. 20—Sun.—Chicago 131 at Boston **135
Apr. 22—Tue.—Boston 122 at Chicago 104

Milwaukee 3, New Jersey 0
Apr. 18—Fri.—New Jersey 107 at Milwaukee 119
Apr. 20—Sun.—New Jersey 97 at Milwaukee 111
Apr. 22—Tue.—Milwaukee 118 at New Jersey 113

Philadelphia 3, Washington 2
Apr. 18—Fri.—Washington 95 at Philadelphia 94
Apr. 20—Sun.—Washington 97 at Philadelphia 102
Apr. 22—Tue.—Philadelphia 91 at Washington 86
Apr. 24—Thur.—Philadelphia 111 at Washington 116
Apr. 27—Sun.—Washington 109 at Philadelphia 134

Atlanta 3, Detroit 1
Apr. 17—Thur.—Detroit 122 at Atlanta 140
Apr. 19—Sat.—Detroit 125 at Atlanta 137
Apr. 22—Tue.—Atlanta 97 at Detroit 106
Apr. 25—Fri.—Atlanta 114 at Detroit..................**113

EASTERN CONFERENCE SEMIFINALS
Boston 4, Atlanta 1
Apr. 27—Sun.—Atlanta 91 at Boston 103
Apr. 29—Tue.—Atlanta 108 at Boston 119
May 2—Fri.—Boston 111 at Atlanta 107
May 4—Sun.—Boston 94 at Atlanta 106
May 6—Tue.—Atlanta 99 at Boston 132

Milwaukee 4, Philadelphia 3
Apr. 29—Tue.—Philadelphia 118 at Milwaukee 112
May 1—Thur.—Philadelphia 107 at Milwaukee 119
May 3—Sat.—Milwaukee 103 at Philadelphia 107
May 5—Mon.—Milwaukee 109 at Philadelphia 104
May 7—Wed.—Philadelphia 108 at Milwaukee 113
May 9—Fri.—Milwaukee 108 at Philadelphia 126
May 11—Sun.—Philadelphia 112 at Milwaukee 113

EASTERN CONFERENCE FINALS
Boston 4, Milwaukee 0
May 13—Tue.—Milwaukee 96 at Boston 128
May 15—Thur.—Milwaukee 111 at Boston 122
May 17—Sat.—Boston 111 at Milwaukee 107
May 18—Sun.—Boston 111 at Milwaukee 98

WESTERN CONFERENCE FIRST ROUND
L.A. Lakers 3, San Antonio 0
Apr. 17—Thur.—San Antonio 88 at L.A. Lakers........................135
Apr. 19—Sat.—San Antonio 94 at L.A. Lakers............................122
Apr. 23—Wed.—L.A. Lakers 114 at San Antonio......................94

Houston 3, Sacramento 0
Apr. 17—Thur.—Sacramento 87 at Houston 107
Apr. 19—Sat.—Sacramento 103 at Houston 111
Apr. 22—Tue.—Houston 113 at Sacramento.............................98

Denver 3, Portland 1
Apr. 18—Fri.—Portland 126 at Denver 133
Apr. 20—Sun.—Portland 108 at Denver.......................106
Apr. 22—Tue.—Denver 115 at Portland........................104
Apr. 24—Thur.—Denver 116 at Portland 112

Dallas 3, Utah 1
Apr. 18—Fri.—Utah 93 at Dallas 101
Apr. 20—Sun.—Utah 106 at Dallas 113
Apr. 23—Wed.—Dallas 98 at Utah 100
Apr. 25—Fri.—Dallas 117 at Utah 113

WESTERN CONFERENCE SEMIFINALS
L.A. Lakers 4, Dallas 2
Apr. 27—Sun.—Dallas 116 at L.A. Lakers.......................130
Apr. 30—Wed.—Dallas 113 at L.A. Lakers......................117
May 2—Fri.—L.A. Lakers 108 at Dallas 110
May 4—Sun.—L.A. Lakers 118 at Dallas 120
May 6—Tue.—Dallas 113 at L.A. Lakers.......................116
May 8—Thur.—L.A. Lakers 120 at Dallas 107

Houston 4, Denver 2
Apr. 26—Sat.—Denver 119 at Houston 126
Apr. 29—Tue.—Denver 101 at Houston 119
May 2—Fri.—Houston 115 at Denver 116
May 4—Sun.—Houston 111 at Denver *114
May 6—Tue.—Denver 103 at Houston 131
May 8—Thur.—Houston 126 at Denver **122

WESTERN CONFERENCE FINALS
Houston 4, L.A. Lakers 1
May 10—Sat.—Houston 107 at L.A. Lakers 119
May 13—Tue.—Houston 112 at L.A. Lakers 102
May 16—Fri.—L.A. Lakers 109 at Houston 117
May 18—Sun.—L.A. Lakers 95 at Houston 105
May 21—Wed.—Houston 114 at L.A. Lakers...............112

NBA FINALS
Boston 4, Houston 2
May 26—Mon.—Houston 100 at Boston.....................112
May 29—Thur.—Houston 95 at Boston 117
June 1—Sun.—Boston 104 at Houston.......................106
June 3—Tue.—Boston 106 at Houston.......................103
June 5—Thur.—Boston 96 at Houston 111
June 8—Sun.—Houston 97 at Boston.........................114

1984-85 NBA STATISTICS

1984-85 NBA CHAMPION LOS ANGELES LAKERS

Front row (left to right): Owner Dr. Jerry Buss, Mike McGee, Kurt Rambis, Jamaal Wilkes, Kareem Abdul-Jabbar, Bob McAdoo, Magic Johnson, Michael Cooper, assistant coach Bill Bertka. Back row: Coach Pat Riley, Byron Scott, Larry Spriggs, James Worthy, Mitch Kupchak, Ronnie Lester, assistant coach Dave Wohl, trainer Gary Vitti.

FINAL STANDINGS

ATLANTIC DIVISION

Team	Atl.	Bos.	Chi.	Cle.	Dal.	Den.	Det.	G.S.	Hou.	Ind.	K.C.	L.A.C.	L.A.L.	Mil.	N.J.	N.Y.	Phi.	Pho.	Por.	S.A.	Sea.	Uta.	Was.	W.	L.	Pct.	G.B.
Boston	4	..	4	6	2	1	4	2	2	5	2	2	1	1	5	6	3	2	1	2	1	2	5	63	19	.768	....
Philadelphia	5	3	5	2	1	1	5	2	1	5	1	2	1	3	4	4	..	2	2	1	2	2	4	58	24	.707	5
New Jersey	3	1	4	3	1	0	5	1	1	3	0	2	0	3	..	6	2	1	0	0	2	0	4	42	40	.512	21
Washington	3	1	2	3	1	0	3	1	2	4	1	1	1	0	2	2	6	2	1	1	2	0	..	40	42	.488	23
New York	3	0	2	3	0	1	2	1	0	4	1	1	0	0	0	..	2	0	0	1	2	1	0	24	58	.293	39

CENTRAL DIVISION

Team	Atl.	Bos.	Chi.	Cle.	Dal.	Den.	Det.	G.S.	Hou.	Ind.	K.C.	L.A.C.	L.A.L.	Mil.	N.J.	N.Y.	Phi.	Pho.	Por.	S.A.	Sea.	Uta.	Was.	W.	L.	Pct.	G.B.
Milwaukee	4	4	3	5	1	1	3	2	2	5	2	2	1	..	3	5	3	1	2	2	2	2	4	59	23	.720	....
Detroit	5	2	3	4	2	2	..	2	1	6	1	1	1	3	1	3	1	2	1	1	1	0	3	46	36	.561	13
Chicago	3	2	..	2	2	1	3	1	0	2	2	2	1	3	2	2	3	4	1	1	1	0	3	38	44	.463	21
Cleveland	3	0	4	..	1	0	1	1	0	4	2	2	0	1	2	3	4	1	1	1	1	1	3	36	46	.439	23
Atlanta	..	1	3	3	0	0	1	2	0	6	0	2	0	2	3	3	0	2	0	0	1	2	3	34	48	.415	25
Indiana	0	1	4	2	0	0	0	2	1	..	1	0	1	1	2	2	1	0	0	1	0	2	1	22	60	.268	37

MIDWEST DIVISION

Team	Atl.	Bos.	Chi.	Cle.	Dal.	Den.	Det.	G.S.	Hou.	Ind.	K.C.	L.A.C.	L.A.L.	Mil.	N.J.	N.Y.	Phi.	Pho.	Por.	S.A.	Sea.	Uta.	Was.	W.	L.	Pct.	G.B.
Denver	2	1	1	2	4	..	0	5	2	2	4	2	2	1	2	1	1	4	4	3	3	4	2	52	30	.634	....
Houston	2	0	2	2	4	4	1	3	..	1	5	2	1	0	1	2	1	4	3	4	3	3	0	48	34	.585	4
Dallas	2	0	0	1	..	2	0	4	2	2	5	3	1	1	1	2	1	2	4	4	5	1	1	44	38	.537	8
San Antonio	2	0	1	1	2	3	1	4	2	1	4	3	2	0	2	1	1	4	2	..	4	1	0	41	41	.500	11
Utah	0	0	2	1	5	2	2	4	3	0		3	0	0	2	1	1	2	2	5	2	..	1	41	41	.500	11
Kansas City	2	0	0	0	1	2	1	3	1	1	..	3	0	0	2	1	1	2	3	2	3	2	1	31	51	.378	21

PACIFIC DIVISION

Team	Atl.	Bos.	Chi.	Cle.	Dal.	Den.	Det.	G.S.	Hou.	Ind.	K.C.	L.A.C.	L.A.L.	Mil.	N.J.	N.Y.	Phi.	Pho.	Por.	S.A.	Sea.	Uta.	Was.	W.	L.	Pct.	G.B.
L.A. Lakers	2	1	1	2	4	3	1	5	4	1	5	6	..	1	2	2	1	5	5	3	3	4	1	62	20	.756	....
Portland	2	1	1	1	1	1	1	4	2	2	5	1	0	2	2	0	3		..	3	4	3	1	42	40	.512	20
Phoenix	0	0	1	3	1	0	4	1	2	3	2	1	1	1	2	0		..	3	1	5	3	1	36	46	.439	26
L.A. Clippers	0	0	0	0	2	3	1	4	3	2	2	..	0	0	0	4	1	2	2	3	1	3	1	31	51	.378	31
Seattle	1	1	0	1	0	2	1	3	2	2	4	3	0	0	0	1	2	1		3	..	2	1	31	51	.378	31
Golden State	0	0	1	1	1	0	0	..	2	0	2	2	1	0	1	1	0	2	2	1	3	1	1	22	60	.268	40

HOME-ROAD RECORDS OF ALL TEAMS

Team	Home	Road	Total	Team	Home	Road	Total
Atlanta	19- 22	15- 26	34- 48	L.A. Lakers	36- 5	26- 15	62- 20
Boston	35- 6	28- 13	63- 19	Milwaukee	36- 5	23- 18	59- 23
Chicago	26- 15	12- 29	38- 44	New Jersey	27- 14	15- 26	42- 40
Cleveland	20- 21	16- 25	36- 46	New York	19- 22	5- 36	24- 58
Dallas	24- 17	20- 21	44- 38	Philadelphia	34- 7	24- 17	58- 24
Denver	34- 7	18- 23	52- 30	Phoenix	26- 15	10- 31	36- 46
Detroit	26- 15	20- 21	46- 36	Portland	30- 11	12- 29	42- 40
Golden State	17- 24	5- 36	22- 60	San Antonio	30- 11	11- 30	41- 41
Houston	29- 12	19- 22	48- 34	Seattle	20- 21	11- 30	31- 51
Indiana	16- 25	6- 35	22- 60	Utah	26- 15	15- 26	41- 41
Kansas City	23- 18	8- 33	31- 51	Washington	28- 13	12- 29	40- 42
L.A. Clippers	20- 21	11- 30	31- 51	Total	601- 342	342- 601	943- 943

OFFENSIVE TEAM STATISTICS

Team	G.	FIELD GOALS Att.	Made	Pct.	FREE THROWS Att.	Made	Pct.	REBOUNDS Off.	Def.	Tot.	Ast.	MISCELLANEOUS PF	Disq.	Stl.	Turn Over	Blk. Sh.	SCORING Pts.	Avg.
Denver	82	7976	3876	.486	2568	2016	.785	1331	2303	3634	2266	2152	18	894	1382	424	9841	120.0
L.A. Lakers	82	7254	3952	.545	2232	1702	.763	1063	2550	3613	2575	1931	7	695	1537	481	9696	118.2
Detroit	82	7999	3840	.480	2262	1783	.788	1403	2534	3937	2302	2076	21	691	1341	397	9508	116.0
Portland	82	7374	3708	.503	2667	2002	.751	1202	2298	3500	2225	1957	21	821	1481	516	9469	115.5
Kansas City	82	7275	3664	.504	2595	2022	.779	1167	2327	3494	2342	2169	19	661	1593	300	9413	114.8
Boston	82	7325	3721	.508	2307	1860	.806	1116	2630	3746	2287	1781	17	645	1332	414	9412	114.8
San Antonio	82	7202	3698	.513	2571	1961	.763	1127	2470	3597	2316	2180	23	757	1542	443	9412	114.8
Philadelphia	82	6992	3443	.492	2883	2316	.803	1301	2364	3665	1999	1971	11	817	1575	534	9261	112.9
Houston	82	7440	3748	.504	2261	1581	.699	1325	2395	3720	2239	2033	27	683	1605	597	9118	111.2
Dallas	82	7280	3560	.489	2324	1844	.793	1095	2345	3440	2152	1796	12	575	1184	335	9116	111.2
Milwaukee	82	7256	3564	.491	2473	1873	.757	1256	2353	3609	2164	2239	37	689	1382	486	9090	110.9
Golden State	82	7555	3498	.463	2531	1944	.768	1327	2139	3466	1759	2136	28	803	1460	284	9052	110.4
New Jersey	82	7445	3646	.490	2237	1631	.729	1233	2325	3558	2163	2011	33	772	1355	415	8975	109.5
Utah	82	7302	3478	.476	2434	1878	.772	1081	2554	3635	2143	1961	16	712	1575	697	8937	109.0
Chicago	82	6909	3453	.500	2526	1981	.784	1074	2366	3440	1992	2071	21	622	1463	468	8916	108.7
Cleveland	82	7364	3470	.471	2491	1867	.749	1203	2445	3648	2096	2173	41	622	1387	472	8903	108.6
Indiana	82	7324	3489	.476	2516	1871	.744	1198	2623	3821	1945	2237	25	625	1622	366	8879	108.3
Phoenix	82	7144	3507	.491	2280	1757	.771	1026	2425	3451	2335	2034	13	727	1583	349	8858	108.0
L.A. Clippers	82	7119	3527	.495	2208	1674	.758	1163	2434	3597	1934	1840	14	534	1587	497	8784	107.1
Atlanta	82	7119	3444	.484	2371	1782	.752	1161	2345	3506	2009	2047	28	665	1475	541	8743	106.6
Washington	82	7383	3534	.479	1989	1478	.743	1012	2395	3407	2088	1869	26	709	1282	393	8655	105.5
New York	82	7101	3435	.484	2350	1706	.726	1116	2102	3218	1999	2398	48	754	1458	267	8627	105.2
Seattle	82	6910	3277	.474	2305	1777	.771	1019	2287	3306	2185	1974	18	649	1493	343	8376	102.1

DEFENSIVE TEAM STATISTICS

Team	FIELD GOALS Att.	Made	Pct.	FREE THROWS Att.	Made	Pct.	REBOUNDS Off.	Def.	Tot.	Ast.	MISCELLANEOUS PF	Disq.	Stl.	Turn Over	Blk. Sh.	SCORING Pts.	Avg.	Pt. Dif.
Milwaukee	6972	3214	.461	2700	2020	.748	1236	2293	3529	1904	2104	33	642	1562	389	8528	104.0	+ 6.9
Washington	7179	3494	.487	2172	1623	.747	1119	2673	3792	1988	1833	7	630	1467	397	8677	105.8	− 0.3
Seattle	7142	3520	.493	2212	1703	.770	1113	2379	3492	2220	2020	13	732	1383	458	8822	107.6	− 5.4
Atlanta	7267	3504	.482	2384	1808	.758	1332	2411	3743	2087	1972	22	614	1488	373	8862	108.1	− 1.5
Boston	7642	3642	.477	1922	1512	.787	1105	2287	3392	2041	1964	20	641	1222	315	8867	108.1	+ 6.6
Philadelphia	7157	3494	.488	2397	1857	.775	1183	2173	3356	2139	2209	32	753	1534	391	8925	108.8	+ 4.1
Dallas	7200	3626	.504	2080	1588	.763	1062	2470	3532	2113	2066	17	572	1340	430	8938	109.0	+ 2.2
Utah	7604	3532	.464	2375	1810	.762	1360	2645	4005	2069	2076	21	806	1606	443	8946	109.1	− 0.1
New Jersey	7040	3514	.499	2454	1849	.753	1084	2405	3489	1975	1933	22	680	1496	352	8956	109.2	+ 0.2
Houston	7274	3500	.481	2425	1887	.778	1159	2222	3381	2117	1903	22	773	1495	415	8977	109.5	+ 1.7
Chicago	7210	3521	.488	2394	1852	.774	1137	2260	3397	2045	2040	25	668	1323	447	8985	109.6	− 0.8
New York	6732	3329	.495	3006	2282	.759	1219	2401	3620	2143	2038	17	667	1589	446	9007	109.8	− 4.6
Phoenix	7309	3605	.493	2295	1756	.765	1125	2416	3541	2181	2019	25	771	1468	410	9031	110.1	− 2.1
L.A. Lakers	7639	3665	.480	2244	1679	.748	1248	2078	3326	2313	1905	18	756	1365	370	9093	110.9	+ 7.4
Cleveland	7415	3547	.478	2554	1965	.769	1210	2451	3661	2215	2101	23	612	1357	429	9129	111.3	− 2.8
L.A. Clippers	7630	3737	.490	2115	1604	.758	1248	2282	3530	2264	1887	14	770	1242	422	9152	111.6	− 4.5
Portland	7494	3697	.493	2269	1737	.766	1268	2336	3604	2235	2160	29	726	1607	459	9190	112.1	+ 3.4
Detroit	7457	3700	.496	2404	1826	.760	1109	2563	3672	2107	2017	30	642	1486	508	9304	113.5	+ 2.5
San Antonio	7348	3644	.496	2548	1977	.776	1136	2265	3401	2283	2154	26	749	1489	472	9337	113.9	+ 0.9
Indiana	7332	3628	.495	2707	2068	.764	1098	2583	3681	2242	2072	25	777	1424	523	9388	114.5	− 6.2
Kansas City	7461	3805	.510	2546	1957	.769	1166	2267	3433	2344	2205	30	761	1424	512	9632	117.5	− 2.7
Denver	7379	3775	.512	2648	2027	.765	1181	2628	3809	2154	2178	28	670	1744	589	9641	117.6	+ 2.4
Golden State	7165	3839	.536	2530	1919	.758	1101	2521	3622	2336	2180	25	650	1583	469	9654	117.7	− 7.3

Disq.—Individual player disqualified (fouled out of game).

INDIVIDUAL LEADERS

POINTS

Minimum 70 games played or 1,400 points

Player	G.	FG	FT	Pts.	Avg.	Player	G.	FG	FT	Pts.	Avg.
King, New York	55	691	426	1809	32.9	Natt, Denver	78	685	447	1817	23.3
Bird, Boston	80	918	403	2295	28.7	Woolridge, Chicago	77	679	409	1767	22.9
Jordan, Chicago	82	837	630	2313	28.2	Johnson, Kansas City	82	769	325	1876	22.9
Short, Golden State	78	819	501	2186	28.0	Griffith, Utah	78	728	216	1764	22.6
English, Denver	81	939	383	2262	27.9	Free, Cleveland	71	609	308	1597	22.5
Wilkins, Atlanta	81	853	486	2217	27.4	Vandeweghe, Portland	72	618	369	1616	22.4
Dantley, Utah	55	512	438	1462	26.6	Mitchell, San Antonio	82	775	269	1824	22.2
Aguirre, Dallas	80	794	440	2055	25.7	Smith, L.A. Clippers	80	682	400	1767	22.1
Malone, Philadelphia	79	602	737	1941	24.6	Sampson, Houston	82	753	303	1809	22.1
Cummings, Milwaukee	79	759	343	1861	23.6	Abdul-Jabbar, L.A. Lakers	79	723	289	1735	22.0

FIELD GOALS
Minimum 300 FG made

	FGA	FGM	Pct.
Donaldson, L.A. Clippers	551	351	.637
Gilmore, San Antonio	854	532	.623
Thorpe, Kansas City	685	411	.600
Abdul-Jabbar, L.A. Lakers	1207	723	.599
Nance, Phoenix	877	515	.587
Worthy, L.A. Lakers	1066	610	.572
McHale, Boston	1062	605	.570
Cheeks, Philadelphia	741	422	.570
Johnson, L.A. Lakers	899	504	.561
Woolridge, Chicago	1225	679	.554

FREE THROWS
Minimum 125 FT made

	FTA	FTM	Pct.
Macy, Phoenix	140	127	.907
Vandeweghe, Portland	412	369	.896
Davis, Dallas	178	158	.888
Tripucka, Detroit	288	255	.885
Adams, Phoenix	283	250	.883
Bird, Boston	457	403	.882
Cheeks, Philadelphia	199	175	.879
Bridgeman, L.A. Clippers	206	181	.879
Johnson, Kansas City	373	325	.871
Green, Utah	267	232	.869

ASSISTS
Minimum 70 games or 400 assists

	G.	No.	Avg.
Thomas, Detroit	81	1123	13.9
Johnson, L.A. Lakers	77	968	12.6
Moore, San Antonio	82	816	10.0
Nixon, L.A. Clippers	81	711	8.8
Bagley, Cleveland	81	697	8.6
Richardson, New Jersey	82	669	8.2
Theus, Kansas City	82	656	8.0
Johnson, Atlanta	73	566	7.8
Green, Utah	77	597	7.8
Gus Williams, Washington	79	608	7.7

STEALS
Minimum 70 games or 125 steals

	G.	No.	Avg.
Richardson, New Jersey	82	243	2.96
Moore, San Antonio	82	229	2.79
Lever, Denver	82	202	2.46
Jordan, Chicago	82	196	2.39
Rivers, Atlanta	69	163	2.36
Thomas, Detroit	81	187	2.31
Gus Williams, Washington	79	178	2.25
Drexler, Portland	80	177	2.21
Cheeks, Philadelphia	78	169	2.17
Conner, Golden State	79	161	2.04

REBOUNDS
Minimum 70 games or 800 rebounds

	G.	Off.	Def.	Tot.	Avg.
Malone, Philadelphia	79	385	646	1031	13.1
Laimbeer, Detroit	82	295	718	1013	12.4
Williams, New Jersey	82	323	682	1005	12.3
Olajuwon, Houston	82	440	534	974	11.9
Eaton, Utah	82	207	720	927	11.3
Smith, Golden State	80	405	464	869	10.9
Parish, Boston	79	263	577	840	10.6
Bird, Boston	80	164	678	842	10.5
Gilmore, San Antonio	81	231	615	846	10.4
Thompson, Kansas City	82	274	580	854	10.4

BLOCKED SHOTS
Minimum 70 games or 100 blocked shots

	G.	No.	Avg.
Eaton, Utah	82	456	5.56
Olajuwon, Houston	82	220	2.68
Bowie, Portland	76	203	2.67
Cooper, Denver	80	197	2.46
Rollins, Atlanta	70	167	2.39
Hinson, Cleveland	76	173	2.28
Gilmore, San Antonio	81	173	2.14
Walton, L.A. Clippers	67	140	2.09
Lister, Milwaukee	81	167	2.06
Abdul-Jabbar, L.A. Lakers	79	162	2.05

3-PT. FIELD GOALS
Minimum 25 made

	FGA	FGM	Pct.
Scott, L.A. Lakers	60	26	.433
Bird, Boston	131	56	.427
Davis, Dallas	115	47	.409
Tucker, New York	72	29	.403
Ellis, Dallas	109	42	.385
Toney, Philadelphia	105	39	.371
Free, Cleveland	193	71	.368
Evans, Denver	157	57	.363
Griffith, Utah	257	92	.358
Buse, Kansas City	87	31	.356

TEAM-BY-TEAM INDIVIDUAL STATISTICS

ATLANTA HAWKS

Player	G.	Min.	FGA	FGM	Pct.	FTA	FTM	Pct.	Off. Reb.	Def. Reb.	Tot. Reb.	Ast.	PF	Dsq.	Stl.	Blk. Sh.	Pts.	Avg.	Hi.
Wilkins	81	3023	1891	853	.451	603	486	.806	226	331	557	200	170	0	135	54	2217	27.4	48
Johnson	73	2367	946	453	.479	332	265	.798	38	154	192	566	184	1	43	7	1193	16.3	34
Rivers	69	2126	701	334	.476	378	291	.770	66	148	214	410	250	7	163	53	974	14.1	30
Williams	34	867	380	167	.439	123	79	.642	45	123	168	94	83	1	28	8	417	12.3	22
Wittman	41	1168	352	187	.531	41	30	.732	16	57	73	125	58	0	28	7	406	9.9	28
Levingston	74	2017	552	291	.527	222	145	.653	230	336	566	104	231	3	70	69	727	9.8	22
Willis	82	1785	690	322	.467	181	119	.657	177	345	522	36	226	4	31	49	765	9.3	24
Glenn	60	1126	388	228	.588	76	62	.816	20	61	81	122	74	0	27	0	518	8.6	21
Carr	62	1195	375	198	.528	128	101	.789	79	153	232	80	219	4	29	78	499	8.0	17
Rollins	70	1750	339	186	.549	93	67	.720	113	329	442	52	213	6	35	167	439	6.3	19
Criss	4	115	17	7	.412	6	4	.667	2	12	14	22	5	0	3	0	18	4.5	8
Russell	21	377	63	34	.540	17	14	.824	8	32	40	66	37	1	17	4	83	4.0	10
Hastings	64	825	188	89	.473	81	63	.778	59	100	159	46	135	1	24	23	241	3.8	16
Eaves	3	37	6	3	.500	6	5	.833	0	0	0	4	6	0	0	0	11	3.7	6
Brown	69	814	192	78	.406	68	39	.574	76	147	223	25	117	0	19	22	195	2.8	12
Granger	9	92	17	6	.353	8	4	.500	1	5	6	12	13	0	2	0	16	1.8	5
Lowe (Tot)	21	190	27	10	.370	8	8	81.000	4	12	16	50	28	0	11	0	28	1.3	6
Lowe (Atl)	15	159	20	8	.400	8	8	81.000	4	11	15	42	23	0	11	0	24	1.6	6
Rautins	4	12	2	0	.000	0	0	---	1	1	2	3	3	0	0	0	0	0.0	

3-Pt. FG: Atlanta 73-235 (.311)—Wilkins 25-81 (.309); Johnson 22-72 (.306); Rivers 15-36 (.417); Williams 4-15 (.267); Wittman 2-7 (.286); Levingston 0-2 (.000); Willis 2-9 (.222); Glenn 0-2 (.000); Carr 2-6 (.333); Criss 0-2 (.000); Russell 1-1 (1.000); Granger 0-1 (.000); Lowe 0-1 (.000). Opponents 46-212 (.217).

BOSTON CELTICS

Player	G.	Min.	FGA	FGM	Pct.	FTA	FTM	Pct.	Off. Reb.	Def. Reb.	Tot. Reb.	Ast.	PF	Dsq.	Stl.	Blk. Sh.	Pts.	Avg.	Hi.
Bird	80	3161	1760	918	.522	457	403	.882	164	678	842	531	208	0	129	98	2295	28.7	60
McHale	79	2653	1062	605	.570	467	355	.760	229	483	712	141	234	3	28	120	1565	19.8	56
Parish	79	2850	1016	551	.542	393	292	.743	263	577	840	125	223	2	56	101	1394	17.6	38
Johnson	80	2976	1066	493	.462	306	261	.853	91	226	317	543	224	2	96	39	1254	15.7	29
Ainge	75	2564	792	419	.529	136	118	.868	76	192	268	399	228	4	122	6	971	12.9	26
Maxwell	57	1495	377	201	.533	278	231	.831	98	144	242	102	140	2	36	15	633	11.1	30
Wedman	78	1127	460	220	.478	55	42	.764	57	102	159	94	111	0	23	10	499	6.4	31
Williams	23	459	143	55	.385	46	31	.674	16	41	57	90	56	1	30	5	147	6.4	16
Carr	47	397	149	62	.416	17	17	1.000	21	22	43	24	44	0	21	6	150	3.2	13
Clark	62	562	152	64	.421	53	41	.774	29	40	69	48	66	0	35	2	169	2.7	12
Buckner	75	858	193	74	.383	50	32	.640	26	61	87	148	142	0	63	2	180	2.4	13
Carlisle	38	179	67	26	.388	17	15	.882	8	13	21	25	21	0	3	0	67	1.8	8
Kite	55	424	88	33	.375	32	22	.688	38	51	89	17	84	3	3	10	88	1.6	14

3-Pt. FG: Boston 110-309 (.356)—Bird 56-131 (.427); McHale 0-6 (.000); Johnson 7-26 (.269); Ainge 15-56 (.268); Maxwell 0-2 (.000); Wedman 17-34 (.500); Williams 6-23 (.261); Carr 9-23 (.391); Clark 0-5 (.000); Buckner 0-1 (.000); Carlisle 0-2 (.000). Opponents 71-269 (.264).

CHICAGO BULLS

Player	G.	Min.	FGA	FGM	Pct.	FTA	FTM	Pct.	Off. Reb.	Def. Reb.	Tot. Reb.	Ast.	PF	Dsq.	Stl.	Blk. Sh.	Pts.	Avg.	Hi.
Jordan	82	3144	1625	837	.515	746	630	.845	167	367	534	481	285	4	196	69	2313	28.2	49
Woolridge	77	2816	1225	679	.554	521	409	.785	158	277	435	135	185	0	58	38	1767	22.9	37
Dailey	79	2101	1111	525	.473	251	205	.817	57	151	208	191	192	0	71	5	1262	16.0	30
Johnson	74	1659	516	281	.545	252	181	.718	146	291	437	64	265	7	37	62	743	10.0	31
Corzine	82	2062	568	276	.486	200	149	.745	130	292	422	140	189	2	32	64	701	8.5	23
Green	48	740	250	108	.432	98	79	.806	72	174	246	29	102	0	11	14	295	6.1	16
Greenwood	61	1523	332	152	.458	94	67	.713	108	280	388	78	190	1	34	18	371	6.1	20
Matthews	78	1523	386	191	.495	85	59	.694	16	51	67	354	133	0	73	12	443	5.7	21
Whatley	70	1385	313	140	.447	86	68	.791	34	67	101	381	141	1	66	10	349	5.0	12
Higgins	68	942	270	119	.441	90	60	.667	55	92	147	73	91	0	21	13	308	4.5	15
Ca. Jones	42	885	115	53	.461	47	36	.766	49	162	211	34	125	3	12	31	142	3.4	12
Oldham	63	993	192	89	.464	50	34	.680	79	157	236	31	166	3	11	127	212	3.4	12
Ch. Jones	3	29	4	2	.500	6	4	.667	2	4	6	1	6	0	0	5	8	2.7	4
Engler	3	3	2	1	.500	0	0	---	1	1	2	0	2	0	0	0	2	0.7	2

3-Pt. FG: Chicago 29-161 (.180)—Jordan 9-52 (.173); Woolridge 0-5 (.000); Dailey 7-30 (.233); Johnson 0-3 (.000); Corzine 0-1 (.000); Green 0-4 (.000); Greenwood 0-1 (.000); Matthews 2-16 (.125); Whatley 1-9 (.111); Higgins 10-37 (.270); Ca. Jones 0-2 (.000); Oldham 0-1 (.000). Opponents 91-292 (.312).

CLEVELAND CAVALIERS

Player	G.	Min.	FGA	FGM	Pct.	FTA	FTM	Pct.	Off. Reb.	Def. Reb.	Tot. Reb.	Ast.	PF	Dsq.	Stl.	Blk. Sh.	Pts.	Avg.	Hi.
Free	71	2249	1328	609	.459	411	308	.749	61	150	211	320	163	0	75	16	1597	22.5	45
Hinson	76	2344	925	465	.503	376	271	.721	186	410	596	68	311	13	51	173	1201	15.8	37
Hubbard	76	2249	822	415	.505	494	371	.751	214	265	479	114	258	8	81	9	1201	15.8	37
Davis	76	1920	791	337	.426	300	255	.850	35	84	119	426	136	1	43	4	941	12.4	33
Turpin	79	1949	711	363	.511	139	109	.784	155	297	452	36	211	3	38	87	835	10.6	24
Thompson	33	715	354	148	.418	53	45	.849	36	80	116	58	77	1	41	20	347	10.5	24
Bagley	81	2401	693	338	.488	167	125	.749	54	237	291	697	132	0	129	5	804	9.9	35
Jones (Tot)	44	769	275	130	.473	111	82	.739	50	121	171	29	123	2	20	29	342	7.8	15
Jones (Clev)	26	447	184	86	.467	60	41	.683	34	75	109	11	71	1	11	11	213	8.2	15
Wilson	11	175	54	27	.500	30	23	.767	10	8	18	24	14	0	10	3	77	7.0	13
Poquette	79	1656	457	210	.460	137	109	.796	148	325	473	79	220	3	47	58	532	6.7	22
Shelton	57	1244	363	158	.435	77	51	.662	82	185	267	96	187	3	44	18	367	6.4	16
Cook	18	440	105	46	.438	27	17	.630	41	63	104	23	53	0	5	9	109	6.1	14
Anderson	36	520	195	84	.431	50	41	.820	39	49	88	34	40	0	9	7	210	5.8	27
West (Tot)	66	888	194	106	.546	87	43	.494	90	161	251	15	197	7	13	49	255	3.9	16
West (Clev)	65	882	193	106	.549	85	41	.482	89	161	250	15	193	7	13	48	253	3.9	16
Williams	46	413	134	58	.433	64	47	.734	19	44	63	61	86	1	22	4	163	3.5	13
Huston	8	93	25	12	.480	3	2	.667	0	1	1	23	8	0	0	0	26	3.3	10
Smith	7	48	17	4	.235	10	8	.800	0	4	4	7	6	0	2	0	16	2.3	7
Russell	3	24	7	2	.286	3	2	.667	0	5	5	3	3	0	0	0	6	2.0	4
Graves	4	51	3	2	.333	5	1	.200	0	5	5	2	1	0	0	0	5	1.3	3

3-Pt. FG: Cleveland 96-335 (.287)—Free 71-193 (.368); Hinson 0-3 (.000); Hubbard 0-4 (.000); Davis 12-46 (.261); Thompson 6-23 (.261); Bagley 3-26 (.115); Jones 0-3 (.000); Poquette 3-17 (.176); Shelton 0-5 (.000); Cook 0-1 (.000); Anderson 1-2 (.500); West 0-1 (.000); Williams 0-5 (.000); Smith 0-4 (.000); Russell 0-1 (.000); Graves 0-1 (.000). Opponents 70-253 (.277).

DALLAS MAVERICKS

Player	G.	Min.	FGA	FGM	Pct.	FTA	FTM	Pct.	Off. Reb.	Def. Reb.	Tot. Reb.	Ast.	PF	Dsq.	Stl.	Blk. Sh.	Pts.	Avg.	Hi.
Aguirre	80	2699	1569	794	.506	580	440	.759	188	289	477	249	250	3	60	24	2055	25.7	49
Blackman	81	2834	1230	625	.508	413	342	.828	107	193	300	289	96	0	61	16	1598	19.7	36
Vincent	79	2543	1138	545	.479	420	351	.836	185	519	704	169	226	0	48	22	1441	18.2	39
Perkins	82	2317	736	347	.471	244	200	.820	189	416	605	135	236	1	63	63	903	11.0	29
Davis	82	2539	614	310	.505	178	158	.888	39	154	193	581	219	1	91	10	825	10.1	19
Harper	82	2218	633	329	.520	154	111	.721	47	152	199	360	194	1	144	37	790	9.6	22
Ellis	72	1314	603	274	.454	104	77	.740	100	138	238	56	131	1	46	7	667	9.3	29
Nimphius	82	2010	434	196	.452	140	108	.771	136	272	408	183	262	4	30	126	500	6.1	16
Bryant	56	860	148	67	.453	44	30	.682	74	167	241	84	110	1	21	24	164	2.9	14
Sluby	31	151	58	30	.517	21	13	.619	5	7	12	16	18	0	3	0	73	2.4	8
Sitton	43	304	94	39	.415	25	13	.520	24	36	60	26	50	0	7	6	91	2.1	8
Carter	11	66	23	4	.174	1	1	1.000	1	2	3	4	4	0	1	0	9	0.8	3

3-Pt. FG: Dallas 152-443 (.343)—Aguirre 27-85 (.318); Blackman 6-20 (.300); Vincent 0-4 (.000); Perkins 9-36 (.250); Davis 47-115 (.409); Harper 21-61 (.344); Ellis 42-109 (.385); Nimphius 0-6 (.000); Sluby 0-2 (.000); Sitton 0-2 (.000); Carter 0-3 (.000). Opponents 98-318 (.308).

DENVER NUGGETS

Player	G.	Min.	FGA	FGM	Pct.	FTA	FTM	Pct.	Off. Reb.	Def. Reb.	Tot. Reb.	Ast.	PF	Dsq.	Stl.	Blk. Sh.	Pts.	Avg.	Hi.
English	81	2924	1812	939	.518	462	383	.829	203	255	458	344	259	1	101	46	2262	27.9	45
Natt	78	2657	1255	685	.546	564	447	.793	209	401	610	238	182	1	75	33	1817	23.3	37
Lever	82	2559	985	424	.430	256	197	.770	147	264	411	613	226	1	202	30	1051	12.8	26
Issel	77	1684	791	363	.459	319	257	.806	80	251	331	137	171	1	65	31	984	12.8	27
Cooper	80	2031	856	404	.472	235	161	.685	229	402	631	86	304	2	28	197	969	12.1	26
Evans	81	1437	661	323	.489	131	113	.863	26	93	119	231	174	2	65	12	816	10.1	38
Hanzlik	80	1673	522	220	.421	238	180	.756	88	119	207	210	291	5	84	26	621	7.8	17
Dunn	81	2290	358	175	.489	116	84	.724	169	216	385	153	213	3	140	14	434	5.4	15
Turner	81	1491	388	181	.466	65	51	.785	88	128	216	158	152	0	96	7	414	5.1	13
Schayes	56	542	129	60	.465	97	79	.814	48	96	144	38	98	2	20	25	199	3.6	23
Kopicki	42	308	95	50	.526	54	43	.796	29	57	86	29	58	0	13	1	145	3.5	14
White	39	234	124	52	.419	31	21	.677	15	21	36	29	24	0	5	2	129	3.3	21

3-Pt. FG: Denver 73-235 (.311)—English 1-5 (.200); Natt 0-3 (.000); Lever 6-24 (.250); Issel 1-7 (.143); Cooper 0-2 (.000); Evans 57-157 (.363); Hanzlik 1-15 (.067); Dunn 0-2 (.000); Turner 1-6 (.167); Kopicki 2-3 (.667); White 4-11 (.364). Opponents 64-254 (.252).

DETROIT PISTONS

Player	G.	Min.	FGA	FGM	Pct.	FTA	FTM	Pct.	Off. Reb.	Def. Reb.	Tot. Reb.	Ast.	PF	Dsq.	Stl.	Blk. Sh.	Pts.	Avg.	Hi.
Thomas	81	3089	1410	646	.458	493	399	.809	114	247	361	1123	288	8	187	25	1720	21.2	38
Tripucka	55	1675	831	396	.477	288	255	.885	66	152	218	135	118	1	49	14	1049	19.1	45
Laimbeer	82	2892	1177	595	.506	306	244	.797	295	718	1013	154	308	4	69	71	1438	17.5	35
Long	66	1820	885	431	.487	123	106	.862	81	109	190	130	139	0	71	14	973	14.7	28
Johnson	82	2093	942	428	.454	247	190	.769	134	118	252	325	205	2	71	20	1051	12.8	28
Tyler	82	2004	855	422	.494	148	106	.716	148	275	423	63	192	0	49	90	950	11.6	28
Roundfield	56	1492	505	236	.467	178	139	.781	175	278	453	102	147	0	26	54	611	10.9	27
Benson	72	1401	397	201	.506	94	76	.809	103	221	324	93	207	4	53	44	478	6.6	15
Cureton	81	1642	428	207	.484	144	82	.569	169	250	419	83	216	1	56	42	496	6.1	18
Campbell	56	625	262	130	.496	70	56	.800	41	48	89	24	107	1	28	3	316	5.6	17
Steppe	54	486	178	83	.466	104	87	.837	25	32	57	36	61	0	16	4	253	4.7	13
Thirdkill	10	115	23	12	.522	11	5	.455	4	4	8	1	16	0	3	2	29	2.9	8
Jones	47	418	87	48	.552	51	33	.647	48	80	128	15	58	0	9	14	129	2.7	15
Romar (Tot)	9	51	16	3	.188	5	5	1.000	0	0	0	12	7	0	4	0	11	1.2	5
Romar (Det)	5	35	8	2	.250	5	5	1.000	0	0	0	10	5	0	4	0	9	1.8	5
Teagle	2	5	2	1	.500	0	0	.....	0	0	0	2	0	0	0	2	1.0	2
Lowe	6	31	7	2	.286	0	0	.....	0	1	1	8	5	0	0	0	4	0.7	4
Wilkinson	2	7	2	0	.000	0	0	.....	0	1	1	0	2	0	0	0	0	0.0	0

3-Pt. FG: Detroit 45-199 (.226)—Thomas 29-113 (.257); Tripucka 2-5 (.400); Laimbeer 4-18 (.222); Long 5-15 (.333); Johnson 5-27 (.185); Tyler 0-8 (.000); Roundfield 0-2 (.000); Benson 0-3 (.000); Cureton 0-3 (.000); Campbell 0-1 (.000); Steppe 0-1 (.000); Thirdkill 0-1 (.000); Romar 0-2 (.000). Opponents 78-249 (.313).

GOLDEN STATE WARRIORS

Player	G.	Min.	FGA	FGM	Pct.	FTA	FTM	Pct.	Off. Reb.	Def. Reb.	Tot. Reb.	Ast.	PF	Dsq.	Stl.	Blk. Sh.	Pts.	Avg.	Hi.
Short	78	3081	1780	819	.460	613	501	.817	157	241	398	234	255	4	116	27	2186	28.0	59
Floyd	82	2873	1372	610	.445	415	336	.810	62	140	202	406	226	1	134	41	1598	19.5	33
Johnson	66	1565	714	304	.426	316	260	.823	149	247	396	149	221	5	70	35	875	13.3	27
Whitehead	79	2536	825	421	.510	235	184	.783	219	403	622	53	322	8	45	43	1026	13.0	27
Smith	80	2497	690	366	.530	256	155	.605	405	464	869	96	285	5	78	54	887	11.1	21
Teagle (Tot)	21	349	137	74	.540	35	25	.714	22	21	43	14	36	0	13	5	175	8.3	24
Teagle (GS)	19	344	135	73	.541	35	25	.714	22	21	43	14	34	0	13	5	173	9.1	24
Conner	79	2258	546	246	.451	192	144	.750	87	159	246	369	136	1	161	13	640	8.1	21
Bratz	56	746	250	106	.424	82	69	.841	11	47	58	122	76	1	47	4	287	5.1	19
Aleksinas	74	1114	337	161	.478	75	55	.733	87	183	270	36	171	1	15	15	377	5.1	15
Thibeaux	51	461	195	94	.482	67	43	.642	29	40	69	17	85	1	11	17	231	4.5	22
Wilson	74	1260	291	134	.460	76	54	.711	35	96	131	217	122	0	77	12	325	4.4	15
Burtt	47	418	188	72	.383	77	53	.688	10	18	28	20	76	0	21	4	197	4.2	14
Plummer	66	702	232	92	.397	92	65	.707	54	80	134	26	127	1	15	14	250	3.8	16

3-Pt. FG: Golden State 112-397 (.282)—Short 47-150 (.313); Floyd 42-143 (.294); Johnson 7-30 (.233); Teagle 2-4 (.500); Conner 4-20 (.200); Bratz 6-26 (.231); Alexsinas 0-1 (.000); Thibeaux 0-2 (.000); Wilson 3-16 (.188); Burtt 0-1 (.000); Plummer 1-4 (.250). Opponents 57-220 (.259).

HOUSTON ROCKETS

Player	G.	Min.	FGA	FGM	Pct.	FTA	FTM	Pct.	Off. Reb.	Def. Reb.	Tot. Reb.	Ast.	PF	Dsq.	Stl.	Blk. Sh.	Pts.	Avg.	Hi.
Sampson	82	3086	1499	753	.502	448	303	.676	227	626	853	224	306	10	81	168	1809	22.1	43
Olajuwon	82	2914	1258	677	.538	551	338	.613	440	534	974	111	344	10	99	220	1692	20.6	42
McCray	82	3001	890	476	.535	313	231	.738	201	338	539	355	215	2	90	75	1183	14.4	25
Lloyd	82	2128	869	457	.526	220	161	.732	98	133	231	280	196	1	73	28	1077	13.1	28
Lucas	47	1158	446	206	.462	129	103	.798	21	64	85	318	78	0	62	2	536	11.4	28
Wiggins	82	1575	657	318	.484	131	96	.733	110	125	235	119	195	1	83	13	738	9.0	23
Reid	82	1763	648	312	.481	126	88	.698	81	192	273	171	196	1	48	22	713	8.7	23
Hollins	80	1950	540	249	.461	136	108	.794	33	140	173	417	187	1	78	10	609	7.6	23
Leavell	42	536	209	88	.421	57	44	.772	8	29	37	102	61	0	23	4	228	5.4	18
Micheaux (Tot)	57	565	157	91	.580	43	29	.674	62	81	143	30	75	0	20	21	211	3.7	16
Micheaux (Hou)	39	394	122	74	.607	26	17	.654	44	55	99	17	49	0	12	14	165	4.2	14
Petersen	60	714	144	70	.486	66	50	.758	44	103	147	29	125	1	14	32	190	3.2	13
Ehlo	45	189	69	34	.493	30	19	.633	8	17	25	26	26	0	11	3	87	1.9	10
Ford	25	290	47	14	.298	18	16	.889	3	24	27	61	33	0	6	1	44	1.8	8
McDowell	34	132	42	20	.476	10	7	.700	7	15	22	9	22	0	3	5	47	1.4	6

3-Pt. FG: Houston 41-186 (.220)—Sampson 0-6 (.000); McCray 0-6 (.000); Lloyd 2-8 (.250); Lucas 21-66 (.318); Wiggins 6-23 (.261); Reid 1-16 (.063); Hollins 3-13 (.231); Leavell 8-37 (.216); Micheaux 0-3 (.000); Ehlo 0-3 (.000); Ford 0-4 (.000); McDowell 0-1 (.000). Opponents 90-258 (.349).

INDIANA PACERS

Player	G.	Min.	FGA	FGM	Pct.	FTA	FTM	Pct.	Off. Reb.	Def. Reb.	Tot. Reb.	Ast.	PF	Dsq.	Stl.	Blk. Sh.	Pts.	Avg.	Hi.
Kellogg	77	2449	1112	562	.505	396	301	.760	224	500	724	244	247	2	86	26	1432	18.6	37
Williams	75	2557	1211	575	.475	341	224	.657	154	480	634	252	218	1	54	134	1375	18.3	33
Fleming	80	2486	922	433	.470	339	260	.767	148	175	323	247	232	4	99	8	1126	14.1	29
Stipanovich	82	2315	871	414	.475	372	297	.798	141	473	614	199	265	4	71	78	1126	13.7	34
Thomas	80	2059	726	347	.478	234	183	.782	74	187	261	234	195	2	76	5	885	11.1	26
Sichting	70	1808	624	325	.521	128	112	.875	24	90	114	264	116	0	47	4	771	11.0	28
Stansbury	74	1278	458	210	.459	126	102	.810	39	75	114	127	205	2	47	12	526	7.1	25
Brown	82	1586	465	214	.460	171	116	.678	146	142	288	159	212	3	59	12	544	6.6	25
Garnett	65	1123	310	149	.481	174	120	.690	98	188	286	67	196	3	28	15	418	6.4	21
Kelser	10	114	53	21	.396	28	20	.714	6	13	19	13	16	0	7	0	62	6.2	19
Durrant	59	756	274	114	.416	102	72	.706	49	75	124	80	106	0	19	10	300	5.1	17
Waiters	62	703	190	85	.447	50	29	.580	57	113	170	30	107	2	16	44	199	3.2	14
Jackson	1	12	3	1	.333	0	0	.....	1	0	1	4	1	0	2	0	2	2.0	2
Gray	52	391	92	35	.380	47	32	.681	29	94	123	15	82	1	9	14	102	2.0	7
Edelin	10	143	13	4	.308	8	18	.25	8	18	26	10	39	1	5	4	11	1.1	2

3-Pt. FG: Indiana 30-155 (.194)—Kellogg 7-14 (.500); Williams 1-9 (.111); Fleming 0-4 (.000); Stipanovich 1-11 (.091); Thomas 8-42 (.190); Sichting 9-37 (.243); Stansbury 4-25 (.160); Brown 0-6 (.000); Garnett 0-2 (.000); Kelser 0-1 (.000); Durrant 0-3 (.000); Waiters 0-1 (.000). Opponents 64-200 (.320).

KANSAS CITY KINGS

Player	G.	Min.	FGA	FGM	Pct.	FTA	FTM	Pct.	Off. Reb.	Def. Reb.	Tot. Reb.	Ast.	PF	Dsq.	Stl.	Blk. Sh.	Pts.	Avg.	Hi.
Johnson	82	3029	1565	769	.491	373	325	.871	151	256	407	273	237	2	83	22	1876	22.9	40
Woodson	78	1998	1068	530	.496	330	264	.800	69	129	198	143	216	1	117	28	1329	17.0	35
Theus	82	2543	1029	501	.487	387	334	.863	106	164	270	656	250	0	95	18	1341	16.4	34
Drew	72	2373	913	457	.501	194	154	.794	39	125	164	484	147	0	93	8	1075	14.9	30
Thorpe	82	1918	685	411	.600	371	230	.620	187	369	556	111	256	2	34	37	1052	12.8	31
Thompson	82	2458	695	369	.531	315	227	.721	274	580	854	130	328	4	98	128	965	11.8	26
Olberding	81	2277	528	265	.502	352	293	.832	139	374	513	243	298	8	56	11	823	10.2	26
Knight	16	189	69	31	.449	16	13	.813	10	12	22	21	14	0	2	1	76	4.8	12
Meriweather	76	1061	243	121	.498	124	96	.774	94	169	263	27	181	1	17	28	339	4.5	20
Buse	65	939	203	82	.404	30	23	.767	21	40	61	203	75	0	38	1	218	3.4	17
Nealy	22	225	44	26	.591	19	10	.526	15	29	44	18	26	0	3	1	62	2.8	11
McNamara (Tot).	45	273	76	40	.526	62	32	.516	31	43	74	6	27	0	7	8	112	2.5	13
McNamara (KC)	33	210	58	28	.483	44	23	.523	24	33	57	6	22	0	5	7	79	2.4	13
Suttle	6	24	13	6	.462	2	2	1.000	0	3	3	2	3	0	1	0	14	2.3	6
Verhoeven	54	366	108	51	.472	25	21	.840	28	35	63	17	85	1	15	7	123	2.3	10
Pope	22	129	53	17	.321	13	7	.538	9	9	18	5	30	0	3	3	41	1.9	11
Natt (Tot)	8	29	6	2	.333	4	2	.500	2	1	3	3	3	0	2	0	6	0.8	4
Natt (KC)	4	16	1	0	.000	0	0	.....	1	0	1	3	1	0	1	0	0	0.0	0

3-Pt. FG: Kansas City 63-238 (.265)—Johnson 13-54 (.241); Woodson 5-21 (.238); Theus 5-38 (.132); Drew 7-28 (.250); Thorpe 0-2 (.000); Olberding 0-3 (.000); Knight 1-1 (1.000); Meriweather 1-2 (.500); Buse 31-87 (.356); Suttle 0-1 (.000); Pope 0-1 (.000). Opponents 65-259 (.251).

LOS ANGELES CLIPPERS

Player	G.	Min.	FGA	FGM	Pct.	FTA	FTM	Pct.	Off. Reb.	Def. Reb.	Tot. Reb.	Ast.	PF	Dsq.	Stl.	Blk. Sh.	Pts.	Avg.	Hi.
Smith	80	2762	1271	682	.537	504	400	.794	174	253	427	216	317	8	77	52	1767	22.1	41
Nixon	81	2894	1281	596	.465	218	170	.780	55	163	218	711	175	2	95	4	1395	17.2	39
Johnson	72	2448	1094	494	.452	260	190	.731	188	240	428	248	193	2	72	30	1181	16.4	32
Bridgeman	80	2042	990	460	.465	206	181	.879	55	175	230	171	128	0	47	18	1115	13.9	30
Donaldson	82	2392	551	351	.637	303	227	.749	168	500	668	48	217	1	28	130	929	11.3	24
Walton	67	1647	516	269	.521	203	138	.680	168	432	600	156	184	0	50	140	676	10.1	23
Cage	75	1610	398	216	.543	137	101	.737	126	266	392	51	164	1	41	32	533	7.1	22
Edwards	16	198	66	36	.545	24	19	.792	3	11	14	38	10	0	17	0	91	5.7	12
White	80	1106	279	144	.516	130	90	.692	94	101	195	34	115	0	35	20	378	4.7	15
Gordon	63	682	287	110	.383	49	37	.755	26	35	61	88	61	0	33	6	259	4.1	22
Warrick	58	713	173	85	.491	57	44	.772	10	48	58	153	85	0	23	6	215	3.7	18
Catchings	70	1049	149	72	.483	89	59	.663	89	173	262	14	162	0	15	57	203	2.9	11
Murphy	23	149	50	8	.160	21	12	.571	6	35	41	4	21	0	1	2	28	1.2	6
Wilkinson (Tot)	12	45	16	4	.250	7	6	.857	1	3	4	2	10	0	0	0	14	1.2	8
Wilkinson (LAC)	10	38	14	4	.286	7	6	.857	1	2	3	2	8	0	0	0	14	1.4	8

3-Pt. FG: L.A. Clippers 56-188 (.298)—Smith 3-19 (.158); Nixon 33-99 (.333); Johnson 3-13 (.231); Bridgeman 14-39 (.359); Walton 0-2 (.000); Gordon 2-9 (.222); Warrick 1-4 (.250); Catchings 0-1 (.000); Murphy 0-1 (.000); Wilkinson 0-1 (.000). Opponents 74-263 (.281).

LOS ANGELES LAKERS

Player	G.	Min.	FGA	FGM	Pct.	FTA	FTM	Pct.	Off. Reb.	Def. Reb.	Tot. Reb.	Ast.	PF	Dsq.	Stl.	Blk. Sh.	Pts.	Avg.	Hi.
Abdul-Jabbar	79	2630	1207	723	.599	395	289	.732	162	460	622	249	238	3	63	162	1735	22.0	40
Johnson	77	2781	899	504	.561	464	391	.843	90	386	476	968	155	0	113	25	1406	18.3	39
Worthy	80	2696	1066	610	.572	245	190	.776	169	342	511	201	196	0	87	67	1410	17.6	32
Scott	81	2305	1003	541	.539	228	187	.820	57	153	210	244	197	1	100	17	1295	16.0	30
McAdoo	66	1254	546	284	.520	162	122	.753	79	216	295	67	170	0	18	53	690	10.5	22
McGee	76	1170	612	329	.538	160	94	.588	97	68	165	71	147	1	39	7	774	10.2	41
Cooper	82	2189	593	276	.465	133	115	.865	56	199	255	429	208	0	93	49	702	8.6	19
Wilkes	42	761	303	148	.488	66	51	.773	35	59	94	41	65	0	19	3	347	8.3	24
Spriggs	75	1292	354	194	.548	146	112	.767	77	150	227	132	195	2	47	13	500	6.7	20
Kupchak	58	716	244	123	.504	91	60	.659	68	116	184	21	104	0	19	20	306	5.3	29
Rambis	82	1617	327	181	.554	103	68	.660	164	364	528	69	211	0	82	47	430	5.2	18
Lester	32	278	82	34	.415	31	21	.677	4	22	26	80	25	0	15	3	89	2.8	15
Nevitt	11	59	17	5	.294	8	2	.250	5	15	20	3	20	0	0	15	12	1.1	4
Jones	2	7	1	0	.000	0	0	.....	0	0	0	0	0	0	0	0	0	0.0	0

3-Pt. FG: L.A. Lakers 90-295 (.305)—Abdul-Jabbar 0-1 (.000); Johnson 7-37 (.189); Worthy 0-7 (.000); Scott 26-60 (.433); McAdoo 0-1 (.000); McGee 22-61 (.361); Cooper 35-123 (.285); Wilkes 0-1 (.000); Spriggs 0-3 (.000); Lester 0-1 (.000). Opponents 84-297 (.283).

MILWAUKEE BUCKS

Player	G.	Min.	FGA	FGM	Pct.	FTA	FTM	Pct.	Off. Reb.	Def. Reb.	Tot. Reb.	Ast.	PF	Dsq.	Stl.	Blk. Sh.	Pts.	Avg.	Hi.
Cummings	79	2722	1532	759	.495	463	343	.741	244	472	716	228	264	4	117	67	1861	23.6	39
Moncrief	73	2734	1162	561	.483	548	454	.828	149	242	391	382	197	1	117	39	1585	21.7	35
Pressey	80	2876	928	480	.517	418	317	.758	149	280	429	543	258	4	129	56	1284	16.1	30
Hodges	82	2496	732	359	.490	130	106	.815	74	112	186	349	262	8	96	1	871	10.6	21
Lister	81	2091	598	322	.538	262	154	.588	219	428	647	127	287	5	49	167	798	9.9	30
Pierce	44	882	307	165	.537	124	102	.823	49	68	117	94	117	0	34	5	433	9.8	24
Thompson (Tot)	49	942	459	189	.412	87	69	.793	57	101	158	78	119	1	56	25	453	9.2	24
Thompson (Mil)	16	227	105	41	.390	34	24	.706	21	21	42	20	42	0	15	5	106	6.6	16
Dunleavy	19	433	135	64	.474	29	25	.862	6	25	31	85	55	1	15	3	169	8.9	16
Mokeski	79	1586	429	205	.478	116	81	.698	107	303	410	99	266	6	28	35	491	6.2	21
Grevey	78	1182	424	190	.448	107	88	.822	27	76	103	94	85	1	30	2	476	6.1	23
Davis (Tot)	61	774	356	153	.430	62	51	.823	59	94	153	51	113	1	22	5	358	5.9	25
Davis (Mil)	57	746	346	151	.436	58	48	.828	57	92	149	50	110	1	21	5	351	6.2	25
Breuer	78	1083	317	162	.511	127	89	.701	92	164	256	40	179	4	21	82	413	5.3	18
Fields	51	535	191	84	.440	36	27	.750	41	43	84	38	84	2	9	10	195	3.8	21
Micheaux	18	171	35	17	.486	17	12	.706	18	26	44	13	26	0	8	7	46	2.6	16
Thirdkill	6	16	4	3	.750	2	1	.500	1	1	2	0	1	0	0	0	7	1.2	5
West	1	6	1	0	.000	2	2	1.000	1	0	1	0	4	0	0	1	2	2.0	2
Engler (Tot)	11	82	20	8	.400	9	5	.556	12	18	30	0	5	0	2	5	21	1.9	14
Engler (Mil)	1	3	2	0	.000	0	0	.....	0	1	1	0	0	0	0	1	0	0.0	0
Romar	4	16	8	1	.125	0	0	.....	0	0	0	2	2	0	0	0	2	0.5	2

3-Pt. FG: Milwaukee 89-294 (.303)—Cummings 0-1 (.000); Moncrief 9-33 (.273); Pressey 7-20 (.350); Hodges 47-135 (.348); Lister 0-1 (.000); Pierce 1-4 (.250); Thompson 0-7 (.000); Dunleavy 16-47 (.340); Mokeski 0-2 (.000); Grevey 8-33 (.242); Davis 1-10 (.100); Romar 0-1 (.000). Opponents 80-308 (.260).

NEW JERSEY NETS

Player	G.	Min.	FGA	FGM	Pct.	FTA	FTM	Pct.	Off. Reb.	Def. Reb.	Tot. Reb.	Ast.	PF	Dsq.	Stl.	Blk. Sh.	Pts.	Avg.	Hi.
Birdsong	56	1842	968	495	.511	259	161	.622	60	88	148	232	145	1	84	7	1155	20.6	42
Richardson	82	3127	1470	690	.469	313	240	.767	156	301	457	669	277	3	243	22	1649	20.1	36
Williams	82	3182	1089	577	.530	538	336	.625	323	682	1005	167	293	7	63	110	1491	18.2	33
Dawkins	39	972	339	192	.566	201	143	.711	55	126	181	45	171	11	14	35	527	13.5	30
Gminski	81	2418	818	380	.465	328	276	.841	229	404	633	158	135	0	38	92	1036	12.8	28
King	42	860	460	226	.491	104	85	.817	70	89	159	58	110	0	41	9	537	12.8	28
O'Koren	43	1119	393	194	.494	67	42	.627	46	120	166	102	115	1	32	16	438	10.2	27
Ransey	81	1689	654	300	.459	142	122	.859	40	90	130	355	134	0	87	7	724	8.9	24
Cook	58	1063	453	212	.468	54	47	.870	21	71	92	160	96	0	74	10	473	8.2	22
Brewer (Tot)	20	326	118	62	.525	25	23	.920	9	12	21	17	23	0	6	6	147	7.4	17
Brewer (NJ)	11	245	84	49	.583	18	16	.889	8	10	18	11	15	0	5	5	114	10.4	17
Turner	72	1429	377	171	.454	92	79	.859	88	130	218	108	243	8	29	7	421	5.8	14
McKenna	29	535	134	61	.455	43	38	.884	20	29	49	58	63	0	30	7	165	5.7	17
Wilson (Tot)	19	267	77	36	.468	36	27	.750	14	17	31	35	21	0	14	5	99	5.2	13
Wilson (NJ)	8	92	23	9	.391	6	4	.667	4	9	13	11	7	0	4	2	22	2.8	8
Sappleton	33	298	87	41	.471	34	14	.412	28	47	75	7	50	0	7	4	96	2.9	9
Engler	7	76	16	7	.438	9	5	.556	10	17	27	0	4	0	2	4	19	2.7	14
Johnson	65	800	79	42	.532	27	22	.815	74	111	185	22	151	2	19	78	107	1.6	7
LaGarde	1	8	1	0	.000	2	1	.500	1	1	2	0	2	0	0	0	1	1.0	1

3-Pt. FG: New Jersey 52-224 (.232)—Birdsong 4-21 (.190); Richardson 29-115 (.252); Williams 1-4 (.250); Dawkins 0-1 (.000); Gminski 0-1 (.000); King 0-8 (.000); O'Koren 8-21 (.381); Ransey 2-11 (.182); Cook 2-23 (.087); Brewer 0-2 (.000); Turner 0-3 (.000); McKenna 5-13 (.385); Johnson 1-1 (1.000). Opponents 79-262 (.302).

NEW YORK KNICKERBOCKERS

Player	G.	Min.	FGA	FGM	Pct.	FTA	FTM	Pct.	Off. Reb.	Def. Reb.	Tot. Reb.	Ast.	PF	Dsq.	Stl.	Blk. Sh.	Pts.	Avg.	Hi.
King	55	2063	1303	691	.530	792	426	.772	114	203	317	204	191	3	71	15	1809	32.9	60
Cummings	63	2069	797	410	.514	227	177	.780	139	379	518	109	247	6	50	17	997	15.8	34
Walker	82	2489	989	430	.435	347	243	.700	128	150	278	408	244	2	167	21	1103	13.5	31
Orr	79	2452	766	372	.486	334	262	.784	171	220	391	134	195	1	100	27	1007	12.7	28
Sparrow	79	2292	662	326	.492	141	122	.865	38	131	169	557	200	2	81	9	781	9.9	21
Tucker	77	1819	606	293	.483	48	38	.792	74	114	188	199	195	0	75	15	653	8.5	27
Carter	69	1279	476	214	.450	134	109	.813	36	59	95	167	151	1	57	5	548	7.9	22
Bannister	75	1404	445	209	.470	192	91	.474	108	222	330	39	279	16	38	40	509	6.8	24
Grunfeld	69	1061	384	188	.490	104	77	.740	41	110	151	105	129	2	50	7	455	6.6	30
Wilkins	54	917	233	116	.498	122	66	.541	86	176	262	16	155	3	21	16	298	5.5	24
Bailey	74	1297	349	156	.447	108	73	.676	122	222	344	39	286	10	30	50	385	5.2	18
Robinson	2	35	5	2	.400	2	0	.000	6	3	9	3	3	0	2	3	4	2.0	4
Cavenall	53	653	86	28	.326	39	22	.564	53	113	166	19	123	2	12	42	78	1.5	7

3-Pt. FG: New York 51-198 (.258)—King 1-10 (.100); Cummings 0-4 (.000); Walker 0-17 (.000); Orr 1-10 (.100); Sparrow 7-31 (.226); Tucker 29-72 (.403); Carter 11-43 (.256); Grunfeld 2-8 (.250); Wilkins 0-2 (.000); Bailey 0-1 (.000). Opponents 67-229 (.293).

PHILADELPHIA 76ers

Player	G.	Min.	FGA	FGM	Pct.	FTA	FTM	Pct.	Off. Reb.	Def. Reb.	Tot. Reb.	Ast.	PF	Dsq.	Stl.	Blk. Sh.	Pts.	Avg.	Hi.
Malone	79	2957	1284	602	.469	904	737	.815	385	646	1031	130	216	0	67	123	1941	24.6	51
Erving	78	2535	1236	610	.494	442	338	.765	172	242	414	233	199	0	135	109	1561	20.0	35
Toney	70	2237	914	450	.492	355	306	.862	35	142	177	363	211	1	65	24	1245	17.8	43
Barkley	82	2347	783	427	.545	400	293	.733	266	437	703	155	301	5	95	80	1148	14.0	29
Cheeks	78	2616	741	422	.570	199	175	.879	54	163	217	497	184	0	169	14	1025	13.1	25
Jones	80	1633	385	207	.538	216	186	.861	105	192	297	155	183	2	84	50	600	7.5	17
Richardson	74	1531	404	183	.453	89	76	.854	60	95	155	157	143	0	37	15	443	6.0	17
Threatt	82	1304	416	188	.452	90	66	.733	21	78	99	175	171	2	80	16	446	5.4	19
G. Johnson	55	756	263	107	.407	56	49	.875	48	116	164	38	99	0	31	16	264	4.8	21
C. Johnson	58	875	235	117	.498	49	36	.735	92	129	221	33	112	0	15	44	270	4.7	12
Wood	38	269	134	50	.373	26	18	.692	3	15	18	45	17	0	8	0	122	3.2	16
Williams	46	488	148	58	.392	47	28	.596	38	68	106	11	92	1	26	26	144	3.1	10

Player	G.	Min.	FGA	FGM	Pct.	FTA	FTM	Pct.	Off. Reb.	Def. Reb.	Tot. Reb.	Ast.	PF	Disq.	Stl.	Blk. Sh.	Pts.	Avg.	Hi.
Iavaroni	12	156	31	12	.387	6	6	1.000	11	18	29	6	24	0	4	3	30	2.5	6
Hayes	11	101	18	10	.556	4	2	.500	11	23	34	1	19	0	1	4	22	2.0	5

3-Pt. FG: Philadelphia 59-224 (.263)—Malone 0-2 (.000); Erving 3-14 (.214); Toney 39-105 (.371); Barkley 1-6 (.167); Cheeks 6-26 (.231); Jones 0-4 (.000); Richardson 1-3 (.333); Threatt 4-22 (.182); G. Johnson 1-10 (.100); C. Johnson 0-1 (.000); Wood 4-30 (.133); Williams 0-1 (.000). Opponents 80-311 (.257).

PHOENIX SUNS

Player	G.	Min.	FGA	FGM	Pct.	FTA	FTM	Pct.	Off. Reb.	Def. Reb.	Tot. Reb.	Ast.	PF	Dsq.	Stl.	Blk. Sh.	Pts.	Avg.	Hi.
Nance	61	2202	877	515	.587	254	180	.709	195	341	536	159	185	2	88	104	1211	19.9	44
Davis	23	570	309	139	.450	73	64	.877	6	29	35	98	42	0	18	0	345	15.0	22
Edwards	70	1787	766	384	.501	370	276	.746	95	292	387	153	237	5	26	52	1044	14.9	30
Adams	82	2136	915	476	.520	283	250	.883	153	347	500	308	254	2	115	48	1202	14.7	36
Lucas	63	1670	727	346	.476	200	150	.750	138	419	557	145	183	0	39	17	842	13.4	28
Macy	65	2018	582	282	.485	140	127	.907	33	146	179	380	128	0	85	3	714	11.0	30
Sanders	21	418	181	75	.486	59	45	.763	38	51	89	29	59	0	23	4	215	10.2	21
Foster	79	1318	636	286	.450	110	83	.755	27	53	80	186	171	1	61	0	696	8.8	24
Humphries	80	2062	626	279	.446	170	141	.829	32	132	164	350	209	2	107	8	703	8.8	25
Holton	74	1761	576	257	.446	118	96	.814	30	102	132	198	141	0	59	6	624	8.4	25
Jones	78	1565	454	236	.520	281	182	.648	139	255	394	128	149	0	45	61	654	8.4	27
Pittman	68	1001	227	107	.471	146	109	.747	90	137	227	69	144	1	20	21	323	4.8	20
Scott	77	1238	259	111	.429	74	53	.716	46	115	161	127	125	0	39	25	276	3.6	10
Young	2	11	6	2	.333	0	0	.....	1	1	2	0	0	0	0	0	4	2.0	4
Robey	4	48	9	2	.222	2	1	.500	3	5	8	5	7	0	2	0	5	1.3	3

3-Pt. FG: Phoenix 87-307 (.283)—Nance 1-2 (.500); Davis 3-10 (.300); Edwards 0-3 (.000); Lucas 0-4 (.000); Macy 23-85 (.271); Foster 41-126 (.325); Humphries 4-20 (.200); Holton 14-45 (.311); Jones 0-4 (.000); Pittman 0-2 (.000); Scott 1-5 (.200); Young 0-1 (.000). Opponents 65-224 (.290).

PORTLAND TRAIL BLAZERS

Player	G.	Min.	FGA	FGM	Pct.	FTA	FTM	Pct.	Off. Reb.	Def. Reb.	Tot. Reb.	Ast.	PF	Dsq.	Stl.	Blk. Sh.	Pts.	Avg.	Hi.
Vandeweghe	72	2502	1158	618	.534	412	369	.896	74	154	228	106	116	0	37	22	1616	22.4	47
M. Thompson	79	2616	1111	572	.515	449	307	.684	211	407	618	205	216	0	78	104	1451	18.4	33
Paxson	68	2253	988	508	.514	248	196	.790	69	153	222	264	115	0	101	5	1218	17.9	40
Drexler	80	2555	1161	573	.494	294	223	.759	217	259	476	441	265	3	177	68	1377	17.2	37
Valentine	75	2278	679	321	.473	290	230	.793	54	165	219	522	189	1	143	5	872	11.6	26
Carr	48	1120	363	190	.523	164	118	.720	90	233	323	56	141	0	25	17	498	10.4	30
Bowie	76	2216	557	299	.537	225	160	.711	207	449	656	215	278	9	55	203	758	10.0	26
Colter	78	1462	477	216	.453	130	98	.754	40	110	150	243	142	0	75	9	556	7.1	35
Kersey	77	958	372	178	.478	181	117	.646	95	111	206	63	147	1	49	29	473	6.1	21
Norris	78	1117	245	133	.543	203	135	.665	90	160	250	47	221	7	42	33	401	5.1	20
B. Thompson	59	535	212	79	.373	51	39	.765	37	39	76	52	79	0	31	10	197	3.3	13
Scheffler	39	268	51	21	.412	20	10	.500	18	58	76	11	48	0	8	11	52	1.3	10

3-Pt. FG: Portland 51-202 (.252)—Vandeweghe 11-33 (.333); Paxson 6-39 (.154); Drexler 8-37 (.216); Valentine 0-2 (.000); Carr 0-3 (.000); Colter 26-74 (.351); Kersey 0-3 (.000); Norris 0-3 (.000); B. Thompson 0-8 (.000). Opponents 59-232 (.254).

SAN ANTONIO SPURS

Player	G.	Min.	FGA	FGM	Pct.	FTA	FTM	Pct.	Off. Reb.	Def. Reb.	Tot. Reb.	Ast.	PF	Dsq.	Stl.	Blk. Sh.	Pts.	Avg.	Hi.
Mitchell	82	2853	1558	775	.497	346	269	.777	145	272	417	151	219	1	61	27	1824	22.2	40
Gervin	72	2091	1182	600	.508	384	324	.844	79	155	234	178	208	2	66	48	1524	21.2	47
Gilmore	81	2756	854	532	.623	646	484	.749	231	615	846	131	306	4	40	173	1548	19.1	35
Moore	82	2689	910	416	.457	248	189	.762	94	284	378	816	247	3	229	18	1046	12.8	27
Banks	82	2091	493	289	.586	257	199	.774	133	312	445	234	220	3	65	13	778	9.5	32
Robertson	79	1685	600	299	.498	169	124	.734	116	149	265	275	217	1	127	24	726	9.2	27
E. Jones	18	322	91	44	.484	51	41	.804	16	46	62	18	52	1	9	18	129	7.2	15
Paxson	78	1259	385	196	.509	100	84	.840	19	49	68	215	117	0	45	3	486	6.2	21
Iavaroni (Tot)	69	1334	354	162	.458	128	87	.680	95	209	304	119	217	5	35	35	411	6.0	17
Iavaroni (SA)	57	1178	323	150	.464	122	81	.664	84	191	275	113	193	5	31	32	381	6.7	17
Knight (Tot)	68	800	354	156	.441	73	64	.877	50	68	118	80	62	0	16	2	387	5.7	21
Knight (SA)	52	611	285	125	.439	57	51	.895	40	56	96	59	48	0	14	1	311	6.0	21
Roberts	22	305	98	44	.449	38	29	.763	10	25	35	22	45	0	10	12	117	5.3	12
Cook (Tot)	72	1288	279	138	.495	64	47	.734	122	192	314	62	203	2	30	23	323	4.5	14
Cook (SA)	54	848	174	92	.529	37	30	.811	81	129	210	39	150	2	25	14	214	4.0	13
Brewer	9	81	34	13	.382	7	7	1.000	1	2	3	6	8	0	1	1	33	3.7	6
O. Jones	67	888	180	106	.589	83	33	.398	65	173	238	56	139	1	30	57	245	3.7	19
Thirdkill (Tot)	18	183	38	20	.526	19	11	.579	10	7	17	4	22	0	5	3	51	2.8	9
Thirdkill (SA)	2	52	11	5	.455	6	5	.833	5	2	7	3	5	0	2	1	15	7.5	9
McNamara	12	63	18	12	.667	18	9	.500	7	10	17	0	5	0	2	1	33	2.8	9
Townes	1	8	6	0	.000	2	2	1.000	1	0	1	0	1	0	0	0	2	2.0	2

3-Pt. FG: San Antonio 55-202 (.272)—Mitchell 5-23 (.217); Gervin 0-10 (.000); Gilmore 0-2 (.000); Moore 25-89 (.281); Banks 1-3 (.333); Robertson 4-11 (.364); E. Jones 0-1 (.000); Paxson 10-34 (.294); Iavaroni 0-4 (.000); Knight 10-24 (.417); O. Jones 0-1 (.000). Opponents 72-242 (.298).

SEATTLE SUPERSONICS

Player	G.	Min.	FGA	FGM	Pct.	FTA	FTM	Pct.	Off. Reb.	Def. Reb.	Tot. Reb.	Ast.	PF	Dsq.	Stl.	Blk. Sh.	Pts.	Avg.	Hi.
Chambers	81	2923	1302	629	.483	571	475	.832	164	415	579	209	312	4	70	57	1739	21.5	38
Sikma	68	2403	943	461	.489	393	335	.852	164	559	723	285	239	1	83	91	1259	18.5	34
Wood	80	2545	1061	515	.485	214	166	.776	99	180	279	236	187	3	84	52	1203	15.0	35
Henderson	79	2648	891	427	.479	255	199	.780	71	119	190	559	196	1	140	9	1062	13.4	31
Sobers	71	1940	628	280	.446	162	132	.815	27	76	103	252	156	0	49	9	700	9.9	26
McCormick	78	1584	483	269	.557	263	188	.715	146	252	398	78	207	2	18	33	726	9.3	29
Vranes	76	2163	402	186	.463	127	67	.528	154	282	436	152	256	4	76	57	440	5.8	24
Cooper	3	45	15	7	.467	6	3	.500	3	6	9	2	7	1	2	1	17	5.7	14

1984-85 STATISTICS

Player	G.	Min.	FGA	FGM	Pct.	FTA	FTM	Pct.	Off. Reb.	Def. Reb.	Tot. Reb.	Ast.	PF	Disq.	Stl.	Blk Sh.	Pts.	Avg.	Hi.
Sundvold	73	1150	400	170	.425	59	48	.814	17	53	70	206	87	0	36	1	400	5.5	24
Brickowski	78	1115	305	150	.492	127	85	.669	76	184	260	100	171	1	34	15	385	4.9	22
Blackwell	60	551	237	87	.367	55	28	.509	42	54	96	26	55	0	25	3	202	3.4	11
Schweitz	19	110	74	25	.338	10	7	.700	6	15	21	18	12	0	0	1	57	3.0	11
King	60	860	149	63	.423	59	41	.695	44	78	122	53	74	1	28	11	167	2.8	13
McCray	6	93	10	6	.600	4	3	.750	6	11	17	7	13	0	1	3	15	2.5	5
Young	3	26	10	2	.200	0	0	.....	0	3	3	2	2	0	3	0	4	1.3	4

3-Pt. FG: Seattle 45-185 (.243)—Chambers 6-22 (.273); Sikma 2-10 (.200); Wood 7-33 (.212); Henderson 9-38 (.237); Sobers 8-28 (.286); McCormick 0-1 (.000); Vranes 1-4 (.250); Sundvold 12-38 (.316); Brickowski 0-4 (.000); Blackwell 0-2 (.000); Schweitz 0-4 (.000); Young 0-1 (.000). Opponents 79-253 (.312).

UTAH JAZZ

Player	G.	Min.	FGA	FGM	Pct.	FTA	FTM	Pct.	Off. Reb.	Def. Reb.	Tot. Reb.	Ast.	PF	Dsq.	Stl.	Blk. Sh.	Pts.	Avg.	Hi.
Dantley	55	1971	964	512	.531	545	438	.804	148	175	323	186	133	0	57	8	1462	26.6	42
Griffith	78	2776	1593	728	.457	298	216	.725	124	220	344	243	178	1	133	30	1764	22.6	41
Drew	19	463	260	107	.412	122	94	.770	36	46	82	35	65	0	22	2	308	16.2	38
Bailey	80	2481	1034	507	.490	234	197	.842	153	372	525	138	215	2	51	105	1212	15.2	27
Green	77	2431	798	381	.477	267	232	.869	37	152	189	597	131	0	132	3	1000	13.0	26
Eaton	82	2813	673	302	.449	267	190	.712	207	720	927	124	312	5	36	456	794	9.7	20
Wilkins	79	1505	582	285	.490	80	61	.763	78	288	366	81	173	0	35	18	631	8.0	22
Roberts (Tot.)	74	1178	418	208	.498	182	150	.824	78	108	186	87	141	0	28	22	567	7.7	25
Roberts (Utah)	52	873	320	164	.513	144	121	.840	68	83	151	65	96	0	18	10	450	8.7	25
Stockton	82	1490	333	157	.471	193	142	.736	26	79	105	415	203	3	109	11	458	5.6	19
Hansen	54	646	225	110	.489	72	40	.556	20	50	70	75	88	0	25	1	261	4.8	22
Kelley	77	1276	216	103	.477	112	84	.750	118	232	350	120	227	5	42	30	290	3.8	16
Anderson	44	457	149	61	.409	45	27	.600	29	53	82	21	70	0	29	9	149	3.4	11
Mannion	34	190	63	27	.429	23	16	.696	12	11	23	27	17	0	16	3	70	2.1	8
Natt	4	13	5	2	.400	4	2	.500	1	1	2	0	2	0	1	0	6	1.5	4
Paultz	62	370	87	32	.368	28	18	.643	24	72	96	16	51	0	6	11	82	1.3	10

3-Pt. FG: Utah 103-307 (.336)—Griffith 92-257 (.358); Drew 0-4 (.000); Bailey 1-1 (1.000); Green 6-20 (.300); Wilkins 0-1 (.000); Roberts 1-1 (1.000); Stockton 2-11 (.182); Hansen 1-7 (.143); Kelley 0-2 (.000); Anderson 0-2 (.000); Mannion 0-1 (.000). Opponents 72-280 (.257).

WASHINGTON BULLETS

Player	G.	Min.	FGA	FGM	Pct.	FTA	FTM	Pct.	Off. Reb.	Def. Reb.	Tot. Reb.	Ast.	PF	Dsq.	Stl.	Blk. Sh.	Pts.	Avg.	Hi.
Gus Williams	79	2960	1483	638	.430	346	251	.725	72	123	195	608	159	1	178	32	1578	20.0	37
Ruland	37	1436	439	250	.569	292	200	.685	127	283	410	162	128	2	31	27	700	18.9	31
Malone	76	2613	1213	605	.499	250	211	.844	60	146	206	184	176	1	52	9	1436	18.9	40
Robinson	60	1870	896	422	.471	213	158	.742	141	405	546	149	187	4	51	47	1003	16.7	32
Ballard	82	2664	978	469	.480	151	120	.795	150	381	531	208	221	0	100	3	1072	13.1	31
Johnson	46	925	358	175	.489	96	72	.750	23	40	63	143	72	0	43	3	428	9.3	21
McMillen	69	1547	534	252	.472	135	112	.830	64	146	210	52	163	3	8	17	616	8.9	37
Daye	80	1573	504	258	.512	249	178	.715	93	179	272	240	164	1	53	19	695	8.7	21
Mahorn	77	2072	413	206	.499	104	71	.683	150	458	608	121	308	11	59	104	483	6.3	25
Jones (Tot)	31	667	127	67	.528	58	40	.690	71	113	184	26	107	3	22	79	174	5.6	15
Jones (Wash)	28	638	123	65	.528	52	36	.692	69	109	178	25	101	3	22	74	166	5.9	15
Bradley	73	1232	299	142	.475	79	54	.684	34	100	134	173	152	0	96	21	358	4.9	22
Collins	11	91	34	12	.353	9	8	.889	10	9	19	7	5	0	7	4	32	2.9	7
Guy Williams	21	119	63	29	.460	5	2	.400	15	12	27	9	17	0	5	2	61	2.9	13
Davis	4	28	10	2	.200	4	3	.750	2	2	4	1	3	0	1	0	7	1.8	5
Sewell	21	87	36	9	.250	4	2	.500	2	2	4	6	13	0	3	1	20	1.0	4

3-Pt. FG: Washington 109-398 (.274)—Gus Williams 51-176 (.290); Ruland 0-2 (.000); Malone 15-72 (.208); Robinson 1-3 (.333); Ballard 14-46 (.304); Johnson 6-17 (.353); McMillen 0-5 (.000); Daye 1-7 (.143); Bradley 20-64 (.313); Guy Williams 1-4 (.250); Sewell 0-2 (.000). Opponents 66-232 (.284).

PLAYOFF RESULTS

EASTERN CONFERENCE FIRST ROUND
Boston 3, Cleveland 1
Apr. 18—Thur.—Cleveland 123 at Boston 126
Apr. 20—Sat.—Cleveland 106 at Boston 108
Apr. 23—Tue.—Boston 98 at Cleveland..105
Apr. 25—Thur.—Boston 117 at Cleveland 115

Milwaukee 3, Chicago 1
Apr. 19—Fri.—Chicago 100 at Milwaukee 109
Apr. 21—Sun.—Chicago 115 at Milwaukee....................................122
Apr. 24—Wed.—Milwaukee 107 at Chicago 109
Apr. 26—Fri.—Milwaukee 105 at Chicago 97

Philadelphia 3, Washington 1
Apr. 17—Wed.—Washington 97 at Philadelphia 104
Apr. 21—Sun.—Washington 94 at Philadelphia 113
Apr. 24—Wed.—Philadelphia 100 at Washington.......................118
Apr. 26—Fri.—Philadelphia 106 at Washington.........................,. 98

Detroit 3, New Jersey 0
Apr. 18—Thur.—New Jersey 105 at Detroit 125
Apr. 21—Sun.—New Jersey 111 at Detroit 121
Apr. 24—Wed.—Detroit 116 at New Jersey 115

EASTERN CONFERENCE SEMIFINALS
Boston 4, Detroit 2
Apr. 28—Sun.—Detroit 99 at Boston 133
Apr. 30—Tue.—Detroit 114 at Boston 121
May   2—Thur.—Boston 117 at Detroit 125
May   5—Sun.—Boston 99 at Detroit 102
May   8—Wed.—Detroit 123 at Boston 130
May 10—Fri.—Boston 123 at Detroit 113

Philadelphia 4, Milwaukee 0
Apr. 28—Sun.—Philadelphia 127 at Milwaukee 105
Apr. 30—Tue.—Philadelphia 112 at Milwaukee 108
May   3—Fri.—Milwaukee 104 at Philadelphia 109
May   5—Sun.—Milwaukee 112 at Philadelphia 121

EASTERN CONFERENCE FINALS
Boston 4, Philadelphia 1
May 12—Sun.—Philadelphia 93 at Boston 108
May 14—Tue.—Philadelphia 98 at Boston 106
May 18—Sat.—Boston 105 at Philadelphia 94
May 19—Sun.—Boston 104 at Philadelphia 115
May 22—Wed.—Philadelphia 100 at Boston.................................102

WESTERN CONFERENCE FIRST ROUND
L.A. Lakers 3, Phoenix 0
Apr. 18—Thur.—Phoenix 114 at L.A. Lakers.................................142
Apr. 20—Sat.—Phoenix 130 at L.A. Lakers....................................147
Apr. 23—Tue.—L.A. Lakers 119 at Phoenix....................................103

Denver 3, San Antonio 2
Apr. 18—Thur.—San Antonio 111 at Denver 141
Apr. 20—Sat.—San Antonio 113 at Denver.....................................111
Apr. 23—Tue.—Denver 115 at San Antonio...................................112
Apr. 26—Fri.—Denver 111 at San Antonio 116
Apr. 28—Sun.—San Antonio   99 at Denver....................................126

Utah 3, Houston 2
Apr. 19—Fri.—Utah 115 at Houston..101
Apr. 21—Sun.—Utah   96 at Houston...122
Apr. 24—Wed.—Houston 104 at Utah 112
Apr. 26—Fri.—Houston   96 at Utah 94
Apr. 28—Sun.—Utah 104 at Houston 97

Portland 3, Dallas 1
Apr. 18—Thur.—Portland 131 a Dallas...............................**139
Apr. 20—Sat.—Portland 124 at Dallas............................*121
Apr. 23—Tue.—Dallas 109 at Portland 122
Apr. 25—Thur.—Dallas 113 at Portland..115

WESTERN CONFERECE SEMIFINALS
L.A. Lakers 4, Portland 1
Apr. 27—Sat.—Portland 101 at L.A. Lakers....................................125
Apr. 30—Tue.—Portland 118 at L.A. Lakers....................................134
May   3—Fri.—L.A. Lakers 130 at Portland.....................................126
May   5—Sun.—L.A. Lakers 107 at Portland 115
May   7—Tue.—Portland 120 at L.A. Lakers 139

Denver 4, Utah 1
Apr. 30—Tue.—Utah 113 at Denver 130
May   2—Thur.—Utah 123 at Denver..............................*131
May   4—Sat.—Denver 123 at Utah 131
May   5—Sun.—Denver 125 at Utah 118
May   7—Tue.—Utah 104 to Denver 116

WESTERN CONFERENCE FINALS
L.A. Lakers 4, Denver 1
May 11—Sat.—Denver 122 at L.A. Lakers.......................................139
May 14—Tue.—Denver 136 at L.A. Lakers.......................................114
May 17—Fri.—L.A. Lakers 136 at Denver 118
May 19—Sun.—L.A. Lakers 120 at Denver......................................116
May 22—Wed.—Denver 109 at L.A. Lakers.....................................153

WORLD CHAMPIONSHIP SERIES
L.A. Lakers 4, Boston 2
May 27—Mon.—L.A. Lakers 114 at Boston 148
May 30—Thur.—L.A. Lakers 109 at Boston 102
Jun.   2—Sun.—Boston 111 at L.A. Lakers.................................136
Jun.   5—Wed.—Boston 107 at L.A. Lakers................................105
Jun.   7—Fri.—Boston 111 at L.A. Lakers 120
Jun.   9—Sun.—L.A. Lakers 111 at Boston.................................100
      *Overtime

1983-84 NBA STATISTICS

1983-84 NBA CHAMPION BOSTON CELTICS

Front row (left to right): Quinn Buckner, Cedric Maxwell, Vice Chairman of the Board Paul Dupee, Chairman of the Board Don Gaston, President and General Manager Arnold (Red) Auerbach, Coach K.C. Jones, Vice Chairman of the Board Alan Cohen, Larry Bird, M.L. Carr. Back row: Team Physician Dr. Thomas Silva, assistant coach Jimmy Rodgers, Gerald Henderson, Scott Wedman, Greg Kite, Robert Parish, Kevin McHale, Dennis Johnson, Danny Ainge, Carlos Clark, assistant coach Chris Ford, Trainer Ray Melchiorre.

FINAL STANDINGS

ATLANTIC DIVISION

Team	Atl.	Bos.	Chi.	Cle.	Dal.	Den.	Det.	G.S.	Hou.	Ind.	K.C.	L.A.	Mil.	N.J.	N.Y.	Phi.	Pho.	Por.	S.A.	S.D.	Sea.	Uta.	Was.	W.	L.	Pct.	G.B.
Boston	5	..	5	6	2	2	4	2	1	5	2	0	5	4	3	2	2	2	2	1	2	1	4	62	20	.756	....
Philadelphia	1	4	3	4	1	1	3	1	2	5	2	1	4	3	4	..	1	1	2	2	1	2	4	52	30	.634	10
New York	1	3	4	3	2	1	2	1	2	4	2	2	1	3	..	2	1	0	2	2	1	2	4	47	35	.573	15
New Jersey	3	2	4	3	2	1	1	4	1	2	5	0	1	..	3	3	2	0	0	2	1	1	1	45	37	.549	17
Washington	2	2	4	1	2	2	3	0	2	4	0	1	1	2	2	2	0	1	1	1	1	1	..	35	47	.427	27

CENTRAL DIVISION

Team	Atl.	Bos.	Chi.	Cle.	Dal.	Den.	Det.	G.S.	Hou.	Ind.	K.C.	L.A.	Mil.	N.J.	N.Y.	Phi.	Pho.	Por.	S.A.	S.D.	Sea.	Uta.	Was.	W.	L.	Pct.	G.B.
Milwaukee	3	1	4	5	2	1	2	2	1	5	2	0	..	4	4	2	2	1	1	1	1	1	5	50	32	.610	....
Detroit	4	2	5	5	2	1	..	4	1	1	4	1	3	1	4	3	2	1	1	2	1	1	3	49	33	.598	1
Atlanta	..	0	4	3	1	0	2	1	1	4	0	0	3	3	4	5	1	0	1	1	1	1	4	40	42	.488	10
Cleveland	3	0	4	..	1	0	1	1	1	2	0	0	1	2	1	2	1	1	1	1	0	0	4	28	54	.341	22
Chicago	2	0	..	2	1	0	1	2	0	3	1	0	2	2	2	2	1	2	0	1	0	1	2	27	55	.329	23
Indiana	2	1	3	4	0	2	2	0	1	..	0	1	1	1	2	0	1	0	1	1	1	1	1	26	56	.317	24

MIDWEST DIVISION

Team	Atl.	Bos.	Chi.	Cle.	Dal.	Den.	Det.	G.S.	Hou.	Ind.	K.C.	L.A.	Mil.	N.J.	N.Y.	Phi.	Pho.	Por.	S.A.	S.D.	Sea.	Uta.	Was.	W.	L.	Pct.	G.B.
Utah	1	1	1	2	2	3	1	4	5	1	3	1	1	1	0	0	4	4	2	3	4	..	1	45	37	.549	....
Dallas	1	0	1	1	..	4	0	4	4	2	3	3	0	1	0	1	3	2	4	4	1	4	0	43	39	.524	2
Denver	2	0	2	2	2	..	1	2	4	0	4	1	1	1	1	1	2	1	3	3	2	3	0	38	44	.463	7
Kansas City	2	0	1	2	3	2	1	1	4	2	..	0	0	2	0	0	2	2	5	3	1	3	0	38	44	.463	7
San Antonio	1	0	2	1	2	3	1	2	4	2	1	3	1	2	0	0	0	1	..	4	2	4	1	37	45	.451	8
Houston	1	1	2	1	2	2	1	3	..	1	2	1	1	0	0	0	2	1	2	2	3	1	0	29	53	.354	16

PACIFIC DIVISION

Team	Atl.	Bos.	Chi.	Cle.	Dal.	Den.	Det.	G.S.	Hou.	Ind.	K.C.	L.A.	Mil.	N.J.	N.Y.	Phi.	Pho.	Por.	S.A.	S.D.	Sea.	Uta.	Was.	W.	L.	Pct.	G.B.
Los Angeles	2	2	2	2	2	4	1	3	4	1	5	..	2	1	0	1	3	5	2	4	3	4	1	54	28	.659	....
Portland	2	0	0	1	3	4	1	4	4	1	3	1	1	2	2	1	4	..	4	4	4	1	1	48	34	.585	6
Seattle	1	0	2	1	4	3	1	2	2	1	4	3	1	1	1	1	4	2	3	4	..	1	1	42	40	.512	12
Phoenix	1	0	1	1	2	3	0	5	3	1	3	3	0	0	1	1	..	2	5	4	2	1	2	41	41	.500	13
Golden State	1	0	0	1	3	1	1	..	2	2	4	3	0	1	1	1	1	2	3	3	4	1	2	37	45	.451	17
San Diego	1	1	1	1	1	2	0	3	3	1	2	1	2	0	1	0	0	2	1	..	3	2	1	30	52	.366	24

HOME-ROAD RECORDS OF ALL TEAMS

Team	Home	Road	Total	Team	Home	Road	Total
Atlanta	31- 10	9- 32	40- 42	Milwaukee	30- 11	20- 21	50- 32
Boston	33- 8	29- 12	62- 20	New Jersey	29- 12	16- 25	45- 37
Chicago	18- 23	9- 32	27- 55	New York	29- 12	18- 23	47- 35
Cleveland	23- 18	5- 36	28- 54	Philadelphia	32- 9	20- 21	52- 30
Dallas	31- 10	12- 29	43- 39	Phoenix	31- 10	10- 31	41- 41
Denver	27- 14	11- 30	38- 44	Portland	33- 8	15- 26	48- 34
Detroit	30- 11	19- 22	49- 33	San Antonio	28- 13	9- 32	37- 45
Golden State	27- 14	10- 31	37- 45	San Diego	25- 16	5- 36	30- 52
Houston	21- 20	8- 33	29- 53	Seattle	32- 9	10- 31	42- 40
Indiana	20- 21	6- 35	26- 56	Utah	31- 10	14- 27	45- 37
Kansas City	26- 15	12- 29	38- 44	Washington	25- 16	10- 31	35- 47
Los Angeles	28- 13	26- 15	54- 28	Total	640-303	303-640	943-943

OFFENSIVE TEAM STATISTICS

Team	G.	FIELD GOALS Att.	Made	Pct.	FREE THROWS Att.	Made	Pct.	REBOUNDS Off.	Def.	Tot.	Ast.	MISCELLANEOUS PF	Disq.	Stl.	Turn Over	Blk. Sh.	SCORING Pts.	Avg.
Denver	82	7983	3935	.493	2690	2200	.818	1133	2444	3577	2482	2279	29	711	1344	352	10147	123.7
San Antonio	82	7721	3909	.506	2604	1965	.755	1230	2528	3758	2361	2146	37	685	1447	491	9862	120.3
Detroit	82	7910	3798	.480	2547	1974	.775	1427	2434	3861	2256	2177	30	697	1310	417	9602	117.1
Los Angeles	82	7250	3854	.532	2272	1712	.754	1095	2499	3594	2455	2054	12	726	1578	478	9478	115.6
Utah	82	7242	3606	.498	2708	2115	.781	1096	2522	3618	2230	1978	16	695	1510	604	9428	115.0
Portland	82	7189	3632	.505	2637	1988	.754	1251	2194	3445	2082	2134	16	814	1483	397	9277	113.1
Boston	82	7235	3616	.500	2407	1907	.792	1159	2538	3697	2122	1949	25	673	1420	430	9194	112.1
Phoenix	82	7220	3677	.509	2204	1673	.759	1066	2298	3364	2214	2147	13	693	1451	388	9101	111.0
San Diego	82	7325	3634	.496	2424	1785	.736	1307	2382	3689	1981	2020	20	567	1515	385	9077	110.7
Houston	82	7533	3729	.495	2139	1583	.740	1200	2483	3683	2204	2317	52	621	1562	515	9071	110.6
Dallas	82	7235	3618	.500	2350	1774	.755	1090	2265	3355	2164	1906	21	579	1303	360	9052	110.4
Kansas City	82	7230	3516	.486	2495	1939	.777	1144	2273	3417	2229	2200	33	715	1504	383	9023	110.0
New Jersey	82	7258	3614	.498	2488	1742	.700	1221	2313	3534	2148	2243	46	814	1608	499	9019	110.0
Golden State	82	7534	3519	.467	2577	1915	.743	1390	2171	3561	1837	2108	23	830	1518	348	9008	109.9
Seattle	82	7083	3460	.488	2460	1918	.780	1064	2332	3396	2233	1884	24	636	1360	350	8865	108.1
Philadelphia	82	6833	3384	.495	2706	2041	.754	1181	2382	3563	2032	2040	13	807	1628	653	8838	107.8
New York	82	6837	3386	.495	2510	1944	.775	1088	2230	3318	2041	2281	27	803	1587	360	8763	106.9
Milwaukee	82	6970	3432	.492	2354	1743	.740	1135	2385	3520	2113	2167	35	642	1415	489	8666	105.7
Indiana	82	7130	3447	.483	2119	1624	.766	1002	2398	3400	2169	2061	20	834	1525	398	8566	104.5
Chicago	82	6972	3305	.474	2508	1871	.746	1141	2300	3441	2095	2196	48	687	1578	454	8501	103.7
Washington	82	6907	3344	.484	2201	1664	.756	1027	2387	3414	2192	1989	37	556	1448	320	8423	102.7
Cleveland	82	7232	3362	.465	2178	1619	.743	1213	2388	3601	1930	2206	38	630	1332	375	8386	102.3
Atlanta	82	6809	3230	.474	2414	1838	.761	1112	2232	3344	1827	2091	35	626	1329	558	8321	101.5

DEFENSIVE TEAM STATISTICS

Team	FIELD GOALS Att.	Made	Pct.	FREE THROWS Att.	Made	Pct.	REBOUNDS Off.	Def.	Tot.	Ast.	MISCELLANEOUS PF	Disq.	Stl.	Turn Over	Blk. Sh.	SCORING Pts.	Avg.	Pt. Dif.
Milwaukee	7033	3207	.456	2489	1869	.751	1252	2235	3487	1959	2093	32	653	1404	319	8325	101.5	+ 4.2
Atlanta	6845	3277	.479	2380	1834	.771	1191	2410	3601	2026	2087	21	579	1409	424	8427	102.8	− 1.3
New York	6687	3260	.488	2474	1876	.758	1045	2171	3216	2049	2197	31	721	1683	397	8448	103.0	+ 3.8
Boston	7372	3463	.470	2143	1659	.774	1101	2227	3328	1957	2090	29	703	1329	328	8656	105.6	+ 6.6
Philadelphia	7136	3427	.480	2367	1757	.742	1235	2237	3472	2062	2237	42	805	1559	483	8658	105.6	+ 2.2
Washington	7086	3465	.489	2218	1693	.763	1037	2381	3418	2038	2021	24	706	1277	492	8660	105.6	− 2.9
Cleveland	6930	3373	.487	2541	1939	.763	983	2405	3388	2141	1906	21	579	1224	395	8735	106.5	− 4.3
Seattle	7337	3585	.489	2168	1655	.763	1167	2404	3571	2278	2097	19	663	1330	388	8879	108.3	− 0.2
Chicago	7082	3502	.494	2471	1885	.763	1125	2388	3513	2235	2110	35	786	1513	514	8926	108.9	− 5.2
New Jersey	6974	3422	.491	2675	2037	.761	1097	2307	3404	1913	2161	30	781	1674	416	8929	108.9	+ 1.1
Indiana	7175	3552	.495	2415	1828	.757	1194	2564	3758	2117	1930	15	761	1587	444	8961	109.3	− 4.8
Portland	6943	3566	.514	2366	1797	.760	1059	2185	3244	2119	2184	23	649	1633	440	8986	109.6	+ 3.5
Dallas	7282	3633	.499	2198	1688	.768	1180	2346	3526	2131	2213	23	632	1386	417	9017	110.0	+ 0.4
Phoenix	7061	3509	.497	2540	1956	.770	1065	2333	3398	2059	2038	24	675	1480	298	9028	110.1	+ 0.9
Kansas City	7169	3601	.502	2510	1909	.761	1126	2387	3513	2108	2191	30	660	1584	493	9144	111.5	− 1.5
Los Angeles	7600	3672	.483	2346	1763	.751	1253	2154	3407	2261	1973	28	797	1443	376	9170	111.8	+ 3.8
Golden State	7210	3725	.517	2377	1801	.758	1211	2513	3724	2150	2246	31	691	1694	494	9287	113.3	− 3.4
Detroit	7369	3657	.496	2577	1941	.753	1163	2457	3620	2193	2187	46	621	1480	527	9308	113.5	− 3.6
Houston	7412	3583	.483	2803	2116	.755	1197	2458	3655	2023	1916	19	782	1421	426	9324	113.7	− 3.1
Utah	7872	3745	.476	2414	1799	.745	1458	2461	3919	2237	2194	31	747	1438	466	9335	113.8	+ 1.1
San Diego	7406	3771	.509	2233	1749	.783	1112	2163	3275	2370	2043	25	727	1242	458	9344	114.0	− 3.3
San Antonio	7910	3996	.505	2427	1840	.758	1293	2455	3748	2518	2187	39	652	1427	464	9884	120.5	− 0.3
Denver	7747	4016	.518	2860	2143	.749	1228	2737	3965	2453	2272	32	671	1538	545	10237	124.8	− 1.1

Disq.—Individual player disqualified (fouled out of game).

INDIVIDUAL LEADERS

POINTS

Minimum 70 games played or 1,400 points

Player	G.	FG	FT	Pts.	Avg.	Player	G.	FG	FT	Pts.	Avg.
Dantley, Utah	79	802	813	2418	30.6	Malone, Philadelphia	71	532	545	1609	22.7
Aguirre, Dallas	79	925	465	2330	29.5	Erving, Philadelphia	77	678	364	1727	22.4
Vandeweghe, Denver	78	895	494	2295	29.4	Blackman, Dallas	81	721	372	1815	22.4
English, Denver	82	907	352	2167	26.4	Free, Cleveland	75	626	395	1669	22.3
King, New York	77	795	437	2027	26.3	Ruland, Washington	75	599	466	1665	22.2
Gervin, San Antonio	76	765	427	1967	25.9	E. Johnson, Kansas City	82	753	268	1794	21.9
Bird, Boston	79	758	374	1908	24.2	Wilkins, Atlanta	81	684	382	1750	21.6
Mitchell, San Antonio	79	779	275	1839	23.3	Abdul-Jabbar, Los Angeles	80	716	285	1717	21.5
Cummings, San Diego	81	737	380	1854	22.9	Thomas, Detroit	82	669	388	1748	21.3
Short, Golden State	79	714	353	1803	22.8	Tripucka, Detroit	76	595	426	1618	21.3

FIELD GOALS
Minimum 300 FG made

	FGA	FGM	Pct.
Gilmore, San Antonio	556	351	.631
Donaldson, San Diego	604	360	.596
McGee, Los Angeles	584	347	.594
Dawkins, New Jersey	855	507	.593
Natt, Portland	857	500	.583
Ruland, Washington	1035	599	.579
Abdul-Jabbar, Los Angeles	1238	716	.578
Nance, Phoenix	1044	601	.576
Lanier, Milwaukee	685	392	.572
King, New York	1391	795	.572

FREE THROWS
Minimum 125 FT made

	FTA	FTM	Pct.
Bird, Boston	421	374	.888
Long, Detroit	275	243	.884
Laimbeer, Detroit	365	316	.866
Davis, Phoenix	270	233	.863
Pierce, San Diego	173	149	.861
Dantley, Utah	946	813	.859
Knight, Kansas City	283	243	.859
Sikma, Seattle	480	411	.856
Vandeweghe, Denver	580	494	.852
Johnson, Boston	330	281	.852

ASSISTS
Minimum 70 games or 400 assists

	G.	No.	Avg.
Johnson, Los Angeles	67	875	13.1
Nixon, San Diego	82	914	11.1
Thomas, Detroit	82	914	11.1
Lucas, San Antonio	63	673	10.7
Moore, San Antonio	59	566	9.6
Green, Utah	81	748	9.2
Williams, Seattle	80	675	8.4
Whatley, Chicago	80	662	8.3
Drew, Kansas City	73	558	7.6
Davis, Dallas	81	561	6.9

STEALS
Minimum 70 games or 125 steals

	G.	No.	Avg.
Green, Utah	81	215	2.65
Thomas, Detroit	82	204	2.49
Williams, Seattle	80	189	2.36
Cheeks, Philadelphia	75	171	2.28
Johnson, Los Angeles	67	150	2.24
Dunn, Denver	80	173	2.16
Williams, New York	76	162	2.13
Cook, New Jersey	82	164	2.00
Conner, Golden State	82	162	1.98
Erving, Philadelphia	77	141	1.83

REBOUNDS
Minimum 70 games or 800 rebounds

	G.	Off.	Def.	Tot.	Avg.
Malone, Philadelphia	71	352	598	950	13.4
Williams, New Jersey	81	355	645	1000	12.3
Ruland, Washington	75	265	657	922	12.3
Laimbeer, Detroit	82	329	674	1003	12.2
Sampson, Houston	82	293	620	913	11.1
Sikma, Seattle	82	225	686	911	11.1
Parish, Boston	80	243	614	857	10.7
Robinson, Cleveland	73	156	597	753	10.3
Greenwood, Chicago	78	214	572	786	10.1
Bird, Boston	79	181	615	796	10.1

BLOCKED SHOTS
Minimum 70 games or 100 blocked shots

	G.	No.	Avg.
Eaton, Utah	82	351	4.28
Rollins, Atlanta	77	277	3.60
Sampson, Houston	82	197	2.40
Nance, Phoenix	82	173	2.11
Gilmore, San Antonio	64	132	2.06
Hinson, Cleveland	80	145	1.81
Thompson, Kansas City	80	145	1.81
Erving, Philadelphia	77	139	1.81
Abdul-Jabbar, Los Angeles	80	143	1.79
Carroll, Golden State	80	142	1.78

3-PT. FIELD GOALS
Minimum 25 made

	FGA	FGM	Pct.
Griffith, Utah	252	91	.361
Evans, Denver	89	32	.360
Moore, San Antonio	87	28	.322
Cooper, Los Angeles	121	38	.314
Williams, New York	81	25	.309
Sobers, Washington	111	29	.261

TEAM-BY-TEAM INDIVIDUAL STATISTICS

ATLANTA HAWKS

Player	G.	Min.	FGA	FGM	Pct.	FTA	FTM	Pct.	Off. Reb.	Def. Reb.	Tot. Reb.	Ast.	PF	Dsq.	Stl.	Blk. Sh.	Pts.	Avg.	Hi.
Wilkins	81	2961	1429	684	.479	496	382	.770	254	328	582	126	197	1	117	87	1750	21.6	39
Roundfield	73	2610	1038	503	.485	486	374	.770	206	515	721	184	221	2	61	74	1380	18.9	37
Johnson	67	1893	798	353	.442	213	164	.770	31	115	146	374	155	2	58	7	886	13.2	29
Davis	75	2079	800	354	.443	256	217	.848	53	86	139	326	146	0	62	6	925	12.3	29
Rivers	81	1938	541	250	.462	325	255	.785	72	148	220	314	286	8	127	30	757	9.3	21
Rollins	77	2351	529	274	.518	190	118	.621	200	393	593	62	297	9	35	277	666	8.6	22
Glenn	81	1503	554	312	.563	70	56	.800	17	87	104	171	146	1	46	5	681	8.4	24
Matthews	6	96	30	16	.533	22	18	.818	1	3	4	21	13	0	5	1	50	8.3	15
Williams	13	258	114	34	.298	46	36	.783	19	31	50	16	33	0	14	1	105	8.1	14
Wittman	78	1071	318	160	.503	46	28	.609	14	57	71	71	82	0	17	0	350	4.5	14
Hastings	68	1135	237	111	.468	104	82	.788	96	174	270	46	220	7	40	36	305	4.5	16
Criss (Tot)	15	215	52	20	.385	16	12	.750	5	15	20	38	11	0	8	0	53	3.5	8
Criss (Atl)	9	108	22	9	.409	5	5	1.000	3	8	11	21	4	0	3	0	23	2.6	6
Brown	68	785	201	94	.468	65	48	.738	67	114	181	29	161	4	18	23	236	3.5	11
Hill	15	181	46	14	.304	21	17	.810	2	8	10	35	30	1	7	0	45	3.0	8
Pinone	7	65	13	7	.538	10	6	.600	0	10	10	3	11	0	2	1	20	2.9	6
Paultz	40	486	88	36	.409	33	17	.515	35	78	113	18	57	0	8	7	89	2.2	9
Landsberger	35	335	51	19	.373	26	15	.577	42	77	119	10	32	0	6	3	53	1.5	7

3-Pt. FG: Atlanta 23-106 (.217)—Wilkins 0-11 (.000); Roundfield 0-11 (.000); Johnson 16-43 (.372); Davis 0-8 (.000); Rivers 2-12 (.167); Glenn 1-2 (.500); Matthews 0-1 (.000); Williams 1-9 (.111); Wittman 2-5 (.400); Hastings 1-4 (.250) Opponents 39-185 (.211).

BOSTON CELTICS

Player	G.	Min.	FGA	FGM	Pct.	FTA	FTM	Pct.	Off. Reb.	Def. Reb.	Tot. Reb.	Ast.	PF	Dsq.	Stl.	Blk. Sh.	Pts.	Avg.	Hi.
Bird	79	3028	1542	758	.492	421	374	.888	181	615	796	520	197	0	144	69	1908	24.2	41
Parish	80	2867	1140	623	.546	368	274	.745	243	614	857	139	266	7	55	116	1520	19.0	36
McHale	82	2577	1055	587	.556	439	336	.765	208	402	610	104	243	5	23	126	1511	18.4	33
Johnson	80	2665	878	384	.437	330	281	.852	87	193	280	338	251	6	93	57	1053	13.2	26
Maxwell	80	2502	596	317	.532	425	320	.753	201	260	461	205	224	4	63	24	955	11.9	24
Henderson	78	2088	718	376	.524	177	136	.768	68	79	147	300	209	1	117	14	908	11.6	22
Ainge	71	1154	361	166	.460	56	46	.821	29	87	116	162	143	2	41	4	384	5.4	18
Wedman	68	916	333	148	.444	35	29	.829	41	98	139	67	107	0	27	7	327	4.8	19
Buckner	79	1249	323	138	.427	74	48	.649	41	96	137	214	187	0	84	3	324	4.1	16
Carr	60	585	171	70	.409	48	42	.875	26	49	75	49	67	0	17	4	185	3.1	22
Kite	35	197	66	30	.455	16	5	.313	27	35	62	7	42	0	1	5	65	1.9	13
Clark	31	127	52	19	.365	18	16	.889	7	10	17	17	13	0	8	1	54	1.7	6

3-Pt. FG: Boston 55-229 (.240)—Bird 18-73 (.247); McHale 1-3 (.333); Johnson 4-32 (.125); Maxwell 1-6 (.167); Henderson 20-57 (.351); Ainge 6-22 (.273); Wedman 2-13 (.154); Buckner 0-6 (.000); Carr 3-15 (.200); Clark 0-2 (.000). Opponents 71-219 (.324).

CHICAGO BULLS

Player	G.	Min.	FGA	FGM	Pct.	FTA	FTM	Pct.	Off. Reb.	Def. Reb.	Tot. Reb.	Ast.	PF	Dsq.	Stl.	Blk. Sh.	Pts.	Avg.	Hi.
Woolridge	75	2544	1086	570	.525	424	303	.715	130	239	369	136	253	6	71	60	1444	19.3	33
Dailey	82	2449	1229	583	.474	396	321	.811	61	174	235	254	218	4	109	11	1491	18.2	44
Wiggins	82	2123	890	399	.448	287	213	.742	138	190	328	187	278	8	106	11	1018	12.4	28
Corzine	82	2674	824	385	.467	275	231	.840	169	406	575	202	227	3	58	120	1004	12.2	29
Greenwood	78	2718	753	369	.490	289	213	.737	214	572	786	139	265	9	67	72	951	12.2	32
Johnson (Tot.)	81	1487	540	302	.559	287	165	.575	162	256	418	81	307	15	37	69	769	9.5	24
Johnson (Chi)	31	594	198	113	.571	110	64	.582	68	98	166	18	119	8	15	21	290	9.4	23
Theus	31	601	237	92	.388	108	84	.778	21	25	46	142	78	2	21	3	271	8.7	22
Whatley	80	2159	556	261	.469	200	146	.730	63	134	197	662	223	4	119	17	668	8.4	21
Higgins	78	1577	432	193	.447	156	113	.724	87	119	206	116	161	0	49	29	500	6.4	18
Lester	43	687	188	78	.415	87	75	.862	20	26	46	168	59	1	30	6	232	5.4	16
Green	49	667	228	100	.439	77	55	.714	58	116	174	25	128	1	18	17	255	5.2	18
Bryant	29	317	133	52	.391	33	14	.424	37	43	80	13	48	0	9	11	118	4.1	18
Oldham	64	870	218	110	.505	66	39	.591	75	158	233	33	139	2	15	76	259	4.0	15

3-Pt. FG: Chicago 20-117 (.171)—Woolridge 1-2 (.500); Dailey 4-32 (.125); Wiggins 7-29 (.241); Corzine 3-9 (.333); Greenwood 0-1 (.000); Theus 3-15 (.200); Whatley 0-2 (.000); Higgins 1-22 (.045); Lester 1-5 (.200). Opponents 37-182 (.203).

CLEVELAND CAVALIERS

Player	G.	Min.	FGA	FGM	Pct.	FTA	FTM	Pct.	Off. Reb.	Def. Reb.	Tot. Reb.	Ast.	PF	Dsq.	Stl.	Blk. Sh.	Pts.	Avg.	Hi.
Free	75	2375	1407	626	.445	504	395	.784	89	128	217	226	214	2	94	8	1669	22.3	40
Robinson	73	2402	1185	533	.450	334	234	.701	156	597	753	185	195	2	51	32	1301	17.8	32
Hubbard	80	1799	628	321	.511	299	221	.739	172	208	380	86	244	3	71	6	863	10.8	31
Shelton	79	2101	779	371	.476	140	107	.764	140	241	381	179	279	9	76	55	850	10.8	33
Huston	77	2041	699	348	.498	154	110	.714	32	64	96	413	126	0	38	1	808	10.5	24
Thompson	82	1731	662	309	.467	149	115	.772	120	192	312	122	192	2	70	37	742	9.0	26
Bagley	76	1712	607	257	.423	198	157	.793	49	107	156	333	113	1	78	4	673	8.9	26
Cook	81	1950	387	188	.486	130	94	.723	174	310	484	123	282	7	68	47	471	5.8	18
Hinson	80	1858	371	184	.496	117	69	.590	175	324	499	69	306	11	31	145	437	5.5	22
Granger	56	738	226	97	.429	70	53	.757	8	47	55	134	97	0	24	0	251	4.5	16
Garris	33	267	102	52	.510	34	27	.794	35	42	77	10	40	0	8	6	131	4.0	20
Poquette	51	858	171	75	.439	43	34	.791	57	125	182	49	114	1	20	33	185	3.6	10
Crompton	7	23	8	1	.125	6	3	.500	6	3	9	1	4	0	1	1	5	0.7	2

3-Pt. FG: Cleveland 43-164 (.262)—Free 22-69 (.319); Robinson 1-2 (.500); Hubbard 0-1 (.000); Shelton 1-5 (.200); Huston 2-11 (.182); Thompson 9-39 (.231); Bagley 2-17 (.118); Cook 1-2 (.500); Granger 4-13 (.308); Poquette 1-5 (.200). Opponents 50-190 (.263).

DALLAS MAVERICKS

Player	G.	Min.	FGA	FGM	Pct.	FTA	FTM	Pct.	Off. Reb.	Def. Reb.	Tot. Reb.	Ast.	PF	Dsq.	Stl.	Blk. Sh.	Pts.	Avg.	Hi.
Aguirre	79	2900	1765	925	.524	621	465	.749	161	308	469	358	246	5	80	22	2330	29.5	46
Blackman	81	3025	1320	721	.546	458	372	.812	124	249	373	288	127	0	56	37	1815	22.4	43
Cummings	80	2492	915	452	.494	190	141	.742	151	507	658	158	282	2	64	23	1045	13.1	28
Davis	81	2665	651	345	.530	238	199	.836	41	146	187	561	218	4	94	13	896	11.1	24
Vincent	61	1421	579	252	.435	215	168	.781	81	166	247	114	159	1	30	10	672	11.0	33
Ellis	67	1059	493	225	.456	121	87	.719	106	144	250	56	118	0	41	9	549	8.2	31
Nimphius	82	2284	523	272	.520	162	101	.623	182	331	513	176	283	5	41	144	646	7.9	24
Harper	82	1712	451	200	.443	98	66	.673	53	119	172	239	143	0	95	21	469	5.7	19
Garnett	80	1529	299	141	.472	176	129	.733	123	208	331	128	217	4	44	66	411	5.1	13
Spanarkel	7	54	16	7	.438	13	9	.692	5	2	7	5	8	0	6	0	24	3.4	8
Turner	47	536	150	54	.360	34	28	.824	42	51	93	59	40	0	26	0	137	2.9	12
Phegley (Tot.)	13	87	35	11	.314	4	4	1.000	2	9	11	11	11	0	1	0	28	2.2	9
Phegley (Dal.)	10	76	31	9	.290	2	2	1.000	2	7	9	9	10	0	1	0	21	2.1	9
West	34	202	42	15	.357	22	7	.318	19	27	46	13	55	0	1	15	37	1.1	6

3-Pt. FG: Dallas 42-184 (.228)—Aguirre 15-56 (.268); Blackman 1-11 (.091); Cummings 0-2 (.000); Davis 7-38 (.184); Vincent 0-1 (.000); Ellis 12-29 (.414); Nimphius 1-4 (.250); Harper 3-26 (.115); Garnett 0-2 (.000); Spanarkel 1-2 (.500); Turner 1-9 (.111); Phegley (Tot.) 2-5 (.400); Phegley (Dal.) 1-4 (.250). Opponents 63-222 (.284).

DENVER NUGGETS

Player	G.	Min.	FGA	FGM	Pct.	FTA	FTM	Pct.	Off. Reb.	Def. Reb.	Tot. Reb.	Ast.	PF	Dsq.	Stl.	Blk. Sh.	Pts.	Avg.	Hi.
Vandeweghe	78	2734	1603	895	.558	580	494	.852	84	289	373	238	187	1	53	50	2295	29.4	51
English	82	2870	1714	907	.529	427	352	.824	216	248	464	406	252	3	83	95	2167	26.4	47
Issel	76	2076	1153	569	.493	428	364	.850	112	401	513	173	182	2	60	44	1506	19.8	37
Williams	79	1924	671	309	.461	209	171	.818	54	140	194	464	268	4	84	5	804	10.2	24
Anderson	78	1380	638	272	.426	150	116	.773	136	270	406	193	183	0	46	28	663	8.5	23
Evans	78	1687	564	243	.431	131	111	.847	23	115	138	288	175	2	61	4	629	8.1	31
Edmonson (Tot.)	55	622	321	158	.492	126	94	.746	46	42	88	34	83	1	26	7	410	7.5	30
Edmonson (Den.)	15	101	47	23	.489	25	18	.720	6	12	18	7	16	0	4	1	64	4.3	30
Schayes	82	1420	371	183	.493	272	215	.790	145	288	433	91	308	5	32	60	581	7.1	26
Carter	55	688	316	145	.459	61	47	.770	38	48	86	71	81	0	19	4	342	6.2	25
Dunn	80	2705	370	174	.470	145	106	.731	195	379	574	228	233	5	173	32	454	5.7	14
Hanzlik	80	1469	306	132	.431	207	167	.807	66	139	205	252	255	6	68	19	434	5.4	19
Roberts	19	197	91	34	.374	18	13	.722	20	31	51	13	43	1	5	1	81	4.3	14
Dennard	43	413	99	36	.364	24	15	.625	37	64	101	45	83	0	23	8	90	2.1	7
Robisch	19	141	40	13	.325	13	11	.846	1	20	21	13	13	0	0	1	37	1.9	9

3-Pt. FG: Denver 77-255 (.302)—Vandeweghe 11-30 (.367); English 1-7 (.143); Issel 4-19 (.211); Williams 15-47 (.319); Anderson 3-19 (.158); Evans 32-89 (.360); Schayes 0-2 (.000); Carter 5-19 (.263); Dunn 0-1 (.000); Hanzlik 3-12 (.250); Dennard 3-10 (.300). Opponents 62-205 (.302).

DETROIT PISTONS

Player	G.	Min.	FGA	FGM	Pct.	FTA	FTM	Pct.	Off. Reb.	Def. Reb.	Tot. Reb.	Ast.	PF	Dsq.	Stl.	Blk. Sh.	Pts.	Avg.	Hi.
Thomas	82	3007	1448	669	.462	529	388	.733	103	224	327	914	324	8	204	33	1748	21.3	47
Tripucka	76	2493	1296	595	.459	523	426	.815	119	187	306	228	190	0	65	17	1618	21.3	44
Laimbeer	82	2864	1044	553	.530	365	316	.866	329	674	1003	149	273	4	49	84	1422	17.3	33
Long	82	2514	1155	545	.472	275	243	.884	139	150	289	205	199	1	93	18	1334	16.3	41
Johnson	82	1909	901	426	.473	275	207	.753	130	107	237	271	196	1	44	19	1063	13.0	28
Tyler	82	1602	691	313	.453	132	94	.712	104	181	285	76	151	1	63	59	722	8.8	20
Levingston	80	1746	436	229	.525	186	125	.672	234	311	545	109	281	7	44	78	583	7.3	22
Benson	82	1734	451	248	.550	101	83	.822	117	292	409	130	230	4	71	53	579	7.1	23
Tolbert	49	475	121	64	.529	45	23	.511	45	53	98	26	88	1	12	20	151	3.1	10
Cureton	73	907	177	81	.458	59	31	.525	86	201	287	36	143	3	24	31	193	2.6	13
Russell	16	119	42	14	.333	13	12	.923	6	13	19	22	25	0	4	0	41	2.6	10
Hollins	32	216	63	24	.381	13	11	.846	4	18	22	62	26	0	13	1	59	1.8	8
Austin	7	28	13	6	.462	0	0	.....	2	1	3	1	7	0	1	1	12	1.7	6
Thirdkill	46	291	72	31	.431	31	15	.484	9	22	31	27	44	0	10	3	77	1.7	9

3-Pt. FG: Detroit 32-141 (.227)—Thomas 22-65 (.338); Tripucka 2-17 (.118); Laimbeer 0-11 (.000); Long 1-5 (.200); Johnson 4-19 (.211); Tyler 2-13 (.154); Levingston 0-3 (.000); Benson 0-1 (.000); Tolbert 0-1 (.000); Cureton 0-1 (.000); Russell 1-2 (.500); Hollins 0-2 (.000); Thirdkill 0-1 (.000). Opponents 53-202 (.262).

GOLDEN STATE WARRIORS

Player	G.	Min.	FGA	FGM	Pct.	FTA	FTM	Pct.	Off. Reb.	Def. Reb.	Tot. Reb.	Ast.	PF	Dsq.	Stl.	Blk. Sh.	Pts.	Avg.	Hi.
Short	79	2945	1509	714	.473	445	353	.793	184	254	438	246	252	2	103	11	1803	22.8	57
Carroll	80	2962	1390	663	.477	433	313	.723	235	401	636	198	244	9	103	142	1639	20.5	32
Floyd	77	2555	1045	484	.463	386	315	.816	87	184	271	269	216	0	103	31	1291	16.8	35
Johnson	78	2122	852	359	.421	432	339	.785	198	320	518	219	290	3	101	30	1062	13.6	40
Conner	82	2573	730	360	.493	259	186	.718	132	173	305	401	176	1	162	12	907	11.1	24
Smith	75	2091	436	244	.560	168	94	.560	282	390	672	72	274	6	61	22	582	7.8	25
Collins	61	957	387	187	.483	89	65	.730	62	67	129	67	119	1	43	14	440	7.2	22
Bratz	82	1428	521	213	.409	137	120	.876	41	102	143	252	155	0	84	6	561	6.8	23
Brewer	13	210	58	27	.466	17	11	.647	5	8	13	6	10	0	6	5	65	5.0	10
Williams	7	59	26	11	.423	7	6	.857	4	9	13	2	6	0	3	2	28	4.0	11
Cross	45	354	112	64	.571	91	38	.418	35	47	82	22	58	0	12	7	166	3.7	15
Tillis	72	730	254	108	.425	63	41	.651	75	109	184	24	176	1	12	60	257	3.6	15
Mannion	57	469	126	50	.397	23	18	.783	23	36	59	47	63	0	25	2	121	2.1	14
Romar	3	15	5	2	.400	4	2	.500	0	1	1	1	1	0	0	0	6	2.0	4
Engler	46	360	83	33	.398	23	14	.609	27	70	97	11	60	0	9	3	80	1.7	10

3-Pt FG: Golden State 55-226 (.243)—Short 22-72 (.306); Carroll 0-1 (.000); Floyd 8-45 (.178); Johnson 5-29 (.172); Conner 1-6 (.167); Collins 1-5 (.200); Bratz 15-51 (.294); Brewer 0-1 (.000); Tillis 0-2 (.000); Mannion 3-13 (.231); Romar 0-1 (.000). Opponents 36-171 (.211).

HOUSTON ROCKETS

Player	G.	Min.	FGA	FGM	Pct.	FTA	FTM	Pct.	Off. Reb.	Def. Reb.	Tot. Reb.	Ast.	PF	Dsq.	Stl.	Blk. Sh.	Pts.	Avg.	Hi.
Sampson	82	2693	1369	716	.523	434	287	.661	293	620	913	163	339	16	70	197	1720	21.0	41
Lloyd	82	2578	1182	610	.516	298	235	.789	128	167	295	321	211	4	102	44	1458	17.8	36
Reid	64	1936	857	406	.474	123	81	.659	97	244	341	217	243	5	88	30	895	14.0	32
Leavell	82	2009	731	349	.477	286	238	.832	31	86	117	459	199	2	107	12	947	11.5	28
McCray	79	2081	672	335	.499	249	182	.731	173	277	450	176	205	1	53	54	853	10.8	28
C. Jones	81	2506	633	318	.502	196	164	.837	168	414	582	156	335	7	46	80	801	9.9	24
Bailey	73	1174	517	254	.491	192	138	.719	104	190	294	79	197	8	33	40	646	8.8	27
Ford	81	2020	470	236	.502	117	98	.838	28	109	137	410	243	7	59	8	572	7.1	18
Teagle	68	616	315	148	.470	44	37	.841	28	50	78	63	81	1	13	4	340	5.0	27
Hayes	81	994	389	158	.406	132	86	.652	87	173	260	71	123	1	16	28	402	5.0	22
Walker	58	612	241	118	.490	18	6	.333	26	66	92	55	65	0	17	4	244	4.2	18
Ehlo	7	63	27	11	.407	1	1	1.000	4	5	9	6	13	0	3	0	23	3.3	14
M. Jones	57	473	130	70	.538	49	30	.612	33	82	115	28	63	0	14	14	170	3.0	13

3-Pt. FG: Houston 30-154 (.195)—Sampson 1-4 (.250); Lloyd 3-13 (.231); Reid 2-8 (.250); Leavell 11-71 (.155); McCray 1-4 (.250); C. Jones 1-3 (.333); Bailey 0-1 (.000); Ford 2-15 (.133); Teagle 7-27 (.259); Hayes 0-2 (.000); Walker 2-6 (.333). Opponents 42-157 (.268).

INDIANA PACERS

Player	G.	Min.	FGA	FGM	Pct.	FTA	FTM	Pct.	Off. Reb.	Def. Reb.	Tot. Reb.	Ast.	PF	Dsq.	Stl.	Blk. Sh.	Pts.	Avg.	Hi.
Kellogg	79	2676	1193	619	.519	340	261	.768	230	489	719	234	242	2	121	28	1506	19.1	37
Williams	69	2279	860	411	.478	295	207	.702	154	400	554	215	193	4	60	108	1029	14.9	32
Carter	73	2045	862	413	.479	178	136	.764	70	83	153	206	211	1	128	13	977	13.4	42
Johnson	81	2073	884	411	.465	270	223	.826	139	321	460	195	256	3	82	49	1056	13.0	32
Stipanovich	81	2426	816	392	.480	243	183	.753	116	446	562	170	303	4	73	67	970	12.0	29
Sichting	80	2497	746	397	.532	135	117	.867	44	127	171	457	179	0	90	8	917	11.5	29
Steppe	61	857	314	148	.471	161	134	.832	43	79	122	79	93	0	34	6	430	7.0	21
McKenna	61	923	371	152	.410	98	80	.816	30	65	95	114	133	3	46	5	387	6.3	21
Thomas	72	1219	403	187	.464	110	80	.727	59	90	149	130	115	1	60	6	455	6.3	21
Combs	48	446	163	81	.497	91	56	.615	19	37	56	38	49	0	23	18	218	4.5	17
Lowe	78	1238	259	107	.413	139	108	.777	30	92	122	269	112	0	93	5	324	4.2	11
Waiters	78	1040	238	123	.517	51	31	.608	64	163	227	60	164	2	24	85	277	3.6	12
Jackson	2	10	4	1	.250	4	4	1.000	1	0	1	0	3	0	0	0	6	3.0	4
Kuczenski (Tot.)	15	119	37	10	.270	12	8	.667	7	16	23	8	18	0	1	1	28	1.9	6
Kuczenski (Ind.)	5	51	17	5	.294	4	4	1.000	3	6	9	2	8	0	0	0	14	2.8	6

3-Pt. FG: Indiana 48-207 (.232)—Kellogg 7-21 (.333); Williams 0-4 (.000); Carter 15-46 (.326); Johnson 11-47 (.234); Stipanovich 3-16 (.188); Sichting 6-20 (.300); Steppe 0-3 (.000); McKenna 3-17 (.176); Thomas 1-11 (.091); Combs 0-3 (.000); Lowe 2-18 (.111); Waiters 0-1 (.000). Opponents 29-146 (.199).

KANSAS CITY KINGS

Player	G.	Min.	FGA	FGM	Pct.	FTA	FTM	Pct.	Off. Reb.	Def. Reb.	Tot. Reb.	Ast.	PF	Dsq.	Stl.	Blk. Sh.	Pts.	Avg.	Hi.
E. Johnson	82	2920	1552	753	.485	331	268	.810	165	290	455	296	266	4	76	21	1794	21.9	40
Drew	73	2363	1026	474	.462	313	243	.776	33	113	146	558	170	0	121	10	1194	16.4	29
Woodson	71	1838	816	389	.477	302	247	.818	62	113	175	175	174	2	83	24	1027	14.5	33
Knight	75	1885	729	358	.491	283	243	.859	89	166	255	160	122	0	54	6	963	12.8	33
Theus (Tot.)	61	1498	625	262	.419	281	214	.762	50	79	129	352	171	3	50	12	745	12.2	36
Theus (K.C.)	30	897	388	170	.438	173	130	.751	29	54	83	210	93	1	29	9	474	15.8	36
Thompson	80	1915	637	333	.523	223	160	.717	260	449	709	86	327	8	71	145	826	10.3	28
S. Johnson	50	893	342	189	.553	177	101	.571	94	158	252	63	188	7	22	48	479	9.6	24
Olberding	81	2160	504	249	.494	318	261	.821	119	326	445	192	291	2	50	28	759	9.4	26
Meriweather	73	1501	363	193	.532	123	94	.764	111	242	353	51	247	8	35	61	480	6.6	18
Suttle	40	469	214	109	.509	47	40	.851	21	25	46	46	46	0	20	0	258	6.5	26
Buse	76	1327	352	150	.426	80	63	.788	29	87	116	303	62	0	86	1	381	5.0	15
Loder	10	133	43	19	.442	13	9	.692	7	11	18	14	15	0	3	5	48	4.8	13
Micheaux	39	332	90	49	.544	39	21	.538	40	73	113	19	46	0	11	11	119	3.1	15
Robisch (Tot.)	31	340	96	35	.365	26	22	.846	15	43	58	20	36	1	3	2	92	3.0	9
Robisch (K.C.)	8	162	48	18	.375	13	11	.846	12	17	29	6	15	0	3	1	47	5.9	9
Nealy	71	960	126	63	.500	60	48	.800	73	149	222	50	138	1	41	9	174	2.5	11

3-Pt. FG: Kansas City 52-189 (.275)—E. Johnson 20-64 (.313); Drew 3-10 (.300); Woodson 2-8 (.250); Knight 4-14 (.286); Theus (Tot.) 7-42 (.167); Theus (K.C.) 4-27 (.148); Olberding 0-1 (.000); Suttle 0-3 (.000); Buse 18-59 (.305); Loder 1-3 (.333). Opponents 33-164 (.201).

LOS ANGELES LAKERS

Player	G.	Min.	FGA	FGM	Pct.	FTA	FTM	Pct.	Off. Reb.	Def. Reb.	Tot. Reb.	Ast.	PF	Dsq.	Stl.	Blk. Sh.	Pts.	Avg.	Hi.
Abdul-Jabbar	80	2622	1238	716	.578	394	285	.723	169	418	587	211	211	1	55	143	1717	21.5	35
Johnson	67	2567	780	441	.565	358	290	.810	99	392	491	875	169	1	150	49	1178	17.6	33
Wilkes	75	2507	1055	542	.514	280	208	.743	130	210	340	214	205	0	72	41	1294	17.3	31
Worthy	82	2415	890	495	.556	257	195	.759	157	358	515	207	244	5	77	70	1185	14.5	37
McAdoo	70	1456	748	352	.471	264	212	.803	82	207	289	74	182	0	42	50	916	13.1	32
Scott	74	1637	690	334	.484	139	112	.806	50	114	164	177	174	0	81	19	788	10.6	32
McGee	77	1425	584	347	.594	113	61	.540	117	76	193	81	176	0	49	6	757	9.8	33
Cooper	82	2387	549	273	.497	185	155	.838	53	209	262	482	267	3	113	67	739	9.0	20
Garrett	41	478	152	78	.513	39	30	.769	24	47	71	31	62	2	12	2	188	4.6	16
Nater	69	829	253	124	.490	91	63	.692	81	183	264	27	150	0	25	7	311	4.5	19
Rambis	47	743	113	63	.558	66	42	.636	82	184	266	34	108	0	30	14	168	3.6	10
Spriggs	38	363	82	44	.537	50	36	.720	16	45	61	30	55	0	12	4	124	3.3	18
Kupchak	34	324	108	41	.380	34	22	.647	35	52	87	7	46	0	4	6	104	3.1	12
Jordan (Tot.)	16	210	49	17	.347	12	8	.667	3	14	17	44	37	0	25	0	42	2.6	8
Jordan (L.A.)	3	27	8	4	.500	2	1	.500	0	4	4	5	5	0	4	0	9	3.0	4

3-Pt. FG: Los Angeles 58-226 (.257)—Abdul-Jabbar 0-1 (.000); Johnson 6-29 (.207); Wilkes 2-8 (.250); Worthy 0-6 (.000); McAdoo 0-5 (.000); Scott 8-34 (.235); McGee 2-12 (.167); Cooper 38-121 (.314); Garrett 2-6 (.333); Nater 0-1 (.000); Spriggs 0-2 (.000); Kupchak 0-1 (.000); Jordan (Tot.) 0-3 (.000). Opponents 63-223 (.283).

MILWAUKEE BUCKS

Player	G.	Min.	FGA	FGM	Pct.	FTA	FTM	Pct.	Off. Reb.	Def. Reb.	Tot. Reb.	Ast.	PF	Dsq.	Stl.	Blk. Sh.	Pts.	Avg.	Hi.
Moncrief	79	3075	1125	560	.498	624	529	.848	215	313	528	358	204	2	108	27	1654	20.9	43
Johnson	74	2715	1288	646	.502	340	241	.709	173	307	480	315	194	1	115	45	1535	20.7	36
Bridgeman	81	2431	1094	509	.465	243	196	.807	80	252	332	265	224	2	53	14	1220	15.1	31
Lanier	72	2007	685	392	.572	274	194	.708	141	314	455	186	228	8	58	51	978	13.6	25
Dunleavy	17	404	127	70	.551	40	32	.800	6	22	28	78	51	0	12	1	191	11.2	17
Pressey	81	1730	528	276	.523	200	120	.600	102	180	282	252	241	6	86	50	674	8.3	21
Lister	82	1955	512	256	.500	182	114	.626	156	447	603	110	327	11	41	140	626	7.6	19
Archibald	46	1038	279	136	.487	101	64	.634	16	60	76	160	78	0	33	0	340	7.4	16
Grevey	64	923	395	178	.451	84	75	.893	30	51	81	75	95	0	27	4	446	7.0	25
White	9	45	17	7	.412	5	2	.400	5	3	8	1	3	0	2	1	16	2.0	8
Romar (Tot.)	68	1022	351	161	.459	94	67	.713	21	72	93	193	77	0	55	8	393	5.8	17
Romar (Mil.)	65	1007	346	159	.460	90	65	.722	21	71	92	192	76	0	55	8	387	6.0	17
Criss	6	107	30	11	.367	11	7	.636	2	7	9	17	7	0	5	0	30	5.0	8
Mokeski	68	838	213	102	.479	72	50	.694	51	115	166	44	168	1	11	29	255	3.8	14
Breuer	57	472	177	68	.384	46	32	.696	48	61	109	17	98	1	11	38	168	2.9	10
Catchings	69	1156	153	61	.399	42	22	.524	89	182	271	43	172	3	25	81	144	2.1	8
Townes	2	2	1	1	1.000	0	0		0	0	0	1	0	0	0	0	2	1.0	2

3-Pt. FG: Milwaukee 59-232 (.254)—Moncrief 5-18 (.278); Johnson 2-13 (.154); Bridgeman 6-31 (.194); Lanier 0-3 (.000); Dunleavy 19-45 (.422); Pressey 2-9 (.222); Archibald 4-18 (.222); Grevey 15-53 (.283); Romar (Tot.) 4-33 (.121); Romar (Milw.) 4-32 (.125); Criss 1-6 (.167); Mokeski 1-3 (.333); Catchings 0-1 (.000). Opponents 42-203 (.207).

NEW JERSEY NETS

Player	G.	Min.	FGA	FGM	Pct.	FTA	FTM	Pct.	Off. Reb.	Def. Reb.	Tot. Reb.	Ast.	PF	Dsq.	Stl.	Blk. Sh.	Pts.	Avg.	Hi.
Birdsong	69	2168	1147	583	.508	319	194	.608	74	96	170	266	180	2	86	17	1365	19.8	38
Dawkins	81	2417	855	507	.593	464	341	.735	159	382	541	123	386	22	60	136	1357	16.8	36
Williams	81	3003	926	495	.535	498	284	.570	355	645	1000	130	298	3	81	125	1274	15.7	27
King	79	2103	946	465	.492	295	232	.786	125	263	388	203	258	6	91	33	1165	14.7	31
Richardson	48	1285	528	243	.460	108	76	.704	56	116	172	214	156	4	103	20	576	12.0	25
Ransey	80	1937	700	304	.434	183	145	.792	28	99	127	483	182	2	91	6	760	9.5	21
Cook	82	1870	687	304	.443	126	95	.754	51	105	156	356	184	3	164	36	714	8.7	21
Gminski	82	1655	462	237	.513	184	147	.799	161	272	433	92	162	0	37	70	621	7.6	18
O'Koren	73	1191	385	186	.483	87	53	.609	71	104	175	95	148	3	34	11	430	5.9	20
Johnson	72	818	256	127	.496	126	92	.730	53	85	138	40	141	1	24	18	346	4.8	14
Willoughby	67	936	258	124	.481	63	55	.873	75	118	193	56	106	0	23	24	303	4.5	15
Walker	34	378	90	32	.356	27	24	.889	8	23	31	81	37	0	20	3	90	2.6	10
Kuczenski	7	28	12	4	.333	6	3	.500	3	5	8	4	3	0	0	0	11	1.6	3
Jones	6	16	6	3	.500	2	1	.500	2	0	2	5	2	0	0	0	7	1.2	4

3-Pt. FG: New Jersey 49-232 (.211)—Birdsong 5-20 (.250); Dawkins 2-5 (.400); Williams 0-4 (.000); King 3-22 (.136); Richardson 14-58 (.241); Ransey 7-32 (.219); Cook 11-46 (.239); Gminski 0-3 (.000); O'Koren 5-28 (.179); Johnson 0-1 (.000); Willoughby 0-7 (.000); Walker 2-5 (.400); Jones 0-1 (.000). Opponents 48-181 (.265).

NEW YORK KNICKERBOCKERS

Player	G.	Min.	FGA	FGM	Pct.	FTA	FTM	Pct.	Off. Reb.	Def. Reb.	Tot. Reb.	Ast.	PF	Dsq.	Stl.	Blk. Sh.	Pts.	Avg.	Hi.
King	77	2667	1391	795	.572	561	437	.779	123	271	394	164	273	2	75	17	2027	26.3	50
Cartwright	77	2487	808	453	.561	502	404	.805	195	454	649	107	262	4	44	97	1310	17.0	38
Williams	76	2230	939	418	.445	318	263	.827	67	200	267	449	274	5	162	26	1124	14.8	36
Robinson	65	2135	581	284	.489	206	133	.646	171	374	545	94	217	6	43	27	701	10.8	31
Sparrow	79	2436	738	350	.474	131	108	.824	48	141	189	539	230	4	100	8	818	10.4	24
Orr	78	1640	572	262	.458	211	173	.820	101	127	228	61	142	0	66	17	697	8.9	25
Walker	82	1324	518	216	.417	263	208	.791	74	93	167	284	202	1	127	15	644	7.9	20
Tucker	63	1228	450	225	.500	33	25	.758	43	87	130	138	124	0	63	8	481	7.6	20
Grunfeld	76	1119	362	166	.459	83	64	.771	24	97	121	108	151	0	43	7	398	5.2	16
Macklin	8	65	30	12	.400	13	11	.846	5	6	11	3	17	0	1	0	35	4.4	10
Webster	76	1290	239	112	.469	117	66	.564	146	220	366	53	187	2	34	100	290	3.8	13
Fernsten	32	402	52	29	.558	34	25	.735	29	57	86	11	49	0	16	8	83	2.6	11
Elmore	65	832	157	64	.408	38	27	.711	62	103	165	30	153	3	29	30	155	2.4	8

3-Pt. FG: New York 47-165 (.285)—King 0-4 (.000); Cartwright 0-1 (.000); Williams 25-81 (.309); Sparrow 10-39 (.256); Walker 4-15 (.267); Tucker 6-16 (.375); Grunfeld 2-9 (.222). Opponents 52-189 (.275).

PHILADELPHIA 76ers

Player	G.	Min.	FGA	FGM	Pct.	FTA	FTM	Pct.	Off. Reb.	Def. Reb.	Tot. Reb.	Ast.	PF	Dsq.	Stl.	Blk. Sh.	Pts.	Avg.	Hi.
Malone	71	2613	1101	532	.483	727	545	.750	352	598	950	96	188	0	71	110	1609	22.7	38
Erving	77	2683	1324	678	.512	483	364	.754	190	342	532	309	217	3	141	139	1727	22.4	42
Toney	78	2556	1125	593	.527	465	390	.839	57	136	193	373	251	1	70	23	1588	20.4	40
Cheeks	75	2494	702	386	.550	232	170	.733	44	161	205	478	196	1	171	20	950	12.7	24
B. Jones	75	1761	432	226	.523	213	167	.784	92	231	323	187	199	1	107	103	619	8.3	19
Richardson	69	1571	473	221	.467	103	79	.767	62	103	165	155	145	0	49	23	521	7.6	17
Matthews (Tot.)	20	388	131	61	.466	36	27	.750	7	20	27	83	45	0	16	3	150	7.5	18
Matthews (Phil.)	14	292	101	45	.446	14	9	.643	6	17	23	62	32	0	11	2	100	7.1	18
Williams (Tot.)	77	1434	431	204	.473	140	92	.657	121	218	339	62	209	3	68	106	500	6.5	18
Williams (Phil.)	70	1375	405	193	.477	133	86	.647	117	209	326	60	203	3	62	103	472	6.7	18
Johnson	80	1721	412	193	.468	113	69	.611	131	267	398	55	205	1	35	65	455	5.7	16
Iavaroni	78	1532	322	149	.463	131	97	.740	91	219	310	95	222	1	36	55	395	5.1	12
Edwards	60	654	221	84	.380	48	34	.708	12	47	59	90	78	1	31	5	202	3.4	16
Threatt	45	464	148	62	.419	28	23	.821	17	23	40	41	65	1	13	2	148	3.3	12
Rautins	28	196	58	21	.362	10	6	.600	9	24	33	29	31	0	9	2	48	1.7	13
Kuczenski	3	40	8	1	.125	2	1	.500	1	5	6	2	7	0	1	1	3	1.0	3
C. Jones	1	3	1	0	.000	4	1	.250	0	0	0	1	0	0	0	1	1	1.0	1

3-Pt. FG: Philadelphia 29-107 (.271)—Malone 0-4 (.000); Erving 7-21 (.333); Toney 12-38 (.316); Cheeks 8-20 (.400); B. Jones 0-1 (.000); Richardson 0-4 (.000); Matthews (Tot.) 1-8 (.125); Matthews (Phil.) 1-7 (.143); Williams (Tot.) 0-1 (.000); Williams (Phil.) 0-1 (.000); Iavaroni 0-2 (.000); Edwards 0-1 (.000); Threatt 1-8 (.125). Opponents 47-207 (.227).

PHOENIX SUNS

Player	G.	Min.	FGA	FGM	Pct.	FTA	FTM	Pct.	Off. Reb.	Def. Reb.	Tot. Reb.	Ast.	PF	Dsq.	Stl.	Blk. Sh.	Pts.	Avg.	Hi.
Davis	78	2546	1274	652	.512	270	233	.863	38	164	202	429	202	0	107	12	1557	20.0	43
Nance	82	2899	1044	601	.576	352	249	.707	227	451	678	214	274	5	86	173	1451	17.7	36
Lucas	75	2309	908	451	.497	383	293	.765	208	517	725	203	235	2	55	39	1195	15.9	29
Edwards	72	1897	817	438	.536	254	183	.720	108	240	348	184	254	3	23	30	1059	14.7	33
Macy	82	2402	713	357	.501	114	95	.833	49	137	186	353	181	0	123	6	832	10.1	26
Adams	70	1452	582	269	.462	160	132	.825	118	201	319	219	195	1	73	32	670	9.6	26
Foster	80	1424	580	260	.448	155	122	.787	39	81	120	172	193	0	54	9	664	8.3	27
White	22	308	144	69	.479	42	24	.571	30	32	62	14	25	0	13	2	162	7.4	18
Westphal	59	865	313	144	.460	142	117	.824	8	35	43	148	69	0	41	6	412	7.0	22
Robey	61	856	257	140	.545	88	61	.693	80	118	198	65	120	0	20	14	342	5.6	20
Pittman	69	989	209	126	.603	101	69	.683	76	138	214	70	129	1	16	22	321	4.7	18
Sanders	50	586	203	97	.478	42	29	.690	40	63	103	44	101	0	23	12	223	4.5	14
Scott	65	735	124	55	.444	72	56	.778	29	71	100	48	85	0	19	20	167	2.6	9
High	29	512	52	18	.346	29	10	.345	16	50	66	51	84	1	40	11	46	1.6	6

3-Pt. FG: Phoenix 74-291 (.254)—Davis 20-87 (.230); Nance 0-7 (.000); Lucas 0-5 (.000); Edwards 0-1 (.000); Macy 23-70 (.329); Adams 0-4 (.000); Foster 22-84 (.262); Westphal 7-26 (.269); Robey 1-1 (1.000); Pittman 0-2 (.000); Scott 1-2 (.500); High 0-2 (.000). Opponents 54-219 (.247).

PORTLAND TRAIL BLAZERS

Player	G.	Min.	FGA	FGM	Pct.	FTA	FTM	Pct.	Off. Reb.	Def. Reb.	Tot. Reb.	Ast.	PF	Dsq.	Stl.	Blk. Sh.	Pts.	Avg.	Hi.
Paxson	81	2686	1322	680	.514	410	345	.841	68	105	173	251	165	0	122	10	1722	21.3	41
Natt	79	2638	857	500	.583	345	275	.797	166	310	476	179	218	3	69	22	1277	16.2	33
Thompson	79	2648	929	487	.524	399	266	.667	235	453	688	308	237	2	84	108	1240	15.7	28
Carr	82	2455	923	518	.561	367	247	.673	208	434	642	157	274	3	68	33	1283	15.6	31
Valentine	68	1893	561	251	.447	246	194	.789	49	78	127	395	179	1	107	6	696	10.2	24
Cooper	81	1662	663	304	.459	230	185	.804	176	300	476	76	247	2	26	106	793	9.8	26
Lever	81	2010	701	313	.447	214	159	.743	96	122	218	372	178	1	135	31	788	9.7	28
Drexler	82	1408	559	252	.451	169	123	.728	112	123	235	153	209	2	107	29	628	7.7	21
Lamp	64	660	261	128	.490	67	60	.896	23	40	63	51	67	0	22	4	318	5.0	19
Norris	79	1157	246	124	.504	149	104	.698	82	175	257	76	231	2	30	34	352	4.5	12
Verhoeven	43	327	100	50	.500	25	17	.680	27	34	61	20	75	0	22	11	117	2.7	9
Jordan	13	183	41	13	.317	10	7	.700	3	10	13	39	32	0	21	0	33	2.5	8
Piotrowski	18	78	26	12	.462	6	6	1.000	6	10	16	5	22	0	1	3	30	1.7	10

3-Pt. FG: Portland 25-129 (.194)—Paxson 17-59 (.288); Natt 2-17 (.118); Thompson 0-2 (.000); Carr 0-5 (.000); Valentine 0-3 (.000); Cooper 0-7 (.000); Lever 3-15 (.200); Drexler 1-4 (.250); Lamp 2-13 (.154); Verhoeven 0-1 (.000); Jordan 0-3 (.000). Opponents 57-208 (.274).

SAN ANTONIO SPURS

Player	G.	Min.	FGA	FGM	Pct.	FTA	FTM	Pct.	Off. Reb.	Def. Reb.	Tot. Reb.	Ast.	PF	Dsq.	Stl.	Blk. Sh.	Pts.	Avg.	Hi.
Gervin	76	2584	1561	765	.490	507	427	.842	106	207	313	220	219	3	79	47	1967	25.9	44
Mitchell	79	2853	1597	779	.488	353	275	.779	188	382	570	93	251	6	62	73	1839	23.3	47
Gilmore	64	2034	556	351	.631	390	280	.718	213	449	662	70	229	4	36	132	982	15.3	30
Banks	80	2600	747	424	.568	270	200	.740	204	378	582	254	256	5	105	23	1049	13.1	28
Lucas	63	1807	595	275	.462	157	120	.764	23	157	180	673	123	1	92	5	689	10.9	29
Jones	81	1770	644	322	.500	242	176	.727	143	306	449	85	298	7	64	107	826	10.2	22
Moore	59	1650	518	231	.446	139	105	.755	37	141	178	566	168	2	123	20	595	10.1	24
Edmonson	40	521	274	135	.493	101	76	.752	40	30	70	27	67	1	22	6	346	8.7	22
Brewer (Tot.)	53	992	403	179	.444	67	52	.776	22	41	63	50	64	0	24	21	413	7.8	23
Brewer (SA)	40	782	345	152	.441	50	41	.820	17	33	50	44	54	0	18	16	348	8.7	23
Roberts	79	1531	399	214	.536	172	144	.837	102	202	304	98	219	4	52	38	573	7.3	17
McNamara	70	1037	253	157	.621	157	74	.471	137	180	317	31	138	2	14	12	388	5.5	22
Williams	19	200	58	25	.431	32	25	.781	4	9	13	43	42	1	8	4	75	3.9	10
Paxson	49	458	137	61	.445	26	16	.615	4	29	33	149	47	0	10	2	142	2.9	25
Batton	4	31	10	5	.500	0	0	.....	1	3	4	3	5	0	0	3	10	2.5	6
Phegley	3	11	4	2	.500	2	2	1.000	0	2	2	2	1	0	0	0	7	2.3	7
Lockhart	2	14	2	2	1.000	0	0	.....	0	3	3	0	5	0	0	0	4	2.0	4
Miller	2	8	3	2	.667	0	0	.....	2	3	5	1	5	0	0	1	4	2.0	4
Robisch	4	37	8	4	.500	0	0	.....	2	6	8	1	8	1	0	0	8	2.0	6
Weidner	8	38	9	2	.222	4	4	1.000	4	7	11	0	5	0	2	0	8	1.0	2
Lingenfelter	3	14	1	1	1.000	2	0	.000	3	1	4	1	6	0	0	0	2	0.7	2

3-Pt. FG: San Antonio 79-263 (.300)—Gervin 10-24 (.417); Mitchell 6-14 (.429); Gilmore 0-3 (.000); Banks 1-6 (.167); Lucas 19-69 (.275); Jones 6-19 (.316); Moore 28-87 (.322); Brewer (Tot.) 3-14 (.214); Brewer (S.A.) 3-13 (.231); Roberts 1-4 (.250); Williams 0-1 (.000); Paxson 4-22 (.182); Phegley 1-1 (1.000). Opponents 52-216 (.241).

SAN DIEGO CLIPPERS

Player	G.	Min.	FGA	FGM	Pct.	FTA	FTM	Pct.	Off. Reb.	Def. Reb.	Tot. Reb.	Ast.	PF	Dsq.	Stl.	Blk. Sh.	Pts.	Avg.	Hi.
Cummings	81	2907	1491	737	.494	528	380	.720	323	454	777	139	298	6	92	57	1854	22.9	37
Nixon	82	3053	1270	587	.462	271	206	.760	56	147	203	914	180	1	94	4	1391	17.0	35
Walton	55	1476	518	288	.556	154	92	.597	132	345	477	183	153	1	45	88	668	12.1	25
Donaldson	82	2525	604	360	.596	327	249	.761	165	484	649	90	214	1	40	139	969	11.8	24
Brooks	47	1405	445	213	.479	151	104	.689	142	200	342	88	125	1	50	14	530	11.3	31
Kelser	80	1783	603	313	.519	356	250	.702	188	203	391	91	249	3	68	31	878	11.0	37
Pierce	69	1280	570	268	.470	173	149	.861	59	76	135	60	143	1	27	13	685	9.9	30
Smith	61	1297	436	238	.546	163	123	.755	54	116	170	82	165	2	33	22	600	9.8	26
Hodges	76	1571	573	258	.450	88	66	.750	22	64	86	116	166	2	58	1	592	7.8	22
Whitehead	70	921	294	144	.490	107	88	.822	94	151	245	19	159	2	17	12	376	5.4	19
White (Tot.)	36	372	170	80	.471	47	26	.553	37	37	74	15	31	0	15	3	186	5.2	18
White (S.D.)	6	19	9	4	.444	0	0	.....	2	2	4	0	3	0	0	0	8	1.3	4
Loder (Tot.)	11	137	43	19	.442	13	9	.692	7	11	18	14	16	0	3	5	48	4.4	13
Loder (S.D.)	1	4	0	0	.....	0	0	.....	0	0	0	1	0	0	0	0	0	0.0	0
McKinney	80	843	305	136	.446	46	39	.848	7	47	54	161	84	0	27	0	311	3.9	13
McDowell	57	611	197	85	.431	56	38	.679	63	92	155	37	77	0	14	2	208	3.6	15
Townes (Tot.)	4	19	8	4	.500	0	0	.....	0	1	1	4	0	1	2	8	2.0	6
Townes (S.D.)	2	17	7	3	.429	0	0	.....	0	1	1	3	0	1	2	6	3.0	6
Jones	4	18	3	0	.000	4	1	.250	0	0	0	0	0	1	0	1	0	1	0.3	1

3-Pt. FG:San Diego 24-128 (.188)—Cummings 0-3 (.000); Nixon 11-46 (.239); Walton 0-2 (.000); Brooks 0-5 (.000); Kelser 2-6 (.333); Pierce 0-9 (.000); Smith 1-6 (.167); Hodges 10-46 (.217); McKinney 0-2 (.000); McDowell 0-3 (.000). Opponents 53-187 (.283).

SEATTLE SUPERSONICS

Player	G.	Min.	FGA	FGM	Pct.	FTA	FTM	Pct.	Off. Reb.	Def. Reb.	Tot. Reb.	Ast.	PF	Dsq.	Stl.	Blk. Sh.	Pts.	Avg.	Hi.
Sikma	82	2993	1155	576	.499	480	411	.856	225	686	911	327	301	6	95	92	1563	19.1	35
Williams	80	2818	1306	598	.458	396	297	.750	67	137	204	675	151	0	189	25	1497	18.7	37
Chambers	82	2570	1110	554	.499	469	375	.800	219	313	532	133	309	8	47	51	1483	18.1	34
Wood	81	2236	945	467	.494	271	223	.823	94	181	275	166	207	1	64	32	1160	14.3	29
Thompson	19	349	165	89	.539	73	62	.849	18	26	44	13	30	0	10	13	240	12.6	32
Brown	71	1129	506	258	.510	86	77	.895	14	48	62	194	84	0	49	2	602	8.5	27
Vranes	80	2174	495	258	.521	236	153	.648	150	245	395	132	263	4	51	54	669	8.4	20
King	77	2086	448	233	.520	206	136	.660	134	336	470	179	159	2	54	24	602	7.8	20
Sundvold	73	1284	488	217	.445	72	64	.889	23	68	91	239	81	0	29	1	507	6.9	24
Hawes	79	1153	237	114	.481	78	62	.782	50	170	220	99	144	2	24	16	290	3.7	14
McCray	47	520	121	47	.388	50	35	.700	45	70	115	44	73	1	11	19	129	2.7	13
Johnson	25	176	50	20	.400	22	14	.636	6	6	12	14	24	0	8	2	55	2.2	9
Bradley	8	39	7	3	.429	7	4	.714	0	3	3	5	6	0	0	1	11	1.4	6
Hayes	43	253	50	26	.520	14	5	.357	19	43	62	13	52	0	5	18	57	1.3	6

3-Pt. FG: Seattle 27-140 (.193)—Sikma 0-2 (.000); Williams 4-25 (.160); Chambers 0-12 (.000); Wood 3-21 (.143); Thompson 0-1 (.000); Brown 9-34 (.265); Vranes 0-1 (.000); King 0-2 (.000); Sundvold 9-37 (.243); Hawes 1-4 (.250); Johnson 1-1 (1.000). Opponents 54-228 (.237).

Utah's Darrell Griffith was the NBA's most prolific three-point field goal shooter in 1983-84, leading the league with a .361 percentage.

UTAH JAZZ

Player	G.	Min.	FGA	FGM	Pct.	FTA	FTM	Pct.	Off. Reb.	Def. Reb.	Tot. Reb.	Ast.	PF	Dsq.	Stl.	Blk. Sh.	Pts.	Avg.	Hi.
Dantley	79	2984	1438	802	.558	946	813	.859	179	269	448	310	201	0	61	4	2418	30.6	47
Griffith	82	2650	1423	697	.490	217	151	.696	95	243	338	283	202	1	114	23	1636	20.0	36
Drew	81	1797	1067	511	.479	517	402	.778	146	192	338	135	208	1	88	2	1430	17.7	42
Green	81	2768	904	439	.486	234	192	.821	56	174	230	748	155	1	215	13	1072	13.2	45
Bailey	81	2009	590	302	.512	117	88	.752	115	349	464	129	193	1	38	122	692	8.5	22
Wilkins	81	1734	520	249	.479	182	134	.736	109	346	455	73	205	1	27	42	632	7.8	22
Eaton	82	2139	416	194	.466	123	73	.593	148	447	595	113	303	4	25	351	461	5.6	17
Kelley	75	1674	264	132	.500	162	124	.765	140	350	490	157	273	6	55	29	388	5.2	14
Eaves	80	1034	293	132	.451	132	92	.697	29	56	85	200	90	0	33	5	356	4.5	21
Hansen	55	419	145	65	.448	28	18	.643	13	35	48	44	62	0	15	4	148	2.7	15
Anderson	48	311	130	55	.423	29	12	.414	38	25	63	22	28	0	15	9	122	2.5	15
Boswell	38	261	52	28	.538	21	16	.762	28	36	64	16	58	1	9	0	73	1.9	15

3-Pt. FG: Utah 101-317 (.310)—Dantley 1-4 (.250); Griffith 91-252 (.361); Drew 6-22 (.273); Green 2-17 (.118); Wilkins 0-3 (.000); Eaton 0-1 (.000); Eaves 0-6 (.000); Hansen 0-8 (.000); Anderson 0-3 (.000); Boswell 1-1 (1.000). Opponents 46-208 (.221).

WASHINGTON BULLETS

Player	G.	Min.	FGA	FGM	Pct.	FTA	FTM	Pct.	Off. Reb.	Def. Reb.	Tot. Reb.	Ast.	PF	Dsq.	Stl.	Blk. Sh.	Pts.	Avg.	Hi.
Ruland	75	3082	1035	599	.579	636	466	.733	265	657	922	296	285	8	68	72	1665	22.2	38
Sobers	81	2624	1115	508	.456	264	221	.837	51	128	179	377	278	10	117	17	1266	15.6	29
Ballard	82	2701	1061	510	.481	208	166	.798	140	348	488	290	214	1	94	35	1188	14.5	33
Malone	81	1976	918	408	.444	172	142	.826	57	98	155	151	162	1	23	13	982	12.1	30
Johnson	82	2686	840	392	.467	252	187	.742	58	126	184	567	174	1	96	6	982	12.0	28
McMillen	62	1294	447	222	.497	156	127	.814	64	135	199	73	162	0	14	17	572	9.2	27
Mahorn	82	2701	605	307	.507	192	125	.651	169	569	738	131	358	14	62	123	739	9.0	21
Daye	75	1174	408	180	.441	133	95	.714	90	98	188	176	154	0	38	12	455	6.1	16
Davis	46	467	218	103	.472	39	24	.615	34	69	103	30	58	1	14	10	231	5.0	14
Kopicki	59	678	132	64	.485	112	91	.813	64	102	166	46	71	0	15	5	220	3.7	19
Scales	2	13	5	3	.600	2	0	.000	0	3	3	0	1	0	1	0	6	3.0	6
Warrick	32	254	66	27	.409	16	8	.500	5	17	22	43	37	0	9	3	63	2.0	12
Gibson	32	229	55	21	.382	17	11	.647	29	37	66	9	30	1	5	7	53	1.7	8
Wilson	6	26	2	0	.000	2	1	.500	1	0	1	3	5	0	0	0	1	0.2	1

3-Pt. FG: Washington 71-282 (.252)—Ruland 1-7 (.143); Sobers 29-111 (.261); Ballard 2-15 (.133); Malone 24-74 (.324); Johnson 11-43 (.256); McMillen 1-6 (.167); Daye 0-6 (.000); Davis 1-9 (.111); Kopicki 1-7 (.143); Warrick 1-3 (.333); Wilson 0-1 (.000). Opponents 37-172 (.215).

PLAYOFF RESULTS

EASTERN CONFERENCE FIRST ROUND
Boston 3, Washington 1
Apr. 17—Tue.—Washington 83 at Boston.................................. 91
Apr. 19—Thur.—Washington 85 at Boston............................... 88
Apr. 21—Sat.—Boston 108 at Washington.........................°111
Apr. 24—Tue.—Boston 99 at Washington........................... 96

Milwaukee 3, Atlanta 2
Apr. 17—Tue.—Atlanta 89 at Milwaukee.....................................105
Apr. 19—Thur.—Atlanta 87 at Milwaukee...................................101
Apr. 21—Sat.—Milwaukee 94 at Atlanta 103
Apr. 24—Tue.—Milwaukee 97 at Atlanta 100
Apr. 26—Thur.—Atlanta 89 at Milwaukee....................................118

New York 3, Detroit 2
Apr. 17—Tue.—New York 94 at Detroit 93
Apr. 19—Thur.—New York 105 at Detroit 113
Apr. 22—Sun.—Detroit 113 at New York 120
Apr. 25—Wed.—Detroit 119 at New York 112
Apr. 27—Fri.—New York 127 at Detroit............................°123

New Jersey 3, Philadelphia 2
Apr. 18—Wed.—New Jersey 116 at Philadelphia 101
Apr. 20—Fri.—New Jersey 116 at Philadelphia.........................102
Apr. 22—Sun.—Philadelphia 108 at New Jersey 100
Apr. 24—Tue.—Philadelphia 110 at New Jersey 102
Apr. 26—Thur.—New Jersey 101 at Philadelphia 98

EASTERN CONFERENCE SEMIFINALS
Boston 4, New York 3
Apr. 29—Sun.—New York 92 at Boston..............................110
May   2—Wed.—New York 102 at Boston 116
May   4—Fri.—Boston 92 at New York 100
May   6—Sun.—Boston 113 at New York...........................118
May   9—Wed.—New York 99 at Boston.............................121
May 11—Fri.—Boston 104 at New York............................106
May 13—Sun.—New York 104 at Boston...........................121

Milwaukee 4, New Jersey 2
Apr. 29—Sun.—New Jersey 106 at Milwaukee 100
May   1—Tue.—New Jersey 94 at Milwaukee 98
May   3—Thur.—Milwaukee 100 at New Jersey........................ 93
May   5—Sat.—Milwaukee 99 at New Jersey.........................106
May   8—Tue.—New Jersey 82 at Milwaukee...........................94
May 10—Thur.—Milwaukee 98 at New Jersey 97

EASTERN CONFERENCE FINALS
Boston 4, Milwaukee 1
May 15—Tue.—Milwaukee 96 at Boston................................119
May 17—Thur.—Milwaukee 110 at Boston 125
May 19—Sat.—Boston 109 at Milwaukee................................100
May 21—Mon.—Boston 113 at Milwaukee...............................122
May 23—Wed.—Milwaukee 108 at Boston...............................115

WESTERN CONFERENCE FIRST ROUND
Utah 3, Denver 2
Apr. 17—Tue.—Denver 121 at Utah..123
Apr. 19—Thur.—Denver 132 at Utah...116
Apr. 22—Sun.—Utah 117 at Denver...121
Apr. 24—Tue.—Utah 129 at Denver 124
Apr. 26—Thur.—Denver 111 at Utah...127

Dallas 3, Seattle 2
Apr. 17—Tue.—Seattle 86 at Dallas.. 88
Apr. 19—Thur.—Seattle 95 at Dallas 92
Apr. 21—Fri.—Dallas 94 at Seattle...104
Apr. 24—Tue.—Dallas 107 at Seattle 96
Apr. 26—Thur.—Seattle 104 at Dallas......................................°105

Phoenix 3, Portland 2
Apr. 18—Wed.—Phoenix 113 at Portland 106
Apr. 20—Fri.—Phoenix 116 at Portland 122
Apr. 22—Sun.—Portland 103 at Phoenix 106
Apr. 24—Tue.—Portland 113 at Phoenix....................................110
Apr. 26—Thur.—Phoenix 117 at Portland 105

Los Angeles 3, Kansas City 0
Apr. 18—Wed.—Kansas City 105 at Los Angeles........................116
Apr. 20—Fri.—Kansas City 102 at Los Angeles.........................109
Apr. 22—Sun.—Los Angeles 108 at Kansas City 102

WESTERN CONFERENCE SEMIFINALS
Los Angeles 4, Dallas 1
Apr. 28—Sat.—Dallas 91 at Los Angeles....................................134
May   1—Tue.—Dallas 101 at Los Angeles................................117
May   4—Fri.—Los Angeles 115 at Dallas................................125
May   6—Sun.—Los Angeles 122 at Dallas................................°115
May   8—Tue.—Dallas 99 at Los Angeles.................................115

Phoenix 4, Utah 2
Apr. 29—Sun.—Phoenix 95 at Utah 105
May   2—Wed.—Phoenix 102 at Utah 97
May   4—Fri.—Utah 94 at Phoenix 106
May   6—Sun.—Utah 110 at Phoenix..°111
May   8—Tue.—Phoenix 106 at Utah 118
May 10—Thur.—Utah 82 at Phoenix..102

WESTERN CONFERENCE FINALS
Los Angeles 4, Phoenix 2
May 12—Sat.—Phoenix 94 at Los Angeles.................................110
May 15—Tue.—Phoenix 102 at Los Angeles...............................118
May 18—Fri.—Los Angeles 127 at Phoenix............................°135
May 20—Sun.—Los Angeles 126 at Phoenix............................115
May 23—Wed.—Phoenix 126 at Los Angeles.............................121
May 25—Fri.—Los Angeles 99 at Phoenix 97

WORLD CHAMPIONSHIP SERIES
Boston 4, Los Angeles 3
May 27—Sun.—Los Angeles 115 at Boston 109
May 31—Thur.—Los Angeles 121 at Boston............................°124
Jun.   3—Sun.—Boston 104 at Los Angeles 137
Jun.   6—Wed.—Boston 129 at Los Angeles ....°125
Jun.   8—Fri.—Los Angeles 103 at Boston.................................121
Jun. 10—Sun.—Boston 108 at Los Angeles 119
Jun. 12—Tue.—Los Angeles 102 at Boston 111

°Overtime

1982-83 NBA STATISTICS

1982-83 NBA CHAMPION PHILADELPHIA 76ers

Front row (left to right): Maurice Cheeks, Bobby Jones, Earl Cureton, Julius Erving, Reggie Johnson, Clint Richardson, Franklin Edwards. Back row: Trainer Al Domenico, Director of Player Personnel Jack McMahon, assistant coach Matt Guokas, Head Coach Billy Cunningham, Clemon Johnson, Mark McNamara, Moses Malone, Marc Iavaroni, Andrew Toney, General Manager Pat Williams, conditioning coach John Kilbourne, Owner Harold Katz, Assistant General Manager John Nash.

FINAL STANDINGS

ATLANTIC DIVISION

Team	Atl.	Bos.	Chi.	Cle.	Dal.	Den.	Det.	G.S.	Hou.	Ind.	K.C.	L.A.	Mil.	N.J.	N.Y.	Phi.	Pho.	Por.	S.A.	S.D.	Sea.	Uta.	Was.	W.	L.	Pct.	G.B.
Philadelphia	4	3	5	5	2	2	6	2	2	4	2	2	5	3	5	..	2	0	1	2	2	2	4	65	17	.793	....
Boston	5	..	3	5	2	2	3	1	2	4	1	2	3	5	3	3	2	1	2	1	1	2	3	56	26	.683	9
New Jersey	4	1	4	6	2	1	2	2	1	6	1	1	2	..	4	3	1	1	0	1	2	1	3	49	33	.598	16
New York	2	3	5	2	2	1	2	0	1	5	0	1	3	3	..	2	2	1	0	2	1	1	4	44	38	.537	21
Washington	2	3	5	2	2	1	2	0	1	5	0	1	3	3	2	2	1	0	2	1	2	..		42	40	.512	23

CENTRAL DIVISION

Team	Atl.	Bos.	Chi.	Cle.	Dal.	Den.	Det.	G.S.	Hou.	Ind.	K.C.	L.A.	Mil.	N.J.	N.Y.	Phi.	Pho.	Por.	S.A.	S.D.	Sea.	Uta.	Was.	W.	L.	Pct.	G.B.
Milwaukee	4	3	5	5	2	0	3	1	2	5	1	0	..	3	4	1	1	2	2	2	0	2	3	51	31	.622	....
Atlanta	..	1	5	6	1	1	3	0	2	6	0	0	1	2	3	2	1	1	0	1	1	2	4	43	39	.524	8
Detroit	3	3	4	5	0	0	..	2	2	4	0	0	3	3	1	0	1	1	1	1	0	0	3	37	45	.451	14
Chicago	1	2	..	5	1	1	2	2	1	4	0	0	1	2	1	1	0	1	0	0	1	1		28	54	.341	23
Cleveland	0	1	1	..	2	0	1	2	2	5	1	0	1	0	1	0	0	1	0	1	1	0	3	23	59	.280	28
Indiana	0	1	2	1	0	1	2	1	0	..	1	0	1	0	3	1	1	0	0	1	1	2	1	20	62	.244	31

MIDWEST DIVISION

Team	Atl.	Bos.	Chi.	Cle.	Dal.	Den.	Det.	G.S.	Hou.	Ind.	K.C.	L.A.	Mil.	N.J.	N.Y.	Phi.	Pho.	Por.	S.A.	S.D.	Sea.	Uta.	Was.	W.	L.	Pct.	G.B.
San Antonio	2	0	2	2	4	4	1	4	5	2	3	4	0	2	0	1	2	3	..	4	1	5	2	53	29	.646	....
Denver	1	0	1	2	3	..	2	4	5	1	3	1	2	1	0	0	4	2	2	3	3	4	1	45	37	.549	8
Kansas City	2	1	2	1	3	3	2	3	5	1	..	1	1	1	1	0	1	2	3	4	1	4	2	45	37	.549	8
Dallas	1	0	1	0	..	3	2	3	5	2	3	2	0	0	0	0	2	3	2	5	2	2	0	38	44	.463	15
Utah	0	0	1	2	4	2	2	2	6	0	2	1	0	1	1	0	0	2	1	3	0	..	0	30	52	.366	23
Houston	0	0	1	0	1	1	0	2	..	2	1	0	0	1	0	0	0	0	1	2	1	0	1	14	68	.171	39

PACIFIC DIVISION

Team	Atl.	Bos.	Chi.	Cle.	Dal.	Den.	Det.	G.S.	Hou.	Ind.	K.C.	L.A.	Mil.	N.J.	N.Y.	Phi.	Pho.	Por.	S.A.	S.D.	Sea.	Uta.	Was.	W.	L.	Pct.	G.B.
Los Angeles	2	0	2	2	3	4	2	5	5	2	4	..	2	1	2	0	3	3	1	5	5	4	1	58	24	.707	....
Phoenix	1	0	2	2	3	1	1	4	5	1	4	3	1	1	2	0	..	5	3	4	5	5	0	53	29	.646	5
Seattle	1	1	2	1	3	2	2	3	4	1	4	1	2	0	1	0	1	3	4	6	..	5	1	48	34	.585	10
Portland	1	1	1	1	2	3	1	4	5	2	3	3	0	1	1	2	1	..	2	5	3	3	1	46	36	.561	12
Golden State	2	1	0	0	2	1	0	..	3	1	1	1	0	1	0	2	2	1	3	3	3	2	0	30	52	.366	28
San Diego	1	1	1	1	0	2	1	3	3	1	1	1	0	1	2	0	2	1	1	..	0	2	0	25	57	.305	33

HOME-ROAD RECORDS OF ALL TEAMS

	Home	Road	Total		Home	Road	Total
Atlanta	26- 15	17- 24	43- 39	Milwaukee	31- 10	20- 21	51- 31
Boston	33- 8	23- 18	56- 26	New Jersey	30- 11	19- 22	49- 33
Chicago	18- 23	10- 31	28- 54	New York	26- 15	18- 23	44- 38
Cleveland	15- 26	8- 33	23- 59	Philadelphia	35- 6	30- 11	65- 17
Dallas	23- 18	15- 26	38- 44	Phoenix	32- 9	21- 20	53- 29
Denver	29- 12	16- 25	45- 37	Portland	31- 10	15- 26	46- 36
Detroit	23- 18	14- 27	37- 45	San Antonio	31- 10	22- 19	53- 29
Golden State	21- 20	9- 32	30- 52	San Diego	18- 23	7- 34	25- 57
Houston	9- 32	5- 36	14- 68	Seattle	29- 12	19- 22	48- 34
Indiana	14- 27	6- 35	20- 62	Utah	21- 20	9- 32	30- 52
Kansas City	30- 11	15- 26	45- 37	Washington	27- 14	15- 26	42- 40
Los Angeles	33- 8	25- 16	58- 24	Total	585- 358	358- 585	943- 943

OFFENSIVE TEAM STATISTICS

		FIELD GOALS			FREE THROWS			REBOUNDS				MISCELLANEOUS				Turn	Blk.	SCORING	
Team	G.	Att.	Made	Pct.	Att.	Made	Pct.	Off.	Def.	Tot.	Ast.	PF	Disq.	Stl.	Over	Sh.	Pts.	Avg.
Denver	82	7999	3951	.494	2696	2179	.808	1214	2524	3738	2336	2091	16	789	1496	352	10105	123.2
Los Angeles	82	7512	3964	.528	2031	1495	.736	1235	2433	3668	2519	1931	10	844	1584	479	9433	115.0
San Antonio	82	7340	3697	.504	2468	1887	.765	1232	2599	3831	2261	2095	26	675	1504	469	9375	114.3
Kansas City	82	7485	3719	.497	2530	1839	.727	1256	2407	3663	2155	2432	28	715	1691	409	9328	113.8
Dallas	82	7550	3674	.487	2462	1852	.752	1296	2381	3677	2227	2067	35	552	1348	348	9243	112.7
Detroit	82	7602	3623	.477	2588	1921	.742	1312	2477	3789	2108	2122	31	679	1557	572	9239	112.7
Boston	82	7547	3711	.492	2348	1730	.737	1273	2532	3805	2216	2062	23	589	1541	521	9191	112.1
Philadelphia	82	7212	3600	.499	2650	1966	.742	1334	2596	3930	2016	2041	11	812	1677	577	9191	112.1
Chicago	82	7373	3537	.480	2690	1983	.737	1267	2527	3794	2086	2192	32	666	1743	400	9102	111.0
Seattle	82	7277	3597	.494	2459	1796	.730	1152	2569	3721	2278	1969	21	677	1533	437	9019	110.0
Utah	82	7342	3525	.480	2440	1844	.756	1093	2550	3643	2176	2017	34	758	1683	595	8938	109.0
Indiana	82	7723	3707	.480	1910	1447	.758	1299	2294	3593	2150	2086	27	755	1535	411	8911	108.7
Golden State	82	7508	3627	.483	2199	1620	.737	1281	2284	3565	1964	2138	32	856	1606	430	8908	108.6
San Diego	82	7634	3625	.475	2195	1589	.724	1394	2108	3502	2087	2284	48	820	1600	408	8903	108.6
Portland	82	7124	3459	.486	2512	1855	.738	1180	2380	3560	2030	1960	23	749	1495	384	8808	107.4
Phoenix	82	7158	3555	.497	2189	1626	.743	1094	2518	3612	2300	2062	22	749	1545	495	8776	107.0
Milwaukee	82	7133	3486	.489	2299	1731	.753	1095	2477	3572	2116	2131	38	662	1447	532	8740	106.6
New Jersey	82	7140	3510	.492	2301	1622	.705	1266	2427	3693	2143	2166	44	911	1873	592	8672	105.8
Atlanta	82	7146	3352	.469	2111	1586	.751	1139	2433	3572	1945	2022	22	573	1424	665	8335	101.6
New York	82	6793	3272	.482	2282	1621	.710	1080	2263	3343	2034	2180	30	701	1509	378	8198	100.0
Houston	82	7446	3338	.448	1934	1402	.725	1206	2260	3466	1931	2131	22	646	1571	422	8145	99.3
Washington	82	7059	3306	.468	2059	1452	.705	1099	2430	3529	2046	1958	41	733	1588	400	8134	99.2
Cleveland	82	6995	3252	.465	1983	1430	.721	1173	2414	3587	1738	2236	56	617	1538	290	7964	97.1

DEFENSIVE TEAM STATISTICS

		FIELD GOALS			FREE THROWS			REBOUNDS				MISCELLANEOUS				Turn	Blk.	SCORING		Pt.
Team	Att.	Made	Pct.	Att.	Made	Pct.	Off.	Def.	Tot.	Ast.	PF	Disq.	Stl.	Over	Sh.	Pts.	Avg.	Dif.
New York	6592	3132	.475	2260	1695	.750	1073	2337	3410	1873	2116	36	694	1682	399	7997	97.5	+ 2.5
Washington	7044	3299	.468	2084	1510	.725	1114	2514	3628	1871	1975	27	698	1543	555	8145	99.3	- 0.1
Phoenix	7265	3305	.455	2268	1707	.753	1210	2326	3536	1988	2039	30	712	1560	343	8361	102.0	+ 5.1
Milwaukee	7318	3338	.456	2243	1665	.742	1303	2343	3646	2043	2145	25	623	1523	300	8379	102.2	+ 4.4
Atlanta	7201	3383	.470	2235	1608	.719	1303	2571	3874	1927	1981	21	656	1468	388	8413	102.6	- 1.0
New Jersey	6962	3327	.478	2370	1746	.737	1102	2176	3278	1978	2129	32	860	1871	495	8445	103.0	+ 2.8
Philadelphia	7470	3442	.461	2253	1624	.721	1325	2263	3588	2089	2246	54	755	1590	511	8562	104.4	+ 7.7
Cleveland	6911	3381	.489	2396	1780	.743	974	2382	3356	2005	1830	14	621	1275	431	8574	104.6	- 7.4
Portland	7211	3503	.486	2046	1572	.768	1126	2364	3490	2072	2232	32	658	1546	500	8633	105.3	+ 2.1
Boston	7401	3477	.470	2307	1750	.759	1186	2393	3579	2027	2137	40	699	1607	340	8752	106.7	+ 5.4
Seattle	7703	3546	.460	2184	1615	.739	1314	2397	3711	2146	2152	23	726	1443	360	8756	106.8	+ 3.2
Los Angeles	7617	3734	.490	2008	1455	.725	1294	2166	3460	2389	1863	14	766	1562	380	8978	109.5	+ 5.5
San Antonio	7531	3654	.485	2239	1716	.766	1160	2263	3423	2329	2199	37	654	1430	457	9075	110.7	+ 3.7
Houston	7244	3641	.503	2375	1781	.750	1198	2710	3908	2252	1933	13	772	1504	406	9096	110.9	- 11.6
Golden State	7260	3706	.510	2391	1751	.732	1249	2495	3744	2170	2026	23	758	1690	489	9205	112.3	- 3.6
Kansas City	7250	3531	.487	2885	2107	.730	1250	2403	3653	1997	2245	37	809	1716	439	9209	112.3	+ 1.5
Detroit	7679	3802	.495	2287	1647	.720	1266	2594	3860	2252	2326	43	761	1580	561	9272	113.1	- 0.4
Dallas	7481	3758	.502	2347	1708	.728	1217	2433	3650	2291	2227	39	607	1383	562	9277	113.1	- 0.4
Utah	7932	3794	.478	2288	1646	.719	1439	2671	4110	2202	2102	18	826	1601	448	9282	113.2	- 4.2
San Diego	6910	3652	.529	2626	1963	.748	1095	2365	3460	2105	1962	22	789	1723	519	9299	113.4	- 4.8
Indiana	7284	3768	.517	2413	1815	.752	1206	2564	3770	2237	1886	17	761	1643	439	9391	114.5	- 5.9
Chicago	7712	3816	.495	2438	1825	.749	1197	2456	3653	2230	2266	39	845	1462	633	9503	115.9	- 4.9
Denver	8120	4098	.505	2393	1787	.747	1369	2697	4066	2389	2356	36	728	1636	611	10054	122.6	+ 0.6

Disq.—Individual players disqualified (fouled out of game)

INDIVIDUAL LEADERS

POINTS
Minimum 70 games played or 1,400 points

	G.	FG	FT	Pts.	Avg.		G.	FG	FT	Pts.	Avg.
English, Denver	82	959	406	2326	28.4	Bird, Boston	79	747	351	1867	23.6
Vandeweghe, Denver	82	841	489	2186	26.7	Thomas, Detroit	81	725	368	1854	22.9
Tripucka, Detroit	58	565	392	1536	26.5	Moncrief, Milwaukee	76	606	499	1712	22.5
Gervin, San Antonio	78	757	517	2043	26.2	Griffith, Utah	77	752	167	1709	22.2
Malone, Philadelphia	78	654	600	1908	24.5	King, New York	68	603	280	1486	21.9
Aguirre, Dallas	81	767	429	1979	24.4	Abdul-Jabbar, L.A.	79	722	278	1722	21.8
Carroll, Golden State	79	785	337	1907	24.1	Paxson, Portland	81	682	388	1756	21.7
Free, Golden State-Cleve.	73	649	430	1743	23.9	Issel, Denver	80	661	400	1726	21.6
Theus, Chicago	82	749	434	1953	23.8	Short, Golden State	67	589	255	1437	21.4
Cummings, San Diego	70	684	292	1660	23.7	Ma. Johnson, Milwaukee	80	723	264	1714	21.4

FIELD GOALS
Minimum 300 FG Made

	FGA	FGM	Pct.
Gilmore, San Antonio	888	556	.626
S. Johnson, Kansas City	595	371	.624
Dawkins, New Jersey	669	401	.599
Abdul-Jabbar, Los Angeles	1228	722	.588
B. Williams, New Jersey	912	536	.588
Woolridge, Chicago	622	361	.580
Worthy, Los Angeles	772	447	.579
B. Davis, Dallas	628	359	.572
Cartwright, New York	804	455	.566
Ruland, Washington	1051	580	.552

FREE THROWS
Minimum 125 FT Made

	FTA	FTM	Pct.
Murphy, Houston	150	138	.920
Vandeweghe, Denver	559	489	.875
Macy, Phoenix	148	129	.872
Gervin, San Antonio	606	517	.853
Dantley, Utah	248	210	.847
B. Davis, Dallas	220	186	.845
Tripucka, Detroit	464	392	.845
Knight, Indiana	408	343	.841
Bird, Boston	418	351	.840
Sikma, Seattle	478	400	.837

ASSISTS
Minimum 70 games or 400 assists

	G.	No.	Avg.
E. Johnson, Los Angeles	79	829	10.5
Moore, San Antonio	77	753	9.8
Green, Utah	78	697	8.9
Drew, Kansas City	75	610	8.1
F. Johnson, Washington	68	549	8.1
G. Williams, Seattle	80	643	8.0
R. Williams, Kansas City	72	569	7.9
Thomas, Detroit	81	634	7.8
Nixon, Los Angeles	79	566	7.2
B. Davis, Dallas	79	565	7.2

STEALS
Minimum 70 games or 125 steals

	G.	No.	Avg.
Richardson, Golden State-New Jersey	64	182	2.84
Green, Utah	78	220	2.82
Moore, San Antonio	77	194	2.52
Thomas, Detroit	81	199	2.46
D. Cook, New Jersey	82	194	2.37
Cheeks, Philadelphia	79	184	2.33
G. Williams, Seattle	80	182	2.28
E. Johnson, Los Angeles	79	176	2.23
Leavell, Houston	79	165	2.09
Lever, Portland	81	153	1.89

REBOUNDS
Minimum 70 games or 800 rebounds

	G.	Off.	Def.	Tot.	Avg.
Malone, Philadelphia	78	445	749	1194	15.3
B. Williams, New Jersey	82	365	662	1027	12.5
Laimbeer, Detroit	82	282	711	993	12.1
Gilmore, San Antonio	82	299	685	984	12.0
Sikma, Seattle	75	213	645	858	11.4
Roundfield, Atlanta	77	259	621	880	11.4
C. Robinson, Cleveland	77	190	666	856	11.1
Ruland, Washington	79	293	578	871	11.0
Bird, Boston	79	193	677	870	11.0
Cummings, San Diego	70	303	441	744	10.6

BLOCKED SHOTS
Minimum 70 games or 100 blocked shots

	G.	No.	Avg.
Rollins, Atlanta	80	343	4.29
Walton, San Diego	33	119	3.61
Eaton, Utah	81	275	3.40
Nance, Phoenix	82	217	2.65
Gilmore, San Antonio	82	192	2.34
McHale, Boston	82	192	2.34
Lister, Milwaukee	80	177	2.21
H. Williams, Indiana	78	171	2.19
Abdul-Jabbar, Los Angeles	79	170	2.15
Malone, Philadelphia	78	157	2.01

3-PT. FIELD GOALS
Minimum 25 made

	FGA	FGM	Pct.
Dunleavy, San Antonio	194	67	.345
Thomas, Detroit	125	36	.288
Griffith, Utah	132	38	.288
Leavell, Houston	175	42	.240

TEAM-BY-TEAM INDIVIDUAL STATISTICS

°Did not finish season with team.

ATLANTA HAWKS

Player	G.	Min.	FGA	FGM	Pct.	FTA	FTM	Pct.	Off. Reb.	Def. Reb.	Tot. Reb.	Ast.	PF	Dsq.	Stl.	Blk. Sh.	Pts.	Avg.	Hi.
Roundfield	77	2811	1193	561	.470	450	337	.749	259	621	880	225	239	1	60	115	1464	19.0	36
Wilkins	82	2697	1220	601	.493	337	230	.682	226	252	478	129	210	1	84	63	1434	17.5	34
E. Johnson	61	1813	858	389	.453	237	186	.785	26	98	124	318	138	2	61	6	978	16.0	32
Davis	53	1465	567	258	.455	206	164	.796	37	91	128	315	100	0	43	7	685	12.9	31
°Sparrow	49	1548	512	264	.516	113	84	.743	39	102	141	238	162	2	70	1	615	12.6	30
Smith (Tot.)	80	1406	565	273	.483	131	114	.870	37	59	96	206	139	1	56	0	663	8.3	29
Smith (Atl.)	15	142	66	29	.439	14	13	.929	2	6	8	14	17	0	2	0	71	4.7	18
McMillen	61	1364	424	198	.467	133	108	.812	57	160	217	76	143	2	17	24	504	8.3	26
Rollins	80	2472	512	261	.510	135	98	.726	210	533	743	75	294	7	49	343	620	7.8	22
Glenn	73	1124	444	230	.518	89	74	.831	16	74	90	125	132	0	30	9	534	7.3	25
Matthews	64	1187	424	171	.403	112	86	.768	25	66	91	249	129	0	60	8	442	6.9	26
Macklin	73	1171	360	170	.472	131	101	.771	85	105	190	71	189	4	41	10	441	6.0	19
Brown (Tot.)	76	1048	349	167	.479	105	65	.619	91	175	266	25	172	1	13	26	399	5.3	21
Brown (Atl.)	26	305	104	49	.471	40	25	.625	35	53	88	9	46	1	5	5	123	4.7	16
°Hawes	46	860	244	91	.373	62	46	.742	53	175	228	59	110	2	29	8	230	5.0	20
Edmonson	32	309	139	48	.345	27	16	.593	20	19	39	22	41	0	11	6	112	3.5	14
°Pellom	2	9	6	2	.333	0	0	.000	0	0	0	1	0	0	0	0	4	2.0	4
G. Johnson	37	461	57	25	.439	19	14	.737	44	73	117	17	69	0	10	59	64	1.7	4
Hastings (Tot.)	31	140	38	13	.342	20	11	.550	15	26	41	3	34	0	6	1	37	1.2	4
Hastings (Atl.)	10	42	16	5	.313	6	4	.667	5	5	10	2	3	0	1	1	14	1.4	4

3-Pt. FG: Atlanta 45-188 (.239)—Roundfield 5-27 (.185); Wilkins 2-11 (.182); E. Johnson 14-41 (.341); Davis 5-18 (.278); °Sparrow 3-15 (.200); Smith (Tot.) 3-18 (.167); Smith (Atl.) 0-2 (.000); McMillen 0-1 (.000); Rollins 0-1 (.000); Glenn 0-1 (.000); Matthews 14-48 (.292); Macklin 0-4 (.000); Brown (Tot.) 0-3 (.000); Brown (Atl.) 0-1 (.000); °Hawes 2-14 (.143); Edmonson 0-2 (.000); Hastings (Tot.) 0-3 (.000); Hastings (Atl.) 0-2 (.000). Opponents 39-166 (.235).

BOSTON CELTICS

Player	G.	Min.	FGA	FGM	Pct.	FTA	FTM	Pct.	Off. Reb.	Def. Reb.	Tot. Reb.	Ast.	PF	Dsq.	Stl.	Blk. Sh.	Pts.	Avg.	Hi.
Bird	79	2982	1481	747	.504	418	351	.840	193	677	870	458	197	0	148	71	1867	23.6	53
Parish	78	2459	1125	619	.550	388	271	.698	260	567	827	141	222	4	79	148	1509	19.3	36
McHale	82	2345	893	483	.541	269	193	.717	215	338	553	104	241	3	34	192	1159	14.1	30
Maxwell	79	2252	663	331	.499	345	280	.812	185	237	422	186	202	3	65	39	942	11.9	30
Wedman (Tot.)	75	1793	788	374	.475	107	85	.794	98	184	282	117	228	6	43	17	843	11.2	30
Wedman (Bos.)	40	503	205	94	.459	30	20	.667	29	45	74	31	83	1	20	6	209	5.2	14
Archibald	66	1811	553	235	.425	296	220	.743	25	66	91	409	110	1	38	4	695	10.5	23
Ainge	80	2048	720	357	.496	97	72	.742	83	131	214	251	259	2	109	6	791	9.9	24
Henderson	82	1551	618	286	.463	133	96	.722	57	67	124	195	190	6	95	3	671	8.2	22
Buckner	72	1565	561	248	.442	117	74	.632	62	125	187	275	195	2	108	5	570	7.9	20
Carr	77	883	315	135	.429	81	60	.741	51	86	137	71	140	0	48	10	333	4.3	17
Robey	59	855	214	100	.467	78	45	.577	79	140	219	65	131	1	13	8	245	4.2	18
Bradley	51	532	176	69	.392	90	46	.511	30	48	78	28	84	0	32	27	184	3.6	14
°Tillis	15	44	23	7	.304	6	2	.333	4	5	9	2	8	0	2	16	1.1	4

3-Pt. FG: Boston 39-186 (.210)—Bird 22-77 (.286); Parish 0-1 (.000); McHale 0-1 (.000); Maxwell 0-1 (.000); Wedman (Tot.) 10-32 (.313); Wedman (Bos.) 1-10 (.100); Archibald 5-24 (.208); Ainge 5-29 (.172); Henderson 3-16 (.188); Buckner 0-4 (.000); Carr 3-19 (.158); Bradley 0-3 (.000); °Tillis 0-1 (.000). Opponents 48-180 (.267).

CHICAGO BULLS

Player	G.	Min.	FGA	FGM	Pct.	FTA	FTM	Pct.	Off. Reb.	Def. Reb.	Tot. Reb.	Ast.	PF	Dsq.	Stl.	Blk. Sh.	Pts.	Avg.	Hi.
Theus	82	2856	1567	749	.478	542	434	.801	91	209	300	484	281	6	143	17	1953	23.8	46
Woolridge	57	1627	622	361	.580	340	217	.638	122	176	298	97	177	1	38	44	939	16.5	34
Dailey	76	2081	1008	470	.466	282	206	.730	87	173	260	280	248	7	72	10	1151	15.1	30
Corzine	82	2496	920	457	.497	322	232	.720	243	474	717	154	242	4	47	109	1146	14.0	35
Higgins	82	2196	698	313	.448	264	209	.792	159	207	366	175	248	3	66	65	848	10.3	25
Greenwood	79	2355	686	312	.455	233	165	.708	217	548	765	151	261	5	54	90	789	10.0	27
Olberding	80	1817	522	251	.481	248	194	.782	108	250	358	131	246	3	50	9	698	8.7	28
Lester	65	1437	446	202	.453	171	124	.725	46	126	172	332	121	2	51	6	528	8.1	21
Jackson	78	1309	426	199	.467	126	92	.730	87	92	179	105	132	0	64	11	492	6.3	17
Oldham	16	171	58	31	.534	22	12	.545	18	29	47	5	30	1	5	13	74	4.6	17
°Jones	49	673	193	86	.446	75	47	.627	56	139	195	40	90	0	18	14	219	4.5	19
Bradley	58	683	159	82	.516	45	36	.800	27	78	105	106	91	0	49	10	201	3.5	19
Bratz	15	140	42	14	.333	13	10	.769	3	16	19	23	20	0	7	0	39	2.6	10
Spriggs	9	39	20	8	.400	7	5	.714	2	7	9	3	3	0	1	2	21	2.3	6
°Kenon	5	25	6	2	.333	0	0	.000	1	3	4	3	2	0	1	0	4	0.8	2

3-Pt. FG: Chicago 45-209 (.215)—Theus 21-91(.231); Woolridge 0-3 (.000); Dailey 5-25 (.200); Corzine 0-2 (.000); Higgins 13-41 (.317); Greenwood 0-4 (.000); Olberding 2-12 (.167); Lester 0-5 (.000); Jackson 2-13 (.154); Bradley 1-5 (.200); Bratz 1-8 (.125). Opponents 46-176 (.261).

CLEVELAND CAVALIERS

Player	G.	Min.	FGA	FGM	Pct.	FTA	FTM	Pct.	Off. Reb.	Def. Reb.	Tot. Reb.	Ast.	PF	Dsq.	Stl.	Blk. Sh.	Pts.	Avg.	Hi.
Free (Tot.)	73	2638	1423	649	.456	583	430	.738	92	109	201	290	241	4	97	15	1743	23.9	38
Free (Clev.)	54	1938	1059	485	.458	434	324	.747	67	157	157	201	175	3	82	12	1309	24.2	37
°Wedman	35	1290	583	280	.480	77	65	.844	69	139	208	86	145	5	23	11	634	18.1	30
Robinson	77	2601	1230	587	.477	301	213	.708	190	666	856	145	272	7	61	58	1387	18.0	40
°Edwards	15	382	150	73	.487	61	38	.623	37	59	96	13	61	3	7	14	184	12.3	25
Huston	80	2716	832	401	.482	245	168	.686	41	118	159	487	215	1	74	4	974	12.2	31
°Brewer	21	563	245	98	.400	51	44	.863	9	28	37	27	27	0	20	6	240	11.4	33
Hubbard	82	1953	597	288	.482	296	204	.689	222	249	471	89	271	11	87	8	780	9.5	22
Nicks	9	148	59	26	.441	17	11	.647	8	18	26	11	17	0	6	0	63	7.0	22
Wilkerson	77	1702	511	213	.417	124	93	.750	62	180	242	189	157	0	68	16	519	6.7	21
°Kenon (Tot.)	48	770	257	119	.463	57	42	.737	66	81	147	39	64	0	23	9	280	5.8	22
Kenon (Clev.)	32	624	212	100	.472	46	35	.761	52	65	117	34	49	0	21	9	235	7.3	22
Bagley	68	990	373	161	.432	84	64	.762	17	79	96	167	74	0	54	5	386	5.7	29
°Mokeski	23	539	121	55	.455	26	16	.615	47	91	138	26	85	6	12	23	126	5.5	13
Cook (Tot.)	75	1333	304	148	.487	104	79	.760	119	216	335	102	181	3	39	31	375	5.0	14
Cook (Clev.)	30	782	162	87	.537	50	38	.760	75	131	206	44	92	3	27	18	212	7.1	14
Flowers	53	699	206	110	.534	53	41	.774	71	109	180	47	99	2	19	12	261	4.9	14
Lacey	60	1232	264	111	.420	37	29	.784	62	169	231	118	209	3	29	25	253	4.2	16
Hayes	65	1058	217	104	.479	51	29	.569	102	134	236	36	215	9	17	41	237	3.6	15
Tillis (Tot.)	52	526	181	76	.420	28	16	.571	41	89	130	18	76	3	8	30	168	3.2	22
Tillis (Clev.)	37	482	158	69	.437	22	14	.636	37	84	121	16	86	3	8	28	152	4.1	22
°Magley	14	56	16	4	.250	8	4	.500	2	8	10	2	5	0	2	0	12	0.9	4

3-Pt. FG: Cleveland 30-120 (.250)—Free (Tot.) 15-45 (.333); Free (Clev.) 15-42 (.357); °Wedman 9-22 (.409); Robinson 0-5 (.000); Huston 4-12 (.333); °Brewer 0-3 (.000); Hubbard 0-2 (.000); Nicks 0-1 (.000); Wilkerson 0-4 (.000); Kenon (Tot.) 0-1 (.000); Kenon (Clev.) 0-1 (.000); Bagley 0-14 (.000); Cook (Tot.) 0-3 (.000); Cook (Clev.) 0-1 (.000); Flowers 0-2 (.000); Lacey 2-9 (.222); Hayes 0-1 (.000); Tillis (Tot.) 0-1 (.000); Tillis (Clev.) 0-0 (.000); Magley 0-1 (.000). Opponents 32-146 (.219).

DALLAS MAVERICKS

Player	G.	Min.	FGA	FGM	Pct.	FTA	FTM	Pct.	Off. Reb.	Def. Reb.	Tot. Reb.	Ast.	PF	Dsq.	Stl.	Blk. Sh.	Pts.	Avg.	Hi.
Aguirre	81	2784	1589	767	.483	578	429	.728	191	317	508	332	247	5	80	26	1979	24.4	44
Vincent	81	2726	1272	622	.489	343	269	.784	217	375	592	212	295	4	70	45	1513	18.7	32
Blackman	75	2349	1042	513	.492	381	297	.780	108	185	293	185	116	0	37	29	1326	17.7	38
Cummings	81	2317	878	433	.493	196	148	.755	225	443	668	144	296	9	57	35	1014	12.5	27
Davis	79	2323	628	359	.572	220	186	.845	34	164	198	565	176	2	80	11	915	11.6	21
Ransey	76	1607	746	343	.460	199	152	.764	44	103	147	280	109	1	58	4	840	11.1	35
Garnett	75	1411	319	170	.533	174	129	.741	141	265	406	103	245	3	48	70	469	6.3	15
Spanarkel	48	722	197	91	.462	113	88	.779	27	57	84	78	59	0	27	3	272	5.7	18
Nimphius	81	1515	355	174	.490	140	77	.550	157	247	404	115	287	11	24	111	426	5.3	20
Turner	59	879	238	96	.403	30	20	.667	68	84	152	88	75	0	47	0	214	3.6	14
°Lloyd	15	206	50	19	.380	17	11	.647	19	27	46	21	24	0	6	6	49	3.3	12
Bristow	37	371	99	44	.444	14	10	.714	24	35	59	70	46	0	6	1	104	2.8	10
Thompson	44	520	137	43	.314	46	36	.783	41	79	120	34	92	0	12	7	122	2.8	9

3-Pt. FG: Dallas 43-185 (.232)—Aguirre 16-76 (.211); Vincent 0-3 (.000); Blackman 3-15 (.200); Cummings 0-1 (.000); Davis 11-43 (.250); Ransey 2-16 (.125); Garnett 0-3 (.000); Spanarkel 2-10 (.200); Nimphius 1-1 (1.000); Turner 2-3 (.667); Lloyd 0-1 (.000); Bristow 6-13 (.462). Opponents 53-202 (.262).

DENVER NUGGETS

Player	G.	Min.	FGA	FGM	Pct.	FTA	FTM	Pct.	Off. Reb.	Def. Reb.	Tot. Reb.	Ast.	PF	Dsq.	Stl.	Blk. Sh.	Pts.	Avg.	Hi.
English	82	2988	1857	959	.516	490	406	.829	263	338	601	397	235	1	116	126	2326	28.4	45
Vandeweghe	82	2909	1537	841	.547	559	489	.875	124	313	437	203	198	0	66	38	2186	26.7	49
Issel	80	2431	1296	661	.510	479	400	.835	151	445	596	223	227	0	83	43	1726	21.6	38
Schayes (Tot.)	82	2284	749	342	.457	295	228	.773	200	435	635	205	325	8	54	98	912	11.1	28
Schayes (Den.)	32	646	235	111	.472	100	71	.710	63	123	186	40	109	1	15	30	293	9.2	18
McKinney	68	1559	546	266	.487	167	136	.814	21	100	121	288	142	0	39	5	668	9.8	30
Dunn	82	2640	527	254	.482	163	119	.730	231	384	615	189	218	2	147	25	627	7.6	20
Williams	74	1443	468	191	.408	174	131	.753	37	99	136	361	221	4	89	12	515	7.0	18
Evans	42	695	243	115	.473	41	33	.805	4	54	58	113	94	3	23	3	263	6.3	16
Hanzlik	82	1547	437	187	.428	160	125	.781	80	156	236	268	220	0	75	15	500	6.1	18
Robisch	61	711	251	96	.382	118	92	.780	34	117	151	53	61	0	10	9	284	4.7	15
Gondrezick	76	1130	294	134	.456	114	82	.719	108	193	301	100	161	0	80	9	350	4.6	16
☆Kelley	38	565	141	59	.418	70	55	.786	61	111	172	59	115	3	21	18	173	4.6	10
☆Anderson	5	33	14	7	.500	10	7	.700	0	2	2	3	7	0	1	0	21	4.2	9
Ray	45	433	153	70	.458	51	33	.647	37	89	126	39	83	2	24	19	173	3.8	11

3-Pt. FG: Denver 24-126 (.190)—English 2-12 (.167); Vandeweghe 15-51 (.294); Issel 4-19 (.211); Schayes (Tot.) 0-1 (.000); Schayes (Den.) 0-0 (.000); McKinney 0-7 (.000); Dunn 0-1 (.000); Williams 2-15 (.133); Evans 0-9 (.000); Hanzlik 1-7 (.143); Robisch 0-1 (.000); Gondrezick 0-3 (.000); Ray 0-1 (.000). Opponents 71-253 (.281).

DETROIT PISTONS

Player	G.	Min.	FGA	FGM	Pct.	FTA	FTM	Pct.	Off. Reb.	Def. Reb.	Tot. Reb.	Ast.	PF	Dsq.	Stl.	Blk. Sh.	Pts.	Avg.	Hi.
Tripucka	58	2252	1156	565	.489	464	392	.845	126	138	264	237	157	0	67	20	1536	26.5	56
Thomas	81	3093	1537	725	.472	518	368	.710	105	223	328	634	318	8	199	29	1854	22.9	46
Johnson	82	2511	1013	520	.513	315	245	.778	167	186	353	301	263	2	93	49	1296	15.8	33
Laimbeer	82	2871	877	436	.497	310	245	.790	282	711	993	263	320	9	51	118	1119	13.6	30
Tyler	82	2543	880	421	.478	196	146	.745	180	360	540	157	221	3	103	160	990	12.1	32
Long	70	1485	692	312	.451	146	111	.760	56	124	180	105	130	1	44	12	737	10.5	29
Benson	21	599	182	85	.467	50	38	.760	53	102	155	49	61	0	14	17	208	9.9	18
☆Jones	49	1036	294	145	.493	172	117	.680	80	191	271	69	160	5	28	77	409	8.3	19
☆May	9	155	50	21	.420	21	17	.810	10	16	26	12	24	1	5	2	59	6.6	11
Levingston	62	879	270	131	.485	147	84	.571	104	128	232	52	125	2	23	36	346	5.6	24
Tolbert (Tot.)	73	1107	314	157	.500	103	52	.505	72	170	242	50	153	1	26	47	366	5.0	20
Tolbert (Det.)	28	395	124	57	.460	59	28	.475	26	65	91	19	56	0	10	23	142	5.1	20
Owens	49	725	192	81	.422	66	45	.682	66	120	186	44	115	0	12	14	207	4.2	12
☆Wilkes	9	129	34	11	.324	15	12	.800	9	10	19	10	22	0	3	1	34	3.8	8
Russell	68	757	184	67	.364	58	47	.810	19	54	73	131	71	0	16	1	183	2.7	16
Pierce	39	265	88	33	.375	32	18	.563	15	20	35	14	42	0	8	4	85	2.2	13
☆Smith	4	18	4	3	.750	4	2	.500	0	5	5	0	4	0	0	0	8	2.0	5
Johnstone (Tot.)	23	191	30	11	.367	20	9	.450	15	31	46	11	33	0	7	31	31	1.3	4
Johnstone (Det.)	16	137	20	9	.450	15	6	.400	11	19	30	10	24	0	2	6	24	1.5	4
☆Zoet	7	30	5	1	.200	0	0	.000	3	5	8	1	9	0	1	3	2	0.3	2

3-Pt. FG: Detroit 72-272 (.265)—Tripucka 14-37 (.378); Thomas 36-125 (.288); Johnson 11-40 (.275); Laimbeer 2-13 (.154); Tyler 2-15 (.133); Long 2-7 (.286); Benson 0-1 (.000); ☆Jones 2-6 (.333); Levingston 0-1 (.000); Tolbert (Tot.) 0-3 (.000); Tolbert (Det.) 0-1 (.000); Wilkes 0-1 (.000); Russell 2-18 (.111); Pierce 1-7 (.143). Opponents 21-182 (.115).

GOLDEN STATE WARRIORS

Player	G.	Min.	FGA	FGM	Pct.	FTA	FTM	Pct.	Off. Reb.	Def. Reb.	Tot. Reb.	Ast.	PF	Dsq.	Stl.	Blk. Sh.	Pts.	Avg.	Hi.
Carroll	79	2988	1529	785	.513	469	337	.719	220	468	688	169	260	7	108	155	1907	24.1	52
☆Free	19	700	364	164	.451	149	106	.711	22	22	44	89	66	1	15	3	434	22.8	38
Short	67	2397	1209	589	.487	308	255	.828	145	209	354	228	242	3	94	14	1437	21.4	40
Johnson (Tot.)	78	2053	921	391	.425	380	312	.821	163	331	494	255	288	10	82	46	1097	14.1	32
Johnson (G.S.)	30	899	359	162	.451	170	141	.829	88	157	245	100	131	6	25	23	466	15.5	28
☆Richardson	33	1074	427	176	.412	87	55	.632	45	100	145	245	124	2	101	9	411	12.5	31
Brewer (Tot.)	74	1807	807	344	.426	170	142	.835	59	85	144	96	123	0	90	25	837	11.3	33
Brewer (G.S.)	53	1401	562	246	.438	119	98	.824	50	57	107	69	96	0	70	19	597	11.3	28
Lloyd	73	1350	566	293	.518	139	100	.719	77	183	260	130	109	0	61	31	687	9.4	30
L. Smith	49	1433	306	180	.588	99	53	.535	209	276	485	46	186	5	36	20	413	8.4	23
Williams	75	1533	479	252	.526	171	123	.719	153	240	393	45	244	4	71	89	627	8.4	26
Floyd (Tot.)	76	1248	527	226	.429	180	150	.833	56	81	137	138	134	3	58	17	612	8.1	28
Floyd (G.S.)	33	754	311	134	.431	135	112	.830	40	55	95	71	78	2	39	8	386	11.7	28
Romar	82	2130	572	266	.465	105	78	.743	23	115	138	455	142	0	98	5	620	7.6	22
☆Hassett	6	139	44	19	.432	0	0	.000	3	8	11	21	14	0	2	0	39	6.5	10
☆Brown	50	743	245	118	.482	65	40	.615	56	122	178	16	126	0	8	21	276	5.5	21
Conner	75	1416	303	145	.479	113	79	.699	69	152	221	253	141	1	116	7	369	4.9	16
☆Duerod	5	49	19	9	.474	0	0	.000	0	3	3	5	5	0	2	1	18	3.6	8
☆McDowell	14	130	29	13	.448	18	14	.778	15	15	30	4	26	0	2	4	40	2.9	12
D. Smith	27	154	51	21	.412	25	17	.680	10	28	38	2	40	0	0	4	59	2.2	10
Engler	54	369	94	38	.404	16	5	.313	43	61	104	11	95	1	7	17	81	1.5	8

3-Pt. FG: Golden State 34-150 (.227)—Carroll 0-3 (.000); ☆Free 0-3 (.000); Short 4-15 (.267); Johnson (Tot.) 3-36 (.083); Johnson (G.S.) 1-17 (.059); ☆Richardson 4-31 (.129); Brewer (Tot.) 7-18 (.389); Brewer (G.S.) 7-15 (.467); Lloyd 1-4 (.250); Williams 0-1 (.000); Floyd (Tot.) 10-25 (.400); Floyd (G.S.) 6-11 (.545); Romar 10-33 (.303); Hassett 1-9 (.111); ☆Brown 0-2 (.000); Conner 0-4 (.000); D. Smith 0-2 (.000). Opponents 42-167 (.251).

HOUSTON ROCKETS

Player	G.	Min.	FGA	FGM	Pct.	FTA	FTM	Pct.	Off. Reb.	Def. Reb.	Tot. Reb.	Ast.	PF	Dsq.	Stl.	Blk. Sh.	Pts.	Avg.	Hi.
Leavell	79	2602	1059	439	.415	297	247	.832	64	131	195	530	215	0	165	14	1167	14.8	42
Bailey (Tot.)	75	1765	774	385	.497	322	226	.702	171	303	474	67	271	7	43	60	996	13.3	34
Bailey (Hou.)	69	1715	756	376	.497	320	224	.700	168	300	468	65	256	7	42	59	976	14.1	34
Hayes	81	2302	890	424	.476	287	196	.683	199	417	616	158	232	2	50	81	1046	12.9	35
Murphy	64	1423	754	337	.447	150	138	.920	34	40	74	158	163	3	59	4	816	12.8	32
Teagle	73	1708	776	332	.428	125	87	.696	74	120	194	150	171	0	53	18	761	10.4	34
Bryant	81	2055	768	344	.448	165	116	.703	88	189	277	186	258	4	82	30	812	10.0	28
Walker	82	2251	806	362	.449	116	72	.621	137	236	373	199	202	3	37	22	797	9.7	23
C. Jones	82	2440	677	307	.453	206	162	.786	222	446	668	138	278	2	46	131	776	9.5	29
M. Jones	60	878	311	142	.457	102	56	.549	114	149	263	39	104	0	22	22	340	5.7	21
Henderson	51	789	263	107	.407	57	45	.789	18	51	69	138	57	0	37	2	259	5.1	17
Nevitt	6	64	15	11	.733	4	1	.250	6	11	17	0	14	0	1	12	23	3.8	8
Taylor	44	774	160	64	.400	46	30	.652	25	53	78	110	82	1	40	15	158	3.6	12
☆Paultz	57	695	200	89	.445	57	26	.456	54	113	167	57	95	0	12	12	204	3.6	12
☆Garrett	4	34	11	4	.364	2	2	1.000	3	4	7	3	4	0	0	0	10	2.5	4

3 Pt. FG: Houston 67-271 (.247)—Leavell 42-175 (.240); Bailey (Tot.) 0-1 (.000); Bailey (Hou.) 0-1 (.000); Hayes 2-4 (.500); Murphy 4-14 (.286); Teagle 10-29 (.345); Bryant 8-36 (.222); Walker 1-4 (.250); C. Jones 0-2 (.000); M. Jones 0-2 (.000); Henderson 0-2 (.000); Taylor 0-1 (.000); Garrett 0-1 (.000). Opponents 33-125 (.264).

INDIANA PACERS

Player	G.	Min.	FGA	FGM	Pct.	FTA	FTM	Pct.	Off. Reb.	Def. Reb.	Tot. Reb.	Ast.	PF	Dsq.	Stl.	Blk. Sh.	Pts.	Avg.	Hi.
Kellogg	81	2761	1420	680	.479	352	261	.741	340	520	860	223	298	6	141	43	1625	20.1	36
Knight	80	2262	984	512	.520	408	343	.841	152	172	324	192	143	0	66	8	1370	17.1	41
Williams	78	2513	1163	580	.499	220	155	.705	151	432	583	262	230	4	54	171	1315	16.9	34
G. Johnson	82	2297	858	409	.477	172	126	.733	176	369	545	220	279	6	77	53	951	11.6	25
Carter	81	1716	706	354	.501	154	124	.805	62	88	150	194	207	5	78	13	849	10.5	42
☆C. Johnson	51	1216	399	208	.521	122	77	.631	115	204	319	115	137	2	51	63	493	9.7	22
Sichting	78	2435	661	316	.478	107	92	.860	33	122	155	433	185	0	104	2	727	9.3	18
Schoene (Tot.)	77	1222	435	207	.476	83	61	.735	96	159	255	59	192	3	25	23	476	6.2	25
Schoene (Ind.)	31	520	228	101	.443	55	40	.727	44	57	101	27	74	1	12	14	243	7.8	15
Branson	62	680	308	131	.425	108	76	.704	73	100	173	46	81	0	27	26	338	5.5	30
Byrnes	80	1436	374	157	.420	95	71	.747	75	116	191	179	149	1	41	6	391	4.9	17
Duren	82	1433	360	163	.453	54	43	.796	38	69	107	200	203	2	66	5	369	4.5	14
Slaughter	63	515	238	89	.374	59	38	.644	34	34	68	52	93	0	36	7	225	3.6	11
☆Morgan	8	46	24	7	.292	4	1	.250	6	11	17	7	7	0	2	0	15	1.9	8

3-Pt. FG: Indiana 50-236 (.212)—Kellogg 4-18 (.222); Knight 3-19 (.158); Williams 0-7 (.000); G. Johnson 7-38 (.184); Carter 17-51 (.333); ☆C. Johnson 0-1 (.000); Sichting 3-18 (.167); Schoene (Tot.) 1-4 (.250); Schoene (Ind.) 1-3 (.333); Branson 0-1 (.000); Byrnes 6-26 (.231); Duren 0-13 (.000); Slaughter 9-41 (.220). Opponents 40-142 (.282).

KANSAS CITY KINGS

Player	G.	Min.	FGA	FGM	Pct.	FTA	FTM	Pct.	Off. Reb.	Def. Reb.	Tot. Reb.	Ast.	PF	Dsq.	Stl.	Blk. Sh.	Pts.	Avg.	Hi.
Drew	75	2690	1218	599	.492	378	310	.820	44	163	207	610	207	1	126	10	1510	20.1	33
E. Johnson	82	2933	1370	677	.494	317	247	.779	191	310	501	216	259	3	70	20	1621	19.8	39
Woodson	81	2426	1154	584	.506	377	298	.790	84	164	248	254	203	0	137	59	1473	18.2	48
Williams	72	2170	1068	419	.392	333	256	.769	93	234	327	569	248	3	120	26	1109	15.4	36
S. Johnson	79	1544	595	371	.624	324	186	.574	140	258	398	95	323	9	40	83	928	11.7	27
☆R. Johnson	50	992	355	178	.501	100	73	.730	75	126	201	48	150	2	18	26	430	8.6	18
Meriweather	78	1706	453	258	.570	163	102	.626	150	274	424	64	285	4	47	86	618	7.9	21
Thompson	71	987	287	147	.512	137	89	.650	133	242	375	33	186	1	40	61	383	5.4	16
Loder	66	818	300	138	.460	80	53	.663	37	88	125	72	98	0	29	8	334	5.1	25
King	58	995	225	104	.462	96	73	.760	91	149	240	58	94	1	28	11	281	4.8	17
Nealy	82	1643	247	147	.595	114	70	.614	170	315	485	62	247	4	68	12	364	4.4	16
Steppe	62	606	176	84	.477	100	76	.760	25	48	73	68	92	0	26	3	245	4.0	16
Dennard	22	224	34	11	.324	9	6	.667	20	32	52	6	27	0	16	1	28	1.3	6
☆Douglas	5	46	3	2	.667	2	0	.000	3	4	7	0	13	0	3	0	4	0.8	4

3-Pt. FG: Kansas City 51-215 (.237)—Drew 2-16 (.125); E. Johnson 20-71 (.282); Woodson 7-33 (.212); Williams 15-74 (.203); ☆R. Johnson 1-4 (.250); Thompson 0-1 (.000); Loder 5-9 (.556); Steppe 1-7 (.143). Opponents 40-188 (.213).

LOS ANGELES LAKERS

Player	G.	Min.	FGA	FGM	Pct.	FTA	FTM	Pct.	Off. Reb.	Def. Reb.	Tot. Reb.	Ast.	PF	Dsq.	Stl.	Blk. Sh.	Pts.	Avg.	Hi.
Abdul-Jabbar	79	2554	1228	722	.588	371	278	.749	167	425	592	200	220	1	61	170	1722	21.8	38
Wilkes	80	2552	1290	684	.530	268	203	.757	146	197	343	182	221	0	65	17	1571	19.6	36
E. Johnson	79	2907	933	511	.548	380	304	.800	214	469	683	829	200	1	176	47	1326	16.8	36
Nixon	79	2711	1123	533	.475	168	125	.744	61	144	205	566	176	1	104	9	1191	15.1	27
McAdoo	47	1019	562	292	.520	163	119	.730	76	171	247	39	153	2	40	40	703	15.0	26
Worthy	77	1970	772	447	.579	221	138	.624	157	242	399	132	221	2	91	64	1033	13.4	28
M. Cooper	82	2148	497	266	.535	130	102	.785	82	192	274	315	208	0	115	50	639	7.8	20
Rambis	78	1806	413	235	.569	166	114	.687	164	367	531	90	233	2	105	63	584	7.5	21
☆Bates (Tot.)	19	304	145	55	.379	22	11	.500	11	8	19	14	19	0	14	3	123	6.5	17
☆Bates (L.A.)	4	27	16	2	.125	2	1	.500	1	0	1	0	1	0	1	0	5	1.3	3
Mix (Tot.)	58	809	283	137	.484	88	75	.852	38	99	137	70	71	0	33	3	350	6.0	20
Mix (L.A.)	1	17	10	4	.400	1	1	1.000	1	0	1	2	1	0	0	0	9	9.0	9
Jones (Tot.)	81	1164	325	148	.455	123	79	.642	84	225	309	62	172	0	31	23	375	4.6	19
Jones (L.A.)	32	491	132	62	.470	48	32	.667	28	86	114	22	82	0	13	9	156	4.9	14
McGee	39	381	163	69	.423	23	17	.739	33	20	53	26	50	1	11	5	156	4.0	19
C. Johnson	48	447	135	53	.393	48	38	.792	40	29	69	24	62	0	22	4	144	3.0	13
Jordan	35	333	132	40	.303	17	11	.647	8	18	26	80	52	0	31	1	94	2.7	12
Landsberger	39	356	102	43	.422	25	12	.480	55	73	128	12	48	0	8	4	98	2.5	8
☆J. Cooper	2	11	4	1	.250	0	0		4	4	8	1	1	0	0	0	2	1.0	2

3-Pt. FG: Los Angeles 10-96 (.104)—Abdul-Jabbar 0-2 (.000); Wilkes 0-6 (.000); E. Johnson 0-21 (.000); Nixon 0-13 (.000); McAdoo 0-1 (.000); Worthy 1-4 (.250); M. Cooper 5-21 (.238); Rambis 0-2 (.000); Mix (Tot.) 1-4 (.250); Jones (Tot.) 0-1 (.000); Jones (L.A.) 0-1 (.000); McGee 1-7 (.143); C. Johnson 0-2 (.000); Jordan 3-16 (.188). Opponents 55-212 (.259).

MILWAUKEE BUCKS

Player	G.	Min.	FGA	FGM	Pct.	FTA	FTM	Pct.	Off. Reb.	Def. Reb.	Tot. Reb.	Ast.	PF	Dsq.	Stl.	Blk. Sh.	Pts.	Avg.	Hi.
Moncrief	76	2710	1156	606	.524	604	499	.826	192	245	437	300	180	1	113	23	1712	22.5	42
Ma. Johnson	80	2853	1420	723	.509	359	264	.735	196	366	562	363	211	0	100	56	1714	21.4	39
Bridgeman	70	1855	856	421	.492	196	164	.837	44	202	246	207	155	0	40	9	1007	14.4	31
°Mi. Johnson	6	153	66	30	.455	9	7	.778	9	16	25	11	22	0	1	2	67	11.2	17
Lanier	39	978	332	163	.491	133	91	.684	58	142	200	105	125	2	34	24	417	10.7	26
Winters	57	1361	587	255	.434	85	73	.859	35	75	110	156	132	2	45	4	605	10.6	30
Lister	80	1885	514	272	.529	242	130	.537	168	400	568	111	328	18	50	177	674	8.4	27
Cowens	40	1014	306	136	.444	63	52	.825	73	201	274	82	137	4	30	15	324	8.1	16
Ford (Tot.)	77	1610	445	213	.479	123	97	.789	18	85	103	290	190	2	52	3	524	6.8	21
Ford (Mil.)	70	1447	410	193	.471	113	90	.796	18	78	96	252	168	2	46	3	477	6.8	21
Pressey	79	1528	466	213	.457	176	105	.597	83	198	281	207	174	2	99	47	532	6.7	23
Criss	66	922	375	169	.451	76	68	.895	14	65	79	127	44	0	27	0	412	6.2	20
°Mix	57	792	273	133	.487	87	74	.851	37	99	136	68	70	0	33	3	341	6.0	20
Mokeski (Tot.)	73	1128	260	119	.458	68	50	.735	76	184	260	49	223	9	21	44	288	3.9	13
Mokeski (Mil.)	50	589	139	64	.460	42	34	.810	29	93	122	23	138	3	9	21	162	3.2	10
°Hill	14	169	26	14	.538	22	18	.818	5	15	20	27	20	0	9	0	46	3.3	10
Catchings	74	1554	197	90	.457	92	62	.674	132	276	408	77	224	4	26	148	242	3.3	12
°Pellom (Tot.)	6	29	16	6	.375	0	0	.000	2	6	8	1	3	0	0	0	12	2.0	4
°Pellom (Mil.)	4	20	10	4	.400	0	0	.000	2	6	8	0	3	0	0	0	8	2.0	4

3-Pt. FG: Milwaukee 37-169 (.219)—Moncrief 1-10 (.100); Ma. Johnson 4-20 (.200); Bridgeman 1-13 (.077); °Mi. Johnson 0-2 (.000); Lanier 0-1 (.000); Winters 22-68 (.324); Cowens 0-2 (.000); Ford (Tot.) 1-9 (.111); Ford (Mil.) 1-8 (.125); Pressey 1-9 (.111); Criss 6-31 (.194); °Mix 1-4 (.250); Mokeski (Tot.) 0-1 (.000); Mokeski (Mil.) 0-1 (.000). Opponents 38-209 (.182).

NEW JERSEY NETS

Player	G.	Min.	FGA	FGM	Pct.	FTA	FTM	Pct.	Off. Reb.	Def. Reb.	Tot. Reb.	Ast.	PF	Dsq.	Stl.	Blk. Sh.	Pts.	Avg.	Hi.
King	79	2447	1226	582	.475	227	176	.775	157	299	456	291	278	5	95	41	1346	17.0	31
Williams	82	2961	912	536	.588	523	324	.620	365	662	1027	125	270	4	91	110	1396	17.0	30
Birdsong	62	1885	834	426	.511	145	82	.566	53	97	150	239	155	0	85	16	936	15.1	29
Cook	82	2625	986	443	.449	242	186	.769	73	167	240	448	213	2	194	48	1080	13.2	24
°Johnson	42	1001	496	199	.401	201	164	.816	66	158	224	144	135	4	56	21	564	13.4	32
Richardson (Tot.)	64	2076	815	346	.425	163	106	.650	113	182	295	432	240	4	182	24	806	12.6	31
Richardson (N.J.)	31	1002	388	170	.438	76	51	.671	68	82	150	187	116	2	81	15	395	12.7	27
Dawkins	81	2093	669	401	.599	257	166	.646	127	293	420	114	379	23	67	152	968	12.0	25
Gminski	80	1255	426	213	.500	225	175	.778	154	228	382	61	118	0	35	116	601	7.5	18
°Ford	7	163	35	20	.571	10	7	.700	0	7	7	38	22	0	6	0	47	6.7	11
O'Koren	46	803	259	136	.525	48	34	.708	42	72	114	82	67	0	42	11	308	6.7	23
Willoughby (Tot.)	62	1146	324	147	.454	55	43	.782	63	138	201	64	139	0	25	17	343	5.5	18
Willoughby (N.J.)	10	84	29	11	.379	2	2	1.000	2	9	11	8	16	0	1	1	24	2.4	6
°Floyd	43	494	216	92	.426	45	38	.844	16	26	42	67	56	1	19	9	226	5.3	13
Walker	79	1388	250	114	.456	149	116	.779	30	106	136	264	134	1	78	3	346	4.4	15
Elmore	74	975	244	97	.398	84	54	.643	81	157	238	39	125	2	44	38	248	3.4	13
°Bailey	6	50	18	9	.500	2	2	1.000	3	3	6	2	15	0	1	2	20	3.3	6
Phillips	48	416	138	56	.406	59	40	.678	27	50	77	29	58	0	14	8	152	3.2	12
Van Breda Kolff	13	63	14	5	.357	6	5	.833	2	11	13	5	9	0	2	2	15	1.2	4

3-Pt. FG: New Jersey 30-149 (.201)—King 6-23 (.261); Williams 0-4 (.000); Birdsong 2-6 (.333); Cook 8-38 (.211); °Johnson 2-17 (.118); Richardson (Tot.) 8-51 (.157); Richardson (N.J.) 4-20 (.200); Gminski 0-1 (.000); °Ford 0-1 (.000); O'Koren 2-9 (.222); Willoughby (Tot.) 6-14 (.429); Willoughby (N.J.) 0-1 (.000); °Floyd 4-14 (.286); Walker 2-12 (.167); Elmore 0-1 (.000); Phillips 0-2 (.000). Opponents 45-208 (.216).

NEW YORK KNICKERBOCKERS

Player	G.	Min.	FGA	FGM	Pct.	FTA	FTM	Pct.	Off. Reb.	Def. Reb.	Tot. Reb.	Ast.	PF	Dsq.	Stl.	Blk. Sh.	Pts.	Avg.	Hi.
King	68	2207	1142	603	.528	388	280	.722	99	227	326	195	233	5	90	13	1486	21.9	43
Cartwright	82	2468	804	455	.566	511	380	.744	185	405	590	136	315	7	41	127	1290	15.7	32
Williams	68	1385	647	314	.485	259	176	.680	94	196	290	133	166	3	73	3	806	11.9	23
Sparrow (Tot.)	81	2428	810	392	.484	199	147	.739	61	169	230	397	255	4	107	5	936	11.6	30
Sparrow (N.Y.)	32	880	298	128	.430	86	63	.733	22	67	89	159	93	2	37	4	321	10.0	24
Westphal	80	1978	693	318	.459	184	148	.804	19	96	115	439	180	1	87	16	798	10.0	25
Robinson	81	2426	706	326	.462	201	118	.587	199	458	657	145	241	4	57	24	770	9.5	26
Tucker	78	1830	647	299	.462	64	43	.672	75	141	216	195	235	1	56	6	655	8.4	27
Orr	82	1666	593	274	.462	175	140	.800	94	134	228	94	134	0	64	24	688	8.4	28
Sherod	64	1624	421	171	.406	80	52	.650	43	106	149	311	112	2	96	14	395	6.2	20
Webster	82	1472	331	168	.508	180	106	.589	176	267	443	49	210	3	35	131	442	5.4	22
Grunfeld	77	1422	377	167	.443	98	81	.827	42	121	163	136	172	1	40	10	415	5.4	14
Taylor	31	321	102	37	.363	32	21	.656	19	17	36	41	54	1	20	2	95	3.1	12
Davis	8	28	10	4	.400	10	6	.600	3	7	10	0	4	0	0	4	14	1.8	5
°Hastings	21	98	22	8	.364	14	7	.500	10	21	31	1	31	1	0	5	0	23	1.1	4

3-Pt. FG: New York 33-131 (.252)—King 0-6 (.000); Williams 2-19 (.105); Sparrow (Tot.) 5-22 (.227); Sparrow (N.Y.) 2-7 (.286); Westphal 14-48 (.292); Tucker 14-30 (.467); Orr 0-2 (.000); Sherod 1-13 (.077); Webster 0-1 (.000); Grunfeld 0-4 (.000); °Hastings 0-1 (.000). Opponents 38-166 (.229).

PHILADELPHIA 76ers

Player	G.	Min.	FGA	FGM	Pct.	FTA	FTM	Pct.	Off. Reb.	Def. Reb.	Tot. Reb.	Ast.	PF	Dsq.	Stl.	Blk. Sh.	Pts.	Avg.	Hi.
Malone	78	2922	1305	654	.501	788	600	.761	445	749	1194	101	206	0	89	157	1908	24.5	38
Erving	72	2421	1170	605	.517	435	330	.759	173	318	491	263	202	1	112	131	1542	21.4	44
Toney	81	2474	1250	626	.501	411	324	.788	42	183	225	365	255	0	80	17	1598	19.7	42
Cheeks	79	2465	745	404	.542	240	181	.754	53	156	209	543	182	0	184	31	990	12.5	32
Jones	74	1749	460	250	.543	208	165	.793	102	242	344	142	199	4	85	91	665	9.0	17
C. Johnson (Tot.)	83	1914	581	299	.515	180	111	.617	190	334	524	139	221	3	67	92	709	8.5	22
C. Johnson (Phil.)	32	698	182	91	.500	58	34	.586	75	130	205	24	84	1	16	29	216	6.8	13
Richardson	77	1755	559	259	.463	111	71	.640	98	149	247	168	164	0	71	18	589	7.6	18

Player	G.	Min.	FGA	FGM	Pct.	FTA	FTM	Pct.	Off. Reb.	Def. Reb.	Tot. Reb.	Ast.	PF	Disq.	Stl.	Blk. Sh.	Pts.	Avg.	Hi.
R. Johnson (Tot.)..	79	1541	509	247	.485	130	95	.731	107	184	291	71	232	3	26	43	590	7.5	18
R. Johnson (Phil.)..	29	549	154	69	.448	30	22	.733	32	58	90	23	82	1	8	17	160	5.5	16
Edwards	81	1266	483	228	.472	113	86	.761	23	62	85	221	119	0	81	6	542	6.7	18
☆Schoene	46	702	207	106	.512	28	21	.750	52	102	154	32	118	2	13	9	233	5.1	25
Iavaroni	80	1612	353	163	.462	113	78	.690	117	212	329	83	238	0	32	44	404	5.1	19
Cureton	73	987	258	108	.419	67	33	.493	84	185	269	43	144	1	37	24	249	3.4	19
McNamara	36	182	64	29	.453	45	20	.444	34	42	76	7	42	1	3	3	78	2.2	7
☆Anderson	13	48	22	8	.364	3	1	.333	4	8	12	1	6	0	1	0	17	1.3	8

3-Pt. FG: Philadelphia 25-109 (.229)—Malone 0-1 (.000); Erving 2-7 (.286); Toney 22-76 (.289); Cheeks 1-6 (.167); Jones 0-1 (.000); C. Johnson (Tot.) 0-1 (.000); Richardson 0-6 (.000); R. Johnson (Tot.) 1-4 (.250); Edwards 0-8 (.000); ☆Schoene 0-1 (.000); Iavaroni 0-2 (.000); ☆Anderson 0-1 (.000). Opponents 54-249 (.217).

PHOENIX SUNS

Player	G.	Min.	FGA	FGM	Pct.	FTA	FTM	Pct.	Off. Reb.	Def. Reb.	Tot. Reb.	Ast.	PF	Dsq.	Stl.	Blk. Sh.	Pts.	Avg.	Hi.
Davis	80	2491	1289	665	.516	225	184	.818	63	134	197	397	186	2	117	12	1521	19.0	38
Nance	82	2914	1069	588	.550	287	193	.672	239	471	710	197	254	4	99	217	1370	16.7	31
Lucas	77	2586	1045	495	.474	356	278	.781	201	598	799	219	274	5	56	43	1269	16.5	33
Johnson	77	2551	861	398	.462	369	292	.791	92	243	335	388	204	1	97	39	1093	14.2	27
Adams	80	2447	981	477	.486	217	180	.829	161	387	548	376	287	7	114	74	1135	14.2	30
Edwards (Tot.)	31	667	263	128	.487	108	69	.639	56	99	155	40	110	5	12	19	325	10.5	25
Edwards (Phoe.)	16	285	113	55	.487	47	31	.660	19	40	59	27	49	2	5	5	141	8.8	17
Macy	82	1836	634	328	.517	148	129	.872	41	124	165	278	130	0	64	8	808	9.9	25
White	65	626	234	127	.543	109	70	.642	47	58	105	30	54	0	16	2	324	5.0	16
Scott	81	1139	259	124	.479	110	81	.736	60	164	224	97	133	0	48	31	329	4.1	14
Thirdkill	49	521	170	74	.435	78	45	.577	28	44	72	36	93	1	19	4	194	4.0	15
☆Cook	45	551	142	61	.430	54	41	.759	44	85	129	58	89	0	12	13	163	3.6	12
High	82	1155	217	100	.461	136	63	.463	45	105	150	153	205	0	85	34	264	3.2	14
Pittman	28	170	40	19	.475	37	25	.676	13	18	31	7	41	0	2	7	63	2.3	10
Kramer	54	458	104	44	.423	16	14	.875	41·	47	88	37	63	0	15	6	102	1.9	8

3-Pt. FG: Phoenix 40-158 (.253)—Davis 7-23 (.304); Nance 1-3 (.333); Lucas 1-3 (.333); Johnson 5-31 (.161); Adams 1-3 (.333); Macy 23-76 (.303); White 0-1 (.000); Scott 0-2 (.000); Thirdkill 1-7 (.143); ☆Cook 0-2 (.000); High 1-5 (.200); Pittman 0-1 (.000); Kramer 0-1 (.000). Opponents 44-199 (.221).

PORTLAND TRAIL BLAZERS

Player	G.	Min.	FGA	FGM	Pct.	FTA	FTM	Pct.	Off. Reb.	Def. Reb.	Tot. Reb.	Ast.	PF	Dsq.	Stl.	Blk. Sh.	Pts.	Avg.	Hi.
Paxson	81	2740	1323	682	.515	478	388	.812	68	106	174	231	160	0	140	17	1756	21.7	35
Natt	80	2879	1187	644	.543	428	339	.792	214	385	599	171	184	2	63	29	1630	20.4	34
Thompson	80	3017	1033	505	.489	401	249	.621	183	570	753	380	213	1	68	110	1259	15.7	26
Valentine	47	1298	460	209	.454	213	169	.793	34	83	117	293	139	1	101	5	587	12.5	24
Carr	82	2331	717	362	.505	366	255	.697	182	407	589	116	306	10	62	42	981	12.0	28
Cooper	80	2099	723	320	.443	197	135	.685	214	397	611	116	318	5	27	136	775	9.7	23
Lever	81	2020	594	256	.431	159	116	.730	85	140	225	426	179	2	153	15	633	7.8	19
Buse	41	643	182	72	.396	46	41	.891	19	35	54	115	60	0	44	2	194	4.7	20
Townes	55	516	234	105	.449	38	28	.737	30	35	65	31	81	0	19	5	247	4.5	20
Lamp	59	690	252	107	.425	52	42	.808	25	51	76	58	67	0	20	3	257	4.4	14
Verhoeven	48	527	171	87	.509	31	21	.677	44	52	96	32	95	2	18	9	195	4.1	16
Judkins	34	309	88	39	.443	30	25	.833	18	25	43	17	39	0	15	2	105	3.1	9
McDowell (Tot.)	56	505	126	58	.460	61	47	.770	54	65	119	24	84	0	8	11	163	2.9	12
McDowell (Port.)	42	375	97	45	.464	43	33	.767	39	50	89	20	58	0	6	7	123	2.9	11
Norris	30	311	63	26	.413	30	14	.467	25	44	69	24	53	0	13	2	66	2.2	8

3-Pt. FG: Portland 35-150 (.233)—Paxson 4-25 (.160); Natt 3-20 (.150); Thompson 0-1 (.000); Valentine 0-1 (.000); Carr 2-6 (.333); Cooper 0-5 (.000); Lever 5-15 (.333); Buse 9-35 (.257); Townes 9-25 (.360); Lamp 1-6 (.167); Verhoeven 0-1 (.000); Judkins 0-2 (.000); McDowell (Tot.) 0-2 (.000); McDowell (Port.) 0-2 (.000). Opponents 55-188 (.293).

SAN ANTONIO SPURS

Player	G.	Min.	FGA	FGM	Pct.	FTA	FTM	Pct.	Off. Reb.	Def. Reb.	Tot. Reb.	Ast.	PF	Dsq.	Stl.	Blk. Sh.	Pts.	Avg.	Hi.
Gervin	78	2830	1553	757	.487	606	517	.853	111	246	357	264	243	5	88	67	2043	26.2	47
Mitchell	80	2803	1342	686	.511	289	219	.758	188	349	537	98	248	6	57	52	1591	19.9	33
Gilmore	82	2797	888	556	.626	496	367	.740	299	685	984	126	273	4	40	192	1479	18.0	40
Banks	81	2722	919	505	.550	278	196	.705	222	390	612	279	229	3	78	21	1206	14.9	43
Moore	77	2552	841	394	.468	199	148	.744	65	212	277	753	247	2	194	32	941	12.2	29
Jones (Tot.)	77	1658	479	237	.495	286	201	.703	136	312	448	89	267	10	42	108	677	8.8	25
Jones (S.A.)	28	622	185	92	.497	114	84	.737	56	121	177	20	107	5	14	31	268	9.6	25
Dunleavy	79	1619	510	213	.418	154	120	.779	18	116	134	437	210	4	74	4	613	7.8	24
Sanders	26	393	157	76	.484	43	31	.721	31	63	94	19	57	0	18	6	183	7.0	16
☆Willoughby	52	1062	295	136	.461	53	41	.774	61	129	190	56	123	0	24	16	319	6.1	18
Phegley	62	599	267	120	.449	56	43	.768	39	45	84	60	92	0	30	8	286	4.6	18
Paultz (Tot.)	64	820	227	101	.445	59	27	.458	64	136	200	61	109	0	17	18	229	3.6	12
Paultz (S.A.)	7	125	27	12	.444	2	1	.500	10	23	33	4	14	0	5	6	25	3.6	8
Griffin	53	956	116	60	.517	76	53	.697	77	139	216	86	153	0	33	25	173	3.3	14
Robinson	35	147	97	35	.361	45	30	.667	6	11	17	21	18	0	4	2	101	2.9	9
Rains	34	292	83	33	.398	43	29	.674	25	19	44	22	35	0	10	1	95	2.8	13
Crompton	14	148	34	14	.412	5	3	.600	18	30	48	7	25	0	3	5	31	2.2	8
Smith (Tot.)	12	68	24	7	.292	10	9	.900	1	5	6	8	13	0	5	0	23	1.9	6
Smith (S.A.)	7	25	11	5	.455	2	2	1.000	0	3	3	2	6	0	1	0	12	1.7	6
☆Johnstone	7	54	10	2	.200	4	4	1.000	4	12	16	1	9	0	1	1	7	1.0	4
☆Dietrick	8	34	5	1	.200	2	0	.000	2	6	8	1	6	0	1	0	2	0.3	2

3-Pt. FG: San Antonio 94-308 (.305)—Gervin 12-33 (.364); Mitchell 0-3 (.000); Gilmore 0-6 (.000); Banks 0-5 (.000); Moore 5-22 (.227); Jones (Tot.) 2-9 (.222); Jones (S.A.) 0-3 (.000); Dunleavy 67-194 (.345); Sanders 0-2 (.000); ☆Willoughby 6-13 (.462); Phegley 3-14 (.214); Robinson 1-11 (.091); Rains 0-1 (.000); Smith (Tot.) 0-2 (.000); Smith (S.A.) 0-1 (.000). Opponents 51-201 (.254).

SAN DIEGO CLIPPERS

Player	G.	Min.	FGA	FGM	Pct.	FTA	FTM	Pct.	Off. Reb.	Def. Reb.	Tot. Reb.	Ast.	PF	Dsq.	Stl.	Blk. Sh.	Pts.	Avg.	Hi.
Cummings	70	2531	1309	684	.523	412	292	.709	303	441	744	177	294	10	129	62	1660	23.7	39
Chambers	79	2665	1099	519	.472	488	353	.723	218	301	519	192	333	15	79	57	1391	17.6	37
Walton	33	1099	379	200	.528	117	65	.556	75	248	323	120	113	0	34	119	465	14.1	30
Hollins	56	1844	717	313	.437	179	129	.721	30	98	128	373	155	2	111	14	758	13.5	25
Brooks	82	2457	830	402	.484	277	193	.697	239	282	521	262	297	6	112	39	1002	12.2	32
Wood	76	1822	740	343	.464	161	124	.770	96	140	236	134	188	5	55	36	825	10.9	27
Hodges	76	2022	704	318	.452	130	94	.723	53	69	122	275	192	3	82	4	750	9.9	24
°Ra. Smith	65	1264	499	244	.489	117	101	.863	35	53	88	192	122	1	54	0	592	9.1	29
Whitehead	46	905	306	164	.536	87	72	.828	105	156	261	42	139	2	21	15	400	8.7	29
Moore	37	642	190	81	.426	56	42	.750	15	40	55	73	72	1	22	1	210	5.7	19
Anderson	78	1274	431	174	.404	69	48	.696	111	161	272	120	170	2	57	26	403	5.2	21
Cooper (Tot.)	20	333	72	37	.514	29	16	.552	42	44	86	17	49	0	9	20	90	4.5	14
Cooper (S.D.)	13	275	59	31	.525	20	11	.550	36	35	71	15	39	0	8	19	73	5.6	14
°Jones	9	85	37	17	.459	6	6	1.000	10	7	17	4	14	0	3	0	40	4.4	12
Brogan	58	466	213	91	.427	43	34	.791	33	29	62	66	79	0	26	9	219	3.8	16
Gross	27	373	82	35	.427	19	12	.632	32	34	66	34	69	1	22	7	83	3.1	9
Nater	7	51	20	6	.300	4	4	1.000	2	11	13	1	1	0	1	0	16	2.3	4
°Ro. Smith	5	43	13	2	.154	8	7	.875	1	2	3	6	7	0	4	0	11	2.2	6
°Douglas	3	12	6	1	.167	2	2	1.000	0	1	1	1	0	0	0	0	5	1.7	3

3-Pt. FG: San Diego 64-262 (.244)—Cummings 0-1 (.000); Chambers 0-8 (.000); Hollins 3-21 (.143); Brooks 5-15 (.333); Wood 15-50 (.300); Hodges 20-90 (.222); °Ra. Smith 3-16 (.188); Moore 6-23 (.261); Anderson 7-19 (.368); Brogan 3-13 (.231); Gross 1-3 (.333); °Ro. Smith 0-1 (.000); Douglas 1-2 (.500). Opponents 32-130 (.246).

SEATTLE SUPERSONICS

Player	G.	Min.	FGA	FGM	Pct.	FTA	FTM	Pct.	Off. Reb.	Def. Reb.	Tot. Reb.	Ast.	PF	Dsq.	Stl.	Blk. Sh.	Pts.	Avg.	Hi.
Williams	80	2761	1384	660	.477	370	278	.751	72	133	205	643	117	0	182	26	1600	20.0	38
Sikma	75	2564	1043	484	.464	478	400	.837	213	645	858	233	263	4	87	65	1368	18.2	31
Thompson	75	2155	925	445	.481	380	298	.784	94	174	270	222	142	0	47	33	1190	15.9	38
Shelton	82	2572	915	437	.478	187	141	.754	158	337	495	237	310	8	75	72	1016	12.4	23
Brown	80	1432	714	371	.520	72	58	.806	32	65	97	242	98	0	59	13	814	10.2	25
Donaldson	82	1789	496	289	.583	218	150	.688	131	370	501	97	171	1	19	101	728	8.9	29
Kelser	80	1507	450	247	.549	257	173	.673	158	245	403	97	243	5	52	35	667	8.3	30
Vranes	82	2054	429	226	.527	209	115	.550	177	248	425	120	254	2	53	49	567	6.9	21
Smith	79	1238	400	175	.438	133	101	.759	27	103	130	216	113	0	44	8	454	5.7	16
Hawes (Tot.)	77	1416	390	163	.418	94	69	.734	81	280	361	95	189	2	38	14	400	5.2	20
Hawes (Sea.)	31	556	146	72	.493	32	23	.719	28	105	133	36	79	0	9	6	170	5.5	16
°Tolbert	45	712	190	100	.526	44	24	.545	46	105	151	31	97	1	16	24	224	5.0	13
Radford	54	439	172	84	.488	73	30	.411	12	35	47	104	78	0	34	4	202	3.7	22
Greig	9	26	13	7	.538	6	5	.833	2	4	6	0	4	0	0	1	19	2.1	8

3-Pt. FG: Seattle 29-138 (.210)—Williams 2-43 (.047); Sikma 0-8 (.000); Thompson 2-10 (.200); Shelton 1-6 (.167); Brown 14-32 (.438); Kelser 0-3 (.000); Vranes 0-1 (.000); Smith 3-8 (.375); Hawes (Tot.) 5-21 (.238); Hawes (Sea.) 3-7 (.429); °Tolbert 0-2 (.000); Radford 4-18 (.222). Opponents 49-197 (.249).

UTAH JAZZ

Player	G.	Min.	FGA	FGM	Pct.	FTA	FTM	Pct.	Off. Reb.	Def. Reb.	Tot. Reb.	Ast.	PF	Dsq.	Stl.	Blk. Sh.	Pts.	Avg.	Hi.
Dantley	22	887	402	233	.580	248	210	.847	58	82	140	105	62	2	20	0	676	30.7	57
Griffith	77	2787	1554	752	.484	246	167	.679	100	204	304	270	184	0	138	33	1709	22.2	38
Drew	44	1206	671	318	.474	392	296	.755	98	137	235	97	152	8	35	7	932	21.2	40
Green	78	2783	942	464	.493	232	185	.797	62	161	223	697	154	0	220	4	1115	14.3	28
°Schayes	50	1638	514	231	.449	195	157	.805	137	312	449	165	216	7	39	68	619	12.4	28
Wilkins	81	2307	816	389	.477	200	156	.780	154	442	596	132	251	4	41	42	934	11.5	35
Poquette	75	2331	697	329	.472	221	166	.751	155	366	521	168	264	5	64	116	825	11.0	30
Eaves	82	1588	575	280	.487	247	200	.810	34	88	122	210	116	0	51	3	761	9.3	35
Anderson (Tot.)	65	1202	379	190	.501	175	100	.571	119	175	294	67	153	1	63	21	480	7.4	21
Anderson (Utah)	52	1154	357	182	.510	172	99	.576	103	167	282	66	147	1	62	21	463	8.9	21
Kelley (Tot.)	70	1345	293	130	.444	175	142	.811	131	273	404	138	221	4	54	39	402	5.7	18
Kelley (Utah)	32	780	152	71	.467	105	87	.829	70	162	232	79	106	1	33	21	229	7.2	18
°F. Williams	18	210	101	36	.356	25	18	.720	3	14	17	10	30	0	6	1	92	5.1	23
Eaton	81	1528	353	146	.414	90	59	.656	86	376	462	112	257	6	24	275	351	4.3	16
Natt	22	210	73	38	.521	14	9	.643	6	16	22	28	36	0	5	0	85	3.9	16
R. Williams	44	346	135	56	.415	53	35	.660	15	23	38	37	42	0	20	4	147	3.3	13

3-Pt. FG: Utah 44-183 (.240)—Griffith 38-132 (.288); Drew 0-5 (.000); Green 2-13 (.154); °Schayes 0-1 (.000); Wilkins 0-3 (.000); Poquette 1-5 (.200); Eaves 1-8 (.125); Anderson (Tot.) 0-4 (.000); Anderson (Utah) 0-3 (.000); F. Williams 2-7 (.286); Eaton 0-1 (.000); Natt 0-2 (.000); R. Williams 0-3 (.000). Opponents 48-199 (.241).

WASHINGTON BULLETS

Player	G.	Min.	FGA	FGM	Pct.	FTA	FTM	Pct.	Off. Reb.	Def. Reb.	Tot. Reb.	Ast.	PF	Dsq.	Stl.	Blk. Sh.	Pts.	Avg.	Hi.
Ruland	79	2862	1051	580	.552	544	375	.689	293	578	871	234	312	12	74	77	1536	19.4	37
Ballard	78	2840	1274	603	.473	233	182	.781	123	385	508	262	176	2	135	25	1401	18.0	37
Sobers	41	1438	534	234	.438	185	154	.832	35	67	102	218	158	3	61	14	645	15.7	29
Johnson	68	2324	786	321	.408	261	196	.751	46	132	178	549	170	1	110	6	852	12.5	36
Collins	65	1575	635	332	.523	136	101	.743	116	94	210	132	166	1	87	30	765	11.8	31
Mahorn	82	3023	768	376	.490	254	146	.575	171	608	779	115	335	13	86	148	898	11.0	27
Haywood	38	775	312	125	.401	87	63	.724	77	106	183	30	94	2	12	27	313	8.2	21
°Bates	15	277	129	53	.411	20	10	.500	10	8	18	14	18	0	13	3	118	7.9	17
Davis	74	1161	534	251	.470	89	56	.629	83	130	213	73	120	0	32	22	560	7.6	33
Grevey	41	756	294	114	.388	69	54	.783	18	31	49	49	61	0	18	7	297	7.2	24
°Porter	11	210	40	21	.525	6	5	.833	2	3	5	46	30	0	10	0	47	4.3	7
°Cox	7	78	37	13	.351	6	3	.500	7	3	10	6	16	0	0	1	29	4.1	10
°Lucas	35	386	131	62	.473	42	21	.500	8	21	29	102	18	0	25	1	145	4.1	14
Warrick	43	727	171	65	.380	57	42	.737	15	54	69	126	103	5	21	8	172	4.0	14

Player	G.	Min.	FGA	FGM	Pct.	FTA	FTM	Pct.	Off. Reb.	Def. Reb.	Tot. Reb.	Ast.	PF	Disq.	Stl.	Blk. Sh.	Pts.	Avg.	Hi.
Kopicki	17	201	51	23	.451	25	21	.840	18	44	62	9	21	0	9	2	67	3.9	16
Batton	54	558	191	85	.445	17	8	.471	45	74	119	29	56	0	15	13	178	3.3	15
°Cooper	5	47	9	5	.556	9	5	.556	4	9	13	2	7	0	0	0	15	3.0	5
Terry	55	514	106	39	.368	15	10	.667	27	72	99	46	79	1	24	13	88	1.6	15
°Lingenfelter	7	53	6	4	.667	4	0	.000	1	11	12	4	16	1	1	3	8	1.1	4

3-Pt. FG: Washington 70-237 (.295)—Ruland 1-3 (.333); Ballard 13-37 (.351); Sobers 23-55 (.418); Johnson 14-61 (.230); Collins 0-6 (.000); Mahorn 0-3 (.000); Haywood 0-1 (.000); °Bates 2-5 (.400); Davis 2-10 (.200); Grevey 15-38 (.395); Cox 0-2 (.000); Lucas 0-5 (.000); Warrick 0-5 (.000); Kopicki 0-1 (.000); Batton 0-3 (.000); Terry 0-2 (.000). Opponents 37-163 (.227).

PLAYOFF RESULTS

EASTERN CONFERENCE FIRST ROUND
New York 2, New Jersey 0
Apr. 20—Wed.—New York 118 at New Jersey.............107
Apr. 21—Thur.—New Jersey 99 at New York...............105

Boston 2, Atlanta 1
Apr. 19—Tue.—Atlanta 95 at Boston.........................103
Apr. 22—Fri.—Boston 93 at Atlanta 95
Apr. 24—Sun.—Atlanta 79 at Boston 98

EASTERN CONFERENCE SEMIFINALS
Philadelphia 4, New York 0
Apr. 24—Sun.—New York 102 at Philadelphia.............112
Apr. 27—Wed.—New York 91 at Philadelphia...............98
Apr. 30—Sat.—Philadelphia 107 at New York.............105
May 1—Sun.—Philadelphia 105 at New York.............102

Milwaukee 4, Boston 0
Apr. 27—Wed.—Milwaukee 116 at Boston...................95
Apr. 29—Fri.—Milwaukee 95 at Boston.......................91
May 1—Sun.—Boston 99 at Milwaukee.....................107
May 2—Mon.—Boston 93 at Milwaukee 107

EASTERN CONFERENCE FINALS
Philadelphia 4, Milwaukee 1
May 8—Sun.—Milwaukee 109 at Philadelphia............111
May 11—Wed.—Milwaukee 81 at Philadelphia..............87
May 14—Sat.—Philadelphia 104 at Milwaukee..............96
May 15—Sun.—Philadelphia 94 at Milwaukee.............100
May 18—Wed.—Milwaukee 103 at Philadelphia...........115

WESTERN CONFERENCE FIRST ROUND
Portland 2, Seattle 0
Apr. 20—Wed.—Portland 108 at Seattle......................97
Apr. 22—Fri.—Seattle 96 at Portland........................105

Denver 2, Phoenix 1
Apr. 19—Tue.—Denver 108 at Phoenix......................121
Apr. 21—Thur.—Phoenix 99 at Denver.......................113
Apr. 24—Sun.—Denver 117 at Phoenix....................°112

WESTERN CONFERENCE SEMIFINALS
Los Angeles 4, Portland 1
Apr. 24—Sun.—Portland 97 at Los Angeles.................118
Apr. 26—Tue.—Portland 106 at Los Angeles...............112
Apr. 29—Fri.—Los Angeles 115 at Portland...............°109
May 1—Sun.—Los Angeles 95 at Portland.................108
May 3—Tue.—Portland 108 at Los Angeles................116

San Antonio 4, Denver 1
Apr. 26—Tue.—Denver 133 at San Antonio.................152
Apr. 27—Wed.—Denver 109 at San Antonio 126
Apr. 29—Fri.—San Antonio 127 at Denver.................°126
May 2—Mon.—San Antonio 114 at Denver 124
May 4—Wed.—Denver 105 at San Antonio 145

WESTERN CONFERENCE FINALS
Los Angeles 4, San Antonio 2
May 8—Sun.—San Antonio 107 at Los Angeles 119
May 10—Tue.—San Antonio 122 at Los Angeles 113
May 13—Fri.—Los Angeles 113 at San Antonio 100
May 15—Sun.—Los Angeles 129 at San Antonio 121
May 18—Wed.—San Antonio 117 at Los Angeles 112
May 20—Fri.—Los Angeles 101 at San Antonio 100

WORLD CHAMPIONSHIP SERIES
Philadelphia 4, Los Angeles 0
May 22—Sun.—Los Angeles 107 at Philadelphia..........113
May 26—Thur.—Los Angeles 93 at Philadelphia 103
May 29—Sun.—Philadelphia 111 at Los Angeles...........94
May 31—Tue.—Philadelphia 115 at Los Angeles 108

°Overtime

1981-82 NBA STATISTICS

1981-82 NBA CHAMPION LOS ANGELES LAKERS

Front row (left to right): Owner Dr. Jerry Buss, Jim Brewer, Kurt Rambis, Jamaal Wilkes, Kareem Abdul-Jabbar, Michael Cooper, Norm Nixon, Earvin (Magic) Johnson, General Manager Bill Sharman. Back row: Head Coach Pat Riley, assistant coach Bill Bertka, Eddie Jordan, Kevin McKenna, Mitch Kupchak, Bob McAdoo, Mark Landsberger, Mike McGee, assistant coach Mike Thibault, trainer Jack Curran.

FINAL STANDINGS

ATLANTIC DIVISION

Team	Atl.	Bos.	Chi.	Cle.	Dal.	Den.	Det.	G.S.	Hous.	Ind.	K.C.	L.A.	Mil.	N.J.	N.Y.	Phi.	Pho.	Por.	S.A.	S.D.	Sea.	Ut.	Wash.	W.	L.	Pct.	G.B.
Boston	5	..	4	5	2	1	6	1	1	4	2	1	3	5	5	4	1	1	2	2	..	2	6	63	19	.768	....
Philadelphia	3	2	5	5	2	1	3	2	1	6	2	1	2	3	5	..	1	2	..	2	2	2	6	58	24	.707	5
New Jersey	2	1	4	6	..	1	4	1	2	1	1	1	..	4	3	2	1	1	2	..	2	4		44	38	.537	19
Washington	4	..	4	5	1	..	4	1	..	5	2	..	2	2	5	..	1	2	1	2	1	1	..	43	39	.524	20
New York	1	1	2	6	1	1	3	1	1	2	..	2	3	2	..	1	..	1	..	2	..	2	1	33	49	.402	30

CENTRAL DIVISION

Team	Atl.	Bos.	Chi.	Cle.	Dal.	Den.	Det.	G.S.	Hous.	Ind.	K.C.	L.A.	Mil.	N.J.	N.Y.	Phi.	Pho.	Por.	S.A.	S.D.	Sea.	Ut.	Wash.	W.	L.	Pct.	G.B.
Milwaukee	3	3	5	6	1	1	4	..	1	6	1	2	..	4	3	4	1	2	1	2	..	2	3	55	27	.671	....
Atlanta	..	1	2	4	1	1	2	..	2	4	1	..	3	3	5	3	1	2	1	1	1	2	2	42	40	.512	13
Detroit	4	..	6	5	1	1	..	2	2	2	2	..	2	2	3	2	..	..	2	1	1	1		39	43	.476	16
Indiana	2	1	3	5	1	2	4	..	..	..	1	..	4	3	..	1	1	2	2	1	1	1		35	47	.427	20
Chicago	3	2	..	5	1	1	..	1	3	1	2	1	2	3	1	..	1	1	2	1	1	2		34	48	.415	21
Cleveland	2	..	1	..	2	..	1	1	1	1	1	..	..	..	1	..	1	..	2	1				15	67	.183	40

MIDWEST DIVISION

Team	Atl.	Bos.	Chi.	Cle.	Dal.	Den.	Det.	G.S.	Hous.	Ind.	K.C.	L.A.	Mil.	N.J.	N.Y.	Phi.	Pho.	Por.	S.A.	S.D.	Sea.	Ut.	Wash.	W.	L.	Pct.	G.B.
San Antonio	1	..	1	2	5	4	2	2	3	..	5	3	1	1	2	2	1	2	..	3	4	3	1	48	34	.585	....
Denver	1	1	1	2	5	..	1	3	5	..	4	1	1	1	1	1	2	2	2	5	2	3	2	46	36	.561	2
Houston	..	1	1	1	4	1	..	4	..	2	3	1	1	1	1	1	3	4	3	4	2	6	2	46	36	.561	2
Kansas City	1	..	1	1	2	2	..	2	3	1	..	1	1	1	2	..	2	..	1	4	2	3	..	30	52	.366	18
Dallas	1	..	1	..	..	1	1	..	2	1	4	1	1	2	1	..	2	2	1	2	1	3	1	28	54	.341	20
Utah	..	..	1	..	3	3	1	2	..	1	3	..	..	..	..	2	1	3	4	..	..	1		25	57	.305	23

PACIFIC DIVISION

Team	Atl.	Bos.	Chi.	Cle.	Dal.	Den.	Det.	G.S.	Hous.	Ind.	K.C.	L.A.	Mil.	N.J.	N.Y.	Phi.	Pho.	Por.	S.A.	S.D.	Sea.	Ut.	Wash.	W.	L.	Pct.	G.B.
Los Angeles	2	1	..	2	4	4	2	3	4	2	4	..	..	1	4	5	2	5	4	5	2	57	25	.695	....
Seattle	1	2	1	2	4	3	1	5	3	1	3	2	2	2	..	3	3	1	5	..	5	1	52	30	.634	5
Phoenix	1	1	2	2	3	2	2	2	1	3	2	1	..	2	1	..	3	4	4	3	3	1	46	36	.561	11
Golden State	2	1	2	1	5	2	..	1	2	3	3	2	1	1	..	4	2	3	5	1	3	1	45	37	.549	12
Portland	..	1	1	1	3	3	2	4	1	1	5	1	..	1	1	..	3	..	3	4	3	4	..	42	40	.512	15
San Diego	1	..	..	1	3	..	..	1	1	..	1	1	..	..	..	2	2	2	..	1	1	..	17	65	.207	40

HOME-ROAD RECORDS OF ALL TEAMS

	Home	Road	Total		Home	Road	Total
Atlanta	24- 17	18- 23	42- 40	Milwaukee	31- 10	24- 17	55- 27
Boston	35- 6	28- 13	63- 19	New Jersey	25- 16	19- 22	44- 38
Chicago	22- 19	12- 29	34- 48	New York	19- 22	14- 27	33- 49
Cleveland	9- 32	6- 35	15- 67	Philadelphia	32- 9	26- 15	58- 24
Dallas	16- 25	12- 29	28- 54	Phoenix	31- 10	15- 26	46- 36
Denver	29- 12	17- 24	46- 36	Portland	27- 14	15- 26	42- 40
Detroit	23- 18	16- 25	39- 43	San Antonio	29- 12	19- 22	48- 34
Golden State	28- 13	17- 24	45- 37	San Diego	11- 30	6- 35	17- 65
Houston	25- 16	21- 20	46- 36	Seattle	31- 10	21- 20	52- 30
Indiana	25- 16	10- 31	35- 47	Utah	18- 23	7- 34	25- 57
Kansas City	23- 18	7- 34	30- 52	Washington	22- 19	21- 20	43- 39
Los Angeles	30- 11	27- 14	57- 25	Total	565-378	378-565	943-943

OFFENSIVE TEAM STATISTICS

		FIELD GOALS			FREE THROWS			REBOUNDS				MISCELLANEOUS			Turn	Blk.	SCORING	
Team	G.	Att.	Made	Pct.	Att.	Made	Pct.	Off.	Def.	Tot.	Ast.	PF	Disq.	Stl.	Over	Sh.	Pts.	Avg.
Denver	82	7656	3980	.520	2978	2371	.796	1149	2443	3592	2272	2131	18	664	1470	368	10371	126.5
Los Angeles	82	7585	3919	.517	2161	1549	.717	1258	2505	3763	2356	1999	11	848	1468	517	9400	114.6
San Antonio	82	7613	3698	.486	2335	1812	.776	1253	2537	3790	2257	2217	28	600	1293	555	9272	113.1
Boston	82	7334	3657	.499	2457	1817	.740	1253	2489	3742	2126	2014	21	652	1452	568	9180	112.0
Philadelphia	82	6974	3616	.518	2471	1846	.747	1031	2389	3420	2264	2183	18	856	1474	622	9119	111.2
Detroit	82	7391	3561	.482	2581	1938	.751	1298	2345	3643	2027	2160	16	741	1629	564	9112	111.1
Utah	82	7446	3679	.494	2282	1714	.751	1147	2362	3509	1895	2196	20	700	1435	357	9094	110.9
Golden State	82	7349	3646	.496	2382	1709	.717	1282	2452	3734	1820	2225	32	685	1424	391	9092	110.9
Portland	82	7187	3629	.505	2387	1719	.720	1142	2355	3497	2054	2012	22	706	1390	367	9006	109.8
San Diego	82	7101	3552	.500	2341	1693	.723	1131	2196	3327	1878	2353	58	636	1570	299	8896	108.5
Milwaukee	82	7015	3544	.505	2329	1753	.753	1167	2415	3582	2233	2281	30	763	1589	455	8890	108.4
Seattle	82	7178	3505	.488	2362	1747	.740	1103	2544	3647	2103	2057	26	691	1351	460	8795	107.3
Kansas City	82	7284	3604	.495	2158	1551	.719	1086	2276	3362	2056	2359	50	743	1507	402	8785	107.1
New Jersey	82	7227	3501	.484	2354	1714	.728	1194	2320	3514	2096	2295	33	918	1650	481	8746	106.7
Chicago	82	6728	3369	.501	2545	1951	.767	1125	2525	3650	2043	2008	16	580	1636	483	8743	106.6
New York	82	7178	3523	.491	2171	1603	.738	1168	2273	3441	2075	2195	18	719	1486	338	8707	106.2
Phoenix	82	7140	3508	.491	2157	1635	.758	1123	2517	3640	2223	2029	34	753	1528	429	8705	106.2
Houston	82	7366	3504	.476	2225	1622	.729	1403	2284	3687	1977	1871	9	648	1321	429	8680	105.9
Dallas	82	7224	3390	.469	2366	1740	.735	1213	2228	3441	2117	2193	40	566	1317	313	8575	104.6
Washington	82	7168	3400	.474	2105	1626	.772	1047	2583	3630	1983	2072	32	643	1390	397	8485	103.5
Cleveland	82	7334	3405	.464	2179	1628	.747	1190	2170	3360	1871	2193	35	634	1319	357	8463	103.2
Indiana	82	7164	3332	.465	2176	1612	.741	1141	2372	3513	1897	2041	23	753	1393	494	8379	102.2
Atlanta	82	6776	3210	.474	2387	1833	.768	1135	2368	3503	1815	2268	29	608	1343	485	8281	101.0

DEFENSIVE TEAM STATISTICS

	FIELD GOALS			FREE THROWS			REBOUNDS				MISCELLANEOUS			Turn	Blk.	SCORING		Pt.
Team	Att.	Made	Pct.	Att.	Made	Pct.	Off.	Def.	Tot.	Ast.	PF	Disq.	Stl.	Over	Sh.	Pts.	Avg.	Dif.
Atlanta	6709	3150	.470	2482	1891	.762	1135	2388	3523	2179	21	578	1444	434	8237	100.5	+ 0.5
Washington	7229	3362	.465	2237	1645	.735	1110	2516	3626	1889	1907	18	624	1325	543	8413	102.6	+ 0.9
Phoenix	7186	3350	.466	2215	1671	.754	1158	2366	3524	1949	2064	18	775	1391	360	8422	102.7	+ 3.5
Milwaukee	7066	3297	.467	2470	1790	.725	1172	2155	3327	2016	2189	25	720	1538	350	8441	102.9	+ 5.5
Seattle	7407	3411	.461	2183	1586	.727	1241	2420	3661	1994	2150	26	660	1405	311	8456	103.1	+ 4.1
Indiana	7062	3470	.491	2133	1558	.730	1204	2598	3802	2053	2016	14	648	1517	397	8532	104.0	- 1.9
Philadelphia	7083	3371	.476	2496	1852	.742	1289	2344	3633	1965	2216	44	702	1615	470	8649	105.5	+ 5.7
Boston	7429	3490	.470	2172	1638	.754	1193	2247	3440	1972	2240	31	681	1432	367	8657	105.6	+ 6.4
Houston	7180	3566	.497	2011	1503	.747	1170	2304	3474	2128	2047	36	678	1341	353	8683	105.9	- 0.0
New Jersey	6934	3343	.482	2597	1946	.749	1142	2346	3488	1931	2164	22	832	1809	539	8690	106.0	+ 0.7
Chicago	7388	3659	.495	2053	1533	.747	1134	2225	3359	2043	2220	25	807	1257	469	8909	108.6	- 2.0
New York	7018	3541	.505	2369	1793	.757	1125	2366	3491	2089	2017	27	703	1462	358	8926	108.9	- 2.7
Dallas	6953	3530	.508	2491	1847	.741	1108	2361	3469	1984	2243	23	643	1370	509	8938	109.0	- 4.4
Portland	7293	3637	.499	2149	1629	.758	1221	2367	3588	2114	2142	31	708	1452	427	8957	109.2	+ 0.6
Los Angeles	7679	3745	.488	2008	1433	.714	1275	2255	3530	2319	2004	25	718	1483	435	9001	109.8	+ 4.9
Golden State	7250	3555	.490	2466	1857	.753	1112	2407	3519	2079	2156	26	661	1368	393	9007	109.8	+ 1.0
Kansas City	6984	3493	.500	2653	2005	.756	1171	2552	3723	1853	2136	30	707	1609	450	9039	110.2	- 3.1
San Antonio	7385	3566	.483	2497	1893	.758	1151	2434	3585	2036	2179	30	661	1352	429	9083	110.8	+ 2.3
Cleveland	7044	3608	.512	2529	1906	.754	1125	2529	3654	2169	2071	17	655	1405	480	9161	111.7	- 8.5
Detroit	7362	3749	.509	2211	1648	.745	1159	2434	3593	2191	2383	40	782	1637	581	9187	112.0	- 0.9
San Diego	7105	3739	.526	2647	1988	.751	1033	2276	3309	2129	2124	19	772	1334	487	9502	115.9	- 7.4
Utah	7530	3835	.509	2466	1837	.745	1253	2599	3852	2148	2052	23	663	1413	420	9558	116.6	- 5.7
Denver	8142	4265	.524	2354	1734	.737	1358	2459	3817	2516	2453	48	749	1476	569	10328	126.0	- 0.5

Disq—Individual players disqualified (fouled out of game)

INDIVIDUAL LEADERS

POINTS
Minimum 70 games played or 1,400 points

	G.	FG	FT	Pts.	Avg.		G.	FG	FT	Pts.	Avg.
Gervin, San Antonio	79	993	555	2551	32.3	Issel, Denver	81	651	546	1852	22.9
Malone, Houston	81	945	630	2520	31.1	Long, Detroit	69	637	238	1514	21.9
Dantley, Utah	81	904	648	2457	30.3	Tripucka, Detroit	82	636	495	1772	21.6
English, Denver	82	855	372	2082	25.4	Vandeweghe, Denver	82	706	347	1760	21.5
Erving, Philadelphia	81	780	411	1974	24.4	Vincent, Dallas	81	719	293	1732	21.4
Abdul-Jabbar, L.A.	76	753	312	1818	23.9	Wilkes, Los Angeles	82	744	246	1734	21.1
Williams, Seattle	80	773	320	1875	23.4	Thompson, Portland	79	681	280	1642	20.8
King, Golden State	79	740	352	1833	23.2	Mitchell, Clev.-S.A.	84	753	220	1726	20.5
Free, Golden State	78	650	479	1789	22.9	R. Williams, New Jersey	82	639	387	1674	20.4
Bird, Boston	77	711	328	1761	22.9	Parish, Boston	80	669	252	1590	19.9

FIELD GOALS
Minimum 300 FG Made

	FGA	FGM	Pct.
Gilmore, Chicago	837	546	.652
S. Johnson, Kansas City	644	395	.613
B. Williams, New Jersey	881	513	.582
Abdul-Jabbar, Los Angeles	1301	753	.579
Natt, Portland	894	515	.576
Dantley, Utah	1586	904	.570
King, Golden State	1307	740	.566
B. Jones, Philadelphia	737	416	.564
Cartwright, New York	694	390	.562
Ruland, Washington	749	420	.561

FREE THROWS
Minimum 125 FT Made

	FTA	FTM	Pct.
Macy, Phoenix	169	152	.899
Criss, Atlanta-San Diego	159	141	.887
Long, Detroit	275	238	.865
Gervin, San Antonio	642	555	.864
Bird, Boston	380	328	.863
Silas, Cleveland	286	246	.860
Newlin, New York	147	126	.857
Vandeweghe, Denver	405	347	.857
Grevey, Washington	193	165	.855
Sikma, Seattle	523	447	.855

ASSISTS
Minimum 70 games or 400 assists

	G.	No.	Avg.
Moore, San Antonio	79	762	9.6
E. Johnson, Los Angeles	78	743	9.5
Cheeks, Philadelphia	79	667	8.4
Archibald, Boston	68	541	8.0
Nixon, Los Angeles	82	652	8.0
Thomas, Detroit	72	565	7.8
Green, Utah	81	630	7.8
Huston, Cleveland	78	590	7.6
Ransey, Portland	78	555	7.1
Richardson, New York	82	572	7.0

STEALS
Minimum 70 games or 125 steals

	G.	No.	Avg.
E. Johnson, Los Angeles	78	208	2.67
Cheeks, Philadelphia	79	209	2.65
Richardson, New York	82	213	2.60
Buckner, Milwaukee	70	174	2.49
R. Williams, New Jersey	82	199	2.43
Green, Utah	81	185	2.28
Williams, Seattle	80	172	2.15
Thomas, Detroit	72	150	2.08
Moore, San Antonio	79	163	2.06
Buse, Indiana	82	164	2.00

REBOUNDS
Minimum 70 games or 800 rebounds

	G.	Off.	Def.	Tot.	Avg.
Malone, Houston	81	558	630	1188	14.7
Sikma, Seattle	82	223	815	1038	12.7
B. Williams, New Jersey	82	347	658	1005	12.3
Thompson, Portland	79	258	663	921	11.7
Lucas, New York	80	274	629	903	11.3
Smith, Golden State	74	279	534	813	11.0
Bird, Boston	77	200	637	837	10.9
Parish, Boston	80	288	578	866	10.8
Gilmore, Chicago	82	224	611	835	10.2
Robinson, Phoenix	74	202	519	721	9.7

BLOCKED SHOTS
Minimum 70 games or 100 blocked shots

	G.	No.	Avg.
G. Johnson, San Antonio	75	234	3.12
Rollins, Atlanta	79	224	2.84
Abdul-Jabbar, Los Angeles	76	207	2.72
Gilmore, Chicago	82	221	2.70
Parish, Boston	80	192	2.40
McHale, Boston	82	185	2.26
Williams, Indiana	82	178	2.17
Tyler, Detroit	82	160	1.95
C. Jones, Philadelphia	81	146	1.80
Erving, Philadelphia	81	141	1.74

3-PT. FIELD GOALS
Minimum 25 made

	FGA	FGM	Pct.
Russell, New York	57	25	.439
Toney, Philadelphia	59	25	.424
Macy, Phoenix	100	39	.390
Winters, Milwaukee	93	36	.387
Buse, Indiana	189	73	.386
Dunleavy, Houston	86	33	.384
Aguirre, Dallas	71	25	.352
Grevey, Washington	82	28	.341
Bratz, San Antonio	138	46	.333
Hassett, Golden State	214	71	.332

TEAM-BY-TEAM INDIVIDUAL STATISTICS

°Did not finish season with team.

ATLANTA HAWKS

Player	G.	Min.	FGA	FGM	Pct.	FTA	FTM	Pct.	Off. Reb.	Def. Reb.	Tot. Reb.	Ast.	PF	Dsq.	Stl.	Blk. Sh.	Pts.	Avg.	Hi.
Roundfield	61	2217	910	424	.466	375	285	.760	227	494	721	162	210	3	64	93	1134	18.6	35
Drew	70	2040	957	465	.486	491	364	.741	169	206	375	96	250	6	64	3	1298	18.5	35
Johnson	68	2314	1011	455	.450	385	294	.764	63	128	191	358	188	1	102	16	1211	17.8	35
Williams (Tot)	60	997	623	276	.443	166	140	.843	23	39	62	86	103	1	29	0	720	12.0	32
Williams (Atl)	23	189	110	42	.382	26	22	.846	2	10	12	9	18	0	6	0	110	4.8	15
Sparrow	82	2610	730	366	.501	148	124	.838	53	171	224	424	240	2	87	13	857	10.5	22
McMillen	73	1792	572	291	.509	170	140	.824	102	234	336	129	202	1	25	24	723	9.9	26
Hawes	49	1317	370	178	.481	126	96	.762	89	231	320	142	156	4	36	34	456	9.3	19
°Criss	27	552	210	84	.400	73	65	.890	6	32	38	75	40	0	23	2	235	8.7	31
Glenn	49	833	291	158	.543	67	59	.881	5	56	61	87	80	0	26	3	376	7.7	26
Macklin	79	1516	484	210	.434	173	134	.775	113	150	263	47	225	5	40	20	554	7.0	30
Matthews	47	837	298	131	.440	79	60	.759	19	39	58	139	129	3	53	2	324	6.9	27
McElroy	20	349	125	52	.416	36	29	.806	6	11	17	39	44	0	8	3	134	6.7	16
Rollins	79	2018	346	202	.584	129	79	.612	168	443	611	59	285	4	35	224	483	6.1	26
°Wood	19	238	105	36	.343	28	20	.714	22	22	44	11	34	0	9	1	92	4.8	17
Pellom	69	1037	251	114	.454	79	61	.772	90	139	229	28	164	0	29	47	289	4.2	17
°Shelton	4	21	6	2	.333	2	1	.500	2	1	3	0	3	0	1	0	5	1.3	4

3-Pt. FG: Atlanta 28-128 (.219)—Roundfield 1-5 (.200); Drew 4-12 (.333); Johnson 7-30 (.233); Williams (Tot.) 28-94 (.298); Williams (Atl.) 4-20 (.200); Sparrow 1-15 (.067); McMillen 1-3 (.333); Hawes 4-10 (.400); °Criss 2-8 (.250); Glenn 1-2 (.500); Macklin 0-3 (.000); Matthews 2-8 (.250); McElroy 1-5 (.200); °Wood 0-6 (.000); Pellom 0-1 (.000). Opponents 46-186 (.247).

BOSTON CELTICS

Player	G.	Min.	FGA	FGM	Pct.	FTA	FTM	Pct.	Off. Reb.	Def. Reb.	Tot. Reb.	Ast.	PF	Dsq.	Stl.	Blk. Sh.	Pts.	Avg.	Hi.
Bird	77	2923	1414	711	.503	380	328	.863	200	637	837	447	244	0	143	66	1761	22.9	40
Parish	80	2534	1235	669	.542	355	252	.710	288	578	866	140	267	5	68	192	1590	19.9	37
Maxwell	78	2590	724	397	.548	478	357	.747	218	281	499	183	263	6	79	49	1151	14.8	31
McHale	82	2332	875	465	.531	248	187	.754	191	365	556	91	264	1	30	185	1117	13.6	28
Archibald	68	2167	652	308	.472	316	236	.747	25	91	116	541	131	1	52	3	858	12.6	26
Henderson	82	1844	705	353	.501	172	125	.727	47	105	152	252	199	3	82	11	833	10.2	27
Carr	56	1296	409	184	.450	116	82	.707	56	94	150	128	136	2	67	21	455	8.1	22
Ford	76	1591	450	188	.418	56	39	.696	52	56	108	142	143	0	42	10	435	5.7	15
Robey	80	1186	375	185	.493	157	84	.535	114	181	295	68	183	2	27	14	454	5.7	17
Ainge	53	564	221	79	.357	65	56	.862	25	31	56	87	86	1	37	3	219	4.1	17
Duerod	21	146	77	34	.442	12	4	.333	6	9	15	12	9	0	3	1	72	3.4	12
Bradley	51	339	122	55	.451	62	42	.677	12	26	38	22	61	0	14	6	152	3.0	10
☆Jackson	11	66	26	10	.385	10	6	.600	7	5	12	5	5	0	3	0	26	2.4	4
Fernsten	43	202	49	19	.388	30	19	.633	12	30	42	8	23	0	5	7	57	1.3	6

3-Pt. FG: Boston 49-184 (.266)—Bird 11-52 (.212); Maxwell 0-3 (.000); Archibald 6-16 (.375); Henderson 2-12 (.167); Carr 5-17 (.294); Ford 20-63 (.317); Robey 0-2 (.000); Ainge 5-17 (.294); Duerod 0-1 (.000); Bradley 0-1 (.000). Opponents 39-203 (.192).

CHICAGO BULLS

Player	G.	Min.	FGA	FGM	Pct.	FTA	FTM	Pct.	Off. Reb.	Def. Reb.	Tot. Reb.	Ast.	PF	Dsq.	Stl.	Blk. Sh.	Pts.	Avg.	Hi.
Gilmore	82	2796	837	546	.652	552	424	.768	224	611	835	136	287	4	49	221	1517	18.5	33
Theus	82	2838	1194	560	.469	449	363	.808	115	197	312	476	243	1	87	16	1508	18.4	36
Greenwood	82	2914	1014	480	.473	291	240	.825	192	594	786	262	292	1	70	92	1200	14.6	35
Sobers	80	1938	801	363	.453	254	195	.768	37	105	142	301	238	6	73	18	940	11.8	28
Lester	75	2252	657	329	.501	256	208	.813	75	138	213	362	158	2	80	14	870	11.6	27
Jones	78	2040	572	303	.530	238	172	.723	156	351	507	114	217	0	49	36	779	10.0	21
Woolridge	75	1188	394	202	.513	206	144	.699	82	145	227	81	152	1	23	24	548	7.3	24
Kenon	60	1036	412	192	.466	88	50	.568	72	108	180	65	71	0	30	7	434	7.2	22
Wilkes	57	862	266	128	.481	80	58	.725	62	97	159	64	112	0	30	18	314	5.5	20
Blume	49	546	222	102	.459	28	18	.643	14	27	41	68	57	0	23	2	226	4.6	18
Jackson (Tot.)	49	478	172	79	.459	49	38	.776	35	28	63	27	48	0	14	3	196	4.0	17
Jackson (Chi.)	38	412	146	69	.473	39	32	.821	28	23	51	22	43	0	11	3	170	4.5	17
☆Robinson	3	29	9	3	.333	4	4	1.000	3	0	3	0	1	0	0	0	10	3.3	6
Dietrick	74	999	200	92	.460	54	38	.704	63	125	188	87	131	1	49	30	222	3.0	12
☆Burkman	6	30	4	0	.000	6	5	.833	2	4	6	5	6	0	6	2	5	0.8	2

3-Pt. FG: Chicago 54-213 (.254);—Gilmore 1-1 (1.000); Theus 25-100 (.250); Greenwood 0-3 (.000); Sobers 19-76 (.250); Lester 4-8 (.500); Jones 1-1 (1.000); Woolridge 0-3 (.000); Wilkes 0-1 (.000); Blume 4-18 (.222); Dietrick 0-1 (.000); ☆Burkman 0-1 (.000). Opponents 58-194 (.299).

CLEVELAND CAVALIERS

Player	G.	Min.	FGA	FGM	Pct.	FTA	FTM	Pct.	Off. Reb.	Def. Reb.	Tot. Reb.	Ast.	PF	Dsq.	Stl.	Blk. Sh.	Pts.	Avg.	Hi.
☆Mitchell	27	·973	504	229	.454	100	72	.720	71	70	141	39	77	0	27	15	530	19.6	36
Brewer (Tot.)	72	2319	1194	569	.477	260	211	.812	55	106	161	188	151	0	82	30	1357	18.8	44
Brewer (Clev.)	47	1724	833	387	.465	172	134	.779	42	69	111	121	114	0	59	23	913	19.4	32
Robinson (Tot)	68	2175	1143	518	.453	313	222	.709	174	435	609	120	222	4	88	103	1258	18.5	38
Robinson (Clev)	30	946	435	196	.451	133	97	.729	91	196	287	49	102	3	42	43	489	16.3	34
Edwards	77	2539	1033	528	.511	339	232	.684	189	392	581	123	347	17	24	117	1288	16.7	31
☆Carr	46	1482	524	271	.517	220	145	.659	114	280	394	63	180	0	58	16	688	15.0	32
Moore	4	70	38	19	.500	8	6	.750	1	3	4	15	15	1	6	1	45	11.3	20
Silas	67	1447	573	251	.438	286	246	.860	26	83	109	222	109	0	40	6	748	11.2	31
Wilkerson	65	1805	679	284	.418	185	145	.784	60	190	250	237	188	3	92	25	716	11.0	28
Wedman	54	1638	589	260	.441	90	66	.733	128	176	304	133	189	4	73	14	591	10.9	30
Huston	78	2409	672	325	.484	200	153	.765	53	97	150	590	169	1	70	11	806	10.3	26
Hubbard (Tot.)	83	1839	665	326	.490	280	191	.682	187	286	473	91	292	3	65	19	843	10.2	21
Hubbard (Clev)	31	735	255	119	.467	117	85	.726	86	115	201	24	116	2	27	3	323	10.4	21
☆Johnson	23	617	175	94	.537	44	35	.795	43	82	125	22	73	1	6	17	223	9.7	19
☆Phegley	27	566	214	104	.486	45	36	.800	28	43	71	53	63	0	16	2	248	9.2	18
☆Laimbeer	50	894	253	119	.470	120	93	.775	124	153	277	45	170	5	22	30	334	6.7	30
Washington	18	313	115	50	.435	15	9	.600	32	43	75	15	51	0	8	2	109	6.1	12
Branson	10	176	52	21	.404	12	11	.917	-14	19	33	6	17	0	5	4	53	5.3	13
Evans (Tot.)	22	270	86	35	.407	20	13	.650	5	17	22	42	36	1	13	0	83	3.8	12
Evans (Clev.)	8	74	35	11	.314	8	5	.625	2	8	10	20	10	0	4	0	27	3.4	12
Mokeski (Tot.)	67	868	193	84	.435	63	48	.762	59	149	208	35	171	2	33	40	216	3.2	11
Mokeski (Cle.)	28	345	82	35	.427	30	23	.767	24	62	86	11	68	0	20	17	93	3.3	11
Herron	30	269	106	39	.368	8	7	.875	10	11	21	23	25	0	8	2	85	2.8	12
☆Dillard	33	221	79	29	.367	23	15	.652	6	9	15	34	40	0	8	2	73	2.2	8
☆Bennett	3	23	4	2	.500	6	1	.167	1	2	3	0	2	0	1	0	5	1.7	4
Restani (Tot.)	47	483	88	32	.364	16	10	.625	39	73	112	22	56	0	11	11	74	1.6	10
Restani (Clev)	34	338	60	23	.383	12	7	.583	31	46	77	15	40	0	10	7	53	1.6	10
☆Ford	21	201	24	9	.375	6	5	.833	14	21	35	11	30	0	8	0	23	1.1	6

3-Pt. FG: Cleveland 25-137 (.182)—☆Mitchell 0-6 (.000); Brewer (Tot.) 8-31 (.258); Brewer (Clev.) 5-21 (.238); Robinson (Tot.) 0-4 (.000); Robinson (Clev.) 0-1 (.000); Edwards 0-4 (.000); ☆Carr 1-9 (.111); Moore 1-5 (.200); Silas 0-5 (.000); Wilkerson 3-18 (.167); Wedman 5-23 (.217); Huston 3-10 (.300); Hubbard (Tot.) 0-4 (.000); Hubbard (Clev.) 0-1 (.000); ☆Phegley 4-13 (.308); ☆Laimbeer 3-6 (.500); Washington 0-2 (.000); Evans (Tot.) 0-6 (.000); Evans (Clev.) 0-4 (.000); Mokeski (Tot.) 0-3 (.000); Mokeski (Clev.) 0-2 (.000); Herron 0-1 (.000); ☆Dillard 0-4 (.000); Restani (Tot.) 0-2 (.000); Restani (Clev.) 0-1 (.000); ☆Ford 0-1 (.000). Opponents 39-131 (.298).

DALLAS MAVERICKS

Player	G.	Min.	FGA	FGM	Pct.	FTA	FTM	Pct.	Off. Reb.	Def. Reb.	Tot. Reb.	Ast.	PF	Dsq.	Stl.	Blk. Sh.	Pts.	Avg.	Hi.
Vincent	81	2626	1448	719	.497	409	293	.716	182	383	565	176	308	8	89	22	1732	21.4	41
Aguirre	51	1468	820	381	.465	247	168	.680	89	160	249	164	152	0	37	22	955	18.7	42
Blackman	82	1979	855	439	.513	276	212	.768	97	157	254	105	122	0	46	30	1091	13.3	27
Davis	82	2614	771	397	.515	230	185	.804	35	191	226	509	218	5	73	6	993	12.1	32
Spanarkel	82	1755	564	270	.479	327	279	.853	99	111	210	206	140	0	86	9	827	10.1	24
Cooper	76	1818	669	281	.420	160	119	.744	200	350	550	115	285	10	37	106	682	9.0	22
Turner	80	1996	639	282	.441	138	97	.703	143	158	301	189	182	1	75	2	661	8.3	19
Bristow	82	2035	499	218	.437	164	134	.817	119	220	339	448	222	2	65	6	573	7.0	16
LaGarde	47	909	269	113	.420	166	86	.518	63	147	210	49	138	3	17	17	312	6.6	18
Nimphius	63	1085	297	137	.461	108	63	.583	92	203	295	61	190	5	17	82	337	5.3	20
Lloyd	74	1047	285	108	.379	91	69	.758	60	103	163	67	175	6	15	7	287	3.9	15
°Mack	13	150	59	19	.322	8	6	.750	8	10	18	14	6	0	5	1	44	3.4	12
Kea	35	248	49	26	.531	42	29	.690	26	35	61	14	55	0	4	3	81	2.3	10

3-Pt. FG: Dallas 55-190 (.289)—Vincent 1-4 (.250); Aguirre 25-71 (.352); Blackman 1-4 (.250); Davis 14-49 (.286); Spanarkel 8-24 (.333); Cooper 1-8 (.125); Turner 0-4 (.000); Bristow 3-18 (.167); LaGarde 0-2 (.000); Lloyd 2-4 (.500); °Mack 0-2 (.000). Opponents 31-138 (.225).

DENVER NUGGETS

Player	G.	Min.	FGA	FGM	Pct.	FTA	FTM	Pct.	Off. Reb.	Def. Reb.	Tot. Reb.	Ast.	PF	Dsq.	Stl.	Blk. Sh.	Pts.	Avg.	Hi.
English	82	3015	1553	855	.551	443	372	.840	210	348	558	433	261	2	87	120	2082	25.4	38
Issel	81	2472	1236	651	.527	655	546	.834	174	434	608	179	245	4	67	55	1852	22.9	39
Vandeweghe	82	2775	1260	706	.560	405	347	.857	149	312	461	247	217	1	52	29	1760	21.5	40
Thompson	61	1246	644	313	.486	339	276	.814	57	91	148	117	149	1	34	29	906	14.9	41
Robisch	12	257	106	48	.453	55	48	.873	14	49	63	32	29	0	3	4	144	12.0	18
McKinney	81	1963	699	369	.528	170	137	.806	29	113	142	338	186	0	69	16	875	10.8	26
Gondrezick	80	1699	495	250	.505	217	160	.737	140	283	423	152	229	0	92	36	660	8.3	24
Dunn	82	2519	504	258	.512	215	153	.712	211	348	559	188	210	1	135	36	669	8.2	23
Higgs	76	1696	468	202	.432	197	161	.817	23	121	144	395	263	8	72	6	569	7.5	27
Hordges	77	1372	414	204	.493	199	116	.583	119	276	395	65	230	1	26	19	527	6.8	19
Roche	39	501	150	68	.453	38	28	.737	4	19	23	89	40	0	15	2	187	4.8	24
Ray	40	262	116	51	.440	36	21	.583	18	47	65	26	59	0	10	16	124	3.1	11
°Burns (Tot.)	9	87	16	7	.438	15	9	.600	1	4	5	15	17	0	3	0	23	2.6	7
°Burns (Den.)	6	53	11	5	.455	9	6	.667	1	2	3	11	13	0	2	0	16	2.7	7

3-Pt. FG: Denver 40-149 (.268)—English 0-8 (.000); Issel 4-6 (.667); Vandeweghe 1-13 (.077); Thompson 4-14 (.286); McKinney 0-17 (.000); Gondrezick 0-3 (.000); Dunn 0-1 (.000); Higgs 4-21 (.190); Hordges 3-13 (.231); Roche 23-52 (.442); Ray 1-1 (1.000). Opponents 64-227 (.282).

DETROIT PISTONS

Player	G.	Min.	FGA	FGM	Pct.	FTA	FTM	Pct.	Off. Reb.	Def. Reb.	Tot. Reb.	Ast.	PF	Dsq.	Stl.	Blk. Sh.	Pts.	Avg.	Hi.
Long	69	2211	1294	637	.492	275	238	.865	95	162	257	148	173	0	65	25	1514	21.9	41
Tripucka	82	3077	1281	636	.496	621	495	.797	219	224	443	270	241	0	89	16	1772	21.6	49
Thomas	72	2433	1068	453	.424	429	302	.704	57	152	209	565	253	2	150	17	1225	17.0	34
Benson	75	2467	802	405	.505	158	127	.804	219	434	653	159	214	2	66	98	940	12.5	27
Carr (Tot.)	74	1926	692	348	.503	302	198	.656	167	364	531	86	249	0	64	22	895	12.1	32
Carr (Det.)	28	444	168	77	.458	82	53	.646	53	84	137	23	69	0	6	6	207	7.4	16
°Hubbard	52	1104	410	207	.505	163	106	.650	101	171	272	67	176	1	38	16	520	10.0	20
Tyler	82	1989	643	336	.523	192	142	.740	154	339	493	126	182	1	77	160	815	9.9	22
Laimbeer (Tot.)	80	1829	536	265	.494	232	184	.793	234	383	617	100	296	5	39	64	718	9.0	30
Laimbeer (Det.)	30	935	283	146	.516	112	91	.813	110	230	340	55	126	2	17	34	384	12.8	24
°Kelser	11	183	86	35	.407	41	27	.659	13	26	39	12	32	0	5	7	97	8.8	14
Jones	48	802	259	142	.548	129	90	.698	70	137	207	40	149	3	28	92	375	7.8	25
Johnson (Tot.)	74	1295	444	217	.489	142	107	.754	82	77	159	171	101	0	56	25	544	7.4	20
Johnson (Det.)	67	1191	422	208	.493	130	98	.754	75	69	144	160	93	0	50	23	517	7.7	20
Hayes (Tot.)	35	487	111	54	.486	53	32	.604	39	78	117	28	71	0	7	20	140	4.0	10
Hayes (Det.)	26	412	93	46	.495	41	25	.610	32	68	100	24	54	0	3	18	117	4.5	9
Hardy	38	310	136	62	.456	29	18	.621	14	20	34	20	32	0	9	4	142	3.7	13
Lee	81	1467	246	88	.358	119	84	.706	35	120	155	312	221	3	116	20	278	3.4	11
°Mokeski	39	523	111	49	.441	33	25	.758	35	87	122	24	103	2	13	23	123	3.2	9
Judkins	30	251	81	31	.383	26	16	.615	14	20	34	14	33	0	6	5	79	2.6	8
°Hagan	4	25	7	3	.429	1	1	1.000	2	2	4	8	7	0	3	0	7	1.8	5
°Wright	1	6	1	0	.000	0	0	.000	0	0	0	0	2	0	0	0	0	0.0	—

3-Pt. FG: Detroit 52-213 (.244)—Long 2-15 (.133); Tripucka 5-22 (.227); Thomas 17-59 (.288); Benson 3-11 (.273); Carr (Tot.) 1-10 (.100); Carr (Det.) 0-1 (.000); °Hubbard 0-3 (.000); Tyler 1-4 (.250); Laimbeer (Tot.) 4-13 (.308); Laimbeer (Det.) 1-7 (.143); °Kelser 0-3 (.000); Jones 1-2 (.500); Johnson (Tot.) 3-12 (.250); Johnson (Det.) 3-11 (.273); Hardy 0-5 (.000); Lee 18-59 (.305); °Mokeski 0-1 (.000); Judkins 1-10 (.100). Opponents 41-175 (.234).

GOLDEN STATE WARRIORS

Player	G.	Min.	FGA	FGM	Pct.	FTA	FTM	Pct.	Off. Reb.	Def. Reb.	Tot. Reb.	Ast.	PF	Dsq.	Stl.	Blk. Sh.	Pts.	Avg.	Hi.
King	79	2861	1307	740	.566	499	352	.705	140	329	469	282	285	6	78	23	1833	23.2	45
Free	78	2796	1452	650	.448	647	479	.740	118	130	248	419	222	1	71	8	1789	22.9	37
Carroll	76	2627	1016	527	.519	323	235	.728	210	423	633	64	265	8	64	127	1289	17.0	33
Short	76	1782	935	456	.488	221	177	.801	123	143	266	209	220	3	65	10	1095	14.4	35
Smith	74	2213	412	220	.534	159	88	.553	279	534	813	83	291	7	65	54	528	7.1	20
Romar	79	1259	403	203	.504	96	79	.823	12	86	98	226	103	0	60	13	488	6.2	17
Williams	59	1073	277	154	.556	89	49	.551	91	217	308	38	156	0	45	76	357	6.1	23
Hassett	68	787	382	144	.377	37	31	.838	13	40	53	104	94	1	30	3	390	5.7	20
Brown	82	1260	418	192	.459	122	86	.705	136	228	364	19	243	4	36	29	470	5.7	20
Gale	75	1793	373	185	.496	65	51	.785	37	152	189	261	173	1	121	28	421	5.6	14
Parker	71	899	245	116	.473	72	48	.667	73	104	177	89	101	0	39	11	280	3.9	15
Lloyd	16	95	45	25	.556	11	7	.636	9	7	16	6	20	0	5	1	57	3.6	11
McDowell	30	335	84	34	.405	41	27	.659	41	59	100	20	52	1	6	8	95	3.2	9

3-Pt. FG: Golden State 91-325 (.280)—King 1-5 (.200); Free 10-56 (.179); Carroll 0-1 (.000); Short 6-28 (.214); Smith 0-1 (.000); Romar 3-15 (.200); Hassett 71-214 (.332); Gale 0-5 (.000). Opponents 40-172 (.233).

HOUSTON ROCKETS

Player	G.	Min.	FGA	FGM	Pct.	FTA	FTM	Pct.	Off. Reb.	Def. Reb.	Tot. Reb.	Ast.	PF	Dsq.	Stl.	Blk. Sh.	Pts.	Avg.	Hi.
Malone	81	3398	1822	945	.519	827	630	.762	558	630	1188	142	208	0	76	125	2520	31.1	53
Hayes	82	3032	1100	519	.472	422	280	.664	267	480	747	144	287	4	62	104	1318	16.1	31
Reid	77	2913	958	437	.456	214	160	.748	175	336	511	314	297	2	115	48	1035	13.4	29
Leavell	79	2150	793	370	.467	135	115	.852	49	119	168	457	182	2	150	15	864	10.9	32
Murphy	64	1204	648	277	.427	110	100	.909	20	41	61	163	142	0	43	1	655	10.2	33
Willoughby	69	1475	464	240	.517	77	56	.727	107	157	264	75	146	1	31	59	539	7.8	19
Dunleavy	70	1315	450	206	.458	106	75	.708	24	80	104	227	161	0	45	3	520	7.4	19
Henderson	75	1721	403	183	.454	150	105	.700	33	105	138	306	120	0	55	7	471	6.3	19
Garrett	51	858	242	105	.434	26	17	.654	27	67	94	76	94	0	32	6	230	4.5	18
Jones	60	746	213	113	.531	77	42	.545	80	122	202	25	100	0	20	29	268	4.5	15
Spriggs	4	37	11	7	.636	2	0	.000	2	4	6	4	7	0	2	0	14	3.5	8
Paultz	65	807	226	89	.394	65	34	.523	54	126	180	41	99	0	15	22	212	3.3	12
Oldham	22	124	36	13	.361	14	8	.571	7	17	24	3	28	0	2	10	34	1.5	5

3-Pt. FG: Houston 50-176 (.284)—Malone 0-6 (.000); Hayes 0-5 (.000); Reid 1-10 (.100); Leavell 9-31 (.290); Murphy 1-16 (.063); Willoughby 3-7 (.429); Dunleavy 33-86 (.384); Henderson 0-2 (.000); Garrett 3-10 (.300); Jones 0-3 (.000). Opponents 48-202 (.238).

INDIANA PACERS

Player	G.	Min.	FGA	FGM	Pct.	FTA	FTM	Pct.	Off. Reb.	Def. Reb.	Tot. Reb.	Ast.	PF	Dsq.	Stl.	Blk. Sh.	Pts.	Avg.	Hi.
Davis	82	2664	1153	538	.467	394	315	.799	72	106	178	346	176	1	76	11	1396	17.0	34
Knight	81	1803	764	378	.495	282	233	.826	97	160	257	118	132	0	63	14	998	12.3	34
°Bantom	39	1037	406	178	.438	153	101	.660	87	127	214	68	139	5	38	24	458	11.7	28
Williams	82	2277	854	407	.477	188	126	.670	175	430	605	139	200	0	53	178	942	11.5	26
Orr	80	1951	719	357	.497	254	203	.799	127	204	331	134	182	1	56	26	918	11.5	24
Owens	74	1599	636	299	.470	226	181	.801	142	230	372	127	259	7	41	37	780	10.5	26
Buse	82	2529	685	312	.455	123	100	.813	46	177	223	407	176	0	164	27	797	9.7	23
C. Johnson	79	1979	641	312	.487	189	123	.651	184	387	571	127	241	3	60	112	747	9.5	20
Carter	75	1035	402	188	.468	70	58	.829	30	49	79	60	110	0	34	11	442	5.9	20
G. Johnson	59	720	291	120	.412	80	60	.750	72	145	217	40	147	2	36	25	300	5.1	15
McGinnis	76	1341	378	141	.373	159	72	.453	93	305	398	204	198	4	96	28	354	4.7	17
Sichting	51	800	194	91	.469	38	29	.763	14	41	55	117	63	0	33	1	212	4.2	16
°Townsend	14	95	41	11	.268	20	11	.550	2	11	13	10	18	0	3	0	35	2.5	6

3-Pt. FG: Indiana 103-316 (.326)—Davis 5-27 (.185); Knight 9-32 (.281); °Bantom 1-3 (.333); Williams 2-7 (.286); Orr 1-8 (.125); Owens 1-2 (.500); Buse 73-189 (.386); Carter 8-25 (.320); G. Johnson 0-2 (.000); McGinnis 0-3 (.000); Sichting 1-9 (.111); °Townsend 2-9 (.222). Opponents 34-183 (.186).

KANSAS CITY KINGS

Player	G.	Min.	FGA	FGM	Pct.	FTA	FTM	Pct.	Off. Reb.	Def. Reb.	Tot. Reb.	Ast.	PF	Dsq.	Stl.	Blk. Sh.	Pts.	Avg.	Hi.
°Robinson (Tot.)	38	1229	708	322	.455	180	125	.694	83	239	322	71	120	1	46	60	769	20.2	38
Woodson (Tot.)	83	2221	1069	538	.503	286	221	.773	102	145	247	222	220	3	142	35	1304	15.7	28
Woodson (K.C.)	76	2186	1001	508	.507	254	198	.780	97	137	234	206	199	2	135	33	1221	16.1	28
S. Johnson	78	1741	644	395	.613	330	212	.642	152	307	459	91	372	25	39	89	1002	12.8	33
Grunfeld	81	1892	822	420	.511	229	188	.821	55	127	182	276	191	0	72	39	1030	12.7	26
King	80	2609	752	383	.509	285	201	.705	162	361	523	173	221	6	84	29	967	12.1	33
R. Johnson (Tot.)	75	1904	662	351	.530	156	118	.756	140	311	451	73	257	5	33	60	820	10.9	27
R. Johnson (K.C.)	31	783	293	163	.556	72	51	.708	54	135	189	31	117	4	20	27	377	12.2	27
Drew	81	1973	757	358	.473	189	150	.794	30	119	149	419	150	0	110	1	874	10.8	28
Ford	72	1952	649	285	.439	166	136	.819	24	81	105	451	160	0	63	1	713	9.9	24
E. Johnson	74	1517	643	295	.459	149	99	.664	128	194	322	109	210	6	50	14	690	9.3	23
Meriweather	18	380	91	47	.516	40	31	.775	25	63	88	17	68	1	13	21	125	6.9	18
Loder	71	1139	448	208	.464	107	77	.720	69	126	195	88	147	0	35	30	493	6.9	25
Dennard	30	607	121	62	.512	40	26	.650	47	86	133	42	81	0	35	8	150	5.0	13
°Lambert	42	493	139	60	.432	28	21	.750	36	91	127	24	80	0	12	10	142	3.4	13
°Lacey	2	20	5	3	.600	2	0	.000	0	4	4	4	2	0	2	1	6	3.0	6
Douglas	63	1093	140	70	.500	80	32	.400	111	179	290	35	210	5	15	38	172	2.7	15
Whitney	23	266	71	25	.352	7	4	.571	13	27	40	19	31	0	12	1	54	2.3	9

3-Pt. FG: Kansas City 26-130 (.200)—°Robinson 0-3 (.000); Woodson (Tot.) 7-25 (.280); Woodson (K.C.) 7-24 (.292); Grunfeld 2-14 (.143); R. Johnson (Tot.) 0-1 (.000); R. Johnson (K.C.) 0-1 (.000); Drew 8-27 (.296); Ford 7-32 (.219); E. Johnson 1-11 (.091); Loder 0-11 (.000); °Lambert 1-6 (.167); Whitney 0-1 (.000). Opponents 48-158 (.304).

LOS ANGELES LAKERS

Player	G.	Min.	FGA	FGM	Pct.	FTA	FTM	Pct.	Off. Reb.	Def. Reb.	Tot. Reb.	Ast.	PF	Dsq.	Stl.	Blk. Sh.	Pts.	Avg.	Hi.
Abdul-Jabbar	76	2677	1301	753	.579	442	312	.706	172	487	659	225	224	0	63	207	1818	23.9	41
Wilkes	82	2906	1417	744	.525	336	246	.732	153	240	393	143	240	1	89	24	1734	21.1	36
E. Johnson	78	2991	1036	556	.537	433	329	.760	252	499	751	743	223	1	208	34	1447	18.6	40
Nixon	82	3024	1274	628	.493	224	181	.808	38	138	176	652	264	3	132	7	1440	17.6	28
Kupchak	26	821	267	153	.573	98	65	.663	64	146	210	33	80	1	12	10	371	14.3	25
Cooper	76	2197	741	383	.517	171	139	.813	84	185	269	230	216	1	120	61	907	11.9	31
McAdoo	41	746	330	151	.458	126	90	.714	45	114	159	32	109	1	22	36	392	9.6	30
McGee	39	352	172	80	.465	53	31	.585	34	15	49	16	59	0	18	3	191	4.9	27
Rambis	64	1131	228	118	.518	117	59	.504	116	232	348	56	167	2	60	76	295	4.6	16
Landsberger	75	1134	329	144	.438	65	33	.508	164	237	401	32	134	0	10	7	321	4.3	17
Jordan	58	608	208	89	.428	54	43	.796	4	39	43	131	98	0	62	1	222	3.8	17
C. Johnson	7	65	20	11	.550	6	3	.500	8	4	12	7	13	0	3	5	25	3.6	14
Brewer	71	966	175	81	.463	19	7	.368	106	158	264	42	127	1	39	46	170	2.4	10
McKenna	36	237	87	28	.322	17	11	.647	18	11	29	14	45	0	10	2	67	1.9	8

3-Pt. FG: Los Angeles 13-94 (.138)—Abdul-Jabbar 0-3 (.000); Wilkes 0-4 (.000); E. Johnson 6-29 (.207); Nixon 3-12 (.250); Cooper 2-17 (.118); McAdoo 0-5 (.000); McGee 0-4 (.000); Rambis 0-1 (.000); Landsberger 0-2 (.000); Jordan 1-9 (.111); Brewer 1-6 (.167); McKenna 0-2 (.000). Opponents 78-213 (.366).

MILWAUKEE BUCKS

Player	G.	Min.	FGA	FGM	Pct.	FTA	FTM	Pct.	Off. Reb.	Def. Reb.	Tot. Reb.	Ast.	PF	Dsq.	Stl.	Blk. Sh.	Pts.	Avg.	Hi.
Moncrief	80	2980	1063	556	.523	573	468	.817	221	313	534	382	206	3	138	22	1581	19.8	39
Ma. Johnson	60	1900	760	404	.532	260	182	.700	153	211	364	213	142	1	59	35	990	16.5	32
Winters	61	1829	806	404	.501	156	123	.788	51	119	170	253	187	1	57	9	967	15.9	42
Lanier	74	1986	729	407	.558	242	182	.752	92	296	388	219	211	3	72	56	996	13.5	29
Buckner	70	2156	822	396	.482	168	110	.655	77	173	250	328	218	2	174	3	906	12.9	27
Mi. Johnson	76	1934	757	372	.491	291	233	.801	133	321	454	215	240	4	72	45	978	12.9	35
Bridgeman	41	924	433	209	.483	103	89	.864	37	88	125	109	91	0	28	3	511	12.5	31
May	65	1187	417	212	.508	193	159	.824	85	133	218	133	151	2	50	6	583	9.0	27
Smith	17	316	110	52	.473	12	10	.833	1	13	14	44	35	0	10	1	116	6.8	15
Cummings	78	1132	430	219	.509	91	67	.736	61	184	245	99	227	6	22	8	505	6.5	20
°Dandridge	11	174	55	21	.382	17	10	.588	4	13	17	13	25	0	5	2	52	4.7	11
Lister	80	1186	287	149	.519	123	64	.520	108	279	387	84	239	4	18	118	362	4.5	18
°Stacom	7	90	34	14	.412	2	1	.500	2	5	7	6	6	0	1	0	30	4.3	10
Holland (Tot.)	14	194	78	27	.346	6	3	.500	6	7	13	18	13	0	11	1	57	4.1	12
Holland (Mil.)	1	9	5	0	.000	2	0	.000	0	0	0	2	1	0	0	0	0	0.0	0
°Evans	14	196	51	24	.471	12	8	.667	3	9	12	22	26	1	9	0	56	4.0	12
Catchings	80	1603	224	94	.420	69	41	.594	129	227	356	97	237	3	42	135	229	2.9	9
Crompton	35	203	32	11	.344	15	6	.400	10	31	41	13	39	0	6	12	28	0.8	4

3-Pt. FG.: Milwaukee 49-164 (.299)—Moncrief 1-14 (.071); Ma. Johnson 0-4 (.000); Winters 36-93 (.387); Lanier 0-2 (.000); Buckner 4-15 (.267); Mi. Johnson 1-7 (.143); Bridgeman 4-9 (.444); May 0-4 (.000); Smith 2-10 (.200); Cummings 0-2 (.000); °Stacom 1-2 (.500); Holland (Tot.) 0-3 (.000); °Evans 0-2 (.000). Opponents 57-224 (.254).

NEW JERSEY NETS

Player	G.	Min.	FGA	FGM	Pct.	FTA	FTM	Pct.	Off. Reb.	Def. Reb.	Tot. Reb.	Ast.	PF	Dsq.	Stl.	Blk. Sh.	Pts.	Avg.	Hi.
R. Williams	82	2732	1383	639	.462	465	387	.832	117	208	325	488	302	9	199	43	1674	20.4	52
B. Williams	82	2825	881	513	.582	388	242	.624	347	658	1005	107	285	5	84	84	1268	15.5	29
Birdsong	37	1025	480	225	.469	127	74	.583	30	67	97	124	74	0	30	5	524	14.2	37
King	76	1694	812	391	.482	171	133	.778	105	207	312	142	261	4	64	36	918	12.1	24
°Woodson	7	145	68	30	.441	32	23	.719	5	8	13	16	21	1	7	2	83	11.9	19
O'Koren	80	2018	778	383	.492	189	135	.714	111	194	305	192	175	0	83	13	909	11.4	25
Cook	82	2090	803	387	.482	162	118	.728	52	103	155	319	196	2	146	24	899	11.0	29
Elmore	81	2100	652	300	.460	170	135	.794	167	274	441	100	280	6	92	92	735	9.1	25
Bailey (Tot.)	77	1468	505	261	.517	224	137	.612	127	264	391	65	270	5	42	83	659	8.6	22
Bailey (N.J.)	67	1288	440	230	.523	213	133	.624	110	233	343	52	228	3	39	76	593	8.9	22
Walker	77	1861	378	156	.413	194	141	.727	31	119	150	398	179	1	120	6	456	5.9	18
Gminski	64	740	270	119	.441	118	97	.822	70	116	186	41	69	0	17	48	335	5.2	20
°Tolbert	12	115	44	20	.455	8	4	.500	11	16	27	8	19	0	4	2	44	3.7	11
van Breda Kolff	41	452	82	41	.500	76	62	.816	17	31	48	32	63	1	12	13	144	3.5	12
Lacey (Tot.)	56	670	154	67	.435	37	27	.730	20	87	107	77	139	1	22	38	161	2.9	10
Lacey (N.J.)	54	650	149	64	.430	35	27	.771	20	83	103	73	137	1	20	37	155	2.9	10
°Burns	3	34	5	2	.400	6	3	.500	0	2	2	4	4	0	1	0	7	2.3	4
°Cooper	1	11	2	1	.500	0	0	.....	1	1	2	0	2	0	0	0	2	2.0	2

3-Pt. FG: New Jersey 30-146 (.205)—R. Williams 9-54 (.167); B. Williams 0-1 (.000); Birdsong 0-10 (.000); King 3-13 (.231); °Woodson 0-1 (.000); O'Koren 8-23 (.348); Cook 7-31 (.226); Walker 3-9 (.333); °Tolbert 0-1 (.000); van Breda Kolff 0-2 (.000); Lacey (Tot.) 0-1 (.000); Lacey (N.J.) 0-1 (.000). Opponents 58-187 (.310).

NEW YORK KNICKERBOCKERS

Player	G.	Min.	FGA	FGM	Pct.	FTA	FTM	Pct.	Off. Reb.	Def. Reb.	Tot. Reb.	Ast.	PF	Dsq.	Stl.	Blk. Sh.	Pts.	Avg.	Hi.
Richardson	82	3044	1343	619	.461	303	212	.700	177	388	565	572	317	3	213	41	1469	17.9	33
Lucas	80	2671	1001	505	.504	349	253	.725	274	629	903	179	309	4	68	70	1263	15.8	35
Cartwright	72	2060	694	390	.562	337	257	.763	116	305	421	87	208	2	48	65	1037	14.4	31
Russell	77	2358	858	410	.478	294	228	.776	86	150	236	284	221	1	77	12	1073	13.9	29
Williams	60	1521	628	349	.556	173	131	.757	100	127	227	142	153	0	77	16	831	13.9	34
Westphal	18	451	194	86	.443	47	36	.766	9	13	22	100	61	1	19	8	210	11.7	19
Smith	82	2033	748	348	.465	151	122	.808	53	102	155	255	199	1	91	1	821	10.0	26
Newlin	76	1507	615	286	.465	147	126	.857	36	55	91	170	194	2	33	3	705	9.3	31
Webster	82	1883	405	199	.491	170	108	.635	184	306	490	99	211	2	22	91	506	6.2	20
Knight	40	550	183	102	.557	25	17	.680	33	49	82	23	74	0	14	11	221	5.5	19
Carter	75	923	280	119	.425	80	64	.800	35	60	95	130	124	1	36	6	302	4.0	12
Bradley	39	331	103	54	.524	48	29	.604	31	34	65	11	37	0	12	5	137	3.5	17
Copeland	18	118	38	16	.421	6	5	.833	3	2	5	9	19	0	4	2	37	2.1	7
Demic	48	356	83	39	.470	39	14	.359	29	50	79	14	65	1	4	6	92	1.9	10
°Scales	3	24	5	1	.200	2	1	.500	2	3	5	0	3	0	1	1	3	1.0	2

3-Pt. FG: New York 58-214 (.271)—Richardson 19-101 (.188); Lucas 0-3 (.000); Russell 25-57 (.439); Williams 2-9 (.222); Westphal 2-8 (.250); Smith 3-11 (.273); Newlin 7-23 (.304); Bradley 0-1 (.000); Demic 0-1 (.000). Opponents 51-168 (.304).

PHILADELPHIA 76ers

Player	G.	Min.	FGA	FGM	Pct.	FTA	FTM	Pct.	Off. Reb.	Def. Reb.	Tot. Reb.	Ast.	PF	Dsq.	Stl.	Blk. Sh.	Pts.	Avg.	Hi.
Erving	81	2789	1428	780	.546	539	411	.763	220	337	557	319	229	1	161	141	1974	24.4	38
Toney	77	1909	979	511	.522	306	227	.742	43	91	134	283	269	5	64	17	1274	16.5	46
B. Jones	76	2181	737	416	.564	333	263	.790	109	284	393	189	211	3	99	112	1095	14.4	25
Cheeks	79	2498	676	352	.521	220	171	.777	51	197	248	667	247	0	209	33	881	11.2	27
Hollins	81	2257	797	380	.477	188	132	.702	35	152	187	316	198	1	103	20	894	11.0	25
Dawkins	48	1124	367	207	.564	164	114	.695	68	237	305	55	193	5	19	55	528	11.0	22
Bantom (Tot.)	82	2016	712	334	.469	267	168	.629	174	266	440	114	272	6	63	61	838	10.2	28
Bantom (Phil.)	43	979	306	156	.510	114	67	.588	87	139	226	46	133	0	25	37	380	8.8	22
C. Jones	81	2446	465	231	.497	219	179	.817	164	544	708	100	301	3	38	146	641	7.9	20
Mix	75	1235	399	202	.506	172	136	.791	92	133	225	93	86	0	42	17	541	7.2	21
Cureton	66	956	306	149	.487	94	51	.543	90	180	270	32	142	0	31	27	349	5.3	23
Richardson	77	1040	310	140	.452	88	69	.784	55	63	118	109	109	0	36	9	351	4.6	12
Edwards	42	291	150	65	.433	27	20	.741	10	17	27	45	37	0	16	5	150	3.6	13
Johnson	26	150	54	27	.500	7	6	.857	7	15	22	10	28	0	13	3	61	2.3	8

3-Pt. FG: Philadelphia 41-139 (.295)—Erving 3-11 (.273); Toney 25-59 (.424); B. Jones 0-3 (.000); Cheeks 6-22 (.273); Hollins 2-16 (.125); Dawkins 0-2 (.000); Bantom (Tot.) 2-6 (.333); Bantom (Phil.) 1-3 (.333); C. Jones 0-3 (.000); Mix 1-4 (.250); Cureton 0-2 (.000); Richardson 2-2 (1.000); Edwards 0-9 (.000); Johnson 1-3 (.333). Opponents 55-212 (.259).

PHOENIX SUNS

Player	G.	Min.	FGA	FGM	Pct.	FTA	FTM	Pct.	Off. Reb.	Def. Reb.	Tot. Reb.	Ast.	PF	Dsq.	Stl.	Blk. Sh.	Pts.	Avg.	Hi.
Johnson	80	2937	1228	577	.470	495	399	.806	142	268	410	369	253	6	105	55	1561	19.5	37
Robinson	74	2745	1128	579	.513	371	255	.687	202	519	721	179	215	2	42	28	1414	19.1	38
Adams	79	2393	1027	507	.494	233	182	.781	138	448	586	356	269	7	114	78	1196	15.1	32
Davis	55	1182	669	350	.523	111	91	.820	21	82	103	162	104	1	46	3	794	14.4	28
Macy	82	2845	945	486	.514	169	152	.899	78	183	261	384	185	1	143	9	1163	14.2	31
Kelley	81	1892	505	236	.467	223	167	.749	168	329	497	293	292	14	64	71	639	7.9	23
Nance	80	1186	436	227	.521	117	75	.641	95	161	256	82	169	2	42	71	529	6.6	29
Scott	81	1740	380	189	.497	148	108	.730	97	197	294	149	169	0	59	70	486	6.0	17
Cook	76	1298	358	151	.422	134	89	.664	112	189	301	100	174	1	37	23	391	5.1	16
Bradley	64	937	281	125	.445	100	74	.740	30	57	87	80	115	0	78	10	325	5.1	20
☆McCullough	8	23	13	9	.692	5	3	.600	1	3	4	3	3	0	2	0	21	2.6	7
Kramer	56	549	133	55	.414	42	33	.786	36	72	108	51	62	0	19	11	143	2.6	9
Dykema	32	103	37	17	.459	9	7	.778	3	9	12	15	19	0	2	0	43	1.3	6

3-Pt. FG: Phoenix 54-174 (.310)—Johnson 8-42 (.190); Robinson 1-1 (1.000); Adams 0-1 (.000); Davis 3-16 (.188); Macy 39-100 (.390); Kelley 0-1 (.000); Nance 0-1 (.000); Scott 0-2 (.000); Cook 0-2 (.000); Bradley 1-4 (.250); Dykema 2-4 (.500). Opponents 51-200 (.255).

PORTLAND TRAIL BLAZERS

Player	G.	Min.	FGA	FGM	Pct.	FTA	FTM	Pct.	Off. Reb.	Def. Reb.	Tot. Reb.	Ast.	PF	Dsq.	Stl.	Blk. Sh.	Pts.	Avg.	Hi.
Thompson	79	3129	1303	681	.523	446	280	.628	258	663	921	319	233	2	69	107	1642	20.8	38
Paxson	82	2756	1258	662	.526	287	220	.767	75	146	221	276	159	0	129	12	1552	18.9	33
Natt	75	2599	894	515	.576	392	294	.750	193	420	613	150	175	1	62	36	1326	17.7	34
Ransey	78	2418	1095	504	.460	318	242	.761	39	147	186	555	169	1	97	4	1253	16.1	33
Bates	75	1229	692	327	.473	211	166	.787	53	55	108	111	100	0	41	5	832	11.1	29
Gross	59	1377	322	173	.537	104	78	.750	101	158	259	125	162	2	75	41	427	7.2	18
Harper	68	1433	370	184	.497	153	96	.627	127	212	339	54	229	7	55	82	464	6.8	20
Valentine	82	1387	453	187	.413	200	152	.760	48	101	149	270	187	1	94	3	526	6.4	20
☆Washington	20	418	78	38	.487	41	24	.585	40	77	117	29	56	0	9	16	100	5.0	17
Verhoeven	71	1207	296	149	.503	72	51	.708	106	148	254	52	215	4	42	22	349	4.9	28
Lamp	54	617	196	100	.510	61	50	.820	24	40	64	28	83	0	16	1	250	4.6	21
Gudmundsson	68	845	166	83	.500	76	52	.684	51	135	186	59	163	2	13	30	219	3.2	18
Kunnert	21	237	48	20	.417	17	9	.529	20	46	66	18	51	1	3	6	49	2.3	9
Bailey	1	7	1	1	1.000	0	0	.000	0	0	0	2	0	0	0	0	2	2.0	2
☆Awtrey	10	121	15	5	.333	9	5	.556	7	7	14	8	28	1	1	2	15	1.5	5

3-Pt. FG: Portland 29-140 (.207)—Paxson 8-35 (.229); Natt 2-8 (.250); Ransey 3-38 (.079); Bates 12-41 (.293); Gross 3-6 (.500); Harper 0-1 (.000); Valentine 0-9 (.000); Lamp 0-1 (.000); Gudmundsson 1-1 (1.000). Opponents 54-206 (.262).

SAN ANTONIO SPURS

Player	G.	Min.	FGA	FGM	Pct.	FTA	FTM	Pct.	Off. Reb.	Def. Reb.	Tot. Reb.	Ast.	PF	Dsq.	Stl.	Blk. Sh.	Pts.	Avg.	Hi.
Gervin	79	2817	1987	993	.500	642	555	.864	138	254	392	187	215	2	77	45	2551	32.3	50
Mitchell (Tot.)	84	3063	1477	753	.510	302	220	.728	244	346	590	82	277	4	60	43	1726	20.5	45
Mitchell (S.A.)	57	2090	973	524	.539	202	148	.733	173	276	449	43	200	4	33	28	1196	21.0	45
☆Brewer	25	595	361	182	.504	88	77	.875	13	37	50	67	37	0	23	7	444	17.8	44
Olberding	68	2098	705	333	.472	338	273	.808	118	321	439	202	253	5	57	29	941	13.8	30
☆R. Johnson	21	504	194	94	.485	40	32	.800	43	94	137	20	67	0	7	16	220	10.5	20
Corzine	82	2189	648	336	.519	213	159	.746	211	418	629	130	235	3	33	126	832	10.1	25
Banks	80	1700	652	311	.477	212	145	.684	157	254	411	147	199	2	55	17	767	9.6	23
Moore	79	2294	667	309	.463	182	122	.670	62	213	275	762	254	6	163	12	741	9.4	27
Bratz	81	1616	565	230	.407	152	119	.783	40	126	166	438	183	0	65	11	625	7.7	28
Phegley (Tot.)	81	1183	507	233	.460	109	85	.780	61	93	154	114	152	0	36	8	556	6.9	18
Phegley (S.A.)	54	617	293	129	.440	64	49	.766	33	50	83	61	91	0	20	6	308	5.7	17
Rains	49	637	177	77	.435	64	38	.594	37	43	80	40	74	0	18	2	192	3.9	21
Griffin	23	459	66	32	.485	37	24	.649	29	66	95	54	67	0	20	8	88	3.8	16
Yonakor	10	70	26	14	.538	7	5	.714	13	14	27	3	7	0	1	2	33	3.3	11
Lambert (Tot.)	63	764	197	86	.437	42	34	.810	55	123	178	37	123	0	18	16	207	3.3	13
Lambert (S.A.)	21	271	58	26	.448	14	13	.929	19	32	51	13	43	0	6	6	65	3.1	10
G. Johnson	75	1578	195	91	.467	64	43	.672	152	302	454	79	259	6	20	234	225	3.0	10
☆Hayes	9	75	18	8	.444	12	7	.583	7	10	17	4	17	0	1	2	23	2.6	10
☆Restani	13	145	28	9	.321	4	3	.750	8	27	35	7	16	0	1	4	21	1.6	6

3-Pt. FG: San Antonio 64-252 (.254)—Gervin 10-36 (.278); Mitchell (Tot.) 0-7 (.000); Mitchell (S.A.) 0-1 (.000); ☆Brewer 3-10 (.300); Olberding 2-12 (.167); Corzine 1-4 (.250); Banks 0-8 (.000); Moore 1-21 (.048); Bratz 46-138 (.333); Phegley (Tot.) 5-31 (.161); Phegley (S.A.) 1-18 (.056); Rains 0-2 (.000); Lambert (Tot.) 1-7 (.143); Lambert (S.A.) 0-1 (.000); ☆Restani 0-1 (.000). Opponents 58-199 (.291).

SAN DIEGO CLIPPERS

Player	G.	Min.	FGA	FGM	Pct.	FTA	FTM	Pct.	Off. Reb.	Def. Reb.	Tot. Reb.	Ast.	PF	Dsq.	Stl.	Blk. Sh.	Pts.	Avg.	Hi.
Chambers	81	2682	1056	554	.525	458	284	.620	211	350	561	146	341	17	58	46	1392	17.2	39
☆Williams	37	808	513	234	.456	140	118	.843	21	29	50	67	85	1	23	0	610	16.5	32
Brooks	82	2750	1066	537	.504	267	202	.757	107	417	624	236	285	7	113	39	1276	15.6	37
Whitehead	72	2214	726	406	.559	241	184	.763	231	433	664	102	290	16	48	44	996	13.8	31
☆P. Smith	48	1446	575	253	.440	168	123	.732	34	83	117	233	151	0	45	19	634	13.2	30
Nater	21	575	175	101	.577	79	59	.747	46	146	192	30	64	1	6	9	262	12.5	20
Bryant	75	1988	701	341	.486	247	194	.785	79	195	274	189	250	1	78	29	884	11.8	32
Criss (Tot.)	55	1392	498	222	.446	159	141	.887	13	69	82	187	96	0	44	6	595	10.8	34
Criss (S.D.)	28	840	288	138	.479	86	76	.884	7	37	44	112	56	0	21	4	360	12.9	34
Taylor	41	1274	328	165	.503	110	90	.818	26	70	96	229	113	1	47	9	443	10.8	32
Wood (Tot.)	48	930	381	179	.470	119	93	.782	51	83	134	58	108	4	31	9	454	9.5	29
Wood (S.D.)	29	692	276	143	.518	91	73	.802	29	61	90	47	74	4	22	8	362	12.5	29
Wiley	61	1013	359	203	.565	141	98	.695	67	115	182	52	127	1	40	16	504	8.3	28
Douglas	64	1031	389	181	.465	102	67	.657	27	63	90	146	147	2	48	9	447	7.0	28
Brogan	63	1027	364	165	.453	84	61	.726	61	59	120	156	123	2	49	13	400	6.3	24
Hill (Tot.)	40	723	126	53	.421	55	39	.709	12	40	52	106	88	0	21	5	145	3.6	13
Hill (S.D.)	19	480	89	34	.382	32	22	.688	6	21	27	81	51	0	16	3	90	4.7	13
☆Davis	7	67	25	10	.400	6	3	.500	7	6	13	4	8	0	0	0	23	3.3	16

Player	G.	Min.	FGA	FGM	Pct.	FTA	FTM	Pct.	Off. Reb.	Def. Reb.	Tot. Reb.	Ast.	PF	Dsq.	Stl.	Blk. Sh.	Pts.	Avg.	Hi.
J. Smith	72	858	169	86	.509	85	39	.459	72	110	182	46	185	5	22	51	211	2.9	13
Lee	2	10	2	1	.500	4	0	.000	0	1	1	2	3	0	0	0	2	1.0	2

3-Pt. FG: San Diego 99-338 (.293)—Chambers 0-2 (.000); *Williams 24-74 (.324); Brooks 0-7 (.000); *P. Smith 5-24 (.208); Nater 1-1 (1.000); Bryant 8-30 (.267); Criss (Tot.) 10-29 (.345); Criss (S.D.) 8-21 (.381); Taylor 23-63 (.365); Wood (Tot.) 3-24 (.125); Wood (S.D.) 3-18 (.167); Wiley 0-5 (.000); Douglas 18-59 (.305); Brogan 9-32 (.281); Hill (Tot.) 0-2 (.000); Hill (S.D.) 0-2 (.000). Opponents 36-146 (.247).

SEATTLE SUPERSONICS

Player	G.	Min.	FGA	FGM	Pct.	FTA	FTM	Pct.	Off. Reb.	Def. Reb.	Tot. Reb.	Ast.	PF	Dsq.	Stl.	Blk. Sh.	Pts.	Avg.	Hi.
Williams	80	2876	1592	773	.486	436	320	.734	92	152	244	549	163	0	172	36	1875	23.4	42
Sikma	82	3049	1212	581	.479	523	447	.855	223	815	1038	277	268	5	102	107	1611	19.6	39
Shelton	81	2667	1046	508	.486	240	188	.783	161	348	509	252	317	12	99	43	1204	14.9	37
Smith (Tot.)	74	2042	761	340	.447	223	163	.731	51	135	186	307	213	0	67	27	848	11.5	30
Smith (Sea.)	26	596	186	87	.468	55	40	.727	17	52	69	74	62	0	22	8	214	8.2	17
Brown	82	1785	863	393	.455	129	111	.860	42	98	140	238	111	0	69	4	922	11.2	24
Walker	70	1965	629	302	.480	134	90	.672	108	197	305	218	215	2	36	28	694	9.9	24
Donaldson	82	1710	419	255	.609	240	151	.629	138	352	490	51	186	2	27	139	661	8.1	23
*Bailey	10	180	65	31	.477	11	4	.364	17	31	48	13	42	2	3	7	66	6.6	12
Hanzlik	81	1974	357	167	.468	176	138	.784	99	167	266	183	250	3	81	30	472	5.8	25
Kelser (Tot.)	60	741	271	116	.428	160	105	.656	80	113	193	57	131	0	18	21	337	5.6	19
Kelser (Sea.)	49	558	185	81	.438	119	78	.655	67	87	154	45	99	0	13	14	240	4.9	19
Vranes	77	1075	262	143	.546	148	89	.601	71	127	198	56	150	0	28	21	375	4.9	15
J. Johnson	14	187	45	22	.489	20	15	.750	3	15	18	29	20	0	4	3	59	4.2	8
*V. Johnson	7	104	22	9	.409	12	9	.750	7	8	15	11	8	0	6	2	27	3.9	9
Tolbert (Tot.)	64	607	202	100	.495	35	19	.543	50	76	126	33	83	0	12	16	219	3.4	11
Tolbert (Sea.)	52	492	158	80	.506	27	15	.556	39	60	99	25	64	0	8	14	175	3.4	11
Radford	43	369	100	54	.540	69	35	.507	13	16	29	57	65	0	16	2	145	3.4	15
*Hill	21	243	37	19	.514	23	17	.739	6	19	25	25	37	0	5	2	55	2.6	11

3-Pt. FG: Seattle 38-153 (.248)—Williams 9-40 (.225); Sikma 2-13 (.154); Shelton 0-8 (.000); Smith (Tot.) 5-27 (.185); Smith (Sea.) 0-3 (.000); Brown 25-77 (.325); Walker 0-2 (.000); Hanzlik 0-4 (.000); Kelser (Tot.) 0-3 (.000); Vranes 0-1 (.000); *V. Johnson 0-1 (.000); Tolbert (Tot.) 0-2 (.000); Tolbert (Sea.) 0-1 (.000); Radford 2-3 (.667). Opponents 48-201 (.239).

UTAH JAZZ

Player	G.	Min.	FGA	FGM	Pct.	FTA	FTM	Pct.	Off. Reb.	Def. Reb.	Tot. Reb.	Ast.	PF	Dsq.	Stl.	Blk. Sh.	Pts.	Avg.	Hi.
Dantley	81	3222	1586	904	.570	648	512	.792	231	283	514	324	252	1	95	14	2457	30.3	53
Griffith	80	2597	1429	689	.482	271	189	.697	128	177	305	187	213	0	95	34	1582	19.8	39
Green	81	2822	1015	500	.493	264	202	.765	85	158	243	630	183	0	185	9	1202	14.8	35
Wilkins	82	2274	718	314	.437	176	137	.778	120	491	611	90	248	4	32	77	765	9.3	37
Schayes	82	1623	524	252	.481	185	140	.757	131	296	427	146	292	4	46	72	644	7.9	22
Nicks	80	1322	555	252	.454	150	85	.567	67	94	161	89	184	0	66	4	589	7.4	19
Poquette	82	1698	428	220	.514	120	97	.808	117	294	411	94	235	4	51	65	540	6.6	20
Robinzine	56	651	294	131	.446	75	61	.813	56	88	144	49	156	5	37	5	323	5.8	18
Hardy	82	1814	369	179	.485	93	64	.688	153	317	470	110	192	2	58	67	422	5.1	19
Duren	79	1056	268	121	.451	37	27	.730	14	70	84	157	143	0	20	4	272	3.4	16
Wood	42	342	120	55	.458	52	34	.654	22	43	65	9	37	0	8	6	144	3.4	16
Cattage	49	337	135	60	.444	41	30	.732	22	51	73	7	58	0	7	0	150	3.1	15
*Worthen	5	22	5	2	.400	0	0	.000	1	0	1	3	3	0	0	0	4	0.8	4

3-Pt. FG: Utah 22-97 (.227)—Dantley 1-3 (.333); Griffith 15-52 (.288); Green 0-8 (.000); Wilkins 0-3 (.000); Schayes 0-1 (.000); Nicks 0-5 (.000); Poquette 3-10 (.300); Hardy 0-1 (.000); Duren 3-11 (.273); Wood 0-1 (.000); Cattage 0-2 (.000). Opponents 51-200 (.255).

WASHINGTON BULLETS

Player	G.	Min.	FGA	FGM	Pct.	FTA	FTM	Pct.	Off. Reb.	Def. Reb.	Tot. Reb.	Ast.	PF	Dsq.	Stl.	Blk. Sh.	Pts.	Avg.	Hi.
Ballard	79	2946	1307	621	.475	283	235	.830	136	497	633	250	204	0	137	22	1486	18.8	33
Ruland	82	2214	749	420	.561	455	342	.752	253	509	762	134	319	7	44	58	1183	14.4	28
Grevey	71	2164	857	376	.439	193	165	.855	57	138	195	149	151	1	44	23	945	13.3	26
Haywood	76	2086	829	395	.476	260	219	.842	144	278	422	64	249	6	45	68	1009	13.3	27
Mahorn	80	2664	816	414	.507	234	148	.632	149	555	704	150	349	12	57	138	976	12.2	26
Johnson	79	2027	812	336	.414	204	153	.750	34	113	147	380	196	1	76	7	842	10.7	27
Collins	79	1609	653	334	.511	169	121	.716	101	95	196	148	195	3	89	24	790	10.0	32
Lucas	79	1940	618	263	.426	176	138	.784	40	126	166	551	105	0	95	6	666	8.4	24
*Holland	13	185	73	27	.370	4	3	.750	6	7	13	16	12	0	11	1	57	4.4	12
Davis	54	575	184	88	.478	37	30	.811	54	79	133	31	89	0	13	6	206	3.8	20
Chones	59	867	171	74	.433	46	36	.783	39	146	185	64	114	1	15	32	184	3.1	19
Witts	46	493	84	49	.583	40	33	.825	29	33	62	38	74	1	17	4	132	2.9	13
Terry	13	60	15	3	.200	4	3	.750	5	7	12	8	15	0	3	1	9	0.7	2

3-Pt. FG: Washington 59-236 (.250)—Ballard 9-22 (.409); Ruland 1-3 (.333); Grevey 28-82 (.341); Haywood 0-3 (.000); Mahorn 0-3 (.000); Johnson 17-79 (.215); Collins 1-12 (.083); Lucas 2-22 (.091); *Holland 0-3 (.000); Davis 0-2 (.000); Witts 1-2 (.500); Terry 0-3 (.000). Opponents 44-183 (.240).

PLAYOFF RESULTS

EASTERN CONFERENCE FIRST ROUND
Philadelphia 2, Atlanta 0
Apr. 21—Wed.—Atlanta 76 at Philadelphia 111
Apr. 23—Fri.—Philadelphia 98 at Atlanta 95

Washington 2, New Jersey 0
Apr. 20—Tue.—Washington 96 at New Jersey 83
Apr. 23—Fri.—New Jersey 92 at Washington 103

EASTERN CONFERENCE SEMIFINALS
Boston 4, Washington 1
Apr. 25—Sun.—Washington 91 at Boston 109
Apr. 28—Wed.—Washington 103 at Boston...............................102
May 1—Sat.—Boston 92 at Washington 83
May 2—Sun.—Boston 103 at Washington *99
May 5—Wed.—Washington 126 at Boston...........................**131

Philadelphia 4, Milwaukee 2
Apr. 25—Sun.—Milwaukee 122 at Philadelphia 125
Apr. 28—Wed.—Milwaukee 108 at Philadelphia..........................120
May 1—Sat.—Philadelphia 91 at Milwaukee...............................92
May 2—Sun.—Philadelphia 100 at Milwaukee 93
May 5—Wed.—Milwaukee 110 at Philadelphia 98
May 7—Fri.—Philadelphia 102 at Milwaukee 90

EASTERN CONFERENCE FINALS
Philadelphia 4, Boston 3
May 9—Sun.—Philadelphia 81 at Boston 121
May 12—Wed.—Philadelphia 121 at Boston................................113
May 15—Sat.—Boston 97 at Philadelphia 99
May 16—Sun.—Boston 94 at Philadelphia 119
May 19—Wed.—Philadelphia 85 at Boston...................................114
May 21—Fri.—Boston 88 at Philadelphia......................................75
May 23—Sun.—Philadelphia 120 at Boston..................................106

WESTERN CONFERENCE FIRST ROUND
Seattle 2, Houston 1
Apr. 21—Wed.—Houston 87 at Seattle......................................102
Apr. 23—Fri.—Seattle 70 at Houston...91
Apr. 25—Sun.—Houston 83 at Seattle 104

Phoenix 2, Denver 1
Apr. 20—Tue.—Phoenix 113 at Denver 129
Apr. 23—Fri.—Denver 110 at Phoenix.......................................126
Apr. 24—Sat.—Phoenix 124 at Denver.......................................119

WESTERN CONFERENCE SEMIFINALS
Los Angeles 4, Phoenix 0
Apr. 27—Tue.—Phoenix 96 at Los Angeles 115
Apr. 28—Wed.—Phoenix 98 at Los Angeles 117
Apr. 30—Fri.—Los Angeles 114 at Phoenix................................106
May 2—Sun.—Los Angeles 112 at Phoenix 107

San Antonio 4, Seattle 1
Apr. 27—Tue.—San Antonio 95 at Seattle 93
Apr. 28—Wed.—San Antonio 99 at Seattle 114
Apr. 30—Fri.—Seattle 97 at San Antonio....................................99
May 2—Sun.—Seattle 113 at San Antonio.................................115
May 5—Wed.—San Antonio 109 at Seattle.................................103

WESTERN CONFERENCE FINALS
Los Angeles 4, San Antonio 0
May 9—Sun.—San Antonio 117 at Los Angeles 128
May 11—Tue.—San Antonio 101 at Los Angeles 110
May 14—Fri.—Los Angeles 118 at San Antonio.........................108
May 15—Sat.—Los Angeles 128 at San Antonio.........................123

WORLD CHAMPIONSHIP SERIES
Los Angeles 4, Philadelphia 2
May 27—Thur.—Los Angeles 124 at Philadelphia.......................117
May 30—Sun.—Los Angeles 94 at Philadelphia..........................110
June 1—Tue.—Philadelphia 108 at Los Angeles 129
June 3—Thur.—Philadelphia 101 at Los Angeles.........................111
June 6—Sun.—Los Angeles 102 at Philadelphia.........................135
June 8—Tue.—Philadelphia 104 at Los Angeles 114

*Overtime

1980-81 NBA STATISTICS

1980-81 NBA CHAMPION BOSTON CELTICS

Front row (left to right): Chris Ford, Cedric Maxwell, President and General Manager Red Auerbach, Coach Bill Fitch, Chairman of the Board Harry T. Mangurian, Jr., Larry Bird, Nate Archibald. Back row: Assistant coach K. C. Jones, Wayne Kreklow, M. L. Carr, Rick Robey, Robert Parish, Kevin McHale, Eric Fernsten, Gerald Henderson, assistant coach Jimmy Rodgers, trainer Ray Melchiorre.

FINAL STANDINGS

ATLANTIC DIVISION

Team	Atl.	Bos.	Chi.	Clev.	Dall.	Den.	Det.	G.S.	Hou.	Ind.	K.C.	L.A.	Mil.	N.J.	N.Y.	Phil.	Pho.	Por.	S.A.	S.D.	Sea.	Utah	Wash.	W.	L.	Pct.	G.B.
Boston	4	..	5	4	2	2	4	1	2	3	1	2	3	6	5	3	2	2	2	1	1	5		62	20	.756	....
Philadelphia	5	3	4	6	2	1	4	2	2	6	2	1	2	5	3	..	1	1	2	2	2	2	4	62	20	.756	....
New York	4	1	3	5	1	2	5	..	2	2	1	..	3	6	..	3	1	1	..	2	2	2	4	50	32	.610	12
Washington	4	1	1	2	2	2	5	1	2	2	1	1	1	3	2	2	1	..	1	2	1	2		39	43	.476	23
New Jersey	2	..	2	3	1	1	3	1	..	1	..	..	1	..	..	1	1	2	..	..	1	1	3	24	58	.293	38

CENTRAL DIVISION

Team	Atl.	Bos.	Chi.	Clev.	Dall.	Den.	Det.	G.S.	Hou.	Ind.	K.C.	L.A.	Mil.	N.J.	N.Y.	Phil.	Pho.	Por.	S.A.	S.D.	Sea.	Utah	Wash.	W.	L.	Pct.	G.B.
Milwaukee	5	3	3	6	2	1	5	1	2	4	1	2	3	3	3	1	2	1	2	2	2	4		60	22	.732	....
Chicago	4	1	..	5	1	1	5	1	1	3	2	1	3	3	3	2	..	..	1	1	2	5		45	37	.549	15
Indiana	5	3	2	4	2	1	4	1	1	..	2	..	2	5	3	..	1	..	2	1	..	1	4	44	38	.537	16
Atlanta	..	2	2	1	2	1	4	2	1	1	1	..	1	3	2	1	..	1	1	1	2	1	4	31	51	.378	29
Cleveland	5	1	1	..	2	1	3	1	..	2	..	..	..	3	..	..	1	1	1	1	..	1	4	28	54	.341	32
Detroit	2	1	1	3	2	..	..	..	1	2	1	..	1	3	1	1	..	..	1	..	..	1		21	61	.256	39

MIDWEST DIVISION

Team	Atl.	Bos.	Chi.	Clev.	Dall.	Den.	Det.	G.S.	Hou.	Ind.	K.C.	L.A.	Mil.	N.J.	N.Y.	Phil.	Pho.	Por.	S.A.	S.D.	Sea.	Utah	Wash.	W.	L.	Pct.	G.B.
San Antonio	1	..	2	1	5	4	2	4	3	..	4	3	1	2	2	..	2	3	..	4	3	5	1	52	30	.634	....
Kansas City	1	1	..	2	6	2	1	..	4	..	..	..	1	2	1	..	3	3	2	3	2	5	1	40	42	.488	12
Houston	1	..	1	2	6	4	1	2	..	1	2	2	..	2	1	..	1	3	3	1	4	4	..	40	42	.488	12
Denver	1	..	1	1	3	..	2	3	2	1	4	3	1	1	..	1	1	2	2	3	3	2	..	37	45	.451	15
Utah	..	1	..	1	5	4	2	1	2	1	1	2	..	1	..	..	3	1	2	1	..			28	54	.341	24
Dallas	..	..	1	..	..	3	..	2	..	..	..	..	..	..	..	1	1	1	2	1	1	..		15	67	.183	37

PACIFIC DIVISION

Team	Atl.	Bos.	Chi.	Clev.	Dall.	Den.	Det.	G.S.	Hou.	Ind.	K.C.	L.A.	Mil.	N.J.	N.Y.	Phil.	Pho.	Por.	S.A.	S.D.	Sea.	Utah	Wash.	W.	L.	Pct.	G.B.
Phoenix	2	..	2	1	4	4	2	4	4	1	2	4	1	1	1	1	..	3	3	6	5	5	1	57	25	.695	....
Los Angeles	2	..	1	2	5	2	2	5	3	2	5	..	..	2	2	1	2	3	2	3	6	3	1	54	28	.659	3
Portland	1	..	2	1	4	3	2	4	2	2	2	3	..	..	1	1	3	..	2	4	4	2	2	45	37	.549	12
Golden State	..	1	1	1	3	2	2	..	3	1	5	1	1	1	2	..	2	2	1	2	3	4	1	39	43	.476	18
San Diego	1	..	1	1	3	2	1	4	4	1	2	3	..	2	..	..	2	1	..	5	3	..		36	46	.439	21
Seattle	1	1	1	2	4	2	2	3	1	2	3	..	..	1	..	1	2	2	1	..	4	1		34	48	.415	23

HOME-ROAD RECORDS OF ALL TEAMS

Team	Home	Road	Total
Atlanta	20- 21	11- 30	31- 51
Boston	35- 6	27- 14	62- 20
Chicago	26- 15	19- 22	45- 37
Cleveland	20- 21	8- 33	28- 54
Dallas	11- 30	4- 37	15- 67
Denver	23- 18	14- 27	37- 45
Detroit	14- 27	7- 34	21- 61
Golden State	26- 15	13- 28	39- 43
Houston	25- 16	15- 26	40- 42
Indiana	27- 14	17- 24	44- 38
Kansas City	24- 17	16- 25	40- 42
Los Angeles	30- 11	24- 17	54- 28
Milwaukee	34- 7	26- 15	60- 22
New Jersey	16- 25	8- 33	24- 58
New York	28- 13	22- 19	50- 32
Philadelphia	37- 4	25- 16	62- 20
Phoenix	36- 5	21- 20	57- 25
Portland	30- 11	15- 26	45- 37
San Antonio	34- 7	18- 23	52- 30
San Diego	22- 19	14- 27	36- 46
Seattle	22- 19	12- 29	34- 48
Utah	20- 21	8- 33	28- 54
Washington	26- 15	13- 28	39- 43
Total	586- 357	357- 586	943- 943

OFFENSIVE TEAM STATISTICS

Team	G.	FIELD GOALS Att.	Made	Pct.	FREE THROWS Att.	Made	Pct.	REBOUNDS Off.	Def.	Tot.	Ast.	PF	Disq.	Stl.	Turn Over	Blk. Sh.	SCORING Pts.	Avg.
Denver	82	7960	3784	.475	3051	2388	.783	1325	2497	3822	2030	2108	24	720	1444	380	9986	121.8
Milwaukee	82	7472	3722	.498	2340	1802	.770	1261	2408	3669	2048	2114	25	685	1533	643	9276	113.1
San Antonio	82	7276	3571	.491	2668	2052	.769	1304	2582	3886	2369	2061	21	857	1702	591	9209	112.3
Philadelphia	82	7073	3636	.514	2427	1865	.768	1091	2618	3709	2363	1955	17	808	1557	551	9156	111.7
Los Angeles	82	7382	3780	.512	2113	1540	.729	1165	2491	3656	2244	2034	30	769	1518	480	9117	111.2
Portland	82	7535	3741	.496	2191	1573	.718	1243	2388	3631	2205	1996	13	876	1733	416	9080	110.7
Phoenix	82	7326	3587	.490	2430	1810	.745	1234	2490	3724	2202	1990	22	683	1577	594	9019	110.0
Boston	82	7099	3581	.504	2369	1781	.752	1155	2424	3579	2026	2158	36	611	1547	501	9008	109.9
Golden State	82	7284	3560	.489	2513	1826	.727	1403	2366	3769	1925	2058	15	729	1672	514	9006	109.8
Chicago	82	6903	3457	.501	2563	1985	.774	1227	2475	3702	2099	1901	8	705	1451	390	8937	109.0
Houston	82	7335	3573	.487	2223	1711	.770	1216	2347	3563	2091	2006	26	833	1491	484	8878	108.3
New York	82	7255	3505	.483	2386	1783	.747	1137	2205	3342	1976	1917	12	861	1461	314	8849	107.9
Indiana	82	7245	3491	.482	2540	1815	.715	1325	2262	3587	2271	2092	23	719	1448	385	8827	107.6
Kansas City	82	7151	3572	.500	2206	1576	.714	1037	2450	3487	2068	2204	35	750	1664	458	8769	106.9
New Jersey	82	7314	3477	.475	2371	1780	.751	1092	2374	3466	2068	2078	21	764	1407	292	8768	106.9
San Diego	82	7283	3477	.477	2246	1651	.735	1169	2144	3313	2098	2078	23	632	1396	322	8737	106.5
Cleveland	82	7609	3556	.467	1909	1486	.778	1258	2243	3501	2007	1995	31	641	1422	392	8670	105.7
Washington	82	7517	3549	.472	2072	1499	.723	1201	2224	3425	2151	1895	21	749	1605	469	8662	105.6
Atlanta	82	6866	3291	.479	2590	2012	.777	1201	2224	3425	1846	2276	54	628	1524	438	8604	104.9
Seattle	82	7145	3343	.468	2376	1813	.763	1167	2434	3601	1984	2008	32	561	1439	214	8531	104.0
Dallas	82	6928	3204	.462	2487	1868	.751	1109	2177	3286	1945	1986	23	637	1423	386	8322	101.5
Utah	82	6825	3332	.488	2080	1595	.767	962	2325	3287	1948	2110	39	637	1423	386	8301	101.2
Detroit	82	6986	3236	.463	2330	1689	.725	1201	2111	3312	1819	2125	35	884	1759	492	8174	99.7

DEFENSIVE TEAM STATISTICS

Team	FIELD GOALS Att.	Made	Pct.	FREE THROWS Att.	Made	Pct.	REBOUNDS Off.	Def.	Tot.	Ast.	PF	Disq.	Stl.	Turn Over	Blk. Sh.	SCORING Pts.	Avg.	Pt. Dif.
Philadelphia	7337	3307	.451	2487	1850	.744	1286	2287	3573	2033	2044	32	818	1642	379	8512	103.8	+ 7.9
Boston	7296	3372	.462	2277	1752	.769	1192	2174	3366	1890	2059	33	736	1473	351	8526	104.0	+ 5.9
Phoenix	7221	3368	.466	2383	1762	.739	1160	2284	3444	1970	2116	26	912	1752	401	8568	104.5	+ 5.5
Washington	7491	3518	.470	2161	1588	.735	1204	2638	3842	2060	1888	13	739	1410	469	8661	105.6	even
Seattle	7421	3453	.465	2323	1718	.740	1247	2357	3604	2044	2044	23	747	1348	387	8666	105.7	- 1.7
Milwaukee	7220	3311	.459	2701	2023	.749	1265	2209	3474	2033	2050	25	735	1670	400	8692	106.0	+ 7.2
Detroit	6869	3499	.509	2217	1663	.750	1090	2396	3486	2113	2064	27	695	1655	439	8712	106.2	- 6.3
Indiana	7071	3457	.489	2290	1757	.767	1246	2407	3653	2088	1994	14	689	1660	452	8716	106.3	+ 1.4
New York	7092	3555	.501	2082	1563	.751	1147	2457	3604	2088	2015	20	717	1520	383	8768	106.9	+ 1.0
Kansas City	7117	3424	.481	2500	1889	.756	1138	2510	3648	1857	2015	20	717	1520	383	8775	107.0	even
Chicago	7209	3527	.489	2211	1669	.755	1145	2096	3241	1950	2135	42	784	1502	441	8784	107.1	+ 1.9
Utah	7018	3430	.489	2472	1879	.760	1154	2440	3594	1985	1855	24	596	1303	406	8802	107.3	- 5.9
Los Angeles	7701	3581	.465	2158	1598	.741	1378	2274	3652	2191	1869	11	754	1473	357	8851	107.9	+ 3.3
Houston	7341	3617	.493	2108	1568	.744	1177	2367	3544	1977	1977	18	689	1430	367	8858	108.0	- 3.1
Atlanta	6867	3401	.495	2641	2024	.766	1207	2318	3525	1935	2097	26	683	1553	392	8867	108.1	- 1.6
San Diego	6951	3508	.505	2433	1818	.747	1091	2377	3468	2097	2006	19	683	1575	481	8973	109.4	+ 2.9
San Antonio	7582	3581	.472	2387	1766	.740	1214	2177	3391	2206	2198	37	700	1422	422	9007	109.8	+ 0.9
Portland	7351	3584	.488	2377	1805	.759	1249	2419	3668	2039	1932	30	802	1575	480	9011	109.9	- 8.4
Dallas	7060	3622	.513	2297	1731	.754	1173	2498	3671	2098	2187	31	713	1433	480	9068	110.6	- 4.9
Cleveland	7174	3608	.503	2395	1800	.752	1158	2499	3657	2223	2093	19	714	1385	386	9103	111.0	- 1.2
Golden State	7204	3631	.504	2411	1804	.748	1137	2210	3347	2144	2092	23	815	1637	502	9262	113.0	- 6.1
New Jersey	7159	3612	.505	2663	2010	.755	1059	2499	3558	2144	2092	23	815	1637	502	10025	122.3	- 0.5
Denver	8017	4059	.506	2507	1863	.743	1320	2680	4000	2529	2387	52	704	1555	547	10025	122.3	- 0.5

Disq.—Individual players disqualified (fouled out of game)

INDIVIDUAL LEADERS

POINTS

(Minimum of 70 games played or 1400 points)

Player	G.	FG	FT	Pts.	Avg.
Dantley, Utah	80	909	632	2452	30.7
Malone, Houston	80	806	609	2222	27.8
Gervin, San Antonio	82	850	512	2221	27.1
Abdul-Jabbar, L.A.	80	836	423	2095	26.2
Thompson, Denver	77	734	489	1967	25.5
Birdsong, K.C.	71	710	317	1747	24.6
Erving, Philadelphia	82	794	422	2014	24.6
Mitchell, Cleveland	82	853	302	2012	24.5
Free, Golden State	65	516	528	1565	24.1
English, Denver	81	768	390	1929	23.8
Wilkes, Los Angeles	81	786	254	1827	22.6
King, Golden State	81	731	307	1771	21.9
Issel, Denver	80	614	519	1749	21.9
Drew, Atlanta	67	500	454	1454	21.7
Newlin, New Jersey	79	632	414	1688	21.4
Bird, Boston	82	719	283	1741	21.2
Griffith, Utah	81	716	229	1671	20.6
Ma. Johnson, Mil.	76	636	269	1541	20.3
Cartwright, N.Y.	82	619	408	1646	20.1
R. Williams, N.Y.	79	616	312	1560	19.7

FIELD GOALS
Minimum 300 FG Made

	FGA	FGM	Pct.
Gilmore, Chicago	816	547	.670
Dawkins, Philadelphia	697	423	.607
Maxwell, Boston	750	441	.588
King, Golden State	1244	731	.588
Abdul-Jabbar, Los Angeles	1457	836	.574
Washington, Portland	571	325	.569
Dantley, Utah	1627	909	.559
Cartwright, New York	1118	619	.554
Nater, San Diego	935	517	.553
Ma. Johnson, Milwaukee	1153	636	.552

FREE THROWS
Minimum 125 FT Made

	FTA	FTM	Pct.
Murphy, Houston	215	206	.958
Sobers, Chicago	247	231	.935
Newlin, New Jersey	466	414	.888
Spanarkel, Dallas	423	375	.887
Bridgeman, Milwaukee	241	213	.884
Long, Detroit	184	160	.870
Criss, Atlanta	214	185	.864
Bird, Boston	328	283	.863
McKinney, Utah-Denver	188	162	.862
Bates, Portland	199	170	.854

ASSISTS
Minimum 70 games or 400 assists

	G.	No.	Avg.
Porter, Washington	81	734	9.1
Nixon, Los Angeles	79	696	8.8
Ford, Kansas City	66	580	8.8
Richardson, New York	79	627	7.9
Archibald, Boston	80	618	7.7
Lucas, Golden State	66	464	7.0
Ransey, Portland	80	555	6.9
Cheeks, Philadelphia	81	560	6.9
Davis, Indiana	76	480	6.3
Higgs, Denver	72	408	5.7

STEALS
Minimum 70 games or 125 steals

	G.	No.	Avg.
Johnson, Los Angeles	37	127	3.43
Richardson, New York	79	232	2.94
Buckner, Milwaukee	82	197	2.40
Cheeks, Philadelphia	81	193	2.38
R. Williams, New York	79	185	2.34
Bradley, Indiana	82	186	2.27
Erving, Philadelphia	82	173	2.11
Lee, Detroit	82	166	2.02
Reid, Houston	82	163	1.99
Bird, Boston	82	161	1.96

REBOUNDS
Minimum 70 games or 800 rebounds

	G.	Off.	Def.	Tot.	Avg.
Malone, Houston	80	474	706	1180	14.8
Nater, San Diego	82	295	722	1017	12.4
Smith, Golden State	82	433	561	994	12.1
Bird, Boston	82	191	704	895	10.9
Sikma, Seattle	82	184	668	852	10.4
Carr, Cleveland	81	260	575	835	10.3
Abdul-Jabbar, L.A.	80	197	624	821	10.3
Gilmore, Chicago	82	220	608	828	10.1
C. Jones, Phila.	81	200	613	813	10.0
Hayes, Washington	81	235	554	789	9.7

BLOCKED SHOTS
Minimum 70 games or 100 blocked shots

	G.	No.	Avg.
G. Johnson, San Antonio	82	278	3.39
Rollins, Atlanta	40	117	2.93
Abdul-Jabbar, Los Angeles	80	228	2.85
Parish, Boston	82	214	2.61
Gilmore, Chicago	82	198	2.41
Catchings, Milwaukee	77	184	2.39
Tyler, Detroit	82	180	2.20
Thompson, Portland	79	170	2.15
Poquette, Utah	82	174	2.12
Hayes, Washington	81	171	2.11

3-PT. FIELD GOALS
Minimum 25 made

	FGA	FGM	Pct.
Taylor, San Diego	115	44	.383
Williams, San Diego	141	48	.340
Hassett, Dall.-G.S.	156	53	.340
Bratz, Cleveland	169	57	.337
Bibby, San Diego	95	32	.337
Grevey, Washington	136	45	.331
Ford, Boston	109	36	.330
Wedman, Kansas City	77	25	.325

TEAM-BY-TEAM INDIVIDUAL STATISTICS

*Did not finish season with team.

ATLANTA HAWKS

Player	G.	Min.	FGA	FGM	Pct.	FTA	FTM	Pct.	Off. Reb.	Def. Reb.	Tot. Reb.	Ast.	PF	Dsq.	Stl.	Blk. Sh.	Pts.	Avg.	Hi.
Drew	67	2075	1096	500	.456	577	454	.787	145	238	383	79	264	9	98	15	1454	21.7	47
Johnson	75	2693	1136	573	.504	356	279	.784	60	119	179	407	188	2	126	11	1431	19.1	40
Roundfield	63	2128	808	426	.527	355	256	.721	231	403	634	161	258	8	76	119	1108	17.6	29
Matthews (Tot.)	79	2266	779	385	.494	252	202	.802	46	93	139	411	242	2	107	17	977	12.4	26
Matthews (Atl.)	34	1105	330	161	.488	123	103	.837	16	56	72	212	122	2	61	7	425	12.5	26
Hawes	74	2309	637	333	.523	278	222	.799	165	396	561	168	289	13	73	32	889	12.0	32
Criss	66	1708	485	220	.454	214	185	.864	26	74	100	283	87	0	61	3	626	9.5	21
McMillen	79	1564	519	253	.487	108	80	.741	96	199	295	72	165	0	23	25	587	7.4	21
Rollins	40	1044	210	116	.552	57	46	.807	102	184	286	35	151	7	29	117	278	7.0	13
Pellom	77	1472	380	186	.489	116	81	.698	122	234	356	48	228	6	50	92	453	5.9	20
Shelton	55	586	219	100	.457	58	35	.603	59	79	138	27	128	1	18	5	235	4.3	22
McElroy	54	680	202	78	.386	59	48	.814	10	38	48	84	62	0	20	9	205	3.8	12
Burleson	31	363	99	41	.414	41	20	.488	44	50	94	12	73	2	8	19	102	3.3	12
A. Collins	29	395	99	35	.354	36	24	.667	19	22	41	25	35	0	11	1	94	3.2	15
*D. Collins	47	1184	530	230	.434	162	137	.846	96	91	187	115	166	5	69	11	597	12.7	25
*Hill	24	624	116	39	.336	50	42	.840	10	41	51	118	60	0	26	3	120	5.0	14

3-Pt. FG: Atlanta 10-82 (.122)—Drew 0-7 (.000); Johnson 6-20 (.300); Roundfield 0-1 (.000); Matthews (Tot.) 5-21 (.238); Matthews (Atl.) 0-6 (.000); Hawes 1-4 (.250); Criss 1-21 (.048); McMillen 1-6 (.167); Rollins 0-1 (.000); Pellom 0-1 (.000); Shelton 0-1 (.000); McElroy 1-8 (.125); A. Collins 0-2 (.000); D. Collins 0-3 (.000); Hill 0-1 (.000). Opponents 32-152 (.211).

BOSTON CELTICS

Player	G.	Min.	FGA	FGM	Pct.	FTA	FTM	Pct.	Off. Reb.	Def. Reb.	Tot. Reb.	Ast.	PF	Dsq.	Stl.	Blk. Sh.	Pts.	Avg.	Hi.
Bird	82	3239	1503	719	.478	328	283	.863	191	704	895	451	239	2	161	63	1741	21.2	36
Parish	82	2298	1166	635	.545	397	282	.710	245	532	777	144	310	9	81	214	1552	18.9	40
Maxwell	81	2730	750	441	.588	450	352	.782	222	303	525	219	256	5	79	68	1234	15.2	34
Archibald	80	2820	766	382	.499	419	342	.816	36	140	176	618	201	1	75	18	1106	13.8	26
McHale	82	1645	666	355	.533	159	108	.679	155	204	359	55	260	3	27	151	818	10.0	23
Robey	82	1569	547	298	.545	251	144	.574	132	258	390	126	204	0	38	19	740	9.0	24
Ford	82	2723	707	314	.444	87	64	.736	72	91	163	295	212	2	100	23	728	8.9	23
Henderson	82	1608	579	261	.451	157	113	.720	43	89	132	213	177	0	79	12	636	7.8	19
Carr	41	655	216	97	.449	67	53	.791	26	57	83	56	74	0	30	18	248	6.0	25
Duerod (Tot.)	50	451	234	104	.444	41	31	.756	17	27	44	36	27	0	17	4	247	4.9	22
Duerod (Bos.)	32	114	73	30	.411	14	13	.929	2	3	5	6	8	0	5	0	79	2.5	12
Fernsten	45	279	79	38	.481	30	20	.667	29	33	62	10	29	0	6	7	96	2.1	9
☆Kreklow	25	100	47	11	.234	10	7	.700	2	10	12	9	20	0	2	1	30	1.2	4

3-Pt. FG: Boston 65-241 (.270)—Bird 20-74 (.270); Parish 0-1 (.000); Maxwell 0-1 (.000); Archibald 0-9 (.000); McHale 0-2 (.000); Robey 0-1 (.000); Ford 36-109 (.330); Henderson 1-16 (.063); Carr 1-14 (.071); Duerod (Tot.) 8-16 (.500), Duerod (Bos.) 6-10 (.600); Kreklow 1-4 (.250). Opponents 30-139 (.216).

CHICAGO BULLS

Player	G.	Min.	FGA	FGM	Pct.	FTA	FTM	Pct.	Off. Reb.	Def. Reb.	Tot. Reb.	Ast.	PF	Dsq.	Stl.	Blk. Sh.	Pts.	Avg.	Hi.
Theus	82	2820	1097	543	.495	550	445	.809	124	163	287	426	258	1	122	20	1549	18.9	32
Gilmore	82	2832	816	547	.670	532	375	.705	220	608	828	172	295	2	47	198	1469	17.9	31
Greenwood	82	2710	989	481	.486	290	217	.748	243	481	724	218	282	5	77	124	1179	14.4	28
Kenon	77	2161	946	454	.480	245	180	.735	179	219	398	120	160	2	75	18	1088	14.1	32
Sobers	71	1803	769	355	.462	247	231	.935	46	98	144	284	225	3	98	17	958	13.5	27
Wilkerson	80	2238	715	330	.462	163	137	.840	86	196	282	272	170	0	102	23	798	10.0	28
Jones	81	1574	507	245	.483	161	125	.776	127	274	401	99	200	1	40	36	615	7.6	29
May	63	815	338	165	.488	149	113	.758	62	93	155	63	83	0	35	7	443	7.0	20
Dietrick	82	1243	320	146	.456	111	77	.694	79	186	265	118	176	1	48	53	371	4.5	16
Wilkes	48	540	184	85	.462	46	29	.690	36	60	96	30	86	0	25	12	199	4.1	21
Lester	8	83	24	10	.417	11	10	.909	3	3	6	7	5	0	2	0	30	3.8	9
Worthen	64	945	192	95	.495	60	45	.750	22	93	115	115	115	0	57	6	235	3.7	18
☆Mack	3	16	6	1	.167	2	1	.500	0	1	1	1	3	0	1	0	3	1.0	2

3-Pt. FG: Chicago 38-179 (.212)—Theus 18-90 (.200); Greenwood 0-2 (.000); Sobers 17-66 (.258); Wilkerson 1-10 (.100); Dietrick 2-6 (.333); Wilkes 0-1 (.000); Worthen 0-4 (.000). Opponents 52-223 (.233).

CLEVELAND CAVALIERS

Player	G.	Min.	FGA	FGM	Pct.	FTA	FTM	Pct.	Off. Reb.	Def. Reb.	Tot. Reb.	Ast.	PF	Dsq.	Stl.	Blk. Sh.	Pts.	Avg.	Hi.
Mitchell	82	3194	1791	853	.476	385	302	.784	215	287	502	139	199	0	63	52	2012	24.5	42
Carr	81	2615	918	469	.511	409	292	.714	260	575	835	192	290	3	76	42	1230	15.2	31
Ra. Smith	82	2199	1043	486	.466	271	221	.815	46	147	193	357	132	0	113	14	1194	14.6	33
Phegley	82	2269	965	474	.491	267	224	.839	90	156	246	184	262	7	65	15	1180	14.4	30
Huston (Tot.)	81	2434	942	461	.489	212	150	.708	45	93	138	394	148	1	58	7	1073	13.2	29
Huston (Clev.)	25	542	153	76	.497	27	22	.815	12	27	39	117	35	0	13	1	174	7.0	19
Bratz	80	2595	817	319	.390	132	107	.811	66	132	198	452	194	1	136	17	802	10.0	22
Wash'gton (Tot.)	80	1812	747	340	.455	159	119	.748	158	295	453	129	273	3	46	61	800	10.0	24
Washington (Clev.)	69	1505	630	289	.459	136	102	.750	133	236	369	113	246	3	41	54	681	9.9	24
Laimbeer	81	2460	670	337	.503	153	117	.765	266	427	693	216	332	14	59	78	791	9.8	26
Ford	64	996	224	100	.446	24	22	.917	74	90	164	84	100	1	15	12	222	3.5	14
Calvin	21	128	39	13	.333	35	25	.714	2	10	12	28	13	0	5	0	52	2.5	6
Jordan	30	207	75	29	.387	17	10	.588	23	19	42	11	35	0	11	5	68	2.3	8
Hughes (Tot.)	53	490	70	27	.386	2	1	.500	48	79	127	35	106	2	28	35	55	1.0	6
Hughes (Clev.)	45	331	45	16	.356	0	0		29	48	77	24	73	0	17	21	32	0.7	6
☆Robisch	11	372	98	37	.378	36	29	.806	27	58	85	44	21	0	7	6	103	9.4	17
Ro. Smith	1	20	5	2	.400	4	4	1.000	1	2	3	3	6	1	0	0	8	8.0	8
☆Robinzine	8	84	32	14	.438	8	5	.625	4	9	13	5	19	1	4	0	33	4.1	10
☆Whitehead (Clev.)	3	8	3	1	.333	0	0		2	1	3	0	6	0	1	0	2	0.7	2
☆Kinch	29	247	96	38	.396	5	4	.800	7	17	24	35	24	0	9	5	80	2.8	10
☆Lambert	3	8	5	3	.600	0	0		1	2	3	2	0	0	0	0	6	2.0	4

3-Pt. FG: Cleveland 72-249 (.289)—Mitchell 4-9 (.444); Carr 0-4 (.000); Ra. Smith 1-28 (.036); Phegley 8-28 (.286); Huston (Tot.) 1-5 (.200), Huston (Clev.) 0-1 (.000); Bratz 57-169 (.337); Washington (Clev.) 1-2 (.500); Ford 0-3 (.000); Calvin 1-5 (.200). Opponents 52-168 (.310).

DALLAS MAVERICKS

Player	G.	Min.	FGA	FGM	Pct.	FTA	FTM	Pct.	Off. Reb.	Def. Reb.	Tot. Reb.	Ast.	PF	Dsq.	Stl.	Blk. Sh.	Pts.	Avg.	Hi.
Spanarkel	82	2317	866	404	.467	423	375	.887	142	155	297	232	230	3	117	20	1184	14.4	28
LaGarde	82	2670	888	417	.470	444	288	.649	177	488	665	237	293	6	35	45	1122	13.7	26
Robinzine (Tot)	78	2016	826	392	.475	281	218	.776	168	365	533	118	275	6	75	9	1003	12.9	26
Robinzine (Dal)	70	1932	794	378	.476	273	213	.780	164	356	520	113	256	5	71	9	970	13.9	26
B. Davis	56	1686	410	230	.561	204	163	.799	29	122	151	385	156	2	52	11	626	11.2	31
Mack (Tot)	65	1682	606	279	.460	125	80	.640	92	138	230	163	117	0	60	7	638	9.8	28
Mack (Dal)	62	1666	600	278	.463	123	79	.642	92	137	229	162	114	0	55	7	635	10.2	28
Lloyd	72	2186	547	245	.448	205	147	.717	161	293	454	159	269	8	34	25	637	8.8	28
Jeelani	66	1108	440	187	.425	220	179	.814	83	147	230	65	123	2	44	31	553	8.4	31
Byrnes	72	1360	451	216	.479	157	120	.764	74	103	177	113	126	0	29	17	561	7.8	25
Kea	16	199	81	37	.457	62	43	.694	28	39	67	5	44	2	6	1	117	7.3	22
P'tk'wicz(Tot)	42	461	138	57	.413	14	11	.786	13	29	42	77	28	0	15	2	144	3.4	10
P'tk'w'z (Dal)	36	433	133	55	.414	14	11	.786	13	28	41	75	26	0	15	2	140	3.9	10
Kinch (Tot)	41	353	141	52	.369	18	14	.778	7	26	33	45	33	0	11	6	118	2.9	10
Kinch (Dal)	12	106	45	14	.311	13	10	.769	0	9	9	9	9	0	2	1	38	3.2	7
☆Huston	56	1892	789	385	.488	185	128	.692	33	66	99	277	113	1	45	6	899	16.1	29
☆Washington	11	307	117	51	.436	23	17	.739	25	59	84	16	37	0	5	7	119	10.8	24
☆Duerod	18	337	161	74	.460	27	18	.667	15	24	39	30	19	0	12	4	168	9.3	22

Player	G.	Min.	FGA	FGM	Pct.	FTA	FTM	Pct.	Off. Reb.	Def. Reb.	Tot. Reb.	Ast.	PF	Dsq.	Stl.	Blk. Sh.	Pts.	Avg.	Hi.
°Hassett	17	280	142	59	.415	13	10	.769	11	14	25	18	21	0	5	0	138	8.1	15
°Boynes	44	757	313	121	.387	55	45	.818	24	51	75	37	79	1	23	16	287	6.5	22
°Whitehead	7	118	38	16	.421	11	5	.455	8	20	28	2	16	0	4	1	37	5.3	14
°Allums	22	276	67	23	.343	22	13	.591	19	46	65	25	51	2	5	8	59	2.7	11
°Drollinger	6	67	14	7	.500	4	1	.250	5	14	19	14	16	0	1	2	15	2.5	8
°Carr	8	77	28	7	.250	4	2	.500	4	5	9	9	10	0	1	0	16	2.0	5
°M. Davis (Tot.)	2	10	5	1	.200	5	1	.200	2	2	4	0	0	0	1	3	3	1.5	2
°M. Davis (Dal.)	1	8	4	0	.000	5	1	.200	2	1	3	0	0	0	1	1	1	1.0	1

3-Pt. FG: Dallas 46-165 (.279)—Spanarkel 1-10 (.100); Robinzine 1-6 (.167); B. Davis 3-17 (.176); Mack 0-9 (.000); Lloyd 0-2 (.000); Jeelani 0-1 (.000); Byrnes 9-20 (.450); Kea 0-1 (.000); Pietkiewicz 19-48 (.396); Huston 1-4 (.250); Duerod 2-6 (.333); Hassett 10-40 (.250); Allums 0-1 (.000). Opponents 36-137 (.263).

DENVER NUGGETS

Player	G.	Min.	FGA	FGM	Pct.	FTA	FTM	Pct.	Off. Reb.	Def. Reb.	Tot. Reb.	Ast.	PF	Dsq.	Stl.	Blk. Sh.	Pts.	Avg.	Hi.
Thompson	77	2620	1451	734	.506	615	489	.795	107	180	287	231	231	3	53	60	1967	25.5	44
English	81	3093	1555	768	.494	459	390	.850	273	373	646	290	255	2	106	100	1929	23.8	42
Issel	80	2641	1220	614	.503	684	519	.759	229	447	676	158	249	6	83	53	1749	21.9	37
Vandeweghe	51	1376	537	229	.426	159	130	.818	86	184	270	94	116	0	29	24	588	11.5	30
Robisch (Tot)	84	2116	740	330	.446	247	200	.810	157	342	499	173	173	0	37	34	860	10.2	27
Robisch (Den)	73	1744	642	293	.456	211	171	.810	130	284	414	129	152	0	30	28	757	10.4	27
McKinney (Tot.)	84	2166	645	327	.507	188	162	.862	36	148	184	360	231	3	99	11	818	9.7	21
McKinney (Den)	49	1134	412	203	.493	140	118	.843	24	86	110	203	124	0	61	7	525	10.7	21
Roche	26	611	179	82	.458	77	58	.753	5	32	37	140	44	0	17	8	231	8.9	30
Hordges	68	1599	480	221	.460	186	130	.699	120	338	458	104	226	4	33	19	572	8.4	21
Higgs	72	1689	474	209	.441	172	140	.814	24	121	145	408	243	5	101	6	562	7.8	21
Gondrezick	73	1077	329	155	.471	137	112	.818	136	171	307	83	185	2	91	20	422	5.8	27
Dunn	82	1427	354	146	.412	121	79	.653	133	168	301	81	141	0	66	29	371	4.5	16
Valentine	24	123	98	37	.378	19	9	.474	10	20	30	7	23	0	7	4	84	3.5	9
Ray	18	148	49	15	.306	10	7	.700	13	24	37	11	31	0	4	4	37	2.1	7
°Nicks	27	493	149	65	.436	59	35	.593	13	36	49	80	52	0	28	2	165	6.1	17
°Hughes	8	159	25	11	.440	2	1	.500	19	31	50	11	33	2	11	14	23	2.9	6
°Oldham	4	21	6	2	.333	0	0	.....	1	1	2	0	2	0	4	1	4	1.0	2

3-Pt. FG: Denver 30-145 (.207)—Thompson 10-39 (.256); English 3-5 (.600); Issel 2-12 (.167); Vandeweghe 0-7 (.000); McKinney (Tot.) 2-12 (.167); McKinney (Den.) 1-10 (.100); Roche 9-27 (.333); Hordges 0-3 (.000); Higgs 4-34 (.118); Gondrezick 0-2 (.000); Dunn 0-2 (.000); Valentine 1-2 (.500); Ray 0-1 (.000); Nicks 0-1 (.000). Opponents 44-162 (.272).

DETROIT PISTONS

Player	G.	Min.	FGA	FGM	Pct.	FTA	FTM	Pct.	Off. Reb.	Def. Reb.	Tot. Reb.	Ast.	PF	Dsq.	Stl.	Blk. Sh.	Pts.	Avg.	Hi.
Long	59	1750	957	441	.461	184	160	.870	95	102	197	106	164	3	95	22	1044	17.7	40
Benson	59	1956	770	364	.473	254	196	.772	124	276	400	172	184	1	72	67	924	15.7	27
Hubbard	80	2289	880	433	.492	426	294	.690	236	350	586	150	317	14	80	20	1161	14.5	29
Herron	80	2270	954	432	.453	267	228	.854	98	113	211	148	154	1	91	26	1094	13.7	29
Tyler	82	2549	895	476	.532	250	148	.592	198	369	567	136	215	2	112	180	1100	13.4	31
Kelser	25	654	285	120	.421	106	68	.642	53	67	120	45	89	0	34	29	308	12.3	33
Robinson	81	1592	509	234	.460	240	175	.729	117	177	294	112	186	2	46	24	643	7.9	19
Wright	45	997	303	140	.462	66	53	.803	26	62	88	153	114	1	42	7	335	7.4	19
Mokeski	80	1815	458	224	.489	200	120	.600	141	277	418	135	267	7	38	73	568	7.1	18
Drew	76	1581	484	197	.407	133	106	.797	24	96	120	249	125	0	88	7	504	6.6	23
Lee	82	1829	323	113	.350	156	113	.724	65	155	220	362	260	4	166	29	341	4.2	15
°McAdoo	6	168	82	30	.366	20	12	.600	9	32	41	20	16	0	8	7	72	12.0	16
°Fuller	15	248	66	24	.364	16	12	.750	13	29	42	28	25	0	10	1	60	4.0	9
°Lawrence	3	19	8	5	.625	4	2	.500	2	2	4	1	6	0	1	0	12	4.0	6
°Black	3	28	10	3	.300	8	2	.250	0	2	2	2	2	0	1	0	8	2.7	4
°Johnson (Tot)	12	90	25	7	.280	0	0	.....	6	16	22	1	18	0	0	5	17	1.4	6
°Johnson (Det)	2	10	2	0	.000	0	0	.....	0	0	0	0	0	0	0	0	0	0.0	0

3-Pt. FG: Detroit 13-84 (.155)—Long 2-11 (.182); Benson 0-4 (.000); Hubbard 1-3 (.333); Herron 2-11 (.182); Tyler 0-8 (.000); Kelser 0-2 (.000); Robinson 0-6 (.000); Wright 2-7 (.286); Mokeski 0-1 (.000); Drew 4-17 (.235); Lee 2-13 (.154); Fuller 0-1 (.000). Opponents 31-127 (.244).

GOLDEN STATE WARRIORS

Player	G.	Min.	FGA	FGM	Pct.	FTA	FTM	Pct.	Off. Reb.	Def. Reb.	Tot. Reb.	Ast.	PF	Dsq.	Stl.	Blk. Sh.	Pts.	Avg.	Hi.
Free	65	2370	1157	516	.446	649	528	.814	48	111	159	361	183	1	85	11	1565	24.1	40
King	81	2914	1244	731	.588	437	307	.703	178	373	551	287	304	5	72	34	1771	21.9	50
Carroll	82	2919	1254	616	.491	440	315	.716	274	485	759	117	313	10	50	121	1547	18.9	46
Short	79	2309	1157	549	.475	205	168	.820	151	240	391	249	244	3	78	19	1269	16.1	45
Smith	82	2578	594	304	.512	301	177	.588	433	561	994	93	316	10	70	63	785	9.6	23
Hassett (Tot)	41	714	340	143	.421	21	17	.810	24	44	68	74	65	0	13	2	356	8.7	23
Hassett (G.S.)	24	434	198	84	.424	8	7	.875	13	30	43	56	44	0	8	2	218	9.1	23
Parker	73	1317	388	191	.492	128	94	.734	101	93	194	106	112	0	67	13	476	6.5	18
Romar	53	726	211	87	.412	63	43	.683	10	46	56	136	64	0	27	3	219	4.1	14
Brown	45	580	162	83	.512	21	16	.762	5	161	166	21	103	4	9	14	182	4.0	15
Reid	59	597	185	84	.454	39	22	.564	27	33	60	71	111	0	33	5	190	3.2	14
Ray	66	838	152	64	.421	62	29	.468	73	144	217	52	194	2	24	13	157	2.4	18
Mayfield	7	54	18	8	.444	2	1	.500	7	2	9	1	8	0	0	1	17	2.4	6
Mengelt	2	11	4	0	.000	0	0	.....	0	0	0	2	0	0	0	0	0	0.0	0
°Lucas	66	1919	506	222	.439	145	107	.738	34	120	154	464	140	1	83	2	555	8.4	23
°White	4	43	18	9	.500	4	4	1.000	0	0	0	2	7	0	4	0	22	5.5	12
°Chenier	9	82	33	11	.333	6	6	1.000	1	7	8	7	10	0	0	0	29	3.2	6
°Abernethy	10	39	3	1	.333	3	2	.667	1	7	8	1	5	0	1	0	4	0.4	2

3-Pt. FG: Golden State 60-210 (.286)—Free 5-31 (.161); King 2-6 (.333); Carroll 0-2 (.000); Short 3-17 (.176); Hassett (Tot.) 53-156 (.340); Hassett (G.S.) 43-116 (.371); Romar 2-6 (.333); Reid 0-5 (.000); Lucas 4-24 (.167); Chenier 1-3 (.333) Opponents 37-160 (.231).

HOUSTON ROCKETS

Player	G.	Min.	FGA	FGM	Pct.	FTA	FTM	Pct.	Off. Reb.	Def. Reb.	Tot. Reb.	Ast.	PF	Dsq.	Stl.	Blk. Sh.	Pts.	Avg.	Hi.
Malone	80	3245	1545	806	.522	804	609	.757	474	706	1180	141	223	0	83	150	2222	27.8	51
Murphy	76	2014	1074	528	.492	215	206	.958	33	54	87	222	209	0	111	6	1266	16.7	42
Reid	82	2963	1113	536	.482	303	229	.756	164	419	583	344	325	4	163	66	1301	15.9	32
Tomjanovich	52	1264	563	263	.467	82	65	.793	78	130	208	81	121	0	19	6	603	11.6	25
Dunleavy	74	1609	632	310	.491	186	156	.839	28	90	118	268	165	1	64	2	777	10.5	48
Leavell	79	1686	548	258	.471	149	124	.832	30	104	134	384	160	1	97	15	642	8.1	24
Paultz	81	1659	517	262	.507	153	75	.490	111	280	391	105	182	1	28	72	599	7.4	25
Willoughby	55	1145	287	150	.523	64	49	.766	74	153	227	64	102	0	18	31	349	6.3	21
Garrett	70	1638	415	188	.453	62	50	.806	85	179	264	132	167	0	50	10	427	6.1	22
Henderson	66	1411	332	137	.413	95	78	.821	30	74	104	307	111	1	53	4	352	5.3	16
Jones	68	1003	252	117	.464	101	64	.634	96	138	234	41	112	0	18	23	298	4.4	18
Stroud	9	88	34	11	.324	4	3	.750	7	6	13	9	7	0	1	0	25	2.8	11
*Johnson	10	80	23	7	.304	5	3	.600	4	14	20	1	17	0	0	5	17	1.7	6

3-Pt. FG: Houston 21-118 (.178)—Malone 1-3 (.333); Murphy 4-17 (.235); Reid 0-4 (.000); Tomjanovich 12-51 (.235); Dunleavy 1-16 (.063); Leavell 2-17 (.118); Paultz 0-3 (.000); Garrett 1-3 (.333); Henderson 0-3 (.000); Jones 0-1 (.000). Opponents 49-171 (.287).

INDIANA PACERS

Player	G.	Min.	FGA	FGM	Pct.	FTA	FTM	Pct.	Off. Reb.	Def. Reb.	Tot. Reb.	Ast.	PF	Dsq.	Stl.	Blk. Sh.	Pts.	Avg.	Hi.
Knight	82	2385	1025	546	.533	410	341	.832	191	219	410	157	155	1	84	12	1436	17.5	52
Edwards	81	2375	1004	511	.509	347	244	.703	191	380	571	212	304	7	32	128	1266	15.6	39
Davis	76	2536	917	426	.465	299	238	.796	56	114	170	480	179	2	95	14	1094	14.4	30
Bantom	76	2375	882	431	.489	281	199	.708	150	277	427	240	284	9	80	85	1061	14.0	29
McGinnis	69	1845	768	348	.453	385	207	.538	164	364	528	210	242	3	99	28	903	13.1	27
G. Johnson	43	930	394	182	.462	122	93	.762	99	179	278	86	120	1	47	23	457	10.6	26
Orr	82	1787	709	348	.491	202	163	.807	172	189	361	132	153	0	55	25	859	10.5	22
Bradley	82	1867	559	265	.474	178	125	.702	70	123	193	188	236	2	186	37	657	8.0	20
C. Johnson	81	1643	466	235	.504	189	112	.593	173	295	468	144	185	1	44	119	582	7.2	17
Buse	58	1095	287	114	.397	65	50	.769	19	65	84	140	61	0	74	8	297	5.1	13
Sichting	47	450	95	34	.358	32	25	.781	11	32	43	70	38	0	23	1	93	2.0	12
Abernethy(Tot.)	39	298	59	25	.424	22	13	.591	20	28	48	19	34	0	7	3	63	1.6	6
Abernethy(Ind.)	29	259	56	24	.429	19	11	.579	19	21	40	18	29	0	6	3	59	2.0	6
*Natt	19	149	77	25	.325	11	7	.636	9	6	15	10	18	0	5	1	59	3.1	15
*Miller	5	34	6	2	.333	0	0		1	3	4	4	2	0	3	0	4	0.8	2

3-Pt. FG: Indiana 30-169 (.178)—Knight 3-19 (.158); Edwards 0-3 (.000); Davis 4-33 (.121); Bantom 0-6 (.000); McGinnis 0-7 (.000); G. Johnson 0-5 (.000); Orr 0-6 (.000); Bradley 2-16 (.125); C. Johnson 0-1 (.000); Buse 19-58 (.328); Sichting 0-5 (.000); Abernethy (Ind.) 0-1 (.000); Natt 2-8 (.250); Miller 0-1 (.000). Opponents 41-179 (.229).

KANSAS CITY KINGS

Player	G.	Min.	FGA	FGM	Pct.	FTA	FTM	Pct.	Off. Reb.	Def. Reb.	Tot. Reb.	Ast.	PF	Dsq.	Stl.	Blk. Sh.	Pts.	Avg.	Hi.
Birdsong	71	2593	1306	710	.544	455	317	.766	119	139	258	233	172	2	93	18	1747	24.6	42
Wedman	81	2902	1437	685	.477	204	140	.686	128	305	433	226	294	4	97	46	1535	19.0	41
Ford	66	2287	887	424	.478	354	294	.831	26	102	128	580	190	3	99	6	1153	17.5	38
King	81	2743	867	472	.544	386	264	.684	235	551	786	122	227	2	102	41	1208	14.9	33
Meriweather	74	1514	415	206	.496	213	148	.695	126	267	393	77	219	4	27	80	560	7.6	24
Grunfeld	79	1584	486	260	.535	101	75	.743	31	175	206	205	155	1	60	15	595	7.5	30
Whitney	47	782	306	149	.487	65	50	.769	29	77	106	68	98	0	47	6	350	7.4	20
Lacey	82	2228	536	237	.442	117	92	.786	131	453	584	399	302	5	95	120	567	6.9	16
Douglas	79	1356	323	185	.573	186	102	.548	150	234	384	69	251	2	25	38	472	6.0	17
Sanders	23	186	72	34	.442	22	20	.909	6	15	21	17	20	0	16	1	88	3.8	13
Walton	61	821	218	90	.413	33	26	.788	13	35	48	208	45	0	32	2	206	3.4	18
Lambert (Tot.)	46	483	165	68	.412	23	18	.783	28	65	93	27	76	0	12	5	154	3.3	12
Lambert (K.C.)	43	475	160	65	.406	23	18	.783	27	63	90	24	74	0	12	5	148	3.4	12
*White	13	236	82	36	.439	18	11	.611	3	18	21	37	21	0	11	1	83	6.4	12
*Gerard	16	123	51	19	.373	29	19	.655	13	16	29	6	24	0	3	6	57	3.6	9

3-Pt. FG: Kansas City 49-168 (.292)—Birdsong 10-35 (.286); Wedman 25-77 (.325); Ford 11-36 (.306); Whitney 2-6 (.333); Lacey 1-5 (.200); Douglas 0-3 (.000); Walton 0-1 (.000); Lambert (K.C.) 0-2 (.000); Gerard 0-3 (.000). Opponents 31-153 (.203).

LOS ANGELES LAKERS

Player	G.	Min.	FGA	FGM	Pct.	FTA	FTM	Pct.	Off. Reb.	Def. Reb.	Tot. Reb.	Ast.	PF	Dsq.	Stl.	Blk. Sh.	Pts.	Avg.	Hi.
Abdul-Jabbar	80	2976	1457	836	.574	552	423	.766	197	624	821	272	244	4	59	228	2095	26.2	42
Wilkes	81	3028	1495	786	.526	335	254	.758	146	289	435	235	223	1	121	29	1827	22.6	34
Johnson	37	1371	587	312	.532	225	171	.760	101	219	320	317	100	0	127	27	798	21.6	41
Nixon	79	2962	1210	576	.476	252	196	.778	64	168	232	696	226	2	146	9	1350	17.1	30
Chones	82	2562	751	378	.503	193	126	.653	180	477	657	153	324	4	39	96	882	10.8	23
Cooper	81	2625	654	321	.491	149	117	.785	121	215	336	332	249	4	133	78	763	9.4	20
Landsberger	69	1086	327	164	.502	116	62	.534	152	225	377	27	135	0	19	6	390	5.7	22
Carter	54	672	247	114	.462	95	70	.740	34	31	65	52	99	0	23	1	301	5.6	16
Jordan (Tot.)	74	1226	352	150	.426	127	87	.685	30	68	98	241	165	0	98	6	393	5.3	18
Jordan (L.A.)	60	987	279	120	.430	95	63	.663	25	55	80	195	136	0	74	7	306	5.1	18
Holland	41	295	111	47	.423	49	35	.714	9	20	29	23	44	0	21	1	130	3.2	10
Brewer	78	1107	197	107	.513	40	15	.375	127	154	281	55	158	2	43	58	217	2.8	14
Hardy	22	111	59	22	.373	10	7	.700	8	11	19	3	13	0	1	9	51	2.3	8
*Patrick	3	9	5	2	.400	2	1	.500	1	1	2	1	3	0	0	9	5	1.7	3
*Jackson	2	14	3	1	.333	0	0		0	2	2	2	1	0	0	0	2	1.0	2

3-Pt. FG: Los Angeles 17-94 (.181)—Abdul-Jabbar 0-1 (.000); Wilkes 1-13 (.077); Johnson 3-17 (.176); Nixon 2-12 (.167); Chones 0-4 (.000); Cooper 4-19 (.211); Landsberger 0-1 (.000); Carter 3-10 (.300); Jordan (Tot.) 6-22 (.273); Jordan (L.A.) 3-12 (.250); Holland 1-3 (.333); Brewer 0-2 (.000). Opponents 42-184 (.228).

MILWAUKEE BUCKS

Player	G.	Min.	FGA	FGM	Pct.	FTA	FTM	Pct.	Off. Reb.	Def. Reb.	Tot. Reb.	Ast.	PF	Dsq.	Stl.	Blk. Sh.	Pts.	Avg.	Hi.
Ma. Johnson	76	2542	1153	636	.552	381	269	.706	225	293	518	346	196	1	115	41	1541	20.3	40
Bridgeman	77	2215	1102	537	.487	241	213	.884	78	211	289	234	182	2	88	28	1290	16.8	34
Lanier	67	1753	716	376	.525	277	208	.751	128	285	413	179	184	0	73	81	961	14.3	29
Moncrief	80	2417	739	400	.541	398	320	.804	186	220	406	264	156	1	90	37	1122	14.0	27
Buckner	82	2384	956	471	.493	203	149	.734	88	210	298	384	271	3	197	3	1092	13.3	31
Mi. Johnson	82	2118	846	379	.448	332	262	.789	183	362	545	286	256	4	94	71	1023	12.5	23
Winters	69	1771	697	331	.475	137	119	.869	32	108	140	229	185	2	70	10	799	11.6	26
Cummings	74	1084	460	248	.539	140	99	.707	97	195	292	62	192	4	31	19	595	8.0	30
Evans	71	911	291	134	.460	64	50	.781	22	65	87	167	114	0	34	4	320	4.5	16
Catchings	77	1635	300	134	.447	92	59	.641	154	319	473	99	284	7	33	184	327	4.2	14
Elmore	72	925	212	76	.358	75	54	.720	48	140	208	69	178	3	37	52	206	2.9	12

3-Pt. FG: Milwaukee 30-131 (.229)—Ma. Johnson 0-9 (.000); Bridgeman 3-21 (.143); Lanier 1-1 (1.000); Moncrief 2-9 (.222); Buckner 1-6 (.167); Mi. Johnson 3-18 (.167); Winters 18-51 (.353); Cummings 0-2 (.000); Evans 2-14 (143). Opponents 35-199 (.176).

NEW JERSEY NETS

Player	G.	Min.	FGA	FGM	Pct.	FTA	FTM	Pct.	Off. Reb.	Def. Reb.	Tot. Reb.	Ast.	PF	Dsq.	Stl.	Blk. Sh.	Pts.	Avg.	Hi.
Newlin	79	2911	1272	632	.497	466	414	.888	78	141	219	299	237	2	87	9	1688	21.4	43
Robinson	63	1822	1070	525	.491	248	178	.718	120	361	481	105	216	6	58	52	1229	19.5	38
Lucas	68	2162	835	404	.484	254	191	.752	153	422	575	173	260	3	57	59	999	14.7	39
Gminski	56	1579	688	291	.423	202	155	.767	137	282	419	72	127	1	54	100	737	13.2	31
Cook	81	1980	819	383	.468	180	132	.733	96	140	236	297	197	4	141	34	904	11.2	35
O'Koren	79	2473	751	365	.486	212	135	.637	179	299	478	252	243	8	86	27	870	11.0	28
McAdoo (Tot.)	16	321	157	68	.433	41	29	.707	17	50	69	30	38	0	17	13	165	10.3	17
McAdoo (N.J.)	10	153	75	38	.507	21	17	.810	8	18	26	10	22	0	9	6	93	9.3	17
Jones	60	950	357	189	.529	218	146	.670	92	171	263	43	185	4	36	81	524	8.7	27
Elliott	73	1320	419	214	.511	202	121	.599	104	157	261	129	175	3	34	16	550	7.5	22
Moore	71	1406	478	212	.444	92	69	.750	43	125	168	228	179	1	61	17	497	7.0	19
Walker	41	1172	169	72	.426	111	88	.793	22	80	102	253	105	0	52	1	234	5.7	25
van B. Kolff	78	1426	245	100	.408	117	98	.838	48	154	202	129	214	3	38	50	300	3.8	11
Sparrow	15	212	63	22	.349	16	12	.750	7	11	18	32	15	0	13	3	56	3.7	14
°Jordan	14	239	73	30	.411	32	24	.750	5	13	18	46	29	0	24	1	87	6.2	14

3-Pt. FG: New Jersey 34-138 (.246)—Newlin 10-30 (.333); Robinson 1-1 (1.000); Lucas 0-2 (.000); Gminski 0-1 (.000); Cook 6-25 (240); O'Koren 5-18 (.278); McAdoo 0-1 (.000); Jones 0-4 (.000); Elliott 1-2 (.500); Moore 4-27 (.148); Walker 2-9 (.222); van Breda Kolff 2-8 (.250); Jordan 3-10 (.300). Opponents 28-130 (.215).

NEW YORK KNICKERBOCKERS

Player	G.	Min.	FGA	FGM	Pct.	FTA	FTM	Pct.	Off. Reb.	Def. Reb.	Tot. Reb.	Ast.	PF	Dsq.	Stl.	Blk. Sh.	Pts.	Avg.	Hi.
Cartwright	82	2925	1118	619	.554	518	408	.788	161	452	613	111	259	2	48	83	1646	20.1	33
R. Williams	79	2742	1335	616	.461	382	312	.817	122	199	321	432	270	4	185	37	1560	19.7	42
Richardson	79	3175	1116	523	.469	338	224	.663	173	372	545	627	258	2	232	35	1293	16.4	28
Russell	79	2865	1095	508	.464	343	268	.781	109	244	353	257	248	2	99	8	1292	16.4	36
S. Williams	67	1976	708	349	.493	268	185	.690	159	257	416	180	199	0	116	18	885	13.2	27
Glenn	82	1506	511	285	.558	110	98	.891	27	61	88	108	126	0	72	5	672	8.2	29
Webster	82	1708	341	159	.466	163	104	.638	162	303	465	72	187	2	27	97	423	5.2	16
Scales	44	484	225	94	.418	39	26	.667	47	85	132	10	54	0	12	4	215	4.9	20
Woodson	81	949	373	165	.442	64	49	.766	33	64	97	75	95	0	36	12	380	4.7	25
Demic	76	964	254	128	.504	92	58	.630	114	129	243	28	153	0	12	13	314	4.1	17
Carter	60	536	179	59	.330	69	51	.739	30	39	69	76	68	0	22	2	169	2.8	11

3-Pt. FG: New York 56-236 (.237)—Cartwright 0-1 (.000); R. Williams 16-68 (.235); Richardson 23-102 (.225); Russell 8-26 (.308); S. Williams 2-8 (.250); Glenn 4-11 (.364); Webster 1-4 (.250); Scales 1-6 (.167); Woodson 1-5 (.200); Demic 0-2 (.000); Carter 0-3 (.000). Opponents 43-172 (.250).

PHILADELPHIA 76ers

Player	G.	Min.	FGA	FGM	Pct.	FTA	FTM	Pct.	Off. Reb.	Def. Reb.	Tot. Reb.	Ast.	PF	Dsq.	Stl.	Blk. Sh.	Pts.	Avg.	Hi.
Erving	82	2874	1524	794	.521	536	422	.787	244	413	657	364	233	0	173	147	2014	24.6	45
Dawkins	76	2088	697	423	.607	304	219	.720	106	439	545	109	316	9	38	112	1065	14.0	26
B. Jones	81	2046	755	407	.539	347	282	.813	142	293	435	226	226	2	95	74	1096	13.5	26
Toney	75	1768	806	399	.495	226	161	.712	32	111	143	273	234	5	59	10	968	12.9	35
Collins	12	329	126	62	.492	29	24	.828	6	23	29	42	23	0	7	4	148	12.3	19
Mix	72	1327	575	288	.501	240	200	.833	105	159	264	114	107	0	59	18	776	10.8	28
Hollins	82	2154	696	332	.470	171	125	.731	47	144	191	352	205	2	104	18	781	9.5	23
Cheeks	81	2415	581	310	.534	178	140	.787	67	178	245	560	231	1	193	39	763	9.4	27
C. Jones	81	2639	485	218	.449	193	148	.767	200	613	813	122	271	2	53	134	584	7.2	15
Richardson	77	1313	464	227	.489	108	84	.778	83	93	176	152	102	0	36	10	538	7.0	19
Johnson	40	372	158	87	.551	31	27	.871	8	47	55	30	45	0	20	2	202	5.1	20
Cureton	52	528	205	93	.454	64	33	.516	51	104	155	25	68	0	20	23	219	4.2	16
°Davis	1	2	1	1	1.000	0	0	.....	0	1	1	0	0	0	0	0	2	2.0	2

3-Pt. FG: Philadelphia 19-84 (.226)—Erving 4-18 (.222); B. Jones 0-3 (.000); Toney 9-29 (.310); Mix 0-3 (.000); Hollins 2-15 (.133); Cheeks 3-8 (.375); Richardson 0-1 (.000); Johnson 1-6 (.167); Cureton 0-1 (.000). Opponents 48-200 (.240).

PHOENIX SUNS

Player	G.	Min.	FGA	FGM	Pct.	FTA	FTM	Pct.	Off. Reb.	Def. Reb.	Tot. Reb.	Ast.	PF	Dsq.	Stl.	Blk. Sh.	Pts.	Avg.	Hi.
Robinson	82	3088	1280	647	.505	396	249	.629	216	573	789	206	220	1	68	38	1543	18.8	40
Johnson	79	2615	1220	532	.436	501	411	.820	160	203	363	291	244	2	136	61	1486	18.8	39
Davis	78	2182	1101	593	.539	250	209	.836	63	137	200	302	192	3	97	12	1402	18.0	32
Adams	75	2054	870	458	.526	259	199	.768	157	389	546	344	226	2	106	69	1115	14.9	31
Cook	79	2192	616	286	.464	155	100	.645	170	297	467	201	236	3	82	54	672	8.5	16
High	81	1750	576	246	.427	264	183	.693	89	139	228	202	251	2	129	26	677	8.4	20

Player	G.	Min.	FGA	FGM	Pct.	FTA	FTM	Pct.	Off. Reb.	Def. Reb.	Tot. Reb.	Ast.	PF	Dsq.	Stl.	Blk. Sh.	Pts.	Avg.	Hi.
Macy	82	1469	532	272	.511	119	107	.899	44	88	132	160	120	0	76	5	663	8.1	21
Kelley	81	1686	387	196	.506	231	175	.758	131	310	441	282	210	0	79	63	567	7.0	17
Scott	82	1423	348	173	.497	127	97	.764	101	167	268	114	124	0	60	70	444	5.4	14
Kramer	82	1065	258	136	.527	91	63	.692	77	155	232	88	132	0	35	17	335	4.1	17
Niles	44	231	138	48	.348	37	17	.459	26	32	58	15	41	0	8	1	115	2.6	10

3-Pt. FG: Phoenix 35-161 (.217)—Johnson 11-51 (.216); Davis 7-17 (.412); Cook 0-5 (.000); High 2-24 (.083); Macy 12-51 (.235); Kelley 0-2 (.000); Scott 1-6 (.167); Kramer 0-1 (.000); Niles 2-4 (.500). Opponents 69-209 (.330).

PORTLAND TRAIL BLAZERS

Player	G.	Min.	FGA	FGM	Pct.	FTA	FTM	Pct.	Off. Reb.	Def. Reb.	Tot. Reb.	Ast.	PF	Dsq.	Stl.	Blk. Sh.	Pts.	Avg.	Hi.
Paxson	79	2701	1092	585	.536	248	182	.734	74	137	211	299	172	1	140	9	1354	17.1	32
Thompson	79	2790	1151	569	.494	323	207	.641	223	463	686	284	260	5	62	170	1345	17.0	33
Ransey	80	2431	1162	525	.452	219	164	.749	42	153	195	555	201	1	88	9	1217	15.2	35
Bates	77	1560	902	439	.487	199	170	.854	71	86	157	196	120	0	82	6	1062	13.8	40
Natt	74	2111	794	395	.497	283	200	.707	149	282	431	159	188	2	73	18	994	13.4	29
Washington	73	2120	571	325	.569	288	181	.628	236	450	686	149	258	5	85	86	831	11.4	27
Owens	79	1843	630	322	.511	250	191	.764	165	291	456	140	273	10	36	47	835	10.6	27
Gross	82	1934	479	253	.528	159	135	.849	126	202	328	251	238	5	90	67	641	7.8	17
Gale (Tot.)	77	1112	309	157	.508	68	55	.809	16	83	99	169	117	0	94	7	371	4.8	19
Gale (Port.)	42	476	145	71	.490	42	36	.857	9	38	47	70	61	0	39	5	179	4.3	19
Kunnert	55	842	216	101	.468	54	42	.778	98	189	287	67	143	1	17	32	244	4.4	19
Harper	55	461	136	56	.412	85	37	.435	28	65	93	17	73	0	23	20	149	2.7	12
Crompton	6	33	8	4	.500	5	1	.200	7	11	18	2	4	0	0	2	9	1.5	6
*Brewer	29	548	246	95	.386	34	26	.765	13	20	33	55	42	0	34	9	217	7.5	26
*Hamilton	1	5	3	1	.333	2	1	.500	2	1	3	0	1	0	0	0	3	3.0	3

3-Pt. FG: Portland 25-148 (.169)—Paxson 2-30 (.067); Thompson 0-1 (.000); Ransey 3-31 (.097); Bates 14-54 (.259); Natt 4-8 (.500); Washington 0-1 (.000); Owens 0-4 (.000); Gross 0-9 (.000); Gale (Tot.) 2-7 (.286); Gale (Port.) 1-4 (.250); Harper 0-3 (.000); Brewer 1-3 (.333). Opponents 34-149 (.228).

SAN ANTONIO SPURS

Player	G.	Min.	FGA	FGM	Pct.	FTA	FTM	Pct.	Off. Reb.	Def. Reb.	Tot. Reb.	Ast.	PF	Dsq.	Stl.	Blk. Sh.	Pts.	Avg.	Hi.
Gervin	82	2765	1729	850	.492	620	512	.826	126	293	419	260	212	4	94	56	2221	27.1	49
Silas	75	2055	997	476	.477	440	374	.850	44	187	231	285	129	0	51	12	1326	17.7	34
Olberding	82	2408	685	348	.508	380	315	.829	146	325	471	277	307	6	75	31	1012	12.3	28
Corzine	82	1960	747	366	.490	175	125	.714	228	408	636	117	212	0	42	99	857	10.5	24
R. Johnson	79	1716	682	340	.499	193	128	.663	132	226	358	78	283	8	45	48	808	10.2	27
Brewer (Tot.)	75	1452	631	275	.436	114	91	.798	34	52	86	148	95	0	61	34	642	8.6	26
Brewer (S.A.)	46	904	385	180	.468	80	65	.813	21	32	53	93	53	0	27	25	425	9.2	20
Moore	82	1578	520	249	.479	172	105	.610	58	138	196	373	178	0	120	22	604	7.4	22
Restani	64	999	369	192	.520	88	62	.705	71	103	174	81	103	0	16	14	449	7.0	22
Griffin	82	1930	325	166	.511	253	170	.672	184	321	505	249	207	3	77	38	502	6.1	12
Wiley	33	271	138	76	.551	48	36	.750	22	42	64	11	38	1	8	6	188	5.7	17
G. Johnson	82	1935	347	164	.473	109	80	.734	215	387	602	92	273	3	47	278	408	5.0	15
*Shumate	22	519	128	56	.438	73	53	.726	33	54	87	24	46	0	21	9	165	7.5	15
*Gale	35	636	164	86	.524	26	19	.731	7	45	52	99	56	0	55	2	192	5.5	15
*Gerard (Tot.)	27	252	111	42	.369	40	27	.675	30	37	67	15	41	0	10	9	109	4.0	12
*Gerard (S.A.)	11	129	60	22	.367	11	8	.727	17	21	38	9	17	0	7	3	52	4.7	12

3-Pt. FG: San Antonio 15-85 (.176)—Gervin 9-35 (.257); Silas 0-2 (.000); Olberding 1-7 (.143); Corzine 0-3 (.000); R. Johnson 0-1 (.000); Brewer (Tot.) 1-7 (.143), Brewer (S.A.) 0-4 (.000); Moore 1-19 (.053); Restani 3-8 (.375); Wiley 0-2 (.000); Gale 1-3 (.333); Gerard (Tot.) 0-3 (.000); Gerard (S.A.) 0-1 (.000). Opponents 45-168 (.268).

SAN DIEGO CLIPPERS

Player	G.	Min.	FGA	FGM	Pct.	FTA	FTM	Pct.	Off. Reb.	Def. Reb.	Tot. Reb.	Ast.	PF	Dsq.	Stl.	Blk. Sh.	Pts.	Avg.	Hi.
Williams	82	1976	1381	642	.465	297	253	.852	75	54	129	164	157	0	91	5	1585	19.3	41
Smith	76	2378	1057	519	.491	313	237	.757	49	107	156	372	231	1	84	18	1279	16.8	35
Nater	82	2809	935	517	.553	307	244	.795	295	722	1017	199	295	8	49	46	1278	15.6	30
Brooks	82	2479	1018	488	.479	320	226	.706	210	232	442	208	234	2	99	31	1202	14.7	35
Bryant	82	2359	791	379	.479	244	193	.791	146	294	440	189	264	4	72	34	953	11.6	34
Taylor	80	2312	591	310	.525	185	146	.789	58	93	151	440	212	0	118	23	810	10.1	31
Davis	64	817	314	139	.443	158	94	.595	47	72	119	47	98	0	36	11	374	5.8	18
Heard	78	1631	396	149	.376	101	79	.782	120	228	348	122	196	0	104	12	377	4.8	16
Bibby	73	1112	306	118	.386	98	67	.684	25	49	74	200	85	0	47	2	335	4.6	18
Whitehead (Tot.)	48	688	180	83	.461	56	28	.500	58	156	214	26	122	2	20	9	194	4.0	16
Whitehead (S.D.)	38	562	139	66	.475	45	23	.511	48	135	183	24	100	2	15	8	155	4.1	16
Rank	25	153	57	21	.368	28	13	.464	17	13	30	17	33	1	7	1	55	2.2	6
*Pietkiewicz	6	30	5	2	.400	0	0	.....	0	1	1	2	2	0	0	0	4	0.7	2
*Wicks	49	1083	286	125	.437	150	76	.507	79	144	223	111	168	3	40	40	326	6.7	18
*Price	5	29	7	2	.286	0	0	.....	0	0	0	3	3	0	2	1	4	0.8	2

3-Pt. FG: San Diego 132-407 (.324)—Williams 48-141 (.340); Smith 4-18 (.222); Brooks 0-6 (.000); Bryant 2-15 (.133); Taylor 44-115 (.383); Davis 2-8 (.250); Heard 0-7 (.000); Bibby 32-95 (.337); Whitehead (S.D.) 0-1 (.000); Wicks 0-1 (.000). Opponents 33-153 (.216).

SEATTLE SUPERSONICS

Player	G.	Min.	FGA	FGM	Pct.	FTA	FTM	Pct.	Off. Reb.	Def. Reb.	Tot. Reb.	Ast.	PF	Dsq.	Stl.	Blk. Sh.	Pts.	Avg.	Hi.
Sikma	82	2920	1311	595	.454	413	340	.823	184	668	852	248	282	5	78	93	1530	18.7	38
Westphal	36	1078	500	221	.442	184	153	.832	11	57	68	148	70	0	46	14	601	16.7	32
Brown	78	1986	1035	505	.488	208	173	.832	53	122	175	233	141	0	88	13	1206	15.5	28
Bailey	82	2539	889	444	.499	361	256	.709	192	415	607	98	332	11	74	143	1145	14.0	27
V. Johnson	81	2311	785	419	.534	270	214	.793	193	173	366	341	198	0	78	20	1053	13.0	31
Shelton	14	440	174	73	.420	55	36	.655	31	47	78	35	48	0	22	3	182	13.0	30

Player	G.	Min.	FGA	FGM	Pct.	FTA	FTM	Pct.	Off. Reb.	Def. Reb.	Tot. Reb.	Ast.	PF	Dsq.	Stl.	Blk. Sh.	Pts.	Avg.	Hi.
J. Johnson	80	2324	866	373	.431	214	173	.808	135	227	362	312	202	2	57	25	919	11.5	26
Walker	82	1796	626	290	.463	169	109	.645	105	210	315	122	168	1	53	15	689	8.4	21
Hanzlik	74	1259	289	138	.478	150	119	.793	67	86	153	111	168	1	58	20	396	5.4	21
Donaldson	68	980	238	129	.542	170	101	.594	107	202	309	42	79	0	8	74	359	5.3	20
Hill (Tot)	75	1738	335	117	.349	172	141	.820	41	118	159	292	207	3	66	11	375	5.0	17
Hill (Sea.)	51	1114	219	78	.356	122	99	.811	31	77	108	174	147	3	40	8	255	5.0	17
Awtrey	47	607	93	44	.473	20	14	.700	33	75	108	54	85	0	12	8	102	2.2	8
Dorsey	29	253	70	20	.286	25	13	.520	23	65	88	9	47	0	9	1	53	1.8	8
°White (Tot)	16	208	65	23	.354	16	15	.938	1	10	11	20	23	0	9	1	61	3.8	13
°White (Sea.)	12	165	47	14	.298	12	11	.917	1	10	11	18	16	0	5	1	39	3.3	13
°Shumate(Tot)	24	527	131	56	.427	76	55	.724	34	54	88	24	49	0	21	9	167	7.0	15
°Shumate(Sea)	2	8	3	0	.000	3	2	.667	1	0	1	0	3	0	0	0	2	1.0	2

3-Pt. FG: Seattle 32-117 (.274)—Sikma 0-5 (.000); Westphal 6-25 (.240); Brown 23-64 (.359); Bailey 1-2 (.500); V. Johnson 1-5 (.200); J. Johnson 0-1 (.000); Walker 0-3 (.000); Hanzlik 1-5 (.200); Hill (Tot.) 0-7 (.000); Hill (Sea.) 0-6 (.000); White 0-1 (.000). Opponents 42-157 (.268).

UTAH JAZZ

Player	G.	Min.	FGA	FGM	Pct.	FTA	FTM	Pct.	Off. Reb.	Def. Reb.	Tot. Reb.	Ast.	PF	Dsq.	Stl.	Blk. Sh.	Pts.	Avg.	Hi.
Dantley	80	3417	1627	909	.559	784	632	.806	192	317	509	322	245	1	109	18	2452	30.7	55
Griffith	81	2867	1544	716	.464	320	229	.716	79	209	288	194	219	0	106	50	1671	20.6	38
Poquette	82	2808	614	324	.528	162	126	.778	160	469	629	161	342	18	67	174	777	9.5	20
Green	47	1307	366	176	.481	97	70	.722	30	86	116	235	123	2	75	1	422	9.0	20
Bristow	82	2001	611	271	.444	198	166	.838	103	327	430	383	190	1	63	3	713	8.7	18
Cooper	71	1420	471	213	.452	90	62	.689	166	274	440	52	219	8	18	51	489	6.9	22
Nicks (Tot)	67	1109	359	172	.479	126	71	.563	37	73	110	149	141	0	60	3	415	6.2	24
Nicks (Utah)	40	616	210	107	.510	67	36	.537	24	37	61	69	89	0	32	1	250	6.3	24
Wilkins	56	1058	260	117	.450	40	27	.675	62	212	274	40	169	3	32	46	261	4.7	22
Judkins	62	666	216	92	.426	51	45	.882	29	64	93	59	84	0	16	2	238	3.8	13
Bennett	28	313	60	26	.433	81	53	.654	33	60	93	15	56	0	3	11	105	3.8	12
Duren	40	458	101	33	.327	9	5	.556	8	27	35	54	54	0	18	2	71	1.8	10
°McKinney	35	1032	233	124	.532	48	44	.917	12	62	74	157	107	3	38	4	293	8.4	21
°Boone	52	1146	371	160	.431	94	75	.798	17	67	84	161	126	0	33	8	406	7.8	18
°Hardy	23	509	111	52	.468	20	11	.550	39	94	133	36	58	2	21	20	115	5.0	13
°Vroman	11	93	27	10	.370	19	14	.737	7	18	25	9	26	1	5	5	34	3.1	9
°Miller (Tot)	8	53	9	4	.444	0	0	.....	2	5	7	5	5	0	4	0	8	1.0	4
°Miller (Utah)	3	19	3	2	.667	0	0	.....	1	2	3	1	3	0	1	0	4	1.3	4

3-Pt. FG: Utah 42-163 (.258)—Dantley 2-7 (.286); Griffith 10-52 (.192); Poquette 3-6 (.500); Green 0-1 (.000); Bristow 5-18 (.278); Cooper 1-3 (.333); Nicks (Tot) 0-4 (.000); Nicks (Utah) 0-3 (.000); Judkins 9-28 (.321); Bennett 0-2 (.000); Duren 0-1 (.000); McKinney 1-2 (.500); Boone 11-39 (.282); Vroman 0-1 (.000); Miller (Tot) 0-1 (.000). Opponents 45-147 (.306).

WASHINGTON BULLETS

Player	G.	Min.	FGA	FGM	Pct.	FTA	FTM	Pct.	Off. Reb.	Def. Reb.	Tot. Reb.	Ast.	PF	Dsq.	Stl.	Blk. Sh.	Pts.	Avg.	Hi.
Hayes	81	2931	1296	584	.451	439	271	.617	235	554	789	98	300	6	68	171	1439	17.8	34
Grevey	75	2616	1103	500	.453	290	244	.841	67	152	219	300	161	1	68	17	1289	17.2	36
Ballard	82	2610	1186	549	.463	196	166	.847	167	413	580	195	194	1	118	39	1271	15.5	38
Porter	81	2577	859	446	.519	247	191	.773	35	89	124	734	257	4	110	10	1086	13.4	31
Kupchak	82	1934	747	392	.525	340	240	.706	198	371	569	62	195	1	36	26	1024	12.5	30
Dandridge	23	545	237	101	.426	39	28	.718	19	64	83	60	54	1	16	9	230	10.0	20
Collins (Tot)	81	1845	811	360	.444	272	211	.776	129	139	268	190	259	6	104	25	931	11.5	27
Collins (Wash)	34	661	281	130	.463	110	74	.673	33	48	81	75	93	1	35	14	334	9.8	27
Unseld	63	2032	429	225	.524	86	55	.640	207	466	673	170	171	1	52	36	507	8.0	22
Terry	26	504	160	80	.500	42	28	.667	43	73	116	70	68	1	27	13	188	7.2	16
Roberts	26	350	144	54	.375	29	19	.655	18	50	68	20	52	0	11	0	127	4.9	18
Mahorn	52	696	219	111	.507	40	27	.675	67	148	215	25	134	3	21	44	249	4.8	28
Carr (Tot)	47	657	234	87	.372	54	34	.630	22	39	61	58	53	0	15	2	208	4.4	17
Carr (Wash)	39	580	206	80	.388	50	32	.640	18	34	52	49	43	0	14	2	192	4.9	17
McCarter	43	448	135	51	.378	24	18	.750	16	23	39	73	36	0	14	0	122	2.8	14
°Matthews	45	1161	449	224	.499	129	99	.767	30	37	67	199	120	1	46	10	552	12.3	24
°Williamson	9	112	56	18	.321	6	5	.833	0	7	7	17	13	0	4	1	42	4.7	12
°Britton	2	9	3	2	.667	0	0	.....	0	2	2	3	2	0	1	0	4	2.0	2
°McCord	2	9	4	2	.500	0	0	.....	1	1	2	1	0	0	0	0	4	2.0	2
°Brown	2	5	3	0	.000	5	2	.400	1	1	2	0	0	0	0	0	2	1.0	2

3-Pt. FG: Washington 65-241 (.270)—Hayes 0-10 (.000); Grevey 45-136 (.331); Ballard 7-32 (.219); Porter 3-12 (.250); Kupchak 0-1 (.000); Dandridge 0-1 (.000); Collins (Tot) 0-6 (.000); Collins (Wash) 0-3 (.000); Unseld 2-4 (.500); Carlos 0-6 (.000); Carr 0-7 (.000); McCarter 2-8 (.250); Matthews 5-15 (.333); Williamson 1-6 (.167). Opponents 37-176 (.210).

PLAYOFF RESULTS

EASTERN CONFERENCE FIRST ROUND
Chicago 2, New York 0
Mar. 31—Tue.—Chicago 90 at New York 80
Apr. 3—Fri.—New York 114 at Chicago...................................*115

Philadelphia 2, Indiana 0
Mar. 31—Tue.—Indiana 108 at Philadelphia 124
Apr. 2—Thu.—Philadelphia 96 at Indiana....................................85

EASTERN CONFERENCE SEMIFINALS
Philadelphia 4, Milwaukee 3
Apr. 5—Sun.—Milwaukee 122 at Philadelphia 125
Apr. 7—Tue.—Milwaukee 109 at Philadelphia...........................99
Apr. 10—Fri.—Philadelphia 108 at Milwaukee.......................103
Apr. 12—Sun.—Philadelphia 98 at Milwaukee.......................109
Apr. 15—Wed.—Milwaukee 99 at Philadelphia......................116
Apr. 17—Fri.—Philadelphia 86 at Milwaukee.......................109
Apr. 19—Sun.—Milwaukee 98 at Philadelphia.......................99

Boston 4, Chicago 0
Apr. 5—Sun.—Chicago 109 at Boston 121
Apr. 7—Tue.—Chicago 97 at Boston 106
Apr. 10—Fri.—Boston 113 at Chicago.....................................107
Apr. 12—Sun.—Boston 109 at Chicago 103

EASTERN CONFERENCE FINALS
Boston 4, Philadelphia 3
Apr. 21—Tue.—Philadelphia 105 at Boston.......................104
Apr. 22—Wed.—Philadelphia 99 at Boston...........................118
Apr. 24—Fri.—Boston 100 at Philadelphia 110
Apr. 26—Sun.—Boston 105 at Philadelphia 107
Apr. 29—Wed.—Philadelphia 109 at Boston...........................111
May 1—Fri.—Boston 100 at Philadelphia...........................98
May 3—Sun.—Philadelphia 90 at Boston...........................91

WESTERN CONFERENCE FIRST ROUND
Houston 2, Los Angeles 1
Apr. 1—Wed.—Houston 111 at Los Angeles 107
Apr. 3—Fri.—Los Angeles 111 at Houston.........................106
Apr. 5—Sun.—Houston 89 at Los Angeles 86

Kansas City 2, Portland 1
Apr. 1—Wed.—Kansas City 98 at Portland...........................*97
Apr. 3—Fri.—Portland 124 at Kansas City *119
Apr. 5—Sun.—Kansas City 104 at Portland 95

WESTERN CONFERENCE SEMIFINALS
Kansas City 4, Phoenix 3
Apr. 7—Tue.—Kansas City 80 at Phoenix...............................102
Apr. 8—Wed.—Kansas City 88 at Phoenix 83
Apr. 10—Fri.—Phoenix 92 at Kansas City 93
Apr. 12—Sun.—Phoenix 95 at Kansas City.............................102
Apr. 15—Wed.—Kansas City 89 at Phoenix.............................101
Apr. 17—Fri.—Phoenix 81 at Kansas City 76
Apr. 19—Sun.—Kansas City 95 at Phoenix.............................88

Houston 4, San Antonio 3
Apr. 7—Tue.—Houston 107 at San Antonio...............................98
Apr. 8—Wed.—Houston 113 at San Antonio...............................125
Apr. 10—Fri.—San Antonio 99 at Houston...............................112
Apr. 12—Sun.—San Antonio 114 at Houston...............................112
Apr. 14—Tue.—Houston 123 at San Antonio...............................117
Apr. 15—Wed.—San Antonio 101 at Houston...............................96
Apr. 17—Fri.—Houston 105 at San Antonio 100

WESTERN CONFERENCE FINALS
Houston 4, Kansas City 1
Apr. 21—Tue.—Houston 97 at Kansas City...............................78
Apr. 22—Wed.—Houston 79 at Kansas City...............................88
Apr. 24—Fri.—Kansas City 88 at Houston...............................92
Apr. 26—Sun.—Kansas City 89 at Houston...............................100
Apr. 29—Wed.—Houston 97 at Kansas City 88

WORLD CHAMPIONSHIP SERIES
Boston 4, Houston 2
May 5—Tue.—Houston 95 at Boston.......................................98
May 7—Thu.—Houston 92 at Boston.......................................90
May 9—Sat.—Boston 94 at Houston 71
May 10—Sun.—Boston 86 at Houston 91
May 12—Tue.—Houston 80 at Boston.......................................109
May 14—Thu.—Boston 102 at Houston.......................................91

*Denotes overtime period.

1979-80 NBA STATISTICS

LOS ANGELES LAKERS 1979-80 NBA WORLD CHAMPIONS

Seated: Chairman of the Board Dr. Jerry Buss, Spencer Haywood, Jamaal Wilkes, Kareem Abdul-Jabbar, Earvin Johnson, Jim Chones, General Manager Bill Sharman. Back Row (left to right): Head Coach Paul Westhead, Butch Lee, Brad Holland, Mark Landsberger, Marty Byrnes, Michael Cooper, Norm Nixon, Trainer Jack Curran, Assistant Coach Pat Riley.

FINAL STANDINGS

ATLANTIC DIVISION

Team	Atl.	Bos.	Chi.	Cle.	Den.	Det.	G.S.	Hou.	Ind.	K.C.	L.A.	Mil.	N.J.	N.Y.	Phi.	Pho.	Por.	S.A.	S.D.	Sea.	Utah	Was.	W.	L.	Pct.	G.B.
Boston	4	..	2	4	2	6	2	6	4	1	..	2	5	5	3	1	2	4	2	..	2	4	61	21	.744	....
Philadelphia	2	3	1	5	2	5	2	4	5	1	1	2	5	6	..	1	2	4	1	1	1	5	59	23	.720	2
Washington	3	2	2	3	1	4	2	4	2	..	1	1	3	3	1	..	1	2	1	1	2	..	39	43	.476	22
New York	2	1	2	3	1	4	2	3	2	1	..	1	4	..	..	2	2	4	1	..	1	3	39	43	.476	22
New Jersey	2	1	1	3	1	4	..	3	4	1	..	1	..	2	1	1	..	3	1	1	1	3	34	48	.415	27

CENTRAL DIVISION

Team	Atl.	Bos.	Chi.	Cle.	Den.	Det.	G.S.	Hou.	Ind.	K.C.	L.A.	Mil.	N.J.	N.Y.	Phi.	Pho.	Por.	S.A.	S.D.	Sea.	Utah	Was.	W.	L.	Pct.	G.B.
Atlanta	..	2	1	4	1	6	2	2	4	..	1	1	4	4	4	1	2	5	1	..	2	3	50	32	.610	....
Houston	4	..	1	4	1	5	1	..	4	..	..	1	3	3	2	1	1	3	2	1	2	2	41	41	.500	9
San Antonio	1	2	2	2	1	4	2	3	4	1	..	2	3	2	2	1	1	..	2	1	1	4	41	41	.500	9
Indiana	2	2	2	4	1	5	1	2	..	1	..	..	2	4	1	..	2	2	1	..	1	4	37	45	.451	13
Cleveland	2	2	..	..	1	6	2	2	2	2	1	..	3	3	1	1	..	4	1	..	1	3	37	45	.451	13
Detroit	..	..	1	..	1	..	..	1	1	1	..	..	1	2	2	1	..	2	..	..	1	2	16	66	.195	34

MIDWEST DIVISION

Team	Atl.	Bos.	Chi.	Cle.	Den.	Det.	G.S.	Hou.	Ind.	K.C.	L.A.	Mil.	N.J.	N.Y.	Phi.	Pho.	Por.	S.A.	S.D.	Sea.	Utah	Was.	W.	L.	Pct.	G.B.
Milwaukee	1	..	5	2	3	1	6	1	2	3	3	..	1	1	..	4	5	..	4	2	4	1	49	33	.598	....
Kansas City	2	1	3	..	6	2	3	2	1	..	2	3	1	1	1	1	1	5	3	6	2	1	47	35	.573	2
Denver	1	..	4	1	..	1	3	1	1	..	1	3	1	1	..	1	2	1	3	1	3	1	30	52	.366	19
Chicago	1	..	..	2	2	1	4	1	..	3	1	1	1	..	1	1	3	..	4	2	2	..	30	52	.366	19
Utah	..	..	4	1	3	1	3	..	1	..	..	2	1	1	1	..	3	1	1	1	..	..	24	58	.293	25

PACIFIC DIVISION

Team	Atl.	Bos.	Chi.	Cle.	Den.	Det.	G.S.	Hou.	Ind.	K.C.	L.A.	Mil.	N.J.	N.Y.	Phi.	Pho.	Por.	S.A.	S.D.	Sea.	Utah	Was.	W.	L.	Pct.	G.B.
Los Angeles	1	2	5	1	5	2	5	2	2	4	..	3	2	2	1	3	2	2	5	4	6	1	60	22	.732	....
Seattle	2	2	4	2	5	2	6	1	2	3	2	4	1	2	1	2	5	1	3	..	5	1	56	26	.683	4
Phoenix	1	1	5	1	5	2	4	1	2	5	3	2	1	..	1	..	6	1	2	4	6	2	55	27	.671	5
Portland	..	..	3	2	4	2	4	1	..	5	4	1	2	..	..	..	1	4	1	3	1	8	38	44	.463	22
San Diego	1	..	2	1	3	2	3	..	1	1	1	2	1	1	1	4	2	..	..	3	5	1	35	47	.427	25
Golden State	..	..	2	..	3	1	..	1	1	3	1	..	2	..	..	2	2	..	3	..	3	..	24	58	.293	36

HOME-ROAD RECORDS OF ALL TEAMS

Team	Home	Road	Total
Atlanta	32- 9	18- 23	50- 32
Boston	35- 6	26- 15	61- 21
Chicago	21- 20	9- 32	30- 52
Cleveland	28- 13	9- 32	37- 45
Denver	24- 17	6- 35	30- 52
Detroit	13- 28	3- 38	16- 66
Golden State	15- 26	9- 32	24- 58
Houston	29- 12	12- 29	41- 41
Indiana	26- 15	11- 30	37- 45
Kansas City	30- 11	17- 24	47- 35
Los Angeles	37- 4	23- 18	60- 22
Milwaukee	28- 13	21- 20	49- 33
New Jersey	22- 19	12- 29	34- 48
New York	25- 16	14- 27	39- 43
Philadelphia	36- 5	23- 18	59- 23
Phoenix	36- 5	19- 22	55- 27
Portland	26- 15	12- 29	38- 44
San Antonio	27- 14	14- 27	41- 41
San Diego	24- 17	11- 30	38- 44
Seattle	33- 8	23- 18	56- 26
Utah	17- 24	7- 34	24- 58
Washington	24- 17	15- 26	39- 43
Totals	588- 314	314- 588	902- 902

OFFENSIVE TEAM STATISTICS

Team	G.	FIELD GOALS Att.	Made	Pct.	FREE THROWS Att.	Made	Pct.	REBOUNDS Off.	Def.	Tot.	Ast.	MISCELLANEOUS PF	Disq.	Stl.	Turn Over	Blk. Sh.	SCORING Pts.	Avg.
San Antonio	82	7738	3856	.498	2528	2024	.801	1153	2515	3668	2326	2103	29	771	1589	333	9788	119.4
Los Angeles	82	7368	3898	.529	2092	1622	.775	1085	2653	3738	2413	1784	15	774	1639	546	9438	115.1
Cleveland	82	8041	3811	.474	2205	1702	.772	1307	2381	3688	2108	1934	18	764	1370	342	9360	114.1
New York	82	7672	3802	.496	2274	1698	.747	1236	2303	3539	2265	2168	33	881	1613	457	9344	114.0
Boston	82	7387	3617	.490	2449	1907	.779	1227	2457	3684	2198	1974	19	809	1539	308	9303	113.5
Indiana	82	7689	3639	.473	2333	1753	.751	1398	2326	3724	2148	1973	37	900	1517	530	9119	111.2
Phoenix	82	7235	3570	.493	2466	1906	.773	1071	2458	3529	2283	1853	9	908	1629	344	9114	111.1
Houston	82	7496	3599	.480	2326	1782	.766	1394	2217	3611	2149	1927	11	782	1565	373	9084	110.8
Milwaukee	82	7553	3685	.488	2102	1605	.764	1245	2396	3641	2277	1937	12	778	1496	510	9025	110.1
Philadelphia	82	7156	3523	.492	2431	1876	.772	1187	2635	3822	2226	1860	17	792	1708	652	8949	109.1
Detroit	82	7596	3643	.480	2149	1590	.740	1226	2415	3641	1950	2069	47	783	1742	562	8933	108.9
Seattle	82	7565	3554	.470	2253	1730	.768	1380	2550	3930	2043	1865	27	750	1496	428	8897	108.5
New Jersey	82	7504	3456	.461	2406	1882	.782	1229	2535	3764	2094	2181	38	869	1702	581	8879	108.3
Denver	82	7470	3462	.463	2539	1871	.737	1311	2524	3835	2079	1917	24	746	1533	404	8878	108.3
Kansas City	82	7489	3582	.478	2250	1671	.743	1187	2429	3616	2123	2135	20	863	1439	356	8860	108.0
San Diego	82	7494	3524	.470	2167	1595	.736	1294	2308	3602	1688	1896	24	664	1443	288	8820	107.6
Chicago	82	6943	3362	.484	2592	2019	.779	1115	2465	3580	2152	2146	26	704	1684	392	8813	107.5
Washington	82	7796	3574	.458	2048	1552	.758	1334	2723	4057	2201	1893	24	530	1380	443	8773	107.0
Atlanta	82	7027	3261	.464	2645	2038	.771	1369	2406	3775	1913	2293	46	782	1495	539	8573	104.5
Golden State	82	7318	3527	.482	1914	1412	.738	1155	2437	3592	2028	2082	28	779	1492	339	8493	103.6
Portland	82	7167	3408	.476	2100	1560	.743	1295	2408	3703	1898	1956	23	708	1552	472	8402	102.5
Utah	82	6817	3382	.496	1943	1571	.809	967	2359	3326	2005	2006	33	656	1543	362	8394	102.4

DEFENSIVE TEAM STATISTICS

Team	FIELD GOALS Att.	Made	Pct.	FREE THROWS Att.	Made	Pct.	REBOUNDS Off.	Def.	Tot.	Ast.	MISCELLANEOUS PF	Disq.	Stl.	Turn Over	Blk. Sh.	SCORING Pts.	Avg.	Pt. Dif.
Atlanta	6872	3144	.458	2616	2000	.765	1261	2339	3600	1758	2171	35	682	1660	554	8334	101.6	+ 2.9
Portland	7008	3349	.478	2281	1716	.752	1138	2358	3496	2008	1880	23	756	1450	395	8469	103.3	− 0.8
Seattle	7424	3408	.459	2147	1640	.764	1203	2409	3612	2016	1997	24	728	1519	393	8515	103.8	+ 4.7
Kansas City	6992	3328	.476	2497	1906	.763	1140	2644	3784	1778	2072	17	695	1762	425	8603	104.9	+ 3.1
Philadelphia	7561	3444	.455	2145	1640	.765	1318	2352	3670	2089	2100	39	876	1561	388	8603	104.9	+ 4.2
Boston	7313	3439	.470	2222	1712	.770	1168	2294	3462	1867	2059	34	686	1635	419	8664	105.7	+ 7.8
Milwaukee	7487	3456	.462	2275	1714	.753	1360	2293	3653	2154	1912	15	717	1638	358	8702	106.1	+ 4.0
Phoenix	7480	3563	.476	2119	1593	.752	1216	2447	3663	2026	2051	32	882	1663	389	8819	107.5	+ 3.6
Golden State	6975	3438	.493	2544	1905	.749	1056	2564	3620	2091	1785	14	720	1486	361	8853	108.0	− 4.4
Utah	7182	3559	.496	2205	1702	.772	1159	2288	3447	1997	1782	15	710	1274	398	8887	108.4	− 6.0
Los Angeles	7921	3723	.470	1884	1430	.759	1312	2242	3554	2324	1860	27	797	1420	382	8954	109.2	+ 5.9
New Jersey	7427	3480	.469	2572	1957	.761	1285	2596	3881	2189	2042	27	849	1692	514	8975	109.5	− 1.2
Washington	7771	3615	.465	2184	1696	.777	1197	2672	3869	2120	1901	24	734	1222	519	8982	109.5	− 2.5
Chicago	7222	3585	.496	2358	1811	.768	1159	2345	3504	2109	2203	38	846	1543	498	9035	110.2	− 2.7
Houston	7382	3658	.496	2153	1696	.788	1290	2317	3607	2223	2049	29	778	1597	428	9070	110.6	+ 0.2
San Diego	7508	3752	.500	2086	1613	.773	1222	2487	3709	2012	1889	16	764	1391	408	9160	111.7	− 4.1
Indiana	7545	3693	.489	2295	1734	.756	1394	2552	3946	2323	2028	26	738	1758	470	9176	111.9	− 0.7
Denver	7591	3736	.492	2235	1698	.760	1197	2587	3784	2289	2033	22	812	1438	455	9240	112.7	− 4.4
Cleveland	7610	3811	.501	2150	1645	.765	1230	2638	3868	2208	2033	30	708	1667	490	9332	113.8	+ 0.3
New York	7492	3707	.495	2556	1969	.770	1293	2432	3725	2143	2042	31	813	1694	390	9439	115.1	− 1.1
Detroit	7761	3847	.496	2405	1858	.773	1319	2572	3891	2306	1871	14	874	1583	470	9609	117.2	− 8.3
San Antonio	7997	4000	.500	2283	1731	.758	1248	2472	3720	2537	2192	28	828	1513	457	9819	119.7	− 0.3

Disq.—Individual players disqualified (fouled out of game).

INDIVIDUAL LEADERS

POINTS
(Minimum of 70 games played or 1400 points)

Player	G.	FG	FT	Pts.	Avg.	Player	G.	FG	FT	Pts.	Avg.
Gervin, San Antonio	78	1024	505	2585	33.1	Williams, Seattle	82	739	331	1816	22.1
Free, San Diego	68	737	572	2055	30.2	Westphal, Phoenix	82	692	382	1792	21.9
Dantley, Utah	68	730	443	1903	28.0	Cartwright, New York	82	665	451	1781	21.7
Erving, Philadelphia	78	838	420	2100	26.9	Johnson, Milwaukee	77	689	291	1671	21.7
Malone, Houston	82	778	563	2119	25.8	Davis, Phoenix	75	657	299	1613	21.5
Abdul-Jabbar, L. A.	82	835	364	2034	24.8	Bird, Boston	82	693	301	1745	21.3
Issel, Denver	82	715	517	1951	23.8	Newlin, New Jersey	78	611	367	1634	20.9
Hayes, Washington	81	761	334	1859	23.0	R. Williams, New York	82	687	333	1714	20.9
Birdsong, Kansas City	82	781	286	1858	22.7	Theus, Chicago	82	566	500	1660	20.2
Mitchell, Cleveland	82	775	270	1820	22.2	Kenon, San Antonio	78	647	270	1565	20.1

FIELD GOALS
Minimum 300 FG Made

	FGA	FGM	Pct.
Maxwell, Boston	750	457	.609
Abdul-Jabbar, Los Angeles	1383	835	.604
Gilmore, Chicago	513	305	.595
Dantley, Utah	1267	730	.576
Boswell, Denver-Utah	613	346	.564
Davis, Phoenix	1166	657	.563
Nater, San Diego	799	443	.554
Washington, Portland	761	421	.553
Cartwright, New York	1215	665	.547
Johnson, Milwaukee	1267	689	.544

FREE THROWS
Minimum 125 FT Made

	FTA	FTM	Pct.
Barry, Houston	153	143	.935
Murphy, Houston	302	271	.897
Boone, Los Angeles-Utah	196	175	.893
Silas, San Antonio	382	339	.887
Newlin, New Jersey	415	367	.884
Furlow, Atlanta-Utah	196	171	.872
Phegley, Washington-New Jersey	203	177	.872
Bratz, Phoenix	162	141	.870
Grevey, Washington	249	216	.867
Roche, Denver	202	175	.866

ASSISTS
Minimum 70 games or 400 assists

	G.	No.	Avg.
Richardson, New York	82	832	10.1
Archibald, Boston	80	671	8.4
Walker, Cleveland	76	607	8.0
Nixon, Los Angeles	82	642	7.8
Lucas, Golden State	80	602	7.5
Ford, Kansas City	82	610	7.4
Johnson, Los Angeles	77	563	7.3
Cheeks, Philadelphia	79	556	7.0
Jordan, New Jersey	82	557	6.8
Porter, Washington	70	457	6.5

STEALS
Minimum 70 games or 125 steals

	G.	No.	Avg.
Richardson, New York	82	265	3.23
Jordan, New Jersey	82	223	2.72
Bradley, Indiana	82	211	2.57
Williams, Seattle	82	200	2.44
Johnson, Los Angeles	77	187	2.43
Cheeks, Philadelphia	79	183	2.32
Erving, Philadelphia	78	170	2.18
Parker, Golden State	82	173	2.11
Walker, Cleveland	76	155	2.04
R. Williams, New York	82	167	2.04

REBOUNDS
Minimum 70 games or 800 rebounds

	G.	Off.	Def.	Tot.	Avg.
Nater, San Diego	81	352	864	1216	15.0
Malone, Houston	82	573	617	1190	14.5
Unseld, Washington	82	334	760	1094	13.3
C. Jones, Philadelphia	80	219	731	950	11.9
Sikma, Seattle	82	198	710	908	11.1
Hayes, Washington	81	269	627	896	11.1
Parish, Golden State	72	247	536	783	10.9
Abdul-Jabbar, L. A.	82	190	696	886	10.8
Washington, Portland	80	325	517	842	10.5
Bird, Boston	82	216	636	852	10.4

BLOCKED SHOTS
Minimum 70 games or 100 blocked shots

	G.	No.	Avg.
Abdul-Jabbar, Los Angeles	82	280	3.41
Johnson, New Jersey	81	258	3.19
Rollins, Atlanta	82	244	2.98
Tyler, Detroit	82	220	2.68
Hayes, Washington	81	189	2.33
Catchings, Milwaukee	72	162	2.25
C. Jones, Philadelphia	80	162	2.03
Poquette, Utah	82	162	1.98
Meriweather, New York	65	120	1.85
Erving, Philadelphia	78	140	1.79

3 PT. FIELD GOALS
Minimum 25 Made

	FGA	FGM	Pct.
Brown, Seattle	88	39	.443
Ford, Boston	164	70	.427
Bird, Boston	143	58	.406
Roche, Denver	129	49	.380
Taylor, San Diego	239	90	.377
Winters, Milwaukee	102	38	.373
Grevey, Washington	92	34	.370
Hassett, Indiana	198	69	.348
Barry, Houston	221	73	.330
Williams, San Diego	128	42	.328

TEAM-BY-TEAM INDIVIDUAL STATISTICS

ATLANTA HAWKS

Player	G.	Min.	FGA	FGM	Pct.	FTA	FTM	Pct.	Off. Reb.	Def. Reb.	Tot. Reb.	Ast.	PF	Dsq.	Stl.	Blk. Sh.	Pts.	Avg.	Hi.
Drew	80	2306	1182	535	.453	646	489	.757	203	268	471	101	313	10	91	23	1559	19.5	40
Johnson	79	2622	1212	590	.487	338	280	.828	95	105	200	370	216	2	120	24	1465	18.5	36
Roundfield	81	2588	1007	502	.499	465	330	.710	293	544	837	184	317	6	101	139	1334	16.5	31
Hawes	82	1885	605	304	.502	182	150	.824	148	348	496	144	205	4	74	29	761	9.3	24
Rollins	82	2123	514	287	.558	220	157	.714	283	491	774	76	322	12	54	244	731	8.9	20
McElroy (Tot)	67	1528	527	228	.433	172	132	.767	32	67	99	227	123	2	46	19	593	8.9	33
McElroy (Atl)	31	516	171	66	.386	53	37	.698	20	29	49	65	45	1	21	5	171	5.5	20
McMillen	53	1071	382	191	.500	107	81	.757	70	150	220	62	126	2	36	14	463	8.7	24
Furlow	21	404	161	66	.410	51	44	.863	23	19	42	72	19	0	19	9	177	8.4	22
Criss	81	1794	578	249	.431	212	172	.811	27	89	116	246	133	0	74	4	671	8.3	26
Hill	79	2092	431	177	.411	146	124	.849	31	107	138	424	261	7	107	8	479	6.1	17
Givens	82	1254	473	182	.385	128	106	.828	114	128	242	59	132	1	51	19	470	5.7	20
Brown (Tot)	32	385	105	37	.352	48	38	.792	26	45	71	18	70	0	3	4	112	3.5	12
Brown (Atl)	28	361	98	37	.378	44	34	.773	21	41	62	14	66	0	3	4	108	3.9	12
Pellom	44	373	108	44	.407	30	21	.700	28	64	92	18	70	0	12	12	109	2.5	10
Lee	30	364	91	29	.319	17	9	.529	11	22	33	67	65	1	15	4	67	2.2	8
Wilson	5	59	14	2	.143	6	4	.667	2	1	3	11	3	0	4	1	8	1.6	3

3-Pt. FG: Atlanta 13-75 (.173)—Drew 0-7 (.000); Johnson 5-13 (.385); Roundfield 0-4 (.000); Hawes 3-8 (.375); McElroy (Tot) 5-21 (.238); (Atl) 2-7 (.286); McMillen 0-1 (.000); Furlow 1-9 (.111); Criss 1-17 (.059); Hill 1-4 (.250); Givens 0-2 (.000); Lee 0-3 (.000). Opponents 46-183 (.251).

BOSTON CELTICS

Player	G.	Min.	FGA	FGM	Pct.	FTA	FTM	Pct.	Off. Reb.	Def. Reb.	Tot. Reb.	Ast.	PF	Dsq.	Stl.	Blk. Sh.	Pts.	Avg.	Hi.
Bird	82	2955	1463	693	.474	360	301	.836	216	636	852	370	279	4	143	53	1745	21.3	45
Maxwell	80	2744	750	457	.609	554	436	.787	284	420	704	199	266	6	76	61	1350	16.9	29
Cowens	66	2159	932	422	.453	122	95	.779	126	408	534	206	216	2	69	61	940	14.2	32
Archibald	80	2864	794	383	.482	435	361	.830	59	138	197	671	218	2	106	10	1131	14.1	29
Maravich (Tot)	43	964	543	244	.449	105	91	.867	17	61	78	83	79	1	24	6	589	13.7	31
Maravich (Bos)	26	442	249	123	.494	55	50	.909	10	28	38	29	49	1	9	2	299	11.5	31
Robey	82	1918	727	379	.521	269	184	.684	209	321	530	92	244	2	53	15	942	11.5	27
Ford	73	2115	709	330	.465	114	86	.754	77	104	181	215	178	0	111	27	816	11.2	27
Carr	82	1994	763	362	.474	241	178	.739	106	224	330	156	214	1	120	36	914	11.1	25
Henderson	76	1061	382	191	.500	129	89	.690	37	46	83	147	96	0	45	15	473	6.2	17
Judkins	65	674	276	139	.504	76	62	.816	32	34	66	47	91	0	29	5	351	5.4	17
Fernsten	56	431	153	71	.464	52	33	.635	40	56	96	28	43	0	17	12	175	3.1	11
Chaney	60	523	189	67	.354	42	32	.762	31	42	73	38	80	1	31	11	167	2.8	8

3-Pt. FG: Boston 162-422 (.384)—Bird 58-143 (.406); Cowens 1-12 (.083); Archibald 4-18 (.222); Maravich (Tot) 10-15 (.667), (Bos) 3-4 (.750); Robey 0-1 (.000); Ford 70-164 (.427); Carr 12-41 (.293); Henderson 2-6 (.333); Judkins 11-27 (.407); Chaney 1-6 (.167). Opponents 74-259 (.286).

CHICAGO BULLS

Player	G.	Min.	FGA	FGM	Pct.	FTA	FTM	Pct.	Off. Reb.	Def. Reb.	Tot. Reb.	Ast.	PF	Dsq.	Stl.	Blk. Sh.	Pts.	Avg.	Hi.
Theus	82	3029	1172	566	.483	597	500	.838	143	186	329	515	262	4	114	20	1660	20.2	33
Gilmore	48	1568	513	305	.595	344	245	.712	108	324	432	133	167	5	29	59	855	17.8	32
Greenwood	82	2791	1051	498	.474	416	337	.810	223	550	773	182	313	8	60	129	1334	16.3	31
Sobers	82	2673	1002	470	.469	239	200	.837	75	167	242	426	294	4	136	17	1161	14.2	33
May	54	1298	587	264	.450	172	144	.837	78	140	218	104	126	2	45	5	672	12.4	26
Jones (Tot)	74	1448	506	257	.508	201	146	.726	114	254	368	101	207	0	28	42	660	8.9	24
Jones (Chi)	53	1170	387	207	.535	165	119	.721	83	213	296	90	159	0	24	37	533	10.1	24
Smith	30	496	230	97	.422	63	57	.905	22	32	54	42	54	0	25	7	259	8.6	22
Landsberger	54	1136	346	183	.529	166	87	.524	157	293	450	32	113	1	23	17	453	8.4	25
Johnson	79	1535	527	262	.497	93	82	.882	50	113	163	161	165	0	59	24	607	7.7	21
Dietrick	79	1830	500	227	.454	118	90	.763	101	262	363	216	230	2	89	51	545	6.9	19
Mengelt	36	387	166	90	.542	49	39	.796	3	20	23	38	54	0	10	0	219	6.1	21
Mack (Tot)	50	681	199	98	.492	51	38	.745	32	39	71	53	50	0	24	3	234	4.7	18
Mack (Chi)	23	526	149	77	.517	33	29	.879	25	24	49	33	34	0	20	3	183	8.0	18
Beshore	68	869	250	88	.352	87	58	.667	16	47	63	139	105	0	58	5	244	3.6	15
Awtrey	26	560	60	27	.450	50	32	.640	29	86	115	40	66	0	12	15	86	3.3	9
Brown	4	37	3	1	.333	0	0	.000	2	8	10	3	4	0	2	0	2	0.5	2

3-Pt. FG: Chicago 70-275 (.255)—Theus 28-105 (.267); Greenwood 1-7 (.143); Sobers 21-68 (.309); May 0-4 (.000); Smith 8-35 (.229); Johnson 1-11 (.091); Dietrick 1-9 (.111); Mengelt 0-6 (.000); Mack (Tot) 0-5 (.000); (Chi) 0-4 (.000); Beshore 10-26 (.385). Opponents 54-199 (.271).

CLEVELAND CAVALIERS

Player	G.	Min.	FGA	FGM	Pct.	FTA	FTM	Pct.	Off. Reb.	Def. Reb.	Tot. Reb.	Ast.	PF	Dsq.	Stl.	Blk. Sh.	Pts.	Avg.	Hi.
Mitchell	82	2802	1482	775	.523	343	270	.787	206	385	591	93	259	4	70	77	1820	22.2	46
Russell	41	1331	630	284	.451	239	178	.745	76	149	225	173	113	1	72	20	747	18.2	33
R. Smith	82	2677	1326	599	.452	283	233	.823	93	163	256	363	190	1	125	7	1441	17.6	36
Robisch	82	2620	940	489	.520	329	277	.842	225	433	658	192	211	2	53	53	1255	15.3	36
A. Carr	77	1595	839	390	.465	172	127	.738	81	84	165	150	120	0	39	3	909	11.8	32
K. Carr (Tot)	79	1838	768	378	.492	263	173	.658	199	389	588	77	246	3	66	52	929	11.8	32
K. Carr (Clev)	74	1781	752	371	.493	261	171	.655	194	377	571	76	240	3	64	51	913	12.3	32
Walker	76	2422	568	258	.454	243	195	.802	78	209	287	607	202	2	155	12	712	9.4	23
B. Smith	8	135	72	33	.458	8	7	.875	2	12	14	7	21	0	3	2	74	9.3	17
Willoughby	78	1447	457	219	.479	127	96	.756	122	207	329	72	189	0	32	62	535	6.9	20
Lambert	74	1324	400	165	.413	101	73	.723	138	214	352	56	203	4	47	42	403	5.4	18
W. Smith	62	1051	315	121	.384	52	40	.769	56	65	121	259	110	1	75	1	299	4.8	14
Ford (Tot)	73	999	274	131	.478	53	45	.849	44	141	185	65	131	0	22	21	308	4.2	17
Ford (Clev)	21	419	144	65	.451	25	22	.880	21	66	87	29	45	0	11	6	153	7.3	17
Frazier	3	27	11	4	.364	2	2	1.000	1	2	3	8	2	0	2	1	10	3.3	6
Tatum	33	225	94	36	.383	19	11	.579	11	15	26	20	29	0	16	5	85	2.6	11
Lee	3	24	11	2	.182	1	0	.000	3	0	3	3	0	0	0	4	4	1.3	2

3-Pt. FG: Cleveland 36-187 (.193)—Mitchell 0-6 (.000); Russell 1-9 (.111); R. Smith 10-53 (.189); Robisch 0-3 (.000); A. Carr 2-6 (.333); K. Carr (Clev.) 0-4 (.000); Walker 1-9 (.111); B. Smith 1-5 (.200); Willoughby 1-9 (.111); Lambert 0-3 (.000); W. Smith 17-71 (.239); Ford (Tot) 1-3 (.333), Ford (Clev) 1-2 (.500); Frazier 0-1 (.000); Tatum 2-6 (.333). Opponents 65-223 (.291).

DENVER NUGGETS

Player	G.	Min.	FGA	FGM	Pct.	FTA	FTM	Pct.	Off. Reb.	Def. Reb.	Tot. Reb.	Ast.	PF	Dsq.	Stl.	Blk. Sh.	Pts.	Avg.	Hi.
Issel	82	2938	1416	715	.505	667	517	.775	236	483	719	198	190	1	88	54	1951	23.8	47
Thompson	39	1239	617	289	.468	335	254	.758	56	118	174	124	106	0	39	38	839	21.5	38
English (Tot)	78	2401	1113	553	.497	266	210	.789	269	336	605	224	206	0	73	62	1318	16.9	40
English(Den)	24	875	427	207	.485	126	96	.762	102	123	225	82	78	0	28	29	512	21.3	40
McGinnis	45	1424	584	268	.459	307	166	.541	134	328	462	221	187	8	69	17	703	15.6	43
Wilkerson	75	2381	1030	430	.417	222	166	.748	85	231	316	243	194	1	93	27	1033	13.8	31
Roche	82	2286	741	354	.478	202	175	.866	24	91	115	405	139	0	82	12	932	11.4	33
Boswell	18	522	135	72	.533	70	58	.829	40	74	114	46	56	1	5	8	203	11.3	24
Johnson	75	1938	649	309	.476	189	148	.783	190	394	584	157	260	4	84	67	768	10.2	30
Scott	69	1868	668	276	.401	118	85	.720	51	115	166	250	197	3	47	23	639	9.3	30
Roberts	23	486	181	69	.381	60	39	.650	54	55	109	20	52	1	13	3	177	7.7	18
Gondrezick	59	1020	286	148	.517	121	92	.760	107	152	259	81	119	0	68	16	390	6.6	20
Garland	78	1106	356	155	.435	26	18	.692	50	88	138	145	80	1	54	4	334	4.3	17
Ellis	48	502	136	61	.449	53	40	.755	65	51	116	30	67	1	10	24	162	3.4	12
Hughes	70	1208	202	102	.505	41	15	.366	125	201	326	74	184	3	66	77	219	3.1	14
Kramer	8	45	22	7	.318	2	2	1.000	6	6	12	3	8	0	0	5	16	2.0	10

3-Pt. FG: Denver 83-255 (.325)—Issel 4-12 (.333); Thompson 7-19 (.368); English (Tot.) 2-6 (.333), English (Den.) 2-3 (.667); McGinnis 1-7 (.143); Wilkerson 7-34 (.206); Roche 49-129 (.380); Boswell 1-2 (.500); Johnson 2-9 (.222); Scott 2-11 (.182); Roberts 0-1 (.000); Gondrezick 2-6 (.333); Garland 6-19 (.316); Ellis 0-3 (.000). Opponents 70-214 (.327).

DETROIT PISTONS

Player	G.	Min.	FGA	FGM	Pct.	FTA	FTM	Pct.	Off. Reb.	Def. Reb.	Tot. Reb.	Ast.	PF	Dsq.	Stl.	Blk. Sh.	Pts.	Avg.	Hi.
Lanier	37	1392	584	319	.546	210	164	.781	108	265	373	122	130	2	38	60	802	21.7	34
McAdoo	58	2097	1025	492	.480	322	235	.730	100	367	467	200	178	3	73	65	1222	21.7	37
Long	69	2364	1164	588	.505	194	160	.825	152	185	337	206	221	4	129	26	1337	19.4	38
Kelser	50	1233	593	280	.472	203	146	.719	124	152	276	108	176	5	60	34	709	14.2	34
Tyler	82	2670	925	430	.465	187	143	.765	228	399	627	129	237	3	107	220	1005	12.3	29
McElroy	36	1012	356	162	.455	119	95	.798	12	38	50	162	78	1	25	14	422	11.7	33
Money(Tot)	61	1549	546	273	.500	106	83	.783	31	73	104	254	146	3	53	11	629	10.3	26
Money(Det)	55	1467	510	259	.508	104	81	.779	28	69	97	238	135	3	53	10	599	10.9	26
Shumate	9	228	65	35	.538	25	17	.680	18	52	70	9	16	0	9	5	87	9.7	20
Benson(Tot)	73	1891	618	299	.484	141	99	.702	126	327	453	178	246	4	73	92	698	9.6	26
Benson(Det)	17	502	187	86	.460	44	33	.750	30	90	120	51	68	3	19	18	206	12.1	26
Duerod	67	1331	598	282	.472	66	45	.682	29	69	98	117	102	0	41	11	624	9.3	28
Hubbard	64	1189	451	210	.466	220	165	.750	114	206	320	70	202	9	48	10	585	9.1	30
Douglas	70	1782	455	221	.486	185	125	.676	171	330	501	121	249	10	30	62	567	8.1	26
Lee(Tot)	61	1167	305	113	.370	70	44	.629	40	83	123	241	172	5	99	17	292	4.8	23
Lee(Det)	31	803	214	84	.393	53	35	.660	29	61	90	174	107	4	84	13	225	7.3	23
Hamilton	72	1116	287	115	.401	150	103	.687	45	62	107	192	82	0	48	5	333	4.6	17
Evans	36	381	140	63	.450	42	24	.571	26	49	75	37	64	0	14	1	157	4.4	16
Robinson	7	51	17	9	.529	11	9	.818	3	2	5	0	8	0	3	3	27	3.9	10
Malovic(Tot)	39	445	67	31	.463	27	18	.667	36	50	86	26	51	0	8	6	80	2.1	9
Malovic(Det)	10	162	25	8	.320	14	10	.714	9	19	28	14	16	0	2	5	26	2.6	9

3-Pt. FG: Detroit 57-219 (.260)—Lanier (Tot.) 0-5 (.000); (Det.) 0-5 (.000); McAdoo 3-24 (.125); Long 1-12 (.083); Kelser 3-15 (.200); Tyler 2-12 (.167); McElroy 3-14 (.214); Benson (Tot.) 1-5 (.200); (Det.) 1-4 (.250); Duerod 15-53 (.283); Hubbard 0-2 (.000); Douglas 0-1 (.000); Lee (Tot.) 22-59 (.373); (Det.) 22-56 (.393); Hamilton 0-2 (.000); Evans 7-18 (.389); Robinson 0-1 (.000). Opponents 57-206 (.277).

GOLDEN STATE WARRIORS

Player	G.	Min.	FGA	FGM	Pct.	FTA	FTM	Pct.	Off. Reb.	Def. Reb.	Tot. Reb.	Ast.	PF	Dsq.	Stl.	Blk. Sh.	Pts.	Avg.	Hi.
Short	62	1636	916	461	.503	165	134	.812	119	197	316	123	186	4	63	9	1056	17.0	37
Parish	72	2119	1006	510	.507	284	203	.715	247	536	783	122	248	6	58	115	1223	17.0	29
Smith	51	1552	685	325	.474	171	135	.789	28	118	146	187	154	1	62	15	792	15.5	29
Parker	82	2849	988	483	.489	302	237	.785	166	298	464	254	195	2	173	32	1203	14.7	36
Lucas	80	2763	830	388	.467	289	222	.768	61	159	220	602	196	2	138	3	1010	12.6	27
Cooper	79	1781	750	367	.489	181	136	.751	202	305	507	42	246	5	20	79	871	11.0	30
White	78	2052	706	336	.476	114	97	.851	42	139	181	239	186	0	88	13	770	9.9	21
Ray	81	1683	383	203	.530	149	84	.564	122	344	466	183	266	6	51	32	490	6.0	19
Townsend	75	1159	421	171	.406	84	60	.714	33	56	89	116	113	0	60	4	406	5.4	17
Abernethy	67	1222	318	153	.481	82	56	.683	62	129	191	87	118	0	35	12	362	5.4	20
Hillman	49	708	179	82	.458	68	34	.500	59	121	180	47	128	2	21	24	198	4.0	19
Johnson	9	53	30	12	.400	5	3	.600	6	8	14	2	11	0	1	0	27	3.0	6
Coughran	24	160	81	29	.358	14	8	.571	2	17	19	12	24	0	7	1	68	2.8	11
Wilson	16	143	25	7	.280	6	3	.500	4	12	16	12	11	0	2	0	17	1.1	4

3-Pt. FG: Golden State 27-121 (.223)—Short 0-6 (.000); Parish 0-1 (.000); Smith 7-22 (.318); Parker 0-2 (.000); Lucas 12-42 (.286); Cooper 1-4 (.250); White 1-6 (.167); Ray 0-2 (.000); Townsend 4-26 (.154); Abernethy 0-1 (.000); Coughran 2-9 (.222). Opponents 72-219 (.329).

HOUSTON ROCKETS

Player	G.	Min.	FGA	FGM	Pct.	FTA	FTM	Pct.	Off. Reb.	Def. Reb.	Tot. Reb.	Ast.	PF	Dsq.	Stl.	Blk. Sh.	Pts.	Avg.	Hi.
Malone	82	3140	1549	778	.502	783	563	.719	573	617	1190	147	210	0	80	107	2119	25.8	45
Murphy	76	2676	1267	624	.493	302	271	.897	68	82	150	299	269	3	143	9	1520	20.0	38
Tomjanovich	62	1834	778	370	.476	147	118	.803	132	226	358	109	161	2	32	10	880	14.2	27
Reid	76	2304	861	419	.487	208	153	.736	140	301	441	244	281	2	132	57	991	13.0	31
Barry	72	1816	771	325	.422	153	143	.935	53	183	236	268	182	0	88	28	866	12.0	30
Leavell	77	2123	656	330	.503	221	180	.814	57	127	184	417	197	1	127	28	843	10.9	22
Paultz(Tot)	84	2193	673	327	.486	182	109	.599	187	399	586	188	213	3	69	84	764	9.1	28
Paultz(Hou)	37	980	292	138	.473	82	43	.524	92	173	265	70	86	0	22	39	319	8.6	28
Dunleavy	51	1036	319	148	.464	134	111	.828	26	74	100	210	120	2	40	4	410	8.0	31
D.Jones	21	278	119	50	.420	36	27	.750	31	41	72	11	48	0	4	5	127	6.0	23
Henderson	66	1551	323	154	.477	77	56	.727	34	77	111	274	107	1	55	4	364	5.5	19
M. Jones	82	1545	392	188	.480	108	61	.565	147	234	381	67	186	0	50	67	438	5.3	17
Shumate	29	332	64	34	.531	44	33	.750	25	54	79	23	39	0	8	9	101	3.5	12
White	9	106	24	13	.542	13	10	.769	0	9	9	5	8	0	5	0	36	4.0	11
Mokeski	12	113	33	11	.333	9	7	.778	14	15	29	2	24	0	1	6	29	2.4	6
Bradley	22	96	48	17	.354	9	6	.667	2	4	6	3	9	0	3	0	41	1.9	7

3-Pt. FG: Houston 104-379 (.274)—Malone 0-6 (.000); Murphy 1-25 (.040); Tomjanovich 22-79 (.278); Reid 0-3 (.000); Barry 73-221 (.330); Leavell 3-19 (.158); Dunleavy 3-20 (.150); Henderson 0-2 (.000); M. Jones 1-3 (.333); Bradley 1-1 (1.000). Opponents 58-215 (.270).

INDIANA PACERS

Player	G.	Min.	FGA	FGM	Pct.	FTA	FTM	Pct.	Off. Reb.	Def. Reb.	Tot. Reb.	Ast.	PF	Dsq.	Stl.	Blk. Sh.	Pts.	Avg.	Hi.
M. Johnson	82	2647	1271	588	.463	482	385	.799	258	423	681	344	291	11	153	112	1566	19.1	41
J. Davis	82	2912	1159	496	.428	352	304	.864	102	124	226	440	178	0	110	23	1300	15.9	32
Edwards	82	2314	1032	528	.512	339	231	.681	179	399	578	127	324	12	55	104	1287	15.7	35
English	54	1526	686	346	.504	140	114	.814	167	213	380	142	128	0	45	33	806	14.9	37
McGinnis(Tot)	73	2208	886	400	.451	448	270	.553	222	477	699	333	303	12	101	23	1072	14.7	43
McGinnis(Ind)	28	784	302	132	.437	181	104	.575	88	149	237	112	116	4	32	6	369	13.2	31
Knight	75	1910	722	385	.533	262	212	.809	136	225	361	155	96	0	82	9	986	13.1	44
Bantom	77	2330	760	384	.505	209	139	.665	192	264	456	279	268	7	85	49	908	11.8	27
Bradley	82	2027	609	275	.452	174	136	.782	69	154	223	252	194	1	211	48	688	8.4	22
Chenier(Tot)	43	850	349	136	.390	67	49	.731	19	59	78	89	55	0	33	15	326	7.6	22

Player	G.	Min.	FGA	FGM	Pct.	FTA	FTM	Pct.	Off. Reb.	Def. Reb.	Tot. Reb.	Ast.	PF	Dsq.	Stl.	Blk. Sh.	Pts.	Avg.	Hi.
Chenier (Ind)	23	380	135	52	.385	26	18	.692	9	26	35	47	29	0	15	10	124	5.4	14
Hassett	74	1135	509	215	.422	29	24	.828	35	59	94	104	85	0	46	8	523	7.1	23
C. Johnson	79	1541	396	199	.503	117	74	.632	145	249	394	115	211	2	48	121	472	6.0	22
Carter	13	117	37	15	.405	7	2	.286	5	14	19	9	19	0	2	3	32	2.5	6
Zeno	8	59	21	6	.286	2	2	1.000	3	11	14	1	13	0	4	3	14	1.8	4
B. Davis	5	43	7	2	.286	4	3	.750	0	2	2	5	7	0	3	0	7	1.4	5
Kuester	24	100	34	12	.353	7	5	.714	3	11	14	16	8	0	7	1	29	1.2	6
Calhoun	7	30	9	4	.444	2	0	.000	7	3	10	0	6	0	2	0	8	1.1	2

3-Pt. FG: Indiana 88-314 (.280)—M. Johnson 5-32 (.156); J. Davis 4-42 (.095); Edwards 0-1 (.000); English 0-3 (.000); McGinnis (Tot.) 2-15 (.133); (Ind.) 1-8 (.125); Knight 4-15 (.267); Bantom 1-3 (.333); Bradley 2-5 (.400); Chenier (Tot.) 5-12 (.417); (Ind.) 2-6 (.333); Hassett 69-198 (.348); Kuester 0-1 (.000). Opponents 56-228 (.246).

KANSAS CITY KINGS

Player	G.	Min.	FGA	FGM	Pct.	FTA	FTM	Pct.	Off. Reb.	Def. Reb.	Tot. Reb.	Ast.	PF	Dsq.	Stl.	Blk. Sh.	Pts.	Avg.	Hi.
Birdsong	82	2885	1546	781	.505	412	286	.694	170	161	331	202	226	2	136	22	1858	22.7	49
Wedman	68	2347	1112	569	.512	181	145	.801	114	272	386	145	230	1	84	45	1290	19.0	45
Ford	82	2621	1058	489	.462	423	346	.818	29	143	172	610	208	0	136	4	1328	16.2	35
Robinzine	81	1917	723	362	.501	274	200	.730	184	342	526	62	311	5	106	23	925	11.4	28
Lacey	81	2412	677	303	.448	185	137	.741	172	473	645	460	307	8	111	109	743	9.2	24
King	82	2052	499	257	.515	219	159	.726	184	382	566	106	230	2	69	31	673	8.2	21
Green	21	459	159	69	.434	42	24	.571	35	78	113	28	55	0	13	21	162	7.7	21
McKinney	76	1333	459	206	.449	133	107	.805	20	66	86	248	87	0	58	5	520	6.8	26
Grunfeld	80	1397	420	186	.443	131	101	.771	87	145	232	109	151	1	56	9	474	5.9	18
Redmond	24	298	138	59	.428	34	24	.706	18	34	52	19	27	0	4	9	142	5.9	19
Gerard	73	869	348	159	.457	100	66	.660	77	100	177	43	96	1	41	26	385	5.3	25
Elmore	58	915	242	104	.430	74	51	.689	74	183	257	64	154	0	41	39	259	4.5	23
Burleson	37	272	36	36	.346	40	23	.575	23	49	72	20	49	0	8	13	95	2.6	12
Crosby	4	28	4	2	.500	2	2	1.000	0	1	1	7	4	0	0	0	6	1.5	4

3-Pt. FG: Kansas City 25-114 (.219)—Birdsong 10-36 (.278); Wedman 7-22 (.318); Ford 4-23 (.174); Robinzine 1-2 (.500); Lacey 0-1 (.000); King 0-1 (.000); Green 0-2 (.000); McKinney 1-10 (.100); Grunfeld 1-2 (.500); Redmond 0-9 (.000); Gerard 1-3 (.333); Burleson 0-3 (.000). Opponents 41-172 (.238).

LOS ANGELES LAKERS

Player	G.	Min.	FGA	FGM	Pct.	FTA	FTM	Pct.	Off. Reb.	Def. Reb.	Tot. Reb.	Ast.	PF	Dsq.	Stl.	Blk. Sh.	Pts.	Avg.	Hi.
Abdul-Jabbar	82	3143	1383	835	.604	476	364	.765	190	696	886	371	216	2	81	280	2034	24.8	42
Wilkes	82	3111	1358	726	.535	234	189	.808	176	349	525	250	220	1	129	28	1644	20.0	30
Johnson	77	2795	949	503	.530	462	374	.810	166	430	596	563	218	1	187	41	1387	18.0	31
Nixon	82	3226	1209	624	.516	253	197	.779	52	177	229	642	241	1	147	14	1446	17.6	30
Chones	82	2394	760	372	.489	169	125	.740	143	421	564	151	271	5	56	65	869	10.6	23
Haywood	76	1544	591	288	.487	206	159	.772	132	214	346	93	197	2	35	54	736	9.7	25
Cooper	82	1973	578	303	.524	143	111	.776	101	128	229	221	215	3	86	38	722	8.8	20
Landsb'r (Tot)	77	1510	483	249	.516	222	116	.523	226	387	613	46	140	1	33	22	614	8.0	25
Landsb'r (LA)	23	374	137	66	.482	56	29	.518	69	94	163	14	27	0	10	5	161	7.0	14
Boone	6	106	40	14	.350	7	6	.857	7	4	11	7	13	0	5	0	34	5.7	10
Carr	5	57	16	7	.438	2	2	1.000	5	12	17	1	6	0	2	1	16	3.2	6
Ford	52	580	130	66	.508	28	23	.821	23	75	98	36	86	0	11	15	155	3.0	15
Holland	38	197	104	44	.423	16	15	.938	4	13	17	22	24	0	15	1	106	2.8	12
Byrnes	32	194	50	25	.500	15	13	.867	9	18	27	13	32	0	5	1	63	2.0	11
Mack	27	155	50	21	.420	18	9	.500	7	15	22	20	16	0	4	0	51	1.9	10
Lee (Tot)	14	55	24	6	.250	8	6	.750	7	4	11	12	2	0	1	0	18	1.3	4
Lee (LA)	11	31	13	4	.308	4	4	.857	4	4	8	9	2	0	1	0	14	1.3	4

3-Pt. FG: Los Angeles 20-100 (.200)—Abdul-Jabbar 0-1 (.000); Wilkes 3-17 (.176); Johnson 7-31 (.226); Nixon 1-8 (.125); Chones 0-2 (.000); Haywood 1-4 (.250); Cooper 5-20 (.250); Ford 0-1 (.000); Holland 3-15 (.200); Mack 0-1 (.000). Opponents 78-274 (.285).

MILWAUKEE BUCKS

Player	G.	Min.	FGA	FGM	Pct.	FTA	FTM	Pct.	Off. Reb.	Def. Reb.	Tot. Reb.	Ast.	PF	Dsq.	Stl.	Blk. Sh.	Pts.	Avg.	Hi.
Johnson	77	2686	1267	689	.544	368	291	.791	217	349	566	273	173	0	100	70	1671	21.7	37
Lanier (Tot)	63	2131	867	466	.537	354	277	.782	152	400	552	184	200	3	74	89	1210	19.2	34
Lanier (Mil)	26	739	283	147	.519	144	113	.785	44	135	179	62	70	1	36	29	408	15.7	32
Bridgeman	81	2316	1243	594	.478	266	230	.865	104	197	301	237	216	3	94	20	1423	17.6	35
Winters	80	2623	1116	535	.479	214	184	.860	48	175	223	362	208	0	101	28	1292	16.2	34
Meyers	79	2204	830	399	.481	246	156	.634	140	308	448	225	218	3	72	40	955	12.1	28
Buckner	67	1690	655	306	.467	143	105	.734	69	169	238	383	202	1	135	4	719	10.7	40
Benson	56	1389	431	213	.494	97	66	.680	96	237	333	127	178	1	54	74	492	8.8	19
Moncrief	77	1557	451	211	.468	292	232	.795	154	184	338	133	106	0	72	16	654	8.5	23
Cummings	71	900	370	187	.505	123	94	.764	81	157	238	53	141	0	22	17	468	6.6	30
Washington	75	1092	421	197	.468	76	46	.605	95	181	276	55	166	2	26	48	440	5.9	20
Walton	76	1243	242	110	.455	71	49	.690	33	58	91	285	68	0	43	2	270	3.6	18
Catchings	72	1366	244	97	.398	64	39	.629	144	246	410	82	191	1	23	162	233	3.2	12

3-Pt. FG: Milwaukee 50-155 (.323)—Johnson 2-9 (.222); Lanier (Tot.) 1-6 (.167); (Mil.) 1-1 (1.000); Bridgeman 5-27 (.185); Winters 38-102 (.373); Meyers 1-5 (.200); Buckner 2-5 (.400); Benson 0-1 (.000); Moncrief 0-1 (.000); Walton 1-3 (.333); Catchings 0-1 (.000). Opponents 76-305 (.249).

NEW JERSEY NETS

Player	G.	Min.	FGA	FGM	Pct.	FTA	FTM	Pct.	Off. Reb.	Def. Reb.	Tot. Reb.	Ast.	PF	Dsq.	Stl.	Blk. Sh.	Pts.	Avg.	Hi.
Newlin	78	2510	1329	611	.460	415	367	.884	101	163	264	314	195	1	115	4	1634	20.9	52
Natt	53	2046	879	421	.479	280	199	.711	173	340	513	112	148	1	78	22	1042	19.7	33
Williamson	28	771	461	206	.447	88	76	.864	24	30	54	87	71	1	26	9	496	17.7	32
Lucas(Tot)	63	1884	813	371	.456	239	179	.749	143	394	537	208	223	2	42	62	923	14.7	32
Lucas(NJ)	22	708	261	128	.490	102	79	.775	58	154	212	83	82	1	19	27	335	15.2	32

Player	G.	Min.	FGA	FGM	Pct.	FTA	FTM	Pct.	Off. Reb.	Def. Reb.	Tot. Reb.	Ast.	PF	Dsq.	Stl.	Blk. Sh.	Pts.	Avg.	Hi.
Robinson	70	1661	833	391	.469	242	168	.694	174	332	506	98	178	1	61	34	951	13.6	45
Jordan	82	2657	1017	437	.430	258	201	.779	62	208	270	557	238	7	223	27	1087	13.3	28
Phegley(Tot)	78	1512	733	350	.477	203	177	.872	75	110	185	102	158	1	34	7	881	11.3	35
Phegley(NJ)	28	541	260	126	.485	83	73	.880	26	44	70	32	52	0	15	4	327	11.7	26
Kelley	57	1466	399	186	.466	250	197	.788	156	241	397	128	215	5	50	79	569	10.0	26
Boynes	64	1102	467	221	.473	136	104	.765	51	82	133	95	132	1	59	19	546	8.5	32
Johnson	81	2119	543	248	.457	126	89	.706	192	410	602	173	312	7	53	258	585	7.2	22
van B. Kolff	82	2399	458	212	.463	155	130	.839	103	326	429	247	307	11	100	76	564	6.8	18
Elliott	54	722	228	101	.443	152	104	.684	67	118	185	53	97	0	29	14	307	5.7	18
Simpson	8	81	47	18	.383	10	5	.500	6	5	11	14	3	0	9	0	41	5.1	12
Smith(Tot)	65	809	269	118	.439	92	80	.870	20	59	79	92	105	1	26	4	324	5.0	17
Smith(NJ)	59	736	254	113	.445	87	75	.862	17	59	76	85	102	1	22	4	309	5.2	17
Jackson	16	194	46	29	.630	10	7	.700	12	12	24	12	35	1	5	4	65	4.1	14
Bassett	7	92	22	8	.364	12	8	.667	7	11	18	4	14	0	5	0	24	3.4	11

3-Pt. FG: 85-298 (.285)—Newlin 45-152 (.296); Natt 1-5 (.200); Williamson 8-19 (.421); Lucas (Tot.) 2-9 (.222), (NJ) 0-4 (.000); Robinson 1-4 (.250); Jordan 12-48 (.250); Phegley (Tot.) 4-9 (.444), (NJ) 2-4 (.500); Kelley 0-3 (.000); Boynes 0-4 (.000); Johnson 0-1 (.000); van Breda Kolff 7-20 (.350); Elliott 1-4 (.250); Simpson 0-2 (.000); Smith (Tot.) 8-26 (.308), (NJ) 8-26 (.308); Jackson 0-2 (.000). Opponents 58-208 (.279).

NEW YORK KNICKERBOCKERS

Player	G.	Min.	FGA	FGM	Pct.	FTA	FTM	Pct.	Off. Reb.	Def. Reb.	Tot. Reb.	Ast.	PF	Dsq.	Stl.	Blk. Sh.	Pts.	Avg.	Hi.
Cartwright	82	3150	1215	665	.547	566	451	.797	194	532	726	165	279	2	48	101	1781	21.7	37
R. Williams	82	2582	1384	687	.496	423	333	.787	149	263	412	512	295	5	167	24	1714	20.9	39
Knight	81	2945	1265	669	.529	261	211	.808	201	292	493	150	302	4	117	86	1549	19.1	34
Richardson	82	3060	1063	502	.472	338	223	.660	151	388	539	832	260	3	265	35	1254	15.3	28
Meriweather	65	1565	477	252	.528	121	78	.645	122	228	350	66	239	8	37	120	582	9.0	24
Monroe	51	633	352	161	.457	64	56	.875	16	20	36	67	46	0	21	3	378	7.4	25
Demic	82	1872	528	230	.436	183	110	.601	195	288	483	64	306	10	56	30	570	7.0	19
Glenn	75	800	364	188	.516	73	63	.863	21	45	66	85	79	0	35	7	441	5.9	19
Copeland	75	1142	368	182	.495	86	63	.733	70	86	156	80	154	0	61	25	427	5.7	19
S. Williams	57	556	267	104	.390	90	58	.644	65	56	121	36	73	0	19	8	266	4.7	21
Webster	20	298	79	38	.481	16	12	.750	28	52	80	9	39	1	3	11	88	4.4	13
Cleamons	22	254	69	30	.435	15	12	.800	10	9	19	40	13	0	13	2	75	3.4	13
Huston	71	923	241	94	.390	38	28	.737	14	44	58	159	83	0	39	5	219	3.1	14

3-Pt. FG: New York 42-191 (.220); R. Williams 7-37 (.189); Knight 0-2 (.000); Richardson 27-110 (.245); Meriweather 0-1 (.000); Glenn 2-10 (.200); Copeland 0-2 (.000); S. Williams 0-4 (.000); Cleamons 3-8 (.375); Huston 3-17 (.176). Opponents 55-198 (.278).

PHILADELPHIA 76ers

Player	G.	Min.	FGA	FGM	Pct.	FTA	FTM	Pct.	Off. Reb.	Def. Reb.	Tot. Reb.	Ast.	PF	Dsq.	Stl.	Blk. Sh.	Pts.	Avg.	Hi.
Erving	78	2812	1614	838	.519	534	420	.787	215	361	576	355	208	0	170	140	2100	26.9	44
Dawkins	80	2541	946	494	.522	291	190	.653	197	496	693	149	238	8	49	142	1178	14.7	34
Collins	36	963	410	191	.466	124	113	.911	29	65	94	100	76	0	30	7	495	13.8	33
B. Jones	81	2125	748	398	.532	329	257	.781	152	298	450	146	223	3	102	118	1053	13.0	26
Mix	81	1543	703	363	.516	249	207	.831	114	176	290	149	114	0	67	9	937	11.6	25
Cheeks	79	2623	661	357	.540	231	180	.779	75	199	274	556	197	1	183	32	898	11.4	24
Hollins(Tot)	47	1209	526	212	.403	140	101	.721	29	60	89	162	103	0	76	10	528	11.2	26
Hollins(Phil)	27	796	313	130	.415	87	67	.770	24	45	69	112	68	0	46	9	329	12.2	26
Bibby	82	2035	626	251	.401	286	226	.790	65	143	208	307	161	0	62	6	739	9.0	21
C. Jones	80	2771	532	232	.426	178	124	.697	219	731	950	164	298	5	43	162	588	7.4	20
Richardson	52	988	348	159	.457	45	28	.622	55	68	123	107	97	0	24	15	347	6.7	24
Spanarkel	40	442	153	72	.471	65	54	.831	27	27	54	51	58	0	12	6	198	5.0	19
Money	6	82	36	14	.389	2	2	1.000	3	4	7	16	11	0	0	1	30	5.0	10
Toone	23	124	64	23	.359	10	8	.800	12	22	34	12	20	0	4	5	55	2.4	8
Skinner	2	10	2	1	.500	0	0	.000	0	0	0	2	1	0	0	0	2	1.0	2

3-Pt. FG: Philadelphia 27-125 (.216); Erving 4-20 (.200); Dawkins 0-6 (.000); Collins 0-1 (.000); B. Jones 0-3 (.000); Mix 4-10 (.400); Cheeks (.444); Hollins (Tot.) 3-20 (.150); (Phil.) 2-10 (.200); Bibby 11-52 (.212); C. Jones 0-2 (.000); Richardson 1-3 (.333); Spanarkel 0-2 (.000); Toone 1-7 (.143). Opponents 75-277 (.271).

PHOENIX SUNS

Player	G.	Min.	FGA	FGM	Pct.	FTA	FTM	Pct.	Off. Reb.	Def. Reb.	Tot. Reb.	Ast.	PF	Dsq.	Stl.	Blk. Sh.	Pts.	Avg.	Hi.
Westphal	82	2665	1317	692	.526	443	382	.862	46	141	187	416	162	0	119	35	1792	21.9	49
Davis	75	2309	1166	657	.563	365	299	.819	75	197	272	337	202	2	114	19	1613	21.5	40
Robinson	82	2710	1064	545	.512	487	325	.667	213	557	770	142	262	2	58	59	1415	17.3	34
Adams	75	2168	875	468	.531	236	188	.797	158	451	609	322	237	4	108	55	1118	14.9	32
Kelley(Tot)	80	1839	484	229	.473	310	244	.787	200	315	515	178	273	5	78	96	702	8.8	26
Kelley(Phoe)	23	373	85	43	.506	60	47	.783	44	74	118	50	58	0	28	17	133	5.8	10
Bratz	82	1589	687	269	.392	162	141	.870	50	117	167	223	165	0	93	9	700	8.5	21
Buse	81	2499	589	261	.443	128	85	.664	70	163	233	320	111	0	132	10	626	7.7	17
Cook	66	904	275	129	.469	129	104	.806	90	151	241	84	102	0	28	18	362	5.5	16
High	82	1121	323	144	.446	178	120	.674	69	104	173	119	172	1	71	15	409	5.0	18
Heard	62	1403	410	171	.417	86	64	.744	118	262	380	97	177	0	84	49	406	5.0	18
Scott	79	1303	301	127	.422	122	95	.779	89	139	228	98	101	0	47	53	350	4.4	10
Kramer	54	711	143	67	.469	70	56	.800	49	102	151	75	104	0	26	5	190	3.5	13

3-Pt. FG: Phoenix 68-280 (.243); Westphal 26-93 (.280); Davis 0-4 (.000); Adams 0-2 (.000); Kelley (Tot.) 0-3 (.000); Phoe. 0-0 (.000); Bratz 21-86 (.244); Buse 19-79 (.241); Cook 0-3 (.000); High 1-7 (.143); Heard 0-2 (.000); Scott 1-3 (.333); Kramer 0-1 (.000). Opponents 100-297 (.337).

PORTLAND TRAIL BLAZERS

Player	G.	Min.	FGA	FGM	Pct.	FTA	FTM	Pct.	Off. Reb.	Def. Reb.	Tot. Reb.	Ast.	PF	Dsq.	Stl.	Blk. Sh.	Pts.	Avg.	Hi.
Natt (Tot)	78	2857	1298	622	.479	419	306	.730	239	452	691	169	205	1	102	34	1553	19.9	39
Natt (Port)	25	811	419	201	.480	139	107	.770	66	112	178	57	57	0	24	12	511	20.4	39
Owens	76	2337	1008	518	.514	283	213	.753	189	384	573	194	270	5	45	53	1250	16.4	32
R. Brewer	82	2815	1182	548	.464	219	184	.840	54	160	214	216	154	0	98	48	1286	15.7	33
Lucas	41	1176	552	243	.440	137	100	.730	85	240	325	125	141	1	23	35	588	14.3	30
Washington	80	2657	761	421	.553	360	231	.642	325	517	842	167	307	8	73	131	1073	13.4	27
Bates	16	235	146	72	.493	39	28	.718	13	16	29	31	26	0	14	2	180	11.3	26
Hollins	20	413	213	82	.385	53	34	.642	5	15	20	50	35	0	30	1	199	10.0	24
Jeelani	77	1286	565	288	.510	204	161	.789	114	156	270	95	155	0	40	40	737	9.6	28
Steele	16	446	146	62	.425	27	22	.815	13	32	45	67	53	0	25	1	146	9.1	18
Gross	62	1581	472	221	.468	114	95	.833	84	165	249	228	179	3	60	47	538	8.7	22
Twardzik	67	1594	394	183	.464	252	197	.782	52	104	156	273	149	2	77	1	567	8.5	23
Kunnert	18	302	114	50	.439	43	26	.605	37	75	112	29	59	1	7	22	126	7.0	16
Dunn	82	1841	551	240	.436	111	84	.757	132	192	324	147	145	1	102	31	564	6.9	23
Paxson	72	1270	460	189	.411	90	64	.711	25	84	109	144	97	0	48	5	443	6.2	21
J. Brewer	67	1016	184	90	.489	29	14	.483	101	156	257	75	129	2	42	43	194	2.9	17

3-Pt. FG: Portland 26-132 (.197)—Natt (Tot) 3-9 (.333); (Port) 2-4 (.500); Owens 1-2 (.500); R. Brewer 6-32 (.188); Washington 0-3 (.000); Bates 8-19 (.421); Jeelani 0-6 (.000); Steele 0-4 (.000); Gross 1-10 (.100); Twardzik 4-7 (.571); Dunn 0-3 (.000); Paxson 1-22 (.045); J. Brewer 0-5 (.000); Lucas 2-5 (.400); Hollins 1-10 (.100). Opponents 55-186 (.296).

SAN ANTONIO SPURS

Player	G.	Min.	FGA	FGM	Pct.	FTA	FTM	Pct.	Off. Reb.	Def. Reb.	Tot. Reb.	Ast.	PF	Dsq.	Stl.	Blk. Sh.	Pts.	Avg.	Hi.
Gervin	78	2934	1940	1024	.528	593	505	.852	154	249	403	202	208	0	110	79	2585	33.1	55
Kenon	78	2798	1333	647	.485	345	270	.783	258	517	775	231	192	0	111	18	1565	20.1	51
Silas	77	2293	999	513	.514	382	339	.887	45	122	167	347	206	2	61	14	1365	17.7	35
Restani	82	1966	727	369	.508	161	131	.814	142	244	386	189	186	0	54	12	874	10.7	24
Olberding	75	2111	609	291	.478	264	210	.795	83	335	418	327	274	7	67	22	792	10.6	22
Paultz	47	1213	381	189	.496	100	66	.660	95	226	321	118	127	3	47	45	444	9.4	26
Shumate (Tot)	65	1337	392	207	.528	216	165	.764	108	255	363	84	126	1	40	45	579	8.9	29
Shumate (SA)	27	777	263	138	.525	147	115	.782	65	149	214	52	71	1	23	31	391	14.5	29
Gale	67	1474	377	171	.454	120	97	.808	34	118	152	312	134	2	123	13	441	6.6	22
Griffin	82	1812	313	173	.553	240	174	.725	154	284	438	250	306	9	81	53	520	6.3	18
Evans	79	1246	464	208	.448	85	58	.682	29	78	107	230	194	2	60	9	486	6.2	21
Peck	52	628	169	73	.432	55	34	.618	66	117	183	33	100	2	17	23	180	3.5	13
Davis	4	30	12	6	.500	2	1	.500	2	4	6	0	8	0	1	0	13	3.3	9
Kiffin	26	212	96	32	.333	25	18	.720	12	28	40	19	43	0	10	2	82	3.2	12
Bassett (Tot)	12	164	34	12	.353	15	10	.667	11	22	33	14	27	0	8	0	34	2.8	11
Bassett (SA)	5	72	12	4	.333	3	2	.667	4	11	15	10	13	0	3	0	10	2.0	4
Norris	17	189	43	18	.419	6	4	.667	10	33	43	6	41	1	3	12	40	2.4	8

3-Pt. FG: San Antonio 52-206 (.252)—Gervin 32-102 (.314); Kenon 1-9 (.111); Silas 0-4 (.000); Restani 5-29 (.172); Olberding 0-3 (.000); Paultz 0-1 (.000); Shumate (Tot) 0-1 (.000); (SA) 0-1 (.000); Gale 2-13 (.154); Evans 12-42 (.286); Peck 0-2 (.000). Opponents 88-288 (.306).

SAN DIEGO CLIPPERS

Player	G.	Min.	FGA	FGM	Pct.	FTA	FTM	Pct.	Off. Reb.	Def. Reb.	Tot. Reb.	Ast.	PF	Dsq.	Stl.	Blk. Sh.	Pts.	Avg.	Hi.
Free	68	2585	1556	737	.474	760	572	.753	129	109	238	283	195	0	81	32	2055	30.2	49
Williams	82	2118	1343	645	.480	238	194	.815	103	89	192	166	145	0	72	9	1526	18.6	51
Walton	14	337	161	81	.503	54	32	.593	28	98	126	34	37	0	8	38	194	13.9	23
Taylor	78	2754	895	418	.467	162	130	.802	76	112	188	335	246	6	147	25	1056	13.5	28
Nater	81	2860	799	443	.554	273	196	.718	352	864	1216	233	259	3	45	37	1082	13.4	28
Smith (Tot)	78	2123	891	385	.432	115	100	.870	94	165	259	100	209	4	62	17	893	11.4	23
Smith (SD)	70	1988	819	352	.430	107	93	.869	92	153	245	93	188	4	59	15	819	11.7	23
Bryant	81	2328	682	294	.431	217	161	.742	171	345	516	144	258	4	102	39	754	9.3	23
Wicks	71	2146	496	210	.423	152	83	.546	138	271	409	213	241	5	76	52	503	7.1	17
Weatherspoon	57	1124	378	164	.434	91	63	.692	83	125	208	54	136	1	34	17	391	6.9	23
Pietkiewicz	50	577	179	91	.508	46	37	.804	26	19	45	94	52	1	25	4	228	4.6	20
Carrington	10	134	37	15	.405	8	6	.750	6	7	13	3	18	0	4	1	36	3.6	9
Whitehead	18	225	45	27	.600	18	5	.278	29	41	70	6	32	0	1	6	59	3.3	11
Barnes	20	287	60	24	.400	32	16	.500	34	43	77	18	52	0	5	12	64	3.2	8
Malovic	28	277	42	23	.548	9	7	.778	27	31	58	12	35	0	5	1	53	1.9	6
Olive	1	15	2	0	.000	0	0	....	0	1	1	0	2	0	0	0	0	0.0	0

3-Pt. FG: San Diego 177-543 (.326)—Free 9-25 (.360); Williams 42-128 (.328); Taylor 90-239 (.377); Nater 0-2 (.000); Smith (Tot) 23-81 (.284); (SD) 22-76 (.289); Bryant 5-34 (.147); Wicks 0-1 (.000); Pietkiewicz 9-36 (.250); Carrington 0-2 (.000). Opponents 43-187 (.230).

SEATTLE SUPERSONICS

Player	G.	Min.	FGA	FGM	Pct.	FTA	FTM	Pct.	Off. Reb.	Def. Reb.	Tot. Reb.	Ast.	PF	Dsq.	Stl.	Blk. Sh.	Pts.	Avg.	Hi.
Williams	82	2969	1533	739	.482	420	331	.788	127	148	275	397	160	1	200	37	1816	22.1	41
D. Johnson	81	2937	1361	574	.422	487	380	.780	173	241	444	332	267	6	144	82	1540	19.0	36
Sikma	82	2793	989	470	.475	292	235	.805	198	710	908	279	232	5	68	77	1175	14.3	32
Shelton	76	2243	802	425	.530	241	184	.763	199	383	582	145	292	11	92	79	1035	13.6	30
Brown	80	1701	843	404	.479	135	113	.837	35	120	155	174	117	0	65	17	960	12.0	27
J. Johnson	81	2533	772	377	.488	201	161	.801	163	263	426	424	213	1	76	35	915	11.3	22
LaGarde	82	1164	306	146	.477	137	90	.657	127	185	312	91	206	2	19	34	382	4.7	13
Walker	70	844	274	139	.507	64	48	.750	64	106	170	53	102	0	21	4	326	4.7	14
Bailey	67	726	271	122	.450	101	68	.673	71	126	197	28	116	1	21	54	312	4.7	23
Silas	82	1595	299	113	.378	136	89	.654	204	232	436	66	120	0	25	5	315	3.8	14
V. Johnson	38	325	115	45	.391	39	31	.795	19	36	55	54	40	0	19	4	121	3.2	12

3-Pt. FG: Seattle 59-189 (.312)—Williams 7-36 (.194); D. Johnson 12-58 (.207); Sikma 0-1 (.000); Shelton 1-5 (.200); Brown 39-88 (.443) V. Johnson 0-1 (.000). Opponents 59-240 (246).

Utah's Adrian Dantley finished third in the NBA in scoring with a 28.0 average in 1979-80.

UTAH JAZZ

Player	G.	Min.	FGA	FGM	Pct.	FTA	FTM	Pct.	Off. Reb.	Def. Reb.	Tot. Reb.	Ast.	PF	Dsq.	Stl.	Blk. Sh.	Pts.	Avg.	Hi.
Dantley	68	2674	1267	730	.576	526	443	.842	183	333	516	191	211	2	96	14	1903	28.0	50
Maravich	17	522	294	121	.412	50	41	.820	7	33	40	54	30	0	15	4	290	17.1	31
Furlow (Tot)	76	2122	926	430	.464	196	171	.872	70	124	194	293	98	0	73	23	1055	13.9	37
Furlow (Utah)	55	1718	765	364	.476	145	127	.876	47	105	152	221	79	0	54	14	878	16.0	37
Boone (Tot)	81	2392	915	405	.443	196	175	.893	54	173	227	309	232	3	97	3	1004	12.4	35
Boone (Utah)	75	2286	875	391	.447	189	169	.894	50	166	216	302	219	3	92	3	970	12.9	35
Bristow	82	2304	785	377	.480	243	197	.811	170	342	512	341	211	2	88	6	953	11.6	31
Boswell (Tot)	79	2077	613	346	.564	273	206	.755	146	296	442	161	270	9	29	37	903	11.4	25
Boswell (Ut)	61	1555	478	274	.573	203	148	.729	106	222	328	115	214	8	24	29	700	11.5	25
King	19	419	137	71	.518	63	34	.540	24	64	88	52	66	3	7	4	176	9.3	24
Poquette	82	2349	566	296	.523	167	139	.832	124	436	560	131	283	8	45	162	731	8.9	27
Williams	77	1794	519	232	.447	60	42	.700	21	85	106	183	166	0	100	11	506	6.6	22
Calvin	48	772	227	100	.440	117	105	.897	13	71	84	134	72	0	27	0	306	6.4	17
Hardy	76	1600	363	184	.507	66	51	.773	124	275	399	104	207	4	47	87	420	5.5	22
Dawkins	57	776	300	141	.470	48	33	.688	42	83	125	77	112	0	33	9	316	5.5	30
Davis (Tot)	18	268	63	35	.556	16	13	.813	4	13	17	50	28	0	13	1	83	4.6	17
Davis (Utah)	13	225	56	33	.586	12	10	.833	4	11	15	45	21	0	10	1	76	5.8	17
Gianelli	17	285	66	23	.348	16	9	.563	14	48	62	17	26	0	6	7	55	3.2	10
Whitehead (Tot)	50	553	114	58	.509	35	10	.286	56	111	167	24	97	3	8	17	126	2.5	11
Whitehead (Ut)	32	328	69	31	.449	17	5	.294	27	70	97	18	65	3	7	11	67	2.1	8
Smith	6	73	15	5	.333	5	5	1.000	3	0	3	7	3	0	4	0	15	2.5	5
Wakefield	8	47	15	6	.400	3	3	1.000	0	4	4	3	13	0	1	0	15	1.9	5
Kilpatrick	2	6	2	1	.500	2	1	.500	1	3	4	0	1	0	0	0	3	1.5	3
Deane	7	48	11	2	.182	7	5	.714	2	4	6	6	3	0	0	0	10	1.4	3
Brown	4	24	7	0	.000	4	4	1.000	5	4	9	4	4	0	0	0	4	1.0	2

3-Pt. FG: Utah 59-185 (.319)—Dantley 0-2 (.000); Maravich 7-11 (.636); Furlow (Tot.) 24-82 (.293) (Utah) 23-73 (.315); Boone (Utah) 19-50 (.380); Bristow 2-7 (.286); Boswell (Tot) 5-10 (.500); (Utah) 4-8 (.500); Poquette 0-2 (.000); Williams 0-12 (.000); Calvin 1-11 (.091) Hardy 1-2 (.500); Dawkins 1-5 (.200); Davis (Utah) 0-1 (.000); Deane 1-1 (1.000). Opponents 59-185 (.319).

WASHINGTON BULLETS

Player	G.	Min.	FGA	FGM	Pct.	FTA	FTM	Pct.	Off. Reb.	Def. Reb.	Tot. Reb.	Ast.	PF	Dsq.	Stl.	Blk. Sh.	Pts.	Avg.	Hi.
Hayes	81	3183	1677	761	.454	478	334	.699	269	627	896	129	309	9	62	189	1859	23.0	43
Dandridge	45	1457	729	329	.451	152	123	.809	63	183	246	178	112	1	29	36	783	17.4	31
Ballard	82	2438	1101	545	.495	227	171	.753	240	398	638	159	197	2	90	36	1277	15.6	32
Williamson (Tot)	58	1374	817	359	.439	138	116	.841	38	61	99	126	137	1	36	19	845	14.6	32
Williamson (Wa)	30	603	356	153	.430	50	40	.800	14	31	45	39	66	0	10	10	349	11.6	24
Grevey	65	1818	804	331	.412	249	216	.867	80	107	187	177	158	0	56	16	912	14.0	32
Phegley	50	971	473	224	.474	120	104	.867	49	66	115	70	106	1	19	3	554	11.1	35
Chenier	20	470	214	84	.393	41	31	.756	10	33	43	42	26	0	18	5	202	10.1	22
Unseld	82	2973	637	327	.513	209	139	.665	334	760	1094	366	249	5	65	61	794	9.7	24
Wright	76	1286	500	229	.458	108	96	.889	40	82	122	222	144	3	49	18	558	7.3·	25
Porter	70	1494	438	201	.459	137	110	.803	25	57	82	457	180	1	59	11	512	7.3	24
Cleamons (Tot)	79	1789	450	214	.476	113	84	.743	53	99	152	288	133	0	57	11	519	6.6	20
Cleamons (Wa)	57	1535	381	184	.483	98	72	.735	43	90	133	248	120	0	44	9	444	7.8	20
Kupchak	40	451	160	67	.419	75	52	.693	32	73	105	16	49	1	8	8	186	4.7	20
Boston	13	125	52	24	.462	13	8	.615	19	20	39	2	25	0	4	2	56	4.3	15
Behagen	6	64	23	9	.391	6	5	.833	6	8	14	7	14	0	4	0	23	3.8	9
Corzine	78	826	216	90	.417	68	45	.662	104	166	270	63	120	1	9	31	225	2.9	13
Bailey	20	180	35	16	.457	13	5	.385	6	22	28	26	18	0	7	4	38	1.9	6
Malovic	1	6	0	0	....	4	1	.250	0	0	0	0	0	0	1	0	1	1.0	1

3-Pt. FG: Washington 73-238 (.307)—Hayes 3-13 (.231); Dandridge 2-11 (.182); Ballard 16-47 (.340); Williamson (Tot) 11-35 (.314); Williamson (Wash) 3-16 (.188); Grevey 34-92 (.370); Phegley 2-5 (.400); Chenier 3-6 (.500); Unseld 1-2 (.500); Wright 4-16 (.250); Porter 0-4 (.000); Cleamons (Tot) 7-31 (.226), Cleamons (Wash) 4-23 (.174); Kupchak 0-2 (.000); Bailey 1-1 (1.000). Opponents 56-214 (.262).

PLAYOFF RESULTS

EASTERN CONFERENCE FIRST ROUND

Philadelphia 2, Washington 0

Apr. 2—Wed.—Washington 96 at Philadelphia 111
Apr. 4←Fri.—Philadelphia 112 at Washington...........104

Houston 2, San Antonio 1

Apr. 2—Wed.—San Antonio 85 at Houston.............. 95
Apr. 4—Fri.—Houston 101 at San Antonio 106
Apr. 6—Sun.—San Antonio 120 at Houston..............141

EASTERN CONFERENCE SEMIFINALS

Boston 4, Houston 0

Apr. 9—Wed.—Houston 101 at Boston 119
Apr. 11—Fri.—Houston 75 at Boston..................... 95
Apr. 13—Sun.—Boston 100 at Houston................... 81
Apr. 14—Mon.—Boston 138 at Houston..................121

Philadelphia 4, Atlanta 1

Apr. 6—Sun.—Atlanta 104 at Philadelphia 107
Apr. 9—Wed.—Atlanta 92 at Philadelphia 99
Apr. 10—Thu.—Philadelphia 93 at Atlanta 105
Apr. 13—Sun.—Philadelphia 107 at Atlanta 83
Apr. 15—Tue.—Atlanta 100 at Philadelphia 105

EASTERN CONFERENCE FINALS

Philadelphia 4, Boston 1

Apr. 18—Fri.—Philadelphia 96 at Boston................. 93
Apr. 20—Sun.—Philadelphia 90 at Boston................ 96
Apr. 23—Wed.—Boston 97 at Philadelphia 99
Apr. 24—Thu.—Boston 90 at Philadelphia 102
Apr. 27—Sun.—Philadelphia 105 at Boston............... 94

WESTERN CONFERENCE FIRST ROUND

Phoenix 2, Kansas City 1

Apr. 2—Wed.—Kansas City 93 at Phoenix 96
Apr. 4—Fri.—Phoenix 96 at Kansas City 106
Apr. 6—Sun.—Kansas City 99 at Phoenix................114

Seattle 2, Portland 1

Apr. 2—Wed.—Portland 110 at Seattle 120
Apr. 4—Fri.—Seattle 95 at Portland ....°105
Apr. 6—Sun.—Portland 86 at Seattle 103

WESTERN CONFERENCE SEMIFINALS

Los Angeles 4, Phoenix 1

Apr. 8—Tue.—Phoenix 110 at Los Angeles...............°119
Apr. 9—Wed.—Phoenix 128 at Los Angeles ....°131
Apr. 11—Fri.—Los Angeles 108 at Phoenix 105
Apr. 13—Sun.—Los Angeles 101 at Phoenix 127
Apr. 15—Tue.—Phoenix 101 at Los Angeles 126

Seattle 4, Milwaukee 3

Apr. 8—Tue.—Milwaukee 113 at Seattle.................°114
Apr. 9—Wed.—Milwaukee 114 at Seattle ....°112
Apr. 11—Fri.—Seattle 91 at Milwaukee.................. 95
Apr. 13—Sun.—Seattle 112 at Milwaukee 107
Apr. 15—Tue.—Milwaukee 108 at Seattle 97
Apr. 18—Fri.—Seattle 86 at Milwaukee 85
Apr. 20—Sun.—Milwaukee 94 at Seattle 98

WESTERN CONFERENCE FINALS

Los Angeles 4, Seattle 1

Apr. 22—Tue.—Seattle 108 at Los Angeles 107
Apr. 23—Wed.—Seattle 99 at Los Angeles................108
Apr. 25—Fri.—Los Angeles 104 at Seattle 100
Apr. 27—Sun.—Los Angeles 98 at Seattle 93
Apr. 30—Wed.—Seattle 105 at Los Angeles 111

WORLD CHAMPIONSHIP SERIES

Los Angeles 4, Philadelphia 2

May 4—Sun.—Philadelphia 102 at Los Angeles..........109
May 7—Wed.—Philadelphia 107 at Los Angeles 104
May 10—Sat.—Los Angeles 111 at Philadelphia..........101
May 11—Sun.—Los Angeles 102 at Philadelphia.........105
May 14—Wed.—Philadelphia 103 at Los Angeles 108
May 16—Fri.—Los Angeles 123 at Philadelphia 107

1978-79 NBA STATISTICS

1978-79 NBA CHAMPION SEATTLE SUPERSONICS

Front row (left to right): Trainer Frank Furtado, Dick Snyder, Jackie Robinson, Fred Brown, Joe Hassett, Dennis Johnson, Gus Williams. Second row: Coach Lenny Wilkens, Dennis Awtrey, Tom LaGarde, John Johnson, Lonnie Shelton, Paul Silas, Scout Mike Uporsky, Assistant Coach Les Habegger. Back row: Jack Sikma, General Manager Zollie Volchok. Missing from photo: Wally Walker.

FINAL STANDINGS

ATLANTIC DIVISION

Team	Atl.	Bos.	Chi.	Cle.	Den.	Det.	G.S.	Hou.	Ind.	K.C.	L.A.	Mil.	N.J.	N.O.	N.Y.	Phi.	Pho.	Por.	S.A.	S.D.	Sea.	Was.	W.	L.	Pct.	G.B.
Washington	2	4	3	4	3	3	2	2	3	..	2	3	3	4	3	1	3	1	3	3	2	..	54	28	.659	..
Philadelphia	2	2	3	2	3	3	1	4	2	2	3	2	2	2	2	..	1	1	3	3	1	3	47	35	.573	7
New Jersey	2	3	2	1	..	4	3	1	2	1	2	2	..	3	1	2	3	2	..	2	..	1	37	45	.451	17
New York	2	1	1	2	1	3	1	..	2	1	..	3	3	2	..	2	..	1	1	2	2	1	31	51	.378	23
Boston	2	..	1	2	1	2	2	1	3	1	1	1	1	2	3	2	..	1	..	1	2	..	29	53	.354	25

CENTRAL DIVISION

Team	Atl.	Bos.	Chi.	Cle.	Den.	Det.	G.S.	Hou.	Ind.	K.C.	L.A.	Mil.	N.J.	N.O.	N.Y.	Phi.	Pho.	Por.	S.A.	S.D.	Sea.	Was.	W.	L.	Pct.	G.B.
San Antonio	1	4	3	4	1	3	3	1	1	3	2	3	4	2	3	1	1	1	..	4	2	1	48	34	.585	..
Houston	1	3	2	2	3	2	2	..	..	3	2	2	3	4	4	..	2	3	3	2	2	2	47	35	.573	1
Atlanta	..	2	3	3	3	1	3	1	3	1	2	1	3	2	2	2	2	2	3	3	1	2	46	36	.561	2
Cleveland	1	2	3	..	1	1	2	1	1	2	1	3	2	2	2	..	..	2	2	..	30	52	.366	18
Detroit	1	2	2	3	2	..	1	2	2	2	2	2	..	2	1	1	..	1	1	2	..	1	30	52	.366	18
New Orleans	2	2	2	2	1	2	1	..	1	1	2	1	..	2	2	1	1	2	..	..	..	26	56	.317	22

MIDWEST DIVISION

Team	Atl.	Bos.	Chi.	Cle.	Den.	Det.	G.S.	Hou.	Ind.	K.C.	L.A.	Mil.	N.J.	N.O.	N.Y.	Phi.	Pho.	Por.	S.A.	S.D.	Sea.	Was.	W.	L.	Pct.	G.B.
Kansas City	2	3	4	3	3	2	2	1	3	..	2	2	3	3	2	2	1	1	2	2	3	48	34	.585	...
Denver	1	3	2	2	..	2	4	1	3	1	3	2	4	3	3	..	3	1	3	2	3	1	47	35	.573	1
Indiana	3	1	2	3	1	2	2	4	..	1	..	2	1	2	2	2	2	3	3	1	..	1	38	44	.463	10
Milwaukee	..	3	3	3	2	1	2	2	2	1	..	2	3	1	2	2	2	1	1	2	1	38	44	.463	10
Chicago	1	2	..	1	2	2	3	2	2	..	1	1	2	2	3	1	1	4	..	..	..	1	31	51	.378	17

PACIFIC DIVISION

Team	Atl.	Bos.	Chi.	Cle.	Den.	Det.	G.S.	Hou.	Ind.	K.C.	L.A.	Mil.	N.J.	N.O.	N.Y.	Phi.	Pho.	Por.	S.A.	S.D.	Sea.	Was.	W.	L.	Pct.	G.B.
Seattle	3	2	4	2	1	3	1	2	4	2	2	2	4	3	2	3	3	3	2	2	..	2	52	30	.634	...
Phoenix	1	4	3	4	1	4	3	2	2	2	2	..	3	4	3	..	3	3	2	1	1	50	32	.610	2
Los Angeles	3	3	3	2	1	2	3	1	4	2	..	3	2	2	3	1	2	2	2	2	2	47	35	.573	5
Portland	2	3	..	4	3	3	2	1	1	3	2	2	3	2	1	..	2	2	1	3	45	37	.549	7
San Diego	1	3	4	2	2	2	3	1	3	2	2	3	2	4	2	1	2	2	..	..	2	43	39	.524	9
Golden State	3	1	1	1	..	3	..	2	2	2	1	2	1	3	3	3	1	2	1	1	3	2	38	44	.463	14

HOME-ROAD RECORDS OF ALL TEAMS

Team	Home	Road	Total	Team	Home	Road	Total
Atlanta	34- 7	12- 29	46- 36	New Jersey	25- 16	12- 29	37- 45
Boston	21- 20	8- 33	29- 53	New Orleans	22- 19	4- 37	26- 56
Chicago	19- 22	12- 29	31- 51	New York	23- 18	8- 33	31- 51
Cleveland	20- 21	10- 31	30- 52	Philadelphia	31- 10	16- 25	47- 35
Denver	29- 12	18- 23	47- 35	Phoenix	32- 9	18- 23	50- 32
Detroit	22- 19	8- 33	30- 52	Portland	33- 8	12- 29	45- 37
Golden State	23- 18	15- 26	38- 44	San Antonio	29- 12	19- 22	48- 34
Houston	30- 11	17- 24	47- 35	San Diego	29- 12	14- 27	43- 39
Indiana	25- 16	13- 28	38- 44	Seattle	31- 10	21- 20	52- 30
Kansas City	32- 9	16- 25	48- 34	Washington	31- 10	23- 18	54- 28
Los Angeles	31- 10	16- 25	47- 35	Total	600-302	302-600	902-902
Milwaukee	28- 13	10- 31	38- 44				

OFFENSIVE TEAM STATISTICS

		FIELD GOALS			FREE THROWS			REBOUNDS			MISCELLANEOUS				Turn	Blk.	SCORING	
Team	G.	Att.	Made	Pct.	Att.	Made	Pct.	Off.	Def.	Tot.	Ast.	PF	Disq.	Stl.	Over	Sh.	Pts.	Avg.
San Antonio	82	7760	3927	.506	2423	1926	.795	1096	2619	3715	2313	2071	25	829	1652	509	9780	119.3
Phoenix	82	7516	3847	.512	2299	1765	.768	1083	2379	3462	2500	1944	19	915	1760	337	9459	115.4
Washington	82	7873	3819	.485	2428	1785	.735	1309	2768	4077	2169	1804	18	614	1420	401	9423	114.9
Milwaukee	82	7773	3906	.503	2021	1541	.762	1157	2370	3527	2562	2106	25	862	1574	435	9353	114.1
Houston	82	7498	3726	.497	2330	1845	.792	1256	2504	3760	2302	2001	19	632	1510	286	9297	113.4
San Diego	82	7706	3721	.483	2471	1836	.743	1392	2413	3805	1539	2127	43	703	1623	392	9278	113.1
Kansas City	82	7644	3764	.492	2392	1746	.730	1191	2404	3595	2239	2419	53	825	1631	390	9274	113.1
Los Angeles	82	7397	3827	.517	2088	1606	.769	949	2557	3506	2338	1851	16	793	1569	500	9260	112.9
Denver	82	7311	3517	.481	2841	2046	.720	1307	2596	3903	2166	2106	45	673	1666	416	9080	110.7
Detroit	82	7802	3708	.475	2242	1607	.717	1303	2380	3683	2092	2141	37	847	1599	550	9023	110.0
Philadelphia	82	7338	3584	.488	2411	1815	.753	1149	2712	3861	2253	2072	26	779	1771	599	8983	109.5
Atlanta	82	7410	3505	.473	2534	1940	.766	1381	2341	3722	1938	2424	72	801	1523	596	8950	109.1
Indiana	82	7525	3575	.475	2317	1759	.759	1225	2530	3755	2005	2093	41	687	1536	416	8909	108.6
Portland	82	7338	3541	.483	2362	1806	.765	1256	2435	3691	1946	2187	49	776	1658	512	8888	108.4
New Orleans	82	7511	3517	.468	2409	1848	.767	1234	2676	3910	2079	1940	27	760	1764	559	8882	108.3
Boston	82	7347	3527	.480	2321	1820	.785	1119	2396	3515	1995	1977	39	710	1713	283	8874	108.2
New Jersey	82	7523	3464	.460	2613	1904	.729	1241	2370	3611	1907	2329	43	853	1861	619	8832	107.7
New York	82	7554	3676	.487	2111	1478	.700	1200	2430	3630	2121	2154	34	699	1605	397	8830	107.7
Seattle	82	7484	3504	.468	2298	1732	.754	1310	2591	3901	1973	1914	23	690	1586	398	8740	106.6
Cleveland	82	7602	3556	.468	2103	1620	.770	1229	2256	3485	1796	2027	21	688	1376	334	8732	106.5
Golden State	82	7453	3627	.487	1872	1367	.730	1169	2513	3682	2064	2023	25	774	1500	420	8621	105.1
Chicago	82	7108	3478	.489	2184	1632	.747	1224	2544	3768	2169	1970	30	576	1813	324	8588	104.7

DEFENSIVE TEAM STATISTICS

		FIELD GOALS			FREE THROWS			REBOUNDS			MISCELLANEOUS				Turn	Blk.	SCORING		Pt.
Team	Att.	Made	Pct.	Att.	Made	Pct.	Off.	Def.	Tot.	Ast.	PF	Disq.	Stl.	Over	Sh.	Pts.	Avg.	Dif.	
Seattle	7509	3475	.463	2108	1567	.743	1156	2453	3609	1910	2057	27	755	1493	407	8517	103.9	+ 2.7	
Golden State	7255	3493	.481	2155	1604	.744	1147	2533	3680	2094	1854	20	637	1580	362	8590	104.8	+ 0.3	
Atlanta	6886	3367	.489	2727	2045	.750	1176	2440	3616	1928	2135	45	646	1799	559	8779	107.1	+ 2.0	
Portland	7059	3448	.488	2501	1889	.755	1080	2350	3430	1963	2206	48	797	1650	422	8785	107.1	+ 1.3	
Philadelphia	7626	3542	.464	2331	1747	.749	1252	2506	3758	2094	2128	35	795	1627	353	8831	107.7	+ 1.8	
Chicago	7408	3682	.497	2029	1549	.763	1095	2377	3472	2146	2093	38	844	1468	503	8913	108.7	- 4.0	
Denver	7616	3631	.477	2277	1713	.752	1218	2429	3647	2173	2262	56	738	1529	471	8975	109.5	+ 1.2	
Los Angeles	7848	3797	.484	1415	1391	.733	1288	2486	3774	2234	1958	28	737	1542	359	9009	109.9	+ 3.0	
Washington	8011	3804	.475	1897	1406	.741	1178	2541	3719	2180	2144	37	726	1380	434	9014	109.9	+ 5.0	
Cleveland	7150	3600	.503	2423	1837	.758	1123	2587	3710	2062	2001	21	658	1557	503	9037	110.2	- 3.7	
Kansas City	7061	3434	.486	2897	2170	.749	1156	2547	3703	1776	2223	41	678	1879	435	9038	110.2	+ 2.9	
Indiana	7499	3586	.478	2416	1868	.773	1299	2605	3904	2178	2091	30	677	1618	437	9040	110.2	- 1.6	
New York	7457	3600	.483	2506	1907	.761	1225	2489	3714	2114	1961	29	751	1558	378	9107	111.1	- 3.4	
Phoenix	7626	3775	.495	2127	1606	.755	1238	2424	3662	2091	2144	33	890	1841	402	9156	111.7	+ 3.7	
Milwaukee	7505	3676	.490	2415	1819	.753	1229	2437	3666	2301	1928	17	763	1748	462	9171	111.8	+ 2.3	
New Jersey	7306	3507	.480	2861	2160	.755	1234	2667	3901	2185	2208	37	861	1919	492	9174	111.9	- 4.2	
Houston	7625	3795	.498	2211	1627	.736	1186	2315	3501	2278	2055	43	660	1400	431	9217	112.4	+ 1.0	
Detroit	7623	3755	.493	2295	1732	.755	1301	2628	3929	2197	1914	21	666	1744	504	9242	112.7	- 2.7	
Boston	7593	3855	.508	2079	1578	.759	1122	2453	3575	2170	2025	25	717	1603	438	9288	113.3	- 5.1	
San Antonio	7970	3798	.477	2343	1759	.751	1297	2531	3828	2232	2168	41	788	1700	405	9355	114.1	+ 5.2	
New Orleans	8039	3864	.481	2246	1666	.742	1486	2664	4150	2264	2061	28	955	1600	566	9394	114.6	- 6.3	
San Diego	7801	3832	.491	2295	1760	.767	1294	2322	3616	1896	2064	30	747	1517	350	9424	114.9	- 1.8	

Disq.—Individual players disqualified (fouled out of game).

INDIVIDUAL LEADERS

POINTS

(Minimum of 70 games played or 1400 points)

Player	G.	FG	FT	Pts.	Avg.	Player	G.	FG	FT	Pts.	Avg.
Gervin, S.A.	80	947	471	2365	29.6	Drew, Atl.	79	650	495	1795	22.7
Free, S.D.	78	795	654	2244	28.8	McGinnis, Den.	76	603	509	1715	22.6
M. Johnson, Mil.	77	820	332	1972	25.6	Williamson, N.J.	74	635	373	1643	22.2
McAdoo, N.Y.-Bos	60	596	295	1487	24.8	Kenon, S.A.	81	748	295	1791	22.1
Malone, Hou.	82	716	599	2031	24.8	Russell, Clev.	74	603	417	1623	21.9
Thompson, Den.	76	693	439	1825	24.0	Hayes, Wash.	82	720	349	1789	21.8
Westphal, Phoe.	81	801	339	1941	24.0	Birdsong, K.C.	82	741	296	1778	21.7
Abdul-Jabbar, L.A.	80	777	349	1903	23.8	King, N.J.	82	710	349	1769	21.6
Gilmore, Chi.	82	753	434	1940	23.7	Robinson, N.O.-Phoe.	69	566	324	1456	21.1
Davis, Phoe.	79	764	340	1868	23.6						
Erving, Phil.	78	715	373	1803	23.1						

FIELD GOALS
Minimum 300 FG Made

	FGA	FGM	Pct.
Maxwell, Boston	808	472	.584
Abdul-Jabbar, Los Angeles	1347	777	.577
Unseld, Washington	600	346	.577
Gilmore, Chicago	1310	753	.575
Nater, San Diego	627	357	.569
Washington, San Diego	623	350	.562
Davis, Phoenix	1362	764	.561
M. Johnson, Milwaukee	1491	820	.550
Robinzine, Kansas City	837	459	.548
Owens, Portland	1095	600	.548

FREE THROWS
Minimum 125 FT Made

	FTA	FTM	Pct.
Barry, Houston	169	160	.947
Murphy, Houston	265	246	.928
Brown, Seattle	206	183	.888
Smith, Denver	180	159	.883
Sobers, Indiana	338	298	.882
White, Boston-Golden State	158	139	.880
Twardzik, Portland	299	261	.873
Newlin, Houston	243	212	.872
Dunleavy, Houston	184	159	.864
Winters, Milwaukee	277	237	.856

ASSISTS
Minimum 70 games or 400 assists

	G.	No.	Avg.
Porter, Detroit	82	1099	13.4
Lucas, Golden State	82	762	9.3
Nixon, Los Angeles	82	737	9.0
Ford, Kansas City	79	681	8.6
Westphal, Phoenix	81	529	6.5
Barry, Houston	80	502	6.3
Williams, New York	81	504	6.2
Henderson, Washington	70	419	6.0
Hill, Atlanta	82	480	5.9
Buckner, Milwaukee	81	468	5.8

STEALS
Minimum 70 games or 125 steals

	G.	No.	Avg.
Carr, Detroit	80	197	2.46
Jordan, New Jersey	82	201	2.45
Nixon, Los Angeles	82	201	2.45
Walker, Cleveland	55	130	2.36
Ford, Kansas City	79	174	2.20
Smith, San Diego	82	177	2.16
Cheeks, Philadelphia	82	174	2.12
Williams, Seattle	76	158	2.08
Porter, Detroit	82	158	1.93
Buckner, Milwaukee	81	156	1.93

REBOUNDS
Minimum 70 games or 800 rebounds

	G.	Off.	Def.	Tot.	Avg.
Malone, Houston	82	587	857	1444	17.6
Kelley, New Orleans	80	303	723	1026	12.8
Abdul-Jabbar, Los Angeles	80	207	818	1025	12.8
Gilmore, Chicago	82	293	750	1043	12.7
Sikma, Seattle	82	232	781	1013	12.4
Hayes, Washington	82	312	682	994	12.1
Parish, Golden State	76	265	651	916	12.1
Robinson, N.O.-Phoenix	69	195	607	802	11.6
McGinnis, Denver	76	256	608	864	11.4
Roundfield, Atlanta	80	326	539	865	10.8

BLOCKED SHOTS
Minimum 70 games or 100 blocked shots

	G.	No.	Avg.
Abdul-Jabbar, Los Angeles	80	316	3.95
Johnson, New Jersey	78	253	3.24
Rollins, Atlanta	81	254	3.14
Parish, Golden State	76	217	2.86
Tyler, Detroit	82	201	2.45
Hayes, Washington	82	190	2.32
Roundfield, Atlanta	80	176	2.20
Kelley, New Orleans	80	166	2.08
C. Jones, Philadelphia	78	157	2.01
Gilmore, Chicago	82	156	1.90

TEAM-BY-TEAM INDIVIDUAL STATISTICS

ATLANTA HAWKS

Player	G.	Min.	FGA	FGM	Pct.	FTA	FTM	Pct.	Off. Reb.	Def. Reb.	Tot. Reb.	Ast.	PF	Dsq.	Stl.	Blk. Sh.	Pts.	Avg.	Hi.
Drew	79	2410	1375	650	.473	677	495	.731	225	297	522	119	332	19	128	16	1795	22.7	50
Johnson	78	2413	982	501	.510	292	243	.832	65	105	170	360	241	6	121	11	1245	16.0	30
Roundfield	80	2539	916	462	.504	420	300	.714	326	539	865	131	358	16	87	176	1224	15.3	38
Furlow (Tot)	78	1686	804	388	.483	195	163	.836	76	91	167	184	122	1	58	30	939	12.0	30
Furlow (Atl)	29	576	235	113	.481	70	60	.857	32	39	71	81	42	0	18	13	286	9.9	30
Hawes	81	2205	756	372	.492	132	108	.818	190	401	591	184	264	1	79	47	852	10.5	27
Hill	82	2527	682	296	.434	288	246	.854	41	123	164	480	292	8	102	16	838	10.2	26
Rollins	81	1900	555	297	.535	141	89	.631	219	369	588	49	328	19	46	254	683	8.4	24
Givens	74	1347	564	234	.415	135	102	.756	98	116	214	83	121	0	72	17	570	7.7	22
Lee	49	997	313	144	.460	117	88	.752	11	48	59	169	88	0	56	1	376	7.7	21
McMillen	82	1392	498	232	.466	119	106	.891	131	201	332	69	211	2	15	32	570	7.0	22
Criss	54	879	289	109	.377	86	67	.779	19	41	60	138	70	0	41	3	285	5.3	17
Wilson	61	589	197	81	.411	44	24	.545	20	56	76	72	66	1	30	8	186	3.0	10
Herron	14	81	48	14	.292	13	12	.923	4	6	10	3	11	0	6	2	40	2.9	7

BOSTON CELTICS

Player	G.	Min.	FGA	FGM	Pct.	FTA	FTM	Pct.	Off. Reb.	Def. Reb.	Tot. Reb.	Ast.	PF	Dsq.	Stl.	Blk. Sh.	Pts.	Avg.	Hi.
McAdoo (Tot)	60	2231	1127	596	.529	450	295	.656	130	390	520	168	189	3	74	67	1487	24.8	45
McAdoo (Bos)	20	637	334	167	.500	115	77	.670	36	105	141	40	55	1	12	20	411	20.6	42
Maxwell	80	2969	808	472	.584	716	574	.802	272	519	791	228	266	4	98	74	1518	19.0	35
Cowens	68	2517	1010	488	.483	187	151	.807	152	500	652	242	263	16	76	51	1127	16.6	32
Ford (Tot)	81	2737	1142	538	.471	227	172	.758	124	150	274	374	209	3	115	25	1248	15.4	34
Ford (Bos)	78	2629	1107	525	.474	219	165	.753	115	141	256	369	200	2	114	24	1215	15.6	34
Knight	40	1119	436	219	.502	146	118	.808	41	132	173	66	86	1	31	3	556	13.9	37
White	47	1455	596	255	.428	89	79	.888	22	106	128	214	100	1	54	4	589	12.5	28
Archibald	69	1662	573	259	.452	307	242	.788	25	78	103	324	132	2	55	6	760	11.0	25
Robey (Tot)	79	1763	673	322	.478	224	174	.777	168	345	513	132	232	4	48	15	818	10.4	28
Robey (Bos)	36	914	378	182	.481	103	84	.816	88	171	259	79	121	3	23	3	448	12.4	27
Judkins	81	1521	587	295	.503	146	119	.815	70	121	191	145	184	1	81	12	709	8.8	29
Barnes	38	796	271	133	.491	66	43	.652	57	120	177	53	144	3	38	39	309	8.1	29
Rowe	53	1222	346	151	.436	75	52	.693	79	163	242	69	105	2	15	13	354	6.7	21
Tatum	3	38	20	8	.400	5	4	.800	1	3	4	1	7	0	0	1	20	6.7	11
Williams	20	273	123	54	.439	24	14	.583	41	64	105	12	41	0	12	9	122	6.7	27
Chaney	65	1074	414	174	.420	42	36	.857	63	78	141	75	167	3	72	11	384	5.9	20
Sanders (Tot)	46	479	246	105	.427	68	54	.794	35	75	110	52	69	1	21	6	264	5.7	16
Sanders (Bos)	24	216	119	55	.462	27	22	.815	22	29	51	17	25	0	7	3	132	5.5	14
Stacom (Tot)	68	831	342	128	.374	60	44	.733	30	55	85	112	47	0	29	1	300	4.4	16
Stacom (Bos)	24	260	133	52	.391	19	13	.684	10	14	24	35	18	0	15	0	117	4.9	15
Barker	14	131	48	21	.438	15	11	.733	12	18	30	6	26	0	4	4	53	4.4	14
Awtrey	23	247	44	17	.386	20	16	.800	13	34	47	20	37	0	3	6	50	2.2	7

CHICAGO BULLS

Player	G.	Min.	FGA	FGM	Pct.	FTA	FTM	Pct.	Off. Reb.	Def. Reb.	Tot. Reb.	Ast.	PF	Dsq.	Stl.	Blk. Sh.	Pts.	Avg.	Hi.
Gilmore	82	3265	1310	753	.575	587	434	.739	293	750	1043	274	280	2	50	156	1940	23.7	41
Theus	82	2753	1119	537	.480	347	264	.761	92	136	228	429	270	0	93	18	1338	16.3	30
M. Johnson	82	2594	1105	496	.449	329	273	.830	193	434	627	380	286	9	88	59	1265	15.4	33
Holland	82	2483	940	445	.473	176	141	.801	78	176	254	330	240	9	122	12	1031	12.6	32
Mengelt	75	1705	689	338	.491	182	150	.824	25	93	118	187	148	1	46	4	826	11.0	26
O. Johnson	71	1734	540	281	.520	110	88	.800	58	169	227	163	182	2	54	33	650	9.2	24
Landsberger	80	1959	585	278	.475	194	91	.469	292	450	742	68	125	0	27	22	647	8.1	21
Brown	77	1265	317	152	.479	98	84	.857	83	155	238	104	180	5	18	10	388	5.0	14
May	37	403	136	59	.434	40	30	.750	14	50	64	39	51	0	22	1	148	4.0	15
Dudley	43	684	125	45	.360	42	28	.667	25	61	86	116	82	0	32	1	118	2.7	14
Sheppard	22	203	51	24	.471	19	12	.632	16	12	28	15	16	0	5	0	60	2.7	11
Armstrong	26	259	70	28	.400	13	10	.769	7	13	20	31	22	0	10	0	66	2.5	8
Lloyd (Tot)	72	496	122	42	.344	47	27	.574	49	47	96	32	92	0	10	8	111	1.5	11
Lloyd (Chi)	67	465	120	42	.350	47	27	.574	48	45	93	32	86	0	9	8	111	1.7	11
Wakefield	2	8	1	0	.000	0	0	.....	0	0	0	1	2	0	0	0	0	0.0	0

CLEVELAND CAVALIERS

Player	G.	Min.	FGA	FGM	Pct.	FTA	FTM	Pct.	Off. Reb.	Def. Reb.	Tot. Reb.	Ast.	PF	Dsq.	Stl.	Blk. Sh.	Pts.	Avg.	Hi.
Russell	74	2859	1268	603	.476	523	417	.797	147	356	503	348	222	2	98	25	1623	21.9	41
Carr	82	2714	1161	551	.475	358	292	.861	155	135	290	217	210	1	77	14	1394	17.0	30
Chones	82	2850	1073	472	.440	215	158	.735	260	582	842	181	278	4	47	102	1102	13.4	28
Furlow	49	1110	569	275	.483	125	103	.824	44	52	96	103	80	1	40	17	653	13.3	25
B. Smith	72	1650	784	361	.460	106	83	.783	77	129	206	121	188	2	43	7	805	11.2	23
Frazier	12	279	122	54	.443	27	21	.778	7	13	20	32	22	0	13	2	129	10.8	18
Mitchell	80	1576	706	362	.513	178	131	.736	127	202	329	60	215	6	51	29	855	10.7	32
Walker	55	1753	448	208	.464	175	137	.783	59	139	198	321	153	0	130	18	553	10.1	26
Lee (Tot)	82	1779	634	290	.457	230	175	.761	33	93	126	295	146	0	86	1	755	9.2	22
Lee (Clev)	33	782	321	146	.455	113	87	.770	22	45	67	126	58	0	30	0	379	11.5	22
E. Smith	24	332	130	69	.531	26	18	.692	45	61	106	13	60	0	7	16	156	6.5	16
Higgs	68	1050	279	127	.455	111	85	.766	18	84	102	141	176	2	66	11	339	5.0	21
Lambert	70	1030	329	148	.450	55	35	.636	116	174	290	43	163	0	25	29	331	4.7	16
Brewer	55	1301	259	114	.440	48	23	.479	125	245	370	74	136	2	48	56	251	4.6	14
Davis	40	394	153	66	.431	43	30	.698	27	39	66	16	66	1	13	8	162	4.1	12

DENVER NUGGETS

Player	G.	Min.	FGA	FGM	Pct.	FTA	FTM	Pct.	Off. Reb.	Def. Reb.	Tot. Reb.	Ast.	PF	Dsq.	Stl.	Blk. Sh.	Pts.	Avg.	Hi.
Thompson	76	2670	1353	693	.512	583	439	.753	109	165	274	225	180	2	70	82	1825	24.0	44
McGinnis	76	2552	1273	603	.474	765	509	.665	256	608	864	283	321	16	129	52	1715	22.6	41
Issel	81	2742	1030	532	.517	419	316	.754	240	498	738	255	233	6	61	46	1380	17.0	29
Scott	79	2617	854	393	.460	215	161	.749	54	156	210	428	284	12	78	30	947	12.0	28
Wilkerson	80	2425	869	396	.456	173	119	.688	100	314	414	284	190	0	118	21	911	11.4	26
Boswell	79	2201	603	321	.532	284	198	.697	248	290	538	242	263	4	50	51	840	10.6	22
Roberts	63	1236	498	211	.424	110	76	.691	106	152	258	107	142	2	20	2	498	7.9	18
Smith	82	1479	436	184	.422	180	159	.883	41	105	146	208	165	1	58	13	527	6.4	19
Ellis	42	268	92	42	.457	36	29	.806	17	45	62	10	45	0	10	13	113	2.7	10
Hughes	81	1086	182	98	.538	45	18	.400	112	223	335	74	215	2	56	102	214	2.6	14
Hicks	20	128	43	18	.419	5	3	.600	13	15	28	8	20	0	5	0	39	2.0	15
Kuester	33	212	52	16	.308	14	13	.929	5	8	13	37	29	0	18	1	45	1.4	8
Crompton	20	88	26	10	.385	12	6	.500	6	17	23	5	19	0	0	3	26	1.3	6

DETROIT PISTONS

Player	G.	Min.	FGA	FGM	Pct.	FTA	FTM	Pct.	Off. Reb.	Def. Reb.	Tot. Reb.	Ast.	PF	Dsq.	Stl.	Blk. Sh.	Pts.	Avg.	Hi.
Lanier	53	1835	950	489	.515	367	275	.749	164	330	494	140	181	5	50	75	1253	23.6	38
Carr	80	3207	1143	587	.514	435	323	.743	219	370	589	262	279	2	197	46	1497	18.7	36
Long	82	2498	1240	581	.469	190	157	.826	127	139	266	121	224	1	102	19	1319	16.1	28
Porter	82	3064	1110	534	.481	266	192	.722	62	147	209	1099	302	5	158	5	1260	15.4	32
Tyler	82	2560	946	456	.482	219	144	.658	211	437	648	89	254	3	104	201	1056	12.9	32
Douglas	78	2215	698	342	.490	328	208	.634	248	416	664	74	319	13	39	55	892	11.4	24
Ford	3	108	35	13	.371	8	7	.875	9	9	18	5	9	1	1	1	33	11.0	22
Tatum (Tot)	79	1233	627	280	.447	71	52	.732	41	84	125	73	165	3	78	34	612	7.7	20
Tatum (Det)	76	1195	600	272	.448	66	48	.727	40	81	121	72	158	3	78	33	592	7.8	20
Poquette	76	1337	464	198	.427	142	111	.782	99	237	336	57	198	4	38	98	507	6.7	28
Green	27	431	177	67	.379	67	45	.672	15	25	40	63	37	0	25	1	179	6.6	17
Hawkins	4	28	16	6	.375	6	6	1.000	3	3	6	4	7	0	5	0	18	4.5	10
Howard (Tot)	14	113	56	24	.429	23	11	.478	18	23	41	5	24	0	2	0	59	4.2	16
Howard (Det)	11	91	45	19	.422	23	11	.478	13	21	34	4	16	0	2	2	49	4.5	16
Brewer (Tot)	80	1611	319	141	.442	63	26	.413	159	316	475	87	174	2	61	66	308	3.9	14
Brewer (Det)	25	310	60	27	.450	15	3	.200	34	71	105	13	38	0	13	10	57	2.3	7
Hollis	25	154	75	30	.400	12	9	.750	21	24	45	6	28	0	11	1	69	2.8	10
McNeill	11	46	20	9	.450	12	11	.917	3	7	10	3	7	0	0	0	29	2.6	19
Wakef'd (Tot)	73	586	177	62	.350	69	48	.696	25	51	76	70	70	0	19	2	172	2.4	17
Wakef'd (Det)	71	578	176	62	.352	69	48	.696	25	51	76	69	68	0	19	2	172	2.4	17
Shepp'd (Tot)	42	279	76	36	.474	34	20	.588	25	22	47	19	26	0	8	1	92	2.2	15
Shepp'd (Det)	20	76	25	12	.480	15	8	.533	9	10	19	4	10	0	3	1	32	1.6	15
Gerard	2	6	3	1	.333	2	1	.500	1	0	1	0	0	0	2	0	3	1.5	3
Boyd	5	40	12	3	.250	0	0	.....	0	2	2	7	5	0	0	0	6	1.2	2
Behagen	1	1	0	0	.....	0	0	.....	0	0	0	0	1	0	0	0	0	0.0	0

GOLDEN STATE WARRIORS

Player	G.	Min.	FGA	FGM	Pct.	FTA	FTM	Pct.	Off. Reb.	Def. Reb.	Tot. Reb.	Ast.	PF	Dsq.	Stl.	Blk. Sh.	Pts.	Avg.	Hi.
Smith	59	2288	977	489	.501	255	194	.761	48	164	212	261	159	3	101	23	1172	19.9	37
Parish	76	2411	1110	554	.499	281	196	.698	265	651	916	115	303	10	100	217	1304	17.2	33
Lucas	82	3095	1146	530	.462	321	264	.822	65	182	247	762	229	1	152	9	1324	16.1	35

Player	G.	Min.	FGA	FGM	Pct.	FTA	FTM	Pct.	Off. Reb.	Def. Reb.	Tot. Reb.	Ast.	PF	Dsq.	Stl.	Blk. Sh.	Pts.	Avg.	Hi.
Parker	79	2893	1019	512	.502	222	175	.788	164	280	444	291	187	0	144	33	1199	15.2	28
White (Tot.)	76	2338	910	404	.444	158	139	.880	42	158	200	347	173	1	80	7	947	12.5	30
White (GS)	29	883	314	149	.475	69	60	.870	20	52	72	133	73	0	26	3	358	12.3	30
Short	75	1703	771	369	.479	85	57	.671	127	220	347	97	233	6	54	12	795	10.6	27
Williams	81	1299	567	284	.501	117	102	.872	68	139	207	61	169	0	55	5	670	8.3	27
Ray	82	1917	439	231	.526	190	106	.558	213	395	608	136	264	4	47	50	568	6.9	21
Abernethy	70	1219	342	176	.515	94	70	.745	74	142	216	79	133	1	39	13	422	6.0	21
Cox	31	360	123	53	.431	92	40	.435	18	45	63	11	68	0	13	5	146	4.7	16
Townsend	65	771	289	127	.439	68	50	.735	11	44	55	91	70	0	27	6	304	4.7	24
Cooper	65	795	293	128	.437	61	41	.672	90	190	280	21	118	0	7	44	297	4.6	22
Robertson	12	74	40	15	.375	9	6	.667	6	4	10	4	10	0	8	0	36	3.0	8
Epps	13	72	23	10	.435	8	6	.750	0	5	5	2	7	0	1	0	26	2.0	10

HOUSTON ROCKETS

Player	G.	Min.	FGA	FGM	Pct.	FTA	FTM	Pct.	Off. Reb.	Def. Reb.	Tot. Reb.	Ast.	PF	Dsq.	Stl.	Blk. Sh.	Pts.	Avg.	Hi.
Malone	82	3390	1325	716	.540	811	599	.739	587	857	1444	147	223	0	79	119	2031	24.8	45
Murphy	82	2941	1424	707	.496	265	246	.928	78	95	173	351	288	5	117	6	1660	20.2	38
Tomjanovich	74	2641	1200	620	.517	221	168	.760	170	402	572	137	186	0	44	18	1408	19.0	33
Barry	80	2566	1000	461	.461	169	160	.947	40	237	277	502	195	0	95	38	1082	13.5	38
Reid	82	2259	777	382	.492	186	131	.704	129	354	483	230	302	7	75	48	895	10.9	21
Newlin	76	1828	581	283	.487	243	212	.872	51	119	170	291	218	3	51	79	778	10.2	24
Dunleavy	74	1486	425	215	.506	184	159	.864	28	100	128	324	168	2	56	5	589	8.0	22
Jones	81	1215	395	181	.458	132	96	.727	110	218	328	57	204	1	34	26	458	5.7	16
Watts	61	1046	227	92	.405	67	41	.612	35	68	103	243	143	1	73	14	225	3.7	16
Dorsey	20	108	43	24	.558	16	8	.500	12	11	23	2	25	0	1	2	56	2.8	8
Bradley	34	245	88	37	.420	33	22	.667	13	33	46	17	33	0	5	1	96	2.8	17
Coleman	6	39	7	5	.714	1	1	1.000	1	6	7	1	11	0	2	0	11	1.8	9
Barker	5	16	6	3	.500	2	2	1.000	2	4	6	0	5	0	0	0	8	1.6	4

INDIANA PACERS

Player	G.	Min.	FGA	FGM	Pct.	FTA	FTM	Pct.	Off. Reb.	Def. Reb.	Tot. Reb.	Ast.	PF	Dsq.	Stl.	Blk. Sh.	Pts.	Avg.	Hi.
J. Davis	79	2971	1240	565	.456	396	314	.793	70	121	191	453	177	1	95	22	1444	18.3	35
Sobers	81	2825	1194	553	.463	338	298	.882	118	183	301	450	315	8	138	23	1404	17.3	34
Edwards	82	2546	1065	534	.501	441	298	.676	179	514	693	92	363	16	60	109	1366	16.7	36
English	81	2696	1102	563	.511	230	173	.752	253	402	655	271	214	3	70	78	1299	16.0	32
Bantom	81	2528	1036	482	.465	338	227	.672	225	425	650	223	316	8	99	62	1191	14.7	29
Knight (Tot)	79	2095	835	441	.528	296	249	.841	94	253	347	152	160	1	63	8	1131	14.3	37
Knight (Ind)	39	976	399	222	.556	150	131	.873	53	121	174	86	74	0	32	5	575	14.7	37
Robey	43	849	295	140	.475	121	90	.744	80	174	254	53	111	1	25	12	370	8.6	28
Calhoun	81	1332	335	153	.457	86	72	.837	64	174	238	104	189	1	37	19	378	4.7	19
Elmore	80	1264	342	139	.406	78	56	.718	115	287	402	75	183	3	62	79	334	4.2	17
Stacom	44	571	209	76	.364	41	31	.756	20	41	61	77	29	0	14	1	183	4.2	16
Radford	52	649	175	83	.474	45	36	.800	25	43	68	57	61	0	30	1	202	3.9	15
B. Davis(Tot)	27	298	55	31	.564	23	16	.696	1	16	17	52	32	0	16	2	78	2.9	11
B. Davis (Ind)	22	233	44	23	.523	19	13	.684	1	15	16	43	22	0	14	2	59	2.7	11
Green	39	265	89	42	.472	34	20	.588	22	30	52	21	39	0	11	3	104	2.7	13

KANSAS CITY KINGS

Player	G.	Min.	FGA	FGM	Pct.	FTA	FTM	Pct.	Off. Reb.	Def. Reb.	Tot. Reb.	Ast.	PF	Dsq.	Stl.	Blk. Sh.	Pts.	Avg.	Hi.
Birdsong	82	2839	1456	741	.509	408	296	.725	176	178	354	281	255	2	125	17	1778	21.7	39
Wedman	73	2498	1050	561	.534	271	216	.797	135	251	386	144	239	4	76	30	1338	18.3	35
Ford	79	2723	1004	467	.465	401	326	.813	33	149	182	681	245	3	174	6	1260	15.9	33
Robinzine	82	2179	837	459	.548	246	180	.732	218	420	638	104	367	16	105	15	1098	13.4	32
Lacey	82	2627	697	350	.502	226	167	.739	179	523	702	430	309	11	106	141	867	10.6	26
McKinney	78	1242	477	240	.503	162	129	.796	20	65	85	253	121	0	58	3	609	7.8	30
Burleson	56	927	342	157	.459	169	121	.716	84	197	281	50	183	3	26	58	435	7.8	18
Redmond	49	736	375	162	.432	50	31	.620	57	51	108	57	93	2	28	16	355	7.2	18
Hillman	78	1618	428	211	.493	224	125	.558	138	293	431	91	228	11	50	66	547	7.0	16
Nash	82	1307	522	227	.435	86	69	.802	76	130	206	71	135	0	29	15	523	6.4	24
Allen	31	413	174	69	.397	33	19	.576	14	32	46	44	52	0	21	6	157	5.1	16
Behagen (Tot)	15	165	62	28	.452	13	10	.769	13	29	42	7	36	0	4	1	66	4.4	12
Behagen (KC)	9	126	50	23	.460	11	8	.727	11	20	31	5	27	0	2	1	54	6.0	12
Gerard (Tot)	58	465	194	84	.433	91	50	.549	40	58	98	21	74	14	20	13	218	3.8	11
Gerard (KC)	56	459	191	83	.435	89	49	.551	39	58	97	21	74	1	18	13	215	3.8	11
Washington	18	161	41	14	.341	16	10	.625	11	37	48	7	31	0	7	3	38	2.1	12

LOS ANGELES LAKERS

Player	G.	Min.	FGA	FGM	Pct.	FTA	FTM	Pct.	Off. Reb.	Def. Reb.	Tot. Reb.	Ast.	PF	Dsq.	Stl.	Blk. Sh.	Pts.	Avg.	Hi.
Abdul-Jabbar	80	3157	1347	777	.577	474	349	.736	207	818	1025	431	230	3	76	316	1903	23.8	40
Wilkes	82	2915	1242	626	.504	362	272	.751	164	445	609	227	275	2	134	27	1524	18.6	31
Dantley	60	1775	733	374	.510	342	292	.854	131	211	342	138	162	0	63	12	1040	17.3	40
Nixon	82	3145	1149	623	.542	204	158	.775	48	183	231	737	250	6	201	17	1404	17.1	29
Hudson	78	1686	636	329	.517	124	110	.887	64	76	140	141	133	1	58	17	768	9.8	23
Boone	82	1583	569	259	.455	104	90	.865	53	92	145	154	171	1	66	11	608	7.4	18
Carr	72	1149	450	225	.500	137	83	.606	70	222	292	60	152	0	38	31	533	7.4	17
Ford	79	1540	450	228	.507	89	72	.809	83	185	268	101	177	2	51	25	528	6.7	22
Price	75	1207	344	171	.497	79	55	.696	26	97	123	218	128	0	66	12	397	5.3	19
Robisch	80	1219	336	150	.446	115	86	.748	82	203	285	97	108	0	20	25	386	4.8	15
Davis	5	65	11	8	.727	4	3	.750	0	1	1	9	10	0	2	0	19	3.8	9
Carter	46	332	124	54	.435	54	36	.667	21	24	45	25	54	1	17	7	144	3.1	14
Cooper	3	7	6	3	.500	0	0	....	0	0	0	0	1	0	1	0	6	2.0	4

MILWAUKEE BUCKS

Player	G.	Min.	FGA	FGM	Pct.	FTA	FTM	Pct.	Off. Reb.	Def. Reb.	Tot. Reb.	Ast.	PF	Dsq.	Stl.	Blk. Sh.	Pts.	Avg.	Hi.
M. Johnson	77	2779	1491	820	.550	437	332	.760	212	374	586	234	186	1	116	89	1972	25.6	40
Winters	79	2575	1343	662	.493	277	237	.856	48	129	177	383	243	1	83	40	1561	19.8	37
Bridgeman	82	1963	1067	540	.506	228	189	.829	113	184	297	163	184	2	88	41	1269	15.5	37
Benson	82	2132	798	413	.518	245	180	.735	187	397	584	204	280	4	89	81	1006	12.3	28
Grunfeld	82	1778	661	326	.493	251	191	.761	124	236	360	216	220	3	58	15	843	10.3	27
Buckner	81	1757	553	251	.454	125	79	.632	57	153	210	468	224	1	156	17	581	7.2	19
Gianelli	82	2057	527	256	.486	102	72	.706	122	286	408	160	196	4	44	67	584	7.1	16
Restani	81	1598	529	262	.495	73	51	.699	141	244	385	122	155	0	30	27	575	7.1	22
G. Johnson	67	1157	342	165	.482	117	84	.718	106	254	360	81	187	5	75	49	414	6.2	20
Walton	75	1381	327	157	.480	90	61	.678	34	70	104	356	103	0	72	9	375	5.0	20
Smith	16	125	47	19	.404	24	18	.750	0	9	9	16	12	0	8	7	56	3.5	10
Howard	3	22	11	5	.455	0	0	.000	5	2	7	1	8	0	0	0	10	3.3	6
Van Lier	38	555	77	30	.390	52	47	.904	8	32	40	158	108	4	43	3	107	2.8	16
Beshore	1	1	0	0	.000	0	0	.....	0	0	0	0	0	0	0	0	0	0.0	0

NEW JERSEY NETS

Player	G.	Min.	FGA	FGM	Pct.	FTA	FTM	Pct.	Off. Reb.	Def. Reb.	Tot. Reb.	Ast.	PF	Dsq.	Stl.	Blk. Sh.	Pts.	Avg.	Hi.
Williamson	74	2451	1367	635	.465	437	373	.854	53	143	196	255	215	3	89	12	1643	22.2	48
King	82	2859	1359	710	.522	619	349	.564	251	418	669	295	326	10	118	39	1769	21.6	41
Money	47	1434	676	325	.481	183	136	.743	55	70	125	249	132	0	74	10	786	16.7	40
Jordan	82	2260	960	401	.418	274	213	.777	74	141	141	365	209	0	201	40	1015	12.4	29
Boynes	69	1176	595	256	.430	169	133	.787	60	95	155	75	117	1	43	7	645	9.3	29
Elliott	14	282	73	41	.562	56	41	.732	16	40	56	22	34	2	6	4	123	8.8	16
Washington	62	1139	434	218	.502	104	66	.635	88	206	294	47	186	5	31	67	502	8.1	26
Skinner	23	334	125	55	.440	82	72	.878	12	30	42	49	53	0	22	2	182	7.9	19
van B Kolff	80	1998	423	196	.463	183	146	.798	108	274	382	180	235	4	85	74	538	6.7	25
Johnson	78	2058	483	206	.427	138	105	.761	201	415	616	88	315	6	68	253	517	6.6	25
Jackson	59	1070	303	144	.475	105	86	.819	59	119	178	85	168	7	45	22	374	6.3	20
Simpson (Tot)	68	979	433	174	.402	111	76	.685	35	61	96	126	57	0	37	5	424	6.2	20
Simpson (NJ)	32	527	237	87	.367	71	48	.676	19	42	61	68	30	0	12	4	222	6.9	17
Cat'ngs (Tot)	56	948	243	102	.420	78	60	.769	101	201	302	48	132	3	23	91	264	4.7	16
Cat'ngs (NJ)	32	659	175	74	.423	61	47	.770	71	133	204	30	90	2	15	56	195	6.1	16
Bassett	82	1508	313	116	.371	131	89	.679	174	244	418	99	219	1	44	29	321	3.9	16

NEW ORLEANS JAZZ

Player	G.	Min.	FGA	FGM	Pct.	FTA	FTM	Pct.	Off. Reb.	Def. Reb.	Tot. Reb.	Ast.	PF	Dsq.	Stl.	Blk. Sh.	Pts.	Avg.	Hi.
Robinson	43	1781	819	397	.485	339	245	.723	139	438	577	74	130	1	29	63	1039	24.2	51
Maravich	49	1824	1035	436	.421	277	233	.841	33	88	121	243	104	2	60	18	1105	22.6	41
Haywood(Tot)	68	2361	1205	595	.494	292	231	.791	172	361	533	127	236	8	40	82	1421	20.9	46
Haywood(NO)	34	1338	696	346	.497	146	124	.849	106	221	327	71	128	6	30	53	816	24.0	33
McElroy	79	2698	1097	539	.491	340	259	.762	61	154	215	453	183	0	148	49	1337	16.9	40
Kelley	80	2705	870	440	.506	458	373	.814	303	723	1026	285	309	8	126	166	1253	15.7	30
Goodrich	74	2130	850	382	.449	204	174	.853	68	115	183	357	177	1	90	13	938	12.7	26
James	73	1417	630	311	.494	140	105	.750	97	151	248	78	202	1	28	21	727	10.0	29
Lee (Tot)	60	1346	507	218	.430	141	98	.695	63	105	168	205	182	3	107	6	534	8.9	24
Lee (N.O.)	17	398	124	45	.363	37	24	.649	21	34	55	73	44	1	38	2	114	6.7	14
Hardy	68	1456	426	196	.460	88	61	.693	121	189	310	65	133	1	52	61	453	6.7	19
Byrnes(Tot)	79	1264	389	187	.481	154	106	.688	90	101	191	104	111	0	27	10	480	6.1	16
Byrnes(N.O.)	36	530	166	78	.470	54	33	.611	41	53	94	43	42	0	12	8	189	5.3	16
Meriweather	36	640	187	84	.449	78	51	.654	62	122	184	31	105	2	17	41	219	6.1	24
Terrell	31	572	144	63	.438	38	27	.711	34	75	109	26	73	0	15	22	153	4.9	12
Green	59	809	237	92	.388	63	48	.762	20	48	68	140	111	0	61	6	232	3.9	16
Griffin	77	1398	223	106	.475	147	91	.619	126	265	391	138	198	3	54	36	303	3.9	14
Bailey	2	9	7	2	.286	0	0	.....	2	0	2	2	1	0	0	4	2.0	2

NEW YORK KNICKERBOCKERS

Player	G.	Min.	FGA	FGM	Pct.	FTA	FTM	Pct.	Off. Reb.	Def. Reb.	Tot. Reb.	Ast.	PF	Dsq.	Stl.	Blk. Sh.	Pts.	Avg.	Hi.
McAdoo	40	1594	793	429	.541	335	218	.651	94	285	379	128	134	2	62	47	1076	26.9	45
Haywood	34	1023	509	249	.489	146	107	.733	66	140	206	56	108	2	10	29	605	17.8	46
Williams	81	2370	1257	575	.457	313	251	.802	104	187	291	504	274	4	128	19	1401	17.3	37
Knight	82	2667	1174	609	.519	206	145	.704	201	347	548	124	309	7	61	60	1363	16.6	43
Monroe	64	1393	699	329	.471	154	129	.838	26	48	74	189	123	0	48	6	787	12.3	34
Webster	60	2027	558	264	.473	262	150	.573	198	457	655	172	183	6	24	112	678	11.3	23
Cleamons	79	2390	657	311	.473	171	130	.760	65	160	225	376	147	1	73	11	752	9.5	24
Meriw'ther(T)	77	1693	500	242	.484	187	126	.674	143	266	409	79	283	10	40	94	610	7.9	24
Meriw'r(NY)	41	1053	313	158	.505	109	75	.688	81	144	225	48	178	8	23	53	391	9.5	22
Glenn	75	1171	486	263	.541	63	57	.905	28	54	82	136	113	0	37	6	583	7.8	31
Richardson	72	1218	483	200	.414	128	69	.539	78	155	233	213	188	2	100	18	469	6.5	19
Gondrezick	75	1602	326	161	.494	97	55	.567	147	277	424	106	226	1	98	18	377	5.0	16
Barker (Tot)	39	476	156	68	.436	37	27	.730	45	74	119	15	76	0	10	11	163	4.2	14
Barker (NY)	22	329	102	44	.431	20	14	.700	31	52	83	9	45	0	6	7	102	4.6	13
Rudd	58	723	133	59	.444	93	66	.710	69	98	167	35	95	1	17	8	184	3.2	17
Beard	7	85	26	11	.423	0	0	.....	1	9	10	19	13	0	7	0	22	3.1	6
Behagen	5	38	12	5	.417	2	2	1.000	2	9	11	2	8	0	2	0	12	2.4	6
Bunch	12	97	26	9	.346	12	10	.833	9	8	17	4	10	0	3	3	28	2.3	7

PHILADELPHIA 76ers

Player	G.	Min.	FGA	FGM	Pct.	FTA	FTM	Pct.	Off. Reb.	Def. Reb.	Tot. Reb.	Ast.	PF	Dsq.	Stl.	Blk. Sh.	Pts.	Avg.	Hi.
Erving	78	2802	1455	715	.491	501	373	.745	198	366	564	357	207	0	133	100	1803	23.1	37
Collins	47	1595	717	358	.499	247	201	.814	36	87	123	191	139	1	52	20	917	19.5	32
Money (Tot)	69	1979	893	444	.497	237	170	.717	70	92	162	331	202	2	87	12	1058	15.3	40
Money (Phil)	23	545	217	119	.548	54	34	.630	15	22	37	82	70	2	13	2	272	11.8	21
Dawkins	78	2035	831	430	.517	235	158	.672	123	508	631	128	295	5	32	143	1018	13.1	30

Player	G.	Min.	FGA	FGM	Pct.	FTA	FTM	Pct.	Off. Reb.	Def. Reb.	Tot. Reb.	Ast.	PF	Dsq.	Stl.	Blk. Sh.	Pts.	Avg.	Hi.
Bibby	82	2538	869	368	.423	335	266	.794	72	172	244	371	199	0	72	7	1002	12.2	27
B. Jones	80	2304	704	378	.537	277	209	.755	199	332	531	201	245	2	107	96	965	12.1	33
Mix	74	1269	493	265	.538	201	161	.801	109	184	293	121	112	0	57	16	691	9.3	34
C. Jones	78	2171	637	302	.474	162	121	.747	177	570	747	151	303	10	39	157	725	9.3	22
Cheeks	82	2409	572	292	.510	140	101	.721	63	191	254	431	198	2	174	12	685	8.4	27
Bryant	70	1064	478	205	.429	170	123	.724	96	163	259	103	171	1	49	9	533	7.6	27
Redm'd(Tot)	53	759	387	163	.421	50	31	.620	57	52	109	58	96	2	28	16	357	6.7	18
Redm'd(Phil)	4	23	12	1	.083	0	0	.....	0	1	1	1	3	0	0	0	2	0.5	2
Skinner(Tot)	45	643	214	91	.425	114	99	.868	27	59	86	89	114	2	40	3	281	6.2	22
Skinner(Phil)	22	309	89	36	.404	32	27	.844	15	29	44	40	61	2	18	1	99	4.5	22
Simpson	37	452	196	87	.444	40	28	.700	16	19	35	58	27	8	25	1	202	5.5	20
Catchings	25	289	68	28	.412	17	13	.765	30	68	98	18	42	1	8	35	69	2.8	12

PHOENIX SUNS

Player	G.	Min.	FGA	FGM	Pct.	FTA	FTM	Pct.	Off. Reb.	Def. Reb.	Tot. Reb.	Ast.	PF	Dsq.	Stl.	Blk. Sh.	Pts.	Avg.	Hi.
Westphal	81	2641	1496	801	.535	405	339	.837	35	124	159	529	159	1	111	26	1941	24.0	43
Davis	79	2437	1362	764	.561	409	340	.831	111	262	373	339	250	50	147	26	1868	23.6	42
Robinson(Tot)	69	2537	1152	566	.491	462	324	.701	195	607	802	113	206	2	46	75	1456	21.1	51
Robinson(Phoe)	26	756	333	169	.508	123	79	.642	56	169	225	39	76	1	17	12	417	16.0	28
Adams	77	2364	1073	569	.530	289	231	.799	220	485	705	360	246	4	110	63	1369	17.8	33
Lee	43	948	383	173	.452	104	74	.712	42	71	113	132	138	2	69	4	420	9.8	24
Bratz	77	1297	533	242	.454	170	139	.818	55	86	141	179	151	0	64	7	623	8.1	20
Buse	82	2544	576	285	.495	91	70	.769	44	173	217	356	149	0	156	18	640	7.8	21
Byrnes	43	734	223	109	.489	100	73	.730	49	48	97	61	69	0	15	2	291	6.8	16
Scott	81	1737	396	212	.535	168	120	.714	104	256	360	126	139	2	80	62	544	6.7	18
Heard	63	1213	367	162	.441	103	71	.689	98	253	351	60	141	1	53	57	395	6.3	18
Kramer	82	1401	370	181	.489	176	125	.710	134	203	337	92	224	2	45	23	487	5.9	18
McClain	36	465	132	62	.470	46	42	.913	25	44	69	60	51	0	19	0	166	4.6	16
Forrest	75	1243	272	118	.434	115	62	.539	110	205	315	167	151	1	29	37	298	4.0	15

PORTLAND TRAIL BLAZERS

Player	G.	Min.	FGA	FGM	Pct.	FTA	FTM	Pct.	Off. Reb.	Def. Reb.	Tot. Reb.	Ast.	PF	Dsq.	Stl.	Blk. Sh.	Pts.	Avg.	Hi.
Lucas	69	2462	1208	568	.470	345	270	.783	192	524	716	215	254	3	66	81	1406	20.4	46
Owens	82	2791	1095	600	.548	403	320	.794	263	477	740	301	329	15	59	58	1520	18.5	37
Hollins	64	1967	886	402	.454	221	172	.778	32	117	149	325	199	3	114	24	976	15.3	33
Thompson	73	2144	938	460	.490	269	154	.572	198	406	04	176	270	10	67	134	1074	14.7	37
Brewer	81	2454	878	434	.494	256	210	.820	88	141	229	165	181	3	102	79	1078	13.3	30
Twardzik	64	1570	381	203	.533	299	261	.873	39	80	119	176	185	5	84	4	667	10.4	23
Gross	53	1441	443	209	.472	119	96	.807	106	144	250	184	161	4	70	47	514	9.7	19
Dunn	80	1828	549	246	.448	158	122	.772	145	199	344	103	166	1	86	23	614	7.7	18
Steele	72	1488	483	203	.420	136	112	.824	58	113	171	142	208	4	74	10	518	7.2	29
Terrell(Tot)	49	732	198	93	.470	53	35	.660	44	102	146	41	100	0	22	28	221	4.5	12
Terrell(Port)	18	160	54	30	.556	15	8	.533	10	27	37	15	27	0	7	6	68	3.8	11
Smith	13	131	44	23	.523	17	12	.706	7	6	13	9	19	0	10	1	58	4.5	14
McMillian	23	278	74	33	.446	21	17	.810	16	23	39	33	18	0	10	3	83	3.6	12
Johnson	74	794	217	102	.470	74	36	.486	83	143	226	78	121	1	23	36	240	3.2	8
Anderson	21	224	77	24	.312	28	15	.536	17	28	45	15	42	0	4	5	63	3.0	10
Neal	4	48	11	4	.364	1	1	1.000	2	7	9	1	7	0	0	1	9	2.3	5

SAN ANTONIO SPURS

Player	G.	Min.	FGA	FGM	Pct.	FTA	FTM	Pct.	Off. Reb.	Def. Reb.	Tot. Reb.	Ast.	PF	Dsq.	Stl.	Blk. Sh.	Pts.	Avg.	Hi.
Gervin	80	2888	1749	947	.541	570	471	.826	142	258	400	219	275	5	137	91	2365	29.6	52
Kenon	81	2947	1484	748	.504	349	295	.845	260	530	790	335	192	1	154	19	1791	22.1	39
Silas	79	2171	922	466	.505	402	334	.831	35	148	183	273	215	1	76	20	1266	16.0	31
Paultz	79	2122	758	399	.526	194	114	.588	169	456	625	178	204	4	35	125	912	11.5	28
Olberding	80	1885	551	261	.474	290	233	.803	96	333	429	211	282	2	53	18	755	9.4	25
Gale	82	2121	612	284	.464	108	91	.843	40	146	186	374	192	1	152	40	659	8.0	19
Green	76	1641	477	235	.493	144	101	.701	131	223	354	116	230	3	37	122	571	7.5	21
Dietrick	76	1487	400	209	.523	99	79	.798	88	227	315	198	206	7	72	38	497	6.5	16
Bristow	74	1324	354	174	.492	149	124	.832	80	167	247	231	154	0	56	15	472	6.4	19
Sanders	22	263	127	50	.394	41	32	.780	13	46	59	35	44	1	14	3	132	6.0	16
Dampier	70	760	251	123	.490	39	29	.744	15	48	63	124	42	0	35	8	275	3.9	11
Mosley	26	221	75	31	.413	38	23	.605	27	37	64	19	35	0	8	10	85	3.3	11

SAN DIEGO CLIPPERS

Player	G.	Min.	FGA	FGM	Pct.	FTA	FTM	Pct.	Off. Reb.	Def. Reb.	Tot. Reb.	Ast.	PF	Dsq.	Stl.	Blk. Sh.	Pts.	Avg.	Hi.
Free	78	2954	1653	795	.481	865	654	.756	127	174	301	340	253	8	111	35	2244	28.8	49
Smith	82	3111	1523	693	.455	359	292	.813	102	193	295	395	177	1	177	5	1678	20.5	37
Weatherspoon	82	2642	998	479	.480	238	176	.739	179	275	454	135	287	6	80	37	1134	13.8	38
Washington	82	2764	623	350	.562	330	227	.688	296	504	800	125	317	11	85	121	927	11.3	29
Nater	79	2006	627	357	.569	165	132	.800	218	483	701	140	244	6	38	29	846	10.7	22
Williams	72	1195	683	335	.490	98	76	.776	48	50	98	83	88	0	42	2	746	10.4	26
Wicks	79	2022	676	312	.462	226	147	.650	159	246	405	126	274	4	70	36	771	9.8	22
Norman	22	323	165	71	.430	23	19	.826	13	19	32	24	35	0	10	3	161	7.3	21
Kunnert	81	1684	501	234	.467	85	56	.659	202	367	569	113	309	7	45	118	524	6.5	16
Taylor	20	212	83	30	1861	18	16	.889	13	13	26	20	34	0	24	0	76	3.8	13
Bigelow	29	413	90	36	.400	21	13	.619	15	31	46	25	37	0	12	2	85	2.9	11
Olive	34	189	40	13	.325	23	18	.783	3	16	19	3	32	0	4	0	44	1.3	7
Whitehead	31	152	34	15	.441	18	8	.444	16	34	50	7	29	0	3	4	38	1.2	6
Pietkiewicz	4	32	8	1	.125	2	2	1.000	0	6	6	3	5	0	1	0	4	1.0	2
Lloyd	5	31	2	0	.....	0	0	.000	1	2	3	0	6	0	1	0	0	0.0	0

SEATTLE SUPERSONICS

Player	G.	Min.	FGA	FGM	Pct.	FTA	FTM	Pct.	Off. Reb.	Def. Reb.	Tot. Reb.	Ast.	PF	Dsq.	Stl.	Blk. Sh.	Pts.	Avg.	Hi.
Williams	76	2266	1224	606	.495	316	245	.775	111	134	245	307	162	3	158	29	1457	19.2	38
D. Johnson	80	2717	1110	482	.434	392	306	.781	146	228	374	280	209	2	100	97	1270	15.9	30
Sikma	82	2958	1034	476	.460	404	329	.814	232	781	1013	261	295	4	82	67	1281	15.6	30
Brown	77	1961	951	446	.469	206	183	.888	38	134	172	260	142	0	119	23	1075	14.0	28
Shelton	76	2158	859	446	.519	189	131	.693	182	286	468	110	266	7	76	75	1023	13.5	28
J. Johnson	82	2386	821	356	.434	250	190	.760	127	285	412	358	245	2	59	25	902	11.0	21
LaGarde	23	575	181	98	.541	95	57	.600	61	129	190	32	75	2	6	18	253	11.0	32
Walker	60	969	343	167	.490	96	58	.604	66	111	177	69	127	0	12	26	394	6.6	19
Silas	82	1957	402	170	.423	194	116	.598	259	316	575	115	177	3	31	19	456	5.6	16
Hansen	15	205	57	29	.509	31	18	.581	22	37	59	14	28	0	1	1	76	5.1	19
Hassett	55	463	211	100	.474	23	23	1.000	13	32	45	42	58	0	14	4	223	4.1	18
Robinson	12	105	41	19	.463	15	8	.533	9	10	19	13	9	0	5	1	46	3.8	10
Snyder	56	536	187	81	.433	51	43	.843	15	33	48	63	52	0	14	6	205	3.7	16
Awtrey (Tot)	63	746	107	44	.411	56	41	.732	42	109	151	69	106	0	16	13	129	2.0	8
Awtrey (Sea)	40	499	63	27	.429	36	25	.694	29	75	104	49	69	0	13	7	79	2.0	8

WASHINGTON BULLETS

Player	G.	Min.	FGA	FGM	Pct.	FTA	FTM	Pct.	Off. Reb.	Def. Reb.	Tot. Reb.	Ast.	PF	Dsq.	Stl.	Blk. Sh.	Pts.	Avg.	Hi.
Hayes	82	3105	1477	720	.487	534	349	.654	312	682	994	143	308	5	75	190	1789	21.8	36
Dandridge	78	2629	1260	629	.499	401	331	.825	109	338	447	365	259	4	71	57	1589	20.4	38
Grevey	65	1856	922	418	.453	224	173	.772	90	142	232	153	159	1	46	14	1009	15.5	28
Kupchak	66	1604	685	369	.539	300	223	.743	152	278	430	88	141	0	23	23	961	14.6	32
Unseld	77	2406	600	346	.577	235	151	.643	274	556	830	315	204	2	71	37	843	10.9	28
Henderson	70	2081	641	299	.466	195	156	.800	51	112	163	419	123	0	87	10	754	10.8	24
Wright	73	1658	589	276	.469	168	125	.744	48	92	140	298	166	3	69	13	677	9.3	30
Johnson	82	1819	786	342	.435	79	67	.848	70	132	202	177	161	0	95	6	751	9.2	28
Ballard	82	1552	559	260	.465	172	119	.692	143	307	450	116	167	3	58	30	639	7.8	24
Chenier	27	385	158	69	.437	28	18	.643	3	17	20	31	28	0	4	5	156	5.8	20
Corzine	59	532	118	63	.534	63	49	.778	52	95	147	49	67	0	10	14	175	3.0	15
Phegley	29	153	78	28	.359	29	24	.828	5	17	22	15	21	0	5	2	80	2.8	14

PLAYOFF RESULTS

EASTERN CONFERENCE FIRST ROUND
Philadelphia 2, New Jersey 0

Apr. 11—Wed.—New Jersey 114 at Philadelphia 122
Apr. 13—Fri.—Philadelphia 111 at New Jersey 101

Atlanta 2, Houston 0

Apr. 11—Wed.—Atlanta 109 at Houston 106
Apr. 13—Fri.—Houston 91 at Atlanta 100

EASTERN CONFERENCE SEMIFINALS
Washington 4, Atlanta 3

Apr. 15—Sun.—Atlanta 89 at Washington 103
Apr. 17—Tue.—Atlanta 107 at Washington 99
Apr. 20—Fri.—Washington 89 at Atlanta 77
Apr. 22—Sun.—Washington 120 at Atlanta 118*
Apr. 24—Tue.—Atlanta 107 at Washington 103
Apr. 26—Thu.—Washington 86 at Atlanta 104
Apr. 29—Sun.—Atlanta 94 at Washington 100

San Antonio 4, Philadelphia 3

Apr. 15—Sun.—Philadelphia 106 at San Antonio 119
Apr. 17—Tue.—Philadelphia 120 at San Antonio 121
Apr. 20—Fri.—San Antonio 115 at Philadelphia 123
Apr. 22—Sun.—San Antonio 115 at Philadelphia 112
Apr. 26—Thu.—Philadelphia 123 at San Antonio 97
Apr. 29—Sun.—San Antonio 90 at Philadelphia 92
May 2—Wed.—Philadelphia 108 at San Antonio 111

EASTERN CONFERENCE FINALS
Washington 4, San Antonio 3

May 4—Fri.—San Antonio 118 at Washington 97
May 6—Sun.—San Antonio 95 at Washington 115
May 9—Wed.—Washington 114 at San Antonio 116
May 11—Fri.—Washington 102 at San Antonio 118
May 13—Sun.—San Antonio 103 at Washington 107
May 16—Wed.—Washington 108 at San Antonio 100
May 18—Fri.—San Antonio 105 at Washington 107

WESTERN CONFERENCE FIRST ROUND
Phoenix 2, Portland 1

Apr. 10—Tue.—Portland 103 at Phoenix 107
Apr. 13—Fri.—Phoenix 92 at Portland.. 96
Apr. 15—Sun.—Portland 91 at Phoenix 101

Los Angeles 2, Denver 1

Apr. 10—Tue.—Los Angeles 105 at Denver 110
Apr. 13—Fri.—Denver 109 at Los Angeles 121
Apr. 15—Sun.—Los Angeles 112 at Denver 111

WESTERN CONFERENCE SEMIFINALS
Seattle 4, Los Angeles 1

Apr. 17—Tue.—Los Angeles 101 at Seattle 112
Apr. 18—Wed.—Los Angeles 103 at Seattle 108*
Apr. 20—Fri.—Seattle 112 at Los Angeles 118*
Apr. 22—Sun.—Seattle 117 at Los Angeles 115
Apr. 25—Wed.—Los Angeles 100 at Seattle 106

Phoenix 4, Kansas City 1

Apr. 17—Tue.—Kansas City 99 at Phoenix 102
Apr. 20—Fri.—Phoenix 91 at Kansas City 111
Apr. 22—Sun.—Kansas City 93 at Phoenix 108
Apr. 25—Wed.—Phoenix 108 at Kansas City 94
Apr. 27—Fri.—Kansas City 99 at Phoenix 120

WESTERN CONFERENCE FINALS
Seattle 4, Phoenix 3

May 1—Tue.—Phoenix 93 at Seattle 108
May 4—Fri.—Phoenix 97 at Seattle..103
May 6—Sun.—Seattle 103 at Phoenix 113
May 8—Tue.—Seattle 91 at Phoenix 100
May 11—Fri.—Phoenix 99 at Seattle 93
May 13—Sun.—Seattle 106 at Phoenix 105
May 17—Thu.—Phoenix 110 at Seattle..114

WORLD CHAMPIONSHIP SERIES
Seattle 4, Washington 1

May 20—Sun.—Seattle 97 at Washington 99
May 24—Thu.—Seattle 92 at Washington 82
May 27—Sun.—Washington 95 at Seattle 105
May 29—Tue.—Washington 112 at Seattle 114*
June 1—Fri.—Seattle 97 at Washington 93

*Denotes overtime period.

1977-78 NBA STATISTICS

1977-78 NBA CHAMPION WASHINGTON BULLETS

Seated (Left to Right): General Manager Bob Ferry, Coach Dick Motta, Larry Wright, Phil Chenier, Tom Henderson, Phil Walker, Owner Abe Pollin, Vice President Jerry Sachs. Standing: Assistant Coach Bernie Bickerstaff, Kevin Grevey, Greg Ballard, Elvin Hayes, Wes Unseld, Mitch Kupchak, Joe Pace, Bob Dandridge, Trainer John Lally. Inset: Charles Johnson.

FINAL STANDINGS

ATLANTIC DIVISION

Team	Atl.	Bos.	Buf.	Chi.	Cle.	Den.	Det.	G.S.	Hou.	Ind.	K.C.	L.A.	Mil.	N.J.	N.O.	N.Y.	Phi.	Pho.	Por.	S.A.	Sea.	Was.	W.	L.	Pct.	G.B.
Philadelphia	2	4	3	1	3	3	4	3	2	2	3	2	2	4	2	3	-	2	2	3	3	2	55	27	.671	--
New York	2	2	1	3	1	3	2	2	3	4	1	1	3	3	-	1	1	1	2	2	2	2	43	39	.524	12
Boston	2	-	3	1	1	1	1	1	2	2	2	2	1	3	3	2	2	-	2	1	-	1	32	50	.390	23
Buffalo	1	1	-	3	1	1	1	1	-	3	1	1	1	1	2	2	3	1	-	1	1	1	27	55	.329	28
New Jersey	1	1	2	2	1	1	1	1	2	2	2	-	1	-	-	1	2	-	-	2	2	2	24	58	.293	31

CENTRAL DIVISION

Team	Atl.	Bos.	Buf.	Chi.	Cle.	Den.	Det.	G.S.	Hou.	Ind.	K.C.	L.A.	Mil.	N.J.	N.O.	N.Y.	Phi.	Pho.	Por.	S.A.	Sea.	Was.	W.	L.	Pct.	G.B.
San Antonio	3	4	3	2	4	1	2	1	3	3	4	2	2	4	3	2	1	2	2	-	2	2	52	30	.634	--
Washington	3	3	3	1	2	1	2	2	3	1	2	2	1	2	4	2	2	2	1	2	3	-	44	38	.537	8
Cleveland	3	3	3	1	-	3	2	2	2	2	2	2	3	3	2	3	1	1	-	-	3	2	43	39	.524	9
Atlanta	-	2	3	1	1	1	2	1	3	2	3	2	3	2	3	2	3	1	1	2	1	2	41	41	.500	11
New Orleans	2	2	2	2	2	1	1	4	3	2	2	1	1	4	-	1	2	1	3	1	2	-	39	43	.476	13
Houston	1	2	1	1	2	-	1	1	-	3	2	1	1	2	1	2	2	1	2	1	-	1	28	54	.341	24

MIDWEST DIVISION

Team	Atl.	Bos.	Buf.	Chi.	Cle.	Den.	Det.	G.S.	Hou.	Ind.	K.C.	L.A.	Mil.	N.J.	N.O.	N.Y.	Phi.	Pho.	Por.	S.A.	Sea.	Was.	W.	L.	Pct.	G.B.
Denver	3	3	3	2	1	-	2	2	3	2	2	3	3	3	3	1	1	2	3	2	1	3	48	34	.585	--
Milwaukee	2	1	3	3	1	1	2	2	3	4	4	1	-	3	2	3	1	1	1	2	1	3	44	38	.537	4
Chicago	3	3	1	-	3	2	2	1	3	3	-	2	1	1	2	1	3	2	1	2	2	2	40	42	.488	8
Detroit	2	3	3	2	2	2	-	2	3	1	1	2	2	3	3	-	2	1	1	1	2	2	38	44	.463	10
Indiana	1	1	3	1	1	2	3	1	1	-	2	1	-	2	2	1	2	1	1	1	1	3	31	51	.378	17
Kansas City	1	2	2	4	2	2	3	1	2	2	-	2	-	2	2	-	1	-	-	-	1	2	31	51	.378	17

PACIFIC DIVISION

Team	Atl.	Bos.	Buf.	Chi.	Cle.	Den.	Det.	G.S.	Hou.	Ind.	K.C.	L.A.	Mil.	N.J.	N.O.	N.Y.	Phi.	Pho.	Por.	S.A.	Sea.	Was.	W.	L.	Pct.	G.B.
Portland	3	3	3	3	4	1	3	3	2	3	4	4	3	3	1	3	2	3	-	2	3	2	58	24	.707	--
Phoenix	1	2	4	2	2	2	2	2	3	3	4	3	3	2	3	3	1	-	1	2	2	2	49	33	.598	9
Seattle	1	4	3	2	1	3	3	2	4	3	3	3	3	2	1	1	2	1	2	-	1	2	47	35	.573	11
Los Angeles	1	2	3	2	2	1	2	4	3	3	2	-	3	4	2	3	2	1	-	2	1	2	45	37	.549	13
Golden State	3	2	3	3	2	2	2	-	2	3	3	-	2	3	-	2	1	2	1	3	2	2	43	39	.524	15

HOME-ROAD RECORDS OF ALL TEAMS

	Home	Road	Total		Home	Road	Total
Atlanta	29- 12	12- 29	41- 41	Milwaukee	28- 13	16- 25	44- 38
Boston	24- 17	8- 33	32- 50	New Jersey	18- 23	6- 35	24- 58
Buffalo	20- 21	7- 34	27- 55	New Orleans	27- 14	12- 29	39- 43
Chicago	29- 12	11- 30	40- 42	New York	29- 12	14- 27	43- 39
Cleveland	27- 14	16- 25	43- 39	Philadelphia	37- 4	18- 23	55- 27
Denver	33- 8	15- 26	48- 34	Phoenix	34- 7	15- 26	49- 33
Detroit	24- 17	14- 27	38- 44	Portland	36- 5	22- 19	58- 24
Golden State	30- 11	13- 28	43- 39	San Antonio	32- 9	20- 21	52- 30
Houston	21- 20	7- 34	28- 54	Seattle	31- 10	16- 25	47- 35
Indiana	21- 20	10- 31	31- 51	Washington	29- 12	15- 26	44- 38
Kansas City	22- 19	9- 32	31- 51	Total	610-292	292-610	902- 902
Los Angeles	29- 12	16- 25	45- 37				

OFFENSIVE TEAM STATISTICS

		FIELD GOALS			FREE THROWS			REBOUNDS			MISCELLANEOUS					SCORING	
Team	G.	Att.	Made	Pct.	Att.	Made	Pct.	Off.	Def.	Tot.	Ast.	PF	Disq.	Stl.	Turn Over	Blk. Sh.	Pts.	Avg.
Philadelphia	82	7471	3628	.486	2863	2153	.752	1299	2694	3993	2220	2188	20	800	1752	548	9409	114.7
San Antonio	82	7594	3794	.500	2234	1797	.804	1030	2594	3624	2240	1871	16	797	1665	553	9385	114.5
New York	82	7822	3815	.488	2225	1670	.751	1180	2689	3869	2338	2193	26	818	1764	442	9300	113.4
Milwaukee	82	7883	3801	.482	2220	1612	.726	1239	2480	3719	2306	2038	23	867	1680	472	9214	112.4
Phoenix	82	7836	3731	.476	2329	1749	.751	1166	2579	3745	2338	1956	16	1059	1766	372	9211	112.3
Denver	82	7441	3548	.477	2705	2068	.765	1177	2736	3913	2187	2116	20	824	1748	422	9164	111.8
Washington	82	7772	3580	.461	2655	1887	.711	1349	2815	4164	1948	1879	25	668	1613	386	9047	110.3
Los Angeles	82	7672	3734	.487	2095	1576	.752	1136	2647	3783	2229	1964	18	802	1548	409	9044	110.3
Kansas City	82	7731	3601	.466	2262	1775	.785	1208	2632	3840	1992	2228	37	794	1690	370	8977	109.5
Detroit	82	7424	3552	.478	2490	1832	.736	1229	2601	3830	1840	1980	29	866	1858	330	8936	109.0
Indiana	82	7783	3500	.450	2564	1904	.743	1386	2624	4010	1982	2230	53	808	1642	456	8904	108.6
Portland	82	7367	3556	.483	2259	1717	.760	1187	2686	3873	2067	2068	30	798	1625	390	8829	107.7
New Orleans	82	7717	3568	.462	2331	1690	.725	1309	2907	4216	2079	1938	35	662	1694	514	8826	107.6
New Jersey	82	8004	3547	.443	2304	1652	.717	1306	2595	3901	1879	2312	72	857	1774	631	8746	106.7
Golden State	82	7654	3574	.467	2081	1550	.745	1183	2629	3812	2097	2113	29	873	1518	405	8698	106.1
Boston	82	7635	3494	.458	2159	1682	.779	1235	2850	4085	1969	2033	32	643	1652	295	8670	105.7
Buffalo	82	7323	3413	.466	2314	1808	.781	1083	2538	3621	1975	2017	31	650	1575	327	8634	105.3
Seattle	82	7715	3445	.447	2352	1675	.712	1456	2601	4057	1799	2008	24	782	1636	429	8565	104.5
Cleveland	82	7707	3496	.454	2116	1569	.741	1187	2676	3863	1740	1832	15	692	1382	455	8561	104.4
Chicago	82	7041	3330	.473	2471	1863	.754	1248	2577	3825	2119	1930	30	665	1667	322	8523	103.9
Houston	82	7691	3523	.458	1896	1467	.774	1301	2421	3722	1942	2025	32	683	1376	319	8513	103.8
Atlanta	82	7253	3335	.460	2316	1836	.793	1160	2359	3519	1901	2470	80	916	1592	408	8506	103.7

DEFENSIVE TEAM STATISTICS

	FIELD GOALS			FREE THROWS			REBOUNDS			MISCELLANEOUS					SCORING		
Team	Att.	Made	Pct.	Att.	Made	Pct.	Off.	Def.	Tot.	Ast.	PF	Disq.	Stl.	Turn Over	Blk. Sh.	Pts.	Avg.	Pt. Dif.
Portland	7318	3289	.449	2282	1747	.766	1187	2523	3710	1818	2093	36	748	1624	390	8325	101.5 + 6.2
Seattle	7377	3384	.459	2203	1670	.758	1121	2600	3721	1956	2067	26	735	1646	410	8438	102.9 + 1.6
Atlanta	6671	3162	.474	2930	2193	.748	1160	2606	3766	1774	2122	36	750	1980	484	8517	103.9 - 0.2
Cleveland	7620	3474	.456	2113	1574	.745	1214	2779	3993	1915	1952	16	690	1475	446	8522	103.9 + 0.5
Chicago	7273	3565	.490	1980	1466	.740	1065	2367	3432	2076	2199	46	777	1479	451	8596	104.8 - 0.9
Golden State	7368	3425	.465	2408	1820	.756	1185	2794	3979	2037	1975	21	728	1738	408	8670	105.7 + 0.3
Los Angeles	7880	3648	.463	2050	1529	.746	1365	2599	3964	2073	1919	30	756	1570	379	8825	107.6 + 2.7
Boston	7761	3539	.456	2278	1752	.769	1142	2575	3717	1981	1871	24	763	1412	374	8830	107.7 - 2.0
Houston	7704	3571	.482	2238	1699	.759	1195	2525	3720	1990	1752	18	605	1410	360	8841	107.8 - 4.0
Phoenix	7622	3578	.469	2319	1749	.754	1202	2743	3945	1988	2178	41	937	1969	372	8905	108.6 + 3.7
Buffalo	7609	3623	.476	2250	1695	.753	1178	2587	3765	2137	2003	25	722	1476	375	8941	109.0 - 3.7
Washington	8065	3767	.467	1895	1437	.758	1166	2683	3849	2144	2312	50	779	1437	427	8971	109.4 + 0.9
New Orleans	7938	3659	.461	2213	1661	.751	1273	2747	4020	2084	2062	28	851	1511	476	8979	109.5 - 1.9
Detroit	7706	3608	.479	2177	1662	.763	1244	2494	3738	2105	2088	27	902	1719	395	9038	110.2 - 1.2
Denver	7799	3678	.472	2365	1740	.736	1267	2546	3813	2248	2220	49	877	1620	524	9096	110.9 + 0.9
Indiana	7663	3634	.474	2455	1841	.750	1350	2793	4143	2259	2135	39	727	1762	466	9109	111.1 - 2.5
San Antonio	8063	3808	.472	1996	1494	.748	1345	2576	3921	2145	2059	25	837	1662	379	9110	111.1 + 3.4
Kansas City	7521	3564	.474	2635	2004	.761	1232	2684	3916	1928	2088	18	796	1694	408	9132	111.4 - 1.9
New Jersey	7620	3544	.465	2830	2135	.754	1312	2996	4308	2073	1999	29	852	1864	560	9223	112.5 - 5.8
Milwaukee	7728	3715	.481	2404	1832	.762	1234	2617	3851	2248	2019	28	790	1783	468	9262	113.0 - 0.6
New York	7742	3658	.472	2785	2029	.729	1254	2623	3877	2113	1989	31	879	1677	357	9345	114.0 - 0.6

Disq.—Individual players disqualified (fouled out of game)

INDIVIDUAL LEADERS

POINTS

(Minimum of 70 games played or 1400 points)

	G.	FG	FT	Pts.	Avg.		G.	FG	FT	Pts.	Avg.
Gervin, S.A.	82	864	504	2232	27.22	Williamson, Ind.-N.J.	75	723	331	1777	23.7
Thompson, Den.	80	826	520	2172	27.15	Drew, Atl.	70	593	437	1623	23.2
McAdoo, N.Y.	79	814	469	2097	26.5	Barry, G.S.	82	760	378	1898	23.1
Abdul-Jabbar, L.A.	62	663	274	1600	25.8	Gilmore, Chi.	82	704	471	1879	22.9
Murphy, Hou.	76	852	245	1949	25.6	Robinson, N.O.	82	748	366	1862	22.7
Westphal, Phoe.	80	809	396	2014	25.2	Dantley, Ind.-L.A.	79	578	541	1697	21.5
Smith, Buff.	82	789	443	2021	24.6	Issel, Den.	82	659	428	1746	21.3
Lanier, Det.	63	622	298	1542	24.5	Erving, Phila.	74	611	306	1528	20.6
Davis, Phoe.	81	786	387	1959	24.2	Kenon, S.A.	81	698	276	1672	20.6
King, N.J.	79	798	313	1909	24.2	McGinnis, Phil.	78	588	411	1587	20.3

FIELD GOALS
(Minimum 300 FG Made)

	FGA	FGM	Pct.
Jones, Den.	761	440	.578
Dawkins, Phil.	577	332	.575
Gilmore, Chi.	1260	704	.559
Abdul-Jabbar, L.A.	1205	663	.550
English, Mil.	633	343	.542
Lanier, Det.	1159	622	.537
Gervin, S.A.	1611	864	.536
Gross, Port.	720	381	.529
Paultz, S.A.	979	518	.529
Davis, Phoe.	1494	786	.526

FREE THROWS
(Minimum 125 FT Made)

	FTA	FTM	Pct.
Barry, G.S.	409	378	.924
Murphy, Hou.	267	245	.918
Brown, Sea.	196	176	.898
Newlin, Hou.	174	152	.874
Wedman, K.C.	254	221	.870
Maravich, N.O.	276	240	.870
Havlicek, Bos.	269	230	.855
Kenon, S.A.	323	276	.854
Boone, K.C.	377	322	.854
Frazier, Clev.	180	153	.850

ASSISTS
Minimum 70 games or 400 assists

	G.	No.	Avg.
K. Porter, Det.-N.J.	82	837	10.2
Lucas, Hou.	82	768	9.4
Sobers, Ind.	79	584	7.4
Nixon, L.A.	81	553	6.8
Van Lier, Chi.	78	531	6.8
Bibby, Phil.	82	464	5.7
Walker, Clev.	81	453	5.6
Smith, Buff.	82	458	5.6
Buckner, Mil.	82	456	5.6
Westphal, Phoe.	80	437	5.5

STEALS
Minimum 70 games or 125 steals

	G.	No.	Avg.
Lee, Phoe.	82	225	2.74
Williams, Sea.	79	185	2.34
Buckner, Mil.	82	188	2.29
Gale, S.A.	70	159	2.27
Buse, Phoe.	82	185	2.26
Walker, Clev.	81	176	2.17
Sobers, Ind.	79	170	2.15
Smith, Buff.	82	172	2.10
Ford, Det.	82	166	2.02
Holland, Chi.	82	164	2.00

REBOUNDS
Minimum 70 games or 800 rebounds

	G.	Off.	Def.	Tot.	Avg.
Robinson, N.O.	82	298	990	1288	15.7
Malone, Hou.	59	380	506	886	15.0
Cowens, Bos.	77	248	830	1078	14.0
Hayes, Wash.	81	335	740	1075	13.3
Nater, Buff.	78	278	751	1029	13.2
Gilmore, Chi.	82	318	753	1071	13.1
Abdul-Jabbar, L.A.	62	186	615	801	12.9
McAdoo, N.Y.	79	236	774	1010	12.8
Webster, Sea.	82	361	674	1035	12.6
Unseld, Wash.	80	286	669	955	11.9

BLOCKED SHOTS
Minimum 70 games or 100 blocked shots

	G.	No.	Avg.
Johnson, N.J.	81	274	3.38
Abdul-Jabbar, L.A.	62	185	2.98
Rollins, Atl.	80	218	2.73
Walton, Port.	58	146	2.52
Paultz, S.A.	80	194	2.43
Gilmore, Chi.	82	181	2.21
Meriweather, N.O.	54	118	2.19
E. Smith, Clev.	81	176	2.17
Webster, Sea.	82	162	1.98
Hayes, Wash.	81	159	1.96

TEAM-BY-TEAM INDIVIDUAL STATISTICS

ATLANTA HAWKS

Player	G.	Min.	FGA	FGM	Pct.	FTA	FTM	Pct.	Off. Reb.	Def. Reb.	Tot. Reb.	Ast.	PF	Disq.	Stl.	Blk. Sh.	Pts.	Avg.	Hi.
Drew	70	2203	1236	593	.480	575	437	.760	213	298	511	141	247	8	119	27	1623	23.2	48
Hawes	75	2325	854	387	.453	214	175	.818	180	510	690	190	230	4	78	57	949	12.7	27
Criss	77	1935	751	319	.425	294	236	.797	24	97	121	294	143	0	108	5	874	11.4	30
Behagen	26	571	249	117	.470	70	51	.729	53	120	173	34	97	3	30	12	285	11.0	22
E. Johnson	79	1875	686	332	.484	201	164	.816	51	102	153	235	232	4	100	4	828	10.5	29
McMillen	68	1683	568	280	.493	145	116	.800	151	265	416	84	233	8	33	16	676	9.9	23
Hill	82	2530	732	304	.415	223	189	.848	59	172	231	427	302	15	151	15	797	9.7	21
Charles	21	520	184	73	.397	50	42	.840	6	18	24	82	53	0	25	5	188	9.0	17
O. Johnson	82	1704	619	292	.472	130	111	.854	89	171	260	120	180	2	80	36	695	8.5	22
Rollins	80	1795	520	253	.487	148	104	.703	179	373	552	79	326	16	57	218	610	7.6	21
Brown	75	1594	405	192	.474	200	165	.825	137	166	303	105	280	18	55	8	549	7.3	27
Robertson	63	929	381	168	.441	53	37	.698	15	55	70	103	133	2	74	5	373	5.9	18
Terry	27	166	68	25	.368	11	9	.818	3	12	15	7	14	0	6	0	59	2.2	6

BOSTON CELTICS

Player	G.	Min.	FGA	FGM	Pct.	FTA	FTM	Pct.	Off. Reb.	Def. Reb.	Tot. Reb.	Ast.	PF	Disq.	Stl.	Blk. Sh.	Pts.	Avg.	Hi.
Cowens	77	3215	1220	598	.490	284	239	.842	248	830	1078	351	297	5	120	67	1435	18.6	36
Scott	31	1080	485	210	.433	118	84	.712	24	77	101	143	97	2	51	6	504	16.3	30
Havlicek	82	2797	1217	546	.449	269	230	.855	93	239	332	328	185	2	90	22	1322	16.1	32
White	46	1641	690	289	.419	120	103	.858	53	127	180	209	109	2	49	7	681	14.8	27
Bing	80	2256	940	422	.449	296	244	.824	76	136	212	300	247	2	79	18	1088	13.6	30
Wicks	81	2413	927	433	.467	329	217	.660	223	450	673	171	318	9	67	46	1083	13.4	35
Wash'ngton (Tot)	57	1617	507	247	.487	246	170	.691	215	399	614	72	188	3	47	64	664	11.6	22
Wash'ngton (Bs)	32	866	263	137	.521	136	102	.750	105	230	335	42	114	2	28	40	376	11.8	18
Stacom	55	1006	484	206	.426	71	54	.761	26	80	106	111	60	0	28	3	466	8.5	22
Maxwell	72	1213	316	170	.538	250	188	.752	138	241	379	68	151	2	53	48	528	7.3	21
Boswell	65	1149	357	185	.518	123	93	.756	117	171	288	71	204	5	25	14	463	7.1	22
Rowe	51	911	273	123	.451	89	66	.742	74	129	203	45	94	1	14	8	312	6.1	20
Chaney (Tot)	51	835	269	104	.387	45	38	.844	40	76	116	66	107	0	44	13	246	4.8	17
Chaney (Bs)	42	702	233	91	.391	39	33	.846	36	69	105	49	93	0	36	10	215	5.1	17
Abdul-Aziz	2	24	13	3	.231	3	2	.667	6	9	15	3	4	0	1	1	8	4.0	6
DiGregorio (Tot)	52	606	209	88	.421	33	28	.848	7	43	50	137	44	0	18	1	204	3.9	24
DiGregorio (Bos)	27	274	109	47	.431	13	12	.923	2	25	27	66	22	0	12	1	106	3.9	24
Saunders	26	243	91	30	.330	17	14	.824	11	26	37	11	34	0	7	4	74	2.8	12
Bigelow (Tot)	5	24	13	4	.308	0	0	....	3	6	9	0	3	0	0	0	8	1.6	4
Bigelow (Bos)	4	17	12	3	.250	0	0	....	1	3	4	0	1	0	0	0	6	1.5	4
Ard	1	9	1	0	.000	2	1	.500	1	3	4	1	1	0	1	0	1	1.0	1
Kuberski	3	14	4	1	.250	0	0	....	1	5	6	0	2	0	1	0	2	0.7	2

BUFFALO BRAVES

Player	G.	Min.	FGA	FGM	Pct.	FTA	FTM	Pct.	Off. Reb.	Def. Reb.	Tot. Reb.	Ast.	PF	Disq.	Stl.	Blk. Sh.	Pts.	Avg.	Hi.
Smith	82	3314	1697	789	.465	554	443	.800	110	200	310	458	224	2	172	11	2021	24.6	40
Knight	53	2155	926	457	.494	372	301	.809	126	257	383	161	137	0	82	13	1215	22.9	41
Nater	78	2778	994	501	.504	272	208	.765	278	751	1029	216	274	3	40	47	1210	15.5	35
Shumate	18	590	151	75	.497	99	74	.747	32	96	128	58	58	1	14	9	224	12.4	26
Barnes (Tot)	60	1646	661	279	.422	182	128	.703	135	304	439	136	241	9	64	83	686	11.4	27
Barnes (Bf)	48	1377	543	226	.416	153	114	.745	107	241	348	117	198	7	57	72	566	11.8	27
McNeill (Tot)	46	940	356	162	.455	175	145	.829	80	122	202	47	114	1	18	11	469	10.2	31
McNeill (Buff)	37	873	338	156	.462	156	130	.833	78	110	188	45	100	1	18	10	442	11.9	31
Averitt (Tot)	55	1085	484	198	.409	141	100	.709	17	66	83	196	123	3	39	9	496	9.0	32
Averitt (Buff)	34	676	296	129	.436	96	64	.667	10	40	50	128	86	2	22	8	322	9.5	24
Glenn	56	947	370	195	.527	65	51	.785	14	65	79	78	98	0	35	5	441	7.9	25
Williams	73	2002	436	208	.477	138	114	.826	29	108	137	317	137	0	48	4	530	7.3	22
Jones	79	1711	514	226	.440	119	84	.706	106	228	334	116	255	7	70	43	536	6.8	18
Willoughby	56	1079	363	156	.430	80	64	.800	76	143	219	38	131	2	24	47	376	6.7	20
McDaniels	42	694	234	100	.427	42	36	.857	46	135	181	44	112	3	4	37	236	5.6	26
McClain	41	727	184	81	.440	63	50	.794	11	64	75	123	88	2	42	2	212	5.2	17
Gerard	10	85	40	16	.400	15	11	.733	6	8	14	9	13	0	2	3	43	4.3	13
Brokaw	13	130	43	18	.419	24	18	.750	3	9	12	20	11	0	3	5	54	4.2	16
Lloyd (Tot)	70	678	193	80	.415	68	49	.721	52	93	145	44	105	1	14	14	209	3.0	10
Lloyd (Buff)	56	566	160	68	.425	58	43	.741	45	74	119	35	83	1	11	9	179	3.2	10
Owens	8	63	21	9	.429	6	3	.500	5	5	10	5	9	0	1	0	21	2.6	8
Johnson	4	38	13	3	.231	2	0	.000	1	4	5	7	3	0	5	2	6	1.5	6

CHICAGO BULLS

Player	G.	Min.	FGA	FGM	Pct.	FTA	FTM	Pct.	Off. Reb.	Def. Reb.	Tot. Reb.	Ast.	PF	Disq.	Stl.	Blk. Sh.	Pts.	Avg.	Hi.
Gilmore	82	3067	1260	704	.559	669	471	.704	318	753	1071	263	261	4	42	181	1879	22.9	38
Johnson	81	2870	1215	561	.462	446	362	.812	218	520	738	267	317	8	92	68	1484	18.3	39
Holland	82	2884	1285	569	.443	279	223	.799	105	189	294	313	258	4	164	14	1361	16.6	36
May	55	1802	612	280	.454	216	175	.810	118	214	332	114	170	4	50	6	735	13.4	27
Mengelt	81	1767	675	325	.481	238	184	.773	41	88	129	232	169	0	51	4	834	10.3	27
Russell	36	789	304	133	.438	57	49	.860	31	52	83	61	63	1	19	4	315	8.8	24
Van Lier	78	2524	477	200	.419	229	172	.751	86	198	284	531	279	9	144	5	572	7.3	23
Landsberger	62	926	251	127	.506	157	91	.580	110	191	301	41	78	0	21	6	345	5.6	25
Weatherspoon	41	611	194	86	.443	42	37	.881	57	68	125	32	74	0	19	10	209	5.1	17
Sheppard	64	698	262	119	.454	56	37	.661	67	64	131	43	72	0	14	3	275	4.3	22
Armstrong	66	716	280	131	.468	27	22	.815	24	44	68	74	42	0	23	0	284	4.3	22
Dickey (Tot)	47	493	198	87	.439	36	30	.833	36	61	97	21	56	0	14	4	204	4.3	18
Dickey (Chi)	25	220	68	27	.397	19	14	.737	15	33	48	10	27	0	4	2	68	2.7	11
Boerwinkle	22	227	50	23	.460	13	10	.769	14	45	59	44	36	0	3	4	56	2.5	10
Pondexter	44	534	85	37	.435	20	14	.700	36	94	130	87	66	0	19	15	88	2.0	14
Ard (Tot)	15	125	17	8	.471	5	3	.600	9	27	36	8	19	0	0	0	19	1.3	4
Ard (Chi)	14	116	16	8	.500	3	2	.667	8	24	32	7	18	0	0	0	18	1.3	4
Hansen	2	4	2	0	.000	0	0	......	0	0	0	0	0	0	0	0	0	0.0	0

CLEVELAND CAVALIERS

Player	G.	Min.	FGA	FGM	Pct.	FTA	FTM	Pct.	Off. Reb.	Def. Reb.	Tot. Reb.	Ast.	PF	Disq.	Stl.	Blk. Sh.	Pts.	Avg.	Hi.
Russell	72	2520	1168	523	.448	469	352	.751	154	304	458	278	193	3	88	12	1398	19.4	38
Frazier	51	1664	714	336	.471	180	153	.850	54	155	209	209	124	1	77	13	825	16.2	29
Chones	82	2906	1113	525	.472	250	180	.720	219	625	844	131	235	4	52	58	1230	15.0	31
E. Smith	81	1996	809	402	.497	309	205	.663	178	500	678	57	241	4	50	176	1009	12.5	32
Carr	82	2186	945	414	.438	225	183	.813	76	111	187	225	168	1	68	19	1011	12.3	30
B. Smith	82	1581	840	369	.439	135	108	.800	65	142	207	91	155	1	38	21	846	10.3	30
Walker	81	2496	641	287	.448	221	159	.719	76	218	294	453	218	0	176	24	733	9.0	20
Furlow	53	827	443	192	.433	99	88	.889	47	60	107	72	67	0	21	14	472	8.9	23
Brewer	80	1798	390	175	.449	100	46	.460	182	313	495	98	178	1	60	48	396	5.0	20
Snyder	58	640	252	112	.444	64	56	.875	9	40	49	56	74	0	23	19	280	4.8	17
Lambert	76	1075	336	142	.423	48	27	.563	125	199	324	38	169	0	27	50	311	4.1	16
Jordan	22	171	56	19	.339	16	12	.750	2	9	11	32	10	0	12	1	50	2.3	11

DENVER NUGGETS

Player	G.	Min.	FGA	FGM	Pct.	FTA	FTM	Pct.	Off. Reb.	Def. Reb.	Tot. Reb.	Ast.	PF	Disq.	Stl.	Blk. Sh.	Pts.	Avg.	Hi.
Thompson	80	3025	1584	826	.521	668	520	.778	156	234	390	362	213	1	92	99	2172	27.2	73
Issel	82	2851	1287	659	.512	547	428	.782	253	577	830	304	279	5	100	41	1746	21.3	40
Jones	75	2440	761	440	.578	277	208	.751	164	472	636	252	221	2	137	126	1088	14.5	29
Taylor	39	1222	403	182	.452	115	88	.765	30	68	98	132	120	1	71	9	452	11.6	23
Wilkerson	81	2780	936	382	.408	210	157	.748	98	376	474	439	275	3	126	21	921	11.4	24
Hillman (Tot)	78	1966	710	340	.479	286	167	.584	199	378	577	102	290	11	63	81	847	10.9	28
Hillman (Den)	33	746	209	104	.498	81	49	.605	73	166	239	53	130	4	14	37	257	7.8	16
Roberts	82	1598	736	311	.423	212	153	.722	135	216	351	105	212	1	40	7	775	9.5	27
Simpson (Tot)	64	1323	576	216	.375	104	85	.817	53	104	157	159	90	1	75	7	517	8.1	23
Simpson (Den)	32	584	230	73	.317	40	31	.775	26	49	75	72	42	0	43	4	177	5.5	21
Price	49	1090	293	141	.481	66	51	.773	30	129	159	158	118	0	69	4	333	6.8	22
Calvin	77	988	333	147	.441	206	173	.840	11	73	84	148	87	0	46	5	467	6.1	20
Ellis	78	1213	320	133	.416	104	72	.692	114	190	304	73	208	2	49	47	338	4.3	13
LaGarde	77	868	237	96	.405	150	114	.760	75	139	214	47	146	1	17	17	306	4.0	14
Smith	45	378	97	50	.515	24	21	.875	6	30	36	39	52	0	18	3	121	2.7	10
Dorsey	7	37	12	3	.250	5	3	.600	5	15	20	2	9	0	2	2	9	1.3	3
Cook	2	10	3	1	.333	0	0	......	1	2	3	1	4	0	0	0	2	1.0	2

DETROIT PISTONS

Player	G.	Min.	FGA	FGM	Pct.	FTA	FTM	Pct.	Off. Reb.	Def. Reb.	Tot. Reb.	Ast.	PF	Disq.	Stl.	Blk. Sh.	Pts.	Avg.	Hi.
Lanier	63	2311	1159	622	.537	386	298	.772	197	518	715	216	185	2	82	93	1542	24.5	41
Money	76	2557	1200	600	.500	298	214	.718	90	119	209	356	237	5	123	12	1414	18.6	39
Shumate (Tot)	80	2760	773	391	.506	508	400	.787	157	525	682	180	200	2	90	52	1182	14.8	31
Shumate (Det)	62	2170	622	316	.508	409	326	.797	125	429	554	122	142	1	76	43	958	15.5	31
Carr	79	2556	857	390	.455	271	200	.738	202	355	557	185	243	4	147	27	980	12.4	28
Douglas	79	1993	667	321	.481	345	221	.641	181	401	582	112	295	6	57	48	863	10.9	28
Simpson	32	739	346	143	.413	64	54	.844	27	55	82	87	48	1	32	3	340	10.6	23
Ford	82	2582	777	374	.481	154	113	.734	117	151	268	381	182	2	166	17	861	10.5	25
Barnes	12	269	118	53	.449	29	14	.483	28	63	91	19	43	2	7	11	120	10.0	15
Price (Tot)	83	1929	656	294	.448	169	135	.799	57	203	260	260	200	0	114	9	723	8.7	26
Price (Det)	34	839	363	153	.421	103	84	.816	27	74	101	102	82	0	45	5	390	11.5	26
Skinner (Tot)	77	1551	488	222	.455	203	162	.798	67	157	224	146	242	6	65	20	606	7.9	28
Skinner (Det)	69	1274	387	181	.468	159	123	.774	53	119	172	113	208	4	52	15	485	7.0	27
Gerard (Tot)	57	890	395	170	.430	108	75	.694	55	105	160	53	109	1	36	25	415	7.3	20
Gerard (Det)	47	805	355	154	.434	93	64	.688	49	97	146	44	96	1	34	22	372	7.9	20
Bostic	4	48	22	12	.545	5	2	.400	8	8	16	3	5	0	0	0	26	6.5	12
Norwood	16	260	82	34	.415	29	20	.690	27	27	54	14	45	0	13	3	88	5.5	13
Eberhard	37	576	160	71	.444	61	41	.672	37	65	102	26	64	0	13	4	183	4.9	20
K. Porter	8	127	31	14	.452	13	9	.692	5	10	15	36	18	0	5	0	37	4.6	14
Poquette	52	626	225	95	.422	60	42	.700	50	95	145	20	69	1	10	22	232	4.5	18
H. Porter	8	107	43	16	.372	7	4	.571	5	12	17	2	15	0	3	5	36	4.5	10
Britt	7	16	10	3	.300	4	3	.750	1	3	4	2	3	0	1	0	9	1.3	4

GOLDEN STATE WARRIORS

Player	G.	Min.	FGA	FGM	Pct.	FTA	FTM	Pct.	Off. Reb.	Def. Reb.	Tot. Reb.	Ast.	PF	Disq.	Stl.	Blk. Sh.	Pts.	Avg.	Hi.
Barry	82	3024	1686	760	.451	409	378	.924	75	374	449	446	188	1	158	45	1898	23.1	51
Smith	82	2940	1373	648	.472	389	316	.812	100	200	300	393	219	2	108	27	1612	19.7	33
Parish	82	1969	911	430	.472	264	165	.625	211	469	680	95	291	10	79	123	1025	12.5	28
Parker	82	2069	783	406	.519	173	122	.705	167	222	389	155	186	0	135	36	934	11.4	26
Williams (Tot)	73	1249	724	312	.431	121	101	.835	65	139	204	74	181	3	57	34	725	9.9	27
Williams (GS)	46	815	510	222	.435	84	70	.833	38	76	114	40	120	2	36	22	514	11.2	27
Ray	79	2268	476	272	.571	243	148	.609	236	522	758	147	291	9	74	90	692	8.8	21
Coleman	72	1801	446	212	.475	55	40	.727	117	259	376	100	253	4	66	23	464	6.4	18
Johnson	32	492	235	96	.409	10	7	.700	23	39	62	48	53	0	31	4	199	6.2	23
Dickey	22	273	130	60	.462	17	16	.941	21	28	49	11	29	0	10	2	136	6.2	18
Dudley	78	1660	249	127	.510	195	138	.708	86	201	287	409	181	0	68	2	392	5.0	14
Cox	43	453	173	69	.399	100	58	.580	42	101	143	12	82	1	21	10	196	4.6	23
Marsh	60	851	289	123	.426	33	23	.697	16	59	75	90	111	0	29	19	269	4.5	23
Green	76	1098	375	143	.381	90	54	.600	49	67	116	149	95	0	58	1	340	4.5	22
McNeill	9	67	18	6	.333	19	15	.789	2	12	14	2	14	0	1	0	27	3.0	6

HOUSTON ROCKETS

Player	G.	Min.	FGA	FGM	Pct.	FTA	FTM	Pct.	Off. Reb.	Def. Reb.	Tot. Reb.	Ast.	PF	Disq.	Stl.	Blk. Sh.	Pts.	Avg.	Hi.
Murphy	76	2900	1737	852	.491	267	245	.918	57	107	164	259	241	4	112	3	1949	25.6	57
Tomjanovich	23	849	447	217	.485	81	61	.753	40	98	138	32	63	0	15	5	495	21.5	35
Malone	59	2107	828	413	.499	443	318	.718	380	506	886	31	179	3	48	76	1144	19.4	39
Newlin	45	1181	495	216	.436	174	152	.874	36	84	120	203	128	1	52	9	584	13.0	27
Lucas	82	2933	947	412	.435	250	193	.772	51	204	255	768	208	1	160	9	1017	12.4	28
D. Jones	82	2476	777	346	.445	233	181	.777	215	426	641	109	265	2	77	39	873	10.6	22
Kunnert	80	2152	842	368	.437	135	93	.689	262	431	693	97	315	13	44	90	829	10.4	27
Reid	80	1849	574	261	.455	96	63	.656	111	248	359	121	277	8	67	51	585	7.3	29
Bradley	43	798	304	130	.428	59	43	.729	24	75	99	54	83	1	16	6	303	7.0	20
Behagen	3	33	11	7	.636	1	0	.000	2	5	7	2	6	0	0	0	14	4.7	8
Ratleff	68	1163	310	130	.419	47	39	.830	56	106	162	153	109	0	60	22	299	4.4	16
Johnson	1	11	4	1	.250	3	2	.667	2	1	3	1	3	0	0	0	4	4.0	4
Kupec	49	626	197	84	.426	33	27	.818	27	64	91	50	54	0	10	3	195	4.0	14
Abdul-Aziz (T)	16	158	60	23	.383	23	17	.739	19	31	50	10	29	0	3	3	63	3.9	8
Abdul-Aziz (H)	14	134	47	20	.426	20	15	.750	13	22	35	7	25	0	2	2	55	3.9	8
White	21	219	85	31	.365	18	14	.778	8	13	21	22	24	0	8	0	76	3.6	10
Dunleavy (Tot)	15	119	50	20	.400	18	13	.722	1	9	10	28	12	0	9	1	53	3.5	9
Dunleavy (H)	11	102	43	17	.395	16	11	.688	1	8	9	22	12	0	8	1	45	4.1	9
R. Jones	12	66	20	11	.550	10	4	.400	5	9	14	2	16	0	1	1	26	2.2	6
Moffett	20	110	17	5	.294	10	6	.600	10	11	21	7	16	0	2	2	16	0.8	6
Bond	7	21	6	2	.333	0	0	......	1	3	4	2	1	0	1	0	4	0.6	2

INDIANA PACERS

Player	G.	Min.	FGA	FGM	Pct.	FTA	FTM	Pct.	Off. Reb.	Def. Reb.	Tot. Reb.	Ast.	PF	Disq.	Stl.	Blk. Sh.	Pts.	Avg.	Hi.
Dantley	23	948	403	201	.499	263	207	.787	94	122	216	65	76	1	48	17	609	26.5	37
Williamson	42	1449	795	335	.421	161	134	.832	34	86	120	132	131	4	47	0	804	19.1	43
Sobers	79	3019	1221	553	.453	400	330	.825	92	235	327	584	308	10	170	23	1436	18.2	31
Bantom	82	2775	1047	502	.479	342	254	.743	184	426	610	238	333	13	100	50	1258	15.3	38
Edwards (Tot)	83	2405	1093	495	.453	421	272	.646	197	418	615	85	322	12	53	78	1262	15.2	33
Edwards (Ind)	58	1682	777	350	.450	296	192	.649	153	282	435	56	233	9	36	50	892	15.4	33
Tatum (Tot)	82	2522	1087	510	.469	196	153	.781	79	216	295	296	257	5	140	40	1173	14.3	25
Tatum (Ind)	57	1859	773	357	.462	137	108	.788	56	149	205	226	172	4	103	30	822	14.4	25
Roundfield	79	2423	861	421	.489	300	218	.727	275	527	802	196	297	4	81	149	1060	13.4	36
Behagen (Tot)	80	1735	804	346	.430	247	179	.725	201	312	513	101	263	4	62	31	871	10.9	24
Behagen (Ind)	51	1131	544	222	.408	176	128	.727	146	187	333	65	160	1	32	19	572	11.2	24
Car'ton (Tot)	72	1653	589	253	.430	171	130	.760	70	104	174	117	205	6	65	23	636	8.8	28
Car'ton (Ind)	35	621	197	96	.487	74	58	.784	28	34	62	62	73	1	22	11	250	7.1	17
Robisch	23	598	181	73	.403	64	50	.781	47	126	173	49	59	1	20	15	196	8.5	16
Elmore	69	1327	386	142	.368	132	88	.667	139	281	420	80	174	4	74	71	372	5.4	19
Flynn	71	955	267	120	.449	97	55	.567	47	70	117	142	52	0	41	10	295	4.2	14
Neumann	20	216	86	35	.407	18	13	.722	5	9	14	27	24	0	6	1	83	4.2	15
Green	44	449	128	56	.438	56	39	.696	31	40	71	30	67	0	14	2	151	3.4	13

Player	G.	Min.	FGA	FGM	Pct.	FTA	FTM	Pct.	Off. Reb.	Def. Reb.	Tot. Reb.	Ast.	PF	Disq.	Stl.	Blk. Sh.	Pts.	Avg.	Hi.
Wilson	12	86	36	14	.389	3	2	.667	6	6	12	8	16	0	2	1	30	2.5	12
Bennett	31	285	81	23	.284	45	28	.622	49	44	93	22	54	1	11	7	74	2.4	8
Smith	1	7	0	0	....	0	0	....	0	0	0	1	1	0	0	0	0	0.0	0

KANSAS CITY KINGS

Player	G.	Min.	FGA	FGM	Pct.	FTA	FTM	Pct.	Off. Reb.	Def. Reb.	Tot. Reb.	Ast.	PF	Disq.	Stl.	Blk. Sh.	Pts.	Avg.	Hi.
Wedman	81	2961	1192	607	.509	254	221	.870	144	319	463	201	242	2	99	22	1435	17.7	35
Boone	82	2653	1271	563	.443	377	322	.854	112	157	269	311	233	3	105	11	1448	17.7	40
Birdsong	73	1878	955	470	.492	310	216	.697	70	105	175	174	179	1	74	12	1156	15.8	37
Washington	78	2231	891	425	.477	199	150	.754	188	466	654	118	324	12	74	73	1000	12.8	29
Allen	77	2147	846	373	.441	220	174	.791	66	163	229	360	180	0	93	28	920	11.9	30
Robinzine	82	1748	677	305	.451	271	206	.760	173	366	539	72	281	5	74	11	816	10.0	28
Lacey	77	2131	590	265	.449	187	134	.717	155	487	642	300	264	7	120	108	664	8.6	24
Burleson	76	1525	525	228	.434	248	197	.794	170	312	482	131	259	6	62	81	653	8.6	20
Nash	66	800	304	157	.516	69	50	.725	75	94	169	46	75	0	27	18	364	5.5	33
Kuester	78	1215	319	145	.455	105	87	.829	19	95	114	252	143	1	58	1	377	4.8	21
Restani (Tot)	54	547	167	72	.431	13	9	.692	36	72	108	30	41	0	5	5	153	2.8	10
Restani (KC)	46	463	139	59	.424	11	9	.818	32	62	94	21	37	0	5	4	127	2.8	10
Bigelow	1	7	1	1	1.000	0	0	....	2	3	5	0	2	0	0	2	2	2.0	2
Nelson	8	53	14	3	.214	11	9	.818	1	2	3	5	5	0	2	1	15	1.9	4
McCarter	1	9	2	0	.000	0	0	....	0	1	1	0	1	0	0	0	0	0.0	0
Hansen (Tot)	5	13	7	0	.000	1	0	....	1	0	1	1	3	0	1	0	0	0.0	0
Hansen (KC)	3	9	5	0	.000	0	0	....	1	0	1	1	3	0	1	0	0	0.0	0

LOS ANGELES LAKERS

Player	G.	Min.	FGA	FGM	Pct.	FTA	FTM	Pct.	Off. Reb.	Def. Reb.	Tot. Reb.	Ast.	PF	Disq.	Stl.	Blk. Sh.	Pts.	Avg.	Hi.
Abdul-Jabbar	62	2265	1205	663	.550	350	274	.783	186	615	801	269	182	1	103	185	1600	25.8	43
Dantley (Tot)	79	2933	1128	578	.512	680	541	.796	265	355	620	253	233	2	118	24	1697	21.5	37
Dantley (LA)	56	1985	725	377	.520	417	334	.801	171	233	404	188	157	1	70	7	1088	19.4	37
Edwards	25	723	316	145	.459	125	80	.640	44	136	180	29	89	3	16	28	370	14.8	32
Tatum	25	663	314	153	.487	59	45	.763	23	67	90	70	85	1	37	10	351	14.0	25
Hudson	82	2283	992	493	.497	177	137	.774	80	108	188	193	196	0	94	14	1123	13.7	30
Nixon	81	2779	998	496	.497	161	115	.714	41	198	239	553	259	3	138	1	1107	13.7	28
Scott (Tot)	79	2473	994	435	.438	260	194	.746	62	187	249	378	252	6	110	17	1064	13.5	30
Scott (LA)	48	1393	509	225	.442	142	110	.775	38	110	148	235	155	4	59	11	560	11.7	24
Wilkes	51	1490	630	277	.440	148	106	.716	113	267	380	182	162	1	77	22	660	12.9	29
Washington	25	751	244	110	.451	110	68	.618	110	169	279	30	74	1	19	24	288	11.5	22
Ford	79	1945	576	272	.472	90	68	.756	106	247	353	142	210	1	68	46	612	7.7	22
Abernethy	73	1317	404	201	.498	111	91	.820	105	160	265	101	122	1	55	22	493	6.8	24
Carr	52	733	302	134	.444	85	55	.647	53	155	208	26	127	0	18	14	323	6.2	15
Robisch (Tot)	78	1277	430	177	.412	129	100	.775	100	252	352	88	130	1	39	29	454	5.8	16
Robisch (LA)	55	679	249	104	.418	65	50	.769	53	126	179	40	71	0	19	14	258	4.7	16
DiGregorio	25	332	100	41	.410	20	16	.800	5	18	23	71	22	0	6	0	98	3.9	11
Chaney	9	133	36	13	.361	6	5	.833	4	7	11	17	14	0	8	3	31	3.4	11
Davis	33	334	72	30	.417	29	22	.759	4	31	35	83	39	1	15	2	82	2.5	10

MILWAUKEE BUCKS

Player	G.	Min.	FGA	FGM	Pct.	FTA	FTM	Pct.	Off. Reb.	Def. Reb.	Tot. Reb.	Ast.	PF	Disq.	Stl.	Blk. Sh.	Pts.	Avg.	Hi.
Winters	80	2751	1457	674	.463	293	246	.840	87	163	250	393	239	4	124	27	1594	19.9	37
Johnson	80	2765	1204	628	.522	409	301	.736	292	555	847	190	221	3	92	103	1557	19.5	32
Meyers	80	2416	938	432	.461	435	314	.722	144	393	537	241	240	2	86	46	1178	14.7	34
Bridgeman	82	1876	947	476	.503	205	166	.810	114	176	290	175	202	1	72	30	1118	13.6	35
English	82	1552	633	343	.542	143	104	.727	144	251	395	129	178	1	41	55	790	9.6	21
Buckner	82	2072	671	314	.468	203	131	.645	78	169	247	456	287	6	188	19	759	9.3	27
Gianelli	82	2327	629	307	.488	123	79	.642	166	343	509	192	189	4	54	92	693	8.5	21
Benson	69	1288	473	220	.465	141	92	.652	89	206	295	99	177	1	69	54	532	7.7	21
Grunfeld	73	1261	461	204	.443	143	94	.657	70	124	194	145	150	1	54	19	502	6.9	22
Walton	76	1264	344	154	.448	83	54	.651	26	50	76	253	94	0	77	13	362	4.8	14
Eakins (Tot)	33	406	86	44	.512	60	50	.833	29	46	75	29	71	0	7	17	138	4.2	10
Eakins (Mil)	17	155	34	14	.411	26	21	.808	28	17	29	12	25	0	4	7	49	2.9	9
Restani	8	84	28	13	.464	2	0	.000	4	10	14	9	4	0	1	6	26	3.3	8
Laurel	10	57	31	10	.323	4	4	1.000	6	4	10	3	10	0	3	1	24	2.4	8
Lloyd	14	112	33	12	.364	10	6	.600	7	19	26	9	22	0	3	5	30	2.1	5

NEW JERSEY NETS

Player	G.	Min.	FGA	FGM	Pct.	FTA	FTM	Pct.	Off. Reb.	Def. Reb.	Tot. Reb.	Ast.	PF	Disq.	Stl.	Blk. Sh.	Pts.	Avg.	Hi.
King	79	3092	1665	798	.479	462	313	.677	265	486	751	193	302	5	122	36	1909	24.2	44
Williamson (Tot)	75	2731	1649	723	.438	391	331	.847	66	161	227	214	236	6	94	10	1777	23.7	50
Williamson (NJ)	33	1282	854	388	.454	230	197	.857	32	75	107	82	105	2	47	10	973	29.5	50
Skinner	8	277	101	41	.406	44	39	.886	14	38	52	33	34	2	13	5	121	15.1	28
K. Porter (Tot)	82	2813	1055	495	.469	320	244	.763	53	161	214	837	283	6	123	15	1234	15.0	40
K. Porter (NJ)	74	2686	1024	481	.470	307	235	.765	48	151	199	801	265	6	118	15	1197	16.2	40
Hillman	45	1220	501	236	.471	205	118	.576	126	212	338	49	160	7	49	44	590	13.1	29
H. Porter (Tot)	63	1323	635	309	.487	155	124	.800	100	179	279	42	134	0	29	38	742	11.8	29
H. Porter (NJ)	55	1216	592	293	.495	148	120	.811	95	167	262	40	119	0	26	33	706	12.8	29
Hawkins	15	343	150	69	.460	29	25	.862	21	29	50	37	51	1	22	13	163	10.9	25
Carrington	37	1032	392	157	.401	97	72	.742	42	70	112	55	132	5	43	12	386	10.4	28
Johnson	81	2411	721	285	.395	185	133	.719	245	534	779	111	339	20	78	274	703	8.7	24
Averitt	21	409	188	69	.367	45	36	.800	7	26	33	68	37	1	17	1	174	8.3	32
Jordan (Tot)	73	1213	538	215	.400	167	131	.784	35	84	119	177	94	0	126	19	561	7.7	30
Jordan (NJ)	51	1042	482	196	.407	151	119	.788	33	75	108	145	84	0	114	18	511	10.0	30
Nelson (Tot)	33	406	211	85	.403	84	57	.679	13	39	52	34	33	0	22	7	227	6.9	22
Nelson (NJ)	25	353	197	82	.416	73	48	.658	12	37	49	29	28	0	20	6	212	8.5	22
Washington (Tot)	38	561	206	100	.485	53	29	.547	50	106	156	10	75	2	18	37	229	6.0	19
Washington (NJ)	24	523	187	92	.492	47	26	.553	48	94	142	9	72	2	17	35	210	8.8	19

Truck Robinson of New Orleans led the NBA in rebounding in 1977-78 with an average of 15.7 a game.

Player	G.	Min.	FGA	FGM	Pct.	FTA	FTM	Pct.	Off. Reb.	Def. Reb.	Tot. Reb.	Ast.	PF	Disq.	Stl.	Blk. Sh.	Pts.	Avg.	Hi.
Crow	15	154	80	35	.438	20	14	.700	14	13	27	8	24	0	5	1	84	5.6	16
Bassett	65	1474	384	149	.388	97	50	.515	142	262	404	63	181	5	62	33	348	5.4	17
van B Kolff	68	1419	292	107	.366	123	87	.707	66	178	244	105	192	7	52	46	301	4.4	13
Wohl	10	118	34	12	.353	12	11	.917	1	3	4	13	24	0	3	0	35	3.5	17
Hughes	56	854	160	57	.356	29	9	.310	95	145	240	38	163	9	49	49	123	2.2	13

NEW ORLEANS JAZZ

Player	G.	Min.	FGA	FGM	Pct.	FTA	FTM	Pct.	Off. Reb.	Def. Reb.	Tot. Reb.	Ast.	PF	Disq.	Stl.	Blk. Sh.	Pts.	Avg.	Hi.
Maravich	50	2041	1253	556	.444	276	240	.870	49	129	178	335	116	1	101	8	1352	27.0	42
Robinson	82	3638	1683	748	.444	572	366	.640	298	990	1288	171	265	5	73	79	1862	22.7	39
Goodrich	81	2553	1050	520	.495	332	264	.795	75	102	177	388	186	0	82	22	1304	16.1	38
James	80	2118	861	428	.497	157	117	.745	163	258	421	112	254	5	36	22	973	12.2	30
Kelley	82	2119	602	304	.505	289	225	.779	249	510	759	233	293	6	89	129	833	10.2	33
McElroy	74	1760	607	287	.473	167	123	.737	44	104	148	292	110	0	58	34	697	9.4	27
Meriweather	54	1277	411	194	.472	133	87	.654	135	237	372	58	188	8	18	118	475	8.8	21
Williams	27	434	214	90	.421	37	31	.838	27	63	90	34	61	1	21	12	211	7.8	23
Watts (Tot)	71	1584	558	219	.392	156	92	.590	60	119	179	294	184	1	108	31	530	7.5	26
Watts (NO)	39	775	286	109	.381	103	62	.602	39	59	98	161	96	0	55	17	280	7.2	26
Griffin	82	1853	358	160	.447	157	112	.713	157	353	510	172	228	6	88	45	432	5.3	15
Boyd	21	363	110	44	.400	22	14	.636	2	17	19	48	23	0	9	3	102	4.9	14
S'nders (Tot)	56	643	234	99	.423	36	26	.722	38	73	111	46	106	3	21	14	224	4.0	18
S'nders (NO)	30	400	143	69	.483	19	12	.632	27	47	74	35	72	3	14	10	150	5.0	18
Bailey	48	449	139	59	.424	67	37	.552	44	38	82	40	46	0	18	15	155	3.2	20

NEW YORK KNICKERBOCKERS

Player	G.	Min.	FGA	FGM	Pct.	FTA	FTM	Pct.	Off. Reb.	Def. Reb.	Tot. Reb.	Ast.	PF	Disq.	Stl.	Blk. Sh.	Pts.	Avg.	Hi.
McAdoo	79	3182	1564	814	.520	645	469	.727	236	774	1010	298	297	6	105	126	2097	26.5	40
Monroe	76	2369	1123	556	.495	291	242	.832	47	135	182	361	189	0	60	19	1354	17.8	37
Shelton	82	2319	988	508	.514	276	203	.736	204	376	580	195	350	11	109	112	1219	14.9	41
Haywood	67	1765	852	412	.484	135	96	.711	141	301	442	126	188	1	37	72	920	13.7	37
Beard	79	1979	614	308	.502	160	129	.806	76	188	264	339	201	2	117	3	745	9.4	32
Williams	81	1550	689	305	.443	207	146	.705	85	124	209	363	211	4	108	15	756	9.3	29
McMillian	81	1977	623	288	.462	134	115	.858	80	209	289	205	116	0	76	17	691	8.5	24
Cleamons	79	2009	448	215	.480	103	81	.786	69	143	212	283	142	1	68	17	511	6.5	18
Knight	80	1169	465	222	.477	97	63	.649	121	200	321	38	211	1	50	28	507	6.3	22
Gondrezick	72	1017	339	131	.386	121	83	.686	92	158	250	83	181	0	56	18	345	4.8	17
Jackson	63	654	115	55	.478	56	43	.768	29	81	110	46	106	0	31	15	153	2.4	16
Burden	2	15	2	1	.500	0	0	......	0	0	0	1	1	0	1	0	2	1.0	2

PHILADELPHIA 76ers

Player	G.	Min.	FGA	FGM	Pct.	FTA	FTM	Pct.	Off. Reb.	Def. Reb.	Tot. Reb.	Ast.	PF	Disq.	Stl.	Blk. Sh.	Pts.	Avg.	Hi.
Erving	74	2429	1217	611	.502	362	306	.845	179	302	481	279	207	0	135	97	1528	20.6	43
McGinnis	78	2533	1270	588	.463	574	411	.716	282	528	810	294	287	6	137	27	1587	20.3	37
Collins	79	2770	1223	643	.526	329	267	.812	87	143	230	320	228	2	128	25	1553	19.7	37
Free	76	2050	857	390	.455	562	411	.731	92	120	212	306	199	0	68	41	1191	15.7	29
Dawkins	70	1722	577	332	.575	220	156	.709	117	438	555	85	268	5	34	125	820	11.7	23
Mix	82	1819	560	291	.520	220	175	.795	96	201	297	174	158	1	87	3	757	9.2	27
Bibby	82	2518	659	286	.434	219	171	.781	62	189	251	464	207	0	91	6	743	9.1	22
Bryant	81	1236	436	190	.436	144	111	.771	103	177	280	129	185	1	56	24	491	6.1	28
Jones	81	1636	359	169	.471	153	96	.627	165	405	570	92	281	4	26	127	434	5.4	18
McClain (Tot)	70	1020	280	123	.439	73	57	.781	20	92	112	157	124	2	58	6	303	4.3	17
McClain (Phil)	29	293	96	42	.438	10	7	.700	9	28	37	34	36	0	16	4	91	3.1	16
Catchings	61	748	178	70	.393	55	34	.618	105	145	250	34	124	1	20	67	174	2.9	10
Mosley	6	21	13	5	.385	7	3	.429	0	5	5	2	5	0	0	0	13	2.2	6
Dunleavy	4	17	7	3	.429	2	2	1.000	0	1	1	6	0	0	1	0	8	2.0	4
Washington	14	38	19	8	.421	6	3	.500	2	12	14	1	3	0	1	2	19	1.4	4

PHOENIX SUNS

Player	G.	Min.	FGA	FGM	Pct.	FTA	FTM	Pct.	Off. Reb.	Def. Reb.	Tot. Reb.	Ast.	PF	Disq.	Stl.	Blk. Sh.	Pts.	Avg.	Hi.
Westphal	80	2481	1568	809	.516	487	396	.813	41	123	164	437	162	0	138	31	2014	25.2	48
Davis	81	2590	1494	786	.526	466	387	.830	158	326	484	273	242	2	113	20	1959	24.2	40
Adams	70	1914	895	434	.485	293	214	.730	158	407	565	225	242	8	86	63	1082	15.5	35
Lee	82	1928	950	417	.439	228	170	.746	95	159	254	305	257	3	225	17	1004	12.2	30
Buse	82	2547	626	287	.458	136	112	.824	59	190	249	391	144	0	185	14	686	8.4	19
Heard	80	2099	625	265	.424	147	90	.612	166	486	652	132	213	0	129	101	620	7.8	24
Scott	81	1538	369	180	.488	191	132	.691	135	222	357	88	158	0	52	40	492	6.1	16
Perry	45	818	243	110	.453	65	51	.785	87	163	250	48	120	2	34	22	271	6.0	18
Bratz	80	933	395	159	.403	68	56	.824	42	73	115	123	104	1	39	5	374	4.7	16
Forrest	64	887	238	111	.466	103	49	.476	84	166	250	129	105	0	23	34	271	4.2	23
Griffin	36	422	169	61	.361	36	23	.639	44	59	103	24	56	0	16	0	145	4.0	15
Awtrey	81	1623	264	112	.424	109	69	.633	97	205	302	163	153	0	19	25	293	3.6	16

PORTLAND TRAIL BLAZERS

Player	G.	Min.	FGA	FGM	Pct.	FTA	FTM	Pct.	Off. Reb.	Def. Reb.	Tot. Reb.	Ast.	PF	Disq.	Stl.	Blk. Sh.	Pts.	Avg.	Hi.
Walton	58	1929	882	460	.522	246	177	.720	118	648	766	291	145	3	60	146	1097	18.9	34
Lucas	68	2119	989	453	.458	270	207	.767	186	435	621	173	221	3	61	56	1113	16.4	35
Hollins	81	2741	1202	531	.442	300	223	.743	81	196	277	380	268	4	157	29	1285	15.9	38
Gross	72	2163	720	381	.529	190	152	.800	180	220	400	254	234	5	100	52	914	12.7	27
Neal	61	1174	540	272	.504	177	127	.718	116	257	373	81	128	0	29	21	671	11.0	35
Davis	82	2188	756	343	.454	227	188	.828	65	108	173	217	173	0	81	14	874	10.7	23
Owens	82	1714	639	313	.490	278	206	.741	195	346	541	160	263	7	33	37	832	10.1	27
Twardzik	75	1820	409	242	.592	234	183	.782	36	98	134	244	186	2	107	4	667	8.9	22
Steele	65	1132	447	210	.470	122	100	.820	34	79	113	87	138	2	59	5	520	8.0	21
Norwood (Tot)	35	611	181	74	.409	75	50	.667	49	70	119	33	101	1	31	3	198	5.7	14
Norwood (Po)	19	351	99	40	.404	46	30	.652	22	43	65	19	56	1	18	0	110	5.8	14
Calhoun	79	1370	365	175	.479	76	66	.868	73	142	215	87	141	3	42	15	416	5.3	24
Walker	9	101	41	19	.463	8	5	.625	7	10	17	8	13	0	2	0	43	4.8	12
Dunn	63	768	240	100	.417	56	37	.661	63	84	147	45	74	0	46	8	237	3.8	13
Dorsey (Tot)	11	88	31	12	.387	16	10	.625	11	19	30	5	17	0	2	3	34	3.1	9
Dorsey (Po)	4	51	19	9	.474	11	7	.636	6	4	10	3	8	0	0	1	25	6.3	9
Schlueter	10	109	19	8	.421	18	9	.500	5	16	21	18	20	0	3	2	25	2.5	10

SAN ANTONIO SPURS

Player	G.	Min.	FGA	FGM	Pct.	FTA	FTM	Pct.	Off. Reb.	Def. Reb.	Tot. Reb.	Ast.	PF	Disq.	Stl.	Blk. Sh.	Pts.	Avg.	Hi.
Gervin	82	2857	1611	864	.536	607	504	.830	118	302	420	302	255	3	136	110	2232	27.2	63
Kenon	81	2869	1426	698	.489	323	276	.854	245	528	773	268	209	2	115	24	1672	20.6	42
Paultz	80	2479	979	518	.529	306	230	.752	172	503	675	213	222	3	42	194	1266	15.8	29
Dampier	82	2037	660	336	.509	101	76	.752	24	98	122	285	84	0	87	13	748	9.1	21
Gale	70	2091	581	275	.473	100	87	.870	57	166	223	376	170	2	159	25	637	9.1	22
Olberding	79	1773	480	231	.481	227	184	.811	104	269	373	131	235	1	45	26	646	8.2	22
Bristow	82	1481	538	257	.478	208	152	.731	99	158	257	194	150	0	69	4	666	8.1	27
Green (Tot)	72	1382	514	238	.463	142	107	.754	130	229	359	76	193	1	30	100	583	8.1	20
Green (S.A.)	63	1132	427	195	.457	111	86	.775	108	196	304	66	167	1	24	87	476	7.6	20
Dietrick	79	1876	543	250	.460	114	89	.781	73	285	358	217	231	4	81	55	589	7.5	18
Eakins	16	251	52	30	.577	34	29	.853	17	29	46	17	46	0	3	10	89	5.6	10
Layton	41	498	168	85	.506	13	12	.923	4	28	32	108	51	0	21	4	182	4.4	14
Silas	37	311	97	43	.443	73	60	.822	4	19	23	38	29	0	11	1	146	3.9	15
Sims	12	95	26	10	.385	15	10	.667	5	8	13	20	16	0	3	0	30	2.5	11
Karl	4	30	6	2	.333	2	2	1.000	0	5	5	5	6	0	1	0	6	1.5	4

SEATTLE SUPERSONICS

Player	G.	Min.	FGA	FGM	Pct.	FTA	FTM	Pct.	Off. Reb.	Def. Reb.	Tot. Reb.	Ast.	PF	Disq.	Stl.	Blk. Sh.	Pts.	Avg.	Hi.
Williams	79	2572	1335	602	.451	278	227	.817	83	173	256	294	198	2	185	41	1431	18.1	37
Brown	72	1965	1042	508	.488	196	176	.898	61	127	188	240	145	0	110	25	1192	16.6	37
Webster	82	2910	851	427	.502	461	290	.629	361	674	1035	203	262	8	48	162	1144	14.0	26
D. Johnson	81	2209	881	367	.417	406	297	.732	152	142	294	230	213	2	118	51	1031	12.7	27
Green	9	250	87	43	.494	31	21	.677	22	33	55	10	26	0	6	13	107	11.9	20
Sikma	82	2238	752	342	.455	247	192	.777	196	482	678	134	300	6	68	40	876	10.7	28
J. Johnson (Tot)	77	1823	824	342	.415	177	133	.751	102	208	310	211	197	0	43	19	817	10.6	26
J. Johnson (Sea)	76	1812	820	341	.416	174	131	.753	100	207	307	210	194	0	43	19	813	10.7	26
Seals	73	1322	551	230	.417	175	111	.634	62	164	226	81	210	4	41	33	571	7.8	28
Watts	32	809	272	110	.404	53	30	.566	21	60	81	133	88	1	53	14	250	7.8	18
Walker (Tot)	77	1104	461	204	.443	120	75	.625	87	132	219	77	138	1	26	10	483	6.3	18
Walker (Sea)	68	1003	420	185	.440	112	70	.625	80	122	202	69	125	1	24	10	440	6.5	18
Silas	82	2172	464	187	.397	186	109	.586	289	377	666	145	182	0	65	16	477	5.8	17
Hassett	48	404	205	91	.444	12	10	.833	14	22	36	41	45	0	21	0	192	4.0	14
Fleming	20	97	31	15	.484	17	10	.588	13	17	30	7	16	0	0	5	40	2.0	8
Wise	2	10	3	0	.000	4	1	.250	2	1	3	0	2	0	0	0	1	0.5	1
Tolson	1	7	1	0	.000	0	0		0	0	0	2	2	0	0	0	0	0.0	0

WASHINGTON BULLETS

Player	G.	Min.	FGA	FGM	Pct.	FTA	FTM	Pct.	Off. Reb.	Def. Reb.	Tot. Reb.	Ast.	PF	Disq.	Stl.	Blk. Sh.	Pts.	Avg.	Hi.
Hayes	81	3246	1409	636	.451	514	326	.634	335	740	1075	149	313	7	96	159	1598	19.7	37
Dandridge	75	2777	1190	560	.471	419	330	.788	137	305	442	287	262	6	101	44	1450	19.3	37
Kupchak	67	1759	768	393	.512	402	280	.697	162	298	460	71	196	1	28	42	1066	15.9	32
Grevey	81	2121	1128	505	.448	308	243	.789	124	166	290	155	203	4	61	17	1253	15.5	43
Chenier	36	937	451	200	.443	138	109	.790	15	87	102	73	54	0	36	9	509	14.1	28
Henderson	75	2315	784	339	.432	240	179	.746	66	127	193	406	131	0	93	15	857	11.4	24
Wright	70	1466	570	283	.496	107	76	.710	31	71	102	260	195	3	68	15	642	9.2	43
Unseld	80	2644	491	257	.523	173	93	.538	286	669	955	326	234	2	98	45	607	7.6	25
Johnson (Tot)	71	1299	581	237	.408	61	49	.803	43	112	155	130	129	0	62	5	523	7.4	29
Johnson (Wsh)	39	807	346	141	.408	51	42	.824	20	73	93	82	76	0	31	1	324	8.3	29
Ballard	76	936	334	142	.425	114	88	.772	102	164	266	62	90	1	30	13	372	4.9	19
Walker	40	384	161	57	.354	96	64	.667	21	31	52	54	39	0	14	5	178	4.5	23
Pace	49	438	140	67	.479	93	57	.613	50	84	134	23	86	1	12	21	191	3.9	18

PLAYOFF RESULTS

EASTERN CONFERENCE FIRST ROUND
New York 2, Cleveland 0
Apr. 12—Wed.—New York 132 at Cleveland 114
Apr. 14—Fri.—Cleveland 107 at New York 109

Washington 2, Atlanta 0
Apr. 12—Wed.—Atlanta 94 at Washington.................................103
Apr. 14—Fri.—Washington 107 at Atlanta 103*

EASTERN CONFERENCE SEMIFINALS
Philadelphia 4, New York 0
Apr. 16—Sun.—New York 90 at Philadelphia 130
Apr. 18—Tue.—New York 100 at Philadelphia.........................119
Apr. 20—Thu.—Philadelphia 137 at New York.........................126
Apr. 23—Sun.—Philadelphia 112 at New York 107

Washington 4, San Antonio 2
Apr. 16—Sun.—Washington 103 at San Antonio 114
Apr. 18—Tue.—Washington 121 at San Antonio......................117
Apr. 21—Fri.—San Antonio 105 at Washington.......................118
Apr. 23—Sun.—San Antonio 95 at Washington.........................98
Apr. 25—Tue.—Washington 105 at San Antonio......................116
Apr. 28—Fri.—San Antonio 100 at Washington.......................103

EASTERN CONFERENCE FINALS
Washington 4, Philadelphia 2
Apr. 30—Sun.—Washington 122 at Philadelphia 117
May 3—Wed.—Washington 104 at Philadelphia.......................110
May 5—Fri.—Philadelphia 108 at Washington.......................123
May 7—Sun.—Philadelphia 105 at Washington.......................121
May 10—Wed.—Washington 94 at Philadelphia........................107
May 12—Fri.—Philadelphia 99 at Washington.........................101

WESTERN CONFERENCE FIRST ROUND
Milwaukee 2, Phoenix 0
Apr. 11—Tue.—Milwaukee 111 at Phoenix 103
Apr. 14—Fri.—Phoenix 90 at Milwaukee..................................94

Seattle 2, Los Angeles 1
Apr. 12—Wed.—Los Angeles 90 at Seattle..............................102
Apr. 14—Fri.—Seattle 99 at Los Angeles 105
Apr. 16—Sun.—Los Angeles 102 at Seattle.............................111

WESTERN CONFERENCE SEMIFINALS
Seattle 4, Portland 2
Apr. 18—Tue.—Seattle 104 at Portland 95
Apr. 21—Fri.—Seattle 93 at Portland 96
Apr. 23—Sun.—Portland 84 at Seattle 99
Apr. 26—Wed.—Portland 98 at Seattle 100
Apr. 30—Sun.—Seattle 89 at Portland 113
May 1—Mon.—Portland 94 at Seattle.....................................105

Denver 4, Milwaukee 3
Apr. 18—Tue.—Milwaukee 103 at Denver................................119
Apr. 21—Fri.—Milwaukee 111 at Denver.................................127
Apr. 23—Sun.—Denver 112 at Milwaukee...............................143
Apr. 25—Tue.—Denver 118 at Milwaukee...............................104
Apr. 28—Fri.—Milwaukee 117 at Denver.................................112
Apr. 30—Sun.—Denver 91 at Milwaukee.................................119
May 3—Wed.—Milwaukee 110 at Denver................................116

WESTERN CONFERENCE FINALS
Seattle 4, Denver 2
May 5—Fri.—Seattle 107 at Denver.......................................116
May 7—Sun.—Seattle 121 at Denver......................................111
May 10—Wed.—Denver 91 at Seattle.....................................105
May 12—Fri.—Denver 94 at Seattle.......................................100
May 14—Sun.—Seattle 114 at Denver....................................123
May 17—Wed.—Denver 108 at Seattle...................................123

WORLD CHAMPIONSHIP SERIES
Washington 4, Seattle 3
May 21—Sun.—Washington 102 at Seattle...............................106
May 25—Thur.—Seattle 98 at Washington................................106
May 28—Sun.—Seattle 93 at Washington..................................92
May 30—Tue.—Washington 120 at Seattle..............................116*
June 2—Fri.—Washington 94 at Seattle....................................98
June 4—Sun.—Seattle 82 at Washington.................................117
June 7—Wed.—Washington 105 at Seattle.................................99

*Denotes overtime period.

1976-77 NBA STATISTICS

1976-77 NBA CHAMPION PORTLAND TRAIL BLAZERS

Seated (Left to Right): President Larry Weinberg, General Manager Harry Glickman, Herm Gilliam, Dave Twardzik, Johnny Davis, Lionel Hollins, Coach Jack Ramsay, Assistant Coach Jack McKinney. Second row: Lloyd Neal, Larry Steele, Corky Calhoun, Bill Walton, Maurice Lucas, Wally Walker, Robin Jones, Bob Gross. Back row: Bill Schonley, radio announcer; Dr. Robert Cook, team physician; Ron Culp, trainer; Wallace Scales, promotions director; Dr. Larry Mudrick, team dentist; George Rickles, business manager; Berlyn Hodges, administative assistant.

FINAL STANDINGS

ATLANTIC DIVISION

Team	Atl.	Bos.	Buf.	Chi.	Cle.	Den.	Det.	G.S.	Hou.	Ind.	K.C.	L.A.	Mil.	N.O.	NYK	NYN	Phi.	Pho.	Por.	S.A.	Sea.	Was.	W.	L.	Pct.	G.B.
Philadelphia	3	3	2	2	3	3	2	2	2	4	3	3	3	1	2	1	..	2	1	2	1	3	50	32	.610	....
Boston	4	..	3	2	1	3	2	1	2	1	3	2	3	2	2	3	1	2	1	4	2	1	44	38	.537	6
N.Y. Knicks	3	2	3	2	2	2	2	3	2	2	1	3	3	1	..	2	1	2	1	1	1	2	40	42	.488	10
Buffalo	..	1	..	1	2	2	3	..	1	1	..	1	3	3	1	2	2	3	1	..	3	..	30	52	.366	20
N.Y. Nets	1	1	2	1	1	1	1	1	2	..	..	..	1	2	2	..	1	2	..	1	1	1	22	60	.268	28

CENTRAL DIVISION

Team	Atl.	Bos.	Buf.	Chi.	Cle.	Den.	Det.	G.S.	Hou.	Ind.	K.C.	L.A.	Mil.	N.O.	NYK	NYN	Phi.	Pho.	Por.	S.A.	Sea.	Was.	W.	L.	Pct.	G.B.
Houston	3	2	3	3	3	..	2	1	..	4	2	2	3	2	2	2	1	3	3	2	3	3	49	33	.598	....
Washington	3	4	4	2	3	2	3	1	1	4	2	..	3	2	2	3	1	3	2	2	1	..	48	34	.585	1
San Antonio	..	..	4	1	2	2	2	2	2	3	1	1	3	3	3	3	3	2	..	..	3	2	44	38	.537	5
Cleveland	2	3	2	1	..	2	1	2	1	2	3	2	4	2	2	3	1	2	2	3	1	1	43	39	.524	6
New Orleans	3	2	1	..	2	1	1	3	2	2	2	2	1	..	2	3	2	1	1	2	1	2	35	47	.427	14
Atlanta	..	..	4	2	2	2	2	..	1	..	1	2	2	1	1	3	1	..	3	4	1	1	31	51	.378	18

MIDWEST DIVISION

Team	Atl.	Bos.	Buf.	Chi.	Cle.	Den.	Det.	G.S.	Hou.	Ind.	K.C.	L.A.	Mil.	N.O.	NYK	NYN	Phi.	Pho.	Por.	S.A.	Sea.	Was.	W.	L.	Pct.	G.B.
Denver	2	1	2	3	2	..	3	2	3	3	3	2	3	3	2	3	3	3	2	1	4	2	50	32	.610	....
Detroit	4	2	1	2	3	2	..	3	2	2	4	1	3	3	1	3	2	2	2	1	1	1	44	38	.537	6
Chicago	2	2	3	..	3	1	2	2	1	2	2	3	3	4	2	2	2	2	..	3	2	1	44	38	.537	6
Kansas City	2	1	3	2	1	1	..	3	2	2	..	1	2	2	4	4	1	3	2	1	1	2	40	42	.488	10
Indiana	4	2	3	2	1	2	..	2	1	..	1	2	2	2	4	2	2	2	..	2	2	1	36	46	.439	14
Milwaukee	2	1	1	1	..	1	1	3	1	2	2	2	..	1	1	3	1	1	2	3	1	1	30	52	.366	20

PACIFIC DIVISION

Team	Atl.	Bos.	Buf.	Chi.	Cle.	Den.	Det.	G.S.	Hou.	Ind.	K.C.	L.A.	Mil.	N.O.	NYK	NYN	Phi.	Pho.	Por.	S.A.	Sea.	Was.	W.	L.	Pct.	G.B.
Los Angeles	2	1	3	1	2	2	3	2	2	3	3	..	3	1	4	2	3	3	3	3	3	4	53	29	.646	....
Portland	1	3	3	4	2	2	2	3	1	4	2	1	2	2	3	3	2	3	..	2	3	1	49	33	.598	4
Golden State	4	3	3	2	2	2	1	..	2	4	1	2	1	1	1	3	3	4	1	2	1	3	46	36	.561	7
Seattle	2	2	1	2	1	..	3	3	1	2	3	1	3	3	2	2	1	1	1	..	..	3	40	42	.488	13
Phoenix	4	2	1	2	1	1	2	..	1	2	1	1	3	1	2	2	2	..	1	1	3	1	34	48	.415	19

HOME-ROAD RECORDS OF ALL TEAMS

	Home	Road	Total		Home	Road	Total
Atlanta	19- 22	12- 29	31- 51	Los Angeles	37- 4	16- 25	53- 29
Boston	28- 13	16- 25	44- 38	Milwaukee	24- 17	6- 35	30- 52
Buffalo	23- 18	7- 34	30- 52	New Orleans	26- 15	9- 32	35- 47
Chicago	31- 10	13- 28	44- 38	New York Knicks	26- 15	14- 27	40- 42
Cleveland	29- 12	14- 27	43- 39	New York Nets	10- 31	12- 29	22- 60
Denver	36- 5	14- 27	50- 32	Philadelphia	32- 9	18- 23	50- 32
Detroit	30- 11	14- 27	44- 38	Phoenix	26- 15	8- 33	34- 48
Golden State	29- 12	17- 24	46- 36	Portland	35- 6	14- 27	49- 33
Houston	34- 7	15- 26	49- 33	San Antonio	31- 10	13- 28	44- 38
Indiana	25- 16	11- 30	36- 46	Seattle	27- 14	13- 28	40- 42
Kansas City	28- 13	12- 29	40- 42	Washington	32- 9	16- 25	48- 34
				Total	618-284	284-618	902- 902

OFFENSIVE TEAM STATISTICS

		FIELD GOALS			FREE THROWS			REBOUNDS			MISCELLANEOUS				Turn	Blk.	SCORING	
Team	G.	Att.	Made	Pct.	Att.	Made	Pct.	Off.	Def.	Tot.	Ast.	PF	Disq.	Stl.	Over	Sh.	Pts.	Avg.
San Antonio	82	7657	3711	.485	2522	2010	.797	1110	2550	3660	2115	1966	35	857	1770	499	9432	115.0
Denver	82	7471	3590	.481	2783	2053	.738	1288	2700	3988	2262	2142	29	953	2011	471	9233	112.6
Portland	82	7537	3623	.481	2515	1917	.762	1260	2703	3963	1990	2220	38	868	1757	492	9163	111.7
Golden State	82	7832	3724	.475	2172	1649	.759	1300	2639	3939	2120	2058	24	904	1624	432	9097	110.9
Philadelphia	82	7322	3511	.480	2732	2012	.736	1293	2752	4045	1966	2074	18	814	1915	561	9034	110.2
Detroit	82	7792	3764	.483	1960	1442	.736	1169	2495	3664	2004	2200	39	877	1718	459	8970	109.4
Knicks	82	7530	3659	.486	2078	1587	.764	974	2680	3654	1956	2007	16	714	1680	304	8905	108.6
Milwaukee	82	7840	3668	.468	2072	1553	.750	1220	2519	3739	1970	2094	27	790	1648	342	8889	108.4
Kansas City	82	7733	3561	.460	2140	1706	.797	1222	2593	3815	1982	2173	36	849	1576	386	8828	107.7
Los Angeles	82	7657	3663	.478	1941	1437	.740	1177	2628	3805	2057	1867	14	801	1538	445	8763	106.9
Indiana	82	7840	3522	.449	2297	1714	.746	1409	2584	3993	2009	2030	37	924	1609	458	8758	106.8
Houston	82	7325	3535	.483	2103	1656	.787	1254	2632	3886	1913	2132	35	616	1600	411	8726	106.4
Washington	82	7479	3514	.470	2264	1622	.716	1185	2758	3943	1935	1940	19	642	1677	433	8650	105.5
Buffalo	82	7475	3366	.450	2492	1880	.754	1213	2623	3836	1883	1842	15	683	1699	392	8612	105.0
Phoenix	82	7249	3406	.470	2345	1791	.764	1059	2493	3552	2100	2089	24	750	1830	346	8603	104.9
New Orleans	82	7602	3443	.453	2183	1688	.773	1249	2828	4077	1854	2099	32	613	1706	357	8574	104.6
Boston	82	7775	3462	.445	2181	1648	.756	1241	2966	4207	2010	2039	49	506	1673	263	8572	104.5
Seattle	82	7639	3439	.450	2386	1646	.690	1355	2433	3788	1772	2198	23	932	1759	503	8524	104.0
Atlanta	82	7176	3279	.457	2451	1836	.749	1244	2512	3756	1882	2302	71	733	1779	330	8394	102.4
Cleveland	82	7688	3451	.449	1993	1468	.737	1312	2563	3875	1845	1951	24	579	1356	472	8370	102.1
Chicago	82	7186	3249	.452	2159	1613	.747	1292	2705	3997	1989	1871	26	699	1552	364	8111	98.9
Nets	82	7222	3096	.429	2274	1673	.736	1157	2547	3704	1422	2187	43	802	1630	435	7865	95.9

DEFENSIVE TEAM STATISTICS

	FIELD GOALS			FREE THROWS			REBOUNDS			MISCELLANEOUS				Turn	Blk.	SCORING		Pt.
Team	Att.	Made	Pct.	Att.	Made	Pct.	Off.	Def.	Tot.	Ast.	PF	Disq.	Stl.	Over	Sh.	Pts.	Avg.	Dif.
Chicago	7095	3306	.466	1907	1425	.747	1055	2559	3614	1917	2166	51	723	1598	460	8037	98.0 +	0.9
Cleveland	7268	3265	.449	2325	1748	.752	1202	2711	3913	1736	1908	23	660	1542	389	8278	101.0 +	1.1
Nets	7074	3279	.464	2488	1863	.749	1149	2937	4086	1910	1970	21	778	1735	512	8421	102.7 –	6.8
Los Angeles	7781	3515	.452	1990	1510	.759	1348	2625	3973	1900	1816	21	763	1599	362	8540	104.1 +	2.8
Phoenix	7192	3320	.462	2525	1903	.754	1180	2594	3774	1856	2325	39	897	1835	440	8543	104.2 +	0.7
Washington	7751	3552	.458	1943	1462	.752	1167	2565	3732	1893	2088	31	815	1506	348	8566	104.5 +	1.0
Houston	7356	3424	.465	2252	1746	.775	1121	2232	3353	1883	1978	27	547	1395	350	8594	104.8 +	1.6
Seattle	7339	3394	.462	2474	1863	.753	1257	2651	3908	2046	2104	24	726	1905	476	8651	105.5 –	1.5
Portland	7404	3408	.460	2514	1889	.751	1197	2510	3707	1817	2242	37	840	1765	478	8705	106.2 +	5.5
Philadelphia	7920	3575	.451	2074	1561	.753	1416	2448	3864	2012	2232	44	823	1769	371	8711	106.2 +	4.0
Atlanta	7137	3409	.478	2527	1909	.755	1121	2533	3654	2020	2174	44	803	1692	442	8727	106.4 –	4.0
Boston	7904	3559	.450	2180	1616	.741	1110	2753	3863	1918	1954	24	699	1369	349	8734	106.5 –	2.0
Kansas City	7244	3422	.472	2513	1912	.761	1097	2739	3836	1744	2030	35	722	1755	392	8756	106.8 +	0.9
Denver	7743	3585	.463	2231	1635	.733	1269	2481	3750	2082	2285	41	941	1944	470	8805	107.4 +	5.2
New Orleans	7712	3486	.452	2448	1833	.749	1318	2781	4099	1748	2125	35	835	1615	361	8805	107.4 –	2.8
Golden State	7584	3567	.470	2282	1699	.745	1256	2640	3896	2114	1939	26	577	1778	420	8833	107.7 +	3.2
Indiana	7629	3599	.472	2252	1705	.757	1378	2770	4148	2097	2043	23	715	1792	466	8903	108.6 –	1.8
Knicks	7610	3577	.470	2327	1752	.735	1163	2716	3879	1847	2008	20	793	1612	412	8906	108.6	Even
Buffalo	7917	3786	.478	1859	1404	.755	1268	2721	3989	2192	2129	31	729	1607	446	8976	109.5 –	4.5
Detroit	7539	3561	.472	2543	1933	.760	1317	2637	3954	1952	1827	15	793	1828	381	9015	110.4 –	1.0
Milwaukee	7753	3712	.479	2330	1721	.739	1265	2613	3878	2193	1940	22	736	1644	410	9145	111.5 –	3.1
San Antonio	8075	3955	.487	2059	1512	.734	1329	2687	4016	2159	2189	40	811	1822	420	9382	114.4 +	0.6

Disq.—Individual players disqualified (fouled out of game).

INDIVIDUAL LEADERS

POINTS

(Minimum 70 games played or 1400 points)

	G.	FG	FT	Pts.	Avg.		G.	FG	FT	Pts.	Avg.
Maravich, N.O.	73	886	501	2273	31.1	Boone, K.C.	82	747	324	1818	22.2
Knight, Ind.	78	831	413	2075	26.6	Kenon, S.A.	78	706	293	1705	21.9
Abdul-Jabbar, L.A.	82	888	376	2152	26.2	Barry, G.S.	79	682	359	1723	21.8
Thompson, Den.	82	824	477	2125	25.9	Erving, Phil.	82	685	400	1770	21.6
McAdoo, Buff.-Knicks	72	740	381	1861	25.8	Tomjanovich, Hou.	81	733	287	1753	21.6
Lanier, Det.	64	678	260	1616	25.3	McGinnis, Phil.	79	659	372	1690	21.4
Drew, Atl.	74	689	412	1790	24.2	Westphal, Phoe.	81	682	362	1726	21.3
Hayes, Wash.	82	760	422	1942	23.7	Williamson, Nets-Ind.	72	618	259	1495	20.8
Gervin, S.A.	82	726	443	1895	23.1	Dandridge, Mil.	70	585	283	1453	20.8
Issel, Den.	79	660	445	1765	22.3	Smith, Buff.	82	702	294	1698	20.7

FIELD GOALS
(Minimum 300 FG Made)

	FGA	FGM	Pct.
Abdul-Jabbar, L.A.	1533	888	.579
Kupchak, Wash.	596	341	.572
Jones, Den.	879	501	.570
Gervin, S.A.	1335	726	.544
Lanier, Det.	1269	678	.534
Gross, Port.	711	376	.529
Nater, Mil.	725	383	.528
Walton, Port.	930	491	.528
Meriweather, Atl.	607	319	.526
Gilmore, Chi.	1091	570	.522

FREE THROWS
(Minimum 125 FT Made)

	FTA	FTM	Pct.
DiGregorio, Buff.	146	138	.945
Barry, G.S.	392	359	.916
Murphy, Hou.	307	272	.886
Newlin, Hou.	304	269	.885
Brown, Sea.	190	168	.884
D. Van Arsdale, Phoe.	166	145	.873
White, Bos.	383	333	.869
Bridgeman, Mil.	228	197	.864
Russell, L.A.	219	188	.858
van Breda Kolff, Nets	228	195	.855

ASSISTS
Minimum 70 games or 400 assists

	G.	No.	Avg.
Buse, Ind.	81	685	8.5
Watts, Sea.	79	630	8.0
Van Lier, Chi.	82	636	7.8
K. Porter, Det.	81	592	7.3
Henderson, Atl.-Wash.	87	598	6.9
Barry, G.S.	79	475	6.0
White, Bos.	82	492	6.0
Gale, S.A.	82	473	5.8
Westphal, Phoe.	81	459	5.7
Lucas, Hou.	82	463	5.6

STEALS
Minimum 70 games or 125 steals

	G.	No.	Avg.
Buse, Ind.	81	281	3.47
Taylor, K.C.	72	199	2.76
Watts, Sea.	79	214	2.71
Buckner, Mil.	79	192	2.43
Gale, S.A.	82	191	2.33
Jones, Den.	82	186	2.27
Hollins, Port.	76	166	2.18
Ford, Det.	82	179	2.18
Barry, G.S.	79	172	2.18
Smith, Buff.	82	176	2.15

REBOUNDS
Minimum 70 games or 800 rebounds

	G.	Off.	Def.	Tot.	Avg.
Walton, Port.	65	211	723	934	14.4
Abdul-Jabbar, L.A.	82	266	824	1090	13.3
Malone, Buff.-Hou.	82	437	635	1072	13.1
Gilmore, Chi.	82	313	757	1070	13.0
McAdoo, Buff.-Knicks	72	199	727	926	12.9
Hayes, Wash.	82	289	740	1029	12.5
Nater, Mil.	72	266	599	865	12.0
McGinnis, Phil.	79	324	587	911	11.5
Lucas, Port.	79	271	628	899	11.4
Kenon, S.A.	78	282	597	879	11.3

BLOCKED SHOTS
Minimum 70 games or 100 blocked shots

	G.	No.	Avg.
Walton, Port.	65	211	3.25
Abdul-Jabbar, L.A.	82	261	3.18
Hayes, Wash.	82	220	2.68
Gilmore, Chi.	82	203	2.48
Jones, Phil.	82	200	2.44
Johnson, G.S.-Buff.	78	177	2.27
Malone, Buff.-Hou.	82	181	2.21
Roundfield, Ind.	61	131	2.15
Paultz, S.A.	82	173	2.11
E. Smith, Mil.-Clev.	70	144	2.06

TEAM-BY-TEAM INDIVIDUAL STATISTICS

ATLANTA HAWKS

Player	G.	Min.	FGA	FGM	Pct.	FTA	FTM	Pct.	Off. Reb.	Def. Reb.	Tot. Reb.	Ast.	PF	Disq.	Stl.	Blk. Sh.	Pts.	Avg.	Hi.
Drew	74	2688	1416	689	.487	577	412	.714	280	395	675	133	275	9	102	29	1790	24.2	42
Robinson (Tot)	77	2777	1200	574	.478	430	314	.730	252	576	828	142	253	3	66	38	1462	19.0	34
Robinson (Atl)	36	1449	648	310	.478	241	186	.772	133	329	462	97	130	3	38	20	806	22.4	34
Hudson	58	1745	905	413	.456	169	142	.840	48	81	129	155	160	2	67	19	968	16.7	39
Charles	82	2487	855	354	.414	256	205	.801	41	127	168	295	240	4	141	45	913	11.1	27
Henderson	46	1568	453	196	.433	168	126	.750	18	106	124	386	74	0	79	6	518	11.3	27
Meriweather	74	2068	607	319	.526	255	182	.714	216	380	596	82	324	21	41	82	820	11.1	27
Hawes	44	945	305	147	.480	88	67	.761	78	183	261	63	141	4	36	24	361	8.2	19
Barker	59	1354	436	182	.417	164	112	.683	111	290	401	60	223	11	33	41	476	8.1	21
Hill	81	1825	439	175	.399	174	139	.799	39	104	143	403	245	8	85	6	489	6.0	26
Brown	77	1405	350	160	.457	150	121	.807	75	161	236	103	217	7	46	7	441	5.7	20
Denton	45	700	256	103	.402	47	33	.702	81	137	218	33	100	1	14	16	239	5.3	25
Terry (Tot)	45	545	191	96	.503	44	36	.818	12	34	46	58	48	0	20	1	228	5.1	22
Terry (Atl)	12	241	87	47	.540	21	18	.857	8	10	18	25	21	0	9	1	112	9.3	22
Willoughby	39	549	169	75	.444	63	43	.683	65	105	170	13	64	1	19	23	193	4.9	16
Sojourner	51	551	203	95	.468	57	41	.719	49	97	146	21	66	0	15	9	231	4.5	18
Davis	7	67	35	8	.229	13	4	.308	2	5	7	2	9	0	7	0	20	2.9	6
Dickerson	6	63	12	6	.500	8	5	.625	0	2	2	11	13	0	1	0	17	2.8	6

BOSTON CELTICS

Player	G.	Min.	FGA	FGM	Pct.	FTA	FTM	Pct.	Off. Reb.	Def. Reb.	Tot. Reb.	Ast.	PF	Disq.	Stl.	Blk. Sh.	Pts.	Avg.	Hi.
White	82	3333	1488	638	.429	383	333	.869	87	296	383	492	193	5	118	22	1609	19.6	41
Scott	43	1581	734	326	.444	173	129	.746	52	139	191	196	155	3	60	12	781	18.2	31
Havlicek	79	2913	1283	580	.452	288	235	.816	109	273	382	400	208	4	84	18	1395	17.7	33
Cowens	50	1888	756	328	.434	198	162	.818	147	550	697	248	181	7	46	49	818	16.4	33
Wicks	82	2642	1012	464	.458	464	310	.668	268	556	824	169	331	14	64	61	1238	15.1	25
Rowe	79	2190	632	315	.489	240	170	.708	188	375	563	107	215	3	24	47	800	10.1	22
Boswell	70	1083	340	175	.515	135	96	.711	111	195	306	85	237	9	27	8	446	6.4	22
Saunders	68	1051	395	184	.466	53	35	.660	73	150	223	85	191	3	26	7	403	5.9	21
Stacom	79	1051	438	179	.409	58	46	.793	40	57	97	117	65	0	19	3	404	5.1	16
Kuberski	76	860	312	131	.420	83	63	.759	76	133	209	39	89	0	7	5	325	4.3	16
Ard	63	969	254	96	.378	76	49	.645	77	219	296	53	128	1	18	28	241	3.8	14
Cook	25	138	72	27	.375	17	9	.529	10	17	27	5	27	0	10	3	63	2.5	10
Wilson	25	131	59	19	.322	13	11	.846	3	6	9	14	19	0	3	0	49	2.0	10

BUFFALO BRAVES

Player	G.	Min.	FGA	FGM	Pct.	FTA	FTM	Pct.	Off. Reb.	Def. Reb.	Tot. Reb.	Ast.	PF	Disq.	Stl.	Blk. Sh.	Pts.	Avg.	Hi.
McAdoo	20	767	400	182	.455	158	110	.696	66	198	264	65	74	1	16	34	474	23.7	42
Smith	82	3094	1504	702	.467	386	294	.762	134	323	457	441	264	2	176	8	1698	20.7	41
Dantley	77	2816	1046	544	.520	582	476	.818	251	336	587	144	215	2	91	15	1564	20.3	39

Player	G.	Min.	FGA	FGM	Pct.	FTA	FTM	Pct.	Off. Reb.	Def. Reb.	Tot. Reb.	Ast.	PF	Dsq.	Stl.	Blk. Sh.	Pts.	Avg.	Hi.
Shumate	74	2601	810	407	.502	450	302	.671	163	538	701	159	197	1	90	84	1116	15.1	26
DiGregorio	81	2267	875	365	.417	146	138	.945	52	132	184	378	150	1	57	3	868	10.7	36
Neumann	4	49	34	15	.441	6	5	.833	5	4	9	4	7	0	3	2	35	8.8	21
Gianelli (Tot)	76	1913	579	257	.444	125	90	.720	154	321	475	83	171	0	35	98	604	7.9	19
Gianelli (Buf)	57	1283	397	171	.431	77	55	.714	94	203	297	57	117	0	21	70	397	7.0	16
Averitt	75	1136	619	234	.378	169	121	.716	20	58	78	134	127	2	30	5	589	7.9	26
Gerard (Tot)	65	1048	454	201	.443	117	78	.667	89	128	217	92	164	1	44	62	480	7.4	21
Gerard (Buf)	41	592	244	100	.410	61	40	.656	51	66	117	43	91	0	23	32	240	5.9	18
Adams	77	1710	526	216	.411	173	129	.746	130	241	371	150	201	0	74	16	561	7.3	28
Johnson (Tot)	78	1652	429	198	.462	98	71	.724	204	407	611	104	246	8	37	177	467	6.0	16
Johnson (Buf)	39	1055	279	125	.448	67	46	.687	117	283	400	78	141	6	22	104	296	7.6	16
Price	20	333	104	44	.423	20	17	.850	5	29	34	38	52	0	25	5	105	5.3	17
McMillen	20	270	92	45	.489	36	26	.722	29	43	72	16	29	0	1	2	116	5.8	19
Foster	59	689	247	99	.401	44	30	.682	33	43	76	48	92	0	16	0	228	3.9	14
Abdul-Aziz	22	195	74	25	.338	43	33	.767	41	49	90	7	21	0	3	9	83	3.8	16
Terry	33	304	104	49	.471	23	18	.783	4	24	28	33	27	0	11	0	116	3.5	14
Williams (Tot)	65	867	210	78	.371	87	68	.782	26	75	101	132	60	0	32	3	224	3.4	14
Williams (Buf)	44	556	117	43	.368	48	38	.792	18	49	67	88	34	0	24	3	124	2.8	8
Mayes	2	7	3	0	.000	3	2	.667	0	3	3	0	2	0	0	0	2	1.0	2
Malone	2	6	0	0	....	0	0	......	0	1	1	0	1	0	0	0	0	0.0	0

CHICAGO BULLS

Player	G.	Min.	FGA	FGM	Pct.	FTA	FTM	Pct.	Off. Reb.	Def. Reb.	Tot. Reb.	Ast.	PF	Dsq.	Stl.	Blk. Sh.	Pts.	Avg.	Hi.
Gilmore	82	2877	1091	570	.522	586	387	.660	313	757	1070	199	266	4	44	203	1527	18.6	42
Johnson	81	2847	1205	538	.446	407	324	.796	297	531	828	195	315	10	103	64	1400	17.3	37
Holland	79	2453	1120	509	.454	192	158	.823	78	175	253	253	201	3	169	16	1176	14.9	30
May	72	2369	955	431	.451	227	188	.828	141	296	437	145	185	2	78	17	1050	14.6	25
Love	14	496	201	68	.338	46	35	.761	38	35	73	23	47	1	8	2	171	12.2	22
Van Lier	82	3097	729	300	.412	306	238	.778	108	262	370	636	268	3	129	16	838	10.2	27
Mengelt	61	1178	458	209	.456	113	89	.788	29	81	110	114	102	2	37	4	507	8.3	26
Marin	54	869	359	167	.465	39	31	.795	27	64	91	62	85	0	13	6	365	6.8	18
McCracken	9	119	47	18	.383	18	11	.611	6	10	16	14	17	0	6	0	47	5.2	13
Laskowski	47	562	212	75	.354	30	27	.900	16	47	63	44	22	0	32	2	177	3.8	15
Boerwinkle	82	1070	273	134	.491	63	34	.540	101	211	312	189	147	0	19	19	302	3.7	19
Kropp	53	480	152	73	.480	41	28	.683	21	26	47	39	77	1	18	1	174	3.3	18
Pondexter	78	996	257	107	.416	65	42	.646	77	159	236	41	82	0	34	11	256	3.3	12
Fernsten	5	61	15	3	.200	11	8	.727	9	7	16	6	9	0	1	3	14	2.8	5
Hicks (Tot)	37	262	89	41	.461	13	11	.846	26	40	66	24	37	0	8	0	93	2.5	12
Hicks (Chi)	35	255	87	41	.471	13	11	.846	25	40	65	23	36	0	7	0	93	2.7	12
Starr	17	65	24	6	.250	2	2	1.000	6	4	10	6	11	0	1	0	14	0.8	4
Smith	2	11	1	0	.000	0	0	......	0	0	0	0	1	0	0	0	0	0.0	0

CLEVELAND CAVALIERS

Player	G.	Min.	FGA	FGM	Pct.	FTA	FTM	Pct.	Off. Reb.	Def. Reb.	Tot. Reb.	Ast.	PF	Dsq.	Stl.	Blk. Sh.	Pts.	Avg.	Hi.
Russell	70	2109	1003	435	.434	370	288	.778	144	275	419	189	196	3	70	24	1158	16.5	36
Carr	82	2409	1221	558	.457	268	213	.795	120	120	240	220	221	3	57	10	1329	16.2	42
B. Smith	81	2135	1149	513	.446	181	148	.818	92	225	317	152	211	3	61	30	1174	14.5	34
Chones	82	2378	972	450	.463	212	155	.731	208	480	688	104	258	3	32	77	1055	12.9	24
Cleamons	60	2045	592	257	.434	148	112	.757	99	174	273	308	126	0	66	23	626	10.4	25
Snyder	82	1685	693	316	.456	149	127	.852	47	102	149	160	177	2	45	30	759	9.3	18
E.Smith(Tot)	70	1464	507	241	.475	213	117	.549	114	325	439	43	207	4	35	144	599	8.6	30
E.Smith(Cle)	36	675	254	128	.504	108	56	.519	62	169	231	13	98	2	16	75	312	8.7	30
Brewer	81	2672	657	296	.451	178	97	.545	275	487	762	195	214	3	94	82	689	8.5	20
Brokaw (Tot)	80	1487	564	242	.429	219	163	.744	22	101	123	228	164	2	36	36	647	8.1	27
Brokaw (Clev)	39	596	240	112	.467	82	58	.707	12	47	59	117	79	2	14	13	282	7.2	21
Walker	62	1216	349	157	.450	115	89	.774	55	105	160	254	124	1	83	4	403	6.5	23
Thurmond	49	997	246	100	.407	106	68	.642	121	253	374	83	128	2	16	81	268	5.5	13
Garrett	29	215	93	40	.430	22	18	.818	10	30	40	7	30	0	7	3	98	3.4	12
Lambert	63	555	157	67	.427	36	25	.694	62	92	154	31	75	0	16	18	159	2.5	11
Howard	9	28	15	8	.533	6	5	.833	2	3	5	5	7	0	1	2	21	2.3	8
Williams	22	65	47	14	.298	12	9	.750	3	1	4	7	7	0	1	0	37	1.7	6

DENVER NUGGETS

Player	G.	Min.	FGA	FGM	Pct.	FTA	FTM	Pct.	Off. Reb.	Def. Reb.	Tot. Reb.	Ast.	PF	Dsq.	Stl.	Blk. Sh.	Pts.	Avg.	Hi.
Thompson	82	3001	1626	824	.507	623	477	.766	138	196	334	337	236	1	114	53	2125	25.9	44
Issel	79	2507	1282	660	.515	558	445	.797	211	485	696	177	246	7	91	29	1765	22.3	40
Jones	82	2419	879	501	.570	329	236	.717	174	504	678	264	238	3	186	162	1238	15.1	27
Gerard	24	456	210	101	.481	56	38	.679	38	62	100	49	73	1	21	30	240	10.0	21
Calvin (Tot)	76	1438	544	220	.404	338	287	.849	36	60	96	240	127	0	61	3	727	9.6	26
Calvin (Den)	29	625	225	100	.444	144	123	.854	19	30	49	115	53	0	27	1	323	11.1	26
Wise	75	1403	513	237	.462	218	142	.651	76	177	253	142	180	2	60	18	616	8.2	20
McClain	72	2002	551	245	.445	133	99	.744	52	177	229	324	255	9	106	13	589	8.2	18
Price (Tot)	81	1828	567	253	.446	103	83	.806	50	181	231	261	247	3	128	20	589	7.3	20
Price (Den)	55	1384	422	188	.445	74	59	.797	41	143	184	208	181	3	96	14	435	7.9	20
Silas	81	1959	572	206	.360	255	170	.667	236	370	606	132	183	0	58	23	582	7.2	20
Webster	80	1276	400	198	.495	220	143	.650	152	332	484	62	149	2	23	118	539	6.7	17
Williams	21	311	93	35	.376	39	30	.769	8	26	34	44	26	0	8	0	100	4.8	14
Beck	53	480	246	107	.435	44	36	.818	45	51	96	33	59	1	15	1	250	4.7	16
Taylor	79	1548	314	132	.420	65	37	.569	90	121	211	288	202	0	132	9	301	3.8	11
Towe	51	409	138	56	.406	25	18	.720	8	26	34	87	61	0	16	0	130	2.5	8

DETROIT PISTONS

Player	G.	Min.	FGA	FGM	Pct.	FTA	FTM	Pct.	Off. Reb.	Def. Reb.	Tot. Reb.	Ast.	PF	Disq.	Stl.	Blk. Sh.	Pts.	Avg.	Hi.
Lanier	64	2446	1269	678	.534	318	260	.818	200	545	745	214	174	0	70	126	1616	25.3	40
Carr	82	2643	931	443	.476	279	205	.735	211	420	631	181	287	8	165	58	1091	13.3	29
H. Porter	78	2200	962	465	.483	120	103	.858	155	303	458	53	202	0	50	73	1033	13.2	27
Ford	82	2539	918	437	.476	170	131	.771	96	174	270	337	192	1	179	26	1005	12.3	33
Simpson	77	1597	834	356	.427	195	138	.708	48	133	181	180	100	0	68	5	850	11.0	25
Money	73	1586	631	329	.521	114	90	.789	43	81	124	243	199	3	91	14	748	10.2	32
Barnes	53	989	452	202	.447	156	106	.679	69	184	253	45	139	1	38	33	510	9.6	33
K. Porter	81	2117	605	310	.512	133	97	.729	28	70	98	592	271	8	88	8	717	8.9	28
Douglas	82	1626	512	245	.479	229	127	.555	181	345	526	68	294	10	44	81	617	7.5	30
Eberhard	68	1219	380	181	.476	138	109	.790	76	145	221	50	197	4	45	15	471	6.9	24
Trapp	6	68	29	15	.517	4	3	.750	4	6	10	3	13	0	0	1	33	5.5	15
Sellers	44	329	190	73	.384	72	52	.722	19	22	41	25	56	0	22	0	198	4.5	17
Cash	6	49	23	9	.391	6	3	.500	8	8	16	1	8	0	2	1	21	3.5	11
Brown	43	322	56	21	.375	26	18	.692	31	59	90	12	68	4	15	18	60	1.4	10

GOLDEN STATE WARRIORS

Player	G.	Min.	FGA	FGM	Pct.	FTA	FTM	Pct.	Off. Reb.	Def. Reb.	Tot. Reb.	Ast.	PF	Disq.	Stl.	Blk. Sh.	Pts.	Avg.	Hi.
Barry	79	2904	1551	682	.440	392	359	.916	73	349	422	475	194	2	172	58	1723	21.8	42
Smith	82	2880	1318	631	.479	376	295	.785	101	231	332	328	227	0	98	29	1557	19.0	51
Wilkes	76	2579	1147	548	.478	310	247	.797	155	423	578	211	222	1	127	16	1343	17.7	32
Williams	82	1930	701	325	.464	150	112	.747	72	161	233	292	218	4	121	19	762	9.3	26
Parish	77	1384	573	288	.503	171	121	.708	201	342	543	74	224	7	55	94	697	9.1	30
Ray	77	2018	450	263	.584	199	105	.528	199	416	615	112	242	5	74	81	631	8.2	23
Dickey	49	856	345	158	.458	61	45	.738	100	140	240	63	101	1	20	11	361	7.4	20
Dudley	79	1682	421	220	.523	203	129	.635	119	177	296	347	169	0	67	6	569	7.2	19
C. Johnson	79	1196	583	255	.437	69	49	.710	50	91	141	91	134	1	77	7	559	7.1	22
McNeill (Tot)	24	230	112	47	.420	61	52	.852	28	47	75	6	32	1	10	2	146	6.1	23
McNeill (G.S.)	16	137	61	29	.475	31	28	.903	18	31	49	3	19	0	6	1	86	5.4	17
Parker	65	889	292	154	.527	92	71	.772	85	88	173	59	77	0	53	26	379	5.8	20
Davis	33	552	124	55	.444	72	49	.681	34	61	95	59	93	1	11	8	159	4.8	12
G. Johnson	39	597	150	73	.487	31	25	.806	87	124	211	26	105	2	15	73	171	4.4	13
Rogers	26	176	116	43	.371	15	14	.933	6	5	11	10	33	0	8	3	100	3.8	10

HOUSTON ROCKETS

Player	G.	Min.	FGA	FGM	Pct.	FTA	FTM	Pct.	Off. Reb.	Def. Reb.	Tot. Reb.	Ast.	PF	Disq.	Stl.	Blk. Sh.	Pts.	Avg.	Hi.
Tomjanovich	81	3130	1437	733	.510	342	287	.839	172	512	684	172	198	1	57	27	1753	21.6	40
Murphy	82	2764	1216	596	.490	307	272	.886	54	118	172	386	281	6	144	8	1464	17.9	34
Malone (Tot)	82	2506	810	389	.480	440	305	.693	437	635	1072	89	275	3	67	181	1083	13.2	26
Malone (Hou)	80	2500	810	389	.480	440	305	.693	437	634	1071	89	274	3	67	181	1083	13.5	26
Newlin	82	2119	850	387	.455	304	269	.885	53	151	204	320	226	2	60	3	1043	12.7	38
Lucas	82	2531	814	388	.477	171	135	.789	55	164	219	463	174	0	125	19	911	11.1	25
Kunnert	81	2050	685	333	.486	126	93	.738	210	459	669	154	361	17	35	105	759	9.4	31
Johnson	79	1738	696	319	.458	132	94	.712	75	191	266	163	199	1	47	24	732	9.3	30
Jones	74	1239	338	167	.494	126	101	.802	98	186	284	48	175	1	38	19	435	5.9	18
Ratleff	37	533	161	70	.435	42	26	.619	24	53	77	43	45	0	20	6	166	4.5	12
Owens	46	462	135	68	.504	76	52	.684	47	95	142	18	96	2	4	13	188	4.1	13
White	46	368	106	47	.443	25	15	.600	13	28	41	35	39	0	11	1	109	2.4	14
Kennedy	32	277	58	31	.534	8	3	.375	14	37	51	6	45	1	7	5	65	2.0	10
Wohl	14	62	17	7	.412	4	4	1.000	1	4	5	15	18	1	0	1	18	1.3	4
Hicks	2	7	2	0	.000	0	0	......	1	0	1	1	1	0	1	0	0	0.0	0

INDIANA PACERS

Player	G.	Min.	FGA	FGM	Pct.	FTA	FTM	Pct.	Off. Reb.	Def. Reb.	Tot. Reb.	Ast.	PF	Disq.	Stl.	Blk. Sh.	Pts.	Avg.	Hi.
Knight	78	3117	1687	831	.493	506	413	.816	223	359	582	260	197	0	117	19	2075	26.6	43
Williamson (Tot.)	72	2481	1347	618	.459	329	259	.787	42	151	193	201	246	4	107	13	1495	20.8	37
Williamson (Ind.)	30	1055	544	261	.480	125	98	.784	18	56	74	111	103	1	48	7	620	20.7	33
Roundfield	61	1645	734	342	.466	239	164	.686	179	339	518	69	243	8	61	131	848	13.9	33
Jones	80	2709	1019	438	.430	223	166	.744	218	386	604	189	305	10	102	80	1042	13.0	26
Robisch	80	1900	811	369	.455	256	213	.832	171	383	554	158	169	1	55	37	951	11.9	30
Hillman	82	2302	811	359	.443	244	161	.660	228	465	693	166	353	15	95	106	879	10.7	27
Flynn	73	1324	573	250	.436	142	101	.711	76	111	187	179	106	0	57	6	601	8.2	24
Buse	81	2947	639	266	.416	145	114	.786	66	204	270	685	129	0	281	16	646	8.0	19
Lewis	32	552	199	81	.407	77	62	.805	17	30	47	56	58	0	18	2	224	7.0	20
Green	70	918	424	183	.432	113	84	.743	79	98	177	46	157	2	46	12	450	6.4	24
Bennett	67	911	294	101	.344	187	112	.599	110	127	237	70	155	0	37	33	314	4.7	19
Mayes	2	21	7	3	.429	4	1	.250	4	3	7	3	5	0	0	2	7	3.5	4
Elmore	6	46	17	7	.412	5	4	.800	7	8	15	2	11	0	4	4	18	3.0	7
Anderson	27	164	59	26	.441	20	14	.700	9	3	12	10	26	0	6	2	66	2.4	14
Hackett (Tot.)	6	46	10	3	.300	14	8	.571	4	9	13	3	8	0	0	1	14	2.3	3
Hackett (Ind.)	5	38	8	3	.375	9	6	.667	3	7	10	3	7	0	0	1	12	2.4	3
Elston	5	40	14	2	.143	2	1	.500	1	5	6	2	6	0	1	0	5	1.0	5

KANSAS CITY KINGS

Player	G.	Min.	FGA	FGM	Pct.	FTA	FTM	Pct.	Off. Reb.	Def. Reb.	Tot. Reb.	Ast.	PF	Disq.	Stl.	Blk. Sh.	Pts.	Avg.	Hi.
Boone	82	3021	1577	747	.474	384	324	.844	128	193	321	338	258	1	119	19	1818	22.2	43
Taylor	72	2488	995	501	.504	275	225	.818	88	150	238	320	206	1	199	16	1227	17.0	38
Wedman	81	2743	1133	521	.460	241	206	.855	187	319	506	227	226	3	100	23	1248	15.4	38
Washington	82	2265	1034	446	.431	254	177	.697	201	497	698	85	324	13	63	90	1069	13.0	30
Lacey	82	2595	774	327	.422	282	215	.762	189	545	734	386	292	9	119	133	869	10.6	28
Robinzine	75	1594	677	307	.453	216	159	.736	164	310	474	95	283	7	86	13	773	10.3	27
Johnson	81	1386	446	218	.489	115	101	.878	68	144	212	105	169	1	43	21	537	6.6	18
Eakins	82	1338	336	151	.449	222	188	.847	112	249	361	119	195	1	29	49	490	6.0	23
McCarter	59	725	257	119	.463	45	32	.711	16	39	55	99	63	0	23	0	270	4.6	22

Player	G.	Min.	FGA	FGM	Pct.	FTA	FTM	Pct.	Off. Reb.	Def. Reb.	Tot. Reb.	Ast.	PF	Disq.	Stl.	Blk. Sh.	Pts.	Avg.	Hi.
Barr	73	1224	279	122	.437	57	41	.719	33	97	130	175	96	0	52	18	285	3.9	14
Hansen	41	289	155	67	.432	32	23	.719	28	31	59	25	44	0	13	3	157	3.8	13
Bigelow	29	162	70	35	.500	17	15	.882	8	19	27	8	17	0	3	1	85	2.9	11

LOS ANGELES LAKERS

Player	G.	Min.	FGA	FGM	Pct.	FTA	FTM	Pct.	Off. Reb.	Def. Reb.	Tot. Reb.	Ast.	PF	Disq.	Stl.	Blk. Sh.	Pts.	Avg.	Hi.
Abdul-Jabbar	82	3016	1533	888	.579	536	376	.701	266	824	1090	319	262	4	101	261	2152	26.2	40
Russell	82	2583	1179	578	.490	219	188	.858	86	208	294	210	163	1	86	7	1344	16.4	35
Allen	78	2482	1035	472	.456	252	195	.774	58	193	251	405	183	0	116	19	1139	14.6	30
Washington	53	1342	380	191	.503	187	132	.706	182	310	492	48	183	1	43	52	514	9.7	20
Tatum	68	1249	607	283	.466	100	72	.720	83	153	236	118	168	1	85	22	638	9.4	23
Calvin	12	207	82	27	.329	48	41	.854	6	10	16	21	16	0	11	1	95	7.9	20
Ford	82	1782	570	262	.460	102	73	.716	105	248	353	133	170	0	60	21	597	7.3	19
Lamar	71	1165	561	228	.406	68	46	.676	30	62	92	177	73	0	59	3	502	7.1	22
Abernethy	70	1378	349	169	.484	134	101	.754	113	178	291	98	118	1	49	10	439	6.3	19
Chaney	81	2408	522	213	.408	94	70	.745	120	210	330	308	224	4	140	33	496	6.1	16
Neumann (Tot)	63	937	397	161	.406	87	59	.678	24	48	72	141	134	2	31	10	381	6.0	24
Neumann (LA)	59	888	363	146	.402	81	54	.667	19	44	63	137	127	2	28	8	346	5.9	24
Kupec	82	908	342	153	.447	101	78	.772	76	123	199	53	113	0	18	4	384	4.7	14
Warner	14	170	53	25	.472	6	4	.667	21	48	69	11	28	0	1	2	54	3.9	10
Murphy	2	18	5	1	.200	7	3	.429	3	1	4	0	5	0	0	0	5	2.5	3
Roberts	28	209	76	27	.355	6	4	.667	9	16	25	19	34	0	4	2	58	2.1	12

MILWAUKEE BUCKS

Player	G.	Min.	FGA	FGM	Pct.	FTA	FTM	Pct.	Off. Reb.	Def. Reb.	Tot. Reb.	Ast.	PF	Disq.	Stl.	Blk. Sh.	Pts.	Avg.	Hi.
Dandridge	70	2501	1253	585	.467	367	283	.771	146	294	440	268	222	1	95	28	1453	20.8	37
Winters	78	2717	1308	652	.498	242	205	.847	64	167	231	337	228	1	114	29	1509	19.3	43
Bridgeman	82	2410	1094	491	.449	228	197	.864	129	287	416	205	221	3	82	26	1179	14.4	41
Nater	72	1960	725	383	.528	228	172	.754	266	599	865	108	214	6	54	51	938	13.0	30
Meyers	50	1262	383	179	.467	192	127	.661	122	219	341	86	152	4	42	32	485	9.7	31
Brokaw	41	891	324	130	.401	137	105	.766	10	54	64	111	85	0	22	23	365	8.9	27
Buckner	79	2095	689	299	.434	154	83	.539	91	173	264	372	291	5	192	21	681	8.6	21
E. Smith	34	789	253	113	.447	105	61	.581	52	156	208	30	109	2	19	69	287	8.4	21
Price	6	111	41	21	.512	9	7	.778	4	9	13	15	14	0	7	1	49	8.2	20
Carter (Tot)	61	1112	500	209	.418	96	68	.708	55	62	117	125	125	0	39	9	486	8.0	27
Carter (Mil)	47	875	399	166	.416	77	58	.753	45	48	93	104	96	0	28	7	390	8.3	27
Lloyd	69	1025	324	153	.472	126	95	.754	81	129	210	33	158	5	21	13	401	5.8	22
Restani	64	1116	334	173	.518	24	12	.500	81	181	262	88	102	0	33	11	358	5.6	22
English	60	648	277	132	.477	60	46	.767	68	100	168	25	78	0	17	18	310	5.2	21
Walton	53	678	188	88	.468	65	53	.815	15	36	51	141	52	0	40	2	229	4.3	13
Davis	19	165	68	29	.426	25	23	.920	11	18	29	20	11	0	6	4	81	4.3	9
Garrett (Tot)	62	598	239	106	.444	51	41	.804	37	75	112	27	80	0	21	10	253	4.1	12
Garrett (Mil)	33	383	146	66	.452	29	23	.739	27	45	72	20	50	0	14	7	155	4.7	12
McDonald	9	79	34	8	.235	4	3	.750	8	4	12	7	11	0	4	0	19	2.1	12

NEW ORLEANS JAZZ

Player	G.	Min.	FGA	FGM	Pct.	FTA	FTM	Pct.	Off. Reb.	Def. Reb.	Tot. Reb.	Ast.	PF	Disq.	Stl.	Blk. Sh.	Pts.	Avg.	Hi.
Maravich	73	3041	2047	886	.433	600	501	.835	90	284	374	392	191	1	84	22	2273	31.1	68
Goodrich	27	609	305	136	.446	85	68	.800	25	36	61	74	43	0	22	2	340	12.6	28
Williams	79	1776	917	414	.451	194	146	.753	107	199	306	92	200	0	76	16	974	12.3	41
James	52	1059	486	238	.490	114	89	.781	56	130	186	55	127	1	20	5	565	10.9	36
McElroy	73	2029	640	301	.470	217	169	.779	55	128	183	260	119	3	60	8	771	10.6	37
Boyd	47	1212	406	194	.478	98	79	.806	19	71	90	147	78	0	44	6	467	9.9	24
Behagen	60	1170	509	213	.418	126	90	.714	144	287	431	83	166	1	41	19	516	8.6	24
Coleman	77	2369	628	290	.462	112	82	.732	149	399	548	103	280	9	62	32	662	8.2	22
Kelley	76	1505	386	184	.477	197	156	.792	210	377	587	208	244	7	45	63	524	6.9	21
Stallworth	40	526	272	126	.463	29	17	.586	19	52	71	23	76	1	19	11	269	6.7	26
Moore	81	2084	477	193	.405	134	91	.679	170	466	636	181	231	3	54	117	477	5.9	17
Griffin	81	1645	256	140	.547	201	145	.721	167	328	495	167	241	6	50	43	425	5.2	20
Howard (Tot)	32	345	132	64	.485	35	24	.686	17	22	39	42	51	0	17	8	152	4.8	17
Howard (N.O.)	23	317	117	56	.479	29	19	.655	15	19	34	37	44	0	16	6	131	5.7	17
Walker	40	438	156	72	.462	47	36	.766	23	52	75	32	59	0	20	7	180	4.5	17

NEW YORK KNICKERBOCKERS

Player	G.	Min.	FGA	FGM	Pct.	FTA	FTM	Pct.	Off. Reb.	Def. Reb.	Tot. Reb.	Ast.	PF	Disq.	Stl.	Blk. Sh.	Pts.	Avg.	Hi.
McAdoo (Tot)	72	2798	1445	740	.512	516	281	.738	199	727	926	205	262	3	77	99	1861	25.8	43
McAdoo (Ks)	52	2031	1045	558	.534	358	271	.757	133	529	662	140	188	2	61	65	1387	26.7	43
Monroe	77	2656	1185	613	.517	366	307	.839	45	178	223	366	197	0	91	23	1533	19.9	37
Frazier	76	2687	1089	532	.489	336	259	.771	52	241	293	403	194	0	132	9	1323	17.4	41
Haywood	31	1021	449	202	.450	131	109	.832	77	203	280	50	72	0	14	29	513	16.5	35
Shelton	82	2104	836	398	.476	225	159	.707	220	413	633	149	363	10	125	98	955	11.6	31
Gianelli	19	630	182	86	.473	48	35	.729	60	118	178	26	54	0	14	28	207	10.9	19
McMillian	67	2158	642	298	.464	86	67	.779	66	241	307	139	103	0	63	5	663	9.9	25
McMillen (Tot)	76	1492	563	274	.487	123	96	.780	114	275	389	67	163	0	11	6	644	8.5	31
McMillen (Ks)	56	1222	471	229	.486	87	70	.805	85	232	317	51	134	0	10	4	528	9.4	31
Layton	56	765	277	134	.484	73	58	.795	11	36	47	154	87	0	21	6	326	5.8	24
Burden	61	608	352	148	.420	85	51	.600	26	40	66	62	88	0	47	1	347	5.7	21
Walk	11	135	57	28	.491	7	6	.857	5	22	27	6	22	0	4	3	62	5.6	17
Beard	70	1082	293	148	.505	109	75	.688	50	113	163	144	137	0	57	5	371	5.3	18
Davis	22	342	110	41	.373	31	22	.710	30	70	100	24	45	0	9	1	104	4.7	13
Bradley	67	1027	274	127	.464	42	34	.810	27	76	103	128	122	0	25	8	288	4.3	20
Jackson	76	1033	232	102	.440	71	51	.718	75	154	229	85	184	4	33	18	255	3.4	19
Meminger	32	254	36	15	.417	23	13	.565	12	14	26	29	17	0	8	1	43	1.3	10

With George McGinnis (above) and Julius Erving on the same team, Philadelphia was favored to win the title in 1976-77. But the 76ers lost, in six games, to Portland in the finals.

NEW YORK NETS

Player	G.	Min.	FGA	FGM	Pct.	FTA	FTM	Pct.	Off. Reb.	Def. Reb.	Tot. Reb.	Ast.	PF	Disq.	Stl.	Blk. Sh.	Pts.	Avg.	Hi.
Williamson	42	1426	803	357	.445	204	161	.789	24	95	119	90	143	3	59	6	875	20.8	37
Archibald	34	1277	560	250	.446	251	197	.785	22	58	80	254	77	1	59	11	697	20.5	34
Hawkins	52	1481	909	406	.447	282	194	.688	67	87	154	93	163	2	77	26	1006	19.3	44
Skinner	79	2256	887	382	.431	292	231	.791	112	251	363	289	279	7	103	53	995	12.6	24
Bantom (Tot)	77	1909	755	361	.478	310	224	.723	184	287	471	102	233	7	63	49	946	12.3	32
Bantom (Nts)	33	1114	474	224	.473	226	166	.735	101	184	285	50	120	4	28	28	614	18.6	32
Love (Tot)	27	724	307	117	.381	85	68	.800	53	58	111	27	70	1	9	4	302	11.2	22
Love (Nets)	13	228	106	49	.462	39	33	.846	15	23	38	4	23	0	1	2	131	10.1	20
Jones	34	877	348	134	.385	121	92	.760	48	146	194	46	109	2	38	11	360	10.6	20
van B. Kolff	72	2398	609	271	.445	228	195	.855	156	304	460	117	205	2	74	68	737	10.2	24
Bassett	76	2442	739	293	.396	177	101	.571	175	466	641	109	246	10	95	53	687	9.0	24
McNeill	8	93	51	18	.353	30	24	.800	10	16	26	3	13	1	4	1	60	7.5	23

Player	G.	Min.	FGA	FGM	Pct.	FTA	FTM	Pct.	Off. Reb.	Def. Reb.	Tot. Reb.	Ast.	PF	Disq.	Stl.	Blk. Sh.	Pts.	Avg.	Hi.
Davis (Tot)	56	1094	464	168	.362	91	64	.703	98	195	293	71	130	0	31	5	400	7.1	25
Davis (Nets)	34	752	354	127	.359	60	42	.700	68	125	193	47	85	0	22	4	296	8.7	25
Fox	71	1165	398	184	.462	114	95	.833	100	229	329	49	158	1	20	25	463	6.5	21
Wohl (Tot)	51	986	290	116	.400	89	61	.685	16	65	81	142	115	2	39	6	293	5.7	22
Wohl (Nets)	37	924	273	109	.399	85	57	.671	15	61	76	127	97	1	39	6	275	7.4	22
Terry	61	1075	318	128	.403	62	48	.774	43	100	143	39	120	0	58	10	304	5.0	19
Hughes	81	2081	354	151	.427	69	19	.275	189	375	564	98	308	9	122	119	321	4.0	14
Daniels	11	126	35	13	.371	23	13	.565	10	24	34	6	29	0	3	11	39	3.5	7
Williams	1	7	2	0	.000	6	3	.500	1	1	2	1	2	0	1	3	3	3.0	3
Hackett	1	8	2	0	.000	5	2	.400	1	2	3	0	1	0	0	0	2	2.0	2

PHILADELPHIA 76ers

Player	G.	Min.	FGA	FGM	Pct.	FTA	FTM	Pct.	Off. Reb.	Def. Reb.	Tot. Reb.	Ast.	PF	Disq.	Stl.	Blk. Sh.	Pts.	Avg.	Hi.
Erving	82	2940	1373	685	.499	515	400	.777	192	503	695	306	251	1	159	113	1770	21.6	40
McGinnis	79	2769	1349	659	.458	546	372	.681	324	587	911	302	299	4	163	37	1690	21.4	37
Collins	58	2037	823	426	.518	250	210	.840	64	131	195	271	174	2	70	15	1062	18.3	33
Free	78	2253	1022	467	.457	464	334	.720	97	140	237	266	207	2	75	25	1268	16.3	39
Mix	75	1958	551	288	.523	263	215	.817	127	249	376	152	167	0	90	20	791	10.5	37
Bibby	81	2639	702	302	.430	282	221	.784	86	187	273	356	200	2	108	5	825	10.2	28
Carter	14	237	101	43	.426	19	10	.526	10	14	24	21	29	0	11	2	96	6.9	19
Jones	82	2023	424	215	.507	116	64	.552	190	476	666	92	301	3	43	200	494	6.0	16
Dawkins	59	684	215	135	.628	79	40	.506	59	171	230	24	129	1	12	49	310	5.3	20
Dunleavy	32	359	145	60	.414	45	34	.756	10	24	34	56	64	1	13	2	154	4.8	32
Bryant	61	612	240	107	.446	70	53	.757	45	72	117	48	84	1	36	13	267	4.4	22
Barnett	16	231	64	28	.438	18	10	.556	7	7	14	23	28	0	4	0	66	4.1	10
Catchings	53	864	123	62	.504	47	33	.702	64	170	234	30	130	1	23	78	157	3.0	16
Furlow	32	174	100	34	.340	18	16	.889	18	21	39	19	11	0	7	2	84	2.6	13

PHOENIX SUNS

Player	G.	Min.	FGA	FGM	Pct.	FTA	FTM	Pct.	Off. Reb.	Def. Reb.	Tot. Reb.	Ast.	PF	Disq.	Stl.	Blk. Sh.	Pts.	Avg.	Hi.
Westphal	81	2600	1317	682	.518	439	362	.825	57	133	190	459	171	1	134	21	1726	21.3	40
Adams	72	2278	1102	522	.474	334	252	.754	180	472	652	322	260	4	95	87	1296	18.0	47
Sobers	79	2005	834	414	.496	289	243	.841	82	152	234	238	258	3	93	14	1071	13.6	32
Perry	44	1391	414	834	.432	142	112	.789	149	246	395	79	163	3	49	28	472	10.7	20
Lee	82	1849	786	347	.441	210	142	.676	99	200	299	263	276	10	156	33	836	10.2	33
Heard	46	1363	457	173	.379	138	100	.725	120	320	440	89	139	2	55	55	446	9.7	28
Terrell	78	1751	545	277	.508	176	111	.631	99	288	387	103	165	0	41	47	665	8.5	22
D. Van Arsdale	78	1535	498	227	.456	166	145	.873	31	86	117	120	94	0	35	5	599	7.7	19
Erickson	50	949	294	142	.483	50	37	.740	36	108	144	104	122	0	30	7	321	6.4	19
T. Van Arsdale	77	1425	395	171	.433	145	102	.703	47	137	184	67	163	0	20	3	444	5.8	20
Awtrey	72	1760	373	160	.429	126	91	.722	111	245	356	182	170	1	23	31	411	5.7	17
Feher	48	487	162	86	.531	99	76	.768	18	56	74	36	46	0	11	7	248	5.2	23
Schlueter	39	337	72	26	.361	31	18	.581	30	50	80	38	62	0	8	8	70	1.8	7

PORTLAND TRAIL BLAZERS

Player	G.	Min.	FGA	FGM	Pct.	FTA	FTM	Pct.	Off. Reb.	Def. Reb.	Tot. Reb.	Ast.	PF	Disq.	Stl.	Blk. Sh.	Pts.	Avg.	Hi.
Lucas	79	2863	1357	632	.466	438	335	.765	271	628	899	229	294	6	83	56	1599	20.2	41
Walton	65	2264	930	491	.528	327	228	.697	211	723	934	245	174	5	66	211	1210	18.6	30
Hollins	76	2224	1046	4526	.432	287	215	.749	52	158	210	313	265	5	166	38	1119	14.7	43
Gross	82	2232	711	376	.529	183	215	.851	173	221	394	242	255	7	107	57	935	11.4	25
Twardzik	74	1937	430	263	.612	284	239	.842	75	127	202	247	228	6	128	15	765	10.3	28
Steele	81	1680	652	326	.500	227	183	.806	71	117	188	172	216	3	118	13	835	10.3	28
Gilliam	80	1665	744	326	.438	120	92	.767	64	137	201	170	168	1	76	6	744	9.3	23
Davis	79	1451	531	234	.441	209	166	.794	62	64	126	148	128	1	41	11	634	8.0	25
Neal	58	955	340	160	.471	117	77	.675	87	168	255	58	148	0	8	35	397	6.8	20
Jones	63	1065	299	139	.465	66	109	.606	103	193	296	80	124	3	37	38	344	5.5	21
Walker	66	627	305	137	.449	100	67	.670	45	63	108	51	92	0	14	2	341	5.2	19
Calhoun	70	743	183	85	.464	85	66	.776	40	104	144	35	123	1	24	8	236	3.4	16
Mayes (Tot)	9	52	19	5	.263	7	3	.429	10	6	16	3	12	0	0	4	13	1.4	4
Mayes (Port.)	5	24	9	2	.222	0	0	......	6	0	6	0	5	0	0	2	4	0.4	2

SAN ANTONIO SPURS

Player	G.	Min.	FGA	FGM	Pct.	FTA	FTM	Pct.	Off. Reb.	Def. Reb.	Tot. Reb.	Ast.	PF	Disq.	Stl.	Blk. Sh.	Pts.	Avg.	Hi.
Gervin	82	2705	1335	726	.544	532	443	.833	134	320	454	238	286	12	105	104	1895	23.1	42
Kenon	78	2936	1435	706	.492	356	293	.823	282	597	879	229	190	0	167	60	1705	21.9	43
Paultz	82	2694	1102	521	.473	320	238	.744	192	495	687	223	262	5	55	173	1280	15.6	31
Bristow	82	2017	747	365	.489	258	206	.798	119	229	348	240	195	1	89	2	936	11.4	25
Olberding	82	1949	598	301	.503	316	251	.794	162	287	449	119	277	6	59	29	853	10.4	23
Gale	82	2598	754	353	.468	167	137	.820	54	219	273	473	224	3	191	50	843	10.3	24
Silas	22	356	142	61	.430	107	87	.813	7	25	32	50	36	0	13	3	209	9.5	28
Galvin	35	606	237	93	.392	146	123	.842	11	20	31	104	58	0	23	1	309	8.8	24
Dietrick	82	1772	620	285	.460	166	119	.717	111	261	372	148	267	8	88	57	689	8.4	24
Dampier	80	1634	507	233	.460	86	64	.744	22	54	76	234	93	0	49	15	530	6.6	21
Nelson	4	57	14	7	.500	7	4	.571	2	5	7	3	9	0	2	0	18	4.5	7
Ward	27	171	90	34	.378	17	15	.882	10	23	33	6	30	0	6	5	83	3.1	16
Karl	29	251	73	25	.342	42	29	.690	4	13	17	46	36	0	10	0	79	2.7	9
D'Antoni	2	9	3	1	.333	2	1	.500	0	2	2	2	3	0	0	0	3	1.5	2

SEATTLE SUPERSONICS

Player	G.	Min.	FGA	FGM	Pct.	FTA	FTM	Pct.	Off. Reb.	Def. Reb.	Tot. Reb.	Ast.	PF	Disq.	Stl.	Blk. Sh.	Pts.	Avg.	Hi.
Brown	72	2098	1114	534	.479	190	168	.884	68	164	232	176	140	1	124	19	1236	17.2	42
Watts	79	2627	1015	428	.422	293	172	.587	81	226	307	630	256	5	214	25	1028	13.0	37
Gray	25	643	262	114	.435	78	59	.756	23	84	107	55	84	1	27	13	287	11.5	23

Player	G.	Min.	FGA	FGM	Pct.	FTA	FTM	Pct.	Off. Reb.	Def. Reb.	Tot. Reb.	Ast.	PF	Disq.	Stl.	Blk. Sh.	Pts.	Avg.	Hi.
Weatherspoon (T)..	62	1657	690	310	.449	144	91	.632	120	308	428	53	168	1	52	28	711	11.5	25
Weatherspoon (S)..	51	1505	614	283	.461	136	86	.632	109	295	404	51	149	1	49	23	652	12.8	25
Seals	81	1977	851	378	.444	195	138	.708	118	236	354	93	262	6	49	58	864	11.0	38
Green	76	1928	658	290	.441	235	166	.706	191	312	503	120	201	1	45	129	746	9.8	31
Burleson	82	1803	652	288	.442	301	220	.731	184	367	551	93	259	1	74	117	796	9.7	26
Johnson	81	1667	566	285	.504	287	179	.624	161	141	302	123	221	3	123	57	749	9.2	24
Norwood	76	1647	461	216	.469	206	151	.733	127	165	292	99	191	1	62	6	583	7.7	21
Bantom	44	795	281	137	.488	84	58	.690	83	103	186	52	113	3	35	21	332	7.5	18
Love (Tot)	59	1174	428	162	.379	132	109	.826	79	119	198	48	120	1	22	6	433	7.3	22
Love (Sea.)	32	450	121	45	.372	47	41	.872	26	61	87	21	50	0	13	2	131	4.1	14
Wilkerson	78	1552	573	221	.386	122	84	.689	96	162	258	171	136	0	72	8	526	6.7	20
Tolson	60	587	242	137	.566	159	85	.535	73	84	157	27	83	0	32	21	359	6.0	19
Oleynick	50	516	223	81	.363	53	39	.736	13	32	45	60	48	0	13	4	201	4.0	19
Barnhill	4	10	6	2	.333	0	0	......	2	1	3	1	5	0	0	0	4	1.0	2

WASHINGTON BULLETS

Player	G.	Min.	FGA	FGM	Pct.	FTA	FTM	Pct.	Off. Reb.	Def. Reb.	Tot. Reb.	Ast.	PF	Disq.	Stl.	Blk. Sh.	Pts.	Avg.	Hi.
Hayes	82	3364	1516	760	.501	614	422	.687	289	740	1029	158	312	1	87	220	1942	23.7	47
Chenier	78	2842	1472	654	.444	321	270	.841	56	243	299	294	166	0	120	39	1578	20.2	38
Robinson	41	1328	522	264	.478	189	128	.677	119	247	366	45	123	0	28	18	656	16.0	33
Henderson (Tot)	87	2791	826	371	.449	313	233	.744	43	196	239	598	148	0	138	17	975	11.2	27
Henderson (Wash.)	41	1223	373	175	.469	145	107	.738	25	90	115	212	74	0	59	9	457	11.1	23
Bing	64	1516	597	271	.454	176	136	.773	54	89	143	275	150	1	61	5	678	10.6	32
Kupchak	82	1513	596	341	.572	246	170	.691	183	311	494	62	204	3	22	34	852	10.4	26
Wright	78	1421	595	262	.440	115	88	.765	32	66	98	232	170	0	55	5	612	7.8	27
Unseld	82	2860	551	270	.490	166	100	.602	243	634	877	363	253	5	87	45	640	7.8	18
Gray (Tot)	83	1639	592	258	.436	158	118	.747	84	209	293	124	273	9	58	31	634	7.6	23
Gray (Wash.)	58	996	330	144	.436	80	59	.738	61	125	186	69	189	8	31	18	347	6.0	18
Grevey	76	1306	530	224	.423	119	79	.664	73	105	178	68	148	1	29	9	527	6.9	22
Weatherspoon	11	152	76	27	.355	8	5	.625	11	13	24	2	19	0	3	5	59	5.4	14
Weiss	62	768	133	62	.466	37	29	.784	15	54	69	130	66	0	53	7	153	2.5	10
Pace	30	119	55	24	.436	29	16	.552	16	18	34	4	29	0	2	17	64	2.1	12
Jones	3	33	9	2	.222	4	2	.500	1	3	4	1	4	0	2	0	6	2.0	4
Riordan	49	289	94	34	.362	15	11	.733	7	20	27	20	33	0	3	2	79	1.6	8

PLAYOFF RESULTS

EASTERN CONFERENCE FIRST ROUND

Boston 2, San Antonio 0

Apr. 12—Tue.—San Antonio 94 at Boston.................................104
Apr. 15—Fri.—Boston 113 at San Antonio 109

Washington 2, Cleveland 1

Apr. 13—Wed.—Cleveland 100 at Washington.............................109
Apr. 15—Fri.—Washington 83 at Cleveland 91
Apr. 17—Sun.—Cleveland 98 at Washington 104

EASTERN CONFERENCE SEMIFINALS

Philadelphia 4, Boston 3

Apr. 17—Sun.—Boston 113 at Philadelphia 111
Apr. 20—Wed.—Boston 101 at Philadelphia 113
Apr. 22—Fri.—Philadelphia 109 at Boston 100
Apr. 24—Sun.—Philadelphia 119 at Boston 124
Apr. 27—Wed.—Boston 91 at Philadelphia 110
Apr. 29—Fri.—Philadelphia 108 at Boston 113
May 1—Sun.—Boston 77 at Philadelphia 83

Houston 4, Washington 2

Apr. 19—Tue.—Washington 111 at Houston 101
Apr. 21—Thur.—Washington 118 at Houston 124*
Apr. 24—Sun.—Houston 90 at Washington 93
Apr. 26—Tue.—Houston 107 at Washington 103
Apr. 29—Fri.—Washington 115 at Houston 123
May 1—Sun.—Houston 108 at Washington 103

EASTERN CONFERENCE FINALS

Philadelphia 4, Houston 2

May 5—Thur.—Houston 117 at Philadelphia 128
May 8—Sun.—Houston 97 at Philadelphia 106
May 11—Wed.—Philadelphia 94 at Houston 118
May 13—Fri.—Philadelphia 107 at Houston 95
May 15—Sun.—Houston 118 at Philadelphia 115
May 17—Tue.—Philadelphia 112 at Houston 109

WESTERN CONFERENCE FIRST ROUND

Golden State 2, Detroit 1

Apr. 12—Tue.—Detroit 95 at Golden State 90
Apr. 14—Thur.—Golden State 138 at Detroit 108
Apr. 17—Sun.—Detroit 101 at Golden State...............................109

Portland 2, Chicago 1

Apr. 12—Tue.—Chicago 83 at Portland 96
Apr. 15—Fri.—Portland 104 at Chicago 107
Apr. 17—Sun.—Chicago 98 at Portland 106

WESTERN CONFERENCE SEMIFINALS

Los Angeles 4, Golden State 3

Apr. 20—Wed.—Golden State 106 at Los Angeles 115
Apr. 22—Fri.—Golden State 86 at Los Angeles 95
Apr. 24—Sun.—Los Angeles 105 at Golden State 109
Apr. 26—Tue.—Los Angeles 103 at Golden State 114
Apr. 29—Fri.—Golden State 105 at Los Angeles..........................112
May 1—Sun.—Los Angeles 106 at Golden State 115
May 4—Wed.—Golden State 84 at Los Angeles 97

Portland 4, Denver 2

Apr. 20—Wed.—Portland 101 at Denver 100
Apr. 22—Fri.—Portland 110 at Denver 121
Apr. 24—Sun.—Denver 106 at Portland 110
Apr. 26—Tue.—Denver 96 at Portland 105
May 1—Sun.—Portland 105 at Denver 114*
May 2—Mon.—Denver 92 at Portland 108

WESTERN CONFERENCE FINALS

Portland 4, Los Angeles 0

May 6—Fri.—Portland 121 at Los Angeles 109
May 8—Sun.—Portland 99 at Los Angeles 97
May 10—Tue.—Los Angeles 97 at Portland.................................102
May 13—Fri.—Los Angeles 101 at Portland 105

WORLD CHAMPIONSHIP SERIES

Portland 4, Philadelphia 2

May 22—Sun.—Portland 101 at Philadelphia 107
May 26—Thur.—Portland 89 at Philadelphia 107
May 29—Sun.—Philadelphia 107 at Portland 129
May 31—Tue.—Philadelphia 98 at Portland 130
June 3—Fri.—Portland 110 at Philadelphia 104
June 5—Sun.—Philadelphia 107 at Portland 109

*Denotes overtime period.

1975-76 NBA STATISTICS

1975-76 NBA CHAMPION BOSTON CELTICS

Seated (Left to Right): Charlie Scott, Paul Silas, Dave Cowens, Irving Levin, Chairman of the Board; Coach Tom Heinsohn, President Arnold (Red) Auerbach, Captain John Havlicek, Jo Jo White, Don Nelson. Standing (Left to Right): Dr. Tom Silva, Mark Volk, assistant trainer; Kevin Stacom, Glenn McDonald, Tom Boswell, Jim Ard, Steve Kuberski, Jerome Anderson, Frank Challant, trainer; Dr. Sam Kane. Inset: John Killilea, assistant coach and chief scout.

FINAL STANDINGS

ATLANTIC DIVISION

Team	Atl.	Bos.	Buf.	Chi.	Cle.	Det.	G.S.	Hou.	KC	L.A.	Mil.	N.O.	N.Y.	Phi.	Pho.	Por.	Sea.	Was.	W.	L.	Pct.	G.B.
Boston	3	..	4	2	3	4	2	4	2	4	2	4	5	4	4	2	2	3	54	28	.659	..
Buffalo	3	3	..	3	3	1	1	3	4	2	3	4	4	3	3	2	2	2	46	36	.561	8
Philadelphia	3	3	4	4	2	3	1	2	3	2	2	4	2	..	3	4	2	2	46	36	.561	8
New York	2	2	3	4	2	1	..	2	3	1	2	3	..	5	2	3	..	3	38	44	.463	16

CENTRAL DIVISION

Team	Atl.	Bos.	Buf.	Chi.	Cle.	Det.	G.S.	Hou.	KC	L.A.	Mil.	N.O.	N.Y.	Phi.	Pho.	Por.	Sea.	Was.	W.	L.	Pct.	G.B.
Cleveland	5	2	2	4	..	2	1	2	1	2	4	4	3	3	3	4	3	4	49	33	.598	..
Washington	5	2	3	4	2	2	1	4	3	3	2	3	2	3	4	2	3	..	48	34	.585	1
Houston	5	1	2	3	4	2	2	..	2	1	2	2	3	3	1	3	1	4	40	42	.488	9
New Orleans	4	1	1	2	3	3	2	4	3	1	2	..	2	3	2	1	2	1	38	44	.463	11
Atlanta	..	2	2	2	2	1	2	2	2	1	2	2	3	2	2	2	1	1	29	53	.354	20

MIDWEST DIVISION

Team	Atl.	Bos.	Buf.	Chi.	Cle.	Det.	G.S.	Hou.	KC	L.A.	Mil.	N.O.	N.Y.	Phi.	Pho.	Por.	Sea.	Was.	W.	L.	Pct.	G.B.
Milwaukee	2	2	1	4	4	4	3	2	5	3	..	2	2	3	2	2	2	2	38	44	.463	..
Detroit	3	0	3	4	2	..	0	0	2	5	1	3	1	1	2	3	2	2	36	46	.439	2
Kansas City	2	2	..	6	3	2	1	2	..	2	1	3	3	1	2	1	2	1	31	51	.378	7
Chicago	2	2	1	..	3	1	1	1	3	2	2	2	2	2	1	2	1	1	24	58	.293	14

PACIFIC DIVISION

Team	Atl.	Bos.	Buf.	Chi.	Cle.	Det.	G.S.	Hou.	KC	L.A.	Mil.	N.O.	N.Y.	Phi.	Pho.	Por.	Sea.	Was.	W.	L.	Pct.	G.B.
Golden State	2	2	3	4	3	5	..	2	4	5	5	2	4	3	4	4	4	3	59	23	.720	..
Seattle	3	2	2	3	1	2	3	2	3	3	3	4	2	3	3	3	..	1	43	39	.524	16
Phoenix	4	2	1	3	1	4	2	4	2	4	2	3	2	1	..	5	4	1	42	40	.512	17
Los Angeles	3	2	2	2	2	4	2	3	3	..	2	3	3	2	2	3	3	1	40	42	.488	19
Portland	2	2	2	4	3	3	2	1	5	4	3	1	1	3	2	..	3	2	37	45	.451	22

HOME-ROAD RECORDS OF ALL TEAMS

Team	Home	Road	Total	Team	Home	Road	Total
Atlanta	20- 21	9- 32	29- 53	Milwaukee	22- 19	16- 25	38- 44
Boston	31- 10	23- 18	54- 28	New Orleans	22- 19	16- 25	38- 44
Buffalo	28- 13	18- 23	46- 36	New York	24- 17	14- 27	38- 44
Chicago	15- 26	9- 32	24- 58	Philadelphia	34- 7	12- 29	46- 36
Cleveland	29- 12	20- 21	49- 33	Phoenix	27- 14	15- 26	42- 40
Detroit	24- 17	12- 29	36- 46	Portland	26- 15	11- 30	37- 45
Golden State	36- 5	23- 18	59- 23	Seattle	31- 10	12- 29	43- 39
Houston	28- 13	12- 29	40- 42	Washington	31- 10	17- 24	48- 34
Los Angeles	31- 10	9- 32	40- 42	Total	484- 254	254- 484	738- 738

OFFENSIVE TEAM STATISTICS

		FIELD GOALS			FREE THROWS			REBOUNDS			MISCELLANEOUS				Turn	Blk.	SCORING	
Team	G.	Att.	Made	Pct.	Att.	Made	Pct.	Off.	Def.	Tot.	Ast.	PF	Disq.	Stl.	Over	Sh.	Pts.	Avg.
Golden State	82	7982	3691	.462	2158	1620	.751	1349	2912	4261	2041	2022	13	928	1613	416	9002	109.8
Buffalo	82	7307	3481	.476	2368	1833	.774	1002	2719	3721	2112	2017	22	720	1743	366	8795	107.3
Los Angeles	82	7622	3547	.465	2164	1670	.772	1132	2870	4002	1939	2025	24	674	1612	528	8764	106.9
Philadelphia	82	7752	3462	.447	2469	1811	.733	1385	2685	4069	1658	2187	35	809	1729	367	8735	106.5
Seattle	82	7730	3542	.458	2309	1642	.711	1217	2498	3715	1935	2133	38	866	1615	355	8726	106.4
Boston	82	7901	3527	.446	2120	1654	.780	1369	2972	4341	1980	2002	37	561	1609	260	8708	106.2
Houston	82	7304	3546	.485	2046	1616	.790	1059	2644	3703	2213	2045	36	656	1665	359	8708	106.2
Phoenix	82	7251	3420	.472	2337	1780	.762	1108	2558	3666	2083	2018	31	853	1852	349	8620	105.1
Detroit	82	7598	3524	.464	2049	1557	.760	1205	2545	3750	1751	2086	26	786	1619	332	8605	104.9
New Orleans	82	7491	3352	.447	2415	1831	.758	1189	2779	3968	1765	2175	30	750	1659	343	8535	104.1
Portland	82	7292	3417	.469	2350	1699	.723	1116	2843	3959	2094	2091	35	776	1867	408	8533	104.1
Kansas City	82	7379	3341	.453	2335	1792	.767	1133	2668	3801	1864	2056	44	751	1607	324	8474	103.3
Washington	82	7234	3416	.472	2215	1595	.720	1019	2812	3831	1823	1921	20	696	1672	485	8427	102.8
New York	82	7555	3443	.456	1985	1532	.772	1022	2723	3745	1660	2006	14	575	1403	259	8418	102.7
Atlanta	82	7338	3301	.450	2467	1809	.733	1225	2540	3765	1666	1983	39	790	1553	277	8411	102.6
Milwaukee	82	7435	3456	.465	1952	1437	.736	1094	2688	3782	1817	2041	30	715	1624	468	8349	101.8
Cleveland	82	7709	3497	.454	1827	1346	.737	1192	2588	3780	1844	1871	10	638	1330	397	8340	101.7
Chicago	82	7499	3106	.414	2197	1651	.751	1375	2726	4101	1704	1977	37	627	1413	255	7863	95.9

DEFENSIVE TEAM STATISTICS

	FIELD GOALS			FREE THROWS			REBOUNDS			MISCELLANEOUS				Turn	Blk.	SCORING		Pt.
Team	Att.	Made	Pct.	Att.	Made	Pct.	Off.	Def.	Tot.	Ast.	PF	Disq.	Stl.	Over	Sh.	Pts.	Avg.	Dif.
Chicago	6946	3246	.467	2137	1609	.753	930	2809	3739	1669	2081	615	31	1485	461	8101	98.8	− 2.9
Cleveland	7188	3262	.454	2152	1610	.748	1134	2792	3926	1728	1860	610	17	1579	325	8134	99.2	+ 2.5
Washington	7636	3377	.442	1992	1482	.744	1145	2687	3832	1705	1988	810	33	1510	338	8236	100.4	+ 2.4
Golden State	7742	3437	.444	2150	1583	.736	1288	2730	4018	2006	1946	743	22	1761	395	8457	103.1	+ 6.7
Milwaukee	7624	3402	.446	2182	1664	.763	1229	2604	3833	1897	1828	683	21	1503	325	8468	103.3	− 1.5
Boston	7772	3489	.449	2074	1538	.742	1037	2659	3696	1835	1895	650	25	1422	334	8516	103.9	+ 2.3
New York	7426	3407	.459	2274	1705	.750	1068	2891	3959	1812	1954	608	31	1453	335	8519	103.9	− 1.2
Phoenix	7357	3444	.468	2265	1682	.743	1143	2513	3656	1979	2163	912	41	1746	336	8570	104.5	− 0.6
New Orleans	7413	3396	.458	2464	1816	.737	1182	2846	4028	1684	2162	777	40	1748	405	8608	105.0	− 0.9
Portland	7531	3405	.452	2333	1825	.782	1121	2657	3778	1920	2128	917	29	1613	386	8635	105.3	− 1.2
Atlanta	7357	3529	.480	2102	1592	.757	1186	2728	3914	1778	2177	779	30	1663	427	8650	105.5	− 2.9
Detroit	7479	3492	.467	2211	1707	.772	1218	2690	3908	2014	1914	724	21	1671	437	8691	106.0	− 1.1
Kansas City	7454	3477	.466	2310	1753	.759	1153	2778	3931	1825	2124	680	26	1639	321	8707	106.2	− 2.9
Philadelphia	7737	3467	.448	2334	1780	.763	1435	2717	4152	1849	2151	730	37	1794	342	8714	106.3	+ 0.2
Buffalo	7722	3558	.461	2156	1611	.747	1183	2645	3828	2079	2137	729	38	1660	319	8727	106.4	+ 0.9
Seattle	7464	3486	.467	2407	1777	.738	1239	2713	3952	2109	2111	745	34	1852	388	8749	106.7	− 0.3
Los Angeles	7980	3592	.450	2148	1573	.732	1384	2837	4221	2032	1987	775	22	1564	363	8757	106.8	+ 0.1
Houston	7551	3603	.477	2072	1568	.757	1116	2473	3589	2028	2050	684	23	1522	311	8774	107.0	− 0.8

Dsq.—Individual players disqualified (fouled out of game).

INDIVIDUAL LEADERS

POINTS
Minimum: 70 games played or 1400 points

	G.	FG	FT	Pts.	Avg.		G.	FG	FT	Pts.	Avg.
McAdoo, Buff.	78	934	559	2427	31.1	Murphy, Hou.	82	675	372	1722	21.0
Abdul-Jabbar, L.A.	82	914	447	2275	27.7	Collins, Phil.	77	614	372	1600	20.8
Maravich, N.O.	62	604	396	1604	25.9	Monroe, N.Y.	76	647	280	1574	20.7
Archibald, K.C.	78	717	501	1935	24.8	Westphal, Phoe.	82	657	365	1679	20.5
F. Brown, Sea.	76	742	273	1757	23.1	P. Smith, G.S.	82	659	323	1641	20.0
McGinnis, Phil.	77	647	475	1769	23.0	Chenier, Wash.	80	654	282	1590	19.9
R. Smith, Buff.	82	702	383	1787	21.8	Haywood, N.Y.	78	605	339	1549	19.9
Drew, Atl.	77	586	488	1660	21.6	Hayes, Wash.	80	649	287	1585	19.8
Dandridge, Mil.	73	650	271	1571	21.5	Goodrich, L.A.	75	583	293	1459	19.5
Barry, G.S.	81	707	287	1701	21.0	Love, Chi.	76	543	362	1448	19.1

FIELD GOALS
Minimum: 300 FG Made

	FGA	FGM	Pct.
Unseld, Wash.	567	318	.56085
Shumate, Phoe.-Buff.	592	332	.56081
McMillian, Buff.	918	492	.536
Lanier, Det.	1017	541	.532
Abdul-Jabbar, L.A.	1728	914	.529
E. Smith, Mil.	962	498	.518
Tomjanovich, Hou.	1202	622	.517
Collins, Phil.	1196	614	.513
O. Johnson, K.C.	678	348	.513
Newlin, Hou.	1123	569	.507

FREE THROWS
Minimum: 125 FT Made

	FTA	FTM	Pct.
Barry, G.S.	311	287	.923
Murphy, Hou.	410	372	.907
C. Russell, L.A.	148	132	.892
Bradley, N.Y.	148	130	.878
F. Brown, Sea.	314	273	.869
Newlin, Hou.	445	385	.865
J. Walker, K.C.	267	231	.865
McMillian, Buff.	219	188	.858
Marin, Buff.-Chi.	188	161	.856
Erickson, Phoe.	157	134	.854

ASSISTS
Minimum: 70 games or 400 assists

	G.	No.	Avg.
Watts, Sea.	82	661	8.1
Archibald, K.C.	78	615	7.9
Murphy, Hou.	82	596	7.3
Van Lier, Chi.	76	500	6.6
Barry, G.S.	81	496	6.1
Bing, Wash.	82	492	6.0
R. Smith, Buff.	82	484	5.9
A. Adams, Phoe.	80	450	5.6
Goodrich, L.A.	75	421	5.6
Newlin, Hou.	82	457	5.6

STEALS
Minimum: 70 games or 125 steals

	G.	No.	Avg.
Watts, Sea.	82	261	3.18
McGinnis, Phil.	77	198	2.57
Westphal, Phoe.	82	210	2.56
Barry, G.S.	81	202	2.49
C. Ford, Det.	82	178	2.17
Steele, Port.	81	170	2.10
Chenier, Wash.	80	158	1.98
Van Lier, Chi.	76	150	1.97
Mix, Phil.	81	158	1.95
F. Brown, Sea.	76	143	1.88

REBOUNDS
Minimum: 70 games or 800 rebounds

	G.	Off.	Def.	Tot.	Avg.
Abdul-Jabbar, L.A.	82	272	1111	1383	16.9
Cowens, Bos.	78	335	911	1246	16.0
Unseld, Wash.	78	271	765	1036	13.3
Silas, Bos.	81	365	660	1025	12.7
Lacey, K.C.	81	218	806	1024	12.6
McGinnis, Phil.	77	260	707	967	12.6
McAdoo, Buff.	78	241	724	965	12.4
E. Smith, Mil.	78	201	692	893	11.4
Haywood, N.Y.	78	234	644	878	11.3
Hayes, Wash.	80	210	668	878	11.0

BLOCKED SHOTS
Minimum: 70 games or 100 blocked shots

	G.	No.	Avg.
Abdul-Jabbar, L.A.	82	338	4.12
E. Smith, Mil.	78	238	3.05
Hayes, Wash.	80	202	2.53
Catchings, Phil.	75	164	2.19
G. Johnson, G.S.	82	174	2.12
McAdoo, Buff.	78	160	2.05
Burleson, Sea.	82	150	1.83
Moore, N.O.	81	136	1.68
Lacey, K.C.	81	134	1.65
Neal, Port.	68	107	1.57

TEAM-BY-TEAM INDIVIDUAL STATISTICS

ATLANTA HAWKS

Player	G.	Min.	FGA	FGM	Pct.	FTA	FTM	Pct.	Off. Reb.	Def. Reb.	Tot. Reb.	Ast.	PF	Disq.	Stl.	Blk. Sh.	Pts.	Avg.	Hi.
Drew	77	2351	1168	586	.502	656	488	.744	286	374	660	150	261	11	138	30	1660	21.6	42
Hudson	81	2558	1205	569	.472	291	237	.814	104	196	300	214	241	3	124	17	1375	17.0	42
Henderson	81	2900	1136	469	.413	305	216	.708	58	207	265	374	195	1	137	10	1154	14.2	33
T. Van Arsdale	75	2026	785	346	.441	166	126	.759	35	151	186	146	202	5	57	7	818	10.9	26
D. Jones	66	1762	542	251	.463	219	163	.744	171	353	524	83	214	8	52	61	665	10.1	24
Sojourner	67	1602	524	248	.473	119	80	.672	126	323	449	58	174	2	38	40	576	8.6	22
C. Hawkins	74	1907	530	237	.447	191	136	.712	102	343	445	212	172	2	80	46	610	8.2	22
J. Brown	75	1758	486	215	.442	209	162	.775	146	257	403	126	235	7	45	16	592	7.9	22
Meminger	68	1418	379	155	.409	152	100	.658	65	86	151	222	116	0	54	8	410	6.0	27
Holland	33	351	213	85	.399	34	22	.647	15	26	41	26	48	0	20	2	192	5.8	21
Willoughby	62	870	284	113	.398	100	66	.660	103	185	288	31	87	0	37	29	292	4.7	20
DuVal	13	130	43	15	.349	9	6	.667	1	7	8	20	15	0	6	2	36	2.8	10
Creighton	32	172	43	12	.279	16	7	.438	13	32	45	4	23	0	2	9	31	1.0	5

BOSTON CELTICS

Player	G.	Min.	FGA	FGM	Pct.	FTA	FTM	Pct.	Off. Reb.	Def. Reb.	Tot. Reb.	Ast.	PF	Disq.	Stl.	Blk. Sh.	Pts.	Avg.	Hi.
Cowens	78	3101	1305	611	.468	340	257	.756	335	911	1246	325	314	10	94	71	1479	19.0	39
J. White	82	3257	1492	670	.449	253	212	.838	61	252	313	445	183	2	107	20	1552	18.9	34
Scott	82	2913	1309	588	.449	335	267	.797	106	252	358	341	356	17	103	24	1443	17.6	32
Havlicek	76	2598	1121	504	.450	333	281	.844	116	198	314	278	204	1	97	29	1289	17.0	38
Silas	81	2662	740	315	.426	333	236	.709	365	660	1025	203	227	3	56	33	866	10.7	19
D. Nelson	75	943	379	175	.462	161	127	.789	56	126	182	77	115	0	14	7	477	6.4	27
McDonald	75	1019	456	191	.419	56	40	.714	56	79	135	68	123	0	39	20	422	5.6	18
Stacom	77	1114	387	170	.439	91	68	.747	62	99	161	128	117	0	23	5	408	5.3	16
Kuberski (Tot)	70	967	291	135	.464	79	71	.899	90	169	259	47	133	1	12	13	341	4.9	20
Kuberski (Bos)	60	882	274	128	.467	76	68	.895	86	148	234	44	123	1	11	11	324	5.4	20
Ard	81	853	294	107	.364	100	71	.710	96	193	289	48	141	2	12	36	285	3.5	18
J. Anderson	22	126	45	25	.556	16	11	.688	4	9	13	6	25	0	3	3	61	2.8	8
Boswell	35	275	93	41	.441	24	14	.583	26	45	71	16	70	1	2	1	96	2.7	9
Searcy	4	12	6	2	.333	2	2	1.000	0	0	0	1	4	0	0	0	6	1.5	2

BUFFALO BRAVES

Player	G.	Min.	FGA	FGM	Pct.	FTA	FTM	Pct.	Off. Reb.	Def. Reb.	Tot. Reb.	Ast.	PF	Disq.	Stl.	Blk. Sh.	Pts.	Avg.	Hi.
McAdoo	78	3328	1918	934	.487	734	559	.762	241	724	965	315	298	5	160	160	2427	31.1	52
R. Smith	82	3167	1422	702	.494	469	383	.817	104	313	417	484	274	5	153	4	1787	21.8	37
McMillian	74	2610	918	492	.536	219	188	.858	134	256	390	205	141	0	88	14	1172	15.8	35
Shumate (Tot)	75	1976	592	332	.561	326	212	.650	143	411	554	127	159	2	82	34	876	11.7	28
Shumate (Buf)	32	1046	254	146	.575	143	97	.678	82	232	314	65	83	1	38	18	389	12.2	25
Charles	81	2247	719	328	.456	205	161	.785	58	161	219	204	257	5	123	48	817	10.1	29
Heard	50	1527	492	207	.421	135	82	.607	138	373	511	126	183	0	66	55	496	9.9	20
Marin	12	278	94	41	.436	33	27	.818	10	30	40	23	30	0	7	6	109	9.1	23
DiGregorio	67	1364	474	182	.384	94	86	.915	15	97	112	265	158	1	37	1	450	6.7	22
McMillen	50	708	222	96	.432	54	41	.759	64	122	186	69	87	1	7	6	233	4.7	18
Gibbs	72	866	301	129	.429	93	77	.828	42	64	106	49	133	2	16	14	335	4.7	19
Weiss	66	995	183	89	.486	48	35	.729	13	53	66	150	94	0	48	14	213	3.2	17
D. Adams	56	704	170	67	.394	57	40	.702	38	107	145	73	128	1	30	7	174	3.1	20
Schlueter	71	773	122	61	.500	81	54	.667	58	166	224	80	141	1	13	17	176	2.5	9
Kuberski	10	85	17	7	.412	3	3	1.000	4	21	25	3	10	0	1	2	17	1.7	5
J. Washington	1	7	1	0	.000	0	0	.000	1	0	1	1	0	0	0	0	0	0.0	0

CHICAGO BULLS

Player	G.	Min.	FGA	FGM	Pct.	FTA	FTM	Pct.	Off. Reb.	Def. Reb.	Tot. Reb.	Ast.	PF	Disq.	Stl.	Blk. Sh.	Pts.	Avg.	Hi.
Love	76	2823	1391	543	.390	452	362	.801	191	319	510	145	233	3	63	10	1448	19.1	40
M. Johnson	81	2390	1033	478	.463	360	283	.786	279	479	758	130	292	8	93	66	1239	15.3	30
Van Lier	76	3026	987	361	.366	319	235	.737	138	272	410	500	298	9	150	26	957	12.6	28
Marin (Tot)	79	1909	812	343	.422	188	161	.856	69	183	252	141	164	0	45	11	847	10.7	34
Marin (Chi)	67	1631	718	302	.421	155	134	.865	59	153	212	118	134	0	38	5	738	11.0	34
Garrett	14	324	131	57	.435	44	38	.864	27	48	75	7	32	0	8	4	152	10.9	22
Sloan	22	617	210	84	.400	78	55	.705	40	76	116	22	77	1	27	5	223	10.1	21
Laskowski	71	1570	690	284	.412	120	87	.725	52	167	219	55	90	0	56	10	655	9.2	29
Boerwinkle	74	2045	530	265	.500	177	118	.667	263	529	792	283	263	9	47	52	648	8.8	31
Wilson	58	856	489	197	.403	58	43	.741	32	62	94	52	96	1	25	2	437	7.5	28
Benbow	76	1586	551	219	.397	140	105	.750	65	111	176	158	186	1	62	11	543	7.1	19
Pondexter	75	1326	380	156	.411	182	122	.670	113	268	381	90	134	4	28	26	434	5.8	22
Guokas	18	278	74	36	.486	11	9	.818	4	12	16	28	23	0	5	1	81	4.5	12
Thurmond	13	260	45	20	.444	18	8	.444	14	57	71	26	15	0	4	12	48	3.7	8
Patterson (Tot)	66	918	220	84	.382	54	34	.630	80	148	228	80	93	1	16	16	202	3.1	13
Patterson (Chi)	52	782	182	69	.379	44	26	.591	73	127	200	71	82	1	13	11	164	3.2	13
Fernsten (Tot)	37	268	86	33	.384	37	26	.703	25	45	70	19	21	0	7	14	92	2.5	8
Fernsten (Chi)	33	259	84	33	.393	37	26	.703	25	44	69	19	20	0	7	14	92	2.8	8
Block	2	7	4	2	.500	2	0	.000	0	2	2	0	2	0	1	0	4	2.0	4

CLEVELAND CAVALIERS

Player	G.	Min.	FGA	FGM	Pct.	FTA	FTM	Pct.	Off. Reb.	Def. Reb.	Tot. Reb.	Ast.	PF	Disq.	Stl.	Blk. Sh.	Pts.	Avg.	Hi.
Chones	82	2741	1258	563	.448	260	172	.662	197	542	739	163	241	2	42	93	1298	15.8	29
M. Russell	82	1961	1003	483	.482	344	266	.773	134	211	345	107	231	5	69	10	1232	15.0	35
B. Smith	81	2338	1121	495	.442	136	111	.816	83	258	341	155	231	0	58	36	1101	13.6	30
Snyder	82	2274	881	441	.501	188	155	.824	50	148	198	220	215	0	59	33	1037	12.6	36
Cleamons	82	2835	887	413	.466	218	174	.798	124	230	354	428	214	2	124	20	1000	12.2	29
Brewer	82	2913	874	400	.458	214	140	.654	298	593	891	209	214	0	94	89	940	11.5	25
Carr	65	1282	625	276	.442	134	106	.791	67	65	132	122	92	0	37	2	658	10.1	27
Beard	15	255	90	35	.389	37	27	.730	14	29	43	45	36	0	10	2	97	6.5	16
Garrett (Tot)	55	540	258	108	.419	65	53	.815	45	72	117	17	68	0	25	7	269	4.9	22
Garrett (Clev)	41	216	127	51	.402	21	15	.714	18	24	42	10	36	0	17	3	117	2.9	15
C. Walker	81	1280	369	143	.388	108	84	.778	53	129	182	288	136	0	98	5	370	4.6	17
Thurmond (Tot)	78	1393	337	142	.421	123	62	.504	115	300	415	94	160	1	22	98	346	4.4	15
Thurmond (Clev)	65	1133	292	122	.418	105	54	.514	101	243	344	68	145	1	18	86	298	4.6	15
Patterson	14	136	38	15	.395	10	8	.800	7	21	28	9	11	0	3	5	38	2.7	8
Lambert	54	333	110	49	.445	37	25	.676	37	65	102	16	54	0	8	12	123	2.3	10
Witte	22	99	32	11	.344	15	9	.600	9	29	38	4	14	0	1	1	31	1.4	6
Fernsten	4	9	2	0	.000	0	0	.000	0	1	1	0	1	0	0	1	0	0.0	0

DETROIT PISTONS

Player	G.	Min.	FGA	FGM	Pct.	FTA	FTM	Pct.	Off. Reb.	Def. Reb.	Tot. Reb.	Ast.	PF	Disq.	Stl.	Blk. Sh.	Pts.	Avg.	Hi.
Lanier	64	2363	1017	541	.532	370	284	.768	217	529	746	217	203	2	79	86	1366	21.3	41
Rowe	80	2998	1098	514	.468	342	252	.737	231	466	697	183	209	3	47	45	1280	16.0	29
Money	80	2267	947	449	.474	180	145	.806	77	130	207	338	243	4	137	11	1043	13.0	26
K. Porter	19	687	235	99	.421	56	42	.750	14	30	44	193	83	3	35	3	240	12.6	23
Mengelt	67	1105	540	264	.489	237	192	.810	27	88	115	108	138	1	40	5	720	10.7	32
Eberhard	81	2066	683	283	.414	229	191	.834	139	251	390	83	250	5	87	15	757	9.3	30
H. Porter	75	1482	635	298	.469	97	73	.753	81	214	295	25	133	0	31	36	669	8.9	28
C. Ford	82	2198	707	301	.426	115	83	.722	80	211	291	272	222	0	178	24	685	8.4	24
Trapp	76	1091	602	278	.462	88	63	.716	79	150	229	50	167	3	33	23	619	8.1	27
W. Jones	1	19	11	4	.364	0	0	.000	0	0	0	2	2	0	2	0	8	8.0	8
Clark	79	1589	577	250	.433	116	100	.862	27	110	137	218	157	0	62	4	600	7.6	18
Hairston	47	651	228	104	.456	112	65	.580	65	114	179	21	84	2	21	32	273	5.8	25
E. Williams	46	562	152	73	.480	44	22	.500	103	148	251	18	81	0	22	20	168	3.7	13
Thomas	28	136	65	28	.431	29	21	.724	15	21	36	3	21	1	4	2	77	2.8	18
R. Brown	29	454	72	29	.403	18	14	.778	47	83	130	12	76	1	6	25	72	2.5	11
Dickerson	17	112	29	9	.310	16	10	.625	3	0	3	8	17	1	2	1	28	1.6	11

GOLDEN STATE WARRIORS

Player	G.	Min.	FGA	FGM	Pct.	FTA	FTM	Pct.	Off. Reb.	Def. Reb.	Tot. Reb.	Ast.	PF	Disq.	Stl.	Blk. Sh.	Pts.	Avg.	Hi.
Barry	81	3122	1624	707	.435	311	287	.923	74	422	496	496	215	1	202	27	1701	21.0	41
P. Smith	82	2793	1383	659	.477	410	323	.788	133	243	376	362	223	0	108	18	1641	20.0	51
Wilkes	82	2716	1334	617	.463	294	227	.772	193	527	720	167	222	0	102	31	1461	17.8	34
G. Williams	77	1728	853	365	.428	233	173	.742	62	97	159	240	143	2	140	26	903	11.7	27
C. Johnson	81	1549	732	342	.467	79	60	.759	77	125	202	122	178	1	100	7	744	9.2	26
Ray	82	2184	404	212	.525	230	140	.609	270	506	776	149	247	2	78	83	564	6.9	20
Dickey	79	1207	473	220	.465	79	62	.785	114	235	349	83	141	1	26	11	502	6.4	20
Dudley	82	1456	345	182	.528	245	157	.641	112	157	269	239	170	0	77	2	521	6.4	18
G. Johnson	82	1745	341	165	.484	104	70	.673	200	427	627	82	275	6	51	174	400	4.9	16
Mullins	29	311	120	58	.483	29	23	.793	12	20	32	39	36	0	14	1	139	4.8	18
D. Davis	72	866	269	111	.413	113	78	.690	86	139	225	46	141	0	20	28	300	4.2	12
R. Hawkins	32	153	104	53	.510	31	20	.645	16	14	30	16	31	0	10	8	126	3.9	15

HOUSTON ROCKETS

Player	G.	Min.	FGA	FGM	Pct.	FTA	FTM	Pct.	Off. Reb.	Def. Reb.	Tot. Reb.	Ast.	PF	Disq.	Stl.	Blk. Sh.	Pts.	Avg.	Hi.
Murphy	82	2995	1369	675	.493	410	372	.907	52	157	209	596	294	3	151	6	1722	21.0	40
Newlin	82	3065	1123	569	.507	445	385	.865	72	264	336	457	263	5	106	5	1523	18.6	34
Tomjanovich	79	2912	1202	622	.517	288	221	.767	167	499	666	188	206	1	42	19	1465	18.5	32
Kunnert	80	2335	954	465	.487	156	102	.654	267	520	787	155	315	14	57	105	1032	12.9	29
Ratleff	72	2401	647	314	.485	206	168	.816	107	272	379	260	234	4	114	37	796	11.1	33
Meriweather	81	2042	684	338	.494	239	154	.644	163	353	516	82	219	4	36	120	830	10.2	29
J. Johnson (Tot)	76	1697	697	316	.453	155	120	.774	94	238	332	217	194	1	57	36	752	9.9	23
J. Johnson (Hou)	67	1485	609	275	.452	128	97	.758	81	211	292	197	163	0	50	28	647	9.7	23

Player	G.	Min.	FGA	FGM	Pct.	FTA	FTM	Pct.	Off. Reb.	Def. Reb.	Tot. Reb.	Ast.	PF	Disq.	Stl.	Blk. Sh.	Pts.	Avg.	Hi.
Meely	14	174	81	32	.395	16	9	.563	12	40	52	10	31	1	9	4	73	5.2	15
R. Riley	65	1049	280	115	.411	56	38	.679	91	213	304	75	137	1	32	21	268	4.1	21
Wohl	50	700	163	66	.405	49	38	.776	9	47	56	112	112	2	26	1	170	3.4	10
R. White	32	284	102	42	.412	25	18	.720	13	25	38	30	32	0	19	5	102	3.2	14
Bailey	30	262	77	28	.364	28	14	.500	20	30	50	41	33	1	14	8	70	2.3	10
Hawes	6	51	13	5	.385	0	0	.000	5	13	18	10	6	0	0	0	10	1.7	8

KANSAS CITY KINGS

Player	G.	Min.	FGA	FGM	Pct.	FTA	FTM	Pct.	Off. Reb.	Def. Reb.	Tot. Reb.	Ast.	PF	Disq.	Stl.	Blk. Sh.	Pts.	Avg.	Hi.
Archibald	78	3184	1583	717	.453	625	501	.802	67	146	213	615	169	0	126	15	1935	24.8	39
J. Walker	73	2490	950	459	.483	267	231	.865	49	128	177	176	186	2	87	14	1149	15.7	32
Wedman	82	2968	1181	538	.456	245	191	.780	199	407	606	199	280	8	103	36	1267	15.5	28
Lacey	81	3083	1019	409	.401	286	217	.759	218	806	1024	378	286	7	132	134	1035	12.8	26
O. Johnson	81	2150	678	348	.513	149	125	.839	116	241	357	146	217	4	67	42	821	10.1	23
McNeill	82	1613	610	295	.484	273	207	.758	157	353	510	72	244	2	51	32	797	9.7	25
Robinzine	75	1327	499	229	.459	198	145	.732	128	227	355	60	290	19	80	8	603	8.0	21
Hansen	66	1145	420	173	.412	117	85	.726	77	110	187	67	144	1	47	13	431	6.5	26
Winfield	22	214	66	32	.485	14	9	.643	8	16	24	19	14	0	10	6	73	3.3	14
Guokas (Tot)	56	793	173	73	.422	27	18	.667	22	41	63	70	76	0	18	3	164	2.9	12
Guokas (KC)	38	515	99	37	.374	16	9	.563	18	29	47	42	53	0	13	2	83	2.2	9
Roberson	74	709	180	73	.406	103	42	.408	74	159	233	53	126	1	18	17	188	2.5	13
Kosmalski	9	93	20	8	.400	7	4	.571	9	16	25	12	11	0	3	4	20	2.2	11
Bigelow	31	163	47	16	.340	33	24	.727	9	20	29	9	18	0	4	1	56	1.8	8
D'Antoni	9	101	27	7	.259	2	2	1.000	4	10	14	16	18	0	10	0	16	1.8	6

LOS ANGELES LAKERS

Player	G.	Min.	FGA	FGM	Pct.	FTA	FTM	Pct.	Off. Reb.	Def. Reb.	Tot. Reb.	Ast.	PF	Disq.	Stl.	Blk. Sh.	Pts.	Avg.	Hi.
Abdul-Jabbar	82	3379	1728	914	.529	636	447	.703	272	1111	1383	413	292	6	119	338	2275	27.7	48
Goodrich	75	2646	1321	583	.441	346	293	.847	94	120	214	421	238	3	123	17	1459	19.5	37
Allen	76	2388	1004	461	.459	254	197	.776	64	150	214	357	241	2	101	20	1119	14.7	28
C. Russell	74	1625	802	371	.463	148	132	.892	50	133	183	122	122	0	53	3	874	11.8	33
Freeman	64	1480	606	263	.434	199	163	.819	72	108	180	171	160	1	57	11	689	10.8	25
D. Ford	76	1838	710	311	.438	139	104	.748	118	215	333	111	186	3	50	14	726	9.6	25
Warner	81	2512	524	251	.479	128	89	.695	223	499	722	106	283	3	55	46	591	7.3	24
P. Riley	2	23	13	5	.385	3	1	.333	1	2	3	0	5	0	1	1	11	5.5	9
Calhoun	76	1816	368	172	.467	83	65	.783	117	224	341	85	216	4	62	35	409	5.4	18
R. Williams	9	158	43	17	.395	13	10	.769	2	17	19	21	15	0	3	0	44	4.9	12
Lantz	53	853	204	85	.417	89	80	.899	28	71	99	76	105	1	27	3	250	4.7	19
Meely (Tot)	34	313	132	52	.394	48	33	.688	22	75	97	19	61	1	14	8	137	4.0	15
Meely (LA)	20	139	51	20	.392	32	24	.750	10	35	45	9	30	0	5	4	64	3.2	11
Wesley	1	7	2	1	.500	4	2	.500	0	1	1	1	2	0	0	0	4	4.0	4
Washington	36	492	90	39	.433	66	45	.682	51	114	165	20	76	0	11	26	123	3.4	14
McDaniels	35	242	102	41	.402	9	9	1.000	26	48	74	15	40	1	4	10	91	2.6	12
Kupec	16	55	40	10	.250	11	7	.636	4	19	23	5	7	0	3	0	27	1.7	6
Roche	15	52	14	3	.214	4	2	.500	0	3	3	6	7	0	0	0	8	0.5	4

MILWAUKEE BUCKS

Player	G.	Min.	FGA	FGM	Pct.	FTA	FTM	Pct.	Off. Reb.	Def. Reb.	Tot. Reb.	Ast.	PF	Disq.	Stl.	Blk. Sh.	Pts.	Avg.	Hi.
Dandridge	73	2735	1296	650	.502	329	271	.824	171	369	540	206	263	5	111	38	1571	21.5	40
Winters	78	2795	1334	618	.464	217	180	.829	66	183	249	366	240	0	124	25	1416	18.2	34
E. Smith	78	2809	962	498	.518	351	222	.632	201	692	893	97	268	7	78	238	1218	15.6	31
Price	80	2525	958	398	.415	166	141	.849	74	187	261	395	264	3	148	32	937	11.7	26
Bridgeman	81	1646	651	286	.439	161	128	.795	113	181	294	157	235	3	52	21	700	8.6	28
Brokaw	75	1468	519	237	.457	227	159	.700	26	99	125	246	138	1	37	17	633	8.4	28
Meyers	72	1589	472	198	.419	210	135	.643	121	324	445	100	145	0	72	25	531	7.4	28
Restani	82	1650	493	234	.475	42	24	.571	115	261	376	96	151	3	36	12	492	6.0	18
Mayes	65	948	248	114	.460	97	56	.577	97	166	263	37	154	7	9	42	284	4.4	19
McGlocklin	33	336	148	63	.426	10	9	.900	3	14	17	38	18	0	8	0	135	4.1	12
Fox	70	918	203	105	.517	79	62	.785	82	153	235	42	129	1	27	16	272	3.9	21
Mi. Davis	45	411	152	55	.362	63	50	.794	25	59	84	37	36	0	13	2	160	3.6	12

NEW ORLEANS JAZZ

Player	G.	Min.	FGA	FGM	Pct.	FTA	FTM	Pct.	Off. Reb.	Def. Reb.	Tot. Reb.	Ast.	PF	Disq.	Stl.	Blk. Sh.	Pts.	Avg.	Hi.
Maravich	62	2373	1316	604	.459	488	396	.811	46	254	300	332	197	3	87	23	1604	25.9	49
N. Williams	81	1935	948	421	.444	239	197	.824	135	225	360	107	253	6	109	17	1039	12.8	33
L. Nelson	66	2030	755	327	.433	230	169	.735	81	121	202	169	147	1	82	6	823	12.5	27
Behagen	66	1733	691	308	.446	179	144	.804	190	363	553	139	222	6	67	26	760	11.5	27
Bibby	79	1772	622	266	.428	251	200	.797	58	121	179	225	165	0	62	3	732	9.3	24
Stallworth	56	1051	483	211	.437	124	85	.685	42	103	145	53	135	1	30	17	507	9.1	22
James	75	1346	594	262	.441	204	153	.750	93	156	249	59	172	1	33	6	677	9.0	24
Moore	81	2407	672	293	.436	226	144	.637	162	631	793	216	250	3	85	136	730	9.0	20
McElroy	51	1134	296	151	.510	110	81	.736	34	76	110	107	70	0	44	4	383	7.5	20
Coleman	67	1850	479	216	.451	89	59	.663	124	295	419	87	227	3	56	30	491	7.3	20
Kelley	75	1346	379	184	.485	205	159	.776	193	335	528	155	209	5	52	60	527	7.0	20
Boyd (Tot)	36	617	171	74	.433	51	29	.569	4	28	32	80	59	0	28	7	177	4.9	18
Boyd (NO)	30	584	165	72	.436	49	28	.571	4	26	30	78	54	0	27	7	172	5.7	18
Counts	30	319	91	37	.407	21	16	.762	27	73	100	38	74	1	16	8	90	3.0	16

NEW YORK KNICKERBOCKERS

Player	G.	Min.	FGA	FGM	Pct.	FTA	FTM	Pct.	Off. Reb.	Def. Reb.	Tot. Reb.	Ast.	PF	Disq.	Stl.	Blk. Sh.	Pts.	Avg.	Hi.
Monroe	76	2889	1354	647	.478	356	280	.787	48	225	273	304	209	1	111	22	1574	20.7	37
Haywood	78	2892	1360	605	.445	448	339	.757	234	644	878	92	255	1	53	80	1549	19.9	35
Frazier	59	2427	969	470	.485	226	186	.823	79	321	400	351	163	1	106	9	1126	19.1	38

Player	G.	Min.	FGA	FGM	Pct.	FTA	FTM	Pct.	Off. Reb.	Def. Reb.	Tot. Reb.	Ast.	PF	Disq.	Stl.	Blk. Sh.	Pts.	Avg.	Hi.
Bradley	82	2709	906	392	.433	148	130	.878	47	187	234	247	256	2	68	18	914	11.1	25
Gianelli	82	2332	687	325	.473	160	114	.713	187	365	552	115	194	1	25	62	764	9.3	24
Beard (Tot)	75	1704	496	228	.460	192	144	.750	103	207	310	218	216	2	81	8	600	8.0	21
Beard (N.Y.)	60	1449	406	193	.475	155	117	.755	89	178	267	173	180	2	71	6	503	8.4	21
Walk	82	1340	607	262	.432	99	79	.798	98	291	389	119	209	3	26	22	603	7.4	21
Jackson	80	1461	387	185	.478	150	110	.733	80	263	343	105	275	3	41	20	480	6.0	17
Barnett	71	1026	371	164	.442	114	90	.789	48	40	88	90	86	0	24	3	418	5.9	18
Mel Davis	42	408	193	76	.394	29	22	.759	43	105	148	31	56	0	16	5	174	4.1	20
Wingo	57	533	163	72	.442	60	40	.667	46	61	107	18	59	0	19	8	184	3.2	13
Mayfield	13	64	46	17	.370	3	3	1.000	1	7	8	4	18	0	0	0	37	2.8	8
Short (Tot)	34	222	91	32	.352	32	20	.625	19	29	48	10	36	0	8	3	84	2.5	10
Short (N.Y.)	27	185	80	26	.325	30	19	.633	17	24	41	8	31	0	8	3	71	2.6	10
Bell	10	76	21	8	.381	7	3	.429	4	10	14	3	11	0	6	1	19	1.9	8
Fogle	2	14	5	1	.200	0	0	.000	1	2	3	0	4	0	1	0	2	1.0	2

PHILADELPHIA 76ers

Player	G.	Min.	FGA	FGM	Pct.	FTA	FTM	Pct.	Off. Reb.	Def. Reb.	Tot. Reb.	Ast.	PF	Disq.	Stl.	Blk. Sh.	Pts.	Avg.	Hi.
McGinnis	77	2946	1552	647	.417	642	475	.740	260	707	967	359	334	13	198	41	1769	23.0	39
Collins	77	2995	1196	614	.513	445	372	.836	126	181	307	191	249	2	110	24	1600	20.8	38
Carter	82	2992	1594	665	.417	312	219	.702	113	186	299	372	286	5	137	13	1549	18.9	35
Mix	81	3039	844	421	.499	351	287	.818	215	447	662	216	288	6	158	29	1129	13.9	33
Cunningham	20	640	251	103	.410	88	68	.773	29	118	147	107	57	1	24	10	274	13.7	26
Free	71	1121	533	239	.448	186	112	.602	64	61	125	104	107	0	37	6	590	8.3	29
Bryant	75	1203	552	233	.422	147	92	.626	97	181	278	61	165	0	44	23	558	7.4	26
Norman	65	818	422	183	.434	24	20	.833	51	50	101	66	87	1	28	7	386	5.9	20
Ellis	29	489	132	61	.462	28	17	.607	47	75	122	21	62	0	16	9	139	4.8	14
Lee	79	1421	282	123	.436	95	63	.663	164	289	453	59	188	0	23	27	309	3.9	14
Catchings	75	1731	242	103	.426	96	58	.604	191	329	520	63	262	6	21	164	264	3.5	13
W. Jones (Tot)	17	176	49	23	.469	13	9	.692	0	9	9	33	27	0	6	0	55	3.2	10
W. Jones (Phil)	16	157	38	19	.500	13	9	.692	0	9	9	31	25	0	4	0	47	2.9	10
Dawkins	37	165	82	41	.500	24	8	.333	15	34	49	3	40	1	2	9	90	2.4	12
Baskerville	21	105	26	8	.308	16	10	.625	13	15	28	3	32	0	6	5	26	1.2	4
Boyd	6	33	6	2	.333	2	1	.500	0	2	2	2	5	0	1	0	5	0.8	2

PHOENIX SUNS

Player	G.	Min.	FGA	FGM	Pct.	FTA	FTM	Pct.	Off. Reb.	Def. Reb.	Tot. Reb.	Ast.	PF	Disq.	Stl.	Blk. Sh.	Pts.	Avg.	Hi.
Westphal	82	2960	1329	657	.494	440	365	.830	74	185	259	440	218	3	210	38	1679	20.5	39
A. Adams	80	2656	1341	629	.469	355	261	.735	215	512	727	450	274	6	121	116	1519	19.0	35
Perry	71	2353	776	386	.497	239	175	.732	197	487	684	182	269	5	84	66	947	13.3	27
D. Van Arsdale	58	1870	570	276	.484	235	195	.830	39	98	137	140	113	2	52	11	747	12.9	26
Shumate	43	930	338	186	.550	183	115	.628	61	179	240	62	76	1	44	16	487	11.3	28
Heard (Tot)	86	2747	901	392	.435	248	158	.637	247	622	869	190	303	2	117	96	942	11.0	27
Heard (Phoe)	36	1220	409	185	.452	113	76	.673	109	249	358	64	120	2	51	41	446	12.4	27
Erickson	74	1850	649	305	.470	157	134	.854	106	226	332	185	196	4	79	6	744	10.1	26
Sobers	78	1898	623	280	.449	192	158	.823	80	179	259	215	253	6	106	7	718	9.2	27
Hawthorne	79	1144	423	182	.430	170	115	.676	86	123	209	46	147	0	33	15	479	6.1	25
Awtrey	74	1376	304	142	.467	109	75	.688	93	200	293	159	153	1	21	22	359	4.9	12
Riley (Tot)	62	813	301	117	.389	77	55	.714	16	34	50	57	112	0	22	6	289	4.7	16
Riley (Phoe)	60	790	288	112	.389	74	54	.730	15	32	47	57	107	0	21	5	278	4.6	16
Saunders	17	146	64	28	.438	11	6	.545	11	26	37	13	23	0	5	1	62	3.6	12
Bantom	7	68	26	8	.308	5	5	1.000	7	16	23	3	13	1	2	2	21	3.0	9
Lumpkin	34	370	65	22	.338	30	26	.867	7	16	23	48	26	0	15	0	70	2.1	10
Wetzel	37	249	46	22	.478	24	20	.833	8	30	38	19	30	0	9	3	64	1.7	6

PORTLAND TRAIL BLAZERS

Player	G.	Min.	FGA	FGM	Pct.	FTA	FTM	Pct.	Off. Reb.	Def. Reb.	Tot. Reb.	Ast.	PF	Disq.	Stl.	Blk. Sh.	Pts.	Avg.	Hi.
Wicks	79	3044	1201	580	.483	512	345	.674	245	467	712	244	250	5	77	53	1505	19.1	35
Petrie	72	2557	1177	543	.461	334	277	.829	38	130	168	330	194	0	82	5	1363	18.9	34
Walton	51	1687	732	345	.471	228	133	.583	132	549	681	220	144	3	49	82	823	16.1	36
Neal	68	2320	904	435	.481	268	186	.694	145	440	585	118	254	4	53	107	1056	15.5	31
J. Johnson	9	212	88	41	.466	27	23	.852	13	27	40	20	31	1	7	8	105	11.7	21
Hollins	74	1891	738	311	.421	247	178	.721	39	136	175	306	235	5	131	28	800	10.8	25
Steele	81	2382	651	322	.495	203	154	.759	77	215	292	324	289	8	170	19	798	9.9	30
Gross	76	1474	400	209	.523	142	97	.683	138	169	307	163	186	3	91	43	515	6.8	24
Hawes (Tot)	72	1411	403	199	.494	120	87	.725	171	326	497	115	169	5	44	25	485	6.7	23
Hawes (Port)	68	1360	390	194	.497	120	87	.725	166	313	479	105	163	5	44	25	475	7.2	23
S. Jones	64	819	380	168	.442	94	78	.830	13	62	75	63	96	0	17	6	414	6.5	23
D. Anderson	52	614	181	88	.486	61	51	.836	15	47	62	85	58	0	20	2	227	4.4	17
Martin	63	889	302	109	.361	77	57	.740	68	243	311	72	126	1	6	23	275	4.4	18
Clemens	49	443	143	70	.490	35	31	.886	27	43	70	33	57	0	27	7	171	3.5	20
G. Lee	5	35	4	2	.500	2	2	1.000	0	2	2	11	6	0	2	0	6	1.2	4
G. Smith	1	3	1	0	.000	0	0	.000	0	0	0	2	0	0	0	0	0	0.0	0

SEATTLE SUPERSONICS

Player	G.	Min.	FGA	FGM	Pct.	FTA	FTM	Pct.	Off. Reb.	Def. Reb.	Tot. Reb.	Ast.	PF	Disq.	Stl.	Blk. Sh.	Pts.	Avg.	Hi.
F. Brown	76	2516	1522	742	.488	314	273	.869	111	206	317	207	186	0	143	18	1757	23.1	41
Burleson	82	2647	1032	496	.481	388	291	.750	258	484	742	180	273	1	70	150	1283	15.6	35
Gray	66	2139	831	394	.474	169	126	.746	109	289	398	203	260	10	75	36	914	13.8	32
Watts	82	2776	1015	433	.427	344	199	.578	112	253	365	661	270	3	261	16	1065	13.0	26
Seals	81	2435	889	388	.436	267	181	.678	157	350	507	119	314	11	64	49	957	11.8	29
Gilliam	81	1644	676	299	.442	116	90	.776	56	164	220	202	139	0	82	12	688	8.5	24
Bantom (Tot)	73	1571	476	220	.462	199	136	.683	140	251	391	105	221	4	28	28	576	7.9	21
Bantom (Sea)	66	1503	450	212	.471	194	131	.675	133	235	368	102	208	3	26	26	555	8.4	21
Norwood	64	1004	301	146	.485	203	152	.749	91	138	229	59	139	3	42	4	444	6.9	24
Oleynick	52	650	316	127	.402	77	53	.688	10	35	45	53	62	0	21	6	307	5.9	22

Player	G.	Min.	FGA	FGM	Pct.	FTA	FTM	Pct.	Off. Reb.	Def. Reb.	Tot. Reb.	Ast.	PF	Disq.	Stl.	Blk. Sh.	Pts.	Avg.	Hi.
Skinner	72	1224	285	132	.463	80	49	.613	89	175	264	67	116	1	50	7	313	4.3	26
Derline	49	339	181	73	.403	56	45	.804	8	19	27	26	22	0	11	1	191	3.9	16
Abdul-Aziz	27	223	75	35	.467	29	16	.552	30	46	76	16	29	0	8	15	86	3.2	11
Hummer	29	364	67	32	.478	41	17	.415	21	56	77	25	71	5	6	9	81	2.8	14
Carlson	28	279	79	27	.342	29	18	.621	30	43	73	13	39	1	7	11	72	2.6	7
Short	7	37	11	6	.545	2	1	.500	2	5	7	2	5	0	0	0	13	1.9	6

WASHINGTON BULLETS

Player	G.	Min.	FGA	FGM	Pct.	FTA	FTM	Pct.	Off. Reb.	Def. Reb.	Tot. Reb.	Ast.	PF	Disq.	Stl.	Blk. Sh.	Pts.	Avg.	Hi.
Chenier	80	2952	1355	654	.483	341	282	.827	84	236	320	255	186	2	158	45	1590	19.9	44
Hayes	80	2975	1381	649	.470	457	287	.628	210	668	878	121	293	5	104	202	1585	19.8	37
Bing	82	2945	1113	497	.447	422	332	.787	94	143	237	492	262	0	118	23	1326	16.2	34
Robinson	82	2055	779	354	.454	314	211	.672	139	418	557	113	239	3	42	107	919	11.2	29
Unseld	78	2922	567	318	.561	195	114	.585	271	765	1036	404	203	3	84	59	750	9.6	25
Riordan	78	1943	662	291	.440	96	71	.740	44	143	187	122	201	2	54	13	653	8.4	22
Weatherspoon	64	1083	458	218	.476	137	96	.701	85	189	274	55	172	2	46	16	532	8.3	31
Haskins	55	737	269	148	.550	65	54	.831	12	42	54	73	79	2	23	8	350	6.4	25
J. Jones	64	1133	308	153	.497	94	72	.766	32	99	131	120	127	1	33	5	378	5.9	16
Grevey	56	504	213	79	.371	58	52	.897	24	36	60	27	65	0	13	3	210	3.8	19
Kozelko	67	584	99	48	.485	30	19	.633	19	63	82	33	74	0	19	4	115	1.7	15
Kropp	25	72	30	7	.233	6	5	.833	5	10	15	8	20	0	2	0	19	0.8	5

PLAYOFF RESULTS

EASTERN CONFERENCE FIRST ROUND
Buffalo 2, Philadelphia 1
Apr. 15—Thu.—Buffalo 95 at Philadelphia 89
Apr. 16—Fri.—Philadelphia 131 at Buffalo 106
Apr. 18—Sun.—Buffalo 124 at Philadelphia 123*

WESTERN CONFERENCE FIRST ROUND
Detroit 2, Milwaukee 1
Apr. 13—Tue.—Detroit 107 at Milwaukee 110
Apr. 15—Thu.—Milwaukee 123 at Detroit 126
Apr. 18—Sun.—Detroit 107 at Milwaukee 104

EASTERN CONFERENCE SEMIFINALS
Boston 4, Buffalo 2
Apr. 21—Wed.—Buffalo 98 at Boston 107
Apr. 23—Fri.—Buffalo 96 at Boston 101
Apr. 25—Sun.—Boston 93 at Buffalo 98
Apr. 28—Wed.—Boston 122 at Buffalo 124
Apr. 30—Fri.—Buffalo 88 at Boston 99
May 2—Sun.—Boston 104 at Buffalo 100

WESTERN CONFERENCE SEMIFINALS
Golden State 4, Detroit 2
Apr. 20—Tue.—Detroit 103 at Golden State 127
Apr. 22—Thu.—Detroit 123 at Golden State 111
Apr. 24—Sat.—Golden State 113 at Detroit 96
Apr. 26—Mon.—Golden State 102 at Detroit 106
Apr. 28—Wed.—Detroit 109 at Golden State 128
Apr. 30—Fri.—Golden State 118 at Detroit 116*

Cleveland 4, Washington 3
Apr. 13—Tue.—Washington 100 at Cleveland 95
Apr. 15—Thu.—Cleveland 80 at Washington 79
Apr. 17—Sat.—Washington 76 at Cleveland 88
Apr. 21—Wed.—Cleveland 98 at Washington 109
Apr. 22—Thu.—Wash. 91 at Cleveland 92
Apr. 26—Mon.—Cleveland 98 at Washington 102*
Apr. 29—Thu.—Washington 85 at Cleveland 87

Phoenix 4, Seattle 2
Apr. 13—Tue.—Phoenix 99 at Seattle 102
Apr. 15—Thu.—Phoenix 116 at Seattle 111
Apr. 18—Sun.—Seattle 91 at Phoenix 103
Apr. 20—Tue.—Seattle 114 at Phoenix 130
Apr. 25—Sun.—Phoenix 108 at Seattle 114
Apr. 27—Tue.—Seattle 112 at Phoenix 123

EASTERN CONFERENCE FINALS
Boston 4, Cleveland 2
May 6—Thu.—Cleveland 99 at Boston 111
May 9—Sun.—Cleveland 89 at Boston 94
May 11—Tue.—Boston 78 at Cleveland 83
May 14—Fri.—Boston 87 at Cleveland 106
May 16—Sun.—Cleveland 94 at Boston 99
May 18—Tue.—Boston 94 at Cleveland 87

WESTERN CONFERENCE FINALS
Phoenix 4, Golden State 3
May 2—Sun.—Phoenix 103 at Golden State 128
May 5—Wed.—Phoenix 108 at Golden State 101
May 7—Fri.—Golden State 99 at Phoenix 91
May 9—Sun.—Golden State 129 at Phoenix 133**
May 12—Wed.—Phoenix 95 at Golden State 111
May 14—Fri.—Golden State 104 at Phoenix 105
May 16—Sun.—Phoenix 94 at Golden State 86

WORLD CHAMPIONSHIP SERIES
Boston 4, Phoenix 2
May 23—Sun.—Phoenix 87 at Boston 98
May 27—Thu.—Phoenix 90 at Boston 105
May 30—Sun.—Boston 98 at Phoenix 105
June 2—Wed.—Boston 107 at Phoenix 109
June 4—Fri.—Phoenix 126 at Boston 128***
June 6—Sun.—Boston 87 at Phoenix 80

*Denotes overtime period.

1974-75 NBA STATISTICS

1974-75 NBA CHAMPION GOLDEN STATE WARRIORS

Front Row (Left to Right): Charles Johnson; Jeff Mullins; Joe Roberts, Assistant Coach; Al Attles, Head Coach; Franklin Mieuli, Owner; Rick Barry, Captain; Butch Beard; Phil Smith; Dick D'Oliva, Trainer. Back Row (Left to Right): Hal Childs, Assistant General Manager; Charles Dudley; Bill Bridges; Clifford Ray; George Johnson; Derrek Dickey; Keith Wilkes; Steve Bracey; Bob Feerick, Director of Player Personnel; Dick Vertlieb, General Manager.

FINAL STANDINGS

ATLANTIC DIVISION

Team	Atl.	Bos.	Buf.	Chi.	Cle.	Det.	G.S.	Hou.	KC-O	L.A.	Mil.	N.O.	N.Y.	Phi.	Pho.	Por.	Sea.	Was.	W.	L.	Pct.	G.B.
Boston	4	..	5	3	3	3	1	4	2	4	4	4	7	5	3	4	2	2	60	22	.732	....
Buffalo	3	4	..	1	3	2	3	2	1	4	1	4	5	6	3	2	3	2	49	33	.598	11
New York	4	2	3	1	3	2	1	3	2	4	1	2	..	4	3	2	2	1	40	42	.488	20
Philadelphia	2	3	3	2	1	1	1	2	3	1	1	2	5	..	2	2	2	1	34	48	.415	26

CENTRAL DIVISION

Team	Atl.	Bos.	Buf.	Chi.	Cle.	Det.	G.S.	Hou.	KC-O	L.A.	Mil.	N.O.	N.Y.	Phi.	Pho.	Por.	Sea.	Was.	W.	L.	Pct.	G.B.
Washington	5	2	2	3	5	3	3	5	3	3	4	7	3	3	3	3	3	..	60	22	.732	....
Houston	5	..	2	2	4	2	2	..	4	2	3	5	1	2	2	2	1	2	41	41	.500	19
Cleveland	4	1	1	2	..	2	2	4	2	2	1	6	1	3	2	2	2	3	40	42	.488	20
Atlanta	..	..	1	..	3	2	1	2	2	2	2	3	..	2	4	1	3	3	31	51	.378	29
New Orleans	5	..	..	..	1	..	2	3	2	1	1	..	2	2	1	2	1	..	23	59	.280	37

MIDWEST DIVISION

Team	Atl.	Bos.	Buf.	Chi.	Cle.	Det.	G.S.	Hou.	KC-O	L.A.	Mil.	N.O.	N.Y.	Phi.	Pho.	Por.	Sea.	Was.	W.	L.	Pct.	G.B.
Chicago	4	1	3	..	2	4	3	2	4	3	3	4	3	2	2	2	4	1	47	35	.573	....
KC-Omaha	2	2	3	5	2	6	2	..	..	3	6	2	2	1	3	3	1	1	44	38	.537	3
Detroit	2	1	2	5	2	..	1	2	2	3	3	4	2	3	2	3	2	1	40	42	.488	7
Milwaukee	2	..	3	5	3	6	1	1	3	..	..	3	3	3	2	2	1	..	38	44	.463	9

PACIFIC DIVISION

Team	Atl.	Bos.	Buf.	Chi.	Cle.	Det.	G.S.	Hou.	KC-O	L.A.	Mil.	N.O.	N.Y.	Phi.	Pho.	Por.	Sea.	Was.	W.	L.	Pct.	G.B.
Golden State	3	3	1	1	2	3	..	2	2	5	3	2	3	3	5	5	4	1	48	34	.585	....
Seattle	1	2	1	..	2	2	3	3	6	3	3	2	2	3	6	..	..	1	43	39	.524	5
Portland	3	..	2	2	2	1	3	2	1	5	2	2	2	6	..	..	2	1	38	44	.463	10
Phoenix	..	1	1	2	2	2	3	2	1	4	2	3	1	2	..	1	4	1	32	50	.390	16
Los Angeles	2	..	..	1	2	1	2	2	1	..	4	3	..	3	4	2	2	1	30	52	.366	18

HOME-ROAD RECORDS OF ALL TEAMS

	Home	Road	Total		Home	Road	Total
Atlanta	22- 19	9- 32	31- 51	Milwaukee	25- 16	13- 28	38- 44
Boston	28- 13	32- 9	60- 22	New Orleans	20- 21	3- 38	23- 59
Buffalo	30- 11	19- 22	49- 33	New York	23- 18	17- 24	40- 42
Chicago	29- 12	18- 23	47- 35	Philadelphia	20- 21	14- 27	34- 48
Cleveland	29- 12	11- 30	40- 42	Phoenix	22- 19	10- 31	32- 50
Detroit	26- 15	14- 27	40- 42	Portland	28- 13	10- 31	38- 44
Golden State	31- 10	17- 24	48- 34	Seattle	24- 17	19- 22	43- 39
Houston	29- 12	12- 29	41- 41	Washington	36- 5	24- 17	60- 22
K.C.-Omaha	29- 12	15- 26	44- 38	Totals	472- 266	266- 472	738- 738
Los Angeles	21- 20	9- 32	30- 52				

OFFENSIVE TEAM STATISTICS

Team	G.	FIELD GOALS Att.	Made	Pct.	FREE THROWS Att.	Made	Pct.	REBOUNDS Off.	Def.	Tot.	MISCELLANEOUS Ast.	PF	Disq.	Stl.	Turn Over	Blk. Sh.	SCORING Pts.	Avg.
Golden State	82	7981	3714	.465	1915	1470	.768	1416	2854	4270	2076	2109	22	972	1716	365	8898	108.5
Buffalo	82	7469	3552	.476	2224	1735	.780	1108	2735	3843	2063	1879	18	718	1710	456	8839	107.8
Boston	82	7825	3587	.458	1971	1560	.791	1315	2949	4264	2159	1913	23	662	1625	288	8734	106.5
Atlanta	82	7824	3424	.438	2435	1772	.728	1441	2653	4094	1878	1964	33	744	1550	227	8620	105.1
Washington	82	7697	3555	.462	1962	1475	.752	1133	2764	3897	2005	1961	26	929	1594	409	8585	104.7
Houston	82	7231	3448	.477	2034	1625	.799	1177	2495	3672	2155	2068	30	746	1759	351	8521	103.9
Portland	82	7113	3414	.480	2265	1680	.742	1049	2758	3807	2209	2055	29	755	1853	399	8508	103.8
Los Angeles	82	7577	3409	.450	2182	1641	.752	1312	2763	4075	2091	2079	23	755	1785	423	8459	103.2
Seattle	82	7653	3488	.456	1970	1475	.749	1142	2579	3721	1997	1977	27	837	1610	378	8451	103.1
New Orleans	82	7509	3301	.440	2247	1717	.764	1144	2616	3760	1818	2222	34	725	1802	256	8319	101.5
KC-Omaha	82	7258	3257	.449	2190	1797	.821	991	2745	3736	1853	1968	19	724	1542	347	8311	101.4
Phoenix	82	7561	3381	.447	2082	1535	.737	1349	2684	4033	1879	2090	45	664	1760	317	8297	101.2
Milwaukee	82	7367	3450	.468	1746	1354	.775	1021	2766	3787	1932	1949	30	596	1540	400	8254	100.7
New York	82	7464	3359	.450	1967	1518	.772	981	2652	3633	1675	2001	22	652	1374	300	8236	100.4
Philadelphia	82	7476	3325	.445	2043	1530	.749	1200	2706	3906	1709	1974	34	576	1591	263	8180	99.8
Cleveland	82	7371	3408	.462	1753	1301	.742	1058	2502	3560	1903	1881	16	600	1462	348	8117	99.0
Detroit	82	7053	3289	.466	1975	1533	.776	1002	2515	3517	1916	1866	13	679	1557	380	8111	98.9
Chicago	82	7085	3167	.447	2203	1711	.777	1107	2786	3893	1840	1952	23	668	1482	379	8045	98.1

DEFENSIVE TEAM STATISTICS

Team	FIELD GOALS Att.	Made	Pct.	FREE THROWS Att.	Made	Pct.	REBOUNDS Off.	Def.	Tot.	MISCELLANEOUS Ast.	PF	Disq.	Stl.	Turn Over	Blk. Sh.	SCORING Pts.	Avg.	Pt. Dif.
Chicago	7070	3167	.448	1900	1457	.767	1008	2647	3655	1686	2168	37	625	1580	404	7791	95.0	+ 3.1
Washington	7415	3249	.438	1967	1499	.762	1184	2819	4003	1811	2004	25	710	1842	259	7997	97.5	+ 7.2
Cleveland	7243	3263	.451	2102	1621	.771	1235	2694	3929	1746	1932	26	711	1618	277	8147	99.4	− 0.4
Detroit	7257	3409	.470	1793	1410	.786	1104	2550	3654	2012	1875	24	663	1523	306	8228	100.3	− 1.4
Milwaukee	7600	3371	.444	1910	1495	.783	1153	2645	3798	1960	1704	11	660	1379	298	8237	100.5	+ 0.2
Boston	7726	3432	.444	1882	1401	.744	1060	2622	3682	1833	1869	24	599	1475	283	8265	100.8	+ 5.7
KC-Omaha	7400	3410	.461	1972	1515	.768	1060	2812	3872	1840	2029	25	606	1605	312	8335	101.6	− 0.2
New York	7357	3361	.457	2082	1615	.776	1070	2856	3926	1668	1912	15	572	1493	369	8337	101.7	− 1.3
Philadelphia	7466	3445	.461	1979	1541	.779	1167	2748	3915	1959	2036	26	742	1577	343	8431	102.8	− 3.0
Houston	7127	3429	.481	2127	1576	.741	1036	2380	3416	2024	2063	37	750	1685	308	8434	102.9	+ 1.0
Portland	7502	3379	.450	2178	1714	.787	1207	2572	3779	2090	2085	34	727	1607	383	8472	103.3	+ 0.5
Phoenix	7323	3356	.458	2350	1730	.757	1112	2564	3676	2062	1992	20	870	1586	412	8492	103.6	− 2.4
Seattle	7606	3490	.459	2090	1560	.746	1286	2754	4040	2188	1948	24	692	1755	349	8540	104.1	− 1.0
Golden State	7628	3481	.456	2209	1666	.754	1185	2658	3843	2084	1855	17	794	1644	387	8628	105.2	+ 3.3
Buffalo	7943	3575	.450	1943	1513	.779	1295	2619	3914	2151	2030	31	730	1670	383	8663	105.6	+ 2.2
Atlanta	7504	3563	.475	2098	1606	.765	1169	2851	4020	1914	2265	33	746	1723	422	8732	106.5	− 1.4
Los Angeles	7914	3595	.454	2117	1603	.757	1422	2807	4229	2239	2015	25	822	1606	442	8793	107.2	− 4.0
New Orleans	7433	3553	.478	2465	1857	.753	1193	2924	4117	1891	2126	33	783	1924	349	8963	109.3	− 7.8

Disq—Individual players disqualified (fouled out of game).

INDIVIDUAL LEADERS

POINTS

(Minimum of 70 games played or 1400 points)

	G.	FG	FT	Pts.	Avg.		G.	FG	FT	Pts.	Avg.
McAdoo, Buff	82	1095	641	2831	34.5	Chenier, Wash.	77	690	301	1681	21.8
Barry, G.S.	80	1028	394	2450	30.6	Wicks, Port.	82	692	394	1778	21.7
Abdul-Jabbar, Mil.	65	812	325	1949	30.0	Maravich, N.O.	79	655	390	1700	21.5
Archibald, KC-O.	82	759	652	2170	26.5	Frazier, N.Y.	78	672	331	1675	21.5
Scott, Phoe.	69	703	274	1680	24.3	F. Brown, Sea.	81	737	226	1700	21.0
Lanier, Det.	76	731	361	1823	24.0	Monroe, N.Y.	78	668	297	1633	20.9
Hayes, Wash.	82	739	409	1887	23.0	Tomjanovich, Hou	81	694	289	1677	20.7
Goodrich, L.A.	72	656	318	1630	22.6	Dandridge, Mil.	80	691	211	1593	19.9
Haywood, Sea.	68	608	309	1525	22.4	Cunningham, Phil.	80	609	345	1563	19.5
Carter, Phil.	77	715	256	1686	21.9	Ch. Walker, Chi.	76	524	413	1461	19.2

FIELD GOALS

Minimum: 300 FGM

	FGA	FGM	Pct.
D. Nelson, Bos.	785	423	.539
Beard, G.S.	773	408	.528
Tomjanovich, Hou.	1323	694	.525
Abdul-Jabbar, Mil.	1584	812	.513
McAdoo, Buff.	2138	1095	.512
Kunnert, Hou.	676	346	.512
Westphal, Bos.	670	342	.510
Lanier, Det.	1433	731	.510
Snyder, Clev.	988	498	.504
McMillian, Buff.	695	347	.499

FREE THROWS

Minimum: 125 FTM

	FTA	FTM	Pct.
Barry, G.S.	436	394	.904
Murphy, Hou.	386	341	.883
Bradley, N.Y.	165	144	.873
Archibald, KC-O.	748	652	.872
Price, L.A.-Mil.	194	169	.871
Havlicek, Bos.	332	289	.870
Marin, Buff.	222	193	.869
Newlin, Hou.	305	265	.869
Ch. Walker, Chi.	480	413	.860
J. Walker, KC-O.	289	247	.855

ASSISTS
Minimum: 70 games or 400 assists

	G.	No.	Avg.
K. Porter, Wash.	81	650	8.0
Bing, Det.	79	610	7.7
Archibald, KC-O.	82	557	6.8
R. Smith, Buff.	82	534	6.5
Maravich, N.O.	79	488	6.2
Barry, G.S.	80	492	6.2
Watts, Sea.	82	499	6.1
Frazier, N.Y.	78	474	6.1
Goodrich, L.A.	72	420	5.8
Van Lier, Chi.	70	403	5.8

STEALS
Minimum: 70 games or 125 steals

	G.	No.	Avg.
Barry, G.S.	80	228	2.85
Frazier, N.Y.	78	190	2.44
Steele, Port.	76	183	2.41
Watts, Sea.	82	190	2.32
F. Brown, Sea.	81	187	2.31
Chenier, Wash.	77	176	2.29
Sloan, Chi.	78	171	2.19
Allen, Mil.-L.A.	66	136	2.06
Van Lier, Chi.	70	139	1.99
Hayes, Wash.	82	158	1.93

REBOUNDS
Minimum: 70 games or 800 rebounds

	G.	Off.	Def.	Tot.	Avg.
Unseld, Wash.	73	318	759	1077	14.8
Cowens, Bos.	65	229	729	958	14.7
Lacey, KC-O.	81	228	921	1149	14.2
McAdoo, Buff.	82	307	848	1155	14.1
Abdul-Jabbar, Mil.	65	194	718	912	14.0
Hairston, L.A.	74	304	642	946	12.8
Silas, Bos.	82	348	677	1025	12.5
Hayes, Wash.	82	221	783	1004	12.2
Lanier, Det.	76	225	689	914	12.0
Perry, Phoe.	79	347	593	940	11.9

BLOCKED SHOTS
Minimum: 70 games or 100 blocked shots

	G.	No.	Avg.
Abdul-Jabbar, Mil.	65	212	3.26
E. Smith, L.A.	74	216	2.92
Thurmond, Chi.	80	195	2.44
Hayes, Wash.	82	187	2.28
Lanier, Det.	76	172	2.26
McAdoo, Buff.	82	174	2.12
Lacey, KC-O.	81	168	2.07
Burleson, Sea.	82	153	1.87
Heard, Buff.	67	120	1.79
Chones, Clev.	72	120	1.67

TEAM-BY-TEAM INDIVIDUAL STATISTICS

ATLANTA HAWKS

Player	G.	Min.	FGA	FGM	Pct.	FTA	FTM	Pct.	Off. Reb.	Def. Reb.	Tot. Reb.	Ast.	PF	Disq.	Stl.	Blk. Sh.	Pts.	Avg.	Hi.
Hudson	11	380	225	97	.431	57	48	.842	14	33	47	40	33	1	13	2	242	22.0	36
Drew	78	2289	1230	527	.428	544	388	.713	357	479	836	138	274	4	119	39	1442	18.5	44
T. V. Arsdale (Tot)	82	2843	1385	593	.428	424	322	.759	77	201	278	223	257	5	91	3	1508	18.1	35
T. V. Arsdale (Atl)	73	2570	1269	544	.429	383	294	.768	70	179	249	207	231	5	78	3	1382	18.9	35
Gilliam	60	1393	736	314	.427	113	94	.832	76	128	204	170	124	1	77	13	722	12.0	26
Sojourner	73	2129	775	378	.488	146	95	.651	196	446	642	93	217	10	35	57	851	11.7	29
Henderson	79	2131	893	367	.411	241	168	.697	51	161	212	314	149	0	105	7	902	11.4	32
J. Brown	73	1986	684	315	.461	250	185	.740	180	254	434	133	228	7	54	15	815	11.2	28
D. Jones	75	2086	752	323	.430	183	132	.721	236	461	697	152	226	1	51	51	778	10.4	24
Meminger	80	2177	500	233	.466	263	168	.639	84	130	214	397	160	0	118	11	634	7.9	26
J. Washington	38	905	259	114	.440	55	41	.745	52	141	193	68	86	2	23	13	269	7.1	19
Lee	9	177	36	12	.333	39	32	.821	24	46	70	8	25	0	1	4	56	6.2	16
Kauffman	73	797	261	113	.433	84	59	.702	67	115	182	81	103	1	19	4	285	3.9	17
Wetzel	63	785	204	87	.426	77	68	.883	34	80	114	77	108	1	51	8	242	3.8	14

BOSTON CELTICS

Player	G.	Min.	FGA	FGM	Pct.	FTA	FTM	Pct.	Off. Reb.	Def. Reb.	Tot. Reb.	Ast.	PF	Disq.	Stl.	Blk. Sh.	Pts.	Avg.	Hi.
Cowens	65	2632	1199	569	.475	244	191	.783	229	729	958	296	243	7	87	73	1329	20.4	38
Havlicek	82	3132	1411	642	.455	332	289	.870	154	330	484	432	231	2	110	16	1573	19.2	40
White	82	3220	1440	658	.457	223	186	.834	44	227	311	458	207	1	128	17	1502	18.3	33
D. Nelson	79	2052	785	423	.539	318	263	.827	127	342	469	181	239	2	32	15	1109	14.0	35
Silas	82	2661	749	312	.417	344	244	.709	348	677	1025	224	229	3	60	22	868	10.6	22
Westphal	82	1581	670	342	.510	156	119	.763	44	119	163	235	192	0	78	33	803	9.8	27
Chaney	82	2208	750	321	.428	165	133	.806	171	199	370	181	244	5	122	66	775	9.5	28
Hankinson	3	24	11	6	.545	0	0	.000	1	6	7	2	3	0	1	0	12	4.0	6
Ard	59	719	266	89	.335	65	48	.738	59	140	199	40	96	2	13	32	226	3.8	19
Stacom	61	447	159	72	.453	33	29	.879	30	25	55	49	65	0	11	3	173	2.8	10
Clyde	25	157	72	31	.431	9	7	.778	15	26	41	5	34	1	5	3	69	2.8	16
McDonald	62	395	182	70	.385	37	28	.757	20	48	68	24	58	0	8	5	168	2.7	14
Finkel	62	518	129	52	.403	43	23	.535	33	79	112	32	72	0	7	3	127	2.0	10
Downing	3	9	2	0	.000	2	0	.000	0	2	2	0	0	0	0	0	0	0.0	0

BUFFALO BRAVES

Player	G.	Min.	FGA	FGM	Pct.	FTA	FTM	Pct.	Off. Reb.	Def. Reb.	Tot. Reb.	Ast.	PF	Disq.	Stl.	Blk. Sh.	Pts.	Avg.	Hi.
McAdoo	82	3539	2138	1095	.512	796	641	.805	307	848	1155	179	278	3	92	174	2831	34.5	51
R. Smith	82	3001	1261	610	.484	295	236	.800	95	249	344	534	247	2	137	3	1456	17.8	35
McMillian	62	2132	695	347	.499	231	194	.840	127	258	385	156	129	0	69	15	888	14.3	28
Marin	81	2147	836	380	.455	222	193	.869	104	259	363	133	238	7	51	16	953	11.8	26
Heard	67	2148	819	318	.388	188	106	.564	185	481	666	190	242	2	106	120	742	11.1	24
DiGregorio	31	712	234	103	.440	45	35	.778	6	39	45	151	62	0	19	0	241	7.8	33
Charles	79	1690	515	240	.466	146	120	.822	68	96	164	171	165	0	87	20	600	7.6	19
Washington (Tot)	80	1579	421	191	.454	93	62	.667	110	280	390	111	167	5	34	26	444	5.6	19
Washington (Buf)	42	674	162	77	.475	38	21	.553	58	139	197	43	81	3	11	13	175	4.2	16
Winfield	68	1259	312	164	.526	68	49	.721	48	81	126	134	106	1	43	30	377	5.5	16
Schlueter	76	962	178	92	.517	121	84	.694	78	186	264	104	163	0	18	42	268	3.5	13
Weiss	76	1338	261	102	.391	67	54	.806	21	83	104	260	146	0	82	19	258	3.4	14
Ruffner	22	103	47	22	.468	5	1	.200	12	10	22	7	22	0	3	3	45	2.0	8
Harris	11	25	11	2	.182	2	1	.500	2	6	8	1	0	0	0	1	5	0.5	2

CHICAGO BULLS

Player	G.	Min.	FGA	FGM	Pct.	FTA	FTM	Pct.	Off. Reb.	Def. Reb.	Tot. Reb.	Ast.	PF	Disq.	Stl.	Blk. Sh.	Pts.	Avg.	Hi.
B. Love	61	2401	1256	539	.429	318	264	.830	99	286	385	102	209	3	63	12	1342	22.0	39
Ch. Walker	76	2452	1076	524	.487	480	413	.860	114	318	432	169	181	0	49	6	1461	19.2	39
VanLier	70	2590	970	407	.420	298	236	.792	86	242	328	403	246	5	139	14	1050	15.0	42
Sloan	78	2577	865	380	.439	258	193	.748	177	361	538	161	265	5	171	17	953	12.2	27
Adelman	12	340	104	43	.413	39	28	.718	6	20	26	35	31	0	16	1	114	9.5	16
Block (Tot)	54	939	346	159	.460	144	114	.792	69	163	232	51	121	0	42	32	432	8.0	29
Block (Chi)	50	882	317	150	.473	134	105	.784	63	151	214	44	110	0	38	31	405	8.1	29
Thurmond	80	2756	686	250	.364	224	132	.589	259	645	904	328	271	6	46	195	632	7.9	25
Garrett	70	1183	474	228	.481	97	77	.794	80	167	247	43	124	0	24	13	533	7.6	21
Guokas	82	2089	500	255	.510	103	78	.757	24	115	139	178	154	1	45	17	588	7.2	20
Hewitt	18	467	129	56	.434	23	14	.609	30	86	116	24	46	1	9	10	126	7.0	17
Wilson	48	425	225	115	.511	58	46	.793	18	34	52	36	54	1	22	1	276	5.8	20
Boerwinkle	80	1175	271	132	.487	95	73	.768	105	275	380	272	163	0	25	45	337	4.2	17
W. Johnson	38	291	118	53	.449	58	37	.638	32	62	94	20	57	1	10	11	143	3.8	16
Benbow	39	252	94	35	.372	18	15	.833	14	24	38	25	41	0	11	6	85	2.2	8

CLEVELAND CAVALIERS

Player	G.	Min.	FGA	FGM	Pct.	FTA	FTM	Pct.	Off. Reb.	Def. Reb.	Tot. Reb.	Ast.	PF	Disq.	Stl.	Blk. Sh.	Pts.	Avg.	Hi.
R. Smith	82	2636	1212	585	.483	160	132	.825	108	299	407	229	227	1	80	26	1302	15.9	41
Chones	72	2427	916	446	.487	224	152	.679	156	521	677	132	247	5	49	120	1044	14.5	28
Carr	41	1081	538	252	.468	106	89	.840	51	56	107	154	57	0	48	2	593	14.5	34
Snyder	82	2590	988	498	.504	195	165	.846	37	201	238	281	226	3	69	43	1161	14.2	30
Cleamons	74	2691	768	369	.480	181	144	.796	97	232	329	381	194	0	84	21	882	11.9	29
D. Davis	78	1964	666	295	.443	245	176	.718	108	356	464	150	254	3	45	39	766	9.8	24
Brewer	82	1991	639	291	.455	159	103	.648	205	304	509	128	150	2	77	43	685	8.4	26
Foster	73	1136	521	217	.417	97	69	.711	56	54	110	103	130	1	22	2	503	6.9	23
M. Russell	68	754	365	150	.411	165	124	.752	43	109	152	45	100	0	21	3	424	6.2	18
Patterson	81	1269	387	161	.416	73	48	.658	112	217	329	93	128	1	21	20	370	4.6	23
Cl. Walker	72	1070	275	111	.404	117	80	.684	47	99	146	192	126	0	80	7	302	4.2	18
Witte	39	271	96	33	.344	31	19	.613	38	54	92	15	42	0	4	22	85	2.2	9

DETROIT PISTONS

Player	G.	Min.	FGA	FGM	Pct.	FTA	FTM	Pct.	Off. Reb.	Def. Reb.	Tot. Reb.	Ast.	PF	Disq.	Stl.	Blk. Sh.	Pts.	Avg.	Hi.
Lanier	76	2987	1433	731	.510	450	361	.802	225	689	914	350	237	1	75	172	1823	24.0	45
Bing	79	3222	1333	578	.434	424	343	.809	86	200	286	610	222	3	116	26	1499	19.0	32
Rowe	82	2787	874	422	.483	227	171	.753	174	411	585	121	190	0	50	44	1015	12.4	26
Mengelt	80	1995	701	336	.479	248	211	.851	38	153	191	201	198	2	72	4	883	11.0	33
Trapp	78	1472	652	288	.442	131	99	.756	71	205	276	63	210	1	37	14	675	8.7	24
Porter (Tot)	58	1163	412	201	.488	79	66	.835	79	175	254	19	93	0	23	26	468	8.1	22
Porter (Det)	41	1030	376	188	.500	70	59	.843	66	150	216	17	76	0	20	25	435	10.6	22
Norwood	24	347	123	64	.520	42	31	.738	31	57	88	16	51	0	23	0	159	6.6	18
Ford	80	1962	435	206	.474	95	63	.663	93	176	269	230	187	0	113	26	475	5.9	18
Adams	51	1376	315	127	.403	78	45	.577	63	181	244	75	179	1	69	20	299	5.9	19
Money	66	889	319	144	.451	45	31	.689	27	61	88	101	121	3	33	2	319	4.8	21
J. Davis	79	1078	260	118	.454	117	85	.726	96	189	285	90	129	2	50	36	321	4.1	21
Ligon	38	272	143	55	.385	25	16	.640	14	12	26	25	31	0	8	9	126	3.3	15
Eberhard	34	277	85	31	.365	21	17	.810	18	29	47	16	33	0	13	1	79	2.3	11
Moore	2	11	4	1	.250	2	1	.500	0	2	2	1	2	0	1	1	3	1.5	3

GOLDEN STATE WARRIORS

Player	G.	Min.	FGA	FGM	Pct.	FTA	FTM	Pct.	Off. Reb.	Def. Reb.	Tot. Reb.	Ast.	PF	Disq.	Stl.	Blk Sh.	Pts.	Avg.	Hi.
Barry	80	3235	2217	1028	.464	436	394	.904	92	364	456	492	225	0	228	33	2450	30.6	55
Wilkes	82	2515	1135	502	.442	218	160	.734	203	468	671	183	222	0	107	22	1164	14.2	31
Beard	82	2521	773	408	.528	279	232	.832	116	200	316	345	297	9	132	11	1048	12.8	29
C. Johnson	79	2171	957	394	.412	102	75	.735	134	177	311	233	204	2	138	8	863	10.9	25
Ray	82	2519	573	299	.522	284	171	.602	259	611	870	178	305	5	95	116	769	9.4	20
Mullins	66	1141	514	234	.455	87	71	.816	46	77	123	153	123	0	57	14	539	8.2	24
P. Smith	74	1055	464	221	.476	158	127	.804	51	89	140	135	141	0	62	0	569	7.7	26
Dickey	80	1859	569	274	.482	99	66	.667	190	360	550	125	199	0	52	19	614	7.7	20
G. Johnson	82	1439	319	152	.476	91	60	.659	217	357	574	67	206	1	32	136	364	4.4	16
Dudley	67	756	217	102	.470	97	70	.722	61	84	145	103	105	1	40	2	274	4.1	15
Kendrick	24	121	77	31	.403	22	18	.818	19	17	36	6	22	0	11	3	80	3.3	10
Bracey	42	340	130	54	.415	38	25	.658	10	28	38	52	41	0	14	1	133	3.2	13
Bridges (Tot)	32	415	93	35	.376	34	17	.500	64	70	134	31	65	1	11	5	87	2.7	15
Bridges (G.S.)	15	108	36	15	.417	4	1	.250	18	22	40	4	19	0	4	0	31	2.1	8

HOUSTON ROCKETS

Player	G.	Min.	FGA	FGM	Pct.	FTA	FTM	Pct.	Off. Reb.	Def. Reb.	Tot. Reb.	Ast.	PF	Disq.	Stl.	Blk. Sh.	Pts.	Avg.	Hi.
Tomjanovich	81	3134	1323	694	.525	366	289	.790	184	429	613	236	230	1	76	24	1677	20.7	41
Murphy	78	2513	1152	557	.484	386	341	.883	52	121	173	381	281	8	128	4	1455	18.7	45
Newlin	79	2709	905	436	.482	305	265	.869	55	205	260	403	288	4	111	7	1137	14.4	37
Ratleff	80	2563	851	392	.461	190	157	.826	185	274	459	259	231	5	146	51	941	11.8	31
Kunnert	75	1801	676	346	.512	169	116	.686	214	417	631	108	223	2	34	84	808	10.8	27
Abdul-Aziz	65	1450	538	235	.437	203	159	.783	154	334	488	84	128	1	37	74	629	9.7	26
Meely	48	753	349	156	.447	94	68	.723	55	109	164	45	117	4	21	11	380	7.9	21
Wohl	75	1722	462	203	.439	106	79	.745	26	86	112	340	184	1	75	9	485	6.5	29
R. Riley	77	1578	470	196	.417	97	71	.732	137	243	380	130	197	3	56	22	463	6.0	16
Hawes	55	897	279	140	.502	55	45	.818	80	195	275	88	99	1	36	36	325	5.9	20
Wells	33	214	100	42	.420	22	15	.682	12	23	35	22	38	0	9	3	99	3.0	12
Bailey	47	446	126	51	.405	41	20	.488	23	59	82	59	52	0	17	16	122	2.6	14

KANSAS CITY-OMAHA KINGS

Player	G.	Min.	FGA	FGM	Pct.	FTA	FTM	Pct.	Off. Reb.	Def. Reb.	Tot. Reb.	Ast.	PF	Disq.	Stl.	Blk. Sh.	Pts.	Avg.	Hi.
Archibald	82	3244	1664	759	.456	748	652	.872	48	174	222	557	187	0	119	7	2170	26.5	41
J. Walker	81	3122	1164	553	.475	289	247	.855	51	188	239	226	222	2	85	13	1353	16.7	32
N. Williams	50	1131	584	265	.454	118	97	.822	58	121	179	78	152	2	53	24	627	12.5	27
Lacey	81	3378	917	392	.427	191	144	.754	228	921	1149	428	274	4	139	168	928	11.5	23
Wedman	80	2554	806	375	.465	170	139	.818	202	288	490	129	270	2	81	27	889	11.1	26
Behagen	81	2205	834	333	.399	264	199	.754	146	446	592	153	301	8	60	42	865	10.7	23
McNeill	80	1749	645	296	.459	241	189	.784	149	348	497	73	229	1	69	27	781	9.8	26
O. Johnson (Tot)	73	1667	429	203	.473	114	95	.833	87	156	243	110	172	1	59	33	501	6.9	20
O. Johnson (KC-O)	30	508	130	64	.492	37	33	.892	27	39	66	30	69	0	17	13	161	5.4	15
Adelman (Tot)	58	1074	291	123	.423	103	73	.709	25	70	95	112	101	1	70	8	319	5.5	16
Adelman (KC-O)	18	121	28	13	.464	5	4	.800	6	8	14	8	12	0	7	1	30	1.7	9
Kojis	21	232	98	46	.469	30	20	.667	14	25	39	10	31	0	12	1	112	5.3	18
Durrett	21	175	78	32	.410	20	11	.550	14	26	40	8	30	0	5	4	75	3.6	9
D'Antoni	67	759	173	69	.399	36	28	.778	13	64	77	107	106	0	67	12	166	2.5	14
May	29	139	54	27	.500	12	10	.833	4	9	13	5	21	0	4	2	64	2.2	12
Kosmalski	67	413	83	33	.398	29	24	.828	31	88	119	41	64	0	6	6	90	1.3	7

LOS ANGELES LAKERS

Player	G.	Min.	FGA	FGM	Pct.	FTA	FTM	Pct.	Off. Reb.	Def. Reb.	Tot. Reb.	Ast.	PF	Disq.	Stl.	Blk. Sh.	Pts.	Avg.	Hi.
Goodrich	72	2668	1429	656	.459	378	318	.841	96	123	219	420	214	1	102	6	1630	22.6	53
Price	9	339	167	75	.449	45	41	.911	17	26	43	63	36	1	21	3	191	21.2	27
Allen (Tot)	66	2353	1170	511	.437	306	238	.778	90	188	278	372	217	4	136	29	1260	19.1	39
Allen (L.A.)	56	2011	1006	443	.440	269	207	.770	81	166	247	319	194	4	122	28	1093	19.5	39
C. Russell	40	1055	580	264	.455	113	101	.894	34	81	115	109	56	0	27	2	629	15.7	30
Winters	68	1516	810	359	.443	92	76	.826	39	99	138	195	168	1	74	18	794	11.7	30
P. Riley	46	1016	523	219	.419	93	69	.742	25	60	85	121	128	0	36	4	507	11.0	38
E. Smith	74	2341	702	346	.493	231	112	.485	210	600	810	145	255	6	84	216	804	10.9	30
Hairston	74	2283	536	271	.506	271	217	.801	304	642	946	173	218	2	52	11	759	10.3	21
Lantz (Tot)	75	1783	561	228	.406	229	192	.838	88	106	194	188	162	1	56	12	648	8.6	26
Lantz (L.A.)	56	1430	446	189	.424	176	145	.824	81	89	170	158	134	1	44	10	523	9.3	26
Hawkins	43	1026	324	139	.429	99	68	.687	54	144	198	120	116	1	51	23	346	8.0	24
S. Love	30	431	194	85	.438	66	47	.712	31	66	97	26	69	1	16	13	217	7.2	18
Beaty	69	1213	310	136	.439	135	108	.800	93	234	327	74	130	1	45	29	380	5.5	19
Calhoun (Tot)	70	1378	318	132	.415	77	58	.753	109	160	269	79	180	1	55	25	322	4.6	13
Calhoun (LA)	57	1270	286	120	.420	62	44	.710	95	141	236	75	160	1	49	23	284	5.0	13
K. Washington	55	949	207	87	.420	122	72	.590	106	244	350	66	155	2	25	32	246	4.5	12
Bridges	17	307	57	20	.351	30	16	.533	46	48	94	27	46	1	7	5	56	3.3	15

MILWAUKEE BUCKS

Player	G.	Min.	FGA	FGM	Pct.	FTA	FTM	Pct.	Off. Reb.	Def. Reb.	Tot. Reb.	Ast.	PF	Disq.	Stl.	Blk. Sh.	Pts.	Avg.	Hi.
Abdul-Jabbar	65	2747	1584	812	.513	426	325	.763	194	718	912	264	205	2	65	212	1949	30.0	52
Dandridge	80	3031	1460	691	.473	262	211	.805	142	409	551	243	330	7	122	48	1593	19.9	33
Allen	10	342	164	68	.415	37	31	.838	9	22	31	53	23	0	14	1	167	16.7	23
Price (Tot)	50	1870	717	317	.442	194	169	.871	62	136	198	286	182	1	111	24	803	16.1	43
Price (Mil)	41	1531	550	242	.440	149	128	.859	45	110	155	223	146	0	90	21	612	14.9	43
Thompson	73	1983	691	306	.443	214	168	.785	50	131	181	225	203	5	66	6	780	10.7	24
McGlocklin	79	1853	651	323	.496	72	63	.875	25	94	119	255	142	2	51	6	709	9.0	24
Brokaw	73	1639	514	234	.455	184	126	.685	36	111	147	221	176	3	31	18	594	8.1	24
Warner	79	2519	541	248	.458	155	106	.684	238	574	812	127	267	8	49	54	602	7.6	19
Mi. Davis	75	1077	363	174	.479	88	78	.886	68	169	237	79	103	0	30	5	426	5.7	18
Restani	76	1755	427	188	.440	49	35	.714	131	272	403	119	172	1	36	19	411	5.4	18
R. Williams	46	526	165	62	.376	29	24	.828	10	33	43	71	70	2	23	2	148	3.2	15
Kuberski	59	517	159	62	.390	56	44	.786	52	71	123	35	59	0	11	3	168	2.8	10
Wesley (Tot)	45	247	93	42	.452	27	16	.593	18	45	63	12	51	0	7	5	100	2.2	10
Wesley (Mil)	41	214	84	37	.440	23	14	.609	14	41	55	11	43	0	7	5	88	2.1	10
Driscoll	11	52	13	3	.231	2	1	.500	7	9	16	3	7	0	1	0	7	0.6	3
D. Cunningham	2	8	0	0	.000	0	0	.000	0	2	2	1	1	0	0	0	0	0.0	0
Rule	1	11	1	0	.000	0	0	.000	0	0	0	2	2	0	0	0	0	0.0	0

NEW ORLEANS JAZZ

Player	G.	Min.	FGA	FGM	Pct.	FTA	FTM	Pct.	Off. Reb.	Def. Reb.	Tot. Reb.	Ast.	PF	Disq.	Stl.	Blk. Sh.	Pts.	Avg.	Hi.
Maravich	79	2853	1562	655	.419	481	390	.811	93	329	422	488	227	4	120	18	1700	21.5	47
N. Williams (Tot)	85	1945	988	474	.480	220	181	.823	102	235	337	145	251	3	97	30	1129	13.3	28
N. Williams (N.O.)	35	814	404	209	.517	102	84	.824	44	114	158	67	99	1	44	6	502	14.3	28
Barnett	45	1238	480	215	.448	188	156	.830	45	83	128	137	109	1	35	16	586	13.0	30
James	76	1731	776	370	.477	189	147	.778	140	226	366	66	217	4	41	15	887	11.7	34
L. Nelson	72	1898	679	307	.452	250	192	.768	75	121	196	178	186	1	65	6	806	11.2	29
B. Stallworth	73	1668	710	298	.420	182	125	.687	78	168	246	46	208	4	59	11	721	9.9	24
Walk	37	851	358	151	.422	80	64	.800	73	189	262	101	122	3	30	20	366	9.9	23
Bibby (Tot)	75	1400	619	270	.436	189	137	.725	47	90	137	181	157	0	54	3	677	9.0	27
Bibby (N.O.)	28	524	219	91	.416	93	68	.731	18	32	50	76	61	0	25	0	250	8.9	20
Coleman	77	2176	568	253	.445	166	116	.699	189	360	549	105	277	10	82	37	622	8.1	23
O. Johnson	43	1159	299	139	.465	77	62	.805	60	117	177	80	103	1	42	20	340	7.9	20
Roberson	16	339	108	48	.444	40	23	.575	39	79	118	23	49	0	7	8	119	7.4	20
Counts	75	1421	495	217	.438	113	86	.761	102	339	441	182	196	0	49	43	520	6.9	20
Block	4	57	29	9	.310	10	9	.900	6	12	18	7	11	0	4	1	27	6.8	12
Moore (Tot)	42	1066	262	118	.450	69	46	.667	92	238	330	83	148	3	21	40	282	6.7	16
Moore (N.O.)	40	1055	258	117	.453	67	45	.672	92	236	328	82	146	3	21	39	279	7.0	16
Kimball	3	90	23	7	.304	7	6	.857	8	18	26	4	12	0	2	0	20	6.7	8
Lantz	19	353	115	39	.339	53	47	.887	7	17	24	30	28	0	12	2	125	6.6	22
Adelman	28	613	159	67	.421	59	41	.695	13	42	55	69	58	1	47	6	175	6.3	16
Bellamy	1	14	2	2	1.000	2	2	1.000	0	5	5	0	2	0	0	0	6	6.0	6
R. Lee	15	139	76	29	.382	14	7	.500	15	16	31	7	17	1	11	3	65	4.3	11
Fryer	31	432	106	47	.443	43	33	.767	16	30	46	52	54	0	22	0	127	4.1	17
Green	15	280	70	24	.343	20	9	.450	28	81	109	16	38	0	4	5	57	3.8	10
K. Boyd	6	25	13	7	.538	11	5	.455	3	2	5	2	2	0	3	0	19	3.2	7

NEW YORK KNICKERBOCKERS

Player	G.	Min.	FGA	FGM	Pct.	FTA	FTM	Pct.	Off. Reb.	Def. Reb.	Tot. Reb.	Ast.	PF	Disq.	Stl.	Blk. Sh.	Pts.	Avg.	Hi.
Frazier	78	3204	1391	672	.483	400	331	.828	90	375	465	474	205	2	190	14	1675	21.5	43
Monroe	78	2814	1462	668	.457	359	297	.827	56	271	327	270	200	0	108	29	1633	20.9	38
Bradley	79	2787	1036	452	.436	165	144	.873	65	186	251	247	283	5	74	18	1048	13.3	32
P. Jackson	78	2285	712	324	.455	253	193	.763	137	463	600	136	330	10	84	53	841	10.8	29
Barnett (Tot)	73	1776	652	285	.437	238	199	.836	60	119	179	176	160	1	47	16	769	10.5	30
Barnett (N.Y.)	28	538	172	70	.407	50	43	.860	15	36	51	39	51	0	12	0	183	6.5	22
Gianelli	80	2797	726	343	.472	195	135	.692	214	475	689	163	263	3	38	118	821	10.3	23
Bibby	47	876	400	179	.448	96	69	.719	29	58	87	105	96	0	29	3	427	9.1	27
Wingo	82	1686	506	233	.460	187	141	.754	163	293	456	84	215	2	48	35	607	7.4	19
Walk (Tot)	67	1125	473	198	.419	105	86	.819	91	248	339	123	177	3	37	23	482	7.2	23
Walk (N.Y.)	30	274	115	47	.409	25	22	.880	18	59	77	22	55	0	7	3	116	3.9	12
Mel Davis	62	903	395	154	.390	70	48	.686	70	251	321	54	105	0	16	8	356	5.7	24
Dark	47	401	157	74	.471	40	22	.550	15	22	37	30	48	0	3	1	170	3.6	13
Bell	52	465	181	68	.376	36	20	.556	48	57	105	25	54	0	22	9	156	3.0	20
Riker	51	483	147	53	.361	82	46	.561	40	67	107	19	64	0	15	5	152	3.0	12
H. Porter	17	133	36	13	.361	9	7	.778	13	25	38	2	17	0	3	1	33	1.9	7
G. Jackson	5	27	10	4	.400	0	0	.000	2	0	2	3	5	0	0	0	8	1.6	6
D. Stallworth	7	57	18	5	.278	0	0	.000	6	14	20	2	10	0	3	3	10	1.4	6

PHILADELPHIA 76ers

Player	G.	Min.	FGA	FGM	Pct.	FTA	FTM	Pct.	Off. Reb.	Def. Reb.	Tot. Reb.	Ast.	PF	Disq.	Stl.	Blk. Sh.	Pts.	Avg.	Hi.
Carter	77	3046	1598	715	.447	347	256	.738	73	267	340	336	257	5	82	20	1686	21.9	37
Cunningham	80	2859	1423	609	.428	444	345	.777	130	596	726	442	270	4	91	35	1563	19.5	38
Collins	81	2820	1150	561	.488	392	331	.844	104	211	315	213	291	6	108	17	1453	17.9	39
Mix	46	1748	582	280	.481	205	159	.776	155	345	500	99	175	6	79	21	719	15.6	36
T. V. Arsdale	9	273	116	49	.422	41	28	.683	7	22	29	16	26	0	13	0	126	14.0	21
Ellis	82	2183	623	287	.461	99	72	.727	195	387	582	117	178	1	44	55	646	7.9	27
F. Boyd	66	1362	495	205	.414	115	55	.478	16	73	89	161	134	0	43	4	465	7.0	35
Bristow	72	1101	393	163	.415	153	121	.791	111	143	254	99	101	0	25	2	447	6.2	23
Lee (Tot)	80	2456	427	176	.412	177	119	.672	288	469	757	105	285	9	30	20	471	5.9	19
Lee (Phil)	71	2279	391	164	.419	138	87	.630	264	423	687	97	260	9	29	16	415	5.8	19
D. Smith	54	538	321	131	.408	21	21	1.000	14	16	30	47	45	0	20	3	283	5.2	19
Norman	12	72	44	23	.523	3	2	.667	3	9	12	4	9	0	3	1	48	4.0	10
Durrett (Tot)	48	445	166	67	.404	52	31	.596	35	67	102	18	72	0	9	8	165	3.4	9
Durrett (Phil)	27	270	88	35	.398	32	20	.625	21	41	62	10	42	0	4	4	90	3.3	9
Tschogl	39	623	148	53	.358	22	13	.591	52	59	111	30	80	2	25	25	119	3.1	13
Wesley	4	33	9	5	.556	4	2	.500	4	4	8	1	8	0	0	0	12	3.0	10
Catchings	37	528	74	41	.554	25	16	.640	49	104	153	21	82	1	10	60	98	2.6	8
Warbington	5	70	21	4	.190	2	2	1.000	2	6	8	16	16	0	0	0	10	2.0	4

PHOENIX SUNS

Player	G.	Min.	FGA	FGM	Pct.	FTA	FTM	Pct.	Off. Reb.	Def. Reb.	Tot. Reb.	Ast.	PF	Disq.	Stl.	Blk. Sh.	Pts.	Avg.	Hi.
Scott	69	2592	1594	703	.441	351	274	.781	72	201	273	311	296	11	111	24	1680	24.3	41
D. Van Arsdale	70	2419	895	421	.470	339	282	.832	52	137	189	195	177	2	81	11	1124	16.1	46
Perry	79	2688	917	437	.477	256	184	.719	347	593	940	186	288	10	108	78	1058	13.4	26
Bantom	82	2239	907	418	.461	259	185	.714	211	342	553	159	273	8	62	47	1021	12.5	29
Erickson	49	1469	557	237	.425	156	130	.833	70	173	243	170	150	3	50	12	604	12.3	29
Awtrey	82	2837	722	339	.470	195	132	.677	242	462	704	342	227	2	60	52	810	9.9	24
Melchionni	68	1529	539	232	.430	141	114	.809	45	142	187	156	116	1	48	12	578	8.5	23
Saunders	69	1059	406	176	.433	95	66	.695	82	171	253	80	151	3	41	15	418	6.1	21
Hawthorne	50	618	287	118	.411	94	61	.649	34	58	92	39	94	0	30	21	297	5.9	20
E. Williams	79	1040	394	163	.414	103	45	.437	156	300	456	95	146	0	28	32	371	4.7	22
G. Jackson (Tot)	49	802	176	73	.415	62	36	.581	19	50	69	96	130	5	23	9	182	3.7	18
G. Jackson (Pho)	44	775	166	69	.416	62	36	.581	17	50	67	93	125	5	23	9	174	4.0	18
Owens	41	432	145	56	.386	16	12	.750	7	36	43	49	27	0	16	2	124	3.0	12
Calhoun	13	108	32	12	.375	15	14	.933	14	19	33	4	20	0	6	2	38	2.9	13

PORTLAND TRAIL BLAZERS

Player	G.	Min.	FGA	FGM	Pct.	FTA	FTM	Pct.	Off. Reb.	Def. Reb.	Tot. Reb.	Ast.	PF	Disq.	Stl.	Blk. Sh.	Pts.	Avg.	Hi.
Wicks	82	3162	1391	692	.497	558	394	.706	231	646	877	287	289	5	108	80	1778	21.7	36
Petrie	80	3109	1319	602	.456	311	261	.839	38	171	209	424	215	1	81	13	1465	18.3	37
J. Johnson	80	2540	1082	527	.487	301	236	.784	162	339	501	240	249	3	75	39	1290	16.1	35
Walton	35	1153	345	177	.513	137	94	.686	92	349	441	167	115	4	29	94	448	12.8	25
Neal	82	2278	869	409	.471	295	189	.641	186	501	687	139	239	2	43	87	1007	12.3	29
Steele	76	2389	484	265	.548	146	122	.836	86	140	226	287	254	6	183	16	652	8.6	23
Martin	81	1372	522	236	.452	142	99	.697	136	272	408	69	239	5	33	49	571	7.0	22
Wilkens	65	1161	305	134	.439	198	152	.768	38	82	120	235	96	1	77	9	420	6.5	20
Clemens	77	952	355	168	.473	60	45	.750	33	128	161	76	139	0	68	2	381	4.9	24
Lumpkin	48	792	190	86	.453	39	30	.769	10	49	59	177	80	1	20	3	202	4.2	14
G. Smith	55	519	146	71	.486	48	32	.667	29	60	89	27	96	1	22	6	174	3.2	16
Anderson	43	453	105	47	.448	30	26	.867	8	21	29	81	44	0	16	1	120	2.8	10

SEATTLE SUPERSONICS

Player	G.	Min.	FGA	FGM	Pct.	FTA	FTM	Pct.	Off. Reb.	Def. Reb.	Tot. Reb.	Ast.	PF	Disq.	Stl.	Blk. Sh.	Pts.	Avg.	Hi.
Haywood	68	2529	1325	608	.459	381	309	.811	198	432	630	137	173	1	54	108	1525	22.4	40
F. Brown	81	2669	1537	737	.480	272	226	.831	113	230	343	284	227	2	187	14	1700	21.0	40
Clark	77	2481	919	455	.495	193	161	.834	59	176	235	433	188	4	110	5	1071	13.9	31
Gray	75	2280	773	378	.489	144	104	.722	133	345	478	163	292	9	63	24	860	11.5	33
Burleson	82	1888	772	322	.417	265	182	.687	155	417	572	115	221	1	64	153	826	10.1	29
Fox	75	1766	540	253	.469	212	170	.802	128	363	491	137	168	1	48	17	676	9.0	28
Brisker	21	276	141	60	.426	49	42	.857	15	18	33	19	33	0	7	3	162	7.7	28
Watts	82	2056	551	232	.421	153	93	.608	95	167	262	499	254	7	190	12	557	6.8	23
Derline	58	666	332	142	.428	56	43	.768	12	47	59	45	47	0	23	4	327	5.6	20
Skinner	73	1574	347	142	.409	97	63	.649	135	209	344	85	161	0	49	17	347	4.8	22

Player	G.	Min.	FGA	FGM	Pct.	FTA	FTM	Pct.	Off. Reb.	Def. Reb.	Tot. Reb.	Ast.	PF	Disq.	Stl.	Blk. Sh.	Pts.	Avg.	Hi.
W. Jackson	56	939	242	96	.397	71	51	.718	53	80	133	30	126	2	26	5	243	4.3	23
McIntosh	6	101	29	6	.207	9	6	.667	6	9	15	7	12	0	4	3	18	3.0	6
Tolson	19	87	37	16	.432	17	11	.647	12	10	22	5	12	0	4	6	43	2.3	14
Hummer	43	568	108	41	.380	51	14	.275	28	76	104	38	63	0	8	7	96	2.2	13

WASHINGTON BULLETS

Player	G.	Min.	FGA	FGM	Pct.	FTA	FTM	Pct.	Off. Reb.	Def. Reb.	Tot. Reb.	Ast.	PF	Disq.	Stl.	Blk. Sh.	Pts.	Avg.	Hi.
Hayes	82	3465	1668	739	.443	534	409	.766	221	783	1004	206	238	0	158	187	1887	23.0	39
Chenier	77	2869	1533	690	.450	365	301	.825	74	218	292	248	158	3	176	58	1681	21.8	38
Riordan	74	2191	1057	520	.492	117	98	.838	90	194	284	198	238	4	72	6	1138	15.4	39
K. Porter	81	2589	827	406	.491	186	131	.704	55	97	152	650	320	12	152	11	943	11.6	29
Unseld	73	2904	544	273	.502	184	126	.685	318	759	1077	297	180	1	115	68	672	9.2	26
Weatherspoon	82	1347	562	256	.456	138	103	.746	132	214	346	51	212	2	65	21	615	7.5	24
J. Jones	73	1424	400	207	.518	142	103	.725	36	101	137	162	190	0	76	10	517	7.1	24
Robinson	76	995	393	191	.486	115	60	.522	94	207	301	40	132	0	36	32	442	5.8	18
Haskins	70	702	290	115	.397	63	53	.841	29	51	80	79	73	0	23	6	283	4.0	18
Gibbs	59	424	190	74	.389	64	48	.750	26	35	61	19	60	0	12	3	196	3.3	13
Kozelko	73	754	167	60	.359	36	31	.861	50	90	140	41	125	4	28	5	151	2.1	14
DuVal	37	137	65	24	.369	18	12	.667	8	15	23	14	34	0	16	2	60	1.6	5
S. Washington	1	4	1	0	.000	0	0	.000	0	0	0	0	1	0	0	0	0	0.0	0

PLAYOFF RESULTS

EASTERN CONFERENCE FIRST ROUND
Houston 2, New York 1

Apr. 8—Tue.—New York 84 at Houston 99
Apr. 10—Thu.—Houston 96 at New York 106
Apr. 12—Sat.—New York 86 at Houston 118

EASTERN CONFERENCE SEMIFINALS
Boston 4, Houston 1

Apr. 14—Mon.—Houston 106 at Boston 123
Apr. 16—Wed.—Houston 100 at Boston 112
Apr. 19—Sat.—Boston 102 at Houston 117
Apr. 22—Tue.—Boston 122 at Houston 117
Apr. 24—Thu.—Houston 115 at Boston 128

Washington 4, Buffalo 3

Apr. 10—Thu.—Buffalo 113 at Washington 102
Apr. 12—Sat.—Washington 120 at Buffalo 106
Apr. 16—Wed.—Buffalo 96 at Washington 111
Apr. 18—Fri.—Washington 102 at Buffalo 108
Apr. 20—Sun.—Buffalo 93 at Washington 97
Apr. 23—Wed.—Washington 96 at Buffalo 102
Apr. 25—Fri.—Buffalo 96 at Washington 115

EASTERN CONFERENCE FINALS
Washington 4, Boston 2

Apr. 27—Sun.—Washington 100 at Boston 95
Apr. 30—Wed.—Boston 92 at Washington 117
May 3—Sat.—Washington 90 at Boston 101
May 7—Wed.—Boston 108 at Washington 119
May 9—Fri.—Washington 99 at Boston 103
May 11—Sun.—Boston 92 at Washington 98

WESTERN CONFERENCE FIRST ROUND
Seattle 2, Detroit 1

Apr. 8—Tue.—Detroit 77 at Seattle 90
Apr. 10—Thu.—Seattle 106 at Detroit 122
Apr. 12—Sat.—Detroit 93 at Seattle 100

WESTERN CONFERENCE SEMIFINALS
Golden State 4, Seattle 2

Apr. 14—Mon.—Seattle 96 at Golden State 123
Apr. 16—Wed.—Seattle 100 at Golden State 99
Apr. 17—Thu.—Golden State 105 at Seattle 96
Apr. 19—Sat.—Golden State 89 at Seattle 111
Apr. 22—Tue.—Seattle 100 at Golden State 124
Apr. 24—Thu.—Golden State 105 at Seattle 96

Chicago 4, K.C-Omaha 2

Apr. 9—Wed.—K.C.-Omaha 89 at Chicago 95
Apr. 13—Sun.—Chicago 95 at K.C.-Omaha 102
Apr.♦16—Wed.—K.C.-Omaha 90 at Chicago 93
Apr. 18—Fri.—Chicago 100 at K.C.-Omaha 104*
Apr. 20—Sun.—K.C.-Omaha 77 at Chicago 104
Apr. 23—Wed.—Chicago 101 at K.C.-Omaha 89

WESTERN CONFERENCE FINALS
Golden State 4, Chicago 3

Apr. 27—Sun.—Chicago 89 at Golden State 107
Apr. 30—Wed.—Golden State 89 at Chicago 90
May 4—Sun.—Golden State 101 at Chicago 108
May 6—Tue.—Chicago 106 at Golden State 111
May 8—Thu.—Chicago 89 at Golden State 79
May 11—Sun.—Golden State 86 at Chicago 72
May 14—Wed.—Chicago 79 at Golden State 83

WORLD CHAMPIONSHIP SERIES
Golden State 4, Washington 0

May 18—Sun.—Golden State 101 at Washington 95
May 20—Tue.—Washington 91 at Golden State 92
May 23—Fri.—Washington 101 at Golden State 109
May 25—Sun.—Golden State 96 at Washington 95

*Denotes overtime period.

1973-74 NBA STATISTICS

1973-74 NBA CHAMPION BOSTON CELTICS

Seated from left, Jo Jo White, Don Chaney, John Havlicek, President and General Manager Arnold (Red) Auerbach, Chairman of the Board Robert Schmertz, Coach Tom Heinsohn, Dave Cowens, Paul Silas and Assistant Coach John Killilea. Standing from left, Assistant Trainer Mark Volk, Team Dentist Dr. Samuel Kane, Paul Westphal, Phil Hankinson, Steve Downing, Don Nelson, Hank Finkel, Steve Kuberski, Art Williams, Team Physician Dr. Thomas Silva and Trainer Frank Challant.

FINAL STANDINGS

ATLANTIC DIVISION

Team	Atl.	Bos.	Buf.	Cap.	Chi.	Clv.	Det.	G.S.	Hou.	KC	L.A.	Mil.	N.Y.	Phil.	Pho.	Prt.	Sea.	W.	L.	Pct.	G.B.
Boston	5	..	5	2	2	4	3	3	4	3	2	2	5	7	3	4	2	56	26	.683	....
New York	5	2	4	3	2	5	3	3	2	3	2	2	..	4	3	2	4	49	33	.598	7
Buffalo	4	2	..	3	1	5	1	1	4	2	0	1	4	6	3	3	2	42	40	.512	14
Philadelphia	3	1	1	2	1	1	2	1	2	3	0	0	3	..	3	2	0	25	57	.305	31

CENTRAL DIVISION

Team	Atl.	Bos.	Buf.	Cap.	Chi.	Clv.	Det.	G.S.	Hou.	KC	L.A.	Mil.	N.Y.	Phil.	Pho.	Prt.	Sea.	W.	L.	Pct.	G.B.
Capital	4	4	3	..	1	6	2	3	4	3	2	1	3	4	2	3	2	47	35	.573	....
Atlanta	..	1	2	4	1	4	0	1	5	1	4	1	1	3	1	2	4	35	47	.427	12
Houston	2	2	2	3	0	4	1	0	..	2	2	0	4	4	2	3	1	32	50	.390	15
Cleveland	3	2	1	1	0	..	2	0	4	0	3	0	1	5	1	4	2	29	53	.354	18

MIDWEST DIVISION

Team	Atl.	Bos.	Buf.	Cap.	Chi.	Clv.	Det.	G.S.	Hou.	KC	L.A.	Mil.	N.Y.	Phil.	Pho.	Prt.	Sea.	W.	L.	Pct.	G.B.
Milwaukee	3	2	3	3	3	4	4	3	4	7	2	..	2	4	5	6	4	59	23	.720	....
Chicago	3	2	3	3	..	4	5	4	4	5	1	3	2	3	4	4		54	28	.659	5
Detroit	4	1	3	2	2	2	..	5	3	4	4	3	1	2	6	5	5	52	30	.634	7
K.C.-Omaha	3	1	2	1	2	4	2	3	2	..	1	0	1	1	4	4	2	33	49	.402	26

PACIFIC DIVISION

Team	Atl.	Bos.	Buf.	Cap.	Chi.	Clv.	Det.	G.S.	Hou.	KC	L.A.	Mil.	N.Y.	Phil.	Pho.	Prt.	Sea.	W.	L.	Pct.	G.B.
Los Angeles	0	2	4	2	5	1	2	2	2	5	..	4	2	4	4	4	4	47	35	.573	....
Golden State	3	1	3	1	2	4	1	..	4	3	4	3	1	3	5	3	3	44	38	.537	3
Seattle	0	2	2	2	2	2	1	3	3	4	3	2	0	4	3	3	..	36	46	.439	11
Phoenix	3	1	1	2	2	3	0	2	2	2	2	1	1	1	..	3	4	30	52	.366	17
Portland	2	0	1	1	2	1	1	4	1	2	3	0	2	2	3	..	3	27	55	.329	20

HOME-ROAD-NEUTRAL RECORDS OF ALL TEAMS

Team	Home	Road	Neutral	Total	Team	Home	Road	Neutral	Total
Atlanta	23-18	12-25	0-4	35-47	K.C.-Omaha	20-21	13-28	0-0	33-49
Boston	26-6	21-18	9-2	56-26	Los Angeles	30-11	17-24	0-0	47-35
Buffalo	19-13	17-21	6-6	42-40	Milwaukee	31-7	24-16	4-0	59-23
Capital	31-10	15-25	1-0	47-35	New York	28-13	21-19	0-1	49-33
Chicago	32-9	21-19	1-0	54-28	Philadelphia	14-23	9-30	2-4	25-57
Cleveland	18-23	11-28	0-2	29-53	Phoenix	24-17	6-34	0-1	30-52
Detroit	29-12	23-17	0-1	52-30	Portland	22-19	5-34	0-2	27-55
Golden State	23-18	20-20	1-0	44-38	Seattle	22-19	14-27	0-0	36-46
Houston	18-23	13-25	1-2	32-50	Total	410-262	262-410	25-25	697-697

OFFENSIVE TEAM STATISTICS

Team	G.	FIELD GOALS Att.	Made	Pct.	FREE THROWS Att.	Made	Pct.	REBOUNDS Off.	Def.	Tot.	MISCELLANEOUS Ast.	PF	Disq.	Stl.	Turn Over	Blk. Sh.	SCORING Pts.	Avg.
Buffalo	82	7763	3728	.480	2221	1699	.765	1150	2830	3980	2165	1875	17	786	1828	600	9155	111.6
Golden State	82	8020	3721	.464	2018	1569	.778	1379	3035	4414	1989	1893	33	668	1667	450	9011	109.9
Los Angeles	82	7803	3536	.453	2443	1879	.769	1365	2970	4335	2179	2032	26	794	1913	653	8951	109.2
Boston	82	7969	3630	.456	2097	1677	.800	1378	3074	4452	2187	1868	22	561	1796	305	8937	109.0
Atlanta	82	7744	3602	.465	2264	1703	.752	1240	2712	3952	1993	2073	33	758	1823	332	8907	108.6
Phoenix	82	7726	3555	.460	2235	1737	.777	1090	2723	3813	2052	2123	46	658	1666	305	8847	107.9
Houston	82	7426	3564	.480	2071	1682	.812	1063	2588	3651	2212	2104	36	727	1681	407	8810	107.4
Milwaukee	82	7571	3726	.492	1741	1328	.763	1133	2881	4014	2225	1864	26	726	1694	519	8780	107.1
Seattle	82	8056	3584	.445	2095	1606	.767	1323	2706	4029	2106	2074	31	689	1622	294	8774	107.0
Portland	82	7684	3585	.467	2112	1591	.753	1254	2598	3852	2106	2050	23	797	1823	341	8761	106.8
Detroit	82	7515	3453	.459	2164	1654	.764	1200	2681	3881	1956	1930	19	793	1763	419	8560	104.4
Chicago	82	7378	3292	.446	2314	1784	.771	1143	2616	3759	1868	1874	17	764	1690	316	8368	102.0
KC-Omaha	82	7342	3369	.459	2104	1628	.774	1112	2554	3666	1744	1916	22	796	1791	384	8366	102.0
Capital	82	7886	3480	.441	1869	1393	.745	1286	2887	4173	1770	1746	24	703	1568	441	8353	101.9
New York	82	7483	3478	.465	1738	1350	.777	959	2725	3684	1937	1884	14	554	1463	277	8306	101.3
Philadelphia	82	7702	3331	.432	2118	1633	.771	1182	2626	3808	1799	1964	25	756	1665	220	8295	101.2
Cleveland	82	7782	3420	.439	1788	1381	.772	1275	2492	3767	2048	1925	22	598	1545	293	8221	100.3

DEFENSIVE TEAM STATISTICS

Team	FIELD GOALS Att.	Made	Pct.	FREE THROWS Att.	Made	Pct.	REBOUNDS Off.	Def.	Tot.	MISCELLANEOUS Ast.	PF	Disq.	Stl.	Turn Over	Blk. Sh.	SCORING Pts.	Avg.	Pt. Dif.
New York	7377	3292	.446	1974	1496	.758	1042	2790	3832	1580	1792	13	479	1555	348	8080	98.5	+2.8
Chicago	7246	3336	.460	1847	1425	.772	1136	2734	3870	1830	2200	34	614	1880	406	8097	98.7	+3.3
Milwaukee	7799	3311	.425	1969	1499	.761	1269	2487	3756	1909	1707	12	719	1554	312	8121	99.0	+8.1
Detroit	7499	3376	.450	1932	1475	.763	1173	2632	3805	1980	1996	30	772	1822	410	8227	100.3	+4.1
Capital	7760	3496	.451	1639	1239	.756	1206	2915	4121	1900	1840	9	651	1651	350	8231	100.4	+1.5
Cleveland	7342	3440	.469	2163	1696	.784	1137	2802	3939	2120	1853	27	630	1654	343	8576	104.6	-4.3
Boston	8047	3561	.443	1936	1494	.772	1131	2604	3735	1934	1858	29	540	1599	309	8616	105.1	+3.9
KC-Omaha	7514	3580	.476	1950	1512	.775	1210	2650	3860	1916	1907	22	723	1765	373	8672	105.8	-3.8
Golden State	7995	3619	.453	2054	1563	.761	1227	2702	3929	2027	1826	15	714	1463	465	8801	107.3	+2.6
Philadelphia	7685	3600	.468	2066	1617	.783	1311	3107	4418	1930	1991	23	755	1830	446	8817	107.5	-6.3
Houston	7433	3551	.478	2337	1719	.736	1162	2619	3781	2122	1994	29	707	1737	375	8821	107.6	-0.2
Los Angeles	8364	3667	.438	2044	1546	.756	1525	2786	4311	2061	2135	37	797	1719	430	8880	108.3	+0.9
Seattle	7675	3554	.463	2427	1875	.773	1173	2932	4105	2255	2012	34	730	1796	355	8983	109.5	-2.5
Atlanta	7628	3573	.468	2386	1878	.787	1142	2754	3896	2028	2128	40	823	1846	388	9024	110.0	-1.4
Phoenix	7809	3648	.467	2356	1843	.782	1220	2773	3993	2180	2003	25	810	1637	396	9139	111.5	-3.6
Portland	7571	3664	.484	2299	1825	.794	1197	2678	3875	2308	1961	20	866	1713	415	9153	111.6	-4.8
Buffalo	8106	3786	.467	2013	1592	.791	1271	2733	4004	2256	1992	37	798	1763	435	9164	111.8	-0.2

Disq.—Individual players disqualified (fouled out of game).

INDIVIDUAL LEADERS

POINTS
(Minimum 70 Games Played)

	G.	FG	FT	Pts.	Avg.
McAdoo, Buff	74	901	459	2261	30.6
Maravich, Atl	76	819	469	2107	27.7
Abdul-Jabbar, Mil	81	948	295	2191	27.0
†Hudson, Atl	65	678	295	1651	25.4
Goodrich, L.A.	82	784	508	2076	25.3
Barry, G.S.	80	796	417	2009	25.1
Tomjanovich, Hou	80	788	385	1961	24.5
Petrie, Port	73	740	291	1771	24.3
Haywood, Sea	75	694	373	1761	23.5
Havlicek, Bos	76	685	346	1716	22.6
Lanier, Det	81	748	326	1822	22.5

	G.	FG	FT	Pts.	Avg.
Wicks, Port	75	685	314	1684	22.5
Chenier, Cap	76	697	274	1668	21.9
Carr, Clev	81	748	279	1775	21.9
B. Love, Chi	82	731	323	1785	21.8
Hayes, Cap	81	689	357	1735	21.4
Carter, Phil	78	706	254	1666	21.4
Frazier, N.Y.	80	674	295	1643	20.5
Russell, G.S.	82	738	208	1684	20.5
Murphy, Hou	81	671	310	1652	20.4
T. Van Arsdale, Phil	78	614	298	1526	19.6

FIELD GOALS
(Minimum 560 Attempts)

	FGA	FGM	Pct.
McAdoo, Buff	1647	901	.547
Abdul-Jabbar, Mil	1759	948	.539
Tomjanovich, Hou	1470	788	.536
Murphy, Hou	1285	671	.522
Beard, G.S.	617	316	.512
Ray, Chi	612	313	.511
D. Nelson, Bos	717	364	.508
Hairston, L.A.	759	385	.507
Lanier, Det	1483	748	.504
Dandridge, Mil	1158	583	.503

FREE THROWS
(Minimum 160 Attempts)

	FTA	FTM	Pct.
DiGregorio, Buff	193	174	.902
Barry, G.S.	464	417	.899
Mullins, G.S.	192	168	.875
C. Walker, Chi	502	439	.875
Bradley, N.Y.	167	146	.874
Murphy, Hou	357	310	.868
Snyder, Sea	224	194	.866
Goodrich, L.A.	588	508	.864
F. Brown, Sea	226	195	.863
McMillian, Buff	379	325	.858

ASSISTS
(Minimum 70 Games)

Player	G.	No.	Avg.
DiGregorio, Buff	81	663	8.2
Murphy, Hou	81	603	7.4
Wilkens, Clev	74	522	7.1
Frazier, N.Y.	80	551	6.9
Bing, Det	81	555	6.9
Van Lier, Chi	80	548	6.9
Robertson, Mil	70	446	6.4
Barry, G.S.	80	484	6.1
Havlicek, Bos	76	447	5.9
K. Porter, Cap	81	469	5.8

STEALS*
(Minimum 70 Games)

Player	G.	No.	Avg.
Steele, Port	81	217	2.68
Mix, Phil	82	212	2.59
R. Smith, Buff	82	203	2.48
†Hudson, Atl	65	160	2.46
Sloan, Chi	77	183	2.38
†Gilliam, Atl.	62	134	2.16
Barry, G.S.	80	169	2.11
Chenier, Cap	76	155	2.04
Van Lier, Chi	80	162	2.03
Frazier, N.Y.	80	161	2.01
Murphy, Hou	81	157	1.94
Price, L.A.	82	157	1.91

REBOUNDS
(Minimum 70 Games)

Player	G.	Off.	Def.	Tot.	Avg.
Hayes, Cap	81	354	1109	1463	18.1
Cowens, Bos	80	264	993	1257	15.7
McAdoo, Buff	74	281	836	1117	15.1
Abdul-Jabbar, Mil	81	287	891	1178	14.5
Hairston, L.A.	77	335	705	1040	13.5
Haywood, Sea	75	318	689	1007	13.4
Lacey, K.C.-O.	79	293	762	1055	13.4
Lanier, Det	81	269	805	1074	13.3
Ray, Chi.	80	285	692	977	12.2
Heard, Buff	81	270	677	947	11.7

BLOCKED SHOTS*
(Minimum 70 Games)

Player	G.	No.	Avg.
E. Smith, L.A.	81	393	4.85
Abdul-Jabbar, Mil	81	283	3.49
McAdoo, Buff	74	246	3.32
Lanier, Det	81	247	3.05
Hayes, Cap	81	240	2.96
Heard, Buff	81	230	2.84
Lacey, K.C.-O	79	184	2.33
Ray, Chi	80	173	2.16
Haywood, Sea	75	106	1.41
D. Smith, Hou	79	104	1.32

*Beginning in the 1973-74 season, the NBA started keeping statistics for steals and blocked shots.

TEAM-BY-TEAM INDIVIDUAL STATISTICS

ATLANTA HAWKS

Player	G.	Min.	FGA	FGM	Pct.	FTA	FTM	Pct.	Off. Reb.	Def. Reb.	Tot. Reb.	Ast.	PF	Disq.	Stl.	Blk. Sh.	Pts.	Avg.	Hi.
Maravich	76	2903	1791	819	.457	568	469	.826	98	276	374	396	261	4	111	13	2107	27.7	42
Hudson	65	2588	1356	678	.500	353	295	.836	126	224	350	213	205	3	160	29	1651	25.4	44
Gilliam	62	2003	846	384	.454	134	106	.791	61	206	267	355	190	5	134	18	874	14.1	35
Bellamy	77	2440	801	389	.486	383	233	.608	264	476	740	189	232	2	52	48	1011	13.1	34
J. Washington	73	2519	612	297	.485	196	134	.684	207	528	735	156	249	5	49	74	728	10.0	23
J. Brown	77	1715	632	277	.438	217	163	.751	177	264	441	114	239	10	29	16	717	9.3	25
D. Jones	74	1448	502	238	.474	156	116	.744	145	309	454	86	197	3	29	64	592	8.0	33
Bracey	75	1463	520	241	.463	96	69	.719	26	120	146	231	157	0	60	5	551	7.3	25
Wetzel	70	1232	252	107	.425	57	41	.719	39	131	170	138	147	1	73	19	255	3.6	17
Schlueter	57	547	135	63	.467	50	38	.760	54	101	155	45	84	0	25	22	164	2.9	12
Ingelsby	48	398	131	50	.382	37	29	.784	10	34	44	37	43	0	19	4	129	2.7	10
Tschogl	64	499	166	59	.355	17	10	.588	33	43	76	33	69	0	17	20	128	2.0	14

BOSTON CELTICS

Player	G.	Min.	FGA	FGM	Pct.	FTA	FTM	Pct.	Off. Reb.	Def. Reb.	Tot. Reb.	Ast.	PF	Disq.	Stl.	Blk. Sh.	Pts.	Avg.	Hi.
Havlicek	76	3091	1502	685	.456	416	346	.832	138	349	487	447	196	1	95	32	1716	22.6	34
Cowens	80	3352	1475	645	.437	274	228	.832	264	993	1257	354	294	7	95	101	1518	19.0	35
White	82	3238	1445	649	.449	227	190	.837	100	251	351	448	185	1	105	25	1488	18.1	37
Silas	82	2599	772	340	.440	337	264	.783	334	581	915	186	246	3	63	20	944	11.5	31
D. Nelson	82	1748	717	364	.508	273	215	.788	90	255	345	162	189	1	19	13	943	11.5	34
Chaney	81	2258	750	348	.464	180	149	.828	210	168	378	176	247	7	83	62	845	10.4	26
Westphal	82	1165	475	238	.501	153	112	.732	49	94	143	171	173	1	39	34	588	7.2	28
Kuberski	78	985	368	157	.427	111	86	.775	96	141	237	38	125	0	7	7	400	5.1	21
Hankinson	28	163	103	50	.485	13	10	.769	22	28	50	4	18	0	3	1	110	3.9	13
Downing	24	137	64	21	.328	38	22	.579	14	25	39	11	33	0	5	0	64	2.7	4
A. Williams	67	617	168	73	.435	32	27	.844	20	95	115	163	100	0	44	3	173	2.6	14
Finkel	60	427	130	60	.462	43	28	.651	41	94	135	27	62	1	3	7	148	2.5	14

BUFFALO BRAVES

Player	G.	Min.	FGA	FGM	Pct.	FTA	FTM	Pct.	Off. Reb.	Def. Reb.	Tot. Reb.	Ast.	PF	Disq.	Stl.	Blk. Sh.	Pts.	Avg.	Hi.
McAdoo	74	3185	1647	901	.547	579	459	.793	281	836	1117	170	252	3	88	246	2261	30.6	52
McMillian	82	3322	1214	600	.494	379	325	.858	216	394	610	256	186	0	129	26	1525	18.6	48
R. Smith	82	2745	1079	531	.492	288	205	.712	87	228	315	383	261	4	203	4	1267	15.5	32
Heard	81	2889	1205	524	.435	294	191	.650	270	677	947	180	300	3	136	230	1239	15.3	36
DiGregorio	81	2910	1260	530	.421	193	174	.902	48	171	219	663	242	0	59	9	1234	15.2	32
Marin (Tot.)	74	1782	709	355	.501	179	153	.855	59	169	228	167	213	5	46	26	863	11.7	26
Marin (Buff.)	27	680	266	145	.545	81	71	.877	30	92	122	46	93	2	23	18	361	13.4	24
Kauffman	74	1304	366	171	.467	150	107	.713	97	229	326	142	155	0	37	18	449	6.1	16
Guokas (Tot.)	75	1871	396	195	.492	60	39	.650	31	90	121	238	150	3	54	21	429	5.7	23
Guokas (Buff.)	27	549	110	61	.555	20	10	.500	12	28	40	69	56	1	19	6	132	4.9	23
Wohl	41	606	150	60	.400	60	42	.700	7	22	29	127	72	1	33	1	162	4.0	16
Charles	59	693	185	88	.476	79	53	.671	25	40	65	54	91	0	31	10	229	3.9	16
Winfield	36	433	105	37	.352	52	33	.635	19	24	43	47	42	0	15	5	107	3.0	9
Kunnert	39	340	101	49	.485	16	11	.688	43	63	106	25	83	0	5	25	109	2.8	9
Macaluso	30	112	44	19	.432	17	10	.588	10	15	25	3	31	0	7	1	48	1.6	8
Ruffner	20	51	27	11	.407	13	8	.615	4	7	11	0	10	0	1	1	30	1.5	7
Garvin	6	11	4	1	.250	0	0	.000	1	4	5	0	1	0	0	0	2	0.3	2

CAPITAL BULLETS

Player	G.	Min.	FGA	FGM	Pct.	FTA	FTM	Pct.	Off. Reb.	Def. Reb.	Tot. Reb.	Ast.	PF	Disq.	Stl.	Blk. Sh.	Pts.	Avg.	Hi.
Chenier	76	2942	1607	697	.434	334	274	.820	114	274	388	239	135	0	155	67	1668	21.9	38
Hayes	81	3602	1627	689	.423	495	357	.721	354	1109	1463	163	252	1	86	240	1735	21.4	43
Riordan	81	3230	1223	577	.472	174	136	.782	120	260	380	264	237	2	102	14	1290	15.9	33
K. Porter	81	2339	997	477	.478	249	180	.723	79	100	179	469	319	14	95	9	1134	14.0	28
Clark	56	1786	675	315	.467	131	103	.786	44	97	141	285	122	0	59	6	733	13.1	28
Weatherspoon	65	1216	483	199	.412	139	96	.691	133	264	397	38	179	1	48	16	494	7.6	19
Unseld	56	2632	612	273	.446	55	36	.655	152	365	517	159	121	1	56	16	328	5.9	14
L. Nelson	49	556	215	93	.433	73	53	.726	26	44	70	52	62	0	31	2	239	4.9	17
D. Stallworth	45	458	187	75	.401	55	47	.855	52	73	125	25	61	0	28	4	197	4.4	19
Wesley	39	400	151	71	.470	43	26	.605	63	73	136	14	74	1	9	20	168	4.3	20
Leaks	53	845	232	79	.341	83	58	.699	94	150	244	25	95	1	10	39	216	4.1	19
Kozelko	49	573	133	59	.444	32	23	.719	52	72	124	25	82	3	21	7	141	2.9	15
Rinaldi	7	48	22	3	.136	4	3	.750	2	5	7	10	7	0	3	1	9	1.3	3
T. Patterson	2	8	1	0	.000	2	1	.500	1	1	2	2	0	0	0	0	1	0.5	1

CHICAGO BULLS

Player	G.	Min.	FGA	FGM	Pct.	FTA	FTM	Pct.	Off. Reb.	Def. Reb.	Tot. Reb.	Ast.	PF	Disq.	Stl.	Blk. Sh.	Pts.	Avg.	Hi.
B. Love	82	3292	1752	731	.417	395	323	.818	183	309	492	130	221	1	84	28	1785	21.8	43
C. Walker	82	2661	1178	572	.486	502	439	.875	131	275	406	200	201	1	68	4	1583	19.3	39
Van Lier	80	2863	1051	427	.406	370	288	.778	114	263	377	548	282	4	162	7	1142	14.3	30
Sloan	77	2860	921	412	.447	273	194	.711	150	406	556	149	273	3	183	10	1018	13.2	25
H. Porter	73	1229	658	296	.450	115	92	.800	86	199	285	32	116	0	23	39	684	9.4	25
Ray	80	2632	612	313	.511	199	121	.608	285	692	977	246	281	5	58	173	747	9.3	24
Weiss	79	1708	564	263	.466	170	142	.835	32	71	103	303	156	0	104	12	668	8.5	24
R. Garrett	41	373	184	68	.370	32	21	.656	31	39	70	11	43	0	5	9	157	3.8	16
Boerwinkle	46	602	119	58	.487	60	42	.700	53	160	213	94	80	0	16	18	158	3.4	16
Adelman	55	618	170	64	.376	76	54	.711	16	53	69	56	63	0	36	1	182	3.3	12
Hummer	18	186	46	23	.500	28	14	.500	13	24	37	13	30	0	3	1	60	3.3	12
Awtrey	68	756	123	65	.528	94	54	.574	49	125	174	86	128	3	22	14	184	2.7	10

CLEVELAND CAVALIERS

Player	G.	Min.	FGA	FGM	Pct.	FTA	FTM	Pct.	Off. Reb.	Def. Reb.	Tot. Reb.	Ast.	PF	Disq.	Stl.	Blk. Sh.	Pts.	Avg.	Hi.
Carr	81	3100	1682	748	.445	326	279	.856	139	150	289	305	189	2	92	14	1775	21.9	39
Wilkens	74	2483	994	462	.465	361	289	.801	80	197	277	522	165	2	97	17	1213	16.4	34
B. Smith	82	2612	1179	536	.455	169	139	.822	134	301	435	198	242	4	89	30	1211	14.8	34
D. Davis	76	2477	862	376	.436	274	197	.719	174	470	644	186	291	6	63	74	949	12.5	25
S. Patterson	76	1910	599	262	.437	112	69	.616	223	396	619	165	193	3	48	58	593	7.8	22
Rule	26	540	192	76	.396	46	34	.739	43	60	103	47	71	0	12	10	186	7.2	22
Cleamons	81	1642	545	236	.433	133	93	.699	63	167	230	227	152	1	61	17	565	7.0	21
Brewer	82	1862	548	210	.383	123	80	.650	207	317	524	149	192	1	46	35	500	6.1	18
Clemens	71	913	346	163	.471	73	62	.849	42	124	166	80	136	2	36	2	388	5.5	18
Foster	58	649	288	112	.389	64	54	.844	43	65	108	62	79	0	19	6	278	4.8	21
Witte	57	728	243	105	.432	62	46	.742	80	147	227	41	91	0	8	22	256	4.5	17
Warren	69	790	291	132	.454	41	35	.854	42	86	128	62	117	1	27	6	299	4.3	24
Warner	5	49	13	2	.154	4	4	1.000	5	12	17	4	7	0	0	2	8	1.6	4

DETROIT PISTONS

Player	G.	Min.	FGA	FGM	Pct.	FTA	FTM	Pct.	Off. Reb.	Def. Reb.	Tot. Reb.	Ast.	PF	Disq.	Stl.	Blk. Sh.	Pts.	Avg.	Hi.
Lanier	81	3047	1483	748	.504	409	326	.797	269	805	1074	343	273	7	110	247	1822	22.5	45
Bing	81	3124	1336	582	.436	438	356	.813	108	173	281	555	216	1	109	17	1520	18.8	33
Rowe	82	2499	769	380	.494	169	118	.698	167	348	515	136	177	1	49	36	878	10.7	28
Adams	74	2298	742	303	.408	201	153	.761	133	315	448	141	242	2	110	12	759	10.3	25
Trapp	82	1489	693	333	.481	134	99	.739	97	216	313	81	226	2	47	33	765	9.3	22
Lantz	50	980	361	154	.427	163	139	.848	34	79	113	97	79	0	38	3	447	8.9	24
Mengelt	77	1555	558	249	.446	229	182	.795	40	166	206	148	164	2	68	7	680	8.8	30
Norwood	74	1178	484	247	.510	143	95	.664	95	134	229	58	156	2	60	9	589	8.0	29
Ford	82	2059	595	264	.444	77	57	.740	109	195	304	279	159	1	148	14	585	7.1	24
J. Davis	78	947	283	117	.413	139	90	.647	102	191	293	86	158	1	39	30	324	4.2	15
Nash	35	281	115	41	.357	39	24	.615	31	43	74	14	35	0	3	10	106	3.0	16
Kelso	46	298	96	35	.365	22	15	.682	15	16	31	18	45	0	12	1	85	1.8	8

GOLDEN STATE WARRIORS

Player	G.	Min.	FGA	FGM	Pct.	FTA	FTM	Pct.	Off. Reb.	Def. Reb.	Tot. Reb.	Ast.	PF	Disq.	Stl.	Blk. Sh.	Pts.	Avg.	Hi.
Barry	80	2918	1746	796	.456	464	417	.899	103	437	540	484	265	4	169	40	2009	25.1	64
Russell	82	2574	1531	738	.482	249	208	.835	142	211	353	192	194	1	54	17	1684	20.5	49
Mullins	77	2498	1144	541	.473	192	168	.875	86	190	276	305	214	2	69	22	1250	16.2	32
Thurmond	62	2463	694	308	.444	287	191	.666	249	629	878	165	179	4	41	179	807	13.0	31
J. Barnett	77	1689	755	350	.464	226	184	.814	76	146	222	209	146	1	56	11	884	11.5	30
Beard	79	2134	617	316	.512	234	173	.739	136	253	389	300	241	11	105	9	805	10.2	30
C. Johnson	59	1051	468	194	.415	55	38	.691	49	126	175	102	111	1	62	7	426	7.2	20
G.T. Johnson	66	1297	358	173	.483	107	59	.551	190	332	522	73	176	3	35	124	405	6.1	23
C. Lee	54	1642	284	129	.454	107	62	.579	188	410	598	68	179	3	27	17	320	5.9	14
Dickey	66	930	233	115	.494	66	51	.773	123	216	339	54	112	1	17	15	281	4.3	17
J. Ellis	50	515	190	61	.321	31	18	.581	37	85	122	37	76	2	33	9	140	2.8	17

HOUSTON ROCKETS

Player	G.	Min.	FGA	FGM	Pct.	FTA	FTM	Pct.	Off. Reb.	Def. Reb.	Tot. Reb.	Ast.	PF	Disq.	Stl.	Blk. Sh.	Pts.	Avg.	Hi.
Tomjanovich	80	3227	1470	788	.536	454	385	.848	230	487	717	250	230	0	89	66	1961	24.5	42
Murphy	81	2922	1285	671	.522	357	310	.868	51	137	188	603	310	8	157	4	1652	20.4	39
Newlin	76	2591	1139	510	.448	444	380	.856	77	185	262	363	259	5	87	9	1400	18.4	36
D. Smith	79	2459	732	336	.459	240	193	.804	259	664	923	166	227	3	80	104	865	10.9	27

Player	G.	Min.	FGA	FGM	Pct.	FTA	FTM	Pct.	Off. Reb.	Def. Reb.	Tot. Reb.	Ast.	PF	Disq.	Stl.	Blk. Sh.	Pts.	Avg.	Hi.
Marin	47	1102	443	210	.474	98	82	.837	29	77	106	121	120	2	23	8	502	10.7	26
Meely	77	1754	773	330	.427	140	90	.643	103	336	439	124	234	5	53	77	750	9.7	22
Ratleff	81	1773	585	254	.434	129	103	.798	93	193	286	181	182	2	90	27	611	7.5	18
Guokas	39	1007	203	93	.458	28	21	.750	17	43	60	133	73	1	27	14	207	5.3	14
Coleman	58	1075	250	128	.512	74	47	.635	81	171	252	76	162	4	37	20	303	5.2	19
Moore	13	313	69	32	.464	8	4	.500	20	64	84	18	37	2	10	18	68	5.2	14
Wohl (Tot.)	67	1055	277	121	.437	102	75	.735	11	35	46	236	136	3	76	2	317	4.7	18
Wohl (Hou.)	26	449	127	61	.480	42	33	.786	4	13	17	109	64	2	43	1	155	6.0	18
J. Walker	3	38	12	7	.583	1	0	.000	0	2	2	4	4	0	0	0	14	4.7	6
R.Riley(Tot.)	48	591	202	81	.401	38	24	.632	48	129	177	37	95	0	18	24	186	3.9	15
R.Riley(Hou.)	36	421	145	57	.393	14	10	.714	35	86	121	29	68	0	15	22	124	3.4	13
Kunnert (Tot.)	64	701	215	105	.488	33	21	.636	83	134	217	43	151	1	10	54	231	3.6	12
Kunnert (Hou.)	25	361	114	56	.491	17	10	.588	40	71	111	18	68	1	5	29	122	4.9	12
G.E. Johnson	26	238	51	23	.451	17	8	.471	20	41	61	9	46	1	8	8	54	2.1	8
McKenzie	11	112	24	7	.292	8	6	.750	3	13	16	6	17	0	3	0	20	1.8	9
McCracken	4	13	4	1	.250	0	0	.000	1	5	6	2	3	0	0	0	2	0.5	2

KANSAS CITY-OMAHA KINGS

Player	G.	Min.	FGA	FGM	Pct.	FTA	FTM	Pct.	Off. Reb.	Def. Reb.	Tot. Reb.	Ast.	PF	Disq.	Stl.	Blk. Sh.	Pts.	Avg.	Hi.
J. Walker (Tot.)	75	2958	1240	582	.469	333	273	.820	39	165	204	307	170	0	81	9	1437	19.2	38
J. Walker(KC-O)	72	2920	1228	575	.468	332	273	.822	39	163	202	303	166	0	81	9	1423	19.8	38
Archibald	35	1272	492	222	.451	211	173	.820	21	64	85	266	76	0	56	7	617	17.6	42
N. Williams	82	2513	1165	538	.462	236	193	.818	118	226	344	182	290	5	149	34	1269	15.5	30
Lacey	79	3107	982	467	.476	247	185	.749	293	762	1055	299	254	3	126	184	1119	14.2	26
Kojis	77	2091	836	400	.478	272	210	.772	126	257	383	110	157	2	77	15	1010	13.1	30
Behagen	80	2059	827	357	.432	212	162	.764	188	379	567	134	291	9	56	37	876	11.0	27
Guokas	9	315	83	41	.494	12	8	.667	2	19	21	36	21	1	8	1	90	10.0	18
Block	82	1777	634	275	.434	206	164	.796	129	260	389	94	229	2	68	35	714	8.7	27
McNeill	54	516	220	106	.482	140	99	.707	60	86	146	24	76	0	35	6	311	5.8	21
R. Riley	12	170	57	24	.421	24	14	.583	13	43	56	8	27	0	3	2	62	5.2	15
D'Antoni	52	989	266	107	.402	47	33	.702	24	69	93	123	112	0	75	15	247	4.8	15
Durrett	45	462	176	86	.489	69	42	.609	28	50	78	19	68	0	13	5	214	4.8	24
Komives	44	830	192	78	.406	38	33	.868	10	33	43	97	83	0	32	3	189	4.3	18
Moore (Tot.)	78	946	240	120	.500	62	39	.629	80	204	284	65	99	2	26	49	279	3.6	15
Moore (KC-O)	65	633	171	88	.515	54	35	.648	60	140	200	47	62	0	16	31	211	3.2	15
Manakas	5	45	10	4	.400	4	4	1.000	0	3	3	2	4	0	1	0	12	2.4	4
Thigpen	1	2	3	1	.333	0	0	.000	1	0	1	0	0	0	0	0	2	2.0	2
Ratliff	2	4	0	0	.000	0	0	.000	0	0	0	0	0	0	0	0	0	0.0	0

LOS ANGELES LAKERS

Player	G.	Min.	FGA	FGM	Pct.	FTA	FTM	Pct.	Off. Reb.	Def. Reb.	Tot. Reb.	Ast.	PF	Disq.	Stl.	Blk. Sh.	Pts.	Avg.	Hi.
Goodrich	82	3061	1773	784	.442	588	508	.864	95	155	250	427	227	3	126	12	2076	25.3	49
West	31	967	519	232	.447	198	165	.833	30	86	116	206	80	0	81	23	629	20.3	35
Price	82	2628	1197	538	.449	234	187	.799	120	258	378	369	229	2	157	29	1263	15.4	31
Hairston	77	2634	759	385	.507	445	343	.771	335	705	1040	208	264	2	64	17	1113	14.5	29
Hawkins (Tot.)	79	2761	807	404	.501	251	191	.761	176	389	565	407	223	1	113	81	999	12.6	26
Hawkins (L.A.)	71	2538	733	368	.502	224	173	.772	162	360	522	379	203	1	105	78	909	12.8	26
E. Smith	81	2922	949	434	.457	249	147	.590	204	702	906	150	309	8	71	393	1015	12.5	37
P. Riley	72	1361	667	287	.430	144	110	.764	38	90	128	148	173	1	54	3	684	9.5	22
Bridges	65	1812	513	216	.421	164	116	.707	193	306	499	148	219	3	58	31	548	8.4	28
S. Love	51	698	278	119	.428	64	49	.766	54	116	170	48	132	3	28	20	287	5.6	21
K. Washington	45	400	151	73	.483	49	26	.531	62	85	147	19	77	0	21	18	172	3.8	18
Counts	45	499	167	61	.365	33	24	.727	56	90	146	54	85	2	20	23	146	3.2	16
Hawthorne	33	229	93	38	.409	48	30	.625	16	16	32	23	33	1	9	6	106	3.2	13
Grant	3	6	4	1	.250	3	1	.333	0	1	1	0	1	0	0	0	3	1.0	3

MILWAUKEE BUCKS

Player	G.	Min.	FGA	FGM	Pct.	FTA	FTM	Pct.	Off. Reb.	Def. Reb.	Tot. Reb.	Ast.	PF	Disq.	Stl.	Blk. Sh.	Pts.	Avg.	Hi.
Abdul-Jabbar	81	3548	1759	948	.539	420	295	.702	287	891	1178	386	238	2	112	283	2191	27.0	44
Dandridge	71	2521	1158	583	.503	214	175	.818	117	362	479	201	271	4	111	41	1341	18.9	32
Allen	72	2388	1062	526	.495	274	216	.788	89	202	291	374	215	2	137	22	1268	17.6	39
Robertson	70	2477	772	338	.438	254	212	.835	71	208	279	446	132	0	77	4	888	12.7	24
McGlocklin	79	1910	693	329	.475	80	72	.900	33	106	139	241	128	1	43	7	730	9.2	29
Perry	81	2386	729	325	.446	134	78	.582	242	461	703	183	301	8	104	97	728	9.0	23
R. Williams	71	1130	393	192	.489	68	60	.882	19	50	69	153	114	1	49	2	444	6.3	21
Warner (Tot.)	72	1405	349	174	.499	114	85	.746	106	291	397	71	204	8	27	42	433	6.0	21
Warner (Mil.)	67	1356	336	172	.512	110	81	.736	101	279	380	67	197	8	27	40	425	6.3	21
Mick Davis	73	1012	335	169	.504	112	93	.830	78	146	224	87	94	0	27	5	431	5.9	22
Driscoll	64	697	187	88	.471	46	30	.652	73	126	199	54	121	0	21	16	206	3.2	15
D. Garrett (Tot.)	40	326	126	43	.341	19	15	.789	15	25	40	23	56	0	10	1	101	2.5	14
D. Garrett (Mil.)	15	87	35	11	.314	6	5	.833	5	9	14	9	15	0	3	0	27	1.8	8
R. Lee	36	166	94	38	.404	16	11	.688	16	24	40	20	29	0	11	0	87	2.4	10
Terry	7	32	12	4	.333	0	0	.000	1	2	3	4	4	0	2	0	8	1.1	4
Cunningham	8	45	6	3	.500	7	0	.000	1	15	16	0	5	0	2	0	6	0.8	4

NEW YORK KNICKERBOCKERS

Player	G.	Min.	FGA	FGM	Pct.	FTA	FTM	Pct.	Off. Reb.	Def. Reb.	Tot. Reb.	Ast.	PF	Disq.	Stl.	Blk. Sh.	Pts.	Avg.	Hi.
Frazier	80	3338	1429	674	.472	352	295	.838	120	416	536	551	212	2	161	15	1643	20.5	44
DeBusschere	71	2699	1212	559	.461	217	164	.756	134	623	757	253	222	2	67	39	1282	18.1	41
Bradley	82	2813	1112	502	.451	167	146	.874	59	194	253	242	278	2	42	21	1150	14.0	31
Monroe	41	1194	513	240	.468	113	93	.823	22	99	121	110	97	0	34	19	573	14.0	29
Jackson	82	2050	757	361	.477	246	191	.776	123	355	478	134	227	7	42	67	913	11.1	30
Reed	19	500	184	84	.457	53	42	.792	47	94	141	30	49	0	12	21	210	11.1	25
Meminger	78	2079	539	274	.508	160	103	.644	125	156	281	162	161	0	62	8	651	8.3	27

In only his second pro season, Buffalo's Bob McAdoo led the NBA in scoring with a 30.6 average in 1973-74.

Player	G.	Min.	FGA	FGM	Pct.	FTA	FTM	Pct.	Off. Reb.	Def. Reb.	Tot. Reb.	Ast.	PF	Disq.	Stl.	Blk. Sh.	Pts.	Avg.	Hi.
Bibby	66	986	465	210	.452	88	73	.830	48	85	133	91	123	0	65	2	493	7.5	22
Gianelli	70	1423	434	208	.479	121	92	.760	110	233	343	77	159	1	23	42	508	7.3	25
Lucas	73	1627	420	194	.462	96	67	.698	62	312	374	230	134	0	28	24	455	6.2	17
D. Barnett	5	58	26	10	.385	3	2	.667	1	3	4	6	2	0	1	0	22	4.4	10
Wingo	60	536	172	82	.477	76	48	.632	72	94	166	25	85	0	7	14	212	3.5	14
D. Garrett	25	239	91	32	.352	13	10	.769	10	16	26	14	41	0	7	1	74	3.0	14
Mel Davis	30	167	95	33	.347	16	12	.750	17	37	54	8	36	0	3	4	78	2.6	12
Riker	17	57	29	13	.448	17	12	.706	9	6	15	3	6	0	0	0	38	2.2	11
McGuire	2	10	4	2	.500	0	0	.000	0	2	2	1	2	0	0	0	4	2.0	2
Bell	1	4	1	0	.000	0	0	.000	0	0	0	0	0	0	0	0	0	0.0	0

PHILADELPHIA 76ers

Player	G.	Min.	FGA	FGM	Pct.	FTA	FTM	Pct.	Off. Reb.	Def. Reb.	Tot. Reb.	Ast.	PF	Disq.	Stl.	Blk. Sh.	Pts.	Avg.	Hi.
Carter	78	3044	1641	706	.430	358	254	.709	82	289	371	443	276	4	113	23	1666	21.4	35
T. Van Arsdale	78	3041	1433	614	.428	350	361	.851	88	305	393	202	300	6	62	3	1526	19.6	35
Mix	82	2969	1042	495	.475	288	228	.792	305	559	864	152	305	9	212	37	1218	14.9	38
L. Jones	72	1876	622	263	.423	235	197	.838	71	113	184	230	116	0	85	18	723	10.0	22
L. Ellis	81	2831	722	326	.452	196	147	.750	292	598	890	189	224	2	86	87	799	9.9	24
Boyd	75	1818	712	286	.402	195	141	.723	16	77	93	249	173	1	60	9	713	9.5	24
Collins	25	436	194	72	.371	72	55	.764	7	39	46	40	65	1	13	2	199	8.0	17
Kimball	75	1592	456	216	.474	185	127	.686	185	367	552	73	199	1	49	23	559	7.5	22
May	56	812	367	152	.414	102	89	.873	25	111	136	63	137	0	25	8	393	7.0	28
Cannon	19	335	127	49	.386	28	19	.679	16	20	36	52	48	0	7	4	117	6.2	17
Bristow	55	643	270	108	.400	57	42	.737	68	99	167	92	68	1	29	1	258	4.7	20
Freeman	35	265	103	39	.379	41	28	.683	22	32	54	14	42	0	12	1	106	3.0	11
Rackley	9	68	13	5	.385	11	8	.727	5	17	22	0	11	0	3	4	18	2.0	5

PHOENIX SUNS

Player	G.	Min.	FGA	FGM	Pct.	FTA	FTM	Pct.	Off. Reb.	Def. Reb.	Tot. Reb.	Ast.	PF	Disq.	Stl.	Blk. Sh.	Pts.	Avg.	Hi.
Scott	52	2003	1171	538	.459	315	246	.781	64	158	222	271	194	6	99	22	1322	25.4	44
D. Van Arsdale	78	2832	1028	514	.500	423	361	.853	66	155	221	324	241	2	96	17	1389	17.8	37
Walk	82	2549	1245	573	.460	297	235	.791	235	602	837	331	255	9	73	57	1381	16.8	32
Erickson	66	2033	824	393	.477	221	177	.801	94	320	414	205	193	3	63	20	963	14.6	40
Hawkins	8	223	74	36	.486	27	18	.667	14	29	43	28	20	0	8	3	90	11.3	21
Haskins	81	1822	792	364	.460	203	171	.842	78	144	222	259	166	1	50	16	899	11.1	36
Bantom	76	1982	787	314	.399	213	141	.662	172	347	519	163	289	15	50	47	769	10.1	26
Calhoun	77	2207	581	268	.461	129	98	.760	115	292	407	135	253	4	71	30	634	8.2	25
Melchionni	69	1251	439	202	.460	107	92	.860	46	96	142	142	85	1	41	9	496	7.2	23
Chamberlain	28	367	130	57	.438	56	39	.696	33	47	80	37	74	2	20	12	153	5.5	19
Christian	81	1244	288	140	.486	151	106	.702	85	254	339	98	191	3	19	32	386	4.8	21
Green	72	1103	317	129	.407	68	38	.559	85	265	350	43	150	1	32	38	296	4.1	14
Owens	17	101	39	21	.538	14	11	.786	1	8	9	15	6	0	5	0	53	3.1	10
Reaves	7	38	11	6	.545	11	4	.364	2	6	8	1	6	0	0	2	16	2.3	4

PORTLAND TRAIL BLAZERS

Player	G.	Min.	FGA	FGM	Pct.	FTA	FTM	Pct.	Off. Reb.	Def. Reb.	Tot. Reb.	Ast.	PF	Disq.	Stl.	Blk. Sh.	Pts.	Avg.	Hi.
Petrie	73	2800	1537	740	.481	341	291	.853	64	144	208	315	199	2	84	15	1771	24.3	43
Wicks	75	2853	1492	685	.459	412	314	.762	196	488	684	326	214	2	90	63	1684	22.5	38
J. Johnson	69	2287	990	459	.464	261	212	.812	160	355	515	284	221	1	69	29	1130	16.4	32
Roberson	69	2060	797	364	.457	316	205	.649	251	450	701	133	252	4	65	55	933	13.5	37
Steele	81	2648	680	325	.478	171	135	.789	89	221	310	323	295	10	217	32	785	9.7	28
Neal	80	1517	502	246	.490	168	117	.696	150	344	494	89	190	0	45	73	609	7.6	22
Fryer	80	1674	491	226	.460	135	107	.793	60	99	159	279	187	1	92	10	559	7.0	27
O. Johnson	79	1718	434	209	.482	94	77	.819	116	208	324	167	179	2	60	30	495	6.3	23
Layton	22	327	112	55	.491	26	14	.538	7	26	33	51	45	0	9	1	124	5.6	19
Verga	21	216	93	42	.452	32	20	.625	11	7	18	17	22	0	12	0	104	5.0	22
Martin	50	538	232	101	.435	66	42	.636	74	107	181	20	90	0	7	26	244	4.9	17
C. Davis	8	90	40	14	.350	4	3	.750	2	9	11	11	7	0	2	0	31	3.9	11
G. Smith	67	878	228	99	.434	79	48	.608	65	124	189	78	126	1	41	6	246	3.7	12
Sibley	28	124	56	20	.357	7	6	.857	9	16	25	13	23	0	4	1	46	1.6	8

SEATTLE SUPERSONICS

Player	G.	Min.	FGA	FGM	Pct.	FTA	FTM	Pct.	Off. Reb.	Def. Reb.	Tot. Reb.	Ast.	PF	Disq.	Stl.	Blk. Sh.	Pts.	Avg.	Hi.
Haywood	75	3039	1520	694	.457	458	373	.814	318	689	1007	240	198	2	65	106	1761	23.5	37
Snyder	74	2670	1189	572	.481	224	194	.866	90	216	306	265	257	4	90	26	1338	18.1	41
F. Brown	82	2501	1226	578	.471	226	195	.863	114	287	401	414	276	6	136	18	1351	16.5	58
Brisker	35	717	396	178	.449	100	82	.820	59	87	146	56	70	0	28	6	438	12.5	47
Fox	78	2179	673	322	.478	293	241	.823	244	470	714	227	247	5	56	21	885	11.3	29
Gibbs	71	1528	700	302	.431	201	162	.806	91	132	223	79	195	1	39	18	766	10.8	30
Watts	62	1424	510	198	.388	155	100	.645	72	110	182	351	207	8	115	13	496	8.0	24
McIntosh	69	2056	573	223	.389	107	65	.607	111	250	361	94	178	4	52	29	511	7.4	22
Hummer (Tot.)	53	1119	305	144	.472	124	59	.476	84	199	283	107	119	0	28	22	347	6.5	16
Hummer (Sea.)	35	933	259	121	.467	96	45	.469	71	175	246	94	89	0	25	21	287	8.2	16
B. Stallworth	67	1019	479	188	.392	77	48	.623	51	123	174	33	129	0	21	12	424	6.3	23
McDaniels	27	439	173	63	.364	43	23	.535	51	77	128	24	48	0	7	15	149	5.5	29
Abdul-Rahman	49	571	180	76	.422	45	34	.756	18	39	57	122	78	0	26	6	186	3.8	24
M. Williams	53	505	149	62	.416	63	41	.651	19	28	47	103	82	1	25	0	165	3.1	22
Marshall	13	174	29	7	.241	7	3	.429	14	23	37	4	20	0	4	3	17	1.3	5

PLAYOFF RESULTS

EASTERN CONFERENCE SEMIFINALS
Boston 4, Buffalo 2

Mar. 30—Buffalo 97 at Boston..................................107
Apr. 2—Boston 105 at Buffalo.................................115
Apr. 3—Buffalo 107 at Boston.................................120
Apr. 6—Boston 102 at Buffalo.................................104
Apr. 9—Buffalo 97 at Boston..................................100
Apr. 12—Boston 106 at Buffalo.................................104

New York 4, Capital 3

Mar. 29—Capital 91 at New York...............................102
Mar. 31—New York 87 at Capital............................... 99
Apr. 2—Capital 88 at New York............................... 79
Apr. 5—New York 101 at Capital...............................93*
Apr. 7—Capital 105 at New York..............................106
Apr. 10—New York 92 at Capital...............................109
Apr. 12—Capital 81 at New York............................... 91

EASTERN CONFERENCE FINALS
Boston 4, New York 1

Apr. 14—New York 88 at Boston................................113
Apr. 16—Boston 111 at New York............................... 99
Apr. 19—New York 103 at Boston...............................100
Apr. 21—Boston 98 at New York................................ 91
Apr. 24—New York 94 at Boston................................105

WESTERN CONFERENCE SEMIFINALS
Milwaukee 4, Los Angeles 1

Mar. 29—Los Angeles 95 at Milwaukee........................ 99
Mar. 31—Los Angeles 90 at Milwaukee........................109
Apr. 2—Milwaukee 96 at Los Angeles........................ 98
Apr. 4—Milwaukee 112 at Los Angeles....................... 90
Apr. 7—Los Angeles 92 at Milwaukee........................114

Chicago 4, Detroit 3

Mar. 30—Detroit 97 at Chicago................................ 88
Apr. 1—Chicago 108 at Detroit...............................103
Apr. 5—Detroit 83 at Chicago................................ 84
Apr. 7—Chicago 87 at Detroit................................102
Apr. 9—Detroit 94 at Chicago................................ 98
Apr. 11—Chicago 88 at Detroit................................ 92
Apr. 13—Detroit 94 at Chicago................................ 96

WESTERN CONFERENCE FINALS
Milwaukee 4, Chicago 0

Apr. 16—Chicago 85 at Milwaukee.............................101
Apr. 18—Milwaukee 113 at Chicago............................111
Apr. 20—Chicago 90 at Milwaukee.............................113
Apr. 22—Milwaukee 115 at Chicago............................ 99

WORLD CHAMPIONSHIP SERIES
Boston 4, Milwaukee 3

Apr. 28—Boston 98 at Milwaukee.............................. 83
Apr. 30—Boston 96 at Milwaukee.............................105*
May 3—Milwaukee 83 at Boston.............................. 95
May 5—Milwaukee 97 at Boston.............................. 89
May 7—Boston 96 at Milwaukee.............................. 87
May 10—Milwaukee 102 at Boston.............................101**
May 12—Boston 102 at Milwaukee............................. 87

*Denotes overtime period.

1972-73 NBA STATISTICS

1972-73 NBA CHAMPION NEW YORK KNICKERBOCKERS

Seated from left: Henry Bibby, Walt Frazier, President Ned Irish, Chairman of the Board Irving Mitchell Felt, General Manager and Coach Red Holzman, Earl Monroe, Dick Barnett. Standing: Bill Bradley, Phil Jackson, John Gianelli, Dave DeBusschere, Willis Reed, Jerry Lucas, Tom Riker, Dean Meminger, Trainer Danny Whalen.

FINAL STANDINGS

ATLANTIC DIVISION

Team	Atl.	Balt.	Bos.	Buf.	Chi.	Clv.	Det.	G.S.	Hou.	KCO.	L.A.	Mil.	N.Y.	Phil.	Pho.	Prt.	Sea.	W.	L.	Pct.	G.B.
Boston	5	5	..	7	3	5	3	3	5	3	4	2	4	7	4	4	4	68	14	.829	....
New York	3	3	4	6	1	6	3	2	5	4	2	2	..	6	3	3	4	57	25	.695	11
Buffalo	1	1	..	2	1	1	1	..	1	1	..	..	1	7	1	2	2	21	61	.256	47
Philadelphia	..	1	..	1	..	..	1	..	1	1	..	1	1	..	..	1	1	9	73	.110	59

CENTRAL DIVISION

Team	Atl.	Balt.	Bos.	Buf.	Chi.	Clv.	Det.	G.S.	Hou.	KCO.	L.A.	Mil.	N.Y.	Phil.	Pho.	Prt.	Sea.	W.	L.	Pct.	G.B.
Baltimore	4	..	1	5	..	8	2	3	5	3	1	2	3	5	2	4	4	52	30	.634	....
Atlanta	..	3	1	5	2	3	3	1	4	2	3	1	1	6	3	4	3	46	36	.561	6
Houston	4	2	1	5	..	3	3	1	..	1	1	1	..	5	2	2	2	33	49	.402	19
Cleveland	4	..	1	5	1	..	1	1	4	2	1	1	..	6	1	1	3	32	50	.390	20

MIDWEST DIVISION

Team	Atl.	Balt.	Bos.	Buf.	Chi.	Clv.	Det.	G.S.	Hou.	KCO.	L.A.	Mil.	N.Y.	Phil.	Pho.	Prt.	Sea.	W.	L.	Pct.	G.B.
Milwaukee	3	2	2	4	4	3	5	5	5	6	3	..	2	3	5	5	5	60	22	.732	....
Chicago	2	4	1	2	..	3	3	3	4	5	1	2	3	4	4	5	5	51	31	.622	9
Detroit	2	2	1	3	4	3	..	2	1	3	1	2	1	3	4	6	2	40	42	.488	20
KC-Omaha	2	1	1	3	2	2	3	2	4	..	1	1	..	3	3	4	4	36	46	.439	24

PACIFIC DIVISION

Team	Atl.	Balt.	Bos.	Buf.	Chi.	Clv.	Det.	G.S.	Hou.	KCO.	L.A.	Mil.	N.Y.	Phil.	Pho.	Prt.	Sea.	W.	L.	Pct.	G.B.
Los Angeles	1	3	..	4	5	3	5	4	3	5	..	3	2	4	6	6	6	60	22	.732	....
Golden State	3	1	1	4	3	3	4	..	3	4	3	1	2	4	2	5	4	47	35	.573	13
Phoenix	1	2	..	3	2	3	2	4	2	3	1	1	1	4	..	5	4	38	44	.463	22
Seattle	1	..	..	2	1	1	4	3	2	2	..	1	..	3	2	4	..	26	56	.317	34
Portland	..	..	..	2	1	3	..	1	2	2	..	1	1	3	2	..	3	21	61	.256	39

HOME-ROAD-NEUTRAL RECORDS OF ALL TEAMS

Team	Home	Road	Neutral	Total
Atlanta	28-13	17-23	1-0	46-36
Baltimore	24-9	21-17	7-4	52-30
Boston	33-6	32-8	3-0	68-14
Buffalo	14-27	6-31	1-3	21-61
Chicago	29-12	20-19	2-0	51-31
Cleveland	20-21	10-27	2-2	32-50
Detroit	26-15	13-25	1-2	40-42
Golden State	27-14	18-20	2-1	47-35
Houston	14-14	10-28	9-7	33-49
K.C.-Omaha	24-17	12-29	0-0	36-46
Los Angeles	30-11	28-11	2-0	60-22
Milwaukee	33-5	25-15	2-2	60-22
New York	35-6	21-18	1-1	57-25
Philadelphia	5-26	2-36	2-11	9-73
Phoenix	22-19	15-25	1-0	38-44
Portland	13-28	8-32	0-1	21-61
Seattle	16-25	10-29	0-2	26-56
Total	393-268	268-393	36-36	697-697

OFFENSIVE TEAM STATISTICS

Team	G.	FIELD GOALS Att.	Made	Pct.	FREE THROWS Att.	Made	Pct.	Reb.	MISCELLANEOUS Ast.	PF	Disq.	SCORING Pts.	Avg.
Houston	82	8249	3772	.457	2152	1706	.793	4060	1939	1949	25	9250	112.8
Boston	82	8511	3811	.448	2073	1616	.780	4802	2320	1805	19	9238	112.7
Atlanta	82	8033	3700	.461	2482	1819	.733	4174	2074	1916	30	9219	112.4
Los Angeles	82	7819	3740	.478	2264	1679	.742	4562	2302	1636	9	9159	111.7
Phoenix	82	7942	3612	.455	2437	1931	.792	4003	1944	2012	40	9155	111.6
Detroit	82	7916	3666	.463	2294	1710	.745	4105	1882	1812	10	9042	110.3
Golden State	82	8163	3715	.455	1871	1493	.798	4405	1985	1693	15	8923	108.8
Kansas City-Omaha	82	7581	3621	.478	2036	1580	.776	3628	2118	2054	33	8822	107.6
Milwaukee	82	7808	3759	.481	1687	1271	.753	4245	2226	1763	13	8789	107.2
Portland	82	7842	3588	.458	2129	1531	.719	3928	2102	1970	33	8707	106.2
New York	82	7764	3627	.467	1739	1356	.780	3382	2187	1775	10	8610	105.0
Baltimore	82	7883	3656	.464	1742	1294	.743	4205	2051	1672	14	8606	105.0
Philadelphia	82	8264	3471	.420	2130	1598	.750	4174	1688	1984	28	8540	104.1
Chicago	82	7835	3480	.444	2073	1574	.759	4000	2023	1881	26	8534	104.1
Seattle	82	7681	3447	.449	2080	1606	.772	4161	1958	1877	24	8500	103.7
Buffalo	82	7877	3536	.449	1966	1399	.712	4158	2218	2034	40	8471	103.3
Cleveland	82	7884	3431	.435	2084	1556	.747	4063	2106	1941	21	8418	102.7

DEFENSIVE TEAM STATISTICS

Team	FIELD GOALS Att.	Made	Pct.	FREE THROWS Att.	Made	Pct.	MISCELLANEOUS Reb.	Ast.	PF	Disq.	SCORING Pts.	Avg.	Pt. Dif.
New York	7561	3291	.435	1961	1471	.750	4100	1714	1781	18	8053	98.2	+ 6.8
Milwaukee	8028	3385	.422	1783	1345	.754	3916	1906	1601	13	8115	99.0	+ 8.2
Chicago	7098	3343	.471	2080	1562	.751	3915	1910	2002	38	8248	100.6	+ 3.5
Baltimore	8010	3531	.441	1702	1269	.746	4226	1852	1682	11	8266	101.6	+ 3.4
Los Angeles	8409	3646	.434	1583	1167	.737	4101	1963	1941	27	8459	103.2	+ 8.5
Boston	8095	3513	.434	2032	1540	.758	3958	1957	1821	23	8566	104.5	+ 8.2
Cleveland	7673	3465	.452	2230	1707	.765	4115	2311	1932	25	8637	105.3	— 2.6
Golden State	8163	3603	.441	1891	1463	.774	4265	2034	1766	14	8669	105.7	+ 3.1
Seattle	8093	3678	.454	2156	1628	.755	4158	2145	1875	25	8984	109.6	— 5.9
Detroit	8064	3803	.472	1862	1418	.762	4019	2263	1891	22	9024	110.0	+ 0.3
Kansas City-Omaha	7640	3698	.484	2174	1665	.766	3961	1885	1816	9	9061	110.5	— 2.9
Atlanta	8152	3758	.461	2193	1696	.773	4147	2020	2104	35	9212	112.3	+ 0.1
Portland	7780	3709	.477	2327	1800	.774	4236	2271	1885	18	9218	112.4	— 6.2
Buffalo	7947	3745	.471	2299	1733	.754	4278	2383	1822	23	9223	112.5	— 9.2
Phoenix	8005	3758	.469	2318	1744	.752	4139	2166	2068	46	9260	112.9	— 1.3
Houston	8119	3824	.471	2290	1744	.762	4338	2104	1902	22	9302	113.4	— 1.7
Philadelphia	8215	3882	.473	2358	1767	.749	4683	2239	1885	21	9531	116.2	— 12.1

Disq.—Individual players disqualified (fouled out of game).

INDIVIDUAL LEADERS

POINTS
(Minimum 70 Games Played)

	G.	FG	FT	Pts.	Avg.
Archibald, Kan. City-Omaha	80	1028	663	2719	34.0
Abdul-Jabbar, Milwaukee	76	982	328	2292	30.2
Haywood, Seattle	77	889	473	2251	29.2
Hudson, Atlanta	75	816	397	2029	27.1
Maravich, Atlanta	79	789	485	2063	26.1
Scott, Phoenix	81	806	436	2048	25.3
Petrie, Portland	79	836	298	1970	24.9
Goodrich, Los Angeles	76	750	314	1814	23.9
Wicks, Portland	80	761	384	1906	23.8
Lanier, Detroit	81	810	307	1927	23.8
Havlicek, Boston	80	766	370	1902	23.8

	G.	FG	FT	Pts.	Avg.
B. Love, Chicago	82	774	347	1895	23.1
Bing, Detroit	82	692	456	1840	22.4
Barry, Golden State	82	737	358	1832	22.3
Hayes, Baltimore	81	713	291	1717	21.2
Frazier, New York	78	681	286	1648	21.1
Carr, Cleveland	82	702	281	1685	20.5
Cowens, Boston	82	740	204	1684	20.5
Wilkens, Cleveland	75	572	394	1538	20.5
Dandridge, Milwaukee	73	638	198	1474	20.2
Walk, Phoenix	81	678	279	1635	20.2

FIELD GOALS
(Minimum 560 Attempts)

	FGA	FGM	Pct.
Chamberlain, Los Angeles	586	426	.727
Guokas, Kansas City-Omaha	565	322	.570
Abdul-Jabbar, Milwaukee	1772	982	.554
Rowe, Detroit	1053	547	.519
J. Fox, Seattle	613	316	.515
Lucas, New York	608	312	.513
Riordan, Baltimore	1278	652	.510
Clark, Baltimore	596	302	.507
Kauffman, Buffalo	1059	535	.505
Bellamy, Atlanta	901	455	.505

FREE THROWS
(Minimum 160 Attempts)

	FTA	FTM	Pct.
Barry, Golden State	397	358	.902
Murphy, Houston	269	239	.888
Newlin, Houston	369	327	.886
J. Walker, Houston	276	244	.884
Bradley, New York	194	169	.871
C. Russell, Golden State	199	172	.864
Snyder, Seattle	216	186	.861
D. Van Arsdale, Phoenix	496	426	.859
Havlicek, Boston	431	370	.858
Marin, Houston	292	248	.849

ASSISTS (Minimum 70 Games)	G.	No.	Avg.
Archibald, Kansas City-Omaha	80	910	11.4
Wilkens, Cleveland	75	628	8.4
Bing, Detroit	82	637	7.8
Robertson, Milwaukee	73	551	7.5
Van Lier, Chicago	80	567	7.1
Maravich, Atlanta	79	546	6.9
Havlicek, Boston	80	529	6.6
Gilliam, Atlanta	76	482	6.3
Scott, Phoenix	81	495	6.1
White, Boston	82	498	6.1

REBOUNDS (Minimum 70 Games)	G.	No.	Avg.
Chamberlain, Los Angeles	82	1526	18.6
Thurmond, Golden State	79	1349	17.1
Cowens, Boston	82	1329	16.2
Abdul-Jabbar, Milwaukee	76	1224	16.1
Unseld, Baltimore	79	1260	15.9
Lanier, Detroit	81	1205	14.9
Hayes, Baltimore	81	1177	14.5
Bellamy, Atlanta	74	964	13.0
Silas, Boston	80	1039	13.0
Haywood, Seattle	77	995	12.9

TEAM-BY-TEAM INDIVIDUAL STATISTICS

ATLANTA HAWKS

Player	G.	Min.	FGA	FGM	Pct.	FTA	FTM	Pct.	Reb.	Ast.	PF	Disq.	Pts.	Avg.
Lou Hudson	75	3027	1710	816	.477	481	397	.825	467	258	197	1	2029	27.1
Pete Maravich	79	3089	1788	789	.441	606	485	.800	346	546	245	1	2063	26.1
Walt Bellamy	74	2802	901	455	.505	526	283	.538	964	179	244	1	1193	16.1
Herm Gilliam	76	2741	1007	471	.468	150	123	.820	399	482	257	8	1065	14.0
George Trapp	77	1853	824	359	.436	194	150	.773	455	127	274	11	868	11.3
Jim Washington	75	2833	713	308	.432	224	163	.728	801	174	252	5	779	10.4
Steve Bracey	70	1050	395	192	.486	110	73	.664	107	125	125	0	457	6.5
Don Adams*	4	76	38	8	.211	8	7	.875	22	5	11	0	23	5.8
Jeff Halliburton*	24	238	116	50	.431	22	21	.955	26	28	29	0	121	5.0
Don May*	32	317	134	61	.455	31	22	.710	67	21	55	0	144	4.5
Bob Christian	55	759	155	85	.548	79	60	.759	305	47	111	2	230	4.2
John Wetzel	28	504	94	42	.447	17	14	.824	58	39	41	1	98	3.5
John Tschogl	10	94	40	14	.350	4	2	.500	21	6	25	0	30	3.0
Eddie Mast	42	447	118	50	.424	30	19	.633	136	37	50	0	119	2.8

BALTIMORE BULLETS

Player	G.	Min.	FGA	FGM	Pct.	FTA	FTM	Pct.	Reb.	Ast.	PF	Disq.	Pts.	Avg.
Elvin Hayes	81	3347	1607	713	.444	434	291	.671	1177	127	232	3	1717	21.2
Phil Chenier	71	2776	1332	602	.452	244	194	.795	288	301	160	0	1398	19.7
Archie Clark	39	1477	596	302	.507	137	111	.810	129	275	111	1	715	18.3
Mike Riordan	82	3466	1278	652	.510	218	179	.821	404	426	216	0	1483	18.1
Wes Unseld	79	3085	854	421	.493	212	149	.703	1260	347	168	0	991	12.5
Mike Davis	13	283	118	50	.424	25	23	.920	35	19	45	4	123	9.5
Rich Rinaldi	33	646	284	116	.408	64	48	.750	68	48	40	0	280	8.5
Flynn Robinson***	44	630	288	133	.462	39	32	.821	62	85	71	0	298	6.8
Flynn Robinson**	38	583	260	119	.458	31	26	.839	55	77	60	0	264	6.9
Kevin Porter	71	1217	451	205	.455	101	62	.614	72	237	206	5	472	6.6
Stan Love	72	995	436	190	.436	100	79	.790	300	46	175	0	459	6.4
Dave Stallworth	73	1217	435	180	.414	101	78	.772	236	112	139	1	438	6.0
John Tresvant	55	541	182	85	.467	59	41	.695	156	33	101	0	211	3.8
Tom Patterson	23	92	49	21	.429	16	13	.813	22	3	18	0	55	2.4
Terry Driscoll*	1	5	1	0	.000	0	0	.000	3	0	1	0	0	0.0

BOSTON CELTICS

Player	G.	Min.	FGA	FGM	Pct.	FTA	FTM	Pct.	Reb.	Ast.	PF	Disq.	Pts.	Avg.
John Havlicek	80	3367	1704	766	.450	431	370	.858	567	529	195	1	1902	23.8
Dave Cowens	82	3425	1637	740	.452	262	204	.779	1329	333	311	7	1684	20.5
Jo Jo White	82	3250	1655	717	.431	228	178	.781	414	498	185	2	1612	19.7
Paul Silas	80	2618	851	400	.470	380	266	.700	1039	251	197	1	1066	13.3
Don Chaney	79	2488	859	414	.482	267	210	.787	449	221	276	6	1038	13.1
Don Nelson	72	1425	649	309	.476	188	159	.846	315	102	155	1	777	10.8
Steve Kuberski	78	762	347	140	.403	84	65	.774	197	26	92	0	345	4.4
Paul Westphal	60	482	212	89	.420	86	67	.779	67	69	88	0	245	4.1
Art Williams	81	974	261	110	.421	56	43	.768	182	236	136	1	263	3.2
Hank Finkel	76	496	173	78	.451	52	28	.538	151	26	83	0	184	2.4
Tom Sanders	59	423	149	47	.315	35	23	.657	88	27	82	0	117	2.0
Mark Minor	4	20	4	1	.250	4	3	.750	4	2	5	0	5	1.3

BUFFALO BRAVES

Player	G.	Min.	FGA	FGM	Pct.	FTA	FTM	Pct.	Reb.	Ast.	PF	Disq.	Pts.	Avg.
Elmore Smith	76	2829	1244	600	.482	337	188	.558	946	192	295	16	1388	18.3
Bob McAdoo	80	2562	1293	585	.452	350	271	.774	728	139	256	6	1441	18.0
Bob Kauffman	77	3049	1059	535	.505	359	280	.780	855	396	211	1	1350	17.5
Randy Smith	82	2603	1154	511	.443	264	192	.727	391	422	247	1	1214	14.8
Dick Garrett	78	1805	813	341	.419	110	96	.873	209	217	217	4	778	10.0
John Hummer	66	1546	464	206	.444	205	115	.561	323	138	185	5	527	8.0
Dave Wohl***	78	1933	568	254	.447	133	103	.774	109	326	227	3	611	7.8
Dave Wohl**	56	1540	454	207	.456	100	79	.790	89	258	182	3	493	8.8
Fred Hilton	59	731	494	191	.387	53	41	.774	98	74	100	0	423	7.2
Howard Komives	67	1468	429	163	.380	98	85	.867	118	239	155	1	411	6.1
M. Abdul-Rahman*	9	134	60	25	.417	6	3	.500	10	17	19	0	53	5.9
Bill Hewitt	73	1332	364	152	.418	74	41	.554	368	110	154	3	345	4.7
Cornell Warner*	4	47	17	8	.471	2	1	.500	15	6	6	0	17	4.3
Harold Fox	10	84	32	12	.375	8	7	.875	8	10	7	0	31	3.1

CHICAGO BULLS

Player	G.	Min.	FGA	FGM	Pct.	FTA	FTM	Pct.	Reb.	Ast.	PF	Disq.	Pts.	Avg.
Bob Love	82	3033	1794	774	.431	421	347	.824	532	119	240	1	1895	23.1
Chet Walker	79	2455	1248	597	.478	452	376	.832	395	179	166	1	1570	19.9
Norm Van Lier	80	2882	1064	474	.445	211	166	.787	438	567	269	5	1114	13.9
Garfield Heard***	81	1552	824	350	.425	178	116	.652	453	60	171	1	816	10.1
Garfield Heard**	78	1535	815	346	.425	177	115	.650	447	58	167	1	807	10.3
Jerry Sloan	69	2412	733	301	.411	133	94	.707	475	151	235	5	696	10.1
Bob Weiss	82	2086	655	279	.426	189	159	.841	148	295	151	1	717	8.7
Clifford Ray	73	2009	516	254	.492	189	117	.619	797	271	232	5	625	8.6
Kennedy McIntosh*	3	33	13	8	.615	2	0	.000	9	1	4	0	16	5.3
Howard Porter	43	407	217	98	.452	29	22	.759	118	16	52	1	218	5.1
Dennis Awtrey***	82	1687	305	146	.479	153	86	.562	447	224	234	6	378	4.6
Dennis Awtrey**	79	1650	298	143	.480	149	85	.570	433	222	226	6	371	4.7
Jim King	65	785	263	116	.441	52	44	.846	76	81	76	0	276	4.2
Tom Boerwinkle	8	176	24	9	.375	20	12	.600	54	40	22	0	30	3.8
Rowland Garrett	35	211	118	52	.441	31	21	.677	61	8	29	0	125	3.6
Frank Russell	23	131	77	29	.377	18	16	.889	17	15	12	0	74	3.2

CLEVELAND CAVALIERS

Player	G.	Min.	FGA	FGM	Pct.	FTA	FTM	Pct.	Reb.	Ast.	PF	Disq.	Pts.	Avg.
Austin Carr	82	3097	1575	702	.446	342	281	.822	369	279	185	1	1685	20.5
Lenny Wilkens	75	2973	1275	572	.449	476	394	.828	346	628	221	2	1538	20.5
John Johnson	82	2815	1143	492	.430	271	199	.734	552	309	246	3	1183	14.4
Rick Roberson	62	2127	709	307	.433	290	167	.576	693	134	249	5	781	12.6
Dwight Davis	81	2151	748	293	.392	222	176	.793	563	118	297	5	762	9.4
Bobby Smith	73	1068	603	268	.444	81	64	.790	199	108	80	0	600	8.2
Charlie Davis*	6	86	41	20	.488	7	4	.571	5	10	20	1	44	7.3
Barry Clemens	72	1119	405	209	.516	68	53	.779	211	115	136	0	471	6.5
Jim Cleamons	80	1392	423	192	.454	101	75	.743	167	205	108	0	459	5.7
Cornell Warner***	72	1370	421	174	.413	90	59	.656	522	72	178	3	407	5.7
Cornell Warner**	68	1323	404	166	.411	88	58	.659	507	66	172	3	390	5.7
John Warren	40	290	111	54	.486	19	18	.947	42	34	45	0	126	3.2
Walt Wesley*	12	110	47	14	.298	12	8	.667	38	7	21	0	36	3.0
Steve Patterson	62	710	198	71	.359	65	34	.523	228	51	79	1	176	2.8
Bob Rule***	52	452	158	60	.380	31	20	.645	108	38	68	0	140	2.7
Bob Rule**	49	440	157	60	.382	31	20	.645	106	37	66	0	140	2.9
Dave Sorenson*	10	129	45	11	.244	11	5	.455	37	5	16	0	27	2.7

DETROIT PISTONS

Player	G.	Min.	FGA	FGM	Pct.	FTA	FTM	Pct.	Reb.	Ast.	PF	Disq.	Pts.	Avg.
Bob Lanier	81	3150	1654	810	.490	397	307	.773	1205	260	278	4	1927	23.8
Dave Bing	82	3361	1545	692	.448	560	456	.814	298	637	229	1	1840	22.4
Curtis Rowe	81	3009	1053	547	.519	327	210	.642	760	172	191	0	1304	16.1
John Mengelt***	79	1647	651	320	.492	160	127	.794	181	153	148	0	767	9.7
John Mengelt**	67	1435	583	294	.504	141	116	.823	159	128	124	0	704	10.5
Stu Lantz	51	1603	455	185	.407	150	120	.800	172	138	117	0	490	9.6
Don Adams***	74	1874	678	265	.391	184	145	.788	441	117	231	2	675	9.1
Don Adams**	70	1798	640	257	.402	176	138	.784	419	112	220	2	652	9.3
Fred Foster	63	1460	627	243	.388	87	61	.701	183	94	150	0	547	8.7
Willie Norwood	79	1282	504	249	.494	225	154	.684	324	56	182	0	652	8.3
Chris Ford	74	1537	434	208	.479	93	60	.645	266	194	133	1	476	6.4
Jim Davis	73	771	257	131	.510	114	72	.632	261	56	126	2	334	4.6
Justus Thigpen	18	99	57	23	.404	0	0	.000	9	8	18	0	46	2.6
Bob Nash	36	169	72	16	.222	17	11	.647	34	16	30	0	43	1.2
Erwin Mueller	21	80	31	9	.290	7	5	.714	14	7	13	0	23	1.1
Harvey Marlatt	7	26	4	2	.500	0	0	.000	1	4	1	0	4	0.6

GOLDEN STATE WARRIORS

Player	G.	Min.	FGA	FGM	Pct.	FTA	FTM	Pct.	Reb.	Ast.	PF	Disq.	Pts.	Avg.
Rick Barry	82	3075	1630	737	.452	397	358	.902	728	399	245	2	1832	22.3
Jeff Mullins	81	3005	1321	651	.493	172	143	.831	363	337	201	2	1445	17.8
Nate Thurmond	79	3419	1159	517	.446	439	315	.718	1349	280	240	2	1349	17.1
Cazzie Russell	80	2429	1182	541	.458	199	172	.864	255	187	171	0	1254	15.7
Jim Barnett	82	2215	844	394	.467	217	183	.843	255	301	150	1	971	11.8
Joe Ellis	74	1054	487	199	.409	93	69	.742	282	88	143	2	467	6.3
Clyde Lee	66	1476	365	170	.464	131	74	.565	598	34	183	5	414	6.3
Ron Williams	73	1016	409	180	.440	83	75	.904	81	114	108	0	435	6.0
Charles Johnson	70	887	400	171	.428	46	33	.717	132	118	105	0	375	5.4
M. Abdul-Rahman***	55	763	256	107	.418	57	47	.825	88	129	110	1	261	4.7
M. Abdul-Rahman**	46	629	196	82	.418	51	44	.863	78	112	91	1	208	4.5
Bob Portman	32	176	70	32	.457	26	20	.769	51	7	16	0	84	2.6
George T. Johnson	56	349	100	41	.410	17	7	.412	138	8	40	0	89	1.6

HOUSTON ROCKETS

Player	G.	Min.	FGA	FGM	Pct.	FTA	FTM	Pct.	Reb.	Ast.	PF	Disq.	Pts.	Avg.
Rudy Tomjanovich	81	2972	1371	655	.478	335	205	.746	938	178	225	1	1560	19.3
Jack Marin	81	3019	1334	624	.468	292	248	.849	499	291	247	4	1496	18.5
Jimmy Walker	81	3079	1301	605	.465	276	244	.884	268	442	207	0	1454	18.0
Mike Newlin	82	2658	1206	534	.443	369	327	.886	340	409	301	5	1395	17.0
Calvin Murphy	77	1697	820	381	.465	269	239	.888	149	262	211	3	1001	13.0
Otto Moore	82	2712	859	418	.487	211	127	.602	868	167	239	4	963	11.7
Don Smith	48	900	375	149	.397	162	119	.735	304	53	108	2	417	8.7
Cliff Meely	82	1694	657	268	.408	137	92	.672	496	91	263	6	628	7.7
Paul McCracken	24	305	89	44	.494	39	23	.590	51	17	32	0	111	4.6
Stan McKenzie***	33	294	119	48	.403	37	30	.811	55	23	43	1	126	3.8
Stan McKenzie**	26	187	83	35	.422	21	16	.762	34	15	28	0	86	3.3
Greg Smith*	4	41	16	5	.313	0	0	.000	8	5	8	0	10	2.5
George E. Johnson	19	169	39	20	.513	4	3	.750	45	3	33	0	43	2.3
Eric McWilliams	44	245	98	34	.347	37	18	.486	60	5	46	0	86	2.0
Dick Gibbs*	1	2	1	1	.000	0	0	.000	0	1	1	0	0	0.0

Nate Archibald of Kansas City-Omaha became the first player in league history to lead the NBA in both points (34.0) and assists (11.4) in the same season in 1972-73.

KANSAS CITY-OMAHA KINGS

Player	G.	Min.	FGA	FGM	Pct.	FTA	FTM	Pct.	Reb.	Ast.	PF	Disq.	Pts.	Avg.
Nate Archibald	80	3681	2106	1028	.488	783	663	.847	223	910	207	2	2719	34.0
John Block°°°	73	2041	886	391	.441	378	300	.794	562	113	242	5	1082	14.8
John Block°°	25	483	180	80	.444	76	64	.842	120	19	69	1	224	9.0
Sam Lacey	79	2930	994	471	.474	178	126	.708	933	189	283	6	1068	13.5
Tom Van Arsdale°	49	1282	547	250	.457	140	110	.786	173	90	123	1	610	12.4
Nate Williams	80	1079	874	417	.477	133	106	.797	339	128	272	9	940	11.8
Matt Guokas	79	2846	565	322	.570	90	74	.822	245	403	190	0	718	9.1
Don Kojis	77	1240	575	276	.480	137	106	.774	198	80	128	0	658	8.5
Ron Riley	74	1634	634	273	.431	116	79	.681	507	76	226	3	625	8.4
Johnny Green	66	1245	317	190	.599	131	89	.679	361	59	185	7	469	7.1
John Mengelt°	12	212	68	26	.382	19	11	.579	22	25	24	0	63	5.3
Mike Ratliff	58	681	235	98	.417	84	45	.536	194	38	111	1	241	4.2
Toby Kimball	67	743	220	96	.436	67	44	.657	191	27	86	2	236	3.5
Dick Gibbs°°°	67	735	222	80	.360	63	47	.746	94	62	114	1	207	3.1
Dick Gibbs°°	66	733	221	80	.362	63	47	.746	94	61	113	1	207	3.1
Ken Durrett	8	65	21	8	.381	8	6	.750	14	3	16	0	22	2.8
Sam Sibert	5	26	13	4	.308	5	4	.800	4	0	4	0	12	2.4
Frank Schade	9	76	7	2	.286	6	6	1.000	6	10	12	0	10	1.1
Pete Cross°	3	24	4	0	.000	0	0	.000	4	0	5	0	0	0.0

LOS ANGELES LAKERS

Player	G.	Min.	FGA	FGM	Pct.	FTA	FTM	Pct.	Reb.	Ast.	PF	Disq.	Pts.	Avg.
Gail Goodrich	76	2697	1615	750	.464	374	314	.840	263	332	193	1	1814	23.9
Jerry West	69	2460	1291	618	.479	421	339	.805	289	607	138	0	1575	22.8
Jim McMillian	81	2953	1431	655	.458	264	223	.845	447	221	176	0	1533	18.9
Harold Hairston	28	939	328	158	.482	178	140	.787	370	68	77	0	456	16.3
Wilt Chamberlain	82	3542	586	426	.727	455	232	.510	1526	365	191	0	1084	13.2
Bill Bridges°°°	82	2867	722	333	.461	255	179	.702	904	219	296	3	845	10.3
Bill Bridges°°	72	2491	597	286	.479	190	133	.700	782	196	261	3	705	9.8
Keith Erickson	76	1920	696	299	.430	110	89	.809	337	242	190	3	687	9.0
Pat Riley	55	801	390	167	.428	82	65	.793	65	81	126	0	399	7.3
Jim Price	59	828	359	158	.440	73	60	.822	115	97	119	1	376	6.4
Flynn Robinson°	6	47	28	14	.500	8	6	.750	7	8	11	0	34	5.7

Player	G.	Min.	FGA	FGM	Pct.	FTA	FTM	Pct.	Reb.	Ast.	PF	Disq.	Pts.	Avg.
Mel Counts***	66	658	294	132	.449	58	39	.672	253	65	106	1	303	4.6
Mel Counts**	59	611	278	127	.457	58	39	.672	237	62	98	1	293	5.0
Travis Grant	33	153	116	51	.440	26	23	.885	52	7	19	0	125	3.8
Leroy Ellis*	10	156	40	11	.275	5	4	.800	33	3	13	0	26	2.6
John Q. Trapp*	5	35	12	3	.250	10	7	.700	14	2	10	0	13	2.6
Bill Turner***	21	125	58	19	.328	7	4	.571	27	11	16	0	42	2.0
Bill Turner**	19	117	52	17	.327	7	4	.571	25	11	13	0	38	2.0
Roger Brown	1	5	0	0	.000	3	1	.333	0	0	1	0	1	1.0

MILWAUKEE BUCKS

Player	G.	Min.	FGA	FGM	Pct.	FTA	FTM	Pct.	Reb.	Ast.	PF	Disq.	Pts.	Avg.
Kareem Abdul-Jabbar	76	3254	1772	982	.554	460	328	.713	1224	379	208	0	2292	30.2
Bob Dandridge	73	2852	1353	638	.472	251	198	.789	600	207	279	2	1474	20.2
Lucius Allen	80	2693	1130	547	.484	200	143	.715	279	426	188	1	1237	15.5
Oscar Robertson	73	2737	983	446	.454	281	238	.847	360	551	167	0	1130	15.5
John McGlocklin	80	1951	699	351	.502	73	63	.863	158	236	119	0	765	9.6
Curtis Perry	67	2094	575	265	.461	126	83	.659	644	123	246	6	613	9.1
Terry Driscoll***	60	964	327	140	.428	62	43	.694	300	55	144	3	323	5.4
Terry Driscoll**	59	959	326	140	.429	62	43	.694	297	55	143	3	323	5.5
Mickey Davis	74	1046	347	152	.438	92	76	.826	226	72	119	0	380	5.1
Wali Jones	27	419	145	59	.407	18	16	.889	29	56	39	0	134	5.0
Gary Gregor	9	88	33	11	.333	7	5	.714	32	9	9	0	27	3.0
Russell Lee	46	277	127	49	.386	43	32	.744	43	38	36	0	130	2.8
Dick Cunningham	72	692	156	64	.410	50	29	.580	208	34	94	0	157	2.1
Chuck Terry	67	693	162	55	.340	24	17	.708	145	40	116	1	127	1.9

NEW YORK KNICKERBOCKERS

Player	G.	Min.	FGA	FGM	Pct.	FTA	FTM	Pct.	Reb.	Ast.	PF	Disq.	Pts.	Avg.
Walt Frazier	78	3181	1389	681	.490	350	286	.817	570	461	186	0	1648	21.1
Dave DeBusschere	77	2827	1224	532	.435	260	194	.746	787	259	215	1	1258	16.3
Bill Bradley	82	2998	1252	575	.459	194	169	.871	301	367	273	5	1319	16.1
Earl Monroe	75	2370	1016	496	.488	208	171	.822	245	288	195	1	1163	15.5
Willis Reed	69	1876	705	334	.474	124	92	.742	590	126	205	0	760	11.0
Jerry Lucas	71	2001	608	312	.513	100	80	.800	510	317	157	0	704	9.9
Phil Jackson	80	1393	553	245	.443	195	154	.790	344	94	218	2	644	8.1
Dean Meminger	80	1453	365	188	.515	129	81	.628	229	133	109	1	457	5.7
Henry Bibby	55	475	205	78	.380	86	73	.849	82	64	67	0	229	4.2
Dick Barnett	51	514	226	88	.389	30	16	.533	41	50	52	0	192	3.8
John Gianelli	52	516	175	79	.451	33	23	.697	150	25	72	0	181	3.5
Tom Riker	14	65	24	10	.417	24	15	.625	16	2	15	0	35	2.5
Harthorne Wingo	13	59	22	9	.409	6	2	.333	16	1	9	0	20	1.5
Luther Rackley	1	2	0	0	.000	0	0	.000	1	0	2	0	0	0.0

PHILADELPHIA 76ers

Player	G.	Min.	FGA	FGM	Pct.	FTA	FTM	Pct.	Reb.	Ast.	PF	Disq.	Pts.	Avg.
Fred Carter	81	2993	1614	679	.421	368	259	.704	485	349	252	8	1617	20.0
John Block*	48	1558	706	311	.441	302	236	.781	442	94	173	4	858	17.9
Tom Van Arsdale***	79	2311	1043	445	.427	308	250	.812	358	152	224	2	1140	14.4
Tom Van Arsdale**	30	1029	496	195	.393	168	140	.833	185	62	101	1	530	17.7
Bill Bridges*	10	376	125	47	.376	65	46	.708	122	23	35	0	140	14.0
Kevin Loughery	32	955	427	169	.396	130	107	.823	113	148	104	0	445	13.9
Leroy Ellis***	79	2600	969	421	.434	161	129	.801	777	139	199	2	971	12.3
Leroy Ellis**	69	2444	929	410	.441	156	125	.801	744	136	186	2	945	13.7
Manny Leaks	82	2530	933	377	.404	200	144	.720	677	95	191	5	898	11.0
Fred Boyd	82	2351	923	362	.392	200	136	.680	210	301	184	1	860	10.5
John Q. Trapp***	44	889	420	171	.407	122	90	.738	200	49	150	4	432	9.8
John Q. Trapp**	39	854	408	168	.412	112	83	.741	186	47	140	4	419	10.7
Don May***	58	919	424	189	.446	93	75	.806	210	64	135	1	453	7.8
Don May**	26	602	290	128	.441	62	53	.855	143	43	80	1	309	11.9
Jeff Halliburton***	55	787	396	172	.434	88	71	.807	108	96	107	1	415	7.5
Jeff Halliburton**	31	549	280	122	.436	66	50	.758	82	68	78	1	294	9.5
Hal Greer	38	848	232	91	.392	39	32	.821	106	111	76	1	214	5.6
Dale Schlueter	78	1136	317	166	.524	123	86	.699	354	103	166	0	418	5.4
Dave Sorenson***	58	755	293	124	.423	90	64	.711	210	36	107	0	312	5.4
Dave Sorenson**	48	626	248	113	.456	79	59	.747	173	31	91	0	285	5.9
Mike Price	57	751	301	125	.415	47	38	.809	117	71	106	0	288	5.1
Dennis Awtrey*	3	37	7	3	.429	4	1	.250	14	2	8	0	7	2.3
Mel Counts*	7	47	16	5	.313	0	0	.000	16	3	8	0	10	1.4
Luther Green	5	32	11	0	.000	9	3	.333	3	0	3	0	3	0.6
Bob Rule*	3	12	1	0	.000	0	0	.000	2	1	2	0	0	0.0

PHOENIX SUNS

Player	G.	Min.	FGA	FGM	Pct.	FTA	FTM	Pct.	Reb.	Ast.	PF	Disq.	Pts.	Avg.
Charlie Scott	81	3062	1809	806	.446	556	436	.784	342	495	306	5	2048	25.3
Neal Walk	81	3114	1455	678	.466	355	279	.786	1006	287	323	11	1635	20.2
Dick Van Arsdale	81	2979	1118	532	.476	496	426	.859	326	268	221	2	1490	18.4
Connie Hawkins	75	2768	920	441	.479	404	322	.797	641	304	229	5	1204	16.1
Clem Haskins	77	1581	731	339	.464	156	130	.833	173	203	143	2	808	10.5
Gus Johnson	21	417	181	69	.381	36	25	.694	136	31	55	0	163	7.8
Dennis Layton	65	990	434	187	.431	119	90	.756	77	139	127	2	464	7.1
Lamar Green	80	2048	520	224	.431	118	89	.754	746	89	263	10	537	6.7
Corky Calhoun	82	2025	450	211	.469	96	71	.740	338	76	214	2	493	6.0
Walt Wesley***	57	474	202	77	.381	46	26	.565	141	31	77	1	180	3.2
Walt Wesley**	45	364	155	63	.406	34	18	.529	113	24	56	1	144	3.2
Scott English	29	196	93	36	.387	29	21	.724	44	15	38	0	93	3.2
Paul Stovall	25	211	76	26	.342	38	24	.632	61	13	37	0	76	3.0

PORTLAND TRAIL BLAZERS

Player	G.	Min.	FGA	FGM	Pct.	FTA	FTM	Pct.	Reb.	Ast.	PF	Disq.	Pts.	Avg.
Geoff Petrie	79	3134	1801	836	.464	383	298	.778	273	350	163	2	1970	24.9
Sidney Wicks	80	3152	1684	761	.452	531	384	.723	870	440	253	3	1906	23.8
Lloyd Neal	82	2723	921	455	.494	293	187	.638	967	146	305	6	1097	13.4
Ollie Johnson	78	2138	620	308	.497	206	156	.757	417	200	166	0	772	9.9
Charlie Davis***	75	1419	631	263	.417	168	130	.774	116	185	194	7	656	8.7
Charlie Davis**	69	1333	590	243	.412	161	126	.783	111	175	174	6	612	8.9
Greg Smith***	76	1610	485	234	.482	128	75	.586	383	122	218	8	543	7.1
Greg Smith**	72	1569	469	229	.488	128	75	.586	375	117	210	8	533	7.4
Rick Adelman	76	1822	525	214	.408	102	73	.716	157	294	155	2	501	6.6
Terry Dischinger	63	970	338	161	.476	96	64	.667	190	103	125	1	386	6.1
Larry Steele	66	1301	329	159	.483	89	71	.798	154	156	181	4	389	5.9
Stan McKenzie*	7	107	36	13	.361	16	14	.875	21	8	15	1	40	5.7
Dave Wohl*	22	393	114	47	.412	33	24	.727	20	68	45	0	118	5.4
LaRue Martin	77	996	366	145	.396	77	50	.649	358	42	162	0	340	4.4
Bill Smith	8	43	15	9	.600	8	5	.625	8	1	8	0	23	2.9
Bill Turner*	2	8	6	2	.333	0	0	.000	2	0	3	0	4	2.0
Bob Davis	9	41	28	6	.214	6	4	.667	5	2	5	0	16	1.8

SEATTLE SUPERSONICS

Player	G.	Min.	FGA	FGM	Pct.	FTA	FTM	Pct.	Reb.	Ast.	PF	Disq.	Pts.	Avg.
Spencer Haywood	77	3259	1868	889	.476	564	473	.839	995	196	213	2	2251	29.2
Dick Snyder	82	3060	1022	473	.463	216	186	.861	323	311	216	2	1132	13.8
Fred Brown	79	2320	1035	471	.455	148	121	.818	318	438	226	5	1063	13.5
John Brisker	70	1633	809	352	.435	236	194	.822	319	150	169	1	898	12.8
Jim Fox	74	2439	613	316	.515	265	214	.808	827	176	239	6	846	11.4
Butch Beard	73	1403	435	191	.439	140	100	.714	174	247	139	0	482	6.6
Lee Winfield	53	1061	332	143	.431	108	62	.574	126	186	92	3	348	6.6
Bud Stallworth	77	1225	522	198	.379	114	86	.754	225	58	138	0	482	6.3
Jim McDaniels	68	1095	386	154	.399	100	70	.700	345	78	140	4	378	5.6
Kennedy McIntosh***	59	1138	341	115	.337	67	40	.597	231	54	102	1	270	4.6
Kennedy McIntosh**	56	1105	328	107	.326	65	40	.615	222	53	98	1	254	4.5
Joby Wright	77	931	278	133	.478	89	37	.416	218	36	164	0	303	3.9
Garfield Heard*	3	17	9	4	.444	1	1	1.000	6	2	4	0	9	3.0
Charlie Dudley	12	99	23	10	.435	16	14	.875	6	16	15	0	34	2.8
Pete Cross***	29	157	25	6	.240	18	8	.444	61	11	29	0	20	0.7
Pete Cross**	26	133	21	6	.286	18	8	.444	57	11	24	0	20	0.8

*Finished season with another team.
**Player total with this club only.
***Player total with all clubs.

PLAYOFF RESULTS

EASTERN CONFERENCE SEMIFINALS
Boston 4, Atlanta 2

Apr. 1	Atlanta 109 at Boston	134
Apr. 4	Boston 126 at Atlanta	113
Apr. 6	Atlanta 118 at Boston	105
Apr. 8	Boston 94 at Atlanta	97
Apr. 11	Atlanta 101 at Boston	108
Apr. 13	Boston 121 at Atlanta	103

New York 4, Baltimore 1

Mar. 30	Baltimore 83 at New York	95
Apr. 1	Baltimore 103 at New York	123
Apr. 4	New York 103 at Baltimore	96
Apr. 6	New York 89 at Baltimore	97
Apr. 8	Baltimore 99 at New York	109

EASTERN CONFERENCE FINALS
New York 4, Boston 3

Apr. 15	New York 108 at Boston	134
Apr. 18	Boston 96 at New York	129
Apr. 20	New York 98 at Boston	91
Apr. 22	Boston 110 at New York	117*
Apr. 25	New York 97 at Boston	98
Apr. 27	Boston 110 at New York	100
Apr. 29	New York 94 at Boston	78

WESTERN CONFERENCE SEMIFINALS
Golden State 4, Milwaukee 2

Mar. 30	Golden State 90 at Milwaukee	110
Apr. 1	Golden State 95 at Milwaukee	92
Apr. 5	Milwaukee 113 at Golden State	93
Apr. 7	Milwaukee 97 at Golden State	102
Apr. 10	Golden State 100 at Milwaukee	97
Apr. 13	Milwaukee 86 at Golden State	100

Los Angeles 4, Chicago 3

Mar. 30	Chicago 104 at Los Angeles	107*
Apr. 1	Chicago 93 at Los Angeles	108
Apr. 6	Los Angeles 86 at Chicago	96
Apr. 8	Los Angeles 94 at Chicago	98
Apr. 10	Chicago 102 at Los Angeles	123
Apr. 13	Los Angeles 93 at Chicago	101
Apr. 15	Chicago 92 at Los Angeles	95

WESTERN CONFERENCE FINALS
Los Angeles 4, Golden State 1

Apr. 17	Golden State 99 at Los Angeles	101
Apr. 19	Golden State 93 at Los Angeles	104
Apr. 21	Los Angeles 126 at Golden State	70
Apr. 23	Los Angeles 109 at Golden State	117
Apr. 25	Golden State 118 at Los Angeles	128

WORLD CHAMPIONSHIP SERIES
New York 4, Los Angeles 1

May 1	New York 112 at Los Angeles	115
May 3	New York 99 at Los Angeles	95
May 6	Los Angeles 83 at New York	87
May 8	Los Angeles 98 at New York	103
May 10	New York 102 at Los Angeles	93

*Denotes overtime period.

1971-72 NBA STATISTICS

1971-72 NBA CHAMPION LOS ANGELES LAKERS

Front row (left to right): Jim McMillian, Jim Cleamons, Pat Riley, Wilt Chamberlain, Coach Bill Sharman, Leroy Ellis, Willie McCarter, Earnie Killum, Flynn Robinson. Back row: Assistant Coach K.C. Jones, Elgin Baylor, Keith Erickson, Gail Goodrich, Fred Hetzel, Roger Brown, Rick Roberson, Malkin Strong, Jerry West, Happy Hairston, trainer Frank O'Neill.

FINAL STANDINGS

ATLANTIC DIVISION

Team	Atl.	Balt.	Bos.	Buf.	Chi.	Cin.	Clv.	Det.	G.S.	Hou.	L.A.	Mil.	N.Y.	Phil.	Pho.	Prt.	Sea.	W.	L.	Pct.	G.B.
Boston	4	2	..	6	3	4	5	5	2	5	1	2	3	6	3	4	3	56	26	.683	..
New York	1	4	3	5	2	2	5	4	3	5	1	3	..	3	1	3	3	48	34	.585	8
Philadelphia	3	0	0	3	1	2	4	4	1	1	0	1	3	..	1	2	4	30	52	.366	26
Buffalo	2	3	0	..	1	3	4	2	0	0	0	0	1	3	0	2	0	22	60	.268	34

CENTRAL DIVISION

Team	Atl.	Balt.	Bos.	Buf.	Chi.	Cin.	Clv.	Det.	G.S.	Hou.	L.A.	Mil.	N.Y.	Phil.	Pho.	Prt.	Sea.	W.	L.	Pct.	G.B.
Baltimore	4	..	2	3	1	4	1	3	1	3	1	0	2	4	4	3	2	38	44	.463	..
Atlanta	..	2	0	4	0	3	4	3	3	1	0	2	3	3	4		1	36	46	.439	2
Cincinnati	3	2	2	3	1	..	6	2	2	0	1	0	2	2	2	2	0	30	52	.366	8
Cleveland	2	5	1	2	0	2	..	1	0	2	1	0	1	2	0	4	0	23	59	.280	15

MIDWEST DIVISION

Team	Atl.	Balt.	Bos.	Buf.	Chi.	Cin.	Clv.	Det.	G.S.	Hou.	L.A.	Mil.	N.Y.	Phil.	Pho.	Prt.	Sea.	W.	L.	Pct.	G.B.
Milwaukee	3	5	3	4	4	5	4	5	2	5	1	..	2	4	4	6	6	63	19	.768	..
Chicago	5	4	2	3	..	3	4	5	3	5	1	2	3	4	5	6	2	57	25	.695	6
Phoenix	2	1	3	4	1	3	4	4	3	3	2	2	4	4	..	6	3	49	33	.598	14
Detroit	2	2	0	4	1	3	3	..	0	3	1	1	1	1	2	2	0	26	56	.317	37

PACIFIC DIVISION

Team	Atl.	Balt.	Bos.	Buf.	Chi.	Cin.	Clv.	Det.	G.S.	Hou.	L.A.	Mil.	N.Y.	Phil.	Pho.	Prt.	Sea.	W.	L.	Pct.	G.B.
Los Angeles	5	4	4	4	3	4	3	4	5	5	..	4	4	5	4	6	5	69	13	.841	..
Golden State	2	4	3	3	3	3	4	5	..	5	1	2	2	4	2	4	4	51	31	.622	18
Seattle	4	3	3	4	3	5	4	4	2	3	1	0	2	1	2	6	..	47	35	.573	22
Houston	4	2	0	4	1	4	2	3	1	..	1	0	0	4	1	4	3	34	48	.415	35
Portland	0	1	0	4	0	2	2	2	2	2	0	0	1	2	0	..	0	18	64	.220	51

HOME-ROAD-NEUTRAL RECORDS OF ALL TEAMS

Team	Home	Road	Neutral	Total	Team	Home	Road	Neutral	Total
Atlanta	22- 19	13- 26	1- 1	36- 46	Houston	15- 20	14- 23	5- 5	34- 48
Baltimore	18- 15	16- 24	4- 5	38- 44	Los Angeles	36- 5	31- 7	2- 1	69- 13
Boston	32- 9	21- 16	3- 1	56- 26	Milwaukee	31- 5	27- 12	5- 2	63- 19
Buffalo	13- 27	8- 31	1- 2	22- 60	New York	27- 14	20- 19	1- 1	48- 34
Chicago	29- 12	26- 12	2- 1	57- 25	Philadelphia	14- 23	14- 26	2- 3	30- 52
Cincinnati	20- 18	8- 32	2- 2	30- 52	Phoenix	30- 11	19- 20	0- 2	49- 33
Cleveland	13- 28	8- 30	2- 1	23- 59	Portland	14- 26	4- 35	0- 3	18- 64
Detroit	16- 25	9- 30	1- 1	26- 56	Seattle	28- 12	18- 22	1- 1	47- 35
Golden State	27- 8	21- 20	3- 3	51- 31	Total	385-277	277-385	35-35	697-697

OFFENSIVE TEAM STATISTICS

Team	G.	FIELD GOALS Att.	Made	Pct.	FREE THROWS Att.	Made	Pct.	Reb.	MISCELLANEOUS Ast.	PF	Disq.	SCORING Pts.	Avg.
Los Angeles	82	7998	3920	.490	2833	2080	.734	4628	2232	1636	7	9920	121.0
Phoenix	82	7877	3599	.457	2999	2336	.779	4301	1976	2026	20	9534	116.3
Boston	82	8431	3819	.453	2367	1839	.777	4462	2230	2030	36	9477	115.6
Milwaukee	82	7653	3813	.498	2399	1774	.739	4269	2160	1862	29	9400	114.6
Philadelphia	82	8057	3577	.444	2825	2049	.725	4318	1920	2203	50	9203	112.2
Chicago	82	7853	3539	.451	2700	2039	.755	4371	2087	1964	24	9117	111.2
Houston	82	8277	3590	.434	2424	1813	.748	4433	1777	1992	32	8993	109.7
Atlanta	82	7570	3482	.460	2725	2018	.741	1080	1897	1967	14	8982	109.5
Seattle	82	7457	3461	.464	2659	2035	.765	4123	1976	1738	18	8957	109.2
Detroit	82	7665	3482	.454	2653	1981	.747	3970	1687	1954	26	8945	109.1
Golden State	82	7923	3477	.439	2500	1917	.767	4450	1854	1840	16	8871	108.2
Cincinnati	82	7496	3444	.459	2578	1948	.756	3754	2020	2079	40	8836	107.8
New York	82	7673	3521	.459	2303	1743	.757	3909	1985	1899	15	8785	107.1
Baltimore	82	7748	3490	.450	2378	1804	.759	4159	1816	1858	16	8784	107.1
Portland	82	7840	3462	.442	2494	1835	.736	3996	2090	1873	24	8759	106.8
Cleveland	82	8074	3458	.428	2390	1758	.736	4098	2060	1936	23	8674	105.8
Buffalo	82	7560	3409	.451	2219	1549	.698	3978	1759	2110	42	8367	102.0

DEFENSIVE TEAM STATISTICS

Team	FIELD GOALS Att.	Made	Pct.	FREE THROWS Att.	Made	Pct.	Reb.	MISCELLANEOUS Ast.	PF	Disq.	SCORING Pts.	Avg.	Pt. Dif.
Chicago	7189	3263	.454	2617	1914	.731	3928	1853	2041	32	8440	102.9	+ 8.3
Milwaukee	8025	3370	.420	2358	1745	.740	3922	1843	1788	10	8485	103.5	+11.1
New York	7513	3332	.443	2565	1920	.749	4169	1626	1892	28	8584	104.7	+ 2.4
Golden State	8082	3560	.440	2265	1688	.745	4381	1968	1912	25	8808	107.4	+ 0.8
Baltimore	7842	3545	.452	2412	1790	.742	4244	1844	1869	28	8880	108.3	- 1.2
Los Angeles	8553	3699	.432	1972	1515	.768	4290	1994	1997	29	8913	108.7	+12.3
Seattle	8029	3619	.451	2248	1681	.748	4183	2037	1975	29	8919	108.8	+ 0.4
Phoenix	7896	3568	.452	2658	1947	.733	4009	1929	2182	45	9083	110.8	+ 5.5
Boston	7886	3498	.444	2766	2089	.755	4179	1798	1842	16	9085	110.8	+ 4.8
Houston	7817	3542	.453	2737	2037	.744	4298	1945	1944	19	9121	111.2	- 1.5
Buffalo	7557	3479	.460	2842	2167	.762	4187	1918	1728	9	9125	111.3	- 9.3
Atlanta	7744	3601	.465	2530	1925	.761	4004	1890	1996	25	9127	111.3	- 1.8
Cincinnati	7588	3537	.466	2829	2093	.740	4228	2028	1971	36	9167	111.8	- 4.0
Cleveland	7537	3653	.485	2611	1994	.764	4034	2322	1937	24	9300	113.4	- 7.6
Philadelphia	7882	3614	.459	3063	2276	.743	4427	2005	2059	33	9504	115.9	- 3.7
Detroit	8106	3822	.472	2474	1862	.753	4377	2214	1931	25	9506	115.9	- 6.8
Portland	7906	3841	.486	2499	1875	.750	4439	2312	1903	19	9557	116.5	- 9.7

Disq.—Individual player disqualified (fouled out of game).

INDIVIDUAL LEADERS

POINTS
(Minimum 70 Games Played)

	G.	FG	FT	Pts.	Avg.		G.	FG	FT	Pts.	Avg.
Abdul-Jabbar, Mil.	81	1159	504	2822	34.8	Hudson, Atl.	77	775	349	1899	24.7
Archibald, Cin.	76	734	677	2145	28.2	Wicks, Port.	82	784	441	2009	24.5
Havlicek, Bos.	82	897	458	2252	27.5	Cunningham, Phila.	75	658	428	1744	23.3
Haywood, Sea.	73	717	480	1914	26.2	Frazier, N. Y.	77	669	450	1788	23.2
Goodrich, L. A.	82	826	475	2127	25.9	White, Bos.	79	770	285	1825	23.1
Love, Chi.	79	819	399	2037	25.8	Marin, Balt.	78	690	356	1736	22.3
West, L. A.	77	735	515	1985	25.8	Walker, Chi.	78	619	481	1719	22.0
Lanier, Det.	80	834	388	2056	25.7	Mullins, G. S.	80	685	350	1720	21.5
Clark, Phil.-Balt.	77	712	514	1938	25.2	Thurmond, G. S.	78	628	417	1673	21.4
Hayes, Hou.	82	832	399	2063	25.2	Russell, G. S.	79	689	315	1693	21.4

FREE THROWS
(Minimum 350 Attempts)

	FTA	FTM	Pct.
Marin, Baltimore	398	356	.894
Murphy, Houston	392	349	.890
Goodrich, Los Angeles	559	475	.850
Walker, Chicago	568	481	.847
Van Arsdale, Phoenix	626	529	.845
Lantz, Houston	462	387	.838
Havlicek, Boston	549	458	.834
Russell, Golden State	378	315	.833
McKenzie, Portland	379	315	.831
Walker, Detroit	480	397	.827

FIELD GOALS
(Minimum 700 Attempts)

	FGA	FGM	Pct.
Chamberlain, Los Angeles	764	496	.649
Abdul-Jabbar, Milwaukee	2019	1159	.574
Bellamy, Atlanta	1089	593	.545
Snyder, Seattle	937	496	.529
Lucas, New York	1060	543	.512
Frazier, New York	1307	669	.512
McGlocklin, Milwaukee	733	374	.510
Walker, Chicago	1225	619	.505
Allen, Milwaukee	874	441	.505
Hudson, Atlanta	1540	775	.503

ASSISTS
(Minimum 70 Games)

	G.	No.	Avg.
West, Los Angeles	77	747	9.7
Wilkens, Seattle	80	766	9.6
Archibald, Cincinnati	76	701	9.2
Clark, Phil.-Balt.	77	613	8.0
Havlicek, Boston	82	614	7.5
Van Lier, Cin.-Chi.	79	542	6.9
Cunningham, Philadelphia	75	443	5.9
Mullins, Golden State	80	471	5.9
Frazier, New York	77	446	5.8
Hazzard, Buffalo	72	406	5.6

REBOUNDS
(Minimum 70 Games)

	G.	No.	Avg.
Chamberlain, Los Angeles	82	1572	19.2
Unseld, Baltimore	76	1336	17.6
Abdul-Jabbar, Milwaukee	81	1346	16.6
Thurmond, Golden State	78	1252	16.1
Cowens, Boston	79	1203	15.2
E. Smith, Buffalo	78	1184	15.2
Hayes, Houston	82	1197	14.6
Lee, Golden State	78	1132	14.5
Lanier, Detroit	80	1132	14.2
Bridges, Atl.-Phil.	78	1051	13.5

TEAM-BY-TEAM INDIVIDUAL STATISTICS

ATLANTA HAWKS

Player	G.	Min.	FGA	FGM	Pct.	FTA	FTM	Pct.	Reb.	Ast.	PF	Disq.	Pts.	Avg.
Lou Hudson	77	3042	1540	775	.503	430	349	.812	385	309	225	0	1899	24.7
Pete Maravich	66	2302	1077	460	.427	438	355	.811	256	393	207	0	1275	19.3
Walt Bellamy	82	3187	1089	593	.545	581	340	.585	1049	262	255	2	1526	18.6
Jim Washington***	84	2961	885	393	.444	323	256	.793	736	146	276	3	1042	12.4
Jim Washington**	67	2416	729	325	.446	256	201	.785	601	121	217	0	851	12.7
Don Adams***	73	2071	798	313	.392	275	205	.745	502	140	266	6	831	11.4
Don Adams**	70	2030	779	307	.394	273	204	.747	494	137	259	5	818	11.7
Herm Gilliam	82	2337	774	345	.446	173	145	.838	335	377	232	3	835	10.2
Bill Bridges*	14	546	134	51	.381	44	31	.705	190	40	50	1	133	9.5
Don May	75	1285	476	234	.492	164	126	.768	217	55	133	0	594	7.9
Milt Williams	10	127	53	23	.434	29	21	.724	4	20	18	0	67	6.7
George Trapp	60	890	388	144	.371	139	105	.755	183	51	144	2	393	6.6
John Vallely*	9	110	43	20	.465	20	13	.650	11	9	13	0	53	5.9
Tom Payne	29	227	103	45	.437	46	29	.630	69	15	40	0	119	4.1
Jeff Halliburton	37	288	133	61	.459	30	25	.833	37	20	50	1	147	4.0
Larry Siegfried***	31	558	123	43	.350	37	32	.865	42	72	53	0	118	3.8
Larry Siegfried**	21	335	77	25	.325	23	20	.870	32	52	32	0	70	3.3
Bob Christian	56	485	142	66	.465	61	44	.721	181	28	77	0	176	3.1
Jim Davis*	11	119	33	8	.242	18	10	.556	36	8	14	0	26	2.4
Shaler Halimon	1	4	0	0	.000	0	0	.000	0	0	1	0	0	0.0

BALTIMORE BULLETS

Player	G.	Min.	FGA	FGM	Pct.	FTA	FTM	Pct.	Reb.	Ast.	PF	Disq.	Pts.	Avg.
Archie Clark***	77	3285	1516	712	.470	667	514	.771	268	613	194	0	1938	25.2
Archie Clark**	76	3243	1500	701	.467	656	507	.773	265	606	191	0	1909	25.1
Jack Marin	78	2927	1444	690	.478	398	356	.894	528	169	240	2	1736	22.3
Earl Monroe*	3	103	64	26	.406	18	13	.722	8	10	9	0	65	21.7
Wes Unseld	76	3171	822	409	.498	272	171	.629	1336	278	218	1	989	13.0
Phil Chenier	81	2481	981	407	.415	247	182	.737	268	205	191	2	996	12.3
Dave Stallworth**	64	1815	690	303	.439	153	123	.804	398	133	186	3	729	11.4
Dave Stallworth***	78	2040	778	336	.432	188	152	.809	433	158	217	3	824	10.6
Mike Riordan**	54	1344	488	229	.469	123	84	.683	127	124	127	0	542	10.0
Mike Riordan***	58	1377	499	233	.467	124	84	.677	128	126	129	0	550	9.5
Stan Love	74	1327	536	242	.451	140	103	.736	338	52	202	0	587	7.9
Fred Carter*	2	68	27	6	.222	9	3	.333	19	12	7	0	15	7.5
John Tresvant	65	1227	360	162	.450	148	121	.818	323	83	175	6	445	6.8
Gary Zeller	28	471	229	83	.362	35	22	.629	65	30	62	0	188	6.7
Kevin Loughery*	2	42	17	4	.235	8	5	.625	5	8	5	0	13	6.5
Gus Johnson	39	668	269	103	.383	63	43	.683	226	51	91	0	249	6.4
Terry Driscoll	40	313	104	40	.385	39	27	.692	109	23	53	0	107	2.7
Dorie Murrey	51	421	113	43	.381	39	24	.615	126	17	76	2	110	2.2
Rich Rinaldi	39	159	104	42	.404	30	20	.667	18	15	25	0	104	2.7

BOSTON CELTICS

Player	G.	Min.	FGA	FGM	Pct.	FTA	FTM	Pct.	Reb.	Ast.	PF	Disq.	Pts.	Avg.
John Havlicek	82	3698	1957	897	.458	549	458	.834	672	614	183	1	2252	27.5
Jo Jo White	79	3261	1788	770	.431	343	285	.831	446	416	227	1	1825	23.1
Dave Cowens	79	3186	1357	657	.484	243	175	.720	1203	245	314	10	1489	18.8
Don Nelson	82	2086	811	389	.480	452	356	.788	453	192	220	3	1134	13.8
Don Chaney	79	2275	786	373	.475	255	197	.773	395	202	295	7	943	11.9
Tom Sanders	82	1631	524	215	.410	136	111	.816	353	98	257	7	541	6.6
Steve Kuberski	71	1128	444	185	.417	102	80	.784	320	46	130	1	450	6.3
Art Williams	81	1326	339	161	.475	119	90	.756	256	327	204	2	412	5.1
Hank Finkel	78	736	254	103	.406	74	43	.581	251	61	118	4	249	3.2
Clarence Glover	25	119	55	25	.455	32	15	.469	46	4	26	0	65	2.6
Garfield Smith	26	134	66	28	.424	31	6	.194	37	8	22	0	62	2.4
Rex Morgan	28	150	50	16	.320	31	23	.742	30	17	34	0	55	2.0

BUFFALO BRAVES

Player	G.	Min.	FGA	FGM	Pct.	FTA	FTM	Pct.	Reb.	Ast.	PF	Disq.	Pts.	Avg.
Bob Kauffman	77	3205	1123	558	.497	429	341	.795	787	297	273	7	1457	18.9
Elmore Smith	78	3186	1275	579	.454	363	194	.534	1184	111	306	10	1352	17.3
Walt Hazzard	72	2389	998	450	.451	303	237	.782	213	406	230	2	1137	15.8
Randy Smith	76	2094	896	432	.482	254	158	.622	368	189	202	2	1022	13.4
Fred Hilton	61	1349	795	309	.389	122	90	.738	156	116	145	0	708	11.6
Dick Garrett	73	1905	735	325	.442	157	136	.866	225	165	225	5	786	10.8

Player	G.	Min.	FGA	FGM	Pct.	FTA	FTM	Pct.	Reb.	Ast.	PF	Disq.	Pts.	Avg.
Mike Davis	62	1068	501	213	.425	180	138	.767	120	82	141	5	564	9.1
Jerry Chambers	26	369	180	78	.433	32	22	.688	67	23	39	0	178	6.8
Cornell Warner	62	1239	366	162	.443	78	58	.714	379	54	125	2	382	6.2
John Hummer	55	1186	290	113	.390	124	58	.468	229	72	178	4	284	5.2
Em Bryant	54	1223	220	101	.459	125	75	.600	127	206	167	5	277	5.1
Bill Hosket	44	592	181	89	.492	52	42	.808	123	38	79	0	220	5.0

CHICAGO BULLS

Player	G.	Min.	FGA	FGM	Pct.	FTA	FTM	Pct.	Reb.	Ast.	PF	Disq.	Pts.	Avg.
Bob Love	79	3108	1854	819	.442	509	399	.784	518	125	235	2	2037	25.8
Chet Walker	78	2588	1225	619	.505	568	481	.847	473	178	171	0	1719	22.0
Jerry Sloan	82	3035	1206	535	.444	391	258	.660	691	211	309	8	1328	16.2
Norm Van Lier***	79	2415	761	334	.439	300	237	.790	357	542	239	5	905	11.5
Norm Van Lier**	69	2140	671	306	.456	278	220	.791	299	491	207	4	832	12.1
Bob Weiss	82	2450	832	358	.430	254	212	.835	170	377	212	1	928	11.3
Clifford Ray	82	1872	445	222	.499	218	134	.615	869	254	296	5	578	7.0
Tom Boerwinkle	80	2022	500	219	.438	180	118	.656	897	281	253	4	556	7.0
Howard Porter	67	730	403	171	.424	77	59	.766	183	24	88	0	401	6.0
Jim Fox*	10	133	53	20	.377	28	20	.714	54	6	21	0	60	6.0
Jim King	73	1017	356	162	.455	113	89	.788	81	101	103	0	413	5.7
Jim Collins	19	134	71	26	.366	11	10	.909	12	10	11	0	62	3.3
Charlie Paulk	7	60	28	8	.286	9	7	.778	15	4	7	0	23	3.3
Kennedy McIntosh	43	405	168	57	.339	44	21	.477	89	18	41	0	135	3.1
Jackie Dinkins	18	89	41	17	.415	20	11	.550	20	7	10	0	45	2.5

CINCINNATI ROYALS

Player	G.	Min.	FGA	FGM	Pct.	FTA	FTM	Pct.	Reb.	Ast.	PF	Disq.	Pts.	Avg.
Nate Archibald	76	3272	1511	734	.486	824	677	.822	222	701	198	3	2145	28.2
Tom Van Arsdale	73	2598	1205	550	.456	396	299	.755	350	198	241	1	1399	19.2
Nate Williams	81	2173	968	418	.432	172	127	.738	372	174	300	11	963	11.9
Sam Lacey	81	2832	972	410	.422	169	119	.704	968	173	284	6	939	11.6
Jim Fox***	81	2180	788	354	.449	297	227	.764	713	86	257	8	935	11.5
Jim Fox**	71	2047	735	334	.454	269	207	.770	659	80	236	8	875	12.3
John Mengelt	78	1438	605	287	.474	252	208	.825	148	146	163	0	782	10.0
Johnny Green	82	1914	582	331	.569	250	141	.564	560	120	238	5	803	9.8
Matt Guokas	61	1975	385	191	.496	83	64	.771	142	321	150	0	446	7.3
Norm Van Lier*	10	275	90	28	.311	22	17	.773	58	51	32	1	73	7.3
Jake Jones***	17	202	72	28	.389	31	20	.645	26	12	22	0	76	4.5
Jake Jones**	11	161	54	22	.407	21	13	.619	20	10	19	0	57	5.2
Ken Durrett	19	233	79	31	.392	28	21	.750	39	14	41	0	83	4.4
Gil McGregor	42	532	182	66	.363	56	39	.696	148	18	120	4	171	4.1
Fred Taylor***	34	283	117	36	.308	32	15	.469	54	18	40	0	87	2.6
Fred Taylor**	21	214	90	30	.333	19	11	.579	37	11	32	0	71	3.4
Darrall Imhoff*	9	76	29	10	.345	8	3	.375	27	2	22	1	23	2.6
Sid Catlett	9	40	9	2	.222	9	2	.222	4	1	3	0	6	0.7

CLEVELAND CAVALIERS

Player	G.	Min.	FGA	FGM	Pct.	FTA	FTM	Pct.	Reb.	Ast.	PF	Disq.	Pts.	Avg.
Austin Carr	43	1539	894	381	.426	196	149	.760	150	148	99	0	911	21.2
John Johnson	82	3041	1286	557	.433	353	277	.785	631	415	268	2	1391	17.0
Butch Beard	68	2434	849	394	.464	342	260	.760	276	456	213	2	1048	15.4
Bobby Smith	82	2734	1190	527	.443	224	178	.795	502	247	222	3	1232	15.0
Rick Roberson	63	2207	688	304	.442	366	215	.587	801	109	251	7	823	13.1
Walt Wesley	82	2185	1006	412	.409	291	196	.674	711	76	245	4	1020	12.4
Charlie Davis	61	1144	569	229	.402	169	142	.840	92	123	143	3	600	9.8
Dave Sorenson	76	1162	475	213	.448	136	106	.779	301	81	120	1	532	7.0
Bobby Washington	69	967	309	123	.398	128	104	.813	129	223	135	1	350	5.1
John Warren	68	969	345	144	.417	58	49	.845	133	91	92	0	337	5.0
Steve Patterson	65	775	263	94	.357	46	23	.500	228	54	80	0	211	3.2
Greg Howard	48	426	131	50	.382	51	39	.765	108	27	50	0	139	2.9
Luther Rackley*	9	65	25	11	.440	4	1	.250	21	3	3	0	23	2.6
Jackie Ridgle	32	107	44	19	.432	26	19	.731	15	7	15	0	57	1.8

DETROIT PISTONS

Player	G.	Min.	FGA	FGM	Pct.	FTA	FTM	Pct.	Reb.	Ast.	PF	Disq.	Pts.	Avg.
Bob Lanier	80	3092	1690	834	.493	505	388	.768	1132	248	297	6	2056	25.7
Dave Bing	45	1936	891	369	.414	354	278	.785	186	317	138	3	1016	22.6
Jimmy Walker	78	3083	1386	634	.457	480	397	.827	231	315	198	2	1665	21.3
Curtis Rowe	82	2661	802	369	.460	287	192	.669	699	99	171	1	930	11.3
Terry Dischinger	79	2062	574	295	.514	200	156	.780	338	92	289	7	746	9.4
Howard Komives	79	2071	702	262	.373	203	164	.808	172	291	196	0	688	8.7
Willie Norwood	78	1272	440	222	.505	215	140	.651	316	43	229	4	584	7.5
Bob Quick	18	204	82	39	.476	45	34	.756	51	11	29	0	112	6.2
Jim Davis***	75	983	338	147	.435	154	100	.649	276	51	138	1	394	5.3
Jim Davis**	52	684	251	121	.428	98	64	.653	196	38	106	1	306	5.9
Harvey Marlatt	31	506	149	60	.403	42	36	.857	62	60	64	1	156	5.0
Steve Mix	8	104	47	15	.319	12	7	.583	23	4	7	0	37	4.6
Bill Hewitt	68	1203	277	131	.473	82	41	.500	370	71	134	1	303	4.5
Erwin Mueller	42	605	197	68	.345	74	43	.581	147	57	64	0	179	4.3
Isaiah Wilson	48	322	177	63	.356	56	41	.732	47	41	32	0	167	3.5

Milwaukee's Kareem Abdul-Jabbar was most valuable player and league scoring champion in 1971-72.

GOLDEN STATE WARRIORS

Player	G.	Min.	FGA	FGM	Pct.	FTA	FTM	Pct.	Reb.	Ast.	PF	Disq.	Pts.	Avg.
Jeff Mullins	80	3214	1466	685	.467	441	350	.794	444	471	260	5	1720	21.5
Cazzie Russell	79	2902	1514	689	.455	378	315	.833	428	248	176	0	1693	21.4
Nate Thurmond	78	3362	1454	628	.432	561	417	.743	1252	230	214	1	1673	21.4
Jim Barnett	80	2200	915	374	.409	292	244	.836	250	309	189	0	992	12.4
Ron Williams	80	1932	614	291	.474	234	195	.833	147	308	232	1	777	9.7
Joe Ellis	78	1462	681	280	.411	132	95	.720	389	97	224	4	655	8.4
Clyde Lee	78	2674	544	256	.471	222	120	.541	1132	85	244	4	632	8.1
Bob Portman	61	553	221	89	.403	60	53	.883	133	26	69	0	231	3.8
Nick Jones	65	478	196	82	.418	61	51	.836	39	45	109	0	215	3.3
Bill Turner	62	597	181	71	.392	53	40	.755	131	22	67	1	182	2.9
Odis Allison	36	166	78	17	.218	61	33	.541	45	10	34	0	67	1.9
Vic Bartolome	38	165	59	15	.254	5	4	.800	60	3	22	0	34	0.9

HOUSTON ROCKETS

Player	G.	Min.	FGA	FGM	Pct.	FTA	FTM	Pct.	Reb.	Ast.	PF	Disq.	Pts.	Avg.
Elvin Hayes	82	3461	1918	832	.434	615	399	.649	1197	270	233	1	2063	25.2
Stu Lantz	81	3097	1279	557	.435	462	387	.838	345	337	211	2	1501	18.5
Calvin Murphy	82	2538	1255	571	.455	392	349	.890	258	393	298	6	1491	18.2
Rudy Tomjanovich	78	2689	1010	500	.495	238	172	.723	923	117	193	2	1172	15.0
Cliff Meely	77	1815	776	315	.406	197	133	.675	507	119	254	9	763	9.9
Greg Smith°°°	82	2256	671	309	.461	168	111	.661	661	483	222	259	4	729	8.9
Greg Smith°°	54	1519	473	212	.448	110	70	.636	322	159	167	3	494	9.1
Mike Newlin	82	1495	618	256	.414	144	108	.750	228	135	233	6	620	7.6
Larry Siegfried°	10	223	46	18	.391	14	12	.857	10	20	21	0	48	4.8
Don Adams°	3	41	19	6	.316	2	1	.500	8	3	7	1	13	4.3
Jim Davis°	12	180	54	18	.333	38	26	.684	44	5	18	0	62	5.2
Dick Gibbs	64	757	265	90	.340	66	55	.833	140	51	127	0	235	3.7
Curtis Perry°	25	355	115	38	.330	24	12	.500	122	22	47	1	88	3.5
John Valley°°°	49	366	171	69	.404	45	30	.667	32	37	50	0	168	3.4
John Valleley°°	40	256	128	49	.383	25	17	.680	21	28	37	0	115	2.9
John Egan	38	437	104	42	.404	32	26	.813	26	51	55	0	110	2.9
McCoy McLemore°°°	27	246	71	28	.394	24	20	.833	73	22	33	1	76	2.8
McCoy McLemore°°	17	147	43	19	.442	12	9	.750	39	10	15	1	47	2.8
Dick Cunningham	63	720	174	67	.385	53	37	.698	243	57	76	0	171	2.7

LOS ANGELES LAKERS

Player	G.	Min.	FGA	FGM	Pct.	FTA	FTM	Pct.	Reb.	Ast.	PF	Disq.	Pts.	Avg.
Gail Goodrich	82	3040	1695	826	.487	559	475	.850	295	365	210	0	2127	25.9
Jerry West	77	2973	1540	735	.477	633	515	.814	327	747	209	0	1985	25.8
Jim McMillian	80	3050	1331	642	.482	277	219	.791	522	209	209	0	1503	18.8
Wilt Chamberlain	82	3469	764	496	.649	524	221	.422	1572	329	196	0	1213	14.8
Happy Hairston	80	2748	798	368	.461	399	311	.779	1045	193	251	2	1047	13.1
Elgin Baylor	9	239	97	42	.433	27	22	.815	57	18	20	0	106	11.8
Flynn Robinson	64	1007	535	262	.490	129	111	.860	115	138	139	2	635	9.9
Pat Riley	67	926	441	197	.447	74	55	.743	127	75	110	0	449	6.7
John Trapp	58	759	314	139	.443	73	51	.699	180	42	130	3	329	5.7
Keith Erickson	15	262	83	40	.482	7	6	.857	39	35	26	0	86	5.7
Leroy Ellis	74	1081	300	138	.460	95	66	.695	310	46	115	0	342	4.6
Jim Cleamons	38	201	100	35	.350	36	28	.778	39	35	21	0	98	2.6

MILWAUKEE BUCKS

Player	G.	Min.	FGA	FGM	Pct.	FTA	FTM	Pct.	Reb.	Ast.	PF	Disq.	Pts.	Avg.
Kareem Abdul-Jabbar	81	3583	2019	1159	.574	732	504	.689	1346	370	235	1	2822	34.8
Bob Dandridge	80	2957	1264	630	.498	291	215	.739	613	249	297	7	1475	18.4
Oscar Robertson	64	2390	887	419	.472	330	276	.836	323	491	116	0	1114	17.4
Lucius Allen	80	2316	874	441	.505	259	198	.764	254	333	214	2	1080	13.5
Jon McGlocklin	80	2213	733	374	.510	126	109	.865	181	231	146	0	857	10.7
John Block	79	1524	530	233	.440	275	206	.749	410	95	213	4	672	8.5
Greg Smith*	28	737	198	97	.490	58	41	.707	161	63	92	1	235	8.4
Wally Jones	48	1030	354	144	.407	90	74	.822	75	141	112	0	362	7.5
Curtis Perry***	75	1826	486	181	.372	119	76	.639	593	100	261	14	438	5.8
Curtis Perry**	50	1471	371	143	.385	95	64	.674	471	78	214	13	350	7.0
Toby Kimball	74	971	229	107	.467	81	44	.543	312	60	137	0	258	3.5
McCoy McLemore*	10	99	28	9	.321	12	11	.917	34	12	18	0	29	2.9
Charles Lowery	20	134	38	17	.447	18	11	.611	19	14	16	1	45	2.3
Bill Dinwiddie	23	144	57	16	.281	9	5	.556	32	9	23	0	37	1.6
Jeff Webb*	19	109	35	9	.257	13	11	.846	18	7	8	0	29	1.5
Barry Nelson	28	102	36	15	.417	10	5	.500	20	7	21	0	35	1.3

NEW YORK KNICKERBOCKERS

Player	G.	Min.	FGA	FGM	Pct.	FTA	FTM	Pct.	Reb.	Ast.	PF	Disq.	Pts.	Avg.
Walt Frazier	77	3126	1307	669	.512	557	450	.808	513	446	185	0	1788	23.2
Jerry Lucas	77	2926	1060	543	.512	249	197	.791	1011	318	218	1	1283	16.7
Dave DeBusschere	80	3072	1218	520	.427	265	193	.728	901	291	219	1	1233	15.4
Bill Bradley	78	2780	1085	504	.465	199	169	.849	250	315	254	4	1177	15.1
Willis Reed	11	363	137	60	.438	39	27	.692	96	22	30	0	147	13.4
Dick Barnett	79	2256	918	401	.437	215	162	.753	153	198	229	4	964	12.2
Earl Monroe***	63	1337	662	287	.434	224	175	.781	100	142	139	1	749	11.9
Earl Monroe**	60	1234	598	261	.436	206	162	.786	92	132	130	1	684	11.4
Phil Jackson	80	1273	466	205	.440	228	167	.732	326	72	224	4	577	7.2
Dave Stallworth*	14	225	88	33	.375	35	29	.829	35	25	31	0	95	6.8
Dean Meminger	78	1173	293	139	.474	140	79	.564	185	103	137	0	357	4.6
Luther Rackley***	71	683	240	103	.429	88	50	.568	208	21	107	0	256	3.6
Luther Rackley**	62	618	215	92	.428	84	49	.583	187	18	104	0	233	3.8
Mike Price	6	40	14	5	.357	11	9	.818	6	6	10	0	19	3.2
Eddie Mast	40	270	112	39	.348	41	25	.610	73	10	39	0	103	2.6
Mike Riordan	4	33	11	4	.364	1	0	.000	1	2	2	0	8	2.0
Charlie Paulk***	35	211	88	24	.273	21	15	.714	64	11	31	0	63	1.8
Charlie Paulk**	28	151	60	16	.267	12	8	.667	49	7	24	0	40	1.4
Eddie Miles	42	198	64	23	.359	18	16	.889	16	17	46	0	62	1.5
Greg Fillmore	10	67	27	7	.259	3	1	.333	15	3	17	0	15	1.5

PHILADELPHIA 76ers

Player	G.	Min.	FGA	FGM	Pct.	FTA	FTM	Pct.	Reb.	Ast.	PF	Disq.	Pts.	Avg.
Archie Clark*	1	42	16	11	.688	11	7	.636	3	7	3	0	29	29.0
Billy Cunningham	75	2900	1428	658	.461	601	428	.712	918	443	295	12	1744	23.3
Bob Rule***	76	2230	1058	461	.436	335	226	.675	534	116	189	4	1148	15.1
Bob Rule**	60	1987	934	416	.445	292	203	.695	479	110	162	4	1035	17.3
Fred Carter***	79	2215	1018	446	.438	293	182	.621	326	211	242	4	1074	13.6
Fred Carter**	77	2147	991	440	.444	284	179	.630	307	199	235	4	1059	13.8
Bill Bridges***	78	2756	779	379	.487	316	222	.703	1051	198	269	6	980	12.6
Bill Bridges**	64	2210	645	328	.509	272	191	.702	861	158	219	5	847	13.2
Kevin Loughery***	76	1771	809	341	.422	320	263	.822	183	196	213	3	945	12.4
Kevin Loughery**	74	1829	792	337	.426	312	258	.827	178	188	208	3	932	12.6
Fred Foster	74	1699	837	347	.415	243	185	.761	276	90	184	3	879	11.9
Hal Greer	81	2410	866	389	.449	234	181	.774	271	316	268	10	959	11.8
Jim Washington*	17	545	156	68	.436	67	55	.821	135	25	59	3	191	11.2
Dave Wohl	79	1628	567	243	.429	206	156	.757	150	228	229	2	642	8.1
Lucious Jackson	63	1083	346	137	.396	133	92	.692	309	88	141	1	366	5.8
Al Henry	43	421	156	68	.436	73	51	.699	137	8	42	0	187	4.3
Dennis Awtrey	58	794	222	98	.441	76	49	.645	248	51	141	3	245	4.2
Jake Jones*	6	41	18	6	.333	10	7	.700	6	2	3	0	19	3.2
Barry Yates	24	144	83	31	.373	11	7	.636	40	7	14	0	69	2.9

PHOENIX SUNS

Player	G.	Min.	FGA	FGM	Pct.	FTA	FTM	Pct.	Reb.	Ast.	PF	Disq.	Pts.	Avg.
Connie Hawkins	76	2798	1244	571	.459	565	456	.807	633	296	235	2	1598	21.0
Dick Van Arsdale	82	3096	1178	545	.463	626	529	.845	334	297	232	1	1619	19.7
Charlie Scott	6	177	113	48	.425	21	17	.810	23	26	19	0	113	18.8
Paul Silas	80	3082	1031	485	.470	560	433	.773	955	343	201	0	1403	17.5
Neal Walk	81	2142	1057	506	.479	344	256	.744	665	151	295	9	1268	15.7

Player	G.	Min.	FGA	FGM	Pct.	FTA	FTM	Pct.	Reb.	Ast.	PF	Disq.	Pts.	Avg.
Clem Haskins	79	2453	1054	509	.483	258	220	.853	270	290	194	1	1238	15.7
Dennis Layton	80	1849	717	304	.424	165	122	.739	164	247	219	0	730	9.1
Otto Moore	81	1624	597	260	.436	156	94	.603	540	88	212	2	614	7.6
Mel Counts	76	906	344	147	.427	140	101	.721	257	96	159	2	395	5.2
Lamar Green	67	991	298	133	.446	90	66	.733	348	45	134	1	332	5.0
Art Harris	21	145	70	23	.329	21	9	.429	13	18	26	0	55	2.6
Jeff Webb°°°	46	238	100	40	.400	23	16	.696	35	23	29	0	96	2.1
Jeff Webb°°	27	129	65	31	.477	10	5	.500	17	16	21	0	67	2.5
John Wetzel	51	419	82	31	.378	30	24	.800	65	56	71	0	86	1.7
Fred Taylor°	13	69	27	6	.222	13	4	.308	17	7	8	0	16	1.2

PORTLAND TRAIL BLAZERS

Player	G.	Min.	FGA	FGM	Pct.	FTA	FTM	Pct.	Reb.	Ast.	PF	Disq.	Pts.	Avg.
Sidney Wicks	82	3245	1837	784	.427	621	441	.710	943	350	186	1	2009	24.5
Geoff Petrie	60	2155	1115	465	.417	256	202	.789	133	248	108	0	1132	18.9
Stan McKenzie	82	2036	834	410	.492	379	315	.831	272	148	240	2	1135	13.8
Dale Schlueter	81	2693	672	353	.525	326	241	.739	860	285	277	3	947	11.7
Gary Gregor	82	2371	884	399	.451	151	114	.755	591	187	201	2	912	11.1
Rick Adelman	80	2445	753	329	.437	201	151	.751	229	413	209	2	809	10.1
Bill Smith	22	448	173	72	.416	64	38	.594	135	19	73	3	182	8.3
Charlie Yelverton	69	1227	530	206	.389	188	133	.707	201	81	145	2	545	7.9
Willie McCarter	39	612	257	103	.401	55	37	.673	43	45	58	0	243	6.2
Ron Knight	49	483	257	112	.436	62	31	.500	116	33	52	0	225	5.2
Larry Steele	72	1311	308	148	.481	97	70	.722	282	161	198	8	366	5.1
Jim Marsh	39	375	117	39	.333	59	41	.695	84	30	50	0	119	3.1
Darrall Imhoff°°°	49	480	132	52	.394	43	24	.558	134	52	98	2	128	2.6
Darrall Imhoff°°	40	404	103	42	.408	35	21	.600	107	50	76	1	105	2.6

SEATTLE SUPERSONICS

Player	G.	Min.	FGA	FGM	Pct.	FTA	FTM	Pct.	Reb.	Ast.	PF	Disq.	Pts.	Avg.
Spencer Haywood	73	3167	1557	717	.461	586	480	.819	926	148	208	0	1914	26.2
Lenny Wilkens	80	2989	1027	479	.466	620	480	.774	338	766	209	4	1438	18.0
Dick Snyder	73	2534	937	496	.529	259	218	.842	228	283	200	3	1210	16.6
Don Smith	58	1780	751	322	.429	214	154	.720	654	124	178	1	798	13.8
Don Kojis	73	1857	687	322	.469	237	188	.793	335	82	168	1	832	11.4
Lee Winfield	81	2040	692	343	.496	262	175	.668	218	290	198	1	861	10.6
Jim McDaniels	12	235	123	51	.415	18	11	.611	82	9	26	0	113	9.4
Garfield Heard	58	1499	474	190	.401	128	79	.617	442	55	126	2	459	7.9
Barry Clemens	82	1447	484	252	.521	90	76	.844	288	64	198	4	580	7.1
Bob Rule°	16	243	124	45	.363	43	23	.535	55	6	27	0	113	7.1
Pete Cross	74	1424	355	152	.428	140	103	.736	509	63	135	2	407	5.5
Fred Brown	33	359	180	59	.328	29	22	.759	37	60	44	0	140	4.2
Jake Ford	26	181	66	33	.500	33	26	.788	11	26	21	0	92	3.5

°Finished season with another team.
°°Player total with this club only.
°°°Player total with all clubs.

PLAYOFF RESULTS

EASTERN CONFERENCE SEMIFINALS
Boston 4, Atlanta 2

Mar. 29—Atlanta 108 at Boston	126
Mar. 31—Boston 104 at Atlanta	113
Apr. 2—Atlanta 113 at Boston	136
Apr. 4—Boston 110 at Atlanta	112
Apr. 7—Atlanta 114 at Boston	124
Apr. 9—Boston 127 at Atlanta	118

New York 4, Baltimore 2

Mar. 31—New York 105 at Baltimore	108°
Apr. 2—Baltimore 88 at New York	110
Apr. 4—New York 103 at Baltimore	104
Apr. 6—Baltimore 98 at New York	104
Apr. 9—New York 106 at Baltimore	82
Apr. 11—Baltimore 101 at New York	107

WESTERN CONFERENCE SEMIFINALS
Milwaukee 4, Golden State 1

Mar. 28—Golden State 117 at Milwaukee	106
Mar. 30—Golden State 93 at Milwaukee	118
Apr. 1—Milwaukee 122 at Golden State	94
Apr. 4—Milwaukee 106 at Golden State	99
Apr. 6—Golden State 100 at Milwaukee	108

Los Angeles 4, Chicago 0

Mar. 28—Chicago 80 at Los Angeles	95
Mar. 30—Chicago 124 at Los Angeles	131
Apr. 2—Los Angeles 108 at Chicago	101
Apr. 4—Los Angeles 108 at Chicago	97

EASTERN CONFERENCE FINALS
New York 4, Boston 1

Apr. 13—New York 116 at Boston	94
Apr. 16—Boston 105 at New York	106
Apr. 19—New York 109 at Boston	115
Apr. 21—Boston 98 at New York	116
Apr. 23—New York 111 at Boston	103

WESTERN CONFERENCE FINALS
Los Angeles 4, Milwaukee 2

Apr. 9—Milwaukee 93 at Los Angeles	72
Apr. 12—Milwaukee 134 at Los Angeles	135
Apr. 14—Los Angeles 108 at Milwaukee	105
Apr. 16—Los Angeles 88 at Milwaukee	114
Apr. 18—Milwaukee 90 at Los Angeles	115
Apr. 22—Los Angeles 104 at Milwaukee	100

WORLD CHAMPIONSHIP SERIES
Los Angeles 4, New York 1

Apr. 26—New York 114 at Los Angeles	92
Apr. 30—New York 92 at Los Angeles	106
May 3—Los Angeles 107 at New York	96
May 5—Los Angeles 116 at New York	111°
May 7—New York 100 at Los Angeles	114

°Denotes overtime period.

1970-71 NBA STATISTICS

1970-71 WORLD CHAMPION MILWAUKEE BUCKS

Seated: Bob Boozer, Greg Smith, Bob Dandridge, Oscar Robertson, Kareem Abdul-Jabbar, Jon McGlocklin, Lucius Allen, Coach Larry Costello; Standing: Trainer Arnie Garber, Jeff Webb, Marvin Winkler, Dick Cunningham, Bob Greacen, McCoy McLemore, Assistant Coach Tom Nissalke.

FINAL STANDINGS

ATLANTIC DIVISION

Team	Atl.	Balt.	Bos.	Buf.	Chi.	Cin.	Clv.	Det.	L.A.	Mil.	N.Y.	Phil.	Pho.	Prt.	S.D.	S.F.	Sea.	W.	L.	Pct.	G.B.
New York	3	4	6	2	2	4	4	3	2	4	..	2	4	3	4	3	2	52	30	.634	....
Philadelphia	2	3	2	4	2	5	3	3	2	1	4	..	3	4	3	3	3	47	35	.573	5
Boston	4	3	..	4	4	4	3	2	3	0	0	4	2	2	3	3	3	44	38	.537	8
Buffalo	1	1	0	..	0	0	5	1	2	0	2	0	1	6	1	1	1	22	60	.268	30

CENTRAL DIVISION

Team	Atl.	Balt.	Bos.	Buf.	Chi.	Cin.	Clv.	Det.	L.A.	Mil.	N.Y.	Phil.	Pho.	Prt.	S.D.	S.F.	Sea.	W.	L.	Pct.	G.B.
Baltimore	3	..	3	3	2	3	4	2	2	1	2	3	3	2	4	2	3	42	40	.512	....
Atlanta	..	2	3	1	2	4	0	3	1	3	4	1	2	2	2		3	36	46	.439	6
Cincinnati	4	3	2	4	0	..	5	1	1	1	2	1	1	4	1	2	1	33	49	.402	9
Cleveland	0	0	1	7	0	1	..	2	0	0	0	1	0	2	0	1	0	15	67	.183	27

MIDWEST DIVISION

Team	Atl.	Balt.	Bos.	Buf.	Chi.	Cin.	Clv.	Det.	L.A.	Mil.	N.Y.	Phil.	Pho.	Prt.	S.D.	S.F.	Sea.	W.	L.	Pct.	G.B.
Milwaukee	4	4	5	4	5	4	4	5	4	..	1	4	4	3	4	6	5	66	16	.805	....
Chicago	4	3	1	4	..	4	4	3	2	1	3	3	3	3	6	4	3	51	31	.622	15
Phoenix	4	2	3	3	3	4	4	4	4	2	1	2	..	4	2	3	3	48	34	.585	18
Detroit	5	2	3	5	3	4	2	..	2	1	2	2	2	3	4	1	3	45	37	.549	21

PACIFIC DIVISION

Team	Atl.	Balt.	Bos.	Buf.	Chi.	Cin.	Clv.	Det.	L.A.	Mil.	N.Y.	Phil.	Pho.	Prt.	S.D.	S.F.	Sea.	W.	L.	Pct.	G.B.
Los Angeles	2	3	2	4	4	4	3	3	..	1	3	3	2	4		3	4	48	34	.585	....
San Francisco	3	2	3	2	3	3	3	2	4	0	2	2	3	4	..		3	41	41	.500	7
San Diego	3	1	2	3	0	3	4	2	3	1	1	2	4	4	..	2	5	40	42	.488	8
Seattle	2	2	2	3	2	4	4	1	2	1	3	2	4	1	3	..		38	44	.463	10
Portland	2	2	2	6	1	0	10	1	0	1	1	0	0	..	0	1	2	29	53	.354	19

HOME-ROAD-NEUTRAL RECORDS OF ALL TEAMS

Team	Home	Road	Neutral	Total
Atlanta	21- 20	14- 26	1- 0	36- 46
Baltimore	24- 13	16- 25	2- 2	42- 40
Boston	25- 14	18- 22	1- 2	44- 38
Buffalo	14- 23	6- 30	2- 7	22- 60
Chicago	30- 11	17- 19	4- 1	51- 31
Cincinnati	17- 16	11- 28	5- 5	33- 49
Cleveland	11- 30	2- 37	2- 0	15- 67
Detroit	24- 17	20- 19	1- 1	45- 37
Los Angeles	30- 11	17- 22	1- 1	48- 34
Milwaukee	34- 2	28- 13	4- 1	66- 16
New York	32- 9	19- 20	1- 1	52- 30
Philadelphia	24- 15	21- 18	2- 2	47- 35
Phoenix	27- 14	19- 20	2- 0	48- 34
Portland	18- 21	9- 26	2- 6	29- 53
San Diego	24- 15	15- 26	1- 1	40- 42
San Francisco	20- 18	19- 21	2- 2	41- 41
Seattle	27- 13	11- 30	0- 1	38- 44
Totals	402-262	262-402	33-33	697-697

OFFENSIVE TEAM STATISTICS

Team	G.	FIELD GOALS Att.	Made	Pct.	FREE THROWS Att.	Made	Pct.	Reb.	MISCELLANEOUS Ast.	PF	Disq.	SCORING Pts.	Avg.
Milwaukee	82	7803	3972	.509	2379	1766	.742	4344	2249	1847	15	9710	118.4
Boston	82	8616	3804	.442	2648	2000	.755	4833	2052	2138	43	9608	117.2
Cincinnati	82	8374	3805	.454	2622	1901	.725	4151	2022	2126	45	9511	116.0
Portland	82	8562	3721	.435	2671	2025	.758	4210	2227	2024	23	9467	115.5
Seattle	82	8034	3664	.456	2790	2101	.753	4456	2049	1917	20	9429	115.0
Philadelphia	82	8026	3608	.450	2967	2199	.741	4437	1976	2168	34	9415	114.8
Los Angeles	82	7857	3739	.476	2717	1933	.711	4269	2205	1709	14	9411	114.8
Atlanta	82	7779	3614	.465	2975	2120	.713	4472	1906	1958	23	9348	114.0
Phoenix	82	8021	3503	.437	3078	2327	.756	4442	1927	2132	30	9333	113.8
San Diego	82	8426	3547	.421	2921	2188	.749	4686	1921	2128	39	9282	113.2
Baltimore	82	8331	3684	.442	2500	1886	.754	4550	1772	1966	20	9254	112.9
Chicago	82	7660	3460	.452	2721	2150	.790	4325	2142	1797	12	9070	110.6
Detroit	82	7730	3468	.449	2808	2093	.745	3923	1696	1969	18	9029	110.1
New York	82	8076	3633	.450	2377	1760	.740	4075	1779	1916	13	9026	110.1
San Francisco	82	7709	3454	.448	2468	1875	.760	4643	1893	1833	25	8783	107.1
Buffalo	82	7860	3424	.436	2504	1805	.721	4261	1962	2232	55	8653	105.5
Cleveland	82	7778	3299	.424	2380	1775	.746	3982	2065	2114	37	8373	102.1

DEFENSIVE TEAM STATISTICS

Team	FIELD GOALS Att.	Made	Pct.	FREE THROWS Att.	Made	Pct.	Reb.	MISCELLANEOUS Ast.	PF	Disq.	SCORING Pts.	Avg.	Pt. Dif.
New York	7752	3343	.431	2565	1928	.752	4591	1509	1889	22	8614	105.0	+ 5.1
Chicago	7709	3491	.453	2216	1658	.748	4031	1914	2099	36	8640	105.4	+ 5.2
Milwaukee	8224	3489	.424	2322	1727	.744	4004	1923	1770	11	8705	106.2	+12.2
San Francisco	8371	3583	.428	2318	1735	.748	4305	1949	1882	16	8901	108.5	– 1.4
Detroit	7713	3525	.457	2703	2040	.755	4292	1912	2087	30	9090	110.9	– 0.8
Los Angeles	8511	3796	.446	2107	1567	.744	4552	2078	1951	23	9159	111.7	+ 3.1
Phoenix	7828	3506	.448	2923	2165	.741	4173	2069	2202	42	9177	111.9	+ 1.9
Buffalo	7666	3486	.455	3018	2224	.737	4447	1998	1956	25	9196	112.1	– 6.6
Baltimore	8164	3640	.446	2584	1926	.745	4435	1862	1897	20	9206	112.3	+ 0.6
Philadelphia	7806	3514	.450	3076	2260	.735	4372	1970	2089	39	9288	113.3	+ 1.5
Cleveland	7480	3476	.465	3024	2337	.773	4175	2307	1899	15	9289	113.3	–11.2
San Diego	8102	3639	.449	2745	2024	.737	4345	2135	2141	41	9302	113.4	– 0.2
Boston	8211	3612	.440	2982	2214	.742	4342	1910	1962	27	9438	115.1	+ 2.1
Atlanta	8525	3801	.446	2515	1893	.753	4279	1996	2074	30	9495	115.8	– 1.8
Seattle	8117	3803	.469	2679	1985	.741	4156	1994	2062	20	9591	117.0	– 2.0
Cincinnati	8130	3795	.467	2991	2184	.730	4675	2050	1979	37	9774	119.2	– 3.2
Portland	8333	3900	.468	2758	2037	.739	4885	2267	2035	32	9837	120.0	– 4.5

Disq.—Individual players disqualified (fouled out of game).

INDIVIDUAL LEADERS

POINTS
(Minimum of 70 games played)

	G.	FG	FT	Pts.	Avg.		G.	FG	FT	Pts.	Avg.
Abdul-Jabbar, Mil	82	1063	470	2596	31.7	Walker, Chi	81	650	480	1780	22.0
Havlicek, Bos	81	892	554	2338	28.9	Van Arsdale, Phoe	81	609	553	1771	21.9
Hayes, S. D.	82	948	454	2350	28.7	Frazier, N. Y.	80	651	434	1736	21.7
Bing, Det	82	799	615	2213	27.0	Monroe, Balt	81	663	406	1732	21.4
Hudson, Atl	76	829	381	2039	26.8	Clark, Phil	82	662	422	1746	21.3
Love, Chi	81	765	513	2043	25.2	White, Bos	75	693	215	1601	21.3
Petrie, Port	82	784	463	2031	24.8	Reed, N. Y.	73	614	299	1527	20.9
Maravich, Atl	81	738	404	1880	23.2	Hawkins, Phoe	71	512	457	1481	20.9
Cunningham, Phil	81	702	455	1859	23.0	Mullins, S. F.	75	630	302	1562	20.8
Van Arsdale, Cin	82	749	377	1875	22.9	Chamberlain, L. A.	82	668	360	1696	20.7

FIELD GOALS
(Minimum 700 Attempts)

	FGA	FGM	Pct.
Johnny Green, Cincinnati	855	502	.587
Kareem Abdul-Jabbar, Milwaukee	1843	1063	.577
Wilt Chamberlain, Los Angeles	1226	668	.545
Jon McGlocklin, Milwaukee	1073	574	.535
Dick Snyder, Seattle	1215	645	.531
Greg Smith, Milwaukee	799	409	.512
Bob Dandridge, Milwaukee	1167	594	.509
Wes Unseld, Baltimore	846	424	.501
Jerry Lucas, San Francisco	1250	623	.498
Archie Clark, Philadelphia	1334	662	.496
Oscar Robertson, Milwaukee	1193	592	.496

ASSISTS
(Minimum 70 Games)

	G.	No.	Avg.
Norm Van Lier, Cincinnati	82	832	10.1
Len Wilkens, Seattle	71	654	9.2
Oscar Robertson, Milwaukee	81	668	8.2
John Havlicek, Boston	81	607	7.5
Walt Frazier, New York	80	536	6.7
Walt Hazzard, Atlanta	82	514	6.3
Ron Williams, San Francisco	82	480	5.9
Nate Archibald, Cincinnati	82	450	5.5
Archie Clark, Philadelphia	82	440	5.4
Dave Bing, Detroit	82	408	5.0

FREE THROWS
(Minimum 350 Attempts)

	FTA	FTM	Pct.
Chet Walker, Chicago	559	480	.859
Oscar Robertson, Milwaukee	453	385	.850
Ron Williams, San Francisco	392	331	.844
Jeff Mullins, San Francisco	358	302	.844
Dick Snyder, Seattle	361	302	.837
Stan McKenzie, Portland	396	331	.836
Jerry West, Los Angeles	631	525	.832
Jimmy Walker, Detroit	414	344	.831
Bob Love, Chicago	619	513	.829
Calvin Murphy, San Diego	434	356	.820

REBOUNDS
(Minimum 70 Games)

	G.	No.	Avg.
Wilt Chamberlain, Los Angeles	82	1493	18.2
Wes Unseld, Baltimore	74	1253	16.9
Elvin Hayes, San Diego	82	1362	16.6
Kareem Abdul-Jabbar, Milwaukee	82	1311	16.0
Jerry Lucas, San Francisco	80	1265	15.8
Bill Bridges, Atlanta	82	1233	15.0
Dave Cowens, Boston	81	1216	15.0
Tom Boerwinkle, Chicago	82	1133	13.8
Nate Thurmond, San Francisco	82	1128	13.8
Willis Reed, New York	73	1003	13.7

TEAM-BY-TEAM INDIVIDUAL STATISTICS

ATLANTA HAWKS

Player	G.	Min.	FGA	FGM	Pct.	FTA	FTM	Pct.	Reb.	Ast.	PF	Disq.	Pts.	Avg.
Lou Hudson	76	3113	1713	829	.484	502	381	.759	386	257	186	0	2039	26.8
Pete Maravich	81	2926	1613	738	.458	505	404	.800	298	355	238	1	1880	23.2
Walt Hazzard	82	2877	1126	517	.459	415	315	.759	300	514	276	2	1349	16.5
Walt Bellamy	82	2908	879	433	.493	556	336	.604	1060	230	271	4	1202	14.7
Bill Bridges	82	3140	834	382	.458	330	211	.639	1233	240	317	7	975	11.9
Jerry Chambers	65	1168	526	237	.451	134	106	.791	245	61	119	0	580	8.9
Jim Davis	82	1864	503	241	.479	288	195	.677	546	108	253	5	677	8.3
Len Chappell°°°	48	537	199	86	.432	88	71	.807	151	17	72	2	243	5.1
Len Chappell°°	42	451	161	71	.441	74	60	.811	133	16	63	2	202	4.8
John Vallely	51	430	204	73	.358	59	45	.763	34	47	50	0	191	3.7
Bob Christian	54	524	127	55	.433	64	40	.625	177	30	118	0	150	2.8
Herb White	38	315	84	34	.405	39	22	.564	48	47	62	2	90	2.4
Bob Riley	7	39	9	4	.444	9	5	.556	12	1	5	0	13	1.9

BALTIMORE BULLETS

Player	G.	Min.	FGA	FGM	Pct.	FTA	FTM	Pct.	Reb.	Ast.	PF	Disq.	Pts.	Avg.
Earl Monroe	81	2843	1501	663	.442	506	406	.802	213	354	220	3	1732	21.4
Jack Marin	82	2920	1360	626	.460	342	290	.848	513	217	261	3	1542	18.8
Gus Johnson	66	2538	1090	494	.453	290	214	.738	1128	192	227	4	1202	18.2
Kevin Loughery	82	2260	1193	481	.403	331	275	.831	219	301	246	2	1237	15.1
Wes Unseld	74	2904	846	424	.501	303	199	.657	1253	293	235	2	1047	14.1
Fred Carter	77	1707	815	340	.417	183	119	.650	251	165	165	0	799	10.4
Eddie Miles	63	1541	591	252	.426	147	118	.803	167	110	119	0	622	9.9
John Tresvant°°°	75	1517	436	202	.463	205	146	.712	382	86	196	1	550	7.3
John Tresvant°°	67	1451	401	184	.459	195	139	.713	359	76	185	1	507	7.6
Al Tucker	31	276	115	52	.452	31	25	.806	73	7	33	0	129	4.2
George Johnson	24	337	100	41	.410	30	11	.367	114	10	63	1	93	3.9
Jim Barnes	11	100	28	15	.536	11	7	.636	16	8	23	0	37	3.4
Dorie Murrey°°°	71	716	178	78	.438	112	75	.670	221	32	149	4	231	3.3
Dorie Murrey°°	69	696	172	77	.448	101	66	.653	214	31	146	4	220	3.2
Dennis Stewart	2	6	4	1	.240	2	2	1.000	3	1	0	0	4	2.0
Gary Zeller	50	226	115	34	.296	28	15	.536	27	7	43	0	83	1.7

BOSTON CELTICS

Player	G.	Min.	FGA	FGM	Pct.	FTA	FTM	Pct.	Reb.	Ast.	PF	Disq.	Pts.	Avg.
John Havlicek	81	3678	1982	892	.450	677	554	.818	730	607	200	0	2338	28.9
Jo Jo White	75	2787	1494	693	.464	269	215	.799	376	361	255	5	1601	21.3
Dave Cowens	81	3076	1302	550	.422	373	273	.732	1216	228	350	15	1373	17.0
Don Nelson	82	2254	881	412	.468	426	317	.744	565	153	232	2	1141	13.9
Don Chaney	81	2289	766	348	.454	313	234	.748	463	235	288	11	930	11.5
Steve Kuberski	82	1867	745	313	.420	183	133	.727	538	78	198	1	759	9.3
Rich Johnson	1	13	5	4	.800	0	0	.000	5	0	3	0	8	8.0
Henry Finkel	80	1234	489	214	.438	127	93	.732	343	79	196	5	521	6.5
Art Williams	74	1141	330	150	.455	83	60	.723	205	233	182	1	360	4.9
Bill Dinwiddie	61	717	328	123	.375	74	54	.730	209	34	90	1	300	4.9
Rex Morgan	34	266	102	41	.402	54	35	.648	61	22	58	2	117	3.4
Garfield Smith	37	281	116	42	.362	56	22	.393	95	9	53	0	106	2.9
Tom Sanders	17	121	44	16	.364	8	7	.875	17	11	25	0	39	2.3
Willie Williams°	16	56	32	6	.188	5	3	.600	10	2	8	0	15	0.9

BUFFALO BRAVES

Player	G.	Min.	FGA	FGM	Pct.	FTA	FTM	Pct.	Reb.	Ast.	PF	Disq.	Pts.	Avg.
Bob Kauffman	78	2778	1309	616	.471	485	359	.740	837	354	263	8	1591	20.4
Don May	76	2666	1336	629	.471	350	277	.791	567	150	219	4	1535	20.2
Dick Garrett	75	2375	902	373	.414	251	218	.869	295	264	290	9	964	12.9
Mike Davis	73	1617	744	317	.410	262	199	.760	187	153	220	7	833	11.4
John Hummer	81	2637	764	339	.444	405	235	.580	717	163	284	10	913	11.3
Herm Gilliam	80	2082	896	378	.422	189	142	.751	334	291	246	4	898	11.2
Emmette Bryant	73	2137	684	288	.421	203	151	.744	262	352	266	7	727	10.0
Bill Hosket	13	217	90	47	.522	17	11	.647	75	20	27	1	105	8.1
Cornell Warner	65	1293	376	156	.415	143	79	.552	452	53	140	2	391	6.0
Fred Crawford°	15	203	106	36	.340	26	16	.615	35	24	18	0	88	5.9
George Wilson	46	713	269	92	.342	69	56	.812	230	48	99	1	240	5.2
Paul Long	30	213	120	57	.475	24	20	.833	31	25	23	0	134	4.5
Nate Bowman	44	483	148	58	.392	38	20	.526	173	41	91	2	136	3.1
Mike Silliman	36	366	79	36	.456	39	19	.487	62	23	37	0	91	2.5
Mike Lynn	5	25	7	2	.286	3	3	1.000	4	1	9	0	7	1.4

CHICAGO BULLS

Player	G.	Min.	FGA	FGM	Pct.	FTA	FTM	Pct.	Reb.	Ast.	PF	Disq.	Pts.	Avg.
Bob Love	81	3482	1710	765	.447	619	513	.829	690	185	259	0	2043	25.2
Chet Walker	81	2927	1398	650	.465	559	480	.859	588	179	187	2	1780	22.0
Jerry Sloan	80	3140	1342	592	.441	389	278	.715	701	281	289	5	1462	18.3
Tom Boerwinkle	82	2370	736	357	.485	232	168	.724	1133	397	275	3	882	10.8
Jim Fox	82	1628	611	280	.458	321	239	.745	598	196	213	0	799	9.7
Bob Weiss	82	2237	659	278	.422	269	226	.840	189	387	216	1	782	9.5
Matt Guokas°°°	79	2213	418	206	.493	138	101	.732	158	342	189	1	513	6.5
Matt Guokas°°	78	2208	418	206	.493	138	101	.732	157	342	189	1	513	6.6
Jim King	55	645	228	100	.439	79	64	.810	68	78	55	0	264	4.8
John Baum	62	543	293	123	.420	58	40	.690	125	31	55	0	286	4.6
Jim Collins	55	478	214	92	.430	45	35	.778	54	60	43	0	219	4.0
Paul Ruffner	10	60	35	15	.429	8	4	.500	16	2	10	0	34	3.4
Shaler Halimon°	2	23	8	1	.125	1	0	.000	2	4	5	0	2	1.0
A. W. Holt	6	14	8	1	.125	3	2	.667	4	0	1	0	4	0.7

CINCINNATI ROYALS

Player	G.	Min.	FGA	FGM	Pct.	FTA	FTM	Pct.	Reb.	Ast.	PF	Disq.	Pts.	Avg.
Tom Van Arsdale	82	3146	1642	749	.456	523	377	.721	499	181	294	3	1875	22.9
Johnny Green	75	2147	855	502	.587	402	248	.617	656	89	233	7	1252	16.7
Norm Van Lier	82	3324	1138	478	.420	440	359	.816	583	832	343	12	1315	16.0
Nate Archibald	82	2867	1095	486	.444	444	336	.757	242	450	218	2	1308	16.0
Sam Lacey	81	2648	1117	467	.418	227	156	.687	913	117	270	8	1090	13.5
Flynn Robinson	71	1368	817	374	.458	228	195	.855	143	138	161	0	943	13.3
Charlie Paulk	68	1213	637	274	.430	131	79	.603	320	27	186	6	627	9.2
Darrall Imhoff	34	826	258	119	.461	73	37	.507	233	79	120	5	275	8.1
Fred Foster°	1	21	8	3	.375	3	1	.333	4	0	2	0	7	7.0
Connie Dierking°	1	23	16	3	.188	0	0	.000	7	1	5	0	6	6.0
Bob Arnzen	55	594	277	128	.462	52	45	.865	152	24	54	0	301	5.5
Greg Hyder	77	1359	409	183	.477	71	51	.718	332	48	187	2	417	5.4
Tom Black°°°	71	873	301	121	.402	88	57	.648	259	44	136	1	299	4.2
Tom Black°°	16	100	33	10	.303	15	6	.400	34	2	20	0	26	1.6
Moe Barr	31	145	62	25	.403	13	11	.846	20	28	27	0	61	2.0
Willie Williams°°°	25	105	42	10	.238	5	3	.600	23	8	14	0	23	0.9
Willie Williams°°	9	49	10	4	.400	0	0	.000	13	6	6	0	8	0.9

CLEVELAND CAVALIERS

Player	G.	Min.	FGA	FGM	Pct.	FTA	FTM	Pct.	Reb.	Ast.	PF	Disq.	Pts.	Avg.
Walt Wesley	82	2425	1241	565	.455	473	325	.687	713	83	295	5	1455	17.7
John Johnson	67	2310	1032	435	.422	298	240	.805	453	323	251	3	1110	16.6
Bob Smith	77	2332	1106	495	.448	234	178	.761	429	258	175	4	1168	15.2
McCoy McLemore°	58	1839	654	254	.388	220	170	.773	463	176	169	1	678	11.7
John Warren	82	2610	899	380	.423	217	180	.829	344	347	299	13	940	11.5
Dave Sorenson	79	1940	794	353	.445	229	184	.803	486	163	181	3	890	11.3
Luther Rackley	74	1434	470	219	.466	190	121	.637	394	66	186	3	559	7.6
Bob Washington	47	823	310	123	.397	140	104	.743	105	190	105	0	350	7.4
Len Chappell°	6	86	38	15	.395	14	11	.786	18	1	9	0	41	6.8
Bob Lewis	79	1852	484	179	.370	152	109	.717	206	244	176	1	467	5.9
Joe Cooke	73	725	341	134	.393	59	48	.814	114	93	135	2	316	4.3
Johnny Egan°	26	410	98	40	.408	28	25	.893	32	58	31	0	105	4.0
Cliff Anderson°	23	171	59	19	.322	60	41	.683	37	16	22	1	79	3.4
Gary Freeman°°°	52	382	134	69	.515	40	29	.725	106	35	67	0	167	3.2
Gary Freeman°°	11	47	12	7	.583	2	1	.500	8	4	4	0	15	1.4
Larry Mikan	53	536	186	62	.333	55	34	.618	139	41	56	1	158	3.0
Gary Suiter	30	140	54	19	.352	9	4	.444	41	2	20	0	42	1.4

DETROIT PISTONS

Player	G.	Min.	FGA	FGM	Pct.	FTA	FTM	Pct.	Reb.	Ast.	PF	Disq.	Pts.	Avg.
Dave Bing	82	3065	1710	799	.467	772	615	.797	364	408	228	4	2213	27.0
Jimmy Walker	79	2765	1201	524	.436	414	344	.831	207	268	173	0	1392	17.6
Bob Lanier	82	2017	1108	504	.455	376	273	.726	665	146	272	4	1281	15.6
Terry Dischinger	65	1855	568	304	.535	211	161	.763	339	113	189	2	769	11.8
Otto Moore	82	1926	696	310	.445	219	121	.553	700	88	182	0	741	9.0
Steve Mix	35	731	294	111	.446	89	68	.764	164	34	72	0	290	8.3
Howard Komives	82	1932	715	275	.385	151	121	.801	152	262	184	0	671	8.2
Bob Quick	56	1146	341	155	.455	176	138	.784	230	56	142	1	448	8.0
Bill Hewitt	62	1725	435	203	.467	120	69	.575	454	124	189	5	475	7.7
Erwin Mueller	52	1224	309	126	.408	108	60	.556	223	113	99	0	312	6.0
Terry Driscoll	69	1255	318	132	.415	154	108	.701	402	54	212	2	372	5.4
Harvey Marlatt	23	214	80	25	.313	18	15	.833	23	30	27	0	65	2.8

LOS ANGELES LAKERS

Player	G.	Min.	FGA	FGM	Pct.	FTA	FTM	Pct.	Reb.	Ast.	PF	Disq.	Pts.	Avg.
Jerry West	69	2845	1351	667	.494	631	525	.832	320	655	180	0	1859	26.9
Wilt Chamberlain	82	3630	1226	668	.545	669	360	.538	1493	352	174	0	1696	20.7
Harold Hairston	80	2921	1233	574	.466	431	337	.782	797	168	256	2	1485	18.6
Gail Goodrich	79	2808	1174	558	.475	343	264	.770	260	380	258	3	1380	17.5
Keith Erickson	73	2272	783	369	.471	112	85	.759	404	223	241	4	823	11.3
Elgin Baylor	2	57	19	8	.421	6	4	.667	11	2	6	0	20	10.0
Jim McMillian	81	1747	629	289	.459	130	100	.769	330	133	122	1	678	8.4
Willie McCarter	76	1369	592	247	.417	77	46	.597	122	126	152	0	540	7.1
John Tresvant°	8	66	35	18	.514	10	7	.700	23	10	11	0	43	5.4
Rick Roberson	65	909	301	125	.415	143	88	.615	304	47	125	1	338	5.2
Pat Riley	54	506	254	105	.413	87	56	.644	54	72	84	0	266	4.9
Fred Hetzel	59	613	256	111	.434	77	60	.779	149	37	99	3	282	4.8
Earnie Killum	4	12	4	0	.000	1	1	1.000	2	0	1	0	1	0.3

MILWAUKEE BUCKS

Player	G.	Min.	FGA	FGM	Pct.	FTA	FTM	Pct.	Reb.	Ast.	PF	Disq.	Pts.	Avg.
Kareem Abdul-Jabbar	82	3288	1843	1063	.577	681	470	.690	1311	272	264	4	2596	31.7
Oscar Robertson	81	3194	1193	592	.496	453	385	.850	462	668	203	0	1569	19.4
Bob Dandridge	79	2862	1167	594	.509	376	264	.702	632	277	287	4	1452	18.4
Jon McGlocklin	82	2891	1073	574	.535	167	144	.862	223	305	189	0	1292	15.8
Greg Smith	82	2428	799	409	.512	213	141	.662	589	227	284	5	959	11.7
McCoy McLemore°°°	86	2254	787	303	.385	261	204	.782	568	206	235	2	810	9.4
McCoy McLemore°°	28	415	133	49	.368	41	34	.829	105	30	66	1	132	4.7
Bob Boozer	80	1775	645	290	.450	181	148	.818	435	128	216	0	728	9.1
Lucius Allen	61	1162	398	178	.447	110	77	.700	152	161	108	0	433	7.1
Gary Freeman°	41	335	122	62	.508	38	28	.737	98	31	63	0	152	3.7
Marvin Winkler	3	14	10	3	.300	2	2	1.000	4	2	3	0	8	2.7
Dick Cunningham	76	675	195	81	.415	59	39	.661	257	43	90	1	201	2.6
Bob Greacen	2	43	12	1	.083	7	3	.429	6	13	7	0	5	2.5
Bill Zopf	53	398	135	49	.363	36	20	.556	46	73	34	0	118	2.2
Jeff Webb	29	300	78	27	.346	15	11	.733	24	19	33	0	65	2.2

NEW YORK KNICKERBOCKERS

Player	G.	Min.	FGA	FGM	Pct.	FTA	FTM	Pct.	Reb.	Ast.	PF	Disq.	Pts.	Avg.
Walt Frazier	80	3455	1317	651	.494	557	434	.779	544	536	240	1	1736	21.7
Willis Reed	73	2855	1330	614	.462	381	299	.785	1003	148	228	1	1527	20.9
Dave DeBusschere	81	2891	1243	523	.421	312	217	.696	901	220	237	2	1263	15.6
Dick Barnett	82	2843	1184	540	.456	278	193	.694	238	225	232	1	1273	15.5
Bill Bradley	78	2300	912	413	.453	175	144	.823	260	280	245	3	970	12.4
Dave Stallworth	81	1565	685	295	.431	230	169	.735	352	106	175	1	759	9.4
Cazzie Russell	57	1056	504	216	.429	119	92	.773	192	77	74	0	524	9.2
Mike Riordan	82	1320	388	162	.418	108	67	.620	169	121	151	0	391	4.8
Phil Jackson	71	771	263	118	.449	133	95	.714	238	31	169	4	331	4.7
Greg Fillmore	39	271	102	45	.441	27	13	.481	93	17	80	0	103	2.6
Eddie Mast	30	164	66	25	.379	20	11	.550	56	4	25	0	61	2.0
Mike Price	56	251	81	30	.370	34	24	.706	29	12	57	0	84	1.5
Milt Williams	5	13	1	1	1.000	3	2	.667	0	2	3	0	4	0.8

PHILADELPHIA 76ers

Player	G.	Min.	FGA	FGM	Pct.	FTA	FTM	Pct.	Reb.	Ast.	PF	Disq.	Pts.	Avg.
Billy Cunningham	81	3090	1519	702	.462	620	455	.734	946	395	328	5	1859	23.0
Archie Clark	82	3245	1334	662	.496	536	422	.787	391	440	217	2	1746	21.3
Hal Greer	81	3060	1371	591	.431	405	326	.805	364	369	289	4	1508	18.6
Jim Washington	78	2501	829	395	.476	340	259	.762	747	97	258	6	1049	13.4
Bailey Howell	82	1589	686	324	.472	315	230	.730	441	115	234	2	878	10.7
Wally Jones	41	962	418	168	.402	101	79	.782	64	128	110	1	415	10.1
Dennis Awtrey	70	1292	421	200	.475	157	104	.662	430	89	211	7	504	7.2
Luke Jackson	79	1774	529	199	.376	189	131	.693	568	148	211	3	529	6.7
Connie Dierking°°°	54	737	322	125	.388	89	61	.685	234	60	114	1	311	5.8
Connie Dierking°°	53	714	306	122	.399	89	61	.685	227	59	109	1	305	5.8
Fred Foster°°°	67	909	368	148	.402	106	73	.689	151	61	115	3	369	5.5
Fred Foster°°	66	888	360	145	.403	103	72	.699	147	61	113	3	362	5.5
Fred Crawford°°°	51	652	281	110	.391	98	48	.490	104	78	77	0	268	5.3
Fred Crawford°°	36	449	175	74	.423	72	32	.444	69	54	59	0	180	5.0
Cliff Anderson°°°	28	198	65	20	.308	67	46	.687	48	20	29	1	86	3.1
Cliff Anderson°°	5	27	6	1	.167	7	5	.714	11	4	7	0	7	1.4
Bud Ogden	27	133	66	24	.364	26	18	.692	20	17	21	0	66	2.4
Al Henry	6	26	6	1	.167	7	5	.714	11	0	1	0	7	1.2
Matt Guokas°	1	5	0	0	.000	0	0	.000	1	0	0	0	0	0.0

PHOENIX SUNS

Player	G.	Min.	FGA	FGM	Pct.	FTA	FTM	Pct.	Reb.	Ast.	PF	Disq.	Pts.	Avg.
Dick Van Arsdale	81	3157	1346	609	.452	682	553	.811	316	329	246	1	1771	21.9
Connie Hawkins	71	2662	1181	512	.434	560	457	.816	643	322	197	2	1481	20.9
Clem Haskins	82	2764	1277	562	.440	431	338	.784	324	383	207	2	1462	17.8
Neal Walk	82	2033	945	426	.451	268	205	.765	674	117	282	8	1057	12.9
Paul Silas	81	2944	789	338	.428	416	285	.685	1015	247	227	3	961	11.9
Mel Counts	80	1669	799	365	.457	198	149	.753	503	136	279	8	879	11.0
Art Harris	56	952	484	199	.411	113	69	.611	100	132	137	0	467	8.3
Lamar Green	68	1326	369	167	.453	106	64	.604	466	53	202	5	398	5.9
Fred Taylor	54	552	284	110	.387	125	78	.624	86	51	113	0	298	5.5
John Wetzel	70	1091	288	124	.431	101	83	.822	153	114	156	1	331	4.7
Greg Howard	44	426	173	68	.393	58	37	.638	119	26	67	0	173	3.9
Joe Thomas	39	204	86	23	.267	20	9	.450	43	17	19	0	55	1.4

PORTLAND TRAIL BLAZERS

Player	G.	Min.	FGA	FGM	Pct.	FTA	FTM	Pct.	Reb.	Ast.	PF	Disq.	Pts.	Avg.
Geoff Petrie	82	3032	1770	784	.443	600	463	.772	280	390	196	1	2031	24.8
Jim Barnett	78	2371	1283	559	.436	402	326	.811	376	323	190	1	1444	18.5
LeRoy Ellis	74	2581	1095	485	.443	261	209	.801	907	235	258	5	1179	15.9
Stan McKenzie	82	2290	902	398	.441	396	331	.836	309	235	238	2	1127	13.7
Rick Adelman	81	2303	895	378	.422	369	267	.724	282	380	214	2	1023	12.6
Gary Gregor	44	1153	421	181	.430	89	59	.663	334	81	120	2	421	9.6
Shaler Halimon°°°	81	1652	783	301	.384	162	107	.660	417	215	183	1	709	8.8
Shaler Halimon°°	79	1629	775	300	.387	161	107	.665	415	211	178	1	707	8.9
Dale Schlueter	80	1823	527	257	.488	218	143	.656	629	192	265	4	657	8.2
Ed Manning	79	1558	559	243	.435	93	75	.806	411	111	198	3	561	7.1
Dorie Murrey°	2	20	6	1	.167	11	9	.818	7	1	3	0	11	5.5
Ron Knight	52	662	230	99	.430	38	19	.500	167	50	99	1	217	4.2
Bill Stricker	1	2	3	2	.667	0	0	.000	0	0	1	0	4	4.0
Walt Gilmore	27	261	54	23	.426	26	12	.462	73	12	49	1	58	2.1
Claude English	18	70	42	11	.262	7	5	.714	20	6	15	0	27	1.5

SAN DIEGO ROCKETS

Player	G.	Min.	FGA	FGM	Pct.	FTA	FTM	Pct.	Reb.	Ast.	PF	Disq.	Pts.	Avg.
Elvin Hayes	82	3633	2215	948	.428	676	454	.672	1362	186	225	1	2350	28.7
Stu Lantz	82	3102	1305	585	.448	644	519	.806	406	344	230	3	1689	20.6
Calvin Murphy	82	2020	1029	471	.458	434	356	.820	245	329	263	4	1298	15.8
Don Adams	82	2374	957	391	.409	212	155	.731	581	173	344	11	937	11.4
John Trapp	82	2080	766	322	.420	188	142	.755	510	138	337	16	786	9.6
John Block	73	1464	584	245	.420	270	212	.785	442	98	193	2	702	9.6

Player	G.	Min.	FGA	FGM	Pct.	FTA	FTM	Pct.	Reb.	Ast.	PF	Disq.	Pts.	Avg.
Larry Siegfried	53	1673	378	146	.386	153	130	.850	207	346	146	0	422	8.0
Rudy Tomjanovich	77	1062	439	168	.383	112	73	.652	381	73	124	0	409	5.3
Bernie Williams	56	708	338	112	.331	81	68	.840	85	113	76	1	292	5.2
Toby Kimball	80	1100	287	111	.387	108	51	.472	406	62	128	1	273	3.4
Curtis Perry	18	100	48	21	.438	20	11	.550	30	5	22	0	53	2.9
Johnny Egan°°°	62	824	178	67	.376	51	42	.824	63	112	71	0	176	2.8
Johnny Egan°°	36	414	80	27	.338	23	17	.739	31	54	40	0	71	2.0

SAN FRANCISCO WARRIORS

Player	G.	Min.	FGA	FGM	Pct.	FTA	FTM	Pct.	Reb.	Ast.	PF	Disq.	Pts.	Avg.
Jeff Mullins	75	2909	1308	630	.482	358	302	.844	341	332	246	5	1562	20.8
Nate Thurmond	82	3351	1401	623	.445	541	395	.730	1128	257	192	1	1641	20.0
Jerry Lucas	80	3251	1250	623	.498	367	289	.787	1265	293	197	0	1535	19.2
Ron Williams	82	2809	977	426	.436	392	331	.844	244	480	301	9	1183	14.4
Joe Ellis	80	2275	898	356	.396	203	151	.744	511	161	287	6	863	10.8
Bob Portman	68	1395	483	221	.458	106	77	.726	321	67	130	0	519	7.6
Nick Jones	81	1183	523	225	.430	151	111	.735	110	113	192	2	561	6.9
Clyde Lee	82	1392	428	194	.453	199	111	.558	570	63	137	0	499	6.1
Adrian Smith	21	247	89	38	.427	41	35	.854	24	30	24	0	111	5.3
Levi Fontaine	35	210	145	53	.366	37	28	.757	15	22	27	0	134	3.8
Bill Turner	18	200	82	26	.317	20	13	.650	42	8	24	0	65	3.6
Al Attles	34	321	54	22	.407	41	24	.585	40	58	59	2	68	2.0
Ralph Ogden	32	162	71	17	.239	12	8	.667	32	9	17	0	42	1.3

SEATTLE SUPERSONICS

Player	G.	Min.	FGA	FGM	Pct.	FTA	FTM	Pct.	Reb.	Ast.	PF	Disq.	Pts.	Avg.
Bob Rule	4	142	98	47	.480	30	25	.833	46	7	14	0	119	29.8
Spencer Haywood	33	1162	579	260	.449	218	160	.733	396	48	84	1	680	20.6
Len Wilkens	71	2641	1125	471	.419	574	461	.803	319	654	201	3	1403	19.8
Dick Snyder	82	2824	1215	645	.531	361	302	.837	257	352	246	6	1592	19.4
Don Kojis	79	2143	1018	454	.446	320	249	.778	435	130	220	3	1157	14.6
Don Smith	61	1276	597	263	.441	188	139	.739	468	42	118	0	665	10.9
Lee Winfield	79	1605	716	334	.466	244	162	.664	193	225	135	1	830	10.5
Tom Meschery	79	1822	615	285	.463	216	162	.750	485	108	202	2	732	9.3
Pete Cross	79	2194	554	245	.442	203	140	.690	949	113	212	2	630	8.0
Barry Clemens	78	1286	526	247	.470	114	83	.728	243	92	169	1	577	7.4
Jake Ford	5	68	25	9	.360	22	16	.727	9	9	11	0	34	6.8
Garfield Heard	65	1027	399	152	.381	125	82	.656	328	45	126	0	386	5.9
Rod Thorn	63	767	299	141	.472	102	69	.676	103	182	60	0	351	5.6
Tom Black°	55	773	268	111	.414	73	51	.699	225	42	116	1	273	5.0

°Finished season with another team.
°°Player total with this club only.
°°°Player total with all clubs.

PLAYOFF RESULTS

EASTERN CONFERENCE SEMIFINALS
New York 4, Atlanta 1

Mar. 25—Atlanta 101 at New York..112
Mar. 27—Atlanta 113 at New York..104
Mar. 28—New York 110 at Atlanta..95
Mar. 30—New York 113 at Atlanta..107
Apr. 1—Atlanta 107 at New York...111

Baltimore 4, Philadelphia 3

Mar. 24—Philadelphia 126 at Baltimore 112
Mar. 26—Baltimore 119 at Philadelphia.......................................107
Mar. 28—Philadelphia 103 at Baltimore.......................................111
Mar. 30—Baltimore 120 at Philadelphia.......................................105
Apr. 1—Philadelphia 104 at Baltimore..103
Apr. 3—Baltimore 94 at Philadelphia...98
Apr. 4—Philadelphia 120 at Baltimore..128

EASTERN CONFERENCE FINALS
Baltimore 4, New York 3

Apr. 6—Baltimore 111 at New York...112
Apr. 9—Baltimore 88 at New York..107
Apr. 11—New York 88 at Baltimore..114
Apr. 14—New York 80 at Baltimore..101
Apr. 16—New York 84 at New York..89
Apr. 18—New York 96 at Baltimore..113
Apr. 19—Baltimore 93 at New York..91

WESTERN CONFERENCE SEMIFINALS
Milwaukee 4, San Francisco 1

Mar. 27—Milwaukee 107 at San Francisco......................................96
Mar. 29—San Francisco 90 vs. Milwaukee at Madison.....................104
Mar. 30—San Francisco 102 vs. Milwaukee at Madison....................114
Apr 1—Milwaukee 104 at San Francisco......................................106
Apr. 4—San Francisco 86 vs. Milwaukee at Madison.......................136

Los Angeles 4, Chicago 3

Mar. 24—Chicago 99 at Los Angeles..100
Mar. 26—Chicago 95 at Los Angeles..105
Mar. 28—Los Angeles 98 at Chicago..106
Mar. 30—Los Angeles 102 at Chicago..112
Apr. 1—Chicago 86 at Los Angeles..115
Apr. 4—Los Angeles 99 at Chicago..113
Apr. 6—Chicago 98 at Los Angeles..109

WESTERN CONFERENCE FINALS
Milwaukee 4, Los Angeles 1

Apr. 9—Los Angeles 85 at Milwaukee...106
Apr. 11—Los Angeles 73 at Milwaukee..91
Apr. 14—Milwaukee 107 at Los Angeles.......................................118
Apr. 16—Milwaukee 117 at Los Angeles..94
Apr. 18—Los Angeles 98 at Milwaukee..116

WORLD CHAMPIONSHIP SERIES
Milwaukee 4, Baltimore 0

Apr. 21—Baltimore 88 at Milwaukee...98
Apr. 25—Milwaukee 102 at Baltimore...83
Apr. 28—Baltimore 99 at Milwaukee...107
Apr. 30—Milwaukee 118 at Baltimore..106

1969-70 NBA STATISTICS

1969-70 NBA CHAMPION NEW YORK KNICKERBOCKERS

Seated (left to right)—John Warren, Don May, Walt Frazier, President Ned Irish, Chairman of the Board Irving Mitchell Felt, General Manager Ed Donovan, Dick Barnett, Mike Riordan, and Cazzie Russell. Standing (left to right)—Phil Jackson, Dave Stallworth, Dave DeBusschere, Capt. Willis Reed, Bill Hosket, Nate Bowman, Bill Bradley and Chief Scout Dick McGuire. Not shown: Coach William (Red) Holzman.

FINAL STANDINGS

EASTERN DIVISION

Team	N.Y.	Mil.	Balt.	Phil.	Cin.	Bos.	Det.	Atl.	L.A.	Chi.	Pho.	Sea.	S.F.	S.D.	W.	L.	Pct.	G.B.
New York	-	4	5	5	5	3	6	2	4	6	6	4	5	5	60	22	.732	....
Milwaukee	2	-	3	5	5	6	6	3	3	2	6	5	4	6	56	26	.683	4
Baltimore	1	3	-	3	4	5	5	4	4	5	3	2	5	6	50	32	.610	10
Philadelphia	2	2	4	-	3	4	5	3	2	3	4	-	6	4	42	40	.512	18
Cincinnati	2	2	3	4	-	3	4	3	2	3	3	1	2	4	36	46	.439	24
Boston	4	1	2	2	3	-	4	-	2	3	2	5	2	4	34	48	.415	26
Detroit	1	1	2	1	2	3	-	3	3	3	3	3	3	3	31	51	.378	29

WESTERN DIVISION

Team	N.Y.	Mil.	Balt.	Phil.	Cin.	Bos.	Det.	Atl.	L.A.	Chi.	Pho.	Sea.	S.F.	S.D.	W.	L.	Pct.	G.B.
Atlanta	4	3	2	3	3	6	3	-	4	5	2	5	4	4	48	34	.585	....
Los Angeles	2	3	2	4	4	4	3	3	-	2	3	6	5	5	46	36	.561	2
Chicago	-	4	1	3	3	3	3	2	4	-	5	4	4	3	39	43	.476	9
Phoenix	-	-	3	2	3	4	3	4	4	2	-	4	3	7	39	43	.476	9
Seattle	2	1	4	6	5	1	3	2	-	3	3	-	4	2	36	46	.439	12
San Francisco	1	2	1	-	4	4	3	3	2	2	3	3	-	2	30	52	.366	18
San Diego	1	-	-	2	2	2	3	2	2	4	-	4	5	-	27	55	.329	21

HOME-ROAD-NEUTRAL RECORDS OF ALL TEAMS

	Home	Road	Neutral	Total		Home	Road	Neutral	Total
Atlanta	25-13	18-16	5-5	48-34	New York	30-11	27-10	3-1	60-22
Baltimore	25-12	19-18	6-2	50-32	Philadelphia	22-16	16-22	4-2	42-40
Boston	16-21	13-27	5-0	34-48	Phoenix	22-15	12-25	5-3	39-43
Chicago	23-10	9-25	7-8	39-43	San Diego	21-17	4-33	2-5	27-55
Cincinnati	19-13	14-25	3-8	36-46	San Francisco	16-20	14-26	0-6	30-52
Detroit	18-20	10-25	3-6	31-51	Seattle	22-14	10-26	4-6	36-46
Los Angeles	27-14	17-21	2-1	46-36	Total	313-207	207-313	54-54	574-574
Milwaukee	27-11	24-14	5-1	56-26					

TEAM STATISTICS

Team	G.	FGA	FGM	Pct.	FTA	FTM	Pct.	Reb.	Ast.	PF	Disq.	For	Agst.	Pt.Dif.
New York	82	7975	3803	.477	2484	1821	.733	4006	2135	2016	10	115.0	105.9	9.1
Milwaukee	82	8041	3923	.488	2589	1895	.732	4419	2168	1971	27	118.8	114.2	4.6
Philadelphia	82	8345	3915	.469	2884	2168	.752	4463	2127	2196	47	121.9	118.5	3.4
Baltimore	82	8567	3925	.458	2652	2050	.773	4679	1881	1896	21	120.7	118.6	2.1
Los Angeles	82	7952	3668	.461	2641	1991	.754	4154	2030	1896	41	113.7	111.8	1.9
Atlanta	82	7907	3817	.483	2669	2012	.754	4210	2142	2016	29	117.6	117.2	0.4
Phoenix	82	7856	3676	.468	3270	2434	.744	4183	2076	2183	33	119.3	121.1	−1.8
Chicago	82	8133	3607	.444	2861	2209	.772	4383	2133	1863	13	114.9	116.7	−1.8
Boston	82	8235	3645	.443	2711	2132	.786	4336	1875	2320	41	114.9	116.8	−1.9
Seattle	82	8029	3709	.462	2851	2171	.761	4312	2214	2175	42	116.9	119.5	−2.6
Cincinnati	82	8271	3767	.455	2841	2082	.733	4163	1992	2215	52	117.3	120.2	−2.9
San Diego	82	8867	3866	.436	2728	2000	.733	4786	2036	2096	17	118.7	121.8	−3.1
Detroit	82	7657	3565	.466	2881	2116	.734	3831	1709	1930	22	112.8	116.1	−3.3
San Francisco	82	8224	3555	.432	2646	2004	.757	4772	1861	2050	32	111.1	115.6	−4.5

INDIVIDUAL LEADERS

POINTS
(Minimum of 70 Games Played)

	G.	FG	FT	Pts.	Avg.		G.	FG	FT	Pts.	Avg.
West, L.A.	74	647	2309	31.2		Van Arsdale, Cinc	71	620	381	1621	22.8
Abdul-Jabbar, Mil.	82	938	485	2361	28.8	Mullins, S. F.	74	656	320	1632	22.1
Hayes, S. D.	82	914	428	2256	27.5	Greer, Phil.	80	705	352	1762	22.0
Cunningham, Phil.	81	802	510	2114	26.1	Robinson, Mil.	81	663	439	1765	21.8
Hudson, Atl.	80	830	371	2031	25.4	Reed, N. Y.	81	702	351	1755	21.7
Hawkins, Phoe.	81	709	577	1995	24.6	Walker, Chi.	78	596	483	1675	21.5
Rule, Sea.	80	789	387	1965	24.6	Van Arsdale, Phoe.	77	592	459	1643	21.3
Havlicek, Bos.	81	736	488	1960	24.2	Caldwell, Atl.	82	674	379	1727	21.1
Monroe, Balt.	82	695	532	1922	23.4	Love, Chi.	82	640	442	1722	21.0
Bing, Det.	70	575	454	1604	22.9	Frazier, N. Y.	77	600	409	1609	20.9

FIELD GOALS
(Minimum 700 or More Attempts in 70 Games)

	FGA	FGM	Pct.
Johnny Green, Cincinnati	860	481	.559
Darrall Imhoff, Phila.	796	430	.540
Lou Hudson, Atlanta	1564	830	.531
Jon McGlocklin, Milw.	1206	639	.530
Dick Snyder, Phoe.-Sea.	863	456	.528
Jim Fox, Phoenix	788	413	.524
Lew Alcindor, Milwaukee	1810	938	.518
Wes Unseld, Baltimore	1015	526	.518
Walt Frazier, New York	1158	600	.518
Dick Van Arsdale, Phoe.	1166	592	.508

ASSISTS
(Minimum 70 Games or More)

	G.	No.	Avg.
Lenny Wilkens, Seattle	75	683	9.1
Walt Frazier, New York	77	629	8.2
Clem Haskins, Chicago	82	624	7.6
Jerry West, Los Angeles	74	554	7.5
Gail Goodrich, Phoenix	81	605	7.5
Walt Hazzard, Atlanta	82	561	6.8
John Havlicek, Boston	81	550	6 8
Art Williams, San Diego	80	503	6.3
Norm VanLier, Cincinnati	81	500	6.2
Dave Bing, Detroit	70	418	6.0

FREE THROWS
(Minimun 350 or More Attempts in 70 Games)

	FTA	FTM	Pct.
Flynn Robinson, Milwaukee	489	439	.898
Chet Walker, Chicago	568	483	.850
Jeff Mullins, San Francisco	378	320	.847
John Havlicek, Boston	578	488	.844
Bob Love, Chicago	525	442	.842
Earl Monroe, Baltimore	641	532	.830
Lou Hudson, Atlanta	450	371	.824
Jerry West, Los Angeles	785	647	.824
Hal Greer, Philadelphia	432	352	.815
Jimmy Walker, Detroit	440	355	.807

REBOUNDS
(Minimum 70 Games or More)

	G.	No.	Avg.
Elvin Hayes, San Diego	82	1386	16.9
Wes Unseld, Baltimore	82	1370	16.7
Kareem Abdul-Jabbar, Milwaukee	82	1190	14.5
Bill Bridges, Atlanta	82	1181	14.4
Gus Johnson, Baltimore	78	1086	13.9
Willis Reed, New York	81	1126	13.9
Billy Cunningham, Philadelphia	81	1101	13.6
Tom Boerwinkle, Chicago	81	1016	12.5
Paul Silas, Phoenix	78	916	11.7
Clyde Lee, San Francisco	82	929	11.3

TEAM-BY-TEAM INDIVIDUAL STATISTICS

ATLANTA HAWKS

Player	G.	Min.	FGA	FGM	Pct.	FTA	FTM	Pct.	Reb.	Ast.	PF	Disq.	Pts.	Avg.
Lou Hudson	80	3091	1564	830	.531	450	371	.824	373	276	225	1	2031	25.4
Joe Caldwell	82	2857	1329	674	.507	551	379	.688	407	287	255	3	1727	21.1
Walt Hazzard	82	2757	1056	493	.467	330	267	.809	329	561	264	3	1253	15.3
Bill Bridges	82	3269	932	443	.475	451	331	.734	1181	345	292	6	1217	14.8
Jim Davis	82	2623	943	438	.464	318	240	.755	796	238	335	5	1116	13.6
Walt Bellamy°°°	79	2028	671	351	.523	373	215	.576	707	143	260	5	917	11.6
Walt Bellamy°°	23	855	287	141	.491	124	75	.605	310	88	97	2	357	15.5
Gary Gregor	81	1603	661	286	.433	113	88	.779	397	63	159	5	660	8.1
Al Beard	72	941	392	183	.467	163	135	.828	140	121	124	0	501	7.0
Don Ohl	66	984	372	176	.473	72	58	.806	71	98	113	1	410	6.2
Dave Newmark	64	612	296	127	.429	77	59	.766	174	42	128	3	313	4.9
Grady O'Malley	24	113	60	21	.350	19	8	.421	26	10	12	0	50	2.1
Gene Tormohlen	2	11	4	2	.500	0	0	.000	4	1	3	0	4	2.0
Richie Guerin	8	64	11	3	.273	1	1	1.000	2	12	9	0	7	0.9

BALTIMORE BULLETS

Player	G.	Min.	FGA	FGM	Pct.	FTA	FTM	Pct.	Reb.	Ast.	PF	Disq.	Pts.	Avg.
Earl Monroe	82	3051	1557	695	.446	641	532	.830	257	402	258	3	1922	23.4
Kevin Loughery	55	2037	1082	477	.441	298	253	.849	168	292	183	3	1207	21.9
Jack Marin	82	2947	1363	666	.489	339	286	.844	537	217	248	6	1618	19.7
Gus Johnson	78	2919	1282	578	.451	272	197	.724	1086	264	269	6	1353	17.3
Wes Unseld	82	3234	1015	526	.518	428	273	.638	1370	291	250	2	1325	16.2
Eddie Miles***	47	1295	541	238	.440	175	133	.760	177	86	107	0	609	13.0
Eddie Miles**	3	52	10	7	.700	5	3	.600	4	4	8	0	17	5.7
Mike Davis	56	1330	586	260	.444	192	149	.776	128	111	174	1	669	12.0
Ray Scott	73	1393	605	257	.425	173	139	.803	457	114	147	0	653	8.9
Leroy Ellis	72	1163	414	194	.469	116	86	.741	376	47	129	0	474	6.6
Al Tucker***	61	819	285	146	.512	87	70	.805	166	38	86	0	362	5.9
Al Tucker**	28	262	96	49	.510	42	33	.786	53	7	34	0	131	4.7
Fred Carter	76	1219	439	157	.358	116	80	.690	192	121	137	0	394	5.2
Bob Quick	15	67	28	14	.500	18	12	.667	12	3	9	0	40	2.7
Ed Manning	29	161	66	32	.485	8	5	.625	35	2	33	0	69	2.4
Brian Heaney	14	70	24	13	.542	4	2	.500	4	6	17	0	28	2.0

BOSTON CELTICS

Player	G.	Min.	FGA	FGM	Pct.	FTA	FTM	Pct.	Reb.	Ast.	PF	Disq.	Pts.	Avg.
John Havlicek	81	3369	1585	736	.464	578	488	.844	635	550	211	1	1960	24.2
Don Nelson	82	2224	920	461	.501	435	337	.775	601	148	238	3	1259	15.4
Larry Siegfried	78	2081	902	382	.424	257	220	.856	212	299	187	2	984	12.6
Bailey Howell	82	2078	931	399	.429	308	235	.763	550	120	261	4	1033	12.6
Jo Jo White	60	1328	684	309	.452	135	111	.822	169	145	132	1	729	12.2
Tom Sanders	57	1616	555	246	.443	183	161	.880	314	92	199	5	653	11.5
Henry Finkel	80	1866	683	310	.454	233	156	.670	613	103	292	13	776	9.7
Emmette Bryant	71	1617	520	210	.404	181	135	.746	269	231	201	5	555	7.8
Steve Kuberski	51	797	335	130	.388	92	64	.696	257	29	87	0	324	6.4
Jim Barnes	77	1049	434	178	.410	128	95	.742	350	52	229	4	451	5.9
Rich Johnson	65	898	361	167	.411	70	46	.657	208	32	155	3	380	5.8
Don Chaney	63	839	320	115	.359	109	82	.752	152	72	118	0	312	5.0
Rich Nieman	6	18	5	2	.400	2	2	1.000	6	2	10	0	6	1.0

CHICAGO BULLS

Player	G.	Min.	FGA	FGM	Pct.	FTA	FTM	Pct.	Reb.	Ast.	PF	Disq.	Pts.	Avg.
Chet Walker	78	2726	1249	596	.477	568	483	.850	604	192	203	1	1675	21.5
Bob Love	82	3123	1373	640	.466	525	442	.842	712	148	260	2	1722	21.0
Clem Haskins	82	3214	1486	668	.450	424	332	.783	378	624	237	0	1668	20.3
Jerry Sloan	53	1822	737	310	.421	318	207	.651	372	165	179	3	827	15.6
Bob Weiss	82	2544	855	365	.427	253	213	.842	227	474	206	0	943	11.5
Tom Boerwinkle	81	2335	775	348	.449	226	150	.664	1016	229	255	4	846	10.4
Walt Wesley	72	1407	648	270	.417	219	145	.662	455	68	184	1	685	9.5
Al Tucker	33	557	189	97	.513	45	37	.822	113	31	52	0	231	7.0
Shaler Halimon	38	517	244	96	.393	73	49	.671	68	69	58	0	241	6.3
Bob Kauffman	64	775	221	94	.425	123	88	.715	211	76	117	1	276	4.3
Ed Manning***	67	777	321	119	.371	56	42	.750	232	36	122	1	280	4.2
Ed Manning**	38	616	255	87	.341	48	37	.771	197	34	89	1	211	5.6
Loy Petersen	31	231	90	33	.367	39	26	.667	26	23	22	0	92	3.0
John Baum	3	13	11	3	.273	0	0	.000	4	0	1	0	6	2.0

CINCINNATI ROYALS

Player	G.	Min.	FGA	FGM	Pct.	FTA	FTM	Pct.	Reb.	Ast.	PF	Disq.	Pts.	Avg.
Oscar Robertson	69	2865	1267	647	.511	561	454	.809	422	558	175	1	1748	25.3
Tom VanArsdale	71	2544	1376	620	.451	492	381	.774	463	155	247	3	1621	22.8
Connie Dierking	76	2448	1243	521	.419	306	230	.752	624	169	275	7	1272	16.7
Johnny Green	78	2278	860	481	.559	429	254	.592	841	112	268	6	1216	15.6
Fred Foster	74	2077	1026	461	.449	243	176	.724	310	107	209	2	1098	14.8
Jerry Lucas	4	118	35	18	.514	7	5	.714	45	9	5	0	41	10.3
Norm VanLier	81	2895	749	302	.403	224	166	.741	409	500	329	18	770	9.5
Luther Rackley	66	1256	423	190	.449	195	124	.636	378	56	204	5	504	7.6
Herm Gilliam	57	1161	441	179	.406	91	68	.747	215	178	163	6	426	7.5
Bill Turner***	72	1170	468	197	.421	167	123	.737	304	43	193	3	517	7.2
Bill Turner**	69	1095	451	188	.417	157	118	.752	290	42	187	3	494	7.2
Adrian Smith	32	453	148	60	.405	60	52	.864	33	45	56	0	172	5.4
Jim King***	34	391	129	53	.411	41	33	.805	62	52	47	0	139	4.1
Jim King**	31	286	83	34	.410	27	22	.815	46	42	39	0	90	2.9
Wally Anderzunas	44	370	166	65	.392	46	29	.630	82	9	47	1	159	3.9
Bob Cousy	7	34	3	1	.333	3	3	1.000	5	10	11	0	5	0.7

DETROIT PISTONS

Player	G.	Min.	FGA	FGM	Pct.	FTA	FTM	Pct.	Reb.	Ast.	PF	Disq.	Pts.	Avg.
Dave Bing	70	2334	1295	575	.440	580	454	.783	299	418	196	0	1604	22.9
Jimmy Walker	81	2869	1394	666	.478	440	355	.807	242	248	203	4	1687	21.0
Eddie Miles	44	1243	531	231	.435	170	130	.765	173	82	99	0	592	13.5
Otto Moore	81	2523	805	383	.476	305	194	.636	900	104	232	3	960	11.9
Terry Dischinger	75	1754	650	342	.526	241	174	.722	369	106	213	5	858	11.4
Howard Komives	82	2418	878	363	.413	234	190	.812	193	312	247	2	916	11.2
Harold Hairston	15	282	103	57	.553	63	45	.714	88	11	36	0	159	10.0
Erwin Mueller***	78	2353	646	300	.464	263	189	.719	483	205	192	1	789	10.1
Erwin Mueller**	74	2284	614	287	.467	254	185	.728	469	199	186	1	759	10.3
Walt Bellamy	56	1173	384	210	.547	249	140	.562	397	55	163	3	560	10.0
McCoy McLemore	73	1421	500	233	.466	145	119	.821	336	83	159	3	585	8.0
Steve Mix	18	276	100	48	.480	39	23	.590	64	15	31	0	119	6.6
Bob Quick***	34	364	139	63	.453	71	49	.690	75	14	50	0	175	5.1
Bob Quick**	19	297	111	49	.441	53	37	.698	63	11	41	0	135	7.1
Bill Hewitt***	65	1279	298	110	.369	94	54	.574	356	64	130	1	274	4.2
Bill Hewitt**	45	801	210	85	.405	63	38	.603	213	36	91	1	208	4.6
Paul Long	25	130	62	28	.452	38	27	.711	11	17	22	0	83	3.3
Geroge Reynolds	10	44	19	8	.421	7	5	.714	14	12	10	0	21	2.1
Tom Workman	2	6	1	0	.000	0	0	.000	0	0	1	0	0	0.0

LOS ANGELES LAKERS

Player	G.	Min.	FGA	FGM	Pct.	FTA	FTM	Pct.	Reb.	Ast.	PF	Disq.	Pts.	Avg.
Jerry West	74	3106	1673	831	.497	785	647	.824	338	554	160	3	2309	31.2
Wilt Chamberlain	12	505	227	129	.568	157	70	.446	221	49	31	0	328	27.3
Elgin Baylor	54	2213	1051	511	.486	357	276	.773	559	292	132	1	1298	24.0
Harold Hairston***	70	2427	973	483	.496	413	326	.789	775	121	230	9	1292	18.5
Harold Hairston**	55	2145	870	426	.490	350	281	.803	687	110	194	9	1133	20.6
Mel Counts	81	2193	1017	434	.427	201	156	.776	683	160	304	7	1024	12.6
Dick Garrett	73	2318	816	354	.434	162	138	.852	235	180	236	5	846	11.6
John Tresvant***	69	1499	595	264	.444	284	206	.725	425	112	204	4	734	10.6
John Tresvant**	20	221	88	47	.534	35	23	.657	63	17	40	0	117	5.9
Keith Erickson	68	1755	563	258	.458	122	91	.746	304	209	175	3	607	8.9
Rick Roberson	74	2005	586	262	.447	212	120	.566	672	92	256	7	644	8.7
Willie McCarter	40	861	349	132	.378	60	43	.717	83	93	71	0	307	7.7
John Egan	72	1627	491	215	.438	121	99	.818	104	216	171	2	529	7.3
Bill Hewitt	20	478	88	25	.284	31	16	.516	141	28	39	0	66	3.3
Mike Lynn	44	403	133	44	.331	48	31	.646	64	30	87	4	119	2.7

MILWAUKEE BUCKS

Player	G.	Min.	FGA	FGM	Pct.	FTA	FTM	Pct.	Reb.	Ast.	PF	Disq.	Pts.	Avg.
Kareem Abdul-Jabbar	82	3534	1810	938	.518	743	485	.653	1190	337	283	8	2361	28.8
Flynn Robinson	81	2762	1391	663	.477	489	439	.898	263	449	254	5	1765	21.8
Jon McGlocklin	82	2966	1206	639	.530	198	169	.854	252	303	164	0	1447	17.6
Bob Dandridge	81	2461	895	434	.485	264	199	.754	625	292	279	1	1067	13.2
Greg Smith	82	2368	664	339	.511	174	125	.718	712	156	304	8	803	9.8
Lennie Chappell	75	1134	523	243	.465	211	135	.640	276	56	127	1	621	8.3
Fred Crawford	77	1331	506	243	.480	148	101	.682	184	225	181	1	587	7.6
Don Smith	80	1637	546	237	.434	185	119	.643	603	62	167	2	593	7.4
John Arthurs	11	86	35	12	.343	15	11	.733	14	17	15	0	35	3.2
Guy Rodgers	64	749	191	68	.356	90	67	.744	74	213	73	1	203	3.2
Bob Greacen	41	292	109	44	.404	28	18	.643	59	27	49	0	106	2.6
Sam Williams	11	44	24	11	.454	11	5	.455	7	3	5	0	27	2.5
Dick Cunningham	60	416	141	52	.369	33	22	.667	160	28	70	0	126	2.1

NEW YORK KNICKERBOCKERS

Player	G.	Min.	FGA	FGM	Pct.	FTA	FTM	Pct.	Reb.	Ast.	PF	Disq.	Pts.	Avg.
Willis Reed	81	3089	1385	702	.507	464	351	.756	1126	161	287	2	1755	21.7
Walt Frazier	77	3040	1158	600	.518	547	409	.748	465	629	203	1	1609	20.9
Dick Barnett	82	2772	1039	494	.475	325	232	.714	221	298	220	0	1220	14.9
Dave DeBusschere	79	2627	1082	488	.451	256	176	.688	790	194	244	2	1152	14.6
Bill Bradley	67	2098	897	413	.460	176	145	.824	239	268	219	0	971	14.5
Cazzie Russell	78	1563	773	385	.498	160	124	.775	236	135	137	0	894	11.5
Dave Stallworth	82	1375	557	239	.429	225	161	.716	323	139	194	2	639	7.8
Mike Riordan	81	1677	549	255	.464	165	114	.691	194	201	192	1	624	7.7
Bill Hosket	36	235	91	46	.505	33	26	.788	63	17	36	0	118	3.3
Nate Bowman	81	744	235	98	.417	79	41	.519	257	46	189	2	237	2.9
Don May	37	238	101	39	.386	19	18	.947	52	17	42	0	96	2.6
John Warren	44	272	108	44	.407	35	24	.686	40	30	53	0	112	2.5

PHILADELPHIA 76ers

Player	G.	Min.	FGA	FGM	Pct.	FTA	FTM	Pct.	Reb.	Ast.	PF	Disq.	Pts.	Avg.
Billy Cunningham	81	3194	1710	802	.469	700	510	.729	1101	352	331	15	2114	26.1
Hal Greer	80	3024	1551	705	.455	432	352	.815	376	405	300	8	1762	22.0
Archie Clark	76	2772	1198	594	.496	396	311	.785	301	380	201	2	1499	19.7
Darrall Imhoff	79	2474	796	430	.540	331	215	.650	754	211	294	7	1075	13.6
Jim Washington	79	2459	842	401	.476	273	204	.747	734	104	262	5	1006	12.7
Wally Jones	78	1740	851	366	.430	226	190	.841	173	276	210	2	922	11.8
Fred Hetzel	63	757	323	156	.483	85	71	.835	207	44	110	3	383	6.1
Matt Guokas	80	1558	416	189	.454	149	106	.711	216	222	201	0	484	6.1
Luke Jackson	37	583	181	71	.392	81	60	.741	198	50	80	0	202	5.5
George Wilson	67	836	304	118	.388	172	122	.709	317	52	145	3	358	5.3
Bud Ogden	47	357	172	82	.477	39	27	.692	86	31	62	2	191	4.1
Dave Scholz	1	1	1	1	1.000	0	0	.000	0	0	0	0	2	2.0

PHOENIX SUNS

Player	G.	Min.	FGA	FGM	Pct.	FTA	FTM	Pct.	Reb.	Ast.	PF	Disq.	Pts.	Avg.
Connie Hawkins	81	3312	1447	709	.490	741	577	.779	846	391	287	4	1995	24.6
Dick Van Arsdale	77	2966	1166	592	.508	575	459	.798	264	338	282	5	1643	21.3
Gail Goodrich	81	3234	1251	568	.454	604	488	.808	340	605	251	3	1624	20.0
Jim Fox	81	2041	788	413	.524	283	218	.770	570	93	261	7	1044	12.9
Paul Silas	78	2836	804	373	.464	412	250	.607	916	214	266	5	996	12.8
Dick Snyder	6	147	45	22	.489	8	7	.875	15	9	20	1	51	8.5
Jerry Chambers	79	1139	658	283	.430	125	91	.728	219	54	162	3	657	8.3
Neal Walk	82	1394	547	257	.470	242	155	.640	455	80	225	2	669	8.2
Art Harris***	81	1553	723	285	.394	134	86	.642	161	231	220	0	656	8.1
Art Harris**	76	1375	650	257	.395	125	82	.656	142	211	209	0	596	7.8
Lamar Green	58	700	234	101	.432	70	41	.586	276	17	115	2	243	4.2
Stan McKenzie	58	525	206	81	.393	73	58	.795	93	52	67	1	220	3.8
Neil Johnson	28	136	60	20	.333	12	8	.667	47	12	38	0	48	1.7

SAN DIEGO ROCKETS

Player	G.	Min.	FGA	FGM	Pct.	FTA	FTM	Pct.	Reb.	Ast.	PF	Disq.	Pts.	Avg.
Elvin Hayes	82	3665	2020	914	.452	622	428	.688	1386	162	270	5	2256	27.5
Don Kojis	56	1578	756	338	.447	241	181	.751	388	78	135	1	857	15.3
Jim Barnett	80	2105	998	450	.451	366	289	.790	305	287	222	3	1189	14.9
John Block	82	2152	1025	453	.442	367	287	.782	609	137	275	2	1193	14.5
Stu Lantz	82	2471	1027	455	.443	361	278	.770	255	287	238	2	1188	14.5
Bernie Williams	72	1228	641	251	.392	122	96	.787	155	165	124	0	598	8.3
Rick Adelman	35	717	247	96	.389	91	68	.747	81	113	90	0	260	7.4

Player	G.	Min.	FGA	FGM	Pct.	FTA	FTM	Pct.	Reb.	Ast.	PF	Disq.	Pts.	Avg.
Bobby Smith	75	1198	567	242	.427	96	66	.68	328	75	119	0	550	7.3
Toby Kimball	77	1622	508	218	.429	185	107	.578	621	95	187	1	543	7.1
John Trapp	70	1025	434	185	.426	104	72	.692	309	49	200	3	442	6.3
Art Williams	80	1545	464	189	.407	118	88	.746	292	503	168	0	466	5.8
Pat Riley	36	474	180	75	.417	55	40	.727	57	85	68	0	190	5.3

SAN FRANCISCO WARRIORS

Player	G.	Min.	FGA	FGM	Pct.	FTA	FTM	Pct.	Reb.	Ast.	PF	Disq.	Pts.	Avg.
Jeff Mullins	74	2861	1426	656	.460	378	320	.847	382	360	240	4	1632	22.1
Nate Thurmond	43	1919	824	341	.414	346	261	.754	762	150	110	1	943	21.9
Jim King	3	105	46	19	.413	14	11	.786	16	10	8	0	49	16.3
Joe Ellis	76	2380	1223	501	.410	270	200	.741	594	139	281	13	1202	15.8
Jerry Lucas***	67	2420	799	405	.507	255	200	.784	951	173	166	2	1010	15.1
Jerry Lucas**	63	2302	764	387	.507	248	195	.786	906	166	159	2	969	15.4
Ron Williams	80	2435	1046	452	.432	337	277	.822	190	424	287	7	1181	14.8
Clyde Lee	82	2641	822	362	.440	300	178	.593	929	80	263	5	902	11.0
Bill Turner	3	75	17	9	.529	10	5	.500	14	1	7	0	23	7.7
Dave Gambee	73	951	464	185	.399	186	156	.839	244	55	172	0	526	7.2
Bobby Lewis	73	1353	557	213	.382	152	100	.658	157	194	170	0	526	7.2
Bob Portman	60	813	398	177	.445	85	66	.776	224	28	77	0	420	7.0
Adrian Smith***	77	1087	416	153	.368	170	152	.894	82	133	122	0	258	5.9
Adrian Smith**	45	634	268	93	.347	110	100	.909	49	87	66	0	286	6.4
Al Attles	45	676	202	78	.386	113	75	.664	74	142	103	0	231	5.1
Dale Schlueter	63	685	167	82	.491	97	60	.619	231	25	108	0	224	3.6

SEATTLE SUPERSONICS

Player	G.	Min.	FGA	FGM	Pct.	FTA	FTM	Pct.	Reb.	Ast.	PF	Disq.	Pts.	Avg.
Bob Rule	80	2959	1705	789	.463	542	387	.714	825	144	278	6	1965	24.6
Len Wilkens	75	2802	1066	448	.420	556	438	.788	378	683	212	5	1334	17.8
Bob Boozer	82	2549	1005	493	.491	320	263	.822	717	110	237	2	1249	15.2
Dick Snyder***	82	2437	863	456	.528	208	169	.813	323	342	277	8	1081	13.2
Dick Snyder**	76	2290	818	434	.531	200	162	.810	308	333	257	7	1030	13.6
John Tresvant	49	1278	507	217	.428	249	183	.735	362	95	164	4	617	12.6
Tom Meschery	80	2294	818	394	.482	248	196	.790	666	157	317	13	984	12.3
Art Harris	5	178	73	28	.384	9	4	.444	19	20	11	0	60	12.0
Lucius Allen	81	1817	692	306	.442	249	182	.731	211	342	201	0	794	9.8
Barry Clemens	78	1487	595	270	.454	140	111	.793	316	116	188	1	651	8.3
Erwin Mueller	4	69	32	13	.406	9	4	.444	14	6	6	0	30	7.5
Lee Winfield	64	771	288	138	.479	116	87	.750	98	102	95	0	363	5.7
Dorie Murrey	81	1079	343	153	.446	186	136	.731	357	76	191	4	442	5.5
Rod Thorn	19	105	45	20	.444	24	15	.625	16	17	8	0	55	2.9
Al Hairston	3	20	8	3	.375	1	1	1.000	5	6	3	0	7	2.3
Joe Kennedy	14	82	34	3	.088	2	2	1.000	20	7	7	0	8	0.6

**Team Total.
***Combined Player Total.

PLAYOFF RESULTS

EASTERN DIVISION SEMIFINALS
Milwaukee 4, Philadelphia 1

Mar. 25—Philadelphia 118 at Milwaukee 125
Mar. 27—Philadelphia 112 at Milwaukee 105
Mar. 30—Milwaukee 156 at Philadelphia 120
Apr. 1—Milwaukee 118 at Philadelphia 111
Apr. 3—Philadelphia 106 at Milwaukee 115

New York 4, Baltimore 3

Mar. 26—Baltimore 117 at New York......................120**
Mar. 27—New York 106 at Baltimore 99
Mar. 29—Baltimore 127 at New York.............................113
Mar. 31—New York 92 at Baltimore 102
Apr. 2—Baltimore 80 at New York...............................101
Apr. 5—New York 87 at Baltimore 96
Apr. 6—Baltimore 114 at New York..............................127

EASTERN DIVISION FINALS
New York 4, Milwaukee 1

Apr. 11—Milwaukee 102 at New York............................110
Apr. 13—Milwaukee 111 at New York............................112
Apr. 17—New York 96 at Milwaukee 101
Apr. 19—New York 117 at Milwaukee 105
Apr. 20—Milwaukee 96 at New York..............................132

WESTERN DIVISION
Atlanta 4, Chicago 1

Mar. 25—Chicago 111 at Atlanta.................................129
Mar. 28—Chicago 104 at Atlanta.................................124
Mar. 31—Atlanta 106 at Chicago.................................101
Apr. 3—Atlanta 120 at Chicago.................................131
Apr. 5—Chicago 107 at Atlanta.................................113

Los Angeles 4, Phoenix 3

Mar. 25—Phoenix 112 at Los Angeles.........................128
Mar. 29—Phoenix 114 at Los Angeles.........................101
Apr. 2—Los Angeles 98 at Phoenix............................112
Apr. 4—Los Angeles 102 at Phoenix..........................112
Apr. 5—Phoenix 121 at Los Angeles.........................138
Apr. 7—Los Angeles 104 at Phoenix........................... 93
Apr. 9—Phoenix 94 at Los Angeles...........................129

WESTERN DIVISION FINALS
Los Angeles 4, Atlanta 0

Apr. 12—Los Angeles 119 at Atlanta...........................115
Apr. 14—Los Angeles 105 at Atlanta............................. 94
Apr. 16—Atlanta 114 at Los Angeles..........................115*
Apr. 19—Atlanta 114 at Los Angeles..........................133

WORLD CHAMPIONSHIP SERIES
New York 4, Los Angeles 3

Apr. 24—Los Angeles 112 at New York....................124
Apr. 27—Los Angeles 105 at New York....................103
Apr. 29—New York 111 at Los Angeles....................108*
May 1—New York 115 at Los Angeles....................121*
May 4—Los Angeles 100 at New York....................107
May 6—New York 113 at Los Angeles....................135
May 8—Los Angeles 99 at New York....................113

*Denotes overtime period.

1968-69 NBA STATISTICS

1968-69 NBA CHAMPION BOSTON CELTICS

Front row (left to right): Don Nelson, Sam Jones, Coach Bill Russell, President Jack Waldron, General Manager Red Auerbach, John Havlicek, Team Physician Dr. Thomas Silva, Larry Siegfried. Back row: Trainer Joe DeLaurl, Emmette Bryant, Don Chaney, Tom Sanders, Rich Johnson, Jim Barnes, Bailey Howell, Mal Graham.

FINAL STANDINGS

EASTERN DIVISION

Team	Bal.	Phil.	N.Y.	Bos.	Cin.	Det.	Mil.	L.A.	Atl.	S.F.	S.D.	Chi.	Sea.	Pho.	W.	L.	Pct.	G.B.
Baltimore	..	2	3	5	4	7	5	3	4	3	5	6	4	6	57	25	.695	....
Philadelphia	4	..	3	2	4	4	6	5	5	2	4	5	6	5	55	27	.671	2
New York	4	4	..	6	2	4	6	1	4	5	3	4	6	5	54	28	.659	3
Boston	2	5	1	..	5	5	5	2	3	3	4	4	3	6	48	34	.585	9
Cincinnati	3	3	4	2	..	3	5	2	2	3	2	5	3	4	41	41	.500	16
Detroit	-	3	3	1	4	..	2	3	-	2	3	3	4	4	32	50	.390	25
Milwaukee	1	-	-	1	1	4	..	1	2	3	4	1	3	6	27	55	.329	30

WESTERN DIVISION

Team	Bal.	Phil.	N.Y.	Bos.	Cin.	Det.	Mil.	L.A.	Atl.	S.F.	S.D.	Chi.	Sea.	Pho.	W.	L.	Pct.	G.B.
Los Angeles	3	1	5	4	4	3	5	..	4	4	7	4	5	6	55	27	.671	....
Atlanta	2	1	2	3	4	6	4	3	..	4	3	6	4	6	48	34	.585	7
San Francisco	3	4	1	3	3	4	3	3	3	..	3	3	4	4	41	41	.500	14
San Diego	1	2	3	2	4	3	2	-	4	3	..	3	3	7	37	45	.451	18
Chicago	-	1	2	2	1	3	5	3	1	4	3	..	4	4	33	49	.402	22
Seattle	2	-	-	3	3	2	5	1	2	3	3	3	..	3	30	52	.366	25
Phoenix	-	1	1	-	2	2	2	-	-	2	1	2	3	..	16	66	.195	39

HOME-ROAD-NEUTRAL RECORDS OF ALL TEAMS

Team	Home	Road	Neutral	Total	Team	Home	Road	Neutral	Total
Atlanta	28-12	18-21	2-1	48-34	New York	30-7	19-20	5-1	54-28
Baltimore	29-9	24-15	4-1	57-25	Philadelphia	26-8	24-16	5-3	55-27
Boston	24-12	21-19	3-3	48-34	Phoenix	11-26	4-28	1-12	16-66
Chicago	19-21	12-25	2-3	33-49	San Diego	25-16	8-25	4-4	37-45
Cincinnati	15-13	16-21	10-7	41-41	San Francisco	22-19	18-21	1-1	41-41
Detroit	21-17	7-30	4-3	32-50	Seattle	18-18	6-29	6-5	30-52
Los Angeles	32-9	21-18	2-0	55-27	Totals	315-206	206-315	53-53	574-574
Milwaukee	15-19	8-27	4-9	27-55					

TEAM STATISTICS

Team	G.	FGA	FGM	Pct.	FTA	FTM	Pct.	Reb.	Ast.	PF	Disq.	For	Agst.	Pt.Dif.
New York	82	7813	3588	.459	2596	1911	.736	4246	2071	2175	35	110.8	105.2	5.6
Boston	82	8316	3583	.431	2657	1936	.729	4840	1953	2073	27	111.0	105.4	5.6
Philadelphia	82	8274	3754	.454	3087	2238	.725	4513	1914	2145	44	118.9	113.8	5.1
Baltimore	82	8567	3770	.440	2734	2002	.732	4963	1682	2038	17	116.4	112.1	4.3
Los Angeles	82	7620	3574	.469	3161	2056	.650	4749	2068	1773	16	112.2	108.1	4.1
Atlanta	82	7844	3605	.460	2785	1913	.687	4599	2069	2082	28	111.3	109.4	1.9
San Diego	82	8631	3691	.428	3039	2074	.682	5026	1925	2110	19	115.3	115.5	−0.2
Cincinnati	82	7742	3565	.460	3012	2262	.751	4525	1983	2031	29	114.5	115.6	−1.1
San Francisco	82	8218	3414	.415	2949	2119	.719	5109	1822	2087	43	109.1	110.7	−1.6
Chicago	82	8021	3355	.418	2577	1877	.728	4550	1597	2064	29	104.7	106.9	−2.2
Detroit	82	7997	3609	.451	3025	2141	.707	4471	1757	2105	24	114.1	117.3	−3.2
Seattle	82	8149	3543	.435	2979	2105	.707	4498	1927	2281	54	112.1	116.9	−4.8
Milwaukee	82	8258	3537	.428	2638	1966	.745	4727	1882	2187	50	110.2	115.4	−5.2
Phoenix	82	8242	3541	.430	2950	2080	.705	4508	1918	2086	30	111.7	120.5	−8.8

INDIVIDUAL LEADERS

POINTS

Player	G.	FG	FT	Pts.	Avg.	Player	G.	FG	FT	Pts.	Avg.
Hayes, San Diego	82	930	467	2327	28.4	Loughery, Balt	80	717	372	1806	22.6
Monroe, Baltimore	80	809	447	2065	25.8	Bing, Detroit	77	678	444	1800	23.4
Cunningham, Phil	82	739	556	2034	24.8	Mullins, San Fran	78	697	381	1775	22.8
Rule, Seattle	82	776	413	1965	24.0	Havlicek, Boston	82	692	387	1771	21.6
Robertson, Cin	79	656	643	1955	24.7	Hudson, Atlanta	81	716	338	1770	21.9
Goodrich, Phoenix	81	718	495	1931	23.8	Reed, New York	82	704	325	1733	21.1
Greer, Philadelphia	82	732	432	1896	23.1	Boozer, Chicago	79	661	394	1716	21.7
Baylor, Los Angeles	76	730	421	1881	24.8	Van Arsdale, Pho	80	612	454	1678	21.0
Wilkens, Seattle	82	644	547	1835	22.4	Chamberlain, L.A.	81	641	382	1664	20.5
Kojis, San Diego	81	687	446	1820	22.5	Robinson, Chi.-Mil	83	625	412	1662	20.0

FIELD GOALS
(Minimum 230 FGM)

Player	FGA	FGM	Pct.
Wilt Chamberlain, Los Angeles	1099	641	.583
Jerry Lucas, Cincinnati	1007	555	.551
Willis Reed, New York	1351	704	.521
Terry Dischinger, Detroit	513	264	.515
Walt Bellamy, N.Y.-Det	1103	563	.510
Joe Caldwell, Atlanta	1106	561	.507
Walt Frazier, New York	1052	531	.505
Tom Hawkins, Los Angeles	461	230	.499
Lou Hudson, Atlanta	1455	716	.492
Jon McGlocklin, Milwaukee	1358	662	.487

ASSISTS

Player	G.	No.	Avg.
Oscar Robertson, Cincinnati	79	772	9.8
Lennie Wilkens, Seattle	82	674	8.2
Walt Frazier, New York	80	635	7.9
Guy Rodgers, Milwaukee	81	561	6.9
Dave Bing, Detroit	77	546	7.1
Art Williams, San Diego	79	524	6.6
Gail Goodrich, Phoenix	81	518	6.4
Walt Hazzard, Atlanta	80	474	5.9
John Havlicek, Boston	82	441	5.4
Jerry West, Los Angeles	61	423	6.9

FREE THROWS
(Minimum 230 FTM)

Player	FTA	FTM	Pct.
Larry Siegfried, Boston	389	336	.864
Jeff Mullins, San Francisco	452	381	.843
Jon McGlocklin, Milwaukee	292	246	.842
Flynn Robinson, Chi.-Mil	491	412	.839
Oscar Robertson, Cincinnati	767	643	.838
Fred Hetzel, Mil.-Cin	357	299	.838
Jack Marin, Baltimore	352	292	.830
Jerry West, Los Angeles	597	490	.821
Bob Boozer, Chicago	489	394	.806
Chet Walker, Philadelphia	459	369	.804

REBOUNDS

Player	G.	No.	Avg.
Wilt Chamberlain, Los Angeles	81	1712	21.1
Wes Unseld, Baltimore	82	1491	18.2
Bill Russell, Boston	77	1484	19.3
Elvin Hayes, San Diego	82	1406	17.1
Nate Thurmond, San Francisco	71	1402	19.7
Jerry Lucas, Cincinnati	74	1360	18.4
Willis Reed, New York	82	1191	14.5
Bill Bridges, Atlanta	80	1132	14.2
Walt Bellamy, N.Y.-Det	88	1101	12.5
Bill Cunningham, Philadelphia	82	1050	12.8

TEAM-BY-TEAM INDIVIDUAL STATISTICS

ATLANTA HAWKS

Player	G.	Min.	FGA	FGM	Pct.	FTA	FTM	Pct.	Reb.	Ast.	PF	Disq.	Pts.	Avg.
Lou Hudson	81	2869	1455	716	.492	435	338	.777	533	216	248	0	1770	21.9
Zelmo Beaty	72	2578	1251	586	.470	506	370	.731	798	131	272	7	1546	21.5
Joe Caldwell	81	2720	1106	561	.507	296	159	.537	303	320	231	1	1281	15.8
Bill Bridges	80	2930	775	351	.453	353	239	.677	1132	298	290	3	941	11.8
Don Ohl	76	1995	901	385	.427	208	147	.707	170	221	232	5	917	12.1
Walt Hazzard	80	2420	869	345	.397	294	208	.707	266	474	264	6	898	11.2
Paul Silas	79	1853	575	241	.419	333	204	.613	745	140	166	0	686	8.7
Jim Davis	78	1367	568	265	.467	231	154	.667	529	97	239	6	684	8.8
Richie Guerin	27	472	111	47	.423	74	57	.770	59	99	66	0	151	5.6
Skip Harlicka	26	218	90	41	.456	31	24	.774	16	37	29	0	106	4.1
Dennis Hamilton	25	141	67	37	.552	5	2	.400	29	8	19	0	76	3.0
George Lehmann	11	138	67	26	.388	12	8	.667	9	27	18	0	60	5.5
Dwight Waller	11	29	9	2	.222	7	3	.429	10	1	8	0	7	0.6

BALTIMORE BULLETS

Player	G.	Min.	FGA	FGM	Pct.	FTA	FTM	Pct.	Reb.	Ast.	PF	Disq.	Pts.	Avg.
Earl Monroe	80	3075	1837	809	.440	582	447	.768	280	392	261	1	2065	25.8
Kevin Loughery	80	3135	1636	717	.438	463	372	.803	266	384	299	3	1806	22.6
Jack Marin	82	2710	1109	505	.455	352	292	.830	608	231	275	4	1302	15.9
Wes Unseld	82	2970	897	427	.476	458	277	.605	1491	213	276	4	1131	13.8
Ray Scott	82	2168	929	386	.416	257	195	.759	722	133	212	1	967	11.8
Gus Johnson	49	1671	782	359	.459	223	160	.717	568	97	176	1	878	17.9
Leroy Ellis	80	1603	527	229	.435	155	117	.755	510	73	168	0	575	7.2
Ed Manning	63	727	288	129	.448	54	35	.648	246	21	120	0	293	4.7
John Barnhill	30	504	175	76	.434	65	39	.600	53	71	63	0	191	6.4
Barry Orms	64	916	246	76	.309	60	29	.483	158	49	155	3	181	2.8
Bob Quick	28	154	73	30	.411	44	27	.614	25	12	14	0	87	3.1
Tom Workman	21	86	54	22	.407	15	9	.600	27	2	16	0	53	2.5
Bob Ferry	7	36	14	5	.357	6	3	.500	9	4	3	0	13	1.9

BOSTON CELTICS

Player	G.	Min.	FGA	FGM	Pct.	FTA	FTM	Pct.	Reb.	Ast.	PF	Disq.	Pts.	Avg.
John Havlicek	82	3174	1709	692	.405	496	387	.780	570	441	247	0	1771	21.6
Bailey Howell	78	2527	1257	612	.487	426	313	.735	685	137	285	3	1537	19.7
Sam Jones	70	1820	1103	496	.450	189	148	.783	265	182	121	0	1140	16.3
Larry Siegfried	79	2560	1031	392	.380	389	336	.864	282	370	222	0	1120	14.2
Don Nelson	82	1773	771	374	.485	259	201	.776	458	92	198	2	949	11.6
Tom Sanders	82	2184	847	364	.430	255	187	.733	574	110	293	9	915	11.2
Bill Russell	77	3291	645	279	.433	388	204	.526	1484	374	231	2	762	9.9
Em Bryant	80	1388	488	197	.404	100	65	.650	192	176	264	2	459	5.7
Jim Barnes (Tot.)	59	606	261	115	.441	111	75	.676	224	28	122	2	305	5.2
Jim Barnes (Bos.)	49	595	202	92	.455	92	65	.707	194	27	107	2	249	5.1
Don Chaney	20	209	113	36	.319	20	8	.400	46	19	32	0	80	4.0
Rich Johnson	31	163	76	29	.382	23	11	.478	52	7	40	0	69	2.2
Mal Graham	22	103	55	13	.236	14	11	.786	24	14	27	0	37	1.7
Bud Olsen*	7	43	19	7	.368	6	0	.000	14	4	6	0	14	2.0

CHICAGO BULLS

Player	G.	Min.	FGA	FGM	Pct.	FTA	FTM	Pct.	Reb.	Ast.	PF	Disq.	Pts.	Avg.
Bob Boozer	79	2872	1375	661	.481	489	394	.806	614	156	218	2	1716	21.7
Clem Haskins	79	2874	1275	537	.421	361	282	.781	359	306	230	0	1356	17.2
Jerry Sloan	78	2939	1170	488	.417	447	333	.745	619	276	313	6	1309	16.8
Jim Washington	80	2705	1023	440	.430	356	241	.677	847	104	226	0	1121	14.0
Tom Boerwinkle	80	2365	831	318	.383	222	145	.653	889	178	317	11	781	9.8
Barry Clemens	75	1444	628	235	.374	125	82	.656	318	125	163	1	552	7.4
Bob Weiss (Tot.)	77	1478	499	189	.379	160	128	.800	162	199	174	1	506	6.6
Bob Weiss (Chi.)	62	1236	385	153	.397	126	101	.802	135	172	150	0	407	6.6
Dave Newmark	81	1159	475	185	.389	139	86	.619	347	58	205	7	456	5.6
Flynn Robinson*	18	550	293	124	.423	114	95	.833	69	57	52	1	343	19.1
Bob Love (Tot.)	49	542	272	108	.397	96	71	.740	150	17	59	0	287	5.9
Bob Love (Chi.)	35	315	166	69	.416	58	42	.724	86	14	37	0	180	5.1
Erwin Mueller*	52	872	224	75	.335	90	46	.511	193	124	98	1	196	3.8
Loy Peterson	38	299	109	44	.404	27	19	.704	41	25	39	0	107	2.8
Jim Barnes*	10	111	59	23	.390	19	10	.526	30	1	15	0	56	5.6
Ken Wilburn	4	14	8	3	.375	4	1	.250	3	1	1	0	7	1.8

CINCINNATI ROYALS

Player	G.	Min.	FGA	FGM	Pct.	FTA	FTM	Pct.	Reb.	Ast.	PF	Disq.	Pts.	Avg.
Oscar Robertson	79	3461	1351	656	.486	767	643	.838	502	772	231	2	1955	24.7
Tom Van Arsdale	77	3059	1233	547	.444	533	398	.747	356	208	300	6	1492	19.4
Jerry Lucas	74	3075	1007	555	.551	327	247	.755	1360	306	206	0	1357	18.3
Connie Dierking	82	2540	1232	546	.443	319	243	.762	739	222	305	9	1335	16.3
Fred Hetzel (Tot.)	84	2276	1047	456	.436	357	299	.838	613	112	287	9	1211	14.4
Fred Hetzel (Cin.)	31	685	287	140	.488	105	88	.838	140	29	94	3	368	11.9
Al Tucker (Tot.)	84	1885	809	361	.446	244	158	.648	439	74	186	2	880	10.5
Al Tucker (Cin.)	28	626	265	126	.475	73	49	.671	122	19	75	2	301	10.8
Adrian Smith	73	1336	562	243	.432	269	217	.807	105	127	166	1	703	9.6
Walt Wesley	82	1334	534	245	.459	207	134	.647	403	47	191	0	624	7.6
John Tresvant*	51	1681	531	239	.450	223	130	.583	419	103	193	5	608	11.9
Bill Dinwiddie	69	1028	352	124	.352	87	45	.517	242	55	146	0	293	4.2
Fred Foster	56	497	193	74	.383	66	43	.652	61	36	49	0	191	3.4
Pat Frink	48	363	147	50	.340	29	23	.793	41	55	54	1	123	2.6
Don Smith*	20	108	43	18	.419	7	2	.286	31	4	17	0	38	1.9
Doug Sims	4	12	5	2	.400	0	0	.000	4	0	4	0	4	1.0

DETROIT PISTONS

Player	G.	Min.	FGA	FGM	Pct.	FTA	FTM	Pct.	Reb.	Ast.	PF	Disq.	Pts.	Avg.
Dave Bing	77	3039	1594	678	.425	623	444	.713	382	546	256	3	1800	23.4
Walt Bellamy (Tot.)	88	3159	1103	563	.510	618	401	.649	1101	176	320	5	1527	17.4
Walt Bellamy (Det.)	53	2023	701	359	.512	416	276	.663	716	99	197	4	994	18.8
Harold Hairston	81	2889	1131	530	.469	553	404	.731	959	109	255	3	1464	18.1
Eddie Miles	80	2252	983	441	.449	273	182	.667	283	180	201	0	1064	13.3
Howard Komives (Tot.)	85	2562	974	379	.389	264	211	.799	299	403	274	1	969	11.4
Howard Komives (Det.)	53	1726	665	272	.409	178	138	.775	204	266	178	1	682	12.9
Jim Walker	69	1639	670	312	.466	229	182	.795	157	221	172	1	806	11.7
McCoy McLemore (Tot.)	81	1620	722	282	.391	214	169	.790	404	94	186	4	733	9.0
McCoy McLemore (Det.)	50	910	356	141	.396	104	84	.808	236	44	113	3	366	7.3
Terry Dischinger	75	1456	513	264	.515	178	130	.730	323	93	230	5	658	8.8
Dave Gambee (Tot.)	59	926	465	210	.452	195	159	.815	257	47	159	4	579	9.8
Dave Gambee (Det.)	25	302	142	60	.423	62	49	.790	78	15	60	0	169	6.8
Otto Moore	74	1605	544	241	.443	168	88	.524	524	68	182	2	570	7.7
Dave DeBusschere*	29	1092	423	189	.447	130	94	.723	353	63	111	1	472	16.3
Jim Fox*	25	375	96	45	.469	53	34	.642	139	23	56	1	124	5.0
Sonny Dove	29	236	100	47	.470	36	24	.667	62	12	49	0	118	4.1
Rich Niemann*	16	123	47	20	.426	10	8	.800	41	9	30	0	48	3.0
Bud Olsen (Tot.)	17	113	42	15	.357	18	4	.222	25	11	14	0	34	2.0
Bud Olsen (Det.)	10	70	23	8	.348	12	4	.333	11	7	8	0	20	2.0
Cliff Williams	3	18	9	2	.222	0	0	.000	3	2	7	0	4	1.3

LOS ANGELES LAKERS

Player	G.	Min.	FGA	FGM	Pct.	FTA	FTM	Pct.	Reb.	Ast.	PF	Disq.	Pts.	Avg.
Elgin Baylor	76	3064	1632	730	.447	567	421	.743	805	408	204	0	1881	24.8
Wilt Chamberlain	81	3669	1099	641	.583	857	382	.446	1712	366	142	0	1664	20.5
Jerry West	61	2394	1156	545	.471	597	490	.821	262	423	156	1	1580	25.9
Mel Counts	77	1866	867	390	.450	221	178	.805	600	109	223	5	958	12.4
John Egan	82	1805	597	246	.412	240	204	.850	147	215	206	1	696	8.5
Keith Erickson	77	1974	629	264	.420	175	120	.686	308	194	222	6	648	8.4
Bill Hewitt	75	1455	528	239	.453	105	61	.575	332	76	139	1	539	7.2
Tom Hawkins	74	1507	461	230	.499	151	62	.411	266	81	168	1	522	7.1
Fred Crawford	81	1690	454	211	.465	154	83	.539	215	154	224	1	505	6.2
Cliff Anderson	35	289	108	44	.407	82	47	.573	44	31	58	0	135	3.9
Jay Carty	28	192	89	34	.382	11	8	.727	58	11	31	0	76	2.7

MILWAUKEE BUCKS

Player	G.	Min.	FGA	FGM	Pct.	FTA	FTM	Pct.	Reb.	Ast.	PF	Disq.	Pts.	Avg.
Flynn Robinson (Tot.)	83	2616	1442	625	.433	491	412	.839	306	377	261	7	1662	20.0
Flynn Robinson (Milw.)	65	2066	1149	501	.436	377	317	.841	237	320	209	6	1319	20.3
Jon McGlocklin	80	2888	1358	662	.487	292	246	.842	343	312	186	1	1570	19.6
Lennie Chappell	80	2207	1011	459	.454	339	250	.737	637	95	247	3	1168	14.6
Wayne Embry	78	2355	894	382	.427	390	259	.664	672	149	302	8	1023	13.1
Fred Hetzel°	53	1591	760	316	.416	252	211	.837	473	83	193	6	843	15.9
Guy Rodgers	81	2157	862	325	.377	232	184	.793	226	561	207	2	834	10.3
Greg Smith	79	2207	613	276	.450	155	91	.587	804	137	264	12	643	8.1
Dave Gambee°	34	624	323	150	.464	133	110	.827	179	32	99	4	410	12.1
Don Smith (Tot.)	49	945	390	144	.369	113	70	.619	409	37	115	3	358	7.3
Don Smith (Milw.)	29	837	347	126	.363	106	68	.642	378	33	98	3	320	11.0
Dick Cunningham	77	1236	332	141	.425	106	69	.651	438	58	166	2	351	4.6
Sam Williams	55	628	228	78	.342	134	72	.537	109	61	106	1	228	4.1
Bob Love°	14	227	106	39	.368	38	29	.763	64	3	22	0	107	7.6
Rich Neimann (Tot.)	34	272	106	44	.415	25	19	.760	100	16	61	1	107	3.1
Rich Neimann (Milw.)	18	149	59	24	.407	15	11	.733	59	7	31	1	59	3.3
Bob Weiss°	15	242	114	36	.316	34	27	.794	27	27	24	1	99	6.6
Charlie Paulk	17	217	84	19	.226	23	13	.565	78	3	26	0	51	3.0
Jay Miller	3	27	10	2	.200	7	5	.714	2	0	4	0	9	3.0
Bob Warlick°	3	22	8	1	.125	5	4	.800	1	1	3	0	6	2.0

NEW YORK KNICKERBOCKERS

Player	G.	Min.	FGA	FGM	Pct.	FTA	FTM	Pct.	Reb.	Ast.	PF	Disq.	Pts.	Avg.
Willis Reed	82	3108	1351	704	.521	435	325	.747	1191	190	314	7	1733	21.1
Dick Barnett	82	2953	1220	565	.463	403	312	.774	251	291	239	4	1442	17.6
Walt Frazier	80	2949	1052	531	.505	457	341	.746	499	635	245	2	1403	17.5
Dave DeBusschere (Tot.)	76	2943	1140	506	.444	328	229	.698	888	191	290	6	1241	16.3
Dave DeBusschere (N.Y.)	47	1851	717	317	.442	198	135	.682	535	128	179	5	769	16.4
Bill Bradley	82	2413	948	407	.429	253	206	.814	350	302	295	4	1020	12.4
Cazzie Russell	50	1645	804	362	.450	240	191	.796	209	115	140	1	915	18.3
Walt Bellamy°	35	1136	402	204	.507	202	125	.619	385	77	123	1	533	15.2
Phil Jackson	47	924	294	126	.429	119	80	.672	246	43	168	6	332	7.1
Howard Komives°	32	836	309	107	.346	86	73	.849	95	137	96	0	287	9.0
Don May	48	560	223	81	.363	58	42	.724	114	35	64	0	204	4.3
Nate Bowman	67	607	226	82	.363	61	29	.475	220	53	142	4	193	2.9
Bill Hosket	50	351	123	53	.431	42	24	.571	94	19	77	0	130	2.6
Mike Riordan	54	397	144	49	.340	42	28	.667	57	46	93	1	126	2.3

PHILADELPHIA 76ers

Player	G.	Min.	FGA	FGM	Pct.	FTA	FTM	Pct.	Reb.	Ast.	PF	Disq.	Pts.	Avg.
Bill Cunningham	82	3345	1736	739	.426	754	556	.737	1050	287	329	10	2034	24.8
Hal Greer	82	3311	1595	732	.459	543	432	.796	435	414	294	8	1896	23.1
Chet Walker	82	2753	1145	554	.484	459	369	.804	640	144	244	0	1477	18.0
Archie Clark	82	2144	928	444	.478	314	219	.697	265	296	188	1	1107	13.5
Wally Jones	81	2340	1005	432	.430	256	207	.809	251	292	280	5	1071	13.2
Darrall Imhoff	82	2360	593	279	.470	325	194	.597	792	218	310	12	752	9.2
George Wilson (Tot.)	79	1846	663	272	.410	235	153	.651	721	108	232	5	697	8.8
George Wilson (Phila.)	38	552	182	81	.445	84	60	.714	216	32	87	1	222	5.8
Lucious Jackson	25	840	332	145	.437	97	69	.711	286	54	102	3	359	14.4
John Green	74	795	282	146	.518	125	57	.456	330	47	110	1	349	4.7
Matt Guokas	72	838	216	92	.426	81	54	.667	94	104	121	1	238	3.3
Shaler Halimon	50	350	196	88	.449	32	10	.313	86	18	34	0	186	3.7
Craig Raymond	27	177	64	22	.344	17	11	.647	68	8	46	2	55	2.0

PHOENIX SUNS

Player	G.	Min.	FGA	FGM	Pct.	FTA	FTM	Pct.	Reb.	Ast.	PF	Disq.	Pts.	Avg.
Gail Goodrich	81	3236	1746	718	.411	663	495	.747	437	518	253	3	1931	23.8
Dick Van Arsdale	80	3388	1386	612	.442	644	454	.705	548	385	245	2	1678	21.0
Dick Snyder	81	2108	846	399	.472	255	185	.725	328	211	213	2	983	12.1
Gary Gregor	80	2182	963	400	.415	131	85	.649	711	96	249	2	885	11.1
Jim Fox (Tot.)	76	2354	677	318	.470	267	191	.715	818	166	266	6	827	10.9
Jim Fox (Phoe.)	51	1979	581	273	.470	214	157	.734	679	143	210	5	703	13.8
Stan McKenzie	80	1569	618	264	.427	287	219	.763	251	123	191	3	747	9.3
Bob Warlick (Tot.)	66	997	509	213	.418	142	87	.613	152	132	122	0	513	7.8
Bob Warlick (Phoe.)	63	975	501	212	.423	137	83	.606	151	131	119	0	507	8.0
George Wilson°	41	1294	481	191	.397	151	93	.616	505	76	145	4	475	11.6
Neil Johnson	80	1319	368	177	.481	177	110	.621	396	134	214	3	464	5.8
Dave Lattin	68	987	366	150	.410	172	109	.634	323	48	163	5	409	6.2
McCoy McLemore°	31	710	366	141	.385	110	85	.773	168	50	73	1	367	11.8
Rodney Knowles	8	40	14	4	.286	3	1	.333	9	0	10	0	9	1.1
Ed Biedenbach	7	18	6	0	.000	6	4	.667	2	3	1	0	4	0.6

SAN DIEGO ROCKETS

Player	G.	Min.	FGA	FGM	Pct.	FTA	FTM	Pct.	Reb.	Ast.	PF	Disq.	Pts.	Avg.
Elvin Hayes	82	3695	2082	930	.447	746	467	.626	1406	113	266	2	2327	28.4
Don Kojis	81	3130	1582	687	.434	596	446	.748	776	214	303	6	1820	22.5
John Block	78	2489	1061	448	.422	400	299	.748	703	141	249	0	1195	15.3
Jim Barnett	80	2346	1093	465	.425	310	233	.752	362	339	240	2	1163	14.5
Toby Kimball	76	1680	537	239	.445	250	117	.468	669	90	216	6	595	7.8
Stuart Lautz	73	1378	482	220	.456	167	129	.772	236	99	178	0	569	7.8
Art Williams	79	1987	592	227	.383	149	105	.705	364	524	238	0	559	7.1
Pat Riley	56	1027	498	202	.406	134	90	.672	112	136	146	1	494	8.8
Rick Adelman	77	1448	449	177	.394	204	131	.642	216	238	158	1	485	6.3
Henry Finkel	35	332	111	49	.441	41	31	.756	107	21	53	1	129	3.7
John Trapp	25	142	80	29	.363	29	19	.655	49	5	38	0	77	3.1
Harry Barnes	22	126	64	18	.281	13	7	.538	26	5	25	0	43	2.0

SAN FRANCISCO WARRIORS

Player	G.	Min.	FGA	FGM	Pct.	FTA	FTM	Pct.	Reb.	Ast.	PF	Disq.	Pts.	Avg.
Jeff Mullins	78	2916	1517	697	.459	452	381	.843	460	339	251	4	1775	22.8
Rudy LaRusso	75	2782	1349	553	.410	559	444	.794	624	159	268	9	1550	20.7
Nate Thurmond	71	3208	1394	571	.410	621	382	.615	1402	253	171	0	1524	21.5
Joe Ellis	74	1731	939	371	.395	201	147	.731	481	130	258	13	889	12.0
Clyde Lee	65	2237	674	268	.398	256	160	.625	897	82	225	1	696	10.7
Bill Turner	79	1486	535	222	.415	230	175	.761	380	67	231	6	619	7.8
Ron Williams	75	1472	567	238	.420	142	109	.768	178	247	176	3	585	7.8
Al Attles	51	1516	359	162	.451	149	95	.638	181	306	183	3	419	8.2
Jim King	46	1010	394	137	.348	108	78	.722	120	123	99	1	352	7.7
Bob Lewis	62	756	290	113	.390	113	83	.735	114	76	117	0	309	5.0
Dale Schlueter	31	559	157	68	.433	82	45	.549	216	30	81	3	181	5.8
Bob Allen	27	232	43	14	.326	36	20	.556	56	10	27	0	48	1.8

SEATTLE SUPERSONICS

Player	G.	Min.	FGA	FGM	Pct.	FTA	FTM	Pct.	Reb.	Ast.	PF	Disq.	Pts.	Avg.
Bob Rule	82	3104	1655	776	.469	606	413	.682	941	141	322	8	1965	24.0
Lennie Wilkens	82	3463	1462	644	.440	710	547	.770	511	674	294	8	1835	22.4
Tom Meschery	82	2673	1019	462	.453	299	220	.736	822	194	304	7	1144	14.0
Art Harris	80	2556	1054	416	.395	251	161	.641	301	258	326	14	993	12.4
John Tresvant (Tot.)	77	2482	820	380	.463	330	202	.612	686	166	300	9	962	12.5
John Tresvant (Sea.)	26	801	289	141	.488	107	72	.673	267	63	107	4	354	13.6
Bob Kauffman	82	1660	496	219	.442	289	203	.702	484	83	252	8	641	7.8
Al Tucker°	56	1259	544	235	.432	171	109	.637	317	55	111	0	579	10.3
Joe Kennedy	72	1241	411	174	.395	124	98	.790	241	60	158	2	446	6.2
Tom Kron	76	1124	372	146	.392	137	96	.701	212	191	179	2	388	5.1
Erwin Mueller (Tot.)	78	1355	384	144	.375	162	89	.549	297	186	143	1	377	4.8
Erwin Mueller (Sea.)	26	483	160	69	.431	72	43	.597	104	62	45	0	181	7.0
Rod Thorn	29	567	283	131	.463	97	71	.732	83	80	58	0	333	11.5
Dorie Murrey	38	465	194	75	.387	97	62	.639	149	21	81	1	212	5.6
Al Hairston	39	274	114	38	.333	14	8	.571	36	38	35	0	84	2.2
Plummer Lott	23	160	66	17	.258	5	2	.400	30	7	9	0	36	1.6

°Finished season with another team.

PLAYOFF RESULTS

EASTERN DIVISION SEMIFINALS

New York 4, Baltimore 0

Mar. 27—New York 113 at Baltimore 101
Mar. 29—Baltimore 91 at New York................................107
Mar. 30—New York 119 at Baltimore 116
Apr. 2—Baltimore 108 at New York 115

WESTERN DIVISION SEMIFINALS

Los Angeles 4, San Francisco 2

Mar. 26—San Francisco 99 at Los Angeles 94
Mar. 28—San Francisco 107 at Los Angeles................................101
Mar. 31—Los Angeles 115 at San Francisco................................98
Apr. 2—Los Angeles 103 at San Francisco................................88
Apr. 4—San Francisco 98 at Los Angeles................................103
Apr. 5—Los Angeles 118 at San Francisco................................78

Boston 4, Philadelphia 1

Mar. 26—Boston 114 at Philadelphia 100
Mar. 28—Philadelphia 103 at Boston 134
Mar. 30—Boston 125 at Philadelphia 118
Apr. 1—Philadelphia 119 at Boston 116
Apr. 4—Boston 93 at Philadelphia 90

Atlanta 4, San Diego 2

Mar. 27—San Diego 98 at Atlanta 107
Mar. 29—San Diego 114 at Atlanta................................116
Apr. 1—Atlanta 97 at San Diego................................104
Apr. 4—Atlanta 112 at San Diego................................114
Apr. 6—San Diego 101 at Atlanta................................112
Apr. 7—Atlanta 108 at San Diego................................106

EASTERN DIVISION FINALS

Boston 4, New York 2

Apr. 6—Boston 108 at New York................................100
Apr. 9—New York 97 at Boston................................112
Apr. 10—Boston 91 at New York................................101
Apr. 13—New York 96 at Boston................................97
Apr. 14—Boston 104 at New York................................112
Apr. 18—New York 105 at Boston................................106

WESTERN DIVISION FINALS

Los Angeles 4, Atlanta 1

Apr. 11—Atlanta 93 at Los Angeles 95
Apr. 13—Atlanta 102 at Los Angeles................................104
Apr. 15—Los Angeles 80 at Atlanta................................99
Apr. 17—Los Angeles 100 at Atlanta................................85
Apr. 20—Atlanta 96 at Los Angeles................................104

WORLD CHAMPIONSHIP SERIES

Boston 4, Los Angeles 3

Apr. 23—Boston 118 at Los Angeles................................120
Apr. 25—Boston 112 at Los Angeles................................118
Apr. 27—Los Angeles 105 at Boston................................111
Apr. 29—Los Angeles 88 at Boston................................89
May 1—Boston 104 at Los Angeles................................117
May 3—Los Angeles 90 at Boston................................99
May 5—Boston 108 at Los Angeles................................106

1967-68 NBA STATISTICS

1967-68 NBA CHAMPION BOSTON CELTICS

Front row (left to right): Sam Jones, Larry Siegfried, General Manager Red Auerbach, Chairman of Board Marvin Kratter, President Clarence Adams, Coach Bill Russell, John Havlicek. Back row: Trainer Joe DeLauri, Rick Weitzman, Tom Thacker, Tom Sanders, Bailey Howell, Wayne Embry, Don Nelson, John Jones, Mal Graham.

FINAL STANDINGS

EASTERN DIVISION

Team	Phil.	Bos.	N.Y.	Det.	Cin.	Balt.	St.L.	L.A.	S.F.	Chi.	Sea.	S.D.	W.	L.	Pct.	G.B.
Philadelphia	..	4	5	7	5	8	5	5	4	6	7	6	62	20	.756	....
Boston	4	..	6	6	3	5	4	4	4	5	6	7	54	28	.659	8
New York	3	2	..	4	5	5	1	3	5	5	4	6	43	39	.524	19
Detroit	1	2	4	..	4	4	4	2	4	4	6	5	40	42	.488	22
Cincinnati	3	5	3	4	..	3	1	1	4	2	6	7	39	43	.476	23
Baltimore	0	3	3	4	5	..	2	3	2	2	5	7	36	46	.439	26

WESTERN DIVISION

St. Louis	2	3	6	3	6	5	..	2	7	7	8	7	56	26	.683	....
Los Angeles	2	3	4	5	6	4	6	..	4	7	4	7	52	30	.634	4
San Francisco	3	3	2	3	3	5	1	4	..	6	7	6	43	39	.524	13
Chicago	1	2	2	3	5	5	1	1	2	..	3	4	29	53	.354	27
Seattle	0	1	3	1	1	2	0	4	1	5	..	5	23	59	.280	33
San Diego	1	0	1	2	0	0	1	1	2	4	3	..	15	67	.183	41

HOME-ROAD-NEUTRAL RECORDS OF ALL TEAMS

	Home	Road	Neutral	Total		Home	Road	Neutral	Total
Baltimore	17- 19	12- 23	7- 4	36- 46	Philadelphia	27- 8	25- 12	10- 0	62- 20
Boston	28- 9	20- 16	6- 3	54- 28	St. Louis	25- 7	22- 13	9- 6	56- 26
Chicago	11- 22	12- 23	6- 8	29- 53	San Diego	8- 33	4- 26	3- 8	15- 67
Cincinnati	18- 12	13- 23	8- 8	39- 43	San Francisco	27- 14	16- 23	0- 2	43- 39
Detroit	21- 11	12- 23	7- 8	40- 42	Seattle	9- 19	7- 24	7-16	23- 59
Los Angeles	30- 11	18- 19	4- 0	52- 30	Total	241-182	182-241	69-69	492-492
New York	20- 17	21- 16	2- 6	43- 39					

TEAM STATISTICS

Team	G.	FGA	FGM	Pct.	FTA	FTM	Pct.	Reb.	Ast.	PF	Disq.	For	Agst.	Pt.Dif.
Philadelphia	82	8414	3965	.471	3338	2121	.635	5914	2197	1851	23	122.6	114.0	+8.6
Los Angeles	82	8031	3827	.477	3143	2283	.726	5225	1983	2152	30	121.2	115.6	+5.6
Boston	82	8371	3686	.440	2983	2151	.721	5666	1798	2147	26	116.1	112.0	+4.1
St. Louis	82	7765	3504	.451	3111	2258	.726	5325	1988	2046	36	113.0	110.3	+2.7
New York	82	8070	3682	.456	3042	2159	.710	5122	1967	2364	25	116.1	114.3	+1.8
Baltimore	82	8428	3691	.438	2994	2245	.750	5431	1534	2127	38	117.4	117.8	−0.4
San Francisco	82	8587	3632	.423	3153	2334	.740	6029	1901	2265	52	117.0	117.6	−0.6
Cincinnati	82	7864	3679	.468	2892	2204	.762	5129	2048	2016	29	116.6	117.4	−0.8
Detroit	82	8386	3755	.448	3129	2215	.708	5452	1700	2240	52	116.6	118.6	−2.0
Chicago	82	8138	3488	.429	2718	2006	.738	5117	1527	2130	42	109.5	113.5	−4.0
Seattle	82	8593	3772	.439	3042	2188	.719	5338	1998	2372	49	118.7	125.1	−6.4
San Diego	82	8547	3466	.417	2929	2083	.711	5418	1837	2188	27	112.4	121.0	−8.6

INDIVIDUAL LEADERS

POINTS

Player	G.	FG	FT	Pts.	Avg.	Player	G.	FG	FT	Pts.	Avg.
Bing, Detroit	79	835	472	2142	27.1	Havlicek, Boston	82	666	368	1700	20.7
Baylor, Los Angeles	77	757	488	2002	26.0	Reed, New York	81	659	367	1685	20.8
Chamberlain, Phila.	82	819	354	1992	24.3	Boozer, Chicago	77	622	411	1655	21.5
Monroe, Baltimore	82	742	507	1991	24.3	Wilkens, St. Louis	82	546	546	1638	20.0
Greer, Philadelphia	82	777	422	1976	24.1	Howell, Boston	82	643	335	1621	19.8
Robertson, Cinn.	65	660	576	1896	29.2	Clark, Los Angeles	81	628	356	1612	19.9
Hazzard, Seattle	79	733	428	1894	23.9	S. Jones, Boston	73	621	311	1553	21.3
Lucas, Cincinnati	82	707	346	1760	21.4	Mullins, San Fran.	79	610	273	1493	18.9
Beaty, St. Louis	82	639	455	1733	21.1	Rule, Seattle	82	568	348	1484	18.1
LaRusso, San Fran.	79	602	522	1726	21.8	Walker, Phila.	82	539	387	1465	17.9

FIELD GOALS
(Minimum 220 FGM)

Player	FGA	FGM	Pct.
Wilt Chamberlain, Philadelphia	1377	819	.595
Walt Bellamy, New York	944	511	.541
Jerry Lucas, Cincinnati	1361	707	.519
Jerry West, Los Angeles	926	476	.514
Len Chappell, Cin.-Det.	458	235	.513
Oscar Robertson, Cincinnati	1321	660	.500
Tom Hawkins, Los Angeles	779	389	.499
Terry Dischinger, Detroit	797	394	.494
Don Nelson, Boston	632	312	.494
Henry Finkel, San Diego	492	242	.492

ASSISTS

Player	G.	No.	Avg.
Wilt Chamberlain, Phila.	82	702	8.6
Lenny Wilkens, St. Louis	82	679	8.3
Oscar Robertson, Cincinnati	65	633	9.7
Dave Bing, Detroit	79	509	6.4
Walt Hazzard, Seattle	79	493	6.2
Art Williams, San Diego	79	391	4.9
Al Attles, San Francisco	67	390	5.8
John Havlicek, Boston	82	384	4.7
Guy Rodgers, Chi.-Cinn.	79	380	4.8
Hal Greer, Philadelphia	82	372	4.5

FREE THROWS
(Minimum 220 FTM)

Player	FTA	FTM	Pct.
Oscar Robertson, Cincinnati	660	576	.873
Larry Siegfried, Boston	272	236	.868
Dave Gambee, San Diego	379	321	.847
Fred Hetzel, San Francisco	474	395	.833
Adrian Smith, Cincinnati	386	320	.829
Sam Jones, Boston	376	311	.827
Flynn Robinson, Cin.-Chi.	351	288	.821
John Havlicek, Boston	453	368	.812
Jerry West, Los Angeles	482	391	.811
Cazzie Russell, New York	349	282	.808

REBOUNDS

Player	G.	No.	Avg.
Wilt Chamberlain, Phila.	82	1952	23.8
Jerry Lucas, Cincinnati	82	1560	19.0
Bill Russell, Boston	78	1451	18.6
Clyde Lee, San Francisco	82	1141	13.9
Nate Thurmond, San Francisco	51	1121	22.0
Ray Scott, Baltimore	81	1111	13.7
Bill Bridges, St. Louis	82	1102	13.4
Dave DeBusschere, Detroit	80	1081	13.5
Willis Reed, New York	81	1073	13.2
Walt Bellamy, New York	82	961	11.7

TEAM-BY-TEAM INDIVIDUAL STATISTICS

BALTIMORE BULLETS

Player	G.	Min.	FGA	FGM	Pct.	FTA	FTM	Pct.	Reb.	Ast.	PF	Disq.	Pts.	Avg.
Earl Monroe	82	3012	1637	742	.453	649	507	.781	465	349	282	3	1991	24.3
Ray Scott	81	2924	1189	490	.412	447	348	.779	1111	167	252	2	1328	16.4
Kevin Loughery	77	2297	1127	458	.406	392	305	.778	247	256	301	13	1221	15.9
Gus Johnson	60	2271	1033	482	.467	270	180	.667	782	159	223	7	1144	19.1
Jack Marin	82	2037	932	429	.460	314	250	.796	473	110	246	4	1108	13.5
Leroy Ellis	78	2719	800	380	.475	286	207	.724	862	158	256	5	967	12.4
Don Ohl*	39	1096	536	232	.433	148	114	.770	113	84	91	0	578	14.8
John Egan	67	930	415	163	.393	183	142	.776	112	134	127	0	468	7.0
Bob Ferry	59	841	311	128	.412	117	73	.624	186	61	92	0	329	5.6
Earl Manning	71	951	259	112	.432	99	60	.606	375	32	153	3	284	4.0
Stan McKenzie	50	653	182	73	.401	88	58	.659	121	24	98	1	204	4.1
Tom Workman (Tot.)	20	95	40	19	.475	23	18	.783	25	3	17	0	56	2.8
Tom Workman (Balt.)	1	10	2	0	.000	1	1	1.000	1	0	3	0	1	1.0
Roland West	4	14	5	2	.400	0	0	.000	5	0	3	0	4	1.0

BOSTON CELTICS

Player	G.	Min.	FGA	FGM	Pct.	FTA	FTM	Pct.	Reb.	Ast.	PF	Disq.	Pts.	Avg.
John Havlicek	82	2921	1551	666	.429	453	368	.812	546	384	237	2	1700	20.7
Bailey Howell	82	2801	1336	643	.481	461	335	.727	805	133	285	4	1621	19.8
Sam Jones	73	2408	1348	621	.461	376	311	.827	357	216	181	0	1553	21.3
Bill Russell	78	2953	858	365	.425	460	247	.537	1451	357	242	2	977	12.5
Don Nelson	82	1498	632	312	.494	268	195	.728	431	103	178	1	819	10.0
Tom Sanders	78	1981	691	296	.428	255	200	.784	454	100	300	12	792	10.2
Larry Siegfried	62	1937	629	261	.415	272	236	.868	215	289	194	2	758	12.2
Wayne Embry	78	1088	483	193	.400	185	109	.589	321	52	174	1	495	6.3
Mal Graham	78	786	272	117	.430	88	56	.636	94	61	123	0	290	6.0
Tom Thacker	65	782	272	114	.419	84	43	.512	161	69	165	2	271	4.2
John Jones	51	475	253	86	.340	68	42	.618	114	26	60	0	214	4.2
Rick Weitzman	25	75	46	12	.261	13	9	.692	10	8	8	0	33	1.3

CHICAGO BULLS

Player	G.	Min.	FGA	FGM	Pct.	FTA	FTM	Pct.	Reb.	Ast.	PF	Disq.	Pts.	Avg.
Bob Boozer	77	2988	1265	622	.492	535	411	.768	756	121	229	1	1655	21.5
Flynn Robinson (Tot.)	75	2046	1010	444	.440	351	288	.821	272	219	184	1	1176	15.7
Flynn Robinson (Chi.)	73	2030	1000	441	.441	344	285	.828	268	214	180	1	1167	16.0
Jerry Sloan	77	2454	959	369	.385	386	289	.749	591	229	291	11	1027	13.3
Jim Washington	82	2525	915	418	.457	274	187	.682	825	113	233	1	1023	12.5
McCoy McLemore	76	2040	940	374	.398	276	215	.779	430	130	219	4	963	12.7
Keith Erickson	78	2257	940	377	.401	257	194	.755	423	267	276	15	948	12.2
Barry Clemens	78	1631	670	301	.449	170	123	.724	375	98	223	4	725	9.3
Clem Haskins	76	1477	650	273	.420	202	133	.658	227	165	175	1	679	8.9

Player	G.	Min.	FGA	FGM	Pct.	FTA	FTM	Pct.	Reb.	Ast.	PF	Disq.	Pts.	Avg.
Jim Barnes (Tot.)	79	1425	499	221	.443	191	133	.696	415	55	262	7	575	7.3
Jim Barnes (Chi.)	37	712	264	120	.455	103	74	.718	204	28	128	3	314	8.5
Dave Schellhase	42	301	138	47	.341	38	20	.526	47	37	43	0	114	2.7
Guy Rodgers*	4	129	54	16	.296	11	9	.818	14	28	11	0	41	10.3
Craig Spitzer	10	44	21	8	.381	3	2	.667	24	0	4	0	18	1.8
Ken Wilburn	3	26	9	5	.556	4	1	.250	10	2	4	0	11	3.3
Jim Burns	3	11	7	2	.286	0	0	.000	2	1	1	0	4	1.3
Erwin Mueller*	35	815	235	91	.387	82	46	.561	167	76	78	1	228	6.5
Reggie Harding	14	305	71	27	.338	33	17	.515	94	18	35	0	65	4.6

CINCINNATI ROYALS

Player	G.	Min.	FGA	FGM	Pct.	FTA	FTM	Pct.	Reb.	Ast.	PF	Disq.	Pts.	Avg.
Oscar Robertson	65	2765	1321	660	.500	660	576	.873	391	633	199	2	1896	29.2
Jerry Lucas	82	3619	1361	707	.519	445	346	.778	1560	251	243	3	1760	21.4
Connie Dierking	81	2637	1164	544	.467	310	237	.765	766	191	315	6	1325	16.4
Adrian Smith	82	2783	1035	480	.464	386	320	.829	185	272	259	6	1280	15.6
John Tresvant (Tot.)	85	2473	867	396	.457	384	250	.651	709	160	344	18	1042	12.3
John Tresvant (Cin.)	30	802	270	121	.448	106	67	.632	169	46	105	3	309	10.3
Harold Hairston*	48	1625	630	317	.503	296	203	.686	355	58	127	1	837	17.4
Tom Van Arsdale (Tot.)	77	1514	545	211	.387	252	188	.746	225	155	202	5	610	7.9
Tom Van Arsdale (Cin.)	27	682	238	97	.408	116	87	.750	93	76	83	2	281	10.4
Bob Love	72	1068	455	193	.424	114	78	.684	209	55	141	1	464	6.4
Walt Wesley	66	918	404	188	.465	152	76	.500	281	34	168	2	452	6.8
Guy Rodgers (Tot.)	79	1546	426	148	.347	133	107	.805	150	380	167	1	403	5.1
Guy Rodgers (Cin.)	75	1417	372	132	.355	122	98	.803	136	352	156	1	362	4.8
Bill Dinwiddie	67	871	358	141	.394	102	62	.608	237	31	122	2	344	5.1
Gary Gray	44	276	134	49	.366	10	7	.700	23	26	48	0	105	2.4
Jim Fox*	31	244	79	32	.405	56	36	.643	95	12	34	0	100	3.2
Len Chappell*	10	65	30	15	.500	10	8	.800	15	5	6	0	38	3.8
Flynn Robinson*	2	16	10	3	.300	7	3	.429	4	5	4	0	9	4.5
Al Jackson	2	17	3	0	.000	0	0	.000	0	1	6	0	0	0.0

DETROIT PISTONS

Player	G.	Min.	FGA	FGM	Pct.	FTA	FTM	Pct.	Reb.	Ast.	PF	Disq.	Pts.	Avg.
Dave Bing	79	3209	1893	835	.441	668	472	.707	373	509	254	2	2142	27.1
Dave DeBusschere	80	3125	1295	573	.442	435	289	.664	1081	181	304	3	1435	17.9
Eddie Miles	76	2303	1180	561	.475	369	282	.764	264	215	200	3	1404	18.5
Harold Hairston (Tot.)	74	2517	987	481	.487	522	365	.699	617	95	199	1	1327	17.9
Harold Hairston (Det.)	26	892	357	164	.459	226	162	.717	262	37	72	0	490	18.8
Terry Dischinger	78	1936	797	394	.494	311	237	.762	483	114	247	6	1025	13.1
John Tresvant*	55	1671	597	275	.461	278	183	.658	540	114	239	15	733	13.3
Jim Walker	81	1585	733	289	.394	175	134	.766	135	226	204	1	712	8.8
Len Chappell (Tot.)	67	1064	458	235	.513	194	138	.711	361	53	119	1	608	9.1
Len Chappell (Det.)	57	999	428	220	.514	184	130	.707	346	48	113	1	570	10.0
Joe Strawder	73	2029	456	206	.452	215	139	.647	685	85	312	18	551	7.5
Tom Van Arsdale*	50	832	307	114	.371	136	101	.743	132	79	119	3	329	6.6
Jim Fox (Tot.)	55	624	161	66	.410	108	66	.611	230	29	85	0	198	3.6
Jim Fox (Det.)	24	380	82	34	.415	52	30	.577	135	17	51	0	98	4.1
George Patterson	59	559	133	44	.331	38	32	.835	159	51	85	0	120	2.0
Paul Long	16	93	51	23	.451	15	11	.733	15	12	13	0	57	3.6
Sonny Dove	28	162	75	22	.293	26	12	.462	52	11	27	0	56	2.0
George Carter	1	5	2	1	.500	1	1	1.000	0	1	0	0	3	3.0

LOS ANGELES LAKERS

Player	G.	Min.	FGA	FGM	Pct.	FTA	FTM	Pct.	Reb.	Ast.	PF	Disq.	Pts.	Avg.
Elgin Baylor	77	3029	1709	757	.443	621	488	.786	941	355	232	0	2002	26.0
Archie Clark	81	3039	1309	628	.480	481	356	.740	342	353	235	3	1612	19.9
Jerry West	51	1919	926	476	.514	482	391	.811	294	310	152	1	1343	26.3
Gail Goodrich	79	2057	812	395	.486	392	302	.770	199	205	228	2	1092	13.8
Mel Counts	82	1739	808	384	.475	254	190	.748	732	139	309	6	958	11.7
Tom Hawkins	78	2463	779	389	.499	229	125	.546	458	117	289	7	903	11.6
Darrall Imhoff	82	2271	613	293	.478	286	177	.619	893	206	264	3	763	9.3
Fred Crawford (Tot.)	69	1182	507	224	.442	179	111	.620	195	141	171	1	559	8.1
Fred Crawford (L.A.)	38	756	330	159	.482	120	74	.617	112	95	104	1	392	10.3
Erwin Mueller (L.A.)	39	973	254	132	.520	103	61	.592	222	78	86	2	325	8.3
Erwin Mueller (Tot.)	74	1788	489	223	.456	185	107	.578	389	154	164	3	553	7.5
Jim Barnes*	42	713	235	101	.430	88	59	.670	211	27	134	4	261	6.2
John Wetzel	38	434	119	52	.437	46	35	.761	84	51	55	0	139	3.7
Dennis Hamilton	44	378	108	54	.500	13	13	1.000	72	30	46	0	121	2.8
Cliff Anderson	18	94	29	7	.241	28	12	.429	11	17	18	1	26	1.4

NEW YORK KNICKERBOCKERS

Player	G.	Min.	FGA	FGM	Pct.	FTA	FTM	Pct.	Reb.	Ast.	PF	Disq.	Pts.	Avg.
Willis Reed	81	2879	1346	659	.490	509	367	.721	1073	159	343	12	1685	20.8
Dick Barnett	81	2488	1159	559	.482	440	343	.780	238	242	222	0	1461	18.0
Cazzie Russell	82	2296	1192	551	.462	349	282	.808	374	195	223	2	1384	16.9
Walt Bellamy	82	2695	944	511	.541	529	350	.662	961	164	259	3	1372	16.7
Dick Van Arsdale	78	2348	725	316	.436	339	227	.670	424	230	225	0	859	11.0
Walt Frazier	74	1588	568	256	.451	235	154	.655	313	305	199	2	666	9.0
Howard Komives	78	1660	631	233	.369	161	132	.820	168	246	170	1	598	7.7
Phil Jackson	75	1093	455	182	.400	168	99	.589	338	55	212	3	463	6.2
Bill Bradley	45	874	341	142	.416	104	76	.731	113	137	138	2	360	8.0
Emmett Bryant	77	968	291	112	.385	86	59	.686	133	134	173	0	283	3.7
Fred Crawford*	31	426	177	65	.367	59	37	.627	83	46	67	0	167	5.4
Nate Bowman	42	272	134	52	.388	15	10	.667	113	20	69	0	114	2.7
Neil Johnson	43	286	106	44	.415	48	23	.479	75	33	63	0	111	2.6
Jim Caldwell	2	7	1	0	.000	0	0	.000	1	1	1	0	0	0.0

Detroit's Dave Bing led the NBA in scoring with a 27.1 average in 1967-68.

PHILADELPHIA 76ers

Player	G.	Min.	FGA	FGM	Pct.	FTA	FTM	Pct.	Reb.	Ast.	PF	Disq.	Pts.	Avg.
Wilt Chamberlain	82	3836	1377	819	.595	932	354	.380	1952	702	160	0	1992	24.3
Hal Greer	82	3263	1626	777	.478	549	422	.769	444	372	289	6	1976	24.1
Chet Walker	82	2623	1172	539	.460	533	387	.726	607	157	252	3	1465	17.9
Bill Cunningham	74	2076	1178	516	.438	509	368	.723	562	187	260	3	1400	18.9
Wally Jones	77	2058	1040	413	.397	202	159	.787	219	245	225	5	985	12.8
Lucious Jackson	82	2570	927	401	.433	231	166	.719	872	139	287	6	968	11.8
John Green (Tot.)	77	1440	676	310	.459	295	139	.471	545	80	163	3	759	9.9
John Green (Phila.)	35	367	150	69	.460	83	39	.470	122	21	51	0	177	5.1
Matt Guokas	82	1612	393	190	.483	152	118	.776	185	191	172	0	498	6.1
Bill Melchionni	71	758	336	146	.435	47	33	.702	104	105	75	0	325	4.6
Larry Costello	28	492	148	67	.453	81	67	.827	51	68	62	0	201	7.2
Ron Filipek	19	73	47	18	.383	14	7	.500	25	7	12	0	43	2.3
Jim Reid	6	52	20	10	.500	5	1	.200	11	3	6	0	21	3.5

ST. LOUIS HAWKS

Player	G.	Min.	FGA	FGM	Pct.	FTA	FTM	Pct.	Reb.	Ast.	PF	Disq.	Pts.	Avg.
Zelmo Beaty	82	3068	1310	639	.488	573	455	.794	959	174	295	6	1733	21.1
Len Wilkens	82	3169	1246	546	.438	711	546	.768	438	679	255	3	1638	20.0
Joe Caldwell	79	2641	1219	564	.463	290	165	.569	338	240	208	1	1293	16.4
Bill Bridges	82	3197	1009	466	.462	484	347	.717	1102	253	366	12	1279	15.6
Paul Silas	82	2652	871	399	.458	424	299	.705	958	162	243	4	1097	13.4
Don Ohl (Tot.)	70	1919	891	393	.441	254	197	.776	175	157	184	1	983	14.0
Don Ohl (St.L.)	31	823	355	161	.454	106	83	.783	62	73	93	1	405	13.1
Dick Snyder	75	1622	613	257	.419	167	129	.772	194	164	215	5	643	8.6
Lou Hudson	46	966	500	227	.454	164	120	.732	193	65	113	2	574	12.5
Gene Tormohlen	77	714	262	98	.374	56	33	.589	226	68	94	0	229	3.0
George Lehman	55	497	172	59	.343	43	35	.814	44	93	54	0	153	2.8
Jim Davis	50	394	139	61	.439	64	25	.391	123	13	85	2	147	2.9
Tom Workman°	19	85	38	19	.500	22	17	.773	24	3	14	0	55	2.9
Jay Miller	8	52	31	8	.258	7	4	.571	7	1	11	0	20	2.5

SAN DIEGO ROCKETS

Player	G.	Min.	FGA	FGM	Pct.	FTA	FTM	Pct.	Reb.	Ast.	PF	Disq.	Pts.	Avg.
Don Kojis	69	2548	1189	530	.446	413	300	.726	710	176	259	5	1360	19.7
Dave Gambee	80	1755	853	375	.440	379	321	.847	464	93	253	5	1071	13.4
John Block	52	1805	865	366	.423	394	316	.802	571	71	189	3	1048	20.2
Toby Kimball	81	2519	894	354	.396	306	181	.592	947	147	273	3	889	11.0
Jon McGlocklin	65	1876	757	316	.417	180	156	.867	199	178	117	0	788	12.1
John Barnhill	75	1883	700	295	.421	234	154	.658	173	259	143	1	744	9.9
Art Williams	79	1739	718	265	.369	165	113	.685	286	391	204	0	643	8.1
Pat Riley	80	1263	660	250	.379	202	128	.634	177	138	205	1	628	7.9
Henry Finkel	53	1116	492	242	.492	191	131	.686	375	72	175	5	615	11.6
John Green*	42	1073	526	241	.458	212	100	.472	423	59	112	3	582	13.9
Jim Barnett	47	1068	456	179	.393	118	84	.712	155	134	101	0	442	9.4
Nick Jones	42	603	232	86	.371	69	55	.797	67	89	84	0	227	5.4
Charles Acton	23	195	74	29	.392	29	19	.655	47	11	35	0	77	3.3
Jim Ware	30	228	97	25	.258	34	23	.676	77	7	28	1	73	2.4
Tyrone Britt	11	84	34	13	.382	3	2	.667	15	12	10	0	28	2.5

SAN FRANCISCO WARRIORS

Player	G.	Min.	FGA	FGM	Pct.	FTA	FTM	Pct.	Reb.	Ast.	PF	Disq.	Pts.	Avg.
Rudy LaRusso	79	2819	1389	602	.433	661	522	.790	741	182	337	14	1726	21.8
Jeff Mullins	79	2805	1391	610	.439	344	273	.794	447	351	271	2	1493	18.9
Fred Hetzel	77	2394	1287	533	.414	474	395	.833	546	131	262	7	1461	19.0
Nate Thurmond	51	2222	929	382	.411	438	282	.644	1121	215	137	1	1046	20.5
Clyde Lee	82	2699	894	373	.417	335	229	.684	1141	135	331	10	975	11.9
Jim King	54	1743	800	340	.425	268	217	.810	243	226	172	1	897	16.6
Al Attles	67	1992	540	252	.467	216	150	.694	276	390	284	9	654	9.8
Bob Warlick	69	1320	610	257	.421	171	97	.567	264	159	164	1	611	8.9
Joe Ellis	51	624	302	111	.368	50	32	.640	195	37	83	2	254	5.0
Bob Lewis	41	342	151	59	.391	79	61	.772	56	41	40	0	179	4.4
Bill Turner	42	482	157	68	.433	60	36	.600	155	16	74	1	172	4.1
Dave Lattin	44	257	102	37	.363	33	23	.697	104	14	94	4	97	2.2
George Lee	10	106	35	8	.229	24	17	.708	27	4	16	0	33	3.3

SEATTLE SUPERSONICS

Player	G.	Min.	FGA	FGM	Pct.	FTA	FTM	Pct.	Reb.	Ast.	PF	Disq.	Pts.	Avg.
Walt Hazzard	79	2666	1662	733	.441	553	428	.774	332	493	246	3	1894	23.9
Bob Rule	82	2424	1162	568	.489	529	348	.658	776	99	316	10	1484	18.1
Tom Meschery	82	2857	1008	473	.469	345	244	.707	840	193	323	14	1190	14.5
Al Tucker	81	2368	989	437	.442	263	186	.707	605	111	262	6	1060	13.1
Rod Thorn	66	1668	835	377	.451	342	252	.737	265	230	117	1	1006	15.2
Bob Weiss	82	1614	686	295	.430	254	213	.839	150	342	137	0	803	9.8
Tom Kron	76	1794	699	277	.396	233	184	.790	355	281	231	4	738	9.7
Dorie Murrey	81	1494	484	211	.436	244	168	.689	600	68	273	7	590	7.3
George Wilson	77	1236	498	179	.359	155	109	.703	470	56	218	1	467	6.1
Bud Olsen	73	897	285	130	.456	62	17	.274	204	75	136	1	277	3.8
Henry Akin	36	259	137	46	.336	31	20	.645	57	14	48	1	112	3.1
Plummer Lott	44	478	148	46	.311	31	19	.613	93	36	65	1	111	2.5

*Finished season with another team.

PLAYOFF RESULTS

EASTERN DIVISION SEMIFINALS
Philadelphia 4, New York 2

Mar. 22—New York 110 at Philadelphia 118
Mar. 23—Philadelphia 117 at New York 128
Mar. 27—New York 132 at Philadelphia **138
Mar. 30—Philadelphia 98 at New York.......................................107
Mar. 31—New York 107 at Philadelphia.................................123
Apr. 1—Philadelphia 113 at New York.......................................97

Boston 4, Detroit 2

Mar. 24—Detroit 116 at Boston 123
Mar. 25—Boston 116 at Detroit 126
Mar. 27—Detroit 109 at Boston...98
Mar. 28—Boston 135 at Detroit 110
Mar. 31—Detroit 96 at Boston...110
Apr. 1—Boston 111 at Detroit 103

EASTERN DIVISION FINALS
Boston 4, Philadelphia 3

Apr. 5—Boston 127 at Philadelphia...118
Apr. 10—Philadelphia 115 at Boston 106
Apr. 11—Boston 114 at Philadelphia...122
Apr. 14—Philadelphia 110 at Boston.......................................105
Apr. 15—Boston 122 at Philadelphia...104
Apr. 17—Philadelphia 106 at Boston.......................................114
Apr. 19—Boston 100 at Philadelphia...96

WESTERN DIVISION SEMIFINALS
San Francisco 4, St. Louis 2

Mar. 22—San Francisco 111 at St. Louis................106
Mar. 23—San Francisco 103 at St. Louis.................111
Mar. 26—St. Louis 109 at San Francisco.................124
Mar. 29—St. Louis 107 at San Francisco.................108
Mar. 31—San Francisco 103 at St. Louis.................129
Apr. 2—St. Louis 106 at San Francisco..................111

Los Angeles 4, Chicago 1

Mar. 24—Chicago 101 at Los Angeles 109
Mar. 25—Chicago 106 at Los Angeles 111
Mar. 27—Los Angeles 98 at Chicago.........................104
Mar. 29—Los Angeles 93 at Chicago.........................87
Mar. 31—Chicago 99 at Los Angeles.........................122

WESTERN DIVISION FINALS
Los Angeles 4, San Francisco 0

Apr. 5—San Francisco 105 at Los Angeles................133
Apr. 10—San Francisco 112 at Los Angeles.............115
Apr. 11—Los Angeles 128 at San Francisco.............124
Apr. 13—Los Angeles 106 at San Francisco.............100

WORLD CHAMPIONSHIP SERIES
Boston 4, Los Angeles 2

Apr. 21—Los Angeles 101 at Boston.............................107
Apr. 24—Los Angeles 123 at Boston.............................113
Apr. 26—Boston 127 at Los Angeles.............................119
Apr. 28—Boston 105 at Los Angeles.............................119
Apr. 30—Los Angeles 117 at Boston.............................*120
May 2—Boston 124 at Los Angeles.............................109

*Denotes overtime period.

1966-67 NBA STATISTICS

1966-67 NBA CHAMPION PHILADELPHIA 76ers

Front row (left to right): Wilt Chamberlain, Dave Gambee, Luke Jackson, Billy Cunning-ham, Chet Walker. Back row: Trainer Al Domenico, Coach Alex Hannum, Wally Jones, Bill Melchionni, Matt Guokas, Hal Greer, Larry Costello, Owner Irv Kosloff, General Manager Jack Ramsay.

FINAL STANDINGS

EASTERN DIVISION

Team	Phil.	Bos.	Cin.	N.Y.	Balt.	S.F.	St.L.	L.A.	Chi.	Det.	W.	L.	Pct.	G.B.
Philadelphia	..	4	8	8	8	7	8	8	8	9	68	13	.840	....
Boston	5	..	8	9	8	6	5	5	8	6	60	21	.741	8
Cincinnati	1	1	..	6	6	5	6	3	4	7	39	42	.481	29
New York	1	0	3	..	7	5	4	5	6	5	36	45	.444	32
Baltimore	1	1	3	2	..	2	4	2	3	2	20	61	.247	48

WESTERN DIVISION

Team	Phil.	Bos.	Cin.	N.Y.	Balt.	S.F.	St.L.	L.A.	Chi.	Det.	W.	L.	Pct.	G.B.
San Francisco	2	3	4	4	7		5	6	6	7	44	37	.543	....
St. Louis	1	4	3	5	5	4	..		5	7	39	42	.481	5
Los Angeles	1	4	6	4	7	3	4	..	3	3	36	45	.444	8
Chicago	1	1	5	3	6	3	4	6	..	4	33	48	.407	11
Detroit	0	3	2	4	7	2	2	5	5	..	30	51	.370	14

HOME-ROAD-NEUTRAL RECORDS OF ALL TEAMS

	Home	Road	Neutral	Total		Home	Road	Neutral	Total
Baltimore	12- 20	3- 30	5-11	20- 61	New York	20- 15	9- 24	7- 6	36- 45
Boston	27- 4	25- 11	8- 6	60- 21	Philadelphia	28- 2	26- 8	14- 3	68- 13
Chicago	17- 19	9- 17	7-12	33- 48	St. Louis	18- 11	12- 21	9-10	39- 42
Cincinnati	20- 11	12- 24	7- 7	39- 42	San Francisco	18- 10	11- 19	15- 8	44- 37
Detroit	12- 18	9- 19	9-14	30- 51	Total	193-128	128-193	84-84	405-405
Los Angeles	21- 18	12- 20	3- 7	36- 45					

TEAM STATISTICS

Team	G.	FGA	FGM	Pct.	FTA	FTM	Pct.	Reb.	Ast.	PF	Disq.	For	Agst.	Pt.Dif.
Philadelphia	81	8103	3912	.483	3411	2319	.680	5701	2138	1906	30	125.2	115.8	+9.4
Boston	81	8325	3724	.447	2963	2216	.748	5703	1962	2138	23	119.3	111.3	+8.0
San Francisco	81	8818	3814	.433	3021	2283	.758	5974	1876	2120	48	122.4	119.5	+2.9
Los Angeles	81	8466	3786	.447	2917	2192	.751	5415	1906	2168	31	120.5	120.2	+0.3
Cincinnati	81	8137	3654	.449	2806	2179	.777	5198	1858	2073	25	117.1	117.4	-0.3
St. Louis	81	8004	3547	.443	2979	2110	.708	5219	1708	2173	40	113.6	115.2	-1.6
New York	81	8025	3637	.453	2980	2151	.722	5178	1782	2110	29	116.4	119.4	-3.0
Chicago	81	8505	3565	.419	2784	2037	.732	5295	1827	2205	21	113.2	116.9	-3.7
Detroit	81	8542	3523	.412	2725	1969	.723	5511	1465	2198	49	111.3	116.8	-5.5
Baltimore	81	8578	3664	.427	2771	2025	.731	5342	1652	2153	51	115.5	122.0	-6.5

INDIVIDUAL LEADERS

POINTS

	G.	FG	FT	Pts.	Avg.		G.	FG	FT	Pts.	Avg.
Rick Barry, San Francisco	78	1011	753	2775	35.6	Sam Jones, Boston	72	638	318	1594	22.1
Oscar Robertson, Cincinnati	79	838	736	2412	30.5	Chet Walker, Philadelphia	81	561	445	1567	19.3
Wilt Chamberlain, Phila.	81	785	386	1956	24.1	Gus Johnson, Baltimore	73	620	271	1511	20.7
Jerry West, Los Angeles	66	645	602	1892	28.7	Walt Bellamy, New York	79	565	369	1499	19.0
Elgin Baylor, Los Angeles	70	711	440	1862	26.6	Bill Cunningham, Phila.	81	556	383	1495	18.5
Hal Greer, Philadelphia	80	699	367	1765	22.1	Lou Hudson, St. Louis	80	620	231	1471	18.4
John Havlicek, Boston	81	684	365	1733	21.4	Guy Rodgers, Chicago	81	538	383	1459	18.0
Willis Reed, New York	78	635	358	1628	20.9	Jerry Lucas, Cincinnati	81	577	284	1438	17.8
Bailey Howell, Boston	81	636	349	1621	20.0	Bob Boozer, Chicago	80	538	360	1436	18.0
Dave Bing, Detroit	80	664	273	1601	20.0	Eddie Miles, Detroit	81	582	261	1425	17.6

FIELD GOALS
(Minimum 220 FGM)

	FGA	FGM	Pct.
Wilt Chamberlain, Phila.	1150	785	.683
Walt Bellamy, New York	1084	565	.521
Bailey Howell, Boston	1242	636	.512
Oscar Robertson, Cincinnati	1699	838	.493
Willis Reed, New York	1298	635	.489
Chet Walker, Philadelphia	1150	561	.488
Bob Boozer, Chicago	1104	538	.487
Tom Hawkins, Los Angeles	572	275	.481
Harold Hairston, Cincinnati	962	461	.479
Dick Barnett, New York	949	454	.478

FREE THROWS
(Minimum 220 FTM)

	FTA	FTM	Pct.
Adrian Smith, Cincinnati	380	343	.903
Rick Barry, San Francisco	852	753	.884
Jerry West, Los Angeles	686	602	.878
Oscar Robertson, Cincinnati	843	736	.873
Sam Jones, Boston	371	318	.857
Larry Siegfried, Boston	347	294	.847
Wally Jones, Philadelphia	266	223	.838
John Havlicek, Boston	441	365	.828
Kevin Loughery, Baltimore	412	340	.825
Elgin Baylor, Los Angeles	541	440	.813

ASSISTS

	G.	No.	Avg.
Guy Rodgers, Chicago	81	908	11.2
Oscar Robertson, Cincinnati	79	845	10.7
Wilt Chamberlain, Phila.	81	630	7.8
Bill Russell, Boston	81	472	5.8
Jerry West, Los Angeles	66	447	6.8
Len Wilkens, St. Louis	78	442	5.7
Howard Komives, New York	65	401	6.2
K. C. Jones, Boston	78	389	5.0
Richie Guerin, St. Louis	80	345	4.3
Paul Neumann, San Francisco	78	342	4.4

REBOUNDS

	G.	No.	Avg.
Wilt Chamberlain, Phila.	81	1957	24.2
Bill Russell, Boston	81	1700	21.0
Jerry Lucas, Cincinnati	81	1547	19.1
Nate Thurmond, San Francisco	65	1382	21.3
Bill Bridges, St. Louis	79	1190	15.1
Willis Reed, New York	78	1136	14.6
Darrall Imhoff, Los Angeles	81	1080	13.3
Walt Bellamy, New York	79	1064	13.5
Leroy Ellis, Baltimore	81	970	12.0
Dave DeBusschere, Detroit	78	924	11.8

TEAM-BY-TEAM INDIVIDUAL STATISTICS

BALTIMORE BULLETS

Player	G.	Min.	FGA	FGM	Pct.	FTA	FTM	Pct.	Reb.	Ast.	PF	Disq.	Pts.	Avg.
Gus Johnson	73	2626	1377	620	.450	383	271	.708	855	194	281	7	1511	20.7
Kevin Loughery	76	2577	1306	520	.398	412	340	.825	349	288	294	10	1380	18.2
Leroy Ellis	81	2938	1166	496	.425	286	211	.738	970	170	258	1	1203	14.9
Don Ohl	58	2024	1002	452	.451	354	276	.780	189	168	1	1	1180	20.3
Ray Scott (Tot.)	72	2446	1144	458	.400	366	256	.699	760	160	225	2	1172	16.3
Ray Scott (Balt.)	27	969	463	206	.445	160	100	.625	356	76	83	1	512	19.0
John Egan	71	1743	624	267	.428	219	185	.845	180	275	190	3	719	10.1
Jack Marin	74	1323	632	283	.448	187	145	.775	313	75	199	6	711	9.6
John Green	61	948	437	203	.465	207	96	.464	394	57	139	7	502	8.2
John Barnhill	53	1214	447	187	.418	103	66	.641	157	136	80	0	440	8.3
Ben Warley	62	1037	312	125	.401	170	134	.788	325	51	176	6	384	6.2
Bob Ferry	51	991	315	132	.419	110	70	.636	258	92	97	0	334	6.5
Wayne Hightower	43	746	308	103	.334	124	89	.718	241	36	110	5	295	6.9
Mel Counts	25	343	167	65	.389	40	29	.725	155	30	81	2	159	6.4
John Austin	4	61	22	5	.227	16	13	.813	7	4	12	0	23	5.9

BOSTON CELTICS

Player	G.	Min.	FGA	FGM	Pct.	FTA	FTM	Pct.	Reb.	Ast.	PF	Disq.	Pts.	Avg.
John Havlicek	81	2602	1540	684	.444	441	365	.828	532	278	210	0	1733	21.4
Bailey Howell	81	2503	1242	636	.512	471	349	.741	677	103	296	4	1621	20.0
Sam Jones	72	2325	1406	638	.454	371	318	.857	338	217	191	1	1594	22.1
Bill Russell	81	3297	870	395	.454	467	285	.610	1700	472	258	4	1075	13.4
Larry Siegfried	73	1891	833	368	.442	347	294	.847	228	250	207	1	1030	14.1
Tom Sanders	81	1926	755	323	.428	218	178	.817	439	91	304	6	824	10.2
Don Nelson	79	1202	509	227	.446	190	141	.742	295	65	143	0	595	7.5
K. C. Jones	78	2446	459	182	.397	189	119	.630	239	389	273	7	483	6.2
Wayne Embry	72	729	359	147	.409	144	82	.569	294	42	137	0	376	5.2
Jim Barnett	48	383	211	78	.370	62	42	.677	53	41	61	0	198	4.1
Toby Kimball	38	222	97	35	.361	40	27	.675	146	13	42	0	97	2.6
Ron Watts	27	89	44	11	.250	23	16	.696	38	1	16	0	38	1.4

CHICAGO BULLS

Player	G.	Min.	FGA	FGM	Pct.	FTA	FTM	Pct.	Reb.	Ast.	PF	Disq.	Pts.	Avg.
Guy Rodgers	81	3063	1377	538	.391	475	383	.806	346	908	243	1	1459	18.0
Bob Boozer	80	2451	1104	538	.487	461	360	.781	679	90	212	0	1436	18.0
Jerry Sloan	80	2942	1214	525	.432	427	340	.796	726	170	293	7	1390	17.4
Erwin Mueller	80	2136	957	422	.441	260	171	.658	497	131	223	2	1015	12.7
Don Kojis	78	1655	773	329	.426	222	134	.604	479	70	204	3	792	10.2
McCoy McLemore	79	1382	670	258	.385	272	210	.772	374	62	189	2	726	9.2
Jim Washington	77	1475	604	252	.417	159	88	.553	468	56	181	1	592	7.7

Player	G.	Min.	FGA	FGM	Pct.	FTA	FTM	Pct.	Reb.	Ast.	PF	Disq.	Pts.	Avg.
Keith Erickson	76	1454	641	235	.367	159	117	.736	339	119	199	2	587	7.7
Barry Clemens	60	986	444	186	.419	90	68	.756	201	39	143	1	440	7.3
Gerry Ward	76	1042	307	117	.381	138	87	.630	179	130	169	2	321	4.2
George Wilson (Tot.)	55	573	234	85	.363	86	58	.674	206	15	92	0	228	4.1
George Wilson (Chi.)	43	448	193	77	.399	70	45	.643	163	15	73	0	199	4.6
Len Chappell	19	179	89	40	.449	21	14	.667	38	12	31	0	94	4.9
Dave Schellhase	31	212	111	40	.360	22	14	.636	29	23	27	0	94	3.0
Nate Bowman	9	65	21	8	.381	8	6	.750	28	2	18	0	22	2.4

CINCINNATI ROYALS

Player	G.	Min.	FGA	FGM	Pct.	FTA	FTM	Pct.	Reb.	Ast.	PF	Disq.	Pts.	Avg.
Oscar Robertson	79	3468	1699	838	.493	843	736	.873	486	845	226	2	2412	30.5
Jerry Lucas	81	3558	1257	577	.459	359	284	.791	1547	268	280	2	1438	17.8
Adrian Smith	81	2636	1147	502	.438	380	343	.903	205	187	272	0	1347	16.6
Harold Hairston	79	2442	962	461	.479	382	252	.660	631	62	273	5	1174	14.9
Connie Dierking	77	1905	729	291	.399	180	134	.744	603	158	251	7	716	9.3
Flynn Robinson	76	1140	599	274	.457	154	120	.779	133	110	197	3	668	8.8
Jon McGlocklin	60	1194	493	217	.440	104	74	.712	164	93	84	0	508	8.5
Bob Love	66	1074	403	173	.429	147	93	.633	257	49	153	3	439	6.7
Len Chappell (Tot.)	73	708	313	132	.422	81	53	.654	189	33	104	0	316	4.3
Len Chappell (Cin.)	54	529	224	92	.411	60	39	.650	151	21	73	0	223	4.1
Walt Wesley	64	909	333	131	.393	123	52	.423	329	19	161	2	314	4.9
Fred Lewis	32	334	153	60	.392	41	29	.707	44	40	49	1	149	4.7
Jim Ware	33	201	97	30	.309	17	10	.588	69	6	35	0	70	2.1
George Wilson	12	125	41	8	.195	16	13	.813	43	0	19	0	29	2.4

DETROIT PISTONS

Player	G.	Min.	FGA	FGM	Pct.	FTA	FTM	Pct.	Reb.	Ast.	PF	Disq.	Pts.	Avg.
Dave Bing	80	2762	1522	664	.436	370	273	.738	359	330	217	2	1601	20.0
Eddie Miles	81	2419	1363	582	.427	338	261	.772	298	181	216	2	1425	17.6
Dave DeBusschere	78	2897	1278	531	.415	512	361	.705	924	216	297	7	1423	18.2
Tom Van Arsdale	79	2134	887	347	.391	347	272	.784	341	193	241	3	966	12.2
Joe Strawder	79	2156	660	281	.426	262	188	.718	791	82	344	19	750	9.5
John Tresvant	68	1553	585	256	.438	234	164	.701	483	88	246	8	676	9.9
Ray Scott	45	1477	681	252	.370	206	156	.757	404	84	132	1	660	14.7
Wayne Hightower (Tot.)	72	1310	567	195	.344	210	153	.729	405	64	190	6	543	7.5
Wayne Hightower (Det.)	29	564	259	92	.355	86	64	.744	164	28	80	1	248	8.6
Ron Reed	61	1248	600	223	.372	133	79	.594	423	81	145	2	525	8.6
Reggie Harding	74	1367	383	172	.449	103	63	.612	455	94	164	2	407	5.5
Charlie Vaughn	50	680	226	85	.376	74	50	.676	67	75	54	0	220	4.4
Dorrie Murrey	35	311	82	33	.402	54	32	.593	102	12	57	2	98	2.8
Bob Hogsett	7	22	16	5	.313	6	6	1.000	3	1	5	0	16	2.3

LOS ANGELES LAKERS

Player	G.	Min.	FGA	FGM	Pct.	FTA	FTM	Pct.	Reb.	Ast.	PF	Disq.	Pts.	Avg.
Jerry West	66	2670	1389	645	.464	686	602	.878	392	447	160	1	1892	28.7
Elgin Baylor	70	2706	1658	711	.429	541	440	.813	898	215	211	1	1862	26.6
Gail Goodrich	77	1780	776	352	.454	337	253	.751	251	210	294	3	957	12.4
Darrall Imhoff	81	2725	780	370	.474	207	127	.614	1080	222	281	7	867	10.7
Archie Clark	76	1763	732	331	.452	192	136	.708	218	205	193	1	798	10.5
Walt Hazzard	79	1642	706	301	.426	177	129	.729	231	323	203	1	731	9.3
Tom Hawkins	76	1798	572	275	.481	173	82	.474	434	83	207	1	632	8.3
Rudy LaRusso	45	1292	509	211	.415	224	156	.696	351	78	149	6	578	12.8
Jim Barnes	80	1398	497	217	.437	187	128	.684	450	47	266	5	562	7.0
Jerry Chambers	68	1015	496	224	.452	93	68	.731	208	44	143	0	516	7.6
Mel Counts (Tot.)	56	860	419	177	.422	94	69	.734	344	52	183	6	423	7.6
Mel Counts (L.A.)	31	517	252	112	.444	54	40	.741	189	22	102	4	264	8.5
John Block	22	118	52	20	.385	34	24	.706	45	5	20	0	64	2.9
Henry Finkel	27	141	47	17	.362	12	7	.583	64	5	39	1	41	1.5

NEW YORK KNICKERBOCKERS

Player	G.	Min.	FGA	FGM	Pct.	FTA	FTM	Pct.	Reb.	Ast.	PF	Disq.	Pts.	Avg.
Willis Reed	78	2824	1298	635	.489	487	358	.735	1136	126	293	9	1628	20.9
Walt Bellamy	79	3010	1084	565	.521	580	369	.637	1064	206	275	5	1499	19.0
Dick Van Arsdale	79	2892	913	410	.449	509	371	.729	555	247	264	3	1191	15.1
Dick Barnett	67	1969	949	454	.478	295	231	.783	226	161	185	2	1139	17.0
Howard Komives	65	2282	995	402	.404	253	217	.858	183	401	213	1	1021	15.7
Dave Stallworth	76	1889	816	380	.466	320	229	.716	472	144	226	4	989	13.0
Cazzie Russell	77	1696	789	344	.436	228	179	.785	251	187	174	1	867	11.3
Emmette Bryant	63	1593	577	236	.409	114	74	.539	273	218	231	4	546	8.7
Henry Akin	50	453	230	83	.361	37	26	.703	120	25	82	0	192	3.8
Neil Johnson	51	522	171	59	.345	86	57	.663	167	38	102	0	175	3.4
Fred Crawford	19	192	116	44	.379	38	24	.632	48	12	39	0	112	5.9
Wayne Molis	13	75	51	19	.373	13	7	.538	22	2	9	0	45	3.5
Dave Deutsch	19	93	36	6	.167	20	9	.450	21	15	17	0	21	1.1

PHILADELPHIA 76ers

Player	G.	Min.	FGA	FGM	Pct.	FTA	FTM	Pct.	Reb.	Ast.	PF	Disq.	Pts.	Avg.
Wilt Chamberlain	81	3682	1150	785	.683	875	386	.441	1957	630	143	0	1956	24.1
Hal Greer	80	3086	1524	699	.459	466	367	.788	422	303	302	5	1765	22.1
Chet Walker	81	2691	1150	561	.488	581	445	.766	660	188	232	4	1567	19.3
Billy Cunningham	81	2168	1211	556	.459	558	383	.686	589	205	260	2	1495	18.5
Wally Jones	81	2249	982	423	.431	266	223	.838	265	303	246	6	1069	13.2
Lucious Jackson	81	2377	882	386	.438	261	198	.759	724	114	276	6	970	12.0
Dave Gambee	63	757	345	150	.435	125	107	.856	197	42	143	5	407	6.5
Larry Costello	49	976	293	130	.444	133	120	.902	103	140	141	2	380	7.8
Bill Melchionni	73	692	353	138	.391	60	39	.650	98	98	73	0	315	4.3
Matt Guokas	69	808	203	79	.389	81	49	.605	83	105	82	0	207	3.0
Bob Weiss	6	29	10	5	.500	5	2	.400	3	10	8	0	12	2.0

ST. LOUIS HAWKS

Player	G.	Min.	FGA	FGM	Pct.	FTA	FTM	Pct.	Reb.	Ast.	PF	Disq.	Pts.	Avg.
Lou Hudson	80	2446	1328	620	.467	327	231	.706	435	95	277	3	1471	18.4
Bill Bridges	79	3130	1106	503	.455	523	367	.702	1190	222	325	12	1373	17.4
Len Wilkens	78	2974	1036	448	.432	583	459	.787	412	442	280	6	1355	17.4
Joe Caldwell	81	2256	1076	458	.426	308	200	.649	442	166	230	4	1116	13.8
Richie Guerin	80	2275	904	394	.436	416	304	.731	192	345	247	2	1092	13.7
Zelmo Beaty	48	1661	694	328	.473	260	197	.758	515	60	189	3	853	17.8
Rod Thorn	67	1166	524	233	.445	172	125	.727	160	118	88	0	591	8.8
Paul Silas	77	1570	482	207	.429	213	113	.531	669	74	208	4	527	6.8
Gene Tormohlen	63	1036	403	172	.427	84	50	.595	347	73	177	4	394	6.3
Dick Snyder	55	676	333	144	.432	61	46	.754	91	59	82	1	334	6.1
Tom Kron	32	221	87	27	.310	19	13	.684	36	46	35	0	67	2.1
Tom Hoover	17	129	31	13	.419	13	5	.385	36	8	35	1	31	1.8

SAN FRANCISCO WARRIORS

Player	G.	Min.	FGA	FGM	Pct.	FTA	FTM	Pct.	Reb.	Ast.	PF	Disq.	Pts.	Avg.
Rick Barry	78	3175	2240	1011	.451	852	753	.884	714	282	258	1	2775	35.6
Nate Thurmond	65	2755	1068	467	.437	445	280	.629	1382	166	183	3	1214	18.7
Paul Neumann	78	2421	911	386	.424	390	312	.800	272	342	266	4	1084	13.9
Jeff Mullins	77	1835	919	421	.458	214	150	.701	388	226	195	5	992	12.9
Fred Hetzel	77	2123	932	373	.400	237	192	.810	639	111	228	3	938	12.2
Tom Meschery	72	1846	706	293	.415	244	175	.717	549	94	264	8	761	10.6
Jim King	67	1667	685	286	.418	221	174	.787	319	240	193	5	746	11.1
Clyde Lee	74	1247	503	205	.408	166	105	.633	551	77	168	5	515	7.0
Al Attles	69	1764	467	212	.454	151	88	.583	321	269	265	13	512	7.4
Bud Olsen	40	348	167	75	.449	58	23	.397	103	32	51	1	173	4.3
Joe Ellis	41	333	164	67	.409	25	19	.760	112	27	45	0	153	3.7
Bob Warlick	12	65	52	15	.280	11	6	.545	20	10	4	0	36	3.0
George Lee	1	5	4	3	.750	7	6	.857	0	0	0	0	12	12.0

PLAYOFF RESULTS

EASTERN DIVISION SEMIFINALS
Boston 3, New York 1

Mar. 21—New York 110 at Boston 140
Mar. 25—Boston 115 at New York 108
Mar. 26—New York 123 at Boston 112
Mar. 28—Boston 118 at New York 109

Philadelphia 3, Cincinnati 1

Mar. 21—Cincinnati 120 at Philadelphia...............................116
Mar. 22—Philadelphia 123 at Cincinnati................................102
Mar. 24—Cincinnati 106 at Philadelphia.................................121
Mar. 25—Philadelphia 112 at Cincinnati....................................94

EASTERN DIVISION FINALS
Philadelphia 4, Boston 1

Mar. 31—Boston 113 at Philadelphia 127
Apr. 2—Philadelphia 107 at Boston 102
Apr. 5—Boston 104 at Philadelphia 115
Apr. 9—Philadelphia 117 at Boston 121
Apr. 11—Boston 116 at Philadelphia 140

WESTERN DIVISION SEMIFINALS
St. Louis 3, Chicago 0

Mar. 21—Chicago 100 at St. Louis 114
Mar. 23—St. Louis 113 at Chicago 107
Mar. 25—Chicago 106 at St. Louis 119

San Francisco 3, Los Angeles 0

Mar. 21—Los Angeles 108 at San Francisco.................................124
Mar. 23—San Francisco 113 at Los Angeles..................................102
Mar. 26—Los Angeles 115 at San Francisco................................122

WESTERN DIVISION FINALS
San Francisco 4, St. Louis 2

Mar. 30—St. Louis 115 at San Francisco..................................117
Apr. 1—St. Louis 136 at San Francisco.................................143
Apr. 5—San Francisco 109 at St. Louis................................115
Apr. 8—San Francisco 104 at St. Louis................................109
Apr. 10—St. Louis 102 at San Francisco................................123
Apr. 12—San Francisco 112 at St. Louis...............................107

WORLD CHAMPIONSHIP SERIES
Philadelphia 4, San Francisco 2

Apr. 14—San Francisco 135 at Philadelphia *141
Apr. 16—San Francisco 95 at Philadelphia 126
Apr. 18—Philadelphia 124 at San Francisco 130
Apr. 20—Philadelphia 122 at San Francisco 108
Apr. 23—San Francisco 117 at Philadelphia 109
Apr. 24—Philadelphia 125 at San Francisco 122

*Denotes overtime period.

1965-66 NBA STATISTICS

1965-66 NBA CHAMPION BOSTON CELTICS

Seated (left to right): John Havlicek, K. C. Jones, Marvin Kratter, chairman of board; Coach Red Auerbach, President John J. Waldron, Bill Russell. Standing: Ron Bonham, Don Nelson, Tom Sanders, Mel Counts, John Thompson, Woody Sauldsberry, Willie Naulls, Sam Jones, Larry Siegfried, Trainer Buddy LeRoux.

FINAL STANDINGS

EASTERN DIVISION

Team	Phil.	Bos.	Cin.	N.Y.	L.A.	Balt.	St.L.	S.F.	Det.	W.	L.	Pct.	G.B.
Philadelphia	..	6	6	8	8	5	7	8	7	55	25	.688	....
Boston	4	..	5	10	7	7	7	8	6	54	26	.675	1
Cincinnati	4	5	..	7	4	7	5	5	8	45	35	.563	10
New York	2	0	3	..	5	3	4	5	8	30	50	.375	25

WESTERN DIVISION

Team	Phil.	Bos.	Cin.	N.Y.	L.A.	Balt.	St.L.	S.F.	Det.	W.	L.	Pct.	G.B.
Los Angeles	2	3	6	5	..	6	8	7	8	45	35	.563	....
Baltimore	5	3	3	7	4	..	7	4	5	38	42	.475	7
St. Louis	3	3	5	6	2	3	..	6	8	36	44	.450	9
San Francisco	2	2	5	5	3	6	4	..	8	35	45	.438	10
Detroit	3	4	2	2	2	5	2	2	..	22	58	.275	23

HOME-ROAD-NEUTRAL RECORDS OF ALL TEAMS

Team	Home	Road	Neutral	Total	Team	Home	Road	Neutral	Total
Baltimore	29- 9	4- 25	5- 8	38- 42	New York	20- 14	4- 30	6- 6	30- 50
Boston	26- 5	19- 18	9- 3	54- 26	Philadelphia	22- 3	20- 17	13- 5	55- 25
Cincinnati	25- 6	11- 23	9- 6	45- 35	St. Louis	22- 10	6- 22	8-12	36- 44
Detroit	13- 17	4- 22	5-19	22- 58	San Francisco	12- 14	8- 19	15-12	35- 45
Los Angeles	28- 11	13- 21	4- 3	45- 35	Totals	197- 89	89-197	74-74	360-360

TEAM STATISTICS

Team	G.	FGA	FGM	Pct.	FTA	FTM	Pct.	Reb.	Ast.	PF	Disq.	For	Agst.	Pt.Dif.
Boston	80	8367	3488	.417	2758	2038	.739	5591	1795	2012	39	112.7	107.8	4.9
Philadelphia	80	8189	3650	.446	2087	2087	.664	5652	1905	2095	39	117.3	112.7	4.6
Los Angeles	80	8109	3597	.444	3057	2363	.773	5334	1936	2035	25	119.5	116.4	3.1
Cincinnati	80	8123	3610	.444	2906	2204	.758	5559	1818	2033	24	117.8	116.6	1.2
St. Louis	80	7836	3379	.431	2870	2155	.751	5167	1782	2179	47	111.4	112.0	—0.6
Baltimore	80	8210	3599	.438	3186	2267	.712	5542	1890	2199	52	118.3	119.5	—1.2
New York	80	7910	3559	.450	3078	2217	.720	5119	1896	2227	48	116.7	119.3	—2.6
San Francisco	80	8512	3557	.418	2879	2129	.730	5727	1872	2069	37	115.5	118.2	—2.7
Detroit	80	8502	3475	.409	2734	1877	.687	5427	1569	2016	27	110.3	117.2	—6.9

INDIVIDUAL LEADERS

POINTS

	G.	FG	FT	Pts.	Avg.		G.	FG	FT	Pts.	Avg.
Wilt Chamberlain, Phila.	79	1074	501	2649	33.5	Eddie Miles, Detroit	80	634	298	1566	19.6
Jerry West, Los Angeles	79	818	840	2476	31.3	Don Ohl, Baltimore	73	593	316	1502	20.6
Oscar Robertson, Cinn.	76	818	742	2378	31.3	Adrian Smith, Cincinnati	80	531	408	1470	18.4
Rick Barry, San Fran.	80	745	569	2059	25.7	Guy Rodgers, San Fran.	79	586	296	1468	18.6
Walt Bellamy, Balt.-N.Y.	80	695	430	1820	22.8	Ray Scott, Detroit	79	544	323	1411	17.9
Hal Greer, Philadelphia	80	703	413	1819	22.7	Bailey Howell, Baltimore	78	481	402	1364	17.5
Dick Barnett, New York	75	631	467	1729	23.1	Kevin Loughery, Baltimore	74	526	297	1349	18.2
Jerry Lucas, Cincinnati	79	690	317	1697	21.5	John Havlicek, Boston	71	530	274	1334	18.8
Zelmo Beaty, St. Louis	80	616	424	1656	20.7	Dave DeBusschere, Detroit	79	524	249	1297	16.4
Sam Jones, Boston	67	626	325	1577	23.5	Len Wilkens, St. Louis	69	411	422	1244	18.0

FIELD GOALS
(Minimum 210 FGM)

	FGA	FGM	Pct.
Wilt Chamberlain, Phila.	1990	1074	.540
John Green, N.Y.-Balt.	668	358	.536
Walt Bellamy, Balt.-N.Y.	1373	695	.506
Al Attles, San Francisco	724	364	.503
Happy Hairston, Cincinnati	814	398	.489
Bailey Howell, Baltimore	986	481	.488
Bob Boozer, Los Angeles	754	365	.484
Oscar Robertson, Cincinnati	1723	818	.475
Zelmo Beaty, St. Louis	1301	616	.473
Jerry West, Los Angeles	1731	818	.473

ASSISTS

	G.	No.	Avg.
Oscar Roberston, Cincinnati	76	847	11.1
Guy Rodgers, San Francisco	79	846	10.7
K. C. Jones, Boston	80	503	6.3
Jerry West, Los Angeles	79	480	6.1
Len Wilkens, St. Louis	69	429	6.2
Howard Komives, New York	80	425	5.3
Wilt Chamberlain, Philadelphia	79	414	5.2
Walt Hazzard, Los Angeles	80	393	4.9
Richie Guerin, St. Louis	80	388	4.9
Hal Greer, Philadelphia	80	384	4.8

FREE THROWS
(Minimum 210 FTM)

	FTA	FTM	Pct.
Larry Siegfried, Boston	311	274	.881
Rick Barry, San Francisco	660	569	.862
Howard Komives, New York	280	241	.861
Jerry West, Los Angeles	977	840	.860
Adrian Smith, Cincinnati	480	408	.850
Oscar Robertson, Cincinnati	881	742	.842
Paul Neumann, San Francisco	317	265	.836
Kevin Loughery, Baltimore	358	297	.830
Richie Guerin, St. Louis	446	362	.812
Hal Greer, Philadelphia	514	413	.804

REBOUNDS

	G.	No.	Avg.
Wilt Chamberlain, Philadelphia	79	1943	24.6
Bill Russell, Boston	78	1779	22.8
Jerry Lucas, Cincinnati	79	1668	21.1
Nate Thurmond, San Francisco	73	1312	18.0
Walt Bellamy, Balt.-N.Y.	80	1254	15.7
Zelmo Beaty, St. Louis	80	1086	13.6
Bill Bridges, St. Louis	78	951	12.2
Dave DeBusschere, Detroit	79	916	11.6
Willis Reed, New York	76	883	11.6
Rick Barry, San Francisco	80	850	10.6

TEAM-BY-TEAM INDIVIDUAL STATISTICS

BALTIMORE BULLETS

Player	G.	Min.	FGA	FGM	Pct.	FTA	FTM	Pct.	Reb.	Ast.	PF	Disq.	Pts.	Avg.
Don Ohl	73	2645	1334	593	.445	430	316	.734	280	290	208	1	1502	20.6
Bailey Howell	78	2328	986	481	.488	551	402	.730	773	155	306	12	1364	17.5
Kevin Loughery	74	2455	1264	526	.416	358	297	.830	227	356	273	8	1349	18.2
John Green (Tot.)	79	1645	668	358	.536	388	202	.521	645	107	183	3	918	11.6
John Green (Balt.)	72	1437	589	315	.535	357	187	.524	571	96	162	3	817	11.3
Jim Barnes (Tot.)	73	2191	818	348	.425	310	212	.684	755	94	283	10	908	12.4
Jim Barnes (Balt.)	66	1928	728	308	.423	268	182	.679	683	85	250	10	798	12.1
John Kerr	71	1770	692	286	.413	272	209	.768	586	225	148	0	781	11.0
John Egan (Tot.)	76	1644	574	259	.451	227	173	.762	183	273	167	1	691	9.1
John Egan (Balt.)	69	1586	558	254	.455	217	166	.765	181	259	163	1	674	9.8
Gus Johnson	41	1284	661	273	.413	178	131	.736	546	114	136	3	677	16.5
Bob Ferry	66	1229	457	188	.411	157	105	.669	334	111	134	1	481	7.3
Jerry Sloan	59	952	289	120	.415	139	98	.705	230	110	176	7	338	5.7
Ben Warley (Tot.)	57	773	284	116	.408	97	64	.660	217	25	129	2	296	5.2
Ben Warley (Balt.)	56	767	281	115	.409	97	64	.660	215	25	128	2	294	5.3
Wayne Hightower	24	460	186	63	.339	78	57	.731	131	35	61	2	183	7.6
Walt Bellamy	8	268	124	56	.452	67	40	.597	102	18	32	2	152	19.0
Willie Somerset	7	98	43	18	.419	11	9	.818	15	9	21	0	45	6.4
Gary Bradds	3	15	6	2	.333	4	3	.750	8	1	1	0	7	2.3
Thales McReynolds	5	28	12	1	.083	2	1	.500	6	1	0	0	3	0.6

BOSTON CELTICS

Player	G.	Min.	FGA	FGM	Pct.	FTA	FTM	Pct.	Reb.	Ast.	PF	Disq.	Pts.	Avg.
Sam Jones	67	2155	1335	626	.469	407	325	.799	347	216	170	0	1577	23.5
John Havlicek	71	2175	1328	530	.399	349	274	.785	423	210	158	1	1334	18.8
Bill Russell	78	3386	943	391	.415	405	223	.551	1779	371	221	4	1005	12.9
Larry Siegfried	71	1675	825	349	.423	311	274	.881	196	165	157	1	972	13.7
Tom Sanders	72	1896	816	349	.428	276	211	.764	508	90	317	19	909	12.6
Don Nelson	75	1765	618	271	.439	326	223	.684	403	79	187	1	765	10.2
Willie Naulls	71	1433	815	328	.402	131	104	.794	319	72	197	4	760	10.7
K. C. Jones	80	2710	619	240	.388	303	209	.690	304	503	243	4	689	8.6
Mel Counts	67	1021	549	221	.403	145	120	.828	432	50	207	5	562	8.4
Ron Bonham	39	312	207	76	.367	61	52	.852	35	11	29	0	204	5.2
Woody Sauldsberry	39	530	249	80	.321	22	11	.500	142	15	94	0	171	4.4
John Thompson	10	72	30	14	.467	6	4	.667	30	3	15	0	32	3.2
Sihugo Green	10	92	31	12	.387	16	8	.500	11	9	16	0	32	3.2
Ron Watts	1	3	2	1	.500	0	0	.000	1	1	1	0	2	2.0

CINCINNATI ROYALS

Player	G.	Min.	FGA	FGM	Pct.	FTA	FTM	Pct.	Reb.	Ast.	PF	Disq.	Pts.	Avg.
Oscar Robertson	76	3493	1723	818	.475	881	742	.842	586	847	227	1	2378	31.3
Jerry Lucas	79	3517	1523	690	.453	402	317	.787	1668	213	274	5	1697	21.5
Adrian Smith	80	2982	1310	531	.405	480	408	.850	287	256	276	1	1470	18.4
Harold Hairston	72	1794	814	398	.489	321	220	.685	546	44	216	3	1016	14.1
Tom Hawkins	79	2123	604	273	.452	209	116	.555	575	99	274	4	662	8.4
Wayne Embry	80	1882	564	232	.411	234	141	.603	525	81	287	9	605	7.6
Jack Twyman	73	943	498	224	.450	117	95	.812	168	60	122	1	543	7.4
Jon McGlocklin	72	852	363	153	.421	79	62	.785	133	88	77	0	368	5.1
Connie Dierking	57	782	322	134	.416	82	50	.610	245	43	113	0	318	5.6
Tom Thacker	50	478	207	84	.406	38	15	.395	119	61	85	0	183	3.7
George Wilson	47	276	138	54	.391	42	27	.643	98	17	56	0	135	2.9
Art Heyman	11	100	43	15	.349	17	10	.588	13	7	19	0	40	3.6
Enoch Olsen	4	36	8	3	.375	3	1	.333	13	2	4	0	7	1.8
Jay Arnette	3	14	6	1	.167	0	0	.000	0	0	3	0	2	0.7

DETROIT PISTONS

Player	G.	Min.	FGA	FGM	Pct.	FTA	FTM	Pct.	Reb.	Ast.	PF	Disq.	Pts.	Avg.
Eddie Miles	80	2788	1418	634	.447	402	298	.741	302	221	203	2	1566	19.6
Ray Scott	79	2652	1309	544	.416	435	323	.743	755	238	209	1	1411	17.9
Dave DeBusschere	79	2696	1284	524	.408	378	249	.659	916	209	252	5	1297	16.4
Tom Van Arsdale	79	2041	834	312	.374	290	209	.721	309	205	251	1	833	10.5
Joe Strawder	79	2180	613	250	.408	256	176	.688	820	78	305	10	676	8.6
John Barnhill (Tot.)	76	1617	606	243	.401	184	113	.614	203	196	134	0	599	7.9
John Barnhill (Det.)	45	926	363	139	.383	98	59	.602	112	113	76	0	337	7.5
John Tresvant (Tot.)	61	969	400	171	.428	190	142	.747	364	72	179	2	484	7.9
John Tresvant (Det.)	46	756	322	134	.416	158	115	.736	279	62	136	2	383	8.3
Charles Vaughn (Tot.)	56	1219	474	182	.384	144	106	.726	109	140	99	1	470	8.4
Charles Vaughn (Det.)	37	774	282	110	.390	82	60	.732	63	104	60	0	280	7.6
Don Kojis	60	783	439	182	.415	141	76	.539	260	42	94	0	440	7.3
Ron Reed	57	997	524	186	.355	100	54	.540	339	92	133	1	426	7.5
Rod Thorn	27	815	343	143	.417	123	90	.732	101	64	67	0	376	13.9
Joe Caldwell	33	716	338	143	.423	88	60	.682	190	65	63	0	346	10.5
Bill Buntin	42	713	299	118	.395	143	88	.615	252	36	119	4	324	7.7
Donnis Butcher	15	285	96	45	.469	34	18	.529	33	30	40	1	108	7.2
Bob Warlick	10	78	38	11	.289	6	2	.333	16	10	8	0	24	2.4

LOS ANGELES LAKERS

Player	G.	Min.	FGA	FGM	Pct.	FTA	FTM	Pct.	Reb.	Ast.	PF	Disq.	Pts.	Avg.
Jerry West	79	3218	1731	818	.473	977	840	.860	562	480	243	1	2476	31.3
Rudy LaRusso	76	2316	897	410	.457	445	350	.787	660	165	261	9	1170	15.4
Walt Hazzard	80	2198	1003	458	.457	257	182	.708	219	393	224	0	1098	13.7
Elgin Baylor	65	1975	1034	415	.401	337	249	.739	621	224	157	0	1079	16.6
LeRoy Ellis	80	2219	927	393	.424	256	186	.727	735	74	232	3	972	12.2
Bob Boozer	78	1847	754	365	.484	289	225	.779	548	87	196	0	955	12.2
Jim King	76	1499	545	238	.437	115	94	.817	204	223	181	1	570	7.5
Gail Goodrich	65	1008	503	203	.404	149	103	.691	130	103	103	1	509	7.8
Darrall Imhoff	77	1413	337	151	.448	136	77	.566	509	113	234	7	379	4.9
Gene Wiley	67	1386	289	123	.426	76	43	.566	490	63	171	3	289	4.3
John Fairchild	30	171	89	23	.258	20	14	.700	45	11	33	0	60	2.0

NEW YORK KNICKERBOCKERS

Player	G.	Min.	FGA	FGM	Pct.	FTA	FTM	Pct.	Reb.	Ast.	PF	Disq.	Pts.	Avg.
Walt Bellamy (Tot.)	80	3352	1373	695	.506	689	430	.624	1254	235	294	9	1820	22.8
Walt Bellamy (N.Y.)	72	3084	1249	639	.512	622	390	.627	1152	217	262	7	1668	23.2
Dick Barnett	75	2589	1344	631	.469	605	467	.772	310	259	235	6	1729	23.1
Willis Reed	76	2537	1009	438	.434	399	302	.757	883	91	323	13	1178	15.5
Howard Komives	80	2612	1116	436	.391	280	241	.861	281	425	278	5	1113	13.9
Dave Stallworth	80	1893	820	373	.455	376	258	.686	492	186	237	4	1004	12.6
Dick Van Arsdale	79	2289	838	359	.428	351	251	.715	376	184	235	5	969	12.3
Emmette Bryant	71	1193	449	212	.472	101	74	.733	170	216	215	4	498	7.0
Barry Clemens	70	877	391	161	.412	78	54	.692	183	67	113	0	376	5.4
Tom Gola	74	1127	271	122	.450	105	82	.781	289	191	207	3	326	4.4
Len Chappell	46	545	238	100	.420	78	46	.590	127	26	64	1	246	5.3
Jim Barnes	7	263	90	40	.444	42	30	.714	72	9	33	0	110	15.7
John Green	7	208	79	43	.544	31	15	.484	74	11	21	0	101	14.4
John Egan	7	58	16	5	.313	10	7	.700	2	14	4	0	17	2.4

PHILADELPHIA 76ers

Player	G.	Min.	FGA	FGM	Pct.	FTA	FTM	Pct.	Reb.	Ast.	PF	Disq.	Pts.	Avg.
Wilt Chamberlain	79	3737	1990	1074	.540	976	501	.513	1943	414	171	0	2649	33.5
Hal Greer	80	3326	1580	703	.445	514	413	.804	473	384	315	6	1819	22.7
Chet Walker	80	2603	982	443	.451	468	335	.716	636	201	238	3	1221	15.3
Bill Cunningham	80	2134	1011	431	.426	443	281	.634	599	207	301	12	1143	14.3
Wally Jones	80	2196	799	296	.370	172	128	.744	169	273	250	6	720	9.0
Lucious Jackson	79	1966	614	246	.401	214	158	.738	676	132	216	2	650	8.2
Dave Gambee	72	1068	437	168	.384	187	159	.850	273	71	189	3	495	6.9
Al Bianchi	78	1312	560	214	.382	98	66	.673	134	134	232	4	494	6.3
Gerry Ward	65	838	189	67	.354	60	39	.650	89	80	163	3	173	2.7
Art Heyman (Tot.)	17	120	52	18	.346	22	14	.636	17	11	23	0	50	2.9
Art Heyman (Phil.)	6	20	9	3	.333	5	4	.800	4	4	4	0	10	1.7
Bob Weiss	7	30	9	3	.333	0	0	.000	7	4	10	0	6	0.9
Jesse Branson	5	14	6	1	.167	4	3	.750	9	1	4	0	5	1.0
Ben Warley	1	6	3	1	.333	0	0	.000	2	0	1	0	2	2.0

ST. LOUIS HAWKS

Player	G.	Min.	FGA	FGM	Pct.	FTA	FTM	Pct.	Reb.	Ast.	PF	Disq.	Pts.	Avg.
Zelmo Beaty	80	3072	1301	616	.473	559	424	.758	1086	125	344	15	1656	20.7
Len Wilkens	69	2692	954	411	.431	532	422	.793	322	429	248	4	1244	18.0
Richie Guerin	80	2363	998	414	.415	446	362	.812	314	388	256	4	1190	14.9
Cliff Hagan	74	1851	942	419	.445	206	176	.854	234	164	177	1	1014	13.7
Bill Bridges	78	2677	927	377	.407	364	257	.706	951	208	333	11	1011	13.0
Joe Caldwell (Tot.)	79	1857	938	411	.438	254	179	.705	436	126	203	3	1001	12.7
Joe Caldwell (St.L.)	46	1141	600	268	.447	166	119	.717	246	61	140	3	655	14.2
Rod Thorn (Tot.)	73	1739	728	306	.420	236	168	.712	210	145	144	0	780	10.7
Rod Thorn (St.L.)	46	924	385	163	.423	113	78	.690	109	81	77	0	404	8.8
Jim Washington	65	1104	393	158	.402	120	68	.567	353	43	176	4	384	5.9
Gene Tormohlen	71	775	324	144	.444	82	54	.659	314	60	138	3	342	4.8
John Barnhill	31	691	243	104	.428	86	54	.628	91	83	58	0	262	8.5
Jeff Mullins	44	587	296	113	.382	36	29	.806	69	66	68	1	255	5.8
Charles Vaughn	19	445	192	72	.375	62	46	.742	46	36	39	1	190	10.0
Paul Silas	46	586	173	70	.405	61	35	.574	236	22	72	0	185	3.8
John Tresvant	15	213	78	37	.474	32	27	.844	85	10	43	0	101	6.7
Mike Farmer	9	79	30	13	.433	5	4	.800	18	6	10	0	30	3.3

SAN FRANCISCO WARRIORS

Player	G.	Min.	FGA	FGM	Pct.	FTA	FTM	Pct.	Reb.	Ast.	PF	Disq.	Pts.	Avg.
Rick Barry	80	2990	1698	745	.439	660	569	.862	850	173	297	2	2059	25.7
Guy Rodgers	79	2902	1571	586	.373	407	296	.727	421	846	241	6	1468	18.6
Nate Thurmond	73	2891	1119	454	.406	428	280	.654	1312	111	223	7	1188	16.3
Tom Meschery	80	2383	895	401	.448	293	224	.765	716	81	285	7	1026	12.8
Paul Neumann	66	1729	817	343	.420	317	265	.836	208	184	174	0	951	14.4
Al Attles	79	2053	724	364	.503	252	154	.611	322	225	265	7	882	11.2
McCoy McLemore	80	1467	528	225	.426	191	142	.743	488	55	197	4	592	7.4
Fred Hetzel	56	722	401	160	.399	92	63	.685	290	27	121	2	383	6.8
Gary Phillips	67	867	303	106	.350	87	54	.621	134	113	97	0	266	4.0
Keith Erickson	64	646	267	95	.356	65	43	.662	162	38	91	1	233	3.6
Enoch Olsen (Tot.)	59	602	193	81	.420	88	39	.443	192	20	81	1	201	3.4
Enoch Olsen (S.F.)	55	566	185	78	.422	85	38	.447	179	18	77	1	194	3.4
Wilbert Frazier	2	9	4	0	.000	2	1	.500	5	1	1	0	1	5.5

PLAYOFF RESULTS

EASTERN DIVISION SEMIFINALS
Boston 3, Cincinnati 2

Mar. 23—Cincinnati 107 at Boston 103
Mar. 26—Boston 132 at Cincinnati 125
Mar. 27—Cincinnati 113 at Boston 107
Mar. 30—Boston 120 at Cincinnati 103
Apr.   1—Cincinnati 103 at Boston 112

EASTERN DIVISION FINALS
Boston 4, Philadelphia 1

Apr.   3—Boston 115 at Philadelphia.................96
Apr.   6—at Boston 114 Philadelphia..................93
Apr.   7—at Philadelphia 111 Boston 105
Apr. 10—at Boston 114 Philadelphia ....°108
Apr. 12—Boston 120 at Philadelphia 112
°Overtime

WESTERN DIVISION SEMIFINALS
St. Louis 3, Baltimore 0

Mar. 24—St. Louis 113 at Baltimore 111
Mar. 27—St. Louis 105 at Baltimore 100
Mar. 30—at St. Louis 121 Baltimore 112

WESTERN DIVISION FINALS
Los Angeles 4, St. Louis 3

Apr.   1—St. Louis 106 at Los Angeles...............129
Apr.   3—St. Louis 116 at Los Angeles...............125
Apr.   6—Los Angeles 113 at St. Louis...............120
Apr.   9—Los Angeles 107 at St. Louis.................95
Apr. 10—St. Louis 112 at Los Angeles...............100
Apr. 13—Los Angeles 127 at St. Louis...............131
Apr. 15—St. Louis 121 at Los Angeles...............130

WORLD CHAMPIONSHIP SERIES
Boston 4, Los Angeles 3

Apr. 17—Los Angeles 133 at Boston.......................°129
Apr. 19—Los Angeles 109 at Boston.......................129
Apr. 20—Boston 120 at Los Angeles.......................106
Apr. 22—Boston 122 at Los Angeles.......................117
Apr. 24—Los Angeles 121 at Boston.......................117
Apr. 26—Boston 115 at Los Angeles.......................123
Apr. 28—Los Angeles 93 at Boston 95

°Denotes overtime period.

1964-65 NBA STATISTICS

1964-65 NBA CHAMPION BOSTON CELTICS

Seated (left to right): K. C. Jones, Tom Heinsohn, President Louis Pieri, Coach Red Auerbach, Bill Russell, Sam Jones. Standing: Ron Bonham, Larry Siegfried, Willie Naulls, Mel Counts, John Thompson, Tom Sanders, John Havlicek, Trainer Buddy LeRoux.

FINAL STANDINGS

EASTERN DIVISION

Team	Bos.	Cin.	Phil.	N.Y.	L.A.	St.L.	Balt.	Det.	S.F.	W.	L.	Pct.	G.B.
Boston	..	8	5	7	7	9	7	10	9	62	18	.775	....
Cincinnati	2	..	6	8	6	8	4	6	8	48	32	.600	14
Philadelphia	5	4	..	5	3	5	6	6	6	40	40	.500	22
New York	3	2	5	..	0	1	8	5	7	31	49	.388	31

WESTERN DIVISION

Los Angeles	3	4	7	10	..	4	6	7	8	49	31	.613	....
St. Louis	1	2	5	9	6	..	5	7	10	45	35	.563	4
Baltimore	3	6	4	2	4	5	..	6	7	37	43	.463	12
Detroit	0	4	4	5	3	3	4	..	8	31	49	.388	18
San Francisco	1	2	4	3	2	0	3	2	..	17	63	.213	32

HOME-ROAD-NEUTRAL RECORDS OF ALL TEAMS

	Home	Road	Neutral	Total		Home	Road	Neutral	Total
Baltimore	23- 14	12- 19	2-10	37- 43	New York	16- 19	8- 22	7- 8	31- 49
Boston	27- 3	27- 11	8- 4	62- 18	Philadelphia	13- 12	9- 21	18- 7	40- 40
Cincinnati	25- 7	17- 21	6- 4	48- 32	St. Louis	26- 14	15- 17	4- 4	45- 35
Detroit	13- 17	11- 20	7-12	31- 49	San Francisco	10- 26	5- 31	2- 6	17- 63
Los Angeles	25- 13	21- 16	3- 2	49- 31	Total	178-125	125-178	57-57	360-360

TEAM STATISTICS

Team	G.	FGA	FGM	Pct.	FTA	FTM	Pct.	Reb.	Ast.	PF	Disq.	For	Agst.	Pt.Dif.
Boston	80	8609	3567	.414	2587	1890	.731	5748	1772	2065	36	112.8	104.5	8.3
St. Louis	80	7710	3269	.424	2947	2168	.736	5208	1691	2069	26	108.8	105.8	3.0
Cincinnati	80	7797	3482	.447	2866	2170	.757	5387	1843	1992	30	114.2	111.9	2.3
Los Angeles	80	7628	3336	.437	2984	2276	.763	5231	1601	1998	28	111.9	109.9	2.0
Philadelphia	80	8028	3391	.422	3011	2221	.738	5246	1692	2096	53	112.5	112.7	—0.2
Baltimore	80	7734	3421	.442	3144	2245	.714	5298	1676	2119	41	113.6	115.8	—2.2
Detroit	80	8297	3467	.418	2537	1747	.689	5394	1609	2058	35	108.5	111.9	—3.4
New York	80	7834	3339	.426	2684	1915	.713	5206	1550	2283	40	107.4	111.1	—3.7
San Francisco	80	8245	3323	.403	2844	1819	.640	5715	1653	2002	34	105.8	112.0	—6.2

INDIVIDUAL LEADERS

POINTS

	G.	FG	FT	Pts.	Avg.		G.	FG	FT	Pts.	Avg.
W. Chamberlain, SF-Phil	73	1063	408	2534	34.7	Gus Johnson, Baltimore	76	577	261	1415	18.6
Jerry West, Los Angeles	74	822	648	2292	31.0	Jerry Lucas, Cincinnati	66	558	298	1414	21.4
Oscar Robertson, Cincinnati	75	807	665	2279	30.4	Hal Greer, Philadelphia	70	539	335	1413	20.2
Sam Jones, Boston	80	821	428	2070	25.9	John Havlicek, Boston	75	570	235	1375	18.3
Elgin Baylor, Los Angeles	74	763	483	2009	27.1	Zelmo Beaty, St. Louis	80	505	341	1351	16.9
Walt Bellamy, Baltimore	80	733	515	1981	24.8	Dave DeBusschere, Detroit	79	508	306	1322	16.7
Willis Reed, New York	80	629	302	1560	19.5	Len Wilkens, St. Louis	78	434	416	1284	16.5
Bailey Howell, Baltimore	80	515	504	1534	19.2	Nate Thurmond, San Fran	77	519	235	1273	16.5
Terry Dischinger, Detroit	80	568	320	1456	18.2	Adrian Smith, Cincinnati	80	463	284	1210	15.1
Don Ohl, Baltimore	77	568	284	1420	18.4	Jim Barnes, New York	75	454	251	1159	15.5

FIELD GOALS
(Minimum 220 FGM)

	FGA	FGM	Pct.
Wilt Chamberlain, SF-Phila	2083	1063	.510
Walt Bellamy, Baltimore	1441	733	.509
Jerry Lucas, Cincinnati	1121	558	.498
Jerry West, Los Angeles	1655	822	.497
Bailey Howell, Baltimore	1040	515	.495
Terry Dischinger, Detroit	1153	568	.493
John Egan, New York	529	258	.488
Zelmo Beaty, St. Louis	1047	505	.482
Oscar Robertson, Cincinnati	1681	807	.480
Paul Neumann, Phila-SF	772	365	.473

ASSISTS

	G.	No.	Avg.
Oscar Robertson, Cincinnati	75	861	11.5
Guy Rodgers, San Francisco	79	565	7.2
K. C. Jones, Boston	78	437	5.6
Len Wilkens, St. Louis	78	431	5.5
Bill Russell, Boston	78	410	5.3
Jerry West, Los Angeles	74	364	4.9
Hal Greer, Philadelphia	70	313	4.5
Kevin Loughery, Baltimore	80	296	3.7
Elgin Baylor, Los Angeles	74	280	3.8
Larry Costello, Philadelphia	64	275	4.3

FREE THROWS
(Minimum 210 FTM)

	FTA	FTM	Pct.
Larry Costello, Philadelphia	277	243	.877
Oscar Robertson, Cincinnati	793	665	.839
Howard Komives, New York	254	212	.835
Adrian, Smith, Cincinnati	342	284	.830
Jerry West, Los Angeles	789	648	.821
Sam Jones, Boston	522	428	.820
Bob Pettit, St. Louis	405	332	.820
Jerry Lucas, Cincinnati	366	298	.814
Dave Gambee, Philadelphia	368	299	.813
Hal Greer, Philadelphia	413	335	.811

REBOUNDS

	G.	No.	Avg.
Bill Russell, Boston	78	1878	24.1
Wilt Chamberlain, SF-Phila.	73	1673	22.9
Nate Thurmond, San Fran.	77	1395	18.1
Jerry Lucas, Cincinnati	66	1321	20.0
Willis Reed, New York	80	1175	14.7
Walt Bellamy, Baltimore	80	1166	14.6
Gus Johnson, Baltimore	76	988	13.0
Lucious Jackson, Phila.	76	980	12.9
Zelmo Beaty, St. Louis	80	966	12.1
Elgin Baylor, Los Angeles	74	950	12.8

TEAM-BY-TEAM INDIVIDUAL STATISTICS

BALTIMORE BULLETS

Player	G.	Min.	FGA	FGM	Pct.	FTA	FTM	Pct.	Reb.	Ast.	PF	Disq.	Pts.	Avg.
Walt Bellamy	80	3301	1441	733	.509	752	515	.685	1166	191	260	2	1981	24.8
Bailey Howell	80	2975	1040	515	.495	629	504	.801	869	208	345	10	1534	19.2
Don Ohl	77	2821	1297	568	.438	388	284	.732	336	250	274	7	1420	18.4
Gus Johnson	76	2899	1379	577	.418	386	261	.676	988	270	258	4	1415	18.6
Kevin Loughery	80	2417	957	406	.424	281	212	.754	235	296	320	13	1024	12.8
Wayne Hightower (Tot.)	75	1547	570	196	.344	254	195	.768	420	54	204	2	587	7.8
Wayne Hightower (Balt.)	27	510	174	60	.345	81	62	.765	173	16	61	1	182	6.7
Bob Ferry	77	1280	338	143	.423	199	122	.613	355	60	156	2	408	5.3
Wally Jones	77	1250	411	154	.375	136	99	.728	140	200	196	1	407	5.3
Sihugo Green	70	1086	368	152	.413	161	101	.627	169	140	134	1	405	5.8
Gary Bradds	41	335	111	46	.414	63	45	.714	84	19	36	0	137	3.3
Charles Hardnett	20	200	80	25	.313	39	23	.590	77	2	37	0	73	3.7
Al Butler	25	172	73	24	.329	15	11	.733	21	12	25	0	59	2.4
Les Hunter	24	114	64	18	.281	14	6	.429	50	11	16	0	42	1.8
Gary Hill°°°	12	103	36	10	.278	14	7	.500	16	7	11	0	27	2.3
Gary Hill°°	3	15	1	0	.000	0	0	.000	1	1	1	0	0	0.0

BOSTON CELTICS

Player	G.	Min.	FGA	FGM	Pct.	FTA	FTM	Pct.	Reb.	Ast.	PF	Disq.	Pts.	Avg.
Sam Jones	80	2885	1818	821	.452	522	428	.820	411	223	176	0	2070	25.9
John Havlicek	75	2169	1420	570	.401	316	235	.744	371	199	200	2	1375	18.3
Bill Russell	78	3466	980	429	.438	426	244	.573	1878	410	204	1	1102	14.1
Tom Sanders	80	2459	871	374	.429	259	193	.745	661	92	318	15	941	11.8
Tom Heinsohn	67	1706	954	365	.383	229	182	.795	399	157	252	5	912	13.6
Willie Naulls	71	1465	786	302	.384	176	143	.813	336	72	225	5	747	10.5
K. C. Jones	78	2434	639	253	.396	227	143	.630	318	437	263	5	649	8.3
Larry Siegfried	72	996	417	173	.415	140	109	.779	134	119	108	1	455	6.3
Ron Bonham	37	369	220	91	.414	112	92	.821	78	19	33	0	274	7.4
Mel Counts	54	572	272	100	.368	74	58	.784	265	19	134	1	258	4.8
John Thompson	64	699	209	84	.402	105	62	.590	230	16	141	0	230	3.6
Bob Nordmann	3	25	5	3	.600	0	0	.000	8	3	5	0	6	2.0
Gerry Ward	3	30	18	2	.111	1	1	1.000	5	6	6	0	5	1.7

CINCINNATI ROYALS

Player	G.	Min.	FGA	FGM	Pct.	FTA	FTM	Pct.	Reb.	Ast.	PF	Disq.	Pts.	Avg.
Oscar Robertson	75	3421	1681	807	.480	793	665	.839	674	861	205	2	2279	30.4
Jerry Lucas	66	2864	1121	558	.498	366	298	.814	1321	157	214	1	1414	21.4
Adrian Smith	80	2745	1016	463	.456	342	284	.830	220	240	199	2	1210	15.1
Jack Twyman	80	2236	1081	479	.443	239	198	.828	383	137	239	4	1156	14.5
Wayne Embry	74	2243	772	352	.456	371	239	.644	741	92	297	10	943	12.7
Bud Olsen	79	1372	512	224	.438	195	144	.738	333	84	203	5	592	7.5
Tom Hawkins	79	1864	538	220	.409	204	116	.569	475	80	240	4	556	7.0
Harold Hairston	61	736	351	131	.373	165	110	.667	293	27	95	0	372	6.1
Jay Arnette	63	662	245	91	.371	75	56	.747	62	68	125	1	238	3.8
Arlen Bockhorn	19	424	157	60	.382	39	28	.718	55	45	52	1	148	7.8
Tom Thacker	55	470	168	56	.333	47	23	.489	127	41	64	0	135	2.5
George Wilson	39	288	155	41	.265	30	9	.300	102	11	59	0	91	2.3

DETROIT PISTONS

Player	G.	Min.	FGA	FGM	Pct.	FTA	FTM	Pct.	Reb.	Ast.	PF	Disq.	Pts.	Avg.
Terry Dischinger	80	2698	1153	568	.493	424	320	.755	479	198	253	5	1456	18.2
Dave DeBusschere	79	2769	1196	508	.425	437	306	.700	874	253	242	5	1322	16.7
Eddie Miles	76	2074	994	439	.442	223	166	.744	258	157	201	1	1044	13.7
Ray Scott	66	2167	1092	402	.368	314	220	.701	634	239	209	5	1024	15.5
Reggie Harding	78	2699	987	405	.410	209	128	.612	906	179	258	5	938	12.0
Rod Thorn	74	1770	750	320	.427	243	176	.724	266	161	122	0	816	11.0
Joe Caldwell	66	1543	776	290	.374	210	129	.614	441	118	171	3	709	10.7
Don Kojis	65	836	416	180	.433	98	62	.633	243	63	115	1	422	6.5
Donnie Butcher	71	1157	353	143	.405	204	126	.618	200	122	183	4	412	5.8
Jack Moreland	54	732	296	103	.348	104	66	.635	183	69	151	4	272	5.0
Hub Reed	62	753	221	84	.380	58	40	.690	206	38	136	2	208	3.4
Willie Jones	12	101	52	21	.404	6	2	.333	10	7	13	0	44	3.7
Bob Duffy	4	26	11	4	.364	7	6	.857	4	5	4	0	14	3.5

LOS ANGELES LAKERS

Player	G.	Min.	FGA	FGM	Pct.	FTA	FTM	Pct.	Reb.	Ast.	PF	Disq.	Pts.	Avg.
Jerry West	74	3066	1655	822	.497	789	648	.821	447	364	221	2	2292	31.0
Elgin Baylor	74	3056	1903	763	.401	610	483	.792	950	280	235	0	2009	27.1
Rudy LaRusso	77	2588	827	381	.461	415	321	.773	725	198	258	3	1083	14.1
Dick Barnett	74	2026	908	375	.413	338	270	.799	200	159	209	1	1020	13.8
Leroy Ellis	80	2026	700	311	.444	284	198	.697	652	49	196	1	820	10.3
Jim King	77	1671	469	184	.392	151	118	.781	214	178	193	2	486	6.3
Gene Wiley	80	2002	376	175	.465	111	56	.505	690	105	235	11	406	5.1
Darrall Imhoff	76	1521	311	145	.466	154	88	.571	500	87	238	7	378	4.8
Walt Hazzard	66	919	306	117	.382	71	46	.648	111	140	132	0	280	4.2
Don Nelson	39	238	85	36	.424	26	20	.769	73	24	40	1	92	2.4
Bill McGill (Tot.)	24	133	65	21	.323	17	13	.765	36	9	32	1	55	2.3
Bill McGill (L.A.)	8	37	20	7	.350	1	1	1.000	12	3	6	0	15	1.9
Cotton Nash	25	167	57	14	.246	32	25	.781	35	10	30	0	53	2.1
Jerry Grote	11	33	11	6	.545	2	2	1.000	4	4	5	0	14	1.3

NEW YORK KNICKERBOCKERS

Player	G.	Min.	FGA	FGM	Pct.	FTA	FTM	Pct.	Reb.	Ast.	PF	Disq.	Pts.	Avg.
Willis Reed	80	3042	1457	629	.432	407	302	.742	1175	133	339	14	1560	19.5
Jim Barnes	75	2586	1070	454	.424	379	251	.662	729	93	312	8	1159	15.5
Bob Boozer	80	2139	963	424	.440	375	288	.768	604	108	183	0	1136	14.2
Howard Komives	80	2376	1020	381	.374	254	212	.835	195	265	246	2	974	12.2
John Green	78	1720	737	346	.469	301	165	.548	545	129	194	3	857	11.0
John Egan	74	1664	529	258	.488	199	162	.814	143	252	139	0	678	9.2
Tom Gola	77	1727	455	204	.448	180	133	.739	319	220	269	8	541	7.0
Dave Budd	62	1188	407	196	.482	170	121	.712	310	62	147	1	513	8.3
Emmette Bryant	77	1332	436	145	.333	133	87	.654	167	167	212	3	377	4.9
Len Chappell	43	655	367	145	.395	100	68	.680	140	15	73	0	358	8.3
Art Heyman	55	663	267	114	.427	132	88	.667	99	79	96	0	316	5.7
Barry Kramer (Tot.)	52	507	186	63	.339	84	60	.714	100	41	67	1	186	3.6
Barry Kramer (N.Y.K.)	19	231	86	27	.314	40	30	.750	41	15	31	1	81	4.4
Tom Hoover	24	153	32	13	.406	14	8	.571	58	12	37	0	34	1.4
John Rudometkin	1	22	8	3	.375	0	0	.000	7	0	5	0	6	6.0

PHILADELPHIA 76ers

Player	G.	Min.	FGA	FGM	Pct.	FTA	FTM	Pct.	Reb.	Ast.	PF	Disq.	Pts.	Avg.
Wilt Chamberlain (Tot.)	73	3301	2083	1063	.510	880	408	.464	1673	250	146	0	2534	34.7
Wilt Chamberlain (Phi.)	35	1558	808	427	.528	380	200	.526	780	133	70	0	1054	30.1
Hal Greer	70	2600	1245	539	.433	413	335	.811	355	313	254	7	1413	20.2
Lucious Jackson	76	2590	1013	419	.414	404	288	.713	980	93	251	4	1126	14.8
Chet Walker	79	2187	936	377	.403	388	288	.742	528	132	200	2	1042	13.2
Dave Gambee	80	1993	864	356	.412	368	299	.813	468	113	277	7	1011	12.6
Larry Costello	64	1967	695	309	.445	277	243	.877	169	275	242	10	861	13.5
John Kerr	80	1810	714	264	.370	181	126	.696	551	197	132	1	654	8.2
Paul Neumann	40	1100	434	213	.491	184	148	.804	102	139	119	1	574	14.4
Al Bianchi	60	1116	486	175	.360	76	54	.711	95	140	178	10	404	6.7
Ben Warley	64	900	253	94	.372	176	124	.705	277	53	170	6	312	4.9
Connie Dierking	38	729	311	121	.389	83	54	.651	239	42	101	3	296	7.8
Larry Jones	23	359	153	47	.307	52	37	.712	57	40	46	2	131	5.7
Steve Courtin	24	317	103	42	.408	21	17	.810	22	22	44	0	101	4.2
Jerry Greenspan	5	49	13	8	.615	8	8	1.000	11	0	12	0	24	4.8

ST. LOUIS HAWKS

Player	G.	Min.	FGA	FGM	Pct.	FTA	FTM	Pct.	Reb.	Ast.	PF	Disq.	Pts.	Avg.
Bob Pettit	50	1754	923	396	.429	405	332	.820	621	128	167	0	1124	22.5
Zelmo Beaty	80	2916	1047	505	.482	477	341	.715	966	111	328	11	1351	16.9
Len Wilkens	78	2854	1048	434	.414	558	416	.746	365	431	283	7	1284	16.5
Cliff Hagan	77	1739	901	393	.436	268	214	.799	276	136	182	0	1000	13.0
Bill Bridges	79	2362	938	362	.386	275	186	.676	853	187	276	3	910	11.5
Charles Vaughn	75	1965	811	344	.424	242	182	.752	173	157	192	2	870	11.6
Richie Guerin	57	1678	662	295	.446	301	231	.767	149	271	193	1	821	14.4
Mike Farmer	60	1272	408	167	.409	94	75	.798	258	88	123	0	409	6.8
Paul Silas	79	1243	375	140	.373	164	83	.506	576	48	161	1	363	4.6
John Barnhill	41	777	312	121	.388	70	45	.643	91	76	56	0	287	7.0
Jeff Mullins	44	492	209	87	.416	61	41	.672	102	44	60	0	215	4.9
Bill McGill	16	96	45	14	.311	16	12	.750	24	6	26	1	40	2.5
Ed Burton	7	42	20	7	.350	7	4	.571	13	2	13	0	18	2.6
John Tresvant	4	35	11	4	.364	9	6	.667	18	6	9	0	14	3.5

SAN FRANCISCO WARRIORS

Player	G.	Min.	FGA	FGM	Pct.	FTA	FTM	Pct.	Reb.	Ast.	PF	Disq.	Pts.	Avg.
Wilt Chamberlain	38	1743	1275	636	.499	500	208	.416	893	117	76	0	1480	38.9
Nate Thurmond	77	3173	1240	519	.419	357	235	.658	1395	157	232	3	1273	16.5
Guy Rodgers	79	2699	1225	465	.380	325	223	.686	323	565	256	4	1153	14.6
Tom Meschery	79	2408	917	361	.394	370	278	.751	655	106	279	6	1000	12.7
Paul Neumann (Tot.)	76	2034	772	365	.473	303	234	.772	198	233	218	3	964	12.7
Paul Neumann (S.F.)	36	934	338	152	.450	119	86	.723	96	94	99	2	390	10.8
Al Attles	73	1733	662	254	.384	274	171	.624	239	205	242	7	679	9.3
McCoy McLemore	78	1731	725	244	.337	220	157	.714	488	81	224	6	645	8.3
Connie Dierking (Tot.)	68	1294	538	218	.405	168	100	.595	435	72	165	4	536	7.9
Connie Dierking (S.F.)	30	565	227	97	.427	85	46	.541	196	30	64	1	240	8.0
Gary Phillips	73	1541	553	198	.358	199	120	.603	189	148	184	3	516	7.1
Wayne Hightower	48	1037	396	136	.343	173	133	.769	247	38	143	1	405	8.4
Bud Koper	54	631	241	106	.440	42	35	.833	61	43	59	1	247	4.6
John Rudometkin (Tot.)	23	376	154	52	.338	50	34	.680	99	16	54	0	138	6.0
John Rudometkin (S.F.)	22	354	146	49	.336	50	34	.680	92	16	49	0	132	6.0
Cotton Nash (Tot.)	45	357	145	47	.324	52	43	.827	83	19	57	0	137	3.0
Cotton Nash (S.F.)	20	190	88	33	.375	20	18	.900	48	9	27	0	84	4.2
Barry Kramer	33	276	100	36	.360	44	30	.682	59	26	36	0	102	3.1
George Lee	19	247	77	27	.351	52	38	.731	55	12	22	0	92	4.8
Gary Hill	9	88	35	10	.286	14	7	.500	15	6	10	0	27	3.0

PLAYOFF RESULTS

EASTERN DIVISION SEMIFINALS
Philadelphia 3, Cincinnati 1

Mar. 24—Philadelphia 119 at Cincinnati..117
Mar. 26—Cincinnati 121 at Philadelphia......................................120
Mar. 28—Philadelphia 108 at Cincinnati.. 94
Mar. 31—Cincinnati 112 at Philadelphia......................................119

WESTERN DIVISION SEMIFINALS
Baltimore 3, St. Louis 1

Mar. 24—Baltimore 108 at St. Louis 105
Mar. 26—Baltimore 105 at St. Louis 129
Mar. 27—St. Louis 99 at Baltimore...131
Mar. 30—St. Louis 103 at Baltimore...109

EASTERN DIVISION FINALS
Boston 4, Philadelphia 3

Apr.   4—Philadelphia 98 at Boston...108
Apr.   6—Boston 103 at Philadelphia...109
Apr.   8—Philadelphia 94 at Boston...112
Apr.   9—Boston 131 at Philadelphia...*134
Apr. 11—Philadelphia 108 at Boston...114
Apr. 13—Boston 106 at Philadelphia...112
Apr. 15—Philadelphia 109 at Boston...110

WESTERN DIVISION FINALS
Los Angeles 4, Baltimore 2

Apr.   3—Baltimore 115 at Los Angeles.......................................121
Apr.   5—Baltimore 115 at Los Angeles.......................................118
Apr.   7—Los Angeles 115 at Baltimore.......................................122
Apr.   9—Los Angeles 112 at Baltimore.......................................114
Apr. 11—Baltimore 112 at Los Angeles.......................................120
Apr. 13—Los Angeles 117 at Baltimore.......................................115

WORLD CHAMPIONSHIP SERIES
Boston 4, Los Angeles 1

Apr. 18—Los Angeles 110 at Boston...142
Apr. 19—Los Angeles 123 at Boston...129
Apr. 21—Boston 105 at Los Angeles...126
Apr. 23—Boston 112 at Los Angeles... 99
Apr. 25—Los Angeles 96 at Boston...129

*—Denotes overtime period.

1963-64 NBA STATISTICS

1963-64 NBA CHAMPION BOSTON CELTICS

Seated (left to right): Sam Jones, Frank Ramsey, K. C. Jones, Coach Red Auerbach, President Walter A. Brown, Bill Russell, John Havlicek. Standing: Jack McCarthy, Tom Sanders, Tom Heinsohn, Clyde Lovellette, Willie Naulls, Jim Loscutoff, Larry Siegfried, Trainer Buddy LeRoux. Inset: Vice-President Lou Pieri.

FINAL STANDINGS

EASTERN DIVISION

Team	Bos.	Cin.	Phil.	N.Y.	S.F.	S.L.	L.A.	Balt.	Det.	W.	L.	Pct.	G.B.
Boston	..	5	10	10	5	7	6	9	7	59	21	.738	....
Cincinnati	7	..	9	11	5	4	4	8	7	55	25	.688	4
Philadelphia	2	3	..	8	4	3	4	5	5	34	46	.425	25
New York	2	1	4	..	1	4	2	3	5	22	58	.275	37

WESTERN DIVISION

Team	Bos.	Cin.	Phil.	N.Y.	S.F.	S.L.	L.A.	Balt.	Det.	W.	L.	Pct.	G.B.
San Francisco	3	4	4	8	..	6	7	7	9	48	32	.600	....
St. Louis	2	4	6	4	6	..	7	7	10	46	34	.575	2
Los Angeles	3	4	5	6	5	5	..	7	7	42	38	.525	6
Baltimore	1	2	5	7	3	3	3	..	7	31	49	.388	17
Detroit	1	2	3	4	3	2	5	3	..	23	57	.288	25

HOME-ROAD-NEUTRAL RECORDS OF ALL TEAMS

	Home	Road	Neutral	Total		Home	Road	Neutral	Total
Baltimore	20- 19	8- 21	3- 9	31- 49	New York	10- 25	8- 27	4- 6	22- 58
Boston	26- 4	21- 17	12- 0	59- 21	Philadelphia	18- 12	12- 22	4-12	34- 46
Cincinnati	26- 7	18- 18	11- 0	55- 25	St. Louis	27- 12	17- 19	2- 3	46- 34
Detroit	9- 21	6- 25	8-11	23- 57	San Francisco	25- 14	21- 15	2- 3	48- 32
Los Angeles	24- 12	15- 21	3- 5	42- 38	Totals	185-126	126-185	49-49	360-360

TEAM STATISTICS

Team	G.	FGA	FGM	Pct.	FTA	FTM	Pct.	Reb.	Ast.	PF	Disq.	For	Agst.	Pt.Dif.
Boston	80	8770	3619	.413	2489	1804	.725	5736	1760	2125	19	113.0	105.1	+7.9
San Francisco	80	7779	3407	.438	2821	1800	.638	5499	1899	1978	33	107.7	102.6	+5.1
Cincinnati	80	7761	3516	.453	2828	2146	.759	5400	1916	2139	35	114.7	109.7	+5.0
St. Louis	80	7776	3341	.430	2795	2115	.757	4959	1901	2266	39	110.0	108.4	+1.6
Los Angeles	80	7438	3272	.440	2910	2230	.766	5025	1676	1997	26	109.7	108.7	+1.0
Baltimore	80	7862	3456	.440	2958	2036	.688	5460	1423	2073	45	111.9	113.6	—1.7
Philadelphia	80	8116	3394	.418	2851	2184	.766	5132	1643	2251	39	112.2	116.5	—4.3
New York	80	7888	3512	.445	2852	1952	.684	5067	1563	2222	33	112.2	119.6	—7.4
Detroit	80	7943	3346	.421	2685	1928	.718	5145	1633	2235	50	107.8	115.5	—7.7

INDIVIDUAL LEADERS

POINTS

	G.	FG	FT	Pts.	Avg.		G.	FG	FT	Pts.	Avg.
Wilt Chamberlain, S. Fran.	80	1204	540	2948	36.9	Sam Jones, Boston	76	612	249	1473	19.4
Oscar Robertson, Cincinnati	79	840	800	2480	31.4	Dick Barnett, Los Angeles	78	541	351	1433	18.4
Bob Pettit, St. Louis	80	791	608	2190	27.4	Cliff Hagan, St. Louis	77	572	269	1413	18.4
Walt Bellamy, Baltimore	80	811	537	2159	27.0	Ray Scott, Detroit	80	539	328	1406	17.6
Jerry West, Los Angeles	72	740	584	2064	28.7	Jerry Lucas, Cincinnati	79	545	310	1400	17.7
Elgin Baylor, Los Angeles	78	756	471	1983	25.4	Wayne Embry, Cincinnati	80	556	271	1383	17.3
Hal Greer, Philadelphia	80	715	435	1865	23.3	Gus Johnson, Baltimore	78	571	210	1352	17.3
Bailey Howell, Detroit	77	598	470	1666	21.6	Len Chappell, Phila.-N.Y.	79	531	288	1350	17.1
Terry Dischinger, Baltimore	80	604	454	1662	20.8	John Kerr, Philadelphia	80	536	268	1340	16.8
John Havlicek, Boston	80	640	315	1595	19.9	Chet Walker, Philadelphia	76	492	330	1314	17.3

FIELD GOALS
(Minimum 210 FGM)

	FGA	FGM	Pct.
Jerry Lucas, Cincinnati	1035	545	.527
Wilt Chamberlain, San Francisco	2298	1204	.524
Walt Bellamy, Baltimore	1582	811	.513
Terry Dischinger, Baltimore	1217	604	.496
Bill McGill, Balt.-N.Y.	937	456	.487
Jerry West, Los Angeles	1529	740	.484
Oscar Robertson, Cincinnati	1740	840	.483
Bailey Howell, Detroit	1267	598	.472
John Green, New York	1026	482	.470
Bob Pettit, St. Louis	1708	791	.463

ASSISTS

	G.	No.	Avg.
Oscar Robertson, Cincinnati	79	868	11.0
Guy Rodgers, San Francisco	79	556	7.0
K. C. Jones, Boston	80	407	5.1
Jerry West, Los Angeles	72	403	5.6
Wilt Chamberlain, San Francisco	80	403	5.0
Richie Guerin, N.Y.-St. Louis	80	375	4.7
Hal Greer, Philadelphia	80	374	4.7
Bill Russell, Boston	78	370	4.7
Len Wilkens, St. Louis	78	359	4.6
John Egan, Det.-N.Y.	66	358	5.4

FREE THROWS
(Minimum 210 FTM)

	FTA	FTM	Pct.
Oscar Robertson, Cincinnati	938	800	.853
Jerry West, Los Angeles	702	584	.832
Hal Greer, Philadelphia	525	435	.829
Tom Heinsohn, Boston	342	283	.827
Richie Guerin, N.Y.-St. Louis	424	347	.818
Cliff Hagan, St. Louis	331	269	.813
Bailey Howell, Detroit	581	470	.809
Elgin Baylor, Los Angeles	586	471	.804
Wayne Hightower, San Francisco	329	260	.790
Paul Neumann, Philadelphia	266	210	.789

REBOUNDS

	G.	No.	Avg.
Bill Russell, Boston	78	1930	24.7
Wilt Chamberlain, San Francisco	80	1787	22.3
Jerry Lucas, Cincinnati	79	1375	17.4
Walt Bellamy, Baltimore	80	1361	17.0
Bob Pettit, St. Louis	80	1224	15.3
Ray Scott, Detroit	80	1078	13.5
Gus Johnson, Baltimore	78	1064	13.6
John Kerr, Philadelphia	80	1017	12.7
Elgin Baylor, Los Angeles	78	936	12.0
Wayne Embry, Cincinnati	80	925	11.6

TEAM-BY-TEAM INDIVIDUAL STATISTICS

BALTIMORE BULLETS

Player	G.	Min.	FGA	FGM	Pct.	FTA	FTM	Pct.	Reb.	Ast.	PF	Disq.	Pts.	Avg.
Walt Bellamy	80	3394	1582	811	.513	825	537	.651	1361	126	300	7	2159	27.0
Terry Dischinger	80	2816	1217	604	.496	585	454	.776	667	157	321	10	1662	20.8
Gus Johnson	78	2847	1329	571	.430	319	210	.658	1064	169	321	11	1352	17.3
Rod Thorn	75	2594	1015	411	.405	353	258	.731	360	281	187	3	1080	14.4
Sihugo Green	75	2064	691	287	.415	290	198	.683	282	215	224	5	772	10.3
Kevin Loughery*	66	1459	631	236	.374	177	126	.712	138	182	175	2	598	9.1
Don Kojis	78	1148	484	203	.419	146	82	.562	309	57	123	0	488	6.3
Charles Hardnett	66	617	260	107	.412	125	84	.672	251	27	114	1	298	4.5
Barney Cable	71	1125	290	116	.400	42	28	.667	301	47	166	3	260	3.7
Gene Shue	47	963	276	81	.293	61	36	.590	94	150	98	2	198	4.2
Paul Hogue*	15	147	30	12	.400	7	2	.286	31	6	35	1	26	1.7
Larry Comley	12	89	37	8	.216	16	9	.563	19	12	11	0	25	2.1
Mel Peterson	2	3	1	1	1.000	0	0	.000	1	0	2	0	2	1.0
Roger Strickland	1	4	3	1	.333	0	0	.000	0	0	1	0	2	2.0

*Loughery—1 Detroit, 65 Baltimore.
Hogue—6 New York, 9 Baltimore.

BOSTON CELTICS

Player	G.	Min.	FGA	FGM	Pct.	FTA	FTM	Pct.	Reb.	Ast.	PF	Disq.	Pts.	Avg.
John Havlicek	80	2587	1535	640	.417	422	315	.746	428	238	227	1	1595	19.9
Sam Jones	76	2381	1359	612	.450	318	249	.783	349	202	192	1	1473	19.4
Tom Heinsohn	76	2040	1223	487	.398	342	283	.827	460	183	268	3	1257	16.5
Bill Russell	78	3482	1077	466	.433	429	236	.550	1930	370	190	0	1168	15.0
Tom Sanders	80	2370	836	349	.417	280	213	.761	667	102	277	6	911	11.4
Willie Naulls	78	1409	769	321	.417	157	125	.796	356	64	208	0	767	9.8
K. C. Jones	80	2424	722	283	.392	168	88	.524	372	407	253	0	654	8.2
Frank Ramsey	75	1227	604	226	.374	233	196	.841	223	81	245	7	648	8.6
Clyde Lovellette	45	437	305	128	.420	57	45	.789	126	24	100	0	301	6.7
Jim Loscutoff	53	451	182	56	.308	31	18	.581	131	25	90	1	130	2.5
Larry Siegfried	31	261	110	35	.318	39	31	.795	51	40	33	0	101	3.3
Jack McCarthy	28	206	48	16	.333	13	5	.385	35	24	42	0	37	1.3

CINCINNATI ROYALS

Player	G.	Min.	FGA	FGM	Pct.	FTA	FTM	Pct.	Reb.	Ast.	PF	Disq.	Pts.	Avg.
Oscar Robertson	79	3559	1740	840	.483	938	800	.853	783	868	280	3	2480	31.4
Jerry Lucas	79	3273	1035	545	.527	398	310	.779	1375	204	300	6	1400	17.7
Wayne Embry	80	2915	1213	556	.458	417	271	.650	925	113	325	7	1383	17.3
Jack Twyman	68	1996	993	447	.450	228	189	.829	364	137	267	7	1083	15.9
Tom Hawkins	73	1770	580	256	.441	188	113	.601	435	74	198	4	625	8.6
Adrian Smith	66	1524	576	234	.406	197	154	.782	147	145	164	1	622	9.4
Arlen Bockhorn	70	1670	587	242	.412	126	96	.762	205	173	227	4	580	8.3
Larry Staverman°	60	674	212	98	.462	90	69	.767	176	32	118	3	265	4.4
Bud Olsen	49	513	210	85	.405	57	32	.561	149	29	78	0	202	4.1
Jay Arnette	48	501	196	71	.362	54	42	.778	54	71	105	2	184	3.8
Tom Thacker	48	457	181	53	.293	53	26	.491	115	51	51	0	132	2.8

°Staverman—6 Baltimore, 20 Detroit, 34 Cincinnati.

DETROIT PISTONS

Player	G.	Min.	FGA	FGM	Pct.	FTA	FTM	Pct.	Reb.	Ast.	PF	Disq.	Pts.	Avg.
Bailey Howell	77	2700	1267	598	.472	581	470	.809	776	205	290	9	1666	21.6
Ray Scott	80	2964	1307	539	.412	456	328	.719	1078	244	296	7	1406	17.6
Don Ohl	71	2366	1224	500	.408	331	225	.680	180	225	219	3	1225	17.3
Bob Ferry	74	1522	670	298	.445	279	186	.667	428	94	174	2	782	10.6
Jack Moreland	78	1780	639	272	.426	210	164	.781	405	121	268	9	708	9.1
Willie Jones	77	1539	680	265	.390	141	100	.709	253	172	211	5	630	8.2
Don Butcher°	78	1971	507	202	.398	256	159	.621	329	244	249	4	563	7.2
Reggie Harding	39	1158	460	184	.400	98	61	.622	410	52	119	1	429	11.0
Eddie Miles	60	811	371	131	.353	87	62	.713	95	58	92	0	324	5.4
Darrall Imhoff	58	871	251	104	.414	114	69	.605	283	56	167	5	277	4.3
Bob Duffy°	48	662	229	94	.410	65	44	.677	61	79	48	0	232	4.8
Dave DeBusschere	15	304	133	52	.391	43	25	.581	105	23	32	1	129	8.6

°Butcher—26 New York, 52 Detroit.
Duffy—2 St. Louis, 4 New York, 42 Detroit.

LOS ANGELES LAKERS

Player	G.	Min.	FGA	FGM	Pct.	FTA	FTM	Pct.	Reb.	Ast.	PF	Disq.	Pts.	Avg.
Jerry West	72	2906	1529	740	.484	702	584	.832	433	403	200	2	2064	28.7
Elgin Baylor	78	3164	1778	756	.425	586	471	.804	936	347	235	1	1983	25.4
Dick Barnett	78	2620	1197	541	.452	454	351	.773	250	238	233	3	1433	18.4
Rudy LaRusso	79	2746	776	337	.434	397	298	.751	800	190	268	5	972	12.3
LeRoy Ellis	78	1459	473	200	.423	170	112	.659	498	41	192	3	512	6.6
Don Nelson	80	1406	323	135	.418	201	149	.741	323	76	181	1	419	5.2
Frank Selvy	73	1286	423	160	.378	122	78	.639	139	149	115	1	398	5.5
Gene Wiley	78	1510	273	146	.535	75	45	.600	510	44	225	4	337	4.3
Jim Krebs	68	975	357	134	.375	85	65	.765	283	49	166	6	333	4.9
Jim King	60	762	198	84	.424	101	66	.653	113	110	99	0	234	3.9
Hub Reed	46	386	91	33	.363	15	10	.667	107	23	73	0	76	1.7
Mel Gibson	8	53	20	6	.800	2	1	.500	4	6	10	0	13	1.4

NEW YORK KNICKERBOCKERS

Player	G.	Min.	FGA	FGM	Pct.	FTA	FTM	Pct.	Reb.	Ast.	PF	Disq.	Pts.	Avg.
Len Chappell°	79	2505	1185	531	.448	403	288	.715	771	83	214	1	1350	17.1
Bob Boozer°°	81	2379	1096	468	.427	376	272	.723	596	96	231	1	1208	14.9
John Green	80	2134	1026	482	.470	392	195	.497	799	157	246	4	1159	14.5
Art Heyman	75	2236	1003	432	.431	422	289	.685	298	256	229	2	1153	15.4
Bill McGill°°°	74	1784	937	456	.487	282	204	.723	414	121	217	7	1116	15.1
John Egan°°°°	66	2325	758	334	.441	243	193	.794	191	358	181	3	861	13.0
Tom Gola	74	2156	602	258	.429	212	154	.726	469	257	278	7	670	9.1
Al Butler	76	1379	616	260	.422	187	138	.738	168	157	167	3	658	8.7
John Rudometkin	52	696	326	154	.472	116	87	.750	164	26	86	0	395	4.6
Dave Budd	73	1031	297	128	.431	115	84	.730	276	57	130	1	340	4.7
Tom Hoover	59	988	247	102	.413	132	81	.614	331	36	185	4	285	4.8
Gene Conley	46	551	189	74	.392	65	44	.677	156	21	124	2	192	4.2
Jerry Harkness	5	59	30	13	.433	8	3	.375	6	6	4	0	29	5.8

°Played 1 game with Philadelphia—Played 78 games with New York.
°°Played 32 games with Cincinnati—Played 49 games with New York.
°°°Played 6 games with Baltimore—Played 68 games with New York.
°°°°Played 24 games with Detroit—Played 42 games with New York.

PHILADELPHIA 76ers

Player	G.	Min.	FGA	FGM	Pct.	FTA	FTM	Pct.	Reb.	Ast.	PF	Disq.	Pts.	Avg.
Hal Greer	80	3157	1611	715	.444	525	435	.829	484	374	291	6	1865	23.3
John Kerr	80	2938	1250	536	.429	357	268	.751	1017	275	187	2	1340	16.8
Chet Walker	76	2775	1118	492	.440	464	330	.711	784	124	232	3	1314	17.3
Paul Neumann	74	1973	732	324	.443	266	210	.789	246	291	211	1	858	11.6
Ben Warley	79	1740	494	215	.435	305	220	.721	619	71	274	5	650	8.2
Al Bianchi	78	1437	684	257	.376	141	109	.773	147	149	248	6	623	8.0
Lee Shaffer	41	1013	587	217	.370	133	102	.767	205	36	116	1	536	13.1
Larry Costello	45	1137	408	191	.476	170	147	.865	105	167	150	3	529	11.8
Connie Dierking	76	1286	514	191	.372	169	114	.675	422	50	221	3	496	6.5
Dave Gambee	41	927	378	149	.394	185	151	.816	256	35	161	6	449	11.0
Dolph Schayes	24	350	143	44	.308	57	46	.807	110	48	76	3	134	5.6
Jerry Greenspan	20	280	90	32	.356	50	34	.680	72	11	54	0	98	4.9
Hubie White	23	196	105	31	.295	28	17	.607	42	12	28	0	79	3.4

ST. LOUIS HAWKS

Player	G.	Min.	FGA	FGM	Pct.	FTA	FTM	Pct.	Reb.	Ast.	PF	Disq.	Pts.	Avg.
Bob Pettit	80	3296	1708	791	.463	771	608	.789	1224	259	300	3	2190	27.4
Cliff Hagan	77	2279	1280	572	.447	331	269	.813	377	193	273	4	1413	18.4
Richie Guerin°	80	2366	846	351	.415	424	347	.818	256	375	276	4	1049	13.1
Len Wilkens	78	2526	808	334	.413	365	270	.740	335	359	287	7	938	12.0
Zelmo Beaty	59	1922	647	287	.444	270	200	.741	633	79	262	11	774	13.1
Bill Bridges	80	1949	675	268	.397	224	146	.652	680	181	269	6	682	8.5
Charlie Vaughn	68	1340	538	238	.442	148	107	.723	126	129	166	0	583	8.6
John Barnhill	74	1367	505	208	.412	115	70	.609	157	145	107	0	486	6.6
Mike Farmer	76	1361	438	178	.406	83	68	.819	225	109	140	0	424	5.6
Gene Tormohlen	51	640	250	94	.376	46	22	.478	216	50	128	3	210	4.1
Bob Nordmann°°	19	259	66	27	.409	19	9	.474	65	5	51	1	63	3.3
Gerry Ward	24	139	53	16	.302	17	11	.647	21	21	26	0	43	1.8
Ken Rohloff	2	7	1	0	.000	0	0	.000	0	1	4	0	0	0.0

°Played 2 games with New York—Played 78 games with St. Louis.
°°Played 7 games with New York—Played 12 games with St. Louis.

SAN FRANCISCO WARRIORS

Player	G.	Min.	FGA	FGM	Pct.	FTA	FTM	Pct.	Reb.	Ast.	PF	Disq.	Pts.	Avg.
Wilt Chamberlain	80	3689	2298	1204	.524	1016	540	.531	1787	403	182	0	2948	36.9
Tom Meschery	80	2422	951	436	.458	295	207	.702	612	149	288	6	1079	13.5
Wayne Hightower	79	2536	1022	393	.385	329	260	.790	566	133	269	7	1046	13.2
Guy Rodgers	79	2695	923	337	.365	280	198	.707	328	556	245	4	872	11.0
Al Attles	70	1883	640	289	.452	275	185	.673	236	197	249	4	763	10.9
Gary Phillips	66	2010	691	256	.370	218	146	.670	248	203	245	8	658	10.0
Nate Thurmond	76	1966	554	219	.395	173	95	.549	790	86	184	2	533	7.0
Gary Hill	67	1015	384	146	.380	77	51	.662	114	103	165	2	343	5.1
George Lee	54	522	169	64	.379	71	47	.662	97	25	67	0	175	3.2
Ken Sears	51	519	120	53	.442	79	64	.810	94	42	71	0	170	3.3
John Windsor	11	68	27	10	.370	8	7	.875	26	2	13	0	27	2.5

PLAYOFF RESULTS

EASTERN DIVISION SEMIFINALS
Cincinnati 3, Philadelphia 2

Mar. 22—Philadelphia 102 at Cincinnati 127
Mar. 24—Cincinnati 114 at Philadelphia 122
Mar. 25—Philadelphia 89 at Cincinnati 101
Mar. 28—Cincinnati 120 at Philadelphia 129
Mar. 29—Philadelphia 124 at Cincinnati 130

WESTERN DIVISION SEMIFINALS
St. Louis 3, Los Angeles 2

Mar. 21—Los Angeles 104 at St. Louis 115
Mar. 22—Los Angeles 90 at St. Louis 106
Mar. 25—St.Louis 105 at Los Angeles 107
Mar. 28—St. Louis 88 at Los Angeles 97
Mar. 30—Los Angeles 108 at St. Louis 121

EASTERN DIVISION FINALS
Boston 4, Cincinnati 1

Mar. 31—Cincinnati 87 at Boston 103
Apr. 2—Cincinnati 90 at Boston 101
Apr. 5—Boston 102 at Cincinnati 92
Apr. 7—Boston 93 at Cincinnati 102
Apr. 9—Cincinnati 95 at Boston 109

WESTERN DIVISION FINALS
San Francisco 4, St. Louis 3

Apr. 1—St. Louis 116 at San Francisco 111
Apr. 3—St. Louis 85 at San Francisco 120
Apr. 5—San Francisco 109 at St. Louis 113
Apr. 8—San Francisco 111 at St. Louis 109
Apr. 10—St. Louis 97 at San Francisco 121
Apr. 12—San Francisco 95 at St. Louis 123
Apr. 16—St. Louis 95 at San Francisco 105

WORLD CHAMPIONSHIP SERIES
Boston 4, San Francisco 1

Apr. 18—San Francisco 96 at Boston 108
Apr. 20—San Francisco 101 at Boston 124
Apr. 22—Boston 91 at San Francisco 115
Apr. 24—Boston 98 at San Francisco 95
Apr. 26—San Francisco 99 at Boston 105

1962-63 NBA STATISTICS

1962-63 NBA CHAMPION BOSTON CELTICS

Seated (left to right): K. C. Jones, Bill Russell, President Walter A. Brown, Coach Red Auerbach, Treasurer Lou Pieri, Captain Bob Cousy, Sam Jones. Standing: Frank Ramsey, Gene Guarilia, Tom Sanders, Tom Heinsohn, Clyde Lovellette, John Havlicek, Jim Loscutoff, Dan Swartz, Trainer Buddy LeRoux.

FINAL STANDINGS

EASTERN DIVISION

Team	Bos.	Syr.	Cin.	N.Y.	L.A.	S.L.	Det.	S.F.	Chi.	W.	L.	Pct.	G.B.
Boston	..	6	9	10	4	5	8	8	8	58	22	.725	....
Syracuse	6	..	5	10	4	4	6	5	8	48	32	.600	10
Cincinnati	3	7	..	10	3	3	4	6	6	42	38	.525	16
New York	2	2	2	..	3	3	1	2	6	21	59	.263	37

WESTERN DIVISION

Team	Bos.	Syr.	Cin.	N.Y.	L.A.	S.L.	Det.	S.F.	Chi.	W.	L.	Pct.	G.B.
Los Angeles	5	4	6	5	..	7	11	8	7	53	27	.663	....
St. Louis	3	5	5	6	5	..	8	9	7	48	32	.600	5
Detroit	0	3	4	8	1	4	..	7	7	34	46	.425	19
San Francisco	1	3	3	6	4	3	5	..	6	31	49	.388	22
Chicago	2	2	4	4	3	3	3	4	..	25	55	.313	28

HOME-AWAY-NEUTRAL RECORDS OF ALL TEAMS

	Home	Road	Neutral	Total		Home	Road	Neutral	Total
Boston	25- 5	21- 16	12- 1	58- 22	New York	12- 22	5- 28	4- 9	21- 59
Chicago	17- 17	3- 23	5-15	25- 55	St. Louis	30- 7	13- 18	5- 7	48- 32
Cincinnati	23- 10	15- 19	4- 9	42- 38	San Francisco	13- 20	11- 25	7- 4	31- 49
Detroit	14- 16	8- 19	12-11	34- 46	Syracuse	23- 5	13- 19	12- 8	48- 32
Los Angeles	27- 7	20- 17	6- 3	53- 27	Totals	184-109	109-184	67-67	360-360

TEAM STATISTICS

Team	G.	FGA	FGM	Pct.	FTA	FTM	Pct.	Reb.	Ast.	PF	Disq.	For	Agst.	Pt.Dif.
Boston	80	8779	3746	.427	2777	2012	.725	5818	1960	2090	30	118.8	111.6	+7.2
Syracuse	80	8290	3690	.445	3005	2350	.782	5516	1742	2277	33	121.6	117.8	+3.8
Los Angeles	80	7948	3506	.441	2931	2230	.761	5282	1739	1775	18	115.5	112.4	+3.1
St. Louis	80	7780	3355	.431	2820	2056	.729	5096	1902	2077	35	109.6	107.8	+1.8
Cincinnati	80	7998	3672	.459	2923	2183	.747	5561	1931	2203	39	119.0	117.8	+1.2
San Francisco	80	8449	3805	.450	2797	1870	.669	5359	1906	1882	45	118.5	120.6	-2.1
Detroit	80	8188	3534	.432	2852	2044	.717	5315	1731	2181	40	113.9	117.6	-3.7
Chicago	80	7448	3371	.453	2944	2053	.697	5145	1773	2065	33	109.9	113.9	-4.0
New York	80	8007	3433	.429	2778	1971	.710	4952	1658	2144	49	110.5	117.7	-7.2

INDIVIDUAL LEADERS

POINTS

	G.	FG	FT	Pts.	Avg.		G.	FG	FT	Pts.	Avg.
Wilt Chamberlain, S. Fran.	80	1463	660	3586	44.8	Sam Jones, Boston	76	621	257	1499	19.7
Elgin Baylor, Los Angeles	80	1029	661	2719	34.0	Jerry West, Los Angeles	55	559	371	1489	27.1
Oscar Robertson, Cinn.	80	825	614	2264	28.3	Lee Shaffer, Syracuse	80	597	294	1488	18.6
Bob Pettit, St. Louis	79	778	685	2241	28.4	Terry Dischinger, Chicago	57	525	402	1452	25.5
Walt Bellamy, Chicago	80	840	553	2233	27.9	John Green, New York	80	582	280	1444	18.1
Bailey Howell, Detroit	79	637	519	1793	22.7	Tom Heinsohn, Boston	76	550	340	1440	18.9
Richie Guerin, New York	79	596	509	1701	21.5	Dick Barnett, Los Angeles	80	547	343	1437	18.0
Jack Twyman, Cincinnati	80	641	304	1586	19.8	Wayne Embry, Cincinnati	76	434	343	1411	18.6
Hal Greer, Syracuse	80	600	362	1562	19.5	Bill Russell, Boston	78	511	287	1309	16.8
Don Ohl, Detroit	80	636	275	1547	19.3	John Kerr, Syracuse	80	507	241	1255	15.7

FIELD GOALS
(Minimum 210 FGM)

	FGA	FGM	Pct.
Wilt Chamberlain, San. Fran.	2770	1463	.528
Walt Bellamy, Chicago	1595	840	.527
Oscar Robertson, Cincinnati	1593	825	.518
Bailey Howell, Detroit	1235	637	.516
Terry Dischinger, Chicago	1026	525	.512
Dave Budd, New York	596	294	.493
Jack Twyman, Cincinnati	1335	641	.480
Al Attles, San Francisco	630	301	.478
Sam Jones, Boston	1305	621	.476
John Kerr, Syracuse	1069	507	.474

ASSISTS

	G.	No.	Avg.
Guy Rodgers, San Francisco	79	825	10.4
Oscar Robertson, Cincinnati	80	758	9.5
Bob Cousy, Boston	76	515	6.8
Sihugo Green, Chicago	73	422	5.8
Elgin Baylor, Los Angeles	80	386	4.8
Len Wilkens, St. Louis	75	381	5.1
Bill Russell, Boston	78	348	4.5
Richie Guerin, New York	79	348	4.4
Larry Costello, Syracuse	78	334	4.3
John Barnhill, St. Louis	77	322	4.2

FREE THROWS
(Minimum 210 FTM)

	FTA	FTM	Pct.
Larry Costello, Syracuse	327	288	.881
Richie Guerin, New York	600	509	.848
Elgin Baylor, Los Angeles	790	661	.837
Tom Heinsohn, Boston	407	340	.835
Hal Greer, Syracuse	434	362	.834
Frank Ramsey, Boston	332	271	.816
Dick Barnett, Los Angeles	421	343	.815
Adrian Smith, Cincinnati	275	223	.811
Jack Twyman, Cincinnati	375	304	.811
Oscar Robertson, Cincinnati	758	614	.810

REBOUNDS

	G.	No.	Avg.
Wilt Chamberlain, San Francisco	80	1946	24.3
Bill Russell, Boston	78	1843	23.6
Walt Bellamy, Chicago	80	1309	16.4
Bob Pettit, St. Louis	79	1191	15.1
Elgin Baylor, Los Angeles	80	1146	14.3
John Kerr, Syracuse	80	1039	13.0
John Green, New York	80	964	12.1
Wayne Embry, Cincinnati	76	936	12.3
Bailey Howell, Detroit	79	910	11.5
Bob Boozer, Cincinnati	79	878	11.1

TEAM-BY-TEAM INDIVIDUAL STATISTICS

BOSTON CELTICS

Player	G.	Min.	FGA	FGM	Pct.	FTA	FTM	Pct.	Reb.	Ast.	PF	Disq.	Pts.	Avg.
Sam Jones	76	2323	1305	621	.476	324	257	.793	396	241	162	1	1499	19.7
Tom Heinsohn	76	2004	1300	550	.423	407	340	.835	569	95	270	4	1440	18.9
Bill Russell	78	3500	1182	511	.432	517	287	.555	1843	348	189	1	1309	16.8
John Havlicek	80	2200	1085	483	.445	239	174	.728	534	179	189	2	1140	14.3
Bob Cousy	76	1975	988	392	.397	298	219	.735	193	515	175	0	1003	13.2
Tom Sanders	80	2148	744	339	.456	252	186	.738	576	95	262	5	864	10.8
Frank Ramsey	77	1541	743	284	.382	332	271	.816	288	95	259	13	839	10.9
K. C. Jones	79	1945	591	230	.389	177	112	.633	263	317	221	3	572	7.2
Clyde Lovellette	61	568	376	161	.428	98	73	.745	177	95	137	0	395	6.5
Jim Luscutoff	63	607	251	94	.375	42	22	.524	157	25	126	1	210	3.3
Gene Guarilia	11	83	38	11	.289	11	4	.364	14	2	5	0	26	2.4
Dan Swartz	39	335	150	57	.380	72	61	.847	88	21	92	0	175	4.5

CHICAGO ZEPHYRS

Player	G.	Min.	FGA	FGM	Pct.	FTA	FTM	Pct.	Reb.	Ast.	PF	Disq.	Pts.	Avg.
Walt Bellamy	80	3306	1595	840	.527	821	553	.674	1309	233	283	7	2233	27.9
Terry Dischinger	57	2294	1026	525	.512	522	402	.770	458	175	188	2	1452	25.5
Sihugo Green	73	2648	783	322	.411	306	209	.683	335	422	274	5	853	11.7
Charles Hardnett	78	1657	683	301	.441	349	225	.645	602	74	225	4	827	10.6
John Cox	73	1685	568	239	.412	135	95	.704	280	142	149	4	573	7.8
Bill McGill	60	590	353	181	.513	119	80	.672	161	38	118	1	442	7.4
Don Nelson	62	1071	293	129	.440	221	161	.729	279	72	136	3	419	6.8
Barney Cable*	61	1200	380	173	.455	96	62	.646	242	82	136	0	408	6.7
Larry Staverman	33	602	194	94	.485	62	49	.790	158	43	94	3	237	7.2
Mel Nowell	39	589	237	92	.388	66	48	.727	67	84	86	0	232	5.9
Bob Leonard	32	879	245	84	.343	85	59	.694	68	143	84	1	227	7.1
Maurice King	37	954	241	94	.390	34	28	.824	102	142	87	0	216	5.8
Nick Mantis*	32	684	244	94	.385	49	27	.551	85	83	94	0	215	5.1
Al Ferrari	18	138	37	12	.324	17	14	.824	12	14	21	0	38	2.1
Jeff Slade	3	20	5	2	.400	1	0	.000	7	0	3	0	4	1.3
Ralph Wells	3	48	7	1	.143	7	0	.000	6	7	6	0	2	0.7

*Cable—42 St. Louis, 19 Chicago; Mantis—9 St. Louis, 23 Chicago.

CINCINNATI ROYALS

Player	G.	Min.	FGA	FGM	Pct.	FTA	FTM	Pct.	Reb.	Ast.	PF	Disq.	Pts.	Avg.
Oscar Robertson	80	3521	1593	825	.518	758	614	.810	835	758	293	1	2264	28.3
Jack Twyman	80	2623	1335	641	.480	375	304	.811	598	214	286	7	1586	19.8
Wayne Embry	76	2511	1165	534	.458	514	343	.667	936	177	286	7	1411	18.6
Bob Boozer	79	2488	992	449	.414	353	252	.714	878	102	299	8	1132	14.3
Arlen Bockhorn	80	2612	954	375	.393	242	183	.756	322	261	260	6	933	11.7
Tom Hawkins	79	1721	635	299	.471	241	147	.610	543	100	197	2	745	9.4
Adrian Smith	79	1522	544	241	.443	275	223	.811	174	141	157	1	705	8.9
Hub Reed	80	1299	427	199	.466	98	74	.755	398	83	261	7	472	5.9
Dave Piontek	48	457	158	60	.380	16	10	.625	96	26	67	0	130	2.7
Bud Olsen	52	373	133	43	.323	39	27	.692	105	42	78	0	113	2.2
Dave Tieman	29	176	57	15	.263	10	4	.400	22	27	18	0	34	1.2
Joseph Buckhalter	2	12	5	0	.000	2	2	1.000	3	0	1	0	2	1.0

DETROIT PISTONS

Player	G.	Min.	FGA	FGM	Pct.	FTA	FTM	Pct.	Reb.	Ast.	PF	Disq.	Pts.	Avg.
Bailey Howell	79	2971	1235	637	.516	650	519	.798	910	232	300	9	1793	22.7
Don Ohl	80	2961	1450	636	.439	380	275	.724	239	325	234	3	1547	19.3
Ray Scott	76	2538	1110	460	.414	457	308	.674	772	191	263	9	1228	16.2
Bob Ferry	79	2479	984	426	.433	339	220	.649	537	170	246	1	1072	13.6
Dave DeBusschere	80	2352	944	406	.430	287	206	.718	694	207	247	2	1018	12.7
Willie Jones	79	1470	730	305	.418	164	118	.720	233	188	207	4	728	9.2
Jack Moreland	78	1516	622	271	.436	214	145	.678	449	114	226	5	687	8.8
Kevin Loughery	57	845	397	146	.368	100	71	.710	109	104	135	1	363	6.4
Jack Egan	46	752	296	110	.372	69	53	.768	59	114	70	0	273	5.9
Walt Dukes	62	913	255	83	.325	137	101	.737	360	55	183	5	267	4.3
Darrall Imhoff	45	458	153	48	.314	50	24	.480	155	28	66	1	120	2.7
Dan Doyle	4	25	12	6	.500	5	4	.800	8	3	4	0	16	4.0

LOS ANGELES LAKERS

Player	G.	Min.	FGA	FGM	Pct.	FTA	FTM	Pct.	Reb.	Ast.	PF	Disq.	Pts.	Avg.
Elgin Baylor	80	3370	2273	1029	.453	790	661	.837	1146	386	226	1	2719	34.0
Jerry West	55	2163	1213	559	.461	477	371	.778	384	307	150	1	1489	27.1
Dick Barnett	80	2544	1162	547	.471	421	343	.815	242	224	189	3	1437	18.0
Rudy LaRusso	75	2505	761	321	.422	393	282	.718	747	187	255	5	924	12.3
Frank Selvy	80	2369	747	317	.424	269	192	.714	289	281	149	0	826	10.3
Jim Krebs	79	1913	627	272	.434	154	115	.747	502	87	256	2	659	8.3
LeRoy Ellis	80	1628	530	222	.419	202	133	.658	518	46	194	1	577	7.2
Rod Hundley	65	785	262	88	.336	119	84	.706	106	151	81	0	260	4.0
Gene Wiley	75	1488	236	109	.462	68	23	.338	504	40	180	4	241	3.2
Ron Horn	28	289	82	27	.329	29	20	.690	71	10	46	0	74	2.6
Howie Joliff	28	293	55	15	.273	9	6	.667	62	20	49	1	36	1.3

NEW YORK KNICKERBOCKERS

Player	G.	Min.	FGA	FGM	Pct.	FTA	FTM	Pct.	Reb.	Ast.	PF	Disq.	Pts.	Avg.
Richie Guerin	79	2712	1380	596	.432	600	509	.848	331	348	228	2	1701	21.5
John Green	80	2553	1261	582	.462	439	280	.638	964	152	243	5	1444	18.1
Gene Shue	78	2288	894	354	.396	302	208	.689	191	259	171	0	916	11.7
Tom Gola*	73	2670	791	363	.459	219	170	.776	517	298	295	9	896	12.3
Dave Budd	78	1725	596	294	.493	202	151	.748	395	87	204	3	739	9.5
Al Butler	74	1488	676	297	.439	187	144	.770	170	156	145	3	738	10.0
Gene Conley	70	1544	651	254	.390	186	122	.656	469	70	263	10	630	9.0
Donnis Butcher	68	1193	424	172	.406	194	131	.675	180	138	164	1	475	7.6
Paul Hogue	50	1340	419	152	.363	174	79	.454	430	42	220	12	383	7.7
Bob Nordmann*	53	1000	319	156	.489	122	59	.484	316	47	156	6	371	7.0
John Rudometkin	56	572	307	108	.352	95	73	.768	149	30	58	0	289	5.2
Tom Stith	25	209	110	37	.336	10	3	.300	39	18	23	0	77	3.1
Jack Foley*	11	83	51	20	.392	15	13	.867	16	5	8	0	53	4.8
Cleveland Buckner	6	27	10	5	.500	4	2	.500	4	5	6	0	12	2.0

*Gola—21 San Francisco, 52 New York; Nordmann—27 St. Louis, 26 New York; Foley—5 Boston, 6 New York.

ST. LOUIS HAWKS

Player	G.	Min.	FGA	FGM	Pct.	FTA	FTM	Pct.	Reb.	Ast.	PF	Disq.	Pts.	Avg.
Bob Pettit	79	3090	1746	778	.446	885	685	.774	1191	245	282	8	2241	28.4
Cliff Hagan	79	1716	1055	491	.465	305	244	.800	341	193	211	2	1226	15.5
John Barnhill	77	2692	838	360	.430	255	181	.710	359	322	168	0	901	11.7
Len Wilkens	75	2569	834	333	.399	319	222	.696	403	381	256	6	888	11.8
Woody Sauldsberry*	77	2034	966	366	.379	163	107	.656	447	78	241	4	839	10.9
Zelmo Beaty	80	1918	677	297	.439	307	220	.717	665	85	312	12	814	10.2
Charles Vaughn	77	1845	708	295	.417	261	188	.720	258	252	201	3	778	10.1
Mike Farmer	80	1724	562	239	.425	139	117	.842	369	143	155	0	595	7.4
Phil Jordon	73	1420	527	211	.400	101	56	.554	319	103	172	3	478	6.5
Bill Bridges	27	374	160	66	.413	51	32	.627	144	23	58	0	164	6.1
Bob Duffy	42	435	174	66	.379	39	22	.564	39	83	42	0	154	3.7
Gene Tormohlen	7	47	10	5	.500	10	2	.200	15	5	11	0	12	1.7

*Sauldsberry—54 Chicago, 23 St. Louis.

SAN FRANCISCO WARRIORS

Player	G.	Min.	FGA	FGM	Pct.	FTA	FTM	Pct.	Reb.	Ast.	PF	Disq.	Pts.	Avg.
Wilt Chamberlain	80	3806	2770	1463	.528	1113	660	.593	1946	275	136	0	3586	44.8
Guy Rodgers	79	3249	1150	445	.387	286	208	.727	394	825	296	7	1098	13.9
Tom Meschery	64	2245	935	397	.425	313	228	.728	624	104	249	11	1022	16.0
Willie Naulls*	70	1901	887	370	.417	207	166	.802	515	102	205	3	906	12.9
Al Attles	71	1876	630	301	.478	206	133	.646	205	184	253	7	735	10.4
Gary Phillips	75	1801	643	256	.398	152	97	.638	225	137	185	7	609	8.1

Player	G.	Min.	FGA	FGM	Pct.	FTA	FTM	Pct.	Reb.	Ast.	PF	Disq.	Pts.	Avg.
Wayne Hightower	66	1387	543	192	.354	157	105	.669	354	51	181	5	489	7.4
Ken Sears*	77	1141	304	161	.530	168	131	.780	206	95	128	0	453	5.9
George Lee	64	1192	394	149	.378	193	152	.788	217	64	113	0	450	7.0
Howard Montgomery	20	364	153	65	.455	23	14	.609	69	21	35	1	144	7.2
Hubie White	29	271	111	40	.360	18	12	.667	35	28	47	0	92	3.2
Fred LaCour	16	171	73	28	.384	16	9	.563	24	19	27	0	65	4.1
Tom Luckenbill	20	201	68	26	.382	20	9	.450	56	8	34	0	61	3.1
Dave Fedor	7	27	10	3	.300	1	0	.000	6	1	4	0	6	0.9
Dave Gunther	1	5	2	1	.500	0	0	.000	3	3	1	0	2	2.6

*Naulls—23 New York, 47 San Francisco; Sears—23 New York, 54 San Francisco.

SYRACUSE NATIONALS

Player	G.	Min.	FGA	FGM	Pct.	FTA	FTM	Pct.	Reb.	Ast.	PF	Disq.	Pts.	Avg.
Hal Greer	80	2631	1293	600	.464	434	362	.834	457	275	286	4	1562	19.5
Lee Shaffer	80	2392	1393	597	.429	375	294	.784	524	97	249	5	1488	18.6
John Kerr	80	2561	1069	507	.474	320	241	.753	1039	214	208	3	1255	15.7
Chet Walker	78	1992	751	352	.469	362	253	.699	561	83	220	3	957	12.3
Larry Costello	78	2066	660	285	.432	327	288	.881	237	334	263	4	858	11.0
Len Chappell	80	1241	604	281	.465	238	148	.622	461	56	171	1	710	8.9
Dave Gambee	60	1234	537	235	.438	238	199	.836	289	48	190	2	669	11.2
Paul Neumann	80	1581	503	237	.471	222	181	.815	200	227	221	5	655	8.2
Dolph Schayes	66	1438	575	223	.388	206	181	.879	375	175	177	2	627	9.5
Al Bianchi	61	1159	476	202	.424	164	120	.732	134	170	165	2	524	8.6
Ben Warley	26	206	111	50	.450	35	25	.714	86	4	42	1	125	4.8
Joe Roberts	33	466	196	73	.372	51	35	.686	155	16	66	1	181	5.5
Porter Meriwether	31	268	122	48	.393	33	23	.697	29	43	19	0	119	3.8

PLAYOFF RESULTS

EASTERN DIVISION SEMIFINALS
Cincinnati 3, Syracuse 2

Mar. 19—Cincinnati 120 at Syracuse 123
Mar. 21—Syracuse 115 at Cincinnati 133
Mar. 23—Cincinnati 117 at Syracuse 121
Mar. 24—Syracuse 118 at Cincinnati 125
Mar. 26—Cincinnati 131 at Syracuse *127

WESTERN DIVISION SEMIFINALS
St. Louis 3, Detroit 1

Mar. 20—Detroit 99 at St. Louis 118
Mar. 22—Detroit 108 at St. Louis 122
Mar. 24—St. Louis 103 at Detroit 107
Mar. 26—St. Louis 104 at Detroit 100

EASTERN DIVISION FINALS
Boston 4, Cincinnati 3

Mar. 28—Cincinnati 135 at Boston 132
Mar. 29—Boston 125 at Cincinnati 102
Mar. 31—Cincinnati 121 at Boston 116
Apr. 3—Boston 128 at Cincinnati 110
Apr. 6—Cincinnati 120 at Boston 125
Apr. 7—Boston 99 at Cincinnati 109
Apr. 10—Cincinnati 131 at Boston 142

WESTERN DIVISION FINALS
Los Angeles 4, St. Louis 3

Mar. 31—St. Louis 104 at Los Angeles 112
Apr. 2—St. Louis 99 at Los Angeles 101
Apr. 4—Los Angeles 112 at St. Louis 125
Apr. 6—Los Angeles 114 at St. Louis 124
Apr. 7—St. Louis 100 at Los Angeles 123
Apr. 9—Los Angeles 113 at St. Louis 121
Apr. 11—St. Louis 100 at Los Angeles 115

WORLD CHAMPIONSHIP SERIES
Boston 4, Los Angeles 2

Apr. 14—Los Angeles 114 at Boston 117
Apr. 16—Los Angeles 106 at Boston 113
Apr. 17—Boston 99 at Los Angeles 119
Apr. 19—Boston 108 at Los Angeles 105
Apr. 21—Los Angeles 126 at Boston 119
Apr. 24—Boston 112 at Los Angeles 109

*Denotes overtime period.

1961-62 NBA STATISTICS

1961-62 NBA CHAMPION BOSTON CELTICS

Seated (left to right): K. C. Jones, Gary Phillips, President Walter A. Brown, Coach Red Auerbach, Treasurer Lou Pieri, Captain Bob Cousy, Sam Jones. Standing: Frank Ramsey, Tom Sanders, Tom Heinsohn, Bill Russell, Gene Guarilia, Jim Loscutoff, Carl Braun, Trainer Buddy LeRoux.

FINAL STANDINGS

EASTERN DIVISION

Team	Bos.	Phil.	Syr.	N.Y.	L.A.	Cinn.	Det.	S.L.	Chi.	W.	L.	Pct.	G.B.
Boston	..	8	10	8	6	7	5	7	9	60	20	.750	....
Philadelphia	4	..	6	8	3	5	7	6	10	49	31	.613	11
Syracuse	2	6	..	9	2	4	5	4	9	41	39	.513	19
New York	4	4	3	..	2	4	4	4	4	29	51	.363	31

WESTERN DIVISION

Team	Bos.	Phil.	Syr.	N.Y.	L.A.	Cinn.	Det.	S.L.	Chi.	W.	L.	Pct.	G.B.
Los Angeles	3	6	6	6	..	7	8	10	8	54	26	.675	....
Cincinnati	1	3	5	5	5	..	6	9	9	43	37	.538	11
Detroit	3	1	4	5	4	6	..	7	7	37	43	.463	17
St. Louis	2	3	4	4	2	3	5	..	6	29	51	.363	25
Chicago	1	0	1	6	2	1	3	4	..	18	62	.225	36

HOME-ROAD-NEUTRAL RECORDS OF ALL TEAMS

	Home	Road	Neutral	Total		Home	Road	Neutral	Total
Boston	23- 5	26- 12	11- 3	60- 20	New York	19- 14	2- 23	8-14	29- 51
Chicago	9- 19	3- 20	6-23	18- 62	Philadelphia	18- 11	18- 19	13- 1	49- 31
Cincinnati	18- 13	14- 16	11- 8	43- 37	St. Louis	19- 16	7- 27	3- 8	29- 51
Detroit	16- 14	8- 17	13-12	37- 43	Syracuse	18- 10	11- 19	12-10	41- 39
Los Angeles	26- 5	18- 13	10- 8	54- 26	Totals	166-107	107-166	87-87	360-360

TEAM STATISTICS

Team	G.	FGA	FGM	Pct.	FTA	FTM	Pct.	Reb.	Ast.	PF	Disq.	For	Agst.	Pt.Dif.
Boston	80	9109	3855	.423	2715	1977	.728	6080	2049	1909	28	121.1	111.9	+9.2
Philadelphia	80	8929	3917	.439	3207	2201	.686	5939	2073	2013	71	125.4	122.7	+2.7
Syracuse	80	8875	3706	.418	2880	2246	.780	5764	1791	2344	53	120.7	118.4	+2.3
Cincinnati	80	8414	3806	.452	2969	2233	.752	5665	2154	2081	31	123.1	121.3	+1.8
Los Angeles	80	8315	3552	.427	3240	2378	.734	5600	1878	2057	39	118.5	120.0	—1.5
Detroit	80	8366	3472	.415	3142	2290	.729	5823	1723	2040	46	115.4	117.1	—1.7
St. Louis	80	8461	3641	.430	2939	2226	.757	5557	1996	2166	51	118.9	122.1	—3.2
New York	80	8696	3638	.418	2693	1911	.710	5440	1765	2056	39	114.8	119.7	—4.9
Chicago	80	8405	3461	.412	2901	1952	.673	5547	1802	1954	30	110.9	119.4	—8.5

INDIVIDUAL LEADERS

POINTS

	G.	FG	FT	Pts.	Avg.
Wilt Chamberlain, Phila.	80	1597	835	4029	50.4
Walt Bellamy, Chicago	79	973	549	2495	31.6
Oscar Robertson, Cinn.	79	866	700	2432	30.8
Bob Pettit, St. Louis	78	867	695	2429	31.1
Jerry West, Los Angeles	75	799	712	2310	30.8
Richie Guerin, New York	78	839	625	2303	29.5
Willie Naulls, New York	75	747	383	1877	25.0
Elgin Baylor, Los Angeles	48	680	476	1836	38.3
Jack Twyman, Cincinnati.	80	739	353	1831	22.9
Cliff Hagan, St. Louis	77	701	362	1764	22.9

	G.	FG	FT	Pts.	Avg.
Tom Heinsohn, Boston	79	692	358	1742	22.1
Paul Arizin, Philadelphia	78	611	484	1706	21.9
Hal Greer, Syracuse	71	644	331	1619	22.8
Bailey Howell, Detroit	79	553	470	1576	19.9
Gene Shue, Detroit	80	580	362	1522	19.0
Wayne Embry, Cincinnati	75	564	356	1484	19.8
Bill Russell, Boston	76	575	286	1436	18.9
Sam Jones, Boston	78	596	243	1435	18.4
Rudy LaRusso, Los Angeles	80	516	342	1374	17.2
Dave Gambee, Syracuse	80	477	384	1338	16.7

FIELD GOALS
(Minimum 200 FGM)

	FGA	FGM	Pct.
Walt Bellamy, Chicago	1875	973	.519
Wilt Chamberlain, Philadelphia	3159	1597	.506
Jack Twyman, Cincinnati	1542	739	.479
Oscar Robertson, Cincinnati	1810	866	.478
Al Attles, Philadelphia	724	343	.474
Clyde Lovellette, St. Louis	724	341	.471
Larry Foust, St. Louis	433	204	.471
Cliff Hagan, St. Louis	1490	701	.470
Rudy LaRusso, Los Angeles	1108	516	.466
Wayne Embry, Cincinnati	1210	564	.466

ASSISTS

	G.	No.	Avg.
Oscar Robertson, Cincinnati	79	899	11.4
Guy Rodgers, Philadelphia	80	643	8.0
Bob Cousy, Boston	75	584	7.8
Richie Guerin, New York	78	539	6.9
Gene Shue, Detroit	80	465	5.8
Jerry West, Los Angeles	75	402	5.4
Frank Selvy, Los Angeles	79	381	4.8
Bob Leonard, Chicago	70	378	5.4
Cliff Hagan, St. Louis	77	370	4.8
Arlen Bockhorn, Cincinnati	80	366	4.6

FREE THROWS
(Minimum 200 FTM)

	FTA	FTM	Pct.
Dolph Schayes, Syracuse	319	286	.896
Willie Naulls, New York	455	383	.842
Larry Costello, Syracuse	295	247	.837
Frank Ramsey, Boston	405	334	.825
Cliff Hagan, St. Louis	439	362	.825
Tom Meschery, Philadelphia	262	216	.824
Richie Guerin, New York	762	625	.820
Tom Heinsohn, Boston	437	358	.819
Hal Greer, Syracuse	404	331	.819
Sam Jones, Boston	297	243	.818

REBOUNDS

	G.	No.	Avg.
Wilt Chamberlain, Philadelphia	80	2052	25.7
Bill Russell, Boston	76	1790	23.6
Walt Bellamy, Chicago	79	1500	19.0
Bob Pettit, St. Louis	78	1459	18.7
John Kerr, Syracuse	80	1176	14.7
John Green, New York	80	1066	13.3
Bailey, Howell, Detroit	79	996	12.6
Oscar Robertson, Cincinnati	79	985	12.5
Wayne Embry, Cincinnati	75	977	13.0
Elgin Baylor, Los Angeles	48	892	18.6

TEAM-BY-TEAM INDIVIDUAL STATISTICS

BOSTON CELTICS

Player	G.	Min.	FGA	FGM	Pct.	FTA	FTM	Pct.	Reb.	Ast.	PF	Disq.	Pts.	Avg.
Tom Heinsohn	79	2383	1613	692	.429	437	358	.819	747	165	280	2	1742	22.1
Bill Russell	76	3433	1258	575	.457	481	286	.595	1790	341	207	3	1436	18.9
Sam Jones	78	2388	1284	596	.464	297	243	.818	458	232	149	0	1435	18.4
Frank Ramsey	79	1913	1019	436	.428	405	334	.825	387	109	245	10	1206	15.3
Bob Cousy	75	2114	1181	462	.391	333	251	.754	261	584	135	0	1175	15.7
Tom Sanders	80	2325	804	350	.435	263	197	.749	762	74	279	9	897	11.2
K. C. Jones	80	2054	724	294	.406	232	147	.634	298	343	206	1	735	9.2
Jim Loscutoff	79	1146	519	188	.362	84	45	.536	329	51	185	3	421	5.3
Gary Phillips	67	713	310	110	.355	86	50	.581	107	64	109	0	270	4.0
Carl Braun	48	414	207	78	.377	27	20	.741	50	71	49	0	176	3.7
Gene Guarilia	45	367	161	61	.379	64	41	.641	124	11	56	0	163	3.6

CHICAGO PACKERS

Player	G.	Min.	FGA	FGM	Pct.	FTA	FTM	Pct.	Reb.	Ast.	PF	Disq.	Pts.	Avg.
Walt Bellamy	79	3344	1875	973	.519	853	549	.644	1500	210	281	6	2495	31.6
Bob Leonard	70	2464	1128	423	.375	371	279	.752	199	378	186	0	1125	16.1
Andy Johnson	71	2193	814	365	.448	452	284	.628	351	228	247	5	1014	14.3
Sihugo Green*	71	2388	905	341	.377	311	218	.701	399	318	226	3	900	12.7
Ralph Davis	77	1992	881	364	.413	103	71	.689	162	247	187	1	799	10.4
Woody Sauldsberry*	63	1765	869	298	.343	123	79	.642	536	90	179	5	675	10.7
Charlie Tyra	78	1606	534	193	.361	214	133	.621	610	86	210	7	519	6.7
Horace Walker	65	1331	439	149	.339	193	140	.725	466	69	194	2	438	6.7
Dave Piontek	45	614	225	83	.369	59	39	.661	155	31	89	1	205	4.6
Jack Turner	42	567	221	84	.380	42	32	.762	85	44	51	0	200	4.8
Howie Carl	31	382	201	67	.333	51	36	.706	39	57	41	1	170	5.5
George BonSalle	3	9	8	2	.250	0	0	.000	2	0	0	0	4	1.3

*Green—14 St. Louis, 57 Chicago. Sauldsberry—14 St. Louis, 49 Chicago.

CINCINNATI ROYALS

Player	G.	Min.	FGA	FGM	Pct.	FTA	FTM	Pct.	Reb.	Ast.	PF	Disq.	Pts.	Avg.
Oscar Robertson	79	3503	1810	866	.478	872	700	.803	985	899	258	1	2432	30.8
Jack Twyman	80	2991	1542	739	.479	435	353	.811	638	215	323	5	1831	22.9
Wayne Embry	75	2623	1210	564	.466	516	356	.690	977	182	286	6	1484	19.8
Arlen Bockhorn	80	3062	1234	531	.430	251	198	.789	376	366	280	5	1260	15.8
Bob Boozer	79	2488	936	410	.438	372	263	.707	804	130	275	3	1083	13.7
Adrian Smith	80	1462	499	202	.405	222	172	.775	151	167	101	0	576	7.2

Player	G.	Min.	FGA	FGM	Pct.	FTA	FTM	Pct.	Reb.	Ast.	PF	Disq.	Pts.	Avg.
Hub Reed	80	1446	460	203	.441	82	60	.732	440	53	267	9	466	5.8
Joe Buckhalter	63	728	334	153	.458	108	67	.620	262	43	123	1	373	5.9
Bob Nordmann	58	344	126	51	.405	57	29	.509	128	18	81	1	131	2.8
Bob Wieseharn	60	326	161	51	.317	30	17	.567	112	23	50	0	119	2.0
Dave Zeller	61	278	102	36	.353	24	18	.750	27	58	37	0	90	1.5

DETROIT PISTONS

Player	G.	Min.	FGA	FGM	Pct.	FTA	FTM	Pct.	Reb.	Ast.	PF	Disq.	Pts.	Avg.
Bailey Howell	79	2857	1193	553	.464	612	470	.768	996	186	317	10	1576	19.9
Gene Shue	80	3143	1422	580	.408	447	362	.810	372	465	192	1	1522	19.0
Don Ohl	77	2526	1250	555	.444	280	201	.718	267	244	173	2	1311	17.0
Bob Ferry	80	1918	939	411	.438	422	286	.678	503	145	199	2	1108	13.9
Ray Scott	75	2087	956	370	.387	388	255	.657	865	132	232	6	995	13.3
Walt Dukes	77	1896	647	256	.396	291	208	.715	803	125	327	20	720	9.4
George Lee	75	1351	500	179	.358	280	213	.761	349	64	128	1	571	7.6
Jack Moreland	74	1219	487	205	.421	186	139	.747	427	76	179	2	549	7.4
Willie Jones	69	1006	475	177	.373	101	64	.634	177	115	137	1	418	6.1
Jack Egan	58	696	301	128	.425	84	64	.762	86	102	64	0	320	5.5
Chuck Noble	26	361	113	32	.283	15	8	.533	43	63	55	1	72	2.8

LOS ANGELES LAKERS

Player	G.	Min.	FGA	FGM	Pct.	FTA	FTM	Pct.	Reb.	Ast.	PF	Disq.	Pts.	Avg.
Jerry West	75	3087	1795	799	.445	926	712	.769	591	402	173	4	2310	30.8
Elgin Baylor	48	2129	1588	680	.428	631	476	.754	892	222	155	1	1836	38.3
Rudy LaRusso	80	2754	1108	516	.466	448	342	.763	828	179	255	5	1374	17.2
Frank Selvy	79	2806	1032	433	.420	404	298	.738	412	381	232	0	1164	14.7
Jim Krebs	78	2012	701	312	.445	208	156	.750	616	110	290	9	780	10.0
Tom Hawkins	79	1903	704	289	.411	222	143	.644	514	95	244	7	721	9.1
Ray Felix	80	1478	398	171	.430	130	90	.692	473	55	266	6	432	5.4
Rod Hundley	78	1492	509	173	.340	127	83	.654	199	290	129	1	429	5.5
Howie Jolliff	64	1094	253	104	.411	78	41	.526	383	76	175	4	249	3.9
Bob McNeill*	50	441	136	56	.412	34	26	.765	56	89	56	0	138	2.8
Wayne Yates	37	263	105	31	.295	22	10	.455	94	16	72	1	72	1.9
Robert Smith	3	7	1	0	.000	0	0	.000	0	0	1	0	0	0.0

*McNeill—21 Philadelphia, 29 Los Angeles.

NEW YORK KNICKERBOCKERS

Player	G.	Min.	FGA	FGM	Pct.	FTA	FTM	Pct.	Reb.	Ast.	PF	Disq.	Pts.	Avg.
Richie Guerin	78	3348	1897	839	.442	762	625	.820	501	539	299	3	2303	29.5
Willie Naulls	75	2978	1798	747	.415	455	383	.842	867	192	260	6	1877	25.0
John Green	80	2789	1164	507	.436	434	261	.601	1066	191	265	4	1275	15.9
Phil Jordon	76	2195	1028	403	.392	168	96	.571	482	156	258	7	902	11.9
Al Butler*	59	2016	754	349	.463	182	129	.709	337	205	156	0	827	14.0
Dave Budd	79	1370	431	188	.436	231	138	.597	345	86	162	4	514	6.5
Darrall Imhoff	76	1481	482	186	.386	139	80	.576	470	82	230	10	452	5.9
Cleveland Buckner	62	696	367	158	.431	133	83	.624	236	39	114	1	399	6.4
Whitey Martin	66	1018	292	95	.325	55	37	.673	158	115	158	4	227	3.4
Sam Stith	32	440	162	59	.364	38	23	.605	51	60	55	0	141	4.4
Donnis Butcher	47	479	155	48	.310	69	42	.609	79	51	63	0	138	2.9
George Blaney	36	363	142	54	.380	17	9	.529	36	45	34	0	117	3.3
Bill Smith	9	83	33	8	.242	8	7	.875	16	7	6	0	23	2.6
Ed Burton	8	28	14	7	.500	4	1	.250	5	1	3	0	15	1.9
Doug Kistler	5	13	6	3	.500	4	2	.500	1	0	2	0	8	1.6

*Butler—5 Boston, 54 New York.

PHILADELPHIA WARRIORS

Player	G.	Min.	FGA	FGM	Pct.	FTA	FTM	Pct.	Reb.	Ast.	PF	Disq.	Pts.	Avg.
Wilt Chamberlain	80	3882	3159	1597	.506	1363	835	.613	2052	192	123	0	4029	50.4
Paul Arizin	78	2785	1490	611	.410	601	484	.805	527	201	307	18	1706	21.9
Tom Meschery	80	2509	929	375	.404	262	216	.824	729	145	330	15	966	12.1
Al Attles	75	2468	724	343	.474	267	158	.592	355	333	279	8	844	11.3
Tom Gola	60	2462	765	322	.421	230	176	.765	587	295	267	16	820	13.7
Guy Rodgers	80	2650	749	267	.356	182	121	.665	348	643	312	12	655	8.2
Ed Conlin	70	963	371	128	.345	89	66	.742	155	85	118	1	322	4.6
York Larese*	59	703	327	122	.373	72	58	.805	77	94	104	0	302	5.1
Tom Luckenbill	67	396	120	43	.358	76	49	.645	110	27	67	0	135	2.0
Joe Ruklick	46	302	147	48	.326	26	12	.461	87	14	56	1	108	2.3
Frank Radovich	37	175	93	37	.398	26	13	.500	51	4	27	0	87	2.3

*Larese—8 Chicago, 51 Philadelphia.

ST. LOUIS HAWKS

Player	G.	Min.	FGA	FGM	Pct.	FTA	FTM	Pct.	Reb.	Ast.	PF	Disq.	Pts.	Avg.
Bob Pettit	78	3282	1928	867	.450	901	695	.771	1459	289	296	4	2429	31.1
Cliff Hagan	77	2786	1490	701	.470	439	362	.825	633	370	282	8	1764	22.9
Clyde Lovellette	40	1192	724	341	.471	187	155	.829	350	68	136	4	837	20.9
Barney Cable*	67	1861	749	305	.407	181	118	.652	563	115	211	4	728	10.9
Shellie McMillon*	62	1225	591	265	.448	182	108	.593	368	59	202	10	638	10.3
Al Ferrari	79	2046	582	208	.357	219	175	.799	213	313	278	9	591	7.5
Fred LaCour	73	1507	536	230	.429	130	106	.815	272	166	168	3	566	7.8
Larry Foust	57	1153	433	204	.471	178	145	.815	328	78	186	3	553	9.7
Bob Sims*	65	1345	491	193	.393	216	123	.549	183	154	187	4	509	7.8
Len Wilkens	20	870	364	140	.385	110	84	.764	131	116	63	0	364	18.2
Cleo Hill	58	1050	309	107	.346	137	106	.774	178	114	98	1	320	5.5
Vern Hatton*	40	898	331	112	.338	125	98	.784	102	99	63	0	322	8.1
Archie Dees*	21	288	115	51	.443	46	35	.761	77	16	33	0	137	6.5
Stacey Arceneaux	7	110	56	22	.393	13	6	.461	32	4	10	0	50	7.1
Jack McCarthy	15	333	73	18	.246	27	12	.444	56	70	50	1	48	3.2

Player	G.	Min.	FGA	FGM	Pct.	FTA	FTM	Pct.	Reb.	Ast.	PF	Disq.	Pts.	Avg.
Jim Darrow	5	34	15	3	.200	7	6	.857	7	6	9	0	12	2.4
Ron Horn	3	25	12	1	.083	2	1	.500	6	1	4	0	3	1.0
Richard Eichhorst	1	10	2	1	.500	0	0	.000	1	3	1	0	2	2.0

*Cable—15 Chicago, 52 St. Louis. Dees—13 Chicago, 8 St. Louis. Hatton—15 Chicago, 25 St. Louis. McMillon—14 Detroit, 48 St. Louis. Sims—19 Los Angeles, 46 St. Louis.

SYRACUSE NATIONALS

Player	G.	Min.	FGA	FGM	Pct.	FTA	FTM	Pct.	Reb.	Ast.	PF	Disq.	Pts.	Avg.
Hal Greer	71	2705	1442	644	.446	404	331	.819	524	313	252	2	1619	22.8
Dave Gambee	80	2301	1126	477	.424	470	384	.817	631	114	275	10	1338	16.7
John Kerr	80	2768	1220	541	.443	302	222	.735	1176	243	272	7	1304	16.3
Lee Shaffer	75	2083	1180	514	.436	310	239	.771	511	99	266	6	1267	16.9
Larry Costello	63	1854	726	310	.427	295	247	.837	245	359	220	5	867	13.7
Al Bianchi	80	1925	847	336	.397	221	154	.697	281	263	232	5	826	10.3
Dolph Schayes	56	1480	751	268	.357	319	286	.896	439	120	167	4	822	14.7
Joe Roberts	80	1642	619	243	.393	194	129	.665	538	50	230	4	615	7.7
Paul Neumann	77	1265	401	172	.429	172	133	.773	194	176	203	3	477	6.2
Swede Halbrook	64	908	422	152	.360	151	96	.636	399	33	179	7	400	6.3
Joe Graboski	38	468	221	77	.348	65	39	.600	154	28	62	0	193	5.1
Charles Osborne	4	21	8	1	.125	4	3	.750	9	1	3	0	5	1.2

*Graboski—3 St. Louis, 12 Chicago, 23 Syracuse.

PLAYOFF RESULTS

EASTERN DIVISION SEMIFINALS
Philadelphia 3, Syracuse 2

Mar. 16—Syracuse 103 at Philadelphia 110
Mar. 18—Philadelphia 97 at Syracuse 82
Mar. 19—Syracuse 101 at Philadelphia 100
Mar. 20—Philadelphia 99 at Syracuse 106
Mar. 22—Syracuse 104 at Philadelphia 121

WESTERN DIVISION SEMIFINALS
Detroit 3, Cincinnati 1

Mar. 16—Cincinnati 122 at Detroit 123
Mar. 17—Detroit 107 at Cincinnati 129
Mar. 18—Cincinnati 107 at Detroit 118
Mar. 20—Detroit 112 at Cincinnati 111

EASTERN DIVISION FINALS
Boston 4, Philadelphia 3

Mar. 24—Philadelphia 89 at Boston 117
Mar. 27—Boston 106 at Philadelphia 113
Mar. 28—Philadelphia 114 at Boston 129
Mar. 31—Boston 106 at Philadelphia 110
Apr. 1—Philadelphia 104 at Boston 119
Apr. 3—Boston 99 at Philadelphia 109
Apr. 5—Philadelphia 107 at Boston 109

WESTERN DIVISION FINALS
Los Angeles 4, Detroit 2

Mar. 24—Detroit 108 at Los Angeles 132
Mar. 25—Detroit 112 at Los Angeles 127
Mar. 27—Los Angeles 111 at Detroit 106
Mar. 29—Los Angeles 117 at Detroit 118
Mar. 31—Detroit 132 at Los Angeles 125
Apr. 3—Los Angeles 123 at Detroit 117

WORLD CHAMPIONSHIP FINALS
Boston 4, Los Angeles 3

Apr. 7—Los Angeles 108 at Boston 122
Apr. 8—Los Angeles 129 at Boston 122
Apr. 10—Boston 115 at Los Angeles 117
Apr. 11—Boston 115 at Los Angeles 103
Apr. 14—Los Angeles 126 at Boston 121
Apr. 16—Boston 119 at Los Angeles 105
Apr. 18—Los Angeles 107 at Boston *110

*Denotes overtime period.

1960-61 NBA STATISTICS

1960-61 NBA CHAMPION BOSTON CELTICS

Seated (left to right): K. C. Jones, Bob Cousy, Coach Red Auerbach, President Walter A. Brown, Bill Sharman, Frank Ramsey; standing, Trainer Buddy LeRoux, Tom Sanders, Tom Heinsohn, Gene Conley, Bill Russell, Gene Guarilia, Jim Loscutoff, Sam Jones. Inset: Treasurer Lou Pieri.

FINAL STANDINGS

EASTERN DIVISION

Team	Bos.	Phil.	Syr.	N.Y.	S.L.	L.A.	Det.	Cinn.	W.	L.	Pct.	G.B.
Boston	..	8	10	10	6	8	8	7	57	22	.722	....
Philadelphia	5	..	6	11	3	8	5	8	46	33	.582	11
Syracuse	3	7	..	8	4	4	6	8	38	41	.481	19
New York	3	2	5	..	1	3	5	2	21	58	.266	36

WESTERN DIVISION

Team	Bos.	Phil.	Syr.	N.Y.	S.L.	L.A.	Det.	Cinn.	W.	L.	Pct.	G.B.
St. Louis	4	7	6	9	..	8	10	7	51	28	.646	....
Los Angeles	2	2	6	7	5	..	9	5	36	43	.456	15
Detroit	2	5	4	5	3	4	..	11	34	45	.430	17
Cincinnati	3	2	4	8	6	8	2	..	33	46	.418	18

HOME-ROAD-NEUTRAL RECORDS OF ALL TEAMS

	Home	Road	Neutral	Total		Home	Road	Neutral	Total
Boston	21- 7	24- 11	12- 4	57- 22	New York	10- 22	7- 25	4-11	21- 58
Cincinnati	18- 13	8- 19	7-14	33- 46	Philadelphia	23- 6	12- 21	11- 6	46- 33
Detroit	20- 11	3- 19	11-15	34- 45	St. Louis	29- 5	15- 20	7- 3	51- 28
Los Angeles	16- 12	8- 20	12-11	36- 43	Syracuse	19- 9	8- 21	11-11	38- 41
					Totals	156- 85	85-156	75-75	316-316

TEAM STATISTICS

Team	G.	FGA	FGM	Pct.	FTA	FTM	Pct.	Reb.	Ast.	PF	Disq.	For	Agst.	Pt.Dif.
Boston	79	9295	3697	.398	2804	2062	.735	6131	1872	2032	46	119.7	114.1	+5.6
St. Louis	79	8795	3618	.411	2921	2147	.735	5994	2136	2135	36	118.8	115.2	+3.6
Syracuse	79	8746	3654	.418	2948	2278	.773	5726	1786	2280	43	121.3	119.2	+2.1
Philadelphia	79	8883	3768	.424	3108	2022	.651	5938	1959	1936	38	121.0	120.1	+0.9
Los Angeles	79	8430	3401	.403	2999	2204	.735	5816	1728	2043	32	114.0	114.1	—0.1
Detroit	79	8357	3481	.417	3240	2408	.743	5813	1866	2157	47	118.6	120.1	—1.5
Cincinnati	79	8281	3626	.438	2761	2060	.746	5581	2107	2159	40	117.9	121.3	—3.4
New York	79	8347	3422	.410	2838	2135	.752	5315	1822	2223	37	113.7	120.1	—6.4

INDIVIDUAL LEADERS

POINTS

	G.	FG	FT	Pts.	Avg.		G.	FG	FT	Pts.	Avg.
Wilt Chamberlain, Phila.	79	1251	531	3033	38.4	Richie Guerin, New York	79	612	496	1720	21.8
Elgin Baylor, Los Angeles	73	931	676	2538	34.8	Cliff Hagan, St. Louis	77	661	383	1705	22.1
Oscar Robertson, Cincinnati	71	756	653	2165	30.5	Tom Heinsohn, Boston	74	627	325	1579	21.3
Bob Pettit, St. Louis	76	769	582	2120	27.9	Hal Greer, Syracuse	79	623	305	1551	19.6
Jack Twyman, Cincinnati	79	796	405	1997	25.3	Clyde Lovellette, St. Louis	67	599	273	1471	22.0
Dolph Schayes, Syracuse	79	594	680	1868	23.6	Jerry West, Los Angeles	79	529	331	1389	17.6
Willie Naulls, New York	79	737	372	1846	23.4	Bob Cousy, Boston	76	513	352	1378	18.1
Paul Arizin, Philadelphia	79	650	532	1832	23.2	Bill Russell, Boston	78	532	258	1322	16.9
Bailey Howell, Detroit	77	607	601	1815	23.6	Dick Barnett, Syracuse	78	540	240	1320	16.9
Gene Shue, Detroit	78	650	465	1765	22.6	Frank Ramsey, Boston	79	448	295	1191	15.1

FIELD GOALS
(Minimum 200 FGM)

	FGA	FGM	Pct.
Wilt Chamberlain, Philadelphia	2457	1251	.509
Jack Twyman, Cincinnati	1632	796	.488
Larry Costello, Syracuse	844	407	.482
Oscar Robertson, Cincinnati	1600	756	.473
Bailey Howell, Detroit	1293	607	.469
Barney Cable, Syracuse	574	266	.463
Clyde Lovellette, St. Louis	1321	599	.453
Dick Barnett, Syracuse	1194	540	.452
Wayne Embry, Cincinnati	1015	458	.451
Hal Greer, Syracuse	1381	623	.451

ASSISTS

	G.	No.	Avg.
Oscar Robertson, Cincinnati	71	690	9.7
Guy Rodgers, Philadelphia	78	677	8.7
Bob Cousy, Boston	76	587	7.7
Gene Shue, Detroit	78	530	6.8
Richie Guerin, New York	79	503	6.4
Jack McCarthy, St. Louis	79	430	5.4
Larry Costello, Syracuse	75	413	5.5
Cliff Hagan, St. Louis	77	381	4.9
Elgin Baylor, Los Angeles	73	371	5.1
Rod Hundley, Los Angeles	79	350	4.4

FREE THROWS
(Minimum 200 FTM)

	FTA	FTM	Pct.
Bill Sharman, Boston	228	210	.921
Dolph Schayes, Syracuse	783	680	.868
Gene Shue, Detroit	543	465	.856
Frank Ramsey, Boston	354	295	.833
Paul Arizin, Philadelphia	639	532	.833
Clyde Lovellette, St. Louis	329	273	.830
Dave Gambee, Syracuse	352	291	.827
Ken Sears, New York	325	268	.825
Oscar Robertson, Cincinnati	794	653	.822
Cliff Hagan, St. Louis	467	383	.820

REBOUNDS

	G.	No.	Avg.
Wilt Chamberlain, Philadelphia	79	2149	27.2
Bill Russell, Boston	78	1868	23.9
Bob Pettit, St. Louis	76	1540	20.3
Elgin Baylor, Los Angeles	73	1447	19.8
Bailey Howell, Detroit	77	1111	14.4
Willie Naulls, New York	79	1055	13.4
Walter Dukes, Detroit	73	1028	14.1
Dolph Schayes, Syracuse	79	960	12.2
John Kerr, Syracuse	79	951	12.0
Wayne Embry, Cincinnati	79	864	10.9

TEAM-BY-TEAM INDIVIDUAL STATISTICS

BOSTON CELTICS

Player	G.	Min.	FGA	FGM	Pct.	FTA	FTM	Pct.	Reb.	Ast.	PF	Disq.	Pts.	Avg.
Tom Heinsohn	74	2256	1566	627	.400	424	325	.767	732	141	260	7	1579	21.3
Bob Cousy	76	2468	1382	513	.371	452	352	.779	331	587	196	0	1378	18.1
Bill Russell	78	3458	1250	532	.426	469	258	.550	1868	268	155	0	1322	16.9
Frank Ramsey	79	2019	1100	448	.407	354	295	.833	431	146	284	14	1191	15.1
Sam Jones	78	2028	1069	480	.449	268	211	.664	421	217	148	1	1171	15.0
Bill Sharman	61	1538	908	383	.422	228	210	.921	223	146	127	0	976	16.0
K. C. Jones	78	1605	601	203	.338	280	186	.664	279	253	190	3	592	7.6
Gene Conley	75	1242	495	183	.370	153	106	.693	550	40	275	15	472	6.3
Tom Sanders	68	1084	352	148	.420	100	67	.670	385	44	131	1	363	5.3
Jim Loscutoff	76	1153	478	144	.310	76	49	.645	291	25	238	5	337	4.4
Gene Guarilia	25	209	94	38	.404	10	3	.300	71	5	28	0	79	3.2

CINCINNATI ROYALS

Player	G.	Min.	FGA	FGM	Pct.	FTA	FTM	Pct.	Reb.	Ast.	PF	Disq.	Pts.	Avg.
Oscar Robertson	71	3032	1600	756	.473	794	653	.822	716	690	219	3	2165	30.5
Jack Twyman	79	2920	1632	796	.488	554	405	.731	672	225	279	5	1997	25.3
Wayne Embry	79	2233	1015	458	.451	331	221	.668	864	127	286	7	1137	14.4
Arlen Bockhorn	79	2669	1059	420	.397	208	152	.731	434	338	282	9	992	12.6
Bob Boozer	79	1573	603	250	.415	247	166	.672	488	109	193	1	666	8.4
Mike Farmer*	59	1301	461	180	.390	94	69	.734	380	81	130	1	429	7.3
Hub Reed	75	1216	364	156	.429	122	85	.697	367	69	199	7	397	5.3
Ralph Davis	73	1210	451	181	.401	52	34	.654	86	177	127	1	396	5.4
Larry Staverman	66	944	249	111	.446	93	79	.849	287	86	164	4	301	4.6
Win Wilfong	62	717	305	106	.348	89	72	.809	147	87	119	1	284	4.6

*Farmer—2 New York, 57 Cincinnati.

DETROIT PISTONS

Player	G.	Min.	FGA	FGM	Pct.	FTA	FTM	Pct.	Reb.	Ast.	PF	Disq.	Pts.	Avg.
Bailey Howell	77	2952	1293	607	.469	798	601	.753	1111	196	297	10	1815	23.6
Gene Shue	78	3361	1545	650	.421	543	465	.856	334	530	207	1	1765	22.6
Don Ohl	79	2172	1085	427	.394	278	200	.719	256	265	224	3	1054	13.3
George Lee	74	1735	776	310	.399	394	276	.701	490	89	158	1	896	12.1
Bob Ferry	79	1657	776	350	.451	255	189	.741	500	129	205	1	889	11.3
Walter Dukes	73	2044	706	286	.405	400	281	.703	1028	139	313	16	853	11.7
Shelly McMillon	78	1636	752	322	.428	201	140	.697	487	98	238	6	784	10.1
Chuck Noble	75	1655	566	196	.346	115	82	.713	180	287	195	4	474	6.3
Jack Moreland	64	1003	477	191	.400	132	86	.652	315	52	174	3	468	7.3
Willie Jones	35	452	216	78	.361	63	40	.635	94	63	90	2	196	5.6
Archie Dees	28	308	135	53	.393	47	39	.830	94	17	50	0	145	5.2

Cincinnati's Oscar Robertson led the league in 1960-61 in assists, was third in scoring, fourth in field goals and ninth in free throws—and was only a rookie.

LOS ANGELES LAKERS

Player	G.	Min.	FGA	FGM	Pct.	FTA	FTM	Pct.	Reb.	Ast.	PF	Disq.	Pts.	Avg.
Elgin Baylor	73	3133	2166	931	.430	863	676	.783	1447	371	279	3	2538	34.8
Jerry West	79	2797	1264	529	.419	497	331	.666	611	333	213	1	1389	17.6
Rudy LaRusso	79	2593	992	416	.419	409	323	.790	781	135	280	8	1155	14.6
Rod Hundley	79	2179	921	323	.351	296	223	.753	289	350	144	0	869	11.0
Frank Selvy	77	2153	767	311	.405	279	210	.753	299	246	219	3	832	10.8
Tom Hawkins	78	1846	719	310	.431	235	140	.596	479	88	209	2	760	9.7
James Krebs	75	1655	692	271	.392	93	75	.806	456	68	223	2	617	8.2
Ray Felix	78	1510	508	189	.372	193	135	.699	539	37	302	12	513	6.6
Bob Leonard	55	600	207	61	.295	100	71	.710	70	81	70	0	193	3.5
Howard Jolliff	46	352	141	46	.326	23	11	.478	141	16	53	0	103	2.2
Ron Johnson*	14	92	43	13	.302	17	11	.647	29	2	10	0	37	2.6
Gary Alcorn	20	174	40	12	.300	8	7	.875	50	2	47	1	31	1.6

*Johnson—6 Detroit, 8 Los Angeles.

NEW YORK KNICKERBOCKERS

Player	G.	Min.	FGA	FGM	Pct.	FTA	FTM	Pct.	Reb.	Ast.	PF	Disq.	Pts.	Avg.
Willie Naulls	79	2976	1723	737	.428	456	372	.816	1055	191	268	5	1846	23.4
Richie Guerin	79	3023	1545	612	.396	626	496	.792	628	503	310	3	1720	21.8
Dick Garmaker	71	2238	943	415	.440	358	275	.768	277	220	240	2	1105	15.6
Phil Jordon*	79	2064	932	360	.386	297	208	.700	674	181	273	5	928	11.7
John Green	78	1784	758	326	.430	278	145	.522	838	97	194	3	797	10.2

Player	G.	Min.	FGA	FGM	Pct.	FTA	FTM	Pct.	Reb.	Ast.	PF	Disq.	Pts.	Avg.
Kenny Sears	52	1396	568	241	.424	325	268	.825	293	102	165	6	750	14.4
Charlie Tyra	59	1404	549	199	.362	173	120	.694	394	82	164	7	518	8.8
Bob McNeill	75	1387	427	166	.389	126	105	.833	123	238	148	2	437	5.8
David Budd	61	1075	361	156	.432	134	87	.649	297	45	171	2	399	6.5
Jim Palmer	55	688	310	125	.403	65	44	.677	179	30	128	0	294	5.3
Darrall Imhoff	62	994	310	122	.394	96	49	.510	296	51	143	2	293	4.7
Phil Rollins°	61	816	293	109	.372	88	58	.659	97	123	121	1	276	4.6
Carl Braun	15	218	79	37	.468	14	11	.786	31	48	29	0	85	5.7
Jack George	16	268	93	31	.333	30	20	.667	32	39	37	0	82	5.1
Whitey Bell	5	45	18	7	.389	3	1	.333	7	1	7	0	15	3.0

°Jordan—48 Cincinnati, 31 New York. Rollins—7 St. Louis, 40 New York, 14 Cincinnati.

PHILADELPHIA WARRIORS

Player	G.	Min.	FGA	FGM	Pct.	FTA	FTM	Pct.	Reb.	Ast.	PF	Disq.	Pts.	Avg.
Wilt Chamberlain	79	3773	2457	1251	.509	1054	531	.504	2149	148	130	0	3033	38.4
Paul Arizin	79	2935	1529	650	.425	639	532	.833	681	188	335	11	1832	23.2
Tom Gola	74	2712	940	420	.447	281	210	.747	692	292	321	13	1050	14.2
Guy Rodgers	78	2905	1029	397	.386	300	206	.687	509	677	262	3	1000	12.8
Andy Johnson	79	2000	834	299	.359	275	157	.571	345	205	249	3	755	9.6
Al Attles	77	1544	543	222	.409	162	97	.599	214	174	235	5	541	7.0
Ed Conlin	77	1294	599	216	.361	139	104	.748	262	123	153	1	536	7.0
Joe Graboski	68	1011	507	169	.333	183	127	.694	262	74	148	2	465	6.8
Vern Hatton	54	610	304	97	.319	56	46	.821	92	59	59	0	240	4.4
Joe Ruklick	29	223	120	43	.358	13	8	.615	62	10	38	0	94	3.2
Bill Kennedy	7	52	21	4	.190	6	4	.667	8	9	6	0	12	1.7

ST. LOUIS HAWKS

Player	G.	Min.	FGA	FGM	Pct.	FTA	FTM	Pct.	Reb.	Ast.	PF	Disq.	Pts.	Avg.
Bob Pettit	76	3027	1720	769	.447	804	582	.724	1540	262	217	1	2120	27.9
Cliff Hagan	77	2701	1490	661	.444	467	383	.820	715	381	286	9	1705	22.1
Clyde Lovellette	67	2111	1321	599	.453	329	273	.830	677	172	248	4	1471	22.0
Len Wilkens	75	1898	783	333	.425	300	214	.713	335	212	215	5	880	11.7
Sihugo Green	76	1968	718	263	.366	247	174	.704	380	258	234	2	700	9.2
John McCarthy	79	2519	746	266	.357	226	122	.540	325	430	272	8	654	8.3
Larry Foust	68	1208	489	194	.397	208	164	.788	389	77	185	0	552	8.1
Woody Sauldsberry	69	1491	768	230	.299	100	56	.560	491	74	197	3	516	7.5
Al Ferrari	63	1031	328	117	.357	116	95	.819	115	143	157	4	329	5.2
Fred LaCour	55	722	295	123	.417	84	63	.750	178	84	73	0	309	5.6
Dave Piontek	29	254	96	47	.490	31	16	.516	68	19	31	0	110	3.8

SYRACUSE NATIONALS

Player	G.	Min.	FGA	FGM	Pct.	FTA	FTM	Pct.	Reb.	Ast.	PF	Disq.	Pts.	Avg.
Dolph Schayes	79	3007	1595	594	.372	783	680	.868	960	296	296	9	1868	23.6
Hal Greer	79	2763	1381	623	.451	394	305	.774	455	302	242	0	1551	19.6
Dick Barnett	78	2070	1194	540	.452	337	240	.712	283	218	169	0	1320	16.9
Dave Gambee	79	2090	947	397	.419	352	291	.827	581	101	276	6	1085	13.7
Larry Costello	75	2167	844	407	.482	338	270	.799	292	413	286	9	1084	14.5
John Kerr	79	2676	1056	419	.397	299	218	.729	951	199	230	4	1056	13.4
Barney Cable	75	1642	574	266	.463	108	73	.676	469	85	246	1	605	8.1
Swede Halbrook	79	1131	463	155	.335	140	76	.543	550	31	262	9	386	4.9
Joe Roberts	68	800	351	130	.370	104	62	.596	243	43	125	0	322	4.7
Al Bianchi	52	667	342	118	.345	87	60	.690	105	93	137	5	296	5.7
Ernie Beck°	10	82	29	10	.345	7	6	.857	23	15	10	0	26	2.6
Cal Ramsey	2	27	11	2	.182	4	2	.500	7	3	7	0	6	3.0

°Beck—7 St. Louis, 3 Syracuse

PLAYOFF RESULTS

EASTERN DIVISION SEMIFINALS
Syracuse 3, Philadelphia 0

Mar. 14—Syracuse 115 at Philadelphia..107
Mar. 16—Philadelphia 114 at Syracuse..115
Mar. 18—Syracuse 106 at Philadelphia..103

WESTERN DIVISION SEMIFINALS
Los Angeles 3, Detroit 2

Mar. 14—Detroit 102 at Los Angeles 120
Mar. 15—Detroit 118 at Los Angeles 120
Mar. 17—Los Angeles 113 at Detroit 124
Mar. 18—Los Angeles 114 at Detroit 123
Mar. 19—Detroit 120 at Los Angeles 137

EASTERN DIVISION FINALS
Boston 4, Syracuse 1

Mar. 19—Syracuse 115 at Boston 128
Mar. 21—Boston 98 at Syracuse...115
Mar. 23—Syracuse 110 at Boston 133
Mar. 25—Boston 120 at Syracuse..107
Mar. 26—Syracuse 101 at Boston 123

WESTERN DIVISION FINALS
St. Louis 4, Los Angeles 3

Mar. 21—Los Angeles 122 at St. Louis..118
Mar. 22—Los Angeles 106 at St. Louis..121
Mar. 24—St. Louis 112 at Los Angeles..118
Mar. 25—St. Louis 118 at Los Angeles..117
Mar. 27—Los Angeles 121 at St. Louis..112
Mar. 29—St. Louis 114 at Los Angeles..°113
Apr. 1—Los Angeles 103 at St. Louis..105

WORLD CHAMPIONSHIP SERIES
Boston 4, St. Louis 1

Apr. 2—St. Louis 95 at Boston 129
Apr. 5—St. Louis 108 at Boston 116
Apr. 8—Boston 120 at St. Louis..124
Apr. 9—Boston 119 at St. Louis..104
Apr. 11—St. Louis 112 at Boston..121

°Denotes overtime period.

1959-60 NBA STATISTICS

1959-60 NBA CHAMPION BOSTON CELTICS

Seated (left to right): Frank Ramsey, Bob Cousy, Coach Red Auerbach, President Walter Brown, Treasurer Lou Pieri, K. C. Jones, Bill Sharman; standing: Gene Guarilia, Tom Heinsohn, John Richter, Bill Russell, Gene Conley, Jim Loscutoff, Sam Jones, Trainer Buddy LeRoux.

FINAL STANDINGS

EASTERN DIVISION

Team	Bos.	Phil.	Syr.	N.Y.	St.L.	Det.	Minn.	Cin.	W.	L.	Pct.	G.B.
Boston	..	8	8	12	6	9	8	8	59	16	.787	....
Philadelphia	5	..	8	9	4	7	7	9	49	26	.653	10
Syracuse	5	5	..	11	4	5	8	7	45	30	.600	14
New York	1	4	2	..	3	5	5	7	27	48	.360	32

WESTERN DIVISION

Team	Bos.	Phil.	Syr.	N.Y.	St.L.	Det.	Minn.	Cin.	W.	L.	Pct.	G.B.
St. Louis	3	5	5	6	..	8	10	9	46	29	.613	....
Detroit	0	2	4	4	5	..	7	8	30	45	.400	16
Minneapolis	1	2	1	4	3	6	..	8	25	50	.333	21
Cincinnati	1	0	2	2	4	5	5	..	19	56	.253	27

HOME-ROAD-NEUTRAL RECORDS OF ALL TEAMS

	Home	Road	Neutral	Total		Home	Road	Neutral	Total
Boston	25- 2	23- 9	11- 5	59- 16	New York	13- 18	9- 19	5-11	27- 48
Cincinnati	9- 22	2- 20	8-14	19- 56	Philadelphia	22- 6	12- 19	15- 1	49- 26
Detroit	17- 14	6- 21	7-10	30- 45	St. Louis	28- 5	12- 20	6- 4	46- 29
Minneapolis	9- 13	9- 22	7-15	25- 50	Syracuse	26- 4	11- 19	8- 7	45- 30
					Totals	149- 84	84-149	67-67	300-300

TEAM STATISTICS

Team	G.	FGA	FGM	Pct.	FTA	FTM	Pct.	Reb.	Ast.	PF	Disq.	For	Agst.	Pt.Dif.
Boston	75	8971	3744	.417	2519	1849	.734	6014	1849	1856	42	124.5	116.2	+8.3
St. Louis	75	7580	3179	.419	2885	2148	.745	5343	1881	1995	40	113.4	110.7	+2.7
Syracuse	75	8232	3406	.414	2662	2105	.791	5406	1676	1939	39	118.9	116.4	+2.5
Philadelphia	75	8678	3549	.409	2686	1797	.669	5916	1796	1715	21	118.6	116.4	+2.2
New York	75	8153	3429	.415	2539	1942	.765	5251	1667	1940	32	117.3	119.6	—2.3
Detroit	75	7920	3146	.397	2847	2075	.729	5491	1472	1983	49	111.6	115.0	—3.4
Minneapolis	75	7884	3040	.386	2691	1965	.730	5432	1444	1813	37	107.3	111.4	—4.1
Cincinnati	75	7786	3210	.412	2672	1913	.716	5251	1747	2097	38	111.1	117.4	—6.3

INDIVIDUAL LEADERS

POINTS

	G.	FG	FT	Pts.	Avg.		G.	FG	FT	Pts.	Avg.
Wilt Chamberlain, Philadelphia	72	1065	577	2707	37.6	George Yardley, Syracuse	73	546	381	1473	20.2
Jack Twyman, Cincinnati	75	870	598	2338	31.2	Bob Cousy, Boston	75	568	319	1455	19.4
Elgin Baylor, Minneapolis	70	755	564	2074	29.6	Clyde Lovellette, St. Louis	68	550	316	1416	20.8
Bob Pettit, St. Louis	72	669	544	1882	26.1	Willie Naulls, New York	65	551	286	1388	21.4
Cliff Hagan, St. Louis	75	719	421	1859	24.8	Bill Sharman, Boston	71	559	252	1370	19.3
Gene Shue, Detroit	75	620	472	1712	22.8	Bill Russell, Boston	74	555	240	1350	18.2
Dolph Schayes, Syracuse	75	578	533	1689	22.5	Bailey Howell, Detroit	75	510	312	1332	17.8
Tom Heinsohn, Boston	75	673	283	1629	21.7	Kenny Sears, New York	64	412	363	1187	18.5
Richie Guerin, New York	74	579	457	1615	21.8	Tom Gola, Philadelphia	75	426	270	1122	15.0
Paul Arizin, Philadelphia	72	593	420	1606	22.3	Frank Ramsey, Boston	73	422	273	1117	15.3

FIELD GOALS
(Minimum 190 FGM)

	FGA	FGM	Pct.
Ken Sears, New York	863	412	.477
Hal Greer, Syracuse	815	388	.476
Clyde Lovellette, St. Louis	1174	550	.468
Bill Russell, Boston	1189	555	.467
Cliff Hagan, St. Louis	1549	719	.464
Wilt Chamberlain, Philadelphia	2311	1065	.461
Bill Sharman, Boston	1225	559	.456
Bailey Howell, Detroit	1119	510	.456
Sam Jones, Boston	782	355	.454
George Yardley, Syracuse	1205	546	.453

ASSISTS

	G.	No.	Avg.
Bob Cousy, Boston	75	715	9.5
Guy Rodgers, Philadelphia	68	482	7.1
Richie Guerin, New York	74	468	6.3
Larry Costello, Syracuse	71	449	6.3
Tom Gola, Philadelphia	75	409	5.5
Dick McGuire, Detroit	68	358	5.3
Rod Hundley, Minneapolis	73	338	4.6
Slater Martin, St. Louis	64	330	5.2
Jack McCarthy, St. Louis	75	328	4.4
Cliff Hagan, St. Louis	75	299	4.0

FREE THROWS
(Minimum 185 FTM)

	FTA	FTM	Pct.
Dolph Schayes, Syracuse	597	533	.893
Gene Shue, Detroit	541	472	.872
Ken Sears, New York	418	363	.868
Bill Sharman, Boston	291	252	.866
Larry Costello, Syracuse	289	249	.862
Willie Naulls, New York	342	286	.836
Clyde Lovellette, St. Louis	385	316	.821
George Yardley, Syracuse	467	381	.816
Cliff Hagan, St. Louis	524	421	.803
Paul Arizin, Philadelphia	526	420	.798

REBOUNDS

	G.	No.	Avg.
Wilt Chamberlain, Philadelphia	72	1941	27.0
Bill Russell, Boston	74	1778	24.0
Bob Pettit, St. Louis	72	1221	17.0
Elgin Baylor, Minneapolis	70	1150	16.4
Dolph Schayes, Syracuse	75	959	12.8
Willie Naulls, New York	65	921	14.2
John Kerr, Syracuse	75	913	12.2
Walter Dukes, Detroit	66	883	13.4
Ken Sears, New York	64	876	13.7
Cliff Hagan, St. Louis	75	803	10.7

TEAM-BY-TEAM INDIVIDUAL STATISTICS

BOSTON CELTICS

Player	G.	Min.	FGA	FGM	Pct.	FTA	FTM	Pct.	Reb.	Ast.	PF	Disq.	Pts.	Avg.
Tom Heinsohn	75	2420	1590	673	.423	386	283	.733	794	171	275	8	1629	21.7
Bob Cousy	75	2588	1481	568	.384	403	319	.792	352	715	146	2	1455	19.4
Bill Sharman	71	1916	1225	559	.456	291	252	.866	262	144	154	2	1370	19.3
Bill Russell	74	3146	1189	555	.467	392	240	.612	1778	277	210	0	1350	18.2
Frank Ramsey	73	2009	1062	422	.397	347	273	.787	506	137	251	10	1117	15.3
Sam Jones	74	1512	782	355	.454	220	168	.764	375	125	101	1	878	11.9
Maurice King	1	19	8	5	.625	1	0	.000	4	2	3	0	10	10.0
Gene Conley	71	1330	539	201	.373	114	76	.667	590	32	270	10	478	6.7
K. C. Jones	74	1274	414	169	.408	170	128	.753	199	189	109	1	466	6.3
Jim Loscutoff	28	536	205	66	.322	36	22	.611	108	12	108	6	154	5.5
John Richter	66	808	332	113	.340	117	59	.504	312	27	158	1	285	4.3
Gene Guarilia	48	423	154	58	.377	41	29	.707	85	18	57	1	145	3.0

CINCINNATI ROYALS

Player	G.	Min.	FGA	FGM	Pct.	FTA	FTM	Pct.	Reb.	Ast.	PF	Disq.	Pts.	Avg.
Jack Twyman	75	3023	2063	870	.422	762	598	.785	664	260	275	10	2338	31.2
Phil Jordon	75	2066	970	381	.393	338	242	.716	624	207	227	7	1004	13.4
Wayne Embry	73	1594	690	303	.439	325	167	.514	692	83	226	1	773	10.6
Arlen Bockhorn	75	2103	812	323	.398	194	145	.747	382	256	249	8	791	10.5
Win Wilfong	72	1992	764	283	.370	207	161	.778	352	265	229	1	727	10.1
Hub Reed°	71	1820	601	270	.449	184	134	.728	614	69	230	6	674	9.5
Med Park	74	1849	582	226	.388	260	189	.727	301	214	180	2	641	8.7
Phil Rollins	72	1235	386	158	.409	127	77	.606	180	233	150	1	393	5.5
Dave Gambee°	61	656	291	117	.402	106	69	.651	229	38	83	1	303	5.0
Larry Staverman	49	479	149	70	.470	64	47	.734	180	36	98	0	187	3.8
Wayne Stevens	8	49	19	3	.158	10	7	.700	16	4	4	0	13	1.6

°Gambee—42 St. Louis, 19 Cincinnati; Reed—2 St. Louis, 69 Cincinnati.

DETROIT PISTONS

Player	G.	Min.	FGA	FGM	Pct.	FTA	FTM	Pct.	Reb.	Ast.	PF	Disq.	Pts.	Avg.
Gene Shue	75	3338	1501	620	.413	541	472	.872	409	295	146	2	1712	22.8
Bailey Howell	75	2346	1119	510	.456	422	312	.739	790	63	282	13	1332	17.8
Walter Dukes	66	2140	871	314	.361	508	376	.740	883	80	310	20	1004	15.2
Chuck Noble	58	1621	774	276	.357	138	101	.732	201	265	172	2	653	11.3
Ed Conlin	70	1636	831	300	.361	238	181	.761	346	126	158	2	781	11.2
Archie Dees	73	1244	617	271	.439	204	165	.809	397	43	188	3	707	9.7
Shellie McMillon	75	1416	627	267	.426	199	132	.663	431	49	198	3	666	8.9
Earl Lloyd	68	1610	665	237	.356	160	128	.800	322	89	226	1	602	8.9

Player	G.	Min.	FGA	FGM	Pct.	FTA	FTM	Pct.	Reb.	Ast.	PF	Disq.	Pts.	Avg.
Dick McGuire	68	1466	402	179	.445	201	124	.617	264	358	112	0	482	7.1
Billy Kenville	25	365	131	47	.359	41	33	.805	71	46	31	0	127	5.1
Tony Windis	9	193	60	16	.267	6	4	.667	47	32	20	0	36	4.0
Gary Alcorn	58	670	312	91	.292	84	48	.571	279	22	123	4	230	4.0

MINNEAPOLIS LAKERS

Player	G.	Min.	FGA	FGM	Pct.	FTA	FTM	Pct.	Reb.	Ast.	PF	Disq.	Pts.	Avg.
Elgin Baylor	70	2873	1781	755	.424	770	564	.732	1150	243	234	2	2074	29.6
Rudy LaRusso	71	2092	913	355	.389	357	265	.742	679	83	222	8	975	13.7
Rod Hundley	73	2279	1019	365	.358	273	203	.744	390	338	194	0	933	12.8
Frank Selvy*	62	1308	521	205	.393	208	153	.736	175	111	101	1	563	9.1
Bob Leonard	73	2074	717	231	.322	193	136	.705	245	252	171	3	598	8.2
Tom Hawkins	69	1467	579	220	.380	164	106	.646	428	54	188	3	546	7.9
Jim Krebs	75	1269	605	237	.392	136	98	.721	327	38	210	2	572	7.6
Ray Felix*	47	883	355	136	.383	112	70	.625	338	23	177	5	342	7.3
Ron Sobie*	16	234	108	37	.343	37	31	.838	48	21	32	0	105	6.6
Ed Fleming	27	413	141	59	.418	69	53	.768	87	38	46	0	171	6.3
Steve Hamilton	15	247	77	29	.377	23	18	.783	58	7	39	1	76	5.1
Charlie Share*	41	651	151	59	.391	80	53	.663	221	62	142	9	171	4.2
Boo Ellis	46	671	185	64	.346	76	51	.671	236	27	64	2	179	3.9
Bob Smith	10	130	54	13	.241	16	11	.688	33	14	10	0	37	3.7
Nick Mantis	10	71	39	10	.256	2	1	.500	6	9	8	0	21	2.1

*Felix—16 New York, 31 Minneapolis; Selvy—19 Syracuse, 43 Minneapolis; Share—38 St. Louis, 3 Minneapolis; Sobie—15 New York, 1 Minneapolis.

NEW YORK KNICKERBOCKERS

Player	G.	Min.	FGA	FGM	Pct.	FTA	FTM	Pct.	Reb.	Ast.	PF	Disq.	Pts.	Avg.
Richie Guerin	74	2420	1379	579	.420	591	457	.773	505	468	242	3	1615	21.8
Willie Naulls	65	2250	1286	551	.428	342	286	.836	921	138	214	4	1388	21.4
Kenny Sears	64	2099	863	412	.477	418	363	.868	876	127	191	2	1187	18.5
Carl Braun	54	1514	659	285	.432	154	129	.838	168	270	127	2	699	12.9
Charlie Tyra	74	2033	952	406	.426	189	133	.704	598	80	258	8	945	12.8
Dick Garmaker*	70	1932	815	323	.396	263	203	.772	313	206	186	4	849	12.1
Jack George	69	1604	650	250	.385	202	155	.767	197	240	148	1	655	9.5
Cal Ramsey*	11	195	96	39	.406	33	19	.576	66	9	25	1	97	8.8
Jim Palmer*	74	1482	574	246	.429	174	119	.684	389	70	224	6	611	8.3
Mike Farmer	67	1536	568	212	.373	83	70	.843	385	57	130	1	494	7.4
Johnny Green	69	1232	468	209	.447	155	63	.406	539	52	195	3	481	7.0
Whitey Bell	31	449	185	70	.378	43	28	.651	87	55	59	0	168	5.4
Bob Anderegg	33	373	143	55	.385	42	23	.548	69	29	32	0	133	4.0
Brendan McCann	4	29	10	1	.100	3	3	1.000	4	10	2	0	5	1.3

*Garmaker—44 Minneapolis, 26 New York; Ramsey—4 St. Louis, 7 New York; Palmer—20 Cincinnati, 54 New York.

PHILADELPHIA WARRIORS

Player	G.	Min.	FGA	FGM	Pct.	FTA	FTM	Pct.	Reb.	Ast.	PF	Disq.	Pts.	Avg.
Wilt Chamberlain	72	3338	2311	1065	.461	991	577	.582	1941	168	150	0	2707	37.6
Paul Arizin	72	2618	1400	593	.423	526	420	.798	621	165	263	6	1606	22.3
Tom Gola	75	2870	983	426	.433	340	270	.794	779	409	311	9	1122	15.0
Guy Rodgers	68	2483	870	338	.389	181	111	.613	391	482	196	3	787	11.6
Woody Sauldsberry	71	1848	974	325	.334	103	55	.534	447	112	203	2	705	9.9
Andy Johnson	75	1421	648	245	.378	208	125	.601	282	152	196	5	615	8.2
Joe Graboski	73	1269	583	217	.372	174	131	.753	358	111	147	1	565	7.7
Joe Ruklick	39	384	214	85	.397	36	26	.722	137	24	70	0	196	5.0
Vern Hatton	67	1049	356	127	.357	87	53	.609	159	82	61	0	307	4.6
Ernie Beck	66	809	294	114	.388	32	27	.844	127	72	90	0	255	3.9
Guy Sparrow	11	80	45	14	.311	8	2	.250	23	6	20	0	30	2.7

ST. LOUIS HAWKS

Player	G.	Min.	FGA	FGM	Pct.	FTA	FTM	Pct.	Reb.	Ast.	PF	Disq.	Pts.	Avg.
Bob Pettit	72	2896	1526	669	.438	722	544	.753	1221	257	204	0	1882	26.1
Cliff Hagan	75	2798	1549	719	.464	524	421	.803	803	299	270	4	1859	24.8
Clyde Lovellette	68	1953	1174	550	.468	385	316	.821	721	127	248	6	1416	20.8
Larry Foust*	72	1964	766	312	.407	320	253	.791	621	96	241	7	877	12.2
Dave Piontek*	77	1833	728	292	.401	202	129	.639	461	118	211	5	713	9.3
Al Ferrari	71	1567	523	216	.413	225	176	.782	162	188	205	7	608	8.6
John McCarthy	75	2383	730	240	.329	226	149	.659	301	328	233	3	629	8.4
Slater Martin	64	1756	383	142	.371	155	113	.729	187	330	174	2	397	6.2
Sihugo Green	70	1354	427	159	.372	175	111	.634	257	133	150	3	429	6.1
Bob Ferry	62	875	338	144	.426	119	76	.639	233	40	132	2	364	5.9
Jack McMahon	25	334	93	33	.355	29	16	.552	24	49	42	1	82	3.3

*Foust—47 Minneapolis, 25 St. Louis; Piontek—52 Cincinnati, 25 St. Louis.

SYRACUSE NATIONALS

Player	G.	Min.	FGA	FGM	Pct.	FTA	FTM	Pct.	Reb.	Ast.	PF	Disq.	Pts.	Avg.
Dolph Schayes	75	2741	1440	578	.401	597	533	.893	959	256	263	10	1689	22.5
George Yardley	73	2402	1205	546	.453	467	381	.816	579	122	227	3	1473	20.2
John Kerr	75	2372	1111	436	.392	310	233	.752	913	167	207	4	1105	14.7
Larry Costello	71	2469	822	372	.453	289	249	.862	388	449	234	4	993	14.0
Hal Greer	70	1979	815	388	.476	189	148	.783	303	188	208	4	924	13.2
Dick Barnett	57	1235	701	289	.412	180	128	.711	155	160	98	0	706	12.4
Bob Hopkins	75	1616	660	257	.389	174	136	.782	465	55	193	2	650	8.7
Al Bianchi	69	1256	576	211	.366	155	109	.703	179	169	231	5	531	7.7
Connie Dierking	71	1119	526	192	.365	188	108	.574	456	54	168	4	492	6.9
Barney Cable*	57	715	290	109	.376	67	44	.657	225	39	93	1	262	4.6
Togo Palazzi	7	70	41	13	.317	8	4	.500	14	3	7	0	30	4.3
Jim Ray	4	21	6	1	.167	0	0	.000	0	2	3	0	2	0.5
Paul Seymour	4	7	4	0	.000	0	0	.000	1	0	1	0	0	0.0

*Cable—7 Detroit, 50 Syracuse.

Perhaps the NBA's most dominant player ever, Wilt Chamberlain was the league's scoring and rebound champ as well as a first-team All-Star in his rookie season.

PLAYOFF RESULTS

EASTERN DIVISION SEMIFINALS
Philadelphia 2, Syracuse 1

Mar. 11—Syracuse 92 at Philadelphia 115
Mar. 13—Philadelphia 119 at Syracuse..........................125
Mar. 14—Syracuse 112 at Philadelphia..........................132

WESTERN DIVISION SEMIFINALS
Minneapolis 2, Detroit 0

Mar. 12—Minneapolis 113 at Detroit 112
Mar. 13—Detroit 99 at Minneapolis 114

EASTERN DIVISION FINALS
Boston 4, Philadelphia 2

Mar. 16—Philadelphia 105 at Boston 111
Mar. 18—Boston 110 at Philadelphia 115
Mar. 19—Philadelphia 90 at Boston................................120
Mar. 20—Boston 112 at Philadelphia 104
Mar. 22—Philadelphia 128 at Boston 107
Mar. 24—Boston 119 at Philadelphia 117

WESTERN DIVISION FINALS
St. Louis 4, Minneapolis 3

Mar. 16—Minneapolis 99 at St. Louis..............................112
Mar. 17—Minneapolis 120 at St. Louis 113
Mar. 19—St. Louis 93 at Minneapolis..............................89
Mar. 20—St. Louis 101 at Minneapolis 103
Mar. 22—Minneapolis 117 at St. Louis ....°110
Mar. 24—St. Louis 117 at Minneapolis............................96
Mar. 26—Minneapolis 86 at St. Louis...............................97

WORLD CHAMPIONSHIP SERIES
Boston 4, St. Louis 3

Mar. 27—St. Louis 122 at Boston.................................140
Mar. 29—St. Louis 113 at Boston.................................103
Apr. 2—Boston 102 at St. Louis.................................86
Apr. 3—Boston 96 at St. Louis.................................106
Apr. 5—St. Louis 102 at Boston.................................127
Apr. 7—Boston 102 at St. Louis.................................105
Apr. 9—St. Louis 103 at Boston.................................122

°Denotes overtime period.

1958-59 NBA STATISTICS

1958-59 NBA CHAMPION BOSTON CELTICS

Seated (left to right): Gene Conley, Bob Cousy, Coach Red Auerbach, President Walter A. Brown, Bill Sharman, Bill Russell; standing: Trainer Buddy LeRoux, K. C. Jones, Lou Tsioropoulos, Tommy Heinsohn, Ben Swain, Jim Loscutoff, Sam Jones, Frank Ramsey. Inset: Treasurer Lou Pieri.

FINAL STANDINGS

EASTERN DIVISION

Team	Bos.	N.Y.	Syr.	Phil.	St.L.	Mpls.	Det.	Cinn.	W.	L.	Pct.	G.B.
Boston	..	7	7	9	4	9	8	8	52	20	.722	....
New York	5	..	9	5	4	5	6	6	40	32	.556	12
Syracuse	5	3	..	8	2	4	7	6	35	37	.486	17
Philadelphia	3	7	4	..	4	4	3	7	32	40	.444	20

WESTERN DIVISON

St. Louis	5	5	7	5	..	8	8	11	49	23	.681	....
Minneapolis	0	4	5	6	4	..	8	6	33	39	.458	16
Detroit	1	3	2	5	4	4	..	9	28	44	.389	21
Cincinnati	1	3	3	2	1	6	3	..	19	53	.264	30

HOME-ROAD-NEUTRAL RECORDS OF ALL TEAMS

	Home	Road	Neutral	Total		Home	Road	Neutral	Total
Boston	26- 4	13- 15	13- 1	52- 20	New York	21- 9	15- 15	4- 8	40- 32
Cincinnati	9- 19	2- 25	8- 9	19- 53	Philadelphia	17- 9	7- 24	8- 7	32- 40
Detroit	13- 17	8- 20	7- 7	28- 44	St. Louis	28- 3	14- 15	7- 5	49- 23
Minneapolis	15- 7	9- 17	9-15	33- 39	Syracuse	19- 12	12- 17	4- 8	35- 37
					Total	148- 80	80-148	60-60	288-288

TEAM STATISTICS

Team	G.	FGA	FGM	Pct.	FTA	FTM	Pct.	Reb.	Ast.	PF	Disq.	For	Agst.	Pt.Dif.
Boston	72	8116	3208	.395	2563	1963	.766	5601	1568	1769	46	116.4	109.9	+6.5
Syracuse	72	7490	3050	.407	2642	2046	.775	4900	1340	1961	44	113.1	109.1	+4.0
St. Louis	72	7015	2879	.410	2757	2072	.752	5045	1567	1937	35	108.8	105.1	+3.7
New York	72	7170	2863	.399	2802	2217	.791	4091	1383	1899	34	110.3	110.1	+0.2
Minneapolis	72	7084	2779	.392	2718	2071	.762	5149	1373	1874	27	106.0	107.3	−1.3
Detroit	72	7305	2811	.385	2627	1943	.740	4860	1317	1881	58	105.1	106.6	−1.5
Philadelphia	72	7423	2826	.381	2425	1783	.735	4910	1375	1776	36	103.3	106.3	−3.0
Cincinnati	72	7340	2854	.389	2375	1713	.721	4887	1369	1855	36	103.1	112.0	−8.9

INDIVIDUAL LEADERS

POINTS

	G.	FG	FT	Pts.	Avg.		G.	FG	FT	Pts.	Avg.
Bob Pettit, St. Louis	72	719	667	2105	29.2	John Kerr, Syracuse	72	502	281	1285	17.8
Jack Twyman, Cincinnati	72	710	437	1857	25.8	Gene Shue, Detroit	72	464	338	1266	17.6
Paul Arizin, Philadelphia	70	632	587	1851	26.4	Tom Heinsohn, Boston	66	465	312	1242	18.8
Elgin Baylor, Minneapolis	70	605	532	1742	24.9	George Yardley, Det.-Syr.	61	446	317	1209	19.8
Cliff Hagan, St. Louis	72	646	415	1707	23.7	Bill Russell, Boston	70	456	256	1168	16.7
Dolph Schayes, Syracuse	72	504	526	1534	21.3	Woody Sauldsberry, Phila.	72	501	110	1112	15.4
Ken Sears, New York	71	491	506	1488	21.0	Larry Costello, Syracuse	70	414	280	1108	15.8
Bill Sharman, Boston	72	562	342	1466	20.4	Frank Ramsey, Boston	72	383	341	1107	15.4
Bob Cousy, Boston	65	484	329	1297	20.0	Willie Naulls, New York	68	405	258	1068	15.7
Richie Guerin, New York	71	443	405	1291	18.2	Joe Graboski, Philadelphia	72	394	270	1058	14.7

FIELD GOALS
(Minimum 230 FGM)

	FGA	FGM	Pct.
Ken Sears, New York	1002	491	.490
Bill Russell, Boston	997	456	.457
Cliff Hagan, St. Louis	1417	646	.456
Hal Greer, Syracuse	679	308	.454
Clyde Lovellette, St. Louis	885	402	.454
John Kerr, Syracuse	1139	502	.441
Bob Pettit, St. Louis	1640	719	.438
Larry Costello, Syracuse	948	414	.437
Sam Jones, Boston	703	305	.434
Paul Arizin, Philadelphia	1466	632	.431

ASSISTS

	G.	No.	Avg.
Bob Cousy, Boston	65	557	8.6
Dick McGuire, Detroit	71	443	6.2
Larry Costello, Syracuse	70	379	5.4
Richie Guerin, New York	71	364	5.1
Carl Braun, New York	72	349	4.8
Slater Martin, St. Louis	71	336	4.7
Jack McMahon, St. Louis	72	298	4.1
Elgin Baylor, Minneapolis	70	287	4.1
Tom Gola, Philadelphia	64	269	4.2
Guy Rodgers, Philadelphia	45	261	5.8

FREE THROWS
(Minimum 190 FTM)

	FTA	FTM	Pct.
Bill Sharman, Boston	367	342	.932
Dolph Schayes, Syracuse	609	526	.864
Ken Sears, New York	588	506	.861
Bob Cousy, Boston	385	329	.855
Willie Naulls, New York	311	258	.830
Clyde Lovellette, St. Louis	250	205	.820
Paul Arizin, Philadelphia	722	587	.813
Vern Mikkelsen, Minneapolis	355	286	.806
Gene Shue, Detroit	421	338	.803
Richie Guerin, New York	505	405	.802
Larry Costello, Syracuse	349	280	.802

REBOUNDS

	G.	No.	Avg.
Bill Russell, Boston	70	1612	23.0
Bob Pettit, St. Louis	72	1182	16.4
Elgin Baylor, Minneapolis	70	1050	15.0
John Kerr, Syracuse	72	1008	14.0
Dolph Schayes, Syracuse	72	962	13.4
Walter Dukes, Detroit	72	958	13.3
Woody Sauldsberry, Phila	72	826	11.5
Cliff Hagan, St. Louis	72	783	10.9
Joe Graboski, Philadelphia	72	751	10.4
Willie Naulls, New York	68	723	10.6

TEAM-BY-TEAM INDIVIDUAL STATISTICS

BOSTON CELTICS

Player	G.	Min.	FGA	FGM	Pct.	FTA	FTM	Pct.	Reb.	Ast.	PF	Disq.	Pts.	Avg.
Bill Sharman	72	2382	1377	562	.408	367	342	.932	292	179	173	1	1466	20.4
Bob Cousy	65	2403	1260	484	.384	385	329	.855	359	557	135	0	1297	20.0
Tom Heinsohn	66	2089	1192	465	.390	391	312	.798	638	164	271	11	1242	18.8
Bill Russell	70	2979	997	456	.457	428	256	.598	1612	222	161	3	1168	16.7
Frank Ramsey	72	2013	1013	383	.378	436	341	.782	491	147	266	11	1107	15.4
Sam Jones	71	1466	703	305	.434	196	151	.770	428	101	102	0	761	10.7
Jim Loscutoff	66	1680	686	242	.353	84	62	.738	460	60	285	15	546	8.3
Ben Swain	58	708	244	99	.400	110	67	.609	262	29	127	3	265	4.6
Gene Conley	50	663	262	86	.328	64	37	.578	276	19	117	2	209	4.2
K. C. Jones	49	609	192	65	.339	68	41	.603	127	70	58	0	171	3.5
Lou Tsioropoulos	35	488	190	60	.316	33	25	.758	110	20	74	0	145	4.1

CINCINNATI ROYALS

Player	G.	Min.	FGA	FGM	Pct.	FTA	FTM	Pct.	Reb.	Ast.	PF	Disq.	Pts.	Avg.
Jack Twyman	72	2713	1691	710	.420	558	437	.783	653	209	277	6	1857	25.8
Dave Piontek	72	1974	813	305	.375	227	156	.687	385	124	162	3	766	10.6
Wayne Embry	66	1590	702	272	.387	314	206	.656	597	96	232	9	750	11.4
Arlen Bockhorn	71	2251	771	294	.381	196	138	.704	460	206	215	6	726	10.2
Jim Palmer	67	1624	633	256	.404	246	178	.724	472	65	211	7	690	10.3
John McCarthy	47	1827	657	245	.373	174	116	.667	227	225	158	4	606	12.9
Archie Dees	68	1252	562	200	.356	204	159	.779	339	56	114	0	559	8.2
Med Park (29 St. L.-33 Cin.)	62	1126	361	145	.402	150	115	.767	188	108	93	0	405	6.5
Jack Parr	66	1037	307	109	.355	73	44	.603	278	51	138	1	262	4.0
Larry Staverman	57	681	215	101	.470	59	45	.763	218	54	103	0	247	4.3
Phil Rollins (23 Phila.-21 Cin.)	44	691	231	83	.359	90	63	.700	118	102	49	0	229	5.2
Tom Marshall	18	272	79	23	.291	29	18	.621	52	27	22	0	64	3.6

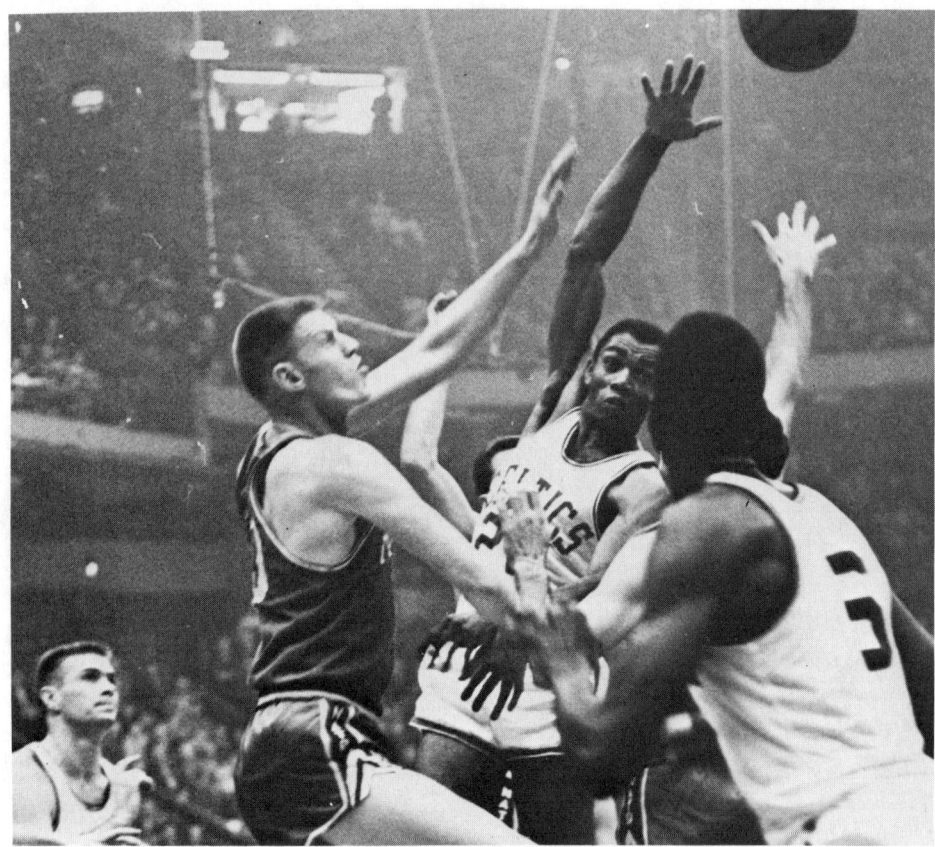

Boston defeated Syracuse four games to three in the Eastern Conference finals. In this photograph, the Nats' Johnny Kerr (in the dark jersey) battles Boston's Sam Jones and Bill Russell for a rebound.

DETROIT PISTONS

Player	G.	Min.	FGA	FGM	Pct.	FTA	FTM	Pct.	Reb.	Ast.	PF	Disq.	Pts.	Avg.
Gene Shue	72	2745	1197	464	.388	421	338	.803	335	231	129	1	1266	17.6
Phil Jordon	72	2058	967	399	.413	303	231	.762	594	83	193	1	1029	14.3
Walter Dukes	72	2338	904	318	.352	452	297	.657	958	64	332	22	933	13.0
Ed Conlin (57 Syr.-15 Det.)	72	1955	891	329	.369	274	197	.719	394	132	188	6	855	11.9
Dick McGuire	71	2063	543	232	.427	258	191	.740	285	443	147	1	655	9.2
Earl Lloyd	72	1796	670	234	.349	182	137	.753	500	90	291	15	605	8.4
Joe Holup	68	1502	580	209	.360	200	152	.760	352	73	239	12	570	8.4
Dick Farley	70	1280	448	177	.395	186	137	.737	195	124	130	2	491	7.0
Chuck Noble	65	939	560	189	.338	113	83	.735	115	114	126	0	461	7.1
Shellie McMillon	48	700	289	127	.439	104	55	.529	285	26	110	2	309	6.4
Barney Cable	31	271	126	43	.341	29	23	.793	88	12	30	0	109	3.5

MINNEAPOLIS LAKERS

Player	G.	Min.	FGA	FGM	Pct.	FTA	FTM	Pct.	Reb.	Ast.	PF	Disq.	Pts.	Avg.
Elgin Baylor	70	2855	1482	605	.408	685	532	.777	1050	287	270	4	1742	24.9
Vern Mikkelsen	72	2139	904	353	.390	355	286	.806	570	159	246	8	992	13.8
Dick Garmaker	72	2493	885	350	.395	368	284	.772	325	211	226	3	984	13.7
Larry Foust	72	1933	771	301	.390	366	280	.765	627	91	233	5	882	12.3
Rod Hundley	71	1664	719	259	.360	218	164	.752	250	205	139	0	682	9.6
Jim Krebs	72	1578	679	271	.399	123	92	.748	491	50	212	4	634	8.8
Bob Leonard	58	1598	552	206	.373	160	120	.750	178	186	119	0	532	9.2
Ed Fleming	71	1132	419	192	.387	190	137	.721	281	89	148	1	461	6.5
Boo Ellis	72	1202	379	163	.430	144	102	.708	380	59	137	0	428	5.9
Steve Hamilton	67	847	294	109	.371	109	74	.679	220	36	144	2	292	4.4

NEW YORK KNICKERBOCKERS

Player	G.	Min.	FGA	FGM	Pct.	FTA	FTM	Pct.	Reb.	Ast.	PF	Disq.	Pts.	Avg.
Kenny Sears	71	2498	1002	491	.490	588	506	.861	658	136	237	6	1488	21.0
Richie Guerin	71	2558	1046	443	.424	505	405	.802	518	364	255	1	1291	18.2
Willie Naulls	68	2061	1072	405	.378	311	258	.830	723	102	233	8	1068	15.7
Carl Braun	72	1959	684	287	.420	218	180	.826	251	349	178	3	754	10.5
Ray Felix	72	1588	700	260	.371	321	229	.713	569	49	275	9	749	10.4
Frank Selvy	68	1448	605	233	.385	262	201	.767	248	96	113	1	667	9.8
Jack George (46 Phil.-25 N.Y.)	71	1881	674	233	.346	203	153	.754	293	221	149	0	619	8.7
Charlie Tyra	69	1586	606	240	.396	190	129	.679	485	33	180	2	609	8.8
Mike Farmer	72	1545	498	176	.353	99	83	.838	315	66	152	1	435	6.0
Ron Sobie	50	857	400	144	.360	133	112	.842	154	78	84	0	400	8.0
Pete Brennan	16	136	43	13	.302	25	14	.560	31	6	15	0	40	2.5
Jerry Bird	11	45	32	12	.375	1	1	1.000	12	4	7	0	25	2.3
Brendan McCann	1	7	3	0	.000	0	0	.000	1	1	1	0	0	0.0

PHILADELPHIA WARRIORS

Player	G.	Min.	FGA	FGM	Pct.	FTA	FTM	Pct.	Reb.	Ast.	PF	Disq.	Pts.	Avg.
Paul Arizin	70	2799	1466	632	.431	722	587	.813	637	119	264	7	1851	26.4
Woody Sauldsberry	72	2743	1380	501	.363	176	110	.625	826	71	276	12	1112	15.4
Joe Graboski	72	2482	1116	394	.353	360	270	.750	751	148	249	5	1058	14.7
Tom Gola	64	2333	773	310	.401	357	281	.787	710	269	243	7	901	14.1
Guy Rodgers	45	1565	535	211	.394	112	61	.545	281	261	132	1	483	10.7
Andy Johnson	67	1158	466	174	.373	191	115	.602	212	90	176	4	463	6.9
Vern Hatton (24 Cin-40 Phi)	64	1109	418	149	.356	105	77	.733	178	70	111	0	375	5.9
Ernie Beck	70	1017	418	163	.390	65	43	.662	176	89	124	0	369	5.3
Guy Sparrow (44 NY-23 Phi)	67	842	406	129	.318	138	78	.565	244	67	158	3	336	5.0
Neil Johnston	28	393	164	54	.329	88	69	.784	139	21	50	0	177	6.3
Len Rosenbluth	29	205	145	43	.297	29	21	.724	54	6	20	0	107	3.7

ST. LOUIS HAWKS

Player	G.	Min.	FGA	FGM	Pct.	FTA	FTM	Pct.	Reb.	Ast.	PF	Disq.	Pts.	Avg.
Bob Pettit	72	2873	1640	719	.438	879	667	.758	1182	221	200	3	2105	29.2
Cliff Hagan	72	2702	1417	646	.456	536	415	.774	783	245	275	10	1707	23.7
Clyde Lovellette	70	1599	885	402	.454	250	205	.820	605	91	216	1	1009	14.4
Slater Martin	71	2504	706	245	.347	254	197	.776	253	336	230	8	687	9.7
Jack McMahon	72	2235	692	248	.358	156	96	.615	164	298	221	2	592	8.2
Charlie Share	72	1713	381	147	.386	184	139	.755	657	103	261	6	433	6.0
Al Ferrari	72	1189	385	134	.348	199	145	.729	142	122	155	1	413	5.7
Sihugo Green (20 Cin-26 StL)	46	1109	415	146	.352	160	104	.650	252	113	127	1	396	8.6
Hub Reed	65	950	317	136	.429	71	53	.746	317	32	171	2	325	5.0
Win Wilfong	63	741	285	99	.347	82	62	.756	121	50	102	0	260	4.1
Ed Macauley	14	196	75	22	.293	35	21	.600	40	13	20	1	65	4.6
Dave Gambee	2	7	1	1	1.000	0	0	.000	2	0	2	0	2	1.0

SYRACUSE NATIONALS

Player	G.	Min.	FGA	FGM	Pct.	FTA	FTM	Pct.	Reb.	Ast.	PF	Disq.	Pts.	Avg.
Dolph Schayes	72	2645	1304	504	.387	609	526	.864	962	178	280	9	1534	21.3
John Kerr	72	2671	1139	502	.441	367	281	.706	1008	142	183	1	1285	17.8
George Yardley (46 De-15 Sy)	61	1839	1042	446	.428	407	317	.779	431	65	159	2	1209	19.8
Larry Costello	70	2750	948	414	.437	349	280	.802	365	379	263	7	1108	15.8
Hal Greer	68	1625	679	308	.454	176	137	.778	196	101	189	1	753	11.1
Al Bianchi	72	1779	756	285	.377	206	149	.723	199	159	260	8	719	10.0
Bob Hopkins	67	1518	611	246	.403	234	176	.752	436	67	181	5	688	10.0
Togo Palazzi	71	1053	612	240	.392	158	115	.728	266	67	174	5	595	8.4
Connie Dierking	64	726	260	105	.362	140	83	.593	233	34	148	2	293	4.6
Geo. Dempsey (23 Phi-34 Syr)	57	694	215	92	.428	106	81	.764	160	68	95	0	265	4.6
Paul Seymour	21	266	98	32	.327	29	26	.897	39	36	25	0	90	4.3
Tom Kearns	1	7	1	1	1.000	0	0	.000	0	0	1	0	2	2.0

PLAYOFF RESULTS

EASTERN DIVISION SEMIFINALS
Syracuse 2, New York 0

Mar. 13—Syracuse 129 at New York 123
Mar. 15—New York 115 at Syracuse 131

WESTERN DIVISION SEMIFINALS
Minneapolis 2, Detroit 1

Mar. 14—Detroit 89 at Minneapolis...............................92
Mar. 15—Minneapolis 103 at Detroit 117
Mar. 18—Detroit 102 at Minneapolis..............................129

EASTERN DIVISION FINALS
Boston 4, Syracuse 3

Mar. 18—Syracuse 109 at Boston 131
Mar. 21—Boston 118 at Syracuse 120
Mar. 22—Syracuse 111 at Boston 133
Mar. 25—Boston 107 at Syracuse 119
Mar. 28—Syracuse 108 at Boston 129
Mar. 29—Boston 121 at Syracuse 133
Apr.   1—Syracuse 125 at Boston 130

WESTERN DIVISION FINALS
Minneapolis 4, St. Louis 2

Mar. 21—Minneapolis 90 at St. Louis.............................124
Mar. 22—St. Louis 98 at Minneapolis.............................106
Mar. 24—Minneapolis 97 at St. Louis.............................127
Mar. 26—St. Louis 98 at Minneapolis.............................108
Mar. 28—Minneapolis 98 at St. Louis...........................*97
Mar. 29—St. Louis 104 at Minneapolis...........................106

WORLD CHAMPIONSHIP SERIES
Boston 4, Minneapolis 0

Apr. 4—Minneapolis 115 at Boston 118
Apr. 5—Minneapolis 108 at Boston 128
Apr. 7—Boston 123, Mpls. at St. Paul 110
Apr. 9—Boston 118 at Minneapolis 113

*Denotes overtime period.

1957-58 NBA STATISTICS

1957-58 NBA CHAMPION ST. LOUIS HAWKS

Front Row (left to right): Coach Alex Hannum, Cliff Hagan, Jack Coleman, Captain Charley Share, Bob Pettit, Walt Davis, Ed Macauley. Rear row: Max Shapiro, ball boy; Slater Martin, Win Wilfong, Jack McMahon, Med Park, Frank Selvy, Trainer Bernie Ebert.

FINAL STANDINGS

EASTERN DIVISION

Team	Bos.	Syr.	Phil.	N.Y.	St.L.	Det.	Cinn.	Mpls.	W.	L.	Pct.	G.B.
Boston	..	7	6	7	5	8	7	9	49	23	.681	....
Syracuse	5	..	9	7	4	4	5	7	41	31	.569	8
Philadelphia	6	3	..	8	7	4	3	6	37	35	.514	12
New York	5	5	4	..	3	5	5	8	35	37	.486	14

WESTERN DIVISION

Team	Bos.	Syr.	Phil.	N.Y.	St.L.	Det.	Cinn.	Mpls.	W.	L.	Pct.	G.B.
St. Louis	4	5	2	6	..	6	9	9	41	31	.569	....
Detroit	1	5	5	4	6	..	6	6	33	39	.458	*8
Cincinnati	2	4	6	4	3	6	..	8	33	39	.458	*8
Minneapolis	0	2	3	1	3	6	4	..	19	53	.264	22

*Detroit and Cincinnati tied for second place. Detroit won coin flip for home court advantage in playoff.

HOME-ROAD-NEUTRAL RECORDS OF ALL TEAMS

Team	Home	Road	Neutral	Total	Team	Home	Road	Neutral	Total
Boston	25- 4	17- 13	7- 6	49- 23	New York	16- 13	11- 19	8- 5	35- 37
Cincinnati	17- 12	10- 19	6- 8	33- 39	Philadelphia	16- 12	12- 19	9- 4	37- 35
Detroit	14- 14	13- 18	6- 7	33- 39	St. Louis	23- 8	9- 19	9- 4	41- 31
Minneapolis	13- 17	4- 22	2-14	19- 53	Syracuse	26- 5	9- 21	6- 5	41- 31
					Totals	150- 85	85-150	53-53	288-288

TEAM STATISTICS

Team	G.	FGA	FGM	Pct.	FTA	FTM	Pct.	Reb.	Ast.	PF	Disq.	For	Agst.	Pt.Dif.
Boston	72	7759	3006	.387	2585	1904	.737	5402	1508	1723	34	109.9	104.4	+5.5
Syracuse	72	7336	2823	.385	2617	2075	.793	4895	1298	1820	28	107.2	105.1	+2.1
New York	72	7307	2884	.395	3056	2300	.753	5385	1359	1865	41	112.1	110.8	+1.3
St. Louis	72	7162	2779	.388	3047	2180	.715	5445	1541	1875	40	107.5	106.2	+1.3
Cincinnati	72	7339	2817	.384	2372	1688	.712	4959	1578	1835	30	101.7	100.6	+1.1
Philadelphia	72	7276	2765	.380	2596	1977	.762	4836	1441	1763	31	104.3	104.4	—0.1
Detroit	72	7295	2746	.376	2774	2093	.755	5168	1264	1807	32	105.3	107.7	—2.4
Minneapolis	72	7192	2660	.370	3007	2246	.747	5189	1322	1982	60	105.1	111.5	—6.4

INDIVIDUAL LEADERS

POINTS

	G.	FG	FT	Pts.	Avg.
George Yardley, Detroit	72	673	655	2001	27.8
Dolph Schayes, Syracuse	72	581	629	1791	24.9
Bob Pettit, St. Louis	70	581	557	1719	24.6
Clyde Lovellette, Cincinnati	71	679	301	1659	23.4
Paul Arizin, Philadelphia	68	483	440	1406	20.7
Bill Sharman, Boston	63	550	302	1402	22.3
Cliff Hagan, St. Louis	70	503	385	1391	19.9
Neil Johnston, Philadelphia	71	473	442	1388	19.5
Ken Sears, New York	72	445	452	1342	18.6
Vern Mikkelsen, Minn.	72	439	370	1248	17.3

	G.	FG	FT	Pts.	Avg.
Jack Twyman, Cincinnati	72	465	307	1237	17.2
Tom Heinsohn, Boston	69	468	294	1230	17.8
Willie Naulls, New York	68	472	284	1228	18.1
Larry Foust, Minneapolis	72	391	428	1210	16.8
Carl Braun, New York	71	426	321	1173	16.5
Bob Cousy, Boston	65	445	277	1167	18.0
Bill Russell, Boston	69	456	230	1142	16.6
Frank Ramsey, Boston	69	377	383	1137	16.5
Dick Garmaker, Minneapolis	68	390	314	1094	16.1
John Kerr, Syracuse	72	407	280	1094	15.2

FIELD GOALS
(Minimum 230 FGM)

	FGA	FGM	Pct.
Jack Twyman, Cincinnati	1028	465	.452
Cliff Hagan, St. Louis	1135	503	.443
Bill Russell, Boston	1032	456	.442
Ray Felix, New York	688	304	.442
Clyde Lovellette, Cincinnati	1540	679	.441
Ken Sears, New York	1014	445	.439
Neil Johnston, Philadelphia	1102	473	.429
Ed Macauley, St. Louis	879	376	.428
Larry Costello, Syracuse	888	378	.426
Bill Sharman, Boston	1297	550	.424

REBOUNDS

	G.	No.	Avg.
Bill Russell, Boston	69	1564	22.7
Bob Pettit, St. Louis	70	1216	17.4
Maurice Stokes, Cincinnati	63	1142	18.1
Dolph Schayes, Syracuse	72	1022	14.2
John Kerr, Syracuse	72	963	13.4
Walter Dukes, Detroit	72	954	13.3
Larry Foust, Minneapolis	72	876	12.2
Clyde Lovellette, Cincinnati	71	862	12.1
Vern Mikkelsen, Minneapolis	72	805	11.2
Willie Naulls, New York	68	799	11.8

FREE THROWS
(Minimum 190 FTM)

	FTA	FTM	Pct.
Dolph Schayes, Syracuse	696	629	.904
Bill Sharman, Boston	338	302	.893
Bob Cousy, Boston	326	277	.850
Carl Braun, New York	378	321	.849
Dick Schnittker, Minneapolis	237	201	.848
Larry Costello, Syracuse	378	320	.847
Gene Shue, Detroit	327	276	.844
Willie Naulls, New York	344	284	.826
Ken Sears, New York	550	452	.822
Ron Sobie, New York	239	196	.820

ASSISTS

	G.	No.	Avg.
Bob Cousy, Boston	65	463	7.1
Dick McGuire, Detroit	69	454	6.6
Maurice Stokes, Cincinnati	63	403	6.4
Carl Braun, New York	71	393	5.5
George King, Cincinnati	63	337	5.3
Jack McMahon, St. Louis	72	333	4.6
Tom Gola, Philadelphia	59	327	5.5
Richie Guerin, New York	63	317	5.0
Larry Costello, Syracuse	72	317	4.4
Jack George, Philadelphia	72	234	3.3

TEAM-BY-TEAM INDIVIDUAL STATISTICS

BOSTON CELTICS

Player	G.	Min.	FGA	FGM	Pct.	FTA	FTM	Pct.	Reb.	Ast.	PF	Disq.	Pts.	Avg.
Bill Sharman	63	2214	1297	550	.424	338	302	.893	295	167	156	3	1402	22.3
Tom Heinsohn	69	2206	1226	468	.382	394	294	.746	705	125	274	6	1230	17.8
Bob Cousy	65	2222	1262	445	.353	326	277	.850	463	136	1	1167	18.0
Bill Russell	69	2640	1032	456	.442	443	230	.519	1564	202	181	2	1142	16.6
Frank Ramsey	69	2047	900	377	.419	472	383	.811	504	167	245	8	1137	16.5
Lou Tsioropoulos	70	1819	624	198	.317	207	142	.686	434	112	242	8	538	7.7
Jack Nichols	69	1224	484	170	.351	80	59	.738	302	63	123	1	399	5.8
Arnie Risen	63	1119	397	134	.338	267	114	.683	360	59	195	5	382	6.1
Sam Jones	56	594	233	100	.429	84	60	.714	160	37	42	0	260	4.6
Andy Phillip	70	1164	273	97	.355	71	42	.592	158	121	121	0	236	3.4
Jim Loscutoff	5	56	31	11	.355	3	1	.333	20	1	8	0	23	4.6

CINCINNATI ROYALS

Player	G.	Min.	FGA	FGM	Pct.	FTA	FTM	Pct.	Reb.	Ast.	PF	Disq.	Pts.	Avg.
Clyde Lovellette	71	2589	1540	679	.441	405	301	.743	862	134	236	3	1659	23.4
Jack Twyman	72	2178	1028	465	.452	396	307	.775	464	110	224	3	1237	17.2
Maurice Stokes	63	2460	1181	414	.351	333	238	.715	1142	403	226	9	1066	16.9
Jim Paxson	67	1795	639	225	.352	285	209	.733	350	139	183	2	659	9.8
George King	63	2272	645	235	.364	227	140	.617	306	337	124	0	610	9.7
Dick Ricketts	72	1620	664	215	.324	196	132	.673	410	114	277	8	562	7.8
Richie Regan	72	1648	569	202	.355	172	120	.698	175	185	174	0	524	7.3
Dave Piontek	71	1032	397	150	.378	151	95	.629	254	52	134	2	395	5.6
Don Meineke	67	792	351	125	.356	119	77	.647	226	38	155	3	327	4.9
Tom Marshall	38	518	166	52	.313	63	48	.762	101	19	43	0	152	4.0
(9 Det., 29 Cinn.)														
Dick Duckett	34	424	158	54	.342	27	24	.889	56	47	60	0	132	3.9
Gerald Paulson	6	68	23	8	.348	6	4	.667	10	4	5	0	20	3.3

DETROIT PISTONS

Player	G.	Min.	FGA	FGM	Pct.	FTA	FTM	Pct.	Reb.	Ast.	PF	Disq.	Pts.	Avg.
George Yardley	72	2843	1624	673	.414	808	655	.811	768	97	226	3	2001	27.8
Harry Gallatin	72	1990	898	340	.379	498	392	.787	749	86	217	6	1072	14.9
Gene Shue	63	2333	919	353	.384	327	276	.844	333	172	150	1	982	15.6
Walt Dukes	72	2184	796	278	.349	366	247	.675	954	52	311	17	803	11.2
Dick McGuire	69	2311	544	203	.373	255	150	.667	291	454	178	0	556	8.1
Nat Clifton	68	1435	597	217	.363	146	91	.623	403	76	202	3	525	7.7
Chuck Noble	61	1363	601	199	.331	77	56	.727	140	153	166	0	454	7.4
Phil Jordon	58	898	467	193	.413	93	64	.688	301	37	108	1	450	7.8
(12 N.Y., 46 Det.)														
Bill Kenville	35	649	280	106	.379	75	46	.613	102	66	68	0	258	7.4

Player	G.	Min.	FGA	FGM	Pct.	FTA	FTM	Pct.	Reb.	Ast.	PF	Disq.	Pts.	Avg.
Joe Holup	53	740	278	91	.327	94	71	.755	221	36	99	2	253	4.8
(16 Syr., 37 Det.)														
Bob Houbregs	17	302	137	49	.358	43	30	.698	65	19	36	0	128	7.5
Bill Thieben	27	243	154	42	.294	27	16	.593	65	7	44	0	100	3.7
Dick Atha	18	160	47	17	.362	12	10	.833	24	19	24	0	44	2.4
Bill Ebben	8	50	28	6	.214	4	3	.750	8	4	5	0	15	1.9
Doug Bolstorff	3	21	5	2	.400	0	0	.000	0	0	1	0	4	1.3

MINNEAPOLIS LAKERS

Player	G.	Min.	FGA	FGM	Pct.	FTA	FTM	Pct.	Reb.	Ast.	PF	Disq.	Pts.	Avg.
Vern Mikkelsen	72	2390	1070	439	.410	471	370	.786	805	166	299	20	1248	17.3
Larry Foust	72	2200	982	391	.398	566	428	.756	876	108	299	11	1210	16.8
Dick Garmaker	68	2216	988	390	.395	411	314	.764	365	183	190	2	1094	16.1
Bob Leonard	66	2074	794	266	.335	268	205	.765	237	218	145	0	737	11.2
Ed Fleming	72	1686	655	226	.345	255	181	.710	492	139	222	5	633	8.8
Jim Krebs	68	1259	527	199	.378	176	135	.767	502	27	182	4	533	7.8
Corky Devlin	70	1248	489	170	.348	172	133	.773	132	167	104	1	473	6.8
Dick Schnittker	50	979	357	128	.359	237	201	.848	211	71	126	5	457	9.1
Rod Hundley	65	1154	548	174	.318	162	104	.642	186	121	99	0	452	7.0
Bo Erias	18	401	170	59	.347	47	30	.638	83	26	52	1	148	8.2
Frank Selvy	38	426	167	44	.263	77	47	.610	88	35	44	0	135	3.6
(26 St.L., 12 Minn.)														
McCoy Ingram	24	267	103	27	.262	28	13	.464	116	20	44	1	67	2.8
Bob Burrow	14	171	70	22	.314	33	11	.333	64	6	15	0	55	3.9
George Brown	1	6	2	0	.000	2	1	.500	1	0	1	0	1	1.0

NEW YORK KNICKERBOCKERS

Player	G.	Min.	FGA	FGM	Pct.	FTA	FTM	Pct.	Reb.	Ast.	PF	Disq.	Pts.	Avg.
Kenny Sears	72	2685	1014	445	.439	550	452	.822	785	126	251	7	1342	18.6
Willie Naulls	68	2369	1189	472	.397	344	284	.826	799	97	220	4	1228	18.1
Carl Braun	71	2475	1018	426	.418	378	321	.849	330	393	183	2	1173	16.5
Richie Guerin	63	2368	973	344	.354	511	353	.691	489	317	202	3	1041	16.5
Ray Felix	72	1709	688	304	.442	389	271	.697	747	52	283	12	879	12.2
Guy Sparrow	72	1661	838	318	.379	257	165	.642	461	69	232	6	801	11.1
Ron Sobie	55	1399	539	217	.403	239	196	.820	263	125	147	3	630	11.5
Charlie Tyra	68	1182	490	175	.357	224	150	.670	480	34	175	3	500	7.4
Art Spoelstra	67	1305	419	161	.384	187	127	.679	332	57	225	11	449	6.7
(50 Min., 17 N.Y.)														
Larry Friend	44	569	226	74	.327	41	27	.659	106	47	54	0	175	4.0
Mel Hutchins	18	384	131	51	.389	43	24	.558	86	34	31	0	126	7.0
Brendan McCann	36	295	100	22	.220	37	25	.676	45	54	34	0	69	1.9
Ron Shavlik	1	2	1	0	.000	0	0	.000	1	0	0	0	0	0.0

PHILADELPHIA WARRIORS

Player	G.	Min.	FGA	FGM	Pct.	FTA	FTM	Pct.	Reb.	Ast.	PF	Disq.	Pts.	Avg.
Paul Arizin	68	2377	1229	483	.393	544	440	.809	503	135	235	7	1406	20.7
Neil Johnston	71	2408	1102	473	.429	540	442	.819	790	166	233	4	1388	19.5
Woody Sauldsberry	71	2377	1082	389	.360	218	134	.615	729	58	245	3	912	12.8
Joe Graboski	72	2077	1017	341	.335	303	227	.749	570	125	249	3	909	12.6
Tom Gola	59	2126	711	295	.415	299	223	.746	639	327	225	11	813	13.8
Ernie Beck	71	1974	683	272	.398	203	170	.837	307	190	173	2	714	10.1
Jack George	72	1910	627	232	.370	242	178	.736	288	234	140	1	642	8.9
George Dempsey	67	1048	311	112	.360	105	70	.667	214	128	113	0	294	4.4
Lennie Rosenbluth	53	373	265	91	.343	84	53	.631	91	23	39	0	235	4.4
Pat Dunn	28	206	90	28	.311	17	14	.824	31	28	20	0	70	2.5
Jim Walsh	10	72	27	5	.185	17	10	.588	15	8	9	0	20	2.0
Ray Radziszewski	1	6	3	0	.000	0	0	.000	2	1	1	0	0	0.0

ST. LOUIS HAWKS

Player	G.	Min.	FGA	FGM	Pct.	FTA	FTM	Pct.	Reb.	Ast.	PF	Disq.	Pts.	Avg.
Bob Pettit	70	2528	1418	581	.410	744	557	.745	1216	157	222	6	1719	24.6
Cliff Hagan	70	2190	1135	503	.443	501	385	.768	707	175	267	9	1391	19.9
Ed Macauley	72	1908	879	376	.428	369	267	.723	478	143	156	2	1019	14.2
Slater Martin	60	2098	768	258	.336	276	206	.746	228	218	187	0	722	12.0
Chuck Share	72	1824	545	216	.396	293	190	.648	749	130	279	15	622	8.6
Jack McMahon	72	2239	719	216	.300	221	134	.606	195	333	184	2	566	7.9
Win Wilfong	71	1360	543	196	.361	238	163	.685	290	163	199	3	555	7.8
Jack Coleman	72	1506	590	231	.413	131	84	.641	485	117	169	3	546	7.6
Med Park	71	1103	363	133	.366	162	118	.728	184	76	106	0	384	5.4
Walt Davis (35 Phil.-26 St.L.)	61	663	244	85	.348	82	61	.744	174	29	143	0	231	3.8
Red Morrison	13	79	26	9	.346	4	3	.750	26	0	12	0	21	1.6
Worthy Patterson	4	13	8	3	.375	2	1	.500	2	2	3	0	7	1.8

SYRACUSE NATIONALS

Player	G.	Min.	FGA	FGM	Pct.	FTA	FTM	Pct.	Reb.	Ast.	PF	Disq.	Pts.	Avg.
Dolph Schayes	72	2918	1458	581	.398	696	629	.904	1022	224	244	6	1791	24.9
John Kerr	72	2384	1020	407	.399	422	280	.664	963	88	197	4	1094	15.2
Larry Costello	72	2746	888	378	.426	378	320	.847	378	317	246	3	1076	14.9
Ed Conlin	60	1871	877	343	.391	270	215	.796	436	133	168	2	901	15.0
Togo Palazzi	67	1001	579	228	.394	171	123	.719	243	42	125	0	579	8.6
Al Bianchi	69	1421	625	215	.344	205	140	.683	221	114	188	4	570	8.3
Bob Hopkins	69	1224	554	221	.399	161	123	.764	392	45	162	5	565	8.2
Bob Harrison	72	1799	604	210	.348	122	97	.795	166	169	200	1	517	7.2
Earl Lloyd	61	1045	359	119	.331	106	79	.745	287	60	179	3	317	5.2
Paul Seymour	64	763	315	107	.340	63	53	.841	107	93	88	0	267	4.2

The St. Louis Hawks won their first and only NBA championship in 1957-58 behind All-Star forward Bob Pettit.

PLAYOFF RESULTS

EASTERN DIVISION SEMIFINALS
Philadelphia 2, Syracuse 1

Mar. 15—Philadelphia 82 at Syracuse 86
Mar. 16—Syracuse 93 at Philadelphia 95
Mar. 18—Philadelphia 101 at Syracuse 88

WESTERN DIVISION SEMIFINALS
Detroit 2, Cincinnati 0

Mar. 15—Cincinnati 93 at Detroit 100
Mar. 16—Detroit 124 at Cincinnati...104

EASTERN DIVISION FINALS
Boston 4, Philadelphia 1

Mar. 19—Philadelphia 98 at Boston...107
Mar. 22—Boston 109 at Philadelphia..87
Mar. 23—Philadelphia 92 at Boston...106
Mar. 26—Boston 97 at Philadelphia..111
Mar. 27—Philadelphia 88 at Boston...93

WESTERN DIVISION FINALS
St. Louis 4, Detroit 1

Mar. 19—Detroit 111 at St. Louis 114
Mar. 22—St. Louis 99 at Detroit 96
Mar. 23—Detroit 109 at St. Louis...89
Mar. 25—St. Louis 145 at Detroit 101
Mar. 27—Detroit 96 at St. Louis...120

WORLD CHAMPIONSHIP SERIES
St. Louis 4, Boston 2

Mar. 29—St. Louis 104 at Boston..102
Mar. 30—St. Louis 112 at Boston..136
Apr. 2—Boston 108 at St. Louis..111
Apr. 5—Boston 109 at St. Louis..98
Apr. 9—St. Louis 102 at Boston..100
Apr. 12—Boston 109 at St. Louis..110

1956-57 NBA STATISTICS

1956-57 NBA CHAMPION BOSTON CELTICS

Front row (left to right): Lou Tsioropoulos, Andy Phillip, Frank Ramsey, Coach Red Auerbach, Captain Bob Cousy, Bill Sharman, Jim Loscutoff. Standing: President Walter A. Brown, Dick Hemric, Jack Nichols, Bill Russell, Arnold Risen, Tom Heinsohn, Trainer Harvey Cohn, Treasurer Lou Pieri.

FINAL STANDINGS

EASTERN DIVISION

Team	Bos.	Syr.	Phil.	N.Y.	St.L.	Minn.	Ft.W.	Roch.	W.	L.	Pct.	G.B.
Boston	..	5	8	7	7	5	6	6	44	28	.611	....
Syracuse	7	..	7	6	4	5	4	5	38	34	.528	6
Philadelphia	4	5	..	8	7	4	5	4	37	35	.514	7
New York	5	6	4	..	6	6	4	5	36	36	.500	8

WESTERN DIVISION

Team	Bos.	Syr.	Phil.	N.Y.	St.L.	Minn.	Ft.W.	Roch.	W.	L.	Pct.	G.B.
St. Louis	2	5	2	3	..	8	8	6	34	38	.472	....
Minneapolis	4	4	5	3	4	..	5	9	34	38	.472	....
Ft. Wayne	3	5	4	5	4	7	..	6	34	38	.472	....
Rochester	3	4	5	4	6	3	6	..	31	41	.431	3

HOME-ROAD-NEUTRAL RECORDS OF ALL TEAMS

	Home	Road	Neutral	Total		Home	Road	Neutral	Total
Boston	27- 4	12- 19	5- 5	44- 28	Philadelphia	26- 5	5- 26	6- 4	37- 35
Ft. Wayne	23- 8	7- 24	4- 6	34- 38	Rochester	19- 12	9- 22	3- 7	31- 41
Minneapolis	18- 13	9- 22	7- 3	34- 38	St. Louis	18- 13	11- 20	5- 5	34- 38
New York	19- 12	11- 20	6- 4	36- 36	Syracuse	22- 9	12- 19	4- 6	38- 34
					Totals	172- 76	76-172	40-40	288-288

TEAM STATISTICS

Team	G.	FGA	FGM	Pct.	FTA	FTM	Pct.	Reb.	Ast.	PF	Disq.	For	Agst.	Pt.Dif.
Boston	72	7326	2808	.383	2644	1983	.750	4963	1464	1851	38	105.5	100.2	+5.3
Philadelphia	72	6533	2584	.396	2658	2062	.776	4305	1467	1732	36	100.4	98.8	+1.6
New York	72	6645	2569	.387	2844	2117	.744	4723	1312	1824	20	100.8	100.9	—0.1
St. Louis	72	6669	2557	.383	2710	1977	.730	4566	1454	1848	36	98.5	98.6	—0.1
Minneapolis	72	6965	2584	.371	2899	2195	.757	4581	1195	1887	49	102.3	103.1	—0.8
Syracuse	72	6915	2550	.369	2613	2075	.794	4350	1282	1809	34	99.7	101.1	—1.4
Rochester	72	6807	2515	.369	2402	1698	.707	4171	1298	1866	38	93.4	95.6	—2.2
Ft. Wayne	72	6612	2532	.383	2510	1874	.747	4289	1398	1643	17	96.4	98.7	—2.3

INDIVIDUAL LEADERS

POINTS

	G.	FG	FT	Pts.	Avg.		G.	FG	FT	Pts.	Avg.
Paul Arizin, Philadelphia	71	613	591	1817	25.6	Jack Twyman, Rochester	72	449	276	1174	16.3
Bob Pettit, St. Louis	71	613	529	1755	24.7	Tom Heinsohn, Boston	72	446	271	1163	16.2
Dolph Schayes, Syracuse	72	496	625	1617	22.5	Maurice Stokes, Rochester	72	434	256	1124	15.6
Neil Johnston, Philadelphia	69	520	535	1575	22.8	Harry Gallatin, New York	72	332	415	1079	15.0
George Yardley, Ft. Wayne	72	522	503	1547	21.5	Ken Sears, New York	72	343	383	1069	14.8
Clyde Lovellette, Minn.	69	574	286	1434	20.8	Joe Graboski, Philadelphia	72	390	252	1032	14.3
Bill Sharman, Boston	67	516	381	1413	21.1	Carl Braun, New York	72	378	245	1001	13.9
Bob Cousy, Boston	64	478	363	1319	20.6	Vern Mikkelsen, Minn.	72	322	342	986	13.7
Ed Macauley, St. Louis	72	414	359	1187	16.5	Ed Conlin, Syracuse	71	335	283	953	13.4
Dick Garmaker, Minn.	72	406	365	1177	16.3	John Kerr, Syracuse	72	333	225	891	12.4

FIELD GOALS
(Minimum 230 FGM)

	FGA	FGM	Pct.
Neil Johnston, Philadelphia	1163	520	.447
Charles Share, St. Louis	535	235	.439
Jack Twyman, Rochester	1023	449	.439
Bob Houbregs, Ft. Wayne	585	253	.432
Bill Russell, Boston	649	277	.427
Clyde Lovellette, Minneapolis	1348	574	.426
Paul Arizin, Philadelphia	1451	613	.422
Ed Macauley, St. Louis	987	414	.419
Ken Sears, New York	821	343	.418
Ray Felix, New York	709	295	.416

ASSISTS

	G.	No.	Avg.
Bob Cousy, Boston	64	478	7.5
Jack McMahon, St. Louis	72	367	5.1
Maurice Stokes, Rochester	72	331	4.6
Jack George, Philadelphia	67	307	4.6
Slater Martin, N.Y.-St.L.	66	269	4.1
Carl Braun, New York	72	256	3.6
Gene Shue, Ft. Wayne	72	238	3.3
Bill Sharman, Boston	67	236	3.5
Larry Costello, Philadelphia	72	236	3.3
Dolph Schayes, Syracuse	72	229	3.2

FREE THROWS
(Minimum 190 FTM)

	FTA	FTM	Pct.
Bill Sharman, Boston	421	381	.905
Dolph Schayes, Syracuse	691	625	.904
Dick Garmaker, Minneapolis	435	365	.839
Paul Arizin, Philadelphia	713	591	.829
Neil Johnston, Philadelphia	648	535	.826
Bob Cousy, Boston	442	363	.821
Carl Braun, New York	303	245	.808
Vern Mikkelsen, Minnesota	424	342	.807
Joseph Holup, Syracuse	253	204	.806
Harry Gallatin, New York	519	415	.800

REBOUNDS

	G.	No.	Avg.
Maurice Stokes, Rochester	72	1256	17.4
Bob Pettit, St. Louis	71	1037	14.6
Dolph Schayes, Syracuse	72	1008	14.0
Bill Russell, Boston	48	943	19.6
Clyde Lovellette, Minneapolis	69	932	13.5
Neil Johnston, Philadelphia	69	855	12.4
John Kerr, Syracuse	72	807	11.2
Walter Dukes, Minneapolis	71	794	11.2
George Yardley, Ft. Wayne	72	755	10.5
Jim Loscutoff, Boston	70	730	10.4

TEAM-BY-TEAM INDIVIDUAL STATISTICS

BOSTON CELTICS

Player	G.	Min.	FGA	FGM	Pct.	FTA	FTM	Pct.	Reb.	Ast.	PF	Disq.	Pts.	Avg.
William Sharman	67	2403	1241	516	.416	421	381	.905	286	236	188	1	1413	21.1
Robert Cousy	64	2364	1264	478	.378	442	363	.821	309	478	134	0	1319	20.6
Thomas Heinsohn	72	2150	1123	446	.397	343	271	.790	705	117	304	12	1163	16.2
James Loscutoff	70	2220	888	306	.345	187	132	.706	730	89	244	5	744	10.6
William Russell	48	1695	649	277	.427	309	152	.492	943	88	143	2	706	14.7
Jack Nichols	61	1372	537	195	.363	136	108	.794	374	85	185	4	498	8.2
Frank Ramsey	35	807	349	137	.393	182	144	.791	178	67	113	3	418	11.9
Dixon Hemric	67	1055	317	109	.344	210	146	.695	304	42	98	0	364	5.4
Arnold Risen	43	935	307	119	.388	156	106	.679	286	53	163	4	344	8.0
Andrew Phillip	67	1476	277	105	.379	137	88	.642	181	168	121	1	298	4.4
Louis Tsioropoulos	52	670	256	79	.309	89	69	.775	207	33	135	6	227	4.4

FORT WAYNE PISTONS

Player	G.	Min.	FGA	FGM	Pct.	FTA	FTM	Pct.	Reb.	Ast.	PF	Disq.	Pts.	Avg.
George Yardley	72	2691	1273	522	.410	639	503	.787	755	147	231	2	1547	21.5
Mel Hutchins	72	2647	953	369	.387	206	152	.738	571	210	182	0	890	12.4
Eugene Shue	72	2470	710	273	.385	316	241	.763	421	238	137	0	787	10.9
Larry Foust	61	1533	617	243	.394	380	273	.718	555	71	221	7	759	12.4
Robert Houbregs	60	1592	585	253	.432	234	167	.714	401	113	118	2	673	11.2
William Kenville	71	1701	608	204	.336	218	174	.798	324	172	169	3	582	8.2
Walter Devlin	71	1242	502	190	.378	143	97	.678	146	141	114	0	477	6.7
Charles Noble	54	1260	556	200	.360	102	76	.745	135	180	161	2	476	8.8
Red Rocha	72	1154	390	136	.349	144	109	.757	272	81	162	1	381	5.3
William Thieben	58	633	256	90	.352	87	57	.655	207	17	78	0	237	4.1
Richard Rosenthal	18	188	79	21	.266	17	9	.529	52	17	22	0	51	2.8

MINNEAPOLIS LAKERS

Player	G.	Min.	FGA	FGM	Pct.	FTA	FTM	Pct.	Reb.	Ast.	PF	Disq.	Pts.	Avg.
Clyde Lovellette	69	2492	1348	574	.426	399	286	.717	932	139	251	4	1434	20.8
Richard Garmaker	72	2406	1015	406	.400	435	365	.839	336	190	199	1	1177	16.3
Vern Mikkelsen	72	2198	854	322	.377	424	342	.807	630	121	312	18	986	13.7
Robert Leonard	72	1943	867	303	.349	241	186	.772	220	169	140	0	792	11.0
Walter Dukes	71	1866	626	228	.364	383	264	.689	794	54	273	10	720	10.1
Charles Mencel	72	1848	688	243	.353	240	179	.746	237	201	95	0	665	9.2
Ed Kalafat	65	1617	507	178	.351	298	197	.661	425	105	243	9	553	8.5
James Paxson	71	1274	485	138	.285	196	170	.720	266	86	163	3	446	6.3
Richard Schnittker	70	997	351	113	.322	193	160	.829	185	52	144	3	386	5.5
Myer Skoog	23	656	220	78	.355	47	44	.936	72	76	65	1	200	8.7
Robert Williams	4	20	4	1	.250	3	2	.667	5	0	2	0	4	1.0

After San Francisco University All-America Bill Russell joined the Boston Celtics in 1956, 11 NBA titles were to follow—the first coming in Russell's rookie year. Here, Russell is shown signing his first Celtic contract as team owner Walter Brown (left) and treasurer Lou Pieri look on.

NEW YORK KNICKERBOCKERS

Player	G.	Min.	FGA	FGM	Pct.	FTA	FTM	Pct.	Reb.	Ast.	PF	Disq.	Pts.	Avg.
Harry Gallatin	72	1943	817	332	.406	519	415	.800	725	85	202	1	1079	15.0
Kenneth Sears	72	2516	821	343	.418	485	383	.790	614	101	226	2	1069	14.8
Carl Braun	72	2345	993	378	.381	303	245	.808	259	256	195	1	1001	13.9
Ray Felix	72	1622	709	295	.416	371	277	.747	587	36	284	8	867	12.0
Nat Clifton	71	2231	818	308	.377	217	146	.673	557	164	243	5	762	10.7
Willie Naulls (StL-NY)	71	1778	820	293	.357	195	132	.677	617	84	186	1	718	10.1
Richie Guerin	72	1793	699	257	.368	292	181	.620	334	182	186	3	695	9.7
Ron Sobieszczyk	71	1378	442	166	.376	199	152	.764	326	129	158	0	484	6.8
Richard McGuire	72	1191	366	140	.383	163	105	.644	146	222	103	0	385	5.3
James Baechtold	45	462	197	75	.381	88	66	.750	80	33	39	0	216	4.8
Phillip Jordon	9	91	49	18	.367	12	8	.667	34	2	15	0	44	4.9
Ron Shavlik	7	7	22	4	.182	5	2	.400	22	0	12	0	10	1.4
Gary Bergen	6	6	11	3	.273	2	2	1.000	8	1	4	0	8	1.3

PHILADELPHIA WARRIORS

Player	G.	Min.	FGA	FGM	Pct.	FTA	FTM	Pct.	Reb.	Ast.	PF	Disq.	Pts.	Avg.
Paul Arizin	71	2767	1451	613	.422	713	591	.829	561	150	274	13	1817	25.6
Neil Johnston	69	2531	1163	520	.447	648	535	.826	855	203	231	2	1575	22.8
Joseph Graboski	72	2501	1118	390	.349	322	252	.783	614	140	244	5	1032	14.3
Jack George	67	2229	750	253	.337	293	200	.683	318	307	165	3	706	10.5
Lawrence Costello	72	2111	497	186	.374	222	175	.788	323	236	182	2	547	7.6
Ernest Beck	72	1743	508	195	.384	157	111	.707	312	190	155	1	501	7.0
Walter Davis	65	1250	437	178	.407	106	74	.698	306	52	235	9	430	6.6
George Dempsey	71	1147	302	134	.444	102	55	.539	251	136	107	0	323	4.5
Lew Hitch (Minn-Phil)	68	1133	296	111	.375	88	63	.716	253	40	103	0	285	4.2
Jack Moore	57	400	106	43	.406	46	37	.804	116	21	75	1	123	2.2
Robert Armstrong	19	110	37	11	.297	12	6	.500	39	3	13	0	28	1.5
Hal Lear	3	14	6	2	.333	0	0	.000	1	1	3	0	4	1.3

ROCHESTER ROYALS

Player	G.	Min.	FGA	FGM	Pct.	FTA	FTM	Pct.	Reb.	Ast.	PF	Disq.	Pts.	Avg.
Jack Twyman	72	2338	1023	449	.439	363	276	.760	354	123	251	4	1174	16.3
Maurice Stokes	72	2761	1249	434	.347	385	256	.665	1256	331	287	12	1124	15.6
Richard Ricketts	72	2114	869	299	.344	297	206	.694	437	127	307	12	804	11.2
Richie Regan	71	2100	780	257	.329	235	182	.774	205	222	179	1	696	9.8
David Piontek	71	1759	637	257	.403	183	122	.667	351	108	141	1	636	9.0
Arthur Spoelstra	69	1176	559	217	.388	120	88	.733	220	56	168	5	522	7.6
John McCarthy	72	1560	460	173	.376	193	130	.674	201	107	130	0	476	6.6
Robert Burrow	67	1028	366	137	.374	211	130	.616	293	41	165	2	404	6.0
Ed Fleming	51	927	364	109	.299	191	139	.728	183	81	94	0	357	7.0
Thomas Marshall	40	460	163	56	.344	58	47	.810	83	31	33	0	159	4.0
Sihugo Green	13	423	143	50	.350	69	49	.710	37	67	36	1	149	11.5
Robert Wanzer	21	159	49	23	.469	46	36	.783	25	9	20	0	82	3.9

ST. LOUIS HAWKS

Player	G.	Min.	FGA	FGM	Pct.	FTA	FTM	Pct.	Reb.	Ast.	PF	Disq.	Pts.	Avg.
Robert Pettit	71	2491	1477	613	.415	684	529	.773	1037	133	181	1	1755	24.7
Edward Macauley	72	2582	987	414	.419	479	359	.749	440	202	206	2	1187	16.5
Jack Coleman	72	2145	775	316	.408	161	123	.764	645	159	235	7	755	10.5
Charles Share	72	1673	535	235	.439	393	269	.686	642	79	269	15	739	10.3
Slater Martin (NY-St.L.)	66	2401	736	244	.332	291	230	.790	288	269	193	1	718	10.9
Jack McMahon	72	2344	725	239	.330	225	142	.631	222	367	213	2	620	8.6
Cliff Hagan	67	971	371	134	.361	145	100	.690	247	86	165	3	368	5.5
Medford Park	66	1130	324	118	.364	146	108	.740	200	94	137	2	344	5.2
Irv Bemoras	62	983	385	124	.322	103	70	.680	127	46	76	0	318	5.1
Alex Hannum (Ft. W.-St.L.)	59	642	223	77	.345	56	37	.661	158	28	135	2	191	3.2
Marion Spears (Ft. W.-St.L.)	11	118	38	12	.316	22	19	.864	15	7	24	0	43	3.9
Norman Stewart	5	37	15	4	.267	6	2	.333	5	2	9	0	10	2.0
John Barber	5	5	8	2	.250	6	3	.500	6	0	4	0	7	1.4

SYRACUSE NATIONALS

Player	G.	Min.	FGA	FGM	Pct.	FTA	FTM	Pct.	Reb.	Ast.	PF	Disq.	Pts.	Avg.
Dolph Schayes	72	2851	1308	496	.379	691	625	.904	1008	229	219	5	1617	22.5
Edward Conlin	71	2250	896	335	.374	368	283	.769	430	205	170	0	953	13.4
John Kerr	72	2191	827	333	.403	313	225	.719	807	90	190	3	891	12.4
Earl Lloyd	72	1965	687	256	.373	179	134	.749	435	114	282	10	646	9.0
Robert Harrison	66	1810	629	243	.386	130	93	.715	156	161	220	5	579	8.8
Al Bianchi	68	1577	567	199	.351	239	165	.690	227	106	198	5	563	8.3
Togo Palazzi (Bos.-Syr.)	63	1013	571	210	.368	175	136	.777	262	49	117	1	556	8.8
Joseph Holup	71	1284	487	160	.329	253	204	.806	279	84	177	5	524	7.4
Paul Seymour	65	1235	442	143	.324	123	101	.821	130	193	91	0	387	6.0
Robert Hopkins	62	764	343	130	.379	126	94	.746	233	22	106	0	354	5.7
Lawrence Hennessy	21	373	175	56	.320	32	23	.719	45	27	28	0	135	6.4
Robert Schafer	11	167	66	19	.288	13	11	.846	11	15	16	0	49	4.5
James Tucker	9	110	44	17	.386	1	0	.000	20	2	26	0	34	3.8
Don Savage	5	55	19	6	.316	7	6	.857	7	2	7	0	18	3.6
James Ray	4	43	11	2	.182	5	3	.600	5	3	4	0	7	1.8
Forest Able	1	1	2	0	.000	0	0	.000	1	1	1	0	0	0.0

PLAYOFF RESULTS

EASTERN DIVISION SEMIFINALS
Syracuse 2, Philadelphia 0
Mar. 16—Syracuse 103 at Philadelphia 96
Mar. 18—Philadelphia 80 at Syracuse 91

EASTERN DIVISION FINALS
Boston 3, Syracuse 0
Mar. 21—Syracuse 90 at Boston 108
Mar. 23—Boston 120 at Syracuse 105
Mar. 24—Syracuse 80 at Boston 83

WESTERN DIVISION TIEBREAKERS
Mar. 14—Ft. Wayne 103 at St. Louis 115
Mar. 16—Minneapolis 111 at St. Louis 114

WESTERN DIVISION SEMIFINALS
Minneapolis 2, Ft. Wayne 0
Mar. 17—Ft. Wayne 127 at Minneapolis 131
Mar. 19—Minneapolis 110 at Ft. Wayne 108

WESTERN DIVISION FINALS
St. Louis 3, Minneapolis 0
Mar. 21—Minneapolis 109 at St. Louis 118
Mar. 24—Minneapolis 104 at St. Louis 106
Mar. 25—St. Louis 143 at Minneapolis **135

WORLD CHAMPIONSHIP SERIES
Boston 4, St. Louis 3
Mar. 30—St. Louis 125 at Boston *123
Mar. 31—St. Louis 99 at Boston 119
Apr. 6—Boston 98 at St. Louis 100
Apr. 7—Boston 123 at St. Louis 118
Apr. 9—St. Louis 109 at Boston 124
Apr. 11—Boston 94 at St. Louis 96
Apr. 13—St. Louis 123 at Boston **125

*Denotes overtime period.

1955-56 NBA STATISTICS

1955-56 NBA CHAMPION PHILADELPHIA WARRIORS

Front row (left to right): Coach George Senesky, Larry Hennessy, Paul Arizin, Jack George, George Dempsey, President Eddie Gottlieb. Standing: Ernie Beck, Neil Johnston, Joe Graboski, Walter Davis, Tom Gola, Jackie Moore.

FINAL STANDINGS

EASTERN DIVISION

Team	Phil.	Bos.	N.Y.	Syr.	Ft.W.	Minn.	St.L.	Roch.	W.	L.	Pct.	G.B.
Philadelphia	..	7	6	9	5	6	6	6	45	27	.625	....
Boston	5	..	5	8	4	7	5	5	39	33	.542	6
New York	6	7	..	4	4	4	4	6	35	37	.486	10
Syracuse	3	4	8	..	5	5	6	4	35	37	.486	10

WESTERN DIVISION

Team	Phil.	Bos.	N.Y.	Syr.	Ft.W.	Minn.	St.L.	Roch.	W.	L.	Pct.	G.B.
Ft. Wayne	4	5	5	4	..	5	7	7	37	35	.514	....
Minneapolis	3	2	5	4	7	..	5	7	33	39	.458	4
St. Louis	3	4	5	3	5	7	..	6	33	39	.458	4
Rochester	3	4	3	5	5	5	6	..	31	41	.431	6

HOME-ROAD-NEUTRAL RECORDS OF ALL TEAMS

	Home	Road	Neutral	Total		Home	Road	Neutral	Total
Boston	20- 7	12- 15	7-11	39- 33	Philadelphia	21- 7	11- 17	13- 3	45- 27
Ft. Wayne	19- 8	10- 17	8-10	37- 35	Rochester	15- 14	7- 21	9- 6	31- 41
Minneapolis	13- 12	6- 21	14- 6	33- 39	St. Louis	16- 10	10- 17	7-12	33- 39
New York	14- 14	15- 14	6- 9	35- 37	Syracuse	23- 8	9- 19	3-10	35- 37
					Totals	141- 80	80-141	67-67	288-288

TEAM STATISTICS

Team	G.	FGA	FGM	Pct.	FTA	FTM	Pct.	Reb.	Ast.	PF	Disq.	For	Agst.	Pt.Dif.
Philadelphia	72	6437	2641	.410	2829	2142	.757	4362	1886	1872	45	103.1	98.8	+4.3
Boston	72	6913	2745	.397	2785	2142	.769	4583	1834	1874	44	106.0	105.3	+0.7
Ft. Wayne	72	6174	2396	.388	2729	2002	.734	3974	1752	1789	20	94.4	93.7	+0.7
Syracuse	72	6661	2466	.370	2703	2044	.756	4060	1710	1783	32	96.9	96.9	....
New York	72	6395	2508	.392	2913	2196	.754	4562	1610	1923	43	100.2	100.6	-0.4
Minneapolis	72	6543	2541	.388	2627	2066	.786	4133	1689	1978	43	99.3	100.2	-0.9
St. Louis	72	6628	2506	.378	2761	1941	.703	4493	1748	1971	42	96.6	98.0	-1.4
Rochester	72	6890	2551	.370	2567	1798	.700	4449	1747	1990	46	95.8	98.7	-2.9

INDIVIDUAL LEADERS

POINTS

	G.	FG	FT	Pts.	Avg.		G.	FG	FT	Pts.	Avg.
Bob Pettit, St. Louis	72	646	557	1849	25.7	Maurice Stokes, Rochester	67	403	319	1125	16.8
Paul Arizin, Philadelphia	72	617	507	1741	24.2	Carl Braun, New York	72	396	320	1112	15.4
Neil Johnston, Philadelphia	70	499	549	1547	22.1	Jack Twyman, Rochester	72	417	204	1038	14.4
Clyde Lovellette, Minneapolis	71	594	338	1526	21.5	Joe Graboski, Philadelphia	72	397	240	1034	14.4
Dolph Schayes, Syracuse	72	465	542	1472	20.4	Harry Gallatin, New York	72	322	358	1002	13.9
Bill Sharman, Boston	72	538	358	1434	19.9	Jack George, Philadelphia	72	352	296	1000	13.9
Bob Cousy, Boston	72	440	476	1356	18.8	Charles Share, St. Louis	72	315	346	976	13.6
Ed Macauley, Boston	71	420	400	1240	17.5	Vern Mikkelsen, Minneapolis	72	317	328	962	13.4
George Yardley, Ft. Wayne	71	434	365	1233	17.4	John Kerr, Syracuse	72	377	207	961	13.3
Larry Foust, Ft. Wayne	72	367	432	1166	16.2	Jack Coleman, Roch.-St.L.	75	390	177	957	12.8

FIELD GOALS
(Minimum 230 FGM)

	FGA	FGM	Pct.
Neil Johnston, Philadelphia	1092	499	.457
Paul Arizin, Philadelphia	1378	617	.448
Larry Foust, Ft. Wayne	821	367	.447
Ken Sears, New York	728	319	.438
Bill Sharman, Boston	1229	538	.438
Clyde Lovellette, Minneapolis	1370	594	.434
Charles Share, St. Louis	733	315	.430
Bob Houbregs, Ft. Wayne	575	247	.430
Bob Pettit, St. Louis	1507	646	.429
Mel Hutchins, Ft. Wayne	764	325	.425

ASSISTS

	G.	No.	Avg.
Bob Cousy, Boston	72	642	8.9
Jack George, Philadelphia	72	457	6.3
Slater Martin, Minneapolis	72	445	6.2
Tom Gola, Philadelphia	68	404	5.9
Andy Phillip, Ft. Wayne	70	410	5.9
George King, Syracuse	72	410	5.7
Dick McGuire, New York	62	362	5.8
Bill Sharman, Boston	72	339	4.7
Maurice Stokes, Rochester	67	328	4.9
Carl Braun, New York	72	298	4.1

FREE THROWS
(Minimum 190 FTM)

	FTA	FTM	Pct.
Bill Sharman, Boston	413	358	.867
Dolph Schayes, Syracuse	632	542	.858
Dick Schnittker, Minneapolis	355	304	.856
Bob Cousy, Boston	564	476	.844
Carl Braun, New York	382	320	.838
Slater Martin, Minneapolis	395	329	.833
Paul Arizin, Philadelphia	626	507	.810
Vern Mikkelsen, Minneapolis	408	328	.804
Neil Johnston, Philadelphia	685	549	.801
Jim Baechtold, New York	291	233	.801

REBOUNDS

	G.	No.	Avg.
Bob Pettit, St. Louis	72	1164	16.2
Maurice Stokes, Rochester	67	1094	16.3
Clyde Lovellette, Minneapolis	71	992	14.0
Dolph Schayes, Syracuse	72	891	12.4
Neil Johnston, Philadelphia	70	872	12.5
Charles Share, St. Louis	72	774	10.8
Harry Gallatin, New York	72	740	10.3
Jack Coleman, Roch.-St.L.	75	688	9.2
George Yardley, Ft. Wayne	71	686	9.7
Larry Foust, Ft. Wayne	72	648	9.0

TEAM-BY-TEAM INDIVIDUAL STATISTICS

BOSTON CELTICS

Player	G.	Min.	FGA	FGM	Pct.	FTA	FTM	Pct.	Reb.	Ast.	PF	Disq.	Pts.	Avg.
William Sharman	72	2698	1229	538	.438	413	358	.867	259	339	197	1	1434	19.9
Robert Cousy	72	2767	1223	440	.360	564	476	.844	492	642	206	2	1356	18.8
Edward Macauley	71	2354	995	420	.422	504	400	.794	422	211	158	2	1240	17.5
Jack Nichols	60	1964	799	330	.413	253	200	.791	625	160	228	7	860	14.3
James Loscutoff	71	1582	628	226	.360	207	139	.671	622	65	213	4	591	8.3
Arnold Risen	68	1597	493	189	.383	240	170	.708	553	88	300	17	548	8.1
Ernie Barrett	72	1451	533	207	.388	118	93	.788	243	174	184	4	507	7.0
Dixon Hemric	71	1329	400	161	.403	273	177	.648	399	60	142	2	499	7.0
Togo Palazzi	63	703	373	145	.389	124	85	.685	182	42	87	0	375	6.0
Dwight Morrison	71	910	240	89	.346	89	44	.494	345	53	159	5	222	3.1

FORT WAYNE PISTONS

Player	G.	Min.	FGA	FGM	Pct.	FTA	FTM	Pct.	Reb.	Ast.	PF	Disq.	Pts.	Avg.
George Yardley	71	2353	1067	434	.407	492	365	.742	686	159	212	2	1233	17.4
Larry Foust	72	2024	821	367	.447	555	432	.778	648	127	263	7	1166	16.2
Mel Hutchins	66	2240	764	325	.425	221	142	.643	496	180	166	1	792	12.0
Robert Houbregs	70	1535	575	247	.430	383	283	.739	414	159	147	0	777	11.1
Charles Noble	72	2013	767	270	.352	195	146	.749	261	282	253	3	686	9.5
Walter Devlin	69	1535	541	200	.370	192	146	.760	171	138	119	0	546	7.9
Marion Spears	72	1378	468	166	.355	201	159	.791	231	121	191	2	491	6.8
Andrew Phillip	70	2078	405	148	.365	199	112	.563	257	410	155	2	408	5.8
Charles Cooper (StL-FtW)	67	1144	308	101	.328	133	100	.752	239	89	140	0	302	4.5
Frank Brian	37	680	263	78	.297	88	72	.818	88	74	62	0	228	6.2
Jesse Arnelle	31	409	164	52	.317	69	43	.623	170	18	60	0	147	4.7
Max Zaslofsky	9	182	81	29	.358	35	30	.857	16	16	18	1	88	9.8
James Holstein (Minn-Ft.W)	27	352	89	24	.270	37	24	.649	76	38	51	1	72	2.7
Don Bielke	7	38	9	5	.556	7	4	.571	9	1	9	0	14	2.0

Philadelphia captured the NBA title behind forward Paul Arizin in 1955-56.

MINNEAPOLIS LAKERS

Player	G.	Min.	FGA	FGM	Pct.	FTA	FTM	Pct.	Reb.	Ast.	PF	Disq.	Pts.	Avg.
Clyde Lovellette	71	2518	1370	594	.434	469	338	.721	992	164	245	5	1526	21.5
Vern Mikkelsen	72	2100	821	317	.386	408	328	.804	608	173	319	17	962	13.4
Slater Martin	72	2838	863	309	.358	395	329	.833	260	445	202	2	947	13.2
Myer Skoog	72	2311	854	340	.398	193	155	.803	291	255	232	5	835	11.6
Richard Schnittker	72	1930	647	254	.393	355	304	.856	296	142	253	4	812	11.3
Ed Kalafat	72	1639	540	194	.359	252	186	.738	440	130	236	2	574	8.0
George Mikan	37	765	375	148	.395	122	94	.770	308	53	153	6	390	10.5
Richard Garmaker	68	870	373	138	.370	139	112	.806	132	104	127	0	388	5.7
Charles Mencel	69	973	375	120	.320	96	78	.813	110	132	74	1	318	4.6
Lew Hitch	69	1129	235	94	.400	132	100	.758	283	77	85	0	288	4.2
Robert Williams	20	173	46	21	.457	45	24	.533	54	7	36	1	66	3.3
John Horan (Ft.W-Minn)	19	93	42	12	.286	11	10	.909	10	2	21	0	34	1.8
Ron Feireisel	10	59	28	8	.286	16	14	.875	6	6	9	0	30	3.0

NEW YORK KNICKERBOCKERS

Player	G.	Min.	FGA	FGM	Pct.	FTA	FTM	Pct.	Reb.	Ast.	PF	Disq.	Pts.	Avg.
Carl Braun	72	2316	1064	396	.372	382	320	.838	259	298	215	3	1112	15.4
Harry Gallatin	72	2378	834	322	.386	455	358	.787	740	168	220	6	1002	13.9
Kenneth Sears	70	2069	728	319	.438	324	258	.796	616	114	201	4	896	12.8
Ray Felix	72	1702	668	277	.415	469	331	.706	623	47	293	13	885	12.3
James Baechtold	70	1738	695	268	.386	291	233	.801	220	163	156	2	769	11.0
Eugene Shue	72	1750	625	240	.384	237	181	.764	212	179	111	0	661	9.2
Nat Clifton	64	1537	541	213	.394	191	135	.707	386	151	189	4	561	8.8
Walter Dukes	60	1290	370	149	.403	236	167	.708	443	39	211	11	465	7.8
Richard McGuire	62	1685	438	152	.347	193	121	.627	220	362	146	0	425	6.9
Robert Peterson	58	779	303	121	.399	104	68	.654	223	44	123	0	310	5.3
Richard Atha	25	288	88	36	.409	27	21	.778	42	32	39	0	93	3.7
Ernest Vandeweghe	5	77	31	10	.323	2	2	1.000	13	12	15	0	22	4.4
Robert Santini	4	23	10	5	.500	2	1	.500	3	1	4	0	11	2.8

PHILADELPHIA WARRIORS

Player	G.	Min.	FGA	FGM	Pct.	FTA	FTM	Pct.	Reb.	Ast.	PF	Disq.	Pts.	Avg.
Paul Arizin	72	2724	1378	617	.448	626	507	.810	530	189	282	11	1741	24.2
Neil Johnston	70	2594	1092	499	.457	685	549	.801	872	225	251	8	1547	22.1
Joseph Graboski	72	2375	1075	397	.369	340	240	.706	642	190	272	5	1034	14.4
Jack George	72	2840	940	352	.374	391	296	.757	313	457	202	1	1000	13.9
Thomas Gola	68	2346	592	244	.412	333	244	.733	616	404	272	11	732	10.8
Ernest Beck	67	1007	351	136	.387	106	76	.717	196	79	86	0	348	5.2
George Dempsey	72	1444	265	126	.475	139	88	.633	264	205	146	7	340	4.7
Walter Davis	70	1097	333	123	.369	112	77	.688	276	56	230	7	323	4.6
Lawrence Hennessy	53	444	247	85	.344	32	26	.813	49	46	37	0	196	3.7
Jack Moore	54	402	129	50	.388	53	32	.604	117	26	80	1	132	2.4

ROCHESTER ROYALS

Player	G.	Min.	FGA	FGM	Pct.	FTA	FTM	Pct.	Reb.	Ast.	PF	Disq.	Pts.	Avg.
Maurice Stokes	67	2323	1137	403	.354	447	319	.714	1094	328	276	11	1125	16.8
Jack Twyman	72	2186	987	417	.422	298	204	.685	466	171	239	4	1038	14.4
Ed Fleming	71	2028	824	306	.371	372	277	.745	489	197	178	1	889	12.5
Robert Wanzer	72	1980	651	245	.376	360	259	.719	272	225	151	0	749	10.4
Arthur Spoelstra	72	1640	576	226	.392	238	163	.685	436	95	248	11	615	8.5
Rich. Ricketts (StL-Roch)	68	1943	752	235	.313	195	138	.708	490	206	287	14	608	8.9
Richie Regan	72	1746	681	240	.352	133	85	.639	174	222	179	4	565	7.8
Don Meineke	69	1248	414	154	.372	232	181	.780	316	102	191	4	489	7.1
Connie Simmons	68	903	428	144	.336	129	78	.605	235	82	142	2	366	5.4
Chris Harris (St.L-Roch)	41	420	149	37	.248	45	27	.600	44	44	43	0	101	2.5
James Davis	3	16	6	0	.000	2	2	1.000	4	1	2	0	2	0.7

ST. LOUIS HAWKS

Player	G.	Min.	FGA	FGM	Pct.	FTA	FTM	Pct.	Reb.	Ast.	PF	Disq.	Pts.	Avg.
Robert Pettit	72	2794	1507	646	.429	757	557	.736	1164	189	202	1	1849	25.7
Charles Share	72	1975	733	315	.430	498	346	.695	774	131	318	13	976	13.6
Jack Coleman (Roch.-St. L.)	75	2738	946	390	.412	249	177	.711	688	294	242	2	957	12.8
Jack Stephens	72	2219	643	248	.386	357	247	.692	377	207	144	6	743	10.3
Robert Harrison	72	2219	725	260	.359	146	97	.664	195	277	246	6	617	8.6
Al Ferrari	68	1611	534	191	.358	236	164	.695	186	163	192	3	546	8.0
Jack McMahon (Roch.-St. L.)	70	1713	615	202	.328	185	110	.595	180	222	170	1	514	7.3
Alex Hannum	71	1480	453	146	.322	154	93	.604	344	157	271	10	385	5.4
Robert Schafer (Phila.-St. L.)	54	578	270	81	.300	81	62	.765	71	53	75	0	224	4.1
Frank Selvy	17	444	183	67	.366	71	53	.746	54	35	38	1	187	11.0
Medford Park	40	424	152	53	.349	70	44	.629	94	40	64	0	150	3.8

SYRACUSE NATIONALS

Player	G.	Min.	FGA	FGM	Pct.	FTA	FTM	Pct.	Reb.	Ast.	PF	Disq.	Pts.	Avg.
Dolph Schayes	72	2517	1202	465	.387	632	542	.858	891	200	251	9	1472	20.4
John Kerr	72	2114	935	377	.403	316	207	.655	607	84	168	3	961	13.3
George King	72	2343	763	284	.372	275	176	.640	250	410	150	2	744	10.3
Red Rocha	72	1883	692	250	.361	281	220	.783	416	131	244	6	729	10.0
Paul Seymour	57	1826	670	227	.339	233	188	.807	152	276	130	1	642	11.3
Earl Lloyd	72	1837	636	213	.335	241	186	.772	492	116	267	6	612	8.5
Ed Conlin	66	1423	574	211	.368	178	121	.680	326	145	121	1	543	8.2
William Kenville	72	1278	448	170	.379	257	195	.759	215	159	132	0	535	7.4
Richard Farley	72	1429	451	168	.373	207	143	.691	165	151	154	2	470	6.7
James Tucker	70	895	290	101	.348	83	66	.795	232	38	166	2	268	3.8

PLAYOFF RESULTS

EASTERN DIVISION 3rd PLACE GAME:

Mar. 15—New York 77 at Syracuse 82

WESTERN DIVISION 2nd PLACE GAME:

Mar. 16—Minneapolis 103 at St. Louis 97

EASTERN DIVISION SEMIFINALS
Syracuse 2, Boston 1

Mar. 17—Syracuse 93 at Boston 110
Mar. 19—Boston 98 at Syracuse 101
Mar. 21—Syracuse 102 at Boston 97

WESTERN DIVISION SEMIFINALS
St. Louis 2, Minneapolis 1

Mar. 17—Minneapolis 115 at St. Louis 116
Mar. 19—St. Louis 75 at Minneapolis..133
Mar. 21—St. Louis 116 at Minneapolis 115

EASTERN DIVISION FINALS
Philadelphia 3, Syracuse 2

Mar. 23—Syracuse 87 at Philadelphia 109
Mar. 25—Philadelphia 118 at Syracuse...122
Mar. 27—Syracuse 96 at Philadelphia 119
Mar. 28—Philadelphia 104 at Syracuse...108
Mar. 29—Syracuse 104 at Philadephia 109

WESTERN DIVISION FINALS
Ft. Wayne 3, St. Louis 2

Mar. 22—St. Louis 86 at Ft. Wayne 85
Mar. 24—Ft. Wayne 74 at St. Louis 84
Mar. 25—St. Louis 84 at Ft. Wayne 107
Mar. 27—Ft. Wayne 93 at St. Louis 84
Mar. 29—St. Louis 97 at Ft. Wayne 102

WORLD CHAMPIONSHIP SERIES
Philadelphia 4, Ft. Wayne 1

Mar. 31—Ft. Wayne 94 at Philadelphia 98
Apr. 1—Philadelphia 83 at Ft. Wayne...............................84
Apr. 3—Ft. Wayne 96 at Philadelphia..............................100
Apr. 5—Philadelphia 107 at Ft. Wayne 105
Apr. 7—Ft. Wayne 88 at Philadelphia 99

1954-55 NBA STATISTICS

1954-55 NBA CHAMPION SYRACUSE NATIONALS

Front row (left to right): Dick Farley, Billy Kenville. Center row: Earl Lloyd, Captain Paul Seymour, Coach Al Cervi, George King, Jim Tucker. Rear row: President Daniel Biasone, Wally Osterkorn, Business Manager Bob Sexton, Dolph Schayes, John Kerr, Billy Gabor, Red Rocha, Trainer Art Van Auken.

FINAL STANDINGS

EASTERN DIVISION

Team	Syr.	N.Y.	Bos.	Phil.	Ft.W.	Minn.	Roch.	Mil.	W.	L.	Pct.	G.B.
Syracuse	..	8	6	7	7	3	7	5	43	29	.597	....
New York	4	..	6	5	7	5	5	6	38	34	.528	5
Boston	6	6	..	7	4	3	4	6	36	36	.500	7
Philadelphia	5	7	5	..	3	3	5	5	33	39	.458	10

WESTERN DIVISION

Team	Syr.	N.Y.	Bos.	Phil.	Ft.W.	Minn.	Roch.	Mil.	W.	L.	Pct.	G.B.
Ft. Wayne	2	2	5	6	..	9	8	11	43	29	.597	....
Minneapolis	6	4	6	6	3	..	8	7	40	32	.556	3
Rochester	2	4	5	4	4	4	..	6	29	43	.403	14
Milwaukee	4	3	3	4	1	5	6	..	26	46	.361	17

HOME-ROAD-NEUTRAL RECORDS OF ALL TEAMS

	Home	Road	Neutral	Total		Home	Road	Neutral	Total
Boston	20- 5	5- 22	11- 9	36- 36	New York	17- 8	8- 19	13- 7	38- 34
Ft. Wayne	20- 6	9- 14	14- 9	43- 29	Philadelphia	16- 5	4- 19	13-15	33- 39
Milwaukee	6- 11	9- 16	11-19	26- 46	Rochester	17- 11	4- 19	8-13	29- 43
Minneapolis	18- 6	10- 14	12-12	40- 32	Syracuse	25- 7	10- 16	8- 6	43- 29
					Totals	139- 59	59-139	90-90	288-288

TEAM STATISTICS

Team	G.	FGA	FGM	Pct.	FTA	FTM	Pct.	Reb.	Ast.	PF	Disq.	For	Agst.	Pt.Dif.
Ft. Wayne	72	5980	2333	.390	2710	1986	.733	3826	1737	1753	26	92.4	90.0	+2.4
Syracuse	72	6343	2360	.372	2450	1837	.750	3933	1778	1658	20	91.1	89.7	+1.4
Minneapolis	72	6465	2506	.388	2517	1873	.744	3865	1468	1935	56	95.6	94.5	+1.1
New York	72	6149	2392	.389	2593	1887	.728	4379	1744	1587	23	92.7	92.6	+0.1
Boston	72	6533	2604	.399	2704	2097	.776	4203	1905	1859	48	101.4	101.5	—0.1
Philadelphia	72	6234	2392	.384	2625	1928	.734	4238	1744	,1716	29	93.2	93.5	—0.3
Rochester	72	6020	2399	.399	2420	1737	.718	3904	1695	1865	26	90.8	92.4	—1.6
Milwaukee	72	6041	2187	.362	2672	1917	.717	3854	1544	1904	59	87.4	90.4	—3.0

INDIVIDUAL LEADERS

POINTS

	G.	FG	FT	Pts.	Avg.		G.	FG	FT	Pts.	Avg.
Neil Johnston, Philadelphia	72	521	589	1631	22.7	Larry Foust, Ft. Wayne	70	398	393	1189	17.0
Paul Arizin, Philadelphia	72	529	454	1512	21.0	Carl Braun, New York	71	400	274	1074	15.1
Bob Cousy, Boston	71	522	460	1504	21.2	Harry Gallatin, New York	72	330	393	1053	14.6
Bob Pettit, Milwaukee	72	520	426	1466	20.4	Paul Seymour, Syracuse	72	375	300	1050	14.6
Frank Selvy, Balt.-Mil.	71	452	444	1348	19.0	Ray Felix, New York	72	364	310	1038	14.4
Dolph Schayes, Syracuse	72	422	489	1333	18.5	George Yardley, Ft. Wayne	60	363	310	1036	17.3
Vern Mikkelsen, Minneapolis	71	440	447	1327	18.7	Jim Baechtold, New York	72	362	279	1003	13.9
Clyde Lovellette, Minneapolis	70	519	273	1311	18.7	Slater Martin, Minneapolis	72	350	276	976	13.6
Bill Sharman, Boston	68	453	347	1253	18.4	Joe Graboski, Philadelphia	70	373	208	954	13.6
Ed Macauley, Boston	71	403	442	1248	17.6	Nat Clifton, New York	72	360	224	944	13.1

FIELD GOALS
(Minimum 210 FGM)

	FGA	FGM	Pct.
Larry Foust, Ft. Wayne	818	398	.487
Jack Coleman, Rochester	866	400	.462
Neil Johnston, Philadelphia	1184	521	.440
Ray Felix, New York	832	364	.438
Clyde Lovellette, Minneapolis	1192	519	.435
Bill Sharman, Boston	1062	453	.427
Ed Macauley, Boston	951	403	.424
Vern Mikkelsen, Minneapolis	1043	440	.422
John Kerr, Syracuse	718	301	.419
George Yardley, Ft. Wayne	869	363	.418

ASSISTS

	G.	No.	Avg.
Bob Cousy, Boston	71	557	7.8
Dick McGuire, New York	71	542	7.6
Andy Phillip, Ft. Wayne	64	491	7.7
Paul Seymour, Syracuse	72	483	6.7
Slater Martin, Minneapolis	72	427	5.9
Jack George, Philadelphia	68	359	5.3
Bob Davies, Rochester	72	355	4.9
George King, Syracuse	67	331	4.9
Bill Sharman, Boston	68	280	4.1
Ed Macauley, Boston	71	275	3.9

FREE THROWS
(Minimum 180 FTM)

	FTA	FTM	Pct.
Bill Sharman, Boston	387	347	.897
Frank Brian, Ft. Wayne	255	217	.851
Dolph Schayes, Syracuse	587	489	.833
Dick Schnittker, Minneapolis	362	298	.823
Jim Baechtold, New York	339	279	.823
Harry Gallatin, New York	483	393	.814
Odie Spears, Rochester	271	220	.812
Paul Seymour Syracuse	370	300	.811
Bob Cousy, Boston	560	460	.807
Carl Braun, New York	342	274	.801

REBOUNDS

	G.	No.	Avg.
Neil Johnston, Philadelphia	72	1085	15.1
Harry Gallatin, New York	72	995	13.8
Bob Pettit, Milwaukee	72	994	13.8
Dolph Schayes, Syracuse	72	887	12.3
Ray Felix, New York	72	818	11.4
Clyde Lovellette, Minneapolis	70	802	11.5
Jack Coleman, Rochester	72	729	10.1
Vern Mikkelsen, Minneapolis	72	722	10.0
Arnie Risen, Rochester	69	703	10.2
Larry Foust, Ft. Wayne	70	700	10.0

TEAM-BY-TEAM INDIVIDUAL STATISTICS

BALTIMORE BULLETS

Player	G.	Min.	FGA	FGM	Pct.	FTA	FTM	Pct.	Reb.	Ast.	PF	Disq.	Pts.	Avg.
Rollen Hans	13	178	67	30	.448	25	13	.520	16	26	20	0	73	5.6
Ebberle Neal	13	194	59	12	.203	22	15	.682	47	9	27	0	39	3.0
Daniel King	12	103	22	7	.318	10	5	.500	25	3	5	0	19	1.6
Al McGuire	10	98	32	9	.281	7	5	.714	9	8	15	0	23	2.3

(Team disbanded November 27; players assigned to other clubs.)

BOSTON CELTICS

Player	G.	Min.	FGA	FGM	Pct.	FTA	FTM	Pct.	Reb.	Ast.	PF	Disq.	Pts.	Avg.
Robert Cousy	71	2747	1316	522	.397	570	460	.807	424	557	165	1	1504	21.2
William Sharman	68	2453	1062	453	.427	387	347	.897	302	280	212	2	1253	18.4
Edward Macauley	71	2706	951	403	.424	558	442	.792	600	275	171	0	1248	17.6
Don Barksdale	72	1790	699	267	.382	338	220	.651	545	129	225	7	754	10.5
Frank Ramsey	64	1754	592	236	.399	322	243	.755	402	185	250	11	715	11.2
Jack Nichols	64	1910	656	249	.380	177	138	.780	533	144	238	10	636	9.9
Robert Brannum	71	1623	465	176	.378	127	90	.709	492	127	232	6	442	6.2
Dwight Morrison	71	1227	284	120	.423	115	72	.626	451	82	222	10	312	4.4
Togo Palazzi	53	504	253	101	.399	60	45	.750	146	30	60	1	247	4.7
Fred Scolari	59	619	249	76	.305	49	39	.796	77	93	76	0	191	3.2
Lucian Whittaker	3	15	6	1	.167	0	0	.000	1	1	4	0	2	0.7

FORT WAYNE PISTONS

Player	G.	Min.	FGA	FGM	Pct.	FTA	FTM	Pct.	Reb.	Ast.	PF	Disq.	Pts.	Avg.
Larry Foust	70	2264	818	398	.487	513	393	.766	700	118	264	9	1189	17.0
George Yardley	60	2150	869	363	.418	416	310	.745	594	126	205	7	1036	17.3
Mel Hutchins	72	2860	903	341	.378	257	182	.708	665	247	232	0	864	12.0
Max Zaslofsky	70	1862	821	269	.328	352	247	.702	191	203	130	0	785	11.2
Frank Brian	71	1381	623	237	.380	255	217	.851	127	142	133	0	691	9.7
Andrew Phillip	64	2332	545	202	.371	308	213	.692	290	491	166	1	617	9.6
Richard Rosenthal	67	1406	523	197	.377	181	130	.718	300	153	179	2	524	7.8
Robert Houbregs (Bal-Bo-FW)	64	1326	386	148	.383	182	129	.709	297	86	180	5	425	6.6
Don Meineke	68	1026	366	136	.372	170	119	.700	246	64	153	1	391	5.8
Paul Walther	68	820	161	56	.348	88	54	.614	155	131	115	1	166	2.4
Al Roges (Balt.-Ft.W.)	17	201	61	23	.377	24	15	.625	24	19	20	0	61	3.6
James Fritsche	16	151	48	16	.333	16	13	.813	32	4	28	0	45	2.8

Syracuse's Dolph Schayes led the Nats to their only title in 1954-55.

MILWAUKEE HAWKS

Player	G.	Min.	FGA	FGM	Pct.	FTA	FTM	Pct.	Reb.	Ast.	PF	Disq.	Pts.	Avg.
Robert Pettit	72	2659	1279	520	.407	567	426	.751	994	229	258	5	1466	20.4
Frank Selvy (Balt.-Milw.)	71	2668	1195	452	.378	610	444	.728	394	245	230	3	1348	19.0
Charles Share	69	1685	577	235	.407	492	351	.713	684	84	273	17	821	11.9
Robert Harrison	72	2300	875	299	.342	185	126	.681	226	252	291	14	724	10.1
Charles Cooper	70	1749	569	193	.339	249	187	.751	385	151	210	8	573	8.2
William Calhoun	69	2109	480	144	.300	236	166	.703	290	235	181	4	454	6.6
Alex Hannum	53	1088	358	126	.352	107	61	.570	245	105	206	9	313	5.9
Frank Saul	65	1139	303	96	.317	123	95	.772	134	104	126	0	287	4.4
Robert Watson	63	702	223	72	.323	45	31	.689	87	79	67	0	175	2.8
Kenneth McBride	12	249	147	48	.327	29	21	.724	31	14	31	0	117	9.8
George Ratkovicz	9	102	19	3	.158	23	10	.435	17	13	15	0	16	1.8
Philip Martin	7	47	19	5	.263	2	2	1.000	10	6	7	0	12	1.7
Fred Diute	7	72	21	2	.095	12	7	.583	13	4	12	0	11	1.6
Ron McGilvray	6	57	12	2	.167	7	4	.571	9	11	5	0	8	1.3
Carl McNulty	1	14	6	1	.167	0	0	.000	0	0	1	0	2	2.0

MINNEAPOLIS LAKERS

Player	G.	Min.	FGA	FGM	Pct.	FTA	FTM	Pct.	Reb.	Ast.	PF	Disq.	Pts.	Avg.
Vern Mikkelsen	71	2559	1043	440	.422	598	447	.747	722	145	319	14	1327	18.7
Clyde Lovellette	70	2361	1192	519	.435	398	273	.686	802	100	262	6	1311	18.7
Slater Martin	72	2784	919	350	.381	359	276	.769	260	427	221	7	976	13.6
Myer Skoog	72	2365	836	330	.395	155	125	.806	303	251	265	10	785	10.9
Richard Schnittker	72	1798	583	226	.388	362	298	.823	349	114	231	7	750	10.4
James Pollard	63	1960	749	265	.354	186	151	.812	458	160	147	3	681	10.8
Lew Hitch (Milw.-Mpls.)	74	1774	417	167	.400	169	115	.680	438	125	110	0	449	6.1
Ed Kalafat	72	1102	375	118	.315	168	111	.661	317	75	205	9	347	4.8
James Holstein	62	980	330	107	.324	94	67	.713	206	58	107	0	281	4.5
Don Sunderlage	45	404	133	33	.248	73	48	.658	56	37	57	0	114	2.5
Robert Carney	19	244	64	24	.375	40	21	.525	45	16	36	0	69	3.6

NEW YORK KNICKERBOCKERS

Player	G.	Min.	FGA	FGM	Pct.	FTA	FTM	Pct.	Reb.	Ast.	PF	Disq.	Pts.	Avg.
Carl Braun	71	2479	1032	400	.388	342	274	.801	295	274	208	3	1074	15.1
Harry Gallatin	72	2548	859	330	.384	483	393	.814	995	176	206	5	1053	14.6
Ray Felix	72	2024	832	364	.438	498	310	.622	818	67	286	11	1038	14.4
James Baechtold	72	2536	898	362	.403	339	279	.823	307	218	202	0	1003	13.9
Nat Clifton	72	2390	932	360	.386	328	224	.683	612	198	221	2	944	13.1
Richard McGuire	71	2310	581	226	.389	303	195	.643	322	542	143	0	647	9.1
Jack Turner	65	922	308	111	.360	76	60	.789	154	77	76	0	282	4.3
Eugene Shue (Phila.-N.Y.)	62	947	289	100	.346	78	59	.756	154	89	64	0	259	4.2
Robert Peterson	37	503	169	62	.367	45	30	.667	154	31	80	2	154	4.2
Bert Cook	37	424	133	42	.316	50	34	.680	72	33	39	0	118	3.2
Fred Christ	6	48	18	5	.278	11	10	.909	8	7	3	0	20	3.3
Charles Grigsby	7	45	19	7	.368	8	2	.250	11	7	9	0	16	2.3
Robert Knight	2	29	7	3	.429	1	1	1.000	1	8	6	0	7	3.5
Norman Hedderick	5	23	9	2	.222	1	0	.000	4	2	3	0	4	0.8
Don Anielak	1	10	4	0	.000	4	3	.750	2	0	0	0	3	3.0

PHILADELPHIA WARRIORS

Player	G.	Min.	FGA	FGM	Pct.	FTA	FTM	Pct.	Reb.	Ast.	PF	Disq.	Pts.	Avg.
Neil Johnston	72	2917	1184	521	.440	769	589	.766	1085	215	255	4	1631	22.7
Paul Arizin	72	2953	1325	529	.399	585	454	.776	675	210	270	5	1512	21.0
Joseph Graboski	70	2515	1096	373	.340	303	208	.686	636	182	259	8	954	13.6
Jack George	68	2480	756	291	.385	291	192	.660	302	359	191	2	774	11.4
Kenneth Murray (Balt.-Phila.)	66	1590	535	187	.350	120	98	.760	179	224	126	1	472	7.2
Robert Zawoluk	67	1117	375	138	.368	199	155	.779	256	87	147	3	431	6.4
George Dempsey	48	1387	360	127	.353	141	98	.695	236	174	141	1	352	7.3
Daniel Finn	43	820	265	77	.291	86	53	.616	157	155	114	3	207	4.8
Paul Hoffman (Balt.-N.Y.)	38	670	216	65	.301	93	64	.688	124	94	93	0	194	5.1
Walter Davis	61	766	182	70	.385	48	35	.729	206	36	100	0	175	2.9
Larry Costello	19	463	139	46	.331	32	26	.813	49	78	37	0	118	6.2
Jack Moore	23	376	115	44	.383	47	22	.468	105	20	62	2	110	4.8
Thomas Brennan	11	52	11	5	.455	0	0	.000	5	2	5	0	10	0.9
Michael Kearns	6	25	5	0	.000	4	1	.250	3	5	1	0	1	0.2

ROCHESTER ROYALS

Player	G.	Min.	FGA	FGM	Pct.	FTA	FTM	Pct.	Reb.	Ast.	PF	Disq.	Pts.	Avg.
Robert Wanzer	72	2376	820	324	.395	374	294	.786	374	247	163	2	942	13.1
Jack Coleman	72	2482	866	400	.462	183	124	.678	729	232	201	1	924	12.8
Robert Davies	72	1870	785	326	.415	293	220	.751	205	355	220	2	872	12.1
Arnold Risen	69	1970	699	259	.371	375	279	.744	703	112	253	10	797	11.6
Marion Spears	71	1888	585	226	.386	271	220	.812	299	148	252	6	672	9.5
Jack McMahon	72	1807	721	251	.348	225	143	.636	211	246	179	1	645	9.0
Thomas Marshall	72	1337	505	223	.442	194	131	.675	256	111	99	0	577	8.0
Arthur Spoelstra	70	1127	399	159	.398	156	108	.692	285	58	170	2	426	6.1
Don Henriksen (Balt.-Roch.)	70	1664	406	139	.342	195	137	.703	484	111	190	2	415	5.9
Cal Christensen	71	1204	305	114	.374	206	124	.602	388	104	174	2	352	5.0
Boris Nachamkin	6	59	20	6	.306	13	8	.615	19	3	6	0	20	3.3

SYRACUSE NATIONALS

Player	G.	Min.	FGA	FGM	Pct.	FTA	FTM	Pct.	Reb.	Ast.	PF	Disq.	Pts.	Avg.
Dolph Schayes	72	2526	1103	422	.383	587	489	.833	887	213	247	6	1333	18.5
Paul Seymour	72	2950	1036	375	.362	370	300	.811	300	483	137	0	1050	14.6
Red Rocha	72	2473	801	295	.368	284	222	.782	489	178	242	5	812	11.3
John Kerr	72	1529	718	301	.419	223	152	.682	474	80	165	2	754	10.5
Earl Lloyd	72	2212	784	286	.365	212	159	.750	553	151	283	4	731	10.2
George King	67	2015	605	228	.377	229	140	.611	227	331	148	0	596	8.9
William Kenville	70	1380	482	172	.357	201	154	.766	247	150	132	1	498	7.1
Richard Farley	69	1113	353	136	.385	201	136	.677	167	111	145	1	408	5.9
Connie Simmons (Balt.-Syr.)	36	862	384	137	.357	114	72	.632	220	61	109	2	346	9.6
James Tucker	20	287	116	39	.336	38	27	.711	97	12	50	0	105	5.3
Wally Osterkorn	19	286	97	20	.206	32	16	.500	70	17	32	0	56	2.9
William Gabor	3	47	22	7	.318	5	3	.600	5	11	6	0	17	5.7

PLAYOFF RESULTS

EASTERN DIVISION SEMIFINALS
Boston 2, New York 1

Mar. 15—New York 101 at Boston 122
Mar. 16—Boston 95 at New York 102
Mar. 19—Boston 116 at New York 109

WESTERN DIVISION SEMIFINALS
Minneapolis 2, Rochester 1

Mar. 16—Rochester 78, Minneapolis at St. Paul............................82
Mar. 18—Minneapolis 92 at Rochester 94
Mar. 19—Rochester 110, Minneapolis at St. Paul 119

EASTERN DIVISION FINALS
Syracuse 3, Boston 1

Mar. 22—Boston 100 at Syracuse 110
Mar. 24—Boston 110 at Syracuse 116
Mar. 26—Syracuse 97 at Boston...*100
Mar. 27—Syracuse 110 at Boston..94

WESTERN DIVISION FINALS
Ft. Wayne 3, Minneapolis 1

Mar. 20—Minneapolis 79, Ft. Wayne at Elkhart, Ind...................96
Mar. 22—Minneapolis 97, Ft. Wayne at Indianapolis *98
Mar. 23—Ft. Wayne 91 at Minneapolis...*99
Mar. 27—Ft. Wayne 105 at Minneapolis 96

WORLD CHAMPIONSHIP SERIES
Syracuse 4, Ft. Wayne 3

Mar. 31—Ft. Wayne 82 at Syracuse 86
Apr. 2—Ft. Wayne 84 at Syracuse 87
Apr. 3—Syracuse 89, Ft. Wayne at Indianapolis.........................96
Apr. 5—Syracuse 102, Ft. Wayne at Indianapolis......................109
Apr. 7—Syracuse 71, Ft. Wayne at Indianapolis.........................74
Apr. 9—Ft. Wayne 104 at Syracuse 109
Apr. 10—Ft. Wayne 91 at Syracuse 92

*Denotes overtime period.

1953-54 NBA STATISTICS

1953-54 NBA CHAMPION MINNEAPOLIS LAKERS

Left to right: Slater Martin, Frank Saul, Jim Holstein, Jim Pollard, Clyde Lovellette, George Mikan, Vern Mikkelsen, Dick Schnittker, Whitey Skoog, Coach John Kundla.

FINAL STANDINGS

EASTERN DIVISION

Team	N.Y.	Bos.	Syr.	Phil.	Balt.	Minn.	Rock.	Ft.W.	Mil.	W.	L.	Pct.	G.B.
New York	..	5	5	7	7	3	7	5	5	44	28	.611	....
Boston	5	..	5	6	9	3	4	4	6	42	30	.583	2
Syracuse	5	5	..	4	7	3	5	6	7	42	30	.583	2
Philadelphia	3	4	6	..	6	2	1	2	5	29	43	.403	15
Baltimore	3	1	3	4	..	2	1	0	2	16	56	.222	28

WESTERN DIVISION

Team	N.Y.	Bos.	Syr.	Phil.	Balt.	Minn.	Rock.	Ft.W.	Mil.	W.	L.	Pct.	G.B.
Minneapolis	5	5	5	6	6	..	6	5	8	46	26	.639	....
Rochester	1	4	3	7	7	5	..	8	9	44	28	.611	2
Ft. Wayne	3	4	2	6	8	5	3	..	9	40	32	.556	6
Milwaukee	3	2	1	3	6	3	1	2	..	21	51	.292	25

HOME-ROAD-NEUTRAL RECORDS OF ALL TEAMS

Team	Home	Road	Neutral	Total	Team	Home	Road	Neutral	Total
Baltimore	12- 20	0- 20	4-16	16- 56	New York	18- 8	15- 13	11- 7	44- 28
Boston	16- 6	11- 19	15- 5	42- 30	Philadelphia	10- 9	6- 16	13-18	29- 43
Ft. Wayne	19- 8	11- 17	10- 7	40- 32	Rochester	18- 10	12- 15	14- 3	44- 28
Milwaukee	10- 14	6- 17	5-20	21- 51	Syracuse	27- 5	10- 19	5- 6	42- 30
Minneapolis	21- 4	13- 15	12- 7	46- 26	Totals	151- 84	84-151	89-89	324-324

TEAM STATISTICS

Team	G.	FGA	FGM	Pct.	FTA	FTM	Pct.	Reb.	Ast.	PF	Disq.	For	Agst.	Pt.Dif.
Syracuse	72	5579	2054	.368	2650	1905	.719	3652	1541	1852	28	83.5	78.6	+4.9
Minneapolis	72	5803	2184	.376	2067	1512	.731	3752	1323	1918	31	81.7	78.3	+3.4
Rochester	72	5451	2010	.369	2518	1722	.684	3494	1454	1904	44	79.8	77.3	+2.5
Boston	72	5580	2232	.400	2550	1851	.726	3867	1773	1969	46	87.7	85.4	+2.3
Ft. Wayne	72	5187	1952	.376	2315	1689	.730	3785	1474	1669	27	77.7	76.1	+1.6
New York	72	5177	1934	.374	2525	1820	.721	3830	1469	1832	23	79.0	79.1	-0.1
Philadelphia	72	5431	2023	.372	2272	1586	.698	3589	1468	1741	42	78.2	80.4	-2.2
Milwaukee	72	5087	1757	.345	2202	1524	.692	3202	1298	1771	45	70.0	75.3	-5.3
Baltimore	72	5539	2036	.368	2312	1566	.677	3816	1385	1777	24	78.3	85.1	-6.8

INDIVIDUAL LEADERS

POINTS

Player	G.	FG	FT	Pts.	Avg.	Player	G.	FG	FT	Pts.	Avg.
Neil Johnston, Philadelphia	72	591	577	1759	24.4	Harry Gallatin, New York	72	258	433	949	13.2
Bob Cousy, Boston	72	486	411	1383	19.2	Arnie Risen, Rochester	72	321	307	949	13.2
Ed Macauley, Boston	71	462	420	1344	18.9	Joe Graboski, Philadelphia	71	354	236	944	13.3
George Mikan, Minneapolis	72	441	424	1306	18.1	Paul Seymour, Syracuse	71	316	299	931	13.1
Ray Felix, Baltimore	72	410	449	1269	17.6	Bob Davies, Rochester	72	288	311	887	12.3
Dolph Schayes, Syracuse	72	370	488	1228	17.1	Jim Pollard, Minn.	71	326	179	831	11.7
Bill Sharman, Boston	72	412	331	1155	16.0	George King, Syracuse	72	280	257	817	11.3
Larry Foust, Ft. Wayne	72	376	338	1090	15.1	Max Zaslofsky, Balt.-Mil.-Ft.W.	65	278	255	811	12.5
Carl Braun, New York	72	354	354	1062	14.8	Vern Mikkelsen, Minn.	72	288	221	797	11.1
Bob Wanzer, Rochester	72	322	314	958	13.3	Don Sunderlage, Milw.	68	254	252	760	11.2

FIELD GOALS
(Minimum 210 FGM)

Player	FGA	FGM	Pct.
Ed Macauley, Boston	950	462	.486
Bill Sharman, Boston	915	412	.450
Neil Johnston, Philadelphia	1317	591	.449
Clyde Lovellette, Minneapolis	560	237	.423
Ray Felix, Baltimore	983	410	.417
Larry Foust, Ft. Wayne	919	376	.409
Eddie Miller, Baltimore	600	244	.407
Jack Coleman, Rochester	714	289	.405
Harry Gallatin, New York	639	258	.404
Mel Hutchins, Ft. Wayne	736	295	.401

ASSISTS

Player	G.	No.	Avg.
Bob Cousy, Boston	72	518	7.2
Andy Phillip, Ft. Wayne	71	449	6.3
Paul Seymour, Syracuse	71	364	5.1
Dick McGuire, New York	68	354	5.2
Bob Davies, Rochester	72	323	4.5
Jack George, Philadelphia	71	312	4.4
Paul Hoffman, Baltimore	72	285	4.0
George King, Syracuse	72	272	3.8
Ed Macauley, Boston	71	271	3.8
Daniel Finn, Philadelphia	68	265	3.9

FREE THROWS
(Minimum 180 FTM)

Player	FTA	FTM	Pct.
Bill Sharman, Boston	392	331	.844
Dolph Schayes, Syracuse	590	488	.827
Carl Braun, New York	429	354	.825
Paul Seymour, Syracuse	368	299	.813
Bob Zawoluk, Philadelphia	230	186	.809
Bob Cousy, Boston	522	411	.787
Harry Gallatin, New York	552	433	.784
George Mikan, Minneapolis	546	424	.777
Odie Spears, Rochester	238	183	.769
Ed Macauley, Boston	554	420	.758

REBOUNDS

Player	G.	No.	Avg.
Harry Gallatin, New York	72	1098	15.3
George Mikan, Minneapolis	72	1028	14.3
Larry Foust, Ft. Wayne	72	967	13.4
Ray Felix, Baltimore	72	958	13.3
Dolph Schayes, Syracuse	72	870	12.1
Neil Johnston, Philadelphia	72	797	11.1
Arnie Risen, Rochester	72	728	10.1
Mel Hutchins, Ft. Wayne	72	695	9.7
Lew Hitch, Milwaukee	72	691	9.6
Joe Graboski, Philadelphia	71	670	9.4

TEAM-BY-TEAM INDIVIDUAL STATISTICS

BALTIMORE BULLETS

Player	G.	Min.	FGA	FGM	Pct.	FTA	FTM	Pct.	Reb.	Ast.	PF	Disq.	Pts.	Avg.
Ray Felix	72	2672	983	410	.417	704	449	.638	958	82	253	5	1269	17.6
Paul Hoffman	72	2505	761	253	.332	303	217	.716	486	285	271	10	723	10.0
Edward Miller	72	1657	600	244	.407	317	231	.729	375	123	209	1	719	10.0
Robert Houbregs (Mil-Balt)	70	1970	562	209	.372	266	190	.714	213	160	177	1	570	8.7
Albert Roges	67	1937	614	220	.358	179	130	.726	213	160	172	1	570	8.5
Rollen Hans	67	1556	515	191	.371	180	101	.561	160	181	172	1	483	7.2
James Fritsche (Min-Balt)	68	1221	379	116	.306	68	49	.721	217	73	103	0	281	4.1
Joseph Smyth	40	495	138	48	.348	65	35	.538	98	49	53	0	131	3.3
James Luisi	31	367	95	31	.326	41	27	.659	25	35	45	0	89	2.9
Hal Uplinger	23	268	94	33	.351	22	20	.909	31	26	42	0	86	3.7
Mark Workman	14	151	60	25	.417	10	6	.600	37	7	31	0	56	4.0
William Bolger	20	202	59	24	.407	13	8	.615	36	11	27	0	56	2.8
Connie Rea	20	154	43	9	.209	16	5	.313	31	16	13	0	23	1.2
Don Asmonga	7	46	15	2	.133	1	1	1.000	1	5	12	1	5	0.7
Francis Mahoney	2	11	2	0	.000	0	0	.000	2	1	0	0	0	0.0
Paul Nolen	1	2	1	0	.000	0	0	.000	1	0	1	0	0	0.0

BOSTON CELTICS

Player	G.	Min.	FGA	FGM	Pct.	FTA	FTM	Pct.	Reb.	Ast.	PF	Disq.	Pts.	Avg.
Robert Cousy	72	2857	1262	486	.385	522	411	.787	394	518	201	3	1383	19.2
Edward Macauley	71	2792	950	462	.486	554	420	.758	571	271	168	1	1344	18.9
William Sharman	72	2467	915	412	.450	392	331	.844	255	229	211	4	1155	16.0
Don Barksdale	63	1358	415	156	.376	225	149	.662	345	117	213	4	461	7.3
Jack Nichols (Mil-Bos)	75	1607	528	163	.309	152	113	.743	363	104	187	2	439	5.9
Robert Harris	71	1898	409	156	.381	172	108	.628	517	94	224	8	420	5.9
Robert Brannum	71	1729	453	140	.309	206	129	.626	509	144	280	10	409	5.8
Robert Donham	68	1451	315	141	.448	213	118	.554	267	186	235	11	400	5.9
Charles Cooper	70	1101	261	78	.299	116	78	.672	304	74	150	1	234	3.3
Ernie Barrett	59	641	191	60	.314	25	14	.560	100	55	116	2	134	2.3
Edward Mikan	9	71	24	8	.333	9	5	.556	20	3	15	0	21	2.3

FORT WAYNE PISTONS

Player	G.	Min.	FGA	FGM	Pct.	FTA	FTM	Pct.	Reb.	Ast.	PF	Disq.	Pts.	Avg.
Larry Foust	72	2693	919	376	.409	475	338	.712	967	161	258	4	1090	15.1
Max Zaslofsky (Balt-Mil-FtW)	65	1881	756	278	.368	357	255	.714	160	154	142	1	811	12.5
Andrew Phillip	71	2705	680	255	.375	330	241	.730	265	449	204	4	751	10.6
Mel Hutchins	72	2934	736	295	.401	223	151	.677	695	210	229	4	741	10.3
George Yardley	63	1489	492	209	.425	205	146	.712	407	99	166	3	564	9.0
Fred Scolari	64	1589	491	159	.324	180	144	.800	139	131	155	1	462	7.2
Leo Barnhorst (Balt-FtW)	72	2064	588	199	.338	88	63	.716	297	226	203	4	461	6.4

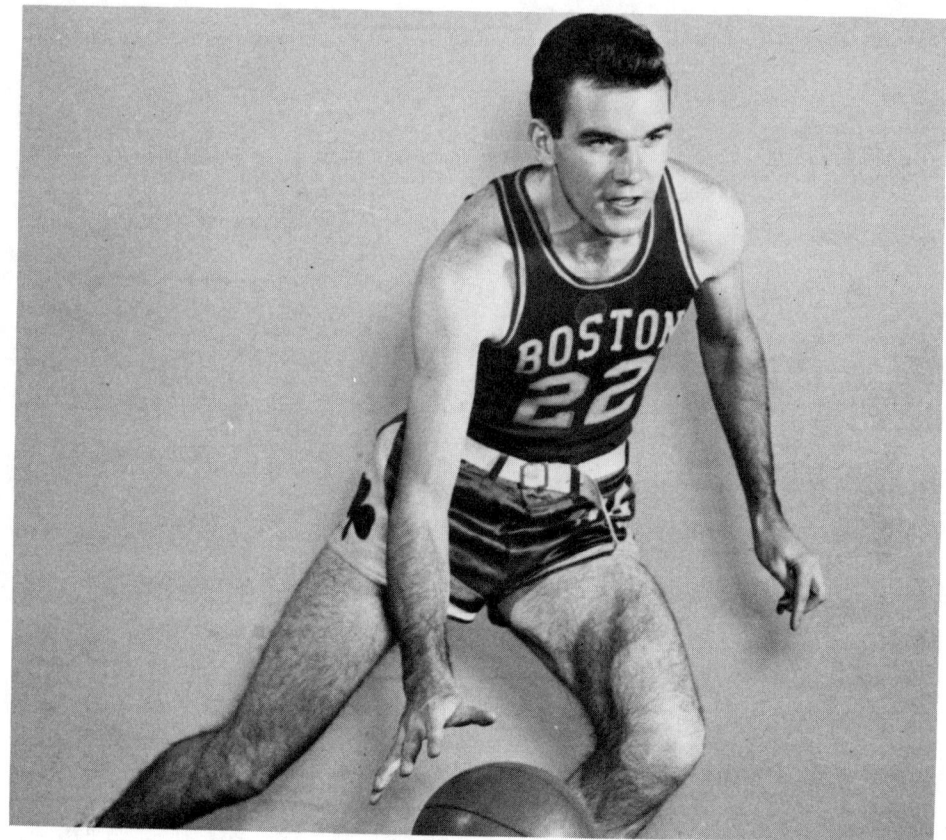

"Easy" Ed Macauley was one of the first great Boston Celtics.

Player	G.	Min.	FGA	FGM	Pct.	FTA	FTM	Pct.	Reb.	Ast.	PF	Disq.	Pts.	Avg.
Don Meineke	71	1466	393	135	.344	169	136	.805	372	81	214	6	406	5.7
Frank Brian	64	973	352	132	.375	182	137	.753	79	92	100	2	491	6.3
Jack Molinas	29	993	278	108	.388	176	134	.761	209	47	74	2	350	12.1
Kenneth Murray	49	528	195	53	.272	60	43	.717	65	56	60	0	149	3.0
Emilio Sinicoa	9	53	16	4	.250	6	3	.500	1	3	8	0	11	1.2

MILWAUKEE HAWKS

Player	G.	Min.	FGA	FGM	Pct.	FTA	FTM	Pct.	Reb.	Ast.	PF	Disq.	Pts.	Avg.
Don Sunderlage	68	2232	748	254	.340	337	252	.748	225	187	263	8	760	11.2
William Calhoun	72	2370	545	190	.349	292	214	.733	274	189	151	3	594	8.3
Lew Hitch	72	2452	603	221	.367	208	133	.639	691	141	176	3	575	8.0
George Ratkovicz	69	2170	501	197	.393	273	176	.645	523	154	255	11	570	8.3
Charles Share (FtW-Mil)	68	1576	493	188	.381	275	188	.684	555	80	210	8	564	8.3
Irving Bemoras	69	1496	505	185	.366	208	139	.668	214	79	152	2	509	7.4
William Tosheff	71	1825	578	168	.291	210	156	.743	163	196	207	3	492	6.9
Robert Harrison (Min-Mil)	64	1443	449	144	.321	158	94	.595	130	139	218	9	382	6.0
William Holzman	51	649	224	74	.330	73	48	.658	46	75	73	1	196	3.8
Richard Surhoff	32	358	129	43	.333	62	47	.758	69	23	53	0	133	4.2
Don Lofgran	21	380	112	35	.313	49	32	.653	64	26	34	0	102	4.9
Eugene Dyker	11	91	26	6	.231	8	4	.500	16	5	21	0	16	1.5
Robert Peterson (Balt-Mil)	8	60	10	3	.300	11	9	.818	12	3	15	1	15	1.9
Isaac Walthour	4	30	6	1	.167	0	0	.000	1	2	6	0	2	0.5

MINNEAPOLIS LAKERS

Player	G.	Min.	FGA	FGM	Pct.	FTA	FTM	Pct.	Reb.	Ast.	PF	Disq.	Pts.	Avg.
George Mikan	72	2362	1160	441	.380	546	424	.777	1028	174	268	4	1306	18.1
James Pollard	71	2483	882	326	.370	230	179	.778	500	214	161	0	831	11.7
Vern Mikkelsen	72	2247	771	288	.374	298	221	.742	615	119	264	7	797	11.1
Slater Martin	69	2472	654	254	.388	243	176	.724	166	253	198	3	684	9.9
Clyde Lovellette	72	1255	560	237	.423	164	114	.695	419	51	210	2	588	8.2
Myer Skoog	71	1877	530	212	.400	97	72	.742	224	179	234	5	496	7.0
Frank Saul	71	1805	467	162	.347	170	128	.753	159	139	149	3	452	6.4
Richard Schnittker	71	1040	307	122	.397	132	86	.652	178	59	178	3	330	4.6
James Holstein	70	1155	288	88	.306	112	64	.571	204	79	140	0	240	3.4

NEW YORK KNICKERBOCKERS

Player	G.	Min.	FGA	FGM	Pct.	FTA	FTM	Pct.	Reb.	Ast.	PF	Disq.	Pts.	Avg.
Carl Braun	72	2373	884	354	.400	429	354	.825	246	209	259	6	1062	14.8
Harry Gallatin	72	2690	639	258	.404	552	433	.784	1098	153	208	2	949	13.2
Connie Simmons	72	2006	713	255	.358	305	210	.689	484	128	234	1	720	10.0
Nat Clifton	72	2179	699	257	.368	277	174	.628	528	176	215	0	688	9.6
Richard McGuire	68	2343	493	201	.408	345	220	.638	310	354	190	3	622	9.1
Fred Schaus	67	1515	415	161	.388	195	153	.785	267	109	176	3	475	7.1
James Baechtold	70	1627	465	170	.366	177	134	.757	183	117	195	5	474	6.8
Vincent Boryla	52	1522	525	175	.333	81	70	.864	130	77	128	0	420	8.1
Al McGuire	64	849	177	58	.328	133	58	.436	121	103	144	2	174	6.1
Ernest Vandeweghe	15	271	103	37	.359	31	25	.806	20	29	38	1	99	6.6
Buddy Ackerman	28	220	63	14	.222	28	15	.536	15	23	43	0	43	1.5
Edward Smith	11	104	45	11	.244	10	6	.600	26	9	15	0	28	2.5

PHILADELPHIA WARRIORS

Player	G.	Min.	FGA	FGM	Pct.	FTA	FTM	Pct.	Reb.	Ast.	PF	Disq.	Pts.	Avg.
Neil Johnston	72	3296	1317	591	.449	772	577	.747	797	203	259	7	1759	24.4
Joseph Graboski	71	2759	1000	354	.354	350	236	.674	670	163	223	4	944	13.3
Jack George	71	2648	736	259	.352	266	157	.590	386	312	210	4	675	9.5
Robert Zawoluk	71	1795	540	203	.376	230	186	.809	330	99	220	6	592	8.3
Daniel Finn	68	1562	495	170	.343	196	126	.643	216	265	215	7	466	6.9
Paul Walther	64	2067	392	138	.352	206	145	.704	257	220	199	5	421	6.6
Walter Davis	68	1568	455	167	.367	101	65	.644	435	58	207	9	399	5.9
Joseph Fulks	61	501	229	61	.266	49	28	.571	101	28	90	0	150	2.5
Ernest Beck	15	422	142	39	.275	43	34	.791	50	34	29	0	112	7.5
George Senesky	58	771	119	41	.345	53	29	.457	66	84	79	0	111	1.9
James Phelan	4	33	6	0	.000	6	3	.500	5	2	9	0	3	0.8
Norman Grekin	1	1	0	0	.000	0	0	.000	0	0	1	0	0	0.0

ROCHESTER ROYALS

Player	G.	Min.	FGA	FGM	Pct.	FTA	FTM	Pct.	Reb.	Ast.	PF	Disq.	Pts.	Avg.
Robert Wanzer	72	2538	835	322	.386	428	314	.734	392	254	171	2	958	13.3
Arnold Risen	72	2385	872	321	.368	430	307	.714	728	120	284	9	949	13.2
Robert Davies	72	2137	777	288	.371	433	311	.718	194	323	224	4	887	12.3
Jack McMahon	71	1891	691	250	.362	303	211	.696	211	238	221	6	711	10.0
Jack Coleman	71	2377	714	289	.405	181	108	.597	589	158	201	3	686	9.7
Marion Spears	72	1633	505	184	.364	238	183	.769	310	109	211	5	551	7.7
Alex Hannum	72	1707	503	175	.348	164	102	.622	350	105	279	11	452	6.3
Cal Christensen	70	1654	395	137	.347	261	138	.529	395	107	196	1	412	5.9
Norman Swanson	63	611	137	31	.226	64	38	.594	110	33	91	3	100	1.6
Frank Reddout	7	18	6	5	.833	4	3	.750	9	0	6	0	13	1.9

SYRACUSE NATIONALS

Player	G.	Min.	FGA	FGM	Pct.	FTA	FTM	Pct.	Reb.	Ast.	PF	Disq.	Pts.	Avg.
Dolph Schayes	72	2655	973	370	.380	590	488	.827	870	214	232	4	1228	17.1
Paul Seymour	71	2727	838	316	.377	368	299	.813	291	364	187	2	931	13.1
George King	72	2370	744	280	.376	410	257	.627	268	272	179	2	817	11.3
Earl Lloyd	72	2206	666	249	.374	209	156	.746	529	115	303	12	654	9.1
Wally Osterkorn	70	2164	586	203	.346	361	209	.579	487	151	209	1	615	8.8
William Gabor	61	1211	551	204	.370	194	139	.716	96	162	183	4	547	9.0
William Kenville	72	1405	388	149	.384	182	136	.747	247	122	138	0	434	6.0
Robert Lavoy (Milw-Syr)	68	1277	356	135	.379	129	94	.729	317	78	215	2	364	5.4
Ebberle Neal	67	899	369	117	.317	132	78	.591	257	24	139	0	312	4.7
Al Masino (Roch-Syr)	27	181	62	26	.419	49	30	.612	28	22	44	0	82	3.0
Bato Govedarica	23	258	79	25	.316	37	25	.676	18	24	44	1	75	3.3
Richard Knostman	5	47	10	3	.300	11	7	.636	17	6	9	0	13	2.6
Ed Earle	2	12	2	1	.500	4	2	.500	2	0	0	0	4	2.0
Michael Novak	5	24	7	0	.000	2	1	.500	2	2	9	0	1	0.2

PLAYOFF RESULTS

EASTERN DIVISION ROUND ROBIN

Mar. 16—Boston 93 at New York 71
Mar. 17—Syracuse 96 at Boston *95
Mar. 18—New York 68 at Syracuse 75
Mar. 20—New York 78 at Boston 79
Mar. 21—Syracuse 103 at New York 99
Mar. 22—Boston 85 at Syracuse 98

WESTERN DIVISION ROUND ROBIN

Mar. 16—Ft. Wayne 75 at Rochester 82
Mar. 17—Rochester 88 at Minneapolis 109
Mar. 18—Minneapolis 90 at Ft. Wayne 85
Mar. 20—Ft. Wayne 73 at Minneapolis 78
Mar. 21—Rochester 89 at Ft. Wayne 71
Mar. 23—Minneapolis at Rochester (cancelled)

EASTERN DIVISION FINALS
Syracuse 2, Boston 0

Mar. 25—Boston 94 at Syracuse 109
Mar. 27—Syracuse 83 at Boston 76

WESTERN DIVISION FINALS
Minneapolis 2, Rochester 1

Mar. 24—Rochester 76 at Minneapolis 89
Mar. 27—Minneapolis 73 at Rochester 74
Mar. 28—Rochester 72 at Minneapolis 82

WORLD CHAMPIONSHIP SERIES
Minneapolis 4, Syracuse 3

Mar. 31—Syracuse 68 at Minneapolis 79
Apr. 3—Syracuse 62 at Minneapolis 60
Apr. 4—Minneapolis 81 at Syracuse 67
Apr. 8—Minneapolis 69 at Syracuse 80
Apr. 10—Minneapolis 84 at Syracuse 73
Apr. 11—Syracuse 65 at Minneapolis 63
Apr. 12—Syracuse 80 at Minneapolis 87

*Denotes overtime period.

1952-53 NBA STATISTICS

1952-53 NBA CHAMPION MINNEAPOLIS LAKERS
Left to right: Coach John Kundla, Slater Martin, Frank Saul, Jim Holstein, Vern Mikkelsen, Lew Hitch, George Mikan, Jim Pollard, Bob Harrison, Whitey Skoog, Assistant Coach Dave McMillan.

FINAL STANDINGS

EASTERN DIVISION

Team	N.Y.	Syr.	Bos.	Balt.	Phil.	Minn.	Roch.	Ft.W.	Ind.	Mil.	W.	L.	Pct.	G.B.
New York	..	6	4	10	10	2	3	2	5	5	47	23	.671	....
Syracuse	4	..	6	8	8	4	4	5	5	3	47	24	.662	.5
Boston	6	5	..	8	9	1	4	4	4	5	46	25	.648	1.5
Baltimore	0	2	2	..	6	1	0	0	2	3	16	54	.229	31
Philadelphia	0	2	1	4	..	0	2	0	1	2	12	57	.174	34.5

WESTERN DIVISION

Team	N.Y.	Syr.	Bos.	Balt.	Phil.	Minn.	Roch.	Ft.W.	Ind.	Mil.	W.	L.	Pct.	G.B.
Minneapolis	4	2	5	5	6	..	4	9	6	7	48	22	.686	....
Rochester	3	2	2	6	4	6	..	7	7	7	44	26	.629	4
Ft. Wayne	4	1	2	5	5	1	3	..	7	7	36	33	.522	11.5
Indianapolis	1	1	2	4	5	4	3	3	..	5	28	43	.394	20.5
Milwaukee	1	3	1	3	4	3	3	3	6	..	27	44	.380	21.5

HOME-ROAD-NEUTRAL RECORDS OF ALL TEAMS

Team	Home	Road	Neutral	Total	Team	Home	Road	Neutral	Total
Baltimore	11- 20	1- 19	4-15	16- 54	Minneapolis	24- 2	16- 15	8- 5	48- 22
Boston	21- 3	11- 18	14- 4	46- 25	New York	21- 4	15- 14	11- 5	47- 23
Ft. Wayne	25- 9	8- 19	3- 5	36- 33	Philadelphia	4- 13	1- 28	7-16	12- 57
Indianapolis	19- 14	4- 23	5- 6	28- 43	Rochester	24- 8	13- 16	7- 2	44- 26
Milwaukee	14- 8	4- 24	9-12	27- 44	Syracuse	32- 2	10- 19	5- 3	47- 24
					Totals	195- 83	83-195	73-73	351-351

TEAM STATISTICS

Team	G.	FGA	FGM	Pct.	FTA	FTM	Pct.	Reb.	Ast.	PF	Disq.	For	Agst.	Pt.Dif.
Minneapolis	70	5559	2166	.390	2221	1611	.739	3406	1351	1917	58	85.3	79.2	+6.1
New York	70	5339	2059	.386	2652	1867	.704	4007	1575	2053	68	85.5	80.3	+5.2
Syracuse	71	5329	1942	.364	2950	2197	.745	3472	1459	2132	49	85.6	81.3	+4.3
Rochester	70	5432	2019	.372	2747	2005	.730	3625	1520	2210	107	86.3	83.5	+2.8
Boston	71	5555	2177	.392	2617	1904	.728	3865	1666	1911	56	88.1	85.8	+2.3
Ft. Wayne	69	5230	1876	.359	2491	1839	.738	3548	1438	2119	97	81.0	81.1	—0.1
Indianapolis	71	5204	1829	.351	2277	1637	.719	3326	1281	1765	60	74.6	77.4	—2.8
Milwaukee	71	5320	1873	.352	2400	1643	.685	3429	1427	2120	93	75.9	78.8	—2.9
Baltimore	70	5615	2083	.371	2542	1745	.686	3727	1514	2141	93	84.4	90.1	—5.7
Philadelphia	69	5546	1987	.358	2298	1560	.679	3763	1513	1860	70	80.2	88.9	—8.7

INDIVIDUAL LEADERS

POINTS

	G.	FG	FT	Pts.	Avg.		G.	FG	FT	Pts.	Avg.
Neil Johnston, Philadelphia	70	504	556	1564	22.3	Carl Braun, New York	70	323	331	977	14.0
George Mikan, Minneapolis	70	500	442	1442	20.6	Leo Barnhorst, India'lis	71	402	163	967	13.6
Bob Cousy, Boston	71	464	479	1407	19.8	Larry Foust, Ft. Wayne	67	311	336	958	14.3
Ed Macauley, Boston	69	451	500	1402	20.3	Paul Seymour, Syracuse	67	306	340	952	14.2
Dolph Schayes, Syracuse	71	375	512	1262	17.8	Don Barksdale, Baltimore	65	321	257	899	13.8
Bill Sharman, Boston	71	403	341	1147	16.2	Joe Graboski, India'lis	69	272	350	894	13.0
Jack Nichols, Milwaukee	69	425	240	1090	15.8	Arnie Risen, Rochester	68	295	294	884	13.0
Vern Mikkelsen, Minneapolis	70	378	291	1047	15.0	Harry Gallatin, New York	70	282	301	865	12.4
Bob Davies, Rochester	66	339	351	1029	15.6	Jim Pollard, Minn.	66	333	193	859	13.0
Bob Wanzer, Rochester	70	318	384	1020	14.6	Joe Fulks, Philadelphia	70	332	168	832	11.9

FIELD GOALS
(Minimum 210 FGM)

	FGA	FGM	Pct.
Neil Johnston, Philadelphia	1114	504	.4524
Ed Macauley, Boston	997	451	.4523
Harry Gallatin, New York	635	282	.444
Bill Sharman, Boston	925	403	.436
Vern Mikkelsen, Minneapolis	868	378	.435
Ernie Vandeweghe, New York	625	272	.435
Jack Coleman, Rochester	748	314	.420
Slater Martin, Minneapolis	634	260	.410
George King, Syracuse	635	255	.402
Bob Lavoy, Indianapolis	560	225	.402

ASSISTS

	G.	No.	Avg.
Bob Cousy, Boston	71	547	7.7
Andy Phillip, Phil.-Ft.W.	70	397	5.7
George King, Syracuse	71	364	5.1
Dick McGuire, New York	61	296	4.9
Paul Seymour, Syracuse	67	294	4.4
Ed Macauley, Boston	69	280	4.1
Bob Davies, Rochester	66	280	4.2
Leo Barnhorst, Indianapolis	71	277	3.9
George Senesky, Philadelphia	69	264	3.8
Bob Wanzer, Rochester	70	252	3.6

FREE THROWS
(Minimum 180 FTM)

	FTA	FTM	Pct.
Bill Sharman, Boston	401	341	.850
Fred Scolari, Fort Wayne	327	276	.844
Dolph Schayes, Syracuse	619	512	.827
Carl Braun, New York	401	331	.825
Fred Schaus, Fort Wayne	296	243	.821
Odie Spears, Rochester	243	199	.819
Paul Seymour, Syracuse	416	340	.817
Bob Cousy, Boston	587	479	.816
Bob Wanzer, Rochester	473	384	.812
Bill Tosheff, Indianapolis	314	253	.806

REBOUNDS

	G.	No.	Avg.
George Mikan, Minneapolis	70	1007	14.4
Neil Johnston, Philadelphia	70	976	13.9
Dolph Schayes, Syracuse	71	920	13.0
Harry Gallatin, New York	70	916	13.1
Mel Hutchins, Milwaukee	71	793	11.2
Jack Coleman, Rochester	70	774	11.1
Larry Foust, Fort Wayne	67	769	11.5
Nat Clifton, New York	70	761	10.9
Arnie Risen, Rochester	68	745	11.0
Joe Graboski, Indianapolis	69	687	10.0

TEAM-BY-TEAM INDIVIDUAL STATISTICS

BALTIMORE BULLETS

Player	G.	Min.	FGA	FGM	Pct.	FTA	FTM	Pct.	Reb.	Ast.	PF	Disq.	Pts.	Avg.
Don Barksdale	65	2298	829	321	.387	401	257	.641	597	166	273	13	899	13.8
Edward Miller	70	2018	781	273	.350	287	187	.652	669	115	250	12	733	10.5
Paul Hoffman	69	1955	656	240	.366	342	224	.655	317	237	282	13	704	10.2
James Baechtold	64	1893	621	242	.390	240	177	.738	219	154	203	8	661	10.3
Don Henricksen	68	2263	475	199	.419	281	176	.626	506	129	242	12	574	8.4
Ray Lumpp (N.Y.-Balt)	55	1422	506	188	.372	206	153	.743	141	168	178	5	529	9.6
Jack Kerris	69	1424	256	93	.363	140	88	.629	295	156	165	7	274	4.0
Ralph O'Brien	55	758	286	96	.336	92	78	.848	70	56	74	0	270	4.9
Kevin O'Shea	46	643	189	71	.376	81	48	.593	76	87	82	1	190	4.1
George Kaftan	23	380	142	45	.317	67	44	.657	75	31	59	2	134	5.8
Richard Bunt	26	271	107	29	.271	48	33	.708	28	17	40	0	92	3.5
Robert Priddy	16	149	38	14	.368	14	8	.571	36	7	36	3	36	2.3
George McLeod	10	85	16	2	.125	15	8	.533	21	4	16	0	12	1.2
Blaine Denning	1	9	5	2	.400	1	1	1.000	4	0	3	0	5	5.0

BOSTON CELTICS

Player	G.	Min.	FGA	FGM	Pct.	FTA	FTM	Pct.	Reb.	Ast.	PF	Disq.	Pts.	Avg.
Robert Cousy	71	2945	1320	464	.352	587	479	.816	449	547	227	4	1407	19.8
Edward Macauley	69	2902	997	451	.452	667	500	.750	629	280	188	0	1402	20.3
William Sharman	71	2333	925	403	.436	401	341	.850	288	191	240	7	1147	16.2
Robert Harris	70	1971	459	192	.418	226	133	.588	485	95	238	6	517	7.4
Robert Brannum	71	1900	541	188	.348	185	110	.595	537	147	287	17	486	6.8
Charles Cooper	70	1994	466	157	.337	190	144	.758	439	112	258	11	458	6.5
Robert Donham	71	1435	353	169	.479	240	113	.471	239	153	213	8	451	6.4
John Mahnken	69	771	252	76	.302	56	38	.696	182	75	110	1	191	2.8
Kenneth Rollins	43	426	115	38	.330	27	22	.815	45	46	63	1	98	2.3
Eugene Conley	39	461	108	35	.324	31	18	.581	171	19	74	1	88	2.3
Francis Mahoney	6	34	10	4	.400	5	4	.800	7	1	7	0	12	2.0

FORT WAYNE PISTONS

Player	G.	Min.	FGA	FGM	Pct.	FTA	FTM	Pct.	Reb.	Ast.	PF	Disq.	Pts.	Avg.
Larry Foust	67	2303	865	311	.360	465	336	.723	769	151	267	16	958	14.3
Fred Scolari	62	2123	809	277	.342	327	276	.844	209	233	212	4	830	13.4
Don Meineke	68	2250	630	240	.381	313	245	.783	466	148	334	26	735	10.8
Frank Brian	68	1910	699	245	.351	297	236	.795	133	142	205	8	726	10.7
Fred Schaus	69	2541	719	240	.334	296	243	.821	413	245	261	11	723	10.5
Andrew Phillip (Phil-Ft. W)	70	2690	629	250	.397	301	222	.737	364	397	229	9	722	10.3
Dwight Eddleman	69	1571	687	241	.351	237	133	.561	236	104	220	5	616	8.9
Don Boven	67	1373	427	153	.358	209	145	.694	217	79	227	13	451	6.7
Charles Share	67	1044	254	91	.358	234	172	.735	373	74	213	13	354	5.3
Richard Groat	26	663	272	100	.368	138	109	.790	86	69	90	7	309	11.9
Jake Fendley	45	380	80	32	.400	60	40	.667	46	36	82	3	104	2.3
Ray Corley	8	65	24	3	.125	6	5	.833	5	5	18	0	11	1.4
Ralph Johnson	3	30	9	3	.333	3	2	.667	1	5	6	0	8	2.7
Jack Kiley	6	27	10	2	.200	2	2	1.000	2	3	7	0	6	1.0

INDIANAPOLIS OLYMPIANS

Player	G.	Min.	FGA	FGM	Pct.	FTA	FTM	Pct.	Reb.	Ast.	PF	Disq.	Pts.	Avg.
Leo Barnhorst	71	2871	1034	402	.389	259	163	.629	483	277	245	8	967	13.6
Joseph Graboski	69	2769	799	272	.340	513	350	.682	687	156	303	18	894	13.0
William Tosheff	67	2459	783	253	.323	314	253	.806	229	243	243	5	759	11.3
Paul Walther	67	2468	645	227	.352	354	264	.746	284	205	260	7	718	10.7
Robert Lavoy	70	2327	560	225	.402	242	168	.694	528	130	274	18	618	8.8
Mel Payton	66	1424	485	173	.357	161	120	.745	313	81	118	0	466	7.1
Eugene Rhodes	65	1162	342	109	.319	169	119	.704	98	91	78	2	337	5.2
Edward Mikan (Phil-Ind)	62	927	292	78	.267	98	79	.806	237	39	124	0	235	3.8
Robert Zawoluk	41	622	150	55	.367	116	77	.664	146	31	83	1	187	4.6
Don Hanrahan	18	121	32	11	.344	15	11	.733	30	11	24	1	33	1.8
Clarence Hermsen	10	62	31	4	.129	5	3	.600	19	4	18	0	11	1.1
Robert Naber	4	11	4	0	.000	2	1	.500	5	1	6	0	1	0.3

MILWAUKEE HAWKS

Player	G.	Min.	FGA	FGM	Pct.	FTA	FTM	Pct.	Reb.	Ast.	PF	Disq.	Pts.	Avg.
Jack Nichols	69	2626	1170	425	.363	339	240	.708	533	196	237	9	1090	15.8
Mel Hutchins	71	2891	842	319	.379	295	193	.654	793	227	214	5	831	11.7
George Ratkovicz	71	2235	619	208	.336	373	262	.702	522	217	287	16	678	9.5
William Calhoun	62	2148	534	180	.337	292	211	.723	277	156	136	4	571	9.2
Stanley Miasek	65	1584	488	178	.365	248	156	.629	360	122	229	13	512	7.9
John Payak	68	1470	373	128	.343	248	180	.726	114	140	194	7	436	6.4
Davage Minor	59	1610	420	154	.367	132	98	.742	252	128	211	11	406	6.9
Al Masino	71	1773	400	134	.335	204	128	.627	177	160	252	12	396	5.5
Dillard Crocker	61	776	284	100	.352	189	130	.688	104	63	199	11	330	5.4
Don Otten	24	384	87	34	.391	91	64	.703	89	21	68	4	132	5.5
James Brasco	20	248	94	25	.266	34	27	.794	24	21	30	2	77	3.9
Bucky McConnell	14	297	71	27	.380	29	14	.483	34	41	39	0	68	4.9
John O'Boyle	5	97	26	8	.308	7	5	.714	10	5	20	1	21	4.2
George Feigenbaum	5	79	22	4	.182	15	8	.533	7	9	14	1	16	3.2
Michael O'Neil	4	50	17	4	.235	4	4	1.000	9	3	10	1	12	3.0
Peter Darcey	12	90	18	3	.167	9	5	.556	10	2	29	2	11	0.9
Andrew Levane	7	68	24	3	.125	3	2	.667	9	9	15	0	8	1.1

MINNEAPOLIS LAKERS

Player	G.	Min.	FGA	FGM	Pct.	FTA	FTM	Pct.	Reb.	Ast.	PF	Disq.	Pts.	Avg.
George Mikan	70	2651	1252	500	.399	567	442	.780	1007	201	290	12	1442	20.6
Vern Mikkelsen	70	2465	868	378	.435	387	291	.752	654	148	289	14	1047	15.0
James Pollard	66	2403	933	333	.357	251	193	.769	452	231	194	3	859	13.0
Slater Martin	70	2556	634	260	.410	287	224	.780	186	250	246	4	744	10.6
Frank Saul	70	1796	471	187	.397	200	142	.710	141	110	174	3	516	7.4
Robert Harrison	70	1643	518	195	.376	165	107	.648	153	160	264	16	497	7.1
James Holstein	66	989	274	98	.358	105	70	.667	173	74	128	1	266	4.0
Lew Hitch	70	1027	255	89	.349	136	83	.610	275	66	122	2	261	3.7
Myer Skoog	68	996	264	102	.386	61	46	.754	121	82	137	2	250	3.7
Howard Schultz	40	474	90	24	.267	62	43	.694	80	29	73	1	91	2.3

NEW YORK KNICKERBOCKERS

Player	G.	Min.	FGA	FGM	Pct.	FTA	FTM	Pct.	Reb.	Ast.	PF	Disq.	Pts.	Avg.
Carl Braun	70	2316	807	323	.400	401	331	.825	233	243	287	14	977	14.0
Harry Gallatin	70	2333	635	282	.444	430	301	.700	916	126	224	6	865	12.4
Nat Clifton	70	2496	794	272	.343	343	200	.583	761	231	274	6	744	10.6
Ernest Vandeweghe	61	1745	625	272	.435	244	187	.766	342	144	242	11	731	12.0
Connie Simmons	65	1707	637	240	.377	340	249	.732	458	127	252	9	729	11.2
Vincent Boryla	66	2200	686	254	.370	201	165	.821	233	166	226	8	673	10.2
Richard McGuire	61	1783	373	142	.381	269	153	.569	280	296	172	3	437	7.2
Al McGuire	58	1231	287	112	.390	201	128	.637	167	145	206	8	352	6.1
Max Zaslofsky	29	722	320	123	.384	142	98	.690	75	55	81	1	344	11.9
Richard Surhoff	26	187	61	13	.213	30	19	.633	25	9	36	1	45	1.7
Sherwin Raiken	6	63	21	3	.143	8	3	.375	8	6	10	0	9	1.5

PHILADELPHIA WARRIORS

Player	G.	Min.	FGA	FGM	Pct.	FTA	FTM	Pct.	Reb.	Ast.	PF	Disq.	Pts.	Avg.
Neil Johnston	70	3166	1114	504	.452	794	556	.700	976	197	248	6	1564	22.3
Joseph Fulks	70	2085	960	332	.346	231	168	.727	387	138	319	20	832	11.9
Don Lofgran	64	1788	525	173	.330	173	126	.728	339	106	178	6	472	7.4
George Senesky	69	2336	485	160	.330	146	93	.637	254	264	166	1	413	6.0
Daniel Finn	31	1015	409	135	.330	182	99	.544	175	146	124	9	369	11.9
Nelson Bobb	55	1286	318	119	.374	162	105	.648	157	192	161	7	343	6.2
Mark Workman	65	1030	408	130	.319	113	70	.619	193	37	166	5	330	5.1
Jerry Fleishman	33	882	303	100	.330	140	96	.686	152	108	118	7	296	9.0
Ralph Polson (N.Y.-Phil.)	49	810	179	65	.363	96	61	.635	211	24	102	5	191	3.9
William Mlkvy	31	608	246	75	.305	48	31	.646	101	62	54	1	181	5.8
Frank Kudelka	36	567	193	59	.306	68	44	.647	88	70	109	2	162	4.5
Jim Mooney (Balt.-Phil.)	18	529	148	54	.365	40	27	.675	70	35	50	1	135	7.5
Claude Overton	15	182	75	19	.253	30	20	.667	25	15	25	0	58	3.9
Moe Radovich	4	33	13	5	.385	4	4	1.000	1	8	5	0	14	3.5
Jack McCloskey	1	16	9	3	.333	0	0	.000	3	1	2	0	6	6.0

ROCHESTER ROYALS

Player	G.	Min.	FGA	FGM	Pct.	FTA	FTM	Pct.	Reb.	Ast.	PF	Disq.	Pts.	Avg.
Robert Davies	66	2216	880	339	.385	466	351	.753	195	280	261	7	1029	15.6
Robert Wanzer	70	2577	866	318	.367	473	384	.812	351	252	206	7	1020	14.6
Arnold Risen	68	2288	802	295	.368	429	294	.685	745	135	274	10	884	13.0
Jack Coleman	70	2625	748	314	.420	208	135	.649	774	231	245	12	763	10.9
Marion Spears	62	1414	494	198	.401	243	199	.819	251	113	227	15	595	9.6
Arnitz Johnson	70	1984	369	140	.379	405	303	.748	419	153	282	14	583	8.3
Jack McMahon	70	1665	534	176	.330	236	155	.657	183	186	253	16	507	7.2
Alex Hannum	68	1288	360	129	.358	133	88	.662	279	81	258	18	346	5.1
Cal Christensen	59	777	230	72	.313	114	68	.596	199	54	148	6	212	3.6
William Holzman	46	392	149	38	.255	38	27	.711	40	35	56	2	103	2.2

SYRACUSE NATIONALS

Player	G.	Min.	FGA	FGM	Pct.	FTA	FTM	Pct.	Reb.	Ast.	PF	Disq.	Pts.	Avg.
Dolph Schayes	71	2668	1022	375	.367	619	512	.827	920	227	271	9	1262	17.8
Paul Seymour	67	2684	798	306	.383	416	340	.817	246	294	210	3	952	14.2
George King	71	2519	635	255	.402	442	284	.643	281	364	244	2	794	11.2
Red Rocha	69	2454	690	268	.388	310	234	.755	510	137	257	5	770	11.2
William Gabor	69	1337	614	215	.350	284	217	.764	104	134	262	11	647	9.4
Earl Lloyd	64	1806	453	156	.344	231	160	.693	444	64	241	6	472	7.4
Noble Jorgensen	70	1355	436	145	.333	199	146	.734	236	76	247	7	436	6.2
Wally Osterkorn	49	1016	262	85	.324	168	106	.631	217	61	129	2	276	5.6
Robert Lochmueller	62	802	245	79	.322	122	74	.607	162	47	143	1	232	3.7
Al Cervi	38	301	71	31	.437	100	81	.810	22	28	90	2	143	3.8
James Brasco	10	111	48	11	.229	14	11	.786	15	12	18	1	33	3.3

PLAYOFF RESULTS

EASTERN DIVISION SEMIFINALS
New York 2, Baltimore 0

Mar. 17—Baltimore 62 at New York 80
Mar. 20—New York 90 at Baltimore 81

Boston 2, Syracuse 0

Mar. 19—Boston 87 at Syracuse 81
Mar. 21—Syracuse 105 at Boston ****111

EASTERN DIVISION FINALS
New York 3, Boston 1

Mar. 25—Boston 91 at New York 95
Mar. 26—New York 70 at Boston 86
Mar. 28—Boston 82 at New York 101
Mar. 29—New York 82 at Boston 75

WESTERN DIVISION SEMIFINALS
Ft. Wayne 2, Rochester 1

Mar. 20—Ft. Wayne 84 at Rochester 77
Mar. 22—Rochester 83 at Ft. Wayne 71
Mar. 24—Ft. Wayne 67 at Rochester 65

Minneapolis 2, Indianapolis 0

Mar. 22—Indianapolis 69 at Minneapolis 85
Mar. 23—Minneapolis 81 at Indianapolis 79

WESTERN DIVISION FINALS
Minneapolis 3, Ft. Wayne 2

Mar. 26—Ft. Wayne 73 at Minneapolis 83
Mar. 28—Ft. Wayne 75 at Minneapolis 82
Mar. 30—Minneapolis 95 at Ft. Wayne 98
Apr. 1—Minneapolis 82 at Ft. Wayne 85
Apr. 2—Ft. Wayne 58 at Minneapolis 74

WORLD CHAMPIONSHIP SERIES
Minneapolis 4, New York 1

Apr. 4—New York 96 at Minneapolis 88
Apr. 5—New York 71 at Minneapolis 73
Apr. 7—Minneapolis 90 at New York 75
Apr. 8—Minneapolis 71 at New York 69
Apr. 10—Minneapolis 91 at New York 84

*—Denotes overtime period.

1951-52 NBA STATISTICS

1951-52 NBA CHAMPION MINNEAPOLIS LAKERS
Left to right: Slater Martin, Joe Hutton, Frank Saul, Bob Harrison, Jim Pollard, Howie Schultz, Vern Mikkelsen, Lew Hitch, George Mikan. (Coach John Kundla). Absent: Whitey Skoog.

FINAL STANDINGS

EASTERN DIVISION

Team	Syr.	Bos.	N.Y.	Phil.	Balt.	Roch.	Minn.	Ind.	Ft.W.	Mil.	W.	L.	Pct.	G.B.
Syracuse	..	5	4	6	6	2	5	2	6	4	40	26	.606	....
Boston	4	..	4	4	8	3	3	3	3	5	39	27	.591	1
New York	5	5	..	6	7	2	2	3	3	4	37	29	.561	3
Philadelphia	3	3	3	..	5	2	4	4	4	5	33	33	.500	7
Baltimore	3	1	2	4	..	2	0	2	2	4	20	46	.303	20

WESTERN DIVISION

Team	Syr.	Bos.	N.Y.	Phil.	Balt.	Roch.	Minn.	Ind.	Ft.W.	Mil.	W.	L.	Pct.	G.B.
Rochester	4	3	4	4	4	..	2	6	6	8	41	25	.621	....
Minneapolis	1	3	2	2	6	7	..	5	4	8	40	26	.606	1
Indianapolis	4	3	3	2	4	3	4	..	4	7	34	32	.515	7
Ft. Wayne	0	3	3	2	4	3	5	5	..	4	29	37	.439	12
Milwaukee	2	1	2	1	2	1	1	2	5	..	17	49	.258	24

HOME-ROAD-NEUTRAL RECORDS OF ALL TEAMS

Team	Home	Road	Neutral	Total	Team	Home	Road	Neutral	Total
Baltimore	17- 15	2- 22	1- 9	20- 46	Minneapolis	21- 5	13- 19	6- 2	40- 26
Boston	22- 7	10- 19	7- 1	39- 27	New York	21- 4	12- 22	4- 3	37- 29
Ft. Wayne	22- 11	6- 24	1- 2	29- 37	Philadelphia	24- 7	6- 25	3- 1	33- 33
Indianapolis	25- 6	4- 24	5- 2	34- 32	Rochester	28- 5	12- 18	1- 2	41- 25
Milwaukee	7- 13	3- 22	7-14	17- 49	Syracuse	26- 7	12- 18	2- 1	40- 26
					Totals	213- 80	80-213	37-37	330-330

TEAM STATISTICS

Team	G.	FGA	FGM	Pct.	FTA	FTM	Pct.	Reb.	Ast.	PF	Disq.	For	Agst.	Pt.Dif.
Minneapolis	66	5733	2106	.367	1921	1436	.748	3543	1389	1763	60	85.6	79.5	+6.1
Syracuse	66	5207	1894	.364	2589	1933	.747	3603	1373	1970	49	86.7	82.2	+4.5
Boston	66	5510	2131	.387	2406	1765	.734	3750	1606	1734	47	87.3	87.3	+4.0
Rochester	66	5172	2014	.389	2150	1661	.773	3373	1590	1804	62	86.2	82.9	+3.3
New York	66	5282	2022	.383	2185	1565	.716	3834	1567	1770	16	85.0	84.2	+0.8
Indianapolis	66	5513	2026	.367	1965	1422	.724	3288	1290	1586	37	82.9	82.8	+0.1
Philadelphia	66	5367	2039	.380	2143	1634	.762	3647	1593	1806	57	86.5	87.8	—1.3
Ft. Wayne	66	5013	1771	.353	2194	1609	.733	3619	1403	1751	70	78.0	80.1	—2.1
Baltimore	66	5495	1882	.342	2211	1614	.730	3780	1417	1719	55	81.5	89.0	—7.5
Milwaukee	66	5055	1674	.331	2177	1485	.682	3540	1229	1848	68	73.2	81.2	—7.9

INDIVIDUAL LEADERS

POINTS

	G.	FG	FT	Pts.	Avg.		G.	FG	FT	Pts.	Avg.
Paul Arizin, Philadelphia	66	548	578	1674	25.4	Jim Pollard, Minneapolis	65	411	183	1005	15.5
George Mikan, Minneapolis	64	545	433	1523	23.8	Fred Scolari, Baltimore	64	290	353	933	14.6
Bob Cousy, Boston	66	512	409	1433	21.7	Max Zaslofsky, New York	66	322	287	931	14.1
Ed Macauley, Boston	66	384	496	1264	19.2	Joe Fulks, Philadelphia	61	336	250	922	15.1
Bob Davies, Rochester	65	379	294	1052	16.2	Joe Graboski, Indianapolis	66	320	264	904	13.7
Frank Brian, Ft. Wayne	66	342	367	1051	15.9	Fred Schaus, Ft. Wayne	62	281	310	872	14.1
Larry Foust, Ft. Wayne	66	390	267	1047	15.9	Dolph Schayes, Syracuse	63	263	342	868	13.8
Bob Wanzer, Rochester	66	328	377	1033	15.7	Red Rocha, Syracuse	66	300	254	854	12.9
Arnie Risen, Rochester	66	365	302	1032	15.6	Leo Barnhorst, Indianapolis	66	349	122	820	12.4
Vern Mikkelsen, Minneapolis	66	363	283	1009	15.3	Andy Phillip, Philadelphia	66	279	232	790	12.0

FIELD GOALS
(Minimum 210 FGM)

	FGA	FGM	Pct.
Paul Arizin, Philadelphia	1222	548	.448
Harry Gallatin, New York	527	233	.442
Ed Macauley, Boston	888	384	.432
Bob Wanzer, Rochester	772	328	.425
Vern Mikkelsen, Minneapolis	866	363	.419
Jack Coleman, Rochester	742	308	.415
George King, Syracuse	579	235	.406
Red Rocha, Syracuse	749	300	.401
Paul Walther, Indianapolis	549	220	.401
Bob Lavoy, Indianapolis	604	240	.397

ASSISTS

	G.	No.	Avg.
Andy Phillip, Philadelphia	66	539	8.2
Bob Cousy, Boston	66	441	6.7
Bob Davies, Rochester	65	390	6.0
Dick McGuire, New York	64	388	6.1
Fred Scolari, Baltimore	64	303	4.7
George Senesky, Philadelphia	57	280	4.9
Bob Wanzer, Rochester	66	262	4.0
Leo Barnhorst, Indianapolis	66	255	3.9
Slater Martin, Minneapolis	66	249	3.8
Fred Schaus, Fort Wayne	62	247	4.0

FREE THROWS
(Minimum 180 FTM)

	FTA	FTM	Pct.
Bob Wanzer, Rochester	417	377	.904
Al Cervi, Syracuse	248	219	.883
Bill Sharman, Boston	213	183	.859
Frank Brian, Fort Wayne	433	367	.848
Fred Scolari, Baltimore	423	353	.835
Fred Schaus, Fort Wayne	372	310	.833
Joe Fulks, Philadelphia	303	250	.825
Bill Tosheff, Indianapolis	221	182	.824
Paul Arizin, Philadelphia	707	578	.818
Bob Cousy, Boston	506	409	.808

REBOUNDS

	G.	No.	Avg.
Larry Foust, Ft. Wayne	66	880	13.3
Mel Hutchins, Milwaukee	66	880	13.3
George Mikan, Minneapolis	64	866	13.5
Arnie Risen, Rochester	66	841	12.7
Dolph Schayes, Syracuse	63	773	12.3
Paul Arizin, Philadelphia	66	745	11.3
Nat Clifton, New York	62	731	11.8
Jack Coleman, Rochester	66	692	10.5
Vern Mikkelsen, Minneapolis	66	681	10.3
Harry Gallatin, New York	66	661	10.0

TEAM-BY-TEAM INDIVIDUAL STATISTICS

BALTIMORE BULLETS

Player	G.	Min.	FGA	FGM	Pct.	FTA	FTM	Pct.	Reb.	Ast.	PF	Disq.	Pts.	Avg.
Fred Scolari	64	2242	867	290	.334	423	353	.835	214	303	213	6	933	14.6
Don Barksdale	62	2014	804	272	.338	343	237	.691	601	137	230	13	781	12.6
Stanley Miasek	66	2174	707	258	.365	372	263	.707	639	140	257	12	779	11.8
Frank Kudelka	65	1583	614	204	.332	258	198	.770	275	183	220	11	606	9.3
Davage Minor	57	1558	522	185	.354	132	101	.765	275	160	161	2	471	8.3
Kevin O'Shea (Mil.-Balt.)	65	1725	466	153	.328	210	144	.686	201	171	175	7	450	6.9
William Calhoun	55	1594	409	129	.315	183	125	.683	252	117	84	0	383	7.0
Brady Walker	35	699	217	89	.410	34	26	.765	195	40	38	0	204	5.8
Joseph McNamee (Roch.-Balt.)	58	695	222	68	.306	50	30	.600	137	40	108	4	166	2.9
James Slaughter	28	525	165	53	.321	68	41	.603	148	25	81	0	147	5.3

BOSTON CELTICS

Player	G.	Min.	FGA	FGM	Pct.	FTA	FTM	Pct.	Reb.	Ast.	PF	Disq.	Pts.	Avg.
Robert Cousy	66	2681	1388	512	.369	506	409	.808	421	441	190	5	1433	21.7
Edward Macauley	66	2631	888	384	.432	621	496	.799	529	232	174	0	1264	19.2
William Sharman	63	1389	628	244	.389	213	183	.859	221	151	181	3	671	10.7
Robert Donham	66	1980	413	201	.487	293	149	.509	330	228	223	9	551	8.3
Charles Cooper	66	1976	545	197	.361	201	149	.741	502	134	219	8	543	8.2
Robert Harris	66	1899	463	190	.410	209	134	.641	531	120	194	5	514	7.8
Robert Brannum	66	1324	404	149	.369	171	107	.626	406	76	235	9	405	6.1
Horace McKinney	63	1083	418	136	.325	80	65	.813	175	111	148	4	337	5.3
John Mahnken	60	581	227	78	.344	43	26	.605	132	63	91	2	182	3.0
Richard Dickey	45	440	136	40	.294	69	47	.681	81	50	79	2	127	2.8

FORT WAYNE PISTONS

Player	G.	Min.	FGA	FGM	Pct.	FTA	FTM	Pct.	Reb.	Ast.	PF	Disq.	Pts.	Avg.
Frank Brian	66	2672	972	342	.352	433	367	.848	232	233	220	5	1051	15.9
Larry Foust	66	2615	989	390	.394	394	267	.678	880	200	245	10	1047	15.9
Fred Schaus	62	2581	778	281	.361	372	310	.833	434	247	221	7	872	14.1
D. Eddleman (Milw.-Ft. W.)	65	1893	809	269	.333	329	202	.614	267	134	249	9	740	11.4
Jack Kerris	66	2148	480	186	.388	325	217	.667	514	212	265	16	589	8.9
Ralph Johnson	66	2265	592	211	.356	140	101	.721	222	210	243	6	523	7.9
William Closs	57	1120	389	120	.309	157	107	.682	204	76	125	2	347	6.1
Charles Share	63	882	236	76	.322	155	96	.619	331	66	141	9	248	3.9
Jake Fendley	58	651	170	54	.318	95	75	.789	80	58	118	3	183	3.2
Jack Kiley	47	477	193	44	.228	54	30	.556	49	62	54	2	118	2.5
Emilio Sinicola	3	15	4	1	.250	2	0	.000	1	0	2	0	2	0.7

INDIANAPOLIS OLYMPIANS

Player	G.	Min.	FGA	FGM	Pct.	FTA	FTM	Pct.	Reb.	Ast.	PF	Disq.	Pts.	Avg.
Joseph Graboski	66	2439	827	320	.387	396	264	.667	655	130	254	10	904	13.7
Leo Barnhorst	66	2344	897	349	.389	187	122	.652	430	255	196	3	820	12.4
Paul Walther	55	1903	549	220	.401	308	231	.750	246	137	171	6	671	12.2
Robert Lavoy	63	1829	604	240	.397	223	168	.753	479	107	210	5	648	10.3
William Tosheff	65	2055	651	213	.327	221	182	.824	216	222	204	7	608	9.4
Ralph O'Brien	64	1577	613	228	.372	149	122	.819	122	124	115	0	578	9.0
Don Lofgran	63	1254	417	149	.357	219	156	.712	257	48	147	3	454	7.2
Wallace Jones	58	1320	524	164	.313	136	102	.750	283	150	137	3	430	7.4
Joseph Holland	55	737	265	93	.351	69	40	.580	166	47	90	0	226	4.1
Clifford Barker	44	494	161	48	.298	51	30	.588	81	70	56	0	126	2.9

MILWAUKEE HAWKS

Player	G.	Min.	FGA	FGM	Pct.	FTA	FTM	Pct.	Reb.	Ast.	PF	Disq.	Pts.	Avg.
Don Otten (Ft. W.-Milw.)	64	1789	636	222	.349	418	323	.773	435	123	218	11	767	12.0
Richard Mehen	65	2294	824	293	.356	167	117	.701	282	171	209	10	703	10.8
Don Boven	66	1982	668	200	.299	350	256	.731	336	177	271	18	656	9.9
Mel Hutchins	66	2618	633	231	.365	225	145	.644	880	190	192	5	607	9.2
Dillard Crocker (Ind.-Milw.)	38	783	279	98	.351	145	97	.669	111	57	132	7	293	7.7
Robert Wilson	63	1308	264	79	.299	135	78	.578	210	108	172	8	236	3.7
Walton Kirk	11	396	101	28	.277	78	55	.705	44	28	47	3	111	10.1
Arthur Burris (Ft. W.-Milw.)	41	514	156	42	.269	39	26	.667	99	27	49	3	110	2.7
Nate DeLong	17	132	142	20	.476	35	24	.686	31	14	47	3	64	3.8
Gene Vance	7	118	26	7	.269	14	9	.643	15	9	18	0	23	3.3
James Owens (Balt.-Milw.)	29	626	252	83	.329	114	64	.561	102	64	92	5	230	7.9
Don Rehfeldt (Balt.-Milw.)	39	788	285	99	.347	80	63	.788	243	50	102	2	261	6.7
Elmer Behnke	4	55	22	6	.273	7	4	.571	17	4	13	1	16	4.0
Charles Black	13	117	31	6	.194	12	5	.417	31	9	31	2	17	1.3
Cal Christensen	24	374	96	29	.302	57	30	.526	82	34	47	2	88	3.7
Jerry Fowler	6	41	13	4	.308	4	1	.250	10	2	9	0	9	1.5
John McConathy	11	106	29	4	.138	14	6	.429	20	8	7	0	14	1.3
John Rennicke	6	54	18	4	.222	9	3	.333	9	1	7	0	11	1.8

MINNEAPOLIS LAKERS

Player	G.	Min.	FGA	FGM	Pct.	FTA	FTM	Pct.	Reb.	Ast.	PF	Disq.	Pts.	Avg.
George Mikan	64	2572	1414	545	.385	555	433	.780	866	194	286	14	1523	23.8
Vern Mikkelsen	66	2345	866	363	.419	372	283	.761	681	180	282	16	1009	15.3
James Pollard	65	2545	1155	411	.356	260	183	.704	593	234	199	4	1005	15.5
Slater Martin	66	2480	632	237	.375	190	142	.747	228	249	226	9	616	9.3
Frank Saul (Balt.-Mpls.)	64	1479	436	157	.360	153	119	.778	165	147	120	3	433	6.8
Robert Harrison	65	1712	487	156	.320	124	89	.718	160	188	203	9	401	6.2
Howard Schultz	66	1301	315	89	.283	119	90	.756	246	102	197	13	268	4.1
Myer Skoog	35	988	296	102	.345	38	30	.789	122	60	94	4	234	6.7
Lew Hitch	61	849	215	77	.358	94	63	.670	243	50	89	3	217	3.6
Joseph Hutton	60	723	158	53	.335	70	49	.700	85	62	110	1	155	2.6
John Pilch	9	41	10	1	.100	6	3	.500	9	2	10	0	5	0.6

NEW YORK KNICKERBOCKERS

Player	G.	Min.	FGA	FGM	Pct.	FTA	FTM	Pct.	Reb.	Ast.	PF	Disq.	Pts.	Avg.
Max Zaslofsky	66	2113	958	322	.336	380	287	.755	194	156	183	5	931	14.1
Harry Gallatin	66	1931	527	233	.442	341	275	.807	661	115	223	6	741	11.2
Nat Clifton	62	2101	729	244	.335	256	170	.664	731	209	227	8	658	10.6
Connie Simmons	66	1558	600	227	.378	254	175	.689	471	121	214	8	629	9.5
Richard McGuire	64	2018	474	204	.430	290	183	.631	332	388	181	4	591	9.2
Ernest Vandeweghe	57	1507	457	200	.438	160	124	.775	264	164	188	3	524	9.2
Vincent Boryla	42	1440	522	202	.387	115	96	.835	219	90	121	2	500	11.9
Ray Lumpp	62	1317	476	184	.387	119	90	.756	125	123	165	4	458	7.4
George Kaftan	52	955	307	115	.375	134	92	.687	196	88	107	0	322	6.2
Al McGuire	59	788	167	72	.431	122	64	.525	121	107	136	8	208	3.5
Herbert Scherer	12	167	65	19	.292	14	9	.643	26	6	25	0	47	3.9
Thomas Smith	1	3	6	0	.000	6	4	.667	0	2	2	0	4	4.0

PHILADELPHIA WARRIORS

Player	G.	Min.	FGA	FGM	Pct.	FTA	FTM	Pct.	Reb.	Ast.	PF	Disq.	Pts.	Avg.
Paul Arizin	66	2939	1222	548	.448	707	578	.818	745	170	250	5	1674	25.4
Joseph Fulks	61	1904	1078	336	.312	303	250	.825	368	123	255	13	922	15.1
Andrew Phillip	66	2933	762	279	.366	308	232	.753	434	539	218	6	790	12.0
Edward Mikan	66	1781	571	202	.354	148	116	.784	492	87	252	7	520	7.9
George Senesky	57	1925	454	164	.361	194	146	.743	232	280	123	0	474	8.3
Neil Johnston	64	993	299	141	.472	151	100	.662	342	39	154	5	382	6.0
Nelson Bobb	62	1192	306	110	.359	167	99	.593	147	168	182	9	319	5.1
Walter Budko	63	1126	240	97	.404	89	60	.674	232	91	196	10	254	4.0
Vernon Gardner	27	507	194	72	.371	23	15	.652	112	37	60	2	159	5.9
Mel Payton	45	471	140	54	.386	28	21	.750	83	45	68	2	129	2.9
Stanley Brown	15	141	63	22	.349	18	10	.556	17	9	32	0	54	3.6
Ed Dahler	14	112	38	14	.368	7	7	1.000	22	5	16	0	35	2.5

ROCHESTER ROYALS

Player	G.	Min.	FGA	FGM	Pct.	FTA	FTM	Pct.	Reb.	Ast.	PF	Disq.	Pts.	Avg.
Robert Davies	65	2394	990	379	.383	379	294	.776	189	390	269	10	1052	16.2
Robert Wanzer	66	2498	772	328	.425	417	377	.904	333	262	201	5	1033	15.7
Arnold Risen	66	2396	926	365	.394	431	302	.701	841	150	258	3	1032	15.6
Jack Coleman	66	2606	742	308	.415	169	120	.710	692	208	218	7	736	11.2
Arnitz Johnson	66	2158	411	178	.433	387	301	.775	404	182	259	9	657	10.0
Marlon Spears	66	1673	570	225	.395	152	116	.763	303	163	225	8	566	8.6
Alex Hannum (Balt.-Roch.)	66	1508	462	170	.368	137	98	.710	336	133	271	16	438	6.6
William Holzman	65	1065	372	104	.280	85	61	.718	106	115	95	1	269	4.1
Sam Ranzino	39	234	90	30	.333	37	26	.703	39	25	63	2	86	2.2
Ray Ragelis	51	337	96	25	.260	29	18	.621	76	31	62	1	68	1.3
Paul Noel	8	32	9	2	.222	3	2	.667	4	3	6	0	6	0.8

SYRACUSE NATIONALS

Player	G.	Min.	FGA	FGM	Pct.	FTA	FTM	Pct.	Reb.	Ast.	PF	Disq.	Pts.	Avg.
Dolph Schayes	63	2004	740	263	.355	424	342	.807	773	182	213	5	868	13.8
Red Rocha	66	2543	749	300	.401	330	254	.770	549	128	249	4	854	12.9
George King	66	1889	579	235	.406	264	188	.712	274	244	199	6	658	10.0
Paul Seymour	66	2209	615	206	.335	245	186	.759	225	220	165	4	598	9.1
Noble Jorgensen	66	1318	460	190	.413	187	149	.797	288	63	190	2	529	8.0
George Ratkovicz	66	1356	473	165	.349	242	163	.674	328	90	235	8	493	7.5
Wally Osterkorn	66	1721	413	145	.351	335	199	.594	444	117	226	8	489	7.4
William Gabor	57	1085	538	173	.322	183	142	.776	93	86	188	5	488	8.6
Al Cervi	55	850	280	99	.354	248	219	.883	87	148	176	7	417	7.6
Gerry Calabrese	58	937	317	109	.344	103	73	.709	84	83	107	0	291	5.0
Don Savage	12	118	43	9	.209	28	18	.643	24	12	22	0	36	3.0

PLAYOFF RESULTS

EASTERN DIVISION SEMIFINALS
Syracuse 2, Philadelphia 1

Mar. 20—Philadelphia 83 at Syracuse 102
Mar. 22—Syracuse 95 at Philadelphia 100
Mar. 23—Philadelphia 73 at Syracuse 84

New York 2, Boston 1

Mar. 19—New York 94 at Boston 105
Mar. 23—Boston 97 at New York 101
Mar. 26—New York 88 at Boston **87

WESTERN DIVISION SEMIFINALS
Minneapolis 2, Indianapolis 0

Mar. 23—Indianapolis 70 at Minneapolis 78
Mar. 25—Minneapolis 94 at Indianapolis 87

Rochester 2, Ft. Wayne 0

Mar. 18—Ft. Wayne 78 at Rochester 95
Mar. 20—Rochester 92 at Ft. Wayne 86

EASTERN DIVISION FINALS
New York 3, Syracuse 1

Apr. 2—New York 87 at Syracuse 85
Apr. 3—New York 92 at Syracuse 102
Apr. 4—Syracuse 92 at New York 99
Apr. 8—Syracuse 93 at New York 100

WESTERN DIVISION FINALS
Minneapolis 3, Rochester 1

Mar. 29—Minneapolis 78 at Rochester 88
Mar. 30—Minneapolis 83 at Rochester 78
Apr. 5—Rochester 67 at Minneapolis 77
Apr. 6—Rochester 80 at Minneapolis 82

WORLD CHAMPIONSHIP SERIES
Minneapolis 4, New York 3

Apr. 12—New York 79, Minn. at St. Paul *83
Apr. 13—New York 80, Minn. at St. Paul 72
Apr. 16—Minneapolis 82 at New York 77
Apr. 18—Minneapolis 89 at New York *90
Apr. 20—New York 89, Minn. at St. Paul 102
Apr. 23—Minneapolis 68 at New York 76
Apr. 25—New York 65 at Minneapolis 82

*Denotes overtime period.

1950-51 NBA STATISTICS

1950-51 NBA CHAMPION ROCHESTER ROYALS

Front row (left to right): Bob Davies, Bob Wanzer, William Holzman, Paul Noel, Frank Saul. Rear row: Bill Calhoun, Joe McNamee, Arnold Risen, Jack Coleman, Arnold Johnson. Inset: Coach Lester Harrison.

FINAL STANDINGS

EASTERN DIVISION

Teams	Phil.	Bos.	N.Y.	Syr.	Balt.	Wash.	Mpls.	Roch.	Ft.W.	Ind.	T-C	W.	L.	Pct.	G.B.
Philadelphia	..	4	3	6	6	3	2	4	3	5	4	40	26	.606	.....
Boston	4	..	4	3	6	4	3	2	5	4	4	39	30	.565	2.5
New York	5	4	..	5	5	2	3	3	4	1	4	36	30	.545	4
Syracuse	2	5	5	..	5	2	2	2	3	3	3	32	34	.485	8
Baltimore	3	3	2	3	..	1	2	1	4	2	3	24	42	.364	16
Washington	0	3	1	0	2	..	0	0	1	2	1	10	25	.286	*

WESTERN DIVISION

Teams	Phil.	Bos.	N.Y.	Syr.	Balt.	Wash.	Mpls.	Roch.	Ft.W.	Ind.	T-C	W.	L.	Pct.	G.B.
Minneapolis	4	3	3	4	4	2	..	4	3	7	10	44	24	.647	.....
Rochester	2	4	3	4	5	5	4	..	5	4	5	41	27	.603	3
Ft. Wayne	3	1	2	3	2	3	5	3	..	5	5	32	36	.471	12
Indianapolis	1	1	5	3	4	2	3	5	3	..	4	31	37	.456	13
Tri-Cities	2	2	2	3	3	1	0	3	5	4	..	25	43	.368	19

*The Washington team was disbanded January 9; players assigned to other clubs.

HOME-ROAD-NEUTRAL RECORDS OF ALL TEAMS

	Home	Road	Neutral	Total		Home	Road	Neutral	Total
Baltimore	21- 11	3- 25	0- 6	24- 42	Philadelphia	29- 3	10- 22	1- 1	40- 26
Boston	26- 6	9- 22	4- 2	39- 30	Rochester	29- 5	12- 22	0- 0	41- 27
Ft. Wayne	27- 7	5- 27	0- 2	32- 36	Syracuse	24- 9	8- 25	0- 0	32- 34
Indianapolis	19- 12	10- 24	2- 1	31- 37	Tri-Cities	22- 13	2- 28	1- 2	25- 43
Minneapolis	29- 3	12- 21	3- 0	44- 24	Washington	6- 11	4- 13	0- 1	10- 25
New York	22- 5	10- 25	4- 0	36- 30	Totals	254- 85	85- 254	15-15	354-354

TEAM STATISTICS

Team	G.	FGA	FGM	Pct.	FTA	FTM	Pct.	Reb.	Ast.	PF	Disq.	For	Agst.	Pt.Dif.
Minneapolis	68	5590	2084	.373	1989	1464	.736	3409	1408	1801	49	82.8	77.4	+5.4
Philadelphia	66	5665	1985	.350	2181	1664	.763	3586	1432	1710	61	85.4	81.6	+3.8
Rochester	68	5377	2032	.378	2248	1692	.753	3015	1368	1534	35	84.6	81.7	+2.9
Syracuse	66	5365	1884	.351	2634	1912	.726	3259	1493	1995	64	86.1	85.5	+0.6

Team	G.	FGA	FGM	Pct.	FTA	FTM	Pct.	Reb.	Ast.	PF	Disq.	For	Agst.	Pt.Dif.
New York	66	5380	2037	.379	2231	1592	.714	3421	1551	1810	47	85.8	85.4	+0.4
Boston	69	5607	2065	.368	2415	1751	.725	3499	1579	1881	52	85.2	85.5	—0.3
Ft. Wayne	68	5927	2002	.338	2387	1718	.720	3725	1142	1961	79	84.1	86.0	—1.9
Indianapolis	68	5779	2096	.363	1902	1363	.717	2779	1455	1569	35	81.7	84.0	—2.3
Baltimore	66	5542	1955	.353	2020	1504	.745	3044	1345	1736	53	82.0	84.3	—2.3
Tri-Cities	68	6041	1988	.329	2425	1754	.723	3715	1476	2092	79	84.3	88.0	—3.7
*Washington	35	2893	967	.334	1244	910	.731	1567	584	1050	26	81.3	86.0	—4.7

*Disbanded January 9

INDIVIDUAL LEADERS

POINTS

	G.	FG	FT	Pts.	Avg.		G.	FG	FT	Pts.	Avg.
George Mikan, Minneapolis	68	678	576	1932	28.4	Dwight Eddleman, Tri-Cities	68	398	244	1040	15.3
Alex Groza, Indianapolis	66	492	445	1429	21.7	Fred Schaus, Ft. Wayne	68	312	404	1028	15.1
Ed Macauley, Boston	68	459	466	1384	20.4	Vince Boryla, New York	66	352	278	982	14.9
Joe Fulks, Philadelphia	66	429	378	1236	18.7	Bob Davies, Rochester	63	326	303	955	15.2
Frank Brian, Tri-Cities	68	363	418	1144	16.8	Larry Foust, Ft. Wayne	68	327	261	915	13.5
Paul Arizin, Philadelphia	65	352	417	1121	17.2	Vern Mikkelsen, Minneapolis	64	359	186	904	14.1
Dolph Schayes, Syracuse	66	332	457	1121	17.0	Fred Scolari, Wash.-Syr.	66	302	279	883	13.4
Ralph Beard, Indianapolis	66	409	293	1111	16.8	Ken Murray, Balt.-Ft. Wayne	66	301	248	850	12.9
Bob Cousy, Boston	69	401	276	1078	15.6	George Ratkovicz, Syracuse	66	264	321	849	12.9
Arnie Risen, Rochester	66	377	323	1077	16.3	Harry Gallatin, New York	66	293	259	845	12.8

FIELD GOALS
(Minimum 200 FGM)

	FGA	FGM	Pct.
Alex Groza, Indianapolis	1046	492	.470
Ed Macauley, Boston	985	459	.466
George Mikan, Minneapolis	1584	678	.428
Jack Coleman, Rochester	749	315	.421
Harry Gallatin, New York	705	293	.416
George Ratkovicz, Syracuse	636	264	.415
Paul Arizin, Philadelphia	864	352	.407
Vince Boryla, New York	867	352	.406
Vern Mikkelsen, Minneapolis	893	359	.402
Bob Wanzer, Rochester	628	252	.401

FREE THROWS
(Minimum 170 FTM)

	FTA	FTM	Pct.
Joe Fulks, Philadelphia	442	378	.855
Bob Wanzer, Rochester	273	232	.850
Belus Smawley, Syr.-Balt.	267	227	.850
Fred Scolari, Wash.-Syr.	331	279	.843
Vince Boryla, New York	332	278	.837
Fred Schaus, Ft. Wayne	484	404	.835
Sonny Hertzberg, Boston	270	223	.826
Frank Brian, Tri-Cities	508	418	.823
Al Cervi, Syracuse	237	194	.819
Red Rocha, Baltimore	299	242	.809

ASSISTS

	G.	No.	Avg.
Andy Phillip, Philadelphia	66	414	6.3
Dick McGuire, New York	64	400	6.3
George Senesky, Philadelphia	65	342	5.3
Bob Cousy, Boston	69	341	4.9
Ralph Beard, Indianapolis	66	318	4.8
Bob Davies, Rochester	63	287	4.6
Frank Brian, Tri-Cities	68	266	3.9
Fred Scolari, Wash.-Syr.	66	255	3.9
Ed Macauley, Boston	68	252	3.7
Dolph Schayes, Syracuse	66	251	3.8

REBOUNDS*

	G.	No.	Avg.
Dolph Schayes, Syracuse	66	1080	16.4
George Mikan, Minneapolis	68	958	14.1
Harry Gallatin, New York	66	800	12.1
Arnie Risen, Rochester	66	795	12.0
Alex Groza, Indianapolis	66	709	10.7
Larry Foust, Ft. Wayne	68	681	10.0
Vern Mikkelsen, Minneapolis	64	655	10.2
Paul Arizin, Philadelphia	65	640	9.8
Ed Macauley, Boston	68	616	9.1
Jack Coleman, Rochester	67	584	8.7

*Beginning in the 1950-51 season, the NBA started keeping statistics for rebounds.

TEAM-BY-TEAM INDIVIDUAL STATISTICS

BALTIMORE BULLETS

Player	G.	FGA	FGM	Pct.	FTA	FTM	Pct.	Reb.	Ast.	PF	Disq.	Pts.	Avg.
Red Rocha	64	843	297	.352	299	242	.809	511	147	242	9	836	13.1
Belus Smawley (Syr.-Bal.)	60	663	252	.380	267	227	.850	178	161	145	4	731	12.2
Charles Halbert (Wash.-Bal.)	68	449	164	.365	248	172	.694	539	158	216	7	500	7.4
Walter Budko	64	464	165	.356	223	166	.744	452	135	203	7	496	7.8
Kenneth Sailors (Bos.-Bal.)	60	533	181	.340	180	131	.728	120	150	196	8	493	8.2
Don Rehfeldt	59	426	164	.385	139	103	.741	251	68	146	4	431	7.3
Brady Walker (Bos.-Bal.)	66	416	164	.394	103	72	.699	354	111	82	2	400	6.1
Paul Hoffman	41	399	127	.318	156	105	.673	202	111	135	2	359	8.8
Gene James (N.Y.-Bal.)	48	235	79	.338	71	44	.620	141	70	118	2	202	4.2
William Hassett	30	156	45	.288	60	40	.667	34	46	68	1	130	4.3
Norman Mager	22	126	32	.254	48	37	.771	44	22	56	3	101	4.6
Joseph Dolhon	11	50	15	.300	13	9	.692	15	15	28	1	39	3.5
Ray Ellefson	3	4	0	.000	4	4	1.000	8	0	6	0	4	1.3

BOSTON CELTICS

Player	G.	FGA	FGM	Pct.	FTA	FTM	Pct.	Reb.	Ast.	PF	Disq.	Pts.	Avg.
Ed Macauley	68	985	459	.466	614	466	.759	616	252	205	4	1384	20.4
Robert Cousy	69	1138	401	.352	365	276	.756	474	341	185	2	1078	15.6
Sidney Hertzberg	65	651	206	.316	270	223	.826	260	244	156	4	635	9.8
Charles Cooper	66	601	207	.344	267	201	.753	562	174	219	7	615	9.3
Clarence Hermsen (Tri-C.-Bos.)	71	644	189	.293	237	155	.654	448	92	261	8	533	7.5
Frank Kudelka (Wash.-Bos.)	62	518	179	.346	119	83	.697	158	105	211	8	441	7.1
Robert Donham	68	298	151	.507	229	114	.498	235	139	179	3	416	6.1
Edward Leede	57	370	119	.322	189	140	.741	118	95	144	3	378	6.6
Robert Harris (Ft.W.-Bos.)	56	295	98	.332	127	86	.677	291	64	157	4	282	5.0
Horace McKinney (Wash.-Bos.)	44	327	102	.312	81	58	.716	198	85	136	6	262	6.0
Andrew Duncan	14	40	7	.175	22	15	.682	30	8	27	0	29	2.1
Edward Stanczak	17	48	11	.229	43	35	.814	34	6	6	0	57	3.4

FORT WAYNE PISTONS

Player	G.	FGA	FGM	Pct.	FTA	FTM	Pct.	Reb.	Ast.	PF	Disq.	Pts.	Avg.
Fred Schaus	68	918	312	.340	484	404	.835	495	184	240	11	1028	15.1
Larry Foust	68	944	327	.346	296	261	.659	681	90	247	6	915	13.5
Kenneth Murray (Bal.-Ft.W.)	66	887	301	.339	332	248	.747	355	202	164	7	850	12.9
Jack Kerris	68	689	255	.370	295	201	.681	477	181	253	12	711	10.5
Ralph Johnson	68	737	235	.319	162	114	.704	275	183	247	11	584	8.6
Don Otten (Wash.-Bal.-Ft.W.)	67	479	162	.338	308	246	.799	404	62	255	15	570	8.5
John Oldham	68	597	199	.333	292	171	.586	242	127	242	15	569	8.4
Richard Mehen (Bal.-Bos.-Ft.W.)	66	532	192	.361	123	90	.732	223	188	149	4	474	7.2
Duane Klueh	61	458	157	.343	184	135	.734	183	82	143	5	449	7.4
Paul Armstrong	38	232	72	.310	90	58	.644	89	77	97	2	202	5.3
James Riffey	35	185	65	.351	26	20	.769	61	16	54	0	150	4.3
Arthur Burris	33	113	28	.248	36	21	.583	106	27	51	0	77	2.3

INDIANAPOLIS OLYMPIANS

Player	G.	FGA	FGM	Pct.	FTA	FTM	Pct.	Reb.	Ast.	PF	Disq.	Pts.	Avg.
Alex Groza	66	1046	492	.470	566	445	.786	709	156	237	8	1429	21.7
Ralph Beard	66	1110	409	.368	378	293	.775	251	318	96	0	1111	16.8
Paul Walther	63	634	213	.336	209	145	.694	226	225	201	8	571	9.1
Leo Barnhorst	68	671	232	.346	119	82	.689	296	218	197	1	546	8.0
Robert Lavoy	63	619	221	.357	133	84	.632	310	76	190	2	526	8.3
Joseph Holland	67	594	196	.330	137	78	.569	344	150	228	8	470	7.0
John Mahnken (Bos.-Ind.)	58	351	111	.316	70	45	.643	219	77	164	6	267	4.6
Wallace Jones	22	237	93	.393	77	61	.792	125	85	74	4	247	11.2
Don Lofgran (Syr.-Ind.)	61	270	79	.293	127	79	.622	157	36	132	4	237	3.9
Malcolm McMullan	51	277	78	.282	82	48	.585	128	33	109	2	204	4.0
Clifford Barker	56	202	51	.252	77	50	.649	100	115	98	0	152	2.7
Bruce Hale	26	135	40	.296	23	14	.609	49	42	30	0	94	3.6
Charles Mrazcvich	23	73	24	.329	46	28	.609	33	12	48	1	76	3.3
Carl Shaeffer	10	22	6	.273	3	3	1.000	10	6	15	0	15	1.5
Leon Blevins	3	4	1	.250	1	0	.000	2	1	3	0	2	0.7

MINNEAPOLIS LAKERS

Player	G.	FGA	FGM	Pct.	FTA	FTM	Pct.	Reb.	Ast.	PF	Disq.	Pts.	Avg.
George Mikan	68	1584	678	.428	717	576	.803	958	208	308	14	1932	28.4
Vern Mikkelsen	64	893	359	.402	275	186	.676	655	181	260	13	904	14.1
James Pollard	54	728	256	.352	156	117	.750	484	184	157	4	629	11.6
Slater Martin	68	627	227	.362	177	121	.684	246	235	199	3	575	8.5
Robert Harrison	68	432	150	.347	128	101	.789	172	195	218	5	401	5.9
Arnold Ferrin	68	373	119	.319	164	114	.695	271	107	220	8	352	5.2
Kevin O'Shea	63	267	87	.326	134	97	.724	125	100	99	1	271	4.3
Tony Jaros	63	287	88	.307	103	65	.631	131	72	131	0	241	3.8
Harry Grant	61	184	53	.288	83	52	.627	115	71	106	0	159	2.6
Joseph Hutton	60	180	59	.328	43	29	.674	102	53	89	1	147	2.5

NEW YORK KNICKERBOCKERS

Player	G.	FGA	FGM	Pct.	FTA	FTM	Pct.	Reb.	Ast.	PF	Disq.	Pts.	Avg.
Vincent Boryla	66	867	352	.406	332	278	.837	249	182	244	6	982	14.9
Harry Gallatin	66	705	293	.416	354	259	.732	800	180	244	4	845	12.8
Max Zaslofsky	66	853	302	.354	298	231	.775	228	136	150	3	835	12.7
Connie Simmons	66	613	229	.374	208	146	.702	426	117	222	8	604	9.2
Nat Clifton	65	656	211	.322	263	140	.532	491	162	269	13	562	8.6
Richard McGuire	64	482	179	.371	276	179	.649	334	400	154	2	537	8.4
Ray Lumpp	64	379	153	.404	160	124	.775	125	115	160	2	430	6.7
Ernest Vandeweghe	44	336	135	.402	97	68	.701	195	121	144	6	338	7.7
George Kaftan	61	286	111	.388	125	78	.624	153	74	102	1	300	4.9
Goebel Ritter	34	297	100	.379	71	49	.690	65	37	52	1	127	3.7
Tony Lavelli	30	93	32	.344	41	35	.854	59	23	56	1	99	3.3

PHILADELPHIA WARRIORS

Player	G.	FGA	FGM	Pct.	FTA	FTM	Pct.	Reb.	Ast.	PF	Disq.	Pts.	Avg.
Joseph Fulks	66	1358	429	.316	442	378	.855	523	117	247	8	1236	18.7
Paul Arizin	65	864	352	.407	526	417	.793	640	138	284	18	1121	17.2
Andrew Phillip	66	690	275	.399	253	190	.751	446	414	221	8	740	11.2
George Senesky	65	703	249	.354	238	181	.761	326	342	144	1	679	10.4
William Closs	65	631	202	.320	223	166	.744	401	110	156	4	570	8.8
Edward Mikan (Roch.-Wash.-Phil.)	61	556	193	.347	189	137	.725	344	63	194	6	523	8.6
Vern Gardner	61	383	129	.337	97	69	.711	237	89	149	6	327	5.4
Ron Livingstone	63	353	104	.295	109	76	.697	297	76	220	10	284	4.5
Nelson Bobb	53	158	52	.329	79	44	.557	101	82	83	1	148	2.8
Leo Mogus	57	122	43	.353	86	53	.616	102	32	60	0	139	2.4
Costic Borsavage	24	74	26	.351	18	12	.667	24	4	34	1	64	2.7
Easy Parham	7	7	3	.429	9	4	.444	12	3	5	0	10	1.4

ROCHESTER ROYALS

Player	G.	FGA	FGM	Pct.	FTA	FTM	Pct.	Reb.	Ast.	PF	Disq.	Pts.	Avg.
Arnold Risen	66	940	377	.401	440	323	.734	795	158	278	9	1077	16.3
Robert Davies	63	877	326	.372	381	303	.795	197	287	208	7	955	15.2
Jack Coleman	67	749	315	.421	172	134	.779	584	197	193	4	764	11.4
Robert Wanzer	68	628	252	.401	273	232	.850	232	181	129	0	736	10.8
Arnitz Johnson	68	403	185	.459	371	269	.725	449	175	290	11	639	9.4
William Calhoun	66	506	175	.346	228	161	.706	199	99	87	1	511	7.7
William Holzman	68	561	183	.326	179	130	.726	152	147	94	0	496	7.3
Frank Saul	65	310	105	.339	105	72	.686	84	68	85	0	282	4.3
Paul Noel	52	174	49	.282	45	32	.711	81	34	61	1	130	2.5
Joseph McNamee	60	167	48	.287	42	27	.643	101	18	88	2	123	2.1

SYRACUSE NATIONALS

Player	G.	FGA	FGM	Pct.	FTA	FTM	Pct.	Reb.	Ast.	PF	Disq.	Pts.	Avg.
Dolph Schayes	66	930	332	.357	608	457	.752	1080	251	271	9	1121	17.0
Fred Scolari (Wash.-Syr.)	66	923	302	.327	331	279	.843	218	255	183	1	883	13.4
George Ratkovicz	66	636	264	.415	439	321	.731	547	193	256	11	849	12.9
William Gabor	61	745	255	.342	242	179	.740	150	125	213	7	689	11.3
Noble Jorgensen (Tri-C.-Syr.)	63	600	223	.372	265	182	.687	338	91	237	8	628	10.0
Alex Hannum	63	494	182	.368	197	107	.543	301	119	271	16	471	7.5
Al Cervi	53	346	132	.382	237	194	.819	152	208	180	9	458	8.6
John Macknowski	58	435	131	.301	170	122	.718	110	69	134	3	384	6.6
Paul Seymour	51	385	125	.325	159	117	.736	194	187	138	0	367	7.2
Gerry Calabrese	46	197	70	.355	88	61	.693	65	65	80	0	201	4.4
Leroy Chollet	14	51	6	.118	19	12	.632	15	12	29	0	24	1.7

TRI-CITIES BLACKHAWKS

Player	G.	FGA	FGM	Pct.	FTA	FTM	Pct.	Reb.	Ast.	PF	Disq.	Pts.	Avg.
Frank Brian	68	1127	363	.322	508	418	.823	244	266	215	4	1144	16.8
Dwight Eddleman	68	1120	398	.355	349	244	.699	410	170	231	5	1040	15.3
Marko Todorovich	66	715	221	.309	301	211	.701	455	179	197	5	653	9.9
Cal Christensen	67	445	134	.301	245	175	.714	523	161	266	19	443	6.6
Warren Perkins	66	428	135	.315	195	126	.646	319	143	232	13	396	6.0
Edward Peterson (Syr.-Tri-C.)	53	384	130	.339	150	99	.660	288	66	188	9	359	6.8
Harry Boykoff (Bos.-Tri-C.)	48	336	126	.375	100	74	.740	220	60	197	12	326	6.8
Robert Carpenter (Ft. W.-Tri-C.)	56	355	109	.307	128	105	.820	229	79	115	2	323	5.8
John Logan	29	257	81	.315	83	62	.747	134	127	66	2	224	7.7
Thomas Byrnes (Bal-Wash-T-C)	48	275	83	.302	84	55	.655	72	69	86	0	221	4.6
Ray Corley	18	85	29	.341	29	16	.552	43	38	26	0	74	4.1
Herbert Scherer	20	84	24	.286	35	20	.571	50	17	56	1	68	3.4
John Hargis (Ft. W.-Tri-C.)	14	66	25	.379	24	17	.708	30	9	26	0	67	4.8
Edward Beach (Mpls.-Tri-C.)	12	38	8	.211	9	6	.667	25	3	14	0	22	1.8
Jack Nichols	5	48	18	.375	13	10	.769	52	14	18	0	46	9.2
Gene Vance	28	110	44	.400	61	43	.705	88	53	91	0	131	4.7
Hank DeZonie	5	25	6	.240	7	5	.714	18	9	6	0	17	3.4
Edward Gayda	14	42	18	.429	23	18	.783	38	13	32	0	54	3.9

WASHINGTON CAPITOLS

Player	G.	FGA	FGM	Pct.	FTA	FTM	Pct.	Reb.	Ast.	PF	Disq.	Pts.	Avg.
William Sharman	31	361	141	.391	108	96	.889	96	39	86	3	378	12.2
Richard Schnittker	29	219	85	.388	139	123	.866	153	42	76	0	293	10.1
Ariel Maughan	35	250	78	.312	120	101	.842	141	48	91	2	257	7.3
Alan Sawyer	33	215	87	.405	54	43	.796	125	25	75	1	217	6.6
Edward Bartels	17	97	24	.247	46	24	.522	84	12	54	0	72	4.2
Richard O'Keefe	17	102	21	.206	39	25	.641	37	25	48	0	67	3.9
Charles Gilmur	16	61	17	.279	32	17	.531	75	17	57	3	51	3.2
Earl Lloyd	7	35	16	.457	13	11	.846	47	11	26	0	43	6.1
Don Carlson	9	46	17	.370	16	8	.500	15	19	23	0	42	4.7
Thomas O'Keefe	6	28	10	.357	4	3	.750	7	10	5	0	23	3.8
John Norlander	9	19	6	.316	14	9	.643	9	5	14	0	21	2.3

(Washington team disbanded January 9; players assigned to other clubs.)

PLAYOFF RESULTS

EASTERN DIVISION SEMIFINALS
New York 2, Boston 0
Mar. 20—New York 83 at Boston 69
Mar. 22—Boston 78 at New York 92

Syracuse 2, Philadelphia 0
Mar. 20—Syracuse 91 at Philadelphia *89
Mar. 22—Philadelphia 78 at Syracuse 90

WESTERN DIVISION SEMIFINALS
Rochester 2, Fort Wayne 1
Mar. 20—Fort Wayne 81 at Rochester 110
Mar. 22—Rochester 78 at Fort Wayne 83
Mar. 24—Fort Wayne 78 at Rochester 97

Minneapolis 2, Indianapolis 1
Mar. 21—Indianapolis 81 at Minneapolis.......................................95
Mar. 23—Minneapolis 88 at Indianapolis......................................108
Mar. 25—Indianapolis 80 at Minneapolis..85

EASTERN DIVISION FINALS
New York 3, Syracuse 2
Mar. 28—Syracuse 92 at New York 103
Mar. 29—New York 80 at Syracuse..............................102
Mar. 31—Syracuse 75 at New York..............................97
Apr. 1—New York 83 at Syracuse 90
Apr. 4—Syracuse 81 at New York 83

WESTERN DIVISION FINALS
Rochester 3, Minneapolis 1
Mar. 29—Rochester 73 at Minneapolis 76
Mar. 31—Rochester 70 at Minneapolis 66
Apr. 1—Minneapolis 70 at Rochester 83
Apr. 3—Minneapolis 75 at Rochester...80

WORLD CHAMPIONSHIP SERIES
Rochester 4, New York 3
Apr. 7—New York 65 at Rochester 92
Apr. 8—New York 84 at Rochester 99
Apr. 11—Rochester 78 at New York 71
Apr. 13—Rochester 73 at New York 79
Apr. 15—New York 92 at Rochester 89
Apr. 18—Rochester 73 at New York 80
Apr. 21—New York 75 at Rochester 79

*Denotes overtime period.

1949-50 NBA STATISTICS

1949-50 NBA CHAMPION MINNEAPOLIS LAKERS

Left to right: Slater Martin, Billy Hassett, Don Carlson, Herm Schaefer, Bob Harrison, Tony Jaros, Coach John Kundla, Bud Grant, Arnie Ferrin, Jim Pollard, Vern Mikkelsen, George Mikan.

FINAL STANDINGS

EASTERN DIVISION

Team	Syr.	N.Y.	Was.	Phil.	Balt.	Bos.	Mpls.	Roch.	Ft.W.	Chi.	St.L.	Ind.	And.	TriC.	Sheb.	Wat.	Den.	W.	L.	Pct.	G.B.
Syracuse	..	2	1	2	2	2	1	1	2	2	1	7	4	6	6	6	6	51	13	.797	....
New York	0	..	5	5	5	5	1	1	2	4	4	1	1	1	1	2	2	40	28	.588	13
Washington	0	1	..	4	3	3	2	1	2	2	2	0	1	1	2	2	2	32	36	.471	21
Philadelphia	1	1	2	..	4	3	0	0	4	3	6	1	1	1	0	1	2	26	42	.382	27
Baltimore	0	1	2	3	..	2	1	3	3	1	3	1	1	0	2	1	1	25	43	.368	28
Boston	0	1	3	3	4	..	1	0	2	0	2	1	2	0	1	1	1	22	46	.324	31

CENTRAL DIVISION

Team	Syr.	N.Y.	Was.	Phil.	Balt.	Bos.	Mpls.	Roch.	Ft.W.	Chi.	St.L.	Ind.	And.	TriC.	Sheb.	Wat.	Den.	W.	L.	Pct.	G.B.
Minneapolis	1	5	6	4	5	5	..	3	4	4	5	1	1	2	1	2	2	51	17	.750	....
Rochester	1	5	6	5	3	6	3	..	3	4	5	1	2	2	1	2	2	51	17	.750	....
Fort Wayne	0	4	2	4	3	4	2	3	..	4	5	1	1	2	2	1	2	40	28	.588	11
Chicago	0	2	3	4	5	6	2	2	2	..	5	1	1	1	2	2	2	40	28	.588	11
St. Louis	1	2	0	4	3	4	1	1	1	1	..	1	0	2	2	1	2	26	42	.382	25

WESTERN DIVISION

Team	Syr.	N.Y.	Was.	Phil.	Balt.	Bos.	Mpls.	Roch.	Ft.W.	Chi.	St.L.	Ind.	And.	TriC.	Sheb.	Wat.	Den.	W.	L.	Pct.	G.B.
Indianapolis	2	1	1	2	1	1	1	1	1	1	1	..	5	4	5	5	7	39	25	.609	....
Anderson	3	1	1	1	1	0	1	0	1	1	2	2	..	7	5	7	4	37	27	.578	2
Tri-Cities	1	1	1	1	2	2	0	0	0	1	0	3	2	..	4	4	7	29	35	.453	10
Sheboygan	1	1	2	0	0	1	1	1	0	0	0	2	2	3	..	4	4	22	40	.355	16
Waterloo	1	0	1	0	1	1	0	0	1	0	1	2	0	3	3	..	5	19	43	.306	19
Denver	1	0	0	0	1	1	0	0	0	0	0	0	3	0	3	2	..	11	51	.177	27

HOME-ROAD-NEUTRAL RECORDS OF ALL TEAMS

	Home	Road	Neutral	Total		Home	Road	Neutral	Total
Anderson	23- 9	11- 18	3- 0	37- 27	Philadelphia	15- 15	8- 23	3- 4	26- 42
Baltimore	16- 15	8- 25	1- 3	25- 43	Rochester	33- 1	17- 16	1- 0	51- 17
Boston	12- 14	5- 28	5- 4	22- 46	St. Louis	17- 14	7- 26	2- 2	26- 42
Chicago	18- 6	14- 21	8- 1	40- 28	Sheboygan	17- 14	5- 22	0- 4	22- 40
Denver	9- 15	1- 26	1-10	11- 51	Syracuse	31- 1	15- 12	5- 0	51- 13
Ft. Wayne	28- 6	12- 22	0- 0	40- 28	Tri-Cities	22- 13	4- 20	3- 2	29- 35
Indianapolis	23- 5	13- 18	3- 2	39- 25	Washington	21- 13	10- 20	1- 3	32- 36
Minneapolis	30- 1	18- 16	3- 0	51- 17	Waterloo	17- 15	1- 22	1- 6	19- 43
New York	19- 10	18- 16	3- 2	40- 28	Totals	351-167	167-351	43-43	561-561

TEAM STATISTICS

Team	G	FGA	FGM	Pct.	FTA	FTM	Pct.	Ast.	PF	For	Agst.	Pt.Dif.
Minneapolis	68	5832	2139	.367	1943	1439	.741	1406	1672	84.1	75.7	+ 8.4
Syracuse	64	5276	1869	.354	2396	1691	.706	1473	1833	84.8	76.7	+ 8.1
Rochester	68	5247	1956	.373	2319	1690	.729	1383	1585	82.4	74.6	+ 7.8
Anderson	64	6254	1943	.311	2343	1703	.727	1240	1806	87.3	83.6	+ 3.7
Indianapolis	64	5283	1982	.375	2145	1529	.713	1342	1676	85.8	82.1	+ 3.7
New York	68	5351	1889	.353	2404	1710	.711	1308	1718	80.7	78.6	+ 2.1
Chicago	68	5892	2003	.340	1934	1346	.696	1366	1977	78.7	77.1	+ 1.6
Ft. Wayne	68	5901	1878	.318	2331	1634	.701	1364	2065	79.3	77.9	+ 1.4
Tri-Cities	64	5515	1818	.330	2308	1677	.727	1330	2057	83.0	83.6	− 0.6
Washington	68	5493	1813	.330	2111	1575	.746	1057	1837	76.5	77.4	− 0.9
Boston	68	5756	1945	.338	2163	1530	.707	1473	1644	79.7	82.2	− 2.5
St. Louis	68	5086	1741	.342	2149	1528	.711	1285	1596	73.7	76.5	− 2.8
Philadelphia	68	5711	1779	.312	2037	1425	.700	1142	1768	73.3	76.4	− 3.1
Sheboygan	62	5022	1727	.344	2338	1654	.707	1279	1766	82.4	87.8	− 5.4
Waterloo	62	4904	1746	.356	2002	1429	.714	1324	1780	79.4	84.9	− 5.5
Baltimore	68	5516	1712	.310	2123	1549	.730	1189	1792	73.1	78.7	− 5.6
Denver	62	5182	1731	.334	1999	1355	.678	1044	1692	77.7	89.1	−11.4

INDIVIDUAL LEADERS

POINTS

	G.	FG	FT	Pts.	Avg.		G.	FG	FT	Pts.	Avg.
George Mikan, Minneapolis	68	649	567	1865	27.4	Joe Fulks, Philadelphia	68	336	293	965	14.2
Alex Groza, Indianapolis	64	521	454	1496	23.4	Ralph Beard, Indianapolis	60	340	215	895	14.9
Frank Brian, Anderson	64	368	402	1138	17.8	Bob Davies, Rochester	64	317	261	895	14.0
Max Zaslofsky, Chicago	68	397	321	1115	16.4	Dick Mehen, Waterloo	62	347	198	892	14.4
Ed Macauley, St. Louis	67	351	379	1081	16.1	Jack Nichols, Wash.-Tri-C	67	310	259	879	13.1
Dolph Schayes, Syracuse	64	348	376	1072	16.8	Ed Sadowski, Phila.-Balt.	69	299	274	872	12.6
Carl Braun, New York	67	373	285	1031	15.4	Paul Hoffman, Baltimore	60	312	242	866	14.4
Ken Sailors, Denver	57	329	329	987	17.3	Fred Scolari, Washington	66	312	236	860	13.0
Jim Pollard, Minneapolis	66	394	185	973	14.7	Vern Gardner, Philadelphia	63	313	227	853	13.5
Fred Schaus, Ft. Wayne	68	351	270	972	14.3	Belus Smawley, St. Louis	61	287	260	834	13.7

FIELD GOALS
(Minimum 200 FGM)

	FGA	FGM	Pct.
Alex Groza, Indianapolis	1090	521	.478
Dick Mehen, Waterloo	826	347	.420
Bob Wanzer, Rochester	614	254	.414
Harry Boykoff, Waterloo	698	288	.413
George Mikan, Minneapolis	1595	649	.407
Red Rocha, St. Louis	679	275	.405
John Hargis, Anderson	550	223	.405
Vern Mikkelsen, Minneapolis	722	288	.399
Ed Macauley, St. Louis	882	351	.398
Jack Toomay, Denver	514	204	.397

FREE THROWS
(Minimum 170 FTM)

	FTA	FTM	Pct.
Max Zaslofsky, Chicago	381	321	.843
Chick Reiser, Washington	254	212	.835
Al Cervi, Syracuse	346	287	.829
Belus Smawley, St. Louis	314	260	.828
Francis Curran, Rochester	241	199	.826
Frank Brian, Anderson	488	402	.824
Fred Scolari, Washington	287	236	.822
Fred Schaus, Ft. Wayne	330	270	.818
Leo Kubiak, Waterloo	236	192	.814
Bob Wanzer, Rochester	351	283	.806

ASSISTS

	G.	No.	Avg.
Dick McGuire, New York	68	386	5.7
Andy Phillip, Chicago	65	377	5.8
Bob Davies, Rochester	64	294	4.6
George Senesky, Philadelphia	68	264	3.9
Al Cervi, Syracuse	56	264	4.7
Dolph Schayes, Syracuse	64	259	4.0
Jim Pollard, Minneapolis	66	252	3.8
Jim Seminoff, Boston	65	249	3.8
Carl Braun, New York	67	247	3.7
John Logan, St. Louis	62	240	3.9

TEAM-BY-TEAM INDIVIDUAL STATISTICS

ANDERSON PACKERS

Player	G.	FGA	FGM	Pct.	FTA	FTM	Pct.	Ast.	PF	Pts.	Avg.
Frank Brian	64	1156	368	.318	488	402	.824	189	192	1138	17.8
William Closs	64	898	283	.315	259	186	.718	160	190	752	11.8
Charles Black (36 Ft.W.-29 And.)	65	813	226	.278	321	209	.651	163	273	661	10.2
John Hargis	60	550	223	.405	277	197	.711	102	170	643	10.7
Milo Komenich	64	861	244	.283	250	146	.584	124	246	634	9.9
Edward Stanczak	57	456	159	.349	270	203	.752	67	166	521	9.1
Richard Niemiera (31 Ft.W.-29 And.)	60	350	110	.314	139	104	.748	116	77	324	5.4
Frank Gates	64	402	113	.281	98	61	.622	91	147	287	4.5
Rollie Seltz	34	309	93	.301	104	80	.769	64	72	266	7.8
James Owens (26 Tri. C.-35 And.)	61	288	86	.299	101	68	.673	73	152	240	3.9
Jake Carter (13 Den.-11 And.)	24	75	23	.307	53	36	.679	24	59	82	3.4
Murray Mitchell	2	3	1	.333	0	0	.000	2	1	2	1.0

BALTIMORE BULLETS

Player	G.	FGA	FGM	Pct.	FTA	FTM	Pct.	Ast.	PF	Pts.	Avg.
Edward Sadowski (17 Phil.-52 Balt.)	69	922	299	.324	373	274	.735	136	244	872	12.6
Paul Hoffman	60	914	312	.341	364	242	.665	161	234	866	14.4
William Towery	68	678	222	.327	202	153	.757	142	244	597	8.8
Walter Budko	66	652	198	.304	263	199	.757	146	259	595	9.0
Joseph Dolhon	64	458	143	.312	214	157	.734	155	193	443	6.9

Player	G.	FGA	FGM	Pct.	FTA	FTM	Pct.	Ast.	PF	Pts.	Avg.
Thomas Byrnes	53	397	120	.302	124	87	.702	88	76	327	6.2
Stanley Von Nieda	59	336	120	.357	115	73	.635	143	127	313	5.3
Les Pugh	56	273	68	.249	136	115	.846	16	118	251	4.5
Harry Jeannette	37	148	42	.284	133	109	.820	93	82	193	5.2
Marvin Schatzman	34	174	43	.247	50	29	.580	38	49	115	3.4
Andrew O'Donnell	25	108	38	.352	18	14	.778	17	32	90	3.6
John Mandic (22 Wash.-3 Balt.)	25	75	22	.293	32	22	.688	8	54	66	2.6
George Feigenbaum	12	57	14	.246	18	8	.444	10	15	36	3.0
Tony Janotta	9	30	9	.300	16	13	.813	4	10	31	3.4
Paul Gordon	4	6	0	.000	5	3	.600	3	3	3	0.8
Richard Triptow	4	5	0	.000	2	2	1.000	1	5	2	0.5
Lee Knorek	1	2	0	.000	0	0	.000	0	4	0	0.0

BOSTON CELTICS

Player	G.	FGA	FGM	Pct.	FTA	FTM	Pct.	Ast.	PF	Pts.	Avg.
Sidney Hertzberg	68	865	275	.318	191	143	.749	200	153	693	10.2
Robert Kinney	60	621	233	.375	320	201	.628	100	251	667	11.1
Howard Shannon	67	646	222	.344	182	143	.786	174	148	587	8.8
Edward Leede	64	507	174	.343	316	223	.706	130	167	571	8.9
George Kaftan	55	535	199	.372	208	136	.654	145	92	534	9.7
Brady Walker	68	583	218	.374	114	72	.632	109	100	508	7.5
Tony Lavelli	56	436	162	.372	197	168	.853	40	107	492	8.8
James Seminoff	65	283	85	.300	188	142	.755	249	154	312	4.8
John Mahnken (2 Ft.W.-36 Tri C.-24 Bos.)	62	495	132	.267	115	77	.670	108	231	341	5.5
Robert Doll	47	347	120	.346	114	75	.658	108	117	315	6.7
John Ezersky (38 Balt.-16 Bos.)	54	487	143	.294	183	127	.694	86	139	413	7.6
Joseph Mullaney	37	70	9	.129	15	12	.800	52	30	30	0.8
Arthur Spector	7	12	2	.167	4	1	.250	3	4	5	0.7

CHICAGO STAGS

Player	G.	FGA	FGM	Pct.	FTA	FTM	Pct.	Ast.	PF	Pts.	Avg.
Max Zaslofsky	68	1132	397	.351	381	321	.843	155	185	1115	16.4
Andrew Phillip	65	814	284	.349	270	190	.704	377	210	758	11.7
Marion Spears	68	775	277	.357	230	158	.687	159	250	712	10.5
Clarence Hermsen	67	615	196	.319	247	153	.619	98	267	545	8.1
Stanley Miasek	68	462	176	.381	221	146	.661	75	264	498	7.3
Leo Barnhorst	67	499	174	.349	129	90	.698	140	192	438	6.5
Frank Kudelka	65	528	172	.326	140	89	.636	132	198	433	6.7
Kenneth Rollins	66	421	144	.342	89	66	.742	131	129	354	5.4
Joseph Graboski	57	247	75	.304	89	53	.596	37	95	203	3.6
George Nostrand (18 Bos-1 Tri C-36 Chi)	55	255	78	.306	99	56	.566	29	118	212	3.9
Joseph Bradley	46	134	36	.269	38	15	.395	36	51	87	1.9
Robert Hahn	10	13	4	.308	7	2	.286	1	17	10	1.0

DENVER NUGGETS

Player	G.	FGA	FGM	Pct.	FTA	FTM	Pct.	Ast.	PF	Pts.	Avg.
Kenneth Sailors	57	944	329	.349	456	329	.721	229	242	987	17.3
Robert Brown	62	764	276	.361	252	172	.683	101	269	724	11.7
Dillard Crocker	53	740	245	.292	317	233	.735	85	223	723	13.6
Jack Toomay	62	514	204	.397	264	186	.705	94	213	594	9.6
Floyd Volker (17 Ind.-37 Den.)	54	527	163	.309	129	71	.550	112	169	397	7.4
Jack Cotton	54	332	97	.292	161	82	.509	65	184	276	5.1
James Darden	26	243	78	.321	80	55	.688	67	67	211	8.1
Robert Royer	42	231	78	.338	58	41	.707	85	72	197	4.7
William Herman	13	65	25	.385	11	6	.545	15	13	56	4.3
James Browne	31	48	17	.354	27	13	.481	8	16	47	1.5
Earl Dodd	9	27	6	.222	5	3	.600	6	13	15	1.7

FT. WAYNE PISTONS

Player	G.	FGA	FGM	Pct.	FTA	FTM	Pct.	Ast.	PF	Pts.	Avg.
Fred Schaus	68	996	351	.352	330	270	.818	176	232	972	14.3
Robert Carpenter	66	617	212	.344	256	190	.742	92	168	614	9.3
Ralph Johnson (35 And.-32 Ft.W.)	67	779	243	.312	129	104	.806	171	207	590	8.8
Howard Schultz (35 And.-32 Ft.W.)	67	771	179	.232	282	196	.695	169	244	554	8.3
Jack Kerris (4 Tri C.-64 Ft.W.)	68	481	157	.326	260	169	.650	119	175	483	7.1
Robert Harris	62	465	168	.361	223	140	.628	129	190	476	7.7
Duane Klueh (33 Den.-19 Ft.W.)	52	414	159	.384	222	157	.707	91	111	475	9.1
Paul Armstrong	63	516	144	.279	241	170	.705	170	217	458	7.3
Leo Klier	66	516	157	.304	190	141	.742	121	177	455	6.9
John Oldham	59	426	127	.298	145	103	.710	99	192	357	6.1
Clint Wager	63	203	57	.281	47	29	.617	90	175	143	2.3
Jerry Nagel	14	28	6	.214	4	1	.250	18	11	13	0.9

INDIANAPOLIS OLYMPIANS

Player	G.	FGA	FGM	Pct.	FTA	FTM	Pct.	Ast.	PF	Pts.	Avg.
Alex Groza	64	1090	521	.478	623	454	.729	162	221	1496	23.4
Ralph Beard	60	936	340	.363	282	215	.762	233	132	895	14.9
Wallace Jones	60	706	264	.374	297	223	.751	194	241	751	12.5
Bruce Hale	64	614	217	.353	285	223	.782	226	143	657	10.3
Joseph Holland	64	453	145	.320	142	98	.690	130	220	388	6.1
Malcolm McMullan	58	380	123	.324	141	77	.546	87	212	323	5.6
Paul Walther (22 Mpls.-31 Ind.)	53	290	114	.393	109	63	.578	56	123	291	5.5
Clifford Barker	49	274	102	.372	106	75	.708	109	99	279	5.7
Marshall Hawkins	39	195	55	.282	61	42	.689	51	87	152	3.9
Carl Shaeffer	43	160	59	.369	57	32	.561	40	103	150	3.5
Robert Evans	47	200	56	.280	44	30	.682	55	99	142	3.0
Jack Parkinson	4	12	1	.083	1	1	1.000	2	3	3	0.8

MINNEAPOLIS LAKERS

Player	G.	FGA	FGM	Pct.	FTA	FTM	Pct.	Ast.	PF	Pts.	Avg.
George Mikan	68	1595	649	.407	728	567	.779	197	297	1865	27.4
James Pollard	66	1140	394	.346	242	185	.764	252	143	973	14.7
Vern Mikkelsen	68	722	288	.399	286	215	.752	123	222	791	11.6
Arnold Ferrin	63	396	132	.333	109	76	.697	95	147	340	5.4
Herman Schaefer	65	314	122	.389	101	86	.851	203	104	330	5.1
Robert Harrison	66	348	125	.359	74	50	.676	131	175	300	4.5
William Hassett (18 Tri C.-42 Mpls.)	60	302	84	.278	161	104	.646	137	136	272	4.5
Slater Martin	67	302	106	.351	93	59	.634	148	162	271	4.0
Don Carlson	57	290	99	.341	95	69	.726	76	126	267	4.7
Tony Jaros	61	289	84	.291	96	72	.750	60	106	240	3.9
Harry Grant	35	115	42	.365	17	7	.412	19	36	91	2.6
Norman Glick	1	1	1	1.000	0	0	.000	1	2	2	2.0

NEW YORK KNICKERBOCKERS

Player	G.	FGA	FGM	Pct.	FTA	FTM	Pct.	Ast.	PF	Pts.	Avg.
Carl Braun	67	1024	373	.364	374	285	.762	247	188	1031	15.4
Harry Gallatin	68	664	263	.396	366	277	.757	56	215	803	11.8
Connie Simmons	60	729	241	.331	299	198	.662	102	203	680	11.3
Vincent Boryla	59	600	204	.340	267	204	.764	95	203	612	10.4
Richard McGuire	68	563	190	.337	313	204	.652	386	160	584	8.6
Ernest Vandeweghe	42	390	164	.421	140	93	.664	78	126	421	10.0
Goebel Ritter	62	297	100	.337	176	125	.710	51	101	325	5.2
Ray Lumpp	58	283	91	.322	108	86	.796	90	117	268	4.6
Harry Donovan	45	275	90	.327	106	73	.689	38	107	253	5.6
Paul Noel	65	291	98	.337	87	53	.609	67	132	249	3.8
Wm. Van Breda Kolff	56	167	55	.329	134	96	.716	78	111	206	3.7
Gene James	29	64	19	.297	31	14	.452	20	53	52	1.8
Edward Bartels (13 Den.-2 N.Y.)	15	86	22	.256	33	19	.576	20	29	63	4.3

PHILADELPHIA WARRIORS

Player	G.	FGA	FGM	Pct.	FTA	FTM	Pct.	Ast.	PF	Pts.	Avg.
Joseph Fulks	68	1209	336	.278	421	293	.696	56	240	965	14.2
Vern Gardner	63	916	313	.342	296	227	.767	119	236	853	13.5
George Senesky	68	709	227	.320	223	157	.704	264	164	611	9.0
Leo Mogus	64	434	172	.396	300	218	.727	99	169	562	8.8
Francis Crossin	64	574	185	.322	101	79	.782	148	139	449	7.0
Ron Livingstone (16 Balt.-38 Phil.)	54	579	163	.282	177	122	.689	141	260	448	8.3
Jerry Fleishman	65	353	102	.289	151	93	.616	118	129	297	4.6
Jake Bornheimer	60	305	88	.289	117	78	.667	40	111	254	4.2
Nelson Bobb	57	248	80	.323	131	82	.626	46	97	242	4.2
Al Guokas (41 Den.-16 Phil.)	57	299	93	.331	50	28	.560	95	143	214	3.8
Fred Lewis (18 Balt.-16 Phil.)	34	184	46	.250	32	25	.781	25	40	117	3.4
Michael Novak (5 Roch.-55 Phil.)	60	149	37	.248	47	25	.532	61	139	99	1.7
Charles Parsley	9	31	8	.258	7	6	.857	8	7	22	2.4
James Nolan	5	21	4	.190	0	0	.000	4	14	8	1.6
Jerry Rullo	4	9	3	.333	1	1	1.000	2	2	7	1.8

ROCHESTER ROYALS

Player	G.	FGA	FGM	Pct.	FTA	FTM	Pct.	Ast.	PF	Pts.	Avg.
Robert Davies	64	887	317	.357	347	261	.752	294	187	895	14.0
Robert Wanzer	67	614	254	.414	351	283	.806	214	102	791	11.8
Arnold Risen	62	598	206	.344	321	213	.664	92	228	625	10.1
Jack Coleman	68	663	250	.377	121	90	.744	153	223	590	8.7
William Calhoun	62	549	207	.377	203	146	.719	115	100	560	9.0
William Holzman	68	625	206	.330	210	144	.686	200	67	556	8.2
Arnitz Johnson	68	376	149	.396	294	200	.680	141	260	498	7.3
Francis Curran	66	235	98	.417	241	199	.826	71	113	395	6.0
Andrew Duncan	67	289	125	.433	108	60	.556	42	160	310	4.6
Edward Mikan (21 Chi.-44 Roch.)	65	321	89	.277	120	92	.767	42	143	270	4.2
Frank Saul	49	183	74	.404	47	34	.723	28	33	182	3.7
Price Brookfield	7	23	11	.478	13	12	.923	1	7	34	4.9

ST. LOUIS BOMBERS

Player	G.	FGA	FGM	Pct.	FTA	FTM	Pct.	Ast.	PF	Pts.	Avg.
Edward Macauley	67	882	351	.398	528	379	.718	200	221	1081	16.1
Belus Smawley	61	832	287	.345	314	260	.828	215	160	834	13.7
Red Rocha	65	679	275	.405	313	220	.703	155	257	770	11.8
John Logan	62	759	251	.331	323	253	.783	240	206	755	12.2
Ariel Maughan	68	574	160	.279	205	157	.766	101	174	477	7.0
Easy Parham	66	421	137	.325	178	88	.494	132	158	362	5.5
Dermott O'Connell (37 Bos.-24 St. L.)	61	425	111	.261	89	47	.528	91	91	269	4.4
William Roberts	67	222	77	.347	39	28	.718	24	90	182	2.7
Mac Otten (12 Tri C.-47 St.L.)	59	155	51	.329	81	40	.494	36	119	142	2.4
Don Putnam	57	200	51	.255	52	33	.635	90	116	135	2.4
D. C. Wilcutt	37	73	24	.329	42	29	.690	49	27	77	2.1
Michael McCarron (3 Bal.-5 St. L.)	8	15	3	.200	5	3	.600	3	5	9	1.1

SHEBOYGAN REDSKINS

Player	G.	FGA	FGM	Pct.	FTA	FTM	Pct.	Ast.	PF	Pts.	Avg.
Max Morris	62	694	252	.363	415	277	.667	194	172	781	12.6
Robert Brannum	59	718	234	.326	355	245	.690	205	279	713	12.1
Noble Jorgensen	54	618	218	.353	350	268	.766	90	201	704	13.0
Jack Burmaster	61	711	237	.333	182	124	.681	179	237	598	9.8
Robert Cook	51	620	222	.358	181	143	.790	158	114	587	11.5
Milt Schoon	62	366	150	.410	300	196	.653	84	190	496	8.0
George Sobek	60	251	95	.378	205	156	.761	95	158	346	5.8
Stanley Patrick (34 Wat.-19 Shey.)	53	294	116	.395	147	89	.605	74	76	321	6.1
Walter Lautenbach	55	332	100	.301	55	38	.691	73	122	238	4.3

Alex Groza of Indianapolis was a first-team All-Star in 1949-50 when he averaged 23.4 points a game.

Player	G.	FGA	FGM	Pct.	FTA	FTM	Pct.	Ast.	PF	Pts.	Avg.
Jack Phelan (15 Wat.-40 Shey.)	55	268	87	.325	90	52	.578	57	151	226	4.1
Richard Schulz (13 Wash-8 TriC-29 Shey)	50	212	63	.297	110	83	.755	66	106	209	4.2
Matthew Mazza	26	110	33	.300	45	32	.711	27	34	98	3.8
John Chaney (6 Tri C.-10 Shey.)	16	86	25	.291	29	20	.690	20	23	70	4.4
Daniel Wagner	11	54	19	.352	35	31	.886	18	22	69	6.3
Glen Selbo	13	51	10	.196	29	22	.759	23	15	42	3.2
Robert Wood	6	14	3	.214	1	1	1.000	1	6	7	1.2
Don Grate	2	6	1	.167	2	2	1.000	3	3	4	2.0

SYRACUSE NATIONALS

Player	G.	FGA	FGM	Pct.	FTA	FTM	Pct.	Ast.	PF	Pts.	Avg.
Dolph Schayes	64	903	348	.385	486	376	.774	259	225	1072	16.8
William Gabor	56	671	226	.337	228	157	.689	108	198	609	10.9
Al Cervi	56	431	143	.332	346	287	.829	264	223	573	10.2
George Ratkovicz	62	439	162	.369	348	211	.606	124	201	535	8.6
Alex Hannum	64	488	177	.363	186	128	.688	129	264	482	7.5
Paul Seymour	62	524	175	.334	176	126	.716	189	157	476	7.7
Edward Peterson	62	390	167	.428	185	111	.600	33	198	445	7.2
John Macknowski	59	463	154	.333	178	131	.736	65	128	439	7.4
Andrew Levane	60	418	139	.333	85	54	.635	156	106	332	5.5
Ray Corley	60	370	117	.316	122	75	.615	109	81	309	5.2
Leroy Chollet	49	179	61	.341	56	35	.625	37	52	157	3.2

TRI-CITIES BLACKHAWKS

Player	G.	FGA	FGM	Pct.	FTA	FTM	Pct.	Ast.	PF	Pts.	Avg.
Dwight Eddleman	64	906	332	.366	260	162	.623	142	254	826	12.9
Marko Todorovich (14 St.L.-51 Tri-C.)	65	852	263	.309	370	266	.719	207	230	792	12.2
Jack Nichols (49 Wash.-18 Tri-C.)	67	848	310	.366	344	259	.753	142	179	879	13.1
Murray Wier	56	480	157	.327	166	115	.693	107	141	429	7.7
Warren Perkins	60	422	128	.303	195	115	.590	114	260	371	6.2
Don Ray	61	403	130	.323	149	104	.698	60	147	364	6.0
Gene Englund (24 Bos.-22 Tri-C.)	46	274	104	.380	192	152	.792	41	167	360	7.8
Walton Kirk (26 And.-32 Tri-C.)	58	361	97	.269	216	155	.718	103	155	349	6.0
Gene Vance	35	325	110	.338	120	86	.717	121	145	306	8.7
William Henry (44 Ft.W.-19 Tri-C.)	63	278	89	.320	176	118	.670	48	122	296	4.7
Dee Gibson	44	245	77	.314	177	127	.718	126	113	281	6.4
Gene Berce	3	16	5	.313	5	0	.000	0	6	10	3.3

WATERLOO HAWKS

Player	G.	FGA	FGM	Pct.	FTA	FTM	Pct.	Ast.	PF	Pts.	Avg.
Richard Mehen	62	826	347	.420	281	198	.705	191	203	892	14.4
Harry Boykoff	61	698	288	.413	262	203	.775	149	229	779	12.8
Leo Kubiak	62	794	259	.326	236	192	.814	201	250	710	11.5
Don Boven	62	558	208	.373	349	240	.688	137	255	656	10.6
Jack Smiley (12 And.-47 Wat.)	59	364	98	.269	201	136	.677	161	193	332	5.6
Wayne See	61	303	113	.373	135	94	.696	143	147	320	5.2
John Payak (17 Phil.-35 Wat.)	52	331	98	.296	173	121	.699	86	113	317	6.1
Ward Gibson (2 Bos.-30 Wat.)	32	195	67	.344	64	42	.656	37	106	176	5.5
Eugene Stump (23 Mpls.-26 Wat.)	49	213	63	.296	54	37	.685	44	59	163	3.3
Robert Tough (8 Bal.-21 Wat.)	29	153	43	.281	40	37	.925	38	40	123	4.2
Charles Shipp	23	137	35	.255	51	37	.725	46	46	107	4.7
John Orr (21 St.L.-13 Wat.)	34	118	40	.339	14	12	.857	20	34	92	2.7
Gene Ollrich	14	72	17	.236	14	10	.714	24	34	44	3.1
Al Miksis	8	21	5	.238	21	17	.810	4	22	27	3.3
Dale Hamilton	14	33	8	.242	19	9	.474	17	30	25	1.8
Elmer Gainer	15	35	9	.257	8	6	.750	7	28	24	1.6
John Pritchard	7	29	9	.310	11	4	.364	8	14	22	3.1
Paul Cloyd (3 Bal.-4 Wat.)	7	26	7	.269	8	5	.625	2	5	19	2.7
Kenneth Menke	6	17	6	.353	8	3	.375	7	7	15	2.5

WASHINGTON CAPITOLS

Player	G.	FGA	FGM	Pct.	FTA	FTM	Pct.	Ast.	PF	Pts.	Avg.
Fred Scolari	66	910	312	.343	287	236	.822	175	181	860	13.0
Don Otten (46 Tri-C.-18 Wash.)	64	648	242	.373	463	341	.737	91	246	825	12.9
Joseph Reiser	67	646	197	.305	254	212	.835	174	223	606	9.0
Horace McKinney	53	631	187	.296	152	118	.776	88	185	492	9.3
Robert Feerick	60	500	172	.344	174	139	.799	127	140	483	8.1
Richard O'Keefe	68	529	162	.306	203	150	.739	74	217	474	7.0
Charles Gilmur (Chi.-Wash.)	68	379	127	.335	241	164	.680	108	275	418	6.1
Charles Halbert	68	284	108	.380	175	112	.640	89	136	328	4.8
John Norlander	40	293	99	.338	85	53	.624	33	71	251	6.3
Leo Katkaveck (Bal.-Wash.)	54	330	101	.306	56	34	.607	68	102	236	4.4
John Dillon	22	55	10	.182	22	16	.727	5	19	36	1.6

PLAYOFF RESULTS

CENTRAL DIVISION 1st PLACE GAME
Mar. 21—Minneapolis 78 at Rochester 76

CENTRAL DIVISION 3rd PLACE GAME
Mar. 20—Chicago 69 at Ft. Wayne................................86

EASTERN DIVISION SEMIFINALS
Syracuse 2, Philadelphia 0
Mar. 22—Philadelphia 76 at Syracuse 93
Mar. 23—Syracuse 59 at Philadelphia 53

New York 2, Washington 0
Mar. 21—New York 90 at Washington 87
Mar. 22—Washington 83 at New York 103

CENTRAL DIVISION SEMIFINALS
Minneapolis 2, Chicago 0
Mar. 22—Chicago 75 at Minneapolis 85
Mar. 25—Minneapolis 75 at Chicago 67

Ft. Wayne 2, Rochester 0
Mar. 23—Ft. Wayne 90 at Rochester 84
Mar. 25—Rochester 78 at Ft. Wayne *79

WESTERN DIVISION SEMIFINALS
Indianapolis 2, Sheboygan 1
Mar. 21—Sheboygan 85 at Indianapolis 86
Mar. 23—Indianapolis 85 at Sheboygan 95
Mar. 25—Sheboygan 84 at Indianapolis 91

Anderson 2, Tri-Cities 1
Mar. 21—Tri-Cities 77 at Anderson 89
Mar. 23—Anderson 75 at Tri-Cities 76
Mar. 24—Tri-Cities 71 at Anderson 94

EASTERN DIVISION FINALS
Syracuse 2, New York 1
Mar. 26—New York 83 at Syracuse *91
Mar. 30—Syracuse 76 at New York 80
Apr. 2—New York 80 at Syracuse 91

CENTRAL DIVISION FINALS
Minneapolis 2, Ft. Wayne 0
Mar. 27—Ft. Wayne 79 at Minneapolis 93
Mar. 28—Minneapolis 89 at Ft. Wayne 82

WESTERN DIVISION FINALS
Anderson 2, Indianapolis 1
Mar. 28—Anderson 74 at Indianapolis 77
Mar. 30—Indianapolis 67 at Anderson 84
Apr. 1—Anderson 67 at Indianapolis 65

NBA SEMIFINALS
Minneapolis 2, Anderson 0
Apr. 5—Anderson 50 at Minneapolis 75
Apr. 6—Minneapolis 90 at Anderson 71

WORLD CHAMPIONSHIP SERIES
Minneapolis 4, Syracuse 2
Apr. 8—Minneapolis 68 at Syracuse 66
Apr. 9—Minneapolis 85 at Syracuse 91
Apr. 14—Syracuse 77, Minn. at St. Paul 91
Apr. 16—Syracuse 69, Minn. at St. Paul 77
Apr. 20—Minneapolis 76 at Syracuse 83
Apr. 23—Syracuse 95 at Minneapolis 110

*Denotes overtime period.

1948-49 NBA STATISTICS

1948-49 NBA CHAMPION MINNEAPOLIS LAKERS

Left to right: Don Forman, Herman Schaefer, Don Carlson, Don Smith, Tony Jaros, John Jorgensen, Earl Gardner, Arnie Ferrin, Jack Dwan, Jim Pollard, George Mikan. (Coach John Kundla.)

FINAL STANDINGS

EASTERN DIVISION

Team	Wash.	N.Y.	Balt.	Phil.	Bos.	Prov.	Roch.	Mpls.	Chi.	St.L.	Ft.W.	Ind.	W.	L.	Pct.	G.B.
Washington	..	3	3	4	5	6	3	3	2	3	3	3	38	22	.633	......
New York	3	..	4	2	3	5	1	1	2	3	4	4	32	28	.533	6
Baltimore	3	2	..	4	4	2	1	1	1	2	4	5	29	31	.483	9
Philadelphia	2	4	2	..	3	6	0	1	3	3	0	4	28	32	.467	10
Boston	1	3	2	3	..	3	1	2	0	3	4	3	25	35	.417	13
Providence	0	1	4	0	3	..	2	0	0	0	1	1	12	48	.200	26

WESTERN DIVISION

Team	Wash.	N.Y.	Balt.	Phil.	Bos.	Prov.	Roch.	Mpls.	Chi.	St.L.	Ft.W.	Ind.	W.	L.	Pct.	G.B.
Rochester	2	4	4	5	4	3	..	2	4	6	6	5	45	15	.750	......
Minneapolis	2	4	4	4	3	5	4	..	4	4	4	6	44	16	.733	1
Chicago	3	3	4	2	5	5	2	2	..	3	4	5	38	22	.633	7
St. Louis	2	2	3	2	2	5	0	2	3	..	5	3	29	31	.483	16
Ft. Wayne	2	1	1	5	1	4	0	2	2	1	..	3	22	38	.367	23
Indianapolis	2	1	0	1	2	4	1	0	1	3	3	..	18	42	.300	27

HOME-ROAD-NEUTRAL RECORDS OF ALL TEAMS

	Home	Road	Neutral	Total		Home	Road	Neutral	Total
Baltimore	17- 12	11- 17	1- 2	29- 31	New York	18- 11	12- 17	2- 0	32- 28
Boston	17- 12	7- 20	1- 3	25- 35	Philadelphia	19- 10	9- 21	0- 1	28- 32
Chicago	16- 8	18- 14	4- 0	38- 22	Providence	7- 23	5- 23	0- 2	12- 48
Ft. Wayne	15- 14	5- 23	2- 1	22- 38	Rochester	24- 5	20- 10	1- 0	45- 15
Indianapolis	14- 15	4- 22	0- 5	18- 42	St. Louis	17- 12	10- 18	2- 1	29- 31
Minneapolis	26- 3	16- 13	2- 0	44- 16	Washington	22- 7	15- 14	1- 1	38- 22
					Totals	212-132	132-212	16-16	360-360

TEAM STATISTICS

Team	G	FGA	FGM	Pct.	FTA	FTM	Pct.	Ast.	PF	For	Agst.	Pt.Dif.
Minneapolis	60	5146	1885	.366	1759	1272	.723	1134	1386	84.0	76.7	+7.3
Rochester	60	4869	1811	.372	2060	1420	.689	1259	1539	84.0	77.4	+6.6
Chicago	60	5750	1905	.331	1775	1228	.692	1220	1731	84.0	80.0	+4.0
Washington	60	5472	1751	.320	1914	1408	.736	972	1710	81.8	79.4	+2.4
New York	60	5237	1688	.322	1959	1376	.702	1017	1559	79.2	77.7	+1.5
Baltimore	60	5162	1736	.336	2053	1545	.753	1000	1730	83.6	82.2	+1.4
Philadelphia	60	5695	1831	.322	1897	1360	.717	1043	1459	83.7	83.4	+0.3
Boston	60	5483	1706	.311	1856	1181	.636	1135	1382	76.6	79.5	—2.9
Ft. Wayne	60	5370	1536	.286	1979	1385	.700	1082	1722	74.3	77.5	—3.2
St. Louis	60	4858	1659	.341	1770	1229	.694	1269	1480	75.8	79.4	—3.6
Indianapolis	60	5367	1621	.302	1798	1240	.690	1225	1393	74.7	79.4	—4.7
Providence	60	5427	1750	.322	1742	1207	.693	1026	1349	78.5	87.1	—8.6

INDIVIDUAL LEADERS

POINTS

	G.	FG	FT	Pts.	Avg.		G.	FG	FT	Pts.	Avg.
George Mikan, Minneapolis	60	583	532	1698	28.3	Jim Pollard, Minneapolis	53	314	156	784	14.8
Joe Fulks, Philadelphia	60	529	502	1560	26.0	Connie Simmons, Baltimore	60	299	181	779	13.0
Max Zaslofsky, Chicago	58	425	347	1197	20.6	Ray Lumpp, Indianapolis-N.Y.	61	279	219	777	12.7
Arnie Risen, Rochester	60	345	305	995	16.6	Bob Feerick, Washington	58	248	256	752	13.0
Ed Sadowski, Philadelphia	60	340	240	920	15.3	Howie Shannon, Providence	55	292	152	736	13.4
Belus Smawley, St. Louis	59	352	210	914	15.5	Horace McKinney, Wash.	57	263	197	723	12.7
Bob Davies, Rochester	60	317	270	904	15.1	Andy Phillip, Chicago	60	285	148	718	12.0
Ken Sailors, Providence	57	309	281	899	15.8	John Palmer, New York	58	240	234	714	12.3
Carl Braun, New York	57	299	212	810	14.2	Kleg Hermsen, Washington	60	248	212	708	11.8
John Logan, St. Louis	57	282	239	803	14.1	Walter Budko, Baltimore	60	224	244	692	11.5

FIELD GOALS
(Minimum 200 FGM)

	FGA	FGM	Pct.
Arnie Risen, Rochester	816	345	.423
George Mikan, Minneapolis	1403	583	.416
Ed Sadowski, Philadelphia	839	340	.405
Jim Pollard, Minneapolis	792	314	.396
Red Rocha, St. Louis	574	223	.389
Bob Wanzer, Rochester	533	202	.379
Connie Simmons, Baltimore	794	299	.377
Herm Schaefer, Minneapolis	572	214	.374
Belus Smawley, St. Louis	946	352	.372
Howie Shannon, Providence	802	292	.364
Bob Davies, Rochester	871	317	.364

FREE THROWS
(Minimum 150 FTM)

	FTA	FTM	Pct.
Bob Feerick, Washington	298	256	.859
Max Zaslofsky, Chicago	413	347	.840
Bob Wanzer, Rochester	254	209	.823
Herm Schaefer, Minneapolis	213	174	.817
Howie Shannon, Providence	189	152	.804
Harold Tidrick, Ind.-Balt.	205	164	.800
John Logan, St. Louis	302	239	.791
Walter Budko, Baltimore	309	244	.790
John Pelkington, Ft.W.-Balt.	267	211	.790
Joe Fulks, Philadelphia	638	502	.787

ASSISTS

	G.	No.	Avg.
Bob Davies, Rochester	60	321	5.4
Andy Phillip, Chicago	60	319	5.3
John Logan, St. Louis	57	276	4.8
Ernie Calverley, Providence	59	251	4.3
George Senesky, Philadelphia	60	233	3.9
Jim Seminoff, Boston	58	229	3.9
George Mikan, Minneapolis	60	218	3.6
Ken Sailors, Providence	57	209	3.7
Bob Feerick, Washington	58	188	3.2
Bob Wanzer, Rochester	60	186	3.1

TEAM-BY-TEAM INDIVIDUAL STATISTICS

BALTIMORE BULLETS

Player	G.	FGA	FGM	Pct.	FTA	FTM	Pct.	Ast.	PF	Pts.	Avg.
Connie Simmons	60	794	299	.377	265	181	.683	116	215	779	13.0
Walter Budko	60	644	224	.348	309	244	.790	99	201	692	11.5
Fred Lewis (8 Ind.-53 Balt.)	61	834	272	.326	181	138	.762	107	167	682	11.2
Joseph Reiser	57	653	219	.335	257	188	.732	132	202	626	11.0
John Pelkington (14 Ft.W.-40 Balt.)	54	469	193	.412	267	211	.790	131	216	597	11.1
Harold Tidrick (8 Ind.-53 Balt.)	61	616	194	.315	205	164	.800	101	191	552	9.0
Sidney Tannenbaum (32 N.Y.-14 Balt.)	46	501	146	.291	120	99	.825	125	74	391	8.5
Stanley Stutz	59	431	121	.281	159	131	.824	82	149	373	6.3
John Ezersky (11 Prov.-18 Bos.-27 Balt.)	56	407	128	.314	160	109	.681	67	98	365	6.5
Harry Jeannette	56	199	73	.367	213	167	.784	124	157	313	5.6
James Martin (37 St.L.-7 Balt.)	44	170	52	.306	47	30	.638	25	115	134	3.0
Daniel Kraus	13	35	5	.143	24	11	.458	7	24	21	1.6
Howard Rader	13	45	7	.156	10	3	.300	14	25	17	1.3
Douglas Holcomb	3	12	3	.250	14	9	.643	5	5	15	5.0
Herbert Krautblatt	10	18	4	.222	11	5	.455	4	14	13	1.3
Darrell Brown	3	6	2	.333	2	0	.000	0	3	4	1.3
Ray Ramsey	2	1	0	.000	2	2	1.000	0	0	2	1.0

BOSTON CELTICS

Player	G.	FGA	FGM	Pct.	FTA	FTM	Pct.	Ast.	PF	Pts.	Avg.
George Nostrand (33 Prov.-27 Bos.)	60	651	212	.326	284	165	.581	94	164	589	9.8
Edward Ehlers	59	583	182	.312	225	150	.667	133	119	514	8.7
Eugene Stump	56	580	193	.333	129	92	.713	56	102	478	8.5
Robert Kinney (37 Ft. W.-21 Bos.)	58	495	161	.325	234	136	.581	77	224	458	7.9
James Seminoff	58	487	153	.314	219	151	.689	229	195	457	7.9
Robert Doll	47	438	145	.331	117	80	.684	117	118	370	7.9
Arthur Spector	59	434	130	.300	116	64	.552	77	111	324	5.5
George Kaftan	21	315	116	.368	115	72	.626	61	28	304	14.5
Dermott O'Connell	21	315	87	.276	56	30	.536	65	40	204	9.7
Thomas Kelly	27	218	73	.335	73	45	.616	38	73	191	7.1
Philip Farbman (27 Phil.-21 Bos.)	48	163	50	.307	81	55	.679	36	86	155	3.2
Earl Shannon (27 Prov.-5 Bos.)	32	127	34	.268	58	39	.672	44	33	107	3.3
John Bach	34	119	34	.286	75	51	.680	25	24	119	3.5
Stanley Noszka	30	123	30	.244	30	15	.500	25	56	75	2.5
Jack Garfinkle	9	70	12	.171	14	10	.714	17	19	34	3.8
Henry Beenders	8	28	6	.214	9	7	.778	3	9	19	2.4
John Hazen	6	17	6	.353	7	6	.857	3	10	18	3.0
Al Lucas	2	3	1	.333	0	0	.000	2	0	2	1.0

CHICAGO STAGS

Player	G.	FGA	FGM	Pct.	FTA	FTM	Pct.	Ast.	PF	Pts.	Avg.
Max Zaslofsky	58	1216	425	.350	413	347	.840	149	156	1197	20.6
Andrew Phillip	60	818	285	.348	219	148	.676	319	205	718	12.0
Edward Mikan	60	729	229	.314	183	136	.743	62	191	594	9.9
Gene Vance	56	657	222	.338	181	131	.724	167	217	575	10.3
Marion Spears	57	631	200	.317	197	131	.665	97	200	531	9.3
Stanley Miasek	58	488	169	.346	216	113	.523	57	208	451	7.8
Kenneth Rollins	59	520	144	.277	104	77	.740	167	150	365	6.2
Charles Gilmur	56	281	110	.391	121	66	.545	125	194	286	5.1
Joseph Graboski	45	157	54	.344	49	17	.347	18	86	125	2.8
Michael Bloom (24 Mpls.-21 Chi.)	45	181	35	.193	74	56	.757	32	53	126	2.8
James Browne	4	2	1	.500	2	1	.500	0	4	3	0.8
Jack Eskridge	3	0	0	.000	0	0	.000	0	1	0	0.0

FT. WAYNE PISTONS

Player	G.	FGA	FGM	Pct.	FTA	FTM	Pct.	Ast.	PF	Pts.	Avg.
Charles Black (41 Ind.-17 Ft. W.)	58	691	203	.294	291	161	.553	140	247	567	9.8
Bruce Hale (18 Ind.-34 Ft. W.)	52	585	187	.320	228	172	.754	156	112	546	10.5
John Mahnken (7 Balt.-13 Ind.-37 Ft. W.)	57	830	215	.259	167	104	.623	125	215	534	9.4
Robert Tough	53	661	183	.277	138	100	.725	99	101	466	8.8
Jack Smiley	59	571	141	.247	164	112	.683	138	202	394	6.7
Paul Armstrong	52	428	131	.306	169	118	.698	105	152	380	7.3
Richard Niemiera	55	331	115	.347	165	132	.800	96	115	362	6.6
Leo Klier	47	492	125	.254	137	97	.708	56	124	347	7.4
Richard Triptow	55	417	116	.278	141	102	.723	96	107	334	6.1
William Henry	32	300	96	.320	203	125	.616	55	110	317	9.9
Ward Williams	53	257	61	.237	124	93	.750	82	158	215	4.1
Dillard Crocker	2	4	1	.250	6	4	.667	0	3	6	3.0

INDIANAPOLIS JETS

Player	G.	FGA	FGM	Pct.	FTA	FTM	Pct.	Ast.	PF	Pts.	Avg.
Carlisle Towery (22 Ft. W.-38 Ind.)	60	771	203	.263	263	195	.741	171	243	601	10.0
Leo Mogus (13 Balt.-20 Ft. W.-19 Ind.)	52	509	172	.338	243	177	.728	104	170	521	10.0
Walter Kirk (14 Ft. W.-35 Ind.)	49	406	140	.345	231	167	.723	118	127	447	9.1
Price Brookfield	54	638	176	.276	125	90	.720	136	145	442	8.2
Thomas Byrnes (35 N.Y.-22 Ind.)	57	525	160	.305	149	92	.617	102	84	412	7.2
Ralph Hamilton (10 Ft. W.-38 Ind.)	48	447	114	.255	91	61	.670	83	67	289	6.0
John Mandic	56	302	97	.321	115	75	.652	80	151	269	4.8
Andrew Kostecka	21	110	46	.418	70	43	.614	14	48	135	6.4
Fritz Nagy	50	271	94	.347	97	65	.670	68	84	253	5.1
George Glamack	11	121	30	.248	55	42	.764	19	28	102	9.3
Jack Eskridge	20	69	25	.362	20	14	.700	14	24	64	3.2
Martin Passaglia	10	57	14	.246	4	3	.750	17	17	31	1.6
Richard Wehr	9	21	5	.238	6	2	.333	3	12	12	1.3
James Spruill	1	3	1	.333	0	0	.000	0	3	2	2.0
James Springer	2	0	0	.000	1	1	1.000	0	0	1	0.5
Jack Maddox	1	0	0	.000	0	0	.000	1	0	0	0.0
Paul Napolitano	1	0	0	.000	0	0	.000	0	0	0	0.0

MINNEAPOLIS LAKERS

Player	G.	FGA	FGM	Pct.	FTA	FTM	Pct.	Ast.	PF	Pts.	Avg.
George Mikan	60	1403	583	.416	689	532	.772	218	260	1698	28.3
James Pollard	53	792	314	.396	227	156	.687	142	144	784	14.8
Herman Schaefer	58	572	214	.374	213	174	.817	185	121	602	10.4
Don Carlson	55	632	211	.334	130	86	.662	170	180	508	9.3
Arnold Ferrin	47	378	130	.344	128	85	.664	76	142	345	7.3
Tony Jaros	59	385	132	.343	110	79	.718	58	114	343	5.8
Jack Dwan	60	380	121	.318	69	34	.493	129	157	276	4.6
Don Forman	44	231	68	.294	67	43	.642	74	94	179	4.1
Ed Kachan (33 Chi.-19 Mpls.)	52	142	38	.208	56	36	.643	37	81	112	2.2
John Jorgensen	48	114	41	.360	33	24	.727	33	68	106	2.2
Earl Gardner	50	101	38	.376	28	13	.464	19	50	89	1.8
Don Smith	8	13	2	.154	3	2	.667	2	6	6	0.8
Jack Tingle	2	6	1	.167	0	0	.000	1	2	2	1.0
Ray Ellefson	3	5	1	.200	0	0	.000	0	2	2	0.7

NEW YORK KNICKERBOCKERS

Player	G.	FGA	FGM	Pct.	FTA	FTM	Pct.	Ast.	PF	Pts.	Avg.
Carl Braun	57	906	299	.330	279	212	.760	173	144	810	14.2
Ray Lumpp (37 Ind.-24 N.Y.)	61	800	279	.349	283	219	.774	158	173	777	12.7
John Palmer	58	685	240	.350	307	234	.762	108	206	714	12.3
Lee Knorek	60	457	156	.341	183	131	.716	135	258	443	7.4
Harry Gallatin	52	479	157	.328	169	120	.710	63	127	434	8.3
Wm. Van Breda Koeff	59	401	127	.317	240	161	.671	143	148	415	7.0
Goebel Ritter	55	353	123	.348	146	91	.623	57	71	337	6.1
Irving Rothenberg	53	367	101	.275	174	112	.644	68	174	314	5.9
Paul Noel	47	277	70	.253	60	37	.617	33	84	177	3.8
Mel McGaha	51	195	62	.318	88	52	.591	51	104	176	3.5
Joe Colone	15	113	35	.310	19	13	.684	9	25	83	5.5
Gene James	11	48	18	.375	12	6	.500	5	20	42	3.8
Ray Kuka	8	36	10	.278	9	5	.556	11	16	25	3.1
Richard Shrider	4	0	0	.000	3	1	.333	2	2	1	0.3

PHILADELPHIA WARRIORS

Player	G.	FGA	FGM	Pct.	FTA	FTM	Pct.	Ast.	PF	Pts.	Avg.
Joseph Fulks	60	1689	529	.313	638	502	.787	74	262	1560	26.0
Edward Sadowski	60	839	340	.405	350	240	.686	160	273	920	15.3
Angelo Musi	58	618	194	.314	119	90	.756	81	108	478	8.2

The Minneapolis Lakers won their first of five NBA championships in 1948-49 as George Mikan captured the scoring title.

Player	G.	FGA	FGM	Pct.	FTA	FTM	Pct.	Ast.	PF	Pts.	Avg.
George Senesky	60	516	138	.267	152	111	.730	233	133	387	6.4
Gale Bishop	56	523	170	.325	195	127	.651	92	137	467	8.3
Jerry Fleishman	59	424	123	.290	118	77	.653	120	137	323	5.5
Howard Dallmar	38	342	105	.307	116	83	.716	116	104	293	7.7
Francis Crossin	44	212	74	.347	42	26	.619	55	53	174	4.0
Irving Torgoff (29 Balt.-13 Phil.)	42	226	59	.261	64	50	.781	44	110	168	7.2
Jerry Rullo	39	183	53	.290	45	31	.689	48	71	137	3.5
Jerry Bornheimer	15	109	34	.312	29	20	.690	13	47	88	5.9
Elmore Morgenthaler	20	39	15	.385	18	12	.667	7	18	35	2.1
Roy Pugh (4 Ft. W.-6 Ind.-13 Phil.)	23	51	13	.255	19	6	.316	9	17	32	1.4

PROVIDENCE STEAMROLLERS

Player	G.	FGA	FGM	Pct.	FTA	FTM	Pct.	Ast.	PF	Pts.	Avg.
Kenneth Sailors	57	906	309	.341	367	281	.766	209	239	899	15.8
Howard Shannon	55	802	292	.364	189	152	.804	125	154	736	13.4
Charles Halbert (33 Bos.-27 Prov.)	60	647	202	.312	345	214	.620	113	175	618	10.3
Ernie Calverley	59	696	218	.313	160	121	.756	251	183	557	9.4
Brady Walker	59	556	202	.363	155	87	.561	68	100	491	8.3
Les Pugh	60	556	168	.302	167	125	.749	59	168	461	7.7

Player	G.	FGA	FGM	Pct.	FTA	FTM	Pct.	Ast.	PF	Pts.	Avg.
Mel Riebe (33 Bos.-10 Prov.)	43	589	172	.292	133	79	.594	104	110	423	9.8
Carl Meinhold (15 Chi.-35 Prov.)	50	306	101	.330	96	61	.635	47	60	263	5.2
Francis O'Grady (30 St.L.-17 Prov.)	47	293	85	.290	71	49	.690	68	57	219	4.7
Robert Brown	20	111	37	.333	47	34	.723	14	67	108	5.4
Gifford Roux (19 St.L.-26 Prov.)	45	118	29	.246	44	29	.659	20	30	87	1.9
Robert Hubbard	34	135	25	.185	34	22	.647	18	39	72	2.1
Andrew Tonkovich	17	71	19	.268	9	6	.667	10	12	44	2.6
Lee Robbins	16	25	9	.360	17	11	.647	12	24	29	1.8
Fred Paine	3	19	3	.158	5	1	.200	1	3	7	2.3
Ben Scharnus	1	1	0	.000	1	0	.000	0	0	0	0.0

ROCHESTER ROYALS

Player	G.	FGA	FGM	Pct.	FTA	FTM	Pct.	Ast.	PF	Pts.	Avg.
Arnold Risen	60	816	345	.423	462	305	.660	100	216	995	16.6
Robert Davies	60	871	317	.364	348	270	.776	321	197	904	15.1
Robert Wanzer	60	533	202	.379	254	209	.823	186	132	613	10.2
William Holzman	60	691	225	.326	157	96	.611	149	93	546	9.1
Arnitz Johnson	60	375	156	.416	284	199	.701	80	247	511	8.5
Andrew Duncan	55	391	162	.414	135	83	.615	51	179	407	7.4
William Calhoun	56	408	146	.358	131	75	.573	125	97	367	6.6
Michael Novak	60	363	124	.342	124	72	.581	112	188	320	5.3
Lionel Malamed (35 Ind.-9 Roch.)	44	290	97	.334	77	64	.831	61	53	258	5.9
Francis Curran	57	168	61	.363	126	85	.675	78	118	207	3.6
Andrew Levane	36	193	55	.285	21	13	.619	39	37	123	3.4
Robert Fitzgerald	18	29	6	.207	10	7	.700	12	26	19	1.1

ST. LOUIS BOMBERS

Player	G.	FGA	FGM	Pct.	FTA	FTM	Pct.	Ast.	PF	Pts.	Avg.
Belus Smawley	59	946	352	.372	281	210	.747	183	145	914	15.5
John Logan	57	816	282	.346	302	239	.791	276	191	803	14.1
Red Rocha	58	574	223	.389	211	162	.768	157	251	608	10.5
Ariel Maughan	55	650	206	.317	285	184	.646	99	134	596	10.8
Easy Parham	60	404	124	.307	172	96	.558	151	134	344	5.7
Otto Schnellbacher (23 Prov.-20 St.L.)	43	280	93	.332	133	89	.669	64	109	275	6.4
Don Putnam	59	330	98	.297	97	52	.536	140	132	248	4.2
William Roberts (2 Chi.-26 Bos.-22 St.L.)	50	267	89	.333	63	44	.698	41	113	222	4.4
Coulby Gunther	32	181	57	.315	71	45	.634	33	64	159	5.0
Grady Lewis	34	137	53	.387	70	42	.600	37	104	148	4.4
William Miller (14 Chi.-14 St.L.)	28	72	21	.292	20	11	.550	20	32	53	1.9
D. C. Wilcutt	22	51	18	.353	18	15	.833	31	9	51	2.3
Robert O'Brien (16 Phil.-8 St.L.)	24	50	10	.200	32	12	.375	9	32	32	1.3
Lou Eggleston	2	4	1	.250	3	2	.667	1	3	4	2.0

WASHINGTON CAPITOLS

Player	G.	FGA	FGM	Pct.	FTA	FTM	Pct.	Ast.	PF	Pts.	Avg.
Robert Feerick	58	708	248	.350	298	256	.859	188	171	752	13.0
Horace McKinney	57	801	263	.328	279	197	.706	114	216	723	12.7
Clarence Hermsen	60	794	248	.312	311	212	.682	99	257	708	11.8
Fred Scolari	48	633	196	.31	183	146	.798	100	150	538	11.2
John Norlander	60	454	164	.361	171	116	.678	86	124	444	7.4
Sidney Hertzberg	60	541	154	.285	164	134	.817	114	140	442	7.4
Jack Nichols	34	392	153	.390	126	92	.730	56	118	398	11.7
Matthew Zunic	56	323	98	.303	109	77	.706	50	182	273	4.9
Leo Katkaveck	53	253	84	.332	71	53	.746	68	110	221	4.8
Richard Schulz	50	278	65	.234	91	65	.714	53	107	195	3.9
Richard O'Keefe	50	274	70	.255	99	51	.515	43	119	191	3.8
John Toomay (23 Balt.-13 Wash.)	36	84	32	.381	53	36	.679	12	65	100	2.8

PLAYOFF RESULTS

EASTERN DIVISION SEMIFINALS
Washington 2, Philadelphia 0
Mar. 23—Washington 92 at Philadelphia 70
Mar. 24—Philadelphia 78 at Washington 80

New York 2, Baltimore 1
Mar. 23—New York 81 at Baltimore 82
Mar. 24—Baltimore 82 at New York 84
Mar. 26—Baltimore 99 at New York *103

EASTERN DIVISION FINALS
Washington 2, New York 1
Mar. 29—New York 71 at Washington 77
Mar. 31—Washington 84 at New York *86
Apr. 2—New York 76 at Washington 84

WESTERN DIVISION SEMIFINALS
Rochester 2, St. Louis 0
Mar. 22—St. Louis 64 at Rochester 93
Mar. 23—Rochester 66 at St. Louis 64

Minneapolis 2, Chicago 0
Mar. 23—Chicago 77 at Minneapolis 84
Mar. 24—Minneapolis 101 at Chicago 85

WESTERN DIVISION FINALS
Minneapolis 2, Rochester 0
Mar. 27—Minneapolis 80 at Rochester 79
Mar. 29—Rochester 55, Minneapolis at St. Paul 67

WORLD CHAMPIONSHIP SERIES
Minneapolis 4, Washington 2
Apr. 4—Washington 84 at Minneapolis 88
Apr. 6—Washington 62 at Minneapolis 76
Apr. 8—Minneapolis 94 at Washington 74
Apr. 9—Minneapolis 71 at Washington 83
Apr. 11—Minneapolis 66 at Washington 74
Apr. 13—Washington 56, Minneapolis at St. Paul 77

*Denotes overtime period.

1947-48 NBA STATISTICS

1947-48 NBA CHAMPION BALTIMORE BULLETS

Left to right: Connie Simmons, Clarence Hermsen, Grady Lewis, Carl Meinhold, Paul Hoffman, Dick Schulz, Herman Feutsch, Chick Reiser, Herman Klotz, Player-Coach Buddy Jeannette.

FINAL STANDINGS

EASTERN DIVISION

Team	Phil.	N.Y.	Bos.	Prov.	St.L.	Balt.	Chi.	Wash.	W.	L.	Pct.	G.B.
Philadelphia	..	4	4	8	3	4	2	2	27	21	.563	....
New York	4	..	7	7	4	1	0	3	26	22	.542	1
Boston	4	1	..	6	2	1	3	3	20	28	.417	7
Providence	0	1	2	..	0	0	2	1	6	42	.125	21

WESTERN DIVISION

St. Louis	3	2	4	6	..	5	5	4	29	19	.604	....
Baltimore	2	5	5	6	3	..	5	2	28	20	.583	1
Chicago	4	6	3	4	3	3	..	5	28	20	.583	1
Washington	4	3	3	5	4	6	3	..	28	20	.583	1

HOME-ROAD RECORDS OF ALL TEAMS

	Home	Road	Total		Home	Road	Total
Baltimore	17- 7	11- 13	28- 20	Philadelphia	14- 10	13- 11	27- 21
Boston	11- 13	9- 15	20- 28	Providence	3- 21	3- 21	6- 42
Chicago	14- 10	14- 10	28- 20	St. Louis	17- 7	12- 12	29- 19
New York	12- 12	14- 10	26- 22	Washington	19- 5	9- 15	28- 20
				Totals	107- 85	85-107	192-192

TEAM STATISTICS

Team	G	FGA	FGM	Pct.	FTA	FTM	Pct.	Ast.	PF	For	Agst.	Pt.Dif.
Baltimore	48	4283	1288	.301	1443	994	.689	320	1080	74.4	70.5	+ 3.9
New York	48	4724	1355	.287	1291	868	.672	376	1076	74.5	71.4	+ 3.1
Chicago	48	4683	1390	.297	1305	860	.659	432	1138	75.8	73.2	+ 2.6
Washington	48	4785	1336	.279	1203	865	.719	305	1084	73.7	71.1	+ 2.6
St. Louis	48	4551	1297	.285	1244	838	.674	218	1050	71.5	69.5	+ 2.0
Philadelphia	48	4875	1279	.262	1349	963	.714	335	934	73.4	72.1	+ 1.3
Boston	48	4323	1241	.287	1246	821	.659	364	1065	68.8	72.7	- 3.9
Providence	48	4630	1268	.274	1275	782	.613	347	1105	69.1	80.1	-11.0

INDIVIDUAL LEADERS

POINTS

	G.	FG	FT	Pts.	Avg.		G.	FG	FT	Pts.	Avg.
Max Zaslofsky, Chicago	48	373	261	1007	21.0	Howard Dallmar, Philadelphia..	48	215	157	587	12.2
Joe Fulks, Philadelphia	43	326	297	949	22.1	Kleg Hermsen, Baltimore	48	212	151	575	12.0
Ed Sadowski, Boston	47	308	294	910	19.4	Ernie Calverley, Providence....	47	226	107	559	11.9
Bob Feerick, Washington	48	293	189	775	16.1	Joe Reiser, Baltimore	47	202	137	541	11.5
Stan Miasek, Chicago	48	263	190	716	14.9	Belus Smawley, St. Louis	48	212	111	535	11.1
Carl Braun, New York	47	276	119	671	14.3	Ken Sailors, Chi.-Phil.-Prov....	44	207	110	524	11.9
John Logan, St. Louis	48	221	202	644	13.4	George Nostrand, Providence.	45	196	129	521	11.6
John Palmer, New York	48	224	174	622	13.0	Mike Bloom, Balt.-Boston	48	174	160	508	10.6
Red Rocha, St. Louis	48	232	147	611	12.7	Dick Holub, New York	48	195	114	504	10.5
Fred Scolari, Washington	47	229	131	589	12.5	Bud Jeannette, Baltimore	46	150	191	491	10.7

FIELD GOALS
(Minimum 200 FGM)

	FGA	FGM	Pct.
Bob Feerick, Washington	861	293	.340
Ed Sadowski, Boston	953	308	.323
Max Zaslofsky, Chicago	1156	373	.323
Carl Braun, New York	854	276	.323
Chick Reiser, Baltimore	628	202	.322
John Palmer, New York	710	224	.315
Red Rocha, St. Louis	740	232	.314
Mel Riebe, Boston	653	202	.309
Belus Smawley, St. Louis	688	212	.308
Stan Miasek, Chicago	867	263	.303

FREE THROWS
(Minimum 125 FTM)

	FTA	FTM	Pct.
Bob Feerick, Washington	240	189	.788
Max Zaslofsky, Chicago	333	261	.784
Joe Fulks, Philadelphia	390	297	.762
Buddy Jeannette, Baltimore	252	191	.758
Howie Dallmar, Philadelphia	211	157	.744
John Palmer, New York	234	174	.744
John Logan, St. Louis	272	202	.743
John Norlander, Washington	182	135	.742
Chick Reiser, Baltimore	185	137	.741
Fred Scolari, Washington	179	131	.732

ASSISTS

	G.	No.	Avg.
Howie Dallmar, Philadelphia	48	120	2.5
Ernie Calverley, Providence	47	119	2.5
Jim Seminoff, Chicago	48	89	1.9
Chuck Gilmur, Chicago	48	77	1.6
Ed Sadowski, Boston	47	74	1.6
Andy Philip, Chicago	32	74	2.3
Buddy Jeannette, Baltimore	46	70	1.5
John Logan, St. Louis	48	62	1.3
Carl Braun, New York	47	61	1.3
Saul Mariaschin, Boston	43	60	1.4

TEAM-BY-TEAM INDIVIDUAL STATISTICS

BALTIMORE BULLETS

Player	G.	FGA	FGM	Pct.	FTA	FTM	Pct.	Ast.	PF	Pts.	Avg.
Clarence Hermsen	48	765	212	.277	227	151	.665	48	154	575	12.0
Joseph Reiser	47	628	202	.322	185	137	.741	40	175	541	11.5
Harry Jeannette	46	430	150	.349	252	191	.758	70	147	491	10.7
Paul Hoffman	37	408	142	.348	157	104	.662	23	123	388	10.5
Connie Simmons (32 Bos.-13 Balt.)	45	545	162	.297	108	62	.574	24	122	386	8.6
Richard Schulz	48	469	133	.284	160	117	.731	28	116	383	8.0
Grady Lewis (24 St. L.-21 Balt.)	45	425	114	.268	135	87	.644	41	151	315	7.0
Carl Meinhold	48	356	108	.303	60	37	.617	16	64	253	5.3
Herman Feutsch	42	140	42	.300	40	25	.625	17	39	109	2.6
Paul Seymour	22	101	27	.267	37	22	.595	6	34	76	3.5
Herman Klotz	11	31	7	.226	3	1	.333	7	3	15	1.4
John Jorgensen (1 Chi.-2 Balt.)	3	9	4	.444	1	1	1.000	0	2	9	3.0
Elmer Gainer	5	9	1	.111	6	3	.500	3	8	5	1.0
John Abramovic (4 St. L.-5 Balt.)	9	21	1	.048	7	4	.571	2	10	6	0.7
Chester McNabb	2	1	0	.000	0	0	.000	0	1	0	0.0
Jerry Rullo	2	4	0	.000	0	0	.000	0	1	0	0.0

BOSTON CELTICS

Player	G.	FGA	FGM	Pct.	FTA	FTM	Pct.	Ast.	PF	Pts.	Avg.
Edward Sadowski	47	953	308	.323	422	294	.697	74	182	910	19.4
Michael Bloom (34 Balt.-14 Bos.)	48	640	174	.272	229	160	.699	38	116	508	10.6
Mel Riebe	48	653	202	.309	137	85	.620	41	137	489	10.2
Saul Mariaschin	43	463	125	.270	117	83	.709	60	121	333	7.7
Ed Ehlers	40	417	104	.249	144	78	.542	44	92	286	7.2
Jack Garfinkle	43	380	114	.300	46	35	.761	59	78	263	6.1
Arthur Spector	48	243	67	.276	92	60	.652	17	106	194	4.0
Eugene Stump	43	247	59	.239	38	24	.632	18	66	142	3.3
Stanley Noszka	22	97	27	.278	35	24	.686	4	52	78	3.5
George Munroe	21	91	27	.297	26	17	.654	3	20	71	3.4
Cecil Hankins	25	116	23	.198	35	24	.686	8	28	70	2.8
Jack Hewson	24	89	22	.247	30	21	.700	1	9	65	2.7
Kevin Connors	4	13	5	.385	3	2	.667	1	5	12	3.0
Charles Hoefer	7	19	5	.158	8	4	.500	3	17	10	1.4

CHICAGO STAGS

Player	G.	FGA	FGM	Pct.	FTA	FTM	Pct.	Ast.	PF	Pts.	Avg.
Max Zaslofsky	48	1156	373	.323	333	261	.784	29	125	1007	21.0
Stan Miasek	48	867	263	.303	310	190	.613	31	192	716	14.9
Charles Gilmur	48	597	181	.303	148	97	.655	77	231	459	9.6
Gene Vance	48	617	163	.264	126	76	.603	49	193	402	8.4
Andrew Phillip	32	425	143	.336	103	60	.583	74	75	346	10.8
James Seminoff	48	381	113	.297	105	73	.695	89	105	299	6.2
Paul Huston	46	215	51	.237	89	62	.697	27	82	164	3.6
Marvin Rottner	44	184	53	.288	34	11	.324	46	49	117	2.7
Ben Schadler	37	116	23	.198	13	10	.769	6	40	56	1.5
Gene Rock	11	18	4	.222	4	2	.500	0	8	10	0.9

NEW YORK KNICKERBOCKERS

Player	G.	FGA	FGM	Pct.	FTA	FTM	Pct.	Ast.	PF	Pts.	Avg.
Carl Braun	47	854	276	.323	183	119	.650	61	102	671	14.3
John Palmer	48	710	224	.315	234	174	.744	45	149	622	13.0
Richard Holub	48	662	195	.295	180	114	.633	37	159	504	10.5
Stanley Stutz	47	501	109	.218	135	113	.837	57	121	331	7.0
Thomas Byrnes	47	410	117	.285	103	65	.631	17	56	299	6.4
Lee Knorek	48	369	99	.268	120	61	.508	50	171	259	5.4
Sidney Tannenbaum	24	360	90	.250	74	62	.838	37	33	242	10.1
Ray Kuka	44	273	89	.326	84	50	.595	27	117	228	5.2
Wm. Van Breda Kolff	44	192	53	.276	120	74	.617	29	81	180	4.1
Leo Gottlieb	27	288	59	.205	21	13	.619	12	36	131	4.9
Paul Noel	29	138	40	.290	30	19	.633	3	41	99	3.4
Wat Misaka	3	13	3	.231	3	1	.333	0	7	7	2.3

PHILADELPHIA WARRIORS

Player	G.	FGA	FGM	Pct.	FTA	FTM	Pct.	Ast.	PF	Pts.	Avg.
Joseph Fulks	43	1258	326	.259	390	297	.762	26	162	949	22.1
Howard Dallmar	48	781	215	.275	211	157	.744	120	141	587	12.2
Charles Halbert (6 Chi.-40 Phil.)	46	605	156	.258	220	140	.636	32	126	452	9.8
George Senesky	47	570	158	.277	147	98	.667	52	90	414	8.8
Jerry Fleishman	46	501	119	.238	138	95	.688	43	122	333	7.2
Angelo Musi	43	485	134	.276	73	51	.699	10	56	319	7.4
Henry Beenders (21 Prov.-24 Phil.)	45	269	76	.283	82	51	.622	13	99	203	4.5
Ralph Kaplowitz	48	292	71	.243	60	47	.783	19	100	189	3.9
Francis Crossin	39	121	29	.240	23	13	.565	20	28	71	1.8
Arthur Hillhouse	11	71	14	.197	37	30	.811	3	30	58	5.3
Stanley Brown	19	71	19	.268	19	12	.632	1	16	50	2.6
Robert O'Brien	22	81	17	.210	26	15	.577	1	40	49	2.2
Jack Rocker	9	22	8	.364	1	1	1.000	3	2	17	1.9

PROVIDENCE STEAMROLLERS

Player	G.	FGA	FGM	Pct.	FTA	FTM	Pct.	Ast.	PF	Pts.	Avg.
Ernie Calverley	47	835	226	.271	161	107	.665	119	168	559	11.9
George Nostrand	45	660	196	.297	239	129	.540	30	148	521	11.6
Kenneth Sailors (1 Chi.-2 Phil.-41 Prov.)	44	689	207	.300	159	110	.692	59	162	524	11.9
Earl Shannon	45	469	123	.262	183	116	.634	49	106	362	8.0
John Ezersky	25	376	95	.253	104	63	.606	16	62	253	10.1
Lee Robbins	31	260	72	.277	93	51	.548	7	93	195	6.3
John Toomay (19 Chi.-14 Prov.)	33	191	61	.319	91	60	.659	7	71	182	5.5
Robert Hubbard	28	199	58	.291	52	36	.692	11	34	152	5.4
Donald Martin	32	193	46	.238	20	9	.450	14	17	101	3.2
William Goodwin	24	155	36	.232	27	19	.704	7	36	91	3.8
Mel Thurston	14	113	32	.283	28	14	.500	4	42	78	5.6
George Mearns	24	115	23	.200	31	15	.484	10	65	61	2.5
John Janisch (3 Bos.-7 Prov.)	10	50	14	.280	16	9	.563	2	5	37	3.7
Ray Wertis	7	72	13	.181	14	6	.429	6	13	32	4.6
Gerard Kelly	3	10	3	.300	1	0	.000	0	3	6	2.0
Nat Hickey	1	3	0	.000	0	0	.000	0	1	0	0.0
Richard Fitzgerald	1	3	0	.000	0	0	.000	0	0	0	0.0
Bill Downey	3	2	0	.000	0	0	.000	0	0	0	0.0

ST. LOUIS BOMBERS

Player	G.	FGA	FGM	Pct.	FTA	FTM	Pct.	Ast.	PF	Pts.	Avg.
John Logan	48	734	221	.301	272	202	.743	62	141	644	13.4
Red Rocha	48	740	232	.314	213	147	.690	39	209	611	12.7
Belus Smawley	48	688	212	.308	150	111	.740	18	88	535	11.1
Robert Doll	42	658	174	.264	148	98	.662	26	107	446	10.6
Don Putnam	42	399	105	.263	84	57	.679	25	95	267	6.4
Irwin Rothenberg (11 Wsh-14 Blt-24 StL)	49	364	103	.283	150	87	.580	7	115	293	6.0
Ariel Maughan (14 Prov.-28 St.L.)	42	256	76	.297	53	32	.604	6	89	184	4.4
Gifford Roux	46	258	68	.264	68	40	.588	12	60	176	3.8
Francis O'Grady	44	257	67	.261	54	36	.667	9	61	170	3.9
James Martin	39	150	35	.233	33	15	.455	2	61	85	2.2
Wyndol Gray (1 Prov.-11 St.L.)	12	37	6	.162	4	1	.250	3	16	13	1.1

WASHINGTON CAPITOLS

Player	G.	FGA	FGM	Pct.	FTA	FTM	Pct.	Ast.	PF	Pts.	Avg.
Robert Feerick	48	861	293	.340	240	189	.788	56	139	775	16.1
Fred Scolari	47	780	229	.294	179	131	.732	58	153	589	12.5
Horace McKinney	43	680	182	.268	188	121	.644	36	176	485	11.3
John Norlander	48	543	167	.308	182	135	.742	44	102	469	9.8
Irving Torgoff	47	541	111	.205	144	117	.813	32	153	339	7.2
John Mahnken	48	526	131	.249	88	54	.614	31	151	316	6.6
Sidney Hertzberg (4 N.Y.-37 Wash.)	41	414	110	.266	73	58	.795	23	61	278	6.8
Richard O'Keefe	37	257	63	.245	59	30	.508	18	85	156	4.2
Jack Tingle	37	137	36	.263	33	17	.515	7	45	89	2.4

All-Star Joe Fulks had another great season, but Philadelphia failed to defend its title, losing to Baltimore in six games in the finals.

PLAYOFF RESULTS

WESTERN DIVISION TIEBREAKERS

Mar. 23—Washington 70 at Chicago 74
Mar. 25—Baltimore 75 at Chicago 72

QUARTERFINALS
Baltimore 2, New York 1

Mar. 27—New York 81 at Baltimore..85
Mar. 28—Baltimore 69 at New York 79
Apr.   1—New York 77 at Baltimore 84

Chicago 2, Boston 1

Mar. 28—Chicago 79 at Boston 72
Mar. 31—Chicago 77 at Boston 81
Apr.   2—Chicago 81 at Boston 74

SEMIFINALS
Philadelphia 4, St. Louis 3

Mar. 23—Philadelphia 58 at St. Louis 60
Mar. 25—Philadelphia 65 at St. Louis 64
Mar. 27—St. Louis 56 at Philadelphia 84
Mar. 30—St. Louis 56 at Philadelphia 51
Apr.   1—Philadelphia 62 at St. Louis 69
Apr.   3—St. Louis 61 at Philadelphia 84
Apr.   6—Philadelphia 85 at St. Louis...46

Baltimore 2, Chicago 0

Apr.   7—Baltimore 73 at Chicago 67
Apr.   8—Chicago 72 at Baltimore...89

WORLD CHAMPIONSHIP SERIES
Baltimore 4, Philadelphia 2

Apr. 10—Baltimore 60 at Philadelphia 71
Apr. 13—Baltimore 66 at Philadelphia 63
Apr. 15—Philadelphia 70 at Baltimore 72
Apr. 17—Philadelphia 75 at Baltimore 78
Apr. 20—Baltimore 82 at Philadelphia 91
Apr. 21—Philadelphia 73 at Baltimore 88

1946-47 NBA STATISTICS

1946-47 NBA CHAMPION PHILADELPHIA WARRIORS

Front row (left to right): Jerry Rullo, Angelo Musi, Peter A. Tyrell, General Manager; Pete Rosenberg, Jerry Fleishman. Back row: Assistant Coach Cy Kaselman, George Senesky, Ralph Kaplowitz, Howard Dallmar, Art Hillhouse, Joe Fulks, Matt Guokas, Coach Ed Gottlieb.

FINAL STANDINGS

EASTERN DIVISION

Teams	Wash.	Phil.	N.Y.	Prov.	Tor.	Bos.	Chi.	St.L.	Clev.	Det.	Pitt.	W.	L.	Pct.	G.B.
Washington	..	5	4	6	5	5	5	4	5	5	5	49	11	.817	...
Philadelphia	1	..	4	4	5	5	1	3	3	4	5	35	25	.583	14
New York	2	2	..	4	3	2	3	4	2	5	6	33	27	.550	16
Providence	0	2	2	..	3	5	3	2	4	4	3	28	32	.467	21
Toronto	1	1	3	3	..	2	2	4	0	3	3	22	38	.367	27
Boston	1	1	4	1	4	..	0	1	2	3	5	22	38	.367	27

WESTERN DIVISION

Teams	Wash.	Phil.	N.Y.	Prov.	Tor.	Bos.	Chi.	St.L.	Clev.	Det.	Pitt.	W.	L.	Pct.	G.B.
Chicago	1	5	3	3	4	6	..	3		3	6	39	22	.639	...
St. Louis	2	3	2	4	2	5	4	..	5	6	5	38	23	.623	1
Cleveland	1	3	4	2	6	4	1	1	..	4	4	30	30	.500	8.5
Detroit	1	2	1	2	3	3	3	0	2	..	3	20	40	.333	18.5
Pittsburgh	1	1	0	3	3	1	0	1	2	3	..	15	45	.250	23.5

HOME-ROAD RECORDS OF ALL TEAMS

	Home	Road	Total		Home	Road	Total
Boston	14- 16	8- 22	22- 38	Pittsburgh	11- 19	4- 26	15- 45
Chicago	22- 9	17- 13	39- 22	Providence	19- 11	9- 21	28- 32
Cleveland	17- 13	13- 17	30- 30	St. Louis	22- 8	16- 15	38- 28
Detroit	12- 18	8- 22	20- 40	Toronto	15- 15	7- 23	22- 38
New York	18- 12	15- 15	33- 27	Washington	29- 1	20- 10	49- 11
Philadelphia	23- 7	12- 18	35- 25	Totals	202-129	129-202	331-331

TEAM STATISTICS

Team	G	FGA	FGM	Pct.	FTA	FTM	Pct.	Ast.	PF	For	Agst.	Pt.Dif.
Washington	60	5794	1723	.297	1391	982	.706	378	1144	73.8	63.9	+9.9
Chicago	61	6309	1879	.297	1550	939	.606	436	1473	77.0	73.3	+3.7
Philadelphia	60	5384	1510	.280	1596	1098	.688	343	1082	68.6	65.2	+3.4
St. Louis	61	5877	1601	.272	1400	862	.616	292	1234	66.6	64.1	+2.5
New York	60	5255	1465	.279	1438	951	.661	457	1218	64.7	64.0	+0.7
Cleveland	60	5699	1674	.294	1428	903	.632	494	1246	70.9	71.8	—0.9
Providence	60	5582	1629	.292	1666	1092	.655	481	1215	72.5	74.2	—1.7
Detroit	60	5843	1437	.246	1494	923	.618	482	1351	63.3	65.3	—2.0
Toronto	60	5672	1515	.267	1552	966	.622	463	1271	66.6	71.0	—4.4
Boston	60	5133	1397	.272	1375	811	.590	470	1202	60.1	65.0	—4.9
Pittsburgh	60	4961	1345	.271	1507	984	.653	272	1360	61.2	67.6	—6.4

INDIVIDUAL LEADERS

POINTS

	G.	FG	FT	Pts.	Avg.		G.	FG	FT	Pts.	Avg.
Joe Fulks, Philadelphia	60	475	439	1389	23.2	Don Martin, Providence	60	311	111	733	12.2
Bob Feerick, Washington	55	364	198	926	16.8	Fred Scolari, Washington	58	291	146	728	12.6
Stan Miasek, Detroit	60	331	233	895	14.9	Henry Beenders, Providence	58	266	181	713	12.3
Ed Sadowski, Toronto-Cleve.	53	329	219	877	16.5	John Janisch, Detroit	60	283	131	697	11.6
Max Zaslofsky, Chicago	61	336	205	877	14.4	Horace McKinney, Wash.	58	275	145	695	12.0
Ernie Calverley, Providence	59	323	199	845	14.3	Earl Shannon, Providence	57	245	197	687	12.1
Charles Halbert, Chicago	61	280	213	773	12.7	Mel Riebe, Cleveland	55	276	111	663	12.1
John Logan, St. Louis	61	290	190	770	12.6	Mike McCarron, Toronto	60	236	177	649	10.8
Leo Mogus, Cleve.-Toronto	58	259	235	753	13.0	Frank Baumholtz, Cleveland	45	255	121	631	14.0
Coulby Gunther, Pittsburgh	52	254	226	734	14.1	Don Carlson, Chicago	59	272	86	630	10.7

FIELD GOALS
(Minimum 200 FGM)

	FGA	FGM	Pct.
Bob Feerick, Washington	908	364	.401
Ed Sadowski, Toronto-Cleve.	891	329	.369
Earl Shannon, Providence	722	245	.339
Coulby Gunther, Pittsburgh	756	254	.336
Max Zaslofsky, Chicago	1020	336	.329
Don Carlson, Chicago	845	272	.322
Connie Simmons, Boston	768	246	.320
John Norlander, Washington	698	223	.319
Ken Sailors, Cleveland	741	229	.309
Mel Riebe, Cleveland	898	276	.307

FREE THROWS
(Minimum 125 FTM)

	FTA	FTM	Pct.
Fred Scolari, Washington	180	146	.811
Tony Kappen, Pitt.-Boston	161	128	.795
Stan Stutz, New York	170	133	.782
Bob Feerick, Washington	260	198	.762
John Logan, St. Louis	254	190	.748
Max Zaslofsky, Chicago	278	205	.737
Joe Fulks, Philadelphia	601	439	.730
Leo Mogus, Cleve.-Toronto	325	235	.723
George Mearns, Providence	175	126	.720
Tony Jaros, Chicago	181	128	.707

ASSISTS

	G.	No.	Avg.
Ernie Calverley, Providence	59	202	3.4
Ken Sailors, Cleveland	58	134	2.3
Ossie Schectman, New York	54	109	2.0
Howie Dallmar, Philadelphia	60	104	1.7
Marv Rottner, Chicago	56	93	1.7
Stan Miasek, Detroit	60	93	1.6
Earl Shannon, Providence	57	84	1.5
Leo Mogus, Clev.-Tor.	58	84	1.4
John Logan, St. Louis	61	78	1.3
Bob Feerick, Washington	55	69	1.3
Horace McKinney, Washington	58	69	1.2

TEAM-BY-TEAM INDIVIDUAL STATISTICS

BOSTON CELTICS

Player	G.	FGA	FGM	Pct.	FTA	FTM	Pct.	Ast.	PF	Pts.	Avg.
Connie Simmons	60	768	246	.320	189	128	.677	62	130	620	10.3
Albert Brightman	58	870	223	.256	193	121	.627	60	115	567	9.8
Tony Kappen (41 Pitts.-18 Bos.)	59	537	128	.238	161	128	.795	28	78	384	6.5
Wyndol Gray	55	476	139	.292	124	72	.581	47	105	350	6.4
Charlie Hoefer (23 Tor.-35 Bos.)	58	514	130	.253	139	91	.655	33	142	351	6.1
Art Spector	55	460	123	.267	150	83	.553	46	130	329	6.0
John Simmons	60	429	120	.280	127	78	.614	29	78	318	5.3
Gerard Kelly	43	313	91	.291	111	74	.667	21	128	256	6.0
Kevin Connors	49	380	94	.247	84	39	.464	40	129	227	4.6
Jack Garfinkle	40	304	81	.266	28	17	.607	58	62	179	4.5
Harold Kottman	53	188	59	.314	101	47	.465	17	58	165	3.1
Bill Fenley	33	138	31	.225	45	23	.511	16	59	85	3.7
Virgil Vaughn	17	78	15	.192	28	15	.536	10	18	45	2.6
Richard Murphy (24 N.Y.-7 Bos.)	31	75	15	.200	9	4	.444	8	15	34	1.1
Robert Duffy (11 Chi.-6 Bos.)	17	32	7	.219	7	5	.714	0	17	19	1.1
Mel Hirsch	13	45	9	.200	2	1	.500	10	18	19	1.5
Herbert Crisler	4	6	2	.333	2	2	1.000	0	6	6	1.5
Bob Eliason	1	1	0	.000	0	0	.000	0	1	0	0.0

CHICAGO STAGS

Player	G.	FGA	FGM	Pct.	FTA	FTM	Pct.	Ast.	PF	Pts.	Avg.
Max Zaslofsky	61	1020	336	.329	278	205	.737	40	121	877	14.4
Charles Halbert	61	915	280	.306	356	213	.598	46	161	773	12.7
Donald Carlson	59	845	272	.322	159	86	.541	59	182	630	10.7
Tony Jaros	59	613	177	.289	181	128	.707	28	156	482	8.2
James Seminoff	60	586	184	.314	130	71	.546	63	155	439	7.3
Marvin Rottner	56	655	190	.290	79	43	.544	93	109	423	7.6
Doyle Parrack	58	413	110	.266	80	52	.650	20	77	272	4.7
Chester Carlisle	51	373	100	.268	92	56	.609	17	136	256	5.0
Wilbert Kautz	50	420	107	.255	73	39	.534	37	114	253	5.1
Charles Gilmur	51	253	76	.300	66	26	.394	21	139	178	3.5
William Davis	47	146	35	.240	41	14	.341	11	92	84	1.8
Wallace Sydnor	15	26	5	.192	10	5	.500	0	6	15	1.0
Garland O'Shields	9	11	2	.182	2	0	.000	1	8	4	0.4
Norman Baker	4	1	0	.000	0	0	.000	0	0	0	0.0
Robert Rensberger	3	7	0	.000	0	0	.000	0	4	0	0.0

CLEVELAND REBELS

Player	G.	FGA	FGM	Pct.	FTA	FTM	Pct.	Ast.	PF	Pts.	Avg.
Edward Sadowski (10 Tor-43 Clev)	53	891	329	.369	328	219	.668	46	194	877	16.5
Frank Baumholtz	45	856	255	.298	156	121	.776	54	93	631	14.0
Melvin Riebe	55	898	276	.307	173	111	.642	67	169	663	12.1
Kenneth Sailors	58	741	229	.309	200	119	.595	134	177	577	9.9
George Nostrand (13 Tor-48 Clev)	61	656	192	.293	210	98	.467	31	145	482	7.9
Robert Faught	51	478	141	.295	106	61	.575	33	97	343	6.7
Nicholas Shaback	53	385	102	.265	53	38	.717	29	75	242	4.6
Ben Scharnus	51	165	33	.200	59	37	.627	19	83	103	2.0
Irving Rothenberg	29	167	36	.216	54	30	.556	15	62	102	3.5
Henry Lefkowitz	24	114	22	.193	13	7	.538	4	35	51	2.1
Ray Wertis (18 Tor-43 Clev)	61	366	79	.216	91	56	.615	39	82	214	3.5
Leon Brown	5	3	0	.000	0	0	.000	0	2	0	0.0
Kenneth Corley	3	0	0	.000	0	0	.000	0	0	0	0.0
Ned Endress	16	25	3	.120	15	8	.533	4	13	14	0.9
Peter Lalich	7	1	0	.000	0	0	.000	0	1	0	0.0

DETROIT LIONS

Player	G.	FGA	FGM	Pct.	FTA	FTM	Pct.	Ast.	PF	Pts.	Avg.
Stanley Miasek	60	1154	331	.287	385	233	.605	93	208	895	14.9
John Janisch	60	983	283	.288	198	131	.662	49	132	697	11.6
Ariel Maughan	59	929	224	.241	114	84	.737	57	180	532	9.0
Robert Dille	57	563	111	.197	111	74	.667	40	92	296	5.2
Thomas King	58	410	97	.237	160	101	.631	32	102	295	5.1
Grady Lewis	60	520	106	.204	138	75	.543	54	166	287	4.8
Harold Brown	54	383	95	.248	117	74	.632	39	122	264	4.9
Moe Becker (17-Pitt-6 Bos-20 Det)	43	358	70	.196	44	22	.500	30	98	162	3.8
Milt Schoon	41	199	43	.216	80	34	.425	12	75	120	2.9
Arthur Stolkey	23	164	36	.220	44	30	.682	38	72	102	4.4
George Pearcy	37	130	31	.238	44	32	.727	13	68	94	2.5
Henry Pearcy	29	108	24	.222	34	25	.735	7	20	73	2.5
Chet Aubuchon	30	91	23	.253	35	19	.543	20	46	65	2.2
Howard McCarthy	19	82	10	.122	10	1	.100	2	22	21	1.1
Harold Johnson	27	20	4	.200	14	7	.500	11	13	15	0.6

NEW YORK KNICKERBOCKERS

Player	G.	FGA	FGM	Pct.	FTA	FTM	Pct.	Ast.	PF	Pts.	Avg.
Sidney Hertzberg	59	695	201	.289	149	113	.758	37	109	515	8.7
Stanley Stutz	60	641	172	.268	170	133	.782	49	127	477	8.0
Thomas Byrnes	60	583	175	.300	160	103	.644	35	90	453	7.6
Ossie Schectman	54	588	162	.276	179	111	.620	109	115	435	8.1
John Palmer	42	521	160	.307	121	81	.669	34	110	401	9.5
Leo Gottlieb	57	494	149	.302	55	36	.655	24	71	334	5.9
Robert Cluggish	54	356	93	.261	91	52	.571	22	113	238	4.4
Robert Fitzgerald (31 Tor-29 NY)	60	362	70	.193	130	81	.623	35	153	221	3.7
Lee Knorek	22	219	62	.283	72	47	.653	21	64	171	7.8
Frido Frey	23	97	28	.289	56	32	.571	14	37	88	3.8
Audley Brindley	12	49	14	.286	7	6	.857	1	16	34	2.8
William Van Breda Kolff	16	34	7	.206	17	11	.647	6	10	25	1.6
Frank Mangiapane	6	13	2	.154	3	1	.333	0	6	5	0.8

PHILADELPHIA WARRIORS

Player	G.	FGA	FGM	Pct.	FTA	FTM	Pct.	Ast.	PF	Pts.	Avg.
Joseph Fulks	60	1557	475	.305	601	439	.730	25	199	1389	23.2
Angelo Musi	60	818	230	.281	123	102	.829	26	120	562	9.4
Howard Dallmar	60	710	199	.280	203	130	.640	104	141	528	8.8
Ralph Kaplowitz (27 NY-30 Phil)	57	523	146	.274	151	111	.735	38	122	403	7.1
George Senesky	58	531	142	.267	124	82	.661	34	83	366	6.3
Arthur Hillhouse	60	412	120	.291	166	120	.723	41	139	360	6.0
Jerry Fleishman	59	372	97	.261	127	69	.543	40	101	263	4.5
Alexander Rosenberg	51	287	60	.209	49	30	.612	27	64	150	2.9
Jerry Rullo	50	174	52	.299	47	23	.489	20	61	127	2.5
Matthew Guokas	47	104	28	.269	47	26	.553	9	70	82	1.7
Fred Sheffield	22	146	29	.199	26	16	.615	4	34	74	3.4
John Murphy (9 NY-11 Phil)	20	40	11	.275	15	10	.667	0	8	32	1.6

PITTSBURGH IRONMEN

Player	G.	FGA	FGM	Pct.	FTA	FTM	Pct.	Ast.	PF	Pts.	Avg.
Coulby Gunther	52	756	254	.336	351	226	.644	32	117	734	14.1
John Abramovic	47	834	202	.242	178	123	.691	35	161	527	11.2
Stanley Noszka	58	693	199	.287	157	109	.694	39	163	507	8.7
Harry Zeller	48	382	120	.314	177	122	.689	31	177	362	7.5
Edward Melvin	57	376	99	.263	127	83	.654	37	150	281	4.9
Press Maravich	51	375	102	.272	58	30	.517	6	102	234	4.6
Michael Bytzura	60	356	87	.244	72	36	.500	31	108	210	3.5
John Mills	47	187	55	.294	129	71	.550	9	94	181	3.9
Noble Jorgensen	15	112	25	.223	25	16	.640	4	40	66	4.4
Joseph Fabel	30	96	25	.260	26	13	.500	2	64	63	2.1
Roger Jorgensen	28	54	14	.259	19	13	.684	1	36	41	1.5
Walter Miller	12	21	7	.333	18	9	.500	6	16	23	1.9
Nat Frankel	6	27	4	.148	12	8	.667	3	6	16	2.7
Zigmund Mihalik	7	9	3	.333	0	0	.000	0	10	6	0.9
Gorham Getchell	16	8	0	.000	9	5	1.000	0	5	5	0.3

PROVIDENCE STEAMROLLERS

Player	G.	FGA	FGM	Pct.	FTA	FTM	Pct.	Ast.	PF	Pts.	Avg.
Ernest Calverley	59	1102	323	.293	283	199	.703	202	191	845	14.3
Don Martin	60	1022	311	.304	168	111	.661	59	98	733	12.2
Henry Beenders	58	1016	266	.262	257	181	.704	37	196	713	12.3

Player	G.	FGA	FGM	Pct.	FTA	FTM	Pct.	Ast.	PF	Pts.	Avg.
Earl Shannon	57	722	245	.339	348	197	.566	84	169	687	12.1
George Mearns	57	478	128	.268	175	126	.720	35	137	382	6.7
Henry Rosenstein (31 NY-29 Prov)	60	390	119	.305	225	144	.640	36	172	382	6.4
Wilfred Goodwin	55	348	98	.282	75	60	.800	15	94	256	4.7
Forest Weber (11 NY-39 Prov)	50	202	59	.292	79	55	.696	4	111	173	3.5
George Pastushok	39	183	48	.262	46	25	.543	15	42	121	3.1
Robert Shea	43	153	37	.242	33	19	.576	6	42	93	2.2
George Grimshaw	21	56	20	.357	44	21	.477	1	25	61	2.9
Kenneth Keller (25 Wash- 3 Prov)	28	30	10	.333	5	2	.400	1	15	22	0.8
Thomas Callahan	13	29	6	.207	12	5	.417	4	9	17	1.3
Elmore Morgenthaler	11	13	4	.308	12	7	.583	3	3	15	1.4
Robert Dehnert	10	15	6	.400	6	2	.333	0	8	14	1.4
Armand Cure	12	15	4	.267	3	2	.667	0	5	10	0.8
Lou Spicer	4	7	0	.000	2	1	.500	0	3	1	0.3

ST. LOUIS BOMBERS

Player	G.	FGA	FGM	Pct.	FTA	FTM	Pct.	Ast.	PF	Pts.	Avg.
John Logan	61	1043	290	.278	254	190	.748	78	136	770	12.6
Robert Doll	60	768	194	.253	206	134	.650	22	167	522	8.7
George Munroe	59	623	164	.263	133	86	.647	17	91	414	7.0
Donald Putnam	58	635	156	.246	105	68	.648	30	106	380	6.6
Gifford Roux	60	478	142	.297	160	70	.438	17	95	354	5.9
Cecil Hankins	55	391	117	.299	150	90	.600	14	49	324	5.9
John Barr	58	438	124	.283	79	47	.595	54	164	295	5.1
Aubrey Davis	59	381	107	.281	115	73	.635	14	136	287	4.9
Belus Smawley	22	352	113	.321	47	36	.766	10	37	262	11.9
James Martin	54	304	89	.293	31	13	.419	9	75	191	3.5
Herschel Baltimore	58	263	53	.202	69	32	.464	16	98	138	2.4
Deb Smith	48	119	32	.269	21	9	.429	6	47	73	1.5
Fred Jacobs	18	69	19	.275	25	12	.480	5	25	50	2.8

TORONTO HUSKIES

Player	G.	FGA	FGM	Pct.	FTA	FTM	Pct.	Ast.	PF	Pts.	Avg.
Leo Mogus (17 Clev.-41 Tor.)	58	879	259	.295	325	235	.723	84	176	753	13.0
Michael McCarron	60	838	236	.282	288	177	.615	59	184	649	10.8
Michael Wallace (24 Bos.-37 Tor.)	61	809	225	.278	196	106	.541	58	167	556	9.1
Richard Schultz (36 Clev.-21 Tor.)	57	548	130	.237	138	94	.681	56	123	354	6.2
Robert Mullen (26 N.Y.-28 Tor.)	54	445	125	.281	102	64	.627	54	94	314	5.8
Clarence Hermsen (11 Clev.-21 Tor.)	32	394	113	.287	112	71	.634	25	86	297	9.3
Richard Fitzgerald	60	495	118	.238	60	41	.683	40	89	277	4.6
Nathan Milltzok (36 N.Y.-21 Tor.)	57	343	90	.262	112	64	.571	42	120	244	4.3
Roy Hurley	46	447	100	.224	64	39	.609	34	85	239	5.2
Harry Miller	53	260	58	.223	82	36	.439	42	119	152	2.9
Frank Fucarino	28	198	53	.268	60	34	.567	7	38	140	5.0
Ralph Siewert (7 St.L.-14 Tor.)	21	44	6	.136	15	8	.533	4	18	20	1.0
Edward Kasid	8	21	6	.286	6	0	.000	6	8	12	1.5
Gino Sovran	6	15	5	.333	2	1	.500	1	5	11	1.8
Henry Biasatti	6	5	2	.400	4	2	.500	0	3	6	1.0

WASHINGTON CAPITOLS

Player	G.	FGA	FGM	Pct.	FTA	FTM	Pct.	Ast.	PF	Pts.	Avg.
Robert Feerick	55	908	364	.401	260	198	.762	69	142	926	16.8
Fred Scolari	58	989	291	.294	180	146	.811	58	159	728	12.6
Horace McKinney	58	987	275	.279	210	145	.690	69	162	695	12.0
John Norlander	60	698	223	.319	276	180	.652	50	122	626	10.4
John Mahnken	60	876	223	.255	163	111	.681	60	181	557	9.3
Irving Torgoff	58	684	187	.273	159	116	.730	30	173	490	8.4
Francis O'Grady	55	231	55	.238	53	38	.717	20	60	148	2.7
Martin Passaglia	43	221	51	.231	32	18	.563	9	44	120	2.8
Robert Gantt	23	89	29	.326	28	13	.464	5	45	71	3.1
Albert Negratti	11	69	13	.188	8	5	.625	5	20	31	2.8
Eugene Gillette	14	11	1	.091	9	6	.667	2	13	8	0.6
Al Lujack	5	8	1	.125	5	2	.400	0	6	4	0.8
Ben Goldfaden	2	2	0	.000	4	2	.500	0	3	2	1.0

PLAYOFF RESULTS

QUARTERFINALS
Philadelphia 2, St. Louis 1

Apr. 2—St. Louis 68 at Philadelphia 73
Apr. 5—Philadelphia 51 at St. Louis 73
Apr. 6—Philadelphia 75 at St. Louis 59

New York 2, Cleveland 1

Apr. 2—New York 51 at Cleveland 77
Apr. 5—Cleveland 74 at New York 86
Apr. 9—Cleveland 71 at New York 93

SEMIFINALS
Chicago 4, Washington 2

Apr. 2—Chicago 81 at Washington 65
Apr. 3—Chicago 69 at Washington 53
Apr. 8—Washington 55 at Chicago 67
Apr. 10—Chicago 69 at Washington 76
Apr. 12—Washington 67 at Chicago 55
Apr. 13—Washington 61 at Chicago 66

Philadelphia 2, New York 0

Apr. 12—New York 70 at Philadelphia 82
Apr. 14—Philadelphia 72 at New York 53

WORLD CHAMPIONSHIP SERIES
Philadelphia 4, Chicago 1

Apr. 16—Chicago 71 at Philadelphia 84
Apr. 17—Chicago 75 at Philadelphia 85
Apr. 19—Philadelphia 75 at Chicago 72
Apr. 20—Philadelphia 73 at Chicago 74
Apr. 22—Chicago 80 at Philadelphia 83

OFFICIAL RULES

OF THE

NATIONAL BASKETBALL

ASSOCIATION

1992-93

NBA OPERATIONS DEPT.

Rod Thorn, Vice President, Operations

Matt Winick, Director of Scheduling
and Game Operations

Gary Brokaw, Manager, Basketball Operations

Darell Garretson, Chief of Officiating Staff

Published by The Sporting News, St. Louis, Missouri 63166

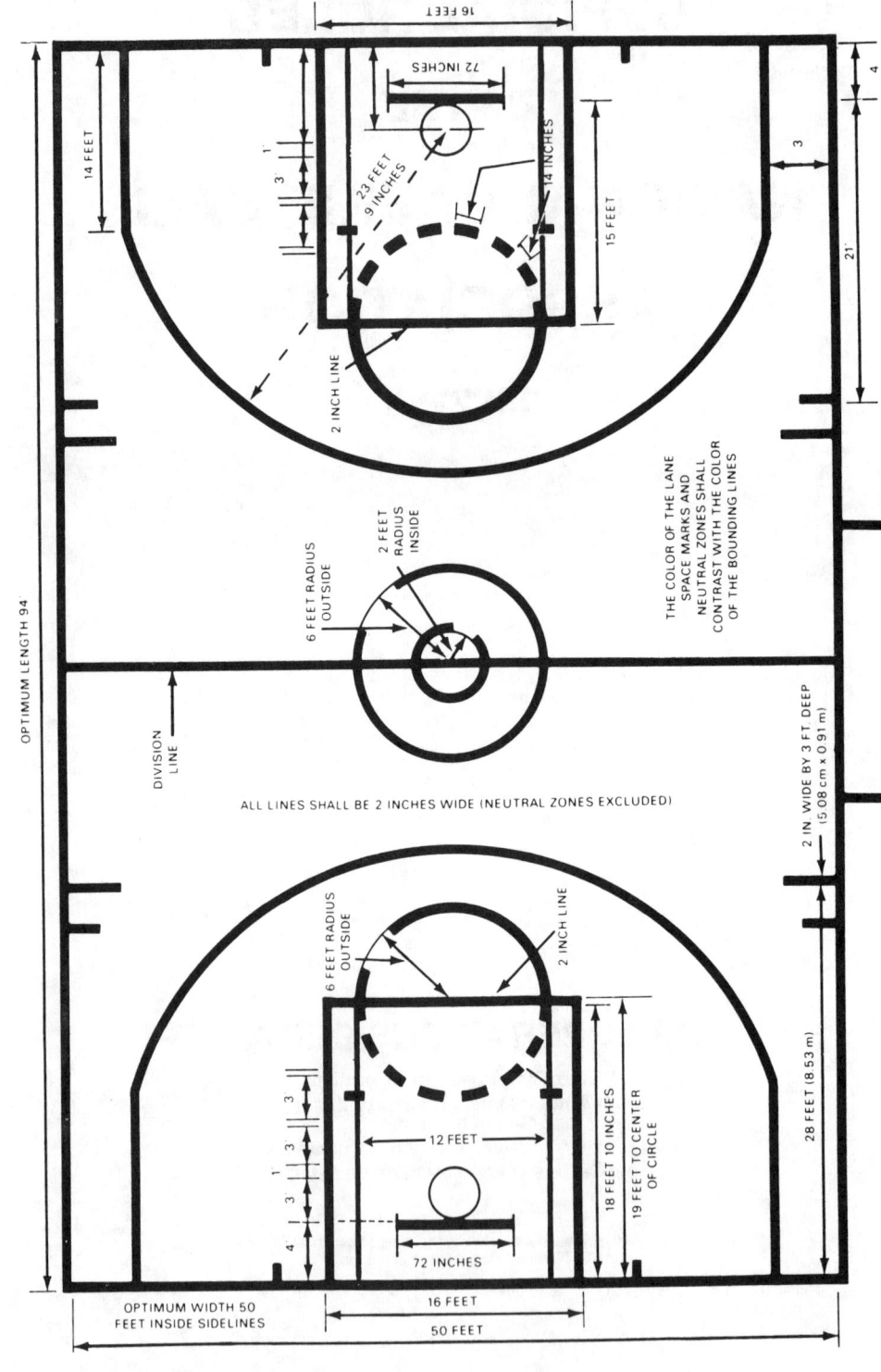

OPTIMUM LENGTH 94

16 FEET

72 INCHES

14 INCHES

23 FEET 9 INCHES

14 FEET

15 FEET

3' 1'

2 INCH LINE

4

3

21'

THE COLOR OF THE LANE SPACE MARKS AND NEUTRAL ZONES SHALL CONTRAST WITH THE COLOR OF THE BOUNDING LINES

2 FEET RADIUS INSIDE

6 FEET RADIUS OUTSIDE

DIVISION LINE

ALL LINES SHALL BE 2 INCHES WIDE (NEUTRAL ZONES EXCLUDED)

2 IN. WIDE BY 3 FT. DEEP (5.08 cm x 0.91 m)

6 FEET RADIUS OUTSIDE

2 INCH LINE

18 FEET 10 INCHES

19 FEET TO CENTER OF CIRCLE

28 FEET (8.53 m)

12 FEET

3

3

3

3

1'

4'

72 INCHES

16 FEET

OPTIMUM WIDTH 50 FEET INSIDE SIDELINES

50 FEET

RULES INDEX

Official Rules

RULE NO. 1—COURT DIMENSIONS—EQUIPMENT

Section I—Court and Dimensions

a. The playing court shall be measured and marked as shown in the court diagram. (See page 8)

b. A free throw lane shall be marked at each end of the court with dimensions and markings as shown on the court diagram. All boundary lines are part of the lane; lane space marks and neutral zone marks are **not.** The color of the lane space marks and neutral zones shall contrast with the color of the boundary lines. The areas identified by the lane space markings are 2" by 8" inches and the neutral zone marks are 12" by 8".

c. A free throw line shall be drawn (2" wide) across each of the circles indicated in the court diagram. It shall be parallel to the end line and shall be 15' from the plane of the face of the backboard.

d. The three-point field goal area has parallel lines 3' from the sidelines, extending from the baseline, and an arc of 23'9" from the middle of the basket which intersects the parallel lines.

e. Four hash marks shall be drawn (2" wide) perpendicular to the sideline on each side of the court and 28' from the baseline. These hash marks shall extend 3' onto the court.

f. Four hash marks shall be drawn (2" wide) perpendicular to the sideline on each side of the court and 25' from the baseline. These hash marks shall extend 6" onto the court.

g. Four hash marks shall be drawn (2" wide) perpendicular to the baseline on each side of the free throw lane line. These hash marks shall be 3' from the free throw lane line and extend 6" onto the court.

h. Four hash marks shall be drawn (2" wide) parallel to the baseline on each side of the free throw circle. These hash marks shall be 13' from the baseline and 3' from the free throw lane lines and shall be 6" in length.

i. Two hash marks shall be drawn (2" wide) perpendicular to the sideline, in front of the scorer's table, and 4' on each side of the midcourt line. This will designate the Substitution Box area.

Section II—Equipment

a. The backboard shall be a rectangle measuring 6' horizontally and 3½' vertically. The front surface shall be flat and transparent.

b. A transparent backboard shall be marked with a 2" white rectangle centered behind the ring. This rectangle shall have outside dimensions of 24" horizontally and 18" vertically.

c. Home management is required to have a spare board with supporting unit on hand for emergencies, and a steel tape or extension ruler and a level for use if necessary.

d. Each basket shall consist of a pressure-release NBA approved metal safety ring 18" in inside diameter with a white cord net 15" to 18" in length. The cord of the net shall not be less than 30 thread nor more than 120 thread and shall be constructed to check the ball momentarily as it passes through the basket.

e. Each basket ring shall be securely attached to the backboard with its upper edge 10' above and parallel to the floor and equidistant from the vertical edges of the board. The nearest point of the inside edge of the ring shall be 6" from the plane of the face of the board. The ring shall be painted orange.

f. (1) The ball shall be an officially approved NBA ball between 7½ and 8½ pounds pressure.

(2) Six balls must be made available to each team for pre-game warmup.

g. At least one electric light is to be placed behind the backboard, obvious to officials and synchronized to light up when the horn sounds at the expiration of time for each period. The electric light is to be "red."

RULE NO. 2—OFFICIALS AND THEIR DUTIES

Section I—The Game Officials

a. The game officials shall be a crew chief, referee and umpire. They will be assisted by an official scorer and two trained timers. One timer will operate the game clock and the other will operate the 24-second clock. All officials shall be approved by the Operations Department.

b. The officials shall wear the uniform prescribed by the NBA.

Section II—Duties of the Officials

a. The officials shall, prior to the start of the game, inspect and approve all equipment, including court, baskets, balls, backboards, timers and scorer's equipment.

b. The officials shall not permit players to play with any type of hand, arm, face, nose, ear, head or neck jewelry.

c. The officials shall not permit any player to wear equipment which, in his judgment, is dangerous to other players. Any equipment which is of hard substance (casts, splints, guards and braces) must be padded or foam covered and have no exposed sharp or cutting edge. All the face masks and eye or nose protectors must conform to the contour of the face and have no sharp or protruding edges. Approval is on a game-to-game basis.

d. All equipment used must be appropriate for basketball. Equipment that is unnatural and designed to increase a player's height or reach, or to gain an advantage, shall not be used.

e. The officials must check the three game balls to see that they are properly inflated. The recommended ball pressure should be between 7½ and 8½ pounds.

f. The crew chief shall be the official in charge.

g. If a coach desires to discuss a rule or interpretation of a rule prior to the start of a game or between periods, it will be mandatory for the officials to ask the other coach to be present during the discussion. The same procedure shall be followed if the officials wish to discuss a game situation with either coach.

h. The designated official shall toss the ball at the start of the game. The crew chief shall decide whether or not a goal shall count if the officials disagree, and he shall decide matters upon which scorers and timers disagree.

i. All officials shall be present during the 20-minute pre-game warm-up period to observe and report to the Operations Department any infractions of Rule 12A-Section VIII—j (hanging on the rim) and to review scoring and timing procedures with table personnel. Officials may await the on-court arrival of the first team.

j. Officials must meet with team captains prior to start of game.

k. Officials must report any atypical or unique incident to the Operations Department by datagram. Flagrant, punching, fighting fouls or a team's failure to have eight players to begin the game must also be reported.

Section III—Elastic Power

The officials shall have the power to make decisions on any point not specifically covered in the rules. The Operations Department will be advised of all such decisions at the earliest possible moment.

Section IV—Different Decisions By Officials

a. The crew chief shall have the authority to set aside or question decisions regarding rules made by the other officials.

b. It is the primary duty of the trail official to signal if goals count. If for any reason he does not know if the goal is made, he should ask the other officials. If none of them saw the goal made they should refer to the timer. If the timer saw the goal scored, it shall count.

EXCEPTION: Period Ending Score or No-Score in Official's Manual.

c. If the officials disagree as to who caused the ball to go out-of-bounds, a jump ball shall be called between the two players involved.

d. In the event that a violation and foul occur at the same time, the foul will take precedence.

e. Double Foul (See Rule 12-B—Section VI-f).

Section V—Time and Place for Decisions

a. The officials shall have the power to render decisions for infractions of rules committed either within or outside the boundary lines. This includes periods when the game may be stopped for any reason.

b. When a foul or violation occurs, an official shall blow his whistle to terminate play and signal the timer to stop the game clock. If it is a personal foul, he shall also designate the number of the offender to the scorer and indicate with his fingers the number of free throws to be attempted.

c. When a team is entitled to a throw-in, an official shall clearly signal the act which caused the ball to become dead, the throw-in spot and the team entitled to the throw-in, unless it follows a successful goal or an awarded goal.

Section VI—Correcting Errors
A. FREE THROWS

Officials may correct an error if a rule is inadvertently set aside and results in the following:

(1) A team not shooting a merited free throw

EXCEPTION: If the offensive team scores or shoots earned free throws on the next possession which occurred due to not attempting a merited free throw, the error shall be ignored.

(2) A team shooting an unmerited free throw

(3) Permitting the wrong player to attempt a free throw
a. Officials shall be notified of a possible error at the first dead ball.

b. Errors which occur in the first, second or third periods must be discovered and rectified prior to the start of the next period.

c. Errors which occur in the fourth period or overtime(s) must be discovered and rectified prior to the end of the period.

d. The ball is not in play on corrected free throw attempt(s). Play is resumed at the same spot and under the same conditions as would have prevailed had the error not been discovered.

e. All play that occurs is to be nullified if the error is discovered within a 24-second time period. The game clock shall be reset to the time that the error occurred.

EXCEPTION (1): Acts of unsportsmanlike conduct, and points scored therefrom, shall not be nullified.

EXCEPTION (2): Free throw attempt resulting from an illegal defense violation.

EXCEPTION (3): Free throw attempt(s) resulting from a personal foul which is a clear path to the basket, or a flagrant foul—penalty (1).

NOTE: The game clock shall not be reset in (2) and (3) above.

B. LINEUP POSITIONS

If the first period or overtime(s) begins with jumpers lined up incorrectly, and the error is discovered:

(1) After more than 24 seconds has elapsed, the teams will continue to shoot for that basket.

(2) If 24 seconds or less has elapsed, all play shall be nullified.

EXCEPTION: Acts of unsportsmanlike conduct, and points scored therefrom, shall not be nullified.

a. The game clock shall be reset to 12:00 or 5:00, respectively.

b. The 24-second clock shall be reset to 24.

(EXAMPLE: 12:00 to 11:36 or 5:00 to 4:36—Restart; 12:00 to 11:35 or 5:00 to 4:35—Do not restart).

C. START OF PERIOD—POSSESSION

If the second, third or fourth period begins with the wrong team being awarded possession, and the error is discovered:

(1) after 24 seconds has elapsed, the error cannot be corrected.

(2) with 24 seconds or less having elapsed, all play shall be nullified.

EXCEPTION: Acts of unsportsmanlike conduct, and points scored therefrom, shall not be nullified.

D. RECORD KEEPING

A record keeping error by the official scorer which involves the score, number of personal fouls and/or timeouts may be corrected by the officials at any time prior to the end of the fourth period. Any such error which occurs in overtime must be corrected prior to the end of that period.

Section VII—Duties of Scorers

a. The scorers shall record the field goals made, the free throws made and missed and shall keep a running summary of the points scored. They shall record the personal and technical fouls called on each player and shall notify the officials immediately when a sixth personal foul is called on any player. They shall record the timeouts charged to each team, shall notify a team and its coach through an official whenever that team takes a sixth and seventh charged timeout and shall notify the nearest official each time a team is granted a charged timeout in excess of the legal number. In case there is a question about an error in the scoring, the scorer shall check with the crew chief at once to find the discrepancy. If the error cannot be found, the official shall accept the record of the official scorer, unless he has knowledge that forces him to decide otherwise.

b. The scorers shall keep a record of the names, numbers and positions of the players who are to start the game and of all substitutes who enter the game. When there is an infraction of the rules pertaining to submission of the lineup, substitutions or numbers of players, they shall notify the nearest official immediately if the ball is dead, or as soon as it becomes dead if it is in play when the infraction is discovered. The scorer shall mark the time at which players are disqualified by reason of receiving six personal fouls, so that it may be easy to ascertain the order in which the players are eligible to go back into the game in accordance with Rule 3—Section I.

c. The scorers shall use a horn or other device unlike that used by the officials or timers to signal the officials. This may be used when the ball is dead or in certain specified situations when the ball is in control of a given team. The scorer shall signal the coach on the bench on every personal foul, designating the number of personal fouls a player has, and number of team fouls. NOTE: White paddles—team fouls; Red paddles—personal fouls.

d. When a player is disqualified from the game, or whenever a penalty free throw is being awarded, a buzzer, siren or some other clearly audible sound must be used by the scorer or timer to notify the game officials. It is the duty of the scorekeeper to be certain the officials have acknowledged the sixth personal foul buzzer and the penalty shot buzzer.

e. The scorer shall not signal the officials while the ball is in play, except to notify them of the necessity to correct an error.

f. Should the scorer sound the horn while the ball is in play, it shall be ignored by the players on the court. The officials must use their judgment in stopping play to consult with the scorer's table.

g. Scorers shall record on the scoreboard the number of team fouls up to a total of five, which will indicate that the team is in a penalty situation.

h. Scorers shall immediately record the name of the team which secures the first possession of the jump ball which opens the game.

i. Scorers shall record all illegal defense violations and notify the officials every time AFTER the first violation charged to each team.

Section VIII—Duties of Timers

a. The timers shall note when each half is to start and shall notify the crew chief and both coaches five minutes before this time, or cause them to be notified at least five minutes before the half is to start. They shall signal the scorers two minutes before starting time. They shall record playing time and time of stoppages as provided in the rules. The timers shall be provided with an extra stop watch to be used in timeouts, etc., other than the official game clock or watch. The official clock or scoreboard should show 12 minute periods.

b. At the beginning of the first period, any overtime period or whenever play is resumed by a jump ball, the game clock shall be started when the ball is legally tapped by either of the jumpers.

c. If, after time has been out, the ball is put in play by a throw-in or by a free throw, the game clock shall be started when the ball is legally touched by a player on the court.

d. During a jump ball, time may not be reduced from the 24-second clock or game clock if there is an illegal tap.

e. The game clock shall be stopped at the expiration of time for each period and when an official signals timeout. For a charged timeout, the timer shall start a timeout watch and shall signal the official when it is time to resume play.

f. The timers shall indicate with a controlled game horn the expiration of playing time. If the timer's signal fails to sound, or is not heard, the timer shall use other means to notify the officials immediately. If, in the meantime, a goal has been made or a foul has occurred, the crew chief shall consult the timer. If the timer agrees that time expired before the ball was in flight, the goal shall not count. If he agrees that the period ended before the foul occurred, the foul shall be disregarded unless it was unsportsmanlike. If there is a disagreement, the goal shall count or the foul shall be penalized unless the official has other knowledge.

g. In a dead ball situation, if the clock shows :00.0, the period or game is considered to have ended although the buzzer may not have sounded.

h. Record only the actual playing time in the last minute of the first, second and third periods.

i. Record only the actual playing time in the last two minutes of the fourth period and the last two minutes of any overtime period or periods.

j. Timers are responsible for contents in Comments On The Rules—Section N.

RULE NO. 3—PLAYERS, SUBSTITUTES AND COACHES

Section I—Team

a. Each team shall consist of five players. No team may be reduced to less than five players. If a player in the game receives his sixth personal foul and all substitutes have already been disqualified, said player shall remain in the game and shall be charged with a personal and team foul. A technical foul also shall be assessed against his team. All subsequent personal fouls, including offensive fouls, shall be treated similarly. All players who have six or more personal fouls and remain in the game shall be treated similarly.

b. In the event that there are only five eligible players remaining and one of these players is injured and must leave the game or is ejected, he must be replaced by the last player who was disqualified by reason of receiving six personal fouls. Each subsequent requirement to replace an injured or ejected player will be treated in this inverse order. Any such re-entry into a game by a disqualified player shall be penalized by a technical foul.

c. In the event that a player becomes ill and must leave the court while the ball is in play, the official will stop play immediately upon that team gaining new possession. The player will be immediately replaced and no technical foul will be assessed.

Section II—Starting Line-Ups

At least ten minutes before the game is scheduled to begin, the scorers shall be supplied with the name and number of each player who may participate in the game. Starting line-ups will be indicated. Failure to comply with this provision shall be reported to the Operations Department.

Section III—The Captain

a. A team may have a captain and a co-captain numbering a maximum of two. The designated captain may be anyone on the squad who is in uniform, except a player-coach.

b. The designated captain is the only player who may talk to an official during a regular or 20-

second timeout charged to his team. He may discuss a rule interpretation, but not a judgment decision.

c. If the designated captain continues to sit on the bench, he remains the captain for the entire game.

d. In the event that the captain is absent from the court or bench, his coach shall immediately designate a new captain.

Section IV—The Coach and Others

a. The coach's position may be on or off the bench from the 28' hash mark to the baseline. All assistants and trainers must remain on the bench. Coaches and trainers may not leave this restricted 28' area unless specifically requested to do so by the officials. Coaches and trainers are not permitted to go to the scorer's table, for any reason, except during a timeout or between periods, and then only to check statistical information. The penalty for violation of this rule is a technical foul.

b. Coaches are not permitted to talk to an official during any timeout. (See Rule 3—Sec. III—(b) for captain's rights).

c. A player-coach will have no special privileges. He is to conduct himself in the same manner as any other player.

d. Any club personnel not seated on the bench must conduct themselves in a manner that would reflect favorably on the dignity of the game or that of the officials. Violations by any of the personnel indicated shall require a written report to the Operations Department for subsequent action.

e. The bench shall be occupied only by a league-approved coach, assistant coaches, players and trainer.

f. If a player, coach or assistant coach is ejected or suspended from a game or games, he shall not at any time before, during or after such game or games appear in any part of the arena or stands where his team is playing. A player, coach or assistant coach may only remain in the dressing room of his team during such suspension, or leave the building. A violation of this rule shall call for an automatic fine of $500.

Section V—Substitutes

a. A substitute shall report to the scorer and position himself in the 8' Substitution Box located in front of the scorer's table. He shall give his name, number and whom he is to replace. The scorer shall sound the horn as soon as the ball is dead to indicate a substitution. The horn does not have to be sounded if the substitution occurs between periods or during timeouts. No substitute may enter the game after a successful field goal by either team, unless the ball is dead due to a personal foul, technical foul, timeout or violation. He may enter the game after the first of multiple free throws, whether made or missed.

b. The substitute shall remain in the Substitution Box until he is beckoned onto the court by an official. If the ball is about to become live, the beckoning signal shall be withheld. Any player who enters the court prior to being beckoned by an official shall be assessed a technical foul.

c. A substitute must be ready to enter the game when beckoned. No delays for removal of warm-up clothing will be permitted.

d. The substitute shall not replace a free throw shooter or a player involved in a jump ball unless dictated to do so by an injury whereby he is selected by the opposing coach. At no time may he be allowed to attempt a free throw awarded as a result of a technical foul.

e. A substitute shall be considered as being in the game when he is beckoned onto the court or recognized as being in the game by an official. Once a player is in the game, he cannot be removed until the next dead ball.

EXCEPTION: Rule 3—Section V—f and Comments on the Rules-P.

f. Any substitute may be removed after a successful free throw attempt which is to remain in play, if the offensive team requests and is granted a regular timeout.

g. A substitute may be recalled from the scorer's table prior to being beckoned onto the court by an official.

h. A player may be replaced and allowed to re-enter the game as a substitute during the same dead ball.

i. A player must be in the Substitution Box at the time a violation occurs if the throw-in is to be administered in the backcourt. If a substitute fails to meet this requirement, he may not enter the game until the next dead ball.

EXCEPTION: In the last two minutes of each period or overtime, a reasonable amount of time will be allowed for a substitution.

j. Notification of all above infractions and ensuing procedures shall be in accordance with Rule 2—Section VII.

k. No substitutes are allowed to enter the game during an official's suspension of play for (1) delay of game warning, (2) retrieving an errant ball or (3) any other unusual circumstance.

Section VI—Uniforms (Players Jerseys)

a. Each player shall be numbered on the front and back of his jersey with a number of solid color contrasting with the color of the shirt.

b. Each number must be not less than ¾" in width and not less than 6" in height on both the front and back. Each player shall have his surname affixed to the back of his game jersey in letters at least 2" in height. If a team has more than one player with the same surname, each such player's first initial must appear before the surname on the back of the game jersey.

c. The home team shall wear light color jerseys, and the visitors dark jerseys. For neutral court games and doubleheaders, the second team named in the official schedule shall be regarded as the home team and shall wear the light colored jerseys.

RULE NO. 4—DEFINITIONS

Section I—Basket/Backboard

a. A team's own basket is the ring and net through which its players try to shoot the ball. The visiting team has the choice of baskets for the first half. The basket selected by the visiting team when it first enters onto the court shall be its basket for the first half.

b. The teams change baskets for the second half. All overtime periods are considered extensions of the second half.

c. All parts of the backboard (front, sides, bottom and top) are considered in play when struck by the basketball except the back of the backboard, which is not in play.

Section II—Blocking

Blocking is illegal personal contact which impedes the progress of an opponent.

Section III—Dribble

A dribble is ball movement caused by a player in control, who throws or taps the ball into the air or to the floor, and then touches it once before it touches the floor.

a. The dribble ends when the dribbler:

(1) Touches the ball simultaneously with both hands

(2) Permits the ball to come to rest while he is in control of it

(3) Tries for a field goal

(4) Throws a pass

(5) Touches the ball more than once while dribbling, before it touches the floor

(6) Loses control

(7) Allows the ball to become dead

Section IV—Fouls

a. A personal foul is a foul which involves illegal contact with an opponent.

b. A technical foul is the penalty for unsportsmanlike conduct by a team member on the floor or seated on the bench which, in the opinion of the official, is detrimental to the game.

c. A double foul is a situation in which two opponents commit personal or technical fouls against each other at approximately the same time.

d. An offensive foul is illegal contact committed by an offensive player while team control exists.

e. A loose ball foul is illegal contact committed by either team when possession does not exist.

f. An elbow foul is making contact with the elbow in an unsportsmanlike manner.

g. A flagrant foul is unnecessary and/or excessive contact committed by a player against an opponent.

h. An away-from-the-play foul is illegal contact by the defense in the last two minutes of the game, which occurs (1) deliberately away from the immediate area of the ball, and/or (2) prior to the ball being released on a throw-in.

Section V—Free Throw

A free throw is the privilege given a player to score one point by an unhindered attempt for the goal from a position directly behind the free throw line. This attempt must be made within 10 seconds.

Section VI—Frontcourt/Backcourt

a. A team's frontcourt consists of that part of the court between its endline and the nearer edge of the midcourt line, including the basket and inbounds part of the backboard.

b. A team's backcourt consists of the entire midcourt line and the rest of the court to include the opponent's basket and inbounds part of the backboard.

c. A ball which is in contact with a player or with the court is in the backcourt if either the ball or the player is touching the backcourt. It is in the frontcourt if neither the ball nor the player is touching the backcourt.

d. A ball which is not in contact with a player or the court retains the same status as when it was last in contact with a player or the court.

EXCEPTION: Rule 4—Section VI—f.

e. The team on the offense must bring the ball across the midcourt line within 10 seconds. No additional 10 second count is permitted in the backcourt.

EXCEPTION: (1) kicked ball, or (2) punched ball, or (3) technical foul on the defensive team, or (4) delay of game warning on the defensive team.

f. The ball is considered in the frontcourt once it has broken the plane of the midcourt line and not in player control.

g. The defensive team has no "frontcourt/backcourt."

Section VII—Held Ball

A held ball occurs when two opponents have one or both hands firmly on the ball.

a. A held ball should not be called until both players have both hands so firmly on the ball that neither can gain sole possession without undue roughness. If a player is lying or sitting on the floor while in possession, he should have an opportunity to throw the ball, but a held ball should be called if there is danger of injury.

Section VIII—Pivot

A pivot takes place when a player who is holding the ball steps once or more than once in any direction with the same foot, while the other foot—called the pivot foot—is being kept at its point of contact with the floor.

Section IX—Traveling

Traveling is progressing in any direction while in possession of the ball, which is in excess of prescribed limits as noted in Rule 10—Section XIV.

Section X—Screen

A screen is the legal action of a player who, without causing undue contact, delays or prevents an opponent from reaching a desired position.

Section XI—Field Goal Attempt

A field goal attempt is a player's attempt to shoot the ball into his basket for a field goal. The attempt starts when the player begins the motion which habitually precedes the actual shot. It continues until the shooting effort ceases and he returns to a normal floor position. The term is also used to include the movement of the ball in flight until it has become dead or has been touched by a player.

Section XII—Throw-In

A throw-in is a method of putting the ball in play from out-of-bounds in accordance with Rule 8—Section III. The throw-in begins when the ball is at the disposal of the team or player entitled to it, and ends when the ball is released by the thrower-in.

Section XIII—Last Two Minutes

When the game clock shows 2:00, the game is considered to be in the two-minute period.

Section XIV—Disconcertion of Free Throw Shooter

Disconcertion of the free throw shooter is any of the following:

a. During the first of multiple free throw attempts, an opponent may not, while located on the lane lines, be allowed to raise arms above his head.

b. During any free throw attempt, an opponent who is in the visual field of the free throw shooter, may not (1) wave his arms, (2) make a sudden dash upcourt, (3) talk to the free throw shooter, or (4) talk loudly to a teammate or coach.

RULE NO. 5—SCORING AND TIMING

Section I—Scoring

a. A legal goal is made when a live ball enters the basket from above and remains in or passes through the net.

b. A successful field goal attempt from the area on or inside the three-point field goal line shall count two points.

c. A successful field goal attempt from the area outside the three-point field goal line shall count three points.

(1) The shooter must have at least one foot on the floor outside the three-point field goal line prior to the attempt.

(2) The shooter may not be touching the floor on or inside the three-point field goal line.

(3) The shooter may contact the three-point field goal line, or land in the two-point field goal area, after the ball is released.

d. A field goal accidentally scored in an opponent's basket shall be added to the opponent's score, credited to the opposing player nearest the shooter, and shall be mentioned in a footnote.

e. A field goal that, in the opinion of the officials, is intentionally scored in the wrong basket shall be disallowed. The ball shall be awarded to the opposing team out-of-bounds at the free throw line extended.

f. A successful free throw attempt shall count one point.

g. An unsuccessful free throw attempt which is tapped into the basket shall count two points and shall be credited to the player who tapped the ball in.

h. If there is a discrepancy in the score and it cannot be resolved, the running score shall be official.

Section II—Timing

a. All periods of regulation play in the NBA will be twelve minutes.

b. All overtime periods of play will be five minutes.

c. Fifteen minutes will be permitted between halves of all games.

d. 100 seconds will be permitted for regular timeouts and between the fourth period and/or any overtime periods. 130 seconds will be permitted between the first and second periods and the third and fourth periods.

e. A team is permitted 30 seconds to replace a disqualified player.

f. The game is considered to be in the two-minute part when the game clock shows 2:00 or less time remaining in the period.

g. The public address operator is required to announce that there are two minutes remaining in regulation and any overtime periods.

h. The game clock shall be equipped to show tenths-of-a-second during the last minute of regulation or overtime periods.

Section III—End of Period

a. Each period ends when time expires.

EXCEPTIONS:

(1) If a live ball is in flight, the period ends when the goal is made, missed or touched by an offensive player.

(2) If a personal or technical foul occurs at :00.0, but prior to the horn sounding, the period officially ends after the free throw(s) are attempted. The free throw(s) will be attempted immediately.

(3) If the ball is in the air when the buzzer sounds ending a period, and it subsequently is touched by: (a) a defensive player, the goal, if successful, shall count; or (b) an offensive player, the period has ended.

(4) If a timeout request is made at approximately the instant time expires for a period, the period ends and the timeout shall not be granted.

b. If the ball is dead and the game clock shows :00.0, the period has ended even though the buzzer may not have sounded.

Section IV—Tie Score—Overtime

If the score is tied at the end of the 4th period, play shall resume in 100 seconds without change of baskets for any of the overtime periods required. (See Rule 5—Section II—d for the amount of time between overtime periods.)

Section V—Stoppage of Timing Devices

a. The timing devices shall be stopped whenever the official's whistle sounds indicating one of the following:

(1) A foul (personal or technical).

(2) A jump ball.

(3) A floor violation.

(4) An unusual delay.

(5) A timeout for any other emergency (Official's time—no substitutions are permitted.)

(6) A regular or 20-second timeout.

b. The timing devices shall be stopped:

(1) During the last minute of the first, second and third periods following a successful field goal attempt.

(2) During the last two minutes of regulation play and/or overtime(s) following a successful field goal attempt.

c. Officials may not use official time to permit a player to change or repair equipment.

Section VI—20-Second Timeout

A player's request for a 20-second timeout shall be granted only when the ball is dead or in control of the team making the request. A request at any other time shall be ignored.

a. Each team is entitled to one (1) 20-second timeout per half for a total of two (2) per game, including overtimes.

b. During a 20-second timeout a team may only substitute for one player. If the team calling the 20-second timeout replaces a player, the opposing team may also replace one player.

c. Only one player per team may be replaced during a 20-second timeout. If two players on the same team are injured at the same time and must be replaced, the coach must call a regular (100-second) timeout.

d. If a second 20-second timeout is requested during a half (including overtimes), it shall be granted. It will automatically become a charged regular timeout. Overtimes are considered to be an extension of the second half.

e. The official shall instruct the timer to record the 20 seconds and to inform him when the time has expired. An additional regular timeout will be charged if play is unable to resume at the expiration of that 20-second time limit.

EXCEPTION: No regular timeout remaining.

f. This rule may be used for any reason, including a request for a rule interpretation. If the correction is sustained, no time-out shall be charged.

g. Players should say "20-second timeout" when requesting this time.

h. A team is not entitled to any options during the last two minutes of the game or the overtime when a 20-second timeout is called.

EXCEPTION: Rule 5—Section VII—d.

i. If a 20-second timeout has been granted and a mandatory timeout by the same team is due, only the mandatory timeout will be charged.

j. A 20-second timeout shall not be granted to the defensive team during an official's suspension of play for (1) delay of game warning, (2) retrieving an errant ball, (3) any other unusual circumstance.

Section VII—Regular Timeout—100 Seconds

A player's request for a timeout shall be granted only when the ball is dead or in control of the team making the request. A request at any other time shall be ignored.

A team is in control when one of its players has possession of the ball on the floor, in the air or following a successful field goal by the opposing team. A request at any other time is to be ignored. Timeouts are considered regular unless the player called, "20-second timeout."

a. Each team is entitled to seven (7) charged timeouts during regulation play. Each team is limited to no more than four (4) timeouts in the fourth period and no more than three (3) timeouts in the last two minutes of regulation play. (This is in addition to one 20-second timeout per half.)

b. In overtime periods each team shall be allowed three (3) timeouts regardless of the number of timeouts called or remaining during regulation play or previous overtimes. There is no restriction as to when a team must call its timeouts during any overtime period.

c. There must be two timeouts per period. If neither team has taken a timeout prior to 6:59 in each of the four regulation periods, it shall be mandatory for the Official Scorer to take it at the first dead ball, and to charge it to the home team.

If neither team has taken a second timeout prior to 2:59 in each of the four regulation periods, it shall be mandatory for the Official Scorer to take it at the first dead ball and charge it to the team not previously charged in that period.

The official scorer shall notify a team when it has been charged with a mandatory timeout.

No mandatory timeout shall be taken during an official's suspension of play for (1) a delay of game warning, or (2) retrieving an errant ball, or (3) any other unusual circumstance.

d. If a regular or mandatory timeout is awarded the offensive team during the last two minutes of regulation play or overtime and (1) the ball is out of bounds in the backcourt, or (2) after securing the ball from a rebound and prior to any advance of the ball, or (3) after securing the ball from a change of possession and prior to any advance of the ball, the timeout shall be granted. Upon resumption of play, they shall have the option of putting the ball into play at the midcourt line, with the ball having to be passed into the frontcourt, or at the designated spot out-of-bounds.

However, once the ball is (1) thrown in from out-of-bounds, or (2) dribbled or passed after receiving it from a rebound or a change of possession, the timeout shall be granted, and, upon resumption of play, the ball shall be in-bounded at the spot nearest where the ball was when the timeout was called.

The time on the game clock and the 24-second clock shall remain as when the timeout was called. In order for the option to be available under the conditions in paragraph #2 above, the offensive team must call a 20-second timeout followed by a regular timeout, or call two successive regular timeouts.

EXCEPTION: Rule 12A—Section II—Excessive Timeouts.

In the last two minutes of the fourth period or overtime, the official shall ask the head coach the type of timeout desired—(regular or 20-second)—prior to notifying the scorer's table. This applies **only** to a requested timeout.

e. No timeout shall be charged if it is called to question a rule interpretation and the correction is sustained.

f. Additional timeouts may be granted at the expense of a technical foul and all privileges apply.

EXCEPTION: see Rule 12A—Section II.

Section VIII—Timeout Requests

a. If an official, upon receiving a timeout request (regular or 20-second) by the defensive team, inadvertently signals while the play is in progress, play shall be suspended and the team in possession shall put the ball in play immediately at the sideline nearest where the ball was when the signal was given. The team in possession shall have only the time remaining of the original ten seconds in which to move the ball into the frontcourt. The 24-second clock shall remain the same.

b. If an official, upon receiving a timeout request (regular or 20-second) from the defensive team, inadvertently signals for a timeout during: (1) a successful field goal or free throw attempt, the point(s) shall be scored; (2) an unsuccessful field goal attempt, play shall be resumed with a jump ball at the center circle between any two opponents; (3) an unsuccessful free throw attempt, the official shall rule disconcerting and award a substitute free throw.

c. If an official inadvertently blows his whistle during (1) a successful field goal or free throw attempt, the points shall be scored, or (2) an unsuccessful field goal or free throw attempt, play shall be resumed with a jump ball at the center circle between any two opponents.

d. Whenever a team is granted a regular or 20-second timeout, play shall not resume until the full 100 seconds, or the full 20 seconds, have elapsed. The throw-in shall be nearest the spot where play was suspended.

Section IX—Time-In

a. After time has been out, the game clock shall be started when the official signals time-in. The timer is authorized to start the game clock if officials neglect to signal.

b. On a free throw that is unsuccessful and the ball continues in play, the clock shall be started when the missed free throw is touched by any player.

c. If play is resumed by a throw-in from out-of-bounds, the clock shall be started when the ball is legally touched by any player within the playing area of the court.

d. If play is resumed with a jump ball, the clock shall be started when the ball is legally tapped.

RULE NO. 6—PUTTING BALL IN PLAY—LIVE/DEAD BALL

Section I—Start of Games/Periods and Others

a. The game and overtimes shall be started with a jump ball in the center circle.

b. The team which gains possession after the opening tap will put the ball into play at their opponent's endline to begin the fourth period. The team losing the opening tap will put the ball into play at their opponent's endline at the beginning of the second and third periods.

c. In putting the ball into play, the thrower-in may run along the endline or pass it to a teammate who is also out-of-bounds at the endline—as after a score.

d. After any dead ball, play shall be resumed by a jump ball, a throw-in or by placing the ball at the disposal of a free-thrower.

e. On the following floor violations, the ball shall be awarded to the opposing team out-of-bounds on the nearest sideline at the free throw line extended:

    (1) Three-seconds

    (2) Ball entering basket from below

    (3) Illegal assist in scoring

    (4) Offensive screen set out-of-bounds

    (5) Free throw violation by the offensive team

    (6) Flagrant foul-penalty (1) or (2)

    (7) Illegal defense

    (8) Jump ball at free throw circle

    (9) Ball over backboard

    (10) Offensive basket interference

    (11) Ball hitting horizontal basket support

    (12) Loose ball fouls which occur inside the free throw line extended

f. On the following floor violations, the ball shall be awarded to the opposing team on the baseline at the nearest spot:

(1) Ball out-of-bounds on baseline

(2) Ball hitting vertical basket support

(3) Defensive goaltending

(4) During a throw-in on the baseline

(5) Inadvertent whistle which is prior to a baseline throw-in

g. On the following floor violations, the ball shall be awarded to the opposing team on the sideline at the nearest spot:

(1) Where ball is out-of-bounds on sideline

(2) Traveling

(3) Double-dribble

(4) Striking or kicking the ball

(5) Swinging of elbows

(6) 24-second violation

(7) Inadvertent whistle when player control exists and the ball is in play

h. Upon resumption of play, the ball shall be awarded out-of-bounds at the nearest spot following a regular or 20-second timeout.

EXCEPTION: Rule 5—Section VII—d.

i. On a violation which requires putting the ball in play in the backcourt, the official will give the ball to the offensive player as soon as he is in a position out-of-bounds and ready to accept the ball.

EXCEPTION: In the last two minutes of each period or overtime, a reasonable amount of time shall be allowed for a substitution.

Section II—Live Ball

a. The ball becomes live when:

(1) It is tossed by an official on any jump ball.

(2) It is at the disposal of the offensive player for a throw-in.

(3) It is placed at the disposal of a free throw shooter.

Section III—Jump Balls in Center Circle

a. The ball shall be put into play in the center circle by a jump between two opponents:

(1) At the start of the game

(2) At the start of each overtime period

(3) A double free-throw violation

(4) Double foul during a loose ball situation

(5) The ball becomes dead when neither team is in control and no field goal or infraction is involved

(6) The ball comes to rest on the basket flange or becomes lodged between the basket ring and the backboard

(7) A double foul which occurs as a result of a difference in opinion between officials

(8) An inadvertent whistle occurs during a loose ball

(9) A fighting foul occurs during a loose ball situation

b. In all cases above, the jump ball shall be between any two opponents in the game at that time. If injury, ejection or disqualification makes it necessary for any player to be replaced, his substitute may not participate in the jump ball.

Section IV—Other Jump Balls

a. The ball shall be put into play by a jump ball at the circle which is closest to the spot where:

(1) A held ball occurs

(2) A ball out-of-bounds caused by both teams

(3) An official is in doubt as to who last touched the ball

b. The jump ball shall be between the two involved players unless injury or ejection precludes one of the jumpers from participation. If the injured or ejected player must leave the game, the coach of the opposing team shall select from his opponent's bench a player who will replace the injured or ejected player. The injured player will not be permitted to re-enter the game.

Section V—Restrictions Governing Jump Balls

a. Each jumper must have at least one foot on or inside that half of the jumping circle which is farthest from his own basket. Each jumper must have both feet within the restraining circle.

b. The ball must be tapped by one or both of the players participating in the jump ball after it reaches its highest point. If the ball falls to the floor without being tapped by at least one of the jumpers, the official off the ball shall whistle the ball dead and signal another toss.

c. Neither jumper may tap the tossed ball before it reaches its highest point.

d. Neither jumper may leave the jumping circle until the ball has been tapped.

e. Neither jumper may catch the tossed ball nor tapped ball until such time as it has been touched by one of the eight non-jumpers, the floor, the basket or the backboard.

f. Neither jumper is permitted to tap the ball more than twice on any jump ball.

g. The eight non-jumpers will remain outside the restraining circle until the ball has been tapped. Teammates may not occupy adjacent positions around the restraining circle if an opponent desires one of the positions.

Penalty for c., d., e., f., g.: Ball awarded out-of-bounds to the opponent.

h. Player position on the restraining circle is determined by the direction of a player's basket. The player whose basket is nearest shall have first choice of position, with position being alternated thereafter.

Section VI—Dead Ball

a. The ball becomes dead and/or remains dead when the following occurs:

(1) Held ball

(2) Ball comes to rest on the basket flange or becomes lodged between the basket ring and the backboard

(3) Time expires for the end of any period

(4) Free throw attempt for a technical foul

(5) Personal foul (punching, away-from-the-play)

(6) Free throw which is the first of multiple attempts

(7) Floor violation (traveling, 3-sec, 24-sec, 10-sec, etc.)

(8) Fighting foul

(9) Inadvertent whistle

(10) Prior to player possession out-of-bounds following a successful field goal or free throw, whereby ball is going to be put into play by a throw-in. Contact which is not considered unsportsmanlike shall be ignored. (Rule 12A—Section VI—i)

EXCEPTION: The ball does not become dead when (3) occurs with a live ball in flight.

RULE NO. 7—24-SECOND CLOCK

Section I—Definition

For the purpose of clarification the 24-second device shall be referred to as "the 24-second clock."

Section II—Starting and Stopping of 24-Second Clock

a. The 24-second clock will start when a team gains new possession of a ball which is in play.

b. On a throw-in, the 24-second clock shall start when the ball is legally touched on the court by a player.

c. A team in possession of the ball must attempt a field goal within 24 seconds after gaining possession of the ball. To constitute a legal field goal attempt, the following conditions must be compiled with:

(1) The ball must leave the player's hand prior to the expiration of 24 seconds.

(2) After leaving the player's hand, the ball must hit the basket ring or legal surface of the backboard. If the ball fails to hit one or the other and seconds have expired, a 24-second violation has been committed.

d. A team is considered in possession of the ball when holding, passing or dribbling. The team is considered in possession of the ball even though the ball has been batted away but the opponent has not gained possession. No 3-second violation can occur under these conditions.

e. Team control ends when:

(1) There is a try for a field goal

(2) The opponent gains possession

(3) The ball becomes dead

f. If a ball is touched by a defensive player who does not gain possession of the ball, the 24-second clock shall continue to run.

g. If a defensive player causes the ball to go out-of-bounds or causes the ball to enter the basket ring from below, the 24-second clock is stopped and the offensive team shall be awarded the ball on the sideline for a throw-in.

The offensive team shall have only the unexpired time remaining on the 24-second clock in which to attempt a field goal. If the 24-second clock reads 0, a 24-second violation has occurred, even though the horn may not have sounded.

h. If during any period there are 24 seconds OR LESS left to play in the period, the 24-second clock shall not function.

i. If an official inadvertently blows his whistle and the 24-second clock buzzer sounds while the ball is in the air, play shall be suspended and play resumed by a jump ball between any two opponents at the center circle, if the shot is unsuccessful. If the shot is successful, the goal shall count and the whistle is ignored. It should be noted that even though the official blows his whistle, all provisions of the above rule apply.

j. If there is a question whether or not an attempt to score has been made within the 24 seconds allowed, the final decision shall be made by the officials.

k. Whenever the 24-second clock reads 0 and the ball is dead for any reason other than an Illegal Defense violation, kicking violation, punched ball violation, personal foul or a technical foul by the defensive team, the allotted 24 seconds have expired even though the horn may not have sounded.

Section III—Putting Ball In Play After Violation

If a team fails to attempt a field goal within the time allotted, a 24-second violation shall be called. The ball is awarded to the defensive team at the sideline, nearest the spot where play was suspended.

Section IV—Resetting 24-Second Clock

a. The 24-second clock shall be reset when a special situation occurs which warrants such action.

b. The 24-second clock shall remain the same as when play was stopped, or reset to 10 seconds, whichever is greater, on all technical fouls or delay of game warnings called on the defensive team.

EXCEPTION: Fighting foul

c. The 24-second clock is never reset on technical fouls called on the offensive team.

EXCEPTION: Fighting foul

d. The 24-second clock shall be reset to 24 seconds anytime the following occurs:

(1) Change of possession

(2) Illegal defense violation

(3) Personal foul

(4) Fighting foul

(5) Kicking the ball or blocking the ball with any part of the leg

(6) Punching the ball with fist

(7) Ball hitting the basket ring or legal surface of backboard of team which is in possession

RULE NO. 8—OUT-OF-BOUNDS AND THROW-IN

Section I—Player

The player is out-of-bounds when he touches the floor or any object on or outside a boundary. For location of a player in the air, his position is that from which he last touched the floor.

Section II—Ball

a. The ball is out-of-bounds when it touches a player who is out-of-bounds or any other person, the floor, or any object on, above or outside of a boundary or the supports or back of the backboard.

b. Any ball that rebounds or passes behind the backboard, in either direction, from any point is considered out-of-bounds.

c. The ball is caused to go out-of-bounds by the last player to touch it before it goes out, provided it is out-of-bounds because of touching something other than a player. If the ball is out-of-bounds because of touching a player who is on or outside a boundary, such player caused it to go out.

d. If the ball goes out-of-bounds and was last touched simultaneously by two opponents, both of whom are inbounds or out-of-bounds, or if the official is in doubt as to who last touched the ball, or if the officials disagree, play shall be resumed by a jump ball between the two involved players in the nearest restraining circle.

e. After the ball is out-of-bounds, the team shall designate a player to make the throw-in. He shall make the throw-in at the spot out-of-bounds nearest where the ball crossed the boundary. The designated thrower-in or his substitute shall not be changed except following a regular or 20-second timeout.

f. After any playing floor violation, the ball is to be put into play on the sideline.

g. If the ball is interfered with by an opponent seated on the bench (Rule 12A—Section III—c), it shall be awarded to the offended team out-of-bounds at the free throw line extended.

Section III—The Throw-In

a. The throw-in starts when the ball is at the disposal of a player entitled to the throw-in. He shall release the ball inbounds within 5 seconds from the time the throw-in starts. Until the passed ball has crossed the plane of the boundary, no player shall have any part of his person over the boundary line and teammates shall not occupy positions paralled or adjacent to the baseline if an opponent desires one of those positions. The defensive man shall have the right to be between his man and the basket.

b. On a throw-in which is not touched inbounds, the ball is returned to the original throw-in spot.

c. After a score, field goal or free throw, the latter coming as the result of a personal foul, any player of the team not credited with the score shall put the ball into play from any point out-of-bounds at the endline of the court where the point(s) were scored. He may pass the ball to a teammate behind the endline; however, the five-second throw-in rule applies.

d. After a free throw violation by the shooter or his teammate, the throw-in is made from out-of-bounds at either end of the free throw line extended.

e. Any ball out-of-bounds in a team's frontcourt or at the midcourt line cannot be passed into the backcourt. On all backcourt violations, and midcourt violations, the ball shall be given to the opposing team at the midcourt line, and must be passed into the frontcourt.

f. A throw-in which touches the floor, or any object on or outside the boundary line, or touches anything above the playing surface is a violation. The ball must be thrown directly inbounds.

EXCEPTION: Rule 8—Section III—c.

PENALTY: Violation of this rule is loss of possession, and the ball must be inbounded at the previous spot of the throw-in.

RULE NO. 9—FREE THROW

Section I—Positions

a. When a free throw is awarded, an official shall put the ball in play by placing it at the disposal of the free throw shooter. The shooter shall be within the upper half of the free throw circle. The same procedure shall be followed each time a free throw is administered.

b. During a free throw for a personal foul, each of the spaces nearest the endline must be occupied by an opponent of the free throw shooter. Teammates of the free throw shooter must occupy the next adjacent spaces on each side. Only one of the third adjacant spaces may be occupied by an opponent of the free throw shooter. It is not mandatory that either of the third adjacent spaces be occupied. No teammates of the free throw shooter are permitted in these spaces.

c. All other players not stationed on the free throw lane must be at least six feet from the free throw lane lines and three feet from the free throw circle.

d. If the ball is to become dead after the last free throw, players shall not take positions along the free throw lane. No players shall be allowed inside the free throw line extended while a free throw is being attempted under these conditions.

PENALTY:

(1) If the violation is by either team and the free throw attempt is successful or occurs on the first of multiple free throw attempts, it is ignored.

(2) If the violation is by an opponent of the free throw shooter and the free throw attempt is unsuccessful, a substitute free throw attempt is awarded.

(3) If the violation is by a teammate of the free throw shooter, it is a violation as soon as the free throw is attempted. The ball is awarded to his opponent at the free throw line extended.

Section II—Shooting of Free Throw

a. The free throw(s) awarded because of a personal foul shall be attempted by the offended player.

EXCEPTIONS: (1) If the offended player is fouled and is subsequently ejected from the game, before shooting the awarded free throw(s), he must immediately leave the court and another of the four players on the court will be designated by the opposing coach to shoot such free throw(s).

(2) If the offended player is injured and cannot shoot the awarded free throw(s), the opposing coach shall select, from his opponent's bench, the player who will replace the injured player. That player will attempt the free throw(s) and the injured player will not be permitted to re-enter the game. The substitute must remain in the game until the next dead ball.

(3) If the offended player is injured and unable to shoot the awarded free throw(s) due to any unsportsmanlike act, his coach may designate any eligible member of the squad to attempt the free throw(s). The injured player will be permitted to re-enter the game.

(4) If the offended player is disqualified and unable to shoot the awarded free throw(s), his coach shall designate an eligible substitute from the bench. That substitute will attempt the free throw(s) and cannot be removed until the next dead ball.

(5) Away from play foul—Rule 12B—Section X-a(1).

b. A free throw attempt, personal or technical, shall neither be legal nor count unless an official handles the ball and is also in the free throw area when foul try is attempted.

c. A player awarded two free throws must attempt both even though the first attempt is nullified by a violation by an offensive player.

Section III—Time Limit

Each free throw attempt shall be made within 10 seconds after the ball has been placed at the disposal of the free-thrower.

Section IV—Next Play

After a successful free throw which is not followed by another free throw, the ball shall be put into play by a throw-in, as after a field goal if the try is successful.

EXCEPTION: After a free throw for a foul which occurs during a dead ball which immediately precedes any period, the ball shall be put into play by the team entitled to the throw-in in the period which follows. (See Rule 6—Section I—b).

RULE NO. 10—VIOLATIONS AND PENALTIES

Section I—Free Throw

a. After the ball is placed at the disposal of a free throw shooter, his attempt shall be within 10 seconds in such a way that the ball enters the basket or touches the ring before it is touched by a player. The free throw attempt shall be within that part of the free throw circle behind the free throw line.

b. A player shall not touch the ball or basket while the ball is on or within the basket.

c. A player who occupies a free throw lane space shall not touch the floor on or across the free throw lane line, nor shall any player 'back out' more than 3' from the free throw lane line. A player who does not occupy a lane space must remain 6' from the free throw line and/or 3' from the free throw circle. This restriction applies until the ball leaves the free thrower's hands.

d. The free throw shooter may not cross the plane of the free throw line until the ball touches the ring or backboard, or the free throw ends.

e. No player shall deflect or catch the ball before it reaches the basket or backboard on a free throw attempt.

f. The free throw shooter shall not purposely fake a free throw attempt.

g. An opponent shall not disconcert the free thrower in any way, once the ball has been placed at the disposal of the shooter.

h. No violation can occur if the ball is not released by the free throw shooter.

EXCEPTION: Rule 10—Section I—f.

PENALTY:

1. In (a-f) above, if the violation is by the offense, no point can be scored. The ball is awarded out-of-bounds to opponents at the free throw line extended.

2. In (b), (c), and (g), if the violation is by the defense and the throw is successful, disregard violation; if the throw is unsuccessful, a substitute free throw shall be awarded.

3. In (e), if the violation is by the defensive team, the point is scored and the same player receives another free throw attempt. The additional free throw attempt is considered a new play. This can only occur when the ball will remain in play after the free throw attempt. If it occurs on the first attempt of multiple free throws, only the single point is awarded, and the second free throw shall be attempted.

4. If there is a free throw violation by each team, on a free throw which is to remain in play, the ball becomes dead, no point can be scored and play shall be resumed by a jump ball between any two opponents at the center circle.

5. The "out-of-bounds" and "jump ball" provisions above do not apply if the free throw is to be followed by another free throw, or if there are free throws to be attempted by both teams.

6. If a violation by the free thrower as in (a) above follows disconcertion, a substitute free throw shall be awarded.

Section II—Out of Bounds

a. A player shall not cause the ball to go out-of-bounds.

PENALTY: Loss of ball. The ball is awarded to opponents at boundary line nearest the spot of the violation.

EXCEPTION: On a throw-in which is not touched inbounds, the ball is returned to the original throw-in spot.

Section III—Dribble:

a. A player shall not run with the ball without dribbling it.

b. A player in control of a dribble who steps on or outside a boundary line, even though not touching the ball while on or outside that boundary line, shall not be allowed to return inbounds and continue his dribble. He may not even be the first player to touch the ball after he has re-established a position inbounds.

c. A player may not dribble a second time after he has voluntarily ended his first dribble.

d. A player may dribble a second time if he lost control of the ball because of:
    (1) A try for a field goal at his own basket (ball must touch backboard or rim)
    (2) A bat by an opponent
    (3) A pass or fumble which has then touched another player

PENALTY: Loss of ball. Ball is awarded to opponent at the sideline nearest the spot of the violation.

Section IV—Thrower-in

a. A thrower-in shall not (1) carry the ball onto the court; (2) fail to release the ball within 5 seconds; (3) touch it on the court before it has touched another player; (4) leave the designated throw-in spot; (5) throw the ball so that it enters the basket before touching anyone on the court; (6) step over the boundary line while inbounding the ball; (7) cause the ball to go out-of-bounds without being touched inbounds; (8) leave the playing surface to gain an advantage on a throw-in.

b. After a team has designated a player to throw the ball in, there shall be no change of player (or his substitute) unless a regular or 20-second timeout has subsequently been called.

PENALTY: Loss of ball. The ball is awarded to the opponent at the original spot of the throw-in.

Section V—Strike the Ball

a. A player shall not kick the ball or strike it with the fist.

b. Kicking the ball or striking it with any part of the leg is a violation when it is an intentional act. The ball accidently striking the foot, the leg or fist is not a violation.

PENALTY: 1. If the violation is by the offense, the ball is awarded to the opponent at the sideline nearest the spot of the violation.

2. If the violation is by the defense, the offensive team retains possession of the ball at the sideline nearest the spot of the violation. The 24-second clock is reset to 24 seconds and if the violation occurred in the backcourt, a new 10-second count is awarded.

Section VI—Jump Ball

a. A player shall not violate the jump ball rule (Rule 6—Section V).

b. A foul committed during any jump ball shall be ruled a "loose ball" foul.

PENALTY: 1. In (a) above, the ball is awarded to the opponent at the sideline nearest the spot of the violation.

2. In (a) above, if there is a violation by each team, or if the official makes a bad toss, the toss shall be repeated.

3. In (b) above, free throws may or may not be awarded, consistent with whether the penalty is in effect (Rule 12B—Section VIII).

In all violations of this rule, neither the game clock nor the 24-second clock shall be started.

Section VII—Three-Second Rule

a. A player shall not remain for more than 3 seconds in that part of his free throw lane between the endline and extended 4' (imaginary) off the court and the farther edge of the free throw line while the ball is in control of his team.

b. Allowance may be made for a player who, having been in the restricted area for less than 3 seconds, is in the act of shooting at the end of the third second.

c. The 3-second count shall not begin until the ball is in control in the offensive team's frontcourt.

PENALTY: Loss of ball. The ball is awarded to the opponent at the sideline at the free throw line extended.

Section VIII—Ten-Second Rule

A team shall not be in continuous control of a ball which is in its backcourt for more than 10 consecutive seconds.

EXCEPTION: A new 10 seconds is awarded if the defense: (1) kicks or punches the ball, (2) is assessed a technical foul, or (3) is issued a delay of game warning.

PENALTY: Loss of ball. The ball is awarded to the opponent at the midcourt line, with the ball having to be passed into the frontcourt.

Section IX—Ball in Backcourt

a. A player shall not be the first to touch a ball which he or a teammate caused to go from frontcourt to backcourt while his team was in control of the ball.

b. During a jump ball, a try for a goal, or a situation in which a player taps the ball away from a congested area, as during rebounding, in an attempt to get the ball out where player control may be secured, the ball is not in control of either team. Hence, the restriction on first touching does not apply.

c. Following a jump ball, a player who secures a positive position and control of the ball in his frontcourt cannot pass the ball to a teammate or dribble the ball into the backcourt.

PENALTY: Loss of ball. The ball is awarded to the opponent at the midcourt line, with the ball having to be passed into the frontcourt. If the violation occurs on a throw-in, the game clock shall not start.

Section X—Swinging of Elbows

A player shall not be allowed excessive and/or vigorous swinging of the elbows in a swinging motion (no contact). When a defensive player is nearby and the offensive player has the ball, it is considered a violation.

PENALTY: Loss of ball. The ball is awarded to the opponent at the sideline, nearest the spot of the violation. If the violation occurs on a throw-in, the game clock shall not be started.

Section XI—Entering Basket From Below

A player shall not cause the ball to enter the basket from below.

PENALTY: Loss of ball. The ball is awarded to the opponent at the sideline, at the free line extended.

Section XII—STICK-UM

A player is not to use "STICK-UM" or any similar substance.

PENALTY: Fine of $25 for the first violation, doubled for each subsequent violation upon notification to the Operations Department by an official.

Section XIII—Illegal Assist in Scoring

a. A player may not assist himself to score by using the ring or backboard to lift, hold or raise himself.

b. A player may not assist a teammate to gain height while attempting to score.

PENALTY: Loss of ball. The ball is awarded to the opponent at the free throw line extended.

Section XIV—Traveling

a. A player who receives the ball while standing still may pivot, using either foot as the pivot foot.

b. A player who receives the ball while he is progressing or upon completion of a dribble, may use a two-count rhythm in coming to a stop, passing or shooting the ball.

The first count occurs:

(1) As he receives the ball, if either foot is touching the floor at the time he receives it.

(2) As the foot touches the floor, or as both feet touch the floor simultaneously after he receives the ball, if both feet are off the floor when he receives it.

The second occurs:

(1) After the count of one when either foot touches the floor, or both feet touch the floor simultaneously.

c. A player who comes to a stop on the count of one may pivot, using either foot as the pivot foot.

d. A player who comes to a stop on the count of two, with one foot in advance of the other, may pivot using only the rear foot as the pivot foot.

e. A player who comes to a stop on the count of two, with neither foot in advance of the other, may use either foot as the pivot foot.

f. A player who receives the ball while standing still, or who comes to a legal stop while holding the ball, may lift the pivot foot or jump when he shoots for the goal or passes, but the ball must leave his hands before the pivot foot again touches the floor, or before either foot again touches the floor if the player has jumped.

g. In starting a dribble after receiving the ball while standing still, or after coming to a legal stop, a player may not jump before the ball leaves his hands, nor may he lift the pivot from the floor before the ball leaves his hands.

h. A player who leaves the floor with the ball must pass or shoot before he returns to the floor. If he drops the ball while in the air, he may not be the first to touch the ball.

i. A player who falls to the floor while holding the ball, or while coming to a stop, may not make progress by sliding.

j. A player who attempts a field goal may not be the first to touch the ball if it fails to touch the backboard, rim or another player.

PENALTY: Loss of ball. The ball is awarded to the opponent at the sideline, nearest spot of the violation.

Section XV—Isolation

If the offensive team positions three or more players above the tip of the circle, on the weakside, a violation shall be called.

PENALTY: Loss of ball. The ball is awarded to the opponent at the tip of the circle extended.

Section XVI—Offensive Screen Set Out-of-Bounds

An offensive player shall not leave the playing area of the floor on the endline in the frontcourt for the purpose of setting a screen.

PENALTY: Loss of ball. The ball is awarded to the opponent at the sideline at the free throw line extended.

RULE NO. 11—BASKETBALL INTERFERENCE—GOALTENDING

Section I—A Player Shall Not:

a. Touch the ball or the basket ring when the ball is on or within either basket.

b. Touch the ball when it is touching the cylinder having the basket ring as its lower base.

EXCEPTION: In (a) or (b) above if a player near his own basket has his hand legally in contact with the ball, it is not a violation if his contact with the ball continues after the ball enters the cylinder, or if, in such action, he touches the basket.

c. Touch the ball when it is above the basket ring and touching the imaginary cylinder.

d. Touch the ball when it is on its downward flight during a field goal attempt, while the entire ball is above the basket ring level and before the ball has touched the basket ring or the attempt has ended.

e. For goaltending to occur, the ball, in the judgment of the official, must have a chance to score.

f. During a field goal attempt, touch a ball after it has touched any part of the backboard above ring level, whether the ball is considered on its upward or downward flight. The offensive player must have caused the ball to touch the backboard.

g. During a field goal attempt, touch a ball after it has touched the backboard below the ring level and while the ball is on its upward flight.

h. Trap the ball against the face of the backboard. (To be a trapped ball, three elements must exist simultaneously. The hand, the ball and the backboard must all occur at the same time. A batted ball against the backboard is not a trapped ball.)

i. Touch any live ball from within the playing area that is on its downward flight with an opportunity to touch the basket ring. This is considered to be a "field goal attempt" or trying for a goal (except a "tap" from a jump ball situation.)

j. Touch the ball at any time with a hand which is through the basket ring.

PENALTY: If violation is at the opponent's basket, the offended team is awarded two points, if the attempt is from the two point zone and three points if it is from the three point zone. The crediting of the score and subsequent procedure is the same as if the awarded score has resulted from the ball having gone through the basket, except that the official shall hand the ball to a player of the team entitled to the throw-in. If the violation is at a team's own basket, no points can be scored and the ball is awarded to the offended team at the out-of-bounds spot on the side at either end of the free throw line extended. If there is a violation by both teams, play shall be resumed by a jump ball between any two opponents at the center circle.

RULE NO. 12—FOULS AND PENALTIES
A. Technical Foul

Section I—Illegal Defenses

a. Illegal defenses which violate the rules and accepted guidelines set forth are not permitted in the NBA.

b. When the offensive team is in its backcourt with the ball, no illegal defense violation may occur.

1. Penalties for Illegal Defenses.

On the first violation, the 24-second clock is reset to 24. On the second and succeeding violations, the clock is reset to 24 and one free throw (technical) is attempted. When a violation occurs during the last 24 seconds of any period (including overtime), regardless of the number of prior offenses, one free throw is awarded for the violation. (On all violations, the ball is awarded to the offended team out-of-bounds at the free throw line extended on either side of the court).

EXCEPTION: If a field goal attempt is simultaneous with a whistle for an illegal violation, and that attempt is successful, the basket shall count and the violation is nullified.

2. Guidelines for Defensive Coverage

a. Weakside defenders may be in a defensive position within the "outside lane" with no time limit, and within the "inside lane" for 2.9 seconds. The defensive player must re-establish a position with both feet out of the "inside -lane" to be considered as having legally cleared the restricted area.

b. When a defensive player is guarding an offensive player who is adjacent (posted-up) to the 3-second lane, the defensive player may be within the "inside lane" area with no time limitations.

An offensive player shall be ruled as "posted-up" when he is within 3' of the free throw lane line. Hash mark on the baseline denotes the 3' area.

c. An offensive player without the ball **may not** be double-teamed from the weakside. **Only** the player with the ball may be double-teamed by a weakside defensive player.

Weakside and strongside restrictions shall extend from the baseline to the midcourt line.

d. When an offensive player, with or without the ball, takes a position above the foul line, the defensive player may be no farther (toward the baseline) than the "middle defensive area." Defensive player(s) may enter and re-enter the "lower defensive area" as many times as desired, so long as he does not exceed 2.9 seconds.

e. When a weakside offensive player is above the free throw line extended, his defensive man may be no lower than the "middle defensive area" extended for more than 2.9 seconds.

When a weakside offensive player is below the free throw line extended, his defensive man must vacate the "inside lane" unless his man is positioned adjacent (posted up) to the 3-second lane extended.

When a weakside offensive player is above the tip of the circle, his defensive man must be no lower than the "upper defensive area" for more than 2.9 seconds.

When a strongside offensive player is above the tip of the circle extended, his defensive man may be no lower than the free throw line extended (upper defensive area) for more than 2.9 seconds.

When a strongside offensive player is above the free throw line extended "upper defensive area," his defensive man may be no lower than the "middle defensive area" for more than 2.9 seconds.

When an offensive player on the strongside is below the free throw line extended "middle defensive area," his defender must take a position below the free throw line extended immediately or double-team the ball as soon as the ball crosses midcourt. There is no 2.9 time limit.

If the offensive player relocates to a position above the free throw line extended, his defender may take a similar position no farther than one defensive area away within 2.9 seconds.

In all of the situations above, a defensive player may always aggressively double-team the ball regardless of his previous position on the floor.

f. When an offensive player takes a position above the tip of the circle, with or without the ball, the defensive player may be no farther (toward the baseline) from him than the "upper defensive area."

g. A defensive player must follow **his weakside offensive man,** switch to another man at an area of intersection, or double-team the ball. There is no 2.9-second time limit on this play. A defensive player must execute one of those three options or he is guilty of an illegal defense **immediately.**

h. A defensive player must follow his **strongside offensive man,** switch to another man at an area of intersection, or double-team the ball. There is a 2.9 second time limit on this play which commences when the defensive player reaches the weakside and "opens up."

i. A double team is when two or more defenders aggressively pursue a player with the ball to a position close enough for a held ball to occur.

Failure to comply with paragraphs (a) through (i) above will result in an Illegal Defense violation.

Section II—Excessive Timeouts

Requests for timeout in excess of the authorized number shall be granted. However, a technical foul penalty shall be assessed. A team is entitled to all regular timeout privileges.

EXCEPTION: During the last two minutes of the fourth period and/or overtime(s), the offensive team shall not have the option of putting the ball into play at the midcourt line.

Section III—Delay of Game

a. A player shall not delay the game by preventing the ball from being promptly put into play such as:

(1) Attempting to gain an advantage by interfering with the ball after a goal.

(2) Failing to immediately pass the ball to the nearest official when a violation is called.

(3) Batting the ball away from an opponent before the player has the opportunity to inbounds the ball.

(4) Crossing the plane of the boundary line, as a defensive player, prior to the ball being inbounded.

b. A team shall not prevent play from commencing at any time.

c. Any person seated on the bench shall not interfere with a ball which is determined to be in play. (Rule 8—Section II—g).

PENALTY: First offense is a warning, with each successive offense to be penalized by a technical foul which is charged to the team. Each offense will be announced by the Public Address Announcer. On each offense, the 24-second clock shall remain the same, or reset to 10 seconds, whichever is greater. The offensive team shall be awarded a new 10 seconds if the ball is in the backcourt. If repeated acts become a travesty, the coach shall be held responsible upon being notified of same.

Section IV—Substitutions

a. A substitute shall not enter the court without reporting to the scorer (standing in the 8' box) and being beckoned by an official.

b. A substitute shall not be allowed to re-enter the game after having been disqualified.

EXCEPTION: Rule 3—Section I—b.

c. It is the responsibility of each team to have the proper number of players on the court at all times.

EXCEPTION: If the violation occurs on the first of multiple free throw attempts, it shall be ignored.

d. Penalty for failure to report to the scorer is a $25 fine. No technical foul is assessed.

Section V—Basket Ring, Backboard or Support

a. Any player who, in the opinion of the officials, has deliberately hung onto the basket ring, backboard or support during the game shall be assessed a non-unsportsmanlike technical foul and a $100 fine.

EXCEPTION: A player may hang on the basket ring, backboard or support to prevent an injury to himself or another player, with no penalty.

b. Should a defensive player use the basket ring, backboard or support to successfully touch a loose ball which may have an opportunity to score, the offensive team shall be awarded a successful field goal. An unsportsmanlike technical shall be assessed whether or not the ball is touched.

c. See Rule 10—Section XIII—with regard to an offensive player assisting himself to score.

Section VI—Conduct

a. An official may assess a technical foul, without prior warning, at any time. A technical foul(s) may be assessed to any player on the court or anyone seated on the bench for conduct which, in the opinion of an official, is detrimental to the game.

b. A maximum of two technicals for unsportsmanlike acts may be assessed any player, coach or trainer. Any of these offenders may be ejected for committing only one unsportsmanlike act, and they must be ejected for committing two unsportsmanlike acts.

c. A technical foul called for (1) delay of game, (2) coaches box violations, (3) illegal defensive violation, or (4) hanging on the rim or backboard is not considered an act of unsportsmanlike conduct.

EXCEPTION: Rule 12A—Section V—b.

d. A technical foul shall be assessed for unsportsmanlike tactics such as:

(1) Disrespectfully addressing an official

(2) Physically contacting an official

(3) Overt actions indicating resentment to a call

(4) Use of profanity

(5) A coach entering onto the court without permission of an official

(6) A deliberately-thrown elbow or any attempted physical act with no contact involved

e. Cursing or blaspheming an official shall not be considered the only cause for imposing technical fouls. Running tirades, continuous criticism or griping may be sufficient cause to assess a technical. Excessive misconduct shall result in ejection from the game.

f. Assessment of a technical foul shall be avoided whenever and wherever possible; but, when necessary they are to be assessed without delay or procrastination. Once a player has been ejected or the game is over, technicals cannot be assessed regardless of the provocation. Any additional unsportsmanlike conduct shall be reported by datagram immediately to the Operations Department.

g. If a technical foul is assessed on a team following a personal foul on the same team, the free throw attempt for the technical foul shall be administered first.

h. The ball shall be awarded to the team which had possession at the time the technical foul was assessed, whether the free throw attempt is successful or not. Play shall be resumed by a throw-in nearest the spot where play was interrupted.

i. Anyone guilty of illegal contact which occurs during a dead ball may be assessed (1) a technical foul, if the contact is deemed to be unsportsmanlike in nature, or (2) a flagrant foul, if unnecessary and/or excessive contact occurs.

j. Free throws awarded for a technical foul must be attempted by a player in the game when the technical foul is assessed.

(1) If a substitute is beckoned into the game prior to the technical foul being assessed, he is eligible to attempt the free throw(s).

(2) If the technical foul is assessed before the opening tap, any player listed in the scorebook as a starter is eligible to attempt the free throw(s).

(3) If a technical foul is assessed before the starting lineup is indicated, any player on the squad may attempt the free throw(s).

k. A technical foul, unsportsmanlike act or flagrant foul must be called for a participant to be ejected. A player, coach or trainer may be ejected for:

(1) An elbow foul which makes contact shoulder level or below

(2) Any unsportsmanlike conduct where a technical foul is assessed

(3) A flagrant foul where unnecessary and/or excessive contact occurs

EXCEPTION: Rule 12A—Section VI—I(5)

l. A player, coach or trainer must be ejected for:

    (1) A punching foul

    (2) A fighting foul

    (3) An elbow foul which makes contact above shoulder level

    (4) An attempted punch which does not make contact

    (5) Deliberately entering the stands other than as a continuance of play

m. Eye guarding (placing a hand in front of the opponent's eyes when guarding from the rear) a player who does not have possession of the ball is illegal and an unsportsmanlike technical shall be assessed.

n. No free throw attempts are awarded when a double technical foul is called. A free throw attempt is awarded when all other technical fouls are assessed.

o. The deliberate act of throwing the ball or any object at an official by a player, coach or trainer is a technical foul and violators are subject to ejection from the game.

p. Punching fouls and elbow fouls, although recorded as both personal and team fouls, are unsportsmanlike acts and shall be counted toward a total of two for ejection. The player may be ejected immediately. (See Comments on Rules—M).

Section VII—Fighting Fouls

a. Technical fouls shall be assessed players, coaches or trainers for fighting. No free throws will be attempted as in any other double foul situation. The participants will be ejected immediately.

b. This rule applies whether play is in progress or the ball is dead.

c. A fine not exceeding $20,000 and/or suspension may be imposed upon such person(s) by the Commissioner at his sole discretion.

Section VIII—Fines

a. Recipients of technical fouls for unsportsmanlike conduct will be assessed a $100 fine for the first offense, and an additional $150 for the second offense in any one given game, for a minimum total of $250. If a player is ejected on (1) the first technical foul for unsportsmanlike conduct, (2) a punching foul, (3) a fighting foul, (4) an elbow foul, or (5) a flagrant foul, he shall be fined a minimum of $250.

b. Whether or not said player(s) are ejected, a fine not exceeding $20,000 and/or suspension may be imposed upon such player(s) by the Commissioner at his sole discretion.

c. During a fight all players not in the game must remain in the vicinity of their bench. Violators will be assessed a $500 fine.

d. A player, coach or assistant coach, upon being notified by an official that he has been ejected from the game, must leave the playing area IMMEDIATELY and remain in the dressing room of his team during such suspension until completion of the game or leave the building. Violation of this rule shall call for an automatic fine of $500. A fine not to exceed $20,000 and possible forfeiture of the game may be imposed for any violation of this rule.

e. Any player who in the opinion of the officials has deliberately hung on the basket shall be assessed a technical foul and a fine of $100.

EXCEPTION: A player fouled in the act of dunking or shooting, may hang on the rim to prevent an injury to himself or another player with no penalty.

f. Penalty for the use of "stickum" is a fine of $25 for the first violation, doubled for each subsequent violation. (Rule 10—Section XII).

g. Any player who fails to properly report to the scorer (Rule 3—Section V—a.) shall be subject to a $25 fine on recommendation of the official scorer.

h. At halftime and the end of each game, the coach and his players are to leave the court and go directly to their dressing room, without pause or delay. There is to be **absolutely** no talking to game officials.

PENALTY—$500 fine to be doubled for any additional violation.

i. Each player, when introduced prior to the start of the game, must be uniformly dressed.

PENALTY—$100 fine.

j. A $250 fine shall be assessed to any player(s) hanging on the rim during pre-game warm-up. Officials shall be present during warm-up to observe violations.

k. Any player who is assessed a flagrant foul—penalty (2) must be ejected and will be fined a minimum of $250. The incident will be reported to the Operations Department.

B. Personal Foul

Section I—Types

a. A player shall not hold, push, charge into, impede the progress of an opponent by extending an arm, leg or knee or by bending the body into a position that is not normal.

b. Contact caused by a defensive player approaching the ball holder from the rear is a form of pushing or holding.

c. Two free throw attempts are awarded for an elbow foul. It is also an unsportsmanlike act. If the elbow contact is above shoulder level, the player will be ejected. If the elbow contact is shoulder level or below, the player may be ejected at the discretion of the official.

Contact must occur for an elbow foul to be called. (See Rule 12A—Section VI—d(6) for non-contact by an elbow)

d. A defensive player is not permitted to retain hand contact with an offensive player when the player is in his "sights." Hand checking will be eliminated by rigid enforcement of this rule by all officials. The illegal use of hands will not be permitted.

e. Any player whose actions against an opponent cause illegal contact with yet another offensive player is guilty of a personal foul and will be penalized accordingly.

f. Contact which occurs on the shooting hand of the offensive player, while that hand is in contact with the ball, is not illegal.

Section II—By Dribbler

a. A dribbler shall not (1) charge into an opponent who has established a legal guarding position or (2) attempt to dribble between two opponents, or between an opponent and a boundary, where sufficient space is not available for contact to be avoided.

b. If a dribbler has sufficient space between two opponents, or between an opponent and a boundary, to have his head and shoulders in advance of them, the responsibility for illegal contact is on the opponent.

c. If a dribbler in his progress has established a straight line path, he may not be crowded out of that path.

d. If an opponent is able to establish a legal defensive position in that path, the dribbler must avoid contact by changing his direction or ending his dribble.

e. The dribbler must be in control of his body at all times.

f. A dribbler may not legally dribble again after a personal foul has been called.

Section III—By Screening

A player who sets a screen shall not (1) take a position closer than a normal step from an opponent, if that opponent is stationary and unaware of the screener's position (2) make illegal contact with an opponent when he assumes a position at the side or front of an opponent, (3) take a position so close to a moving opponent that illegal contact cannot be avoided by that opponent without changing direction or stopping, or (4) move laterally or toward an opponent being screened, after having assumed a legal screening position. The screener may move in the same direction and path of the opponent being screened.

In (3) above, the speed of the opponent being screened will determine what the screener's stationary position may be. This position will vary and may be one to two normal steps or strides from his opponent.

Section IV—Penalties for Sections, I, II, III

The penalty for any violation of the sections above will be as follows:

a. The offender is charged with a personal foul. The offended team is awarded; (1) Ball out-of-bounds if an offensive foul is assessed, (2) Ball out-of-bounds if penalty situation is not in effect, (3) One free throw attempt if there is a successful field goal on the play, or (4) One free throw attempt plus a penalty free throw attempt if the offended player was not in the act of shooting.

b. If contact committed against a player, with or without the ball, is judged flagrant, the infraction shall be penalized as follows:
PENALTY:

(1) Two free throw attempts and possession of the ball out-of-bounds at the free throw line extended.

EXCEPTION: Rule 12B—Section V—Articles b and c.

(2) Offender may also be ejected if there is no apparent effort to play the ball, and/or if in the official's judgment, the contact was of such an excessive nature that an injury could have occurred.

(3) A personal foul is charged to the player and a team foul to the team.

(4) If the offended player is unable to attempt his free throws, his coach may select any player, on or off the floor, to do so. His coach will also select the substitute to replace the offended player. This penalty can be assessed only if the offender is ejected as in (2) above.

(5). The flagrant foul is considered an unsportsmanlike act if the player is ejected.

(6) The flagrant foul may be assessed whether the ball is dead or alive. Contact must occur.

c. A second free throw shall be awarded if the personal foul is:

(1) Committed against an offensive player attempting a field goal which is unsuccessful.

(2) For illegal contact with an elbow. Free throw attempt(s) are awarded whether the ball is dead, in possession, loose, or away from the play in the last two minutes of regulation or overtime(s). Contact must occur.

(3) Committed by a defensive player whose team has exceeded the limit for team fouls in the period.

(4) Committed by a defensive player prior to the ball being released on a throw-in from out-of-bounds.

EXCEPTION: Rule 12B—Section X.

(5) Committed against an offensive player in the frontcourt, if either he or a teammate has a clear path to the basket and thereby is deprived of the opportunity to score. The new possession must originate in the backcourt.

(6) For intentionally undercutting an opponent.

d. If a personal foul is committed on a player who is subsequently ejected from the game before attempting any or all of the awarded free throw(s), the ejected player must leave the court immediately. The opposing coach will select one of the four remaining players on the floor to attempt the remaining free throw(s). The ejected player's coach will select the substitute.

e. When a personal foul is committed on an offensive player who, as part of a continuous motion which started before the illegal contact occurred, attempt a field goal, that field goal shall be scored if successful, even if the ball leaves his hands after the whistle has sounded.

The offensive player must be attempting a field goal or starting his motion at the time the personal foul occurs. The field goal will not be scored if time on the game clock expires before the ball leaves the player's hand.

f. A personal foul committed by the offensive team during a throw-in shall be an offensive foul, regardless of whether the ball has been released or not.

EXCEPTION: Flagrant, elbow, and punching fouls.

Section V—Free Throw Penalty Situations

a. Each team shall be limited to four team fouls per regulation period without additional penalties. Common team fouls charged to a team in excess of four will be penalized by one free throw attempt plus an additional free throw attempt.

(1) The first four fouls committed by a team in any regulation period, if non-shooting, shall result in the ball being awarded to the opponent at the sideline nearest where the personal foul occurred. The ball shall be awarded no nearer to the baseline than the free throw line extended.

(2) The first three fouls committed by a team in any overtime period, if non-shooting, shall result in the ball being awarded to the opponent at the sideline nearest where the personal foul occurred. The ball shall be awarded no nearer to the baseline than the free throw line extended.

(3) If a team has not committed its quota of four team fouls during the first ten minutes of any regulation period, or its quota of three team fouls during the first three minutes of any overtime period, it shall be permitted to incur one team foul during the last two minutes without penalty.

(4) During each regulation or overtime period an additional penalty free throw will be awarded when the quota of team fouls has been reached.

(5) Personal fouls which are flagrant, punching, elbowing or away from the play will carry their own separate penalties and are included in the team foul total.

(6) Personal fouls committed against an offensive player in the act of shooting will result in two free throw attempts being awarded. No additional free throws shall be awarded if a penalty situation exists.

(7) Personal fouls committed during a successful field goal attempt, which result in one free throw attempt being awarded, will not result in an additional free throw attempt if the penalty situation exists.

b. A maximum of three points may be scored by the same team on a successful two-point field goal attempt.

c. A maximum of four points may be scored by the same team on a successful 3-point field goal attempt.

Section VI—Double Fouls

a. No free throw attempts will be awarded on double fouls, whether they are personal or technical.

b. Double personal fouls shall add to a player's total, but not to the team total.

c. If a double or fighting foul occurs, the team in possession of the ball at the time of the call shall retain possession. Play is resumed out-of-bounds on the sideline, nearest the point where play was interrupted. The 24-second clock is reset to 24 seconds.

d. If a double or fighting foul occurs with neither team in possession, or when the ball is in the air on an unsuccessful field goal attempt, play will be resumed with a jump ball at the center circle between any two opponents in the game at that time. If injury, ejection or disqualification makes it necessary for any player to be replaced, no substitute may participate in the jump ball.

e. If a double or fighting foul occurs on a successful field goal attempt, the team that has been scored upon will inbound the ball at the baseline as after any other score.

f. If a double foul occurs as a result of a difference in opinion by the officials, no points can be scored and play shall resume with a jump ball at the center circle between any two opponents in the game at that time. No substitute may participate in the jump ball.

Section VII—Offensive Fouls

A personal foul assessed against an offensive player which is neither an elbow, punching or flagrant foul shall be penalized in the following manner:

(1) No points can be scored by the offensive team

(2) The offending player is charged with a personal foul

(3) The offending team is not charged with a team foul

EXCEPTION: Rule 3—Section I—a. No free throws are awarded.

Section VIII—Loose Ball Fouls

a. A personal foul, which is neither a punching, flagrant or an elbow foul, committed while there is no team possession shall be administered in the following manner:

(1) Offending team is charged with a team foul

(2) Offending player is charged with a personal foul

(3) Offended team will be awarded possession at the sideline, nearest the spot of foul, if no penalty exists

(4) Offended player is awarded one free throw attempt plus a penalty free throw attempt if the offending team is in a penalty situation

b. If a "loose ball" foul called against the defensive team is then followed by a successful field goal/free throw attempt, a free throw attempt will be awarded to the offended team, allowing for the three point or four point play. This interpretation applies:

(1) Regardless of which offensive player is fouled

(2) Whether or not the penalty situation exists. The ball can never be awarded to the scoring team out-of-bounds following a personal foul which occurs on the same play

c. If a "loose ball" foul called against the offensive team is then followed by a successful field goal attempt by an offensive player, no points may be scored.

Section IX—Punching Fouls

a. Illegal contact called on a player for punching is a personal foul and a team foul. One free throw attempt shall be awarded, regardless of the number of previous fouls in the period. The ball shall be awarded to the offended team out-of-bounds at midcourt, whether the free throw is successful or unsuccessful.

b Any player who throws a punch which makes contact has committed an unsportsmanlike act and will be ejected immediately.

c. Any player who throws a punch, whether it connects or not, will be ejected immediately.

d. This rule applies whether play is in progress or the ball is dead.

e. In the case where one punching foul is followed by another, all aspects of the rule are applied in both cases, and the team last offended is awarded possession at midcourt.

f. A fine not exceeding $20,000 and/or suspension may be imposed upon such player(s) by the Commissioner at his sole discretion. (See Rule 12A—Section VIII)

Section X—Away-From-The-Play Foul

a. During the last two minutes of the fourth period or overtime period(s) with the offensive team in possession of the ball, all personal fouls which are assessed against the defensive team prior to the ball being released on a throw-in and/or away-from-the-play, shall be administered as follows:

(1) A personal foul and team foul shall be assessed and one free throw attempt shall be awarded. The free throw may be attempted by any player in the game at the time the personal foul was committed.

(2) The offended team shall be awarded the ball at the nearest point where play was interrupted with all privileges remaining.

EXCEPTION: Rule 12-B—Section X-b.

b. In the event that the personal foul committed is an elbow foul, the play shall be administered as follows:

(1) A personal foul and team foul shall be assessed and the free throw shooter shall be awarded two free throw attempts. The free throw(s) may be attempted by any player in the game at the time the personal foul was committed.

(2) In the event that the offended player is unable to participate in the game, the free throw shooter may be selected by his coach from any eligible player on the team. Any substitute must remain in the game until the next dead ball.

c. In the event that the personal foul committed is a flagrant foul, the play shall be administered as follows:

(1) A personal foul and team foul shall be assessed and the free throw shooter shall be awarded two free throw attempts. The free throws may be attempted by any player in the game at the time the flagrant foul was committed.

(2) If a flagrant foul—penalty (1) is assessed and the offended player is unable to participate in the game, the substitute will be selected by his coach. The two free throws may be attempted by any of the four remaining players in the game. The ball will be awarded to the offended team at the free throw line extended in the frontcourt. The injured player may return to the game.

(3) If a flagrant foul—penatly (2) is assessed and the offended player is unable to participate in the game, the substitute will be selected by his coach. The two free throws may be attempted by the substitute or any of the four remaining players in the game. The ball will be awarded to the offended team at the free throw line extended in the frontcourt. The injured player may return to the game.

COMMENTS ON THE RULES
I. GUIDES FOR ADMINISTRATION AND APPLICATION OF THE RULES

Each official should have a definite and clear conception of his overall responsibility to include the intent and purpose of each rule. If all officials possess the same conception there will be a guaranteed uniformity in the administration of all contests.

The restrictions placed upon the player by the rules are intended to create a balance of play, equal opportunity for the defense and the offense, to provide reasonable safety and protection, and to emphasize cleverness and skill without unduly limiting freedom of action of player or team.

The primary purpose of penalties is to compensate a player who has been placed at a disadvantage through an illegal act of an opponent. A secondary purpose is to restrain players from committing acts which, if ignored, might lead to roughness even though they do not affect the immediate play. To implement this philosophy, many of the rules are written in general terms while the need for the rule may have been created by specific play situations. This practice eliminates the necessity for many additional rules and provides the officials the latitude and authority to adapt application of the rules to fit conditions of play in any particular game.

II. BASIC PRINCIPLES
A. CONTACT SITUATIONS
1. Incidental Contact

a. The mere fact that contact occurs does not necessarily constitute a foul. Contact which is incidental to an effort by a player to play an opponent, reach a loose ball, or perform normal defensive or offensive movements, should not be considered illegal. If, however, a player attempts to play an opponent from a position where he has no reasonable chance to perform without making contact with his opponent, the responsibility is on the player in this position.

b. The hand is considered "part of the ball" when it is in contact with the ball. Therefore, contact on that hand by a defender while it is in contact with the ball is not illegal.

2. Guarding an Opponent

In all guarding situations, a player is entitled to any spot on the court he desires, provided he gets to that spot first and without contact with an opponent.

In all guarding situations during a live ball, a player is entitled to any spot on the court he desires, provided that he gets to the spot first without contact with an opponent.

In all guarding situations during a dead ball, the defensive player(s) must be allowed to take a position between his man and the basket.

a. In most guarding situations, the guard must be facing his opponent at the moment he assumes a guarding position after which no particular facing is required.

b. A player may continue to move after gaining a guarding position in the path of an opponent provided he is not moving directly or obliquely toward his opponent when contact occurs. A player is never permitted to move into the path of an opponent after the opponent has jumped into the air.

c. A player who extends an arm, shoulder, hip or leg into the path of an opponent and thereby causes contact is not considered to have a legal position in the path of an opponent.

d. A player is entitled to an erect (vertical) position even to the extent of holding his arms above his shoulders, as in post play or when double-teaming in pressing tactics.

e. A player is not required to maintain any specific distance from an opponent.

f. Any player who conforms to the above is absolved from responsibility for any contact by an opponent which may dislodge or tend to disloge such player from the position which he has attained and is maintaining legally. If contact occurs, the official must decide whether the contact is incidental or a foul has been committed.

The following are the usual situations to which the foregoing principles apply:

a. Guarding a player with the ball

b. Guarding a player who is trying for a goal

c. Switching to a player with the ball

d. Guarding a dribbler

e. Guarding a player without the ball

f. Guarding a post player with or without the ball

g. Guarding a rebounder

3. Screening

When a player screens in front of or at the side of a stationary opponent, he may be as close as he desires providing he does not make contact. His opponent can see him and, therefore, is expected to detour around the screen.

If he screens behind a stationary opponent, the opponent must be able to take a normal step backward without contact. Because the opponent is not expected to see a screener behind him, the player screened is given latitude of movement.

To screen a moving opponent, the player must stop soon enough to permit his opponent to stop or change direction. The distance between the player screening and his opponent will depend upon the speed at which the players are moving.

If two opponents are moving in the same direction and path, the player who is behind is responsible for contact. The player in front may stop or slow his pace, but he may not move backward or sidewards into his opponent. The player in front may or may not have the ball. This situation assumes the two players have been moving in identically the same direction and path before contact.

4. The Dribble

If the dribbler's path is blocked, he is expected to pass or shoot; that is, he should not try to dribble by an opponent unless there is a reasonable chance of getting by without contact.

B. FIELD GOAL ATTEMPT

A player is attempting a field goal when he has the ball and is (in the judgment of the official) in the act of shooting or trying to attempt to shoot. It is not essential that the ball leave the shooter's hand. His arm(s) might be held so that he cannot actually make an attempt. He is thus deprived of an opportunity to score and is entitled to two free throw attempts.

If a player is fouled when tapping a tossed ball or a rebound toward or into the basket, he is not considered to be "trying for goal." If a live ball is in flight when time expires, the goal, if made, shall count.

C. FOULS: FLAGRANT—UNSPORTSMANLIKE

To be unsportsmanlike is to act in a manner unbecoming to the image of professional basketball. It consists of acts of deceit, disrespect of officials and profanity. The penalty for such action is a technical foul. Repeated acts shall result in expulsion from the game and a minimum fine of $250.

A flagrant foul—penalty (1) is unnecessary contact committed by a player against an opponent.

A flagrant foul—penalty (2) is unnecessary and excessive contact committed by a player against an opponent. It is an unsportsmanlike act and the offender is ejected immediately.

The offender will be subject to a fine not exceeding $20,000 and/or suspension by the Commissioner.

See Rule 12B—Section IV—b (1) for interpretation and penalties.

D. ILLEGAL DEFENSIVE ALIGNMENTS

The term Illegal Defense has replaced Zone Defense in NBA usage. The rule now in place, supported by guidelines, defines approved coverage by defensive players and teams. Violations of these rules and guidelines will be noted as Illegal Defense.

E. CHARGING-BLOCKING

A defensive player shall not be permitted to move into the path of an offensive player once he has picked up the ball in an effort to either pass or shoot.

If contact occurs on this play, and it is anything but negligible and/or incidental, a blocking foul shall be called on the defensive player. Any field goal attempt, if successful, shall count, as long as the ball has not been returned to the floor following the official's whistle.

If a defensive player acquires a position directly under the basket/backboard on anything but a "baseline drive," he shall be responsible if contact occurs. An offensive foul should never be called under these conditions. The offensive player remains a shooter until he has regained a normal playing position on the floor. Many times this type of play is allowed to continue if the goal is successful.

The opposite is also true. If an offensive player causes contact with a defensive player, who has established a legal position prior to the offensive player having picked up the ball in an effort to either pass or shoot, and it is anything but negligible and/or incidental, an offensive foul shall be called, and no points may be scored. A defensive player may turn slightly to protect himself, but is never allowed to bend over and submarine an opponent.

On a "drive-in" shot, if the defensive player has established a legal position in front of the basket/backboard, the offensive player shall be responsible for any illegal contact which occurs prior to his having regained his balance on the floor. An offensive foul shall be called and no points are to be awarded if the field goal is successful.

The mere fact that contact occurs on these type of plays, or any other similar play, does not necessarily mean that a personal foul has been committed. The officials must decide whether the contact is negligible and/or incidental, judging each situation separately.

In judging this play, the officials must be aware that if EITHER player has been placed at a disadvantage by the contact which has occurred, then a personal foul MUST be called on the player responsible for that contact.

F. GAME CANCELLATION

For the purpose of game cancellation, the officials' jurisdiction begins with the opening tip-off. Prior to this, it shall be the decision of the home management whether or not playing conditions are such to warrant postponement.

However, once the game begins, if because of extremely hazardous playing conditions the question arises whether or not the game should be cancelled, the crew chief shall see that EVERY effort is made to continue the game before making the decision to terminate it.

G. PHYSICAL CONTACT—SUSPENSION

Any player or coach guilty of intentional physical contact with an official shall automatically be suspended without pay for one game. A fine and/or longer period of suspension will result if circumstances so dictate.

H. PROTEST

Protests are not permitted during the course of a game. In order to file a protest, the procedure, as set forth in the NBA constitution, is as follows: "In order to protest against or appeal from the result of a game, notice thereof must be given to the Commissioner within forty-eight (48) hours after the conclusion of said game, by telegram, stating therein the grounds for such protest. No protest may be filed in connection with any game played during the regular season after midnight of the day of the last game of the regular schedule. A protest in connection with a playoff game must be filed not later than midnight of the day of the game protested. A game may be protested only by a Governor, Alternate Governor or Head Coach. The right of protest shall inure not only to the immediately allegedly aggrieved contestants, but to any other member who can show an interest in the grounds of protest and the results that might be attained if the protest were allowed. Each telegram of protest shall be immediately confirmed by letter and no protest shall be valid unless the letter of confirmation is accompanied by a check in the sum of $1,500 payable to the Association. If the member filing the protest prevails, the $1,500 is to be refunded. If the member does not prevail, the $1,500 is to be forfeited and retained in the Association treasury.

Upon receipt of a protest, the Commissioner shall at once notify the member operating the opposing team in the game protested and require both of said members within five (5) days to file with him such evidence as he may desire bearing upon the issue. The Commissioner shall decide the question raised within five (5) days after receipt of such evidence.

I. SHATTERING BACKBOARDS

Any player whose contact with the basket ring or backboard causes the backboard to shatter will be penalized in the following manner:

(1) Pre-game and/or Half-time warm-ups—No penalty to be assessed by officials.

(2) During the game—Non-unsportsmanlike conduct technical foul. Under NO circumstances will that player be ejected from the game.

The Commissioner will review all actions and plays involved in the shattering of a backboard.

J. PLAYER/TEAM CONDUCT AND DRESS

(1) Each player when introduced, prior to the game, must be uniformly dressed.

(2) Players, coaches and trainers are to stand and line up in a dignified posture along the sidelines or on the foul line during the playing of the National Anthem.

(3) Coaches and assistant coaches must wear a sport coat or suit coat.

(4) While playing, players must keep their uniform shirts tucked into their pants, and no T-shirts are allowed.

(5) The only article bearing a commerical 'logo' which can be worn by players is their shoes.

K. OFFENSIVE 3-SECONDS

The offensive player cannot be allowed in the 3-second lane for more than the allotted time. This causes the defensive player to 'hand-check' because he cannot control the offensive player for that extended period of time.

If the offensive player is in the 3-second lane for less than three seconds and receives the ball, he must make a move toward the hoop for the official to discontinue his three second count. If he attempts to back the defensive player down, attempting to secure a better position in relation to the basket, offensive three seconds or an offensive foul must be called. If he passes off and immediately makes a move out of the lane, there should be no whistle. The basic concern in this situation is that the offensive player not be allowed any advantage that is not allowed the defensive player by the illegal defensive guidelines.

L. PLAYER CONDUCT—SPECTATORS

Any coach, player or trainer who deliberately enters the spectator stands during the game will be automatically ejected and the incident reported by datagram to the Commissioner. Entering the stands to keep a ball in play by a player or the momentum which carries the player into the stands is not considered deliberate. The first row of seats is considered the beginning of the stands.

M. PUNCHING, FIGHTING AND ELBOW FOULS

Violent acts of any nature on the court will not be tolerated. Players involved in altercations will be ejected, fined and/or suspended.

Officials have been instructed to eject a player who throws a punch, whether or not it connects, or an elbow which makes contact above shoulder level. If elbow contact is shoulder level or below, it shall be left to the discretion of the official as to whether the player is ejected. Even if a punch or an elbow goes undetected by the officials during the game, but is detected during a review of a videotape, that player will be penalized.

There is absolutely no justification for fighting in an NBA game. The fact that you may feel provoked by another player is not an acceptable excuse. If a player takes it upon himself to retaliate, he can expect to be subject to appropriate penalties.

N. EXPIRATION OF TIME

NO LESS THAN :00.3 must expire on the game clock when a ball is thrown inbounds and then hit instantly out-of-bounds. If less than :00.3 expires in such a situation, the timer will be instructed to deduct AT LEAST :00.3 from the game clock. If, in the judgment of the official, the play took longer than :00.3, he will instruct the timer to deduct more time. If less than :00.3 remain on the game clock when this situation occurs, the period is over.

NO LESS THAN :00.3 must expire on the game clock when a player secures possession of an inbounds pass and then attempts a field goal. If less than :00.3 expires in such a situation, the timer will be instructed to deduct AT LEAST :00.3 from the game clock. If less than :00.3 remain on the game clock when this situation occurs, the period is over, and the field goal attempt will be disallowed immediately whether successful or unsuccessful.

This guideline shall apply to any field goal attempted by a player after he receives an inbounds pass, OTHER THAN what will be called, for this purpose, a "tip-in" or "alley oop."

A "tip-in" is defined as any action in which the ball is deflected, not controlled, by a player and then enters the basket ring. This type of action shall be deemed legal if :00.1 or more remains in a period.

A "high lob" is defined as a pass which is received by an offensive player while in mid-air, and is followed instantaneously by a field goal attempt. If the reception of the pass and the subsequent "slam dunk" is immediately adjacent to the basket ring, this type of action shall be deemed legal if :00.1 or more remains in a period. However, if the "high lob" attempt is a distance from the basket ring whereby the ball must be controlled in mid-air, either one-handed or two-handed, a minimum of :00.3 is necessary for a field goal to score if successful.

NO LESS than :00.3 must expire on the game clock when a player secures possession of an unsuccessful free throw attempt and immediately requests a timeout. If LESS than :00.3 expires in such a circumstance, the time on the game clock shall be reduced by at least :00.3. Therefore, if :00.3 OR LESS remain on the game clock when the above situation exists, and a player requests a timeout upon securing possession of the ball, the period is over.

During ANY regular or 20-second timeout taken during the FINAL minute of ANY period, the crew chief must meet with his fellow officials to discuss possible timing scenarios, fouls being taken if either team is under the penalty limit, number of timeouts, assistance by all officials on 3-point field goal attempts, rotation or away-from-the play foul.

Regardless of when the horn or red light operates to signify the end of period, the officials will ultimately make the final decision whether to allow or disallow a successful field goal. THE CREW CHIEF MUST TAKE CHARGE OF THE SITUATION.

O. VERBAL FAN INTERFERENCE

Any spectator who verbally abuses players and/or coaches in a manner which, in the opinion of the game officials, interferes with the ability of a coach to communicate with his players during the game and/or huddles, will, at the direction of the crew chief, be given one warning by a building security officer. If the same spectator continues to behave in a like manner, the crew chief shall direct a building security officer to eject the spectator from the arena.

P. GUIDELINES FOR INFECTION CONTROL

If a player suffers a laceration or a wound where bleeding occurs, the officials shall suspend the game at the earliest appropriate time and remove the injured player from the game. The opposing team shall be allowed to substitute one player. The injured player may return to the game when he has received appropriate treatment by medical staff personnel.

If the player returns to the game, the officials shall make certain that any lesion, wound or dermatitis is covered with a dressing that will prevent contamination to and/or from other sources.

If the injured player is awarded a free throw attempt(s) as a result of a personal foul, play shall be suspended as soon as the final attempt is successful or unsuccessful. If the player is involved in a jump ball, play shall be suspended as soon as possession is gained by either team. Caution shall be used when suspending play, so as not to halt a fast break situation.

Mandatory timeouts shall not be granted at any time play is suspended. The offensive team may call a 20-second or regular timeout.

Alphabetical Index to Contents